The Norton Anthology
of English Literature

REVISED

VOLUME 2

The Norton Anthology of English Literature

REVISED

M. H. Abrams, *General Editor*
Professor of English, Cornell University

E. Talbot Donaldson
Professor of English, Columbia University

Hallett Smith
*Professor of English and Chairman, Division of the Humanities,
California Institute of Technology*

Robert M. Adams
Professor of English, University of California at Los Angeles

Samuel Holt Monk
Professor Emeritus, University of Minnesota

George H. Ford
*Professor of English and Chairman, Department of English,
University of Rochester*

David Daiches
*Professor of English and Dean of the School of English
and American Studies, University of Sussex*

VOLUME 2

W · W · NORTON & COMPANY · INC · New York

SBN 393 09807 9 *Cloth Edition*
SBN 393 09792 7 *Paper Edition*
Library of Congress Catalog Card No. 68-12176
Book design by John Woodlock
PRINTED IN THE UNITED STATES OF AMERICA

8 9 0

Contents

The Twentieth Century   1373
(1890 to the Present)

Preface
to the Revised Edition

The first edition of the *Norton Anthology* was the result of two decades of experimentation with the indispensable course that introduces students to the greatness and variety of English literature. The response to that edition has amply justified the principles that guided its design. These are: that an introductory anthology ought to make possible a study in depth of all the major writers (other than novelists) in the historical context of the chief literary modes and traditions of their times; that the student deserves the most accurate texts of these writers, edited to make them immediately accessible and printed in a format manageable to the hand and inviting to the eye; and that the editorial materials should make the anthology self-sufficient, assist precise and sensitive reading, and enhance an intelligent delight in literature as literature.

Out of their experience with this book, many teachers and scholars volunteered comments, suggestions, and corrections; many others answered requests for information about their procedures and preferences generously and in detail. As the result of this accumulating information, based on actual use of the anthology in teaching, the editors are now able to provide in this revised edition a substantial improvement on the first.

A few selections (assigned very little or not at all) have been eliminated; a far greater number have been added. A number of works originally represented only in part are now complete, among them *Beowulf*, Book I of *The Faerie Queene*, *Absalom and Achitophel*, and *The Marriage of Heaven and Hell*. New titles have been added for all the major writers and for most of the lesser writers. Many of these are long works, reprinted *in toto*: Chaucer's *Wife of Bath's Tale*, Milton's *Samson Agonistes* (in addition to a larger representation of *Paradise Lost*), Swift's *Argument against Abolishing Christianity* and Part IV (in addition to Part II) of *Gulliver's Travels*, Blake's *Book of Thel*, Wordsworth's *Ruined Cottage*, Coleridge's *Eolian Harp*, Byron's *Vision of Judgment*, Shelley's *Mont Blanc* and *Triumph of Life*, and Keat's *Fall of Hyperion*. Other important additions have been made to the work of many poets—especially to Skelton, Wyatt, Sidney, Spenser, Ralegh, and Shakespeare in the Elizabethan age; to Tennyson's *In Memoriam* and the poems of Browning and Arnold; and to Hardy, Hopkins, Yeats, Housman, Edward Thomas, Owen, and Dylan Thomas among other more recent poets. New prose selections are included for Caxton, Browne, Johnson, Lamb, Carlyle, Newman, Mill, Conrad, and Eliot. D. H. Lawrence (as befits a major writer) is now represented by substantial examples of his writing in a variety of genres. The list of contemporary poets has been augmented by Edwin Muir and Robert Graves.

The "Topics" in literary, critical, or intellectual history appended to the selections for each period have proved widely useful in various ways—as additional reading, as convenient illustrations for points made in lectures, as materials for discussion, or as starting places for written reports. In the second edition we add three new Topics: one on "Medieval Views of Life on Earth"; another, in the Restoration and Eighteenth Century, on "The General and the Particular," which is documented by writings from Aristotle and Horace to William Blake; and a third, on "Literature Since Mid-Century: Anti-Culture and the New Traditionalism," which illustrates, through the writings of Samuel Beckett and some contemporary British poets, a central opposition in the literature of the present day.

By an improvement in the quality of the paper, these and many other additions have been made without increasing appreciably the bulk of the volumes and without impairing the visibility and open layout of the texts. Poetry in this anthology can still be read as it was written to be read: in a single column and with comfortable margins.

We also continue faithful to the principle that texts for undergraduates should be no less scrupulously chosen and edited than texts for the scholar. Accordingly we offer new, more sensitive, and more accurate translations of *Beowulf* and of *Sir Gawain and the Green Knight*. We use William Ringler's edition of Sir Philip Sidney's poetry and the David Erdman and Harold Bloom edition of William Blake. Shelley's *Triumph of Life* is the revised version recently published by Donald H. Reiman, and Wordsworth's great but neglected narrative poem, *The Ruined Cottage*, is a new and improved version edited from an unpublished manuscript by Jonathan Wordsworth.

Each editor has reconsidered all his introductory essays and footnotes and has rewritten many of them in the light of recent scholarship and criticism. The comprehensive introductions and the full glossing of archaisms and allusions have freed the student from reliance on a reference library and enabled him to carry and read the book anywhere—in class, at home in his own room, or under a tree. Actual use of the anthology in teaching has confirmed our original opinion that, in selected instances, the notes should also provide a modicum of guidance in interpretation; for some of the works here are among the most complex and difficult in the language, and of those assigned to the student, only a fraction can be discussed adequately in class. Experience has shown that these editorial aids do not displace the teacher but open possibilities to the student's own judgment and suggest points of departure for commentary and dialogue in the classroom. All the bibliographical guides at the end of the volumes, designed to encourage students to read further on their own, have been brought up to date. As a convenience to the student wishing to develop his own library of literary history and criticism, a dagger symbol indicates the books currently available in paperback.

We have continued the editorial procedures which have proved their utility in the earlier edition. In each of the historical and biographical introductions we list and identify the dates of crucial importance at the beginning and limit further chronological references to those the student needs to orient himself. In order, however, to specify the interrelations of individual works, we place after each selection, where the facts are known, the date of composition on the left and the date of first publication in book form on the right; the latter is sometimes preceded by the date of first appearance in a periodical publication. The writings of authors such as Chaucer, Skelton, Spenser, or Burns, which contain a large proportion of unfamiliar words, have been glossed in the margin, where the translation can be assimilated with least impediment to the flow of the reading. Whenever a portion of text has been omitted, the omission is indicated by three asterisks. Titles supplied by the editors are enclosed in square brackets.

All texts are printed in the form which makes them most immediately available to their particular audience. We have thus normalized spellings and capitalization according to modern American usage, but only in those instances in which the change does not alter semantic, phonological, or metric qualities. The verse of Spenser and of Hopkins and the prose of Joyce, Shaw, Carlyle, and Keats (in his letters) have been reproduced in their original form; only the minimal changes necessary for ready intelligibility have been made in the writings etched by William Blake; and in all writers, significant deviations from the norm (Keats's "faery," for example) have been left unaltered. The works of Chaucer and other writers in Middle English not too difficult for diately available to their particular audience. We have normalized spellings and capitalization according to modern American usage, but only in those instances in which the change does not alter semantic, phonological, or metric qualities. The verse of Spenser and Hopkins and the prose of Joyce, Shaw, Carlyle, and Keats (in his letters) have been reproduced in their original form; only the minimal changes necessary for ready intelligibility have been made in the writings of William Blake; and in all writers, significant deviations from the norm (Keats's "faery," for example) have been left unaltered. The writings of Chaucer have also been left in the original language, but each word is consistently spelled in that variant of its scribal forms which is closest to modern English. When we have altered punctuation, it has been on the conservative principle that a change should be made only when the old punctuation would mislead a modern reader.

In the process of compiling and revising this anthology, the editors incurred obligations to scores of teachers throughout the country who volunteered useful suggestions or gave essential information when asked. To each of these—too numerous to list here— we owe our thanks. We wish especially to acknowledge the wise counsel, in preparing the first edition, of W. R. Keast, now president of Wayne State University, and the detailed and helpful critiques toward revising that edition provided by a number of teacher-scholars: William Alfred (Harvard University); Harold Bloom (Yale University); Jack M. Davis (University of Connecticut); Peter Elbow (University of California, Berkeley); James Gindin (University of Michigan); David D. Harvey (State University of New York at Albany); Robert W. Hill, Jr. (Middlebury College); Arthur Hoffman (Syracuse University); David Kalstone (Rutgers, The State University); Robert Kimbrough (University of Wisconsin); R. M. Lumiansky (University of Pennsylvania); Hugh Maclean (State University of New York at Albany); Thomas Moser (Stanford University); Stephen M. Parrish (Cornell University); S. P. Rosenbaum (University of Toronto); and Clarence Tracy (University of British Columbia). Howard L. Anderson (Michigan State University) was of special assistance on the bibliography for the Eighteenth Century, and Richard L. Greene (Wesleyan University, Connecticut) provided the editors with a comprehensive and most helpful list of corrections and suggestions. George P. Brockway and John Benedict, of W. W. Norton & Company, Inc. —assisted ably by Eleanor Brooks, Kathleen Calkins, and S. H. Dammacco—have contributed immensely, by encouragement, caveats, and hard editorial work, to mitigate the chronic dilemmas in the endeavor to represent, justly and accurately, the work of all the major English writers in a single volume.

M. H. Abrams

The Romantic Period

(1798-1832)

1789–1815: Revolutionary and Napoleonic period in France. 1789: The Revolution begins with the assembly of the States-General in May and the storming of the Bastille on July 14.—1793: King Louis XVI executed; England joins the alliance against France.—1793–94: The Reign of Terror under Robespierre.—1804: Napoleon crowned emperor. 1815: Napoleon defeated at Waterloo.

1798: *Lyrical Ballads* published anonymously by William Wordsworth and Samuel Taylor Coleridge.

1811–20: The Regency—George, Prince of Wales, acts as regent for George III, who was declared incurably insane.

1820: Accession of George IV.

1832: The Reform Bill carried in Parliament.

THE POLITICAL BACKGROUND: REVOLUTION AND REACTION

Following the common usage of historians of English literature, we will denote by the "Romantic period" the span between the year 1798, in which Wordsworth and Coleridge published their *Lyrical Ballads*, and 1832, when Sir Walter Scott died, when other major writers of the earlier century were either dead or no longer productive, and when the passage of the first Reform Bill, after more than three decades of political stagnation and repression, inaugurated the Victorian era of cautious readjustment of political power to conform to the economic and social realities of a new industrial age. This was a turbulent period in political and economic history, during which England was experiencing the ordeal of the change from its former status as a primarily agricultural society, where wealth and power had been largely concentrated in the landholding aristocracy, to a recognizably modern industrial nation, in which the balance of economic power was shifted to large-scale employers, who found themselves ranged against an immensely enlarging and increasingly restive working class. And this change occurred in a context first of the American and then of the much more radical French Revolution, of wars, of economic cycles of inflation and depression, and of the constant threat to the social structure

1

from imported revolutionary ideologies to which the ruling classes responded by heresy-hunts and the repression of traditional liberties.

The early period of the French Revolution, marked by the Declaration of the Rights of Man and the storming of the Bastille to release the imprisoned political offenders, evoked enthusiastic support from English liberals and radicals alike. Two influential books indicate the radical social thinking stimulated by the Revolution. Tom Paine's *Rights of Man* (1791–92) justified the French Revolution against Edmund Burke's attack in his *Reflections on the Revolution in France* (1790), and advocated for England a democratic republic which was to be achieved, if lesser pressures failed, by popular revolution. More important for its influence on Wordsworth, Shelley, and other poets was William Godwin's *Inquiry Concerning Political Justice* (1793), which foretold an inevitable but peaceful evolution of society to a final stage in which all property would be equally distributed and all government would wither away. Later, however, English sympathizers dropped off as the Revolution followed its increasingly grim and violent course: the accession to power by the Jacobin extremists; the "September Massacres" of the imprisoned and helpless nobility in 1792, followed by the execution of the royal family; the invasion by the French Republic of the Rhineland and Netherlands, and its offer of armed assistance to all countries desiring to overthrow their governments, which brought England into the war against France; the guillotining of thousands in the Reign of Terror under Robespierre; and after the execution in their turn of the men who had directed the Terror, the emergence of Napoleon first as dictator and then as emperor of France. As Wordsworth wrote in *The Prelude* (XI.206–9),

> become oppressors in their turn,
> Frenchmen had changed a war of self-defense
> For one of conquest, losing sight of all
> Which they had struggled for * * *

For Wordsworth and all the English of liberal inclinations, these events posed a dilemma which has become familiar since the 1920's, in our parallel era of wars, revolutions, and the struggle by competing social ideologies—liberals had no clear choice, and no side they could wholeheartedly espouse. Napoleon, the child and champion of the French Revolution, had become an arch-aggressor, a despot, and the founder of a new dynasty; yet almost all those who opposed him did so for the wrong reasons, so that his final defeat at Waterloo in 1815 proved to be the triumph, not of progress and reform, but of reactionary despotisms throughout continental Europe.

In England this period of the wars against France and of the terrifying threat of the revolutionary spirit at home was one of harsh repressive measures. Public meetings were prohibited, habeas corpus suspended for the first time in over a hundred years, and advocates of even moderate measures of political change were persecuted as Jacobins, exponents of regicide and political terror, and were charged with high treason in time of war. In effect the Napoleonic wars put an end to reform, and to almost all genuine political life in England, for more than three decades. Although George III's attempt to revive the personal power of the Crown had been defeated by what G. M. Trevelyan calls "the new Tory oligarchy" under William Pitt the younger (1759–1806), the ruling classes—Whig and Tory—were still constituted much as they had been throughout the earlier part of the 18th century: aristocratic landholders and the higher Anglican clergy, with a popular leavening. And the Tories of this period saw themselves protecting the English constitution against the dangerous inroads of the democratic spirit of the French Revolution, much as the Whigs of 1689 had seen themselves as protectors of the same constitution against the Jacobites.

Yet this was the very time when profound economic and social changes were creating a desperate need for corresponding changes in political arrangements and politics, and new classes—manufacturing, rather than agricultural—were beginning to demand a power in government proportionate to their wealth. The "Industrial Revolution"—the shift in methods of manufacturing which resulted from the invention of power-driven machinery to replace hand labor—had begun in the mid-18th century with improvements in machines for processing textiles, and was given immense impetus when James Watt perfected the steam engine in 1765. In the succeeding decades steam replaced wind and water as the primary source of power in one after another type of manufacturing; and at once, after centuries of almost imperceptibly slow change, there began that constantly accelerating and still continuing alteration in economic and social conditions which shows no signs of slowing down in the foreseeable future. The application of steam power to manufacturing led to the massing of a new laboring population in the sprawling mill towns which burgeoned in central and northern England. In rural communities the destruction of home industry was accompanied by a rapid acceleration of the process—lamented by Oliver Goldsmith in *The Deserted Village* as early as 1770—of enclosing the old open-field and communally worked farms into privately owned agricultural holdings. This process was necessary for the more efficient methods of agriculture and animal breeding required to supply a growing population (although some of the land thus acquired was turned into vast private parks); in any case, it was achieved at the cost of creating a new landless class which either migrated to the industrial towns or remained as farm laborers, barely subsisting on starvation wages eked out by an inadequate dole. The landscape of England began to take on its modern appearance: the hitherto open rural areas subdivided into a checkerboard of fields enclosed by hedges and stone walls, and the factories of the mushrooming industrial and trading cities casting a pall of smoke over vast new areas of monotonous jerry-built houses and slum tenements. Meanwhile, the population was becoming increasingly polarized into what Disraeli later called the "Two Nations"—the two classes of capital and labor, the large owner or trader and the possessionless wageworker, the rich and the poor.

No attempt was made to regulate this movement from the old economic world to the new, not only because of the inertia of tradition and the power of vested interests, but because even the liberal reformers were dominated by the social philosophy of laissez faire. This theory of "let alone" holds that the general welfare can be ensured only by the free operation of economic laws; the government must maintain a policy of strict noninterference and leave each man to pursue his own private interests. For the great majority of the laboring class the results of this policy were inadequate wages, long hours of work under harsh discipline in sordid conditions, and the large-scale employment of women and children for tasks which destroyed both the body and the spirit. Reports by investigating committees on conditions in the coal mines, with male and female children of ten or even five years of age harnessed by the waist to heavy coal-sledges which they dragged by crawling on their hands and knees, read like lurid scenes from Dante's *Inferno*. The protracted French war, like other wars, was accompanied by high taxes, inflated prices, and shortages of food. In 1815 the conclusion of this war, when the enlargement of the working force by demobilized troops coincided with the fall in the wartime demand for goods, brought on the first modern industrial depression. Since the workers had no vote and were prevented by law from combining into labor unions, their sole recourse was to petitions, protest meetings, agitation, and hunger riots, which only frightened the ruling class into more repressive measures. In addition the introduction of new machines caused technological unemployment, and this provoked sporadic attempts by dispossessed workers to destroy the machines. After one such outbreak the House of Lords—despite Lord Byron's eloquent protest—passed a bill (1821) substituting death for transportation as the penalty for destroying the frames used for weaving in the stocking industry. In 1819 meetings of workers were organized to demand Parliamentary reform. In August of that year, a huge but orderly assembly at St. Peter's Fields, Manchester, was wantonly charged by troops, who killed nine and severely injured hundreds more; this was the notorious "Peterloo Massacre," so named as a parody on the Battle of Waterloo. The quick approval of this military action by the government evoked Percy Bysshe Shelley's scalding satire *The Masque of Anarchy* and inspired his poems for the working class, *England in 1819* and *Song to the Men of England*.

Suffering was largely confined to the poor, however, for all the while the landed classes, the industrialists, and many of the merchants prospered. In London the Regency period was for the leisure class a time of lavish display and moral laxity. In the provinces, the gentry in their great country houses carried on their familial and social concerns—so fully reflected in the novels of Jane Austen—almost untouched by great national and international events.

But the pressures for reform, while they might be repressed, could not be eliminated, especially since political disabilities were not limited to the working class. The right to vote was held by very few of the newly well-to-do; the shifts of population had increased the number of "rotten boroughs" (localities which, although now depopulated, kept their seats in the House of Commons, usually at the disposal of a single wealthy nobleman); while great new industrial cities such as Manchester had no representation at all. Gradually the working-class reformers acquired the support of the middle classes and the liberal Whigs. Finally, at a time of acute economic distress, and after a period of unprecedented agitation and disorders that threatened to break out into revolution, the first Reform Bill was carried in 1832, amid widespread rejoicing. It eliminated the rotten boroughs, redistributed parliamentary representation, and extended the vote. Although about half the middle class and almost all the working class remained still without a franchise, the principle of peaceful adjustment of conflicting interests by Parliamentary majority had been firmly established; and reform was to go on until, by stages, England acquired universal adult suffrage.

"THE SPIRIT OF THE AGE"

"Romanticism" has often been used by literary historians as though it were the name for a single essence or quality shared, in varying proportions, by all the principal writers of the Romantic period. But all attempts at a single definition of Romanticism fall far short of matching the variegated facts of a time which exceeds almost all ages of English literature in the range and diversity of its achievements. No writer in Wordsworth's lifetime thought of himself as a "Romantic," or as sharing an essential literary quality with all his important contemporaries; the word "Romantic" was not applied until half a century later, by English historians. Critics and reviewers contemporary with these writers treated them as independent individuals, or else grouped them (often invidiously, but with some basis in literary fact) into a number of separate schools: "the Lake School" of Wordsworth, Coleridge, and Robert Southey; "the Cockney School" of Leigh Hunt, Hazlitt, and associated writers, including John Keats; and "the Satanic School" of Byron, Shelley, and their followers.

Many of the major writers, however, did feel that there was something distinctive about their time—not a shared doctrine or literary quality, but a pervasive intellectual climate, which some of them called "the spirit of the age." They had the sense that (as Keats said in one of his sonnets) "Great spirits now on earth are sojourning," and that there was evidence all about of that release of energy, experimental boldness, and creative power which marks a literary renaissance. In his *Defense of Poetry* Shelley claimed that the literature of the age "has arisen as it were from a new birth. * * * It is impossible to read the compositions of the most celebrated writers of the present day without being startled with the electric life which burns within their words," and this is "less their spirit than the spirit of the age." Shelley explained this literary spirit as the inescapable accompaniment of political and social revolution; and other writers agreed. Francis Jeffrey, foremost conservative reviewer of the day, connected "the revolution in our literature" with "the agitations of the French Revolution, and the discussions as well as the hopes and terrors to which it gave occasion." William Hazlitt, who published a book of essays called *The Spirit of the Age*, described how, in his early youth, the French Revolution seemed "the dawn of a new era, a new impulse had been given to men's minds," so that "philosophy took a higher, poetry could afford a deeper range." The new poetry of the school of Wordsworth, he maintained, "had its origin in the French Revolution. * * * There was a mighty ferment in the heads of statesmen and poets, kings and people. * * * It was a time of promise, a renewal of the world—and of letters."

The imagination of Romantic writers was, indeed, preoccupied with the fact and idea of revolution. First the American and later, and to a much greater degree, the French Revolution seemed to promise that, by breaking free from outmoded concepts and institutions, man might also escape the oppression and sufferings which had hitherto seemed the inescapable condition of his existence, and establish a new and joyous world of liberty, equality, and fraternity. In the early period of the Revolution all the leading English writers except Edmund Burke were in sympathy with it, and Robert Burns, William Blake, Wordsworth, Coleridge, and Southey were among its most fervent adherents. Later, even after the first boundless expectations had been disappointed by the events in France, the younger writers, including Hazlitt, Hunt, Shelley, and Byron, felt that its example, when purged of its errors, still comprised man's best hope. The Revolution generated a feeling that this was a great age of new beginnings, when, by discarding inherited procedures and outworn customs, everything was possible; and not only in political and social arrangements, but in intellectual and literary enterprises as well. In his *Prelude* Wordsworth wrote the classic description of the intoxicating spirit of the early 1790's, with "France standing on the top of golden hours, / And human nature seeming born again," so that "not favored spots alone, but the whole Earth, / The beauty wore of promise." Something of this sense of suddenly expanding horizons and of limitless possibilities through new beginnings survived the shock of first disappointment at events in France and carried over to the year 1797, when Wordsworth and Coleridge, in excited daily communion, set out to revolutionize the theory and practice of poetry. The product of these discussions was the *Lyrical Ballads* of 1798.

POETIC THEORY AND POETIC PRACTICE

Wordsworth undertook to justify the new poetry by a critical manifesto or statement of poetic principles, in the form of an extended Preface to the second edition of *Lyrical Ballads* in 1800. In it he set himself in opposition to the literary *ancien régime*, those writers of the preceding century who, to his view, had imposed on poetry artificial conventions which distorted its free and natural development. Wordsworth's later critical writings were largely attempts to clarify, buttress, or qualify points made in his first declaration. Coleridge declared that the Preface was "half a child of my own brain"; and although he soon developed doubts about certain of Wordsworth's unguarded statements, and undertook to correct them in *Biographia Literaria* (1817), he did not question the necessity of Wordsworth's attempt to overturn the reigning tradition. In the fashion of innovators, Wordsworth was more concerned with justifying his program against what he regarded as the poetic Establishment than with doing strict historical justice to his predecessors. In the course of the 18th century there had been increasing opposition to the neoclassic tradition of Dryden, Pope, and Dr. Johnson and to the dominance of satire, verse essay, and the poetry of wit; and especially in the 1740's and later, there had emerged many of the critical concepts, as well as a number of the poetic subjects and forms, which were later exploited by Wordsworth and his contemporaries. Wordsworth's Preface nevertheless deserves its reputation as marking a turning point in English literature, for Wordsworth gathered up largely isolated ideas, organized them into a coherent theory based on explicit critical principles, and made them the rationale for his own massive achievements as a poet. We can conveniently use some of the concepts in this extremely influential essay as points of departure for a survey of distinctive elements in the theory and poetry of the Romantic period.

1. *The Concept of Poetry.*

In neoclassic theory, poetry had been regarded as primarily an imitation of human life—in a favorite figure, "a mirror held up to nature"—in a form designed to instruct and give artistic pleasure to the reader. Wordsworth, in a reiterated statement, defined all good poetry as "the spontaneous overflow of powerful feelings." In a reversal of earlier aesthetic theory, he thus located the source of poetry not in the outer world, but in the individual poet, and identified as its essential material not men and their actions, but the fluid feelings of the writer himself. Other Romantic theories, however various, concurred in this crucial point by referring to the mind and feelings of the individual writer, instead of to the outer world, for the source and substance of a poem. Many writers identified poetry (in metaphors parallel to Wordsworth's "overflow") as the "expression" or "utterance" or "exhibition" of emotion. Blake and Shelley described a poem as the poet's private imaginative vision, which they opposed to the ordinary world of public experience. Coleridge regarded poetry as the product of the poet's imagination which—by a process that Coleridge called "a dim analogue" of God's own creative activity—assimilates the materials of sense into an organic entity that does not imitate the created world, but constitutes an equivalent creation of its own.

In accordance with the view that poetry expresses the poet's own mind and feelings, Romantic poems to an extraordinary extent take as their subject matter, not the actions of other men, but the personal experiences, thoughts, and feelings of the poets who wrote them. The lyric poem written in the first person, which had earlier been regarded as a minor poetic kind, became a major Romantic form and was usually described as the most essentially poetic of all the genres. And in the Romantic lyric the "I" is often not a mere *dramatis persona*, a typical lyric speaker such as the Petrarchan lover or Cavalier gallant of Elizabethan and 17th-century love poems, but is recognizably the poet in his private person. In the poems of Coleridge and Keats, for example, the experiences and states of mind expressed by the lyric speaker often accord closely with the personal confessions in the poets' letters and journals. Even in his ostensibly fictional writings, narrative and dramatic, Byron usually invites his readers to identify the hero with the author, whether the hero is presented romantically (as in *Childe Harold, Manfred*, or the Oriental tales) or in an ironic perspective (as in *Don Juan*). An extreme example of this subjective tendency is Wordsworth's *Prelude*, which is a poem of epic length and epic seriousness about the growth of the poet's own mind, while Wordsworth's projected but incompleted poem *The Recluse* was to have been a huge trilogy concerning "the sensations and opinions of a poet living in retirement," the first and third parts to consist "chiefly of meditations in the Author's own person." In contemporary prose, the equivalent development was the vogue of the personal essays of Charles Lamb, Hazlitt, and Leigh Hunt, and the currency of the intellectual or spiritual autobiography, whether fictionalized (Thomas Carlyle's *Sartor Resartus*) or presented as unaltered fact (Coleridge's *Biographia Literaria*, Thomas De Quincey's *Confessions of an English Opium Eater* and *Autobiographic Sketches*).

Naturally enough, in the applied criticism of an age which viewed poetry as an expressive activity, there emerged for the first time the peculiarly modern tendency to read the great poetry of the past—including the poetry of Milton, Shakespeare, Dante, and even Homer—as a revelation, more or less disguised, of the deep inner personality of the poet. By 1827 Carlyle could say, with considerable truth, that the great question usually raised by "the best of our own critics at present is a question mainly of a psychological sort, to be answered by discovering and delineating the peculiar nature of the poet from his poetry."

2. *Poetic Spontaneity and Freedom*.

It will be noted that Wordsworth defined good poetry not merely as the overflow but as "the *spontaneous* overflow" of feelings. In traditional aesthetic theory, poetry had been regarded as supremely an art; an art perfected by painstaking endeavor, which in modern times could be practiced successfully only by a craftsman who had assimilated classical precedents, was aware of the "rules" governing the kind of poem he was writing, and (except for the felicities which, as Pope said, are "beyond the reach of art") deliberately employed tested means to achieve foreknown effects upon his audience. But to Wordsworth, although the writing of a poem may be preceded by reflection and followed by second thoughts and revisions, the immediate act of composition must be spontaneous— that is, unforced, arising from impulse, and free from all rules and the artful manipulation of means to foreseen ends—if the product is to be a genuine poem and not an artificial sham. Other important Romantic critics also voiced declarations of artistic independence. Keats listed as an "axiom" that "if poetry comes not as naturally as the leaves to a tree it had better not come at all." Blake insisted that he wrote from "Inspiration and Vision," and that his long "prophetic" poem, *Milton*, was given to him by an agency not himself, and "produced without Labor or Study." Shelley also maintained that it is "an error to assert that the finest passages of poetry are produced by labor and study," and suggested instead that they are the products of an unconscious creativity: "A great statue or picture grows under the power of the artist as a child in the mother's womb." "The definition of genius," Hazlitt remarked, "is that it acts unconsciously." Despite their theoretical insistence on the total autonomy and spontaneity of poetic activity, however, the surviving work-sheets of the Romantic poets, as well as the testimony of observers, show that they worked and reworked their texts no less arduously—if perhaps more immediately and intensely under the impetus of first conception—than the craftsmen of earlier ages. Coleridge, who believed that truth lies in a union of opposites, came closer to the facts of Romantic practice when he claimed that the act of composing poetry involves the psychological contraries "of passion and of will, of *spontaneous* impulse and of *voluntary* purpose."

The emphasis in this period on the free activity of the imagination is related to a characteristic insistence that the products of the precise and systematic intellect fall far short of matching the complexity, nuances, and ambiguities of concrete human experience. It is also in accord with the contemporary insistence on the essential role of instinct, intuition, and the feelings of "the heart" to supplement the judgments of the purely logical faculty, "the head," whether in the province of artistic beauty, philosophical and religious truth, or moral goodness. "Deep thinking," Coleridge wrote, "is attainable only by a man of deep feeling, and all truth is a species of revelation"; hence, "a metaphysical solution that does not tell you something in the heart is grievously to be suspected as apocryphal."

3. *Romantic "Nature Poetry."*
In his Preface Wordsworth wrote that "I have at all times endeavored to look steadily at my subject"; and in a supplementary Essay later attached to *Lyrical Ballads,* although he paid handsome tribute to James Thomson's descriptive poem *The Seasons,* he complained that, from Dryden through Pope, there is scarcely an image from external nature "from which it can be inferred that the eye of the poet had been steadily fixed on his object." A glance at the table of contents of any collection of Romantic poems will indicate the astonishing degree to which the natural scene and its flora and fauna have become a primary poetic subject; while Wordsworth, Shelley, and even more Coleridge and Keats, described natural phenomena with an accuracy of observation which, although it profited from the many descriptive poems that had followed upon *The Seasons,* exceeded 18th-century precedent in its ability to capture the sensuous nuance.

As a consequence of the prominence of landscape in this period, "Romantic poetry" has to the popular mind become almost synonymous with "nature poetry." Neither Romantic theory nor Romantic practice, however, justifies the opinion that the aim of this poetry was description for its own sake. Wordsworth in fact insisted that the ability to observe and describe objects accurately, "though indispensable to a Poet, is one which he employs only in submission to necessity, and never for a continuance of time: as its exercise supposes all the higher qualities of the mind to be passive, and in a state of subjection to external objects." And while most of the great Romantic lyrics—Wordsworth's *Tintern Abbey* and *Ode: Intimations of Immortality,* Coleridge's *Frost at Midnight* and *Dejection,* Shelley's *Ode to the West Wind,* Keats's *Nightingale*—begin with an aspect or change of aspect in the natural scene, this serves only as stimulus to the most characteristic human activity, that of thinking. Romantic "nature poems" are in fact descriptive-meditative poems, in which the presented scene usually serves to raise an emotional problem whose development and resolution constitute the organizing principle of the poem. As Wordsworth said, not nature, but "the Mind of Man" is "my haunt, and the main region of my song."

In addition, Romantic poems habitually imbue the landscape with human life, passion, and expressiveness. In part such descriptions represent the poetic equivalent of the current metaphysical concept of nature, which had developed in deliberate revolt against the world views of Descartes and other scientific philosophers of the 17th and 18th centuries, who had posited as the ultimate reality a mechanical world consisting of physical particles in motion. What is needed in philosophy, Coleridge wrote, is "the substitution of life and intelligence * * * for the philosophy of mechanism, which, in everything that is most worthy of the human intellect, strikes *Death*. * * * " But for many Romantic poets it was clearly also a matter of immediate, unthinking experience to respond to the outer universe as to a living entity which shares the feelings of the observer. James Thomson and other descriptive poets had described the physical universe as giving direct access to God, and even as itself possessing the attributes of divinity; in *Tintern Abbey* and other poems Wordsworth exhibits toward the landscape attitudes and sentiments which men had earlier felt not only for God, but also for a father, a mother, or a beloved woman. Elsewhere, as in the great passage on crossing Simplon Pass (see *The Prelude* VI.624 ff.), Wordsworth also revives the ancient theological concept that God's creation constitutes a symbol system, in a huge book of physical revelation parallel to the Revelation in the Scriptures—

> Characters of the great Apocalypse,
> The types and symbols of Eternity,
> Of first, and last, and midst, and without end.

This view of natural objects as symbols possessing a natural correspondence to the spiritual world (which had persisted in many esoteric philosophies as well as in Christian theology), served also as the theoretical understructure for a Romantic tendency, exhibited in its extreme form by Blake and Shelley, to write a symbolist poetry in which a rose, a sunflower, a mountain, a cave, or a cloud are presented as objects instinct with a significance beyond themselves. "I always seek in what I see," Shelley said, "the likeness of something beyond the present and tangible object."

4. The Glorification of the Commonplace.

In two lectures on Wordsworth, one in a series on *The English Poets* (1815) and another in *The Spirit of the Age* (1825), Hazlitt declared that the school of poetry founded by Wordsworth was the literary equivalent of the French Revolution, translating political changes into poetical experiments. The parallel between the political and poetical revolution was especially evident in the leveling tendency of Wordsworth's subject matter: "Kings and queens were dethroned from their rank and station in legitimate tragedy or epic poetry, as they were decapitated elsewhere. * * * The paradox [these poets] set out with was that all things are by nature equally fit subjects for poetry; or that if there is any preference to be given, those that are the meanest and most unpromising are the best. * * * They claimed kindred only with the commonest of the people. * * * "

What Hazlitt had in mind was Wordsworth's statement that the aim of *Lyrical Ballads* was "to choose incidents and situations from common life," and to use a "selection of language really spoken by men"; the special source of this subject matter and the principal model for this language, Wordsworth went on to say, is "humble and rustic life." As Hazlitt shrewdly saw, this was more a social than a distinctively literary definition of the proper materials and language for poetry. What Hazlitt failed to observe, however, was that Wordsworth represented not so much an abrupt break with tradition as the culmination of a tendency through the preceding century to dissolve the traditional hierarchy of the genres and the traditional theory of poetic decorum, according to which an appropriate level of style—high, middle, or low—had to be matched to the status of the poetic kinds, ranging from epic and tragedy at the top down to the pastoral and short lyric forms at the base. Versifiers of the later decades of the 18th century had experimented in the simple treatment of simple subjects, and Robert Burns—like Wordsworth, a sympathizer with the French Revolution—had achieved great poetic success in the serious representation of humble life in a language really spoken by rustics. But Wordsworth buttressed his poetic practice by a theory which inverted the old hierarchy by elevating humble and rustic life and the plain style, earlier appropriate to the lowly pastoral, into the principal subject and medium for poetry in general. And in his own practice, as Hazlitt also noted, Wordsworth went even further, and turned for the subjects of his serious poems not only to humble people but to the ignominious, the outcast, the delinquent—to "convicts, female vagrants, gypsies * * * idiot boys and mad mothers," as well as to "peasants, peddlers, and village barbers." Hence the outrage of Lord Byron, who alone among his great Romantic contemporaries insisted that Dryden and Pope had laid out the proper road for poetry, and who—in spite of his liberalism in politics—maintained allegiance both to aristocratic proprieties and traditional poetic decorum:

> "Peddlers," and "Boats," and "Wagons"! Oh! ye shades
> Of Pope and Dryden, are we come to this?

But in his democratization of poetry, Hazlitt insisted, Wordsworth was "the most original poet now living, and the one whose writings could the least be spared." And certainly it was Wordsworth, far more than any 18th-century predecessor, who effected an immense enlargement of our imaginative sympathies and brought into the province of serious literature a range of materials and interests which are still being diligently explored by major writers of the present day.

It should be noted, however, that Wordsworth's aim in *Lyrical Ballads* was not a mere reproductive realism, but as he announced in his Preface, to throw over "situations from common life * * * a certain coloring of imagination, whereby ordinary things should be presented to the mind in an unusual aspect." Or as Coleridge expanded this statement in *Biographia Literaria*, Chapter XIV, Wordsworth's object was "to give the charm of novelty to things of every day, and to excite a feeling analogous to the supernatural, by awakening the mind's attention from the lethargy of custom, and directing it to the loveliness and wonders of the world before us." As these passages indicate, Wordsworth's concern in his poetry was not only with "common life" but with "ordinary *things*"; no one can read *The Prelude*, for example, without noticing the extraordinary reverence which he attaches to such words as "common," "ordinary," "everyday," "humble," whether applied to people, to events, or to the visible scene. His aim throughout is to shake us out of the lethargy of custom so as to refresh our sense of wonder in the everyday, the trivial, and the familiar.

Dr. Johnson had said that "wonder is a pause of reason," and that "all wonder is the effect of novelty upon ignorance." But for many Romantic critics, to arouse in the sophisticated mind that sense of wonder felt by the ignorant and the naïve was a primary power of imagination and a major function of poetry. Commenting on the special imaginative quality of Wordworth's early poetry (*Biographia,* Chapter VI), Coleridge commented: "To carry on the feelings of childhood into the powers of manhood; to combine the child's sense of wonder and novelty with the appearances, which every day for perhaps forty years had rendered familiar * * * this is the character and privilege of genius," and its effect on the reader is to awaken "freshness of sensation" in the representation of "familiar objects." Poetry, said Shelley in his *Defense of Poetry,* "reproduces the common universe" but "purges from our inward sight the film of familiarity which obscures from us the wonder of our being," and "creates anew the universe, after it has been blunted by reiteration." And in Carlyle's *Sartor Resartus* (1833–34), the chief—indeed the only—effect of the conversion of the protagonist from despairing unbelief is that he is able to sustain a sense of the "Natural Supernaturalism" in ordinary experience and so overcome the "custom" which "blinds us to the miraculousness of daily-recurring miracles."

Carlyle's terminology suggests that the Romantic attempt to apotheosize the lowly and the commonplace had a religious origin; it is a secular or nontheologial form of a central Christian doctrine: "the last shall be first." Wordsworth constantly endeavors to present a seemingly trivial person or thing or moment and show it suddenly transfigured, rendered luminous by an enduring and quasireligious significance. When he fails, as in the poem *We Are Seven,* the result verges on bathos. But often he wonderfully succeeds, as in his descriptions of such ordinary events as ice-skating, borrowing a rowboat without permission, and meeting an old blind beggar or a solitary leech-gatherer. In one of the events Wordsworth called "a spot of time," when he entered London for the first time, he describes how the "vulgar men about me, trivial forms * * * mean shapes" suddenly assumed a "weight and power" that lasted only a moment, "yet with Time it dwells, / And grateful memory, as a thing divine" (*The Prelude* VIII.543–59).

5. *The Supernatural and "Strangeness in Beauty."*

In most of his poems Coleridge, like Wordsworth, dealt with the everyday things of this world, and in *Frost at Midnight,* written in February of 1798, he showed how well he too could manage a natural supernaturalism and achieve the effect of wonder in the familiar. But according to the agreed division of labor between Wordsworth and Coleridge in writing *Lyrical Ballads,* Coleridge's special function, he tells us, was to achieve wonder by a frank violation of natural laws and the ordinary course of events, in poems of which "the incidents and agents were to be, in part at least, supernatural." And in *The Ancient Mariner, Christabel*, and *Kubla Khan*, Coleridge opened up to English poetry the realm of mystery and magic, in which ancient folklore, superstition, and demonology are used to startle and enthrall sophisticated readers by impressing them with the sense of occult powers and unknown modes of being. Such poems are usually set in the distant past or in faraway places, or both; the milieu of *Kubla Khan*, for example, exploits the exoticism both of the Middle Ages and of the Orient. Next to Coleridge, the greatest master of this Romantic mode was John Keats. In *La Belle Dame sans Merci* and *The Eve of St. Agnes* he adapted the old forms of ballad and romance to modern sophisticated use and, like Coleridge, exploited the charm of "the far away and long ago" by establishing a medieval setting for the events of magic and mystery. Hence the term "the medieval revival," frequently attached to the Romantic period, which comprehends also the ballad imitations and some of the verse tales and historical novels of Sir Walter Scott.

Another side of the tendency which Walter Pater later called "the addition of strangeness to beauty" was the Romantic interest in unusual modes of experience, of a kind which earlier writers had largely ignored as either too trivial or too aberrant for serious literary concern. Blake, Wordsworth, and Coleridge in their poetry explored aspects of those visionary states of consciousness which are common among children but which violate the standard categories of adult judgment. Coleridge was interested in mesmerism (what we now call hypnotism), shared with De Quincey a concern with dreams, nightmares, and the distortion of perception caused by drugs, and like Blake and Shelley, steeped himself in occult and esoteric doctrines—in "all the strange phantasms," as he called them, "that ever possessed your philosophy dreamers from Thoth the Egyptian to [Thomas] Taylor, the English Pagan." Byron exploited the fascination of the forbidden and the appeal of the terrifying Satanic hero. And Keats was extraordinarily sensitive to the ambivalence of human experience—to the mingling, at their highest intensity, of pleasure and pain, to the destructiveness of love, and to the erotic quality of the longing for death. Most of these phenomena had already been crudely explored by 18th-century writers of terror tales and Gothic fiction, and later in the 19th century all of them, sometimes exaggerated to the point of blatant abnormality, became the special literary province of Charles Baudelaire, Algernon Charles Swinburne, and other writers of the European Decadence.

INDIVIDUALISM, NONCONFORMITY, AND APOCALYPTIC EXPECTATION

Through the greater part of the 18th century, man had for the most part been viewed as a limited being in a strictly ordered and essentially unchanging world. A variety of philosophical and religious systems in this century coincided in a distrust of radical innovation, an emphasis on tradition and respect for the precedents established through the ages by the common sense of mankind, and the recommendation to man to set accessible goals and avoid extremes, whether in matters of politics, intellect, morality, or art. Many of the great literary works of the period, whatever their philosophical or religious differences, joined in attacking "pride," or man's persistent aspiration beyond the limits natural to his species. "The bliss of man," Pope wrote in *An Essay on Man*, "(could pride that blessing find) / Is not to act or think beyond mankind."

> This kind, this due degree
> Of blindness, weakness, Heaven bestows on thee.
> Submit.

The Romantic period, the age of burgeoning free enterprise and revolutionary hope, was also an age of radical individualism, in which both the philosophers and poets put an immensely higher estimate on man's potentialities and on his proper aims. In German post-Kantian philosophy, which generated many of the characteristic ideas of European Romanticism, the mind of man—what was called the "Subject" or "Ego"—took over various functions which had hitherto been the sole prerogative of Divinity. Most prominent was the rejection of a central 18th-century concept of the mind as a mirrorlike recipient of a universe already created and its replacement by the new concept of the mind as itself the creator of the universe it perceives. In the extreme version of the German idealist J. G. Fichte, all existence is a creation of the Ego, which sets up an external world merely to serve as a limit to itself, which it can then strive ceaselessly to overcome. The English founders of the new poetry also described the mind as creating its own experience, although they usually held that it performs this function in collaboration with the divine Creator, or with something given to it from without. Mind, wrote Coleridge in 1801, is "not passive" but "made in God's Image, and that too in the sublimest sense—the Image of the *Creator*." And Wordsworth declared in *The Prelude* (II.257–60) that the individual mind

> Doth, like an agent of the one great Mind
> Create, creator and receiver both,
> Working but in alliance with the works
> Which it beholds. * * *

Many Romantic writers also agreed that man's mind has an access beyond sense to the infinite, through a special faculty they called either Reason or Imagination. In *The Prelude* (VI.592 ff.) Wordsworth describes a flash of imagination "that has revealed / The invisible world," and affirms:

> Our destiny, our being's heart and home,
> Is with infinitude, and only there;
> With hope it is, hope that can never die,
> Effort, and expectation, and desire,
> And something evermore about to be.

The aspect of man which, to the moralists of the preceding age, had been his essential sin, or his tragic error, now becomes his glory and his triumph: he refuses to submit to his limitations and, though finite, persists in setting infinite, hence inaccessible goals. Wordsworth characteristically goes on to declare that "under such banners militant, the soul / Seeks for no trophies, struggles for no spoils"; for him, the militant striving is entirely spiritual, and ends in physical quietism and moral fortitude. But for other writers, especially in Germany, man's proper destiny is ceaseless activity—

a *"Streben nach dem Unendlichen,"* a striving for the infinite. This view is epitomized by Goethe's *Faust,* who in his quest for the unattainable violates ordinary moral limits, yet wins salvation by his very insatiability, which never stoops to contentment with any possibilities offered by this finite world. Man's infinite longing—in Shelley's phrase, "the desire of the moth for a star"—was a common theme also in the English literature of the day. "Less than everything," Blake announced, "cannot satisfy man." Shelley's *Alastor* and Keats's *Endymion* both represent the quest for an indefinable and inaccessible goal, and Byron's *Manfred* has for its hero a man whose "powers and will" reach beyond the limits of that human clay "which clogs the ethereal essence," so that "his aspirations / Have been beyond the dwellers of the earth."

In the contemporary theory of art, we find critics rejecting the neoclassic ideal of a limited intention, perfectly accomplished, in favor of "the glory of the imperfect," in which the artist's very failure attests the largeness of his aim. In a classic author like Sophocles, Coleridge said, "there is a completeness, a satisfying, an excellence, on which the mind can rest," but in Shakespeare there is "a dissatisfying, or falling short of perfection, yet so promising of our progression that we would not exchange it for that repose of mind * * * " And in their own work, Romantic writers often set themselves ambitious goals and experimented boldly in poetic language, versification, and design. They continued to cultivate a number of forms current in the later 18th century, including the sonnet, the extended lyric combining regional description and meditation, verse narratives of domestic and rural life, and songs written on the traditional themes of love, drink, and war. But especially in their longer poems, they struck out in new directions, and in the space of a few decades produced an astonishing variety of forms constructed on novel principles of organization and style. Blake's symbolic lyrics and visionary "prophetic" poems; Coleridge's strange ballad-narrative of sin and retribution, *The Ancient Mariner*; Wordsworth's epiclike spiritual autobiography, *The Prelude*; Shelley's cosmic symbolic drama, *Prometheus Unbound*; Keats's great sequence of *Odes* on the irreconcilable conflict in basic human desires; Byron's ironic survey of all European civilization, *Don Juan*—these depart sufficiently from their closest literary antecedents so that one might say of each of them, as Shelley said of *Don Juan*, that it was "something wholly new and relative to the age."

The great neoclassic writers had typically dealt with men as members of an organized, and usually an urban, society; of this society the author regarded himself as an integral part, its highest standards were those he spoke for, and to it as his audience he addressed himself. Some Romantic writers, on the other hand, deliberately isolated themselves from society. Wordsworth's projected masterwork he entitled *The Recluse,* and he described himself as "musing in solitude" on its subject, "the individual Mind that keeps her own / Inviolate retirement." And in almost all Wordsworth's poems, long or short, the words "single," "solitary," "by oneself," "alone" constitute a leitmotif; again and again his imagination is released by the sudden apparition of a single figure or object, standing out starkly against an undifferentiated background. Coleridge also, and still more strikingly, Byron and Shelley, liked to deal with a solitary protagonist who is separated from society because he has rejected it, or because it has rejected him; these poets thus introduced what developed into a persistent theme in many Victorian and modern writers, from Matthew Arnold through Thomas Mann, T. S. Eliot, and James Joyce—the theme of exile, of the disinherited mind which cannot find a spiritual home in its native land and society or in the whole modern world. The solitary Romantic nonconformist was sometimes also a great sinner. Writers of that time were fascinated by the outlaws of myth, legend, or history—Cain, Satan, Faust, the Wandering Jew or the great, flawed figure of Napoleon—about whom they wrote and on whom they modeled a number of their villains or their heroes. In Coleridge's *Ancient Mariner* (as in Wordsworth's *Guilt and Sorrow* and *Peter Bell*) the guilty outcast—"alone, alone, all, all alone"—is made to realize and expiate his sin against the community of living things, so that he may reassume his place in the social order. But in Byron the violator of conventional laws and limits remains proudly unrepentant. His hero Manfred, a compound of guilt and superhuman greatness, cannot be defeated by death, and wins the admiration even of the holy abbot by successfully defying the demons who, in the tradition of Marlowe's *Dr. Faustus,* have come to drag his soul to hell: I "was my own destroyer, and will be / My own hereafter * * * / Back, ye baffled fiends!" A more reputable Romantic hero, who turns up frequently in Byron and other writers and is made the protagonist of Shelley's greatest poem, is the Prometheus of Greek mythology. He shares with Satan the status of superlative nonconformity, since he sets himself in opposition to deity itself; unlike Satan, however, he is an unflawed nonconformist, because he acts as the champion rather than the enemy of the human race.

Nowhere is the Romantic combination of boundless aspiration and the reliance on the power of the individual mind better exhibited than in their literary treatment of the ultimate hope of mankind. The French Revolution had aroused in many sympathizers the millennial expectations which are deeply rooted in Hebrew and Christian tradition. "Few persons but those who have lived in it," Robert Southey reminisced in 1824, "can conceive or comprehend what the memory of the French Revolution was, nor what a visionary world seemed to open upon those who were just entering it. Old things seemed passing away, and nothing was dreamt of but the regeneration of the human race." Southey's language—like that of Wordsworth in *The Prelude* and Hazlitt in his autobiographical essays, when these writers described their early Revolutionary fervor—is Biblical; and it reflects the extent to which, in England, the Revolution was championed especially by members of radical Protestant sects, who envisioned it more or less explicitly on the model of Biblical prophecy. For the Biblical canon, which begins with the Creation, the felicity of Eden, and the abrupt Fall of Man, ends with the Apocalypse (literally, "Revelation" —the vision of the last things) of an equally abrupt return to felicity at Christ's Second Coming, first in an interim millennium (literally "one thousand years") of an earthly kingdom, and then, after the destruction of the original creation, in the eternity of "a new heaven and a new earth." The Biblical Book of Revelation symbolizes this ultimate event as a marriage between the holy city of New Jerusalem and Christ the Lamb. In 1794 Joseph Priestley, chemist, political radical, and leader of the Unitarian sect, published a sermon in which he interpreted the French Revolution as the stage preceding the millennium prophesied in Revelation. Coleridge in his *Religious Musings* (1794–96) followed Priestley in seeing the Revolution as the violent preliminary to the thousand years of earthly happiness, to be "followed by the passing away of this earth" in a new earth and heaven. And Blake's poems, *The French Revolution* (1791) and *America, a Prophecy* (1793), represent both these events, in apocalyptic terms, as portents of the last days of the fallen world.

The later course of the French Revolution, as we have seen, dashed the faith of most writers in violent political revolution as a way to the millennium. But a number of English poets did not abandon their apocalyptic hope; they salvaged it by giving it a new interpretation. They transferred the agency of apocalypse from mass action to the individual mind—from a political to a spiritual revolution—and proposed that "the new earth and new heaven" of Revelation is available here, now, to each man, if only he can make his visionary imagination triumph over his senses and logic-chopping understanding. Hence the extraordinary Romantic emphasis on a new way of *seeing* (which is the restoration of a lost earlier way of seeing) as man's chief aim in life. Blake's "Prophetic Books," for example, all deal with some aspect of the Fall and Redemption, and represent apocalypse as the recovery of the imaginative vision of things as they really are, seen "through and not with the eye." "The Last Judgment," he wrote, "is not Fable or Allegory, but Vision. * * * Vision or Imagination is a Representation of what Eternally Exists, Really and Unchangeably." "The Nature of my Work is Visionary or Imaginative; it is an Endeavor to Restore what the Ancients called the Golden Age." In some writers, this concept of the imaginative recreation of the old earth into a new earth is still expressed in the original Biblical metaphor of a marriage—although now it is not a marriage of the New Jerusalem with the Lamb, but a reintegration of man's inner faculties into spiritual unity, or else a marriage between man's mind and the external world. Coleridge put this latter version most succinctly, in *Dejection: An Ode*; it is the inner condition of "Joy," at life's highest moments, "Which, wedding nature to us, gives in dower / A new earth and new heaven." Wordsworth announced as the "high argument" for *The Recluse* (the same theme serves as underpattern for *The Prelude*) that "Paradise, and groves Elysian" are not "a history only of departed things"—

> For the discerning intellect of Man
> When wedded to this goodly universe
> In love and holy passion, shall find these
> A simple produce of the common day.

In Shelley's *Prometheus Unbound*, Prometheus represents archetypal man, whose total change of heart frees his imaginative capacity to envision a regenerate world; the fourth act symbolizes this event in the mode of a prodigious marriage celebration in which the whole cosmos participates. Carlyle's *Sartor Resartus*, to mention one more example, is the history of an individual's savage spiritual crisis and conversion, which turns out to be in fact the achievement of an individual apocalypse: "And I awoke to a new Heaven and a new Earth." But, as Carlyle goes on to indicate, this new earth is the same old earth, merely seen by his protagonist as though miraculously recreated, because he has learned to substitute the "Imaginative" faculty for what Carlyle represents as the chief faculty of the 18th-century Enlightenment, the "Logical, Mensurative faculty," or "Understanding." Writing in 1830–31, at the close of the period historians have labeled "Romantic," Carlyle thus summed up the tendency of a generation of writers to retain the ancient faith in apocalypse, but to interpret it not as a change in the world, but as a change in man's world view.

THE FAMILIAR ESSAY

At the close of the 18th century the reviews and magazines, written largely by hacks who acceded to the political bias and financial interests of the publisher and advertisers, had been mainly depositories of ill-assorted facts, news reports, reviews, letters, and general commentary. The essays they included were weak imitations of the type established nearly a century earlier by the single-essay periodicals, the *Tatler* and the *Spectator*; that is, they were uniformly short, primarily didactic, employed standard devices of stereotyped characters and anecdotes in the attempt to enliven morality with wit, and were preoccupied with the life and concerns of the leisure class and the "Town." In 1802, however, the *Edinburgh Review* inaugurated the modern type of periodical publication. It was established as an organ of the Whig reformers, but allowed considerable latitude to its writers, set its literary standards high, and was able to meet these standards by paying for contributions at rates good enough to command the best talents of the day. Francis Jeffrey, its editor, also contributed literary critiques to the journal; he was the chief of the "Scotch reviewers" in Byron's satire on *English Bards and Scotch Reviewers* (1809). Jeffrey's influence was so potent that it was said that one of his articles could affect the stock market. But his criticism has historical rather than permanent value, for Jeffrey, as he himself admitted, deliberately suppressed his own tastes in order to voice what he judged to be the common denominator of popular literary preferences.

The great and immediate success of this new enterprise stimulated the Tories to start the rival *Quarterly Review* in 1809 and *Blackwood's Edinburgh Magazine* in 1817. (A "review," usually issued four times yearly, consisted primarily of essays on important books and discussions of contemporary issues; a "magazine" was a monthly publication which printed more miscellaneous materials, including a high proportion of original essays, poems, and stories.) In 1820 appeared the *London Magazine*, liberal in politics and contemporary in literary interests; in its short but notable career until 1829, at which point it ceased publication, it printed the work of a group of brilliant writers, including the three men who soon established themselves as the greatest essayists of the age—Lamb, Hazlitt, and De Quincey. These magazines, and others like them, elevated the essay in literary dignity and quality and revolutionized its form and substance. They competed strenuously for talent, paying well enough so that an author (at least if he were as prolific as Hazlitt) could earn a living as a free-lance essayist. Since allotment of space was flexible, each topic could find its appropriate length, instead of being held to the Procrustean brevity of the earlier essays modeled on Addison and Steele; in consequence, the new essays tended to be from two to four times as long as the 18th-century form. And writers were treated as serious craftsmen who were competent, within broad limits, to write as they pleased.

Under these new conditions the familiar essay—a commentary on a nontechnical subject written in a relaxed and intimate manner—flourished, and in a fashion that to some degree paralleled the course of Romantic poetry. Each of the major essayists was in fact closely associated with important poets and supported at least some of the new poetic developments in critical commentaries whose perceptiveness and discrimination render them permanently valuable. Like the poets, these essayists were personal and subjective; their essays are often candidly autobiographical, reminiscent, self-analytic; and when the writers treated other matters than themselves, they did so impressionistically, so that the material is seen reflected in the particular temperament of the essayist. The subject matter of the essays, like that of the poetry, exhibits an extension of range and sympathy far beyond the earlier limits of the leisure class and its fashionable concerns, to comprehend clerks, chimney sweeps, poor relations, handball players, prizefighters, and murderers. Most strikingly, the essayists resemble the poets in rebelling against 18th-century conventions to revive prose forms long disused and to develop new prose styles and structural principles. The result was a notable variety of achievement, ranging from Hazlitt's hard-hitting plain style and seemingly casual order of topics, through Lamb's delicately contrived rhetoric and meticulously controlled organization, to De Quincey's elaborate experiments in applying to prose the rhythms, harmonies, and thematic structure of music.

DRAMA

Although favorable to the essay, literary conditions in the early 19th century were unfavorable in the extreme to writing for the stage. By a licensing act which was not repealed until 1843, only the Drury Lane and Covent Garden theaters had the right to produce "legitimate"—that is to say, spoken—drama; the other theaters were restricted by law to entertainments in which there could be no dialogue except to music, and so put on mainly dancing, pantomime, and various types of musical plays. The two monopoly theaters were vast and ill-lighted, and their audiences, constituted in large part by the more disreputable representatives of the lower classes, were noisy and unruly; as a result, actors played in a grandiose, elaborate, and orotund style. To succeed under such conditions, plays had also to be blatant and magniloquent, so that the drama of that period (fettered also by rigid moral and political censorship) tended to the extremes of either farce or melodrama. None of the plays written by the professional playwrights of the time have survived, except in the literary limbo of scholarly monographs on the history of the theater.

Nonetheless, attracted irresistibly by the example of their idolized Shakespeare, all the major Romantic poets, and many minor ones, tried their hand at poetic plays. Some of these were deliberate closet dramas—Byron's *Manfred* and Shelley's *Prometheus Unbound*, for example, can hardly be visualized, much less produced—but others were expressly written for the stage. The poets, however, lacked experience with the hard necessities of the practical theater, and they were unable to throw off the archaism and artificiality of a style dominated by Elizabethan and Jacobean models.

Above all, the genius of an age which excelled in the more subjective and expressive literary forms—lyric, spiritual autobiography, quasi-mythical narratives of magic and mystery, visionary and symbolic poems—was ill adapted to writing for the theater, which is a peculiarly social genre and must represent a variety of men other than the author himself. Even Byron, the only important poet of his generation to produce major work in a literary kind—satire—which requires a highly developed social sensibility, did not succeed as a practical dramatist. His stage plays, while readable, mainly exhibit various aspects of the Byronic hero; they lack theatrical vigor and variety, and their thin-skinned author wisely refused to let them be put on before the merciless and demonstrative audiences of his day. Coleridge achieved a minor hit with his tragedy *Remorse*, which ran for twenty nights at the Drury Lane in 1813. But the Romantic dramatist who came closest to theatrical and literary success was, surprisingly, Shelley. He hesitated for a long time to write his tragedy, *The Cenci* (1820), because, he said, he was as a poet "too metaphysical and abstract * * * to succeed as a tragedian." But in the play, with extraordinary tact and genuine theatrical acumen, Shelley converts a true Renaissance story— of a monstrous father who violates his daughter and is in turn murdered by her—into a powerful version of his own central fable of the instinctive desire of evil to destroy, by degrading, the defiant individual, and of the moral triumph of the unconquerable single spirit, even in death. The play was not acted until long after Shelley had died.

THE NOVEL

Two new types of fiction were prominent in the late 18th century. One was the "Gothic novel," which had been inaugurated in 1764 by Horace Walpole's *Castle of Otranto, A Gothic Story*. The term derives from the frequent setting of these tales in a gloomy castle of the Middle Ages, but it has been extended to a larger group of novels, set somewhere in the past, which exploit the possibilities of mystery and terror in sullen, craggy landscapes; decaying mansions with dank dungeons, secret passages, and stealthy ghosts; chilling supernatural phenomena; and often, persecution of a beautiful maiden by an obsessed and haggard villain. In her *Mysteries of Udolpho* (1794), and better still in *The Italian* (1797), Ann Radcliffe developed the figure of the mysterious and solitary *homme fatal*, torturing others because himself tortured by unspeakable guilt, who, though a villain, usurps the place of the hero in the reader's interest. Matthew Gregory Lewis, in *The Monk* (1797), which he wrote at the age of 20, has a similar protagonist, and brings to the fore the elements of diabolism, sensuality, and sadistic perversion which were pungent but discreetly submerged components in Mrs. Radcliffe's Gothic formula. The effects of Gothicism are apparent also in Romantic poetry: in Coleridge's medieval terror poem *Christabel*, in Byron's recurrent hero-villain, and in Shelley's inclinations (fostered by his early love for Gothic tales and his own youthful trials in that form) toward the fantastic and the macabre.

The second fictional mode popular at the turn of the century was the novel of purpose, often written to propagate the new social and political theories current in the period of the French Revolution. The best and most readable examples combine didactic intention with elements of Gothic terror. William Godwin, the political philosopher, wrote *Caleb*

Williams (1794) to illustrate the thesis that the lower classes are helplessly subject to the power and privilege of the ruling class, but he did
so in the form of a chilling story concerning the relentless pursuit and
persecution by a wealthy squire of the young secretary who has come
upon evidence that his employer has committed murder. And *Franken-
stein*, written in 1817 by Shelley's wife, Mary Godwin, fuses a horror
story about a fabricated monster with the social theme of the moral distortion imposed on an individual who, because he differs from the norm,
is rejected by society.

The Romantic period produced two great novelists, Jane Austen and
Sir Walter Scott. Jane Austen (1775–1817) was the one major author
who, untouched by the political, intellectual and artistic revolutions of
the age, stayed serenely within the cultural and literary traditions of the
neoclassic past. Charlotte Brontë, speaking for the Romantic sensibility,
complained that Jane Austen's novels lack warmth, enthusiasm, energy;
"she ruffles her reader by nothing vehement, disturbs him by nothing profound. The passions are perfectly unknown to her. * * * " But Jane
Austen deliberately elected to stay within the circumference of her own
experience—the life of provincial English gentlefolk—and to maintain
the decorum of the aloof and ironic novel of manners, based on such
18th-century antecedents as the comedy of manners of William Congreve and Richard Brinsley Sheridan and the comic fiction of Henry Fielding and his later followers, Fanny Burney and Maria Edgeworth. Within
these limits of both subject and form, Jane Austen achieved a fully particularized setting within which to examine the values men and women
live by in their everyday social lives.

Sense and Sensibility and *Northanger Abbey* poke fun at two latter
18th-century deviations from the humanistic norm, the cult of sensibility
and the taste for Gothic terrors. Her other novels, published between 1813
and 1818—*Mansfield Park, Persuasion*, and best of all, *Pride and Prejudice*
and *Emma*—all deal with the subject of getting married. Not only was
this in fact the central preoccupation and problem for the young leisure-
class lady of that age; it also afforded Jane Austen her best opportunities
for testing her heroines' practical sense and moral integrity, their degree of
knowledge of the world and of themselves, and their capacity to demonstrate grace under pressure.

Sir Walter Scott (1771–1832) was almost exactly contemporary with
Jane Austen, and admired her greatly, but his work in fiction was at the
opposite extreme from hers. In 1814, with the anonymous *Waverly*, he
turned from narrative verse (in which Byron had displaced him in popularity) to narrative prose, and managed to write almost thirty long works
of fiction in the eighteen years before he died. They are in the mode which
he himself defined as romance, "the interest of which turns upon marvelous
and uncommon incidents," in contrast to the novel such as Jane Austen
wrote, in which "the events are accommodated to the ordinary train of
human events, and the modern state of society." Scott's great originality
lay in opening up to fiction the realm of history; he does not scruple sometimes to alter the order of events for novelistic purposes, yet he maintains fidelity to the spirit of the past and a meticulous accuracy in antiquarian detail. His great series of Scottish novels, including *Guy Manner-*

ing, The Antiquary, Old Mortality, Rob Roy and (best of all) *The Heart of Midlothian,* are rooted in historical events from the 17th century up to his own time; *Ivanhoe* is set in 13th-century England and *Kenilworth* in the age of Elizabeth; and *Quentin Durward,* the best of his Continental romances, has for background the French Court of the 15th century.

Like his friend Byron, Scott wrote with dash and grandiosity in a kind of sustained improvisation; his plotting is often slovenly, his romantic lovers pallid, and his kings and chieftains large-scale puppets. But in his great scenes of action there is a scope and sweep that was not to be exceeded in fiction until the appearance of Leo Tolstoy's *War and Peace* in the 1860's. And although, unlike his liberal Romantic contemporaries, Scott's political sympathies were aristocratic and feudal, his most vivid and convincing characters belong in the middle and lower classes. His tradesmen, servants, peasantry, social outcasts, and demented old women, speaking a rich Scottish vernacular (Scott's dialogue, like Robert Burns's in verse, tended to become stilted and conventional when he wrote in standard English), compose a populous world in which each person is an individual, rooted in the circumstances of his time and place and class and occupation. Scott had an immense international vogue, equaling that of Byron and Goethe, and became the acknowledged master of some of the greatest 19th-century novelists, including Honoré de Balzac and Tolstoy. Jane Austen, on the other hand, during her lifetime was admired only by a limited group of English readers. But her novels have demonstrated greater staying power. Scott's combination of casualness in design and prodigality in detail puts off many readers who have formed their sensibilities on the well-made novel of the last 75 years. But even after the achievements of such craftsmen in the form as Henry James, Jane Austen remains the sovereign of the intricate, spare, and graceful art of the novel of manners.

ROBERT BURNS
(1759–1796)

1786: *Poems, Chiefly in the Scottish Dialect* (Kilmarnock edition).
1787: Begins collecting, editing, and writing songs for *The Scots Musical Museum.*

A favorite myth of later 18th-century primitivists was that there existed natural poets who warbled their native woodnotes wild, independent of art or literary tradition. These artless poets were sought among peasants and proletarians, whose caste or rural habitation, it was thought, protected them from contamination by the artificialities of civilized life and culture. When Robert Burns published his first volume of *Poems,* in 1786, he was at once hailed by the literati of Edinburgh as an instance of the natural genius, a "Heaven-taught plowman" whose poems were the spontaneous overflow of his native feelings. Burns himself sometimes fostered this belief, and rather enjoyed playing the role of the poet by instinct. But in fact he was a well-read (although largely self-educated) man, whose quick intelligence and sensibility enabled him to make the most of limited opportunities. And although he broke clear of the contemporary conventions of decayed English neoclassicism, he did so not by instinct but as a deliberate craftsman who turned to two earlier traditions for his models —the Scottish oral tradition of folklore and folk song, and the highly developed Scottish literary tradition, which goes back to the late Middle Ages.

His father—William Burnes, as he spelled his name—was a God-fearing and hard-working farmer of Ayrshire, a county in southwestern Scotland, who could not make a go of it in a period of hard times and high rents, and died in 1784, broken in body and spirit. Robert, with his brother Gilbert, was forced to do the toil of a man while still a boy, and began to develop the heart trouble of which he was to die when only 37. Although his father had the Scotsman's esteem for education and saw to it that his sons attended school whenever they could, Burns's education in literature, theology, politics, and philosophy came mainly from his own reading. At the age of 15 he fell in love, and was immediately inspired by that event to write his first song. "Thus," Burns said, "with me began Love and Poesy." After he reached maturity, Burns cultivated assiduously both these propensities. He began a series of amorous affairs, producing in 1785 the first of a number of illegitimate children; he also extended greatly the range and quantity of his attempts at poetry. So rapid was his development as a poet that by the time he published the Kilmarnock edition, at the age of 27, he had written all but a few of his greatest long poems.

The Kilmarnock volume (so named from the town in which it was published) was one of the most extraordinary first volumes by any British poet, and it had a great and immediate success. Burns was at once acclaimed "Caledonia's Bard" and was lionized by the intellectuals and gentlefolk when he visited Edinburgh soon after his book came out. In this milieu the peasant-poet soon demonstrated that he could more than hold his own as a brilliant conversationalist and debater. But he was also wise enough to realize that once the novelty wore off, his eminence in this society would not endure. He had a fierce pride which was quick to resent any hint of contempt or condescension toward himself as a man of low degree. His sympathies were democratic, and he was an outspoken admirer of the American Revolution and of the republican experiment in France. In religion, too, he was a radical, professing "the Religion of Sentiment and Reason" in opposition to the strict Calvinism in which he had been raised, and he offended many pious Presbyterians by his devastating satires against the rigid tenets and the moral authoritarianism of the Scottish kirk. Furthermore, his sexual irregularities were notorious, less because they were out of the common order at that time than because of his bravado in flaunting them before the "unco guid"—as his biographer, DeLancey Ferguson, has said, "it was not so much that he was conspicuously sinful as that he sinned conspicuously." Most of Burns's friends in high station quickly fell away, and his later visits to Edinburgh did not repeat the social success of the first.

In 1788 Burns was given a commission as Excise officer, or tax inspector, and he settled down with Jean Armour, his former mistress—now his wife—at Ellisland, near Dumfries, combining his official duties with farming. This was the fourth farm on which Burns had worked; and when it, like the others, failed, he moved his family to the lively country town of Dumfries. Here he was fairly happy, despite recurrent illness and a chronic shortage of money. He performed his official duties efficiently and was respected by his fellow townspeople and esteemed by his superiors; he was a devoted family man and father; and he accumulated a circle of intimates to whom he could repair for conversation and conviviality. In 1787 James Johnson, an engraver, had enlisted Burns's aid in collecting Scottish folk songs for an anthology called *The Scots Musical Museum*. Burns soon became the real editor for several volumes of this work, devoting all of his free time to collecting, editing, restoring, and imitating traditional songs, or writing verses of his own to traditional dance tunes. Almost all of his creative work, during the last twelve years of his life, went into the writing of songs for the *Musical Museum* and for George Thomson's *Select Collection of Original Scottish Airs*. This was for Burns a devoted labor of love and patriotism, done anonymously, for which he refused to accept any pay, although badly in need of money; and he continued the work when he was literally on his deathbed.

Burns's best work was written in Scots, a northern dialect of English spoken by Scottish peasants and (on other than formal occasions) by most 18th-century Scottish gentlemen as well. When Burns attempted to write in standard English the result—except in an occasional lyric such as the lucid and graceful *Afton Water*—was stilted and conventional, with all the stock phrasing, sententiousness, and sentimentality of the genteel poetic tradition of his day. He is often considered a "pre-Romantic" who, anticipating Wordsworth, revived the English lyric, exploited the literary forms and legends of folk culture, and wrote in the language really spoken by the common man. But this reputation is based primarily on his songs. By far the major portion of the poems Burns published under his own name are concerned with men and manners and fall, technically, in the favorite genres of 18th-century poets; they include brilliant satire in a variety of forms, a number of fine verse epistles to friends and fellow poets, and one masterpiece of mock-heroic (or at least, seriocomic) narrative, *Tam o' Shanter*. The claim could be supported that, next to Pope, Burns is the greatest 18th-century master of these literary types. Yet Burns's writings in satire, epistle, and mock-heroic are very remote from Pope's, in their heartiness and verve, no less than in their dialect and intricate stanza forms. The reason for the difference is that Burns turned for his models not to Horace and the English neoclassic tradition, but to the native tradition which had been established in the golden age of Scottish poetry by Robert Henryson, William Dunbar, Gavin Douglas, and other Scottish Chaucerians of the 15th and 16th centuries. He knew this literature through his 18th-century Scottish predecessors, especially Allan Ramsay and Robert Fergusson, who had collected some of the ancient poems and written new ones based on the ancient models. Burns improved on these predecessors, but he derived from them much that is characteristic in his literary forms, subjects, diction, and stanzas.

Burns's songs, however, are more widely known than his longer poems, and have in themselves been adequate to sustain his reputation as a major poet. He wrote over 300 of them, in unequaled abundance and variety. In them he surrenders himself wholeheartedly to the emotion of the moment, evoked by all the great lyric subjects: love, drink, work, friendship, patriotism, and bawdry. His poetic character is hearty, generous, rollicking, tender, with a sympathy that encompasses men of all types, from national heroes to tavern roarers; like all the great poets of humanity, Burns had that poetical character which Keats described: "It lives in gusto, be it foul or fair, high or low, rich or poor, mean or elevated. It has as much delight in conceiving an Iago as an Imogen." Burns is not only the national poet of Scotland but also a song writer for all English-speaking people. Everywhere in the world on New Year's Eve when, helped by drink and the reminder of their bondage to time, men indulge their instinct of a common humanity, they join hands and sing a song of Burns.

Corn Rigs[1] an' Barley Rigs

It was upon a Lammas night,[2]
   When corn rigs are bonnie,
Beneath the moon's unclouded light
   I held awa to Annie:
5 The time flew by wi' tentless° heed,   *careless*
   Till 'tween the late and early,

1. "Ridges," the space between plowed furrows.   2. I.e., early in August.

Wi' sma' persuasion she agreed
To see me through the barley.

      Chorus
Corn rigs, an' barley rigs,
10   An' corn rigs are bonnie:
I'll ne'er forget that happy night
Amang the rigs wi' Annie.

The sky was blue, the wind was still,
   The moon was shining clearly;
15 I set her down wi' right good will,
   Amang the rigs o' barley;
I kent° her heart was a' my ain;   *knew*
   I loved her most sincerely;
I kissed her owre and owre again
20   Amang the rigs o' barley.
             (*Chorus*)

I locked her in my fond embrace;
   Her heart was beating rarely;
My blessings on that happy place,
   Amang the rigs o' barley!
25 But by the moon and stars so bright,
   That shone that hour so clearly,
She ay° shall bless that happy night   *always*
   Amang the rigs o' barley.
             (*Chorus*)

I hae been blythe wi' comrades dear;
30   I hae been merry drinking;
I hae been joyfu' gath'rin gear;°   *possessions*
   I hae been happy thinking:
But a' the pleasures e'er I saw,
   Though three times doubled fairly,
35 That happy night was worth them a',
   Amang the rigs o' barley.
             (*Chorus*)
1783   1786

To a Mouse

ON TURNING HER UP IN HER NEST WITH THE PLOW, NOVEMBER, 1785[1]

Wee, sleekit,° cow'rin', tim'rous beastie,   *sleek*
O, what a panic's in thy breastie!
Thou need na start awa sae hasty,
       Wi' bickering brattle![2]

1. Burns's brother said that this poem was composed on the occasion it de-scribes.
2. With headlong scamper.

5 I wad be laith° to rin an' chase thee   *loath*
          Wi' murd'ring pattle!°   *plowstaff*

I'm truly sorry man's dominion
Has broken Nature's social union,
An' justifies that ill opinion
10   Which makes thee startle
At me, thy poor, earth-born companion,
          An' fellow mortal!

I doubt na, whiles,° but thou may thieve;   *sometimes*
What then? poor beastie, thou maun° live!   *must*
15 A daimen-icker in a thrave³
          'S a sma' request:
I'll get a blessin' wi' the lave,°   *remainder*
          And never miss 't!

Thy wee-bit housie, too, in ruin!
20 Its silly° wa's the win's are strewin'!   *feeble*
An' naething, now, to big° a new ane,   *build*
          O' foggage° green!   *moss*
An' bleak December's winds ensuin',
          Baith snell° an' keen!   *bitter*

25 Thou saw the fields laid bare and waste,
An' weary winter comin' fast,
An' cozie here, beneath the blast,
          Thou thought to dwell,
Till crash! the cruel coulter° passed   *cutter-blade*
30   Out-through thy cell.

That wee-bit heap o' leaves an' stibble°   *stubble*
Has cost thee mony a weary nibble!
Now thou's turned out, for a' thy trouble,
          But° house or hald,⁴   *without*
35 To thole° the winter's sleety dribble,   *endure*
          An' cranreuch° cauld!   *hoarfrost*

But Mousie, thou art no thy lane,⁵
In proving foresight may be vain:
The best-laid schemes o' mice an' men
40   Gang aft a-gley,⁶
An' lea'e us nought but grief an' pain,
          For promised joy.

Still thou art blest compared wi' me!
The present only toucheth thee:
45 But och! I backward cast my e'e
          On prospects drear!
An' forward though I canna see,
          I guess an' fear!

1785   1786

3. An occasional ear in 24 sheaves.   5. Not alone.
4. Hold, holding (i.e., land).   6. Go oft awry.

Green Grow the Rashes[7]

Chorus
Green grow the rashes, O;
  Green grow the rashes, O;
The sweetest hours that e'er I spend,
Are spent amang the lasses, O!

5 There's nought but care on ev'ry han',
  In ev'ry hour that passes, O:
What signifies the life o' man,
  An' 'twere na for the lasses, O.
      (Chorus)

The warly° race may riches chase,   *worldly*
10 An' riches still may fly them, O;
An' though at last they catch them fast,
  Their hearts can ne'er enjoy them, O.
      (Chorus)

But gie me a canny° hour at e'en,   *quiet*
  My arms about my dearie, O;
15 An' warly cares, an' warly men,
  May a' gae tapsalteerie,° O!   *topsy-turvy*
      (Chorus)

For you sae douce,° ye sneer at this,   *sober*
  Ye're nought but senseless asses, O:
The wisest man[8] the warl' saw,
20 He dearly loved the lasses, O.
      (Chorus)

Auld nature swears, the lovely dears
  Her noblest work she classes, O:
Her prentice han' she tried on man,
  An' then she made the lasses, O.
      (Chorus)

1784   1787

Holy Willie's Prayer[1]

O thou, wha in the Heavens dost dwell,
Wha, as it pleases best thysel',

7. Burns's revision of a song long current in a number of versions, most of them bawdy. "Rashes": rushes.
8. King Solomon.

1. This satire, in the form of a dramatic monologue, was inspired by one William Fisher, a self-righteous elder in the parish of Mauchline, and is directed

Sends ane to heaven and ten to hell,
   A' for thy glory,
5 And no for ony guid or ill
    They've done afore thee!

I bless and praise thy matchless might,
Whan thousands thou hast left in night,
That I am here afore thy sight,
10   For gifts an' grace
A burnin' an' a shinin' light,
   To a' this place.

What was I, or my generation,
That I should get sic exaltation?
15 I, wha deserve most just damnation,
   For broken laws,
Sax° thousand years 'fore my creation,   *six*
   Through Adam's cause.

When frae my mither's womb I fell,
20 Thou might hae plungéd me in hell,
To gnash my gums, to weep and wail,
   In burnin' lakes,
Where damnéd devils roar and yell,
   Chained to their stakes;

25 Yet I am here a chosen sample,
To show thy grace is great and ample;
I'm here a pillar in thy temple,
   Strong as a rock,
A guide, a buckler, an example
30   To a' thy flock.

O Lord, thou kens what zeal I bear,
When drinkers drink, and swearers swear,
And singin' there and dancin' here,
   Wi' great an' sma':
35 For I am keepit by thy fear
   Free frae them a'.

But yet, O Lord! confess I must
At times I'm fashed° wi' fleshly lust;   *troubled*
An' sometimes too, in warldly trust,
40   Vile self gets in;
But thou remembers we are dust,
   Defiled in sin.

O Lord! yestreen, thou kens, wi' Meg—
Thy pardon I sincerely beg;
45 O! may't ne'er be a livin' plague

against a basic Calvinist tenet of the old Scottish kirk. Holy Willie assumes that he is one of the small minority, God's "elect"; in other words, that he has been predestined for grace, no matter what he does in this vale of tears.

> To my dishonor,
> An' I'll ne'er lift a lawless leg
> Again upon her.
>
> Besides I farther maun° allow,   *must*
> 50 Wi' Lizzie's lass, three times I trow—
> But, Lord, that Friday I was fou,°   *drunk*
> When I cam near her,
> Or else thou kens thy servant true
> Wad never steer°her.   *molest*
>
> 55 May be thou lets this fleshly thorn
> Beset thy servant e'en and morn
> Lest he owre high and proud should turn,
> That he's sae gifted;
> If sae, thy hand maun e'en be borne,
> 60 Until thou lift it.
>
> Lord, bless thy chosen in this place,
> For here thou hast a chosen race;
> But God confound their stubborn face,
> And blast their name,
> 65 Wha bring thy elders to disgrace
> An' public shame.
>
> Lord, mind Gawn Hamilton's² deserts,
> He drinks, an' swears, an' plays at cartes,°   *cards*
> Yet has sae mony takin' arts
> 70 Wi' grit° an' sma',   *great*
> Frae God's ain priest the people's hearts
> He steals awa'.
>
> An' when we chastened him therefor,
> Thou kens how he bred sic a splore°   *disturbance*
> 75 As set the warld in a roar
> O' laughin' at us;
> Curse thou his basket and his store,
> Kail° and potatoes.   *broth*
>
> Lord, hear my earnest cry an' pray'r,
> 80 Against that presbyt'ry o' Ayr;
> Thy strong right hand, Lord, make it bare
> Upo' their heads;
> Lord, weigh it down, and dinna spare,
> For their misdeeds.
>
> 85 O Lord my God, that glib-tongued Aiken,
> My very heart and soul are quakin',
> To think how we stood sweatin', shakin',
> An' pissed wi' dread,
> While he, wi' hingin'° lips and snakin',°   *hanging / sneering*
> 90 Held up his head.

2. Burns's friend Gavin Hamilton, whom "Holy Willie" had brought up on moral charges before the Kirk Session of the Presbytery of Ayr; Hamilton was successfully defended by his counsel, Robert Aiken (referred to in line 85).

Lord, in the day of vengeance try him;
Lord, visit them wha did employ him,
And pass not in thy mercy by them,
      No hear their pray'r:
95 But, for thy people's sake, destroy them,
      And dinna spare.

But, Lord, remember me and mine
Wi' mercies temp'ral and divine,
That I for gear° and grace may shine   *goods, wealth*
100   Excelled by nane,
And a' the glory shall be thine,
      Amen, Amen!
1785   1789, 1799

Willie Brewed a Peck o' Maut[1]

O Willie brewed a peck o' maut,
    And Rob and Allan cam to see:
Three blither hearts, that lee-lang° night,   *livelong*
    Ye wad na found in Christendie.

    Chorus
5 We are na fou,° we're no that fou,   *drunk*
    But just a drappie° in our e'e;   *drop*
The cock may craw, the day may daw,
    And ay we'll taste the barley bree.°   *brew*

Here are we met, three merry boys,
10   Three merry boys, I trow, are we;
And mony a night we've merry been,
    And mony mae° we hope to be!   *more*
      (Chorus)

It is the moon, I ken her horn,
    That's blinkin' in the lift° sae hie;°   *air / high*
15 She shines sae bright to wyle° us hame,   *entice*
    But, by my sooth she'll wait a wee.
      (Chorus)

Wha first shall rise to gang awa,
    A cuckold, coward loun° is he!   *scoundrel*
Wha first beside his chair shall fa',
20   He is the king amang us three!
      (Chorus)

1790

1. This best-known of Burns's many efforts in the ancient tradition of the drinking song was written on the occasion of a "joyous meeting" of Burns and Allan Masterton "with Mr. Wm. Nicol, of the High School, Edinburgh." "Maut" is malt—i.e., barley allowed to germinate in water, a basic ingredient both in beer and in Scotch whisky.

Tam o' Shanter[1]

Of Brownyis and of Bogillis full is this Buke.
—Gavin Douglas

When chapman billies[2] leave the street,
And drouthy° neebors neebors meet,   *thirsty*
As market days are wearing late,
An' folk begin to tak the gate;°   *road*
5 While we sit bousing at the nappy,°   *strong ale*
An' getting fou° and unco° happy,   *drunk / very*
We think na on the lang Scots miles,
The mosses, waters, slaps,° and stiles,   *gaps (in walls)*
That lie between us and our hame,
10 Where sits our sulky sullen dame,
Gathering her brows like gathering storm,
Nursing her wrath to keep it warm.
This truth fand° honest Tam o' Shanter,   *found*
As he frae Ayr ae night did canter
15 (Auld Ayr, wham ne'er a town surpasses
For honest men and bonnie lasses).
O Tam! hadst thou but been sae wise
As ta'en thy ain wife Kate's advice!
She tauld thee weel thou was a skellum,[3]
20 A bletherin', blusterin', drunken blellum;°   *babbler*
That frae November till October,
Ae market day thou was na sober;
That ilka melder[4] wi' the miller
Thou sat as lang as thou had siller;°   *silver, money*
25 That every naig° was ca'd° a shoe on,   *nag / driven*
The smith and thee gat roarin' fou on;
That at the Lord's house, even on Sunday,
Thou drank wi' Kirkton Jean till Monday.
She prophesied that, late or soon,
30 Thou would be found deep drowned in Doon;

1. This poem was written to order for a book on Scottish antiquities, and was based on a witch story told about Alloway Kirk, an old ruin near Burns's house in Ayr. As a mock-heroic rendering of folk material, *Tam o' Shanter* is comparable to the Nun's Priest's Tale of Chaucer, in excellence as well as genre. Burns recognized that the poem was his most sustained and finished artistic performance; it discovers "a spice of roguish waggery," but also shows "a force of genius and a finishing polish that I despair of ever excelling." The verve and seriocomic sympathy with which Burns manages this misadventure of a confirmed tippler won Wordsworth, a water-drinker, to passionate advocacy against the moralists who objected to Burns's ribaldry: "Who but some impenetrable dunce or narrow-minded puritan in works of art ever read without delight the picture which he has drawn of the convivial exaltation of the rustic adventurer, Tam o' Shanter? * * * I pity him who cannot perceive that, in all this, though there was no moral purpose, there is a moral effect" (letter to a friend of Burns, 1816).
2. Peddler fellows.
3. Good-for-nothing; "bletherin' ": chattering.
4. A "melder" is the amount of corn processed at a single grinding. "Ilka": every.

Or catched wi' warlocks° in the mirk°   *wizards / night*
By Alloway's auld haunted kirk.
    Ah, gentle dames! it gars° me greet°   *makes / weep*
To think how mony counsels sweet,
₃₅ How mony lengthened sage advices,
The husband frae the wife despises!
    But to our tale: Ae market night,
Tam had got planted unco right,
Fast by an ingle,° bleezing° finely,   *fireplace / blazing*
₄₀ Wi' reaming swats,[5] that drank divinely;
And at his elbow, Souter° Johnny,   *Cobbler*
His ancient, trusty, drouthy crony;
Tam lo'ed him like a very brither;
They had been fou for weeks thegither.
₄₅ The night drave on wi' sangs and clatter,
And ay the ale was growing better:
The landlady and Tam grew gracious,
Wi' favors secret, sweet, and precious;
The souter tauld his queerest stories;
₅₀ The landlord's laugh was ready chorus:
The storm without might rair° and rustle,   *roar*
Tam did na mind the storm a whistle.
    Care, mad to see a man sae happy,
E'en drowned himsel amang the nappy.
₅₅ As bees flee hame wi' lades o' treasure,
The minutes winged their way wi' pleasure;
Kings may be blest, but Tam was glorious,
O'er a' the ills o' life victorious!
    But pleasures are like poppies spread—
₆₀ You seize the flow'r, its bloom is shed;
Or like the snow falls in the river—
A moment white, then melts forever;
Or like the borealis race,
That flit ere you can point their place;
₆₅ Or like the rainbow's lovely form
Evanishing amid the storm.
Nae man can tether time nor tide;
The hour approaches Tam maun° ride;   *must*
That hour, o' night's black arch the keystane,
₇₀ That dreary hour, he mounts his beast in;
And sic a night he taks the road in,
As ne'er poor sinner was abroad in.
    The wind blew as 'twad blawn its last;
The rattling show'rs rose on the blast;
₇₅ The speedy gleams the darkness swallowed;
Loud, deep, and lang, the thunder bellowed:
That night, a child might understand,
The Deil had business on his hand.
    Weel mounted on his gray mare, Meg,

5. Foaming new ale.

80 A better never lifted leg,
    Tam skelpit° on through dub° and mire,   *slapped / puddle*
    Despising wind, and rain, and fire;
    Whiles holding fast his gude blue bonnet;
    Whiles crooning o'er some auld Scots sonnet;
85 Whiles glowring° round wi' prudent cares,   *staring*
    Lest bogles° catch him unawares.   *hobgoblins*
    Kirk-Alloway was drawing nigh,
    Whare ghaists° and houlets° nightly cry.   *ghosts / owls*
      By this time he was cross the ford,
90 Where in the snaw the chapman smoored;[6]
    And past the birks° and meikle stane,[7]   *birches*
    Where drunken Charlie brak 's neck bane;
    And through the whins,[8] and by the cairn,[8a]
    Where hunters fand the murdered bairn;
95 And near the thorn, aboon the well,
    Where Mungo's mither hanged hersel.
    Before him Doon pours all his floods;
    The doubling storm roars through the woods;
    The lightnings flash from pole to pole;
100 Near and more near the thunders roll:
    When, glimmering through the groaning trees,
    Kirk-Alloway seemed in a bleeze;
    Through ilka bore° the beams were glancing;   *hole*
    And loud resounded mirth and dancing.
105   Inspiring bold John Barleycorn!
    What dangers thou canst make us scorn!
    Wi' tippenny,[9] we fear nae evil;
    Wi' usquebae,° we'll face the devil!   *whisky*
    The swats sae reamed in Tammie's noddle,
110 Fair play, he cared na deils a boddle![1]
    But Maggie stood right sair astonished,
    Till, by the heel and hand admonished,
    She ventured forward on the light;
    And, vow! Tam saw an unco° sight!   *strange*
115 Warlocks and witches in a dance!
    Nae cotillon brent° new frae France,   *brand*
    But hornpipes, jigs, strathspeys,[2] and reels,
    Put life and mettle in their heels.
    A winnock-bunker° in the east,   *window seat*
120 There sat auld Nick, in shape o' beast—
    A touzie tyke,[3] black, grim, and large!
    To gie them music was his charge:
    He screwed the pipes and gart° them skirl.°   *made / screech*
    Till roof and rafters a' did dirl.°   *rattle*
125 Coffins stood round like open presses,

6. The peddler smothered.
7. Big stone.
8. Furze (an evergreen shrub).
8a. Stones heaped up as a memorial.
9. Twopenny (of drink).

1. I.e., he didn't care a farthing about devils (a "boddle" is a very small copper coin).
2. Slow Highland dance.
3. Shaggy dog.

That shawed the dead in their last dresses;
And by some devilish cantraip° sleight   *charm, trick*
Each in its cauld hand held a light,
By which heroic Tam was able
130 To note upon the haly° table   *holy*
A murderer's banes in gibbet airns;°   *irons*
Twa span-lang,[4] wee, unchristened bairns;
A thicf new-cutted frae the rape°—   *rope*
Wi' his last gasp his gab° did gape;   *mouth*
135 Five tomahawks, wi' blude red rusted;
Five scimitars, wi' murder crusted;
A garter, which a babe had strangled;
A knife, a father's throat had mangled,
Whom his ain son o' life bereft—
140 The gray hairs yet stack to the heft;
Wi' mair of horrible and awfu',
Which even to name wad be unlawfu'.
     As Tammie glowred, amazed, and curious,
The mirth and fun grew fast and furious:
145 The piper loud and louder blew;
The dancers quick and quicker flew;
They reeled, they set, they crossed, they cleekit,°   *joined hands*
Till ilka carlin° swat and reekit,   *old woman*
And coost her duddies to the wark,[5]
150 And linkit° at it in her sark!°   *tripped lightly / shirt*
     Now Tam, O Tam! had thae been queans,°   *girls*
A' plump and strapping in their teens;
Their sarks, instead o' crecshic flannen,[6]
Been snaw-white seventeen hunder ' linen!
155 Thir° breeks o' mine, my only pair,   *these*
That ance were plush, o' gude blue hair,
I wad hae gi'en them off my hurdies,°   *buttocks*
For ae blink o' the bonnie burdies!°   *maidens*
     But withered beldams, auld and droll,
160 Rigwoodie° hags wad spean° a foal,   *bony / wean*
Louping° and flinging on a crummock,°   *leaping / staff*
I wonder didna turn thy stomach.
     But Tam kent what was what fu' brawlie°   *finely*
There was ae winsome wench and walie°   *strapping*
165 That night enlisted in the core,°   *corps*
Lang after kent on Carrick shore!
(For mony a beast to dead she shot,
And perished mony a bonnie boat,
And shook baith meikle corn and bear,°   *barley*
170 And kept the countryside in fear.)
Her cutty° sark, o' Paisley harn,°   *short / yarn*
That while a lassie she had worn,
In longitude though sorely scanty,

---

4. Span-long (i.e., the distance from outstretched thumb to little finger).
5. Cast off her clothes for the work.
6. Greasy flannel.
7. Very fine linen, woven on a loom with 1700 strips.

It was her best, and she was vauntie.°   *proud*
175 Ah! little kent thy reverend grannie
    That sark she coft° for her wee Nannie   *bought*
    Wi' twa pund Scots ('twas a' her riches)
    Wad ever graced a dance of witches!
       But here my muse her wing maun cour;°   *lower*
180 Sic flights are far beyond her pow'r—
    To sing how Nannie lap and flang
    (A souple jade she was, and strang);
    And how Tam stood, like ane bewitched,
    And thought his very een enriched;
185 Even Satan glowred, and fidged fu' fain,[8]
    And hotched° and blew wi' might and main: *jerked*
    Till first ae caper, syne° anither,   *then*
    Tam tint° his reason a' thegither,   *lost*
    And roars out, "Weel done, Cutty-sark!"
190 And in an instant all was dark!
    And scarcely had he Maggie rallied,
    When out the hellish legion sallied.
      As bees bizz out wi' angry fyke°   *fuss*
    When plundering herds° assail their byke,°   *herdsmen / hive*
195 As open° pussie's mortal foes   *begin to bark*
    When pop! she starts before their nose,
    As eager runs the market crowd,
    When "Catch the thief!" resounds aloud.
    So Maggie runs; the witches follow,
200 Wi' mony an eldritch° skriech and hollow.   *unearthly*
      Ah, Tam! ah, Tam! thou'll get thy fairin'!°   *deserts*
    In hell they'll roast thee like a herrin'!
    In vain thy Kate awaits thy comin'!
    Kate soon will be a woefu' woman!
205 Now do thy speedy utmost, Meg,
    And win the keystane o' the brig:°   *bridge*
    There at them thou thy tail may toss,
    A running stream they darena cross.
    But ere the keystane she could make,
210 The fient a tail she had to shake![9]
    For Nannie, far before the rest,
    Hard upon noble Maggie pressed,
    And flew at Tam wi' furious ettle;°   *intent*
    But little wist she Maggie's mettle!
215 Ae spring brought off her master hale,°   *whole*
    But left behind her ain gray tail:
    The carlin claught° her by the rump,   *clutched*
    And left poor Maggie scarce a stump.
      Now, wha this tale o' truth shall read,
220 Each man and mother's son, take heed;
    Whene'er to drink you are inclined,
    Or cutty-sarks rin in your mind,

8. Fidgeted with pleasure.   9. I.e., she had no tail left at all.

Think! ye may buy the joys o'er dear;
Remember Tam o' Shanter's mare.
1790   1791

Afton Water[1]

Flow gently, sweet Afton, among thy green braes,
Flow gently, I'll sing thee a song in thy praise;
My Mary's asleep by thy murmuring stream,
Flow gently, sweet Afton, disturb not her dream.

Thou stock-dove whose echo resounds through the glen,   5
Ye wild whistling blackbirds in yon thorny den,
Thou green-crested lapwing, thy screaming forbear,
I charge you disturb not my slumbering fair.

How lofty, sweet Afton, thy neighboring hills,
Far marked with the courses of clear winding rills;   10
There daily I wander as noon rises high,
My flocks and my Mary's sweet cot[2] in my eye.

How pleasant thy banks and green valleys below,
Where wild in the woodlands the primroses blow;
There oft as mild evening weeps over the lea,   15
The sweet-scented birk[3] shades my Mary and me.

Thy crystal stream, Afton, how lovely it glides,
And winds by the cot where my Mary resides;
How wanton thy waters her snowy feet lave,
As gathering sweet flowerets she stems thy clear wave.   20

Flow gently, sweet Afton, among thy green braes,
Flow gently, sweet river, the theme of my lays;
My Mary's asleep by thy murmuring stream,
Flow gently, sweet Afton, disturb not her dream.
1789   1792

Ae Fond Kiss[4]

Ae fond kiss, and then we sever!
Ae fareweel, and then forever!
Deep in heart-wrung tears I'll pledge thee,
Warring sighs and groans I'll wage thee.
Who shall say that fortune grieves him   5

1. The Afton is a small river in Ayrshire. "Braes": slopes, hillsides.
2. Cottage.
3. Birch.
4. Written to Mrs. M'Lehose, with
whom Burns had been engaged in a
sentimental correspondence, on the occasion of her departure to rejoin her husband in the West Indies.

While the star of hope she leaves him?
Me, nae cheerfu' twinkle lights me,
Dark despair around benights me.

I'll ne'er blame my partial fancy,
Naething could resist my Nancy; 10
But to see her was to love her,
Love but her, and love forever.
Had we never loved sae kindly,
Had we never loved sae blindly,
Never met—or never parted, 15
We had ne'er been broken-hearted.

Fare thee weel, thou first and fairest!
Fare thee weel, thou best and dearest!
Thine be ilka joy and treasure,
Peace, enjoyment, love, and pleasure! 20
Ae fond kiss, and then we sever;
Ae fareweel, alas, forever!
Deep in heart-wrung tears I'll pledge thee,
Warring sighs and groans I'll wage thee.

1791   1792

Ye Flowery Banks[1]

Ye flowery banks o' bonnie Doon,
    How can ye blume sae fair?
How can ye chant, ye little birds,
    And I sae fu' o' care?

5 Thou'll break my heart, thou bonnie bird,
    That sings upon the bough;
Thou minds me o' the happy days,
    When my fause° luve was true.   *false*

Thou'll break my heart, thou bonnie bird,
10   That sings beside thy mate;
For sae I sat, and sae I sang,
    And wist na o' my fate.

Aft hae I roved by bonnie Doon,
    To see the woodbine twine,
15 And ilka° bird sang o' its luve,   *every*
    And sae did I o' mine.

Wi' lightsome heart I pu'd° a rose   *pulled*
    Frae aff its thorny tree;
But my fause luver staw° my rose,   *stole*
20   And left the thorn wi' me.

1. Burns wrote several versions of this song; the present one is the simplest and the best.

Wi' lightsome heart I pu'd a rose
  Upon a morn in June;
And sae I flourished on the morn,
  And sae was pu'd ere noon.

1792, 1808

Scots, Wha Hae[2]

Scots, wha hae wi' Wallace[3] bled,
Scots, wham Bruce has aften led,
Welcome to your gory bed,
    Or to victorie.

Now's the day, and now's the hour;   5
See the front o' battle lour;
See approach proud Edward's power—
    Chains and slaverie!

Wha will be a traitor-knave?
Wha can fill a coward's grave?   10
Wha sae base as be a slave?
    Let him turn and flee!

Wha for Scotland's King and law
Freedom's sword will strongly draw,
Freeman stand, or freeman fa',   15
    Let him follow me!

By oppression's woes and pains!
By your sons in servile chains!
We will drain our dearest veins,
    But they shall be free!   20

Lay the proud usurpers low!
Tyrants fall in every foe!
Liberty's in every blow!
    Let us do, or die!

1793   1794, 1815

For A' That and A' That[1]

Is there, for honest poverty,
  That hangs his head, and a' that?

2. In this best-known of Burns's patriotic songs, Robert Bruce is addressing his army before the great victory at Bannockburn (1314), at which the English were driven from Scotland.
3. Sir William Wallace (ca. 1272–1305), the great Scottish warrior in the wars against the English.
1. Burns's vigorous affirmation of the radical ideas of liberty, equality, and fraternity may have been based on Tom Paine's *Rights of Man.*

The coward slave, we pass him by,
  We dare be poor for a' that!
5   For a' that, and a' that,
      Our toils obscure, and a' that;
  The rank is but the guinea's stamp,
    The man's the gowd° for a' that.   *gold*

What though on hamely fare we dine,
10 Wear hodden-gray,[2] and a' that;
Gie fools their silks, and knaves their wine,
  A man's a man for a' that:
    For a' that, and a' that,
      Their tinsel show, and a' that;
15   The honest man, though e'er sae poor,
      Is king o' men for a' that.

Ye see yon birkie,° ca'd a lord,   *brisk young fellow*
  Wha struts, and stares, and a' that;
Though hundreds worship at his word,
20 He's but a coof° for a' that: *dolt*
    For a' that, and a' that,
      His riband, star, and a' that,
  The man of independent mind,
      He looks and laughs at a' that.

25 A prince can mak a belted knight,
  A marquis, duke, and a' that;
But an honest man's aboon° his might,   *above*
  Guid faith he mauna fa' that![3]
    For a' that, and a' that,
30   Their dignities, and a' that,
  The pith o' sense, and pride o' worth,
    Are higher rank than a' that.

Then let us pray that come it may,
  As come it will for a' that,
35 That sense and worth, o'er a' the earth,
  May bear the gree,[4] and a' that.
    For a' that, and a' that,
      It's coming yet, for a' that,
  That man to man the warld o'er
40   Shall brothers be for a' that.

1794   1795, 1799

A Red, Red Rose[1]

O My Luve's like a red, red rose,
  That's newly sprung in June;

2. A coarse cloth of undyed wool.
3. Must not claim that.
4. Win the prize.

1. Like many of Burns's songs, this
one incorporates elements from several
current folk songs.

O My Luve's like the melodie
   That's sweetly played in tune.

As fair art thou, my bonnie lass,   5
   So deep in luve am I;
And I will luve thee still, my dear,
   Till a' the seas gang dry.

'Till a' the seas gang dry, my dear,
   And the rocks melt wi' the sun: 10
O I will love thee still, my dear,
   While the sands o' life shall run.

And fare thee weel, my only luve,
   And fare thee weel awhile!
And I will come again, my luve,   15
   Though it were ten thousand mile.

1796

Auld Lang Syne[1]

Should auld acquaintance be forgot,
   And never brought to min'?
Should auld acquaintance be forgot,
   And days o' lang syne?

       Chorus
5   For auld lang syne, my dear,
       For auld lang syne,
       We'll tak a cup o' kindness yet,
       For auld lang syne.

We twa hae run about the braes,°   *slopes*
10   And pu'd the gowans° fine,   *daisies*
But we've wandered mony a weary foot,
   Sin' auld lang syne.
       (*Chorus*)

We twa hae paidled i' the burn,°   *stream*
   From morning sun till dine;°   *dinner, noon*
15 But seas between us braid° hae roared,   *broad*
   Sin' auld lang syne.
       (*Chorus*)

And there's a hand, my trusty fiere,°   *friend*
   And gie's a hand o' thine;
And we'll tak a right gude-willie waught,[2]
20   For auld lang syne.
       (*Chorus*)

And surely ye'll be° your pint-stowp,°   *pay for / pint-cup*
   And surely I'll be mine;

1. Long ago.   2. A very hearty swig.

And we'll tak a cup o' kindness yet,
For auld lang syne.
(*Chorus*)
1788   1796

WILLIAM BLAKE

(1757–1827)

1783: *Poetical Sketches*, his first book of poems.
1794: *Songs of Innocence and of Experience*.
1804–20: The two last and greatest "prophetic" poems, *Milton* and *Jerusalem*.

What Blake called his "Spiritual Life" was as varied, free, and dramatic as his "Corporeal Life" was simple, limited, and unadventurous. His father was a London haberdasher. His only formal education was in art: at the age of 10 he entered a drawing school and later studied for a time at the school of the Royal Academy of Arts. At 14 he was apprenticed for seven years to a well-known engraver, James Basire, read widely in his free time, and began to try his hand at poetry. At 24 he married Catherine Boucher, daughter of a market gardener. She was then illiterate, but Blake taught her to read and to help him in his engraving and printing. In the early and somewhat sentimentalized biographies, Catherine is represented as an ideal wife for an unorthodox and impecunious genius—gentle, forbearing, and resourceful, with an unswerving faith in her husband's visions and God-given powers. Blake, however, must have been a trying domestic partner, and his vehement attacks on the oppression and torment caused by a possessive, jealous female will, which reached a climax in 1793 and remained prominent in his writings for another decade, may well reflect a troubled period at home. The couple were childless.

The Blakes for a time enjoyed a moderate prosperity while Blake gave drawing lessons, illustrated books, and engraved designs made by other artists. When the demand for his work slackened, Blake in 1800 moved to a cottage at Felpham, on the Sussex seacoast, under the patronage of the wealthy poetaster, biographer, and amateur of the arts, William Hayley, who with the best of narrow intentions tried to transform Blake into a conventional artist and breadwinner. But the caged eagle soon rebelled. Hayley, Blake wrote, "is the Enemy of my Spiritual Life while he pretends to be the Friend of my Corporeal."

At Felpham in 1803 occurred an event that left a permanent mark on Blake's mind and art. He had an altercation with one John Scholfield, a private in the Royal Dragoons. Blake ordered the soldier out of his garden and, when the soldier replied with threats and curses against Blake and his wife, pushed him the fifty yards to the inn where he was quartered. Scholfield brought charges that Blake had uttered seditious statements about King and country. Despite Blake's insistence that Scholfield had perjured himself, he was indicted and brought to trial. Since England was at war with France, sedition was a hanging offense. Blake was acquitted; an event, according to a newspaper account, "which so gratified the auditory that the court was * * * thrown into an uproar by their noisy exultations." Nevertheless Scholfield, his fellow-soldier Cock, and other participants in the trial haunted Blake's imagination and were enlarged to demonic characters who play a sinister role in *Jerusalem*. The event exacerbated Blake's sense that ominous forces were at work in the contemporary world and led him to complicate the symbolic obliquities by which he veiled the unorthodoxy of his political, religious, and moral opinions, and the radicalism of the many allusions to contemporary affairs that he worked into his poems.

After three years at Felpham Blake moved back to London, determined to follow his "Divine Vision" though it meant a life of isolation, misunderstanding, and poverty. When his one great bid for public recognition, a one-man show put on in 1809, proved a total failure, Blake passed into almost complete obscurity. Only when he was in his 60's did he finally attract a small but devoted group of young painters who served as an audience for his work and his talk. Blake's old age was serene, self-confident, and joyous, largely free from the bursts of irascibility with which he had earlier responded to the shallowness and blindness of the English public. He died in his seventieth year.

Blake's first book of poems, *Poetical Sketches*, which he had printed when he was 26 years old, demonstrated his dissatisfaction with the reigning poetic tradition and his restless quest for new forms and techniques. For lyric models he turned back to the Elizabethan and early 17th-century poets, to the Ossianic poems, Collins, Thomas Chatterton, and other 18th-century writers outside the tradition of Pope; he also experimented with partial rhymes and novel rhythms and employed bold figures of speech that at times approximate the status of symbols. In *Songs of Innocence* (1789) Blake inaugurated the method of publication he used for all his later original works, a procedure he had partly invented. He drew text and illustrations as a total pictorial design with an acid-proof substance directly on the copper plate, then applied acid so that the design was left in relief. With this plate he printed a page, which he later colored with water colors by hand and bound with the other pages to make up a volume. The procedure of making the plates was laborious and time-consuming, and Blake struck off very few copies of his works; for example, of *Songs of Innocence and Experience* 27 copies (both complete and incomplete) are known to exist; of *The Book of Thel*, 15; of *The Marriage of Heaven and Hell*, 9; of *Milton*, 4; and of *Jerusalem*, 5. The existing works are a unique fusion of text, picture, and decoration; it must be remembered that to read Blake's poem in a printed text is to see only an abstraction from what, in its original version, was an integral and mutually illuminating combination of words and design.

In the *Songs of Innocence* Blake assumes the stance that he is writing "happy songs / Every child may joy to hear." They show the fallen world, however, as it appears to the limited view of a naïve and acquiescent innocence; and some of the songs, such as "The Chimney Sweeper" and "Holy Thursday," are deeply equivocal, hinting the possibility of a different evaluation of the events they represent. This "contrary" vision is expressed in *Songs of Experience* (1794), which reveal an ugly and terrifying world of poverty, disease, prostitution, war, exploitation, and social, institutional, and sexual repression. In the best of these Songs, such as *The Tyger* and *London*, Blake achieved his mature lyric technique of compressed metaphor and symbol which explode into a multiplicity of reference.

Gradually Blake's symbolic thinking about human history and his personal experience of life and suffering articulated themselves in the "Giant Forms" and their actions, which constitute a complete mythology. As Los said, speaking for all imaginative artists, "I must Create a System or be enslaved by another Man's." This coherent but constantly altering and enlarging system composed the subject matter, first of Blake's "minor prophecies," completed by 1795, and then of the major prophetic books on which he continued working until about 1820: *The Four Zoas, Milton,* and *Jerusalem.*

In his 60's Blake gave up poetry to devote himself to pictorial art. In the course of his life he produced hundreds of paintings and engravings, many of them illustrations for the work of other poets, including a representation of Chaucer's Canterbury pilgrims, a superb set of designs for the Book of Job, and a series of illustrations of Dante, on which he was still hard at work when he died. At the time of his death Blake was little known as an artist and almost entirely unknown as a poet. In the mid-19th century he acquired a group of admirers among the Pre-Raphaelites, who regarded him as a precursor, and since then his reputation and influence have been growing steadily both in England and abroad. Since the mid 1920's, Blake has finally come into his own, both in poetry and painting, as one of the most dedicated, intellectually challenging, and astonishingly original of artists.

The explication of Blake's large, cryptic, and complex prophetic books has been the preoccupation of many scholars. Blake wrote them in the persona, or "voice," of "the Bard / Who Present, Past, & Future sees"— that is, as a British poet who follows Spenser, and especially Milton, in a lineage going back to the poet-prophets of the Bible. "The Nature of my Work," he said, "is Visionary or Imaginative." What Blake meant by the key terms "vision" and "imagination," however, is often misrepresented by taking literally what he, speaking the traditional language of his great predecessors, intended in a figurative sense. "That which can be made Explicit to the Idiot," Blake declared, "is not worth my care." Blake was a born ironist who enjoyed mystifying his well-meaning but literal-minded friends and who took a defiant pleasure in shocking the dull and complacent "angels" of his day by being deliberately outrageous in representing his work and opinions.

Blake declared "warmly" that "all he knew was in the Bible," and that "The Old & New Testaments are the Great Code of Art." This is an exaggeration of the truth that all his prophetic writings deal, in various formulations, with some aspects of the over-all Biblical plot of the creation and fall of man, the history of the generations of man in the fallen world, redemption, and the promise of a recovery of Eden and of a New Jerusalem. These events, however, Blake interprets in his own way—a way for which he had considerable precedent, not so much in the Neoplatonic and occult thinkers with which some modern commentators align him as in the "spiritual" interpreters of the Bible among the radical Protestant sects in 17th- and 18th-century England. In *The French Revolution, America: A Proph-*

ecy, *Europe: A Prophecy,* and the trenchant prophetic satire, *A Marriage of Heaven and Hell*—all of which Blake wrote in the early 1790's while he was an ardent supporter of the French Revolution—he, like Wordsworth, Coleridge, Southey, and a number of radical English theologians, represented the contemporary Revolution as the purifying violence that, according to Biblical prophecy, was the portent of the imminent redemption of man and the world. In Blake's later writings, however, Orc, the fiery spirit of revolution, gives way as central personage to Los, the type of the visionary imagination in the fallen world—an index of Blake's shift of emphasis from apocalypse by revolution to apocalypse by imagination.

BLAKE'S MATURE MYTH

Blake's first attempt to articulate his full myth of mankind's present, past, and future was *The Four Zoas,* begun in 1796 or 1797—later than any of the works represented here. A passage from the opening statement of its theme will exemplify the long verse line (what Blake called "the march of long resounding strong heroic verse") in which he wrote all his Prophetic Books and will serve also to indicate in broad outline the myth, or visualizable imaginative form, in which Blake's thought embodied itself:

> Four Mighty Ones are in every Man: a Perfect Unity
> Cannot Exist, but from the Universal Brotherhood of Eden,
> The Universal Man. To Whom be Glory Evermore, Amen. * * *
> Los was the fourth immortal starry one, & in the Earth
> Of a bright Universe Empery attended day & night
> Days & nights of revolving joy, Urthona was his name
> In Eden; in the Auricular Nerves of Human life
> Which is the Earth of Eden, he his Emanations propagated. * * *
> 　　　　　　　　　Daughter of Beulah, Sing
> His fall into Division & his Resurrection to Unity.

Blake's mythical premise, or starting point, is not a transcendent God but "The Universal Man" who is himself God and who incorporates the cosmos as well. (Blake elsewhere describes this founding image as "the Human Form Divine" and names him "Albion.") The fall, in this myth, is not the fall of man away from God but a falling apart of primal man, a "fall into Division." In this event the original sin is what Blake calls "selfhood," the attempt of an isolated part to be self-sufficient. The break-up of the all-inclusive Universal Man in Eden into exiled parts, it is evident, identifies the fall of man with the creation—both of man and of nature, as we ordinarily know them. Universal Man divides first into the "Four Mighty Ones" who are the Zoas, or chief faculties of man, and these in turn divide sexually into male Spectres and female Emanations. (Thus in the quoted passage the Zoa known in the unfallen state as Urthona, the imaginative power, separates into the form of Los in the fallen world.) In addition to Eden there are three successively lower "states" of being in the fallen world, which Blake calls Beulah (a pastoral condition of easy and relaxed innocence, without clash of "contraries"), Generation (the realm of common human experience, suffering, and conflicting contraries), and Ulro (Blake's hell, the lowest state, or limit, of bleak rationality, tyranny, static negation, and isolated selfhood). The fallen world moves through the cycles of its history, successively approaching and falling away from redemption, until, by the agency of the Redeemer (who is equated

with the human imagination and is most potently operative in the poet),
it will culminate in an apocalypse. In terms of his controlling image of the
Universal Man, Blake describes this apocalypse as a return to the original,
undivided condition, "his Resurrection to Unity."

Blake, although he did not know it, shared with a number of contemporary German philosophers the point of view—it has in our own time
become the prevailing point of view—that man's fall, and the malaise of
modern culture, is essentially a mode of psychic disintegration, and that
man's hope of recovery lies in a process of reintegration. As an imaginative
poet, however, Blake does not present this view in abstract conceptual
terms, but embodies it in picturable agents acting out an epic plot. What is
confusing to many readers is that Blake uses different ways of representing
the same vision of man in the world. For example, Blake alternates with
his image of the division of Primal Man, the representation of the fall as a
catastrophic alteration of vision in individual human beings. The result of
this alteration was that the cosmos, which in the original mode of unified
perception had been beheld as human and one, came to be seen as a multitude
of isolated individuals in a de-humanized and alien nature. Conversely, the
apocalypse toward which Blake—the imaginative artist who as an individual
represents the mythical type-figure Los—is always working, is to enable all
men to break through to a restored unity of vision. To such a vision all
beings, together with the world they inhabit, will again be perceived as
sharing the one life and the one humanity of that "Universal Brotherhood,"
the Human Form Divine, who is imaged as creating such a universe by the
very act of so envisioning it. Although Blake decries, as the mythical being
"Vala," what we ordinarily mean by "nature," it is a mistake to equate his
views with any form of ascetic otherworldliness; he does not look forward
to a consummation that will wipe out the fleshly and the natural world and
replace it by a transcendental substitute. Blake maintained, on the contrary,
that we achieve redemption by liberating and intensifying the bodily
senses—as he said, by "an improvement of sensual enjoyment"—and by
attaining and sustaining that mode of vision that does not cancel the fallen
world, but transfigures it, by revealing the lineaments of its eternal imaginative form. That is what Blake means when, in *A Vision of the Last Judgment* (included below), he says that "The Nature of my Work is Visionary
or Imaginative; it is an Endeavour to Restore what the Ancients called the
Golden Age"; that "All Things are comprehended in their Eternal Forms
in the Divine body of the Saviour . . . The Human Imagination"; and
that in the moment of apocalyptic redemption "Error or Creation will be
Burnt Up & then & not till then Truth or Eternity will appear. It is Burnt
up the Moment Men cease to behold it." Accordingly, in the apocalypse
that concludes *Jerusalem*, the reunion of Albion the Universal Man with
Jerusalem, his emanation, is accompanied by a freeing of man's senses and
the annihilation of his selfhood and results in the recovery of a lost mode
of vision that sees all men in brotherhood, dwelling in a nature which,
because it is humanized, is a place where individual men, united as One
Man, can feel at home: "& they walked / To & fro in Eternity as One Man
reflecting each in each & clearly seen / And seeing," in a setting which consists of "Human Forms identified, even Tree Metal Earth & Stone."

The text for all of Blake's writings is that of *The Poetry and Prose of*

William Blake, edited by David V. Erdman and Harold Bloom (New York, 1965). Blake's often erratic spelling and punctuation have been altered when the original form might mislead the modern reader.

From POETICAL SKETCHES[1]

Song

How sweet I roam'd from field to field,
 And tasted all the summer's pride,
'Till I the prince of love beheld,
 Who in the sunny beams did glide!

He shew'd me lilies for my hair,   5
 And blushing roses for my brow;
He led me through his gardens fair,
 Where all his golden pleasures grow.

With sweet May dews my wings were wet,
 And Phoebus fir'd my vocal rage;[2]   10
He caught me in his silken net,
 And shut me in his golden cage.

He loves to sit and hear me sing,
 Then, laughing, sports and plays with me;
Then stretches out my golden wing,   15
 And mocks my loss of liberty.

                                                    1783

To the Evening Star

Thou fair-hair'd angel of the evening,
Now, while the sun rests on the mountains, light
Thy bright torch of love; thy radiant crown
Put on, and smile upon our evening bed!
Smile on our loves; and, while thou drawest the   5
Blue curtains of the sky, scatter thy silver dew
On every flower that shuts its sweet eyes
In timely sleep. Let thy west wind sleep on

1. *Poetical Sketches*, Blake's only volume of poems to be set in type, went to press in 1783, but was never put on sale. A preface written by an anonymous friend apologized for the poems on the ground that they had been composed between the ages of 12 and 20. Although, like the work of other youthful poets, they echo earlier writers, many of them show remarkable originality. Some are radical experiments in meter and rhyme; *To the Evening Star* shows Blake's boldness in metaphor (lines 8–10); while in this same sonnet (lines 11–14) and in the *Song* ("How sweet I roam'd"), the images begin to assume the added reach of meaning that characterizes Blake's mature symbolism.
2. Fervor.

The lake; speak silence with thy glimmering eyes,
And wash the dusk with silver. Soon, full soon,   10
Dost thou withdraw; then the wolf rages wide,
And the lion glares thro' the dun forest:
The fleeces of our flocks are cover'd with
Thy sacred dew: protect them with thine influence.[3]

1783

Song[4]

Memory, hither come,
    And tune your merry notes;
And, while upon the wind,
    Your music floats,
I'll pore upon the stream,   5
Where sighing lovers dream,
And fish for fancies as they pass
Within the watery glass.

I'll drink of the clear stream,
    And hear the linnet's song;   10
And there I'll lie and dream
    The day along:
And, when night comes, I'll go
    To places fit for woe;
Walking along the darken'd valley,   15
    With silent Melancholy.

1783

Mad Song[5]

The wild winds weep,
    And the night is a-cold;
Come hither, Sleep,
    And my griefs infold:
But lo! the morning peeps   5
    Over the eastern steeps,
And the rustling birds of dawn
The earth do scorn.

---

3. In astrology, the technical term for the occult power of stars over men.
4. Cf. *Under the Greenwood Tree* in *As You Like It* II.v.
5. Cf. the songs of the Fool in Shakespeare's great scene of madness and incipient madness in *King Lear*, Act. III. In a marginal comment on Spurzheim's *Observations on Insanity* (1817), Blake wrote: "Cowper came to me & said, 'O that I were insane always; I will never rest. * * * You retain health & yet are as mad as any of us all—over us all—mad as a refuge from unbelief—from Bacon Newton & Locke.' " (Cowper, like the other 18th-century poets, Christopher Smart and William Collins, went genuinely insane.)

Lo! to the vault
   Of pavéd heaven,   10
With sorrow fraught
   My notes are driven:
They strike the ear of night,
   Make weep the eyes of day;
They make mad the roaring winds,   15
   And the tempests play.

Like a fiend in a cloud
   With howling woe,
After night I do croud,
   And with night will go;   20
I turn my back to the east,
From whence comforts have increas'd;
For light doth seize my brain
   With frantic pain.

                 1783

To the Muses

Whether on Ida's [6] shady brow,
   Or in the chambers of the East,
The chambers of the sun, that now
   From antient melody have ceas'd;

Whether in Heav'n ye wander fair,   5
   Or the green corners of the earth,
Or the blue regions of the air,
   Where the melodious winds have birth;

Whether on chrystal rocks ye rove,
   Beneath the bosom of the sea   10
Wand'ring in many a coral grove,
   Fair Nine,[7] forsaking Poetry!

How have you left the antient love
   That bards of old enjoy'd in you! [8]
The languid strings do scarcely move!   15
   The sound is forc'd, the notes are few!

                 1783

---

6. Ida is a mountain in southern Phrygia, celebrated in classical mythology.
7. The nine Muses.

8. The poem is Blake's lament, in the diction of latter 18th-century poetry, over the failure of the inspiration of the "bards," the older British poet-prophets.

From SONGS OF INNOCENCE AND OF EXPERIENCE

SHEWING THE TWO CONTRARY STATES OF THE HUMAN SOUL

From Songs of Innocence[1]

1789

The Author & Printer   W Blake

Introduction

Piping down the valleys wild
Piping songs of pleasant glee
On a cloud I saw a child,
And he laughing said to me,

"Pipe a song about a Lamb";   5
So I piped with merry chear;
"Piper pipe that song again"—
So I piped, he wept to hear.

"Drop thy pipe thy happy pipe
Sing thy songs of happy chear";   10
So I sung the same again
While he wept with joy to hear.

"Piper sit thee down and write
In a book that all may read"—
So he vanish'd from my sight.   15
And I pluck'd a hollow reed,

And I made a rural pen,
And I stain'd the water clear,
And I wrote my happy songs
Every child may joy to hear.   20

1789

1. *Songs of Innocence* was etched in 1789 and in 1794 was combined with other poems under the title above. Innocence is the state of the soul which, in these poems, is represented by the naïve outlook of the child who believes what he is told by his elders, and takes appearance for the reality and the best aspect of things for the whole truth. A number of the Songs represent this state in the mode of a pastoral or protected world. In other Songs, however, such as *The Chimney Sweeper* and *Holy Thursday,* a contrary possibility intrudes its ironic perspective, to reveal how precarious is the ignorantly innocent outlook upon the world.

But children need to grow up, and the state of innocence needs to yield to that of experience, which sees as real the world of materialism, poverty, oppression, prostitution, disease, and war, epitomized in the ghastly city of modern London. Some of the individual songs of innocence have a matched counterpart, or "contrary," in a terrifying song of experience; thus the meek lamb is replaced by the flaming, wrathful tiger. In Blake's later writings the "contrary states" become a dialectic of contraries, according to which naïve innocence must necessarily pass through and assimilate the opposing state of experience if it is to move on, by an act of imagination, to the third state, comprehending but transcending both the others, which he called "organized innocence."

The Lamb

Little Lamb, who made thee?
Dost thou know who made thee?
Gave thee life & bid thee feed,
By the stream & o'er the mead;
Gave thee clothing of delight,   5
Softest clothing wooly bright;
Gave thee such a tender voice,
Making all the vales rejoice!
  Little Lamb who made thee?
  Dost thou know who made thee?   10

Little Lamb I'll tell thee,
Little Lamb I'll tell thee!
He is calléd by thy name,
For he calls himself a Lamb:
He is meek & he is mild,   15
He became a little child:
I a child & thou a lamb,
We are calléd by his name.
  Little Lamb God bless thee.
  Little Lamb God bless thee.   20

1789

The Divine Image

To Mercy, Pity, Peace, and Love,
All pray in their distress:
And to these virtues of delight
Return their thankfulness.

For Mercy, Pity, Peace, and Love,   5
Is God, our father dear:
And Mercy, Pity, Peace, and Love,
Is Man, his child and care.

For Mercy has a human heart,
Pity, a human face: 10
And Love, the human form divine,
And Peace, the human dress.

Then every man of every clime,
That prays in his distress,
Prays to the human form divine,   15
Love, Mercy, Pity, Peace.

And all must love the human form,
In heathen, Turk, or Jew.
Where Mercy, Love, & Pity dwell,
There God is dwelling too.   20

1789

The Chimney Sweeper

When my mother died I was very young,
And my father sold me while yet my tongue
Could scarcely cry " 'weep! 'weep! 'weep! 'weep!" [2]
So your chimneys I sweep & in soot I sleep.

There's little Tom Dacre, who cried when his head   5
That curl'd like a lambs back, was shav'd, so I said,
"Hush, Tom! never mind it, for when your head's bare,
You know that the soot cannot spoil your white hair."

And so he was quiet, & that very night,
As Tom was a-sleeping he had such a sight!   10
That thousands of sweepers, Dick, Joe, Ned, & Jack,
Were all of them lock'd up in coffins of black;

And by came an Angel who had a bright key,
And he open'd the coffins & set them all free;
Then down a green plain, leaping, laughing they run,   15
And wash in a river and shine in the Sun;

Then naked & white, all their bags left behind,
They rise upon clouds, and sport in the wind.
And the Angel told Tom, if he'd be a good boy,
He'd have God for his father & never want joy.   20

And so Tom awoke; and we rose in the dark
And got with our bags & our brushes to work.
Tho' the morning was cold, Tom was happy & warm;
So if all do their duty, they need not fear harm.

1789

Nurse's Song

When the voices of children are heard on the green
And laughing is heard on the hill,
My heart is at rest within my breast
And everything else is still.

"Then come home my children, the sun is gone down   5
And the dews of night arise;
Come, come, leave off play, and let us away
Till the morning appears in the skies."

2. The child's lisping attempt at the chimney sweeper's street cry, "Sweep! Sweep!"

"No, no, let us play, for it is yet day
And we cannot go to sleep;   10
Besides, in the sky, the little birds fly
And the hills are all coverd with sheep."

"Well, well, go & play till the light fades away
And then go home to bed."
The little ones leapéd & shouted & laugh'd   15
And all the hills ecchoéd.

ca. 1784   1789

Holy Thursday[3]

'Twas on a Holy Thursday, their innocent faces clean,
The children walking two & two, in red & blue & green,
Grey headed beadles[4] walkd before with wands as white as snow,
Till into the high dome of Paul's they like Thames' waters flow.

O what a multitude they seemd, these flowers of London town!   5
Seated in companies they sit with radiance all their own.
The hum of multitudes was there, but multitudes of lambs,
Thousands of little boys & girls raising their innocent hands.

Now like a mighty wind they raise to heaven the voice of song,
Or like harmonious thunderings the seats of heaven among.   10
Beneath them sit the aged men, wise guardians of the poor;
Then cherish pity, lest you drive an angel from your door.[5]

ca. 1784   1789

The Little Black Boy

My mother bore me in the southern wild,
And I am black, but O! my soul is white;
White as an angel is the English child:
But I am black as if bereav'd of light.

My mother taught me underneath a tree,   5
And sitting down before the heat of day,
She took me on her lap and kisséd me,
And pointing to the east, began to say:

"Look on the rising sun: there God does live,
And gives his light, and gives his heat away;   10

3. In the English church, the Thursday celebrating the ascension of Jesus (forty days after Easter). It was the custom on this day to march the children from the charity schools of London to a service at St. Paul's Cathedral.

4. Lower church officers, one of whose duties is to keep order.
5. Hebrews xiii.2:"Be not forgetful to entertain strangers: for thereby some have entertained angels unawares."

And flowers and trees and beasts and men receive
Comfort in morning, joy in the noon day.

"And we are put on earth a little space,
That we may learn to bear the beams of love,
And these black bodies and this sun-burnt face   15
Is but a cloud, and like a shady grove.

"For when our souls have learn'd the heat to bear,
The cloud will vanish; we shall hear his voice,
Saying: 'Come out from the grove, my love & care,
And round my golden tent like lambs rejoice.' "   20

Thus did my mother say, and kisséd me;
And thus I say to little English boy:
When I from black and he from white cloud free,
And round the tent of God like lambs we joy,

I'll shade him from the heat till he can bear   25
To lean in joy upon our father's knee;
And then I'll stand and stroke his silver hair,
And be like him, and he will then love me.

                                                                  1789

From Songs of Experience

1794

The Author & Printer   W Blake

Introduction

Hear the voice of the Bard!
Who Present, Past, & Future sees;
Whose ears have heard
The Holy Word
That walk'd among the ancient trees;[6]   5

Calling the lapséd Soul
And weeping in the evening dew;
That might controll
The starry pole,
And fallen, fallen light renew!   10

6. Genesis iii.8: "And [Adam and Eve] heard the voice of the Lord God walking in the garden in the cool of the day." The Bard, whose imagination is not bound by time, has heard the voice of the Lord in Eden and calls to the fallen ("lapsed") soul and to the fallen Earth to turn full to the light and stop its endless cycle of alternating light and darkness. In Blake's symbolism the starry sky ("floor") and the margin of the sea ("watery shore")—see the final stanza—are symbols of the rigid rational order and the temporal and spatial bondage imposed on the free imagination by the material world known through the "corporeal eye."

"O Earth, O Earth, return!
Arise from out the dewy grass;
Night is worn,
And the morn
Rises from the slumberous mass.   15

"Turn away no more;
Why wilt thou turn away?
The starry floor
The watry shore
Is giv'n thee till the break of day."   20

1794

Earth's Answer

Earth rais'd up her head,
From the darkness dread & drear.
Her light fled:
Stony dread!
And her locks cover'd with grey despair.   5

"Prison'd on watry shore
Starry Jealousy does keep my den,
Cold and hoar
Weeping o'er
I hear the Father of the ancient men.[7]   10

"Selfish father of men,
Cruel, jealous, selfish fear!
Can delight
Chain'd in night
The virgins of youth and morning bear?   15

"Does spring hide its joy
When buds and blossoms grow?
Does the sower
Sow by night,
Or the plowman in darkness plow?   20

"Break this heavy chain
That does freeze my bones around;
Selfish! vain!
Eternal bane!
That free Love with bondage bound."   25

1790–92

1794

7. The character Blake called "Urizen" in his later prophetic works. He represents perceptual, rational, and moral tyranny that binds the mind to the sensible order of time and space and imposes upon sexual desire (as upon all forms of creative human energy) the stultifying and distorting bondage of selfishness, fear, secrecy, shame, and jealousy.

The Clod & the Pebble

"Love seeketh not Itself to please,
Nor for itself hath any care;
But for another gives its ease,
And builds a Heaven in Hell's despair."

So sang a little Clod of Clay,   5
Trodden with the cattle's feet;
But a Pebble of the brook,
Warbled out these metres meet:

"Love seeketh only Self to please,
To bind another to its delight;   10
Joys in another's loss of ease,
And builds a Hell in Heaven's despite."

1790–92   1794

Holy Thursday

Is this a holy thing to see,
In a rich and fruitful land,
Babes reducd to misery,
Fed with cold and usurous hand?

Is that trembling cry a song?   5
Can it be a song of joy?
And so many children poor?
It is a land of poverty!

And their sun does never shine,
And their fields are bleak & bare,   10
And their ways are fill'd with thorns;
It is eternal winter there.

For where-e'er the sun does shine,
And where-e'er the rain does fall,
Babe can never hunger there,   15
Nor poverty the mind appall.

1790–92   1794

The Chimney Sweeper

A little black thing among the snow
Crying "'weep, 'weep," in notes of woe!
"Where are thy father & mother? say?"
"They are both gone up to the church to pray.

"Because I was happy upon the heath,   5
And smil'd among the winter's snow;
They clothéd me in the clothes of death,
And taught me to sing the notes of woe.

"And because I am happy, & dance & sing,
They think they have done me no injury,   10
And are gone to praise God & his Priest & King,
Who make up a heaven of our misery."
1790–92   1794

Nurse's Song

When the voices of children, are heard on the green
And whisprings are in the dale,
The days of my youth rise fresh in my mind,
My face turns green and pale.

Then come home my children, the sun is gone down   5
And the dews of night arise;
Your spring & your day are wasted in play,
And your winter and night in disguise.
1790–92   1794

The Sick Rose

O Rose, thou art sick.
The invisible worm
That flies in the night
In the howling storm

Has found out thy bed   5
Of crimson joy,
And his dark secret love
Docs thy life destroy.
1790–92   1794

The Tyger

Tyger! Tyger! burning bright
In the forests of the night,
What immortal hand or eye
Could frame thy fearful symmetry?

In what distant deeps or skies   5
Burnt the fire of thine eyes?
On what wings dare he aspire?
What the hand, dare seize the fire?

And what shoulder, & what art,
Could twist the sinews of thy heart?   10

And when thy heart began to beat,
What dread hand? & what dread feet?

What the hammer? what the chain?
In what furnace was thy brain?
What the anvil? what dread grasp   15
Dare its deadly terrors clasp?

When the stars threw down their spears,
And water'd heaven with their tears,
Did he smile his work to see?
Did he who made the Lamb make thee?   20

Tyger! Tyger! burning bright
In the forests of the night,
What immortal hand or eye
Dare frame thy fearful symmetry?

1790–92   1794

Ah Sun-Flower

Ah Sun-flower! weary of time,
Who countest the steps of the Sun,
Seeking after that sweet golden clime
Where the traveller's journey is done;

Where the Youth pined away with desire,   5
And the pale Virgin shrouded in snow,
Arise from their graves and aspire,
Where my Sun-flower wishes to go.

1794

The Garden of Love

I went to the Garden of Love,
And saw what I never had seen:
A Chapel was built in the midst,
Where I used to play on the green.

And the gates of this Chapel were shut,   5
And "Thou shalt not" writ over the door;
So I turn'd to the Garden of Love,
That so many sweet flowers bore,

And I saw it was filled with graves,
And tomb-stones where flowers should be: 10
And Priests in black gowns were walking their rounds,
And binding with briars my joys & desires.

1790–92   1794

London

I wander thro' each charter'd [1] street,
Near where the charter'd Thames does flow,
And mark in every face I meet
Marks of weakness, marks of woe.

In every cry of every Man,   5
In every Infant's cry of fear,
In every voice, in every ban,[2]
The mind-forg'd manacles I hear.

How the Chimney-sweeper's cry
Every blackning Church appalls;   10
And the hapless Soldier's sigh
Runs in blood down Palace walls.

But most thro' midnight streets I hear
How the youthful Harlot's curse
Blasts the new-born Infant's tear,[3]   15
And blights with plagues the Marriage hearse.[4]

1790–92   1794

The Human Abstract[5]

Pity would be no more,
If we did not make somebody Poor;
And Mercy no more could be,
If all were as happy as we;

And mutual fear brings peace,   5
Till the selfish loves increase;
Then Cruelty knits a snare,
And spreads his baits with care.

He sits down with holy fears,
And waters the ground with tears;   10
Then Humility takes its root
Underneath his foot.

1. "Given liberty," but also, ironically, "pre-empted as private property, and rented out."
2. The various meanings of "ban" are relevant (political and legal prohibition, curse, public condemnation) as well as "banns" (marriage proclamation).
3. Implying prenatal blindness, resulting from a parent's venereal disease (the "plagues" of line 16) by earlier infection from the harlot.
4. In the older sense of "hearse": converts the marriage bed into a bier. Or possibly, since the current sense of the word had also come into use in Blake's day, "converts the marriage coach into a funeral hearse."
5. The matched contrary to *The Divine Image* in *Songs of Innocence*. The virtues of the earlier poem, "Mercy, Pity, Peace, and Love," are now seen as exploitation, cruelty, conflict, and hypocritical humility—the seed in the human brain of the Tree of Mystery, which darkens the natural world.

Soon spreads the dismal shade
Of Mystery over his head;
And the Catterpiller and Fly   15
Feed on the Mystery.

And it bears the fruit of Deceit,
Ruddy and sweet to eat;
And the Raven his nest has made
In its thickest shade.   20

The Gods of the earth and sea,
Sought thro' Nature to find this Tree,
But their search was all in vain:
There grows one in the Human Brain.

1790–92   1794

Infant Sorrow

My mother groand! my father wept.
Into the dangerous world I leapt:
Helpless, naked, piping loud;
Like a fiend hid in a cloud.

Struggling in my father's hands,   5
Striving against my swadling bands,
Bound and weary I thought best
To sulk upon my mother's breast.

1790–92   1794

A Poison Tree

I was angry with my friend:
I told my wrath, my wrath did end.
I was angry with my foe:
I told it not, my wrath did grow.

And I waterd it in fears,   5
Night & morning with my tears;
And I sunnéd it with smiles,
And with soft deceitful wiles.

And it grew both day and night,
Till it bore an apple bright.
And my foe beheld it shine,   10
And he knew that it was mine,

And into my garden stole,
When the night had veild the pole;
In the morning glad I see   15
My foe outstretchd beneath the tree.

1790–92   1794

To Tirzah[6]

Whate'er is Born of Mortal Birth
Must be consuméd with the Earth
To rise from Generation free;
Then what have I to do with thee?

The Sexes sprung from Shame & Pride,   5
Blow'd[7] in the morn: in evening died;
But Mercy changd Death into Sleep;
The Sexes rose to work & weep.

Thou, Mother of my Mortal part,
With cruelty didst mould my Heart,   10
And with false self-deceiving tears
Didst bind my Nostrils, Eyes, & Ears.

Didst close my Tongue in senseless clay
And me to Mortal Life betray.
The Death of Jesus set me free,   15
Then what have I to do with thee?

ca. 1805

A Divine Image[8]

Cruelty has a Human Heart
And Jealousy a Human Face,
Terror, the Human Form Divine,
And Secrecy, the Human Dress.

The Human Dress is forgéd Iron,   5
The Human Form, a fiery Forge,
The Human Face, a Furnace seal'd,
The Human Heart, its hungry Gorge.[9]

1790–91

6. Tirzah was the capital of the Northern Kingdom of Israel and is conceived by Blake in opposition to Jerusalem, capital of the Southern Kingdom of Judah, whose tribes had been redeemed from captivity. In this poem, which was added to late versions of *Songs of Experience*, Tirzah represents that necessity inherent in nature, the realm of "generation," from which the "mortal part" of man derives, and which enslaves his heart and senses. Blake antici-pates his emancipation from this bondage to the cycle of generation by the triumph of the imaginative over the natural body.
7. Blossomed.
8. After etching this poem Blake omitted it from *Songs of Experience*, probably because *The Human Abstract* served as a more comprehensive and subtle contrary to *The Divine Image*, in *Songs of Innocence*.
9. Throat.

The Book of Thel [1]

The Author & Printer Willm Blake, 1789

PLATE i [2]

THEL'S MOTTO

Does the Eagle know what is in the pit?
Or wilt thou go ask the Mole?
Can Wisdom be put in a silver rod?
Or Love in a golden bowl? [3]

PLATE 1

I

The daughters of Mne [4] Seraphim led round their sunny flocks,
All but the youngest; she in paleness sought the secret air,

1. Although Blake dated the engraved poem 1789, its composition probably extended to 1791, so that he was working on it at the time he was writing the *Songs of Innocence* and some of the *Songs of Experience. The Book of Thel* treats the same two "states" and implies the need to pass from primitive innocence through experience in order to achieve a higher, organized innocence; now, however, Blake employs the narrative instead of the lyrical mode and embodies aspects of the developing myth which was fully enacted in his later prophetic books. And like the major prophecies, this poem is written in the fourteener, a long line of seven stresses and (for the most part) fourteen syllables.

Thel—her name probably derives from a Greek word for "wish" or "will" and suggests the timid failure of a desire to fulfil itself—is a virgin dwelling in the Vales of Har, which is equivalent to the sheltered condition of pastoral peace and naïve innocence in Blake's *Songs of Innocence* and will develop into the "Beulah" of his prophetic books. In the fragile beauty of this realm of unrealized potentiality, Thel lives a two-dimensional mirror image of existence (line 9), a diaphanous, fading half-life. The Lily of the Valley and the Cloud—elements of the milieu in this mild realm without opposition or conflict—try to comfort her by describing their content with their roles in the cycle of innocent existence. Thel, however, since she is a human potentiality, finds such comfort inapplicable to her condition of unfulfillment and uselessness, as a virgin without a male contrary and as a shepherdess whose sheep run no risks and need no care. The Clod of Clay then speaks for her child, the voiceless

Worm, an emblem of phallic generation and a devourer of the mortal body in the fallen world; but the maternal Clay sees the role of the Worm, as well as her own, only from the perspective of primal innocence, hence of essential ignorance: "But how this is, sweet maid, I know not, and I cannot know." In her capacity, however, as the substance from which is formed the mortal body of man, the Clay invites Thel to try the experiment of dying into embodied life. With an abrupt and brutal shift in language and tone, Part IV expresses the shock of the revelation to Thel of the world of Generation and Experience—a revelation from which she flees in terror back to her sheltered, if inadequate, paradise.

The reader does not need to be an adept in Blakean mythology to recognize the symbolic reach of this poem over a large area of ordinary human experience—the elemental failure of nerve to meet the challenge of life as it is, the timid incapacity to risk the conflict, suffering, loss, and defeat without which there is no possibility either of growth or of any kind of creativity.

2. The plate numbers identify the page, each with its own pictorial design, as originally printed by Blake. They are reproduced here because they are frequently used for reference to Blake's writings.

3. Ecclesiastes xii.5–6 describes a time when "fears shall be in the way * * * and desire shall fail: because man goeth to his long home, and the mourners go about the streets: Or ever the silver cord be loosed, or the golden bowl be broken." Blake presumably changed the silver cord to a rod in order to make it, with the golden bowl, a sexual symbol.

To fade away like morning beauty from her mortal day;
Down by the river of Adona [5] her soft voice is heard,
And thus her gentle lamentation falls like morning dew: 5

"O life of this our spring! why fades the lotus of the water?
Why fade these children of the spring? born but to smile & fall.
Ah! Thel is like a watry bow, and like a parting cloud,
Like a reflection in a glass, like shadows in the water,
Like dreams of infants, like a smile upon an infant's face,   10
Like the dove's voice, like transient day, like music in the air.
Ah! gentle may I lay me down, and gentle rest my head,
And gentle sleep the sleep of death and gentle hear the voice
Of him that walketh in the garden in the evening time."[6]

The Lilly of the valley, breathing in the humble grass,   15
Answer'd the lovely maid and said: "I am a watry weed,
And I am very small, and love to dwell in lowly vales;
So weak, the gilded butterfly scarce perches on my head;
Yet I am visited from heaven, and he that smiles on all
Walks in the valley and each morn over me spreads his hand,   20
Saying: 'Rejoice, thou humble grass, thou new-born lilly flower,
Thou gentle maid of silent valleys and of modest brooks;
For thou shall be clothed in light, and fed with morning manna,
Till summer's heat melts thee beside the fountains and the springs
To flourish in eternal vales.' Then why should Thel complain?   25

PLATE 2

Why should the mistress of the vales of Har utter a sigh?"

She ceasd & smild in tears, then sat down in her silver shrine.

Thel answerd: "O thou little virgin of the peaceful valley,
Giving to those that cannot crave, the voiceless, the o'ertired;
Thy breath doth nourish the innocent lamb, he smells thy milky
   garments,   5
He crops thy flowers, while thou sittest smiling in his face,
Wiping his mild and meekin [7] mouth from all contagious taints.
Thy wine doth purify the golden honey; thy perfume,
Which thou dost scatter on every little blade of grass that springs,
Revives the milkéd cow, & tames the fire-breathing steed.   10
But Thel is like a faint cloud kindled at the rising sun:
I vanish from my pearly throne, and who shall find my place?"

---

4. If not simply a misprint for "the," this may be, as Geoffrey Keynes says, a variation upon "the mystical name, Bne Seraphim." In the Bible, Seraphim are the highest order of angels.
5. Possibly suggesting an equation of the Vales of Har to Spenser's Garden of Adonis in *The Faerie Queene* III.vi, as well as to the paradisal garden in Genesis (in line 14).
6. Genesis iii.8.
7. Humble.

"Queen of the vales," the Lilly answered, "ask the tender cloud,
And it shall tell thee why it glitters in the morning sky,
And why it scatters its bright beauty thro' the humid air.   15
Descend, O little cloud, & hover before the eyes of Thel."

The Cloud descended, and the Lilly bowd her modest head,
And went to mind her numerous charge among the verdant grass.

PLATE 3

II

"O little Cloud," the virgin said, "I charge thee tell to me,
Why thou complainest not when in one hour thou fade away:
Then we shall seek thee but not find; ah, Thel is like to Thee.
I pass away, yet I complain, and no one hears my voice."

The Cloud then shew'd his golden head & his bright form emerg'd,   5
Hovering and glittering on the air before the face of Thel.

"O virgin, know'st thou not our steeds drink of the golden springs
Where Luvah[8] doth renew his horses? Look'st thou on my youth,
And fearest thou, because I vanish and am seen no more,
Nothing remains? O maid, I tell thee, when I pass away,   10
It is to tenfold life, to love, to peace, and raptures holy:
Unseen descending, weigh my light wings upon balmy flowers,
And court the fair eyed dew, to take me to her shining tent;
The weeping virgin trembling kneels before the risen sun,
Till we arise link'd in a golden band, and never part,   15
But walk united, bearing food to all our tender flowers."

"Dost thou O little Cloud? I fear that I am not like thee;
For I walk through the vales of Har and smell the sweetest flowers,
But I feed not the little flowers; I hear the warbling birds,
But I feed not the warbling birds; they fly and seek their food;   20
But Thel delights in these no more, because I fade away,
And all shall say, 'Without a use this shining woman liv'd,
Or did she only live to be at death the food of worms?' "

The Cloud reclind upon his airy throne and answer'd thus:

"Then if thou art the food of worms, O virgin of the skies,   25
How great thy use, how great thy blessing! Every thing that lives
Lives not alone, nor for itself; fear not, and I will call
The weak worm from its lowly bed, and thou shalt hear its voice.
Come forth, worm of the silent valley, to thy pensive queen."

The helpless worm arose, and sat upon the Lilly's leaf,   30
And the bright Cloud saild on, to find his partner in the vale.

---

8. The earliest mention in Blake's work
of one of his "Giant Forms," the Zoas.
Luvah, the mythical embodiment of the
passional and sexual aspect of man, repairs to the Vales of Har simply in
order to rest and water his horses.

PLATE 4

III

Then Thel astonish'd view'd the Worm upon its dewy bed.

"Art thou a Worm? Image of weakness, art thou but a Worm?
I see thee like an infant wrapped in the Lilly's leaf;
Ah, weep not, little voice, thou can'st not speak, but thou can'st weep.
Is this a Worm? I see thee lay helpless & naked, weeping,   5
And none to answer, none to cherish thee with mother's smiles."

The Clod of Clay heard the Worm's voice, & raisd her pitying head;
She bow'd over the weeping infant, and her life exhal'd
In milky fondness; then on Thel she fix'd her humble eyes.

"O beauty of the vales of Har! we live not for ourselves;   10
Thou seest me the meanest thing, and so I am indeed.
My bosom of itself is cold, and of itself is dark;

PLATE 5

But he that loves the lowly, pours his oil upon my head,
And kisses me, and binds his nuptial bands around my breast,
And says: 'Thou mother of my children, I have lovéd thee,
And I have given thee a crown that none can take away.'
But how this is, sweet maid, I know not, and I cannot know;   5
I ponder, and I cannot ponder; yet I live and love."

The daughter of beauty wip'd her pitying tears with her white veil,
And said: "Alas! I knew not this, and therefore did I weep.
That God would love a Worm, I knew, and punish the evil foot
That, wilful, bruis'd its helpless form; but that he cherish'd it   10
With milk and oil I never knew; and therefore did I weep,
And I complaind in the mild air, because I fade away,
And lay me down in thy cold bed, and leave my shining lot."

"Queen of the vales," the matron Clay answerd, "I heard thy sighs,
And all thy moans flew o'er my roof, but I have call'd them down. 15
Wilt thou, O Queen, enter my house? 'Tis given thee to enter
And to return; fear nothing, enter with thy virgin feet."

PLATE 6

IV

The eternal gates' terrific porter lifted the northern bar: [9]
Thel enter'd in & saw the secrets of the land unknown.
She saw the couches of the dead, & where the fibrous roots

9. Homer, in *Odyssey* XIII, described the Cave of the Naiades, of which the northern gate is for men and the southern gate for gods. The Neoplatonist Porphyro had allegorized it as an account of the descent of the soul into matter. Blake has Thel use the northern gate to pass from the state before birth into incarnate life.

Of every heart on earth infixes deep its restless twists:
A land of sorrows & of tears where never smile was seen.   5

She wanderd in the land of clouds thro' valleys dark, listning
Dolours & lamentations; waiting oft beside a dewy grave,
She stood in silence, listning to the voices of the ground,
Till to her own grave plot she came, & there she sat down,
And heard this voice of sorrow breathéd from the hollow pit: 10

"Why cannot the Ear be closed to its own destruction?
Or the glistning Eye to the poison of a smile?
Why are Eyelids stord with arrows ready drawn,
Where a thousand fighting men in ambush lie?
Or an Eye of gifts & graces, show'ring fruits & coinéd gold?   15
Why a Tongue impress'd with honey from every wind?
Why an Ear, a whirlpool fierce to draw creations in?
Why a Nostril wide inhaling terror, trembling, & affright?
Why a tender curb upon the youthful burning boy?
Why a little curtain of flesh on the bed of our desire?" [1]   20

The Virgin started from her seat, & with a shriek
Fled back unhinderd till she came into the vales of Har.
                              THE END

                                                      1789–91

1. From Thel's grave issues, apparently, the voice of Thel herself, expressing how experience would seem to her timid and shrinking temperament, should she elect to live out her life in the human world. The catalogue of experience runs through the various senses to end with touch, the primary sexual sense.

The Marriage of Heaven and Hell

This, the most immediately accessible of Blake's longer works, is a vigorous, deliberately outrageous, and at times comic, onslaught against the timidly conventional and self-righteous members of society, as well as against many of the stock opinions of orthodox Christian piety and morality. The seeming simplicity of Blake's satiric attitude, however, is deceptive.

Initially, Blake accepts the terminology of middle-class Christian morality ("what the religious call Good & Evil") but reverses its values. In this conventional use Evil, which is manifested by the class of beings called Devils and which consigns a man to the orthodox Hell, is everything associated with the body and its desires and consists essentially of energy, abundance, act, freedom. And conventional Good, which is manifested by Angels and guarantees its adherents a place in the orthodox Heaven, is associated with the Soul (regarded as entirely separate from the body) and consists of the contrary qualities of reason, restraint, passivity, and prohibition. Blandly adopting this current nomenclature, Blake elects to assume the diabolic persona—what he calls "the voice of the Devil"—and to utter "Proverbs of Hell." This ironic stance produces a vein of satire which is in the great 18th-century tradition of sustained ironic reversal, represented by works such as Jonathan Swift's *Modest Proposal.*

But the transvaluation of standard criteria is only a first stage in Blake's complex irony, designed to startle the reader into recognizing the inadequacy of standard moral categories and stock responses. As he also says in the opening summary of his total argument, "Without Contraries is no progression," and "Reason and Energy" are both "necessary to Human existence." It turns out that Blake subordinates his satiric reversal of conventional values under a more inclusive point of view, according to which the real Good, as distinguished from the merely ironic Good, is not simply freedom from restraint, but a "marriage" of the contrary extremes of desire and restraint, energy and reason, the promptings of Hell and the limitations of Heaven—or as Blake calls these contraries, in the comprehensive terms he introduces in Plate 16, "the Prolific" and "the Devouring." These two classes, he adds, "should be enemies," and "whoever tries to reconcile them seeks to destroy existence." When Blake speaks not as moral satirist but as serious moralist, the good life is that abundant and strenuous life he describes as the sustained conflict, without victory or suppression, of simultaneous opposites.

Blake was stimulated to write this unique work in response to the books of the visionary Swedish theologian, Emanuel Swedenborg, whom he had at first admired but then had come to recognize as a conventional Angel in the disguise of a radical Devil. In Plate 3, the writings of Swedenborg are described as the winding clothes Blake discards as he is resurrected from the tomb of his past self, as a poet-prophet who heralds the apocalyptic promise of his age. For Blake wrote *The Marriage of Heaven and Hell* during the bright early years of the French Revolution, when he shared the expectations of a number of radical Englishmen, including the young poets Wordsworth, Coleridge, and Southey, that the Revolution was the universal violence which had been predicted by the Biblical prophets as a stage immediately preceding the millennium. The double role of *The Marriage* as both satire and revolutionary prophecy is made explicit in *A Song of Liberty*, which Blake engraved in 1792 and added as a coda.

The Marriage of Heaven and Hell

PLATE 2

The Argument

Rintrah [1] roars & shakes his fires in the burdend air;
Hungry clouds swag on the deep.

Once meek, and in a perilous path,
The just man kept his course along
The vale of death.   5

1. Rintrah plays the role of the angry Old Testament prophet Elijah as well as of John the Baptist, the voice "crying in the wilderness" (Matthew iii), preparing the way for Christ the Messiah. The "Argument" is a summary of the subject matter of the poem. The villain, who hypocritically assumes a "mild humility," represents the class of Angels in the *Marriage;* the just man is represented by Blake himself, a raging poet-prophet in the guise of a "Devil," who announces the apocalyptic possibility of imaginative redemption.

Roses are planted where thorns grow,
And on the barren heath
Sing the honey bees.

Then the perilous path was planted,
And a river, and a spring,   10
On every cliff and tomb;
And on the bleached bones
Red clay ² brought forth;

Till the villain left the paths of ease,
To walk in perilous paths, and drive   15
The just man into barren climes.

Now the sneaking serpent walks
In mild humility,
And the just man rages in the wilds
Where lions roam.   20

Rintrah roars & shakes his fires in the burdend air;
Hungry clouds swag ³ on the deep.

PLATE 3

As a new heaven is begun, and it is now thirty-three years since
its advent, the Eternal Hell revives.⁴ And lo! Swedenborg is the
Angel sitting at the tomb; his writings are the linen clothes folded
up. Now is the dominion of Edom, & the return of Adam into
Paradise; see Isaiah xxxiv & XXXV Chap.⁵

Without Contraries is no progression. Attraction and Repulsion,
Reason and Energy, Love and Hate, are necessary to Human existence.

2. In Hebrew, the literal meaning of "Adam," or created man. There is also a probable reference to the Redeemer, the new Adam.
3. Sag or sway (or both).
4. The Swedish scientist and religious philosopher, Emanuel Swedenborg (1688–1772) had predicted, on the basis of his visions, that the Last Judgment and the coming of the Kingdom of Heaven would occur in 1757. This was precisely the year of Blake's birth. Now, in 1790, Blake is thirty-three, the age at which Christ had been resurrected from the tomb; appropriately, Blake rises from the tomb of his past life in his new role as imaginative artist who will redeem his age. But, Blake ironically comments, the works he will engrave in his resurrection will constitute the Eternal Hell, the contrary inevitably brought into simultaneous being by Swedenborg's limited New Heaven.
5. Isaiah xxxiv prophesies "the day of the Lord's vengeance," a time of violent destruction and bloodshed; Isaiah xxxv prophesies the redemption to follow, in which "the desert shall * * * blossom as the rose," "in the wilderness shall waters break out, and streams in the desert," and "no lion shall be there," but "an highway shall be there * * * and it shall be called the way of holiness." (Cf. "The Argument," lines 3–11, 20.) Blake combines with these chapters Isaiah lxiii, in which "Edom" is the place from which comes the man whose garments are red with the blood he has spilled; for as he says, "the day of vengeance is in mine heart, and the year of my redeemed is come." Blake interprets this last phrase as predicting the time when Adam would regain his lost Paradise.

With reference to affairs in 1790, Edom represents France, and the red man coming from Edom (to England) is the spirit of the French Revolution, which Blake represents as a portent of apocalyptic redemption and of the recovery of Paradise.

From these contraries spring what the religious call Good & Evil. Good is the passive that obeys Reason. Evil is the active springing from Energy.
Good is Heaven. Evil is Hell.

PLATE 4

The voice of the Devil

All Bibles or sacred codes have been the causes of the following Errors:

1. That Man has two real existing principles; Viz: a Body & a Soul.
2. That Energy, calld Evil, is alone from the Body, & that Reason, calld Good, is alone from the Soul.
3. That God will torment Man in Eternity for following his Energies. But the following Contraries to these are True:

1. Man has no Body distinct from his Soul; for that calld Body is a portion of Soul discernd by the five Senses, the chief inlets of Soul in this age.
2. Energy is the only life, and is from the Body; and Reason is the bound or outward circumference of Energy.
3. Energy is Eternal Delight

PLATE 5

Those who restrain desire, do so because theirs is weak enough to be restrained; and the restrainer or reason usurps its place & governs the unwilling.

And being restraind, it by degrees becomes passive, till it is only the shadow of desire.

The history of this is written in *Paradise Lost*,[6] & the Governor or Reason is call'd Messiah.

And the original Archangel, or possessor of the command of the heavenly host, is calld the Devil or Satan, and his children are call'd Sin & Death.[7]

But in the Book of Job, Milton's Messiah is call'd Satan.[8]

For this history has been adopted by both parties.

It indeed appear'd to Reason as if Desire was cast out; but the Devil's account is, that the Messi[PL. 6]ah fell, & formed a heaven of what he stole from the Abyss.

This is shewn in the Gospel, where he prays to the Father to send the comforter or Desire that Reason may have Ideas to build

----

6. What follows, to the end of this section, is Blake's "diabolical" reading of Milton's *Paradise Lost*.
7. Satan's giving birth to Sin and then incestuously begetting Death upon her is described in II.745 ff.; the war in heaven, referred to three lines below, in which the Messiah defeated Satan and drove him out of heaven, is described in VI.824 ff.
8. Satan plays the role of the moral accuser and physical tormentor of Job.

on; [9] the Jehovah of the Bible being no other than he who dwells in flaming fire. Know that after Christ's death, he became Jehovah.

But in Milton, the Father is Destiny, the Son, a Ratio of the five senses,[1] & the Holy-ghost, Vacuum!

Note. The reason Milton wrote in fetters when he wrote of Angels & God, and at liberty when of Devils & Hell, is because he was a true Poet and of the Devil's party without knowing it.

A Memorable Fancy [2]

As I was walking among the fires of hell, delighted with the enjoyments of Genius, which to Angels look like torment and insanity, I collected some of their Proverbs; thinking that as the sayings used in a nation mark its character, so the Proverbs of Hell shew the nature of Infernal wisdom better than any description of buildings or garments.

When I came home, on the abyss of the five senses, where a flat sided steep frowns over the present world, I saw a mighty Devil folded in black clouds, hovering on the sides of the rock; with cor-[PL 7]roding fires he wrote the following sentence [3] now perceived by the minds of men, & read by them on earth:

> How do you know but ev'ry Bird that cuts the airy way,
> Is an immense world of delight, clos'd by your senses five?

Proverbs of Hell [4]

In seed time learn, in harvest teach, in winter enjoy.
Drive your cart and your plow over the bones of the dead.
The road of excess leads to the palace of wisdom.
Prudence is a rich ugly old maid courted by Incapacity.
He who desires but acts not, breeds pestilence.
The cut worm forgives the plow.
Dip him in the river who loves water.
A fool sees not the same tree that a wise man sees.
He whose face gives no light, shall never become a star.
Eternity is in love with the productions of time.
The busy bee has no time for sorrow.
The hours of folly are measur'd by the clock; but of wisdom, no

9. Possibly John xiv.16–17, where Christ says he "will pray the Father, and he shall give you another Comforter * * * even the Spirit of truth."
1. The Latin *ratio* means both "reason" and "sum." Blake applies the term to the 18th-century view, following the empirical philosophy of John Locke, that the content of the mind is limited to the sum of the experience acquired by the five senses.

2. A parody of what Swedenborg called "memorable relations" of his literal-minded visions of the eternal world.
3. The "mighty Devil" is Blake, as he sees himself reflected in the shiny plate on which he is etching this very passage with "corroding fires"—i.e., acid. See also the third from last sentence in Plate 14.
4. A "diabolic" version of the Book of Proverbs in the Old Testament.

clock can measure.
All wholsom food is caught without a net or a trap.
Bring out number, weight, & measure in a year of dearth.
No bird soars too high, if he soars with his own wings.
A dead body revenges not injuries.
The most sublime act is to set another before you.
If the fool would persist in his folly hc would bccome wise.
Folly is the cloke of knavery.
Shame is Pride's cloke.

PLATE 8

Prisons are built with stones of Law, Brothels with bricks of Religion.
The pride of the peacock is the glory of God.
The lust of the goat is the bounty of God.
The wrath of the lion is the wisdom of God.
The nakedness of woman is the work of God.
Excess of sorrow laughs. Excess of joy weeps.
The roaring of lions, the howling of wolves, the raging of the stormy
    sea, and the destructive sword, are portions of eternity too great
    for the eye of man.
The fox condemns the trap, not himself.
Joys impregnate. Sorrows bring forth.
Lct man wear the fell of the lion, woman the fleece of the sheep.
The bird a nest, the spider a web, man friendship.
The selfish, smiling fool & the sullen, frowning fool shall be both
    thought wise, that they may be a rod.
What is now proved was once only imagin'd.
The rat, the mouse, the fox, the rabbit watch the roots; the lion, the
    tyger, the horse, the elephant, watch the fruits.
The cistern contains: the fountain overflows.
One thought fills immensity.
Always be ready to speak your mind, and a base man will avoid you.
Every thing possible to be believ'd is an image of truth.
The eagle never lost so much time as when he submitted to learn of
    the crow.

PLATE 9

The fox provides for himself, but God provides for the lion.
Think in the morning, Act in the noon, Eat in the evening, Sleep in
    the night.
He who has sufferd you to impose on him knows you.
As the plow follows words, so God rewards prayers.
The tygers of wrath are wiser than the horses of instruction.
Expect poison from the standing water.
You never know what is enough unless you know what is more than
    enough.
Listen to the fools reproach! it is a kingly title!
The eyes of fire, the nostrils of air, the mouth of water, the beard of
    earth.
The weak in courage is strong in cunning.

The apple tree never asks the beech how he shall grow, nor the lion the horse, how he shall take his prey.
The thankful reciever bears a plentiful harvest.
If others had not been foolish, we should be so.
The soul of sweet delight can never be defil'd.
When thou seest an Eagle, thou seest a portion of Genius; lift up thy head!
As the catterpiller chooses the fairest leaves to lay her eggs on, so the priest lays his curse on the fairest joys.
To create a little flower is the labour of ages.
Damn braces: Bless relaxes.
The best wine is the oldest, the best water the newest.
Prayers plow not! Praises reap not!
Joys laugh not! Sorrows weep not!

PLATE 10
The head Sublime, the heart Pathos, the genitals Beauty, the hands & feet Proportion.
As the air to a bird or the sea to a fish, so is contempt to the contemptible.
The crow wish'd every thing was black, the owl that every thing was white.
Exuberance is Beauty.
If the lion was advised by the fox, he would be cunning.
Improvement makes strait roads, but the crooked roads without Improvement are roads of Genius.
Sooner murder an infant in its cradle than nurse unacted desires.
Where man is not, nature is barren.
Truth can never be told so as to be understood, and not be believ'd.
Enough! or Too much.

PLATE 11
    The ancient Poets animated all sensible objects with Gods or Geniuses, calling them by the names and adorning them with the properties of woods, rivers, mountains, lakes, cities, nations, and whatever their enlarged & numerous senses could percieve.
    And particularly they studied the genius of each city & country, placing it under its mental deity.
    Till a system was formed, which some took advantage of & enslav'd the vulgar by attempting to realize or abstract the mental deities from their objects; thus began Priesthood,
    Choosing forms of worship from poetic tales.
    And at length they pronounced that the Gods had ordered such things.
    Thus men forgot that All deities reside in the human breast.

PLATE 12

A Memorable Fancy

The Prophets Isaiah and Ezekiel dined with me, and I asked them how they dared so roundly to assert that God spake to them; and whether they did not think at the time that they would be misunderstood, & so be the cause of imposition.

Isaiah answer'd: "I saw no God, nor heard any, in a finite organical perception; but my senses discover'd the infinite in every thing, and as I was then perswaded, & remain confirm'd, that the voice of honest indignation is the voice of God, I cared not for consequences, but wrote."

Then I asked: "Does a firm perswasion that a thing is so, make it so?"

He replied: "All poets believe that it does, & in ages of imagination this firm perswasion removed mountains; but many are not capable of a firm perswasion of any thing."

Then Ezekiel said: "The philosophy of the East taught the first principles of human perception. Some nations held one principle for the origin & some another; we of Israel taught that the Poetic Genius (as you now call it) was the first principle and all the others merely derivative, which was the cause of our despising the Priests & Philosophers of other countries, and prophecying that all Gods |PL 13| would at last be proved to originate in ours & to be the tributaries of the Poetic Genius; it was this that our great poet, King David, desired so fervently & invokes so patheticly, saying by this he conquers enemies & governs kingdoms; and we so loved our God, that we cursed in his name all the deities of surrounding nations, and asserted that they had rebelled; from these opinions the vulgar came to think that all nations would at last be subject to the Jews."

"This," said he, "like all firm perswasions, is come to pass, for all nations believe the Jews' code and worship the Jews' god, and what greater subjection can be?"

I heard this with some wonder, & must confess my own conviction. After dinner I ask'd Isaiah to favour the world with his lost works; he said none of equal value was lost. Ezekiel said the same of his.

I also asked Isaiah what made him go naked and barefoot three years? He answerd, "the same that made our friend Diogenes, the Grecian." [5]

I then asked Ezekiel why he eat dung, & lay so long on his right & left side? [6] He answered, "the desire of raising other men into a

5. In Isaiah xx.2–3, the Lord commanded Isaiah to go "naked and barefoot" for three years. Diogenes was the 4th-century Greek Cynic, whose extreme repudiation of civilized customs gave rise to anecdotes that he had renounced clothing.

6. The Lord gave these instructions to the prophet Ezekiel, iv.4–6.

perception of the infinite; this the North American tribes practise, & is he honest who resists his genius or conscience only for the sake of present ease or gratification?"

PLATE 14

The ancient tradition that the world will be consumed in fire at the end of six thousand years is true, as I have heard from Hell.

For the cherub with his flaming sword is hereby commanded to leave his guard at tree of life; [7] and when he does, the whole creation will be consumed, and appear infinite and holy, whereas it now appears finite & corrupt.

This will come to pass by an improvement of sensual enjoyment.

But first the notion that man has a body distinct from his soul is to be expunged; this I shall do, by printing in the infernal method, by corrosives, which in Hell are salutary and medicinal, melting apparent surfaces away, and displaying the infinite which was hid. [8]

If the doors of perception were cleansed every thing would appear to man as it is, infinite.

For man has closed himself up, till he sees all things thro' narrow chinks of his cavern.

PLATE 15

A Memorable Fancy

I was in a Printing house in Hell & saw the method in which knowledge is transmitted from generation to generation.

In the first chamber was a Dragon-Man, clearing away the rubbish from a cave's mouth; within, a number of Dragons were hollowing the cave.

In the second chamber was a Viper folding round the rock & the cave, and others adorning it with gold, silver, and precious stones.

In the third chamber was an Eagle with wings and feathers of air; he caused the inside of the cave to be infinite; around were numbers of Eagle-like men, who built palaces in the immense cliffs.

In the fourth chamber were Lions of flaming fire, raging around & melting the metals into living fluids.

In the fifth chamber were Unnam'd forms, which cast the metals into the expanse.

There they were receiv'd by Men who occupied the sixth chamber, and took the forms of books & were arranged in libraries. [9]

---

7. In Genesis iii.24, when the Lord drove Adam and Eve from the Garden of Eden, he had placed Cherubims and a flaming sword at the eastern end "to keep the way of the tree of life."

8. See the preceding "Memorable Fancy," and footnote.

9. This Memorable Fancy is Blake's allegorical rendering of the creation and printing of works of imagination.

PLATE 16

The Giants who formed this world into its sensual existence, and now seem to live in it in chains, are in truth the causes of its life & the sources of all activity; but the chains are the cunning of weak and tame minds which have power to resist energy; according to the proverb, the weak in courage is strong in cunning.

Thus one portion of being is the Prolific, the other, the Devouring: to the Devourer it seems as if the producer was in his chains; but it is not so, he only takes portions of existence and fancies that the whole.

But the Prolific would cease to be Prolific unless the Devourer as a sea received the excess of his delights.[1]

Some will say, "Is not God alone the Prolific?" I answer, "God only Acts & Is, in existing beings or Men."

These two classes of men are always upon earth, & they should be enemies; whoever tries [PL 17] to reconcile them seeks to destroy existence.

Religion is an endeavour to reconcile the two.

Note. Jesus Christ did not wish to unite but to separate them, as in the Parable of sheep and goats! & he says, "I came not to send Peace but a Sword." [2]

Messiah or Satan or Tempter was formerly thought to be one of the Antediluvians [3] who are our Energies.

A Memorable Fancy

An Angel came to me and said: "O pitiable foolish young man! O horrible! O dreadful state! consider the hot burning dungeon thou art preparing for thyself to all eternity, to which thou art going in such career."

I said: "Perhaps you will be willing to shew me my eternal lot, & we will contemplate together upon it and see whether your lot or mine is most desirable."

So he took me thro' a stable & thro' a church & down into the church vault at the end of which was a mill; thro' the mill we went, and came to a cave; down the winding cavern we groped our tedious way till a void boundless as a nether sky appeard beneath us, & we held by the roots of trees and hung over this immensity, but I said: "If you please, we will commit ourselves to this void, and see whether Providence is here also, if you will not I will." But he answerd: "Do not presume, O young man, but as we here remain, behold thy lot which will soon appear when the darkness passes

---

1. The "Giants" in this section are man's creative energies, called "the Prolific," which are necessarily limited by their contrary, "the Devourer."

2. The parable of the sheep and the goats is in Matthew xxv.32–33; the saying of Christ, in Matthew x.34.
3. Men who lived before Noah's flood.

away." [4]

So I remaind with him sitting in the twisted [PL 18] root of an oak; he was suspended in a fungus which hung with the head downward into the deep.

By degrees we beheld the infinite Abyss, fiery as the smoke of a burning city; beneath us at an immense distance was the sun, black but shining; round it were fiery tracks on which revolv'd vast spiders, crawling after their prey, which flew, or rather swum in the infinite deep, in the most terrific shapes of animals sprung from corruption; & the air was full of them, & seemd composed of them; these are Devils, and are called Powers of the air. I now asked my companion which was my eternal lot? he said, "Between the black & white spiders."

But now, from between the black & white spiders a cloud and fire burst and rolled thro the deep, blackning all beneath, so that the nether deep grew black as a sea & rolled with a terrible noise; beneath us was nothing now to be seen but a black tempest, till looking east between the clouds & the waves, we saw a cataract of blood mixed with fire, and not many stones throw from us appeard and sunk again the scaly fold of a monstrous serpent. At last to the east, distant about three degrees, appeard a fiery crest above the waves. Slowly it reared like a ridge of golden rocks till we discovered two globes of crimson fire, from which the sea fled away in clouds of smoke; and now we saw it was the head of Leviathan; his forehead was divided into streaks of green & purple like those on a tyger's forehead: soon we saw his mouth & red gills hang just above the raging foam, tinging the black deep with beams of blood, advancing toward [PL 19] us with all the fury of a spiritual existence.

My friend the Angel climb'd up from his station into the mill; I remain'd alone, & then this appearance was no more, but I found myself sitting on a pleasant bank beside a river by moon light, hearing a harper who sung to the harp, & his theme was: "The man who never alters his opinion is like standing water, & breeds reptiles of the mind."

But I arose, and sought for the mill, & there I found my Angel, who surprised asked me how I escaped?

I answerd: "All that we saw was owing to your metaphysics: for when you ran away, I found myself on a bank by moonlight hearing

4. The "stable" is that where Jesus was born, which, allegorically, leads to the "church" founded in his name and to the "vault" where this institution effectually buried him. The "mill" in Blake is a symbol of mechanical and analytic philosophy; through this the pilgrims pass into the twisting cave of rationalistic theology and descend to an underworld which is an empty abyss. The point of this Blakean equivalent of a carnival fun house is that only after you have thoroughly confused yourself by this tortuous approach, and only if you then (as in the next two paragraphs) stare at this topsy-turvy emptiness long enough, will the void gradually assume the semblance of the comic horrors of the fantasied hell of angelic orthodoxy.

a harper. But now we have seen my eternal lot, shall I shew you yours? He laughd at my proposal; but I by force suddenly caught him in my arms, & flew westerly thro' the night, till we were elevated above the earth's shadow; then I flung myself with him directly into the body of the sun; here I clothed myself in white, & taking in my hand Swedenborg's volumes, sunk from the glorious clime, and passed all the planets till we came to Saturn; here I staid to rest & then leap'd into the void between Saturn & the fixed stars.

"Here," said I, "is your lot, in this space, if space it may be calld." Soon we saw the stable and the church, & I took him to the altar and open'd the Bible, and lo! it was a deep pit, into which I descended, driving the Angel before me; soon we saw seven houses of brick;[5] one we enterd; in it were a [PL 20] number of monkeys, baboons, & all of that species, chaind by the middle, grinning and snatching at one another, but withheld by the shortness of their chains: however, I saw that they sometimes grew numerous, and then the weak were caught by the strong, and with a grinning aspect, first coupled with & then devourd, by plucking off first one limb and then another till the body was left a helpless trunk. This, after grinning & kissing it with seeming fondness, they devourd too; and here & there I saw one savourily picking the flesh off of his own tail; as the stench terribly annoyd us both, we went into the mill, & I in my hand brought the skeleton of a body, which in the mill was Aristotle's Analytics.[6]

So the Angel said: "Thy phantasy has imposed upon me, & thou oughtest to be ashamed."

I answerd: "We impose on one another, & it is but lost time to converse with you whose works are only Analytics."

Opposition is true Friendship.

PLATE 21

I have always found that Angels have the vanity to speak of themselves as the only wise; this they do with a confident insolence sprouting from systematic reasoning.

Thus Swedenborg boasts that what he writes is new; tho' it is only the Contents or Index of already publish'd books.

A man carried a monkey about for a shew, & because he was a little wiser than the monkey, grew vain, and conciev'd himself as much wiser than seven men. It is so with Swedenborg; he shews the folly of churches & exposes hypocrites, till he imagines that all are religious, & himself the single [PL 22] one on earth that ever broke

5. The "seven churches which are in Asia," to which John addresses the Book of Revelation i.4. Blake now forces upon the angel his own diabolic view of angelic Biblical exegesis, theological speculation and disputation, and Hell— a view, Harold Bloom has remarked, which "makes monkeys out of the theologians."

6. Aristotle's treatises on logic.

a net.

Now hear a plain fact: Swedenborg has not written one new truth. Now hear another: he has written all the old falshoods.

And now hear the reason: He conversed with Angels who are all religious, & conversed not with Devils, who all hate religion, for he was incapable thro' his conceited notions.

Thus Swedenborg's writings are a recapitulation of all superficial opinions, and an analysis of the more sublime, but no further.

Have now another plain fact: Any man of mechanical talents may from the writings of Paracelsus or Jacob Behmen [7] produce ten thousand volumes of equal value with Swedenborg's, and from those of Dante or Shakespear, an infinite number.

But when he has done this, let him not say that he knows better than his master, for he only holds a candle in sunshine.

A Memorable Fancy

Once I saw a Devil in a flame of fire, who arose before an Angel that sat on a cloud, and the Devil utterd these words:

"The worship of God is, Honouring his gifts in other men, each according to his genius, and loving the [PL 23] greatest men best; those who envy or calumniate great men hate God, for there is no other God."

The Angel hearing this became almost blue; but mastering himself, he grew yellow, & at last white, pink, & smiling, and then replied:

"Thou Idolater, is not God One? & is not he visible in Jesus Christ? and has not Jesus Christ given his sanction to the law of ten commandments, and are not all other men fools, sinners, & nothings?"

The Devil answer'd; "Bray [8] a fool in a mortar with wheat, yet shall not his folly be beaten out of him; if Jesus Christ is the greatest man, you ought to love him in the greatest degree; now hear how he has given his sanction to the law of ten commandments: did he not mock at the sabbath, and so mock the sabbath's God? murder those who were murderd because of him? turn away the law from the woman taken in adultery? steal the labor of others to support him? bear false witness when he omitted making a defence before Pilate? covet when he pray'd for his disciples, and when he bid them shake off the dust of their feet against such as refused to lodge them? I tell you, no virtue can exist without breaking these ten commandments.˙. Jesus was all virtue, and acted from im[PL

7. Paracelsus (1493–1541), a Swiss physician and a pioneer in empirical medicine, was also a prominent theorist of the occult. Behmen is Jakob Boehme (1575–1624), a German shoemaker who developed a theosophical system which has had great and persisting influence both on theological and metaphysical speculation.
8. Pound into small pieces.

24]pulse, not from rules."

When he had so spoken, I beheld the Angel, who stretched out his arms, embracing the flame of fire, & he was consumed and arose as Elijah.[9]

Note. This Angel, who is now become a Devil, is my particular friend; we often read the Bible together in its infernal or diabolical sense, which the world shall have if they behave well.

I have also The Bible of Hell,[1] which the world shall have whether they will or no.

One Law for the Lion & Ox is Oppression.

1790–93   1790–93

PLATE 25

A Song of Liberty [2]

1. The Eternal Female groand! it was heard over all the Earth.

2. Albion's [3] coast is sick, silent; the American meadows faint!

3. Shadows of Prophecy shiver along by the lakes and the rivers and mutter across the ocean: France, rend down thy dungeon!

4. Golden Spain, burst the barriers of old Rome!

5. Cast thy keys, O Rome, into the deep down falling, even to eternity down falling,

6. And weep.

7. In her trembling hands she took the new born terror, howling.

8. On those infinite mountains of light now barr'd out by the Atlantic sea,[4] the new born fire stood before the starry king!

9. Flag'd with grey brow'd snows and thunderous visages, the jealous wings wav'd over the deep.

10. The speary hand burned aloft, unbuckled was the shield, forth went the hand of jealousy among the flaming hair, and [PL 26] hurl'd the new born wonder thro' the starry night.

11. The fire, the fire, is falling!

12. Look up! look up! O citizen of London, enlarge thy countenance! O Jew, leave counting gold! return to thy oil and wine. O African! black African! (Go, wingéd thought, widen his forehead.)

---

9. The angry Old Testament prophet; see the opening "Argument," footnote.
1. I.e., the poems and designs that Blake is working on.
2. Blake etched this poem in 1792 and sometimes bound it as an appendix to *The Marriage of Heaven and Hell*. It recounts the birth, manifested in the contemporary events in France, of the flaming Spirit of Revolution (whom Blake later called Orc), and describes his conflict with the tyrannical sky-god (whom Blake later called Urizen). The poem ends with the portent of the Spirit of Revolution shattering the ten commandments, or prohibitions against political, religious, and moral liberty, and bringing in a free and joyous new world.
3. England's.
4. The legendary continent of Atlantis, sunk beneath the sea; Blake uses it to represent the condition before the fall.

13. The fiery limbs, the flaming hair, shot like the sinking sun into the western sea.

14. Wak'd from his eternal sleep, the hoary element roaring fled away:

15. Down rushd, beating his wings in vain, the jealous king; his grey brow'd councellors, thunderous warriors, curl'd veterans, among helms, and shields, and chariots, horses, elephants; banners, castles, slings and rocks,

16. Falling, rushing, ruining! buried in the ruins, on Urthona's [5] dens;

17. All night beneath the ruins; then, their sullen flames, faded, emerge round the gloomy king,

18. With thunder and fire, leading his starry hosts thro' the waste wilderness [PL 27] he promulgates his ten commands, glancing his beamy eyelids over the deep in dark dismay,

19. Where the son of fire in his eastern cloud, while the morning plumes her golden breast,

20. Spurning the clouds written with curses, stamps the stony law to dust, loosing the eternal horses from the dens of night, crying:

Empire is no more! and now the lion & wolf shall cease.[6]

CHORUS

Let the Priests of the Raven of dawn, no longer in deadly black, with hoarse note curse the sons of joy. Nor his accepted brethren, whom, tyrant, he calls free, lay the bound or build the roof. Nor pale religious letchery call that virginity, that wishes but acts not!

For every thing that lives is Holy.

1792   1792

For the Sexes: The Gates of Paradise[1]

[*Prologue*]
Mutual Forgiveness of each Vice,
Such are the Gates of Paradise.
Against the Accuser's chief desire
Who walkd among the Stones of Fire
Jehovah's Finger Wrote the Law,   5
Then Wept! then rose in Zeal & Awe
And the Dead Corpse from Sinai's heat
Buried beneath his Mercy Seat.

5. In the later Prophetic Books, Urthona is the unfallen form of Los, who in the fallen world represents the poetic imagination, the agent working for the regeneration of humanity.
6. Cf. Isaiah's prophecy, lxv.17–25, of "new heavens and a new earth," when "the wolf and the lamb shall feed together, and the lion shall eat straw like the bullock."
1. The two poems reprinted here introduce and conclude a series of emblems (drawings with explanatory captions) that Blake issued first under the title *For Children: The Gates of Paradise* and later amplified and reissued under the present title.

O Christians, Christians! tell me Why
You rear it on your Altars high.   10

[*Epilogue*]
To The Accuser who is
The God of This World

Truly My Satan thou art but a Dunce,
And dost not know the Garment from the Man;
Every Harlot was a Virgin once,
Nor canst thou ever change Kate into Nan.

Tho thou art Worshipd by the Names Divine   5
Of Jesus & Jehovah: thou art still
The Son of Morn in weary Night's decline,
The lost Traveller's Dream under the Hill.

1793–ca. 1818   1793–ca. 1818

Poems from BLAKE'S NOTEBOOK[1]

Never Pain to Tell Thy Love

Never pain to tell thy love
Love that never told can be,
For the gentle wind does move
Silently, invisibly.

I told my love, I told my love,   5
I told her all my heart,
Trembling, cold, in ghastly fears—
Ah, she doth depart.

Soon as she was gone from me
A traveller came by
Silently, invisibly—   10
O, was no deny.

I Askéd a Thief

I askéd a thief to steal me a peach,
He turned up his eyes;
I ask'd a lithe lady to lie her down,
Holy & meek she cries.

1. A commonplace book in which Blake drew sketches and jotted down verses and memoranda between the late 1780's and 1810. It is known as the "Rossetti Notebook" because it later came into the possession of the poet and painter Dante Gabriel Rossetti. The manuscript was published by Geoffrey Keynes in 1935.

As soon as I went   5
An angel came.
He wink'd at the thief
And smil'd at the dame—

And without one word said
Had a peach from the tree   10
And still as a maid
Enjoy'd the lady.

1796

Mock on, Mock on, Voltaire, Rousseau

Mock on, Mock on, Voltaire, Rousseau;
Mock on, Mock on, 'tis all in vain.
You throw the sand against the wind,
And the wind blows it back again.

And every sand becomes a Gem   5
Reflected in the beams divine;
Blown back, they blind the mocking Eye,
But still in Israel's paths they shine.

The Atoms of Democritus
And Newton's Particles of light   10
Are sands upon the Red sea shore,
Where Israel's tents do shine so bright.

Morning

To find the Western path
Right thro the Gates of Wrath
I urge my way;
Sweet Mercy leads me on,
With soft repentant moan   5
I see the break of day.

The war of swords & spears
Melted by dewy tears
Exhales on high;
The Sun is freed from fears   10
And with soft grateful tears
Ascends the sky.

And Did Those Feet[1]

And did those feet in ancient time
Walk upon England's mountains green?

1. These quatrains occur in the Preface to Blake's prophetic poem *Milton*.
There is an ancient belief, still current
in parts of England, that Jesus came

And was the holy Lamb of God
On England's pleasant pastures seen?

And did the Countenance Divine 5
Shine forth upon our clouded hills?
And was Jerusalem builded here,
Among these dark Satanic Mills? 2

Bring me my Bow of burning gold:
Bring me my Arrows of desire: 10
Bring me my Spear: O clouds unfold!
Bring me my Chariot of fire!

I will not cease from Mental Fight,
Nor shall my Sword sleep in my hand,
Till we have built Jerusalem 15
In England's green & pleasant Land.

ca. 1804–10   ca. 1804–10

A Vision of The Last Judgment 1

For the Year 1810
Additions to Blake's Catalogue of Pictures &c

The Last Judgment [will be] when all those are Cast away who trouble Religion with Questions concerning Good & Evil or Eating of the Tree of those Knowledges or Reasonings which hinder the Vision of God turning all into a Consuming fire. When Imaginative Art & Science & all Intellectual Gifts, all the Gifts of the Holy Ghost, are lookd upon as of no use & only Contention remains to Man then the Last Judgment begins & its Vision is seen by the Imaginative Eye of Every one according to the situation he holds.

[PAGE 68] The Last Judgment is not Fable or Allegory but Vision. Fable or Allegory are a totally distinct & inferior kind of

to England with Joseph of Arimathea. Blake adapts the legend to his own conception of a spiritual Israel, in which the significance of Biblical events are as relevant to England as to Palestine. By a particularly Blakean irony, this poem of mental war in the service of apocalyptic desire is widely used as a hymn by those of us whom Blake called "angels."
2. There may be an allusion here to industrial England; but the mill is primarily Blake's symbol for a mechanistic and utilitarian world view, according to which, as he said elsewhere, "the same dull round, even of a universe" becomes "a mill with complicated wheels."
1. In this essay Blake describes and comments on his painting of the Last Judgment, now lost, which is said to have measured seven by five feet and

to have included a thousand figures. The text has been transcribed and rearranged, as the sequence of the pages indicate, from the scattered fragments in Blake's Notebook. The opening and closing parts are reprinted here as Blake's fullest, although cryptic, statements of what he means by vision. These sections deal with the relations of imaginative vision to allegory, Greek fable, and the Biblical story; to uncurbed human passion and intellectual power; to conventional and coercive virtue; to what is seen by the "corporeal" eye; to the arts; and to the Last Judgment and the apocalyptic redemption of man and the created world —an apocalypse which is to be achieved by the triumph over the bodily eye of human imagination, as manifested in the creative artist.

Poetry. Vision or Imagination is a Representation of what Eternally Exists, Really & Unchangeably. Fable or Allegory is Formd by the daughters of Memory. Imagination is Surrounded by the daughters of Inspiration who in the aggregate are calld Jerusalem. [P 69] Fable is Allegory but what Critics call The Fable is Vision itself. [P 68] The Hebrew Bible & the Gospel of Jesus are not Allegory but Eternal Vision or Imagination of All that Exists. Note here that Fable or Allegory is Seldom without some Vision. Pilgrim's Progress is full of it, the Greek Poets the same; but Allegory & Vision ought to be known as Two Distinct Things & so calld for the Sake of Eternal Life. Plato has made Socrates say that Poets & Prophets do not know or Understand what they write or Utter; this is a most Pernicious Falshood. If they do not, pray is an inferior Kind to be calld Knowing? Plato confutes himself.

The Last Judgment is one of these Stupendous Visions. I have represented it as I saw it. To different People it appears differently as [P 69] every thing else does for tho on Earth things seem Permanent they are less permanent than a Shadow as we all know too well.

The Nature of Visionary Fancy or Imagination is very little Known & the Eternal nature & permanence of its ever Existent Images is considered as less permanent than the things of Vegetative & Generative Nature; yet the Oak dies as well as the Lettuce, but Its Eternal ·Image & Individuality never dies, but renews by its seed. Just so the Imaginative Image returns by the seed of Contemplative Thought. The Writings of the Prophets illustrate these conceptions of the Visionary Fancy by their various sublime & Divine Images as seen in the Worlds of Vision. * * *

Let it here be Noted that the Greek Fables originated in Spiritual Mystery [P 72] and Real Visions Which are lost & clouded in Fable & Allegory while the Hebrew Bible & the Greek Gospel are Genuine, Preservd by the Saviour's Mercy. The Nature of my Work is Visionary or Imaginative. It is an Endeavour to Restore what the Ancients calld the Golden Age.

[PAGE 69] This world of Imagination is the World of Eternity; it is the Divine bosom into which we shall all go after the death of the Vegetated body. This World of Imagination is Infinite & Eternal whereas the world of Generation or Vegetation is Finite & for a small moment Temporal. There Exist in that Eternal World the Permanent Realities of Every Thing which we see reflected in this Vegetable Glass of Nature.

All Things are comprehended in their Eternal Forms in the Divine [P 70] body of the Saviour, the True Vine of Eternity, The Human Imagination, who appeard to Me as Coming to Judgment among his Saints & throwing off the Temporal that the Eternal

might be Establishd. Around him were seen the Images of Existences according to a certain order suited to my Imaginative Eye.
* * *

[PAGE 87] Men are admitted into Heaven not because they have curbed & governd their Passions or have No Passions but because they have Cultivated their Understandings. The Treasures of Heaven are not Negations of Passion but Realities of Intellect from which All the Passions Emanate Uncurbed in their Eternal Glory. The Fool shall not enter into Heaven let him be ever so Holy. Holiness is not The Price of Enterance into Heaven. Those who are cast out Are All Those who, having no Passions of their own because No Intellect, Have spent their lives in Curbing & Governing other People's by the Various arts of Poverty & Cruelty of all kinds. Wo Wo Wo to you Hypocrites. Even Murder the Courts of Justice, more merciful than the Church, are compelld to allow is not done in Passion but in Cool Blooded Design & Intention.

The Modern Church Crucifies Christ with the Head Downwards.

[PAGE 92] Many Persons such as Paine & Voltaire with some of the Ancient Greeks say we will not converse concerning Good & Evil we will live in Paradise & Liberty. You may do so in Spirit but not in the Mortal Body as you pretend, till after the Last Judgment; for in Paradise they have no Corporeal & Mortal Body; that originated with the Fall & was calld Death & cannot be removed but by a Last Judgment; while we are in the world of Mortality we Must Suffer. The Whole Creation Groans to be deliverd; there will always be as many Hypocrites born as Honest Men & they will always have superior Power in Mortal Things. You cannot have Liberty in this World without what you call Moral Virtue & you cannot have Moral Virtue without the Slavery of that half of the Human Race who hate what you call Moral Virtue.

The Nature of Hatred & Envy & of All the Mischiefs in the World are here depicted. No one Envies or Hates one of his Own Party; even the devils love one another in their Way; they torment one another for other reasons than Hate or Envy; these are only employd against the Just. Neither can Seth Envy Noah, or Elijah Envy Abraham, but they may both of them Envy the Success [P 93] of Satan or of Og or Molech. The Horse never Envies the Peacock nor the Sheep the Goat but they Envy a Rival in Life & Existence whose ways & means exceed their own, let him be of what Class of Animals he will; a Dog will envy a Cat who is pamperd at the expense of his comfort, as I have often seen. The Bible never tells us that Devils torment one another thro Envy; it is thro this that they torment the Just; but for what do they torment one another? I answer, For the Coercive Laws of Hell, Moral Hypocrisy. They torment a Hypocrite when he is discovered; they Punish a Failure in the tormentor who has suffered the Subject of his torture to Escape. In Hell all is Self Righteousness; there is no such thing there as Forgiveness of Sin; he who does Forgive Sin is Crucified as an Abettor of Criminals, & he who performs Works of Mercy in Any shape whatever is punishd & if possible destroyd, not thro Envy or Hatred or Malice but thro Self Righteousness that thinks it does God service, which God is Satan. They do not Envy one another; they contemn & despise one another.

Forgiveness of Sin is only at the Judgment Seat of Jesus the Saviour, where the Accuser is cast out, not because he Sins but because he torments the Just & makes them do what he condemns as Sin & what he knows is opposite to their own Identity.

It is not because Angels are Holier than Men or Devils that makes them Angels but because they do not Expect Holiness from one another but from God only.

The Player is a liar when he Says Angels are happier than [P 94] Men because they are better. Angels are happier than Men & Devils because they are not always Prying after Good & Evil in one Another & eating the Tree of Knowledge for Satan's Gratification.

Thinking as I do that the Creator of this World is a very Cruel Being, & being a Worshipper of Christ, I cannot help saying: "the Son O how unlike the Father!" First God Almighty comes with a Thump on the Head. Then Jesus Christ comes with a balm to heal it.

The Last Judgment is an Overwhelming of Bad Art & Science. Mental Things are alone Real; what is Calld Corporeal Nobody Knows of its dwelling Place; it is in Fallacy & its Existence an Imposture. Where is the Existence Out of Mind or Thought? Where is it but in the Mind of a Fool? Some People flatter themselves that there will be No Last Judgment & [P 95] that Bad Art will be adopted & mixed with Good Art, That Error or Experiment will make a Part of Truth, & they Boast that it is its Foundation. These People flatter themselves; I will not Flatter them. Error is Created. Truth is Eternal. Error or Creation will be Burned Up, & then & not till then Truth or Eternity will appear. It is Burnt up the Moment Men cease to behold it. I assert for My self that I do not behold the Outward Creation & that to me it is hindrance & not Action; it is as the Dirt upon my feet, No part of Me. "What," it will be Questiond, "When the Sun rises do you not see a round Disk of fire somewhat like a Guinea?" O no no, I see an Innumerable company of the Heavenly host crying "Holy Holy Holy is the Lord God Almighty." I question not my Corporeal or Vegetative Eye any more than I would Question a Window concerning a Sight. I look thro it & not with it.

1810   1810

WILLIAM WORDSWORTH
(1770–1850)

1791–92: In France during the early period of the Revolution.
1797: With his sister Dorothy at Alfoxden, Somersetshire, near Coleridge at Nether Stowey.
1798: First edition of *Lyrical Ballads*.
1799: William and Dorothy settle at Grasmere, in the Lake District.
1800: Second edition of *Lyrical Ballads* in two volumes, with the famous Preface.
1807: *Poems in Two Volumes;* end of the great decade.

Wordsworth was born in Cockermouth in West Cumberland, just on the northern fringe of the English Lake District; when his mother died, the 8-year-old boy was sent to school at Hawkshead, near Esthwaite Lake, in the heart of that thinly settled region which he and Coleridge were to transform into the poetic center of England. William and his three brothers boarded in the cottage of Ann Tyson, who gave the boys simple comfort, ample affection, and freedom to roam the countryside at will. A vigorous, willful, and sometimes moody boy, William spent his free days and sometimes "half the night" in the sports and rambles described in the first two books of *The Prelude*, "drinking in" (to use one of his favorite metaphors) the natural sights and sounds, and getting to know the cottagers, shepherds, and solitary wanderers who moved through his imagination and dreams into his later poetry. He also found time to read voraciously in the books owned by his young headmaster, William Taylor, who encouraged him in his inclination to poetry.

John Wordsworth, the poet's father, died suddenly when William was 13, leaving to his five children mainly the substantial sum owed him by Lord Lonsdale, whom he had served as attorney and as steward of the huge Lonsdale estate. That harsh and litigious nobleman managed to keep from paying the debt until he died in 1802. Wordsworth was nevertheless able to go up to St. John's College, Cambridge, in 1787, where he found very little in the limited curriculum of that time to appeal to him; he took his A.B. degree in 1791 without distinction.

During the summer vacation of his third year at Cambridge (1790), Wordsworth and his closest college friend, the Welshman Robert Jones, made a walking tour through France and the Alps (described in *The Prelude* VI) at the time when Frenchmen were joyously celebrating the first anniversary of the fall of the Bastille. Upon completing his course at Cambridge, Wordsworth spent four months in London, set off on another walking tour with Robert Jones through Wales (the time of the memorable ascent of Mount Snowdon in *The Prelude* XIV), and then went back alone to France in order to master the language and qualify as a traveling tutor.

In that year (between November, 1791, and December, 1792) Wordsworth became a fervent "democrat" and proselyte of the French Revolution —which seemed to him, as to many other generous spirits, to promise a "glorious renovation"—and he had a passionate love affair with Annette Vallon, the impetuous and warm-hearted daughter of a French surgeon at Blois. It seems clear that Wordsworth and Annette planned to marry, despite their difference in religion and political inclinations (Annette belonged to an old Catholic family whose sympathies were Royalist). But almost immediately after a daughter, Caroline, was born, lack of funds forced Wordsworth back to England. The outbreak of war between England and France made it impossible for him to rejoin Annette until they had drifted so far apart in sympathies that a permanent union no longer seemed practicable. Wordsworth's agonies of guilt, his divided loyalties between England and France, his gradual disillusion with the course of the Revolution in France—as he describes them in *The Prelude* X and XI —brought him to the verge of an emotional breakdown, when "sick, wearied out with contrarieties," he "yielded up moral questions in despair." His suffering, his near-collapse, and the successful effort, after his sharp break with his own past, to re-establish "a saving intercourse with my true self" are the experiences which underlie many of Wordsworth's greatest poems.

At this critical point a young friend, Raisley Calvert, died and left Wordsworth a sum of money just sufficient to enable him to live solely by his poetry. He settled in a rent-free cottage at Racedown, Dorsetshire, with his beloved sister Dorothy, who now began her long career as confidante, inspirer, and secretary. At that same time Wordsworth met Samuel Taylor Coleridge; two years later he moved to Alfoxden to be near Coleridge, who lived four miles away at Nether Stowey. Here, his recovery complete, he entered at the age of 27 upon the delayed spring-time of his poetic career.

Even while he had been an undergraduate at Cambridge, Coleridge had detected signs of genius in Wordsworth's rather conventional poem about his tour in the Alps, *Descriptive Sketches*, published in 1793. Now he hailed Wordsworth unreservedly as "the best poet of the age." The two men met almost daily, talked for hours about poetry, and composed prolifically. So close was their association that they lost almost all sense of individual proprietorship in a composition. We find the same phrases occurring in poems of Wordsworth and Coleridge, as well as in the delightful journals that Dorothy kept at the time; the two poets collaborated in some writings and freely traded thoughts and passages for others; and Coleridge even undertook to complete a few poems that Wordsworth had left unfinished.

The result of their joint efforts was a small volume, published anonymously in 1798, *Lyrical Ballads, With a Few Other Poems*. It opened with Coleridge's *Ancient Mariner*, included three other poems by Coleridge, a number of Wordsworth's verse anecdotes and psychological studies of humble people, some lyrics in which Wordsworth celebrated impulses from a vernal wood, and closed with Wordsworth's great descriptive and meditative poem in blank verse (not a "lyrical ballad," but one of the "other poems" of the title), *Tintern Abbey*. No other book of poems in

English so plainly announces a new literary departure. William Hazlitt wrote that when he heard Coleridge read some of these newly written poems aloud, "the sense of a new style and a new spirit in poetry came over me," with something of the effect "that arises from the turning up of the fresh soil, or of the first welcome breath of spring." The professional reviewers were less enthusiastic. Nevertheless *Lyrical Ballads* sold out in two years, and Wordsworth published over his own name a new edition, dated 1800, to which he added a second volume of poems, many of them written in homesickness during a long, cold, and friendless winter he and Dorothy had spent in Goslar, Germany, 1798–99. In his famous Preface to this edition, planned, like so many of the poems, in close consultation with Coleridge, Wordsworth enunciated the principles of the new criticism which served as rationale for the new poetry. Notable among the other works written in this prolific period is the austere and powerful tragic poem *The Ruined Cottage*.

Late in 1799 Wordsworth and Dorothy moved back permanently to their native lakes, settling at Grasmere in the little house later named Dove Cottage; Coleridge, following them, rented Greta Hall at Keswick, thirteen miles away. In 1802 Wordsworth finally came into his father's inheritance and, after an amicable settlement with Annette Vallon, married Mary Hutchinson, a Lake Country girl whom he had known since childhood. The course of his existence after that time was broken by various disasters: the drowning in 1805 of his favorite brother John, a sea captain whose ship was wrecked in a storm; the death of two of his five children in 1812; a gradual estrangement from Coleridge, culminating in an open quarrel (1810) from which they were not completely reconciled for almost two decades; and, from the 1830's on, the physical and mental decline of his sister Dorothy. The life of his middle age, however, was one of steadily increasing prosperity and reputation, as well as of political and religious conservatism. In 1813 an appointment as Stamp Distributor (that is, revenue collector) for Westmoreland was concrete evidence of his recognition as a national poet. Gradually Wordsworth's residences, as he moved into more and more commodious quarters, became standard places of resort for tourists; he was awarded honorary degrees and, in 1843, appointed poet laureate. He died in 1850 at the age of 80; only then did his executors publish his masterpiece, *The Prelude*, the autobiographical poem which he had begun in 1798 and completed, in its first version, in 1805, but which he had continued to revise and re-revise up to the last decade of his life.

Most of Wordsworth's greatest poetry had been written by 1807, when he published *Poems in Two Volumes*; and after *The Excursion* (1814) and the first collected edition of his poems (1815), although he continued to write voluminously, there is a conspicuous decline in his powers as a poet. The causes of what is often called "Wordsworth's anti-climax" have been much debated; the principal cause seems to be inherent in the very nature of his most characteristic writing. Wordsworth is above all the poet of the remembrance of things past, or as he himself put it, of "emotion recollected in tranquility." Some object or event in the present triggers a sudden renewal of feelings he had experienced in youth; the result is a poem exhibiting the sharp discrepancy between what Wordsworth called "two consciousnesses": himself as he is now and as he once was. But one's early emotional experience is not an inexhaustible resource for poetry. As Basil Willey has said, Wordsworth as a poet "was living upon capital"; and he knew it. As he says in *The Prelude* XII, while describing the recurrence of "spots of time" from his memories of childhood:

> The days gone by
> Return upon me almost from the dawn
> Of life: the hiding places of man's power
> Open; I would approach them, but they close.
> I see by glimpses now; when age comes on,
> May scarcely see at all. * * *

The past which Wordsworth recollected was one of emotional turmoil which is ordered, in the calmer present, into a hard-won equilibrium. The result was a poetry of excitation in calm; genius, as Wordsworth said, is "born to thrive by interchange / Of peace and excitation" (*Prelude* XIII.1–10). As time went on, however, the precarious equilibrium of his great creative period became a habit, and Wordsworth finally gained what, in the *Ode to Duty* (composed in 1804), he longed for, "a repose which ever is the same"—but at the expense of the agony and excitation which, under the calm surface, empowers his best and most characteristic poems.

Occasionally in his middle and later life a jolting experience would revive the intensity of Wordsworth's remembered emotion, and also his earlier poetic strength. The moving sonnet *Surprised by Joy*, for example, was written in his forties at the abrupt realization that time was beginning to diminish his grief at the death some years earlier of his little daughter Catharine. And when Wordsworth was 65 years old, the sudden report of the death of James Hogg called up the memory of other and greater poets whom Wordsworth had loved and outlived; the result was an "Extempore Effusion," written in a return to the simple quatrains of the early *Lyrical Ballads* and with a recovery of the great elegiac voice which had uttered the dirges to Lucy, 35 years before.

From LYRICAL BALLADS
We Are Seven[1]

—A simple Child,
That lightly draws its breath,
And feels its life in every limb,
What should it know of death?

I met a little cottage Girl: 5
She was eight years old, she said;
Her hair was thick with many a curl
That clustered round her head.

---

1. "Written at Alfoxden in the spring of 1798. * * * The little girl who is the heroine I met within the area of Goodrich Castle in the year 1793" (Wordsworth). Wordsworth also tells us that he composed the last line of the last stanza first, and that Coleridge contributed the initial stanza.

She had a rustic, woodland air,
And she was wildly clad:
Her eyes were fair, and very fair; 10
—Her beauty made me glad.

"Sisters and brothers, little Maid,
How many may you be?"
"How many? Seven in all," she said, 15
And wondering looked at me.

"And where are they? I pray you tell."
She answered, "Seven are we;
And two of us at Conway dwell,
And two are gone to sea. 20

"Two of us in the churchyard lie,
My sister and my brother;
And, in the churchyard cottage, I
Dwell near them with my mother."

"You say that two at Conway dwell, 25
And two are gone to sea,
Yet ye are seven! I pray you tell,
Sweet Maid, how this may be."

Then did the little Maid reply,
"Seven boys and girls are we; 30
Two of us in the churchyard lie,
Beneath the churchyard tree."

"You run about, my little Maid,
Your limbs they are alive;
If two are in the churchyard laid, 35
Then ye are only five."

"Their graves are green, they may be seen,"
The little Maid replied,
"Twelve steps or more from my mother's door,
And they are side by side. 40

"My stockings there I often knit,
My kerchief there I hem;
And there upon the ground I sit,
And sing a song to them.

"And often after sunset, sir, 45
When it is light and fair,
I take my little porringer,[2]
And eat my supper there.

"The first that died was sister Jane;
In bed she moaning lay, 50
Till God released her of her pain;
And then she went away.

2. Bowl for porridge.

"So in the churchyard she was laid;
And, when the grass was dry,
Together round her grave we played,   55
My brother John and I.

"And when the ground was white with snow,
And I could run and slide,
My brother John was forced to go,
And he lies by her side."   60

"How many are you, then," said I,
"If they two are in heaven?"
Quick was the little Maid's reply,
"O master! we are seven."

"But they are dead; those two are dead!   65
Their spirits are in heaven!"
'Twas throwing words away; for still
The little Maid would have her will,
And said, "Nay, we are seven!"

1798   1798

Lines Written in Early Spring

I heard a thousand blended notes,
While in a grove I sate reclined,
In that sweet mood when pleasant thoughts
Bring sad thoughts to the mind.

To her fair works did Nature link   5
The human soul that through me ran;
And much it grieved my heart to think
What man has made of man.

Through primrose tufts, in that green bower,
The periwinkle³ trailed its wreaths;   10
And 'tis my faith that every flower
Enjoys the air it breathes.

The birds around me hopped and played,
Their thoughts I cannot measure—
But the least motion which they made,   15
It seemed a thrill of pleasure.

The budding twigs spread out their fan,
To catch the breezy air;
And I must think, do all I can,
That there was pleasure there.   20

If this belief from heaven be sent,
If such be Nature's holy plan,⁴

---

3. A trailing evergreen plant with small blue flowers (U.S. myrtle).
4. The version of these lines printed in the *Lyrical Ballads* of 1798 mentioned neither heaven nor holiness: "If I these thoughts may not prevent, / If such be of my creed the plan."

Have I not reason to lament
What man has made of man?

1798   1798

Expostulation and Reply[1]

"Why, William, on that old gray stone,
Thus for the length of half a day,
Why, William, sit you thus alone,
And dream your time away?

"Where are your books?—that light bequeathed   5
To beings else forlorn and blind!
Up! up! and drink the spirit breathed
From dead men to their kind.

"You look round on your Mother Earth,
As if she for no purpose bore you;   10
As if you were her first-born birth,
And none had lived before you!"

One morning thus, by Esthwaite lake,
When life was sweet, I knew not why,
To me my good friend Matthew[2] spake,   15
And thus I made reply:

"The eye—it cannot choose but see;
We cannot bid the ear be still;
Our bodies feel, where'er they be,
Against or with our will.   20

"Nor less I deem that there are Powers
Which of themselves our minds impress;
That we can feed this mind of ours
In a wise passiveness.

"Think you, 'mid all this mighty sum   25
Of things forever speaking,
That nothing of itself will come,
But we must still be seeking?

"—Then ask not wherefore, here, alone,
Conversing[3] as I may,   30
I sit upon this old gray stone,
And dream my time away."

1798   1798

1. This and the following companion-poem have often been attacked—and defended—as Wordsworth's solemn deliverance on the comparative merits of nature and of books. But they are a dialogue between two friends who are intimate enough to rally one another by the usual device of overstating parts of a whole truth. Wordsworth said that the pieces originated in a conversation "with a friend who was somewhat unreasonably attached to modern books of moral philosophy," and also that the lore of "a wise passiveness" made the poem a favorite among Quakers.
2. A fictitious schoolmaster who plays a role in others of Wordsworth's early poems.
3. In the old sense of "communing" (with the "things forever speaking").

The Tables Turned

AN EVENING SCENE ON THE SAME SUBJECT

Up! up! my friend, and quit your books,
Or surely you'll grow double;
Up! up! my friend, and clear your looks;
Why all this toil and trouble?

The sun, above the mountain's head,   5
A freshening luster mellow
Through all the long green fields has spread,
His first sweet evening yellow.

Books! 'tis a dull and endless strife;
Come, hear the woodland linnet,[1]   10
How sweet his music! on my life,
There's more of wisdom in it.

And hark! how blithe the throstle[2] sings!
He, too, is no mean preacher;
Come forth into the light of things,   15
Let Nature be your teacher.

She has a world of ready wealth,
Our minds and hearts to bless—
Spontaneous wisdom breathed by health,
Truth breathed by cheerfulness.   20

One impulse from a vernal wood
May teach you more of man,
Of moral evil and of good,
Than all the sages can.

Sweet is the lore which Nature brings;   25
Our meddling intellect
Misshapes the beauteous forms of things—
We murder to dissect.

Enough of Science and of Art;
Close up those barren leaves;   30
Come forth, and bring with you a heart
That watches and receives.

1798   1798

To My Sister[1]

It is the first mild day of March:
Each minute sweeter than before,

---

1. A small finch, common in Europe.
2. The song thrush.
1. "Composed in front of Alfoxden House. * * * The larch mentioned in the first stanza was standing when I revisited the place in May, 1841, more than forty years after" (Wordsworth). The "Sister" is, of course, Dorothy, and "Edward" (named in line 13) is the boy Basil Montagu, then living with the Wordsworths.

The redbreast sings from the tall larch
That stands beside our door.

There is a blessing in the air,   5
Which seems a sense of joy to yield
To the bare trees, and mountains bare,
And grass in the green field.

My Sister! ('tis a wish of mine)
Now that our morning meal is done,   10
Make haste, your morning task resign;
Come forth and feel the sun.

Edward will come with you—and, pray,
Put on with speed your woodland dress,
And bring no book; for this one day   15
We'll give to idleness.

No joyless forms shall regulate
Our living calendar;
We from today, my Friend, will date
The opening of the year.   20

Love, now a universal birth,
From heart to heart is stealing,
From earth to man, from man to earth:
—It is the hour of feeling.

One moment now may give us more   25
Than years of toiling reason;
Our minds shall drink at every pore
The spirit of the season.

Some silent laws our hearts will make,
Which they shall long obey,   30
We for the year to come may take
Our temper from today.

And from the blessed power that rolls
About, below, above,
We'll frame the measure of our souls: 35
They shall be tuned to love.

Then come, my Sister! come, I pray,
With speed put on your woodland dress;
And bring no book: for this one day
We'll give to idleness.   40

1798   1798

Lines[1]

COMPOSED A FEW MILES ABOVE TINTERN ABBEY
ON REVISITING THE BANKS OF THE WYE
DURING A TOUR. JULY 13, 1798

Five years have passed; five summers, with the length
Of five long winters! and again I hear
These waters, rolling from their mountain-springs
With a soft inland murmur. Once again
Do I behold these steep and lofty cliffs,   5
That on a wild secluded scene impress
Thoughts of more deep seclusion; and connect
The landscape with the quiet of the sky.
The day is come when I again repose
Here, under this dark sycamore, and view   10
These plots of cottage ground, these orchard tufts,
Which at this season, with their unripe fruits,
Are clad in one green hue, and lose themselves
'Mid groves and copses. Once again I see
These hedgerows, hardly hedgerows, little lines   15
Of sportive wood run wild; these pastoral farms,
Green to the very door; and wreaths of smoke
Sent up, in silence, from among the trees!
With some uncertain notice, as might seem
Of vagrant dwellers in the houseless woods,   20
Or of some Hermit's cave, where by his fire
The Hermit sits alone.

          These beauteous forms,
Through a long absence, have not been to me
As is a landscape to a blind man's eye;
But oft, in lonely rooms, and 'mid the din   25
Of towns and cities, I have owed to them,
In hours of weariness, sensations sweet,
Felt in the blood, and felt along the heart;
And passing even into my purer mind,
With tranquil restoration—feelings too   30
Of unremembered pleasure; such, perhaps,
As have no slight or trivial influence
On that best portion of a good man's life,

1. "No poem of mine was composed under circumstances more pleasant for me to remember than this. I began it upon leaving Tintern, after crossing the Wye, and concluded it just as I was entering Bristol in the evening, after a ramble of 4 or 5 days, with my sister. Not a line of it was altered, and not any part of it written down till I reached Bristol" (Wordsworth). The poem was printed as the last item in *Lyrical Ballads.*

    Wordsworth had first visited the Wye valley and the ruins of Tintern Abbey, in Monmouthshire, while on a solitary walking tour in August of 1793, when he was 23 years old. The puzzling difference between the present landscape and the remembered "picture of the mind" (line 61) gives rise to an intricately organized meditation, in which the poet reviews his past, evaluates the present, and (through his sister as intermediary) anticipates the future, until he ends by rounding back quietly upon the scene which had been his point of departure.

His little, nameless, unremembered, acts
Of kindness and of love. Nor less, I trust,   35
To them I may have owed another gift,
Of aspect more sublime; that blessed mood,
In which the burthen of the mystery,
In which the heavy and the weary weight
Of all this unintelligible world,   40
Is lightened—that serene and blessed mood,
In which the affections gently lead us on—
Until, the breath of this corporeal frame
And even the motion of our human blood
Almost suspended, we are laid asleep   45
In body, and become a living soul;
While with an eye made quiet by the power
Of harmony, and the deep power of joy,
We see into the life of things.

              If this
Be but a vain belief, yet, oh! how oft—   50
In darkness and amid the many shapes
Of joyless daylight; when the fretful stir
Unprofitable, and the fever of the world,
Have hung upon the beatings of my heart—
How oft, in spirit, have I turned to thee,   55
O sylvan Wye! thou wanderer through the woods,
How often has my spirit turned to thee!

   And now, with gleams of half-extinguished thought
With many recognitions dim and faint,
And somewhat of a sad perplexity,   60
The picture of the mind revives again;
While here I stand, not only with the sense
Of present pleasure, but with pleasing thoughts
That in this moment there is life and food
For future years. And so I dare to hope,   65
Though changed, no doubt, from what I was when first
I came among these hills; when like a roe
I bounded o'er the mountains, by the sides
Of the deep rivers, and the lonely streams,
Wherever nature led—more like a man   70
Flying from something that he dreads than one
Who sought the thing he loved. For nature then
(The coarser pleasures of my boyish days,
And their glad animal movements all gone by)
To me was all in all.—I cannot paint   75
What then I was. The sounding cataract
Haunted me like a passion; the tall rock,
The mountain, and the deep and gloomy wood,
Their colors and their forms, were then to me
An appetite; a feeling and a love,   80

That had no need of a remoter charm,
By thought supplied, nor any interest
Unborrowed from the eye.—That time is past,
And all its aching joys are now no more,
And all its dizzy raptures.[2] Not for this   85
Faint[3] I, nor mourn nor murmur; other gifts
Have followed; for such loss, I would believe,
Abundant recompense. For I have learned
To look on nature, not as in the hour
Of thoughtless youth; but hearing oftentimes   90
The still, sad music of humanity,
Nor harsh nor grating, though of ample power
To chasten and subdue. And I have felt
A presence that disturbs me with the joy
Of elevated thoughts; a sense sublime   95
Of something far more deeply interfused,
Whose dwelling is the light of setting suns,
And the round ocean and the living air,
And the blue sky, and in the mind of man:
A motion and a spirit, that impels   100
All thinking things, all objects of all thought,
And rolls through all things. Therefore am I still
A lover of the meadows and the woods,
And mountains; and of all that we behold
From this green earth; of all the mighty world   105
Of eye, and ear—both what they half create,[4]
And what perceive; well pleased to recognize
In nature and the language of the sense
The anchor of my purest thoughts, the nurse,
The guide, the guardian of my heart, and soul   110
Of all my moral being.

                Nor perchance,
If I were not thus taught, should I the more
Suffer my genial spirits[5] to decay:
For thou art with me here upon the banks
Of this fair river; thou my dearest Friend,[6]   115

2. Lines 76 ff. contain Wordsworth's famous description of the three stages of his growing up, defined in terms of his evolving relations to the natural scene: the young boy's purely physical responsiveness (lines 73–74); the post-adolescent's aching, dizzy, and equivocal passions—a love which is more like dread (lines 67–72, 75–85: this was his state of mind on the occasion of his first visit); his present state (lines 85 ff.), in which for the first time he adds thought to sense. All his knowledge of human suffering, so painfully acquired in the interim, chastens him while it enriches the visible scene like a chord of music, and he has gained also awareness of an immanent "presence" which links his mind and all the elements of the external world.
3. Lose heart.
4. The fact that apparent changes in the sensible world have turned out to be projected by the changing mind of the observer gives evidence that the faculties "half create" the world; the part that is "perceived" (line 107) is what has remained unchanged between the two visits. This view that the "creative sensibility" contributes to its own perceptions is often reiterated in the early books of *The Prelude*.
5. "Genial" is here the adjectival form of the noun "genius" ("native powers").
6. His sister Dorothy.

My dear, dear Friend; and in thy voice I catch
The language of my former heart, and read
My former pleasures in the shooting lights
Of thy wild eyes. Oh! yet a little while
May I behold in thee what I was once,   120
My dear, dear Sister! and this prayer I make,
Knowing that Nature never did betray
The heart that loved her; 'tis her privilege,
Through all the years of this our life, to lead
From joy to joy: for she can so inform   125
The mind that is within us, so impress
With quietness and beauty, and so feed
With lofty thoughts, that neither evil tongues,
Rash judgments, nor the sneers of selfish men,
Nor greetings where no kindness is, nor all   130
The dreary intercourse of daily life,
Shall e'er prevail against us, or disturb
Our cheerful faith, that all which we behold
Is full of blessings. Therefore let the moon
Shine on thee in thy solitary walk;   135
And let the misty mountain winds be free
To blow against thee: and, in after years,
When these wild ecstasies shall be matured
Into a sober pleasure; when thy mind
Shall be a mansion for all lovely forms,   140
Thy memory be as a dwelling place
For all sweet sounds and harmonies; oh! then,
If solitude, or fear, or pain, or grief
Should be thy portion, with what healing thoughts
Of tender joy wilt thou remember me,   145
And these my exhortations! Nor, perchance —
If I should be where I no more can hear
Thy voice, nor catch from thy wild eyes these gleams
Of past existence[7]— wilt thou then forget
That on the banks of this delightful stream   150
We stood together; and that I, so long
A worshiper of Nature, hither came
Unwearied in that service; rather say
With warmer love—oh! with far deeper zeal
Of holier love. Nor wilt thou then forget,   155
That after many wanderings, many years
Of absence, these steep woods and lofty cliffs,
And this green pastoral landscape, were to me
More dear, both for themselves and for thy sake!

1798

7. I.e., his own "past experience" five years before; see lines 116–19.

From Preface to the Second Edition
OF SEVERAL OF THE FOREGOING POEMS, PUBLISHED, WITH AN ADDITIONAL VOLUME, UNDER THE TITLE OF "LYRICAL BALLADS"[1]

The first volume of these poems has already been submitted to general perusal. It was published as an experiment, which I hoped might be of some use to ascertain how far, by fitting to metrical arrangement a selection of the real language of men in a state of vivid sensation, that sort of pleasure and that quantity of pleasure may be imparted, which a poet may rationally endeavor to impart.

I had formed no very inaccurate estimate of the probable effect of those poems: I flattered myself that they who should be pleased with them would read them with more than common pleasure; and, on the other hand, I was well aware that by those who should dislike them they would be read with more than common dislike. The result has differed from my expectation in this only, that a greater number have been pleased than I ventured to hope I should please.

Several of my friends are anxious for the success of these poems, from a belief that, if the views with which they were composed were indeed realized, a class of poetry would be produced, well adapted to interest mankind permanently, and not unimportant in the

---

1. The "Advertisement" prefixed to the first edition of *Lyrical Ballads* in 1798 said that the majority of the poems were "to be considered as experiments" to determine "how far the language of conversation in the middle and lower classes of society is adapted to the purposes of poetic pleasure." In the second edition of 1800 Wordsworth, relying in part on discussions with Coleridge, expanded this Advertisement into a justification of the new poetry on the basis of what he considered to be the principles of all good poetry. This Preface was enlarged in 1802, and altered later; the extract printed here includes these revisions.

Though the Preface has been one of the most discussed and influential of all critical essays, commentators still do not agree about precisely what were Wordsworth's major claims, or about the structure of his argument. It is clear, however, that Wordsworth tried to overthrow the basic theory, as well as the practice, of neoclassic poetry. When Wordsworth said that his principal object was "to choose incidents and situations from common life," he attacked the strict neoclassic view that the highest and most serious poetic kinds, such as epic and tragedy, were limited to the actions of kings, nobles, and heroes, and that only the lower poetic kinds, such as comedy and sat-

ire, might concern themselves with the lower social classes. Wordsworth thus translated his democratic sympathies into critical terms, overturning the precepts of traditional poetic "decorum" in order to justify the serious poetic treatment of peasants, children, criminals, and idiot boys. In addition Wordsworth undertook to write in "a selection of language really used by men," on the grounds that there can be no "*essential* difference between the language of prose and metrical composition." Here he opposed the basic neoclassic principle that in order to give its proper pleasure, the language of a poem must be artfully elevated over standard prose, by a special diction and figures of speech, in order to match itself to the height and dignity of its particular poetic kind. Wordsworth's own view of poetic diction is based on the new critical premise, at the heart of his theory, that "all good poetry is the spontaneous overflow of powerful feeling." The equivalence, therefore, between the language proper to a poet and the prose language "really spoken by men" is not one of vocabulary or grammar, but an equivalence in psychological origin—both, according to Wordsworth, ought to originate instinctively, as the words and figures of speech naturally prompted by the feelings of the speaker.

quality and in the multiplicity of its moral relations; and on this account they have advised me to prefix a systematic defense of the theory upon which the poems were written. But I was unwilling to undertake the task, knowing that on this occasion the reader would look coldly upon my arguments, since I might be suspected of having been principally influenced by the selfish and foolish hope of *reasoning* him into an approbation of these particular poems; and I was still more unwilling to undertake the task, because adequately to display the opinions, and fully to enforce the arguments, would require a space wholly disproportionate to a preface. For to treat the subject with the clearness and coherence of which it is susceptible, it would be necessary to give a full account of the present state of the public taste in this country, and to determine how far this taste is healthy or depraved; which, again, could not be determined, without pointing out in what manner language and the human mind act and react on each other, and without retracing the revolutions, not of literature alone, but likewise of society itself. I have therefore altogether declined to enter regularly upon this defense; yet I am sensible that that there would be something like impropriety in abruptly obtruding upon the public, without a few words of introduction, poems so materially different from those upon which general approbation is at present bestowed.

It is supposed that by the act of writing in verse an author makes a formal engagement that he will gratify certain known habits of association; that he not only thus apprises the reader that certain classes of ideas and expressions will be found in his book, but that others will be carefully excluded. This exponent or symbol held forth by metrical language must in different eras of literature have excited very different expectations: for example, in the age of Catullus, Terence, and Lucretius, and that of Statius or Claudian;[2] and in our own country, in the age of Shakespeare and Beaumont and Fletcher, and that of Donne and Cowley, or Dryden, or Pope. I will not take upon me to determine the exact import of the promise which, by the act of writing in verse, an author in the present day makes to his reader; but it will undoubtedly appear to many persons that I have not fulfilled the terms of an engagement thus voluntarily contracted. They who have been accustomed to the gaudiness and inane phraseology of many modern writers, if they persist in reading this book to its conclusion, will, no doubt, frequently have to struggle with feelings of strangeness and awkwardness; they will look round for poetry, and will be induced to inquire by what species of courtesy these attempts can be permitted to assume that title. I hope, therefore, the reader will not censure

2. Wordsworth has in mind the difference between the naturalness and simplicity of the first three Roman poets (who wrote in the last two centuries B.C.) and the elaborate artifice of the last two Roman poets (Statius wrote in the 1st and Claudian in the 4th century A.D.).

me for attempting to state what I have proposed to myself to perform; and also (as far as the limits of a preface will permit) to explain some of the chief reasons which have determined me in the choice of my purpose: that at least he may be spared any unpleasant feeling of disappointment, and that I myself may be protected from one of the most dishonorable accusations which can be brought against an author; namely, that of an indolence which prevents him from endeavoring to ascertain what is his duty, or, when his duty is ascertained, prevents him from performing it.

The principal object, then, proposed in these poems was to choose incidents and situations from common life, and to relate or describe them, throughout, as far as was possible, in a selection of language really used by men, and, at the same time, to throw over them a certain coloring of imagination, whereby ordinary things should be presented to the mind in an unusual aspect;[3] and further, and above all, to make these incidents and situations interesting by tracing in them, truly though not ostentatiously, the primary laws of our nature: chiefly, as far as regards the manner in which we associate ideas in a state of excitement. Humble and rustic life was generally chosen, because in that condition the essential passions of the heart find a better soil in which they can attain their maturity, are less under restraint, and speak a plainer and more emphatic language; because in that condition of life our elementary feelings co-exist in a state of greater simplicity, and consequently may be more accurately contemplated and more forcibly communicated; because the manners of rural life germinate from those elementary feelings, and, from the necessary character of rural occupations, are more easily comprehended, and are more durable; and, lastly, because in that condition the passions of men are incorporated with the beautiful and permanent forms of nature. The language, too, of these men has been adopted (purified indeed from what appear to be its real defects, from all lasting and rational causes of dislike or disgust) because such men hourly communicate with the best objects from which the best part of language is originally derived; and because, from their rank in society and the sameness and narrow circle of their intercourse, being less under the influence of social vanity, they convey their feelings and notions in simple and unelaborated expressions. Accordingly, such a language, arising out of repeated experience and regular feelings, is a more permanent and a far more philosophical language than that which is frequently substituted for it by poets, who think that they are conferring honor upon themselves and their art, in proportion as they separate themselves from the sympathies of men, and indulge in arbitrary and capricious habits of expression, in

3. Cf. Coleridge's account of their plan in *Biographia Literaria*, Chapter XIV.

order to furnish food for fickle tastes, and fickle appetites, of their own creation.[4]

I cannot, however, be insensible to the present outcry against the triviality and meanness, both of thought and language, which some of my contemporaries have occasionally introduced into their metrical compositions; and I acknowledge that this defect, where it exists, is more dishonorable to the writer's own character than false refinement or arbitrary innovation, though I should contend at the same time that it is far less pernicious in the sum of its consequences. From such verses the poems in these volumes will be found distinguished at least by one mark of difference, that each of them has a worthy *purpose*. Not that I always began to write with a distinct purpose formally conceived; but habits of meditation have, I trust, so prompted and regulated my feelings that my descriptions of such objects as strongly excite those feelings will be found to carry along with them a *purpose*. If this opinion be erroneous, I can have little right to the name of a poet. For all good poetry is the spontaneous overflow of powerful feelings; and though this be true, poems to which any value can be attached were never produced on any variety of subjects but by a man who, being possessed of more than usual organic sensibility, had also thought long and deeply. For our continued influxes of feeling are modified and directed by our thoughts, which are indeed the representatives of all our past feelings; and, as by contemplating the relation of these general representatives to each other, we discover what is really important to men, so, by the repetition and continuance of this act, our feelings will be connected with important subjects, till at length, if we be originally possessed of much sensibility, such habits of mind will be produced that, by obeying blindly and mechanically the impulses of those habits, we shall describe objects, and utter sentiments, of such a nature, and in such connection with each other, that the understanding of the reader must necessarily be in some degree enlightened, and his affections strengthened and purified.

It has been said that each of these poems has a purpose. Another circumstance must be mentioned which distinguishes these poems from the popular poetry of the day; it is this, that the feeling therein developed gives importance to the action and situation, and not the action and situation to the feeling.

A sense of false modesty shall not prevent me from asserting that the reader's attention is pointed to this mark of distinction, far less for the sake of these particular poems than from the general importance of the subject. The subject is indeed important! For

4. "It is worth while here to observe that the affecting parts of Chaucer are almost always expressed in language pure and universally intelligible even to this day" [Wordsworth's note].

the human mind is capable of being excited without the application of gross and violent stimulants; and he must have a very faint perception of its beauty and dignity who does not know this, and who does not further know that one being is elevated above another in proportion as he possesses this capability. It has therefore appeared to me that to endeavor to produce or enlarge this capability is one of the best services in which, at any period, a writer can be engaged; but this service, excellent at all times, is especially so at the present day. For a multitude of causes, unknown to former times, are now acting with a combined force to blunt the discriminating powers of the mind, and, unfitting it for all voluntary exertion, to reduce it to a state of almost savage torpor. The most effective of these causes are the great national events which are daily taking place, and the increasing accumulation of men in cities, where the uniformity of their occupations produces a craving for extraordinary incident, which the rapid communication of intelligence hourly gratifies.[5] To this tendency of life and manners the literature and theatrical exhibitions of the country have conformed themselves. The invaluable works of our elder writers, I had almost said the works of Shakespeare and Milton, are driven into neglect by frantic novels, sickly and stupid German tragedies,[6] and deluges of idle and extravagant stories in verse. When I think upon this degrading thirst after outrageous stimulation, I am almost ashamed to have spoken of the feeble endeavor made in these volumes to counteract it; and, reflecting upon the magnitude of the general evil, I should be oppressed with no dishonorable melancholy, had I not a deep impression of certain inherent and indestructible qualities of the human mind, and likewise of certain powers in the great and permanent objects that act upon it, which are equally inherent and indestructible; and were there not added to this impression a belief that the time is approaching when the evil will be systematically opposed by men of greater powers, and with far more distinguished success.

Having dwelt thus long on the subjects and aim of these poems, I shall request the reader's permission to apprise him of a few circumstances relating to their *style*, in order, among other reasons, that he may not censure me for not having performed what I never attempted. The reader will find the personifications of abstract ideas rarely occur in these volumes, and are utterly rejected, as an ordinary device to elevate the style, and raise it above prose. My purpose was to imitate, and, as far as possible, to adopt the very language of men; and assuredly such personifications do not make any

---

5. This was the period of the French Revolution, of the Industrial Revolution, and of the Napoleonic Wars.
6. Wordsworth probably had in mind the "Gothic" terror novels by writers such as Ann Radcliffe and M. G. Lewis, and the sentimental melodramas, then exceedingly popular in England, of August von Kotzebue and his German contemporaries.

natural or regular part of that language. They are, indeed, a figure of speech occasionally prompted by passion, and I have made use of them as such; but have endeavored utterly to reject them as a mechanical device of style, or as a family language which writers in meter seem to lay claim to by prescription. I have wished to keep the reader in the company of flesh and blood, persuaded that by so doing I shall interest him. Others who pursue a different track will interest him likewise; I do not interfere with their claim, but wish to prefer a claim of my own. There will also be found in these volumes little of what is usually called poetic diction; as much pains has been taken to avoid it as is ordinarily taken to produce it; this has been done for the reason already alleged, to bring my language near to the language of men; and further, because the pleasure which I have proposed to myself to impart is of a kind very different from that which is supposed by many persons to be the proper object of poetry. Without being culpably particular, I do not know how to give my reader a more exact notion of the style in which it was my wish and intention to write than by informing him that I have at all times endeavored to look steadily at my subject; consequently there is, I hope, in these poems little falsehood of description, and my ideas are expressed in language fitted to their respective importance. Something must have been gained by this practice, as it is friendly to one property of all good poetry, namely, good sense; but it has necessarily cut me off from a large portion of phrases and figures of speech which from father to son have long been regarded as the common inheritance of poets. I have also thought it expedient to restrict myself still further, having abstained from the use of many expressions, in themselves proper and beautiful, but which have been foolishly repeated by bad poets, till such feelings of disgust are connected with them as it is scarcely possible by any art of association to overpower.

If in a poem there should be found a series of lines, or even a single line, in which the language, though naturally arranged, and according to the strict laws of meter, does not differ from that of prose, there is a numerous class of critics, who, when they stumble upon these prosaisms, as they call them, imagine that they have made a notable discovery, and exult over the poet as over a man ignorant of his own profession. Now these men would establish a canon of criticism which the reader will conclude he must utterly reject, if he wishes to be pleased with these volumes. And it would be a most easy task to prove to him that not only the language of a large portion of every good poem, even of the most elevated character, must necessarily, except with reference to the meter, in no respect differ from that of good prose, but likewise that some of the most interesting parts of the best poems will be found to be strictly the language of prose when prose is well written. The truth of this assertion might be demonstrated by innumerable passages from almost all the poetical writings, even of Milton himself. To illustrate the subject in a general manner, I will here adduce a short composition of Gray, who was at the head of those who, by their reasonings, have attempted to widen the space of separation betwixt prose and metrical composition, and was more than any other man curiously elaborate in the structure of his own poetic diction.[7]

> In vain to me the smiling mornings shine,
> And reddening Phoebus lifts his golden fire:
> The birds in vain their amorous descant join,
> Or cheerful fields resume their green attire.
> These ears, alas! for other notes repine;
> *A different object do these eyes require;*
> *My lonely anguish melts no heart but mine;*
> *And in my breast the imperfect joys expire;*
> Yet morning smiles the busy race to cheer,
> And newborn pleasure brings to happier men;
> The fields to all their wonted tribute bear;
> To warm their little loves the birds complain.
> *I fruitless mourn to him that cannot hear,*
> *And weep the more because I weep in vain.*

It will easily be perceived that the only part of this sonnet which is of any value is the lines printed in italics; it is equally obvious that, except in the rhyme, and in the use of the single word "fruitless" for fruitlessly, which is so far a defect, the language of these lines does in no respect differ from that of prose.

By the foregoing quotation it has been shown that the language of prose may yet be well adapted to poetry; and it was previously asserted that a large portion of the language of every good poem can in no respect differ from that of good prose. We will go further. It may be safely affirmed that there neither is, nor can be, any *essential* difference between the language of prose and metrical composition. We are fond of tracing the resemblance between poetry and painting, and, accordingly, we call them sisters; but where shall we find bonds of connection sufficiently strict to typify the affinity betwixt metrical and prose composition? They both speak by and to the same organs; the bodies in which both of them are clothed may be said to be of the same substance, their affections are kindred, and almost identical, not necessarily differing even in degree; poetry[8] sheds no tears "such as angels weep," but natural

---

7. Thomas Gray had written that "the language of the age is never the language of poetry." The poem Wordsworth reproduces here is Gray's *Sonnet on the Death of Richard West.*
8. "I here use the word 'poetry' (though against my own judgment) as opposed to the word 'prose,' and synonymous with metrical composition. But much confusion has been introduced into criticism by this contradistinction of poetry and prose, instead of

and human tears; she can boast of no celestial ichor[9] that distinguishes her vital juices from those of prose; the same human blood circulates through the veins of them both. * * *

Taking up the subject, then, upon general grounds, let me ask what is meant by the word Poet? What is a poet? To whom does he address himself? And what language is to be expected from him? —He is a man speaking to men: a man, it is true, endowed with more lively sensibility, more enthusiasm and tenderness, who has a greater knowledge of human nature, and a more comprehensive soul, than are supposed to be common among mankind; a man pleased with his own passions and volitions, and who rejoices more than other men in the spirit of life that is in him; delighting to contemplate similar volitions and passions as manifested in the goings on of the universe, and habitually impelled to create them where he does not find them. To these qualities he has added a disposition to be affected more than other men by absent things as if they were present; an ability of conjuring up in himself passions which are indeed far from being the same as those produced by real events, yet (especially in those parts of the general sympathy which are pleasing and delightful) do more nearly resemble the passions produced by real events than anything which, from the motions of their own minds merely, other men are accustomed to feel in themselves—whence, and from practice, he has acquired a greater readiness and power in expressing what he thinks and feels, and especially those thoughts and feelings which, by his own choice, or from the structure of his own mind, arise in him without immediate external excitement.

But whatever portion of this faculty we may suppose even the greatest poet to possess, there cannot be a doubt that the language which it will suggest to him must often, in liveliness and truth, fall short of that which is uttered by men in real life under the actual pressure of those passions, certain shadows of which the poet thus produces, or feels to be produced, in himself.

However exalted a notion we would wish to cherish of the character of a poet, it is obvious that while he describes and imitates passions, his employment is in some degree mechanical, compared with the freedom and power of real and substantial action and suffering. So that it will be the wish of the poet to bring his feelings near to those of the persons whose feelings he describes; nay, for short spaces of time, perhaps, to let himself slip into an entire delusion, and even confound and identify his own feelings with theirs;

the more philosophical one of poetry and matter of fact, or science. The only strict antithesis to prose is meter; nor is this, in truth, a *strict* antithesis, because lines and passages of meter so naturally occur in writing prose that it would be scarcely possible to avoid them, even if it were desirable" [Wordsworth's note]. The quotation in the text is from *Paradise Lost* I.620.

9. In Greek mythology, the fluid in the veins of the gods.

modifying only the language which is thus suggested to him by a consideration that he describes for a particular purpose, that of giving pleasure. Here, then, he will apply the principle of selection which has been already insisted upon. He will depend upon this for removing what would otherwise be painful or disgusting in the passion; he will feel that there is no necessity to trick out or to elevate nature; and the more industriously he applies this principle the deeper will be his faith that no words which *his* fancy or imagination can suggest will be to be compared with those which are the emanations of reality and truth. * * *

The knowledge both of the poet and the man of science is pleasure; but the knowledge of the one cleaves to us as a necessary part of our existence, our natural and unalienable inheritance; the other is a personal and individual acquisition, slow to come to us, and by no habitual and direct sympathy connecting us with our fellow beings. The man of science seeks truth as a remote and unknown benefactor; he cherishes and loves it in his solitude; the poet, singing a song in which all human beings join with him, rejoices in the presence of truth as our visible friend and hourly companion. Poetry is the breath and finer spirit of all knowledge; it is the impassioned expression which is in the countenance of all science. Emphatically may it be said of the poet, as Shakespeare hath said of man, that "he looks before and after."[1] He is the rock of defense for human nature; an upholder and preserver, carrying everywhere with him relationship and love. In spite of difference of soil and climate, of languagè and manners, of laws and customs, in spite of things silently gone out of mind, and things violently destroyed, the poet binds together by passion and knowledge the vast empire of human society, as it is spread over the whole earth and over all time. The objects of the poet's thoughts are everywhere; though the eyes and senses of man are, it is true, his favorite guides, yet he will follow wheresoever he can find an atmosphere of sensation in which to move his wings. Poetry is the first and last of all knowledge—it is as immortal as the heart of man. If the labors of men of science should ever create any material revolution, direct or indirect, in our condition, and in the impressions which we habitually receive, the poet will sleep then no more than at present; he will be ready to follow the steps of the man of science, not only in those general indirect effects, but he will be at his side, carrying sensation into the midst of the objects of the science itself.[2] The remotest discoveries of the chemist, the botanist, or mineralogist will be as proper objects of the poet's art as any upon which it can be employed, if the time should ever come when these things shall be

---

1. *Hamlet* IV.iv.37.
2. Wordsworth heralds here, among other things, the modern poetry of the machine; he himself wrote an early example in the sonnet *Steamboats, Viaducts, and Railways.*

familiar to us, and the relations under which they are contemplated by the followers of these respective sciences shall be manifestly and palpably material to us as enjoying and suffering beings. If the time should ever come when what is now called science, thus familiarized to men, shall be ready to put on, as it were, a form of flesh and blood, the poet will lend his divine spirit to aid the transfiguration, and will welcome the being thus produced, as a dear and genuine inmate of the household of man.—It is not, then, to be supposed that anyone who holds that sublime notion of poetry which I have attempted to convey will break in upon the sanctity and truth of his pictures by transitory and accidental ornaments, and endeavor to excite admiration of himself by arts the necessity of which must manifestly depend upon the assumed meanness of his subject.

What has been thus far said applies to poetry in general, but especially to those parts of composition where the poet speaks through the mouths of his characters; and upon this point it appears to authorize the conclusion that there are few persons of good sense who would not allow that the dramatic parts of composition are defective, in proportion as they deviate from the real language of nature, and are colored by a diction of the poet's own, either peculiar to him as an individual poet or belonging simply to poets in general; to a body of men who, from the circumstance of their compositions being in meter, it is expected will employ a particular language.

It is not, then, in the dramatic parts of composition that we look for this distinction of language; but still it may be proper and necessary where the poet speaks to us in his own person and character. To this I answer by referring the reader to the description before given of a poet. Among the qualities there enumerated as principally conducing to form a poet, is implied nothing differing in kind from other men, but only in degree. The sum of what was said is that the poet is chiefly distinguished from other men by a greater promptness to think and feel without immediate external excitement, and a greater power in expressing such thoughts and feelings as are produced in him in that manner. But these passions and thoughts and feelings are the general passions and thoughts and feelings of men. And with what are they connected? Undoubtedly with our moral sentiments and animal[3] sensations, and with the causes which excite these; with the operations of the elements, and the appearances of the visible universe; with storm and sunshine, with the revolutions of the seasons, with cold and heat, with loss of friends and kindred, with injuries and resentments, gratitude and hope, with fear and sorrow. These, and the like, are the sensations and objects which the poet describes, as they are the sensations of

3. In the old sense: that which pertains to man's senses, as distinguished from his intellectual and moral aspects.

other men, and the objects which interest them. The poet thinks and feels in the spirit of human passions. How, then, can his language differ in any material degree from that of all other men who feel vividly and see clearly? It might be *proved* that it is impossible. But supposing that this were not the case, the poet might then be allowed to use a peculiar language when expressing his feelings for his own gratification, or that of men like himself. But poets do not write for poets alone, but for men. Unless, therefore, we are advocates for that admiration which subsists upon ignorance, and that pleasure which arises from hearing what we do not understand, the poet must descend from this supposed height; and, in order to excite rational sympathy, he must express himself as other men express themselves. To this it may be added that while he is only selecting from the real language of men, or, which amounts to the same thing, composing accurately in the spirit of such selection, he is treading upon safe ground, and we know what we are to expect from him. Our feelings are the same with respect to meter; for, as it may be proper to remind the reader, the distinction of meter is regular and uniform, and not, like that which is produced by what is usually called POETIC DICTION, arbitrary, and subject to infinite caprices upon which no calculation whatever can be made. In the one case, the reader is utterly at the mercy of the poet, respecting what imagery or diction he may choose to connect with the passion; whereas in the other, the meter obeys certain laws, to which the poet and reader both willingly submit because they are certain, and because no interference is made by them with the passion but such as the concurring testimony of ages has shown to heighten and improve the pleasure which coexists with it. * * *

I have said that poetry is the spontaneous overflow of powerful feelings: it takes its origin from emotion recollected in tranquillity: the emotion is contemplated till, by a species of reaction, the tranquillity gradually disappears, and an emotion, kindred to that which was before the subject of contemplation, is gradually produced, and does itself actually exist in the mind. In this mood successful composition generally begins, and in a mood similar to this it is carried on; but the emotion, of whatever kind, and in whatever degree, from various causes, is qualified by various pleasures, so that in describing any passions whatsoever, which are voluntarily described, the mind will, upon the whole, be in a state of enjoyment. If Nature be thus cautious to preserve in a state of enjoyment a being so employed, the poet ought to profit by the lesson held forth to him, and ought especially to take care that, whatever passions he communicates to his reader, those passions, if his reader's mind be sound and vigorous, should always be accompanied with an overbalance of pleasure. Now the music of harmonious metrical language, the sense of difficulty overcome, and the blind association of pleasure which has been previously received from works of rhyme or meter of the same or similar construction, an indistinct perception perpetually renewed of language closely resembling that of real life, and yet, in the circumstance of meter, differing from it so widely—all these imperceptibly make up a complex feeling of delight, which is of the most important use in tempering the painful feeling always found intermingled with powerful descriptions of the deeper passions. This effect is always produced in pathetic and impassioned poetry; while in lighter compositions the ease and gracefulness with which the poet manages his numbers are themselves confessedly a principal source of the gratification of the reader. All that it is *necessary* to say, however, upon this subject, may be effected by affirming, what few persons will deny, that of two descriptions, either of passions, manners, or characters each of them equally well executed, the one in prose and the other in verse, the verse will be read a hundred times where the prose is read once. * * *

If an author, by any single composition, has impressed us with respect for his talents, it is useful to consider this as affording a presumption that on other occasions, where we have been displeased, he nevertheless may not have written ill or absurdly; and further, to give him so much credit for this one composition as may induce us to review what has displeased us with more care than we should otherwise have bestowed upon it. This is not only an act of justice, but, in our decisions upon poetry especially, may conduce in a high degree to the improvement of our own taste; for an *accurate* taste in poetry and in all the other arts, as Sir Joshua Reynolds[4] has observed, is an *acquired* talent, which can only be produced by thought and a long-continued intercourse with the best models of composition. This is mentioned, not with so ridiculous a purpose as to prevent the most inexperienced reader from judging for himself (I have already said that I wish him to judge for himself), but merely to temper the rashness of decision, and to suggest that, if poetry be a subject on which much time has not been bestowed, the judgment may be erroneous; and that, in many cases, it necessarily will be so.

Nothing would, I know, have so effectually contributed to further the end which I have in view, as to have shown of what kind the pleasure is, and how that pleasure is produced, which is confessedly produced by metrical composition essentially different from that which I have here endeavored to recommend: for the reader will say that he has been pleased by such composition; and what more can be done for him? The power of any art is limited; and he will suspect that, if it be proposed to furnish him with new

4. Leading English portrait painter of the 18th century and author of *Discourses on Art* ((1769–1790).

friends, that can be only upon condition of his abandoning his old friends. Besides, as I have said, the reader is himself conscious of the pleasure which he has received from such composition, composition to which he has peculiarly attached the endearing name of poetry; and all men feel an habitual gratitude, and something of an honorable bigotry, for the objects which have long continued to please them: we not only wish to be pleased, but to be pleased in that particular way in which we have been accustomed to be pleased. There is in these feelings enough to resist a host of arguments; and I should be the less able to combat them successfully, as I am willing to allow that, in order entirely to enjoy the poetry which I am recommending, it would be necessary to give up much of what is ordinarily enjoyed. But, would my limits have permitted me to point out how this pleasure is produced, many obstacles might have been removed, and the reader assisted in perceiving that the powers of language are not so limited as he may suppose; and that it is possible for poetry to give other enjoyments, of a purer, more lasting, and more exquisite nature. This part of the subject has not been· altogether neglected, but it has not been so much my present aim to prove that the interest excited by some other kinds of poetry is less vivid, and less worthy of the nobler powers of the mind, as to offer reasons for presuming that, if my purpose were fulfilled, a species of poetry would be produced which is genuine poetry, in its nature well adapted to interest mankind permanently, and likewise important in the multiplicity and quality of its moral relations.

From what has been said, and from a perusal of the poems, the reader will be able clearly to perceive the object which I had in view; he will determine how far it has been attained, and, what is a much more important question, whether it be worth attaining; and upon the decision of these two questions will rest my claim to the approbation of the public.

1800, 1802

Strange Fits of Passion Have I Known[1]

Strange fits of passion have I known:
And I will dare to tell,
But in the Lover's ear alone,
What once to me befell.

1. This and the four following pieces are often known as the "Lucy poems." All but the last were written in 1799, while Wordsworth and Dorothy were in Germany, and homesick. There has been diligent speculation about the identity of Lucy, but it remains speculation; the one certainty is that she is not the girl of Wordsworth's *Lucy Gray*, below. "Fits of passion": in an archaic sense, "sudden moods of intense grief."

When she I loved looked every day   5
Fresh as a rose in June,
I to her cottage bent my way,
Beneath an evening moon.

Upon the moon I fixed my eye,
All over the wide lea;   10
With quickening pace my horse drew nigh
Those paths so dear to me.

And now we reached the orchard plot;
And, as we climbed the hill,
The sinking moon to Lucy's cot   15
Came near, and nearer still.

In one of those sweet dreams I slept,
Kind Nature's gentlest boon!
And all the while my eyes I kept
On the descending moon.   20

My horse moved on; hoof after hoof
He raised, and never stopped:
When down behind the cottage roof,
At once, the bright moon dropped.

What fond and wayward thoughts will slide   25
Into a Lover's head!
"O mercy!" to myself I cried,
"If Lucy should be dead!"[2]

1799   1800

She Dwelt Among the Untrodden Ways

She dwelt among the untrodden ways
    Beside the springs of Dove,[3]
A Maid whom there were none to praise
    And very few to love;

A violet by a mossy stone   5
    Half hidden from the eye!
—Fair as a star, when only one
    Is shining in the sky.

She lived unknown, and few could know
    When Lucy ceased to be;   10
But she is in her grave, and, oh,
    The difference to me!

1799   1800

2. An additional stanza in an earlier MS. version demonstrates how a poem may profit by omitting a passage which is, in itself, excellent poetry: "I told her this: her laughter light / Is ringing in my ears; / And when I think upon that night / My eyes are dim with tears."
3. There are several rivers by this name in England, including one in the Lake Country.

Three Years She Grew

Three years she grew in sun and shower,
Then Nature said, "A lovelier flower
On earth was never sown;
This Child I to myself will take;
She shall be mine, and I will make   5
A Lady of my own.

"Myself will to my darling be
Both law and impulse:[4] and with me
The Girl, in rock and plain,
In earth and heaven, in glade and bower,   10
Shall feel an overseeing power
To kindle or restrain.

"She shall be sportive as the fawn
That wild with glee across the lawn
Or up the mountain springs;   15
And hers shall be the breathing balm,
And hers the silence and the calm
Of mute insensate things.

"The floating clouds their state shall lend
To her; for her the willow bend;   20
Nor shall she fail to see
Even in the motions of the Storm
Grace that shall mold the Maiden's form
By silent sympathy.

"The stars of midnight shall be dear   25
To her; and she shall lean her ear
In many a secret place
Where rivulets dance their wayward round,
And beauty born of murmuring sound
Shall pass into her face.   30

"And vital feelings of delight
Shall rear her form to stately height,
Her virgin bosom swell;
Such thoughts to Lucy I will give
While she and I together live   35
Here in this happy dell."

Thus Nature spake—the work was done—
How soon my Lucy's race was run!
She died, and left to me
This health, this calm, and quiet scene;   40

4. Wordsworth recognizes in the moral tutelage of nature a double influence, "to kindle or restrain." Cf. *The Prel-* *ude* I.301–2, where Wordsworth grows up "fostered alike by beauty and by fear."

The memory of what has been,
And never more will be.

1799   1800

A Slumber Did My Spirit Seal

A slumber did my spirit seal;
    I had no human fears:
She seemed a thing that could not feel
    The touch of earthly years.

No motion has she now, no force;   5
    She neither hears nor sees;
Rolled round in earth's diurnal[2] course,
    With rocks, and stones, and trees.

1799   1800

I Traveled Among Unknown Men

I traveled among unknown men,
    In lands beyond the sea;
Nor, England! did I know till then
    What love I bore to thee.

'Tis past, that melancholy dream!   5
    Nor will I quit thy shore
A second time; for still I seem
    To love thee more and more.

Among thy mountains did I feel
    The joy of my desire;   10
And she I cherished turned her wheel
    Beside an English fire.

Thy mornings showed, thy nights concealed,
    The bowers where Lucy played;
And thine too is the last green field   15
    That Lucy's eyes surveyed.

ca. 1801   1807

Lucy Gray[1]

OR SOLITUDE

Oft I had heard of Lucy Gray:
And, when I crossed the wild,

2. Daily.
1. Written in 1799 while Wordsworth was in Germany, and founded on a true account of a young girl who drowned when she lost her way in a snowstorm. "The body however was found in the canal. The way in which the incident was treated and the spiritualizing of

I chanced to see at break of day
The solitary child.

No mate, no comrade Lucy knew;   5
She dwelt on a wide moor,
—The sweetest thing that ever grew
Beside a human door!

You yet may spy the fawn at play,
The hare upon the green;   10
But the sweet face of Lucy Gray
Will never more be seen.

"Tonight will be a stormy night—
You to the town must go;
And take a lantern, Child, to light   15
Your mother through the snow."

"That, Father! will I gladly do:
'Tis scarcely afternoon—
The minster² clock has just struck two,
And yonder is the moon!"   20

At this the Father raised his hook,
And snapped a faggot band;³
He plied his work—and Lucy took
The lantern in her hand.

Not blither is the mountain roe;   25
With many a wanton stroke
Her feet disperse the powdery snow,
That rises up like smoke.

The storm came on before its time;
She wandered up and down;   30
And many a hill did Lucy climb,
But never reached the town.

The wretched parents all that night
Went shouting far and wide;
But there was neither sound nor sight   35
To serve them for a guide.

At daybreak on a hill they stood
That overlooked the moor;
And thence they saw the bridge of wood,
A furlong⁴ from their door.   40

They wept—and, turning homeward, cried,

the character might furnish hints for
contrasting the imaginative influences
which I have endeavored to throw over
common life with Crabbe's matter-of-
fact style of treating subjects of the
same kind" (Wordsworth). Compare
Wordsworth's statement (in the Preface to *Lyrical Ballads*) of his undertaking to throw over ordinary things
"a certain coloring of imagination."
2. Church.
3. Cord binding a bundle of sticks to
be used for fuel.
4. One eighth of a mile.

"In heaven we all shall meet";
—When in the snow the mother spied
The print of Lucy's feet.

Then downwards from the steep hill's edge   45
They tracked the footmarks small;
And through the broken hawthorn hedge,
And by the long stone wall;

And then an open field they crossed:
The marks were still the same;   50
They tracked them on, nor ever lost;
And to the bridge they came.

They followed from the snowy bank
Those footmarks, one by one,
Into the middle of the plank;   55
And further there were none!

—Yet some maintain that to this day
She is a living child;
That you may see sweet Lucy Gray
Upon the lonesome wild.   60

O'er rough and smooth she trips along,
And never looks behind;
And sings a solitary song
That whistles in the wind.

1799   1800

The Ruined Cottage Wordsworth wrote *The Ruined Cottage* in
1797–98, but revised it several times before he finally published an expanded rendering of the story as Book I of *The Excursion*, in 1814. Not
until 1949 was *The Ruined Cottage*, as an independent poem, made available in the fifth volume of *The Poetical Works of William Wordsworth*,
edited by Ernest de Selincourt and Helen Darbishire, who printed a version
known as "MS. B." The version reprinted here is, however, from "MS. D,"
dating 1799 or 1800, as transcribed by Jonathan Wordsworth in *The Music
of Humanity: A Critical Study of Wordsworth's "Ruined Cottage"* (1969).
    This is a shorter and better poem than the one reprinted in *The Poetical
Works*. The latter lacks the great concluding passage, lines 493–538, and
includes in Part I more than 250 lines describing the youthful development
of the peddler that are extraneous to the narrative proper and soften the
hard naturalism of the story by introducing into it, at considerable length,
the peddler's faith that nature teaches "deeply the lesson deep of love."
The version in the first book of *The Excursion* is longer still, is attenuated
in style, and attempts to mitigate the impact of Margaret's sufferings even
more by attributing to her a Christian piety which is conventional rather
than deeply realized. In the version reprinted here, however, we confront the

blank facts of "a tale of silent suffering"—suffering which is undeserved, unrationalized, and irremissive. Like the narrating poet, we attend in "the impotence of grief" as Margaret's anguish at the loss of her husband slowly bends and then breaks her spirit, before destroying her life. Her deterioration under this relentless pressure is a moral one, measured by the bleak details of the correlative deterioration of her untended garden and cottage. The event is "a common tale," and it poses the implicit question, What are we to make of human life, in which such things happen?

The peddler's recovery of heart turns, unexpectedly, on his recognition that this human tragedy takes place within the unceasing and neutral operation—as the narrator says, "the calm oblivious tendencies"—of nature. This nature, unmindful of man, his aims and suffering and work, quietly goes about the process of assimilating the human artifacts which have been wrought from it back into its own independent and continuing life. In a reversal as extreme as Wordsworth could make it, the peddler declares: "I turned away,/And walked along my road in happiness." By his artistry Wordsworth carries us along in imagination so that we too, whatever our own beliefs, feel what it is to be able to look upon and master the fact of human suffering, unsupported by any consoling creed of a beneficent power, whether in or out of nature.

Beyond any of Wordsworth's writings, even *Michael*, *The Ruined Cottage* demonstrates the distinctive quality of Wordsworth at his best— the quality Walter Raleigh identified more than a half century ago as his "calm and almost terrible strength."

The Ruined Cottage

First Part

'Twas Summer and the sun was mounted high.
Along the south the uplands feebly glared
Through a pale steam, and all the northern downs,
In clearer air ascending, shewed far off
Their surfaces with shadows dappled o'er   5
Of deep embattled clouds. Far as the sight
Could reach those many shadows lay in spots
Determined and unmoved, with steady beams
Of clear and pleasant sunshine interposed—
Pleasant to him who on the soft cool grass   10
Extends his careless limbs beside the root
Of some huge oak whose aged branches make
A twilight of their own, a dewy shade
Where the wren warbles while the dreaming man,
Half conscious of that soothing melody,   15
With sidelong eye looks out upon the scene,
By those impending branches made more soft,
More soft and distant.

Other lot was mine.
Across a bare wide Common I had toiled
With languid feet which by the slipp'ry ground   20
Were baffled still, and when I stretched myself
On the brown earth my limbs from very heat
Could find no rest, nor my weak arm disperse
The insect host which gathered round my face
And joined their murmurs to the tedious noise   25
Of seeds of bursting gorse that crackled round.
I rose and turned towards a group of trees
Which midway in that level stood alone;
And thither come at length, beneath a shade
Of clustering elms that sprang from the same root   30
I found a ruined house, four naked walls
That stared upon each other. I looked round
And near the door I saw an aged Man,
Alone and stretched upon the cottage bench,
An iron-pointed staff lay at his side.   35
With instantaneous joy I recognized
That pride of nature and of lowly life,
The venerable Armytage, a friend
As dear to me as is the setting sun.

                         Two days before   40
We had been fellow travelers. I knew
That he was in this neighborhood, and now
Delighted found him here in the cool shade.
He lay, his pack of rustic merchandise
Pillowing his head. I guess he had no thought   45
Of his way-wandering life. His eyes were shut,
The shadows of the breezy elms above
Dappled his face. With thirsty heat oppressed
At length I hailed him, glad to see his hat
Bedewed with waterdrops, as if the brim   50
Had newly scooped a running stream. He rose
And pointing to a sunflower, bade me climb
The [   ] wall where that same gaudy flower
Looked out upon the road.

                    It was a plot
Of garden ground now wild, its matted weeds   55
Marked with the steps of those whom as they passed,
The gooseberry trees that shot in long lank slips,
Or currants hanging from their leafless stems
In scanty strings, had tempted to o'erleap
The broken wall. Within that cheerless spot,   60
Where two tall hedgerows of thick alder boughs
Joined in a damp cold nook, I found a well
Half covered up with willow flowers and grass.
I slaked my thirst and to the shady bench
Returned, and while I stood unbonneted   65

To catch the motion of the cooler air,
The old Man said, "I see around me here
Things which you cannot see. We die, my Friend,
Nor we alone, but that which each man loved
And prized in his peculiar nook of earth   70
Dies with him, or is changed, and very soon
Even of the good is no memorial left.
The Poets, in their elegies and songs
Lamenting the departed, call the groves,
They call upon the hills and streams to mourn,   75
And senseless rocks—nor idly, for they speak
In these their invocations with a voice
Obedient to the strong creative power
Of human passion. Sympathies there are
More tranquil, yet perhaps of kindred birth,   80
That steal upon the meditative mind
And grow with thought. Beside yon spring I stood,
And eyed its waters till we seemed to feel
One sadness, they and I. For them a bond
Of brotherhood is broken; time has been   85
When every day the touch of human hand
Disturbed their stillness, and they ministered
To human comfort. When I stooped to drink
A spider's web hung to the water's edge,
And on the wet and slimy footstone lay   90
The useless fragment of a wooden bowl.
It moved my very heart.

            The day has been
When I could never pass this road but she
Who lived within these walls, when I appeared,
A daughter's welcome gave me, and I loved her   95
As my own child. Oh Sir, the good die first,
And they whose hearts are dry as summer dust
Burn to the socket. Many a passenger
Has blessed poor Margaret for her gentle looks
When she upheld the cool refreshment drawn   100
From that forsaken spring, and no one came
But he was welcome, no one went away
But that it seemed she loved him. She is dead,
The worm is on her cheek, and this poor hut,
Stripped of its outward garb of household flowers,   105
Of rose and sweetbriar, offers to the wind
A cold bare wall whose earthy top is tricked
With weeds and the rank spear grass. She is dead,
And nettles rot and adders sun themselves
Where we have sate together while she nursed   110
Her infant at her breast. The unshod colt,
The wandring heifer and the Potter's ass,
Find shelter now within the chimney wall
Where I have seen her evening hearthstone blaze

And through the window spread upon the road   115
Its cheerful light. You will forgive me, sir,
But often on this cottage do I muse
As on a picture, till my wiser mind
Sinks, yielding to the foolishness of grief.

She had a husband, an industrious man,   120
Sober and steady. I have heard her say
That he was up and busy at his loom
In summer ere the mower's scythe had swept
The dewy grass, and in the early spring
Ere the last star had vanished. They who passed   125
At evening, from behind the garden fence
Might hear his busy spade, which he would ply
After his daily work till the daylight
Was gone, and every leaf and flower were lost
In the dark hedges. So they passed their days   130
In peace and comfort, and two pretty babes
Were their best hope next to the God in Heaven.

You may remember, now some ten years gone,
Two blighting seasons when the fields were left
With half a harvest. It pleased heaven to add   135
A worse affliction in the plague of war,
A happy land was stricken to the heart,
'Twas a sad time of sorrow and distress.
A wanderer among the cottages,
I with my pack of winter raiment saw   140
The hardships of that season. Many rich
Sunk down as in a dream among the poor,
And of the poor did many cease to be,
And their place knew them not. Meanwhile, abridged
Of daily comforts, gladly reconciled   145
To numerous self-denials, Margaret
Went struggling on through those calamitous years
With cheerful hope. But ere the second autumn
A fever seized her husband. In disease
He lingered long, and when his strength returned   150
He found the little he had stored to meet
The hour of accident, or crippling age,
Was all consumed. As I have said, 'twas now
A time of trouble: shoals of artisans
Were from their daily labor turned away   155
To hang for bread on parish charity,
They and their wives and children, happier far
Could they have lived as do the little birds
That peck along the hedges, or the kite
That makes her dwelling in the mountain rocks.   160

Ill fared it now with Robert, he who dwelt
In this poor cottage. At his door he stood
And whistled many a snatch of merry tunes

That had no mirth in them, or with his knife
Carved uncouth figures on the heads of sticks,   165
Then idly sought about through every nook
Of house or garden any casual task
Of use or ornament, and with a strange
Amusing but uneasy novelty
He blended where he might the various tasks   170
Of summer, autumn, winter, and of spring.
But this endured not, his good humor soon
Became a weight in which no pleasure was,
And poverty brought on a petted mood
And a sore temper. Day by day he drooped,   175
And he would leave his home, and to the town
Without an errand would he turn his steps,
Or wander here and there among the fields.
One while he would speak lightly of his babes
And with a cruel tongue, at other times   180
He played with them wild freaks of merriment,
And 'twas a piteous thing to see the looks
Of the poor innocent children. 'Every smile,'
Said Margaret to me here beneath these trees,
'Made my heart bleed.' "   180

            At this the old Man paused,
And looking up to those enormous elms
He said, " 'Tis now the hour of deepest noon.
At this still season of repose and peace,
This hour when all things which are not at rest
Are cheerful, while this multitude of flies   190
Fills all the air with happy melody,
Why should a tear be in an old man's eye?
Why should we thus with an untoward mind,
And in the weakness of humanity,
From natural wisdom turn our hearts away,   195
To natural comfort shut our eyes and ears,
And, feeding on disquiet, thus disturb
The calm of Nature with our restless thoughts?"
 END OF THE FIRST PART

Second Part

He spake with somewhat of a solemn tone,
But when he ended there was in his face   200
Such easy cheerfulness, a look so mild,
That for a little time it stole away
All recollection, and that simple tale
Passed from my mind like a forgotten sound.
A while on trivial things we held discourse,   205
To me soon tasteless. In my own despite
I thought of that poor woman as of one

Whom I had known and loved. He had rehearsed
Her homely tale with such familiar power,
With such an active countenance, an eye   210
So busy, that the things of which he spake
Seemed present, and, attention now relaxed,
There was a heartfelt chillness in my veins.
I rose, and turning from that breezy shade
Went out into the open air, and stood   215
To drink the comfort of the warmer sun.
Long time I had not stayed ere, looking round
Upon that tranquil ruin, I returned
And begged of the old man that for my sake
He would resume his story.   220

                              He replied,
"It were a wantonness, and would demand
Severe reproof, if we were men whose hearts
Could hold vain dalliance with the misery
Even of the dead, contented thence to draw
A momentary pleasure, never marked   225
By reason, barren of all future good.
But we have known that there is often found
In mournful thoughts, and always might be found,
A power to virtue friendly; were't not so
I am a dreamer among men, indeed   230
An idle dreamer. 'Tis a common tale
By moving accidents uncharactered,
A tale of silent suffering, hardly clothed
In bodily form, and to the grosser sense
But ill adapted, scarcely palpable   235
To him who does not think. But at your bidding
I will proceed.

                      While thus it fared with them
To whom this cottage till that hapless year
Had been a blessed home, it was my chance
To travel in a country far remote;   240
And glad I was when, halting by yon gate
That leads from the green lane, again I saw
These lofty elm trees. Long I did not rest:
With many pleasant thoughts I cheered my way
O'er the flat common. At the door arrived,   245
I knocked, and when I entered, with the hope
Of usual greeting, Margaret looked at me
A little while, then turned her head away
Speechless, and sitting down upon a chair
Wept bitterly. I wist not what to do,   250
Or how to speak to her. Poor wretch, at last
She rose from off her seat, and then, oh Sir,

I cannot tell how she pronounced my name.
With fervent love, and with a face of grief
Unutterably helpless, and a look   255
That seemed to cling upon me, she enquired
If I had seen her husband. As she spake
A strange surprise and fear came to my heart,
Nor had I power to answer ere she told
That he had disappeared—just two months gone.   260
He left his house: two wretched days had passed,
And on the third by the first break of light,
Within her casement full in view she saw
A purse of gold.[1] 'I trembled at the sight,'
Said Margaret, 'for I knew it was his hand   265
That placed it there. And on that very day
By one, a stranger, from my husband sent,
The tidings came that he had joined a troop
Of soldiers going to a distant land.
He left me thus. Poor Man, he had not heart   270
To take farewell of me, and he feared
That I should follow with my babes, and sink
Beneath the misery of a soldier's life.'

This tale did Margaret tell with many tears,
And when she ended I had little power   275
To give her comfort, and was glad to take
Such words of hope from her own mouth as served
To cheer us both. But long we had not talked
Ere we built up a pile of better thoughts,
And with a brighter eye she looked around,   280
As if she had been shedding tears of joy.
We parted. It was then the early spring:
I left her busy with her garden tools,
And well remember, o'er that fence she looked,
And, while I paced along the footway path,   285
Called out and sent a blessing after me,
With tender cheerfulness, and with a voice
That seemed the very sound of happy thoughts.

I roved o'er many a hill and many a dale
With this my weary load, in heat and cold,   290
Through many a wood and many an open ground,
In sunshine or in shade, in wet or fair,
Now blithe, now drooping, as it might befall;
My best companions now the driving winds
And now the 'trotting brooks' and whispering trees, 295
And now the music of my own sad steps,
With many a short-lived thought that passed between
And disappeared.

1. The "bounty" that her husband had been paid for enlisting in the militia. The shortage of volunteers and England's sharply rising military needs had in some counties forced the bounty up from about £1 in 1757 to more than £16 in 1796 (J. R. Western, *English Militia in the Eighteenth Century*, 1965, p. 276).

                        I came this way again
Towards the wane of summer, when the wheat
Was yellow, and the soft and bladed grass   300
Sprang up afresh and o'er the hay field spread
Its tender green. When I had reached the door
I found that she was absent. In the shade,
Where we now sit, I waited her return.
Her cottage in its outward look appeared   305
As cheerful as before, in any shew
Of neatness little changed, but that I thought
The honeysuckle crowded round the door,
And from the wall hung down in heavier tufts,
And knots of worthless stonecrop started out   310
Along the window's edge, and grew like weeds
Against the lower panes. I turned aside
And strolled into her garden. It was changed.
The unprofitable bindweed spread his bells
From side to side, and with unwieldy wreaths   315
Had dragged the rose from its sustaining wall
And bent it down to earth. The border tufts,
Daisy, and thrift, and lowly camomile,
And thyme, had straggled out into the paths
Which they were used to deck.   320

                        Ere this an hour
Was wasted. Back I turned my restless steps,
And as I walked before the door it chanced
A stranger passed, and guessing whom I sought,
He said that she was used to ramble far.
The sun was sinking in the west, and now   325
I sate with sad impatience. From within
Her solitary infant cried aloud.
The spot though fair seemed very desolate,
The longer I remained more desolate;
And looking round I saw the cornerstones,   330
Till then unmarked, on either side the door
With dull red stains discolored, and stuck o'er
With tufts and hairs of wool, as if the sheep
That feed upon the commons thither came
Familiarly, and found a couching place   335
Even at her threshold.

                        The house clock struck eight:
I turned and saw her distant a few steps.
Her face was pale and thin, her figure too
Was changed. As she unlocked the door she said,
'It grieves me you have waited here so long,   340
But in good truth I've wandered much of late,
And sometimes, to my shame I speak, have need
Of my best prayers to bring me back again.'
While on the board she spread our evening meal,

She told me she had lost her elder child,   345
That he for months had been a serving boy,
Apprenticed by the parish. 'I perceive
You look at me, and you have cause. Today
I have been traveling far, and many days
About the fields I wander, knowing this   350
Only, that what I seek I cannot find.
And so I waste my time: for I am changed,
And to myself,' she said, 'have done much wrong,
And to this helpless infant. I have slept
Weeping, and weeping I have waked. My tears   355
Have flowed as if my body were not such
As others are, and I could never die.
But I am now in mind and in my heart
More easy, and I hope,' she said, 'that heaven
Will give me patience to endure the things   360
Which I behold at home.'

                              It would have grieved
Your very soul to see her. Sir, I feel
The story linger in my heart. I fear
'Tis long and tedious, but my spirit clings
To that poor woman. So familiarly   365
Do I perceive her manner and her look
And presence, and so deeply do I feel
Her goodness, that not seldom in my walks
A momentary trance comes over me,
And to myself I seem to muse on one   370
By sorrow laid asleep or borne away,
A human being destined to awake
To human life, or something very near
To human life, when he shall come again
For whom she suffered. Sir, it would have grieved   375
Your very soul to see her: evermore
Her eyelids drooped, her eyes were downward cast,
And when she at her table gave me food
She did not look at me. Her voice was low,
Her body was subdued. In every act   380
Pertaining to her house affairs appeared
The careless stillness which a thinking mind
Gives to an idle matter. Still she sighed,
But yet no motion of the breast was seen,
No heaving of the heart. While by the fire   385
We sate together, sighs came on my ear,
I knew not how, and hardly whence they came.
I took my staff, and when I kissed her babe
The tears stood in her eyes. I left her then
With the best hope and comfort I could give: 390
She thanked me for my will, but for my hope
It seemed she did not thank me.

                                    I returned
And took my rounds along this road again
Ere on its sunny bank the primrose flower
Had chronicled the earliest day of spring.   395
I found her sad and drooping. She had learned
No tidings of her husband; if he lived,
She knew not that he lived; if he were dead,
She knew not he was dead. She seemed the same
In person or appearance, but her house   400
Bespoke a sleepy hand of negligence.
The floor was neither dry nor neat, the hearth
Was comfortless,
The windows too were dim, and her few books,
Which one upon the other heretofore   405
Had been piled up against the corner panes
In seemly order, now with straggling leaves
Lay scattered here and there, open or shut,
As they had chanced to fall. Her infant babe
Had from its mother caught the trick of grief,   410
And sighed among its playthings. Once again
I turned towards the garden gate, and saw
More plainly still that poverty and grief
Were now come nearer to her. The earth was hard,
With weeds defaced and knots of withered grass;   415
No ridges there appeared of clear black mould,
No winter greenness. Of her herbs and flowers
It seemed the better part were gnawed away
Or trampled on the earth. A chain of straw,
Which had been twisted round the tender stem   420
Of a young apple tree, lay at its root;
The bark was nibbled round by truant sheep.
Margaret stood near, her infant in her arms,
And, seeing that my eye was on the tree,
She said, 'I fear it will be dead and gone   425
Ere Robert come again.'

                                  Towards the house
Together we returned, and she inquired
If I had any hope. But for her Babe,
And for her little friendless Boy, she said,
She had no wish to live—that she must die   430
Of sorrow. Yet I saw the idle loom
Still in its place. His Sunday garments hung
Upon the selfsame nail, his very staff
Stood undisturbed behind the door. And when
I passed this way beaten by Autumn winds,   435
She told me that her little babe was dead,
And she was left alone. That very time,
I yet remember, through the miry lane
She walked with me a mile, when the bare trees

Trickled with foggy damps, and in such sort   440
That any heart had ached to hear her, begged
That wheresoe'r I went I still would ask
For him whom she had lost. We parted then,
Our final parting; for from that time forth
Did many seasons pass ere I returned   445
Into this tract again.

               Five tedious years
She lingered in unquiet widowhood,
A wife and widow. Needs must it have been
A sore heart-wasting. I have heard, my friend,
That in that broken arbor she would sit   450
The idle length of half a sabbath day;
There, where you see the toadstool's lazy head;
And when a dog passed by she still would quit
The shade and look abroad. On this old Bench
For hours she sate, and evermore her eye   455
Was busy in the distance, shaping things
Which made her heart beat quick. Seest thou that path?—
The green sward now has broken its gray line—
There to and fro she paced through many a day
Of the warm summer, from a belt of flax   460
That girt her waist, spinning the long-drawn thread
With backward steps. Yet ever as there passed
A man whose garments shewed the Soldier's red,
Or crippled Mendicant in Sailor's garb,
The little child who sate to turn the wheel   465
Ceased from his toil, and she, with faltering voice,
Expecting still to hear her husband's fate,
Made many a fond inquiry; and when they
Whose presence gave no comfort, were gone by,
Her heart was still more sad. And by yon gate,   470
Which bars the traveler's road, she often stood,
And when a stranger horseman came, the latch
Would lift, and in his face look wistfully,
Most happy if from aught discovered there
Of tender feeling she might dare repeat   475
The same sad question.

              Meanwhile her poor hut
Sunk to decay; for he was gone, whose hand
At the first nippings of October frost
Closed up each chink, and with fresh bands of straw
Chequered the green-grown thatch. And so she lived   480
Through the long winter, reckless and alone,
Till this reft house, by frost, and thaw, and rain,
Was sapped; and when she slept, the nightly damps
Did chill her breast, and in the stormy day
Her tattered clothes were ruffled by the wind   485
Even at the side of her own fire. Yet still

She loved this wretched spot, nor would for worlds
Have parted hence; and still that length of road,
And this rude bench, one torturing hope endeared,
Fast rooted at her heart. And here, my friend,   490
In sickness she remained; and here she died,
Last human tenant of these ruined walls."

The old Man ceased: he saw that I was moved.
From that low bench rising instinctively,
I turned aside in weakness, nor had power   495
To thank him for the tale which he had told.
I stood, and leaning o'er the garden gate
Reviewed that Woman's sufferings; and it seemed
To comfort me while with a brother's love
I blessed her in the impotence of grief.   500
At length towards the cottage I returned
Fondly, and traced with milder interest,
That secret spirit of humanity
Which, 'mid the calm oblivious tendencies
Of nature, 'mid her plants, her weeds and flowers,   505
And silent overgrowings, still survived.
The old man seeing this resumed, and said,
"My friend, enough to sorrow have you given,
The purposes of Wisdom ask no more:
Be wise and cheerful, and no longer read   510
The forms of things with an unworthy eye.
She sleeps in the calm earth, and peace is here.
I well remember that those very plumes,
Those weeds, and the high spear grass on that wall,
By mist and silent raindrops silvered o'er,   515
As once I passed, did to my mind convey
So still an image of tranquillity,
So calm and still, and looked so beautiful
Amid the uneasy thoughts which filled my mind,
That what we feel of sorrow and despair   520
From ruin and from change, and all the grief
The passing shews of being leave behind,
Appeared an idle dream that could not live
Where meditation was. I turned away,
And walked along my road in happiness."   525

He ceased. By this the sun declining shot
A slant and mellow radiance, which began
To fall upon us where beneath the trees
We sate on that low bench. And now we felt,
Admonished thus, the sweet hour coming on: 530
A linnet warbled from those lofty elms,
A thrush sang loud, and other melodies
At distance heard, peopled the milder air.
The old man rose and hoisted up his load.
Together casting then a farewell look   535

Upon those silent walls, we left the shade;
And, ere the stars were visible, attained
A rustic inn, our evening resting place.

THE END

1797–ca. 1799   1968

Michael[1]

A PASTORAL POEM

If from the public way you turn your steps
Up the tumultuous brook of Greenhead Ghyll,[2]
You will suppose that with an upright path
Your feet must struggle; in such bold ascent
The pastoral mountains front you, face to face.   5
But, courage! for around that boisterous brook
The mountains have all opened out themselves,
And made a hidden valley of their own.
No habitation can be seen; but they
Who journey thither find themselves alone   10
With a few sheep, with rocks and stones, and kites[3]
That overhead are sailing in the sky.
It is in truth an utter solitude;
Nor should I have made mention of this dell
But for one object which you might pass by,   15
Might see and notice not. Beside the brook
Appears a straggling heap of unhewn stones!
And to that simple object appertains
A story—unenriched with strange events,
Yet not unfit, I deem, for the fireside,   20
Or for the summer shade. It was the first
Of those domestic tales that spake to me
Of Shepherds, dwellers in the valleys, men
Whom I already loved—not verily
For their own sakes, but for the fields and hills   25
Where was their occupation and abode.
And hence this Tale, while I was yet a Boy
Careless of books, yet having felt the power
Of Nature, by the gentle agency
Of natural objects, led me on to feel   30

1. This poem is founded on the actual misfortunes of a family at Grasmere. "The sheepfold," Wordsworth said, "on which so much of the poem turns, remains, or rather the ruins of it." He wrote to Thomas Poole, on April 9, 1801, that he had attempted to picture a man "agitated by two of the most powerful affections of the human heart; the parental affection, and the love of property, *landed* property, including the feelings of inheritance, home, and personal and family independence." The subtitle shows Wordsworth's shift of the term "pastoral" from aristocratic make-believe to the tragic suffering of people in what he called "humble and rustic life."
2. Greenhead Ghyll (a ghyll is a ravine forming the bed of a stream) is not far from Wordsworth's cottage at Grasmere. The other places named in the poem are also in that vicinity.
3. Hawks.

For passions that were not my own, and think
(At random and imperfectly indeed)
On man, the heart of man, and human life.
Therefore, although it be a history
Homely and rude, I will relate the same   35
For the delight of a few natural hearts;
And, with yet fonder feeling, for the sake
Of youthful Poets, who among these hills
Will be my second self when I am gone.

Upon the forest side in Grasmere Vale   40
There dwelt a Shepherd, Michael was his name;
An old man, stout of heart, and strong of limb.
His bodily frame had been from youth to age
Of an unusual strength: his mind was keen,
Intense, and frugal, apt for all affairs,   45
And in his shepherd's calling he was prompt
And watchful more than ordinary men.
Hence had he learned the meaning of all winds,
Of blasts of every tone; and oftentimes,
When others heeded not, he heard the South   50
Make subterraneous music, like the noise
Of bagpipers on distant Highland hills.
The Shepherd, at such warning, of his flock
Bethought him, and he to himself would say,
"The winds are now devising work for me!"   55
And, truly, at all times, the storm, that drives
The traveler to a shelter, summoned him
Up to the mountains: he had been alone
Amid the heart of many thousand mists,
That came to him, and left him, on the heights.   60
So lived he till his eightieth year was past.
And grossly that man errs, who should suppose
That the green valleys, and the streams and rocks,
Were things indifferent to the Shepherd's thoughts.
Fields, where with cheerful spirits he had breathed   65
The common air; hills, which with vigorous step
He had so often climbed; which had impressed
So many incidents upon his mind
Of hardship, skill or courage, joy or fear;
Which, like a book, preserved the memory   70
Of the dumb animals, whom he had saved,
Had fed or sheltered, linking to such acts
The certainty of honorable gain;
Those fields, those hills—what could they less? had laid
Strong hold on his affections, were to him   75
A pleasurable feeling of blind love,
The pleasure which there is in life itself.

His days had not been passed in singleness.
His Helpmate was a comely matron, old—
Though younger than himself full twenty years.   80
She was a woman of a stirring life,
Whose heart was in her house; two wheels she had
Of antique form: this large, for spinning wool;
That small, for flax; and, if one wheel had rest,
It was because the other was at work.   85
The Pair had but one inmate in their house,
An only Child, who had been born to them
When Michael, telling o'er his years, began
To deem that he was old—in shepherd's phrase,
With one foot in the grave. This only Son,   90
With two brave sheep dogs tried in many a storm,
The one of an inestimable worth,
Made all their household. I may truly say,
That they were as a proverb in the vale
For endless industry. When day was gone,   95
And from their occupations out of doors
The Son and Father were come home, even then,
Their labor did not cease; unless when all
Turned to the cleanly supper board, and there,
Each with a mess of pottage and skimmed milk,   100
Sat round the basket piled with oaten cakes,
And their plain homemade cheese. Yet when the meal
Was ended, Luke (for so the Son was named)
And his old Father both betook themselves
To such convenient work as might employ   105
Their hands by the fireside; perhaps to card
Wool for the Housewife's spindle, or repair
Some injury done to sickle, flail, or scythe,
Or other implement of house or field.

Down from the ceiling, by the chimney's edge,   110
That in our ancient uncouth country style
With huge and black projection overbrowed
Large space beneath, as duly as the light
Of day grew dim the Housewife hung a lamp;
An aged utensil, which had performed   115
Service beyond all others of its kind.
Early at evening did it burn—and late,
Surviving comrade of uncounted hours,
Which, going by from year to year, had found,
And left, the couple neither gay perhaps   120
Nor cheerful, yet with objects and with hopes,
Living a life of eager industry.
And now, when Luke had reached his eighteenth year,
There by the light of this old lamp they sate,
Father and Son, while far into the night   125

The Housewife plied her own peculiar work,
Making the cottage through the silent hours
Murmur as with the sound of summer flies.
This light was famous in its neighborhood,
And was a public symbol of the life   130
That thrifty Pair had lived. For, as it chanced,
Their cottage on a plot of rising ground
Stood single, with large prospect, north and south,
High into Easedale, up to Dunmail Raise,
And westward to the village near the lake;   135
And from this constant light, so regular,
And so far seen, the House itself, by all
Who dwelt within the limits of the vale,
Both old and young, was named The Evening Star.

    Thus living on through such a length of years,   140
The Shepherd, if he loved himself, must needs
Have loved his Helpmate; but to Michael's heart
This son of his old age was yet more dear—
Less from instinctive tenderness, the same
Fond spirit that blindly works in the blood of all—   145
Than that a child, more than all other gifts
That earth can offer to declining man,
Brings hope with it, and forward-looking thoughts,
And stirrings of inquietude, when they
By tendency of nature needs must fail.   150
Exceeding was the love he bare to him,
His heart and his heart's joy! For oftentimes
Old Michael, while he was a babe in arms,
Had done him female service, not alone
For pastime and delight, as is the use   155
Of fathers, but with patient mind enforced
To acts of tenderness; and he had rocked
His cradle, as with a woman's gentle hand.

    And in a later time, ere yet the Boy
Had put on boy's attire, did Michael love,   160
Albeit of a stern unbending mind,
To have the Young-one in his sight, when he
Wrought in the field, or on his shepherd's stool
Sate with a fettered sheep before him stretched
Under the large old oak, that near his door   165
Stood single, and, from matchless depth of shade,
Chosen for the Shearer's covert from the sun,
Thence in our rustic dialect was called
The Clipping Tree, a name which yet it bears,
There, while they two were sitting in the shade,   170
With others round them, earnest all and blithe,
Would Michael exercise his heart with looks

Of fond correction and reproof bestowed
Upon the Child, if he disturbed the sheep
By catching at their legs, or with his shouts   175
Scared them, while they lay still beneath the shears.

And when by Heaven's good grace the boy grew up
A healthy Lad, and carried in his cheek
Two steady roses that were five years old;
Then Michael from a winter coppice[4] cut   180
With his own hand a sapling, which he hooped
With iron, making it throughout in all
Due requisites a perfect shepherd's staff,
And gave it to the Boy; wherewith equipped
He as a watchman oftentimes was placed   185
At gate or gap, to stem or turn the flock;
And, to his office prematurely called,
There stood the urchin, as you will divine,
Something between a hindrance and a help;
And for this cause not always, I believe,   190
Receiving from his Father hire of praise;
Though nought was left undone which staff, or voice,
Or looks, or threatening gestures, could perform.

But soon as Luke, full ten years old, could stand
Against the mountain blasts, and to the heights,   195
Not fearing toil, nor length of weary ways,
He with his Father daily went, and they
Were as companions, why should I relate
That objects which the Shepherd loved before
Were dearer now? that from the Boy there came   200
Feelings and emanations—things which were
Light to the sun and music to the wind;
And that the old Man's heart seemed born again?

Thus in his Father's sight the Boy grew up:
And now, when he had reached his eighteenth year,   205
He was his comfort and his daily hope.

While in this sort the simple household lived
From day to day, to Michael's ear there came
Distressful tidings. Long before the time
Of which I speak, the Shepherd had been bound   210
In surety for his brother's son, a man
Of an industrious life, and ample means;
But unforeseen misfortunes suddenly
Had pressed upon him; and old Michael now
Was summoned to discharge the forfeiture,   215
A grievous penalty, but little less
Than half his substance. This unlooked-for claim,
At the first hearing, for a moment took

4. Grove of small trees.

More hope out of his life than he supposed
That any old man ever could have lost.   220
As soon as he had armed himself with strength
To look his trouble in the face, it seemed
The Shepherd's sole resource to sell at once
A portion of his patrimonial fields.
Such was his first resolve; he thought again,   225
And his heart failed him. "Isabel," said he,
Two evenings after he had heard the news,
"I have been toiling more than seventy years,
And in the open sunshine of God's love
Have we all lived; yet, if these fields of ours   230
Should pass into a stranger's hand, I think
That I could not lie quiet in my grave.
Our lot is a hard lot; the sun himself
Has scarcely been more diligent than I;
And I have lived to be a fool at last   235
To my own family. An evil man
That was, and made an evil choice, if he
Were false to us; and, if he were not false,
There are ten thousand to whom loss like this
Had been no sorrow. I forgive him—but   240
'Twere better to be dumb than to talk thus.

    "When I began, my purpose was to speak
Of remedies and of a cheerful hope.
Our Luke shall leave us, Isabel; the land
Shall not go from us, and it shall be free;   245
He shall possess it, free as is the wind
That passes over it. We have, thou know'st,
Another kinsman—he will be our friend
In this distress. He is a prosperous man,
Thriving in trade—and Luke to him shall go,   250
And with his kinsman's help and his own thrift
He quickly will repair this loss, and then
He may return to us. If here he stay,
What can be done? Where everyone is poor,
What can be gained?"   At this the old Man paused,   255
And Isabel sat silent, for her mind
Was busy, looking back into past times.
There's Richard Bateman,[5] thought she to herself,
He was a parish boy—at the church door
They made a gathering for him, shillings, pence,   260
And halfpennies, wherewith the neighbors bought
A basket, which they filled with peddler's wares;

5. "The story alluded to here is well known in the country. The chapel is called Ings Chapel and is on the road leading from Kendal to Ambleside" [Wordsworth's note].

And, with this basket on his arm, the lad
Went up to London, found a master there,
Who, out of many, chose the trusty boy   265
To go and overlook his merchandise
Beyond the seas; where he grew wondrous rich,
And left estates and monies to the poor,
And, at his birthplace, built a chapel floored
With marble, which he sent from foreign lands.   270
These thoughts, and many others of like sort,
Passed quickly through the mind of Isabel,
And her face brightened. The old Man was glad,
And thus resumed: "Well, Isabel! this scheme
These two days has been meat and drink to me.   275
Far more than we have lost is left us yet.
We have enough—I wish indeed that I
Were younger—but this hope is a good hope.
Make ready Luke's best garments, of the best
Buy for him more, and let us send him forth   280
Tomorrow, or the next day, or tonight:
If he *could* go, the Boy should go tonight."

Here Michael ceased, and to the fields went forth
With a light heart. The Housewife for five days
Was restless morn and night, and all day long   285
Wrought on with her best fingers to prepare
Things needful for the journey of her son.
But Isabel was glad when Sunday came
To stop her in her work; for, when she lay
By Michael's side, she through the last two nights   290
Heard him, how he was troubled in his sleep;
And when they rose at morning she could see
That all his hopes were gone. That day at noon
She said to Luke, while they two by themselves
Were sitting at the door, "Thou must not go;   295
We have no other Child but thee to lose,
None to remember—do not go away,
For if thou leave thy Father he will die."
The Youth made answer with a jocund voice;
And Isabel, when she had told her fears,   300
Recovered heart. That evening her best fare
Did she bring forth, and all together sat
Like happy people round a Christmas fire.

With daylight Isabel resumed her work;
And all the ensuing week the house appeared   305
As cheerful as a grove in spring; at length
The expected letter from their kinsman came,
With kind assurances that he would do
His utmost for the welfare of the Boy;

To which requests were added that forthwith   310
He might be sent to him. Ten times or more
The letter was read over; Isabel
Went forth to show it to the neighbors round;
Nor was there at that time on English land
A prouder heart than Luke's. When Isabel   315
Had to her house returned, the old Man said,
"He shall depart tomorrow." To this word
The Housewife answered, talking much of things
Which, if at such short notice he should go,
Would surely be forgotten. But at length   320
She gave consent, and Michael was at ease.

    Near the tumultuous brook of Greenhead Ghyll,
In that deep valley, Michael had designed
To build a Sheepfold;[6] and, before he heard
The tidings of his melancholy loss,   325
For this same purpose he had gathered up
A heap of stones, which by the streamlet's edge
Lay thrown together, ready for the work.
With Luke that evening thitherward he walked;
And soon as they had reached the place he stopped,   330
And thus the old Man spake to him: "My son,
Tomorrow thou wilt leave me: with full heart
I look upon thee, for thou art the same
That wert a promise to me ere thy birth,
And all thy life hast been my daily joy.   335
I will relate to thee some little part
Of our two histories; 'twill do thee good
When thou art from me, even if I should touch
On things thou canst not know of. After thou
First cam'st into the world—as oft befalls   340
To newborn infants—thou didst sleep away
Two days, and blessings from thy Father's tongue
Then fell upon thee. Day by day passed on,
And still I loved thee with increasing love.
Never to living ear came sweeter sounds   345
Than when I heard thee by our own fireside
First uttering, without words, a natural tune;
While thou, a feeding babe, didst in thy joy
Sing at thy Mother's breast. Month followed month,
And in the open fields my life was passed   350
And on the mountains; else I think that thou
Hadst been brought up upon thy Father's knees.
But we were playmates, Luke; among these hills,
As well thou knowest, in us the old and young
Have played together, nor with me didst thou   355
Lack any pleasure which a boy can know."

6. Pen for sheep. "A sheepfold in these   stone walls, with different divisions"
mountains is an unroofed building of   [Wordsworth's note].

Luke had a manly heart; but at these words
He sobbed aloud. The old Man grasped his hand,
And said, "Nay, do not take it so—I see
That these are things of which I need not speak.   360
Even to the utmost I have been to thee
A kind and a good Father: and herein
I but repay a gift which I myself
Received at others' hands; for, though now old
Beyond the common life of man, I still   365
Remember them who loved me in my youth.
Both of them sleep together; here they lived,
As all their Forefathers had done; and, when
At length their time was come, they were not loath
To give their bodies to the family mold.   370
I wished that thou shouldst live the life they lived,
But 'tis a long time to look back, my Son,
And see so little gain from threescore years.
These fields were burthened[7] when they came to me;
Till I was forty years of age, not more   375
Than half of my inheritance was mine.
I toiled and toiled; God blessed me in my work,
And till these three weeks past the land was free.
It looks as if it never could endure
Another master. Heaven forgive me, Luke,   380
If I judge ill for thee, but it seems good
That thou shouldst go."
                 At this the old Man paused;
Then, pointing to the stones near which they stood,
Thus, after a short silence, he resumed:
"This was a work for us; and now, my Son,   385
It is a work for me. But, lay one stone—
Here, lay it for me, Luke, with thine own hands.
Nay, Boy, be of good hope—we both may live
To see a better day. At eighty-four
I still am strong and hale; do thou thy part;   390
I will do mine. I will begin again
With many tasks that were resigned to thee:
Up to the heights, and in among the storms,
Will I without thee go again, and do
All works which I was wont to do alone,   395
Before I knew thy face. Heaven bless thee, Boy!
Thy heart these two weeks has been beating fast
With many hopes; it should be so—yes—yes—
I knew that thou couldst never have a wish
To leave me, Luke; thou hast been bound to me   400
Only by links of love; when thou art gone,
What will be left to us!—But I forget
My purposes. Lay now the cornerstone,
As I requested; and hereafter, Luke,

---

7. I.e., mortgaged.

When thou art gone away, should evil men   405
Be thy companions, think of me, my Son,
And of this moment; hither turn thy thoughts,
And God will strengthen thee; amid all fear
And all temptation, Luke, I pray that thou
May'st bear in mind the life thy Fathers lived,   410
Who, being innocent, did for that cause
Bestir them in good deeds. Now, fare thee well—
When thou return'st, thou in this place wilt see
A work which is not here: a covenant
'Twill be between us; but, whatever fate   415
Befall thee, I shall love thee to the last,
And bear thy memory with me to the grave."

     The Shepherd ended here; and Luke stooped down,
And, as his Father had requested, laid
The first stone of the Sheepfold. At the sight   420
The old Man's grief broke from him; to his heart
He pressed his Son, he kisséd him and wept;
And to the house together they returned.
Hushed was that House in peace, or seeming peace
Ere the night fell; with morrow's dawn the Boy   425
Began his journey, and, when he had reached
The public way, he put on a bold face;
And all the neighbors, as he passed their doors,
Came forth with wishes and with farewell prayers,
That followed him till he was out of sight.   430

     A good report did from their kinsman come,
Of Luke and his well-doing; and the Boy
Wrote loving letters, full of wondrous news,
Which, as the Housewife phrased it, were throughout
"The prettiest letters that were ever seen."   435
Both parents read them with rejoicing hearts.
So, many months passed on; and once again
The Shepherd went about his daily work
With confident and cheerful thoughts; and now
Sometimes when he could find a leisure hour   440
He to that valley took his way, and there
Wrought at the Sheepfold. Meantime Luke began
To slacken in his duty; and, at length,
He in the dissolute city gave himself
To evil courses; ignominy and shame   445
Fell on him, so that he was driven at last
To seek a hiding place beyond the seas.

     There is a comfort in the strength of love;
'Twill make a thing endurable, which else
Would overset the brain, or break the heart;   450
I have conversed with more than one who well
Remember the old Man, and what he was

Years after he had heard this heavy news.
His bodily frame had been from youth to age
Of an unusual strength. Among the rocks   455
He went, and still looked up to sun and cloud,
And listened to the wind; and, as before,
Performed all kinds of labor for his sheep,
And for the land, his small inheritance.
And to that hollow dell from time to time   460
Did he repair, to build the Fold of which
His flock had need. 'Tis not forgotten yet
The pity which was then in every heart
For the old Man—and 'tis believed by all
That many and many a day he thither went,   465
And never lifted up a single stone.

There, by the Sheepfold, sometimes was he seen
Sitting alone, or with his faithful Dog,
Then old, beside him, lying at his feet.
The length of full seven years, from time to time,   470
He at the building of this Sheepfold wrought,
And left the work unfinished when he died.
Three years, or little more, did Isabel
Survive her Husband: at her death the estate
Was sold, and went into a stranger's hand.   475
The Cottage which was named The Evening Star
Is gone—the plowshare has been through the ground
On which it stood; great changes have been wrought
In all the neighborhood; yet the oak is left
That grew beside their door; and the remains   480
Of the unfinished Sheepfold may be seen
Beside the boisterous brook of Greenhead Ghyll.

Oct. 11–Dec. 9, 1800   1800

Written in March[2]

**WHILE RESTING ON THE BRIDGE AT THE FOOT
OF BROTHER'S WATER**

The cock is crowing,
The stream is flowing,
The small birds twitter,
The lake doth glitter,
The green field sleeps in the sun;   5
The oldest and youngest
Are at work with the strongest;
The cattle are grazing,
Their heads never raising;
There are forty feeding like one!   10

---

2. From Dorothy Wordsworth's *Journals* for April 16, 1802: "When we came to Brother's Water I left William sitting on the bridge. * * * When I returned I found William writing a poem descriptive of the sights and

Like an army defeated
The snow hath retreated,
And now doth fare ill
On the top of the bare hill;
The plowboy is whooping—anon—anon: 15
There's joy in the mountains;
There's life in the fountains;
Small clouds are sailing,
Blue sky prevailing;
The rain is over and gone!   20

1802   1807

Resolution and Independence[1]

1

There was a roaring in the wind all night;
The rain came heavily and fell in floods;
But now the sun is rising calm and bright;
The birds are singing in the distant woods;
Over his own sweet voice the stock dove broods;   5
The jay makes answer as the magpie chatters;
And all the air is filled with pleasant noise of waters.

2

All things that love the sun are out of doors;
The sky rejoices in the morning's birth;
The grass is bright with raindrops; on the moors   10
The hare is running races in her mirth;
And with her feet she from the plashy earth
Raises a mist; that, glittering in the sun,
Runs with her all the way, wherever she doth run.

3

I was a Traveler then upon the moor;   15
I saw the hare that raced about with joy;
I heard the woods and distant waters roar;
Or heard them not, as happy as a boy:
The pleasant season did my heart employ:

sounds we saw and heard. There was the gentle flowing of the stream, the glittering, lively lake * * * behind us, a flat pasture with forty-two cattle feeding. * * * William finished the poem before we got to the foot of Kirkstone."
1. "This old man I met a few hundred yards from my cottage at Town End, Grasmere [October 3, 1800]; and the account of him is taken from his own mouth. I was in the state of feeling described in the beginning of the poem, while crossing over Barton Fell from Mr. Clarkson's, at the foot of Ullswater, towards Askam. The image of the hare I then observed on the ridge of the Fell" (Wordsworth). Two years later the trivial events, recollected in tranquillity, were transformed into this splendid example of Wordsworth's spontaneous mythmaking. In stanzas 8 ff., under Wordsworth's visionary stare, the still old man, sent as "by peculiar grace," is metamorphosed into a sequence of figures both more and less than human, until in the end he modulates into the archetypal figure of the eternal and haunted wanderer, of whom Coleridge's Ancient Mariner had been the most recent embodiment. Unlike Coleridge's, however, Wordsworth's is a natural supernaturalism, for the old leech-gatherer remains stubbornly matter-of-fact, and the event realistic.

My old remembrances went from me wholly;   20
And all the ways of men, so vain and melancholy.

4

But, as it sometimes chanceth, from the might
Of joy in minds that can no further go,
As high as we have mounted in delight
In our dejection do we sink as low;   25
To me that morning did it happen so;
And fears and fancies thick upon me came;
Dim sadness—and blind thoughts, I knew not, nor could name.

5

I heard the skylark warbling in the sky;
And I bethought me of the playful hare: 30
Even such a happy Child of earth am I;
Even as these blissful creatures do I fare;
Far from the world I walk, and from all care;
But there may come another day to me—
Solitude, pain of heart, distress, and poverty.   35

6

My whole life I have lived in pleasant thought,
As if life's business were a summer mood;
As if all needful things would come unsought
To genial faith, still rich in genial good;
But how can he expect that others should   40
Build for him, sow for him, and at his call
Love him, who for himself will take no heed at all?

7

I thought of Chatterton,[2] the marvelous Boy,
The sleepless Soul that perished in his pride;
Of him who walked in glory and in joy
Following his plow, along the mountainside;[3]   45
By our own spirits are we deified:
We Poets in our youth begin in gladness,
But thereof come in the end despondency and madness.

8

Now, whether it were by peculiar grace,
A leading from above, a something given,   50
Yet it befell that, in this lonely place,
When I with these untoward thoughts had striven,
Beside a pool bare to the eye of heaven
I saw a Man before me unawares: 55
The oldest man he seemed that ever wore gray hairs.

9

As a huge stone is sometimes seen to lie
Couched on the bald top of an eminence;
Wonder to all who do the same espy,

2. Thomas Chatterton (1752–70), a poet of great talent who, in his loneliness and dire poverty, poisoned himself at the age of 17 and so became the prime Romantic symbol of neglected young genius.
3. Robert Burns, also considered at that time as a natural poet who died young and poor, without adequate recognition.

By what means it could thither come, and whence;   60
So that it seems a thing endued with sense:
Like a sea beast crawled forth, that on a shelf
Of rock or sand reposeth, there to sun itself;

10

Such seemed this Man,[4] not all alive nor dead,
Nor all asleep—in his extreme old age;   65
His body was bent double, feet and head
Coming together in life's pilgrimage;
As if some dire constraint of pain, or rage
Of sickness felt by him in times long past,
A more than human weight upon his frame had cast.   70

11

Himself he propped, limbs, body, and pale face,
Upon a long gray staff of shaven wood;
And, still as I drew near with gentle pace,
Upon the margin of that moorish flood
Motionless as a cloud that old Man stood,   75
That heareth not the loud winds when they call,
And moveth all together, if it move at all.

12

At length, himself unsettling, he the pond
Stirred with his staff, and fixedly did look
Upon the muddy water, which he conned,   80
As if he had been reading in a book;
And now a stranger's privilege I took,
And, drawing to his side, to him did say,
"This morning gives us promise of a glorious day."

13

A gentle answer did the old Man make,   85
In courteous speech which forth he slowly drew;
And him with further words I thus bespake,
"What occupation do you there pursue?
This is a lonesome place for one like you."
Ere he replied, a flash of mild surprise   90
Broke from the sable orbs of his yet-vivid eyes.

14

His words came feebly, from a feeble chest,
But each in solemn order followed each,
With something of a lofty utterance dressed—
Choice word and measured phrase, above the reach   95
Of ordinary men; a stately speech;
Such as grave livers[5] do in Scotland use,
Religious men, who give to God and man their dues.

4. In Wordsworth's own analysis of this passage, he says that the stone is endowed with something of life, the sea beast is stripped of some of its life to assimilate it to the stone, and the old man divested of enough life and motion to make "the two objects unite and coalesce in just comparison"; he used the passage to demonstrate his theory of how the "conferring, the abstracting, and the modifying powers of the Imagination * * * are all brought into conjunction" (Preface to the *Poems* of 1815). Compare Coleridge's analysis of the imagination in *Biographia Literaria*, Chapter XIII.
5. Those who live gravely.

15

He told, that to these waters he had come
To gather leeches,[6] being old and poor: 100
Employment hazardous and wearisome!
And he had many hardships to endure:
From pond to pond he roamed, from moor to moor;
Housing, with God's good help, by choice or chance;
And in this way he gained an honest maintenance.   105

16

The old Man still stood talking by my side;
But now his voice to me was like a stream
Scarce heard; nor word from word could I divide;
And the whole body of the Man did seem
Like one whom I had met with in a dream;   110
Or like a man from some far region sent,
To give me human strength, by apt admonishment.

17

My former thoughts returned: the fear that kills;
And hope that is unwilling to be fed;
Cold, pain, and labor, and all fleshly ills;   115
And mighty Poets in their misery dead.
—Perplexed, and longing to be comforted,
My question eagerly did I renew,
"How is it that you live, and what is it you do?"

18

He with a smile did then his words repeat;   120
And said that, gathering leeches, far and wide
He traveled, stirring thus about his feet
The waters of the pools where they abide.
"Once I could meet with them on every side,
But they have dwindled long by slow decay;   125
Yet still I persevere, and find them where I may."

19

While he was talking thus, the lonely place,
The old Man's shape, and speech—all troubled me:
In my mind's eye I seemed to see him pace   130
About the weary moors continually,
Wandering about alone and silently.
While I these thoughts within myself pursued,
He, having made a pause, the same discourse renewed.

20

And soon with this he other matter blended,   135
Cheerfully uttered, with demeanor kind,
But stately in the main; and, when he ended,
I could have laughed myself to scorn to find
In that decrepit Man so firm a mind.
"God," said I, "be my help and stay[7] secure;   140
I'll think of the Leech Gatherer on the lonely moor!"
May 3–July 4, 1802   1807

6. Leeches were used to draw blood for curative purposes. A leech-gatherer, barelegged in shallow water, stirred the water to rouse them, and then picked them off his skin.
7. Support (a noun).

The Green Linnet[1]

Beneath these fruit-tree boughs that shed
Their snow-white blossoms on my head,
With brightest sunshine round me spread
    Of spring's unclouded weather,
In this sequestered nook how sweet   5
To sit upon my orchard seat!
And birds and flowers once more to greet,
    My last year's friends together.

One have I marked, the happiest guest
In all this covert of the blest: 10
Hail to thee, far above the rest
    In joy of voice and pinion!
Thou, Linnet! in thy green array,
Presiding Spirit here today,
Dost lead the revels of the May;   15
    And this is thy dominion.

While birds, and butterflies, and flowers,
Make all one band of paramours,
Thou, ranging up and down the bowers,
    Art sole in thy employment: 20
A Life, a Presence like the Air,
Scattering thy gladness without care,
Too blest with any one to pair;
    Thyself thy own enjoyment.

Amid yon tuft of hazel trees,   25
That twinkle to the gusty breeze,
Behold him perched in ecstasies,
    Yet seeming still to hover;
There! where the flutter of his wings
Upon his back and body flings   30
Shadows and sunny glimmerings,
    That cover him all over.

My dazzled sight he oft deceives,
A brother of the dancing leaves;
Then flits, and from the cottage eaves   35
    Pours forth his song in gushes;
As if by that exulting strain
He mocked and treated with disdain
The voiceless Form he chose to feign,
    While fluttering in the bushes.   40

1803   1807

1. Coleridge used the last two stanzas to demonstrate Wordsworth's "perfect truth of nature in his images and descriptions." The extent and particularity of this description, however, are rare in Wordsworth, despite his reputation as a "nature poet."

Yew Trees[1]

There is a Yew Tree, pride of Lorton Vale,
Which to this day stands single, in the midst
Of its own darkness, as it stood of yore:
Not loath to furnish weapons for the bands
Of Umfraville or Percy ere they marched   5
To Scotland's heaths; or those that crossed the sea
And drew their sounding bows at Azincour,
Perhaps at earlier Crecy, or Poictiers.
Of vast circumference and gloom profound
This solitary Tree! a living thing   10
Produced too slowly ever to decay;
Of form and aspect too magnificent
To be destroyed. But worthier still of note
Are those fraternal Four of Borrowdale,
Joined in one solemn and capacious grove;   15
Huge trunks! and each particular trunk a growth
Of intertwisted fibers serpentine
Up-coiling, and inveterately convolved;
Nor uninformed with Phantasy, and looks
That threaten the profane—a pillared shade,   20
Upon whose grassless floor of red-brown hue,
By sheddings from the pining umbrage[2] tinged
Perennially—beneath whose sable roof
Of boughs, as if for festal purpose decked
With unrejoicing berries—ghostly Shapes   25
May meet at noontide; Fear and trembling Hope,
Silence and Foresight; Death the Skeleton
And Time the Shadow—there to celebrate,
As in a natural temple scattered o'er
With altars undisturbed of mossy stone,   30
United worship; or in mute repose
To lie, and listen to the mountain flood
Murmuring from Glaramara's[3] inmost caves.

ca. 1803   1815

I Wandered Lonely As a Cloud[4]

I wandered lonely as a cloud
That floats on high o'er vales and hills,

1. An evergreen tree; its wood was used for the bows which won the English victories mentioned in the poem, in the late medieval wars against Scotland and France. In the *Biographia Literaria*, Chapter XXII, Coleridge cited lines 13 ff. as a prime example of the faculty of imagination, in which Wordsworth "stands nearest of all modern writers to Shakespeare and Milton; and yet in a kind perfectly unborrowed and his own."
2. Foliage that casts a shade.
3. Mountain rising from Borrowdale valley, in the Lake Country.
4. The last stanza describes the kind of recollection in tranquillity from which this poem arose, two years after

When all at once I saw a crowd,
A host, of golden daffodils;
Beside the lake, beneath the trees,   5
Fluttering and dancing in the breeze.

Continuous as the stars that shine
And twinkle on the milky way,
They stretched in never-ending line
Along the margin of a bay: 10
Ten thousand saw I at a glance,
Tossing their heads in sprightly dance.

The waves beside them danced; but they
Outdid the sparkling waves in glee;
A poet could not but be gay,   15
In such a jocund company;
I gazed—and gazed—but little thought
What wealth the show to me had brought:

For oft, when on my couch I lie
In vacant or in pensive mood,   20
They flash upon that inward eye
Which is the bliss of solitude;
And then my heart with pleasure fills,
And dances with the daffodils.

1804   1807

My Heart Leaps Up

My heart leaps up when I behold
    A rainbow in the sky:
So was it when my life began;
So is it now I am a man;
So be it when I shall grow old,   5
    Or let me die!
The Child is father of the Man;
And I could wish my days to be
Bound each to each by natural piety.[1]

March 26, 1802   1807

the original experience. This event Dorothy Wordsworth described in her *Journals* for April 15, 1802; the occasion was a walk past the shore of Ullswater: "I never saw daffodils so beautiful. They grew among the mossy stones about and about them; some rested their heads upon these stones, as on a pillow, for weariness; and the rest tossed and reeled and danced, and seemed as if they verily laughed with the wind, that blew upon them over the lake; they looked so gay, ever glancing, ever changing."

1. As distinguished from piety based on the Scriptures; a continuing responsiveness to the miracle of ordinary things is the religious sentiment that binds Wordsworth's maturity to his childhood.

Ode: Intimations of Immortality   "This was composed during my residence at Town End, Grasmere; two years at least passed be-

tween the writing of the four first stanzas and the remaining part. To the attentive and competent reader the whole sufficiently explains itself; but there may be no harm in adverting here to particular feelings or *experiences* of my own mind on which the structure of the poem partly rests. Nothing was more difficult for me in childhood than to admit the notion of death as a state applicable to my own being. I have said elsewhere

> —A simple child,
> That lightly draws its breath,
> And feels its life in every limb,
> What should it know of death!—

But it was not so much from [feelings] of animal vivacity that *my* difficulty came as from a sense of the indomitableness of the spirit within me. I used to brood over the stories of Enoch and Elijah, and almost to persuade myself that, whatever might become of others, I should be translated, in something of the same way, to heaven. With a feeling congenial to this, I was often unable to think of external things as having external existence, and I communed with all that I saw as something not apart from, but inherent in, my own immaterial nature. Many times while going to school have I grasped at a wall or tree to recall myself from this abyss of idealism to the reality. At that time I was afraid of such processes. In later periods of life I have deplored, as we have all reason to do, a subjugation of an opposite character, and have rejoiced over the remembrances, as is expressed in the lines—

> Obstinate questionings
> Of sense and outward things,
> Fallings from us, vanishings; etc.

To that dreamlike vividness and splendor which invest objects of sight in childhood, everyone, I believe, if he would look back, could bear testimony, and I need not dwell upon it here: but having in the Poem regarded it as presumptive evidence of a prior state of existence, I think it right to protest against a conclusion, which has given pain to some good and pious persons, that I meant to inculcate such a belief. It is far too shadowy a notion to be recommended to faith, as more than an element in our instincts of immortality. But let us bear in mind that, though the idea is not advanced in revelation, there is nothing there to contradict it, and the fall of Man presents an analogy in its favor. Accordingly, a pre-existent state has entered into the popular creeds of many nations; and, among all persons acquainted with classic literature, is known as an ingredient in Platonic philosophy. Archimedes said that he could move the world if he had a point whereon to rest his machine. Who has not felt the same aspirations as regards the world of his own mind? Having to wield some of its elements when I was impelled to write this Poem on the 'Immortality of the Soul,' I took hold of the notion of pre-existence as having sufficient foundation in humanity for authorizing me to make for my purpose the best use of it I could as a Poet" (Wordsworth).

As Wordsworth says, Plato held the doctrine that the soul is immortal and exists separately from the body both before birth and after death. But while the *Ode* proposes that the soul only gradually loses "the vision splendid" after birth, Plato maintained the contrary: that the knowledge of the eternal Ideas, which the soul had acquired by direct acquaintance, is totally lost at the instant of birth, and must be gradually "recollected" by philosophical discipline in the course of this life (*Phaedo* 73–77). Wordsworth's concept resembles more closely the view of some Neo-Platonists that the glory of the unborn soul is gradually quenched by its descent into the darkness of matter.

Wordsworth was troubled by objections to the Christian heterodoxy of this apparent claim for the pre-existence, in addition to the orthodox belief in the survival, of the soul. He insisted that he did not intend to assert this as doctrine, but only to use it as a premise, a poetic postulate, not necessarily to be credited outside the poem, enabling him to deal "as a poet" with an experience to which everyone, as he says, "if he would look back, could bear testimony." The basic problem is a universal human one: that the loss of youth involves the loss of a freshness and radiance investing all experience. Coleridge's *Dejection: An Ode,* which he wrote after he had heard the first four stanzas of Wordsworth's poem, employs a similar figurative technique for a comparable, though more devastating, experience of loss. As with all poems so large and rich as this one, there are divergent interpretations of its purport, emphases, and organization; but almost all commentators agree that this poem is the equal of the best in the difficult and elevated form of the irregular Pindaric ode. The Catholic poet G. M. Hopkins remarked. "For my part I should think St. George and St. Thomas of Canterbury wore roses in heaven for England's sake on the day that *Ode,* not without their intercession, was penned."

The original version of this poem had as its title only "Ode," and then as epigraph *"Paulo maiora canamus"* ("Let us sing of somewhat higher things") from Virgil's *Eclogue IV*.

Ode

INTIMATIONS OF IMMORTALITY FROM RECOLLECTIONS OF EARLY CHILDHOOD

The Child is father of the Man;
And I could wish my days to be
Bound each to each by natural piety.[1]

1

There was a time when meadow, grove, and stream,
The earth, and every common sight,
　　　　To me did seem
　　　Apparelled in celestial light,
The glory and the freshness of a dream.　　　　　　　　5
It is not now as it hath been of yore—
　　　　Turn whereso'er I may,
　　　　　　By night or day,
The things which I have seen I now can see no more.

1. The concluding lines of Wordsworth's *My Heart Leaps Up.*

2

The Rainbow comes and goes,   10
    And lovely is the Rose,
    The Moon doth with delight
Look round her when the heavens are bare,
        Waters on a starry night
        Are beautiful and fair;   15
    The sunshine is a glorious birth;
    But yet I know, where'er I go,
That there hath passed away a glory from the earth.

3

Now, while the birds thus sing a joyous song,
    And while the young lambs bound   20
        As to the tabor's sound,[2]
To me alone there came a thought of grief:
A timely utterance[3] gave that thought relief,
    And I again am strong:
The cataracts blow their trumpets from the steep;   25
No more shall grief of mine the season wrong;
I hear the Echoes through the mountains throng,
The Winds come to me from the fields of sleep,[4]
    And all the earth is gay;
        Land and sea   30
    Give themselves up to jollity,
        And with the heart of May
    Doth every Beast keep holiday—
        Thou Child of Joy,
Shout round me, let me hear thy shouts, thou happy   35
    Shepherd-boy!

4

Ye blessed Creatures, I have heard the call
    Ye to each other make; I see
The heavens laugh with you in your jubilee;
    My heart is at your festival,
    My head hath its coronal,[5]   40
The fullness of your bliss, I feel—I feel it all.
        Oh, evil day! if I were sullen
        While Earth herself is adorning,
            This sweet May morning,   45
        And the Children are culling
            On every side,

2. A tabor is a small drum often used to beat time for dancing.
3. Perhaps *My Heart Leaps Up*, perhaps *Resolution and Independence*, perhaps not a poem at all.
4. Of the many suggested interpretations, the simplest is "from the fields where they were sleeping." Wordsworth often associated a rising wind with the revival of spirit and poetic inspiration; see, e.g., the opening passage of *The Prelude*.
5. Circlet of wild flowers, with which the shepherd boys trimmed their hats in May.

In a thousand valleys far and wide,
Fresh flowers; while the sun shines warm,
And the Babe leaps up on his Mother's arm—   50
I hear, I hear, with joy I hear!
—But there's a Tree, of many, one,
A single Field which I have looked upon,
Both of them speak of something that is gone:
      The Pansy at my feet   55
      Doth the same tale repeat:
Whither is fled the visionary gleam?
Where is it now, the glory and the dream?

        5
Our birth is but a sleep and a forgetting:
The Soul that rises with us, our life's Star,[6]   60
      Hath had elsewhere its setting,
        And cometh from afar:
      Not in entire forgetfulness,
      And not in utter nakedness,
But trailing clouds of glory do we come   65
      From God, who is our home:
Heaven lies about us in our infancy!
Shades of the prison-house begin to close
      Upon the growing Boy
        But he   70
Beholds the light, and whence it flows,
      He sees it in his joy;
The Youth, who daily farther from the east
      Must travel, still is Nature's Priest,
      And by the vision splendid   75
      Is on his way attended;
At length the Man perceives it die away,
And fade into the light of common day.

        6
Earth fills her lap with pleasures of her own;
Yearnings she hath in her own natural kind,   80
And, even with something of a Mother's mind,
      And no unworthy aim,
      The homely[7] Nurse doth all she can
To make her foster child, her Inmate Man,
      Forget the glories he hath known,   85
And that imperial palace whence he came.

        7
Behold the Child among his newborn blisses,
A six-years' Darling of a pygmy size!
See, where 'mid work of his own hand he lies,
Fretted[8] by sallies of his mother's kisses,   90
With light upon him from his father's eyes!

6. The sun, as metaphor for the soul.   friendly."
7. In the old sense, "simple and   8. Checkered over.

See, at his feet, some little plan or chart,
Some fragment from his dream of human life,
Shaped by himself with newly-learned art;
  A wedding or a festival,   95
  A mourning or a funeral;
   And this hath now his heart,
   And unto this he frames his song;
    Then will he fit his tongue
To dialogues of business, love, or strife;   100
  But it will not be long
  Ere this be thrown aside,
  And with new joy and pride
The little Actor cons another part;
Filling from time to time his "humorous stage"[9]   105
With all the Persons, down to palsied Age,
That Life brings with her in her equipage;
   As if his whole vocation
   Were endless imitation.

       8

Thou, whose exterior semblance doth belie   110
   Thy Soul's immensity;
Thou best Philosopher, who yet dost keep
Thy heritage, thou Eye among the blind,
That, deaf and silent, read'st the eternal deep,
Haunted forever by the eternal mind—   115
   Mighty Prophet! Seer blest!
   On whom those truths do rest, .
Which we are toiling all our lives to find,
In darkness lost, the darkness of the grave;
Thou, over whom thy Immortality   120
Broods like the Day, a Master o'er a Slave,
A Presence which is not to be put by;
Thou little Child, yet glorious in the might
Of heaven-born freedom on thy being's height,
Why with such earnest pains dost thou provoke   125
The years to bring the inevitable yoke,
Thus blindly with thy blessedness at strife?
Full soon thy Soul shall have her earthly freight,
And custom lie upon thee with a weight,
 ~ Heavy as frost, and deep almost as life!   130

       9

  O joy! that in our embers
  Is something that doth live,
  That nature yet remembers
  What was so fugitive!
The thought of our past years in me doth breed   135
Perpetual benediction: not indeed
For that which is most worthy to be blest;
Delight and liberty, the simple creed

---

9. From a sonnet by Samuel Daniel, Elizabethan poet. In Daniel's age, "humorous" meant "capricious," and also referred to the various characters and temperaments ("humors") represented in drama.

Of Childhood, whether busy or at rest,
With new-fledged hope still fluttering in his breast—   140
      Not for these I raise
      The song of thanks and praise;
   But for those obstinate questionings
   Of sense and outward things,
   Fallings from us, vanishings;   145
   Blank misgivings of a Creature
Moving about in worlds not realized,[1]
High instincts before which our mortal Nature
Did tremble like a guilty Thing surprised;
      But for those first affections,   150
      Those shadowy recollections,
      Which, be they what they may,
Are yet the fountain light of all our day,
Are yet a master light of all our seeing;
      Uphold us, cherish, and have power to make   155
Our noisy years seem moments in the being
Of the eternal Silence: truths that wake,
         To perish never;
Which neither listlessness, nor mad endeavor,
         Nor Man nor Boy,   160
Nor all that is at enmity with joy,
Can utterly abolish or destroy!
      Hence in a season of calm weather
      Though inland far we be,
Our Souls have sight of that immortal sea   165
      Which brought us hither,
      Can in a moment travel thither,
And see the Children sport upon the shore,
And hear the mighty waters rolling evermore.

                    10
Then sing, ye Birds, sing, sing a joyous song!   170
      And let the young Lambs bound
      As to the tabor's sound!
We in thought will join your throng,
      Ye that pipe and ye that play,
      Ye that through your hearts today   175
      Feel the gladness of the May!
What though the radiance which was once so bright
Be now forever taken from my sight,
      Though nothing can bring back the hour
Of splendor in the grass, of glory in the flower;   180
      We will grieve not, rather find
      Strength in what remains behind;
      In the primal sympathy
      Which having been must ever be;
      In the soothing thoughts that spring   185
      Out of human suffering;

---

1. Not seeming real; see Wordsworth's comment in the headnote to the *Ode*.

In the faith that looks through death,
In years that bring the philosophic mind.

11

And O, ye Fountains, Meadows, Hills, and Groves,
Forebode not any severing of our loves!   190
Yet in my heart of hearts I feel your might;
I only have relinquished one delight
To live beneath your more habitual sway.
I love the Brooks which down their channels fret,
Even more than when I tripped lightly as they;   195
The innocent brightness of a newborn Day
  Is lovely yet;
The clouds that gather round the setting sun
Do take a sober coloring from an eye
That hath kept watch o'er man's mortality;   200
Another race hath been, and other palms are won[2].
Thanks to the human heart by which we live,
Thanks to its tenderness, its joys, and fears,
To me the meanest flower that blows can give
Thoughts that do often lie too deep for tears.   205

1802–4   1807

Ode to Duty[1]

Jam non consilio bonus, sed more eo perductus, ut non tantum recte facere possim, sed nisi recte facere non possim.

Stern Daughter of the Voice of God![2]
O Duty! if that name thou love

2. In Greece, foot races were often run for the prize of a branch or wreath of palm.

1. "This Ode * * * is on the model of Gray's *Ode to Adversity* which is copied from Horace's *Ode to Fortune.* Many and many a time have I been twitted by my wife and sister for having forgotten this dedication of myself to the stern lawgiver" (Wordsworth).

This poem merits its reputation as a departure from Wordsworth's earlier poems and ideas. In it he abandons the descriptive-meditative pattern of his *Tintern Abbey* and *Ode: Intimations of Immortality* and reverts to the standard 18th-century form of an ode addressed to a personified abstraction. The moral idea of this poem also represents Wordsworth's reversion from his youthful reliance on natural impulse to a more orthodox ethical tradition. The poem makes no reference to that "Nature" which earlier had constituted for Wordsworth "both law and impulse," and, in *Tintern Abbey,* had been called "The guide, the guardian of my heart, and soul / Of all my moral being." The Duty, "Stern Daughter of the Voice of God," to which Wordsworth now commends himself, is the same concept as Milton's "right reason," God's representative in man, which Christian humanists had developed by combining the stern morality of the pagan Stoics with the concept of the inner voice of the Christian "conscience." (In one MS. variant Wordsworth described Duty as "sent from God" to keep us to the road "which conscience hath pronounced the best.")

The epigraph is translated, "Now I am not good by taking thought, but have been brought by habit to such a point that it is not so much that I am able to act rightly, but that I am unable to act except rightly." Added in 1837, it is an adaptation from *Moral Epistles* CXX.10 by Seneca (4 B.C.– A.D. 65), Stoic philosopher and writer of tragedies.

2. Cf. *Paradise Lost* IX.652–54: "God so commanded, and left that Command / Sole Daughter of his voice; the rest, we live / Law to ourselves, our Reason is our Law."

Who are a light to guide, a rod
To check the erring, and reprove;
Thou, who art victory and law
When empty terrors overawe;
From vain temptations dost set free;
And calm'st the weary strife of frail humanity!

There are who ask not if thine eye
Be on them; who, in love and truth,
Where no misgiving is, rely
Upon the genial sense[3] of youth:
Glad Hearts! without reproach or blot;
Who do thy work, and know it not:
Oh! if through confidence misplaced
They fail, thy saving arms, dread Power! around them cast.

Serene will be our days and bright,
And happy will our nature be,
When love is an unerring light,
And joy its own security.
And they a blissful course may hold
Even now, who, not unwisely bold,
Live in the spirit of this creed;
Yet seek thy firm support, according to their need.

I, loving freedom, and untried,
No sport of every random gust,
Yet being to myself a guide,
Too blindly have reposed my trust;
And oft, when in my heart was heard
Thy timely mandate, I deferred
The task, in smoother walks to stray;
But thee I now would serve more strictly, if I may.

Through no disturbance of my soul,
Or strong compunction[4] in me wrought,
I supplicate for thy control;
But in the quietness of thought:
Me this unchartered freedom tires;
I feel the weight of chance desires:
My hopes no more must change their name,
I long for a repose that ever is the same.

Stern Lawgiver! yet thou dost wear
The Godhead's most benignant grace;
Nor know we anything so fair
As is the smile upon thy face:
Flowers laugh before thee on their beds
And fragrance in thy footing treads;

3. Innate good nature.
4. In the older sense, "sting of conscience," "remorse."

Thou dost preserve the stars from wrong;[5]
And the most ancient heavens, through thee, are fresh and strong.

To humbler functions, awful Power!
I call thee: I myself commend   50
Unto thy guidance from this hour;
Oh, let my weakness have an end!
Give unto me, made lowly wise,[6]
The spirit of self-sacrifice;
The confidence of reason give;   55
And in the light of truth thy Bondman let me live!
ca. 1804   1807

The Solitary Reaper[1]

Behold her, single in the field,
Yon solitary Highland Lass!
Reaping and singing by herself;
Stop here, or gently pass!
Alone she cuts and binds the grain,   5
And sings a melancholy strain;
O listen! for the Vale profound
Is overflowing with the sound.

No Nightingale did ever chaunt
More welcome notes to weary bands   10
Of travelers in some shady haunt,
Among Arabian sands;
A voice so thrilling ne'er was heard
In springtime from the Cuckoo bird,
Breaking the silence of the seas   15
Among the farthest Hebrides.

Will no one tell me what she sings?[2]—
Perhaps the plaintive numbers flow
For old, unhappy, far-off things,
And battles long ago;   20
Or is it some more humble lay,

5. Wordsworth's parallel between the moral law and the laws governing the motion of the stars is illuminated by Kant's famous statement: "Two things fill the mind with ever new and increasing admiration and awe * * * the starry heavens above and the moral law within."
6. Another echo from Milton, whose Christian-humanist ethic pervades this ode. The angel Raphael had advised Adam (*Paradise Lost* VIII.173–74), "Be lowly wise: / Think only what concerns thee and thy being."
1. One of the rare poems not based on Wordsworth's own experience. Wordsworth tells us that it was suggested by a passage in Thomas Wilkinson's *Tour of Scotland* (1824), which he had seen in MS.: "Passed by a female who was reaping alone, she sung in Erse [the Gaelic language of Scotland] as she bended over her sickle, the sweetest human voice I ever heard. Her strains were tenderly melancholy, and felt delicious long after they were heard no more."
2. Wordsworth did not understand Erse, the language in which she sings.

Familiar matter of today?
Some natural sorrow, loss, or pain,
That has been, and may be again?

Whate'er the theme, the Maiden sang   25
As if her song could have no ending;
I saw her singing at her work,
And o'er the sickle bending—
I listened, motionless and still;
And, as I mounted up the hill,   30
The music in my heart I bore,
Long after it was heard no more.

November 5, 1805   1807

Elegiac Stanzas

SUGGESTED BY A PICTURE OF PEELE CASTLE, IN A STORM, PAINTED BY SIR GEORGE BEAUMONT[1]

I was thy neighbor once, thou rugged Pile!
Four summer weeks I dwelt in sight of thee:
I saw thee every day; and all the while
Thy Form was sleeping on a glassy sea.

So pure the sky, so quiet was the air!   5
So like, so very like, was day to day!
Whene'er I looked, thy Image still was there;
It trembled, but it never passed away.

How perfect was the calm! it seemed no sleep;
No mood, which season takes away, or brings: 10
I could have fancied that the mighty Deep
Was even the gentlest of all gentle Things.

Ah! then, if mine had been the Painter's hand,
To express what then I saw; and add the gleam,
The light that never was, on sea or land,   15
The consecration, and the Poet's dream;

I would have planted thee, thou hoary Pile
Amid a world how different from this!
Beside a sea that could not cease to smile;
On tranquil land, beneath a sky of bliss.   20

Thou shouldst have seemed a treasure house divine
Of peaceful years; a chronicle of heaven—
Of all the sunbeams that did ever shine
The very sweetest had to thee been given.

1. Sir George Beaumont, a wealthy landscape painter, was Wordsworth's patron and close friend. Peele Castle is on a promontory opposite Rampside, Lancashire, where Wordsworth had spent a month in 1794, eleven years before he saw Beaumont's painting.

A Picture had it been of lasting ease,   25
Elysian[2] quiet, without toil or strife;
No motion but the moving tide, a breeze,
Or merely silent Nature's breathing life.

Such, in the fond illusion of my heart,
Such Picture would I at that time have made,   30
And seen the soul of truth in every part,
A steadfast peace that might not be betrayed.

So once it would have been—'tis so no more;
I have submitted to a new control:
A power is gone, which nothing can restore;   35
A deep distress hath humanized my Soul.[3]

Not for a moment could I now behold
A smiling sea, and be what I have been:
The feeling of my loss will ne'er be old;
This, which I know, I speak with mind serene.   40

Then, Beaumont, Friend! who would have been the Friend,
If he had lived, of him whom I deplore,
This work of thine I blame not, but commend;
This sea in anger, and that dismal shore.

O 'tis a passionate Work!—yet wise and well,   45
Well chosen is the spirit that is here;
That Hulk which labors in the deadly swell,
This rueful sky, this pageantry of fear!

And this huge Castle, standing here sublime,
I love to see the look with which it braves,   50
Cased in the unfeeling armor of old time,
The lightning, the fierce wind, and trampling waves.

Farewell, farewell the heart that lives alone,
Housed in a dream, at distance from the Kind![4]
Such happiness, wherever it be known,   55
Is to be pitied; for 'tis surely blind.

But welcome fortitude, and patient cheer,
And frequent sights of what is to be borne!
Such sights, or worse, as are before me here.—
Not without hope we suffer and we mourn.   60
1805   1807

---

2. Elysium, in classical mythology, was the peaceful place where those favored by the gods dwelled after death.
3. Captain John Wordsworth, Wil- liam's brother, had been drowned in a shipwreck on February 5, 1805. He is referred to in lines 41–42.
4. Mankind.

SONNETS
Composed upon Westminster Bridge, September 3, 1802[1]

Earth has not anything to show more fair:
Dull would he be of soul who could pass by
A sight so touching in its majesty;
This City now doth, like a garment, wear
The beauty of the morning; silent, bare,   5
Ships, towers, domes, theaters, and temples lie
Open unto the fields, and to the sky;
All bright and glittering in the smokeless air.
Never did sun more beautifully steep
In his first splendor, valley, rock, or hill;   10
Ne'er saw I, never felt, a calm so deep!
The river glideth at his own sweet will:
Dear God! the very houses seem asleep;
And all that mighty heart is lying still!

1802   1807

It Is a Beauteous Evening[2]

It is a beauteous evening, calm and free,
The holy time is quiet as a Nun
Breathless with adoration; the broad sun
Is sinking down in its tranquility;
The gentleness of heaven broods o'er the Sea: 5
Listen! the mighty Being is awake,
And doth with his eternal motion make
A sound like thunder—everlastingly.
Dear Child! dear Girl! that walkest with me here,
If thou appear untouched by solemn thought,   10
Thy nature is not therefore less divine:
Thou liest in Abraham's bosom[3] all the year,
And worship'st at the Temple's inner shrine,
God being with thee when we know it not.

1802   1807

1. "Composed on the roof of a coach, on my way to France" (Wordsworth). The date of this trip, however, was not September 3, but July 31, 1802. The conflict of feelings attending Wordsworth's brief return to France, where he had once been a revolutionist and the lover of Annette Vallon, evoked a number of personal and political sonnets, among them the three which follow.

2. "This was composed on the beach near Calais in the autumn of 1802" (Wordsworth). The girl walking with Wordsworth is Caroline, his natural daughter by Annette Vallon.
3. Where the souls destined for heaven rest after death. Luke xvi.22: "And it came to pass, that the beggar died, and was carried by the angels into Abraham's bosom."

Composed in the Valley Near Dover, On the Day of Landing

Here, on our native soil, we breathe once more.
The cock that crows, the smoke that curls, that sound
Of bells—those boys who in yon meadow ground
In white-sleeved shirts are playing; and the roar
Of the waves breaking on the chalky shore— 5
All, all are English. Oft have I looked round
With joy in Kent's green vales; but never found
Myself so satisfied in heart before.
Europe is yet in bonds; but let that pass,
Thought for another moment. Thou art free, 10
My Country! and 'tis joy enough and pride
For one hour's perfect bliss, to tread the grass
Of England once again, and hear and see,
With such a dear Companion⁴ at my side.

August 30, 1802 1807

London, 1802⁵

Milton! thou shouldst be living at this hour:
England hath need of thee: she is a fen
Of stagnant waters: altar, sword, and pen,
Fireside, the heroic wealth of hall and bower,
Have forefeited their ancient English dower 5
Of inward happiness. We are selfish men;
Oh! raise us up, return to us again;
And give us manners, virtue, freedom, power.
Thy soul was like a Star, and dwelt apart;
Thou hadst a voice whose sound was like the sea: 10
Pure as the naked heavens, majestic, free,
So didst thou travel on life's common way,
In cheerful godliness; and yet thy heart
The lowliest duties on herself did lay.

September, 1802 1807

The World Is Too Much with Us

The world is too much with us; late and soon,
Getting and spending, we lay waste our powers;

4. Dorothy Wordsworth.
5. One of a series "written immediately after my return from France to
London, when I could not but be
struck, as here described, with the
vanity and parade of our own country
* * * as contrasted with the quiet,
and I may say the desolation, that the
revolution had produced in France"
(Wordsworth).

Little we see in Nature that is ours;
We have given our hearts away, a sordid boon![6]
This Sea that bares her bosom to the moon,5
The winds that will be howling at all hours,
And are up-gathered now like sleeping flowers,
_For this, for everything, we are out of tune;
It moves us not.—Great God! I'd rather be
A Pagan suckled in a creed outworn;10
So might I, standing on this pleasant lea,
Have glimpses that would make me less forlorn;
Have sight of Proteus rising from the sea;
Or hear old Triton blow his wreathéd horn.[7]

1807

Surprised by Joy[8]

Surprised by joy—impatient as the Wind
I turned to share the transport—Oh! with whom
But thee, deep buried in the silent tomb,
That spot which no vicissitude can find?
Love, faithful love, recalled thee to my mind—5
But how could I forget thee? Through what power,
Even for the least division of an hour,
Have I been so beguiled as to be blind
To my most grievous loss!—That thought's return
Was the worst pang that sorrow ever bore,10
Save one, one only, when I stood forlorn,
Knowing my heart's best treasure was no more;
That neither present time, nor years unborn
Could to my sight that heavenly face restore.

1815

Composed by the Side of Grasmere Lake

Clouds, lingering yet, extend in solid bars
Through the gray west; and lo! these waters, steeled
By breezeless air to smoothest polish, yield
A vivid repetition of the stars;
Jove, Venus, and the ruddy crest of Mars[9]5
Amid his fellows beauteously revealed
At happy distance from earth's groaning field,
Where ruthless mortals wage incessant wars.
Is it a mirror?—or the nether Sphere[1]

6. Gift; it is the act of giving the heart away that is sordid.
7. Proteus: an old man of the sea who (in the *Odyssey*) can assume a variety of shapes. Triton: a sea deity, usually represented as blowing on a conch shell.
8. "This was in fact suggested by my daughter Catharine, long after her death" (Wordsworth). Catharine Wordsworth died June 4, 1812, at the age of 4.
9. Roman god of war.
1. The earth, region below the sphere of the moon.

Opening to view the abyss in which she feeds
Her own calm fires?—But list! a voice is near;
Great Pan himself low-whispering through the reeds,
"Be thankful, thou; for, if unholy deeds
Ravage the world, tranquillity is here!"

1807   1819

Afterthought[2]

I thought of thee,[3] my partner and my guide,
As being passed away.—Vain sympathies!
For, backward, Duddon! as I cast my eyes,
I see what was, and is, and will abide;
Still glides the Stream, and shall forever glide;   5
The Form remains, the Function never dies;
While we, the brave, the mighty, and the wise,
We Men, who in our morn of youth defied
The elements, must vanish—be it so!
Enough, if something from our hands have power   10
To live, and act, and serve the future hour;
And if, as toward the silent tomb we go,
Through love, through hope, and faith's transcendant dower,[4]
We feel that we are greater than we know.

1820

Mutability[5]

From low to high doth dissolution climb,
And sink from high to low, along a scale
Of awful notes, whose concord shall not fail;
A musical but melancholy chime,
Which they can hear who meddle not with crime,   5
Nor avarice, nor over-anxious care.
Truth fails not; but her outward forms that bear
The longest date do melt like frosty rime,
That in the morning whitened hill and plain
And is no more; drop like the tower sublime   10

2. The last in the sonnet sequence *The River Duddon*, which traces the course of the river from its source in the Lake Country to its terminus in the Irish Sea. The description of the course of a river, combined with the incidental meditations which the changing scene evokes, had been a common poetic formula in the "local poems" of the 18th century, but Wordsworth employs it here for a memorable statement of one of his reiterated topics: the flow of water as an emblem of permanence in change.
3. I.e., the river.
4. Endowment, gift.
5. This great sonnet interrupts a rather pedestrian sequence, *Ecclesiastical Sonnets*, dealing with the history and ceremonies of the church in England.

Of yesterday, which royally did wear
His crown of weeds, but could not even sustain
Some casual shout that broke the silent air,
Or the unimaginable touch of Time.

1821   1822

Steamboats, Viaducts, and Railways[6]

Motions and Means, on land and sea at war
With old poetic feeling, not for this,
Shall ye, by Poets even, be judged amiss!
Nor shall your presence, howsoe'er it mar
The loveliness of Nature, prove a bar   5
To the Mind's gaining that prophetic sense
Of future change, that point of vision, whence
May be discovered what in soul ye are.
In spite of all that beauty may disown
In your harsh features, Nature doth embrace   10
Her lawful offspring in Man's art; and Time,
Pleased with your triumphs o'er his brother Space,
Accepts from your bold hands the proffered crown
Of hope, and smiles on you with cheer sublime.

1833   1835

Extempore Effusion upon the Death of James Hogg[1]

When first, descending from the moorlands,
I saw the Stream of Yarrow[2] glide
Along a bare and open valley,
The Ettrick Shepherd[3] was my guide.

When last along its banks I wandered,   5
Through groves that had begun to shed

---

6. In late middle age Wordsworth demonstrates, as he had predicted in the Preface to *Lyrical Ballads*, that the poet will assimilate to his subject matter the "material revolution" produced by science. Unlike most poets, furthermore, he boldly accepts as evidences of man's progress even the unlovely encroachments of technology upon his beloved natural scene.
1. Wordsworth's niece relates how Wordsworth was deeply moved by finding unexpectedly in a newspaper the account of the death of the poet James Hogg. "Half an hour afterwards he came into the room where the ladies were sitting and asked Miss Hutchinson [his sister-in-law] to write down some lines which he had just composed." All the poets named here, several of Wordsworth's closest friends among them, had died between 1832 and 1835.
2. A river in the southeast of Scotland.
3. James Hogg, the "Ettrick Shepherd" (he was born in Ettrick Forest, and was for a time a shepherd), was discovered as a writer by Sir Walter Scott, and became well known as a poet, essayist, and editor.

Their golden leaves upon the pathways,
My steps the Border-minstrel[4] led.

The mighty Minstrel breathes no longer,
'Mid moldering ruins low he lies;   10
And death upon the braes[5] of Yarrow,
Has closed the Shepherd-poet's eyes:

Nor has the rolling year twice measured,
From sign to sign, its steadfast course,
Since every mortal power of Coleridge   15
Was frozen at its marvelous source;

The rapt One, of the godlike forehead,
The heaven-eyed creature sleeps in earth:
And Lamb, the frolic and the gentle,
Has vanished from his lonely hearth.   20

Like clouds that rake the mountain summits,
Or waves that own no curbing hand,
How fast has brother followed brother,
From sunshine to the sunless land!

Yet I, whose lids from infant slumber   25
Were earlier raised, remain to hear
A timid voice, that asks in whispers,
"Who next will drop and disappear?"

Our haughty life is crowned with darkness,
Like London with its own black wreath,   30
On which with thee, O Crabbe![6] forth-looking,
I gazed from Hampstead's breezy heath.

As if but yesterday departed,
Thou too art gone before; but why,
O'er ripe fruit, seasonably gathered,   35
Should frail survivors heave a sigh?

Mourn rather for that holy Spirit,
Sweet as the spring, as ocean deep;
For her[7] who, ere her summer faded,
Has sunk into a breathless sleep.   40

No more of old romantic sorrows,
For slaughtered Youth or lovelorn Maid!
With sharper grief is Yarrow smitten,
And Ettrick mourns with her their Poet dead.

November 21, 1835   1835

---

4. Sir Walter Scott.
5. The sloping banks of a stream.
6. George Crabbe, the poet of rural and village life.
7. Felicia Hemans, a minor but prolific poetess, who died when only 42. She is best known in America for *The Landing of the Pilgrim Fathers* and *The Boy Stood on the Burning Deck*.

From The Recluse[1]

["*Prospectus*"]

On Man, on Nature, and on Human Life,
Musing in solitude, I oft perceive
Fair trains of imagery before me rise,
Accompanied by feelings of delight
Pure, or with no unpleasing sadness mixed;   5
And I am conscious of affecting thoughts
And dear remembrances, whose presence soothes
Or elevates the Mind, intent to weigh
The good and evil of our mortal state.
—To these emotions, whencesoe'er they come,   10
Whether from breath of outward circumstance,
Or from the Soul—an impulse to herself—
I would give utterance in numerous verse.[2]
Of Truth, of Grandeur, Beauty, Love, and Hope,
And melancholy Fear subdued by Faith;   15
Of blessed consolations in distress;
Of moral strength, and intellectual Power;
Of joy in widest commonalty spread;
Of the individual Mind that keeps her own
Inviolate retirement, subject there   20
To Conscience only, and the law supreme
Of that Intelligence which governs all,
I sing—"fit audience let me find though few!"[3]

---

1. Through most of his poetic life Wordsworth labored intermittently at a long philosophic poem called *The Recluse*, which he intended to be his masterwork. It was to consist of an autobiographical introduction (the poem now called *The Prelude*) and three long parts; of these three he completed only Book I of Part I ("Home at Grasmere") and the whole of Part II, called *The Excursion*. In the Preface to *The Excursion*, published separately in 1814, Wordsworth printed this long extract (the concluding section of "Home at Grasmere") to serve "as a kind of *Prospectus* of the design and scope of the whole Poem"— i.e., of the entire *Recluse*.

The first version of this "Prospectus" was probably drafted as early as 1798. In language thronged with echoes from *Paradise Lost*, Wordsworth announces an undertaking which he conceives to be no less inspired and sublime than Milton's. In it he will move higher than heaven and deeper than hell, past scenes evoking greater fear than Erebus and greater awe than Jehovah; but without ever leaving "the Mind of Man— / My haunt, and the main region of my song" (lines 40–41). And his "high argument" is that Paradise need not remain Paradise lost, for it can be regained; not, however, as in Revelation xxi, by the marriage between the New Jerusalem and Christ the Lamb, but by a marriage between the "intellect of Man" and "this goodly universe," and the resulting new "creation * * * which they with blended might / Accomplish" (lines 47–71). In no other passage does Wordsworth reveal so clearly the extent to which he assimilates to his poetry the Biblical scheme of Milton's epic—assigning, however, the active role, from creation to redemption, to the human faculties, in their vital interaction with the external universe.

2. Harmonious verse; an echo of *Paradise Lost* V.150. The inspiring "breath of outward circumstance" parallels the "correspondent breeze" in the opening passage of *The Prelude*, just below.

3. *Paradise Lost* VII.31.

So prayed, more gaining than he asked, the Bard—
In holiest mood. Urania,[4] I shall need   25
Thy guidance, or a greater Muse, if such
Descend to earth or dwell in highest heaven!
For I must tread on shadowy ground, must sink
Deep—and, aloft ascending, breathe in worlds
To which the heaven of heavens [4a] is but a veil.   30
All strength—all terror, single or in bands,
That ever was put forth in personal form—
Jehovah—with his thunder, and the choir
Of shouting Angels, and the empyreal thrones[5]—
I pass them unalarmed. Not Chaos, not   35
The darkest pit of lowest Erebus,[6]
Nor aught of blinder vacancy, scooped out
By help of dreams—can breed such fear and awe
As fall upon us often when we look
Into our Minds, into the Mind of Man—   40
My haunt, and the main region of my song.
—Beauty—a living Presence of the earth,
Surpassing the most fair ideal Forms
Which craft of delicate Spirits hath composed
From earth's materials—waits upon my steps;   45
Pitches her tents before me as I move,
An hourly neighbor. Paradise, and groves
Elysian,[7] Fortunate Fields—like those of old
Sought in the Atlantic Main—why should they be
A history only of departed things,   50
Or a mere fiction of what never was?
For the discerning intellect of Man,
When wedded to this goodly universe
In love and holy passion, shall find these
A simple produce of the common day.   55
—I, long before the blissful hour arrives,
Would chant, in lonely peace, the spousal[8] verse
Of this great consummation—and, by words
Which speak of nothing more than what we are,
Would I arouse the sensual from their sleep   60
Of Death, and win the vacant and the vain
To noble raptures; while my voice proclaims
How exquisitely the individual Mind
(And the progressive powers perhaps no less
Of the whole species) to the external World   65
Is fitted—and how exquisitely, too—

4. The Muse whom Milton had invoked in *Paradise Lost*. In pagan myth, Urania had been the Muse of astronomy.
4a. In *Paradise Lost* the dwelling place, beyond the visible heaven, of God and his angels.
5. *Paradise Lost* II.430.
6. In classical myth, a dark region of the underworld; often used as a name for hell by Christian writers.

7. Elysium, in Greek myth, was the place where men favored by the gods live a happy life after death. It was sometimes identified with the "Islands of the Blessed," reputed to be located far out in the western sea—hence "sought in the Atlantic Main." See Horace, *Epodes* XVI.
8. Marital; hence a "spousal verse" is an epithalamion.

Theme this but little heard of among men—
The external World is fitted to the Mind;
And the creation (by no lower name
Can it be called) which they with blended might   70
Accomplish—this is our high argument.[9]
—Such grateful haunts foregoing, if I oft
Must turn elsewhere—to travel near the tribes
And fellowships of men, and see ill sights
Of madding passions mutually inflamed;   75
Must hear Humanity in fields and groves
Pipe solitary anguish; or must hang
Brooding above the fierce confederate storm
Of sorrow, barricadoed[1] evermore
Within the walls of cities—may these sounds   80
Have their authentic comment; that even these
Hearing, I be not downcast or forlorn!—
Descend, prophetic Spirit! that inspir'st
The human Soul of universal earth,
Dreaming on things to come;[2] and dost possess   85
A metropolitan[3] temple in the hearts
Of mighty Poets: upon me bestow
A gift of genuine insight; that my Song
With starlike virtue in its place may shine,
Shedding benignant influence, and secure,   90
Itself, from all malevolent effect
Of those mutations that extend their sway
Throughout the nether sphere![4]—And if with this
I mix more lowly matter; with the thing
Contemplated, describe the Mind and Man   95
Contemplating; and who, and what he was—
The transitory Being that beheld
The Vision; when and where, and how he lived—
Be not this labor useless. If such theme
May sort with highest objects, then—dread Power!   100
Whose gracious favor is the primal source
Of all illumination—may my Life
Express the image of a better time,
More wise desires, and simpler manners—nurse
My Heart in genuine freedom—all pure thoughts   105
Be with me—so shall thy unfailing love
Guide, and support, and cheer me to the end!

ca. 1798–1814   1814

---

9. Theme, as in *Paradise Lost* I.24: "the height of this great Argument."
1. Barricaded, as in *Paradise Lost* VIII.241.
2. Cf. "the prophetic soul / Of the wide world dreaming on things to come" (Shakespeare, *Sonnet* CVII).
3. Designating the principal seat of a religion.
4. In the Ptolemaic world picture, the spheres of the heavenly bodies were immutable, and only the earth (the "nether sphere," or region below the sphere of the moon) was subject to change. Compare *Paradise Lost* VII.375 and X.656–64.

The Prelude Wordsworth originally planned, in 1798, to incorporate an account of his own poetic development within his projected philosophical poem, *The Recluse*, but decided in the following year to make these materials into an independent poem, addressed to S. T. Coleridge, which would serve as a prefatory work to *The Recluse*. "The preparatory poem is biographical," Wordsworth wrote in his Preface to *The Excursion* (1814), "and conducts the history of the Author's mind to the point when he was emboldened to hope that his faculties were sufficiently matured for entering upon the arduous labor which he had proposed to himself." Most of Books I and II were written in 1798–99; and by May, 1805, Wordsworth had completed the first version of the entire poem. For the next 35 years, however, he kept tinkering with the text, and it was not published until 1850, three months after Wordsworth's death. The author himself referred to the manuscript only as a poem "on my own earlier life," or "on the growth of my own mind." The apt title, *The Prelude*, was bestowed on it by Mrs. Wordsworth.

Wordsworth was well aware that "it was a thing unprecedented in literary history that a man should talk so much about himself." But it should be recognized that Wordsworth deals with himself only, in Coleridge's term, as the "I-representative." The events of his life are presented, not as they had seemed to him at the time they occurred, but reinterpreted in tranquility and shaped into an artistic pattern; and the protagonist of the poem is not really Wordsworth the private person, but the poet's mind, or more specifically, the poetic imagination. "This faculty," Wordsworth wrote in the last book (XIV.193–94), "hath been the feeding source / Of our long labor"; and the account of its emergence, development, impairment, and restoration, he goes on to say, constitutes the plot, or narrative principle, of the whole of *The Prelude*.

When he had finished *The Prelude* Wordsworth felt, in disappointment, that it was "far below what I had seemed capable of executing"; and at the close of the poem he described it as only preliminary to his "building up a Work that shall endure" (XIV.311). This later work was never finished. But in the sustained treatment of his remembrance of things past, Wordsworth had in fact found his great and original poetic subject; and though he did not realize it, in writing the prelude to his masterpiece he had written the masterpiece itself.

From The Prelude[1]
or
Growth of a Poet's Mind

AN AUTOBIOGRAPHICAL POEM

From *Book I. Introduction—Childhood and Schooltime*

Oh there is blessing in this gentle breeze,[2]
A visitant that while it fans my cheek
Doth seem half-conscious of the joy it brings
From the green fields, and from yon azure sky.
Whate'er its mission, the soft breeze can come   5
To none more grateful than to me; escaped
From the vast city,[3] where I long had pined
A discontented sojourner: now free,
Free as a bird to settle where I will.
What dwelling shall receive me? in what vale   10
Shall be my harbor? underneath what grove
Shall I take up my home? and what clear stream
Shall with its murmur lull me into rest?
The earth is all before me.[4] With a heart
Joyous, nor scared at its own liberty,   15
I look about; and should the chosen guide
Be nothing better than a wandering cloud,
I cannot miss my way. I breathe again!
Trances of thought and mountings of the mind
Come fast upon me: it is shaken off,   20
That burthen of my own unnatural self,
The heavy weight of many a weary day
Not mine, and such as were not made for me.
Long months of peace (if such bold word accord
With any promises of human life),   25

1. The first version of *The Prelude*, completed in 1805, together with variant passages from Wordsworth's later MSS., was published by Ernest de Selincourt in 1926. The text reproduced here is Wordsworth's final version of 1850.
2. Wordsworth says, lines 46–50, that the preceding lines were uttered in the circumstances they describe. Until recently it was the standard opinion that the occasion was September of 1795 when Wordsworth, released from financial worries by a legacy, was on his way to find a home in Racedown, Dorset. It is much more likely, however, that the lines refer primarily to his walk to what was to be his home at Grasmere, late in 1797, deliberately fused with details from an earlier trip to Racedown. In 1804 this passage was adopted as the preamble for *The Prelude,* where it replaces the epic device (as in *Paradise Lost*) of the opening prayer to the Muse for inspiration. To be "inspired" is, in its literal sense, to be blown into by a divinity: Wordsworth begins his poem with a literal wind, the "breath of heaven," which (lines 33–42) becomes the stimulus for a correspondent inner breeze, marking both a springlike revival of the spirit after a wintry season and a burst of poetic power which Wordsworth equates with the inspiration of the Biblical prophets when touched by the Holy Spirit (lines 50–54). The revivifying breeze, material and spiritual, recurs as a kind of leitmotif in *The Prelude,* and also became the radical metaphor of Coleridge's *Dejection: An Ode* and Shelley's *Ode to the West Wind.*
3. London, where Wordsworth had lived February to August, 1795.
4. The first of many echoes of *Paradise Lost:* "The world was all before them" (XII.646).

Long months of ease and undisturbed delight
Are mine in prospect; whither shall I turn,
By road or pathway, or through trackless field,
Uphill or down, or shall some floating thing
Upon the river point me out my course?   30

   Dear Liberty! Yet what would it avail
But for a gift that consecrates the joy?
For I, methought, while the sweet breath of heaven
Was blowing on my body, felt within
A correspondent breeze, that gently moved   35
With quickening virtue,[5] but is now become
A tempest, a redundant energy,
Vexing its own creation. Thanks to both,
And their congenial[6] powers, that, while they join
In breaking up a long-continued frost,   40
Bring with them vernal promises, the hope
Of active days urged on by flying hours—
Days of sweet leisure, taxed with patient thought
Abstruse, nor wanting punctual service high,
Matins and vespers of harmonious verse!   45

   Thus far, O Friend![7] did I, not used to make
A present joy the matter of a song,[8]
Pour forth that day my soul in measured strains
That would not be forgotten, and are here
Recorded: to the open fields I told   50
A prophecy: poetic numbers came
Spontaneously to clothe in priestly robe
A renovated spirit singled out,
Such hope was mine, for holy services.
My own voice cheered me, and, far more, the mind's   55
Internal echo of the imperfect sound;
To both I listened, drawing from them both
A cheerful confidence in things to come.

            * * *

   Fair seedtime had my soul, and I grew up
Fostered alike by beauty and by fear:[9]
Much favored in my birthplace, and no less
In that belovéd Vale[1] to which erelong
We were transplanted—there were we let loose   305
For sports of wider range. Ere I had told

5. Reviving power.
6. Kindred.
7. Here begins *The Prelude* proper, composed 1798–1805. The "Friend" is Samuel Taylor Coleridge, to whom the entire poem is addressed as a kind of immense verse letter. For Coleridge's reply, see *To William Wordsworth*.
8. His poetry, as Wordsworth said in the Preface to *Lyrical Ballads*, usually originates as "emotion recollected in tranquility," not, as in the preamble just preceding, during the actual experience it describes.
9. Wordsworth refers repeatedly to the double impulse of nature, "both law and impulse * * * / To kindle or restrain," as he said in *Three Years She Grew* (lines 8–12).
1. The valley of Esthwaite, the location of Hawkshead, where Wordsworth attended school.

Ten birthdays, when among the mountain slopes
Frost, and the breath of frosty wind, had snapped
The last autumnal crocus, 'twas my joy
With store of springes[2] o'er my shoulder hung   310
To range the open heights where woodcocks run
Along the smooth green turf. Through half the night,
Scudding away from snare to snare, I plied
That anxious visitation—moon and stars
Were shining o'er my head. I was alone,   315
And seemed to be a trouble to the peace
That dwelt among them. Sometimes it befell
In these night wanderings, that a strong desire
O'erpowered my better reason, and the bird
Which was the captive of another's toil   320
Became my prey; and when the deed was done
I heard among the solitary hills
Low breathings coming after me, and sounds
Of undistinguishable motion, steps
Almost as silent as the turf they trod.   325

    Nor less, when spring had warmed the cultured Vale,
Moved we as plunderers where the mother bird
Had in high places built her lodge; though mean
Our object and inglorious, yet the end
Was not ignoble. Oh! when I have hung   330
Above the raven's nest, by knots of grass
And half-inch fissures in the slippery rock
But ill sustained, and almost (so it seemed)
Suspended by the blast that blew amain,
Shouldering the naked crag, oh, at that time   335
While on the perilous ridge I hung alone,
With what strange utterance did the loud dry wind
Blow through my ear! the sky seemed not a sky
Of earth—and with what motion moved the clouds!

    Dust as we are, the immortal spirit grows   340
Like harmony in music; there is a dark
Inscrutable workmanship that reconciles
Discordant elements, makes them cling together
In one society. How strange that all
The terrors, pains, and early miseries,   345
Regrets, vexations, lassitudes interfused
Within my mind, should e'er have borne a part,
And that a needful part, in making up
The calm existence that is mine when I
Am worthy of myself! Praise to the end!   350
Thanks to the means which Nature deigned to employ;
Whether her fearless visitings, or those
That came with soft alarm, like hurtless light
Opening the peaceful clouds; or she may use

2. Bird snares.

Severer interventions, ministry   355
More palpable, as best might suit her aim.[3]

   One summer evening (led by her) I found
A little boat tied to a willow tree
Within a rocky cave, its usual home.
Straight I unloosed her chain, and stepping in   360
Pushed from the shore. It was an act of stealth
And troubled pleasure, nor without the voice
Of mountain echoes did my boat move on;
Leaving behind her still, on either side,
Small circles glittering idly in the moon,   365
Until they melted all into one track
Of sparkling light. But now, like one who rows,
Proud of his skill, to reach a chosen point
With an unswerving line, I fixed my view
Upon the summit of a craggy ridge,   370
The horizon's utmost boundary; for above
Was nothing but the stars and the gray sky.
She was an elfin pinnace;[4] lustily
I dipped my oars into the silent lake,
And, as I rose upon the stroke, my boat   375
Went heaving through the water like a swan;
When, from behind that craggy steep till then
The horizon's bound, a huge peak, black and huge,
As if with voluntary power instinct,
Upreared its head.[5] I struck and struck again,   380
And growing still in stature the grim shape
Towered up between me and the stars, and still,
For so it seemed, with purpose of its own
And measured motion like a living thing,
Strode after me. With trembling oars I turned,   385
And through the silent water stole my way
Back to the covert of the willow tree;
There in her mooring place I left my bark,
And through the meadows homeward went, in grave
And serious mood; but after I had seen   390
That spectacle, for many days, my brain
Worked with a dim and undetermined sense
Of unknown modes of being; o'er my thoughts
There hung a darkness, call it solitude
Or blank desertion. No familiar shapes   395
Remained, no pleasant images of trees,
Of sea or sky, no colors of green fields;
But huge and mighty forms, that do not live

3. A restatement of the double ministry of nature described in line 302; what follows is a second example of discipline by fear.
4. Small boat.
5. In order to direct his boat in a straight line, the rower has fixed his eye on a point in the ridge of the nearby shore, which blocks out the landscape behind. As he moves farther out, the black peak suddenly rears into his altering angle of vision and seems to stride closer with each stroke of the oars.

Like living men, moved slowly through the mind
By day, and were a trouble to my dreams.   400

    Wisdom and Spirit of the universe!
Thou Soul that art the eternity of thought,
That givest to forms and images a breath
And everlasting motion, not in vain
By day or starlight thus from my first dawn   405
Of childhood didst thou intertwine for me
The passions that build up our human soul;
Not with the mean and vulgar works of man,
But with high objects, with enduring things—
With life and nature—purifying thus   410
The elements of feeling and of thought,
And sanctifying, by such discipline,
Both pain and fear, until we recognize
A grandeur in the beatings of the heart.
Nor was this fellowship vouchsafed to me   415
With stinted kindness. In November days,
When vapors rolling down the valley made
A lonely scene more lonesome, among woods,
At noon and 'mid the calm of summer nights,
When, by the margin of the trembling lake,   420
Beneath the gloomy hills homeward I went
In solitude, such intercourse was mine;
Mine was it in the fields both day and night,
And by the waters, all the summer long.

    And in the frosty season, when the sun   425
Was set, and visible for many a mile
The cottage windows blazed through twilight gloom,
I heeded not their summons: happy time
It was indeed for all of us—for me
It was a time of rapture! Clear and loud   430
The village clock tolled six—I wheeled about,
Proud and exulting like an untired horse
That cares not for his home. All shod with steel,
We hissed along the polished ice in games
Confederate, imitative of the chase   435
And woodland pleasures—the resounding horn,
The pack loud chiming, and the hunted hare.
So through the darkness and the cold we flew,
And not a voice was idle; with the din
Smitten, the precipices rang aloud;   440
The leafless trees and every icy crag
Tinkled like iron; while far distant hills
Into the tumult sent an alien sound
Of melancholy not unnoticed, while the stars
Eastward were sparkling clear, and in the west   445
The orange sky of evening died away.
Not seldom from the uproar I retired

Into a silent bay, or sportively
Glanced sideway, leaving the tumultuous throng,
To cut across the reflex[6] of a star   450
That fled, and, flying still before me, gleamed
Upon the glassy plain; and oftentimes,
When we had given our bodies to the wind,
And all the shadowy banks on either side
Came sweeping through the darkness, spinning still   455
The rapid line of motion, then at once
Have I, reclining back upon my heels,
Stopped short; yet still the solitary cliffs
Wheeled by me—even as if the earth had rolled
With visible motion her diurnal round!   460
Behind me did they stretch in solemn train,
Feebler and feebler, and I stood and watched
Till all was tranquil as a dreamless sleep.

　　Ye Presences of Nature in the sky
And on the earth! Ye Visions of the hills!   465
And Souls of lonely places![7] can I think
A vulgar hope was yours when ye employed
Such ministry, when ye, through many a year
Haunting me thus among my boyish sports,
On caves and trees, upon the woods and hills,   470
Impressed upon all forms the characters
Of danger or desire; and thus did make
The surface of the universal earth
With triumph and delight, with hope and fear,
Work like a sea? * * *   475

　　Nor, sedulous as I have been to trace
How Nature by extrinsic passion first   545
Peopled the mind with forms sublime or fair,[8]
And made me love them, may I here omit
How other pleasures have been mine, and joys
Of subtler origin; how I have felt,
Not seldom even in that tempestuous time,   550
Those hallowed and pure motions of the sense
Which seem, in their simplicity, to own
An intellectual[9] charm; that calm delight
Which, if I err not, surely must belong
To those first-born affinities that fit   555
Our new existence to existing things,
And, in our dawn of being, constitute
The bond of union between life and joy.

6. Reflection.
7. In this period Wordsworth referred both to a single "Spirit" or "Soul" of the universe as a whole (e.g., lines 401–2, above) and to plural "Presences" and "Souls" inanimating the various parts of the universe.
8. The passion at first was "extrinsic" because felt not for nature itself, but for nature as associated with the outdoor activities he loved. He now goes on to distinguish other "subtler" pleasures, felt in the very process of sensing the natural objects themselves.
9. As though they were abstract concepts rather than sensations.

Yes, I remember when the changeful earth,
And twice five summers on my mind had stamped   560
The faces of the moving year, even then
I held unconscious intercourse with beauty
Old as creation, drinking in a pure
Organic pleasure from the silver wreaths
Of curling mist, or from the level plain   565
Of waters colored by impending[1] clouds.

The sands of Westmoreland, the creeks and bays
Of Cumbria's[2] rocky limits, they can tell
How, when the Sea threw off his evening shade,
And to the shepherd's hut on distant hills   570
Sent welcome notice of the rising moon,
How I have stood, to fancies such as these
A stranger, linking with the spectacle
No conscious memory of a kindred sight,
And bringing with me no peculiar sense   575
Of quietness or peace; yet have I stood,
Even while mine eye hath moved o'er many a league
Of shining water, gathering as it seemed,
Through every hairbreadth in that field of light,
New pleasure like a bee among the flowers.   580

Thus oft amid those fits of vulgar[3] joy
Which, through all seasons, on a child's pursuits
Are prompt attendants, 'mid that giddy bliss
Which, like a tempest, works along the blood
And is forgotten; even then I felt   585
Gleams like the flashing of a shield—the earth
And common face of Nature spake to me
Rememberable things; sometimes, 'tis true,
By chance collisions and quaint accidents
(Like those ill-sorted unions, work supposed   590
Of evil-minded fairies), yet not vain
Nor profitless, if haply they impressed
Collateral[4] objects and appearances,
Albeit lifeless then, and doomed to sleep
Until maturer seasons called them forth   595
To impregnate and to elevate the mind.
—And if the vulgar joy by its own weight
Wearied itself out of the memory,
The scenes which were a witness of that joy
Remained in their substantial lineaments   600
Depicted on the brain, and to the eye
Were visible, a daily sight; and thus
By the impressive discipline of fear,
By pleasure and repeated happiness,
So frequently repeated, and by force   605

1. Overhanging.   3. Commonplace.
2. Cumberland's.   4. Accompanying but subordinate.

Of obscure feelings representative
Of things forgotten, these same scenes so bright,
So beautiful, so majestic in themselves,
Though yet the day was distant, did become
Habitually dear, and all their forms   610
And changeful colors by invisible links
Were fastened to the affections. * * *

From *Book II. Schooltime (continued)*

Blest the infant Babe
(For with my best conjecture I would trace
Our Being's earthly progress),[1] blest the Babe,
Nursed in his Mother's arms, who sinks to sleep   235
Rocked on his Mother's breast; who with his soul
Drinks in the feelings of his Mother's eye!
For him, in one dear Presence, there exists
A virtue which irradiates and exalts
Objects through widest intercourse of sense.   240
No outcast he, bewildered and depressed:
Along his infant veins are interfused
The gravitation and the filial bond
Of nature that connect him with the world.
Is there a flower, to which he points with hand   245
Too weak to gather it, already love
Drawn from love's purest earthly fount for him
Hath beautified that flower; already shades
Of pity cast from inward tenderness
Do fall around him upon aught that bears   250
Unsightly marks of violence or harm.
Emphatically such a Being lives,
Frail creature as he is, helpless as frail,
An inmate of this active universe.
For feeling has to him imparted power   255
That through the growing faculties of sense
Doth like an agent of the one great Mind
Create, creator and receiver both,[2]
Working but in alliance with the works
Which it beholds.—Such, verily, is the first   260
Poetic spirit of our human life,
By uniform control of after years,
In most, abated or suppressed; in some,
Through every change of growth and of decay,
Pre-eminent till death. * * *   265

---

1. Like the modern psychologist, Wordsworth recognized the importance of earliest infancy in the development of the individual mind and temperament, although he had then to invent the terms with which to analyze infant psychology.
2. Like Coleridge (see *Biographia Lite-*
raria, Chapter XIII), Wordsworth describes the mind in perception as partially creating the world it seems passively to receive. In the succeeding passage (lines 360–74) Wordsworth repeats this concept in various metaphors signifying the give-and-take of outer world and inner mind and emotion.

'Twere long to tell
What spring and autumn, what the winter snows,
And what the summer shade, what day and night,
Evening and morning, sleep and waking, thought   355
From sources inexhaustible, poured forth
To feed the spirit of religious love
In which I walked with Nature. But let this
Be not forgotten, that I still retained
My first creative sensibility;   360
That by the regular action of the world
My soul was unsubdued. A plastic power
Abode with me; a forming hand, at times
Rebellious, acting in a devious mood;
A local spirit of his own, at war   365
With general tendency, but, for the most,
Subservient strictly to external things
With which it communed. An auxiliar light
Came from my mind, which on the setting sun
Bestowed new splendor; the melodious birds,   370
The fluttering breezes, fountains that run on
Murmuring so sweetly in themselves, obeyed
A like dominion, and the midnight storm
Grew darker in the presence of my eye:
Hence my obeisance, my devotion hence,   375
And hence my transport.
                        Nor should this, perchance,
Pass unrecorded, that I still had loved
The exercise and produce of a toil,
Than analytic industry to me
More pleasing, and whose character I deem   380
Is more poetic as resembling more
Creative agency. The song would speak
Of that interminable building reared
By observation of affinities
In objects where no brotherhood exists   385
To passive minds. My seventeenth year was come;
And, whether from this habit rooted now
So deeply in my mind, or from excess
In the great social principle of life
Coercing all things into sympathy,   390
To unorganic natures were transferred
My own enjoyments; or the power of truth
Coming in revelation, did converse
With things that really are;[3] I, at this time,
Saw blessings spread around me like a sea.   395
Thus while the days flew by, and years passed on,

---

3. Wordsworth is careful to indicate that there are two possible explanations for his sense that life pervades the inorganic as well as organic world: it may be the illusory result of a projection of his own inner life, or it may be the perception of an objective truth.

From Nature and her overflowing soul,
I had received so much, that all my thoughts
Were steeped in feeling; I was only then
Contented, when with bliss ineffable   400
I felt the sentiment of Being spread
O'er all that moves and all that seemeth still;
O'er all that, lost beyond the reach of thought
And human knowledge, to the human eye
Invisible, yet liveth to the heart;   405
O'er all that leaps and runs, and shouts and sings,
Or beats the gladsome air; o'er all that glides
Beneath the wave, yea, in the wave itself,
And mighty depth of waters. Wonder not
If high the transport, great the joy I felt,   410
Communing in this sort through earth and heaven
With every form of creature, as it looked
Towards the Uncreated with a countenance
Of adoration, with an eye of love.[4]
One song they sang, and it was audible,   415
Most audible, then, when the fleshly ear,
O'ercome by humblest prelude of that strain,
Forgot her functions, and slept undisturbed.[5]

* * *

From *Book III. Residence at Cambridge*

The Evangelist St. John my patron was:[1]
Three Gothic courts are his, and in the first
Was my abiding place, a nook obscure;
Right underneath, the College kitchens made
A humming sound, less tunable than bees,   50
But hardly less industrious; with shrill notes
Of sharp command and scolding intermixed.
Near me hung Trinity's[2] loquacious clock,
Who never let the quarters, night or day,
Slip by him unproclaimed, and told the hours   55
Twice over with a male and female voice.
Her pealing organ was my neighbor too;
And from my pillow, looking forth by light
Of moon or favoring stars, I could behold
The antechapel where the statue stood   60
Of Newton with his prism and silent face,
The marble index of a mind forever
Voyaging through strange seas of Thought, alone.

4. Wordsworth did not add lines 412–14, giving a Christian frame to his experience of the "one life," until very late, in 1839.
5. Cf. this description of the trance state, like that of religious mystics, with *Tintern Abbey*, lines 41–49.
1. Wordsworth was a student at St. John's College, Cambridge University, from 1787 to 1791.
2. Trinity College adjoins St. John's. Roubiliac's statue of Newton, holding the prism with which he had conducted the experiments described in his *Optics*, stands in the west end of Trinity chapel.

Of College labors, of the Lecturer's room
All studded round, as thick as chairs could stand,   65
With loyal students faithful to their books,
Half-and-half idlers, hardy recusants,
And honest dunces—of important days,
Examinations, when the man was weighed
As in a balance! of excessive hopes,   70
Tremblings withal and commendable fears,
Small jealousies, and triumphs good or bad,
Let others that know more speak as they know.
Such glory was but little sought by me,
And little won. Yet from the first crude days   75
Of settling time in this untried abode,
I was disturbed at times by prudent thoughts,
Wishing to hope without a hope, some fears
About my future worldly maintenance,
And, more than all, a strangeness in the mind,   80
A feeling that I was not for that hour,
Nor for that place. * * *

    It hath been told that when the first delight
That flashed upon me from this novel show
Had failed, the mind returned into herself;
Yet true it is that I had made a change
In climate, and my nature's outward coat   205
Changed also slowly and insensibly.
Full oft the quiet and exalted thoughts
Of loneliness gave way to empty noise
And superficial pastimes; now and then
Forced labor, and more frequently forced hopes;   210
And, worst of all, a treasonable growth
Of indecisive judgments, that impaired
And shook the mind's simplicity.—And yet
This was a gladsome time. Could I behold—
Who, less insensible than sodden clay   215
In a sea river's bed at ebb of tide,
Could have beheld—with undelighted heart,
So many happy youths, so wide and fair
A congregation in its budding time
Of health, and hope, and beauty, all at once   220
So many divers samples from the growth
Of life's sweet season—could have seen unmoved
That miscellaneous garland of wild flowers
Decking the matron temples of a place
So famous through the world? To me, at least,   225
It was a goodly prospect: for, in sooth,
Though I had learnt betimes to stand unpropped,
And independent musings pleased me so
That spells seemed on me when I was alone,
Yet could I only cleave to solitude   230

In lonely places; if a throng was near
That way I leaned by nature; for my heart
Was social, and loved idleness and joy.

* * *

         Companionships,
Friendships, acquaintances, were welcome all.
We sauntered, played, or rioted;[3] we talked
Unprofitable talk at morning hours;
Drifted about along the streets and walks,   250
Read lazily in trivial books, went forth
To gallop through the country in blind zeal
Of senseless horsemanship, or on the breast
Of Cam[4] sailed boisterously, and let the stars
Come forth, perhaps without one quiet thought.   255

* * *

    Thus in submissive idleness, my Friend!
The laboring time of autumn, winter, spring,   630
Eight months! rolled pleasingly away; the ninth
Came and returned me to my native hills.

From *Book IV. Summer Vacation*[1]

            Yes, that heartless chase
Of trivial pleasures was a poor exchange
For books and nature at that early age.
'Tis true some casual knowledge might be gained   300
Of character or life; but at that time,
Of manners put to school I took small note,
And all my deeper passions lay elsewhere.
Far better had it been to exalt the mind
By solitary study, to uphold   305
Intense desire through meditative peace;
And yet, for chastisement of these regrets,
The memory of one particular hour
Doth here rise up against me. 'Mid a throng
Of maids and youths, old men, and matrons staid,   310
A medley of all tempers, I had passed
The night in dancing, gaiety, and mirth,
With din of instruments and shuffling feet,
And glancing forms, and tapers glittering,
And unaimed prattle flying up and down;   315
Spirits upon the stretch, and here and there
Slight shocks of young love-liking interspersed,
Whose transient pleasure mounted to the head,

3. This was a period of low ebb in the intellectual vigor and discipline of Cambridge, so that Wordsworth was able to indulge generously in the fringe activities of university life.
4. The river Cam, which flows through Cambridge.
1. Wordsworth spent his first summer vacation from the university at Hawkshead. In this passage he describes an experience during the walk home after an all-night dance.

And tingled through the veins. Ere we retired,
The cock had crowed, and now the eastern sky   320
Was kindling, not unseen, from humble copse
And open field, through which the pathway wound,
And homeward led my steps. Magnificent
The morning rose, in memorable pomp,
Glorious as e'er I had beheld—in front,   325
The sea lay laughing at a distance; near,
The solid mountains shone, bright as the clouds,
Grain-tinctured,[2] drenched in empyrean light;
And in the meadows and the lower grounds
Was all the sweetness of a common dawn—   330
Dews, vapors, and the melody of birds,
And laborers going forth to till the fields.
Ah! need I say, dear Friend! that to the brim
My heart was full; I made no vows, but vows
Were then made for me; bond unknown to me   335
Was given, that I should be, else sinning greatly,
A dedicated Spirit. On I walked
In thankful blessedness, which yet survives.

* * *

From *Book V. Books*

        Oh! why hath not the Mind   45
Some element to stamp her image on
In nature somewhat nearer to her own?
Why, gifted with such powers to send abroad
Her spirit, must it lodge in shrines so frail?[1]

    One day, when from my lips a like complaint   50
Had fallen in presence of a studious friend,
He with a smile made answer, that in truth
'Twas going far to seek disquietude;
But on the front of his reproof confessed
That he himself had oftentimes given way   55
To kindred hauntings. Whereupon I told,
That once in the stillness of a summer's noon,
While I was seated in a rocky cave
By the seaside, perusing, so it chanced,
The famous history of the errant knight   60
Recorded by Cervantes,[2] these same thoughts
Beset me, and to height unusual rose,
While listlessly I sate, and, having closed
The book, had turned my eyes toward the wide sea.

2. Crimson. The "empyrean" was, in
ancient thought, the outer sphere of the
universe, composed of pure fire.
1. Wordsworth is describing his recurrent fear that some holocaust might
wipe out all books, the frail and perishable repositories of all man's wisdom and poetry.
2. I.e., Don Quixote. Wordsworth's
nightmare involves all the elements of
the poet's last waking experience. Mathematics had flourished among the Arabs
—hence the Arabian rider (lines 75 ff.).

On poetry and geometric truth, 65
And their high privilege of lasting life,
From all internal injury exempt,
I mused upon these chiefly; and at length,
My senses yielding to the sultry air,
Sleep seized me, and I passed into a dream. 70
I saw before me stretched a boundless plain
Of sandy wilderness, all black and void,
And as I looked around, distress and fear
Came creeping over me, when at my side,
Close at my side, an uncouth shape appeared 75
Upon a dromedary, mounted high.
He seemed an Arab of the Bedouin tribes:
A lance he bore, and underneath one arm
A stone, and in the opposite hand a shell
Of a surpassing brightness. At the sight 80
Much I rejoiced, not doubting but a guide
Was present, one who with unerring skill
Would through the desert lead me; and while yet
I looked and looked, self-questioned what this freight
Which the newcomer carried through the waste 85
Could mean, the Arab told me that the stone
(To give it in the language of the dream)
Was "Euclid's Elements";[3] and "This," said he,
"Is something of more worth"; and at the word
Stretched forth the shell, so beautiful in shape, 90
In color so resplendent, with command
That I should hold it to my ear. I did so,
And heard that instant in an unknown tongue,
Which yet I understood, articulate sounds,
A loud prophetic blast of harmony; 95
An Ode, in passion uttered, which foretold
Destruction to the children of the earth
By deluge, now at hand. No sooner ceased
The song, than the Arab with calm look declared
That all would come to pass of which the voice 100
Had given forewarning, and that he himself
Was going then to bury those two books:
The one that held acquaintance with the stars,
And wedded soul to soul in purest bond
Of reason, undisturbed by space or time; 105
The other that was a god, yea, many gods,
Had voices more than all the winds, with power
To exhilarate the spirit, and to soothe,
Through every clime, the heart of human kind.
While this was uttering, strange as it may seem, 110
I wondered not, although I plainly saw
The one to be a stone, the other a shell;

3. Euclid was a Greek mathematician; his celebrated book on plane geometry and the theory of numbers continued to be used as a textbook into the 19th century.

Nor doubted once but that they both were books,
Having a perfect faith in all that passed.
Far stronger, now, grew the desire I felt   115
To cleave unto this man; but when I prayed
To share his enterprise, he hurried on
Reckless[4] of me: I followed, not unseen,
For oftentimes he cast a backward look,
Grasping his twofold treasure.—Lance in rest,   120
He rode, I keeping pace with him; and now
He, to my fancy, had become the knight
Whose tale Cervantes tells; yet not the knight,
But was an Arab of the desert too;
Of these was neither, and was both at once.   125
His countenance, meanwhile, grew more disturbed;
And, looking backwards when he looked, mine eyes
Saw, over half the wilderness diffused,
A bed of glittering light: I asked the cause:
"It is," said he, "the waters of the deep   130
Gathering upon us"; quickening then the pace
Of the unwieldy creature he bestrode,
He left me: I called after him aloud;
He heeded not; but, with his twofold charge
Still in his grasp, before me, full in view,   135
Went hurrying o'er the illimitable waste,
With the fleet waters of a drowning world
In chase of him; whereat I waked in terror,
And saw the sea before me, and the book,
In which I had been reading, at my side.   140

                    * * *

There was a Boy: ye knew him well, ye cliffs
And islands of Winander!—many a time   365
At evening, when the earliest stars began
To move along the edges of the hills,
Rising or setting, would he stand alone
Beneath the trees or by the glimmering lake,
And there, with fingers interwoven, both hands   3°0
Pressed closely palm to palm, and to his mouth
Uplifted, he, as through an instrument,
Blew mimic hootings to the silent owls,
That they might answer him; and they would shout
Across the watery vale, and shout again,   375
Responsive to his call, with quivering peals,
And long halloos and screams, and echoes loud,
Redoubled and redoubled, concourse wild
Of jocund din; and, when a lengthened pause
Of silence came and baffled his best skill,   380
Then sometimes, in that silence while he hung
Listening, a gentle shock of mild surprise

4. Neglectful.

Has carried far into his heart the voice
Of mountain torrents; or the visible scene
Would enter unawares into his mind,   385
With all its solemn imagery, its rocks,
Its woods, and that uncertain heaven, received
Into the bosom of the steady lake.[5]

* * *

Here must we pause: this only let me add,
From heart experience, and in humblest sense   585
Of modesty, that he, who in his youth
A daily wanderer among woods and fields
With living Nature hath been intimate,
Not only in that raw unpracticed time
Is stirred to ecstasy, as others are,   590
By glittering verse; but further, doth receive,
In measure only dealt out to himself,
Knowledge and increase of enduring joy
From the great Nature that exists in works
Of mighty Poets.[6] Visionary power   595
Attends the motions of the viewless winds,
Embodied in the mystery of words:
There, darkness makes abode, and all the host
Of shadowy things work endless changes—there,
As in a mansion like their proper home,   600
Even forms and substances are circumfused
By that transparent veil with light divine,
And, through the turnings intricate of verse,
Present themselves as objects recognized,
In flashes, and with glory not their own.   605

From Book VI. *Cambridge and the Alps*

When the third summer freed us from restraint,[1]
A youthful friend, he too a mountaineer,
Not slow to share my wishes, took his staff,
And sallying forth, we journeyed side by side,   325
Bound to the distant Alps. A hardy slight
Did this unprecedented course imply
Of college studies and their set rewards;[2]

---

5. Coleridge wrote of the last line and a half ("that uncertain heaven * * * lake"): "Had I met these lines running wild in the deserts of Arabia, I should instantly have screamed out, 'Wordsworth.' "
6. Having found a set of symbols in nature, Wordsworth now finds nature in the symbol systems of "mighty poets," in one of his characteristically sonorous passages of splendid obscurity.
1. After reviewing briefly his second and third years at Cambridge, Wordsworth here describes his trip through France and Switzerland with a college friend, Robert Jones, in the succeeding summer vacation, 1790. France was then in the "golden hours" of the early period of the Revolution; the fall of the Bastille had occurred on July 14 of the preceding year.
2. English universities allow much longer vacations than those in America, on the optimistic assumption that they will be used primarily for intensive study. Wordsworth is facing his final examinations in the next college year.

Nor had, in truth, the scheme been formed by me
Without uneasy forethought of the pain,   330
The censures, and ill-omening, of those
To whom my worldly interests were dear.
But Nature then was sovereign in my mind,
And mighty forms, seizing a youthful fancy,
Had given a charter to irregular hopes.   335
In any age of uneventful calm
Among the nations, surely would my heart
Have been possessed by similar desire;
But Europe at that time was thrilled with joy,
France standing on the top of golden hours,   340
And human nature seeming born again.

* * *

When from the Vallais we had turned, and clomb
Along the Simplon's steep and rugged road,[3]
Following a band of muleteers, we reached
A halting place, where all together took   565
Their noontide meal. Hastily rose our guide,
Leaving us at the board; awhile we lingered,
Then paced the beaten downward way that led
Right to a rough stream's edge, and there broke off;
The only track now visible was one   570
That from the torrent's further brink held forth
Conspicuous invitation to ascend
A lofty mountain. After brief delay
Crossing the unbridged stream, that road we took,
And clomb with eagerness, till anxious fears   575
Intruded, for we failed to overtake
Our comrades gone before. By fortunate chance,
While every moment added doubt to doubt,
A peasant met us, from whose mouth we learned
That to the spot which had perplexed us first   580
We must descend, and there should find the road,
Which in the stony channel of the stream
Lay a few steps, and then along its banks;
And, that our future course, all plain to sight,
Was downwards, with the current of that stream.   585
Loath to believe what we so grieved to hear,
For still we had hopes that pointed to the clouds,
We questioned him again, and yet again;
But every word that from the peasant's lips
Came in reply, translated by our feelings,   590
Ended in this—*that we had crossed the Alps.*[4]

3. The Simplon Pass through the Alps.
4. As Dorothy Wordsworth baldly put it later on, "The ambition of youth was disappointed at these tidings." The visionary experience that follows occurred not in the Alps but at the time of writing the passage, as the 1805 text explicitly says: "Imagination! lifting up itself / Before the eye and progress of my Song." Wordsworth goes on to interpret it as a revelation that man's glory consists in the infinite striving of his insatiable spirit.

Imagination—here the Power so called
Through sad incompetence of human speech,
That awful Power rose from the mind's abyss
Like an unfathered vapor[5] that enwraps,   595
At once, some lonely traveler. I was lost;
Halted without an effort to break through;
But to my conscious soul I now can say—
"I recognize thy glory": in such strength
Of usurpation, when the light of sense   600
Goes out, but with a flash that has revealed
The invisible world, doth greatness make abode,
There harbors; whether we be young or old,
Our destiny, our being's heart and home,
Is with infinitude, and only there;   605
With hope it is, hope that can never die,
Effort, and expectation, and desire,
And something evermore about to be.
Under such banners militant, the soul
Seeks for no trophies, struggles for no spoils   610
That may attest her prowess, blest in thoughts
That are their own perfection and reward,
Strong in herself and in beatitude[6]
That hides her, like the mighty flood of Nile
Poured from his fount of Abyssinian clouds   615
To fertilize the whole Egyptian plain.

The melancholy slackening that ensued
Upon those tidings by the peasant given
Was soon dislodged. Downwards we hurried fast,
And, with the half-shaped road which we had missed,   620
Entered a narrow chasm. The brook and road
Were fellow travelers in this gloomy strait,
And with them did we journey several hours
At a slow pace. The immeasurable height
Of woods decaying, never to be decayed,   625
The stationary blasts of waterfalls,
And in the narrow rent at every turn
Winds thwarting winds, bewildered and forlorn,
The torrents shooting from the clear blue sky,
The rocks that muttered close upon our ears,   630
Black drizzling crags that spake by the wayside
As if a voice were in them, the sick sight
And giddy prospect of the raving stream,
The unfettered clouds and region of the Heavens,
Tumult and peace, the darkness and the light—   635
Were all like workings of one mind, the features
Of the same face, blossoms upon one tree;
Characters of the great Apocalypse,[7]

---

5. Sudden vapor from no apparent source.
6. The ultimate blessedness or happiness.
7. The objects in this natural scene, exhibiting a coincidence of all oppo-

The types and symbols of Eternity,
Of first, and last, and midst, and without end.[8] 640

* * *

From *Book VII. Residence in London*

Rise up, thou monstrous anthill on the plain
Of a too busy world![1] Before me flow, 150
Thou endless stream of men and moving things!
Thy everyday appearance, as it strikes—
With wonder heightened, or sublimed by awe—
On strangers, of all ages; the quick dance
Of colors, lights, and forms; the deafening din; 155
The comers and the goers face to face,
Face after face; the string of dazzling wares,
Shop after shop, with symbols, blazoned names,[2]
And all the tradesman's honors overhead:
Here, fronts of houses, like a title page, 160
With letters huge inscribed from top to toe,
Stationed above the door, like guardian saints;
There, allegoric shapes, female or male,
Or physiognomies of real men,
Land warriors, kings, or admirals of the sea, 165
Boyle,[3] Shakespeare, Newton, or the attractive head
Of some quack doctor, famous in his day.

* * *

From these sights 675
Take one—that ancient festival, the Fair,
Holden where martyrs suffered in past time,
And named of St. Bartholomew;[4] there, see
A work completed to our hands, that lays,
If any spectacle on earth can do, 680
The whole creative powers of man asleep!—
For once, the Muse's help will we implore,
And she shall lodge us, wafted on her wings,
Above the press and danger of the crowd,
Upon some showman's platform. What a shock 685

sites, are like the written words of the Apocalypse—i.e., of the Book of Revelation, the last book of the New Testament.
8. In *Paradise Lost* V.153–165 Milton says that the things created declare their Creator, and calls on all to extol "him first, him last, him midst, and without end."
1. This is how London struck the young man from the country in the three and a half months he spent there in 1791.
2. The names ostentatiously inscribed on the shop signs.
3. Robert Boyle, the great 17th-century physicist and chemist. "Attrac-

tive": i.e., drawing people to him.
4. This huge fair was long held in Smithfield, the place where, on St. Bartholomew's Day, August 24, Protestants had been executed in Queen Mary's reign. The scene, which for Wordsworth laid "the whole creative powers of man asleep" (line 681), is exactly the kind that most stimulates those writers (including Chaucer, Shakespeare, and Dickens) who take inspiration from the vigor and bustle of variegated humanity. But "before it could touch [Wordsworth] near," as Walter Raleigh said, "an experience had to be simple and isolated."

For eyes and ears! what anarchy and din,
Barbarian and infernal—a phantasma,[5]
Monstrous in color, motion, shape, sight, sound!
Below, the open space, through every nook
Of the wide area, twinkles, is alive   690
With heads; the midway region, and above,
Is thronged with staring pictures and huge scrolls,
Dumb proclamations of the Prodigies;
With chattering monkeys dangling from their poles,
And children whirling in their roundabouts;[6]   695
With those that stretch the neck and strain the eyes,
And crack the voice in rivalship, the crowd
Inviting; with buffoons against buffoons
Grimacing, writhing, screaming—him who grinds
The hurdy-gurdy, at the fiddle weaves,   700
Rattles the salt box, thumps the kettledrum,
And him who at the trumpet puffs his cheeks,
The silver-collared Negro with his timbrel,
Equestrians, tumblers, women, girls, and boys,
Blue-breeched, pink-vested, with high-towering plumes.   705
All movables of wonder, from all parts,
Are here—Albinos, painted Indians, Dwarfs,
The Horse of knowledge,[7] and the learned Pig,
The Stone-eater, the man that swallows fire,
Giants, Ventriloquists, the Invisible Girl,   710
The Bust that speaks and moves its goggling eyes,
The Waxwork, Clockwork, all the marvelous craft
Of modern Merlins,[8] Wild Beasts, Puppet-shows,
All out-o'-the-way, farfetched, perverted things,
All freaks of nature, all Promethean[9] thoughts   715
Of man, his dullness, madness, and their feats
All jumbled up together, to compose
A Parliament of Monsters. Tents and Booths
Meanwhile, as if the whole were one vast mill,
Are vomiting, receiving on all sides,   720
Men, Women, three-years' Children, Babes in arms.

Oh, blank confusion! true epitome
Of what the mighty City is herself
To thousands upon thousands of her sons,
Living amid the same perpetual whirl   725
Of trivial objects, melted and reduced
To one identity, by differences
That have no law, no meaning, and no end—
Oppression, under which even highest minds
Must labor, whence the strongest are not free.   730
But though the picture weary out the eye,

5. Fantasy of a disordered mind.
6. Merry-go-rounds.
7. A horse trained to tap out answers to numerical questions, etc.
8. Magicians. Merlin was the magician in the Arthurian romances.
9. Creative, or highly inventive. Prometheus, in Greek mythology, made man out of clay and taught him the arts.

By nature an unmanageable sight,
It is not wholly so to him who looks
In steadiness, who hath among least things
An under-sense of greatest; sees the parts   735
As parts, but with a feeling of the whole.

* * *

From *Book VIII. Retrospect—Love of Nature Leading to Love of Man*[1]

For me, when my affections first were led
From kindred, friends, and playmates, to partake
Love for the human creature's absolute self,
That noticeable kindliness of heart
Sprang out of fountains, there abounding most,   125
Where sovereign Nature dictated the tasks
And occupations which her beauty adorned,
And Shepherds were the men that pleased me first.

* * *

A rambling schoolboy, thus
I felt his presence in his own domain,
As of a lord and master, or a power,
Or genius, under Nature, under God,
Presiding; and severest solitude   260
Had more commanding looks when he was there.
When up the lonely brooks on rainy days
Angling I went, or trod the trackless hills
By mists bewildered, suddenly mine eyes
Have glanced upon him distant a few steps,   265
In size a giant, stalking through thick fog,
His sheep like Greenland bears; [1a] or, as he stepped
Beyond the boundary line of some hill-shadow,
His form hath flashed upon me, glorified
By the deep radiance of the setting sun;[2]   270
Or him have I descried in distant sky,
A solitary object and sublime,
Above all height! like an aerial cross
Stationed alone upon a spiry rock
Of the Chartreuse, for worship.[3] Thus was man   275

1. In this book Wordsworth reviews the first 21 years of his life in order to trace the transfer of his earlier feelings for nature to shepherds and other humble people who carry on their lonely duties almost as though they were moving parts of the landscape (cf. *Michael*, lines 1–39). Wordsworth's central concern is to describe the early development in his relatively inexperienced mind of an Image, or conceptual model, of the largeness, worth, and almost sacred dignity of generic Man (lines 256–81); an Image which proved invulnerable to the acid bath of his later experience of the vulgarity, meanness, and evil of which individual men are capable (lines 317–22).
1a. Polar bears.
2. A "glory" is a mountain phenomenon in which the enlarged figure of a man is seen projected by the sun upon the mist, with a radiance about its head. Cf. Coleridge's *Dejection*, line 54.
3. In his tour of the Alps Wordsworth had been deeply impressed by the Chartreuse, a Carthusian monastery in

Ennobled outwardly before my sight,
And thus my heart was early introduced
To an unconscious love and reverence
Of human nature; hence the human form
To me became an index of delight,   280
Of grace and honor, power and worthiness.
Meanwhile this creature—spiritual almost
As those of books, but more exalted far;
Far more of an imaginative form
Than the gay Corin[4] of the groves, who lives   285
For his own fancies, or to dance by the hour,
In coronal, with Phyllis in the midst—
Was, for the purposes of kind,[5] a man
With the most common; husband, father; learned,
Could teach, admonish; suffered with the rest   290
From vice and folly, wretchedness and fear;
Of this I little saw, cared less for it,
But something must have felt.
                              Call ye these appearances—
Which I beheld of shepherds in my youth,
This sanctity of Nature given to man—   295
A shadow, a delusion, ye who pore
On the dead letter, miss the spirit of things;
Whose truth is not a motion or a shape
Instinct with vital functions, but a block
Or waxen image which yourselves have made,   300
And ye adore! But blessed be the God
Of Nature and of Man that this was so;
That men before my inexperienced eyes
Did first present themselves thus purified,
Removed, and to a distance that was fit: 305
And so we all of us in some degree
Are led to knowledge, whencesoever led,
And howsoever; were it otherwise,
And we found evil fast as we find good
In our first years, or think that it is found,   310
How could the innocent heart bear up and live!
But doubly fortunate my lot; not here
Alone, that something of a better life
Perhaps was round me than it is the privilege
Of most to move in, but that first I looked   315
At Man through objects that were great or fair;
First communed with him by their help. And thus
Was founded a sure safeguard and defense
Against the weight of meanness, selfish cares,

the French Alps, with its soaring cross
visible against the sky. There is an
overtone here of the Christlike divinity
investing the "common" man (line
289).
4. "Corin" and "Phyllis," dancing in

their "coronals," or wreaths of flowers,
were stock characters in earlier pastoral literature.
5. I.e., in carrying out the tasks of
humankind.

Coarse manners, vulgar passions, that beat in   320
On all sides from the ordinary world
In which we traffic. * * *

Yet deem not, Friend! that human kind with me   340
Thus early took a place pre-eminent;
Nature herself was, at this unripe time,
But secondary to my own pursuits
And animals activities, and all
Their trivial pleasures;[6] and when these had drooped   345
And gradually expired, and Nature, prized
For her own sake, became my joy, even then—
And upwards through late youth, until not less
Than two-and-twenty summers had been told—
Was Man in my affections and regards   350
Subordinate to her, her visible forms
And viewless agencies: a passion, she,
A rapture often, and immediate love
Ever at hand; he, only a delight
Occasional, an accidental grace,   355
His hour being not yet come. * * *

From *Book IX. Residence in France*[1]

France lured me forth; the realm that I had crossed
So lately, journeying toward the snow-clad Alps.
But now, relinquishing the scrip and staff,[2]   35
And all enjoyment which the summer sun
Sheds round the steps of those who meet the day
With motion constant as his own, I went
Prepared to sojourn in a pleasant town,
Washed by the current of the stately Loire.[3]   40

Through Paris lay my readiest course, and there
Sojourning a few days, I visited,
In haste, each spot of old or recent fame,
The latter chiefly; from the field of Mars   45
Down to the suburbs of St. Antony,
And from Mont Martyr southward to the Dome
Of Geneviève.[4] In both her clamorous Halls,

6. Cf, Wordsworth's account of the stages of his development in *Tintern Abbey*, lines 65–92 and note.
1. Wordsworth's second visit to France, while he was 21 and 22 years of age (1791–92), came during a crucial period of the French Revolution. This book deals with Wordsworth's stay at Paris, Orléans, and Blois, when he developed his passionate partisanship for the French people and the revolutionary cause.
2. The "scrip" (the bag or knapsack) and the "staff" are the traditional emblems of the foot pilgrim.

3. Orléans, on the Loire river, where Wordsworth stayed from late November, 1791, until he moved to Blois early the next year.
4. The "field of Mars" (the Champ de Mars), where Louis XVI swore fidelity to the new constitution. "The suburbs of St. Anthony": Faubourg St. Antoine, near the Bastille, a working-class quarter and center of revolutionary violence. "Mont Martyr": Montmartre, a hill on which revolutionary meetings were held. The "dome of Geneviève" became the Panthéon, a burial place for notable Frenchmen.

The National Synod[5] and the Jacobins,
I saw the Revolutionary Power   50
Toss like a ship at anchor, rocked by storms;
The Arcades I traversed, in the Palace huge
Of Orléans;[6] coasted round and round the line
Of Tavern, Brothel, Gaming-house, and Shop,
Great rendezvous of worst and best, the walk   55
Of all who had a purpose, or had not;
I stared and listened, with a stranger's ears,
To Hawkers and Haranguers, hubbub wild!
And hissing Factionists with ardent eyes,
In knots, or pairs, or single. Not a look   60
Hope takes, or Doubt or Fear is forced to wear,
But seemed there present; and I scanned them all,
Watched every gesture uncontrollable,
Of anger, and vexation, and despite,
All side by side, and struggling face to face,   65
With gaiety and dissolute idleness.

      Where silent zephyrs sported with the dust
Of the Bastille, I sate in the open sun,
And from the rubbish gathered up a stone,
And pocketed the relic, in the guise   70
Of an enthusiast: yet, in honest truth,
I looked for something that I could not find,
Affecting more emotion than I felt;
For 'tis most certain that these various sights,
However potent their first shock, with me   75
Appeared to recompense the traveler's pains
Less than the painted Magdalene of Le Brun,[7]
A beauty exquisitely wrought, with hair
Disheveled, gleaming eyes, and rueful cheek
Pale and bedropped with overflowing tears.   80

                           * * *

                          For myself, I fear   110
Now in connection with so great a theme
To speak (as I must be compelled to do)
Of one so unimportant; night by night
Did I frequent the formal haunts of men,
Whom, in the city, privilege of birth   115
Sequestered from the rest, societies
Polished in arts, and in punctilio[8] versed;
Whence, and from deeper causes, all discourse
Of good and evil of the time was shunned

5. The newly formed National Assembly. "Jacobins": the club of radical democratic revolutionists, named for the ancient convent of St. Jacques, their meeting place.
6. The arcades in the courtyard of the Palais Royal, a shopping center and Parisian rendezvous.
7. A theatrical painting of the weeping Mary Magdalene by Charles Le Brun (1619–90), then regarded as a religious masterpiece.
8. The niceties of social manners.

With scrupulous care; but these restrictions soon   120
Proved tedious, and I gradually withdrew
Into a noisier world, and thus ere long
Became a patriot;[9] and my heart was all
Given to the people, and my love was theirs.

* * *

Among that band of Officers was one,
Already hinted at, of other mold—
A patriot, thence rejected by the rest,   290
And with an oriental loathing spurned,
As of a different caste.[1] A meeker man
Than this lived never, nor a more benign,
Meek though enthusiastic. Injuries
Made *him* more gracious, and his nature then   295
Did breathe its sweetness out most sensibly,
As aromatic flowers on Alpine turf,
When foot hath crushed them. He through the events
Of that great change wandered in perfect faith,
As through a book, an old romance, or tale   300
Of Fairy, or some dream of actions wrought
Behind the summer clouds. By birth he ranked
With the most noble, but unto the poor
Among mankind he was in service bound,
As by some tie invisible, oaths professed   305
To a religious order. Man he loved
As man; and, to the mean and the obscure,
And all the homely[2] in their homely works,
Transferred a courtesy which had no air
Of condescension, but did rather seem   310
A passion and a gallantry, like that
Which he, a soldier, in his idler day
Had paid to woman: somewhat vain he was,
Or seemed so, yet it was not vanity,
But fondness, and a kind of radiant joy   315
Diffused around him, while he was intent
On works of love or freedom, or revolved
Complacently[3] the progress of a cause,
Whereof he was a part: yet this was meek
And placid, and took nothing from the man   320
That was delightful. Oft in solitude
With him did I discourse about the end
Of civil government, and its wisest forms;
Of ancient loyalty, and chartered rights,
Custom and habit, novelty and change;   325
Of self-respect, and virtue in the few

---

9. A republican in politics.
1. This memorable character sketch is
of Michel Beaupuy, fifteen years older
than Wordsworth, and one of the rare
republicans among the officer corps of
the regular army. By doctrine and
force of character he did much to shape
Wordsworth's radical sympathies.
2. Lowly.
3. With quiet satisfaction.

For patrimonial honor set apart,
And ignorance in the laboring multitude.
For he, to all intolerance indisposed,
Balanced these contemplations in his mind;   330
And I, who at that time was scarcely dipped
Into the turmoil, bore a sounder judgment
Than later days allowed; carried about me,
With less alloy to its integrity,
The experience of past ages, as, through help   335
Of books and common life, it makes sure way
To youthful minds, by objects over near
Not pressed upon, nor dazzled or misled
By struggling with the crowd for present ends.

* * *

       Yet not the less,
Hatred of absolute rule, where will of one
Is law for all, and of that barren pride
In them who, by immunities unjust,
Between the sovereign and the people stand,   505
His helper and not theirs, laid stronger hold
Daily upon me, mixed with pity too
And love; for where hope is, there love will be
For the abject multitude. And when we chanced
One day to meet a hunger-bitten girl,   510
Who crept along fitting her languid gait
Unto a heifer's motion, by a cord
Tied to her arm, and picking thus from the lane
Its sustenance, while the girl with pallid hands
Was busy knitting in a heartless mood   515
Of solitude, and at the sight my friend
In agitation said, " 'Tis against *that*
That we are fighting," I with him believed
That a benignant spirit was abroad
Which might not be withstood, that poverty   520
Abject as this would in a little time
Be found no more, that we should see the earth
Unthwarted in her wish to recompense
The meek, the lowly, patient child of toil,
All institutes forever blotted out   525
That legalized exclusion, empty pomp
Abolished, sensual state and cruel power
Whether by edict of the one or few;
And finally, as sum and crown of all,
Should see the people having a strong hand   530
In framing their own laws; whence better days
To all mankind.[4] * * *

4. The following political aims constituted the radicalism of Wordsworth and Beaupuy: elimination of the extreme of poverty; the rewards of tillage to go to the tiller of the land; all careers opened to talents; abolition of absolute power, whether by a monarch or an oligarchy; and a greatly extended franchise.

From *Book X. Residence in France (continued)*[1]

Cheered with this hope,[2] to Paris I returned,
And ranged, with ardor heretofore unfelt,
The spacious city, and in progress passed   50
The prison[3] where the unhappy Monarch lay,
Associate with his children and his wife
In bondage; and the palace, lately stormed
With roar of cannon by a furious host.
I crossed the square (an empty area then!)   55
Of the Carrousel, where so late had lain
The dead, upon the dying heaped, and gazed
On this and other spots, as doth a man
Upon a volume whose contents he knows
Are memorable, but from him locked up,   60
Being written in a tongue he cannot read,
So that he questions the mute leaves with pain,
And half upbraids their silence. But that night
I felt most deeply in what world I was,
What ground I trod on, and what air I breathed.   65
High was my room and lonely, near the roof
Of a large mansion or hotel, a lodge
That would have pleased me in more quiet times;
Nor was it wholly without pleasure then.
With unextinguished taper I kept watch,   70
Reading at intervals; the fear gone by
Pressed on me almost like a fear to come.
I thought of those September massacres,
Divided from me by one little month,
Saw them and touched:[4] the rest was conjured up   75
From tragic fictions or true history,
Remembrances and dim admonishments.
The horse is taught his manage,[5] and no star
Of wildest course but treads back his own steps;
For the spent hurricane the air provides   80
As fierce a successor; the tide retreats
But to return out of its hiding place
In the great deep; all things have second birth;
The earthquake is not satisfied at once;
And in this way I wrought upon myself,   85
Until I seemed to hear a voice that cried,

1. At this period, October, 1792–August, 1794, Wordsworth's revolutionary enthusiasm was at its height.
2. The Parisian mob had stormed the Tuileries; the king had been deposed and imprisoned; and the Commune had organized the "September Massacres," in which 3,000 Royalist suspects were murdered. Wordsworth's "hope" was that the moderates were now taking over and would eliminate further violence.
3. I.e., the "Temple," where Louis XVI was held prisoner. "The palace" is the Tuileries; in front of this is the great square of "the Carrousel," where a number of the mob storming the palace had been killed.
4. I.e., his imagination of the September Massacres was so vivid as to be palpable.
5. The French *manège*, the prescribed action and paces of a trained horse.

To the whole city, "Sleep no more." The trance
Fled with the voice to which it had given birth;
But vainly comments of a calmer mind
Promised soft peace and sweet forgetfulness.   90
The place, all hushed and silent as it was,
Appeared unfit for the repose of night,
Defenseless as a wood where tigers roam.

* * *

     In this frame of mind,
Dragged by a chain of harsh necessity,
So seemed it—now I thankfully acknowledge,
Forced by the gracious providence of Heaven—
To England I returned,[6] else (though assured   225
That I both was and must be of small weight,
No better than a landsman on the deck
Of a ship struggling with a hideous storm)
Doubtless, I should have then made common cause
With some who perished; haply perished too,   230
A poor mistaken and bewildered offering—
Should to the breast of Nature have gone back,
With all my resolutions, all my hopes,
A Poet only to myself, to men
Useless, and even, belovéd Friend! a soul   235
To thee unknown![7] * * *

What, then, were my emotions, when in arms
Britain put forth her freeborn strength in league,
Oh, pity and shame! with those confederate Powers![8]   265
Not in my single self alone I found,
But in the minds of all ingenuous youth,
Change and subversion from that hour. No shock
Given to my moral nature had I known
Down to that very moment; neither lapse   270
Nor turn of sentiment that might be named
A revolution, save at this one time;
All else was progress on the selfsame path
On which, with a diversity of pace,
I had been traveling: this a stride at once   275
Into another region. As a light
And pliant harebell, swinging in the breeze
On some gray rock—its birthplace—so had I

6. Forced by the "harsh necessity" of a lack of money, Wordsworth returned to England late in 1792.
7. Wordsworth did not meet Coleridge, the "belovéd Friend," until 1795.
8. England joined the war against France in February, 1793. The great moral crisis which almost wrecked Wordsworth's life began with this sudden split between his profound attachments to the English land (the development of which he had described in the early books of *The Prelude*) and his later but heartfelt identification with the cause of the French Revolution. What had seemed a single and coherent development suddenly became split into conflicting parts. The moral turmoil he goes on to describe is remarkably parallel to that of many young radicals of the 1930's and later, who had staked their hopes for mankind on the Russian Revolution.

Wantoned, fast rooted on the ancient tower
Of my belovéd country, wishing not   280
A happier fortune than to wither there:
Now was I from that pleasant station torn
And tossed about in whirlwind. I rejoiced,
Yea, afterwards—truth most painful to record!—
Exulted, in the triumph of my soul,   285
When Englishmen by thousands were o'erthrown,
Left without glory on the field, or driven,
Brave hearts! to shameful flight.[9] It was a grief—
Grief call it not, 'twas anything but that—
A conflict of sensations without name,   290
Of which *he* only, who may love the sight
Of a village steeple, as I do, can judge,
When, in the congregation bending all
To their great Father, prayers were offered up,
Or praises for our country's victories;   295
And, 'mid the simple worshipers, perchance
I only, like an uninvited guest
Whom no one owned, sate silent, shall I add,
Fed on the day of vengeance yet to come.

* * *

Most melancholy at that time, O Friend!
Were my day thoughts—my nights were miserable;[10]
Through months, through years, long after the last beat
Of those atrocities, the hour of sleep   400
To me came rarely charged with natural gifts,
Such ghastly visions had I of despair
And tyranny, and implements of death;
And innocent victims sinking under fear,
And momentary hope, and worn-out prayer,   405
Each in his separate cell, or penned in crowds
For sacrifice, and struggling with fond mirth
And levity in dungeons, where the dust
Was laid with tears. Then suddenly the scene
Changed, and the unbroken dream entangled me   410
In long orations, which I strove to plead
Before unjust tribunals—with a voice
Laboring, a brain confounded, and a sense,
Deathlike, of treacherous desertion, felt
In the last place of refuge—my own soul.   415

* * *

From *Book XI. France (concluded)*[1]

O pleasant exercise of hope and joy!   105
For mighty were the auxiliars which then stood

9. The French defeated the English in
the battle of Hondschoote, September
6, 1793.
10. The Reign of Terror, under Robespierre, had begun with the execution
of the moderate Girondist leaders in
October and November, 1793.
1. Book XI deals with the year from

Upon our side, us who were strong in love!
Bliss was it in that dawn to be alive,
But to be young was very Heaven! O times,
In which the meager, stale, forbidding ways   110
Of custom, law, and statute, took at once
The attraction of a country in romance!
When Reason seemed the most to assert her rights
When most intent on making of herself
A prime enchantress—to assist the work,   115
Which then was going forward in her name!
Not favored spots alone, but the whole Earth,
The beauty wore of promise—that which sets
(As at some moments might not be unfelt
Among the bowers of Paradise itself)   120
The budding rose above the rose full blown.[2]
What temper at the prospect did not wake
To happiness unthought of? The inert
Were roused, and lively natures rapt away!
They who had fed their childhood upon dreams,   125
The playfellows of fancy, who had made
All powers of swiftness, subtlety, and strength
Their ministers—who in lordly wise had stirred
Among the grandest objects of the sense,
And dealt with whatsoever they found there   130
As if they had within some lurking right
To wield it—they, too, who of gentle mood
Had watched all gentle motions, and to these
Had fitted their own thoughts, schemers more mild,
And in the region of their peaceful selves—   135
Now was it that *both* found, the meek and lofty
Did both find helpers to their hearts' desire,
And stuff at hand, plastic as they could wish—
Were called upon to exercise their skill,
Not in Utopia, subterranean fields,   140
Or some secreted island, Heaven knows where!
But in the very world, which is the world
Of all of us—the place where, in the end,
We find our happiness, or not at all!

Why should I not confess that Earth was then   145
To me, what an inheritance, new-fallen,
Seems, when the first time visited, to one
Who thither comes to find in it his home?
He walks about and looks upon the spot

August, 1794, through September, 1795: Wordsworth's growing disillusionment with the French Revolution, his recourse to abstract theories of man and politics, his despair and nervous breakdown, and the beginning of his recovery when he moved from London to Racedown.

2. A statement of the Romantic theme of the glory of the imperfect, which sets a higher value on promise than on achievement.

With cordial transport, molds it and remolds,   150
And is half-pleased with things that are amiss,
'Twill be such joy to see them disappear.

* * *

But now, become oppressors in their turn,
Frenchmen had changed a war of self-defense
For one of conquest,[3] losing sight of all
Which they had struggled for: now mounted up,
Openly in the eye of earth and heaven,   210
The scale of liberty.[4] I read her doom.
With anger vexed, with disappointment sore,
But not dismayed, nor taking to the shame
Of a false prophet. While resentment rose,
Striving to hide, what nought could heal, the wounds   215
Of mortified presumption, I adhered
More firmly to old tenets, and, to prove
Their temper, strained them more; and thus, in heat
Of contest, did opinions every day
Grow into consequence, till round my mind   220
They clung, as if they were its life, nay more,
The very being of the immortal soul.

* * *

I summoned my best skill, and toiled, intent
To anatomize the frame of social life,   280
Yea, the whole body of society
Searched to its heart.[5] Share with me, Friend! the wish
That some dramatic tale, endued with shapes
Livelier, and flinging out less guarded words
Than suit the work we fashion, might set forth   285
What then I learned, or think I learned, of truth,
And the errors into which I fell, betrayed
By present objects, and by reasonings false
From their beginnings, inasmuch as drawn
Out of a heart that had been turned aside   290
From Nature's way by outward accidents,
And which was thus confounded, more and more
Misguided, and misguiding. So I fared,
Dragging all precepts, judgments, maxims, creeds,
Like culprits to the bar; calling the mind,   295
Suspiciously, to establish in plain day
Her titles and her honors; now believing,
Now disbelieving; endlessly perplexed

3. In late 1794 and early 1795 French troops had successes in Spain, Italy, Holland, and Germany.
4. I.e., the desire for power now outweighed the love of liberty.
5. Disappointed in the course of the actual Revolution, Wordsworth turned to the theories of William Godwin and other philosophers of the Enlighten-ment. These theorists attempted to deduce the laws of ethics and government from rational premises; they fatally omitted, as Wordsworth later maintained, to take account of the moral promptings and loyalties of man's "heart"—i.e., of his instinctual and feelingful nature (see lines 353–56).

With impulse, motive, right and wrong, the ground
Of obligation, what the rule and whence   300
The sanction; till, demanding formal *proof*,
And seeking it in everything, I lost
All feeling of conviction, and, in fine,[6]
Sick, wearied out with contrarieties,
Yielded up moral questions in despair.   305

   This was the crisis of that strong disease,
This the soul's last and lowest ebb; I drooped,
Deeming our blessed reason of least use
Where wanted most * * *

           Then it was—
Thanks to the bounteous Giver of all good!—
That the belovéd Sister[7] in whose sight   335
Those days were passed, now speaking in a voice
Of sudden admonition—like a brook
That did but *cross* a lonely road, and now
Is seen, heard, felt, and caught at every turn,
Companion never lost through many a league—   340
Maintained for me a saving intercourse
With my true self;[8] for, though bedimmed and changed
Much, as it seemed, I was no further changed
Than as a clouded and a waning moon;
She whispered still that brightness would return;   345
She, in the midst of all, preserved me still
A Poet, made me seek beneath that name,
And that alone, my office upon earth;
And, lastly, as hereafter will be shown,
If willing audience fail not, Nature's self,   350
By all varieties of human love
Assisted, led me back through opening day
To those sweet counsels between head and heart
Whence grew that genuine knowledge, fraught with peace,
Which, through the later sinkings of this cause,   355
Hath still upheld me, and upholds me now
In the catastrophe (for so they dream,
And nothing less), when, finally to close
And seal up all the gains of France, a Pope
Is summoned in, to crown an Emperor[9] * * *   360

6. At last.
7. After a long separation, from 1791 to 1794, Dorothy Wordsworth came to live with her brother at Racedown in 1795, and continued a member of his household until her death.
8. Dorothy and the renewed influence of nature (line 350) healed the inner fracture between his earlier and later self, which Wordsworth had described in Book X, lines 268 ff.
9. The ultimate blow to liberal hopes for France when, on December 2, 1804, Napoleon summoned Pope Pius VII to officiate at the ceremony elevating him to Emperor. At the last moment, Napoleon took the crown and donned it himself.

From *Book XII. Imagination and Taste,
How Impaired and Restored*[1]

There are in our existence spots of time,
That with distinct pre-eminence retain
A renovating virtue, whence—depressed   210
By false opinion and contentious thought,
Or aught of heavier or more deadly weight,
In trivial occupations, and the round
Of ordinary intercourse—our minds
Are nourished and invisibly repaired;   215
A virtue, by which pleasure is enhanced,
That penetrates, enables us to mount,
When high, more high, and lifts us up when fallen.
This efficacious spirit chiefly lurks
Among those passages of life that give   220
Profoundest knowledge to what point, and how,
The mind is lord and master—outward sense
The obedient servant of her will. Such moments
Are scattered everywhere, taking their date
From our first childhood. I remember well,   225
That once, while yet my inexperienced hand
Could scarcely hold a bridle, with proud hopes
I mounted, and we journeyed towards the hills:
An ancient servant of my father's house
Was with me, my encourager and guide;   230
We had not traveled long, ere some mischance
Disjoined me from my comrade; and, through fear
Dismounting, down the rough and stony moor
I led my horse, and, stumbling on, at length
Came to a bottom, where in former times   235
A murderer had been hung in iron chains.
The gibbet-mast had moldered down, the bones
And iron case were gone; but on the turf,
Hard by, soon after that fell deed was wrought,
Some unknown hand had carved the murderer's name.   240
The monumental letters were inscribed
In times long past; but still, from year to year
By superstition of the neighborhood,
The grass is cleared away, and to this hour
The characters are fresh and visible: 245

1. Book XII reviews the "impairment" and gradual recovery of Wordsworth's creative sensibility in response to the natural world; its climax is the famed description of the "spots of time." These are moments of experience of what is in itself ordinary (line 254), but becomes luminous with a profound significance that, since it is bestowed by the perceiver, evidences the imaginative power of the perceiving mind (lines 220–23, 275–77). The recollection of these indelible scenes nourishes and repairs the mind in those periods of depression or distraction when the imagination flags (lines 210–215). Wordsworth also recognizes (lines 277–86) that the recollection of such spots of time from his own early experience is the source of his greatest poetry, and that this source is not inexhaustible.

A casual glance had shown them, and I fled,
Faltering and faint, and ignorant of the road;
Then, reascending the bare common, saw
A naked pool that lay beneath the hills,
The beacon on the summit, and more near,   250
A girl, who bore a pitcher on her head,
And seemed with difficult steps to force her way
Against the blowing wind. It was, in truth,
An ordinary sight; but I should need
Colors and words that are unknown to man,   255
To paint the visionary dreariness
Which, while I looked all round for my lost guide,
Invested moorland waste and naked pool,
The beacon crowning the lone eminence,
The female and her garments vexed and tossed   260
By the strong wind. When, in the blessed hours
Of early love, the loved one at my side,
I roamed, in daily presence of this scene,
Upon the naked pool and dreary crags,
And on the melancholy beacon, fell   265
A spirit of pleasure and youth's golden gleam;
And think ye not with radiance more sublime
For these remembrances, and for the power
They had left behind? So feeling comes in aid
Of feeling, and diversity of strength   270
Attends us, if but once we have been strong.
Oh! mystery of man, from what a depth
Proceed thy honors. I am lost, but see
In simple childhood something of the base
On which thy greatness stands; but this I feel,   275
That from thyself it comes, that thou must give,
Else never canst receive. The days gone by
Return upon me almost from the dawn
Of life: the hiding places of man's power
Open; I would approach them, but they close.   280
I see by glimpses now; when age comes on,
May scarcely see at all; and I would give,
While yet we may, as far as words can give,
Substance and life to what I feel, enshrining,
Such is my hope, the spirit of the Past   285
For future restoration.—Yet another
Of these memorials:
                    One Christmas time,
On the glad eve of its dear holidays,
Feverish, and tired, and restless, I went forth
Into the fields, impatient for the sight   290
Of those led palfreys[2] that should bear us home;
My brothers and myself. There rose a crag,
That, from the meeting point of two highways

2. Small saddle horses.

Ascending, overlooked them both, far stretched;
Thither, uncertain on which road to fix   295
My expectation, thither I repaired,
Scoutlike, and gained the summit; 'twas a day
Tempestuous, dark, and wild, and on the grass
I sate half-sheltered by a naked wall;
Upon my right hand couched a single sheep,   300
Upon my left a blasted hawthorn stood;
With those companions at my side, I watched,
Straining my eyes intensely, as the mist
Gave intermitting prospect of the copse
And plain beneath. Ere we to school returned—   305
That dreary time—ere we had been ten days
Sojourners in my father's house, he died;
And I and my three brothers, orphans then,
Followed his body to the grave. The event,
With all the sorrow that it brought, appeared   310
A chastisement; and when I called to mind
That day so lately passed, when from the crag
I looked in such anxiety of hope,
With trite reflections of morality,
Yet in the deepest passion, I bowed low   315
To God, who thus corrected my desires;
And, afterwards, the wind and sleety rain,
And all the business of the elements,
The single sheep, and the one blasted tree,
And the bleak music from that old stone wall,   320
The noise of wood and water, and the mist
That on the line of each of those two roads
Advanced in such indisputable shapes;[3]
All these were kindred spectacles and sounds
To which I oft repaired, and thence would drink,   325
As at a fountain; and on winter nights,
Down to this very time, when storm and rain
Beat on my roof, or, haply, at noonday,
While in a grove I walk, whose lofty trees,
Laden with summer's thickest foliage, rock   330
In a strong wind, some working of the spirit,
Some inward agitations thence are brought,
Whate'er their office, whether to beguile
Thoughts over busy in the course they took,
Or animate an hour of vacant ease.   335

From *Book XIII. Imagination and Taste, How Impaired and Restored (concluded)*

Here, calling up to mind what then I saw,[1]
A youthful traveler, and see daily now

3. I.e., shapes one didn't dare dispute
with.
1. Wordsworth has described, as part
of his imaginative recovery, his learning to look again with sympathy upon
"the unassuming things that hold / A

In the familiar circuit of my home,
Here might I pause, and bend in reverence
To Nature, and the power of human minds,
To men as they are men within themselves.   225
How oft high service is performed within,
When all the external man is rude in show—
Not like a temple rich with pomp and gold,
But a mere mountain chapel, that protects   230
Its simple worshipers from sun and shower.
Of these, said I, shall be my song; of these,
If future years mature me for the task,
Will I record the praises, making verse
Deal boldly with substantial things; in truth   235
And sanctity of passion, speak of these,
That justice may be done, obeisance paid
Where it is due: thus haply shall I teach,
Inspire; through unadulterated ears
Pour rapture, tenderness, and hope—my theme   240
No other than the very heart of man,
As found among the best of those who live,
Not unexalted by religious faith,
Nor uninformed by books, good books, though few,
In Nature's presence; thence may I select   245
Sorrow, that is not sorrow, but delight;
And miserable love, that is not pain
To hear of, for the glory that redounds
Therefrom to human kind, and what we are.
Be mine to follow with no timid step   250
Where knowledge leads me: it shall be my pride
That I have dared to tread this holy ground,
Speaking no dream, but things oracular;
Matter not lightly to be heard by those
Who to the letter of the outward promise   255
Do read the invisible soul;[2] by men adroit
In speech, and for communion with the world
Accomplished; minds whose faculties are then
Most active when they are most eloquent,
And elevated most when most admired.   260
Men may be found of other mold than these,
Who are their own upholders, to themselves
Encouragement, and energy, and will,
Expressing liveliest thoughts in lively words
As native passion dictates. * * *   265

silent station in this beauteous world," and his finding again "in Man an object of delight." Now he shows how, in reaction against his concern with great actions detached from moral purpose which constituted the French Revolution, he came to embrace the poetic doctrines of the Preface to *Lyrical Ballads*. He will write of simple, lowly men, whose patient endurance of suffering redounds to the glory of human kind, and who speak a language which is the spontaneous overflow of powerful feeling (lines 263–64).

2. I.e., this doctrine will not be lightly accepted by those who judge a man's inner worth by his exterior seeming.

From *Book XIV. Conclusion*

In one of those excursions (may they ne'er
Fade from remembrance!) through the northern tracts
Of Cambria ranging with a youthful friend,[1]
I left Bethgelert's huts at couching time,
And westward took my way, to see the sun   5
Rise, from the top of Snowdon. To the door
Of a rude cottage at the mountain's base
We came, and roused the shepherd who attends
The adventurous stranger's steps, a trusty guide;
Then, cheered by short refreshment, sallied forth.   10

It was a close, warm, breezeless summer night,
Wan, dull, and glaring, with a dripping fog
Low-hung and thick that covered all the sky;
But, undiscouraged, we began to climb
The mountainside. The mist soon girt us round,   15
And, after ordinary travelers' talk
With our conductor, pensively we sank
Each into commerce with his private thoughts;
Thus did we breast the ascent, and by myself
Was nothing either seen or heard that checked   20
Those musings or diverted, save that once
The shepherd's lurcher,[2] who, among the crags,
Had to his joy unearthed a hedgehog, teased
His coiled-up prey with barkings turbulent.
This small adventure, for even such it seemed   25
In that wild place and at the dead of night,
Being over and forgotten, on we wound
In silence as before. With forehead bent
Earthward, as if in opposition set
Against an enemy, I panted up   30
With eager pace, and no less eager thoughts.
Thus might we wear a midnight hour away,
Ascending at loose distance each from each,
And I, as chanced, the foremost of the band;
When at my feet the ground appeared to brighten,   35
And with a step or two seemed brighter still;
Nor was time given to ask or learn the cause,
For instantly a light upon the turf
Fell like a flash, and lo! as I looked up,
The Moon hung naked in a firmament   40

---

1. Wordsworth climbed Mt. Snowdon, the highest peak in Wales ("Cambria"), with Robert Jones, the friend with whom he had also tramped through the Alps (Book VI). The climb started from the village of Bethgelert at "couching time," the time of night when the sheep lie down to sleep. This event had taken place in 1791 (or possibly 1793); Wordsworth presents it out of its chronological order to introduce at this point a great natural "type" or "emblem" (lines 66, 70) for the mind, and especially for the activity of the imagination, whose "restoration" he has described in the two preceding books.

2. A crossbred dog, used to hunt hares.

Of azure without cloud, and at my feet
Rested a silent sea of hoary mist.
A hundred hills their dusky backs upheaved
All over this still ocean; and beyond,
Far, far beyond, the solid vapors stretched,   45
In headlands, tongues, and promontory shapes,
Into the main Atlantic, that appeared
To dwindle, and give up his majesty,
Usurped upon far as the sight could reach.
Not so the ethereal vault; encroachment none   50
Was there, nor loss;[3] only the inferior stars
Had disappeared, or shed a fainter light
In the clear presence of the full-orbed Moon,
Who, from her sovereign elevation, gazed
Upon the billowy ocean, as it lay   55
All meek and silent, save that through a rift—
Not distant from the shore whereon we stood,
A fixed, abysmal, gloomy, breathing-place—
Mounted the roar of waters, torrents, streams
Innumerable, roaring with one voice!   60
Heard over earth and sea, and, in that hour,
For so it seemed, felt by the starry heavens.

When into air had partially dissolved
That vision, given to spirits of the night
And three chance human wanderers, in calm thought   65
Reflected, it appeared to me the type
Of a majestic intellect, its acts
And its possessions, what it has and craves,
What in itself it is, and would become.
There I beheld the emblem of a mind   70
That feeds upon infinity, that broods
Over the dark abyss, intent to hear
Its voices issuing forth to silent light
In one continuous stream; a mind sustained
By recognitions of transcendent power,   75
In sense conducting to ideal form,
In soul of more than mortal privilege.[4]
One function, above all, of such a mind
Had Nature shadowed there, by putting forth,
'Mid circumstances awful and sublime,   80
That mutual domination which she loves
To exert upon the face of outward things,
So molded, joined, abstracted, so endowed
With interchangeable supremacy,
That men, least sensitive, see, hear, perceive,   85

---

3. The mist projected in various shapes over the Atlantic Ocean, but did not "encroach" upon the heavens overhead.
4. The sense of lines 74–77 may be that the mind recognizes its transcendent power to idealize objects in the realm of sense and to exceed the limits of mortality in the realm of soul.

And cannot choose but feel. The power, which all
Acknowledge when thus moved, which Nature thus
To bodily sense exhibits, is the express
Resemblance of that glorious faculty
That higher minds bear with them as their own.[5]   90
This is the very spirit in which they deal
With the whole compass of the universe:
They from their native selves can send abroad
Kindred mutations; for themselves create
A like existence; and, whene'er it dawns   95
Created for them, catch it, or are caught
By its inevitable mastery,
Like angels stopped upon the wing by sound
Of harmony from Heaven's remotest spheres.
Them the enduring and the transient both   100
Serve to exalt; they build up greatest things
From least suggestions; ever on the watch,
Willing to work and to be wrought upon,
They need not extraordinary calls
To rouse them; in a world of life they live,   105
By sensible impressions not enthralled,
But by their quickening impulse made more prompt
To hold fit converse with the spiritual world,
And with the generations of mankind
Spread over time, past, present, and to come,   110
Age after age, till Time shall be no more.
Such minds are truly from the Deity,
For they are Powers; and hence the highest bliss
That flesh can know is theirs—the consciousness
Of Whom they are, habitually infused   115
Through every image and through every thought,
And all affections by communion raised
From earth to heaven, from human to divine;
Hence endless occupation for the Soul,
Whether discursive or intuitive;[6]   120
Hence cheerfulness for acts of daily life,
Emotions which best foresight need not fear,
Most worthy then of trust when most intense.
Hence, amid ills that vex and wrongs that crush
Our hearts—if here the words of Holy Writ   125
May with fit reverence be applied—that peace
Which passeth understanding,[7] that repose

5. The "glorious faculty" is the imagination, which in its exhibition of mastery over sense—through its power to alter and re-create what is given to it in perception (lines 93–106)—is analogous to that aspect of the outer scene, in which the ordinary landscape is transfigured by the moonlit mist. Compare the mind as "lord and master" of outward sense in Book XII, lines 221–23.

6. An echo of *Paradise Lost* V.488. The "discursive" reason undertakes to reach truths through a logical sequence of premises, observations, and conclusions; the "intuitive" reason comprehends truths immediately.

7. Philippians iv.7: "the peace of God, which passeth all understanding." This passage of Christian piety was added by Wordsworth in a late revision.

In moral judgments which from this pure source
Must come, or will by man be sought in vain.

* * *

Never did I, in quest of right and wrong,
Tamper with conscience from a private aim;
Nor was in any public hope the dupe
Of selfish passions; nor did ever yield
Willfully to mean cares or low pursuits,
But shrunk with apprehensive jealousy   155
From every combination which might aid
The tendency, too potent in itself,
Of use and custom to bow down the soul
Under a growing weight of vulgar sense,
And substitute a universe of death   160
For that which moves with light and life informed,
Actual, divine, and true. To fear and love,
To love as prime and chief, for there fear ends,
Be this ascribed;[8] to early intercourse,
In presence of sublime or beautiful forms,   165
With the adverse principles of pain and joy—
Evil as one is rashly named by men
Who know not what they speak. By love subsists
All lasting grandeur, by pervading love;
That gone, we are as dust. * * *   170

    This spiritual Love acts not nor can exist
Without Imagination,[9] which, in truth,
Is but another name for absolute power   190
And clearest insight, amplitude of mind,
And Reason in her most exalted mood.
This faculty hath been the feeding source
Of our long labor: we have traced the stream
From the blind cavern whence is faintly heard   195
Its natal murmur; followed it to light
And open day; accompanied its course
Among the ways of Nature, for a time
Lost sight of it bewildered and engulfed;
Then given it greeting as it rose once more   200
In strength, reflecting from its placid breast
The works of man and face of human life;
And lastly, from its progress have we drawn
Faith in life endless, the sustaining thought
Of human Being, Eternity, and God.[1]   205

8. Wordsworth's mind, he had said early in *The Prelude*, had been "fostered alike by beauty and by fear" (I.302); that is, by the opposing but equally necessary principles of the beautiful and terrifying aspects of nature. Now, in his conclusion, the principles of fear and pain are said to be ultimately transcended by their "adverse principles" of love and joy.
9. Cf. Shelley's *Defense of Poetry:* "The great secret of morals is love; or a going out of our own nature. * * * The great instrument of moral good is the imagination."
1. In the 1805 version, this read: "The feeling of life endless, the great thought / By which we live, Infinity and God."

Imagination having been our theme,
So also hath that intellectual Love,
For they are each in each, and cannot stand
Dividually.[2] * * *

And now, O Friend![3] this history is brought
To its appointed close: the discipline
And consummation of a Poet's mind,
In everything that stood most prominent,   305
Have faithfully been pictured; we have reached
The time (our guiding object from the first)
When we may, not presumptuously, I hope,
Suppose my powers so far confirmed, and such
My knowledge, as to make me capable   310
Of building up a work that shall endure.

* * *

Oh! yet a few short years of useful life,   430
And all will be complete, thy race be run,
Thy monument of glory will be raised;
Then, though (too weak to tread the ways of truth)
This age fall back to old idolatry,
Though men return to servitude as fast   435
As the tide ebbs, to ignominy and shame,
By nations sink together,[4] we shall still
Find solace—knowing what we have learnt to know,
Rich in true happiness if allowed to be
Faithful alike in forwarding a day   440
Of firmer trust, joint laborers in the work
(Should Providence such grace to us vouchsafe)
Of their deliverance, surely yet to come.
Prophets of Nature, we to them will speak
A lasting inspiration, sanctified   445
By reason, blest by faith: what we have loved,
Others will love, and we will teach them how;
Instruct them how the mind of man becomes
A thousand times more beautiful than the earth
On which he dwells, above this frame of things   450
(Which, 'mid all revolution in the hopes
And fears of men, doth still remain unchanged)
In beauty exalted, as it is itself
Of quality and fabric more divine.[5]

1799–1805   1850

2. Separately.
3. Coleridge, to whom the "thy" in lines 431–32 also refers.
4. I.e., though men—whole nations of them together—sink to ignominy and shame.
5. Cf. Wordsworth's statement about "the Mind of Man * * * the main region of my song," in *The Recluse*, lines 40–41.

SAMUEL TAYLOR COLERIDGE
(1772–1834)

1797: At Nether Stowey, Somersetshire; the Wordsworths settle nearby, at Alfoxden.
1798: *Lyrical Ballads*, which included *The Ancient Mariner* and several other poems by Coleridge.
1800: Moves to Greta Hall, Keswick, thirteen miles from the Wordsworths at Grasmere.
1816: Final residence at Highgate, near London, under the care of Dr. James Gillman.
1817: *Biographia Literaria*.

In *The Prelude* Wordsworth, recording his gratitude to the mountains, lakes, and winds "that dwell among the hills where I was born," commiserates with Coleridge because "thou, my Friend! wert reared / In the great city, 'mid far other scenes." Coleridge had in fact been born in the small town of Ottery St. Mary, in rural Devonshire; but upon the death of his father he had been sent to school at Christ's Hospital, in London. He was a dreamy, enthusiastic, and extraordinarily precocious schoolboy; Charles Lamb, his schoolmate and lifelong friend, in his essay on Christ's Hospital has given us a vivid sketch of Coleridge's loneliness, his learning, and his eloquence. When in 1791 Coleridge went up to Jesus College, Cambridge, he was an accomplished scholar; but he found little intellectual stimulation at the university, fell into idleness, dissoluteness, and debt, and in despair fled to London and enlisted in the Light Dragoons under the alias of Silas Tomkyn Comberbacke—probably the most inept cavalryman in the long history of the British army. Although rescued by his brothers and sent back to Cambridge, he left in 1794 without a degree.

In June, 1794, Coleridge met Robert Southey, then a student at Oxford who, like himself, had poetic aspirations, was a radical in religion and politics, and sympathized with the republican experiment in France. Together the two young men planned to establish an ideal democratic community in America for which Coleridge coined the name "Pantisocracy," signifying an equal rule by all. A plausible American real-estate agent persuaded them that the ideal location would be on the banks of the Susquehanna, in Pennsylvania. Twelve men undertook to go; and since perpetuation of the scheme required offspring, hence wives, Coleridge dutifully became engaged to Sara Fricker, conveniently at hand as the sister of Southey's fiancée. The Pantisocracy scheme collapsed, but at Southey's insistence Coleridge went through with the marriage, "resolved," as he said, "but wretched." Later Coleridge's radicalism waned, and he became a conservative—a highly philosophical one—in politics, and a staunch Anglican in religion.

Despite this inauspicious beginning, Coleridge was at first happy in his marriage. When Wordsworth (whom Coleridge met in 1795, and almost immediately judged "the best poet of the age") brought his sister Dorothy to settle at Alfoxden, only three miles from the Coleridges at Nether Stowey, the period of intimate communication and poetic collaboration began which was the golden time of Coleridge's life. An annuity of £150, granted to Coleridge by Thomas and Josiah Wedgwood, sons of the founder of the famous pottery firm, came just in time to deflect him from assuming a post as a Unitarian minister. After their momentous joint publication of *Lyrical Ballads* in 1798, Coleridge and the Wordsworths spent a winter in Germany, where Coleridge attended the University of Göttingen and began the lifelong study of Kant and the post-Kantian German philosophers and critics which helped to alter profoundly his thinking about philosophy, religion, and aesthetics.

Back in England, Coleridge in 1800 followed the Wordsworths to the Lake District, settling at Greta Hall, Keswick. He had become gradually disaffected from his wife, and in 1799 he fell helplessly and hopelessly in love with Sara Hutchinson, whose sister, Mary, Wordsworth married three years later. All his life Coleridge had suffered from numerous painful physical ailments; Wordsworth has described how sometimes, in a sudden spasm of agony, Coleridge would "throw himself down and writhe like a worm upon the ground." According to the standard medical prescription of the time, Coleridge had long been taking laudanum (opium dissolved in alcohol). In 1800–1801 heavy dosages taken for attacks of rheumatism made opium a necessity to him, and Coleridge soon recognized that the drug was a worse evil than the diseases it did not cure. *Dejection: An Ode*, published in 1802, was Coleridge's despairing farewell to health, happiness, and poetic creativity. A two-year sojourn on the Mediterranean island of Malta, intended to restore his health, instead completed his decline. When he returned to England in the late summer of 1806 he was a broken man, an inveterate drug addict, estranged from his wife, suffering from agonies of remorse, and subject to terrifying nightmares of guilt and despair from which his own shrieks awakened him. A bitter quarrel with Wordsworth in 1810 marked the nadir of his life and expectations.

Under these conditions Coleridge's literary efforts, however sporadic and fragmentary, were little short of heroic. In 1808 he gave his first course of public lectures in London, and in the next eleven years followed these with other series on both literary and philosophical topics. He wrote for newspapers and singlehandedly undertook to write, publish, and distribute a periodical, *The Friend*, which lasted for some fourteen months after January, 1809. A tragedy, *Remorse*, had in 1813 a very successful run of twenty performances at the Drury Lane Theatre. In 1816 he took up residence at Highgate, a northern suburb of London, under the supervision of the excellent and endlessly patient physician James Gillman, who managed to control, although not to eliminate, Coleridge's consumption of opium. The next three years were Coleridge's most sustained period of literary activity: while continuing to lecture and to write for the newspapers on a variety of subjects, he published the *Biographia Literaria*, *Zapolya* (a drama), a book consisting of the essays in *The Friend* (revised and greatly enlarged), two collections of poems, and several important treatises on philosophical and religious subjects; in these he undertook to establish a metaphysical basis for the Trinitarian theology to which he had turned after his youthful period of Unitarianism.

The remaining years of his life, which he spent with Dr. and Mrs. Gillman, were quieter and happier than any he had known since the turn of the century. He came to a peaceful understanding with his wife and was reconciled to Wordsworth, with whom he toured the Rhineland in 1828. His rooms at Highgate became a center for friends, for the London literati, and for a steady stream of pilgrims from England and America. They came to hear one of the wonders of the age, the Sage of Highgate's conversation—or monologue—for even in his decline, Coleridge's talk never entirely lost the almost incantatory power which Hazlitt has immortalized in *My First Acquaintance with Poets*. When he died, Coleridge left his friends with the sense that an incomparable intellect had vanished from the world. "The most *wonderful* man that I have ever known," Wordsworth declared, his voice breaking; and Charles Lamb: "His great and dear spirit haunts me. * * * Never saw I his likeness, nor probably the world can see again."

Coleridge's friends, however, abetted by Coleridge's own merciless self-judgments, set current the opinion, still common, that Coleridge was great in promise but not in performance. Even in his buoyant youth, before opium had drained his strength and weakened his will, Coleridge described his own character as "indolence capable of energies"; and it is true that while his mind was incessantly active and fertile, he always lacked application and staying power. After *The Ancient Mariner*, most of the poems he completed were written, like the first version of *Dejection: An Ode*, at a single sitting, in a burst of inspiration or spasm of intense effort. Writings which required sustained planning and application were either left unfinished or, like the *Biographia Literaria*, made up of brilliant sections patched together and eked out with filler, in a desperate effort to meet a deadline. Many of his best speculations Coleridge merely confided to his notebooks and the ears of his friends, incorporated in letters, and poured out upon the margins of his own and other people's books.

Even so, it is only when measured against his own immense potentialities that Coleridge's achievements appear minor. In opposition to the prevailing British philosophy of empiricism and associationism, Coleridge for most of his mature life expounded his views of the mind as creative in perception, intuitive in its discovery of the first premises of metaphysics and religion, and capable of a poetic re-creation of the world of sense by the fusing and shaping power of the "secondary imagination." Within the decade after Coleridge died, John Stuart Mill, the most acute student of contemporary thought, announced that Coleridge was one of "the two great seminal minds of England," the most important instigator and representative of the conservative intellectual movement of the day. Time has proved Mill's estimate of Coleridge to be just, for his influence is strongly evident in 19th-century English and American traditions of philosophical idealism, enlightened political conservatism, and liberal interpretations of Trinitarian theology. By present consensus, Coleridge is also one of the greatest and most influential of literary theorists; his ideas have become central points of reference even in many of the new critics who depreciate the Romantic poetry for which Coleridge, in his criticism, attempted to provide a rationale. And Coleridge's writings in verse, though small in bulk, are the work of a major and notably original poet.

Here, too, we tend to underestimate Coleridge's versatility—this time because of our preoccupation with his three poems of mystery and magic, *The Ancient Mariner*, *Christabel*, and *Kubla Khan*. These are indeed great and unprecedented achievements, but Coleridge wrote them all within a few years, and then dropped the mode. No less impressive in their own way are the blank-verse poems of the lonely and meditative mind which, by an extension of his term for one of them, are called "Conversation Poems"; in the best of these, *Frost at Midnight*, Coleridge perfected that characteristic pattern of integrally related description and meditation which Wordsworth immediately adopted in *Tintern Abbey*. Coleridge himself adapted this pattern to the larger requirements of *Dejection*, a high achievement in a genre in which very few poets have been successful, the irregular Pindaric ode. The verse epistle *To William Wordsworth* is at once a movingly personal poem, the most revealing comment ever made about *The Prelude*, and a noble tribute to a friend whom Coleridge thought the greatest poet since Milton. And even when he had mainly given up poetry, after 1805, Coleridge continued to write occasional short lyrics (represented below) which are remarkable equally for their quality, their diversity, and the extent to which they have been neglected by anthologists.

The Eolian Harp[1]

COMPOSED AT CLEVEDON, SOMERSETSHIRE

My pensive Sara! thy soft cheek reclined
Thus on mine arm, most soothing sweet it is
To sit beside our Cot, our Cot o'ergrown

1. Named for Aeolus, god of the winds, the harp has strings stretched over a rectangular sounding box. The strings are tuned in unison. When placed in an opened window, the harp (also called "Eolian lute," "Eolian lyre," "wind harp") responds to the altering wind by sequences of musical chords. This instrument, which seems to voice nature's own music, was a favorite household furnishing in the period, and was repeatedly alluded to in Romantic poetry; see Geoffrey Grigson, *The Harp of Aeolus and Other Essays* (1947). It served also as one of the recurrent Romantic images for the mind—either the mind in poetic inspiration, as in the last stanza of Shelley's *Ode to the West Wind*, or else the mind in perception, responding to an intellectual breeze by trembling into consciousness, as in this poem.

Coleridge, however, no sooner puts forward this concept than he retracts it, for it comes too close to the heresy of pantheism, which identifies God with the nature that, in the orthodox view, is His creation.

Coleridge wrote this poem to Sara Fricker, whom he married on October 4, 1795, and took to a cottage at Clevedon, overlooking the Bristol Channel. He later made changes in the original version; the famous lines 26–33, for example, were not incorporated until 1817. It was Coleridge's first achievement in the important Romantic form of the sustained blank-verse lyric of description and meditation, in the mode of conversation addressed to a silent auditor, which he perfected in *Frost at Midnight*, and which Wordsworth adopted for *Tintern Abbey*.

With white-flowered Jasmin, and the broad-leaved Myrtle,
(Meet emblems they of Innocence and Love!)   5
And watch the clouds, that late were rich with light,
Slow saddening round, and mark the star of eve
Serenely brilliant (such should Wisdom be)
Shine opposite! How exquisite the scents
Snatched from yon bean-field! and the world so hushed!   10
The stilly murmur of the distant Sea
Tells us of silence.
                          And that simplest Lute,
Placed length-ways in the clasping casement, hark!
How by the desultory breeze caressed,
Like some coy maid half yielding to her lover,   15
It pours such sweet upbraiding, as must needs
Tempt to repeat the wrong! And now, its strings
Boldlier swept, the long sequacious² notes
Over delicious surges sink and rise,
Such a soft floating witchery of sound   20
As twilight Elfins make, when they at eve
Voyage on gentle gales from Fairy-Land,
Where Melodies round honey-dropping flowers,
Footless and wild, like birds of Paradise,³
Nor pause, nor perch, hovering on untamed wing!   25
O! the one Life within us and abroad,
Which meets all motion and becomes its soul,
A light in sound, a sound-like power in light,
Rhythm in all thought, and joyance everywhere—
Methinks, it should have been impossible   30
Not to love all things in a world so filled;
Where the breeze warbles, and the mute still air
Is Music slumbering on her instrument.

And thus, my Love! as on the midway slope
Of yonder hill I stretch my limbs at noon,   35
Whilst through my half-closed eyelids I behold
The sunbeams dance, like diamonds, on the main,
And tranquil muse upon tranquillity:
Full many a thought uncalled and undetained,
And many idle flitting phantasies,   40
Traverse my indolent and passive brain,
As wild and various as the random gales
That swell and flutter on this subject Lute!

And what if all of animated nature
Be but organic Harps diversely framed,   45
That tremble into thought, as o'er them sweeps
Plastic and vast, one intellectual breeze,
At once the Soul of each, and God of all?

---

2. Successive.
3. Brilliantly colored birds, found in New Guinea and adjacent islands. The native practice of removing the legs when preparing the skin led Europeans to believe that the birds were footless and spent their lives hovering in the air and feeding on nectar.

But thy more serious eye a mild reproof
Darts, O belovéd Woman! nor such thoughts   50
Dim and unhallowed dost thou not reject,
And biddest me walk humbly with my God.
Meek Daughter in the family of Christ!
Well hast thou said and holily dispraised
These shapings of the unregeneratc mind;   55
Bubbles that glitter as they rise and break
On vain Philosophy's aye-babbling spring.
For never guiltless may I speak of him,
The Incomprehensible! save when with awe
I praise him, and with Faith that inly *feels*;   60
Who with his saving mercies healéd me,
A sinful and most miserable man,
Wildered and dark, and gave me to possess
Peace, and this Cot, and thee, heart-honored Maid!
1795   1796

The Rime of the Ancient Mariner[1]

IN SEVEN PARTS

*Facile credo, plures esse Naturas invisibiles quam visibiles in rerum universitate.
Sed horum* [sic] *omnium familiam quis nobis enarrabit? et gradus et cognationes
et discrimina et singulorum munera? Quid agunt? quae loca habitant? Harum rerum
notitiam semper ambivit ingenium humanum, nunquam attigit. Juvat, interea, non
diffiteor, quandoque in animo, tanquam in tabulâ, majoris et melioris mundi ima-
ginem contemplari: ne mens assuefacta hodiernae vitae minutiis se contrahat
nimis, et tota subsidat in pusillas cogitationes. Sed veritati interea invigilandum est,
modusque servandus, ut certa ab incertis, diem a nocte, distinguamus.*

T. BURNET, *Archaeol. Phil.* p. 68.[2]

Argument

How a Ship, having first sailed to the Equator, was driven by storms
to the cold Country towards the South Pole; how the Ancient Mari-

1. Coleridge describes the origin of this poem in the opening section of Chapter XIV of *Biographia Literaria*. In a note on his *We Are Seven*, dictated to Isabella Fenwick in 1843, Wordsworth added some details. The poem, based on a dream of Coleridge's friend Cruikshank, was originally planned as a collaboration between the two friends, to pay the expense of a walking tour they took with Dorothy Wordsworth in November of 1797. Before he dropped out of the enterprise, Wordsworth suggested the shooting of the albatross and the navigation of the ship by the dead men; he also contributed lines 13–16 and 226–27.

The version of *The Ancient Mariner* printed in *Lyrical Ballads* (1798) contained many archaic words and spellings. In later editions Coleridge greatly improved the poem by pruning the archaisms, and by other revisions; he also added the Latin epigraph and the marginal glosses.
2. Latin epigraph: "I readily believe that there are more invisible than visible Natures in the universe. But who will explain for us the family of all these beings, and the ranks and relations and distinguishing features and functions of each? What do they do? What places do they inhabit? The human mind has always sought the knowl-

ner cruelly and in contempt of the laws of hospitality killed a Sea-bird and how he was followed by many and strange Judgments: and in what manner he came back to his own Country.

Part I

An ancient Mariner meeteth three Gallants bidden to a wedding feast, and detaineth one.

It is an ancient Mariner
And he stoppeth one of three.
—"By thy long gray beard and glittering eye,
Now wherefore stopp'st thou me?

The Bridegroom's doors are opened wide,   5
And I am next of kin;
The guests are met, the feast is set:
May'st hear the merry din."

He holds him with his skinny hand,
"There was a ship," quoth he.   10
"Hold off! unhand me, graybeard loon!"
Eftsoons³ his hand dropped he.

The Wedding Guest is spellbound by the eye of the old seafaring man, and constrained to hear his tale.

He holds him with his glittering eye—
The Wedding Guest stood still,
And listens like a three years' child: 15
The Mariner hath his will.

The Wedding Guest sat on a stone:
He cannot choose but hear;
And thus spake on that ancient man,
The bright-eyed Mariner.   20

"The ship was cheered, the harbor cleared,
Merrily did we drop
Below the kirk,⁴ below the hill,
Below the lighthouse top.

The Mariner tells how the ship sailed southward with a good wind and fair weather, till it reached the Line.

The Sun came up upon the left,   25
Out of the sea came he!
And he shone bright, and on the right
Went down into the sea.

Higher and higher every day,
Till over the mast at noon⁵—"   30
The Wedding Guest here beat his breast,
For he heard the loud bassoon.

edge of these things, but never attained it. Meanwhile I do not deny that it is helpful sometimes to contemplate in the mind, as on a tablet, the image of a greater and better world, lest the intellect, habituated to the petty things of daily life, narrow itself and sink wholly into trivial thoughts. But at the same time we must be watchful for the truth and keep a sense of proportion, so that we may distinguish the certain from the uncertain, day from night." Adapted by Coleridge from Thomas Burnet, *Archaeologiae philosophicae* (1692).
3. At once.
4. Church.
5. I.e., the ship had reached the equator (the "Line").

The bride hath paced into the hall,
Red as a rose is she;
Nodding their heads before her goes 35
The merry minstrelsy.

*The Wedding
Guest heareth
the bridal music;
but the Mariner
continueth his
tale.*

The Wedding Guest he beat his breast,
Yet he cannot choose but hear;
And thus spake on that ancient man,
The bright-eyed Mariner. 40

*The ship driven
by a storm to-
ward the South
Pole.*

"And now the STORM-BLAST came, and he
Was tyrannous and strong;
He struck with his o'ertaking wings,
And chased us south along.

With sloping masts and dipping prow, 45
As who pursued with yell and blow
Still treads the shadow of his foe,
And forward bends his head,
The ship drove fast, loud roared the blast,
And southward aye we fled. 50

And now there came both mist and snow,
And it grew wondrous cold:
And ice, mast-high, came floating by,
As green as emerald.

*The land of ice,
and of fearful
sounds where no
living thing was
to be seen.*

And through the drifts the snowy clifts[6] 55
Did send a dismal sheen:
Nor shapes of men nor beasts we ken—
The ice was all between.

The ice was here, the ice was there,
The ice was all around: 60
It cracked and growled, and roared and howled,
Like noises in a swound![7]

*Till a great sea
bird, called the
Albatross, came
through the
snow-fog, and
was received
with great joy
and hospitality.*

At length did cross an Albatross,
Thorough the fog it came;
As if it had been a Christian soul,
We hailed it in God's name. 65

It ate the food it ne'er had eat,
And round and round it flew.
The ice did split with a thunder-fit;
The helmsman steered us through! 70

*And lo! the Al-
batross proveth
a bird of good
omen, and fol-
loweth the ship
as it returned
northward
through fog and
floating ice.*

And a good south wind sprung up behind;
The Albatross did follow,
And every day, for food or play,
Came to the mariners' hollo!

In mist or cloud, on mast or shroud,[8] 75
It perched for vespers nine;

6. Cliffs.
7. Swoon.

8. Rope supporting the mast.

Whiles all the night, through fog-smoke white,
Glimmered the white Moon-shine."

The ancient Mariner inhospitably killeth the pious bird of good omen.

"God save thee, ancient Mariner!
From the fiends, that plague thee thus!— 80
Why look'st thou so?"—With my crossbow
I shot the ALBATROSS.

Part II

The Sun now rose upon the right:⁹
Out of the sea came he,
Still hid in mist, and on the left 85
Went down into the sea.

And the good south wind still blew behind,
But no sweet bird did follow,
Nor any day for food or play
Came to the mariners' hollo! 90

His shipmates cry out against the ancient Mariner, for killing the bird of good luck.

And I had done a hellish thing,
And it would work 'em woe:
For all averred, I had killed the bird
That made the breeze to blow.
Ah wretch! said they, the bird to slay, 95
That made the breeze to blow!

But when the fog cleared off, they justify the same, and thus make themselves accomplices in the crime.

Nor dim nor red, like God's own head,
The glorious Sun uprist:
Then all averred, I had killed the bird
That brought the fog and mist. 100
'Twas right, said they, such birds to slay,
That bring the fog and mist.

The fair breeze continues; the ship enters the Pacific Ocean, and sails northward, even till it reaches the Line.

The fair breeze blew, the white foam flew,
The furrow followed free;
We were the first that ever burst 105
Into that silent sea.

The ship hath been suddenly becalmed.

Down dropped the breeze, the sails dropped down,
'Twas sad as sad could be;
And we did speak only to break
The silence of the sea! 110

All in a hot and copper sky,
The bloody Sun, at noon,
Right up above the mast did stand,
No bigger than the Moon.

Day after day, day after day, 115
We stuck, nor breath nor motion;
As idle as a painted ship
Upon a painted ocean.

9. I.e., having rounded Cape Horn, the ship heads north into the Pacific.

And the Alba-
tross begins to
be avenged.

Water, water, everywhere,
And all the boards did shrink;   120
Water, water, everywhere,
Nor any drop to drink.

The very deep did rot: O Christ!
That ever this should be!
Yea, slimy things did crawl with legs   125
Upon the slimy sea.

About, about, in reel and rout
The death-fires[1] danced at night;
The water, like a witch's oils,
Burnt green, and blue and white.   130

And some in dreams assuréd were
Of the Spirit that plagued us so;

A Spirit had
followed them;
one of the invis-
ible inhabitants
of this planet,

Nine fathom deep he had followed us
From the land of mist and snow.

neither departed souls nor angels; concerning whom the learned Jew, Josephus, and
the Platonic Constantinopolitan, Michael Psellus, may be consulted. They are very
numerous, and there is no climate or element without one or more.

And every tongue, through utter drought,   135
Was withered at the root;
We could not speak, no more than if
We had been choked with soot.

Ah! well-a-day! what evil looks

The shipmates,
in their sore dis-
tress, would fain
throw the whole
guilt on the an-
cient Mariner: in

Had I from old and young!   140
Instead of the cross, the Albatross
About my neck was hung.

sign whereof they hang the dead sea bird round his neck.

Part III

There passed a weary time. Each throat
Was parched, and glazed each eye.
A weary time! a weary time!   145
How glazed each weary eye,

The ancient Mar-
iner beholdeth a
sign in the ele-
ment afar off.

When looking westward, I beheld
A something in the sky.

At first it seemed a little speck,
And then it seemed a mist;   150
It moved and moved, and took at last
A certain shape, I wist.[2]

A speck, a mist, a shape, I wist!
And still it neared and neared:

1. The corposant, or St. Elmo's fire, an atmospheric electricity on a ship's mast or rigging, believed by the super- stitious sailor to portend disaster.
2. Knew.

As if it dodged a water sprite,   155
It plunged and tacked and veered.

At its nearer ap-
proach, it seem-
eth him to be a
ship; and at a
dear ransom he
freeth his speech
from the bonds
of thirst.

With throats unslaked, with black lips baked,
We could nor laugh nor wail;
Through utter drought all dumb we stood!
I bit my arm, I sucked the blood,   160
And cried, A sail! a sail!

With throats unslaked, with black lips baked,
Agape they heard me call:

A flash of joy;

Gramercy!³ they for joy did grin,
And all at once their breath drew in,   165
As they were drinking all.

And horror fol-
lows. For can it
be a ship that
comes onward
without wind or
tide?

See! see! (I cried) she tacks no more!
Hither to work us weal;⁴
Without a breeze, without a tide,
She steadies with upright keel!   170

The western wave was all aflame.
The day was well nigh done!
Almost upon the western wave
Rested the broad bright Sun;
When that strange shape drove suddenly   175
Betwixt us and the Sun.

It seemeth him
but the skeleton
of a ship.

And straight the Sun was flecked with bars,
(Heaven's Mother send us grace!)
As if through a dungeon grate he peered
With broad and burning face.   180

And its ribs are
seen as bars on
the face of the
setting Sun.

Alas! (thought I, and my heart beat loud)
How fast she nears and nears!
Are those *her* sails that glance in the Sun,
Like restless gossameres?⁵

The Specter-
Woman and her
Deathmate, and
no other on
board the skele-
ton ship.

Are those *her* ribs through which the Sun   185
Did peer, as through a grate?
And is that Woman all her crew?
Is that a DEATH? and are there two?
Is DEATH that woman's mate?

Like vessel, like
crew!

Her lips were red, *her* looks were free,   190
Her locks were yellow as gold:
Her skin was as white as leprosy,
The Nightmare LIFE-IN-DEATH was she,
Who thicks man's blood with cold.

Death and Life-
in-Death have
diced for the
ship's crew, and
she (the latter)
winneth the an-
cient Mariner.

The naked hulk alongside came,   195
And the twain were casting dice;
"The game is done! I've won! I've won!"
Quoth she, and whistles thrice.

3. From the French *grand-merci*, "great   4. Benefit.
thanks."   5. Filmy cobwebs floating in the air.

*No twilight
within the courts
of the Sun.*
The Sun's rim dips; the stars rush out:
At one stride comes the dark;   200
With far-heard whisper, o'er the sea,
Off shot the specter bark.

*At the rising of
the Moon,*
We listened and looked sideways up!
Fear at my heart, as at a cup,
My lifeblood seemed to sip!   205
The stars were dim, and thick the night,
The steersman's face by his lamp gleamed white;
From the sails the dew did drip—
Till clomb above the eastern bar
The hornéd Moon, with one bright star   210
Within the nether tip.[5a]

*One after an-
other,*
One after one, by the star-dogged Moon,
Too quick for groan or sigh,
Each turned his face with ghastly pang,
And cursed me with his eye.   215

*His shipmates
drop down dead.*
Four times fifty living men,
(And I heard nor sigh nor groan)
With heavy thump, a lifeless lump,
They dropped down one by one.

*But Life-in-
Death begins her
work on the an-
cient Mariner.*
The souls did from their bodies fly—   220
They fled to bliss or woe!
And every soul, it passed me by,
Like the whizz of my crossbow!

Part IV

*The Wedding
Guest feareth
that a Spirit is
talking to him;*
"I fear thee, ancient Mariner!
I fear thy skinny hand!   225
And thou art long, and lank, and brown,
As is the ribbed sea-sand.

I fear thee and thy glittering eye,
And thy skinny hand, so brown."—
*But the ancient
Mariner assureth
him of his bodily
life, and pro-
ceedeth to relate
his horrible pen-
ance.*
Fear not, fear not, thou Wedding Guest!   230
This body dropped not down.

Alone, alone, all, all alone,
Alone on a wide wide sea!
And never a saint took pity on
My soul in agony.   235

*He despiseth the
creatures of the
calm,*
The many men, so beautiful!
And they all dead did lie:
And a thousand thousand slimy things
Lived on; and so did I.

5a. An omen of impending evil.

And envieth that they should live, and so many lie dead.

I looked upon the rotting sea, 240
And drew my eyes away;
I looked upon the rotting deck,
And there the dead men lay.

I looked to heaven, and tried to pray;
But or ever a prayer had gushed, 245
A wicked whisper came, and made
My heart as dry as dust.

I closed my lids, and kept them close,
And the balls like pulses beat;
For the sky and the sea, and the sea and the sky 250
Lay like a load on my weary eye,
And the dead were at my feet.

But the curse liveth for him in the eye of the dead men.

The cold sweat melted from their limbs,
Nor rot nor reek did they:
The look with which they looked on me 255
Had never passed away.

An orphan's curse would drag to hell
A spirit from on high;
But oh! more horrible than that
Is the curse in a dead man's eye! 260
Seven days, seven nights, I saw that curse,
And yet I could not die.

The moving Moon went up the sky,
And nowhere did abide:

In his loneliness and fixedness he yearneth towards the journeying Moon, and the stars that still sojourn, yet still move onward; and everywhere the blue sky belongs to them, and is their appointed rest, and their native country and their own natural homes, which they enter unannounced, as lords that are certainly expected and yet there is a silent joy at their arrival.

Softly she was going up, 265
And a star or two beside—

Her beams bemocked the sultry main,
Like April hoar-frost spread;
But where the ship's huge shadow lay,
The charmèd water burnt alway 270
A still and awful red.

By the light of the Moon he beholdeth God's creatures of the great calm.

Beyond the shadow of the ship,
I watched the water snakes:
They moved in tracks of shining white,
And when they reared, the elfish light 275
Fell off in hoary flakes.

Within the shadow of the ship
I watched their rich attire:
Blue, glossy green, and velvet black,
They coiled and swam; and every track 280
Was a flash of golden fire.

Their beauty and their happiness.

O happy living things! no tongue
Their beauty might declare:

He blesseth them in his heart.

A spring of love gushed from my heart,
And I blessed them unaware: 285
Sure my kind saint took pity on me,
And I blessed them unaware.

The spell begins to break.

The selfsame moment I could pray;
And from my neck so free
The Albatross fell off, and sank   290
Like lead into the sea.

Part V

Oh sleep! it is a gentle thing,
Beloved from pole to pole!
To Mary Queen the praise be given!
She sent the gentle sleep from Heaven,   295
That slid into my soul.

By grace of the holy Mother, the ancient Mariner is refreshed with rain.

The silly[6] buckets on the deck,
That had so long remained,
I dreamt that they were filled with dew;
And when I awoke, it rained.   300

My lips were wet, my throat was cold,
My garments all were dank;
Sure I had drunken in my dreams,
And still my body drank.

I moved, and could not feel my limbs: 305
I was so light—almost
I thought that I had died in sleep,
And was a blessed ghost.

He heareth sounds and seeth strange sights and commotions in the sky and the element.

And soon I heard a roaring wind:
It did not come anear;   310
But with its sound it shook the sails,
That were so thin and sere.

The upper air burst into life!
And a hundred fire-flags sheen,[7]
To and fro they were hurried about!   315
And to and fro, and in and out,
The wan stars danced between.

And the coming wind did roar more loud,
And the sails did sigh like sedge;[8]
And the rain poured down from one black cloud; 320
The Moon was at its edge.

The thick black cloud was cleft, and still
The Moon was at its side:
Like waters shot from some high crag,
The lightning fell with never a jag,   325
A river steep and wide.

6. In the archaic sense: blessed, happy.
7. Shone. These are the Aurora Aus-   tralis, or Southern Lights.
8. A rushlike plant growing in wet soil.

*The bodies of
the ship's crew
are inspirited,
and the ship
moves on;*

The loud wind never reached the ship,
Yet now the ship moved on!
Beneath the lightning and the Moon
The dead men gave a groan.   330

They groaned, they stirred, they all uprose,
Nor spake, nor moved their eyes;
It had been strange, even in a dream,
To have seen those dead men rise.

The helmsman steered, the ship moved on;   335
Yet never a breeze up-blew;
The mariners all 'gan work the ropes,
Where they were wont to do;
They raised their limbs like lifeless tools—
We were a ghastly crew.   340

The body of my brother's son
Stood by me, knee to knee:
The body and I pulled at one rope,
But he said nought to me.

*But not by the
souls of the men,
nor by demons
of earth or mid-
dle air, but by a
blessed troop of
angelic spirits,
sent down by
the invocation of
the guardian
saint.*

"I fear thee, ancient Mariner!"   345
Be calm, thou Wedding Guest!
'Twas not those souls that fled in pain,
Which to their corses[9] came again,
But a troop of spirits blest:

For when it dawned—they dropped their arms,   350
And clustered round the mast;
Sweet sounds rose slowly through their mouths,
And from their bodies passed.

Around, around, flew each sweet sound,
Then darted to the Sun;   355
Slowly the sounds came back again,
Now mixed, now one by one.

Sometimes a-dropping from the sky
I heard the skylark sing;
Sometimes all little birds that are,   360
How they seemed to fill the sea and air
With their sweet jargoning![1]

And now 'twas like all instruments,
Now like a lonely flute;
And now it is an angel's song,   365
That makes the heavens be mute.

It ceased; yet still the sails made on
A pleasant noise till noon,
A noise like of a hidden brook

9. Corpses.   1. In Middle English, "warbling."

In the leafy month of June,   370
That to the sleeping woods all night
Singeth a quiet tune.

Till noon we quietly sailed on,
Yet never a breeze did breathe:
Slowly and smoothly went the ship,   375
Moved onward from beneath.

The lonesome Spirit from the South Pole carries on the ship as far as the Line, in obedience to the angelic troop, but still requireth vengeance.

Under the keel nine fathom deep,
From the land of mist and snow,
The spirit slid: and it was he
That made the ship to go.   380
The sails at noon left off their tune,
And the ship stood still also.

The Sun, right up above the mast,
Had fixed her to the ocean:
But in a minute she 'gan stir,   385
With a short uneasy motion—
Backwards and forwards half her length
With a short uneasy motion.

Then like a pawing horse let go,
She made a sudden bound: 390
It flung the blood into my head,
And I fell down in a swound.

The Polar Spirit's fellow demons, the invisible inhabitants of the element, take part in his wrong; and two of them relate, one to the other, that penance long and heavy for the ancient Mariner hath been accorded to the Polar Spirit, who returneth southward.

How long in that same fit I lay,
I have not[2] to declare;
But ere my living life returned,   395
I heard and in my soul discerned
Two voices in the air.

"Is it he?" quoth one, "Is this the man?
By him who died on cross,
With his cruel bow he laid full low   400
The harmless Albatross.

The spirit who bideth by himself
In the land of mist and snow,
He loved the bird that loved the man
Who shot him with his bow."   405

The other was a softer voice,
As soft as honeydew:
Quoth he, "The man hath penance done,
And penance more will do."

Part VI

FIRST VOICE

"But tell me, tell me! speak again,   410
Thy soft response renewing—

2. I.e., have not the knowledge.

What makes that ship drive on so fast?
What is the ocean doing?"

SECOND VOICE
"Still as a slave before his lord,
The ocean hath no blast;
His great bright eye most silently   415
Up to the Moon is cast—

If he may know which way to go;
For she guides him smooth or grim.
See, brother, see! how graciously   420
She looketh down on him."

FIRST VOICE

The Mariner hath been cast into a trance; for the angelic power causeth the vessel to drive northward faster than human life could endure.

"But why drives on that ship so fast,
Without or wave or wind?"

SECOND VOICE
"The air is cut away before,
And closes from behind.   425

Fly, brother, fly! more high, more high!
Or we shall be belated:
For slow and slow that ship will go,
When the Mariner's trance is abated."

The supernatural motion is retarded; the Mariner awakes, and his penance begins anew.

I woke, and we were sailing on   430
As in a gentle weather:
'Twas night, calm night, the moon was high;
The dead men stood together.

All stood together on the deck,
For a charnel-dungeon fitter: 435
All fixed on me their stony eyes,
That in the Moon did glitter.

The pang, the curse, with which they died,
Had never passed away:
I could not draw my eyes from theirs,   440
Nor turn them up to pray.

The curse is finally expiated.

And now this spell was snapped: once more
I viewed the ocean green,
And looked far forth, yet little saw
Of what had else been seen—   445

Like one, that on a lonesome road
Doth walk in fear and dread,
And having once turned round walks on,
And turns no more his head;
Because he knows, a frightful fiend   450
Doth close behind him tread.

But soon there breathed a wind on me,
Nor sound nor motion made:
Its path was not upon the sea,
In ripple or in shade. 455

It raised my hair, it fanned my cheek
Like a meadow-gale of spring—
It mingled strangely with my fears,
Yet it felt like a welcoming.

Swiftly, swiftly flew the ship, 460
Yet she sailed softly too:
Sweetly, sweetly blew the breeze—
On me alone it blew.

And the ancient Mariner beholdeth his native country.

Oh! dream of joy! is this indeed
The lighthouse top I see? 465
Is this the hill? is this the kirk?
Is this mine own countree?

We drifted o'er the harbor bar,
And I with sobs did pray—
O let me be awake, my God! 470
Or let me sleep alway.

The harbor bay was clear as glass,
So smoothly it was strewn!
And on the bay the moonlight lay,
And the shadow of the Moon. 475

The rock shone bright, the kirk no less,
That stands above the rock:
The moonlight steeped in silentness
The steady weathercock.

And the bay was white with silent light, 480
Till rising from the same,

The angelic spirits leave the dead bodies,

Full many shapes, that shadows were,
In crimson colors came.

And appear in their own forms of light.

A little distance from the prow
Those crimson shadows were: 485
I turned my eyes upon the deck—
Oh, Christ! what saw I there!

Each corse lay flat, lifeless and flat,
And, by the holy rood![3]
A man all light, a seraph man, 490
On every corse there stood.

This seraph band, each waved his hand:
It was a heavenly sight!

3. Cross. "Seraph": a shining celestial being, highest in the ranks of the angels.

They stood as signals to the land,
Each one a lovely light; 495

This seraph band, each waved his hand,
No voice did they impart—
No voice; but oh! the silence sank
Like music on my heart.

But soon I heard the dash of oars, 500
I heard the Pilot's cheer;
My head was turned perforce away
And I saw a boat appear.

The Pilot and the Pilot's boy,
I heard them coming fast: 505
Dear Lord in Heaven! it was a joy
The dead men could not blast.

I saw a third—I heard his voice:
It is the Hermit good!
He singeth loud his godly hymns 510
That he makes in the wood.
He'll shrieve my soul, he'll wash away
The Albatross's blood.

Part VII

*The Hermit of
the Wood*

This Hermit good lives in that wood
Which slopes down to the sea. 515
How loudly his sweet voice he rears!
He loves to talk with marineres
That come from a far countree.

He kneels at morn, and noon, and eve—
He hath a cushion plump: 520
It is the moss that wholly hides
The rotted old oak stump.

The skiff boat neared: I heard them talk,
"Why, this is strange, I trow!
Where are those lights so many and fair, 525
That signal made but now?"

*Approacheth the
ship with won-
der.*

"Strange, by my faith!" the Hermit said—
"And they answered not our cheer!
The planks looked warped! and see those sails,
How thin they are and sere! 530
I never saw aught like to them,
Unless perchance it were

Brown skeletons of leaves that lag
My forest-brook along;
When the ivy tod[4] is heavy with snow, 535

4. Clump of ivy.

And the owlet whoops to the wolf below,
That eats the she-wolf's young."

"Dear Lord! it hath a fiendish look,"
The Pilot made reply,
"I am a-feared"—"Push on, push on!"   540
Said the Hermit cheerily.

The boat came closer to the ship,
But I nor spake nor stirred;
The boat came close beneath the ship,
And straight a sound was heard.   545

The ship sud-
denly sinketh.

Under the water it rumbled on,
Still louder and more dread:
It reached the ship, it split the bay;
The ship went down like lead.

The uncient
Mariner is saved
in the Pilot's
boat.

Stunned by that loud and dreadful sound,   550
Which sky and ocean smote,
Like one that hath been seven days drowned
My body lay afloat;
But swift as dreams, myself I found
Within the Pilot's boat.   555

Upon the whirl, where sank the ship,
The boat spun round and round;
And all was still, save that the hill
Was telling of the sound.

I moved my lips—the Pilot shrieked   560
And fell down in a fit;
The holy Hermit raised his eyes,
And prayed where he did sit.

I took the oars: the Pilot's boy,
Who now doth crazy go,   565
Laughed loud and long, and all the while
His eyes went to and fro.
"Ha! ha!" quoth he, "full plain I see,
The Devil knows how to row."

And now, all in my own countree,   570
I stood on the firm land!
The Hermit stepped forth from the boat,
And scarcely he could stand.

The ancient
Mariner ear-
nestly entreateth
the Hermit to
shrieve him; and
the penance of
life falls on him.

"O shrieve me, shrieve me, holy man!"
The Hermit crossed his brow.[5]
"Say quick," quoth he, "I bid thee say—   575
What manner of man art thou?"

5. Made the sign of the cross on his forehead.

Forthwith this frame of mine was wrenched
With a woeful agony,
Which forced me to begin my tale;　　580
And then it left me free.

And ever and anon throughout his future life an agony constraineth him to travel from land to land;

Since then, at an uncertain hour,
That agony returns:
And till my ghastly tale is told,
This heart within me burns.　　585

I pass, like night, from land to land;
I have strange power of speech;
That moment that his face I see,
I know the man that must hear me:
To him my tale I teach.　　590

What loud uproar bursts from that door!
The wedding guests are there:
But in the garden-bower the bride
And bridemaids singing are:
And hark the little vesper bell,　　595
Which biddeth me to prayer!

O Wedding Guest! this soul hath been
Alone on a wide wide sea:
So lonely 'twas, that God himself
Scarce seeméd there to be.　　600

O sweeter than the marriage feast,
'Tis sweeter far to me,
To walk together to the kirk
With a goodly company!—

To walk together to the kirk,　　605
And all together pray,
While each to his great Father bends,
Old men, and babes, and loving friends
And youths and maidens gay!

And to teach, by his own example, love and reverence to all things that God made and loveth.

Farewell, farewell! but this I tell　　610
To thee, thou Wedding Guest!
He prayeth well, who loveth well
Both man and bird and beast.

He prayeth best, who loveth best
All things both great and small;　　615
For the dear God who loveth us,
He made and loveth all.

The Mariner, whose eye is bright,
Whose beard with age is hoar,
Is gone: and now the Wedding Guest　　620
Turned from the bridegroom's door.

He went like one that hath been stunned,
And is of sense forlorn:[6]
A sadder and a wiser man,
He rose the morrow morn.

1797–98

625

1798

Kubla Khan

OR A VISION IN A DREAM. A FRAGMENT

The following fragment is here published at the request of a poet of great and deserved celebrity,[1] and, as far as the author's own opinions are concerned, rather as a psychological curiosity, than on the ground of any supposed *poetic* merits.

In the summer of the year 1797, the author, then in ill health, had retired to a lonely farmhouse between Porlock and Linton, on the Exmoor confines of Somerset and Devonshire. In consequence of a slight indisposition, an anodyne had been prescribed, from the effects of which he fell asleep in his chair at the moment that he was reading the following sentence, or words of the same substance, in *Purchas's Pilgrimage*: "Here the Khan Kubla commanded a palace to be built, and a stately garden thereunto. And thus ten miles of fertile ground were inclosed with a wall."[2] The author continued for about three hours in a profound sleep, at least of the external senses,[3] during which time he has the most vivid confidence that he could not have composed less than from two to three hundred lines; if that indeed can be called composition in which all the images rose up before him as *things*, with a parallel production of the correspondent expressions, without any sensation or consciousness of effort. On awaking he appeared to himself to have a distinct recollection of the whole, and taking his pen, ink, and paper, instantly and eagerly wrote down the lines that are here preserved. At this moment he was unfortunately called out by a person on business from Porlock, and detained by him above an hour, and on his return to his room, found, to his no small surprise and mortification, that though he still retained some vague and dim

6. Forsaken.
1. Lord Byron.
2. "In Xamdu did Cublai Can build a stately Palace, encompassing sixteene miles of plaine ground with a wall, wherein are fertile Meddowes, pleasant springs, delightfull Streames, and all sorts of beasts of chase and game, and in the middest thereof a sumptuous house of pleasure, which may be removed from place to place." From Samuel Purchas, *Purchas his Pilgrimage* (1613). The historical Kublai Khan founded the Mongol dynasty in China in the 13th century.
3. In a note on a manuscript copy of *Kubla Khan*, Coleridge gave a more precise account of the nature of this "sleep": "This fragment with a good deal more, not recoverable, composed, in a sort of reverie brought on by two grains of opium, taken to check a dysentery, at a farmhouse between Porlock and Linton, a quarter of a mile from Culbone Church, in the fall of the year, 1797."

recollection of the general purport of the vision, yet, with the exception of some eight or ten scattered lines and images, all the rest had passed away like the images on the surface of a stream into which a stone has been cast, but, alas! without the after restoration of the latter!

> Then all the charm
> Is broken—all that phantom world so fair
> Vanishes, and a thousand circlets spread,
> And each misshape[s] the other. Stay awhile,
> Poor youth! who scarcely dar'st lift up thine eyes—
> The stream will soon renew its smoothness, soon
> The visions will return! And lo, he stays,
> And soon the fragments dim of lovely forms
> Come trembling back, unite, and now once more
> The pool becomes a mirror.
> [From Coleridge's *The Picture; or, the Lover's Resolution*,
> lines 91–100]

Yet from the still surviving recollections in his mind, the author has frequently purposed to finish for himself what had been originally, as it were, given to him. Σαμερον αδιον ασω:[4] but the tomorrow is yet to come.

> In Xanadu did Kubla Khan
> A stately pleasure dome decree:
> Where Alph, the sacred river, ran
> Through caverns measureless to man
>   Down to a sunless sea.   5
> So twice five miles of fertile ground
> With walls and towers were girdled round:
> And there were gardens bright with sinuous rills,
> Where blossomed many an incense-bearing tree;
> And here were forests ancient as the hills,   10
> Enfolding sunny spots of greenery.
>
> But oh! that deep romantic chasm which slanted
> Down the green hill athwart a cedarn cover!
> A savage place! as holy and enchanted
> As e'er beneath a waning moon was haunted   15
> By woman wailing for her demon lover!
> And from this chasm, with ceaseless turmoil seething,
> As if this earth in fast thick pants were breathing,
> A mighty fountain momently was forced:
> Amid whose swift half-intermitted burst   20
> Huge fragments vaulted like rebounding hail,
> Or chaffy grain beneath the thresher's flail:

4. "I shall sing a sweeter song today." In the edition of 1834, Σαμερον ("today") was changed to αὔριον ("tomorrow"). Coleridge had in mind Theocritus, *Idyls* I.145: ἐς ὕστερον ἄδιον ᾀσῶ ("I shall sing a sweeter song on a later day").

And 'mid these dancing rocks at once and ever
It flung up momently the sacred river.
Five miles meandering with a mazy motion   25
Through wood and dale the sacred river ran,
Then reached the caverns measureless to man,
And sank in tumult to a lifeless ocean:
And 'mid this tumult Kubla heard from far
Ancestral voices prophesying war!   30
 The shadow of the dome of pleasure
 Floated midway on the waves;
 Where was heard the mingled measure
 From the fountain and the caves.
It was a miracle of rare device,   35
A sunny pleasure dome with caves of ice!

 A damsel with a dulcimer
 In a vision once I saw:
 It was an Abyssinian maid,
 And on her dulcimer she played,   40
 Singing of Mount Abora.
Could I revive within me
Her symphony and song,
To such a deep delight 'twould win me,
That with music loud and long,   45
I would build that dome in air,
That sunny dome! those caves of ice!
And all who heard should see them there,
And all should cry, Beware! Beware!
His flashing eyes, his floating hair!   50
Weave a circle round him thrice,[5]
And close your eyes with holy dread,
For he on honeydew hath fed,
And drunk the milk of Paradise.

ca. 1797–98   1816

Christabel[1]

Preface

 The first part of the following poem was written in the year
1797, at Stowey, in the county of Somerset. The second part, after
my return from Germany, in the year 1800, at Keswick, Cumber-

5. A magic ritual, to protect the inspired poet from intrusion.
1. Coleridge had planned to publish *Christabel* in the second edition of *Lyrical Ballads* (1800), but had not been able to complete the poem. When *Christabel* was finally published in 1816 in its present fragmentary state, Coleridge still had hopes of finishing it, for the Preface contained this sentence (deleted in the edition of 1834): "But as, in my very first conception of the tale, I had the whole present to my mind, with the wholeness, no less than the liveliness of a vision, I trust that I shall be able to embody in verse the three parts yet to come, in the course of the present year."

land. It is probable that if the poem had been finished at either of the former periods, or if even the first and second part had been published in the year 1800, the impression of its originality would have been much greater than I dare at present expect. But for this I have only my own indolence to blame. The dates are mentioned for the exclusive purpose of precluding charges of plagiarism or servile imitation from myself. For there is amongst us a set of critics, who seem to hold that every possible thought and image is traditional; who have no notion that there are such things as fountains in the world, small as well as great; and who would there-fore charitably derive every rill they behold flowing from a perfora-tion made in some other man's tank. I am confident, however, that as far as the present poem is concerned, the celebrated poets[2] whose writings I might be suspected of having imitated, either in partic-ular passages, or in the tone and the spirit of the whole, would be among the first to vindicate me from the charge, and who, on any striking coincidence, would permit me to address them in this dog-gerel version of two monkish Latin hexameters.

> 'Tis mine and it is likewise yours;
> But an if this will not do;
> Let it be mine, good friend! for I
> Am the poorer of the two.

I have only to add that the meter of Christabel is not, properly speaking, irregular, though it may seem so from its being founded on a new principle: namely, that of counting in each line the ac-cents, not the syllables.[3] Though the latter may vary from seven to twelve, yet in each line the accents will be found to be only four. Nevertheless, this occasional variation in number of syllables is not introduced wantonly, or for the mere ends of convenience, but in correspondence with some transition in the nature of the imagery or passion.

Part I

'Tis the middle of night by the castle clock,
And the owls have awakened the crowing cock;
Tu—whit!——Tu—whoo!
And hark, again! the crowing cock,
How drowsily it crew.   5

2. Sir Walter Scott and Lord Byron, who had read and admired *Christabel* while it circulated in manuscript. Cole-ridge has in mind Scott's *Lay of the Last Minstrel* (1805) and Byron's *Siege of Corinth* (1816), which showed the influence of *Christabel*, especially in their meter.
3. Much of the older English versifica-tion had, in practice, been based on the stress, or "accent," and some of it shows as much freedom in varying the number of syllables as does *Christabel*. Coleridge is, however, departing from the 18th-century theory of versification, which maintained that English meter is based on a recurrent number of syl-lables in each line, and not on a recur-rent number of stresses.

Sir Leoline, the Baron rich,
Hath a toothless mastiff bitch;
From her kennel beneath the rock
She maketh answer to the clock,
Four for the quarters, and twelve for the hour;   10
Ever and aye, by shine and shower,
Sixteen short howls, not over loud;
Some say she sees my lady's shroud.

Is the night chilly and dark?
The night is chilly, but not dark.   15
The thin gray cloud is spread on high,
It covers but not hides the sky.
The moon is behind, and at the full;
And yet she looks both small and dull.
The night is chill, the cloud is gray: 20
'Tis a month before the month of May,
And the spring comes slowly up this way.

The lovely lady, Christabel,
Whom her father loves so well,
What makes her in the wood so late,   25
A furlong from the castle gate?
She had dreams all yesternight
Of her own betrothèd knight;
And she in the midnight wood will pray
For the weal⁴ of her lover that's far away.   30

She stole along, she nothing spoke,
The sighs she heaved were soft and low,
And naught was green upon the oak
But moss and rarest mistletoe:
She kneels beneath the huge oak tree,   35
And in silence prayeth she.

The lady sprang up suddenly,
The lovely lady, Christabel!
It moaned as near, as near can be,
But what it is she cannot tell.—   40
On the other side it seems to be,
Of the huge, broad-breasted, old oak tree.

The night is chill; the forest bare;
Is it the wind that moaneth bleak?
There is not wind enough in the air   45
To move away the ringlet curl
From the lovely lady's cheek—
There is not wind enough to twirl
The one red leaf, the last of its clan,
That dances as often as dance it can,   50

4. Well-being.

Hanging so light, and hanging so high,
On the topmost twig that looks up at the sky.

Hush, beating heart of Christabel!
Jesu, Maria, shield her well!
She folded her arms beneath her cloak,   55
And stole to the other side of the oak.
      What sees she there?

There she sees a damsel bright,
Dressed in a silken robe of white,
That shadowy in the moonlight shone: 60
The neck that made that white robe wan,
Her stately neck, and arms were bare;
Her blue-veined feet unsandaled were,
And wildly glittered here and there
The gems entangled in her hair.   65
I guess, 'twas frightful there to see
A lady so richly clad as she—
Beautiful exceedingly!

Mary mother, save me now!
(Said Christabel), And who art thou?   70

The lady strange made answer meet,[5]
And her voice was faint and sweet—
Have pity on my sore distress,
I scarce can speak for weariness:
Stretch forth thy hand, and have no fear!   75
Said Christabel, How camest thou here?
And the lady, whose voice was faint and sweet,
Did thus pursue her answer meet—

My sire is of a noble line,
And my name is Geraldine: 80
Five warriors seized me yestermorn,
Me, even me, a maid forlorn:
They choked my cries with force and fright,
And tied me on a palfrey white.
The palfrey was as fleet as wind,   85
And they rode furiously behind.
They spurred amain,[6] their steeds were white:
And once we crossed the shade of night.
As sure as Heaven shall rescue me,
I have no thought what men they be;   90
Nor do I know how long it is
(For I have lain entranced, I wis[7])
Since one, the tallest of the five,
Took me from the palfrey's back,
A weary woman, scarce alive.   95

5. Appropriate.
6. At top speed.
7. I believe; Coleridge's misinterpre-
tation of the Middle English adverb
"ywis," meaning "certainly."

Some muttered words his comrades spoke:
He placed me underneath this oak;
He swore they would return with haste;
Whither they went I cannot tell—
I thought I heard, some minutes past,   100
Sounds as of a castle bell.
Stretch forth thy hand (thus ended she),
And help a wretched maid to flee.

Then Christabel stretched forth her hand,
And comforted fair Geraldine: 105
O well, bright dame! may you command
The service of Sir Leoline;
And gladly our stout chivalry
Will he send forth and friends withal
To guide and guard you safe and free   110
Home to your noble father's hall.

She rose: and forth with steps they passed
That strove to be, and were not, fast.
Her gracious stars the lady blessed,
And thus spake on sweet Christabel: 115
All our houschold are at rest,
The hall as silent as the cell;
Sir Leoline is weak in health,
And may not well awakened be,
But we will move as if in stealth,   120
And I beseech your courtesy,
This night, to share your couch with me.

They crossed the moat, and Christabel
Took the key that fitted well;
A little door she opened straight,   125
All in the middle of the gate;
The gate that was ironed within and without,
Where an army in battle array had marched out.
The lady sank, belike through pain,
And Christabel with might and main   130
Lifted her up, a weary weight,
Over the threshold of the gate:[8]
Then the lady rose again,
And moved, as she were not in pain.

So free from danger, free from fear,   135
They crossed the court: right glad they were.
And Christabel devoutly cried
To the lady by her side,
Praise we the Virgin all divine
Who hath rescued thee from thy distress!   140

8. She cannot cross the threshold by her own power because it has been blessed against evil spirits; this is the first of several indications that Geraldine is a malign being.

Alas, alas! said Geraldine,
I cannot speak for weariness.
So free from danger, free from fear,
They crossed the court: right glad they were.

Outside her kennel, the mastiff old   145
Lay fast asleep, in moonshine cold.
The mastiff old did not awake,
Yet she an angry moan did make!
And what can ail the mastiff bitch?
Never till now she uttered yell   150
Beneath the eye of Christabel.
Perhaps it is the owlet's scritch:
For what can ail the mastiff bitch?

They passed the hall, that echoes still,
Pass as lightly as you will!   155
The brands were flat, the brands were dying,
Amid their own white ashes lying;
But when the lady passed, there came
A tongue of light, a fit of flame;
And Christabel saw the lady's eye,   160
And nothing else saw she thereby,
Save the boss of the shield of Sir Leoline tall,
Which hung in a murky old niche in the wall.
O softly tread, said Christabel,
My father seldom sleepeth well.   165

Sweet Christabel her feet doth bare,
And jealous of the listening air
They steal their way from stair to stair,
Now in glimmer, and now in gloom,
And now they pass the Baron's room,   170
As still as death, with stifled breath!
And now have reached her chamber door;
And now doth Geraldine press down
The rushes of the chamber floor.

The moon shines dim in the open air,   175
And not a moonbeam enters here.
But they without its light can see
The chamber carved so curiously,
Carved with figures strange and sweet,
All made out of the carver's brain,   180
For a lady's chamber meet:
The lamp with twofold silver chain
Is fastened to an angel's feet.

The silver lamp burns dead and dim;
But Christabel the lamp will trim.   185
She trimmed the lamp, and made it bright,
And left it swinging to and fro,

While Geraldine, in wretched plight,
Sank down upon the floor below.

O weary lady, Geraldine,   190
I pray you, drink this cordial wine!
It is a wine of virtuous powers;
My mother made it of wild flowers.

And will your mother pity me,
Who am a maiden most forlorn?   195
Christabel answered—Woe is me!
She died the hour that I was born.
I have heard the gray-haired friar tell
How on her deathbed she did say,
That she should hear the castle bell   200
Strike twelve upon my wedding day.
O mother dear! that thou wert here!
I would, said Geraldine, she were!
But soon with altered voice, said she—
"Off, wandering mother! Peak and pine!   205
I have power to bid thee flee."
Alas! what ails poor Geraldine?
Why stares she with unsettled eye?
Can she the bodiless dead espy?
And why with hollow voice cries she,   210
"Off, woman, off! this hour is mine—
Though thou her guardian spirit be,
Off, woman, off! 'tis given to me."

Then Christabel knelt by the lady's side,
And raised to heaven her eyes so blue—   215
Alas! said she, this ghastly ride—
Dear lady! it hath 'wildered you!
The lady wiped her moist cold brow,
And faintly said, " 'tis over now!"

Again the wild-flower wine she drank: 220
Her fair large eyes 'gan glitter bright,
And from the floor whereon she sank,
The lofty lady stood upright:
She was most beautiful to see,
Like a lady of a far countree.   225

And thus the lofty lady spake—
"All they who live in the upper sky,
Do love you, holy Christabel!
And you love them, and for their sake
And for the good which me befell.   230
Even I in my degree will try,
Fair maiden, to requite you well.
But now unrobe yourself; for I
Must pray, ere yet in bed I lie."

Quoth Christabel, So let it be!   235
And as the lady bade, did she.
Her gentle limbs did she undress,
And lay down in her loveliness.

But through her brain of weal and woe
So many thoughts moved to and fro,   240
That vain it were her lids to close;
So halfway from the bed she rose,
And on her elbow did recline
To look at the lady Geraldine.

Beneath the lamp the lady bowed,   245
And slowly rolled her eyes around;
Then drawing in her breath aloud,
Like one that shuddered, she unbound
The cincture[9] from beneath her breast:
Her silken robe, and inner vest,   250
Dropped to her feet, and full in view,
Behold! her bosom and half her side——
A sight to dream of, not to tell!
O shield her! shield sweet Christabel!

Yet Geraldine nor speaks nor stirs;   255
Ah! what a stricken look was hers!
Deep from within she seems halfway
To lift some weight with sick assay,
And eyes the maid and seeks delay;
Then suddenly, as one defied,   200
Collects herself in scorn and pride,
And lay down by the maiden's side!—
And in her arms the maid she took,
          Ah well-a-day!
And with low voice and doleful look   265
These words did say:
"In the touch of this bosom there worketh a spell,
Which is lord of thy utterance, Christabel!
Thou knowest tonight, and wilt know tomorrow,
This mark of my shame, this seal of my sorrow;   270
          But vainly thou warrest,
               For this is alone in
          Thy power to declare,
               That in the dim forest
               Thou heard'st a low moaning,   275
And found'st a bright lady, surpassingly fair;
And didst bring her home with thee in love and in charity,
To shield her and shelter her from the damp air."

The Conclusion to Part I

It was a lovely sight to see
The lady Christabel, when she   280

9. Belt.

Was praying at the old oak tree.
Amid the jagged shadows
Of mossy leafless boughs,
Kneeling in the moonlight,
To make her gentle vows;   285
Her slender palms together pressed,
Heaving sometimes on her breast;
Her face resigned to bliss or bale[1]—
Her face, oh call it fair not pale,
And both blue eyes more bright than clear,   290
Each about to have a tear.

With open eyes (ah woe is me!)
Asleep, and dreaming fearfully,
Fearfully dreaming, yet I wis,
Dreaming that alone, which is—   295
O sorrow and shame! Can this be she,
The lady, who knelt at the old oak tree?
And lo! the worker of these harms,
That holds the maiden in her arms,
Seems to slumber still and mild,   300
As a mother with her child.

A star hath set, a star hath risen,
O Geraldine! since arms of thine
Have been the lovely lady's prison.
O Geraldine! one hour was thine—   305
Thou'st had thy will! By tairn[2] and rill,
The night birds all that hour were still.
But now they are jubilant anew,
From cliff and tower, tu—whoo! tu—whoo!
Tu—whoo! tu—whoo! from wood and fell![3]   310

And see! the lady Christabel
Gathers herself from out her trance;
Her limbs relax, her countenance
Grows sad and soft; the smooth thin lids
Close o'er her eyes; and tears she sheds—   315
Large tears that leave the lashes bright!
And oft the while she seems to smile
As infants at a sudden light!

Yea, she doth smile, and she doth weep,
Like a youthful hermitess,   320
Beauteous in a wilderness,
Who, praying always, prays in sleep.
And, if she move unquietly,
Perchance, 'tis but the blood so free
Comes back and tingles in her feet.   325
No doubt, she hath a vision sweet.

1. Evil, sorrow.   3. Elevated moor, or hill.
2. Tarn, a mountain pool.

What if her guardian spirit 'twere,
What if she knew her mother near?
But this she knows, in joys and woes,
That saints will aid if men will call: 330
For the blue sky bends over all!

Part II

Each matin bell, the Baron saith,
Knells us back to a world of death.
These words Sir Leoline first said,
When he rose and found his lady dead: 335
These words Sir Leoline will say
Many a morn to his dying day!

And hence the custom and law began
That still at dawn the sacristan,
Who duly pulls the heavy bell,   340
Five and forty beads must tell[4]
Between each stroke—a warning knell,
Which not a soul can choose but hear
From Bratha Head to Wyndermere.[5]

Saith Bracy the bard, So let it knell!   345
And let the drowsy sacristan
Still count as slowly as he can!
There is no lack of such, I ween,
As well fill up the space between.
In Langdale Pike[6] and Witch's Lair,   350
And Dungeon Ghyll[7] so foully rent,
With ropes of rock and bells of air
Three sinful sextons' ghosts are pent,
Who all give back, one after t'other,
The death note to their living brother;   355
And oft too, by the knell offended,
Just as their one! two! three! is ended,
The devil mocks the doleful tale
With a merry peal from Borodale.

The air is still! through mist and cloud   360
That merry peal comes ringing loud;
And Geraldine shakes off her dread,
And rises lightly from the bed;
Puts on her silken vestments white,
And tricks her hair in lovely plight,[8]   365
And nothing doubting of her spell
Awakens the lady Christabel.

4. Pray while "telling" (keeping count on) the beads of a rosary. "Sacristan": sexton.
5. These and the following names are of localities in the English Lake Country.
6. Peak.
7. Ravine forming the bed of a stream.
8. Plait.

"Sleep you, sweet lady Christabel?
I trust that you have rested well."

And Christabel awoke and spied   370
The same who lay down by her side—
O rather say, the same whom she
Raised up beneath the old oak tree!
Nay, fairer yet! and yet more fair!
For she belike hath drunken deep   375
Of all the blessedness of sleep!
And while she spake, her looks, her air
Such gentle thankfulness declare,
That (so it seemed) her girded vests
Grew tight beneath her heaving breasts.   380
"Sure I have sinned!" said Christabel,
"Now heaven be praised if all be well!"
And in low faltering tones, yet sweet,
Did she the lofty lady greet
With such perplexity of mind   385
As dreams too lively leave behind.

So quickly she rose, and quickly arrayed
Her maiden limbs, and having prayed
That He, who on the cross did groan,
Might wash away her sins unknown,   390
She forthwith led fair Geraldine
To meet her sire, Sir Leoline.

The lovely maid and the lady tall
Are pacing both into the hall,
And pacing on through page and groom,   395
Enter the Baron's presence-room.

The Baron rose, and while he pressed
His gentle daughter to his breast,
With cheerful wonder in his eyes
The lady Geraldine espies,   400
And gave such welcome to the same,
As might beseem so bright a dame!

But when he heard the lady's tale,
And when she told her father's name,
Why waxed Sir Leoline so pale,   405
Murmuring o'er the name again,
Lord Roland de Vaux of Tryermaine?

Alas! they had been friends in youth;
But whispering tongues can poison truth;
And constancy lives in realms above;
And life is thorny; and youth is vain;   410
And to be wroth with one we love
Doth work like madness in the brain.
And thus it chanced, as I divine,

With Roland and Sir Leoline.   415
Each spake words of high disdain
And insult to his heart's best brother:
They parted—ne'er to meet again!
But never either found another
To free the hollow heart from paining—   420
They stood aloof, the scars remaining,
Like cliffs which had been rent asunder;
A dreary sea now flows between—
But neither heat, nor frost, nor thunder,
Shall wholly do away, I ween,   425
The marks of that which once hath been.

Sir Leoline, a moment's space,
Stood gazing on the damsel's face:
And the youthful Lord of Tryermaine
Came back upon his heart again.   430

O then the Baron forgot his age,
His noble heart swelled high with rage;
He swore by the wounds in Jesu's side
He would proclaim it far and wide,
With trump and solemn heraldry,   435
That they, who thus had wronged the dame,
Were base as spotted infamy!
"And if they dare deny the same,
My herald shall appoint a week,
And let the recreant traitors seek   440
My tourney court—that there and then
I may dislodge their reptile souls
From the bodies and forms of men!"
He spake: his eye in lightning rolls!
For the lady was ruthlessly seized; and he kenned   445
In the beautiful lady the child of his friend!

And now the tears were on his face,
And fondly in his arms he took
Fair Geraldine, who met the embrace,
Prolonging it with joyous look.   450
Which when she viewed, a vision fell
Upon the soul of Christabel,
The vision of fear, the touch and pain!
She shrunk and shuddered, and saw again—
(Ah, woe is me! Was it for thee,   455
Thou gentle maid! such sights to see?)

Again she saw that bosom old,
Again she felt that bosom cold,
And drew in her breath with a hissing sound:
Whereat the Knight turned wildly round,   460
And nothing saw, but his own sweet maid
With eyes upraised, as one that prayed.

The touch, the sight, had passed away,
And in its stead that vision blest,
Which comforted her after-rest 465
While in the lady's arms she lay,
Had put a rapture in her breast,
And on her lips and o'er her eyes
Spread smiles like light!
         With new surprise,
"What ails then my belovéd child?" 470
The Baron said—His daughter mild
Made answer, "All will yet be well!"
I ween, she had no power to tell
Aught else: so mighty was the spell.

Yet he, who saw this Geraldine, 475
Had deemed her sure a thing divine:
Such sorrow with such grace she blended,
As if she feared she had offended
Sweet Christabel, that gentle maid!
And with such lowly tones she prayed 480
She might be sent without delay
Home to her father's mansion.
              "Nay!
Nay, by my soul!" said Leoline.
"Ho! Bracy the bard, the charge be thine!
Go thou, with music sweet and loud, 485
And take two steeds with trappings proud,
And take the youth whom thou lov'st best
To bear thy harp, and learn thy song,
And clothe you both in solemn vest,
And over the mountains haste along, 490
Lest wandering folk, that are abroad,
Detain you on the valley road.

"And when he has crossed the Irthing flood,
My merry bard! he hastes, he hastes
Up Knorren Moor, through Halegarth Wood, 495
And reaches soon that castle good
Which stands and threatens Scotland's wastes.

"Bard Bracy! bard Bracy! your horses are fleet,
Ye must ride up the hall, your music so sweet,
More loud than your horses' echoing feet! 500
And loud and loud to Lord Roland call,
Thy daughter is safe in Langdale hall!
Thy beautiful daughter is safe and free—
Sir Leoline greets thee thus through me!
He bids thee come without delay 505
With all thy numerous array
And take thy lovely daughter home:
And he will meet thee on the way

With all his numerous array
White with their panting palfreys' foam: 510
And, by mine honor! I will say,
That I repent me of the day
When I spake words of fierce disdain
To Roland de Vaux of Tryermaine!—
For since that evil hour hath flown,   515
Many a summer's sun hath shone;
Yet ne'er found I a friend again
Like Roland de Vaux of Tryermaine."

The lady fell, and clasped his knees,
Her face upraised, her eyes o'erflowing;   520
And Bracy replied, with faltering voice,
His gracious Hail on all bestowing!—
"Thy words, thou sire of Christabel,
Are sweeter than my harp can tell;
Yet might I gain a boon of thee,   525
This day my journey should not be,
So strange a dream hath come to me,
That I had vowed with music loud
To clear yon wood from thing unblest,
Warned by a vision in my rest!   530
For in my sleep I saw that dove,
That gentle bird, whom thou dost love,
And call'st by thy own daughter's name—
Sir Leoline! I saw the same
Fluttering, and uttering fearful moan,   535
Among the green herbs in the forest alone.
Which when I saw and when I heard,
I wondered what might ail the bird;
For nothing near it could I see,
Save the grass and green herbs underneath the old tree.   540

"And in my dream methought I went
To search out what might there be found;
And what the sweet bird's trouble meant,
That thus lay fluttering on the ground.
I went and peered, and could descry   545
No cause for her distressful cry;
But yet for her dear lady's sake
I stooped, methought, the dove to take,
When lo! I saw a bright green snake
Coiled around its wings and neck.   550
Green as the herbs on which it couched,
Close by the dove's its head it crouched;
And with the dove it heaves and stirs,
Swelling its neck as she swelled hers!
I woke; it was the midnight hour,   555
The clock was echoing in the tower;
But though my slumber was gone by,

This dream it would not pass away—
It seems to live upon my eye!
And thence I vowed this selfsame day   560
With music strong and saintly song
To wander through the forest bare,
Lest aught unholy loiter there."

Thus Bracy said: the Baron, the while,
Half-listening heard him with a smile;   565
Then turned to Lady Geraldine,
His eyes made up of wonder and love;
And said in courtly accents fine,
"Sweet maid, Lord Roland's beauteous dove,
With arms more strong than harp or song,   570
Thy sire and I will crush the snake!"
He kissed her forehead as he spake,
And Geraldine in maiden wise
Casting down her large bright eyes,
With blushing cheek and courtesy fine   575
She turned her from Sir Leoline;
Softly gathering up her train,
That o'er her right arm fell again;
And folded her arms across her chest,
And couched her head upon her breast,   580
And looked askance at Christabel——
Jesu, Maria, shield her well!

A snake's small eye blinks dull and shy;
And the lady's eyes they shrunk in her head,
Each shrunk up to a serpent's eye,   585
And with somewhat of malice, and more of dread,
At Christabel she looked askance!—
One moment—and the sight was fled!
But Christabel in dizzy trance
Stumbling on the unsteady ground   590
Shuddered aloud, with a hissing sound;
And Geraldine again turned round,
And like a thing, that sought relief,
Full of wonder and full of grief,
She rolled her large bright eyes divine   595
Wildly on Sir Leoline.

The maid, alas! her thoughts are gone,
She nothing sees—no sight but one!
The maid, devoid of guile and sin,
I know not how, in fearful wise,   600
So deeply had she drunken in
That look, those shrunken serpent eyes,
That all her features were resigned
To this sole image in her mind:
And passively did imitate   605

That look of dull and treacherous hate!
And thus she stood, in dizzy trance,
Still picturing that look askance
With forced unconscious sympathy
Full before her father's view—   610
As far as such a look could be
In eyes so innocent and blue!

And whence the trance was o'er, the maid
Paused awhile, and inly prayed:
Then falling at the Baron's feet,   615
"By my mother's soul do I entreat
That thou this woman send away!"
She said: and more she could not say:
For what she knew she could not tell,
O'ermastered by the mighty spell.   620

Why is thy cheek so wan and wild,
Sir Leoline? Thy only child
Lies at thy feet, thy joy, thy pride,
So fair, so innocent, so mild;
The same, for whom thy lady died!   625
O by the pangs of her dear mother
Think thou no evil of thy child!
For her, and thee, and for no other,
She prayed the moment ere she died:
Prayed that the babe for whom she died,   630
Might prove her dear lord's joy and pride!
     That prayer her deadly pangs beguiled,
               Sir Leoline!
     And wouldst thou wrong thy only child,
               Her child and thine?   635

Within the Baron's heart and brain
If thoughts, like these, had any share,
They only swelled his rage and pain,
And did but work confusion there.
His heart was cleft with pain and rage,   640
His cheeks they quivered, his eyes were wild,
Dishonored thus in his old age;
Dishonored by his only child,
And all his hospitality
To the wronged daughter of his friend   645
By more than woman's jealousy
Brought thus to a disgraceful end—
He rolled his eye with stern regard
Upon the gentle minstrel bard,
And said in tones abrupt, austere—   650
"Why, Bracy! dost thou loiter here?
I bade thee hence!" The bard obeyed;
And turning from his own sweet maid,

The aged knight, Sir Leoline,
Led forth the lady Geraldine! 655

The Conclusion to Part II

A little child, a limber elf,
Singing, dancing to itself,
A fairy thing with red round cheeks,
That always finds, and never seeks,
Makes such a vision to the sight 660
As fills a father's eyes with light;
And pleasures flow in so thick and fast
Upon his heart, that he at last
Must needs express his love's excess
With words of unmeant bitterness. 665
Perhaps 'tis pretty to force together
Thoughts so all unlike each other;
To mutter and mock a broken charm,
To dally with wrong that does no harm.
Perhaps 'tis tender too and pretty 670
At each wild word to feel within
A sweet recoil of love and pity.
And what, if in a world of sin
(O sorrow and shame should this be true!)
Such giddiness of heart and brain 675
Comes seldom save from rage and pain,
So talks as it's most used to do.

ca. 1797–1801 1816

Frost at Midnight[1]

The Frost performs its secret ministry,
Unhelped by any wind. The owlet's cry
Came loud—and hark, again! loud as before.
The inmates of my cottage, all at rest,
Have left me to that solitude, which suits 5
Abstruser musings: save that at my side
My cradled infant slumbers peacefully.
'Tis calm indeed! so calm, that it disturbs
And vexes meditation with its strange
And extreme silentness. Sea, hill, and wood, 10
This populous village! Sea, and hill, and wood,
With all the numberless goings-on of life,
Inaudible as dreams! the thin blue flame
Lies on my low-burnt fire, and quivers not;
Only that film,[2] which fluttered on the grate, 15

1. The scene is Coleridge's cottage at Nether Stowey; the infant in line 7 is his son Hartley.

2. "In all parts of the kingdom these films are called *strangers* and supposed to portend the arrival of some absent

Still flutters there, the sole unquiet thing.
Methinks its motion in this hush of nature
Gives it dim sympathies with me who live,
Making it a companionable form,
Whose puny flaps and freaks the idling Spirit   20
By its own moods interprets, everywhere
Echo or mirror seeking of itself,
And makes a toy of Thought.

                  But O! how oft,
How oft, at school, with most believing mind,
Presageful, have I gazed upon the bars,   25
To watch that fluttering *stranger!* and as oft
With unclosed lids, already had I dreamt
Of my sweet birthplace,[3] and the old church tower,
Whose bells, the poor man's only music, rang
From morn to evening, all the hot fair-day,   30
So sweetly, that they stirred and haunted me
With a wild pleasure, falling on mine ear
Most like articulate sounds of things to come!
So gazed I, till the soothing things, I dreamt,
Lulled me to sleep, and sleep prolonged my dreams!   35
And so I brooded all the following morn,
Awed by the stern preceptor's face,[4] mine eye
Fixed with mock study on my swimming book:
Save if the door half opened, and I snatched
A hasty glance, and still my heart leaped up,   40
For still I hoped to see the *stranger's* face,
Townsman, or aunt, or sister more beloved,
My playmate when we both were clothed alike![5]

    Dear Babe, that sleepest cradled by my side,
Whose gentle breathings, heard in this deep calm,   45
Fill up the interspersèd vacancies
And momentary pauses of the thought!
My babe so beautiful! it thrills my heart
With tender gladness, thus to look at thee,
And think that thou shalt learn far other lore,   50
And in far other scenes! For I was reared
In the great city, pent 'mid cloisters dim,
And saw nought lovely but the sky and stars.
But *thou*, my babe! shalt wander like a breeze
By lakes and sandy shores, beneath the crags   55
Of ancient mountain, and beneath the clouds,
Which image in their bulk both lakes and shores

friend" [Coleridge's note]. The "film"
is a piece of soot fluttering on the bar
of the grate; it was one of various
signs which, according to popular English belief of the time, foretold an unexpected visitor. See also lines 26 and
41.
3. Coleridge was born at Ottery St.

Mary, Devonshire, but went to school
in London, beginning at the age of 9.
4. The "stern preceptor" at Coleridge's
school, Christ's Hospital, was the Rev.
James Boyer, whom Coleridge describes
in *Biographia Literaria*, Chapter I.
5. I.e., when both Coleridge and his
sister Ann still wore infant clothes.

And mountain crags: so shalt thou see and hear
The lovely shapes and sounds intelligible
Of that eternal language, which thy God   60
Utters, who from eternity doth teach
Himself in all, and all things in himself.
Great universal Teacher! he shall mold
Thy spirit, and by giving make it ask.

    Therefore all seasons shall be sweet to thee,   65
Whether the summer clothe the general earth
With greenness, or the redbreast sit and sing
Betwixt the tufts of snow on the bare branch
Of mossy apple tree, while the nigh thatch
Smokes in the sun-thaw; whether the eave-drops fall   70
Heard only in the trances of the blast,
Or if the secret ministry of frost
Shall hang them up in silent icicles,
Quietly shining to the quiet Moon.

February, 1798   1798

Dejection: An Ode[1]

> Late, late yestreen I saw the new Moon,
> With the old Moon in her arms;
> And I fear, I fear, my master dear!
> We shall have a deadly storm.
>   *Ballad of Sir Patrick Spence*

1

Well! If the bard was weather-wise, who made
The grand old ballad of Sir Patrick Spence,
  This night, so tranquil now, will not go hence
Unroused by winds, that ply a busier trade
Than those which mold yon cloud in lazy flakes,   5
Or the dull sobbing draft, that moans and rakes
  Upon the strings of this Aeolian lute,[2]

---

1. This poem originated in a verse letter of 340 lines, called *A Letter to* ————, which Coleridge wrote on the night of April 4, 1802, after hearing the opening stanzas of *Ode: Intimations of Immortality*, which Wordsworth had just composed. The *Letter* was addressed to Sara Hutchinson (whom Coleridge sometimes called "Asra"), the sister of Wordsworth's fiancée Mary. It picked up the theme of a loss in the quality of perceptual experience which Wordsworth had presented at the beginning of his *Ode*. In his original poem, Coleridge lamented at length his unhappy marriage and the hopelessness of his love for Sara Hutchinson. In the next six months Coleridge deleted more than half the original lines, revised and re-ordered the remaining passages, and so transformed a long verse confession into the compact and dignified *Dejection: An Ode*. He published the *Ode*, in substantially its present form, on October 4, 1802, Wordsworth's wedding day—and also the seventh anniversary of Coleridge's own disastrous marriage to Sara Fricker. Coleridge's implicit concern with the marital relation emerges in the marriage metaphors of lines 49 and 67–70.

2. A stringed instrument played upon by the wind; see Coleridge's *The Eolian Harp*, note 1.

Which better far were mute.
For lo! the New-moon winter-bright!
And overspread with phantom light, 10
(With swimming phantom light o'erspread
But rimmed and circled by a silver thread)
I see the old Moon in her lap, foretelling
    The coming-on of rain and squally blast.
And oh! that even now the gust were swelling, 15
    And the slant night shower driving loud and fast!
Those sounds which oft have raised me, whilst they awed,
    And sent my soul abroad,
Might now perhaps their wonted³ impulse give,
Might startle this dull pain, and make it move and live! 20

        2
A grief without a pang, void, dark, and drear,
    A stifled, drowsy, unimpassioned grief,
    Which finds no natural outlet, no relief,
        In word, or sigh, or tear—
O Lady!⁴ in this wan and heartless mood, 25
To other thoughts by yonder throstle wooed,
All this long eve, so balmy and serene,
Have I been gazing on the western sky,
    And its peculiar tint of yellow green:
And still I gaze—and with how blank an eye! 30
And those thin clouds above, in flakes and bars,
That give away their motion to the stars;
Those stars, that glide behind them or between,
Now sparkling, now bedimmed, but always seen:
Yon crescent Moon, as fixed as if it grew 35
In its own cloudless, starless lake of blue;
I see them all so excellently fair,
I see, not feel, how beautiful they are!

        3
    My genial⁵ spirits fail;
    And what can these avail 40
To lift the smothering weight from off my breast?
    It were a vain endeavor,
    Though I should gaze forever
On that green light that lingers in the west:
I may not hope from outward forms to win 45
The passion and the life, whose fountains are within.

        4
O Lady! we receive but what we give,
And in our life alone does Nature live:

---

3. Customary.
4. In the original version "Sara"—i.e., Sara Hutchinson, with whom Coleridge was hopelessly in love. After intervening versions, in which the poem was addressed first to "William" (Wordsworth) and then to "Edmund," Coleridge introduced the noncommittal "Lady" in 1817.
5. In its old use as the adjective form of "genius": "My innate powers fail."

Ours is her wedding garment, ours her shroud![6]
And would we aught behold, of higher worth,   50
Than that inanimate cold world allowed
To the poor loveless ever-anxious crowd,
   Ah! from the soul itself must issue forth
A light, a glory,[7] a fair luminous cloud
     Enveloping the Earth—   55
And from the soul itself must there be sent
   A sweet and potent voice, of its own birth,
Of all sweet sounds the life and element!

5

O pure of heart! thou need'st not ask of me
What this strong music in the soul may be!   60
What, and wherein it doth exist,
This light, this glory, this fair luminous mist,
This beautiful and beauty-making power.
   Joy,[8] virtuous Lady! Joy that ne'er was given,
Save to the pure, and in their purest hour,   65
Life, and Life's effluence, cloud at once and shower,
Joy, Lady! is the spirit and the power,
Which wedding Nature to us gives in dower
   A new Earth and new Heaven,[9]
Undreamt of by the sensual and the proud—   70
Joy is the sweet voice, Joy the luminous cloud—
     We in ourselves rejoice!
And thence flows all that charms or ear or sight,
   All melodies the echoes of that voice,
All colors a suffusion from that light.   75

6

There was a time when, though my path was rough,
   This joy within me dallied with distress,
And all misfortunes were but as the stuff
   Whence Fancy made me dreams of happiness:
For hope grew round me, like the twining vine,   80
And fruits, and foliage, not my own, seemed mine.
But now afflictions bow me down to earth:
Nor care I that they rob me of my mirth;
     But oh! each visitation
Suspends what nature gave me at my birth,   85
    My shaping spirit of Imagination.

---

6. I.e., whether nature is experienced as "inanimate" (line 51) or in living interchange with the observer depends on the apathy or joyous vitality of the observer's own spirit.

7. Coleridge commonly used "glory" not in the sense of a halo, merely, but as a term for a mountain phenomenon in which a walker sees his own figure projected by the sun in the mist, enlarged, and with a circle of light around its head. See Coleridge's *Constancy to an Ideal Object*, line 30.

8. Coleridge often uses "Joy" for a sense of abounding vitality and of har- mony between one's inner life and the life of nature. He sometimes calls the contrary "exsiccation," or spiritual dryness.

9. The sense of this passage becomes clearer if line 68 is punctuated, as in one of Coleridge's quotations from his own poem in an essay: "Which, wedding Nature to us, gives in dower"; i.e., "Joy" is the condition which (overcoming the alienation between man's mind and its milieu) marries us to "Nature," and gives by way of wedding portion ("dower") the experience of a renovated outer world.

For not to think of what I needs must feel,
 But to be still and patient, all I can;
And happly by abstruse research to steal
 From my own nature all the natural man—   90
 This was my sole resource, my only plan:
Till that which suits a part infects the whole,
And now is almost grown the habit of my soul.

7

Hence, viper thoughts, that coil around my mind,
 Reality's dark dream!   95
I turn from you, and listen to the wind,
 Which long has raved unnoticed. What a scream
Of agony by torture lengthened out
That lute sent forth! Thou Wind, that rav'st without,
 Bare crag, or mountain tairn,[1] or blasted tree,   100
Or pine grove whither woodman never clomb,
Or lonely house, long held the witches' home,
 Methinks were fitter instruments for thee,
Mad lutanist! who in this month of showers,
Of dark-brown gardens, and of peeping flowers,   105
Mak'st devils' yule,[2] with worse than wintry song,
The blossoms, buds, and timorous leaves among.
 Thou actor, perfect in all tragic sounds!
Thou mighty poet, e'en to frenzy bold!
  What tell'st thou now about?   110
 'Tis of the rushing of an host in rout,
With groans, of trampled men, with smarting wounds—
At once they groan with pain, and shudder with the cold!
But hush! there is a pause of deepest silence!
 And all that noise, as of a rushing crowd,   115
With groans, and tremulous shudderings—all is over—
 It tells another tale, with sounds less deep and loud!
  A tale of less affright,
  And tempered with delight,
As Otway's[3] self had framed the tender lay—   120
  'Tis of a little child
  Upon a lonesome wild,
Not far from home, but she hath lost her way:
And now moans low in bitter grief and fear,
And now screams loud, and hopes to make her mother hear. 125

8

'Tis midnight, but small thoughts have I of sleep:
Full seldom may my friend such vigils keep!
Visit her, gentle Sleep! with wings of healing,
 And may this storm be but a mountain birth,[4]
May all the stars hang bright above her dwelling,   130

1. Tarn, or mountain pool.
2. Christmas, in the perverted form in which it is celebrated by devils.
3. Thomas Otway (1652–85), a dramatist noted for the pathos of his tragic passages. The poet originally named was "William," and the allusion was probably to Wordsworth's *Lucy Gray*.
4. Probably, "May this be a typical mountain storm, short though violent," although it is possible that Coleridge intended an allusion to Horace's phrase, "the mountain labored and brought forth a mouse."

Silent as though they watched the sleeping Earth!
  With light heart may she rise,
  Gay fancy, cheerful eyes,
Joy lift her spirit, joy attune her voice;
To her may all things live, from pole to pole,   135
Their life the eddying of her living soul!
  O simple spirit, guided from above,
Dear Lady! friend devoutest of my choice,
Thus mayest thou ever, evermore rejoice.

April 4, 1802   1802, 1817

What Is Life?[5]

Resembles life what once was deemed of light,
Too ample in itself for human sight?
An absolute self—an element ungrounded—
All that we see, all colors of all shade
  By encroach of darkness made?—   5
Is very life by consciousness unbounded?
And all the thoughts, pains, joys of mortal breath,
A war-embrace of wrestling life and death?

1804   1829

Phantom[6]

All look and likeness caught from earth
All accident of kin and birth,
Had passed away. There was no trace
Of aught on that illumined face,
Upraised beneath the rifted stone   5
But of one spirit all her own—
She, she herself, and only she,
Shone through her body visibly.

1804   1834

To William Wordsworth

COMPOSED ON THE NIGHT AFTER HIS RECITATION OF A POEM
ON THE GROWTH OF AN INDIVIDUAL MIND[1]

Friend of the wise! and teacher of the good!
Into my heart have I received that lay

5. Written by Coleridge in a notebook kept at Malta in 1804, in order, he said, "to try a meter." It expresses a conception of life as a sustained opposition between the life principle and the death principle, in which the latter is the inevitable victor.

6. A notebook Coleridge kept at Malta in 1804 makes it clear that the poem describes the appearance of Sara Hutchinson in a dream.

1. This was the poem (later called *The Prelude*) addressed to Coleridge, which Wordsworth had completed in 1805. After Coleridge returned from Malta, very low in health and spirits, Wordsworth read the poem aloud to him on the evenings of almost two weeks. Coleridge wrote most of his poem immediately the reading was completed, on January 7, 1807.

More than historic, that prophetic lay
Wherein (high theme by thee first sung aright)
Of the foundations and the building up   5
Of a Human Spirit thou hast dared to tell
What may be told, to the understanding mind
Revealable; and what within the mind
By vital breathings secret as the soul
Of vernal growth, oft quickens in the heart   10
Thoughts all too deep for words![2]—

                Theme hard as high!
Of smiles spontaneous, and mysterious fears
(The first-born they of Reason and twin birth),
Of tides obedient to external force,
And currents self-determined, as might seem,   15
Or by some inner Power; of moments awful,
Now in thy inner life, and now abroad,
When power streamed from thee, and thy soul received
The light reflected, as a light bestowed—
Of fancies fair, and milder hours of youth,   20
Hyblean[3] murmurs of poetic thought
Industrious in its joy, in vales and glens
Native or outland, lakes and famous hills!
Or on the lonely highroad, when the stars
Were rising; or by secret mountain streams,   25
The guides and the companions of thy way!

Of more than Fancy, of the Social Sense
Distending wide, and man beloved as man,
Where France in all her towns lay vibrating
Like some becalméd bark beneath the burst   30
Of Heaven's immediate thunder, when no cloud
Is visible, or shadow on the main.
For thou wert there, thine own brows garlanded,
Amid the tremor of a realm aglow,
Amid a mighty nation jubilant,   35
When from the general heart of human kind
Hope sprang forth like a full-born deity!
——Of that dear Hope afflicted and struck down,
So summoned homeward, thenceforth calm and sure
From the dread watchtower of man's absolute self,   40
With light unwaning on her eyes, to look
Far on—herself a glory to behold,
The Angel of the vision! Then (last strain)
Of Duty, chosen Laws controlling choice,
Action and joy!—An Orphic song[4] indeed,   45

2. Wordsworth had described the effect
on his mind of the animating breeze
("vital breathings") in *The Prelude*,
I.1-44 "Thoughts * * * words" echoes
the last line of his *Intimations* ode.
Coleridge then summarizes the major
themes and events of *The Prelude*.

3. Sweet.
4. As enchanting and oracular as the
song of the legendary Orpheus. The allusion is probably also to the Orphic
mysteries, involving spiritual death and
rebirth; see lines 61-66.

A song divine of high and passionate thoughts
To their own music chaunted!

              O great bard!
Ere that last strain dying awed the air,
With steadfast eye I viewed thee in the choir
Of ever-enduring men. The truly great   50
Have all one age, and from one visible space
Shed influence! They, both in power and act,
Are permanent, and Time is not with them,
Save as it worketh for them, they in it.
Nor less a sacred roll, than those of old,   55
And to be placed, as they, with gradual fame
Among the archives of mankind, thy work
Makes audible a linkéd lay of Truth,
Of Truth profound a sweet continuous lay,
Not learnt, but native, her own natural notes!   60
Ah! as I listened with a heart forlorn,
The pulses of my being beat anew:
And even as Life returns upon the drowned,[5]
Life's joy rekindling rousèd a throng of pains—
Keen pangs of Love, awakening as a babe   65
Turbulent, with an outcry in the heart;
And fears self-willed, that shunned the eye of Hope;
And Hope that scarce would know itself from Fear;
Sense of past Youth, and Manhood come in vain,
And Genius given, and Knowledge won in vain;   70
And all which I had culled in wood-walks wild,
And all which patient toil had reared, and all,
Commune with thee had opened out—but flowers
Strewed on my corse, and borne upon my bier
In the same coffin, for the selfsame grave!   75

    That way no more! and ill beseems it me,
Who came a welcomer in herald's guise,
Singing of Glory, and Futurity,
To wander back on such unhealthful road,
Plucking the poisons of self-harm! And ill   80
Such intertwine beseems triumphal wreaths
Strewed before thy advancing!

              Nor do thou,
Sage bard! impair the memory of that hour
Of thy communion with my nobler mind[6]
By pity or grief, already felt too long!   85
Nor let my words import more blame than needs.
The tumult rose and ceased: for Peace is nigh
Where Wisdom's voice has found a listening heart.
Amid the howl of more than wintry storms,
The Halcyon[7] hears the voice of vernal hours   90

---

5. A death-in-life is also described in, e.g., *Dejection* and *Epitaph*.
6. I.e., during the early association be-
tween the two poets (1797-98).
7. A fabled bird, able to calm the sea, where it nested in winter.

Already on the wing.

Eve following eve,[8]
Dear tranquil time, when the sweet sense of Home
Is sweetest! moments for their own sake hailed
And more desired, more precious, for thy song,
In silence listening, like a devout child,   95
My soul lay passive, by thy various strain
Driven as in surges now beneath the stars,
With momentary stars of my own birth,
Fair constellated foam, still darting off
Into the darkness; now a tranquil sea,   100
Outspread and bright, yet swelling to the moon.

And when—O friend! my comforter and guide!
Strong in thyself, and powerful to give strength!—
Thy long sustainéd song finally closed,
And thy deep voice had ceased—yet thou thyself   105
Wert still before my eyes, and round us both
That happy vision of belovéd faces—
Scarce conscious, and yet conscious of its close
I sate, my being blended in one thought
(Thought was it? or aspiration? or resolve?)   110
Absorþed, yet hanging still upon the sound—
And when I rose, I found myself in prayer.
January 7, 1807   1817

Recollections of Love

1
How warm this woodland wild recess!
  Love surely hath been breathing here;
  And this sweet bed of heath, my dear!
Swells up, then sinks with faint caress,
  As if to have you yet more near.   5

2
Eight springs have flown since last I lay
  On seaward Quantock's heathy hills,
  Where quiet sounds from hidden rills
Float here and there, like things astray,
  And high o'erhead the skylark shrills.   10

3
No voice as yet had made the air
  Be music with your name; yet why
  That asking look? that yearning sigh?
That sense of promise every where?
  Belovéd! flew your spirit by?   15

4
As when a mother doth explore

8. The evenings during which Wordsworth read his poem aloud.

The rose mark on her long-lost child,
I met, I loved you, maiden mild!
As whom I long had loved before—
So deeply had I been beguiled.   20

5

You stood before me like a thought,
A dream remembered in a dream.
But when those meek eyes first did seem
To tell me, Love within you wrought—
O Greta,[1] dear domestic stream!   25
6

Has not, since then, Love's prompture deep,
Has not Love's whisper evermore
Been ceaseless, as thy gentle roar?
Sole voice, when other voices sleep,
Dear under-song in clamor's hour.   30

ca. 1807   1817

On Donne's Poetry[2]

With Donne, whose muse on dromedary trots,
Wreathe iron pokers into truelove knots;
Rhyme's sturdy cripple, fancy's maze and clue,
Wit's forge and fire-blast, meaning's press and screw.

ca. 1818   1836

Work Without Hope

LINES COMPOSED 21ST FEBRUARY 1825

All Nature seems at work. Slugs leave their lair—
The bees are stirring—birds are on the wing—
And Winter slumbering in the open air
Wears on his smiling face a dream of Spring!
And I the while, the sole unbusy thing,   5
Nor honey make, nor pair, nor build, nor sing.

Yet well I ken the banks where amaranths[3] blow,
Have traced the fount whence streams of nectar flow.
Bloom, O ye amaranths! bloom for whom ye may,
For me ye bloom not! Glide, rich streams, away!   10
With lips unbrightened, wreathless brow, I stroll:
And would you learn the spells that drowse my soul?
Work without Hope draws nectar in a sieve,
And Hope without an object cannot live.

1825   1828

---

1. The river Greta, which flowed past
Coleridge's home in Keswick, in the
Lake Country.
2. Donne as a poet had been in eclipse
for most of the 18th century. This terse
and penetrating comment shows the
Romantic poet's great, though qualified, respect for the master of the metaphysical style.
3. Mythical flowers that bloom perpetually.

Constancy to an Ideal Object

Since all that beat about in Nature's range
Or veer or vanish, why should'st thou remain
The only constant in a world of change,
O yearning Thought! that liv'st but in the brain?
Call to the Hours, that in the distance play,   5
The faery people of the future day——
Fond[1] Thought! not one of all that shining swarm
Will breathe on thee with life-enkindling breath,
Till when, like strangers shelt'ring from a storm,
Hope and Despair meet in the porch of Death!   10
Yet still thou haunt'st me; and though well I see,
She[1a] is not thou, and only thou art she,
Still, still as though some dear embodied Good,
Some living Love before my eyes there stood
With answering look a ready ear to lend,   15
I mourn to thee and say—"Ah! loveliest friend!
That this the meed[2] of all my toils might be,
To have a home, an English home, and thee!"
Vain repetition! Home and thou are one.
The peaceful'st cot the moon shall shine upon,   20
Lulled by the thrush and wakened by the lark,
Without thee were but a becalméd bark,
Whose Helmsman on an ocean waste and wide
Sits mute and pale his moldering helm beside.

And art thou nothing? Such thou art, as when   25
The woodman winding westward up the glen
At wintry dawn, where o'er the sheep-track's maze
The viewless snow-mist weaves a glist'ning haze,
Sees full before him, gliding without tread,
An image with a glory round its head;[3]   30
The enamored rustic worships its fair hues,
Nor knows he makes the shadow he pursues!

                                                        1828

Phantom or Fact

A DIALOGUE IN VERSE

AUTHOR

A lovely form there sate beside my bed,
And such a feeding calm its presence shed,
A tender love so pure from earthly leaven,
That I unnethe[1] the fancy might control,
'Twas my own spirit newly come from heaven,   5
Wooing its gentle way into my soul!
But ah! the change—It had not stirred, and yet—

---

1. Foolish.
1a. Sara Hutchinson.
2. Reward.
3. A projected image of oneself in the mist. See Coleridge's *Dejection: An Ode*, line 54.
1. With difficulty.

Alas! that change how fain would I forget!
That shrinking back, like one that had mistook!
That weary, wandering, disavowing look!   10
'Twas all another, feature, look, and frame,
And still, methought, I knew, it was the same!

FRIEND

This riddling tale, to what does it belong?
Is't history? vision? or an idle song?
Or rather say at once, within what space   15
Of time this wild disastrous change took place?

AUTHOR

Call it a moment's work (and such it seems)
This tale's a fragment from the life of dreams;
But say that years matured the silent strife,
And 'tis a record from the dream of life.   20

ca. 1830   1834

Epitaph[1]

Stop, Christian passer-by!—Stop, child of God,
And read with gentle breast. Beneath this sod
A poet lies, or that which once seemed he.
O lift one thought in prayer for S. T. C.;
That he who many a year with toil of breath   5
Found death in life, may here find life in death!
Mercy for praise—to be forgiven for[2] fame
He asked, and hoped, through Christ. Do thou the same!

1833   1834

From Biographia Literaria[1]
From *Chapter I*

*The discipline of his taste at school—Bowles's sonnets—Compari-
son between the poets before and since Mr. Pope.*

* * * At school I enjoyed the inestimable advantage of a very

---

1. Written by Coleridge the year before he died. One version that he sent in a letter had as title: "Epitaph on a Poet little known, yet better known by the Initials of his name than by the Name Itself."
2. " 'For' in the sense of 'instead of' " [Coleridge's note].
1. In March, 1815, Coleridge was preparing a collected edition of his poems, and planned to include "a general preface * * * on the principles of philosophic and genial criticism." Characteristically, the materials developed as

Coleridge worked on them, until, on July 29, he declared that the preface had been extended into a complete work, "an Autobiographia Literaria"; it was to consist of two main parts, "my literary life and opinions, as far as poetry and *poetical* criticism [are] concerned," and a critique of Wordsworth's theory of poetic diction. This work was ready by 17 September 1815, but the *Biographia Literaria*, in two volumes, was not published until July, 1817. The delay was caused by a series of miscalculations by his printer, which

sensible, though at the same time a very severe master. He[2] early molded my taste to the preference of Demosthenes to Cicero, of Homer and Theocritus to Virgil, and again of Virgil to Ovid. He habituated me to compare Lucretius (in such extracts as I then read), Terence, and, above all, the chaster poems of Catullus not only with the Roman poets of the so-called silver and brazen ages but with even those of the Augustan era; and, on grounds of plain sense and universal logic, to see and assert the superiority of the former in the truth and nativeness both of their thoughts and diction. At the same time that we were studying the Greek tragic poets, he made us read Shakespeare and Milton as lessons; and they were the lessons, too, which required most time and trouble to *bring up*, so as to escape his censure. I learnt from him that poetry, even that of the loftiest and, seemingly, that of the wildest odes, had a logic of its own as severe as that of science; and more difficult, because more subtle, more complex, and dependent on more, and more fugitive, causes. In the truly great poets, he would say, there is a reason assignable, not only for every word, but for the position of every word; and I well remember that, availing himself of the synonyms to the Homer of Didymus,[3] he made us attempt to show, with regard to each, *why* it would not have answered the same purpose, and *wherein* consisted the peculiar fitness of the word in the original text.

In our own English compositions (at least for the last three years of our school education) he showed no mercy to phrase, metaphor, or image unsupported by a sound sense, or where the same sense might have been conveyed with equal force and dignity in plainer words. Lute, harp, and lyre, muse, muses, and inspirations, Pegasus, Parnassus, and Hippocrene were all an abomina-

forced Coleridge to add miscellaneous materials needed to eke out the length of his original manuscript.

The critique of Wordsworth's theory of diction, which Coleridge had been planning ever since 1802, when he had detected "a radical difference in our theoretical opinions respecting poetry," is long, detailed, and subtly reasoned. In the selection from Chapter XVII, below, Coleridge agrees with Wordsworth's general aim of reforming the artifices of modern poetic diction, but he sharply denies Wordsworth's claim that there is no essential difference between the language of poetry and the language really spoken by men. The other selections printed here are devoted mainly to the central principle of Coleridge's own critical theory, the distinction between the mechanical "fancy" and the organic "imagination." Thus the biographical section of the *Biographia* (Chapters I and IV), dealing with the development of his poetic

taste and theory, describes his gradual realization, climaxed by his first exposure to Wordsworth's poetry, "that fancy and imagination were two distinct and widely different faculties." The conclusion to Chapter XIII tersely summarizes this distinction, and the definition of poetry, at the end of Chapter XIV, develops at somewhat greater length the nature of the process and products of the "synthetic and magical power * * * of imagination." These cryptic paragraphs have proved to be the most widely discussed and influential passages ever written by an English critic.

2. "The Rev. James Boyer, many years Head Master of the Grammar School, Christ's Hospital" [Coleridge's note]. See also Charles Lamb's essay, *Christ's Hospital Five-and-Thirty Years Ago*.

3. Didymus of Alexandria (ca. 65 B.C.– A.D. 10) was the author of a commentary on the text of Homer.

tion to him. In fancy I can almost hear him now, exclaiming, "Harp? Harp? Lyre? Pen and ink, boy, you mean! Muse, boy, muse? Your nurse's daughter, you mean! Pierian spring? Oh, aye! the cloister pump, I suppose!" Nay, certain introductions, similes, and examples were placed by name on a list of interdiction. Among the similes there was, I remember, that of the manchincel fruit,[4] as suiting equally well with too many subjects, in which, however, it yielded the palm at once to the example of Alexander and Clytus,[5] which was equally good and apt whatever might be the theme. Was it ambition? Alexander and Clytus! Flattery? Alexander and Clytus! Anger? Drunkenness? Pride? Friendship? Ingratitude? Late repentance? Still, still Alexander and Clytus! At length the praises of agriculture having been exemplified in the sagacious observation that, had Alexander been holding the plow, he would not have run his friend Clytus through with a spear, this tried and serviceable old friend was banished by public edict *in secula seculorum*.[6] I have sometimes ventured to think that a list of this kind or an *index expurgatorius* of certain well-known and ever returning phrases, both introductory and transitional, including the large assortment of modest egotisms and flattering illeisms,[7] etc., etc., might be hung up in our law courts and both Houses of Parliament with great advantage to the public as an important saving of national time, an incalculable relief to his Majesty's ministers; but, above all, as insuring the thanks of country attorneys and their clients, who have private bills to carry through the House.

Be this as it may, there was one custom of our master's which I cannot pass over in silence, because I think it imitable and worthy of imitation. He would often permit our theme exercises, under some pretext of want of time, to accumulate till each lad had four or five to be looked over. Then placing the whole number *abreast* on his desk, he would ask the writer why this or that sentence might not have found as appropriate a place under this or that other thesis; and if no satisfying answer could be returned and two faults of the same kind were found in one exercise, the irrevocable verdict followed, the exercise was torn up, and another on the same subject to be produced, in addition to the tasks of the day. The reader will, I trust, excuse this tribute of recollection to a man whose severities, even now, not seldom furnish the dreams by which the blind fancy would fain interpret to the mind the painful sensations of distempered sleep; but neither lessen nor dim the deep sense of my moral and intellectual obligations. He sent us to the university excellent Latin and Greek scholars and tolerable

---

4. Poisonous, though attractive in appearance.
5. Plutarch's *Life* of Alexander the Great relates that the king killed his friend Clytus in a drunken quarrel.
6. Forever ("for centuries of centuries").
7. Excessive use of the pronoun "he" (in Latin, *ille*).

Hebraists. Yet our classical knowledge was the least of the good gifts which we derived from his zealous and conscientious tutorage. He is now gone to his final reward, full of years and full of honors, even of those honors which were dearest to his heart as gratefully bestowed by that school, and still binding him to the interests of that school in which he had been himself educated and to which during his whole life he was a dedicated thing. * * *

I had just entered on my seventeenth year when the sonnets of Mr. Bowles,[8] twenty in number, and just then published in a quarto pamphlet, were first made known and presented to me by a schoolfellow who had quitted us for the university and who, during the whole time that he was in our first form (or in our school language, a Grecian), had been my patron and protector. I refer to Dr. Middleton, the truly learned and every way excellent Bishop of Calcutta * * *

It was a double pleasure to me, and still remains a tender recollection, that I should have received from a friend so revered the first knowledge of a poet by whose works, year after year, I was so enthusiastically delighted and inspired. My earliest acquaintances will not have forgotten the undisciplined eagerness and impetuous zeal with which I laboured to make proselytes, not only of my companions, but of all with whom I conversed, of whatever rank and in whatever place. As my school finances did not permit me to purchase copies I made, within less than a year and a half, more than forty transcriptions, as the best presents I could offer to those who had in any way won my regard. And with almost equal delight did I receive the three or four following publications of the same author.

Though I have seen and known enough of mankind to be well aware that I shall perhaps stand alone in my creed, and that it will be well if I subject myself to no worse charge than that of singularity, I am not therefore deterred from avowing that I regard and ever have regarded the obligations of intellect among the most sacred of the claims of gratitude. A valuable thought, or a particular train of thoughts, gives me additional pleasure when I can safely refer and attribute it to the conversation or correspondence of another. My obligations to Mr. Bowles were indeed important and for radical good. At a very premature age, even before my fifteenth year, I had bewildered myself in metaphysics and in theological controversy. Nothing else pleased me. History and particular facts lost all interest in my mind. Poetry (though for a

8. William Lisle Bowles (1762–1850) published in 1789 two editions of a collection of sonnets setting forth, in simple and fluent language, the pensive meditations evoked from a traveler by the varying scene. Coleridge's immense admiration for Bowles (which was shared to a lesser degree by Wordsworth) has puzzled literary historians; but Bowles did point the way to the long lyric of description and meditation, in heightened colloquial language, which became a major Romantic genre.

schoolboy of that age I was above par in English versification and
had already produced two or three compositions which, I may venture to say without reference to my age, were somewhat above
mediocrity, and which had gained me more credit than the sound
good sense of my old master was at all pleased with), poetry itself,
yea novels and romances, became insipid to me. In my friendless
wanderings on our leave-days (for I was an orphan, and had scarce
any connections in London), highly was I delighted if any passenger, especially if he were dressed in black,[9] would enter into
conversation with me. For I soon found the means of directing it
to my favorite subjects

> Of providence, foreknowledge, will, and fate,
> Fixed fate, free will, foreknowledge absolute,
> And found no end, in wandering mazes lost.[1]

This preposterous pursuit was, beyond doubt, injurious both to
my natural powers and to the progress of my education. It would
perhaps have been destructive had it been continued; but from this
I was auspiciously withdrawn, partly indeed by an accidental introduction to an amiable family,[2] chiefly however by the genial influence of a style of poetry so tender and yet so manly, so natural
and real, and yet so dignified and harmonious, as the sonnets, etc.,
of Mr. Bowles! Well were it for me, perhaps, had I never relapsed
into the same mental disease; if I had continued to pluck the flower
and reap the harvest from the cultivated surface, instead of delving
in the unwholesome quicksilver mines of metaphysic depths. But
if in after time I have sought a refuge from bodily pain and mis-
managed sensibility in abstruse researches, which exercised the
strength and subtlety of the understanding without awakening the
feelings of the heart; still there was a long and blessed interval, during which my natural faculties were allowed to expand and my original tendencies to develop themselves; my fancy, and the love of
nature, and the sense of beauty in forms and sounds.

The second advantage which I owe to my early perusal and admiration of these poems (to which let me add, though known to
me at a somewhat later period, the *Lewesdon Hill* of Mr. Crow)[3]
bears more immediately on my present subject. Among those with
whom I conversed there were, of course, very many who had formed
their taste and their notions of poetry from the writings of Mr.
Pope and his followers: or to speak more generally, in that school
of French poetry condensed and invigorated by English understanding which had predominated from the last century. I was not blind

9. I.e., if he were a clergyman.
1. *Paradise Lost* II.559–61.
2. The family of Mary Evans, with
whom Coleridge fell deeply in love in
1788.
3. William Crow(e) (1745–1829) pub-

lished in 1788 *Lewesdon Hill*, a long
poem in blank verse which, like
Bowles's sonnets, combined descriptions
of the natural scene with associated
moral and personal reflections.

to the merits of this school, yet as from inexperience of the world and consequent want of sympathy with the general subjects of these poems they gave me little pleasure, I doubtless undervalued the *kind*, and with the presumption of youth withheld from its masters the legitimate name of poets. I saw that the excellence of this kind consisted in just and acute observations on men and manners in an artificial state of society as its matter and substance, and in the logic of wit conveyed in smooth and strong epigrammatic couplets as its *form*. Even when the subject was addressed to the fancy or the intellect, as in the *Rape of the Lock* or the *Essay on Man*; nay, when it was a consecutive narration, as in that astonishing product of matchless talent and ingenuity, Pope's translation of the *Iliad*; still a *point* was looked for at the end of each second line, and the whole was as it were a sorites or, if I may exchange a logical for a grammatical metaphor, a *conjunction disjunctive*,[4] of epigrams. Meantime the matter and diction seemed to me characterized not so much by poetic thoughts as by thoughts *translated* into the language of poetry. On this last point I had occasion to render my own thoughts gradually more and more plain to myself by frequent amicable disputes concerning Darwin's *Botanic Garden*,[5] which for some years was greatly extolled, not only by the *reading* public in general, but even by those whose genius and natural robustness of understanding enabled them afterwards to act foremost in dissipating these "painted mists" that occasionally rise from the marshes at the foot of Parnassus. During my first Cambridge vacation I assisted a friend in a contribution for a literary society in Devonshire, and in this I remember to have compared Darwin's work to the Russian palace of ice, glittering, cold, and transitory. In the same essay too I assigned sundry reasons, chiefly drawn from a comparison of passages in the Latin poets with the original Greek from which they were borrowed, for the preference of Collins's odes to those of Gray, and of the simile in Shakespeare:

> How like a younker or a prodigal
> The scarfed bark puts from her native bay,
> Hugged and embraced by the strumpet wind!
> How like the prodigal doth she return,
> With over-weathered ribs and ragged sails,
> Lean, rent and beggared by the strumpet wind![6]

to the imitation in the *Bard*:

> Fair laughs the morn, and soft the zephyr blows
> While proudly riding o'er the azure realm

4. "Sorites": a procession of logical propositions; *"conjunction disjunctive"*: a word which connects the parts of a sentence but expresses an alternative or opposition: "or," "but," "lest," etc.

5. Published in 1789–91 by Erasmus Darwin (1731–1802); a long poem in closed couplets, presenting the science of botany in elaborate allegories.
6. *Merchant of Venice* II.vi.14–19.

In gallant trim the gilded vessel goes;
YOUTH on the prow, and PLEASURE at the helm;
Regardless of the sweeping whirlwind's sway,
That, hushed in grim repose, expects its evening prey.[7]

(In which, by the bye, the words "realm" and "sway" are rhymes
dearly purchased.) I preferred the original, on the ground that in
the imitation it depended wholly in the compositor's putting, or
not putting, a small capital both in this and in many other passages
of the same poet whether the words should be personifications or
mere abstracts. I mention this because, in referring various lines
in Gray to their original in Shakespeare and Milton, and in the
clear perception how completely all the propriety was lost in the
transfer, I was at that early period led to a conjecture which, many
years afterwards, was recalled to me from the same thought having
been started in conversation, but far more ably, and developed
more fully, by Mr. Wordsworth; namely, that this style of poetry
which I have characterized above as translations of prose thoughts
into poetic language had been kept up by, if it did not wholly
arise from, the custom of writing Latin verses and the great importance attached to these exercises in our public schools. Whatever might have been the case in the fifteenth century, when the
use of the Latin tongue was so general among learned men that
Erasmus is said to have forgotten his native language; yet in the
present day it is not to be supposed that a youth can think in Latin,
or that he can have any other reliance on the force or fitness of his
phrases but the authority of the author from whence he had adopted
them. Consequently he must first prepare his thoughts and then
pick out from Virgil, Horace, Ovid, or perhaps more compendiously,
from his *Gradus*,[8] halves and quarters of lines in which to embody
them.

I never object to a certain degree of disputatiousness in a young
man from the age of seventeen to that of four or five and twenty,
provided I find him always arguing on one side of the question.
The controversies occasioned by my unfeigned zeal for the honor
of a favorite contemporary, then known to me only by his works,
were of great advantage in the formation and establishment of my
taste and critical opinions. In my defense of the lines running into
each other instead of closing at each couplet, and of natural language, neither bookish nor vulgar, neither redolent of the lamp nor
of the kennel, such as I *will remember thee*; instead of the same
thought tricked up in the rag-fair finery of

———Thy image on her wing
Before my Fancy's eye shall Memory bring,

7. Thomas Gray, *The Bard* (1757).
8. *Gradus ad Parnassum* ("Stairway
to Parnassus"), a dictionary of Latin
words, synonyms, and descriptive epithets, illustrated from the Latin poets.
It was long used as a school text in
Latin composition.

I had continually to adduce the meter and diction of the Greek poets from Homer to Theocritus inclusive; and still more of our elder English poets from Chaucer to Milton. Nor was this all. But as it was my constant reply to authorities brought against me from later poets of great name that no authority could avail in opposition to Truth, Nature, Logic, and the Laws of Universal Grammar; actuated too by my former passion for metaphysical investigations, I labored at a solid foundation on which permanently to ground my opinions in the component faculties of the human mind itself and their comparative dignity and importance. According to the faculty or source from which the pleasure given by any poem or passage was derived I estimated the merit of such poem or passage. As the result of all my reading and meditation, I abstracted two critical aphorisms, deeming them to comprise the conditions and criteria of poetic style: first, that not the poem which we have *read*, but that to which we *return* with the greatest pleasure, possesses the genuine power and claims the name of *essential* poetry. Second, that whatever lines can be translated into other words of the same language without diminution of their significance, either in sense of association or in any worthy feeling, are so far vicious in their diction. Be it however observed that I excluded from the list of worthy feelings the pleasure derived from mere novelty in the reader, and the desire of exciting wonderment at his powers in the author. Oftentimes since then, in perusing French tragedies, I have fancied two marks of admiration at the end of each line, as hieroglyphics of the author's own admiration at his own cleverness. Our genuine admiration of a great poet is a continuous undercurrent of feeling; it is everywhere present, but seldom anywhere as a separate excitement. I was wont boldly to affirm that it would be scarcely more difficult to push a stone out from the pyramids with the bare hand than to alter a word, or the position of a word, in Milton or Shakespeare (in their most important works at least), without making the auther say something else, or something worse, than he does say. One great distinction I appeared to myself to see plainly, between even the characteristic faults of our elder poets and the false beauties of the moderns. In the former, from Donne to Cowley, we find the most fantastic out-of-the-way thoughts, but in the most pure and genuine mother English; in the latter, the most obvious thoughts, in language the most fantastic and arbitrary. Our faulty elder poets sacrificed the passion and passionate flow of poetry to the subtleties of intellect and to the starts of wit; the moderns to the glare and glitter of a perpetual yet broken and heterogeneous imagery, or rather to an amphibious something, made up half of image and half of abstract[9] meaning. The one

9. "I remember a ludicrous instance in the poem of a young tradesman: 'No more will I endure Love's pleasing pain, / Or round my *heart's leg* tie his galling chain' " [Coleridge's note].

sacrificed the heart to the head, the other both heart and head to point and drapery. * * *

From *Chapter IV*

Mr. Wordsworth's earlier poems—On fancy and imagination— The investigation of the distinction important to the fine arts.

* * * During the last year of my residence at Cambridge I became acquainted with Mr. Wordsworth's first publication, entitled *Descriptive Sketches;*[1] and seldom, if ever, was the emergence of an original poetic genius above the literary horizon more evidently announced. In the form, style, and manner of the whole poem, and in the structure of the particular lines and periods, there is a harshness and acerbity connected and combined with words and images all aglow which might recall those products of the vegetable world, where gorgeous blossoms rise out of the hard and thorny rind and shell within which the rich fruit was elaborating. The language was not only peculiar and strong, but at times knotty and contorted, as by its own impatient strength; while the novelty and struggling crowd of images acting in conjunction with the difficulties of the style demanded always a greater closeness of attention than poetry (at all events than descriptive poetry) has a right to claim. It not seldom therefore justified the complaint of obscurity. In the following extract I have sometimes fancied that I saw an emblem of the poem itself and of the author's genius as it was then displayed:

'Tis storm; and hid in mist from hour to hour,
All day the floods a deepening murmur pour,
The sky is veiled, and every cheerful sight;
Dark is the region as with coming night;
And yet what frequent bursts of overpowering light!
Triumphant on the bosom of the storm,
Glances the fire-clad eagle's wheeling form;
Eastward, in long perspective glittering, shine
The wood-crowned cliffs that o'er the lake recline;
Wide o'er the Alps a hundred streams unfold,
At once to pillars turned that flame with gold;
Behind his sail the peasant strives to shun
The West, that burns like one dilated sun,
Where in a mighty crucible expire
The mountains, glowing hot, like coals of fire.[2]

The poetic Psyche, in its process to full development, undergoes as many changes as its Greek namesake, the butterfly.[3] And it is

1. Published 1793, the year before Coleridge left Cambridge; a long descriptive-meditative poem in closed couplets.
2. *Descriptive Sketches* (1815 version), lines 332 ff.
3. "In Greek, Psyche is the common name for the soul and the butterfly" [Coleridge's note].

remarkable how soon genius clears and purifies itself from the faults and errors of its earliest products; faults which, in its earliest compositions, are the more obtrusive and confluent because, as heterogeneous elements which had only a temporary use, they constitute the very *ferment* by which themselves are carried off. Or we may compare them to some diseases, which must work on the humors and be thrown out on the surface in order to secure the patient from their future recurrence. I was in my twenty-fourth year when I had the happiness of knowing Mr. Wordsworth personally;[4] and, while memory lasts, I shall hardly forget the sudden effect produced on my mind by his recitation of a manuscript poem which still remains unpublished, but of which the stanza and tone of style were the same as those of *The Female Vagrant* as originally printed in the first volume of the *Lyrical Ballads*.[5] There was here no mark of strained thought or forced diction, no crowd or turbulence of imagery, and, as the poet hath himself well described in his lines on revisiting the Wye, manly reflection and human associations had given both variety and an additional interest to natural objects which in the passion and appetite of the first love they had seemed to him neither to need or permit.[6] The occasional obscurities which had risen from an imperfect control over the resources of his native language had almost wholly disappeared, together with that worse defect of arbitrary and illogical phrases, at once hackneyed and fantastic, which hold so distinguished a place in the *technique* of ordinary poetry and will, more or less, alloy the earlier poems of the truest genius, unless the attention has been specifically directed to their worthlessness and incongruity. I did not perceive anything particular in the mere style of the poem alluded to during its recitation, except indeed such difference as was not separable from the thought and manner; and the Spenserian stanza which always, more or less, recalls to the reader's mind Spenser's own style, would doubtless have authorized in my then opinion a more frequent descent to the phrases of ordinary life than could, without an ill effect, have been hazarded in the heroic couplet. It was not however the freedom from false taste, whether as to common defects or to those more properly his own, which made so unusual an impression on my feelings immediately, and subsequently on my judgment. It was the union of deep feeling with profound thought; the fine balance of truth in observing with the imaginative faculty in modifying the objects observed; and above all the original gift of spreading the tone, the *atmosphere*, and with it the depth and height of the ideal world, around forms,

4. The meeting occurred in September, 1795.

5. *Guilt and Sorrow*, composed between 1791 and 1794; a revised portion of this poem was published as *The Female Vagrant* in *Lyrical Ballads* (1798).

6. Wordsworth's *Tintern Abbey*, lines 76 ff.

incidents, and situations of which, for the common view, custom had bedimmed all the luster, had dried up the sparkle and the dew-drops. "To find no contradiction in the union of old and new, to contemplate the Ancient of Days and all his works with feelings as fresh as if all had then sprang forth at the first creative fiat, characterizes the mind that feels the riddle of the world and may help to unravel it. To carry on the feelings of childhood into the powers of manhood; to combine the child's sense of wonder and novelty with the appearances which every day for perhaps forty years had rendered familiar:

> With sun and moon and stars throughout the year
> And man and woman;[7]

this is the character and privilege of genius, and one of the marks which distinguish genius from talents. And therefore it is the prime merit of genius, and its most unequivocal mode of manifestation, so to represent familiar objects as to awaken in the minds of others a kindred feeling concerning them, and that freshness of sensation which is the constant accompaniment of mental no less than of bodily convalescence. Who has not a thousand times seen snow fall on water? Who has not watched it with a new feeling from the time that he has read Burns' comparison of sensual pleasure:

> To snow that falls upon a river
> A moment white—then gone forever![8]

In poems, equally as in philosophic disquisitions, genius produces the strongest impressions of novelty while it rescues the most ad-mitted truths from the impotence caused by the very circumstance of their universal admission. Truths of all others the most awful and mysterious, yet being at the same time of universal interest, are too often considered as so true, that they lose all the life and efficiency of truth and lie bedridden in the dormitory of the soul side by side with the most despised and exploded errors." *The Friend*, p. 76, No. 5.[9]

This excellence, which in all Mr. Wordsworth's writings is more or less predominant and which constitutes the character of his mind, I no sooner felt than I sought to understand. Repeated medi-tations led me first to suspect (and a more intimate analysis of the human faculties, their appropriate marks, functions, and effects, matured my conjecture into full conviction) that fancy and imagi-nation were two distinct and widely different faculties, instead of being, according to the general belief, either two names with one meaning, or at furthest the lower and higher degree of one and the same power. It is not, I own, easy to conceive a more apposite

7. Altered from Milton's sonnet *To Mr. Cyriack Skinner upon his Blindness.*
8. Altered from Burns, *Tam o' Shanter,* lines 61–62.
9. *The Friend* was a periodical pub-lished by Coleridge (1809–10).

translation of the Greek *phantasia* than the Latin *imaginatio;* but it is equally true that in all societies there exists an instinct of growth, a certain collective unconscious good sense working progressively to desynonymize those words originally of the same meaning which the conflux of dialects had supplied to the more homogeneous languages, as the Greek and German, and which the same cause, joined with accidents of translation from original works of different countries, occasion in mixed languages like our own. The first and most important point to be proved is that two conceptions perfectly distinct are confused under one and the same word, and (this done) to appropriate that word exclusively to one meaning, and the synonym (should there be one) to the other. But if (as will be often the case in the arts and sciences) no synonym exists, we must either invent or borrow a word. In the present instance the appropriation had already begun and been legitimated in the derivative adjective: Milton had a highly *imaginative*, Cowley a very *fanciful*, mind. If therefore I should succeed in establishing the actual existence of two faculties generally different, the nomenclature would be at once determined. To the faculty by which I had characterized Milton we should confine the term *imagination;* while the other would be contra-distinguished as *fancy*. Now were it once fully ascertained that this division is no less grounded in nature than that of delirium from mania, or Otway's

> Lutes, lobsters, seas of milk, and ships of amber,[1]

from Shakespeare's

> What! have his daughters brought him to this pass?[2]

or from the preceding apostrophe to the elements, the theory of the fine arts and of poetry in particular could not, I thought, but derive some additional and important light. It would in its immediate effects furnish a torch of guidance to the philosophical critic, and ultimately to the poet himself. In energetic minds truth soon changes by domestication into power; and from directing in the discrimination and appraisal of the product becomes influencive in the production. To admire on principle is the only way to imitate without loss of originality. * * *

From *Chapter XIII*

On the imagination, or esemplastic[3] power.

* * * The IMAGINATION, then, I consider either as primary, or secondary. The primary IMAGINATION I hold to be the living power and prime agent of all human perception, and as a repetition in

---

1. Thomas Otway, in *Venice Preserved* (1682), wrote "laurels" in place of "lobsters" (V.ii.151).
2. *King Lear* III.iv.63.
3. Coleridge coined this word and used it to mean "molding into unity."

the finite mind of the eternal act of creation in the infinite I AM. The secondary I consider as an echo of the former, coexisting with the conscious will, yet still as identical with the primary in the *kind* of its agency, and differing only in *degree*, and in the *mode* of its operation. It dissolves, diffuses, dissipates, in order to re-create; or where this process is rendered impossible, yet still, at all events, it struggles to idealize and to unify. It is essentially *vital*, even as all objects (*as* objects) are essentially fixed and dead.

FANCY, on the contrary, has no other counters to play with but fixities and definites. The fancy is indeed no other than a mode of memory emancipated from the order of time and space; and blended with, and modified by that empirical phenomenon of the will which we express by the word CHOICE. But equally with the ordinary memory it must receive all its materials ready made from the law of association.[4] * * *

Chapter XIV

Occasion of the Lyrical Ballads, *and the objects originally proposed—Preface to the second edition—The ensuing controversy, its causes and acrimony—Philosophic definitions of a poem and poetry with scholia.*[5]

During the first year that Mr. Wordsworth and I were neighbors[6] our conversations turned frequently on the two cardinal points of poetry, the power of exciting the sympathy of the reader by a faithful adherence to the truth of nature, and the power of giving the interest of novelty by the modifying colors of imagination.[7] The sudden charm which accidents of light and shade, which moonlight or sunset diffused over a known and familiar landscape, appeared to represent the practicability of combining both. These are the poetry of nature. The thought suggested itself (to which of us I do not recollect) that a series of poems might be composed of two sorts. In the one, the incidents and agents were to be, in part at least, supernatural; and the excellence aimed at was to consist in the interesting of the affections by the dramatic truth of such emotions as would naturally accompany such situations, supposing them real. And real in *this* sense they have been to every human being who, from whatever source of delusion, has at any

4. Coleridge conceives God's creation to be a continuous process, which has an analogy in the creative perception ("primary imagination") of all human minds. The creative process is repeated, or "echoed," on still a third level, by the "secondary imagination" of the poet, which dissolves the products of primary perception in order to shape them into a new and unified creation—the imaginative passage or poem. The "fancy," on the other hand, can only manipulate "fixities and definites" which, linked by association, come to it ready-made from perception. Its products, therefore, are not re-creations (echoes of God's original creative process), but mosaic-like reassemblies of existing bits and pieces.
5. Additional remarks, after a philosophic demonstration.
6. At Nether Stowey and Alfoxden, Somerset, in 1797.
7. Cf. Wordsworth's account in his Preface to *Lyrical Ballads*.

time believed himself under supernatural agency. For the second class, subjects were to be chosen from ordinary life; the characters and incidents were to be such as will be found in every village and its vicinity where there is a meditative and feeling mind to seek after them, or to notice them when they present themselves.

In this idea originated the plan of the *Lyrical Ballads*; in which it was agreed that my endeavors should be directed to persons and characters supernatural, or at least romantic; yet so as to transfer from our inward nature a human interest and a semblance of truth sufficient to procure for these shadows of imagination that willing suspension of disbelief for the moment, which constitutes poetic faith. Mr. Wordsworth, on the other hand, was to propose to himself as his object to give the charm of novelty to things of every day, and to excite a feeling analogous to the supernatural, by awakening the mind's attention from the lethargy of custom and directing it to the loveliness and the wonders of the world before us; an inexhaustible treasure, but for which, in consequence of the film of familiarity and selfish solicitude, we have eyes yet see not, ears that hear not, and hearts that neither feel nor understand.[8]

With this view I wrote the *Ancient Mariner*, and was preparing, among other poems, the *Dark Ladie*, and the *Christabel*, in which I should have more nearly realized my ideal than I had done in my first attempt. But Mr. Wordsworth's industry had proved so much more successful and the number of his poems so much greater, that my compositions, instead of forming a balance, appeared rather an interpolation of heterogeneous matter.[9] Mr. Wordsworth added two or three poems written in his own character, in the impassioned, lofty, and sustained diction which is characteristic of his genius. In this form the *Lyrical Ballads* were published; and were presented by him, as an *experiment*,[1] whether subjects which from their nature rejected the usual ornaments and extra-colloquial style of poems in general might not be so managed in the language of ordinary life as to produce the pleasurable interest which it is the peculiar business of poetry to impart. To the second edition[2] he added a preface of considerable length; in which, notwithstanding some passages of apparently a contrary import, he was understood to contend for the extension of this style to poetry of all kinds, and to reject as vicious and indefensible all phrases and forms of style that were not included in what he (unfortunately, I think, adopting an equivocal expression) called the language of *real* life. From this preface, prefixed to poems in which it was impossible to deny the presence of original genius, however mistaken its direction might

8. Cf. Isaiah vi.9–10.
9. The first edition of *Lyrical Ballads*, published anonymously in 1798, contained nineteen poems by Wordsworth, four by Coleridge.

1. "Experiments" was also the word used by Wordsworth in his "Advertisement" to the first edition.
2. Of 1800.

be deemed, arose the whole long continued controversy.[3] For from the conjunction of perceived power with supposed heresy I explain the inveteracy and in some instances, I grieve to say, the acrimonious passions with which the controversy has been conducted by the assailants.

Had Mr. Wordsworth's poems been the silly, the childish things which they were for a long time described as being; had they been really distinguished from the compositions of other poets merely by meanness of language and inanity of thought; had they indeed contained nothing more than what is found in the parodies and pretended imitations of them; they must have sunk at once, a dead weight, into the slough of oblivion, and have dragged the preface along with them. But year after year increased the number of Mr. Wordsworth's admirers. They were found too not in the lower classes of the reading public, but chiefly among young men of strong sensibility and meditative minds; and their admiration (inflamed perhaps in some degree by opposition) was distinguished by its intensity, I might almost say, by its *religious* fervor. These facts, and the intellectual energy of the author, which was more or less consciously felt where it was outwardly and even boisterously denied, meeting with sentiments of aversion to his opinions and of alarm at their consequences, produced an eddy of criticism which would of itself have borne up the poems by the violence with which it whirled them round and round. With many parts of this preface, in the sense attributed to them and which the words undoubtedly seem to authorize, I never concurred; but, on the contrary objected to them as erroneous in principle, and as contradictory (in appearance at least) both to other parts of the same preface and to the author's own practice in the greater number of the poems themselves. Mr. Wordsworth in his recent collection[4] has, I find, degraded this prefatory disquisition to the end of his second volume, to be read or not at the reader's choice. But he has not, as far as I can discover, announced any change in his poetic creed. At all events, considering it as the source of a controversy in which I have been honored more than I deserve by the frequent conjunction of my name with his, I think it expedient to declare once for all in what points I coincide with his opinions, and in what points I altogether differ. But in order to render myself intelligible I must previously, in as few words as possible, explain my ideas, first, of a POEM; and secondly, of POETRY itself, in *kind* and in *essence*.

The office of philosophical *disquisition* consists in just *distinction*; while it is the privilege of the philosopher to preserve himself constantly aware that distinction is not division. In order to ob-

3. The controversy over Wordsworth's theory and poetical practice in the literary journals of the day.

4. Wordsworth's *Poems*, two volumes, 1815.

tain adequate notions of any truth, we must intellectually separate its distinguishable parts; and this is the technical *process* of philosophy. But having so done, we must then restore them in our conceptions to the unity in which they actually coexist; and this is the *result* of philosophy. A poem contains the same elements as a prose composition; the difference therefore must consist in a different combination of them, in consequence of a different object proposed. According to the difference of the object will be the difference of the combination. It is possible that the object may be merely to facilitate the recollection of any given facts or observations by artificial arrangement; and the composition will be a poem, merely because it is distinguished from prose by meter, or by rhyme, or by both conjointly. In this, the lowest sense, a man might attribute the name of a poem to the well-known enumeration of the days in the several months:

> Thirty days hath September
> April, June, and November, etc.

and others of the same class and purpose. And as a particular pleasure is found in anticipating the recurrence of sounds and quantities, all compositions that have this charm superadded, whatever be their contents, *may* be entitled poems.

So much for the superficial *form*. A difference of object and contents supplies an additional ground of distinction. The immediate purpose may be the communication of truths; either of truth absolute and demonstrable, as in works of science; or of facts experienced and recorded, as in history. Pleasure, and that of the highest and most permanent kind, may *result* from the *atttainment* of the end; but it is not itself the immediate end. In other works the communication of pleasure may be the immediate purpose; and though truth, either moral or intellectual, ought to be the *ultimate* end, yet this will distinguish the character of the author, not the class to which the work belongs. Blessed indeed is that state of society in which the immediate purpose would be baffled by the perversion of the proper ultimate end; in which no charm of diction or imagery could exempt the Bathyllus even of an Anacreon, or the Alexis of Virgil,[5] from disgust and aversion!

But the communication of pleasure may be the immediate object of a work not metrically composed; and that object may have been in a high degree attained, as in novels and romances. Would then the mere superaddition of meter, with or without rhyme, entitle *these* to the name of poems? The answer is that nothing can permanently please which does not contain in itself the reason why it is so, and not otherwise. If meter be superadded, all other

---

5. The reference is to poems of homosexual love. "Bathyllus" was a beautiful boy praised by Anacreon, a Greek lyric poet (ca. 560–475 B.C.); "Alexis" was a young man loved by the shepherd Corydon in Virgil's *Eclogues* II.

parts must be made consonant with it. They must be such as to justify the perpetual and distinct attention to each part which an exact correspondent recurrence of accent and sound are calculated to excite. The final definition then, so deduced, may be thus worded. A poem is that species of composition which is opposed to works of science by proposing for its *immediate* object pleasure, not truth; and from all other species (having *this* object in common with it) it is discriminated by proposing to itself such delight from the *whole* as is compatible with a distinct gratification from each component *part*.

Controversy is not seldom excited in consequence of the disputants attaching each a different meaning to the same word; and in few instances has this been more striking than in disputes concerning the present subject. If a man chooses to call every composition a poem which is rhyme, or measure, or both, I must leave his opinion uncontroverted. The distinction is at least competent to characterize the writer's intention. If it were subjoined that the whole is likewise entertaining or affecting as a tale or as a series of interesting reflections, I of course admit this as another fit ingredient of a poem and an additional merit. But if the definition sought for be that of a *legitimate* poem, I answer it must be one the parts of which mutually support and explain each other; all in their proportion harmonizing with, and supporting the purpose and known influences of metrical arrangement. The philosophic critics of all ages coincide with the ultimate judgment of all countries in equally denying the praises of a just poem on the one hand to a series of striking lines or distichs,[6] each of which absorbing the whole attention of the reader to itself disjoins it from its context and makes it a separate whole, instead of a harmonizing part; and on the other hand, to an unsustained composition, from which the reader collects rapidly the general result unattracted by the component parts. The reader should be carried forward, not merely or chiefly by the mechanical impulse of curiosity, or by a restless desire to arrive at the final solution; but by the pleasurable activity of mind excited by the attractions of the journey itself. Like the motion of a serpent, which the Egyptians made the emblem of intellectual power; or like the path of sound through the air; at every step he pauses and half recedes, and from the retrogressive movement collects the force which again carries him onward. *"Praecipitandus est liber spiritus,"* says Petronius Arbiter most happily.[7] The epithet *liber* here balances the preceding verb; and it is not easy to conceive more meaning condensed in fewer words.

But if this should be admitted as a satisfactory character of a poem, we have still to seek for a definition of poetry. The writings

6. Pairs of lines.
7. "The free spirit [of the poet] must be hurled onward." From the *Satyricon,* by the lively Roman satirist, Petronius Arbiter (1st century A.D.).

of Plato, and Bishop Taylor, and the *Theoria Sacra* of Burnet,[8] furnish undeniable proofs that poetry of the highest kind may exist without meter, and even without the contradistinguishing objects of a poem. The first chapter of Isaiah (indeed a very large proportion of the whole book) is poetry in the most emphatic sense; yet it would be not less irrational than strange to assert that pleasure, and not truth, was the immediate object of the prophet. In short, whatever *specific* import we attach to the word poetry, there will be found involved in it, as a necessary consequence, that a poem of any length neither can be, nor ought to be, all poetry.[9] Yet if a harmonious whole is to be produced, the remaining parts must be preserved *in keeping* with the poetry; and this can be no otherwise effected than by such a studied selection and artificial arrangement as will partake of *one*, though not a *peculiar*, property of poetry. And this again can be no other than the property of exciting a more continuous and equal attention than the language of prose aims at, whether colloquial or written.

My own conclusions on the nature of poetry, in the strictest use of the word, have been in part anticipated in the preceding disquisition on the fancy and imagination. What is poetry? is so nearly the same question with, what is a poet? that the answer to the one is involved in the solution of the other. For it is a distinction resulting from the poetic genius itself, which sustains and modifies the images, thoughts, and emotions of the poet's own mind. The poet, described in *ideal* perfection, brings the whole soul of man into activity, with the subordination of its faculties to each other, according to their relative worth and dignity. He diffuses a tone and spirit of unity that blends and (as it were) *fuses*, each into each, by that synthetic and magical power to which we have exclusively appropriated the name of imagination. This power, first put in action by the will and understanding and retained under their irremissive, though gentle and unnoticed, control (*laxis effertur habenis*[1]) reveals itself in the balance or reconciliation of opposite or discordant qualities:[2] of sameness, with difference; of the general, with the concrete; the idea, with the image; the individual, with the representative; the sense of novelty and freshness, with old and familiar objects; a more than usual state of emotion,

---

8. Bishop Jeremy Taylor (1613–67), author of *Holy Living* and *Holy Dying;* Thomas Burnet, author of *The Sacred Theory of the Earth* (1681–89). Coleridge greatly admired the elaborate and sonorous prose of both these writers; he took from a work by Burnet the Latin motto for *The Ancient Mariner*.
9. Coleridge does not use the word "poetry" in the usual way, as a term for the class of all metrical compositions, but to designate those passages, whether in verse or prose, produced by the mind of genius in its supreme mo-

ments of imaginative activity.
1. I.e., driven with loosened reins.
2. Here Coleridge introduces into English criticism the concept that the highest poetry incorporates and reconciles opposite or discordant elements; under the names of "irony" and "paradox," this concept has become a primary criterion of the "new criticism" of our day. Although admittedly derived from Coleridge, the concept, by a further irony, has usually been employed to derogate Romantic poetry.

with more than usual order; judgment ever awake and steady self-possession, with enthusiasm and feeling profound or vehement; and while it blends and harmonizes the natural and the artificial, still subordinates art to nature; the manner to the matter; and our admiration of the poet to our sympathy with the poetry. "Doubtless," as Sir John Davies observes of the soul (and his words may with slight alteration be applied, and even more appropriately, to the poetic IMAGINATION):

> Doubtless this could not be, but that she turns
> Bodies to spirit by sublimation strange,
> As fire converts to fire the things it burns,
> As we our food into our nature change.
>
> From their gross matter she abstracts their forms,
> And draws a kind of quintessence from things;
> Which to her proper nature she transforms
> To bear them light on her celestial wings.
>
> Thus does she, when from individual states
> She doth abstract the universal kinds;
> Which then reclothed in divers names and fates
> Steal access through our senses to our minds.[3]

Finally, GOOD SENSE is the BODY of poetic genius, FANCY its DRAPERY, MOTION its LIFE, and IMAGINATION the SOUL that is everywhere, and in each; and forms all into one graceful and intelligent whole.

From *Chapter XVII*

Examination of the tenets peculiar to Mr. Wordsworth—Rustic life (above all, low and rustic life) especially unfavorable to the formation of a human diction—The best parts of language the products of philosophers, not clowns or shepherds—Poetry essentially ideal and generic—The language of Milton as much the language of real life, yea, incomparably more so than that of the cottager.

As far then as Mr. Wordsworth in his preface contended, and most ably contended, for a reformation in our poetic diction, as far as he has evinced the truth of passion, and the *dramatic* propriety of those figures and metaphors in the original poets which, stripped of their justifying reasons and converted into mere artifices of connection or ornament, constitute the characteristic falsity in the poetic style of the moderns; and as far as he has, with equal acuteness and clearness, pointed out the process by which this change was effected and the resemblances between that state into which the reader's mind is thrown by the pleasurable confusion of

3. Adapted from John Davies' *Nosce Teipsum* ("Know Thyself"), a philosophical poem (1599).

thought from an unaccustomed train of words and images and that state which is induced by the natural language of impassioned feeling, he undertook a useful task and deserves all praise, both for the attempt and for the execution. The provocations to this remonstrance in behalf of truth and nature were still of perpetual recurrence before and after the publication of this preface. I cannot likewise but add that the comparison of such poems of merit as have been given to the public within the last ten or twelve years with the majority of those produced previously to the appearance of that preface leave no doubt on my mind that Mr. Wordsworth is fully justified in believing his efforts to have been by no means ineffectual. Not only in the verses of those who have professed their admiration of his genius, but even of those who have distinguished themselves by hostility to his theory and depreciation of his writings, are the impressions of his principles plainly visible. It is possible that with these principles others may have been blended, which are not equally evident, and some which are unsteady and subvertible from the narrowness or imperfection of their basis. But it is more than possible that these errors of defect or exaggeration, by kindling and feeding the controversy, may have conduced not only to the wider propagation of the accompanying truths, but that, by their frequent presentation to the mind in an excited state they may have won for them a more permanent and practical result. A man will borrow a part from his opponent the more easily, if he feels himself justified in continuing to reject a part. While there remain important points in which he can still feel himself in the right, in which he still finds firm footing for continued resistance, he will gradually adopt those opinions which were the least remote from his own convictions as not less congruous with his own theory than with that which he reprobates. In like manner, with a kind of instinctive prudence, he will abandon by little and little his weakest posts, till at length he seems to forget that they had ever belonged to him, or affects to consider them at most as accidental and "petty annexments," the removal of which leaves the citadel unhurt and unendangered.

My own differences from certain supposed parts of Mr. Wordsworth's theory ground themselves on the assumption that his words had been rightly interpreted, as purporting that the proper diction for poetry in general consists altogether in a language taken, with due exceptions, from the mouths of men in real life, a language which actually constitutes the natural conversation of men under the influence of natural feelings.[4] My objection is, first, that in *any* sense this rule is applicable only to *certain* classes of poetry; secondly, that even to these classes it is not applicable, except in

4. Wordsworth, Preface to *Lyrical Ballads* (1800): "a selection of the real language of men in a state of vivid sensation. * * * " The language of men of "humble and rustic life" has been adopted.

such a sense as hath never by anyone (as far as I know or have read) been denied or doubted; and, lastly, that as far as, and in that degree in which it is *practicable,* yet as a *rule* it is useless, if not injurious, and therefore either need not or ought not to be practiced. * * *

Here let me be permitted to remind the reader that the positions which I controvert are contained in the sentences—"a selection of the REAL language of men"; "the language of these men (i.e., men in low and rustic life) I propose to myself to imitate, and as far as possible to adopt the very language of men." "Between the language of prose and that of metrical composition there neither is, nor can be any essential difference." It is against these exclusively that my opposition is directed.

I object, in the very first instance, to an equivocation in the use of the word "real." Every man's language varies according to the extent of his knowledge, the activity of his faculties and the depth or quickness of his feelings. Every man's language has, first, its *individualities;* secondly, the common properties of the *class* to which he belongs; and thirdly, words and phrases of *universal* use. The language of Hooker, Bacon, Bishop Taylor, and Burke differs from the common language of the learned class only by the superior number and novelty of the thoughts and relations which they had to convey. The language of Algernon Sidney[5] differs not at all from that which every well-educated gentleman would wish to write, and (with due allowances for the undeliberateness and less connected train of thinking natural and proper to conversation) such as he would wish to talk. Neither one or the other differ half as much from the general language of cultivated society as the language of Mr. Wordsworth's homeliest composition differs from that of a common peasant. For "real" therefore we must substitute *ordinary,* or *lingua communis.* And this, we have proved, is no more to be found in the phraseology of low and rustic life than in that of any other class. Omit the peculiarities of each, and the result of course must be common to all. And assuredly the omissions and changes to be made in the language of rustics before it could be transferred to any species of poem, except the drama or other professed imitation, are at least as numerous and weighty as would be required in adapting to the same purpose the ordinary language of tradesmen and manufacturers. Not to mention that the language so highly extolled by Mr. Wordsworth varies in every county, nay, in every village, according to the accidental character of the clergyman, the existence or nonexistence of schools; or even, perhaps, as the exciseman, publican, or barber happen to be, or not to be, zealous politicians and readers of the weekly newspaper *pro*

5. Algernon Sidney (1622–83), republican soldier and statesman, author of *Discourses Concerning Government.*

bono publico.[6] Anterior to cultivation the *lingua communis* of every country, as Dante has well observed, exists everywhere in parts and nowhere as a whole.[7]

Neither is the case rendered at all more tenable by the addition of the words "in a state of excitement."[8] For the nature of a man's words, when he is strongly affected by joy, grief, or anger, must necessarily depend on the number and quality of the general truths, conceptions, and images, and of the words expressing them, with which his mind had been previously stored. For the property of passion is not to *create*, but to set in increased activity. At least, whatever new connections of thoughts or images, or (which is equally, if not more than equally, the appropriate effect of strong excitement) whatever generalizations of truth or experience the heat of passion may produce, yet the terms of their conveyance must have pre-existed in his former conversations, and are only collected and crowded together by the unusual stimulation. It is indeed very possible to adopt in a poem the unmeaning repetitions, habitual phrases, and other blank counters which an unfurnished or confused understanding interposes at short intervals in order to keep hold of his subject which is still slipping from him, and to give him time for recollection; or in mere aid of vacancy, as in the scanty companies of a country stage the same player pops backwards and forwards, in order to prevent the appearance of empty spaces, in the procession of *Macbeth* or *Henry VIIIth.* But what assistance to the poet or ornament to the poem these can supply, I am at a loss to conjecture. Nothing assuredly can differ either in origin or in mode more widely from the apparent tautologies of intense and turbulent feeling in which the passion is greater and of longer endurance than to be exhausted or satisfied by a single representation of the image or incident exciting it. Such repetitions I admit to be a beauty of the highest kind; as illustrated by Mr. Wordsworth himself from the song of Deborah. "At her feet he bowed, he fell, he lay down: at her feet he bowed, he fell: where he bowed, there he fell down dead."[9]

1815   1817

From Lectures on Shakespeare[1]
[*Fancy and Imagination in Shakespeare's Poetry*]

In the preceding lecture we have examined with what armor clothed and with what titles authorized Shakespeare came forward

6. "For the public welfare."
7. In *De vulgari eloquentia* ("On the Vulgar Tongue") Dante discusses—and affirms—the fitness for poetry of the unlocalized Italian vernacular.
8. Wordsworth: "the manner in which we associate ideas in a state of excite-

ment."
9. Judges v.27. Cited by Wordsworth in a note to *The Thorn* as an example of the natural tautology of "impassioned feelings."
1. Although Coleridge's series of public lectures on Shakespeare and other

as a poet to demand the throne of fame as the dramatic poet of England; we have now to observe and retrace the excellencies which compelled even his contemporaries to seat him on that throne, although there were giants in those days contending for the same honor. Hereafter we shall endeavor to make out the title of the English drama, as created by and existing in Shakespeare, and its right to the supremacy of dramatic excellence in general. I have endeavored to prove that he had shown himself a *poet*, previously to his appearance [as] a dramatic poet—and that had no *Lear*, no *Othello*, no *Henry the Fourth*, no *Twelfth Night* appeared, we must have admitted that Shakespeare possessed the chief if not all the requisites of a poet—namely, deep feeling and exquisite sense of beauty, both as exhibited to the eye in combinations of form, and to the ear in sweet and appropriate melody (with the exception of Spenser he is [the sweetest of English poets]); that these feelings were under the command of *his own will*—that in his very first productions he projected his mind out of his own particular being, and felt and made others feel, on subjects [in] no way connected with himself, except by force of contemplation, and that sublime faculty, by which a great mind becomes that which it meditates on. To this we are to add the affectionate love of nature and natural objects, without which no man could have observed so steadily, or painted so truly and passionately the very minutest beauties of the external world. Next, we have shown that he possessed fancy, considered as the faculty of bringing together images dissimilar in the main by some one point or more of likeness distinguished.[2]

> Full gently now she takes him by the hand,
> A lily prisoned in a jail of snow,
> Or ivory in an alabaster band—
> So white a friend engirts so white a foe.

Still mounting, we find undoubted proof in his mind of imagination, or the power by which one image or feeling is made to modify many others and by a sort of *fusion to force many into one*—that which after showed itself in such might and energy in *Lear*, where the deep anguish of a father spreads the feeling of ingratitude and cruelty over the very elements of heaven. Various are the workings

poets contained much of his best criticism, he published none of this material, leaving only fragmentary remains of his lectures in notebooks, scraps of manuscript, and notes written in the margins of books. The following selections, which develop some of the basic ideas presented in *Biographia Literaria*, are taken from T. M. Raysor's edition, based on Coleridge's manuscripts and on contemporary reports, of *Coleridge's Shakespearean Criticism* (1930).

2. Coleridge here applies the distinction between fancy and imagination presented in *Biographia Literaria*, Chapter XIII. This passage from the narrative poem *Venus and Adonis* (lines 361–64) is an instance of fancy because the elements brought together remain an assemblage of recognizable and independent "fixities and definites," despite the isolated points of likeness which form the grounds of the comparison.

of this greatest faculty of the human mind—both passionate and tranquil. In its tranquil and purely pleasurable operation, it acts chiefly by producing out of many things, as they would have appeared in the description of an ordinary mind, described slowly and in unimpassioned succession, a oneness, even as nature, the greatest of poets, acts upon us when we open our eyes upon an extended prospect. Thus the flight of Adonis from the enamored goddess in the dusk of evening—

> Look how a bright star shooteth from the sky—
> So glides he in the night from Venus' eye.[3]

How many images and feelings are here brought together without effort and without discord—the beauty of Adonis—the rapidity of his flight—the yearning yet hopelessness of the enamored gazer—and a shadowy ideal character thrown over the whole.[4]—Or it acts by impressing the stamp of humanity, of human feeling, over inanimate objects * * *

> Lo, here the gentle lark, weary of rest,
> From his moist cabinet mounts up on high
> And wakes the morning, from whose silver breast
> The sun ariseth in his majesty;
> Who doth the world so gloriously behold
> That cedar tops and hills seem burnished gold.

And lastly, which belongs only to a great poet, the power of so carrying on the eye of the reader as to make him almost lose the consciousness of words—to make him *see* everything—and this without exciting any painful or laborious attention, without any *anatomy* of description (a fault not uncommon in descriptive poetry) but with the sweetness and easy movement of nature.

Lastly, he previously to his dramas, gave proof of a most profound, energetic, and philosophical mind, without which he might have been a very delightful poet, but not the great dramatic poet * * * But chance and his powerful instinct combined to lead him to his proper province—in the conquest of which we are to consider both the difficulties that opposed him, and the advantages. ca. 1808

[Mechanic vs. Organic Form][5]

The subject of the present lecture is no less than a question submitted to your understandings, emancipated from national prej-

3. *Venus and Adonis*, lines 815–16.
4. An instance of imagination, Coleridge claims, because the component parts—the shooting star and the flight of Adonis, together with the feelings with which both are perceived—dissolve into a new and seamless unity, different in character from the sum of its parts. In the following instance (lines 853–58), the imagination is said to fuse the neutral and inanimate objects with the human nature and feelings of the observer.
5. Coleridge is opposing the earlier view that, because he violates the critical "rules" based on classical drama,

udice: Are the plays of Shakespeare works of rude uncultivated genius, in which the splendor of the parts compensates, if aught can compensate, for the barbarous shapelessness and irregularity of the whole? To which not only the French critics, but even his own English admirers, say [yes]. Or is the form equally admirable with the matter, the judgment of the great poet not less deserving of our wonder than his genius? Or to repeat the question in other words, is Shakespeare a great dramatic poet on account only of these beauties and excellencies which he possesses in common with the ancients, but with diminished claims to our love and honor to the full extent of his difference from them? Or are these very differences additional proofs of poetic wisdom, at once results and symbols of living power as contrasted with lifeless mechanism, of free and rival originality as contradistinguished from servile imitation, or more accurately, [from] a blind copying of effects instead of a true imitation of the essential principles? Imagine not I am about to oppose genius to rules. No! the comparative value of these rules is the very cause to be tried. The spirit of poetry, like all other living powers, must of necessity circumscribe itself by rules, were it only to unite power with beauty. It must embody in order to reveal itself; but a living body is of necessity an organized one—and what is organization but the connection of parts to a whole, so that each part is at once end and means! This is no discovery of criticism; it is a necessity of the human mind—and all nations have felt and obeyed it, in the invention of meter and measured sounds as the vehicle and involucrum[6] of poetry, itself a fellow growth from the same life, even as the bark is to the tree.

No work of true genius dare want its appropriate form; neither indeed is there any danger of this. As it must not, so neither can it, be lawless! For it is even this that constitutes its genius—the power of acting creatively under laws of its own origination. How then comes it that not only single Zoili,[7] but whole nations have combined in unhesitating condemnation of our great dramatist, as a sort of African nature, fertile in beautiful monsters, as a wild heath where islands of fertility look greener from the surrounding waste, where the loveliest plants now shine out among unsightly weeds and now are choked by their parasitic growth, so intertwined

Shakespeare is a highly irregular dramatist whose occasional successes are the result of innate and untutored genius, operating without artistry or judgment. Coleridge's refutation is based on his distinction between the "mechanical form" conceived by neoclassical criticism, and "organic form." Mechanical form results from imposing a pattern of pre-existing rules on the literary material. Shakespeare's organic form, on the other hand, evolves like a plant by an inner principle, according not to rules but to the laws of its own growth, until it achieves an organic unity—a living interdependence of parts and whole in which, as Coleridge says, "each part is at once end and means." The concept of "organic form," in one or another interpretation, has become a cardinal principle in much modern criticism.

6. Outer covering of part of a plant.
7. Plural of "Zoilus," who in classical times was the standard example of a bad critic.

that we cannot disentangle the weed without snapping the flower. In this statement I have had no reference to the vulgar abuse of Voltaire,[8] save as far as his charges are coincident with the decisions of his commentators and (so they tell you) his almost idolatrous admirers. The true ground of the mistake, as has been well remarked by a continental critic,[9] lies in the confounding mechanical regularity with organic form. The form is mechanic when on any given material we impress a predetermined form, not necessarily arising out of the properties of the material, as when to a mass of wet clay we give whatever shape we wish it to retain when hardened. The organic form, on the other hand, is innate; it shapes as it develops itself from within, and the fulness of its development is one and the same with the perfection of its outward form. Such is the life, such the form. Nature, the prime genial artist, inexhaustible in diverse powers, is equally inexhaustible in forms. Each exterior is the physiognomy of the being within, its true image reflected and thrown out from the concave mirror. And even such is the appropriate excellence of her chosen poet, of our own Shakespeare, himself a nature humanized, a genial understanding directing self-consciously a power and an implicit wisdom deeper than consciousness.[1] 1930

8. Voltaire (1694–1778) wrote critiques treating Shakespeare as a barbarous, irregular, and sometimes indecent natural genius.
9. August Wilhelm Schlegel, German critic and literary historian, whose *Lec-*

tures on Dramatic Art and Literature (1808–9) present many of the ideas Coleridge develops in this lecture.
1. I.e., the organic process of the imagination is in part unconscious.

GEORGE GORDON, LORD BYRON
(1788–1824)

1812:   *Childe Harold,* Cantos I and II.
1813–14: The Oriental tales, including *The Giaour, The Corsair, Lara.*
1816:   Separation from Lady Byron; leaves England, never to return.
1818:   Begins *Don Juan.*
1823:   Joins the Greek war for liberation from the Turks.

In his *History of English Literature,* written in the late 1850's, the French critic Hippolyte Taine gave only a few condescending pages to Wordsworth, Coleridge, Shelley, and Keats, and then devoted a long enthusiastic chapter to Lord Byron, "the greatest and most English of these artists; he is so great and so English that from him alone we shall learn more truths of his country and of his age than from all the rest together." Byron had achieved an immense European reputation during his own lifetime, while his great English contemporaries were admired only by small coteries in England and America, and through much of the 19th century he continued to be rated as one of the greatest of English poets and the very prototype of literary Romanticism. His influence was felt everywhere, not only among minor writers—in the two or three decades after his death, most European poets struck Byronic attitudes—but among the greatest poets and novelists (including Goethe in Germany, Balzac and Stendhal in France, Pushkin and Dostoevsky in Russia, and Melville in America), painters (especially Delacroix), and composers (especially Beethoven and Berlioz).

These facts may startle the contemporary student, who has been brought up in the modern estimate of Byron as the least important and the least Romantic of the five great English poets of his day. Neither Byron's critical theories nor his literary achievements fit easily into the standard categories ascribed to the "Romantic movement" in England, and his poems have little in common with the characteristic innovations of Wordsworth, Coleridge, Keats, or Shelley. Only Shelley, among these writers, thought highly of either Byron or his work; while Byron spoke slightingly of all of them except Shelley, and in fact insisted that, measured against the poetic practice of Pope, he and his contemporaries were "all in the wrong, one as much as another * * * we are upon a wrong revolutionary poetical system, or systems, not worth a damn in itself." Byron's masterpiece, *Don Juan,* is an instance of that favorite neoclassic type, a satire against modern civilization, which has much more in common with the methods and aims of Pope, Swift, Voltaire, or Sterne than with those of his own contemporaries. Even Byron's lyrics are old-fashioned: many are in the 18th-century gentlemanly mode of witty extemporization and epigram (*Written after Swimming from Sestos to Abydos*) or continue the Cavalier tradition of poetic gallantry and the elaborate deployment of a compliment to a lady (*She Walks in Beauty* or *There Be None of Beauty's Daughters*).

Byron's chief claim to be called an arch-Romantic is that he provided his age with what Taine called its "ruling personage; that is, the model that contemporaries invest with their admiration and sympathy." This personage is the "Byronic hero." He occurs in many guises in Byron's romances and dramas, but his central and recurrent attribute is that of a saturnine, passionate, moody, and remorse-torn but unrepentant sinner, who, in proud moral isolation, relies on his absolute self against all institutional and moral trammels on the display of individuality. This figure, infusing the archrebel in a nonpolitical form with a strong erotic interest, gathered together and embodied the implicit yearnings of Byron's time, was imitated in life as well as in art, and helped shape the intellectual as well as the cultural history of the later 19th century. Bertrand Russell, in his *History of Western Philosophy,* gives a chapter to Byron—not because he was a systematic thinker, but because "Byronism," the attitude of "Titanic cosmic self-assertion," established an outlook and way of feeling that entered 19th-century philosophy and eventually helped to form Nietzsche's concept of the Superman, the great hero who stands outside the jurisdiction of the ordinary criteria of good and evil.

Byron's contemporaries insisted on identifying the author with his fictional characters. But Byron's letters and the testimony of his friends show that, except for recurrent moods of black depression, his own temperament was in many respects the antithesis to that of his heroes. He was passionate and willful, but when in good humor he could be very much a man of the world in the 18th-century style—gregarious, lively, tolerant, and a witty conversationalist capable of taking an ironic attitude toward his own foibles as well as those of other men. The aloof hauteur he exhibited in public was largely a mask to hide his painful diffidence when in a strange company; he possessed devoted friends, both men and women, and among them he was usually unassuming, companionable, sometimes even exuberant, and tactful; to his household dependents he was unfailingly generous and tenaciously loyal. But if Byronism was largely a fiction, produced by a collaboration between Byron's imagination and that of his public, then the fiction was historically more important than the poet in his actual person.

Byron was descended from two aristocratic families, both of them colorful, violent, and dissolute. His grandfather was an admiral known as "Foulweather Jack"; his great-uncle was the fifth Baron Byron, known to his rural neighbors as the "Wicked Lord," who was tried by his peers for killing his kinsman, William Chaworth, in a drunken duel; his father, Captain John Byron, was a rake and fortune-hunter who rapidly dissipated the patrimony of two wealthy wives. Byron's mother was a Scotswoman, Catherine Gordon of Gight, the last descendant of a line of lawless Scottish lairds. After her husband died (Byron was then 3), she brought up her son in near poverty in Aberdeen, where he was indoctrinated with the Calvinistic morality of Scottish Presbyterianism. Mrs. Byron was an ill-educated and almost pathologically irascible woman, who nevertheless had an abiding love for her son; they fought violently when together, but corresponded affectionately enough when apart, until her death in 1811. When Byron was 10, the death of his great-uncle, preceded by that of more immediate heirs to the title, made him the sixth Lord Byron. In a fashion suitable to his new eminence he was sent to Harrow School, then to Trinity College, Cambridge. Byron had been born with a clubfoot, which was made worse by inept medical treatment, and this defect all his life caused him physical suffering and agonized embarrassment. His lameness increased his avidity for athletic prowess, and he played cricket and made himself an expert boxer, fencer, and horseman, and a powerful swimmer. He was also sexually precocious; when only 7, he fell in love with a little cousin, Mary Duff, and so violently that ten years later news of her marriage threw him into convulsions. Both at Cambridge and at his ancestral estate of Newstead, he engaged with more than ordinary vigor in the expensive pursuits and fashionable dissipations of a young Regency lord—at college he had richly furnished rooms, a carriage and retinue, a tame bear, and a mistress whom he liked to disguise as a boy. As a result, despite a sizeable and increasing income, Byron got into financial difficulties from which he did not entirely extricate himself until late in his life. In the course of his schooling he formed many close friendships, the most important with John Cam Hobhouse, a sturdy political liberal and common-sense moralist who exerted a steadying influence throughout Byron's turbulent life.

Despite his distractions at the university, Byron found time to try his hand at lyric verse, which was published in 1807 in a slim and conventional volume entitled *Hours of Idleness*. This was treated with unmerited harshness by the pontifical *Edinburgh Review*, and Byron was provoked to write in reply his first important poem, *English Bards and Scotch Reviewers*, a vigorous satire in the couplet style of the late 18th-century followers of Pope, in which he incorporated skillful but tactless ridicule of all his major poetic contemporaries, including Scott, Wordsworth, and Coleridge.

After attaining his M.A. degree and his majority, Byron set out with Hobhouse in 1809 on a tour through Portugal and Spain to Malta, and then to little-known Albania, Greece, and Asia Minor. In this adventurous two-year excursion, Byron accumulated materials which he wove into most of his important poems, including his last work, *Don Juan*. The first literary product was *Childe Harold*; he wrote the opening two cantos while on the tour which the poem describes, published them in 1812 soon after his return to England, and, in his own oft-quoted phrase, "awoke one morning and found myself famous." He became the literary and social celebrity of fashionable London, enjoying an unprecedented success, which he at once increased by his series of highly readable Near-Eastern verse tales; in these the Byronic hero, in various embodiments, flaunts his misanthropy and undergoes a variety of violent and romantic adventures which current gossip attributed to the author himself. In his chronic shortage of money, Byron could well have used the huge income from these publications, but instead maintained his status as an aristocratic amateur by giving the royalties away. Occupying his inherited seat in the House of Lords, Byron also became briefly active on the extreme liberal side of the Whig party and spoke courageously in defense of the Nottingham weavers who, made desperate by technological unemployment, had resorted to destroying the new textile machines; he also supported other liberal measures, including that of Catholic Emancipation.

In the meantime Byron found himself besieged by women. He was extraordinarily handsome—"so beautiful a countenance," Coleridge wrote, "I scarcely ever saw. * * * his eyes the open portals of the sun—things of light, and for light"; because of a constitutional tendency to obesity, however, Byron was able to maintain his beauty only by recurring again and again to a starvation diet of biscuits, soda water, and strong cathartics. Often as a result of female initiative rather than his own, Byron incurred a sequence of liaisons with ladies of fashion. One of these, the flamboyant, eccentric, and hysterical young Lady Caroline Lamb, caused him so much distress by her frenzied pursuit and public tantrums that Byron turned for relief to marriage with Annabella Milbanke, who was in every way Lady Caroline's opposite, for she was naïve, unworldly, intellectual (with a special passion for mathematics), and not a little priggish; she persuaded herself that she could make Byron over in her own image. This ill-starred marriage produced a daughter (Augusta Ada) and many scenes in which Byron, goaded by financial difficulties, behaved so frantically that his wife suspected his sanity; after only one year, the union ended in a legal separation. The final blow came when Lady Byron discovered her husband's incestuous relations with his half sister, Augusta Leigh. The two had been raised apart, so that they were almost strangers when they met as adults; also, Byron seems to have had one attribute in common with the Byronic hero—a compulsion to try forbidden experience (including, as we now know, homosexual love affairs), joined with a tendency to court his own destruction. The facts of the case have long been violently disputed, but now there remains no room for doubt concerning the validity of the charge. Byron's affection for his sister, however guilty, was deep and genuine, and endured all through his life. This affair proved a delicious morsel even to the jaded palate of the dissolute Regency society; Byron was ostracized by all but a few friends, and finally forced to leave England forever on April 25, 1816.

Byron now resumed the travels incorporated in the third and fourth cantos of *Childe Harold*. At Geneva he lived for several months in close and intellectually fruitful relation to Shelley, who was accompanied by his wife, Mary Godwin, and by his wife's stepsister, Claire Clairmont—a misguided girl of 17 who had forced herself upon Byron while he was still in England and who in January, 1817, bore him a daughter, Allegra. In the fall of 1817 Byron established himself in Venice, where he inaugurated various affairs that culminated in a period of frenzied debauchery which, Byron estimated, involved more than 200 women, mainly of the lower classes. This period was nevertheless one of great literary creativity: often working through the later hours of the night, he finished his tragedy *Manfred*, wrote the fourth canto of *Childe Harold*, and after turning out *Beppo*, a short rehearsal in the narrative style and stanza of *Don Juan*, began the composition of *Don Juan* itself. In the colloquial ottava rima, Byron finally learned to write poetry as well as he had written prose.

Exhausted and bored by promiscuity, Byron in 1819 settled into a placid and relatively faithful relationship with Teresa Guiccioli, the young wife of the elderly Count Alessandro Guiccioli; according to the Italian upper-class mores of the times, having contracted a marriage of convenience, she could now with propriety attach Byron to herself as a *cavalier servente*. Through Teresa's nationalistic family, the Gambas, Byron became involved in the Carbonari plot against Austrian control over northern Italy. When the Gambas were forced by the authorities to move to Pisa, Byron followed them there, and for the second time joined Shelley. There grew up about the two friends the "Pisan Circle," which in addition to the Gambas included Shelley's friends Thomas Medwin and Edward and Jane Williams, as well as the Greek nationalist leader Prince Mavrocordatos, the picturesque Irish Couñt Taaffe, and the flamboyant and mendacious adventurer Edward Trelawny, who seems to have stepped out of one of Byron's romances. They were later joined by Leigh Hunt and his family, whom Shelley enlisted in a short-lived scheme to publish a new radical political journal, the *Liberal*. The circle was gradually broken up, first by Shelley's anger over Byron's treatment of his daughter Allegra (Byron, refusing any association with the mother, Claire Clairmont, had sent the child to be brought up as a Catholic in an Italian convent, where she died of a fever in 1822); then by the expulsion of the Gambas, whom Byron followed to Genoa; and finally by the drowning of Shelley and Williams in July, 1822.

Byron meanwhile had been steadily at work on a series of closet tragedies (including *Cain*, *Sardanapalus*, and *Marino Faliero*) and on *The*

Vision of Judgment, a superb satire directed against a sycophantic poem, *A Vision of Judgment*, in which the poet laureate, Robert Southey, had memorialized the death of King George III. He also continued writing his great series of incomparably vivid, informative, and witty letters to his friends in England. But increasingly Byron devoted himself to the continuation of *Don Juan*. He had always been diffident in his self-judgments and easily swayed by literary advice. But now, confident that he had at last found his métier and was accomplishing a masterpiece, Byron kept on, in spite of persistent objections against the supposed immorality of the poem by the English public, by his publisher, John Murray, by his friends and well-wishers, and by his extremely decorous mistress, the Countess Guiccioli—by almost everyone, in fact, except the idealist, Shelley, who thought *Juan* incomparably better than anything he himself could write, and insisted "that every word of it is pregnant with immortality."

Byron finally broke off literature for action: he organized an expedition to assist in the Greek war for independence from the Turks. He knew too well the conditions in Greece, and had too skeptical an estimate of human nature, to entertain great hope of success; but he was bored with love, with the domesticity of his relations to Teresa, and in some moods, with life itself. He had, in addition, by his own writings helped to kindle European enthusiasm for the Greek cause, and now felt honor-bound to try what could be done. In the dismal, marshy town of Missolonghi he lived a Spartan existence, undertaking to train troops whom he had himself subsidized and exhibiting great practical grasp and power of leadership amid an incredible confusion of factionalism, intrigue, and military ineptitude until, worn out, he succumbed to a series of feverish attacks and died just after he had reached his 36th birthday. Harold Nicolson, the historian of these events in *Byron: The Last Journey*, wrote: "Lord Byron accomplished nothing at Missolonghi except his own suicide; but by that single act of heroism he secured the liberation of Greece." To this day Byron is revered by the Greek people as a national hero.

Students of Byron still feel, as his friends had felt, the magnetic attraction of his paradoxical and variable temperament. As Mary Shelley wrote six years after his death, when she read Thomas Moore's edition of his *Letters and Journals*: "The Lord Byron I find there is our Lord Byron—the fascinating—faulty—childish—philosophical being—daring the world—docile to a private circle—impetuous and indolent—gloomy and yet more gay than any other. * * * [I become] reconciled (as I used to in his lifetime) to those waywardnesses which annoyed me when he was away, through the delightful and buoyant tone of his conversation and manners." Of his inner discordances, Byron himself was well aware; he told his friend Lady Blessington: "I am so changeable, being everything by turns and nothing long—I am such a strange *mélange* of good and evil, that it would be difficult to describe me." Yet he remained faithful to his own code: a determination always to tell the truth as he saw it about the world and about himself—his refusal, unlike most of us, to suppress or conceal any of his moods is in fact what made him seem so contradictory—and a passionate dedication to the freedom of nations and individuals. As he went on to say to Lady Blessington: "There are but two sentiments to which I am constant—a strong love of liberty, and a detestation of cant."

Written After Swimming from Sestos to Abydos[1]

1

If, in the month of dark December,
　　Leander, who was nightly wont
(What maid will not the tale remember?)
　　To cross thy stream, broad Hellespont!

2

If, when the wintry tempest roared,　　　　　　　　　　5
　　He sped to Hero, nothing loath,
And thus of old thy current poured,
　　Fair Venus! how I pity both!

3

For *me*, degenerate modern wretch,
　　Though in the genial month of May,　　　　　　　　10
My dripping limbs I faintly stretch,
　　And think I've done a feat today.

4

But since he crossed the rapid tide,
　　According to the doubtful story,
To woo—and—Lord knows what beside,　　　　　　　　15
　　And swam for Love, as I for Glory;

5

'Twere hard to say who fared the best:
　　Sad mortals! thus the gods still plague you!
He lost his labor, I my jest;
　　For he was drowned, and I've the ague.　　　　　　　20

1810　　　　　　　　　　　　　　　　　　　　　　　　1812

When We Two Parted

When we two parted
　　In silence and tears,
Half broken-hearted
　　To sever for years,

1. The Hellespont (now called the Dardanelles) is the narrow strait between Europe and Asia. In the ancient story, retold in Christopher Marlowe's *Hero and Leander*, young Leander of Abydos, on the Asian side, swam nightly to visit Hero, a priestess of the goddess Venus at Sestos, until he was drowned when he made the attempt in a storm. Byron and a young Lt. Ekenhead swam the Hellespont in the reverse direction on May 3, 1810. Byron alternated between complacency and humor in his many references to the event. In a note to the poem, Byron mentions that the distance was "upwards of four English miles, though the actual breadth is barely one. The rapidity of the current is such that no boat can row directly across. * * * The water was extremely cold, from the melting of the mountain snows."

Pale grew thy cheek and cold,   5
    Colder thy kiss;
Truly that hour foretold
    Sorrow to this.

The dew of the morning
    Sunk chill on my brow—   10
It felt like the warning
    Of what I feel now.
Thy vows are all broken,
    And light is thy fame;
I hear thy name spoken,   15
    And share in its shame.

They name thee before me,
    A knell to mine ear;
A shudder comes o'er me—
    Why wert thou so dear?   ·   20
They know not I knew thee,
    Who knew thee too well—
Long, long shall I rue thee,
    Too deeply to tell.

In secret we met—   25
    In silence I grieve,
That thy heart could forget,
    Thy spirit deceive.
If I should meet thee
    After long years,   30
How should I greet thee?—
    With silence and tears.

1813   1816

She Walks in Beauty[1]

1

She walks in beauty, like the night
    Of cloudless climes and starry skies;
And all that's best of dark and bright
    Meet in her aspect and her eyes:
Thus mellowed to that tender light   5
    Which heaven to gaudy day denies.

2

One shade the more, one ray the less,
    Had half impaired the nameless grace

1. One of the lyrics in *Hebrew Melodies* (1815), written to be set to adaptations of traditional Jewish tunes by the young musician Isaac Nathan. Byron wrote the lines the morning after he had met his beautiful young cousin by marriage, Mrs. Robert John Wilmot, who wore a black mourning gown brightened with spangles.

Which waves in every raven tress,
  Or softly lightens o'er her face;   10
Where thoughts serenely sweet express
  How pure, how dear their dwelling place.

3

And on that cheek, and o'er that brow,
  So soft, so calm, yet eloquent,
The smiles that win, the tints that glow,   15
  But tell of days in goodness spent,
A mind at peace with all below,
  A heart whose love is innocent!

June 12, 1814   1815

Stanzas for Music

There Be None of Beauty's Daughters

1

There be none of Beauty's daughters
  With a magic like thee;
And like music on the waters
  Is thy sweet voice to me:
When, as if its sound were causing   5
The charméd ocean's pausing,
The waves lie still and gleaming,
And the lulled winds seem dreaming;

2

And the midnight moon is weaving
  Her bright chain o'er the deep;   10
Whose breast is gently heaving,
  As an infant's asleep:
So the spirit bows before thee,
To listen and adore thee;
With a full but soft emotion,   15
Like the swell of summer's ocean.

1816   1816

They Say That Hope Is Happiness

1

They say that Hope is happiness;
  But genuine Love must prize the past,
And Memory wakes the thoughts that bless:
  They rose the first—they set the last;

2

And all that Memory loves the most   5
  Was once our only Hope to be,
And all that Hope adored and lost
  Hath melted into Memory.

3
Alas! it is delusion all;
  The future cheats us from afar,   10
Nor can we be what we recall,
  Nor dare we think on what we are.

1816   1829

Darkness[1]

I had a dream, which was not all a dream.
The bright sun was extinguished, and the stars
Did wander darkling[2] in the eternal space,
Rayless, and pathless, and the icy earth
Swung blind and blackening in the moonless air;   5
Morn came and went—and came, and brought no day,
And men forgot their passions in the dread
Of this their desolation; and all hearts
Were chilled into a selfish prayer for light:
And they did live by watchfires—and the thrones,   10
The palaces of crownéd kings—the huts,
The habitations of all things which dwell,
Were burnt for beacons; cities were consumed,
And men were gathered round their blazing homes
To look once more into each other's face;   15
Happy were those who dwelt within the eye
Of the volcanoes, and their mountain torch:
A fearful hope was all the world contained;
Forests were set on fire—but hour by hour
They fell and faded—and the crackling trunks   20
Extinguished with a crash—and all was black.
The brows of men by the despairing light
Wore an unearthly aspect, as by fits
The flashes fell upon them; some lay down
And hid their eyes and wept; and some did rest   25
Their chins upon their clenchéd hands, and smiled;
And others hurried to and fro, and fed
Their funeral piles with fuel, and looked up
With mad disquietude on the dull sky,
The pall of a past world; and then again   30
With curses cast them down upon the dust,
And gnashed their teeth and howled: the wild birds shrieked
And, terrified, did flutter on the ground,
And flap their useless wings; the wildest brutes
Came tame and tremulous; and vipers crawled   35
And twined themselves among the multitude,

1. A powerfully imagined blank-verse description of the end of life on earth—a speculation hardly less common in Byron's time than in ours.
2. In the dark.

Hissing, but stingless—they were slain for food;
And War, which for a moment was no more,
Did glut himself again—a meal was bought
With blood, and each sate sullenly apart   40
Gorging himself in gloom: no love was left;
All earth was but one thought—and that was death
Immediate and inglorious; and the pang
Of famine fed upon all entrails—men
Died, and their bones were tombless as their flesh;   45
The meager by the meager were devoured,
Even dogs assailed their masters, all save one,
And he was faithful to a corse, and kept
The birds and beasts and famished men at bay,
Till hunger clung them, or the dropping dead   50
Lured their lank jaws; himself sought out no food,
But with a piteous and perpetual moan,
And a quick desolate cry, licking the hand
Which answered not with a caress—he died.
The crowd was famished by degrees; but two   55
Of an enormous city did survive,
And they were enemies: they met beside
The dying embers of an altar place,
Where had been heaped a mass of holy things
For an unholy usage; they raked up,   60
And shivering scraped with their cold skeleton hands
The feeble ashes, and their feeble breath
Blew for a little life, and made a flame
Which was a mockery; then they lifted up
Their eyes as it grew lighter, and beheld   65
Each other's aspects—saw, and shrieked, and died—
Even of their mutual hideousness they died,
Unknowing who he was upon whose brow
Famine had written Fiend. The world was void,
The populous and the powerful was a lump   70
Seasonless, herbless, treeless, manless, lifeless—
A lump of death—a chaos of hard clay.
The rivers, lakes, and ocean all stood still,
And nothing stirred within their silent depths;
Ships sailorless lay rotting on the sea,   75
And their masts fell down piecemeal: as they dropped
They slept on the abyss without a surge—
The waves were dead; the tides were in their grave,
The Moon, their mistress, had expired before;
The winds were withered in the stagnant air,   80
And the clouds perished; Darkness had no need
Of aid from them—She was the Universe.
1816   1816

From Childe Harold's Pilgrimage[1]

A ROMAUNT[2]

From *Canto I*

1

Oh, thou! in Hellas deemed of heavenly birth,
Muse! formed or fabled at the minstrel's will!
Since shamed full oft by later lyres on earth,
Mine dares not call thee from thy sacred hill:
Yet there I've wandered by thy vaunted rill;   5
Yes! sighed o'er Delphi's long-deserted shrine,
Where, save that feeble fountain, all is still;
Nor mote my shell awake the weary Nine[3]
To grace so plain a tale—this lowly lay of mine.

2

Whilome[4] in Albion's isle there dwelt a youth,   10
Who ne in virtue's ways did take delight;
But spent his days in riot most uncouth,
And vexed with mirth the drowsy ear of Night.
Ah, me! in sooth he was a shameless wight,

1. *Childe Harold* is a travelogue, narrated by a melancholy, passionate, well-read, and very eloquent tourist. Byron wrote most of the first two cantos while on the tour through Spain, Portugal, Albania, and Greece which these cantos describe; when he published them, in 1812, they made him at once stroke the best known and most talked about living English poet. Byron took up *Childe Harold* again in 1816, during the European tour he made after the breakup of his marriage. Canto III, published in 1816, moves through Belgium, up the Rhine, then to Switzerland and the Alps. Canto IV, published in 1818, describes the great cities and monuments of Italy.

Byron chose for his poem the Spenserian stanza, and like James Thomson (in the *Castle of Indolence*) and other 18th-century predecessors, he attempted in the first canto to imitate, in a serio-comic fashion, the archaic language of his Elizabethan model. (The word "Childe" itself is the ancient term for a young noble awaiting knighthood.) But Byron soon dropped the archaisms; and in the last two cantos, he adapts Spenser's mellifluous stanza to his own assured and brassy magniloquence.

In the Preface to his first two cantos, Byron had insisted that the narrator, Childe Harold, was "a fictitious character," merely "the child of imagination." But in the manuscript version of these cantos, he had himself called his hero "Childe Burun," the early form of his own family name; the world insisted on identifying the character as well as the travels of the protagonist with those of the author; and in the fourth canto Byron, abandoning the third-person *dramatis persona*, spoke out frankly in the first person.

In its shock tactics of apostrophes, imperatives, exclamations, hyperbole, and abrupt changes in subject, pace, and mood, the style of *Childe Harold* is without close parallel in English; to it Goethe applied the terms *Keckheit, Kühnheit, und Grandiosität:* "daring, dash, and grandiosity." It is no small feat in the author to have converted a meticulously accurate tourist's record of scenes, memorials, and museums into a dramatic and passionate experience. The result is like seeing Europe by flashes of lightning, for everything is presented, not as it is in itself, but as it affects the violent sensibility of that new cultural phenomenon, the Romantic Man of Feeling.

2. A romance, or narrative of adventure.

3. The "shell" is a lyre (Hermes is fabled to have invented the lyre by stretching strings over the hollow of a tortoise shell); the "Nine" are the Muses, whose "vaunted rill," (line 5) was the Castalian spring. "Mote": may.

4. Once upon a time.

Sore given to revel and ungodly glee;   15
Few earthly things found favor in his sight
Save concubines and carnal companie,
And flaunting wassailers⁵ of high and low degree.

3

Childe Harold was he hight—but whence his name
And lineage long, it suits me not to say;   20
Suffice it that perchance they were of fame,
And had been glorious in another day:
But one sad losel⁶ soils a name for aye,
However mighty in the olden time;
Nor all that heralds rake from coffined clay,   25
Nor florid prose, nor honeyed lies of rhyme,
Can blazon evil deeds, or consecrate a crime.

4

Childe Harold basked him in the noontide sun,
Disporting there like any other fly;
Nor deemed before his little day was done   30
One blast might chill him into misery.
But long ere scarce a third of his passed by,
Worse than adversity the Childe befell;
He felt the fullness of satiety:
Then loathed he in his native land to dwell,   35
Which seemed to him more lone than eremite's⁷ sad cell.

5

For he through Sin's long labyrinth had run,
Nor made atonement when he did amiss;
Had sighed to many though he loved but one,
And that loved one, alas! could ne'er be his.   40
Ah, happy she! to 'scape from him whose kiss
Had been pollution unto aught so chaste;
Who soon had left her charms for vulgar bliss,
And spoiled her goodly lands to gild his waste,
Nor calm domestic peace had ever deigned to taste.   45

6

And now Childe Harold was sore sick at heart,
And from his fellow bacchanals would flee;
'Tis said, at times the sullen tear would start,
But Pride congealed the drop within his ee:⁸
Apart he stalked in joyless reverie,   50
And from his native land resolved to go,
And visit scorching climes beyond the sea;
With pleasure drugged, he almost longed for woe,
And e'en for change of scene would seek the shades below.

* * *

5. Brazen topers.   drunken duel.
6. Rascal. Byron's great-uncle, the 5th   7. A religious hermit.
Lord Byron, had killed a kinsman in a   8. Eye.

From *Canto III*

1

Is thy face like thy mother's, my fair child!
Ada![1] sole daughter of my house and heart?
When last I saw thy young blue eyes they smiled,
And then we parted—not as now we part,
But with a hope.—
       Awaking with a start,   5
The waters heave around me; and on high
The winds lift up their voices: I depart,
Whither I know not; but the hour's gone by,
When Albion's[2] lessening shores could grieve or glad mine eye.

2

Once more upon the waters! yet once more!   10
And the waves bound beneath me as a steed
That knows his rider. Welcome to their roar!
Swift be their guidance, wheresoe'er it lead!
Though the strained mast should quiver as a reed,
And the rent canvas fluttering strew the gale,   15
Still must I on; for I am as a weed,
Flung from the rock on Ocean's foam, to sail
Where'er the surge may sweep, the tempest's breath prevail.

3

In my youth's summer[3] I did sing of One,
The wandering outlaw of his own dark mind;   20
Again I seize the theme, then but begun,
And bear it with me, as the rushing wind
Bears the cloud onwards: in that tale I find
The furrows of long thought, and dried-up tears,
Which, ebbing, leave a sterile track behind,   25
O'er which all heavily the journeying years
Plod the last sands of life—where not a flower appears.

4

Since my young days of passion—joy, or pain—
Perchance my heart and harp have lost a string,
And both may jar:[4] it may be that in vain   30
I would essay as I have sung to sing.
Yet, though a dreary strain, to this I cling,
So that it wean me from the weary dream
Of selfish grief or gladness—so it fling
Forgetfulness around me—it shall seem   35
To me, though to none else, a not ungrateful theme.

5

He, who grown aged in this world of woe,
In deeds, not years, piercing the depths of life,

1. Byron's daughter, Augusta Ada, born December, 1816, a month before her parents separated. Byron's "hope" (line 5) had been for a reconciliation, but he was never to see Ada again.
2. England's.
3. Byron wrote Canto I at 21; he is now 28.
4. Sound discordant.

So that no wonder waits him—nor below
Can love, or sorrow, fame, ambition, strife,   40
Cut to his heart again with the keen knife
Of silent, sharp endurance—he can tell
Why thought seeks refuge in lone caves, yet rife
With airy images, and shapes which dwell
Still unimpaired, though old, in the soul's haunted cell.   45

6

'Tis to create, and in creating live
A being more intense, that we endow
With form our fancy, gaining as we give
The life we image, even as I do now.
What am I? Nothing: but not so art thou,   50
Soul of my thought!⁵ with whom I traverse earth,
Invisible but gazing, as I glow
Mixed with thy spirit, blended with thy birth,
And feeling still with thee in my crushed feelings' dearth.

7

Yet must I think less wildly—I *have* thought   55
Too long and darkly, till my brain became,
In its own eddy boiling and o'erwrought,
A whirling gulf of phantasy and flame:
And thus, untaught in youth my heart to tame,
My springs of life were poisoned. 'Tis too late!   60
Yet am I changed; though still enough the same
In strength to bear what time can not abate,
And feed on bitter fruits without accusing Fate.

8

Something too much of this—but now 'tis past,
And the spell closes with its silent seal.⁶   65
Long absent HAROLD reappears at last;
He of the breast which fain no more would feel,
Wrung with the wounds which kill not but ne'er heal;
Yet Time, who changes all, had altered him
In soul and aspect as in age: years steal   70
Fire from the mind as vigor from the limb,
And life's enchanted cup but sparkles near the brim.

9

His had been quaffed too quickly, and he found
The dregs were wormwood; but he filled again,
And from a purer fount, on holier ground,   75
And deemed its spring perpetual; but in vain!
Still round him clung invisibly a chain
Which galled forever, fettering though unseen,
And heavy though it clanked not; worn with pain,
Which pined although it spoke not, and grew keen,   80
Entering with every step he took through many a scene.

5. I.e., Childe Harold, his literary creation.

6. I.e., he sets the seal of silence on his
personal tale ("spell").

10

Secure in guarded coldness, he had mixed
Again in fancied safety with his kind,
And deemed his spirit now so firmly fixed
And sheathed with an invulnerable mind,   85
That, if no joy, no sorrow lurked behind;
And he, as one, might 'midst the many stand
Unheeded, searching through the crowd to find
Fit speculation—such as in strange land
He found in wonderworks of God and Nature's hand.   90

11

But who can view the ripened rose, nor seek
To wear it? who can curiously behold
The smoothness and the sheen of beauty's cheek,
Nor feel the heart can never all grow old?
Who can contemplate Fame through clouds unfold   95
The star which rises o'er her steep, nor climb?
Harold, once more within the vortex, rolled
On with the giddy circle, chasing Time,
Yet with a nobler aim than in his youth's fond[7] prime.

12

But soon he knew himself the most unfit   100
Of men to herd with Man, with whom he held
Little in common; untaught to submit
His thoughts to others, though his soul was quelled
In youth by his own thoughts; still uncompelled,
He would not yield dominion of his mind   105
To spirits against whom his own rebelled,
Proud though in desolation; which could find
A life within itself, to breathe without mankind.

13

Where rose the mountains, there to him were friends;
Where rolled the ocean, thereon was his home;   110
Where a blue sky, and glowing clime, extends,
He had the passion and the power to roam;
The desert, forest, cavern, breaker's foam,
Were unto him companionship; they spake
A mutual language, clearer than the tome   115
Of his land's tongue, which he would oft forsake
For Nature's pages glassed[8] by sunbeams on the lake.

14

Like the Chaldean,[9] he could watch the stars,
Till he had peopled them with beings bright
As their own beams; and earth, and earth-born jars,   120
And human frailties, were forgotten quite:
Could he have kept his spirit to that flight
He had been happy; but this clay will sink
Its spark immortal, envying it the light

7. Foolish.
8. Made glassy.
9. A people of ancient Babylonia, expert in astronomy.

To which it mounts, as if to break the link 125
That keeps us from yon heaven which woos us to its brink.

15

But in Man's dwellings he became a thing
Restless and worn, and stern and wearisome,
Drooped as a wild-born falcon with clipped wing,
To whom the boundless air alone were home: 130
Then came his fit again, which to o'ercome,
As eagerly the barred-up bird will beat
His breast and beak against his wiry dome
Till the blood tinge his plumage, so the heat
Of his impeded soul would through his bosom eat. 135

16

Self-exiled Harold wanders forth again,
With nought of hope left—but with less of gloom;
The very knowledge that he lived in vain,
That all was over on this side the tomb,
Had made Despair a smilingness assume, 140
Which, though 'twere wild—as on the plundered wreck
When mariners would madly meet their doom
With draughts intemperate on the sinking deck—
Did yet inspire a cheer which he forebore to check.

17

Stop!—for thy tread is on an Empire's dust! 145
An Earthquake's spoil is sepulchered below!
Is the spot marked with no colossal bust,
Nor column trophied for triumphal show?
None;[1] but the moral's truth tells simpler so,
As the ground was before, thus let it be— 150
How that red rain hath made the harvest grow!
And is this all the world has gained by thee,
Thou first and last of fields, king-making Victory?

18

And Harold stands upon this place of skulls,
The grave of France, the deadly Waterloo! 155
How in an hour the power which gave annuls
Its gifts, transferring fame as fleeting too!
In "pride of place" here last the eagle flew,[2]
Then tore with bloody talon the rent plain,
Pierced by the shaft of banded nations through; 160
Ambition's life and labors all were vain;
He wears the shattered links of the world's broken chain.[3]

19

Fit retribution! Gaul[4] may champ the bit
And foam in fetters—but is Earth more free?

1. Napoleon's defeat at Waterloo, near Brussels, had occurred only the year before, on June 18, 1815.
2. The eagle was the standard of Napoleon. "Pride of place" is a term from falconry, meaning the highest point of flight (cf. *Macbeth* II.iv.12).
3. Napoleon was then a prisoner at St. Helena.
4. France. Byron, like Shelley and other liberals, saw the defeat of the Napoleonic tyranny as at the same time a victory for tyrannous kings and the forces of extreme reaction throughout Europe.

Did nations combat to make *One* submit; 165
Or league to teach all kings true sovereignty?
What! shall reviving Thralldom again be
The patched-up idol of enlightened days?
Shall we, who struck the Lion down, shall we
Pay the Wolf homage? proffering lowly gaze 170
And servile knees to thrones? No; *prove*[5] before ye praise!

20

If not, o'er one fallen despot boast no more!
In vain fair cheeks were furrowed with hot tears
For Europe's flowers long rooted up before
The trampler of her vineyards; in vain years 175
Of death, depopulation, bondage, fears,
Have all been borne, and broken by the accord
Of roused-up millions: all that most endears
Glory is when the myrtle wreathes a sword
Such as Harmodius drew on Athens' tyrant lord.[6] 180

21

There was a sound of revelry by night,
And Belgium's capital had gathered then
Her Beauty and her Chivalry, and bright
The lamps shone o'er fair women and brave men;[7]
A thousand hearts beat happily; and when 185
Music arose with its voluptuous swell,
Soft eyes looked love to eyes which spake again,
And all went merry as a marriage bell—
But hush! hark! a deep sound strikes like a rising knell!

22

Did ye not hear it?—No; 'twas but the wind, 190
Or the car rattling o'er the stony street;
On with the dance! let joy be unconfined;
No sleep till morn, when Youth and Pleasure meet
To chase the glowing Hours with flying feet—
But hark!—that heavy sound breaks in once more, 195
As if the clouds its echo would repeat;
And nearer, clearer, deadlier than before!
Arm! Arm! it is—it is—the cannon's opening roar!

23

Within a windowed niche of that high hall
Sate Brunswick's fated chieftain;[8] he did hear 200
That sound the first amidst the festival,
And caught its tone with Death's prophetic ear;
And when they smiled because he deemed it near,

---

5. Await the test (proof) of experience.
6. In 514 B.C. Harmodius and Aristogeiton, hiding their daggers in myrtle (symbol of love), killed Hipparchus, tyrant of Athens.
7. This famous ball, given by the Duchess of Richmond on the eve of the battle of Quatre Bras, which opened the conflict at Waterloo, is also described in Thackeray's *Vanity Fair*, Chapters 29–30.
8. The Duke of Brunswick, nephew of George III of England, was killed in the battle of Quatre Bras, just as his father, commanding the Prussian army against Napoleon, had been killed at Auerstedt in 1806 (line 205).

His heart more truly knew that peal too well
Which stretched his father on a bloody bier,   205
And roused the vengeance blood alone could quell:
He rushed into the field, and, foremost fighting, fell.

24

Ah! then and there was hurrying to and fro,
And gathering tears, and tremblings of distress,
And cheeks all pale, which but an hour ago   210
Blushed at the praise of their own loveliness;
And there were sudden partings, such as press
The life from out young hearts, and choking sighs
Which ne'er might be repeated; who could guess
If ever more should meet those mutual eyes,   215
Since upon night so sweet such awful morn could rise!

25

And there was mounting in hot haste: the steed,
The mustering squadron, and the clattering car,
Went pouring forward with impetuous speed,
And swiftly forming in the ranks of war;   220
And the deep thunder peal on peal afar;
And near, the beat of the alarming drum
Roused up the soldier ere the morning star;
While thronged the citizens with terror dumb,
Or whispering, with white lips—"The foe! They come! they come!"

26

And wild and high the "Cameron's gathering"⁹ rose!   226
The war-note of Lochiel, which Albyn's hills
Have heard, and heard, too, have her Saxon foes—
How in the noon of night that pibroch¹ thrills,
Savage and shrill! But with the breath which fills   230
Their mountain pipe, so fill the mountaineers
With the fierce native daring which instills
The stirring memory of a thousand years,
And Evan's, Donald's fame² rings in each clansman's ears!

27

And Ardennes³ waves above them her green leaves,   235
Dewy with nature's teardrops, as they pass,
Grieving, if aught inanimate e'er grieves,
Over the unreturning brave—alas!
Ere evening to be trodden like the grass
Which now beneath them, but above shall grow   240
In its next verdure, when this fiery mass
Of living valor, rolling on the foe
And burning with high hope, shall molder cold and low.

9. The clan song of the Camerons, whose chief was called "Lochiel," after his estate. "Albyn's": Scotland's.
1. Bagpipe music, usually warlike in character.
2. Sir Evan and Donald Cameron, famous warriors in the Stuart cause in the 17th and 18th centuries.
3. A forested region covering parts of Belgium, France, and Luxembourg, which became a battlefield again in both World Wars.

28

Last noon beheld them full of lusty life,
Last eve in Beauty's circle proudly gay,   245
The midnight brought the signal-sound of strife,
The morn the marshaling in arms—the day
Battle's magnificently-stern array!
The thunderclouds close o'er it, which when rent
The earth is covered thick with other clay,   250
Which her own clay shall cover, heaped and pent,
Rider and horse—friend, foe—in one red burial blent!

* * *

36

There sunk the greatest, nor the worst of men,[4]
Whose spirit antithetically mixed
One moment of the mightiest, and again
On little objects with like firmness fixed,
Extreme in all things! hadst thou been betwixt,   320
Thy throne had still been thine, or never been;
For daring made thy rise as fall: thou seek'st
Even now to reassume the imperial mien,
And shake again the world, the Thunderer of the scene!

37

Conqueror and captive of the earth art thou!   325
She trembles at thee still, and thy wild name
Was ne'er more bruited in men's minds than now
That thou are nothing, save the jest of Fame,
Who wooed thee once, thy vassal, and became
The flatterer of thy fierceness, till thou wert   330
A god unto thyself; nor less the same
To the astounded kingdoms all inert,
Who deemed thee for a time whate'er thou didst assert.

38

Oh, more or less than man—in high or low,
Battling with nations, flying from the field;   335
Now making monarchs' necks thy footstool, now
More than thy meanest soldier taught to yield;
An empire thou couldst crush, command, rebuild,
But govern not thy pettiest passion, nor,
However deeply in men's spirits skilled,   340
Look through thine own, nor curb the lust of war,
Nor learn that tempted Fate will leave the loftiest star.

39

Yet well thy soul hath brooked the turning tide
With that untaught innate philosophy,
Which, be it wisdom, coldness, or deep pride,   345
Is gall and wormwood to an enemy.
When the whole host of hatred stood hard by,
To watch and mock thee shrinking, thou hast smiled

4. I.e., Napoleon.

With a sedate and all-enduring eye—
When Fortune fled her spoiled and favorite child, 350
He stood unbowed beneath the ills upon him piled.

40

Sager than in thy fortunes; for in them
Ambition steeled thee on too far to show
That just habitual scorn, which could contemn
Men and their thoughts; 'twas wise to feel, not so 355
To wear it ever on thy lip and brow,
And spurn the instruments thou wert to use
Till they were turned unto thine overthrow:
'Tis but a worthless world to win or lose;
So hath it proved to thee and all such lot⁵ who choose. 360

41

If, like a tower upon a headlong rock,
Thou hadst been made to stand or fall alone,
Such scorn of man had helped to brave the shock;
But men's thoughts were the steps which paved thy throne,
Their admiration thy best weapon shone; 365
The part of Philip's son⁶ was thine, not then
(Unless aside thy purple had been thrown)
Like stern Diogenes⁷ to mock at men;
For sceptered cynics earth were far too wide a den.

42

But quiet to quick bosoms is a hell, 370
And *there* hath been thy bane; there is a fire
And motion of the soul which will not dwell
In its own narrow being, but aspire
Beyond the fitting medium of desire;
And, but once kindled, quenchless evermore, 375
Preys upon high adventure, nor can tire
Of aught but rest; a fever at the core,
Fatal to him who bears, to all who ever bore.

43

This makes the madmen who have made men mad
By their contagion; Conquerors and Kings, 380
Founders of sects and systems, to whom add
Sophists, Bards, Statesmen, all unquiet things
Which stir too strongly the soul's secret springs,
And are themselves the fools to those they fool;
Envied, yet how unenviable! what stings 385
Are theirs! One breast laid open were a school
Which would unteach mankind the lust to shine or rule.

44

Their breath is agitation, and their life
A storm whereon they ride, to sink at last;

5. Hazard.
6. Alexander the Great, son of Philip of Macedon.
7. The Greek philosopher of Cynicism, contemporary of Alexander. It is related that Alexander was so struck by his independence of mind that he said, "If I were not Alexander, I should wish to be Diogenes"; hence the allusion in line 369.

And yet so nursed and bigoted to strife,   390
That should their days, surviving perils past,
Melt to calm twilight, they feel overcast
With sorrow and supineness, and so die;
Even as a flame unfed which runs to waste
With its own flickering, or a sword laid by,   395
Which eats into itself and rusts ingloriously.

45

He who ascends to mountain tops, shall find
The loftiest peaks most wrapped in clouds and snow;
He who surpasses or subdues mankind,
Must look down on the hate of those below.   400
Though high *above* the sun of glory glow,
And far *beneath* the earth and ocean spread,
Round him are icy rocks, and loudly blow
Contending tempests on his naked head,
And thus reward the toils which to those summits led.[8]   405

* * *

52

Thus Harold inly said, and passed along,   460
Yet not insensibly to all which here
Awoke the jocund birds to early song
In glens which might have made even exile dear:
Though on his brow were graven lines austere,
And tranquil sternness which had ta'en the place   465
Of feelings fierier far but less severe,
Joy was not always absent from his face,
But o'er it in such scenes would steal with transient trace.

53

Nor was all love shut from him, though his days
Of passion had consumed themselves to dust.   470
It is in vain that we would coldly gaze
On such as smile upon us; the heart must
Leap kindly back to kindness, though disgust
Hath weaned it from all wordlings: thus he felt,
For there was soft remembrance, and sweet trust   475
In one fond breast,[3] to which his own would melt,
And in its tenderer hour on that his bosom dwelt.

54

And he had learned to love—I know not why,
For this in such as him seems strange of mood—
The helpless looks of blooming infancy,   480
Even in its earliest nurture; what subdued,
To change like this, a mind so far imbued
With scorn of man, it little boots to know;
But thus it was; and though in solitude

8. In the stanzas here omitted, Harold
is abruptly sent sailing up the Rhine,
meditating on the "thousand battles"
that "have assailed thy banks."

3. Commentators agree that the reference is to Byron's half sister, Augusta
Leigh.

Small power the nipped affections have to grow,   485
In him this glowed when all beside had ceased to glow.

55

And there was one soft breast, as hath been said,
Which unto his was bound by stronger ties
Than the church links withal; and, though unwed,
That love was pure, and, far above disguise,   490
Had stood the test of mortal enmities
Still undivided, and cemented more
By peril, dreaded most in female eyes;
But this was firm, and from a foreign shore
Well to that heart might his these absent greetings pour!   495

* * *

68

Lake Leman[4] woos me with its crystal face,
The mirror where the stars and mountains view   645
The stillness of their aspect in each trace
Its clear depth yields of their far height and hue:
There is too much of man here, to look through
With a fit mind the might which I behold;
But soon in me shall Loneliness renew   650
Thoughts hid, but not less cherished than of old,
Ere mingling with the herd had penned me in their fold.

69

To fly from, need not be to hate, mankind:
All are not fit with them to stir and toil,
Nor is it discontent to keep the mind   655
Deep in its fountain, lest it overboil
In the hot throng, where we become the spoil
Of our infection, till too late and long
We may deplore and struggle with the coil,[5]
In wretched interchange of wrong for wrong   660
Midst a contentious world, striving where none are strong.

70

There, in a moment, we may plunge our years
In fatal penitence, and in the blight
Of our own soul turn all our blood to tears,
And color things to come with hues of night;   665
The race of life becomes a hopeless flight
To those that walk in darkness: on the sea,
The boldest steer but where their ports invite,
But there are wanderers o'er Eternity
Whose bark drives on and on, and anchored ne'er shall be.   670

71

Is it not better, then, to be alone,
And love earth only for its earthly sake?
By the blue rushing of the arrowy Rhone,
Or the pure bosom of its nursing lake,
Which feeds it as a mother who doth make   675

4. The Lake of Geneva, Switzerland.   5. Tumult.

A fair but froward infant her own care,
Kissing its cries away as these awake—
Is it not better thus our lives to wear,
Than join the crushing crowd, doomed to inflict or bear?

72

I live not in myself, but I become   680
Portion of that around me; and to me
High mountains are a feeling, but the hum
Of human cities torture: I can see
Nothing to loathe in nature, save to be
A link reluctant in a fleshly chain,   685
Classed among creatures, when the soul can flee,
And with the sky, the peak, the heaving plain
Of ocean, or the stars, mingle, and not in vain.[6]

73

And thus I am absorbed, and this is life:
I look upon the peopled desert past,   690
As on a place of agony and strife,
Where, for some sin, to sorrow I was cast,
To act and suffer, but remount at last
With a fresh pinion; which I feel to spring,
Though young, yet waxing vigorous, as the blast   695
Which it would cope with, on delighted wing,
Spurning the clay-cold bonds which round our being cling.

74

And when, at length, the mind shall be all free
From what it hates in this degraded form,
Reft of its carnal life, save what shall be   700
Existent happier in the fly and worm—
When elements to elements conform,
And dust is as it should be, shall I not
Feel all I see, less dazzling, but more warm?
The bodiless thought? the Spirit of each spot?   705
Of which, even now, I share at times the immortal lot?

75

Are not the mountains, waves, and skies a part
Of me and of my soul, as I of them?
Is not the love of these deep in my heart
With a pure passion? should I not contemn   710
All objects, if compared with these? and stem
A tide of suffering, rather than forego
Such feelings for the hard and worldly phlegm
Of those whose eyes are only turned below,
Gazing upon the ground, with thoughts which dare not glow?   715

* * *

6. Byron had lived in close contact with Shelley at Geneva and had toured the lake with him. At the time, he was introduced to concepts of nature held by Shelley and Wordsworth, whom Shelley had pressed on Byron's attention; these ideas are reflected in Canto III, but the voice is Byron's. Byron said of this canto: "I was half mad during the time of its composition, between metaphysics, mountains, lakes, love unextinguishable, thoughts unutterable, and the nightmare of my own delinquencies."

85

Clear, placid Leman! thy contrasted lake,
With the wild world I dwelt in, is a thing
Which warns me with its stillness to forsake
Earth's troubled waters for a purer spring.   800
This quiet sail is as a noiseless wing
To waft me from distraction; once I loved
Torn ocean's roar, but thy soft murmuring
Sounds sweet as if a sister's voice reproved,
That I with stern delights should e'er have been so moved.   805

86

It is the hush of night, and all between
Thy margin and the mountains, dusk, yet clear,
Mellowed and mingling, yet distinctly seen,
Save darkened Jura,[7] whose capped heights appear
Precipitously steep; and drawing near,   810
There breathes a living fragrance from the shore,
Of flowers yet fresh with childhood; on the ear
Drops the light drip of the suspended oar,
Or chirps the grasshopper one good-night carol more.

87

He is an evening reveler, who makes   815
His life an infancy, and sings his fill;
At intervals, some bird from out the brakes[8]
Starts into voice a moment, then is still.
There seems a floating whisper on the hill,
But that is fancy, for the starlight dews   820
All silently their tears of love instill,
Weeping themselves away, till they infuse
Deep into Nature's breast the spirit of her hues.

88

Ye stars! which are the poetry of heaven!
If in your bright leaves we would read the fate   825
Of men and empires—'tis to be forgiven,
That in our aspirations to be great,
Our destinies o'erleap their mortal state,
And claim a kindred with you; for ye are
A beauty and a mystery, and create   830
In us such love and reverence from afar
That fortune—fame—power—life have named themselves a Star.

89

All heaven and earth are still—though not in sleep,
But breathless, as we grow when feeling most;
And silent, as we stand in thoughts too deep—   835
All heaven and earth are still. From the high host
Of stars to the lulled lake and mountain coast,
All is concentered in a life intense,
Where not a beam, nor air, nor leaf is lost,

7. The mountain range between Swit-   Lake of Geneva.
zerland and France, visible from the   8. Thickets.

But hath a part of being, and a sense 840
Of that which is of all Creator and defense.

90

Then stirs the feeling infinite, so felt
In solitude, where we are *least* alone;
A truth, which through our being then doth melt
And purifies from self: it is a tone, 845
The soul and source of music, which makes known
Eternal harmony, and sheds a charm,
Like to the fabled Cytherea's zone,[9]
Binding all things with beauty—'twould disarm
The specter Death, had he substantial power to harm. 850

91

Not vainly did the early Persian make
His altar the high places and the peak
Of earth-o'ergazing mountains, and thus take
A fit and unwalled temple, there to seek
The Spirit, in whose honor shrines are weak 855
Upreared of human hands. Come, and compare
Columns and idol-dwellings, Goth or Greek,
With Nature's realms of worship, earth and air,
Nor fix on fond abodes to circumscribe thy prayer!

92

The sky is changed!—and such a change! Oh night, 860
And storm, and darkness, ye are wondrous strong,
Yet lovely in your strength, as is the light
Of a dark eye in woman! Far along,
From peak to peak, the rattling crags among,
Leaps the live thunder! Not from one lone cloud, 865
But every mountain now hath found a tongue,
And Jura answers, through her misty shroud,
Back to the joyous Alps, who call to her aloud!

93

And this is in the night—Most glorious night!
Thou wert not sent for slumber! let me be 870
A sharer in thy fierce and far delight—
A portion of the tempest and of thee!
How the lit lake shines, a phosphoric sea,
And the big rain comes dancing to the earth!
And now again 'tis black—and now, the glee 875
Of the loud hills shakes with its mountain mirth,
As if they did rejoice o'er a young earthquake's birth.

94

Now, where the swift Rhone cleaves his way between
Heights which appear as lovers who have parted
In hate, whose mining depths so intervene 880
That they can meet no more, though brokenhearted!
Though in their souls, which thus each other thwarted,
Love was the very root of the fond rage

9. The sash of Venus, which conferred the power to attract love.

Which blighted their life's bloom, and then departed—
Itself expired, but leaving them an age   885
Of years all winters—war within themselves to wage:

95

Now, where the quick Rhone thus hath cleft his way,
The mightiest of the storms hath ta'en his stand:
For here, not one, but many, make their play,
And fling their thunderbolts from hand to hand,   890
Flashing and cast around: of all the band,
The brightest through these parted hills hath forked
His lightnings—as if he did understand,
That in such gaps as desolation worked,
There the hot shaft should blast whatever therein lurked.   895

96

Sky—mountains—river—winds—lake—lightnings! ye,
With night, and clouds, and thunder, and a soul
To make these felt and feeling, well may be
Things that have made me watchful; the far roll
Of your departing voices, is the knoll[1]   900
Of what in me is sleepless—if I rest.
But where of ye, oh tempests! is the goal?
Are ye like those within the human breast?
Or do ye find at length, like eagles, some high nest?

97

Could I embody and unbosom now   905
That which is most within me—could I wreak
My thoughts upon expression, and thus throw
Soul, heart, mind, passions, feelings, strong or weak,
All that I would have sought, and all I seek,
Bear, know, feel—and yet breathe—into *one* word,   910
And that one word were lightning, I would speak;
But as it is, I live and die unheard,
With a most voiceless thought, sheathing it as a sword.

98

The morn is up again, the dewy morn,
With breath all incense and with cheek all bloom,   915
Laughing the clouds away with playful scorn,
And living as if earth contained no tomb—
And glowing into day; we may resume
The march of our existence; and thus I,
Still on thy shores, fair Leman! may find room   920
And food for meditation, nor pass by
Much, that may give us pause, if pondered fittingly.

* * *

113

I have not loved the world, nor the world me;
I have not flattered its rank breath, nor bowed   1050
To its idolatries a patient knee—
Nor coined my cheek to smiles—nor cried aloud

1. Knell (old form).

In worship of an echo; in the crowd
They could not deem me one of such; I stood
Among them, but not of them; in a shroud   1055
Of thoughts which were not their thoughts, and still could,
Had I not filed[2] my mind, which thus itself subdued.

114

I have not loved the world, nor the world me—
But let us part fair foes; I do believe,
Though I have found them not, that there may be   1060
Words which are things, hopes which will not deceive,
And virtues which are merciful nor weave
Snares for the failing: I would also deem
O'er others' griefs that some sincerely grieve;
That two, or one, are almost what they seem—   1065
That goodness is no name, and happiness no dream.

115

My daughter! with thy name this song begun—
My daughter! with thy name thus much shall end!—
I see thee not—I hear thee not—but none
Can be so wrapped in thee; thou art the friend   1070
To whom the shadows of far years extend:
Albeit my brow thou never shouldst behold,
My voice shall with thy future visions blend,
And reach into thy heart—when mine is cold—
A token and a tone even from thy father's mold.   1075

116

To aid thy mind's development—to watch
Thy dawn of little joys—to sit and see
Almost thy very growth—to view thee catch
Knowledge of objects—wonders yet to thee!
To hold thee lightly on a gentle knee,   1080
And print on thy soft cheek a parent's kiss—
This, it should seem, was not reserved for me;
Yet this was in my nature—as it is,
I know not what is there, yet something like to this.

117

Yet, though dull Hate as duty should be taught,   1085
I know that thou wilt love me; though my name
Should be shut from thee, as a spell still fraught
With desolation, and a broken claim;
Though the grave closed between us—'twere the same;
I know that thou wilt love me; though to drain   1090
My blood from out thy being were an aim
And an attainment—all would be in vain—
Still thou wouldst love me, still that more than life retain.

118

The child of love—though born in bitterness
And nurtured in convulsion! Of thy sire   1095

2. Defiled. In a note Byron refers to *Macbeth* III.i.65 ("For Banquo's issue have I filed my mind").

These were the elements, and thine no less.
As yet such are around thee, but thy fire
Shall be more tempered and thy hope far higher.
Sweet be thy cradled slumbers! O'er the sea,
And from the mountains where I now respire,   1100
Fain would I waft such blessing upon thee,
As, with a sigh, I deem thou mightst have been to me!

From *Canto IV*

1

I stood in Venice, on the Bridge of Sighs,[1]
A palace and a prison on each hand:
I saw from out the wave her structures rise
As from the stroke of the enchanter's wand:
A thousand years their cloudy wings expand   5
Around me, and a dying Glory smiles
O'er the far times, when many a subject land
Looked to the wingéd Lion's[2] marble piles,
Where Venice sate in state, throned on her hundred isles!

2

She looks a sea Cybele,[3] fresh from ocean,   10
Rising with her tiara of proud towers
At airy distance, with majestic motion,
A ruler of the waters and their powers:
And such she was—her daughters had their dowers
From spoils of nations, and the exhaustless East   15
Poured in her lap all gems in sparkling showers:
In purple was she robed, and of her feast
Monarchs partook, and deemed their dignity increased.

3

In Venice Tasso's echoes are no more,
And silent rows the songless gondolier;[4]   20
Her palaces are crumbling to the shore,
And music meets not always now the ear:
Those days are gone—but Beauty still is here;
States fall, arts fade—but Nature doth not die,
Nor yet forget how Venice once was dear,   25
The pleasant place of all festivity,
The revel of the earth, the masque of Italy![5]

4

But unto us she hath a spell beyond
Her name in story, and her long array
Of mighty shadows, whose dim forms despond   30

1. A covered bridge between the Doge's
Palace and the prison of San Marco.
2. The emblem of St. Mark, patron
saint of Venice.
3. A nature goddess, sometimes represented wearing a crown ("tiara") of
towers.
4. The gondoliers once had the custom
of chanting stanzas of Tasso's *Jerusalem Delivered*.
5. "Masques" were lavish dramatic entertainments popular in the courts of
the Renaissance, involving songs,
dances, and elaborate costumes and
staging.

Above the dogeless city's[6] vanished sway:
Ours is a trophy which will not decay
With the Rialto;[7] Shylock and the Moor
And Pierre cannot be swept or worn away—
The keystones of the arch! though all were o'er,   35
For us repeopled were[8] the solitary shore.

* * *

178

There is a pleasure in the pathless woods,
There is a rapture on the lonely shore,   1595
There is society where none intrudes,
By the deep sea, and music in its roar:
I love not Man the less, but Nature more,
From these our interviews, in which I steal
From all I may be, or have been before,   1600
To mingle with the Universe, and feel
What I can ne'er express, yet can not all conceal.

179

Roll on, thou deep and dark blue Ocean—roll!
Ten thousand fleets sweep over thee in vain;
Man marks the earth with ruin—his control   1605
Stops with the shore; upon the watery plain
The wrecks are all thy deed, nor doth remain
A shadow of man's ravage, save his own,
When, for a moment, like a drop of rain,
He sinks into thy depths with bubbling groan,   1610
Without a grave, unknelled, uncoffined, and unknown.

180

His steps are not upon thy paths—thy fields
Are not a spoil for him—thou dost arise
And shake him from thee; the vile strength he wields
For earth's destruction thou dost all despise,   1615
Spurning him from thy bosom to the skies,
And send'st him, shivering in thy playful spray
And howling, to his Gods, where haply lies
His petty hope in some near port or bay,
And dashest him again to earth—there let him lay.[9]   1620

181

The armaments which thunderstrike the walls
Of rock-built cities, bidding nations quake
And monarchs tremble in their capitals,
The oak leviathans,[1] whose huge ribs make
Their clay creator the vain title take   1625
Of lord of thee, and arbiter of war—

6. The last duke ("doge") of Venice was deposed by Napoleon in 1797.
7. The business district in Venice, a setting in *The Merchant of Venice* and *Othello* ("the Moor"), and also in Thomas Otway's tragedy, *Venice Preserved* (1682), in which Pierre (line 34) is a leading character.
8. Would be.
9. For "lie." Denounced by many critics, this has been called the most notorious solecism in English poetry. But Byron, like other English aristocrats of the time, deliberately affected a cavalier indifference to commonplace grammar.
1. Warships.

These are thy toys, and, as the snowy flake,
They melt into thy yeast of waves, which mar
Alike the Armada's pride or spoils of Trafalgar.[2]

182

Thy shores are empires, changed in all save thee—   1630
Assyria, Greece, Rome, Carthage, what are they?
Thy waters washed them power while they were free,
And many a tyrant since; their shores obey
The stranger, slave, or savage; their decay
Has dried up realms to deserts—not so thou,   1635
Unchangeable save to thy wild waves' play;
Time writes no wrinkle on thine azure brow—
Such as creation's dawn beheld, thou rollest now.

183

Thou glorious mirror, where the Almighty's form
Glasses[3] itself in tempests; in all time,   1640
Calm or convulsed—in breeze, or gale, or storm,
Icing the pole, or in the torrid clime
Dark-heaving—boundless, endless, and sublime—
The image of Eternity—the throne
Of the Invisible; even from out thy slime   1645
The monsters of the deep are made; each zone
Obeys thee; thou goest forth, dread, fathomless, alone.

184

And I have loved thee, Ocean! and my joy
Of youthful sports was on thy breast to be
Borne, like thy bubbles, onward: from a boy   1650
I wantoned with thy breakers—they to me
Were a delight; and if the freshening sea
Made them a terror—'twas a pleasing fear,
For I was as it were a child of thee,
And trusted to thy billows far and near,   1655
And laid my hand upon thy mane—as I do here.

185

My task is done—my song hath ceased—my theme
Has died into an echo; it is fit
The spell should break of this protracted dream.
The torch shall be extinguished which hath lit   1660
My midnight lamp—and what is writ, is writ—
Would it were worthier! but I am not now
That which I have been—and my visions flit
Less palpably before me—and the glow
Which in my spirit dwelt is fluttering, faint, and low.   1665

186

Farewell! a word that must be, and hath been—
A sound which makes us linger—yet—farewell!
Ye! who have traced the Pilgrim to the scene

2. The Spanish Armada, defeated by the English in 1588, lost many ships in a storm; another storm was responsible for the loss of a number of French ships that Nelson had captured at Trafalgar (1805).
3. Mirrors.

Which is his last, if in your memories dwell
A thought which once was his, if on ye swell   1670
A single recollection, not in vain
He wore his sandal shoon and scallop shell;[4]
Farewell! with *him* alone may rest the pain,
If such there were—with *you*, the moral of his strain!

1812, 1816, 1818

So We'll Go No More A-Roving[1]

1

So we'll go no more a-roving
    So late into the night,
Though the heart be still as loving,
    And the moon be still as bright.

2

For the sword outwears its sheath,   5
    And the soul wears out the breast,
And the heart must pause to breathe,
    And Love itself have rest.

3

Though the night was made for loving,
    And the day returns too soon,   10
Yet we'll go no more a-roving
    By the light of the moon.

1817   1836

4. Sandals and a scallop shell (worn on the hat) were traditional emblems of pilgrims to holy shrines. of travel by land and travel by sea.

1. Included in a letter to Thomas Moore, February 28, 1817, and written in the Lenten aftermath of a spell of feverish dissipation in the Carnival season at Venice. Byron wrote, "I find 'the sword wearing out the scabbard,' though I have but just turned the corner of twenty-nine." The poem is based on the refrain of a Scottish song, *The Jolly Beggar:* "And we'll gang nae mair a roving / Sae late into the nicht * * * "

Don Juan   Byron began his masterpiece (pronounced in the English fashion, *Don Joó-un*) in July of 1818, published it in installments, beginning with Cantos I and II in 1819, and continued working on it almost until his death. He extemporized the poem from episode to episode; "I *have* no plan," he said, "I *had* no plan; but I had or have materials." The work was composed with remarkable speed (the 888 lines of Canto XIII, for example, were accomplished within a week), and it seeks to give the effect of improvisation and comprehensiveness rather than of compression; it ought to be read rapidly, at a conversational pace.

The poem breaks off in the sixteenth canto, but even in its unfinished state *Don Juan* is the longest satire, and one of the longest of all poems, written in English. Its hero, the Spanish libertine, had in the original legend been superhuman in his sexual energy and wickedness. Throughout

Byron's version the unspoken but persistent joke is that this violent and archetypal *homme fatal* of European legend is in fact more acted upon than active—never the seducer, always the seduced. Unfailingly amiable and well-intentioned, he is guilty largely of youth, charm, and a courteous and compliant spirit. The ladies do all the rest.

The chief models for the poem were the Italian seriocomic versions of medieval chivalric romances; the genre had been introduced by Pulci in the 15th century and achieved its greatest success in Ariosto's *Orlando Furioso* (1516). From these writers Byron caught the mixed moods and violent oscillations between the sublime and the ridiculous, as well as the easy, colloquial management of the complex ottava rima—an eight-line stanza in which the initial interlaced rhymes (*ababab*) build up to the comic turn in the final pat couplet (*cc*). Byron was influenced in the English use of this Italian form by a mildly amusing poem published in 1817, under the pseudonym of "Whistlecraft," by his friend John Hookham Frere. Other recognizable antecedents of *Don Juan* are Swift's *Gulliver's Travels* and Johnson's *Rasselas*, which also employed the naïve traveler as a satiric device, and Laurence Sterne's novel, *Tristram Shandy*, with its comic exploitation of a narrative medium blatantly subject to the whimsy of the author. But even the most original literary works play variations upon inherited conventions. Shelley at once recognized his friend's poem for what it was, "something wholly new and relative to the age."

Byron's most trusted literary advisers thought the poem disgracefully immoral, and John Murray took the precaution of printing the first two installments without identifying either Byron as the author or himself as the publisher. In our own day, however, the most common complaint is not that *Don Juan* is immoral, but that it is morally nihilistic—that the poem is destructive without limit, since it proposes no positive values as a base for the satire, but sees life, in the words of one critic, as "a strange meaningless pageant." Yet Byron insisted that *Don Juan* is "a *satire* on *abuses* of the present state of society," and "the most moral of poems." Though the final phrase exaggerates, it has a foundation of truth. What the poem most frequently attacks, in love, religion, and social relations, are very considerable vices—sham, hypocrisy, complacency, oppression, greed, and lust. Furthermore, the satire constantly, though silently, assumes as moral positives the qualities of courage, loyalty, generosity, and, above all, total candor; it merely implies that these virtues are excessively rare, and that the modern world is not constituted to reward, to encourage, or even to recognize them when they make their appearance. And far from being intimidatingly nihilistic, *Don Juan* is always and zestfully on the side of life, in its abundant variety. "As to *Don Juan*," Byron wrote elatedly to a friend, "confess—confess, you dog and be candid. * * * It may be profligate, but is it not *life*, is it not *the thing*?"

Another critical complaint is that the slender plot of the poem is buried under an excess of authorial digression. It is a mistake, however, to read *Don Juan* primarily for the story. The controlling element is not the narrative but the narrator: his play of mind and volatility of mood constitute the center of interest, and his temperament gives the work its unity. The poem is really an incessant monologue, in the course of which a story manages to be told. It opens with the first-person pronoun and immediately lets us into the story-teller's predicament: "I want a hero * * * " The voice then goes on, for almost two thousand stanzas, with effortless volubility and bewildering shifts of mood and perspective, using the occasion of Juan's misadventures to confide to us the speaker's thoughts and judgments upon all the major institutions, activities, and values of Western society.

What Byron discovered in *Don Juan* was how to give literary expression to that aspect of his temperament which, in real life, his self-consciousness and reserve permitted him to display only in the security of a circle of intimate friends or in his wonderfully vivacious letters to people he trusted. The poet who in his brilliantly successful youth created the gloomy and misanthropic Byronic hero, in his later and sadder life created a character (not the hero, but the narrator of *Don Juan*) who is one of the great comic inventions in literature.

From Don Juan

Fragment[1]

I would to heaven that I were so much clay,
   As I am blood, bone, marrow, passion, feeling—
Because at least the past were passed away—
   And for the future—(but I write this reeling,
Having got drunk exceedingly today,   5
   So that I seem to stand upon the ceiling)
I say—the future is a serious matter—
And so—for God's sake—hock[2] and soda water!

From Canto I

1

I want a hero: an uncommon want,
   When every year and month sends forth a new one,
Till, after cloying the gazettes with cant,
   The age discovers he is not the true one;
Of such as these I should not care to vaunt,   5
   I'll therefore take our ancient friend Don Juan—
We all have seen him, in the pantomime,[1]
Sent to the devil somewhat ere his time.

* * *

5

Brave men were living before Agamemnon[2]
   And since, exceeding valorous and sage,
A good deal like him too, though quite the same none;   35

1. This stanza was written on the back of part of the MS. of Canto I.
2. A white Rhine wine, from the German *Hochheimer*.
1. The Juan legend was a popular subject in English pantomime.
2. In Homer's *Iliad*, the king commanding the Greeks in the siege of Troy. This line is translated from an ode by Horace.

But then they shone not on the poet's page,
And so have been forgotten—I condemn none,
But can't find any in the present age
Fit for my poem (that is, for my new one);
So, as I said, I'll take my friend Don Juan.   40

6

Most epic poets plunge *"in medias res"*[3]
(Horace makes this the heroic turnpike road),
And then your hero tells, whene'er you please,
What went before—by way of episode,
While seated after dinner at his ease,   45
Beside his mistress in some soft abode,
Palace, or garden, paradise, or cavern,
Which serves the happy couple for a tavern.

7

That is the usual method, but not mine—
My way is to begin with the beginning;   50
The regularity of my design
Forbids all wandering as the worst of sinning,
And therefore I shall open with a line
(Although it cost me half an hour in spinning)
Narrating somewhat of Don Juan's father,   55
And also of his mother, if you'd rather.

8

In Seville was he born, a pleasant city,
Famous for oranges and women—he
Who has not seen it will be much to pity,
So says the proverb—and I quite agree;   60
Of all the Spanish towns is none more pretty,
Cadiz perhaps—but that you soon may see—
Don Juan's parents lived beside the river,
A noble stream, and called the Guadalquivir.

9

His father's name was Jóse[4]—*Don*, of course,   65
A true Hidalgo, free from every stain
Of Moor or Hebrew blood, he traced his source
Through the most Gothic gentlemen of Spain;
A better cavalier ne'er mounted horse,
Or, being mounted, e'er got down again,   70
Than Jóse, who begot our hero, who
Begot—but that's to come—Well, to renew:

10

His mother was a learned lady, famed
For every branch of every science known—
In every Christian language ever named,   75
With virtues equaled by her wit alone:
She made the cleverest people quite ashamed,
And even the good with inward envy groan,

---

3. "Into the middle of things" (Horace, *Ars Poetica* 148).

4. Normally "José," of course; Byron transferred the accent for his meter.

Finding themselves so very much exceeded
In their own way by all the things that she did.   80

11

Her memory was a mine: she knew by heart
   All Calderon and greater part of Lopé,[5]
So that if any actor missed his part
   She could have served him for the prompter's copy;
For her Feinagle's[6] were an useless art,   85
   And he himself obliged to shut up shop—he
Could never make a memory so fine as
That which adorned the brain of Donna Inez.

12

Her favorite science was the mathematical,
   Her noblest virtue was her magnanimity,   90
Her wit (she sometimes tried at wit) was Attic[7] all,
   Her serious sayings darkened to sublimity;
In short, in all things she was fairly what I call
   A prodigy—her morning dress was dimity,
Her evening silk, or, in the summer, muslin,   95
And other stuffs, with which I won't stay puzzling.

13

She knew the Latin—that is, "the Lord's prayer,"
   And Greek—the alphabet—I'm nearly sure;
She read some French romances here and there,
   Although her mode of speaking was not pure;   100
For native Spanish she had no great care,
   At least her conversation was obscure;
Her thoughts were theorems, her words a problem,
As if she deemed that mystery would ennoble 'em.

              * * *

22

'Tis pity learned virgins ever wed
   With persons of no sort of education,   170
Or gentlemen, who, though well born and bred,
   Grow tired of scientific conversation:
I don't choose to say much upon this head,
   I'm a plain man, and in a single station,
But—Oh! ye lords of ladies intellectual,   175
Inform us truly, have they not henpecked you all?

23

Don Jóse and his lady quarrelled—*why*,
   Not any of the many could divine,
Though several thousand people chose to try,
   'Twas surely no concern of theirs nor mine;   180
I loathe that low vice, curiosity;
   But if there's anything in which I shine,

5. Lope de Vega and Calderón de la Barca, the great Spanish dramatists of the early 17th century.
6. Gregor von Feinagle, a German expert on mnemonics, who had lectured in England in 1811.
7. Athenian. The common phrase "Attic salt" signifies the famed wit of the Athenians.

'Tis in arranging all my friends' affairs,
Not having, of my own, domestic cares.

24

And so I interfered, and with the best   185
  Intentions, but their treatment was not kind;
I think the foolish people were possessed,
  For neither of them could I ever find,
Although their porter afterwards confessed—
  But that's no matter, and the worst's behind,   100
For little Juan o'er me threw, downstairs,
A pail of housemaid's water unawares.

25

A little curly-headed, good-for-nothing,
  And mischief-making monkey from his birth;
His parents ne'er agreed except in doting   195
  Upon the most unquiet imp on earth;
Instead of quarreling, had they been but both in
  Their senses, they'd have sent young master forth
To school, or had him soundly whipped at home,
To teach him manners for the time to come.   200

26

Don Jóse and the Donna Inez led
  For some time an unhappy sort of life,
Wishing each other, not divorced, but dead;
  They lived respectably as man and wife,
Their conduct was exceedingly well-bred,   205
  And gave no outward signs of inward strife,
Until at length the smothered fire broke out,
And put the business past all kind of doubt.

27

For Inez called some druggists and physicians,
  And tried to prove her loving lord was *mad*,[8]   210
But as he had some lucid intermissions,
  She next decided he was only *bad*;
Yet when they asked her for her depositions,
  No sort of explanation could be had,
Save that her duty both to man and God   215
Required this conduct—which seemed very odd.

28

She kept a journal, where his faults were noted,
  And opened certain trunks of books and letters,
All which might, if occasion served, be quoted;
  And then she had all Seville for abettors,   220
Besides her good old grandmother (who doted);
  The hearers of her case became repeaters,
Then advocates, inquisitors, and judges,
Some for amusement, others for old grudges.

8. Lady Byron had thought her husband might be insane, and sought medical advice on the matter. This and other
passages obviously allude to his wife,
although Byron insisted that Donna
Inez was not intended to be a caricature
of Lady Byron.

29

And then this best and meekest woman bore   225
   With such serenity her husband's woes,
Just as the Spartan ladies did of yore,
   Who saw their spouses killed, and nobly chose
Never to say a word about them more—
   Calmly she heard each calumny that rose,   230
And saw *his* agonies with such sublimity,
That all the world exclaimed, "What magnanimity!"

* * *

32

Their friends had tried at reconciliation,
   Then their relations, who made matters worse   250
('Twere hard to tell upon a like occasion
   To whom it may be best to have recourse—
I can't say much for friend or yet relation);
   The lawyers did their utmost for divorce,
But scarce a fee was paid on either side   255
Before, unluckily, Don Jóse died.

33

He died: and most unluckily, because
   According to all hints I could collect
From counsel learned in those kinds of laws
   (Although their talk's obscure and circumspect),   260
His death contrived to spoil a charming cause;
   A thousand pities also with respect
To public feeling, which on this occasion
Was manifested in a great sensation.

* * *

37

Dying intestate, Juan was sole heir
   To a chancery suit,[9] and messuages, and lands,   290
Which, with a long minority and care,
   Promised to turn out well in proper hands:
Inez became sole guardian, which was fair,
   And answered but to nature's just demands;
An only son left with an only mother   295
Is brought up much more wisely than another.

38

Sagest of women, even of widows, she
   Resolved that Juan should be quite a paragon,
And worthy of the noblest pedigree
   (His sire was of Castile, his dam from Aragon).   300
Then for accomplishments of chivalry,
   In case our lord the king should go to war again,
He learned the arts of riding, fencing, gunnery,
And how to scale a fortress—or a nunnery.

9. A suit in what was then the highest English court, notorious for its delays.   "Messuages": houses and the adjoining lands.

39

But that which Donna Inez most desired,   305
    And saw into herself each day before all
The learned tutors whom for him she hired,
    Was that his breeding should be strictly moral:
Much into all his studies she inquired,
    And so they were submitted first to her, all,   310
Arts, sciences, no branch was made a mystery
To Juan's eyes, excepting natural history.[1]

40

The languages, especially the dead,
    The sciences, and most of all the abstruse,
The arts, at least all such as could be said   315
    To be the most remote from common use,
In all these he was much and deeply read;
    But not a page of anything that's loose,
Or hints continuation of the species,
Was ever suffered, lest he should grow vicious.   320

41

His classic studies made a little puzzle,
    Because of filthy loves of gods and goddesses,
Who in the earlier ages raised a bustle,
    But never put on pantaloons or bodices;
His reverend tutors had at times a tussle,   325
    And for their *Aeneids*, *Iliads*, and *Odysseys*,
Were forced to make an odd sort of apology,
For Donna Inez dreaded the mythology.

42

Ovid's a rake, as half his verses show him,
    Anacreon's morals are a still worse sample,   330
Catullus scarcely has a decent poem,
    I don't think Sappho's *Ode* a good example,
Although Longinus tells us there is no hymn
    Where the sublime soars forth on wings more ample;[2]
But Virgil's songs are pure, except that horrid one   335
Beginning with "*Formosum Pastor Corydon.*"[3]

43

Lucretius' irreligion[4] is too strong
    For early stomachs, to prove wholesome food;
I can't help thinking Juvenal[5] was wrong,
    Although no doubt his real intent was good,   340
For speaking out so plainly in his song,
    So much indeed as to be downright rude;

1. Which includes biology and physiology.
2. The Greek rhetorician Longinus praises a passage from Sappho in *On the Sublime* X.
3. Virgil's *Eclogue II* begins: "The shepherd, Corydon, burned with love for the handsome Alexis."
4. In *De rerum natura* ("On the Nature of Things") Lucretius sets out to show that the universe can be explained without reference to any god.
5. The Latin satires of Juvenal attacked the corruption of Roman society in the first century A.D.

And then what proper person can be partial
To all those nauseous epigrams of Martial?

44

Juan was taught from out the best edition,
    Expurgated by learned men, who place,
Judiciously, from out the schoolboy's vision,
    The grosser parts; but fearful to deface
Too much their modest bard by this omission,
    And pitying sore his mutilated case,
They only add them all in an appendix,[6]
Which saves, in fact, the trouble of an index.

* * *

52

For my part I say nothing—nothing—but
    This I will say—my reasons are my own—
That if I had an only son to put
    To school (as God be praised that I have none)
'Tis not with Donna Inez I would shut
    Him up to learn his catechism alone,
No—no—I'd send him out betimes to college,
For there it was I picked up my own knowledge.

53

For there one learns—'tis not for me to boast,
    Though I acquired—but I pass over *that*,
As well as all the Greek I since have lost:
    I say that there's the place—but *"Verbum sat,"*[7]
I think I picked up too, as well as most,
    Knowledge of matters—but no matter *what*—
I never married—but, I think, I know
That sons should not be educated so.

54

Young Juan now was sixteen years of age,
    Tall, handsome, slender, but well knit: he seemed
Active, though not so sprightly, as a page;
    And everybody but his mother deemed
Him almost man; but she flew in a rage
    And bit her lips (for else she might have screamed)
If any said so, for to be precocious
Was in her eyes a thing the most atrocious.

55

Amongst her numerous acquaintance, all
    Selected for discretion and devotion,
There was the Donna Julia, whom to call
    Pretty were but to give a feeble notion
Of many charms in her as natural
    As sweetness to the flower, or salt to ocean,
Her zone[8] to Venus, or his bow to Cupid
(But this last simile is trite and stupid).

6. "Fact! There is, or was, such an edition, with all the obnoxious epigrams of Martial placed by themselves at the end" [Byron's note].
7. A word [to the wise] is sufficient.
8. Girdle.

56

The darkness of her Oriental eye
  Accorded with her Moorish origin
(Her blood was not all Spanish, by the by;
  In Spain, you know, this is a sort of sin).
When proud Granada fell, and, forced to fly,   445
  Boabdil wept,[9] of Donna Julia's kin
Some went to Africa, some stayed in Spain,
Her great-great-grandmamma chose to remain.

57

She married (I forget the pedigree)
  With an hidalgo,[1] who transmitted down   450
His blood less noble than such blood should be;
  At such alliances his sires would frown,
In that point so precise in each degree
  That they bred *in and in*, as might be shown,
Marrying their cousins—nay, their aunts, and nieces,   455
Which always spoils the breed, if it increases.

58

This heathenish cross restored the breed again,
  Ruined its blood, but much improved its flesh;
For from a root the ugliest in old Spain
  Sprung up a branch as beautiful as fresh;   460
The sons no more were short, the daughters plain:
  But there's a rumor which I fain would hush,
'Tis said that Donna Julia's grandmamma
Produced her Don more heirs at love than law.

59

However this might be, the race went on   465
  Improving still through every generation,
Until it centered in an only son,
  Who left an only daughter; my narration
May have suggested that this single one
  Could be but Julia (whom on this occasion   470
I shall have much to speak about), and she
Was married, charming, chaste, and twenty-three.

60

Her eye (I'm very fond of handsome eyes)
  Was large and dark, suppressing half its fire
Until she spoke, then through its soft disguise   475
  Flashed an expression more of pride than ire,
And love than either; and there would arise
  A something in them which was not desire,
But would have been, perhaps, but for the soul
Which struggled through and chastened down the whole.   480

61

Her glossy hair was clustered o'er a brow
  Bright with intelligence, and fair, and smooth;

9. The last Moorish king of Granada (then a province in Spain) wept when his capital fell to the Spaniards (1492).

1. A Spanish nobleman of the lower class.

Her eyebrow's shape was like the aërial bow,
  Her cheek all purple with the beam of youth,
Mounting, at times, to a transparent glow,   485
  As if her veins ran lightning; she, in sooth,
Possessed an air and grace by no means common:
  Her stature tall—I hate a dumpy woman.

62

Wedded she was some years, and to a man
  Of fifty, and such husbands are in plenty;   490
And yet, I think, instead of such a ONE
  'Twere better to have TWO of five-and-twenty,
Especially in countries near the sun:
  And now I think on't, *"mi vien in mente,"*[2]
Ladies even of the most uneasy virtue   495
  Prefer a spouse whose age is short of thirty.

63

'Tis a sad thing, I cannot choose but say,
  And all the fault of that indecent sun,
Who cannot leave alone our helpless clay,
  But will keep baking, broiling, burning on,   500
That howsoever people fast and pray,
  The flesh is frail, and so the soul undone:
What men call gallantry, and gods adultery,
Is much more common where the climate's sultry.

64

Happy the nations of the moral North!   505
  Where all is virtue, and the winter season
Sends sin, without a rag on, shivering forth
  ('Twas snow that brought St. Anthony to reason);[3]
Where juries cast up what a wife is worth
  By laying whate'er sum, in mulct,[4] they please on   510
The lover, who must pay a handsome price,
Because it is a marketable vice.

65

Alfonso was the name of Julia's lord,
  A man well looking for his years, and who
Was neither much beloved nor yet abhorred: 515
  They lived together as most people do,
Suffering each other's foibles by accord,
  And not exactly either *one* or *two*;
Yet he was jealous, though he did not show it,
For jealousy dislikes the world to know it.

* * *

69

Juan she saw, and, as a pretty child,   545
  Caressed him often—such a thing might be
Quite innocently done, and harmless styled,

2. "It comes to my mind."
3. "For the particulars of St. Anthony's recipe for hot blood in cold weather,
see Mr. Alban Butler's *Lives of the Saints*" [Byron's note].
4. By way of a fine or legal penalty.

When she had twenty years, and thirteen he;
But I am not so sure I should have smiled
   When he was sixteen, Julia twenty-three;
These few short years make wondrous alterations,
Particularly amongst sunburnt nations.

70

Whate'er the cause might be, they had become
   Changed; for the dame grew distant, the youth shy,
Their looks cast down, their greetings almost dumb,
   And much embarrassment in either eye;
There surely will be little doubt with some
   That Donna Julia knew the reason why,
But as for Juan, he had no more notion
Than he who never saw the sea, of ocean.

71

Yet Julia's very coldness still was kind,
   And tremulously gentle her small hand
Withdrew itself from his, but left behind
   A little pressure, thrilling, and so bland
And slight, so very slight, that to the mind
   'Twas but a doubt; but ne'er magician's wand
Wrought change with all Armida's[5] fairy art
Like what this light touch left on Juan's heart.

72

And if she met him, though she smiled no more,
   She looked a sadness sweeter than her smile,
As if her heart had deeper thoughts in store
   She must not own, but cherished more the while,
For that compression in its burning core;
   Even innocence itself has many a wile,
And will not dare to trust itself with truth,
And love is taught hypocrisy from youth.

* * *

76

She vowed she never would see Juan more,
   And next day paid a visit to his mother,
And looked extremely at the opening door,
   Which, by the Virgin's grace, let in another;
Grateful she was, and yet a little sore—
   Again it opens, it can be no other,
'Tis surely Juan now—No! I'm afraid
That night the Virgin was no further prayed.

77

She now determined that a virtuous woman
   Should rather face and overcome temptation,
That flight was base and dastardly, and no man
   Should ever give her heart the least sensation;
That is to say, a thought beyond the common

5. The sorceress who seduces Rinaldo in Tasso's *Jerusalem Delivered*.

Preference, that we must feel upon occasion,
For people who are pleasanter than others,   615
But then they only seem so many brothers.

78

And even if by chance—and who can tell?
  The devil's so very sly—she should discover
That all within was not so very well,
  And, if still free, that such or such a lover   620
Might please perhaps, a virtuous wife can quell
  Such thoughts, and be the better when they're over;
And if the man should ask, 'tis but denial:
I recommend young ladies to make trial.

79

And then there are such things as love divine,   625
  Bright and immaculate, unmixed and pure,
Such as the angels think so very fine,
  And matrons, who would be no less secure,
Platonic, perfect, "just such love as mine":
  Thus Julia said—and thought so, to be sure,   630
And so I'd have her think, were I the man
On whom her reveries celestial ran.

✦ ✹ ✺

86

So much for Julia. Now we'll turn to Juan.
  Poor little fellow! he had no idea
Of his own case, and never hit the true one;
  In feelings quick as Ovid's Miss Medea,[6]
He puzzled over what he found a new one,   685
  But not as yet imagined it could be a
Thing quite in course, and not at all alarming,
Which, with a little patience, might grow charming.

✶ ✶ ✶

90

Young Juan wandered by the glassy brooks,
  Thinking unutterable things; he threw
Himself at length within the leafy nooks   715
  Where the wild branch of the cork forest grew;
There poets find materials for their books,
  And every now and then we read them through,
So that their plan and prosody are eligible,
Unless, like Wordsworth, they prove unintelligible.   720

91

He, Juan (and not Wordsworth), so pursued
  His self-communion with his own high soul,
Until his mighty heart, in its great mood,
  Had mitigated part, though not the whole
Of its disease; he did the best he could   725

6. In *Metamorphoses* VII, Ovid tells the story of Medea's mad infatuation for Jason.

With things not very subject to control,
And turned, without perceiving his condition,
Like Coleridge, into a metaphysician.

92

He thought about himself, and the whole earth,
   Of man the wonderful, and of the stars,   730
And how the deuce they ever could have birth;
   And then he thought of earthquakes, and of wars,
How many miles the moon might have in girth,
   Of air-balloons, and of the many bars
To perfect knowledge of the boundless skies—   735
And then he thought of Donna Julia's eyes.

93

In thoughts like these true wisdom may discern
   Longings sublime, and aspirations high,
Which some are born with, but the most part learn
   To plague themselves withal, they know not why: 740
'Twas strange that one so young should thus concern
   His brain about the action of the sky;
If *you* think 'twas philosophy that this did,
I can't help thinking puberty assisted.

94

He pored upon the leaves, and on the flowers,   745
   And heard a voice in all the winds; and then
He thought of wood nymphs and immortal bowers,
   And how the goddesses came down to men:
He missed the pathway, he forgot the hours,
   And when he looked upon his watch again,   750
He found how much old Time had been a winner—
He also found that he had lost his dinner.

* * *

103

'Twas on a summer's day—the sixth of June—
   I like to be particular in dates,
Not only of the age, and year, but moon;
   They are a sort of post house, where the Fates   820
Change horses, making history change its tune,
   Then spur away o'er empires and o'er states,
Leaving at last not much besides chronology,
Excepting the post-obits[7] of theology.

104

'Twas on the sixth of June, about the hour   825
   Of half-past six—perhaps still nearer seven—
When Julia sate within as pretty a bower
   As e'er held houri in that heathenish heaven
Described by Mahomet, and Anacreon Moore,[8]

7. I.e., post-obit bonds (*post obitum,* "after death"): loans to an heir which fall due after the death of the person whose estate he is to inherit. Byron's meaning is probably that only theology purports to tell us what rewards are due in heaven.
8. Byron's friend, the poet Thomas Moore, who had translated the *Odes* of Anacreon; Byron is alluding to the

To whom the lyre and laurels have been given,   830
With all the trophies of triumphant song—
He won them well, and may he wear them long!

105

She sate, but not alone; I know not well
　How this same interview had taken place,
And even if I knew, I should not tell—   835
　People should hold their tongues in any case;
No matter how or why the thing befell,
　But there she and Juan, face to face—
When two such faces are so, 'twould be wise,
But very difficult, to shut their eyes.   840

106

How beautiful she looked! her conscious[9] heart
　Glowed in her cheek, and yet she felt no wrong.
Oh Love! how perfect is thy mystic art,
　Strengthening the weak, and trampling on the strong,
How self-deceitful is the sagest part   845
　Of mortals whom thy lure hath led along—
The precipice she stood on was immense,
So was her creed[1] in her own innocence.

107

She thought of her own strength, and Juan's youth,
　And of the folly of all prudish fears,   850
Victorious virtue, and domestic truth,
　And then of Don Alfonso's fifty years:
I wish these last had not occurred, in sooth,
　Because that number rarely much endears,
And through all climes, the snowy and the sunny,   855
Sounds ill in love, whate'er it may in money.

*　*　*

113

The sun set, and up rose the yellow moon:
　The devil's in the moon for mischief; they
Who called her CHASTE, methinks, began too soon
　Their nomenclature; there is not a day,   900
The longest, not the twenty-first of June,
　Sees half the business in a wicked way
On which three single hours of moonshine smile—
And then she looks so modest all the while.

114

There is a dangerous silence in that hour,   905
　A stillness, which leaves room for the full soul
To open all itself, without the power
　Of calling wholly back its self-control;
The silver light which, hallowing tree and tower,
　Sheds beauty and deep softness o'er the whole,   910

tale of *Paradise and the Peri* in 　9. Feelingful.
Moore's Oriental poem *Lalla Rookh*.　1. Belief.

Breathes also to the heart, and o'er it throws
A loving languor, which is not repose.

115

And Julia sate with Juan, half embraced
   And half retiring from the glowing arm,
Which trembled like the bosom where 'twas placed;   915
   Yet still she must have thought there was no harm,
Or else 'twere easy to withdraw her waist;
   But then the situation had its charm,
And then——God knows what next—I can't go on;
I'm almost sorry that I e'er begun.   920

116

Oh Plato! Plato! you have paved the way,
   With your confounded fantasies, to more
Immoral conduct by the fancied sway
   Your system feigns o'er the controlless core
Of human hearts, than all the long array   925
   Of poets and romancers: You're a bore,
A charlatan, a coxcomb—and have been,
At best, no better than a go-between.

117

And Julia's voice was lost, except in sighs,
   Until too late for useful conversation;   930
The tears were gushing from her gentle eyes,
   I wish, indeed, they had not had occasion,
But who, alas! can love, and then be wise?
   Not that remorse did not oppose temptation;
A little still she strove, and much repented,   935
And whispering "I will ne'er consent"—consented.

* * *

126

'Tis sweet to win, no matter how, one's laurels
   By blood or ink; 'tis sweet to put an end
To strife; 'tis sometimes sweet to have our quarrels,
   Particularly with a tiresome friend:
Sweet is old wine in bottles, ale in barrels;   1005
   Dear is the helpless creature we defend
Against the world; and dear the schoolboy spot
We ne'er forget, though there we are forgot.

127

But sweeter still than this, than these, than all,
   Is first and passionate love—it stands alone,   1010
Like Adam's recollection of his fall;
   The tree of knowledge has been plucked—all's known—
And life yields nothing further to recall
   Worthy of this ambrosial sin, so shown,
No doubt in fable, as the unforgiven   1015
Fire which Prometheus[2] filched for us from heaven.

* * *

2. The Titan Prometheus incurred the wrath of Jupiter by stealing fire for mankind from heaven.

133

Man's a phenomenon, one knows not what,
  And wonderful beyond all wondrous measure;
'Tis pity though, in this sublime world, that
  Pleasure's a sin, and sometimes sin's a pleasure;   1060
Few mortals know what end they would be at,
  But whether glory, power, or love, or treasure,
The path is through perplexing ways, and when
The goal is gained, we die, you know—and then——

134

What then?—I do not know, no more do you—   1065
  And so good night.—Return we to our story:
'Twas in November, when fine days are few,
  And the far mountains wax a little hoary,
And clap a white cape on their mantles blue;
  And the sea dashes round the promontory,   1070
And the loud breaker boils against the rock,
And sober suns must set at five o'clock.

135

'Twas, as the watchmen say, a cloudy night;
  No moon, no stars, the wind was low or loud
By gusts, and many a sparkling hearth was bright   1073
  With the piled wood, round which the family crowd;
There's something cheerful in that sort of light,
  Even as a summer sky's without a cloud:
I'm fond of fire, and crickets, and all that,
A lobster salad, and champagne, and chat   1080

136

'Twas midnight—Donna Julia was in bed,
  Sleeping, most probably—when at her door
Arose a clatter might awake the dead,
  If they had never been awoke before,
And that they have been so we all have read,   1085
  And are to be so, at the least, once more;
The door was fastened, but with voice and fist
First knocks were heard, then "Madam—Madam—hist!

137

"For God's sake, Madam—Madam—here's my master,
  With more than half the city at his pack—   1090
Was ever heard of such a cursed disaster!
  'Tis not my fault—I kept good watch—Alack!
Do, pray, undo the bolt a little faster—
  They're on the stair just now, and in a crack
Will all be here; perhaps he yet may fly—   1095
Surely the window's not so *very* high!"

138

By this time Don Alfonso was arrived,
  With torches, friends, and servants in great number;
The major part of them had long been wived,
  And therefore paused not to disturb the slumber   1100
Of any wicked woman, who contrived

By stealth her husband's temples to encumber:³
Examples of this kind are so contagious,
Were *one* not punished, *all* would be outrageous.

139

I can't tell how, or why, or what suspicion   1105
  Could enter into Don Alfonso's head;
But for a cavalier of his condition⁴
  It surely was exceedingly ill-bred,
Without a word of previous admonition,
  To hold a levee⁵ round his lady's bed,   1110
And summon lackeys, armed with fire and sword,
To prove himself the thing he most abhorred.

140

Poor Donna Julia! starting as from sleep
  (Mind that I do not say she had not slept),
Began at once to scream, and yawn, and weep;   1115
  Her maid, Antonia, who was an adept,
Contrived to fling the bedclothes in a heap,
  As if she had just now from out them crept:
I can't tell why she should take all this trouble
To prove her mistress had been sleeping double.   1120

141

But Julia mistress, and Antonia maid,
  Appeared like two poor harmless women, who
Of goblins, but still more of men, afraid,
  Had thought one man might be deterred by two,
And therefore side by side were gently laid,   1125
  Until the hours of absence should run through,
And truant husband should return, and say,
"My dear, I was the first who came away."

142

Now Julia found at length a voice, and cried,
  "In heaven's name, Don Alfonso, what d'ye mean?   1130
Has madness seized you? would that I had died
  Ere such a monster's victim I had been!
What may this midnight violence betide,
  A sudden fit of drunkenness or spleen?
Dare you suspect me, whom the thought would kill?   1135
Search, then, the room!"—Alfonso said, "I will."

143

He searched, *they* searched, and rummaged everywhere,
  Closet and clothes-press, chest and window seat,
And found much linen, lace, and several pair
  Of stockings, slippers, brushes, combs, complete,   1140
With other articles of ladies fair,
  To keep them beautiful, or leave them neat:
Arras they pricked and curtains with their swords,
And wounded several shutters, and some boards.

3. Horns growing on the forehead were   4. Rank.
the traditional emblem of the cuckolded   5. Morning reception.
husband.

144

Under the bed they searched, and there they found—   1145
   No matter what—it was not that they sought;
They opened windows, gazing if the ground
   Had signs or footmarks, but the earth said nought;
And then they stared each other's faces round:
   'Tis odd, not one of all these seekers thought,   1150
And seems to me almost a sort of blunder,
Of looking *in* the bed as well as under.

145

During this inquisition Julia's tongue
   Was not asleep—"Yes, search and search," she cried,
"Insult on insult heap, and wrong on wrong!   1155
   It was for this that I became a bride!
For this in silence I have suffered long
   A husband like Alfonso at my side;
But now I'll bear no more, nor here remain,
If there be law or lawyers in all Spain.   1160

146

"Yes, Don Alfonso! husband now no more,
   If ever you indeed deserved the name,
Is't worthy of your years?—you have threescore—
   Fifty, or sixty, it is all the same—
Is't wise or fitting, causeless to explore   1165
   For facts against a virtuous woman's fame?
Ungrateful, perjured, barbarous Don Alfonso,
How dare you think your lady would go on so?"

* * *

159

The Senhor Don Alfonso stood confused;   1265
   Antonia bustled round the ransacked room,
And, turning up her nose, with looks abused
   Her master, and his myrmidons, of whom
Not one, except the attorney, was amused;
   He, like Achates,[6] faithful to the tomb,   1270
So there were quarrels, cared not for the cause,
Knowing they must be settled by the laws.

160

With prying snub nose, and small eyes, he stood,
   Following Antonia's motions here and there,
With much suspicion in his attitude;   1275
   For reputations he had little care;
So that a suit or action were made good,
   Small pity had he for the young and fair,
And ne'er believed in negatives, till these
Were proved by competent false witnesses.   1280

6. The *fidus Achates* ("faithful Achates") of Virgil's *Aeneid*, whose loyalty to
Aeneas has become proverbial.

161

But Don Alfonso stood with downcast looks,
    And, truth to say, he made a foolish figure;
When, after searching in five hundred nooks,
    And treating a young wife with so much rigor,
He gained no point, except some self-rebukes,   1285
    Added to those his lady with such vigor
Had poured upon him for the last half hour,
Quick, thick, and heavy—as a thundershower.

162

At first he tried to hammer an excuse,
    To which the sole reply was tears, and sobs,   1290
And indications of hysterics, whose
    Prologue is always certain throes, and throbs,
Gasps, and whatever else the owners choose—
    Alfonso saw his wife, and thought of Job's;[7]
He saw too, in perspective, her relations,   1295
And then he tried to muster all his patience.

163

He stood in act to speak, or rather stammer,
    But sage Antonia cut him short before
The anvil of his speech received the hammer,
    With "Pray, sir, leave the room, and say no more,   1300
Or madam dies."—Alfonso muttered, "D—n her."
    But nothing else, the time of words was o'er;
He cast a rueful look or two, and did,
He knew not wherefore, that which he was bid.

164

With him retired his *"posse comitatus,"*[8]   1305
    The attorney last, who lingered near the door
Reluctantly, still tarrying there as late as
    Antonia let him—not a little sore
At this most strange and unexplained *"hiatus"*
    In Don Alfonso's facts, which just now wore   1310
An awkward look; as he revolved the case,
The door was fastened in his legal face.

165

No sooner was it bolted, than—Oh shame!
    Oh sin! Oh sorrow! and Oh womankind!
How can you do such things and keep your fame,   1315
    Unless this world, and t'other too, be blind?
Nothing so dear as an unfilched good name!
    But to proceed—for there is more behind:
With much heartfelt reluctance be it said,
Young Juan slipped, half-smothered, from the bed.   1320

7. Job's wife had advised her afflicted husband to "curse God, and die" (Job ii.9).
8. The complete form of the modern word "posse" (*posse comitatus* means literally "power of the county," i.e., the body of citizens summoned by a sheriff to preserve order in the county).

166

He had been hid—I don't pretend to say
  How, nor can I indeed describe the where—
Young, slender, and packed easily, he lay,
  No doubt, in little compass, round or square;
But pity him I neither must nor may   1325
  His suffocation by that pretty pair;
'Twere better, sure, to die so, than be shut
With maudlin Clarence in his malmsey butt.[9]

* * *

169

What's to be done? Alfonso will be back   1345
  The moment he has sent his fools away.
Antonia's skill was put upon the rack,
  But no device could be brought into play—
And how to parry the renewed attack?
  Besides, it wanted but few hours of day: 1350
Antonia puzzled; Julia did not speak,
But pressed her bloodless lip to Juan's cheek.

170

He turned his lip to hers, and with his hand
  Called back the tangles of her wandering hair;
Even then their love they could not all command,
  And half forgot their danger and despair: 1355
Antonia's patience now was at a stand—
  "Come, come, 'tis no time now for fooling there,"
She whispered, in great wrath—"I must deposit
This pretty gentleman within the closet."   1360

* * *

173

Now, Don Alfonso entering, but alone,
  Closed the oration of the trusty maid:
She loitered, and he told her to be gone,
  An order somewhat sullenly obeyed;   1380
However, present remedy was none,
  And no great good seemed answered if she stayed:
Regarding both with slow and sidelong view,
She snuffed the candle, curtsied, and withdrew.

174

Alfonso paused a minute—then begun   1385
  Some strange excuses for his late proceeding;
He would not justify what he had done,
  To say the best, it was extreme ill-breeding;
But there were ample reasons for it, none
  Of which he specified in this his pleading: 1390

9. The Duke of Clarence, brother of Richard III, was reputed to have been assassinated by being drowned in a cask ("butt") of malmsey, a sweet and aromatic wine.

His speech was a fine sample, on the whole,
Of rhetoric, which the learned call *"rigmarole."*[1]

* * *

180

Alfonso closed his speech, and begged her pardon,
   Which Julia half withheld, and then half granted,
And laid conditions, he thought very hard on,   1435
   Denying several little things he wanted:
He stood like Adam lingering near his garden,
   With useless penitence perplexed and haunted,
Beseeching she no further would refuse,
When, lo! he stumbled o'er a pair of shoes.   1440

181

A pair of shoes!—what then? not much, if they
   Are such as fit with ladies' feet, but these
(No one can tell how much I grieve to say)
   Were masculine; to see them, and to seize,
Was but a moment's act.—Ah! well-a-day!   1445
   My teeth begin to chatter, my veins freeze—
Alfonso first examined well their fashion,
And then flew out into another passion.

182

He left the room for his relinquished sword,
   And Julia instant to the closet flew.   1450
"Fly, Juan, fly! for heaven's sake—not a word—
   The door is open—you may yet slip through
The passage you so often have explored—
   Here is the garden key—Fly—fly—Adieu!
Haste—haste! I hear Alfonso's hurrying feet—   1455
Day has not broke—there's no one in the street."

183

None can say that this was not good advice,
   The only mischief was, it came too late;
Of all experience 'tis the usual price,
   A sort of income tax laid on by fate: 1460
Juan had reached the room door in a trice,
   And might have done so by the garden gate,
But met Alfonso in his dressing gown,
Who threatened death—so Juan knocked him down.

184

Dire was the scuffle, and out went the light;   1465
   Antonia cried out "Rape!" and Julia "Fire!"
But not a servant stirred to aid the fight.
   Alfonso, pommeled to his heart's desire,
Swore lustily he'd be revenged this night;
   And Juan, too, blasphemed an octave higher;   1470
His blood was up: though young, he was a Tartar,[2]
And not at all disposed to prove a martyr.

1. Illogical sequence of vague statements.

2. "To catch a Tartar" is to tackle someone too strong for his assailant.

185

Alfonso's sword had dropped ere he could draw it,
  And they continued battling hand to hand.
For Juan very luckily ne'er saw it;   1475
  His temper not being under great command,
If at that moment he had chanced to claw it,
  Alfonso's days had not been in the land
Much longer.—Think of husbands', lover's lives!
And how ye may be doubly widows—wives!   1480

186

Alfonso grappled to detain the foe,
  And Juan throttled him to get away,
And blood ('twas from the nose) began to flow;
  At last, as they more faintly wrestling lay,
Juan contrived to give an awkward blow,   1485
  And then his only garment quite gave way;
He fled, like Joseph,[3] leaving it; but there,
I doubt, all likeness ends between the pair.

187

Lights came at length, and men, and maids, who found
  An awkward spectacle their eyes before;   1490
Antonia in hysterics, Julia swooned,
  Alfonso leaning, breathless, by the door;
Some half-torn drapery scattered on the ground,
  Some blood, and several footsteps, but no more:
Juan the gate gained, turned the key about,   1495
And liking not the inside, locked the out.

188

Here ends this canto.—Need I sing, or say,
  How Juan, naked, favored by the night,
Who favors what she should not, found his way,
  And reached his home in an unseemly plight?   1500
The pleasant scandal which arose next day,
  The nine days' wonder which was brought to light,
And how Alfonso sued for a divorce,
Were in the English newspapers, of course.

189

If you would like to see the whole proceedings,   1505
  The depositions, and the cause at full,
The names of all the witnesses, the pleadings
  Of counsel to nonsuit,[4] or to annul,
There's more than one edition, and the readings
  Are various, but they none of them are dull;   1510
The best is that in shorthand ta'en by Gurney,[5]
Who to Madrid on purpose made a journey.

---

3. In Genesis xxxix.7 ff. the chaste
Joseph flees from the advances of Poti-
phar's wife, leaving "his garment in
her hand."
4. Judgment against the plaintiff for
failure to establish his case.
5. William B. Gurney, official shorthand
writer for the Houses of Parliament and
a famous court reporter.

190

But Donna Inez, to divert the train
　　Of one of the most circulating scandals
That had for centuries been known in Spain,　　　　　　1515
　　At least since the retirement of the Vandals,[6]
First vowed (and never had she vowed in vain)
　　To Virgin Mary several pounds of candles;
And then, by the advice of some old ladies,
She sent her son to be shipped off from Cadiz.　　　　1520

191

She had resolved that he should travel through
　　All European climes, by land or sea,
To mend his former morals, and get new,
　　Especially in France and Italy
(At least this is the thing most people do).　　　　　　1525
　　Julia was sent into a convent; she
Grieved, but, perhaps, her feelings may be better
Shown in the following copy of her letter:

192

"They tell me 'tis decided; you depart:
　　'Tis wise—'tis well, but not the less a pain;　　　1530
I have no further claim on your young heart,
　　Mine is the victim, and would be again;
To love too much has been the only art
　　I used—I write in haste, and if a stain
Be on this sheet, 'tis not what it appears;　　　　　　1535
My eyeballs burn and throb, but have no tears.

193

"I loved, I love you, for this love have lost
　　State, station, heaven, mankind's, my own esteem,
And yet cannot regret what it hath cost,
　　So dear is still the memory of that dream;　　　　1540
Yet, if I name my guilt, 'tis not to boast,
　　None can deem harshlier of me than I deem:
I trace this scrawl because I cannot rest—
I've nothing to reproach, or to request.

194

"Man's love is of man's life a thing apart,　　　　　1545
　　'Tis woman's whole existence; man may range
The court, camp, church, the vessel, and the mart;
　　Sword, gown, gain, glory, offer in exchange
Pride, fame, ambition, to fill up his heart,
　　And few there are whom these cannot estrange;　1550
Men have all these resources, we but one,
To love again, and be again undone."

* * *

6. The Germanic tribe which overran Spain and other parts of southern Europe in the 4th and 5th centuries; notorious for rape and violence.

198

This note was written upon gilt-edged paper
  With a neat little crow-quill, slight and new;
Her small white hand could hardly reach the taper,[7]
  It trembled as magnetic needles do,   1580
And yet she did not let one tear escape her;
  The seal a sunflower; *"Elle vous suit partout,"*[8]
The motto, cut upon a white cornelian;
The wax was superfine, its hue vermilion.

199

This was Don Juan's earliest scrape; but whether   1585
  I shall proceed with his adventures is
Dependent on the public altogether;
  We'll see, however, what they say to this,
Their favor in an author's cap's a feather,
  And no great mischief's done by their caprice;   1590
And if their approbation we experience,
Perhaps they'll have some more about a year hence.

200

My poem's epic, and is meant to be
  Divided in twelve books; each book containing,
With love, and war, a heavy gale at sea,   1595
  A list of ships, and captains, and kings reigning,
New characters; the episodes are three;
  A panoramic view of hell's in training,
After the style of Virgil and of Homer,
So that my name of Epic's no misnomer.   1600

201

All these things will be specified in time,
  With strict regard to Aristotle's rules,
The *Vade Mecum*[9] of the true sublime,
  Which makes so many poets, and some fools:
Prose poets like blank verse, I'm fond of rhyme,   1605
  Good workmen never quarrel with their tools;
I've got new mythological machinery,
And very handsome supernatural scenery.

202

There's only one slight difference between
  Me and my epic brethren gone before,   1610
And here the advantage is my own, I ween
  (Not that I have not several merits more,
But this will more peculiarly be seen):
  They so embellish that 'tis quite a bore
Their labyrinth of fables to thread through,   1615
Whereas this story's actually true.

---

7. The candle (in order to melt wax to seal the letter).
8. "She follows you everywhere."
9. Handbook (Latin, "go with me");

Byron is deriding the interpretation of Aristotle's *Poetics* ("rules") as a guide for writing epic and tragedy.

203

If any person doubt it, I appeal
　To history, tradition, and to facts,
To newspapers, whose truth all know and feel,
　To plays in five, and operas in three acts; 　　　　　　1620
All these confirm my statement a good deal,
　But that which more completely faith exacts
Is that myself, and several now in Seville,
Saw Juan's last elopement with the devil.[1]

204

If ever I should condescend to prose, 　　　　　　　　1625
　I'll write poetical commandments, which
Shall supersede beyond all doubt all those
　That went before; in these I shall enrich
My text with many things that no one knows,
　And carry precept to the highest pitch: 　　　　　　　1630
I'll call the work "Longinus o'er a Bottle,
Or Every Poet his *own* Aristotle."

205

Thou shalt believe in Milton, Dryden, Pope;[2]
　Thou shalt not set up Wordsworth, Coleridge, Southey;
Because the first is crazed beyond all hope,
　The second drunk, the third so quaint and mouthy: 　　　1635
With Crabbe it may be difficult to cope,
　And Campbell's Hippocrene[3] is somewhat drouthy:
Thou shalt not steal from Samuel Rogers, nor
Commit—flirtation with the muse of Moore.[4] 　　　　　1640

206

Thou shalt not covet Mr. Sotheby's Muse,[5]
　His Pegasus, nor anything that's his;
Thou shalt not bear false witness like "the Blues"[6]
　(There's one, at least, is very fond of this);
Thou shalt not write, in short, but what I choose: 　　　1645
　This is true criticism, and you may kiss—
Exactly as you please, or not,—the rod;
But if you don't, I'll lay it on, by G—d!

207

If any person should presume to assert
　This story is not moral, first I pray 　　　　　　　　1650
That they will not cry out before they're hurt,
　Then that they'll read it o'er again, and say

---

1. The usual plays on the Juan legend ended with Juan in hell; a recent version is George Bernard Shaw's *Man and Superman.*
2. This is one of many passages, in prose and verse, in which Byron vigorously defended Dryden and Pope against his Romantic contemporaries.
3. Fountain on Mt. Helicon whose waters supposedly gave inspiration.
4. George Crabbe, whom Byron admired, was the author of *The Village* (1783) and other realistic poems of rural life. Thomas Campbell, Samuel Rogers, and Thomas Moore were minor poets of the Romantic period; the last two were close friends of Byron's (cf. line 829 and note).
5. William Sotheby, contemporary poet and translator, was a wealthy man (see line 1642). Pegasus was the winged horse, symbolizing poetic inspiration.
6. I.e., "bluestockings," a contemporary term for pedantic lady intellectuals, among whom Byron numbered his wife (line 1644).

(But, doubtless, nobody will be so pert)
   That this is not a moral tale, though gay;
Besides, in Canto Twelfth, I mean to show   1655
The very place where wicked people go.

* * *

213
But now at thirty years my hair is gray
   (I wonder what it will be like at forty?
I thought of a peruke[7] the other day)—
   My heart is not much greener; and, in short, I   1700
Have squandered my whole summer while 'twas May,
   And feel no more the spirit to retort; I
Have spent my life, both interest and principal,
And deem not, what I deemed, my soul invincible.

214
No more—no more—Oh! never more on me   1705
   The freshness of the heart can fall like dew,
Which out of all the lovely things we see
   Extracts emotions beautiful and new,
Hived in our bosoms like the bag o' the bee:
   Think'st thou the honey with those objects grew?   1710
Alas! 'twas not in them, but in thy power
To double even the sweetness of a flower.

215
No more—no more—Oh! never more, my heart,
   Canst thou be my sole world, my universe!
Once all in all, but now a thing apart,   1715
   Thou canst not be my blessing or my curse:
The illusion's gone forever, and thou art
   Insensible, I trust, but none the worse,
And in thy stead I've got a deal of judgment,
Though heaven knows how it ever found a lodgment.   1720

216
My days of love are over; me no more
   The charms of maid, wife, and still less of widow
Can make the fool of which they made before—
   In short, I must not lead the life I did do;
The credulous hope of mutual minds is o'er,   1725
   The copious use of claret is forbid too,
So for a good old-gentlemanly vice,
I think I must take up with avarice.

* * *

219
What are the hopes of man? Old Egypt's King   1745
   Cheops erected the first pyramid
And largest, thinking it was just the thing
   To keep his memory whole, and mummy hid:
But somebody or other rummaging

7. Wig.

Burglariously broke his coffin's lid: 1750
Let not a monument give you or me hopes,
Since not a pinch of dust remains of Cheops.

220

But I, being fond of true philosophy,
    Say very often to myself, "Alas!
All things that have been born were born to die,   1755
    And flesh (which Death mows down to hay) is grass;
You've passed your youth not so unpleasantly,
    And if you had it o'er again—'twould pass—
So thank your stars that matters are no worse,
And read your Bible, sir, and mind your purse."   1760

221

But for the present, gentle reader! and
    Still gentler purchaser! the bard—that's I—
Must, with permission, shake you by the hand,
    And so your humble servant, and good-by!
We meet again, if we should understand   1765
    Each other; and if not, I shall not try
Your patience further than by this short sample—
'Twere well if others followed my example.

222

"Go, little book, from this my solitude!
    I cast thee on the waters—go thy ways!
And if, as I believe, thy vein be good,   1770
    The world will find thee after many days."
When Southey's read, and Wordsworth understood,
    I can't help putting in my claim to praise—
The four first rhymes are Southey's, every line:[8]   1775
For God's sake, reader! take them not for mine!

From *Canto II*

8

But to our tale: the Donna Inez sent
    Her son to Cadiz only to embark;
To stay there had not answered her intent,
    But why?—we leave the reader in the dark—   60
'Twas for a voyage the young man was meant,
    As if a Spanish ship were Noah's ark,
To wean him from the wickedness of earth,
And send him like a dove of promise forth.

9

Don Juan bade his valet pack his things   65
    According to direction, then received
A lecture and some money: for four springs
    He was to travel; and though Inez grieved
(As every kind of parting has its stings),
    She hoped he would improve—perhaps believed: 70

8. The lines occur in the last stanza of Southey's *Epilogue to the Lay of the Laureate.*

A letter, too, she gave (he never read it)
Of good advice—and two or three of credit.

* * *

11

Juan embarked—the ship got under way,
  The wind was fair, the water passing rough;
A devil of a sea rolls in that bay,
  As I, who've crossed it oft, know well enough;
And, standing upon deck, the dashing spray   85
  Flies in one's face, and makes it weather-tough:
And there he stood to take, and take again,
His first—perhaps his last—farewell of Spain.

12

I can't but say it is an awkward sight
  To see one's native land receding through   90
The growing waters; it unmans one quite,
  Especially when life is rather new:
I recollect Great Britain's coast looks white,
  But almost every other country's blue,
When gazing on them, mystified by distance,   95
We enter on our nautical existence.

* * *

17

And Juan wept, and much he sighed and thought,
  While his salt tears dropped into the salt sea,   130
"Sweets to the sweet" (I like so much to quote,
  You must excuse this extract—'tis where she,
The Queen of Denmark, for Ophelia brought
  Flowers to the grave);[1] and, sobbing often, he
Reflected on his present situation,   135
And seriously resolved on reformation.

18

"Farewell, my Spain! a long farewell!" he cried,
  "Perhaps I may revisit thee no more,
But die, as many an exiled heart hath died,
  Of its own thirst to see again thy shore: 140
Farewell, where Guadalquiver's waters glide!
  Farewell, my mother! and, since all is o'er,
Farewell, too, dearest Julia!—(here he drew
Her letter out again, and read it through).

19

"And oh! if e'er I should forget, I swear—   145
  But that's impossible, and cannot be—
Sooner shall this blue ocean melt to air,
  Sooner shall earth resolve itself to sea,
Than I resign thine image, oh, my fair!
  Or think of anything, excepting thee;   150

1. Hamlet V.i.266.

A mind diseased no remedy can physic—
(Here the ship gave a lurch, and he grew seasick.)

20

"Sooner shall heaven kiss earth—(here he fell sicker)
    Oh, Julia! what is every other woe?—
(For God's sake let me have a glass of liquor;   155
    Pedro, Battista, help me down below.)
Julia, my love—(you rascal, Pedro, quicker)—
    Oh, Julia!—(this cursed vessel pitches so)—
Beloved Julia, hear me still beseeching!"
(Here he grew inarticulate with retching.)   160

21

He felt that chilling heaviness of heart,
    Or rather stomach, which, alas! attends,
Beyond the best apothecary's art,
    The loss of love, the treachery of friends,
Or death of those we dote on, when a part   165
    Of us dies with them as each fond hope ends:
No doubt he would have been much more pathetic,
But the sea acted as a strong emetic.[2]

* * *

49

'Twas twilight, and the sunless day went down   385
    Over the waste of waters; like a veil,
Which, if withdrawn, would but disclose the frown
    Of one whose hate is masked but to assail.
Thus to their hopeless eyes the night was shown,
    And grimly darkled o'er the faces pale,   390
And the dim desolate deep: twelve days had Fear
Been their familiar, and now Death was here.

50

Some trial had been making at a raft,
    With little hope in such a rolling sea,
A sort of thing at which one would have laughed,   395
    If any laughter at such times could be,
Unless with people who too much have quaffed,
    And have a kind of wild and horrid glee,
Half epileptical, and half hysterical—
    Their preservation would have been a miracle.   400

51

At half-past eight o'clock, booms, hencoops, spars,
    And all things, for a chance, had been cast loose
That still could keep afloat the struggling tars,
    For yet they strove, although of no great use:
There was no light in heaven but a few stars,   405
    The boats put off o'ercrowded with their crews;
She gave a heel, and then a lurch to port,
And, going down head foremost—sunk, in short.

2. In stanzas 22–48 (here omitted) the   violent storm, which leaves her a help-
ship, bound for Leghorn, runs into a   less, sinking wreck.

52

Then rose from sea to sky the wild farewell—
   Then shrieked the timid, and stood still the brave—   410
Then some leaped overboard with dreadful yell,
   As eager to anticipate their grave;
And the sea yawned around her like a hell,
   And down she sucked with her the whirling wave,
Like one who grapples with his enemy,   415
And strives to strangle him before he die.

53

And first one universal shriek there rushed,
   Louder than the loud ocean, like a crash
Of echoing thunder; and then all was hushed,
   Save the wild wind and the remorseless dash   420
Of billows; but at intervals there gushed,
   Accompanied with a convulsive splash,
A solitary shriek, the bubbling cry
Of some strong swimmer in his agony.

* * *

56

Juan got into the longboat, and there
   Contrived to help Pedrillo[3] to a place;
It seemed as if they had exchanged their care,
   For Juan wore the magisterial face
Which courage gives, while poor Pedrillo's pair   445
   Of eyes were crying for their owner's case:
Battista, though (a name called shortly Tita),
Was lost by getting at some aqua-vita.[4]

57

Pedro, his valet, too, he tried to save,
   But the same cause, conducive to his loss,   450
Left him so drunk, he jumped into the wave
   As o'er the cutter's edge he tried to cross,
And so he found a wine-and-watery grave;
   They could not rescue him although so close,
Because the sea ran higher every minute,   455
And for the boat—the crew kept crowding in it.

* * *

103

As they drew nigh the land, which now was seen
   Unequal in its aspect here and there,
They felt the freshness of its growing green,
   That waved in forest tops, and smoothed the air,   820
And fell upon their glazed eyes like a screen
   From glistening waves, and skies so hot and bare—
Lovely seemed any object that should sweep
Away the vast, salt, dread, eternal deep.

3. Juan's tutor.   4. Brandy.

104

The shore looked wild, without a trace of man,   825
    And girt by formidable waves; but they
Were mad for land, and thus their course they ran,
    Though right ahead the roaring breakers lay:
A reef between them also now began
    To show its boiling surf and bounding spray,   830
But finding no place for their landing better,
They ran the boat for shore—and overset her.

105

But in his native stream, the Guadalquiver,
    Juan to lave his youthful limbs was wont;
And having learnt to swim in that sweet river,   835
    Had often turned the art to some account:
A better swimmer you could scarce see ever,
    He could, perhaps, have passed the Hellespont,
As once (a feat on which ourselves we prided)
Leander, Mr. Ekenhead, and I did.[5]   840

106

So, here, though faint, emaciated, and stark,
    He buoyed his boyish limbs, and strove to ply
With the quick wave, and gain, ere it was dark,
    The beach which lay before him, high and dry:
The greatest danger here was from a shark,   845
    That carried off his neighbor by the thigh;
As for the other two, they could not swim,
So nobody arrived on shore but him.

107

Nor yet had he arrived but for the oar,
    Which, providentially for him, was washed   850
Just as his feeble arms could strike no more,
    And the hard wave o'erwhelmed him as 'twas dashed
Within his grasp; he clung to it, and sore
    The waters beat while he thereto was lashed:
At last, with swimming, wading, scrambling, he   855
Rolled on the beach, half senseless, from the sea:

108

There, breathless, with his digging nails he clung
    Fast to the sand, lest the returning wave,
From whose reluctant roar his life he wrung,
    Should suck him back to her insatiate grave: 860
And there he lay, full length, where he was flung,
    Before the entrance of a cliff-worn cave,
With just enough of life to feel its pain,
And deem that it was saved, perhaps, in vain.

109

With slow and staggering effort he arose,   865
    But sunk again upon his bleeding knee

---

5. Like Leander in the myth, Byron and Lt. Ekenhead had swum the Helles-pont on May 3, 1810. See *Written After Swimming from Sestos to Abydos.*

And quivering hand; and then he looked for those
  Who long had been his mates upon the sea;
But none of them appeared to share his woes,
  Save one, a corpse, from out the famished three,   870
Who died two days before, and now had found
An unknown barren beach for burial ground.

110

And as he gazed, his dizzy brain spun fast,
  And down he sunk; and as he sunk, the sand
Swam round and round, and all his senses passed: 875
  He fell upon his side, and his stretched hand
Drooped dripping on the oar (their jurymast),
  And, like a withered lily, on the land
His slender frame and pallid aspect lay,
As fair a thing as e'er was formed of clay.   880

111

How long in his damp trance young Juan lay
  He knew not, for the earth was gone for him,
And time had nothing more of night nor day
  For his congealing blood, and senses dim;
And how this heavy faintness passed away   885
  He knew not, till each painful pulse and limb,
And tingling vein seemed throbbing back to life,
For Death, though vanquished, still retired with strife.

112

His eyes he opened, shut, again unclosed,
  For all was doubt and dizziness; he thought   890
He still was in the boat, and had but dozed,
  And felt again with his despair o'erwrought,
And wished it death in which he had reposed,
  And then once more his feelings back were brought,
And slowly by his swimming eyes was seen   895
A lovely female face of seventeen.

113

'Twas bending close o'er his, and the small mouth
  Seemed almost prying into his for breath;
And chafing him, the soft warm hand of youth
  Recalled his answering spirits back from death;   900
And, bathing his chill temples, tried to soothe
  Each pulse to animation, till beneath
Its gentle touch and trembling care, a sigh
To these kind efforts made a low reply.

114

Then was the cordial poured, and mantle flung   905
  Around his scarce-clad limbs; and the fair arm
Raised higher the faint head which o'er it hung;
  And her transparent cheek, all pure and warm,
Pillowed his deathlike forehead; then she wrung
  His dewy curls, long drenched by every storm;   910

And watched with eagerness each throb that drew
A sigh from his heaved bosom—and hers, too.

115

And lifting him with care into the cave,
    The gentle girl, and her attendant—one
Young, yet her elder, and of brow less grave,   915
    And more robust of figure—then begun
To kindle fire, and as the new flames gave
    Light to the rocks that roofed them, which the sun
Had never seen, the maid, or whatsoe'er
She was, appeared distinct, and tall, and fair.   920

116

Her brow was overhung with coins of gold,
    That sparkled o'er the auburn of her hair,
Her clustering hair, whose longer locks were rolled
    In braids behind; and though her stature were
Even of the highest for a female mold,   925
    They nearly reached her heel; and in her air
There was a something which bespoke command,
As one who was a lady in the land.

117

Her hair, I said, was auburn; but her eyes
    Were black as death, their lashes the same hue,   930
Of downcast length, in whose silk shadow lies
    Deepest attraction; for when to the view
Forth from its raven fringe the full glance flies,
    Ne'er with such force the swiftest arrow flew;
'Tis as the snake late coiled, who pours his length,   935
And hurls at once his venom and his strength.

* * *

123

And these two tended him, and cheered him both
    With food and raiment, and those soft attentions,
Which are (as I must own) of female growth,
    And have ten thousand delicate inventions: 980
They made a most superior mess of broth,
    A thing which poesy but seldom mentions,
But the best dish that e'er was cooked since Homer's
Achilles ordered dinner for newcomers.[6]

124

I'll tell you who they were, this female pair,   985
    Lest they should seem princesses in disguise;
Besides, I hate all mystery, and that air
    Of claptrap, which your recent poets prize;
And so, in short, the girls they really were
    They shall appear before your curious eyes,   990
Mistress and maid; the first was only daughter
Of an old man, who lived upon the water.

6. A reference to the lavish feast with which Achilles entertained Ajax, Phoenix,
and Ulysses (*Iliad* IX.193 ff.).

125

A fisherman he had been in his youth,
    And still a sort of fisherman was he;
But other speculations were, in sooth,
    Added to his connection with the sea,
Perhaps not so respectable, in truth:
    A little smuggling, and some piracy,
Left him, at last, the sole of many masters
Of an ill-gotten million of piasters.[7]

126

A fisher, therefore, was he—though of men,
    Like Peter the Apostle[8]—and he fished
For wandering merchant vessels, now and then,
    And sometimes caught as many as he wished;
The cargoes he confiscated, and gain
    He sought in the slave market too, and dished
Full many a morsel for that Turkish trade,
By which, no doubt, a good deal may be made.

127

He was a Greek, and on his isle had built
    (One of the wild and smaller Cyclades[9])
A very handsome house from out his guilt,
    And there he lived exceedingly at ease;
Heaven knows what cash he got or blood he spilt,
    A sad[1] old fellow was he, if you please;
But this I know, it was a spacious building,
Full of barbaric carving, paint, and gilding.

128

He had an only daughter, called Haidée,
    The greatest heiress of the Eastern Isles;
Besides, so very beautiful was she,
    Her dowry was as nothing to her smiles:
Still in her teens, and like a lovely tree
    She grew to womanhood, and between whiles
Rejected several suitors, just to learn
How to accept a better in his turn.

129

And walking out upon the beach, below
    The cliff, towards sunset, on that day she found,
Insensible—not dead, but nearly so—
    Don Juan, almost famished, and half drowned;
But being naked, she was shocked, you know,
    Yet deemed herself in common pity bound,
As far as in her lay, "to take him in,
A stranger"[2] dying, with so white a skin.

---

7. Near Eastern coins.
8. Christ's words to Peter and Andrew, both fishermen: "Follow me, and I will make you fishers of men" (Matthew iv.19).
9. A group of islands in the Aegean Sea.
1. In the playful sense: "wicked."
2. Cf. Matthew xxv.35: "I was a stranger, and ye took me in."

130

But taking him into her father's house
  Was not exactly the best way to save,
But like conveying to the cat the mouse,   1035
  Or people in a trance into their grave;
Because the good old man had so much "νοῦς,"[3]
  Unlike the honest Arab thieves so brave,
He would have hospitably cured the stranger
And sold him instantly when out of danger.   1040

131

And therefore, with her maid, she thought it best
  (A virgin always on her maid relies)
To place him in the cave for present rest:
  And when, at last, he opened his black eyes,
Their charity increased about their guest;   1045
  And their compassion grew to such a size,
It opened half the turnpike gates to heaven
(St. Paul says 'tis the toll which must be given).[4]

* * *

141

And Haidée met the morning face to face;
  Her own was freshest, though a feverish flush
Had dyed it with the headlong blood, whose race
  From heart to check is curbed into a blush,
Like to a torrent which a mountain's base,   1125
  That overpowers some Alpine river's rush,
Checks to a lake, whose waves in circles spread;
Or the Red Sea—but the sea is not red.

142

And down the cliff the island virgin came,
  And near the cave her quick light footsteps drew,   1130
While the sun smiled on her with his first flame,
  And young Aurora[5] kissed her lips with dew,
Taking her for a sister; just the same
  Mistake you would have made on seeing the two,
Although the mortal, quite as fresh and fair,   1135
Had all the advantage, too, of not being air.

143

And when into the cavern Haidée stepped
  All timidly, yet rapidly, she saw
That like an infant Juan sweetly slept;
  And then she stopped, and stood as if in awe   1140
(For sleep is awful), and on tiptoe crept
  And wrapped him closer, lest the air, too raw,
Should reach his blood, then o'er him still as death
Bent, with hushed lips, that drank his scarce-drawn breath.

* * *

3. Nous, "intelligence"; in England,   4. I Corinthians xiii.13.
pronounced so as to rhyme with "mouse."   5. The dawn.

148

And she bent o'er him, and he lay beneath,
   Hushed as the babe upon its mother's breast,
Drooped as the willow when no winds can breathe,
   Lulled like the depth of ocean when at rest,   1180
Fair as the crowning rose of the whole wreath,
   Soft as the callow cygnet[6] in its nest;
In short, he was a very pretty fellow,
Although his woes had turned him rather yellow.

149

He woke and gazed, and would have slept again,   1185
   But the fair face which met his eyes forbade
Those eyes to close, though weariness and pain
   Had further sleep a further pleasure made;
For woman's face was never formed in vain
   For Juan, so that even when he prayed   1190
He turned from grisly saints, and martyrs hairy,
To the sweet portraits of the Virgin Mary.

150

And thus upon his elbow he arose,
   And looked upon the lady, in whose cheek
The pale contended with the purple rose,   1195
   As with an effort she began to speak;
Her eyes were eloquent, her words would pose,
   Although she told him, in good modern Greek,
With an Ionian accent, low and sweet,
That he was faint, and must not talk, but eat.   1200

* * *

168

And every day by daybreak—rather early
   For Juan, who was somewhat fond of rest—
She came into the cave, but it was merely
   To see her bird reposing in his nest;   1340
And she would softly stir his locks so curly,
   Without disturbing her yet slumbering guest,
Breathing all gently o'er his cheek and mouth,
As o'er a bed of roses the sweet South.[7]

169

And every morn his color freshlier came,   1345
   And every day helped on his convalescence;
'Twas well, because health in the human frame
   Is pleasant, besides being true love's essence,
For health and idleness to passion's flame
   Are oil and gunpowder; and some good lessons   1350
Are also learnt from Ceres[8] and from Bacchus,
Without whom Venus will not long attack us.

6. Young swan.   8. Goddess of the grain.
7. The south wind.

170

While Venus fills the heart (without heart really
   Love, though good always, is not quite so good),
Ceres presents a plate of vermicelli—   1355
   For love must be sustained like flesh and blood—
While Bacchus pours out wine, or hands a jelly:
   Eggs, oysters, too, are amatory food;
But who is their purveyor from above
Heaven knows—it may be Neptune, Pan, or Jove.   1360

171

When Juan woke he found some good things ready,
   A bath, a breakfast, and the finest eyes
That ever made a youthful heart less steady,
   Besides her maid's, as pretty for their size;
But I have spoken of all this already—   1365
   And repetition's tiresome and unwise—
Well—Juan, after bathing in the sea,
Came always back to coffee and Haidée.

172

Both were so young, and one so innocent,
   That bathing passed for nothing; Juan seemed
To her, as 'twere, the kind of being sent,   1370
   Of whom these two years she had nightly dreamed,
A something to be loved, a creature meant
   To be her happiness, and whom she deemed
To render happy; all who joy would win   1375
Must share it—Happiness was born a twin.

173

It was such pleasure to behold him, such
   Enlargement of existence to partake
Nature with him, to thrill beneath his touch,
   To watch him slumbering, and to see him wake: 1380
To live with him forever were too much;
   But then the thought of parting made her quake:
He was her own, her ocean-treasure, cast
Like a rich wreck—her first love, and her last.

174

And thus a moon rolled on, and fair Haidée   1385
   Paid daily visits to her boy, and took
Such plentiful precautions, that still he
   Remained unknown within his craggy nook;
At last her father's prows put out to sea,
   For certain merchantmen upon the look,   1390
Not as of yore to carry off an Io,[9]
But three Ragusan vessels, bound for Scio.[1]

175

Then came her freedom, for she had no mother,
   So that, her father being at sea, she was

9. Io, a mistress of Zeus persecuted by his jealous wife Hera, was kidnaped by Phoenician merchants.

1. Ragusa (or Dubrovnik), is an Adriatic port; Scio is the Italian name for Chios, an island near Turkey.

Free as a married woman, or such other   1395
  Female, as where she likes may freely pass,
Without even the encumbrance of a brother,
  The freest she that ever gazed on glass:
I speak of Christian lands in this comparison,
  Where wives, at least, are seldom kept in garrison.   1400

176

Now she prolonged her visits and her talk
  (For they must talk), and he had learnt to say
So much as to propose to take a walk—
  For little had he wandered since the day
On which, like a young flower snapped from the stalk,   1405
  Drooping and dewy on the beach he lay—
And thus they walked out in the afternoon,
And saw the sun set opposite the moon.

177

It was a wild and breaker-beaten coast,
  With cliffs above, and a broad sandy shore,   1410
Guarded by shoals and rocks as by an host,
  With here and there a creek, whose aspect wore
A better welcome to the tempest-tossed;
  And rarely ceased the haughty billow's roar,
Save on the dead long summer days, which make   1415
The outstretched ocean glitter like a lake.

178

And the small ripple split upon the beach
  Scarcely o'erpass'd the cream of your champagne,
When o'er the brim the sparkling bumpers reach,
  That spring dew of the spirit! the heart's rain!   1420
Few things surpass old wine; and they may preach
  Who please—the more because they preach in vain—
Let us have wine and woman, mirth and laughter,
Sermons and soda water the day after.

179

Man, being reasonable, must get drunk;   1425
  The best of life is but intoxication:
Glory, the grape, love, gold, in these are sunk
  The hopes of all men, and of every nation;
Without their sap, how branchless were the trunk
  Of life's strange tree, so fruitful on occasion: 1430
But to return—Get very drunk; and when
You wake with headache, you shall see what then.

180

Ring for your valet—bid him quickly bring
  Some hock and soda water, then you'll know
A pleasure worthy Xerxes the great king;[2]   1435
  For not the blest sherbet, sublimed with snow,
Nor the first sparkle of the desert spring,

2. Xerxes, 5th-century Persian king, anyone who could discover a new kind
was said to have offered a reward to of pleasure.

Nor Burgundy in all its sunset glow,
After long travel, ennui, love, or slaughter,
Vie with that draught of hock and soda water.　　　　1440

181
The coast—I think it was the coast that I
　　Was just describing—Yes, it *was* the coast—
Lay at this period quiet as the sky,
　　The sands untumbled, the blue waves untossed,
And all was stillness, save the sea bird's cry,　　　　1445
　　And dolphin's leap, and little billow crossed
By some low rock or shelve, that made it fret
Against the boundary it scarcely wet.

182
And forth they wandered, her sire being gone,
　　As I have said, upon an expedition;　　　　1450
And mother, brother, guardian, she had none,
　　Save Zoë, who, although with due precision
She waited on her lady with the sun,
　　Thought daily service was her only mission,
Bringing warm water, wreathing her long tresses,　　　　1455
And asking now and then for cast-off dresses.

183
It was the cooling hour, just when the rounded
　　Red sun sinks down behind the azure hill,
Which then seems as if the whole earth it bounded,
　　Circling all nature, hushed, and dim, and still,　　　　1460
With the far mountain crescent half surrounded
　　On one side, and the deep sea calm and chill
Upon the other, and the rosy sky,
With one star sparkling through it like an eye.

184
And thus they wandered forth, and hand in hand,　　　　1465
　　Over the shining pebbles and the shells,
Glided along the smooth and hardened sand,
　　And in the worn and wild receptacles
Worked by the storms, yet worked as it were planned,
　　In hollow halls, with sparry roofs and cells,　　　　1470
They turned to rest; and, each clasped by an arm,
Yielded to the deep twilight's purple charm.

185
They looked up to the sky, whose floating glow
　　Spread like a rosy ocean, vast and bright;
They gazed upon the glittering sea below,　　　　1475
　　Whence the broad moon rose circling into sight;
They heard the waves splash, and the wind so low,
　　And saw each other's dark eyes darting light
Into each other—and, beholding this,
Their lips drew near, and clung into a kiss;　　　　1480

186

A long, long kiss, a kiss of youth, and love,
    And beauty, all concéntrating like rays
Into one focus, kindled from above;
    Such kisses as belong to early days,
Where heart, and soul, and sense, in concert move,   1485
    And the blood's lava, and the pulse a blaze,
Each kiss a heart-quake—for a kiss's strength,
I think, it must be reckoned by its length.

187

By length I mean duration; theirs endured
    Heaven knows how long—no doubt they never reckoned;   1490
And if they had, they could not have secured
    The sum of their sensations to a second:
They had not spoken; but they felt allured,
    As if their souls and lips each other beckoned,
Which, being joined, like swarming bees they clung—   1495
Their hearts the flowers from whence the honey sprung.

188

They were alone, but not alone as they
    Who shut in chambers think it loneliness;
The silent ocean, and the starlight bay,
    The twilight glow, which momently grew less,   1500
The voiceless sands, and dropping caves, that lay
    Around them, made them to each other press,
As if there were no life beneath the sky
Save theirs, and that their life could never die.

189

They feared no eyes nor ears on that lone beach,   1505
    They felt no terrors from the night, they were
All in all to each other: though their speech
    Was broken words, they *thought* a language there—
And all the burning tongues the passions teach
    Found in one sigh the best interpreter   1510
Of nature's oracle—first love—that all
Which Eve has left her daughters since her fall.

190

Haidée spoke not of scruples, asked no vows,
    Nor offered any; she had never heard
Of plight and promises to be a spouse,   1515
    Or perils by a loving maid incurred;
She was all which pure ignorance allows,
    And flew to her young mate like a young bird;
And never having dreamt of falsehood, she
Had not one word to say of constancy.[3]   1520

191

She loved, and was belovéd—she adored,
    And she was worshiped; after nature's fashion,

3. Byron said, with reference to Haidée:
"I was, and am, penetrated with the
conviction that women only know evil
from men, whereas men have no criterion to judge of purity or goodness but
woman."

Their intense souls, into each other poured,
  If souls could die, had perished in that passion—
But by degrees their senses were restored,   1525
  Again to be o'ercome, again to dash on;
And, beating 'gainst *his* bosom, Haidée's heart
Felt as if never more to beat apart.

192

Alas! they were so young, so beautiful,
  So lonely, loving, helpless, and the hour   1530
Was that in which the heart is always full,
  And, having o'er itself no further power,
Prompts deeds eternity cannot annul,
  But pays off moments in an endless shower
Of hell-fire—all prepared for people giving   1535
Pleasure or pain to one another living.

193

Alas! for Juan and Haidée! they were
  So loving and so lovely—till then never,
Excepting our first parents, such a pair
  Had run the risk of being damned forever;   1540
And Haidée, being devout as well as fair,
  Had, doubtless, heard about the Stygian river,[4]
And hell and purgatory—but forgot
Just in the very crisis she should not.

194

They look upon each other, and their eyes   1545
  Gleam in the moonlight; and her white arm clasps
Round Juan's head, and his around hers lies
  Half buried in the tresses which it grasps;
She sits upon his knee, and drinks his sighs,
  He hers, until they end in broken gasps;   1550
And thus they form a group that's quite antique,
Half naked, loving, natural, and Greek.

195

And when those deep and burning moments passed,
  And Juan sunk to sleep within her arms,
She slept not, but all tenderly, though fast,   1555
  Sustained his head upon her bosom's charms;
And now and then her eye to heaven is cast,
  And then on the pale cheek her breast now warms,
Pillowed on her o'erflowing heart, which pants
With all it granted, and with all it grants.   1560

196

An infant when it gazes on a light,
  A child the moment when it drains the breast,
A devotee when soars the Host[5] in sight,
  An Arab with a stranger for a guest,
A sailor when the prize has struck[6] in fight,   1565

4. The Styx, which flows through Hades.
5. The Eucharistic wafer.
6. Has lowered its flag in token of surrender.

A miser filling his most hoarded chest,
Feel rapture; but not such true joy are reaping
As they who watch o'er what they love while sleeping.

197

For there it lies so tranquil, so beloved,
  All that it hath of life with us is living;
So gentle, stirless, helpless, and unmoved,
  And all unconscious of the joy 'tis giving;
All it hath felt, inflicted, passed, and proved,
  Hushed into depths beyond the watcher's diving;
There lies the thing we love with all its errors
And all its charms, like death without its terrors.

198

The lady watched her lover—and that hour
  Of Love's, and Night's, and Ocean's solitude,
O'erflowed her soul with their united power;
  Amidst the barren sand and rocks so rude
She and her wave-worn love had made their bower,
  Where nought upon their passion could intrude,
And all the stars that crowded the blue space
Saw nothing happier than her glowing face.

199

Alas! the love of women! it is known
  To be a lovely and a fearful thing;
For all of theirs upon that die is thrown,
  And if 'tis lost, life hath no more to bring
To them but mockeries of the past alone,
  And their revenge is as the tiger's spring,
Deadly, and quick, and crushing; yet, as real
Torture is theirs, what they inflict they feel.

200

They are right; for man, to man so oft unjust,
  Is always so to women; one sole bond
Awaits them, treachery is all their trust;
  Taught to conceal, their bursting hearts despond
Over their idol, till some wealthier lust
  Buys them in marriage—and what rests beyond?
A thankless husband, next a faithless lover,
Then dressing, nursing, praying, and all's over.

201

Some take a lover, some take drams or prayers,
  Some mind their household, others dissipation,
Some run away, and but exchange their cares,
  Losing the advantage of a virtuous station;
Few changes e'er can better their affairs,
  Theirs being an unnatural situation,
From the dull palace to the dirty hovel:
Some play the devil, and then write a novel.[7]

7. The impetuous and hysterical Lady Caroline Lamb, having thrown herself at Byron and been after a time rejected, incorporated incidents from the affair in her novel, *Glenarvon* (1816).

Line numbers: 1570, 1575, 1580, 1585, 1590, 1595, 1600, 1605

202

Haidée was Nature's bride, and knew not this;
   Haidée was Passion's child, born where the sun   1610
Showers triple light, and scorches even the kiss
   Of his gazelle-eyed daughters; she was one
Made but to love, to feel that she was his
   Who was her chosen: what was said or done
Elsewhere was nothing. She had nought to fear,   1615
Hope, care, nor love beyond, her heart beat *here*.

203

And oh! that quickening of the heart, that beat!
   How much it costs us! yet each rising throb
Is in its cause as its effect so sweet,
   That Wisdom, ever on the watch to rob   1620
Joy of its alchemy, and to repeat
   Fine truths; even Conscience, too, has a tough job
To make us understand each good old maxim,
So good—I wonder Castlereagh[8] don't tax 'em.

204

And now 'twas done—on the lone shore were plighted   1625
   Their hearts; the stars, their nuptial torches, shed
Beauty upon the beautiful they lighted:
   Ocean their witness, and the cave their bed,
By their own feelings hallowed and united,
   Their priest was Solitude, and they were wed: 1630
And they were happy, for to their young eyes
Each was an angel, and earth paradise.

* * *

208

But Juan! had he quite forgotten Julia?
   And should he have forgotten her so soon?
I can't but say it seems to me mostly truly a
   Perplexing question; but, no doubt, the moon   1660
Does these things for us, and whenever newly a
   Strong palpitation rises, 'tis her boon,
Else how the devil is it that fresh features
Have such a charm for us poor human creatures?

209

I hate inconstancy—I loathe, detest,   1665
   Abhor, condemn, abjure the mortal made
Of such quicksilver clay that in his breast
   No permanent foundation can be laid;
Love, constant love, has been my constant guest—
   And yet last night, being at a masquerade,   1670
I saw the prettiest creature, fresh from Milan,
Which gave me some sensations like a villain.

8. Robert Stewart, Viscount Castlereagh, British Foreign Secretary from 1812 to 1822.

210

But soon Philosophy came to my aid,
   And whispered, "Think of every sacred tie!"
"I will, my dear Philosophy!" I said,   1675
   "But then her teeth, and then, oh, Heaven! her eye!
I'll just inquire if she be wife or maid,
   Or neither—out of curiosity."
"Stop!" cried Philosophy, with air so Grecian
(Though she was masked then as a fair Venetian);   1680

211

"Stop!" so I stopped.—But to return: that which
   Men call inconstancy is nothing more
Than admiration due where nature's rich
   Profusion with young beauty covers o'er
Some favored object; and as in the niche   1685
   A lovely statue we almost adore,
This sort of adoration of the real
Is but a heightening of the "beau ideal."[9]

212

'Tis the perception of the beautiful,
   A fine extension of the faculties,   1690
Platonic, universal, wonderful,
   Drawn from the stars, and filtered through the skies,
Without which life would be extremely dull;
   In short, it is the use of our own eyes,
With one or two small senses added, just   1695
To hint that flesh is formed of fiery dust.

213

Yet 'tis a painful feeling, and unwilling,
   For surely if we always could perceive
In the same object graces quite as killing
   As when she rose upon us like an Eve,   1700
'Twould save us many a heartache, many a shilling
   (For we must get them anyhow, or grieve),
Whereas, if one sole lady pleased forever,
How pleasant for the heart, as well as liver!

* * *

216

In the meantime, without proceeding more
   In this anatomy, I've finished now
Two hundred and odd stanzas as before,
   That being about the number I'll allow
Each canto of the twelve, or twenty-four;   1725
   And, laying down my pen, I make my bow,
Leaving Don Juan and Haidée to plead
For them and theirs with all who deign to read.

9. Ideal beauty.

From *Canto III*

1

Hail, Muse! et cetera.—We left Juan sleeping,
  Pillowed upon a fair and happy breast,
And watched by eyes that never yet knew weeping,
  And loved by a young heart, too deeply blest
To feel the poison through her spirit creeping,   5
  Or know who rested there, a foe to rest,
Had soiled the current of her sinless years,
And turned her pure heart's purest blood to tears!

2

Oh, Love! what is it in this world of ours
  Which makes it fatal to be loved? Ah why   10
With cypress branches[1] hast thou wreathed thy bowers,
  And made thy best interpreter a sigh?
As those who dote on odors pluck the flowers,
  And place them on their breast—but place to die—
Thus the frail beings we would fondly cherish   15
Are laid within our bosoms but to perish.

3

In her first passion woman loves her lover,
  In all the others all she loves is love,
Which grows a habit she can ne'er get over,
  And fits her loosely—like an easy glove,   20
As you may find, whene'er you like to prove her:
  One man alone at first her heart can move;
She then prefers him in the plural number,
Not finding that the additions much encumber.

4

I know not if the fault be men's or theirs;   25
  But one thing's pretty sure; a woman planted[2]
(Unless at once she plunge for life in prayers)
  After a decent time must be gallánted;
Although, no doubt, her first of love affairs
  Is that to which her heart is wholly granted;   30
Yet there are some, they say, who have had *none*,
But those who have ne'er end with only *one*.

5

'Tis melancholy, and a fearful sign
  Of human frailty, folly, also crime,
That love and marriage rarely can combine,   35
  Although they both are born in the same clime;
Marriage from love, like vinegar from wine—
  A sad, sour, sober beverage—by time
Is sharpened from its high celestial flavor,
Down to a very homely household savor.   40

---

1. Signifying sorrow.   2. Abandoned (from the French *planter
là*, to leave in the lurch).

6

There's something of antipathy, as 'twere,
     Between their present and their future state;
A kind of flattery that's hardly fair
     Is used until the truth arrives too late—
Yet what can people do, except despair?   45
     The same things change their names at such a rate;
For instance—passion in a lover's glorious,
But in a husband is pronounced uxorious.

7

Men grow ashamed of being so very fond;
     They sometimes also get a little tired   50
(But that, of course, is rare), and then despond:
     The same things cannot always be admired,
Yet 'tis "so nominated in the bond,"[3]
     That both are tied till one shall have expired.
Sad thought! to lose the spouse that was adorning   55
Our days, and put one's servants into mourning.

8

There's doubtless something in domestic doings
     Which forms, in fact, true love's antithesis;
Romances paint at full length people's wooings,
     But only give a bust of marriages;   60
For no one cares for matrimonial cooings,
     There's nothing wrong in a connubial kiss:
Think you, if Laura had been Petrarch's wife,
He would have written sonnets all his life?

9

All tragedies are finished by a death,   65
     All comedies are ended by a marriage;
The future states of both are left to faith,
     For authors fear description might disparage
The worlds to come of both, or fall beneath,
     And then both worlds would punish their miscarriage; 70
So leaving each their priest and prayer book ready,
They say no more of Death or of the Lady.[4]

10

The only two that in my recollection
     Have sung of heaven and hell, or marriage, are
Dante and Milton, and of both the affection   75
     Was hapless in their nuptials, for some bar
Of fault or temper ruined the connection
     (Such things, in fact, it don't ask much to mar);
But Dante's Beatrice and Milton's Eve
Were not drawn from their spouses, you conceive.   80

11

Some persons say that Dante meant theology
     By Beatrice, and not a mistress—I,

3. Shylock: "Is it so nominated in the   4. Alluding to a popular ballad, *Death*
bond?"   *The   Merchant   of   Venice   and the Lady.*
IV.i.254.

Although my opinion may require apology,
   Deem this a commentator's phantasy,
Unless indeed it was from his own knowledge he   85
   Decided thus, and showed good reason why;
I think that Dante's more abstruse ecstatics
Meant to personify the mathematics.

12

Haidée and Juan were not married, but
   The fault was theirs, not mine: it is not fair,   90
Chaste reader, then, in any way to put
   The blame on me, unless you wish they were;
Then if you'd have them wedded, please to shut
   The book which treats of this erroneous pair,
Before the consequences grow too awful;   95
'Tis dangerous to read of loves unlawful.

13

Yet they were happy—happy in the illicit
   Indulgence of their innocent desires;
But more imprudent grown with every visit,
   Haidée forgot the island was her sire's;   100
When we have what we like, 'tis hard to miss it,
   At least in the beginning, ere one tires;
Thus she came often, not a moment losing,
Whilst her piratical papa was cruising.

14

Let not his mode of raising cash seem strange,   105
   Although he fleeced the flags of every nation,
For into a prime minister but change
   His title, and 'tis nothing but taxation;
But he, more modest, took an humbler range
   Of life, and in an honester vocation   110
Pursued o'er the high seas his watery journey,
And merely practiced as a sea attorney.

15

The good old gentleman had been detained
   By winds and waves, and some important captures;
And, in the hope of more, at sea remained,   115
   Although a squall or two had damped his raptures,
By swamping one of the prizes; he had chained
   His prisoners, dividing them like chapters
In numbered lots; they all had cuffs and collars,
And averaged each from ten to a hundred dollars.   120

* * *

19

Then having settled his marine affairs,   145
   Despatching single cruisers here and there,
His vessel having need of some repairs,
   He shaped his course to where his daughter fair
Continued still her hospitable cares;
   But that part of the coast being shoal and bare,   150

And rough with reefs which ran out many a mile,
His port lay on the other side o' the isle.

20

And there he went ashore without delay,
  Having no customhouse nor quarantine
To ask him awkward questions on the way
  About the time and place where he had been:
He left his ship to be hove down next day,
  With orders to the people to careen;[5]
So that all hands were busy beyond measure,
In getting out goods, ballast, guns, and treasure.

* * *

27

He saw his white walls shining in the sun,
  His garden trees all shadowy and green;
He heard his rivulet's light bubbling run,
  The distant dog-bark; and perceived between
The umbrage of the wood so cool and dun,
  The moving figures, and the sparkling sheen
Of arms (in the East all arm)—and various dyes
Of colored garbs, as bright as butterflies.

28

And as the spot where they appear he nears,
  Surprised at these unwonted signs of idling,
He hears—alas! no music of the spheres,
  But an unhallowed, earthly sound of fiddling!
A melody which made him doubt his ears,
  The cause being past his guessing or unriddling;
A pipe, too, and a drum, and shortly after,
A most unoriental roar of laughter.

* * *

38

He did not know (alas! how men will lie)
  That a report (especially the Greeks)
Avouched his death (such people never die),
  And put his house in mourning several weeks—
But now their eyes and also lips were dry;
  The bloom, too, had returned to Haidée's cheeks.
Her tears, too, being returned into their fount,
She now kept house upon her own account.

39

Hence all this rice, meat, dancing, wine, and fiddling,
  Which turned the isle into a place of pleasure;
The servants all were getting drunk or idling,
  A life which made them happy beyond measure.
Her father's hospitality seemed middling,
  Compared with what Haidée did with his treasure;
'Twas wonderful how things went on improving,
While she had not one hour to spare from loving.

5. To tip a vessel on its side in order to clean and repair its hull.

40

Perhaps you think in stumbling on this feast,
  He flew into a passion, and in fact
There was no mighty reason to be pleased;
  Perhaps you prophesy some sudden act,   315
The whip, the rack, or dungeon at the least,
  To teach his people to be more exact,
And that, proceeding at a very high rate,
He showed the royal penchants of a pirate.   320

41

You're wrong.—He was the mildest mannered man
  That ever scuttled ship or cut a throat;
With such true breeding of a gentleman,
  You never could divine his real thought,
No courtier could, and scarcely woman can   325
  Gird more deceit within a petticoat;
Pity he loved adventurous life's variety,
He was so great a loss to good society.

* * *

48

Not that he was not sometimes rash or so,
  But never in his real and serious mood;
Then calm, concéntrated, and still, and slow,
  He lay coiled like the boa in the wood;   380
With him it never was a word and blow,
  His angry word once o'er, he shed no blood,
But in his silence there was much to rue,
And his *one* blow left little work for *two*.

49

He asked no further questions, and proceeded   385
  On to the house, but by a private way,
So that the few who met him hardly heeded,
  So little they expected him that day;
If love paternal in his bosom pleaded
  For Haidée's sake is more than I can say,   390
But certainly to one deemed dead returning,
This revel seemed a curious mode of mourning.

50

If all the dead could now return to life
  (Which God forbid!), or some, or a great many,
For instance, if a husband or his wife   395
  (Nuptial examples are as good as any),
No doubt whate'er might be their former strife,
  The present weather would be much more rainy—
Tears shed into the grave of the connection
Would share most probably its resurrection.   400

51

He entered in the house no more his home,
  A thing to human feelings the most trying,

And harder for the heart to overcome,
  Perhaps, than even the mental pangs of dying;
To find our hearthstone turned into a tomb,   405
  And round its once warm precincts palely lying
The ashes of our hopes, is a deep grief,
Beyond a single gentleman's belief.

52

He entered in the house—his home no more,
  For without hearts there is no home—and felt   410
The solitude of passing his own door
  Without a welcome: *there* he long had dwelt,
There his few peaceful days Time had swept o'er,
  There his warm bosom and keen eye would melt
Over the innocence of that sweet child,   415
His only shrine of feelings undefiled.

53

He was a man of a strange temperament,
  Of mild demeanor though of savage mood,
Moderate in all his habits, and content
  With temperance in pleasure, as in food,   420
Quick to perceive, and strong to bear, and meant
  For something better, if not wholly good;
His country's wrongs and his despair to save her
Had stung him from a slave to an enslaver.

* * *

96

But let me to my story: I must own,
  If I have any fault, it is digression—
Leaving my people to proceed alone,
  While I soliloquize beyond expression;   860
But these are my addresses from the throne,
  Which put off business to the ensuing session:
Forgetting each omission is a loss to
The world, not quite so great as Ariosto.[6]

* * *

101

T' our tale.—The feast was over, the slaves gone,
  The dwarfs and dancing girls had all retired;
The Arab lore and poet's song were done,
  And every sound of revelry expired;   900
The lady and her lover, left alone,
  The rosy flood of twilight's sky admired—
Ave Maria![7] o'er the earth and sea,
That heavenliest hour of Heaven is worthiest thee!

6. Byron warmly admired this poet, author of *Orlando Furioso* (1532), the greatest of the Italian chivalric romances.
7. "Hail, Mary": these words open a Roman Catholic prayer. *Ave Maria* is sometimes used to refer to evening (or morning), since the prayer is part of the service at these times.

102

Ave Maria! blessed be the hour! 905
   The time, the clime, the spot, where I so oft
Have felt that moment in its fullest power
   Sink o'er the earth so beautiful and soft,
While swung the deep bell in the distant tower,
   Or the faint dying day-hymn stole aloft, 910
And not a breath crept through the rosy air,
And yet the forest leaves seemed stirred with prayer.

103

Ave Maria! 'tis the hour of prayer!
   Ave Maria! 'tis the hour of love!
Ave Maria! may our spirits dare 915
   Look up to thine and to thy Son's above!
Ave Maria! oh that face so fair!
   Those downcast eyes beneath the Almighty dove—
What though 'tis but a pictured image strike—
That painting is no idol—'tis too like. 920

104

Some kinder casuists are pleased to say,
   In nameless print—that I have no devotion;
But set those persons down with me to pray,
   And you shall see who has the properest notion
Of getting into heaven the shortest way; 925
   My altars are the mountains and the ocean,
Earth, air, stars—all that springs from the great Whole,
Who hath produced, and will receive the soul.

* * *

From *Canto IV*

3

As boy, I thought myself a clever fellow,
   And wished that others held the same opinion;
They took it up when my days grew more mellow,
   And other minds acknowledged my dominion: 20
Now my sere fancy "falls into the yellow
   Leaf,"[1] and Imagination droops her pinion,
And the sad truth which hovers o'er my desk
Turns what was once romantic to burlesque.

4

And if I laugh at any mortal thing, 25
   'Tis that I may not weep; and if I weep,
'Tis that our nature cannot always bring
   Itself to apathy, for we must steep
Our hearts first in the depths of Lethe's spring,
   Ere what we least wish to behold will sleep: 30
Thetis baptized her mortal son in Styx;[2]
A mortal mother would on Lethe fix.

1. Cf. *Macbeth* V.iii.22–23: "My way of life / Is fallen into the sere, the yellow leaf."   2. The river in Hades into which the

5

Some have accused me of a strange design
    Against the creed and morals of the land,
And trace it in this poem every line: 35
    I don't pretend that I quite understand
My own meaning when I would be *very* fine;
    But the fact is that I have nothing planned,
Unless it were to be a moment merry,
A novel word in my vocabulary.   40

6

To the kind reader of our sober clime
    This way of writing will appear exotic;
Pulci[3] was sire of the half-serious rhyme,
    Who sang when chivalry was more Quixotic,
And reveled in the fancies of the time,   45
    True knights, chaste dames, huge giants, kings despotic;
But all these, save the last, being obsolete,
I chose a modern subject as more meet.

7

How I have treated it, I do not know;
    Perhaps no better than they have treated me   50
Who have imputed such designs as show
    Not what they saw, but what they wished to see:
But if it gives them pleasure, be it so;
    This is a liberal age, and thoughts are free:
Meantime Apollo plucks me by the ear,   55
And tells me to resume my story here.

* * *

26

Juan and Haidée gazed upon each other
    With swimming looks of speechless tenderness,
Which mixed all feelings, friend, child, lover, brother,
    All that the best can mingle and express
When two pure hearts are poured in one another,   205
    And love too much, and yet cannot love less;
But almost sanctify the sweet excess
By the immortal wish and power to bless.

27

Mixed in each other's arms, and heart in heart,
    Why did they not then die?—they had lived too long   210
Should an hour come to bid them breathe apart;
    Years could but bring them cruel things or wrong;
The world was not for them, nor the world's art
    For beings passionate as Sappho's song;
Love was born *with* them, *in* them, so intense,   215
It was their very spirit—not a sense.

nymph Thetis dipped Achilles, to make
him invulnerable. Lethe, another river
in Hades, brings oblivion of life.
3. Author of the *Morgante Maggiore*,

prototype of the Italian seriocomic romance from which Byron derived the
stanza and manner of *Don Juan*. See the
introduction to *Don Juan*.

28

They should have lived together deep in woods,
   Unseen as sings the nightingale; they were
Unfit to mix in these thick solitudes
   Called social, haunts of Hate, and Vice, and Care: 220
How lonely every freeborn creature broods!
   The sweetest songbirds nestle in a pair;
The eagle soars alone; the gull and crow
Flock o'er their carrion, just like men below.

29

Now pillowed cheek to cheek, in loving sleep,   225
   Haidée and Juan their siesta took,
A gentle slumber, but it was not deep,
   Forever and anon a something shook
Juan, and shuddering o'er his frame would creep;
   And Haidée's sweet lips murmured like a brook   230
A wordless music, and her face so fair
Stirred with her dream, as rose-leaves with the air;

30

Or as the stirring of a deep clear stream
   Within an Alpine hollow, when the wind
Walks o'er it, was she shaken by the dream,   235
   The mystical usurper of the mind—
O'erpowering us to be whate'er may seem
   Good to the soul which we no more can bind;
Strange state of being! (for 'tis still to be)
Senseless to feel, and with sealed eyes to see.   240

31

She dreamed of being alone on the seashore,
   Chained to a rock; she knew not how, but stir
She could not from the spot, and the loud roar
   Grew, and each wave rose roughly, threatening her;
And o'er her upper lip they seemed to pour,   245
   Until she sobbed for breath, and soon they were
Foaming o'er her lone head, so fierce and high—
Each broke to drown her, yet she could not die.

32

Anon—she was released, and then she strayed
   O'er the sharp shingles[4] with her bleeding feet,   250
And stumbled almost every step she made;
   And something rolled before her in a sheet,
Which she must still pursue howe'er afraid;
   'Twas white and indistinct, nor stopped to meet
Her glance nor grasp, for still she gazed and grasped,   255
And ran, but it escaped her as she clasped.

33

The dream changed—in a cave she stood, its walls
   Were hung with marble icicles; the work
Of ages on its water-fretted halls,

4. Loose pebbles.

Where waves might wash, and seals might breed and lurk;
Her hair was dripping, and the very balls   261
  Of her black eyes seemed turned to tears, and murk
The sharp rocks looked below each drop they caught,
Which froze to marble as it fell, she thought.

                              34
And wet, and cold, and lifeless at her feet,   265
  Pale as the foam that frothed on his dead brow,
Which she essayed in vain to clear (how sweet
  Were once her cares, how idle seemed they now!),
Lay Juan, nor could aught renew the beat
  Of his quenched heart; and the sea dirges low   270
Rang in her sad ears like a mermaid's song,
And that brief dream appeared a life too long.

                              35
And gazing on the dead, she thought his face
  Faded, or altered into something new—
Like to her father's features, till each trace   275
  More like and like to Lambro's aspect grew—
With all his keen worn look and Grecian grace;
  And starting, she awoke, and what to view?
Oh! Powers of Heaven! what dark eye meets she there?
'Tis—'tis her father's—fixed upon the pair!   280

                              36
Then shrieking, she arose, and shrieking fell,
  With joy and sorrow, hope and fear, to see
Him whom she deemed a habitant where dwell
  The ocean-buried, risen from death, to be
Perchance the death of one she loved too well: 285
  Dear as her father had been to Haidée,
It was a moment of that awful kind—
I have seen such—but must not call to mind.

                              37
Up Juan sprung to Haidée's bitter shriek,
  And caught her falling, and from off the wall   290
Snatched down his saber, in hot haste to wreak
  Vengeance on him who was the cause of all:
Then Lambro, who till now forebore to speak,
  Smiled scornfully, and said, "Within my call,
A thousand scimitars await the word;   295
Put up, young man, put up your silly sword."

                              38
And Haidée clung around him; "Juan, 'tis—
  'Tis Lambro—'tis my father! Kneel with me—
He will forgive us—yes—it must be—yes.
  Oh! dearest father, in this agony   300
Of pleasure and of pain—even while I kiss
  Thy garment's hem with transport, can it be
That doubt should mingle with my filial joy?
Deal with me as thou wilt, but spare this boy."

39

High and inscrutable the old man stood,   305
    Calm in his voice, and calm within his eye—
Not always signs with him of calmest mood:
    He looked upon her, but gave no reply;
Then turned to Juan, in whose cheek the blood
    Oft came and went, as there resolved to die;   310
In arms, at least, he stood, in act to spring
On the first foe whom Lambro's call might bring.

40

"Young man, your sword"; so Lambro once more said:
    Juan replied, "Not while this arm is free."
The old man's cheek grew pale, but not with dread,   315
    And drawing from his belt a pistol, he
Replied, "Your blood be then on your own head."
    Then looked close at the flint, as if to see
'Twas fresh—for he had lately used the lock[5]—
And next proceeded quietly to cock.   320

41

It has a strange quick jar upon the ear,
    That cocking of a pistol, when you know
A moment more will bring the sight to bear
    Upon your person, twelve yards off, or so;
A gentlemanly distance,[6] not too near,   325
    If you have got a former friend for foe;
But after being fired at once or twice,
The ear becomes more Irish, and less nice.[7]

42

Lambro presented, and one instant more
    Had stopped this Canto, and Don Juan's breath,   330
When Haidée threw herself her boy before;
    Stern as her sire: "On me," she cried, "let death
Descend—the fault is mine; this fatal shore
    He found—but sought not. I have pledged my faith;
I love him—I will die with him: I knew   335
Your nature's firmness—know your daughter's too."

43

A minute past, and she had been all tears,
    And tenderness, and infancy; but now
She stood as one who championed human fears—
    Pale, statue-like, and stern, she wooed the blow;   340
And tall beyond her sex, and their compeers,[8]
    She drew up to her height, as if to show
A fairer mark; and with a fixed eye scanned
Her father's face—but never stopped his hand.

---

5. That part of the gun which explodes the charge.
6. I.e., dueling distance.
7. Finicky. Byron alludes to the propensity of hotheaded young Irishmen to fight duels.
8. I.e., she was the match in height of Lambro and Juan.

44

He gazed on her, and she on him; 'twas strange 345
   How like they looked! the expression was the same;
Serenely savage, with a little change
   In the large dark eye's mutual-darted flame;
For she, too, was as one who could avenge,
   If cause should be—a lioness, though tame; 350
Her father's blood before her father's face
Boiled up, and proved her truly of his race.

45

I said they were alike, their features and
   Their stature differing but in sex and years;
Even to the delicacy of their hand 355
   There was resemblance, such as true blood wears;
And now to see them, thus divided, stand
   In fixed ferocity, when joyous tears,
And sweet sensations, should have welcomed both,
Show what the passions are in their full growth. 360

46

The father paused a moment, then withdrew
   His weapon, and replaced it; but stood still,
And looking on her, as to look her through,
   "Not I," he said, "have sought this stranger's ill;
Not I have made this desolation: few 365
   Would bear such outrage, and forbear to kill;
But I must do my duty—how thou hast
Done thine, the present vouches for the past.

47

"Let him disarm; or, by my father's head,
   His own shall roll before you like a ball!" 370
He raised his whistle as the word he said,
   And blew; another answered to the call,
And rushing in disorderly, though led,
   And armed from boot to turban, one and all,
Some twenty of his train came, rank on rank; 375
He gave the word, "Arrest or slay the Frank."[9]

48

Then, with a sudden movement, he withdrew
   His daughter; while compressed within his clasp,
'Twixt her and Juan interposed the crew;
   In vain she struggled in her father's grasp— 380
His arms were like a serpent's coil: then flew
   Upon their prey, as darts an angry asp,
The file of pirates; save the foremost, who
Had fallen, with his right shoulder half cut through.

49

The second had his cheek laid open; but 385
   The third, a wary, cool old sworder, took
The blows upon his cutlass, and then put

9. Term used in the Near East to designate a western European.

His own well in; so well, ere you could look,
His man was floored, and helpless at his foot,
  With the blood running like a little brook   390
From two smart saber gashes, deep and red—
One on the arm, the other on the head.

50
And then they bound him where he fell, and bore
  Juan from the apartment: with a sign
Old Lambro bade them take him to the shore,   395
  Where lay some ships which were to sail at nine.
They laid him in a boat, and plied the oar
  Until they reached some galliots,[1] placed in line;
On board of one of these, and under hatches,
They stowed him, with strict orders to the watches.   400

51
The world is full of strange vicissitudes,
  And here was one exceedingly unpleasant:
A gentleman so rich in the world's goods,
  Handsome and young, enjoying all the present,
Just at the very time when he least broods   405
  On such a thing is suddenly to sea sent,
Wounded and chained, so that he cannot move,
And all because a lady fell in love.

* * *

56
Afric is all the sun's, and as her earth
  Her human clay is kindled; full of power
For good or evil, burning from its birth,
  The Moorish blood partakes the planet's hour,
And like the soil beneath it will bring forth: 445
  Beauty and love were Haidée's mother's dower;
But her large dark eye showed deep Passion's force,
Though sleeping like a lion near a source.

57
Her daughter, tempered with a milder ray,
  Like summer clouds all silvery, smooth, and fair,   450
Till slowly charged with thunder they display
  Terror to earth, and tempest to the air,
Had held till now her soft and milky way;
  But overwrought with passion and despair,
The fire burst forth from her Numidian[2] veins,   455
Even as the simoom[3] sweeps the blasted plains.

58
The last sight which she saw was Juan's gore,
  And he himself o'ermastered and cut down;
His blood was running on the very floor
  Where late he trod, her beautiful, her own;   460

---

1. A small, fast galley, propelled both
by oars and sails.
2. North African.

3. A violent, hot, dust-laden desert
wind.

Thus much she viewed an instant and no more—
  Her struggles ceased with one convulsive groan;
On her sire's arm, which until now scarce held
  Her writhing, fell she like a cedar felled.

59

A vein had burst, and her sweet lips' pure dyes   465
  Were dabbled with the deep blood which ran o'er;
And her head drooped, as when the lily lies
  O'ercharged with rain: her summoned handmaids bore
Their lady to her couch with gushing eyes;
  Of herbs and cordials they produced their store,   470
But she defied all means they could employ,
Like one life could not hold, nor death destroy.

60

Days lay she in that state unchanged, though chill—
  With nothing livid,[4] still her lips were red;
She had no pulse, but death seemed absent still;   475
  No hideous sign proclaimed her surely dead;
Corruption came not in each mind to kill
  All hope; to look upon her sweet face bred
New thoughts of life, for it seemed full of soul—
She had so much, earth could not claim the whole.   480

* * *

69

Twelve days and nights she withered thus; at last,   515
  Without a groan, or sigh, or glance, to show
A parting pang, the spirit from her passed:
  And they who watched her nearest could not know
The very instant, till the change that cast
  Her sweet face into shadow, dull and slow,   550
Glazed o'er her eyes—the beautiful, the black—
Oh! to possess such luster—and then lack!

70

She died, but not alone; she held within
  A second principle of life, which might
Have dawned a fair and sinless child of sin;   555
  But closed its little being without light,
And went down to the grave unborn, wherein
  Blossom and bough lie withered with one blight;
In vain the dews of Heaven descend above
The bleeding flower and blasted fruit of love.   560

71

Thus lived—thus died she; never more on her
  Shall sorrow light, or shame. She was not made
Through years or moons the inner weight to bear,
  Which colder hearts endure till they are laid
By age in earth; her days and pleasures were   565
  Brief, but delightful—such as had not stayed

4. I.e., she was ashen pale.

Long with her destiny; but she sleeps well
By the seashore, whereon she loved to dwell.

72

That isle is now all desolate and bare,
  Its dwellings down, its tenants passed away;   570
None but her own and father's grave is there,
  And nothing outward tells of human clay;
Ye could not know where lies a thing so fair,
  No stone is there to show, no tongue to say
What was; no dirge, except the hollow sea's,   575
  Mourns o'er the beauty of the Cyclades.

73

But many a Greek maid in a loving song
  Sighs o'er her name; and many an islander
With her sire's story makes the night less long;
  Valor was his, and beauty dwelt with her: 580
If she loved rashly, her life paid for wrong—
  A heavy price must all pay who thus err,
In some shape; let none think to fly the danger,
For soon or late Love is his own avenger.[5]

* * *

1818–23   1819–24

The Vision of Judgment[1]

By Quevedo Redivivus[2]

SUGGESTED BY THE COMPOSITION SO ENTITLED BY THE AUTHOR OF
Wat Tyler

"A Daniel come to judgment! yea, a Daniel!
I thank thee, Jew, for teaching me that word."[3]

5. Juan's adventures continue: he is sold as a slave in Constantinople, has an episode in the harem of the sultana, engages in the Russian siege of Ismail, becomes "man-mistress" to Catherine the Great of Russia, and, in Canto X, is sent on a diplomatic mission to England. He is a guest at a great English country house, a subject of interest to several very beautiful women, when the poem breaks off in the sixteenth canto. 1. Although originally an ardent supporter of the French Revolution, Robert Southey soon turned a Tory and in 1813 was appointed poet laureate. Four years after the appointment he was dismayed by the unauthorized publication of his radical poetical drama *Wat Tyler*, which he had written in 1794 but had prudently left in manuscript. Byron reminds him of it in the subtitle. When King George III died in 1820—Shelley in his *Sonnet: England in 1819* had called him, accurately enough, "an old, mad, blind, despised, and dying king"— Southey did his official duty by writing

A Vision of Judgment (1821). In this fulsome eulogy George III goes to heaven, confounds such detractors as John Wilkes and Junius, and obtains a testimonial of noble character from his old enemy, George Washington. The vision ends with the King, beatified, ceremoniously admitted to heaven.

Byron, responding to reports that Southey was vilifying him, had ridiculed the poet in his "Dedication" to Canto I of *Don Juan*. In the Preface to his *Vision of Judgment*, Southey then exhibited his bad judgment by denouncing Byron as head of the "Satanic School" of poetry, combining "lascivious" passages with "a satanic spirit of pride and audacious impiety." Byron immediately responded with *The Vision of Judgment*, in which he purports to tell the true story of how, with the unwitting help of Southey, King George had really managed to get into heaven. The poem is in the genre of the satiric attack on literary "dunces" by Dryden and Pope, but is written in the ottava

1

Saint Peter sat by the celestial gate:
　His keys were rusty, and the lock was dull,
So little trouble had been given of late;
　Not that the place by any means was full,
But since the Gallic era "eighty-eight"[4]   5
　The devils had ta'en a longer, stronger pull,
And "a pull altogether," as they say
At sea—which drew most souls another way.

2

The angels all were singing out of tune,
　And hoarse with having little else to do,   10
Excepting to wind up the sun and moon,
　Or curb a runaway young star or two,
Or wild colt of a comet, which too soon
　Broke out of bounds o'er th' ethereal blue,
Splitting some planet with its playful tail,   15
As boats are sometimes by a wanton whale.

3

The guardian seraphs had retired on high,
　Finding their charges past all care below;
Terrestrial business filled nought in the sky
　Save the recording angel's black bureau;   20
Who found, indeed, the facts to multiply
　With such rapidity of vice and woe,
That he had stripped off both his wings in quills,
And yet was in arrear of human ills.

4

His business so augmented of late years,   25
　That he was forced, against his will no doubt
(Just like those cherubs, earthly ministers),
　For some resource to turn himself about,
And claim the help of his celestial peers,
　To aid him ere he should be quite worn out   30
By the increased demand for his remarks;
Six angels and twelve saints were named his clerks.

5

This was a handsome board—at least for heaven;
　And yet they had even then enough to do,
So many conquerors' cars were daily driven,   35
　So many kingdoms fitted up anew;
Each day too slew its thousands six or seven,
　Till at the crowning carnage, Waterloo,
They threw their pens down in divine disgust—
The page was so besmeared with blood and dust.   40

rima stanza and the easy colloquial manner of Byron's *Don Juan*. In its quick, sure characterization, the pace and economy of its narrative, its inventiveness in detail, above all in the high spirits and unfailing good humor with which the author demolishes his opponent, this poem represents Byron at his masterful best.

2. "Quevedo Revived." Quevedo was a 17th-century Spanish author of *Sueños*, "Visions," written in prose and predominantly satirical in tone.
3. Quoted, not quite accurately, from *The Merchant of Venice*, IV.i.340–41.
4. The last year of the old régime in France, before the outbreak of the Revolution in 1789.

6

This by the way; 'tis not mine to record
  What angels shrink from: even the very devil
On this occasion his own work abhorred,
  So surfeited with the infernal revel:
Though he himself had sharpened every sword,   45
  It almost quenched his innate thirst of evil.
(Here Satan's sole good work deserves insertion—
'Tis, that he has both generals in reversion.[5])

7

Let's skip a few short years of hollow peace,
  Which peopled earth no better, hell as wont,   50
And heaven none—they form the tyrant's lease,
  With nothing but new names subscribed upon 't;
'Twill one day finish: meantime they increase,
  "With seven heads and ten horns," and all in front,
Like Saint John's foretold beast;[6] but ours are born   55
Less formidable in the head than horn.

8

In the first year of freedom's second dawn[7]
  Died George the Third; although no tyrant, one
Who shielded tyrants, till each sense withdrawn
  Left him nor mental nor external sun: 60
A better farmer ne'er brushed dew from lawn,
  A worse king never left a realm undone!
He died—but left his subjects still behind,
One half as mad—and t'other no less blind.

9

He died! his death made no great stir on earth;   65
  His burial made some pomp; there was profusion
Of velvet, gilding, brass, and no great dearth
  Of aught but tears—save those shed by collusion.
For these things may be bought at their true worth;
  Of elegy there was the due infusion—   70
Bought also; and the torches, cloaks, and banners,
Heralds, and relics of old Gothic manners,

10

Formed a sepulchral melodrame. Of all
  The fools who flocked to swell or see the show,
Who cared about the corpse? The funeral   75
  Made the attraction, and the black the woe.
There throbbed not there a thought which pierced the pall;
  And when the gorgeous coffin was laid low,
It seemed the mockery of hell to fold
The rottenness of eighty years in gold.   80

---

5. Satan has the legal right to the future possession of both Napoleon and Wellington, the commanding officers at the Battle of Waterloo.
6. The Book of Revelation describes such a beast, xiii.1.
7. 1820 was a year of new revolutionary movements in Italy and other countries of southern Europe.

11

So mix his body with the dust! It might
  Return to what it *must* far sooner, were
The natural compound left alone to fight
  Its way back into earth, and fire, and air;
But the unnatural balsams[8] merely blight   85
  What nature made him at his birth, as bare
As the mere million's base unmummied clay—
Yet all his spices but prolong decay.

12

He's dead—and upper earth with him has done;
  He's buried; save the undertaker's bill,   90
Or lapidary scrawl,[9] the world is gone
  For him, unless he left a German will;
But where's the proctor who will ask his son?[1]
  In whom his qualities are reigning still,
Except that household virtue, most uncommon,   95
Of constancy to a bad, ugly woman.

13

"God save the king!" It is a large economy
  In God to save the like; but if he will
Be saving, all the better; for not one am I
  Of those who think damnation better still·   100
I hardly know too if not quite alone am I
  In this small hope of bettering future ill
By circumscribing, with some slight restriction,
The eternity of hell's hot jurisdiction.

14

I know this is unpopular; I know   105
  'Tis blasphemous; I know one may be damned
For hoping no one else may e'er be so;
  I know my catechism; I know we're crammed
With the best doctrines till we quite o'erflow;
  I know that all save England's church have shammed, 110
And that the other twice two hundred churches
And synagogues have made a *damned* bad purchase.

15

God help us all! God help me too! I am,
  God knows, as helpless as the devil can wish,
And not a whit more difficult to damn,   115
  Than is to bring to land a late-hooked fish,
Or to the butcher to purvey the lamb;
  Not that I'm fit for such a noble dish,
As one day will be that immortal fry
Of almost everybody born to die.   120

16

Saint Peter sat by the celestial gate,
  And nodded o'er his keys; when, lo! there came

---

8. I.e., embalming fluids.
9. Inscription cut into a stone monument.
1. A King's Proctor is an official who intervenes in the probate of a will, when chicanery is suspected. Byron alludes to the scandal that the will of George I, of the German House of Hanover, had been hidden by his son, George II, who was the grandfather of the late George III.

A wondrous noise he had not heard of late—
A rushing sound of wind, and stream, and flame;
In short, a roar of things extremely great,   125
Which would have made aught save a saint exclaim;
But he, with first a start and then a wink,
Said, "There's another star gone out, I think!"

                            17
But ere he could return to his repose,
A cherub flapped his right wing o'er his eyes—   130
At which St. Peter yawned, and rubbed his nose:
"Saint porter," said the angel, "prithee rise!"
Waving a goodly wing, which glowed, as glows
An earthly peacock's tail, with heavenly dyes:
To which the saint replied, "Well, what's the matter?   135
"Is Lucifer come back with all this clatter?"

                            18
"No," quoth the cherub; "George the Third is dead."
"And who *is* George the Third?" replied the apostle:
"*What George? what Third?*" "The king of England," said
The angel. "Well! he won't find kings to jostle   140
Him on his way; but does he wear his head;
Because the last we saw here had a tustle,
And ne'er would have got into heaven's good graces,
Had he not flung his head in all our faces.[2]

                            19
"He was, if I remember, king of France;   145
That head of his, which could not keep a crown
On earth, yet ventured in my face to advance
A claim to those of martyrs—like my own:
If I had had my sword, as I had once
When I cut ears off, I had cut him down;[3]   150
But having but my *keys*, and not my brand,
I only knocked his head from out his hand.

                            20
"And then he set up such a headless howl,
That all the saints came out and took him in;
And there he sits by St. Paul, cheek by jowl;   155
That fellow Paul—the parvenu! The skin
Of St. Bartholomew,[4] which makes his cowl
In heaven, and upon earth redeemed his sin
So as to make a martyr, never sped
Better than did this weak and wooden head.   160

                            21
"But had it come up here upon its shoulders,
There would have been a different tale to tell:
The fellow-feeling in the saint's beholders
Seems to have acted on them like a spell;

2. Louis XVI, who had been guillotined in January, 1793.
3. When the officers came to take Jesus, "Simon Peter having a sword drew it, and smote the high priest's servant, and cut off his right ear" (John xviii.10). "Brand," line 151, is archaic for "sword."
4. According to tradition, the martyred St. Bartholomew was flayed alive.

And so this very foolish head heaven solders 165
    Back on its trunk: it may be very well,
And seems the custom here to overthrow
Whatever has been wisely done below."

22

The angel answered, "Peter! do not pout:
    The king who comes has head and all entire, 170
And never knew much what it was about—
    He did as doth the puppet—by its wire,
And will be judged like all the rest, no doubt:
    My business and your own is not to inquire
Into such matters, but to mind our cue— 175
Which is to act as we are bid to do."

23

While thus they spake, the angelic caravan,
    Arriving like a rush of mighty wind,
Cleaving the fields of space, as doth the swan
    Some silver stream (say Ganges, Nile, or Inde, 180
Or Thames, or Tweed), and 'midst them an old man
    With an old soul, and both extremely blind,
Halted before the gate, and in his shroud
Seated their fellow traveler on a cloud.

24

But bringing up the rear of this bright host 185
    A Spirit of a different aspect waved
His wings, like thunder clouds above some coast
    Whose barren beach with frequent wrecks is paved;
His brow was like the deep when tempest-tossed;
    Fierce and unfathomable thoughts engraved 190
Eternal wrath on his immortal face,
And *where* he gazed a gloom pervaded space.

25

As he drew near, he gazed upon the gate
    Ne'er to be entered more by him or Sin,
With such a glance of supernatural hate, 195
    As made Saint Peter wish himself within;
He pattered with his keys at a great rate,
    And sweated through his apostolic skin:
Of course his perspiration was but ichor,[5]
Or some such other spiritual liquor. 200

26

The very cherubs huddled all together,
    Like birds when soars the falcon; and they felt
A tingling to the tip of every feather,
    And formed a circle like Orion's belt
Around their poor old charge; who scarce knew whither 205
    His guards had led him, though they gently dealt
With royal manes[6] (for by many stories,
And true, we learn the angels all are Tories).

5. The fluid in the veins of the gods.
6. In Roman religion, spirits of the dead (pronounced *mā'nēz*).

27

As things were in this posture, the gate flew
  Asunder, and the flashing of its hinges   210
Flung over space an universal hue
  Of many-colored flame, until its tinges
Reached even our speck of earth, and made a new
  Aurora borealis spread its fringes
O'er the North Pole; the same seen, when ice-bound,   215
By Captain Parry's[7] crew, in "Melville's Sound."

28

And from the gate thrown open issued beaming
  A beautiful and mighty Thing of Light,
Radiant with glory, like a banner streaming
  Victorious from some world-o'erthrowing fight: 220
My poor comparisons must needs be teeming
  With earthly likenesses, for here the night
Of clay obscures our best conceptions, saving
Johanna Southcote,[8] or Bob Southey raving.

29

'Twas the archangel Michael: all men know   225
  The make of angels and archangels, since
There's scarce a scribbler has not one to show,
  From the fiends' leader to the angels' prince.
There also are some altarpieces, though
  I really can't say that they much evince   230
One's inner notions of immortal spirits;
But let the connoisseurs explain *their* merits.

30

Michael flew forth in glory and in good;
  A goodly work of him from whom all glory
And good arise; the portal past—he stood;   235
  Before him the young cherubs and saints hoary—
(I say *young*, begging to be understood
  By looks, not years; and should be very sorry
To state, they were not older than St. Peter,
But merely that they seemed a little sweeter).   240

31

The cherubs and the saints bowed down before
  That arch-angelic hierarch, the first
Of essences angelical, who wore
  The aspect of a god; but this ne'er nursed
Pride in his heavenly bosom, in whose core   245
  No thought, save for his Master's service, durst
Intrude, however glorified and high;
He knew him but the viceroy of the sky.

---

7. Captain William Edward Parry, in his account of his *Voyage in 1819–20*, in search of a northwest passage.
8. Joanna Southcott (1750–1814) was a servant girl who, claiming direct communications from the Almighty, became head of a religious sect. In 1813 she proclaimed that she was about to give birth to a son, Shiloh, who would redeem the world. The pregnancy turned out to be a tumor, of which she died the following year.

32

He and the somber silent Spirit met—
    They knew each other both for good and ill;   250
Such was their power, that neither could forget
    His former friend and future foe; but still
There was a high, immortal, proud regret
    In either's eye, as if 'twere less their will
Than destiny to make the eternal years   255
Their date of war, and their "champ clos"[9] the spheres.

33

But here they were in neutral space: we know
    From Job, that Satan hath the power to pay
A heavenly visit thrice a year or so;
    And that the "sons of God," like those of clay,   260
Must keep him company;[1] and we might show
    From the same book, in how polite a way
The dialogue is held between the Powers
Of Good and Evil—but 'twould take up hours.

34

And this is not a theologic tract,   265
    To prove with Hebrew and with Arabic
If Job be allegory or a fact,
    But a true narrative; and thus I pick
From out the whole but such and such an act
    As sets aside the slightest thought of trick.   270
'Tis every tittle true, beyond suspicion,
And accurate as any other vision.

35

The spirits were in neutral space, before
    The gate of heaven; like eastern thresholds is
The place where Death's grand cause is argued o'er,[2]   275
    And souls despatched to that world or to this;
And therefore Michael and the other wore
    A civil aspect: though they did not kiss,
Yet still between his Darkness and his Brightness
There passed a mutual glance of great politeness.   280

36

The Archangel bowed, not like a modern beau,
    But with a graceful oriental bend,
Pressing one radiant arm just where below
    The heart in good men is supposed to tend.
He turned as to an equal, not too low,   285
    But kindly; Satan met his ancient friend
With more hauteur, as might an old Castilian
Poor noble meet a mushroom rich civilian.[3]

9. "Enclosed field," the arena for knightly tournaments.
1. Job i.6. "There was a day when the sons of God came to present themselves before the Lord, and Satan came also among them."
2. The gateways of walled cities in the Middle East were sometimes used for public debates and to administer justice.
3. Byron contrasts ancient Spanish noblemen with *nouveaux riches* who spring up as rapidly as mushrooms.

37

He merely bent his diabolic brow
   An instant; and then raising it, he stood   290
In act to assert his right or wrong, and show
   Cause why King George by no means could or should
Make out a case to be exempt from woe
   Eternal, more than other kings, endued
With better sense and hearts, whom history mentions,   295
Who long have "paved hell with their good intentions."[4]

38

Michael began: "What wouldst thou with this man,
   Now dead, and brought before the Lord? What ill
Hath he wrought since his mortal race began,
   That thou canst claim him? Speak! and do thy will,   300
If it be just: if in this earthly span
   He hath been greatly failing to fulfil
His duties as a king and mortal, say,
And he is thine; if not, let him have way."

39

"Michael!" replied the Prince of Air, "even here,   305
   Before the Gate of him thou servest, must
I claim my subject: and will make appear
   That as he was my worshiper in dust,
So shall he be in spirit, although dear
   To thee and thine, because nor wine nor lust   310
Were of his weaknesses; yet on the throne
He reigned o'er millions to serve me alone.

40

"Look to *our* earth, or rather *mine*; it was,
   Once, *more* thy master's: but I triumph not
In this poor planet's conquest; nor, alas!   315
   Need he thou servest envy me my lot:
With all the myriads of bright worlds which pass
   In worship round him, he may have forgot
Yon weak creation of such paltry things:
I think few worth damnation save their kings—   320

41

"And these but as a kind of quitrent,[5] to
   Assert my right as lord: and even had
I such an inclination, 'twere (as you
   Well know) superfluous; they are grown so bad,
That hell has nothing better left to do   325
   Than leave them to themselves: so much more mad
And evil by their own internal curse,
Heaven cannot make them better, nor I worse.

42

"Look to the earth, I said, and say again:
   When this old, blind, mad, helpless, weak, poor worm   330
Began in youth's first bloom and flush to reign,

4. An old English proverb.
5. A fixed rent, paid in place of services to a feudal lord.

The world and he both wore a different form,
And much of earth and all the watery plain
　　Of ocean called him king: through many a storm
His isles had floated on the abyss of time;　　335
For the rough virtues chose them for their clime.

43

"He came to his scepter young; he leaves it old:
　　Look to the state in which he found his realm,
And left it; and his annals too behold,
　　How to a minion first he gave the helm,[6]　　340
How grew upon his heart a thirst for gold,
　　The beggar's vice, which can but overwhelm
The meanest hearts; and for the rest, but glance
Thine eye along America and France.

44

" 'Tis true, he was a tool from first to last　　345
　　(I have the workmen safe); but as a tool
So let him be consumed. From out the past
　　Of ages, since mankind have known the rule
Of monarchs—from the bloody rolls amassed
　　Of sin and slaughter—from the Caesar's school,　　350
Take the worst pupil; and produce a reign
More drenched with gore, more cumbered with the slain.

45

"He ever warred with freedom and the free:
　　Nations as men, home subjects, foreign foes,
So that[7] they uttered the word 'Liberty!'　　355
　　Found George the Third their first opponent. Whose
History was ever stained as his will be
　　With national and individual woes?
I grant his household abstinence; I grant
His neutral virtues, which most monarchs want;　　360

46

"I know he was a constant consort; own
　　He was a decent sire, and middling lord.
All this is much, and most upon a throne;
　　As temperance, if at Apicius' board,[8]
Is more than at an anchorite's[9] supper shown.　　365
　　I grant him all the kindest can accord;
And this was well for him, but not for those
Millions who found him what oppression chose.

47

"The New World shook him off; the Old yet groans
　　Beneath what he and his prepared, if not　　370
Completed: he leaves heirs on many thrones
　　To all his vices, without what begot
Compassion for him—his tame virtues; drones

---

6. The unpopular Earl of Bute, whom
George III made Prime Minister in
1802.
7. "Provided that."

8. I.e., At the table of Apicius (a famed
Roman gourmet in the time of Augustus).
9. A religious hermit's.

Who sleep, or despots who have now forgot
A lesson which shall be re-taught them, wake   375
Upon the thrones of earth; but let them quake!

48

"Five millions of the primitive,[1] who hold
    The faith which makes ye great on earth, implored
A *part* of that vast *all* they held of old—
    Freedom to worship—not alone your Lord,   380
Michael, but you, and you, Saint Peter! Cold
    Must be your souls, if you have not abhorred
The foe to Catholic participation
In all the license of a Christian nation.

49

"True! he allowed them to pray God; but as   385
    A consequence of prayer, refused the law
Which would have placed them upon the same base
    With those who did not hold the saints in awe."
But here Saint Peter started from his place,
    And cried, "You may the prisoner withdraw: 390
Ere heaven shall ope her portals to this Guelph,[2]
While I am guard, may I be damned myself!

50

"Sooner will I with Cerberus[3] exchange
    My office (and *his* is no sinecure)
Than see this royal Bedlam bigot range   395
    The azure fields of heaven, of that be sure!"
"Saint!" replied Satan, "you do well to avenge
    The wrongs he made your satellites endure;
And if to this exchange you should be given,
I'll try to coax *our* Cerberus up to heaven."   400

51

Here Michael interposed: "Good saint! and devil!
    Pray, not so fast; you both outrun discretion.
Saint Peter! you were wont to be more civil!
    Satan! excuse this warmth of his expression,
And condescension to the vulgar's level: 405
    Even saints sometimes forget themselves in session.
Have you got more to say?"—"No."—"If you please,
I'll trouble you to call your witnesses."

52

Then Satan turned and waved his swarthy hand,
    Which stirred with its electric qualities   410
Clouds farther off than we can understand,
    Although we find him sometimes in our skies;
Infernal thunder shook both sea and land
    In all the planets, and hell's batteries

1. The Irish Catholics. In 1795 George had opposed the Catholic Emancipation Bill, which gave Roman Catholics the right to hold public offices (line 383). 2. The House of Hanover was descended from the German Guelphs. 3. The three-headed dog guarding the entrance to Hades.

Let off the artillery, which Milton mentions   415
As one of Satan's most sublime inventions.[4]

53

This was a signal unto such damned souls
   As have the privilege of their damnation
Extended far beyond the mere controls
   Of worlds past, present, or to come; no station   420
Is theirs particularly in the rolls
   Of hell assigned; but where their inclination
Or business carries them in search of game,
They may range freely—being damned the same.

54

They're proud of this—as very well they may,   425
   It being a sort of knighthood, or gilt key
Stuck in their loins;[5] or like an "entré"
   Up the back stairs, or such freemasonry.
I borrow my comparisons from clay,
   Being clay myself. Let not those spirits be   430
Offended with such base low likenesses;
   We know their posts are nobler far than these.

55

When the great signal ran from heaven to hell—
   About ten million times the distance reckoned
From our sun to its earth, as we can tell   435
   How much time it takes up, even to a second,
For every ray that travels to dispel
   The fogs of London, through which, dimly beaconed,
The weathercocks are gilt some thrice a year,
   If that the *summer* is not too severe—   440

56

I say that I can tell—'twas half a minute:
   I know the solar beams take up more time
Ere, packed up for their journey, they begin it;
   But then their telegraph[6] is less sublime,
And if they ran a race, they would not win it   445
   'Gainst Satan's couriers bound for their own clime.
The sun takes up some years for every ray
To reach its goal—the devil not half a day.

57

Upon the verge of space, about the size
   Of half-a-crown, a little speck appeared   450
(I've seen a something like it in the skies
   In the Aegean, ere a squall); it neared,
And, growing bigger, took another guise;
   Like an aërial ship it tacked, and steered,

---

4. In *Paradise Lost* VI. 469 ff., Satan announced his invention of the cannon for use in the war in heaven.
5. A gold key hung from the belt betokens certain official positions at the English court.
6. In its original sense, any apparatus for transmitting signals at a distance.

Or *was* steered (I am doubtful of the grammar   455
Of the last phrase, which makes the stanza stammer—

58

But take your choice); and then it grew a cloud;
    And so it was—a cloud of witnesses.
But such a cloud! No land e'er saw a crowd
    Of locusts numerous as the heavens saw these;   460
They shadowed with their myriads space; their loud
    And varied cries were like those of wild geese
(If nations may be likened to a goose),
And realized the phrase of "hell broke loose."[7]

59

Here crashed a sturdy oath of stout John Bull,   465
    Who damned away his eyes as heretofore:
There Paddy brogued "By Jasus!"—"What's your wull?"
    The temperate Scot exclaimed: the French ghost swore
In certain terms I shan't translate in full,
    As the first coachman will; and 'midst the war,   470
The voice of Jonathan was heard to express,
"*Our* president is going to war, I guess."[8]

60

Besides there were the Spaniard, Dutch, and Dane;
    In short, an universal shoal of shades,
From Otaheite's isle[9] to Salisbury Plain,   475
    Of all climes and professions, years and trades,
Ready to swear against the good king's reign,
    Bitter as clubs in cards are against spades;
All summoned by this grand "subpoena," to
Try if kings mayn't be damned like me or you.   480

61

When Michael saw this host, he first grew pale,
    As angels can; next, like Italian twilight,
He turned all colors—as a peacock's tail,
    Or sunset streaming through a Gothic skylight
In some old abbey, or a trout not stale,   485
    Or distant lightning on the horizon *by* night,
Or a fresh rainbow, or a grand review
Of thirty regiments in red, green, and blue.

62

Then he addressed himself to Satan: "Why—
    My good old friend, for such I deem you, though   490
Our different parties make us fight so shy,
    I ne'er mistake you for a *personal* foe;
Our difference is *political*, and I
    Trust that, whatever may occur below,
You know my great respect for you: and this   495
Makes me regret whate'er you do amiss—

7. *Paradise Lost* IV. 918.
8. "Brother Jonathan" was the name applied to America and Americans, now replaced by "Uncle Sam"; the "I guess" was used by Byron as an obvious Americanism. This was written during the troubled Anglo-American relations after the War of 1812.
9. The old name for Tahiti.

63

"Why, my dear Lucifer, would you abuse
  My call for witnesses? I did not mean
That you should half of earth and hell produce;
  'Tis even superfluous, since two honest, clean,   500
True testimonies are enough: we lose
  Our time, nay, our eternity, between
The accusation and defense: if we
Hear both, 'twill stretch our immortality."

64

Satan replied, "To me the matter is   505
  Indifferent, in a personal point of view:
I can have fifty better souls than this
  With far less trouble than we have gone through
Already; and I merely argued his
  Late majesty of Britain's case with you   510
Upon a point of form: you may dispose
Of him; I've kings enough below, God knows!"

65

Thus spoke the Demon (late called "multifaced"
  By multo-scribbling Southey[1]). "Then we'll call
One or two persons of the myriads placed   515
  Around our congress, and dispense with all
The rest," quoth Michael: "Who may be so graced
  As to speak first? there's choice enough—who shall
It be?" Then Satan answered, "There are many;
But you may choose Jack Wilkes[2] as well as any."   520

66

A merry, cock-eyed, curious-looking sprite
  Upon the instant started from the throng,
Dressed in a fashion now forgotten quite;
  For all the fashions of the flesh stick long
By people in the next world; where unite   525
  All the costumes since Adam's, right or wrong,
From Eve's fig leaf down to the petticoat,
Almost as scanty, of days less remote.

67

The spirit looked around upon the crowds
  Assembled, and exclaimed, "My friends of all   530
The spheres, we shall catch cold amongst these clouds;
  So let's to business: why this general call?
If those are freeholders I see in shrouds,
  And 'tis for an election that they bawl,
Behold a candidate with unturned coat!   535
Saint Peter, may I count upon your vote?"

1. In *A Vision of Judgment* V. 70.
2. John Wilkes (1727–97), notorious libertine, wit, and courageous political radical, who in 1764 was expelled from the House of Commons and driven into exile for his libelous attack on George III in his weekly periodical, *The North Briton*. He later came back to England, became Lord Mayor of London, and was triumphantly returned to Parliament. For a supreme example of the wit and aplomb for which Byron admired Wilkes, see Boswell's account of Dr. Johnson's dinner with him in Volume 1.

68

"Sir," replied Michael, "you mistake; these things
    Are of a former life, and what we do
Above is more august; to judge of kings
    Is the tribunal met: so now you know."   540
"Then I presume those gentlemen with wings,"
    Said Wilkes, "are cherubs; and that soul below
Looks much like George the Third, but to my mind
A good deal older—Bless me! is he blind?"

69

"He is what you behold him, and his doom   545
    Depends upon his deeds," the Angel said.
"If you have aught to arraign in him, the tomb
    Gives license to the humblest beggar's head
To lift itself against the loftiest."—"Some,"
    Said Wilkes, "don't wait to see them laid in lead,   550
For such a liberty—and I, for one,
Have told them what I thought beneath the sun."

70

"*Above* the sun repeat, then, what thou hast
    To urge against him," said the Archangel. "Why,"
Replied the spirit, "since old scores are past,   555
    Must I turn evidence? In faith, not I.
Besides, I beat him hollow at the last,
    With all his Lords and Commons:³ in the sky
I don't like ripping up old stories, since
His conduct was but natural in a prince.   560

71

"Foolish, no doubt, and wicked, to oppress
    A poor unlucky devil without a shilling;
But then I blame the man himself much less
    Than Bute and Grafton,⁴ and shall be unwilling
To see him punished here for their excess,   565
    Since they were both damned long ago, and still in
Their place below: for me, I have forgiven,
And vote his 'habeas corpus' into heaven."

72

"Wilkes," said the Devil, "I understand all this;
    You turned to half a courtier ere you died,⁵   570
And seem to think it would not be amiss
    To grow a whole one on the other side
Of Charon's ferry;⁶ you forget that *his*
    Reign is concluded; whatsoe'er betide,
He won't be sovereign more: you've lost your labor   575
For at the best he will but be your neighbor.

---

3. In 1782 Wilkes succeeded in getting
the House of Commons to expunge
the record of his expulsion.
4. The Duke of Grafton, like the Earl
of Bute, was a minister subservient to
George III.

5. Wilkes in his latter years softened his
opposition and moved in higher social
circles.
6. In Greek mythology, Charon ferried
the dead to the underworld across the
river Styx.

73

"However, I knew what to think of it,
 When I beheld you in your jesting way
Flitting and whispering round about the spit
 Where Belial, upon duty for the day,   580
With Fox's lard was basting William Pitt,[7]
 His pupil; I knew what to think, I say:
That fellow even in hell breeds farther ills;
I'll have him *gagged*—'twas one of his own bills.[8]

74

"Call Junius!"[9] From the crowd a shadow stalked,   585
 And at the name there was a general squeeze,
So that the very ghosts no longer walked
 In comfort, at their own aërial ease,
But were all rammed, and jammed (but to be balked,
 As we shall see), and jostled hands and knees,   590
Like wind compressed and pent within a bladder,
Or like a human colic, which is sadder.

75

The shadow came—a tall, thin, gray-haired figure,
 That looked as it had been a shade on earth;
Quick in its motions, with an air of vigor,   595
 But nought to mark its breeding or its birth:
Now it waxed little, then again grew bigger,
 With now an air of gloom, or savage mirth;
But as you gazed upon its features, they
Changed every instant—to *what*, none could say.   600

76

The more intently the ghosts gazed, the less
 Could they distinguish whose the features were;
The Devil himself seemed puzzled even to guess;
 They varied like a dream—now here, now there;
And several people swore from out the press,   605
 They knew him perfectly; and one could swear
He was his father: upon which another
Was sure he was his mother's cousin's brother:

77

Another, that he was a duke, or knight,
 An orator, a lawyer, or a priest,   610
A nabob,[1] a man-midwife; but the wight
 Mysterious changed his countenance at least
As oft as they their minds: though in full sight
 He stood, the puzzle only was increased;

7. Charles James Fox, statesman and political opponent of William Pitt, prime minister under George III, was notably corpulent.
8. The Alien and Sedition Bills of 1795 severely restricted freedom of speech and of the press.
9. Pseudonym of the writer of a brilliant series of letters (1769–71), attacking supporters of George III and the King himself. His identity is an unsolved political mystery; among more than fifty possibilities proposed are Edmund Burke, John Horne Tooke, and Sir Philip Francis, mentioned in lines 631–32. When the letters were published as a book, the title-page read: *Letters of Junius, Stat Nominis Umbra* ("he stands, the shadow of a name"); hence the allusions, lines 593 ff., 667. The Latin phrase is from Lucan's *Pharsalia* I.135.
1. A man of great wealth, especially one who has returned to England with a fortune acquired in India.

The man was a phantasmagoria in   615
Himself—he was so volatile and thin.

78

The moment that you had pronounced him *one*,
    Presto! his face changed, and he was another;
And when that change was hardly well put on,
    It varied, till I don't think his own mother   620
(If that he had a mother) would her son
    Have known, he shifted so from one to t'other;
Till guessing from a pleasure grew a task,
At this epistolary "Iron Mask."[2]

79

For sometimes he like Cerberus would seem—   625
    "Three gentlemen at once" (as sagely says
Good Mrs. Malaprop[3]); then you might deem
    That he was not even *one*; now many rays
Were flashing round him; and now a thick steam
    Hid him from sight—like fogs on London days: 630
Now Burke, now Tooke, he grew to people's fancies,
And certes often like Sir Philip Francis.

80

I've an hypothesis—'tis quite my own;
    I never let it out till now, for fear
Of doing people harm about the throne,   635
    And injuring some minister or peer,
On whom the stigma might perhaps be blown;
    It is—my gentle public, lend thine ear!
'Tis, that what Junius we are wont to call
Was *really*, *truly*, nobody at all.   640

81

I don't see wherefore letters should not be
    Written without hands, since we daily view
Them written without heads; and books, we see,
    Are filled as well without the latter too:
And really till we fix on somebody   645
    For certain sure to claim them as his due,
Their author, like the Niger's mouth,[4] will bother
The world to say if *there* be mouth or author.

82

"And who and what art thou?" the Archangel said.
    "For *that* you may consult my title page,"   650
Replied this mighty shadow of a shade:
    "If I have kept my secret half an age,
I scarce shall tell it now."—"Canst thou upbraid,"
    Continued Michael, "George Rex, or allege

---

2. "The Man in the Iron Mask" was a state prisoner in the reign of Louis XIV, whose identity was thus concealed.
3. A character in R. B. Sheridan's *The Rivals*, who comically misused words; the word "malapropism" derives from her name.
4. Several recent British expeditions to explore the course of the river Niger, in western Africa, had ended in failure.

Aught further?" Junius answered, "You had better   655
  First ask him for *his* answer to my letter:

83

"My charges upon record will outlast
  The brass of both his epitaph and tomb."
"Repent'st thou not," said Michael, "of some past
  Exaggeration? something which may doom   660
Thyself if false, as him if true? Thou wast
  Too bitter—is it not so?—in thy gloom
Of passion?"—"Passion!" cried the phantom dim,
"I loved my country, and I hated him.

84

"What I have written, I have written:[5] let   665
  The rest be on his head or mine!" So spoke
Old "Nominis Umbra"; and while speaking yet,
  Away he melted in celestial smoke.
Then Satan said to Michael, "Don't forget
  To call George Washington, and John Horne Tooke,[6]   670
And Franklin"—but at this time there was heard
A cry for room, though not a phantom stirred.

85

At length with jostling, elbowing, and the aid
  Of cherubim appointed to that post,
The devil Asmodeus[7] to the circle made   675
  His way, and looked as if his journey cost
Some trouble. When his burden down he laid,
  "What's this?" cried Michael; "why, 'tis not a ghost?"
"I know it," quoth the incubus; "but he
Shall be one, if you leave the affair to me   680

86

"Confound the renegado! I have sprained
  My left wing, he's so heavy; one would think
Some of his works about his neck were chained.
  But to the point; while hovering o'er the brink
Of Skiddaw (where as usual it still rained),[8]   685
  I saw a taper, far below me, wink,
And stooping, caught this fellow at a libel—
No less on history than the Holy Bible.

87

"The former is the devil's scripture, and
  The latter yours, good Michael: so the affair   690
Belongs to all of us, you understand.
  I snatched him up just as you see him there,
And brought him off for sentence out of hand:
  I've scarcely been ten minutes in the air—
At least a quarter it can hardly be: 695
I dare say that his wife is still at tea."

5. Said by Pilate, John xix.22.
6. A prominent English opponent of the war against the American colonies; see note to line 585.
7. The devil in Le Sage's *Le Diable Boiteux* ("The Lame Devil"), published 1707, who carries Don Cleofas to the summit of San Salvador.
8. Mount Skiddaw, near Southey's home in the Lake Country.

88

Here Satan said, "I know this man of old,
 And have expected him for some time here;
A sillier fellow you will scarce behold,
 Or more conceited in his petty sphere: 700
But surely it was not worth while to fold
 Such trash below your wing, Asmodeus dear:
We had the poor wretch safe (without being bored
With carriage) coming of his own accord.

89

"But since he's here, let's see what he has done."   705
 "Done!" cried Asmodeus, "he anticipates
The very business you are now upon,
 And scribbles as if head clerk to the Fates.
Who knows to what his ribaldry may run,
 When such an ass as this, like Balaam's,[9] prates?"   710
"Let's hear," quoth Michael, "what he has to say:
You know we're bound to that in every way."

90

Now the bard, glad to get an audience, which
 By no means often was his case below,
Began to cough, and hawk, and hem, and pitch   715
 His voice into that awful note of woe
To all unhappy hearers within reach
 Of poets when the tide of rhyme's in flow;
But stuck fast with his first hexameter,
Not one of all whose gouty feet would stir.   720

91

But ere the spavined dactyls[1] could be spurred
 Into recitative, in great dismay
Both cherubim and seraphim were heard
 To murmur loudly through their long array;
And Michael rose ere he could get a word   725
 Of all his foundered verses under way,
And cried, "For God's sake stop, my friend! 'twere best—
Non Di, non homines[2]—you know the rest."

92

A general bustle spread throughout the throng,
 Which seemed to hold all verse in detestation;   730
The angels had of course enough of song
 When upon service; and the generation
Of ghosts had heard too much in life, not long
 Before, to profit by a new occasion:

9. Balaam's ass was granted speech in Numbers xxii.28 ff.
1. Southey's *A Vision of Judgment* was written in dactylic hexameters, a very awkward measure in English. A "spavined" horse is a lame one.

2. Horace, *Art of Poetry*, 372–73: "mediocribus esse poetis / Non homines, non di, non concessere columnae" ("mediocrity in poets has never been tolerated by either men, or gods, or booksellers").

The monarch, mute till then, exclaimed, "What! what!   735
Pye[3] come again? No more—no more of that!"

93

The tumult grew; an universal cough
  Convulsed the skies, as during a debate,
When Castlereagh[4] has been up long enough
  (Before he was first minister of state,   740
I mean—the *slaves hear now*); some cried "Off, off!"
  As at a farce; till, grown quite desperate,
The bard Saint Peter prayed to interpose
(Himself an author)[5] only for his prose.

94

The varlet was not an ill-favored knave;   745
  A good deal like a vulture in the face,
With a hook nose and a hawk's eye, which gave
  A smart and sharper looking sort of grace
To his whole aspect, which, though rather grave,
  Was by no means so ugly as his case;   750
But that, indeed, was hopeless as can be,
Quite a poetic felony "*de se.*"[6]

95

Then Michael blew his trump, and stilled the noise
  With one still greater, as is yet the mode
On earth besides; except some grumbling voice,   755
  Which now and then will make a slight inroad
Upon decorous silence, few will twice
  Lift up their lungs when fairly overcrowed;
And now the bard could plead his own bad cause,
With all the attitudes of self-applause.   760

96

He said—(I only give the heads)—he said,
  He meant no harm in scribbling; 'twas his way
Upon all topics; 'twas, besides, his bread,
  Of which he buttered both sides; 'twould delay
Too long the assembly (he was pleased to dread),   765
  And take up rather more time than a day,
To name his works—he would but cite a few—
"Wat Tyler"—"Rhymes on Blenheim"—"Waterloo."

97

He had written praises of a regicide;[7]
  He had written praises of all kings what ever;
He had written for republics far and wide,   770
  And then against them bitterer than ever:

---

3. Henry James Pye, a bad and much ridiculed poet, Southey's predecessor as poet laureate.
4. Viscount Castlereagh was foreign secretary when Byron wrote his poem. "The slaves hear now": i.e., now that he is Prime Minister members of the House of Commons listen obsequiously.

5. The reference is to the first and second epistles of Peter, very short books in the New Testament.
6. A felony "upon himself"; that is, suicide.
7. In an early poem on Henry Martin, one of the judges who had condemned Charles I to be beheaded.

For pantisocracy[8] he once had cried
   Aloud, a scheme less moral than 'twas clever;
Then grew a hearty anti-jacobin—   775
   Had turned his coat—and would have turned his skin.

98

He had sung against all battles, and again
   In their high praise and glory; he had called
Reviewing "the ungentle craft,"[9] and then
   Become as base a critic as e'er crawled—   780
Fed, paid, and pampered by the very men
   By whom his muse and morals had been mauled:
He had written much blank verse, and blanker prose,
And more of both than anybody knows.

99

He had written Wesley's life—here turning round   785
   To Satan, "Sir, I'm ready to write yours,
In two octavo volumes, nicely bound,
   With notes and preface, all that most allures
The pious purchaser; and there's no ground
   For fear, for I can choose my own reviewers: 790
So let me have the proper documents,
That I may add you to my other saints."

100

Satan bowed, and was silent. "Well, if you,
   With amiable modesty, decline
My offer, what says Michael? There are few   795
   Whose memoirs could be rendered more divine.
Mine is a pen of all work; not so new
   As it was once, but I would make you shine
Like your own trumpet. By the way, my own
Has more of brass in it, and is as well blown.   800

101

"But talking about trumpets, here's my Vision!
   Now you shall judge, all people; yes, you shall
Judge with my judgment, and by my decision
   Be guided who shall enter heaven or fall.
I settle all these things by intuition,   805
   Times present, past, to come, heaven, hell, and all,
Like King Alfonso.[1] When I thus see double,
I save the Deity some worlds of trouble."

102

He ceased, and drew forth an MS.; and no
   Persuasion on the part of devils, saints,   810
Or angels, now could stop the torrent; so

---

8. An ideal community that Southey and Coleridge, in 1794–95, had planned to set up in America on the banks of the Susquehanna. The scheme was utopian, but in no way immoral.
9. In Southey's *The Remains of Henry Kirke White*, Vol. I (1808).

1. "King Alphonso [of Castile, in the 13th century] speaking of the Ptolemean system, said that had he been consulted at the creation of the world, he would have spared the Maker some absurdities" [Byron's note].

He read the first three lines of the contents;
But at the fourth, the whole spiritual show
Had vanished, with variety of scents,
Ambrosial and sulphureous, as they sprang,   815
Like lightning, off from his "melodious twang."[2]

103

Those grand heroics acted as a spell:
    The angels stopped their ears and plied their pinions;
And the devils ran howling, deafened, down to hell;
    The ghosts fled, gibbering, for their own dominions—   820
(For 'tis not yet decided where they dwell,
    And I leave every man to his opinions);
Michael took refuge in his trump—but, lo!
His teeth were set on edge, he could not blow!

104

Saint Peter, who has hitherto been known   825
    For an impetuous saint, upraised his keys,
And at the fifth line knocked the poet down;
    Who fell like Phaëton,[3] but more at ease,
Into his lake, for there he did not drown;
    A different web being by the Destinies   830
Woven for the Laureate's final wreath, whene'er
Reform shall happen either here or there.

105

He first sank to the bottom—like his works,
    But soon rose to the surface—like himself;
For all corrupted things are buoyed like corks,   835
    By their own rottenness, light as an elf,
Or wisp that flits o'er a morass: he lurks,
    It may be, still, like dull books on a shelf,
In his own den, to scrawl some "Life" or "Vision,"
As Welborn says—"the devil turned precisian."[4]   840

106

As for the rest, to come to the conclusion
    Of this true dream, the telescope is gone
Which kept my optics free from all delusion,
    And showed me what I in my turn have shown;
All I saw farther, in the last confusion,   845
    Was, that King George slipped into heaven for one;
And when the tumult dwindled to a calm,
I left him practising the hundredth psalm.[5]

1821   1822

---

2. John Aubrey in his *Miscellanies upon Various Subjects* (1696) had described a ghost that vanished "with a curious perfume, and most melodious twang."
3. Phaethon, son of Apollo, tried to drive his father's chariot, the sun. He could not control the horses and was struck down into the sea by a thunderbolt of Zeus. The satiric point is that Apollo is the god of poetry as well as of the sun.
4. A "precisian" is a Puritan. Spoken by Welborn in Massinger's play, *A New Way to Pay Old Debts* (1626), I.i.6.
5. Which contains the relevant line, "Enter into his gates with thanksgiving."

Stanzas to the Po[1]

River, that rollest by the ancient walls,
    Where dwells the Lady of my love, when she
Walks by thy brink, and there perchance recalls
    A faint and fleeting memory of me;

What if thy deep and ample stream should be   5
    A mirror of my heart, where she may read
The thousand thoughts I now betray to thee,
    Wild as thy wave, and headlong as thy speed!

What do I say—a mirror of my heart?
    Are not thy waters sweeping, dark, and strong?   10
Such as my feelings were and are, thou art;
    And such as thou art were my passions long.

Time may have somewhat tamed them—not forever;
    Thou overflow'st thy banks, and not for aye
Thy bosom overboils, congenial river!   15
    Thy floods subside, and mine have sunk away—

But left long wrecks behind: and now again,
    Borne in our old unchanged career, we move:
Thou tendest wildly onwards to the main.
    And I—to loving *one* I should not love.   20

The current I behold will sweep beneath
    Her native walls, and murmur at her feet;
Her eyes will look on thee, when she shall breathe
    The twilight air, unharmed by summer's heat.

She will look on thee—I have looked on thee,   25
    Full of that thought; and, from that moment, ne'er
Thy waters could I dream of, name, or see,
    Without the inseparable sigh for her!

Her bright eyes will be imaged in thy stream—
    Yes! they will meet the wave I gaze on now: 30
Mine cannot witness, even in a dream,
    That happy wave repass me in its flow!

The wave that bears my tears returns no more:
    Will she return by whom that wave shall sweep?
Both tread thy banks, both wander on thy shore,
    I by thy source, she by the dark-blue deep.   35

1. This powerful lyric was written a month or two after Byron had fallen in love with the 19-year-old Italian Teresa Guiccioli. The Po is a river in northern Italy that flows into the Adriatic.

But that which keepeth us apart is not
   Distance, nor depth of wave, nor space of earth,
But the distraction of a various lot,
   As various as the climates of our birth.   40

A stranger loves the Lady of the land,
   Born far beyond the mountains, but his blood
Is all meridian,[2] as if never fanned
   By the black wind that chills the polar flood.

My blood is all meridian; were it not,   45
   I had not left my clime, nor should I be,
In spite of tortures, ne'er to be forgot,
   A slave again of love—at least of thee.

'Tis vain to struggle—let me perish young—
   Live as I lived, and love as I have loved;   50
To dust if I return, from dust I sprung,
   And then, at least, my heart can ne'er be moved.

1819   1824

When a Man Hath No Freedom to Fight for at Home[1]

When a man hath no freedom to fight for at home,
   Let him combat for that of his neighbors;
Let him think of the glories of Greece and of Rome,
   And get knocked on his head for his labors.

To do good to mankind is the chivalrous plan,   5
   And is always as nobly requited;
Then battle for freedom wherever you can,
   And, if not shot or hanged, you'll get knighted.

November 5, 1820   1824

Stanzas Written on the Road Between Florence and Pisa

Oh, talk not to me of a name great in story—
   The days of our youth are the days of our glory;

2. Southern.
1. The ironist's attitude toward gratuitous enlistment in a foreign war for national freedom—a cause to which Byron gave his own life less than four years later.

And the myrtle and ivy of sweet two-and-twenty
Are worth all your laurels,[1] though ever so plenty.

What are garlands and crowns to the brow that is wrinkled? 5
'Tis but as a dead-flower with May-dew besprinkled:
Then away with all such from the head that is hoary!
What care I for the wreaths that can *only* give glory?

Oh FAME!—if I e'er took delight in thy praises,
'Twas less for the sake of thy high-sounding phrases, 10
Than to see the bright eyes of the dear one discover
She thought that I was not unworthy to love her.

There chiefly I sought thee, *there* only I found thee;
Her glance was the best of the rays that surround thee;
When it sparkled o'er aught that was bright in my story, 15
I knew it was love, and I felt it was glory.

November, 1821   1830

1. Myrtle was sacred to Venus, goddess of love, and ivy to Bacchus, god of wine and revelry; a laurel crown was awarded by the Greeks as a mark of high honor.

PERCY BYSSHE SHELLEY
(1792–1822)

> 1811: Is expelled from Oxford and elopes with Harriet West-
>   brook.
> 1818: Leaves England for Italy, never to return.
> 1819: The great year: *Prometheus Unbound, The Cenci, Ode
>   to the West Wind,* and some of his best lyrics.
> 1820: Settles in Pisa and its vicinity; the "Pisan Circle."

Although he was an extreme heretic and nonconformist in all his life and thought, Shelley emerged from a solidly conservative background. His ancestors had been Sussex aristocrats since early in the 17th century; his grandfather, Sir Bysshe Shelley, made himself the richest man in Horsham, Sussex; his father, Timothy Shelley, was a hardheaded and conventional member of Parliament; Percy Shelley himself was in line for a baronetcy, and as befitted his station, was sent to be educated at Eton and at Oxford. He was slight of build, eccentric in manner, and unskilled in sports or fighting, and as a consequence, was mercilessly baited by older and stronger boys. Even then he saw the petty tyranny of schoolmasters and schoolmates as representative of man's general inhumanity to man, and dedicated his life to a war against all injustice and oppression. He describes the experience in the Dedication to *The Revolt of Islam:*

> So without shame, I spoke: "I will be wise,
> And just, and free, and mild, if in me lies
> Such power, for I grow weary to behold
> The selfish and the strong still tyrannize
> Without reproach or check." I then controlled
> My tears, my heart grew calm, and I was meek and bold.

At Oxford in the autumn of 1810 Shelley's closest friend was Thomas Jefferson Hogg, a self-centered and self-confident young man who shared Shelley's love of philosophy and scorn of orthodoxy. The two collaborated on a pamphlet, *The Necessity of Atheism*, which claimed that God's existence cannot be proved on empirical grounds. Shelley refused to repudiate the document before the authorities and, to his great shock and grief, was peremptorily expelled, terminating a university career that had lasted only six months. This event opened a breach between Shelley and his father that widened over the years.

Shelley went to London where, eager for a test of his zeal for social justice, he took up the cause of Harriet Westbrook, the pretty and warm-hearted daughter of a well-to-do tavern keeper, whose father, Shelley wrote to Hogg, "has persecuted her in a most horrible way by endeavoring to compel her to go to school." Harriet threw herself on Shelley's protection, and "gratitude and admiration," he wrote, "all demand that I shall love her *forever*." He eloped with Harriet to Edinburgh and married her, though against his firm conviction that marriage was a tyrannical and degrading social institution. He was then 18 years of age, and his bride 16. The young couple moved restlessly from place to place, living on a small allowance granted reluctantly by their families. In February of 1812, accompanied by Harriet's sister Eliza, they traveled to Dublin to distribute Shelley's *Address to the Irish People* and otherwise take part in the movement for Catholic emancipation and for the amelioration of the oppressed and poverty-stricken people.

Back in London, Shelley became a disciple of the radical social philosopher William Godwin, author of the *Inquiry Concerning Political Justice*. In 1813 he printed privately his first important work, *Queen Mab*, a long prophetic poem set in the fantastic frame of the journcy of a disembodied soul through space, to whom the fairy Mab reveals in visions the woeful past, the dreadful present, and the utopian future. Announcing that "there is no God!" Mab decries institutional religion and codified morality as the causes of social evil. She predicts, by the action of the all-ruling goddess Necessity, the withering away of all institutions, and the return of man to his natural state of goodness and felicity.

In the following spring Shelley, who had drifted apart from Harriet, fell in love with the beautiful Mary Wollstonecraft Godwin. Acting according to his conviction that cohabitation without love is immoral, he abandoned Harriet, fled to France with Mary (taking along her half sister, Claire Clairmont), and—still acting in accordance with his belief in nonexclusive love—invited Harriet to come live with them in the relationship of a sister. Shelley's elopement with Mary outraged even her father, though his theoretical views of marriage had been no less liberal than Shelley's, and despite the fact that Shelley, himself in financial difficulties, had earlier taken over Godwin's very substantial debts. When he returned to London, Shelley found that the general public, his family, and most of his friends regarded him not only as an atheist and revolutionary, but also as a gross immoralist. When, two years later, Harriet drowned herself in a fit of despair, the courts denied Shelley the custody of their two children. Shelley married Mary Godwin and, in 1818, moved to Italy; thereafter he saw himself in the role of an alien and outcast, scorned and rejected by the mankind to whose welfare he had dedicated his powers and his life.

In Italy he resumed his restless existence, moving from town to town and house to house. His health was usually bad. Although the death of his grandfather in 1815 had provided a substantial income, he dissipated so much of it by his warmhearted but improvident support of William Godwin, Leigh Hunt, and other indigent pensioners that he was constantly short of money and harried by creditors. Within nine months, in 1818–19, Clara and William, the beloved children of Percy and Mary Shelley, both died. This tragedy threw Mary into a state of apathy and self-absorption which destroyed the earlier harmony of her relationship with her husband, and from which even the birth of another son, Percy Florence, could not entirely rescue her.

In these desperate circumstances, in a state sometimes verging on despair, and knowing that he almost entirely lacked a literary audience, Shelley wrote his greatest works. In 1819 he completed his masterpiece, *Prometheus Unbound*, and wrote a fine tragedy, *The Cenci*, as well as a number of lyric poems, two satires (*The Mask of Anarchy* and *Peter Bell the Third*), and a penetrating political essay, *A Philosophical View of Reform*. His works of the next two years include *A Defense of Poetry; Epipsychidion*, a rhapsodic vision of love as a union, beyond earthly limits, with what the title identifies as "the soul out of my soul"; *Adonais*, his noble elegy on the death of Keats; and *Hellas*, a lyrical drama evoked by the Greek war for liberation from the Turks in which he again projected his vision of a new golden age. These writings, unlike the early *Queen Mab*, are the products of a mind enlarged and chastened by tragic experience, deepened by incessant philosophical speculation, and richly stored with the harvest of his reading—which Shelley carried on, as his friend Hogg said, "in season and out of season, at table, in bed, and especially during a walk," until he became one of the most erudite of poets. His delight in scientific discoveries and speculations continued, but his earlier zest for Gothic terrors and the social theories of the radical 18th-century optimists had given way to an absorption in Greek tragedy, Milton's *Paradise Lost*, and the Bible. While he did not give up his hopes for a millennial future (he wore a ring with the motto *Il buon tempo verrà*—"the good time will come"), he now attributed the evils of present society to man's own moral failures, and grounded the possibility of radical social reform upon a prior reform of man's moral nature through the redeeming power of love. Though often thought of as a simple-minded doctrinaire, Shelley in fact possessed a complex and energetically inquisitive intelligence which never halted at a fixed mental position; all his writings represent, not final solutions, but stages in a ceaseless exploration.

The poems of Shelley's maturity also exhibit the effect of his intensive study of Plato and the Neo-Platonists. From his early childhood, Shelley had lived in two worlds. One was the world of his everyday experience, the world of suffering, oppression, and cruelty, which he found intolerable; the other was an imagined world of absolute justice, goodness, and love. To such a mind Platonism was congenial, for it sees the cosmos as divided between the passing and shadowy domain of sense experience and the criterion world of Forms, perfect, eternal, out of time and space, the locus of all Reality, Beauty, and Goodness, of which the world of sense is only a distant and illusory reflection. The earlier interpretations of Shelley as an outright (if somewhat confused) Platonic idealist have been drastically modified by recent investigations of Shelley's reading, and of his philosophical essays, as well as his poetry. He was a close student of the English empirical tradition, which limits knowledge to valid reasoning upon what is given in sense-experience, and felt a special affinity, within this tradition, to the radical scepticism of David Hume. Very early in his career he wrote, in a note to *Queen Mab*, "All that we have a right to infer from our ignorance of any event is that we do not know it"; and later: we quickly reach "the verge where words abandon us, and what wonder if we grow dizzy to look down the dark abyss of how little we know." Shelley was indeed an idealist, but as C. E. Pulos has shown in *The Deep Truth: A Study of Shelley's Scepticism*, his was "a qualified idealism," holding provisionally to the ideas envisioned by an imagination which transcends experience, but refusing to assert of these ideas specific attributes outside the limits of experience. On this ground he steadfastly refused, for example, to affirm the survival of conscious life and personal identity beyond the grave; what we know is that this life ends in death, and what happens thereafter, as he said in *Prometheus Unbound*, however we may imagine it, "is known / But to the uncommunicating dead." The *Hymn to Intellectual Beauty* is often represented as the central instance of Shelley's Platonism; in fact, the poem expressly rejects positive assertions about the nature, controlling causes, and ends of this "unseen Power," which have been proposed either by doctrinaire philosophy or dogmatic religion. Shelley also puts forward the concept of another Power, the ultimate principle that governs all process, the way things actually happen—the Power "in the likeness of the Arve" in *Mont Blanc*, the "mighty darkness" and shapeless form that is Demogorgon in *Prometheus Unbound*; but this principle is represented as inaccessible to the knowing mind and totally indifferent to human ends, so that, although capable of being turned to great good, it is equally capable of bringing destruction to all that we most value. To the mature Shelley the hope that good will triumph in a millennial condition on earth is not an intellectual certainty, but only an essential virtue, a moral *sine qua non*. The indefeasible hope in the ultimate redemption of life by love and the imagination does not guarantee its achievement, but it keeps open the possibility of such achievement, and releases man's imaginative and creative potentialities which are its only available means. We must cling to hope, for its contrary, despair, does guarantee its own validity, by ensuring the permanence of the desperate conditions before which the mind has surrendered its aspirations.

When in 1820 the Shelleys settled finally at Pisa, he came closer to finding contentment than at any time in his adult life. A group of friends, Shelley's "Pisan Circle," gathered around them, including for a while Lord Byron and the swashbuckling young Cornishman, Edward Trelawney. Chief in Shelley's affections, however, were Edward Williams, a retired lieutenant of the army of the East India Company, and his charming common-law wife, Jane, with whom Shelley carried on a flirtation and to whom he addressed some of his best lyrics and verse letters. The end came suddenly, and in a fashion pre-visioned in the ecstatic last stanza of *Adonais*, where Shelley had described his spirit as a ship driven by a violent storm out into the dark unknown to join the disembodied soul of Adonais. On July 8, 1822, Shelley and Edward Williams were sailing their open boat, the *Don Juan*, from Leghorn to their summer house near Lerici, on the Gulf of Spezzia. A violent squall blew up and swamped the boat. When several days later the bodies were washed ashore they were cremated, and Shelley's ashes were buried in the Protestant Cemetery at Rome, near the graves of John Keats and of William Shelley, the poet's young son. He left unfinished *The Triumph of Life* which, in its sustained narrative power, boldness of design, and stylistic concentration was a new departure for Shelley and, in the estimation of many readers, promised to be his greatest poem.

Byron, who did not pay moral compliments lightly, wrote to John Murray at the time of Shelley's death: "You were all brutally mistaken about Shelley, who was, without exception, the *best* and least selfish man I ever knew. I never knew one who was not a beast in comparison." The tragedy of Shelley's short life was that, in attempting to live in this world according to his ideas of what ought to be, he brought disaster and suffering upon himself and those he loved; as he himself recognized when he wrote to Mary the year before he died: "Good, far more than evil impulses, love, far more than hatred, has been to me * * * the source of all sorts of mischief."

To many of the new critics in the decades after 1920 (and despite the reverence toward him of W. B. Yeats, an admitted master of the poetry they most admire), Shelley has served as the very model of what poetry should not be, a favorite resort for supposed examples of intellectual and emotional immaturity, shoddy workmanship, unvisualizable descriptions, and incoherent imagery. But the attack has elicited a number of able defenders, whose close reading of Shelley's poems have increasingly verified Wordsworth's perception that "Shelley is one of the best *artists* of us all: I mean in workmanship of style." Shelley's expansion of the metrical and sonantal resources of verse is without recent parallel in the history of English literature. Furthermore, his successful poems show an astonishing range of voice, from the sovereign order in rage of *Ode to the West Wind*, through the calm and heroic dignity of the utterances of Prometheus, and the near approximation to the inexpressible in the representation of the transfiguration of Asia and in the visionary conclusion of *Adonais*, to—and most surprising, in a poet who almost entirely lacked an audience—the assured urbanity, the effortless command of the tone and the language of a cultivated man of the world, which is exemplified in passages that Shelley wrote all through his mature career, but most sustainedly in the great lyrics and verse letters that he composed during the last year of his life.

Mutability

We are as clouds that veil the midnight moon;
  How restlessly they speed, and gleam, and quiver,
Streaking the darkness radiantly!—yet soon
  Night closes round, and they are lost forever:

Or like forgotten lyres, whose dissonant strings   5
  Give various response to each varying blast,
To whose frail frame no second motion brings
  One mood or modulation like the last.

We rest.—A dream has power to poison sleep;
  We rise.—One wandering thought pollutes the day;   10
We feel, conceive or reason, laugh or weep;
  Embrace fond woe, or cast our cares away:

It is the same!—For, be it joy or sorrow,
  The path of its departure still is free:
Man's yesterday may ne'er be like his morrow;   15
  Nought may endure but Mutability.

1816

Mont Blanc[1]

LINES WRITTEN IN THE VALE OF CHAMOUNI

1

The everlasting universe of things
Flows through the mind, and rolls its rapid waves,

1. Shelley wrote of this poem: "It was composed under the immediate impression of the deep and powerful feelings excited by the objects which it attempts to describe; and, as an indisciplined overflowing of the soul, rests its claim to approbation on an attempt to imitate the untamable wildness and inaccessible solemnity from which those feelings sprang."

Shelley's comment points to two important attributes of *Mont Blanc*. First, he attempts, as in other poems (supremely in *Ode to the West Wind*), to make the poem iconic, or directly imitative—in the over-all impetus, but interpolated *ritardandi*, of its blank verse, syntax, and imagery—of the alternating "wildness" and "solemnity" of the scene and the consonant thought and feelings it evokes. Second, this work belongs to the genre of the "local" poem, a descriptive-meditative presentation of a precisely identified landscape. In this respect it resembles Wordsworth's *Tintern Abbey*, the major influence on *Mont Blanc*. Shelley's poem, like Wordsworth's, emphasizes the interchange between mind and nature in perception and goes on to pose the question of the significance of nature to man; it proposes, however, a very different answer to that question.

The poem raises the central problem about the nature and human significance of "Power," the ultimate principle behind all natural and mental process. The symbol of this Power is the river Arve (lines 16–17), which has its "secret throne" at the summit of Mont Blanc, the highest peak in Europe, and beyond human access. The process of the Arve begins with the ceaseless but unseen fall of snow and the unheard play of winds at the far height of the mountain, becomes the Mer de Glace glacier, moves inexorably down the mountain, and melts into the river, which runs through its ravine into the valley of Chamonix in southeastern France. Shelley's answers to all questions about this Power are austerely skeptical. He postulates only that "the power is there," at the inaccessible peak of Mont Blanc (lines 127 ff.), but it is "remote, serene, and inaccessible" (lines 96–97): Shelly refuses to invest it with anthropomorphic intentions or values.

What we do know is that this Power,

Now dark—now glittering—now reflecting gloom—
Now lending splendor, where from secret springs
The source of human thought its tribute brings   5
Of waters—with a sound but half its own,
Such as a feeble brook will oft assume
In the wild woods, among the mountains lone,
Where waterfalls around it leap forever,
Where woods and winds contend, and a vast river   10
Over its rocks ceaselessly bursts and raves.

2

Thus thou, Ravine of Arve—dark, deep Ravine—
Thou many-colored, many-voicéd vale,
Over whose pines, and crags, and caverns sail
Fast cloud-shadows and sunbeams: awful scene,   15
Where Power in likeness of the Arve comes down
From the ice-gulfs that gird his secret throne,
Bursting through these dark mountains like the flame
Of lightning through the tempest; thou dost lie,
Thy giant brood of pines around thee clinging,   20
Children of elder time, in whose devotion
The chainless winds still come and ever came
To drink their odors, and their mighty swinging
To hear—an old and solemn harmony;
Thine earthly rainbows stretched across the sweep   25
Of the aethereal waterfall, whose veil
Robes some unsculptured image; the strange sleep
Which when the voices of the desert fail
Wraps all in its own deep eternity;
Thy caverns echoing to the Arve's commotion,   30
A loud, lone sound no other sound can tame;
Thou art pervaded with that ceaseless motion,
Thou art the path of that unresting sound—
Dizzy Ravine! and when I gaze on thee
I seem as in a trance sublime and strange   35
To muse on my own separate fantasy,
My own, my human mind, which passively
Now renders and receives fast influencings,
Holding an unremitting interchange
With the clear universe of things around;[2]   40

as, in its embodiment as a glacier, it descends from its secret throne into the human ken, remorselessly destroys all things, animal and human (lines 100–20); yet in its simultaneous form as a river (lines 120–26), it with equal moral indifference is the "breath and blood of distant lands," and the source of life-giving rain. It is the enlightened human will alone which can convert this purposeless destroyer and preserver to moral purposefulness, by harnessing process as means to its own human ends, even to the revolutionary end of total reform by the repeal of "Large codes of fraud and woe" (lines 80–83). The poem ends like *Ode to the West Wind*, with a rhetorical question, of which the implication is that phenomenal nature is in itself but a universal blank, except as it is invested with human significance by the imagination of observing man. Shelley comes close here to the central theme of the modern American poet, Wallace Stevens, for whom the human imagination confronts an alien and neutral nature and creates the order and meaning it does not find.
2. This passage is remarkably parallel

One legion of wild thoughts, whose wandering wings
Now float above thy darkness, and now rest
Where that or thou art no unbidden guest,
In the still cave of the witch Poesy,
Seeking among the shadows that pass by   45
Ghosts of all things that are, some shade of thee,
Some phantom, some faint image; till the breast
From which they fled recalls them, thou art there!

3

Some say that gleams of a remoter world
Visit the soul in sleep, that death is slumber,   50
And that its shapes the busy thoughts outnumber
Of those who wake and live. I look on high;
Has some unknown omnipotence unfurled
The veil of life and death? or do I lie
In dream, and does the mightier world of sleep   55
Spread far around and inaccessibly
Its circles? For the very spirit fails,
Driven like a homeless cloud from steep to steep
That vanishes among the viewless[3] gales!
Far, far above, piercing the infinite sky,   60
Mont Blanc appears—still, snowy, and serene—
Its subject mountains their uncarthly forms
Pile around it, ice and rock; broad vales between
Of frozen floods, unfathomable deeps,
Blue as the overhanging heaven, that spread   65
And wind among the accumulated steeps;
A desert peopled by the storms alone,
Save when the eagle brings some hunter's bone,
And the wolf tracks her there—how hideously
Its shapes are heaped around! rude, bare, and high,   70
Ghastly, and scarred, and riven. Is this the scene
Where the old Earthquake-daemon taught her young
Ruin? Were these their toys? or did a sea
Of fire envelop once this silent snow?[4]
None can reply—all seems eternal now.   75
The wilderness has a mysterious tongue
Which teaches awful doubt, or faith so mild,
So solemn, so serene, that man may be,
But for such faith,[5] with nature reconciled;
Thou hast a voice, great Mountain, to repeal   80
Large codes of fraud and woe; not understood

to a passage in Wordsworth's *Prelude* which (since the poem was not published until 1850) Shelley could not have read. See above, in *The Prelude*, XIV, 63 ff., where in the landscape viewed from Mount Snowdon, Wordsworth discovers the "type" or "emblem" of the human mind.
3. Invisible.
4. An allusion to theories current in Shelley's day that the earth was origi- nally a smooth globe, and that moun- tains were formed by catastrophic earthquakes, by floods, or by a bursting forth of fire from the earth's interior.
5. "Simply by holding such a faith"— such as Wordsworth's "cheerful faith" (lines 133–34) in *Tintern Abbey* "that all which we behold / Is full of bless- ings." In Shelley's balance of possibil- ities, the landscape is equally capable of teaching this faith and "awful doubt."

By all, but which the wise, and great, and good
Interpret, or make felt, or deeply feel.

4

The fields, the lakes, the forests, and the streams,
Ocean, and all the living things that dwell   85
Within the daedal[6] earth; lightning, and rain,
Earthquake, and fiery flood, and hurricane,
The torpor of the year when feeble dreams
Visit the hidden buds, or dreamless sleep
Holds every future leaf and flower; the bound   90
With which from that detested trance they leap;
The works and ways of man, their death and birth,
And that of him and all that his may be;
All things that move and breathe with toil and sound
Are born and die; revolve, subside, and swell.   95
Power dwells apart in its tranquillity,
Remote, serene, and inaccessible:
And *this*, the naked countenance of earth,
On which I gaze, even these primaeval mountains
Teach the adverting mind. The glaciers creep   100
Like snakes that watch their prey, from their far fountains,
Slow rolling on; there, many a precipice,
Frost and the Sun in scorn of mortal power
Have piled: dome, pyramid, and pinnacle,
A city of death, distinct with many a tower   105
And wall impregnable of beaming ice.
Yet not a city, but a flood of ruin
Is there, that from the boundaries of the sky
Rolls its perpetual stream; vast pines are strewing
Its destined path, or in the mangled soil   110
Branchless and shattered stand; the rocks, drawn down
From yon remotest waste, have overthrown
The limits of the dead and living world,
Never to be reclaimed. The dwelling place
Of insects, beasts, and birds, becomes its spoil   115
Their food and their retreat for ever gone,
So much of life and joy is lost. The race
Of man flies far in dread; his work and dwelling
Vanish, like smoke before the tempest's stream,
And their place is not known. Below, vast caves   120
Shine in the rushing torrents' restless gleam,
Which from those secret chasms in tumult welling[7]
Meet in the vale, and one majestic River,
The breath and blood of distant lands, forever
Rolls its loud waters to the ocean waves,   125
Breathes its swift vapors to the circling air.

6. Intricately formed; derived from Daedalus, builder of the labyrinth in Crete.
7. Like lines 9–11, an echo of Coleridge's description of the chasm and sacred river in *Kubla Khan*, lines 11–24. In writing *Mont Blanc* Shelley probably remembered also Coleridge's *Hymn before Sun-Rise, in the Vale of Chamouni.*

5

Mont Blanc yet gleams on high—the power is there,
The still and solemn power of many sights,
And many sounds, and much of life and death.
In the calm darkness of the moonless nights,   130
In the lone glare of day, the snows descend
Upon that Mountain; none beholds them there,
Nor when the flakes burn in the sinking sun,
Or the star-beams dart through them—Winds contend
Silently there, and heap the snow with breath   135
Rapid and strong, but silently! Its home
The voiceless lightning in these solitudes
Keeps innocently, and like vapor broods
Over the snow. The secret Strength of things
Which governs thought, and to the infinite dome   140
Of Heaven is as a law, inhabits thee!
And what were thou,[8] and earth, and stars, and sea,
If to the human mind's imaginings
Silence and solitude were vacancy?
July 23, 1816   1817

Hymn to Intellectual Beauty[1]

1

The awful shadow of some unseen Power
  Floats though unseen among us—visiting
  This various world with as inconstant wing
As summer winds that creep from flower to flower—
Like moonbeams that behind some piny mountain shower,   5
    It visits with inconstant glance
    Each human heart and countenance;
Like hues and harmonies of evening—
    Like clouds in starlight widely spread—
    Like memory of music fled—   10
    Like aught that for its grace may be
Dear, and yet dearer for its mystery.

---

8. Mont Blanc.
1. "Intellectual" here signifies non-material. Intellectual Beauty is an "unseen Power" because it is beyond access by sense experience. It is an entity postulated to account for occasional states of awareness which lend splendor, grace, and truth to both the natural world and to man's moral consciousness. The attempts of philosophy, superstition, and religion (stanza 3) to identify and control the mystery, which is outside the limits of human knowledge, are equally vain. Yet to this mystery (stanzas 5–7), at its first unexpected visitation in his youth, Shelley had dedicated his powers, and to it he now prays as he passes the noon of life.

2

Spirit of BEAUTY, that dost consecrate
　　With thine own hues all thou dost shine upon
　　Of human thought or form—where art thou gone?　　　　15
Why dost thou pass away and leave our state,
This dim vast vale of tears, vacant and desolate?
　　　　Ask why the sunlight not forever
　　　　Weaves rainbows o'er yon mountain river,
Why aught should fail and fade that once is shown,　　20
　　　　Why fear and dream and death and birth
　　　　Cast on the daylight of this earth
　　　　Such gloom—why man has such a scope
For love and hate, despondency and hope?

3

No voice from some sublimer world hath ever　　　　25
　　To sage or poet these responses given—
Therefore the names of Demon, Ghost, and Heaven,
Remain the records of their vain endeavor,
Frail spells—whose uttered charm might not avail to sever,
　　　　From all we hear and all we see,　　　　30
　　　　Doubt, chance, and mutability.
Thy light alone—like mist o'er mountains driven,
　　　　Or music by the night wind sent
　　　　Through strings of some still instrument,
　　　　Or moonlight on a midnight stream,　　　　35
Gives grace and truth to life's unquiet dream.

4

Love, Hope, and Self-esteem, like clouds depart
　　And come, for some uncertain moments lent.
　　Man were immortal, and omnipotent,
Didst thou, unknown and awful as thou art,　　　　40
Keep with thy glorious train firm state within his heart.
　　　　Thou messenger of sympathies,
　　　　That wax and wane in lovers' eyes—
Thou—that to human thought art nourishment,
　　　　Like darkness to a dying flame!　　　　45
　　　　Depart not as thy shadow came,
　　　　Depart not—lest the grave should be,
Like life and fear, a dark reality.

5

While yet a boy I sought for ghosts, and sped
　　Through many a listening chamber, cave and ruin,　　50
　　And starlight wood, with fearful steps pursuing
Hopes of high talk with the departed dead.[2]
I called on poisonous names with which our youth is fed;
　　　　I was not heard—I saw them not—
　　　　When musing deeply on the lot　　　　55

2. A reference to Shelley's youthful attempts to evoke ghosts and to practice
magic. The "poisonous names" in the
following line are probably elements of
the religious rituals he had been taught
as a boy.

Of life, at that sweet time when winds are wooing
    All vital things that wake to bring
    News of birds and blossoming—
    Sudden, thy shadow fell on me;
I shrieked, and clasped my hands in ecstasy!   60
6
I vowed that I would dedicate my powers
    To thee and thine—have I not kept the vow?
    With beating heart and streaming eyes, even now
I call the phantoms of a thousand hours
Each from his voiceless grave: they have in visioned bowers   65
    Of studious zeal or love's delight
    Outwatched with me the envious night[3]—
They know that never joy illumed my brow
    Unlinked with hope that thou wouldst free
    This world from its dark slavery,   70
    That thou—O awful LOVELINESS,
Wouldst give whate'er these words cannot express.
7
The day becomes more solemn and serene
    When noon is past—there is a harmony
    In autumn, and a luster in its sky,   75
Which through the summer is not heard or seen,
As if it could not be, as if it had not been!
    Thus let thy power, which like the truth
    Of nature on my passive youth
Descended, to my onward life supply   80
    Its calm—to one who worships thee,
    And every form containing thee,
    Whom, SPIRIT fair, thy spells did bind
To fear himself, and love all human kind.
1816   1817

Ozymandias[1]

I met a traveler from an antique land
Who said: Two vast and trunkless legs of stone
Stand in the desert . . . Near them, on the sand,
Half sunk, a shattered visage lies, whose frown,
And wrinkled lip, and sneer of cold command,   5
Tell that its sculptor well those passions read

---

3. I.e., watched until the night, envious of their delight, had reluctantly departed.
1. According to a passage in Diodorus Siculus, the Greek historian of the 1st century B.C., the largest statue in Egypt had the inscription: "I am Ozymandias, king of kings; if anyone wishes to know what I am and where I lie, let him surpass me in some of my exploits." Ozymandias was Ramses II of Egypt, 13th century B.C.

Which yet survive, stamped on these lifeless things,
The hand that mocked them, and the heart that fed:[2]
And on the pedestal these words appear:
"My name is Ozymandias, king of kings: 10
Look on my works, ye Mighty, and despair!"
Nothing beside remains. Round the decay
Of that colossal wreck, boundless and bare
The lone and level sands stretch far away.

1817   1818

Sonnet

Lift not the painted veil which those who live
Call Life: though unreal shapes be pictured there,
And it but mimic all we would believe
With colors idly spread—behind, lurk Fear
And Hope, twin Destinies; who ever weave   5
Their shadows, o'er the chasm, sightless and drear.
I knew one who had lifted it—he sought,
For his lost heart was tender, things to love,
But found them not, alas! nor was there aught
The world contains, the which he could approve.   10
Through the unheeding many he did move,
A splendor among shadows, a bright blot
Upon this gloomy scene, a Spirit that strove
For truth, and like the Preacher[3] found it not.

1818   1824

Stanzas Written in Dejection, Near Naples[1]

1

The sun is warm, the sky is clear,
    The waves are dancing fast and bright,
Blue isles and snowy mountains wear
    The purple noon's transparent might,
    The breath of the moist earth is light,   5
    Around its unexpanded buds;

---

2. The sculptured passions survive the hand of the sculptor who had "mocked" (i.e., both represented and derided) them, as well as the heart of the king which had been their source.
3. Author of the skeptical and pessimistic Book of Ecclesiastes in the Old Testament.

1. Shelley's first wife, Harriet, had drowned herself; Clara, his baby daughter by Mary Shelley, had just died; and Shelley himself was plagued by ill health, pain, financial worries, and the sense that he had failed as a poet.

Like many a voice of one delight,
The winds, the birds, the ocean floods,
The City's voice itself is soft like Solitude's.

2

I see the Deep's untrampled floor
    With green and purple seaweeds strown;   10
I see the waves upon the shore,
    Like light dissolved in star-showers, thrown:
I sit upon the sands alone—
The lightning of the noontide ocean   15
    Is flashing round me, and a tone
Arises from its measured motion;
How sweet! did any heart now share in my emotion.

3

Alas! I have nor hope nor health,
    Nor peace within nor calm around,   20
Nor that content surpassing wealth
    The sage in meditation found,
    And walked with inward glory crowned—
Nor fame, nor power, nor love, nor leisure.
    Others I see whom these surround—   25
Smiling they live, and call life pleasure;
To me that cup has been dealt in another measure.

4

Yet now despair itself is mild,
    Even as the winds and waters are;
I could lie down like a tired child,
    And weep away the life of care   30
    Which I have borne and yet must bear,
Till death like sleep might steal on me,
    And I might feel in the warm air
My cheek grow cold, and hear the sea   35
Breathe o'er my dying brain its last monotony.

5

Some might lament that I were cold,
    As I, when this sweet day is gone,
Which my lost heart, too soon grown old,
    Insults with this untimely moan;   40
    They might lament—for I am one
Whom men love not—and yet regret,
    Unlike this day, which, when the sun
Shall on its stainless glory set,
Will linger, though enjoyed, like joy in memory yet.[2]   45

December, 1818   1824

2. I.e., the few men who may lament his passing will find the remembrance flawed by his failings, but this stainless day, even after the enjoyment of it is past, will leave a memory of flawless joy.

Song to the Men of England[1]

1

Men of England, wherefore plow
For the lords who lay ye low?
Wherefore weave with toil and care
The rich robes your tyrants wear?

2

Wherefore feed, and clothe, and save,   5
From the cradle to the grave,
Those ungrateful drones who would
Drain your sweat—nay, drink your blood?

3

Wherefore, Bees of England, forge
Many a weapon, chain, and scourge,   10
That these stingless drones may spoil
The forced produce of your toil?

4

Have ye leisure, comfort, calm,
Shelter, food, love's gentle balm?
Or what is it ye buy so dear   15
With your pain and with your fear?

5

The seed ye sow, another reaps;
The wealth ye find, another keeps;
The robes ye weave, another wears;
The arms ye forge, another bears.   20

6

Sow seed—but let no tyrant reap;
Find wealth—let no impostor heap;
Weave robes—let not the idle wear;
Forge arms—in your defense to bear.

7

Shrink to your cellars, holes, and cells;   25
In halls ye deck another dwells.
Why shake the chains ye wrought? Ye see
The steel ye tempered glance on ye.

8

With plow and spade, and hoe and loom,
Trace your grave, and build your tomb,   30
And weave your winding sheet, till fair
England be your sepulcher.

1819   1839

1. This and the following poem were written at a time of turbulent unrest among English workers, after the return of many thousands of soldiers from the Napoleonic Wars had led to the first great depression of the new industrial age. The poems express Shelley's hope for a proletarian revolution. This song was originally planned as one of a series of poems for workingmen, but Shelley gave up the project. It has become, as Shelley hoped, a hymn of the British labor movement.

England in 1819

An old, mad, blind, despised, and dying king[1]—
Princes, the dregs of their dull race, who flow
Through public scorn—mud from a muddy spring;
Rulers who neither see, nor feel, nor know,
But leechlike to their fainting country cling,   5
Till they drop, blind in blood, without a blow;
A people starved and stabbed in the untilled field—
An army, which liberticide and prey
Makes as a two-edged sword to all who wield;
Golden and sanguine laws[2] which tempt and slay;   10
Religion Christless, Godless—a book sealed;
A Senate—Time's worst statute unrepealed[3]—
Are graves, from which a glorious Phantom[4] may
Burst, to illumine our tempestuous day.

1819   1839

The Indian Serenade[1]

1

I arise from dreams of thee
In the first sweet sleep of night.
When the winds are breathing low,
And the stars are shining bright:
I arise from dreams of thee,   5
And a spirit in my feet
Hath led me—who knows how?
To thy chamber window, Sweet!

2

The wandering airs they faint
On the dark, the silent stream—   10
The Champak[2] odors fail
Like sweet thoughts in a dream;
The nightingale's complaint,
It dies upon her heart—
As I must on thine,   15
Oh, beloved as thou art!

3

Oh lift me from the grass!
I die! I faint! I fail!
Let thy love in kisses rain
On my lips and eyelids pale.   20
My cheek is cold and white, alas!

1. George III, who died in the next year, 1820.
2. Laws bought with gold, and leading to bloodshed.
3. The law imposing disabilities upon Roman Catholics.
4. I.e., the revolution.

1. It is a mistake to read this as an utterance by Shelley himself. The poem is explicitly a dramatic lyric, sung by an imagined East-Indian lover in an exotic landscape, and exhibits the conventional extravagance of a serenade.
2. An Indian species of magnolia.

My heart beats loud and fast—
Oh! press it to thine own again,
Where it will break at last.

1819   1822

Ode to the West Wind[1]

1

O wild West Wind, thou breath of Autumn's being,
Thou, from whose unseen presence the leaves dead
Are driven, like ghosts from an enchanter fleeing,

Yellow, and black, and pale, and hectic red,
Pestilence-stricken multitudes: O thou,   5
Who chariotest to their dark wintry bed

The wingéd seeds, where they lie cold and low,
Each like a corpse within its grave, until
Thine azure sister of the Spring[2] shall blow

Her clarion[3] o'er the dreaming earth, and fill   10
(Driving sweet buds like flocks to feed in air)
With living hues and odors plain and hill:

Wild Spirit, which art moving everywhere;
Destroyer and preserver; hear, oh, hear!

2

Thou on whose stream, mid the steep sky's commotion,   15
Loose clouds like earth's decaying leaves are shed,
Shook from the tangled boughs of Heaven and Ocean,[4]

Angels of rain and lightning: there are spread
On the blue surface of thine aëry surge,
Like the bright hair uplifted from the head   20

1. "This poem was conceived and chiefly written in a wood that skirts the Arno, near Florence, and on a day when that tempestuous wind, whose temperature is at once mild and animating, was collecting the vapors which pour down the autumnal rains" [Shelley's note]. As in other major Romantic poems— see, for example, the opening of Wordsworth's *Prelude*, Coleridge's *Dejection*, and the conclusion to Shelley's *Adonais* —the rising wind, linked with the cycle of the seasons, is presented as the outer correspondent to an inner change from apathy and a deathlike torpor to renewed spiritual vitality, and from imaginative sterility to a burst of creative power which is paralleled to the inspiration of the Biblical prophets. In Hebrew, Greek, and many other languages, the words for wind, breath, soul, and inspiration are all identical or related. Thus Shelley's west wind is a "spirit" (the Latin *spiritus:* wind, breath, soul, and the root word in "inspiration"), the "breath of Autumn's being," which on earth, sky, and sea destroys in the autumn in order to revive in the spring. Around this central image the poem weaves various cycles of death and regeneration—vegetational, human, and divine.

The remarkable stanza used in this ode was developed by Shelley from the interlaced tercets (three-line units) of the Italian *terza rima: aba bcb cdc,* etc. Shelley's stanza consists of a set of four such tercets, closed by a couplet rhyming with the middle line of the preceding tercet: *aba bcb cdc ded ee.*
2. The reviving wind that will blow in the spring.
3. A high, shrill trumpet; compare "the trumpet of a prophecy" in line 69.
4. I.e., the fragmentary clouds ("leaves") are torn by the wind from the larger clouds formed by a union of the air with the water vapor (the

Of some fierce Maenad,[5] even from the dim verge
Of the horizon to the zenith's height,
The locks of the approaching storm. Thou dirge

Of the dying year, to which this closing night
Will be the dome of a vast sepulcher, 25
Vaulted with all thy congregated might

Of vapours, from whose solid atmosphere
Black rain, and fire, and hail will burst: oh, hear!

3

Thou who didst waken from his summer dreams
The blue Mediterranean, where he lay, 30
Lulled by the coil of his crystálline streams,[6]

Beside a pumice[7] isle in Baiae's bay,
And saw in sleep old palaces and towers
Quivering within the wave's intenser day,[8]

All overgrown with azure moss and flowers 35
So sweet, the sense faints picturing them! Thou
For whose path the Atlantic's level powers

Cleave themselves into chasms, while far below
The sea-blooms and the oozy woods which wear
The sapless foliage of the ocean, know 40

Thy voice, and suddenly grow gray with fear,
And tremble and despoil themselves:[9] oh, hear!

4

If I were a dead leaf thou mightest bear;
If I were a swift cloud to fly with thee;
A wave to pant beneath thy power, and share 45

The impulse of thy strength, only less free
Than thou, O uncontrollable! If even
I were as in my boyhood, and could be

The comrade of thy wanderings over Heaven,
As then, when to outstrip thy skyey speed 50
Scarce seemed a vision; I would ne'er have striven

As thus with thee in prayer in my sore need.
Oh, lift me as a wave, a leaf, a cloud!
I fall upon the thorns of life! I bleed!

"tangled boughs of Heaven and Ocean"). "Angels" suggests the old sense: messengers, harbingers.
5. A female votary who danced frenziedly in the worship of Dionysus (or Bacchus), the Greek god of wine and vegetation. As vegetation god, he was fabled to die in the fall and to be resurrected in the spring; hence, there is a glancing allusion here to a mythic cycle of death and rebirth.
6. The currents that flow in the Mediterranean Sea, sometimes with a visible difference in color.
7. Formed of a porous volcanic stone. "Baiae's bay," west of Naples, was the locale of imposing villas erected by Roman emperors.
8. Shelley once observed that, when seen reflected in water, colors are "more vivid yet blended with more harmony."
9. "The phenomenon * * * is well known to naturalists. The vegetation at the bottom of the sea * * * sympathizes with that of the land in the change of seasons" [Shelley's note].

A heavy weight of hours has chained and bowed   55
One too like thee: tameless, and swift, and proud.

5

Make me thy lyre,[1] even as the forest is:
What if my leaves are falling like its own!
The tumult of thy mighty harmonies

Will take from both a deep, autumnal tone,   60
Sweet though in sadness. Be thou, Spirit fierce,
My spirit! Be thou me, impetuous one!

Drive my dead thoughts over the universe
Like withered leaves to quicken a new birth!
And, by the incantation of this verse,   65

Scatter, as from an unextinguished hearth
Ashes and sparks, my words among mankind!
Be through my lips to unawakened earth

The trumpet of a prophecy! O Wind,
If Winter comes, can Spring be far behind?   70
1819   1820

1. The Aeolian lyre, or wind harp, which responds to the wind with a musical chord. This image is also used for the response of the human mind to the wind in Wordsworth's *Prelude* and Coleridge's *Eolian Harp* and *Dejection*.

Prometheus Unbound   Shelley composed this work in Italy between the autumn of 1818 and the close of 1819 and published it the following summer. Upon its completion he wrote in a letter, "It is a drama, with characters and mechanism of a kind yet unattempted; and I think the execution is better than any of my former attempts." It is based upon the *Prometheus Bound* of Aeschylus, which dramatizes the sufferings of Prometheus, unrepentant champion of mankind, who, because he had stolen fire from heaven, was condemned by Zeus to be chained to Mt. Caucasus and to be tortured by a vulture feeding upon his liver. Shelley continued Aeschylus' story, but transformed it into a symbolic drama about the origin of evil and its elimination. In such earlier writings as *Queen Mab* Shelley had expressed his belief that injustice and suffering can be eliminated by an external revolution which will wipe out or radically reform existing social, political, and religious institutions. Implicit in *Prometheus Unbound*, on the other hand, is the view that both the origin of evil and the possibility of reform are the moral responsibility of man himself. Social chaos and wars are a gigantic projection of man's moral disorder and inner division and conflict: tyrants are the outer representatives of the tyranny of man's baser over his better elements; hatred for others is an expression of self-contempt; and successful political reform is impossible unless man has first reformed his own nature at its deep roots, by substituting selfless love for divisive hate. Shelley thus incorporates into his secular myth of universal regeneration by an apocalypse of man's moral imagination, the ethical teaching of Christ on the Mount, as well as the highest classical morality represented in the *Prometheus* of Aeschylus. And Shelley warns (IV.562 ff.) that even should such a victory take place—the reintegration of splintered man, and the consequent restoration of an order which is at once moral and political, and which releases all man's creative powers in art and science—the price of its continuation is an unremitting vigilance lest the serpent deep in human nature should break loose and start the cycle of fall into division and conflict all over again.

Shelley wrote in his Preface that Prometheus is, "as it were, the type of the highest perfection of moral and intellectual nature." But he also warned that it is a mistake to suppose that the poem contains "a reasoned system on the theory of human life. Didactic poetry is my abhorrence." *Prometheus Unbound* is not a dramatized philosophical essay, nor a moral allegory, but a large and very intricate imaginative construction which involves premises about the nature of man and the springs of morality and creativity. The non-Christian poet, Yeats, called it one of "the sacred books of the world," and the Christian critic, C. S. Lewis, found in it many of the powers of Dante. Many readers argue, at any rate, that, with *The Triumph of Life* and some of the longer lyrics, *Prometheus Unbound* constitutes a weighty claim to rank Shelley as among the major poets.

From Prometheus Unbound

A LYRICAL DRAMA

Dramatis Personae

PROMETHEUS	HERCULES
DEMOGORGON	THE PHANTASM OF JUPITER
JUPITER	THE SPIRIT OF THE EARTH
THE EARTH	THE SPIRIT OF THE MOON
OCEAN	SPIRITS OF THE HOURS
APOLLO	SPIRITS
MERCURY	ECHOES
ASIA ⎫	FAUNS
PANTHEA ⎬ *Oceanides*	FURIES
IONE ⎭	

From Act I

SCENE—*A Ravine of Icy Rocks in the Indian Caucasus.* PROMETHEUS *is discovered bound to the Precipice.* PANTHEA *and* IONE *are seated at his feet. Time, night. During the Scene, morning slowly breaks.*

PROMETHEUS. Monarch of Gods and Daemons,[1] and all Spirits
But One, who throng those bright and rolling worlds
Which Thou and I alone of living things
Behold with sleepless eyes! regard this Earth
Made multitudinous with thy slaves, whom thou   5
Requitest for knee-worship, prayer, and praise,
And toil, and hecatombs[2] of broken hearts,
With fear and self-contempt and barren hope.

1. Prometheus is addressing Jupiter.
2. In Greek, "a hundred oxen" (slaughtered as a sacrifice to the gods).

Whilst me, who am thy foe, eyeless in hate,[3]
Hast thou made reign and triumph, to thy scorn,   10
O'er mine own misery and thy vain revenge.
Three thousand years of sleep-unsheltered hours,
And moments aye divided by keen pangs
Till they seemed years, torture and solitude,
Scorn and despair—these are mine empire—   15
More glorious far than that which thou surveyest
From thine unenvied throne, O Mighty God!
Almighty, had I deigned[4] to share the shame
Of thine ill tyranny, and hung not here
Nailed to this wall of eagle-baffling mountain,   20
Black, wintry, dead, unmeasured; without herb,
Insect, or beast, or shape or sound of life.
Ah me! alas, pain, pain ever, forever!

No change, no pause, no hope! Yet I endure.
I ask the Earth, have not the mountains felt?   25
I ask yon Heaven, the all-beholding Sun,
Has it not seen? The Sea, in storm or calm,
Heaven's ever-changing Shadow, spread below,
Have its deaf waves not heard my agony?
Ah me! alas, pain, pain ever, forever!   30

The crawling glaciers pierce me with the spears
Of their moon-freezing crystals, the bright chains
Eat with their burning cold into my bones.
Heaven's wingéd hound,[5] polluting from thy lips
His beak in poison not his own, tears up   35
My heart; and shapeless sights come wandering by,
The ghastly people of the realm of dream,
Mocking me: and the Earthquake-fiends are charged
To wrench the rivets from my quivering wounds
When the rocks split and close again behind: 40
While from their loud abysses howling throng
The genii of the storm, urging the rage
Of whirlwind, and afflict me with keen hail.
And yet to me welcome is day and night,
Whether one breaks the hoar frost of the morn,   45
Or starry, dim, and slow, the other climbs
The leaden-colored east; for then they lead
The wingless, crawling hours, one among whom
—As some dark Priest hales the reluctant victim
Shall drag thee, cruel King, to kiss the blood   50
From these pale feet,[6] which then might trample thee
If they disdained not such a prostrate slave.
Disdain! Ah no! I pity thee.[7] What ruin

3. Blinded by hate.
4. I.e., you would have been all-powerful, if I had deigned.
5. The vulture, tearing daily at Prometheus' heart, was kissed by Jupiter by way of reward.
6. One of a number of implied parallels between the agony of Prometheus and the passion of Christ.
7. At this early point occurs the technical crisis of the play: the beginning of Prometheus' change of heart from hate to compassion, which is consummated in

Will hunt thee undefended through wide Heaven!
How will thy soul, cloven to its depth with terror,   55
Gape like a hell within! I speak in grief,
Not exultation, for I hate no more,
As then ere misery made me wise. The curse
Once breathed on thee I would recall. Ye Mountains,
Whose many-voicéd Echoes, through the mist   60
Of cataracts, flung the thunder of that spell!
Ye icy Springs, stagnant with wrinkling frost,
Which vibrated to hear me, and then crept
Shuddering through India! Thou serenest Air,
Through which the Sun walks burning without beams!   65
And ye swift Whirlwinds, who on poiséd wings
Hung mute and moveless o'er yon hushed abyss,
As thunder, louder than your own, made rock
The orbéd world! If then my words had power,
Though I am changed so that aught evil wish   70
Is dead within; although no memory be
Of what is hate, let them not lose it now!⁸
What was that curse? for ye all heard me speak.⁹

* * *

PHANTASM

Fiend, I defy thee! with a calm, fixed mind,
    All that thou canst inflict I bid thee do;
Foul Tyrant both of Gods and Humankind,
    One only being shalt thou not subdue.   265
Rain then thy plagues upon me here,
Ghastly disease, and frenzying fear;
And let alternate frost and fire
Eat into me, and be thine ire
Lightning, and cutting hail, and legioned forms   270
Of furies, driving by upon the wounding storms.

Aye, do thy worst. Thou art omnipotent.
    O'er all things but thyself I gave thee power,
And my own will. Be thy swift mischiefs sent
    To blast mankind, from yon ethereal tower.   275
Let thy malignant spirit move
In darkness over those I love:
On me and mine I imprecate
The utmost torture of thy hate;
And thus devote to sleepless agony,   280
This undeclining head while thou must reign on high.

lines 303–5. The rest of the symbolic drama gradually unfolds the consequences of this moral triumph—of which Prometheus himself (like Coleridge's Ancient Mariner when he blessed the water snakes) is at this time entirely unaware.
8. I.e., let my words not lose their power now.
9. In the passage here omitted, none dares to repeat the curse Prometheus had proclaimed against Jupiter for fear of that god's vengeance. Prometheus is finally forced to call up the Phantasm of Jupiter himself who, in the next excerpt, repeats the curse.

But thou, who art the God and Lord: O, thou,
  Who fillest with thy soul this world of woe,
To whom all things of Earth and Heaven do bow
  In fear and worship: all-prevailing foe!   285
I curse thee! let a sufferer's curse
Clasp thee, his torturer, like remorse;
Till thine Infinity shall be
A robe of envenomed agony;
And thine Omnipotence a crown of pain,   290
To cling like burning gold round thy dissolving brain.

Heap on thy soul, by virtue of this Curse,
  Ill deeds, then be thou damned, beholding good;
Both infinite as is the universe,
  And thou, and thy self-torturing solitude.   295
An awful image of calm power
Though now thou sittest, let the hour
Come, when thou must appear to be
That which thou art internally;
And after many a false and fruitless crime   300
Scorn track thy lagging fall through boundless space and time.

PROMETHEUS. Were these my words, O Parent?
THE EARTH.   They were thine.
PROMETHEUS. It doth repent me: words are quick and vain;
  Grief for awhile is blind, and so was mine.
I wish no living thing to suffer pain.   305

THE EARTH
  Misery, Oh misery to me,
  That Jove at length should vanquish thee.[1]
  Wail, howl aloud, Land and Sea,
  The Earth's rent heart shall answer ye.
Howl, Spirits of the living and the dead,   310
Your refuge, your defense lies fallen and vanquishéd.

FIRST ECHO
Lies fallen and vanquishéd!

SECOND ECHO
Fallen and vanquishéd!

IONE[2]
Fear not: 'tis but some passing spasm,
The Titan is unvanquished still.   315

* * *

1. In this extreme instance of dramatic irony, Earth mistakes mercy for submission, and therefore interprets Prometheus' victory as his defeat.

2. Ione, Panthea, and Asia (in the following scene) are sisters and Oceanids —i.e., daughters of Oceanus.

From Act II[1]

SCENE IV—*The Cave of* DEMOGORGON. ASIA *and* PANTHEA.

PANTHEA. What veiléd form sits on that ebon throne?
ASIA. The veil has fallen.
PANTHEA.   I see a mighty darkness
  Filling the seat of power, and rays of gloom
  Dart round, as light from the meridian sun.
  —Ungazed upon and shapeless; neither limb,   5
  Nor form, nor outline; yet we feel it is
  A living Spirit.
DEMOGORGON.   Ask what thou wouldst know.
ASIA. What canst thou tell?
DEMOGORGON.   All things thou dar'st demand.
ASIA. Who made the living world?
DEMOGORGON.   God.
ASIA.   Who made all
  That it contains? thought, passion, reason, will,   10
  Imagination?
DEMOGORGON. God: Almighty God.
ASIA. Who made that sense[2] which, when the winds of Spring
  In rarest visitation, or the voice
  Of one beloved heard in youth alone,
  Fills the faint eyes with falling tears which dim   15
  The radiant looks of unbewailing flowers,
  And leaves this peopled earth a solitude
  When it returns no more?
DEMOGORGON.   Merciful God.
ASIA. And who made terror, madness, crime, remorse,
  Which from the links of the great chain of things,   20
  To every thought within the mind of man
  Sway and drag heavily, and each one reels
  Under the load towards the pit of death;
  Abandoned hope, and love that turns to hate;
  And self-contempt, bitterer to drink than blood;   25

1. Act II has opened with Asia, the feminine principle and embodiment of love, who was separated from Prometheus at the moment of his fall into divisive hate, in a lovely Indian valley at the first hour of the first dawn of the spring season of redemption. Asia and her sister Panthea have been led, by a sweet and irresistible compulsion, first to the portal and then down into the depths of the cave of Demogorgon—the central enigma of Shelley's poem.
  Commentators have usually equated Demogorgon with *necessity*, but the interpretation, though pertinent, is too neat and confining. More flexibly, he can be thought of as *process*, the inexorable way in which things evolve. But the ultimate mover of that process —the ultimate reason for things—must remain, Shelley skeptically insists, a mystery beyond the limits of accessible knowledge. Demogorgon, like the inaccessible Power represented by the Arve in *Mont Blanc* (above), is implacable, neutral, and the more terrifying because he himself is ignorant of the principle that controls him. He serves merely to stimulate Asia to ask once more the ultimate and persistent questions about the "why" of creation, good, and evil. But "the deep truth is imageless" (line 116). Demogorgon can give merely riddling answers, which in fact tell Asia only what she herself has thought already (lines 121–23). The one question he can answer unequivocally is not "why," but "when": the hour in the process when Prometheus shall arise. That hour (line 128) is now.
2. Presumably the sense by which one is aware of the "unseen Power" which Shelley calls "Intellectual Beauty"; see *Hymn to Intellectual Beauty*, stanza 2.

Pain, whose unheeded and familiar speech
Is howling, and keen shrieks, day after day;
And Hell, or the sharp fear of Hell?[3]

DEMOGORGON.   He reigns.

ASIA. Utter his name: a world pining in pain
  Asks but his name: curses shall drag him down.   30

DEMOGORGON. He reigns.

ASIA.   I feel, I know it: who?

DEMOGORGON.   He reigns.

ASIA. Who reigns? There was the Heaven and Earth at first,
  And Light and Love; then Saturn,[4] from whose throne
  Time fell, an envious shadow: such the state
  Of the earth's primal spirits beneath his sway,   35
  As the calm joy of flowers and living leaves
  Before the wind or sun has withered them
  And semivital worms; but he refused
  The birthright of their being, knowledge, power,
  The skill which wields the elements, the thought   40
  Which pierces this dim universe like light,
  Self-empire, and the majesty of love;
  For thirst of which they fainted. Then Prometheus
  Gave wisdom, which is strength, to Jupiter,
  And with this law alone, "Let man be free,"   45
  Clothed him with the dominion of wide Heaven.
  To know nor faith, nor love, nor law; to be
  Omnipotent but friendless is to reign;
  And Jove now reigned; for on the race of man
  First famine, and then toil, and then disease,   50
  Strife, wounds, and ghastly death unseen before,
  Fell; and the unseasonable seasons drove
  With alternating shafts of frost and fire,
  Their shelterless, pale tribes to mountain caves:
  And in their desert hearts fierce wants he sent,   55
  And mad disquietudes, and shadows idle
  Of unreal good, which levied mutual war,
  So ruining the lair wherein they raged.
  Prometheus saw, and waked the legioned hopes
  Which sleep within folded Elysian flowers,   60
  Nepenthe, Moly, Amaranth,[5] fadeless blooms,
  That they might hide with thin and rainbow wings
  The shape of Death; and Love he sent to bind
  The disunited tendrils of that vine
  Which bears the wine of life, the human heart;   65
  And he tamed fire which, like some beast of prey,
  Most terrible, but lovely, played beneath
  The frown of man; and tortured to his will

3. The nouns "hope," "love," etc. (lines 24–28), are all objects of the verb "made" (line 19).
4. In Greek myth, Saturn's reign was the golden age. In Asia's version, it was for men the age of happy but totally ignorant innocence.
5. These are medicinal flowers in Greek myth. Asia (lines 59–97) is describing the various sciences and arts given to man by Prometheus, the culture-bringer.

Iron and gold, the slaves and signs of power,
And gems and poisons, and all subtlest forms   70
Hidden beneath the mountains and the waves.
He gave man speech, and speech created thought,
Which is the measure of the universe;
And Science struck the thrones of earth and heaven,
Which shook, but fell not; and the harmonious mind   75
Poured itself forth in all-prophetic song;
And music lifted up the listening spirit
Until it walked, exempt from mortal care,
Godlike, o'er the clear billows of sweet sound;
And human hands first mimicked and then mocked,[6]   80
With molded limbs more lovely than its own,
The human form, till marble grew divine;
And mothers, gazing, drank the love men see
Reflected in their race, behold, and perish.[7]
He told the hidden power of herbs and springs,   85
And Disease drank and slept. Death grew like sleep.
He taught the implicated orbits woven
Of the wide-wandering stars; and how the sun
Changes his lair, and by what secret spell
The pale moon is transformed, when her broad eye   90
Gazes not on the interlunar[8] sea:
He taught to rule, as life directs the limbs,
The tempest-wingéd chariots of the Ocean,
And the Celt knew the Indian.[9] Cities then
Were built, and through their snowlike columns flowed   95
The warm winds, and the azure ether shone,
And the blue sea and shadowy hills were seen.
Such, the alleviations of his state,
Prometheus gave to man, for which he hangs
Withering in destined pain: but who rains down   100
Evil, the immedicable plague,[1] which, while
Man looks on his creation like a God
And sees that it is glorious, drives him on,
The wreck of his own will, the scorn of earth,
The outcast, the abandoned, the alone?   105
Not Jove: while yet his frown shook Heaven, aye, when
His adversary from adamantine chains
Cursed him, he trembled like a slave. Declare
Who is his master? Is he too a slave?
DEMOGORGON. All spirits are enslaved which serve things evil: 110
    Thou knowest if Jupiter be such or no.
ASIA. Whom calledst thou God?

6. I.e., sculptors first merely reproduced, but later improved upon ("mocked"), the beauty of the human form. Cf. *Ozymandias*, line 8.
7. Expectant mothers looked at the beautiful statues so that their children might, by prenatal influence, be born with that beauty which makes beholders die of love.
8. The phase between old and new moon, when the moon is invisible.
9. The reference is to the ships in which the Celtic (here, British) races of Europe were able to sail to India.
1. The disease not curable by medicine.

DEMOGORGON. I spoke but as ye speak,
For Jove is the supreme of living things.
ASIA. Who is the master of the slave?
DEMOGORGON. If the abysm
Could vomit forth its secrets.—But a voice 115
Is wanting, the deep truth is imageless;[2]
For what would it avail to bid thee gaze
On the revolving world? What to bid speak
Fate, Time, Occasion, Chance, and Change? To these
All things are subject but eternal Love. 120
ASIA. So much I asked before, and my heart gave
The response thou hast given; and of such truths
Each to itself must be the oracle.
One more demand; and do thou answer me
As mine own soul would answer, did it know 125
That which I ask. Prometheus shall arise
Henceforth the sun of this rejoicing world:
When shall the destined hour arrive?
DEMOGORGON. Behold![3]
ASIA. The rocks are cloven, and through the purple night
I see cars drawn by rainbow-wingéd steeds 130
Which trample the dim winds: in each there stands
A wild-eyed charioteer urging their flight.
Some look behind, as fiends pursued them there,
And yet I see no shapes but the keen stars:
Others, with burning eyes, lean forth, and drink 135
With eager lips the wind of their own speed,
As if the thing they loved fled on before,
And now, even now, they clasped it. Their bright locks
Stream like a comet's flashing hair: they all
Sweep onward.
DEMOGORGON. These are the immortal Hours, 140
Of whom thou didst demand. One waits for thee.
ASIA. A spirit with a dreadful countenance
Checks its dark chariot by the craggy gulf.
Unlike thy brethren, ghastly charioteer,
Who art thou? Whither wouldst thou bear me? Speak! 145
SPIRIT. I am the shadow of a destiny
More dread than is my aspect: ere yon planet
Has set, the darkness[4] which ascends with me
Shall wrap in lasting night heaven's kingless throne.
ASIA. What meanest thou?
PANTHEA. That terrible shadow floats 150
Up from its throne, as may the lurid smoke
Of earthquake-ruined cities o'er the sea.

2. Three years earlier Shelley had written (*On Life*): "How vain is it to think that words can penetrate the mystery of our being!" And in a note on *Hellas* he was to say, three years later, that "the Gordian knot of the origin of evil" cannot be disentangled by assertions.
3. Demogorgon's answer is a gesture: he points to the approaching chariots ("cars").
4. I.e., Demogorgon, who is ascending (lines 150–55) to effect the dethronement of Jupiter.

Lo! it ascends the car; the coursers fly
Terrified: watch its path among the stars
Blackening the night!
ASIA.   Thus I am answered: strange!   155
PANTHEA. See, near the verge, another chariot stays;
An ivory shell inlaid with crimson fire,
Which comes and goes within its sculptured rim
Of delicate strange tracery; the young spirit
That guides it has the dovelike eyes of hope;   160
How its soft smiles attract the soul! as light
Lures wingéd insects through the lampless air.[5]

SPIRIT
My coursers are fed with the lightning,
    They drink of the whirlwind's stream,
And when the red morning is bright'ning   165
    They bathe in the fresh sunbeam;
    They have strength for their swiftness I deem,
Then ascend with me, daughter of Ocean.

I desire: and their speed makes night kindle;
    I fear: they outstrip the Typhoon;   170
Ere the cloud piled on Atlas can dwindle:
    We encircle the earth and the moon:
    We shall rest from long labors at noon:
Then ascend with me, daughter of Ocean.

SCENE V—*The Car pauses within a Cloud on the top of a snowy
Mountain.* ASIA, PANTHEA, *and the* SPIRIT OF THE HOUR.

SPIRIT
On the brink of the night and the morning
    My coursers are wont to respire;
But the Earth has just whispered a warning
    That their flight must be swifter than fire:
    They shall drink the hot speed of desire!   5

ASIA. Thou breathest on their nostrils, but my breath
Would give them swifter speed.
SPIRIT.   Alas! it could not.
PANTHEA. Oh Spirit! pause, and tell whence is the light
Which fills this cloud? the sun is yet unrisen.
SPIRIT. The sun will rise not until noon.[6] Apollo   10
Is held in heaven by wonder; and the light
Which fills this vapor, as the aërial hue
Of fountain-gazing roses fills the water,
Flows from thy mighty sister.
PANTHEA.   Yes, I feel—
ASIA. What is it with thee, sister? Thou art pale.   15
PANTHEA. How thou art changed! I dare not look on thee;

5. The ancient image of the soul, "psyche," was a moth. The chariot described here by Panthea will carry Asia to a reunion with Prometheus.
6. Noon will be the time of the reunion between Prometheus and Asia.

I feel but see thee not. I scarce endure
The radiance of thy beauty.[7] Some good change
Is working in the elements, which suffer
Thy presence thus unveiled. The Nereids tell   20
That on the day when the clear hyaline
Was cloven at thine uprise, and thou didst stand
Within a veinéd shell,[8] which floated on
Over the calm floor of the crystal sea,
Among the Aegean isles, and by the shores   25
Which bear thy name, love, like the atmosphere
Of the sun's fire filling the living world,
Burst from thee, and illumined earth and heaven
And the deep ocean and the sunless caves
And all that dwells within them, till grief cast   30
Eclipse upon the soul from which it came:[9]
Such art thou now; nor is it I alone,
Thy sister, thy companion, thine own chosen one,
But the whole world which seeks thy sympathy.
Hearest thou not sound i' the air which speak the love   35
Of all articulate beings? Feelest thou not
The inanimate winds enamored of thee? List!   [*Music.*]
ASIA. Thy words are sweeter than aught else but his
Whose echoes they are: yet all love is sweet,
Given or returned. Common as light is love,   40
And its familiar voice wearies not ever.
Like the wide heaven, the all-sustaining air,
It makes the reptile equal to the God:
They who inspire it most are fortunate,
As I am now; but those who feel it most   45
Are happier still, after long sufferings,
As I shall soon become.
PANTHEA.   List! Spirits speak.

VOICE IN THE AIR[1] [*singing*]
Life of Life! thy lips enkindle
   With their love the breath between them;
And thy smiles before they dwindle   50
   Make the cold air fire; then screen them
In those looks, where whoso gazes
Faints, entangled in their mazes.

Child of Light! thy limbs are burning
   Through the vest which seems to hide them;   55
As the radiant lines of morning

7. In an earlier scene, Panthea had envisioned in a dream the radiant and
eternal inner form of Prometheus emerging through his "wound-worn limbs."
The corresponding transfiguration of
Asia, prepared for by her descent to the
underworld, now takes place.
8. The story told by the Nereids (sea
nymphs) serves to associate Asia with
Aphrodite, goddess of love, emerging

(as in Botticelli's painting) from the
Mediterranean on a seashell. "Hyaline": the glassy sea.
9. The inner radiance, now revived, had
been obliterated at the time of Asia's
separation from Prometheus.
1. The voice describes, in a dizzying
whirl of optical paradoxes, what it feels
like to look upon the naked essence of
love and beauty.

Through the clouds ere they divide them;
And this atmosphere divinest
Shrouds thee wheresoe'er thou shinest.

Fair are others; none beholds thee,　　　　　　　　60
　　But thy voice sounds low and tender
Like the fairest, for it folds thee
　　From the sight, that liquid splendor,
And all feel, yet see thee never,
As I feel now, lost forever!　　　　　　　　　　65

Lamp of Earth! where'er thou movest
　　Its dim shapes are clad with brightness,
And the souls of whom thou lovest
　　Walk upon the winds with lightness,
Till they fail, as I am failing,　　　　　　　　70
Dizzy, lost, yet unbewailing!

ASIA

My soul is an enchanted boat,
　　Which, like a sleeping swan, doth float
Upon the silver waves of thy sweet singing;
　　And thine doth like an angel sit　　　　　　75
　　Beside a helm conducting it,
Whilst all the winds with melody are ringing.
　　It seems to float ever, forever,
　　Upon that many-winding river,
　　Between mountains, woods, abysses,　　　　80
　　A paradise of wildernesses!
Till, like one in slumber bound,
Borne to the ocean, I float down, around,
Into a sea profound, of ever-spreading sound:

　　Meanwhile thy spirit lifts its pinions　　　85
　　In music's most serene dominions;
Catching the winds that fan that happy heaven.
　　And we sail on, away, afar,
　　Without a course, without a star,
But, by the instinct of sweet music driven;　　90
　　Till through Elysian garden islets
　　By thee, most beautiful of pilots,
　　Where never mortal pinnace glided,
　　The boat of my desire is guided:
Realms where the air we breathe is love,　　　95
Which in the winds and on the waves doth move,
Harmonizing this earth with what we feel above.

　　We have passed Age's icy caves,
　　And Manhood's dark and tossing waves,
And Youth's smooth ocean, smiling to betray:　　100
　　Beyond the glassy gulfs we flee
　　Of shadow-peopled Infancy,

Through Death and Birth, to a diviner day;[2]
A paradise of vaulted bowers,
Lit by downward-gazing flowers,   105
And watery paths that wind between
Wildernesses calm and green,
Peopled by shapes too bright to see,
And rest, having beheld; somewhat like thee;
Which walk upon the sea, and chant melodiously!   110

From *Act III*

SCENE I—*Heaven.* JUPITER *on his Throne;* THETIS *and the other Deities assembled.*

JUPITER. Ye congregated powers of heaven, who share
The glory and the strength of him ye serve,
Rejoice! henceforth I am omnipotent.
All else had been subdued to me; alone
The soul of man, like unextinguished fire,   5
Yet burns towards heaven with fierce reproach, and doubt,
And lamentation, and reluctant prayer,
Hurling up insurrection, which might make
Our antique empire insecure, though built
On eldest faith, and hell's coeval, fear;   10
And though my curses through the pendulous air,
Like snow on herbless peaks, fall flake by flake,
And cling to it;[1] though under my wrath's night
It climbs the crags of life, step after step,
Which wound it, as ice wounds unsandaled feet,   15
It yet remains supreme o'er misery,
Aspiring, unrepressed, yet soon to fall:
Even now have I begotten a strange wonder,
That fatal child,[2] the terror of the earth,
Who waits but till the destined hour arrive,   20
Bearing from Demogorgon's vacant throne
The dreadful might of ever-living limbs
Which clothed that awful spirit unbeheld,
To redescend, and trample out the spark.[3]
Pour forth heaven's wine, Idaean Ganymede,[4]   25
And let it fill the Daedal cups like fire,
And from the flower-inwoven soil divine
Ye all-triumphant harmonies arise,
As dew from earth under the twilight stars:
Drink! be the nectar circling through your veins   30

2. Asia is describing what it feels like to be transfigured—in the image of moving backward down the stream of time, through youth and infancy and birth itself, in order to die to this life and be born again to a "diviner" existence.
1. I.e., "the soul of man," line 5 (as also in lines 14 and 16).
2. The son of Jupiter and Thetis; Jupiter believes that the "fatal child" will assume the bodily form of the conquered Demogorgon and then return to announce his victory and to trample out the resistance of Prometheus.
3. The "spark" of Prometheus' defiance.
4. Ganymede had been seized on Mt. Ida by an eagle and carried to heaven to be Jupiter's cupbearer. "Daedal": skillfully wrought (from the name of the Greek craftsman, Daedalus).

The soul of joy, ye ever-living Gods,
Till exultation burst in one wide voice
Like music from Elysian winds.
      And thou
Ascend beside me, veiléd in the light
Of the desire which makes thee one with me,   35
Thetis, bright image of eternity!
When thou didst cry, "Insufferable might!⁵
God! Spare me! I sustain not the quick flames,
The penetrating presence; all my being,
Like him whom the Numidian seps⁶ did thaw   40
Into a dew with poison, is dissolved,
Sinking through its foundations": even then
Two mighty spirits, mingling, made a third
Mightier than either, which, unbodied now,
Between us floats, felt, although unbeheld,   45
Waiting the incarnation, which ascends,
(Hear ye the thunder of the fiery wheels
Griding⁷ the winds?) from Demogorgon's throne.
Victory! victory! Feel'st thou not, O world,
The earthquake of his chariot thundering up   50
Olympus?
  [*The Car of the* HOUR *arrives.* DEMOGORGON *descends, and*
  moves towards the Throne of JUPITER.]
    Awful shape, what art thou? Speak!
DEMOGORGON. Eternity. Demand no direr name.
Descend, and follow me down the abyss.
I am thy child,⁸ as thou wert Saturn's child;
Mightier than thee: and we must dwell together   55
Henceforth in darkness. Lift thy lightnings not.
The tyranny of heaven none may retain,
Or reassume, or hold, succeeding thee:
Yet if thou wilt, as 'tis the destiny
Of trodden worms to writhe till they are dead,   60
Put forth thy might.
JUPITER.   Detested prodigy!
Even thus beneath the deep Titanian prisons
I trample thee! thou lingerest?
      Mercy! mercy!
No pity, no release, no respite! Oh,
That thou wouldst make mine enemy my judge,   65
Even where he hangs, seared by my long revenge,
On Caucasus! he would not doom me thus.
Gentle, and just, and dreadless, is he not
The monarch of the world?⁹ What then art thou?

---

5. This description of the union of Jupiter and Thetis is a grotesque parody of the reunion of Prometheus and Asia.
6. A serpent of Numidia (North Africa) whose bite was thought to cause putrefaction.
7. Cutting with a rasping sound.

8. Ironically, and in a figurative sense: Demogorgon's function follows from Jupiter's actions.
9. The ultimate irony: Jupiter appeals to those very qualities of Prometheus for which he has hitherto persecuted him, begging for a mercy which Prome-

No refuge! no appeal!
              Sink with me then,   70
We two will sink on the wide waves of ruin,
Even as a vulture and a snake outspent
Drop, twisted in inextricable fight,
Into a shoreless sea. Let hell unlock
Its mounded oceans of tempestuous fire,   75
And whelm on them into the bottomless void
This desolated world, and thee, and me,
The conqueror and the conquered, and the wreck
Of that for which they combated.
                        Ai! Ai!
The elements obey me not. I sink   80
Dizzily down, ever, forever, down.
And, like a cloud, mine enemy above
Darkens my fall with victory! Ai, Ai!

From SCENE IV—*A Forest. In the Background a Cave.* PROME-
THEUS, ASIA, PANTHEA, IONE, *and the* SPIRIT OF THE EARTH.[1]

            * * *

[*The* SPIRIT OF THE HOUR *enters.*]
PROMETHEUS. We feel what thou hast heard and seen: yet speak.
SPIRIT OF THE HOUR. Soon as the sound had ceased whose thunder
    filled
The abysses of the sky and the wide earth,
There was a change: the impalpable thin air   100
And the all-circling sunlight were transformed,
As if the sense of love dissolved in them
Had folded itself round the spheréd world.
My vision then grew clear, and I could see
Into the mysteries of the universe: 105
Dizzy as with delight I floated down,
Winnowing the lightsome air with languid plumes,
My coursers sought their birthplace in the sun,
Where they henceforth will live exempt from toil,
Pasturing flowers of vegetable fire;   110
And where my moonlike car will stand within
A temple, gazed upon by Phidian forms[2]
Of thee, and Asia, and the Earth, and me,
And you fair nymphs looking the love we feel—
In memory of the tidings it has borne—   115
Beneath a dome fretted with graven flowers,

theus has already granted him; but Prometheus' change from vengefulness to mercy is in fact the cause of Jupiter's present downfall.

1. After Jupiter's annihilation (described in Scene ii), Hercules unbinds Prometheus, who is reunited with Asia and retires to a cave "where we will sit and talk of time and change / * * * ourselves unchanged." In the speech which concludes the act (re-printed here) the Spirit of the Hour describes what happened when he sounded the trumpet of human and social regeneration.

2. The crescent-shaped ("moonlike") chariot, its apocalyptic mission accomplished, will be frozen to the immobility of stone, and will be surrounded by the sculptured forms of other agents in the drama. Phidias (5th century B.C.) was the noblest of Greek sculptors.

Poised on twelve columns of resplendent stone,
And open to the bright and liquid sky.
Yoked to it by an amphisbaenic snake[3]
The likeness of those wingéd steeds will mock[4]   120
The flight from which they find repose. Alas,
Whither has wandered now my partial[5] tongue
When all remains untold which ye would hear?
As I have said, I floated to the earth:
It was, as it is still, the pain of bliss   125
To move, to breathe, to be; I wandering went
Among the haunts and dwellings of mankind,
And first was disappointed not to see
Such mighty change as I had felt within
Expressed in outward things; but soon I looked,   130
And behold, thrones were kingless, and men walked
One with the other even as spirits do,
None fawned, none trampled; hate, disdain, or fear,
Self-love or self-contempt, on human brows
No more inscribed, as o'er the gate of hell,   135
"All hope abandon ye who enter here";[6]
None frowned, none trembled, none with eager fear
Gazed on another's eye of cold command,
Until the subject of a tyrant's will
Became, worse fate, the abject of his own,[7]   140
Which spurred him, like an outspent horse, to death.
None wrought his lips in truth-entangling lines
Which smiled the lie his tongue disdained to speak;
None, with firm sneer, trod out in his own heart
The sparks of love and hope till there remained   145
Those bitter ashes, a soul self-consumed,
And the wretch crept a vampire among men,
Infecting all with his own hideous ill;
None talked that common, false, cold, hollow talk
Which makes the heart deny the *yes* it breathes,   150
Yet question that unmeant hypocrisy
With such a self-mistrust as has no name.
And women, too, frank, beautiful, and kind
As the free heaven which rains fresh light and dew
On the wide earth, past; gentle radiant forms,   155
From custom's evil taint exempt and pure;
Speaking the wisdom once they could not think,
Looking emotions once they feared to feel,
And changed to all which once they dared not be,
Yet being now, made earth like heaven; nor pride,   160
Nor jealousy, nor envy, nor ill shame,

---

3. A mythical snake with a head at either end; it serves here as a symbolic warning that a reversal of the process of redemption is always possible. Cf. IV.561–69.
4. "Imitate" and also, in their statu-esque immobility, "mock at" the flight that they represent.
5. Biased, self-concerned.
6. Dante, *Inferno* III.9.
7. I.e., abjectly subject to his own will.

The bitterest of those drops of treasured gall,
Spoilt the sweet taste of the nepenthe,[8] love.

Thrones, altars, judgment-seats, and prisons; wherein,
And beside which, by wretched men were borne   165
Scepters, tiaras, swords, and chains, and tomes
Of reasoned wrong, glozed on[9] by ignorance,
Were like those monstrous and barbaric shapes,
The ghosts of a no-more-remembered fame,
Which, from their unworn obelisks, look forth   170
In triumph o'er the palaces and tombs
Of those who were their conquerors: moldering round,
These imaged to the pride of kings and priests
A dark yet mighty faith, a power as wide
As is the world it wasted, and are now   175
But an astonishment; even so the tools
And emblems of its last captivity,
Amid the dwellings of the peopled earth,
Stand, not o'erthrown, but unregarded now.
And those foul shapes,[1] abhorred by god and man—   180
Which, under many a name and many a form
Strange, savage, ghastly, dark, and execrable,
Were Jupiter, the tyrant of the world;
And which the nations, panic-stricken, served
With blood, and hearts broken by long hope, and love   185
Dragged to his altars soiled and garlandless,
And slain amid men's unreclaiming tears,
Flattering the thing they feared, which fear was hate—
Frown, moldering fast, o'er their abandoned shrines:
The painted veil, by those who were, called life,[2]   190
Which mimicked, as with colors idly spread,
All men believed or hoped, is torn aside;
The loathsome mask has fallen, the man remains—
Scepterless, free, uncircumscribed—but man:
Equal, unclassed, tribeless, and nationless,   195
Exempt from awe, worship, degree, the king
Over himself; just, gentle, wise: but man
Passionless?—no, yet free from guilt or pain,
Which were, for his will made or suffered them,
Nor yet exempt, though ruling them like slaves,   200
From chance, and death, and mutability,
The clogs of that which else might oversoar
The loftiest star of unascended heaven,
Pinnacled dim in the intense inane.[3]

8. A fabled drug bringing forgetfulness
of pain and sorrow.
9. Annotated.
1. The variously named gods which
claimed human sacrifice—all really
manifestations of Jupiter (line 183).
2. I.e., which was thought to be life
(reality) by men as they were before
their regeneration.
3. I.e., a dim point in the extreme of
empty space. If regenerate man were
to be entirely released from the material conditions of chance, death, and
change (line 201), he would cease to
be man at all, becoming, what even
the stars are not, a pure ideal.

From Act IV[1]

SCENE—A *Part of the Forest near the Cave of Prometheus.*

* * *

THE EARTH

The joy, the triumph, the delight, the madness!
The boundless, overflowing, bursting gladness,   320
The vaporous exultation not to be confined![2]
Ha! ha! the animation of delight
Which wraps me, like an atmosphere of light,
And bears me as a cloud is borne by its own wind.

THE MOON

Brother mine, calm wanderer,   325
Happy globe of land and air,
Some Spirit[3] is darted like a beam from thee,
Which penetrates my frozen frame,
And passes with the warmth of flame,
With love, and odor, and deep melody   330
Through me, through me!

THE EARTH

Ha! ha! the caverns of my hollow mountains,
My cloven fire-crags, sound-exulting fountains
Laugh with a vast and inextinguishable laughter.
The oceans, and the deserts, and the abysses,   335
And the deep air's unmeasured wildernesses,
Answer from all their clouds and billows, echoing after.

They cry aloud as I do. Sceptered curse,[4]
Who all our green and azure universe
Threatenedst to muffle round with black destruction, sending   340
A solid cloud to rain hot thunderstones,
And splinter and knead down my children's bones,
All I bring forth, to one void mass battering and blending—

Until each craglike tower, and storied column,
Palace, and obelisk, and temple solemn,   345

1. The original drama, completed in the spring of 1819, contained only three acts. Later that year Shelley, feeling the need for a more impressive climax, added the fourth act by way of a great choral conclusion. The rejuvenation of man is reflected throughout the universe, and the apocalyptic vision of a new heaven and earth is presented, as in Revelation xxi, in the symbol of a marriage: "And I saw a new heaven and a new earth: for the first heaven and the first earth were passed away; and there was no more sea. And I John saw the holy city, new Jerusalem, coming down from God out of heaven, prepared as a bride adorned for her hus-band." Shelley extends this marital figure to the cosmos (including, in the excerpt here, the earth and moon), in a total renewal of love and relationship that reflects the central reunion of Prometheus and Asia and represents the reintegration of a split and conflicting humanity. In the coda, Demogorgon sums up the meaning of the whole.
2. Literally, the earth's gases are bursting out through its volcanoes.
3. Represented physically by gravitational force, exerted by the moving earth upon its circling satellite.
4. Jupiter.

My imperial mountains crowned with cloud, and snow, and fire;
  My sealike forests, every blade and blossom
  Which finds a grave or cradle in my bosom,.
Were stamped by thy strong hate into a lifeless mire:

  How art thou sunk, withdrawn, covered, drunk up   350
  By thirsty nothing, as the brackish cup
Drained by a desert troop, a little drop for all;
  And from beneath, around, within, above,
  Filling thy void annihilation, love
Burst in like light on caves cloven by the thunder ball.   355

THE MOON
  The snow upon my lifeless mountains
  Is loosened into living fountains,
My solid oceans flow, and sing, and shine:
  A spirit from my heart bursts forth,
  It clothes with unexpected birth   360
My cold bare bosom: Oh! it must be thine
      On mine, on mine!

  Gazing on thee I feel, I know
  Green stalks burst forth, and bright flowers grow,
And living shapes upon my bosom move: 365
  Music is in the sea and air,
  Wingèd clouds soar here and there,
Dark with the rain new buds are dreaming of:
      'Tis love, all love!

THE EARTH
It interpenetrates my granite mass,   370
  Through tangled roots and trodden clay doth pass
Into the utmost leaves and delicatest flowers;
  Upon the winds, among the clouds 'tis spread,
  It wakes a life in the forgotten dead,
They breathe a spirit up from their obscurest bowers.   375

  And like a storm bursting its cloudy prison
  With thunder, and with whirlwind, has arisen
Out of the lampless caves of unimagined being:
  With earthquake shock and swiftness making shiver
  Thought's stagnant chaos, unremoved forever,[5]   380
Till hate, and fear, and pain, light-vanquished shadows, fleeing,

  Leave Man, who was a many-sided mirror,
  Which could distort to many a shape of error,
This true fair world of things, a sea reflecting love;
  Which over all his kind, as the sun's heaven   385
  Gliding o'er ocean, smooth, serene, and even,
Darting from starry depths radiance and life, doth move:

  Leave Man, even as a leprous child is left,
  Who follows a sick beast to some warm cleft

5. I.e., never to be removed.

Of rocks, through which the might of healing springs is poured;   390
  Then when it wanders home with rosy smile,
  Unconscious, and its mother fears awhile
It is a spirit, then, weeps on her child restored.

  Man, oh, not men![6] a chain of linkéd thought,
    Of love and might to be divided not,   395
Compelling the elements with adamantine stress;
  As the sun rules,[7] even with a tyrant's gaze,
  The unquiet republic of the maze
Of planets, struggling fierce towards heaven's free wilderness.

  Man, one harmonious soul of many a soul,   400
    Whose nature is its own divine control,
Where all things flow to all, as rivers to the sea;
  Familiar acts are beautiful through love;
  Labor, and pain, and grief, in life's green grove
Sport like tame beasts, none knew how gentle they could be!   405

  His will, with all mean passions, bad delights,
    And selfish cares, its trembling satellites,
A spirit ill to guide, but mighty to obey,
  Is as a tempest-wingéd ship, whose helm
  Love rules, through waves which dare not overwhelm,   410
Forcing life's wildest shores to own its sovereign sway.

  All things confess his strength. Through the cold mass
    Of marble and of color his dreams pass;
Bright threads whence mothers weave the robes their children wear;
  Language is a perpetual Orphic song,[8]   415
  Which rules with Daedal harmony a throng
Of thoughts and forms, which else senseless and shapeless were.

  The lightning is his slave;[9] heaven's utmost deep
    Gives up her stars, and like a flock of sheep
They pass before his eye, are numbered, and roll on!   420
  The tempest is his steed, he strides the air;
  And the abyss shouts from her depth laid bare,
Heaven, hast thou secrets? Man unveils me; I have none.

THE MOON

  The shadow of white death has passed
    From my path in heaven at last,   425
A clinging shroud of solid frost and sleep;
  And through my newly-woven bowers,
    Wander happy paramours,
Less mighty, but as mild as those who keep
    Thy vales more deep.   430

6. Human society, once splintered into isolated individuals by hate and conflict, is now described as bound by love and commonalty of thought into a single macrocosmic Man.
7 By its gravitational attraction.
8. Like the music of Orpheus, which attracted and controlled beasts, rocks, and trees. "Daedal" (next line): skillful, intricate.
9. The Earth describes the scientific and technological triumphs of regenerate man.

THE EARTH

As the dissolving warmth of dawn may fold
A half unfrozen dew-globe, green, and gold,
And crystalline, till it becomes a wingéd mist,
And wanders up the vault of the blue day,
Outlives the noon, and on the sun's last ray   435
Hangs o'er the sea, a fleece of fire and amethyst.

THE MOON

Thou art folded, thou art lying
In the light which is undying
Of thine own joy, and heaven's smile divine;
All suns and constellations shower   440
On thee a light, a life, a power
Which doth array thy sphere; thou pourest thine
        On mine, on mine!

THE EARTH

I spin beneath my pyramid of night,[1]
Which points into the heavens dreaming delight,   445
Murmuring victorious joy in my enchanted sleep;
As a youth lulled in love-dreams faintly sighing,
Under the shadow of his beauty lying,
Which round his rest a watch of light and warmth doth keep.

THE MOON

As in the soft and sweet eclipse,   450
When soul meets soul on lovers' lips,
High hearts are calm, and brightest eyes are dull;
So when thy shadow falls on me,[1a]
Then am I mute and still, by thee
Covered; of thy love, Orb most beautiful,   455
        Full, oh, too full!

Thou art speeding round the sun
Brightest world of many a one;
Green and azure sphere which shinest
With a light which is divinest   460
Among all the lamps of Heaven
To whom life and light is given;
I, thy crystal paramour
Borne beside thee by a power
Like the polar Paradise,   465
Magnet-like of lovers' eyes;[2]
I, a most enamored maiden
Whose weak brain is overladen
With the pleasure of her love,
Maniac-like around thee move   470
Gazing, an insatiate bride,
On thy form from every side

---

1. The conic shadow cast by the earth as it intercepts the sun's light.
1a. In the eclipse of the moon; cf. line 450.

2. Circling the earth, the moon keeps her face constantly toward it.

Like a Maenad,[3] round the cup
Which Agave lifted up
In the weird Cadmaean forest.   475
Brother, wheresoe'er thou soarest
I must hurry, whirl, and follow
Through the heavens wide and hollow,
Sheltered by the warm embrace
Of thy soul from hungry space,   480
Drinking from thy sense and sight
Beauty, majesty, and might,
As a lover or a chameleon
Grows like what it looks upon,
As a violet's gentle eye   485
Gazes on the azure sky
Until its hue grows like what it beholds,
As a gray and watery mist
Glows like solid amethyst
Athwart the western mountain it enfolds,   490
When the sunset sleeps
    Upon its snow—

THE EARTH
And the weak day weeps[4]
    That it should be so.
Oh, gentle Moon, the voice of thy delight   495
Falls on me like thy clear and tender light
Soothing the seaman, borne the summer night,
    Through isles forever calm;
Oh, gentle Moon, thy crystal accents pierce
The caverns of my pride's deep universe,   500
Charming the tiger joy, whose tramplings fierce
Made wounds which need thy balm.

* * *

DEMOGORGON
Man, who wert once a despot and a slave;
    A dupe and a deceiver; a decay;   550
A traveler from the cradle to the grave
    Through the dim night of this immortal day:

ALL
Speak: thy strong words may never pass away.

DEMOGORGON
This is the day which down the void abysm
At the Earth-born's[5] spell yawns for Heaven's despotism,   555
    And Conquest is dragged captive through the deep:[6]

---

3. The Maenads were female participants in the ecstatic worship of Dionysus, or Bacchus. Agave, daughter of
King Cadmus (lines 474–75), in a
blind frenzy tore her own son Pentheus
to bits when he was caught spying on
the Dionysiac rites.
4. I.e., the dew at nightfall.
5. Prometheus'.
6. Ephesians iv.8: "When [Christ]
ascended up on high, he led captivity
captive."

Love, from its awful throne of patient power
In the wise heart, from the last giddy hour
   Of dread endurance, from the slippery, steep,
And narrow verge of craglike agony, springs   560
And folds over the world its healing wings.

Gentleness, Virtue, Wisdom, and Endurance,
These are the seals of that most firm assurance
   Which bars the pit over Destruction's strength;
And if, with infirm hand, Eternity,   565
Mother of many acts and hours, should free
   The serpent that would clasp her with his length;[7]
These are the spells by which to reassume
An empire o'er the disentangled doom:[8]

To suffer woes which Hope thinks infinite;   570
To forgive wrongs darker than death or night;
   To defy Power, which seems omnipotent;
To love, and bear; to hope till Hope creates
From its own wreck the thing it contemplates;
   Neither to change, nor falter, nor repent;   575
This, like thy glory, Titan, is to be
Good, great and joyous, beautiful and free;
This is alone Life, Joy, Empire, and Victory.
1818–19   1820

The Cloud

I bring fresh showers for the thirsting flowers,
   From the seas and the streams;
I bear light shade for the leaves when laid
   In their noonday dreams.
From my wings are shaken the dews that waken   5
   The sweet buds every one,
When rocked to rest on their mother's breast,
   As she dances about the sun.
I wield the flail of the lashing hail,
   And whiten the green plains under,   10
And then again I dissolve it in rain,
   And laugh as I pass in thunder.

I sift the snow on the mountains below,
   And their great pines groan aghast;
And all the night 'tis my pillow white,   15
   While I sleep in the arms of the blast.

7. A final reminder that the serpent incessantly struggles to break loose and start the cycle of evil all over again. Felicity must continue to be earned.
8. Shelley's four cardinal virtues (line 562), which seal the serpent in the pit, also constitute the magic formulas ("spells") by which to remaster him, should he again break loose. These virtues are expanded upon in the concluding lines (570–75).

Sublime on the towers of my skyey bowers,
 Lightning my pilot[1] sits;
In a cavern under is fettered the thunder,
 It struggles and howls at fits;[2]   20
Over earth and ocean, with gentle motion,
 This pilot is guiding me,
Lured by the love of the genii that move
 In the depths of the purple sea;
Over the rills, and the crags, and the hills,   25
 Over the lakes and the plains,
Wherever he dream, under mountain or stream,
 The Spirit he loves remains;
And I all the while bask in Heaven's blue smile,[3]
 Whilst he is dissolving in rains.   30

The sanguine Sunrise, with his meteor eyes,
 And his burning plumes outspread,
Leaps on the back of my sailing rack,[4]
 When the morning star shines dead;
As on the jag of a mountain crag,   35
 Which an earthquake rocks and swings,
An eagle alit one moment may sit
 In the light of its golden wings.
And when Sunset may breathe, from the lit sea beneath,
 Its ardors of rest and of love,   40
And the crimson pall of eve may fall
 From the depth of Heaven above,
With wings folded I rest, on mine aëry nest,
 As still as a brooding dove.

That orbéd maiden with white fire laden,   45
 Whom mortals call the Moon,
Glides glimmering o'er my fleecelike floor,
 By the midnight breezes strewn;
And wherever the beat of her unseen feet,
 Which only the angels hear,   50
May have broken the woof[5] of my tent's thin roof,
 The stars peep behind her and peer;
And I laugh to see them whirl and flee,
 Like a swarm of golden bees,
When I widen the rent in my wind-built tent, 55
 Till the calm rivers, lakes, and seas,
Like strips of the sky fallen through me on high,
 Are each paved with the moon and these.[6]

I bind the Sun's throne with a burning zone,[7]
 And the Moon's with a girdle of pearl;   60

1. The atmospheric electricity which guides the movements of the cloud; it is "lured" (line 23) by the attraction of an opposite charge.
2. Fitfully.
3. The upper part of the cloud re-mains exposed to the sun.
4. High, broken clouds, driven by the wind.
5. Texture.
6. I.e., the stars.
7. Girdle, belt.

The volcanoes are dim, and the stars reel and swim,
　　When the whirlwinds my banner unfurl.
From cape to cape, with a bridgelike shape,
　　Over a torrent sea,
Sunbeam-proof, I hang like a roof—　　　　　　　　65
　　The mountains its columns be.
The triumphal arch through which I march
　　With hurricane, fire, and snow,
When the Powers of the air are chained to my chair,
　　Is the million-colored bow;　　　　　　　　　　70
The sphere-fire[8] above its soft colors wove,
　　While the moist Earth was laughing below.

I am the daughter of Earth and Water,
　　And the nursling of the Sky;
I pass through the pores of the ocean and shores;　　75
　　I change, but I cannot die.
For after the rain when with never a stain
　　The pavilion of Heaven is bare,
And the winds and sunbeams with their convex gleams
　　Build up the blue dome of air,[9]　　　　　　　80
I silently laugh at my own cenotaph,[1]
　　And out of the caverns of rain,
Like a child from the womb, like a ghost[2] from the tomb,
　　I arise and unbuild it again.

　　　　　　　　　　　　　　　　　　　　　1820

To a Skylark[1]

Hail to thee, blithe Spirit!
　　Bird thou never wert,
That from Heaven, or near it,
　　Pourest thy full heart
In profuse strains of unpremeditated art.　　　　　5

Higher still and higher
　　From the earth thou springest
Like a cloud of fire;
　　The blue deep thou wingest,
And singing still dost soar, and soaring ever singest.　　10

In the golden lightning
　　Of the sunken sun,
O'er which clouds are bright'ning,

8. The sunlight.
9. The blue color of the sky; the phenomenon results from the way "sunbeams" are filtered through the atmosphere.
1. The memorial monument ("cenotaph") of the dead cloud is the cloudless blue dome.

2. Soul, spirit.
1. The bird, freed from the bonds of earth and soaring beyond the reach of all the physical senses except hearing, is made the emblem of a nonmaterial spirit of pure joy, beyond access by human sense; see lines 15, 61.

Thou dost float and run;
Like an unbodied joy whose race is just begun.   15

The pale purple even
    Melts around thy flight
Like a star of Heaven,
    In the broad daylight
Thou art unseen, but yet I hear thy shrill delight,   20

Keen as are the arrows
    Of that silver sphere,[2]
Whose intense lamp narrows
    In the white dawn clear
Until we hardly see—we feel that it is there.   25

All the earth and air
    With thy voice is loud,
As, when night is bare,
    From one lonely cloud
The moon rains out her beams, and Heaven is overflowed.   30

What thou art we know not;
    What is most like thee?
From rainbow clouds there flow not
    Drops so bright to see
As from thy presence showers a rain of melody.   35

Like a Poet hidden
    In the light of thought,
Singing hymns unbidden,
    Till the world is wrought
To sympathy with hopes and fears it heeded not: 40

Like a high-born maiden
    In a palace tower
Soothing her love-laden
    Soul in secret hour
With music sweet as love, which overflows her bower: 45

Like a glowworm golden
    In a dell of dew,
Scattering unbeholden
    Its aërial hue
Among the flowers and grass, which screen it from the view!   50

Like a rose embowered
    In its own green leaves,
By warm winds deflowered,[3]
    Till the scent it gives
Makes faint with too much sweet those heavy-wingéd thieves:[4]   55

2. The morning star.
3. In the double sense: fertilized, and stripped of its petals.
4. The "warm winds," line 53.

Sound of vernal showers
    On the twinkling grass,
Rain-awakened flowers,
    All that ever was
Joyous, and clear, and fresh, thy music doth surpass: 60

Teach us, Sprite[5] or Bird,
    What sweet thoughts are thine:
I have never heard
    Praise of love or wine
That panted forth a flood of rapture so divine.   65

Chorus Hymeneal,[6]
    Or triumphal chant,
Matched with thine would be all
    But an empty vaunt,
A thing wherein we feel there is some hidden want.   70

What objects are the fountains
    Of thy happy strain?
What fields, or waves, or mountains?
    What shapes of sky or plain?
What love of thine own kind? what ignorance of pain?   75

With thy clear keen joyance
    Languor cannot be:
Shadow of annoyance
    Never came near thee:
Thou lovest—but ne'er knew love's sad satiety.   80

Waking or asleep,
    Thou of death must deem
Things more true and deep
    Than we mortals dream,
Or how could thy notes flow in such a crystal stream?   85

We look before and after,
    And pine for what is not:
Our sincerest laughter
    With some pain is fraught;
Our sweetest songs are those that tell of saddest thought.   90

Yet if we could scorn
    Hate, and pride, and fear;
If we were things born
    Not to shed a tear,
I know not how thy joy we ever should come near.   95

Better than all measures
    Of delightful sound,
Better than all treasures

5. Spirit.
6. Celebrating a marriage (from Hymen, Greek god of marriage).

That in books are found,
Thy skill to poet were, thou scorner of the ground! 100

Teach me half the gladness
That thy brain must know,
Such harmonious madness
From my lips would flow
The world should listen then—as I am listening now. 105
1820   1820

Hymn of Apollo[1]

1

The sleepless Hours who watch me as I lie,
  Curtained with star-inwoven tapestries
From the broad moonlight of the sky,
  Fanning the busy dreams from my dim eyes—
Waken me when their Mother, the gray Dawn,   5
Tells them that dreams and that the moon is gone.

2

Then I arise, and climbing Heaven's blue dome,
  I walk over the mountains and the waves,
Leaving my robe upon the ocean foam;
  My footsteps pave the clouds with fire; the caves   10
Are filled with my bright presence, and the air
Leaves the green Earth to my embraces bare.

3

The sunbeams are my shafts, with which I kill
  Deceit, that loves the night and fears the day;
All men who do or even imagine ill
  Fly me, and from the glory of my ray   15
Good minds and open actions take new might,
Until diminished by the reign of Night.

4

I feed the clouds, the rainbows and the flowers
  With their aethereal colors; the moon's globe   20
And the pure stars in their eternal bowers
  Are cinctured[2] with my power as with a robe;
Whatever lamps on Earth or Heaven may shine
Are portions of one power, which is mine.

5

I stand at noon upon the peak of Heaven,   25
  Then with unwilling steps I wander down
Into the clouds of the Atlantic even;

1. Written, with the companion piece that follows, for the opening scene in Mary Shelley's verse drama *Midas*. Apollo, god of the sun, of healing, and of poetry and the other arts, sings this serenely Olympian hymn in a contest with Pan, the goatlike deity of flocks, forests, and wild life. In the play, old Tmolus, a mountain god who judges the contest, awards the prize to Apollo; when Midas, a mortal, objects, preferring Pan's song of natural desire, passions, and suffering, Apollo affixes on him asses' ears.
2. Girdled.

For grief that I depart they weep and frown:
What look is more delightful than the smile
With which I soothe them from the western isle?   30
6
I am the eye with which the Universe
    Beholds itself and knows itself divine;
All harmony of instrument or verse,
    All prophecy, all medicine is mine,
All light of art or nature; to my song   35
Victory and praise in its own right belong.

1820   1824

Hymn of Pan[1]

1
From the forests and highlands
    We come, we come;
From the river-girt islands,
    Where loud waves are dumb
        Listening to my sweet pipings.   5
The wind in the reeds and the rushes,
    The bees on the bells of thyme,
The birds on the myrtle bushes,
    The cicale[2] above in the lime,
And the lizards below in the grass,   10
Were as silent as ever old Tmolus was,
    Listening to my sweet pipings.

2
Liquid Peneus[3] was flowing,
    And all dark Tempe lay
In Pelion's shadow, outgrowing   15
    The light of the dying day,
        Speeded by my sweet pipings.
The Sileni, and Sylvans, and Fauns,[4]
    And the Nymphs of the woods and the waves,
To the edge of the moist river lawns,   20
    And the brink of the dewy caves,
And all that did then attend and follow,
Were silent with love, as you now, Apollo,
    With envy of my sweet pipings.

3
I sang of the dancing stars,   25
    I sang of the daedal[5] Earth,

1. Pan's reply to Apollo in his singing
contest; see *Hymn of Apollo*, note 1.
2. Locust.
3. The river Peneus flows through the
lovely valley of Tempe, not far from
Mt. Pelion; the locale is Thessaly, in
northeastern Greece.
4. The male sileni, sylvans, and fauns,
and the female nymphs, are all minor
rural or woodland deities.
5. Ingeniously formed.

And of Heaven—and the giant wars,[6]
  And Love, and Death, and Birth—
  And then I changed my pipings—
Singing how down the vale of Maenalus   30
  I pursued a maiden and clasped a reed.[7]
Gods and men, we are all deluded thus!
  It breaks in our bosom and then we bleed:
All wept, as I think both ye now would,
If envy or age had not frozen your blood,   35
  At the sorrow of my sweet pipings.

1820   1824

The Two Spirits: An Allegory[1]

FIRST SPIRIT

O thou, who plumed with strong desire
  Wouldst float above the earth, beware!
A Shadow tracks thy flight of fire—
    Night is coming!
Bright are the regions of the air,   5
And among the winds and beams
It were delight to wander there—
    Night is coming!

SECOND SPIRIT

The deathless stars are bright above;
  If I would cross the shade of night,[2]   10
Within my heart is the lamp of love,
    And that is day!
And the moon will smile with gentle light
On my golden plumes where'er they move;
  The meteors will linger round my flight,   15
    And make night day.

FIRST SPIRIT

But if the whirlwinds of darkness waken
  Hail, and lightning, and stormy rain;
See, the bounds of the air are shaken—

---

6. I.e., the ancient wars of the giants, sons of Earth, against the gods of Olympus.
7. Pan pursued the nymph, Syrinx, but as he caught her, she turned into a reed. From it was made Pan's pipe, the "syrinx."
1. The Second Spirit speaks for the poet's unquenchable desire, accepting the risk involved in the attempt to soar above the limits of earth and its cycle of night into the light of the sun; the First Spirit speaks for the timidity that would bind the poet, safe but somnolent, to darkness and the "dull earth." The last two stanzas pose, without resolving, alternate possibilities: that the aspiring spirit ends up in an eddy, trapped amid the frozen mountain heights of the earth, or else that, in the course of an overflight which is successful, his inner light makes night day for other weary but undefeated travelers.
2. The shadow cast by the earth in the light of the sun; cf. *Prometheus Unbound* IV.444–45.

Night is coming!   20
The red swift clouds of the hurricane
Yon declining sun have overtaken,
The clash of the hail sweeps over the plain—
Night is coming!

SECOND SPIRIT
I see the light, and I hear the sound;   25
    I'll sail on the flood of the tempest dark,
With the calm within and the light around
        Which makes night day:
And thou, when the gloom is deep and stark,
Look from thy dull earth, slumber-bound,   30
    My moonlike flight thou then mayst mark
        On high, far away.

Some say there is a precipice
    Where one vast pine is frozen to ruin
O'er piles of snow and chasms of ice   35
        Mid Alpine mountains;
And that the languid storm pursuing
That wingéd shape, forever flies
    Round those hoar branches, aye renewing
        Its aëry fountains.   40

Some say when nights are dry and clear,
    And the death-dews sleep on the morass,
Sweet whispers are heard by the traveler,
        Which make night day:
And a silver shape like his early love doth pass   45
Upborne by her wild and glittering hair,
    And when he awakes on the fragrant grass,
        He finds night day.

1820   1824

The Tower of Famine[1]

Amid the desolation of a city,
    Which was the cradle, and is now the grave
Of an extinguished people—so that Pity

Weeps o'er the shipwrecks of Oblivion's wave,
    There stands the Tower of Famine. It is built   5
Upon some prison-homes, whose dwellers rave

1. At Pisa there still exists the prison of Ugolino, which goes by the name of "La Torre della Fame"; in the adjoining building the galley slaves are confined. It is situated on the Ponte al Marc on the Arno [note either by Shelley or Mary Shelley]. The story of Ugolino is told in Dante's *Inferno*, XXXIII. He was a Guelf of the late 13th century who having made himself master of Pisa by treachery was overthrown and, together with two sons and two grandsons, locked up in the tower and left to starve to death.

For bread, and gold, and blood: Pain, linked to Guilt,
Agitates the light flame of their hours,
Until its vital oil is spent or spilt.

There stands the pile, a tower amid the towers   10
And sacred domes; each marble-ribbéd roof,
The brazen-gated temples, and the bowers

Of solitary wealth—the tempest-proof
Pavilions of the dark Italian air—
Are by its presence dimmed—they stand aloof,   15

And are withdrawn—so that the world is bare;
As if a specter wrapped in shapeless terror
Amid a company of ladies fair

Should glide and glow, till it became a mirror
Of all their beauty, and their hair and hue,   20
The life of their sweet eyes, with all its error,
Should be absorbed, till they to marble grew.

1820   1829

To Night[1]

1

Swiftly walk o'er the western wave,
    Spirit of Night!
Out of the misty eastern cave,
Where, all the long and lone daylight,
Thou wovest dreams of joy and fear,   5
Which make thee terrible and dear—
    Swift be thy flight!

2

Wrap thy form in a mantle gray,
    Star-inwrought!
Blind with thine hair the eyes of Day;   10
Kiss her until she be wearied out,
Then wander o'er city, and sea, and land,
Touching all with thine opiate wand—
    Come, long-sought!

3

When I arose and saw the dawn,   15
    I sighed for thee;
When light rode high, and the dew was gone,
And noon lay heavy on flower and tree,
And the weary Day turned to his rest,
Lingering like an unloved guest,   20
    I sighed for thee.

1. In a number of Shelley's poems night and darkness, as opposed to the clarity of the day, are emblems of the myste-rious and primordial powers of the poetic imagination. See, e.g., the opening of *The Triumph of Life*, below.

4

Thy brother Death came, and cried,
　　"Wouldst thou me?"
Thy sweet child Sleep, the filmy-eyed,
Murmured like a noontide bee,
　　"Shall I nestle near thy side?   25
Wouldst thou me?"—And I replied,
　　"No, not thee!"

5

Death will come when thou art dead,
　　Soon, too soon—   30
Sleep will come when thou art fled;
Of neither would I ask the boon
I ask of thee, belovéd Night—
Swift be thine approaching flight,
　　Come soon, soon!   35

1821   1824

To ——

Music, when soft voices die,
Vibrates in the memory—
Odors, when sweet violets sicken,
Live within the sense they quicken.
Rose leaves, when the rose is dead,   5
Are heaped for the belovéd's bed;[1]
And so thy thoughts,[2] when thou art gone,
Love itself shall slumber on.

1821   1824

A Lament

1

O world! O life! O time!
On whose last steps I climb,
　　Trembling at that where I had stood before;
When will return the glory of your prime?
　　No more—Oh, never more!   5

2

Out of the day and night
A joy has taken flight;
　　Fresh spring, and summer, and winter hoar,
Move my faint heart with grief, but with delight
　　No more—Oh, never more!   10

1821   1824

1. The fallen petals form a bed for   2. I.e., my thoughts of thee.
the dead rose.

When Passion's Trance Is Overpast

1

When passion's trance is overpast,
If tenderness and truth could last,
Or live, whilst all wild feelings keep
Some mortal slumber, dark and deep,
I should not weep, I should not weep!   5

2

It were enough to feel, to see,
Thy soft eyes gazing tenderly,
And dream the rest—and burn and be
The secret food of fires unseen,
Couldst thou but be as thou hast been.   10

3

After the slumber of the year
The woodland violets reappear;
All things revive in field or grove,
And sky and sea, but two, which move
And form all others, life and love.   15

1821   1824

Choruses from Hellas[1]

Worlds on Worlds

Worlds on worlds are rolling ever
　From creation to decay,
Like the bubbles on a river
　Sparkling, bursting, borne away.
But they[2] are still immortal   5
　Who, through birth's orient[3] portal
And death's dark chasm hurrying to and fro,
　Clothe their unceasing flight
　In the brief dust and light

1. *Hellas*, a closet drama written in the autumn of 1821 and published the next year, was inspired by the Greek war for independence against the Turks. In his Preface Shelley declared that he regarded this revolution as only part of a larger pattern in this "age of the war of the oppressed against the oppressors"; he believed that it contained the promise of the final overthrow of all tyranny. The choruses below are sung by Greek captive women. The first chorus describes the emergence of Christ into the revolving cycle of history; the second chorus concludes the drama. Shelley wrote in a note that this final chorus prophesies "darkly a period of regeneration and happiness"—in other words, a return to the golden age, and a final stop to the rolling of the historical cycle. Shelley said that the coming of this millennium is far from certain, but based his hope on the precedent of Isaiah's messianic prophecy and on the prediction of a return to the golden time of Saturn in Virgil's *Eclogues* IV.
2. The immortal "beings which inhabit the planets and * * * clothe themselves in matter" [Shelley's note]. Shelley adopts the ancient notion that each of the planets possesses a supervising spirit.
3. Eastern.

Gathered around their chariots as they go;   10
  New shapes they still may weave,
  New gods, new laws receive,
Bright or dim are they as the robes they last
  On Death's bare ribs had cast.

A power from the unknown God,   15
  A Promethean conqueror,[4] came;
Like a triumphal path he trod
  The thorns of death and shame.
  A mortal shape to him
  Was like the vapor dim   20
Which the orient planet animates with light;
  Hell, Sin, and Slavery came,
  Like bloodhounds mild and tame,
Nor preyed, until their Lord had taken flight;
  The moon of Mahomet[5]   25
  Arose, and it shall set:
While blazoned as on Heaven's immortal noon
  The cross leads generations on.

Swift as the radiant shapes of sleep
  From one whose dreams are Paradise   30
Fly, when the fond wretch wakes to weep,
  And Day peers forth with her blank eyes;
  So fleet, so fain, so fair,
  The Powers of earth and air
Fled from the folding-star[6] of Bethlehem: 35
  Apollo, Pan, and Love,
  And even Olympian Jove
Grew weak, for killing Truth had glared on them;
  Our hills and seas and streams,
  Dispeopled of their dreams,   40
Their waters turned to blood, their dew to tears,
  Wailed for the golden years.

The World's Great Age

The world's great age begins anew,
  The golden years return,[7]
The earth doth like a snake renew
  Her winter weeds[8] outworn:
Heaven smiles, and faiths and empires gleam,   5
  Like wrecks of a dissolving dream.

---

4. Christ, whom Shelley compares to Prometheus, who brought fire and the arts of civilization to mankind.
5. The crescent, emblem of Mohammedanism, which was founded six centuries after the birth of Christ.
6. The star of evening, the time when sheep are driven into the sheepfold; hence, "folding." Shelley goes on to describe the pagan gods of earth and Olympus fleeing before the star of Bethlehem.
7. According to Greek myth, the first period of mankind was the golden age.
8. Clothes, especially mourning garments; "weeds" also suggest the dead vegetation of winter.

A brighter Hellas rears its mountains
　　From waves serener far;
A new Peneus[9] rolls his fountains
　　Against the morning star.　　　　　　　　　10
Where fairer Tempes bloom, there sleep
Young Cyclads[1] on a sunnier deep.

A loftier Argo[2] cleaves the main,
　　Fraught with a later prize;
Another Orpheus[3] sings again,　　　　　　　15
　　And loves, and weeps, and dies.
A new Ulysses leaves once more
Calypso[4] for his native shore.

Oh, write no more the tale of Troy,
　　If earth Death's scroll must be!　　　　　　20
Nor mix with Laian rage[5] the joy
　　Which dawns upon the free:
Although a subtler Sphinx renew
Riddles of death Thebes never knew.

Another Athens shall arise,　　　　　　　　　25
　　And to remoter time
Bequeath, like sunset to the skies,
　　The splendor of its prime;
And leave, if nought so bright may live,
All earth can take or Heaven can give.　　　　30

Saturn and Love their long repose
　　Shall burst, more bright and good
Than all who fell, than One who rose,
　　Than many unsubdued:[6]
Not gold, not blood, their altar dowers,　　　35
But votive tears and symbol flowers.

Oh, cease! must hate and death return?
　　Cease! must men kill and die?
Cease! drain not to its dregs the urn
　　Of bitter prophecy.　　　　　　　　　　　40
The world is weary of the past,
Oh, might it die or rest at last!

　　　　　　　　　　　　　　　　　　　　1822

9. The river that flows through the beautiful vale of Tempe (line 11).
1. The Cyclades, Greek islands in the Aegean Sea.
2. On which Jason sailed in his quest for the Golden Fleece.
3. The legendary player on the lyre who was torn to pieces by the frenzied Thracian women while he was mourning the death of his wife, Eurydice.
4. The nymph deserted by Ulysses on his voyage back from the Trojan War to his native Ithaca.
5. King Laius of Thebes was killed in an angry quarrel by his son Oedipus, who did not recognize his father. Shortly thereafter, Oedipus delivered Thebes from the ravages of the Sphinx by answering its riddle (lines 23–24).
6. "Saturn and Love were among the deities of a real or imaginary state of innocence and happiness. 'All' those 'who fell' [are] the Gods of Greece, Asia, and Egypt; the 'One who rose' [is] Jesus Christ * * * and the 'many unsubdued' [are] the monstrous objects of the idolatry of China, India, the Antarctic islands, and the native tribes of America" [Shelley's note].

Adonais[1]

AN ELEGY ON THE DEATH OF JOHN KEATS, AUTHOR OF ENDYMION, HYPERION, ETC.

[Thou wert the morning star among the living,
    Ere thy fair light had fled—
Now, having died, thou art as Hesperus, giving
    New splendor to the dead.][2]

1

I weep for Adonais—he is dead!
O, weep for Adonais! though our tears
Thaw not the frost which binds so dear a head!
And thou, sad Hour, selected from all years
To mourn our loss, rouse thy obscure compeers,   5
And teach them thine own sorrow, say: "With me
Died Adonais; till the Future dares
Forget the Past, his fate and fame shall be
An echo and a light unto eternity!"

1. John Keats died in Rome February 23, 1821, and was buried there in the Protestant Cemetery. Shelley had met Keats, had invited him to be his guest at Pisa, and had gradually come to recognize him as "among the writers of the highest genius who have adorned our age" (Preface to *Adonais*). The name "Adonais" is derived from Adonis, the handsome youth who had been loved by the goddess Venus and slain by a wild boar; the function of the beast in this poem is attributed to the anonymous author of a vituperative review of Keats's *Endymion* in the *Quarterly Review*, April, 1818 (now known to be John Wilson Croker), whom Shelley mistakenly believed to be responsible for Keats's illness and death. The alteration of "Adonis" to "Adonais" has evoked a good deal of discussion. Recently Earl Wasserman has argued persuasively that it is a fusion of "Adonis" (who had been worshiped as a vegetation deity) with "Adonai," one of the Old Testament names of God; in this procedure Shelley would be following the speculative mythographers of his day, a number of whom identified Adonis with Adonai as god of the sun and of fertility.
   Shelley described *Adonais* in a letter as a "highly wrought piece of art." Its artistry consists in part in the care with which it follows the conventions of the pastoral elegy, established more than two thousand years earlier by the Greek Sicilian poets Theocritus, Bion, and Moschus—Shelley had himself translated into English Bion's *Lament for Adonis* and Moschus' *Lament for Bion*. We recognize the centuries-old poetic ritual in many verbal echoes, and in such devices as the mournful and accusing invocation to a muse (stanzas 2–4), the sympathetic participation of nature in the death of the poet (stanzas 14–17), the procession of appropriate mourners (stanzas 30–35), the denunciation of unworthy practitioners of the pastoral or literary art (stanzas 17, 27–29, 36–37); and above all in the shift from despair at the finality of human death (lines 64, 190: "*He* will awake no more, oh, never more!") to consolation in the sudden and contradictory discovery that the grave is a gate to a higher existence (line 343: "Peace, peace! he is not dead, he doth not sleep"). These familiar elements Shelley reinterprets with astonishing inventiveness and transforms into a densely symbolic poetic construction; *Adonais* ranks with Milton's *Lycidas* among the supreme examples of the exacting form of the pastoral elegy.
2. This is Shelley's own translation of a Greek epigram, attributed to Plato, which he had prefixed to *Adonais* as a motto. (See also *The Triumph of Life*, below, line 256.) The reference is to the planet Venus, which appears both as the morning star, Lucifer, and the evening star, Hesperus or Vesper. Shelley makes of this phenomenon—the hidden identity of a single star under various aspects, and its persistence even when invisible in daylight—a key element in his symbolism for Adonais' triumph over death. See stanzas 44–46.

2

Where wert thou, mighty Mother,[3] when he lay,   10
When thy Son lay, pierced by the shaft which flies
In darkness? where was lorn Urania
When Adonais died? With veiléd eyes,
'Mid listening Echoes, in her Paradise
She sate, while one,[4] with soft enamored breath,   15
Rekindled all the fading melodies,
With which, like flowers that mock the corse[5] beneath,
He had adorned and hid the coming bulk of Death.

3

Oh, weep for Adonais—he is dead!
Wake, melancholy Mother, wake and weep!   20
Yet wherefore? Quench within their burning bed
Thy fiery tears, and let thy loud heart keep
Like his, a mute and uncomplaining sleep;
For he is gone, where all things wise and fair
Descend—oh, dream not that the amorous Deep   25
Will yet restore him to the vital air;
Death feeds on his mute voice, and laughs at our despair.

4

Most musical of mourners, weep again!
Lament anew, Urania!—He[6] died,
Who was the Sire of an immortal strain,   30
Blind, old, and lonely, when his country's pride,
The priest, the slave, and the liberticide,
Trampled and mocked with many a loathéd rite
Of lust and blood; he went, unterrified,
Into the gulf of death; but his clear Sprite[7]   35
Yet reigns o'er earth; the third[8] among the sons of light.

5

Most musical of mourners, weep anew!
Not all to that bright station dared to climb;
And happier they their happiness who knew,
Whose tapers yet burn through that night of time   40
In which suns perished; others more sublime,
Struck by the envious wrath of man or god,
Have sunk, extinct in their refulgent prime;
And some yet live, treading the thorny road,
Which leads, through toil and hate, to Fame's serene abode.   45

6

But now, thy youngest, dearest one, has perished—
The nursling of thy widowhood, who grew,
Like a pale flower by some sad maiden cherished,

3. Urania, originally the Muse of astronomy. But the name was also an epithet for Aphrodite or Venus, and Shelley converts the Venus who, in Greek myth, had been the lover of Adonis into the mother of Adonais and, like the *Venus Genetrix* of Lucretius' *On the Nature of Things*, the "mighty Mother" of all earthly life.
4. I.e., the echo of Keats's own poems.
5. Corpse.
6. Milton, who had already adopted Urania as the muse of *Paradise Lost*.
7. Spirit.
8. The latest of the great epic poets, after Homer and Dante.

And fed with truelove tears, instead of dew;[9]
Most musical of mourners, weep anew!
Thy extreme[1] hope, the loveliest and the last,
The bloom, whose petals nipped before they blew
Died on the promise of the fruit, is waste;
The broken lily lies—the storm is overpast.

                    7

To that high Capital,[2] where kingly Death
Keeps his pale court in beauty and decay,
He came; and bought, with price of purest breath,
A grave among the eternal.—Come away!
Haste, while the vault of blue Italian day
Is yet his fitting charnel-roof! while still
He lies, as if in dewy sleep he lay;
Awake him not! surely he takes his fill
Of deep and liquid rest, forgetful of all ill.

                    8

He will awake no more, oh, never more!—
Within the twilight chamber spreads apace
The shadow of white Death, and at the door
Invisible Corruption waits to trace
His extreme way to her dim dwelling place;
The eternal Hunger sits, but pity and awe
Soothe her pale rage, nor dares she to deface
So fair a prey, till darkness, and the law
Of change, shall o'er his sleep the mortal curtain draw.

                    9

Oh, weep for Adonais!—The quick Dreams,[3]
The passion-wingéd Ministers of thought,
Who were his flocks, whom near the living streams
Of his young spirit he fed, and whom he taught
The love which was its music, wander not—
Wander no more, from kindling brain to brain,
But droop there, whence they sprung; and mourn their lot
Round the cold heart, where, after their sweet pain,
They ne'er will gather strength, or find a home again.

                    10

And one with trembling hands clasps his cold head,
And fans him with her moonlight wings, and cries:
"Our love, our hope, our sorrow, is not dead;
See, on the silken fringe of his faint eyes,
Like dew upon a sleeping flower, there lies
A tear some Dream has loosened from his brain."
Lost Angel of a ruined Paradise![4]
She knew not 'twas her own; as with no stain
She faded, like a cloud which had outwept its rain.

50

55

60

65

70

75

80

85

90

9. An allusion to an incident in Keats's
Isabella.
1. Last.
2. Rome.

3. The products of his poetic imagination.
4. Lost messenger ("angel") from a
destroyed creative imagination.

11

One from a lucid urn of starry dew
Washed his light limbs as if embalming them;
Another clipped her profuse locks, and threw
The wreath upon him, like an anadem,[5]
Which frozen tears instead of pearls begem;   95
Another in her willful grief would break
Her bow and wingéd reeds, as if to stem
A greater loss with one which was more weak,
And dull the barbéd fire against his frozen cheek.

12

Another Splendor on his mouth alit,   100
That mouth, whence it was wont to draw the breath
Which gave it strength to pierce the guarded wit,[6]
And pass into the panting heart beneath
With lightning and with music: the damp death
Quenched its caress upon his icy lips;   105
And, as a dying meteor stains a wreath
Of moonlight vapor, which the cold night clips,[7]
It flushed through his pale limbs, and passed to its eclipse.

13

And others came . . . Desires and Adorations,
Wingéd Persuasions and veiled Destinies,   110
Splendors, and Glooms, and glimmering Incarnations
Of hopes and fears, and twilight Phantasies;
And Sorrow, with her family of Sighs,
And Pleasure, blind with tears, led by the gleam
Of her own dying smile instead of eyes,   115
Came in slow pomp—the moving pomp might seem
Like pageantry of mist on an autumnal stream.

14

All he had loved, and molded into thought,
From shape, and hue, and odor, and sweet sound,
Lamented Adonais. Morning sought   120
Her eastern watch-tower, and her hair unbound,
Wet with the tears which should adorn the ground,
Dimmed the aërial eyes that kindle day;
Afar the melancholy thunder moaned,
Pale Ocean in unquiet slumber lay,   125
And the wild Winds flew round, sobbing in their dismay.

15

Lost Echo sits amid the voiceless mountains,
And feeds her grief with his remembered lay,
And will no more reply to winds or fountains,
Or amorous birds perched on the young green spray,   130
Or herdsman's horn, or bell at closing day;
Since she can mimic not his lips, more dear
Than those for whose disdain she pined away

---

5. A rich garland.
6. The cautious intellect of the listener.
7. "Cuts off," or else, in the older sense, "embraces."

Into a shadow of all sounds[8]—a drear
Murmur, between their songs, is all the woodmen hear.   135

16

Grief made the young Spring wild, and she threw down
Her kindling buds, as if she Autumn were,
Or they dead leaves; since her delight is flown,
For whom should she have waked the sullen year?
To Phoebus was not Hyacinth so dear[9]   140
Nor to himself Narcissus, as to both
Thou, Adonais: wan they stand and sere
Amid the faint companions of their youth,
With dew all turned to tears; odor, to sighing ruth.[1]

17

Thy spirit's sister, the lorn nightingale   145
Mourns not her mate with such melodious pain;
Not so the eagle, who like thee could scale
Heaven, and could nourish in the sun's domain
Her mighty youth with morning,[2] doth complain,
Soaring and screaming round her empty nest,   150
As Albion[3] wails for thee: the curse of Cain
Light on his[4] head who pierced thy innocent breast,
And scared the angel soul that was its earthly guest!

18

Ah, woe is me! Winter is come and gone,
But grief returns with the revolving year;   155
The airs and streams renew their joyous tone;
The ants, the bees, the swallows reappear;
Fresh leaves and flowers deck the dead Seasons' bier;
The amorous birds now pair in every brake,[5]
And build their mossy homes in field and brere;   160
And the green lizard, and the golden snake,
Like unimprisoned flames, out of their trance awake.

19

Through wood and stream and field and hill and Ocean
A quickening life from the Earth's heart has burst
As it has ever done, with change and motion,   165
From the great morning of the world when first
God dawned on Chaos; in its stream immersed,
The lamps of Heaven flash with a softer light;
All baser things pant with life's sacred thirst,
Diffuse themselves, and spend in love's delight,   170
The beauty and the joy of their renewéd might:

8. Because of her unrequited love for
Narcissus, who was enamored of his
own reflection (line 141), the nymph
Echo pined away until she was only a
voice.
9. Young Hyacinthus was loved by
Phoebus Apollo, who accidentally killed
him in a game of quoits. Apollo made
the hyacinth flower spring from his
blood.

1. Pity.
2. In legend, the aged eagle, to renew
his youth, flies toward the sun until his
old plumage is burned off and the film
cleared away from his eyes.
3. England.
4. I.e., the reviewer of Keats's *Endymion* (see title footnote above).
5. Thicket. "Brere": briar.

20

The leprous corpse, touched by this spirit tender,
Exhales itself in flowers of gentle breath;
Like incarnations of the stars, when splendor
Is changed to fragrance, they illumine death   175
And mock the merry worm that wakes beneath;
Nought we know, dies. Shall that alone which knows
Be as a sword consumed before the sheath
By sightless lightning?[6]—the intense atom glows
A moment, then is quenched in a most cold repose.   180

21

Alas! that all we loved of him should be,
But for our grief, as if it had not been,
And grief itself be mortal! Woe is me!
Whence are we, and why are we? of what scene
The actors or spectators? Great and mean   185
Meet massed in death, who lends what life must borrow.[7]
As long as skies are blue, and fields are green,
Evening must usher night, night urge the morrow,
Month follow month with woe, and year wake year to sorrow.

22

He will awake no more, oh, never more!   190
"Wake thou," cried Misery, "childless Mother, rise
Out of thy sleep, and slake, in thy heart's core,
A wound more fierce than his, with tears and sighs."
And all the Dreams that watched Urania's eyes,
And all the Echoes whom their sister's song   195
Had held in holy silence, cried: "Arise!"
Swift as a Thought by the snake Memory stung,
From her ambrosial rest the fading Splendor[8] sprung.

23

She rose like an autumnal Night, that springs
Out of the East, and follows wild and drear   200
The golden Day, which, on eternal wings,
Even as a ghost abandoning a bier,
Had left the Earth a corpse. Sorrow and fear
So struck, so roused, so rapt Urania;
So saddened round her like an atmosphere   205
Of stormy mist; so swept her on her way
Even to the mournful place where Adonais lay.

24

Out of her secret Paradise she sped,
Through camps and cities rough with stone, and steel,
And human hearts, which to her aery tread   210
Yielding not, wounded the invisible
Palms of her tender feet where'er they fell:

---

6. I.e., the material world, which the mind knows, survives. Shall only the knowing mind be destroyed, like a sword melted by invisible ("sightless") lightning, while the sheath (the body, or material vehicle of the mind) survives?
7. I.e., life is a short-term loan from death.
8. Urania.

And barbéd tongues, and thoughts more sharp than they,
Rent the soft Form they never could repel,
Whose sacred blood, like the young tears of May,   215
Paved with eternal flowers that undeserving way.

25

In the death chamber for a moment Death,
Shamed by the presence of that living Might,
Blushed to annihilation, and the breath
Revisited those lips, and Life's pale light   220
Flashed through those limbs, so late her dear delight.
"Leave me not wild and drear and comfortless,
As silent lightning leaves the starless night!
Leave me not!" cried Urania: her distress
Roused Death: Death rose and smiled, and met her vain caress.

26

"Stay yet awhile! speak to me once again;   226
Kiss me, so long but as a kiss may live;
And in my heartless breast[9] and burning brain
That word, that kiss, shall all thoughts else survive,
With food of saddest memory kept alive,   230
Now thou art dead, as if it were a part
Of thee, my Adonais! I would give
All that I am to be as thou now art!
But I am chained to Time, and cannot thence depart!

27

"O gentle child, beautiful as thou wert,   235
Why didst thou leave the trodden paths of men
Too soon, and with weak hands though mighty heart
Dare the unpastured dragon in his den?
Defenseless as thou wert, oh, where was then
Wisdom the mirrored shield, or scorn the spear?[1]   240
Or hadst thou waited the full cycle, when
Thy spirit should have filled its crescent sphere,
The monsters of life's waste had fled from thee like deer.

28

"The herded wolves, bold only to pursue;
The obscene ravens, clamorous o'er the dead;   245
The vultures to the conqueror's banner true
Who feed where Desolation first has fed,
And whose wings rain contagion—how they fled,
When, like Apollo, from his golden bow
The Pythian of the age[2] one arrow sped   250
And smiled!—The spoilers tempt no second blow,
They fawn on the proud feet that spurn them lying low.

9. Because her heart has been given to Adonais.

1. Young defenseless Keats confronting the literary reviewers is paralleled with Perseus in the myth, who attacked Medusa (the "dragon") with his spear, avoiding her direct gaze (which turned men into stone) by looking only at her reflection in his shield.

2. Apollo was called "the Pythian" because he had slain the dragon Python; the allusion here is to Byron, who "slew" the critics in *English Bards and Scotch Reviewers* (1809).

29

"The sun comes forth, and many reptiles spawn;
He sets, and each ephemeral insect then
Is gathered into death without a dawn,   255
And the immortal stars awake again;
So is it in the world of living men:
A godlike mind soars forth, in its delight
Making earth bare and veiling heaven,[3] and when
It sinks, the swarms that dimmed or shared its light   260
Leave to its kindred lamps[4] the spirit's awful night."

30

Thus ceased she: and the mountain shepherds came,
Their garlands sere, their magic mantles rent;
The Pilgrim of Eternity,[5] whose fame
Over his living head like Heaven is bent,   265
An early but enduring monument,
Came, veiling all the lightnings of his song
In sorrow; from her wilds Ierne sent
The sweetest lyrist[6] of her saddest wrong,
And Love taught Grief to fall like music from his tongue.   270

31

Midst others of less note, came one frail Form,[7]
A phantom among men; companionless
As the last cloud of an expiring storm
Whose thunder is its knell; he, as I guess,
Had gazed on Nature's naked loveliness,   275
Actaeon-like,[8] and now he fled astray
With feeble steps o'er the world's wilderness,
And his own thoughts, along that rugged way,
Pursued, like raging hounds, their father and their prey.

32

A pardlike[9] Spirit beautiful and swift—   280
A Love in desolation masked—a Power
Girt round with weakness—it can scarce uplift
The weight of the superincumbent hour;
It is a dying lamp, a falling shower,
A breaking billow—even whilst we speak   285
Is it not broken? On the withering flower
The killing sun smiles brightly: on a cheek
The life can burn in blood, even while the heart may break.

33

His head was bound with pansies overblown,
And faded violets, white, and pied, and blue;
And a light spear topped with a cypress cone,   290

3. As the sun reveals the earth but veils the other stars.
4. The other stars, or divine minds.
5. Byron, who had referred to Childe Harold as one of the "wanderers o'er eternity" (III.669).
6. Thomas Moore (1779–1852) the poet from Ireland ("Ierne").
7. Shelley himself.
8. Actaeon while hunting came upon Diana bathing, and in punishment was turned into a stag and torn to pieces by his own hounds.
9. Leopardlike.

Round whose rude shaft dark ivy tresses grew[1]
Yet dripping with the forest's noonday dew,
Vibrated, as the ever-beating heart
Shook the weak hand that grasped it; of that crew   295
He came the last, neglected and apart;
A herd-abandoned deer struck by the hunter's dart.

34
All stood aloof, and at his partial[2] moan
Smiled through their tears; well knew that gentle band
Who in another's fate now wept his own,   300
As in the accents of an unknown land
He sung new sorrow; sad Urania scanned
The Stranger's mien, and murmured: "Who art thou?"
He answered not, but with a sudden hand
Made bare his branded and ensanguined brow,   305
Which was like Cain's or Christ's[3]—oh! that it should be so!

35
What softer voice is hushed over the dead?
Athwart what brow is that dark mantle thrown?
What form leans sadly o'er the white deathbed,
In mockery[4] of monumental stone,   310
The heavy heart heaving without a moan?
If it be he,[5] who, gentlest of the wise,
Taught, soothed, loved, honored the departed one,
Let me not vex, with inharmonious sighs,
The silence of that heart's accepted sacrifice.   315

36
Our Adonais has drunk poison—oh!
What deaf and viperous murderer could crown
Life's early cup with such a draught of woe?
The nameless worm[6] would now itself disown:
It felt, yet could escape, the magic tone   320
Whose prelude held[7] all envy, hate, and wrong,
But what was howling in one breast alone,
Silent with expectation of the song,
Whose master's hand is cold, whose silver lyre unstrung.

37
Live thou, whose infamy is not thy fame!   325
Live! fear no heavier chastisement from me,
Thou noteless blot on a remembered name!
But be thyself, and know thyself to be!
And ever at thy season be thou free
To spill the venom when thy fangs o'erflow;   330

1. Like the thyrsus, the leaf-entwined staff carried by Dionysus, deity of vegetation.
2. I.e., with reference to himself.
3. His bloody ("ensanguined") brow bore a mark like that with which God had branded Cain for murdering Abel —or like that left by Christ's crown of thorns.
4. Imitation.
5. Leigh Hunt, close friend both of Keats and Shelley.
6. Serpent. In accordance with the journalistic custom of that time, the reviewer of *Endymion* had remained "nameless."
7. Held back, checked.

Remorse and Self-contempt shall cling to thee;
Hot Shame shall burn upon thy secret brow,
And like a beaten hound tremble thou shalt—as now.

38

Nor let us weep that our delight is fled
Far from these carrion kites that scream below;   335
He wakes or sleeps with the enduring dead;
Thou canst not soar where he is sitting now.—
Dust to the dust! but the pure spirit shall flow
Back to the burning fountain whence it came,
A portion of the Eternal,[8] which must glow   340
Through time and change, unquenchably the same,
Whilst thy cold embers[9] choke the sordid hearth of shame.

39

Peace, peace! he is not dead, he doth not sleep—
He hath awakened from the dream of life—
'Tis we, who lost in stormy visions, keep   345
With phantoms an unprofitable strife,
And in mad trance, strike with our spirit's knife
Invulnerable nothings.—We decay
Like corpses in a charnel; fear and grief
Convulse us and consume us day by day,   350
And cold hopes swarm like worms within our living clay.

40

He has outsoared the shadow of our night;[1]
Envy and calumny and hate and pain,
And that unrest which men miscall delight,
Can touch him not and torture not again;   355
From the contagion of the world's slow stain
He is secure, and now can never mourn
A heart grown cold, a head grown gray in vain;
Nor, when the spirit's self has ceased to burn,
With sparkless ashes load an unlamented urn.   360

41

He lives, he wakes—'tis Death is dead, not he;
Mourn not for Adonais.—Thou young Dawn,
Turn all thy dew to splendor, for from thee
The spirit thou lamentest is not gone;
Ye caverns and ye forests, cease to moan!   365
Cease, ye faint flowers and fountains, and thou Air,
Which like a mourning veil thy scarf hadst thrown
O'er the abandoned Earth, now leave it bare
Even to the joyous stars which smile on its despair![2]

8. According to a Neo-Platonic world view, all mortal life is an overflow from the Absolute, imaged as the eternal fountain, and also as the radiant light-source, of life, which emanates down through the dross of matter (stanza 43) and recirculates continuously to its source. The recognition of this fact is the turning point of the poem: it leads to the discovery that our existence in the material world is but "the dream of life"—that it is, in fact, the real death.
9. I.e., the reviewer's ashes.
1. Keats has soared beyond night, which Shelley (it is one of his favorite figures) accurately describes as the shadow cast by the earth as it intercepts the radiance of the sun.
2. Again the science is accurate: it is the envelope of air around the earth

42

He is made one with Nature: there is heard   370
His voice in all her music, from the moan
Of thunder, to the song of night's sweet bird;
He is a presence to be felt and known
In darkness and in light, from herb and stone,
Spreading itself where'er that Power may move   375
Which has withdrawn his being to its own;
Which wields the world with never-wearied love,
Sustains it from beneath, and kindles it above.

43

He is a portion of the loveliness
Which once he made more lovely: he doth bear   380
His part, while the one Spirit's plastic[3] stress
Sweeps through the dull dense world, compelling there
All new successions to the forms they wear;
Torturing th' unwilling dross that checks its flight
To its own likeness, as each mass may bear;[4]   385
And bursting in its beauty and its might
From trees and beasts and men into the Heaven's light.

44

The splendors of the firmament of time
May be eclipsed, but are extinguished not;
Like stars to their appointed height they climb,
And death is a low mist which cannot blot   390
The brightness it may veil.[5] When lofty thought
Lifts a young heart above its mortal lair,
And love and life contend in it, for what
Shall be its earthly doom, the dead live there[6]
And move like winds of light on dark and stormy air.   395

45

The inheritors of unfulfilled renown[7]
Rose from their thrones, built beyond mortal thought,
Far in the Unapparent. Chatterton
Rose pale—his solemn agony had not   400
Yet faded from him; Sidney, as he fought
And as he fell and as he lived and loved

(lines 366–67) which, by diffusing and
reflecting the sunlight, renders the stars
invisible in the daytime.
3. Molding, shaping.
4. I.e. to the degree that a particular
substance will permit. The concept is an
ancient one, that different kinds of matter offer variable resistance to the attempt of Spirit to realize itself on earth.
The stars ("the Heaven's light," line
387) are of such a refined matter that
they can approximate to the pure radiance of the "one Spirit" itself.
5. The spirits of great poets ("splendors of the firmament of time"), like
stars in daylight, continue to exist even
when invisible to earthly eyes because
"eclipsed" or "veiled" by death. In

Shelley's image, the viewpoint is transferred from earth to airless interstellar
space: from this station we see that the
radiance of a star persists, even if it is
temporarily "eclipsed" from the earth
by the intervention of another heavenly body, or "veiled" by the "low
mist" of the atmosphere.
6. I.e., in that "young heart" (line
393).
7. Poets who died young, before achieving their full measure of renown.
Thomas Chatterton (1752–70) committed suicide at 17, Sir Philip Sidney
(1554–86) died in battle at 32, and
Lucan killed himself at 26 to escape
Nero's sentence of death.

Sublimely mild, a Spirit without spot,
Arose; and Lucan, by his death approved:[8]
Oblivion as they rose shrank like a thing reproved.   405

46

And many more, whose names on Earth are dark,
But whose transmitted effluence cannot die
So long as fire outlives the parent spark,
Rose, robed in dazzling immortality.
"Thou art become as one of us," they cry,   410
"It was for thee yon kingless sphere has long
Swung blind in unascended majesty,
Silent alone amid an Heaven of Song.
Assume thy wingéd throne, thou Vesper of our throng!"[9]

47

Who mourns for Adonais? Oh, come forth,   415
Fond wretch! and know thyself and him aright.
Clasp with thy panting soul the pendulous[1] Earth;
As from a center, dart thy spirit's light
Beyond all worlds, until its spacious might
Satiate the void circumference: then shrink   420
Even to a point within our day and night;[2]
And keep thy heart light lest it make thee sink
When hope has kindled hope, and lured thee to the brink.

48

Or go to Rome, which is the sepulcher,
Oh, not of him, but of our joy: 'tis nought   425
That ages, empires, and religions there
Lie buried in the ravage they have wrought;
For such as he can lend—they borrow not
Glory from those who made the world their prey;
And he is gathered to the kings of thought   430
Who waged contention with their time's decay,
And of the past are all that cannot pass away

49

Go thou to Rome—at once the Paradise,
The grave, the city, and the wilderness;
And where its wrecks like shattered mountains rise,   435
And flowering weeds, and fragrant copses dress
The bones of Desolation's nakedness
Pass, till the spirit of the spot shall lead
Thy footsteps to a slope of green access[3]
Where, like an infant's smile, over the dead   440
A light of laughing flowers along the grass is spread;

8. Justified, proved worthy.
9. Adonais assumes his rightful place in the unoccupied sphere of Vesper, the evening star. See the epigraph and cf. lines 35–36. Shelley also adopts here the ancient view of the music of the spheres ("an Heaven of Song").
1. Suspended.
2. Shelley asks the wretch so foolish ("fond") as to mourn Adonais to stretch his imagination to encompass the poet's present cosmic viewpoint (see stanza 55 and note 5) and then contract ("shrink") back to his ordinary tiny station on earth where, unlike Adonais, we have an alternation of day and night (life and death).
3. The Protestant Cemetery, Keats's burial place.

50

And gray walls molder round, on which dull Time
Feeds, like slow fire upon a hoary brand;
And one keen pyramid with wedge sublime,[4]
Pavilioning the dust of him who planned
This refuge for his memory, doth stand   445
Like flame transformed to marble; and beneath,
A field is spread, on which a newer band[5]
Have pitched in Heaven's smile their camp of death,
Welcoming him we lose with scarce extinguished breath.   450

51

Here pause: these graves are all too young as yet
To have outgrown the sorrow which consigned
Its charge to each; and if the seal is set,
Here, on one fountain of a mourning mind,
Break it not thou! too surely shalt thou find   455
Thine own well full, if thou returnest home,
Of tears and gall. From the world's bitter wind
Seek shelter in the shadow of the tomb.
What Adonais is, why fear we to become?

52

The One[6] remains, the many change and pass;   460
Heaven's light forever shines, Earth's shadows fly;
Life, like a dome of many-colored glass,
Stains the white radiance of Eternity,
Until Death tramples it to fragments.—Die,
If thou wouldst be with that which thou dost seek!   465
Follow where all is fled!—Rome's azure sky,
Flowers, ruins, statues, music, words, are weak
The glory they transfuse with fitting truth to speak.

53

Why linger, why turn back, why shrink, my Heart?
Thy hopes are gone before: from all things here   470
They have departed; thou shouldst now depart!
A light is passed from the revolving year,
And man, and woman; and what still is dear
Attracts to crush, repels to make thee wither.
The soft sky smiles—the low wind whispers near: 475
'Tis Adonais calls! oh, hasten thither,
No more let Life divide what Death can join together.

54

That Light whose smile kindles the Universe,
That Beauty in which all things work and move,
That Benediction which the eclipsing Curse   480
Of birth can quench not, that sustaining Love
Which through the web of being blindly wove

---

4. The tomb of Gaius Cestius, a Roman
statesman.
5. The recently buried dead (the cemetery had been established not long before), including Shelley's 3-year-old

son, William, referred to in lines
453–55.
6. The Absolute, the one fountain of
all light, of lines 339–40.

By man and beast and earth and air and sea,
Burns bright or dim, as each are mirrors of [6a]
The fire for which all thirst,[7] now beams on me,   485
Consuming the last clouds of cold mortality.

55

The breath whose might I have invoked in song[8]
Descends on me; my spirit's bark is driven,
Far from the shore, far from the trembling throng
Whose sails were never to the tempest given;   490
The massy earth and spheréd skies are riven!
I am borne darkly, fearfully, afar;
Whilst, burning through the inmost veil of Heaven,
The soul of Adonais, like a star,
Beacons from the abode where the Eternal are.   495
June, 1821   1821

Lines: When the Lamp Is Shattered

1

When the lamp is shattered
The light in the dust lies dead—
When the cloud is scattered
The rainbow's glory is shed.
When the lute is broken,   5
Sweet tones are remembered not;
When the lips have spoken,
Loved accents are soon forgot.

2

As music and splendor
Survive not the lamp and the lute,   10
The heart's echoes render
No song when the spirit is mute—
No song but sad dirges,
Like the wind through a ruined cell,
Or the mournful surges   15
That ring the dead seaman's knell.

3

When hearts have once mingled
Love first leaves the well-built nest;[1]
The weak one is singled
To endure what it once possessed.   20
O Love! who bewailest
The frailty of all things here,

6a. According to the degree that each mirrors.
7. The inordinate "thirst" of the human spirit to return to its source in the "burning fountain" of eternal light, beauty, and love (lines 339–40).
8. The reference is to the "breath of Autumn's being," which Shelley had "invoked," or prayed for, two years before, in the last two stanzas of *Ode to the West Wind*. Lines 488–90 describe what it feels like to be "inspired"—literally, breathed or blown into.
1. I.e., Love first flies away from the stronger heart.

Why choose you the frailest[2]
For your cradle, your home, and your bier?

4

Its passions will rock thee   25
As the storms rock the ravens on high;
  Bright reason will mock thee,
Like the sun from a wintry sky.
  From thy nest every rafter
Will rot, and thine eagle home[3]   30
  Leave thee naked to laughter,
When leaves fall and cold winds come.

1822   1824

A Dirge

Rough wind, that moanest loud
  Grief too sad for song;
Wild wind, when sullen cloud
  Knells all the night long;
Sad storm, whose tears are vain,   5
Bare woods, whose branches strain,
Deep caves and dreary main—
  Wail, for the world's wrong!

1822   1824

To Jane: The Invitation[1]

Best and brightest, come away!
Fairer far than this fair Day,
Which, like thee to those in sorrow,
Comes to bid a sweet good-morrow
To the rough Year just awake   5
In its cradle on the brake.
The brightest hour of unborn Spring,
Through the winter wandering,
Found, it seems, the halcyon Morn
To hoar February born.   10
Bending from Heaven, in azure mirth,
It kissed the forehead of the Earth,
And smiled upon the silent sea,
And bade the frozen streams be free,

2. The heart.
3. The nest of Love (the heart), like that of the eagle, is exposed to the winter sun and vulnerable to the winter weather.
1. "Jane" is Jane Williams, common-law wife of Edward Williams, Shelley's close friend. This invitation to an outdoor excursion exemplifies Shelley's grace and urbanity, writing in the ancient tradition of the verse letter.

And waked to music all their fountains, 15
And breathed upon the frozen mountains,
And like a prophetess of May
Strewed flowers upon the barren way,
Making the wintry world appear
Like one on whom thou smilest, dear. 20
Away, away, from men and towns,
To the wild wood and the downs—
To the silent wilderness
Where the soul need not repress
Its music lest it should not find 25
An echo in another's mind,
While the touch of Nature's art
Harmonizes heart to heart.
I leave this notice on my door
For each accustomed visitor: 30
"I am gone into the fields
To take what this sweet hour yields;
Reflection, you may come tomorrow,
Sit by the fireside with Sorrow.—
You with the unpaid bill, Despair— 35
You, tiresome verse-reciter, Care—
I will pay you in the grave—
Death will listen to your stave.
Expectation too, be off!
Today is for itself enough; 40
Hope, in pity mock not Woe
With smiles, nor follow where I go;
Long having lived on thy sweet food,
At length I find one moment's good
After long pain—with all your love, 45
This you never told me of."

Radiant Sister of the Day,
Awake! arise! and come away!
To the wild woods and the plains,
And the pools where winter rains 50
Image all their roof of leaves,
Where the pine its garland weaves
Of sapless green and ivy dun
Round stems that never kiss the sun;
Where the lawns and pastures be, 55
And the sandhills of the sea;
Where the melting hoarfrost wets
The daisy-star that never sets,
And windflowers, and violets,
Which yet join not scent to hue, 60
Crown the pale year weak and new;
When the night is left behind
In the deep east, dun and blind,

And the blue noon is over us,
And the multitudinous
Billows murmur at our feet,
Where the earth and ocean meet,
And all things seem only one
In the universal sun.

1822   1824

To Jane: The Keen Stars Were Twinkling

1

The keen stars were twinkling,
And the fair moon was rising among them,
   Dear Jane!
The guitar was tinkling,
But the notes were not sweet till you sung them
   Again.

2

As the moon's soft splendor
O'er the faint cold starlight of Heaven
   Is thrown,
So your voice most tender
To the strings without soul had then given
   Its own.

3

The stars will awaken,
Though the moon sleep a full hour later,
   Tonight;
No leaf will be shaken
Whilst the dews of your melody scatter
   Delight.

4

Though the sound overpowers,
Sing again, with your dear voice revealing
   A tone
Of some world far from ours,
Where music and moonlight and feeling
   Are one.

1822   1832

Lines Written in the Bay of Lerici[1]

She left me at the silent time
When the moon had ceased to climb
The azure path of Heaven's steep,
And like an albatross asleep,

1. Another of Shelley's last lyrics, inspired by Jane Williams.

Balanced on her wings of light,   5
Hovered in the purple night,
Ere she sought her ocean nest
In the chambers of the West.
She left me, and I stayed alone
Thinking over every tone   10
Which, though silent to the ear,
The enchanted heart could hear,
Like notes which die when born, but still
Haunt the echoes of the hill;
And feeling ever—oh, too much!—   15
The soft vibration of her touch,
As if her gentle hand, even now,
Lightly trembled on my brow;
And thus, although she absent were,
Memory gave me all of her   20
That even Fancy dares to claim:
Her presence had made weak and tame
All passions, and I lived alone
In the time which is our own;
The past and future were forgot,   25
As they had been, and would be, not.
But soon, the guardian angel gone,
The daemon² reassumed his throne
In my faint heart. I dare not speak
My thoughts, but thus disturbed and weak   30
I sat and saw the vessels glide
Over the ocean bright and wide,
Like spirit-wingéd chariots sent
O'er some serenest element
For ministrations strange and far;   35
As if to some Elysian star
They sailed for drink to medicine
Such sweet and bitter pain as mine.
And the wind that winged their flight
From the land came fresh and light,   40
And the scent of sleeping flowers,
And the coolness of the hours
Of dew, and sweet warmth left by day,
Were scattered o'er the twinkling bay.
And the fisher with his lamp   45
And spear about the low rocks damp
Crept, and struck the fish which came
To worship the delusive flame.
Too happy they, whose pleasure sought
Extinguishes all sense and thought   50
Of the regret that pleasure leaves,
Destroying life alone, not peace!

1822   1862

2. I.e., the passions, with compulsion to look before and after.

The Triumph of Life Shelley left this poem in process when he died in early July, 1822. He took its central event from Petrarch's six *Trionfi*, "triumph" having the meaning of the Latin *triumphus*, the ceremonial entrance of a victorious general into ancient Rome in a procession which included his prisoners of war. The poem is strongly influenced by Dante's *Divine Comedy*, not only in its *terza rima* (the verse form also of Petrarch's *Trionfi*) but also in over-all conception, in a number of narrative details, and in style. It is notable that Shelley, like Keats in *The Fall of Hyperion*, left unfinished at his death a long poem in the form of a Dantean dream-vision, in which the poet faces up to the discovery that human history has been a continuous process of human suffering and defeat —and, in Shelley's version, an almost unrelieved narrative of human weakness and evil-doing.

We ought to be cautious, however, of a current tendency to dramatize Shelley's career by imposing on it the form of a tragic plot, moving inexorably to the dead end of *The Triumph of Life*, from which there was no exit except the poet's own death. The vision in the poem of the frantic, quiescent, or despairing captives in the procession of Life—including all who have in the least degree compromised in spirit or aspiration with the passions, temptations, or values of the fleshly life and the material world— is a desolate one, but its darkness is not unrelieved. There are the "sacred few" among humanity who have not compromised at all. The band of "mighty captives" chained to Life's car represent a full spectrum of relative worth, from mighty villains to mighty heroes. And although we lack Shelley's answer to the question posed at the end of the fragment—"then, what is Life?"—there is no definitive evidence that he planned to depart from the precedent of all his other long poems, in which he allowed some scope of possibility for redeeming life by the cardinal Shelleyan virtues; and above all by that love which, as he says near the close of *The Triumph of Life* (lines 472–76), led Dante safely "from the lowest depths of Hell" through Purgatory to Heaven and back to earth.

But any statement of how Shelley would have ended this fragment is speculative. What is certain is the vitality, the tone, and the timbre of the poetic voice in the portion before us. No other narrative poem quite matches in its opening the puissance, impetus, and assurance of Shelley's forty-line induction, as the sun springs forth like a bridegroom coming out of his chamber, to be greeted with the quiet ceremonies of natural worship by the revolving world, to whom it brings light, heat, and joyous reawakening—to all except the poet who, having waked while the world slept in darkness, now composes himself to sleep as the world awakes, to undergo, in the transparent darkness of a trance, the crisis of his vision. And the promise of this extraordinary opening is fulfilled in the unflagging narrative drive, and in the ease, clarity, and precision of language, of the rest of the poem, which expresses an *élan* even in its grimmest passages.

The Triumph of Life does not sound like the voice of a defeated poet at the end of his tether, but of a poet who, just attaining the height of his powers, was making a masterful new beginning, when fate slit the thin spun life.

The Triumph of Life[1]

Swift as a spirit hastening to his task
  Of glory & of good, the Sun sprang forth
Rejoicing in his splendour, & the mask

  Of darkness fell from the awakened Earth.
The smokeless altars of the mountain snows   5
  Flamed above crimson clouds, & at the birth

Of light, the Ocean's orison[2] arose
  To which the birds tempered their matin lay.
All flowers in field or forest which unclose

  Their trembling eyelids to the kiss of day,   10
Swinging their censers in the element,
  With orient[3] incense lit by the new ray

Burned slow & inconsumably, & sent
  Their odorous sighs up to the smiling air,
And in succession due, did Continent,   15

  Isle, Ocean, & all things that in them wear
The form & character of mortal mould
  Rise as the Sun their father rose, to bear

Their portion of the toil which he of old
  Took as his own & then imposed on them;   20
But I, whom thoughts which must remain untold

  Had kept as wakeful as the stars that gem
The cone of night,[4] now they were laid asleep,
  Stretched my faint limbs beneath the hoary stem

Which an old chestnut flung athwart the steep   25
  Of a green Apennine:[5] before me fled
The night; behind me rose the day; the Deep

  Was at my feet, & Heaven above my head
When a strange trance over my fancy grew
  Which was not slumber, for the shade it spread   30

---

1. The text is that newly edited from Shelley's manuscript by Donald H. Reiman, in *Shelley's "The Triumph of Life": A Critical Study* (Urbana, Illinois, 1965). Shelley left a difficult and uncompleted manuscript draft; as Reiman says, "had Shelley lived, he would have revised and corrected [it] extensively." In the best tradition of modern textual scholarship, the editor has worked out Shelley's final intentions "both from the physical evidence of the manuscript and from the prosodic laws of *terza rima*." We reprint Reiman's text unaltered (without his careful textual notes) as much closer than the earlier published versions to what Shelley actually wrote. Blank spaces in the text reproduce blanks in the manuscript; some marks of punctuation (e.g., quotation marks) are Reiman's.
2. Prayer; to which (in the next line) the birds tuned their chanted morning prayer.
3. Morning.
4. The conical shadow cast by the earth as it intercepts the sunlight.
5. One of the Apennines, the chain of mountains extending down the Italian peninsula.

Was so transparent that the scene came through
  As clear as when a veil of light is drawn
O'er evening hills they glimmer;[6] and I knew

  That I had felt the freshness of that dawn,
Bathed in the same cold dew my brow & hair   35
  And sate as thus upon that slope of lawn

Under the self same bough, & heard as there
  The birds, the fountains & the Ocean hold
Sweet talk in music through the enamoured air.
And then a Vision on my brain was rolled . .   40

As in that trance of wondrous thought I lay
  This was the tenour of my waking dream.
Methought I sate beside a public way

  Thick strewn with summer dust, & a great stream
Of people there was hurrying to & fro   45
  Numerous as gnats upon the evening gleam,

All hastening onward, yet none seemed to know
  Whither he went, or whence he came, or why
He made one of the multitude, yet so

  Was borne amid the crowd as through the sky   50
One of the million leaves of summer's bier.—
  Old age & youth, manhood & infancy,

Mixed in one mighty torrent did appear,
  Some flying from the thing they feared & some
Seeking the object of another's fear,   55

  And others as with steps towards the tomb
Pored on the trodden worms that crawled beneath,
  And others mournfully within the gloom

Of their own shadow walked, and called it death . . .
  And some fled from it[7] as it were a ghost,   60
Half fainting in the affliction of vain breath.

  But more with motions which each other crost
Pursued or shunned the shadows the clouds threw
  Or birds within the noonday ether lost,

Upon that path where flowers never grew;   65
  And weary with vain toil & faint for thirst
Heard not the fountains whose melodious dew

  Out of their mossy cells forever burst
Nor felt the breeze which from the forest told
  Of grassy paths, & wood lawns interspersed   70

6. "They" refers to "hills," in the same   7. I.e., from their own shadow (line 59).
line.

With overarching elms & caverns cold,
  And violet banks where sweet dreams brood, but they
Pursued their serious folly as of old . . . .

And as I gazed methought that in the way
  The throng grew wilder, as the woods of June   75
  When the South wind shakes the extinguished day.—

And a cold glare, intenser than the noon
  But icy cold, obscured with   light
The Sun as he the stars. Like the young moon

  When on the sunlit limits of the night   80
Her white shell trembles amid crimson air
  And whilst the sleeping tempest gathers might

Doth, as a herald of its coming, bear
  The ghost of her dead Mother, whose dim form
Bends in dark ether from her infant's chair,[8]   85

  So came a chariot on the silent storm
Of its own rushing splendour, and a Shape
  So sate within as one whom years deform

Beneath a dusky hood & double cape
  Crouching within the shadow of a tomb,   90
And o'er what seemed the head, a cloud like crape,

  Was bent a dun & faint etherial gloom
Tempering the light, upon the chariot's beam
  A Janus-visaged[9] Shadow did assume

The guidance of that wonder-wingéd team.   95
  The Shapes which drew it in thick lightnings
Were lost: I heard alone on the air's soft stream

  The music of their ever moving wings.
All the four faces of that charioteer
  Had their eyes banded . . . little profit brings   100

Speed in the van & blindness in the rear,
  Nor then avail the beams that quench the Sun
Or that his banded eyes could pierce the sphere

  Of all that is, has been, or will be done.—
So ill was the car guided, but it past   105
  With solemn speed majestically on . . .

8. The crescent new moon bearing the faint outline of the full moon in its arms—the omen of a coming storm, as in Coleridge's *Dejection: An Ode*, epigraph and lines 9–14. The parallel is to the crescent-formed chariot bearing the dark Shape of Life.
9. The Roman god Janus was represented with two faces, looking before and after. The shadowy charioteer guiding his team (which is invisible in the glare), however, has four faces, all of them blindfolded ("banded," line 100). Harold Bloom points out that this description of the chariot of Life is a parodic version of Ezekiel's vision of a divine chariot in the likeness of four living creatures, each having four faces, and in their progress forming rings which "were full of eyes" (Ezekiel i.4–28); echoed in *Paradise Lost* VI. 749–72.

The crowd gave way, & I arose aghast,
  Or seemed to rise, so mighty was the trance,
And saw like clouds upon the thunder blast

    The million with fierce song and maniac dance   110
Raging around; such seemed the jubilee
    As when to greet some conqueror's advance

Imperial Rome poured forth her living sea
    From senatehouse & prison & theatre
When Freedom left those who upon the free   115

    Had bound a yoke which soon they stooped to bear.[1]

Nor wanted here the true similitude
    Of a triumphal pageant, for where'er

The chariot rolled a captive multitude
    Was driven; althose who had grown old in power   120
Or misery,—all who have their age subdued,

    By action or by suffering, and whose hour
Was drained to its last sand in weal or woe,
    So that the trunk survived both fruit & flower;

All those whose fame or infamy must grow   125
    Till the great winter lay the form & name
Of their own earth with them forever low,[2]

    All but the sacred few who could not tame
Their spirits to the Conqueror, but as soon
    As they had touched the world with living flame   130

Fled back like eagles to their native noon,
    Or those who put aside the diadem
Of earthly thrones or gems, till the last one

    Were there;—for they of Athens & Jerusalem[3]
Were neither mid the mighty captives seen   135
    Nor mid the ribald crowd that followed them

Or fled before .. Now swift, fierce & obscene
    The wild dance maddens in the van, & those
Who lead it, fleet as shadows on the green,

    Outspeed the chariot & without repose   140
Mix with each other in tempestuous measure
    To savage music .... Wilder as it grows,

1. I.e., free men who are enslaved become subservient in spirit.
2. Until the world shall end in ice.
3. The "captive multitude" (line 119) following the chariot include all the men whose exceptional power or talent had made them famous or infamous (line 125), except the "sacred few." The latter are divided into two classes: those who having touched the world with their purifying flame had died young, and those who having lived into older age had resisted the corrupting influence of "earthly thrones or gems" (line 133). These few included, doubtless, Socrates and Jesus ("of Athens and Jerusalem," line 134), but how many others the text does not specify.

They, tortured by the agonizing pleasure,
   Convulsed & on the rapid whirlwinds spun
Of that fierce spirit, whose unholy leisure   145

   Was soothed by mischief since the world begun,
Throw back their heads & loose their streaming hair,
   And in their dance round her who dims the Sun

Maidens & youths fling their wild arms in air
   As their feet twinkle; they recede, and now   150
Bending within each other's atmosphere

   Kindle invisibly; and as they glow
Like moths by light attracted & repelled,
   Oft to new bright destruction come & go.

Till like two clouds into one vale impelled   155
   That shake the mountains when their lightnings mingle
And die in rain,—the fiery band which held

   Their natures, snaps . . . ere the shock cease to tingle
One falls and then another in the path
   Senseless, nor is the desolation single,   160

Yet ere I can say *where* the chariot hath
   Past over them; nor other trace I find
But as of foam after the Ocean's wrath

   Is spent upon the desert shore.—Behind,
Old men, and women foully disarrayed   165
   Shake their grey hair in the insulting wind,

Limp in the dance & strain with limbs decayed
   To reach the car of light which leaves them still
Farther behind & deeper in the shade.

   But not the less with impotence of will   170
They wheel, though ghastly shadows interpose
   Round them & round each other, and fulfill

Their work and to the dust whence they arose
   Sink & corruption veils them as they lie
And frost in these performs what fire in those.[4]   175

   Struck to the heart by this sad pageantry,
Half to myself I said, "And what is this?
   Whose shape is that within the car? & why"—

4. The narrator sees three separate companies of captives: (1) the "maidens and youths" who in a Dionysian intoxication, dance in an erotic frenzy, meet, couple, and fall senseless, to be crushed by the onrushing chariot (lines 137–64); (2) the foul and ribald "old men and women" at the rear of the total procession, attempting impotently to perform the same dance as the young (lines 136, 164–75); (3) the "mighty captives," men with high capacities for good who have to various degrees been corrupted by Life, who are chained to the chariot in the middle of the procession (lines 119–27, 135). (In the Roman triumphs, the captive chieftains were bound to the conqueror's chariot, to heighten their dishonor.)

I would have added—"is all here amiss?"
    But a voice answered . . "Life" . . . I turned & knew   180
(O Heaven have mercy on such wretchedness!)

    That what I thought was an old root which grew
To strange distortion out of the hill side
    Was indeed one of that deluded crew,

And that the grass which methought hung so wide   185
    And white, was but his thin discoloured hair,
And that the holes it vainly sought to hide

    Were or had been eyes.—"If thou canst forbear
To join the dance, which I had well forborne,"[5]

    Said the grim Feature, of my thought aware,   190

"I will now tell that which to this deep scorn
    Led me & my companions, and relate
The progress of the pageant since the morn;

    "If thirst of knowledge doth not thus abate,
Follow it even to the night, but I   195
    Am weary" . . . Then like one who with the weight

Of his own words is staggered, wearily
    He paused, and ere he could resume, I cried,
"First who art thou?" . . . "Before thy memory

    "I feared, loved, hated, suffered, did, & died,[6]   200
And if the spark with which Heaven lit my spirit
    Earth had with purer nutriment supplied

"Corruption would not now thus much inherit
    Of what was once Rousseau—nor this disguise
Stained that within which still disdains to wear it.—   205

    "If I have been extinguished, yet there rise
A thousand beacons from the spark I bore."—[7]
    "And who are those chained to the car?" "The Wise,

"The great, the unforgotten: they who wore
    Mitres & helms & crowns, or wreathes of light,[8]   210
Signs of thought's empire over thought; their lore

    "Taught them not this—to know themselves; their might
Could not repress the mutiny within,
    And for the morn of truth they feigned, deep night

5. I.e., which I would have done well
to avoid. "Feature": in the old sense,
"form," "shape."
6. I.e., Rousseau had lived and died before Shelley was born.
7. The sparks of Rousseau's writings
had lighted a thousand signal fires—including that of the French Revolution,
of which one child was Napoleon, described in lines 215–27.
8. I.e., mitered churchmen, helmeted
soldiers, crowned kings, and philosophers
adorned with wreaths composed of light.
With line 208 Rousseau takes up the
description in detail of the captives
chained to the chariot (see footnote for
line 175).

"Caught them ere evening." "Who is he with chin   215
   Upon his breast and hands crost on his chain?"
"The Child of a fierce hour; he sought to win

   "The world, and lost all it did contain
Of greatness, in its hope destroyed; & more
   Of fame & peace than Virtue's self can gain   220

"Without the opportunity which bore
   Him on its eagle's pinion to the peak
From which a thousand climbers have before

   "Fall'n as Napoleon fell."—I felt my cheek
Alter to see the great form pass away   225
   Whose grasp had left the giant world so weak

That every pigmy kicked it as it lay—
   And much I grieved to think how power & will
In opposition rule our mortal day—

   And why God made irreconcilable   230
Good & the means of good;[9] and for despair
   I half disdained mine eye's desire to fill

With the spent vision of the times that were
   And scarce have ceased to be . . . "Dust thou behold,"
Said then my guide, "those spoilers spoiled, Voltaire,   235

   "Frederic, & Kant, Catherine, & Leopold,[1]
Chained hoary anarchs,[2] demagogue & sage
   Whose name the fresh world thinks already old—

"For in the battle Life & they did wage
   She remained conqueror—I was overcome   240
By my own heart alone,[3] which neither age

   "Nor tears nor infamy nor now the tomb
Could temper to its object."—"Let them pass"—
   I cried—"the world & its mysterious doom

"Is not so much more glorious than it was   245
   That I desire to worship those who drew
New figures on its false & fragile glass

   "As the old faded."—"Figures ever new
Rise on the bubble, paint them how you may;
   We have but thrown, as those before us threw,   250

9. I.e., the possession of the will to do good is opposed to the possession of power, the means to accomplish good.

1. Presumably Voltaire (the immensely influential thinker and man of letters of the French Enlightenment) is the "demagogue"; Frederick the Great of Prussia, Catherine the Great of Russia, and Leopold II of the Holy Roman Empire, all influenced by Voltaire's ideas, are the "anarchs"; and Immanuel Kant (the great German philosopher writing at the end of the Enlightenment) is the "sage."

2. Leaders who bring about anarchy.

3. While these others were conquered by Life, Rousseau was self-conquered by his own heart's limitless desires, which no experience could moderate ("temper") to contentment with an achievable object or satisfaction.

"Our shadows on it as it past away.
But mark, how chained to the triumphal chair
The mighty phantoms of an elder day—

"All that is mortal of great Plato there
Expiates the joy & woe his master knew not;[4]   255
That star that ruled his doom was far too fair—

"And Life, where long that flower of Heaven grew not,
Conquered the heart by love which gold or pain
Or age or sloth or slavery could subdue not—

"And near   walk the   twain,   260
The tutor & his pupil,[5] whom Dominion
Followed as tame as vulture in a chain.—

"The world was darkened beneath either pinion
Of him whom from the flock of conquerors
Fame singled as her thunderbearing minion;   265

"The other long outlived both woes & wars,
Throned in new thoughts of men, and still had kept
The jealous keys of truth's eternal doors

"If Bacon's spirit   had not leapt
Like lightning out of darkness; he compelled   270
The Proteus shape of Nature's as it slept

"To wake & to unbar the caves that held
The treasure of the secrets of its reign—
See the great bards of old who inly quelled

"The passions which they sung, as by their strain   275
May well be known:[6] their living melody
Tempers its own contagion to the vein

"Of those who are infected with it—I
Have suffered what I wrote, or viler pain!—

"And so my words were seeds of misery—   280
Even as the deeds of others."—Not as theirs," [6a]
I said—he pointed to a company

4. All that is mortal of Plato (excluding, that is, the immortal powers of the
great philosopher-poet) is expiating the
joy and woe of Life, which Socrates,
"his master," escaped, but to which Plato
succumbed solely because of love. Shelley
alludes to the tradition of Plato's all-
too-earthly love for the Greek youth,
Aster (the Greek means "star," line
256), who died young (line 257). For
the epigram on Aster as the morning
and evening star, ascribed to Plato, see
the motto Shelley prefixed to *Adonais*,
above.
5. Aristotle and his pupil, Alexander the
Great. Shelley represents Aristotle as no
less a tyrant than the conqueror; the
influence of Aristotle's dogmatic philosophy would even now keep us from
access to truth had not the Renaissance
philosopher Francis Bacon opened the
way again by his new method of inquiry
in the natural sciences (lines 267–73).
6. The classical poets who, unlike Rousseau, subdued the passions they expressed.
6a. "Theirs" refers to the deeds of the
evil "company" (the next line) to which
Rousseau is pointing.

In which I recognized amid the heirs
    Of Caesar's crime from him to Constantine,[7]
The Anarchs old whose force & murderous snares   285

    Had founded many a sceptre bearing line
And spread the plague of blood & gold abroad,
    And Gregory & John[8] and men divine

Who rose like shadows between Man & god
    Till that eclipse, still hanging under Heaven,   290
Was worshipped by the world o'er which they strode

    For the true Sun it quenched.—"Their power was given
But to destroy," replied the leader—"I
    Am one of those who have created, even

"If it be but a world of agony."—   295
    "Whence camest thou & whither goest thou?
How did thy course begin," I said, "& why?

    "Mine eyes are sick of this perpetual flow
Of people, & my heart of one sad thought.—
    Speak." [9] "Whence I came, partly I seem to know,   300

"And how & by what paths I have been brought
    To this dread pass, methinks even thou mayst guess;
Why this should be my mind can compass not;

    "Whither the conqueror hurries me still less.
But follow thou, & from spectator turn   305
    Actor or victim in this wretchedness,

"And what thou wouldst be taught I then may learn
    From thee.—Now listen . . . In the April prime
When all the forest tops began to burn

    "With kindling green, touched by the azure clime   310
Of the young year, I found myself asleep
    Under a mountain which from unknown time

"Had yawned into a cavern high & deep,
    And from it came a gentle rivulet
Whose water like clear air in its calm sweep   315

    "Bent the soft grass & kept for ever wet
The stems of the sweet flowers, and filled the grove
    With sound which all who hear must needs forget

7. The crime of destroying the Roman Republic by becoming dictator and so opening the line of Roman emperors extending to Constantine, who inaugurated the Christian rule of Rome early in the 4th century. The "Anarchs" are the founders of later European dynasties in the Christian period.
8. Pope Gregory the Great established the independent political power of the papacy; "John," presumably, simply because it has been a name frequently assumed by Popes.
9. The rest of the fragment consists of Rousseau's allegorical account of his own life, in response to the only two of the narrator's questions (lines 296–97) which, he says, the limitations of his knowledge permit him partially to answer. "April prime": Spring, the first season of the year.

"All pleasure & all pain, all hate & love,
   Which they had known before that hour of rest: 320
A sleeping mother then would dream not of

"The only child who died upon her breast
At eventide, a king would mourn no more
   The crown of which his brow was dispossest

"When the sun lingered o'er the Ocean floor   325
   To gild his rival's new prosperity.—
Thou wouldst forget thus vainly to deplore

"Ills, which if ills, can find no cure from thee,
The thought of which no other sleep will quell
   Nor other music blot from memory—   330

"So sweet & deep is the oblivious[1] spell.—
   Whether my life had been before that sleep
The Heaven which I imagine, or a Hell

"Like this harsh world in which I wake to weep,
I know not. I arose & for a space   335
   The scene of woods & waters seemed to keep,

"Though it was now broad day, a gentle trace
   Of light diviner than the common Sun
Sheds on the common Earth, but all the place

"Was filled with many sounds woven into one   340
Oblivious melody, confusing sense
   Amid the gliding waves & shadows dun;

"And as I looked the bright omnipresence
   Of morning through the orient[2] cavern flowed,
And the Sun's image radiantly intense   345

"Burned on the waters of the well that glowed
Like gold, and threaded all the forest maze
   With winding paths of emerald fire—there stood

"Amid the sun, as he amid the blaze
   Of his own glory, on the vibrating   350
Floor of the fountain, paved with flashing rays,

"A shape all light, which with one hand did fling
Dew on the earth, as if she were the Dawn[3]
   Whose invisible rain forever seemed to sing

1. Causing forgetfulness. Shelley models Rousseau's account of his life in part on Rousseau's own writings and in part on Wordsworth's metaphoric description, in *Intimations Ode*, of the westward course of man's life, substituting his own skepticism for Wordsworth's certainties.
2. Lit from the east. The cavern runs from east to west through the mountain, and as Rousseau grows older he follows the course of its stream westward.
3. "The shape all light," of which the meaning has been much disputed, probably signifies the false Rousseauistic (and in Shelley's view, Wordsworthian) ideal of the state of nature and of trust in the natural human instincts. The attractive feminine shape is formed by a reflection of the sun's light from the earthly medium of water and leads Rousseau on only to betray him (lines 382 ff., 405 ff.).

"A silver music on the mossy lawn,   355
  And still before her on the dusky grass
Iris[4] her many coloured scarf had drawn.—

"In her right hand she bore a crystal glass
Mantling with bright Nepenthe;[5]—the fierce splendour
  Fell from her as she moved under the mass   360

"Of the deep cavern, & with palms so tender
  Their tread broke not the mirror of its billow,
Glided along the river, and did bend her

"Head under the dark boughs, till like a willow
Her fair hair swept the bosom of the stream   365
  That whispered with delight to be their pillow.—

"As one enamoured is upborne in dream
  O'er lily-paven lakes mid silver mist
To wondrous music, so this shape might seem

"Partly to tread the waves with feet which kist   370
The dancing foam, partly to glide along
  The airs that roughened the moist amethyst,

"Or the slant morning beams that fell among
  The trees, or the soft shadows of the trees;
And her feet ever to the ceaseless song   375

"Of leaves & winds & waves & birds & bees
And falling drops moved in a measure new
  Yet sweet, as on the summer evening breeze

"Up from the lake a shape of golden dew
  Between two rocks, athwart the rising moon,
Moves up the east, where eagle never flew.—   380

"And still her feet, no less than the sweet tune
To which they moved, seemed as they moved, to blot
  The thoughts of him who gazed on them, & soon

"All that was seemed as if it had been not,   385
  As if the gazer's mind was strewn beneath
Her feet like embers, & she, thought by thought,

"Trampled its fires into the dust of death,
  As Day upon the threshold of the east
Treads out the lamps of night, until the breath   390

---

4. The rainbow; here it signifies the prismatic colors of the refracted light of the sun.
5. A drug causing total forgetfulness. The sinister suggestion subtly introduced in the description of the shape ("the fierce splendor," line 359) is heightened by echoes from Milton's *Comus*, lines 671 ff., in which the enchanter Comus (born of Circe, "daughter of the Sun") tries to seduce the Lady by a beverage which Milton compared to Nepenthe.

"Of darkness reillumines even the least
　　Of heaven's living eyes[6]—like day she came,
Making the night a dream; and ere she ceased

"To move, as one between desire and shame
　　Suspended, I said—'If, as it doth seem,　　　　395
　　Thou comest from the realm without a name,

" 'Into this valley of perpetual dream,
　　Shew whence I came, and where I am, and why—
Pass not away upon the passing stream.'

" 'Arise and quench thy thirst,' was her reply.　　400
And as a shut lily, stricken by the wand
　　Of dewy morning's vital alchemy,

"I rose; and, bending at her sweet command,
　　Touched with faint lips the cup she raised,
And suddenly my brain became as sand　　　　405

"Where the first wave had more than half erased
The track of deer on desert Labrador,
　　Whilst the fierce wolf from which they fled amazed

"Leaves his stamp visibly upon the shore
　　Until the second bursts—so on my sight　　　　410
Burst a new Vision never seen before.—

"And the fair shape waned in the coming light
As veil by veil the silent splendour drops
　　From Lucifer, amid the chrysolite[7]

"Of sunrise ere it strike the mountain tops—　　415
　　And as the presence of that fairest planet
Although unseen is felt by one who hopes

"That his day's path may end as he began it
In that star's smile, whose light is like the scent
　　Of a jonquil when evening breezes fan it,　　　　420

"Or the soft note in which his dear lament
　　The Brescian shepherd[8] breathes, or the caress
That turned his weary slumber to content.—

"So knew I in that light's severe excess
The presence of that shape which on the stream　　425
　　Moved, as I moved along the wilderness,

"More dimly than a day appearing dream,
　　The ghost of a forgotten form of sleep,
A light from Heaven whose half extinguished beam

6. I.e., the stars.
7. A greenish gem.
8. The favorite song, *Stanco di pascolar le pecorelle,* is a Brescian national air

[Mary Shelley's note]. The title translates, "I am tired of pasturing the sheep." Brescia: a region in northern Italy.

"Through the sick day in which we wake to weep 430
Glimmers, forever sought, forever lost.—
   So did that shape its obscure tenour keep

"Beside my path, as silent as a ghost;[9]
   But the new Vision, and its cold bright car,
With savage music, stunning music, crost 435

   "The forest, and as if from some dread war
Triumphantly returning, the loud million
   Fiercely extolled the fortune of her star.—

"A moving arch of victory the vermilion
   And green & azure plumes of Iris had 440
Built high over her wind-winged pavilion,

   "And underneath aetherial glory clad
The wilderness, and far before her flew
   The tempest of the splendour which forbade

"Shadow to fall from leaf or stone;—the crew 445
   Seemed in that light like atomies[1] that dance
Within a sunbeam.—Some upon the new

   "Embroidery of flowers that did enhance
The grassy vesture of the desart, played,
   Forgetful of the chariot's swift advance; 450

"Others stood gazing till within the shade
   Of the great mountain its light left them dim.—
Others outspeeded it, and others made

   "Circles around it like the clouds that swim
Round the high moon in a bright sea of air, 455
   And more did follow, with exulting hymn,

"The chariot & the captives fettered there,
   But all like bubbles on an eddying flood
Fell into the same track at last & were

   "Borne onward.—I among the multitude 460
Was swept; me sweetest flowers delayed not long,
   Me not the shadow nor the solitude,

"Me not the falling stream's Lethean song,
   Me, not the phantom of that early form
Which moved upon its motion,—but among 465

   "The thickest billows of the living storm
I plunged, and bared my bosom to the clime
   Of that cold light, whose airs too soon deform.—

---

9. In lines 410–33 the brilliance of the chariot of Life makes the fair shape fade until, like the morning (and evening) star, Lucifer (line 414) in the daytime, its presence is felt, although no longer seen. (Cf. *To a Skylark*, above, lines 21–25.)
1. Particles of dust.

"Before the chariot had begun to climb
 The opposing steep of that mysterious dell, 470
Behold a wonder worthy of the rhyme

"Of him[2] whom from the lowest depths of Hell
 Through every Paradise & through all glory
Love led serene, & who returned to tell

"In words of hate & awe the wondrous story 475
 How all things are transfigured, except Love;
For deaf as is a sea which wrath makes hoary

"The world can hear not the sweet notes that move
 The sphere[3] whose light is melody to lovers—
A wonder worthy of his rhyme—the grove 480

"Grew dense with shadows to its inmost covers,
 The earth was grey with phantoms, & the air
Was peopled with dim forms, as when there hovers

"A flock of vampire-bats before the glare
 Of the tropic sun, bringing ere evening 485
Strange night upon some Indian isle,—thus were

"Phantoms diffused around, & some did fling
 Shadows of shadows, yet unlike themselves,
Behind them, some like eaglets on the wing

"Were lost in the white blaze, others like elves 490
Danced in a thousand unimagined shapes
 Upon the sunny streams & grassy shelves;

"And others sate chattering like restless apes
 On vulgar paws and voluble like fire.
Some made a cradle of the ermined capes 495

"Of kingly mantles, some upon the tiar[4]
Of pontiffs sate like vultures, others played
 Within the crown which girt with empire

"A baby's or an idiot's brow, & made
 Their nests in it; the old anatomies[5] 500
Sate hatching their bare brood under the shade

"Of demon wings, and laughed from their dead eyes
To reassume the delegated power
 Arrayed in which these worms did monarchize

---

2. Dante, who in *The Divine Comedy* was kept safe by Love in his pilgrimage.
3. The third sphere of the planet Venus (Love), in Dante's Ptolemaic universe.
4. The tiara, or triple crown of the popes.

5. Skeletonlike monsters.
6. The monarchs who had made the earth one great cemetery ("charnel") were like grave-worms, for they fed upon the corpses they had slaughtered.

"Who make this earth their charnel.[6]—Others more   505
    Humble, like falcons sate upon the fist
Of common men, and round their heads did soar,

"Or like small gnats & flies, as thick as mist
On evening marshes, thronged about the brow
    Of lawyer, statesman, priest & theorist,   510

"And others like discoloured flakes of snow
    On fairest bosoms & the sunniest hair
Fell, and were melted by the youthful glow

"Which they extinguished; for like tears, they were
A veil to those from whose faint lids they rained   515
    In drops of sorrow.—I became aware

"Of whence those forms proceeded which thus stained
    The track in which we moved; after brief space
From every form the beauty slowly waned,

"From every firmest limb & fairest face   520
The strength & freshness fell like dust, & left
    The action & the shape without the grace

"Of life;[7] the marble brow of youth was cleft
    With care, and in the eyes where once hope shone
Desire like a lioness bereft   525

"Of its last cub, glared ere it died; each one
Of that great crowd sent forth incessantly
    These shadows, numerous as the dead leaves blown

"In Autumn evening from a poplar tree—
    Each, like himself & like each other were,   530
At first, but soon distorted, seemed to be

"Obscure clouds moulded by the casual air;
And of this stuff the car's creative ray
    Wrought all the busy phantoms that were there

"As the sun shapes the clouds—thus, on the way   535
    Mask after mask fell from the countenance
And form of all, and long before the day

"Was old, the joy which waked like Heaven's glance
The sleepers in the oblivious valley, died,
    And some grew weary of the ghastly dance   540

"And fell, as I have fallen by the way side,
    Those soonest from whose forms most shadows past
And least of strength & beauty did abide."—

7. In lines 481–523, the shadows and phantoms originate (lines 516–37) in the qualities of beauty, strength, and freshness, which fall like masks away from the men and women in the procession, as their hope degenerates into mere desire. These shadows of lost physical qualities are soon distorted by the currents of the air and miscreated into phantoms by the light from the car of Life.

"Then, what is Life?" I said . . . the cripple cast
His eye upon the car which now had rolled   545
   Onward, as if that look must be the last,

And answered . . . . "Happy those for whom the fold
   Of
1822   1824

From A Defense of Poetry[1]
Part I

According to one mode of regarding those two classes of mental
action, which are called reason and imagination, the former may
be considered as mind contemplating the relations borne by one
thought to another, however produced; and the latter, as mind
acting upon those thoughts so as to color them with its own light,
and composing from them, as from elements, other thoughts, each
containing within itself the principle of its own integrity. The one[2]
is the τὸ ποιεῖν,[3] or the principle of synthesis, and has for its objects

---

1. In 1820 Shelley's good friend
Thomas Love Peacock published an
ironic essay, *The Four Ages of Poetry*,
in which he took the position that poetry is a primitive use of language
which once had a function in a barbarous society, but has become a useless anachronism in this age of science
and technology. Peacock was himself a
poet, as well as the best contemporary
prose satirist, and Shelley saw the joke;
but he also recognized that the position
which Peacock had ironically assumed
was very close to that actually held
in his day by Utilitarian philosophers
and material-minded laymen who either
attacked or contemptuously ignored the
imaginative faculty and its achievements. He therefore undertook, as he
good-humoredly wrote to Peacock, "to
break a lance with you * * * in honor
of my mistress Urania," even though he
was only "the knight of the shield of
shadow and the lance of gossamere."
The result was *The Defense of Poetry*,
planned to consist of three parts. The
last two parts were never written, and
even the existing section, written in
1821, remained unpublished until 1840,
eighteen years after Shelley's death.
   For many decades Shelley's *Defense*
was regarded as one of the very few
classic essays in literary criticism. Its
reputation, however, has diminished in
the recent era of the new criticism. The
chief interest since the 1920's has been
in applied commentary and the kind of
critical theory that is oriented toward
providing useful distinctions for the close
analysis of particular literary texts. But

Shelley's main enterprise, although different, is no less valid and a rarer
achievement in the history of critical
writings. His emphasis is on the universal and permanent forms, qualities, and
values that all great poems, as products
of imagination, possess in common; on
those aspects, as he puts it, in which
time, person, and place "are convertible
with respect to the highest poetry without injuring it as poetry." More than
this: Shelley extends the term "poet"
to comprehend all the creative minds
that break out of the limitations of their
age and place to approximate the enduring and general forms of value—including not only writers in verse and prose,
but artists, legislators, and prophets,
as well as the founders of a new organization of society, morality, or religion.
The very range of the *Defense* gives it
unequaled importance as a ringing claim
for the validity and indispensability of
the visionary and creative imagination
in all the great human concerns. Nor
has any later writer exceeded the co-
gency of the attack, which Shelley includes, on our acquisitive society and
its narrowly material concept of utility
and progress, which has permitted man
to make enormous progress in science
and in his material well-being without
a proportionate development of his "poetical faculty," the moral imagination;
with the grotesque result, as Shelley
says, that "man, having enslaved the
elements, remains himself a slave."
2. I.e., the imagination.
3. "Making." The Greek word from
which "poet" derives means "maker,"

those forms which are common to universal nature and existence itself; the other is the τὸ λογίζειν,[4] or principle of analysis, and its action regards the relations of things simply as relations; considering thoughts, not in their integral unity, but as the algebraical representations which conduct to certain general results. Reason is the enumeration of quantities already known; imagination is the perception of the value of those quantities, both separately and as a whole. Reason respects the differences, and imagination the similitudes of things. Reason is to the imagination as the instrument to the agent, as the body to the spirit, as the shadow to the substance.[5] * * *

In the youth of the world, men dance and sing and imitate natural objects, observing in these actions, as in all others, a certain rhythm or order. And, although all men observe a similar, they observe not the same order, in the motions of the dance, in the melody of the song, in the combinations of language, in the series of their imitations of natural objects. For there is a certain order or rhythm belonging to each of these classes of mimetic representation, from which the hearer and the spectator receive an intenser and purer pleasure than from any other: the sense of an approximation to this order has been called taste by modern writers. Every man in the infancy of art observes an order which approximates more or less closely to that from which this highest delight results; but the diversity is not sufficiently marked, as that its gradations should be sensible, except in those instances where the predominance of this faculty of approximation to the beautiful (for so we may be permitted to name the relation between this highest pleasure and its cause) is very great. Those in whom it exists in excess are poets, in the most universal sense of the word; and the pleasure resulting from the manner in which they express the influence of society or nature upon their own minds communicates itself to others, and gathers a sort of reduplication from that community. Their language is vitally metaphorical; that is, it marks the before unapprehended relations of things and perpetuates their apprehension, until the words which represent them become, through time, signs for portions or classes of thoughts[6] instead of pictures of integral thoughts; and then if no new poets should arise to create afresh the associations which have been thus disorganized, language will be dead to all the nobler purposes of human intercourse. These similitudes or relations are finely said by Lord Bacon to be "the same footsteps of nature impressed upon the various subjects of

and the term "maker" had been adopted by Renaissance defenders of poetry. Sir Philip Sidney, in his *Apology for Poetry* (1595), which Shelley had carefully studied, said: "The Greeks named him poet. * * * It cometh of this word *poiein,* which is *to make;* wherein * * * we Englishmen have met with the Greeks in calling him a maker. * * * "

4. "Calculating," "reasoning."

5. In the paragraph here omitted, Shelley defines poetry as "the expression of the imagination"; it is "connate with the origin of man."

6. I.e., abstract concepts.

the world,"[7] and he considers the faculty which perceives them as the storehouse of axioms common to all knowledge. In the infancy of society every author is necessarily a poet, because language itself is poetry; and to be a poet is to apprehend the true and the beautiful, in a word, the good which exists in the relation, subsisting first, between existence and perception, and secondly, between perception and expression. Every original language near to its source is in itself the chaos of a cyclic poem; the copiousness of lexicography and the distinctions of grammar are the works of a later age, and are merely the catalogue and the form of the creations of poetry.

But poets, or those who imagine and express this indestructible order, are not only the authors of language and of music, of the dance, and architecture, and statuary, and painting; they are the institutors of laws, and the founders of civil society, and the inventors of the arts of life, and the teachers, who draw into a certain propinquity with the beautiful and the true that partial apprehension of the agencies of the invisible world which is called religion.[8] Hence all original religions are allegorical, or susceptible of allegory, and, like Janus,[9] have a double face of false and true. Poets, according to the circumstances of the age and nation in which they appeared, were called, in the earlier epochs of the world, legislators, or prophets;[1] a poet essentially comprises and unites both these characters. For he not only beholds intensely the present as it is, and discovers those laws according to which present things ought to be ordered, but he beholds the future in the present, and his thoughts are the germs of the flower and the fruit of latest time. Not that I assert poets to be prophets in the gross sense of the word, or that they can foretell the form as surely as they foreknow the spirit of events: such is the pretense of superstition, which would make poetry an attribute of prophecy, rather than prophecy an attribute of poetry. A poet participates in the eternal, the infinite, and the one; as far as relates to his conceptions, time and place and number are not. The grammatical forms which express the moods of time, and the difference of persons, and the distinction of place are convertible with respect to the highest poetry without injuring it as poetry; and the choruses of Aeschylus, and the Book of Job, and Dante's *Paradiso*, would afford, more than any other writings, examples of this fact, if the limits of this essay did not forbid citation. The creations of sculpture, painting, and music, are illustrations still more decisive. * * *

A poem is the very image of life expressed in its eternal truth. There is this difference between a story and a poem, that a story

7. "*De augmentis scientiarum*" I.iii" [Shelley's note].

8. Shelley thus deliberately enlarges the discussion to include all creative insights or imaginative break-throughs of mankind in whatever area they may occur.

9. Roman god of doorways, with two heads which face in opposite directions.

1. The term *vates* ("prophet") was sometimes applied to poets by the Romans.

is a catalogue of detached facts, which have no other bond of connection than time, place, circumstance, cause, and effect; the other is the creation of actions according to the unchangeable forms of human nature as existing in the mind of the Creator, which is itself the image of all other minds. The one is partial, and applies only to a definite period of time and a certain combination of events which can never again recur; the other is universal, and contains within itself the germ of a relation to whatever motives or actions have place in the possible varieties of human nature. Time, which destroys the beauty and the use of the story of particular facts, stripped of the poetry which should invest them, augments that of poetry, and forever develops new and wonderful applications of the eternal truth which it contains. Hence epitomes have been called the moths of just history; they eat out the poetry of it.[2] A story of particular facts is a mirror which obscures and distorts that which should be beautiful; poetry is a mirror which makes beautiful that which is distorted.

The parts of a composition may be poetical, without the composition as a whole being a poem. A single sentence may be considered as a whole, though it may be found in the midst of a series of unassimilated portions; a single word even may be a spark of inextinguishable thought. And thus all the great historians, Herodotus, Plutarch, Livy, were poets; and although the plan of these writers, especially that of Livy, restrained them from developing this faculty in its highest degree, they make copious and ample amends for their subjection, by filling all the interstices of their subjects with living images.

Having determined what is poetry, and who are poets, let us proceed to estimate its effects upon society.

Poetry is ever accompanied with pleasure: all spirits on which it falls open themselves to receive the wisdom which is mingled with its delight. In the infancy of the world neither poets themselves nor their auditors are fully aware of the excellence of poetry, for it acts in a divine and unapprehended manner, beyond and above consciousness; and it is reserved for future generations to contemplate and measure the mighty cause and effect in all the strength and splendor of their union. Even in modern times, no living poet ever arrived at the fullness of his fame; the jury which sits in judgment upon a poet, belonging as he does to all time, must be composed of his peers: it must be impaneled by time from the selectest of the wise of many generations. A poet is a nightingale, who sits in darkness and sings to cheer its own solitude with sweet sounds; his auditors are as men entranced by the melody of an unseen musician, who feel that they are moved and softened, yet know not whence or why. The poems of Homer and his contemporaries

2. Cf. Bacon's *Advancement of Learning* II.ii.4; "epitomes" are abstracts or condensations.

were the delight of infant Greece; they were the elements of that
social system which is the column upon which all succeeding civilization has reposed. Homer embodied the ideal perfection of his
age in human character; nor can we doubt that those who read his
verses were awakened to an ambition of becoming like to Achilles,
Hector, and Ulysses; the truth and beauty of friendship, patriotism,
and persevering devotion to an object were unveiled to their depths
in these immortal creations; the sentiments of the auditors must
have been refined and enlarged by a sympathy with such great and
lovely impersonations, until from admiring they imitated, and from
imitation they identified themselves with the objects of their admiration. Nor let it be objected that these characters are remote
from moral perfection and that they can by no means be considered
as edifying patterns for general imitation. Every epoch, under names
more or less specious, has deified its peculiar errors; revenge is the
naked idol of the worship of a semi-barbarous age, and self-deceit
is the veiled image of unknown evil, before which luxury and satiety
lie prostrate. But a poet considers the vices of his contemporaries
as a temporary dress in which his creations must be arrayed and
which cover without concealing the eternal proportions of their
beauty. An epic or dramatic personage is understood to wear them
around his soul, as he may the ancient armor or the modern uniform around his body; whilst it is easy to conceive a dress more
graceful than either. The beauty of the internal nature cannot be
so far concealed by its accidental vesture, but that the spirit of its
form shall communicate itself to the very disguise, and indicate
the shape it hides from the manner in which it is worn. A majestic
form and graceful motions will express themselves through the
most barbarous and tasteless costume. Few poets of the highest
class have chosen to exhibit the beauty of their conceptions in its
naked truth and splendor; and it is doubtful whether the alloy of
costume, habit, etc., be not necessary to temper this planetary
music[3] for mortal ears.

The whole objection, however, of the immorality of poetry[4] rests
upon a misconception of the manner in which poetry acts to produce the moral improvement of man. Ethical science[5] arranges the
elements which poetry has created, and propounds schemes and
proposes examples of civil and domestic life; nor is it for want of
admirable doctrines that men hate, and despise, and censure, and
deceive, and subjugate one another. But poetry acts in another and
diviner manner. It awakens and enlarges the mind itself by rendering it the receptacle of a thousand unapprehended combinations of
thought. Poetry lifts the veil from the hidden beauty of the world,

3. The music of the revolving crystalline spheres of the planets, inaudible
to human ears.
4. In the preceding paragraph Shelley
has been implicitly dealing with the

charge, voiced by Plato, that poetry
is immoral because it presents evil
characters acting evilly.
5. Moral philosophy.

and makes familiar objects be as if they were not familiar; it reproduces all that it represents, and the impersonations clothed in its Elysian light stand thenceforward in the minds of those who have once contemplated them, as memorials of that gentle and exalted content[6] which extends itself over all thoughts and actions with which it coexists. The great secret of morals is love, or a going out of our own nature, and an identification of ourselves with the beautiful which exists in thought, action, or person not our own. A man, to be greatly good, must imagine intensely and comprehensively; he must put himself in the place of another and of many others; the pains and pleasures of his species must become his own. The great instrument of moral good is the imagination;[7] and poetry administers to the effect by acting upon the cause. Poetry enlarges the circumference of the imagination by replenishing it with thoughts of ever new delight, which have the power of attracting and assimilating to their own nature all other thoughts and which form new intervals and interstices whose void forever craves fresh food. Poetry strengthens that faculty which is the organ of the moral nature of man, in the same manner as exercise strengthens a limb. A poet therefore would do ill to embody his own conceptions of right and wrong, which are usually those of his place and time, in his poetical creations, which participate in neither. By this assumption of the inferior office of interpreting the effect, in which perhaps after all he might acquit himself but imperfectly, he would resign a glory in a participation in the cause.[8] There was little danger that Homer, or any of the eternal poets, should have so far misunderstood themselves as to have abdicated this throne of their widest dominion. Those in whom the poetical faculty, though great, is less intense, as Euripides, Lucan, Tasso, Spenser, have frequently affected[9] a moral aim, and the effect of their poetry is diminished in exact proportion to the degree in which they compel us to advert to this purpose.[1] * * *

It is difficult to define pleasure in its highest sense; the definition involving a number of apparent paradoxes. For, from an inexplicable defect of harmony in the constitution of human nature, the pain of the inferior is frequently connected with the pleasures of the

6. Contentment, total satisfaction.

7. Central to Shelley's theory is the concept of the sympathetic imagination—the faculty by which an individual is enabled to overleap the limits of his own nervous system and identify himself with the thoughts and feelings of other men. Shelley claims that the faculty which in poetry enables us to share the joys and sufferings of invented characters is also the basis of all morality, for it compels us to feel for others as we feel for ourselves.

8. The "effect," or the particular moral standards set up by the imagination, is contrasted to the "cause" of all morality, the imagination itself.

9. Assumed, adopted.

1. In the omitted passage Shelley reviews the history of drama and poetry in relation to civilization and morality and proceeds to refute the charge that poets are less useful than "reasoners and merchants." He begins by defining utility in terms of pleasure, and then distinguishes between the lower (physical and material) and the higher (imaginative) pleasures.

superior portions of our being. Sorrow, terror, anguish, despair itself, are often the chosen expressions of an approximation to the highest good. Our sympathy in tragic fiction depends on this principle; tragedy delights by affording a shadow of the pleasure which exists in pain. This is the source also of the melancholy which is inseparable from the sweetest melody. The pleasure that is in sorrow is sweeter than the pleasure of pleasure itself. And hence the saying, "It is better to go to the house of mourning, than to the house of mirth"[2]—not that this highest species of pleasure is necessarily linked with pain. The delight of love and friendship, the ecstasy of the admiration of nature, the joy of the perception and still more of the creation of poetry, is often wholly unalloyed.

The production and assurance of pleasure in this highest sense is true utility. Those who produce and preserve this pleasure are poets or poetical philosophers.

The exertions of Locke, Hume, Gibbon, Voltaire, Rousseau,[3] and their disciples in favor of oppressed and deluded humanity are entitled to the gratitude of mankind. Yet it is easy to calculate the degree of moral and intellectual improvement which the world would have exhibited, had they never lived. A little more nonsense would have been talked for a century or two; and perhaps a few more men, women, and children burnt as heretics. We might not at this moment have been congratulating each other on the abolition of the Inquisition in Spain.[4] But it exceeds all imagination to conceive what would have been the moral condition of the world if neither Dante, Petrarch, Boccaccio, Chaucer, Shakespeare, Calderon, Lord Bacon, nor Milton had ever existed; if Raphael and Michael Angelo had never been born; if the Hebrew poetry had never been translated; if a revival of the study of Greek literature had never taken place; if no monuments of ancient sculpture had been handed down to us; and if the poetry of the religion of the ancient world had been extinguished together with its belief. The human mind could never, except by the intervention of these excitements, have been awakened to the invention of the grosser sciences, and that application of analytical reasoning to the aberrations of society, which it is now attempted to exalt over the direct expression of the inventive and creative faculty itself.

We have more moral, political, and historical wisdom than we know how to reduce into practice; we have more scientific and economical knowledge than can be accommodated to the just distribution of the produce which it multiplies. The poetry in these systems of thought is concealed by the accumulation of facts and calculating processes. There is no want of knowledge respecting

2. Ecclesiastes vii.2.
3. "Although Rousseau has been thus classed, he was essentially a poet. The others, even Voltaire, were mere reasoners" [Shelley's note].
4. In 1820.

what is wisest and best in morals, government, and political economy, or at least, what is wiser and better than what men now practise and endure. But we let "*I dare not* wait upon *I would*, like the poor cat in the adage."[5] We want the creative faculty to imagine that which we know; we want the generous impulse to act that which we imagine; we want the poetry of life; our calculations have outrun our conception; we have eaten more than we can digest. The cultivation of those sciences which have enlarged the limits of the empire of man over the external world has, for want of the poetical faculty, proportionally circumscribed those of the internal world; and man, having enslaved the elements, remains himself a slave. To what but a cultivation of the mechanical arts in a degree disproportioned to the presence of the creative faculty, which is the basis of all knowledge, is to be attributed the abuse of all invention for abridging and combining labor, to the exasperation of the inequality of mankind? From what other cause has it arisen that the discoveries which should have lightened have added a weight to the curse imposed on Adam? Thus poetry and the principle of Self, of which money is the visible incarnation, are the God and Mammon of the world.

The functions of the poetical faculty are twofold: by one it creates new materials of knowledge and power and pleasure; by the other it engenders in the mind a desire to reproduce and arrange them according to a certain rhythm and order which may be called the beautiful and the good. The cultivation of poetry is never more to be desired than at periods when, from an excess of the selfish and calculating principle, the accumulation of the materials of external life exceed the quantity of the power of assimilating them to the internal laws of human nature. The body has then become too unwieldy for that which animates it.

Poetry is indeed something divine. It is at once the center and circumference of knowledge; it is that which comprehends all science, and that to which all science must be referred. It is at the same time the root and blossom of all other systems of thought; it is that from which all spring, and that which adorns all; and that which, if blighted, denies the fruit and the seed, and withholds from the barren world the nourishment and the succession of the scions of the tree of life. It is the perfect and consummate surface and bloom of all things; it is as the odor and the color of the rose to the texture of the elements which compose it, as the form and the splendor of unfaded beauty to the secrets of anatomy and corruption. What were virtue, love, patriotism, friendship; what were the scenery of this beautiful universe which we inhabit; what were our consolations on this side of the grave—and what were our aspirations beyond it, if poetry did not ascend to bring light and fire

5. *Macbeth* I.vii.44–45.

from those eternal regions where the owl-winged faculty of calculation dare not ever soar? Poetry is not like reasoning, a power to be
exerted according to the determination of the will. A man cannot
say, "I will compose poetry." The greatest poet even cannot say
it; for the mind in creation is as a fading coal, which some invisible
influence, like an inconstant wind, awakens to transitory brightness;
this power arises from within, like the color of a flower which fades
and changes as it is developed, and the conscious portions of our
natures are unprophetic either of its approach or its departure.[6]
Could this influence be durable in its original purity and force, it
is impossible to predict the greatness of the results; but when composition begins, inspiration is already on the decline, and the most
glorious poetry that has ever been communicated to the world is
probably a feeble shadow of the original conceptions of the poet.
I appeal to the greatest poets of the present day, whether it be not
an error to assert that the finest passages of poetry are produced by
labor and study. The toil and the delay recommended by critics can
be justly interpreted to mean no more than a careful observation
of the inspired moments, and an artificial connection of the spaces
between their suggestions by the intertexture of conventional expressions—a necessity only imposed by the limitedness of the poetical faculty itself; for Milton conceived the *Paradise Lost* as a
whole before he executed it in portions. We have his own authority
also for the muse having "dictated" to him the "unpremeditated
song."[7] And let this be an answer to those who would allege the
fifty-six various readings of the first line of the *Orlando Furioso*.[8]
Compositions so produced are to poetry what mosaic is to painting.
This instinct and intuition of the poetical faculty is still more observable in the plastic and pictorial arts: a great statue or picture
grows under the power of the artist as a child in the mother's
womb; and the very mind which directs the hands in formation
is incapable of accounting to itself for the origin, the gradations,
or the media of the process.

Poetry is the record of the best and happiest[9] moments of
the happiest and best minds. We are aware of evanescent
visitations of thought and feeling sometimes associated with
place or person, sometimes regarding our own mind alone, and
always arising unforeseen and departing unbidden, but elevating
and delightful beyond all expression: so that even in the desire and
regret they leave, there cannot but be pleasure, participating as it
does in the nature of its object. It is as it were the interpenetration

6. This passage reiterates the ancient
belief that the highest poetry is "inspired," and therefore occurs independently of the intention, effort, or consciousness of the poet. Unlike earlier
critics, however, Shelley attributes such
poetry not to a god or muse outside
the poet, but to the unconscious depths
within the poet's own mind.
7. *Paradise Lost* IX.21–24.
8. The epic romance by the 16th-cen-
tury Italian poet Ariosto.
9. In the double sense of "most joyous" and "most apt or felicitous in invention."

of a diviner nature through our own; but its footsteps are like those of a wind over the sea, which the coming calm erases, and whose traces remain only, as on the wrinkled sand which paves it. These and corresponding conditions of being are experienced principally by those of the most delicate sensibility and the most enlarged imagination; and the state of mind produced by them is at war with every base desire. The enthusiasm of virtue, love, patriotism, and friendship is essentially linked with such emotions; and whilst they last, self appears as what it is, an atom to a universe. Poets are not only subject to these experiences as spirits of the most refined organization, but they can color all that they combine with the evanescent hues of this ethereal world; a word or a trait in the representation of a scene or a passion will touch the enchanted chord, and reanimate, in those who have ever experienced these emotions, the sleeping, the cold, the buried image of the past. Poetry thus makes immortal all that is best and most beautiful in the world; it arrests the vanishing apparitions which haunt the interlunations[1] of life, and, veiling them or in language or in form, sends them forth among mankind, bearing sweet news of kindred joy to those with whom their sisters abide—abide, because there is no portal of expression from the caverns of the spirit which they inhabit into the universe of things. Poetry redeems from decay the visitations of the divinity in man.

Poetry turns all things to loveliness; it exalts the beauty of that which is most beautiful, and it adds beauty to that which is most deformed; it marries exultation and horror, grief and pleasure, eternity and change; it subdues to union, under its light yoke, all irreconcilable things. It transmutes all that it touches, and every form moving within the radiance of its presence is changed by wondrous sympathy to an incarnation of the spirit which it breathes: its secret alchemy turns to potable gold the poisonous waters which flow from death through life; it strips the veil of familiarity from the world, and lays bare the naked and sleeping beauty, which is the spirit of its forms.

All things exist as they are perceived—at least in relation to the percipient. "The mind is its own place, and of itself can make a heaven of hell, a hell of heaven."[2] But poetry defeats the curse which binds us to be subjected to the accident of surrounding impressions. And whether it spreads its own figured curtain, or withdraws life's dark veil from before the scene of things, it equally creates for us a being within our being. It makes us the inhabitants of a world to which the familiar world is a chaos. It reproduces the common universe of which we are portions and percipients, and it purges from our inward sight the film of familiarity which obscures from us the wonder of our being. It compels us to feel that

1. The dark intervals between the old and new moon. 2. Satan's speech, *Paradise Lost* I.254–55.

which we perceive, and to imagine that which we know. It creates anew the universe,[3] after it has been annihilated in our minds by the recurrence of impressions blunted by reiteration. It justifies the bold and true words of Tasso: *Non merita nome di creatore, se non Iddio ed il Poeta.*[4]

A poet, as he is the author to others of the highest wisdom, pleasure, virtue, and glory, so he ought personally to be the happiest, the best, the wisest, and the most illustrious of men. As to his glory, let time be challenged to declare whether the fame of any other institutor of human life be comparable to that of a poet. That he is the wisest, the happiest, and the best, inasmuch as he is a poet, is equally incontrovertible: the greatest poets have been men of the most spotless virtue, of the most consummate prudence, and, if we would look into the interior of their lives, the most fortunate of men; and the exceptions, as they regard those who possessed the poetic faculty in a high yet inferior degree, will be found on consideration to confine rather than destroy the rule. Let us for a moment stoop to the arbitration of popular breath, and usurping and uniting in our own persons the incompatible characters of accuser, witness, judge, and executioner, let us decide without trial, testimony, or form, that certain motives of those who are "there sitting where we dare not soar,"[5] are reprehensible. Let us assume that Homer was a drunkard, that Virgil was a flatterer, that Horace was a coward, that Tasso was a madman, that Lord Bacon was a peculator, that Raphael was a libertine, that Spenser was a poet laureate. It is inconsistent with this division of our subject to cite living poets, but posterity has done ample justice to the great names now referred to. Their errors have been weighed and found to have been dust in the balance; if their sins "were as scarlet, they are now white as snow":[6] they have been washed in the blood of the mediator and redeemer, time. Observe in what a ludicrous chaos the imputations of real or fictitious crime have been confused in the contemporary calumnies against poetry and poets;[7] consider how little is, as it appears—or appears, as it is; look to your own motives, and judge not, lest ye be judged.

Poetry, as has been said, differs in this respect from logic, that it is not subject to the control of the active powers of the mind, and that its birth and recurrence have no necessary connection with

---

3. Shelley's version of a widespread Romantic doctrine: the poetic imagination is, like God, creative, because it re-creates or makes new the old universe. One way in which it does so is by revealing the wonder in the familiar; cf. Coleridge, *Biographia Literaria*, Chapter IV, above, on "freshness of sensation," or "the child's sense of wonder and novelty" combined with the oldest and most familiar appearances.

4. "No one merits the name of Creator except God and the Poet." The sense, though not the exact wording, is to be found in Tasso, the 16th-century Italian poet.
5. *Paradise Lost* IV.829.
6. Isaiah i.18.
7. Shelley's defense of Lord Byron and himself against the charges of immorality frequently voiced by contemporary reviewers.

the consciousness or will. It is presumptuous to determine that these[8] are the necessary conditions of all mental causation, when mental effects are experienced unsusceptible of being referred to them. The frequent recurrence of the poetical power, it is obvious to suppose, may produce in the mind a habit of order and harmony correlative with its own nature and with its effects upon other minds. But in the intervals of inspiration, and they may be frequent without being durable, a poet becomes a man, and is abandoned to the sudden reflux of the influences under which others habitually live. But as he is more delicately organized than other men, and sensible to pain and pleasure, both his own and that of others, in a degree unknown to them, he will avoid the one and pursue the other with an ardor proportioned to this difference. And he renders himself obnoxious to calumny when he neglects to observe the circumstances under which these objects of universal pursuit and flight have disguised themselves in one another's garments.

But there is nothing necessarily evil in this error, and thus cruelty, envy, revenge, avarice, and the passions purely evil have never formed any portion of the popular imputations on the lives of poets.

I have thought it most favorable to the cause of truth to set down these remarks according to the order in which they were suggested to my mind, by a consideration of the subject itself, instead of observing the formality of a polemical reply;[9] but if the view which they contain be just, they will be found to involve a refutation of the arguers against poetry, so far at least as regards the first division of the subject. I can readily conjecture what should have moved the gall of some learned and intelligent writers who quarrel with certain versifiers; I confess myself, like them, unwilling to be stunned by the Theseids[1] of the hoarse Codri of the day. Bavius and Maevius undoubtedly are, as they ever were, insufferable persons. But it belongs to a philosophical critic to distinguish rather than confound.

The first part of these remarks has related to poetry in its elements and principles; and it has been shown, as well as the narrow limits assigned them would permit, that what is called poetry, in a restricted sense, has a common source with all other forms of order and of beauty, according to which the materials of human life are susceptible of being arranged, and which is poetry in a universal sense.

The second part[2] will have for its object an application of these

---

8. I.e., consciousness and will. The concept that some mental processes are "unconscious" (outside our awareness or control) was developed in the late 18th and early 19th centuries.
9. I.e., to Peacock's *Four Ages of Poetry*.
1. Epic poems about Theseus. Codrus

(plural "Codri") was the author of a long, dull *Theseid*, attacked by Juvenal in *Satires* I; "Bavius and Maevius" were would-be poets satirized by Virgil in *Eclogues* III.
2. Shelley completed only the first part of his *Defense*.

principles of the present state of the cultivation of poetry, and a defense of the attempt to idealize the modern forms of manners and opinions, and compel them into a subordination to the imaginative and creative faculty. For the literature of England, an energetic development of which has ever preceded or accompanied a great and free development of the national will, has arisen as it were from a new birth. In spite of the low-thoughted envy which would undervalue contemporary merit, our own will be a memorable age in intellectual achievements, and we live among such philosophers and poets as surpass beyond comparison any who have appeared since the last national struggle for civil and religious liberty.[3] The most unfailing herald, companion, and follower of the awakening of a great people to work a beneficial change in opinion or institution is poetry. At such periods there is an accumulation of the power of communicating and receiving intense and impassioned conceptions respecting man and nature. The persons in whom this power resides may often, as far as regards many portions of their nature, have little apparent correspondence with that spirit of good of which they are the ministers. But even whilst they deny and abjure, they are yet compelled to serve the power which is seated on the throne of their own soul. It is impossible to read the compositions of the most celebrated writers of the present day without being startled with the electric life which burns within their words. They measure the circumference and sound the depths of human nature with a comprehensive and all-penetrating spirit, and they are themselves perhaps the most sincerely astonished at its manifestations; for it is less their spirit than the spirit of the age.[4] Poets are the hierophants[5] of an unapprehended inspiration; the mirrors of the gigantic shadows which futurity casts upon the present; the words which express what they understand not; the trumpets which sing to battle and feel not what they inspire; the influence which is moved not, but moves.[6] Poets are the unacknowledged legislators of the world.

1821   1840

---

3. The age of Milton and the English Civil War.

4. More than any contemporary Shelley recognized the existence and greatness of what we now call "the Romantic movement" in poetry and thought, as well as its relation to the ferment of ideas and aspirations produced by the French Revolution.

5. Priests, the expositors of sacred mysteries.

6. Aristotle had said that God is the "Unmoved Mover" of the universe.

JOHN KEATS
(1795–1821)

1817: *Poems*, Keats's first book.
1818: *Endymion*.
1819: Keats's *annus mirabilis*, in which he writes almost all his greatest poems.
1820: Publishes the volume *Lamia, Isabella, The Eve of St. Agnes, and Other Poems*.

No major poet has had a less propitious origin. Keats's father was head ostler at a London livery stable; he married his employer's daughter and inherited the business. Mrs. Keats, by all reports, was a strongly sensuous woman, and a rather casual but affectionate mother to her four children —John (the first-born), his two brothers, and a sister. Keats was sent to the Reverend John Clarke's private school at Enfield, where he was a noisy, high-spirited boy; despite his small physique (when full-grown, he was barely over five feet in height), he distinguished himself in skylarking and fist-fights. Here Keats had the good fortune to have as a teacher Charles Cowden Clarke, son of the headmaster, who later became himself a man of letters; he encouraged Keats's passion for reading and, both at school and in the course of their later friendship, introduced him to Spenser and other poets, to music, and to the theater.

When Keats was 8 his father was killed by a fall from a horse, and when he was 14, his mother died of tuberculosis. Although the livery stable had prospered, and £8,000 had been left in trust to the children by Keats's grandmother, the estate remained tied up in a Chancery suit for all of Keats's lifetime. The children's guardian, Richard Abbey, was an unimaginative and practical-minded businessman; he took Keats out of school at the age of 15 and bound him apprentice to Thomas Hammond, a surgeon and apothecary at Edmonton. In 1815 Keats carried on his medical studies at Guy's Hospital, London, and the next year qualified to practice as an apothecary—but almost immediately, over his guardian's protests, he abandoned medicine for poetry.

This decision was influenced by Keats's friendship with Leigh Hunt, then editor of the *Examiner* and a leading political radical, a minor poet, and a prolific writer of criticism and periodical essays. Hunt, the first successful author of Keats's acquaintance, added his enthusiastic encouragement of Keat's poetic efforts to that of Clarke. More important, Hunt introduced him to writers greater than himself, Hazlitt, Lamb, and Shelley, as well as to Benjamin Robert Haydon, painter of grandiose historical and religious canvases. Through Hunt Keats also met John Hamilton Reynolds, and then Charles Wentworth Dilke and Charles Brown, men who became his intimate friends and provided him with an essential circumstance for a fledgling poet, a sympathetic and appreciative audience. The rapidity and sureness of Keats's development has no match. He did not even undertake poetry until his 18th year, and for the next few years produced album verse which was at best merely competent and at times exhibited a labored vulgarity of sentiment and phrasing. Suddenly, in 1816, he spoke out loud and bold in *On First Looking into Chapman's Homer*, a major sonnet in the grand style. Later that same year he wrote *Sleep and Poetry*, in which he laid out for himself a poetic program deliberately modeled on the careers of the greatest poets, asking only

> for ten years, that I may overwhelm
> Myself in poesy; so I may do the deed
> That my own soul has to itself decreed.

For even while his health was good, Keats felt a foreboding of early death, and applied himself to his art with a desperate urgency. In 1817 Keats went on to compose *Endymion*, an ambitious undertaking of more than 4,000 lines. It is a profuse and often obscure allegory of the poet's search for the ideal of beauty and happiness, but in a number of single passages, it already exhibits the sure movement and phrasing of his mature poetic style. But Keats's critical judgment and aspiration exceeded his achievement: long before he completed it, he declared impatiently that he carried on with the "slipshod" *Endymion* only as a poetic exercise and "trial of invention" and began to block out the more ambitious *Hyperion*, conceived on the model of Milton's *Paradise Lost* in that most demanding of forms, the epic poem. The extent of his success in achieving the Miltonic manner is what made Keats leave off before *Hyperion* was finished, for he recognized that he was uncommonly susceptible to poetic influences, and regarded this as a threat to his poetic individuality. "I will write independently," he insisted. "The Genius of Poetry must work out its own salvation in a man." He had refused the chance of intimacy with Shelley "that I might have my own unfettered scope"; he had broken away from Leigh Hunt's influence lest he get "the reputation of Hunt's *élève*"; now he shied away from domination by Milton's idiosyncratic and powerfully infectious style.

With the year 1818 began a series of disappointments and disasters which culminated in Keats's mortal illness. Sentimental legend used to fix the blame upon two anonymous articles: a scurrilous attack on Keats as a member of the "Cockney School" (that is, Leigh Hunt's radical literary circle) which appeared in the heavily Tory *Blackwood's Magazine*, and a savage mauling of *Endymion* in the *Quarterly Review*. Shelley gave impetus to this myth by his description of Keats as "a pale flower" in *Adonais*, and Byron, who knew even less about Keats, asserted that he was "snuffed out by an article." But in fact, Keats had the good sense to recognize that the attacks were motivated by Tory bias and class snobbery, and he had already passed his own severe judgment on *Endymion*: "My own domestic criticism," he said, "has given me pain without comparison beyond what *Blackwood* or the *Quarterly* could possibly inflict." More important was the financial distress of his brother George and his young bride, who had just emigrated to Kentucky and lost their money in an ill-advised investment; Keats, himself always short of funds, had now to turn to literary journey-work to eke out the family income. His younger brother Tom contracted tuberculosis, and the poet, in constant attendance upon him through the later months of 1818, helplessly watched him waste away until his death that December. In the spring and summer of that year Keats had taken a strenuous walking tour in the English Lake Country, Scotland, and Ireland; it was a glorious adventure, but a totally exhausting one in wet, cold weather, and Keats returned in August with a chronically ulcerated throat made increasingly ominous by the shadow of the tuberculosis which had killed his mother and brother. And in the late fall of 1818 Keats fell desperately, unwillingly, helplessly in love with Fanny Brawne. This pretty, vivacious, and mildly flirtatious girl of 18 had little interest in poetry, but she possessed an alert and sensible mind and loved Keats sincerely, and might well have made him an excellent wife. They became engaged, but Keats's dedication to poetry, his poverty, and his growing illness made marriage impossible and love a torment.

In this period of acute distress and emotional turmoil, within five years of his first trying his hand at poetry, Keats achieved the culmination of his brief poetic career. Between January and September of 1819, masterpiece followed masterpiece in astonishing succession: *The Eve of St. Agnes*, *La Belle Dame sans Merci*, all six of the great *Odes*, *Lamia*, and a sufficient number of fine sonnets to make him, with Wordsworth, the major Romantic craftsman in that form. All of these poems possess the distinctive qualities of the work of Keats's maturity: a slow-paced, gracious movement; a concreteness of description in which all the senses—tactile, gustatory, kinetic, organic, as well as visual and auditory—combine to give the total apprehension of an experience; an intense delight at the sheer existence of things outside himself, the poet seeming to lose his own identity in the fullness of identification with the object he contemplates; and a concentrated felicity of phrasing which reminded Keats's friends, as it has so many critics since, of the language of Shakespeare. And under the rich sensuous surface we find Keats's characteristic presentation of all experience as a tangle of inseparable but irreconcilable opposites. He finds melancholy in delight, and pleasure in pain; he feels the highest intensity of love as an approximation to death; he inclines equally toward a life of indolence and "sensation" and toward a life of thought; he is aware both of the attraction of an imaginative dream world without "disagreeables" and the remorseless pressure of the actual; he aspires at the same time for aesthetic detachment (what in his letters he called "negative capability") and for social responsibility.

His letters, no less remarkable than his poetry, show that Keats felt on his pulses the conflicts he dramatized in his major poems. Above all, they reveal him wrestling with the problem of evil and suffering in the world— what to make of our lives in the discovery that "the world is full of misery and heartbreak, pain, sickness and oppression." To the end of his life Keats, with stubborn courage, refused to seek comfort by substituting for the complexity and contradictions of experience, and of a life which must find its justification in this world, either the simplicity of inherited philosophical doctrines or the absolutes of a religious creed. At the close of his poetic career, in the latter part of 1819, Keats began to rework the epic *Hyperion* into the form of a dream vision which he called *The*

Fall of Hyperion. In the introductory section of this fragment the poet is told by the prophetess Moneta that he has hitherto been merely a dreamer; he must know that

> The poet and the dreamer are distinct,
> Diverse, sheer opposite, antipodes,

and that the height of poetry can only be reached by

> those to whom the miseries of the world
> Are misery, and will not let them rest.

Keats was seemingly planning to undertake a new direction and subject matter, when death intervened.

On the night of February 3, 1820, he coughed up some blood. He refused to evade the truth: "I cannot be deceived in that color; that drop of blood is my death warrant. I must die." That spring and summer a series of hemorrhages rapidly weakened him. In the autumn he allowed himself to be persuaded to seek a milder climate in Italy in the company of Joseph Severn, a young painter; but these last months were only what he called "a posthumous existence." He died in Rome on February 23, 1821, and was buried in the Protestant Cemetery. At times the agony of his disease, the apparent frustration of his hopes for great poetic achievement, and the despair of his passion for Fanny Brawne combined to compel even Keats's brave spirit to bitterness, resentment, and jealousy, but he always recovered his gallantry. His last letter, written to Charles Brown, concludes: "I can scarcely bid you good-bye, even in a letter. I always made an awkward bow. God bless you! John Keats."

No one can read Keats's poems and letters without an undersense of the immense waste of so extraordinary an intellect and genius cut off so early. What he might have accomplished is beyond conjecture; what we do know is that his achievement, when he stopped writing at the age of 24, greatly exceeds that at the corresponding age of Chaucer, Shakespeare, or Milton.

On First Looking into Chapman's Homer[1]

> Much have I traveled in the realms of gold,
> And many goodly states and kingdoms seen;
> Round many western islands have I been
> Which bards in fealty to Apollo hold.
> Oft of one wide expanse had I been told   5
> That deep-browed Homer ruled as his demesne;[2]
> Yet did I never breathe its pure serene[3]

---

1. Keats's former schoolteacher, Charles Cowden Clarke, introduced him to Homer in the vigorous translation of the Elizabethan poet George Chapman. They read through the night, and Keats walked home at dawn; this sonnet, his first great poem, reached Clarke by the ten o'clock mail that same morning. That it was Balboa, not Cortez, who caught his first sight of the Pacific from the heights of Darien, in Panama, matters to history but not to poetry.
2. Realm, feudal possession.
3. Clear expanse of air.

Till I heard Chapman speak out loud and bold:
Then felt I like some watcher of the skies
   When a new planet swims into his ken;   10
Or like stout Cortez when with eagle eyes
   He stared at the Pacific—and all his men
Looked at each other with a wild surmise—
   Silent, upon a peak in Darien.

October, 1816   1816

From Sleep and Poetry[1]

* * *

O for ten years, that I may overwhelm
Myself in poesy; so I may do the deed
That my own soul has to itself decreed.
Then will I pass the countries that I see
In long perspective, and continually   100
Taste their pure fountains. First the realm I'll pass
Of Flora, and old Pan:[2] sleep in the grass,
Feed upon apples red, and strawberries,
And choose each pleasure that my fancy sees;
Catch the white-handed nymphs in shady places,   105
To woo sweet kisses from averted faces—
Play with their fingers, touch their shoulders white
Into a pretty shrinking with a bite
As hard as lips can make it: till agreed,
A lovely tale of human life we'll read.   110
And one will teach a tame dove how it best
May fan the cool air gently o'er my rest;
Another, bending o'er her nimble tread,
Will set a green robe floating round her head,
And still will dance with ever varied ease,   115
Smiling upon the flowers and the trees:
Another will entice me on, and on
Through almond blossoms and rich cinnamon;
Till in the bosom of a leafy world

1. At the early age of 21, Keats set himself a rigorous regimen of poetic training modeled on the course followed by the greatest poets. Virgil had established the pattern of beginning with pastoral writing and proceeding gradually to the point at which he was ready to undertake the epic, and this pattern had been deliberately followed by Spenser and Milton. Keats's version of this program, as he describes it here, is to begin with the realm of "Flora, and old Pan" (line 102) and, within ten years, to climb up to the level of poetry dealing with "the agonies, the strife / Of human hearts" (lines 124–25). The latter achievement Keats found best represented among his contemporaries by Wordsworth and, less successfully, by Shelley—Keats's vision of the chariot of poesy (lines 125–154) echoes Shelley's allegorical visions. The program Keats set himself is illuminated by his analysis of Wordsworth's progress in his letter to J. H. Reynolds of May 3, 1818.
2. I.e., the carefree pastoral world. Flora was the Roman goddess of flowers, and Pan the Greek god of pastures, woods, and animal life.

We rest in silence, like two gems upcurled   120
In the recesses of a pearly shell.

And can I ever bid these joys farewell?
Yes, I must pass them for a nobler life,
Where I may find the agonies, the strife
Of human hearts: for lo! I see afar   125
O'ersailing the blue cragginess, a car[3]
And steeds with streamy manes—the charioteer
Looks out upon the winds with glorious fear:
And now the numerous tramplings quiver lightly
Along a huge cloud's ridge; and now with sprightly   130
Wheel downward come they into fresher skies,
Tipped round with silver from the sun's bright eyes.
Still downward with capacious whirl they glide;
And now I see them on the green-hill's side
In breezy rest among the nodding stalks.   135
The charioteer with wond'rous gesture talks
To the trees and mountains; and there soon appear
Shapes of delight, of mystery, and fear,
Passing along before a dusky space
Made by some mighty oaks: as they would chase   140
Some ever-fleeting music on they sweep.
Lo! how they murmur, laugh, and smile, and weep:
Some with upholden hand and mouth severe;
Some with their faces muffled to the ear
Between their arms; some, clear in youthful bloom,   145
Go glad and smilingly athwart the gloom;
Some looking back, and some with upward gaze;
Yes, thousands in a thousand different ways
Flit onward—now a lovely wreath of girls
Dancing their sleek hair into tangled curls;   150
And now broad wings. Most awfully intent
The driver of those steeds is forward bent,
And seems to listen: O that I might know
All that he writes with such a hurrying glow.

The visions all are fled—the car is fled   155
Into the light of heaven, and in their stead
A sense of real things comes doubly strong,
And, like a muddy stream, would bear along
My soul to nothingness: but I will strive
Against all doubtings, and will keep alive   160
The thought of that same chariot, and the strange
Journey it went * * *

Nov.–Dec., 1816   1817

3. This chariot, with its "charioteer" (line 127), represents the higher poetic imagination, which bodies forth (line 138), the matters "of delight, of mystery, and fear" that characterize the grander poetic forms.

On Seeing the Elgin Marbles for the First Time[4]

My spirit is too weak; mortality
  Weighs heavily on me like unwilling sleep,
  And each imagined pinnacle and steep
Of godlike hardship tells me I must die
Like a sick eagle looking at the sky.   5
  Yet 'tis a gentle luxury to weep,
  That I have not the cloudy winds to keep
Fresh for the opening of the morning's eye.
Such dim-conceivéd glories of the brain
  Bring round the heart an indescribable feud;   10
So do these wonders a most dizzy pain,
  That mingles Grecian grandeur with the rude
Wasting of old Time—with a billowy main,
A sun, a shadow of a magnitude.

                               1817

On the Sea

It keeps eternal whisperings around
  Desolate shores, and with its mighty swell
  Gluts twice ten thousand Caverns, till the spell
Of Hecate leaves them their old shadowy sound.
Often 'tis in such gentle temper found,   5
  That scarcely will the very smallest shell
  Be moved for days from where it sometime fell,
When last the winds of Heaven were unbound.
Oh ye! who have your eyeballs vexed and tired,
  Feast them upon the wideness of the Sea;   10
  Oh ye! whose ears are dinned with uproar rude,
Or fed too much with cloying melody—
  Sit ye near some old Cavern's Mouth and brood,
Until ye start, as if the sea nymphs quired!

1817   1817

From Endymion[1]

A POETIC ROMANCE

Preface

Knowing within myself the manner in which this Poem has
been produced, it is not without a feeling of regret that I make it

4. Lord Elgin had brought to England
in 1806 the marble statues and friezes
which adorned the Parthenon at Athens; in 1816 they were purchased by
the government for the British Museum.
Keats's response to his first sight of
these time-worn memorials of Grecian
artistry is characteristically intense,
mixed, and subtly analyzed.
1. This poem of more than 4,000 lines
(based on the classical myth of a mortal beloved by the goddess of the moon)

public.

What manner I mean, will be quite clear to the reader, who must soon perceive great inexperience, immaturity, and every error denoting a feverish attempt, rather than a deed accomplished. The two first books, and indeed the two last, I feel sensible are not of such completion as to warrant their passing the press; nor should they if I thought a year's castigation would do them any good— it will not: the foundations are too sandy. It is just that this young ster should die away: a sad thought for me, if I had not some hope that while it is dwindling I may be plotting, and fitting myself for verses fit to live.

This may be speaking too presumptuously, and may deserve a punishment: but no feeling man will be forward to inflict it: he will leave me alone, with the conviction that there is not a fiercer hell than the failure in a great object. This is not written with the least atom of purpose to forestall criticisms of course, but from the desire I have to conciliate men who are competent to look, and who do look with a zealous eye, to the honor of English literature.

The imagination of a boy is healthy, and the mature imagination of a man is healthy; but there is a space of life between, in which the soul is in a ferment, the character undecided, the way of life uncertain, the ambition thick-sighted: thence proceeds mawkishness, and all the thousand bitters which those men I speak of must necessarily taste in going over the following pages.

I hope I have not in too late a day touched the beautiful mythology of Greece, and dulled its brightness: for I wish to try once more,[2] before I bid it farewell.

TEIGNMOUTH, April 10, 1818.

From *Book I*
[A THING OF BEAUTY]

A thing of beauty is a joy forever:
Its loveliness increases; it will never
Pass into nothingness; but still will keep
A bower quiet for us, and a sleep

tells of Endymion's long and agonized search for an immortal goddess whom he had seen in several visions. In the course of his wanderings he comes upon an Indian maid who had been abandoned by the followers of Bacchus, and to his utter despair succumbs to a sensual passion for her, in apparent betrayal of his love for his heavenly ideal. In the resolution, the Indian maid reveals that she is herself Cynthia (Diana), goddess of the moon, and also the celestial goddess of his earlier visions.

Keats set himself to writing a long poem before he was entirely ready in range of knowledge, clarity of thought, or stylistic assurance; the poem reaches a high level only in single passages. The interpretation which seems best to fit the text is that ideal love and imaginative beauty are to be found only by way of instinctual impulses and earthly passion, which the ideal repeats, in one of Keats's phrases, "in a finer tone." The poem's constitution is so cloudy, however, that its purport is disputed. But Keats has disarmed all external criticism by his self-criticism in the candid and insightful Preface, which has become a classic statement of the characteristics of unripe genius.

2. In *Hyperion*, which Keats was already planning.

Full of sweet dreams, and health, and quiet breathing.　　5
Therefore, on every morrow, are we wreathing
A flowery band to bind us to the earth,
Spite of despondence, of the inhuman dearth
Of noble natures, of the gloomy days,
Of all the unhealthy and o'er-darkened ways　　10
Made for our searching: yes, in spite of all,
Some shape of beauty moves away the pall
From our dark spirits. Such the sun, the moon,
Trees old, and young, sprouting a shady boon
For simple sheep; and such are daffodils　　15
With the green world they live in; and clear rills
That for themselves a cooling covert make
'Gainst the hot season; the mid-forest brake,[3]
Rich with a sprinkling of fair musk-rose blooms:
And such too is the grandeur of the dooms[4]　　20
We have imagined for the mighty dead;
All lovely tales that we have heard or read:
An endless fountain of immortal drink,
Pouring unto us from the heaven's brink.[5]

Nor do we merely feel these essences
For one short hour; no, even as the trees　　25
That whisper round a temple become soon
Dear as the temple's self, so does the moon,
The passion poesy, glories infinite,
Haunt us till they become a cheering light　　30
Unto our souls, and bound to us so fast,
That, whether there be shine, or gloom o'ercast,
They always must be with us, or we die.

Therefore, 'tis with full happiness that I
Will trace the story of Endymion.　　35
The very music of the name has gone
Into my being, and each pleasant scene
Is growing fresh before me as the green
Of our own valleys * * *

[THE "PLEASURE THERMOMETER"]

"Peona![6] ever have I longed to slake
My thirst for the world's praises: nothing base,　　770
No merely slumberous phantasm, could unlace
The stubborn canvas for my voyage prepared—
Though now 'tis tattered; leaving my bark bared
And sullenly drifting: yet my higher hope

3. Thicket.
4. Judgments.
5. The poet sets up, and searches to resolve, the basic opposition between the inevitably "mortal" pleasures in this life and the conceived possibility of "immortal" delight. Thus "essences" (line 25) seem to be the things of beauty in this world, purged of the alloy of sadness and mutability that spoils ordinary experience. The central passage dealing with this theme is below, Book I, lines 777 ff.
6. The sister to whom Endymion confides his troubles.

Is of too wide, too rainbow-large a scope,   775
To fret at myriads of earthly wrecks.
Wherein lies happiness?[7] In that which becks
Our ready minds to fellowship divine,
A fellowship with essence; till we shine,
Full alchemized,[8] and free of space. Behold   780
The clear religion of heaven! Fold
A rose leaf round thy finger's taperness,
And soothe thy lips: hist, when the airy stress
Of music's kiss impregnates the free winds,
And with a sympathetic touch unbinds   785
Aeolian[9] magic from their lucid wombs:
Then old songs waken from enclouded tombs;
Old ditties sigh above their father's grave;
Ghosts of melodious prophesyings rave
Round every spot where trod Apollo's foot;   790
Bronze clarions awake, and faintly bruit,[1]
Where long ago a giant battle was;
And, from the turf, a lullaby doth pass
In every place where infant Orpheus slept.
Feel we these things?—that moment have we stepped   795
Into a sort of oneness, and our state
Is like a floating spirit's. But there are
Richer entanglements, enthrallments far
More self-destroying, leading, by degrees,
To the chief intensity: the crown of these   800
Is made of love and friendship, and sits high
Upon the forehead of humanity.
All its more ponderous and bulky worth
Is friendship, whence there ever issues forth
A steady splendor; but at the tiptop,   805
There hangs by unseen film, an orbèd drop
Of light, and that is love: its influence,
Thrown in our eyes, genders a novel sense,
At which we start and fret; till in the end,
Melting into its radiance, we blend,   810
Mingle, and so become a part of it—

7. Of lines 777–857, Keats wrote to his publisher, John Taylor: "When I wrote it, it was the regular stepping of the Imagination towards a Truth. My having written that Argument will perhaps be of the greatest Service to me of anything I ever did—It set before me at once the gradations of Happiness even like a kind of Pleasure Thermometer, and is my first step towards the chief attempt in the Drama—the playing of different Natures with Joy and Sorrow." The gradations on this "Pleasure Thermometer" mark the stages on the way to what Keats calls "happiness" (line 777)—his secular version of the religious concept of "felicity" which, in the orthodox view, is to be achieved by a surrender of oneself to God. For Keats the way to happiness lies through a fusion of ourselves, first sensuously, with the lovely objects of nature and art (lines 781–97), then on a higher level, with other human beings through "love and friendship" (line 801) but in the final degree, only through sexual love. By this "self-destroying," or total loss of personal identity through our imaginative identification with a beloved person outside ourselves, we escape from the material and spatial limits, and from the self-centered condition, of ordinary experience, to achieve a "fellowship with essence," which is a kind of immortality within our mortal existence (line 844).
8. Transformed by alchemy from a base to a precious metal.
9. From Aeolus, god of winds.
1. Make a sound.

Nor with aught else can our souls interknit
So wingedly: when we combine therewith,
Life's self is nourished by its proper pith,[2]
And we are nurtured like a pelican brood.[3]   815
Aye, so delicious is the unsating food,
That men, who might have towered in the van
Of all the congregated world, to fan
And winnow from the coming step of time
All chaff of custom, wipe away all slime   820
Left by men-slugs and human serpentry,
Have been content to let occasion die,
Whilst they did sleep in love's elysium.
And, truly, I would rather be struck dumb,
Than speak against this ardent listlessness: 825
For I have ever thought that it might bless
The world with benefits unknowingly;
As does the nightingale, upperchéd high,
And cloistered among cool and bunchéd leaves—
She sings but to her love, nor e'er conceives   830
How tiptoe Night holds back her dark gray hood.[4]
Just so may love, although 'tis understood
The mere commingling of passionate breath,
Produce more than our searching witnesseth:
What I know not: but who, of men, can tell   835
That flowers would bloom, or that green fruit would swell
To melting pulp, that fish would have bright mail,
The earth its dower of river, wood, and vale,
The meadows runnels, runnels pebble-stones,
The seed its harvest, or the lute its tones,   840
Tones ravishment, or ravishment its sweet
If human souls did never kiss and greet?

　　"Now, if this earthly love has power to make
Men's being mortal, immortal; to shake
Ambition from their memories, and brim   845
Their measure of content: what merest whim,
Seems all this poor endeavor after fame,
To one, who keeps within his steadfast aim
A love immortal, an immortal too.
Look not so 'wildered; for these things are true,   850
And never can be born of atomies[5]
That buzz about our slumbers, like brain-flies,
Leaving us fancy-sick. No, no, I'm sure,
My restless spirit never could endure
To brood so long upon one luxury,   855
Unless it did, though fearfully, espy
A hope beyond the shadow of a dream."

2. Its own elemental substance.
3. Young pelicans were once thought to
feed on their mother's flesh; so our life
be nourished by their mother's blood; so

our life is nourished by another's life,
with which it fuses in love.
4. I.e., in order better to hear.
5. Mites, tiny flying insects.

From *Book IV*

[THE CAVE OF QUIETUDE[1]]

There lies a den,
Beyond the seeming confines of the space
Made for the soul to wander in and trace
Its own existence, of remotest glooms.   515
Dark regions are around it, where the tombs
Of buried griefs the spirit sees, but scarce
One hour doth linger weeping, for the pierce
Of new-born woe it feels more inly smart:
And in these regions many a venomed dart   520
At random flies; they are the proper home
Of every ill: the man is yet to come
Who hath not journeyed in this native hell.
But few have ever felt how calm and well
Sleep may be had in that deep den of all.   525
There anguish does not sting; nor pleasure pall:
Woe-hurricanes beat ever at the gate,
Yet all is still within and desolate.
Beset with painful gusts, within ye hear
No sound so loud as when on curtained bier   530
The death-watch tick[2] is stifled. Enter none
Who strive therefore: on the sudden it is won.
Just when the sufferer begins to burn,
Then it is free to him; and from an urn,
Still fed by melting ice, he takes a draught—   535
Young Semele[3] such richness never quaffed
In her maternal longing! Happy gloom!
Dark Paradise! where pale becomes the bloom
Of health by due; where silence dreariest
Is most articulate; where hopes infest;   540
Where those eyes are the brightest far that keep
Their lids shut longest in a dreamless sleep.
O happy spirit-home! O wondrous soul!
Pregnant with such a den to save the whole

---

1. Endymion, although divided between his heavenly and earthly loves, has surrendered to his passion for the human Indian maiden. A pair of winged horses have carried the couple aloft, but as Endymion turns to his bride, she dissolves in the cold moonlight, leaving him alone. He plunges into the "Cave of Quietude"—a mental state (a "native hell," line 523) of total desolation, a "Dark Paradise" of pain and despair so extreme that they become indistinguishable from their own opposites of pleasure and happiness. Compare this description to the lesson of the nature of "high tragedy"—the aesthetic contemplation of human suffering which has passed beyond the bounds of both pain and pleasure—which the poet reads in the "wan" but "bright-blanched" face of Moneta; below, *The Fall of Hyperion*, I.256–82.

2. The death-watch beetle makes a sound like the ticking of a watch, supposed to portend death.

3. Semele presumptuously prayed that Jove unite with her not as man but as a god. When he did so, she was consumed by flames, but conceived Bacchus who was rescued by Jove from the maternal ashes.

In thine own depth.[4] Hail, gentle Carian![5]   545
For, never since thy griefs and woes began,
Hast thou felt so content: a grievous feud
Hath led thee to this Cave of Quietude.
Aye, his lulled soul was there, although upborne
With dangerous speed: and so he did not mourn   550
Because he knew not whither he was going.
So happy was he, not the aërial blowing
Of trumpets at clear parley[6] from the east
Could rouse from that fine relish, that high feast.
They stung the feathered horse:[7] with fierce alarm   555
He flapped towards the sound. Alas, no charm
Could lift Endymion's head, or he had viewed
A skyey masque,[8] a pinioned multitude—
And silvery was its passing: voices sweet
Warbling the while as if to lull and greet   560
The wanderer in his path. Thus warbled they,
While past the vision went in bright array.[9]

Apr.–Nov., 1817   1818

In Drear-Nighted December

1

In drear-nighted December,
   Too happy, happy tree,
Thy branches ne'er remember
   Their green felicity:
The north cannot undo them   5
   With a sleety whistle through them;
Nor frozen thawings glue them
   From budding at the prime.[1]

2

In drear-nighted December,
   Too happy, happy brook,   10
Thy bubblings ne'er remember
   Apollo's[2] summer look;
But with a sweet forgetting,
   They stay their crystal fretting,
Never, never petting[3]   15
   About the frozen time.

4. The apparent meaning is that the soul, in the utter depth of its suffering, can produce a cave ("den") of quietude in which to heal itself.
5. Endymion was a native of Caria, in Asia Minor.
6. A trumpet call to assembly.
7. The winged horse on whose back Endymion lay.
8. A dramatic entertainment, involving dialogue, song, and dance by masked actors. "Pinioned": winged.
9. The flying chorus in this masque go on to sing a celebration of Diana's coming marriage—to Endymion himself, although he, listening, does not know it.
1. The earliest period; hence, spring.
2. I.e., the sun's.
3. Fretting.

3

Ah! would 'twere so with many
A gentle girl and boy!
But were there ever any
Writhed not of passéd joy?   20
The feel of *not* to feel it,[4]
When there is none to heal it
Nor numbéd sense to steel it,
Was never said in rhyme.

December, 1817   1829

On Sitting Down to Read *King Lear* Once Again[1]

O golden-tongued Romance with serene lute!
Fair pluméd Siren! Queen of far away!
Leave melodizing on this wintry day,
Shut up thine olden pages, and be mute:
Adieu! for once again the fierce dispute   5
Betwixt damnation and impassioned clay
Must I burn through; once more humbly essay
The bitter-sweet of this Shakespearean fruit.
Chief Poet! and ye clouds of Albion,[2]
Begetters of our deep eternal theme,   10
When through the old oak forest I am gone,
Let me not wander in a barren dream,
But when I am consuméd in the fire,
Give me new Phoenix[3] wings to fly at my desire.

January, 1818   1838, 1848

When I Have Fears[4]

When I have fears that I may cease to be
Before my pen has gleaned my teeming brain,
Before high-piléd books, in charact'ry,[5]
Hold like rich garners the full-ripened grain;
When I behold, upon the night's starred face,   5
Huge cloudy symbols of a high romance,

---

4. This version of line 21, from a recently discovered autograph copy, is adopted in preference to the earlier version in the printed form of the poem: "To know the change and feel it."
1. Keats pauses in revising *Endymion: A Poetic Romance* to read again Shakespeare's great tragedy. The word "Siren" (line 2) indicates Keats's feeling that Romance was enticing him from the poet's prime duty, to deal with "the agonies, the strife / Of human hearts" (*Sleep and Poetry*, lines 124–125).

2. Albion is the old Celtic name for England; *King Lear* is set in Celtic Britain. The "oak forest" of line 11 refers either to *King Lear* or (more likely) to the romance, *Endymion*.
3. The fabulous bird which periodically burns itself to death in order to rise anew from the ashes.
4. The first, and one of the most successful, of Keats's attempts at the sonnet in the Shakespearean rhyme scheme.
5. Characters; written or printed letters of the alphabet.

And think that I may never live to trace
  Their shadows, with the magic hand of chance;
And when I feel, fair creature of an hour,
  That I shall never look upon thee more,   10
Never have relish in the faery power
  Of unreflecting love!—then on the shore
Of the wide world I stand alone, and think
Till Love and Fame to nothingness do sink.

January, 1818   1848

To Homer

Standing aloof in giant ignorance,
  Of thee I hear and of the Cyclades,[6]
As one who sits ashore and longs perchance
  To visit dolphin-coral in deep seas.
So thou wast blind!—but then the veil was rent;   5
  For Jove uncurtained Heaven to let thee live,
And Neptune made for thee a spumy tent,
  And Pan made sing for thee his forest-hive;
Aye, on the shores of darkness there is light,
  And precipices show untrodden green;   10
There is a budding morrow in midnight,
  There is a triple sight in blindness keen;
Such seeing hadst thou, as it once befell
To Dian, Queen of Earth, and Heaven, and Hell.[7]

1818   1848

The Eve of St. Agnes[1]

1

St. Agnes' Eve—Ah, bitter chill it was!
The owl, for all his feathers, was a-cold;
The hare limped trembling through the frozen grass,

6. A group of islands in the Aegean Sea, off Greece; Keats's allusion is to his ignorance of the Greek language.
7. In later cults Diana was worshiped as a three-figured goddess, the deity of nature and of the moon, as well as queen of hell. The "triple sight" which blind Homer paradoxically commands is of these three regions, and also of heaven, sea, and earth (the realms of Jove, Neptune, and Pan, lines 6–8).
1. St. Agnes, martyred ca. 303 at the age of 13, is the patron saint of virgins. Legend has it that if a virtuous young girl performs the proper ritual, she will dream of her future husband on the evening before St. Agnes' Day, which falls on January 21. Keats combined this superstition with the Romeo and Juliet theme of young love thwarted by feuding families and told the story in a sequence of sensuously evolving Spenserian stanzas. The luxurious product has been called "a colored dream," but it is a complexly meaningful dream, in which the strong contrasts of heat and cold, crimson and silver, youth and age, revelry and austere penance, sensuality and chastity, life and death, hell and heaven, assume symbolic values, and are used to show forth the extremes of spirituality and grossness which are mediated by a candid physicality, the difference between the dream and the reality of passion, and the ambivalences at the center of human love. The poem is Keats's first complete success in sustained narrative.

And silent was the flock in woolly fold:
Numb were the Beadsman's[2] fingers, while he told   5
His rosary, and while his frosted breath,
Like pious incense from a censer old,
Seemed taking flight for heaven, without a death,
Past the sweet Virgin's picture, while his prayer he saith.

2

His prayer he saith, this patient, holy man;   10
Then takes his lamp, and riseth from his knees,
And back returneth, meager, barefoot, wan,
Along the chapel aisle by slow degrees:
The sculptured dead, on each side, seem to freeze,
Imprisoned in black, purgatorial rails: 15
Knights, ladies, praying in dumb orat'ries,[3]
He passeth by; and his weak spirit fails
To think[4] how they may ache in icy hoods and mails.

3

Northward he turneth through a little door,
And scarce three steps, ere Music's golden tongue   20
Flattered[5] to tears this aged man and poor;
But no—already had his deathbell rung:
The joys of all his life were said and sung:
His was harsh penance on St. Agnes' Eve:
Another way he went, and soon among   25
Rough ashes sat he for his soul's reprieve,
And all night kept awake, for sinner's sake to grieve.

4

That ancient Beadsman heard the prelude soft;
And so it chanced, for many a door was wide,
From hurry to and fro. Soon, up aloft,   30
The silver, snarling trumpets 'gan to chide:
The level chambers, ready with their pride,[6]
Were glowing to receive a thousand guests:
The carvéd angels, ever eager-eyed,
Stared, where upon their heads the cornice rests,   35
With hair blown back, and wings put cross-wise on their breasts.

5

At length burst in the argent revelry,[7]
With plume, tiara, and all rich array,
Numerous as shadows haunting fairily
The brain, new stuffed, in youth, with triumphs gay   40
Of old romance. These let us wish away,
And turn, sole-thoughted, to one Lady there,
Whose heart had brooded, all that wintry day,
On love, and winged St. Agnes' saintly care,
As she had heard old dames full many times declare.   45

2. A "beadsman" is paid to pray for his benefactor. He "tells" (counts) the beads of his rosary, to keep track of his prayers.
3. Silent chapels.
4. I.e., when he thinks.
5. Beguiled, charmed.
6. Ostentation.
7. Silver-clad revelers.

6

They told her how, upon St. Agnes' Eve,
Young virgins might have visions of delight,
And soft adorings from their loves receive
Upon the honeyed middle of the night,
If ceremonies due they did aright;   50
As, supperless to bed they must retire,
And couch supine their beauties, lily white;
Nor look behind, nor sideways, but require
Of Heaven with upward eyes for all that they desire.

7

Full of this whim was thoughtful Madeline: 55
The music, yearning like a God in pain,
She scarcely heard: her maiden eyes divine,
Fixed on the floor, saw many a sweeping train
Pass by—she heeded not at all: in vain
Came many a tiptoe, amorous cavalier,   60
And back retired; not cooled by high disdain;
But she saw not: her heart was otherwhere:
She sighed for Agnes' dreams, the sweetest of the year.

8

She danced along with vague, regardless eyes,
Anxious her lips, her breathing quick and short: 65
The hallowed hour was near at hand: she sighs
Amid the timbrels,[8] and the thronged resort
Of whisperers in anger, or in sport;
'Mid looks of love, defiance, hate, and scorn,
Hoodwinked with faery fancy;[9] all amort,   70
Save to St. Agnes and her lambs unshorn,[1]
And all the bliss to be before tomorrow morn.

9

So, purposing each moment to retire,
She lingered still. Meantime, across the moors,
Had come young Porphyro, with heart on fire   75
For Madeline. Beside the portal doors,
Buttressed from moonlight,[2] stands he, and implores
All saints to give him sight of Madeline,
But for one moment in the tedious hours,
That he might gaze and worship all unseen;   80
Perchance speak, kneel, touch, kiss—in sooth such things have been.

10

He ventures in: let no buzzed whisper tell:
All eyes be muffled, or a hundred swords
Will storm his heart, Love's fev'rous citadel:
For him, those chambers held barbarian hordes,   85
Hyena foemen, and hot-blooded lords,

8. Small drums.
9. She was blinded ("hoodwinked"—as though the eyes were covered by a hood) by her charmed imagination; "all amort": as though dead.
1. On St. Agnes' Day it was the custom to offer lambs' wool at the altar, to be made into cloth by nuns.
2. Sheltered from the moonlight by the buttresses (the supports projecting from the wall).

Whose very dogs would execrations howl
Against his lineage: not one breast affords
Him any mercy, in that mansion foul,
Save one old beldame,[3] weak in body and in soul.   90

11

Ah, happy chance! the aged creature came,
Shuffling along with ivory-headed wand,[4]
To where he stood, hid from the torch's flame,
Behind a broad hall-pillar, far beyond
The sound of merriment and chorus bland:[5]   95
He startled her; but soon she knew his face,
And grasped his fingers in her palsied hand,
Saying, "Mercy, Porphyro! hie thee from this place;
They are all here tonight, the whole bloodthirsty race!

12

"Get hence! get hence! there's dwarfish Hildebrand;   100
He had a fever late, and in the fit
He curséd thee and thine, both house and land:
Then there's that old Lord Maurice, not a whit
More tame for his gray hairs—Alas me! flit!
Flit like a ghost away."—"Ah, Gossip[6] dear,   105
We're safe enough; here in this armchair sit,
And tell me how"—"Good Saints! not here, not here;
Follow me, child, or else these stones will be thy bier."

13

He followed through a lowly archéd way,
Brushing the cobwebs with his lofty plume,   110
And as she muttered "Well-a—well-a-day!"
He found him in a little moonlight room,
Pale, latticed, chill, and silent as a tomb.
"Now tell me where is Madeline," said he,
"O tell me, Angela, by the holy loom   115
Which none but secret sisterhood may see,
When they St. Agnes' wool are weaving piously."

14

"St. Agnes! Ah! it is St. Agnes' Eve—
Yet men will murder upon holy days:
Thou must hold water in a witch's sieve,[7]   120
And be liege lord of all the Elves and Fays,
To venture so: it fills me with amaze
To see thee, Porphyro!—St. Agnes' Eve!
God's help! my lady fair the conjuror plays[8]
This very night: good angels her deceive!   125
But let me laugh awhile, I've mickle[9] time to grieve."

15

Feebly she laugheth in the languid moon,

3. Old (and usually, homely) woman; an ironic development in English from the French meaning, "lovely lady."
4. Staff.
5. Soft.
6. In the old sense: godmother, or old friend.
7. A sieve made to hold water by witch-craft.
8. I.e., in her attempt to evoke the vision of her lover.
9. Much.

While Porphyro upon her face doth look,
Like puzzled urchin on an aged crone
Who keepeth closed a wondrous riddle-book,   130
As spectacled she sits in chimney nook.
But soon his eyes grew brilliant, when she told
His lady's purpose; and he scarce could brook[1]
Tears, at the thought of those enchantments cold,
And Madeline asleep in lap of legends old.   135

16

Sudden a thought came like a full-blown rose,
Flushing his brow, and in his painéd heart
Made purple riot: then doth he propose
A stratagem, that makes the beldame start:
"A cruel man and impious thou art: 140
Sweet lady, let her pray, and sleep, and dream
Alone with her good angels, far apart
From wicked men like thee. Go, go!—I deem
Thou canst not surely be the same that thou didst seem."

17

"I will not harm her, by all saints I swear,"   145
Quoth Porphyro: "O may I ne'er find grace
When my weak voice shall whisper its last prayer,
If one of her soft ringlets I displace,
Or look with ruffian passion in her face:
Good Angela, believe me by these tears;   150
Or I will, even in a moment's space,
Awake, with horrid shout, my foemen's ears,
And beard them, though they be more fanged than wolves and
    bears."

18

"Ah! why wilt thou affright a feeble soul?
A poor, weak, palsy-stricken, churchyard thing,   155
Whose passing bell[2] may ere the midnight toll;
Whose prayers for thee, each morn and evening,
Were never missed."—Thus plaining,[3] doth she bring
A gentler speech from burning Porphyro;
So woeful and of such deep sorrowing,   160
That Angela gives promise she will do
Whatever he shall wish, betide her weal or woe.

19

Which was, to lead him, in close secrecy,
Even to Madeline's chamber, and there hide
Him in a closet, of such privacy   165
That he might see her beauty unespied,
And win perhaps that night a peerless bride,
While legioned faeries paced the coverlet,
And pale enchantment held her sleepy-eyed.

---

1. "Brook" ordinarily means "endure," although Keats apparently uses it for "restrain."
2. Death knell.
3. Complaining.

Never on such a night have lovers met,   170
Since Merlin paid his Demon all the monstrous debt.[4]

20

"It shall be as thou wishest," said the Dame:
"All cates[5] and dainties shall be storéd there
Quickly on this feast night: by the tambour frame[6]
Her own lute thou wilt see: no time to spare,   175
For I am slow and feeble, and scarce dare
On such a catering trust my dizzy head.
Wait here, my child, with patience; kneel in prayer
The while: Ah! thou must needs the lady wed,
Or may I never leave my grave among the dead."   180

21

So saying, she hobbled off with busy fear.
The lover's endless minutes slowly passed:
The dame returned, and whispered in his ear
To follow her; with aged eyes aghast
From fright of dim espial. Safe at last,   185
Through many a dusky gallery, they gain
The maiden's chamber, silken, hushed, and chaste;
Where Porphyro took covert, pleased amain.[7]
His poor guide hurried back with agues in her brain.

22

Her falt'ring hand upon the balustrade,   190
Old Angela was feeling for the stair,
When Madeline, St. Agnes' charméd maid,
Rose, like a missioned spirit,[8] unaware:
With silver taper's light, and pious care,
She turned, and down the aged gossip led   195
To a safe level matting. Now prepare,
Young Porphyro, for gazing on that bed;
She comes, she comes again, like ringdove frayed[9] and fled.

23

Out went the taper as she hurried in;
Its little smoke, in pallid moonshine, died: 200
She closed the door, she panted, all akin
To spirits of the air, and visions wide:
No uttered syllable, or, woe betide!
But to her heart, her heart was voluble,
Paining with eloquence her balmy side;   205
As though a tongueless nightingale should swell
Her throat in vain, and die, heart-stifled, in her dell.

24

A casement high and triple-arched there was,
All garlanded with carven imag'ries
Of fruits, and flowers, and bunches of knot-grass,   210

4. It is not clear what episode in the Arthurian legends this refers to—possibly the one in which Merlin, the magician, paid for his magic with his life when the wily lady Vivien turned one of his own spells against him.

5. Delicacies.
6. A drum-shaped embroidery frame.
7. Mightily.
8. Like an angel sent on a mission.
9. Frightened.

And diamonded with panes of quaint device,
Innumerable of stains and splendid dyes,
As are the tiger moth's deep-damasked wings;
And in the midst, 'mong thousand heraldries,
And twilight saints, and dim emblazonings,   215
A shielded scutcheon blushed with blood of queens and kings.[1]

25

Full on this casement shone the wintry moon,
And threw warm gules[2] on Madeline's fair breast,
As down she knelt for heaven's grace and boon;[3]
Rose-bloom fell on her hands, together pressed,   220
And on her silver cross soft amethyst,
And on her hair a glory, like a saint:
She seemed a splendid angel, newly dressed,
Save wings, for heaven—Porphyro grew faint:
She knelt, so pure a thing, so free from mortal taint.   225

26

Anon his heart revives: her vespers done,
Of all its wreathéd pearls her hair she frees;
Unclasps her warméd jewels one by one;
Loosens her fragrant bodice; by degrees
Her rich attire creeps rustling to her knees: 230
Half-hidden, like a mermaid in sea-weed,
Pensive awhile she dreams awake, and sees,
In fancy, fair St. Agnes in her bed,
But dares not look behind, or all the charm is fled.

27

Soon, trembling in her soft and chilly nest,   235
In sort of wakeful swoon, perplexed[4] she lay,
Until the poppied warmth of sleep oppressed
Her soothéd limbs, and soul fatigued away;
Flown, like a thought, until the morrow-day;
Blissfully havened both from joy and pain;   240
Clasped like a missal where swart Paynims pray;[5]
Blinded alike from sunshine and from rain,
As though a rose should shut, and be a bud again.

28

Stol'n to this paradise, and so entranced,
Porphyro gazed upon her empty dress,   245
And listened to her breathing, if it chanced
To wake into a slumberous tenderness;
Which when he heard, that minute did he bless,
And breathed himself: then from the closet crept,
Noiseless as fear in a wide wilderness,   250

1. In the stained glass are represented many genealogical symbols ("heraldries") and other dim-colored devices ("emblazonings"); among these, a shield-shaped escutcheon signified by its colored symbols that the family was of royal lineage (of the "blood of queens and kings").
2. In heraldry, the color red.
3. Gift, blessing.
4. In a confused state between waking and sleeping.
5. Variously interpreted; perhaps: held tightly, cherished, like a Christian prayer book ("missal") in a land where the religion is that of dark-skinned pagans ("swart Paynims").

And over the hushed carpet, silent, stepped,
And 'tween the curtains peeped, where, lo!—how fast she slept.

29

Then by the bedside, where the faded moon
Made a dim, silver twilight, soft he set
A table, and, half anguished, threw thereon   255
A cloth of woven crimson, gold, and jet—
O for some drowsy Morphean amulet![6]
The boisterous, midnight, festive clarion,[7]
The kettledrum, and far-heard clarinet,
Affray his ears, though but in dying tone—   260
The hall door shuts again, and all the noise is gone.

30

And still she slept an azure-lidded sleep,
In blanchéd linen, smooth, and lavendered,
While he from forth the closet brought a heap
Of candied apple, quince, and plum, and gourd;[8]   265
With jellies soother than the creamy curd,
And lucent syrups, tinct with cinnamon;
Manna and dates, in argosy transferred
From Fez;[9] and spicéd dainties, every one,
From silken Samarcand to cedared Lebanon.   270

31

These delicates he heaped with glowing hand
On golden dishes and in baskets bright
Of wreathéd silver: sumptuous they stand
In the retired quiet of the night,
Filling the chilly room with perfume light.—   275
"And now, my love, my seraph[1] fair, awake!
Thou art my heaven, and I thine eremite:[2]
Open thine eyes, for meek St. Agnes' sake,
Or I shall drowse beside thee, so my soul doth ache."

32

Thus whispering, his warm, unnervéd arm   280
Sank in her pillow. Shaded was her dream
By the dusk curtains: 'twas a midnight charm
Impossible to melt as icéd stream:
The lustrous salvers in the moonlight gleam;
Broad golden fringe upon the carpet lies: 285
It seemed he never, never could redeem
From such a steadfast spell his lady's eyes;
So mused awhile, entoiled in wo-féd fantasies.[3]

33

Awakening up, he took her hollow lute—
Tumultuous—and, in chords that tenderest be,   290

6. Sleep-producing charm.
7. High-pitched trumpet.
8. Melon. According to the legend, the dream lover would bring the virgin a feast of delicacies.
9. I.e., jellies softer ("soother") than the curds of cream, clear ("lucent") syrups tinged with cinnamon, and sweet gums ("manna") and dates transported in a great merchant ship ("argosy") from Fez.
1. One of the highest order of angels.
2. A religious hermit.
3. Entangled in a weave of fantasies.

He played an ancient ditty, long since mute,
In Provence called "*La belle dame sans merci*":[4]
Close to her ear touching the melody;
Wherewith disturbed, she uttered a soft moan:
He ceased—she panted quick—and suddenly   295
Her blue affrayéd eyes wide open shone:
Upon his knees he sank, pale as smooth-sculptured stone.

34

Her eyes were open, but she still beheld,
Now wide awake, the vision of her sleep:
There was a painful change, that nigh expelled   300
The blisses of her dream so pure and deep,
At which fair Madeline began to weep,
And moan forth witless words with many a sigh;
While still her gaze on Porphyro would keep,
Who knelt, with joinéd hands and piteous eye,   305
Fearing to move or speak, she looked so dreamingly.

35

"Ah, Porphyro!" said she, "but even now
Thy voice was at sweet tremble in mine ear,
Made tunable with every sweetest vow;
And those sad eyes were spiritual and clear: 310
How changed thou art! how pallid, chill, and drear!
Give me that voice again, my Porphyro,
Those looks immortal, those complainings dear!
Oh leave me not in this eternal woe,
For if thou diest, my Love, I know not where to go."   315

36

Beyond a mortal man impassioned far
At these voluptuous accents, he arose,
Ethereal, flushed, and like a throbbing star
Seen mid the sapphire heaven's deep repose;
Into her dream he melted, as the rose   320
Blendeth its odor with the violet—
Solution sweet: meantime the frost-wind blows
Like Love's alarum pattering the sharp sleet
Against the windowpanes; St. Agnes' moon hath set.

37

'Tis dark: quick pattereth the flaw-blown[5] sleet: 325
"This is no dream, my bride, my Madeline!"
'Tis dark: the icéd gusts still rave and beat:
"No dream, alas! alas! and woe is mine!
Porphyro will leave me here to fade and pine.—
Cruel! what traitor could thee hither bring?   330
I curse not, for my heart is lost in thine,
Though thou forsakest a deceivéd thing—
A dove forlorn and lost with sick unprunéd wing."

---

4. "The Lovely Lady Without Pity,"   ballad.
by the medieval poet, Alain Chartier.   5. Gust-blown.
Keats later used the title for his own

38

"My Madeline! sweet dreamer! lovely bride!
Say, may I be for aye thy vassal blest?   335
Thy beauty's shield, heart-shaped and vermeil[6] dyed?
Ah, silver shrine, here will I take my rest
After so many hours of toil and quest,
A famished pilgrim—saved by miracle.
Though I have found, I will not rob thy nest   340
Saving of thy sweet self; if thou think'st well
To trust, fair Madeline, to no rude infidel.

39

"Hark! 'tis an elfin-storm from faery land,
Of haggard[7] seeming, but a boon indeed:
Arise—arise! the morning is at hand—   345
The bloated wassaillers[8] will never heed—
Let us away, my love, with happy speed;
There are no ears to hear, or eyes to see—
Drowned all in Rhenish and the sleepy mead:[9]
Awake! arise! my love, and fearless be,   350
For o'er the southern moors I have a home for thee."

40

She hurried at his words, beset with fears,
For there were sleeping dragons all around,
At glaring watch, perhaps, with ready spears—
Down the wide stairs a darkling[1] way they found.—   355
In all the house was heard no human sound.
A chain-drooped lamp was flickering by each door;
The artas, rich with horseman, hawk, and hound,
Fluttered in the besieging wind's uproar;
And the long carpets rose along the gusty floor.   360

41

They glide, like phantoms, into the wide hall;
Like phantoms, to the iron porch, they glide;
Where lay the Porter, in uneasy sprawl,
With a huge empty flagon by his side:
The wakeful bloodhound rose, and shook his hide,   365
But his sagacious eye an inmate owns:[2]
By one, and one, the bolts full easy slide:
The chains lie silent on the footworn stones;
The key turns, and the door upon its hinges groans.

42

And they are gone: aye, ages long ago   370
These lovers fled away into the storm.
That night the Baron dreamt of many a woe,
And all his warrior-guests, with shade and form
Of witch, and demon, and large coffin-worm,
Were long be-nightmared. Angela the old   375

6. Vermilion.
7. Wild, untamed (originally, a wild hawk).
8. Drunken carousers.
9. Rhine wine and the sleep-producing mead (a heavy fermented drink made with honey).
1. In the dark.
2. Acknowledges a member of the household.

Died palsy-twitched, with meager face deform;
The Beadsman, after thousand aves[3] told,
For aye unsought for slept among his ashes cold.
Jan.–Feb., 1819   1820

Bright Star[4]

Bright star, would I were steadfast as thou art—
    Not in lone splendor hung aloft the night
And watching, with eternal lids apart,
    Like nature's patient, sleepless Eremite,[5]
The moving waters at their priestlike task   5
    Of pure ablution[6] round earth's human shores,
Or gazing on the new soft fallen mask
    Of snow upon the mountains and the moors—
No—yet still steadfast, still unchangeable,
    Pillowed upon my fair love's ripening breast,   10
To feel forever its soft fall and swell,
    Awake forever in a sweet unrest,
Still, still to hear her tender-taken breath,
And so live ever—or else swoon to death.[7]

1819   1838

Why Did I Laugh Tonight?[8]

Why did I laugh tonight? No voice will tell:
    No God, no Demon of severe response,
Deigns to reply from Heaven or from Hell.
    Then to my human heart I turn at once.
Heart! Thou and I are here sad and alone;   5
    I say, why did I laugh? O mortal pain!
O Darkness! Darkness! ever must I moan,
    To question Heaven and Hell and Heart in vain.
Why did I laugh? I know this Being's lease,
    My fancy to its utmost blisses spreads;   10
Yet would I on this very midnight cease,
    And the world's gaudy ensigns[9] see in shreds;

3. The prayers beginning *Ave Maria* ("Hail Mary").
4. While on a tour of the Lake Country in 1818, Keats had said that the austere scenes "refine one's sensual vision into a sort of north star which can never cease to be open lidded and steadfast over the wonders of the great Power"; the thought developed into this sonnet. This used to be called Keats's last sonnet, since it was believed that Keats composed it on his way to death in Italy in September, 1820, at which time he copied it into his volume of Shakespeare. But a MS. draft dated 1819 has since been found.
5. Hermit, religious solitary.
6. Washing, as part of a religious rite.
7. In the earlier version: "Half passionless, and so swoon on to death."
8. In the letter to his brother and sister-in-law, George and Georgiana Keats, into which he copied this sonnet, March 19, 1819, Keats wrote: "Though the first steps to it were through my human passions, they went away, and I wrote with my Mind—and perhaps I must confess a little bit of my heart. * * * I went to bed, and enjoyed an uninterrupted sleep. Sane I went to bed and sane I arose."
9. Banners.

Verse, Fame, and Beauty are intense indeed,
But Death intenser—Death is Life's high meed.

March, 1819   1848

La Belle Dame sans Merci[1]

O what can ail thee, Knight at arms,
  Alone and palely loitering?
The sedge has withered from the Lake
  And no birds sing!

O what can ail thee, Knight at arms,   5
  So haggard, and so woebegone?
The squirrel's granary is full
  And the harvest's done.

I see a lily on thy brow
  With anguish moist and fever dew,   10
And on thy cheeks a fading rose
  Fast withereth too.

I met a Lady in the Meads,
  Full beautiful, a faery's child,
Her hair was long, her foot was light   15
  And her eyes were wild.

I made a Garland for her head,
  And bracelets too, and fragrant Zone;[2]
She looked at me as she did love
  And made sweet moan.   20

I set her on my pacing steed
  And nothing else saw all day long,
For sidelong would she bend and sing
  A faery's song.

She found me roots of relish sweet,   25
  And honey wild, and manna dew,
And sure in language strange she said
  "I love thee true."

She took me to her elfin grot
  And there she wept and sighed full sore,   30
And there I shut her wild wild eyes
  With kisses four.

1. The title, though not the subject matter, was taken from a medieval poem by Alain Chartier and means "The Lovely Lady Without Pity." The story of a mortal destroyed by his love for a supernatural *femme fatale* has been told repeatedly in myth, fairy tale, and ballad, but never so hauntingly. The metrical key to its effect is the poignant and richly suggestive suspension achieved by shortening to two stresses the final line of each stanza.

We print here Keats's first version, written in a letter to his brother and sister-in-law. The version published in 1820, "Ah, what can ail thee, wretched wight," is a rare instance in which Keats weakened a poem by revision.

Keats imitates a frequent procedure of folk ballads by casting the poem into the dialogue form. The first three stanzas are addressed to the Knight, and the rest of the poem is his reply.

2. Girdle.

And there she lulléd me asleep,
  And there I dreamed, Ah Woe betide!
The latest[3] dream I ever dreamt   35
  On the cold hill side.

I saw pale Kings, and Princes too,
  Pale warriors, death-pale were they all;
They cried, "La belle dame sans merci
  Thee hath in thrall!"   40

I saw their starved lips in the gloam
  With horrid warning gapéd wide,
And I awoke, and found me here
  On the cold hill's side.

And this is why I sojourn here,   45
  Alone and palely loitering;
Though the sedge is withered from the Lake
  And no birds sing.

April, 1819   1820

On the Sonnet[1]

If by dull rhymes our English must be chained,
  And, like Andromeda,[2] the Sonnet sweet
Fettered, in spite of painéd loveliness;
  Let us find out, if we must be constrained,
Sandals more interwoven and complete   5
  To fit the naked foot of poesy;
Let us inspect the lyre, and weigh the stress
  Of every chord,[3] and see what may be gained
By ear industrious, and attention meet;
  Misers of sound and syllable, no less   10
Than Midas[4] of his coinage, let us be
  Jealous of dead leaves in the bay-wreath crown;
So, if we may not let the Muse be free,
  She will be bound with garlands of her own.

April, 1819   1848

To Sleep

O soft embalmer of the still midnight,
  Shutting, with careful fingers and benign,

---

3. Last.
1. In a letter including this sonnet, Keats wrote that "I have been endeavoring to discover a better sonnet stanza than we have," objecting especially to the "pouncing rhymes" of the Petrarchan form and the inevitable tick of the closing couplet in the Shakespearean stanza. This and the two following poems exemplify Keats's experiments with variations upon these conventional sonnet patterns.
2. Andromeda was chained to a rock in order to placate a sea monster, but was rescued by Perseus.
3. Lyre-string.
4. King Midas was granted his wish that all he touched should turn to gold.

Our gloom-pleased eyes, embowered from the light,
  Enshaded in forgetfulness divine;
O soothest[1] Sleep! if so it please thee, close   5
  In midst of this thine hymn my willing eyes,
Or wait the amen, ere thy poppy[2] throws
  Around my bed its lulling charities;
Then save me, or the passéd day will shine
Upon my pillow, breeding many woes;   10
  Save me from curious[3] conscience, that still lords
Its strength for darkness, burrowing like a mole;
Turn the key deftly in the oiléd wards,[4]
And seal the hushéd casket of my soul.

April, 1819   1838, 1848

On Fame

"You cannot eat your cake and have it too."
                              —*Proverb*

How fevered is the man, who cannot look
  Upon his mortal days with temperate blood,
Who vexes all the leaves of his life's book,
  And robs his fair name of its maidenhood;
It is as if the rose should pluck herself,   5
  Or the ripe plum finger its misty bloom,
As if a Naiad,[5] like a meddling elf,
  Should darken her pure grot with muddy gloom;
But the rose leaves herself upon the briar,
  For winds to kiss and grateful bees to feed,   10
And the ripe plum still wears its dim attire;
  The undisturbéd lake has crystal space;
Why then should man, teasing the world for grace,
  Spoil his salvation for a fierce miscreed?[6]

April, 1819   1848

Ode to Psyche[1]

O Goddess! hear these tuneless numbers, wrung
  By sweet enforcement and remembrance dear,

1. Softest.
2. Opium is made from the dried juice of the opium poppy.
3. Scrupulous. "Lords": marshals, sets in order.
4. The ridges in a lock which determine the pattern of the key.
5. Water nymph.
6. I.e., the false doctrine ("miscreed") that the award of salvation ("grace") can be won by achieving fame in this world. Cf. Milton's *Lycidas*, lines 78 ff.: "Fame is no plant that grows on mortal soil. * * * "
1. This poem initiated the sequence of five great odes that Keats wrote in late April and in May, 1819. Since it is copied into the same journal-letter which included *On the Sonnet*, it is likely that Keats's experiments with sonnet schemes led to the development of the intricate and varied stanzas of his odes, and also that Keats abandoned the sonnet upon discovering the richer possibilities of the more spacious form. In a letter of April 30, 1819, Keats said that of all his poems up to that time, *Psyche* "is the first and the only one with which I have taken even moderate pains. I have for the most part dashed off my

And pardon that thy secrets should be sung
    Even into thine own soft-conchéd[2] ear:
Surely I dreamt today, or did I see
    The wingéd Psyche with awakened eyes?[2a]   5
I wandered in a forest thoughtlessly,
    And, on the sudden, fainting with surprise,
Saw two fair creatures, couchéd side by side
    In deepest grass, beneath the whisp'ring roof   10
Of leaves and trembled blossoms, where there ran
    A brooklet, scarce espied:

'Mid hushed, cool-rooted flowers, fragrant-eyed,
    Blue, silver-white, and budded Tyrian,[3]
They lay calm-breathing on the bedded grass;   15
    Their arms embracéd, and their pinions[4] too;
Their lips touched not, but had not bade adieu,
    As if disjoinéd by soft-handed slumber,
And ready still past kisses to outnumber
    At tender eye-dawn of aurorean love:[5]   20
        The wingéd boy I knew;
    But who wast thou, O happy, happy dove?
        His Psyche true!

O latest born and loveliest vision far
    Of all Olympus' faded hierarchy![6]   25
Fairer than Phoebe's sapphire-regioned star,[7]
    Or Vesper, amorous glowworm of the sky;
Fairer than these, though temple thou hast none,
    Nor altar heaped with flowers;
Nor virgin choir to make delicious moan   30
    Upon the midnight hours;
No voice, no lute, no pipe, no incense sweet
    From chain-swung censer teeming;

lines in a hurry. This I have done leisurely—I think it reads the more richly for it and will I hope encourage me to write other things in even a more peaceable and healthy spirit." In the story told by the Roman author Apuleius in the 2nd century A.D., Psyche was a lovely mortal beloved by Cupid, "the winged boy," son of Venus. After various tribulations, imposed by Venus because she was jealous of Psyche's beauty, Psyche was wedded to Cupid and translated to heaven as an immortal.

    The tendency in recent criticism of Keats is to read the *Ode* as a quasi-allegory, in which Psyche (in Greek: soul, or mind) represents "the human-soul-in-love" (Harold Bloom) or else the modern inward-oriented poetry of the mind (W. J. Bate). To this latter-day goddess, Keats in the last two stanzas promises to establish a place of worship within "some untrodden region" of his own mind, with himself as poet-

priest and prophet.
2. Soft and shaped like a seashell.
2a. Another of Keats's inquiries into the relation of dreams to poetic vision; see, e.g., *Sleep and Poetry*, the concluding section of *Ode to a Nightingale*, the opening section of *The Fall of Hyperion: A Dream*.
3. The purple dye anciently made in Tyre.
4. Wings.
5. Aurora was the goddess of the dawn.
6. The ranks of the classic gods of Mt. Olympus. "You must recollect that Psyche was not embodied as a goddess before the time of Apuleius the Platonist who lived after the Augustan age, and consequently the goddess was never worshiped or sacrificed to with any of the ancient fervor—and perhaps never thought of in the old religion" (Keats, letter of April 30, 1819).
7. The moon, supervised by the goddess Phoebe (Diana). "Vesper": the evening star.

No shrine, no grove, no oracle, no heat
    Of pale-mouthed prophet dreaming.   35

O brightest! though too late for antique vows,
    Too, too late for the fond believing lyre,
When holy were the haunted forest boughs,
    Holy the air, the water, and the fire;
Yet even in these days so far retired   40
    From happy pieties, thy lucent fans,[8]
    Fluttering among the faint Olympians,
I see, and sing, by my own eyes inspired.
So let me be thy choir, and make a moan
        Upon the midnight hours;   45
Thy voice, thy lute, thy pipe, thy incense sweet
    From swingéd censer teeming;
Thy shrine, thy grove, thy oracle, thy heat
    Of pale-mouthed prophet dreaming.
Yes, I will be thy priest, and build a fane[9]   50
    In some untrodden region of my mind,
Where branchéd thoughts, new grown with pleasant pain,
    Instead of pines shall murmur in the wind:
Far, far around shall those dark-clustered trees
    Fledge[1] the wild-ridged mountains steep by steep; 55
And there by zephyrs, streams, and birds, and bees,
    The moss-lain Dryads[2] shall be lulled to sleep;
And in the midst of this wide quietness
A rosy sanctuary will I dress
With the wreathed trellis of a working brain,   60
    With buds, and bells, and stars without a name,
    With all the gardener Fancy e'er could feign,
        Who breeding flowers, will never breed the same:
And there shall be for thee all soft delight
    That shadowy thought can win,   65
A bright torch, and a casement ope at night,
    To let the warm Love[3] in!
April, 1819   1820

Ode on a Grecian Urn[1]

1

Thou still unravished bride of quietness,
    Thou foster child of silence and slow time,

8. Shining wings.
9. Temple.
1. I.e., the trees shall stand, rank against rank, like layers of feathers.
2. Wood nymphs.
3. I.e., Cupid, god of love.
1. This urn, with its sculptured reliefs of Dionysian ecstasies, panting young lovers in flight and pursuit, a pastoral piper under spring foliage, and the quiet celebration of communal pieties, resembles parts of various vases, sculptures, and paintings; but it existed in all its particulars only in Keats's imagination. In the urn—which captures moments of intense experience in attitudes of grace and freezes them into marble immobility—Keats found the perfect correlative for his persistent concern with the longing for permanence in a world of change. The interpretation of the details with which Keats devel-

Sylvan[2] historian, who canst thus express
  A flowery tale more sweetly than our rhyme:
What leaf-fringed legend haunts about thy shape   5
    Of deities or mortals, or of both,
        In Tempe or the dales of Arcady?[3]
What men or gods are these? What maidens loath?
What mad pursuit? What struggle to escape?
     What pipes and timbrels? What wild ecstasy?   10

2

Heard melodies are sweet, but those unheard
  Are sweeter; therefore, ye soft pipes, play on;
Not to the sensual ear,[4] but, more endeared,
    Pipe to the spirit ditties of no tone:
Fair youth, beneath the trees, thou canst not leave   15
  Thy song, nor ever can those trees be bare;
     Bold Lover, never, never canst thou kiss,
Though winning near the goal—yet, do not grieve;
    She cannot fade, though thou hast not thy bliss,
     Forever wilt thou love, and she be fair!   20

3

Ah, happy, happy boughs! that cannot shed
  Your leaves, nor ever bid the Spring adieu;
And, happy melodist, unwearièd,
    Forever piping songs forever new;
More happy love! more happy, happy love!   25
  Forever warm and still to be enjoyed,
     Forever panting, and forever young;
All breathing human passion far above,
    That leaves a heart high-sorrowful and cloyed,
     A burning forehead, and a parching tongue.   30

4

Who are these coming to the sacrifice?
  To what green altar, O mysterious priest,
Lead'st thou that heifer lowing at the skies,
    And all her silken flanks with garlands dressed?
What little town by river or sea shore,   35
  Or mountain-built with peaceful citadel,
     Is emptied of this folk, this pious morn?
And, little town, thy streets forevermore
    Will silent be; and not a soul to tell
     Why thou art desolate, can e'er return.   40

ops this concept, however, is hotly disputed, all the way from the opening phrase—is "still" an adverb ("as yet") or an adjective ("motionless")?—to the two concluding lines, an ending which has already accumulated as much critical discussion as the "two-handed engine" in Milton's *Lycidas* or the cruxes in Shakespeare's plays. But these disputes testify to the enigmatic richness of meaning in the five short stanzas, and show that the ode has become a central point of reference in the criticism of the English lyric.
2. Rustic, representing a woodland scene.
3. Tempe is a beautiful valley in Greece, which has come to represent supreme rural beauty. The "dales of Arcady" are the valleys of Arcadia, a state in ancient Greece often used as a symbol of the pastoral ideal.
4. The ear of sense (as opposed to that of the "spirit," or imagination).

5
O Attic[5] shape! Fair attitude! with brede
  Of marble men and maidens overwrought,[6]
With forest branches and the trodden weed;
  Thou, silent form, dost tease us out of thought
As doth eternity: Cold Pastoral!   45
  When old age shall this generation waste,
    Thou shalt remain, in midst of other woe
Than ours, a friend to man, to whom thou say'st,
  "Beauty is truth, truth beauty,"[7]—that is all
    Ye know on earth, and all ye need to know.   50

May, 1819   1820

Ode to a Nightingale[1]

1
My heart aches, and a drowsy numbness pains
  My sense, as though of hemlock[2] I had drunk,
Or emptied some dull opiate to the drains
  One minute past, and Lethe-wards[3] had sunk:
'Tis not through envy of thy happy lot,   5
  But being too happy in thine happiness—
    That thou, light-wingéd Dryad of the trees,
      In some melodious plot
Of beechen green, and shadows numberless,
  Singest of summer in full-throated ease.   10

2
O, for a draught of vintage! that hath been
  Cooled a long age in the deep-delvéd earth,
Tasting of Flora[4] and the country green,
  Dance, and Provençal song,[5] and sunburnt mirth!

5. Greek. Attica was the region of Greece in which Athens was located.
6. Ornamented all over ("overwrought") with an interwoven pattern ("brede").
7. The quotation marks around this phrase are found in the volume of poems Keats published in 1820; but there are no quotation marks in the version printed in *Annals of the Fine Arts* that same year, or in the four transcripts of the poem made by Keats's friends. This discrepancy has encouraged the diversity of critical interpretations of the last two lines. Leading critics disagree whether the whole of these lines is said by the urn, or "Beauty is truth, truth beauty" by the urn and the rest by Keats or else by an invented lyric speaker; whether the "ye" in the last line is addressed to the lyric speaker, to the readers, to the urn, or to the figures on the urn; whether "all ye know" is that beauty is truth, or this plus the statement in lines 46–48; and whether "beauty is truth" is a universal and profound metaphysical proposition, or an overstatement uttered in the course of a dramatic dialogue, or simply nonsense. (The various commentaries are collected in *Keats's Well-Read Urn*, ed. H. T. Lyon, 1958).
1. Charles Brown, with whom Keats was then living in Hampstead, wrote: "In the spring of 1819 a nightingale had built her nest near my house. Keats felt a tranquil and continual joy in her song; and one morning he took his chair from the breakfast table to the grass plot under a plum tree, where he sat for two or three hours. When he came into the house, I perceived he had some scraps of paper in his hand, and these he was quietly thrusting behind the books. On inquiry, I found those scraps, four or five in number, contained his poetic feeling on the song of our nightingale."
2. A poisonous herb, not the North American evergreen tree.
3. Toward Lethe, the river in Hades whose waters cause forgetfulness.
4. Roman goddess of flowers, or the flowers themselves.
5. Provence, in southern France, was in

O for a beaker full of the warm South,   15
  Full of the true, the blushful Hippocrene,[6]
    With beaded bubbles winking at the brim,
      And purple-stainéd mouth;
  That I might drink, and leave the world unseen,
    And with thee fade away into the forest dim: 20

3

Fade far away, dissolve, and quite forget
  What thou among the leaves hast never known,
The weariness, the fever, and the fret
  Here, where men sit and hear each other groan;
Where palsy shakes a few, sad, last gray hairs,   25
  Where youth grows pale, and specter-thin, and dies;[7]
    Where but to think is to be full of sorrow
      And leaden-eyed despairs,
  Where Beauty cannot keep her lustrous eyes,
    Or new Love pine at them beyond tomorrow.   30

4

Away! away! for I will fly to thee,
  Not charioted by Bacchus and his pards,
But on the viewless wings of Poesy,[8]
  Though the dull brain perplexes and retards:
Already with thee! tender is the night, —   35
  And haply the Queen-Moon is on her throne,
    Clustered around by all her starry Fays;[9]
      But here there is no light,
  Save what from heaven is with the breezes blown
    Through verdurous[1] glooms and winding mossy ways.   40

5

I cannot see what flowers are at my feet,
  Nor what soft incense hangs upon the boughs,
But, in embalméd[2] darkness, guess each sweet
  Wherewith the seasonable month endows
The grass, the thicket, and the fruit tree wild;   45
  White hawthorn, and the pastoral eglantine;[3]
    Fast fading violets covered up in leaves;
      And mid-May's eldest child,
  The coming musk-rose, full of dewy wine,
    The murmurous haunt of flies on summer eves.   50

6

Darkling[4] I listen; and for many a time
  I have been half in love with easeful Death,

---

the late Middle Ages renowned for its troubadours, the writers and singers of love songs.
6. Pronounced *Hip'-ocreen:* fountain of the Muses on Mt. Helicon; hence, the waters of inspiration, here applied metaphorically to a beaker of wine.
7. Keats's brother, Tom, wasted by tuberculosis, had died the previous winter.
8. I.e., not by getting drunk on wine

(the "vintage" of stanza two), but on the invisible ("viewless") wings of the poetic fancy. (Bacchus, god of wine, was sometimes represented in a chariot drawn by "pards"—leopards.)
9. Fairies.
1. Green-foliaged.
2. Perfumed.
3. Sweetbrier, or honeysuckle.
4. In the dark.

Called him soft names in many a muséd[5] rhyme,
　To take into the air my quiet breath;
Now more than ever seems it rich to die,　　　　　　　　55
　To cease upon the midnight with no pain,
　　While thou art pouring forth thy soul abroad
　　　In such an ecstasy!
Still wouldst thou sing, and I have ears in vain—
　To thy high requiem become a sod.　　　　　　　　60

7

Thou wast not born for death, immortal Bird!
No hungry generations tread thee down;
The voice I hear this passing night was heard
　In ancient days by emperor and clown:
Perhaps the selfsame song that found a path　　　　65
　Through the sad heart of Ruth,[7] when, sick for home,
　　She stood in tears amid the alien corn;[8]
　　　The same that ofttimes hath
Charmed magic casements, opening on the foam
　Of perilous seas, in faery lands forlorn.　　　　　70

8

Forlorn![9] the very word is like a bell
　To toll me back from thee to my sole self!
Adieu! the fancy[10] cannot cheat so well
　As she is famed to do, deceiving elf.
Adieu! adieu! thy plaintive anthem[11] fades　　　　75
　Past the near meadows, over the still stream,
　　Up the hill side; and now 'tis buried deep
　　　In the next valley-glades:
Was it a vision, or a waking dream?
　Fled is that music:—Do I wake or sleep?[1]　　　　80

May, 1819　　　　　　　　　　　　　　　1819, 1820

5. Meditated. Two earlier poems ("rhymes") by Keats which called on "easeful Death" are the sonnets *Why Did I Laugh?* and *Bright Star.*
7. The young widow in the Biblical Book of Ruth.
8. I.e., wheat.
9. One critic has said that "forlorn"—which means "long past" as well as "sorrowful"—"has its feet in two worlds," the faeryland of imagination and the woe of reality to which the word reawakens the lyric speaker.
10. I.e., "the viewless wings of Poesy" of line 33.
11. Hymn. As the lyric speaker's own mood changes, the interpreted quality of the bird song alters from the flawless happiness of stanza 1, to the "high requiem" of line 60, to the sadness of the broken vision at the end.
1. See *Ode to Psyche*, above, note to line 6.

Ode on Melancholy This is Keats's best-known statement of his recurrent theme of the inextricable contrarieties of life. The remarkable last stanza, in which Melancholy becomes a veiled goddess in a mystery religion, implies that it is the tragic human destiny that beauty, joy, and life itself take their quality and value from the very fact that they are transitory, and turn into their opposites.

　The poem originally had the following opening stanza, which Keats canceled in MS:

Though you should build a bark of dead men's bones,
And rear a phantom gibbet for a mast,
Stitch creeds together for a sail, with groans
To fill it out, blood-stainéd and aghast;
Although your rudder be a dragon's tail
Long severed, yet still hard with agony,
Your cordage large uprootings from the skull
Of bald Medusa, certes you would fail
To find the Melancholy—whether she
Dreameth in any isle of Lethe dull.

Ode on Melancholy

1

No, no, go not to Lethe,[2] neither twist
Wolfsbane, tight-rooted, for its poisonous wine;
Nor suffer thy pale forehead to be kissed
By nightshade,[3] ruby grape of Proserpine;
Make not your rosary of yew-berries,[4]   5
Nor let the beetle, nor the death-moth be
Your mournful Psyche,[5] nor the downy owl
A partner in your sorrow's mysteries;[6]
For shade to shade will come too drowsily,
And drown the wakeful anguish of the soul.[7]   10

2

But when the melancholy fit shall fall
Sudden from heaven like a weeping cloud,
That fosters the droop-headed flowers all,
And hides the green hill in an April shroud;
Then glut thy sorrow on a morning rose,   15
Or on the rainbow of the salt sand-wave,
Or on the wealth of globéd peonies;
Or if thy mistress some rich anger shows,
Imprison her soft hand, and let her rave,
And feed deep, deep upon her peerless eyes.   20

3

She[8] dwells with Beauty—Beauty that must die;
And Joy, whose hand is ever at his lips
Bidding adieu; and aching Pleasure nigh,
Turning to Poison while the bee-mouth sips:
Aye, in the very temple of Delight   25
Veiled Melancholy has her sov'reign shrine,

2. The waters of forgetfulness in Hades.
3. "Nightshade" and "wolfsbane" (line 2) are poisonous plants. Proserpine is the wife of Pluto and queen of the infernal regions.
4. A symbol of death.
5. In ancient times Psyche (the soul) was sometimes represented as a butterfly or moth, fluttering out of the mouth of a dying man. The allusion may also be to the death's-head moth, which has skull-like markings on its back. The "beetle" of line 6 refers to replicas of the large black beetle, the scarab, which were often placed by Egyptians in their tombs as a symbol of resurrection.
6. Secret religious rites.
7. I.e., the intensity of sorrow is merely dulled when it is put next to other sorrows; it needs contrast to heighten it.
8. I.e., Melancholy, personified as a goddess whose chief place of worship ("shrine," line 26) is located "in the very temple of Delight" (line 25).

Though seen of none save him whose strenuous tongue
Can burst Joy's grape against his palate fine;[9]
His soul shall taste the sadness of her might,
And be among her cloudy trophies hung.[1]

May, 1819   30
                                                                                                                1820

9. Sensitive, subtly discriminative.   practice of hanging trophies in the
1. A reference to the Greek and Roman   temples of the gods.

Lamia   Keats himself cited, as the source of his plot, a story in Robert
Burton's *Anatomy of Melancholy* (1621): "One Menippus Lycius, a young
man twenty-five years of age, that going betwixt Cenchreas and Corinth,
met such a phantasm in the habit of a fair gentlewoman, which, taking
him by the hand, carried him home to her house, in the suburbs of Corinth. * * * The young man, a philosopher, otherwise staid and discreet,
able to moderate his passions, though not this of love, tarried with her a
while to his great content, and at last married her, to whose wedding,
amongst other guests, came Apollonius; who, by some probable conjectures,
found her out to be a serpent, a lamia; and that all her furniture was, like
Tantalus' gold, described by Homer, no substance but mere illusions. When
she saw herself descried, she wept, and desired Apollonius to be silent, but
he would not be moved, and thereupon she, plate, house, and all that was
in it, vanished in an instant: many thousands took notice of this fact, for
it was done in the midst of Greece."

In ancient demonology, a "lamia"—pronounced *lā'-mĭ-a*—was a monster
in woman's form who preyed on human beings. There are various clues
(see especially Part II, 229–38) that Keats invested the ancient legend with
allegorical significance. Its interpretation, however, and even the inclination
of Keats's own sympathies in the contest between Lamia and Apollonius,
have been disputed. It is possible that Keats failed to make up his mind, or
wavered in the course of composition. What seems to be Keats's indecision,
however, may in fact indicate that he intended to present an inevitably
fatal situation, in which no one is entirely blameless or blameworthy, and
no character is meant to monopolize either our sympathy or antipathy.
Lamia is an enchantress, a liar, and a calculating expert in *amour*; but she
apparently intends no harm, is genuinely in love, and is very beautiful. And
both male protagonists exhibit culpable extremes which alienate our sympathy. Lycius, though an attractive young lover, is gullible, a slave to his
passions, and capable of gratuitous cruelty; while Apollonius, though realis-
tically clear-sighted, is rigid, puritanical, and inhumane.

The poem, written between late June and early September, 1819, is a
return, after the Spenserian stanzas of *The Eve of St. Agnes*, to the pen-
tameter couplets Keats had used in *Endymion* and other early narrative
poems. But Keats had in the meantime been studying Dryden's closed and
strong-paced couplets. The initial lines of Dryden's version of Boccaccio's
story *Cymon and Iphigenia* will show the kind of narrative model which
helped Keats make the technical transition from the fluent but sprawling
gracefulness of the opening of *Endymion* to the vigor and economy of the
opening of *Lamia*:

In that sweet isle where Venus keeps her court,
And every grace, and all the loves, resort;
Where either sex is formed of softer earth,
And takes the bent of pleasure from their birth;
There lived a Cyprian lord, above the rest
Wise, wealthy, with a numerous issue blest;

* * *

Lamia

Part I

Upon a time, before the faery broods
Drove Nymph and Satyr from the prosperous woods,[1]
Before King Oberon's bright diadem,
Scepter, and mantle, clasped with dewy gem,
Frighted away the Dryads and the Fauns   5
From rushes green, and brakes,[2] and cowslipped lawns,
The ever-smitten Hermes empty left
His golden throne, bent warm on amorous theft:[3]
From high Olympus had he stolen light,
On this side of Jove's clouds, to escape the sight   10
Of his great summoner, and made retreat
Into a forest on the shores of Crete.
For somewhere in that sacred island dwelt
A nymph, to whom all hooféd Satyrs knelt;
At whose white feet the languid Tritons[4] poured   15
Pearls, while on land they withered and adored.
Fast by the springs where she to bathe was wont,
And in those meads where sometimes she might haunt,
Were strewn rich gifts, unknown to any Muse,
Though Fancy's casket were unlocked to choose.   20
Ah, what a world of love was at her feet!
So Hermes thought, and a celestial heat
Burnt from his wingéd heels to either ear,
That from a whiteness, as the lily clear,
Blushed into roses 'mid his golden hair,   25
Fallen in jealous curls about his shoulders bare.[5]
From vale to vale, from wood to wood, he flew,
Breathing upon the flowers his passion new,
And wound with many a river to its head,
To find where this sweet nymph prepared her secret bed: 30
In vain; the sweet nymph might nowhere be found,
And so he rested, on the lonely ground,
Pensive, and full of painful jealousies

---

1. Nymphs and satyrs—like the dryads and fauns in line 5—were all minor classical deities of the woods and fields, said here to have been driven off by Oberon, king of the fairies, who were supernatural beings of the postclassical era.
2. Thickets.
3. Hermes (or Mercury), wing-footed messenger at the summons of Jove (line 11), was notoriously amorous.
4. Minor sea gods.
5. The curls clung jealously to his bare shoulders. This line is the first of a number of Alexandrines, a device for introducing variety of movement that Keats learned from Dryden. Another such device is the triplet in lines 61–63.

Of the Wood-Gods, and even the very trees.
There as he stood, he heard a mournful voice,   35
Such as once heard, in gentle heart, destroys
All pain but pity: thus the lone voice spake:
"When from this wreathéd tomb shall I awake!
When move in a sweet body fit for life,
And love, and pleasure, and the ruddy strife   40
Of hearts and lips! Ah, miserable me!"
The God, dove-footed,[6] glided silently
Round bush and tree, soft-brushing, in his speed,
The taller grasses and full-flowering weed,
Until he found a palpitating snake,   45
Bright, and cirque-couchant[7] in a dusky brake.

She was a gordian[8] shape of dazzling hue,
Vermilion-spotted, golden, green, and blue;
Striped like a zebra, freckled like a pard,
Eyed like a peacock,[9] and all crimson barred;   50
And full of silver moons, that, as she breathed,
Dissolved, or brighter shone, or interwreathed
Their lusters with the gloomier tapestries—
So rainbow-sided, touched with miseries,
She seemed, at once, some penanced lady elf,   55
Some demon's mistress, or the demon's self.
Upon her crest she wore a wannish[1] fire
Sprinkled with stars, like Ariadne's tiar:[2]
Her head was serpent, but ah, bitter-sweet!
She had a woman's mouth with all its pearls[3] complete: 60
And for her eyes: what could such eyes do there
But weep, and weep, that they were born so fair?
As Proserpine still weeps for her Sicilian air.[4]
Her throat was serpent, but the words she spake
Came, as through bubbling honey, for Love's sake,   65
And thus; while Hermes on his pinions lay,
Like a stooped falcon[5] ere he takes his prey.

"Fair Hermes, crowned with feathers, fluttering light,
I had a splendid dream of thee last night:
I saw thee sitting, on a throne of gold,   70
Among the Gods, upon Olympus old,
The only sad one; for thou didst not hear
The soft, lute-fingered Muses chaunting clear,
Nor even Apollo when he sang alone,
Deaf to his throbbing throat's long, long melodious moan.   75
I dreamt I saw thee, robed in purple flakes,
Break amorous through the clouds, as morning breaks,

6. Quietly as a dove.
7. Lying in a circular coil.
8. Intricately twisted, like the knot tied by King Gordius, which no one could undo.
9. Having multicolored spots, like the "eyes" in a peacock's tail. "Pard": leopard.
1. Rather dark.
2. Ariadne, who was transformed into a constellation, had been represented in a painting by Titian wearing a symbolic crown, or tiara ("tiar"), of stars.
3. "Pearls" had become almost a synonym for teeth in Elizabethan poetry.
4. Proserpine had been carried off to Hades by Pluto from the field of Enna, in Sicily.
5. "Stoop" is the term for the plunge of a falcon upon his prey.

And, swiftly as bright Phoebean dart,[6]
Strike for the Cretan isle; and here thou art!
Too gentle Hermes, hast thou found the maid?"　　　　80
Whereat the star of Lethe[7] not delayed
His rosy eloquence and thus inquired:
"Thou smooth-lipped serpent, surely high inspired!
Thou beauteous wreath, with melancholy eyes,
Possess whatever bliss thou canst devise,　　　　85
Telling me only where my nymph is fled—
Where she doth breathe!" "Bright planet, thou hast said,"
Returned the snake, "but seal with oaths, fair God!"
"I swear," said Hermes, "by my serpent rod,
And by thine eyes, and by thy starry crown!"　　　　90
Light flew his earnest words, among the blossoms blown.
Then thus again the brilliance feminine:
"Too frail of heart! for this lost nymph of thine,
Free as the air, invisibly, she strays
About these thornless wilds; her pleasant days　　　　95
She tastes unseen; unseen her nimble feet
Leave traces in the grass and flowers sweet;
From weary tendrils, and bowed branches green,
She plucks the fruit unseen, she bathes unseen:
And by my power is her beauty veiled　　　　100
To keep it unaffronted, unassailed
By the love-glances of unlovely eyes,
Of Satyrs, Fauns, and bleared Silenus'[8] sighs.
Pale grew her immortality, for woe
Of all these lovers, and she grievéd so　　　　105
I took compassion on her, bade her steep
Her hair in weïrd[9] syrups, that would keep
Her loveliness invisible, yet free
To wander as she loves, in liberty.
Thou shalt behold her, Hermes, thou alone,　　　　110
If thou wilt, as thou swearest, grant my boon!"
Then, once again, the charméd God began
An oath, and through the serpent's ears it ran
Warm, tremulous, devout, psalterian.[1]
Ravished, she lifted her Circean[2] head,　　　　115
Blushed a live damask, and swift-lisping said,
"I was a woman, let me have once more
A woman's shape, and charming as before.
I love a youth of Corinth—O the bliss!
Give me my woman's form, and place me where he is.　　　　120
Stoop, Hermes, let me breathe upon thy brow,
And thou shalt see thy sweet nymph even now."
The God on half-shut feathers sank serene,

6. A ray of Phoebus Apollo, god of the sun.
7. Hermes, when he appeared like a star on the banks of Lethe, in the darkness of Hades. (One of Hermes' offices was to guide the souls of the dead to the lower regions.)
8. Silenus was a satyr, tutor of Bacchus, and always drunk.
9. Magical; Keats makes the word a dissyllable.
1. Either "like a psalm" or "like the sound of the psaltery" (an ancient stringed instrument).
2. Like that of Circe, the enchantress in the *Odyssey*. "Live damask": a living damask rose (large and fragrant pink rose).

She breathed upon his eyes, and swift was seen
Of both the guarded nymph near-smiling on the green.   125
It was no dream; or say a dream it was,
Real are the dreams of Gods, and smoothly pass
Their pleasures in a long immortal dream.
One warm, flushed moment, hovering, it might seem
Dashed by the wood-nymph's beauty, so he burned;   130
Then, lighting on the printless verdure, turned
To the swooned serpent, and with languid arm,
Delicate, put to proof the lithe Caducean charm.[3]
So done, upon the nymph his eyes he bent
Full of adoring tears and blandishment,   135
And towards her stepped: she, like a moon in wane,
Faded before him, cowered, nor could restrain
Her fearful sobs, self-folding like a flower
That faints into itself at evening hour:
But the God fostering her chilléd hand,   140
She felt the warmth, her eyelids opened bland,[4]
And, like new flowers at morning song of bees,
Bloomed, and gave up her honey to the lees.[5]
Into the green-recesséd woods they flew;
Nor grew they pale, as mortal lovers do.   145

    Left to herself, the serpent now began
To change; her elfin blood in madness ran,
Her mouth foamed, and the grass, therewith besprent,[6]
Withered at dew so sweet and virulent;
Her eyes in torture fixed, and anguish drear,   150
Hot, glazed, and wide, with lid-lashes all sear,
Flashed phosphor and sharp sparks, without one cooling tear.
The colors all inflamed throughout her train,
She writhed about, convulsed with scarlet pain:
A deep volcanian[7] yellow took the place   155
Of all her milder-moonéd body's grace;
And, as the lava ravishes the mead,
Spoilt all her silver mail, and golden brede;[8]
Made gloom of all her frecklings, streaks and bars,
Eclipsed her crescents, and licked up her stars: 160
So that, in moments few, she was undressed
Of all her sapphires, greens, and amethyst,
And rubious-argent:[9] of all these bereft,
Nothing but pain and ugliness were left.
Still shone her crown; that vanished, also she   165
Melted and disappeared as suddenly;
And in the air, her new voice luting soft,
Cried, "Lycius! gentle Lycius!"—Borne aloft
With the bright mists about the mountains hoar
These words dissolved: Crete's forests heard no more.   170

3. I.e., put to the test the magic of the flexible Caduceus (Hermes' official staff).
4. Softly.
5. Dregs.
6. Sprinkled.
7. The color of sulphur (thrown up by a volcano), in contrast to her former silvery moon color.
8. "Mail": interlinked rings, as in a coat of armor; "brede": embroidery, interwoven pattern.
9. Silvery red.

Whither fled Lamia, now a lady bright,
A full-born beauty new and exquisite?
She fled into that valley they pass o'er
Who go to Corinth from Cenchreas' shore;[1]
And rested at the foot of those wild hills,   175
The rugged founts of the Peraean rills,
And of that other ridge whose barren back
Stretches, with all its mist and cloudy rack,
Southwestward to Cleone. There she stood
About a young bird's flutter from a wood,   180
Fair, on a sloping green of mossy tread,
By a clear pool, wherein she passionéd[2]
To see herself escaped from so sore ills,
While her robes flaunted with the daffodils.

Ah, happy Lycius!—for she was a maid   185
More beautiful than ever twisted braid,
Or sighed, or blushed, or on spring-flowered lea[3]
Spread a green kirtle to the minstrelsy:
A virgin purest lipped, yet in the lore
Of love deep learnéd to the red heart's core: 190
Not one hour old, yet of sciential brain
To unperplex bliss from its neighbor pain;[4]
Define their pettish limits, and estrange
Their points of contact, and swift counterchange;
Intrigue with the specious chaos,[5] and dispart   195
Its most ambiguous atoms with sure art;
As though in Cupid's college she had spent
Sweet days a lovely graduate, still unshent,[6]
And kept his rosy terms in idle languishment.

Why this fair creature chose so faerily   200
By the wayside to linger, we shall see;
But first 'tis fit to tell how she could muse
And dream, when in the serpent prison-house,
Of all she list[7] strange or magnificent:
How, ever, where she willed, her spirit went;   205
Whether to faint Elysium, or where
Down through tress-lifting waves the Nereids[8] fair
Wind into Thetis' bower by many a pearly stair;
Or where God Bacchus drains his cups divine,
Stretched out, at ease, beneath a glutinous pine;   210
Or where in Pluto's gardens palatine
Mulciber's columns gleam in far piazzian line.[9]

1. Cenchrea (Keats's "Cenchreas") was a harbor of Corinth, in southern Greece.
2. Felt intense excitement.
3. Meadow; "kirtle": gown.
4. I.e., of knowledgeable ("sciential") brain to disentangle ("unperplex") bliss from its closely-related pain, to define their quarreled-over ("pettish") limits, and to separate out ("estrange") their points of contact and the swift changes of each condition into its opposite. Cf. Keats's *Ode on Melancholy*, lines 25–26.
5. I.e., turn to her own artful purpose the seeming ("specious") chaos.
6. Unspoiled. "Rosy terms": the terms spent studying in "Cupid's college."
7. Wished.
8. Sea nymphs, of whom Thetis (the mother of Achilles) was one.
9. I.e., columns made by Mulciber

And sometimes into cities she would send
Her dream, with feast and rioting to blend;
And once, while among mortals dreaming thus,   215
She saw the young Corinthian Lycius
Charioting foremost in the envious race,
Like a young Jove with calm uneager face,
And fell into a swooning love of him.
Now on the moth-time of that evening dim   220
He would return that way, as well she knew,
To Corinth from the shore; for freshly blew
The eastern soft wind, and his galley now
Grated the quaystones with her brazen prow
In port Cenchreas, from Egina isle   225
Fresh anchored; whither he had been awhile
To sacrifice to Jove, whose temple there
Waits with high marble doors for blood and incense rare.
Jove heard his vows, and bettered his desire;
For by some freakful chance he made retire   230
From his companions, and set forth to walk,
Perhaps grown wearied of their Corinth talk:
Over the solitary hills he fared,
Thoughtless at first, but ere eve's star appeared
His phantasy was lost, where reason fades,   235
In the calmed twilight of Platonic shades.[1]
Lamia beheld him coming, near, more near—
Close to her passing, in indifference drear,
His silent sandals swept the mossy green;
So neighbored to him, and yet so unseen   240
She stood: he passed, shut up in mysteries,
His mind wrapped like his mantle, while her eyes
Followed his steps, and her neck regal white
Turned—syllabling thus, "Ah, Lycius bright,
And will you leave me on the hills alone?   245
Lycius, look back! and be some pity shown."
He did; not with cold wonder fearingly,
But Orpheus-like at an Eurydice;[2]
For so delicious were the words she sung,
It seemed he had loved them a whole summer long: 250
And soon his eyes had drunk her beauty up,
Leaving no drop in the bewildering cup,
And still the cup was full—while he, afraid
Lest she should vanish ere his lip had paid
Due adoration, thus began to adore;   255
Her soft look growing coy, she saw his chain so sure:
"Leave thee alone! Look back! Ah, Goddess, see
Whether my eyes can ever turn from thee!
For pity do not this sad heart belie[3]—

(Vulcan, god of fire and metalworking) gleam in long lines around open courts (piazzas). "Palatine": palatial.
1. I.e., he was absorbed in musing about the obscurities of Plato's philosophy.
2. As Orpheus looked at Eurydice in Hades. Orpheus was allowed by Pluto to lead Eurydice back to earth on condition that he not look back at her, but he could not resist doing so, and lost her once more.
3. Be false to.

Even as thou vanishest so shall I die.   260
Stay! though a Naiad of the rivers, stay!
To thy far wishes will thy streams obey:
Stay! though the greenest woods be thy domain,
Alone they can drink up the morning rain:
Though a descended Pleiad,⁴ will not one   265
Of thine harmonious sisters keep in tune
Thy spheres, and as thy silver proxy shine?
So sweetly to these ravished ears of mine
Came thy sweet greeting, that if thou shouldst fade
Thy memory will waste me to a shade—   270
For pity do not melt!"—"If I should stay,"
Said Lamia, "here, upon this floor of clay,
And pain my steps upon these flowers too rough,
What canst thou say or do of charm enough
To dull the nice⁵ remembrance of my home?   275
Thou canst not ask me with thee here to roam
Over these hills and vales, where no joy is—
Empty of immortality and bliss!
Thou art a scholar, Lycius, and must know
That finer spirits cannot breathe below   280
In human climes, and live: Alas! poor youth,
What taste of purer air hast thou to soothe
My essence? What serener palaces,
Where I may all my many senses please,
And by mysterious sleights a hundred thirsts appease?   285
It cannot be—Adieu!" So said, she rose
Tiptoe with white arms spread. He, sick to lose
The amorous promise of her lone complain,
Swooned, murmuring of love, and pale with pain.
The cruel lady, without any show   290
Of sorrow for her tender favorite's woe,
But rather, if her eyes could brighter be,
With brighter eyes and slow amenity,
Put her new lips to his, and gave afresh
The life she had so tangled in her mesh: 295
And as he from one trance was wakening
Into another, she began to sing,
Happy in beauty, life, and love, and everything,
A song of love, too sweet for earthly lyres,
While, like held breath, the stars drew in their panting fires.   300
And then she whispered in such trembling tone,
As those who, safe together met alone
For the first time through many anguished days,
Use other speech than looks; bidding him raise
His drooping head, and clear his soul of doubt,   305
For that she was a woman, and without
Any more subtle fluid in her veins
Than throbbing blood, and that the selfsame pains
Inhabited her frail-strung heart as his.

4. One of the seven sisters composing   5. Detailed, minutely accurate.
the constellation Pleiades.

And next she wondered how his eyes could miss 310
Her face so long in Corinth, where, she said,
She dwelt but half retired, and there had led
Days happy as the gold coin could invent
Without the aid of love; yet in content
Till she saw him, as once she passed him by, 315
Where 'gainst a column he leant thoughtfully
At Venus' temple porch, 'mid baskets heaped
Of amorous herbs and flowers, newly reaped
Late on that eve, as 'twas the night before
The Adonian feast;[6] whereof she saw no more, 320
But wept alone those days, for why should she adore?
Lycius from death awoke into amaze,
To see her still, and singing so sweet lays;
Then from amaze into delight he fell
To hear her whisper woman's lore so well; 325
And every word she spake enticed him on
To unperplexed delight[7] and pleasure known.
Let the mad poets say whate'er they please
Of the sweets of Faeries, Peris,[8] Goddesses,
There is not such a treat among them all, 330
Haunters of cavern, lake, and waterfall,
As a real woman, lineal indeed
From Pyrrha's pebbles[9] or old Adam's seed.
Thus gentle Lamia judged, and judged aright,
That Lycius could not love in half a fright, 335
So threw the goddess off, and won his heart
More pleasantly by playing woman's part,
With no more awe than what her beauty gave,
That, while it smote, still guaranteed to save.
Lycius to all made eloquent reply, 340
Marrying to every word a twinborn sigh;
And last, pointing to Corinth, asked her sweet,
If 'twas too far that night for her soft feet.
The way was short, for Lamia's eagerness
Made, by a spell, the triple league decrease 345
To a few paces; not at all surmised
By blinded Lycius, so in her comprised.[1]
They passed the city gates, he knew not how,
So noiseless, and he never thought to know.

As men talk in a dream, so Corinth all, 350
Throughout her palaces imperial,
And all her populous streets and temples lewd,[2]
Muttered, like tempest in the distance brewed,
To the wide-spreaded night above her towers.
Men, women, rich and poor, in the cool hours, 355

6. The feast of Adonis, beloved by Venus.
7. I.e., delight not mixed with its neighbor, pain; see line 192.
8. Fairylike creatures in Persian mythology.
9. Descended from the pebbles with which, in Greek myth, Pyrrha and Deucalion repeopled the earth after the flood.
1. Bound up.
2. Temples of Venus, whose worship sometimes involved ritual prostitution.

Shuffled their sandals o'er the pavement white,
Companioned or alone; while many a light
Flared, here and there, from wealthy festivals,
And threw their moving shadows on the walls,
Or found them clustered in the corniced shade   360
Of some arched temple door, or dusky colonnade.

Muffling his face, of greeting friends in fear,
Her fingers he pressed hard, as one came near
With curled gray beard, sharp eyes, and smooth bald crown,
Slow-stepped, and robed in philosophic gown: 365
Lycius shrank closer, as they met and passed,
Into his mantle, adding wings to haste,
While hurried Lamia trembled: "Ah," said he,
"Why do you shudder, love, so ruefully?
Why does your tender palm dissolve in dew?"—   370
"I'm wearied," said fair Lamia: "tell me who
Is that old man? I cannot bring to mind
His features—Lycius! wherefore did you blind
Yourself from his quick eyes?" Lycius replied,
" 'Tis Apollonius sage, my trusty guide   375
And good instructor; but tonight he seems
The ghost of folly haunting my sweet dreams."

While yet he spake they had arrived before
A pillared porch, with lofty portal door,
Where hung a silver lamp, whose phosphor glow   380
Reflected in the slabbèd steps below,
Mild as a star in water; for so new,
And so unsullied was the marble hue,
So through the crystal polish, liquid fine,
Ran the dark veins, that none but feet divine   385
Could e'er have touched there. Sounds Aeolian[3]
Breathed from the hinges, as the ample span
Of the wide doors disclosed a place unknown
Some time to any, but those two alone,
And a few Persian mutes, who that same year   390
Were seen about the markets: none knew where
They could inhabit; the most curious
Were foiled, who watched to trace them to their house:
And but the flitter-wingèd verse must tell,
For truth's sake, what woe afterwards befell,   395
'Twould humor many a heart to leave them thus,
Shut from the busy world of more incredulous.

Part II

Love in a hut, with water and a crust,
Is—Love, forgive us!—cinders, ashes, dust;
Love in a palace is perhaps at last
More grievous torment than a hermit's fast:

3. Like sounds from the wind harp (Aeolus is god of winds), which responds
musically to a current of air.

That is a doubtful tale from faery land,   5
Hard for the non-elect to understand.
Had Lycius lived to hand his story down,
He might have given the moral a fresh frown,
Or clenched it quite: but too short was their bliss
To breed distrust and hate, that make the soft voice hiss.   10
Beside, there, nightly, with terrific glare,
Love, jealous grown of so complete a pair,
Hovered and buzzed his wings, with fearful roar,
Above the lintel of their chamber door,
And down the passage cast a glow upon the floor.   15

  For all this came a ruin: side by side
They were enthronéd, in the eventide,
Upon a couch, near to a curtaining
Whose airy texture, from a golden string,
Floated into the room, and let appear   20
Unveiled the summer heaven, blue and clear,
Betwixt two marble shafts: there they reposed,
Where use had made it sweet, with eyelids closed,
Saving a tithe which love still open kept,
That they might see each other while they almost slept;   25
When from the slope side of a suburb hill,
Deafening the swallow's twitter, came a thrill
Of trumpets—Lycius started—the sounds fled,
But left a thought, a buzzing in his head.
For the first time, since first he harbored in   30
That purple-linéd palace of sweet sin,
His spirit passed beyond its golden bourn
Into the noisy world almost forsworn.
The lady, ever watchful, penetrant,
Saw this with pain, so arguing a want   35
Of something more, more than her empery[4]
Of joys; and she began to moan and sigh
Because he mused beyond her, knowing well
That but a moment's thought is passion's passing bell.[5]
"Why do you sigh, fair creature?" whispered he: 40
"Why do you think?" returned she tenderly:
"You have deserted me—where am I now?
Not in your heart while care weighs on your brow:
No, no, you have dismissed me; and I go
From your breast houseless: aye, it must be so."   45
He answered, bending to her open eyes,
Where he was mirrored small in paradise,
"My silver planet, both of eve and morn![6]
Why will you plead yourself so sad forlorn,
While I am striving how to fill my heart   50
With deeper crimson, and a double smart?
How to entangle, trammel up, and snare
Your soul in mine, and labyrinth you there

4. Empire.   6. The planet Venus, which is both the
5. Death knell.   morning and the evening star.

Like the hid scent in an unbudded rose?
Aye, a sweet kiss—you see your mighty woes.[7] 55
My thoughts! shall I unveil them? Listen then!
What mortal hath a prize, that other men
May be confounded and abashed withal,
But lets it sometimes pace abroad majestical,
And triumph, as in thee I should rejoice 60
Amid the hoarse alarm of Corinth's voice.
Let my foes choke, and my friends shout afar,
While through the throngéd streets your bridal car
Wheels round its dazzling spokes."—The lady's cheek
Trembled; she nothing said, but, pale and meek, 65
Arose and knelt before him, wept a rain
Of sorrows at his words; at last with pain
Beseeching him, the while his hand she wrung,
To change his purpose. He thereat was stung,
Perverse, with stronger fancy to reclaim 70
Her wild and timid nature to his aim:
Besides, for all his love, in self-despite,
Against his better self, he took delight
Luxurious in her sorrows, soft and new.
His passion, cruel grown, took on a hue 75
Fierce and sanguineous as 'twas possible
In one whose brow had no dark veins to swell.
Fine was the mitigated fury, like
Apollo's presence when in act to strike
The serpent—Ha, the serpent! certes, she 80
Was none. She burnt, she loved the tyranny,
And, all subdued, consented to the hour
When to the bridal he should lead his paramour.
Whispering in midnight silence, said the youth,
"Sure some sweet name thou hast, though, by my truth, 85
I have not asked it, ever thinking thee
Not mortal, but of heavenly progeny,
As still I do. Hast any mortal name,
Fit appellation for this dazzling frame?
Or friends or kinsfolk on the cited earth, 90
To share our marriage feast and nuptial mirth?"
"I have no friends," said Lamia, "no, not one;
My presence in wide Corinth hardly known:
My parents' bones are in their dusty urns
Sepulchered, where no kindled incense burns, 95
Seeing all their luckless race are dead, save me,
And I neglect the holy rite for thee.
Even as you list invite your many guests;
But if, as now it seems, your vision rests
With any pleasure on me, do not bid 100
Old Apollonius—from him keep me hid."
Lycius, perplexed at words so blind and blank,

---

7. Playfully: "You see how great your troubles were!"

Made close inquiry; from whose touch she shrank,
Feigning a sleep; and he to the dull shade
Of deep sleep in a moment was betrayed.   105

    It was the custom then to bring away
The bride from home at blushing shut of day,
Veiled, in a chariot, heralded along
By strewn flowers, torches, and a marriage song,
With other pageants: but this fair unknown   110
Had not a friend. So being left alone
(Lycius was gone to summon all his kin),
And knowing surely she could never win
His foolish heart from its mad pompousness,
She set herself, high-thoughted, how to dress   115
The misery in fit magnificence.
She did so, but 'tis doubtful how and whence
Came, and who were her subtle servitors.
About the halls, and to and from the doors,
There was a noise of wings, till in short space   120
The glowing banquet room shone with wide-archéd grace.
A haunting music, sole perhaps and lone
Supportress of the faery roof, made moan
Throughout, as fearful the whole charm might fade.
Fresh carvéd cedar, mimicking a glade   125
Of palm and plantain, met from either side,
High in the midst, in honor of the bride:
Two palms and then two plaintains, and so on,
From either side their stems branched one to one
All down the aisléd place; and beneath all   130
There ran a stream of lamps straight on from wall to wall.
So canopied, lay an untasted feast
Teeming with odors. Lamia, regal dressed,
Silently paced about, and as she went,
In pale contented sort of discontent,   135
Missioned her viewless servants to enrich
The fretted⁸ splendor of each nook and niche.
Between the tree stems, marbled plain at first,
Came jasper panels; then, anon, there burst
Forth creeping imagery of slighter trees,   140
And with the larger wove in small intricacies.
Approving all, she faded at self-will,
And shut the chamber up, close, hushed and still,
Complete and ready for the revels rude,
When dreadful⁹ guests would come to spoil her solitude. 145

    The day appeared, and all the gossip rout.
O senseless Lycius! Madman! wherefore flout
The silent-blessing fate, warm cloistered hours,
And show to common eyes these secret bowers?

---

8. Adorned with fretwork (interlaced patterns).   9. Terrifying.

The herd approached; each guest, with busy brain,   150
Arriving at the portal, gazed amain,[1]
And entered marveling: for they knew the street,
Remembered it from childhood all complete
Without a gap, yet ne'er before had seen
That royal porch, that high-built fair demesne;[2]   155
So in they hurried all, 'mazed, curious and keen:
Save one, who looked thereon with eye severe,
And with calm-planted steps walked in austere;
'Twas Apollonius: something too he laughed,
As though some knotty problem, that had daft[3]   160
His patient thought, had now begun to thaw,
And solve and melt—'twas just as he foresaw.

He met within the murmurous vestibule
His young disciple. " 'Tis no common rule,
Lycius," said he, "for uninvited guest   165
To force himself upon you, and infest
With an unbidden presence the bright throng
Of younger friends; yet must I do this wrong,
And you forgive me." Lycius blushed, and led
The old man through the inner doors broad-spread;   170
With reconciling words and courteous mien
Turning into sweet milk the sophist's spleen.

Of wealthy luster was the banquet room,
Filled with pervading brilliance and perfume:
Before each lucid panel fuming stood   175
A censer fed with myrrh and spicéd wood,
Each by a sacred tripod held aloft,
Whose slender feet wide-swerved upon the soft
Wool-wooféd[4] carpets: fifty wreaths of smoke
From fifty censers their light voyage took   180
To the high roof, still mimicked as they rose
Along the mirrored walls by twin-clouds odorous.
Twelve spheréd tables, by silk seats ensphered,
High as the level of a man's breast reared
On libbard's[5] paws, upheld the heavy gold   185
Of cups and goblets, and the store thrice told
Of Ceres' horn[6] and, in huge vessels, wine
Come from the gloomy tun with merry shine.
Thus loaded with a feast the tables stood,
Each shrining in the midst the image of a God.   190

When in an antechamber every guest
Had felt the cold full sponge to pleasure pressed,
By minist'ring slaves, upon his hands and feet,
And fragrant oils with ceremony meet

1. Intently.
2. Estate.
3. Baffled, bewildered.
4. Woven.

5. Leopard's.
6. The horn of plenty, overflowing with the products of Ceres, goddess of vegetation.

Poured on his hair, they all moved to the feast   195
In white robes, and themselves in order placed
Around the silken couches, wondering
Whence all this mighty cost and blaze of wealth could spring.

    Soft went the music the soft air along,
While fluent Greek a voweled undersong   200
Kept up among the guests, discoursing low
At first, for scarcely was the wine at flow;
But when the happy vintage touched their brains,
Louder they talk, and louder come the strains
Of powerful instruments—the gorgeous dyes,   205
The space, the splendor of the draperies,
The roof of awful richness, nectarous cheer,
Beautiful slaves, and Lamia's self, appear,
Now, when the wine has done its rosy deed,
And every soul from human trammels freed,   210
No more so strange; for merry wine, sweet wine,
Will make Elysian shades not too fair, too divine.
Soon was God Bacchus at meridian height;
Flushed were their cheeks, and bright eyes double bright:
Garlands of every green, and every scent   215
From vales deflowered, or forest trees branch-rent,
In baskets of bright osiered[7] gold were brought
High as the handles heaped, to suit the thought
Of every guest; that each, as he did please,
Might fancy-fit his brows, silk-pillowed at his ease.   220

    What wreath for Lamia? What for Lycius?
What for the sage, old Apollonius?
Upon her aching forehead be there hung
The leaves of willow and of adder's tongue;[8]
And for the youth, quick, let us strip for him   225
The thyrsus,[9] that his watching eyes may swim
Into forgetfulness; and, for the sage,
Let spear-grass and the spiteful thistle wage
War on his temples. Do not all charms fly
At the mere touch of cold philosophy?[1]   230
There was an awful[2] rainbow once in heaven:
We know her woof, her texture; she is given
In the dull catalogue of common things.
Philosophy will clip an Angel's wings,
Conquer all mysteries by rule and line,   235
Empty the haunted air, and gnoméd mine[3]—

---

7. Plaited. An "osier" is a willow rod used in weaving baskets.
8. A fern whose spikes resemble a serpent's tongue.
9. The vine-covered staff of Bacchus, used to signify drunkenness.
1. "Philosophy" in the sense of "natural philosophy," or science. Benjamin Haydon tells in his *Autobiography* how, at a hard-drinking and high-spirited dinner party, Keats had agreed with Charles Lamb (to what extent jokingly, is not clear) that Newton's *Optics* "had destroyed all the poetry of the rainbow by reducing it to the prismatic colors."
2. Awe-inspiring.
3. Gnomes were guardians of mines.

Unweave a rainbow, as it erewhile made
The tender-personed Lamia melt into a shade.

By her glad Lycius sitting, in chief place,
Scarce saw in all the room another face,   240
Till, checking his love trance, a cup he took
Full brimmed, and opposite sent forth a look
'Cross the broad table, to beseech a glance
From his old teacher's wrinkled countenance,
And pledge him.[4] The bald-head philosopher   245
Had fixed his eye, without a twinkle or stir
Full on the alarméd beauty of the bride,
Brow-beating her fair form, and troubling her sweet pride.
Lycius then pressed her hand, with devout touch,
As pale it lay upon the rosy couch: 250
'Twas icy, and the cold ran through his veins;
Then sudden it grew hot, and all the pains
Of an unnatural heat shot to his heart.
"Lamia, what means this? Wherefore dost thou start?
Know'st thou that man?" Poor Lamia answered not.   255
He gazed into her eyes, and not a jot
Owned[5] they the lovelorn piteous appeal:
More, more he gazed: his human senses reel:
Some hungry spell that loveliness absorbs;
There was no recognition in those orbs.   260
"Lamia!" he cried—and no soft-toned reply.
The many heard, and the loud revelry
Grew hush; the stately music no more breathes;
The myrtle[5a] sickened in a thousand wreaths.
By faint degrees, voice, lute, and pleasure ceased;   265
A deadly silence step by step increased,
Until it seemed a horrid presence there,
And not a man but felt the terror in his hair.
"Lamia!" he shrieked; and nothing but the shriek
With its sad echo did the silence break.   270
"Begone, foul dream!" he cried, gazing again
In the bride's face, where now no azure vein
Wandered on fair-spaced temples; no soft bloom
Misted the cheek; no passion to illume
The deep-recesséd vision—all was blight;   275
Lamia, no longer fair, there sat a deadly white.
"Shut, shut those juggling[6] eyes, thou ruthless man!
Turn them aside, wretch! or the righteous ban
Of all the Gods, whose dreadful images
Here represent their shadowy presences,   280
May pierce them on the sudden with the thorn
Of painful blindness; leaving thee forlorn,
In trembling dotage to the feeblest fright
Of conscience, for their long offended might,

4. Drink a toast to him.   of love.
5. Acknowledged.   6. Deceiving, full of trickery.
5a. Sacred to Venus, hence an emblem

For all thine impious proud-heart sophistries, 285
Unlawful magic, and enticing lies.
Corinthians! look upon that gray-beard wretch!
Mark how, possessed, his lashless eyelids stretch
Around his demon eyes! Corinthians, see!
My sweet bride withers at their potency." 290
"Fool!" said the sophist, in an undertone
Gruff with contempt; which a death-nighing moan
From Lycius answered, as heart-struck and lost,
He sank supine beside the aching ghost.
"Fool! Fool!" repeated he, while his eyes still 295
Relented not, nor moved; "from every ill
Of life have I preserved thee to this day,
And shall I see thee made a serpent's prey?"
Then Lamia breathed death breath; the sophist's eye,
Like a sharp spear, went through her utterly, 300
Keen, cruel, perceant,[7] stinging: she, as well
As her weak hand could any meaning tell,
Motioned him to be silent; vainly so,
He looked and looked again a level—No!
"A serpent!" echoed he; no sooner said, 305
Than with a frightful scream she vanishéd:
And Lycius' arms were empty of delight,
As were his limbs of life, from that same night.
On the high couch he lay!—his friends came round—
Supported him—no pulse, or breath they found, 310
And, in its marriage robe, the heavy body wound.

July–Aug., 1819   1820

7. Piercing.

The Fall of Hyperion   In September of 1818, at the close of his
twenty-third year and while he was serving as nurse to his dying brother
Tom, Keats undertook an epic poem, modeled on *Paradise Lost*, which he
called *Hyperion*. Its subject, the displacement of Saturn and his fellow
Titans by Zeus and the other Olympians, was taken from Greek mythology,
but the primary epic question, like that in *Paradise Lost*, was *unde
malum?*—whence and why evil? Keats set out to represent an answer,
not in terms of the Christian or any other religious creed, but in humanistic
terms, delimited to man and his natural milieu. The Titans had been
equable and benign gods, ruling in the Saturnian, or golden, age of general
felicity. Yet at the beginning of the poem all the Titans except Hyperion,
god of the sun, have been dethroned; and the uncomprehending Saturn
again and again raises the question, Who? Why? How? Is there blank
unreason and injustice at the heart of the universe? Oceanus, god of the
sea, offers a valid but incomplete solution: the gods, though themselves
blameless, have fallen in the natural progression of things, according to
which each stage of development is fated to give place to a higher excellence, "for 'tis the eternal law / That first in beauty should be first in
might." And it is the part of wisdom and virtue among the Titans to
accept this truth uncomplainingly,

for to bear all naked truths,
And to envisage circumstance, all calm,
That is the top of sovereignty.

In Book III of the original *Hyperion* this is supplemented by the experience of Apollo, still a youth on earth but destined to displace Hyperion among the heavenly powers. He lives in "aching ignorance" of the universe and its processes, but he is aware of his ignorance and avid for knowledge. To him appears Mnemosyne, herself a Titan, but one who has deserted her fellow gods "For prophecies of thee, and for the sake / Of loveliness new born." Suddenly Apollo reads in the face of Mnemosyne—goddess of memory, who will be mother of the muses, and so of all the arts—the silent record of the defeat of the Titans and at once soars to the knowledge that he seeks: the deep understanding, at once intoxicating and agonizing, that life involves process, and process entails change and suffering, and that there can be no creative progress except by the defeat and destruction of the preceding stage. Apollo cries out:

Knowledge enormous makes a god of me.
Names, deeds, gray legends, dire events, rebellions,
Majesties, sovran voices, agonies,
Creations and destroyings, all at once
Pour into the wide hollows of my brain
And deify me, as if of some blithe wine
Or elixir peerless I had drunk,
And so become immortal.

This is an enlargement of Apollo's awareness to encompass the sense of the tragic nature of life which it has been the Titans' deficiency to lack. As the fragment breaks off Apollo is transfigured, like one who should "with fierce convulse / Die into life," not only into the god of the sun, who has earned the right to displace Hyperion, but also into the god of the highest poetry.

This extraordinary fragment Keats wrote mainly in the two months between late September and December, 1818, and he abandoned it entirely by April of 1819. Late that summer, however, he took up the theme again, under the title *The Fall of Hyperion: A Dream*. This time his primary model is Dante, especially the *Purgatorio*, which he had been carefully studying in Cary's translation. In *The Divine Comedy* all the narrated events had been represented as a vision granted to Dante at the beginning of the poem. In similar fashion Keats begins his new poem with a long induction in which the poet, in a dream, earns the right to a vision finally granted him by Moneta (her Latin name suggests "the Admonisher"), who replaces Mnemosyne; this vision incorporates the epic events narrated in the first *Hyperion*. The induction, in effect, shifts the center of poetic concern from the epic action to the evolving consciousness of the narrative poet himself, as he seeks his identity and status; it serves also to displace the earlier ordeal through which Apollo had become god of poetry by the ordeal of this particular poet.

As early as *Sleep and Poetry* (1816), Keats had begun to explore the baffling relation of dreams to insight, of wishful fantasies and illusions to imaginative truth, of the life of actuality and of humane action to the contemplative vision of the poet; and he had worked these matters into his poetic program to move from the realm of "Flora, and old Pan" to the "nobler life" of "the agonies, the strife / Of human hearts." He continued to widen these speculations in *Endymion* and a number of his shorter poems; and his letters show his ceaseless effort to assimilate his ever-enlarging experience, his sharpening sense of suffering humanity, and his awareness of the need for some equivalent of the "salvation" offered by a religious creed he could not accept, into his theory and program of poetry. (See especially the letters, included here, on "The Chambers of Human Life" and on "The Vale of Soul-Making.") Into the induction to the long "Dream" which constitutes *The Fall of Hyperion*, Keats works the results of his sustained attempts to differentiate escapist dreams, as well as the creeds of the religious "fanatic," from the imaginative vision of the poet; he presents these results as progressive discoveries which he had made at the various stages of his own development as a poet. The induction, therefore, is Keats's equivalent of a poem he never saw, Wordsworth's *Prelude*, the account of "the Growth of a Poet's Mind." But whereas Wordsworth had represented his evolution of mind, up to and through the crisis in which he discovered his poetic identity, in the mode of literal autobiography, Keats instead employs the pattern of a ritual initiation. In the course of this agonizing rite of passage the poet progresses, in quantum leaps of expanding awareness of what it is to be human, and a poet of humanity, to the stage at which, having passed through and beyond the sufferings of ordinary experience to achieve aesthetic insight and distance—the power (line 304) "To see as a god sees"— he has defined the kind of poet he is and earned the right to essay his epic poem of tragic suffering.

A number of reasons impelled Keats to abandon *The Fall of Hyperion* at the sixty-first line of the second Canto. Keats wrote to Reynolds on September 21, 1819:

I have given up Hyperion . . . Miltonic verse cannot be written but in an artful or rather artist's humour. I wish to give myself up to other sensations. English ought to be kept up. It may be interesting to you to pick out some lines from Hyperion and put a mark X to the false beauty proceeding from art, and one ‖ to the true voice of feeling.

The two *Hyperions* are astonishing achievements; but they are achievements, as Keats, with his matchless acumen in self-criticism recognized, which have the air of artistic *tours de force*, written in an age in which the high artifice of the epic matter and style had ceased to be the natural voice of the poet. In the same letter Keats mentions having composed two days earlier the ode *To Autumn*; in this, his last and most flawless major poem, the poet had envisaged the circumstance of the cycle of life and death, all calm, and had uttered his experience in the true voice of feeling.

The Fall of Hyperion

A DREAM

Canto I

Fanatics have their dreams, wherewith they weave
A paradise for a sect; the savage too
From forth the loftiest fashion of his sleep

Guesses at Heaven; pity these have not
Traced upon vellum or wild Indian leaf   5
The shadows of melodious utterance.
But bare of laurel they live, dream, and die;
For Poesy alone can tell her dreams,
With the fine spell of words alone can save
Imagination from the sable chain   10
And dumb enchantment. Who alive can say,
"Thou art no Poet—may'st not tell thy dreams"?
Since every man whose soul is not a clod
Hath visions, and would speak, if he had loved,
And been well nurtured in his mother tongue.   15
Whether the dream now purposed to rehearse
Be poet's or fanatic's will be known
When this warm scribe, my hand, is in the grave.

Methought I stood where trees of every clime,
Palm, myrtle, oak, and sycamore, and beech,   20
With plantain, and spice-blossoms, made a screen;
In neighborhood of fountains (by the noise
Soft-showering in my ears), and (by the touch
Of scent) not far from roses. Turning round
I saw an arbor with a drooping roof   25
Of trellis vines, and bells, and larger blooms,
Like floral censers, swinging light in air;
Before its wreathéd doorway, on a mound
Of moss, was spread a feast of summer fruits,
Which, nearer seen, seemed refuse of a meal   30
By angel tasted or our Mother Eve;[1]
For empty shells were scattered on the grass,
And grape-stalks but half bare, and remnants more,
Sweet smelling, whose pure kinds I could not know.
Still was more plenty than the fabled horn[2]   35
Thrice emptied could pour forth, at banqueting
For Proserpine returned to her own fields,[3]
Where the white heifers low. And appetite
More yearning than on Earth I ever felt
Growing within, I ate deliciously;   40
And, after not long, thirsted, for thereby
Stood a cool vessel of transparent juice,
Sipped by the wandered bee, the which I took,
And, pledging all the mortals of the world,
And all the dead whose names are in our lips,   45
Drank. That full draught is parent of my theme.[4]
No Asian poppy nor elixir fine

1. In *Paradise Lost* V.321 ff., Eve serves the visiting angel, Raphael, with a meal of fruits and fruit juices. Keats thus adapts Milton's Eden to represent the early stage of his own experience and poetry.
2. The cornucopia, or horn of plenty.

3. When Proserpine each year is released by her husband, Pluto, god of the underworld, for a sojourn on earth, it is the beginning of spring.
4. The drink puts the poet to sleep and effects the dream within a dream which constitutes the rest of his poem.

Of the soon-fading jealous Caliphat;[5]
No poison gendered in close monkish cell,
To thin the scarlet conclave of old men,[6]   50
Could so have rapt unwilling life away.
Among the fragrant husks and berries crushed,
Upon the grass I struggled hard against
The domineering potion; but in vain:
The cloudy swoon came on, and down I sunk,   55
Like a Silenus[7] on an antique vase.
How long I slumbered 'tis a chance to guess.
When sense of life returned, I started up
As if with wings; but the fair trees were gone,
The mossy mound and arbor were no more: 60
I looked around upon the carvéd sides
Of an old sanctuary with roof august,
Builded so high, it seemed that filméd clouds
Might spread beneath, as o'er the stars of heaven;
So old the place was, I remembered none   65
The like upon the Earth: what I had seen
Of gray cathedrals, buttressed walls, rent towers,
The superannuations of sunk realms,
Or Nature's rocks toiled hard in waves and winds,
Seemed but the faulture of decrepit things   70
To that eternal doméd Monument.—
Upon the marble at my feet there lay
Store of strange vessels and large draperies,
Which needs had been of dyed asbestos wove,
Or in that place the moth could not corrupt,[8]   75
So white the linen, so, in some, distinct
Ran imageries from a somber loom.
All in a mingled heap confused there lay
Robes, golden tongs, censer and chafing dish,
Girdles, and chains, and holy jewelries.[9]   80

Turning from these with awe, once more I raised
My eyes to fathom the space every way;
The embosséd roof, the silent massy range
Of columns north and south, ending in mist
Of nothing; then to eastward, where black gates   85
Were shut against the sunrise evermore.[1]
Then to the west I looked, and saw far off
An image, huge of feature as a cloud,
At level of whose feet an altar slept,
To be approached on either side by steps,   90

5. A council of Caliphs, Mohammedan rulers, who plot to kill each other with a poisonous draft ("elixir").
6. The Cardinals of the Catholic Church.
7. An elderly satyr, usually represented as dead drunk.
8. Matthew vi.20. "Lay up for yourselves treasures in heaven, where neither moth nor rust doth corrupt."
9. Offerings to the gods were spread on the floor of Greek temples.
1. The poet cannot turn back to his origin in the east, and the ways north and south lead nowhere; he must travel the way of mortal life toward the sunset. Cf. the westering course of the sun in Wordsworth's *Ode: Intimations of Immortality.*

And marble balustrade, and patient travail
To count with toil the innumerable degrees.
Towards the altar sober-paced I went,
Repressing haste, as too unholy there;
And, coming nearer, saw beside the shrine   95
One minist'ring;[2] and there arose a flame.
When in mid-May the sickening East wind
Shifts sudden to the south, the small warm rain
Melts out the frozen incense from all flowers,
And fills the air with so much pleasant health   100
That even the dying man forgets his shroud;
Even so that lofty sacrificial fire,
Sending forth Maian[3] incense, spread around
Forgetfulness of everything but bliss,
And clouded all the altar with soft smoke;   105
From whose white fragrant curtains thus I heard
Language pronounced: "If thou canst not ascend
These steps,[4] die on that marble where thou art.
Thy flesh, near cousin to the common dust,
Will parch for lack of nutriment—thy bones   110
Will wither in few years, and vanish so
That not the quickest eye could find a grain
Of what thou now art on that pavement cold.
The sands of thy short life are spent this hour,
And no hand in the universe can turn   115
Thy hourglass, if these gummed leaves be burnt
Ere thou canst mount up these immortal steps."
I heard, I looked: two senses both at once,
So fine, so subtle, felt the tyranny
Of that fierce threat and the hard task proposed.   120
Prodigious seemed the toil, the leaves were yet
Burning—when suddenly a palsied chill
Struck from the paved level up my limbs,
And was ascending quick to put cold grasp
Upon those streams that pulse beside the throat: 125
I shrieked, and the sharp anguish of my shriek
Stung my own ears—I strove hard to escape
The numbness; strove to gain the lowest step.
Slow, heavy, deadly was my pace: the cold
Grew stifling, suffocating, at the heart;   130
And when I clasped my hands I felt them not.
One minute before death, my iced foot touched
The lowest stair; and as it touched, life seemed
To pour in at the toes: I mounted up,
As once fair angels on a ladder flew   135
From the green turf to Heaven.[5] "Holy Power,"

2. Who identifies herself, line 226, as
Moneta.
3. Maia was one of the Pleiades, a
daughter of Atlas and (by Zeus) the
mother of Hermes.
4. These steps which the poet must ascend to knowledge were probably suggested by the stairs going up the steep
side of the Purgatorial Mount, in Dante's
Purgatorio.
5. The ladder by which, in a dream,
Jacob saw angels passing between heaven
and earth; Genesis xxviii.12 and *Paradise Lost* III.510–15.

Cried I, approaching near the hornéd shrine,[6]
"What am I that should so be saved from death?
What am I that another death come not
To choke my utterance sacrilegious, here?"   140
Then said the veiléd shadow: "Thou hast felt
What 'tis to die and live again before
Thy fated hour, that thou hadst power to do so
Is thy own safety; thou hast dated on
Thy doom."[7] "High Prophetess," said I, "purge off,   145
Benign, if so it please thee, my mind's film."
"None can usurp this height," returned that shade,
"But those to whom the miseries of the world
Are misery, and will not let them rest.
All else who find a haven in the world,   150
Where they may thoughtless sleep away their days,
If by a chance into this fane[8] they come,
Rot on the pavement where thou rottedst half."[9]
"Are there not thousands in the world," said I,
Encouraged by the sooth voice of the shade,   155
"Who love their fellows even to the death,
Who feel the giant agony of the world,
And more, like slaves to poor humanity,
Labor for mortal good? I sure should see
Other men here; but I am here alone."   160
"Those whom thou spak'st of are no vision'ries,"
Rejoined that voice. "They are no dreamers weak,
They seek no wonder but the human face;
No music but a happy-noted voice—
They come not here, they have no thought to come—   165
And thou art here, for thou art less than they.
What benefit canst thou, or all thy tribe,
To the great world? Thou art a dreaming thing,
A fever of thyself—think of the earth;
What bliss even in hope is there for thee?   170
What haven? every creature hath its home;
Every sole man hath days of joy and pain,
Whether his labors be sublime or low—
The pain alone, the joy alone, distinct.
Only the dreamer venoms all his days,   175
Bearing more woe than all his sins deserve.
Therefore, that happiness be somewhat shared,
Such things as thou art are admitted oft
Into like gardens thou didst pass erewhile,
And suffered in these temples: for that cause   180
Thou standest safe beneath this statue's knees."
"That I am favored for unworthiness,

6. As e.g., in Exodus xxvii.2, "And thou shalt make the horns of [the altar] upon the four corners thereof." In his description of the temple and its accoutrements. Keats deliberately mingles Hebrew, Christian, and pagan elements, to represent the poet's passage through the stage represented by all religions, which are "dreams" made into the creed for "a sect" (lines 1–18).
7. I.e., you have postponed the time when you will be judged.
8. Temple.
9. I.e., "where you halfway rotted."

By such propitious parley medicined
In sickness not ignoble, I rejoice,
Aye, and could weep for love of such award."   185
So answered I, continuing, "If it please,
1[Majestic shadow, tell me: sure not all
Those melodies sung into the World's ear
Are useless: sure a poet is a sage;
A humanist, physician to all men.   190
That I am none I feel, as vultures feel
They are no birds when eagles are abroad.
What am I then: Thou spakest of my tribe:
What tribe?" The tall shade veiled in drooping white
Then spake, so much more earnest, that the breath   195
Moved the thin linen folds that drooping hung
About a golden censer from the hand
Pendent—"Art thou not of the dreamer tribe?
The poet and the dreamer are distinct,
Diverse, sheer opposite, antipodes.   200
The one pours out a balm upon the World,
The other vexes it." Then shouted I
Spite of myself, and with a Pythia's spleen,2
"Apollo! faded! O far flown Apollo!
Where is thy misty pestilence3 to creep   205
Into the dwellings, through the door crannies
Of all mock lyrists, large self worshipers
And careless Hectorers in proud bad verse?4
Though I breathe death with them it will be life
To see them sprawl before me into graves.]5   210

1. Keats's friend, Richard Woodhouse, crossed out lines 187–210 in a manuscript of the poem, with the marginal comment at the first line, "Keats seems to have intended to erase this and the next twenty-one lines"; perhaps his ground for this opinion is the repetition between lines 187 and 211, and between lines 194–98 and 216–20. Since there is no good evidence, however, that Keats planned to do more than merely revise this crucial passage, it is usually reprinted (as here) in brackets.
2. With the anger ("spleen") of the Pythia, the priestess who served at Delphi as the oracle of Apollo, the god of poetry.
3. Probably the foul vapors which were said to issue from the earth and intoxicate the Delphic oracle.
4. This has been conjectured as referring to Byron, or else to several contemporaries, including Shelley and Wordsworth. But the poetic types, not individuals, are all that matter to Keats's argument.
5. In lines 147–210, we find a series of progressive distinctions: (1) between humanitarians who feel for "the miseries of the world" and those men who are "thoughtless" sleepers (lines 147–53);

(2) within the class of humanitarians, between those who actively "benefit * * * the great world" and the poets who are "visionaries" and "dreamers" (lines 161–69); (3) and within the class of poets, between those who are merely dreamers and those who are sages and healers (lines 187–202). As in the colloquy between Asia and Demogorgon (see above, Shelley's *Prometheus Unbound*, II.1–128), the interchange here represents, in dramatized form, a process of inner analysis and self-discovery on the part of the questing poet. Moneta's charges should not be read as final judgments but as tests to determine the "tribe" to which he belongs—tests he passes by the nature of the responses he makes. The fact that Moneta continuously alters the categories by which she judges him signifies that, in the very course of his self-investigation, he changes and grows into what he is at the end of the process. At this point, the fact that the narrator himself proceeds to bring charges against self-indulgent and irresponsible poets distinguishes him from the class of poets he denounces and thus shows that he is ready for the final stage of his ordeal, his initiation into the realm of the highest poetry,

Majestic shadow, tell me where I am,
Whose altar this; for whom this incense curls;
What image this whose face I cannot see,
For the broad marble knees; and who thou art,
Of accent feminine so courteous?"   215

    Then the tall shade, in drooping linens veiled,
Spoke out, so much more earnest, that her breath
Stirred the thin folds of gauze that drooping hung
About a golden censer from her hand
Pendent; and by her voice I knew she shed   220
Long-treasured tears. "This temple, sad and lone,
Is all spared from the thunder of a war
Foughten long since by giant hierarchy
Against rebellion: this old image here,
Whose carvéd features wrinkled as he fell,   225
Is Saturn's; I Moneta, left supreme,
Sole Priestess of his desolation."
I had no words to answer, for my tongue,
Useless, could find about its rooféd home
No syllable of a fit majesty   230
To make rejoinder to Moneta's mourn.
There was a silence, while the altar's blaze
Was fainting for sweet food. I looked thereon,
And on the pavéd floor, where nigh were piled
Faggots of cinnamon, and many heaps   235
Of other crispéd spice-wood; then again
I looked upon the altar, and its horns
Whitened with ashes, and its lang'rous flame,
And then upon the offerings again;
And so by turns—till sad Moneta cried,   240
"The sacrifice is done, but not the less
Will I be kind to thee for thy good will.
My power, which to me is still a curse,
Shall be to thee a wonder; for the scenes
Still swooning vivid through my globéd brain,   245
With an electral changing misery,
Thou shalt with those dull mortal eyes behold,
Free from all pain, if wonder pain thee not."
As near as an immortal's spheréd words
Could to a mother's soften, were these last: 250
And yet I had a terror of her robes,
And chiefly of the veils, that from her brow
Hung pale, and curtained her in mysteries,
That made my heart too small to hold its blood.
This saw that Goddess, and with sacred hand   255
Parted the veils. Then saw I a wan face,
Not pined by human sorrows, but bright-blanched

through the revelation of the "high tragedy" (line 277) of what it means to be human. This ultimate enlightenment, which begins with line 291 and which was intended to constitute the remainder of the poem, is a vision in a dream within a dream (see line 46 and footnote).

By an immortal sickness which kills not;
It works a constant change, which happy death
Can put no end to; deathwards progressing   260
To no death was that visage; it had passed
The lily and the snow; and beyond these
I must not think now, though I saw that face—
But for her eyes I should have fled away.
They held me back, with a benignant light,   265
Soft mitigated by divinest lids
Half-closed, and visionless entire they seemed
Of all external things; they saw me not,
But in blank splendor, beamed like the mild moon,
Who comforts those she sees not, who knows not   270
What eyes are upward cast. As I had found
A grain of gold upon a mountain's side,
And twinged with avarice strained out my eyes
To search its sullen entrails rich with ore,
So at the view of sad Moneta's brow,   275
I ached to see what things the hollow brain
Behind enwombéd: what high tragedy
In the dark secret chambers of her skull
Was acting, that could give so dread a stress
To her cold lips, and fill with such a light   280
Her planetary eyes; and touch her voice
With such a sorrow. "Shade of Memory!"
Cried I, with act adorant at her feet,
"By all the gloom hung round thy fallen house,
By this last temple, by the golden age,   285
By great Apollo, thy dear Foster Child,
And by thyself, forlorn divinity,
The pale Omega⁶ of a withered race,
Let me behold, according as thou saidst,
What in thy brain so ferments to and fro!"   290
No sooner had this conjuration passed
My devout lips, than side by side we stood
(Like a stunt bramble by a solemn pine)
Deep in the shady sadness of a vale,⁷
Far sunken from the healthy breath of morn,   295
Far from the fiery noon and eve's one star.
Onward I looked beneath the gloomy boughs,
And saw, what first I thought an image huge,
Like to the image pedestaled so high
In Saturn's temple. Then Moneta's voice   300
Came brief upon mine ear: "So Saturn sat
When he had lost his Realms—" whereon there grew
A power within me of enormous ken
To see as a god sees, and take the depth

6. The long *O*, final letter of the Greek alphabet; hence, "last member."
7. This was the opening line of the original *Hyperion*. The rest of the poem is a revised version of part of that first text, with the poet now represented as allowed to envision the course of events which Moneta remembers (lines 282, 289–90).

Of things as nimbly as the outward eye 305
Can size and shape pervade. The lofty theme
At those few words hung vast before my mind,
With half-unraveled web. I set myself
Upon an eagle's watch, that I might see,
And seeing ne'er forget. No stir of life 310
Was in this shrouded vale, not so much air
As in the zoning[8] of a summer's day
Robs not one light seed from the feathered grass,
But where the dead leaf fell there did it rest:
A stream went voiceless by, still deadened more 315
By reason of the fallen Divinity
Spreading more shade; the Naiad[9] 'mid her reeds
Pressed her cold finger closer to her lips.
    Along the margin-sand large footmarks went
No farther than to where old Saturn's feet 320
Had rested, and there slept, how long a sleep!
Degraded, cold, upon the sodden ground
His old right hand lay nerveless, listless, dead,
Unsceptred; and his realmless eyes[1] were closed,
While his bowed head seemed listening to the Earth, 325
His ancient mother,[2] for some comfort yet.

    It seemed no force could wake him from his place;
But there came one who, with a kindred hand
Touched his wide shoulders after bending low
With reverence, though to one who knew it not. 330
Then came the grievéd voice of Mnemosyne,[3]
And grieved I hearkened. "That divinity
Whom thou saw'st step from yon forlornest wood,
And with slow pace approach our fallen King,
Is Thea,[4] softest-natured of our Brood." 335
I marked the Goddess in fair statuary
Surpassing wan Moneta by the head,[5]
And in her sorrow nearer woman's tears.
There was a listening fear in her regard,
As if calamity had but begun; 340
As if the vanward clouds[6] of evil days
Had spent their malice, and the sullen rear
Was with its stored thunder laboring up.
One hand she pressed upon that aching spot
Where beats the human heart, as if just there, 345
Though an immortal, she felt cruel pain;
The other upon Saturn's bended neck
She laid, and to the level of his hollow ear
Leaning with parted lips, some words she spoke

8. Course.
9. Water nymph.
1. Saturn's eyes, when open, express the fact that he has lost his realm.
2. Saturn and the other Titans were the children of Heaven and Earth.

3. A slip; Moneta was Mnemosyne in the first *Hyperion*.
4. Sister and wife of Hyperion.
5. I.e., Thea was a head taller than Moneta.
6. The front line of clouds.

In solemn tenor and deep organ tune;   350
Some mourning words, which in our feeble tongue
Would come in this-like accenting; how frail
To that large utterance of the early Gods!

    "Saturn! look up—and for what, poor lost King?[7]
I have no comfort for thee; no, not one;   355
I cannot cry, 'Wherefore thus sleepest thou?'
For Heaven is parted from thee, and the Earth
Knows thee not, so afflicted, for a God;
And Ocean too, with all its solemn noise,
Has from thy scepter passed, and all the air   360
Is emptied of thine hoary majesty:
Thy thunder, captious at the new command,
Rumbles reluctant o'er our fallen house;
And thy sharp lightning, in unpracticed hands,
Scorches and burns our once serene domain.   365
With such remorseless speed still come new woes,
That unbelief has not a space to breathe.[8]
Saturn! sleep on—me thoughtless,[1] why should I
Thus violate thy slumbrous solitude?
Why should I ope thy melancholy eyes?   370
Saturn! sleep on, while at thy feet I weep."

    As when upon a trancéd summer-night
Forests, branch-charméd by the earnest stars,[2]
Dream, and so dream all night without a noise,
Save from one gradual solitary gust,   375
Swelling upon the silence; dying off;
As if the ebbing air had but one wave;
So came these words, and went; the while in tears
She pressed her fair large forehead to the earth,
Just where her fallen hair might spread in curls,   380
A soft and silken mat for Saturn's feet.
Long, long those two were postured motionless,
Like sculpture builded up upon the grave
Of their own power. A long awful time
I looked upon them: still they were the same;   385
The frozen God still bending to the earth,
And the sad Goddess weeping at his feet,
Moneta silent. Without stay or prop,
But my own weak mortality, I bore
The load of this eternal quietude,   390
The unchanging gloom, and the three fixéd shapes
Ponderous upon my senses, a whole moon.
For by my burning brain I measured sure

7. Keats several times recalls *King Lear*, in representing the condition of Saturn.
8. I.e., that disbelief has not an instant to catch its breath.
1. I.e., how thoughtless I am!
2. Keats here sacrifices to epic severity a notable figure in the first *Hyperion* I, 72 ff., "As when, upon a trancéd summer-night / Those green-robed senators of mighty woods, / Tall oaks, branch-charméd by the earnest stars, / Dream * * *.

Her silver seasons shedded on the night,
And ever day by day methought I grew   395
More gaunt and ghostly. Oftentimes I prayed
Intense, that Death would take me from the Vale
And all its burdens—gasping with despair
Of change, hour after hour I cursed myself;
Until old Saturn raised his faded eyes,   400
And looked around and saw his kingdom gone,
And all the gloom and sorrow of the place,
And that fair kneeling Goddess at his feet.
As the moist scent of flowers, and grass, and leaves,
Fills forest dells with a pervading air,   405
Known to the woodland nostril, so the words
Of Saturn filled the mossy glooms around,
Even to the hollows of time-eaten oaks,
And to the windings of the foxes' holes,
With sad low tones, while thus he spake, and sent   410
Strange musings to the solitary Pan.
"Moan, brethren, moan; for we are swallowed up
And buried from all godlike exercise
Of influence benign on planets pale,
And peaceful sway above man's harvesting,   415
And all those acts which Deity supreme
Doth ease its heart of love in. Moan and wail,
Moan, brethren, moan; for lo, the rebel spheres
Spin round, the stars their ancient courses keep,
Clouds still with shadowy moisture haunt the earth,   420
Still suck their fill of light from sun and moon;
Still buds the tree, and still the sea-shores murmur;
There is no death in all the Universe,
No smell of death—there shall be death[3]—moan, moan;
Moan, Cybele,[4] moan; for thy pernicious Babes   425
Have changed a god into a shaking palsy.
Moan, brethren, moan, for I have no strength left;
Weak as the reed—weak—feeble as my voice—
Oh, oh, the pain, the pain of feebleness.
Moan, moan, for still I thaw—or give me help;   430
Throw down those Imps,[5] and give me victory.
Let me hear other groans, and trumpets blown
Of triumph calm, and hymns of festival,
From the gold peaks of heaven's high-piléd clouds;
Voices of soft proclaim,[6] and silver stir   435
Of strings in hollow shells; and let there be
Beautiful things made new for the surprise
Of the sky-children." So he feebly ceased,
With such a poor and sickly sounding pause,
Methought I heard some old man of the earth   440

---

3. The passing of the Saturnian golden age (paralleled by Keats with the fable of the loss of Eden) has introduced suffering, and will also introduce death.
4. Pronounced Sĭb'elē; the wife of Saturn and mother of the Olympian gods, who have overthrown their parents.
5. I.e., his rebellious children.
6. Used as a noun, "proclamation."

Bewailing earthly loss; nor could my eyes
And ears act with that pleasant unison of sense
Which marries sweet sound with the grace of form,
And dolorous accent from a tragic harp
With large-limbed visions.[7]—More I scrutinized: 445
Still fixed he sat beneath the sable trees,
Whose arms spread straggling in wild serpent forms,
With leaves all hushed; his awful presence there
(Now all was silent) gave a deadly lie
To what I erewhile heard—only his lips   450
Trembled amid the white curls of his beard.
They told the truth, though, round, the snowy locks
Hung nobly, as upon the face of heaven
A mid-day fleece of clouds. Thea arose,
And stretched her white arm through the hollow dark,   455
Pointing some whither: whereat he too rose
Like a vast giant, seen by men at sea
To grow pale from the waves at dull midnight.[8]
They melted from my sight into the woods;
Ere I could turn, Moneta cried, "These twain   460
Are speeding to the families of grief,
Where roofed in by black rocks they waste, in pain
And darkness, for no hope."—And she spake on,
As ye may read who can unwearied pass
Onward from the Antechamber of this dream,   465
Where even at the open doors awhile
I must delay, and glean my memory
Of her high phrase—perhaps no further dare.

Canto II

"Mortal, that thou may'st understand aright,
I humanize my sayings to thine ear,
Making comparisons of earthly things;
Or thou might'st better listen to the wind,
Whose language is to thee a barren noise,   5
Though it blows legend-laden through the trees.—
In melancholy realms big tears are shed,
More sorrow like to this, and suchlike woe,
Too huge for mortal tongue, or pen of scribe.
The Titans fierce, self hid or prison bound,   10
Groan for the old allegiance[9] once more,
Listening in their doom for Saturn's voice.
But one of our whole eagle-brood still keeps
His sov'reignty, and rule, and majesty;
Blazing Hyperion on his orbéd fire   15
Still sits, still snuffs the incense teeming up
From Man to the Sun's God—yet unsecure,
For as upon the earth dire prodigies[1]

7. I.e., he could not attach this speech,
like that of a feebly complaining old
mortal, to the visible form of the large-
limbed god who uttered it.
8. I.e., like a giant who is seen by men

at sea to emerge, pale, from the waves.
9. The meter requires four syllables:
al-lé-gǐ-ánce.
1. Terrifying omens.

Fright and perplex, so also shudders he;
Nor at dog's howl or gloom-bird's even screech,   20
Or the familiar visitings of one
Upon the first toll of his passing bell:[2]
But horrors, portioned to a giant nerve,
Make great Hyperion ache. His palace bright,
Bastioned with pyramids of glowing gold,   25
And touched with shade of bronzéd obelisks,
Glares a blood-red through all the thousand courts,
Arches, and domes, and fiery galleries;
And all its curtains of Aurorian clouds
Flush angerly; when he would taste the wreaths   30
Of incense breathed aloft from sacred hills,
Instead of sweets, his ample palate takes
Savor of poisonous brass and metals sick.
Wherefore when harbored in the sleepy West,
After the full completion of fair day,   35
For rest divine upon exalted couch
And slumber in the arms of melody,
He paces through the pleasant hours of ease
With strides colossal, on from hall to hall,
While far within each aisle and deep recess   40
His wingéd minions in close clusters stand
Amazed, and full of fear; like anxious men,
Who on a wide plain gather in sad troops,
When earthquakes jar their battlements and towers.
Even now, while Saturn, roused from icy trance,   45
Goes, step for step, with Thea from yon woods,
Hyperion, leaving twilight in the rear,
Is sloping to the threshold of the West.—
Thither we tend."—Now in clear light I stood,
Relieved from the dusk vale. Mnemosyne[3]   50
Was sitting on a square-edged polished stone,
That in its lucid depth reflected pure
Her priestess-garments. My quick eyes ran on
From stately nave to nave, from vault to vault,
Through bow'rs of fragrant and enwreathéd light   55
And diamond-pavéd lustrous long arcades.
Anon rushed by the bright Hyperion;
His flaming robes streamed out beyond his heels,
And gave a roar, as if of earthly fire,
That scared away the meek ethereal hours,   60
And made their dove-wings tremble. On he flared.

1819   1856

---

2. Lines 20–22 might be paraphrased: "Not, however, at such portents as a dog's howl or the evening screech of the owl, nor with the well-known feelings ["visitings"] of someone when he hears the first stroke of his own death knell * * *" It had been the English custom to ring the church bell when a person was close to death, to invite hearers to pray for his departing soul. See, e.g., Shakespeare, *Venus and Adonis*, lines 701–2; and for "visitings," *Macbeth* I.v. 46.

3. As in I, 331, a slip for "Moneta."

To Autumn[1]

1

Season of mists and mellow fruitfulness,
　　Close bosom-friend of the maturing sun;
Conspiring with him how to load and bless
　　With fruit the vines that round the thatch-eaves run;
To bend with apples the mossed cottage-trees,　　　　5
　　And fill all fruit with ripeness to the core;
　　　　To swell the gourd, and plump the hazel shells
　　With a sweet kernel; to set budding more,
And still more, later flowers for the bees,
Until they think warm days will never cease,　　　　10
　　For Summer has o'er-brimmed their clammy cells.

2

Who hath not seen thee oft amid thy store?
　　Sometimes whoever seeks abroad may find
Thee sitting careless on a granary floor,
　　Thy hair soft-lifted by the winnowing[2] wind;　　　　15
Or on a half-reaped furrow sound asleep,
　　Drowsed with the fume of poppies, while thy hook[3]
　　　　Spares the next swath and all its twinéd flowers:
And sometimes like a gleaner thou dost keep
　　Steady thy laden head across a brook;　　　　20
　　Or by a cider-press, with patient look,
　　　　Thou watchest the last oozings hours by hours.

3

Where are the songs of Spring? Aye, where are they?
　　Think not of them, thou hast thy music too—
While barred clouds bloom the soft-dying day,　　　　25
　　And touch the stubble-plains with rosy hue;
Then in a wailful choir the small gnats mourn
　　Among the river sallows,[4] borne aloft
　　　　Or sinking as the light wind lives or dies;
And full-grown lambs loud bleat from hilly bourn;[4a]　　　　30
　　Hedge crickets sing; and now with treble soft
　　The redbreast whistles from a garden croft;[5]
　　　　And gathering swallows twitter in the skies.

September 19, 1819　　　　　　　　　　　　　　　　1820

---

1. Two days after this serene and gracious ode was composed, Keats wrote to J. H. Reynolds: "I never liked stubble fields so much as now—Aye, better than the chilly green of the spring. Somehow a stubble plain looks warm— in the same way that some pictures look warm—this struck me so much in my Sunday's walk that I composed upon it."
2. To "winnow" is to fan the chaff from the grain.
3. Scythe.
4. Willows.
4a. Region.
5. A "croft" is an enclosed plot of farm land.

This Living Hand[1]

This living hand, now warm and capable
Of earnest grasping, would, if it were cold
And in the icy silence of the tomb,
So haunt thy days and chill thy dreaming nights
That thou wouldst wish thine own heart dry of blood   5
So in my veins red life might stream again,
And thou be conscience-calmed—see here it is—
I hold it towards you.

Late 1819?   1898

1. Found written in the margin of a page of Keats's unfinished satire, *The Cap and Bells*, and commonly assumed to have been addressed to Fanny Brawne.

Letters   Keats's letters constitute a running commentary on his life, reading, thinking, and writing. They demonstrate an extraordinary intelligence, whose very lack of academic or technical training gives its expression a freedom from jargon and standard categories that is equally challenging and rewarding to the reader. Keats's early reputation as a poet of pure luxury, sensation, and art for art's sake has been revolutionized since, early this century, critics began to pay close attention to his letters. For Keats thought hard and persistently about life and art, and any seed of an ethical or critical idea that he picked up from his intellectual contemporaries (Hazlitt, Coleridge, Wordsworth) instantly germinated and flourished in the rich soil of his imagination. What T. S. Eliot said about the metaphysical poets applies equally to Keats in his letters: his "mode of feeling was directly and freshly altered by [his] reading and thought." And like Donne, he looked not only into the heart, but literally, "into the cerebral cortex, the nervous system, and the digestive tract." A number of Keats's casual comments on the poet and on poetry included below—especially those dealing with what we now call empathy, and with "negative capability"— have become standard points of reference in aesthetic theory. But nothing that Keats said did he himself regard as ultimate; each statement constituted only a stage in his continuing exploration into what he called "the mystery."

The text below is that of the edition of the *Letters* by Hyder E. Rollins (1958), which reproduces the original MSS. precisely, so that the reader may follow Keats's pen as, throwing spelling and grammar to the winds, it strains to keep up with the rush of his thoughts.

To Benjamin Bailey[1]
[*The Authenticity of the Imagination*]

[November 22, 1817]

My dear Bailey,
    * * * O I wish I was as certain of the end of all your troubles as

1. Bailey was one of Keats's closest friends. Keats had stayed with him the month before at Oxford, where Bailey was an undergraduate.

that of your momentary start about the authenticity of the Imagination. I am certain of nothing but of the holiness of the Heart's affections and the truth of Imagination—What the imagination seizes as Beauty must be truth[2]—whether it existed before or not—for I have the same Idea of all our Passions as of Love they are all in their sublime, creative of essential Beauty—In a Word, you may know my favorite Speculation by my first Book and the little song I sent in my last[3]—which is a representation from the fancy of the probable mode of operating in these Matters—The Imagination may be compared to Adam's dream[4]—he awoke and found it truth. I am the more zealous in this affair, because I have never yet been able to perceive how any thing can be known for truth by consequitive reasoning[5]—and yet it must be—Can it be that even the greatest Philosopher ever ~~when~~ arrived at his goal without putting aside numerous objections—However it may be, O ·for a Life of Sensations[6] rather than of Thoughts! It is "a Vision in the form of Youth" a Shadow of reality to come—and this consideration has further conv[i]nced me for it has come as auxiliary to another favorite Speculation of mine, that we shall enjoy ourselves here after by having what we called happiness on Earth repeated in a finer tone and so repeated[7]—And yet such a fate can only befall those who delight in sensation rather than hunger as you do after Truth—Adam's dream will do here and seems to be a conviction that Imagination and its empyreal reflection is the same as human Life and its spiritual repetition. But as I was saying—the simple imaginative Mind may have its rewards in the repeti[ti]on of its own silent Working coming continually on the spirit with a fine suddenness—to compare great things with small—have you never by being surprised with an old Melody—in a delicious place—by a delicious voice, fe[l]t over again your very speculations and surmises at the time it first operated on your soul—do you not remember forming to yourself the singer's face more beautiful that[8] it was possible and yet with the elevation of the Moment you did not think so—even then you were mounted on the Wings of Imagination so high—that the Prototype must be here after—that delicious face you will see— What a time! I am continually running away from the subject— sure this cannot be exactly the case with a complex Mind—one that is imaginative and at the same time careful of its fruits—who would exist partly on sensation partly on thought—to whom it is necessary that years should bring the philosophic Mind[9]—such an one I con-

2. The phrase occurs in a poetic context at the close of *Ode on a Grecian Urn*. Try substituting "real," or "reality," where Keats uses the word "truth."
3. The song was "O Sorrow," from *Endymion.*
4. In *Paradise Lost* VIII.452–90, Adam dreams that Eve has been created, and awakes to find her real.
5. Consecutive   reasoning—reasoning which moves by logical steps.
6. Not only sense experiences, but also the intuitive perceptions of truths, as opposed to truth achieved by consecutive reasoning.
7. Cf. the "Pleasure Thermometer" in *Endymion,* Book I, lines 777 ff.
8. For "than."
9. An echo of Wordsworth, *Ode: Intimations of Immortality,* line 187.

sider your's and therefore it is necessary to your eternal Happiness that you not only have drink this old Wine of Heaven which I shall call the redigestion of our most ethereal Musings on Earth; but also increase in knowledge and know all things. I am glad to hear you are in a fair Way for Easter—you will soon get through your unpleasant reading and then!—but the world is full of troubles and I have not much reason to think myself pesterd with many—I think Jane or Marianne has a better opinion of me than I deserve—for really and truly I do not think my Brothers illness connected with mine—you know more of the real Cause than they do—nor have I any chance of being rack'd as you have been[1]—you perhaps at one time thought there was such a thing as Worldly Happiness to be arrived at, at certain periods of time marked out—you have of necessity from your disposition been thus led away—I scarcely remember counting upon any Happiness—I look not for it if it be not in the present hour—nothing startles me beyond the Moment. The setting sun will always set me to rights—or if a Sparrow come before my Window I take part in its existence and pick about the Gravel. The first thing that strikes me on hea[r]ing a Misfortune having befalled another is this. Well it cannot be helped.—he will have the pleasure of trying the resourses of his spirit, and I beg now my dear Bailey that hereafter should you observe any thing cold in me not to but[2] it to the account of heartlessness but abstraction—for I assure you I sometimes feel not the influence of a Passion or Affection during a whole week—and so long this sometimes continues I begin to suspect myself and the genuiness of my feelings at other times—thinking them a few barren Tragedy-tears * * *

Your affectionate friend
John Keats—

To George and Thomas Keats
[Negative Capability]

[December 21, 27 (?), 1817]

My dear Brothers

I must crave your pardon for not having written ere this * * * I spent Friday evening with Wells[1] & went the next morning to see *Death on the Pale horse*. It is a wonderful picture, when West's age is considered;[2] But there is nothing to be intense upon; no women one feels mad to kiss; no face swelling into reality the excellence of every Art is its intensity, capable of making all disagreeables evapo-

1. Keats's friends Jane and Marianne Reynolds feared that Keats's ill health at this time threatened tuberculosis, from which his brother Tom was suffering. Bailey had recently suffered pain (been "racked") because of an unsuccessful love affair.
2. For "put."
1. Charles Wells, a former schoolmate of Tom Keats and, for a time, a friend of John Keats.
2. Benjamin West (1738–1820), painter of historical pictures, was an American who moved to England and became president of the Royal Academy. The "Christ Rejected" mentioned a few sentences farther on is also by West.

rate, from their being in close relationship with Beauty & Truth[3]—
Examine King Lear & you will find this examplified throughout; but
in this picture we have unpleasantness without any momentous
depth of speculation excited, in which to bury its repulsiveness—
The picture is larger than Christ rejected—I dined with Haydon[4]
the sunday after you left, & had a very pleasant day, I dined too
(for I have been out too much lately) with Horace Smith & met his
two Brothers with Hill & Kingston & one Du Bois,[5] they only served
to convince me, how superior humour is to wit in respect to enjoyment—These men say things which make one start, without making
one feel, they are all alike; their manners are alike; they all know
fashionables; they have a mannerism in their very eating & drinking,
in their mere handling a Decanter—They talked of Kean[6] & his
low company—Would I were with that company instead of yours
said I to myself! I know such like acquaintance will never do for
me & yet I am going to Reynolds, on wednesday—Brown & Dilke[7]
walked with me & back from the Christmas pantomime.[8] I had not
a dispute but a disquisition with Dilke, on various subjects; several
things dovetailed in my mind, & at once it struck me, what quality
went to form a Man of Achievement especially in Literature &
which Shakespeare posessed so enormously—I mean *Negative Capability*,[9] that is when man is capable of being in uncertainties, Mysteries, doubts, without any irritable reaching after fact & reason—
Coleridge, for instance, would let go by a fine isolated verisimilitude
caught from the Penetralium[1] of mystery, from being incapable of
remaining content with half knowledge. This pursued through Volumes would perhaps take us no further than this, that with a great
poet the sense of Beauty overcomes every other consideration, or
rather obliterates all consideration.

3. Keats's solution to a problem at
least as old as Aristotle: why do we
enjoy the aesthetic representation of a
subject which in real life would be ugly
or painful?
4. Keats's close friend, Benjamin Haydon, painter of grandiose historical and
religious pictures.
5. Horace Smith was one of the best
known literary wits of the day; the
others mentioned were men of letters
or of literary interests.
6. Edmund Kean, the noted Shakespearean actor of the early 19th century.
7. John Hamilton Reynolds, 'Charles
Armitage Brown, and Charles Wentworth Dilke were all writers and friends
of Keats.
8. Christmas pantomimes were performed each year at Drury Lane and
Covent Garden.
9. This famous and elusive phrase has
accumulated a heavy body of commentary. Two points may here suffice: (1)
Keats is concerned with a central aesthetic question of his day: to distinguish between what was called the "objective" poet, who simply and imper-
sonally presents his material, and the
"subjective" or "sentimental" poet, who
presents his material as it appears when
viewed through his personal interests,
beliefs, and feelings. The poet of "negative capability" is the objective poet.
(See the letter to Reynolds, Feb. 3,
1818, below.) (2) Keats goes on to
propose that, within a poem, the presentation of matter in an artistic form
that appeals to our "sense of Beauty"
is enough, independently of its truth or
falsity when considered outside the
poem according to nonartistic logical
criteria. T. S. Eliot illuminated an
important aspect of Keats's meaning
when he observed that a theory "which
has entered into poetry is established,
for its truth or falsity in one sense
ceases to matter, and its truth in another sense is proved" (*The Metaphysical Poets*).
1. The Latin *penetralia* signified the
innermost and most secret parts of a
temple.

Shelley's poem[2] is out & there are words about its being objected too, as much as Queen Mab was. Poor Shelley I think he has his Quota of good qualities, in sooth la!! Write soon to your most sincere friend & affectionate Brother

John

To John Hamilton Reynolds[1]
[Wordsworth's Poetry]

[February 3, 1818]

My dear Reynolds,

* * * It may be said that we ought to read our Contemporaries. that Wordsworth &c should have their due from us. but for the sake of a few fine imaginative or domestic passages, are we to be bullied into a certain Philosophy engendered in the whims of an Egotist[2]— Every man has his speculations, but every man does not brood and peacock over them till he makes a false coinage and deceives himself—Many a man can travel to the very bourne[2a] of Heaven, and yet want confidence to put down his halfseeing. Sancho[3] will invent a Journey heavenward as well as any body. We hate poetry that has a palpable design upon us—and if we do not agree, seems to put its hand in its breeches pocket. Poetry should be great & unobtrusive, a thing which enters into one's soul, and does not startle it or amaze it with itself but with its subject.—How beautiful are the retired flowers! how would they lose their beauty were they to throng into the highway crying out, admire me I am a violet! dote upon me I am a primrose! Modern poets differ from the Elizabethans in this. Each of the moderns like an Elector of Hanover governs his petty state, & knows how many straws are swept daily from the Causeways in all his dominions & has a continual itching that all the Housewives should have their coppers well scoured: the antients were Emperors of large Emperors of vast Provinces, they had only heard of the remote ones and scarcely cared to visit them.—I will cut all this—I will have no more of Wordsworth or Hunt[4] in particular—Why should we be of the tribe of Manasseh, when we can wander with Esau?[5] why should we kick against the Pricks, when we

---

2. *Laon and Cythna* (1817), which dealt with incest, and had to be recalled by the author; it was revised and republished as *The Revolt of Islam* (1818). *Queen Mab* (1813) was a youthful poem in which Shelley presented his radical program for the achievement of the millennium by the elimination of "kings, priests, and statesmen," and the reform of human institutions.
1. Reynolds, a close friend, was at this time an insurance clerk and also an able, though minor, poet and man of letters.
2. Keats immensely admired Wordsworth, as succeeding letters will show,

and learned more from him than from any poetic contemporary. He had reservations, however, about the subjective and didactic qualities of Wordsworth's poetry (see the letter to George and Thomas Keats, above)—reservations which, in some moods, he stated in unflattering terms.
2a. Boundary.
3. Sancho Panza, the earthy squire in *Don Quixote.*
4. Leigh Hunt, a poet who earlier had strongly influenced Keats's style.
5. I.e., why should we remain in a conventional way of life (as did the tribe of Manasseh, which followed the

can walk on Roses? Why should we be owls, when we can be Eagles? Why be teased with "nice Eyed wagtails," when we have in sight "the Cherub Contemplation"?[6]—Why with Wordsworths "Matthew with a bough of wilding in his hand" when we can have Jacques "under an oak &c"[7]—The secret of the Bough of Wilding will run through your head faster than I can write it—Old Matthew spoke to him some years ago on some nothing, & because he happens in an Evening Walk to imagine the figure of the old man—he must stamp it down in black & white, and it is henceforth sacred—I don't mean to deny Wordsworth's grandeur & Hunt's merit, but I mean to say we need not be teazed with grandeur & merit—when we can have them uncontaminated & unobtrusive. Let us have the old Poets, & robin Hood[8] Your letter and its sonnets gave me more pleasure than will the 4th Book of Childe Harold[9] & the whole of any body's life & opinions. * * *

> Yr sincere friend and Coscribbler
> John Keats.

To John Taylor[1]
[*Keats's Axioms in Poetry*]

[February 27, 1818]

My dear Taylor,
    Your alteration strikes me as being a great improvement—the page looks much better. * * * It is a sorry thing for me that any one should have to overcome Prejudices in reading my Verses—that affects me more than any hypercriticism on any particular Passage. In *Endymion* I have most likely but moved into the Go-cart from the leading strings. In Poetry I have a few Axioms, and you will see how far I am from their Centre. 1st I think Poetry should surprise by a fine excess and not by Singularity—it should strike the Reader as a wording of his own highest thoughts, and appear almost a Remembrance—2nd Its touches of Beauty should never be half way therby making the reader breathless instead of content: the rise, the progress, the setting of imagery should like the Sun come natural natural too him—shine over him and set soberly although in magnificence leaving him in the Luxury of twilight—but it is easier to think what Poetry should be than to write it—and this leads me on to another axiom. That if Poetry comes not as naturally

conventional paths of Old Testament history) when we can become adventurers (like Esau, who sold his birthright in Genesis xxv.29–34 and became a domestic outlaw).
6. The first phrase is from Hunt's *Nymphs,* the second from Milton's *Il Penseroso* (line 54).
7. The Wordsworth phrase is from his poem *The Two April Mornings* (a "wilding" is an uncultivated tree or plant, especially the wild apple tree).

Jacques is in *As You Like It* (see II.i.31).
8. A reference to two sonnets on Robin Hood by Reynolds which he had sent to Keats.
9. Canto IV of Byron's *Childe Harold* was being eagerly awaited by English readers.
1. Member of the publishing firm of Taylor and Hessey, to whom Keats wrote this letter while *Endymion* was being put through the press.

as the Leaves to a tree it had better not come at all. However it may be with me I cannot help looking into new countries with "O for a Muse of fire to ascend!"[2]—If Endymion serves me as a Pioneer perhaps I ought to be content. I have great reason to be content, for thank God I can read and perhaps understand Shakspeare to his depths, and I have I am sure many friends, who, if I fail, will attribute any change in my Life and Temper to Humbleness rather than to Pride—to a cowering under the Wings of great Poets rather than to a Bitterness that I am not appreciated. I am anxious to get Endymion printed that I may forget it and proceed. * * *

Your sincere and oblig^d friend
John Keats—

P.S. You shall have a sho[r]t *Preface* in good time—

To John Hamilton Reynolds
[*Milton, Wordsworth, and the Chambers of Human Life*]

[May 3, 1818]

My dear Reynolds.

* * * Were I to study physic or rather Medicine again,—I feel it would not make the least difference in my Poetry; when the Mind is in its infancy a Bias ~~in~~ is in reality a Bias, but when we have acquired more strength, a Bias becomes no Bias. Every department of knowledge we see excellent and calculated towards a great whole. I am so convinced of this, that I am glad at not having given away my medical Books, which I shall again look over to keep alive the little I know thitherwards; and moreover intend through you and Rice to become a sort of Pip-civilian.[1] An extensive knowledge is needful to thinking people—it takes away the heat and fever; and helps, by widening speculation, to ease the Burden of the Mystery:[2] a thing I begin to understand a little, and which weighed upon you in the most gloomy and true sentence in your Letter. The difference of high Sensations with and without knowledge appears to me this —in the latter case we are falling continually ten thousand fathoms deep and being blown up again without wings and with all [the] horror of a ~~Case~~ bare shoulderd Creature—in the former case, our shoulders are fledged,[3] and we go thro' the same ~~Fir~~ air and space without fear. * * *

You say "I fear there is little chance of any thing else in this life." You seem by that to have been going through with a more painful and acute ~~test~~ zest the same labyrinth that I have—I have

2. Altered from Shakespeare's *Henry V*, Prologue, line 1.
1. Apparently, "a small-scale layman." James Rice, a lawyer, was one of Keats's favorite friends.
2. *Tintern Abbey*, line 38. Here begins

Keats's wonderfully insightful expansion of the significance of this and other phrases and passages in Wordsworth.
3. Grow wings.

come to the same conclusion thus far. My Branchings out therefrom have been numerous: one of them is the consideration of Wordsworth's genius and as a help, in the manner of gold being the meridian Line of worldly wealth,—how he differs from Milton.[4]—And here I have nothing but surmises, from an uncertainty whether Miltons apparently less anxiety for Humanity proceeds from his seeing further or no than Wordsworth: And whether Wordsworth has in truth epic passion, and martyrs himself to the human heart, the main region of his song[5]—In regard to his genius alone—we find what he says true as far as we have experienced and we can judge no further but by larger experience—for axioms in philosophy are not axioms until they are proved upon our pulses: We read fine—— things but never feel them to thee[6] full until we have gone the same steps as the Author.—I know this is not plain; you will know exactly my meaning when I say, that now I shall relish Hamlet more than I ever have done—Or, better—You are sensible no man can set down Venery[7] as a bestial or joyless thing until he is sick of it and therefore all philosophizing on it would be mere wording. Until we are sick, we understand not;—in fine, as Byron says, "Knowledge is Sorrow";[8] and I go on to say that "Sorrow is Wisdom"—and further for aught we can know for certainty! "Wisdom is folly" * * *

I will return to Wordsworth—whether or no he has an extended vision or a circumscribed grandeur—whether he is an eagle in his nest, or on the wing—And to be more explicit and to show you how tall I stand by the giant, I will put down a simile of human life as far as I now perceive it; that is, to the point to which I say we both have arrived at—Well—I compare human life to a large Mansion of Many Apartments, two of which I can only describe, the doors of the rest being as yet shut upon me—The first we step into we call the infant or thoughtless Chamber, in which we remain as long as we do not think—We remain there a long while, and notwithstanding the doors of the second Chamber remain wide open, showing a bright appearance, we care not to hasten to it; but are at length imperceptibly impelled by the awakening of the thinking principle —within us—we no sooner get into the second Chamber, which I shall call the Chamber of Maiden-Thought,[9] than we become intoxicated with the light and the atmosphere, we see nothing but pleasant wonders, and think of delaying there for ever in delight: However among the effects this breathing is father of is that tremendous one of sharpening one's vision into the ~~head~~ heart and nature of Man—of convincing ones nerves that the World is full

---

4. I.e., as gold is the standard of material wealth (in the way that the meridian line of Greenwich Observatory, England, is the reference for measuring degrees of longitude), so Milton is the standard of poetic value, by which we may measure Wordsworth.

5. Cf. "Prospectus" to *The Recluse,* line 41.
6. For "the."
7. Sexual indulgence.
8. *Manfred* I.i.10: "Sorrow is knowledge."
9. I.e., innocent thought.

of Misery and Heartbreak, Pain, Sickness and oppression—whereby This Chamber of Maiden Thought becomes gradually darken'd and at the same time on all sides of it many doors are set open—but all dark—all leading to dark passages—We see not the ballance of good and evil. We are in a Mist—We are now in that state—We feel the "burden of the Mystery," To this point was Wordsworth come, as far as I can conceive when he wrote "Tintern Abbey" and it seems to me that his Genius is explorative of those dark Passages. Now if we live, and go on thinking, we too shall explore them. he is a Genius and superior [to] us, in so far as he can, more than we, make discoveries, and shed a light in them—Here I must think Wordsworth is deeper than Milton—though I think it has depended more upon the general and gregarious advance of intellect, than individual greatness of Mind—From the Paradise Lost and the other Works of Milton, I hope it is not too presuming, even between ourselves to say, his Philosophy, human and divine, may be tolerably understood by one not much advanced in years, In his time englishmen were just emancipated from a great superstition—and Men had got hold of certain points and resting places in reasoning which were too newly born to be doubted, and too much oppressed opposed by the Mass of Europe not to be thought etherial and authentically divine—who could gainsay his ideas on virtue, vice, and Chastity in Comus, just at the time of the dismissal of Cod-pieces[1] and a hundred other disgraces? who would not rest satisfied with his hintings at good and evil in the Paradise Lost, when just free from the inquisition and burning in Smithfield?[2] The Reformation produced such immediate and great benefits, that Protestantism was considered under the immediate eye of heaven, and its own remaining Dogmas and superstitions, then, as it were, regenerated, constituted those resting places and seeming sure points of Reasoning—from that I have mentioned, Milton, whatever he may have thought in the sequel,[3] appears to have been content with these by his writings—He did not think into the human heart, as Wordsworth has done—Yet Milton as a Philosop[h]er, had sure as great powers as Wordsworth—What is then to be inferr'd? O many things—It proves there is really a grand march of intellect—, It proves that a mighty providence subdues the mightiest Minds to the service of the time being, whether it be in human Knowledge or Religion— * * *

Your affectionate friend
John Keats.

1. In the 15th and 16th centuries the codpiece was a flap, often ornamental, which covered an opening in the front of men's breeches.

2. An open place northwest of the walls of the City of London where, in the 16th century, heretics were burned.
3. I.e., later on.

To Richard Woodhouse[1]
[A Poet Has No Identity]

[October 27, 1818]

My dear Woodhouse,

Your Letter gave me a great satisfaction; more on account of its friendliness, than any relish of that matter in it which is accounted so acceptable in the "genus irritabile"[2] The best answer I can give you is in a clerklike manner to make some observations on two principle points, which seem to point like indices into the midst of the whole pro and con, about genius, and views and atchievements and ambition and cœtera. 1st As to the poetical Character itself, (I mean that sort of which, if I am any thing, I am a Member; that sort distinguished from the wordsworthian or egotistical sublime; which is a thing per se and stands alone) it is not itself—it has no self—it is every thing and nothing—It has no character—it enjoys light and shade; it lives in gusto, be it foul or fair, high or low, rich or poor, mean or elevated—It has as much delight in conceiving an Iago as an Imogen.[3] What shocks the virtuous philosop[h]er, delights the camelion[4] Poet. It does no harm from its relish of the dark side of things any more than from its taste for the bright one; because they both end in speculation.[5] A Poet is the most unpoetical of any thing in existence; because he has no Identity—he is continually in for[6]—and filling some other Body—The Sun, the Moon, the Sea and Men and Women who are creatures of impulse are poetical and have about them an unchangeable attribute—the poet has none; no identity—he is certainly the most unpoetical of all God's Creatures. If then he has no self, and if I am a Poet, where is the Wonder that I should say I would ~~right~~ write no more? Might I not at that very instant [have] been cogitating on the Characters of saturn and Ops?[7] It is a wretched thing to confess; but is a very fact that not one word I ever utter can be taken for granted as an opinion growing out of my identical nature—how can it, when I have no nature? When I am in a room with People if I ever am free from speculating on creations of my own brain, then not myself goes home to myself: but the identity of every one in the room

1. Woodhouse was a young lawyer with literary interests who recognized Keats's talents and prepared, or preserved, manuscript copies of many of his poems and letters.
2. "The irritable race," a phrase Horace had applied to poets.
3. Iago is the villain in Shakespeare's *Othello* and Imogen the virtuous heroine of his *Cymbeline*.
4. The chameleon is a lizard which camouflages itself by matching its color to its surroundings.

5. "In speculation" here means "in contemplation"—i.e., without affecting our practical judgment or actions.
6. Instead of "in for," Keats may have intended to write "informing."
6a. Woodhouse had written Keats a letter, expressing concern at a remark by Keats that, since former writers had preempted the best poetic materials and styles, there was nothing new left for the modern poet.
7. Characters in Keats's *Hyperion*.

begins to to press upon me[8] that, I am in a very little time an[ni]-
hilated—not only among Men; it would be the same in a Nursery
of children: I know not whether I make myself wholly understood:
I hope enough so to let you see that no dependence is to be placed
on what I said that day.

In the second place I will speak of my views, and of the life I
purpose to myself—I am ambitious of doing the world some good:
if I should be spared that may be the work of maturer years—in the
interval I will assay to reach to as high a summit in Poetry as the
nerve[9] bestowed upon me will suffer. The faint conceptions I have
of Poems to come brings the blood frequently into my forehead—
All I hope is that I may not lose all interest in human affairs—that
the solitary indifference I feel for applause even from the finest
Spirits, will not blunt any acuteness of vision I may have. I do not
think it will—I feel assured I should write from the mere yearning
and fondness I have for the Beautiful even if my night's labours
should be burnt every morning and no eye ever shine upon them.
But even now I am perhaps not speaking from myself; but from
some character in whose soul I now live. I am sure however that
this next sentence is from myself. I feel your anxiety, good opinion
and friendliness in the highest degree, and am

Your's most sincerely
John Keats

To George and Georgiana Keats[1]
[*"The Vale of Soul-Making"*]

[February 14–May 3, 1819]

My Dear Brother & Sister——

* * * I have this moment received a note from Haslam[2] in
which he expects the death of his Father who has been for some
time in a state of insensibility—his mother bears up he says very
well—I shall go to twon[3] tommorrow to see him. This is the world
—thus we cannot expect to give way many hours to pleasure—Circumstances are like Clouds continually gathering and bursting—
While we are laughing the seed of some trouble is put into ~~he~~ the
wide arable land of events—while we are laughing it sprouts is[4]
grows and suddenly bears a poison fruit which we must pluck—
Even so we have leisure to reason on the misfortunes of our friends;
our own touch us too nearly for words. Very few men have ever

8. Perhaps "*so* to press upon me."
9. Sinew.
1. Keats's younger brother and his wife, who had emigrated to Louisville, Kentucky, in 1818. This is part of a long letter, which Keats wrote over a period of several months.
2. William Haslam, a young business-man and intimate friend.
3. For "town."
4. For "it."

arrived at a complete disinterestedness of Mind: very few have been influenced by a pure desire of the benefit of others—in the greater part of the Benefactors ~~of~~ & to Humanity some meretricious motive has sullied their greatness—some melodramatic scenery has facinated them—From the manner in which I feel Haslam's misfortune I perceive how far I am from any humble standard of disinterestedness—Yet this feeling ought to be carried to its highest pitch, as there is no fear of its ever injuring society—which it would do I fear pushed to an extremity—For in wild nature the Hawk would loose his Breakfast of Robins and the Robin his of Worms The Lion must starve as well as the swallow—The greater part of Men make their way with the same instinctiveness, the same unwandering eye from their purposes, the same animal eagerness as the Hawk—The Hawk wants a Mate, so does the Man—look at them both they set about it and procure on[e] in the same manner —They want both a nest and they both set about one in the same manner—they get their food in the same manner—The noble animal Man for his amusement smokes his pipe—the Hawk balances about the Clouds—that is the only difference of their leisures. This it is that makes the Amusement of Life—to a speculative Mind. I go among the Feilds and catch a glimpse of a stoat[5] or a fieldmouse peeping out of the withered grass—the creature hath a purpose and its eyes are bright with it—I go amongst the buildings of a city and I see a Man hurrying along—to what? The Creature has a purpose and his eyes are bright with it. But then as Wordsworth says, "we have all one human heart"[6]—there is an ellectric fire in human nature tending to purify—so that among these human creature[s] there is continully some birth of new heroism—The pity is that we must wonder at it: as we should at finding a pearl in rubbish—I have no doubt that thousands of people never heard of have had hearts comp[l]etely disinterested: I can remember but two—Socrates and Jesus—their Histories evince it—What I heard a little time ago, Taylor observe with respect to Socrates, may be said of Jesus— That he was so great as man that though he transmitted no writing of his own to posterity, we have his Mind and his sayings and his greatness handed to us by others. It is to be lamented that the history of the latter was written and revised by Men interested in the pious frauds of Religion. Yet through all this I see his splendour. Even here though I myself am pursueing the same instinctive course as the veriest human animal you can think of—I am however young writing at random—straining at particles of light in the midst of a great darkness—without knowing the bearing of any one assertion of any one opinion. Yet may I not in this be free from sin?[7] May

5. A weasel.
6. *The Old Cumberland Beggar*, line 153.

7. Keats speculates that though his instinctive course is not, any more than an animal's, "disinterested" (free from

there not be superior beings amused with any graceful, though instinctive attitude my mind my[8] fall into, as I am entertained with the alertness of a Stoat or the anxiety of a Deer? Though a quarrel in the streets is a thing to be hated, the energies displayed in it are fine; the commonest Man shows a grace in his quarrel—By a superior being our reasoning[s] may take the same tone—though erroneous they may be fine—This is the very thing in which consists poetry; and if so it is not so fine a thing as philosophy—For the same reason that an eagle is not so fine a thing as a truth—Give me this credit—Do you not think I strive—to know myself? Give me this credit—and you will not think that on my own accou[n]t I repeat Milton's lines

> "How charming is divine Philosophy
> Not harsh and crabbed as dull fools suppose
> But musical as is Apollo's lute"—[9]

No—no for myself—feeling grateful as I do to have got into a state of mind to relish them properly—Nothing ever becomes real till it is experienced—Even a Proverb is no proverb to you till your Life has illustrated it— * * *

The common cognomen of this world among the misguided and superstitious is "a vale of tears" from which we are to be redeemed by a certain arbitary interposition of God and taken to Heaven— What a little circumscribe[d] straightened notion! Call the world if you Please "The vale of Soul-making" Then you will find out the use of the world (I am speaking now in the highest terms for human nature admitting it to be immortal which I will here take for granted for the purpose of showing a thought which has struck me concerning it) I say "Soul making" Soul as distinguished from an Intelligence—There may be intelligences or sparks of the divinity in millions—but they are not Souls ~~the~~ till they acquire identities, till each one is personally itself. I[n]telligences are atoms of perception —they know and they see and they are pure, in short they are God —how then are Souls to be made? How then are these sparks which are God to have identity given them—so as ever to possess a bliss peculiar to each ones individual existence? How, but by the medium of a world like this? This point I sincerely wish to consider because I think it a grander system of salvation than the chrysteain religion —or rather it is a system of Spirit-creation[1]—This is effected by

selfish interests), it may still be, like an animal's, natural, hence innocent and possessed of an innate grace and beauty. He further supposes that this may be the nature of poetry, also, as distinguished from the deliberate and self-conscious process of philosophical reasoning. Compare the letter on "Negative Capability," Dec. 21, 1817, above.
8. For "may."
9. *Comus*, lines 475–77.

1. Keats is struggling magnificently for an analogy which will embody his solution to the ancient riddle of evil, as an alternative to what he understands to be the Christian view: evil exists as a test of man's merit of salvation in heaven, and this world is only a proving ground for a later and better life. Keats proposes that the function of the human experience of sorrow and

three grand materials acting the one upon the other for a series of years—These three Materials are the *Intelligence*—the *human heart* (as distinguished from intelligence or Mind) and the *World* or *Elemental space* suited for the proper action of *Mind and Heart* on each other for the purpose of forming the *Soul* or *Intelligence destined to possess the sense of Identity*. I can scarcely express what I but dimly perceive—and yet I think I perceive it—that you may judge the more clearly I will put it in the most homely form possible— I will call the *world* a School instituted for the purpose of teaching little children to read—I will call the *human heart* the horn Book[2] used in that School—and I will call the *Child able to read, the Soul* made from that *school* and its *hornbook*. Do you not see how necessary a World of Pains and troubles is to school an Intelligence and make it a soul? A Place where the heart must feel and suffer in a thousand diverse ways! Not merely is the Heart a Hornbook, It is the Minds Bible, it is the Minds experience, it is the teat from which the Mind or intelligence sucks its identity—As various as the Lives of Men are—so various become their souls, and thus does God make individual beings, Souls, Identical Souls of the sparks of his own essence—This appears to me a faint sketch of a system of Salvation which does not affront our reason and humanity—I am convinced that many difficulties which christians labour under would vanish before it—There is one wh[i]ch even now Strikes me—the Salvation of Children—In them the Spark or intelligence returns to God without any Identity—It having had no time to learn of, and be altered by, the heart—or seat of the human Passions—It is pretty generally suspected that the chr[i]stian scheme has been coppied from the ancient persian and greek Philosophers. Why may they not have made this simple thing even more simple for common apprehension by introducing Mediators and Personages in the same manner as in the hethen mythology abstractions are personified— Seriously I think it probable that this System of Soul-making—may have been the Parent of all the more palpable and personal Schemes of Redemption, among the Zoroastrians the Christians and the Hindoos. For as one part of the human species must have their carved Jupiter; so another part must have the palpable and named Mediator and saviour, their Christ their Oromanes and their Vishnu[2a]—

pain is to feed and discipline the formless and unstocked "intelligence" that a man possesses at birth, and thus to shape it into a rich and coherent "identity," or "soul." This result provides a justification ("salvation") for our suffering life on its own terms; that is, experience is its own reward, and not in heaven, but on earth. The passage is Keats's version of what Wordsworth says in the last two stanzas of his *Ode: Intimations of Immortality.*

2. A child's primer, which used to consist of a sheet of paper mounted on thin wood, protected by a sheet of transparent horn.

2a. Oromanes (Ahriman) was the principle of evil, locked in a persisting struggle with Ormazd, the principle of good, in the Zoroastrian religion. Vishnu was the deity who creates and preserves the world, in Hindu belief.

If what I have said should not be plain enough, as I fear it may not be, I will but[3] you in the place where I began in this series of thoughts—I mean, I began by seeing how man was formed by circumstances—and what are circumstances?—but touchstones of his heart—? and what are touch stones?—but proovings of his hearrt? —and what are proovings of his heart but fortifiers or alterers of his nature? and what is his altered nature but his soul?—and what was his soul before it came into the world and had These provings and alterations and perfectionings?—An intelligences—without Identity —and how is this Identity to be made? Through the medium of the Heart? And how is the heart to become this Medium but in a world of Circumstances?—There now I think what with Poetry and Theology you may thank your Stars that my pen is not very long winded— * * *

This is the 3ᵈ of May & every thing is in delightful forwardness; the violets are not withered, before the peeping of the first rose; You must let me know every thing, how parcels go & come, what papers you have, & what Newspapers you want, & other things— God bless you my dear Brother & Sister

Your ever Affectionate Brother
John Keats—

To Percy Bysshe Shelley[1]
[*"Load Every Rift with Ore"*]

[August 16, 1820]

My dear Shelley,

I am very much gratified that you, in a foreign country, and with a mind almost over occupied, should write to me in the strain of the Letter beside me. If I do not take advantage of your invitation it will be prevented by a circumstance I have very much at heart to prophesy[2]—There is no doubt that an english winter would put an end to me, and do so in a lingering hateful manner, therefore I must either voyage or journey to Italy as a soldier marches up to a battery. My nerves at present are the worst part of me, yet they feel soothed when I think that come what extreme may, I shall not be destined to remain in one spot long enough to take a hatred of any four particular bed-posts. I am glad you take any pleasure in my poor Poem;[3]—which I would willingly take the trouble to unwrite, if possible, did I care so much as I have done about Reputation. I received a copy of the Cenci,[4] as from yourself from Hunt. There

3. For "put."
1. Written in reply to a letter urging Keats (who was ill) to spend the winter with the Shelleys in Pisa.
2. His own death.
3. Keats's *Endymion*, Shelley had written, contains treasures, "though treasures poured forth with indistinct profusion." Keats here responds with advice in kind.
4. Shelley's blank-verse tragedy, *The Cenci*, had been published in the spring of 1820.

is only one part of it I am judge of; the Poetry, and dramatic effect, which by many spirits now a days is considered the mammon. A modern work it is said must have a purpose, which may be the God —*an artist* must serve Mammon[5]—he must have "self concentration" selfishness perhaps. You I am sure will forgive me for sincerely remarking that you might curb your magnanimity and be more of an artist, and "load every rift"[6] of your subject with ore. The thought of such discipline must fall like cold chains upon you, who perhaps never sat with your wings furl'd for six Months together. And is not this extraordina[r]y talk for the writer of Endymion? whose mind was like a pack of scattered cards—I am pick'd up and sorted to a pip.[7] My Imagination is a Monastry and I am its Monk—you must explain my metap⁰ˢ[8] to yourself. I am in expectation of Prometheus[9] every day. Could I have my own wish for its interest effected you would have it still in manuscript—or be but now putting an end to the second act. I remember you advising me not to publish my first-blights, on Hampstead heath—I am returning advice upon your hands. Most of the Poems in the volume I send you[1] have been written above two years, and would never have been publish'd but from a hope of gain; so you see I am inclined enough to take your advice now. I must exp[r]ess once more my deep sense of your kindness, adding my sincere thanks and respects for Mʳˢ Shelley. In the hope of soon seeing you I remain

most sincerely yours,
John Keats—

5. Matthew vi.24, and Luke xvi.13: "Ye cannot serve God and mammon."
6. Spenser, *Faerie Queene* II.vii.28: "With rich metall loaded every rifte."
7. Perfectly ordered; all the suits in the deck matched up ("pips" are the conventional spots on playing cards).
8. I.e., "metaphysics."
9. *Prometheus Unbound*, of which Shelley had promised Keats a copy.
1. Keats's volume of 1820, including *Lamia, The Eve of St. Agnes*, and the *Odes*. When Shelley drowned, he had this small book open in his pocket.

Romantic Lyric Poets

In the variety and magnitude of the lyric achievement by its major poets, the Romantic period ranks with Elizabethan and Jacobean times as one of the two greatest ages of the English lyric. It cannot approach the earlier period, however, in the number of second-order poets, many of them anonymous, who wrote excellent songs. The late 16th and early 17th centuries had been a great age of English vocal music, when there had been a pressing demand for poetic texts to match to the many exquisite airs and madrigals. In the Romantic period, however, lyric poems were mainly "art lyrics," written not to be sung but to be read, and no doubt the decline in the number of gifted amateurs who turned their hand to this form is related to the decline of England, through the 18th and 19th centuries, as a great singing nation.

This section represents Romantic poets good enough to have kept their places in all representative anthologies of lyric poems. It will be noted that there is no single, identifiable type of "Romantic lyric." The scope of these writers is very wide, ranging from Thomas Moore's tinkling echoes of Cavalier gallantries, through W. S. Landor's revitalization of the tradition of classic epigram, John Clare's successful achievement of Wordsworth's early aim (poems on common or seemingly trivial things, written in language really spoken by the peasant class), Scott's brilliant imitations of the popular ballad and George Darley's of Elizabethan song, Thomas Love Peacock's parody of the contemporary verse romance, the grotesque fantasy of Leigh Hunt's *The Fish, the Man, and the Spirit,* and the crossing of the Jacobean macabre with Gothic horror in the extraordinary songs of Thomas Lovell Beddoes.

SIR WALTER SCOTT
(1771–1832)

Sir Walter Scott (he was made a baronet in 1820) spent a great part of his childhood in the valley of the Tweed River, and at that time and in many later rides along the Border and in the Highlands he absorbed Scottish gossip, history, legend, song, and folklore. He was an inordinate reader with a capacious memory, and even while he was studying law in Edinburgh he spent a great deal of time reading medieval romances, history, travel books, and other documents, which provided him with the antiquarian learning he later poured into his novels. In 1802–3 he published an important three-volume collection of popular ballads, *Minstrelsy of the*

Scottish Border, sometimes piecing out the missing parts of the ballads from his own invention. Between 1805 and 1813 he wrote a series of metrical romances loosely modeled on medieval narrative forms—including *The Lay of the Last Minstrel, Marmion, The Lady of the Lake*—which made him for a time the most widely read of English poets. When his public was won over by Byron's more brilliant narrative romances, Scott turned to writing (until 1827, anonymously) his great series of historical novels. He made a large fortune, but went deeply into debt by building up the huge, pseudo-medieval estate of Abbotsford on the banks of the Tweed, where he attempted to live the antique life of a lord of the manor. In 1826 the failure of the printing firm of James Ballantyne (in which Scott was a silent partner) and of his publisher, Archibald Constable, plunged him into financial disaster, from which he struggled heroically all the rest of his life to extricate himself. Only after his death were his debts finally paid off, with money realized by the sale of his copyrights.

The Dreary Change is Scott's quiet and controlled version of the Romantic theme of an apparent loss of glory in the landscape which is in fact a change in the mind of the observer. And in some of his lyrics deriving from the popular ballad and folk song, Scott (like Keats in *La Belle Dame Sans Merci*) captured from his originals the artistic values of understatement and terse suggestiveness.

The Dreary Change

The sun upon the Weirdlaw Hill,
 In Ettrick's vale, is sinking sweet;
The westland wind is hush and still,
 The lake lies sleeping at my feet.
Yet not the landscape to mine eye   5
 Bears those bright hues that once it bore;
Though evening, with her richest dye,
 Flames o'er the hills of Ettrick's shore.

With listless look along the plain,
 I see Tweed's silver current glide,   10
And coldly mark the holy fane
 Of Melrose rise in ruined pride.
The quiet lake, the balmy air,
 The hill, the stream, the tower, the tree—
Are they still such as once they were?   15
 Or is the dreary change in me?

Alas, the warped and broken board,
 How can it bear the painter's dye!
The harp of strained and tuneless chord,
 How to the minstrel's skill reply!   20
To aching eyes each landscape lowers,
 To feverish pulse each gale blows chill;

And Araby's or Eden's bowers
Were barren as this moorland hill.

1817

Jock of Hazeldean[4]

"Why weep ye by the tide, ladie?
  Why weep ye by the tide?
I'll wed ye to my youngest son,
  And ye sall be his bride:
And ye sall be his bride, ladie,   5
  Sae comely to be seen"—
But ay she loot the tears down fa'
  For Jock of Hazeldean.

"Now let this willfu' grief be done,
  And dry that cheek so pale;   10
Young Frank is chief of Errington
  And lord of Langley Dale;
His step is first in peaceful ha',
  His sword in battle keen"—
But ay she loot the tears down fa'   15
  For Jock of Hazeldean.

"A chain of gold ye sall not lack,
  Nor braid to bind your hair;
Nor mettled hound, nor managed[5] hawk,
  Nor palfrey fresh and fair;   20
And you, the foremost o' them a',
  Shall ride our forest queen"—
But ay she loot the tears down fa'
  For Jock of Hazeldean.

The kirk was decked at morningtide,   25
  The tapers glimmered fair;
The priest and bridegroom wait the bride,
  And dame and knight are there.
They sought her baith by bower and ha';
  The ladie was not seen!   30
She's o'er the Border and awa'
  Wi' Jock of Hazeldean.

1816

---

4. The first stanza is from a traditional   5. Trained.
Scottish ballad.

Proud Maisie[6]

Proud Maisie is in the wood
  Walking so early;
Sweet Robin sits on the bush,
  Singing so rarely.

"Tell me, thou bonny bird,   5
  When shall I marry me?"—
"When six braw[7] gentlemen
  Kirkward shall carry ye."

"Who makes the bridal bed,
  Birdie, say truly?"—   10
"The gray-headed sexton
  That delves the grave duly.

"The glowworm o'er grave and stone
  Shall light thee steady,
The owl from the steeple sing,   15
  'Welcome, proud lady.' "

                                          1818

6. Sung by crazy Madge Wildfire on her   (Chapter 40).
deathbed in *The Heart of Midlothian*   7. Fine.

ROBERT SOUTHEY
(1774–1843)

Time has dealt harshly with Robert Southey, for he is remembered mainly for his close association with poets greater than himself and for Byron's brilliant lampoons in *Don Juan* and *The Vision of Judgment*. He attended Oxford, was for a short time a fervent supporter of the French Revolution, and wrote an epic and two dramas inspired by that event. With Coleridge (who became his brother-in-law) he planned the frustrated "Pantisocracy" on the banks of the Susquehanna and collaborated on several poems. In 1803 he settled at Keswick in the Lake Country, within long walking distance of his friend Wordsworth; with advancing age, he settled into a Tory viewpoint more conservative than either Wordsworth's or Coleridge's. All his life a learned and hard-working professional writer, he produced thousands of pages of epic and shorter poems, history, essays, biographies, and anything else for which there was a market; he was awarded the laureateship in 1813.

The only Southey writings still widely read are a few lyrics, a beautifully lucid short *Life of Nelson* (1813), and—a piece so widely loved and often retold that it has lost its connection with its author and acquired the status of an anonymous "fairy tale"—the story of *The Three Bears*.

My Days Among the Dead Are Passed

My days among the dead are passed;
　Around me I behold,
Where'er these casual eyes are cast,
　The mighty minds of old;
My never-failing friends are they,　　　　　　　5
With whom I converse day by day.

With them I take delight in weal,
　And seek relief in woe;
And while I understand and feel
　How much to them I owe,　　　　　　　　　10
My cheeks have often been bedewed
With tears of thoughtful gratitude.

My thoughts are with the dead, with them
　I live in long-past years,
Their virtues love, their faults condemn,　　　　15
　Partake their hopes and fears,
And from their lessons seek and find
Instruction with an humble mind.

My hopes are with the dead, anon
　My place with them will be,　　　　　　　　20
And I with them shall travel on
　Through all futurity;
Yet leaving here a name, I trust,
That will not perish in the dust.

1818　　　　　　　　　　　　　　　　　　　　　1823

WALTER SAVAGE LANDOR
(1775–1864)

Landor was born well-to-do, and with a violently independent and combative temper: he quarreled with the authorities at Rugby and at Oxford, with his wife and family, with servants and officials, with the governments of Europe (he was a Revolutionary sympathizer, and unlike most of his literary contemporaries never wavered in his republicanism), and with his neighbors, first in Wales and then in Italy; he was constantly embroiled in expensive litigation. But in the course of his long life the generous-hearted and outspoken poet also acquired many friends and admirers, ranging from Southey and Hazlitt in the Romantic generation to Robert Browning, Charles Dickens, and Algernon Charles Swinburne among the Victorians. He lived in Italy from 1815 to 1835. When he returned to England he was lionized for a time as an active Romantic poet when all the others were dead or silent, but a notorious outburst, which led to court action, forced him in 1857 to take up once more his exile in Italy, where he died in his 90th year.

Most of the writings of this greatly irascible man, whether in prose or verse, have characteristics to which critics apply the terms "serene" and "marmoreal." His best-known prose works are the numerous *Imaginary Conversations* (1824–53), mainly between historical figures, and on literary, philosophic, and political topics. These have their strong admirers, but they are written in a style which is so elevated and remote that they sometimes suggest dialogues between heroic-sized Greek statues. He wrote many long narrative and dramatic poems, of which the most durable is the epic *Gebir*, published in the same year as *Lyrical Ballads* (1798). But Landor's supreme achievement, in which he emulated Greek and Roman models, is in the short lyric, usually an elegy or a courtly compliment which is stripped down until it approximates an epigram. He is the master of a form of verse very rare in English—the spare, elegant, and severely formal utterance of lyric passion.

Mother, I Cannot Mind My Wheel

Mother, I cannot mind my wheel;
   My fingers ache, my lips are dry:
Oh! if you felt the pain I feel!
   But oh, who ever felt as I!

No longer could I doubt him true,   5
   All other men may use deceit;
He always said my eyes were blue,
   And often swore my lips were sweet.

1806

Rose Aylmer[1]

Ah, what avails the sceptered race,
   Ah, what the form divine!
What every virtue, every grace!
   Rose Aylmer, all were thine.

Rose Aylmer, whom these wakeful eyes   5
   May weep, but never see,
A night of memories and of sighs
   I consecrate to thee.

1806

1. Rose Aylmer was the daughter of the fourth Baron Aylmer (hence "the sceptered race," line 1). She became a friend of Landor's in 1794 at the age of 17, and died suddenly in Calcutta, six years later.

The Three Roses[2]

When the buds began to burst,
Long ago, with Rose the First
I was walking; joyous then
Far above all other men,
Till before us up there stood   5
Britonferry's[3] oaken wood,
Whispering, "*Happy as thou art,
Happiness and thou must part.*"
Many summers have gone by
Since a Second Rose and I   10
(Rose from that same stem) have told
This and other tales of old.
She upon her wedding day
Carried home my tenderest lay:[4]
From her lap I now have heard   15
Gleeful, chirping, Rose the Third.
Not for *her* this hand of mine
Rhyme with nuptial wreath shall twine;
Cold and torpid it must lie,
Mute the tongue, and closed the eye.   20

1855

On Seeing a Hair of Lucretia Borgia[5]

Borgia, thou once wert almost too august
And high for adoration—now thou'rt dust;
All that remains of thee these plaits infold,
Calm hair, meandering with pellucid gold!

1825, 1846

Past Ruined Ilion

Past ruined Ilion Helen lives,
    Alcestis rises from the shades;[6]
Verse calls them forth; 'tis verse that gives
    Immortal youth to mortal maids.

2. The first Rose was Rose Aylmer, the second her niece, and the third her grandniece.
3. In Wales.
4. Landor's epithalamion, *To a Bride*.
5. 1480–1519; Duchess of Ferrara, whose court became a notable center for scholars, poets, and artists.
6. Helen of Troy ("Ilion"); Alcestis gave her life in exchange for that of her husband, but was rescued from Hades ("the shades") by Hercules.

Soon shall oblivion's deepening veil   5
  Hide all the peopled hills you see,
The gay, the proud, while lovers hail
  These many summers you and me.

The tear for fading beauty check,
  For passing glory cease to sigh;   10
One form shall rise above the wreck,
  One name, Ianthe, shall not die.

1831

Dirce

Stand close around, ye Stygian set,[7]
  With Dirce in one boat conveyed!
Or Charon, seeing, may forget
  That he is old and she a shade.

1831

Twenty Years Hence

Twenty years hence my eyes may grow
If not quite dim, yet rather so,
Still yours from others they shall know
  Twenty years hence.

Twenty years hence though it may hap   5
That I be called to take a nap
In a cool cell where thunderclap
  Was never heard,

There breathe but o'er my arch of grass
A not too sadly sighed *Alas*,   10
And I shall catch, ere you can pass,
  That wingéd word.

1846

On His Seventy-fifth Birthday

I strove with none; for none was worth my strife,
  Nature I loved, and next to Nature, Art;
I warmed both hands before the fire of life,
  It sinks, and I am ready to depart.

1849   1849

7. I.e., the shades of the dead, ferried by Charon over the river Styx to Hades.

Well I Remember How You Smiled

Well I remember how you smiled
  To see me write your name upon
The soft sea-sand. . . "O! *what a child!*
  You think you're writing upon stone!"
I have since written what no tide   5
  Shall ever wash away, what men
Unborn shall read o'er ocean wide
  And find Ianthe's name again.

1863

THOMAS MOORE
(1779–1852)

Although he was the Irish Catholic son of a Dublin grocer, Tom Moore
became the fashionable versifier of Regency England. His *Irish Melodies*,
published between 1807 and 1834 with accompanying music (some of
the tunes were by Moore himself), were an immense success, and for
many years his Irish wit, charm, liberalism, and singing voice made him
a brilliant figure in literary and social circles, especially among the aristocratic Whig reformers. The same qualities made him one of Byron's closest
friends. He wrote numerous satires, lampoons, and prose pieces. He is
chiefly remembered, however, for *Lalla Rookh* (1817), written during the
vogue for Oriental verse romances, which achieved a great European
success; his fine *Life of Byron* (1830); and a handful of songs—most of
them in the tradition of amatory gallantry that goes back to the 17th-
century Cavaliers—which transcend the triviality, prettiness, and easy
pathos of his lyric standard, and have won their way into that repertory which
is sung on a social evening around the piano.

Believe Me, If All Those Endearing Young Charms

Believe me, if all those endearing young charms,
  Which I gaze on so fondly today,
Were to change by tomorrow, and fleet in my arms,
  Like fairy-gifts fading away,
Thou wouldst still be adored, as this moment thou art,   5
  Let thy loveliness fade as it will,
And around the dear ruin each wish of my heart
  Would entwine itself verdantly still.

It is not while beauty and youth are thine own,
 And thy cheeks unprofaned by a tear   10
That the fervor and faith of a soul can be known,
 To which time will but make thee more dear;
No, the heart that has truly loved never forgets,
 But as truly loves on to the close,
As the sunflower turns on her god, when he sets,   15
 The same look which she turned when he rose.

                                                1808

The Harp That Once Through Tara's Halls[1]

The harp that once through Tara's halls
 The soul of music shed,
Now hangs as mute on Tara's walls
 As if that soul were fled.—
So sleeps the pride of former days,   5
 So glory's thrill is o'er,
And hearts that once beat high for praise
 Now feel that pulse no more.

No more to chiefs and ladies bright
 The harp of Tara swells;   10
The chord alone that breaks at night
 Its tale of ruin tells.
Thus Freedom now so seldom wakes,
 The only throb she gives,
Is when some heart indignant breaks,   15
 To show that still she lives.

                                                1834

The Time I've Lost in Wooing

The time I've lost in wooing,
 In watching and pursuing
  The light that lies
  In woman's eyes,
Has been my heart's undoing.   5
Though Wisdom oft has sought me,
I scorned the lore she brought me,
  My only books
  Were woman's looks,
And folly's all they've taught me.   10

1. Tara, northwest of Dublin, was capital of Ireland during the Middle Ages, when that country was a great center of European civilization and learning.

Her smile when Beauty granted,
I hung with gaze enchanted,
    Like him, the sprite,[2]
    Whom maids by night
Oft meet in glen that's haunted.   15
Like him, too, Beauty won me,
But while her eyes were on me;
    If once their ray
    Was turned away,
Oh! winds could not outrun me.   20

And are those follies going?
And is my proud heart growing
    Too cold or wise
    For brilliant eyes
Again to set it glowing?   25
No, vain, alas! th' endeavor
From bonds so sweet to sever;
    Poor Wisdom's chance
    Against a glance
Is now as weak as ever.   30

1834

2. The Irish fairy; he can be controlled by mortals only when their eyes are fixed on him.

LEIGH HUNT
(1784–1859)

James Henry Leigh Hunt was an impulsive, warm-hearted, but improvident man, who begot a large family, was in constant financial difficulties, and often fell back on the charity of his friends. But however inept in managing his personal affairs, Hunt was a fighting liberal journalist. With his brother John he began the *Examiner*, a weekly periodical which ran for fourteen years as the most formidable opponent of the oppressive Tory government. In 1812 the brothers were fined and imprisoned for denouncing the Prince Regent (later George IV) as a liar and "a fat Adonis of fifty." Leigh Hunt spent two rather comfortable years in jail, living with his family and free to write and receive visits from his friends and political admirers. In 1822 he took his family to Pisa to join Shelley and Byron in establishing a quarterly, the *Liberal*, but the drowning of Shelley and Byron's impatience with his collaborator brought the periodical to a close after only four issues. Back in England, Hunt carried on a great variety of activities through a long literary career, and before he died gained the friendship and somewhat qualified esteem of Browning, Thomas Carlyle, and Dickens.

As an informal essayist Hunt is copious, relaxed, and often engaging; but he was overshadowed by his great prose contemporaries, Lamb, Hazlitt, and

De Quincey. He was a voluminous reviewer and critic. His theatrical criticism is the best surviving record of the day-to-day popular theater; his literary criticism, while admirable for the sensitive taste and generosity with which he recognized and championed unpopular new poets, especially Shelley and Keats, lacks the theoretical penetration, the originality, and the distinction which characterized the critical writings of Coleridge and Hazlitt. Hunt also undertook a variety of poems, many of them on Italian and classical themes; the most ambitious, *The Story of Rimini* (1816), is written in loose and freely running couplets, and treats a serious theme in an incongruously arch and familiar style. For a short time this poem strongly influenced Hunt's young disciple, John Keats, who caught from it the relaxed meter and lush sensuousness that mar his early poems and thus gave some grounds for John Gibson Lockhart's grouping of Keats with Hunt in his brutal attack on the lower-class vulgarity of the "Cockney School of Poetry" in *Blackwood's Magazine* (1817).

The Fish, the Man, and the Spirit

TO A FISH

You strange, astonished-looking, angle-faced,
Dreary-mouthed, gaping wretches of the sea,
Gulping salt-water everlastingly,
Cold-blooded, though with red your blood be graced,
And mute, though dwellers in the roaring waste;   5
And you, all shapes beside, that fishy be—
Some round, some flat, some long, all devilry,
Legless, unloving, infamously chaste—

O scaly, slippery, wet, swift, staring wights,
What is't ye do? what life lead? eh, dull goggles?   10
How do ye vary your vile days and nights?
How pass your Sundays? Are ye still but joggles
In ceaseless wash? Still nought but gapes, and bites,
And drinks, and stares, diversified with boggles?[1]

A FISH ANSWERS

Amazing monster! that, for aught I know,   15
With the first sight of thee didst make our race
Forever stare! Oh flat and shocking face,
Grimly divided from the breast below!
Thou that on dry land horribly dost go
With a split body and most ridiculous pace,   20
Prong after prong, disgracer of all grace,
Long-useless-finned, haired, upright, unwet, slow!

O breather of unbreathable, sword-sharp air,
How canst exist? How bear thyself, thou dry
And dreary sloth? What particle canst share   25

1. Sudden movements of alarm.

Of the only blessed life, the watery?
I sometimes see of ye an actual *pair*
Go by! linked fin by fin! most odiously.

THE FISH TURNS INTO A MAN, AND THEN INTO A
SPIRIT, AND AGAIN SPEAKS

Indulge thy smiling scorn, if smiling still,
O man! and loathe, but with a sort of love;
For difference must its use by difference prove,   30
And, in sweet clang, the spheres with music fill.
One of the spirits am I, that at his will
Live in whate'er has life—fish, eagle, dove—
No hate, no pride, beneath nought, nor above,   35
A visitor of the rounds of God's sweet skill.

Man's life is warm, glad, sad, 'twixt loves and graves,
Boundless in hope, honored with pangs austere,
Heaven-gazing; and his angel-wings he craves:
The fish is swift, small-needing, vague yet clear,   40
A cold, sweet, silver life, wrapped in round waves,
Quickened with touches of transporting fear.

1836

Rondeau[2]

Jenny kissed me when we met,
   Jumping from the chair she sat in;
Time, you thief, who love to get
   Sweets into your list, put that in:
Say I'm weary, say I'm sad,   5
   Say that health and wealth have missed me,
Say I'm growing old, but add,
   Jenny kissed me.

1838

2. Jenny is said to be Mrs. Jane Welsh Carlyle. This is a shortened form of the rondeau, an elaborate French verse form which normally has fifteen lines.

THOMAS LOVE PEACOCK
(1785–1866)

Peacock, the son of a London businessman, had a position with the East India Company which allowed him leisure to devote to his writing. Although he was himself a poet, his *Four Ages of Poetry* (1820) was a sly comment on the excesses of his Romantic contemporaries in the ironic guise of a history of the decline of poetry from its golden past; it evoked from his close friend Shelley *The Defense of Poetry* by way of refutation. Peacock's finest achievements are his inimitable novels—including *Headlong Hall* (1816), *Melincourt* (1817), *Nightmare Abbey* (1818), and *Crotchet Castle* (1831)—in which he gathers a group of argumentative eccentrics in a country house and sets them to talking. His protagonists represent extreme or bigoted or visionary points of view on all sides of the important topics of the day; among them are caricatures of his great contemporaries, Wordsworth, Coleridge, Southey, Byron, as well as his friend Shelley—who took no offense. The novels also included satiric songs. The one reprinted here is taken from *The Misfortunes of Elphin* (1829); it explodes the Romantic vogue of the long, pseudohistorical metrical romance in forty devastating lines.

The War Song of Dinas Vawr

The mountain sheep are sweeter,
But the valley sheep are fatter;
We therefore deemed it meeter
To carry off the latter.
We made an expedition;   5
We met a host, and quelled it;
We forced a strong position,
And killed the men who held it.

On Dyfed's richest valley,
Where herds of kine were browsing,   10
We made a mighty sally,
To furnish our carousing.
Fierce warriors rushed to meet us;
We met them, and o'erthrew them:
They struggled hard to beat us;   15
But we conquered them, and slew them.

As we drove our prize at leisure,
The king marched forth to catch us:
His rage surpassed all measure,
But his people could not match us.   20
He fled to his hall pillars;
And, ere our force we led off,
Some sacked his house and cellars,
While others cut his head off.

We there, in strife bewild'ring,   25
Spilt blood enough to swim in:
We orphaned many children,
And widowed many women.
The eagles and the ravens
We glutted with our foemen;   30

The heroes and the cravens,
The spearmen and the bowmen.

We brought away from battle,
And much their land bemoaned them,
Two thousand head of cattle,   35
And the head of him who owned them:
Ednyfed, king of Dyfed,
His head was borne before us;
His wine and beasts supplied our feasts,
And his overthrow, our chorus.   40

1829

JOHN CLARE
(1793–1864)

John Clare was the nearest thing to the pure and artless "natural poet" for whom primitivists had been searching ever since the mid-18th century. An earlier and far greater peasant poet, Robert Burns, had managed to acquire a solid liberal education; Clare, however, was born at Helpston, a Northamptonshire village, of a field laborer who was barely literate and a mother who was entirely illiterate, and himself obtained only sufficient schooling to teach him to read and write. Although he was a sickly and fearful child, he had to work hard in the field, where he found himself composing verse "for downright pleasure in giving vent to my feelings." In 1820 publication of his *Poems Descriptive of Rural Life* attracted critical attention, and on a trip to London he was made much of by leading writers of the day. But his celebrity soon dimmed, and his three later books of verse were failures. Under these and other disappointments his mind gave way in 1837, and he spent almost all the rest of his life in an asylum. The place was for him a refuge as well as a confinement, for he was treated kindly, allowed to wander about the countryside, and encouraged to go on writing his verses; some of his best achievements are the poems composed in his madness.

Clare did not, of course, write independently of a poetic tradition, for he had studied the poetry of James Thomson, Milton, Wordsworth, and Coleridge. But he managed to stay true to his own experience of unspectacular country sights and customs and to capture in his verse the country idiom. Clare's homely mouse, in the poem below, is a bit of pure rustic impressionism in a way that even Robert Burns's moralized mouse is not. And a small proportion of Clare's introspective asylum-poems achieve so haunting a poignancy and are spoken in so quietly distinctive a voice that they have made the great mass of mainly humdrum manuscripts he left at his death an exciting place of discovery for recent editors.

Mouse's Nest

I found a ball of grass among the hay
And progged[1] it as I passed and went away;
And when I looked I fancied something stirred,
And turned again and hoped to catch the bird—
When out an old mouse bolted in the wheats   5
With all her young ones hanging at her teats;
She looked so odd and so grotesque to me,
I ran and wondered what the thing could be,
And pushed the knapweed[2] bunches where I stood;
Then the mouse hurried from the craking[3] brood.   10
The young ones squeaked, and as I went away
She found her nest again among the hay.
The water o'er the pebbles scarce could run
And broad old cesspools[4] glittered in the sun.

ca. 1835–37   1935

I Am

I am: yet what I am none cares or knows,
    My friends forsake me like a memory lost,
I am the self-consumer of my woes—
    They rise and vanish in oblivious host,
Like shadows in love's frenzied stifled throes—   5
And yet I am, and live—like vapors tossed

Into the nothingness of scorn and noise,
    Into the living sea of waking dreams,
Where there is neither sense of life or joys,
    But the vast shipwreck of my life's esteems;   10
And e'en the dearest, that I love the best,
Are strange—nay, rather stranger than the rest.

I long for scenes, where man hath never trod,
    A place where woman never smiled or wept—
There to abide with my Creator, God,   15
    And sleep as I in childhood sweetly slept,
Untroubling, and untroubled where I lie,
The grass below—above the vaulted sky.

1842–64   1848

1. Prodded.
2. A plant with knobs of purple
flowers.
3. Squawking.
4. Low spots where water has collected.

Clock-a-clay[5]

In the cowslip pips[6] I lie
Hidden from the buzzing fly,
While green grass beneath me lies
Pearled with dew like fishes' eyes,
Here I lie, a clock-a-clay,   5
Waiting for the time of day.

While grassy forests quake surprise,
And the wild wind sobs and sighs,
My gold home rocks as like to fall
On its pillar green and tall;   10
When the parting rain drives by
Clock-a-clay keeps warm and dry.

Day by day and night by night
All the week I hide from sight.
In the cowslip pips I lie,   15
In rain and dew still warm and dry.
Day and night, and night and day,
Red, black-spotted clock-a-clay.

My home shakes in wind and showers,
Pale green pillar topped with flowers,   20
Bending at the wild wind's breath
Till I touch the grass beneath;
Here I live, lone clock-a-clay,
Watching for the time of day.

ca. 1848   1873

Song

I peeled bits of straw and I got switches too
From the gray peeling willow as idlers do,
And I switched at the flies as I sat all alone
Till my flesh, blood, and marrow was turned to dry bone.
My illness was love, though I knew not the smart,   5
But the beauty of love was the blood of my heart.
Crowded places, I shunned them as noises too rude
And fled to the silence of sweet solitude,
Where the flower in green darkness buds, blossoms, and fades,
Unseen of all shepherds and flower-loving maids—   10
The hermit bees find them but once and away;
There I'll bury alive and in silence decay.

I looked on the eyes of fair woman too long,
Till silence and shame stole the use of my tongue:

5. The small beetle known as the ladybird or ladybug. The sixth and last lines
probably allude to the children's game
of telling the hour by the number of
taps it takes to make the ladybird fly
off one's hand.
6. The blossoms of the cowslip, a yellow
primrose.

When I tried to speak to her I'd nothing to say,   15
So I turned myself round and she wandered away.
When she got too far off, why, I'd something to tell,
So I sent sighs behind her and walked to my cell.
Willow switches I broke and peeled bits of straws,
Ever lonely in crowds, in nature's own laws—   20
My ballroom the pasture, my music the bees,
My drink was the fountain, my church the tall trees.
Who ever would love or be tied to a wife
When it makes a man mad all the days of his life?

1842–64   1920

Secret Love

I hid my love when young till I
Couldn't bear the buzzing of a fly;
I hid my life to my despite
Till I could not bear to look at light:
I dare not gaze upon her face   5
But left her memory in each place;
Where'er I saw a wild flower lie
I kissed and bade my love good-bye.

I met her in the greenest dells,
Where dewdrops pearl the wood bluebells;   10
The lost breeze kissed her bright blue eye,
The bee kissed and went singing by,
A sunbeam found a passage there,
A gold chain round her neck so fair;
As secret as the wild bee's song   15
She lay there all the summer long.

I hid my love in field and town
Till e'en the breeze would knock me down;
The bees seemed singing ballads o'er,
The fly's bass turned a lion's roar;   20
And even silence found a tongue,
To haunt me all the summer long;
The riddle nature could not prove
Was nothing else but secret love.

1842–64   1920

Invitation to Eternity

Say, wilt thou go with me, sweet maid,
Say, maiden, wilt thou go with me
Through the valley-depths of shade,
Of night and dark obscurity;
Where the path has lost its way,   5
Where the sun forgets the day,

Where there's nor light nor life to see,
Sweet maiden, wilt thou go with me?

Where stones will turn to flooding streams,
Where plains will rise like ocean's waves,   10
Where life will fade like visioned dreams
And mountains darken into caves,
Say, maiden, wilt thou go with me
Through this sad non-identity,
Where parents live and are forgot,   15
And sisters live and know us not?

Say, maiden, wilt thou go with me
In this strange death-in-life to be,
To live in death and be the same,
Without this life or home or name,   20
At once to be and not to be—
That was and is not—yet to see
Things pass like shadows, and the sky
Above, below, around us lie?

The land of shadows wilt thou trace,   25
Nor look nor know each other's face;
The present marred with reason gone,
And past and present all as one?
Say, maiden, can thy life be led
To join the living and the dead?   30
Then trace thy footsteps on with me;
We are wed to one eternity.

1842–64   1920

I Lost the Love of Heaven

I lost the love of heaven above,
    I spurned the lust of earth below,
I felt the sweets of fancied love,
    And hell itself my only foe.

I lost earth's joys, but felt the glow   5
    Of heaven's flame abound in me,
Till loveliness and I did grow
    The bard of immortality.

I loved, but woman fell away;
    I hid me from her faded flame.   10
I snatched the sun's eternal ray
    And wrote till earth was but a name.

In every language upon earth,
    On every shore, o'er every sea,
I gave my name immortal birth   15
    And kept my spirit with the free.

1842–64   1924

GEORGE DARLEY
(1795–1846)

Darley, an Irish mathematician, was one of the poets who figured in the "Elizabethan revival" of the later Romantic period. He wrote prose tales, dramatic criticism, and various dramas in the style of Shakespeare's contemporaries. His long work, *Nepenthe* (1835), includes most of his best lyrics, from which the first of the following poems has been selected; the last poem is from *Syren Songs* (1837). The distinctive charm of Darley's lyrics is that they recall, without merely mimicking, their Elizabethan and 17th-century originals. The stately lyric *It Is Not Beauty I Demand* was for years printed in Palgrave's *Golden Treasury* as a poem of the Caroline period.

The Phoenix[1]

O blest unfabled Incense Tree,
That burns in glorious Araby,
With red scent chalicing the air,
Till earth-life grow Elysian there!

Half-buried to her flaming breast   5
In this bright tree, she makes her nest,
Hundred-sunned Phoenix! when she must
Crumble at length to hoary dust!

Her gorgeous deathbed! her rich pyre
Burnt up with aromatic fire!   10
Her urn, sight high from spoiler men!
Her birthplace when self-born again!

The mountainless green wilds among,
Here ends she her unechoing song!
With amber tears and odorous sighs   15
Mourned by the desert where she dies!

                                                  1835

It Is Not Beauty I Demand

It is not Beauty I demand,
    A crystal brow, the moon's despair,
Nor the snow's daughter, a white hand,
    Nor mermaid's yellow pride of hair.

Tell me not of your starry eyes,   5
    Your lips that seem on roses fed,

---

1. A legendary bird: only one exists at a time; it dies periodically, singing in aromatic flames, and is reborn from the ashes.

Your breasts where Cupid trembling lies,
    Nor sleeps for kissing of his bed.

A bloomy pair of vermeil cheeks,
    Like Hebe's in her ruddiest hours,   10
A breath that softer music speaks
    Than summer winds a-wooing flowers.

These are but gauds; nay, what are lips?
    Coral beneath the ocean-stream,
Whose brink when your adventurer sips   15
    Full oft he perisheth on them.

And what are cheeks but ensigns oft
    That wave hot youth to fields of blood?
Did Helen's breast though ne'er so soft,
    Do Greece or Ilium any good?   20

Eyes can with baleful ardor burn,
    Poison can breath that erst perfumed,
There's many a white hand holds àn urn
    With lovers' hearts to dust consumed.

For crystal brows—there's naught within,   25
    They are but empty cells for pride;
He who the Syren's hair would win
    Is mostly strangled in the tide.

Give me, instead of beauty's bust,
    A tender heart, a loyal mind,   30
Which with temptation I could trust,
    Yet never linked with error find.

One in whose gentle bosom I
    Could pour my secret heart of woes,
Like the care-burdened honey-fly   35
    That hides his murmurs in the rose.

My earthly comforter! whose love
    So indefeasible might be,
That when my spirit won above
    Hers could not stay for sympathy.   40
                                                          1828

The Mermaidens' Vesper Hymn

Troop home to silent grots and caves!
    Troop home! and mimic as you go
The mournful winding of the waves
    Which to their dark abysses flow.

At this sweet hour, all things beside   5
    In amorous pairs to covert creep;

The swans that brush the evening tide
Homeward in snowy couples keep.

In his green den the murmuring seal
   Close by his sleek companion lies;   10
While singly we to bedward steal,
   And close in fruitless sleep our eyes.

In bowers of love men take their rest,
   In loveless bowers we sigh alone,
With bosom friends are others blest—   15
   But we have none! but we have none!

1837

THOMAS LOVELL BEDDOES
(1803–1849)

Beddoes was the most gifted poet of the late Romantic "Elizabethan revival." By profession a physician and anatomist, he studied at Oxford and
Göttingen, then spent most of his mature life as a solitary wanderer among
the universities of Germany and Switzerland, involving himself in various
radical movements. His letters contain shrewd and caustic criticism of
his own and others' writings, but also reveal an eccentricity and a despondency that sometimes verge on madness. His only two published volumes,
The Improvisatore (1821) and *The Bride's Tragedy* (1822), he wrote
while still an undergraduate at Oxford. His later writings consist mainly
of massive fragments of drama and romance. The major work was *Death's
Jest-Book, or The Fool's Tragedy*, begun in the later 1820's, incessantly
patched and revised for the next quarter century, and left still unfinished
at his death. A nightmarish drama of murder, disguise, revenge, and
ghosts, it reveals that his chief models were Jacobean tragedy, English and
German terror tales of the "Gothic" vogue, and the more fantastic among
the writings of Shelley. Beddoes' lyrics, many of which were incorporated
in his dramas, specialize in the sinister and the grotesquely comic effect,
and at their best achieve an exquisite movement and a thrilling felicity
of unexpected phrasing. Beddoes, like his Jacobean masters, John Webster
and Cyril Tourneur—and his contemporary master, Shelley—was much
obsessed by death, as a thing at once terrible and dear. He ended his own
life, after several unsuccessful attempts, by taking poison.

Song

How many times do I love thee, dear?
   Tell me how many thoughts there be

In the atmosphere
Of a new-fall'n year,
Whose white and sable hours appear   5
The latest flake of Eternity—
So many times do I love thee, dear.

How many times do I love again?
Tell me how many beads there are
In a silver chain   10

Of evening rain,
Unraveled from the tumbling main,
And threading the eye of a yellow star—
So many times do I love again.

1824   1851

Song

Old Adam, the carrion crow,
The old crow of Cairo;
He sat in the shower, and let it flow
Under his tail and over his crest;
And through every feather   5
Leaked the wet weather;
And the bough swung under his nest;
For his beak it was heavy with marrow.
Is that the wind dying? O no;
It's only two devils, that blow   10
Through a murderer's bones, to and fro,
In the ghosts' moonshine.

Ho! Eve, my gray carrion wife,
When we have supped on kings' marrow,
Where shall we drink and make merry our life?   15
Our nest it is queen Cleopatra's skull,
'Tis cloven and cracked,
And battered and hacked,
But with tears of blue eyes it is full:
Let us drink then, my raven of Cairo.   20
Is that the wind dying? O no;
It's only two devils, that blow
Through a murderer's bones, to and fro,
In the ghosts' moonshine.

1825–28   1849–50

The Phantom Wooer

A ghost, that loved a lady fair,
Ever in the starry air
  Of midnight at her pillow stood;
And, with a sweetness skies above
The luring words of human love,   5
  Her soul the phantom wooed.
Sweet and sweet is their poisoned note,
The little snakes of silver throat,
In mossy skulls that nest and lie,
Ever singing, "Die, oh! die."   10
  •

Young soul put off your flesh, and come
With me into the quiet tomb,
  Our bed is lovely, dark, and sweet;
The earth will swing us, as she goes,
Beneath our coverlid of snows,   15
  And the warm leaden sheet.
Dear and dear is their poisoned note,
The little snakes of silver throat,
In mossy skulls that nest and lie,
Ever singing, "Die, oh! die."   20

1844–48   1849–50

Song of the Stygian Naiades[1]

"What do you think the mermaids of the Styx were singing as I
watched them bathing the other day"—

1

Proserpine may pull her flowers,
  Wet with dew or wet with tears,
  Red with anger, pale with fears;
Is it any fault of ours,
If Pluto be an amorous king   5
  And come home nightly, laden
Underneath his broad bat-wing
  With a gentle earthly maiden?

1. Water nymphs of the river Styx, which encircles the classical underworld, where Proserpine dwells as the captive bride of Pluto, its amorous king. Beelzebub (line 16) is a devil (sometimes identified with Satan himself) in the Christian hell.

Is it so, Wind, is it so?
All that I and you do know   10
Is that we saw fly and fix
'Mongst the flowers and reeds of Styx,
      Yesterday,
Where the Furies made their hay
For a bed of tiger cubs,   15
A great fly of Beelzebub's,
The bee of hearts, which mortals name
Cupid, Love, and Fie for shame.

2

Proserpine may weep in rage,
   But ere I and you have done   20
   Kissing, bathing in the sun,
What I have in yonder cage,
   She shall guess and ask in vain,
Bird or serpent, wild or tame;
   But if Pluto does 't again,   25
It shall sing out loud his shame.
      What hast caught then? What hast caught?
Nothing but a poet's thought,
   Which so light did fall and fix
   'Mongst the flowers and reeds of Styx,   30
      Yesterday,
Where the Furies made their hay
For a bed of tiger cubs,
A great fly of Beelzebub's,
The bee of hearts, which mortals name   35
Cupid, Love, and Fie for shame.

1830–39   1935

Romantic Essayists

WILLIAM HAZLITT
(1778–1830)

1813–14: Begins writing dramatic criticism and general essays.
1815–22: The height of his powers as essayist and as lecturer
on English poetry and drama.

"I started in life," Hazlitt wrote, "with the French Revolution, and I have
lived, alas! to see the end of it. * * * Since then, I confess, I have no
longer felt myself young, for with that my hopes fell." He was born into
a radical circle, for the elder William Hazlitt, his father, was a Unitarian
minister who declared from the pulpit his advocacy both of American independence and of the French Revolution. When young William was 5
years old, his father took the family to America in search of liberty and
founded the first Unitarian Church in Boston; but four years later he returned to settle at Wem, in Shropshire. Despite the persistent attacks of
reviewers and the backsliding of his once-radical friends, Hazlitt himself
never wavered in his loyalty to liberty, equality, and the principles behind
the overthrow of the monarchy in France. His first literary production, at
the age of 13, was a letter to a newspaper in indignant protest against the
mob which sacked Joseph Priestley's house, when the scientist and preacher
had celebrated publicly the second anniversary of the fall of the Bastille. His
last book, published in the year he died, was a four-volume life of Napoleon, in whom Hazlitt stubbornly insisted on seeing a noble-intentioned
champion of the emancipation of mankind.

Hazlitt was a long time finding his vocation. When he attended the
Hackney College, London, between the age of 15 and 18, he plunged into
philosophical studies with such zeal that he ruined his health. In 1799
he took up the study of painting, and did not give up the ambition to
become a portraitist until 1812. Hazlitt's first books dealt with philosophy,
economics, and politics, and his first job as a journalist was as Parliamentary reporter for the *Morning Chronicle*. It was not until 1813, at the
age of 36, that he began contributing dramatic criticism and miscellaneous
essays to various periodicals, and so discovered what he had been born
to do. Years of wide reading and hard thinking had made him thoroughly
ready: within the next decade Hazlitt demonstrated himself to be a highly
popular lecturer on Shakespeare, Elizabethan drama, and English poetry;
a superb connoisseur of the theater and of painting; one of the two most
important literary critics of the day (Coleridge is the other); and a

master of the familiar essay.

Unlike his contemporaries, Coleridge, Lamb, and De Quincey, whose writings look back to the elaborate prose stylists of the earlier 17th century, Hazlitt developed a fast-moving, hard-hitting prose in what has been aptly called a "literary-colloquial English": it gives the effect of good talk, but heightened. He wrote, indeed, almost as fast as he talked, turning out at a single sitting enough text to fill ten or fifteen printed pages, almost without correction and (despite the density of literary quotations) without reference to books or notes. This rapidity was possible only because his essays are relatively planless. Hazlitt characteristically lays down a topic and then expands upon it by piling up relevant observations and instances, expressed in a sequence of forthright and relatively uncomplicated sentences; the essay accumulates instead of developing, and it does not come to a conclusion, but simply stops. Hazlitt's prose is unfailingly energetic; but his most satisfying essays, considered as rounded and integral works of literary art, are those which, like *My First Acquaintance with Poets* and *The Fight*, have a narrative subject matter to give them a principle of organization.

In his demeanor Hazlitt was excessively bashful, suspicious, and gauche. Coleridge described him in 1803 as "brow-hanging, shoe-contemplative, strange. He is, I verily believe, kindly-natured * * * but he is jealous, gloomy, and of an irritable pride." Hazlitt's gracelessness and lack of talent for domesticity doomed him to be unlucky in love. At the age of 30 he married Sarah Stoddart, three years his senior, separated from her after ten inharmonious years, and several years later secured her consent to a Scottish divorce, in the hope he could marry Sarah Walker, the young daughter of his landlord in London. But the girl was a cold and faithless coquette, who (as Hazlitt himself relates in his confessional *Liber Amoris*) mercilessly teased and then jilted her infatuated lover. When in 1824 he married a widow with a substantial income, she too left him within three years, in part because of the antagonism of young William, Hazlitt's son by his first wife.

Hazlitt, it must be remembered, had grown up as a member of a highly unpopular minority, both in religion and politics; he found his friends deserting to the side of reaction; and his naturally combative disposition was exacerbated by the malignant abuse directed against him in the periodicals of that day. In the course of his life he managed to quarrel violently, in private and in print, with almost all the people he had once most admired and liked, including Coleridge, Wordsworth, and Leigh Hunt; even Charles Lamb, with whom his friendship was the most intimate and enduring, was not always safe from Hazlitt's rasping tongue. But we may let the tolerant Lamb speak for the rare and admirable qualities which emerged when Hazlitt relaxed in company he felt he could trust: "I think W.H. to be, in his natural state, one of the wisest and finest spirits breathing. * * * I think I shall go to my grave without finding, or expecting to find, such another companion."

What appealed to Hazlitt's personal admirers, as to the readers of his essays, was his courage and uncompromising honesty, and above all, his ardor, and his zest for life in all its variety—including even, as he announced in the title of a characteristic essay, *The Pleasure of Hating.*

Hazlitt intensely relished, and could matchlessly communicate, the particular qualities of diverse things—whether a passage of poetry, a painting, a natural prospect, a person, or a well-directed blow in a prize fight. Despite the recurrent frustrations of his 52 years of existence, he was able, on looking back, to say with his last breath: "Well, I've had a happy life."

My First Acquaintance with Poets[1]

My father was a Dissenting Minister, at Wem, in Shropshire; and in the year 1798 (the figures that compose that date are to me like the "dreaded name of Demogorgon"[2]) Mr. Coleridge came to Shrewsbury, to succeed Mr. Rowe in the spiritual charge of a Unitarian congregation there. He did not come till late on the Saturday afternoon before he was to preach; and Mr. Rowe, who himself went down to the coach, in a state of anxiety and expectation, to look for the arrival of his successor, could find no one at all answering the description but a round-faced man, in a short black coat (like a shooting jacket) which hardly seemed to have been made for him, but who seemed to be talking at a great rate to his fellow passengers. Mr. Rowe had scarce returned to give an account of his disappointment, when the round-faced man in black entered, and dissipated all doubts on the subject, by beginning to talk. He did not cease while he stayed; nor has he since, that I know of. He held the good town of Shrewsbury in delightful suspense for three weeks that he remained there, "fluttering the proud *Salopians, like an eagle in a dovecote*";[3] and the Welsh mountains that skirt the horizon with their tempestuous confusion, agree to have heard no such mystic sounds since the days of

High-born Hoel's harp or soft Llewellyn's lay![4]

As we passed along between Wem and Shrewsbury, and I eyed their blue tops seen through the wintry branches, or the red rustling leaves of the sturdy oak trees by the roadside, a sound was in my ears as of a Siren's song; I was stunned, startled with it, as from deep sleep; but I had no notion then that I should ever be able to express my admiration to others in motley imagery or quaint

1. This essay was written a quarter century after the events it describes. Coleridge and Wordsworth had long given up their early radicalism, and both men had since quarreled violently with Hazlitt—hence the essay's elegiac note in dealing with the genius of the two poets. Nevertheless Hazlitt communicates the intense excitement he had felt when Coleridge awakened him to the sense of his own literary possibilities, and the essay remains an incomparable portrait of Wordsworth and Coleridge

early in 1798, the period of their closest collaboration.
2. *Paradise Lost* II.964–65. To mythographers of the Renaissance, Demogorgon was a mysterious and terrifying demon, sometimes described as ancestor of all the gods. He plays a role in Shelley's *Prometheus Unbound.*
3. Adapted from Shakespeare's *Coriolanus* V.vi.114–15. "Salopians" are inhabitants of Shropshire.
4. Gray's *The Bard*, line 28.

allusion, till the light of his genius shone into my soul, like the sun's rays glittering in the puddles of the road. I was at that time dumb, inarticulate, helpless, like a worm by the wayside, crushed, bleeding, lifeless; but now, bursting from the deadly bands that bound them,

With Styx nine times round them,[5]

my ideas float on winged words, and as they expand their plumes, catch the golden light of other years. My soul has indeed remained in its original bondage, dark, obscure, with longings infinite and unsatisfied; my heart, shut up in the prison house of this rude clay, has never found, nor will it ever find, a heart to speak to; but that my understanding also did not remain dumb and brutish, or at length found a language to express itself, I owe to Coleridge. But this is not to my purpose.

My father lived ten miles from Shrewsbury, and was in the habit of exchanging visits with Mr. Rowe, and with Mr. Jenkins of Whitechurch (nine miles farther on) according to the custom of Dissenting Ministers in each other's neighborhood. A line of communication is thus established, by which the flame of civil and religious liberty is kept alive, and nourishes its smoldering fire unquenchable, like the fires in the *Agamemnon* of Aeschylus, placed at different stations, that waited for ten long years to announce with their blazing pyramids the destruction of Troy. Coleridge had agreed to come over to see my father, according to the courtesy of the country, as Mr. Rowe's probable successor; but in the meantime, I had gone to hear him preach the Sunday after his arrival. A poet and a philosopher getting up into a Unitarian pulpit to preach the Gospel was a romance in these degenerate days, a sort of revival of the primitive spirit of Christianity, which was not to be resisted.

It was in January of 1798, that I rose one morning before daylight, to walk ten miles in the mud, and went to hear this celebrated person preach. Never, the longest day I have to live, shall I have such another walk as this cold, raw, comfortless one, in the winter of the year 1798. *Il y a des impressions que ni le temps ni les circonstances peuvent effacer. Dusse-je vivre des siècles entiers, le doux temps de ma jeunesse ne peut renaître pour moi, ni s'effacer jamais dans ma mémoire.*[6] When I got there, the organ was playing the 100th psalm, and when it was done, Mr. Coleridge rose and gave out his text, "And he went up into the mountain to pray, *himself, alone.*"[7] As he gave out this text, his voice "rose like a steam of rich distilled perfume,"[8] and when he

5. Adapted from Pope's *Ode on St. Cecilia's Day*, lines 90–91.
6. "There are some impressions which neither time nor circumstances can efface. Might I live whole centuries, the sweet time of my youth could not be reborn for me, nor ever erased from my memory." Based on Rousseau's epistolary novel, *La Nouvelle Héloise* (1761), Part VI, Letter 7.
7. Cf. Matthew xiv.23; John vi.15.
8. Milton's *Comus,* line 556.

came to the two last words, which he pronounced loud, deep, and distinct, it seemed to me, who was then young, as if the sounds had echoed from the bottom of the human heart, and as if that prayer might have floated in solemn silence through the universe. The idea of St. John came into my mind, "of one crying in the wilderness, who had his loins girt about, and whose food was locusts and wild honey."[9] The preacher then launched into his subject, like an eagle dallying with the wind. The sermon was upon peace and war; upon church and state—not their alliance but their separation—on the spirit of the world and the spirit of Christianity, not as the same, but as opposed to one another. He talked of those who had "inscribed the cross of Christ on banners dripping with human gore." He made a poetical and pastoral excursion—and to show the fatal effects of war, drew a striking contrast between the simple shepherd boy, driving his team afield, or sitting under the hawthorn, piping to his flock, "as though he should never be old,"[1] and the same poor country lad, crimped,[2] kidnapped, brought into town, made drunk, at an alehouse, turned into a wretched drummer boy, with his hair sticking on end with powder and pomatum, a long cue at his back, and tricked out in the loathsome finery of the profession of blood.

Such were the notes our once-loved poet sung.[3]

And for myself, I could not have been more delighted if I had heard the music of the spheres. Poetry and Philosophy had met together. Truth and Genius had embraced, under the eye and with the sanction of Religion. This was even beyond my hopes. I returned home well satisfied. The sun that was still laboring pale and wan through the sky, obscured by thick mists, seemed an emblem of the *good cause*;[4] and the cold dank drops of dew, that hung half melted on the beard of the thistle, had something genial and refreshing in them; for there was a spirit of hope and youth in all nature, that turned everything into good. The face of nature had not then the brand of *Jus Divinum*[5] on it:

Like to that sanguine flower inscribed with woe.[6]

On the Tuesday following, the half-inspired speaker came. I was called down into the room where he was, and went half-hoping, half-afraid. He received me very graciously, and I listened for a long time without uttering a word. I did not suffer in his opinion by my silence. "For those two hours," he afterwards was pleased to say, "he was conversing with W. H.'s forehead!" His appearance

9. See Matthew iii. 3–4 and Mark i.3–6.
1. Sir Philip Sidney's *Arcadia* I.ii.
2. Trapped into enlisting in military service.
3. The first line of Pope's *Epistle to Robert, Earl of Oxford.*
4. The cause of liberty, i.e., the French Revolution.
5. The divine right (of kings).
6. I.e., the hyacinth, believed to be marked with the Greek lament "AI AI"; the line is from Milton's *Lycidas* (106).

was different from what I had anticipated from seeing him before. At a distance, and in the dim light of the chapel, there was to me a strange wildness in his aspect, a dusky obscurity, and I thought him pitted with the smallpox. His complexion was at that time clear, and even bright—

As are the children of yon azure sheen.[7]

His forehead was broad and high, light as if built of ivory, with large projecting eyebrows, and his eyes rolling beneath them, like a sea with darkened luster. "A certain tender bloom his face o'erspread,"[8] a purple tinge as we see it in the pale thoughtful complexions of the Spanish portrait painters, Murillo and Velasquez. His mouth was gross, voluptuous, open, eloquent; his chin good-humored and round; but his nose, the rudder of the face, the index of the will, was small, feeble, nothing—like what he has done. It might seem that the genius of his face as from a height surveyed and projected him (with sufficient capacity and huge aspiration) into the world unknown of thought and imagination, with nothing to support or guide his veering purpose, as if Columbus had launched his adventurous course for the New World in a scallop,[9] without oars or compass. So at least I comment on it after the event. Coleridge in his person was rather above the common size, inclining to the corpulent, or like Lord Hamlet, "somewhat fat and pursy."[1] His hair (now, alas! gray) was then black and glossy as the raven's, and fell in smooth masses over his forehead. This long pendulous hair is peculiar to enthusiasts, to those whose minds tend heavenward; and is traditionally inseparable (though of a different color) from the pictures of Christ. It ought to belong, as a character, to all who preach *Christ crucified*, and Coleridge was at that time one of those!

It was curious to observe the contrast between him and my father, who was a veteran in the cause, and then declining into the vale of years. He had been a poor Irish lad, carefully brought up by his parents, and sent to the University of Glasgow (where he studied under Adam Smith[2]) to prepare him for his future destination. It was his mother's proudest wish to see her son a Dissenting Minister. So if we look back to past generations (as far as eye can reach) we see the same hopes, fears, wishes, followed by the same disappointments, throbbing in the human heart; and so we may see them (if we look forward) rising up forever, and disappearing, like vaporish bubbles, in the human breast! After being tossed about from congregation to congregation in the heats of the Unitarian

7. See James Thomson, *The Castle of Indolence* II.xxxiii.
8. See *ibid.* I.lvii.
9. Probably for "shallop," a small boat.

1. Cf. *Hamlet* V.ii.298.
2. Scottish philosopher and author of the great economic treatise, *The Wealth of Nations* (1776).

controversy, and squabbles about the American war,[3] he had been relegated to an obscure village, where he was to spend the last thirty years of his life, far from the only converse that he loved, the talk about disputed texts of Scripture and the cause of civil and religious liberty. Here he passed his days, repining but resigned, in the study of the Bible, and the perusal of the Commentators—huge folios, not easily got through, one of which would outlast a winter! Why did he pore on these from morn to night (with the exception of a walk in the fields or a turn in the garden to gather broccoli plants or kidney beans of his own rearing, with no small degree of pride and pleasure)? Here were "no figures nor no fantasies"[4]—neither poetry nor philosophy—nothing to dazzle, nothing to excite modern curiosity; but to his lackluster eyes there appeared, within the pages of the ponderous, unwieldy, neglected tomes, the sacred name of JEHOVAH in Hebrew capitals: pressed down by the weight of the style, worn to the last fading thinness of the understanding, there were glimpses, glimmering notions of the patriarchal wanderings, with palm trees hovering in the horizon, and processions of camels at the distance of three thousand years; there was Moses with the Burning Bush, the number of the Twelve Tribes, types, shadows,[5] glosses on the law and the prophets; there were discussions (dull enough) on the age of Methuselah, a mighty speculation! there were outlines, rude guesses at the shape of Noah's Ark and of the riches of Solomon's Temple; questions as to the date of the creation, predictions of the end of all things; the great lapses of time, the strange mutations of the globe were unfolded with the voluminous leaf, as it turned over; and though the soul might slumber with an hieroglyphic veil of inscrutable mysteries drawn over it, yet it was in a slumber ill-exchanged for all the sharpened realities of sense, wit, fancy, or reason. My father's life was comparatively a dream; but it was a dream of infinity and eternity, of death, the resurrection, and a judgment to come!

No two individuals were ever more unlike than were the host and his guest. A poet was to my father a sort of nondescript: yet whatever added grace to the Unitarian cause was to him welcome. He could hardly have been more surprised or pleased if our visitor had worn wings. Indeed, his thoughts had wings; and as the silken sounds rustled round our little wainscoted parlor, my father threw back his spectacles over his forehead, his white hairs mixing with its sanguine hue; and a smile of delight beamed across his rugged cordial face, to think that Truth had found a new ally in Fancy! Besides, Coleridge seemed to take considerable notice of me, and

3. The American Revolution, with which a number of radical Unitarian preachers were in sympathy.
4. *Julius Caesar* II.i.231.
5. "Types" were characters and events in the Old Testament believed to prefigure analogous matters in the New Testament. "Shadows" were Old Testament foreshadowings of later events, or symbols of moral and theological truths.

that of itself was enough. He talked very familiarly, but agreeably, and glanced over a variety of subjects. At dinner time he grew more animated, and dilated in a very edifying manner on Mary Wollstonecraft and Mackintosh.[6] The last, he said, he considered (on my father's speaking of his *Vindiciae Gallicae* as a capital performance) as a clever scholastic[7] man—a master of the topics—or as the ready warehouseman of letters, who knew exactly where to lay his hand on what he wanted, though the goods were not his own. He thought him no match for Burke, either in style or matter. Burke was a metaphysician, Mackintosh a mere logician. Burke was an orator (almost a poet) who reasoned in figures, because he had an eye for nature: Mackintosh, on the other hand, was a rhetorician, who had only an eye to commonplaces. On this I ventured to say that I had always entertained a great opinion of Burke, and that (as far as I could find) the speaking of him with contempt might be made the test of a vulgar democratical mind. This was the first observation I ever made to Coleridge, and he said it was a very just and striking one. I remember the leg of Welsh mutton and the turnips on the table that day had the finest flavor imaginable. Coleridge added that Mackintosh and Tom Wedgwood[8] (of whom, however, he spoke highly) had expressed a very indifferent opinion of his friend Mr. Wordsworth, on which he remarked to them— "He strides on so far before you that he dwindles in the distance!" Godwin[9] had once boasted to him of having carried on an argument with Mackintosh for three hours with dubious success; Coleridge told him—"If there had been a man of genius in the room, he would have settled the question in five minutes." He asked me if I had ever seen Mary Wollstonecraft, and I said I had once for a few moments, and that she seemed to me to turn off Godwin's objections to something she advanced with quite a playful, easy air. He replied, that "this was only one instance of the ascendancy which people of imagination exercised over those of mere intellect." He did not rate Godwin very high (this was caprice or prejudice, real or affected) but he had a great idea of Mrs. Wollstonecraft's powers of conversation, none at all of her talent for book-making. We talked a little about Holcroft.[1] He had been asked if he was not much struck *with* him, and he said, he thought himself in more danger of being struck *by* him. I complained that he would

6. Mary Wollstonecraft was a radical author, the wife of William Godwin and mother of Shelley's second wife. Sir James Mackintosh, Scottish philosopher, wrote *Vindiciae Gallicae* ("Defense of France," 1791), in opposition to Edmund Burke's *Reflections on the French Revolution.*
7. The Scholastics, medieval philosophers and theologians, organized their thought systematically, often under various "topics"—standard headings, or "commonplaces" (see the third sentence following).
8. Son of Josiah Wedgwood (1730–95), who founded the great pottery firm which still exists.
9. William Godwin (1756–1836), radical philosopher and didactic novelist, author of the influential *Inquiry Concerning Political Justice* (1793).
1. Thomas Holcroft, another radical contemporary, author of plays and novels.

not let me get on at all, for he required a definition of even the
commonest word, exclaiming, "What do you mean by a *sensation,*
sir? What do you mean by an *idea?*" This, Coleridge said, was bar-
ricadoing the road to truth: it was setting up a turnpike gate at
every step we took. I forget a great number of things, many more
than I remember; but the day passed off pleasantly, and the next
morning Mr. Coleridge was to return to Shrewsbury. When I came
down to breakfast, I found that he had just received a letter from
his friend, T. Wedgwood, making him an offer of £150 a year if
he chose to waive his present pursuit, and devote himself entirely
to the study of poetry and philosophy. Coleridge seemed to make
up his mind to close with this proposal in the act of tying on one
of his shoes. It threw an additional damp on his departure. It took
the wayward enthusiast quite from us to cast him into Deva's winding vales,[2] or by the shores of old romance. Instead of living at
ten miles' distance, of being the pastor of a Dissenting congregation at Shrewsbury, he was henceforth to inhabit the Hill of Parnassus, to be a Shepherd on the Delectable Mountains.[3] Alas! I knew
not the way thither, and felt very little gratitude for Mr. Wedgwood's bounty. I was presently relieved from this dilemma; for Mr.
Coleridge, asking for a pen and ink, and going to a table to write
something on a bit of card, advanced towards me with undulating
step, and giving me the precious document, said that that was his
address, *Mr. Coleridge, Nether Stowey, Somersetshire;* and that he
should be glad to see me there in a few weeks' time, and, if I chose,
would come half way to meet me. I was not less surprised than the
shepherd boy (this simile is to be found in *Cassandra*[4]) when he
sees a thunderbolt fall close at his feet. I stammered out my ac-
knowledgments and acceptance of this offer (I thought Mr. Wedgwood's annuity a trifle to it) as well as I could; and this mighty
business being settled, the poet-preacher took leave, and I accompanied him six miles on the road. It was a fine morning in the middle of winter, and he talked the whole way. The scholar in Chaucer
is described as going

————sounding on his way.[5]

So Coleridge went on his. In digressing, in dilating, in passing from
subject to subject, he appeared to me to float in air, to slide on ice.
He told me in confidence (going along) that he should have
preached two sermons before he accepted the situation at Shrews-

2. Milton, *Lycidas,* line 55: "Nor yet
where Deva spreads her wizard stream"
("Deva" is the river Dee, in Wales).
Since Milton speaks in that passage of
"Druid bards," Hazlitt means that
Coleridge will devote himself to imaginative writing.
3. An allegorical locale in Bunyan's
Pilgrim's Progress, here used as another periphrasis for the occupation of
poetry.
4. A romance by the 17th-century
French writer La Calprenède.
5. *The Canterbury Tales,* General Prologue, line 309: "Souning in moral
vertu was his speeche" (in Chaucer,
the meaning of "souning" is "resounding").

bury, one on Infant Baptism, the other on the Lord's Supper, showing that he could not administer either, which would have effectually disqualified him for the object in view. I observed that he
continually crossed me on the way by shifting from one side of
the footpath to the other. This struck me as an odd movement;
but I did not at that time connect it with any instability of purpose or involuntary change of principle, as I have done since. He
seemed unable to keep on in a straight line. He spoke slightingly
of Hume[6] (whose *Essay on Miracles* he said was stolen from an
objection started in one of South's[7] sermons—*Credat Judaeus Ap-
pella!*) I was not very much pleased at this account of Hume, for
I had just been reading, with infinite relish, that completest of all
metaphysical *choke-pears*,[8] his *Treatise on Human Nature*, to which
the *Essays*, in point of scholastic subtlety and close reasoning, are
mere elegant trifling, light summer reading. Coleridge even denied
the excellence of Hume's general style, which I think betrayed a
want of taste or candor. He however made me amends by the manner in which he spoke of Berkeley.[9] He dwelt particularly on his
Essay on Vision as a masterpiece of analytical reasoning. So it undoubtedly is. He was exceedingly angry with Dr. Johnson for striking the stone with his foot, in allusion to this author's theory of
matter and spirit, and saying, "Thus I confute him, sir."[1] Coleridge drew a parallel (I don't know how he brought about the
connection) between Bishop Berkeley and Tom Paine.[2] He said
the one was an instance of a subtle, the other of an acute mind,
than which no two things could be more distinct. The one was
a shop-boy's quality, the other the characteristic of a philosopher.
He considered Bishop Butler[3] as a true philosopher, a profound
and conscientious thinker, a genuine reader of nature and of his
own mind. He did not speak of his *Analogy*, but of his *Sermons
at the Rolls' Chapel*, of which I had never heard. Coleridge somehow always contrived to prefer the *unknown* to the *known*. In this
instance he was right. The *Analogy* is a tissue of sophistry, of wire-
drawn, theological special-pleading; the *Sermons* (with the Preface
to them) are in a fine vein of deep, matured reflection, a candid
appeal to our observation of human nature, without pedantry and
without bias. I told Coleridge I had written a few remarks, and
was sometimes foolish enough to believe that I had made a discovery on the same subject (the *Natural Disinterestedness of the*

6. David Hume, 18th-century Scottish
philosopher.
7. Robert South (1634–1716), Anglican divine. The Latin phrase, from
Horace, *Satires* I.v.100, means, "Let
Apella the Jew believe it"—implying
that he himself does not.
8. A very sour variety of pear; hence,
anything hard to take in.
9. Bishop George Berkeley, 18th-cen-
tury idealist philosopher, and author of

an *Essay Toward a New Theory of
Vision* (1709).
1. See Boswell's *Life of Johnson* for
the year 1763.
2. Philosophical supporter of the American and French Revolutions and author of *Common Sense* and *The Rights
of Man.*
3. Joseph Butler, 18th-century theologian and moral philosopher, author of
the *Analogy of Religion* (1736).

Human Mind[4])—and I tried to explain my view of it to Coleridge, who listened with great willingness, but I did not succeed in making myself understood. I sat down to the task shortly afterwards for the twentieth time, got new pens and paper, determined to make clear work of it, wrote a few meager sentences in the skeleton-style of a mathematical demonstration, stopped halfway down the second page; and, after trying in vain to pump up any words, images, notions, apprehensions, facts, or observations, from that gulf of abstraction in which I had plunged myself for four or five years preceding, gave up the attempt as labor in vain, and shed tears of helpless despondency on the blank unfinished paper. I can write fast enough now. Am I better than I was then? Oh no! One truth discovered, one pang of regret at not being able to express it, is better than all the fluency and flippancy in the world. Would that I could go back to what I then was! Why can we not revive past times as we can revisit old places? If I had the quaint Muse of Sir Philip Sidney to assist me, I would write a *Sonnet to the Road between Wem and Shrewsbury*, and immortalize every step of it by some fond enigmatical conceit. I would swear that the very milestones had ears, and that Harmer Hill stooped with all its pines, to listen to a poet, as he passed! I remember but one other topic of discourse in this walk. He mentioned Paley,[5] praised the naturalness and clearness of his style, but condemned his sentiments, thought him a mere time-serving casuist, and said that "the fact of his work on Moral and Political Philosophy being made a textbook in our universities was a disgrace to the national character." We parted at the six-mile stone; and I returned homeward pensive but much pleased. I had met with unexpected notice from a person whom I believed to have been prejudiced against me. "Kind and affable to me had been his condescension, and should be honored ever with suitable regard."[6] He was the first poet I had known, and he certainly answered to that inspired name. I had heard a great deal of his powers of conversation, and was not disappointed. In fact, I never met with anything at all like them, either before or since. I could easily credit the accounts which were circulated of his holding forth to a large party of ladies and gentlemen, an evening or two before, on the Berkeleian Theory, when he made the whole material universe look like a transparency of fine words; and another story (which I believe he has somewhere told himself)[7] of his being asked to a party at Birmingham, of his smoking tobacco and going to sleep after dinner on a sofa, where the company found him, to their no small surprise, which was in-

4. Published as *An Essay on the Principles of Human Action* (1805).
5. William Paley, author of *Evidences of Christianity* (1794), and supporter of a utilitarian theology and morality.
6. Paraphrasing Adam's words about the angel Raphael in *Paradise Lost* VIII.648–50.
7. See *Biographia Literaria*, Chapter X.

creased to wonder when he started up of a sudden, and rubbing
his eyes, looked about him, and launched into a three hours' description of the third heaven, of which he had had a dream, very
different from Mr. Southey's *Vision of Judgment*,[8] and also from
that other *Vision of Judgment*, which Mr. Murray, the secretary
of the Bridge Street Junto, has taken into his especial keeping!

On my way back, I had a sound in my ears, it was the voice
of Fancy: I had a light before me, it was the face of Poetry. The
one still lingers there, the other has not quitted my side! Coleridge
in truth met me half-way on the ground of philosophy, or I should
not have been won over to his imaginative creed. I had an uneasy,
pleasurable sensation all the time, till I was to visit him. During
those months the chill breath of winter gave me a welcoming; the
vernal air was balm and inspiration to me. The golden sunsets, the
silver star of evening, lighted me on my way to new hopes and
prospects. *I was to visit Coleridge in the spring.* This circumstance
was never absent from my thoughts, and mingled with all my feelings. I wrote to him at the time proposed, and received an answer
postponing my intended visit for a week or two, but very cordially
urging me to complete my promise then. This delay did not damp,
but rather increased my ardor. In the meantime, I went to Llangol-
len Vale,[9] by way of initiating myself in the mysteries of natural
scenery; and I must say I was enchanted with it. I had been reading Coleridge's description of England in his fine *Ode on the Departing Year*, and I applied it, *con amore*,[1] to the objects before
me. That valley was to me (in a manner) the cradle of a new existence: in the river that winds through it, my spirit was baptized
in the waters of Helicon![2]

I returned home, and soon after set out on my journey with unworn heart and untired feet. My way lay through Worcester and
Gloucester, and by Upton, where I thought of Tom Jones and the
adventure of the muff.[3] I remember getting completely wet through
one day, and stopping at an inn (I think it was at Tewkesbury)
where I sat up all night to read *Paul and Virginia*.[4] Sweet were the
showers in early youth that drenched my body, and sweet the drops
of pity that fell upon the books I read! I recollect a remark of Coleridge's upon this very book that nothing could show the gross in-
delicacy of French manners and the entire corruption of their imagination more strongly than the behavior of the heroine in the

8. Robert Southey's sycophantic memorial poem describing the entrance into
heaven of George III. "Mr. Murray"
was Charles Murray, solicitor to an
Association, located at New Bridge
Street, for "Opposing Disloyal and
Seditious Principles"; he prosecuted
John Hunt for publishing Byron's
Vision of Judgment, a brilliant parody
of Southey's poem. Hazlitt derisively
refers to the Association as a "junto"—

i.e., a group formed for political intrigue.
9. In north Wales (about 35 miles
from Wem).
1. "With love," fervently.
2. A mountain sacred to Apollo and the
Muses.
3. Henry Fielding's *Tom Jones* X.v. ff.
4. A sentimental love idyll (1788) by
Bernardin de Saint-Pierre.

last fatal scene, who turns away from a person on board the sinking vessel, that offers to save her life, because he has thrown off his clothes to assist him in swimming. Was this a time to think of such a circumstance? I once hinted to Wordsworth, as we were sailing in his boat on Grasmere lake, that I thought he had borrowed the idea of his *Poems on the Naming of Places* from the local inscriptions of the same kind in *Paul and Virginia*. He did not own the obligation, and stated some distinction without a difference in defense to his claim to originality. Any the slightest variation would be sufficient for this purpose in his mind; for whatever *he* added or omitted would inevitably be worth all that any one else had done, and contain the marrow of the sentiment. I was still two days before the time fixed for my arrival, for I had taken care to set out early enough. I stopped these two days at Bridgewater, and when I was tired of sauntering on the banks of its muddy river, returned to the inn and read *Camilla*.[5] So have I loitered my life away, reading books, looking at pictures, going to plays, hearing, thinking, writing on what pleased me best. I have wanted only one thing to make me happy; but wanting that, have wanted everything![6]

I arrived, and was well received. The country about Nether Stowey is beautiful, green and hilly, and near the seashore. I saw it but the other day, after an interval of twenty years, from a hill near Taunton. How was the map of my life spread out before me, as the map of the country lay at my feet! In the afternoon, Coleridge took me over to Alfoxden, a romantic old family mansion of the St. Aubins, where Wordsworth lived. It was then in the possession of a friend of the poet's, who gave him the free use of it.[7] Somehow, that period (the time just after the French Revolution) was not a time when *nothing was given for nothing*. The mind opened and a softness might be perceived coming over the heart of individuals, beneath "the scales that fence" our self-interest. Wordsworth himself was from home, but his sister kept house, and set before us a frugal repast; and we had free access to her brother's poems, the *Lyrical Ballads*, which were still in manuscript, or in the form of *Sybilline Leaves*.[8] I dipped into a few of these with great satisfaction, and with the faith of a novice. I slept that night in an old room wth blue hangings, and covered with the round-faced family portraits of the age of George I and II and from the wooded declivity of the adjoining park that overlooked my window, at the dawn of day, could

———hear the loud stag speak.[9]

5. A novel by Fanny Burney, published 1796.
6. The love of Sarah Walker; see the introduction to Hazlitt, above.
7. A mistake; Wordsworth paid rent.
8. I.e., "prophetic writings"; used by Coleridge as the title for his published poems in 1817.
9. From Ben Jonson's poem *To Sir Robert Wroth*, line 22.

In the outset of life (and particularly at this time I felt it so) our imagination has a body to it. We are in a state between sleeping and waking, and have indistinct but glorious glimpses of strange shapes, and there is always something to come better than what we see. As in our dreams the fullness of the blood gives warmth and reality to the coinage of the brain, so in youth our ideas are clothed, and fed, and pampered with our good spirits; we breathe thick with thoughtless happiness, the weight of future years presses on the strong pulses of the heart, and we repose with undisturbed faith in truth and good. As we advance, we exhaust our fund of enjoyment and of hope. We are no longer wrapped in *lamb's wool*, lulled in Elysium. As we taste the pleasures of life, their spirit evaporates, the sense palls; and nothing is left but the phantoms, the lifeless shadows of what *has been!*

That morning, as soon as breakfast was over, we strolled out into the park, and seating ourselves on the trunk of an old ash tree that stretched along the ground, Coleridge read aloud with a sonorous and musical voice, the ballad of *Betty Foy*.[1] I was not critically or skeptically inclined. I saw touches of truth and nature, and took the rest for granted. But in the *Thorn*, the *Mad Mother*, and the *Complaint of a Poor Indian Woman*, I felt that deeper power and pathos which have been since acknowledged,

> In spite of pride, in erring reason's spite,[2]

as the characteristics of this author; and the sense of a new style and a new spirit in poetry came over me. It had to me something of the effect that arises from the turning up of the fresh soil, or of the first welcome breath of spring,

> While yet the trembling year is unconfirmed.[3]

Coleridge and myself walked back to Stowey that evening, and his voice sounded high

> Of Providence, foreknowledge, will, and fate,
> Fixed fate, free will, foreknowledge absolute,[4]

as we passed through echoing grove, by fairy stream or waterfall, gleaming in the summer moonlight! He lamented that Wordsworth was not prone enough to believe in the traditional superstitions of the place, and that there was a something corporeal, a *matter-of-fact-ness*, a clinging to the palpable, or often to the petty, in his poetry, in consequence. His genius was not a spirit that descended to him through the air; it sprung out of the ground like a flower, or unfolded itself from a green spray, on which the goldfinch sang.

1. Wordsworth's *Idiot Boy;* like the other poems mentioned, it was included in *Lyrical Ballads*.
2. Pope's *Essay on Man* I.293.
3. James Thomson, *The Seasons*, "Spring," line 18.
4. *Paradise Lost* II.559-60.

He said, however (if I remember right) that this objection must be confined to his descriptive pieces, that his philosophic poetry had a grand and comprehensive spirit in it, so that his soul seemed to inhabit the universe like a palace, and to discover truth by intuition, rather than by deduction. The next day Wordsworth arrived from Bristol at Coleridge's cottage. I think I see him now. He answered in some degree to his friend's description of him, but was more gaunt and Don Quixote-like. He was quaintly dressed (according to the *costume* of that unconstrained period) in a brown fustian[5] jacket and striped pantaloons. There was something of a roll, a lounge in his gait, not unlike his own Peter Bell.[6] There was a severe, worn pressure of thought about his temples, a fire in his eye (as if he saw something in objects more than the outward appearance), an intense high narrow forehead, a Roman nose, cheeks furrowed by strong purpose and feeling, and a convulsive inclination to laughter about the mouth, a good deal at variance with the solemn, stately expression of the rest of his face. Chantry's bust wants the marking traits; but he was teased into making it regular and heavy; Haydon's head of him, introduced into the *Entrance of Christ into Jerusalem*, is the most like his drooping weight of thought and expression.[7] He sat down and talked very naturally and freely, with a mixture of clear gushing accents in his voice, a deep guttural intonation, and a strong tincture of the northern *burr*, like the crust on wine. He instantly began to make havoc of the half of a Cheshire cheese on the table, and said triumphantly that "his marriage with experience had not been so unproductive as Mr. Southey's in teaching him a knowledge of the good things of this life." He had been to see the *Castle Specter* by Monk Lewis,[8] while at Bristol, and described it very well. He said "it fitted the taste of the audience like a glove." This *ad captandum*[9] merit was, however, by no means a recommendation of it, according to the severe principles of the new school, which reject rather than court popular effect. Wordsworth, looking out of the low, latticed window, said, "How beautifully the sun sets on that yellow bank!" I thought within myself, "With what eyes these poets see nature!" and ever after, when I saw the sunset stream upon the objects facing it, conceived I had made a discovery, or thanked Mr. Wordsworth for having made one for me! We went over to Alfoxden again the day following, and Wordsworth read us the story of *Peter Bell* in the open air; and the comment made upon it by his face and voice was very different from that of

5. A coarse and heavy cotton cloth.
6. The protagonist in Wordsworth's *Peter Bell*.
7. Sir Francis Chantrey, a sculptor; Benjamin Robert Haydon, painter of grandiose historical and religious pictures.

8. Matthew Gregory Lewis (1775–1818), called "Monk" Lewis from his horror tale, *The Monk* (1795). *The Castle Specter* was a play, also in the Gothic terror-mode.
9. "For the sake of captivating" an audience.

some later critics! Whatever might be thought of the poem, "his face was as a book where men might read strange matters,"[1] and he announced the fate of his hero in prophetic tones. There is a *chaunt* in the recitation both of Coleridge and Wordsworth, which acts as a spell upon the hearer, and disarms the judgment. Perhaps they have deceived themselves by making habitual use of this ambiguous accompaniment. Coleridge's manner is more full, animated, and varied; Wordsworth's more equable, sustained, and internal. The one might be termed more *dramatic*, the other more *lyrical*. Coleridge has told me that he himself liked to compose in walking over uneven ground, or breaking through the straggling branches of a copse wood; whereas Wordsworth always wrote (if he could) walking up and down a straight gravel walk, or in some spot where the continuity of his verse met with no collateral interruption. Returning that same evening, I got into a metaphysical argument with Wordsworth, while Coleridge was explaining the different notes of the nightingale to his sister, in which we neither of us succeeded in making ourselves perfectly clear and intelligible. Thus I passed three weeks at Nether Stowey and in the neighborhood, generally devoting the afternoons to a delightful chat in an arbor made of bark by the poet's friend Tom Poole, sitting under two fine elm trees, and listening to the bees humming round us while we quaffed our flip.[2] It was agreed, among other things, that we should make a jaunt down the Bristol Channel, as far as Linton. We set off together on foot, Coleridge, John Chester, and I. This Chester was a native of Nether Stowey, one of those who were attracted to Coleridge's discourse as flies are to honey, or bees in swarming-time to the sound of a brass pan. He "followed in the chase like a dog who hunts, not like one that made up the cry."[3] He had on a brown cloth coat, boots, and corduroy breeches, was low in stature, bowlegged, had a drag in his walk like a drover, which he assisted by a hazel switch, and kept on a sort of trot by the side of Coleridge, like a running footman by a state coach, that he might not lose a syllable or sound that fell from Coleridge's lips. He told me his private opinion, that Coleridge was a wonderful man. He scarcely opened his lips, much less offered an opinion the whole way: yet of the three, had I to choose during that journey, I would be John Chester. He afterwards followed Coleridge into Germany, where the Kantean philosophers were puzzled how to bring him under any of their categories. When he sat down at table with his idol, John's felicity was complete; Sir Walter Scott's, or Mr. Blackwood's, when they sat down at the same table with the King,[4] was not more so. We passed Dunster on our right, a small town be-

1. See *Macbeth* I.v.63–64.
2. Spiced and sweetened ale.
3. Cf. *Othello* II.iii.369–70.
4. At a banquet given to George IV at Edinburgh, in 1822. William Blackwood, publisher of *Blackwood's Magazine*, was, like Scott, a Tory; hence the irony.

tween the brow of a hill and the sea. I remember eying it wistfully as it lay below us: contrasted with the woody scene around,
it looked as clear, as pure, as *embrowned* and ideal as any landscape
I have seen since, of Gaspar Poussin's or Domenichino's. We had
a long day's march—(our feet kept time to the echoes of Coleridge's tongue)—through Minehead and by the Blue Anchor, and
on to Linton, which we did not reach till near midnight, and where
we had some difficulty in making a lodgment. We however knocked
the people of the house up at last, and we were repaid for our apprehensions and fatigue by some excellent rashers of fried bacon
and eggs. The view in coming along had been splendid. We walked
for miles and miles on dark brown heaths overlooking the channel,
with the Welsh hills beyond, and at times descended into little
sheltered valleys close by the seaside, with a smuggler's face scowling
by us, and then had to ascend conical hills with a path winding
up through a coppice to a barren top, like a monk's shaven crown,
from one of which I pointed out to Coleridge's notice the bare
masts of a vessel on the very edge of the horizon and within the
red-orbed disk of the setting sun, like his own specter-ship in the
Ancient Mariner. At Linton the character of the seacoast becomes
more marked and rugged. There is a place called the Valley of
Rocks (I suspect this was only the poetical name for it) bedded
among precipices overhanging the sea, with rocky caverns beneath,
into which the waves dash, and where the seagull forever wheels
its screaming flight. On the tops of these are huge stones thrown
transverse, as if an earthquake had tossed them there, and behind
these is a fretwork of perpendicular rocks, something like the Giant's
Causeway.[5] A thunderstorm came on while we were at the inn,
and Coleridge was running out bareheaded to enjoy the commotion of the elements in the Valley of Rocks, but as if in spite, the
clouds only muttered a few angry sounds, and let fall a few refreshing drops. Coleridge told me that he and Wordsworth were to have
made this place the scene of a prose tale,[6] which was to have been
in the manner of, but far superior to, the *Death of Abel*, but they
had relinquished the design. In the morning of the second day, we
breakfasted luxuriously in an old-fashioned parlor, on tea, toast,
eggs, and honey, in the very sight of the beehives from which it
had been taken, and a garden full of thyme and wild flowers that
had produced it. On this occasion Coleridge spoke of Virgil's
Georgics, but not well. I do not think he had much feeling for
the classical or elegant. It was in this room that we found a little
worn-out copy of the *Seasons*,[7] lying in a window seat, on which
Coleridge exclaimed, "*That* is true fame!" He said Thomson was

5. A mass of rocks on the northern
Irish coast.
6. The "prose tale" exists as a fragment, *The Wanderings of Cain*. The
Death of Abel (1758) is by the once
celebrated Swiss poet, Salomon Gessner.
7. By James Thomson, published 1726–
30.

626 · *William Hazlitt*

a great poet, rather than a good one; his style was as meretricious
as his thoughts were natural. He spoke of Cowper as the best modern poet. He said the *Lyrical Ballads* were an experiment about to
be tried by him and Wordsworth, to see how far the public taste
would endure poetry written in a more natural and simple style
than had hitherto been attempted; totally discarding the artifices
of poetical diction, and making use only of such words as had probably been common in the most ordinary language since the days
of Henry II. Some comparison was introduced between Shakespeare
and Milton. He said "he hardly knew which to prefer. Shakespeare
appeared to him a mere stripling in the art; he was as tall and as
strong, with infinitely more activity than Milton, but he never appeared to have come to man's estate; or if he had, he would not
have been a man, but a monster." He spoke with contempt of
Gray, and with intolerance of Pope. He did not like the versification
of the latter. He observed that "the ears of these couplet-writers
might be charged with having short memories, that could not retain
the harmony of whole passages." He thought little of Junius[8] as a
writer; he had a dislike of Dr. Johnson; and a much higher opinion
of Burke as an orator and politician, than of Fox or Pitt. He however thought him very inferior in richness of style and imagery to
some of our elder prose writers, particularly Jeremy Taylor.[9] He
liked Richardson, but not Fielding; nor could I get him to enter
into the merits of *Caleb Williams*.[1] In short, he was profound and
discriminating with respect to those authors whom he liked, and
where he gave his judgment fair play; capricious, perverse, and prejudiced in his antipathies and distastes. We loitered on the "ribbed
sea-sands,"[2] in such talk as this, a whole morning, and I recollect
met with a curious seaweed, of which John Chester told us the
country name! A fisherman gave Coleridge an account of a boy
that had been drowned the day before, and that they had tried
to save him at the risk of their own lives. He said "he did not know
how it was that they ventured, but, sir, we have a *nature* towards
one another." This expression, Coleridge remarked to me, was
a fine illustration of that theory of disinterestedness which I (in
common with Butler) had adopted. I broached to him an argument of mine to prove that *likeness* was not mere association of
ideas. I said that the mark in the sand put one in mind of a man's
foot, not because it was part of a former impression of a man's
foot (for it was quite new) but because it was like the shape of a
man's foot. He assented to the justness of this distinction (which

8. The pseudonym of an author (his
identity is still unknown) of a series
of attacks on George III and various
politicians, 1769–72.
9. The 17th-century divine, author of
Holy Living (1650) and *Holy Dying*
(1651).

1. Samuel Richardson and Henry Fielding, the great 18th-century novelists.
Caleb Williams (1794) was a novel
by William Godwin.
2. Echoing *The Ancient Mariner*, line
227.

I have explained at length elsewhere, for the benefit of the curious)
and John Chester listened; not from any interest in the subject,
but because he was astonished that I should be able to suggest
anything to Coleridge that he did not already know. We returned
on the third morning, and Coleridge remarked the silent cottage-
smoke curling up the valleys where, a few evenings before, we had
seen the lights gleaming through the dark.

In a day or two after we arrived at Stowey, we set out, I on my
return home, and he for Germany. It was a Sunday morning, and
he was to preach that day for Dr. Toulmin of Taunton. I asked
him if he had prepared anything for the occasion? He said he had
not even thought of the text, but should as soon as we parted. I
did not go to hear him,—this was a fault—but we met in the
evening at Bridgewater. The next day we had a long day's walk
to Bristol, and sat down, I recollect, by a well-side on the road,
to cool ourselves and satisfy our thirst, when Coleridge repeated
to me some descriptive lines from his tragedy of *Remorse;* which
I must say became his mouth and that occasion better than they,
some years after, did Mr. Elliston's and the Drury Lane boards,[3]

> Oh memory! shield me from the world's poor strife,
> And give those scenes thine everlasting life.

I saw no more of him for a year or two, during which period
he had been wandering in the Hartz Forest in Germany; and his
return was cometary, meteorous, unlike his setting out. It was
not till some time after that I knew his friends Lamb and Southey.
The last always appears to me (as I first saw him) with a common-
place-book under his arm, and the first with a bon mot in his
mouth. It was at Godwin's that I met him with Holcroft and
Coleridge, where they were disputing fiercely which was the best
—*Man as he was, or man as he is to be.* "Give me," says Lamb,
"man as he is *not* to be." This saying was the beginning of a friendship between us, which I believe still continues.—Enough of this
for the present.

> But there is matter for another rhyme,
> And I to this may add a second tale.[4]

1823

3. Robert William Elliston, a well-known actor. Coleridge's *Remorse* was produced at Drury Lane Theatre in 1813.
4. Wordsworth, *Hart-Leap Well,* lines 95–96.

From On Shakespeare and Milton[1]

* * * The striking peculiarity of Shakespeare's mind was its generic quality, its power of communication with all other minds —so that it contained a universe of thought and feeling within itself, and had no one peculiar bias, or exclusive excellence more than another. He was just like any other man, but that he was like all other men. He was the least of an egotist that it was possible to be. He was nothing in himself; but he was all that others were, or that they could become. He not only had in himself the germs of every faculty and feeling, but he could follow them by anticipation, intuitively, into all their conceivable ramifications, through every change of fortune or conflict of passion, or turn of thought. He had "a mind reflecting ages past,"[2] and present—all the people that ever lived are there. There was no respect of persons with him. His genius shone equally on the evil and on the good, on the wise and the foolish, the monarch and the beggar: "All corners of the earth, kings, queens, and states, maids, matrons, nay, the secrets of the grave,"[3] are hardly hid from his searching glance. He was like the genius of humanity, changing places with all of us at pleasure, and playing with our purposes as with his own. He turned the globe round for his amusement, and surveyed the generations of men, and the individuals as they passed, with their different concerns, passions, follies, vices, virtues, actions, and motives—as well those that they knew, as those which they did not know, or acknowledge to themselves. The dreams of childhood, the ravings of despair, were the toys of his fancy. Airy beings waited at his call, and came at his bidding. Harmless fairies "nodded to him, and did him curtesies":[4] and the night hag bestrode the blast at the command of "his so potent art."[5] The world of spirits lay open to him, like the world of real men and women: and there is the

1. This essay constituted the third in a series of *Lectures on the English Poets* that Hazlitt delivered with great success in London during January and February, 1818. It exemplifies Hazlitt's typical procedure in criticism—the unsystematic piling of statement on statement; the emphasis on particular lines or passages; the relish for the brief, intense expression; the sudden flashes of critical insight. It also develops one of Hazlitt's major critical ideas, the distinction between Shakespeare's objectivity and the subjectivity of Wordsworth and the "modern school," who project their own egos and moods into everything they undertake to describe. Milton, according to Hazlitt, falls between. John Keats attended Hazlitt's lectures, and the trace of Hazlitt's ideas can be detected in Keats's own poetic "axioms" and in his opposition of what he called Wordsworth's "egotistical sublime" to the higher poetry exemplified by Shakespeare, who exists in his work only as he identifies himself, by sympathetic self-projection, with the characters that he imagines. See Keats's letters of February 3, February 27, and October 27, 1818.
2. From a poem on Shakespeare prefixed to the Second Folio of his plays (1632).
3. See Shakespeare's *Cymbeline* III.iv. 39–40.
4. Cf. *A Midsummer Night's Dream* III.i.177.
5. See *The Tempest* V.i.50.

same truth in his delineations of the one as of the other; for if the preternatural characters he describes could be supposed to exist, they would speak, and feel, and act, as he makes them. He had only to think of any thing in order to become that thing, with all the circumstances belonging to it. When he conceived of a character, whether real or imaginary, he not only entered into all its thoughts and feelings, but seemed instantly, and as if by touching a secret spring, to be surrounded with all the same objects, "subject to the same skyey influences,"[6] the same local, outward, and unforeseen accidents which would occur in reality. Thus the character of Caliban not only stands before us with a language and manners of its own, but the scenery and situation of the enchanted island he inhabits, the traditions of the place, its strange noises, its hidden recesses, "his frequent haunts and ancient neighborhood,"[7] are given with a miraculous truth of nature, and with all the familiarity of an old recollection. The whole "coheres semblably together"[8] in time, place, and circumstance. In reading this author, you do not merely learn what his characters say—you see their persons. By something expressed or understood, you are at no loss to decipher their peculiar physiognomy, the meaning of a look, the grouping, the by-play, as we might see it on the stage. A word, an epithet, paints a whole scene, or throws us back whole years in the history of the person represented. So (as it has been ingeniously remarked)[9] when Prospero describes himself as left alone in the boat with his daughter, the epithet which he applies to her, "Me and thy *crying* self,"[1] flings the imagination instantly back from the grown woman to the helpless condition of infancy, and places the first and most trying scene of his misfortunes before us, with all that he must have suffered in the interval. How well the silent anguish of Macduff is conveyed to the reader, by the friendly expostulation of Malcolm—"What! man, ne'er pull your hat upon your brows!"[2] Again, Hamlet, in the scene with Rosencrantz and Guildenstern,[3] somewhat abruptly concludes his fine soliloquy on life by saying, "Man delights not me, nor woman neither, though by your smiling you seem to say so." Which is explained by their answer—"My lord, we had no such stuff in our thoughts. But we smiled to think, if you delight not in man, what lenten entertainment the players shall receive from you, whom we met on the way" —as if while Hamlet was making this speech, his two old schoolfellows from Wittenberg had been really standing by, and he had seen them smiling by stealth, at the idea of the players crossing their minds. It is not "a combination and a form"[4] of words, a

6. See *Measure for Measure* III.i.9.
7. Cf. Milton's *Comus*, line 314.
8. See Shakespeare, *2 Henry IV* V.i.73.
9. By Coleridge, in a lecture on Shakespeare given in December, 1811.

1. *The Tempest* I.ii.132.
2. *Macbeth* IV.iii.208.
3. *Hamlet* II.ii.
4. *Ibid.* III.iv.60.

set speech or two, a preconcerted theory of a character, that will do this: but all the persons concerned must have been present in the poet's imagination, as at a kind of rehearsal; and whatever would have passed through their minds on the occasion, and have been observed by others, passed through his, and is made known to the reader. * * *

The account of Ophelia's death begins thus:

> There is a willow hanging o'er a brook,
> That shows its hoary leaves in the glassy stream.[5]

Now this is an instance of the same unconscious power of mind which is as true to nature as itself. The leaves of the willow are, in fact, white underneath, and it is this part of them which would appear "hoary" in the reflection in the brook. The same sort of intuitive power, the same faculty of bringing every object in nature, whether present or absent, before the mind's eye, is observable in the speech of Cleopatra, when conjecturing what were the employments of Antony in his absence: "He's speaking now, or murmuring, where's my serpent of old Nile?"[6] How fine to make Cleopatra have this consciousness of her own character, and to make her feel that it is this for which Antony is in love with her! She says, after the battle of Actium, when Antony has resolved to risk another fight, "It is my birthday; I had thought to have held it poor: but since my lord is Antony again, I will be Cleopatra."[7] What other poet would have thought of such a casual resource of the imagination, or would have dared to avail himself of it? The thing happens in the play as it might have happened in fact.—That which, perhaps, more than any thing else distinguishes the dramatic productions of Shakespeare from all others is this wonderful truth and individuality of conception. Each of his characters is as much itself, and as absolutely independent of the rest, as well as of the author, as if they were living persons, not fictions of the mind. The poet may be said, for the time, to identify himself with the character he wishes to represent, and to pass from one to another, like the same soul successively animating different bodies. By an art like that of the ventriloquist, he throws his imagination out of himself, and makes every word appear to proceed from the mouth of the person in whose name it is given. His plays alone are properly expressions of the passions, not descriptions of them. His characters are real beings of flesh and blood; they speak like men, not like authors. One might suppose that he had stood by at the time, and overheard what passed. As in our dreams we hold conversations with ourselves, make remarks, or communicate intelligence, and have no idea of the answer which we shall receive, and which we

5. *Ibid.* IV.vii.168–69, somewhat misquoted.
6. *Antony and Cleopatra* I.v.24–25.
7. *Ibid.* III.xiii.185–87.

ourselves make, till we hear it: so the dialogues in Shakespeare are carried on without any consciousness of what is to follow, without any appearance of preparation or premeditation. The gusts of passion come and go like sounds of music borne on the wind. Nothing is made out by formal inference and analogy, by climax and antithesis: all comes, or seems to come, immediately from nature. Each object and circumstance exists in his mind, as it would have existed in reality: each several train of thought and feeling goes on of itself, without confusion or effort. In the world of his imagination, everything has a life, a place, and being of its own! * * *

The great fault of a modern school of poetry[8] is that it is an experiment to reduce poetry to a mere effusion of natural sensibility; or what is worse, to divest it both of imaginary splendor and human passion, to surround the meanest objects with the morbid feelings and devouring egotism of the writers' own minds. Milton and Shakespeare did not so understand poetry. They gave a more liberal interpretation both to nature and art. They did not do all they could to get rid of the one and the other, to fill up the dreary void with the Moods of their own Minds.[9] They owe their power over the human mind to their having had a deeper sense than others of what was grand in the objects of nature, or affecting in the events of human life. But to the men I speak of there is nothing interesting, nothing heroical, but themselves. To them the fall of gods or of great men is the same. They do not enter into the feeling. They cannot understand the terms. They are even debarred from the last poor, paltry consolation of an unmanly triumph over fallen greatness; for their minds reject, with a convulsive effort and intolerable loathing, the very idea that there ever was, or was thought to be, anything superior to themselves. All that has ever excited the attention or admiration of the world, they look upon with the most perfect indifference; and they are surprised to find that the world repays their indifference with scorn. "With what measure they mete, it has been meted to them again."[1]

Shakespeare's imagination is of the same plastic kind as his conception of character or passion. "It glances from heaven to earth, from earth to heaven."[2] Its movement is rapid and devious. It unites the most opposite extremes: or, as Puck says, in boasting of his own feats, "puts a girdle round about the earth in forty minutes."[3] He seems always hurrying from his subject, even while describing it; but the stroke, like the lightning's, is sure as it is sud-

8. I.e., what Hazlitt elsewhere called "the Lake school of poetry," of which "Mr. Wordsworth is at the head." Hazlitt's phrase, the "effusion of natural sensibility," may echo Wordsworth's definition of poetry as "the spontaneous overflow of natural feelings."

9. Wordsworth had entitled one section of his *Poems* of 1807, "Moods of My Own Mind."
1. Cf. Mark iv.24; Luke vi.38.
2. Cf. *A Midsummer Night's Dream* V.i.13.
3. Cf. *ibid.* II.i.175–76.

den. He takes the widest possible range, but from that very range he has his choice of the greatest variety and aptitude of materials. He brings together images the most alike, but placed at the greatest distance from each other; that is, found in circumstances of the greatest dissimilitude. From the remoteness of his combinations, and the celerity with which they are effected, they coalesce the more indissolubly together. The more the thoughts are strangers to each other, and the longer they have been kept asunder, the more intimate does their union seem to become. Their felicity is equal to their force. Their likeness is made more dazzling by their novelty. They startle, and take the fancy prisoner in the same instant. * * *

Shakespeare discovers in his writings little religious enthusiasm, and an indifference to personal reputation; he had none of the bigotry of his age, and his political prejudices were not very strong. In these respects, as well as in every other, he formed a direct contrast to Milton. Milton's works are a perpetual invocation to the Muses; a hymn to Fame. He had his thoughts constantly fixed on the contemplation of the Hebrew theocracy, and of a perfect commonwealth; and he seized the pen with a hand just warm from the touch of the ark of faith. His religious zeal infused its character into his imagination; so that he devotes himself with the same sense of duty to the cultivation of his genius, as he did to the exercise of virtue, or the good of his country. The spirit of the poet, the patriot, and the prophet vied with each other in his breast. His mind appears to have held equal communion with the inspired writers, and with the bards and sages of ancient Greece and Rome:

> Blind Thamyris, and blind Maeonides,
> And Tiresias, and Phineus, prophets old.[4]

He had a high standard, with which he was always comparing himself, nothing short of which could satisfy his jealous ambition. He thought of nobler forms and nobler things than those he found about him. He lived apart, in the solitude of his own thoughts, carefully excluding from his mind whatever might distract its purposes or alloy its purity, or damp its zeal. "With darkness and with dangers compassed round,"[5] he had the mighty models of antiquity always present to his thoughts, and determined to raise a monument of equal height and glory, "piling up every stone of luster from the brook,"[6] for the delight and wonder of posterity. He had girded himself up, and as it were, sanctified his genius to this service from his youth. * * *

Milton has borrowed more than any other writer, and exhausted every source of imitation, sacred or profane; yet he is perfectly dis-

4. *Paradise Lost* III.35–36.   6. *Ibid*. XI.324–25.
5. *Ibid*. VII.27.

tinct from every other writer. He is a writer of centos,[7] and yet in originality scarcely inferior to Homer. The power of his mind is stamped on every line. The fervor of his imagination melts down and renders malleable, as in a furnace, the most contradictory materials. In reading his works, we feel ourselves under the influence of a mighty intellect, that the nearer it approaches to others becomes more distinct from them. The quantity of art in him shows the strength of his genius: the weight of his intellectual obligations would have oppressed any other writer. Milton's learning has the effect of intuition. He describes objects, of which he could only have read in books, with the vividness of actual observation. His imagination has the force of nature. He makes words tell as pictures.

> Him followed Rimmon, whose delightful seat
> Was fair Damascus, on the fertile banks
> Of Abbana and Pharphar, lucid streams.[8]

The word *lucid* here gives to the idea all the sparkling effect of the most perfect landscape.

And again:

> As when a vulture on Imaus bred,
> Whose snowy ridge the roving Tartar bounds,
> Dislodging from a region scarce of prey,
> To gorge the flesh of lambs and yeanling kids
> On hills where flocks are fed, flies towards the springs
> Of Ganges or Hydaspes, Indian streams;
> But in his way lights on the barren plains
> Of Sericana, where Chineses drive
> With sails and wind their cany wagons light.[9]

If Milton had taken a journey for the express purpose, he could not have described this scenery and mode of life better. Such passages are like demonstrations of natural history. Instances might be multiplied without end.

We might be tempted to suppose that the vividness with which he describes visible objects was owing to their having acquired an unusual degree of strength in his mind, after the privation of his sight; but we find the same palpableness and truth in the descriptions which occur in his early poems. In *Lycidas* he speaks of "the great vision of the guarded mount,"[1] with that preternatural weight of impression with which it would present itself suddenly to "the pilot of some small night-foundered skiff":[2] and the lines in the *Penseroso*, describing "the wandering moon,"

> Riding near her highest noon,
> Like one that had been led astray
> Through the heaven's wide pathless way,[3]

7. Literary compositions made up of quotations from other works.
8. *Paradise Lost* I.467–69.
9. *Ibid* III.431–39.

1. Line 161.
2. *Paradise Lost* I.204.
3. Lines 67–70.

are as if he had gazed himself blind in looking at her. There is also the same depth of impression in his descriptions of the objects of all the different senses, whether colors, or sounds, or smells—the same absorption of his mind in whatever engaged his attention at the time. It has been indeed objected to Milton, by a common perversity of criticism, that his ideas were musical rather than picturesque, as if because they were in the highest degree musical, they must be (to keep the sage critical balance even, and to allow no one man to possess two qualities at the same time) proportionably deficient in other respects. But Milton's poetry is not cast in any such narrow, commonplace mold; it is not so barren of resources. His worship of the Muse was not so simple or confined. A sound arises "like a steam of rich distilled perfumes";[4] we hear the pealing organ, but the incense on the altars is also there, and the statues of the gods are ranged around! The ear indeed predominates over the eye, because it is more immediately affected, and because the language of music blends more immediately with, and forms a more natural accompaniment to, the variable and indefinite associations of ideas conveyed by words. But where the associations of the imagination are not the principal thing, the individual object is given by Milton with equal force and beauty. The strongest and best proof of this, as a characteristic power of his mind, is that the persons of Adam and Eve, of Satan, etc., are always accompanied, in our imagination, with the grandeur of the naked figure; they convey to us the ideas of sculpture. * * *

Again, nothing can be more magnificent than the portrait of Beelzebub:

> With Atlantean shoulders fit to bear
> The weight of mightiest monarchies:[5]

Or the comparison of Satan, as he "lay floating many a rood," to "that sea beast,"

> Leviathan, which God of all his works
> Created hugest that swim the ocean-stream![6]

What a force of imagination is there in this last expression! What an idea it conveys of the size of that hugest of created beings, as if it shrunk up the ocean to a stream, and took up the sea in its nostrils as a very little thing! Force of style is one of Milton's greatest excellences. Hence, perhaps, he stimulates us more in the reading, and less afterwards. The way to defend Milton against all impugners is to take down the book and read it. * * *

To proceed to a consideration of the merits of *Paradise Lost*, in the most essential point of view, I mean as to the poetry of character

4. *Comus,* line 556. 6. *Ibid.* I.196, 200–202.
5. *Paradise Lost* II.306–7.

and passion. I shall say nothing of the fable, or of other technical objections or excellences; but I shall try to explain at once the foundation of the interest belonging to the poem. I am ready to give up the dialogues in Heaven, where, as Pope justly observes, "God the Father turns a school-divine";[7] nor do I consider the battle of the angels as the climax of sublimity, or the most success-ful effort of Milton's pen. In a word, the interest of the poem arises from the daring ambition and fierce passions of Satan, and from the account of the paradisaical happiness, and the loss of it by our first parents. Three-fourths of the work are taken up with these characters, and nearly all that relates to them is unmixed sublimity and beauty. The two first books alone are like two massy pillars of solid gold.

Satan is the most heroic subject that ever was chosen for a poem; and the execution is as perfect as the design is lofty. He was the first of created beings, who, for endeavoring to be equal with the highest, and to divide the empire of heaven with the Almighty, was hurled down to hell. His aim was no less than the throne of the universe; his means, myriads of angelic armies bright, the third part of the heavens, whom he lured after him with his countenance, and who durst defy the Omnipotent in arms. His ambition was the greatest, and his punishment was the greatest; but not so his despair, for his fortitude was as great as his sufferings. His strength of mind was matchless as his strength of body; the vastness of his designs did not surpass the firm, inflexible determination with which he submitted to his irreversible doom, and final loss of all good. His power of action and of suffering was equal. He was the greatest power that was ever overthrown, with the strongest will left to re-sist or to endure. He was baffled, not confounded. He stood like a tower; or

> As when Heaven's fire
> Hath scathed the forest oaks or mountain pines.[8]

He was still surrounded with hosts of rebel angels, armed warriors, who own him as their sovereign leader, and with whose fate he sym-pathizes as he views them round, far as the eye can reach; though he keeps aloof from them in his own mind, and holds supreme counsel only with his own breast. An outcast from Heaven, Hell trembles beneath his feet, Sin and Death are at his heels, and man-kind are his easy prey.

> All is not lost; th' unconquerable will,
> And study of revenge, immortal hate,
> And courage never to submit or yield,
> And what else is not to be overcome,[9]

---

7. Pope's Horatian *Epistle to Augustus,* lines 101–2. 8. *Paradise Lost* I.612–13.
9. *Ibid.* I.106–9.

are still his. The sense of his punishment seems lost in the magnitude of it; the fierceness of tormenting flames is qualified and made innoxious by the greater fierceness of his pride; the loss of infinite happiness to himself is compensated in thought, by the power of inflicting infinite misery on others. Yet Satan is not the principle of malignity, or of the abstract love of evil—but of the abstract love of power, of pride, of self-will personified, to which last principle all other good and evil, and even his own, are subordinate. From this principle he never once flinches. His love of power and contempt for suffering are never once relaxed from the highest pitch of intensity. His thoughts burn like a hell within him; but the power of thought holds dominion in his mind over every other consideration. The consciousness of a determined purpose, of "that intellectual being, those thoughts that wander through eternity," though accompanied with endless pain, he prefers to nonentity, to "being swallowed up and lost in the wide womb of uncreated night."[1] He expresses the sum and substance of all ambition in one line. "Fallen cherub, to be weak is miserable, doing or suffering!"[2] After such a conflict as his, and such a defeat, to retreat in order, to rally, to make terms, to exist at all, is something; but he does more than this—he founds a new empire in hell, and from it conquers this new world, whither he bends his undaunted flight, forcing his way through nether and surrounding fires. The poet has not in all this given us a mere shadowy outline; the strength is equal to the magnitude of the conception. The Achilles of Homer is not more distinct; the Titans were not more vast; Prometheus chained to his rock was not a more terrific example of suffering and of crime. Wherever the figure of Satan is introduced, whether he walks or flies, "rising aloft incumbent on the dusky air,"[3] it is illustrated with the most striking and appropriate images: so that we see it always before us, gigantic, irregular, portentous, uneasy, and disturbed—but dazzling in its faded splendor, the clouded ruins of a god. The deformity of Satan is only in the depravity of his will; he has no bodily deformity to excite our loathing or disgust. The horns and tail are not there, poor emblems of the unbending, unconquered spirit, of the writhing agonies within. Milton was too magnanimous and open an antagonist to support his argument by the by-tricks of a hump and cloven foot; to bring into the fair field of controversy the good old Catholic prejudices of which Tasso and Dante have availed themselves, and which the mystic German critics would restore. He relied on the justice of his cause, and did not scruple to give the devil his due. Some persons may think that he has carried his liberality too far, and injured the cause he pro-

1. See *ibid*. II.147–50. These words are spoken by Belial, not Satan.
2. *Ibid* I.157–58.
3. *Ibid*. I.225–26.

fes⌐ed to espouse by making him the chief person in his poem. Considering the nature of his subject, he would be equally in danger of running into this fault, from his faith in religion, and his love of rebellion; and perhaps each of these motives had its full share in determining the choice of his subject. * * *

1818

From The Fight[1]

* * * The morning dawns; that dim but yet clear light appears, which weighs like solid bars of metal on the sleepless eyelids; the guests drop down from their chambers one by one—but it was too late to think of going to bed now (the clock was on the stroke of seven), we had nothing for it but to find a barber's (the pole that glittered in the morning sun lighted us to his shop), and then a nine miles' march to Hungerford. The day was fine, the sky was blue, the mists were retiring from the marshy ground, the path was tolerably dry, the sitting up all night had not done us much harm— at least the cause was good; we talked of this and that with amicable difference, roving and sipping of many subjects, but still invariably we returned to the fight. At length, a mile to the left of Hungerford, on a gentle eminence, we saw the ring surrounded by covered carts, gigs, and carriages, of which hundreds had passed us on the road; Toms gave a youthful shout, and we hastened down a narrow lane to the scene of action.

Reader, have you ever seen a fight? If not, you have a pleasure to come, at least if it is a fight like that between the Gas-man and Bill Neate. The crowd was very great when we arrived on the spot; open carriages were coming up, with streamers flying and music playing, and the country people were pouring in over hedge and ditch in all directions, to see their hero beat or be beaten. The odds were still on Gas, but only about five to four. Gully[2] had been down to try Neate, and had backed him considerably, which was a damper to the sanguine confidence of the adverse party. About two hundred thousand pounds were pending. The Gas says he has lost £3000 which were promised him by different gentlemen if he had won. He had presumed too much on himself, which had made others presume on him. This spirited and formidable young fellow

1. The famous prize fight between Tom Hickman, "the Gas-man," and Bill Neate on December 11, 1821, which was fought in the early 19th-century style, with bare fists and no limit on the number of rounds. Hazlitt's report was published a few months later; it has set a standard of excellence for all sports writing since that time. The first part of the essay, which is here omitted, describes how Hazlitt managed to make his way to the vicinity of the fight (its location had to be kept secret from the authorities) and sat up all night at an inn talking with fellow *aficionados* of the sport.

2. John Gully, a notable prizefighter, recently retired.

seems to have taken for his motto the old maxim that "there are three things necessary to success in life—*Impudence! Impudence! Impudence!*" It is so in matters of opinion, but not in the *Fancy*,[3] which is the most practical of all things, though even here confidence is half the battle, but only half. Our friend had vapored[4] and swaggered too much, as if he wanted to grin and bully his adversary out of the fight. "Alas! the Bristol man was not so tamed!"[5]—"This is *the grave-digger*," would Tom Hickman exclaim in the moments of intoxication from gin and success, showing his tremendous right hand, "this will send many of them to their long homes; I haven't done with them yet!" Why should he—though he had licked four of the best men within the hour, yet why should he threaten to inflict dishonorable chastisement on my old master Richmond,[6] a veteran going off the stage, and who has borne his sable honors meekly? Magnanimity, my dear Tom, and bravery, should be inseparable. Or why should he go up to his antagonist, the first time he ever saw him at the Fives Court,[7] and measuring him from head to foot with a glance of contempt, as Achilles surveyed Hector,[8] say to him, "What, are you Bill Neate? I'll knock more blood out of that great carcass of thine, this day fortnight, than you ever knocked out of a bullock's!" It was not manly, 'twas not fighter-like. If he was sure of the victory (as he was not), the less said about it the better. Modesty should accompany the *Fancy* as its shadow. The best men were always the best behaved. Jem Belcher, the Game Chicken[9] (before whom the Gas-man could not have lived) were civil, silent men. So is Cribb, so is Tom Belcher, the most elegant of sparrers, and not a man for every one to take by the nose. I enlarged on this topic in the mail[1] (while Turtle was asleep), and said very wisely (as I thought) that impertinence was a part of no profession. A boxer was bound to beat his man, but not to thrust his fist, either actually or by implication, in everyone's face. Even a highwayman, in the way of trade, may blow out your brains, but if he uses foul language at the same time, I should say he was no gentleman. A boxer, I would infer, need not be a blackguard or a coxcomb, more than another. Perhaps I press this point too much on a fallen man—Mr. Thomas Hickman has by this time learnt that first of all lessons, "That man was made to mourn."[2] He has lost nothing by the late fight but his presumption; and that every man may do as well without! By an over-display of this quality,

3. A slang term for the fighting game.
4. Blustered.
5. Altered from Cowper, *The Task* II.322.
6. Bill Richmond, a colored boxer, now an instructor; he had apparently given boxing lessons to Hazlitt.
7. A building near Leicester Square used for various sports, including boxing. "Fives" is a form of handball.

8. During the single combat of these champions before the walls of Troy (*Iliad* XXII).
9. Henry Pearce, who, like Jem Belcher, his teacher, was a famous fighter.
1. The Bath mail coach, on which Hazlitt had ridden to the fight with Tom Turtle, a trainer.
2. Title of a poem by Robert Burns.

however, the public had been prejudiced against him, and the *knowing-ones* were taken in. Few but those who had bet on him wished Gas to win. With my own prepossessions on the subject, the result of the 11th of December appeared to me as fine a piece of poetical justice as I had ever witnessed. The difference of weight between the two combatants (14 stone to 12)[3] was nothing to the sporting men. Great, heavy, clumsy, long-armed Bill Neate kicked the beam in the scale of the Gas-man's vanity. The amateurs were frightened at his big words, and thought that they would make up for the difference of six feet and five feet nine. Truly, the Fancy are not men of imagination. They judge of what has been, and cannot conceive of anything that is to be. The Gas-man had won hitherto; therefore he must beat a man half as big again as himself —and that to a certainty. Besides, there are as many feuds, factions, prejudices, pedantic notions in the Fancy as in the state or in the schools. Mr. Gully is almost the only cool, sensible man among them, who exercises an unbiased discretion, and is not a slave to his passions in these matters. But enough of reflections, and to our tale. The day, as I have said, was fine for a December morning. The grass was wet, and the ground miry, and plowed up with multitudinous feet, except that, within the ring itself, there was a spot of virgin green closed in and unprofaned by vulgar tread, that shone with dazzling brightness in the midday sun. For it was now noon, and we had an hour to wait. This is the trying time. It is then the heart sickens, as you think what the two champions are about, and how short a time will determine their fate. After the first blow is struck, there is no opportunity for nervous apprehensions; you are swallowed up in the immediate interest of the scene—but

> Between the acting of a dreadful thing
> And the first motion, all the interim is
> Like a phantasma or a hideous dream.[4]

I found it so as I felt the sun's rays clinging to my back, and saw the white wintry clouds sink below the verge of the horizon. "So," I thought, "my fairest hopes have faded from my sight!—so will the Gas-man's glory, or that of his adversary, vanish in an hour." The *swells*[5] were parading in their white box coats, the outer ring was cleared with some bruises on the heads and shins of the rustic assembly (for the *cockneys* had been distanced by the sixty-six miles[6]); the time drew near, I had got a good stand; a bustle, a buzz, ran through the crowd, and from the opposite side entered

---

3. A "stone" is fourteen pounds, so that, in this heavyweight bout, Neate weighed 224 pounds and the Gas-man 196.
4. Shakespeare's *Julius Caesar* II.i.63–65.
5. Gentlemen of fashion, dressed in

"box coats" (heavy overcoats for driving a carriage; the "box"' is the driver's seat).
6. I.e., the Londoners ("cockneys"), having a long distance to come, found that the countrymen had taken the best posts.

Neate, between his second and bottle-holder. He rolled along, swathed in his loose great coat, his knock-knees bending under his huge bulk; and, with a modest cheerful air, threw his hat into the ring. He then just looked round, and began quietly to undress; when from the other side there was a similar rush and an opening made, and the Gas-man came forward with a conscious air of anticipated triumph, too much like the cock-of-the walk. He strutted about more than became a hero, sucked oranges with a supercilious air, and threw away the skin with a toss of his head, and went up and looked at Neate, which was an act of supererogation. The only sensible thing he did was, as he strode away from the modern Ajax, to fling out his arms, as if he wanted to try whether they would do their work that day. By this time they had stripped, and presented a strong contrast in appearance. If Neate was like Ajax, "with Atlantean shoulders, fit to bear"[7] the pugilistic reputation of all Bristol, Hickman might be compared to Diomed,[8] light, vigorous, elastic, and his back glistened in the sun, as he moved about, like a panther's hide. There was now a dead pause—attention was awestruck. Who at that moment, big with a great event, did not draw his breath short—did not feel his heart throb? All was ready. They tossed up for the sun,[9] and the Gas-man won. They were led up to the *scratch*[1]—shook hands, and went at it.

In the first round[2] everyone thought it was all over. After making play a short time, the Gas-man flew at his adversary like a tiger, struck five blows in as many seconds, three first, and then following him as he staggered back, two more, right and left, and down he fell, a mighty ruin. There was a shout, and I said, "There is no standing this." Neate seemed like a lifeless lump of flesh and bone, round which the Gas-man's blows played with the rapidity of electricity or lightning, and you imagined he would only be lifted up to be knocked down again. It was as if Hickman held a sword or a fire in that right hand of his, and directed it against an unarmed body. They met again, and Neate seemed, not cowed, but particularly cautious. I saw his teeth clenched together and his brows knit close against the sun. He held out both his arms at full length straight before him, like two sledge hammers, and raised his left an inch or two higher. The Gas-man could not get over this guard—they struck mutually and fell, but without advantage on either side. It was the same in the next round; but the balance of power was thus restored—the fate of the battle was suspended. No one could tell how it would end. This was the only moment in which opinion

7. *Paradise Lost* II.306; "Atlantean" is the adjectival form of Atlas, the Titan who supports the heavens.
8. A Greek warrior in the *Iliad*.
9. To determine which fighter should face into the sun.
1. The line drawn across the ring, at which boxers formerly joined battle.
2. By the old rules, each "round" was ended by a knockdown. In this match there was a half-minute interval between rounds, and the fight ended when one of the boxers failed to take his feet in time for the next round.

was divided; for, in the next, the Gas-man aiming a mortal blow at his adversary's neck with his right hand, and failing from the length he had to reach, the other returned it with his left at full swing, planted a tremendous blow on his cheek-bone and eyebrow, and made a red ruin of that side of his face. The Gas-man went down, and there was another shout—a roar of triumph as the waves of fortune rolled tumultuously from side to side. This was a settler. Hickman got up, and "grinned horrible a ghastly smile,"[3] yet he was evidently dashed in his opinion of himself; it was the first time he had ever been so punished; all one side of his face was perfect scarlet, and his right eye was closed in dingy blackness, as he advanced to the fight, less confident, but still determined. After one or two rounds, not receiving another such remembrancer, he rallied and went at it with his former impetuosity. But in vain. His strength had been weakened—his blows could not tell at such a distance—he was obliged to fling himself at his adversary, and could not strike from his feet; and almost as regularly as he flew at him with his right hand, Neate warded the blow, or drew back out of its reach, and felled him with the return of his left. There was little cautious sparring—no half-hits—no tapping and trifling, none of the *petit-maîtreship*[4] of the art—they were almost all knock-down blows: the fight was a good stand-up fight. The wonder was the half-minute time. If there had been a minute or more allowed between each round, it would have been intelligible how they should by degrees recover strength and resolution; but to see two men smashed to the ground, smeared with gore, stunned, senseless, the breath beaten out of their bodies; and then, before you recover from the shock, to see them rise up with new strength and courage, stand ready to inflict or receive mortal offense, and rush upon each other "like two clouds over the Caspian"[5]—this is the most astonishing thing of all: this is the high and heroic state of man! From this time forward the event became more certain every round, and about the twelfth it seemed as if it must have been over. Hickman generally stood with his back to me; but in the scuffle, he had changed positions, and Neate just then made a tremendous lunge at him, and hit him full in the face. It was doubtful whether he would fall backwards or forwards; he hung suspended for a second or two, and then fell back, throwing his hands in the air, and with his face lifted up to the sky. I never saw anything more terrific than his aspect just before he fell. All traces of life, of natural expression, were gone from him. His face was like a human skull, a death's-head, spouting blood. The eyes were filled with blood, the nose streamed with blood, the mouth gaped blood. He was not like an actual man, but like a preternatural, spectral appearance, or like

3. A description of Death in *Paradise Lost* II.846.
4. *Petit-maître* ("little master"), the

French term for a dandy or fop.
5. See *Paradise Lost* II.714–16.

one of the figures in Dante's *Inferno*. Yet he fought on after this for several rounds, still striking the first desperate blow, and Neate standing on the defensive, and using the same cautious guard to the last, as if he had still all his work to do; and it was not till the Gas-man was so stunned in the seventeenth or eighteenth round that his senses forsook him, and he could not come to time, that the battle was declared over. Ye who despise the Fancy, do something to show as much *pluck*, or as much self-possession as this, before you assume a superiority which you have never given a single proof of by any one action in the whole course of your lives! When the Gas-man came to himself, the first words he uttered were, "Where am I? What is the matter?" "Nothing is the matter, Tom —you have lost the battle, but you are the bravest man alive." And Jackson whispered to him, "I am collecting a purse for you, Tom." —Vain sounds, and unheard at that moment! Neate instantly went up and shook him cordially by the hand, and seeing some old acquaintance, began to flourish with his fists, calling out, "Ah, you always said I couldn't fight. What do you think now?" But all in good humor, and without any appearance of arrogance; only it was evident Bill Neate was pleased that he had won the fight. When it was over, I asked Cribb if he did not think it was a good one? He said, "*Pretty well!*" The carrier pigeons now mounted into the air, and one of them flew with the news of her husband's victory to the bosom of Mrs. Neate. Alas, for Mrs. Hickman!

Mais au revoir, as Sir Fopling Flutter[6] says. I went down with Toms; I returned with Jack Pigott, whom I met on the ground. Toms is a rattle brain; Pigott is a sentimentalist. Now, under favor, I am a sentimentalist too—therefore I say nothing, but that the interest of the excursion did not flag as I came back. Pigott and I marched along the causeway leading from Hungerford to Newbury, now observing the effect of a brilliant sun on the tawny meads or moss-colored cottages, now exulting in the fight, now digressing to some topic of general and elegant literature. My friend was dressed in character for the occasion, or like one of the FANCY; that is, with a double portion of greatcoats, clogs,[7] and overhauls: and just as we had agreed with a couple of country lads to carry his superfluous wearing apparel to the next town, we were overtaken by a return post-chaise, into which I got, Pigott preferring a seat on the bar. There were two strangers already in the chaise, and on their observing they supposed I had been to the fight, I said I had, and concluded they had done the same. They appeared, however, a little shy and sore on the subject, and it was not till after several hints dropped, and questions put, that it turned out that they had missed it. One of these friends had undertaken to drive the other there in

6. In *The Man of Mode*, by the Restoration dramatist Sir George Etherege.

7. Stout, thick-soled shoes; "overhauls" are overalls.

his gig: they had set out, to make sure work, the day before at three in the afternoon. The owner of the one-horse vehicle scorned to ask his way, and drove right on to Bagshot, instead of turning off at Hounslow: there they stopped all night, and set off the next day across the country to Reading, from whence they took coach, and got down within a mile or two of Hungerford, just half an hour after the fight was over. This might be safely set down as one of the miseries of human life. We parted with these two gentlemen who had been to see the fight, but had returned as they went, at Wolhampton, where we were promised beds (an irresistible temptation, for Pigott had passed the preceding night at Hungerford as we had done at Newbury), and we turned into an old bow-windowed parlor with a carpet and a snug fire; and after devouring a quantity of tea, toast, and eggs, sat down to consider, during an hour of philosophic leisure, what we should have for supper. In the midst of an Epicurean deliberation between a roasted fowl and mutton chops with mashed potatoes, we were interrupted by an inroad of Goths and Vandals[8]—*O procul este profani*—not real flashmen,[9] but interlopers, noisy pretenders, butchers from Tothill Fields, brokers from Whitechapel, who called immediately for pipes and tobacco, hoping it would not be disagreeable to the gentlemen, and began to insist that it was *a cross*.[1] Pigott withdrew from the smoke and noise into another room, and left me to dispute the point with them for a couple of hours *sans intermission* by the dial.[2] The next morning we rose refreshed; and on observing that Jack had a pocket volume in his hand, in which he read in the intervals of our discourse, I inquired what it was, and learned to my particular satisfaction that it was a volume of the *New Eloise*.[3] Ladies, after this, will you contend that a love for the FANCY is incompatible with the cultivation of sentiment? We jogged on as before, my friend setting me up in a genteel drab greatcoat and green silk handkerchief (which I must say became me exceedingly), and after stretching our legs for a few miles, and seeing Jack Randall, Ned Turner, and Scroggins, pass on the top of one of the Bath coaches, we engaged with the driver of the second to take us to London for the usual fee. I got inside, and found three other passengers. One of them was an old gentleman with an aquiline nose, powdered hair, and a pigtail, and who looked as if he had played many a rubber at the Bath rooms.[4] I said to myself, he is very like Mr. Windham; I wish he would enter into conversation, that I might hear what fine observations would come from those finely-turned features. However, nothing passed, till, stopping to dine at Reading, some

8. I.e., barbarian invaders. The Latin tag which follows means, "Away, unhallowed ones!" (*Aeneid* VI.258).
9. Patrons of boxing.
1. I.e., that the fight was fixed.
2. "Without intermission, according to the clock." See *As You Like It* II.vii. 32–33.
3. *La Nouvelle Héloise*, novel by Rousseau.
4. In the card rooms at Bath, a resort town.

inquiry was made by the company about the fight, and I gave (as the reader may believe) an eloquent and animated description of it. When we got into the coach again, the old gentleman, after a graceful exordium,[5] said, he had, when a boy, been to a fight between the famous Broughton and George Stevenson, who was called the *Fighting Coachman,* in the year 1770, with the late Mr. Windham. This beginning flattered the spirit of prophecy within me and riveted my attention. He went on—"George Stevenson was coachman to a friend of my father's. He was an old man when I saw him some years afterwards. He took hold of his own arm and said, 'there was muscle here once, but now it is no more than this young gentleman's.' He added, 'Well, no matter; I have been here long, I am willing to go hence, and I hope I have done no more harm than another man.' Once," said my unknown companion, "I asked him if he had ever beat Broughton? He said yes; that he had fought with him three times, and the last time he fairly beat him, though the world did not allow it. 'I'll tell you how it was, master. When the seconds lifted us up in the last round, we were so exhausted that neither of us could stand, and we fell upon one another, and as Master Broughton fell uppermost, the mob gave it in his favor, and he was said to have won the battle. But,' says he, 'the fact was, that as his second (John Cuthbert) lifted him up, he said to him, "I'll fight no more, I've had enough"; which,' says Stevenson, 'you know gave me the victory. And to prove to you that this was the case, when John Cuthbert was on his deathbed, and they asked him if there was anything on his mind which he wished to confess, he answered, "Yes, that there was one thing he wished to set right, for that certainly Master Stevenson won that last fight with Master Broughton; for he whispered him as he lifted him up in the last round of all, that he had had enough." ' " "This," said the Bath gentleman, "was a bit of human nature"; and I have written this account of the fight on purpose that it might not be lost to the world. He also stated as a proof of the candor of mind in this class of men, that Stevenson acknowledged that Broughton could have beat him in his best day; but that he (Broughton) was getting old in their last rencounter. When we stopped in Piccadilly, I wanted to ask the gentleman some questions about the late Mr. Windham, but had not courage. I got out, resigned my coat and green silk handkerchief to Pigott (loath to part with these ornaments of life), and walked home in high spirits.

P.S. Toms called upon me the next day, to ask me if I did not think the fight was a complete thing? I said I thought it was. I hope he will relish my account of it.

1822

5. The formal opening of an oration.

THOMAS DE QUINCEY
(1785–1859)

1821:   Begins literary career with *Confessions of an Eng-
               lish Opium Eater*.
1853–60: "Collective Edition" of his writings.

De Quincey's father was a wealthy merchant, who died when Thomas
was 7 years old. The boy was a precocious scholar, especially in Latin and
Greek, and a gentle and bookish introvert; he found it difficult to adapt
himself to discipline and routine, and was thrown into panic by any
emergency that called for decisive action. He ran away from Manchester
Grammar School and after a summer spent tramping through Wales,
broke off completely from his family and guardians and went to London
in the hope that he could obtain from moneylenders an advance on his
prospective inheritance. There at the age of 17 he spent a terrible winter
of loneliness and destitution, befriended only by some kindly streetwalkers.
These early experiences with the sinister part of city life later became persistent elements in his dreams of terror.

After a reconciliation with his guardians he entered Worcester College,
Oxford, on an inadequate allowance. He spent the years 1803–8 in sporadic
attendance, isolated as usual, and devoting himself especially to two subjects not then part of the university curriculum: English literature and
the German language. He left abruptly in the middle of his examination
for the B.A. with honors because he could not face the ordeal of the oral
part of the examination.

De Quincey had been an early and fervent admirer of Wordsworth and
Coleridge. No sooner did he come of age and into his inheritance than,
with his usual combination of generosity and improvidence, he made
Coleridge an anonymous gift of £300. He visited with the Wordsworths
at Grasmere, became an intimate friend, and when they left Dove Cottage
for Allan Bank, took up his own residence at Dove Cottage in order to be
near them. Here he built up a fine library and for a time lived the life
of a rural scholar, trying to decide how to eke out his dwindling resources.
In the meantime he fell in love with Margaret Simpson, the daughter
of a small local landholder and farmer and, after she had borne him an
illegitimate son, married her in February, 1817. This affair led to an
estrangement from the Wordsworths and increased the drain on his resources. Worse still, De Quincey at this time became completely enslaved
to opium. He had been taking the drug regularly since 1804, when, in
accordance with the medical practice of the time, he had turned to it for
relief from rheumatic pains in his face. A variety of physical ailments had
led to increasingly large and frequent doses; now, driven by pain, poverty,
and despair, he indulged in huge quantities of laudanum (opium dissolved
in alcohol). From this time on, although he struggled intermittently to

break the habit and often succeeded in reducing the dosage, he was never able to free himself from "the pleasures and pains of opium." It was during his periods of maximum addiction, and especially in the recurrent agonies of cutting down his opium allowance, that he had the grotesque and terrifying dreams which he wove into the pattern of his literary fantasies.

In desperation De Quincey at last, at the age of 36, turned to writing for a livelihood. The *Confessions of an English Opium Eater,* which he contributed in two installments to the *London Magazine,* scored an immediate success and was at once reprinted as a book, but it earned De Quincey very little money. After frequent visits to London, and a number of varied contributions to the *London Magazine,* he moved his family to Edinburgh in 1828, in order to write for *Blackwood's Magazine.* For almost all the rest of his life De Quincey led a frantic existence, beset by rheumatism, toothache, stomach trouble, erysipelas, and finally gout, struggling with his native irresolution and melancholia and the horrors of the opium habit, dodging his creditors and the constant threat of imprisonment for debt. All the while he ground out articles on any salable subject in a ceaseless struggle to keep his eight children from starving to death. Only after his mother died and left him a small income was he able, in his 60's, to live in comparative ease and freedom under the care of his loyal and practical-minded daughters. The last decade of his life De Quincey spent mainly in gathering, revising, and expanding his essays for his "Collective Edition"; the final volume appeared in 1860, the year after his death.

Although De Quincey's life, in its externals, was disorderly, and his best-known writings were sensational in their matter, he was not a Bohemian dabbler in drugs and abnormality, but staunchly conventional and conservative—a rigid moralist, a sturdy Tory, and a faithful champion of the Church of England. Everybody who knew this shy and elusive little man has testified to his gentleness, his courteous and musical speech, and his elaborate and exquisite manners. Less obvious, under the surface timidity and irresolution, were the toughness and courage which sustained him through a long life of seemingly hopeless struggle.

Although more than 150 of De Quincey's anonymous essays have been identified, the great bulk of them were pieces of hasty journalism which are now read only by scholars. These range over history, political economy, and philosophy; while in his commentaries on recent and contemporary German writers and thinkers, together with his translations from the German, De Quincey served for a time as an important avenue of access for Englishmen to the great new literature of the late 18th-century German renaissance. As a literary critic De Quincey was capable of a fine essay in critical impressionism, *On the Knocking at the Gate in Macbeth,* but he was too whimsical and unsystematic to rank with his greater contemporaries, Coleridge and Hazlitt; his best theoretical contributions are essays on "Style" and "Rhetoric." He wrote a number of vivid and candid biographical sketches of writers he knew personally, especially Wordsworth, Coleridge, Southey, and Lamb. His most distinctive and impressive achievements, however, are the writings which start with fact and move into macabre fantasy (*On Murder Considered as One of the Fine Arts*), and especially those that begin as quiet autobiography and develop into an elaborate and lurid construction made up from the materials of his dreams (*Confessions of an English Opium Eater, Autobiographic Sketches, Suspiria de Profundis,* and *The English Mail Coach*). In these last pieces De Quincey revived the ornate prose style of the 17th-century writers, Sir Thomas Browne, Jeremy Taylor, and John Milton. To the modern reader De Quincey's slowly evolving sentences and paragraphs often seem too contrived, in their elaborate patterning of phrases, clauses, and sound sequences, to sustain his earlier reputation as one of the supreme prose stylists. What interests us more today in these fantasies is their subject matter and the novel principles which govern their over-all structure. He opened up to English literature the night-side of human consciousness, with all its grotesque strangeness, its *Angst* (anxiety), and its pervasive sense of guilt and alienation. "In dreams," De Quincey wrote, long before Sigmund Freud, "perhaps under some secret conflict of the midnight sleeper, lighted up to the consciousness at the time, but darkened to the memory as soon as all is finished, each several child of our mysterious race completes for himself the treason of the aboriginal fall." And for these dream writings De Quincey developed a mode of organization which is not based on chronological narrative, or exposition, or argument, but on the statement, variation, development, and counterpoint of thematic imagery, in a pattern derived from the art of music, in which he had a deep and abiding interest. For although by temperament a conservative, De Quincey was in his writings a radical innovator, whose experiments look ahead to the materials and methods of such modern masters in prose and verse as James Joyce, Franz Kafka, and T. S. Eliot.

On the Knocking at the Gate in Macbeth[1]

From my boyish days I had always felt a great perplexity on one point in *Macbeth*. It was this: The knocking at the gate which succeeds to the murder of Duncan produced to my feelings an effect for which I never could account. The effect was that it reflected back upon the murderer a peculiar awfulness and a depth of solemnity; yet, however obstinately I endeavored with my understanding to comprehend this, for many years I never could see *why* it should produce such an effect.

Here I pause for one moment, to exhort the reader never to pay

1. This essay, one of the best-known critiques of Shakespeare, deals with the scene in *Macbeth* (II.ii–iii) in which, just after they have murdered Duncan, Macbeth and his wife are startled by a loud knocking at the gate. De Quincey exhibits the procedure in Romantic criticism of making, as he says, the "understanding" wait upon the "feelings." Instead of judging the success or failure of a passage by its conformity to prior critical theory, De Quincey brings in theory only to explain his impression or immediate emotional response to the passage. The final paragraph demonstrates a weakness of this Romantic position when it is driven to an extreme, for it converts the reasonable view that Shakespeare must be presumed right until shown to be wrong into the untenable view that Shakespeare is an artistic deity who can do no wrong.

any attention to his understanding when it stands in opposition to any other faculty of his mind. The mere understanding, however useful and indispensable, is the meanest faculty in the human mind, and the most to be distrusted; and yet the great majority of people trust to nothing else—which may do for ordinary life, but not for philosophical purposes. Of this out of ten thousand instances that I might produce I will cite one. Ask of any person whatsoever who is not previously prepared for the demand by a knowledge of the perspective to draw in the rudest way the commonest appearance which depends upon the laws of that science—as, for instance, to represent the effect of two walls standing at right angles to each other, or the appearance of the houses on each side of a street as seen by a person looking down the street from one extremity. Now, in all cases, unless the person has happened to observe in pictures how it is that artists produce these effects, he will be utterly unable to make the smallest approximation to it. Yet why? For he has actually seen the effect every day of his life. The reason is that he allows his understanding to overrule his eyes. His understanding, which includes no intuitive knowledge of the laws of vision, can furnish him with no reason why a line which is known and can be proved to be a horizontal line should not *appear* a horizontal line: a line that made any angle with the perpendicular less than a right angle would seem to him to indicate that his houses were all tumbling down together. Accordingly, he makes the line of his houses a horizontal line, and fails, of course, to produce the effect demanded. Here, then, is one instance out of many in which not only the understanding is allowed to overrule the eyes, but where the understanding is positively allowed to obliterate the eyes, as it were; for not only does the man believe the evidence of his understanding in opposition to that of his eyes, but (what is monstrous) the idiot is not aware that his eyes ever gave such evidence. He does not know that he has seen (and therefore *quoad* his consciousness[2] has *not* seen) that which he *has* seen every day of his life.

But to return from this digression. My understanding could furnish no reason why the knocking at the gate in *Macbeth* should produce any effect, direct or reflected. In fact, my understanding said positively that it could *not* produce any effect. But I knew better; I felt that it did; and I waited and clung to the problem until further knowledge should enable me to solve it. At length, in 1812, Mr. Williams made his debut on the stage of Ratcliffe Highway, and executed those unparalleled murders which have procured for him such a brilliant and undying reputation.[3] On which murders,

2. I.e., so far as his consciousness is concerned.
3. John Williams, a sailor, had thrown London into a panic (the date was actually December, 1811) by murdering the Marr family and, twelve days later, the Williamson family. De Quincey described these murders at length in the Postscript to his two essays *On Murder Considered as One of the Fine Arts*.

by the way, I must observe that in one respect they have had an
ill effect, by making the connoisseur in murder very fastidious in
his taste, and dissatisfied by anything that has been since done in
that line. All other murders look pale by the deep crimson of his;
and, as an amateur[4] once said to me in a querulous tone, "There has
been absolutely nothing *doing* since his time, or nothing that's
worth speaking of." But this is wrong; for it is unreasonable to expect all men to be great artists, and born with the genius of Mr.
Williams. Now, it will be remembered that in the first of these
murders (that of the Marrs) the same incident (of a knocking at
the door[5] soon after the work of extermination was complete) did
actually occur which the genius of Shakespeare has invented; and
all good judges, and the most eminent dilettanti,[6] acknowledged the
felicity of Shakespeare's suggestion as soon as it was actually realized. Here, then, was a fresh proof that I was right in relying on
my own feeling, in opposition to my understanding; and I again set
myself to study the problem. At length I solved it to my own
satisfaction; and my solution is this: Murder, in ordinary cases,
where the sympathy is wholly directed to the case of the murdered
person, is an incident of coarse and vulgar horror; and for this
reason—that it flings the interest exclusively upon the natural but
ignoble instinct by which we cleave to life: an instinct which, as
being indispensable to the primal law of self-preservation, is the
same in kind (though different in degree) amongst all living creatures. This instinct, therefore, because it annihilates all distinctions,
and degrades the greatest of men to the level of "the poor beetle
that we tread on,"[7] exhibits human nature in its most abject and
humiliating attitude. Such an attitude would little suit the purposes
of the poet. What then must he do? He must throw the interest on
the murderer. Our sympathy must be with *him* (of course I mean
a sympathy of comprehension, a sympathy by which we enter into
his feelings, and are made to understand them—not a sympathy of
pity or approbation).[8] In the murdered person, all strife of thought,
all flux and reflux of passion and of purpose, are crushed by one
overwhelming panic; the fear of instant death smites him "with its
petrific[9] mace." But in the murderer, such a murderer as a poet
will condescend to, there must be raging some great storm of passion—jealousy, ambition, vengeance, hatred—which will create a
hell within him; and into this hell we are to look.

4. Here, a fancier or follower of an art
or sport.
5. By a maidservant of the Marrs, returning from the purchase of oysters
for supper.
6. Lovers of the fine arts.
7. Shakespeare's *Measure for Measure*
III.i.79.
8. In a note De Quincey decries "the
unscholarlike use of the word sympathy,

at present so general, by which, instead
of taking it in its proper sense, as the
act of reproducing in our minds the
feelings of another, whether for hatred,
indignation, love, pity, or approbation,
it is made a mere synonym of the word
pity * * * "
9. Petrifying, turning to stone (from
Paradise Lost X.294).

In *Macbeth*, for the sake of gratifying his own enormous and teeming faculty of creation, Shakespeare has introduced two murderers: and, as usual in his hands, they are remarkably discriminated; but—though in Macbeth the strife of mind is greater than in his wife, the tiger spirit not so awake, and his feelings caught chiefly by contagion from her—yet, as both were finally involved in the guilt of murder, the murderous mind of necessity is finally to be presumed in both. This was to be expressed; and, on its own account, as well as to make it a more proportionable antagonist to the unoffending nature of their victim, "the gracious Duncan," and adequately to expound "the deep damnation of his taking off,"[1] this was to be expressed with peculiar energy. We were to be made to feel that the human nature—i.e., the divine nature of love and mercy, spread through the hearts of all creatures, and seldom utterly withdrawn from man—was gone, vanished, extinct, and that the fiendish nature had taken its place. And, as this effect is marvelously accomplished in the *dialogues* and *soliloquies* themselves, so it is finally consummated by the expedient under consideration; and it is to this that I now solicit the reader's attention. If the reader has ever witnessed a wife, daughter, or sister in a fainting fit, he may chance to have observed that the most affecting moment in such a spectacle is *that* in which a sigh and a stirring announce the recommencement of suspended life. Or, if the reader has ever been present in a vast metropolis on the day when some great national idol was carried in funeral pomp to his grave, and, chancing to walk near the course through which it passed, has felt powerfully, in the silence and desertion of the streets, and in the stagnation of ordinary business, the deep interest which at that moment was possessing the heart of man—if all at once he should hear the death-like stillness broken up by the sound of wheels rattling away from the scene, and making known that the transitory vision was dissolved, he will be aware that at no moment was his sense of the complete suspension and pause in ordinary human concerns so full and affecting as at that moment when the suspension ceases, and the goings-on of human life are suddenly resumed. All action in any direction is best expounded, measured, and made apprehensible, by reaction. Now, apply this to the case in *Macbeth*. Here, as I have said, the retiring of the human heart and the entrance of the fiendish heart was to be expressed and made sensible. Another world has stepped in; and the murderers are taken out of the region of human things, human purposes, human desires. They are transfigured: Lady Macbeth is "unsexed";[2] Macbeth has forgot that he was born of woman; both are conformed to the image of devils; and the world of devils is suddenly revealed. But how shall this be

---

1. *Macbeth* III.i.66 and I.vii.20.
2. Steeling herself to the murder, Lady

Macbeth calls on the spirits of hell to "unsex me here" (I.v.42).

conveyed and made palpable? In order that a new world may step in, this world must for a time disappear. The murderers and the murder must be insulated—cut off by an immeasurable gulf from the ordinary tide and succession of human affairs—locked up and sequestered in some deep recess; we must be made sensible that the world of ordinary life is suddenly arrested, laid asleep, tranced, racked into a dread armistice; time must be annihilated, relation to things without abolished; and all must pass self-withdrawn into a deep syncope[3] and suspension of earthly passion. Hence it is that, when the deed is done, when the work of darkness is perfect, then the world of darkness passes away like a pageantry in the clouds: the knocking at the gate is heard, and it makes known audibly that the reaction has commenced; the human has made its reflux upon the fiendish; the pulses of life are beginning to beat again; and the re-establishment of the goings-on of the world in which we live first makes us profoundly sensible of the awful parenthesis that had suspended them.

O mighty poet! Thy works are not as those of other men, simply and merely great works of art, but are also like the phenomena of nature, like the sun and the sea, the stars and the flowers, like frost and snow, rain and dew, hailstorm and thunder, which are to be studied with entire submission of our own faculties, and in the perfect faith that in them there can be no too much or too little, nothing useless or inert, but that, the farther we press in our discoveries, the more we shall see proofs of design and self-supporting arrangement where the careless eye had seen nothing but accident!

1823

From The English Mail Coach[1]
From *II. The Vision of Sudden Death*[2]

* * * On this occasion the usual silence and solitude prevailed along the road. Not a hoof nor a wheel was to be heard. And, to

---

3. Fainting spell.
1. The three essays joined under this title were first published anonymously in *Blackwood's Magazine* for 1849. *The Glory of Motion* gave an account of the fast English coaches which

strengthen this false luxurious confidence in the noiseless roads, it happened also that the night was one of peculiar solemnity and peace. For my own part, though slightly alive to the possibilities of peril, I had so far yielded to the influence of the mighty calm as to sink into a profound reverie. The month was August; in the middle of which lay my own birthday—a festival to every thoughtful man suggesting solemn and often sigh-born thoughts. The county was my own native county—upon which, in its southern section, more than upon any equal area known to man past or present, had descended the original curse of labor in its heaviest form, not mastering the bodies only of men, as of slaves, or criminals in mines, but working through the fiery will. Upon no equal space of earth was, or ever had been, the same energy of human power put forth daily. At this particular season also of the assizes,[3] that dreadful hurricane of flight and pursuit, as it might have seemed to a stranger, which swept to and from Lancaster all day long, hunting the county up and down, and regularly subsiding back into silence about sunset, could not fail (when united with this permanent distinction of Lancashire as the very metropolis and citadel of labor) to point the thoughts pathetically upon that counter-vision of rest, of saintly repose from strife and sorrow, towards which, as to their secret haven, the profounder aspirations of man's heart are in solitude continually traveling. Obliquely upon our left we were nearing the sea; which also must, under the present circumstances, be repeating the general state of halcyon repose. The sea, the atmosphere, the light, bore each an orchestral part in this universal lull. Moonlight and the first timid tremblings of the dawn were by this time blending; and the blendings were brought into a still more exquisite

carried both passengers and mail; it emphasized their function in disseminating military news, especially that of the great victory over Napoleon at Waterloo. *The Vision of Sudden Death,* partly reproduced here, describes De Quincey's experience of a near accident. *Dream-Fugue,* reprinted in its entirety, treats this incident as it entered into De Quincey's dreams of terror.

A fugue is a musical composition in which a theme, or "subject," is introduced successively by various voices and then developed in contrapuntal fashion. When he reprinted these essays in his "Collective Edition" (1854), De Quincey undertook to explain the "logic" of his composition for the perplexed critics of his day. He pointed out that the whole of the *Dream-Fugue* "radiates as a natural expansion" of *The Vision of Sudden Death:* "So far as I know, every element in the shifting movements of the Dream derived itself either primarily from the incidents of the actual scene, or from secondary features associated with the mail."

The structure of this essay, though its materials are no doubt derived, as De Quincey says, from his dreams, does not simply reproduce these dreams. Instead, the essay states a thematic subject and then enriches, varies, and develops it until it reaches a grand climax which incorporates the Christian pattern of death, grace, and resurrection. De Quincey was attempting in prose what T. S. Eliot, in *Four Quartets,* was to attempt a century later in verse —the adaptation of a musical form to a literary medium of expression.

2. In the first part of this essay, De Quincey has described his situation as a lone passenger on the top of the mail coach from Manchester to Glasgow on a summer night two or three years after the Battle of Waterloo. To relieve his fatigue he takes a dose of opium and sinks "into a profound reverie"; the one-eyed coachman drowses off; the great coach rushes on unguided through the extraordinarily peaceful night.

3. The sessions of the superior courts in each of the English counties.

state of unity by a slight silvery mist, motionless and dreamy, that covered the woods and fields, but with a veil of equable transparency. Except the feet of our own horses—which, running on a sandy margin of the road, made but little disturbance—there was no sound abroad. In the clouds and on the earth prevailed the same majestic peace; and, in spite of all that the villain of a schoolmaster has done for the ruin of our sublimer thoughts, which are the thoughts of our infancy, we still believe in no such nonsense as a limited atmosphere. Whatever we may swear with our false feigning lips, in our faithful hearts we still believe, and must forever believe, in fields of air traversing the total gulf between earth and the central heavens. Still, in the confidence of children that tread without fear *every* chamber in their father's house, and to whom no door is closed, we, in that Sabbatic vision which sometimes is revealed for an hour upon nights like this, ascend with easy steps from the sorrow-stricken fields of earth upwards to the sandals of God.

Suddenly, from thoughts like these I was awakened to a sullen sound, as of some motion on the distant road. It stole upon the air for a moment; I listened in awe; but then it died away. Once roused, however, I could not but observe with alarm the quickened motion of our horses. Ten years' experience had made my eye learned in the valuing of motion; and I saw that we were now running thirteen miles an hour. I pretend to no presence of mind. On the contrary, my fear is that I am miserably and shamefully deficient in that quality as regards action. The palsy of doubt and distraction hangs like some guilty weight of dark unfathomed remembrances upon my energies when the signal is flying for *action*. But, on the other hand, this accursed gift I have, as regards *thought*, that in the first step towards the possibility of a misfortune I see its total evolution; in the radix[4] of the series I see too certainly and too instantly its entire expansion; in the first syllable of the dreadful sentence I read already the last. It was not that I feared for ourselves. *Us* our bulk and impetus charmed against peril in any collision. And I had ridden through too many hundreds of perils that were frightful to approach, that were matter of laughter to look back upon, the first face of which was horror, the parting face a jest—for any anxiety to rest upon *our* interests. The mail was not built, I felt assured, nor bespoke, that could betray *me* who trusted to its protection. But any carriage that we could meet would be frail and light in comparison of ourselves. And I remarked this ominous accident of our situation—we were on the wrong side of the road. But then, it may be said, the other party, if other there was, might also be on the wrong side; and two wrongs might make a right. *That* was not likely. The same motive which had

4. Root; here used in its mathematical sense, as the basic number of a numerical system.

drawn *us* to the right-hand side of the road—viz., the luxury of the soft beaten sand as contrasted with the paved center—would prove attractive to others. The two adverse carriages would therefore, to a certainty, be traveling on the same side; and from this side, as not being ours in law, the crossing over to the other would, of course, be looked for from *us*. Our lamps, still lighted, would give the impression of vigilance on our part. And every creature that met us would rely upon *us* for quartering.[5] All this, and if the separate links of the anticipation had been a thousand times more, I saw, not discursively, or by effort, or by succession, but by one flash of horrid simultaneous intuition.

Under this steady though rapid anticipation of the evil which *might* be gathering ahead, ah! what a sullen mystery of fear, what a sigh of woe, was that which stole upon the air, as again the far-off sound of a wheel was heard! A whisper it was—a whisper from, perhaps, four miles off—secretly announcing a ruin that, being foreseen, was not the less inevitable; that, being known, was not therefore healed. What could be done—who was it that could do it—to check the storm-flight of these maniacal horses? Could I not seize the reins from the grasp of the slumbering coachman? You, reader, think that it would have been in *your* power to do so. And I quarrel not with your estimate of yourself. But, from the way in which the coachman's hand was vised between his upper and lower thigh, this was impossible. Easy was it? See, then, that bronze equestrian statue. The cruel rider has kept the bit in his horse's mouth for two centuries. Unbridle him for a minute, if you please, and wash his mouth with water. Easy was it? Unhorse me, then, that imperial rider; knock me those marble feet from those marble stirrups of Charlemagne.

The sounds ahead strengthened, and were now too clearly the sounds of wheels. Who and what could it be? Was it industry in a taxed cart? Was it youthful gaiety in a gig?[6] Was it sorrow that loitered, or joy that raced? For as yet the snatches of sound were too intermitting, from distance, to decipher the character of the motion. Whoever were the travelers, something must be done to warn them. Upon the other party rests the active responsibility, but upon *us*—and, woe is me! that *us* was reduced to my frail opium-shattered self—rests the responsibility of warning. Yet, how should this be accomplished? Might I not sound the guard's horn? Already, on the first thought, I was making my way over the roof to the guard's seat. But this, from the accident which I have mentioned, of the foreign mails being piled upon the roof, was a difficult and even dangerous attempt to one cramped by nearly three hundred miles of outside traveling. And, fortunately, before I had lost much

5. I.e., pulling aside in order to yield the right of way.

6. A small two-wheeled carriage, drawn by one horse.

time in the attempt, our frantic horses swept round an angle of the road which opened upon us that final stage where the collision must be accomplished and the catastrophe sealed. All was apparently finished. The court was sitting; the case was heard; the judge had finished; and only the verdict was yet in arrear.

Before us lay an avenue straight as an arrow, six hundred yards, perhaps, in length; and the umbrageous trees, which rose in a regular line from either side, meeting high overhead, gave to it the character of a cathedral aisle. These trees lent a deeper solemnity to the early light; but there was still light enough to perceive, at the farther end of this Gothic aisle, a frail reedy gig, in which were seated a young man, and by his side a young lady. Ah, young sir! what are you about? If it is requisite that you should whisper your communications to this young lady—though really I see nobody, at an hour and on a road so solitary, likely to overhear you—is it therefore requisite that you should carry your lips forward to hers? The little carriage is creeping on at one mile an hour; and the parties within it, being thus tenderly engaged, are naturally bending down their heads. Between them and eternity, to all human calculation, there is but a minute and a half. Oh heavens! what is it that I shall do? Speaking or acting, what help can I offer? Strange it is, and to a mere auditor of the tale might seem laughable, that I should need a suggestion from the *Iliad* to prompt the sole resource that remained. Yet so it was. Suddenly I remembered the shout of Achilles, and its effect.[7] But could I pretend to shout like the son of Peleus, aided by Pallas? No: but then I needed not the shout that should alarm all Asia militant; such a shout would suffice as might carry terror into the hearts of two thoughtless young people and one gig-horse. I shouted—and the young man heard me not. A second time I shouted—and now he heard me, for now he raised his head.

Here, then, all had been done that, by me, *could* be done; more on *my* part was not possible. Mine had been the first step; the second was for the young man; the third was for God. If, said I, this stranger is a brave man, and if indeed he loves the young girl at his side—or, loving her not, if he feels the obligation, pressing upon every man worthy to be called a man, of doing his utmost for a woman confided to his protection—he will at least make some effort to save her. If *that* fails, he will not perish the more, or by a death more cruel, for having made it; and he will die as a brave man should, with his face to the danger, and with his arm about the woman that he sought in vain to save. But, if he makes no effort, shrinking without a struggle from his duty, he himself will not the less certainly perish for this baseness of poltroonery. He will

7. In *Iliad* XVIII the unarmed Achilles, aided by the voice of Pallas Athena, shouts so loudly that he frightens the Trojans away from the corpse of his friend Patroclus.

die no less: and why not? Wherefore should we grieve that there is one craven less in the world? No; *let* him perish, without a pitying thought of ours wasted upon him; and, in that case, all our grief will be reserved for the fate of the helpless girl who now, upon the least shadow of failure in *him*, must by the fiercest of translations—must without time for a prayer—must within seventy seconds—stand before the judgment seat of God.

But craven he was not: sudden had been the call upon him, and sudden was his answer to the call. He saw, he heard, he comprehended, the ruin that was coming down: already its gloomy shadow darkened above him; and already he was measuring his strength to deal with it. Ah! what a vulgar thing does courage seem when we see nations buying it and selling it for a shilling a day: [8] ah! what a sublime thing does courage seem when some fearful summons on the great deeps of life carries a man, as if running before a hurricane, up to the giddy crest of some tumultuous crisis from which lie two courses, and a voice says to him audibly, "One way lies hope; take the other, and mourn forever!" How grand a triumph if, even then, amidst the raving of all around him, and the frenzy of the danger, the man is able to confront his situation—is able to retire for a moment into solitude with God, and to seek his counsel from *Him!*

For seven seconds, it might be, of his seventy, the stranger settled his countenance steadfastly upon us, as if to search and value every element in the conflict before him. For five seconds more of his seventy he sat immovably, like one that mused on some great purpose. For five more, perhaps, he sat with eyes upraised, like one that prayed in sorrow, under some extremity of doubt, for light that should guide him to the better choice. Then suddenly he rose; stood upright; and, by a powerful strain upon the reins, raising his horse's forefeet from the ground, he slewed him round on the pivot of his hind legs, so as to plant the little equipage in a position nearly at right angles to ours. Thus far his condition was not improved; except as a first step had been taken towards the possibility of a second. If no more were done, nothing was done; for the little carriage still occupied the very center of our path, though in an altered direction. Yet even now it may not be too late: fifteen of the seventy seconds may still be unexhausted; and one almighty bound may avail to clear the ground. Hurry, then, hurry! for the flying moments—*they* hurry. Oh, hurry, hurry, my brave young man! for the cruel hoofs of our horses—*they* also hurry! Fast are the flying moments, faster are the hoofs of our horses. But fear not for *him*, if human energy can suffice; faithful was he that drove to his terrific duty; faithful was the horse to *his* command. One blow, one impulse given with voice and hand, by the stranger, one rush from the horse, one bound as if in the act of rising to a fence,

8. The daily pay of the English soldier.

landed the docile creature's forefeet upon the crown or arching center of the road. The larger half of the little equipage had then cleared our over-towering shadow: *that* was evident even to my own agitated sight. But it mattered little that one wreck should float off in safety if upon the wreck that perished were embarked the human freightage. The rear part of the carriage—was *that* certainly beyond the line of absolute ruin? What power could answer the question? Glance of eye, thought of man, wing of angel, which of these had speed enough to sweep between the question and the answer, and divide the one from the other? Light does not tread upon the steps of light more indivisibly than did our all-conquering arrival upon the escaping efforts of the gig. *That* must the young man have felt too plainly. His back was now turned to us; not by sight could he any longer communicate with the peril; but, by the dreadful rattle of our hardness, too truly had his ear been instructed that all was finished as regarded any effort of *his*. Already in resignation he had rested from his struggle; and perhaps in his heart he was whispering, "Father, which art in heaven, do Thou finish above what I on earth have attempted." Faster than ever millrace we ran past them in our inexorable flight. Oh, raving of hurricanes that must have sounded in their young ears at the moment of our transit! Even in that moment the thunder of collision spoke aloud. Either with the swingle-bar,[9] or with the haunch of our near leader, we had struck the off wheel of the little gig; which stood rather obliquely, and not quite so far advanced as to be accurately parallel with the nearwheel. The blow, from the fury of our passage, resounded terrifically. I rose in horror, to gaze upon the ruins we might have caused. From my elevated station I looked down, and looked back upon the scene; which in a moment told its own tale, and wrote all its records on my heart forever.

Here was the map of the passion[10] that now had finished. The horse was planted immovably, with his forefeet upon the paved crest of the central road. He of the whole party might be supposed untouched by the passion of death. The little cany carriage—partly, perhaps, from the violent torsion of the wheels in its recent movement, partly from the thundering blow we had given to it—as if it sympathized with human horror, was all alive with tremblings and shiverings. The young man trembled not, nor shivered. He sat like a rock. But *his* was the steadiness of agitation frozen into rest by horror. As yet he dared not to look round; for he knew that, if anything remained to do, by him it could no longer be done. And as yet he knew not for certain if their safety were accomplished. But the lady——

But the lady——! Oh, heavens! will that spectacle ever depart from my dreams, as she rose and sank upon her seat, sank and rose,

9. The swinging bar to which the traces of a harness are fastened.
10. In the old sense: suffering. De Quincey means to suggest Christ's passion on the cross, preparatory to the concluding section of the fugue.

threw up her arms wildly to heaven, clutched at some visionary object in the air, fainting, praying, raving, despairing? Figure to yourself, reader, the elements of the case; suffer me to recall before your mind the circumstances of that unparalleled situation. From the silence and deep peace of this saintly summer night—from the pathetic blending of this sweet moonlight, dawnlight, dreamlight—from the manly tenderness of this flattering, whispering, murmuring love—suddenly as from the woods and fields—suddenly as from the chambers of the air opening in revelation—suddenly as from the ground yawning at her feet, leaped upon her, with the flashing of cataracts, Death the crowned phantom, with all the equipage of his terrors, and the tiger roar of his voice.

The moments were numbered; the strife was finished; the vision was closed. In the twinkling of an eye, our flying horses had carried us to the termination of the umbrageous aisle; at the right angles we wheeled into our former direction; the turn of the road carried the scene out of my eyes in an instant, and swept it into my dreams forever.

III. Dream-Fugue Founded on the Preceding Theme of Sudden Death

> *Whence the sound*
> *Of instruments, that made melodious chime,*
> *Was heard, of harp and organ; and who moved*
> *Their stops and chords was seen; his volant*[11] *touch*
> *Instinct through all proportions, low and high,*
> *Fled and pursued transverse the resonant fugue.*
> PARADISE LOST XI. 558–63.

TUMULTUOSISSIMAMENTE[1]

Passion of sudden death! that once in youth I read and interpreted by the shadows of thy averted signs![2]—rapture of panic taking the shape (which amongst tombs in churches I have seen) of woman bursting her sepulchral bonds—of woman's Ionic[3] form bending forward from the ruins of her grave with arching foot, with eyes upraised, with clasped adoring hands—waiting, watching, trembling, praying for the trumpet's call to rise from dust forever! Ah, vision too fearful of shuddering humanity on the brink of almighty abysses!—vision that didst start back, that didst reel away, like a shriveling scroll from before the wrath of fire racing on the wings of the wind! Epilepsy so brief of horror, wherefore is it that thou canst not die? Passing so suddenly into darkness, wherefore is it that still thou sheddest thy sad funeral blights upon the gorgeous mosaics of dreams? Fragment of music too passionate, heard once,

11. Flying.
1. "Very tumultuously"—in imitation of a composer's instruction to the performer of a piece of music.
2. In a note De Quincey reminds us that he interpreted the lady's agony from her gestures alone, "never once catching the lady's full face, and even her profile imperfectly."
3. Graceful; from the Greek Ionic column, which is more graceful and feminine than the heavier Doric.

and heard no more, what aileth thee, that thy deep rolling chords come up at intervals through all the worlds of sleep, and after forty years have lost no element of horror?

1

Lo, it is summer—almighty summer! The everlasting gates of life and summer are thrown open wide; and on the ocean, tranquil and verdant as a savannah, the unknown lady from the dreadful vision and I myself are floating—she upon a fairy pinnace,[4] and I upon an English three-decker. Both of us are wooing gales of festal happiness within the domain of our common country, within that ancient watery park, within the pathless chase of ocean, where England takes her pleasure as a huntress through winter and summer, from the rising to the setting sun. Ah, what a wilderness of floral beauty was hidden, or was suddenly revealed, upon the tropic islands through which the pinnace moved! And upon her deck what a bevy of human flowers: young women how lovely, young men how noble, that were dancing together, and slowly drifting towards *us* amidst music and incense, amidst blossoms from forests and gorgeous corymbi[5] from vintages, amidst natural caroling, and the echoes of sweet girlish laughter. Slowly the pinnace nears us, gaily she hails us, and silently she disappears beneath the shadow of our mighty bows. But then, as at some signal from heaven, the music, and the carols, and the sweet echoing of girlish laughter— all are hushed. What evil has smitten the pinnace, meeting or overtaking her? Did ruin to our friends couch within our own dreadful shadow? Was our shadow the shadow of death? I looked over the bow for an answer, and, behold! the pinnace was dismantled; the revel and the revelers were found no more; the glory of the vintage was dust; and the forests with their beauty were left without a witness upon the seas. "But where," and I turned to our crew— "where are the lovely women that danced beneath the awning of flowers and clustering corymbi? Whither have fled the noble young men that danced with *them?*" Answer there was none. But suddenly the man at the masthead, whose countenance darkened with alarm, cried out, "Sail on the weather beam![6] Down she comes upon us: in seventy seconds she also will founder."

2

I looked to the weather side, and the summer had departed. The sea was rocking, and shaken with gathering wrath. Upon its surface sat mighty mists, which grouped themselves into arches and long cathedral aisles. Down one of these, with the fiery pace of a quarrel[7] from a crossbow, ran a frigate right athwart our course. "Are they mad?" some voice exclaimed from our deck. "Do they woo their ruin?" But in a moment, as she was close upon us, some impulse

4. A light sailing vessel.
5. Clusters of grapes or other fruits.
6. To windward, at right angles to the ship.
7. The square-headed arrow for a crossbow.

of a heady current[8] or local vortex gave a wheeling bias to her course, and off she forged without a shock. As she ran past us, high aloft amongst the shrouds[9] stood the lady of the pinnace. The deeps opened ahead in malice to receive her, towering surges of foam ran after her, the billows were fierce to catch her. But far away she was borne into desert spaces of the sea: whilst still by sight I followed her, as she ran before the howling gale, chased by angry sea birds and by maddening billows; still I saw her, as at the moment when she ran past us, standing amongst the shrouds, with her white draperies streaming before the wind. There she stood, with hair disheveled, one hand clutched amongst the tackling—rising, sinking, fluttering, trembling, praying; there for leagues I saw her as she stood, raising at intervals one hand to heaven, amidst the fiery crests of the pursuing waves and the raving of the storm; until at last, upon a sound from afar of malicious laughter and mockery, all was hidden forever in driving showers; and afterwards, but when I know not, nor how,

3

Sweet funeral bells from some incalculable distance, wailing over the dead that die before the dawn, awakened me as I slept in a boat moored to some familiar shore. The morning twilight even then was breaking; and, by the dusky revelations which it spread, I saw a girl, adorned with a garland of white roses about her head for some great festival, running along the solitary strand in extremity of haste. Her running was the running of panic; and often she looked back as to some dreadful enemy in the rear. But, when I leaped ashore, and followed on her steps to warn her of a peril in front, alas! from me she fled as from another peril, and vainly I shouted to her of quicksands that lay ahead. Faster and faster she ran; round a promontory of rocks she wheeled out of sight; in an instant I also wheeled round it, but only to see the treacherous sands gathering above her head. Already her person was buried; only the fair young head and the diadem of white roses around it were still visible to the pitying heavens; and, last of all, was visible one white marble arm. I saw by the early twilight this fair young head, as it was sinking down to darkness—saw this marble arm, as it rose above her head and her treacherous grave, tossing, faltering, rising, clutching, as at some false deceiving hand stretched out from the clouds—saw this marble arm uttering her dying hope, and then uttering her dying despair. The head, the diadem, the arm—these all had sunk; at last over these also the cruel quicksand had closed; and no memorial of the fair young girl remained on earth, except my own solitary tears, and the funeral bells from the desert seas, that, rising again more softly, sang a requiem over the grave

---

8. A current directly opposed to a ship's course. 9. The ropes attached to the top of a mast which help to support it.

of the buried child, and over her blighted dawn.

I sat, and wept in secret the tears that men have ever given to the memory of those that died before the dawn, and by the treachery of earth, our mother. But suddenly the tears and funeral bells were hushed by a shout as of many nations, and by a roar as from some great king's artillery, advancing rapidly along the valleys, and heard afar by echoes from the mountains. "Hush!" I said, as I bent my ear earthwards to listen—"hush!—this either is the very anarchy of strife, or else"—and then I listened more profoundly, and whispered as I raised my head—"or else, oh heavens! it is *victory* that is final, victory that swallows up all strife."

4

Immediately, in trance, I was carried over land and sea to some distant kingdom, and placed upon a triumphal car, amongst companions crowned with laurel. The darkness of gathering midnight, brooding over all the land, hid from us the mighty crowds that were weaving restlessly about ourselves as a center: we heard them, but saw them not. Tidings had arrived, within an hour, of a grandeur that measured itself against centuries; too full of pathos they were, too full of joy, to utter themselves by other language than by tears, by restless anthems, and *Te Deums* [9a] reverberated from the choirs and orchestras of earth. These tidings we that sat upon the laureled car had it for our privilege to publish amongst all nations. And already, by signs audible through the darkness, by snortings and tramplings, our angry horses, that knew no fear of fleshly weariness, upbraided us with delay. Wherefore *was* it that we delayed? We waited for a secret word, that should bear witness to the hope of nations as now accomplished for ever. At midnight the secret word arrived; which word was—*Waterloo and Recovered Christendom!* The dreadful word shone by its own light; before us it went; high above our leaders' heads it rode, and spread a golden light over the paths which we traversed. Every city, at the presence of the secret word, threw open its gates. The rivers were conscious as we crossed. All the forests, as we ran along their margins, shivered in homage to the secret word. And the darkness comprehended it.[9b]

Two hours after midnight we approached a mighty Minster.[1] Its gates, which rose to the clouds, were closed. But, when the dreadful word that rode before us reached them with its golden light, silently they moved back upon their hinges; and at a flying gallop our equipage entered the grand aisle of the cathedral. Headlong was our pace; and at every altar, in the little chapels and oratories to the right hand and left of our course, the lamps, dying or sickening, kindled anew in sympathy with the secret word that was flying past. Forty leagues we might have run in the cathedral, and as yet no strength of morning light had reached us, when before us we

9a. From the hymn, *Te Deum laudamus*, "We praise thee, O God."

9b. An echo from John i.5.
1. A large church.

saw the aerial galleries of organ and choir. Every pinnacle of the fretwork, every station of advantage amongst the traceries, was crested by white-robed choristers that sang deliverance; that wept no more tears, as once their fathers had wept; but at intervals that sang together to the generations, saying,

> Chant the deliverer's praise in every tongue,

and receiving answers from afar,

> Such as once in heaven and earth were sung.

And of their chanting was no end; of our headlong pace was neither pause nor slackening.

Thus as we ran like torrents—thus as we swept with bridal rapture over the Campo Santo² of the cathedral graves—suddenly we became aware of a vast necropolis rising upon the far-off horizon— a city of sepulchers, built within the saintly cathedral for the warrior dead that rested from their feuds on earth. Of purple granite was the necropolis; yet, in the first minute, it lay like a purple stain upon the horizon, so mighty was the distance. In the second minute it trembled through many changes, growing into terraces and towers of wondrous altitude, so mighty was the pace. In the third minute already, with our dreadful gallop, we were entering its suburbs. Vast sarcophagi rose on every side, having towers and turrets that, upon the limits of the central aisle, strode forward with haughty intrusion, that ran back with mighty shadows into answering recesses. Every sarcophagus showed many bas-reliefs³—bas-reliefs of battles and of battlefields; battles from forgotten ages, battles from yesterday; battlefields that, long since, nature had healed and reconciled to herself with the sweet oblivion of flowers; battlefields that were yet angry and crimson with carnage. Where the terraces ran, there did *we* run; where the towers curved, there did *we* curve. With the flight of swallows our horses swept round every angle. Like rivers in flood wheeling round headlands, like hurricanes that ride into the secrets of forests, faster than ever light unwove the mazes of darkness, our flying equipage carried earthly passions, kindled warrior instincts, amongst the dust that lay around us—dust oftentimes of our noble fathers that had slept in God from Crécy to Trafalgar.⁴ And now had we reached the last sarcophagus, now were we abreast of the last bas-relief, already had we recovered the arrow-like flight of the illimitable central aisle, when coming up this aisle to meet us we beheld afar off a female

2. "Holy Field"—i.e., the cemetery. In a note De Quincey points out that the graves within English cathedrals "often form a flat pavement over which carriages and horses *might* run."
3. "Low reliefs": sculptured figures projecting from a background.

4. Crécy, France, was in 1346 the scene of the victory over the French knights by the English archers under Edward III; at Trafalgar Cape, off the coast of Spain, Nelson in 1805 destroyed Napoleon's fleet.

child, that rode in a carriage as frail as flowers. The mists which went before her hid the fawns that drew her, but could not hide the shells and tropic flowers with which she played—but could not hide the lovely smiles by which she uttered her trust in the mighty cathedral, and in the cherubim that looked down upon her from the mighty shafts of its pillars. Face to face she was meeting us; face to face she rode, as if danger there were none. "Oh, baby!" I exclaimed, "shalt thou be the ransom for Waterloo? Must we, that carry tidings of great joy to every people, be messengers of ruin to thee!" In horror I rose at the thought; but then also, in horror at the thought, rose one that was sculptured on a bas-relief—a Dying Trumpeter. Solemnly from the field of battle he rose to his feet; and, unslinging his stony trumpet, carried it, in his dying anguish, to his stony lips—sounding once, and yet once again; proclamation that, in *thy* ears, oh baby! spoke from the battlements of death. Immediately deep shadows fell between us, and aboriginal silence. The choir had ceased to sing. The hoofs of our horses, the dreadful rattle of our harness, the groaning of our wheels, alarmed the graves no more. By horror the bas-relief had been unlocked unto life. By horror we, that were so full of life, we men and our horses, with their fiery forelegs rising in mid air to their everlasting gallop, were frozen to a bas-relief. Then a third time the trumpet sounded; the seals were taken off all pulses; life, and the frenzy of life, tore into their channels again; again the choir burst forth in sunny grandeur, as from the muffling of storms and darkness; again the thunderings of our horses carried temptation into the graves. One cry burst from our lips, as the clouds, drawing off from the aisle, showed it empty before us—"Whither has the infant fled?—is the young child caught up to God?" Lo! afar off, in a vast recess, rose three mighty windows to the clouds; and on a level with their summits, at height insuperable to man, rose an altar of purest alabaster. On its eastern face was trembling a crimson glory. A glory was it from the reddening dawn that now streamed *through* the windows? Was it from the crimson robes of the martyrs painted *on* the windows? Was it from the bloody bas-reliefs of earth? There, suddenly, within that crimson radiance, rose the apparition of a woman's head, and then of a woman's figure. The child it was—grown up to woman's height. Clinging to the horns of the altar, voiceless she stood— sinking, rising, raving, despairing; and behind the volume of incense that, night and day, streamed upwards from the altar, dimly was seen the fiery font, and the shadow of that dreadful being who should have baptized her with the baptism of death. But by her side was kneeling her better angel, that hid his face with wings; that wept and pleaded for *her*; that prayed when *she* could *not*; that fought with Heaven by tears for *her* deliverance; which also, as he raised his immortal countenance from his wings, I saw, by the glory in his eye, that from Heaven he had won at last.

5

Then was completed the passion of the mighty fugue. The golden tubes of the organ, which as yet had but muttered at intervals—gleaming amongst clouds and surges of incense—threw up, as from fountains unfathomable, columns of heart-shattering music. Choir and anti-choir were filling fast with unknown voices. Thou also, Dying Trumpeter, with thy love that was victorious, and thy anguish that was finishing, didst enter the tumult; trumpet and echo—farewell love, and farewell anguish—rang through the dreadful sanctus.[5] Oh, darkness of the grave! that from the crimson altar and from the fiery font wert visited and searched by the effulgence in the angel's eyes—were these indeed thy children? Pomps of life, that, from the burials of centuries, rose again to the voice of perfect joy, did ye indeed mingle with the festivals of Death? Lo! as I looked back for seventy leagues through the mighty cathedral, I saw the quick and the dead that sang together to God, together that sang to the generations of man. All the hosts of jubilation, like armies that ride in pursuit, moved with one step. Us, that, with laureled heads, were passing from the cathedral, they overtook, and, as with a garment, they wrapped us round with thunders greater than our own. As brothers we moved together; to the dawn that advanced, to the stars that fled; rendering thanks to God in the highest—that, having hid His face through one generation behind thick clouds of War, once again was ascending, from the Campo Santo of Waterloo was ascending, in the visions of Peace; rendering thanks for thee, young girl! whom having overshadowed with His ineffable passion of death, suddenly did God relent, suffered thy angel to turn aside His arm, and even in thee, sister unknown! shown to me for a moment only to be hidden forever, found an occasion to glorify His goodness. A thousand times, amongst the phantoms of sleep, have I seen thee entering the gates of the golden dawn, with the secret word riding before thee, with the armies of the grave behind thee, seen thee sinking, rising, raving, despairing; a thousand times in the worlds of sleep have seen thee followed by God's angel through storms, through desert seas, through the darkness of quicksands, through dreams and the dreadful revelations that are in dreams; only that at the last, with one sling of His victorious arm, He might snatch thee back from ruin, and might emblazon in thy deliverance the endless resurrections of His love!

1849

5. The last part of the Preface to the Mass (repeated thrice, "Holy, Holy, Holy").

CHARLES LAMB
(1775–1834)

1782–89: At Christ's Hospital school; Coleridge a fellow student.
1820–25: Contributes "Essays of Elia" to the *London Magazine*.

Lamb was almost the exact contemporary of Wordsworth and Coleridge; he numbered these two poets, as well as Keats, among his close friends, published his own early poems in combination with those of Coleridge in 1796 and 1797, and supported the *Lyrical Ballads* and some of the other avant-garde poetry of his time. Yet Lamb lacks almost all the traits and convictions we think of as characteristically "Romantic." He happily lived all his life in the city and its environs, sharing Dr. Johnson's opinion that he who tires of London tires of life. He could not abide Shelley or his poetry and he distrusted Coleridge's supernaturalism and Wordsworth's oracular sublimities and religion of nature, preferring the elements in their poems which were human and realistic. In an age when many of the important writers were fervent radicals and some became equally fervent reactionaries, Lamb remained uncommitted in both politics and religion; and although on intimate terms with such dedicated reformers as Hazlitt, William Godwin, Thomas Holcroft, and Leigh Hunt, he chose them, as he said, not for their opinions, but "for some individuality of character which they manifested." In his own writings, the one attribute he shared with his great contemporaries was that of *l'étalage du moi*, "the display of one's own personality": many of his best familiar essays, like Wordsworth's poems, are made up of his early experiences and feelings, recollected in tranquility. But it must be remembered that, although personal poetry was a new and distinctive Romantic form, the personal essay was already a well-established genre which had been developed by Montaigne as early as the 16th century.

Lamb was born in the Inner Temple, an ancient section of London where his father was clerk and assistant to a lawyer. At the age of 7 he entered Christ's Hospital, the "Bluecoat School" of his essay *Christ's Hospital Five and Thirty Years Ago*. He left the school before he was 15 and soon thereafter became a clerk in the accounting department of the huge commercial house, The East India Company, where he remained for 33 years. His adult life was quiet and unadventurous, but under its calm surface, as Walter Pater said, lay "something of the fateful domestic horror, of the beautiful heroism and devotedness too, of old Greek tragedy." When he was 22 his beloved sister Mary, ten years his senior, broke under the strain of caring for her invalid parents and in an insane paroxysm stabbed her mother to the heart. Lamb wrote to Coleridge:

My dearest friend—

* * * My poor dear dearest sister in a fit of insanity has been the death of her own mother. I was at hand only time enough to snatch the knife out of her grasp. She is at present in a madhouse, from whence I fear she must be moved to an hospital. God has preserved to me my senses. * * * My poor father was slightly wounded, and I am left to take care of him and my aunt. * * * Write—as religious a letter as possible—but no mention of what is gone and done with—with me former things are passed away, and I have something more to do than to feel— God Almighty have us all in his keeping.—

C. Lamb

Upon her recovery Mary was released to the care of her brother, who devoted to her and to their common household the rest of his life. Mary's attacks recurred, briefly but periodically, and when the terribly familiar symptoms began to manifest themselves, Lamb and Mary would walk arm in arm and weeping to the asylum, carrying a strait jacket with them.

Most of the time, however, Mary was her normally serene and gracious self, and she shared her brother's delight in old books, the theater, art galleries, and the inexhaustible variousness of the great city. She shared also his gregariousness and genius for friendship. The Wednesday (sometimes Thursday) night gatherings at the Lambs attracted a varied company which included many of the leading writers and artists of England. Among his guests Lamb moved with his peculiar shuffling gait, dressed invariably in old-fashioned black of clerical cut, his body fragile, but surmounted by a fine head; everyone remarked on the sad sweetness of his smile. He drew furiously upon a pipe of strong tobacco and drank copiously; as the alcohol eased his habitual stammer, his puns and practical jokes grew ever more outrageous. Occasionally an evening ended with Lamb drunk under the table. But his friends invariably applied to him the epithet "gentle"—to his great indignation. "For God's sake," he exploded to Coleridge, "don't make me ridiculous any more by terming me gentle-hearted in print, or do it in better verses." "Substitute drunken dog, ragged-head, seld-shaven, odd-eyed, stuttering, or any other epithet which truly and properly belongs to the gentleman in question." Lamb had, in fact, a complex temperament, in which the playfulness overlay a somber melancholy and the freakishness sometimes manifested a touch of malice. To requests from Wordsworth and Coleridge for criticism of their poems he replied with a caustic candor not entirely appreciated by its beneficiaries. This charming egotist cherished his prejudices and distastes—he called them his "imperfect sympathies"— no less than he did his sympathies and enjoyments, and he never encountered pretentiousness, complacency, or a solemnity too profound and sustained without puncturing it by a well-honed witticism. "What choice venom!" exclaimed his friend Hazlitt, an expert on the subject—but while Hazlitt managed to antagonize almost everyone by his outspokenness, few could take offense, and none could long sustain it, at Lamb's antic speech and behavior.

To supplement his salary at the East India House, Lamb had early turned to writing in a variety of forms. When in 1818, at the age of 43, he published his *Works*, he apparently thought his major writing had already been accomplished. He had produced a good deal of minor verse; a sentimental novel, *Rosamund Gray*; a blank verse tragedy in the Elizabethan manner, *John Woodvil*; a farce, *Mr. H——*, which was hissed by many (including the honest author) when it was produced at Drury Lane; and, in collaboration with his sister Mary, the excellent children's book, *Tales from Shakespeare*. His most impressive achievements were the brilliant comments incorporated in his anthology, important in the Elizabethan revival of that period, *Specimens of English Dramatic Poets Who Lived About the Time of Shakespeare*, together with two fine critical essays, *The Tragedies of Shakespeare* and *On the Genius and Character of Hogarth*. But not until two years after the appearance of his *Works* did Lamb begin to contribute to the *London Magazine* the *Essays of Elia*, which have elevated him to the rank of a major author.

Lamb's earlier attempts in the fictional forms show that he lacked the power of inventing characters and events, but in the familiar essay (in which he had, in effect, served a long apprenticeship in his letters to his friends) he was able to exploit his one great subject: himself, his connoisseurship of literature and of people, and his strong local attachments— "old chairs, old tables, streets, squares, where I have sunned myself, my old school." Under the pseudonym of an Italian clerk named Elia, whom he had known while briefly employed in the South Sea House, Lamb projects in his essays the character of a man who is whimsical but strong-willed, self-deprecating yet self-absorbed, a specialist in nostalgia and in that humor which balances delicately on the verge of pathos. So engaging is the literary persona which pervades his work that it has attracted a host of devotees who have established what has been called "the Elia industry." But the critical preoccupation with Lamb's seemingly ingenuous self-revelation has obscured the actual cunning of a deliberate and dedicated artist in prose. Lamb's style was not in any contemporary tradition. He wrote, as he said, "for antiquity"; his prose style, like that of Edmund Spenser's in verse, is an invented style. Although its basis is plain modern English, it is colored throughout by archaic words, expressions, and turns of syntax. In the conduct of his essays Lamb is capricious, droll, and (in the manner of earlier literary eccentrics such as Robert Burton and Laurence Sterne) he delights in tricks of words and thought and in the elaborate exploration of a literary conceit. Close imitators of Lamb's style invariably fall into archness and sentimentality. Lamb's inimitable feat was to transform whimsy into a classic type of the personal essay, uttered in one of the distinctive voices in English prose.

Christ's Hospital Five-and-Thirty Years Ago[1]

In Mr. Lamb's *Works*, published a year or two since, I find a magnificent eulogy on my old school, such as it was, or now ap-

1. Christ's Hospital, London (founded in 1552 by Edward VI), was run as a free boarding school for the sons of middle-class parents in straitened financial circumstances. Its students were known as "Bluecoat Boys," from their uniforms of a long blue gown and yellow stockings. Lamb had in 1813 published a magazine article, *Recollections of Christ's Hospital*, which the present essay undertakes to supplement by presenting the less formal side of school life. The "I" or narrator of the essay is Elia—a device which allows Lamb to combine his own circumstances and experiences with those of Coleridge, his older contemporary at the school.

pears to him to have been, between the years 1782 and 1789. It happens very oddly that my own standing at Christ's was nearly corresponding with his; and, with all gratitude to him for his enthusiasm for the cloisters, I think he has contrived to bring together whatever can be said in praise of them, dropping all the other side of the argument most ingeniously.

I remember L. at school, and can well recollect that he had some peculiar advantages, which I and others of his schoolfellows had not. His friends lived in town, and were near at hand; and he had the privilege of going to see them almost as often as he wished, through some invidious distinction, which was denied to us. The present worthy subtreasurer to the Inner Temple can explain how that happened. He had his tea and hot rolls in a morning, while we were battening upon our quarter of a penny loaf—our *crug* [2]—moistened with attenuated small beer, in wooden piggins,[3] smacking of the pitched leathern jack it was poured from. Our Monday's milk porritch, blue and tasteless, and the pease soup of Saturday, coarse and choking, were enriched for him with a slice of "extraordinary bread and butter," from the hot loaf of the Temple. The Wednesday's mess of millet,[4] somewhat less repugnant—(we had three banyan to four meat days in the week [5])—was endeared to his palate with a lump of double-refined, and a smack of ginger (to make it go down the more glibly) or the fragrant cinnamon. In lieu of our *half-pickled* Sundays, or *quite fresh* boiled beef on Thursdays (strong as *caro equina*[6]), with detestable marigolds floating in the pail to poison the broth—our scanty mutton scrags[7] on Friday—and rather more savory, but grudging, portions of the same flesh, rotten-roasted[8] or rare, on the Tuesdays (the only dish which excited our appetites, and disappointed our stomachs, in almost equal proportion)—he had his hot plate of roast veal, or the more tempting griskin[9] (exotics unknown to our palates), cooked in the paternal kitchen (a great thing), and brought him daily by his maid or aunt! I remember the good old relative (in whom love forbade pride) squatting down upon some odd stone in a by-nook of the cloisters, disclosing the viands (of higher regale than those cates which the ravens ministered to the Tishbite[1]); and the contending passions of L. at the unfolding. There was love for the bringer; shame for the thing brought, and the manner of its bringing; sympathy for those who were too many to share in it; and, at top of all, hunger (eldest, strongest of the passions!) predominant, breaking down the stony fences of shame, and awkwardness, and a troubling over-consciousness.

2. Slang for bread.
3. Small wooden pails. The "jack" is a leather vessel coated on the outside with pitch.
4. Cereal.
5. "Banyan days" is a nautical term for days when no meat is served.
6. Horsemeat.
7. Necks.
8. Overdone.
9. The lean part of a loin of pork.
1. The prophet Elijah, fed by the ravens in I Kings xvii. "Cates": delicacies.

I was a poor friendless boy. My parents, and those who should care for me, were far away. Those few acquaintances of theirs, which they could reckon upon being kind to me in the great city, after a little forced notice, which they had the grace to take of me on my first arrival in town, soon grew tired of my holiday visits. They seemed to them to recur too often, though I thought them few enough; and, one after another, they all failed me, and I felt myself alone among six hundred playmates.

O the cruelty of separating a poor lad from his early homestead! The yearnings which I used to have towards it in those unfledged years! How, in my dreams, would my native town (far in the west) come back, with its church, and trees, and faces! How I would wake weeping, and in the anguish of my heart exclaim upon sweet Calne in Wiltshire![8]

To this late hour of my life, I trace impressions left by the recollections of those friendless holidays. The long warm days of summer never return but they bring with them a gloom from the haunting memory of those *whole-day leaves*, when, by some strange arrangement, we were turned out for the livelong day, upon our own hands, whether we had friends to go to or none. I remember those bathing excursions to the New River which L. recalls with such relish, better, I think, than he can—for he was a home seeking lad, and did not much care for such water pastimes: How merrily we would sally forth into the fields; and strip under the first warmth of the sun; and wanton like young dace[9] in the streams; getting us appetites for noon, which those of us that were penniless (our scanty morning crust long since exhausted) had not the means of allaying—while the cattle, and the birds, and the fishes were at feed about us and we had nothing to satisfy our cravings—the very beauty of the day, and the exercise of the pastime, and the sense of liberty, setting a keener edge upon them! How faint and languid, finally, we would return, towards nightfall, to our desired morsel, half-rejoicing, half-reluctant that the hours of our uneasy liberty had expired!

It was worse in the days of winter, to go prowling about the streets objectless—shivering at cold windows of print shops, to extract a little amusement; or haply, as a last resort in the hopes of a little novelty, to pay a fifty-times repeated visit (where our individual faces should be as well known to the warden as those of his own charges) to the Lions in the Tower—to whose levee, by courtesy immemorial, we had a prescriptive title to admission.[1]

L.'s governor (so we called the patron who presented us to the

---

8. Coleridge had come to school from Ottery St. Mary, Devonshire, in the southwest of England.
9. A small quick-darting fish.
1. The Bluecoat Boys had the right of free admission to the royal menagerie, then housed in the Tower of London. A "levee" is a formal morning reception.

foundation[2]) lived in a manner under his paternal roof. Any complaint which he had to make was sure of being attended to. This was understood at Christ's, and was an effectual screen to him against the severity of masters, or worse tyranny of the monitors. The oppressions of these young brutes are heart-sickening to call to recollection. I have been called out of my bed, and *waked for the purpose*, in the coldest winter nights—and this not once, but night after night—in my shirt, to receive the discipline of a leathern thong with eleven other sufferers, because it pleased my callow overseer, when there has been any talking heard after we were gone to bed, to make the six last beds in the dormitory, where the youngest children of us slept, answerable for an offense they neither dared to commit nor had the power to hinder. The same execrable tyranny drove the younger part of us from the fires, when our feet were perishing with snow; and, under the cruelest penalties, forbade the indulgence of a drink of water when we lay in sleepless summer nights fevered with the season and the day's sports.

There was one H——, who, I learned, in after days was seen expiating some maturer offense in the hulks.[3] (Do I flatter myself in fancying that this might be the planter of that name, who suffered—at Nevis, I think, or St. Kitts—some few years since? My friend Tobin was the benevolent instrument of bringing him to the gallows.) This petty Nero actually branded a boy who had offended him with a red-hot iron; and nearly starved forty of us with exacting contributions, to the one-half of our bread, to pamper a young ass, which, incredible as it may seem, with the connivance of the nurse's daughter (a young flame of his) he had contrived to smuggle in, and keep upon the leads[4] of the *ward*, as they called our dormitories. This game went on for better than a week, till the foolish beast, not able to fare well but he must cry roast meat —happier than Caligula's minion,[5] could he have kept his own counsel—but foolisher, alas! than any of his species in the fables —waxing fat, and kicking, in the fullness of bread, one unlucky minute would needs proclaim his good fortune to the world below; and, laying out his simple throat, blew such a ram's-horn blast, as (toppling down the walls of his own Jericho[6]) set concealment any longer at defiance. The client was dismissed, with certain attentions, to Smithfield; but I never understood that the patron underwent any censure on the occasion. This was in the stewardship of L.'s admired Perry.[7]

2. I.e., who vouched for a candidate for entrance to Christ's Hospital. Lamb's patron was Samuel Salt, a lawyer and Member of Parliament, for whom Lamb's father served as clerk.
3. Prison ship. (In Lamb's time the plural "hulks" had come to be used for the singular.)
4. A flat roof.
5. The favorite horse of the Emperor Caligula, who was fed gilded oats and appointed to the post of chief consul.
6. Joshua toppled the walls of Jericho by trumpet blasts (Joshua vi.16–20).
7. John Perry, steward of the school, described in Lamb's earlier essay.

Under the same *facile* administration, can L. have forgotten the cool impunity with which the nurses used to carry away openly, in open platters, for their own tables, one out of two of every hot joint, which the careful matron had been seeing scrupulously weighed out for our dinners? These things were daily practiced in that magnificent apartment which L. (grown connoisseur since, we presume) praises so highly for the grand paintings "by Verrio, and others," with which it is "hung round and adorned." But the sight of sleek, well-fed bluecoat boys in pictures was, at that time, I believe, little consolatory to him, or us, the living ones, who saw the better part of our provisions carried away before our faces by harpies;[8] and ourselves reduced (with the Trojan in the hall of Dido)

> To feed our mind with idle portraiture.[9]

L. has recorded the repugnance of the school to *gags*, or the fat of fresh beef boiled; and sets it down to some superstition. But these unctuous morsels are never grateful to young palates (children are universally fat-haters), and in strong, coarse, boiled meats, *unsalted*, are detestable. A *gag-eater* in our time was equivalent to a *ghoul*, and held in equal detestation.——— suffered under the imputation.

> . . . . . "Twas said
> He ate strange flesh.[1]

He was observed, after dinner, carefully to gather up the remnants left at his table (not many nor very choice fragments, you may credit me)—and, in an especial manner, these disreputable morsels, which he would convey away and secretly stow in the settle that stood at his bedside. None saw when he ate them. It was rumored that he privately devoured them in the night. He was watched, but no traces of such midnight practices were discoverable. Some reported that on leave-days he had been seen to carry out of the bounds a large blue check handkerchief, full of something. This then must be the accursed thing. Conjecture next was at work to imagine how he could dispose of it. Some said he sold it to the beggars. This belief generally prevailed. He went about moping. None spake to him. No one would play with him. He was excommunicated; put out of the pale of the school. He was too powerful a boy to be beaten, but he underwent every mode of that negative punishment which is more grievous than many stripes. Still he persevered. At length he was observed by two of his school-

8. In classical mythology, filthy creatures, part woman and part bird, who carried away or fouled the food of their victims.
9. In Virgil's *Aeneid* I.464; Aeneas is inspecting the paintings in Dido's temple to Juno.
1. Loosely quoted from Shakespeare's *Antony and Cleopatra* I.iv.67.

fellows, who were determined to get at the secret, and had traced him one leave-day for the purpose, to enter a large worn-out building, such as there exist specimens of in Chancery Lane, which are let out to various scales of pauperism, with open door and a common staircase. After him they silently slunk in, and followed by stealth up four flights, and saw him tap at a poor wicket, which was opened by an aged woman, meanly clad. Suspicion was now ripened into certainty. The informers had secured their victim. They had him in their toils. Accusation was formally preferred, and retribution most signal was looked for. Mr. Hathaway, the then steward (for this happened a little after my time), with that patient sagacity which tempered all his conduct, determined to investigate the matter before he proceeded to sentence. The result was that the supposed mendicants, the receivers or purchasers of the mysterious scraps, turned out to be the parents of ————, an honest couple come to decay—whom this seasonable supply had, in all probability, saved from mendicancy; and that this young stork, at the expense of his own good name, had all this while been only feeding the old birds!—The governors on this occasion, much to their honor, voted a present relief to the family of ————, and presented him with a silver medal. The lesson which the steward read upon RASH JUDGMENT, on the occasion of publicly delivering the medal to ————, I believe would not be lost upon his auditory.—I had left school then, but I well remember ————. He was a tall, shambling youth, with a cast in his eye, not at all calculated to conciliate hostile prejudices. I have since seen him carrying a baker's basket. I think I heard he did not do quite so well by himself as he had done by the old folks.

I was a hypochondriac lad;[2] and the sight of a boy in fetters, upon the day of my first putting on the blue clothes, was not exactly fitted to assuage the natural terrors of initiation. I was of tender years, barely turned of seven; and had only read of such things in books, or seen them but in dreams. I was told he had *run away*. This was the punishment for the first offense.—As a novice I was soon after taken to see the dungeons. These were little, square, Bedlam[3] cells, where a boy could just lie at his length upon straw and a blanket—a mattress, I think, was afterwards substituted —with a peep of light, let in askance, from a prison orifice at top, barely enough to read by. Here the poor boy was locked in by himself all day, without sight of any but the porter who brought him his bread and water—who *might not speak to him*—or of the beadle, who came twice a week to call him out to receive his periodical chastisement, which was almost welcome, because it separated him for a brief interval from solitude—and here he

2. From now on Elia speaks as Lamb, rather than as Coleridge.   3. St. Mary of Bethlehem, an insane asylum in London.

was shut up by himself *of nights* out of the reach of any sound, to suffer whatever horrors the weak nerves, and superstition incident to his time of life, might subject him to. This was the penalty for the second offense. Wouldst thou like, reader, to see what became of him in the next degree?

The culprit, who had been a third time an offender, and whose expulsion was at this time deemed irreversible, was brought forth, as at some solemn auto da fé,[4] arrayed in uncouth and most appalling attire—all trace of his late "watchet weeds"[5] carefully effaced, he was exposed in a jacket resembling those which London lamplighters formerly delighted in, with a cap of the same. The effect of this divestiture was such as the ingenious devisers of it could have anticipated. With his pale and frighted features, it was as if some of those disfigurements in Dante[6] had seized upon him. In this disguisement he was brought into the hall (*L.'s favorite state room*), where awaited him the whole number of his schoolfellows, whose joint lessons and sports he was thenceforth to share no more; the awful presence of the steward, to be seen for the last time; of the executioner beadle, clad in his state robe for the occasion; and of two faces more, of direr import, because never but in these extremities visible. These were governors; two of whom by choice, or charter, were always accustomed to officiate at these *Ultima Supplicia;*[7] not to mitigate (so at least we understood it), but to enforce the uttermost stripe. Old Bamber Gascoigne, and Peter Aubert, I remember, were colleagues on one occasion, when the beadle turning rather pale, a glass of brandy was ordered to prepare him for the mysteries. The scourging was, after the old Roman fashion, long and stately. The lictor[8] accompanied the criminal quite round the hall. We were generally too faint, with attending to the previous disgusting circumstances, to make accurate report with our eyes of the degree of corporal suffering inflicted. Report, of course, gave out the back knotty and livid. After scourging, he was made over, in his *San Benito*,[9] to his friends, if he had any (but commonly such poor runagates were friendless), or to his parish officer, who, to enhance the effect of the scene, had his station allotted to him on the outside of the hall gate.

These solemn pageantries were not played off so often as to spoil the general mirth of the community. We had plenty of exercise and recreation *after* school hours; and, for myself, I must confess that I was never happier than *in* them. The Upper and the Lower Grammar Schools were held in the same room; and an imaginary line only divided their bounds. Their character was as different as

4. The ceremony prior to the execution of heretics under the Spanish Inquisition (literally, "act of faith").
5. Blue clothes.
6. I.e., of the sinners in Dante's *Inferno;* see Canto XX.

7. Extreme punishments.
8. A Roman officer who cleared the way for the chief magistrates.
9. The yellow robe worn by the condemned heretic at an auto-da-fé

that of the inhabitants on the two sides of the Pyrenees. The Rev. James Boyer[1] was the Upper Master; but the Rev. Matthew Field presided over that portion of the apartment of which I had the good fortune to be a member. We lived a life as careless as birds. We talked and did just what we pleased, and nobody molested us. We carried an accidence,[2] or a grammar, for form; but, for any trouble it gave us, we might take two years in getting through the verbs deponent, and another two in forgetting all that we had learned about them. There was now and then the formality of saying a lesson, but if you had not learned it, a brush across the shoulders (just enough to disturb a fly) was the sole remonstrance. Field never used the rod; and in truth he wielded the cane with no great good will—holding it "like a dancer." It looked in his hands rather like an emblem than an instrument of authority; and an emblem, too, he was ashamed of. He was a good, easy man, that did not care to ruffle his own peace, nor perhaps set any great consideration upon the value of juvenile time. He came among us, now and then, but often stayed away whole days from us; and when he came it made no difference to us—he had his private room to retire to, the short time he stayed, to be out of the sound of our noise. Our mirth and uproar went on. We had classics of our own, without being beholden to "insolent Greece or haughty Rome,"[3] that passed current among us—*Peter Wilkins*—the *Adventures of the Hon. Captain Robert Boyle*—the *Fortunate Bluecoat Boy*[4]—and the like. Or we cultivated a turn for mechanic and scientific operations; making little sundials of paper; or weaving those ingenious parentheses called *cat cradles*; or making dry peas to dance upon the end of a tin pipe; or studying the art military over that laudable game "French and English,"[4a] and a hundred other such devices to pass away the time—mixing the useful with the agreeable—as would have made the souls of Rousseau and John Locke chuckle to have seen us.[5]

Matthew Field belonged to that class of modest divines who affect to mix in equal proportion the *gentleman*, the *scholar*, and the *Christian*; but, I know not how, the first ingredient is generally found to be the predominating dose in the composition. He was engaged in gay parties, or with his courtly bow at some episcopal levee, when he should have been attending upon us. He had for many years the classical charge of a hundred children, during the four or five first years of their education, and his very highest form seldom proceeded further than two or three of the introductory fables

1. This teacher is also described by Coleridge in *Biographia Literaria*, Chapter I.
2. A table giving lists of Latin or Greek word forms.
3. Ben Jonson's *To the Memory of * * * William Shakespeare*, line 39.
4. All three were popular adventure stories or romances of the day.
4a. A page is covered with dots and the contestants, with eyes closed, try to draw a line which will cover the maximum number of the dots.
5. These two philosophers recommended systems of education which combined theory with practical experience.

of Phaedrus.[6] How things were suffered to go on thus, I cannot guess. Boyer, who was the proper person to have remedied these abuses, always affected, perhaps felt, a delicacy in interfering in a province not strictly his own. I have not been without my suspicions, that he was not altogether displeased at the contrast we presented to his end of the school. We were a sort of Helots to his young Spartans.[7] He would sometimes, with ironic deference, send to borrow a rod of the Under Master, and then, with sardonic grin, observe to one of his upper boys, "how neat and fresh the twigs looked." While his pale students were battering their brains over Xenophon and Plato, with a silence as deep as that enjoined by the Samite,[8] we were enjoying ourselves at our ease in our little Goshen.[9] We saw a little into the secrets of his discipline, and the prospect did but the more reconcile us to our lot. His thunders rolled innocuous for us; his storms came near, but never touched us; contrary to Gideon's miracle, while all around were drenched, our fleece was dry.[1] His boys turned out the better scholars; we, I suspect, have the advantage in temper. His pupils cannot speak of him without something of terror allaying their gratitude; the remembrance of Field comes back with all the soothing images of indolence, and summer slumbers, and work like play, and innocent idleness, and Elysian exemptions, and life itself a "playing holiday."

Though sufficiently removed from the jurisdiction of Boyer, we were near enough (as I have said) to understand a little of his system. We occasionally heard sounds of the *Ululantes*, and caught glances of Tartarus.[2] B. was a rabid pedant. His English style was cramped to barbarism. His Easter anthems (for his duty obliged him to those periodical flights) were grating as scrannel pipes.[3]— He would laugh, aye, and heartily, but then it must be at Flaccus's quibble about *Rex*[4]—or at the *tristis serveritas in vultu*, or *inspicere in patinas*, of Terence[5]—thin jests, which at their first broaching could hardly have had *vis*[6] enough to move a Roman muscle.—

6. A Roman author of the 1st century A.D., author of a collection of beast fables, including such children's favorites as "The Fox and the Sour Grapes" and "King Log and King Watersnake."
7. The Spartans exhibited drunken Helots (slaves) as a warning example to their children.
8. Pythogoras of Samos, Greek mathematician and philosopher of the 6th century B.C., forbade his pupils to speak until they had studied with him five years.
9. Where the Jews dwelt, protected from the swarms of flies with which the Lord plagued the Egyptians in Exodus viii.22.
1. Judges vi.37–38. As a sign to Gideon, the Lord soaked his sheepskin while leaving the earth around it dry.

2. In the *Aeneid* VI.557–58, Aeneas hears the groans and the sound of the lash from Tartarus, the infernal place of punishment for the wicked. "*Ululantes*" means "howling sufferers."
3. "Harsh pipes," an echo of Milton's *Lycidas*, line 124.
4. In *Satires* I.vii of Horace (Quintus Horatius Flaccus), there is a pun on *Rex* as both a surname and the word for "king."
5. In Terence's *Andrea* V.ii one character says of a notorious liar that he has "a sober severity in his countenance." In his *Adelphi* III.iii, after a father has advised his son to look into the lives of men as a mirror, the slave advises the kitchen scullions "to look into the stew pans" as a mirror.
6. Force; a term in rhetorical theory.

He had two wigs, both pedantic, but of different omen. The one serene, smiling, fresh powdered, betokening a mild day. The other, an old, discolored, unkempt, angry caxon,[7] denoting frequent and bloody execution. Woe to the school, when he made his morning appearance in his *passy*, or *passionate wig*. No comet expounded surer.[8]—J. B. had a heavy hand. I have known him double his knotty fist at a poor trembling child (the maternal milk hardly dry upon its lips) with a "Sirrah, do you presume to set your wits at me?"—Nothing was more common than to see him make a headlong entry into the schoolroom, from his inner recess, or library, and, with turbulent eye, singling out a lad, roar out, "Od's my life, sirrah" (his favorite adjuration), "I have a great mind to whip you"—then, with as sudden a retracting impulse, fling back into his lair—and, after a cooling lapse of some minutes (during which all but the culprit had totally forgotten the context) drive headlong out again, piecing out his imperfect sense, as if it had been some Devil's Litany, with the expletory yell—"*and I* WILL, *too.*"—In his gentler moods, when the *rabidus furor*[9] was assuaged, he had resort to an ingenious method, peculiar, for what I have heard, to himself, of whipping the boy, and reading the Debates,[1] at the same time; a paragraph, and a lash between; which in those times, when parliamentary oratory was most at a height and flourishing in these realms, was not calculated to impress the patient with a veneration for the diffuser graces of rhetoric.

Once, and but once, the uplifted rod was known to fall ineffectual from his hand—when droll squinting W——— having been caught putting the inside of the master's desk to a use for which the architect had clearly not designed it, to justify himself, with great simplicity averred, that *he did not know that the thing had been forewarned*. This exquisite irrecognition of any law antecedent to the *oral* or *declaratory* struck so irresistibly upon the fancy of all who heard it (the pedagogue himself not excepted)—that remission was unavoidable.

L. has given credit to B.'s great merits as an instructor. Coleridge, in his literary life, has pronounced a more intelligible and ample encomium on them. The author of the *Country Spectator*[2] doubts not to compare him with the ablest teachers of antiquity. Perhaps we cannot dismiss him better than with the pious ejaculation of C.—when he heard that his old master was on his deathbed: "Poor J. B.!—may all his faults be forgiven; and may he be wafted to bliss by little cherub boys all head and wings, with no *bottoms* to reproach his sublunary infirmities."

---

7. A type of wig.
8. Comets were superstitiously regarded as omens of disaster.
9. Mad rage.
1. The record of debates in Parliament.

2. Thomas Middleton, who was at school with Lamb and Coleridge, edited the magazine *Country Spectator* (1792–93) and later became Bishop of Calcutta.

Under him were many good and sound scholars bred.—First Grecian[3] of my time was Lancelot Pepys Stevens, kindest of boys and men, since Co-grammar-master (and inseparable companion) with Dr. T——e. What an edifying spectacle did this brace of friends present to those who remembered the antisocialities of their predecessors!—You never met the one by chance in the street without a wonder, which was quickly dissipated by the almost immediate sub-appearance of the other. Generally arm-in-arm, these kindly coadjutors lightened for each other the toilsome duties of their profession, and when, in advanced age, one found it convenient to retire, the other was not long in discovering that it suited him to lay down the fasces[4] also. Oh, it is pleasant, as it is rare, to find the same arm linked in yours at forty, which at thirteen helped it to turn over the *Cicero De Amicitia*,[5] or some tale of Antique Friendship, which the young heart even then was burning to anticipate!—Co-Grecian with S. was Th——, who has since executed with ability various diplomatic functions at the Northern courts. Th was a tall, dark, saturnine youth, sparing of speech, with raven locks.—Thomas Fanshaw Middleton followed him (now Bishop of Calcutta), a scholar and a gentleman in his teens. He has the reputation of an excellent critic; and is author (besides the *Country Spectator*) of a *Treatise on the Greek Article*, against Sharpe. M. is said to bear his miter high in India, where the *regni novitas*[6] (I dare say) sufficiently justifies the bearing. A humility quite as primitive as that of Jewel or Hooker[7] might not be exactly fitted to impress the minds of those Anglo-Asiatic diocesans with a reverence for home institutions, and the church which those fathers watered. The manners of M. at school, though firm, were mild and unassuming.—Next to M. (if not senior to him) was Richards, author of the *Aboriginal Britons*, the most spirited of the Oxford Prize Poems; a pale, studious Grecian.—Then followed poor S——, ill-fated M——! of these the Muse is silent.

> Finding some of Edward's race
> Unhappy, pass their annals by.[8]

Come back into memory, like as thou wert in the dayspring of thy fancies, with hope like a fiery column before thee—the dark pillar not yet turned—Samuel Taylor Coleridge—Logician, Metaphysician, Bard!—How have I seen the casual passer through the cloisters stand still, entranced with admiration (while he weighed the disproportion between the *speech* and the *garb* of the young

---

3. The Grecians were the small group of superior scholars selected to be sent to a university (usually Cambridge) on a Christ's Hospital scholarship.
4. The bundle of rods, serving as the handle of an ax, carried before the Roman magistrates as a symbol of office.
5. Cicero's essay "On Friendship."

6. Newness of the reign.
7. Famous divines in the 16th century, during the early period of the Anglican Church.
8. Altered from Matthew Prior's *Carmen Seculare* (1700). "Edward's race" is applied to the students of Christ's hospital, founded by Edward VI.

Mirandola[9]), to hear thee unfold, in thy deep and sweet intonations, the mysteries of Jamblichus, or Plotinus[1] (for even in those years thou waxedst not pale at such philosophic draughts), or reciting Homer in his Greek, or Pindar—while the walls of the old Grey Friars[2] re-echoed to the accents of the *inspired charity-boy!* —Many were the "wit combats" (to dally awhile with the words of old Fuller) between him and C. V. Le G——, "which two I behold like a Spanish great galleon, and an English man-of-war; Master Coleridge, like the former, was built far higher in learning, solid, but slow in his perfromances. C. V. L., with the English man-of-war, lesser in bulk, but lighter in sailing, could turn with all tides, tack about, and take advantage of all winds, by the quickness of his wit and invention."[3]

Nor shalt thou, their compeer, be quickly forgotten, Allen, with the cordial smile, and still more cordial laugh, with which thou wert wont to make the old cloisters shake, in thy cognition of some poignant jest of theirs; or the anticipation of some more material, and, peradventure practical one, of thine own. Extinct are those smiles, with that beautiful countenance, with which (for thou wert the *Nireus formosus*[4] of the school), in the days of thy maturer waggery, thou didst disarm the wrath of infuriated town-damsel, who, incensed by provoking pinch, turning tigress-like round, suddenly converted by thy angel look, exchanged the half-formed terrible "*bl*——," for a gentler greeting—"*bless thy handsome face!*"

Next follow two, who ought to be now alive, and the friends of Elia—the junior Le G—— and F——; who impelled, the former by a roving temper, the latter by too quick a sense of neglect—ill capable of enduring the slights poor Sizars[5] are sometimes subject to in our seats of learning—exchanged their Alma Mater for the camp; perishing, one by climate, and one on the plains of Salamanca: Le G——, sanguine, volatile, sweet-natured; F——, dogged, faithful, anticipative of insult, warmhearted, with something of the old Roman height about him.

Fine, frank-hearted Fr——, the present master of Hertford, with Marmaduke T——, mildest of missionaries—and both my good friends still—close the catalogue of Grecians in my time.

1820

---

9. Pico della Mirandola, the brilliant and charming humanist and philosopher of the Italian Renaissance, who died in 1494 at the age of 31.
1. Neo-Platonic philosophers.
2. Christ's Hospital was located in buildings that had once belonged to the Grey Friars (i.e., Franciscans).
3. Lamb adapts to Coleridge and Charles Valentine Le Grice the famous description of the wit combats between Shakespeare (the "man-of-war") and Ben Jonson (the "great galleon") in Thomas Fuller's *Worthies of England* (1662).
4. "The handsome Nireus," a Greek warrior in Homer's *Iliad* II.
5. An undergraduate at Cambridge University who receives an allowance toward his expenses.

The Two Races of Men[1]

The human species, according to the best theory I can form of it, is composed of two distinct races, *the men who borrow*, and *the men who lend*. To these two original diversities may be reduced all those impertinent classifications of Gothic and Celtic tribes, white men, black men, red men. All the dwellers upon earth, "Parthians, and Medes, and Elamites," [2] flock hither, and do naturally fall in with one or other of these primary distinctions. The infinite superiority of the former, which I choose to designate as the *great race*, is discernible in their figure, port, and a certain instinctive sovereignty. The latter are born degraded. "He shall serve his brethren." [3] There is something in the air of one of this cast, lean and suspicious; contrasting with the open, trusting, generous manners of the other.

Observe who have been the greatest borrowers of all ages—Alcibiades—Falstaff—Sir Richard Steele—our late incomparable Brinsley [4]—what a family likeness in all four!

What a careless, even deportment hath your borrower! what rosy gills! what a beautiful reliance on Providence doth he manifest—taking no more thought than lilies! [5] What contempt for money—accounting it (yours and mine especially) no better than dross! What a liberal confounding of those pedantic distinctions of *meum* and *tuum*! [6] or rather, what a noble simplification of language (beyond Tooke [7]), resolving these supposed opposites into one clear, intelligible pronoun adjective! What near approaches doth he make to the primitive *community* [8]—to the extent of one half of the principle at least!

He is the true taxer who "calleth all the world up to be taxed"; [9] and the distance is as vast between him and *one of us*, as subsisted betwixt the Augustan Majesty and the poorest obolary [1] Jew that paid it tribute pittance at Jerusalem! His exactions, too, have such a cheerful, voluntary air! So far removed from your sour parochial or

1. A small masterpiece in the tradition of the mock encomium, or ironic praise of the unpraiseworthy, such as Erasmus's *The Praise of Folly*. Lamb's oldest and closest friend, Coleridge, figures twice in the essay. In the role of heroic borrower of books almost never returned, he is Comberbatch—a private joke, for the name was identifiable only by Coleridge and a few initiates; in his second role, in which he returns books with the lavish interest of his extraordinary marginalia, he is S. T. C.—initials by which he was already known to many readers.
2. Acts ii.9.
3. Noah's curse upon his youngest son, Ham, in Genesis ix.25.
4. Richard Brinsley Sheridan (1751–1816), dramatist, producer, and statesman.
5. I.e., than "the lilies of the field," in Matthew vi.28 and Luke xii.26–7.
6. Mine and thine.
7. John Horne Tooke, author of *The Diversions of Purley* (1786–98), a book on philology.
8. The community of the Apostles, who held all their possessions in common, Acts ii.44–5.
9. See Luke ii.1; this is the call that brought Joseph and Mary to Bethlehem.
1. Possessing an obolus, a Greek penny.

state-gatherers—those ink-horn varlets, who carry their want of welcome in their faces! He cometh to you with a smile, and troubleth you with no receipt; confining himself to no set season. Every day is his Candlemas, or his Feast of Holy Michael.[2] He applieth the *lene tormentum* [3] of a pleasant look to your purse—which to that gentle warmth expands her silken leaves, as naturally as the cloak of the traveler, for which sun and wind contended! He is the true Propontic which never ebbeth! [4] The sea which taketh handsomely at each man's hand. In vain the victim, whom he delighteth to honor, struggles with destiny; he is in the net. Lend therefore cheerfully, O man ordained to lend—that thou lose not in the end, with thy worldly penny, the reversion [5] promised. Combine not preposterously in thine own person the penalties of Lazarus and of Dives! [6]—but, when thou seest the proper authority coming, meet it smilingly, as it were half-way. Come, a handsome sacrifice! See how light *he* makes of it! Strain not courtesies with a noble enemy.

Reflections like the foregoing were forced upon my mind by the death of my old friend, Ralph Bigod, Esq,[7] who departed this life on Wednesday evening; dying, as he had lived, without much trouble. He boasted himself a descendant from mighty ancestors of that name, who heretofore held ducal dignities in this realm. In his actions and sentiments he belied not the stock to which he pretended. Early in life he found himself invested with ample revenues; which, with that noble disinterestedness which I have noticed as inherent in men of the *great race*, he took almost immediate measures entirely to dissipate and bring to nothing: for there is something revolting in the idea of a king holding a private purse; and the thoughts of Bigod were all regal. Thus furnished, by the very act of disfurnishment; getting rid of the cumbersome luggage of riches, more apt (as one sings)

> To slacken virtue, and abate her edge,
> Than prompt her to do aught may merit praise,[8]

he set forth, like some Alexander, upon his great enterprise, "Borrowing and to borrow!" [9]

In his periegesis,[1] or triumphant progress throughout this island, it has been calculated that he laid a tithe [2] part of the inhabitants

2. Feb. 2 and Sept. 29—English quarter-days, when rents fall due.
3. "Gentle torture"; said by Horace about wine, *Odes* III.xxi.13.
4. See *Othello* III.iii.453–56.
5. The right of future possession—"promised," if you cast your bread upon the waters, Ecclesiastes xi.1, or lend to the poor, Proverbs xix.17.
6. Dives, the "rich man," finds when he dies that he is in hell, while Lazarus, who had been a beggar on earth, after death goes to dwell in "Abraham's bosom"; Luke xvi.19–26.
7. He has been identified as John Fenwick, editor of a newspaper, *Albion*.
8. Milton, *Paradise Regained* II.455–56.
9. Playing upon Revelation vi.2, "and he went forth conquering, and to conquer."
1. Tour.
2. One-tenth.

under contribution. I reject this estimate as greatly exaggerated—but having had the honor of accompanying my friend, divers times, in his perambulations about this vast city, I own I was greatly struck at first with the prodigious number of faces we met, who claimed a sort of respectful acquaintance with us. He was one day so obliging as to explain the phenomenon. It seems, these were his tributaries; feeders of his exchequer; gentlemen, his good friends (as he was pleased to express himself), to whom he had occasionally been beholden for a loan. Their multitudes did no way disconcert him. He rather took a pride in numbering them; and, with Comus, seemed pleased to be "stocked with so fair a herd." [3]

With such sources, it was a wonder how he contrived to keep his treasury always empty. He did it by force of an aphorism, which he had often in his mouth, that "money kept longer than three days stinks." So he made use of it while it was fresh. A good part he drank away (for he was an excellent tosspot), some he gave away, the rest he threw away, literally tossing and hurling it violently from him —as boys do burrs, or as if it had been infectious—into ponds, or ditches, or deep holes—inscrutable cavities of the earth; or he would bury it (where he would never seek it again) by a river's side under some bank, which (he would facetiously observe) paid no interest—but out away from him it must go peremptorily, as Hagar's offspring [4] into the wilderness, while it was sweet. He never missed it. The streams were perennial which fed his fisc. [5] When new supplies became necessary, the first person that had the felicity to fall in with him, friend or stranger, was sure to contribute to the deficiency. For Bigod had an *undeniable* way with him. He had a cheerful, open exterior, a quick jovial eye, a bald forehead, just touched with gray (*cana fides*). [6] He anticipated no excuse, and found none. And, waiving for a while my theory as to the *great race*, I would put it to the most untheorizing reader, who may at times have disposable coin in his pocket, whether it is not more repugnant to the kindliness of his nature to refuse such a one as I am describing, than to say *no* to a poor petitionary rogue (your bastard borrower), who, by his mumping visnomy [7] tells you, that he expects nothing better; and, therefore, whose preconceived notions and expectations you do in reality so much less shock in the refusal.

When I think of this man; his fiery glow of heart; his swell of feeling; how magnificent, how *ideal* he was; how great at the midnight hour; and when I compare with him the companions with whom I have associated since, I grudge the saving of a few idle ducats, and think that I am fallen into the society of *lenders*, and *little men*.

---

3. Adapted from Milton's *Comus* 152.
4. Ishmael, the son of Hagar, in Genesis xxi.9 ff.
5. Public treasury.

6. "Hoary trustworthiness," i.e., of his gray hair; the phrase is in Virgil's *Aeneid* I.292.
7. Dialect or "mumbling physiognomy."

To one like Elia, whose treasures are rather cased in leather covers than closed in iron coffers, there is a class of alienators [8] more formidable than that which I have touched upon; I mean your *borrowers of books*—those mutilators of collections, spoilers of the symmetry of shelves, and creators of odd volumes. There is Comberbatch,[9] matchless in his depredations!

That foul gap in the bottom shelf facing you, like a great eye-tooth knocked out—(you are now with me in my little back study in Bloomsbury, reader!)—with the huge Switzerlike [1] tomes on each side (like the Guildhall giants, in their reformed posture, guardant of nothing) once held the tallest of my folios, *Opera Bonaventurae*,[2] choice and massy divinity, to which its two supporters (school divinity also, but of a lesser caliber—Bellarmine, and Holy Thomas), showed but as dwarfs—itself an Ascapart! [3] *that* Comberbatch abstracted upon the faith of a theory he holds, which is more easy, I confess, for me to suffer by than to refute, namely, that "the title to property in a book (my Bonaventure, for instance), is in exact ratio to the claimant's powers of understanding and appreciating the same." Should he go on acting upon this theory, which of our shelves is safe?

The slight vacuum in the left-hand case—two shelves from the ceiling—scarcely distinguishable but by the quick eye of a loser—— was whilom the commodious resting place of Browne on Urn Burial. C. will hardly allege that he knows more about that treatise than I do, who introduced it to him, and was indeed the first (of the moderns) to discover its beauties—but so have I known a foolish lover to praise his mistress in the presence of a rival more qualified to carry her off than himself. Just below, Dodsley's dramas want their fourth volume, where Vittoria Corombona is! The remainder nine are as distasteful as Priam's refuse sons, when the Fates *borrowed* Hector. [4] Here stood the Anatomy of Melancholy, in sober state. There loitered the Complete Angler; quiet as in life, by some stream side. In yonder nook, John Buncle, a widower-volume, with "eyes closed," mourns his ravished mate.[5]

8. Those who alienate property—i.e., transfer it to another.
9. Coleridge had left college for a brief and disastrous career as a cavalryman in the Light Dragoons, under the alias of Silas Tomkyn Comberbacke.
1. "Switzers" are Swiss guardsmen, selected for their imposing stature.
2. The theological *Works* of St. Bonaventure (1221–74); the "supporters" are St. Robert Bellarmine (1542–1621) and St. Thomas Aquinas (ca. 1225–74).
3. A giant, in the 14th-century verse romance, *Bevis of Hampton*.
4. I.e., the remaining nine volumes of Dodsley's *Collection* are rated as low by the lender as (in Homer's *Iliad*) Priam's nine remaining sons were rated by the Trojan king, after his greatest son, Hector, had been killed in battle.
5. The books in this paragraph: Sir Thomas Browne, *Hydriotaphia, or Urn Burial* (1658); Robert Dodsley's *Select Collection of Old Plays* (1744); John Webster's tragedy, *The White Devil, or Vittoria Corombona* (ca. 1608); Robert Burton, *The Anatomy of Melancholy* (1621); Izaak Walton, *The Compleat Angler* (1653); Thomas Amory, *John Buncle, Esq.* (1756–66)—a novel about a man who successively married seven wives, each of whom died within a few years.

One justice I must do my friend, that if he sometimes, like the sea, sweeps away a treasure, at another time, sealike, he throws up as rich an equivalent to match it. I have a small under-collection of this nature (my friend's gatherings in his various calls), picked up, he has forgotten at what odd places, and deposited with as little memory as mine. I take in these orphans, the twice-deserted. These proselytes of the gate are welcome as the true Hebrews. There they stand in conjunction; natives, and naturalized. The latter seem as little disposed to inquire out their true lineage as I am. I charge no warehouse-room for these deodands,[6] nor shall ever put myself to the ungentlemanly trouble of advertising a sale of them to pay expenses.

To lose a volume to C. carries some sense and meaning in it. You are sure that he will make one hearty meal on your viands, if he can give no account of the platter after it. But what moved thee, wayward, spiteful K,[7] to be so importunate to carry off with thee, in spite of tears and adjurations to thee to forbear, the Letters of that princely woman, the thrice noble Margaret Newcastle?—knowing at the time, and knowing that I knew also, thou most assuredly wouldst never turn over one leaf of the illustrious folio what but the mere spirit of contradiction, and childish love of getting the better of thy friend? Then, worst cut of all! to transport it with thee to the Gallican land—

Unworthy land to harbor such a sweetness,
A virtue in which all ennobling thoughts dwelt,
Pure thoughts, kind thoughts, high thoughts, her sex's wonder![8]

——hadst thou not thy playbooks, and books of jests and fancies, about thee, to keep thee merry, even as thou keepest all companies with thy quips and mirthful tales? Child of the Greenroom,[9] it was unkindly done of thee. Thy wife, too, that part-French, better-part Englishwoman!—that *she* could fix upon no other treatise to bear away, in kindly token of remembering us, than the works of Fulke Greville, Lord Brook [10]—of which no Frenchman, nor woman of France, Italy, or England, was ever by nature constituted to comprehend a tittle! *Was there not Zimmerman on Solitude?*

Reader, if haply thou art blessed with a moderate collection, be shy of showing it; or if thy heart overfloweth to lend them, lend thy books; but let it be to such a one as S. T. C.—he will return them (generally anticipating the time appointed) with usury; enriched with annotations, tripling their value. I have had experience. Many

6. In English law, objects that are forfeited to the crown (because they have caused a human death).
7. James Kenney (1780–1849), an actor, who has borrowed and taken to France the *Sociable Letters* (1664) of Margaret Cavendish, Duchess of Newcastle.
8. Possibly composed by Lamb himself.
9. The room where actors await their cues.
10. Sir Fulke Greville, Baron Brooke (1554–1628). J. G. von Zimmerman's *Solitude* was translated into English about 1791.

are these precious MSS. of his (in *matter* oftentimes, and almost in *quantity* not unfrequently, vying with the originals) in no very clerkly hand—legible in my Daniel; [11] in old Burton; in Sir Thomas Browne; and those abstruser cogitations of the Greville, now, alas! wandering in Pagan lands. I counsel thee, shut not thy heart, nor thy library, against S. T. C.

1820, 1823

New Year's Eve

Every man hath two birthdays: two days, at least, in every year, which set him upon revolving the lapse of time, as it affects his mortal duration. The one is that which in an especial manner he termeth *his*. In the gradual desuetude of old observances, this custom of solemnizing our proper birthday hath nearly passed away, or is left to children, who reflect nothing at all about the matter, nor understand anything in it beyond cake and orange. But the birth of a New Year is of an interest too wide to be pretermitted by king or cobbler. No one ever regarded the first of January with indifference. It is that from which all date their time, and count upon what is left. It is the nativity of our common Adam.

Of all sound of all bells—bells, the music nighest bordering upon heaven—most solemn and touching is the peal which rings out the Old Year. I never hear it without a gathering-up of my mind to a concentration of all the images that have been diffused over the past twelvemonth; all I have done or suffered, performed or neglected—in that regretted time. I begin to know its worth, as when a person dies. It takes a personal color; nor was it a poetical flight in a contemporary, when he exclaimed,

I saw the skirts of the departing Year.[1]

It is no more than what in sober sadness every one of us seems to be conscious of, in that awful leave-taking. I am sure I felt it, and all felt it with me, last night; though some of my companions affected rather to manifest an exhilaration at the birth of the coming year, than any very tender regrets for the decease of its predecessor. But I am none of those who

Welcome the coming, speed the parting guest.[2]

I am naturally, beforehand, shy of novelties; new books, new faces, new years—from some mental twist which makes it difficult in me to face the prospective. I have almost ceased to hope; and am sanguine only in the prospects of other (former) years. I plunge

11. Samuel Daniel, the poet (1562–1619).
1. Coleridge, *Ode to the Departing Year*, line 8, in the version of 1797.
2. This line occurs in Alexander Pope's translation of the *Odyssey* XV.84, and again in his imitation of Horace's *Satires* (II.ii.160).

into foregone visions and conclusions. I encounter pell-mell with
past disappointments. I am armor-proof against old discourage-
ments. I forgive, or overcome in fancy, old adversaries. I play over
again *for love*, as the gamesters phrase it, games, for which I once
paid so dear. I would scarce now have any of those untoward accidents and events of my life reversed. I would no more alter them
than the incidents of some well-contrived novel. Methinks it is
better that I should have pined away seven of my goldenest years,
when I was thrall to the fair hair and fairer eyes of Alice W——n,[3]
than that so passionate a love adventure should be lost. It was
better that our family should have missed that legacy, which old
Dorrell cheated us of, than that I should have at this moment
two thousand pounds *in banco*, and be without the idea of that
specious old rogue.

In a degree beneath manhood, it is my infirmity to look back
upon those early days. Do I advance a paradox, when I say that,
skipping over the intervention of forty years, a man may have leave
to love *himself*, without the imputation of self-love?

If I know aught of myself, no one whose mind is introspective—
and mine is painfully so—can have a less respect for his present
identity than I have for the man Elia. I know him to be light, and
vain, and humorsome; a notorious ——; addicted to ——;
averse from counsel, neither taking it nor offering it; —— besides; a stammering buffoon; what you will; lay it on, and spare
not; I subscribe to it all, and much more, than thou canst be willing to lay at his door—but for the child Elia, that "other me,"
there, in the background—I must take leave to cherish the remembrance of that young master—with as little reference, I protest, to this stupid changeling of five-and-forty, as if it had been
a child of some other house, and not of my parents. I can cry over
its patient smallpox at five, and rougher medicaments. I can lay
its poor fevered head upon the sick pillow at Christ's,[4] and wake
with it in surprise at the gentle posture of maternal tenderness
hanging over it, that unknown had watched its sleep. I know how
it shrank from any the least color of falsehood.—God help thee,
Elia, how art thou changed! Thou art sophisticated.—I know how
honest, how courageous (for a weakling) it was—how religious,
how imaginative, how hopeful! From what have I not fallen, if
the child I remember was indeed myself—and not some dissem-
bling guardian, presenting a false identity, to give the rule to my
unpracticed steps, and regulate the tone of my moral being!

That I am fond of indulging, beyond a hope of sympathy, in such
retrospection may be the symptom of some sickly idiosyncrasy. Or
is it owing to another cause; simply, that being without wife or fam-

3. Elia's Alice Winterton; she may be
the Anne Simmons with whom Lamb
had been in love when a youth.

4. Christ's Hospital school, which
Lamb had attended.

ily, I have not learned to project myself enough out of myself; and
having no offspring of my own to dally with, I turn back upon
memory, and adopt my own early idea, as my heir and favorite?
If these speculations seem fantastical to thee, reader (a busy man
perchance), if I tread out of the way of thy sympathy, and am
singularly-conceited only, I retire, impenetrable to ridicule, under
the phantom cloud of Elia.

The elders, with whom I was brought up, were of a character
not likely to let slip the sacred observance of any old institution;
and the ringing out of the Old Year was kept by them with circumstances of peculiar ceremony.—In those days the sound of
those midnight chimes, though it seemed to raise hilarity in all
around me, never failed to bring a train of pensive imagery into
my fancy. Yet I then scarce conceived what it meant, or thought
of it as a reckoning that concerned me. Not childhood alone, but
the young man till thirty, never feels practically that he is mortal.
He knows it indeed, and, if need were, he could preach a homily
on the fragility of life; but he brings it not home to himself, any
more than in a hot June we can appropriate to our imagination the
freezing days of December. But now, shall I confess a truth?—I
feel these audits but too powerfully. I begin to count the probabilities of my duration, and to grudge at the expenditure of moments and shortest periods, like misers' farthings. In proportion
as the years both lessen and shorten, I set more count upon their
periods, and would fain lay my ineffectual finger upon the spoke
of the great wheel. I am not content to pass away "like a weaver's
shuttle."[5] Those metaphors solace me not, nor sweeten the un-
palatable draught of mortality. I care not to be carried with the
tide that smoothly bears human life to eternity; and reluct at the
inevitable course of destiny. I am in love with this green earth;
the face of town and country; the unspeakable rural solitudes, and
the sweet security of streets. I would set up my tabernacle here.
I am content to stand still at the age to which I am arrived; I, and
my friends: to be no younger, no richer, no handsomer. I do not
want to be weaned by age; or drop, like mellow fruit, as they say,
into the grave.—Any alteration, on this earth of mine, in diet or
in lodging, puzzles and discomposes me. My household gods plant
a terrible fixed foot, and are not rooted up without blood. They
do not willingly seek Lavinian shores.[6] A new state of being stag-
gers me.

Sun, and sky, and breeze, and solitary walks, and summer holidays, and the greenness of fields, and the delicious juices of meats
and fishes, and society, and the cheerful glass, and candlelight, and
fireside conversations, and innocent vanities, and jests, and *irony*

5. Altered from Job vii.6.
6. Italy, so called in the *Aeneid* because
Aeneas, after his wanderings, married
Lavinia there and founded the Roman
race. Since Aeneas transported his
"household gods" with him from Troy
to Italy, Lamb's allusion simply means
that he is disinclined to wander.

itself—do these things go out with life?

Can a ghost laugh, or shake his gaunt sides, when you are pleasant with him?

And you, my midnight darlings, my Folios![7] must I part with the intense delight of having you (huge armfuls) in my embraces? Must knowledge come to me, if it come at all, by some awkward experiment of intuition, and no longer by this familiar process of reading?

Shall I enjoy friendships there, wanting the smiling indications which point me to them here—the recognizable face—the "sweet assurance of a look"?[8]

In winter this intolerable disinclination to dying—to give it its mildest name—does more especially haunt and beset me. In a genial August noon, beneath a sweltering sky, death is almost problematic. At those times do such poor snakes as myself enjoy an immortality. Then we expand and burgeon. Then are we as strong again, as valiant again, as wise again, and a great deal taller. The blast that nips and shrinks me, puts me in thoughts of death. All things allied to the insubstantial wait upon that master feeling: cold, numbness, dreams, perplexity; moonlight itself, with its shadowy and spectral appearances—that cold ghost of the sun, or Phoebus' sickly sister, like that innutritious one denounced in the Canticles.[9]—I am none of her minions—I hold with the Persian.[1]

Whatsoever thwarts, or puts me out of my way, brings death into my mind. All partial evils, like humors, run into that capital plague sore.—I have heard some profess an indifference to life. Such hail the end of their existence as a port of refuge; and speak of the grave as of some soft arms, in which they may slumber as on a pillow. Some have wooed death—but out upon thee, I say, thou foul, ugly phantom! I detest, abhor, execrate, and (with Friar John[2]) give thee to six-score thousand devils, as in no instance to be excused or tolerated, but shunned as an universal viper; to be branded, proscribed, and spoken evil of! In no way can I be brought to digest thee, thou thin, melancholy *Privation*, or more frightful and confounding *Positive!*[3]

Those antidotes, prescribed against the fear of thee, are altogether frigid and insulting, like thyself. For what satisfaction hath a man, that he shall "lie down with kings and emperors in death,"[4] who in his lifetime never greatly coveted the society of such bedfellows?—or, forsooth, that "so shall the fairest face appear"?[5]—

7. The large volumes in which the older English writers were often printed.
8. Altered from Matthew Roydon's elegy on Sir Philip Sidney.
9. The Song of Solomon viii.8: "We have a little sister, and she hath no breasts." Elia's allusion is to the moon, described as the weaker sister of Phoebus, the sun.
1. The ancient Persians were sun-worshipers.

2. A bellicose character in Rabelais's *Gargantua*.
3. I.e., death as the absence of existence or, more terrifying still, an actual being.
4. Job iii.13–14: "Then had I been at rest, with kings and counselors of the earth."
5. Line 9 of *William and Margaret*, a ballad-imitation written in 1724 by David Mallet.

why, to comfort me, must Alice W——n be a goblin? More than all, I conceive disgust at those impertinent and misbecoming familiarities inscribed upon your ordinary tombstones. Every dead man must take upon himself to be lecturing me with his odious truism that "such as he now is, I must shortly be." Not so shortly, friend, perhaps as thou imaginest. In the meantime I am alive. I move about. I am worth twenty of thee. Know thy betters! Thy New Years' days are past. I survive, a jolly candidate for 1821. Another cup of wine—and while that turncoat bell, that just now mournfully chanted the obsequies of 1820 departed, with changed notes lustily rings in a successor, let us attune to its peal the song made on a like occasion, by hearty, cheerful Mr. Cotton.[6]—

The New Year

Hark, the cock crows, and yon bright star
Tells us the day himself's not far;
And see where, breaking from the night,
He gilds the western hills with light.
With him old Janus doth appear,
Peeping into the future year,
With such a look as seems to say,
The prospect is not good that way.
Thus do we rise ill sights to see,
And 'gainst ourselves to prophesy;
When the prophetic fear of things
A more tormenting mischief brings,
More full of soul-tormenting gall,
Than direst mischiefs can befall.
But stay! but stay! methinks my sight,
Better informed by clearer light,
Discerns sereneness in that brow,
That all contracted seemed but now.
His reversed face may show distaste,
And frown upon the ills are past;
But that which this way looks is clear,
And smiles upon the Newborn Year.
He looks too from a place so high,
The year lies open to his eye;
And all the moments open are
To the exact discoverer.
Yet more and more he smiles upon
The happy revolution.
Why should we then suspect or fear
The influences of a year,
So smiles upon us the first morn,
And speaks us good so soon as born?
Plague on't! the last was ill enough,
This cannot but make better proof;
Or, at the worst, as we brushed through

6. Charles Cotton, a genial poet of the mid-17th century.

The last, why so we may this too;
And then the next in reason should
Be superexcellently good:
For the worst ills (we daily see)
Have no more perpetuity
Than the best fortunes that do fall;
Which also bring us wherewithal
Longer their being to support,
Than those do of the other sort:
And who has one good year in three,
And yet repines at destiny,
Appears ungrateful in the case,
And merits not the good he has.
Then let us welcome the New Guest
With lusty brimmers of the best;
Mirth always should Good Fortune meet,
And renders e'en Disaster sweet:
And though the Princess turn her back,
Let us but line ourselves with sack,[7]
We better shall by far hold out,
Till the next Year she face about.

How say you, reader—do not these verses smack of the rough magnanimity of the old English vein? Do they not fortify like a cordial; enlarging the heart, and productive of sweet blood, and generous spirits, in the concoction? Where be those puling fears of death, just now expressed or affected?—Passed like a cloud—absorbed in the purging sunlight of clear poetry—clean washed away by a wave of genuine Helicon,[8] your only spa for these hypochondries—And now another cup of the generous! and a merry New Year, and many of them to you all, my masters!

1821

From On the Artificial Comedy of the Last Century[1]

The Artificial Comedy, or Comedy of Manners, is quite extinct on our stage. Congreve and Farquhar[2] show their heads once in

7. A former name for sherry and other strong white wines from Spain and the Canary Islands.
8. A mountain on which flowed springs sacred to the Muses. A "spa" is a mineral spring, here thought of as curing morbid depression ("hypochondries").
1. This essay, a defense of the moral man's privilege to enjoy the gay immoralties of Restoration comedy, has been the occasion of much discussion and controversy. Thomas Babington Macaulay, for instance, said that Lamb was mistaken because comedy is (in the terms of neoclassic criticism) "an imitation, under whatever conventions, of real life," and therefore subject to ordinary moral criteria. Lamb overstated

his case in implying that the profligate society in Restoration plays had no counterpart in reality, but his central theoretical claim has become an important premise in modern criticism. He proposes that the "artificial comedies" are unlike realistic drama in that they do not imitate the real world, but create "a world of themselves"; the spectator, taking a kind of moral holiday, adapts himself to the conditions of this artificial world and enjoys its characters and events by a suspension of his ordinary sensibilities.
2. George Farquhar (1678–1707), author of a number of comedies; the best known is *The Beaux' Stratagem.*

seven years only; to be exploded and put down instantly. The times cannot bear them. Is it for a few wild speeches, an occasional license or dialogue? I think not altogether. The business of their dramatic characters will not stand the moral test. We screw everything up to that. Idle gallantry in a fiction, a dream, the passing pageant of an evening, startles us in the same way as the alarming indications of profligacy in a son or ward in real life should startle a parent or guardian. We have no such middle emotions as dramatic interests left. We see a stage libertine playing his loose pranks of two hours' duration, and of no after consequence, with the severe eyes which inspect real vices with their bearings upon two worlds. We are spectators to a plot or intrigue (not reducible in life to the point of strict morality), and take it all for truth. We substitute a real for a dramatic person, and judge him accordingly. We try him in our courts, from which there is no appeal to the *dramatis personae*, his peers. We have been spoiled with—not sentimental comedy—but a tyrant far more pernicious to our pleasures which has succeeded to it, the exclusive and all-devouring drama of common life; where the moral point is everything; where, instead of the fictitious half-believed personages of the stage (the phantoms of old comedy), we recognize ourselves, our brothers, aunts, kinsfolk, allies, patrons, enemies—the same as in life—with an interest in what is going on so hearty and substantial, that we cannot afford our moral judgment, in its deepest and most vital results, to compromise or slumber for a moment. What is *there* transacting by no modification is made to affect us in any other manner than the same events or characters would do in our relationships of life. We carry our fireside concerns to the theater with us. We do not go thither, like our ancestors, to escape from the pressure of reality, so much as to confirm our experience of it; to make assurance double, and take a bond of fate. We must live our toilsome lives twice over, as it was the mournful privilege of Ulysses to descend twice to the shades.[3] All that neutral ground of character, which stood between vice and virtue; or which in fact was indifferent to neither, where neither properly was called in question; that happy breathing-place from the burthen of a perpetual moral questioning—the sanctuary and quiet Alsatia of hunted casuistry[4]—is broken up and disfranchised, as injurious to the interests of society. The privileges of the place are taken away by law. We dare not dally with images, or names, of wrong. We bark like foolish dogs at shadows. We dread infection from the scenic representation of disorder, and fear a painted pustule. In our anxiety that our morality should not take cold, we wrap it up in a great

3. In Homer's *Odyssey*, Ulysses visited Hades to interview the shade of the blind soothsayer, Tiresias. He descended a second time, of course, at his death.
4. "Alsatia" was a district near Whitefriars which, until 1697, served as a legal sanctuary for debtors. Lamb's point is that the comedy of manners offers a sanctuary for man, eternally harried by "casuistry" (logical consideration of the problems of right and wrong).

blanket surtout[5] of precaution against the breeze and sunshine.

I confess for myself that (with no great delinquencies to answer for) I am glad for a season to take an airing beyond the diocese of the strict conscience—not to live always in the precincts of the law courts—but now and then, for a dream-while or so, to imagine a world with no meddling restrictions—to get into recesses, whither the hunter cannot follow me—

> secret shades
> Of woody Ida's inmost grove,
> While yet there was no fear of Jove.[6]

I come back to my cage and my restraint the fresher and more healthy for it. I wear my shackles more contentedly for having respired the breath of an imaginary freedom. I do not know how it is with others, but I feel the better always for the perusal of one of Congreve's—nay, why should I not add even of Wycherley's[7]—comedies. I am the gayer at least for it; and I could never connect those sports of a witty fancy in any shape with any result to be drawn from them to imitation in real life. They are a world of themselves almost as much as fairyland. Take one of their characters, male or female (with few exceptions they are alike), and place it in a modern play, and my virtuous indignation shall rise against the profligate wretch as warmly as the Catos of the pit[8] could desire; because in a modern play I am to judge of the right and the wrong. The standard of *police* is the measure of *political justice*. The atmosphere will blight it; it cannot live here. It has got into a moral world, where it has no business, from which it must needs fall headlong; as dizzy, and incapable of making a stand, as a Swedenborgian bad spirit that has wandered unawares into the sphere of one of his Good Men, or Angels.[9] But in its own world do we feel the creature is so very bad?—The Fainalls and the Mirabells, the Dorimants and the Lady Touchwoods,[1] in their own sphere, do not offend my moral sense; in fact they do not appeal to it at all. They seem engaged in their proper element. They break through no laws, or conscientious restraints. They know of none. They have got out of Christendom into the land—what shall I call it?—of cuckoldry—the Utopia of gallantry, where pleasure is duty, and the manners perfect freedom. It is altogether

5. Long and heavy overcoat.
6. Milton, *Il Penseroso*, lines 28–30. Ida is a mountain in Crete where Jove was said to have been born.
7. William Wycherley (1640–1716), whose comedies (e.g., *The Country Wife*) were considered profligate even by Restoration standards.
8. Cato (234–149 B.C.) was noted for his opposition to the luxury and decadence of Rome. The "pit," in an English theater, is that part of the auditorium which is on the main floor, below the stage.
9. Emanuel Swedenborg, the 18th-century Swedish scientist and mystic, held that there are several heavens and hells, peopled by corresponding good and evil spirits.
1. Characters in Restoration comedies: Fainall and Mirabell in Congreve's *Way of the World*, Dorimant in Etherege's *Man of Mode*, and Lady Touchwood in Congreve's *Double-Dealer*.

a speculative scene of things, which has no reference whatever to the world that is. No good person can be justly offended as a specta-tor, because no good person suffers on the stage. Judged morally, every character in these plays—the few exceptions only are *mis-takes*—is alike essentially vain and worthless. The great art of Con-greve is especially shown in this, that he has entirely excluded from his scenes—some little generosities in the part of Angelica[2] perhaps excepted—not only anything like a faultless character, but any pre-tensions to goodness or good feelings whatsoever. Whether he did this designedly, or instinctively, the effect is as happy, as the design (if design) was bold. I used to wonder at the strange power which his *Way of the World* in particular possesses of interesting you all along in the pursuits of characters, for whom you absolutely care nothing—for you neither hate nor love his personages—and I think it is owing to this very indifference for any that you endure the whole. He has spread a privation of moral light, I will call it, rather than by the ugly name of palpable darkness, over his creations; and his shadows flit before you without distinction or preference. Had he introduced a good character, a single gush of moral feeling, a revulsion of the judgment to actual life and actual duties, the im-pertinent Goshen[3] would have only lighted to the discovery of de-formities, which now are none, because we think them none.

Translated into real life, the characters of his and his friend Wycherley's dramas are profligates and strumpets—the business of their brief existence, the undivided pursuit of lawless gallantry. No other spring of action, or possible motive of conduct, is recognized; principles which, universally acted upon, must reduce this frame of things to a chaos. But we do them wrong in so translating them. No such effects are produced, in *their* world. When we are among them, we are amongst a chaotic people. We are not to judge them by our usages. No reverend institutions are insulted by their proceedings—for they have none among them. No peace of families is violated—for no family ties exist among them. No purity of the marriage bed is stained—for none is supposed to have a being. No deep affec-tions are disquieted, no holy wedlock bands are snapped asunder—for affection's depth and wedded faith are not of the growth of that soil. There is neither right nor wrong—gratitude or its oppo-site—claim or duty—paternity or sonship. Of what consequence is it to Virtue, or how is she at all concerned about it, whether Sir Simon or Dapperwit steal away Miss Martha; or who is the father of Lord Froth's or Sir Paul Pliant's children?[4]

The whole is a passing pageant, where we should sit as uncon-

2. In Congreve's *Love for Love.*
3. In Exodus viii.22, the place the Jews dwelt, immune from the swarms of flies with which the Lord plagued the Egyp-tians.
4. Sir Simon, Dapperwit, and Martha are in Wycherley's *Love in a Wood;* Lord Froth and Sir Paul in Congreve's *Double-Dealer.*

cerned at the issues, for life or death, as at a battle of the frogs and mice. But, like Don Quixote, we take part against the puppets, and quite as impertinently. We dare not contemplate an Atlantis,[5] a scheme out of which our coxcombical moral sense is for a little transitory ease excluded. We have not the courage to imagine a state of things for which there is neither reward nor punishment. We cling to the painful necessities of shame and blame. We would indict our very dreams.

Amidst the mortifying circumstances attendant upon growing old, it is something to have seen the *School for Scandal* in its glory. This comedy grew out of Congreve and Wycherley, but gathered some allays of the sentimental comedy which followed theirs. It is impossible that it should be now *acted*, though it continues, at long intervals, to be announced in the bills. Its hero, when Palmer[6] played it at least, was Joseph Surface. When I remember the gay boldness, the graceful solemn plausibility, the measured step, the insinuating voice—to express it in a word—the downright *acted* villainy of the part, so different from the pressure of conscious actual wickedness—the hypocritical assumption of hypocrisy—which made Jack so deservedly a favorite in that character, I must needs conclude the present generation of playgoers more virtuous than myself, or more dense. I freely confess that he divided the palm with me with his better brother; that, in fact, I liked him quite as well. Not but there are passages—like that, for instance, where Joseph is made to refuse a pittance to a poor relation— incongruities which Sheridan was forced upon by the attempt to join the artificial with the sentimental comedy, either of which must destroy the other—but over these obstructions Jack's manner floated him so lightly that a refusal from him no more shocked you than the easy compliance of Charles gave you in reality any pleasure; you got over the paltry question as quickly as you could, to get back into the regions of pure comedy, where no cold moral reigns. The highly artificial manner of Palmer in this character counteracted every disagreeable impression which you might have received from the contrast, supposing them real, between the two brothers. You did not believe in Joseph with the same faith with which you believed in Charles. The latter was a pleasant reality, the former a no less pleasant poetical foil to it. The comedy, I have said, is incongruous; a mixture of Congreve with sentimental incompatibilities; the gaiety upon the whole is buoyant; but it required the consummate art of Palmer to reconcile the discordant elements.[7] * * *

1822

5. A mythical island in the western ocean which is supposed to have sunk beneath the sea.
6. Jack Palmer, famous comic actor of the late 18th century, especially noted for his playing of Joseph Surface.
7. The remainder of the essay is a critique of some of the actors who had appeared in the old comedies of manners.

Old China

I have an almost feminine partiality for old china. When I go to see any great house, I inquire for the china closet, and next for the picture gallery. I cannot defend the order of preference, but by saying that we have all some taste or other, of too ancient a date to admit of our remembering distinctly that it was an acquired one. I can call to mind the first play, and the first exhibition, that I was taken to; but I am not conscious of a time when china jars and saucers were introduced into my imagination.

I had no repugnance then—why should I now have?—to those little, lawless, azure-tinctured grotesques, that under the notion of men and women float about, uncircumscribed by any element, in that world before perspective—a china teacup.

I like to see my old friends—whom distance cannot diminish—figuring up in the air (so they appear to our optics), yet on terra firma still—for so we must in courtesy interpret that speck of deeper blue, which the decorous artist, to present absurdity, had made to spring up beneath their sandals.

I love the men with women's faces, and the women, if possible, with still more womanish expressions.

Here is a young and courtly mandarin, handing tea to a lady from a salver—two miles off. See how distance seems to set off respect! And here the same lady, or another—for likeness is identity on teacups—is stepping into a little fairy boat, moored on the hither side of this calm garden river, with a dainty mincing foot, which in a right angle of incidence (as angles go in our world) must infallibly land her in the midst of a flowery mead—a furlong off on the other side of the same strange stream!

Farther on—if far or near can be predicated of their world—see horses, trees, pagodas, dancing the hays.[1]

Here—a cow and rabbit couchant,[2] and coextensive—so objects show, seen through the lucid atmosphere of fine Cathay.[3]

I was pointing out to my cousin last evening, over our Hyson[4] (which we are old-fashioned enough to drink unmixed still of an afternoon), some of these *speciosa miracula*[5] upon a set of extraordinary old blue china (a recent purchase) which we were now for the first time using; and could not help remarking how favorable circumstances had been to us of late years that we could afford to please the eye sometimes with trifles of this sort—when a passing

---

1. An English country dance with a serpentining movement.
2. Heraldic term: lying down with the head raised.
3. The old European name for China.
4. A Chinese green-tea.
5. "Shining wonders."

sentiment seemed to overshade the brows of my companion. I am quick at detecting these summer clouds in Bridget.[6]

"I wish the good old times would come again," she said, "when we were not quite so rich. I do not mean that I want to be poor; but there was a middle state"—so she was pleased to ramble on— "in which I am sure we were a great deal happier. A purchase is but a purchase, now that you have money enough and to spare. Formerly it used to be a triumph. When we coveted a cheap luxury (and, O! how much ado I had to get you to consent in those times!)—we were used to have a debate two or three days before, and to weigh the *for* and *against*, and think what we might spare it out of, and what saving we could hit upon, that should be an equivalent. A thing was worth buying then, when we felt the money that we paid for it.

"Do you remember the brown suit, which you made to hang upon you, till all your friends cried shame upon you, it grew so threadbare—and all because of that folio Beaumont and Fletcher,[7] which you dragged home late at night from Barker's in Covent Garden? Do you remember how we eyed it for weeks before we could make up our minds to the purchase, and had not come to a determination till it was near ten o'clock of the Saturday night, when you set off from Islington,[8] fearing you should be too late—and when the old bookseller with some grumbling opened his shop, and by the twinkling taper (for he was setting bedwards) lighted out the relic from his dusty treasures—and when you lugged it home, wishing it were twice as cumbersome—and when you presented it to me—and when we were exploring the perfectness of it (*collating*, you called it)—and while I was repairing some of the loose leaves with paste, which your impatience would not suffer to be left till daybreak—was there no pleasure in being a poor man? or can those neat black clothes which you wear now, and are so careful to keep brushed, since we have become rich and finical, give you half the honest vanity with which you flaunted it about in that overworn suit—your old corbeau[9]—for four or five weeks longer than you should have done, to pacify your conscience for the mighty sum of fifteen—or sixteen shillings was it?—a great affair we thought it then—which you had lavished on the old folio. Now you can afford to buy any book that pleases you, but I do not see that you ever bring me home any nice old purchases now.

"When you came home with twenty apologies for laying out a less number of shillings upon that print after Leonardo,[1] which we

6. In Lamb's essays, his name for his sister, Mary.
7. The Elizabethan dramatic collaborators, whose plays were first collected in a large folio volume in 1647.
8. In the north of London, where the Lambs had been living.

9. A dark green cloth, almost black (hence its name, the French for "raven").
1. Leonardo da Vinci (1452–1519), the great Italian painter. The painting is the one known as "Modesty and Vanity."

christened the 'Lady Blanch'; when you looked at the purchase, and thought of the money—and thought of the money, and looked again at the picture—was there no pleasure in being a poor man? Now, you have nothing to do but to walk into Colnaghi's, and buy a wilderness of Leonardos. Yet do you?

"Then, do you remember our pleasant walks to Enfield, and Potter's Bar, and Waltham,[2] when we had a holiday—holidays, and all other fun, are gone now we are rich—and the little hand-basket in which I used to deposit our day's fare of savory cold lamb and salad —and how you would pry about at noontide for some decent house, where we might go in and produce our store—only paying for the ale that you must call for—and speculate upon the looks of the landlady, and whether she was likely to allow us a tablecloth— and wish for such another honest hostess as Izaak Walton has described many a one on the pleasant banks of the Lea, when he went a-fishing—and sometimes they would prove obliging enough, and sometimes they would look grudgingly upon us—but we had cheerful looks still for one another, and would eat our plain food savorily, scarcely grudging Piscator[3] his Trout Hall? Now—when we go out a day's pleasuring, which is seldom, moreover, we *ride* part of the way—and go into a fine inn, and order the best of dinners, never debating the expense—which, after all, never has half the relish of those chance country snaps,[3a] when we were at the mercy of uncertain usage, and a precarious welcome.

"You are too proud to see a play anywhere now but in the pit. Do you remember where it was we used to sit, when we saw the *Battle of Hexham*, and the *Surrender of Calais*,[4] and Bannister and Mrs. Bland in the *Children in the Wood*[5]—when we squeezed out our shillings apiece to sit three or four times in a season in the one-shilling gallery—where you felt all the time that you ought not to have brought me—and more strongly I felt obligation to you for having brought me—and the pleasure was the better for a little shame—and when the curtain drew up, what cared we for our place in the house, or what mattered it where we were sitting, when our thoughts were with Rosalind in Arden, or with Viola at the Court of Illyria.[6] You used to say that the gallery was the best place of all for enjoying a play socially—that the relish of such exhibitions must be in proportion to the infrequency of going—that the company we met there, not being in general readers of plays, were obliged to attend the more, and did attend, to what was going on, on the stage—because a word lost would have been a chasm, which it was impossible for them to fill up. With such reflections we

---

2. All three are suburbs to the north of London.
3. The fisherman in Izaak Walton's *Complete Angler* (1653).
3a. Snacks.

4. Comedies by George Colman (1762–1836).
5. By Thomas Morton (1764–1838).
6. Rosalind in *As You Like It* and Viola in *Twelfth Night*.

consoled our pride then—and I appeal to you whether, as a woman, I met generally with less attention and accommodation than I have done since in more expensive situations in the house? The getting in indeed, and the crowding up those inconvenient stair-cases, was bad enough—but there was still a law of civility to woman recognized to quite as great an extent as we ever found in the other passages—and how a little difficulty overcome heightened the snug seat and the play, afterwards! Now we can only pay our money and walk in. You cannot see, you say, in the galleries now. I am sure we saw, and heard too, well enough then—but sight, and all, I think, is gone with our poverty.

"There was pleasure in eating strawberries, before they became quite common—in the first dish of peas, while they were yet dear—to have them for a nice supper, a treat. What treat can we have now? If we were to treat ourselves now—that is, to have dainties a little above our means, it would be selfish and wicked. It is the very little more that we allow ourselves beyond what the actual poor can get at that makes what I call a treat—when two people living to-gether, as we have done, now and then indulge themselves in a cheap luxury, which both like; while each apologizes, and is willing to take both halves of the blame to his single share. I see no harm in people making much of themselves, in that sense of the word. It may give them a hint how to make much of others. But now—what I mean by the word—we never do make much of ourselves. None but the poor can do it. I do not mean the veriest poor of all, but persons as we were, just above poverty.

"I know what you were going to say, that it is mighty pleasant at the end of the year to make all meet—and much ado we used to have every Thirty-first Night of December to account for our ex-ceedings—many a long face did you make over your puzzled ac-counts, and in contriving to make it out how we had spent so much—or that we had not spent so much—or that it was im-possible we should spend so much next year—and still we found our slender capital decreasing—but then, betwixt ways, and projects, and compromises of one sort or another, and talk of curtailing this charge, and doing without that for the future—and the hope that youth brings, and laughing spirits (in which you were never poor till now), we pocketed up our loss, and in conclusion, with 'lusty brimmers' (as you used to quote it out of *hearty cheerful Mr. Cotton*,[7] as you called him), we used to welcome in 'the coming guest.' Now we have no reckoning at all at the end of the old year—no flat-tering promises about the new year doing better for us."

Bridget is so sparing of her speech on most occasions that when she gets into a rhetorical vein, I am careful how I interrupt it. I

---

7. Charles Cotton, the 17th-century poet, a favorite of Lamb's; the quotations are from his poem *The New Year*.

could not help, however, smiling at the phantom of wealth which her dear imagination had conjured up out of a clear income of poor ——— hundred pounds a year. "It is true we were happier when we were poorer, but we were also younger, my cousin. I am afraid we must put up with the excess, for if we were to shake the superflux into the sea, we should not much mend ourselves. That we had much to struggle with, as we grew up together, we have reason to be most thankful. It strengthened and knit our compact closer. We could never have been what we have been to each other, if we had always had the sufficiency which you now complain of. The resisting power—those natural dilations of the youthful spirit, which circumstances cannot straiten—with us are long since passed away. Competence to age is supplementary youth, a sorry supplement indeed, but I fear the best that is to be had. We must ride where we formerly walked: live better and lie softer—and shall be wise to do so—than we had means to do in those good old days you speak of. Yet could those days return—could you and I once more walk our thirty miles a day—could Bannister and Mrs. Bland again be young, and you and I be young to see them—could the good old one-shilling gallery days return—they are dreams, my cousin, now—but could you and I at this moment, instead of this quiet argument, by our well-carpeted fireside, sitting on this luxurious sofa—be once more struggling up those inconvenient staircases, pushed about, and squeezed, and elbowed by the poorest rabble of poor gallery scramblers—could I once more hear those anxious shrieks of yours—and the delicious *Thank God, we are safe,* which always followed when the topmost stair, conquered, let in the first light of the whole cheerful theater down beneath us—I know not the fathom line that ever touched a descent so deep as I would be willing to bury more wealth in than Croesus had, or the great Jew R——[8] is supposed to have, to purchase it. And now do just look at that merry little Chinese waiter holding an umbrella, big enough for a bed-tester, over the head of that pretty insipid half Madonna-ish chit of a lady in that very blue summerhouse."

1823

---

8. Nathan Meyer Rothschild (1777–1836) founded the English branch of the great European banking house.

A Letter to Wordsworth[1]

[*The* Lyrical Ballads *of 1800*]

[January 30, 1801]

Thanks for your letter and present. I had already borrowed your second volume. What most please me are the *Song of Lucy.*[2] "Simon's sickly daughter" in *The Sexton*[3] made me *cry.* Next to these are the description of the continuous echoes in the story of Joanna's laugh,[4] where the mountains and all the scenery absolutely seem alive—and that fine Shakspearean character of the happy man, in *The Brothers,*

> —that creeps about the fields,
> Following his fancies by the hour, to bring
> Tears down his check, or solitary smiles
> Into his face, *until the setting sun*
> *Write fool upon his forehead.*

I will mention one more: the delicate and curious feeling in the wish for the Cumberland Beggar, that he may have about him the melody of birds, although he hear them not.[5] Here the mind knowingly passes a fiction upon herself, first substituting her own feelings for the Beggar's, and, in the same breath detecting the fallacy, will not part with the wish.—The *Poet's Epitaph* is disfigured, to my taste, by the vulgar satire upon parsons and lawyers in the beginning, and the coarse epithet of pinpoint in the sixth stanza. All the rest is eminently good, and your own. I will just add that it appears to me a fault in the Beggar that the instructions conveyed in it are too direct and like a lecture: they don't slide into the mind of the reader while he is imagining no such matter. An intelligent reader finds a sort of insult in being told: I will teach you how to think upon this subject.[6] This fault, if I am right, is in a ten-

---

1. Written in response to Wordsworth's gift of the *Lyrical Ballads* of 1800, in two volumes. The first volume was a revised version of the first edition of 1798, and the second volume consisted of new poems. Since both Wordsworth and Coleridge were Lamb's close friends, he is faced with the difficult diplomatic task of indicating that he is not equally enthusiastic about all the materials in these volumes. To have picked *The Ancient Mariner, Tintern Abbey,* and *She Dwelt Among the Untrodden Ways* for special commendation is a triumph of contemporary critical judgment.

Lamb's reply to Wordsworth's invitation to a sojourn in the Lake Country is a reminder that one could be a friend and warm admirer of the great Ro-

mantic poets, yet eminently prefer the abundant life of a great city to what Lamb calls "dead Nature." Compare Wordsworth's description of London, *The Prelude,* Book VII.
2. *She Dwelt Among the Untrodden Ways,* which in a letter written two weeks later Lamb called "the best piece" among those added in 1800.
3. *To a Sexton,* line 14.
4. *To Joanna,* lines 51–65.
5. *The Old Cumberland Beggar,* lines 183–85.
6. Commenting on Wordsworth's poetry in his letter of February 3, 1818, Keats similarly objected to "being bullied into a certain philosophy. * * * We hate poetry that has a palpable design upon us."

thousandth worse degree to be found in Sterne and many many novelists and modern poets, who continually put a signpost up to show where you are to feel. They set out with assuming their readers to be stupid. Very different from *Robinson Crusoe, The Vicar of Wakefield, Roderick Random,* and other beautiful bare narratives. There is implied an unwritten compact between author and reader: I will tell you a story, and I suppose you will understand it. Modern novels, *St. Leons* [7] and the like, are full of such flowers as these: "Let not my reader suppose"—"Imagine, *if you can*"—modest!—etc.—I will here have done with praise and blame. I have written so much, only that you may not think I have passed over your book without observation.—I am sorry that Coleridge has christened his *Ancient Mariner* "a Poet's Reverie" [8]—it is as bad as Bottom the Weaver's declaration that he is not a lion but only the scenical representation of a lion.[9] What new idea is gained by this title, but one subversive of all credit, which the tale should force upon us, of its truth? For me, I was never so affected with any human tale. After first reading it, I was totally possessed with it for many days—I dislike all the miraculous part of it, but the feelings of the man under the operation of such scenery dragged me along like Tom Piper's magic whistle. I totally differ from your idea that the Mariner should have had a character and profession.[1] This is a beauty in *Gulliver's Travels,* where the mind is kept in a placid state of little wonderments; but the Ancient Mariner undergoes such trials as overwhelm and bury all individuality or memory of what he was, like the state of a man in a bad dream, one terrible peculiarity of which is that all consciousness of personality is gone. Your other observation is, I think, as well a little unfounded: the Mariner from being conversant in supernatural events *has* acquired a supernatural and strange cast of *phrase,* eye, appearance, etc., which frighten the wedding guest. You will excuse my remarks, because I am hurt and vexed that you should think it necessary with a prose apology to open the eyes of dead men that cannot see. To sum up a general opinion of the second vol.—I do not feel any one poem in it so forcibly as *The Ancient Mariner, The Mad Mother,*[2]

7. *St. Leon* (1799), a didactic novel by William Godwin.
8. Coleridge added this subtitle in the edition of 1800, but fortunately deleted it in a later revision.
9. In *A Midsummer Night's Dream* (III.i.37 ff.) Bottom suggests that Snug, who is to play the part of the lion, make this reassuring comment.
1. Wordsworth had inserted an apologetic note after Coleridge's *Ancient Mar-*
iner, remarking that "the poem of my friend has indeed great defects; first, that the principal person has no distinct character, either in his profession of Mariner, or as a human being who having been long under the control of supernatural impressions might be supposed himself to partake of something supernatural. * * * "
2. I.e., *Her Eyes Are Wild.*

and the *Lines at Tintern Abbey*, in the first.—I could, too, have
wished the critical preface had appeared in a separate treatise. All
its dogmas are true and just, and most of them new, *as* criticism.
But they associate a *diminishing* idea with the poems which follow,
as having been written for *experiment* on the public taste,[3] more
than having sprung (as they must have done) from living and
daily circumstances.—I am prolix, because I am gratified in the
opportunity of writing to you, and I don't well know when to leave
off. I ought before this to have replied to your very kind invitation
into Cumberland. With you and your sister I could gang [4] anywhere; but I am afraid whether I shall ever be able to afford so
desperate a journey. Separate from the pleasure of your company,
I don't much care if I never see a mountain in my life. I have passed
all my days in London, until I have formed as many and intense
local attachments as any of you mountaineers can have done with
dead Nature. The lighted shops of the Strand and Fleet Street;
the innumerable trades, tradesmen and customers, coaches, wagons,
playhouses; all the bustle and wickedness round about Covent
Garden; the very women of the town; [5] the watchmen, drunken
scenes, rattles; life awake, if you awake, at all hours of the night; the
impossibility of being dull in Fleet Street; the crowds, the very dirt
and mud, the sun shining upon houses and pavements, the print
shops, the old bookstalls, parsons cheapening [6] books, coffeehouses,
steams of soups from kitchens, the pantomimes—London itself a
pantomime and a masquerade—all these things work themselves
into my mind and feed me, without a power of satiating me. The
wonder of these sights impels me into night walks about her
crowded streets, and I often shed tears in the motley Strand from
fullness of joy at so much life. All these emotions must be strange
to you. So are your rural emotions to me. But consider, what must
I have been doing all my life, not to have lent great portions of my
heart with usury to such scenes?

My attachments are all local, purely local. I have no passion (or
have had none since I was in love, and then it was the spurious
engendering of poetry and books) to groves and valleys. The rooms
where I was born, the furniture which has been before my eyes all
my life, a bookcase which has followed me about (like a faithful
dog, only exceeding him in knowledge), wherever I have moved, old
chairs, old tables, streets, squares, where I have sunned myself, my

3. In the Preface of 1798, Wordsworth had written that the volume "was published as an experiment."
4. "Go"; probably in playful imitation of Wordsworth's north-country dialect.
5. Streetwalkers.
6. Bargaining over.

old school—these are my mistresses. Have I not enough, without your mountains? I do not envy you. I should pity you, did I not know that the mind will make friends of anything. Your sun and moon and skies and hills and lakes affect me no more, or scarcely come to me in more venerable characters, than as a gilded room with tapestry and tapers, where I might live with handsome visible objects. I consider the clouds above me but as a roof, beautifully painted but unable to satisfy the mind; and at last, like the pictures of the apartment of a connoisseur, unable to afford him any longer a pleasure. So fading upon me, from disuse, have been the beauties of Nature, as they have been confinedly called; so ever fresh, and green, and warm are all the inventions of men and assemblies of men in this great city. I should certainly have laughed with dear Joanna.[7]

Give my kindest love *and my sister's* to D.[8] and your*self*, and a kiss from me to little Barbara Lewthwaite.[9]

C. LAMB

Thank you for liking my play!! [1]

7. In Wordsworth's *To Joanna*, mentioned at the beginning of this letter.
8. Dorothy Wordsworth.
9. Wordsworth's neighbor, who plays a role in his poem *The Pet Lamb*.
1. Lamb had sent Wordsworth a manuscript of his tragedy, *John Woodvil*.

Topics in Romantic Literature

THE SATANIC AND BYRONIC HERO

Not until the age of the American and French Revolutions, more than a century after Milton wrote *Paradise Lost*, did some readers begin to take the side of Satan in the war between Heaven and Hell, admiring him as the archrebel who had taken on no less an antagonist than Omnipotence itself. In his ironic *Marriage of Heaven and Hell* Blake claimed that Milton himself had unconsciously, but justly, taken the part of the Devil (representing rebellious energy) against Jehovah (representing oppressive limitation). Thirty years later, Shelley similarly maintained that Satan is the moral superior to Milton's tyrannical God, but he admitted that Satan's greatness of character is flawed by vengefulness and pride. It was precisely this aspect of flawed grandeur, however, that made Satan so attractive a model for Shelley's friend Byron. Byron's more immediate precedents were the protagonists of some of the Gothic terror novels of the later 18th century—especially Schedoni in Mrs. Radcliffe's *The Italian*, who embodied many of the sinister and terrifying aspects of Milton's Satan—in addition to the towering historical figure of Napoleon Bonaparte, who to the contemporary imagination also combined moral culpability with superhuman power and grandeur. Byron first sketched out his hero in 1812, in the opening stanzas of *Childe Harold's Pilgrimage*, Canto I (see above, p. 297); at this stage he is rather crudely depicted as a young man, prematurely sated by sin, who wanders about in the attempt to escape society and his own memories. Conrad, hero of *The Corsair*, has become more isolated, darker, more complex in his history and inner conflict, and therefore more frightening and compelling to the reader. The hero of *Lara* (1814) is a finished product; he reappears, with variations, in Canto III (1816) of *Childe Harold* (see above, stanzas 2–16, 52–55), and again as the hero of Byron's poetic drama, *Manfred* (1817).

In his developed form the Byronic hero is an alien, mysterious, and gloomy spirit, in all his passions and powers immensely greater than the common run of mankind, whom he regards with contempt as a lesser breed of being than himself. He harbors an inner demon, a torturing memory of an enormous though nameless guilt, which drives him restlessly toward an inevitable doom. He lives according to a simple and rigid code of his own: to the one he truly, though fatally, loves, he is faithful to death, and he will not betray a trust. He is absolutely self-reliant, inflexibly pursuing his own ends against any opposition, human or superhuman, and he exerts on men and women alike an attraction which is the more irresistible because it involves terror at his obliviousness to ordinary human concerns and values.

Coleridge early recognized the disquieting elements in the appeal of the Satanic-Napoleonic-Byronic figure, and in the brilliant passage reproduced below, he warned his age against it; but in vain. This personage immensely affected the life, the art, and even the philosophy of the 19th century. He became the model for the behavior of avant-garde young men and gave focus to the yearnings of emancipated young women. Pale ghosts of the Byronic hero wander through hundreds of second-rate European poems and novels. But among the descendants of this figure we also find the protagonists of masterpieces, including Heathcliff in *Wuthering Heights*, Ahab in *Moby Dick*, and the hero of Pushkin's great poem *Eugene Oniegin.*

JOHN MILTON: [Satan]

* * * He, above the rest
In shape and gesture proudly eminent,
Stood like a tower. His form had yet not lost
All her original brightness, nor appeared
Less then Archangel ruined, and the excess
Of glory obscured: as when the sun new-risen
Looks through the horizontal misty air
Shorn of his beams, or from behind the moon,
In dim eclipse, disastrous twilight sheds
On half the nations, and with fear of change
Perplexes monarchs. Darkened so, yet shone
Above them all the archangel; but his face
Deep scars of thunder had intrenched, and care
Sat on his faded cheek, but under brows
Of dauntless courage, and considerate pride
Waiting revenge. Cruel his eye, but cast
Signs of remorse and passion, to behold
The fellows of his crime, the followers rather
(Far other once beheld in bliss), condemned
Forever now to have their lot in pain * * *
[*Paradise Lost* I.589–608]

ROMANTIC COMMENTS ON MILTON'S SATAN

WILLIAM BLAKE

Those who restrain desire do so because theirs is weak enough to be restrained; and the restrainer or reason usurps its place and governs the unwilling.

And being restrained, it by degrees becomes passive, till it is only the shadow of desire.

The history of this is written in *Paradise Lost*, and the Governor or Reason is called Messiah.

And the original Archangel, or possessor of the command of the heavenly host, is called the Devil or Satan, and his children are called Sin & Death. * * *

But in Milton, the Father is Destiny, the Son a Ratio of the five senses, and the Holy-ghost Vacuum!

Note: The reason Milton wrote in fetters when he wrote of Angels and God, and at liberty when of Devils and Hell, is because he was a true Poet and of the Devil's party without knowing it.

[From *The Marriage of Heaven and Hell*, ca. 1790–93]

PERCY BYSSHE SHELLEY

1

* * * Milton's poem contains within itself a philosophical refutation of that system, of which, by a strange and natural antithesis, it has been a chief popular support. Nothing can exceed the energy and magnificence of the character of Satan as expressed in *Paradise Lost*. It is a mistake to suppose that he could ever have been intended for the popular personification of evil. Implacable hate, patient cunning, and a sleepless refinement of device to inflict the extremest anguish on an enemy, these things are evil; and, although venial in a slave, are not to be forgiven in a tyrant; although redeemed by much that ennobles his defeat in one subdued, are marked by all that dishonors his conquest in the victor. Milton's Devil as a moral being is as far superior to his God, as one who perseveres in some purpose which he has conceived to be excellent in spite of adversity and torture is to one who in the cold security of undoubted triumph inflicts the most horrible revenge upon his enemy, not from any mistaken notion of inducing him to repent of a perseverance in enmity, but with the alleged design of exasperating him to deserve new torments. Milton has so far violated the popular creed (if this shall be judged to be a violation) as to have alleged no superiority of moral virtue to his God over his Devil.

[From *A Defense of Poetry*, 1821]

2

* * * The only imaginary being resembling in any degree Prometheus is Satan; and Prometheus is, in my judgement, a more poetical character than Satan, because, in addition to courage, and majesty, and firm and patient opposition to omnipotent force, he is susceptible of being described as exempt from the taints of ambition, envy, revenge, and a desire for personal aggrandizement, which, in the hero of *Paradise Lost*, interfere with the interest. The character of Satan engenders in the mind a pernicious casuistry

which leads us to weigh his faults with his wrongs, and to excuse the former because the latter exceed all measure. In the minds of those who consider that magnificent fiction with a religious feeling it engenders something worse. But Prometheus is, as it were, the type of the highest perfection of moral and intellectual nature, impelled by the purest and the truest motives to the best and noblest ends.

[From Preface to *Prometheus Unbound*, 1820]

SAMUEL TAYLOR COLERIDGE

But in its utmost abstraction and consequent state of reprobation, the will becomes Satanic pride and rebellious self-idolatry in the relations of the spirit to itself, and remorseless despotism relatively to others; the more hopeless as the more obdurate by its subjugation of sensual impulses, by its superiority to toil and pain and pleasure; in short, by the fearful resolve to find in itself alone the one absolute motive of action, under which all other motives from within and from without must be either subordinated or crushed.

This is the character which Milton has so philosophically as well as sublimely embodied in the Satan of his *Paradise Lost*. Alas! too often has it been embodied in real life. Too often has it given a dark and savage grandeur to the historic page. And wherever it has appeared, under whatever circumstances of time and country, the same ingredients have gone to its composition; and it has been identified by the same attributes. Hope in which there is no cheerfulness; steadfastness within and immovable resolve, with outward restlessness and whirling activity; violence with guile; temerity with cunning; and, as the result of all, interminableness of object with perfect indifference of means; these are the qualities that have constituted the commanding genius; these are the marks that have characterized the masters of mischief, the liberticides, and mighty hunters of mankind, from Nimrod[1] to Bonaparte. And from inattention to the possibility of such a character as well as from ignorance of its elements, even men of honest intentions too frequently become fascinated. Nay, whole nations have been so far duped by this want of insight and reflection as to regard with palliative admiration, instead of wonder and abhorrence, the Molochs[2] of human nature, who are indebted for the larger portion of their meteoric success to their total want of principle, and who surpass the gen-

---

1. In Genesis x.9 Nimrod is described as "a mighty hunter before the Lord." This passage was traditionally interpreted to mean that Nimrod hunted down men, and so was the prototype for all tyrants and bloody conquerors.

2. I.e., monsters of evil (Moloch is an evil idol of the Old Testament to whom first-born children were sacrificed; he is also one of the fallen angels in *Paradise Lost*).

erality of their fellow creatures in one act of courage only, that of daring to say with their whole heart, "Evil, be thou my good!"

[From *The Statesman's Manual*, 1816]

The Evolution of the Byronic Hero
ANN RADCLIFFE: [The Italian Villain]

There lived in the Dominican convent of the Santo Spirito, at Naples, a man called Father Schedoni; an Italian, as his name imported, but whose family was unknown, and from some circumstances, it appeared that he wished to throw an impenetrable veil over his origin. * * * Some few persons in the convent, who had been interested by his appearance, believed that the peculiarities of his manners, his severe reserve and unconquerable silence, his solitary habits and frequent penances, were the effect of misfortune preying upon a haughty and disordered spirit; while others conjectured them the consequence of some hideous crime gnawing upon an awakened conscience. * * *

Among his associates no one loved him, many disliked him, and more feared him. His figure was striking, but not so from grace; it was tall, and, though extremely thin, his limbs were large and uncouth, and as he stalked along, wrapped in the black garments of his order, there was something terrible in its air; something almost superhuman. His cowl, too, as it threw a shade over the livid paleness of his face, increased its severe character, and gave an effect to his large melancholy eye, which approached to horror. His was not the melancholy of a sensible and wounded heart, but apparently that of a gloomy and ferocious disposition. There was something in his physiognomy extremely singular, and that cannot easily be defined. It bore the traces of many passions, which seemed to have fixed the features they no longer animated. An habitual gloom and severity prevailed over the deep lines of his countenance; and his eyes were so piercing that they seemed to penetrate, at a single glance, into the hearts of men, and to read their most secret thoughts; few persons could support their scrutiny, or even endure to meet them twice.

[From *The Italian, or The Confessional of the Black Penitents*, 1797]

LORD BYRON: *From* Lara[1]

17

In him inexplicably mixed appeared
Much to be loved and hated, sought and feared;   290
Opinion varying o'er his hidden lot,
In praise or railing ne'er his name forgot:
His silence formed a theme for others' prate—
They guessed—they gazed—they fain would know his fate.
What had he been? what was he, thus unknown,   295
Who walked their world, his lineage only known?
A hater of his kind? yet some would say,
With them he could seem gay amidst the gay;
But owned that smile, if oft observed and near,
Waned in its mirth, and withered to a sneer;   300
That smile might reach his lip but passed not by,
None e'er could trace its laughter to his eye:
Yet there was softness too in his regard,
At times, a heart as not by nature hard,
But once perceived, his spirit seemed to chide   305
Such weakness as unworthy of its pride,
And steeled itself, as scorning to redeem
One doubt from others' half-withheld esteem;
In self-inflicted penance of a breast
Which tenderness might once have wrung from rest;   310
In vigilance of grief that would compel
The soul to hate for having loved too well.

18

There was in him a vital scorn of all:
As if the worst had fallen which could befall,
He stood a stranger in this breathing world,   315
An erring spirit from another hurled;
A thing of dark imaginings, that shaped
By choice the perils he by chance escaped;
But 'scaped in vain, for in their memory yet
His mind would half exult and half regret.   320
With more capacity for love than earth
Bestows on most of mortal mold and birth,
His early dreams of good outstripped the truth,
And troubled manhood followed baffled youth;
With thought of years in phantom chase misspent,   325
And wasted powers for better purpose lent;
And fiery passions that had poured their wrath
In hurried desolation o'er his path,
And left the better feelings all at strife

1. "Lara" is the assumed name of *The Corsair*'s Conrad, who has given up piracy and retired to his ancestral home. Lady Byron related that Byron once said, with respect to Lara: "There's more [of me] in that than any of them." Saying this he shuddered, and avoided her eye.

In wild reflection o'er his stormy life;　330
But haughty still and loath himself to blame,
He called on Nature's self to share the shame,
And charged all faults upon the fleshly form
She gave to clog the soul, and feast the worm;
Till he at last confounded good and ill,　335
And half mistook for fate the acts of will.
Too high for common selfishness, he could
At times resign his own for others' good,
But not in pity, not because he ought,
But in some strange perversity of thought,　340
That swayed him onward with a secret pride
To do what few or none would do beside;
And this same impulse would, in tempting time,
Mislead his spirit equally to crime;
So much he soared beyond, or sunk beneath,　345
The men with whom he felt condemned to breathe,
And longed by good or ill to separate
Himself from all who shared his mortal state.
His mind abhorring this had fixed her throne
Far from the world, in regions of her own:　350
Thus coldly passing all that passed below,
His blood in temperate seeming now would flow:
Ah! happier if it ne'er with guilt had glowed,
But ever in that icy smoothness flowed!
'Tis true, with other men their path he walked,　355
And like the rest in seeming did and talked,
Nor outraged Reason's rules by flaw nor start,
His madness was not of the head, but heart;
And rarely wandered in his speech, or drew
His thoughts so forth as to offend the view.　360

19

With all that chilling mystery of mien,
And seeming gladness to remain unseen,
He had (if 'twere not nature's boon) an art
Of fixing memory on another's heart:
It was not love perchance, nor hate, nor aught　365
That words can image to express the thought;
But they who saw him did not see in vain,
And once beheld, would ask of him again:
And those to whom he spake remembered well,
And on the words, however light, would dwell:　370
None knew, nor how, nor why, but he entwined
Himself perforce around the hearer's mind;
There he was stamped, in liking, or in hate,
If greeted once; however brief the date
That friendship, pity, or aversion knew,　375
Still there within the inmost thought he grew.
You could not penetrate his soul, but found,
Despite your wonder, to your own he wound;

His presence haunted still; and from the breast
He forced an all unwilling interest: 380
Vain was the struggle in that mental net,
His spirit seemed to dare you to forget!

* * *

1814   1814

THE ART OF ROMANTIC POETRY

In reaction against the neoclassic view that the composition of poetry was primarily a deliberate act, controlled by the explicit rules and implicit principles of "art," most Romantic poets insisted that composition was primarily a matter of spontaneous impulse, or of inspiration, or of unconscious mental processes. But as Richard Aldington recently remarked about poetry, "genius is not enough; one must also work." However much the Romantic poem might be unforced or involuntary in its origin, poetic vision did not obviate revision, nor did spontaneity seem to be incompatible with selecting, eliminating, and making second or third trials, in the very process of composing. Wordsworth, in fact, corrected and recorrected his writings, both before and after first publication, as much as any poet on record: he spent over half his life revising the first version of *The Prelude*. Byron loved to display himself in the role of the noble amateur who dashes off verses with unprofessional casualness and bravura. But though Byron composed very fast, and after he had fixed a poem on paper hated to go back and revise in cold blood, his drafts show that even the easy colloquialism and seeming casualness of *Don Juan* was achieved only after a great deal of trial and error at getting a stanza or passage to work out.

In the first group of the excerpts that follow, the Romantic poets comment on their methods of composition and struggle to explain in what way the poetic process can be said to be spontaneous, even though it permits the play of judgment and afterthought. The second group reveals these poets actually at work. The passages from Wordsworth and Coleridge exemplify revisions which were made some time after the earlier version had already been written out or printed. The selections from Blake, Shelley, Byron, and Keats, on the other hand, reproduce passages from the drafts of some of their best poems, scribbled in the heat of first invention. Here we look on as the poet—whether or not he believes himself inspired, and no matter how rapidly he achieves a result that he is willing to let stand—carries on his inevitably tentative and groping efforts to meet the simultaneous requirements of meaning, syntax, meter, sound pattern, and the limits imposed by the chosen stanza. And because these are very good poets, it will be observed that the seeming conflict between the requirements of meaning and of form often results not in the distortion but in the perfection of the poetic statement.

COMMENTS ON THE POETIC PROCESS

WILLIAM BLAKE

1

Now I may say to you, what perhaps I should not dare to say to
anyone else: That I can alone carry on my visionary studies in
London unannoyed, and that I may converse with my friends in
Eternity, See Visions, Dream Dreams, and prophesy and speak
Parables unobserved and at liberty from the Doubts of other Mortals; perhaps Doubts proceeding from Kindness, but Doubts are
always pernicious, Especially when we Doubt our Friends. Christ
is very decided on this Point: "He who is Not With Me is Against
Me."[1] There is no Medium or Middle state; and if a Man is the
Enemy of my Spiritual Life while he pretends to be the Friend
of my Corporeal, he is a Real Enemy—but the Man may be the
friend of my Spiritual Life while he seems the Enemy of my Corporeal, but Not Vice Versa. * * *

But none can know the Spiritual Acts of my three years' Slumber
on the banks of the Ocean,[2] unless he has seen them in the Spirit,
or unless he should read My long Poem descriptive of those Acts;
for I have in these three years composed an immense number of
verses on One Grand Theme, Similar to Homer's *Iliad* or Milton's
Paradise Lost, the Persons and Machinery entirely new to the Inhabitants of Earth (some of the Persons Excepted). I have written
this poem from immediate Dictation, twelve or sometimes twenty
or thirty lines at a time, without Premeditation and even against
my Will; the Time it has taken in writing was thus rendered Non
Existent, and an immense Poem Exists which seems to be the
Labor of a long Life, all produced without Labor or Study. I mention this to show you what I think the Grand Reason of my being
brought down here. * * *

[From letter to Thomas Butts, April 25, 1803]

2

We who dwell on Earth can do nothing of ourselves; everything
is conducted by Spirits, no less than Digestion or Sleep. * * *
When this Verse was first dictated to me, I considered a Monotonous Cadence, like that used by Milton and Shakespeare and all
writers of English Blank Verse, derived from the modern bondage
of Rhyming, to be a necessary and indispendible part of Verse. But
I soon found that in the mouth of a true Orator such monotony
was not only awkward, but as much a bondage as rhyme itself. I

1. Matthew xii.30.
2. Blake was preparing to return to
London after having lived since September, 1800, at the seaside town of
Felpham, Sussex, under the irksome
patronage of William Hayley. The
"immense Poem" that Blake says he
wrote at that time may have been
Milton, or *The Four Zoas,* or both of
these together.

therefore have produced a variety in every line, both of cadences and number of syllables. Every word and every letter is studied and put into its fit place; the terrific numbers are reserved for the terrific parts, the mild and gentle for the mild and gentle parts, and the prosaic for inferior parts; all are necessary to each other. Poetry Fettered Fetters the Human Race.

[From Preface to *Jerusalem*, 1804–20]

WILLIAM WORDSWORTH

1

* * * [These poems] were composed in front of Rydal Mount[3] and during my walks in the neighborhood. Nine-tenths of my verses have been murmured out in the open air; and here let me repeat what I believe has already appeared in print. One day a stranger having walked round the garden and grounds of Rydal Mount asked one of the female servants who happened to be at the door, permission to see her master's study. "This," said she, leading him forward, "is my master's library, where he keeps his books, but his study is out of doors." After a long absence from home it has more than once happened that some one of my cottage neighbors has said—"Well, there he is; we are glad to hear him *booing* about again."

2

* * * Had I been more intimate with [the Reverend George Crabbe],[4] I should have ventured to touch upon his office as a Minister of the Gospel, and how far his heart and soul were in it so as to make him a zealous and diligent laborer. In poetry, though he wrote much, as we all know, he assuredly was not so. I happened once to speak of pains as necessary to produce merit of a certain kind which I highly valued: his observation was—"It is not worth while." You are quite right, thought I, if the labor encroaches upon the time due to teach truth as a steward of the mysteries of God: if there be cause to fear that, write less: but, if poetry is to be produced at all, make what you do produce as good as you can.

[From notes on his poems dictated to Isabella Fenwick, 1843]

SAMUEL TAYLOR COLERIDGE: [Spontaneous and Controlled Composition]

And, first, from the origin of meter. This I would trace to the balance in the mind effected by that spontaneous effort which

3. A house on Rydal Water, in the English Lake Country, where Wordsworth lived from 1813 until his death.

4. 1754–1832; author of *The Village* and other realistic poems of rural life.

strives to hold in check the workings of passion. It might be easily explained likewise in what manner this salutary antagonism is assisted by the very state which it counteracts; and how this balance of antagonists became organized into meter (in the usual acceptation of that term) by a supervening act of the will and judgment, consciously and for the foreseen purpose of pleasure. Assuming these principles as the date of our argument, we deduce from them two legitimate conditions which the critic is entitled to expect in every metrical work. First, that as the elements of meter owe their existence to a state of increased excitement, so the meter itself should be accompanied by the natural language of excitement. Secondly, that as these elements are formed into meter artificially, by a voluntary act, with the design and for the purpose of blending delight with emotion, so the traces of present volition should throughout the metrical language be proportionally discernible. Now these two conditions must be reconciled and co-present. There must be not only a partnership, but a union; an interpenetration of passion and of will, of spontaneous impulse and of voluntary purpose. * * * But if it be asked by what principles the poet is to regulate his own style, if he do not adhere closely to the sort and order of words which he hears in the market, wake, highroad or plowfield? I reply: by principles, the ignorance or neglect of which would convict him of being no poet, but a silly or presumptuous usurper of the name! By the principles of grammar, logic, psychology! In one word, by such a knowledge of the facts, material and spiritual, that most appertain to his art as, if it have been governed and applied by good sense and rendered instinctive by habit, becomes the representative and reward of our past conscious reasonings, insights, and conclusions, and acquires the name of taste. By what rule that does not leave the reader at the poet's mercy, and the poet at his own, is the latter to distinguish between the language suitable to suppressed, and the language which is characteristic of indulged, anger? Or between that of rage and that of jealousy? Is it obtained by wandering about in search of angry or jealous people in uncultivated society, in order to copy their words? Or not far rather by the power of imagination proceeding upon the *all in each* of human nature? By meditation, rather than by observation? And by the latter in consequence only of the former? As eyes, for which the former has predetermined their field of vision and to which, as to its organ, it communicates a microscopic power? There is not, I firmly believe, a man now living who has from his own inward experience a clearer intuition than Mr. Wordsworth himself that the last mentioned are the true sources of genial discrimination. Through the same process and by the same creative agency will the poet distinguish the degree and kind of the excitement produced by the very act of poetic composition.

As intuitively will he know what differences of style it at once inspires and justifies; what intermixture of conscious volition is natural to that state; and in what instances such figures and colors of speech degenerate into mere creatures of an arbitrary purpose, cold technical artifices of ornament or connection. For even as truth is its own light and evidence, discovering at once itself and falsehood, so is it the prerogative of poetic genius to distinguish by parental instinct its proper offspring from the changelings which the gnomes of vanity or the fairies of fashion may have laid in its cradle or called by its names. Could a rule be given from without poetry would cease to be poetry and sink into a mechanical art. It would be μόρφωσις not ποίησις.[5] The rules of the imagination are themselves the very powers of growth and production. The words to which they are reducible present only the outlines and external appearance of the fruit. A deceptive counterfeit of the superficial form and colors may be elaborated; but the marble peach feels cold and heavy, and children only put it to their mouths.

[From *Biographia Literaria*, Chapter XVIII]

LORD BYRON

1

I told you long ago that the new Cantos [*Don Juan*, Cantos III and IV] were *not* good, and I also *told you a reason*: recollect, I do not oblige you to publish them; you may suppress them, if you like, but I can alter nothing. I have erased the six stanzas about those two impostors, Southey and Wordsworth (which I suppose will give you great pleasure), but I can do no more. I can neither recast, nor replace; but I give you leave to put it all into the fire, if you like, or *not* to publish, and I think that's sufficient. * * * I can't cobble: I must "either make a spoon or spoil a horn"— and there's an end; for there's no remeid: but I leave you free will to suppress the *whole*, if you like it.

[From a letter to his publisher, John Murray, April 23, 1820]

2

* * * With regard to what you say of retouching [*Don Juan*], it is all very well; but I can't *furbish*. I am like the tiger (in poesy), if I miss my first Spring, I go growling back to my Jungle. There is no second. I can't correct; I can't, and I won't. * * * You must take my things as they happen to be: if they are not likely to suit, reduce their *estimate* then accordingly. I would rather give them away than hack and hew them. I don't say that you are not

---

5. *Morphosis*, not *poiesis*," i.e., structuring, not creating.

right: I merely assert that I cannot better them. I must either "make a spoon, or spoil a horn." And there's an end.

[To John Murray, September 18, 1820]

EDWARD J. TRELAWNY: [Shelley on Composing]

The day I found Shelley in the pine forest he was writing verses on a guitar.[6] I picked up a fragment, but could only make out the first two lines:

> Ariel to Miranda: Take
> This slave of music.

It was a frightful scrawl; words smeared out with his finger, and one upon the other, over and over in tiers, and all run together "in most admired disorder";[7] it might have been taken for a sketch of a marsh overgrown with bulrushes, and the blots for wild ducks; such a dashed-off daub as self-conceited artists mistake for a manifestation of genius. On my observing this to him, he answered:

"When my brain gets heated with thought, it soon boils, and throws off images and words faster than I can skim them off. In the morning, when cooled down, out of the rude sketch, as you justly call it, I shall attempt a drawing. If you ask me why I publish what few or none will care to read, it is that the spirits I have raised haunt me until they are sent to the devil of a printer. All authors are anxious to breech their bantlings."[8]

[From *Records of Shelley, Byron, and the Author*, 1858]

THOMAS MEDWIN: [Shelley's Self-Hypercriticism]

But to return to *Charles I*.[9] Other causes besides doubt as to the manner of treating the subject operated to impede its progress. The ever growing fastidiousness of his taste, had, I have often thought, begun to cramp his genius. The opinion of the world too, at times shook his confidence in himself and generated doubts that he was unprofitably wasting his energies, that produce what he might, he was doomed to be unread. I have often been shown the scenes of this tragedy on which he was engaged; like the MS. of Tasso's *Gerusalemme Liberata*, in the library of Ferrara, his were larded with word on word, till they were scarcely decipherable. I remember a printed copy of his *Revolt of Islam*, that was similarly interlined.

6. *With a Guitar: To Jane* (1822).
7. Altered from *Macbeth* III.iv.110. "Admired" here means "strange, extraordinary."

8. Infants, especially illegitimate ones.
9. An unfinished tragedy by Shelley, written 1819–22.

The *Queen Mab* in the possession of Mr. Brooks, which I have spoken of, had innumerable *pentimenti;*[1] and when I one day objected to this self-hypercriticism, he replied, "The source of poetry is native and involuntary, but requires severe labor in its development."

[From *The Life of P. B. Shelley,* 1847]

RICHARD WOODHOUSE: [Keats on Composing]

* * * He has repeatedly said in conversation that he never sits down to write, unless he is full of ideas—and then thoughts come about him in troops as though soliciting to be accepted and he selects—one of his Maxims is that if Poetry does not come naturally it had better not come at all.[2] The moment he feels any dearth he discontinues writing and waits for a happier moment. He is generally more troubled by a redundancy than by a poverty of images, and he culls what appears to him at the time the best. —He never corrects, unless perhaps a word here or there should occur to him as preferable to an expression he has already used.— He is impatient of correcting and says he would rather burn the piece in question and write another or something else. "My judgment," he says, "is as active while I am actually writing as my imagination. In fact all my faculties are strongly excited, and in their full play.—And shall I afterwards, when my imagination is idle, and the heat in which I wrote has gone off, sit down coldly to criticize when in possession of only one faculty what I have written when almost inspired."—This fact explains the reason of the perfectness, fullness, richness, and completion of most that comes from him. He has said that he has often not been aware of the beauty of some thought or expression until after he had composed and written it down.—It has then struck him with astonishment, and seemed rather the production of another person than his own. —He has wondered how he came to hit upon it. This was the case with the description of Apollo in the 3rd book of *Hyperion,* "white melodious throat."[3] . . . It seemed to come by chance or magic —to be as it were something given to him.

[From Notes on Keats]

1. Italian: second thoughts.
2. See Keats's letter to John Taylor, Feb. 27, 1818.
3. The reference is to Keats's *Hyperion*

III.79–82: "Apollo then, / With sudden scrutiny and gloomless eyes, / Thus answered, while his white melodious throat / Throbbed with the syllables."

POEMS IN PROCESS: MANUSCRIPTS AND EARLY VERSIONS

WILLIAM BLAKE: The Tiger[1]

[First Draft]

The Tyger

1　Tyger Tyger burning bright
In the forests of the night
What immortal hand or eye
~~Dare~~ ~~Could~~ frame thy fearful symmetry

2　Burnt in
~~In what~~ distant deeps or skies
~~The cruel~~ ~~Burnt the~~ fire of thine eyes
On what wings dare he aspire
What the hand dare sieze the fire

3　And what shoulder & what art
Could twist the sinews of thy heart
And when thy heart began to beat
What dread hand & what dread feet

~~Could fetch it from the furnace deep~~
~~And in thy horrid ribs dare steep~~
~~In the well of sanguine woe~~
~~In what clay & in what mould~~
~~Were thy eyes of fury rolld~~

4　Where　　　　　　where
~~What~~ the hammer ~~what~~ the chain
In what furnace was thy brain

　　　　　　　　　　　　dread grasp
What the anvil what ~~the arm~~ ~~arm~~ ~~grasp~~ ~~clasp~~
Dare ~~Could~~ its deadly terrors ~~clasp~~ ~~grasp~~ clasp

6　Tyger Tyger burning bright
In the forests of the night
What immortal hand & eye
frame
Dare ~~form~~ thy fearful symmetry

1. These drafts have been taken from a notebook used by William Blake, called "The Rossetti MS." because it was once owned by Dante Gabriel Rossetti, the Victorian poet and painter. The first draft appears on p. 109 of the MS., the trial stanzas and second full draft on p. 108 (Blake worked from back to front of the book). The stanza and line numbers are Blake's own. Geoffrey Keynes's *Notebook of William Blake* (1935) is a photographic facsimile of the MS.

[*Trial Stanzas*]

Burnt in distant deeps or skies
The cruel fire of thine eye,
Could heart descend or wings aspire
What the hand dare sieze the fire

                dare he smile laugh
5 3   And did he laugh his work to see

                ankle
       What the shoulder what the knee

       Dare
4   Did he who made the lamb make thee
1   When the stars threw down their spears
2   And waterd heaven with their tears

[*Second Full Draft*]

Tyger Tyger burning bright
In the forests of the night
What Immortal hand & eye
Dare frame thy fearful symmetry

And what shoulder & what art
Could twist the sinews of thy heart
And when thy heart began to beat
What dread hand & what dread feet

When the stars threw down their spears
And waterd heaven with their tears
Did he smile his work to see
Did he who made the lamb make thee

Tyger Tyger burning bright
In the forests of the night
What immortal hand & eye
Dare frame thy fearful symmetry

[*Final Version*, 1794][2]

Tyger! Tyger! burning bright
In the forests of the night,
What immortal hand or eye
Could frame thy fearful symmetry?

In what distant deeps or skies
Burnt the fire of thine eyes?
On what wings dare he aspire?
What the hand dare sieze the fire?

And what shoulder, & what art,
Could twist the sinews of thy heart?
And when thy heart began to beat,
What dread hand? & what dread feet?

2. As published in *Songs of Experience*.

What the hammer? what the chain?
In what furnace was thy brain?
What the anvil? what dread grasp
Dare its deadly terrors clasp?

When the stars threw down their spears,
And water'd heaven with their tears,
Did he smile his work to see?
Did he who made the Lamb make thee?

Tyger! Tyger! burning bright
In the forests of the night,
What immortal hand or eye,
Dare frame thy fearful symmetry?

WILLIAM WORDSWORTH: She Dwelt
Among the Untrodden Ways

*[Version in a Letter to Coleridge,
December, 1798, or January, 1799]*[3]

My hope was one, from cities far
  Nursed on a lonesome heath:
Her lips were red as roses are,
  Her hair a woodbine wreath.

She lived among the untrodden ways   5
  Beside the springs of Dove,
A maid whom there were none to praise,
  And very few to love;

A violet by a mossy stone
  Half-hidden from the eye!   10
Fair as a star when only one
  Is shining in the sky!

And she was graceful as the broom[4]
  That flowers by Carron's side;
But slow distemper checked her bloom,   15
  And on the Heath she died.

Long time before her head lay low
  Dead to the world was she:
But now she's in her grave, and Oh!
  The difference to me!   20

[Final Version, 1800][5]

She dwelt among the untrodden ways
  Beside the springs of Dove

3. Printed in Ernest de Selincourt's *Early Letters of William and Dorothy Wordsworth* (1935).
4. A shrub with long slender branches and yellow flowers; the Carron is a river in northwestern Scotland.
5. As published in the second edition of *Lyrical Ballads*.

A Maid whom there were none to praise
And very few to love:

A violet by a mossy stone   5
Half hidden from the eye!
—Fair as a star, when only one
Is shining in the sky.

She lived unknown, and few could know
When Lucy ceased to be;   10
But she is in her grave, and, oh,
The difference to me!

SAMUEL TAYLOR COLERIDGE: *From*
Dejection: An Ode[6]
[*From* A Letter to ———, *April 4, 1802*]

'Tis Midnight! and small Thoughts have I of Sleep.
Full seldom may my Friend such Vigils keep—
O breathe She softly in her gentle Sleep!
Cover her, gentle Sleep! with wings of Healing.
And be this Tempest but a Mountain Birth!   220
May all the Stars hang bright above her Dwelling,
Silent, as though they *watch'd* the sleeping Earth!
Healthful and light, my Darling! may'st thou rise
With clear and chearful Eyes—
And of the same good Tidings to me send!   225
For oh! beloved Friend!
I am not the buoyant Thing I was of yore
When like an own Child, I to Joy belong'd:
For others mourning oft, myself oft sorely wrong'd,
Yet bearing all things then, as if I nothing bore!   230

* * *

Sister and Friend of my devoutest Choice
Thou being innocent and full of love,   325
And nested with the Darlings of thy Love,
    And feeling in thy Soul, Heart, Lips, and Arms
Even what the conjugal and mother Dove,
That borrows genial Warmth from those, she warms,
Feels in the thrill'd wings, blessedly outspread—   330
Thou free'd awhile from Cares and human Dread

6. In 1937 Ernest de Selincourt printed from MS. the original version of *Dejection*, which was a confessional verse letter addressed to Sara Hutchinson, Wordsworth's sister-in-law, with whom Coleridge was secretly in love. On October 4, 1802, Coleridge published anonymously in the *Morning Post* a much shortened version, entitled *Dejection: An Ode*, which differs only in details from the final text that he printed in his collected poems, *Sybilline Leaves*, in 1817. The excerpts demonstrate how Coleridge pulled two passages out of the middle and the end of the original verse letter, purged them of embarrassingly candid personal details, and fused them into the impersonal concluding stanza of his great *Ode*.

By the Immenseness of the Good and Fair
   Which thou seest everywhere—
Thus, thus, should'st thou rejoice!
To thee would all things live from Pole to Pole;   335
Their life the Eddying of thy living Soul—
O dear! O Innocent! O full of Love!
A very Friend! A Sister of my Choice—
O dear, as Light and Impulse from above,
Thus may'st thou ever, evermore rejoice!   340

[*From* Dejection: An Ode, *version of 1817*]

8

'Tis midnight, but small thoughts have I of sleep:
Full seldom may my friend such vigils keep!
Visit her, gentle Sleep! with wings of healing,
   And may this storm be but a mountain-birth,
May all the stars hang bright above her dwelling,   130
   Silent as though they watched the sleeping Earth!
     With light heart may she rise,
     Gay fancy, cheerful eyes,
Joy lift her spirit, joy attune her voice;
To her may all things live, from pole to pole,   135
Their life the eddying of her living soul!
   O simple spirit, guided from above,
Dear Lady! friend devoutest of my choice,
Thus mayest thou ever, evermore rejoice.

LORD BYRON: *From* Don Juan[7]
[*First Draft: Canto III, Stanza 9*]

1   ~~Life is a play and men~~
      All tragedies are finished by a death,
2   All Comedies are ended by a marriage,
3   ~~For Life can go no further~~
      ~~These two form the last gasp of Passion's breath~~
4   ~~All further is a blank—I won't disparage~~
5   ~~That holy state—but certainly beneath~~
6   ~~The Sun—of human things—~~
3   ~~These two are levellers, and human breath~~
      ~~So—These point the epigram of human breath~~
      ~~Or any—~~The future states of both are left to faith,
4   ~~Though Life and love I like not to disparage~~
      ~~The~~ For authors ~~think~~ description might disparage
           fear
5   ~~'Tis strange that poets never try to wreathe~~ [sic?]
      ~~With eith~~ ~~'Tis strange that poets of the Catholic faith~~
6   ~~Neer go beyond—and~~ ~~but seem to dread miscarriage~~

7. Reproduced from transcripts made from Byron's manuscripts in T. G. Steffan and W. W. Pratt, *Byron's "Don Juan"* (1957); the line numbers were added by these editors. The stanzas were published by Byron in their amended form.

7 ~~So dramas close with death or settlement for life~~
   ~~Veiling   Leaving the future states of Love and Life~~
   ~~The paradise beyond like that of life~~
8 ~~And ne'er describing either~~
   ~~To mere conjecture of a devil   and   or wife~~
   ~~And don't say much of paradise or wife~~
5 The worlds to come of both—&~~or~~ fall beneath,
6 And ~~all~~   ~~both the worlds would blame them for miscarriage~~
   And then both worlds would punish their miscarriage—
7 ~~So leaving both with priest & prayerbook ready~~
   So leaving ~~Clerg both a~~ each their Priest and prayerbook ready,
8 They say no more of death or of the Lady.

[First Draft: Canto XIV, Stanza 95]

1 Alas! ~~I speak by~~ Experience—~~never~~ yet
     ~~quote~~   seldom
2–4 ~~I had a paramour—and I've had many~~
   ~~To whom I did not cause a deep~~ regret—
            some small
   ~~Whom I had not some reason to~~ regret
   ~~For Whom—I did not feel myself~~ a Zany—
1–4 Alas! by all experience, seldom yet
   (I merely quote what I have heard from many)
   Had lovers not some reason to regret
   The passion which made Solomon a Zany.
5 ~~I also had a wife~~—not to forget—
   I've also seen some wives—not to forget—
6 The marriage state—the best or worst of any—
7 Who ~~was~~ the very ~~paragon~~ of wives,
     were   paragons
8 Yet made the misery of ~~both our~~ lives.
           many
          ~~several~~
     ~~of~~ at least two

PERCY BYSSHE SHELLEY: A Lament[8]
[First Stage]

Ah time, oh night, oh day
~~Ni nal ni na, na ni~~
~~Ni na ni na, ni na~~
Oh life O death, O time
  Time a di
~~Never Time~~

8. The draft versions of this poem, one of Shelley's most concentrated lyrics, are scattered through one of Shelley's notebooks—although apparently in the reverse order from that in which Shelley composed them. These drafts have been transcribed by H. Buxton Forman in *Note Books of Percy Bysshe Shelley* (1911). They show Shelley working with fragmentary words and phrases, and simultaneously with a wordless pattern of pulses which marked out, roughly, the meter of the single lines and the shape of the lyric stanzas. Bennett Weaver has analyzed the evolution of this lyric in "Shelley Works out the Rhythms of *A Lament*," *PMLA* (1932), pp. 570–576. The first two stages appear on pp. 23 and 60 of the notebook, respectively.

Ah time, a time O-time
~~Time!~~

[Second Stage]

Oh time, oh night oh day
~~O day oh night, alas~~
~~O~~ Death time night ~~oh~~
Oh, Time
Oh time o night oh day

[Third Stage][9]

[1]

Na na, na na na′ na
Nă nă na na na—nă nă
Nă nă nă nă nā nā
Na na nā nā nâ ă na

Na na na—nă nă—na na
Na na na na—na na na na na
Na na na na na
Na na
Na na na na na
Na na
Na na na na na ˇ na!

[2]

Oh time, oh night, o day
alas
O day ~~serenest,~~ o day
O day alas the day
That thou shouldst sleep when we awake to say

O time time—o death—o day
O day, o death for life is far from thee
O thou wert never free
For death is now with thee
~~And life is far from~~
O death, o day for life is far from thee

[Published Version, 1824]

O world! O life! O time!
On whose last steps I climb,
    Trembling at that where I had stood before;
When will return the glory of your prime?
    No more—Oh, never more!   5

Out of the day and night
A joy has taken flight;
    Fresh spring, and summer, and winter hoar,

9. The two parts of this stage—Shelley's wordless metrical pattern and his
third version of the poem—appear on
facing pp. 61 and 62 of the notebook.

Move my faint heart with grief, but with delight
No more—Oh, never more! 10

JOHN KEATS: *From* The Eve of St. Agnes[1]

[*Stanza 24*]

1 A Casement ~~ach'd~~ tripple archd and diamonded
2 With many coloured glass fronted the Moon
       wereof
3 In midst ~~of which~~ a shilded scutcheon shed
4   High blushing gules ~~upon she kneeled saintly~~ down
5 And inly prayed for grace and heavenly boon
6 The blood red gules fell on her silver cross
7 And ~~her~~ white(est) hands devout

There was
1 A Casement tripple archd and high
2   All garlanded with carven imageries
3 Of fruits ~~& trailing~~ flowers and sunny corn
                                    ears parchd

1 A Casement high and tripple archd there was
2   All gardneded with carven imageries
3 Of fruits and flowers and bunches of knot grass;
4   And diamonded with panes of quaint device
5 Innumerable of stains and splendid dies
              sunset
   As is the tger moths ~~rich~~ deep ~~damasked~~ wjngs
6 ~~As is the wing of evening tiger moths;~~
         whereft   thousand
7 ~~And in the~~ midst 'momg ~~man~~ heraldries
8 And ~~dim twilight~~ twilight saints and dim emblasonings
9 A shielded scutcheon blushd with Blood of Queens & Kings

[*Stanza 25*]

1 Full on this Casement shone the wintry moon
         ~~warm~~ rich   breast
2 And threw ~~red~~ gules on Madelines fair ~~face~~
3 As down she kneel'd for heavens grace and boon
                              fell
   ~~And~~   rose ~~with red~~   bloom ∧on her hang togeth
4 ~~Tinging her pious~~ hands ~~together~~ prest
       on her
5 And ∧silver cross soft Amethyst
6 And on her hair a glory like a Saint's
7 Shee seem'd ~~like an immortal agel drest~~
        silvery angel newly drest,

1. Transcribed from what is probably the best known of all manuscripts, that which contains Keats's first draft of all but the first seven stanzas of *The Eve of St. Agnes;* it is now in the Harvard University Library. The line numbers are not Keats's.

                                    Lionel
8   Save wings, for heaven—~~Porphyro~~ grew faint
9   She knelt too pure a thing, too free from motal taint

[Stanza 26]

1   But ~~soon~~ his heart revives—her prayers said
2   ~~She lays aside her veil~~
                          pearled
        strips her hair of all its ∧ wreathed ~~pearl~~
3   ~~Unclasps her bosom jewels~~
     ~~And twists it in one knot upon her head~~

1   But soon his heart revives—her prayers (ing) done,
                                             ~~soon~~
2   ~~Sh~~(Of) all her (its) wreathed pearl she strips her hair
3   Unclasps her warmed jewels one by one
                      her bursting
4   Loosens ~~her~~ ∧ ~~boddice from her~~
                 ~~her Boddice lace~~ string
              ~~her Boddice and her bosom bar~~
                      her
                [HERE KEATS BEGINS A NEW SHEET]
     Loosens her fragrant ~~boddice~~ and doth bare
5   Her

          Anon
1   ~~But soon~~ his heart revives—her praying done
                                             frees
2   Of all its wreathéd pearl her hair she ~~strips~~
3   Unclasps her warmed jewels one by one
                                   by degrees
4   Loosens her fragrant boddice: ~~and down slips~~
                                  ~~to her knees~~
5   Her sweet attire ~~falls light creeps down by~~
                  creeps rusteling to her knees
                  Mermaid   in sea weed
6   Half hidden like a ~~Syren of the Sea~~
7   ~~And more melodious~~   dreaming
                       She stands awhile in ∧ thought, and sees
8   In fancy fair Saint Agnes in her bed
9   But dares not look behind or all the charm is ~~fled~~ dead

[Stanza 30]

       ~~But~~
1   ~~And still she slept:~~
     And still she slept an azure-lidded sleep
2   In blanched linen smooth and lavender'd;
3   While he from frorth the closet brought a heap
               fruits
4   Of candied ~~sweets sweets with~~ and plumb and gourd
           apple   Quince
                              creamed
5   With jellies soother than the ~~dairy~~ curd
                       tinct
6   And lucent syrups ~~smooth~~ with crannamon

7   ~~And sugar'd dates from that o'er Euphrates fard~~

~~in Brigantine transferred~~

~~transferred~~

  Manna and daites in Bragine ~~wild transferrd~~

~~and Manna~~

7a   ~~And Manna wild and~~   ~~Bragantine~~

~~sugar'd~~ dates transferrd

argosy [in left margin]

8   ~~In Brigantine from Fez~~

From fez—and spiced danties every one

glutted

9   From ~~wealthy~~ Saxmarchand to cedard lebanon

silken

The Victorian Age

(1832-1901)

1832: The First Reform Bill.
1837: Victoria becomes queen.
1846: The Corn Laws repealed.
1851: The Great Exhibition in London.
1859: Charles Darwin's *Origin of Species* published.
1870–71: Franco-Prussian War.
1901: Death of Victoria.

AN AGE OF EXPANSION

During the long reign of Queen Victoria England reached her highest point of development as a world power. In the 18th century the pivotal city of Western civilization had been Paris; by the second half of the 19th century this center of influence had shifted to London, a city which expanded from about a million inhabitants when Victoria came to the throne to 6.5 million at the time of her death. The rapid growth of London is one of the many indications of the most important development of the age: the shift from a way of life based on the ownership of land to a modern urban economy based on trade and manufacturing. "We have been living, as it were, the life of three hundred years in thirty." This was the impression formed by Dr. Thomas Arnold during the early stages of England's industrialization. By the end of the century—after the resources of steam power had been more fully exploited for fast railways and iron ships, for looms, printing presses, and farmers' combines, and after the introduction of the telegraph, intercontinental cable, anesthetics, and universal compulsory education—an observer might have felt that three thousand years rather than three hundred had been crammed into his lifetime.

Because England was the first country to become industrialized, her transformation was an especially painful one, but being first had a compensation: it was profitable. An early start enabled England to capture markets all over the globe. Her cotton and other manufactured products were exported in English ships, a merchant fleet whose size was without parallel in other countries. The profits gained from her trade led also to extensive capital investments in all continents (especially in the under-developed sections of her own Empire) so that after England had become the world's workshop, London became, from 1870 on, the world's banker.

The effect of these developments on Victorian character has been described by the historian David Thomson. The period, he says in *England and the Nineteenth Century*, "is one of strenuous activity and dynamic change, of ferment of ideas and recurrent social unrest, of great inventiveness and expansion." And he adds:

The whole meaning of Victorian England is lost if it is thought of as a country of stuffy complacency and black top-hatted moral priggery. Its frowsty crinolines and dingy hansom cabs, its gas-lit houses and over-ornate draperies, concealed a people engaged in a tremendously exciting adventure—the daring experiment of fitting industrial man into a democratic society. Their failures, faults, and ludicrous shortcomings are all too apparent: but the days when Mr. Lytton Strachey could afford to laugh at the foibles of the "Eminent Victorians" have passed, and we must ask ourselves the question of whether we *can* laugh at our great-grandfathers' attempts to solve problems to which we have so far failed to find an answer. At least the Victorians found greatness, stability, and peace: and the whole world, marveling, envied them for it.

The reactions of Victorian writers to the fast-paced expansion of England were various. A few, such as Thomas Babington Macaulay (1800–59), relished the spectacle as wholly delightful. During the prosperous 1850's Macaulay's essays and histories, with their recitations of the statistics of industrial growth, constituted a Hymn to Progress as well as a celebration of the superior qualities of the English people—"the greatest and most highly civilized people that ever the world saw," Macaulay wrote. And later in the century there were lesser jingoists whose writings confidently pointed out the reasons for further national self-congratulation. More representative, perhaps, was Tennyson. Such poems as *Locksley Hall* may remind us of Macaulay's confidence in the blessings of progress, yet Tennyson's capacity to relish industrial change was only sporadic. Much of the time he felt instead like those writers in the camp opposite to Macaulay, nostalgic writers who perceived that leadership in commerce and industry was being paid for at a terrible price in human happiness. In their experience a so-called "progress" had been gained only by abandoning the traditional rhythms of life and traditional patterns of human relationships which had sustained mankind for centuries. In the melancholy poetry of Matthew Arnold this note is often struck:

> For what wears out the life of mortal men?
> 'Tis that from change to change their being rolls;
> 'Tis that repeated shocks, again, again,
> Exhaust the energy of strongest souls.

An occasional ride on a roller coaster may be exhilarating, but to be chained aboard for a lifetime is a nightmare.

Despite the industrial and political pre-eminence of England during the period, it is evident that most perceptive Victorians suffered from an anxious sense of something lost, a sense too of being displaced persons in a world made alien by technological changes which had been exploited too quickly for the adaptive powers of the human psyche. In this respect, as in many others, the Victorians may remind us of their English-speaking counterparts in America during the second half of the 20th century who have taken over a leading position in the Western world with similar mixed feelings of satisfaction and anxiety.

CRITICAL REACTIONS AGAINST VICTORIANS IN THE TWENTIETH CENTURY

To suggest a similarity between the Victorians and ourselves (a similarity, not an identity) seems a necessary preliminary for a reading of their writings. Literary history requires of us a double perspective. We should be able to see our predecessors as like ourselves; otherwise they will appear to us as mere monsters. We should also be able to see them as unlike ourselves; otherwise they are stripped of their distinctive coloration in time. In the earlier decades of the 20th century, most literary critics were incapable of exercising this double perspective. In their eyes the Victorian writers were monsters, grotesque and remote as the dinosaurs and yet, paradoxically, still threatening. Having been brought up as children to believe that Tennyson and Thackeray were great writers, they had to assert their independence by demonstrating that Tennyson and Thackeray were sometimes absurd and therefore of no consequence. Lytton Strachey's skillful puncturing of over-inflated Victorian balloons is characteristic of the Edwardian (1901–10) and Georgian (1911–36) attitudes. One encounters these attitudes, in subtler form, in the Georgian novelist Virginia Woolf. Her book *Orlando* is a delightful fictionalized survey of English literature from Elizabethan times to 1928, in which the Victorians are presented in terms of dampness, rain, and proliferating vegetation:

Ivy grew in unparalleled profusion Houses that had been of bare stone were smothered in greenery. * * * And just as the ivy and the evergreen rioted in the damp earth outside, so did the same fertility show itself within. The life of the average woman was a succession of childbirths. * * * Giant cauliflowers towered deck above deck till they rivaled * * * the elm trees themselves. Hens laid incessantly eggs of no special tint. * * * The whole sky itself as it spread wide above the British Isles was nothing but a vast feather bed.

Two comments can be made about this witty description. One is that it accurately identifies a distinguishing quality of Victorian life and literature: creative energy. A second is that the author of the passage did not admire such creative energy. In fact she felt terrified by it as if it might smother her. Mrs. Woolf was the daughter of Sir Leslie Stephen (1832–1904), himself an eminent Victorian. Growing up under such towering shadows, she and her generation had to fight back. And her father himself provided the kind of ammunition needed to attack him. Had he not stated fatuously that Hardy's *Return of the Native*, a novel now discussed in our high schools, was "too passionate" for publication? Yet the demolishing of these Victorian predecessors was achieved by a narrowing of sympathies. As Mrs. Woolf herself says of her heroine, Orlando: "The spirit of the nineteenth century was antipathetic to her in the extreme, and thus it took her and broke her, and she was aware of her defeat at its hands."

The Georgian reaction against the Victorians is perhaps now only a matter of the history of taste, but it needs airing here because its aftereffects have lingered. Most readers today enjoy the writings of Dickens and Browning, Arnold and Newman, George Eliot and Emily Brontë. Yet sometimes these same readers, with curious inconsistency, employ the term "Victorian" in an exclusively pejorative sense. Most of us would rather be called a thief than a prude, and if the connotation of "Victorian" is narrowed down to suggest "prude" and nothing else, we remain seriously hampered in enjoying to the full what the Victorian writers accomplished. Sympathy may not be essential, but condescension is fatal to understanding.

At the opposite extreme is the more recent tendency to sentimentalize minor aspects of the age. The kind of antiquarian zeal that today fosters enthusiasm for Victorian stuffed birds or quaint gables is of little help in approaching Victorian literature. What is required is that we be wary of outmoded suppositions about the nature of the Victorian age and that we see these writers not as smothering monsters but as artists who "lived, felt dawn, saw sunset glow, loved and were loved"—as a poet said of a later generation that perished between 1914 and 1918 on the battlefields of Flanders. In some of the more recent studies of Victorian literature we have admirable instances of how it can best be read, studies in which Browning and T. S. Eliot, instead of being merely pitted against each other, are regarded as adjacent and complementary links in the continuous chain of which English literature is made up.

Before seeking further to characterize the age and its literature, we should consider a second difficulty about the term "Victorian." For a period almost seventy years in length we can hardly expect our generalizations to be uniformly applicable. It may be legitimate to categorize as "Victorian" both the writings of Thomas Carlyle at the beginning of the period and of Oscar Wilde at the end, but we should do so with our eyes open to the gap that stretches between the worlds of these two writers. As a preliminary corrective it is helpful to subdivide the age into three phases: Early Victorian (1832–48); Mid-Victorian (1848–70); and Late Victorian (1870–1901).

THE EARLY PERIOD (1832–48): A TIME OF TROUBLES

The early phase has been sometimes characterized as the Time of Troubles. In 1832 the passing of a Reform Bill had seemed to satisfy many of the demands of the middle classes, who were gradually taking over control of England's economy. The bill extended the right to vote to all men owning property worth ten pounds or more in annual rent. In effect the voting public hereafter included the lower middle classes but not the working classes (the latter had to wait their turn until 1867 when a second Reform Bill was passed). Even more important than the extension of the franchise was the abolition in 1832 of an archaic electoral system whereby some of the new industrial cities were unrepresented in Parliament while "rotten boroughs" (communities which had become depopulated) elected the nominees of the local squire. Because it broke up the monopoly of power that the conservative landowners had so long enjoyed (the Tory party had been in office almost continuously from 1783 until 1830), the Reform Bill represents the beginning of a new age. Yet this celebrated piece of legislation could hardly be expected to solve all of the economic, social, and political problems that had been building up while England was developing into a modern democratic and industrialized state. In the early 1840's a severe depression, with widespread unemployment, led to rioting. Even without the provocation of unemployment, conditions in the new industrial and coal-mining areas were sufficiently inflammatory to create fears of revolution. Workers and their families in the slums of such cities as Manchester lived like packs of rats in a sewer, and the conditions under which women and children toiled in mines and factories were unimaginably brutal. Elizabeth Barrett's poem *The Cry of the Children* (1843) may strike us as hysterical exaggeration, but it was based upon reliable evidence concerning children of five years of age who dragged heavy tubs of coal through low-ceilinged mine-passages for sixteen hours a day. Life in early Victorian mines and factories was much like Thomas Hobbes's "state of nature"—"poor, nasty, brutish, and short."

The owners of mines and factories are invariably blamed for such conditions, yet these owners regarded themselves as innocent, and with some justification, for they were wedded to an economic theory of laissez faire which assumed that unregulated working conditions would ultimately benefit everyone. A sense of the seemingly hopeless complexity of the situation during the Hungry 1840's is provided by an entry for 1842 in the diary of the statesman Charles Greville, an entry written at the same time that Carlyle was making his contribution to the "Condition of England Question," *Past and Present.* Conditions in the north of England, Greville reports, were "appalling."

There is an immense and continually increasing population, no adequate demand for labor, * * * no confidence, but a universal alarm, disquietude, and discontent. Nobody can sell anything. * * * Certainly I have never seen * * * so serious a state of things as that which now stares us in the face; and this after thirty years of uninterrupted peace, and the most ample scope afforded for the development of all our resources. * * * One remarkable feature in the present condition of affairs is that nobody can account for it, and nobody pretends to be able to point out any remedy.

In reality many remedies were being pointed out. One of the most striking was put forward by the Chartists, a large organization of workingmen. In 1838 the organization drew up a "People's Charter" advocating the extension of the right to vote, the use of secret balloting, and other legislative reforms. For ten years the Chartist leaders engaged in agitation to have their program adopted by Parliament. Their fiery speeches, addressed to large mobs of discontented men, alarmed those who were not themselves suffering from hunger. In *Locksley Hall*, Tennyson seems to have had the Chartist mobs in mind when he pictured the threat posed by this time of troubles: "Slowly comes a hungry people, as a lion, creeping nigher, / Glares at one that nods and winks behind a slowly-dying fire." Although in the eyes of posterity the Chartist program seems an eminently reasonable one, it was premature in the 1840's. More immediately feasible was the agitation to abolish the high tariffs on imported grains, tariffs known as the Corn Laws (the word "corn" in England refers to wheat and other grains). These high tariffs had been established to protect English farm products from having to compete with low-priced products imported from abroad. Landowners and farmers fought to keep these tariffs in force so that high prices for their wheat would be assured, but the rest of the population suffered severely from the exorbitant price of bread or, in years of bad crops, from scarcity of food. In 1845 serious crop failures in England and the outbreak of potato blight in Ireland convinced Sir Robert Peel, the Tory Prime Minister, that traditional protectionism must be abandoned. In 1846 the Corn Laws were repealed by Parliament, and the way was paved for the introduction of a system of Free Trade whereby goods could be imported with the payment of only minimal tariff duties. Although Free Trade did not eradicate the slums of Manchester, it worked well for many years and helped to relieve the major crisis of the Victorian economy. In 1848, when armed revolutions were exploding violently in every country of Europe, England was relatively unaffected. A monster Chartist demonstration fizzled out harmlessly in London, and Englishmen settled down to enjoy two decades of prosperity.

This Time of Troubles left its mark on some early Victorian literature. "Insurrection is a most sad necessity," Carlyle writes in his *Past and Present*, "and governors who wait for that to instruct them are surely getting into the fatalest courses." A similar refrain runs through Carlyle's history *The French Revolution* (1837), with its warning that an irresponsible English government might suffer the same fate as the irresponsible government of Louis XVI had suffered. The warning is a reminder that if the Victorians were not so obsessed as we are with the possibilities of the outbreak of an international war, they did feel they were living under the shadow of a possible civil war. Memories of the French Reign of Terror lasted longer than memories of Trafalgar and Waterloo, memories freshened by later outbreaks of civil strife, "the red fool-fury of the Seine" as Tennyson described one of the violent overturnings of government in France. It is the novelists of the 1840's and early 1850's, however, who show the most marked response to the industrial and political scene. Vivid records of these conditions are to be found in the fiction of Charles Kingsley (1819–75), Mrs. Gaskell (1810–65), and Benjamin Disraeli (1804–81), a novelist who became Prime Minister. For his novel *Sybil* (1845) Disraeli chose an appropriate subtitle, *The Two Nations*—a phrase that pointed up the line dividing the England of the rich from the other nation, the England of the poor. The novels of Charles Dickens (1812–70) can also be related to these developments. *Pickwick Papers*, his first novel, appearing in the same year as Victoria's accession, was predominantly a gay-spirited comedy, but each of his later books shows a more somber dissatisfaction with the shortcomings of the Victorian social scene. The indignant social criticism in such late novels as *Our Mutual Friend* indicates how Dickens continued to represent in the 1860's a frame of mind more appropriate for the 1840's.

THE MID-VICTORIAN PERIOD (1848–70): ECONOMIC PROSPERITY
AND RELIGIOUS CONTROVERSY

Dickens' mood of indignation was unrepresentative but not unique after 1848. It was shared, for example, by John Ruskin, who abandoned the criticism of art during this period in order to expose the faults of Victorian industry and commerce, as in his prophetic history of architecture, *The Stones of Venice* (1853) or in his attacks upon laissez-faire economics in *Unto This Last* (1862). Generally speaking, however, the comfortable and commonsensical novels of Anthony Trollope (1815–82) are a more characteristic reflection of the mid-Victorian attitude towards the social and political scene. This second phase of the Victorian age had many harassing problems, but it was a time of prosperity. On the whole its institutions worked well. Even the badly-bungled war against Russia in the Crimea (1854–56) did not seriously affect the growing sense of satisfaction that the challenging difficulties of the 1840's had been solved or would be solved by English wisdom and energy. The monarchy was proving its worth in a modern setting. The queen and her husband, Prince Albert, had more than merely adapted themselves to a state in which the middle class had become dominant; they were themselves models of middle-class domesticity and devotion to duty. The aristocracy was discovering that Free Trade was enriching rather than impoverishing their estates; agriculture flourished together with trade and industry. And through a succession of Factory Acts in Parliament, which restricted child labor and limited hours of employment, the condition of the working classes was also being gradually improved. When we speak of Victorian complacency or stability or optimism, we are usually referring to this mid-Victorian phase—"The Age of Improvement," as the historian Asa Briggs has called it. "Of all the decades in our history," writes G. M. Young, "a wise man would choose the eighteen-fifties to be young in."

In 1851 Prince Albert opened the Great Exhibition in Hyde Park where a gigantic glass greenhouse, the Crystal Palace, had been erected to display the exhibits of modern industry and science. Although the Crystal Palace has been later cited as an example of Victorian bad taste in the arts, it was one of the first buildings constructed according to modern architectural principles in which materials such as glass and iron are employed for purely functional ends (much late Victorian furniture, on the other hand, with its fantastic and irrelevant ornamentation, was constructed according to the opposite principle). The building itself, as well as the exhibits, symbolized the triumphant feats of Victorian technology. As Benjamin Disraeli (later to become Prime Minister) wrote to a friend in 1862: "It is a privilege to live in this age of rapid and brilliant events. What an error to consider it a utilitarian age. It is one of infinite romance."

In the strenuous assertiveness of some of Robert Browning's poetry one might detect parallels to the confident mood inspired by the Great Exhibition. Generally, however, most mid-Victorian poetry and critical prose was less preoccupied with technology, economics, and politics than with the conflict between religion and science. This conflict was not, of course, altogether a new one. Tennyson's *In Memoriam* (1850), like much mid-Victorian literature, carries on the religious debates of earlier decades, debates concerning the role of the church and the authority of the Bible, and the claims of scientific reasoning to be the most reliable method of discovering truth. These debates, in their earlier form, had been generally between the Utilitarians, the followers of Jeremy Bentham (1772–1832) and the philosophical conservatives, the followers of S. T. Coleridge. As John Stuart Mill demonstrates in his excellent essays on Bentham and Coleridge, these two writers divided between them the allegiance of all thoughtful men in England. Bentham and his disciples, such as James Mill (the father of John Stuart Mill), were reformers of a distinctive cast of mind. Their aim was to test all institutions, government or church or the law, in the light of human reason and common sense in order to determine whether such institutions were useful—that is, whether they contributed to the greatest happiness of the greatest numbers of men. This "Utilitarian" test was an extremely effective method of correcting inefficiencies in government administration: the drastic remodeling of the Civil

Service in Victorian England was a tribute to Benthamite thinking. The fact that some procedures in government or law had been established for hundreds of years did not daunt Bentham in the least. Man's traditional customs, the very past itself, were of little interest to his logical mind; everything had to be tested afresh in terms of the Utilitarian formula. Such a test, if applied to a long-established institution like the Church of England, or to religious belief in general, could have, and did have, disruptive effects. Was religious belief useful for the needs of a reasonable man? To the Benthamites the answer was evident: religious belief was merely an outmoded superstition.

Opponents of Utilitarianism, including Coleridge, argued that Bentham's view of human nature was unrealistically narrow, that man had always needed a faith as profoundly as he had needed food, and that if reason seemed to demonstrate the irrelevance of religion then reason must be an inadequate mode of arriving at truth. These anti-Utilitarians were of two types. The first were those such as Carlyle, who abandoned institutional Christianity yet sought to retain some sort of substitute religious belief— a quest that is vividly described in Carlyle's spiritual autobiography, *Sartor Resartus*. Others, led by John Henry Newman, argued that only a power- ful, dogmatic, and traditional religious institution could withstand the at- tacks of irreverent thinkers of the Benthamite stamp. In the 1830's and 1840's (before he was converted to Roman Catholicism), Newman became the leader of an impressive crusade to strengthen the Church of England. The movement he headed is known under various names including "The Oxford Movement," because it originated at Oxford University, or as "Tractarianism," because Newman and his conservative followers developed their arguments in defense of a High Church in a series of pamphlets or tracts, or as "Puseyism," because Edward Pusey, an Oxford clergyman, shared with Newman the leadership in these developments. Whatever name it went by, Newman's campaign produced a lively controversy. When Arthur Hugh Clough and Matthew Arnold were at Oxford in the early 1840's, the university was seething with religious debates, debates that were to have a marked effect on the poetry written by both men in the 1850's.

In mid-Victorian England these controversies continued, but with an added intensification. Leadership in the anticlerical position passed grad- ually from the Utilitarians to some of the leaders of science, in particular to Thomas Henry Huxley, the lieutenant of Charles Darwin. Although many English scientists were themselves men of strong religious convic- tions, the impact of their scientific discoveries seemed consistently damag- ing to established faiths. Complaining about the "flimsiness" of his own religious faith in 1851, Ruskin exclaimed: "If only the Geologists would let me alone, I could do very well, but those dreadful hammers! I hear the clink of them at the end of every cadence of the Bible verses."

The damage lamented by Ruskin was effected in two ways. First was the application of a scientific attitude of mind towards a study of the Bible itself. This kind of investigation, developed especially in Germany, was known as the "Higher Criticism." Instead of treating the Bible as a sacredly infallible document, scientifically-minded scholars examined it as a mere text of history and presented evidence about its composition that believers, especially in Protestant countries, found disconcerting, to say the least. The second kind of damage was effected by the view of man implicit in the discoveries of Geology and Astronomy, the new and "Terrible Muses" of literature, as Tennyson called them in a late poem. Geology, by extending the history of the earth backwards millions of years, reduced the stature of man in time. The revolution effected by geology during the Victorian age was described by John Tyndall, an eminent physicist, in an address at Belfast in 1874. In the 18th century, Tyndall notes, men had an "unwavering trust" in the "chronology of the Old Testament," but in Victorian times men have had to become accustomed to "the idea that not for six thousand, nor for sixty thousand, nor for six thousand thousand, but for aeons embracing untold millions of years, this earth has been the theater of life and death. The riddle of the rocks has been read by the geologist and paleontologist, from sub-Cambrian depths to the deposits thickening over the sea bottoms of today. And upon the leaves of that stone book are * * * stamped the characters, plainer and surer than those formed by the ink of history, which carry the mind back into abysses of past time." And if geology reduced the stature of man in time, astronomy, by extending a knowledge of stellar distances to dizzying expanses, reduced the stature of man in space. To Tennyson's speaker in *Maud* (1855) the stars are "innumerable" tyrants of "iron skies." They are "Cold fires, yet with power to burn and brand / His nothingness into man."

In the mid-Victorian period a further reduction into "nothingness" was effected by Biology. Darwin's great treatise, *The Origin of Species* (1859), was interpreted by the nonscientific public in a variety of ways. Some chose to assume that evolution was synonymous with progress, but most readers recognized that Darwin's theory of natural selection conflicted not only with the concept of creation derived from the Bible but also with long-established assumptions of the values attached to man's special role in the world. Darwin's later treatise, *The Descent of Man* (1871), raised more explicitly the spectral question of man's identification with the animal kingdom. If the principle of survival of the fittest was accepted as the key to conduct, there remained the inquiry: fittest for what?

Disputes about evolutionary science, like the disputes about the Oxford Movement, are a reminder that beneath the placidly prosperous surface of the mid-Victorian age there were serious conflicts and anxieties. In the same year as the Great Exhibition, with its celebration of the triumphs of trade and industry, Charles Kingsley described the painful estrangements in Victorian households that had been brought about by religious differences. "The young men and women of our day are fast parting from their parents and each other; the more thoughtful are wandering either towards Rome, towards sheer materialism, or towards an unchristian and unphilosophic spiritualism."

THE LATE PERIOD (1870–1901): DECAY OF VICTORIAN VALUES

The third phase of the Victorian age is more difficult to categorize. At first glance its point of view seems merely an extension of mid-Victorianism whose golden glow lingered on through the Jubilee years of 1887 and 1897 (years celebrating the fiftieth and sixtieth anniversaries of the queen's accession) down to 1914. For many Victorians, this final phase of the century was a time of serenity and security, the age of house parties and long weekends in the country. In the amber of Henry James's prose is immortalized a sense of the comfortable pace of these pleasant, well-fed gatherings. Life in London, too, was for many an exhilarating heyday. In *My Life and Loves*, the Irish-American Frank Harris, often a severe critic of the English scene, records his recollections of the gaiety of London in the 1880's: "London: who would give even an idea of its varied delights: London, the center of civilization, the queen city of the world without a peer in the multitude of its attractions, as superior to Paris as Paris is to New York." Yet as the leading social critic of the 1860's, Matthew Arnold, had tried to show, there were anomalies in the seemingly smooth-working institutions of mid-Victorian England, and after 1870 flaws became evident. The sudden emergence of Bismarck's Germany after the defeat of France in 1871 was progressively to confront England with powerful threats to her naval and military position and also to her exclusive pre-eminence in trade and industry. The recovery of the United States after the Civil War likewise provided serious competition from a new quarter. In 1873 and 1874 economic depressions occurred of so severe a nature that the rate of emigration rose to an alarming degree. Also threatening to the domestic balance of power was the growth of labor as a political and economic force. In 1867, under Disraeli's guidance, a second Reform Bill had been passed which extended the right to vote to sections of the working classes, and this, together with the subsequent development of trade unions, made labor a political force to be reckoned with. Although Gilbert and Sullivan's comic opera *Iolanthe* had said that "every boy and every gal that's born into the world alive / Is either a little Liberal, or else a little Conserva-tive," it would not be long before this lyric of the year 1882 would require a corrective footnote. A third party, the Labour Party, was about to be added, a party dedicated to a very different conception of the role of the state than that held by the earlier generations of Whigs and Tories. The new party represented a wide variety of shades of socialism. Some labor leaders were disciples of the Tory-Socialism of John Ruskin and shared his idealistic conviction that the middle-class economic and political system, with its distrust of state interference, was irresponsible and immoral. Other labor leaders had been infected instead by the revolutionary theories of Karl Marx and Friedrich Engels as expounded in their *Communist Manifesto* of 1847 and in Marx's *Capital* (1867, 1885, 1895). Perhaps the first English author of note to be connected with Marxism was the poet and painter William Morris. Morris, himself a man of some independent means, was too much of an individualist to follow consistently an orthodox Marxist line, but he did share with Marx a conviction that utopia could be achieved only after the working classes had, by revolution, taken control of government and industry.

In much of the literature of this final phase of Victorianism we can sense an over-all change of attitudes. Some of the late Victorian writers expressed the change openly by simply attacking the major mid-Victorian idols. Samuel Butler (1835–1902), for example, set about demolishing Darwin, Tennyson, and Prime Minister Gladstone, figures whose aura of authority reminded him of his own father. For the more worldly and casual-mannered Prime Minister Disraeli, on the other hand, Butler could express considerable admiration, as can be seen in the following characteristically witty evaluation he made of "Dizzy" in 1881: "Earnestness was his greatest danger, but if he did not quite overcome it (as who indeed can? it is the last enemy that shall be subdued), he managed to veil it with a fair amount of success." In his novel, *The Way of All Flesh*, much of which was written in the 1870's, Butler satirized family life. In particular he made fun of the tyrannical self-righteousness of a Victorian father, his own father (a clergyman) serving as his model. Butler's open revolt was perhaps premature. More typical were Walter Pater and his followers, writers who concluded that the striving of their predecessors was ultimately pointless, that the answers to man's problems are not to be found, and that our role is to enjoy the fleeting moments of beauty in "this short day of frost and sun." It is symptomatic of this shift in point of view that Edward FitzGerald's beautiful translation of the *Rubáiyát of Omar Khayyám* (1859), with its melancholy theme that life's problems are insoluble, went virtually unnoticed in the 1860's but became a popular favorite in subsequent decades. The most dramatic illustration of the shift is provided by the life and works of Pater's disciple, Oscar Wilde. In Dickens' *David Copperfield*, the hero affirms: "I have always been thoroughly in earnest." Forty-four years later, in Wilde's comedy, *The Importance of Being Earnest* (1895), we see what happened to this typical mid-Victorian word, "earnest." In Wilde's deft dialogue the word is reduced to a pun, a key joke in this comic spectacle of earlier Victorian values being turned upside down.

 EARNESTNESS, RESPECTABILITY, AND THE EVANGELICALS

Wilde's decades, the 1880's and 1890's, when being earnest was apparently not important, can be legitimately overlooked if we are trying to categorize the Victorian age as a whole instead of distinguishing the stages of its development. Why has the term "earnest" been so often applied to the typical Victorian writers? It should be noted that the quality of earnestness (or as some historians call it, more appropriately, "eagerness") was not strained. It did not exclude high spirits and humor. An age which relished the comic genius of Dickens and Thackeray, the grotesque humor of Browning and Carlyle, the nonsensical whimsy of Edward Lear and Lewis Carroll, was not exclusively dedicated to mere solemnity. Nevertheless the general Victorian preference was for the mood of *Il Penseroso* rather than *L'Allegro*. This earnestness of spirit can best be accounted for by distinguishing it not from what came after but from what went before it.

The connections between literature in the Romantic and Victorian ages are close. Victorian poets as different as Browning and Swinburne both derive from Shelley. Tennyson is a follower of Keats, Arnold is a follower of Wordsworth, and many other instances of such continuity and influence may be cited. If we are looking for a dividing point, however, we may find one in Carlyle's well-known advice to his contemporaries in 1834: "Close thy *Byron*; open thy *Goethe*." Carlyle's advice could be interpreted in two ways. The first is with reference to literary forms. By ceasing to use Byron as a model, a Victorian writer might avoid the wild excesses, the lack of controlled form of much Romantic writing. Byron himself foresaw that such a reformation was necessary. "We are all on a wrong tack ('Lakers' and all)," he wrote. "Our successors will have to go back to the riding school * * * and learn to ride the great horse." Some of Byron's Victorian successors ignored his prediction; they too rode Pegasus bareback as casually as he had done. The novels of the Brontë sisters, for example, are Byronic; *Wuthering Heights* and *Jane Eyre* (both published in 1847) have affinities with the Gothic novels popular in Byron's day. The prose of Carlyle himself is Byronic. Yet several Victorian poets, Tennyson in particular, do fulfill Byron's prediction. The energy of Romantic literature persists, but it is channeled into a stricter concern for disciplined forms, "Nature still," as Alexander Pope recommended, "but Nature methodized." Tennyson's Virgilian sense of vowel sounds and Dante Gabriel Rossetti's polished polysyllables are symptomatic of the change. Matthew Arnold, too, at least in his literary criticism, is evidently a classical riding master. It is significant that the Romantic poet most influential in the Victorian age was Keats, the most form-conscious of the Romantics, rather than Byron.

As for Carlyle himself, when he advised his contemporaries to close their volumes of Byron he was not primarily concerned with a chastening of literary forms. He was saying, in effect: "Stop moping. There is work to be done, work that requires the earnest efforts of all of us." Byronism, in this context, meant the easy-going aristocratic code that had been dominant during the Regency, with its preference for a happy-go-lucky enjoyment of the physical pleasures of life, for hunting and hard drinking and lounging. Lord Melbourne, Victoria's first Prime Minister, embodied such a view of life and found himself out of place under the new dispensation—an "autumn rose" as Strachey called him. Carlyle's gospel, on the other hand, was soon to be extremely timely for the new generation. From 1830 on there developed what the historian Arnold Toynbee calls a "challenge." The earnest strivings of the Victorians provided the needed "response." The strenuous transformation of English political, social, economic, and literary life is evidence that the volumes of Byron (as thus interpreted) had been closed.

A further indication of the timeliness of Carlyle's call to action in *Sartor Resartus* is its Evangelical tone. "Evangelical," a term commonly used in all discussions of 19th-century literature, requires some explanation. In its strictest sense "Evangelical" refers to part of a branch of the Church of England called the Low Church. In the 18th century many Anglicans had been profoundly affected by the teachings of John Wesley. Without setting up a separate church, they had sought to instill some of Wesley's ideals and religious enthusiasm into the phlegmatic and easy-going Established Church of which they were members. Zealously dedicated to good causes (they were responsible for the emancipation of all the slaves in the British Empire as early as 1833), advocates of a strict puritan code of morality, and righteously censorious of worldliness in others, the Evangelicals became a powerful and active minority in the early part of the 19th century. Much of their power depended on the fact that their view of life and religion was virtually identical with that of a much larger group, the Nonconformists—that is, the Baptists, Methodists, Congregationalists, and other Protestant sects outside the Church of England. When united for action with this large group of sects, whose membership included a generous proportion of successful businessmen, the Evangelicals were a formidable force. For this reason, the term "Evangelical" is often stretched to refer to the puritan code and spiritual zeal shared by this combination of the Protestant sects and the Evangelical wing of the church.

Finally, the term "Evangelical" has been loosely applied to cover any kind of enthusiastic concern for reform. It is thus used to describe anyone infected with the *spirit* of the Evangelical movement even though he does not subscribe to its ethical code or its beliefs. This loose use of the term may be a mere sleight-of-hand trick, but it enables the historian to equate Evangelicalism with early Victorianism. Seen in this light, even secular reformers such as Jeremy Bentham and his Utilitarian followers could be classified as Evangelical in spirit. Bentham was no churchman; as his earnest-minded disciple J. S. Mill described him, he was "the great questioner of things established." Yet because the sober effort of the Utilitarians was responsible for many of the major reforms of government and administration in the Victorian age, it could be said that the Utilitarians showed signs of having been lastingly infected by a religious spirit which they had outwardly rejected. Less incongruously, the spirit of Evangelicalism can be detected among the school of thinkers opposed to Bentham, the conservative school of Coleridge. The revival of conservatism was most dramatically manifested not in politics but in the Oxford Movement in religion. Although Newman and his Tractarian followers of the 1830's and 1840's were of course opposed to the theological position of the true Evangelicals, the fervor with which they set about reforming the Anglican Church by instilling fresh energy into its doctrines and rituals is similar to the fervor of Evangelical theologians such as Thomas Scott, whose teachings left a permanent mark on Newman himself.

Victorian earnestness may therefore be explained partly as a response to a challenging situation and partly as rooted in an active religious movement that left its stamp on agnostics as well as on believers. Arnold's friend Arthur Clough, who became a skeptic, attributed his own persistent obsession with problems of conscience to the Evangelical revival. The movement "beginning with Wesleyanism, and culminating at last in Puseyism" was responsible, he said, for an "over-excitation of the religious sense, resulting in this irrational, almost animal irritability of conscience." George Eliot (pseudonym of Mary Ann Evans; 1819–80) is another example of this Evangelical legacy. After having abandoned Christianity and having flouted convention by living for years with a married man, she devoted her novels to painstaking analyses of problems of conscience and moral choice. It would be difficult to name a Victorian writer of any consequence who remained an Evangelical in the true sense of the term; it would be equally difficult to name one who was not affected by what Evangelicalism had stood for.

If we also consider the puritan code of morality advocated by the Nonconformists and Evangelicals rather than their earnestness of spirit, it is once more apparent why Carlyle's recommendation to close the volumes of Byron was appropriate. During Byron's lifetime those advocating the puritan code had been a minority. After 1832 they gradually came to represent if not a numerical majority at least the most potent voice in Victorian England. And they were not reluctant to make that voice heard.

The code of puritanism and respectability, which the middle classes imposed on England, is symbolized by the joyless Victorian Sunday. In 1837, a new Sunday Observance Bill was introduced into Parliament, a bill that provoked Dickens into protesting against its strict prohibition of harmless entertainments on the Sabbath. Although the Bill did not quite pass, the Sober Sunday ritual became established by custom if not by law. To later generations, even more noteworthy was the puritans' standard of sexual behavior, with its intense concern for female innocence—or, as its opponents contended, for female ignorance. The history of Victorian asceticism is nevertheless much more complex than common supposition allows, as may be suggested by the fact that in 1850 8,000 prostitutes were known by the police to be operating in London. In the city of Leeds, a few years earlier, statistics indicate that there were two churches and 39 chapels or meeting houses to compete with 451 taverns and 98 brothels. For a striking corrective to the commonly accepted suppositions about Victorian asceticism, Steven Marcus' study of the sexual habits of different classes of mid-19th-century English society, *The Other Victorians* (1966), may be consulted.

The middle-class puritan code was largely derived from the Old Testament, but it also reflected commercial experience in which sobriety, hard work, and a joyless abstention from worldly pleasures paid off, paradoxically enough, in worldly success. Intermixed with this ascetic code was an insistence upon respectability—an insistence reflecting the insecurity of a newly powerful class in a fluid society, a class anxious to have a fixed set of manners by which to live and to measure themselves and the families of others. Hence developed the phenomenon of "Mrs. Grundyism": conformity in its worst sense—that is, external conformity.

It is against this background that John Stuart Mill's essay *On Liberty* should be read. The status of liberty in Victorian England was actually one of the most outstanding achievements of the age. For continental agitators of Left, Right, or Center in politics, Victorian England was the land of freedom, an asylum where the policeman was a friendly protector instead of an instrument of tyranny. To this asylum flocked General Torrijos (whose plot against the Spanish monarchy involved Tennyson); Mazzini, the Italian nationalist; Louis Napoleon of France; Kossuth, the Hungarian patriot; Prince Metternich of Austria; and Karl Marx himself, whose major work, *Capital*, was conceived in the Reading Room of the British Museum. The Victorian achievement in religious as well as political freedom is also impressive. Atheist orators such as Charles Bradlaugh enjoyed the privilege of addressing large audiences. As Amy Cruse affirms, "no age has done more towards giving religious freedom in thought and speech and practice."

Under such circumstances, we may wonder why Mill considered liberty a problem worth writing a treatise about in 1859. Mill was inspired by his experience that individuality is threatened not merely by political tyrannies or entrenched religions. It is threatened also by the less tangible pressures exerted by society itself, in particular by the middle-class conventions which weighed upon the nonconformist in society rather than upon the Nonconformist in religion. In Hardy's late-Victorian novel, *Jude the Obscure*, a novel which contributed to the breakdown of the puritan code in literature, it is revealing that when the heroine resolves to leave her husband she justifies her action by citing a passage from Mill's *On Liberty*.

THE DIVERSITY OF VICTORIAN LITERATURE

The weight of the puritan code on the literature of early and mid-Victorian England was, as we might expect, considerable. It was most evident in the novels, for novels were commonly read aloud in family gatherings, and the need to avoid topics which might cause embarrassment to young girls established taboos that the novelist could not dare ignore, although he might sometimes skillfully circumvent them. Thackeray and others offered protests, but it was not until near the end of the century or later that the novelists broke clear of the restrictions imposed on them by the demands of their middle-class public. The poets, and also the writers of that important Victorian form, the extended essay, fared better. When Browning was writing *The Ring and the Book* he was obviously unconcerned about whether his poem might raise blushes on prudish cheeks, and Swinburne's *Poems and Ballads* flouts the taboos in the manner of the French poets whom he admired. Both volumes appeared in the 1860's at the same time as the essays of Matthew Arnold with their attacks on the narrowness of the puritan middle-class mind.

Too much can be made of the importance of these quaint taboos as literary conventions in the Victorian age. A much more significant kind of pressure from the Victorian audience on its writers was one that they were themselves inclined to comply with rather than to repudiate or circumvent. This was the desire on the part of readers to be guided and edified. The desire stems from a combination of the various strands of Victorian character we have been here considering: the earnest preoccupation with problems of a new age, the sense of anxious uncertainty as an established order gives way, and the strain of puritanism which may dismiss entertainment as mere entertainment. The newly expanding reading public, despite its air of solid confidence, wanted help from its authors, and its authors were understandably flattered by the request. Only a few, such as D. G. Rossetti, ignored it; the others all exhibit, in varying degrees, an air of prophecy and mission. Carlyle in his lectures *On Heroes* identifies the writer or "Poet" such as Shakespeare with the great prophets such as Mahomet, and in his own writings it is evident that he sought to make his mark as a seer rather than as a mere man of letters. The very high status that even Matthew Arnold claimed for literature is evident in his statement that "most of what now passes with us for religion and philosophy will be replaced by poetry." Perhaps the most extreme example of a Victorian writer with a sense of mission is, however, John Ruskin, a writer who had opinions on everything from Botticelli to how to build sheepfolds. Tennyson, here as in most instances, is more representative. To provide firm guidance in problems of science and religion, the destiny of nations and daily life, was a task that sometimes appealed to Tennyson and sometimes appalled him. As we might expect, several of his poems are concerned with the dilemma of a writer's divided duty towards his public and his art—a dilemma that has become even more acute in the 20th century as the reading public has further expanded.

The existence of this dilemma may help to explain another characteristic of Victorian literature: its variety both in style and in subject matter. Variety is in part a symptom of the Victorian writer's bold independence and his zest for literary experiment for its own sake, but it is also a symptom of an absence of any final general agreement concerning the function of literature and art in a democratic society. The writer and his audience might usually agree that instruction was a desirable attribute of a work of literature, but what was to constitute the instruction and what was the appropriate mode in which to convey it? Tennyson's poem *The Lotos-Eaters* (1842) and Browning's poem *The Bishop Orders his Tomb* (1845) were published within the space of three years. The one is in the grand manner of English poetry, the culmination of a poetic tradition emphasizing beautiful cadences and vowel sounds: "To watch the crisping ripples on the beach, / And tender curving lines of creamy spray." The colloquial speech of Browning's bishop, as he hisses his hatred of a rival, seems to belong to a different century: "Shrewd was that snatch from out the corner south / He graced his carrion with, God curse the same!" And if we ignore the stylistic differences here and concentrate upon a possible similarity—that both poems, like many Victorian writings, evoke the past of myth and history—what is to be done to align these works with other works of the same period? What resemblance is there to Dickens' *Oliver Twist* (1838) for example, with its realistic scenes of a sordid workhouse, or to Carlyle's *Past and Present* (1843) with its idiosyncratic manner of exposing the sufferings of the Victorian poor, or to John Ruskin's *Modern Painters* (1843) with its rhapsodic celebrations of alpine scenery and romantic sunsets? In one of his early letters Matthew Arnold complained to a friend of the "multitudinousness" of the age, and as a literary critic Arnold sought to provide for himself as a poet, and for his contemporaries in general, a set of classical critical principles which would correct this anarchical diversity and would reimpose some kind of order. Arnold's achievement as a critic and poet is indeed impressive, yet it can hardly be said that he succeeded in persuading his contemporaries to accept him as a Victorian Aristotle. The "multitudinousness" was too overpowering, even for him. As a result, most candid literary historians admit that while we may confidently identify the distinguishing characteristics of individual Victorian writers, of a Browning, a Dickens, or a Newman, it is extremely difficult to devise satisfactory statements about Victorian literature that are generally applicable to most or all of these writers. This admission is distressing to tidy minds, but in itself it tells us something distinctive about Victorian literature as a whole. Variety may frustrate the pleasure of ready classification, but it provides interesting challenges of its own.

What we can perhaps isolate is what Jerome Buckley calls the "temper" of Victorian literature, a state of mind and emotion already described in this introduction as an eager or earnest response to the expanding horizons of 19th-century life. We also encounter some frequently recurring subjects in Victorian literature, including a preoccupation with man's relationship to God. Also shared in common is an awareness of time, a strong sense of past and future times as well as of present time. As for quality, we have to confront another phase of Victorian variety in the very unevenness of the literary achievements of the age. Exaggerated conceptions about the writer's role as prophet may help to account for the more absurd lapses into which Victorian authors seem at times to fall. Moreover, as its interior decorating will illustrate, the Victorian age was not an age of delicate taste, although some of its poets, as we have seen, did succeed in subduing the excesses of Romanticism. In general, instead of taste and decorum, the Victorian age tended to value strenuous energy. Compared with later periods it was less afraid to risk a fall. If it seems in many respects a golden age in literature with a distracting admixture of tinsel, the roll call of some of its major authors remains an impressive summary of achievement. In the novel: Dickens, Thackeray, the Brontës, George Eliot, and Hardy; in nonfictional prose: Carlyle, Mill, Newman, Ruskin, and Arnold; in poetry, Tennyson, Browning, Arnold, and even Gerard Manley Hopkins, a Victorian at present on loan to the 20th-century anthologists. Only in drama is there a conspicuous blank.

THE VICTORIAN NOVEL

Something needs to be said about one great Victorian genre in particular—the novel. When studying Victorian literature in anthologies we tend to overlook the novels of the period because they do not readily lend themselves to representative excerpts. Although some selections from Dickens and Kingsley have been included in the Topics section of the present anthology, it will be evident that a few fragments of stained glass cannot adequately evoke a Gothic cathedral. Fortunately, however, these monumental books, essential to any estimate of Victorian literature, are among the most readily available books in English.

Often the novelist and poet or essayist confront the same issues and employ similar styles (the stylistic affinities between Browning and Dickens, for example, are striking). At other times there are significant differences. For instance, the novelists for the most part do not share the preoccupation of the Victorian poets and essayists with man's relationship to God. Like their greatest predecessors—Fielding, Richardson, and Jane Austen—most of the Victorian novelists were primarily concerned with man in society and with those aspects of experience categorized by the title of Lionel Trilling's essay: "Manners, Morals and the Novel," to which we can add an additional topic—Money. The stories of the governess-heroine of Charlotte Brontë's *Jane Eyre* (1847), Arthur Pendennis in Thackeray's *Pendennis* (1850), Pip in Dickens' *Great Expectations* (1861), or Clara Middleton in Meredith's *The Egoist* (1879) all center on the struggles of a protagonist, male or female, to find himself in relation to other men and women, in love or marriage, with family or neighbors, or with associates in his working career. Occasionally such a search may take on quasi-religious dimensions, as in the later novels of Thomas Hardy or in that unclassifiable sport among Victorian novels, *Wuthering Heights*, and, more indirectly, in George Eliot's novels, with their persistent concern with the role of free will and fate in the lives of their characters. On the whole, however, the Victorian novelists were less occupied with man's relation to God than with his relation to other men.

And for the most part, the other men were the reader's contemporaries. To be sure, the historical novel, as established by Sir Walter Scott, remained popular throughout the post-Romantic period, but it was a form especially congenial to the lesser novelists, such as Bulwer Lytton (*The Last Days of Pompeii*, 1834) or Charles Reade (*The Cloister and the Hearth*, 1861). While the major novelists occasionally tried their hand at historical fiction—for example, Thackeray in *Henry Esmond* (1852), Dickens in *A Tale of Two Cities* (1859), and George Eliot in *Romola* (1863) —their preference was for the contemporary. Whether the story was set in the rural landscapes of Eliot's Warwickshire, Trollope's cathedral towns, or Dickens' fogbound London, readers expected a representation of daily 19th-century life that would be recognizably familiar to them.

To satisfy such expectations they were provided with a rich fare. Charles Dickens, who established himself as the leading Victorian novelist in 1837 and enjoyed triumph after triumph until his death in 1870, was praised by Walter Bagehot for having described London "like a special correspondent for posterity." One of the many pleasures his novels provided was his representation of what seemed to his readers to be ordinary life in Victorian home, tavern, office, or factory. His contemporaries and successors among the novelists were also skillful reporters, and most of them were more scrupulously concerned with detailed realism than he had been. Disputes about the degree of Dickens' realism have persisted among critical readers from his day to ours; the truth is that he was much more than a brilliant reporter. He was a great poet, in his own way a "lord of language" (as Tennyson said of Virgil) with a command of the comic in description and dialogue that produces a heightening and stylization very different in effect from that of straightforward realism. Dickens' habitual construction of his scenes according to the model of the theater added to the stylized quality of his novels. Although the Victorians, despite well-intentioned efforts, were unsuccessful in writing plays of lasting interest, theirs was an age in which theatrical entertainment flourished—especially highly melodramatic plays— and Dickens was an avid patron of the theater. "Every writer of fiction," he said, "although he may not adopt the dramatic form, writes, in effect, for the stage." Among Dickens' rivals and successors there was a common agreement that the stagey aspect of his novels was his most glaring fault, and each novelist in turn set out to correct that fault by his own example of what he believed was a more realistic representation of life. Thackeray's masterpiece, *Vanity Fair* (1848), has to a modern reader many mannerisms of its own, but is much less blatantly mannered than a characteristic Dickens novel. "The Art of Novels," Thackeray affirmed in a letter, "*is* to represent Nature: to convey as strongly as possible the sentiment of reality." In Thackeray's disciple, Anthony Trollope, and later in the drab narratives of George Gissing, a lesser figure, there is a similar reduction of stagelike scenes and effects. In George Eliot this reaction against novelistic theatricalism took a more influential turn: she set out to explore what the theatrical writer rarely explores—the inner lives of her characters. Early in the 20th century, the young D. H. Lawrence, beginning his career as a novelist, noted that among his predecessors it was George Eliot whose novels marked a significant innovation. "You see, it was really George Eliot who started it all," Lawrence remarked to a friend. "And how wild they all were with her for doing it. It was she who started putting all the action inside. Before, you know, with Fielding and the others, it had been outside. Now I wonder which is right?" Lawrence himself decided, as a practicing novelist, that Fielding and his Victorian followers could be as right as George Eliot, but most early 20th-century novelists preferred to emphasize the new areas opened up by Eliot's example. They chose to concentrate on the inner lives of their characters; and critical readers, adapting their tastes to the new mode, were disposed to undervalue Victorian novels which had portrayed man acting rather than man recollecting, or reflecting, or trying to come to a decision.

Contributing to this underevaluation of the Victorian achievement was the assumption that novels published in serial form (as Victorian novels had usually been published) must be slapdash productions altogether deficient in art, or as Henry James characterized them, "large loose baggy monsters." James's affectionate derogation is applicable to such a novel as Dickens' early *Pickwick Papers*, but it should be noted that it does not apply at all to some of Dickens' later novels such as *Bleak House* (a masterpiece of narrative construction), Eliot's *Middlemarch* (1872), Hardy's *Jude the Obscure* (1895), or the tight and intricate plotting of Wilkie Collins' detective novel, *The Moonstone* (1868). Serial publication, as later critics have come to recognize, did not necessarily preclude artful storytelling, and it had advantages to offset the possible disadvantages of fragmentation. Publication by installments challenged the novelist to sustain the interest of his readers; in every single number he had to entertain them or, to use the traditional critical term, to provide delight. Like an actor or public speaker, the Victorian novelist had a sense, during the very process of writing his book, of how his audience was responding to his performance. And it was an audience that offered a special challenge because of its exceptional diversity; Victorian readers ranged from the sophisticated and well-read lawyer to the semiliterate household servant. The present-day division of the novel-reading public into highbrow, middlebrow, and lowbrow existed only in embryonic form in the Victorian age, and did not become a significant controlling influence on the novelist until late in the century.

This popular genre is thus especially representative of all but the religious attitudes that have been emphasized in this account of the Victorian period: the earnest sense of responsibility, the occasional lapses of taste, and the overflowing creative energy of its writers. Near the end of his life Thackeray drew a comparison between himself and Dickens: "I am played out. All I can do now is to bring out my old puppets. * * * But, if he live to be ninety, Dickens will still be creating new characters. In his art that man is marvelous." Wrung from a novelist whose own writings occupy more than twenty thick volumes, this compliment is quintessentially Victorian.

THOMAS CARLYLE
(1795–1881)

1833: *Sartor Resartus* published in *Fraser's Magazine.*
1834: Moves to London from Craigenputtock in Scotland.
1837: *The French Revolution* published.
1843: *Past and Present* published.
1866: Death of Jane Carlyle.

W. B. Yeats once asked William Morris what writers had inspired the socialist movement of the 1880's, and Morris replied: "Oh, Ruskin and Carlyle, but somebody should have been beside Carlyle and punched his head every five minutes." Morris's mixed feelings of admiration and exasperation are typical of the response Carlyle evokes in many readers. Anyone approaching his prose for the first time should expect to be sometimes bewildered. Like George Bernard Shaw, Carlyle discovered, early in life, that exaggeration can be a highly effective way of gaining the attention of an audience. But it can also be a way of distracting an audience unfamiliar with the idiosyncrasies of his rhetoric and unprepared for the distinctive enjoyments his writings can provide.

One of the idiosyncrasies of his prose is that it is meant to be read aloud. As a talker Carlyle was as famous in his day as Dr. Johnson in his. Charles Darwin testified that he was "the best worth listening to of any man I know." No Boswell has adequately recorded this talk, but no Boswell was needed, for Carlyle has contrived to get the sound of his own spoken voice into his writings. It is a noisy and emphatic voice, startling upon first acquaintance. To become familiar with its unusual sounds and rhythms, one can best begin by reading aloud from some of Carlyle's portraits of his contemporaries which are included in the following selections. Many of these colorful portraits are from his letters, and it becomes evident that the mannerisms of the author were simply the mannerisms of the man and were congenial and appropriate for the author's purposes.

Carlyle was 41 years old when Victoria became queen of England. He had been born in the same year as Keats, yet he is rarely grouped with his contemporaries among the Romantic writers. Instead his name is linked with younger men such as Dickens, Browning, and Ruskin, the early generation of Victorian writers. The classification is fitting, for it was Carlyle's role to foresee the problems that were to preoccupy the Victorians and early to report upon his experiences in confronting these problems. After 1837 his loud voice began to attract an audience, and he soon became one of the most influential figures of the age, affecting the attitudes of scientists, statesmen, and especially of men of letters. His wife once complained that Ralph Waldo Emerson had no ideas (except mad ones) that he had not derived from Carlyle. "But pray, Mrs. Carlyle," replied a friend, "*who has?*"

Before attaining such prestige among the Victorians, however, Carlyle had a long wait. His early career is the dramatic story of struggles against narrowness of background, poverty, ill-health, and religious uncertainties.

Carlyle was born in Ecclefechan, a village in Scotland, the eldest child of a large family. His mother, at the time of her marriage, had been illiterate. His father, James Carlyle, a stonemason and later a farmer, was proudly characterized by his son as a peasant. The key to the character of James Carlyle was the Scottish Calvinism which he instilled into the members of his household. Frugality, hard work, a tender but undemonstrative family loyalty, and a peculiar blend of self-denial and self-righteousness were characteristic features of Carlyle's childhood home. The stamp of its discipline, imprinted upon him for life, can be detected even in Carlyle's sense of humor, which was highly developed yet limited. The trivial banter of London's bohemia did not merely bore him; it drove him to furious repudiations. His incapacity to enjoy the fun of Charles Lamb is comparable to his father's stern rejection of workmen who wasted time.

With his father's aid the young Carlyle was educated at Annan Academy and at Edinburgh University, the subject of his special interest being mathematics; he left without taking a degree. It was his parents' hope that their son would become a clergyman, but in this respect Thomas made a severe break with his ancestry. He was a prodigious reader, and his exposure to such skeptical writers as Hume, Voltaire, and Gibbon had undermined his faith. Gibbon's *Decline and Fall of the Roman Empire*, he told Emerson, was "the splendid bridge from the old world to the new." By the time he was 23, Carlyle had crossed the bridge and had abandoned his Christian faith and his proposed career as a clergyman. During the period in which he was thinking through his religious position, he supported himself by teaching school in Scotland, and later by tutoring private pupils, but from 1824 to the end of his life he relied exclusively upon his writings for his livelihood. His early writings consisted of translations, biographies, and critical studies of Goethe and other German authors, to whose view of life he was deeply attracted. The German Romantics (loosely grouped by Carlyle under the label "Mystics") were the second most important influence on his life and character, exceeded only by his early family experiences. Aided by the writings of these German poets and philosophers, he arrived finally at a faith in life that served as a substitute for the Christian faith he had lost.

His most significant early essay, *Characteristics*, appeared in *The Edinburgh Review* in 1831. A year earlier he had begun writing his full-length autobiographical novel, *Sartor Resartus*, a work which he had great difficulty in persuading anyone to publish. In book form *Sartor* first appeared in America in 1836, where Carlyle's follower, Emerson, had prepared an enthusiastic audience for this unusual work. His American following (which was later to become a vast one) did little at first, however, to relieve the poverty in which he still found himself after fifteen years of writing. In 1837 the tide at last turned when he published *The French Revolution*. "O it has been a great success, dear," his wife assured him, but her husband, embittered by the long struggle, was incredulous that the sought-for recognition had at last come to him.

It was in character for his wife, Jane Welsh Carlyle, to be less surprised by his success than he was. That Thomas Carlyle was a genius had been an article of faith to her from her first meeting with him in 1821. A clever girl, the daughter of a doctor of good family, Jane Welsh had many suitors. When in 1826 she finally accepted Carlyle, her family and friends were shocked. This peasant's son, of no fixed employment, seemed a fantastic choice. Subsequent events seemed to confirm her family's verdict. Not long after marriage, Carlyle insisted upon their retiring to a remote farm at Craigenputtock where for six years (1828–34) this sociable woman was obliged to live in isolation and loneliness. After they moved to London in 1834 and settled in a house on Cheyne Walk in Chelsea, Jane Carlyle was considerably happier and enjoyed her role as hostess. Her husband, however, remained a difficult man to live with. His stomach ailments, irascible nerves, and preoccupation with his writings, as well as the lionizing to which he was subjected, left him with little inclination for domestic amenities.

This marriage of the Carlyles has aroused almost as much interest as that of the Brownings. Their friend the Reverend W. H. Brookfield (whose marriage was an unhappy one) once said cynically that marrying is "dipping into a pitcher of snakes for the chance of an eel," and partisan biographers have argued that Jane Welsh drew a snake instead of an eel. Even without such partisanship, it is easy to be sorry for the wife. Yet if we study her letters, before and after her marriage, it is evident that she got what she asked for. She wanted a man of genius who would change the world. She paid for what she wanted by years of comparative poverty, ill health, and loneliness. Just before her death in 1866, she had the satisfaction of enjoying to the full a high point of her husband's triumph when the peasant's son she had chosen returned to Scotland to deliver his inaugural address as Lord Rector of Edinburgh University.

During the first thirty years of Carlyle's residence in London he wrote extensive historical works and many pamphlets concerning contemporary issues. After *The French Revolution* he edited, in 1845, the *Letters and Speeches of Oliver Cromwell*, a Puritan leader of heroic dimensions in Carlyle's eyes, and later wrote a full-length biography, *The History of Friedrich II of Prussia, Called Frederick the Great* (1858–65). Carlyle's pamphleteering is seen at its best in *Past and Present* (1843) and in its most violent phase in his *Latter-Day Pamphlets* (1850). Following the death of his wife, he wrote very little. For the remaining fifteen years of his life he confined himself to reading, or to talking to the stream of visitors who called at Cheyne Walk to listen to the "Sage of Chelsea," as he came to be called. In 1874 he accepted the Prussian Order of Merit from Bismarck but declined an English baronetcy offered by Disraeli. In 1881 he died and was buried near his family in Ecclefechan churchyard.

To understand Carlyle's role as historian, biographer, and social critic, it is essential to understand his attitude towards religion. The qualities of his prose style as well as his mature evaluation of past and present are ultimately attributable to religious experiences undergone in his earlier years. By the time he was 23, he had been shorn of his faith in Christianity. At this stage, as Carlyle observed with dismay, many men seemed content simply to stop. A Utilitarian such as James Mill or some of his common-sensical professors at the University of Edinburgh regarded society and the universe itself as machines. To such men the machines might sometimes seem complex, but they were not mysterious, for machines are subject to man's control and understanding through reason and observation. To Carlyle, and to many others, life without a sense of the divine was a meaningless nightmare. In the first part of "The Everlasting No," a chapter of *Sartor Resartus,* he gives a memorable picture of the horrors of such a soulless world that drove him in 1822 to thoughts of suicide. The 18th-century Enlightenment had left him not in light but in darkness. As William Barrett says of modern man, in his study of 20th-century Existentialism: "The individual is thrust out of the sheltered nest that society has provided. He can no longer hide his nakedness by the old disguises."

Barrett's choice of terms here is identical with Carlyle's metaphor of the "Clothes Philosophy." The naked man seeks clothing for protection. One solution, represented by Coleridge and his followers, was to repudiate the skepticism of Voltaire and Hume and to return to the protective beliefs and rituals of the Christian church. To Carlyle such a return was pointless. The traditional Christian coverings were worn out—"Hebrew Old Clothes" he called them. His own solution, described in "The Everlasting Yea," was to tailor a new suit of beliefs from German philosophy, shreds of Scottish Calvinism, and his own observations. The following summarizes his basic religious attitude: "Gods die with the men who have conceived them. But the god-stuff roars eternally, like the sea. * * * Even the gods must be born again. We must be born again." Although this passage is from *The Plumed Serpent,* by D. H. Lawrence (a writer who resembles Carlyle at almost every point), it might have come from any one of Carlyle's own books—most especially from *Sartor Resartus,* in which he describes his being born again—his "Fire-baptism"—into a new secular faith.

On what evidence was the new faith based? Carlyle and Lawrence might contend that the word "evidence" is irrelevant here. Or Carlyle might cite the religious experience itself, the moment of insight when he saw the realities behind the appearances. He might also cite his realization that all the sciences he had studied had failed to answer the important questions confronting man, which remain what he called "mysteries." From this latter realization there derives what seems an anti-intellectual strain in Carlyle. He speaks often of the limitations of the conscious analytic intellect and praises instead the instinctive responses of the unconsciously healthy soul, responses which include a sense of religious awe.

The most appropriate term to describe Carlyle's central position is *vitalism.* The presence of energy in the world was, in itself, for him, a sign of the godhead. Carlyle therefore judges everything in terms of the presence or absence of some vital spark. The minds of men, books, societies, churches, or even landscapes, are rated as alive or dead, dynamic or merely mechanical. The government of Louis XVI, for example, was obviously moribund, doomed to be swept away by the dynamic forces of the French Revolution. The government of Victorian England seemed likewise to be doomed unless infused with vital energies of leadership and an awareness of the real needs of mankind. When an editor complained that his essay *Characteristics* was "inscrutable," Carlyle remarked: "My own fear was that it might be too *scrutable;* for it indicates decisively enough that Society (in my view) is utterly condemned to destruction, and even now beginning its long travail-throes of Newbirth."

This preoccupation with revolution and the destruction of the old orders suggests that Carlyle's politics were radical, but his position is bewilderingly difficult to classify. During the Hungry 1840's, he was one of the most outspoken critics of middle-class bunglings and of the economic theory of laissez faire which, in his opinion, was ultimately responsible for these bunglings. On behalf of the millions of people suffering from the miseries attendant upon a major breakdown of industry and agriculture he did strenuous work. At other times, because of his insistence upon strong and heroic leadership, Carlyle appears to be a violent conservative, or, as some have argued, virtually a fascist. That some aspects of his political position are similar to fascism is beyond dispute. The theory of democracy seemed to him to be based on an unrealistic premise about the basic needs of mankind, and he had no confidence that democratic institutions could work efficiently. A few men in every age are, in his view, leaders; the rest are followers and are happy only as followers. Society should be organized so that these gifted leaders can have scope to govern effectively. Such leaders are, for Carlyle, heroes. George Bernard Shaw, who learned much from Carlyle, would call them supermen. Liberals and democrats, however, might call them dictators. Although Carlyle was aware that the Western world was committed to a faith in a system of balloting and of legislative debate, he was confident that the system would eventually break down. The democratic assumption that all voters are equally capable of choice and the assumption that men value liberty more than they value order seemed to him nonsense. To all of us nurtured in presuppositions about the virtues of the democratic system of politics, it is instructive to confront this potent Victorian critic of democracy. But it is also instructive to observe how his political authoritarianism became intensified as he grew older. In his earlier writings Carlyle was arguing, in effect, that in politics, as well as in religion, men need the guiding hand of some kind of father. In his later writings, on the other hand, he seems to be arguing for the need of some kind of ruthless commander. His opinions about how governors should treat Negro workers on the Jamaica plantations make painful reading. As he himself said, these fierce *Latter-Day Pamphlets* had "divided me altogether from the mob of 'Progress-of-the-Species' and other vulgar." One distinction should, however, be noted. Concerning the English and Irish laborers thrown out of work by economic circumstances Carlyle writes with affectionate compassion. But toward anyone who does not *want* to work (as he had been informed was the case in Jamaica), he writes with the savage contempt of the hard-working northerner. Once more the test remains for Carlyle the presence or absence of energy.

The effect of vitalism on Carlyle's prose style will also be evident. At the time he began to write, the essayists of the 18th century, Samuel Johnson in particular, were the models of good prose. Carlyle recognized that their style, however admirable an instrument for reasoning, analysis, and generalized exposition, did not suit his purposes. Like a poet, he wanted to convey the sense of experience itself. Like a preacher or prophet, he wanted to exhort or inspire his readers rather than to develop a chain of logical argument. Like a psychoanalyst, he wanted to explore the unconscious and irrational levels of human life, the hidden nine tenths of the iceberg rather than the conscious and rational fraction above the surface. To this end he developed his highly individual manner of writing, with its vivid imagery of fire and barnyard and zoo, its mixture of Biblical rhythms and explosive talk, and its inverted and unorthodox syntax. Classicists may complain, as Landor did, that the result is not English. Carlyle would reply that it is not 18th-century English, but that his style was appropriate for a Victorian who reports of revolutions in society and in thought. In reply to a friend who had protested about his stylistic experiments Carlyle exclaimed: "Do you reckon this really a time for Purism of Style? I do not: with whole ragged battalions of Scott's Novel Scotch, with Irish, German, French, and even Newspaper Cockney * * * storming in on us, and the whole structure of our Johnsonian English breaking up from its foundations—revolution *there* as visible as anywhere else!" Carlyle's defense of his style can be tested by his history, *The French Revolution.* One may agree or disagree with the historian's explanations of how the fire started or how it was extinguished. But the fire itself is unquestionably there before us, roaring, palpable, giving off a heat of its own.

In 1847 Emerson made his second visit to Carlyle in England and recorded his impressions of his writings and talk: "In Carlyle, as in Byron, one is more struck with the rhetoric than with the matter. He has manly superiority rather than intellectuality, and so makes good hard hits all the time. There is more character than intellect in every sentence, herein strongly resembling Samuel Johnson." We should misunderstand Emerson if we took this verdict to be unkind. What he says has the virtue of putting Carlyle into the appropriate company of Byron and Dr. Johnson instead of Immanuel Kant and St. Thomas Aquinas. There are readers in the 20th century, of whom D. H. Lawrence was one, who find Carlyle's religious position, even his political position, worthy of imitation. But for most readers he survives rather as a man of letters, the inventor of a distinctive and extremely effective prose medium which can bring to life for us the very texture of events in scenes such as when a king confronts a guillotine, a young agnostic confronts the devil, or a talker such as Coleridge stupefies an audience of admiring disciples.

[Carlyle's Portraits of His Contemporaries][1]

[KING WILLIAM IV AT 69]

The old King came driving to the ground, near where I was standing: he was in regimentals [2] with a most copious plume of feathers, so that while he sat all shrunk together in the open carriage, you saw little else but a lock of feathers, and might have taken our Defender of the Faith for some singular species of *Clocker* [3] coming thither. On dismounting, he showed an innocent respectable old face; straddled out his legs greatly (which seemed weak), rested on his heels, *stiddering* [4] himself, and looked round with much simplicity what they wanted next with him. The Review itself was a wheeling and marching of foot and horse, several thousands; a flaring and a blaring from trumpet and drum, with artillery-vollies, sham-charges, and then a continued explosion of musketry and cannon from the whole posse of them, like a long explosion of Mount Ætna: all very grand.

[From a letter to his mother, July 19, 1835]

[QUEEN VICTORIA AT 18]

Yesterday, going through one of the Parks, I saw the poor little Queen. She was in an open carriage, preceded by three or four swift red-coated troopers; all off for Windsor just as I happened to pass. Another carriage or carriages followed with maids-of-honour, etc.: the whole drove very fast. It seemed to me the poor little Queen was a bit modest, nice sonsy [5] little lassie; blue eyes, light hair, fine white skin; of extremely small stature: she looked timid, anxious, almost frightened; for the people looked at her in perfect silence; one old liveryman alone touched his hat to her: I was heartily sorry for the poor bairn,—tho' perhaps she might have said as Parson Swan did, "*Greet* [6] not for me brethren; for verily, yea verily, I

---

1. Carlyle once said that "human Portraits, faithfully drawn, are of all pictures the welcomest on human walls." With his pen, rather than with brush, he himself has created a strikingly colorful gallery of his contemporaries.
A few of the following selections (all of them excerpted by the present editor) were written for publication, in particular the elaborate portrait of Coleridge; the majority of them, however, are from his letters. They are thus sketches rather than portraits—sometimes, in fact, caricatures. As Charles Sanders, a biographer, has shown, Carlyle has earned the title of the Victorian Rembrandt. But with his sharp eye for absurdities he is often the Victorian Daumier or Rowlandson. This element of caricature can be partly explained in terms of difference of age. It will be noted that most of the celebrities described were men older than Carlyle, and he had the customary determination of youth to make fun of the pretensions of an older and established generation. In Carlyle's case there was the additional urge to be irreverent in that he was a provincial in a great metropolis with the provincial's need to assert his independence of judgment.

The portraits are not presented chronologically. The first two are sketches of royalty; the others are of English writers. Titles for each portrait have been assigned by the editor.
2. I.e., in military uniform.
3. Clucking hen (Scottish).
4. Steadying (Scottish).
5. Sweet (Scottish).
6. Weep.

greet not for mysel'." It is a strange thing to look at the fashion of this world!

[From a letter to his mother, April 12, 1838]

[CHARLES LAMB AT 56]

Charles Lamb I sincerely believe to be in some considerable degree *insane*. A more pitiful, ricketty, gasping, staggering, stammering Tom fool I do not know. He is witty by denying truisms, and abjuring good manners. His speech wriggles hither and thither with an incessant painful fluctuation; not an opinion in it or a fact or even a phrase that you can thank him for: more like a convulsion fit than natural systole and diastole.—Besides he is now a confirmed shameless drunkard: *asks* vehemently for gin-and-water in strangers' houses; tipples until he is utterly mad, and is only not thrown out of doors because he is too much despised for taking such trouble with him. Poor Lamb! Poor England where such a despicable abortion is named genius!—He said: There are just two things I regret in English History; first that Guy Faux's plot did not take effect (there would have been so glorious an *explosion*); second that the Royalists did not hang Milton (then we might have laughed at them); etc., etc.

[From *Notebooks*, November 2, 1831]

[SAMUEL TAYLOR COLERIDGE AT 53] [7]

Coleridge sat on the brow of Highgate Hill, in those years, looking down on London and its smoke-tumult, like a sage escaped from the inanity of life's battle; attracting towards him the thoughts of innumerable brave souls still engaged there. His express contributions to poetry, philosophy, or any specific province of human literature or enlightenment, had been small and sadly intermittent; but he had, especially among young inquiring men, a higher than literary, a kind of prophetic or magician character. He was thought to hold, he alone in England, the key of German and other Transcendentalisms; knew the sublime secret of believing by "the reason" what "the understanding" had been obliged to fling out as incredible; and could still, after Hume and Voltaire had done their best and worst with him, profess himself an orthodox Christian, and say and print to the Church of England, with its singular old rubrics and surplices at Allhallowtide,[8] *Esto perpetua.* A sublime man; who, alone in those dark days, had saved his crown of spiritual

7. In 1816 Coleridge moved to a London suburb as a permanent guest in the home of James Gillman. Here he received visits from admirers of his philosophy such as Carlyle's friend, John Sterling, from whose biography, by Carlyle, this selection has been taken. Carlyle's visits were made during his first residence in London in 1824–25.
8. November 1, a festival in honor of all the saints, celebrated by the Roman Catholic and Angelican Churches. The Latin means, "Be thou everlasting"— the last words of Paolo Sarpi (1552–1623), theologian and historian, addressed to the city of Venice.

manhood; escaping from the black materialisms, and revolutionary deluges, with "God, Freedom, Immortality" still his: a king of men. The practical intellects of the world did not much heed him, or carelessly reckoned him a metaphysical dreamer: but to the rising spirits of the young generation he had this dusky sublime character; and sat there as a kind of *Magus*,[9] girt in mystery and enigma; his Dodona [1] oak-grove (Mr. Gillman's house at Highgate) whispering strange things, uncertain whether oracles or jargon.

The Gillmans did not encourage much company, or excitation of any sort, round their sage; nevertheless access to him, if a youth did reverently wish it, was not difficult. He would stroll about the pleasant garden with you, sit in the pleasant rooms of the place,—perhaps take you to his own peculiar room, high up, with a rearward view, which was the chief view of all. A really charming outlook, in fine weather. Close at hand, wide sweep of flowery leafy gardens, their few houses mostly hidden, the very chimney-pots veiled under blossomy umbrage, flowed gloriously down hill, gloriously issuing in wide-tufted undulating plain-country, rich in all charms of field and town. Waving blooming country of the brightest green; dotted all over with handsome villas, handsome groves; crossed by roads and human traffic, here inaudible or heard only as a musical hum: and behind all swam, under olive-tinted haze, the illimitable limitary ocean of London, with its domes and steeples definite in the sun, big Paul's and the many memories attached to it hanging high over all. Nowhere, of its kind, could you see a grander prospect on a bright summer day, with the set of the air going southward,—southward, and so draping with the city-smoke not *you* but the city. Here for hours would Coleridge talk, concerning all conceivable or inconceivable things; and liked nothing better than to have an intelligent, or failing that, even a silent and patient human listener. He distinguished himself to all that ever heard him as at least the most surprising talker extant in this world,—and to some small minority, by no means to all, as the most excellent.

The good man, he was now getting old, towards sixty perhaps; and gave you the idea of a life that had been full of sufferings; a life heavy-laden, half-vanquished, still swimming painfully in seas of manifold physical and other bewilderment. Brow and head were round, and of massive weight, but the face was flabby and irresolute. The deep eyes, of a light hazel, were as full of sorrow as of inspiration; confused pain looked mildly from them, as in a kind of mild astonishment. The whole figure and air, good and amiable otherwise, might be called flabby and irresolute; expressive of weakness

9. An oriental magician or sorcerer.
1. An oracle in Greece. Prophecies were voiced by priests who interpreted the rustling sounds made by oak leaves stirred by the wind.

under possibility of strength. He hung loosely on his limbs, with knees bent, and stooping attitude; in walking, he rather shuffled than decisively stept; and a lady once remarked, he never could fix which side of the garden walk would suit him best, but continually shifted, in corkscrew fashion, and kept trying both. A heavy-laden, high-aspiring and surely much-suffering man. His voice, naturally soft and good, had contracted itself into a plaintive snuffle and singsong; he spoke as if preaching,—you would have said, preaching earnestly and also hopelessly the weightiest things. I still recollect his "object" and "subject," terms of continual recurrence in the Kantean province; and how he sang and snuffled them into "om-m-mject" and "sum-m-mject," with a kind of solemn shake or quaver, as he rolled along. No talk, in his century or in any other, could be more surprising. * * *

Nothing could be more copious than his talk; and furthermore it was always, virtually or literally, of the nature of a monologue; suffering no interruption, however reverent; hastily putting aside all foreign additions, annotations, or most ingenuous desires for elucidation, as well-meant superfluities which would never do. Besides, it was talk not flowing anywhither like a river, but spreading everywhither in inextricable currents and regurgitations like a lake or sea; terribly deficient in definite goal or aim, nay often in logical intelligibility; *what* you were to believe or do, on any earthly or heavenly thing, obstinately refusing to appear from it. So that, most times, you felt logically lost; swamped near to drowning in this tide of ingenious vocables, spreading out boundless as if to submerge the world.

To sit as a passive bucket and be pumped into, whether you consent or not, can in the long-run be exhilarating to no creature; how eloquent soever the flood of utterance that is descending. But if it be withal a confused unintelligible flood of utterance, threatening to submerge all known landmarks of thought, and drown the world and you!—I have heard Coleridge talk, with eager musical energy, two stricken hours, his face radiant and moist, and communicate no meaning whatsoever to any individual of his hearers,—certain of whom, I for one, still kept eagerly listening in hope; the most had long before given up, and formed (if the room were large enough) secondary humming groups of their own. He began anywhere: you put some question to him, made some suggestive observation: instead of answering this, or decidedly setting out towards answer of it, he would accumulate formidable apparatus, logical swim-bladders, transcendental life-preservers and other precautionary and vehiculatory gear, for setting out; perhaps did at last get under way, —but was swiftly solicited, turned aside by the glance of some radiant new game on this hand or that, into new courses; and ever into new; and before long into all the Universe, where it was uncertain what game you would catch, or whether any.

His talk, alas, was distinguished, like himself, by irresolution: it disliked to be troubled with conditions, abstinences, definite fulfilments;—loved to wander at its own sweet will, and make its auditor and his claims and humble wishes a mere passive bucket for itself! He had knowledge about many things and topics, much curious reading; but generally all topics led him, after a pass or two, into the high seas of theosophic philosophy, the hazy infinitude of Kantean transcendentalism, with its "sum-m-mjects" and "om-m-mjects." Sad enough; for with such indolent impatience of the claims and ignorances of others, he had not the least talent for explaining this or anything unknown to them; and you swam and fluttered in the mistiest wide unintelligible deluge of things, for most part in a rather profitless uncomfortable manner.

Glorious islets, too, I have seen rise out of the haze; but they were few, and soon swallowed in the general element again. Balmy sunny islets, islets of the blest and the intelligible:—on which occasions those secondary humming groups would all cease humming, and hang breathless upon the eloquent words; till once your islet got wrapt in the mist again, and they could recommence humming. * * * Coleridge was not without what talkers call wit, and there were touches of prickly sarcasm in him, contemptuous enough of the world and its idols and popular dignitaries; he had traits even of poetic humour: but in general he seemed deficient in laughter; or indeed in sympathy for concrete human things either on the sunny or on the stormy side. One right peal of concrete laughter at some convicted flesh-and-blood absurdity, one burst of noble indignation at some injustice or depravity, rubbing elbows with us on this solid Earth, how strange would it have been in that Kantean haze-world, and how infinitely cheering amid its vacant air-castles and dim-melting ghosts and shadows! None such ever came. His life had been an abstract thinking and dreaming, idealistic, passed amid the ghosts of defunct bodies and of unborn ones. The moaning singsong of that theosophico-metaphysical monotony left on you, at last, a very dreary feeling. * * *

But indeed, to the young ardent mind, instinct with pious nobleness, yet driven to the grim deserts of Radicalism for a faith, his speculations had a charm much more than literary, a charm almost religious and prophetic. The constant gist of his discourse was lamentation over the sunk condition of the world; which he recognised to be given-up to Atheism and Materialism, full of mere sordid misbeliefs, mispursuits and misresults. All Science had become mechanical; the science not of men, but of a kind of human beavers. Churches themselves had died away into a godless mechanical condition; and stood there as mere Cases of Articles, mere Forms of Churches; like the dried carcasses of once-swift camels, which you find left withering in the thirst of the universal desert, —ghastly portents for the present, beneficent ships of the desert no more. Men's souls were blinded, hebetated,[2] and sunk under the influence of Atheism and Materialism, and Hume and Voltaire: the world for the present was as an extinct world, deserted of God, and incapable of welldoing till it changed its heart and spirit. This, expressed I think with less of indignation and with more of long-drawn querulousness, was always recognisable as the ground-tone: —in which truly a pious young heart, driven into Radicalism and the opposition party, could not but recognise a too sorrowful truth; and ask of the Oracle, with all earnestness, What remedy, then?

The remedy, though Coleridge himself professed to see it as in sunbeams, could not, except by processes unspeakably difficult, be described to you at all. On the whole, those dead Churches, this dead English Church especially, must be brought to life again. Why not? It was not dead; the soul of it, in this parched-up body, was tragically asleep only. Atheistic Philosophy was true on its side, and Hume and Voltaire could on their own ground speak irrefrag ably for themselves against any Church: but lift the Church and them into a higher sphere of argument, *they* died into inanition, the Church revivified itself into pristine florid vigour,—became once more a living ship of the desert, and invincibly bore you over stock and stone. But how, but how! By attending to the "reason" of man, said Coleridge, and duly chaining-up the "understanding" of man: the *Vernunft* (Reason) and *Verstand* (Understanding) of the Germans, it all turned upon these, if you could well understand them, —which you couldn't. For the rest, Mr. Coleridge had on the anvil various Books, especially was about to write one grand Book *On the Logos*, which would help to bridge the chasm for us. So much appeared, however: Churches, though proved false (as you had imagined), were still true (as you were to imagine): here was an Artist who could burn you up an old Church, root and branch; and then as the Alchymists professed to do with organic substances in general, distil you an "Astral Spirit" from the ashes, which was the very image of the old burnt article, its airdrawn counterpart,— this you still had, or might get, and draw uses from, if you could. Wait till the Book on the Logos were done;—alas, till your own terrene eyes, blind with conceit and the dust of logic, were purged, subtilised and spiritualised into the sharpness of vision requisite for discerning such an "om-m-mject."—The ingenuous young English head, of those days, stood strangely puzzled by such revelations; uncertain whether it were getting inspired, or getting infatuated

2. Dulled.

into flat imbecility; and strange effulgence, of new day or else of deeper meteoric night, coloured the horizon of the future for it.

[From *Life of John Sterling*, 1851]

[WILLIAM WORDSWORTH IN HIS SEVENTIES]

On a summer morning (let us call it 1840 then) I was apprised by Taylor[3] that Wordsworth had come to town, and would meet a small party of us at a certain tavern in St. James's Street, at breakfast, to which I was invited for the given day and hour. We had a pretty little room, quiet though looking street-ward (tavern's name is quite lost to me); the morning sun was pleasantly tinting the opposite houses, a balmy, calm and sunlight morning. Wordsworth, I think, arrived just along with me; we had still five minutes of sauntering and miscellaneous talking before the whole were assembled. I do not positively remember any of them, except that James Spedding[1] was there, and that the others, not above five or six in whole, were polite intelligent quiet persons, and, except Taylor and Wordsworth, not of any special distinction in the world. Breakfast was pleasant, fairly beyond the common of such things. Wordsworth seemed in good tone, and, much to Taylor's satisfaction, talked a great deal; about "poetic" correspondents of his own (i.e. correspondents for the sake of his poetry; especially one such who had sent him, from Canton, an excellent chest of tea; correspondent grinningly applauded by us all); then about ruralities and miscellanies. * * * These were the first topics. Then finally about literature, literary laws, practices, observances, at considerable length, and turning wholly on the mechanical part, including even a good deal of shallow enough etymology, from me and others, which was well received. On all this Wordsworth enlarged with evident satisfaction, and was joyfully reverent of the "wells of English undefiled";[2] though stone dumb as to the deeper rules and wells of Eternal Truth and Harmony, which you were to try and set forth by said undefiled wells of English or what other speech you had! To me a little disappointing, but not much; though it would have given me pleasure had the robust veteran man emerged a little out of vocables into things, now and then, as he never once chanced to do. For the rest, he talked well in his way; with veracity, easy brevity and force, as a wise tradesman would of his tools and workshop,—and as no unwise one could. His voice was good, frank and sonorous, though practically clear distinct and forcible rather than melodious; the tone of him businesslike, sedately confident; no discourtesy, yet no anxiety about being courteous. A fine whole-

3. Henry Taylor, contemporary play-wright.
1. Editor of the works of Francis Ba-con.
2. Spenser, *Faerie Queene* IV.ii.32—referring to Chaucer.

some rusticity, fresh as his mountain breezes, sat well on the stalwart veteran, and on all he said and did. You would have said he was a usually taciturn man; glad to unlock himself to audience sympathetic and intelligent, when such offered itself. His face bore marks of much, not always peaceful, meditation; the look of it not bland or benevolent so much as close impregnable and hard: a man *multa tacere loquive paratus*,[3] in a world where he had experienced no lack of contradictions as he strode along! The eyes were not very brilliant, but they had a quiet clearness; there was enough of brow and well shaped; rather too much of cheek ("horse face" I have heard satirists say); face of squarish shape and decidedly longish, as I think the head itself was (its "length" going horizontal); he was large-boned, lean, but still firm-knit tall and strong-looking when he stood, a right good old steel-grey figure, with rustic simplicity and dignity about him, and a vivacious strength looking through him which might have suited one of those old steel-grey markgrafs[4] whom Henry the Fowler set up to ward the "marches" and do battle with the intrusive heathen in a stalwart and judicious manner.

On this and other occasional visits of his, I saw Wordsworth a number of times, at dinner, in evening parties; and we grew a little more familiar, but without much increase of real intimacy or affection springing up between us. He was willing to talk with me in a corner, in noisy extensive circles, having weak eyes, and little loving the general bubble current in such places. One evening, probably about this time, I got him upon the subject of great poets, who I thought might be admirable equally to us both; but was rather mistaken, as I gradually found. Pope's partial failure I was prepared for; less for the narrowish limits visible in Milton and others. I tried him with Burns, of whom he had sung tender recognition; but Burns also turned out to be a limited inferior creature, any genius he had a theme for one's pathos rather; even Shakespeare himself had his blind sides, his limitations; gradually it became apparent to me that of transcendent unlimited there was, to this critic, probably but one specimen known, Wordsworth himself! He by no means said so, or hinted so, in words; but on the whole it was all I gathered from him in this considerable *tête-à-tête* of ours; and it was not an agreeable conquest. New notion as to poetry or poet I had not in the smallest degree got; but my insight into the depths of Wordsworth's pride in himself had considerably augmented; and it did not increase my love of him; though I did not in the least hate it either, so quiet was it, so fixed, unappealing, like a dim old lichened crag on the wayside, the private meaning of which, in con-

3. "Prepared to speak out or to pass over much in silence."
4. Governors appointed by Henry I of Germany, "the Fowler" (876–936), to guard the borders ("marches") of his kingdom.

trast with any public meaning it had, you recognised with a kind of not wholly melancholy grin. * * *

During the last seven or ten years of his life, Wordsworth felt himself to be a recognised lion, in certain considerable London circles, and was in the habit of coming up to town with his wife for a month or two every season, to enjoy his quiet triumph and collect his bits of tribute *tales quales*.[5] * * * Wordsworth took his bit of lionism very quietly, with a smile sardonic rather than triumphant, and certainly got no harm by it, if he got or expected little good. His wife, a small, withered, puckered, winking lady, who never spoke, seemed to be more in earnest about the affair, and was visibly and sometimes ridiculously assiduous to secure her proper place of precedence at table. * * * The light was always afflictive to his eyes; he carried in his pocket something like a skeleton brass candlestick, in which, setting it on the dinner-table, between him and the most afflictive or nearest of the chief lights, he touched a little spring, and there flirted out, at the top of his brass implement, a small vertical green circle which prettily enough threw his eyes into shade, and screened him from that sorrow. In proof of his equanimity as lion I remember, in connection with this green shade, one little glimpse. * * * Dinner was large, luminous, sumptuous; I sat a long way from Wordsworth; dessert I think had come in, and certainly there reigned in all quarters a cackle as of Babel (only politer perhaps), which far up in Wordsworth's quarter (who was leftward on my side of the table) seemed to have taken a sententious, rather louder, logical and quasi-scientific turn, heartily unimportant to gods and men, so far as I could judge of it and of the other babble reigning. I looked upwards, leftwards, the coast being luckily for a moment clear; there, far off, beautifully screened in the shadow of his vertical green circle, which was on the farther side of him, sate Wordsworth, silent, slowly but steadily gnawing some portion of what I judged to be raisins, with his eye and attention placidly fixed on these and these alone. The sight of whom, and of his rock-like indifference to the babble, quasi-scientific and other, with attention turned on the small practical alone, was comfortable and amusing to me, who felt like him but could not eat raisins. This little glimpse I could still paint, so clear and bright is it, and this shall be symbolical of all.

In a few years, I forget in how many and when, these Wordsworth appearances in London ceased; we heard, not of ill-health perhaps, but of increasing love of rest; at length of the long sleep's coming; and never saw Wordsworth more. One felt his death as the extinction of a public light, but not otherwise.

[From *Reminiscences*, 1867, 1881]

5. Of such a sort.

[ALFRED TENNYSON AT 34]

Alfred is one of the few British or Foreign Figures (a not increasing number I think!) who are and remain beautiful to me;—a true human soul, or some authentic approximation thereto, to whom your own soul can say, Brother!—However, I doubt he will not come; he often skips me, in these brief visits to Town; skips everybody indeed; being a man solitary and sad, as certain men are, dwelling in an element of gloom,—carrying a bit of Chaos about him, in short, which he is manufacturing into Cosmos!

Alfred is the son of a Lincolnshire Gentleman Farmer, I think; indeed, you see in his verses that he is a native of "moated granges," and green, fat pastures, not of mountains and their torrents and storms. He had his breeding at Cambridge, as if for the Law or Church; being master of a small annuity on his Father's decease, he preferred clubbing with his Mother and some Sisters, to live unpromoted and write Poems. In this way he lives still, now here, now there; the family always within reach of London, never in it; he himself making rare and brief visits, lodging in some old comrade's rooms. I think he must be under forty, not much under it. One of the finest-looking men in the world. A great shock of rough dusty-dark hair; bright-laughing hazel eyes; massive aquiline face, most massive yet most delicate; of sallow-brown complexion, almost Indian-looking; clothes cynically loose, free-and-easy;—smokes infinite tobacco. His voice is musical metallic,—fit for loud laughter and piercing wail, and all that may lie between; speech and speculation free and plenteous: I do not meet, in these late decades, such company over a pipe!—We shall see what he will grow to. He is often unwell; very chaotic,—his way is through Chaos and the Bottomless and Pathless; not handy for making out many miles upon.

[From a letter to Emerson, August 5, 1844]

[WILLIAM MAKEPEACE THACKERAY AT 42]

Thackeray has very rarely come athwart me since his return: he is a big fellow, soul and body; of many gifts and qualities (particularly in the Hogarth[6] line, with a dash of Sterne[7] superadded), of enormous *appetite* withal, and very uncertain and chaotic in all points except his *outer breeding*, which is fixed enough, and *perfect* according to the modern English style. I rather dread explosions in his history. A *big*, fierce, weeping, hungry man; not a strong one.

[From a letter to Emerson, September 9, 1853]

---

6. William Hogarth (1697–1764), a realistic and satirical painter of English life.

7. Laurence Sterne (1713–68), whose novels are often sentimental.

From Characteristics[1]

The healthy know not of their health, but only the sick: this is the Physician's Aphorism; and applicable in a far wider sense than he gives it. We may say, it holds no less in moral, intellectual, political, poetical, than in merely corporeal therapeutics; that wherever, or in what shape soever, powers of the sort which can be named *vital* are at work, herein lies the test of their working right or working wrong.

In the Body, for example, as all doctors are agreed, the first condition of complete health is, that each organ perform its function unconsciously, unheeded; let but any organ announce its separate existence, were it even boastfully, and for pleasure, not for pain, then already has one of those unfortunate "false centres of sensibility" established itself, already is derangement there. The perfection of bodily well-being is, that the collective bodily activities seem one; and be manifested, moreover, not in themselves, but in the action they accomplish. * * *

However, without venturing into the abstruse, or too eagerly asking Why and How, in things where our answer must needs prove, in great part, an echo of the question, let us be content to remark farther, in the merely historical way, how that Aphorism of the bodily Physician holds good in quite other departments. Of the Soul, with her activities, we shall find it no less true than of the Body: nay, cry the Spiritualists, is not that very division of the unity, Man, into a dualism of Soul and Body, itself the symptom of disease; as, perhaps, your frightful theory of Materialism, of his being but a Body, and therefore, at least, once more a unity, may be the paroxysm which was critical, and the beginning of cure! But omitting this, we observe, with confidence enough, that the truly strong mind, view it as Intellect, as Morality, or under any other aspect, is nowise the mind acquainted with its strength; that here

1. First published in the *Edinburgh Review*, ostensibly as a review of two books of philosophy which had appeared in 1830 and 1831: *An Essay on the Origin and Prospects of Man* by Thomas Hope, and *Philosophical Lectures* by Friedrich von Schlegel. Hope was a Utilitarian writer, and his analytical treatise may have inspired the first half of the essay, in which Carlyle exposes what seems to him the most characteristic symptom of modern man's diseased state of mind and spirit: self-consciousness. Schlegel's book, an example of the German transcendental philosophy which Carlyle admired, may have inspired the second half of his essay, in which he points out the encouraging prospects for the future if mankind can find a new religious faith. Yet it is only near the end of *Characteristics* that Carlyle finally refers directly to these two books as such, for his real object, as his title suggests, is not to write a mere book review but to describe the state of mind and society characteristic of the age. This early essay, even in the necessarily abridged form adopted here, contains in embryo all the basic religious and political ideas that Carlyle was to develop in his later writings.

as before the sign of health is Unconsciousness. In our inward, as in our outward world, what is mechanical lies open to us; not what is dynamical and has vitality. Of our Thinking, we might say, it is but the mere upper surface that we shape into articulate Thoughts; —underneath the region of argument and conscious discourse, lies the region of meditation; here, in its quiet mysterious depths, dwells what vital force is in us; here, if aught is to be created, and not merely manufactured and communicated, must the work go on. Manufacture is intelligible, but trivial; Creation is great, and cannot be understood. Thus if the Debater and Demonstrator, whom we may rank as the lowest of true thinkers, knows what he has done, and how he did it, the Artist, whom we rank as the highest, knows not; must speak of Inspiration, and in one or the other dialect, call his work the gift of a divinity.

But on the whole "genius is ever a secret to itself";[2] of this old truth we have, on all sides, daily evidence. The Shakespeare takes no airs for writing *Hamlet* and the *Tempest*, understands not that it is anything surprising: Milton, again, is more conscious of his faculty, which accordingly is an inferior one. On the other hand, what cackling and strutting must we not often hear and see, when, in some shape of academical prolusion, maiden speech, review article, this or the other well-fledged goose has produced its goose-egg, of quite measurable value, were it the pink of its whole kind; and wonders why all mortals do not wonder!

Foolish enough, too, was the College Tutor's surprise at Walter Shandy:[3] how, though unread in Aristotle, he could nevertheless argue; and not knowing the name of any dialectic tool, handled them all to perfection. Is it the skilfulest anatomist that cuts the best figure[4] at Sadler's Wells? or does the boxer hit better for knowing that he has a *flexor longus* and a *flexor brevis?*[5] But indeed, as in the higher case of the Poet, so here in that of the Speaker and Inquirer, the true force is an unconscious one. The healthy Understanding, we should say, is not the Logical, argumentative, but the Intuitive; for the end of Understanding is not to prove and find reasons, but to know and believe. Of logic, and its limits, and uses and abuses, there were much to be said and examined; one fact, however, which chiefly concerns us here, has long been familiar: that the man of logic and the man of insight; the Reasoner and the Discoverer, or even Knower, are quite separable, —indeed, for most part, quite separate characters. In practical matters, for example, has it not become almost proverbial that the man of logic cannot prosper? This is he whom business-people call Sys-

2. From an essay by the German poet J. C. F. von Schiller (1759–1805).
3. Laurence Sterne, *Tristram Shandy* I.xix.
4. Makes the most striking appearance. "Sadler's Wells" refers to a London theater.
5. Technical terms for bodily muscles.

tematic and Theoriser and Word-monger; his *vital* intellectual force lies dormant or extinct, his whole force is mechanical, conscious: of such a one it is foreseen that, when once confronted with the infinite complexities of the real world, his little compact theorem of the world will be found wanting; that unless he can throw it overboard and become a new creature, he will necessarily founder. * * * Never since the beginning of Time was there, that we hear or read of, so intensely self-conscious a Society. Our whole relations to the Universe and to our fellow-man have become an Inquiry, a Doubt; nothing will go on of its own accord, and do its function quietly; but all things must be probed into, the whole working of man's world be anatomically studied. Alas, anatomically studied, that it may be medically aided! Till at length indeed, we have come to such a pass, that except in this same *medicine,* with its artifices and appliances, few can so much as imagine any strength or hope to remain for us. The whole Life of Society must now be carried on by drugs: doctor after doctor appears with his nostrum, of Co-operative Societies, Universal Suffrage, Cottage-and-Cow systems, Repression of Population, Vote by Ballot. To such height has the dyspepsia of Society reached; as indeed the constant grinding internal pain, or from time to time the mad spasmodic throes, of all Society do otherwise too mournfully indicate.

Far be it from us to attribute, as some unwise persons do, the disease itself to this unhappy sensation that there is a disease! The Encyclopedists[6] did not produce the troubles of France; but the troubles of France produced the Encyclopedists, and much else. The Self-consciousness is the symptom merely; nay, it is also the attempt towards cure. We record the fact, without special censure; not wondering that Society should feel itself, and in all ways complain of aches and twinges, for it has suffered enough. * * *

But leaving this, let us rather look within, into the Spiritual condition of Society, and see what aspects and prospects offer themselves there. * * * To begin with our highest Spiritual function, with Religion, we might ask, Whither has Religion now fled? Of Churches and their establishments we here say nothing; nor of the unhappy domains of Unbelief, and how innumerable men, blinded in their minds, have grown to "live without God in the world";[7] but, taking the fairest side of the matter, we ask, What is the nature of that same Religion, which still lingers in the hearts of the few who are called, and call themselves, specially the Religious? Is it a healthy religion, vital, unconscious of itself; that shines forth spontaneously in doing of the Work, or even in preaching of the Word? Unhappily, no. Instead of heroic martyr Conduct, and in-

6. Diderot, Voltaire, and other critics of the established order in France who were contributors to the *Encyclopédie*   (1751–52, 1776–80).
7. Cf. Ephesians ii.12.

spired and soul-inspiring Eloquence, whereby Religion itself were brought home to our living bosoms, to live and reign there, we have "Discourses on the Evidences,"[8] endeavouring, with smallest result, to make it probable that such a thing as Religion exists. The most enthusiastic Evangelicals do not preach a Gospel, but keep describing how it should and might be preached: to awaken the sacred fire of faith, as by a sacred contagion, is not their endeavour; but, at most, to describe how Faith shows and acts, and scientifically distinguish true Faith from false. Religion, like all else, is conscious of itself, listens to itself; it becomes less and less creative, vital; more and more mechanical. Considered as a whole, the Christian Religion of late ages has been continually dissipating itself into Metaphysics; and threatens now to disappear, as some rivers do, in deserts of barren sand.

Of Literature, and its deep-seated, wide-spread maladies, why speak? Literature is but a branch of Religion, and always participates in its character: however, in our time, it is the only branch that still shows any greenness; and, as some think, must one day become the main stem. * * * Nay, is not the diseased self-conscious state of Literature disclosed in this one fact, which lies so near us here, the prevalence of Reviewing! Sterne's wish for a reader "that would give-up the reins of his imagination into his author's hands, and be pleased he knew not why, and cared not wherefore,"[9] might lead him a long journey now. Indeed, for our best class of readers, the chief pleasure, a very stinted one, is this same knowing of the Why; which many a Kames and Bossu[1] has been, ineffectually enough, endeavouring to teach us: till at last these also have laid down their trade; and now your Reviewer is a mere *taster*; who tastes, and says, by the evidence of such palate, such tongue, as he has got, It is good, It is bad. Was it thus that the French carried out certain inferior creatures on their Algerine Expedition, to taste the wells for them, and try whether they were poisoned? Far be it from us to disparage our own craft, whereby we have our living! Only we must note these things: that Reviewing spreads with strange vigour; that such a man as Byron reckons the Reviewer and the Poet equal; that at the last Leipzig Fair, there was advertised a Review of Reviews. By and by it will be found that all Literature has become one boundless self-devouring Review; and, as in London routs,[2] we have to *do* nothing, but only to *see* others do nothing.—Thus does Literature also, like a sick thing, superabundantly "listen to itself."

No less is this unhealthy symptom manifest, if we cast a glance

---

8. *Evidences of Christianity* (1794) by William Paley, a Utilitarian theologian.
9. Sterne's *Tristram Shandy* (III.xii).
1. Henry Home, Lord Kames (1696–

1782), author of *Elements of Criticism;* René le Bossu (1631–89), French literary critic.
2. Fashionable gatherings.

on our Philosophy, on the character of our speculative Thinking. Nay already, as above hinted, the mere existence and necessity of a Philosophy is an evil. Man is sent hither not to question, but to work: "the end of man," it was long ago written, "is an Action, not a Thought."[3] In the perfect state, all Thought were but the picture and inspiring symbol of Action; Philosophy, except as Poetry and Religion, would have no being. And yet how, in this imperfect state, can it be avoided, can it be dispensed with? Man stands as in the centre of Nature; his fraction of Time encircled by Eternity, his handbreadth of Space encircled by Infinitude: how shall he forbear asking himself, What am I; and Whence; and Whither? How too, except in slight partial hints, in kind asseverations and assurances, such as a mother quiets her fretfully inquisitive child with, shall he get answer to such inquiries?

The disease of Metaphysics, accordingly, is a perennial one. In all ages, those questions of Death and Immortality, Origin of Evil, Freedom and Necessity, must, under new forms, anew make their appearance; ever, from time to time, must the attempt to shape for ourselves some Theorem of the Universe be repeated. And ever unsuccessfully: for what Theorem of the Infinite can the Finite render complete? We, the whole species of Mankind, and our whole existence and history, are but a floating speck in the illimitable ocean of the All; yet *in* that ocean; indissoluble portion thereof; partaking of its infinite tendencies: borne this way and that by its deep-swelling tides, and grand ocean currents;—of which what faintest chance is there that we should ever exhaust the significance, ascertain the goings and comings? A region of Doubt, therefore, hovers forever in the background; in Action alone can we have certainty. Nay properly Doubt is the indispensable inexhaustible material whereon Action works, which Action has to fashion into Certainty and Reality; only on a canvas of Darkness, such is man's way of being, could the many-coloured picture of our Life paint itself and shine. * * *

Now this is specially the misery which has fallen on man in our Era. Belief, Faith has well-nigh vanished from the world. The youth on awakening in this wondrous Universe no longer finds a competent theory of its wonders. Time was, when if he asked himself, What is man, What are the duties of man? the answer stood ready written for him. But now the ancient "ground-plan of the All" belies itself when brought into contact with reality; Mother Church has, to the most, become a superannuated Step-mother, whose lessons go disregarded; or are spurned at, and scornfully gainsaid. For young Valour and thirst of Action no ideal Chivalry invites to heroism, prescribes what is heroic: the old ideal of Man-

---

3. Aristotle, *Ethics* I.iii.

hood has grown obsolete, and the new is still invisible to us, and we grope after it in darkness, one clutching this phantom, another that; Werterism,[4] Byronism, even Brummelism, each has its day. For Contemplation and love of Wisdom, no Cloister now opens its religious shades; the Thinker must, in all senses, wander homeless, too often aimless, looking up to a Heaven which is dead for him, round to an Earth which is deaf. Action, in those old days, was easy, was voluntary, for the divine worth of human things lay acknowledged; Speculation was wholesome, for it ranged itself as the handmaid of Action; what could not so range itself died out by its natural death, by neglect. Loyalty still hallowed obedience, and made rule noble; there was still something to be loyal to: the Godlike stood embodied under many a symbol in men's interests and business; the Finite shadowed forth the Infinite; Eternity looked through Time. The Life of man was encompassed and overcanopied by a glory of Heaven, even as his dwelling-place by the azure vault.

How changed in these new days! Truly may it be said, the Divinity has withdrawn from the Earth; or veils himself in that widewasting Whirlwind of a departing Era, wherein the fewest can discern his goings. Not Godhead, but an iron, ignoble circle of Necessity embraces all things; binds the youth of these times into a sluggish thrall, or else exasperates him into a rebel. Heroic Action is paralysed; for what worth now remains unquestionable with him? At the fervid period when his whole nature cries aloud for Action, there is nothing sacred under whose banner he can act; the course and kind and conditions of free Action are all but undiscoverable. Doubt storms-in on him through every avenue; inquiries of the deepest, painfulest sort must be engaged with; and the invincible energy of young years waste itself in sceptical, suicidal cavillings; in passionate "questionings of Destiny," whereto no answer will be returned.

For men, in whom the old perennial principle of Hunger (be it Hunger of the poor Day-drudge who stills it with eighteenpence a-day, or of the ambitious Place-hunter who can nowise still it with so little) suffices to fill-up existence, the case is bad; but not the worst. These men have an aim, such as it is; and can steer towards it, with chagrin enough truly; yet, as their hands are kept full, without desperation. Unhappier are they to whom a higher instinct has been given; who struggle to be persons, not machines; to whom the Universe is not a warehouse, or at best a fancy-bazaar, but a mystic temple and hall of doom. For such men there lie properly two courses open. The lower, yet still an estimable class, take up with worn-out Symbols of the Godlike; keep trimming and trucking be-

4. The cultivation of melancholy based on the model of Goethe's novel, *The Sorrows of Young Werther*. "Brum- melism": a fad for wearing elegant clothes in the manner of Beau Brummel, a dandy of George IV's time.

tween these and Hypocrisy, purblindly enough, miserably enough. A numerous intermediate class end in Denial; and form a theory that there is no theory; that nothing is certain in the world, except this fact of Pleasure being pleasant; so they try to realise what trifling modicum of Pleasure they can come at, and to live contented therewith, winking hard. Of these we speak not here; but only of the second nobler class, who also have dared to say No and cannot yet say Yea; but feel that in the No they dwell as in a Golgotha, where life enters not, where peace is not appointed them.

Hard, for most part, is the fate of such men; the harder the nobler they are. In dim forecastings, wrestles within them the "Divine Idea of the World" yet will nowhere visibly reveal itself. They have to realise a Worship for themselves, or live unworshipping. The Godlike has vanished from the world; and they, by the strong cry of their soul's agony, like true wonder-workers, must again evoke its presence. This miracle is their appointed task; which they must accomplish, or die wretchedly: this miracle has been accomplished by such; but not in our land; our land yet knows not of it. Behold a Byron, in melodious tones, "cursing his day": he mistakes earth-born passionate Desire for heaven-inspired Freewill; without heavenly load-star, rushes madly into the dance of meteoric lights that hover on the mad Mahlstrom; and goes down among its eddies. Hear a Shelley filling the earth with inarticulate wail; like the infinite, inarticulate grief and weeping of forsaken infants. A noble Friedrich Schlegel,[5] stupefied in that fearful loneliness, as of a silenced battle-field, flies back to Catholicism; as a child might to its slain mother's bosom, and cling there. In lower regions, how many a poor Hazlitt must wander on God's verdant earth, like the Unblest on burning deserts; passionately dig wells, and draw up only the dry quicksand; believe that he is seeking Truth, yet only wrestle among endless Sophisms, doing desperate battle as with spectre-hosts; and die and make no sign!

To the better order of such minds any mad joy of Denial has long since ceased: the problem is not now to deny, but to ascertain and perform. Once in destroying the False, there was a certain inspiration; but now the genius of Destruction has done its work, there is now nothing more to destroy. The doom of the Old has long been pronounced, and irrevocable; the Old has passed away: but, alas, the New appears not in its stead; the Time is still in pangs of travail with the New. Man has walked by the light of conflagrations, and amid the sound of falling cities; and now there is darkness, and long watching till it be morning. The voice even of the faithful can but exclaim: "As yet struggles the twelfth hour of the Night: birds of darkness are on the wing, spectres uproar,

---

5. German literary critic and leader of the Romantic school (1772–1829). In 1808 he joined the Roman Catholic Church.

the dead walk, the living dream.—Thou, Eternal Providence, wilt cause the day to dawn!"[6]

Such being the condition, temporal and spiritual, of the world at our Epoch, can we wonder that the world "listens to itself," and struggles and writhes, everywhere externally and internally, like a thing in pain? Nay, is not even this unhealthy action of the world's Organisation, if the symptom of universal disease, yet also the symptom and sole means of restoration and cure? The effort of Nature, exerting her medicative force to cast-out foreign impediments, and once more become One, become whole? In Practice, still more in Opinion, which is the precursor and prototype of Practice, there must needs be collision, convulsion; much has to be ground away. Thought must needs be Doubt and Inquiry before it can again be Affirmation and Sacred Precept. Innumerable "Philosophies of Man," contending in boundless hubbub, must annihilate each other, before an inspired Poesy and Faith for Man can fashion itself together. * * *

For ourselves, the loud discord which jars in these two Works,[7] in innumerable works of the like import, and generally in all the Thought and Action of this period, does not any longer utterly confuse us. Unhappy who, in such a time, felt not, at all conjunctures, ineradicably in his heart the knowledge that a God made this Universe, and a Demon not! And shall Evil always prosper, then? Out of all Evil comes Good; and no Good that is possible but shall one day be real. Deep and sad as is our feeling that we stand yet in the bodeful Night; equally deep, indestructible is our assurance that the Morning also will not fail. Nay already, as we look round, streaks of a dayspring are in the east; it is dawning; when the time shall be fulfilled, it will be day. The progress of man towards higher and nobler developments of whatever is highest and noblest in him, lies not only prophesied to Faith, but now written to the eye of Observation, so that he who runs may read.

One great step of progress, for example, we should say, in actual circumstances, was this same; the clear ascertainment that we are in progress. About the grand Course of Providence, and his final Purposes with us, we can know nothing, or almost nothing: man begins in darkness, ends in darkness; mystery is everywhere around us and in us, under our feet, among our hands. Nevertheless so much has become evident to every one, that this wondrous Mankind is advancing somewhither; that at least all human things are, have been and forever will be, in Movement and Change;—as, indeed, for beings that exist in Time, by virtue of Time, and are made

---

6. "Jean Paul's *Hesperus*" [Carlyle's note]. Jean Paul Richter (1763–1825) was a German humorist.

7. Books by Hope and Schlegel. See the title note.

of Time, might have been long since understood. In some provinces, it is true, as in Experimental Science, this discovery is an old one; but in most others it belongs wholly to these latter days. How often, in former ages, by eternal Creeds, eternal Forms of Government and the like, has it been attempted, fiercely enough, and with destructive violence, to chain the Future under the Past; and say to the Providence, whose ways with man are mysterious, and through the great deep: Hitherto shalt thou come, but no farther! A wholly insane attempt; and for man himself, could it prosper, the frightfulest of all enchantments, a very Life-in-Death. Man's task here below, the destiny of every individual man, is to be in turns Apprentice and Workman; or say rather, Scholar, Teacher, Discoverer: by nature he has a strength for learning, for imitating; but also a strength for acting, for knowing on his own account. Are we not in a world seen to be Infinite; the relations lying closest together modified by those latest discovered and lying farthest asunder? Could you ever spell-bind man into a Scholar merely, so that he had nothing to discover, to correct; could you ever establish a Theory of the Universe that were entire, unimprovable, and which needed only to be got by heart; man then were spiritually defunct, the Species we now name Man had ceased to exist. But the gods, kinder to us than we are to ourselves, have forbidden such suicidal acts. As Phlogiston[8] is displaced by Oxygen, and the Epicycles of Ptolemy by the Ellipses of Kepler,[9] so does Paganism give place to Catholicism, Tyranny to Monarchy, and Feudalism to Representative Government,—where also the process does not stop. Perfection of Practice, like completeness of Opinion, is always approaching, never arrived; Truth, in the words of Schiller, *immer wird, nie ist*; never *is*, always *is a-being*.

Sad, truly, were our condition did we know but this, that Change is universal and inevitable. Launched into a dark shoreless sea of Pyrrhonism, what would remain for us but to sail aimless, hopeless; or make madly merry, while the devouring Death had not yet ingulfed us? As indeed, we have seen many, and still see many do. Nevertheless so stands it not. The venerator of the Past (and to what pure heart is the Past, in that "moonlight of memory," other than sad and holy?) sorrows not over its departure, as one utterly bereaved. The true Past departs not, nothing that was worthy in the Past departs; no Truth or Goodness realised by man ever dies, or can die; but is all still here, and, recognised or not, lives and works through endless changes. If all things, to speak in the German dialect, are discerned by us, and exist for us, in an element of

8. A hypothetical substance which, according to older theories of chemistry, was part of all combustible objects and was released in burning.
9. Ptolemy, an astronomer of Alexandria, 2nd century A.D. Johannes Kep-

ler (1571–1630), German astronomer whose theories of planetary orbits (together with the earlier discoveries of Copernicus) supplanted the Ptolemaic theories.

Time, and therefore of Mortality and Mutability; yet Time itself reposes on Eternity: the truly Great and Transcendental has its basis and substance in Eternity; stands revealed to us as Eternity in a vesture of Time. Thus in all Poetry, Worship, Art, Society, as one form passes into another, nothing is lost: it is but the superficial, as it were the *body* only, that grows obsolete and dies; under the mortal body lies a *soul* which is immortal; which anew incarnates itself in fairer revelation; and the Present is the living sum-total of the whole Past.

In Change, therefore, there is nothing terrible, nothing supernatural: on the contrary, it lies in the very essence of our lot and life in this world. To-day is not yesterday: we ourselves change; how can our Works and Thoughts, if they are always to be the fittest, continue always the same? Change, indeed, is painful; yet ever needful; and if Memory have its force and worth, so also has Hope. Nay, if we look well to it, what is all Derangement, and necessity of great Change, in itself such an evil, but the product simply of *increased resources* which the old *methods* can no longer administer; of new wealth which the old cotters will no longer contain? What is it, for example, that in our own day bursts asunder the bonds of ancient Political Systems, and perplexes all Europe with the fear of Change, but even this: the increase of social resources, which the old social methods will no longer sufficiently administer? The new omnipotence of the Steam-engine is hewing asunder quite other mountains than the physical. Have not our economical distresses, those barnyard Conflagrations[1] themselves, the frightfulest madness of our mad epoch, their rise also in what is a real increase: increase of Men; of human Force; properly, in such a Planet as ours, the most precious of all increases? It is true again, the ancient methods of administration will no longer suffice. Must the indomitable millions, full of old Saxon energy and fire, lie cooped-up in this Western Nook, choking one another, as in a Blackhole of Calcutta,[2] while a whole fertile untenanted Earth, desolate for want of the ploughshare, cries: Come and till me, come and reap me?[3] If the ancient Captains can no longer yield guidance, new must be sought after: for the difficulty lies not in nature, but in artifice; the European Calcutta-Blackhole has no walls but air ones and paper ones. —So too, Scepticism itself, with its innumerable mischiefs, what is it but the sour fruit of a most blessed increase, that of Knowledge; a fruit too that will not always continue *sour*?

In fact, much as we have said and mourned about the unproduc-

---

1. Rick-burning in the 1820's and 1830's by disgruntled farm laborers in England.
2. A small room in which 146 European men and women were imprisoned by the Indians in 1756. After one night, only 23 remained alive.
3. Carlyle often urged emigration to America as a solution to the over-crowding of Europe. One of his brothers did emigrate, and became a farmer in Ontario, Canada.

tive prevalence of Metaphysics, it was not without some insight into the use that lies in them. Metaphysical Speculation, if a necessary evil, is the forerunner of much good. The fever of Scepticism must needs burn itself out, and burn out thereby the Impurities that caused it; then again will there be clearness, health. The principle of life, which now struggles painfully, in the outer, thin and barren domain of the Conscious or Mechanical, may then withdraw into its inner sanctuaries, its abysses of mystery and miracle; withdraw deeper than ever into that domain of the Unconscious, by nature infinite and inexhaustible; and creatively work there. From that mystic region, and from that alone, all wonders, all Poesies, and Religions, and Social Systems have proceeded: the like wonders, and greater and higher, lie slumbering there; and, brooded on by the spirit of the waters, will evolve themselves, and rise like exhalations from the Deep. * * *

Remarkable it is, truly, how everywhere the eternal fact begins again to be recognised, that there is a Godlike in human affairs; that God not only made us and beholds us, but is in us and around us; that the Age of Miracles, as it ever was, now is. Such recognition we discern on all hands and in all countries: in each country after its own fashion. In France, among the younger nobler minds, strangely enough; where, in their loud contention with the Actual and Conscious, the Ideal or Unconscious is, for the time, without exponent; where Religion means not the parent of Polity, as of all that is highest, but Polity itself; and this and the other earnest man has not been wanting, who could audibly whisper to himself: "Go to, I will make religion." In England still more strangely; as in all things, worthy England will have its way: by the shrieking of hysterical women,[4] casting out of devils, and other "gifts of the Holy Ghost." Well might Jean Paul say, in this his twelfth hour of the Night, "the living dream"; well might he say, "the dead walk."[5] Meanwhile let us rejoice rather that so much has been seen into, were it through never so diffracting media, and never so madly distorted; that in all dialects, though but half-articulately, this high Gospel begins to be preached: Man is still Man. The genius of Mechanism, as was once before predicted, will not always sit like a choking incubus on our soul; but at length, when by a new magic Word the old spell is broken, become our slave, and as familiar-spirit do all our bidding. "We are near awakening when we dream that we dream."[6]

He that has an eye and a heart can even now say: Why should I falter? Light has come into the world; to such as love Light, so

4. An allusion to followers of Carlyle's friend, the preacher Edward Irving. Women in Irving's congregation asserted that they had acquired the gift of tongues.

5. See note 6 above, Jean Paul's *Hesperus.*
6. Quoted from a work by the German poet Novalis (1772–1801).

as Light must be loved, with a boundless all-doing, all-enduring love. For the rest, let that vain struggle to read the mystery of the Infinite cease to harass us. It is a mystery which, through all ages, we shall only read here a line of, there another line of. Do we not already know that the name of the Infinite is GOOD, is GOD? Here on Earth we are as Soldiers, fighting in a foreign land; that understand not the plan of the campaign, and have no need to understand it; seeing well what is at our hand to be done. Let us do it like Soldiers; with submission, with courage, with a heroic joy. "Whatsoever thy hand findeth to do, do it with all thy might."[7] Behind us, behind each one of us, lie Six Thousand Years of human effort, human conquest: before us is the boundless Time, with its as yet uncreated and unconquered Continents and Eldorados, which we, even we, have to conquer, to create; and from the bosom of Eternity there shine for us celestial guiding stars.

> "My inheritance how wide and fair!
> Time is my fair seed-field, of Time I'm heir."[8]

1831   1831

From Sartor Resartus[1]
Chapter VII. *The Everlasting No*

Under the strange nebulous envelopment, wherein our Professor has now shrouded himself, no doubt but his spiritual nature is nevertheless progressive, and growing: for how can the "Son of

7. Ecclesiastes ix.10.
8. From Goethe's romance, *Wilhelm Meisters Wanderjahre* (1821).
1. *Sartor Resartus* is a combination of novel, autobiography, and essay. To present some of his own experiences, Carlyle invented a hero, Professor Diogenes Teufelsdröckh of Germany, whose name itself (meaning "God-Begotten Devil's Dung") suggests the grotesque and fantastic humor which Carlyle used to expound a serious treatise. Teufelsdröckh tells the story of his unhappiness in love and of his difficulties in religion. He also airs his opinions on a variety of subjects. Interspersed between the Professor's words (which are in quotation marks) are the remarks of an editor, also imaginary, who has the task of putting together the story from assorted documents written by Teufelsdröckh. The title, meaning "The Tailor Re-Tailored," refers to the editor's role of patching the story together. The title also refers to Carlyle's so-called "Clothes Philosophy," which is expounded by the hero in many chapters of *Sartor*. In effect this Clothes Philosophy is an attempt to demonstrate the difference between the appearances of things and their reality. The appearance of a man depends upon the costume he wears; the reality of a man is the body underneath the costume. By analogy, Carlyle suggests that institutions, such as churches or governments, are like clothes. They may be useful "visible emblems" of the spiritual forces which they cover, but they wear out and have to be replaced by new clothes. The Christian church, for example, which once expressed man's permanent religious desires, is, in Carlyle's terms, worn out and must be discarded. But the underlying religious spirit must be recognized and kept alive at all costs. In this respect, the Clothes Philosophy has much in common with the theory of archetypal experiences developed in the 20th century by the psychiatrist Carl Jung. Carlyle extends his analogy, however, into many other areas. Clothes hide the body just as the world of nature cloaks the reality of God and as the body itself cloaks the reality of man's soul. The discovery of these realities behind the appearances is, for Carlyle and for his

Time," in any case, stand still? We behold him, through those dim years, in a state of crisis, of transition: his mad Pilgrimings, and general solution into aimless Discontinuity, what is all this but a mad Fermentation; wherefrom, the fiercer it is, the clearer product will one day evolve itself?

Such transitions are ever full of pain: thus the Eagle when he moults is sickly; and, to attain his new beak, must harshly dash-off the old one upon rocks. What Stoicism soever our Wanderer, in his individual acts and motions, may affect, it is clear that there is a hot fever of anarchy and misery raging within; coruscations of which flash out: as, indeed, how could there be other? Have we not seen him disappointed, bemocked of Destiny, through long years? All that the young heart might desire and pray for has been denied; nay, as in the last worst instance, offered and then snatched away. Ever an "excellent Passivity"; but of useful, reasonable Activity, essential to the former as Food to Hunger, nothing granted: till at length, in this wild Pilgrimage, he must forcibly seize for himself an Activity, though useless, unreasonable. Alas, his cup of bitterness, which had been filling drop by drop, ever since that first "ruddy morning" in the Hinterschlag Gymnasium,[2] was at the very lip; and then with that poison-drop, of the Towgood-and-Blumine business,[3] it runs over, and even hisses over in a deluge of foam.

He himself says once, with more justice than originality: "Man is, properly speaking, based upon Hope, he has no other possession but Hope; this world of his is emphatically the Place of Hope." What, then, was our Professor's possession? We see him, for the present, quite shut-out from Hope; looking not into the golden orient, but vaguely all round into a dim copper firmament, pregnant with earthquake and tornado.

Alas, shut-out from Hope, in a deeper sense than we yet dream of! For, as he wanders wearisomely through this world, he has now lost all tidings of another and higher. Full of religion, or at least of religiosity, as our Friend has since exhibited himself, he hides not that, in those days, he was wholly irreligious: "Doubt had darkened into Unbelief," says he; "shade after shade goes grimly over your soul, till you have the fixed, starless, Tartarean black." To such readers as have reflected, what can be called reflecting, on man's life, and happily discovered, in contradiction to much Profit-

hero, the initial stage of a solution to the dilemmas of life.

Teufelsdröckh's religious development, as described in the following chapters, may be contrasted with J. S. Mill's account of his own crisis of spirit in his *Autobiography*.
2. "Smite-Behind Grammar School";

Teufelsdröckh's unhappiness had begun with his loneliness at this school.
3. Blumine, a girl loved by Teufelsdröckh, had married his friend Towgood. His distress is pictured in the preceding chapter, entitled "Sorrows of Teufelsdröckh."

and-loss Philosophy,[4] speculative and practical, that Soul is *not* synonymous with Stomach; who understand, therefore, in our Friend's words, "that, for man's well-being, Faith is properly the one thing needful; how, with it, Martyrs, otherwise weak, can cheerfully endure the shame and the cross; and without it, Worldlings puke-up their sick existence, by suicide, in the midst of luxury": to such it will be clear that, for a pure moral nature, the loss of his religious Belief was the loss of everything. Unhappy young man! All wounds, the crush of long-continued Destitution, the stab of false Friendship and of false Love, all wounds in thy so genial heart, would have healed again, had not its life-warmth been withdrawn. Well might he exclaim, in his wild way: "Is there no God, then; but at best an absentee God, sitting idle, ever since the first Sabbath, at the outside of his Universe, and seeing it go? Has the word Duty no meaning; is what we call Duty no divine Messenger and Guide, but a false earthly Fantasm, made-up of Desire and Fear, of emanations from the Gallows and from Dr. Graham's Celestial-Bed?[5] Happiness of an approving Conscience! Did not Paul of Tarsus, whom admiring men have since named Saint, feel that *he* was 'the chief of sinners';[6] and Nero of Rome, jocund in spirit (*wohlgemuth*), spend much of his time in fiddling? Foolish Word-monger and Motive-grinder, who in thy Logic-mill hast an earthly mechanism for the Godlike itself, and wouldst fain grind me out Virtue from the husks of Pleasure,—I tell thee, Nay! To the unregenerate Prometheus Vinctus[7] of a man, it is ever the bitterest aggravation of his wretchedness that he is conscious of Virtue, that he feels himself the victim not of suffering only, but of injustice. What then? Is the heroic inspiration we name Virtue but some Passion; some bubble of the blood, bubbling in the direction others *profit* by? I know not: only this I know, If what thou namest Happiness be our true aim, then are we all astray. With Stupidity and sound Digestion man may front much. But what, in these dull unimaginative days, are the terrors of Conscience to the diseases of the Liver! Not on Morality, but on Cookery, let us build our stronghold: there brandishing our frying-pan, as censer, let us offer sweet incense to the Devil, and live at ease on the fat things *he* has provided for his Elect!"

Thus has the bewildered Wanderer to stand, as so many have done,

---

4. Utilitarian theory of ethics that our actions should be based on calculating the sum of pleasures and pains which would result from such actions. This "hedonistic calculus" horrified Carlyle because it left out of account man's religious instincts.
5. James Graham (1745–94), a quack doctor, had invented an elaborate bed which was supposed to cure sterility in couples using it. In this passage the bed is apparently a symbol of sexual desires.
6. See I Timothy i.15.
7. I.e., Prometheus Bound; this is also the title of a play by Aeschylus depicting the sufferings of a hero who defied Zeus.

shouting question after question into the Sibyl-cave of Destiny,[8] and receive no Answer but an Echo. It is all a grim Desert, this once-fair world of his; wherein is heard only the howling of wild-beasts, or the shrieks of despairing, hate-filled men; and no Pillar of Cloud by day, and no Pillar of Fire by night,[9] any longer guides the Pilgrim. To such length has the spirit of Inquiry carried him. "But what boots it (*was thut's*)?" cries he: "it is but the common lot in this era. Not having come to spiritual majority prior to the *Siècle de Louis Quinze*,[1] and not being born purely a Loghead (*Dummkopf*), thou hast no other outlook. The whole world is, like thee, sold to Unbelief, their old Temples of the Godhead, which for long have not been rainproof, crumble down; and men ask now: Where is the Godhead; our eyes never saw him?"

Pitiful enough were it, for all these wild utterances, to call our Diogenes wicked. Unprofitable servants as we all are, perhaps at no era of his life was he more decisively the Servant of Goodness, the Servant of God, than even now when doubting God's existence. "One circumstance I note," says he: "after all the nameless woe that Inquiry, which for me, what it is not always, was genuine Love of Truth, had wrought me, I nevertheless still loved Truth, and would bate no jot of my allegiance to her. 'Truth'! I cried, 'though the Heavens crush me for following her: no Falsehood! though a whole celestial Lubberland[2] were the price of Apostasy.' In conduct it was the same. Had a divine Messenger from the clouds, or miraculous Handwriting on the wall, convincingly proclaimed to me *This thou shalt do*, with what passionate readiness, as I often thought, would I have done it, had it been leaping into the infernal Fire. Thus, in spite of all Motive-grinders, and Mechanical Profit-and-Loss Philosophies, with the sick ophthalmia and hallucination they had brought on, was the Infinite nature of Duty still dimly present to me: living without God in the world, of God's light I was not utterly bereft; if my as yet sealed eyes, with their unspeakable longing, could nowhere see Him, nevertheless in my heart He was present, and His heaven-written Law still stood legible and sacred there."

Meanwhile, under all these tribulations, and temporal and spiritual destitutions, what must the Wanderer, in his silent soul, have endured! "The painfullest feeling," writes he, "is that of your own Feebleness (*Unkraft*); ever, as the English Milton says, to be weak is the true misery.[3] And yet of your Strength there is and can be no clear feeling, save by what you have prospered in, by what you have done. Between vague wavering Capability and fixed indubitable Performance, what a difference! A certain inarticulate Self-conscious-

8. An allusion to Virgil's *Aeneid* VI. 36 ff., where Aeneas questions the Cumaean sibyl.
9. Exodus xiii.21.
1. "The Century of Louis XV," an allusion to Voltaire's history of the skeptical and enquiring spirit of 18th-century France during the reign of Louis XV (1710–74): *Précis du Siècle de Louis XV*.
2. Land of Plenty.
3. *Paradise Lost* I.157: "Fallen cherub, to be weak is miserable."

ness dwells dimly in us; which only our Works can render articulate and decisively discernible. Our Works are the mirror wherein the spirit first sees its natural lineaments. Hence, too, the folly of that impossible Precept, *Know thyself;*[4] till it be translated into this partially possible one, *Know what thou canst work-at.*

"But for. me, so strangely unprosperous had I been, the net-result of my Workings amounted as yet simply to—Nothing. How then could I believe in my Strength, when there was as yet no mirror to see it in? Ever did this agitating, yet, as I now perceive, quite frivolous question, remain to me insoluble: Hast thou a certain Faculty, a certain Worth, such even as the most have not; or art thou the completest Dullard of these modern times? Alas! the fearful Unbelief is unbelief in yourself; and how could I believe? Had not my first, last Faith in myself, when even to me the Heavens seemed laid open, and I dared to love, been all-too cruelly belied? The speculative Mystery of Life grew ever more mysterious to me: neither in the practical Mystery[5] had I made the slightest progress, but been everywhere buffeted, foiled, and contemptuously cast-out. A feeble unit in the middle of a threatening Infinitude, I seemed to have nothing given me but eyes, whereby to discern my own wretchedness. Invisible yet impenetrable walls, as of Enchantment, divided me from all living: was there, in the wide world, any true bosom I could press trustfully to mine? O Heaven, No, there was none! I kept a lock upon my lips: why should I speak much with that shifting variety of so called Friends, in whose withered, vain and too-hungry souls Friendship was but an incredible tradition? In such cases, your resource is to talk little, and that little mostly from the Newspapers. Now when I look back, it was a strange isolation I then lived in. The men and women around me, even speaking with me, were but Figures; I had, practically, forgotten that they were alive, that they were not merely automatic. In midst of their crowded streets and assemblages, I walked solitary; and (except as it was my own heart, not another's, that I kept devouring) savage also, as the tiger in his jungle. Some comfort it would have been, could I, like a Faust,[6] have fancied myself tempted and tormented of the Devil; for a Hell, as I imagine, without Life, though only diabolic Life, were more frightful: but in our age of Down-pulling and Disbelief, the very Devil has been pulled down, you cannot so much as believe in a Devil. To me the Universe was all void of Life, of Purpose, of Volition, even of Hostility: it was one huge, dead, immeasurable Steam-engine, rolling on, in its dead indifference, to grind me limb from limb. O, the vast, gloomy, solitary Golgotha,[7] and Mill of

---

4. This maxim was inscribed in gold letters over the portico of the temple at Delphi.
5. A profession or practical occupation.

6. Faust, the hero of a drama by Goethe, was tempted by the Devil.
7. Calvary, the place where Christ was crucified.

Death! Why was the Living banished thither companionless, conscious? Why, if there is no Devil; nay, unless the Devil is your God?"

A prey incessantly to such corrosions, might not, moreover, as the worst aggravation to them, the iron constitution even of a Teufelsdröckh threaten to fail? We conjecture that he has known sickness; and, in spite of his locomotive habits, perhaps sickness of the chronic sort. Hear this, for example: "How beautiful to die of broken-heart, on Paper! Quite another thing in practice; every window of your Feeling, even of your Intellect, as it were, begrimed and mud-bespattered, so that no pure ray can enter; a whole Drug-shop in your inwards; the fordone soul drowning slowly in quagmires of Disgust!"

Putting all which external and internal miseries together, may we not find in the following sentences, quite in our Professor's still vein, significance enough? "From Suicide a certain aftershine (*Nachschein*) of Christianity withheld me: perhaps also a certain indolence of character; for, was not that a remedy I had at any time within reach? Often, however, was there a question present to me: Should some one now, at the turning of that corner, blow thee suddenly out of Space, into the other World, or other No-World, by pistol-shot,—how were it? On which ground, too, I have often, in sea-storms and sieged cities and other death-scenes, exhibited an imperturbability, which passed, falsely enough, for courage.

"So had it lasted," concludes the Wanderer, "so had it lasted, as in bitter protracted Death-agony, through long years. The heart within me, unvisited by any heavenly dewdrop, was smouldering in sulphurous, slow-consuming fire. Almost since earliest memory I had shed no tear; or once only when I, murmuring half-audibly, recited Faust's Deathsong, that wild *Selig der den er im Siegesglanze findet* (Happy whom *he* finds in Battle's splendour),[8] and thought that of this last Friend[9] even I was not forsaken, that Destiny itself could not doom me not to die. Having no hope, neither had I any definite fear, were it of Man or of Devil: nay, I often felt as if it might be solacing, could the Arch-Devil himself, though in Tartarean terrors, but rise to me, that I might tell him a little of my mind. And yet, strangely enough, I lived in a continual, indefinite, pining fear; tremulous, pusillanimous, apprehensive of I knew not what: it seemed as if all things in the Heavens above and the Earth beneath would hurt me; as if the Heavens and the Earth were but boundless jaws of a devouring monster, wherein I, palpitating, waited to be devoured.

"Full of such humour, and perhaps the miserablest man in the

8. Adapted from Goethe's *Faust* I.iv.   9. Death.
1573–76.

whole French Capital or Suburbs, was I, one sultry Dogday,[1] after much perambulation, toiling along the dirty little *Rue Saint-Thomas de l'Enfer*,[2] among civic rubbish enough, in a close atmosphere, and over pavements hot as Nebuchadnezzar's Furnace; whereby doubtless my spirits were little cheered; when, all at once, there rose a Thought in me, and I asked myself: 'What *art* thou afraid of? Wherefore, like a coward, dost thou forever pip and whimper, and go cowering and trembling? Despicable biped! what is the sum-total of the worst that lies before thee? Death? Well, Death; and say the pangs of Tophet[3] too, and all that the Devil and Man may, will or can do against thee! Hast thou not a heart; canst thou not suffer whatsoever it be; and, as a Child of Freedom, though outcast, trample Tophet itself under thy feet, while it consumes thee? Let it come, then; I will meet it and defy it!' And as I so thought, there rushed like a stream of fire over my whole soul; and I shook base Fear away from me forever. I was strong, of unknown strength; a spirit, almost a god. Ever from that time, the temper of my misery was changed: not Fear or whining Sorrow was it, but Indignation and grim fire-eyed Defiance.

"Thus had the EVERLASTING No[4] (*das ewige Nein*) pealed authoritatively through all the recesses of my Being, of my ME; and then was it that my whole ME stood up, in native God-created majesty, and with emphasis recorded its Protest. Such a Protest, the most important transaction in Life, may that same Indignation and Defiance, in a psychological point of view, be fitly called. The Everlasting No had said: 'Behold, thou art fatherless, outcast, and the Universe is mine (the Devil's)'; to which my whole Me now made answer: '*I* am not thine, but Free, and forever hate thee!'

"It is from this hour that I incline to date my Spiritual New-birth, or Baphometic Fire-baptism;[5] perhaps I directly thereupon began to be a Man."

Chapter VIII. Centre of Indifference

Though, after this "Baphometic Fire-baptism" of his, our Wanderer signifies that his Unrest was but increased; as indeed, "Indignation and Defiance," especially against things in general, are not the most peaceable inmates; yet can the Psychologist surmise that it was no longer a quite hopeless Unrest; that henceforth it had at least a

---

1. A hot and unwholesome summer period, coinciding with the prominence of Sirius, the Dog Star, is called the season of the dog days.
2. "St. Thomas-of-Hell Street." In later life Carlyle admitted that this incident was based upon his own experience during a walk in Edinburgh (rather than in Paris) when he was 26 or 27 years of age. For a period of three weeks, he said, he had been suffering from "total sleeplessness."

3. Hell.
4. This phrase does not signify the hero's protest. It represents the sum of all the forces that had denied meaning to life. These negative forces, which had hitherto held the hero in bondage, are repudiated by his saying, "No!" to the "Everlasting No."
5. A transformation by a flash of spiritual illumination. The term may derive from Baphomet, an idol that inspired such spiritual experiences.

fixed centre to revolve round. For the fire-baptised soul, long so scathed and thunder-riven, here feels its own Freedom, which feeling is its Baphometic Baptism: the citadel of its whole kingdom it has thus gained by assault, and will keep inexpugnable; outwards from which the remaining dominions, not indeed without hard battling, will doubtless by degrees be conquered and pacificated. Under another figure, we might say, if in that great moment, in the *Rue Saint-Thomas de l'Enfer*, the old inward Satanic School[1] was not yet thrown out of doors, it received peremptory judicial notice to quit; —whereby, for the rest, its howl-chantings, Ernulphus-cursings,[2] and rebellious gnashings of teeth, might, in the meanwhile, become only the more tumultuous, and difficult to keep secret.

Accordingly, if we scrutinise these Pilgrimings well, there is perhaps discernible henceforth a certain incipient method in their madness. Not wholly as a Spectre does Teufelsdröckh now storm through the world; at worst as a spectre-fighting Man, nay who will one day be a Spectre-queller. If pilgriming restlessly to so many "Saints' Wells,"[3] and ever without quenching of his thirst, he nevertheless finds little secular wells, whereby from time to time some alleviation is ministered. In a word, he is now, if not ceasing, yet intermitting to "eat his own heart"; and clutches round him outwardly on the NOT-ME for wholesomer food. Does not the following glimpse exhibit him in a much more natural state?

"Towns also and Cities, especially the ancient, I failed not to look upon with interest. How beautiful to see thereby, as through a long vista, into the remote Time; to have as it were, an actual section of almost the earliest Past brought safe into the Present, and set before your eyes! There, in that old City, was a live ember of Culinary Fire put down, say only two-thousand years ago; and there, burning more or less triumphantly, with such fuel as the region yielded, it has burnt, and still burns, and thou thyself seest the very smoke thereof. Ah! and the far more mysterious live ember of Vital Fire was then also put down there; and still miraculously burns and spreads; and the smoke and ashes thereof (in these Judgment-Halls and Church-yards), and its bellows-engines (in these Churches), thou still seest; and its flame, looking out from every kind countenance, and every hateful one, still warms thee or scorches thee.

"Of Man's Activity and Attainment the chief results are aeriform, mystic, and preserved in Tradition only: such are his Forms of Government, with the Authority they rest on; his Customs, or Fashions both of Cloth-habits and of Soul-habits; much more his collec-

---

1. A term coined by Robert Southey to characterize the self-assertive and rebellious temper of the poetry of Byron and Shelley.
2. A curse devised by Ernulf (1040–1124), Bishop of Rochester, when sentencing persons to excommunication. See Sterne's *Tristram Shandy* III.xi.
3. Holy fountains or wells whose waters were reputed to restore health. Here a figurative allusion to Teufelsdröckh's unsuccessful search, at this time, for a religious solution to his problems.

tive stock of Handicrafts, the whole Faculty he has acquired of manipulating Nature: all these things, as indispensable and priceless as they are, cannot in any way be fixed under lock and key, but must flit, spirit-like, on impalpable vehicles, from Father to Son; if you demand sight of them, they are nowhere to be met with. Visible Plowmen and Hammermen there have been, ever from Cain and Tubalcain downwards: [4] but where does your accumulated Agricultural, Metallurgic, and other Manufacturing SKILL lie warehoused? It transmits itself on the atmospheric air, on the sun's rays (by Hearing and by Vision); it is a thing aeriform, impalpable, of quite spiritual sort. In like manner, ask me not. Where are the LAWS where is the GOVERNMENT? In vain wilt thou go to Schönbrunn, to Downing Street, to the Palais Bourbon: [5] thou findest nothing there but brick or stone houses, and some bundles of Papers tied with tape. Where, then, is that same cunningly-devised almighty GOVERNMENT of theirs to be laid hands on? Everywhere, yet nowhere: seen only in its works, this too is a thing aeriform, invisible; or if you will, mystic and miraculous. So spiritual (*geistig*) is our whole daily Life: all that we do springs out of Mystery, Spirit, invisible Force; only like a little Cloud-image, or Armida's Palace,[6] air-built, does the Actual body itself forth from the great mystic Deep.

"Visible and tangible products of the Past, again, I reckon-up to the extent of three. Cities, with their Cabinets and Arsenals; then tilled Fields, to either or to both of which divisions Roads with their Bridges, may belong; and thirdly—Books. In which third truly, the last invented, lies a worth far surpassing that of the two others. Wondrous indeed is the virtue of a true Book. Not like a dead city of stones, yearly crumbling, yearly needing repair; more like a tilled field, but then a spiritual field: like a spiritual tree, let me rather say, it stands from year to year, and from age to age (we have Books that already number some hundred-and-fifty human ages); and yearly comes its new produce of leaves (Commentaries, Deductions, Philosophical, Political Systems; or were it only Sermons, Pamphlets, Journalistic Essays), every one of which is talismanic and thaumaturgic,[7] for it can persuade men. O thou who art able to write a Book, which once in the two centuries or oftener there is a man gifted to do, envy not him whom they name City-builder, and inexpressibly pity him whom they name Conqueror or City-burner! Thou too art a Conqueror and Victor; but of the true sort, namely over the Devil: thou too hast built what will outlast all marble and metal, and be a wonder-bringing City of the Mind, a Temple and Seminary and Prophetic Mount, whereto all kindreds of the Earth will pilgrim. —Fool! why journeyest thou wearisomely, in thy antiquarian fervour, to gaze on the stone pyramids of Geeza, or the clay ones of

4. See Genesis, iv.1–22.
5. Headquarters of government in Vienna, London, and Paris, respectively.
6. The magic palace of a beautiful enchantress in Tasso's *Jerusalem Delivered*.
7. Miracle-working.

Sacchara?[8] These stand there, as I can tell thee, idle and inert, looking over the Desert, foolishly enough, for the last three-thousand years: but canst thou not open thy Hebrew BIBLE, then, or even Luther's Version thereof?"

No less satisfactory is his sudden appearance not in Battle, yet on some Battle-field; which, we soon gather, must be that of Wagram;[9] so that here, for once, is a certain approximation to distinctiveness of date. Omitting much, let us impart what follows:

"Horrible enough! A whole Marchfeld[1] strewed with shell-splinters, cannon-shot, ruined tumbrils, and dead men and horses; stragglers still remaining not so much as buried. And those red mould heaps: ay, there lie the Shells of Men, out of which all the Life and Virtue has been blown; and now are they swept together, and crammed-down out of sight, like blown Egg-shells!—Did Nature, when she bade the Donau bring down his mould-cargoes from the Carinthian and Carpathian Heights, and spread them out here into the softest, richest level,—intend thee, O Marchfeld, for a corn-bearing Nursery, whereon her children might be nursed; or for a Cockpit, wherein they might the more commodiously be throttled and tattered? Were thy three broad Highways, meeting here from the ends of Europe, made for Ammunition-wagons, then? Were thy Wagrams and Stillfrieds[2] but so many ready-built Casemates,[3] wherein the house of Hapsburg might batter with artillery, and with artillery be battered? König Ottokar, amid yonder hillocks, dies under Rodolf's truncheon; here Kaiser Franz falls a-swoon under Napoleon's: within which five centuries, to omit the others, how has thy breast, fair Plain, been defaced and defiled! The greensward is torn-up and trampled-down; man's fond care of it, his fruit-trees, hedge-rows, and pleasant dwellings, blown away with gunpowder; and the kind seedfield lies a desolate, hideous Place of Sculls.— Nevertheless, Nature is at work; neither shall these Powder-Devilkins with their utmost devilry gainsay her: but all that gore and carnage will be shrouded-in, absorbed into manure; and next year the Marchfeld will be green, nay greener. Thrifty unwearied Nature, ever out of our great waste educing some little profit of thy own,— how dost thou, from the very carcass of the Killer, bring Life for the Living![4]

"What, speaking in quite unofficial language, is the net-purport and upshot of war? To my own knowledge, for example, there dwell

---

8. Pyramids at Ghizeh and Sakkara near Cairo.
9. A village in Austria; site of Napoleon's victory over the Austrians, July, 1809.
1. A fertile plain in Austria whose soil (according to Teufelsdröckh) was brought down from the Carpathian mountains by the Danube (Donau) River.
2. Stillfried was the site of a battle in

which Ottokar, King ("könig") of Bohemia, was killed by the forces of Rudolph of Hapsburg in 1278. In 1809 the Hapsburg armies, under Emperor Francis ("Franz") I, were in turn defeated by Napoleon at nearby Wagram.
3. Fortified chambers.
4. Cf. Byron's reflections on the battle-field at Waterloo: "How that red rain hath made the harvest grow!"—*Childe Harold's Pilgrimage*, III.xvii.150.

and toil, in the British village of Dumdrudge, usually some five-hundred souls. From these, by certain 'Natural Enemies'[5] of the French, there are successively selected, during the French war, say thirty able-bodied men: Dumdrudge, at her own expense, has suckled and nursed them: she has, not without difficulty and sorrow, fed them up to manhood, and even trained them to crafts, so that one can weave, another build, another hammer, and the weakest can stand under thirty stone avoirdupois. Nevertheless, amid much weeping and swearing, they are selected; all dressed in red; and shipped away, at the public charges, some two-thousand miles, or say only to the south of Spain;[6] and fed there till wanted. And now to that same spot, in the south of Spain, are thirty similar French artisans, from a French Dumdrudge, in like manner wending: till at length, after infinite effort, the two parties come into actual juxtaposition; and Thirty stands fronting Thirty, each with a gun in his hand. Straightway the word 'Fire!' is given: and they blow the souls out of one another; and in place of sixty brisk useful craftsmen, the world has sixty dead carcasses, which it must bury, and anew shed tears for. Had these men any quarrel? Busy as the Devil is, not the smallest! They lived far enough apart; were the entirest strangers; nay, in so wide a Universe, there was even, unconsciously, by Commerce, some mutual helpfulness between them. How then? Simpleton! their Governors had fallen-out; and, instead of shooting one another, had the cunning to make these poor blockheads shoot.—Alas, so is it in Deutschland, and hitherto in all other lands; still as of old, 'what devilry soever Kings do, the Greeks must pay the piper!'[7]—In that fiction of the English Smollet,[8] it is true, the final Cessation of War is perhaps prophetically shadowed forth; where the two Natural Enemies, in person, take each a Tobacco-pipe, filled with Brimstone; light the same, and smoke in one another's faces, till the weaker gives in: but from such predicted Peace-Era, what blood-filled trenches, and contentious centuries, may still divide us!"

Thus can the Professor, at least in lucid intervals, look away from his own sorrows, over the many-coloured world, and pertinently enough note what is passing there. We may remark, indeed, that for the matter of spiritual culture, if for nothing else, perhaps few periods of his life were richer than this. Internally, there is the most momentous instructive Course of Practical Philosophy, with Experiments, going on; towards the right comprehension of which his Peripatetic[9] habits, favourable to Meditation, might help him rather than hinder. Externally, again, as he wanders to and fro, there are, if for the longing heart little substance, yet for the seeing eye

5. Term often used in English newspapers to account for the frequency of wars between the English and French.
6. Where British armies fought against Napoleon, 1808–14.
7. Cf. Horace, *Epistles*, I.ii.14.
8. See Chapter XLI of *The Adventures of Ferdinand Count Fathom* by Tobias Smollett (1721–71).
9. Walking about, after the manner of Aristotle who delivered his lectures while walking in the Lyceum.

sights enough: in these so boundless Travels of his, granting that the Satanic School was even partially kept down, what an incredible knowledge of our Planet, and its Inhabitants and their Works, that is to say, of all knowable things, might not Teufelsdröckh acquire!

"I have read in most Public Libraries," says he, "including those of Constantinople and Samarcand: in most Colleges, except the Chinese Mandarin ones, I have studied, or seen that there was no studying. Unknown Languages have I oftenest gathered from their natural repertory, the Air, by my organ of Hearing; Statistics, Geographics, Topographics came, through the Eye, almost of their own accord. The ways of Man, how he seeks food, and warmth, and protection for himself, in most regions, are ocularly known to me. Like the great Hadrian,[1] I meted-out much of the terraqueous Globe with a pair of Compasses[2] that belonged to myself only.

"Of great Scenes why speak? Three summer days, I lingered reflecting, and even composing (*dichtete*), by the Pine-chasms of Vaucluse; and in that clear Lakelet[3] moistened my bread. I have sat under the Palm-trees of Tadmor;[4] smoked a pipe among the ruins of Babylon. The great Wall of China I have seen; and can testify that it is of gray brick, coped and covered with granite, and shows only second-rate masonry.—Great Events, also, have not I witnessed? Kings sweated-down (*ausgemergelt*) into Berlin-and-Milan Customhouse-Officers;[5] the World well won, and the World well lost;[6] oftener than once a hundred-thousand individuals shot (by each other) in one day. All kindreds and peoples and nations dashed together, and shifted and shovelled into heaps, that they might ferment there, and in time unite. The birth-pangs of Democracy,[7] wherewith convulsed Europe was groaning in cries that reached Heaven, could not escape me.

"For great Men I have ever had the warmest predilection; and can perhaps boast that few such in this era have wholly escaped me. Great Men are the inspired (speaking and acting) Texts of that divine BOOK OF REVELATION, whereof a Chapter is completed from epoch to epoch, and by some named HISTORY; to which inspired Texts your numerous talented men, and your innumerable untalented men, are the better or worse exegetic Commentaries, and wagonload of too-stupid, heretical or orthodox, weekly Sermons. For my study, the inspired Texts themselves! Thus did not I, in very early days, having disguised me as tavern-waiter, stand behind

---

1. Roman emperor (76–138) who traveled extensively throughout his empire.
2. I.e., legs.
3. A pool at the base of a mountain in Vaucluse in southern France. The adjacent "Pine-chasms" were one of Petrarch's favorite haunts. For Teufelsdröckh the area served as one of the "secular wells" that helped to restore him to spiritual health.

4. Palmyra in Syria.
5. Napoleon reduced some of Europe's kings to the status of mere tax collectors for his regime.
6. Cf. the title of Dryden's play *All for Love, or the World Well Lost.*
7. As manifested in the revolutionary outbreaks in France (1789 and 1830) and in the agitations in England preceding the Reform Bill of 1832.

the field-chairs, under that shady Tree at Treisnitz by the Jena Highway; [8] waiting upon the great Schiller and greater Goethe; and hearing what I have not forgotten. For—"

—But at this point the Editor recalls his principle of caution, some time ago laid down, and must suppress much. Let not the sacredness of Laurelled, still more, of Crowned Heads, be tampered with. Should we, at a future day, find circumstances altered, and the time come for Publication, then may these glimpses into the privacy of the Illustrious be conceded; which for the present were little better than treacherous, perhaps traitorous Eavesdroppings. Of Lord Byron, therefore, of Pope Pius, Emperor Tarakwang, and the "White Water-roses" [9] (Chinese Carbonari) with their mysteries, no notice here! Of Napoleon himself we shall only, glancing from afar, remark that Teufelsdröckh's relation to him seems to have been of very varied character. At first we find our poor Professor on the point of being shot as a spy; then taken into private conversation, even pinched on the ear, yet presented with no money; at last indignantly dismissed, almost thrown out of doors, as an "Ideologist." "He himself," says the Professor, "was among the completest Ideologists, at least Ideopraxists: [1] in the Idea (*in der Idee*) he lived, moved and fought. The man was a Divine Missionary, though unconscious of it; and preached, through the cannon's throat, that great doctrine, *La carrière ouverte aux talens* (The Tools to him that can handle them), which is our ultimate Political Evangel, wherein alone can liberty lie. Madly enough he preached, it is true, as Enthusiasts [2] and first Missionaries are wont, with imperfect utterance, amid much frothy rant; yet as articulately perhaps as the case admitted. Or call him, if you will, an American Backwoodsman, who had to fell unpenetrated forests, and battle with innumerable wolves, and did not entirely forbear strong liquor, rioting, and even theft; whom, notwithstanding, the peaceful Sower will follow, and, as he cuts the boundless harvest, bless."

More legitimate and decisively authentic is Teufelsdröckh's appearance and emergence (we know not well whence) in the solitude of the North Cape, on that June Midnight. He has a "light-blue Spanish cloak" hanging round him, as his "most commodious, principal, indeed sole upper-garment"; and stands there, on the World-promontory, looking over the infinite Brine, like a little blue Belfry (as we figure), now motionless indeed, yet ready, if stirred, to ring quaintest changes.

"Silence as of death," writes he; "for Midnight, even in the Arctic latitudes, has its character: nothing but the granite cliffs ruddy-tinged, the peaceable gurgle of that slow-heaving Polar Ocean, over

---

8. Where Goethe and Schiller met during the 1790's when they were collaborating on their writings.
9. Like the Carbonari in Italy, a secret revolutionary society in China during the regime of Emperor "Tarakwang" (Tao Kuang, 1821–50).
1. Those who put ideas into practice.
2. Religious fanatics.

which in the utmost North the great Sun hangs low and lazy, as if
he too were slumbering. Yet is his cloud-couch wrought of crimson
and cloth-of-gold; yet does his light stream over the mirror of
waters, like a tremulous fire-pillar, shooting downwards to the abyss,
and hide itself under my feet. In such moments, Solitude also is invaluable; for who would speak, or be looked on, when behind him
lies all Europe and Africa, fast asleep, except the watchmen; and
before him the silent Immensity, and Palace of the Eternal, whereof
our Sun is but a porch-lamp?

"Nevertheless, in this solemn moment comes a man, or monster,
scrambling from among the rock-hollows; and, shaggy, huge as the
Hyperborean[3] Bear, hails me in Russian speech: most probably,
therefore, a Russian Smuggler. With courteous brevity, I signify my
indifference to contraband trade, my humane intentions, yet strong
wish to be private. In vain: the monster, counting doubtless on his
superior stature, and minded to make sport for himself, or perhaps
profit, were it with murder, continues to advance; ever assailing me
with his importunate train-oil[4] breath; and now has advanced, till
we stand both on the verge of the rock, the deep Sea rippling
greedily down below. What argument will avail? On the thick
Hyperborean, cherubic reasoning, seraphic eloquence were lost. Prepared for such extremity, I, deftly enough, whisk aside one step;
draw out, from my interior reservoirs, a sufficient Birmingham
Horse-pistol, and say, 'Be so obliging as retire, Friend (*Er ziehe sich
zurück, Freund*), and with promptitude!' This logic even the Hyperborean understands: fast enough, with apologetic, petitionary
growl, he sidles off; and, except for suicidal as well as homicidal
purposes, need not return.

"Such I hold to be the genuine use of Gunpowder: that it makes
all men alike tall. Nay, if thou be cooler, cleverer than I, if thou have
more *Mind*, though all but no *Body* whatever, then canst thou kill
me first, and are the taller. Hereby, at last, is the Goliath powerless,
and the David resistless; savage Animalism is nothing, inventive
Spiritualism is all.

"With respect to Duels, indeed, I have my own ideas. Few things,
in this so surprising world, strike me with more surprise. Two little
visual Spectra of men, hovering with insecure enough cohesion in
the midst of the UNFATHOMABLE, and to dissolve therein, at any
rate, very soon,—make pause at the distance of twelve paces asunder;
whirl round; and, simultaneously by the cunningest mechanism, explode one another into Dissolution; and off-hand become Air, and
Nonextant! Deuce on it (*verdammt*), the little spitfires!—Nay, I
think with old Hugo von Trimberg:[5] 'God must needs laugh outright, could such a thing be, to see his wondrous Manikins here
below.' "

3. From the far North.   5. Medieval poet (1260–1309).
4. Whale oil.

But amid these specialties, let us not forget the great generality, which is our Chief guest here: How prospered the inner man of Teufelsdröckh under so much outward shifting? Does Legion [6] still lurk in him, though repressed; or has he exorcised that Devil's Brood? We can answer that the symptoms continue promising. Experience is the grand spiritual Doctor; and with him Teufelsdröckh has been long a patient, swallowing many a bitter bolus.[7] Unless our poor Friend belong to the numerous class of Incurables, which seems not likely, some cure will doubtless be effected. We should rather say that Legion, or the Satanic School, was now pretty well extirpated and cast out, but next to nothing introduced in its room; whereby the heart remains, for the while, in a quiet but no comfortable state.

"At length, after so much roasting," thus writes our Autobiographer, "I was what you might name calcined. Pray only that it be not rather, as is the more frequent issue, reduced to a *caput-mortuum!*[8] But in any case, by mere dint of practice, I had grown familiar with many things. Wretchedness was still wretched; but I could now partly see through it, and despise it. Which highest mortal, in this inane Existence, had I not found a Shadow-hunter, or Shadow-hunted; and, when I looked through his brave garnitures, miserable enough? Thy wishes have all been sniffed aside, thought I: but what, had they ever been all granted! Did not the Boy Alexander weep because he had not two Planets to conquer; or a whole Solar System, or after that, a whole Universe? *Ach Gott,* when I gazed into these Stars, have they not looked-down on me as if with pity, from their serene spaces; like Eyes glistening with heavenly tears over the little lot of man! Thousands of human generations, all as noisy as our own, have been swallowed-up of Time, and there remains no wreck of them any more; and Arcturus and Orion and Sirius and the Pleiades are still shining in their courses, clear and young, as when the Shepherd first noted them in the plain of Shinar.[9] Pshaw! what is this paltry little Dog-cage[1] of an Earth; what art thou that sittest whining there? Thou art still Nothing, Nobody: true; but who, then, is Something, Somebody? For thee the Family of Man has no use; it rejects thee; thou art wholly as a dissevered limb: so be it; perhaps it is better so!"

Too-heavy-laden Teufelsdröckh! Yet surely his bands are loosening; one day he will hurl the burden far from him, and bound forth free and with a second youth.

6. Unclean spirits as described in Mark v.9.
7. Large pill.
8. Death's head.
9. The shepherd is probably Abraham, who was commanded by the Lord to "tell the stars, if thou be able to number them" (Genesis xv.5). Shinar was a plain in the Sumerian region (in modern times, Iraq). Abraham migrated from the Sumerian city of Ur (Genesis x.10; xi.31).
1. A drum-shaped cage that turns when a dog runs inside the cylinder. This dog-powered device, attached to a kitchen spit, was used for turning joints of meat during roasting.

Chapter IX. The Everlasting Yea

"Temptations in the Wilderness!"[2] exclaims Teufelsdröckh: "Have we not all to be tried with such? Not so easily can the old Adam, lodged in us by birth, be dispossessed. Our Life is compassed round with Necessity; yet is the meaning of Life itself no other than Freedom, than Voluntary Force: thus have we a warfare; in the beginning, especially, a hard-fought battle. For the God-given mandate, *Work thou in Welldoing*, lies mysteriously written, in Promethean[3] Prophetic Characters, in our hearts; and leaves us no rest, night or day, till it be deciphered and obeyed; till it burn forth, in our conduct, a visible, acted Gospel of Freedom. And as the clay-given mandate, *Eat thou and be filled*, at the same time persuasively proclaims itself through every nerve,—must not there be a confusion, a contest, before the better Influence can become the upper?

"To me nothing seems more natural than that the Son of Man, when such God-given mandate first prophetically stirs within him, and the Clay must now be vanquished, or vanquish,—should be carried of the spirit into grim Solitudes, and there fronting the Tempter do grimmest battle with him; defiantly setting him at naught, till he yield and fly. Name it as we choose: with or without visible Devil, whether in the natural Desert of rocks and sands, or in the populous moral Desert of selfishness and baseness,—to such Temptation are we all called. Unhappy if we are not! Unhappy if we are but Half-men, in whom that divine handwriting has never blazed forth, all-subduing, in true sun-splendour; but quivers dubiously amid meaner lights: or smoulders, in dull pain, in darkness, under earthly vapours!—Our Wilderness is the wide World in an Atheistic Century; our Forty Days are long years of suffering and fasting: nevertheless, to these also comes an end. Yes, to me also was given, if not Victory, yet the consciousness of Battle, and the resolve to persevere therein while life or faculty is left. To me also, entangled in the enchanted forests, demon-peopled, doleful of sight and of sound, it was given, after weariest wanderings, to work out my way into the higher sunlit slopes—of that Mountain which has no summit, or whose summit is in Heaven only!"

He says elsewhere, under a less ambitious figure; as figures are, once for all, natural to him: "Has not thy Life been that of most sufficient men (*tüchtigen Männer*) thou hast known in this generation? An outflush of foolish young Enthusiasm, like the first

2. Matthew iv.1.
3. Fiery or fiery-spirited, an allusion to Prometheus, the defiant Titan who brought the secret of fire-making to man.

fallow-crop, wherein are as many weeds as valuable herbs: this all parched away, under the Droughts of practical and spiritual Unbelief, as Disappointment, in thought and act, often-repeated gave rise to Doubt, and Doubt gradually settled into Denial! If I have had a second-crop, and now see the perennial greensward, and sit under umbrageous[4] cedars, which defy all Drought (and Doubt); herein too, be the Heavens praised, I am not without examples, and even exemplars."

So that, for Teufelsdröckh also, there has been a "glorious revolution":[5] these mad shadow-hunting and shadow-hunted Pilgrimings of his were but some purifying "Temptation in the Wilderness," before his Apostolic work (such as it was) could begin; which Temptation is now happily over, and the Devil once more worsted! Was "that high moment in the *Rue de l'Enfer*," then, properly the turning-point of the battle; when the Fiend said, *Worship me or be torn in shreds*; and was answered valiantly with an *Apage Satana?*[6] —Singular Teufelsdröckh, would thou hadst told thy singular story in plain words! But it is fruitless to look there, in those Paper-bags,[7] for such. Nothing but innuendoes, figurative crotchets: a typical Shadow, fitfully wavering, prophetico-satiric; no clear logical Picture. "How paint to the sensual eye," asks he once, "what passes in the Holy-of-Holies of Man's Soul; in what words, known to these profane times, speak even afar-off of the unspeakable?" We ask in turn: Why perplex these times, profane as they are, with needless obscurity, by omission and by commission? Not mystical only is our Professor, but whimsical; and involves himself, now more than ever, in eye-bewildering *chiaroscuro*.[8] Successive glimpses, here faithfully imparted, our more gifted readers must endeavour to combine for their own behoof.

He says: "The hot Harmattan wind[9] had raged itself out; its howl went silent within me; and the long-deafened soul could now hear. I paused in my wild wanderings; and sat me down to wait, and consider; for it was as if the hour of change drew nigh. I seemed to surrender, to renounce utterly, and say: Fly, then, false shadows of Hope; I will chase you no more, I will believe you no more. And ye too, haggard spectres of Fear, I care not for you; ye too are all shadows and a lie. Let me rest here: for I am way-weary and life-weary; I will rest here, were it but to die: to die or to live is alike to me; alike insignificant."—And again: "Here, then, as I lay in that Centre of Indifference; cast, doubtless by benignant upper Influence, into a healing sleep, the heavy dreams rolled gradually away, and I awoke to a new Heaven and a new Earth.[1] The first

4. Shady.
5. The overthrow of James II of England in 1688.
6. "Get thee hence, Satan!" (Matthew iv.8–10).
7. Bags containing documents and writings by Teufelsdröckh.
8. Light and shade.
9. A hot dry wind in Africa.
1. Revelation xxi.1.

preliminary moral Act, Annihilation of Self (*Selbsttödtung*), had been happily accomplished; and my mind's eyes were now unsealed, and its hands ungyved."[2]

Might we not also conjecture that the following passage refers to his Locality, during this same "healing sleep"; that his Pilgrim-staff lies cast aside here, on "the high table-land"; and indeed that the repose is already taking wholesome effect on him? If it were not that the tone, in some parts, has more of riancy,[3] even of levity, than we could have expected! However, in Teufelsdröckh, there is always the strangest Dualism: light dancing, with guitar-music, will be going on in the fore-court, while by fits from within comes the faint whimpering of woe and wail. We transcribe the piece entire:

"Beautiful it was to sit there, as in my skyey Tent, musing and meditating; on the high table-land, in front of the Mountains; over me, as roof, the azure Dome, and around me, for walls, four azure-flowing curtains,—namely, of the Four azure winds, on whose bottom-fringes also I have seen gilding. And then to fancy the fair Castles that stood sheltered in these Mountain hollows; with their green flower-lawns, and white dames and damosels, lovely enough: or better still, the straw-roofed Cottages, wherein stood many a Mother baking bread, with her children round her:—all hidden and protectingly folded-up in the valley-folds; yet there and alive, as sure as if I beheld them. Or to see, as well as fancy, the nine Towns and Villages, that lay round my mountain-seat, which, in still weather, were wont to speak to me (by their steeple-bells) with metal tongue; and, in almost all weather, proclaimed their vitality by repeated Smoke-clouds; whereon, as on a culinary horologe,[4] I might read the hour of the day. For it was the smoke of cookery, as kind housewives at morning, midday, eventide, were boiling their husbands' kettles; and ever a blue pillar rose up into the air, successively or simultaneously, from each of the nine, saying, as plainly as smoke could say: Such and such a meal is getting ready here. Not uninteresting! For you have the whole Borough, with all its love-makings and scandal-mongeries, contentions and content-ments, as in miniature, and could cover it all with your hat.—If, in my wide Wayfarings, I had learned to look into the business of the World in its details, here perhaps was the place for combining it into general propositions, and deducing inferences therefrom.

"Often also could I see the black Tempest marching in anger through the Distance: round some Schreckhorn,[5] as yet grim-blue, would the eddying vapour gather, and there tumultuously eddy, and flow down like a mad witch's hair; till, after a space, it vanished, and, in the clear sunbeam, your Schreckhorn stood smiling grim-

2. Unfettered.
3. Gaiety.
4. Clock.

5. "Peak of Terror." A mountain in Switzerland.

white, for the vapour had held snow. How thou fermentest and elaboratest, in thy great fermenting-vat and laboratory of an Atmosphere, of a World, O Nature!—Or what is Nature? Ha! why do I not name thee GOD? Art not thou the 'Living Garment of God'? O Heavens, is it, in very deed, HE, then, that ever speaks through thee; that lives and loves in thee, that lives and loves in me?

"Fore-shadows, call them rather fore-splendours, of that Truth, and Beginning of Truths, fell mysteriously over my soul. Sweeter than Dayspring to the Shipwrecked in Nova Zembla;[6] ah, like the mother's voice to her little child that strays bewildered, weeping, in unknown tumults; like soft streamings of celestial music to my too-exasperated heart, came that Evangel. The Universe is not dead and demoniacal, a charnel-house with spectres; but godlike, and my Father's!

"With other eyes, too, could I now look upon my fellow man; with an infinite Love, an infinite Pity. Poor, wandering, wayward man! Art thou not tired, and beaten with stripes, even as I am? Ever, whether thou bear the royal mantle or the beggar's gabardine, art thou not so weary, so heavy-laden; and thy Bed of Rest is but a Grave. O my Brother, my Brother, why cannot I shelter thee in my bosom, and wipe away all tears from thy eyes! Truly, the din of many-voiced Life, which, in this solitude, with the mind's organ, I could hear, was no longer a maddening discord, but a melting one; like inarticulate cries, and sobbings of a dumb creature, which in the ear of Heaven are prayers. The poor Earth, with her poor joys, was now my needy Mother, not my cruel Stepdame; man, with his so mad Wants and so mean Endeavours, had become the dearer to me; and even for his sufferings and his sins, I now first named him Brother. Thus I was standing in the porch of that 'Sanctuary of Sorrow';[7] by strange, steep ways had I too been guided thither; and ere long its sacred gates would open, and the 'Divine Depth of Sorrow' lie disclosed to me."

The Professor says, he here first got eye on the Knot that had been strangling him, and straightway could unfasten it, and was free. "A vain interminable controversy," writes he, "touching what is at present called Origin of Evil, or some such thing, arises in every soul, since the beginning of the world; and in every soul, that would pass from idle Suffering into actual Endeavouring, must first be put an end to. The most, in our time, have to go content with a simple, incomplete enough Suppression of this controversy; to a few some Solution of it is indispensable. In every new era, too, such Solution comes-out in different terms; and ever the Solution

6. A Dutch sea captain, whose ship was wrecked off the island of Nova Zembla in the Arctic in 1596, recorded in his journal his thankfulness at the coming of daylight.
7. Adapted from Goethe's *Wilhelm Meister.*

of the last era has become obsolete, and is found unserviceable. For it is man's nature to change his Dialect from century to century; he cannot help it though he would. The authentic *Church-Cate-chism* of our present century has not yet fallen into my hands: meanwhile, for my own private behoof, I attempt to elucidate the matter so. Man's Unhappiness, as I construe, comes of his Great-ness; it is because there is an Infinite in him, which with all his cunning he cannot quite bury under the Finite. Will the whole Finance Ministers and Upholsterers and Confectioners of modern Europe undertake, in joint-stock company, to make one Shoeblack HAPPY? They cannot accomplish it, above an hour or two; for the Shoeblack also has a Soul quite other than his Stomach; and would require, if you consider it, for his permanent satisfaction and satura-tion, simply this allotment, no more, and no less: *God's infinite Universe altogether to himself*, therein to enjoy infinitely, and fill every wish as fast as it rose. Oceans of Hochheimer,[8] a Throat like that of Ophiuchus:[9] speak not of them; to the infinite Shoeblack they are as nothing. No sooner is your ocean filled, than he grum-bles that it might have been of better vintage. Try him with half of a Universe, of an Omnipotence, he sets to quarrelling with the proprietor of the other half, and declares himself the most mal-treated of men.—Always there is a black spot in our sunshine: it is even as I said, the *Shadow of Ourselves*.

"But the whim we have of Happiness is somewhat thus. By cer-tain valuations, and averages, of our own striking, we come upon some sort of average terrestrial lot; this we fancy belongs to us by nature, and of indefeasible right. It is simple payment of our wages, of our deserts; requires neither thanks nor complaint; only such *overplus* as there may be do we account Happiness; any *deficit* again is Misery. Now consider that we have the valuation of our own deserts ourselves, and what a fund of Self-conceit there is in each of us,—do you wonder that the balance should so often dip the wrong way, and many a Blockhead cry: See there, what a payment; was ever worthy gentleman so used!—I tell thee, Blockhead, it all comes of thy Vanity; of what thou *fanciest* those same deserts of thine to be. Fancy that thou deservest to be hanged (as is most likely), thou wilt feel it happiness to be only shot: fancy that thou deservest to be hanged in a hair-halter, it will be a luxury to die in hemp.

"So true is it, what I then say, that *the Fraction of Life can be increased in value not so much by increasing your Numerator as by lessening your Denominator*. Nay, unless my Algebra deceive me, *Unity* itself divided by *Zero* will give *Infinity*. Make thy claim of wages a zero, then; thou hast the world under thy feet. Well did

---

8. Rhine wine or hock from Hochheim.   9. The serpent in the constellation Serpentarius.

the Wisest of our time write: 'It is only with Renunciation (*Entsagen*) that Life, properly speaking, can be said to begin.'[1]

"I asked myself: What is this that, ever since earliest years, thou hast been fretting and fuming, and lamenting and self-tormenting, on account of? Say it in a word: is it not because thou art not HAPPY? Because the THOU (sweet gentleman) is not sufficiently honoured, nourished, soft-bedded, and lovingly cared for? Foolish soul! What Act of Legislature was there that *thou* shouldst be Happy? A little while ago thou hadst no right to *be* at all. What if thou wert born and predestined not to be Happy, but to be Unhappy! Art thou nothing other than a Vulture, then, that fliest through the Universe seeking after somewhat to *eat*; and shrieking dolefully because carrion enough is not given thee? Close thy *Byron*; open thy *Goethe*."

"*Es leuchtet mir ein*,[2] I see a glimpse of it!" cries he elsewhere: "there is in man a HIGHER than Love of Happiness: he can do without Happiness, and instead thereof find Blessedness! Was it not to preach-forth this same HIGHER that sages and martyrs, the Poet and the Priest, in all times, have spoken and suffered; bearing testimony, through life and through death, of the Godlike that is in Man, and how in the Godlike only has he Strength and Freedom? Which God-inspired Doctrine art thou also honoured to be taught; O Heavens! and broken with manifold merciful Afflictions, even till thou become contrite, and learn it! O, thank thy Destiny for these; thankfully bear what yet remain: thou hadst need of them; the Self in thee needed to be annihilated. By benignant fever-paroxysms is Life rooting out the deep-seated chronic Diseases, and triumphs over Death. On the roaring billows of Time, thou art not engulfed, but borne aloft into the azure of Eternity. Love not Pleasure; love God.[3] This is the EVERLASTING YEA, wherein all contradiction is solved: wherein whoso walks and works, it is well with him."

And again: "Small is it that thou canst trample the Earth with its injuries under thy feet, as old Greek Zeno[4] trained thee: thou canst love the Earth while it injures thee, and even because it injures thee; for this a Greater than Zeno was needed, and he too was sent. Knowest thou that '*Worship of Sorrow*'?[5] The Temple thereof, founded some eighteen centuries ago, now lies in ruins, overgrown with jungle, the habitation of doleful creatures: nevertheless, venture forward; in a low crypt, arched out of falling fragments, thou findest the Altar still there, and its sacred Lamp perennially burning."

1. Adapted from *Wilhelm Meister;* "the wisest of our time" is Goethe.
2. An exclamation of Wilhelm Meister's.
3. II Timothy iii.4.
4. Greek Stoic philosopher of the 3rd century B.C. After being injured in a fall Zeno is reputed to have struck the earth with his hand as if the earth were responsible for his injury. Afterwards he committed suicide. Hence he is said to "trample the Earth."
5. Christianity.

Without pretending to comment on which strange utterances, the Editor will only remark, that there lies beside them much of a still more questionable character; unsuited to the general apprehension; nay wherein he himself does not see his way. Nebulous disquisitions on Religion, yet not without bursts of splendour; on the "perennial continuance of Inspiration"; on Prophecy; that there are "true Priests, as well as Baal-Priests,[6] in our own day": with more of the like sort. We select some fractions, by way of finish to this farrago.

"Cease, my much-respected Herr von Voltaire," thus apostrophises the Professor: "shut thy sweet voice; for the task appointed thee seems finished. Sufficiently hast thou demonstrated this proposition, considerable or otherwise: That the Mythus of the Christian Religion looks not in the eighteenth century as it did in the eighth. Alas, were thy six-and-thirty quartos, and the six-and-thirty thousand other quartos and folios, and flying sheets or reams, printed before and since on the same subject, all needed to convince us of so little! But what next? Wilt thou help us to embody the divine Spirit of that Religion in a new Mythus, in a new vehicle and vesture, that our Souls, otherwise too like perishing, may live? What! thou hast no faculty in that kind? Only a torch for burning, no hammer for building? Take our thanks, then, and ———— thyself away.

"Meanwhile what are antiquated Mythuses to me? Or is the God present, felt in my own heart, a thing which Herr von Voltaire will dispute out of me; or dispute into me? To the 'Worship of Sorrow' ascribe what origin and genesis thou pleasest, *has* not that Worship originated, and been generated; is it not *here*? Feel it in thy heart, and then say whether it is of God! This is Belief; all else is Opinion, —for which latter whoso will let him worry and be worried."

"Neither," observes he elsewhere, "shall ye tear-out one another's eyes, struggling over 'Plenary Inspiration,'[7] and suchlike: try rather to get a little even Partial Inspiration, each of you for himself. One BIBLE I know, of whose Plenary Inspiration doubt is not so much as possible; nay with my own eyes I saw the God's-Hand writing it: thereof all other Bibles are but leaves,—say, in Picture-Writing to assist the weaker faculty."

Or, to give the wearied reader relief, and bring it to an end, let him take the following perhaps more intelligible passage:

"To me, in this our life," says the Professor, "which is an internecine warfare with the Time-spirit, other warfare seems questionable. Hast thou in any way a Contention with thy brother, I advise thee, think well what the meaning thereof is. If thou gauge

6. False priests. See I Kings xviii.17–40.
7. Doctrine that all statements in the Bible are supernaturally inspired and authoritative. Voltaire had sought to demonstrate that this doctrine was absurd.

it to the bottom, it is simply this: 'Fellow, see! thou art taking more than thy share of Happiness in the world, something from *my* share: which, by the Heavens, thou shalt not; nay I will fight thee rather.'—Alas, and the whole lot to be divided is such a beggarly matter, truly a 'feast of shells,'[8] for the substance has been spilled out: not enough to quench one Appetite; and the collective human species clutching at them!—Can we not, in all such cases, rather say: 'Take it, thou too-ravenous individual; take that pitiful additional fraction of a share, which I reckoned mine, but which thou so wantest; take it with a blessing: would to Heaven I had enough for thee!'—If Fichte's *Wissenschaftslehre*[9] be, 'to a certain extent, Applied Christianity,' surely to a still greater extent, so is this. We have here not a Whole Duty of Man,[1] yet a Half Duty, namely the Passive half: could we but do it, as we can demonstrate it!

"But indeed Conviction, were it never so excellent, is worthless till it convert itself into Conduct. Nay properly Conviction is not possible till then; inasmuch as all Speculation is by nature endless, formless, a vortex amid vortices: only by a felt indubitable certainty of Experience does it find any centre to revolve round, and so fashion itself into a system. Most true is it, as a wise man teaches us, that 'Doubt of any sort cannot be removed except by Action.'[2] On which ground, too, let him who gropes painfully in darkness or uncertain light, and prays vehemently that the dawn may ripen into day, lay this other precept well to heart, which to me was of invaluable service: '*Do the Duty which lies nearest thee,*' which thou knowest to be a Duty! Thy second Duty will already have become clearer.

"May we not say, however, that the hour of Spiritual Enfranchisement is even this: When your Ideal World, wherein the whole man has been dimly struggling and inexpressibly languishing to work, becomes revealed, and thrown open; and you discover, with amazement enough, like the Lothario in *Wilhelm Meister*, that your 'America is here or nowhere'? The Situation that has not its Duty, its Ideal, was never yet occupied by man. Yes here, in this poor, miserable, hampered, despicable Actual, wherein thou even now standest, here or nowhere is thy Ideal: work it out therefrom; and working, believe, live, be free. Fool! the Ideal is in thyself, the impediment too is in thyself: thy Condition is but the stuff thou art to shape that same Ideal out of: what matters whether such stuff be of this sort or that, so the Form thou give it be heroic, be poetic? O thou that pinest in the imprisonment of the Actual, and criest bitterly to the gods for a kingdom wherein to rule and create, know

8. Empty eggshells.
9. "The Doctrine of Knowledge"; by the German philosopher Johann Gottlieb Fichte (1762–1814).
1. Title of an anonymous book of reli-

gious instruction first published in 1659.
2. This and the following quotation are from Goethe's *Wilhelm Meister*.

this of a truth: the thing thou seekest is already with thee, 'here or nowhere,' couldst thou only see!

"But it is with man's Soul as it was with Nature: the beginning of Creation is—Light.[3] Till the eye have vision, the whole members are in bonds.[4] Divine moment, when over the tempest-tost Soul, as once over the wild-weltering Chaos, it is spoken: Let there be Light! Ever to the greatest that has felt such moment, is it not miraculous and God-announcing; even as, under simpler figures, to the simplest and least. The mad primeval Discord is hushed; the rudely-jumbled conflicting elements bind themselves into separate Firmaments: deep silent rock-foundations are built beneath; and the skyey vault with its everlasting Luminaries above: instead of a dark wasteful Chaos, we have a blooming, fertile, heaven-encompassed World.

"I too could now say to myself: Be no longer a Chaos, but a World, or even Worldkin. Produce! Produce! Were it but the pitifullest infinitesimal fraction of a Product, produce it, in God's name! 'Tis the utmost thou hast in thee: out with it, then. Up, up! Whatsoever thy hand findeth to do, do it with thy whole might. Work while it is called Today; for the Night cometh, wherein no man can work."[5]

1830–31   1833–34

From The French Revolution[1]
September in Paris[2]

The tocsin is pealing its loudest, the clocks inaudibly striking *Three*, when poor Abbé Sicard,[3] with some thirty other Nonjurant

3. Cf. Genesis i.3.
4. Cf. Matthew vi.22–23.
5. Adapted from Ecclesiastes ix.10 and John ix.4.
1. To tell the story of the French Revolution, Carlyle uses an imaginary reporter as his narrator. This reporter voices the feelings of the revolutionary party. At times he expresses pity towards the victims of the revolution, but for the most part he is at one with the force he calls "Patriotism," praising those leaders who are ardently dedicated to overthrowing the corrupt feudal order. He thus speaks appropriately in the first person plural: "Give *us* arms." This method of day-to-day eyewitnessing of events contributes to the effect of immediacy that Carlyle sought in what he himself called his "wild savage Book, itself a kind of French Revolution."
A second feature of his method is the device of weaving into the narrative a number of direct quotations from the sources he had consulted during the three years devoted to writing the history. Although later historians have been able to point out inaccuracies in *The French Revolution*, Carlyle did base his account on extensive researches. G. M. Trevelyan has said of him that he was not only a great writer but also "in his own strange way, a great historian." Perhaps the most satisfactory comment on *The French Revolution* is J. S. Mill's statement in his review of 1837: "This is not so much a history as an epic poem, and nothwithstanding * * * the truest of histories."
2. Part III, Book 1, Chapter iv. In September, 1792, the revolutionary party under Georges Jacques Danton and Jean Paul Marat urged desperate measures to defend Paris from the invading armies of Austria and Prussia. Hysterical fears of a counterrevolutionary "fifth column" in Paris led to the so-called September Massacres, in which 1,400 political prisoners were slaughtered in four days.
3. The head of a school for the deaf and dumb in Paris; he died in 1822.

Priests,[4] in six carriages, fare along the streets, from their preliminary House of Detention at the Townhall, westward towards the Prison of the Abbaye. Carriages enough stand deserted on the streets; these six move on,—through angry multitudes, cursing as they move. Accursed Aristocrat Tartuffes,[5] this is the pass ye have brought us to! And now ye will break the Prisons, and set Capet Veto[6] on horseback to ride over us? Out upon you, Priests of Beelzebub and Moloch; of Tartuffery, Mammon and the Prussian Gallows,—which ye name Mother-Church and God!—Such reproaches have the poor Nonjurants to endure, and worse; spoken in on them by frantic Patriots, who mount even on the carriage-steps; the very Guards hardly refraining. Pull up your carriage-blinds?—No! answers Patriotism, clapping its horny paw on the carriage-blind, and crushing it down again. Patience in oppression has limits: we are close on the Abbaye, it has lasted long: a poor Nonjurant, of quicker temper, smites the horny paw with his cane; nay, finding solacement in it, smites the unkempt head, sharply and again more sharply, twice over,—seen clearly of us and of the world. It is the last that we see clearly. Alas, next moment, the carriages are locked and blocked in endless raging tumults; in yells deaf to the cry for mercy, which answer the cry for mercy with sabre-thrusts through the heart. The thirty Priests are torn out, are massacred about the Prison-Gate, one after one,—only the poor Abbé Sicard, whom one Moton a watchmaker, knowing him, heroically tried to save and secrete in the Prison, escapes to tell;—and it is Night and Orcus,[7] and Murder's snaky-sparkling head *has* risen in the murk!—

From Sunday afternoon (exclusive of intervals and pauses not final) till Thursday evening, there follow consecutively a Hundred Hours. Which hundred hours are to be reckoned with the hours of the Bartholomew Butchery, of the Armagnac Massacres, Sicilian Vespers, or whatsoever is savagest in the annals of this world. Horrible the hour when man's soul, in its paroxysm, spurns asunder the barriers and rules; and shows what dens and depths are in it! For Night and Orcus, as we say, as was long prophesied, have burst forth, here in this Paris, from their subterranean imprisonment: hideous, dim-confused; which it is painful to look on; and yet which cannot, and indeed which should not, be forgotten.

The Reader, who looks earnestly through this dim Phantasmagory of the Pit, will discern few fixed certain objects; and yet still a few.

4. Priests who had refused to swear allegiance to the new church constitution established by the National Assembly in 1791.
5. Hypocrites (from the title of Molière's play).
6. I.e., the king (Louis XVI). The "Nonjurant Priests" were accused of favoring the restoration to the king of his power to veto legislation, a power he had lost after August 10, 1792. At the same time he had been stripped of his royal titles and was thereafter referred to simply as Louis Capet, the family name of an early dynasty of French kings (Louis XVI was a Bourbon).
7. Hades, the underworld of the dead.

He will observe, in this Abbaye Prison, the sudden massacre of the Priests being once over, a strange Court of Justice, or call it Court of Revenge and Wild-Justice, swiftly fashion itself, and take seat round a table, with the Prison-Registers spread before it;—Stanislas Maillard, Bastille-hero, famed Leader of the Menads,[8] presiding. O Stanislas, one hoped to meet thee elsewhere than here; thou shifty Riding-Usher, with an inkling of Law! This work also thou hadst to do; and then—to depart for ever from our eyes. At *La Force*, at the *Châtelet*, the *Conciergerie*, the like Court forms itself, with the like accompaniments: the thing that one man does, other men can do. There are some Seven Prisons in Paris, full of Aristocrats with conspiracies;—nay not even *Bicêtre* and *Salpêtrière* shall escape, with their Forgers of Assignats:[9] and there are seventy times seven hundred Patriot hearts in a state of frenzy. Scoundrel hearts also there are; as perfect, say, as the Earth holds,—if such are needed. To whom, in this mood, law is as no-law; and killing, by what name soever called, is but work to be done.

So sit these sudden Courts of Wild-Justice, with the Prison-Registers before them; unwonted wild tumult howling all round; the Prisoners in dread expectancy within. Swift: a name is called; bolts jingle, a Prisoner is there. A few questions are put; swiftly this sudden Jury decides: Royalist Plotter or not? Clearly not; in that case, Let the Prisoner be enlarged with *Vive la Nation*. Probably yea; then still, Let the Prisoner be enlarged, but without *Vive la Nation*; or else it may run. Let the Prisoner be conducted to La Force. At La Force again their formula is, Let the Prisoner be conducted to the Abbaye.—"To La Force then!" Volunteer bailiffs seize the doomed man; he is at the outer gate; "enlarged," or "conducted," not into La Force, but into a howling sea; forth, under an arch of wild sabres, axes and pikes; and sinks, hewn asunder. And another sinks, and another; and there forms itself a piled heap of corpses, and the kennels begin to run red. Fancy the yells of these men, their faces of sweat and blood; the crueller shrieks of these women, for there are women too; and a fellow-mortal hurled naked into it all! Jourgniac de Saint-Méard has seen battle, has seen an effervescent Regiment du Roi in mutiny; but the bravest heart may quail at this. The Swiss Prisoners, remnants of the Tenth of August,[1] "clasped each other spasmodically, and hung back; grey veterans crying: 'Mercy, Messieuers; ah, mercy!' But there was no mercy. Suddenly, however, one of these men steps forward. He had on a blue frock coat; he seemed about thirty, his stature was above common, his look noble and martial. 'I go first,' said he,

---

8. Frenzied women of Greece, followers of Dionysus. Maillard had led a mob of women in the march to Versailles in October, 1789.
9. Paper money issued by the French revolutionary government. Royalists ac-

cused of forging such currency had been imprisoned.
1. Remnants of the Swiss Guards, most of whom had been massacred on August 10, 1792, when defending the king's palace from a mob.

'since it must be so: adieu!' Then dashing his hat sharply behind
him: 'Which way?' cried he to the Brigands: 'Show it me, then.'
They open the folding gate; he is announced to the multitude. He
stands a moment motionless; then plunges forth among the pikes,
and dies of a thousand wounds."

Man after man is cut down; the sabres need sharpening, the killers refresh themselves from wine-jugs. Onward and onward goes
the butchery; the loud yells wearying down into bass growls. A
sombre-faced shifting multitude looks on; in dull approval, or dull
disapproval; in dull recognition that it is Necessity. "An *Anglais*
in drab greatcoat" was seen, or seemed to be seen, serving liquor
from his own drambottle;—for what purpose, "if not set on by
Pitt," Satan and himself know best! Witty Dr. Moore grew sick
on approaching, and turned into another street.—Quick enough
goes this Jury-Court; and rigorous. The brave are not spared, nor
the beautiful, nor the weak. Old M. de Montmorin, the Minister's
Brother, was acquitted by the Tribunal of the Seventeenth; and
conducted back, elbowed by howling galleries; but is not acquitted
here. Princess de Lamballe[2] has lain down on bed: "Madame, you
are to be removed to the Abbaye." "I do not wish to remove; I
am well enough here." There is a need-be for removing. She will
arrange her dress a little, then; rude voices answer, "You have not
far to go." She too is led to the hell-gate; a manifest Queen's-Friend.
She shivers back, at the sight of bloody sabres; but there is no return: Onwards! That fair hind head is cleft with the axe; the neck
is severed. That fair body is cut in fragments; with indignities, and
obscene horrors of moustachio *grands-lèvres*,[3] which human nature
would fain find incredible,—which shall be read in the original
language only. She was beautiful, she was good, she had known
no happiness. Young hearts, generation after generation, will think
with themselves: O worthy of worship, thou king-descended, god-
descended, and poor sister-woman! why was not I there; and some
Sword Balmung[4] or Thor's Hammer in my hand? Her head is fixed
on a pike; paraded under the windows of the Temple; that a still
more hated, a Marie Antoinette, may see. One Municipal, in the
Temple with the Royal Prisoners at the moment, said, "Look out."
Another eagerly whispered, "Do not look." The circuit of the Temple is guarded, in these hours, by a long stretched tricolor riband:
terror enters, and the clangour of infinite tumult; hitherto not
regicide, though that too may come.

But it is more edifying to note what thrillings of affection, what
fragments of wild virtues turn up in this shaking asunder of man's

2. Great-granddaughter of the King
of Sardinia; she had married a Bourbon, was early widowed, and later became a close friend of Queen Marie
Antoinette, with whom she had been
imprisoned.
3. "Thick lips"—a figure of speech to
characterize the mob.
4. The sharp sword of Siegfried, hero
of the *Nibelungenlied*.

existence; for of these too there is a proportion. Note old Marquis Cazotte: he is doomed to die; but his young Daughter clasps him in her arms, with an inspiration of eloquence, with a love which is stronger than very death: the heart of the killers themselves is touched by it; the old man is spared. Yet he was guilty, if plotting for his King is guilt: in ten days more, a Court of Law condemned him, and he had to die elsewhere; bequeathing his Daughter a lock of his old grey hair. Or note old M. de Sombreuil, who also had a Daughter:—My Father is not an Aristocrat: O good gentlemen, I will swear it, and testify it, and in all ways prove it; we are not; we hate Aristocrats! "Wilt thou drink Aristocrats' blood?" The man lifts blood (if universal Rumour can be credited); the poor maiden does drink. "This Sombreuil is innocent then!" Yes, indeed,—and now note, most of all, how the bloody pikes, at this news, do rattle to the ground; and the tiger-yells become bursts of jubilee over a brother saved; and the old man and his daughter are clasped to bloody bosoms, with hot tears; and borne home in triumph of *Vive la Nation*, the killers refusing even money! Does it seem strange, this temper of theirs? It seems very certain, well proved by Royalist testimony in other instances; and very significant.

Place de la Révolution[1]

To this conclusion, then, hast thou come, O hapless Louis! The Son of Sixty Kings is to die on the Scaffold by form of Law. Under Sixty Kings this same form of Law, form of Society, has been fashioning itself together, these thousand years; and has become, one way and other, a most strange Machine. Surely, if needful, it is also frightful, this Machine; dead, blind; not what it should be; which, with swift stroke, or by cold slow torture, has wasted the lives and souls of innumerable men. And behold now a King himself, or say rather Kinghood in his person, is to expire here in cruel tortures;—like a Phalaris[2] shut in the belly of his own red-heated Brazen Bull! It is ever so; and thou shouldst know it, O haughty tyrannous man: injustice breeds injustice; curses and falsehoods do verily return "always *home*," wide as they may wander. Innocent Louis bears the sins of many generations: he too experiences that man's tribunal is not in this Earth; that if he had no Higher one, it were not well with him.

A King dying by such violence appeals impressively to the imagination; as the like must do, and ought to do. And yet at bottom it is not the King dying, but the man! Kingship is a coat: the grand loss is of the skin. The man from whom you take his Life, to him

1. Part III, Book 2, Chapter viii. On January 20, 1793, by a small majority, the Convention of Delegates in Paris had voted for the death of the king.

2. A Sicilian tyrant whose victims were roasted alive by being confined inside the brass figure of a bull under which a fire was lit.

can the whole combined world do *more?* Lally[3] went on his hurdle; his mouth filled with a gag. Miserablest mortals, doomed for picking pockets, have a whole five-act Tragedy in them, in that dumb pain, as they go to the gallows, unregarded; they consume the cup of trembling down to the lees. For Kings and for Beggars, for the justly doomed and the unjustly, it is a hard thing to die. Pity them all: thy utmost pity, with all aids and appliances and throne-and-scaffold contrasts, how far short is it of the thing pitied!

A Confessor has come; Abbé Edgeworth, of Irish extraction, whom the King knew by good report, has come promptly on this solemn mission. Leave the Earth alone, then, thou hapless King; it with its malice will go its way, thou also canst go thine. A hard scene yet remains: the parting with our loved ones. Kind hearts, environed in the same grim peril with us; to be left *here!* Let the Reader look with the eyes of Valet Cléry,[4] through these glass-doors, where also the Municipality watches; and see the cruellest of scenes:

"At half-past eight, the door of the ante-room opened: the Queen appeared first, leading her Son by the hand; then Madame Royale[5] and Madame Elizabeth: they all flung themselves into the arms of the King. Silence reigned for some minutes; interrupted only by sobs. The Queen made a movement to lead his Majesty towards the inner room, where M. Edgeworth was waiting unknown to them: 'No,' said the King, 'let us go into the dining-room, it is there only that I can see you.' They entered there; I shut the door of it, which was of glass. The King sat down, the Queen on his left hand, Madame Elizabeth on his right, Madame Royale almost in front; the young Prince remained standing between his Father's legs. They all leaned towards him, and often held him embraced. This scene of woe lasted an hour and three quarters; during which we could hear nothing; we could see only that always when the King spoke, the sobbings of the Princesses redoubled, continued for some minutes; and that then the King began again to speak." —And so our meetings and our partings do now end! The sorrows we gave each other; the poor joys we faithfully shared, and all our lovings and our sufferings, and confused toilings under the earthly Sun, are over. Thou good soul, I shall never, never through all ages of Time, see thee any more!—NEVER! O Reader, knowest thou that hard word?

For nearly two hours this agony lasts; then they tear themselves asunder. "Promise that you will see us on the morrow." He promises:—Ah yes, yes; yet once; and go now, ye loved ones; cry to God

---

3. A French general who was accused unjustly of treachery and executed in 1766. The gag in his mouth was presumably to prevent his protesting his innocence.
4. The valet who attended the king dur-

ing his imprisonment and who later published a journal.
5. The king's daughter, the Duchesse d'Angoulême (1778–1851); Madame Elizabeth was the king's sister, guillotined a year later.

for yourselves and me!—It was a hard scene, but it is over. He will not see them on the morrow. The Queen, in passing through the ante-room, glanced at the Cerberus Municipals;[6] and, with woman's vehemence, said through her tears, "*Vous êtes tous des scélérats.*"[7]

King Louis slept sound, till five in the morning, when Cléry, as he had been ordered, awoke him. Cléry dressed his hair: while this went forward, Louis took a ring from his watch, and kept trying it on his finger; it was his wedding-ring, which he is now to return to the Queen as a mute farewell. At half-past six, he took the Sacrament; and continued in devotion, and conference with Abbé Edgeworth. He will not see his Family: it were too hard to bear.

At eight, the Municipals enter: the King gives them his Will, and messages and effects; which they, at first, brutally refuse to take charge of: he gives them a roll of gold pieces, a hundred and twenty-five louis; these are to be returned to Malesherbes,[8] who had lent them. At nine, Santerre[9] says the hour is come. The King begs yet to retire for three minutes. At the end of three minutes, Santerre again says the hour is come. "Stamping on the ground with his right foot, Louis answers: '*Partons,* Let us go.' "—How the rolling of those drums comes in, through the Temple bastions and bulwarks, on the heart of a queenly wife; soon to be a widow! He is gone, then, and has not seen us? A Queen weeps bitterly; a King's Sister and Children. Over all these Four does Death also hover: all shall perish miserably save one; she, as Duchesse d'Angoulême, will live,—not happily.

At the Temple Gate were some faint cries, perhaps from voices of Pitiful women: "*Grâce!*[1] *Grâce!*" Through the rest of the streets there is silence as of the grave. No man not armed is allowed to be there: the armed, did any even pity, dare not express it, each man overawed by all his neighbours. All windows are down, none seen looking through them. All shops are shut. No wheel-carriage rolls, this morning, in these streets but one only. Eighty-thousand armed men stand ranked, like armed statues of men; cannons bristle, cannoneers with match burning, but no word or movement: it is as a city enchanted into silence and stone: one carriage with its escort, slowly rumbling, is the only sound. Louis reads, in his Book of Devotion, the Prayers of the Dying: clatter of this death-march falls sharp on the ear, in the great silence; but the thought would fain struggle heavenward, and forget the Earth.

As the clocks strike ten, behold the Place de la Révolution, once Place de Louis Quinze: the Guillotine, mounted near the old

---

6. Municipal officers, likened to Cerberus, the three-headed dog that guarded the entrance to Hades.
7. "You are all scoundrels."
8. A delegate who had defended the

king. He was guillotined a year later.
9. A Jacobin leader who commanded the troops in Paris.
1. "Mercy!"

Pedestal where once stood the Statue of that Louis! Far round, all bristles with cannons and armed men: spectators crowding in the rear; D'Orléans Égalité[2] there in cabriolet. Swift messengers, *hoquetons*, speed to the Townhall, every three minutes: near by is the Convention sitting,—vengeful for Lepelletier.[3] Heedless of all, Louis reads his Prayers of the Dying; not till five minutes yet has he finished; then the Carriage opens. What temper he is in? Ten different witnesses will give ten different accounts of it. He is in the collision of all tempers; arrived now at the black Mahlstrom and descent of Death: in sorrow, in indignation, in resignation struggling to be resigned. "Take care of M. Edgeworth," he straitly charges the Lieutenant who is sitting with them: then they two descend.

The drums are beating: "*Taisez-vous*, Silence!" he cries "in a terrible voice, *d'une voix terrible.*" He mounts the scaffold, not without delay; he is in puce[4] coat, breeches of grey, white stockings. He strips off the coat; stands disclosed in a sleeve-waistcoat of white flannel. The Executioners approach to bind him: he spurns, resists; Abbé Edgeworth has to remind him how the Saviour, in whom men trust, submitted to be bound. His hands are tied, his head bare; the fatal moment is come. He advances to the edge of the Scaffold, "his face very red," and says: "Frenchmen, I die innocent: it is from the Scaffold and near appearing before God that I tell you so. I pardon my enemies; I desire that France——" A General on horseback, Santerre or another, prances out, with uplifted hand: "*Tambours!*" The drums drown the voice. "Executioners, do your duty!" The Executioners, desperate lest themselves be murdered (for Santerre and his Armed Ranks will strike, if they do not), seize the hapless Louis: six of them desperate, him singly desperate, struggling there; and bind him to their plank. Abbé Edgeworth, stooping, bespeaks him: "Son of Saint Louis,[5] ascend to Heaven." The Axe clanks down; a King's Life is shorn away. It is Monday the 21st of January 1793. He was aged Thirty-eight years four months and twenty-eight days.

Executioner Samson shows the Head: fierce shout of *Vive la République* rises, and swells; caps raised on bayonets, hats waving: students of the College of Four Nations take it up, on the far Quais; fling it over Paris. D'Orléans drives off in his cabriolet: the Townhall Councillors rub their hands, saying, "It is done, It is done." There is dipping of handkerchiefs, of pike-points in the blood. Headsman Samson, though he afterwards denied it, sells locks of the hair: fractions of the puce coat are long after worn in

---

2. The Duc d'Orléans, a Royalist who had become a revolutionary leader, was called Égalité (Equality). Despite his having voted for the king's death, he was himself executed in 1793.
3. A delegate who had voted for the

king's death and was killed by a Royalist sympathizer.
4. Dull red.
5. Louis IX, king of France (reigned 1226–70).

rings.—And so, in some half-hour it is done; and the multitude has all departed. Pastry-cooks, coffee-sellers, milkmen sing out their trivial quotidian cries: the world wags on, as if this were a common day. In the coffee-houses that evening, says Prudhomme, Patriot shook hands with Patriot in a more cordial manner than usual. Not till some days after, according to Mercier, did public men see what a grave thing it was.

From *Cause and Effect*[1]

* * * Yes, Reader, here is the miracle. Out of that putrescent rubbish of Scepticism, Sensualism, Sentimentalism, hollow Machiavelism, such a Faith has verily risen; flaming in the heart of a People. A whole People, awakening as it were to consciousness in deep misery, believes that it is within reach of a Fraternal Heaven-on-Earth. With longing arms, it struggles to embrace the Unspeakable; cannot embrace it, owing to certain causes.—Seldom do we find that a whole People can be said to have any Faith at all; except in things which it can eat and handle. Whensoever it gets any Faith, its history becomes spirit-stirring, noteworthy. But since the time when steel Europe shook itself simultaneously at the word of Hermit Peter,[2] and rushed towards the Sepulchre where God had lain, there was no universal impulse of Faith that one could note. Since Protestantism went silent, no Luther's voice, no Zisca's[3] drum any longer proclaiming that God's truth was *not* the Devil's Lie; and the Last of the Cameronians[4] (Renwick was the name of him; honour to the name of the brave!) sank, shot, on the Castle-hill of Edinburgh, there was no partial impulse of Faith among Nations. Till now, behold, once more, this French Nation believes! Herein, we say, in that astonishing Faith of theirs, lies the miracle. It is a Faith undoubtedly of the more prodigious sort, even among Faiths; and will embody itself in prodigies. It is the soul of that world-prodigy named French Revolution; whereat the world still gazes and shudders.

But, for the rest, let no man ask History to explain by cause and effect how the business proceeded henceforth. This battle of Mountain and Gironde,[5] and what follows, is the battle of Fanaticisms

---

1. Part III, Book 3, Chapter i. Between the execution of the king and the advent of Napoleon, the revolutionary movement in France suffered from dissension and counterrevolutionary outbreaks which led to the Reign of Terror (1793–94). During this period most of the political leaders and thousands of their followers lost their lives. Before recommencing his narrative, Carlyle pauses, in this chapter, to consider some of the forces underlying these developments.
2. Leader of the First Crusade to Palestine in the late 11th century.
3. Ca. 1360–1424; successful general and leader of the Hussites, a religious sect in Bohemia.
4. A 17th-century Scottish sect. See Sir Walter Scott's novel, *The Heart of Midlothian*.
5. The Girondists were a party of moderate revolutionaries, often of middle-class backgrounds. They were liquidated (as the Marxists say) by their opponents, the Jacobins, who were more adept at controlling the populace. Because the Jacobin delegates in the Na-

and Miracles; unsuitable for cause and effect. The sound of it, to the mind, is as a hubbub of voices in distraction; little of articulate is to be gathered by long listening and studying; only battle-tumult, shouts of triumph, shrieks of despair. The Mountain has left no Memoirs; the Girondins have left Memoirs, which are too often little other than long-drawn Interjections, of *Woe is me*, and *Cursed be ye*. So soon as History can philosophically delineate the conflagration of a kindled Fireship,[6] she may try this other task. Here lay the bitumen-stratum, there the brimstone one; so ran the vein of gunpowder, of nitre, terebinth[7] and foul grease: this, were she inquisitive enough, History might partly know. But how they acted and reacted below decks, one fire-stratum playing into the other, by its nature and the art of man, now when all hands ran raging, and the flames lashed high over shrouds and topmast: this let not History attempt.

The Fireship is old France, the old French Form of Life; her crew a Generation of men. Wild are their cries and their ragings there, like spirits tormented in that flame. But, on the whole, are they not *gone*, O Reader? Their Fireship and they, frightening the world, have sailed away; its flames and its thunders quite away, into the Deep of Time. One thing therefore History will do: pity them all; for it went hard with them all. Not even the seagreen Incorruptible[8] but shall have some pity, some human love, though it takes an effort. And now, so much once thoroughly attained, the rest will become easier. To the eye of equal brotherly pity, innumerable perversions dissipate themselves; exaggerations and execrations fall off, of their own accord. Standing wistfully on the safe shore, we will look, and see, what is of interest to us, what is adapted to us.

1834–37   1837

tional Assembly sat in the most elevated place, the party was sometimes called the "Mountain."
6. A ship filled with combustibles (such as gunpowder and brimstone) which is set adrift among enemy shipping to create havoc.
7. Turpentine.
8. Maximilien Robespierre, "the Incorruptible"; chief of the Jacobin party and principal instigator of the Reign of Terror.

From Past and Present[1]

From *Democracy*

If the Serene Highnesses and Majesties do not take note of that,[2] then, as I perceive, *that* will take note of itself! The time for levity, insincerity, and idle babble and play-acting, in all kinds, is gone by; it is a serious, grave time. Old long-vexed questions, not yet solved in logical words or parliamentary laws, are fast solving themselves in facts, somewhat unblessed to behold! This largest of questions, this question of Work and Wages, which ought, had we heeded Heaven's voice, to have begun two generations ago or more, cannot be delayed longer without hearing Earth's voice. "Labour" will verily need to be somewhat "organized," as they say,—God knows with what difficulty. Man will actually need to have his debts and earnings a little better paid by man; which, let Parliaments speak of them, or be silent of them, are eternally his due from man, and cannot, without penalty and at length not without death-penalty,[3] be withheld. How much ought to cease among us straightway; how much ought to begin straightway, while the hours yet are!

Truly they are strange results to which this of leaving all to "Cash"; of quietly shutting up the God's Temple, and gradually opening wide-open the Mammon's Temple, with "Laissez-faire, and Every man for himself,"—have led us in these days! We have Upper, speaking Classes, who indeed do "speak" as never man spake before; the withered flimsiness, godless baseness and barrenness of whose Speech might of itself indicate what kind of Doing and practical Governing went on under it! For Speech is the gaseous element out of which most kinds of Practice and Performance,

1. In 1842 there were reputedly 1.5 million unemployed in England (out of a population of 18 million). The closing of factories and the reduction of wages led to severe rioting in the manufacturing districts. Bread-hungry mobs (as well as the Chartist mobs who demanded political reforms) caused many observers to dread that a large-scale revolution was imminent. Carlyle was himself so appalled by the plight of the industrial workers that he postponed his researches into the life and times of Cromwell in order to air his views on the contemporary crisis. *Past and Present*, a book written in seven weeks, was a call for heroic leadership. Cromwell and other historic leaders are cited, but the principal example from the past is Abbot Samson, a medieval monk who established order in the monasteries under his charge. Carlyle hoped that the "Captains of Industry" might provide a comparable leadership in 1843. He was aware that the spread of democracy was inevitable, but he had little confidence in it as a method of producing leaders. Nor did he have any confidence, at this time, in the landed aristocracy who seemed to him preoccupied with fox-hunting, preserving their game, and upholding the tariffs on grain (the Corn Laws). In place of a "Do nothing Aristocracy" there was need for a "Working Aristocracy." The first selection here printed is from Book III, Chapter 13.

2. The previous chapter, "Reward," had urged that English manufacturers needed the help of everyone, and that Parliament should remove the tariffs (Corn Laws) restricting the growth of trade and industry.

3. I.e., by the outbreak of a revolution, as in France.

especially all kinds of moral Performance, condense themselves, and take shape; as the one is, so will the other be. Descending, accordingly, into the Dumb Class in its Stockport Cellars[4] and Poor-Law Bastilles,[5] have we not to announce that they are hitherto unexampled in the History of Adam's Posterity?

Life was never a May-game for men: in all times the lot of the dumb millions born to toil was defaced with manifold sufferings, injustices, heavy burdens, avoidable and unavoidable; not play at all, but hard work that made the sinews sore and the heart sore. As bond-slaves, *villani, bordarii, sochemanni,* nay indeed as dukes, earls and kings, men were oftentimes made weary of their life; and had to say, in the sweat of their brow and of their soul, Behold, it is not sport, it is grim earnest, and our back can bear no more! Who knows not what massacrings and harryings there have been; grinding, long-continuing, unbearable injustices,—till the heart had to rise in madness, and some "*Eu Sachsen, nimith euer sachses,* You Saxons, out with your gully-knives, then!*" You Saxons, some "arrestment," partial "arrestment of the Knaves and Dastards" has become indispensable!—The page of Dryasdust[6] is heavy with such details.

And yet I will venture to believe that in no time, since the beginnings of Society, was the lot of those same dumb millions of toilers so entirely unbearable as it is even in the days now passing over us. It is not to die, or even to die of hunger, that makes a man wretched; many men have died; all men must die,—the last exit of us all is in a Fire-Chariot of Pain.[7] But it is to live miserable we know not why; to work sore and yet gain nothing; to be heart-worn, weary, yet isolated, unrelated, girt-in with a cold universal Laissez-faire: it is to die slowly all our life long, imprisoned in a deaf, dead, Infinite Injustice, as in the accursed iron belly of a Phalaris' Bull![8] This is and remains for ever intolerable to all men whom God has made. Do we wonder at French Revolutions, Chartisms, Revolts of Three Days? The times, if we will consider them, are really unexampled.

Never before did I hear of an Irish Widow reduced to "prove her sisterhood by dying of typhus-fever and infecting seventeen persons,"—saying in such undeniable way, "You *see,* I was your sister!"[9] Sisterhood, brotherhood, was often forgotten; but not till the rise of these ultimate Mammon and Shotbelt Gospels[1] did I ever

4. In a cellar in the slum district of Stockport, an industrial town near Manchester, three children were poisoned by their starving parents in order to collect insurance benefits from a burial society.
5. I.e. workhouse for the unemployed.
6. An imaginary author of dull histories.
7. Cf. II Kings ii.11–12.
8. Phalaris was a Sicilian tyrant whose

victims were roasted alive by being confined inside the brass figure of a bull under which a fire was lit.
9. An incident referred to several times in *Past and Present.* Dickens in *Bleak House* also showed how indifference to the lack of sanitation in London slums led to the spread of disease to other parts of the city.
1. "Mammon Gospel" signifies the pursuit of wealth according to the eco-

see it so expressly denied. If no pious Lord or *Law-ward* would remember it, always some pious Lady ("*Hlaf dig*," Benefactress, "*Loaf-giveress*," they say she is,—blessings on her beautiful heart!) was there, with mild mother-voice and hand, to remember it; some pious thoughtful *Elder*, what we now call "Prester," *Presbyter* or "Priest," was there to put all men in mind of it, in the name of the God who had made all.

Not even in Black Dahomey[2] was it ever, I think, forgotten to the typhus-fever length. Mungo Park,[3] resourceless, had sunk down to die under the Negro Village-Tree, a horrible White object in the eyes of all. But in the poor Black Woman, and her daughter who stood aghast at him, whose earthly wealth and funded capital consisted of one small calabash of rice, there lived a heart richer than "*Laissez-faire*": they, with a royal munificence, boiled their rice for him; they sang all night to him, spinning assiduous on their cotton distaffs, as he lay to sleep: "Let us pity the poor white man; no mother has he to fetch him milk, no sister to grind him corn!" Thou poor black Noble One,—thou *Lady* too: did not a God make thee too; was there not in thee too something of a God!—

Gurth,[4] born thrall of Cedric the Saxon, has been greatly pitied by Dryasdust and others. Gurth, with the brass collar round his neck, tending Cedric's pigs in the glades of the wood, is not what I call an exemplar of human felicity: but Gurth, with the sky above him, with the free air and tinted boscage and umbrage round him, and in him at least the certainty of supper and social lodging when he came home; Gurth to me seems happy, in comparison with many a Lancashire and Buckinghamshire man, of these days, not born thrall of anybody! Gurth's brass collar did not gall him: Cedric *deserved* to be his Master. The pigs were Cedric's, but Gurth too would get his parings of them. Gurth had the inexpressible satisfaction of feeling himself related indissolubly, though in a rude brass-collar way, to his fellow-mortals in this Earth. He had superiors, inferiors, equals.—Gurth is now "emancipated" long since; has what we call "Liberty." Liberty, I am told, is a Divine thing. Liberty when it becomes the "Liberty to die by starvation" is not so divine!

Liberty? The true liberty of a man, you would say, consisted in his finding out, or being forced to find out, the right path, and to walk thereon. To learn, or to be taught, what work he actually was able for; and then by permission, persuasion, and even compulsion, to set about doing of the same! That is his true blessed-

nomic code of laissez faire, whereby no one took the responsibility of caring for the starving widow. The meaning of "Shotbelt" has not been identified.
2. A state in west Africa where savage customs, such as human sacrifice and

cannibalism, persisted.
3. Explorer and author of *Travels in the Interior of Africa* (1799). In 1806 he was killed by African natives.
4. A swineherd described in Scott's *Ivanhoe*.

ness, honour, "liberty" and maximum of wellbeing: if liberty be not that, I for one have small care about liberty. You do not allow a palpable madman to leap over precipices; you violate his liberty, you that are wise; and keep him, were it in strait-waistcoats, away from the precipices! Every stupid, every cowardly and foolish man is but a less palpable madman: his true liberty were that a wiser man, that any and every wiser man, could, by brass collars, or in whatever milder or sharper way, lay hold of him when he was going wrong, and order and compel him to go a little righter. O, if thou really art my *Senior*, Seigneur, my *Elder*, Presbyter or Priest, —if thou art in very deed my *Wiser*, may a beneficent instinct lead and impel thee to "conquer" me, to command me! If thou do know better than I what is good and right, I conjure thee in the name of God, force me to do it; were it by never such brass collars, whips and handcuffs, leave me not to walk over precipices! That I have been called, by all the Newspapers, a "free man" will avail me little, if my pilgrimage have ended in death and wreck. O that the Newspapers had called me slave, coward, fool, or what it pleased their sweet voices to name me, and I had attained not death, but life!—Liberty requires new definitions.

A conscious abhorrence and intolerance of Folly, of Baseness, Stupidity, Poltroonery and all that brood of things, dwells deep in some men: still deeper in others an *unconscious* abhorrence and intolerance, clothed moreover by the beneficent Supreme Powers in what stout appetites, energies, egoisms so-called, are suitable to it;—these latter are your Conquerors, Romans, Normans, Russians, Indo-English; Founders of what we call Aristocracies. Which indeed have they not the most "divine right" to found;—being themselves very truly *Ἄριστοι*, BRAVEST, BEST; and conquering generally a confused rabble of WORST, or at lowest, clearly enough, of WORSE? I think their divine right, tried, with affirmatory verdict, in the greatest Law-Court known to me, was good! A class of men who are dreadfully exclaimed against by Dryasdust; of whom nevertheless beneficent Nature has oftentimes had need; and may, alas, again have need.

When, across the hundredfold poor scepticisms, trivialisms, and constitutional cobwebberies of Dryasdust, you catch any glimpse of a William the Conqueror,[5] a Tancred of Hauteville[6] or such like,—do you not discern veritably some rude outline of a true God-made King; whom not the Champion of England[7] cased in

---

5. King William I of England (reigned 1066–87), surnamed the Conqueror after the Battle of Hastings in 1066. Being an illegitimate son, he also bore the surname of William the Bastard. Although some historians condemn William as a ruthless ruler, he is ranked by Carlyle as a hero because of his strong and efficient government. Wil-liam fulfilled the requirements of the kingly hero described by Carlyle in his lectures *On Heroes:* a man fittest "to *command* over us * * * to tell us what we are to *do*."
6. Norman hero of the First Crusade.
7. An official who goes through a formality, at coronation ceremonies, of demanding whether anyone challenges

tin, but all Nature and the Universe were calling to the throne? It is absolutely necessary that he get thither. Nature does not mean her poor Saxon children to perish, of obesity, stupor or other malady, as yet: a stern Ruler and Line of Rulers therefore is called in, —a stern but most beneficent *perpetual House-Surgeon* is by Nature herself called in, and even the appropriate *fees* are provided for him! Dryasdust talks lamentably about Hereward[8] and the Fen Counties; fate of Earl Waltheof;[9] Yorkshire and the North reduced to ashes; all of which is undoubtedly lamentable. But even Dryasdust apprises me of one fact: "A child, in this William's reign, might have carried a purse of gold from end to end of England." My erudite friend, it is a fact which outweighs a thousand! Sweep away thy constitutional, sentimental, and other cobwebberies; look eye to eye, if thou still have any eye, in the face of this big burly William Bastard: thou wilt see a fellow of most flashing discernment, of most strong lion-heart;—in whom, as it were, within a frame of oak and iron, the gods have planted the soul of "a man of genius"! Dost thou call that nothing? I call it an immense thing! —Rage enough was in this Willelmus Conquaestor, rage enough for his occasions;—and yet the essential element of him, as of all such men, is not scorching *fire*, but shining illuminative *light*. Fire and light are strangely interchangeable; nay, at bottom, I have found them different forms of the same most godlike "elementary substance" in our world: a thing worth stating in these days. The essential element of this Conquaestor is, first of all, the most suneyed perception of what *is* really what on this God's-Earth;—which, thou wilt find, does mean at bottom "Justice," and "Virtues" not a few: *Conformity* to what the Maker has seen good to make; that, I suppose, will mean Justice and a Virtue or two?—

Dost thou think Willelmus Conquaestor would have tolerated ten years' jargon, one hour's jargon, on the propriety of killing Cotton-manufactures by partridge Corn-Laws?[1] I fancy, this was not the man to knock out of his night's-rest with nothing but a noisy bedlamism in your mouth! "Assist us still better to bush the partridges; strangle Plugson who spins the shirts?"[2]—*"Par la Splendeur de Dieu!"*[3]—Dost thou think Willelmus Conquaestor, in this new time, with Steam-engine Captains of Industry on one hand

---

the right of the monarch to ascend the throne. He wears full armor ("cased in tin"). A symbol for Carlyle of outworn feudal customs.
8. Hereward the Wake, an outlaw whose exploits against William the Conqueror made him seem a romantic figure like Robin Hood.
9. His execution in 1075, on a supposedly trumped-up charge, is cited as a blot on William's record as king.
1. See the title note.

2. This speech sums up the pleas of the High Tariff lobby in Parliament. "Keep the Corn Laws intact so that the aristocratic landlords may continue to enjoy shooting partridges on their estates; subdue the manufacturing leaders by preventing trade." ("Plugson of Undershot" was Carlyle's term to describe the new class of industrial leaders.)
3. "By the splendor of God!"—one of William's oaths.

of him, and Joe-Manton Captains of Idleness[4] on the other, would
have doubted which *was* really the BEST; which did deserve strangling, and which not?

I have a certain indestructible regard for Willelmus Conquaestor.
A resident House-Surgeon, provided by Nature for her beloved English People, and even furnished with the requisite fees, as I said;
for he by no means felt himself doing Nature's work, this Willelmus, but his own work exclusively! And his own work withal it
was; informed *"par la Splendeur de Dieu."*—I say, it is necessary
to get the work out of such a man, however harsh that be! When
a world, not yet doomed for death, is rushing down to ever-deeper
Baseness and Confusion, it is a dire necessity of Nature's to bring
in her ARISTOCRACIES, her BEST, even by forcible methods. When
their descendants or representatives cease entirely to *be* the Best,
Nature's poor world will very soon rush down again to Baseness;
and it becomes a dire necessity of Nature's to cast them out.
Hence French Revolutions, Five-point Charters, Democracies, and
a mournful list of *Etceteras*, in these our afflicted times. * * *

Democracy, the chase of Liberty in that direction, shall go its
full course; unrestrained by him of Pferdefuss-Quacksalber, or any
of *his* household. The Toiling Millions of Mankind, in most vital
need and passionate instinctive desire of Guidance, shall cast away
False-Guidance; and hope, for an hour, that No-Guidance will
suffice them: but it can be for an hour only. The smallest item of
human Slavery is the oppression of man by his Mock-Superiors;
the palpablest, but I say at bottom the smallest. Let him shake off
such oppression, trample it indignantly under his feet; I blame
him not, I pity and commend him. But oppression by your Mock-
Superiors well shaken off, the grand problem yet remains to solve:
That of finding government by your Real-Superiors! Alas, how shall
we ever learn the solution of that, benighted, bewildered, sniffing,
sneering, godforgetting unfortunates as we are? It is a work for
centuries; to be taught us by tribulations, confusions, insurrections,
obstructions; who knows if not by conflagration and despair! It is
a lesson inclusive of all other lessons; the hardest of all lessons
to learn. * * *

Captains of Industry[1]

If I believed that Mammonism with its adjuncts was to continue
henceforth the one serious principle of our existence, I should
reckon it idle to solicit remedial measures from any Government,
the disease being insusceptible of remedy. Government can do
much, but it can in no wise do all. Government, as the most conspicuous object in Society, is called upon to give signal of what

4. The idle aristocracy who wasted
time shooting partridges with guns
made by Joseph Manton, a London
gunsmith.
1. From Book IV, Chapter 4.

shall be done; and, in many ways, to preside over, further, and command the doing of it. But the Government cannot do, by all its signalling and commanding, what the Society is radically indisposed to do. In the long-run every Government is the exact symbol of its People, with their wisdom and unwisdom; we have to say, Like People like Government.—The main substance of this immense Problem of Organizing Labour, and first of all of Managing the Working Classes, will, it is very clear, have to be solved by those who stand practically in the middle of it; by those who themselves work and preside over work. Of all that can be enacted by any Parliament in regard to it, the germs must already lie potentially extant in those two Classes, who are to obey such enactment. A Human Chaos *in* which there is no light, you vainly attempt to irradiate by light shed *on* it: order never can arise there.

But it is my firm conviction that the "Hell of England" will *cease* to be that of "not making money"; that we shall get a nobler Hell and a nobler Heaven! I anticipate light *in* the Human Chaos, glimmering, shining more and more; under manifold true signals from without That light shall shine. Our deity no longer being Mammon,—O Heavens, each man will then say to himself: "Why such deadly haste to make money? I shall not go to Hell, even if I do not make money! There is another Hell, I am told!" Competition, at railway-speed, in all branches of commerce and work will then abate:—good felt-hats for the head, in every sense, instead of seven-feet lath-and-plaster hats on wheels,[2] will then be discoverable! Bubble-periods,[3] with their panics and commercial crises, will again become infrequent; steady modest industry will take the place of gambling speculation. To be a noble Master, among noble Workers, will again be the first ambition with some few; to be a rich Master only the second. How the Inventive Genius of England, with the whirr of its bobbins and billy-rollers[4] shoved somewhat into the backgrounds of the brain, will contrive and devise, not cheaper produce exclusively, but fairer distribution of the produce at its present cheapness! By degrees, we shall again have a Society with something of Heroism in it, something of Heaven's Blessing on it; we shall again have, as my German friend[5] asserts, "instead of Mammon-Feudalism with unsold cotton-shirts and Preservation of the Game, noble just Industrialism and Government by the Wisest!"

It is with the hope of awakening here and there a British man to know himself for a man and divine soul, that a few words of parting admonition, to all persons to whom the Heavenly Powers

---

2. A London hatter's mode of advertising. Carlyle considered most advertisements to be wasteful.
3. Periods of violent fluctuation in the stock market caused by unsound speculating.
4. Machines used to prepare cotton or wool for spinning.
5. Teufelsdröckh, the hero of *Sartor Resartus*.

have lent power of any kind in this land, may now be addressed. And first to those same Master-Workers, Leaders of Industry; who stand nearest, and in fact powerfullest, though not most prominent, being as yet in too many senses a Virtuality rather than an Actuality.

The Leaders of Industry, if Industry is ever to be led, are virtually the Captains of the World; if there be no nobleness in them, there will never be an Aristocracy more. But let the Captains of Industry consider: once again, are they born of other clay than the old Captains of Slaughter; doomed for ever to be not Chivalry, but a mere gold-plated *Doggery*,—what the French well name *Canaille*, "Doggery" with more or less gold carrion at its disposal? Captains of Industry are the true Fighters, henceforth recognizable as the only true ones: Fighters against Chaos, Necessity and the Devils and Jötuns;[6] and lead on Mankind in that great, and alone true, and universal warfare; the stars in their courses fighting for them, and all Heaven and all Earth saying audibly, Well done! Let the Captains of Industry retire into their own hearts, and ask solemnly, If there is nothing but vulturous hunger for fine wines, valet reputation and gilt carriages, discoverable there? Of hearts made by the Almighty God I will not believe such a thing. Deep-hidden under wretchedest god-forgetting Cants, Epicurisms, Dead-Sea Apisms;[7] forgotten as under foullest fat Lethe mud and weeds, there is yet, in all hearts born into this God's-World, a spark of the Godlike slumbering. Awake, O nightmare sleepers; awake, arise, or be for ever fallen! This is not playhouse poetry; it is sober fact. Our England, our world cannot live as it is. It will connect itself with a God again, or go down with nameless throes and fire-consummation to the Devils. Thou who feelest aught of such a Godlike stirring in thee, any faintest intimation of it as through heavy-laden dreams, follow *it*, I conjure thee. Arise, save thyself, be one of those that save thy country.

Bucaniers,[8] Chactaw Indians, whose supreme aim in fighting is that they may get the scalps, the money, that they may amass scalps and money; out of such came no Chivalry, and never will! Out of such came only gore and wreck, infernal rage and misery; desperation quenched in annihilation. Behold it, I bid thee, behold there, and consider! What is it that thou have a hundred thousand-pound bills laid up in thy strong-room, a hundred scalps hung up in thy wigwam? I value not them or thee. Thy scalps and thy thousand-pound bills are as yet nothing, if no nobleness from

6. Giants of Scandinavian mythology.
7. A tribe of men living near the Dead Sea were transformed into apes because they had ignored the prophecies of Moses. This story, of Mohammedan origin, is used by Carlyle to represent the possible fate of nations which are indifferent to their social problems.
8. Buccaneers.

within irradiate them; if no Chivalry, in action, or in embryo ever struggling towards birth and action, be there.

Love of men cannot be bought by cash-payment; and without love, men cannot endure to be together. You cannot lead a Fighting World without having it regimented, chivalried: the thing, in a day, becomes impossible; all men in it, the highest at first, the very lowest at last, discern consciously, or by a noble instinct, this necessity. And can you any more continue to lead a Working World unregimented, anarchic? I answer, and the Heavens and Earth are now answering, No! The thing becomes not "in a day" impossible; but in some two generations it does. Yes, when fathers and mothers, in Stockport hunger-cellars, begin to eat their children, and Irish widows have to prove their relationship by dying of typhus-fever; and amid Governing "Corporations of the Best and Bravest," busy to preserve their game by "bushing," dark millions of God's human creatures start up in mad Chartisms, impracticable Sacred-Months, and Manchester Insurrections;[9]—and there is a virtual Industrial Aristocracy as yet only half-alive, spell-bound amid money-bags and ledgers; and an actual Idle Aristocracy seemingly near dead in somnolent delusions, in trespasses and double-barrels;[1] "sliding," as on inclined-planes, which every new year they *soap* with new Hansard's-jargon[2] under God's sky, and so are "sliding" ever faster, towards a "scale" and balance-scale whereon is written *Thou art found Wanting:*—in such days, after a generation or two, I say, it does become, even to the low and simple, very palpably impossible! No Working World, any more than a Fighting World, can be led on without a noble Chivalry of Work, and laws and fixed rules which follow out of that,—far nobler than any Chivalry of Fighting was. As an anarchic multitude on mere Supply-and-demand, it is becoming inevitable that we dwindle in horrid suicidal convulsion, and self-abrasion, frightful to the imagination, into *Chactaw* Workers. With wigwams and scalps,—with palaces and thousand-pound bills; with savagery, depopulation, chaotic desolation! Good Heavens, will not one French Revolution and Reign of Terror suffice us, but must there be two? There will be two if needed; there will be twenty if needed; there will be precisely as many as are needed. The Laws of Nature will have themselves fulfilled. That is a thing certain to me.

Your gallant battle-hosts and work-hosts, as the others did, will need to be made loyally yours; they must and will be regulated, methodically secured in their just share of conquest under you;—

9. In 1819 a large open-air labor meeting in Manchester was broken up by charging cavalry. Thirteen men and women were massacred, and many others were wounded.
1. Carlyle is suggesting that the only concern of the landed aristocrats is to keep trespassers off their game preserves and reserve shooting rights to themselves.
2. Parliamentary oratory, as in Hansard's printed record of debates in the House of Commons.

joined with you in veritable brotherhood, sonhood, by quite other and deeper ties than those of temporary day's wages! How would mere redcoated regiments, to say nothing of chivalries, fight for you, if you could discharge them on the evening of the battle, on payment of the stipulated shillings,—and they discharge you on the morning of it! Chelsea Hospitals,[3] pensions, promotions, rigorous lasting covenant on the one side and on the other, are indispensable even for a hired fighter. The Feudal Baron, much more, —how could he subsist with mere temporary mercenaries round him, at sixpence a day; ready to go over to the other side, if sevenpence were offered? He could not have subsisted;—and his noble instinct saved him from the necessity of even trying! The Feudal Baron had a Man's Soul in him; to which anarchy, mutiny, and the other fruits of temporary mercenaries, were intolerable: he had never been a Baron otherwise, but had continued a Chactaw and Bucanier. He felt it precious, and at last it became habitual, and his fruitful enlarged existence included it as a necessity, to have men round him who in heart loved him; whose life he watched over with rigour yet with love; who were prepared to give their life for him, if need came. It was beautiful; it was human! Man lives not otherwise, nor can live contented, anywhere or anywhen. Isolation is the sum-total of wretchedness to man. To be cut off, to be left solitary: to have a world alien, not your world; all a hostile camp for you; not a home at all, of hearts and faces who are yours, whose you are! It is the frightfullest enchantment; too truly a work of the Evil One. To have neither superior, nor inferior, nor equal, united manlike to you. Without father, without child, without brother. Man knows no sadder destiny. "How is each of us," exclaims Jean Paul,[4] "so lonely in the wide bosom of the All!" Encased each as in his transparent "ice-palace"; our brother visible in his, making signals and gesticulations to us;—visible, but for ever unattainable: on his bosom we shall never rest, nor he on ours. It was not a God that did this; no!

Awake, ye noble Workers, warriors in the one true war: all this must be remedied. It is you who are already half-alive, whom I will welcome into life; whom I will conjure in God's name to shake off your enchanted sleep, and live wholly! Cease to count scalps, goldpurses; not in these lies your or our salvation. Even these, if you count only these, will not be left. Let bucaniering be put far from you; alter, speedily abrogate all laws of the bucaniers, if you would gain any victory that shall endure. Let God's justice, let pity, nobleness and manly valour, with more gold-purses or with fewer, testify themselves in this your brief Life-transit to all the Eternities, the Gods and Silences. It is to you I call; for ye are not dead, ye

---

3. Home for disabled veterans.   4. Jean Paul Richter (1763–1825), German humorist.

are already half-alive: there is in you a sleepless dauntless energy, the prime-matter of all nobleness in man. Honour to you in your kind. It is to you I call: ye know at least this, That the mandate of God to His creature man is: Work! The future Epic of the World rests not with those that are near dead, but with those that are alive, and those that are coming into life.

Look around you. Your world-hosts are all in mutiny, in confusion, destitution; on the eve of fiery wreck and madness! They will not march farther for you, on the sixpence a day and supply-and-demand principle: they will not; nor ought they, nor can they. Ye shall reduce them to order, begin reducing them. To order, to just subordination; noble loyalty in return for noble guidance. Their souls are driven nigh mad; let yours be sane and ever saner. Not as a bewildered bewildering mob; but as a firm regimented mass, with real captains over them, will these men march any more. All human interests, combined human endeavours, and social growths in this world, have, at a certain stage of their development, required organizing: and Work, the grandest of human interests, does now require it.

God knows, the task will be hard: but no noble task was ever easy. This task will wear away your lives, and the lives of your sons and grandsons: but for what purpose, if not for tasks like this, were lives given to men? Ye shall cease to count your thousand-pound scalps, the noble of you shall cease! Nay, the very scalps, as I say, will not long be left if you count on these. Ye shall cease wholly to be barbarous vulturous Chactaws, and become noble European Nineteenth-Century Men. Ye shall know that Mammon, in never such gigs[5] and flunkey "respectabilities," is not the alone God; that of himself he is but a Devil, and even a Brute-god.

Difficult? Yes, it will be difficult. The short-fibre cotton; that too was difficult. The waste cotton-shrub, long useless, disobedient, as the thistle by the wayside,—have ye not conquered it; made it into beautiful bandana webs; white woven shirts for men; bright-tinted air-garments wherein flit goddesses? Ye have shivered mountains asunder, made the hard iron pliant to you as soft putty: the Forest-giants, Marsh-jötuns bear sheaves of golden grain; Aegir the Sea-demon[6] himself stretches his back for a sleek highway to you, and on Firehorses and Windhorses ye career. Ye are most strong. Thor red-bearded, with his blue sun-eyes, with his cheery heart and strong thunder-hammer, he and you have prevailed. Ye are most strong, ye Sons of the icy North, of the far East,—far marching from your rugged Eastern Wildernesses, hitherward from the grey Dawn of Time! Ye are Sons of the *Jötun*-land; the land of Diffi-

---

5. To own a gig (a light carriage) was a sign of respectable status comparable to owning certain kinds of automobiles today. Carlyle ridiculed the passion for respectability as "gigmanity."
6. From Scandinavian mythology.

culties Conquered. Difficult? You must try this thing. Once try it with the understanding that it will and shall have to be done. Try it as ye try the paltrier thing, making of money! I will bet on you once more, against all Jötuns, Tailor-gods,[7] Double-barrelled Law-wards, and Denizens of Chaos whatsoever!

1843   1843

7. False gods.

ALFRED, LORD TENNYSON
(1809–1892)

1830: *Poems Chiefly Lyrical.*
1833: Death of Arthur Hallam.
1842: *Poems.*
1850: *In Memoriam.* Tennyson appointed poet laureate.
1859: *Idylls of the King* (first four books).

In the earlier years of the 20th century, an easy way to arouse laughter at a gathering of intelligent people was to recite aloud some poem by Tennyson such as *Flower in the Crannied Wall.* A high falsetto voice might add to the effect but was not essential, for the company would laugh not because this was a bad poem but simply because it was a poem by Tennyson. Samuel Butler, who anticipated early 20th-century tastes, has a characteristic entry in his *Notebooks:* "Talking it over, we agreed that Blake was no good because he learnt Italian at 60 in order to study Dante, and we knew Dante was no good because he was so fond of Virgil, and Virgil was no good because Tennyson ran him, and as for Tennyson—well, Tennyson goes without saying." It was inevitable that the almost hysterical repudiation of their Victorian predecessors by the Edwardians and Georgians would be directed most damagingly against Tennyson, the so-called spokesman of the Victorian age, the poet whose works were on the bookshelves of almost every family of readers in England and the United States from 1850 onwards. As Thomas Hardy noted sadly in *An Ancient to Ancients,*

> The bower we shrined to Tennyson,
>   Gentlemen,
> Is roof-wrecked; damps there drip upon
> Sagged seats, the creeper-nails are rust,
> The spider is sole denizen.

Hardy's obituary was premature. Tennyson's "bower" has to a considerable extent been rebuilt. The scale of the vast building has been wisely reduced, but the best of his poems are now established upon foundations of more solid critical appreciation. And when we enjoy such poems as *Ulysses* or *Tears, Idle Tears* we may wonder what perversity of taste led earlier critics to write off the delight to be found in this "lord of language"—as

Tennyson himself addresses his favorite predecessor, Virgil. The Edwardians might reply, however, that they had read other poems by Tennyson than *Ulysses*. They had been brought up to admire such sentimental pieces as *The May Queen*, his popular idyls of rural life, and his newspaper verses. And the Edwardians had here a point, for in such poems, Tennyson was certainly vulnerable. *Enoch Arden* gained him the title that Walt Whitman longed for, "The Poet of the People," but his more enduring reputation, as J. Churton Collins predicted in 1891, was to be as "the poet of the cultured." A year later, Tennyson himself made an accurate prophecy of his status in his lines on *Poets and Critics*:

> What is true at last will tell:
> Few at first will place thee well;
> Some too low would have thee shine,
> Some too high—no fault of thine—
> Hold thine own, and work thy will!

Like his poetry, Tennyson's life and character have been reassessed in the 20th century. To many of his contemporaries he seemed a remote wizard, secure in his laureate's robes, a man whose life had been sheltered, marred only by the loss of his best friend in youth. During much of his career Tennyson may have been isolated, but his was not a sheltered life in the real sense of the word. Although he grew up in a parsonage, it was not the kind of parsonage one encounters in the novels of Jane Austen. His family could have supplied materials instead for one of William Faulkner's novels about the American South. It was a household dominated by frictions and loyalties and broodings over ancestral inheritances, in which the children showed marked strains of instability and eccentricity.

Alfred was the fourth son in a family of twelve children. One of his brothers had to be confined to an insane asylum for life; another was long a victim of the opium habit; another had violent quarrels with his father, who had become a drunkard. This father, the Reverend Dr. George Tennyson, was the eldest son of a wealthy landowner. He had been obliged to become a clergyman, a profession he disliked, because he had been disinherited in favor of his younger brother. George Tennyson therefore settled in a small rectory at Somersby in Lincolnshire where he tutored his sons in classical and modern languages to prepare them for entering the university.

Before leaving this strange household for Cambridge, Alfred had already demonstrated a flair for writing verse—precocious exercises in the manner of Milton or Byron or the Elizabethan dramatists. He had even published a volume in 1827, in collaboration with his brother Charles, *Poems by Two Brothers*. This feat drew him to the attention of a group of gifted undergraduates at Cambridge, the "Apostles," who encouraged him to devote his life to poetry. Up until this time, the young man had known scarcely anyone outside the circle of his own family. Despite his massive frame and powerful physique, he was painfully shy, and the friendships he found at Cambridge, as well as the intellectual and political discussions in which he participated, served to give him confidence and to widen his horizons as a poet. The most important of these friendships was with Arthur Hallam, a leader of the Apostles, who later became engaged to Tennyson's sister. Hallam's sudden death, in 1833, seemed an overwhelming calamity to his friend. Not only the long elegy *In Memoriam* but many of Tennyson's other poems are tributes to this early friendship.

Alfred's career at Cambridge was interrupted and finally broken off in 1831 by family dissensions and financial need, and he returned home to study and practice the craft of poetry. His early volumes (1830 and 1832) were attacked as "obscure" or "affected" by some of the reviewers. Tennyson suffered acutely under hostile criticism, but he also profited from it. His volume of 1842 demonstrated a remarkable advance in taste and technical excellence, and in 1850 he at last attained fame and full critical recognition with *In Memoriam*. In the same year he became poet laureate in succession to Wordsworth. The struggle during the previous twenty years had been made especially painful by the long postponement of his marriage to Emily Sellwood, with whom he had fallen in love in 1836 but could not marry, because of poverty, until 1850.

His life thereafter was a comfortable one. He was as popular as Byron had been, and his fame lasted for much longer. The earnings from his poetry (sometimes exceeding £10,000 a year) enabled him to purchase a house in the country and to enjoy the kind of seclusion he liked. His notoriety was enhanced, like that of G. B. Shaw and Walt Whitman, by his colorful appearance. Huge and shaggy, in cloak and broadbrimmed hat, gruff in manner as a farmer, he impressed everyone as what is called a "character." He also had a booming voice, when reading his poetry, that electrified listeners much as Dylan Thomas electrified audiences in the 20th century: "mouthing out his hollow o's and a's, / Deep-chested music." Moreover, for many Victorian readers, he seemed not only a great poetical phrasemaker and a striking individual but also a wise man whose occasional pronouncements on politics or world affairs represented the national voice itself. In 1884 he accepted a peerage. In 1892 he died and was buried in Westminster Abbey.

It is often said that success was bad for Tennyson, and that after *In Memoriam* his poetic power seriously declined. That in his last 42 years certain of his mannerisms became accentuated is true. One of the difficulties of his dignified blank verse was, as he said himself, that it is hard to describe commonplace objects and "at the same time to retain poetical elevation." The ornateness of his later style sometimes betrayed him into such blunders as describing a basketful of fish as "Enoch's ocean spoil / In ocean-smelling osier." In others of his later poems, those dealing with national affairs, there is also an increased shrillness of tone—a mannerism accentuated by Tennyson's realizing that like Dickens he had a vast public behind him to back up his pronouncements.

It is foolish, however, to try to shelve all of Tennyson's later productions. In 1855 he published his experimental monologue *Maud*, perhaps his finest long poem. In 1859 he published four books of his *Idylls of the King*, a large-scale epic which occupied most of his energies in the second half of his career. About this late poem, completed in twelve books, in 1888, there is less agreement. Some readers consider it to be complacent— mere "lollipops," as Carlyle called it. Yet *Idylls of the King* is not simply a hymn to progress. It records, instead, a cycle of change from a society that has emerged from a wasteland into civilization but which may revert to a wasteland once more. In any event, even if this ambitious epic does not show Tennyson in his best vein, there is no sign of decline in his late lyrics. The 80-year-old poet who wrote *Crossing the Bar* had certainly not lost his touch.

The problem of Tennyson's development is really of more significance for the period before 1850 rather than afterwards. W. H. Auden has stated that Tennyson had "the finest ear, perhaps, of any English poet." The interesting point is that Tennyson did not have such an ear: he developed it. Studies of the original versions of his poems in the 1830 and 1832 volumes demonstrate that not only was his taste uncertain at the outset of his career but that his sense of meter was originally unreliable. The harmonics he was to achieve from 1842 onwards had to be learned just as a pianist with a weak left hand has to overcome his weakness by constant exercise. Like Chaucer or Keats or Pope, Tennyson studied his predecessors assiduously to perfect his technique. Anyone wanting to learn the traditional craft of English verse can study with profit the various stages of revision that such poems as *The Lotos-Eaters* were subjected to by this painstaking and artful poet.

If the early Tennyson was uncertain of meter, he had other skills that were immediately in evidence. One of these was a capacity for linking scenery to states of mind. As early as 1835, J. S. Mill identified the special kind of scene-painting to be found in early poems such as *Mariana:* " * * * not the power of producing that rather vapid species of composition usually termed descriptive poetry * * * but the power of *creating* scenery, in keeping with some state of human feeling so fitted to it as to be the embodied symbol of it, and to summon up the state of feeling itself, with a force not to be surpassed by anything but reality."

A second aspect of Tennyson's early development was his increased preoccupation with problems of his day. If J. S. Mill praised his capacity to render landscape, he also urged, in his review, Tennyson's further responsibilities—to "cultivate, and with no half devotion, philosophy as well as poetry." Advice of this kind Tennyson was already predisposed to heed. The death of Hallam, the religious uncertainties which he had himself experienced, together with his own extensive study of writings by geologists, astronomers, and biologists, led him to confront many of the religious issues that bewildered his generation and later generations. The result was *In Memoriam* (1850), a long elegy written over a period of seventeen years, embodying the poet's reflections on man's relation to God and to nature.

Was Tennyson intellectually equipped to deal with the great questions raised in *In Memoriam?* The answer may depend on a reader's religious and philosophical presuppositions. Some, such as T. H. Huxley, considered Tennyson an intellectual giant, a thinker who had mastered the scientific thought of his century and fully confronted the issues it raised. Others dismissed Tennyson, in this phase, as a lightweight. Auden went so far as to call him the "stupidest" of English poets. We might say more accurately that his mind was slow, ponderous, brooding, and we should add that for the composition of *In Memoriam* such qualities of mind were assets, not liabilities. In these terms we can understand when Tennyson's poetry really fails to measure up: it is when he writes of events of the moment over which his thoughts and feelings have had no time to brood. Several of his poems are essentially newspaper pieces. They are Letters to the Editor, in effect, with the ephemeral heat and simplicity we expect of such productions. *The Charge of the Light Brigade,* inspired by a report in *The Times* of a cavalry charge at Balaclava during the Crimean War, is one of the best of his productions in this category. His *Dedication* of *Idylls of the King* to Prince Albert is also related to this kind of occasional verse and is included in the following selections as a representative example of a Victorian period piece.

Tennyson's poems of contemporary events were inevitably popular in his own day. So too were those poems where, as in *Locksley Hall,* he dipped into the future. The technological changes wrought by Victorian inventors and engineers fascinated him. Sometimes they gave him an assurance of human progress as swaggeringly exultant as that of Macaulay. At other times the horrors of industrialism's by-products in the slums, the bloodshed of war, the greed of the newly rich, destroyed his hopes that man was evolving upwards. Such a late poem as *The Dawn* embodies an attitude which he found in Virgil: "Thou majestic in thy sadness at the doubtful doom of human kind."

For despite Tennyson's fascination with technological developments, he was essentially a poet of the countryside, a man whose whole being was conditioned by the recurring rhythms of rural rather than urban life. He had the countryman's awareness of traditional roots and his sense of the past. It is appropriate that most of his best poems are about the past, not about the present or future. The past is his great theme: his own past (as in *All Along the Valley*), his country's past (as in *The Revenge*), the past of mankind, the past of the world itself:

> There rolls the deep where grew the tree.
> O earth, what changes hast thou seen!
> There where the long street roars hath been
> The stillness of the central sea.

Tennyson is the first major writer to express this awareness of the vast extent of geological time that has haunted human consciousness since Victorian scientists exposed the history of the earth's crust. In his more usual vein, however, it is the recorded past of mankind that inspires him, the classical past in particular. Classical themes, as Douglas Bush has noted, "generally banished from his mind what was timid, parochial, sentimental * * * and evoked his special gifts and most authentic emotions, his rich and wistful sense of the past, his love of nature, and his power of style."

One returns, finally then, to the question of language. At the time of his death, a critic complained that Tennyson was merely "a discoverer of words rather than of ideas." The same complaint has been made by George Bernard Shaw and others—not about Tennyson but about Shakespeare.

The Kraken[1]

Below the thunders of the upper deep,
Far, far beneath in the abysmal sea,

---

1. A mythical sea beast of gigantic size.

His ancient, dreamless, uninvaded sleep
The Kraken sleepeth: faintest sunlights flee
About his shadowy sides; above him swell   5
Huge sponges of millennial growth and height;
And far away into the sickly light,
From many a wondrous grot and secret cell
Unnumbered and enormous polypi[2]
Winnow with giant arms the slumbering green.   10
There hath he lain for ages, and will lie
Battening upon huge sea worms in his sleep,
Until the latter fire[3] shall heat the deep;
Then once by man and angels to be seen,
In roaring he shall rise and on the surface die.   15

                                                             1830

Mariana[1]

"Mariana in the moated grange."
Measure for Measure

With blackest moss the flower plots
    Were thickly crusted, one and all;
The rusted nails fell from the knots
    That held the pear to the gable wall.
The broken sheds looked sad and strange: 5
    Unlifted was the clinking latch;
    Weeded and worn the ancient thatch
Upon the lonely moated grange.
        She only said, "My life is dreary,
            He cometh not," she said;   10
        She said, "I am aweary, aweary,
            I would that I were dead!"

Her tears fell with the dews at even;
    Her tears fell ere the dews were dried;
She could not look on the sweet heaven,   15
    Either at morn or eventide.
After the flitting of the bats,
    When thickest dark did trance the sky,
    She drew her casement curtain by,
And glanced athwart the glooming flats.   20
        She only said, "The night is dreary,
            He cometh not," she said;
        She said, "I am aweary, aweary,
            I would that I were dead!"

---

2. Octopuses.
3. Fire which would finally consume the world. See Revelation xvi.3–9.
1. Mariana, in Shakespeare's *Measure* *for Measure* (III.i.277), waits in a grange (an outlying farmhouse) for her lover who has deserted her.

Upon the middle of the night,   25
  Waking she heard the nightfowl crow;
The cock sung out an hour ere light;
  From the dark fen the oxen's low
Came to her; without hope of change,
  In sleep she seemed to walk forlorn,   30
  Till cold winds woke the gray-eyed morn
About the lonely moated grange.
      She only said, "The day is dreary,
        He cometh not," she said;
      She said, "I am aweary, aweary,   35
        I would that I were dead!"

About a stonecast from the wall
  A sluice with blackened waters slept,
And o'er it many, round and small,
  The clustered marish[2] mosses crept.   40
Hard by a poplar shook alway,
  All silver-green with gnarlèd bark:
For leagues no other tree did mark
The level waste, the rounding gray.
      She only said, "My life is dreary,   45
        He cometh not," she said;
      She said, "I am aweary, aweary,
        I would that I were dead!"

And ever when the moon was low,
  And the shrill winds were up and away,   50
In the white curtain, to and fro,
  She saw the gusty shadow sway.
But when the moon was very low,
  And wild winds bound within their cell,
The shadow of the poplar fell   55
Upon her bed, across her brow.
      She only said, "The night is dreary,
        He cometh not," she said;
      She said, "I am aweary, aweary,
        I would that I were dead!"   60

All day within the dreamy house,
  The doors upon their hinges creaked;
The blue fly sung in the pane; the mouse
  Behind the moldering wainscot shrieked,
Or from the crevice peered about.   65
  Old faces glimmered through the doors,
  Old footsteps trod the upper floors,
Old voices called her from without.
      She only said, "My life is dreary,
        He cometh not," she said;   70
      She said, "I am aweary, aweary,
        I would that I were dead!"

2. Marsh.

The sparrow's chirrup on the roof,
  The slow clock ticking, and the sound
Which to the wooing wind aloof
  The poplar made, did all confound   75
Her sense; but most she loathed the hour
  When the thick-moted sunbeam lay
Athwart the chambers, and the day
  Was sloping toward his western bower.   80
  Then, said she, "I am very dreary,
    He will not come," she said;
  She wept, "I am aweary, aweary,
    Oh God, that I were dead!"

          1830

Sonnet

She took the dappled partridge flecked with blood,
  And in her hand the drooping pheasant bare,
  And by his feet she held the woolly hare,
And like a master painting where she stood,
Looked some new goddess of an English wood.   5
  Nor could I find an imperfection there,
  Nor blame the wanton act that showed so fair—
To me whatever freak[3] she plays is good.
Hers is the fairest Life that breathes with breath,
  And *their* still plumes and azure eyelids closed   10
    Made quiet Death so beautiful to see
That Death lent grace to Life and Life to Death
  And in one image Life and Death reposed,
    To make my love an Immortality.

ca. 1830   1931

The Lady of Shalott

Part I

On either side the river lie
Long fields of barley and of rye,
That clothe the wold[1] and meet the sky;
And through the field the road runs by
    To many-towered Camelot;[2]   5
And up and down the people go,
Gazing where the lilies blow[3]
Round an island there below,
    The island of Shalott.

3. Prank.   Arthur's palace was located.
1. Rolling plains.   3. Bloom.
2. Legendary city in which King

Willows whiten, aspens quiver,   10
Little breezes dusk and shiver
Through the wave that runs forever
By the island in the river
  Flowing down to Camelot.
Four gray walls, and four gray towers,   15
Overlook a space of flowers,
And the silent isle imbowers
  The Lady of Shalott.

By the margin, willow-veiled,
Slide the heavy barges trailed   20
By slow horses; and unhailed
The shallop⁴ flitteth silken-sailed
  Skimming down to Camelot:
But who hath seen her wave her hand?
Or at the casement seen her stand?   25
Or is she known in all the land,
  The Lady of Shalott?

Only reapers, reaping early
In among the bearded barley,
Hear a song that echoes cheerly   30
From the river winding clearly,
  Down to towered Camelot;
And by the moon the reaper weary,
Piling sheaves in uplands airy,
Listening, whispers " 'Tis the fairy   35
  Lady of Shalott."

Part II

There she weaves by night and day
A magic web with colors gay.
She has heard a whisper say,
A curse is on her if she stay   40
  To look down to Camelot.
She knows not what the curse may be,
And so she weaveth steadily,
And little other care hath she,
  The Lady of Shalott.   45

And moving through a mirror clear
That hangs before her all the year,
Shadows of the world appear.
There she sees the highway near
  Winding down to Camelot;   50
There the river eddy whirls,
And there the surly village churls,
And the red cloaks of market girls,
  Pass onward from Shalott.

4. A light open boat.

Sometimes a troop of damsels glad,   55
An abbot on an ambling pad,[5]
Sometimes a curly shepherd lad,
Or long-haired page in crimson clad,
     Goes by to towered Camelot;
And sometimes through the mirror blue   60
The knights come riding two and two:
She hath no loyal knight and true,
     The Lady of Shalott.

But in her web she still delights
To weave the mirror's magic sights,   65
For often through the silent nights
A funeral, with plumes and lights
     And music, went to Camelot;
Or when the moon was overhead,
Came two young lovers lately wed: 70
"I am half sick of shadows," said
     The Lady of Shalott.

Part III

A bowshot from her bower eaves,
He rode between the barley sheaves,
The sun came dazzling through the leaves,   75
And flamed upon the brazen greaves[6]
     Of bold Sir Lancelot.
A red-cross knight[7] forever kneeled
To a lady in his shield,
That sparkled on the yellow field,   80
     Beside remote Shalott.

The gemmy bridle glittered free,
Like to some branch of stars we see
Hung in the golden Galaxy.
The bridle bells rang merrily   85
     As he rode down to Camelot;
And from his blazoned baldric[8] slung
A mighty silver bugle hung,
And as he rode his armor rung,
     Beside remote Shalott.   90

All in the blue unclouded weather
Thick-jeweled shone the saddle leather,
The helmet and the helmet-feather
Burned like one burning flame together,
     As he rode down to Camelot;   95
As often through the purple night,
Below the starry clusters bright,

5. Easy-paced horse.
6. Armor protecting the leg below the knee.
7. Cf. Spenser's *Faerie Queene* I.
8. A richly decorated sash worn diagonally across the breast.

Some bearded meteor, trailing light,
　　Moves over still Shalott.

His broad clear brow in sunlight glowed;　　　100
On burnished hooves his war horse trode;
From underneath his helmet flowed
His coal-black curls as on he rode,
　　As he rode down to Camelot.
From the bank and from the river　　　105
He flashed into the crystal mirror,
"Tirra lirra," by the river
　　Sang Sir Lancelot.

She left the web, she left the loom,
She made three paces through the room,　　　110
She saw the water lily bloom,
She saw the helmet and the plume,
　　She looked down to Camelot.
Out flew the web and floated wide;
The mirror cracked from side to side;　　　115
"The curse is come upon me," cried
　　The Lady of Shalott.

Part IV

In the stormy east wind straining,
The pale yellow woods were waning,
The broad stream in his banks complaining,　　　120
Heavily the low sky raining
　　Over towered Camelot;
Down she came and found a boat
Beneath a willow left afloat,
And round about the prow she wrote　　　125
　　The Lady of Shalott.

And down the river's dim expanse
Like some bold seër in a trance,
Seeing all his own mischance—
With a glassy countenance　　　130
　　Did she look to Camelot.
And at the closing of the day
She loosed the chain, and down she lay;
The broad stream bore her far away,
　　The Lady of Shalott.　　　135

Lying, robed in snowy white
That loosely flew to left and right—
The leaves upon her falling light—
Through the noises of the night
　　She floated down to Camelot;　　　140
And as the boat-head wound along
The willowy hills and fields among,

They heard her singing her last song,
    The Lady of Shalott.

Heard a carol, mournful, holy,   145
Chanted loudly, chanted lowly,
Till her blood was frozen slowly,
And her eyes were darkened wholly,
    Turned to towered Camelot.
For ere she reached upon the tide   150
The first house by the waterside,
Singing in her song she died,
    The Lady of Shalott.

Under tower and balcony,
By garden wall and gallery,
A gleaming shape she floated by,   155
Dead-pale between the houses high,
    Silent into Camelot.
Out upon the wharfs they came,
Knight and burgher, lord and dame,
And round the prow they read her name, 160
    The Lady of Shalott.

Who is this? and what is here?
And in the lighted palace near
Died the sound of royal cheer;   165
And they crossed themselves for fear,
    All the knights at Camelot:
But Lancelot mused a little space;
He said, "She has a lovely face;
God in his mercy lend her grace,   170
    The Lady of Shalott."

                         1832, 1842

The Lotos-Eaters[1]

"Courage!" he[2] said, and pointed toward the land,
"This mounting wave will roll us shoreward soon."
In the afternoon they came unto a land[3]

1. Based on a short episode from the *Odyssey* (IX.82–97) in which the weary Greek veterans of the Trojan War are tempted by a desire to abandon their long voyage homeward. As Odysseus later reported: "On the tenth day we set foot on the land of the lotos-eaters who eat a flowering food. * * * I sent forth certain of my company [who] * * * mixed with the men of the lotos-eaters who * * * gave them of the lotos to taste. Now whosoever of them did eat the honey-sweet fruit of the lotos had no more wish to bring tidings nor to come back, but there he chose to abide * * * forgetful of his homeward way."

Tennyson expands Homer's brief account into an elaborate picture of weariness and the desire for rest and death. The descriptions in the first stanzas are similar to Spenser's *Faerie Queene* (II.vi). The final section derives, in part, from Lucretius' conception of the gods in *De rerum natura*.
2. Odysseus (or Ulysses).
3. The repetition of "land" from line 1 was deliberate; Tennyson said that

In which it seeméd always afternoon.
All round the coast the languid air did swoon,   5
Breathing like one that hath a weary dream.
Full-faced above the valley stood the moon;
And, like a downward smoke, the slender stream
Along the cliff to fall and pause and fall did seem.

A land of streams! some, like a downward smoke,   10
Slow-dropping veils of thinnest lawn,[4] did go;
And some through wavering lights and shadows broke,
Rolling a slumbrous sheet of foam below.
They saw the gleaming river seaward flow
From the inner land; far off, three mountaintops   15
Three silent pinnacles of aged snow,
Stood sunset-flushed; and, dewed with showery drops,
Up-clomb the shadowy pine above the woven copse.

The charméd sunset lingered low adown
In the red West; through mountain clefts the dale   20
Was seen far inland, and the yellow down[5]
Bordered with palm, and many a winding vale
And meadow, set with slender galingale;[6]
A land where all things always seemed the same!
And round about the keel with faces pale,   25
Dark faces pale against that rosy flame,
The mild-eyed melancholy Lotos-eaters came.

Branches they bore of that enchanted stem,
Laden with flower and fruit, whereof they gave
To each, but whoso did receive of them   30
And taste, to him the gushing of the wave
Far far away did seem to mourn and rave
On alien shores; and if his fellow spake,
His voice was thin, as voices from the grave;
And deep-asleep he seemed, yet all awake,   35
And music in his ears his beating heart did make.

They sat them down upon the yellow sand,
Between the sun and moon upon the shore;
And sweet it was to dream of Fatherland,
Of child, and wife, and slave; but evermore   40
Most weary seemed the sea, weary the oar,
Weary the wandering fields of barren foam.
Then some one said, "We will return no more";
And all at once they sang, "Our island home[7]
Is far beyond the wave; we will no longer roam."   45

this "no rhyme" was "lazier" in its
effect. Compare "afternoon" (lines 3–4)
and the rhyming of "adown" and
"down" (lines 19, 21).

4. A fine, thin linen.
5. An open plain on high ground.
6. A plant resembling tall coarse grass.
7. Ithaca.

Choric Song[8]

1

There is sweet music here that softer falls
Than petals from blown roses on the grass,
Or night-dews on still waters between walls
Of shadowy granite, in a gleaming pass;
Music that gentlier on the spirit lies,   50
Than tired eyelids upon tired eyes;
Music that brings sweet sleep down from the blissful skies.
Here are cool mosses deep,
And through the moss the ivies creep,
And in the stream the long-leaved flowers weep,   55
And from the craggy ledge the poppy hangs in sleep.

2

Why are we weighed upon with heaviness,
And utterly consumed with sharp distress,
While all things else have rest from weariness?
All things have rest: why should we toil alone,   60
We only toil, who are the first of things,
And make perpetual moan,
Still from one sorrow to another thrown;
Nor ever fold our wings,
And cease from wanderings,   65
Nor steep our brows in slumber's holy balm;
Nor harken what the inner spirit sings,
"There is no joy but calm!"—
Why should we only toil, the roof and crown of things?

3

Lo! in the middle of the wood,   70
The folded leaf is wooed from out the bud
With winds upon the branch, and there
Grows green and broad, and takes no care,
Sun-steeped at noon, and in the moon
Nightly dew-fed; and turning yellow   75
Falls, and floats adown the air.
Lo! sweetened with the summer light,
The full-juiced apple, waxing over-mellow,
Drops in a silent autumn night.
All its allotted length of days   80
The flower ripens in its place,
Ripens and fades, and falls, and hath no toil,
Fast-rooted in the fruitful soil.

4

Hateful is the dark blue sky,
Vaulted o'er the dark blue sea.   85
Death is the end of life; ah, why

8. Sung by the mariners.

Should life all labor be?
Let us alone. Time driveth onward fast,
And in a little while our lips are dumb.
Let us alone. What is it that will last?   90
All things are taken from us, and become
Portions and parcels of the dreadful past.
Let us alone. What pleasure can we have
To war with evil? Is there any peace
In ever climbing up the climbing wave?   95
All things have rest, and ripen toward the grave
In silence—ripen, fall, and cease:
Give us long rest or death, dark death, or dreamful ease.

5

How sweet it were, hearing the downward stream,
With half-shut eyes ever to seem   100
Falling asleep in a half-dream!
To dream and dream, like yonder amber light,
Which will not leave the myrrh-bush on the height;
To hear each other's whispered speech;
Eating the Lotos day by day,   105
To watch the crisping[9] ripples on the beach,
And tender curving lines of creamy spray;
To lend our hearts and spirits wholly
To the influence of mild-minded melancholy;
To muse and brood and live again in memory,   110
With those old faces of our infancy
Heaped over with a mound of grass,
Two handfuls of white dust, shut in an urn of brass!

6

Dear is the memory of our wedded lives,
And dear the last embraces of our wives   115
And their warm tears; but all hath suffered change;
For surely now our household hearths are cold,
Our sons inherit us, our looks are strange,
And we should come like ghosts to trouble joy.
Or else the island princes[1] overbold   120
Have eat our substance, and the minstrel sings
Before them of the ten years' war in Troy,
And our great deeds, as half-forgotten things.
Is there confusion in the little isle?
Let what is broken so remain.   125
The Gods are hard to reconcile;
'Tis hard to settle order once again.
There *is* confusion worse than death,
Trouble on trouble, pain on pain,
Long labor unto aged breath,   130
Sore tasks to hearts worn out by many wars
And eyes grown dim with gazing on the pilot-stars.

9. Curling.   1. Penelope's suitors.

7

But, propped on beds of amaranth[2] and moly,
How sweet—while warm airs lull us, blowing lowly—
With half-dropped eyelid still,   135
Beneath a heaven dark and holy,
To watch the long bright river drawing slowly
His waters from the purple hill—
To hear the dewy echoes calling
From cave to cave through the thick-twined vine—   140
To watch the emerald-colored water falling
Through many a woven acanthus wreath divine!
Only to hear and see the far-off sparkling brine,
Only to hear were sweet, stretched out beneath the pine.

8

The Lotos blooms below the barren peak,   145
The Lotos blows by every winding creek;
All day the wind breathes low with mellower tone;
Through every hollow cave and alley lone
Round and round the spicy downs the yellow Lotos dust is blown.
We have had enough of action, and of motion we,   150
Rolled to starboard, rolled to larboard, when the surge was seething
    free,
Where the wallowing monster spouted his foam-fountains in the sea.
Let us swear an oath, and keep it with an equal mind,
In the hollow Lotos land to live and lie reclined
On the hills like Gods together, careless of mankind.   155
For they lie beside their nectar, and the bolts[3] are hurled
Far below them in the valleys, and the clouds are lightly curled
Round their golden houses, girdled with the gleaming world;
Where they smile in secret, looking over wasted lands,
Blight and famine, plague and earthquake, roaring deeps and fiery
    sands,   160
Clanging fights, and flaming towns, and sinking ships, and praying
    hands.
But they smile, they find a music centered in a doleful song
Steaming up, a lamentation and an ancient tale of wrong,
Like a tale of little meaning though the words are strong;
Chanted from an ill-used race of men that cleave the soil,   165
Sow the seed, and reap the harvest with enduring toil,
Storing yearly little dues of wheat, and wine and oil;
Till they perish and they suffer—some, 'tis whispered—down in hell
Suffer endless anguish, others in Elysian valleys dwell,
Resting weary limbs at last on beds of asphodel.[4]   170
Surely, surely, slumber is more sweet than toil, the shore
Than labor in the deep mid-ocean, wind and wave and oar;
O, rest ye, brother mariners, we will not wander more.

1832, 1842

2. A legendary unfading flower; "moly": a flower with magical properties, mentioned by Homer.
3. Thunderbolts.
4. A yellow lilylike flower supposed to grow in the Elysian valleys.

You Ask Me, Why, Though Ill at Ease[5]

You ask me, why, though ill at ease,
　Within this region I subsist,
　Whose spirits falter in the mist,
And languish for the purple seas.

It is the land that freemen till,　　　　　　　　　　5
　That sober-suited Freedom chose,
　The land, where girt with friends or foes
A man may speak the thing he will;

A land of settled government,
　A land of just and old renown,　　　　　　　　　10
　Where Freedom slowly broadens down
From precedent to precedent;

Where faction seldom gathers head,
　But, by degrees to fullness wrought,
　The strength of some diffusive thought　　　　　15
Hath time and space to work and spread.

Should banded unions[6] persecute
　Opinion, and induce a time
　When single thought is civil crime,
And individual freedom mute,　　　　　　　　　　20

Though power should make from land to land
　The name of Britain trebly great—
　Though every channel of the State
Should fill and choke with golden sand—

Yet waft me from the harbor-mouth,　　　　　　　25
　Wild wind! I seek a warmer-sky,
　And I will see before I die
The palms and temples of the South.

1833　　　　　　　　　　　　　　　　　　　　　　　1842

Morte d'Arthur[1]
The Epic

At Francis Allen's on the Christmas eve—
The game of forfeits done—the girls all kissed

---

5. Written at the time of the disturbances during and after the passing of the Reform Bill of 1832.
6. Any organized political groups, not necessarily trade unions.

1. At the age of 24, Tennyson proposed to write a long epic poem in twelve books on the subject of King Arthur and the knights of the Round Table, but harsh reviews discouraged

Beneath the sacred bush[2] and passed away—
The parson Holmes, the poet Everard Hall,
The host, and I sat round the wassail-bowl,
Then halfway ebbed; and there we held a talk,   5
How all the old honor had from Christmas gone,
Or gone or dwindled down to some odd games
In some odd nooks like this; till I, tired out
With cutting eights that day upon the pond,   10
Where, three times slipping from the outer edge,
I bumped the ice into three several stars,
Fell in a doze; and half-awake I heard
The parson taking wide and wider sweeps,
Now harping on the church-commissioners,[3]   15
Now hawking at geology and schism;
Until I woke, and found him settled down
Upon the general decay of faith
Right through the world: "at home was little left,
And none abroad; there was no anchor, none,   20
To hold by." Francis, laughing, clapped his hand
On Everard's shoulder, with "I hold by him."
"And I," quoth Everard, "by the wassail-bowl."
"Why yes," I said, "we knew your gift that way
At college; but another which you had—   25
I mean of verse (for so we held it then),
What came of that?" "You know," said Frank, "he burnt
His epic, his King Arthur, some twelve books"—
And then to me demanding why: "O, sir,
He thought that nothing new was said, or else   30
Something so said 'twas nothing—that a truth
Looks freshest in the fashion of the day;
God knows; he has a mint of reasons; ask.
It pleased me well enough." "Nay, nay," said Hall,
"Why take the style of those heroic times?   35
For nature brings not back the mastodon,
Nor we those times; and why should any man
Remodel models? these twelve books of mine
Were faint Homeric echoes, nothing-worth,
Mere chaff and draff, much better burnt." "But I,"   40

him for many years from completing his plan. By 1838 he had completed one book of the twelve, the story of King Arthur's death, which was published in 1842 under the title *Morte d'Arthur*. In this earlier version, the story is framed by a short introductory section called *The Epic* (lines 1–51) and an epilogue (lines 324–54) describing a party on Christmas Eve in modern times, at which a poet reads *Morte d'Arthur* to a group of friends. The facetious and easy conversational style of this introductory section is in marked contrast to the heroic manner of the main story.

Later, in 1869, Tennyson incorporated *Morte d'Arthur* into his long narrative poem, *Idylls of the King*. Under a new title, *The Passing of Arthur*, it appears there as the twelfth book of the *Idylls*. At this time Tennyson discarded *The Epic* framework and added some lines to the main story, but in effect *Morte d'Arthur* may be read as an example of *Idylls of the King*.

2. Mistletoe.
3. Commissioners appointed by the government in 1835 to regulate finances of the Anglican Church.

Said Francis, "picked the eleventh from this hearth,
And have it; keep a thing, its use will come.
I hoard it as a sugarplum for Holmes."
He laughed, and I, though sleepy, like a horse
That hears the corn-bin open, pricked my ears;   45
For I remembered Everard's college fame
When we were Freshmen. Then at my request
He brought it; and the poet, little urged,
But with some prelude of disparagement,
Read, mouthing out his hollow o's and a's,   50
Deep-chested music, and to this result.

Morte d'Arthur

So all day long the noise of battle rolled
Among the mountains by the winter sea,
Until King Arthur's table, man by man,
Had fallen in Lyonnesse[4] about their lord,   55
King Arthur; then, because his wound was deep,
The bold Sir Bedivere uplifted him,
Sir Bedivere, the last of all his knights,
And bore him to a chapel nigh the field,
A broken chancel with a broken cross,   60
That stood on a dark strait of barren land.
On one side lay the ocean, and on one
Lay a great water, and the moon was full.
Then spake King Arthur to Sir Bedivere:
"The sequel of today unsolders all   65
The goodliest fellowship of famous knights
Whereof this world holds record. Such a sleep
They sleep—the men I loved. I think that we
Shall never more, at any future time,
Delight our souls with talk of knightly deeds,   70
Walking about the gardens and the halls
Of Camelot, as in the days that were.
I perish by this people which I made—
Though Merlin sware that I should come again
To rule once more—but let what will be be,   75
I am so deeply smitten through the helm
That without help I cannot last till morn.
Thou therefore take my brand[5] Excalibur,
Which was my pride; for thou rememberest how
In those old days, one summer noon, an arm   80
Rose up from out the bosom of the lake,
Clothed in white samite,[6] mystic, wonderful,
Holding the sword—and how I rowed across
And took it, and have worn it, like a king;
And, wheresoever I am sung or told   85
In aftertime, this also shall be known.

4. Legendary country off the coast of   5. Sword.
Cornwall.   6. A rich, heavy silk.

But now delay not; take Excalibur,
And fling him far into the middle mere;[7]
Watch what thou seest, and lightly[8] bring me word."
    To him replied the bold Sir Bedivere: 90
"It is not meet, Sir King, to leave thee thus,
Aidless, alone, and smitten through the helm.
A little thing may harm a wounded man.
Yet I thy hest will all perform at full,
Watch what I see, and lightly bring thee word."   95
    So saying, from the ruined shrine he stepped
And in the moon athwart the place of tombs,
Where lay the mighty bones of ancient men,
Old knights, and over them the sea wind sang
Shrill, chill, with flakes of foam. He, stepping down   100
By zigzag paths and juts of pointed rock,
Came on the shining levels of the lake.
    There drew he forth the brand Excalibur,
And o'er him, drawing it, the winter moon,
Brightening the skirts of a long cloud, ran forth   105
And sparkled keen with frost against the hilt;
For all the haft twinkled with diamond sparks,
Myriads of topaz-lights, and jacinth-work[9]
Of subtlest jewelry. He gazed so long
That both his eyes were dazzled, as he stood,   110
This way and that dividing the swift mind,
In act to throw; but at the last it seemed
Better to leave Excalibur concealed
There in the many-knotted water-flags,
That whistled stiff and dry about the marge.   115
So strode he back slow to the wounded king.
    Then spake King Arthur to Sir Bedivere:
"Hast thou performed my mission which I gave?
What is it thou hast seen, or what hast heard?"
    And answer made the bold Sir Bedivere: 120
"I heard the ripple washing in the reeds,
And the wild water lapping on the crag."
    To whom replied King Arthur, faint and pale:
"Thou hast betrayed thy nature and thy name,
Not rendering true answer, as beseemed   125
Thy fealty, nor like a noble knight;
For surer sign had followed, either hand,
Or voice, or else a motion of the mere.
This is a shameful thing for men to lie.
Yet now, I charge thee, quickly go again   130
As thou art lief[1] and dear, and do the thing
I bade thee, watch, and lightly bring me word."
    Then went Sir Bedivere the second time
Across the ridge, and paced beside the mere,

---

7. Middle of the lake.
8. Quickly.
9. A "jacinth" is a red-colored gem.
1. Beloved.

Counting the dewy pebbles, fixed in thought; 135
But when he saw the wonder of the hilt,
How curiously[2] and strangely chased, he smote
His palms together, and he cried aloud:
    "And if indeed I cast the brand away,
Surely a precious thing, one worthy note, 140
Should thus be lost forever from the earth,
Which might have pleased the eyes of many men.
What good should follow this, if this were done?
What harm, undone? deep harm to disobey,
Seeing obedience is the bond of rule. 145
Were it well to obey then, if a king demand
An act unprofitable, against himself?
The king is sick, and knows not what he does.
What record, or what relic of my lord
Should be to aftertime, but empty breath 150
And rumors of a doubt? but were this kept,
Stored in some treasure-house of mighty kings,
Some one might show it at a joust of arms,
Saying, 'King Arthur's sword, Excalibur,
Wrought by the lonely maiden of the lake; 155
Nine years she wrought it, sitting in the deeps
Upon the hidden bases of the hills.'
So might some old man speak in the aftertime
To all the people, winning reverence;
But now much honor and much fame were lost." 160
    So spake he, clouded with his own conceit,[3]
And hid Excalibur the second time,
And so strode back slow to the wounded king.
    Then spoke King Arthur, breathing heavily:
"What is it thou hast seen, or what hast heard?" 165
    And answer made the bold Sir Bedivere:
"I heard the water lapping on the crag,
And the long ripple washing in the reeds."
    To whom replied King Arthur, much in wrath:
"Ah, miserable and unkind, untrue, 170
Unknightly, traitor-hearted! Woe is me!
Authority forgets a dying king,
Laid widowed of the power in his eye
That bowed the will. I see thee what thou art,
For thou, the latest-left of all my knights, 175
In whom should meet the offices of all,
Thou wouldst betray me for the precious hilt;
Either from lust of gold, or like a girl
Valuing the giddy pleasure of the eyes.
Yet, for a man may fail in duty twice, 180
And the third time may prosper, get thee hence;
But, if thou spare to fling Excalibur,
I will arise and slay thee with my hands."

2. Skillfully; "chased": adorned.   3. Vain and foolish fancies.

Then quickly rose Sir Bedivere, and ran,
And, leaping down the ridges lightly, plunged   185
Among the bulrush-beds, and clutched the sword,
And strongly wheeled and threw it. The great brand
Made lightnings in the splendor of the moon,
And flashing round and round, and whirled in an arch,
Shot like a streamer of the northern morn,[4]   190
Seen where the moving isles of winter shock[5]
By night, with noises of the northern sea.
So flashed and fell the brand Excalibur;
But ere he dipped the surface, rose an arm
Clothed in white samite, mystic, wonderful,   195
And caught him by the hilt, and brandished him
Three times, and drew him under in the mere.
And lightly went the other to the king.
    Then spoke King Arthur, drawing thicker breath:
"Now see I by thine eyes that this is done.   200
Speak out; what is it thou hast heard, or seen?"
    And answer made the bold Sir Bedivere:
"Sir King, I closed mine eyelids, lest the gems
Should blind my purpose, for I never saw,
Nor shall see, here or elsewhere, till I die,   205
Not though I live three lives of mortal men,
So great a miracle as yonder hilt.
Then with both hands I flung him, wheeling him;
But when I looked again, behold an arm,
Clothed in white samite, mystic, wonderful,   210
That caught him by the hilt, and brandished him
Three times, and drew him under in the mere."
    And answer made King Arthur, breathing hard:
"My end draws nigh; 'tis time that I were gone.
Make broad thy shoulders to receive my weight,   215
And bear me to the margin; yet I fear
My wound hath taken cold, and I shall die."
    So saying, from the pavement he half rose,
Slowly, with pain, reclining on his arm,
And looking wistfully with wide blue eyes   220
As in a picture. Him Sir Bedivere
Remorsefully regarded through his tears,
And would have spoken, but he found not words,
Then took with care, and kneeling on one knee,
O'er both his shoulders drew the languid hands,   225
And rising bore him through the place of tombs.
    But, as he walked, King Arthur panted hard,
Like one that feels a nightmare on his bed
When all the house is mute. So sighed the king,
Muttering and murmuring at his ear, "Quick, quick!   230
I fear it is too late, and I shall die."
But the other swiftly strode from ridge to ridge,

---

4. The northern lights.   5. I.e., where the icebergs collide.

Clothed with his breath, and looking, as he walked,
Larger than human on the frozen hills.
He heard the deep behind him, and a cry   235
Before. His own thought drove him like a goad.
Dry clashed his harness in the icy caves
And barren chasms, and all to left and right
The bare black cliff clanged round him, as he based
His feet on juts of slippery crag that rang   240
Sharp-smitten with the dint of arméd heels—
And on a sudden, lo! the level lake,
And the long glories of the winter moon.
    Then saw they how there hove a dusky barge,
Dark as a funeral scarf from stem to stern,   245
Beneath them; and descending they were ware
That all the decks were dense with stately forms
Black-stoled, black-hooded, like a dream—by these
Three queens with crowns of gold—and from them rose
A cry that shivered to the tingling stars,   250
And, as it were one voice, an agony
Of lamentation, like a wind that shrills
All night in a waste land, where no one comes,
Or hath come, since the making of the world.
    Then murmured Arthur, "Place me in the barge,"   255
And to the barge they came. There those three queens
Put forth their hands, and took the king, and wept.
But she that rose the tallest of them all
And fairest laid his head upon her lap,
And loosed the shattered casque,[6] and chafed his hands,   260
And called him by his name, complaining loud,
And dropping bitter tears against his brow
Striped with dark blood; for all his face was white
And colorless, and like the withered moon
Smote by the fresh beam of the springing east;   265
And all his greaves and cuisses dashed with drops
Of onset;[7] and the light and lustrous curls—
That made his forehead like a rising sun
High from the dais-throne—were parched with dust;
Or, clotted into points and hanging loose,   270
Mixed with the knightly growth that fringed his lips.
So like a shattered column lay the king;
Not like that Arthur who, with lance in rest,
From spur to plume a star of tournament,
Shot through the lists at Camelot, and charged   275
Before the eyes of ladies and of kings.
    Then loudly cried the bold Sir Bedivere:
"Ah! my Lord Arthur, whither shall I go?
Where shall I hide my forehead and my eyes?

---

6. Helmet.
7. "Greaves": armor to protect the leg below the knee, "cuisses": armor to protect the front of the thighs, "onset": blood from the battle.

For now I see the true old times are dead,   280
When every morning brought a noble chance,
And every chance brought out a noble knight.
Such times have been not since the light that led
The holy Elders with the gift of myrrh.[8]
But now the whole ROUND TABLE is dissolved   285
Which was an image of the mighty world;
And I, the last, go forth companionless,
And the days darken round me, and the years,
Among new men, strange faces, other minds."

  And slowly answered Arthur from the barge: 290
"The old order changeth, yielding place to new,
And God fulfills himself in many ways,
Lest one good custom should corrupt the world.
Comfort thyself: what comfort is in me?
I have lived my life, and that which I have done   295
May He within himself make pure! but thou,
If thou shouldst never see my face again,
Pray for my soul. More things are wrought by prayer
Than this world dreams of. Wherefore, let thy voice
Rise like a fountain for me night and day.   300
For what are men better than sheep or goats
That nourish a blind life within the brain,
If, knowing God, they lift not hands of prayer
Both for themselves and those who call them friend?
For so the whole round earth is every way   305
Bound by gold chains about the feet of God.
But now farewell. I am going a long way
With these thou seest—if indeed I go—
For all my mind is clouded with a doubt—
To the island-valley of Avilion;[9]   310
Where falls not hail, or rain, or any snow,
Nor ever wind blows loudly, but it lies
Deep-meadowed, happy, fair with orchard lawns
And bowery hollows crowned with summer sea,
Where I will heal me of my grievous wound."   315

  So said he, and the barge with oar and sail
Moved from the brink, like some full-breasted swan
That, fluting a wild carol ere her death,
Ruffles her pure cold plume, and takes the flood
With swarthy webs. Long stood Sir Bedivere   320
Revolving many memories, till the hull
Looked one black dot against the verge of dawn,
And on the mere the wailing died away.

    Here ended Hall, and our last light, that long
Had winked and threatened darkness, flared and fell;   325

8. I.e., the star that guided the three kings ("Elders") to the Christ Child at Bethlehem.
9. Avalon, in Celtic mythology and medieval romance, the Vale of the Blessed where heroes enjoyed life after death.

At which the parson, sent to sleep with sound,
And waked with silence, grunted "Good!" but we
Sat rapt: it was the tone with which he read—
Perhaps some modern touches here and there
Redeemed it from the charge of nothingness—   330
Or else we loved the man, and prized his work;
I know not; but we sitting, as I said,
The cock crew loud, as at that time of year
The lusty bird takes every hour for dawn.
Then Francis, muttering, like a man ill-used,   335
"There now—that's nothing!" drew a little back,
And drove his heel into the smoldered log,
That sent a blast of sparkles up the flue.
And so to bed, where yet in sleep I seemed
To sail with Arthur under looming shores,   340
Point after point; till on to dawn, when dreams
Begin to feel the truth and stir of day,
To me, methought, who waited with the crowd,
There came a bark that, blowing forward, bore
King Arthur, like a modern gentleman   345
Of stateliest port; and all the people cried,
"Arthur is come again: he cannot die."
Then those that stood upon the hills behind
Repeated—"Come again, and thrice as fair";
And, further inland, voices echoed—"Come   350
With all good things, and war shall be no more."
At this a hundred bells began to peal,
That with the sound I woke, and heard indeed
The clear church bells ring in the Christmas morn.

1833–38   1842

Ulysses[1]

It little profits that an idle king,
By this still hearth, among these barren crags,
Matched with an aged wife, I mete and dole
Unequal laws[2] unto a savage race,
That hoard, and sleep, and feed, and know not me.   5

1. According to Dante, after Ulysses had returned home to Ithaca and had settled down to rule his island kingdom, he became restless and desired to set out on another voyage of exploration to the west. In old age he persuaded a band of his followers to accompany him on such a voyage. "Consider your origin," he addressed them, "ye were not formed to live like brutes, but to follow virtue and knowledge" (*Inferno* XXVI).
The contrast between the conscientious administrator, Telemachus, and the energetic quester, his father, has been variously interpreted. A few readers argue that Ulysses is not represented in the monologue as a great hero but as irresponsible. Tennyson himself stated that the poem expressed his own "need of going forward and braving the struggle of life" after the death of Hallam.
2. Measure out rewards and punishments.

I cannot rest from travel; I will drink
Life to the lees. All times I have enjoyed
Greatly, have suffered greatly, both with those
That loved me, and alone; on shore, and when
Through scudding drifts[3] the rainy Hyades   10
Vexed the dim sea. I am become a name;
For always roaming with a hungry heart
Much have I seen and known—cities of men
And manners, climates, councils, governments,
Myself not least, but honored of them all—   15
And drunk delight of battle with my peers,
Far on the ringing plains of windy Troy.
I am a part of all that I have met;
Yet all experience is an arch wherethrough
Gleams that untraveled world whose margin fades   20
Forever and forever when I move.
How dull it is to pause, to make an end,
To rust unburnished, not to shine in use!
As though to breathe were life! Life piled on life
Were all too little, and of one to me   25
Little remains; but every hour is saved
From that eternal silence, something more,
A bringer of new things; and vile it were
For some three suns to store and hoard myself,
And this gray spirit yearning in desire   30
To follow knowledge like a sinking star,
Beyond the utmost bound of human thought.

    This is my son, mine own Telemachus,
To whom I leave the scepter and the isle—
Well-loved of me, discerning to fulfill   35
This labor, by slow prudence to make mild
A rugged people, and through soft degrees
Subdue them to the useful and the good.
Most blameless is he, centered in the sphere
Of common duties, decent not to fail   40
In offices of tenderness, and pay
Meet adoration to my household gods,
When I am gone. He works his work, I mine.

    There lies the port; the vessel puffs her sail;
There gloom the dark, broad seas. My mariners,   45
Souls that have toiled, and wrought, and thought with me—
That ever with a frolic welcome took
The thunder and the sunshine, and opposed
Free hearts, free foreheads—you and I are old;
Old age hath yet his honor and his toil.   50
Death closes all; but something ere the end,
Some work of noble note, may yet be done,

3. Driving showers of spray and rain; the "Hyades" are a group of stars whose rising was assumed to be followed by rain.

Not unbecoming men that strove with Gods.
The lights begin to twinkle from the rocks;
The long day wanes; the slow moon climbs; the deep   55
Moans round with many voices. Come, my friends,
'Tis not too late to seek a newer world.
Push off, and sitting well in order smite
The sounding furrows; for my purpose holds
To sail beyond the sunset, and the baths   60
Of all the western stars,[4] until I die.
It may be that the gulfs will wash us down;
It may be we shall touch the Happy Isles,[5]
And see the great Achilles, whom we knew.
Though much is taken, much abides; and though   65
We are not now that strength which in old days
Moved earth and heaven, that which we are, we are—
One equal temper of heroic hearts,
Made weak by time and fate, but strong in will
To strive, to seek, to find, and not to yield.   70

1833   1842

Tithonus[1]

The woods decay, the woods decay and fall,
The vapors weep their burthen to the ground,
Man comes and tills the field and lies beneath,
And after many a summer dies the swan.[2]
Me only cruel immortality   5
Consumes; I wither slowly in thine arms,[3]
Here at the quiet limit of the world,
A white-haired shadow roaming like a dream
The ever-silent spaces of the East,
Far-folded mists, and gleaming halls of morn.   10
    Alas! for this gray shadow, once a man —
So glorious in his beauty and thy choice,
Who madest him thy chosen, that he seemed
To his great heart none other than a God!
I asked thee, "Give me immortality."   15
Then didst thou grant mine asking with a smile,
Like wealthy men who care not how they give.
But thy strong Hours indignant worked their wills,

4. The outer ocean or river which, in Greek cosmology, surrounded the flat circle of the earth, and into which the stars descended.

5. Elysium, or the Islands of the Blessed, where heroes such as Achilles were supposed to enjoy life after death. These islands were thought to be in the far-western ocean.

1. Tithonus, a Trojan prince, was loved by the goddess of the dawn, Eos or Aurora, who obtained for him the gift of living forever but neglected to obtain for him the gift of everlasting youth. In the monologue, Tithonus appears as an aged man, dwelling still in the palace of the goddess, and cut off by his frustrating predicament from the normal cycle of human life which culminates in death. To him immortality, not death, is "cruel."

2. Some species of swans live for at least fifty years.

3. I.e., the arms of Eos.

And beat me down and marred and wasted me,
And though they could not end me, left me maimed
To dwell in presence of immortal youth,
Immortal age beside immortal youth,
And all I was in ashes. Can thy love,
Thy beauty, make amends, though even now,
Close over us, the silver star,[4] thy guide,
Shines in those tremulous eyes that fill with tears
To hear me? Let me go; take back thy gift.
Why should a man desire in any way
To vary from the kindly race of men,
Or pass beyond the goal of ordinance[5]
Where all should pause, as is most meet for all?
    A soft air fans the cloud apart; there comes
A glimpse of that dark world where I was born.
Once more the old mysterious glimmer steals
From thy pure brows, and from thy shoulders pure,
And bosom beating with a heart renewed.
Thy cheek begins to redden through the gloom,
Thy sweet eyes brighten slowly close to mine,
Ere yet they blind the stars, and the wild team[6]
Which love thee, yearning for thy yoke, arise,
And shake the darkness from their loosened manes,
And beat the twilight into flakes of fire.
    Lo! ever thus thou growest beautiful
In silence, then before thine answer given
Departest, and thy tears are on my cheek.
    Why wilt thou ever scare me with thy tears,
And make me tremble lest a saying learnt,
In days far-off, on that dark earth, be true?
"The Gods themselves cannot recall their gifts."
    Ay me! ay me! with what another heart
In days far-off, and with what other eyes
I used to watch—if I be he that watched—
The lucid outline forming round thee; saw
The dim curls kindle into sunny rings;
Changed with thy mystic change, and felt my blood
Glow with the glow that slowly crimsoned all
Thy presence and thy portals, while I lay,
Mouth, forehead, eyelids, growing dewy-warm
With kisses balmier than half-opening buds
Of April, and could hear the lips that kissed
Whispering I knew not what of wild and sweet,
Like that strange song I heard Apollo sing,
While Ilion like a mist rose into towers.[7]
    Yet hold me not forever in thine East;

20

25

30

35

40

45

50

55

60

4. The morning star that precedes the dawn.
5. What is decreed or ordained as human destiny.
6. The horses that draw Eos' chariot into the sky at daybreak.
7. The walls of Troy (Ilion) were supposed to have been built to the strains of Apollo's music.

How can my nature longer mix with thine? 65
Coldly thy rosy shadows bathe me, cold
Are all thy lights, and cold my wrinkled feet
Upon thy glimmering thresholds, when the steam
Floats up from those dim fields about the homes
Of happy men that have the power to die, 70
And grassy barrows of the happier dead.
Release me, and restore me to the ground.
Thou seest all things, thou wilt see my grave;
Thou wilt renew thy beauty morn by morn,
I earth in earth forget these empty courts, 75
And thee returning on thy silver wheels.

1833, 1859   1860

Break, Break, Break

Break, break, break,
   On thy cold gray stones, O Sea!
And I would that my tongue could utter
   The thoughts that arise in me.

O, well for the fisherman's boy, 5
   That he shouts with his sister at play!
O, well for the sailor lad,
   That he sings in his boat on the bay!

And the stately ships go on
   To their haven under the hill; 10
But O for the touch of a vanished hand,
   And the sound of a voice that is still!

Break, break, break,
   At the foot of thy crags, O Sea!
But the tender grace of a day that is dead 15
   Will never come back to me.

1834   1842

Locksley Hall[1]

Comrades, leave me here a little, while as yet 'tis early morn;
Leave me here, and when you want me, sound upon the bugle horn.

---

1. The situation in this poem—of a young man's being jilted by a girl who chose to marry a wealthy landowner—may have been suggested to Tennyson by the experience of his brother. Frederick Tennyson, a hot-tempered man, had fallen in love with his cousin, Julia Tennyson, and was similarly unsuccessful. It may also have been inspired by Tennyson's own frustrated courtship of Rosa Baring who rejected the young poet in favor of a wealthy suitor. Concerning the ranting tone of the speaker (a tone accentuated by the heavily marked trochaic meter), Tennyson himself said: "The whole poem represents young life, its good side, its deficiencies, and its yearnings."

'Tis the place, and all around it, as of old, the curlews call,
Dreary gleams[2] about the moorland flying over Locksley Hall;

Locksley Hall, that in the distance overlooks the sandy tracts,   5
And the hollow ocean-ridges roaring into cataracts.

Many a night from yonder ivied casement, ere I went to rest,
Did I look on great Orion sloping slowly to the west.

Many a night I saw the Pleiads,[3] rising through the mellow shade,
Glitter like a swarm of fireflies tangled in a silver braid.   10

Here about the beach I wandered, nourishing a youth sublime
With the fairy tales of science, and the long result of time;

When the centuries behind me like a fruitful land reposed;
When I clung to all the present for the promise that it closed;[4]

When I dipped into the future far as human eye could see,   15
Saw the vision of the world and all the wonder that would be.—

In the spring a fuller crimson comes upon the robin's breast;
In the spring the wanton lapwing gets himself another crest;

In the spring a livelier iris changes on the burnished dove;
In the spring a young man's fancy lightly turns to thoughts of love.   20

Then her cheek was pale and thinner than should be for one so young,
And her eyes on all my motions with a mute observance hung.

And I said, "My cousin Amy, speak, and speak the truth to me,
Trust me, cousin, all the current of my being sets to thee."

On her pallid cheek and forehead came a color and a light,   25
As I have seen the rosy red flushing in the northern night.

And she turned—her bosom shaken with a sudden storm of sighs—
All the spirit deeply dawning in the dark of hazel eyes—

Saying, "I have hid my feelings, fearing they should do me wrong";
Saying, "Dost thou love me, cousin?" weeping, "I have loved thee
     long."   30

Love took up the glass of Time, and turned it in his glowing hands;
Every moment, lightly shaken, ran itself in golden sands.

Love took up the harp of Life, and smote on all the chords with
     might;
Smote the chord of Self, that, trembling, passed in music out of
     sight.

Many a morning on the moorland did we hear the copses ring,   35
And her whisper thronged my pulses with the fullness of the spring.

---

2. Tennyson stated that "gleams" does
not refer to "curlews" flying but to
streaks of light.

3. The Pleiades, a seven-starred constellation.
4. Enclosed.

Many an evening by the waters did we watch the stately ships,
And our spirits rushed together at the touching of the lips.

O my cousin, shallow-hearted! O my Amy, mine no more!
O the dreary, dreary moorland! O the barren, barren shore!   40

Falser than all fancy fathoms, falser than all songs have sung,
Puppet to a father's threat, and servile to a shrewish tongue!

Is it well to wish thee happy?—having known me—to decline
On a range of lower feelings and a narrower heart than mine!

Yet it shall be; thou shalt lower to his level day by day,   45
What is fine within thee growing coarse to sympathize with clay.

As the husband is, the wife is; thou art mated with a clown,⁵
And the grossness of his nature will have weight to drag thee down.

He will hold thee, when his passion shall have spent its novel force,
Something better than his dog, a little dearer than his horse.   50

What is this? his eyes are heavy; think not they are glazed with wine.
Go to him, it is thy duty; kiss him, take his hand in thine.

It may be my lord is weary, that his brain is overwrought;
Soothe him with thy finer fancies, touch him with thy lighter
     thought.

He will answer to the purpose, easy things to understand—   55
Better thou wert dead before me, though I slew thee with my hand!

Better thou and I were lying, hidden from the heart's disgrace,
Rolled in one another's arms, and silent in a last embrace.

Cursed be the social wants that sin against the strength of youth!
Cursed be the social lies that warp us from the living truth!   60

Cursed be the sickly forms that err from honest Nature's rule!
Cursed be the gold that gilds the straitened⁶ forehead of the fool!

Well—'tis well that I should bluster!—Hadst thou less unworthy
     proved—
Would to God—for I had loved thee more than ever wife was loved.

Am I mad, that I should cherish that which bears but bitter fruit?   65
I will pluck it from my bosom, though my heart be at the root.

Never, though my mortal summers to such length of years should
     come
As the many-wintered crow⁷ that leads the clanging rookery home.

Where is comfort? in division of the records of the mind?
Can I part her from herself, and love her, as I knew her, kind?   70

I remember one that perished; sweetly did she speak and move;
Such a one do I remember, whom to look at was to love.

5. Boor.   7. A rook, a long-lived bird.
6. Narrowed.

Can I think of her as dead, and love her for the love she bore?
No—she never loved me truly; love is love for evermore.

Comfort? comfort scorned of devils! this is truth the poet[8] sings,   75
That a sorrow's crown of sorrow is remembering happier things.

Drug thy memories, lest thou learn it, lest thy heart be put to proof,
In the dead unhappy night, and when the rain is on the roof.

Like a dog, he hunts in dreams, and thou art staring at the wall,
Where the dying night-lamp flickers, and the shadows rise and
　　fall.   80

Then a hand shall pass before thee, pointing to his drunken sleep,
To thy widowed[9] marriage-pillows, to the tears that thou wilt weep.

Thou shalt hear the "Never, never," whispered by the phantom years.
And a song from out the distance in the ringing of thine ears;

And an eye shall vex thee, looking ancient kindness on thy pain.   85
Turn thee, turn thee on thy pillow; get thee to thy rest again.

Nay, but Nature brings thee solace; for a tender voice will cry.
'Tis a purer life than thine, a lip to drain thy trouble dry.

Baby lips will laugh me down; my latest rival brings thee rest.
Baby fingers, waxen touches, press me from the mother's breast.   90

O, the child too clothes the father with a dearness not his due.
Half is thine and half is his; it will be worthy of the two.

O, I see thee old and formal, fitted to thy petty part,
With a little hoard of maxims preaching down a daughter's heart.

"They were dangerous guides the feelings—she herself was not ex-
　　empt—   95
Truly, she herself had suffered"—Perish in thy self-contempt!

Overlive it—lower yet—be happy! wherefore should I care?
I myself must mix with action, lest I wither by despair.

What is that which I should turn to, lighting upon days like these?
Every door is barred with gold, and opens but to golden keys.   100

Every gate is thronged with suitors, all the markets overflow.
I have but an angry fancy; what is that which I should do?

I had been content to perish, falling on the foeman's ground,
When the ranks are rolled in vapor, and the winds are laid with
　　sound.[1]

But the jingling of the guinea helps the hurt that Honor feels,   105
And the nations do but murmur, snarling at each other's heels.

---

8. Dante (*Inferno* V.121–23).
9. Presumably figurative. Her marriage having become a mockery, she is widowed.
1. It was once believed that the firing of artillery stilled the winds.

Can I but relive in sadness? I will turn that earlier page.
Hide me from my deep emotion, O thou wondrous Mother-Age![2]

Make me feel the wild pulsation that I felt before the strife,
When I heard my days before me, and the tumult of my life;   110

Yearning for the large excitement that the coming years would yield,
Eager-hearted as a boy when first he leaves his father's field,

And at night along the dusky highway near and nearer drawn,
Sees in heaven the light of London flaring like a dreary dawn;

And his spirit leaps within him to be gone before him then,   115
Underneath the light he looks at, in among the throngs of men;

Men, my brothers, men the workers, ever reaping something new;
That which they have done but earnest[3] of the things that they shall
    do.

For I dipped into the future, far as human eye could see,
Saw the Vision of the world, and all the wonder that would be;   120

Saw the heavens fill with commerce, argosies of magic sails,[4]
Pilots of the purple twilight, dropping down with costly bales;

Heard the heavens fill with shouting, and there rained a ghastly dew
From the nations' airy navies grappling in the central blue;

Far along the world-wide whisper of the south wind rushing
    warm,   125
With the standards of the peoples plunging through the thunder-
    storm;

Till the war drum throbbed no longer, and the battle flags were
    furled
In the Parliament of man, the Federation of the world.

There the common sense of most shall hold a fretful realm in awe,
And the kindly earth shall slumber, lapped in universal law.   130

So I triumphed ere my passion sweeping through me left me dry,
Left me with the palsied heart, and left me with the jaundiced eye;

Eye, to which all order festers, all things here are out of joint.
Science moves, but slowly, slowly, creeping on from point to point;

Slowly comes a hungry people, as a lion, creeping nigher,   135
Glares at one that nods and winks behind a slowly-dying fire.

Yet I doubt not through the ages one increasing purpose runs,
And the thoughts of men are widened with the process of the suns.

What is that to him that reaps not harvest of his youthful joys,
Though the deep heart of existence beat forever like a boy's?   140

2. Perhaps signifying the consolations   3. A pledge.
of a future age of progress. See also   4. Probably airships, such as balloons.
line 185.

Knowledge comes, but wisdom lingers, and I linger on the shore,
And the individual withers, and the world is more and more.

Knowledge comes, but wisdom lingers, and he bears a laden breast,
Full of sad experience, moving toward the stillness of his rest.

Hark, my merry comrades call me, sounding on the bugle horn,   145
They to whom my foolish passion were a target for their scorn.

Shall it not be scorn to me to harp on such a moldered string?
I am shamed through all my nature to have loved so slight a thing.

Weakness to be wroth with weakness! woman's pleasure, woman's
    pain—
Nature made them blinder motions bounded in a shallower brain.   150

Woman is the lesser man, and all thy passions, matched with mine,
Are as moonlight unto sunlight, and as water unto wine—

Here at least, where nature sickens, nothing. Ah, for some retreat
Deep in yonder shining Orient, where my life began to beat,

Where in wild Mahratta-battle[5] fell my father evil-starred—   155
I was left a trampled orphan, and a selfish uncle's ward.

Or to burst all links of habit—there to wander far away,
On from island unto island at the gateways of the day.

Larger constellations burning, mellow moons and happy skies,
Breadths of tropic shade and palms in cluster, knots of Paradise.   160

Never comes the trader, never floats an European flag,
Slides the bird o'er lustrous woodland, swings the trailer[6] from the
    crag;

Droops the heavy-blossomed bower, hangs the heavy-fruited tree—
Summer isles of Eden lying in dark purple spheres of sea.

There methinks would be enjoyment more than in this march of
    mind,
                                                                165
In the steamship, in the railway, in the thoughts that shake man-
    kind.

There the passions cramped no longer shall have scope and breath-
    ing space;
I will take some savage woman, she shall rear my dusky race.

Iron-jointed, supple-sinewed, they shall dive, and they shall run,
Catch the wild goat by the hair, and hurl their lances in the sun;   170

Whistle back the parrot's call, and leap the rainbows of the brooks,
Not with blinded eyesight poring over miserable books—

Fool, again the dream, the fancy! but I *know* my words are wild,
But I count the gray barbarian lower than the Christian child.

5. A reference to wars waged by a   in India (1803 and 1817).
Hindu people against the British forces   6. A vine.

I, to herd with narrow foreheads, vacant of our glorious gains.   175
Like a beast with lower pleasures, like a beast with lower pains!

Mated with a squalid savage—what to me were sun or clime?
I the heir of all the ages, in the foremost files of time—

I that rather held it better men should perish one by one,
Than that earth should stand at gaze like Joshua's moon in
    Ajalon![7]   180

Not in vain the distance beacons. Forward, forward let us range,
Let the great world spin forever down the ringing grooves[8] of change.

Through the shadow of the globe we sweep into the younger day;
Better fifty years of Europe than a cycle of Cathay.[9]

Mother-Age—for mine I knew not—help me as when life begun;   185
Rift the hills, and roll the waters, flash the lightnings, weigh the sun.

O, I see the crescent promise of my spirit hath not set.
Ancient founts of inspiration well through all my fancy yet.

Howsoever these things be, a long farewell to Locksley Hall!
Now for me the woods may wither, now for me the roof-tree fall.   190

Comes a vapor from the margin, blackening over heath and holt,
Cramming all the blast before it, in its breast a thunderbolt.

Let it fall on Locksley Hall, with rain or hail, or fire or snow;
For the mighty wind arises, roaring seaward, and I go.

                                                    1842

Move Eastward, Happy Earth

Move eastward, happy earth, and leave
    Yon orange sunset waning slow;
From fringes of the faded eve,
    O happy planet, eastward go,
Till over thy dark shoulder glow   5
    Thy silver sister-world,[1] and rise
    To glass herself in dewy eyes
That watch me from the glen below.

Ah, bear me with thee, smoothly borne,
    Dip forward under starry light,   10

---

7. At the command of Joshua, the sun and moon stood still while the Israelites completed the slaughter of their enemies in the valley of Ajalon (Joshua x.12–13).
8. Railroad tracks. Tennyson at one time had the impression that train wheels ran in grooved rails.
9. China, regarded in the 19th century as a static, unprogressive country.
1. The planet Venus, or perhaps the moon, which will be reflected in the eyes of the speaker's beloved.

And move me to my marriage morn,
And round again to happy night.

ca. 1836   1842

Lines

Here[2] often, when a child I lay reclined,
    I took delight in this locality.
Here stood the infant Ilion of the mind,
    And here the Grecian ships did seem to be.
And here again I come, and only find   5
    The drain-cut levels of the marshy lea—
Gray sea banks and pale sunsets—dreary wind,
    Dim shores, dense rains, and heavy-clouded sea!

1837   1850

The Eagle: A Fragment

He clasps the crag with crooked hands;
Close to the sun in lonely lands,
Ringed with the azure world, he stands.

The wrinkled sea beneath him crawls;
He watches from his mountain walls,   5
And like a thunderbolt he falls.

1851

Songs from THE PRINCESS[1]
Sweet and Low

Sweet and low, sweet and low,
    Wind of the western sea,
Low, low, breathe and blow,
    Wind of the western sea!
Over the rolling waters go,   5
Come from the dying moon, and blow,
    Blow him again to me;
While my little one, while my pretty one, sleeps.

2. At Mablethorpe, on the Lincolnshire coast.
1. *The Princess* is a story of the role of women in modern society. As a long narrative love poem, *The Princess* has not been highly regarded, and parodies such as Gilbert and Sullivan's *Princess* *Ida* have exposed the flaws in the story. What saves the poem is its use of interludes in which occasional songs were sung. These songs rank among the finest of Tennyson's lyrics, and various 19th- and 20th-century composers have set them to music.

Sleep and rest, sleep and rest,
    Father will come to thee soon;   10
Rest, rest, on mother's breast,
    Father will come to thee soon;
Father will come to his babe in the nest,
Silver sails all out of the west
    Under the silver moon;   15
Sleep, my little one, sleep, my pretty one, sleep.

          1850

The Splendor Falls

The splendor falls on castle walls
    And snowy summits old in story;
The long light shakes across the lakes,
    And the wild cataract leaps in glory.
Blow, bugle, blow, set the wild echoes flying,   5
Blow, bugle; answer, echoes, dying, dying, dying.

O, hark, O, hear! how thin and clear,
    And thinner, clearer, farther going!
O, sweet and far from cliff and scar[2]
    The horns of Elfland faintly blowing!   10
Blow, let us hear the purple glens replying,
Blow, bugle; answer, echoes, dying, dying, dying.

O love, they die in yon rich sky,
    They faint on hill or field or river;
Our echoes roll from soul to soul,   15
    And grow forever and forever.
Blow, bugle, blow, set the wild echoes flying,
And answer, echoes, answer, dying, dying, dying.

          1850

Tears, Idle Tears

    Tears, idle tears, I know not what they mean,
Tears from the depth of some divine despair
Rise in the heart, and gather to the eyes,
In looking on the happy autumn-fields,
And thinking of the days that are no more.   5

    Fresh as the first beam glittering on a sail,
That brings our friends up from the underworld,
Sad as the last which reddens over one

2. Mountainside.

That sinks with all we love below the verge;
So sad, so fresh, the days that are no more.   10

Ah, sad and strange as in dark summer dawns
The earliest pipe of half-awakened birds
To dying ears, when unto dying eyes
The casement slowly grows a glimmering square;
So sad, so strange, the days that are no more.   15

Dear as remembered kisses after death,
And sweet as those by hopeless fancy feigned
On lips that are for others; deep as love,
Deep as first love, and wild with all regret;
O Death in Life, the days that are no more!
                                                                                 20
                                                                           1847

Ask Me No More

Ask me no more: the moon may draw the sea;
    The cloud may stoop from heaven and take the shape,
    With fold to fold, of mountain or of cape;
But O too fond, when have I answered thee?
                    Ask me no more.   5

Ask me no more: what answer should I give?
    I love not hollow cheek or faded eye:
    Yet, O my friend, I will not have thee die!
Ask me no more, lest I should bid thee live;
                    Ask me no more.   10

Ask me no more: thy fate and mine are sealed;
    I strove against the stream and all in vain;
    Let the great river take me to the main.
No more, dear love, for at a touch I yield;
                    Ask me no more.   15
                                                                           1850

Now Sleeps the Crimson Petal

Now sleeps the crimson petal, now the white;
Nor waves the cypress in the palace walk;
Nor winks the gold fin in the porphyry font.
The firefly wakens; waken thou with me.

Now droops the milk-white peacock like a ghost,   5
And like a ghost she glimmers on to me.

Now lies the Earth all Danaë[3] to the stars,
And all thy heart lies open unto me.

Now slides the silent meteor on, and leaves
A shining furrow, as thy thoughts in me.   10

Now folds the lily all her sweetness up,
And slips into the bosom of the lake.
So fold thyself, my dearest, thou, and slip
Into my bosom and be lost in me.

1847

Come Down, O Maid

Come down, O maid, from yonder mountain height.
What pleasure lives in height (the shepherd sang),
In height and cold, the splendor of the hills?
But cease to move so near the heavens, and cease
To glide a sunbeam by the blasted pine,   5
To sit a star upon the sparkling spire;
And come, for Love is of the valley, come,
For Love is of the valley, come thou down
And find him; by the happy threshold, he,
Or hand in hand with Plenty in the maize,   10
Or red with spirted purple of the vats,
Or foxlike in the vine;[4] nor cares to walk
With Death and Morning on the Silver Horns,[5]
Nor wilt thou snare him in the white ravine,
Nor find him dropped upon the firths of ice,[6]   15
That huddling slant in furrow-cloven falls
To roll the torrent out of dusky doors.[7]
But follow; let the torrent dance thee down
To find him in the valley; let the wild
Lean-headed eagles yelp alone, and leave   20
The monstrous ledges there to slope, and spill
Their thousand wreaths of dangling water-smoke,
That like a broken purpose waste in air.
So waste not thou, but come; for all the vales
Await thee; azure pillars of the hearth[8]   25
Arise to thee; the children call, and I
Thy shepherd pipe, and sweet is every sound,
Sweeter thy voice, but every sound is sweet;

3. Danaë, a Greek princess, was confined in a metal tower by her father to prevent suitors from coming near her. Zeus, however, succeeded in visiting her in the form of a shower of gold. Their offspring was the hero, Perseus.
4. This image comes from the Song of Solomon ii.15.

5. Mountain peaks.
6. Glaciers.
7. Heaps of rock and refuse at the base of a glacier through which the mountain torrent forces its way down to the valley below.
8. Columns of smoke from the houses in the valley.

Myriads of rivulets hurrying through the lawn,
The moan of doves in immemorial elms,   30
And murmuring of innumerable bees.

1847

In Memoriam A. H. H. Like most of Tennyson's writings, *In Memoriam* shows his debt to earlier poetry, yet its structure is strikingly different from such traditional elegies as Milton's *Lycidas* or Shelley's *Adonais*. Resembling a song cycle more than a symphony, it is made up of individual lyric units, seemingly self-sustaining, that may be enjoyed by themselves even though the full pleasure to be derived from each component depends upon its relationship to the poem as a whole. The circumstances of the poem's composition help to explain how this new kind of elegy was evolved. The sudden death of Arthur Hallam at the age of 22 had a profound effect on Tennyson. The young poet had cherished Hallam not only as his closest friend and the fiancé of his sister but as an all-wise counselor upon whose judgment he depended for guidance. This fatherly prop having been pulled away, Tennyson was overwhelmed with doubts about the meaning of life and man's role in the universe, doubts reinforced by his own study of geology and other sciences. As a kind of poetic diary recording the variety of his feelings and reflections he began to compose a series of lyrics. These "short swallow-flights of song," as he calls them, written at intervals over a period of seventeen years, were later grouped into one long elegy in which a progressive development from despair to some sort of hope, as in section 95, is recorded.

    Some of the early sections of the poem resemble traditional pastoral elegies, including those portraying the voyage during which Hallam's body was brought to England for burial (sections 9–11, 13–15, 19). Other early sections portraying the speaker's loneliness, in which even Christmas festivities seem joyless (section 28), are more distinctive. With the passage of time, indicated by anniversaries and by recurring changes of the seasons, the speaker comes to accept the loss and to assert his belief in life and in an afterlife. In particular the recurring Christmases (sections 28, 78, 104) indicate the stages of his development, yet the pattern of progress in the poem is not a simple unimpeded movement upwards. Dramatic conflicts recur throughout. Thus the most intense expression of doubt occurs not at the beginning of *In Memoriam* but as late as sections 54, 55, and 56.

    The quatrain form in which the whole poem is written is usually called the "*In Memoriam* stanza," although it had been occasionally used by earlier poets. So rigid a form taxed Tennyson's ingenuity in achieving variety, but it is one of several means by which the diverse parts of the poem are knitted together.

    The introductory section, consisting of eleven stanzas, is commonly referred to as the "Prologue," although Tennyson did not assign a title to it. It was written in 1849 after the rest of the poem was complete.

From In Memoriam A. H. H.

OBIIT MDCCCXXXIII

Strong Son of God, immortal Love,
  Whom we, that have not seen thy face,
  By faith, and faith alone, embrace,
Believing where we cannot prove;[1]

Thine are these orbs[2] of light and shade;   5
  Thou madest Life in man and brute;
  Thou madest Death; and lo, thy foot
Is on the skull which thou hast made.

Thou wilt not leave us in the dust:
  Thou madest man, he knows not why,   10
  He thinks he was not made to die;
And thou hast made him: thou art just.

Thou seemest human and divine,
  The highest, holiest manhood, thou.
  Our wills are ours, we know not how;   15
Our wills are ours, to make them thine.

Our little systems[3] have their day;
  They have their day and cease to be;
  They are but broken lights of thee,
And thou, O Lord, art more than they.   20

We have but faith: we cannot know,
  For knowledge is of things we see;
  And yet we trust it comes from thee,
A beam in darkness: let it grow.

Let knowledge grow from more to more,   25
  But more of reverence in us dwell;
  That mind and soul, according well,
May make one music as before,[4]

But vaster. We are fools and slight;
  We mock thee when we do not fear: 30
  But help thy foolish ones to bear;
Help thy vain worlds to bear thy light.

Forgive what seemed my sin in me,
  What seemed my worth since I began;
  For merit lives from man to man,   35
And not from man, O Lord, to thee.

1. See John xx.24–29, in which Jesus rebukes Thomas for his doubts concerning the Resurrection: "Blessed are they that have not seen, and yet have believed."
2. Planets.
3. Systems of religion and philosophy.
4. As in the days of fixed religious faith.

Forgive my grief for one removed,
  Thy creature, whom I found so fair.
  I trust he lives in thee, and there
I find him worthier to be loved.   40

Forgive these wild and wandering cries,
  Confusions of a wasted [5] youth;
  Forgive them where they fail in truth,
And in thy wisdom make me wise.

1849

1

I held it truth, with him who sings
  To one clear harp in divers tones,[6]
  That men may rise on stepping stones
Of their dead selves to higher things.

But who shall so forecast the years   5
  And find in loss a gain to match?
  Or reach a hand through time to catch
The far-off interest of tears?

Let Love clasp Grief lest both be drowned,
  Let darkness keep her raven gloss.   10
  Ah, sweeter to be drunk with loss,
To dance with Death, to beat the ground,

Than that the victor Hours should scorn
  The long result of love, and boast,
  "Behold the man that loved and lost,   15
But all he was is overworn."

2

Old yew, which graspest at the stones
  That name the underlying dead,
  Thy fibers net the dreamless head,
Thy roots are wrapped about the bones.

The seasons bring the flower again,   5
  And bring the firstling to the flock;
  And in the dusk of thee the clock
Beats out the little lives of men.

O, not for thee the glow, the bloom,
  Who changest not in any gale,   10
  Nor branding summer suns avail
To touch thy thousand years of gloom; [7]

And gazing on thee, sullen tree,
  Sick for [8] thy stubborn hardihood,

---

5. Desolated.
6. Identified by Tennyson as Goethe.
7. The ancient yew tree, growing in the grounds near the clock tower and church where Hallam was to be buried, seems neither to blossom in spring nor change from its dark mournful color in summer.
8. Envying or longing to share.

I seem to fail from out my blood   15
And grow incorporate into thee.

3

O Sorrow, cruel fellowship,
    O Priestess in the vaults of Death,
    O sweet and bitter in a breath,
What whispers from thy lying lip?

"The stars," she whispers, "blindly run;   5
    A web is woven across the sky;
    From out waste places comes a cry,
And murmurs from the dying sun;

"And all the phantom, Nature, stands—
    With all the music in her tone,   10
    A hollow echo of my own—
A hollow form with empty hands."

And shall I take a thing so blind,
    Embrace her [9] as my natural good;
    Or crush her, like a vice of blood,   15
Upon the threshold of the mind?

4

To Sleep I give my powers away;
    My will is bondsman to the dark;
    I sit within a helmless bark,
And with my heart I muse and say:

O heart, how fares it with thee now,   5
    That thou should fail from thy desire,
    Who scarcely darest to inquire,
"What is it makes me beat so low?"

Something it is which thou hast lost,
    Some pleasure from thine early years.   10
    Break thou deep vase of chilling tears,
That grief hath shaken into frost!

Such clouds of nameless trouble cross
    All night below the darkened eyes;
    With morning wakes the will, and cries,   15
"Thou shalt not be the fool of loss."

5

I sometimes hold it half a sin
    To put in words the grief I feel;
    For words, like Nature, half reveal
And half conceal the Soul within.

But, for the unquiet heart and brain,   5
    A use in measured language lies;
    The sad mechanic exercise,
Like dull narcotics, numbing pain.

9. I.e., sorrow.

In words, like weeds,[1] I'll wrap me o'er,
   Like coarsest clothes against the cold;
   But that large grief which these enfold
Is given in outline and no more.   10

* * *

7

Dark house,[2] by which once more I stand
   Here in the long unlovely street,
   Doors, where my heart was used to beat
So quickly, waiting for a hand,

A hand that can be clasped no more—   5
   Behold me, for I cannot sleep,
   And like a guilty thing I creep
At earliest morning to the door.

He is not here; but far away
   The noise of life begins again,   10
   And ghastly through the drizzling rain
On the bald street breaks the blank day.

* * *

9

Fair ship, that from the Italian shore
   Sailest the placid ocean-plains
   With my lost Arthur's loved remains,
Spread thy full wings, and waft him o'er.

So draw him home to those that mourn   5
   In vain; a favorable speed
   Ruffle thy mirrored mast, and lead
Through prosperous floods his holy urn.

All night no ruder air perplex
   Thy sliding keel, till Phosphor,[3] bright   10
   As our pure love, through early light
Shall glimmer on the dewey decks.

Sphere all your lights around, above;
   Sleep, gentle heavens, before the prow;
   Sleep, gentle winds, as he sleeps now,   15
My friend, the brother of my love;

My Arthur, whom I shall not see
   Till all my widowed race be run;
   Dear as the mother to the son,
More than my brothers are to me.   20

10

I hear the noise about thy keel;
   I hear the bell struck in the night;
   I see the cabin window bright;
   I see the sailor at the wheel.

1. Garments.
2. House on Wimpole Street, in London, where Hallam had lived.
3. The morning star.

Thou bring'st the sailor to his wife,　　　　　5
　　And traveled men from foreign lands;
　　And letters unto trembling hands;
And, thy dark freight, a vanished life.

So bring him; we have idle dreams;
　　This look of quiet flatters thus　　　　10
　　Our home-bred fancies. O, to us,
The fools of habit, sweeter seems

To rest beneath the clover sod,
　　That takes the sunshine and the rains,
　　Or where the kneeling hamlet drains　　15
The chalice of the grapes of God; [4]

Than if with thee the roaring wells
　　Should gulf him fathom-deep in brine,
　　And hands so often clasped in mine,
Should toss with tangle [5] and with shells.　　20

11

Calm is the morn without a sound,
　　Calm as to suit a calmer grief,
　　And only through the faded leaf
The chestnut pattering to the ground;

Calm and deep peace on this high wold, [6]　　5
　　And on these dews that drench the furze,
　　And all the silvery gossamers
That twinkle into green and gold;

Calm and still light on yon great plain
　　That sweeps with all its autumn bowers,　　10
　　And crowded farms and lessenings towers,
To mingle with the bounding main;

Calm and deep peace in this wide air,
　　These leaves that redden to the fall,
　　And in my heart, if calm at all,　　15
If any calm, a calm despair;

Calm on the seas, and silver sleep,
　　And waves that sway themselves in rest,
　　And dead calm in that noble breast
Which heaves but with the heaving deep. [7]　　20

* * *

13

Tears of the widower, when he sees
　　A late-lost form that sleep reveals,

4. Referring to a burial inside a church building rather than in the churchyard.
5. Seaweed.
6. High and open countryside.
7. It is now the autumn of 1833, and the poet imagines that Hallam's body was already being brought back by ship to England. The date of the actual voyage seems to have been later in the year.

And moves his doubtful arms, and feels
Her place is empty, fall like these;

Which weep a loss forever new,   5
    A void where heart on heart reposed;
    And, where warm hands have pressed and closed,
Silence, till I be silent too;

Which weep the comrade of my choice,
    An awful thought, a life removed,   10
    The human-hearted man I loved,
A Spirit, not a breathing voice.

Come, Time, and teach me, many years,
    I do not suffer in a dream;
    For now so strange do these things seem,   15
Mine eyes have leisure for their tears,

My fancies time to rise on wing,
    And glance about the approaching sails,
    As though they brought but merchants' bales,
And not the burthen that they bring.[8]   20

14

If one should bring me this report,
    That thou [9] hadst touched the land today,
    And I went down unto the quay,
And found thee lying in the port;

And standing, muffled round with woe,   5
    Should see thy passengers in rank
    Come stepping lightly down the plank
And beckoning unto those they know;

And if along with these should come
    The man I held as half divine,   10
    Should strike a sudden hand in mine,
And ask a thousand things of home;

And I should tell him all my pain,
    And how my life had drooped of late,
    And he should sorrow o'er my state   15
And marvel what possessed my brain;

And I perceived no touch of change,
    No hint of death in all his frame,
    But found him all in all the same,
I should not feel it to be strange.   20

15

Tonight the winds begin to rise
    And roar from yonder dropping day;

8. The speaker asks Time to teach him to confront the awesome fact of what has happened (line 10) so that he will not delude himself by fancying the ship is bearing only merchandise and not the body of his friend. 9. I.e., the ship.

The last red leaf is whirled away,
The rooks are blown about the skies;

The forest cracked, the waters curled,   5
   The cattle huddled on the lea;
   And wildly dashed on tower and tree
The sunbeam strikes along the world:

And but for fancies, which aver
   That all thy [1] motions gently pass   10
   Athwart a plane of molten glass,
I scarce could brook the strain and stir

That makes the barren branches loud;
   And but for fear it is not so,
   The wild unrest that lives in woe   15
Would dote and pore on yonder cloud

That rises upward always higher,
   And onward drags a laboring breast,
   And topples round the dreary west,
A looming bastion fringed with fire.   20

* * *
19
The Danube to the Severn [2] gave
   The darkened heart that beat no more;
   They laid him by the pleasant shore,
And in the hearing of the wave.

There twice a day the Severn fills;   5
   The salt sea water passes by,
   And hushes half the babbling Wye,[3]
And makes a silence in the hills.

The Wye is hushed nor moved along,
   And hushed my deepest grief of all,   10
   When filled with tears that cannot fall,
I brim with sorrow drowning song.

The tide flows down, the wave again
   Is vocal in its wooded walls;
   My deeper anguish also falls,   15
And I can speak a little then.

* * *
21
I sing to him that rests below,
   And, since the grasses round me wave,

1. I.e., the ship's.
2. Hallam died at Vienna on the Danube. His burial place is on the banks of the Severn, a tidal river in the southwest of England.
3. The water of the Wye River, a tributary of the Severn, is dammed up as the tide flows in, and its sound is silenced until, with the turn of the tide, its "wave" once more becomes "vocal" (lines 13–14); these stanzas were written at Tintern Abbey in the Wye River country.

I take the grasses of the grave,[4]
And make them pipes whereon to blow.

The traveler hears me now and then,   5
    And sometimes harshly will he speak:
    "This fellow would make weakness weak,
And melt the waxen hearts of men."

Another answers: "Let him be,
    He loves to make parade of pain,   10
    That with his piping he may gain
The praise that comes to constancy."

A third is wroth: "Is this an hour
    For private sorrow's barren song,
    When more and more the people throng   15
The chairs and thrones of civil power?

"A time to sicken and to swoon,
    When Science reaches forth her arms [5]
    To feel from world to world, and charms
Her secret from the latest moon?" [6]   20

Behold, ye speak an idle thing;
    Ye never knew the sacred dust.
    I do but sing because I must,
And pipe but as the linnets sing;

And one is glad; her note is gay,   25
    For now her little ones have ranged;
    And one is sad; her note is changed,
Because her brood is stolen away.

22

The path by which we twain did go,
    Which led by tracts that pleased us well,
    Through four sweet years arose and fell,
From flower to flower, from snow to snow;

And we with singing cheered the way,   5
    And, crowned with all the season lent,
    From April on to April went,
And glad at heart from May to May.

But where the path we walked began
    To slant the fifth autumnal slope,[7]   10
    As we descended following Hope,
There sat the Shadow feared of man;

4. The speaker assumes that the burial was in the churchyard; in fact, Hallam's body was interred in a vault inside St. Andrews church at Clevedon, Somersetshire, on January 3, 1834. See section 10, lines 11–16.
5. Astronomical instruments such as telescopes.
6. Probably alluding to the discovery, in 1846, of the planet Neptune and its moon.
7. Hallam died in early autumn (September 15, 1833) in the fifth year of the friendship.

Who broke our fair companionship,
   And spread his mantle dark and cold,
   And wrapped thee formless in the fold,   15
And dulled the murmur on thy lip,

And bore thee where I could not see
   Nor follow, though I walk in haste,
   And think that somewhere in the waste
The Shadow sits and waits for me.   20

23

Now, sometimes in my sorrow shut,
   Or breaking into song by fits,
   Alone, alone, to where he sits,
The Shadow cloaked from head to foot,

Who keeps the keys of all the creeds,   5
   I wander, often falling lame,
   And looking back to whence I came,
Or on to where the pathway leads;

And crying, How changed from where it ran
   Through lands where not a leaf was dumb,   10
   But all the lavish hills would hum
The murmur of a happy Pan;

When each by turns was guide to each,
   And Fancy light from Fancy caught,
   And Thought leapt out to wed with Thought   15
Ere Thought could wed itself with Speech;

And all we met was fair and good,
   And all was good that Time could bring,
   And all the secret of the Spring
Moved in the chambers of the blood;   20

And many an old philosophy
   On Argive heights divinely sang,[8]
   And round us all the thicket rang
To many a flute of Arcady.[9]

24

And was the day of my delight
   As pure and perfect as I say?
   The very source and fount of day
Is dashed with wandering isles of night.[1]

If all was good and fair we met,   5
   This earth had been the Paradise
   It never looked to human eyes
Since our first sun arose and set.

And is it that the haze of grief
   Makes former gladness loom so great?   10

8. In classical times the Greek city of Argos was renowned for its music.
9. Sheep-raising region in Greece associated with pastoral poetry.
1. Moving spots on the sun.

The lowness of the present state,
That sets the past in this relief?

Or that the past will always win
  A glory from its being far,
  And orb into the perfect star   15
We saw not when we moved therein? [2]

25

I know that this was Life—the track
  Whereon with equal feet we fared;
  And then, as now, the day prepared
The daily burden for the back.

But this it was that made me move   5
  As light as carrier birds in air;
  I loved the weight I had to bear,
Because it needed help of Love;

Nor could I weary, heart or limb,
  When mighty Love would cleave in twain   10
  The lading of a single pain,
And part it, giving half to him.

26

Still onward winds the dreary way;
  I with it, for I long to prove
  No lapse of moons can canker Love,
Whatever fickle tongues may say.

And if that eye which watches guilt   5
  And goodness, and hath power to see
  Within the green the mouldered tree,
And towers fallen as soon as built—

O, if indeed that eye foresee
  Or see—in Him is no before—   10
  In more of life true life no more
And Love the indifference to be,

Then might I find, ere yet the morn
  Breaks hither over Indian seas,
  That Shadow waiting with the keys,   15
To shroud me from my proper scorn. [3]

27

I envy not in any moods
  The captive void of noble rage,
  The linnet born within the cage,
That never knew the summer woods;

2. The speaker speculates whether past experiences seem so much more "pure and perfect" (line 2) than present ones because they are far distant from us in time just as our planet Earth would have the deceptive appearance of being a perfect orb if we viewed it from a great distance in space, as from another planet. See *Locksley Hall Sixty Years After*, lines 187–92.

3. The Deity, being outside time, sees (rather than foresees) whether or not the rest of life ("more of life," line 11) will be pointless. If pointless then the way for the speaker to deal with his self-scorn ("proper scorn") might be to seek death.

I envy not the beast that takes   5
   His license in the field of time,
   Unfettered by the sense of crime,
To whom a conscience never wakes;

Nor, what may count itself as blest,
   The heart that never plighted troth   10
   But stagnates in the weeds of sloth;
Nor any want-begotten rest.[4]

I hold it true, whate'er befall;
   I feel it, when I sorrow most;
   'Tis better to have loved and lost   15
Than never to have loved at all.

28

The time draws near the birth of Christ.[5]
   The moon is hid, the night is still;
   The Christmas bells from hill to hill
Answer each other in the mist.

Four voices of four hamlets round,   5
   From far and near, on mead and moor,
   Swell out and fail, as if a door
Were shut between me and the sound;

Each voice four changes [6] on the wind,
   That now dilate, and now decrease,   10
   Peace and goodwill, goodwill and peace,
Peace and goodwill, to all mankind.

This year I slept and woke with pain,
   I almost wished no more to wake,
   And that my hold on life would break   15
Before I heard those bells again;

But they my troubled spirit rule,
   For they controlled me when a boy;
   They bring me sorrow touched with joy,
The merry, merry bells of Yule.   20

* * *

30

With trembling fingers did we weave
   The holly round the Christmas hearth;
   A rainy cloud possessed the earth,
And sadly fell our Christmas eve.

At our old pastimes in the hall   5
   We gamboled, making vain pretense
   Of gladness, with an awful sense
Of one mute Shadow watching all.

4. Complacency resulting from some deficiency or "want."
5. The first Christmas after Hallam's death (1833); the setting is Tennyson's family home in Lincolnshire.
6. Different sequences in which church bells are pealed.

We paused: the winds were in the beech;
　　We heard them sweep the winter land;　　　　　10
　　And in a circle hand-in-hand
Sat silent, looking each at each.

Then echo-like our voices rang;
　　We sung, though every eye was dim,
　　A merry song we sang with him　　　　　15
Last year; impetuously we sang.

We ceased; a gentler feeling crept
　　Upon us: surely rest is meet.[7]
　　"They rest," we said, "their sleep is sweet,"
And silence followed, and we wept.　　　　　20

Our voices took a higher range;
　　Once more we sang: "They do not die
　　Nor lose their mortal sympathy,
Nor change to us, although they change;

"Rapt [8] from the fickle and the frail　　　　　25
　　With gathered power, yet the same,
　　Pierces the keen seraphic flame
From orb to orb,[9] from veil to veil."

Rise, happy morn, rise, holy morn,
　　Draw forth the cheerful day from night:　　　　　30
　　O Father, touch the east, and light
The light that shone when Hope was born.

* * *

34

My own dim life should teach me this,
　　That life shall live forevermore,
　　Else earth is darkness at the core,
And dust and ashes all that is;

This round of green, this orb of flame,　　　　　5
　　Fantastic beauty; such as lurks
　　In some wild poet, when he works
Without a conscience or an aim.[1]

What then were God to such as I?
　　'Twere hardly worth my while to choose　　　　　10
　　Of things all mortal, or to use
A little patience ere I die;

'Twere best at once to sink to peace,
　　Like birds the charming serpent draws,[2]

7. Proper or appropriate.
8. Carried away from.
9. The angelic spirit ("flame") of the dead moves from star to star.
1. Perhaps Thomas Lovell Beddoes, a brilliantly promising but erratic poet, admired by Tennyson, who committed suicide in 1849.
2. Some snakes are reputed to capture their prey by casting a charm.

To drop head-foremost in the jaws 15
Of vacant darkness and to cease.

35

Yet if some voice that man could trust
    Should murmur from the narrow house,
    "The cheeks drop in, the body bows;
Man dies, nor is there hope in dust";

Might I not say? "Yet even here, 5
    But for one hour, O Love, I strive
    To keep so sweet a thing alive."
But I should turn mine ears and hear

The moanings of the homeless sea,
    The sound of streams that swift or slow 10
    Draw down Aeonian hills,[3] and sow
The dust of continents to be;

And Love would answer with a sigh,
    "The sound of that forgetful shore
    Will change my sweetness more and more, 15
Half-dead to know that I shall die."

O me, what profits it to put
    An idle case? If Death were seen
    At first as Death, Love had not been,
Or been in narrowest working shut, 20

Mere fellowship of sluggish moods,
    Or in his coarsest Satyr-shape
    Had bruised the herb and crushed the grape,
And basked and battened in the woods.[4]

* * *

39

Old warder of these buried bones,
    And answering now my random stroke
    With fruitful cloud and living smoke,
Dark yew, that graspest at the stones

And dippest toward the dreamless head, 5
    To thee too comes the golden hour
    When flower is feeling after flower;[5]
But Sorrow—fixed upon the dead,

And darkening the dark graves of men—
    What whispered from her lying lips? 10

3. Hills that are aeons old, seemingly
everlasting.
4. Lines 18 ff. may be paraphrased: if
we knew death to be final and that no
afterlife were possible, love could not
exist except on a primitive or bestial
level.

5. The ancient yew tree in the graveyard was described in section 2 as never
changing. Now the speaker discovers
that in the flowering season, if the tree
is struck ("my random stroke," line
2), it gives off a cloud of golden pollen.

Thy gloom is kindled at the tips,[6]
And passes into gloom again.

* * *

44

How fares it with the happy dead?
   For here the man is more and more;
   But he forgets the days before
God closed the doorways of his head.[7]

The days have vanished, tone and tint,   5
   And yet perhaps the hoarding sense [8]
   Gives out at times (he knows not whence)
A little flash, a mystic hint;

And in the long harmonious years
   (If Death so taste Lethean springs [9])   10
   May some dim touch of earthly things
Surprise thee ranging with thy peers.

If such a dreamy touch should fall,
   O turn thee round, resolve the doubt;
   My guardian angel will speak out   15
In that high place, and tell thee all.

* * *

47

That each, who seems a separate whole,
   Should move his rounds,[1] and fusing all
   The skirts [2] of self again, should fall
Remerging in the general Soul,

Is faith as vague as all unsweet.   5
   Eternal form shall still divide
   The eternal soul from all beside;
And I shall know him when we meet;

And we shall sit at endless feast,
   Enjoying each the other's good.   10
   What vaster dream can hit the mood
Of Love on earth? He seeks at least

Upon the last and sharpest height,
   Before the spirits fade away,
   Some landing place, to clasp and say,   15
"Farewell! We lose ourselves in light."

---

6. Only the tips of the yew-branches are in flower.
7. This difficult stanza has been variously interpreted. If "man" (line 2) refers to the dead, the passage means that in our living world the dead man is more and more remembered, but that he, in the afterworld, is shut off through death from remembering past experiences on earth. Alternatively if "man" refers to living mankind rather than to the "happy dead," the passage means that as man grows up (line 2) he forgets his earliest infancy, especially the two-year period before the sutures of his skull are closed.
8. Memory.
9. I.e., springs of forgetfulness.
1. I.e., go through the customary circuit of life.
2. Outer edges or fringes.

48

If these brief lays, of Sorrow born,
    Were taken to be such as closed
    Grave doubts and answers here proposed,
Then these were such as men might scorn.

Her [3] care is not to part and prove;   5
    She takes, when harsher moods remit,
    What slender shade of doubt may flit,
And makes it vassal unto love;

And hence, indeed, she sports with words,
    But better serves a wholesome law,   10
    And holds it sin and shame to draw
The deepest measure from the chords;

Nor dare she trust a larger lay,
    But rather loosens from the lip
    Short swallow-flights of song, that dip   15
Their wings in tears, and skim away.

* * *

50

Be near me when my light is low,
    When the blood creeps, and the nerves prick
    And tingle; and the heart is sick,
And all the wheels of being slow.

Be near me when the sensuous frame   5
    Is racked with pangs that conquer trust;
    And Time, a maniac scattering dust,
And Life, a Fury slinging flame.

Be near me when my faith is dry,
    And men the flies of latter spring,   10
    That lay their eggs, and sting and sing
And weave their petty cells and die.

Be near me when I fade away,
    To point the term of human strife,
    And on the low dark verge of life   15
The twilight of eternal day.

* * *

54

O, yet we trust that somehow good
    Will be the final goal of ill,
    To pangs of nature, sins of will,
Defects of doubt, and taints of blood;

That nothing walks with aimless feet;   5
    That not one life shall be destroyed,

3. I.e., sorrow's.

Or cast as rubbish to the void,
When God hath made the pile complete;

That not a worm is cloven in vain;
  That not a moth with vain desire   10
  Is shriveled in a fruitless fire,
Or but subserves another's gain.

Behold, we know not anything;
  I can but trust that good shall fall
  At last—far off—at last, to all,   15
And every winter change to spring.

So runs my dream; but what am I?
  An infant crying in the night;
  An infant crying for the light,
And with no language but a cry.   20

55

The wish, that of the living whole
  No life may fail beyond the grave,
  Derives it not from what we have
The likest God within the soul?

Are God and Nature then at strife,   5
  That Nature lends such evil dreams?
  So careful of the type [4] she seems,
So careless of the single life,

That I, considering everywhere
  Her secret meaning in her deeds,   10
  And finding that of fifty seeds
She often brings but one to bear,

I falter where I firmly trod,
  And falling with my weight of cares
  Upon the great world's altar-stairs   15
That slope through darkness up to God,

I stretch lame hands of faith, and grope,
  And gather dust and chaff, and call
  To what I feel is Lord of all,
And faintly trust the larger hope.[5]   20

56

"So careful of the type?" but no.
  From scarpéd [6] cliff and quarried stone
  She [7] cries, "A thousand types are gone;
I care for nothing, all shall go.

"Thou makest thine appeal to me: 5
  I bring to life, I bring to death;
  The spirit does but mean the breath:
I know no more." And he, shall he,

4. Species.
5. As expressed in lines 1–2 of this
section.

6. Cut away so that the strata are exposed.
7. Nature.

Man, her last work, who seemed so fair,
    Such splendid purpose in his eyes,
    Who rolled the psalm to wintry skies,
Who built him fanes [8] of fruitless prayer,   10

Who trusted God was love indeed
    And love Creation's final law—
    Though Nature, red in tooth and claw   15
With ravine, shrieked against his creed—

Who loved, who suffered countless ills,
    Who battled for the True, the Just,
    Be blown about the desert dust,
Or sealed within the iron hills? [9]   20

No more? A monster then, a dream,
    A discord. Dragons of the prime,
    That tare [1] each other in their slime,
Were mellow music matched with [2] him.

O life as futile, then, as frail!   25
    O for thy voice to soothe and bless!
    What hope of answer, or redress?
Behind the veil, behind the veil.

57

Peace; come away: [3] the song of woe
    Is after all an earthly song.
    Peace; come away: we do him wrong
To sing so wildly: let us go.

Come; let us go: your cheeks are pale;   5
    But half my life I leave behind.
    Methinks my friend is richly shrined;
But I shall pass, my work will fail.

Yet in these ears, till hearing dies,
    One set slow bell will seem to toll   10
    The passing of the sweetest soul
That ever looked with human eyes.

I hear it now, and o'er and o'er,
    Eternal greetings to the dead;
    And "Ave, [4] Ave, Ave," said,   15
"Adieu, adieu," forevermore.

58

In those sad words I took farewell.
    Like echoes in sepulchral halls,
    As drop by drop the water falls
In vaults and catacombs, they fell;

---

8. Temples.
9. Preserved like fossils in rock.
1. Tore (archaic).
2. In comparison with.

3. Perhaps addressed to Emily Tennyson, the poet's sister and Hallam's fiancée.
4. Hail.

And, falling, idly broke the peace   5
  Of hearts that beat from day to day,
  Half-conscious of their dying clay,
And those cold crypts where they shall cease.

The high Muse answered: "Wherefore grieve
  Thy brethren with a fruitless tear?   10
  Abide a little longer here,
And thou shalt take a nobler leave."

59

O Sorrow, wilt thou live with me
  No casual mistress, but a wife,
  My bosom friend and half of life;
As I confess it needs must be?

O Sorrow, wilt thou rule my blood,   5
  Be sometimes lovely like a bride,
  And put thy harsher moods aside,
If thou wilt have me wise and good?

My centered passion cannot move,
  Nor will it lessen from today;   10
  But I'll have leave at times to play
As with the creature of my love;

And set thee forth, for thou art mine,
  With so much hope for years to come,
  That, howsoe'er I know thee, some   15
Could hardly tell what name were thine.

* * *

64

Dost thou [5] look back on what hath been,
  As some divinely gifted man,
  Whose life in low estate began
And on a simple village green;

Who breaks his birth's invidious bar,   5
  And grasps the skirts of happy chance,
  And breasts the blows of circumstance,
And grapples with his evil star;

Who makes by force his merit known
  And lives to clutch the golden keys,[6]   10
  To mold a mighty state's decrees,
And shape the whisper of the throne;

And moving up from high to higher,
  Becomes on Fortune's crowning slope
  The pillar of a people's hope,   15
The center of a world's desire;

---

5. I.e., Hallam.   6. Badges of high public office.

Yet feels, as in a pensive dream,
　　When all his active powers are still,
　　A distant dearness in the hill,
A secret sweetness in the stream,　　　　　　　　20

The limit of his narrower fate,
　　While yet beside its vocal springs
　　He played at counselors and kings,
With one that was his earliest mate;

Who plows with pain his native lea　　　　　　　25
　　And reaps the labor of his hands,
　　Or in the furrow musing stands:
"Does my old friend remember me?"

* * *
67

When on my bed the moonlight falls,
　　I know that in thy place of rest
　　By that broad water of the west [7]
There comes a glory on the walls:

Thy marble bright in dark appears,　　　　　　　5
　　As slowly steals a silver flame
　　Along the letters of thy name,
And o'er the number of thy years.

The mystic glory swims away,
　　From off my bed the moonlight dies;　　　　　10
　　And closing eaves of wearied eyes
I sleep till dusk is dipped in gray;

And then I know the mist is drawn
　　A lucid veil from coast to coast,
　　And in the dark church like a ghost　　　　　15
Thy tablet glimmers to the dawn.

* * *
70

I cannot see the features right,
　　When on the gloom I strive to paint
　　The face I know; the hues are faint
And mix with hollow masks of night;

Cloud-towers by ghostly masons wrought,　　　　5
　　A gulf that ever shuts and gapes,
　　A hand that points, and palléd [8] shapes
In shadowy thoroughfares of thought;

And crowds that stream from yawning doors,
　　And shoals of puckered faces drive;　　　　　10

7. The Severn River.　　　　　　8. Dim or pale.

Dark bulks that tumble half alive,
And lazy lengths on boundless shores;

Till all at once beyond the will
  I hear a wizard music roll,
  And through a lattice on the soul   15
Looks thy fair face and makes it still.

71

Sleep, kinsman thou to death and trance
  And madness, thou [9] has forged at last
  A night-long present of the past
In which we went through summer France.[1]

Hadst thou such credit with the soul?   5
  Then bring an opiate trebly strong,
  Drug down the blindfold sense of wrong,
That so my pleasure may be whole;

While now we talk as once we talked
  Of men and minds, the dust of change,   10
  The days that grow to something strange,
In walking as of old we walked

Beside the river's wooded reach,
  The fortress, and the mountain ridge,
  The cataract flashing from the bridge,   15
The breaker breaking on the beach.

72

Risest thou thus, dim dawn, again,[2]
  And howlest, issuing out of night,
  With blasts that blow the poplar white,
And lash with storm the streaming pane?

Day, when my crowned estate [3] begun   5
  To pine in that reverse of doom,[4]
  Which sickened every living bloom,
And blurred the splendor of the sun;

Who usherest in the dolorous hour
  With thy quick tears that make the rose   10
  Pull sideways, and the daisy close
Her crimson fringes to the shower;

Who mightst have heaved a windless flame
  Up the deep East, or, whispering, played
  A checker-work of beam and shade   15
Along the hills, yet looked the same,

---

9. I.e., sleep.
1. In the summer of 1830, Hallam and
Tennyson went through southern France
en route to Spain.
2. September 15, 1834, the first anniversary of Hallam's death.
3. State of happiness.
4. The reversal of disaster which doom
brought upon him when Hallam died.

As wan, as chill, as wild as now;
   Day, marked as with some hideous crime,
   When the dark hand struck down through time,
And canceled nature's best: but thou,   20

Lift as thou mayst thy burthened brows
   Through clouds that drench the morning star,
   And whirl the ungarnered sheaf afar,
And sow the sky with flying boughs,

And up thy vault with roaring sound   25
   Climb thy thick noon, disastrous day;
   Touch thy dull goal of joyless gray,
And hide thy shame beneath the ground.

* * *

75

I leave thy praises unexpressed
   In verse that brings myself relief,
   And by the measure of my grief
I leave thy greatness to be guessed.

What practice howsoe'er expert   5
   In fitting aptest words to things,
   Or voice the richest-toned that sings,
Hath power to give thee as thou wert?

I care not in these fading days
   To raise a cry that lasts not long,   10
   And round thee with the breeze of song
To stir a little dust of praise.

Thy leaf has perished in the green,
   And, while we breathe beneath the sun,
   The world which credits what is done   15
Is cold to all that might have been.

So here shall silence guard thy fame;
   But somewhere, out of human view,
   Whate'er thy hands are set to do
Is wrought with tumult of acclaim.   20

* * *

78

Again at Christmas [5] did we weave
   The holly round the Christmas hearth;
   The silent snow possessed the earth,
And calmly fell our Christmas eve.

The yule clog [6] sparkled keen with frost,   5
   No wing of wind the region swept,

---

5. The second Christmas (1834) after Hallam's death.
6. Log.

But over all things brooding slept
The quiet sense of something lost.

As in the winters left behind,
   Again our ancient games had place,   10
   The mimic picture's [7] breathing grace,
And dance and song and hoodman-blind.

Who showed a token of distress?
   No single tear, no mark of pain—
   O sorrow, then can sorrow wane?   15
O grief, can grief be changed to less?

O last regret, regret can die!
   No—mixed with all this mystic frame,
   Her [8] deep relations are the same,
But with long use her tears are dry.   20

* * *
82
I wage not any feud with Death
   For changes wrought on form and face;
   No lower life that earth's embrace
May breed with him can fright my faith.

Eternal process moving on,   5
   From state to state the spirit walks;
   And these are but the shattered stalks,
Or ruined chrysalis of one.

Nor blame I Death, because he bare
   The use of virtue out of earth;   10
   I know transplanted human worth
Will bloom to profit, otherwhere.

For this alone on Death I wreak
   The wrath that garners in my heart:
   He put our lives so far apart   15
We cannot hear each other speak.
83
Dip down upon the northern shore,
   O sweet new-year [9] delaying long;
Thou doest expectant Nature wrong;
   Delaying long, delay no more.

What stays thee from the clouded noons,   5
   Thy sweetness from its proper place?
   Can trouble live with April days,
Or sadness in the summer moons?

---

7. A game in which the participants
pose in the manner of some famous
statue or painting and the spectators
try to guess what work of art is being
mimicked.
8. I.e., sorrow's.
9. Spring of 1835.

Bring orchis, bring the foxglove spire,
   The little speedwell's [1] darling blue,   10
   Deep tulips dashed with fiery dew,
Laburnums, dropping-wells of fire.

O thou, new-year, delaying long,
   Delayest the sorrow in my blood,
   That longs to burst a frozen bud   15
And flood a fresher throat with song.

84

When I contemplate all alone
   The life that had been thine below,
   And fix my thoughts on all the glow
To which thy crescent would have grown,

I see thee sitting crowned with good,   5
   A central warmth diffusing bliss
   In glance and smile, and clasp and kiss,
On all the branches of thy blood;

Thy blood, my friend, and partly mine;
   For now the day was drawing on,   10
   When thou shouldst link thy life with one
Of mine own house, and boys of thine

Had babbled "Uncle" on my knee;
   But that remorseless iron hour
   Made cypress of her orange flower,[2]   15
Despair of hope, and earth of thee.

I seem to meet their least desire,
   To clap their cheeks, to call them mine.
   I see their unborn faces shine
Beside the never-lighted fire.   20

I see myself an honored guest,
   Thy partner in the flowery walk
   Of letters, genial table talk,
Or deep dispute, and graceful jest;

While now thy prosperous labor fills   25
   The lips of men with honest praise,
   And sun by sun the happy days
Descend below the golden hills

With promise of a morn as fair;
   And all the train of bounteous hours   30
   Conduct, by paths of growing powers,
To reverence and the silver hair;

1. A blue spring flower.
2. Orange blossoms are associated with brides—here the poet's sister, Emily Tennyson, to whom Hallam had been engaged.

Till slowly worn her earthly robe,
  Her lavish mission richly wrought,
  Leaving great legacies of thought,   35
Thy spirit should fail from off the globe;

What time mine own might also flee,
  As linked with thine in love and fate,
  And, hovering o'er the dolorous strait
To the other shore, involved in thee,   40

Arrive at last the blessed goal,
  And He that died in Holy Land
  Would reach us out the shining hand,
And take us as a single soul.

What reed was that on which I leant?   45
  Ah, backward fancy, wherefore wake
  The old bitterness again, and break
The low beginnings of content?

* * *

86

Sweet after showers, ambrosial air,
  That rollest from the gorgeous gloom
  Of evening over brake and bloom
And meadow, slowly breathing bare

The round of space,[3] and rapt below   5
  Through all the dewy-tasseled wood,
  And shadowing down the hornéd flood [4]
In ripples, fan my brows and blow

The fever from my cheek, and sigh
  The full new life that feeds thy breath   10
  Throughout my frame, till Doubt and Death,
Ill brethren, let the fancy fly

From belt to belt of crimson seas
  On leagues of odor streaming far,
  To where in yonder orient star   15
A hundred spirits whisper "Peace."

87

I passed beside the reverend walls [5]
  In which of old I wore the gown;
  I roved at random through the town,
And saw the tumult of the halls;

And heard once more in college fanes   5
  The storm their high-built organs make,

---

3. Air that is slowly clearing the clouds from the sky.
4. Crescent-shaped body of water.

5. Of Trinity College, Cambridge University.

And thunder-music, rolling, shake
The prophet blazoned on the panes;

And caught once more the distant shout,
  The measured pulse of racing oars   10
  Among the willows; paced the shores
And many a bridge, and all about

The same gray flats again, and felt
  The same, but not the same; and last
  Up that long walk of limes I passed   15
To see the rooms in which he dwelt.

Another name was on the door.
  I lingered; all within was noise
  Of songs, and clapping hands, and boys
That crashed the glass and beat the floor; 20

Where once we held debate, a band
  Of youthful friends,[6] on mind and art,
  And labor, and the changing mart,
And all the framework of the land;

When one would aim an arrow fair,   25
  But send it slackly from the string;
  And one would pierce an outer ring,
And one an inner, here and there;

And last the master bowman, he,
  Would cleave the mark. A willing ear   30
  We lent him. Who but hung to hear
The rapt oration flowing free

From point to point, with power and grace
  And music in the bounds of law,[7]
  To those conclusions when we saw   35
The God within him light his face,

And seem to lift the form, and glow
  In azure orbits heavenly-wise;
  And over those ethereal eyes
The bar of Michael Angelo?[8]   40

88

Wild bird, whose warble, liquid sweet,
  Rings Eden through the budded quicks,[9]

6. The "Apostles," an undergraduate club to which Tennyson and Hallam had belonged.
7. An essay presented by Hallam at Cambridge in 1831 provides an example of his skill in theological argument (see *The Writings of Arthur Hallam*, edited by T. H. V. Motter, 1943, pp. 198–213). This essay, much admired by Tennyson, may have influenced the main argument of *In Memoriam*. In his essay Hallam develops an idea he had stated in a letter to Tennyson's sister: "It is by the heart, not by the head, that we must all be convinced of the two great fundamental truths, the reality of Love, and the reality of Evil." See also *In Memoriam*, section 109, lines 1–8 below.
8. Hallam, like Michelangelo, had a prominent ridge of bone above his eyes.
9. Hawthorn hedges. The "wild bird" is presumably a nightingale.

O tell me where the senses mix,
O tell me where the passions meet,

Whence radiate: fierce extremes employ   45
  Thy spirits in the darkening leaf,[1]
  And in the midmost heart of grief
Thy passion clasps a secret joy;

And I—my harp would prelude woe—
  I cannot all command the strings;   50
  The glory of the sum of things
Will flash along the chords and go.

                        89
Witch elms that counterchange the floor
Of this flat lawn with dusk and bright;[2]
  And thou, with all thy breadth and height
Of foliage, towering sycamore;

How often, hither wandering down,   5
  My Arthur found your shadows fair,
  And shook to all the liberal air
The dust and din and steam of town!

He brought an eye for all he saw;
  He mixed in all our simple sports;   10
  They pleased him, fresh from brawling courts
And dusty purlieus of the law.[3]

O joy to him in this retreat,
  Immantled in ambrosial dark,
  To drink the cooler air, and mark   15
The landscape winking through the heat!

O sound to rout the brood of cares,
  The sweep of scythe in morning dew,
  The gust that round the garden flew,
And tumbled half the mellowing pears!   20

O bliss, when all in circle drawn
  About him, heart and ear were fed
  To hear him, as he lay and read
The Tuscan poets [4] on the lawn!

Or in the all-golden afternoon   25
  A guest, or happy sister, sung,
  Or here she brought the harp and flung
A ballad to the brightening moon.

Nor less it pleased in livelier moods,
  Beyond the bounding hill to stray,   30

---

1. Cf. Keats' *Ode to a Nightingale* (lines 10 and 60) and his sonnet on *King Lear*, line 5.
2. Shadows of the elm tree checker the lawn at Somersby, the Tennysons' country home.
3. Hallam became a law student in London after leaving Cambridge.
4. Petrarch and Dante.

And break the livelong summer day
  With banquet in the distant woods;

Whereat we glanced from theme to theme,
  Discussed the books to love or hate,
  Or touched the changes of the state,   35
Or threaded some Socratic dream;[5]

But if I praised the busy town,
  He loved to rail against it still,
  For "ground in yonder social mill
We rub each other's angles down,   40

"And merge," he said, "in form and gloss
  The picturesque of man and man."
  We talked: the stream beneath us ran,
The wine-flask lying couched in moss,

Or cooled within the glooming wave;   45
  And last, returning from afar,
  Before the crimson-circled star [6]
Had fallen into her father's grave,

And brushing ankle-deep in flowers,
  We heard behind the woodbine veil   50
  The milk that bubbled in [7] the pail,
And buzzings of the honeyed hours.

*   *   *

91

When rosy plumelets tuft the larch,
  And rarely [8] pipes the mounted thrush,
  Or underneath the barren bush
Flits by the sea-blue bird [9] of March;

Come, wear the form by which I know   5
  Thy spirit in time among thy peers;
  The hope of unaccomplished years
Be large and lucid round thy brow.

When summer's hourly-mellowing change
  May breathe, with many roses sweet,   10
  Upon the thousand waves of wheat
That ripple round the lowly grange,

Come; not in watches of the night,
  But where the sunbeam broodeth warm,
  Come, beauteous in thine after form,   15
And like a finer light in light.

*   *   *

---

5. I.e., worked our way through some discourse of Socrates (as recorded by Plato).
6. Venus, which will sink into the west as the sun has done. According to the nebular hypothesis, planets were flung from the sun into the outer spaces of our solar system; in this sense the sun is the "father" of planets.
7. Into.
8. Exquisitely.
9. Kingfisher.

93

I shall not see thee. Dare I say
  No spirit ever brake the band
  That stays him from the native land
Where first he walked when clasped in clay? [1]

No visual shade of someone lost,   5
  But he, the Spirit himself, may come
  Where all the nerve of sense is numb,
Spirit to Spirit, Ghost to Ghost.

Oh, therefore from thy sightless [2] range
  With gods in unconjectured bliss,   10
  Oh, from the distance of the abyss
Of tenfold-complicated change,

Descend, and touch, and enter; hear
  The wish too strong for words to name,
  That in this blindness of the frame [3]   15
My Ghost may feel that thine is near.

94

How pure at heart and sound in head,
  With what divine affections bold
  Should be the man whose thought would hold
An hour's communion with the dead.

In vain shalt thou, or any, call   5
  The spirits from their golden day,
  Except, like them, thou too canst say,
My spirit is at peace with all.

They haunt the silence of the breast,
  Imaginations calm and fair,   10
  The memory like a cloudless air,
The conscience as a sea at rest;

But when the heart is full of din,
  And doubt beside the portal waits,
  They can but listen at the gates,   15
And hear the household jar within.

95

By night we lingered on the lawn,
  For underfoot the herb was dry;
  And genial warmth; and o'er the sky
The silvery haze of summer drawn;

And calm that let the tapers burn   5
  Unwavering: not a cricket chirred;
  The brook alone far off was heard,
And on the board the fluttering urn. [4]

1. I.e., when he was alive and clothed   3. The living body.
in flesh.   4. Urn to boil water for tea or coffee.
2. Invisible.

And bats went round in fragrant skies,
    And wheeled or lit the filmy shapes [5]
    That haunt the dusk, with ermine capes
And woolly breasts and beaded eyes;

While now we sang old songs that pealed
    From knoll to knoll, where, couched at ease,
    The white kine glimmered, and the trees
Laid their dark arms [6] about the field.

But when those others, one by one,
    Withdrew themselves from me and night,
    And in the house light after light
Went out, and I was all alone,

A hunger seized my heart; I read
    Of that glad year which once had been,
    In those fallen leaves which kept their green,
The noble letters of the dead.

And strangely on the silence broke
    The silent-speaking words, and strange
    Was love's dumb cry defying change
To test his worth; and strangely spoke

The faith, the vigor, bold to dwell
    On doubts that drive the coward back,
    And keen through wordy snares to track
Suggestion to her inmost cell.

So word by word, and line by line,
    The dead man touched me from the past,
    And all at once it seemed at last
The [7] living soul was flashed on mine,

And mine in this was wound, and whirled
    About empyreal heights of thought,
    And came on that which is, and caught
The deep pulsations of the world,

Aeonian music [8] measuring out
    The steps of Time—the shocks of Chance—
    The blows of Death. At length my trance
Was canceled, stricken through with doubt.[9]

10

15

20

25

30

35

40

5. The white-winged night moths called ermine moths.
6. Cast the shadows of their branches.
7. Printed "His" in the first edition; and line 37 read, in the first edition, "And mine in his was wound."
8. The music of the universe which has pulsated for aeons of time.
9. In a letter of 1874 replying to an enquiry about his experience of mystical trances, Tennyson wrote: "A kind of waking trance I have frequently had, quite up from boyhood, when I have been all alone. This has generally come upon me through repeating my own name two or three times to myself silently, till all at once, as it were out of the intensity of the consciousness of individuality, the individuality itself seemed to dissolve and fade away into boundless being, and this not a confused state, but the clearest of the clearest, the surest of the surest, the weirdest of the weirdest, utterly beyond words,

Vague words! but ah, how hard to frame   45
    In matter-molded forms of speech,
    Or even for intellect to reach
Through memory that which I became.

Till now the doubtful dusk revealed
    The knolls once more where, couched at ease,   50
    The white kine glimmered, and the trees
Laid their dark arms about the field;

And sucked from out the distant gloom
    A breeze began to tremble o'er
    The large leaves of the sycamore,   55
And fluctuate all the still perfume,

And gathering freshlier overhead,
    Rocked the full-foliaged elms, and swung
    The heavy-folded rose, and flung
The lilies to and fro, and said,   60

"The dawn, the dawn," and died away;
    And East and West, without a breath,
    Mixed their dim lights, like life and death,
To broaden into boundless day.

96

You say, but with no touch of scorn,
    Sweet-hearted, you,[1] whose light blue eyes
    Are tender over drowning flies,
You tell me, doubt is Devil-born.

I know not: one [2] indeed I knew   5
    In many a subtle question versed,
    Who touched a jarring lyre at first,
But ever strove to make it true;

Perplexed in faith, but pure in deeds,
    At last he beat his music out.   10
    There lives more faith in honest doubt,
Believe me, than in half the creeds.

He fought his doubts and gathered strength,
    He would not make his judgment blind,
    He faced the specters of the mind   15
And laid them; thus he came at length

To find a stronger faith his own,
    And Power was with him in the night,

where death was an almost laughable impossibility, the loss of personality (if so it were) seeming no extinction but the only true life. * * * This might * * * be the state which St. Paul describes, 'Whether in the body I cannot tell, or whether out of the body I cannot tell.' * * * I am ashamed of my feeble description. Have I not said the state is utterly beyond words? But in a moment, when I come back to my normal state of 'sanity,' I am ready to fight for *mein liebes Ich* [my dear self], and hold that it will last for aeons of aeons."—*Alfred Lord Tennyson, A Memoir*, 1897, I, 320.
1. A woman of simple faith.
2. Hallam.

Which makes the darkness and the light,
And dwells not in the light alone,   20

But in the darkness and the cloud,[3]
As over Sinaï's peaks of old,
While Israel made their gods of gold,
Although the trumpet blew so loud.

* * *

99

Risest thou thus, dim dawn, again,[4]
So loud with voices of the birds,
So thick with lowings of the herds,
Day, when I lost the flower of men;

Who tremblest through thy darkling red   5
On yon swollen brook that bubbles fast [5]
By meadows breathing of the past,
And woodlands holy to the dead;

Who murmurest in the foliage eaves
A song that slights the coming care,[6]   10
And Autumn laying here and there
A fiery finger on the leaves;

Who wakenest with thy balmy breath
To myriads on the genial earth,
Memories of bridal, or of birth,[7]   15
And unto myriads more, of death.

Oh, wheresoever those [8] may be,
Betwixt the slumber of the poles,
Today they count as kindred souls;
They know me not, but mourn with me.   20

* * *

103

On that last night before we went
From out the doors where I was bred,[9]
I dreamed a vision of the dead,
Which left my after-morn content.

Methought I dwelt within a hall,   5
And maidens with me; distant hills
From hidden summits fed with rills
A river sliding by the wall.

3. See Exodus xix.16–25. After veiling Mount Sinai in a "cloud" of smoke, God addressed Moses from the darkness.
4. September 15, 1835, the second anniversary of Hallam's death.
5. Reflections of the clouded red light of dawn quiver on the surface of the fast-moving water.
6. I.e., disregards future events such as death or the coming of autumn. Cf. Shelley's *Ode to the West Wind.*

7. Cf. *Epilogue,* below, lines 117–28.
8. I.e., the "myriads" who remember death.
9. In 1837 Tennyson and his family moved away from their home in Lincolnshire, which had been closely associated with his friendship with Hallam. In section 104 the move seems to occur in 1835, the year of the third Christmas after Hallam's death.

The hall with harp and carol rang.
    They sang of what is wise and good   10
    And graceful. In the center stood
A statue veiled, to which they sang;

And which, though veiled, was known to me,
    The shape of him I loved, and love
    Forever. Then flew in a dove   15
And brought a summons from the sea; [1]

And when they learnt that I must go,
    They wept and wailed, but led the way
    To where the little shallop [2] lay
At anchor in the flood below;   20

And on by many a level mead,
    And shadowing bluff that made the banks,
    We glided winding under ranks
Of iris and the golden reed;

And still as vaster grew the shore   25
    And rolled the floods in grander space,
    The maidens gathered strength and grace
And presence, lordlier than before;

And I myself, who sat apart
    And watched them, waxed in every limb;   30
    I felt the thews of Anakim, [3]
The pulses of a Titan's heart;

As one would sing the death of war,
    And one would chant the history
    Of that great race which is to be, [4]   35
And one the shaping of a star;

Until the forward-creeping tides
    Began to foam, and we to draw
    From deep to deep, to where we saw
A great ship lift her shining sides. [5]   40

The man we loved was there on deck,
    But thrice as large as man he bent
    To greet us. Up the side I went,
And fell in silence on his neck;

Whereat those maidens with one mind   45
    Bewailed their lot; I did them wrong:

1. Cf. *Crossing the Bar:* "And one clear call for me."
2. A light open boat.
3. Plural of *Anak;* i.e., a reference to the giant sons of Anak. See Numbers xiii.33. The Titans (line 32) were giants of Greek mythology.
4. See the account of the "crowning race" in *Epilogue,* below, lines 128–44.
5. Cf. *Morte d'Arthur,* lines 255–322, in which Bedivere is left behind as Arthur's barge, the ship of death, sails away. In the present dream vision, not only is the speaker taken aboard but also his companions, who represent the creative arts of this world—"all the human powers and talents that do not pass with life but go along with it," as Tennyson said of this passage.

"We served thee here," they said, "so long,
  And wilt thou leave us now behind?"

So rapt [6] I was, they could not win
  An answer from my lips, but he   50
  Replying, "Enter likewise ye
And go with us:" they entered in.

And while the wind began to sweep
  A music out of sheet and shroud,
  We steered her toward a crimson cloud   55
That landlike slept along the deep.

104

The time draws near the birth of Christ; [7]
  The moon is hid, the night is still;
  A single church below the hill
Is pealing, folded in the mist.

A single peal of bells below,   5
  That wakens at this hour of rest
  A single murmur in the breast,
That these are not the bells I know.

Like strangers' voices here they sound,
  In lands where not a memory strays,   10
  Nor landmark breathes of other days,
But all is new unhallowed ground.

* * *
106

Ring out, wild bells, to the wild sky,
  The flying cloud, the frosty light:
  The year is dying in the night;
Ring out, wild bells, and let him die.

Ring out the old, ring in the new,   5
  Ring, happy bells, across the snow:
  The year is going, let him go;
Ring out the false, ring in the true.

Ring out the grief that saps the mind,
  For those that here we see no more;   10
  Ring out the feud of rich and poor,
Ring in redress to all mankind.

Ring out a slowly dying cause,
  And ancient forms of party strife;
  Ring in the nobler modes of life,   15
With sweeter manners, purer laws.

Ring out the want, the care, the sin,
  The faithless coldness of the times;

---

6. Entranced.   7. See note 9 to section 103.

Ring out, ring out my mournful rhymes,
But ring the fuller minstrel in.   20

Ring out false pride in place and blood,
    The civic slander and the spite;
    Ring in the love of truth and right,
Ring in the common love of good.

Ring out old shapes of foul disease;   25
    Ring out the narrowing lust of gold;
    Ring out the thousand wars of old,
Ring in the thousand years of peace.

Ring in the valiant man and free,
    The larger heart, the kindlier hand;   30
    Ring out the darkness of the land,
Ring in the Christ that is to be.[8]

107

It is the day when he was born,[9]
    A bitter day that early sank
    Behind a purple-frosty bank
Of vapor, leaving night forlorn.

The time admits not flowers or leaves   5
    To deck the banquet. Fiercely flies
    The blast of North and East, and ice
Makes daggers at the sharpened eaves,

And bristles all the brakes and thorns
    To yon hard crescent, as she hangs   10
    Above the wood which grides [1] and clangs
Its leafless ribs and iron horns

Together, in the drifts [2] that pass
    To darken on the rolling brine
    That breaks the coast. But fetch the wine,   15
Arrange the board and brim the glass;

Bring in great logs and let them lie,
    To make a solid core of heat;
    Be cheerful-minded, talk and treat
Of all things even as he were by;   20

We keep the day. With festal cheer,
    With books and music, surely we
    Will drink to him, whate'er he be,
And sing the songs he loved to hear.

* * *

8. These allusions to the second coming of Christ and to the millennium are derived from Revelation xx, but Tennyson has interpreted the Biblical account in his own way. He once told his son of his conviction that "the forms of Christian religion would alter; but that the spirit of Christ would still grow from more to more."
9. February 1.
1. Clashes with a strident noise.
2. Either cloud-drifts or clouds of snow.

109

Heart-affluence in discursive talk
   From household fountains never dry;
   The critic clearness of an eye
That saw through all the Muses' walk; [3]

Seraphic intellect and force   5
   To seize and throw the doubts of man;
   Impassioned logic, which outran
The hearer in its fiery course;

High nature amorous of the good,
   But touched with no ascetic gloom;   10
   And passion pure in snowy bloom
Through all the years of April blood;

A love of freedom rarely felt,
   Of freedom in her regal seat
   Of England; not the schoolboy heat,   15
The blind hysterics of the Celt; [4]

And manhood fused with female grace
   In such a sort, the child would twine
   A trustful hand, unasked, in thine,
And find his comfort in thy face;   20

All these have been, and thee mine eyes
   Have looked on: if they looked in vain,
   My shame is greater who remain,
Nor let thy wisdom make me wise.

* * *

115

Now fades the last long streak of snow,
   Now burgeons every maze of quick [5]
   About the flowering squares,[6] and thick
By ashen roots the violets blow.

Now rings the woodland loud and long,   5
   The distance takes a lovelier hue,
   And drowned in yonder living blue
The lark becomes a sightless song.

Now dance the lights on lawn and lea,
   The flocks are whiter down the vale,   10
   And milkier every milky sail
On winding stream or distant sea;

Where now the seamew pipes, or dives
   In yonder greening gleam, and fly
   The happy birds, that change their sky   15
To build and brood, that live their lives

3. The realm of art and literature.
4. In particular the French at the time
of the Revolution of 1789. See also
section 127, lines 7–8.
5. In hawthorn hedges.
6. Fields.

From land to land; and in my breast
   Spring wakens too, and my regret
   Becomes an April violet,
And buds and blossoms like the rest.   20

* * *

118

Contémplate all this work of Time,
   The giant laboring in his youth;
   Nor dream of human love and truth,
As dying Nature's earth and lime;

But trust that those we call the dead   5
   Are breathers of an ampler day
   For ever nobler ends. They [7] say,
The solid earth whereon we tread

In tracts of fluent heat began,
   And grew to seeming-random forms,   10
   The seeming prey of cyclic storms,
Till at the last arose the man;

Who throve and branched from clime to clime,
   The herald of a higher race,
   And of himself in higher place,   15
If so he type [8] this work of time

Within himself, from more to more;
   Or, crowned with attributes of woe
   Like glories, move his course, and show
That life is not as idle ore,   20

But iron dug from central gloom,
   And heated hot with burning fears,
   And dipped in baths of hissing tears,
And battered with the shocks of doom

To shape and use. Arise and fly   25
   The reeling Faun, the sensual feast;
   Move upward, working out the beast,
And let the ape and tiger die.

119

Doors, where my heart was used to beat
   So quickly, not as one that weeps
   I come once more; the city sleeps;
I smell the meadow in the street;

I hear a chirp of birds; I see   5
   Betwixt the black fronts long-withdrawn
   A light blue lane of early dawn,
And think of early days and thee,

---

7. Geologists and astronomers.   8. Emulate, prefigure as a type.

And bless thee, for thy lips are bland,
   And bright the friendship of thine eye;   10
   And in my thoughts with scarce a sigh
I take the pressure of thine hand.

120

I trust I have not wasted breath:
   I think we are not wholly brain,
   Magnetic mockeries; [9] not in vain,
Like Paul [1] with beasts, I fought with Death;

Not only cunning casts in clay: 5
   Let Science prove we are, and then
   What matters Science unto men,
At least to me? I would not stay.

Let him, the wiser man [2] who springs
   Hereafter, up from childhood shape   10
   His action like the greater ape,
But I was *born* to other things.

121

Sad Hesper [3] o'er the buried sun
   And ready, thou, to die with him,
   Thou watchest all things ever dim
And dimmer, and a glory done.

The team is loosened from the wain, [4]   5
   The boat is drawn upon the shore;
   Thou listenest to the closing door,
And life is darkened in the brain.

Bright Phosphor, [5] fresher for the night,
   By thee the world's great work is heard   10
   Beginning, and the wakeful bird;
Behind thee comes the greater light.

The market boat is on the stream,
   And voices hail it from the brink;
   Thou hear'st the village hammer clink,   15
And see'st the moving of the team.

Sweet Hesper-Phosphor, double name [6]
   For what is one, the first, the last,
   Thou, like my present and my past,
Thy place is changed; thou art the same.   20

* * *

9. Mechanisms operated by responses to electrical forces.
1. I Corinthians xv.32.
2. Spoken ironically.
3. Evening star.
4. Hay wagon.
5. Morning star.
6. The same planet, Venus, is both evening star and morning star.

123

There rolls the deep where grew the tree.
    O earth, what changes hast thou seen!
    There where the long street roars hath been
The stillness of the central sea.[7]

The hills are shadows, and they flow   5
    From form to form, and nothing stands;
    They melt like mist, the solid lands,
Like clouds they shape themselves and go.

But in my spirit will I dwell,
    And dream my dream, and hold it true;   10
    For though my lips may breathe adieu,
I cannot think the thing farewell.

124

That which we dare invoke to bless;
    Our dearest faith; our ghastliest doubt;
    He, They, One, All; within, without;
The Power in darkness whom we guess—

I found Him not in world or sun,   5
    Or eagle's wing, or insect's eye,[8]
    Nor through the questions men may try,
The petty cobwebs we have spun.

If e'er when faith had fallen asleep,
    I heard a voice, "believe no more,"   10
    And heard an ever-breaking shore
That tumbled in the Godless deep,

A warmth within the breast would melt
    The freezing reason's colder part,
    And like a man in wrath the heart   15
Stood up and answered, "I have felt."

No, like a child in doubt and fear:
    But that blind clamor made me wise;
    Then was I as a child that cries,
But, crying, knows his father near;   20

And what I am beheld again
    What is, and no man understands;

<hr>

7. Cf. a passage from Sir Charles Lyell's *The Principles of Geology* (1832), a book well-known to Tennyson. In discussing the "interchange of sea and land" that has occurred "on the surface of our globe" Lyell remarks: "In the Mediterranean alone, many flourishing inland towns and a still greater number of ports now stand where the sea rolled its waves since the era when civilized nations first grew in Europe."

8. He does not discover satisfactory proof of God's existence in the 18th-century argument that because objects in nature are designed there must exist a designer.

And out of darkness came the hands
That reach through nature, molding men.

* * *

126

Love is and was my lord and king,
  And in his presence I attend
  To hear the tidings of my friend,
Which every hour his couriers bring.

Love is and was my king and lord,   5
  And will be, though as yet I keep
  Within the court on earth, and sleep
Encompassed by his faithful guard,

And hear at times a sentinel
  Who moves about from place to place,   10
  And whispers to the worlds of space,
In the deep night, that all is well.

127

And all is well, though faith and form [9]
  Be sundered in the night of fear;
  Well roars the storm to those that hear
A deeper voice across the storm,

Proclaiming social truth shall spread,   5
  And justice, even though thrice again
  The red fool-fury of the Seine
Should pile her barricades with dead.[1]

But ill for him that wears a crown,
  And him, the lazar,[2] in his rags!   10
  They tremble, the sustaining crags;
The spires of ice are toppled down,

And molten up, and roar in flood;
  The fortress crashes from on high,
  The brute earth lightens [3] to the sky,   15
And the great Aeon [4] sinks in blood,

And compassed by the fires of hell,
  While thou, dear spirit, happy star,
  O'erlook'st the tumult from afar,
And smilest, knowing all is well.   20

* * *

9. Traditional institutions through which faith was formerly expressed, such as the Church. See Carlyle's essay, *Characteristics,* above.
1. Revolutionary uprisings in France, in each of which a king lost his throne (line 9): in 1789 against Louis XVI, in 1830 against Charles X, and in 1848 against Louis Philippe. The third (line 6) would have been a prophesy if, as Tennyson recollected, section 126 was finished at a date earlier than 1848.
2. Pauper suffering from disease.
3. Is lit up by fire.
4. A vast tract of time, here perhaps modern western civilization.

129

Dear friend, far off, my lost desire,
   So far, so near in woe and weal,
   O loved the most, when most I feel
There is a lower and a higher;

Known and unknown, human, divine;   5
   Sweet human hand and lips and eye;
   Dear heavenly friend that canst not die,
Mine, mine, forever, ever mine;

Strange friend, past, present, and to be;
   Loved deeplier, darklier understood;   10
   Behold, I dream a dream of good,
And mingle all the world with thee.

130

Thy voice is on the rolling air;
   I hear thee where the waters run;
   Thou standest in the rising sun,
And in the setting thou art fair.

What art thou then? I cannot guess;   5
   But though I seem in star and flower
   To feel thee some diffusive power,
I do not therefore love thee less.

My love involves the love before;
   My love is vaster passion now;   10
   Tho' mix'd with God and Nature thou,
I seem to love thee more and more.

Far off thou art, but ever nigh;
   I have thee still, and I rejoice;
   I prosper, circled with thy voice;   15
I shall not lose thee tho' I die.

131

O living will [5] that shalt endure
   When all that seems shall suffer shock,
   Rise in the spiritual rock,[6]
Flow through our deeds and make them pure,

That we may lift from out of dust   5
   A voice as unto him that hears,
   A cry above the conquered years
To one that with us works, and trust,

With faith that comes of self-control,
   The truths that never can be proved   10
   Until we close with all we loved,
And all we flow from, soul in soul.

---

5. Tennyson later commented that he   6. Christ (see I Corinthians x.4).
meant here the moral will of mankind.

From *Epilogue* [7]

* * *

And rise, O moon, from yonder down,
  Till over down and over dale
  All night the shining vapor sail
And pass the silent-lighted town,

The white-faced halls, the glancing rills,   5
  And catch at every mountain head,
  And o'er the friths [8] that branch and spread
Their sleeping silver through the hills;

And touch with shade the bridal doors,
  With tender gloom the roof, the wall;   10
  And breaking let the splendor fall
To spangle all the happy shores

By which they rest, and ocean sounds,
  And, star and system rolling past,
  A soul shall draw from out the vast   15
And strike his being into bounds,

And, moved through life of lower phase,
  Result in man,[9] be born and think,
  And act and love, a closer link
Betwixt us and the crowning race   20

Of those that, eye to eye, shall look
  On knowledge; under whose command
  Is Earth and Earth's, and in their hand
Is Nature like an open book;

No longer half-akin to brute,   25
  For all we thought and loved and did,
  And hoped, and suffered, is but seed
Of what in them is flower and fruit;

Whereof the man that with me trod
  This planet was a noble type   30
  Appearing ere the times were ripe,
That friend of mine who lives in God,

That God, which ever lives and loves,
  One God, one law, one element,
  And one far-off divine event,   35
To which the whole creation moves.

1833–50   1850

7. The *Epilogue* describes the wedding day of Tennyson's sister Cecilia to Edmund Lushington. At the conclusion (reprinted here) the speaker reflects upon their moonlit wedding night and the kind of offspring which will result from their union.

8. Inlets of the sea.
9. A child will be conceived and will develop in embryo through various stages. This development is similar to the evolution of man from the animal to the human level and perhaps to a future higher stage of development.

The Charge of the Light Brigade[1]

1

Half a league, half a league,
Half a league onward,
All in the valley of Death
   Rode the six hundred.
"Forward the Light Brigade!   5
Charge for the guns!" he said.
Into the valley of Death
   Rode the six hundred.

2

"Forward, the Light Brigade!"
Was there a man dismayed?   10
Not though the soldier knew
   Someone had blundered.
Theirs not to make reply,
Theirs not to reason why,
Theirs but to do and die.   15
Into the valley of Death
   Rode the six hundred.

3

Cannon to right of them,
Cannon to left of them,
Cannon in front of them   20
   Volleyed and thundered;
Stormed at with shot and shell,
Boldly they rode and well,
Into the jaws of Death,
Into the mouth of hell   25
   Rode the six hundred.

4

Flashed all their sabers bare,
Flashed as they turned in air
Sab'ring the gunners there,
Charging an army, while   30
   All the world wondered.
Plunged in the battery smoke
Right through the line they broke;
Cossack and Russian
Reeled from the saber stroke   35
   Shattered and sundered.

1. During the Crimean War, owing to confusion of orders, a brigade of British cavalry charged some entrenched batteries of Russian artillery. This blunder cost the lives of three fourths of the 600 horsemen engaged (see Cecil Woodham-Smith, *The Reason Why*, 1954). Tennyson rapidly composed his "ballad" (as he called the poem) after reading an account of the battle in a newspaper.

Then they rode back, but not,
  Not the six hundred.

        5

Cannon to right of them,
Cannon to left of them,   40
Cannon behind them
  Volleyed and thundered;
Stormed at with shot and shell,
While horse and hero fell,
They that had fought so well   45
Came through the jaws of Death,
Back from the mouth of hell,
All that was left of them,
  Left of six hundred.

        6

When can their glory fade?   50
O the wild charge they made!
  All the world wondered.
Honor the charge they made!
Honor the Light Brigade,
  Noble six hundred!   55

1854   1854

From Maud[1]

VIII

She came to the village church,
And sat by a pillar alone;
An angel watching an urn
Wept over her, carved in stone;
And once, but once, she lifted her eyes,   305
And suddenly, sweetly, strangely blushed
To find they were met by my own;
And suddenly, sweetly, my heart beat stronger
And thicker, until I heard no longer
The snowy-banded, dilettante,   310
Delicate-handed priest intone;
And thought, is it pride? and mused and sighed,
"No surely, now it cannot be pride."

* * *

1. The speaker is a young man, living alone in the country, whose disillusionment after his father's suicide has left him full of a bitterness that borders on madness. He is restored to sanity and intense happiness when he discovers that Maud, the beautiful daughter of a local landowner, accepts his love for him. The following selections tell of his proposal to her and her acceptance of him. Later in the poem he loses Maud after killing her brother in a duel.

    Maud was a poem that Tennyson especially enjoyed reading aloud. He called it "a little *Hamlet*," but it is closer to *Romeo and Juliet* in its picture of love in the midst of family feuds.

XVI

Catch not my breath, O clamorous heart,
Let not my tongue be a thrall to my eye,
For I must tell her before we part,
I must tell her, or die.

* * *

XVIII

1

I have led her home, my love, my only friend.
There is none like her, none.   600
And never yet so warmly ran my blood
And sweetly, on and on
Calming itself to the long-wished-for end,
Full to the banks, close on the promised good.

2

None like her, none.   605
Just now the dry-tongued laurels' pattering talk
Seemed her light foot along the garden walk,
And shook my heart to think she comes once more.
But even then I heard her close the door;
The gates of heaven are closed, and she is gone.   610

3

There is none like her, none,
Nor will be when our summers have deceased.
O, art thou[2] sighing for Lebanon
In the long breeze that streams to thy delicious East,
Sighing for Lebanon,   615
Dark cedar, though thy limbs have here increased,
Upon a pastoral slope as fair,
And looking to the South and fed
With honeyed rain and delicate air,
And haunted by the starry head   620
Of her whose gentle will has changed my fate,
And made my life a perfumed altar-flame;
And over whom thy darkness must have spread
With such delight as theirs of old, thy great
Forefathers of the thornless garden, there   625
Shadowing the snow-limbed Eve from whom she came?

4

Here will I lie, while these long branches sway,
And you fair stars that crown a happy day
Go in and out as if at merry play,
Who am no more so all forlorn   630
As when it seemed far better to be born
To labor and the mattock-hardened hand
Than nursed at ease and brought to understand
A sad astrology,[3] the boundless plan

2. The cedar-of-Lebanon tree in Maud's   3. Astronomy.
garden.

That makes you tyrants in your iron skies,   635
Innumerable, pitiless, passionless eyes,
Cold fires, yet with power to burn and brand
His nothingness into man.

5

But now shine on, and what care I,
Who in this stormy gulf have found a pearl   640
The countercharm of space and hollow sky,[4]
And do accept my madness, and would die
To save from some slight shame one simple girl?—

6

Would die, for sullen-seeming Death may give
More life to Love than is or ever was   645
In our low world, where yet 'tis sweet to live.
Let no one ask me how it came to pass;
It seems that I am happy, that to me
A livelier emerald twinkles in the grass,
A purer sapphire melts into the sea.   650

7

Not die, but live a life of truest breath,
And teach true life to fight with mortal wrongs.
O, why should Love, like men in drinking songs,
Spice his fair banquet with the dust of death?
Make answer, Maud my bliss,   655
Maud made my Maud by that long loving kiss,
Life of my life, wilt thou not answer this?
"The dusky strand of Death inwoven here
With dear Love's tie, makes Love himself more dear."

8

Is that enchanted moan only the swell   660
Of the long waves that roll in yonder bay?
And hark the clock within, the silver knell
Of twelve sweet hours that passed in bridal white,
And died to live, long as my pulses play;
But now by this my love has closed her sight   665
And given false death[5] her hand, and stolen away
To dreamful wastes where footless fancies dwell
Among the fragments of the golden day.
May nothing there her maiden grace affright!
Dear heart, I feel with thee the drowsy spell.   670
My bride to be, my evermore delight,
My own heart's heart, my ownest own, farewell;
It is but for a little space I go.
And ye[6] meanwhile far over moor and fell
Beat to the noiseless music of the night!   675
Has our whole earth gone nearer to the glow
Of your soft splendors that you look so bright?
I have climbed nearer out of lonely hell.

4. Something that offsets his former
fears of the vastness of space revealed
by modern astronomy.
5. I.e., sleep.
6. The stars.

Beat, happy stars, timing with things below,
Beat with my heart more blest than heart can tell,   680
Blest, but for some dark undercurrent woe
That seems to draw—but it shall not be so;
Let all be well, be well.

* * *

1855

In the Valley of Cauteretz[7]

All along the valley, stream that flashest white,
Deepening thy voice with the deepening of the night,
All along the valley, where thy waters flow,
I walked with one I loved two and thirty years ago.
All along the valley, while I walked today,   5
The two and thirty years were a mist that rolls away;
For all along the valley, down thy rocky bed,
Thy living voice to me was as the voice of the dead,
And all along the valley, by rock and cave and tree,
The voice of the dead was a living voice to me.   10

1861   1864

From Idylls of the King
Dedication[1]

These to His Memory—since he held them dear,
Perchance as finding there unconsciously
Some image of himself—I dedicate,
I dedicate, I consecrate with tears—
These Idylls.

            And indeed he seems to me   5
Scarce other than my king's ideal knight,
"Who reverenced his conscience as his king;
Whose glory was, redressing human wrong;
Who spake no slander, no, nor listened to it;
Who loved one only and who clave to her—"[2]   10

7. A valley in the French Pyrenees visited by Tennyson and Hallam in 1830 and revisited by Tennyson in 1861.
1. Tennyson's dedication of his *Idylls* to Prince Albert, Queen Victoria's husband, who had died in 1861, could be dismissed as a mere formality on the part of the poet laureate; but it was more. Because of his earnest dedication to duty, his statesmanship, his work for peace, Albert seemed to Tennyson to have been almost a modern reincarnation of King Arthur.

Concerning the *Idylls* as a poem, see the Tennyson introduction. *Morte d'Arthur*, included above, may be read as a representative *Idyll;* in a slightly revised form, it became the final book of the twelve-book cycle.
2. A paraphrase of King Arthur's words (*Idylls* XI.472) summarizing the ideals of the knights of the Round Table.

Her—over all whose realms to their last isle,
Commingled with the gloom of imminent war,
The shadow of his loss drew like eclipse,
Darkening the world. We have lost him; he is gone.
We know him now; all narrow jealousies   15
Are silent, and we see him as he moved,
How modest, kindly, all-accomplished, wise,
With what sublime repression of himself,
And in what limits, and how tenderly;
Not swaying to this faction or to that;   20
Not making his high place the lawless perch
Of winged ambitions, nor a vantage-ground
For pleasure; but through all this tract of years
Wearing the white flower of a blameless life,
Before a thousand peering littlenesses,   25
In that fierce light which beats upon a throne,
And blackens every blot: for where is he,
Who dares foreshadow for an only son
A lovelier life, a more unstained, than his?
Or how should England dreaming of *his* sons   30
Hope more for these than some inheritance
Of such a life, a heart, a mind as thine,
Thou noble Father of her Kings to be,
Laborious for her people and her poor—
Voice in the rich dawn of an ampler day—   35
Far-sighted summoner of War and Waste
To fruitful strifes and rivalries of peace—
Sweet nature gilded by the gracious gleam
Of letters, dear to Science, dear to Art,
Dear to thy land[3] and ours, a Prince indeed,   40
Beyond all titles, and a household name,
Hereafter, through all times, Albert the Good.

    Break not, O woman's-heart, but still endure;
Break not, for thou art Royal, but endure,
Remembering all the beauty of that star   45
Which shone so close beside Thee that ye made
One light together, but has passed and leaves
The Crown a lonely splendor.

                May all love,
His love, unseen but felt, o'ershadow thee,
The love of all thy sons encompass thee,   50
The love of all thy daughters cherish thee,
The love of all thy people comfort thee,
Till God's love set thee at his side again!

                            1862

---

3. Albert was a native of Saxe-Coburg in Germany.

In Love, If Love Be Love[4]

In love, if love be Love, if love be ours,
Faith and unfaith can ne'er be equal powers:
Unfaith in aught is want of faith in all.

It is the little rift[5] within the lute,
That by and by will make the music mute,   5
And ever widening slowly silence all.

The little rift within the lover's lute
Or little pitted speck in garnered fruit,
That rotting inward slowly molders all.

It is not worth the keeping: let it go: 10
But shall it? answer, darling, answer, no.
And trust me not at all or all in all.

Northern Farmer[1]

NEW STYLE

1

Dosn't thou 'ear my 'erse's[2] legs, as they canters awaäy?
Proputty,[3] proputty, proputty—that's what I 'ears 'em saäy.
Proputty, proputty, proputty—Sam, thou's an ass for thy paaïns;
Theer's moor sense i' one o' 'is legs, nor in all thy braaïns.

2

Woä—theer's a craw[4] to pluck wi' tha, Sam: yon's Parson's 'ouse—
Dosn't thou knaw that a man mun be eäther a man or a mouse? 6
Time to think on it then; for thou'll be twenty to weeäk.[5]
Proputty, proputty—woä then, woä—let ma 'ear mysén[6] speäk.

3

Me an' thy muther, Sammy, 'as beän a-talkin' o' thee;
Thou's beän talkin' to muther, an' she beän a-tellin' it me.   10
Thou'll not marry for munny—thou's sweet upo' Parson's lass—
Noä—thou'll marry for luvv—an' we boäth on us thinks tha an ass.

4

Seeäed her todaäy goä by—Saäint's-daäy—they was ringing the bells.
She's a beauty, thou thinks—an' soä is scoors o' gells,[7]

4. Sung by Vivien in her successful attempt to seduce Merlin, the magician (*Idylls* VI.385 ff.).
5. Crack.
1. This monologue exemplifies the diversity of Tennyson's talents. A passionate attachment to land and property, which was portrayed sympathetically by Wordsworth in *Michael*, is here represented humorously. The harsh common sense of the farmer's attitude towards love and marriage is reinforced by his jaw-breaking north-English dialect.

This is the second of a pair of monologues in dialect. In the first, *Northern Farmer: Old Style*, the speaker is a bailiff who has spent his life supervising the farmlands of a wealthy squire. In the second, the "new style" farmer is himself an independent landowner.
2. Horse's.
3. Property.
4. Crow.
5. This week.
6. Myself.
7. Scores of girls.

Them as 'as munny an' all—wot's a beauty?—the flower as blaws. 15
But proputty, proputty sticks, an' proputty, proputty graws.

5
Do'ant be stunt;[8] taäke time. I knaws what maäkes tha sa mad.
Warn't I craäzed fur the lasses mysén when I wur a lad?
But I knawed a Quaäker feller as often 'as towd[9] ma this:
"Doänt thou marry for munny, but goä wheer munny is!" 20

6
An' I went wheer munny war; an' thy muther coom to 'and,
Wi' lots o' munny laaïd by, an' a nicetish bit o' land.
Maäybe she warn't a beauty—I niver giv it a thowt—
But warn't she as good to cuddle an' kïss as a lass as 'ant nowt?[1]

7
Parson's lass 'ant nowt, an' shc weänt 'a nowt[2] when 'e's deäd, 25
Mun be a guvness, lad, or summut, and addle[3] her breäd.
Why? fur 'e's nobbut[4] a curate, an' weänt niver get hissén clear,
An' 'e maäde the bed as 'e ligs[5] on afoor 'e coomed to thc shere.

8
An' thin 'e coomed to the parish wi' lots o' Varsity debt,
Stook to his taaïl they did, an' 'e 'ant got slut on 'em[6] yet. 30
An' 'e ligs on 'is back i' the grip,[7] wi' noän to lend 'im a shuvv,
Woorse nor a far-weltered yowc;[8] fur, Sammy, 'e married fur luvv.

9
Luvv? what's luvv? thou can luvv thy lass an' 'er munny too,
Maäkin' 'em goä togither, as they've good right to do.
Couldn' I luvv thy muther by cause o' 'er munny laaïd by? 35
Naäy—fur I luvved 'er a vast sight moor fur it; reäson why.

10
Aye, an' thy muther says thou wants to marry the lass,
Cooms of a gentleman burn;[9] an' we boäth on us thinks tha an ass.
Woä then, proputty, wiltha?—an ass as near as mays nowt[1]—
Woä then, wiltha? dangtha!—the bees is as fell as owt.[2] 40

11
Breäk me a bit o' the esh[3] for his 'eäd, lad, out o' the fence!
Gentleman burn! what's gentleman burn? is it shillins an' pence?
Proputty, proputty's ivrything 'ere, an', Sammy, I'm blest
If it isn't the saäme oop yonder, fur them as 'as it's the best.

12
Tis'n them as 'as munny as breäks into 'ouses an' steäls, 45
Them as 'as coäts to their backs an' taäkes their regular meäls.
Noä, but it's them as niver knaws wheer a meäl's to be 'ad.
Taäke my word for it, Sammy, the poor in a loomp is bad.

8. Stubborn.	7. Ditch.
9. Told.	8. Ewe lying on her back.
1. Has nothing.	9. Born.
2. Won't have anything.	1. Makes nothing.
3. Earn.	2. The flies are as mean as anything.
4. Only.	3. A branch of ash leaves (to keep the
5. Lies; "shere": shire.	flies off the horse's head).
6. Rid of them.	

13

Them or thir feythers, tha sees, mun 'a beän a laäzy lot,
Fur work mun 'a gone to the gittin' whiniver munny was got. 50
Feyther 'ad ammost nowt; leästways 'is munny was 'id.
But 'e tued an' moiled[4] issén deäd, an' 'e died a good un, 'e did.

14

Looök thou theer wheer Wrigglesby beck[5] cooms out by the 'ill!
Feyther run oop[6] to the farm, an' I runs oop to the mill;
An' I'll run oop to the brig,[7] an' that thou'll live to see; 55
And if thou marries a good un I'll leäve the land to thee.

15

Thim's my noätions, Sammy, wheerby I meäns to stick;
But if thou marries a bad un, I'll leäve the land to Dick.—
Coom oop, proputty, proputty—that's what I 'ears 'im saäy—
Proputty, proputty, proputty—canter an' canter awaäy. 60

1869

Flower in the Crannied Wall

Flower in the crannied wall,
I pluck you out of the crannies,
I hold you here, root and all, in my hand,
Little flower—but *if* I could understand
What you are, root and all, and all in all, 5
I should know what God and man is.

1869

The Revenge[1]

A BALLAD OF THE FLEET

1

At Flores in the Azores Sir Richard Grenville lay,
And a pinnace, like a fluttered bird, came flying from far away:
"Spanish ships of war at sea! we have sighted fifty-three!"
Then sware Lord Thomas Howard: " 'Fore God I am no coward;
But I cannot meet them here, for my ships are out of gear, 5
And the half my men are sick. I must fly, but follow quick.
We are six ships of the line; can we fight with fifty-three?"

2

Then spake Sir Richard Grenville: "I know you are no coward;
You fly them for a moment to fight with them again.
But I've ninety men and more that are lying sick ashore. 10

---

4. Toiled and drudged.
5. Brook.
6. I.e., father's property ran up.
7. Bridge.
1. Based on Sir Walter Ralegh's account of an engagement in 1591 off
the coast of Flores, one of the islands
of the Azores, in which five Spanish
ships were sunk by the *Revenge* during
a fifteen-hour battle.

I should count myself the coward if I left them, my Lord Howard,
To these Inquisition dogs and the devildoms of Spain."

3

So Lord Howard passed away with five ships of war that day,
Till he melted like a cloud in the silent summer heaven;
But Sir Richard bore in hand all his sick men from the land   15
Very carefully and slow,
Men of Bideford in Devon,
And we laid them on the ballast down below;
For we brought them all aboard,
And they blessed him in their pain, that they were not left to
    Spain,   20
To the thumbscrew and the stake, for the glory of the Lord.

4

He had only a hundred seamen to work the ship and to fight,
And he sailed away from Flores till the Spaniard came in sight,
With his huge sea-castles heaving upon the weather bow.
"Shall we fight or shall we fly?   25
Good Sir Richard, tell us now,
For to fight is but to die!
There'll be little of us left by the time this sun be set."
And Sir Richard said again: "We be all good English men.
Let us bang these dogs of Seville, the children of the devil,   30
For I never turned my back upon Don or devil yet."

5

Sir Richard spoke and he laughed, and we roared a hurrah, and so
The little Revenge ran on sheer into the heart of the foe,
With her hundred fighters on deck, and her ninety sick below;
For half of their fleet to the right and half to the left were seen,   35
And the little Revenge ran on through the long sea lane between.

6

Thousands of their soldiers looked down from their decks and
    laughed,
Thousands of their seamen made mock at the mad little craft
Running on and on, till delayed
By their mountain-like San Philip that, of fifteen hundred tons,   40
And up-shadowing high above us with her yawning tiers of guns,
Took the breath from our sails, and we stayed.

7

And while now the great San Philip hung above us like a cloud
Whence the thunderbolt will fall
Long and loud,   45
Four galleons drew away
From the Spanish fleet that day,
And two upon the larboard and two upon the starboard lay,
And the battle thunder broke from them all.

8

But anon the great San Philip, she bethought herself and went,   50
Having that within her womb that had left her ill content;
And the rest they came aboard us, and they fought us hand to hand,

For a dozen times they came with their pikes and musqueteers,
And a dozen times we shook 'em off as a dog that shakes his ears
When he leaps from the water to the land.   55

9

And the sun went down, and the stars came out far over the summer
    sea,
But never a moment ceased the fight of the one and the fifty-three.
Ship after ship, the whole night long, their high-built galleons came,
Ship after ship, the whole night long, with her battle thunder and
    flame;
Ship after ship, the whole night long, drew back with her dead and
    her shame.   60
For some were sunk and many were shattered, and so could fight us
    no more—
God of battles, was ever a battle like this in the world before?

10

For he said, "Fight on! fight on!"
Though his vessel was all but a wreck;
And it chanced that, when half of the short summer night was
    gone,   65
With a grisly wound to be dressed he had left the deck,
But a bullet struck him that was dressing it suddenly dead,
And himself he was wounded again in the side and the head,
And he said, "Fight on! fight on!"

11

And the night went down, and the sun smiled out far over the
    summer sea,   70
And the Spanish fleet with broken sides lay round us all in a ring;
But they dared not touch us again, for they feared that we still could
    sting,
So they watched what the end would be.
And we had not fought them in vain,
But in perilous plight were we,   75
Seeing forty of our poor hundred were slain,
And half of the rest of us maimed for life
In the crash of the cannonades and the desperate strife;
And the sick men down in the hold were most of them stark and
    cold,
And the pikes were all broken or bent, and the powder was all of
    it spent;   80
And the masts and the rigging were lying over the side;
But Sir Richard cried in his English pride:
"We have fought such a fight for a day and a night
As may never be fought again!
We have won great glory, my men!   85
And a day less or more
At sea or ashore,
We die—does it matter when?
Sink me the ship, Master Gunner—sink her, split her in twain!
Fall into the hands of God, not into the hands of Spain!"   90

12

And the gunner said, "Aye, aye," but the seamen made reply:
"We have children, we have wives,
And the Lord hath spared our lives.
We will make the Spaniard promise, if we yield, to let us go;
We shall live to fight again and to strike another blow." 95
And the lion there lay dying, and they yielded to the foe.

13

And the stately Spanish men to their flagship bore him then,
Where they laid him by the mast, old Sir Richard caught at last,
And they praised him to his face with their courtly foreign grace;
But he rose upon their decks, and he cried: 100
"I have fought for Queen and Faith like a valiant man and true;
I have only done my duty as a man is bound to do.
With a joyful spirit I Sir Richard Grenville die!"
And he fell upon their decks, and he died.

14

And they stared at the dead that had been so valiant and true, 105
And had holden the power and glory of Spain so cheap
That he dared her with one little ship and his English few;
Was he devil or man? He was devil for aught they knew,
But they sank his body with honor down into the deep,
And they manned the Revenge with a swarthier alien crew, 110
And away she sailed with her loss and longed for her own;
When a wind from the lands they had ruined awoke from sleep,
And the water began to heave and the weather to moan,
And or ever that evening ended a great gale blew,
And a wave like the wave that is raised by an earthquake grew, 115
Till it smote on their hulls and their sails and their masts and their
    flags,
And the whole sea plunged and fell on the shot-shattered navy of
    Spain,
And the little Revenge herself went down by the island crags
To be lost evermore in the main.

1878

To Virgil

WRITTEN AT THE REQUEST OF THE MANTUANS[1] FOR THE
NINETEENTH CENTENARY OF VIRGIL'S DEATH

1

Roman Virgil, thou that singest
    Ilion's lofty temples robed in fire,
Ilion falling, Rome arising,
    wars, and filial faith, and Dido's pyre;[2]

1. Inhabitants of Mantua, the city
near which Virgil was born.
2. The allusions in this stanza are to
incidents in Virgil's *Aeneid*, especially
the fall of Troy (Ilion).

2

Landscape-lover, lord of language
    more than he that sang the "Works and Days,"[3]
All the chosen coin of fancy
    flashing out from many a golden phrase;

3

Thou that singest wheat and woodland,
    tilth and vineyard, hive and horse and herd;   5
All the charm of all the Muses
    often flowering in a lonely word;

4

Poet of the happy Tityrus[4]
    piping underneath his beechen bowers;
Poet of the poet-satyr[5]
    whom the laughing shepherd bound with flowers;

5

Chanter of the Pollio,[6] glorying
    in the blissful years again to be,
Summers of the snakeless meadow,
    unlaborious earth and oarless sea;   10

6

Thou that seest Universal
    Nature moved by Universal Mind;
Thou majestic in thy sadness
    at the doubtful doom of human kind;

7

Light among the vanished ages;
    star that gildest yet this phantom shore;
Golden branch[7] amid the shadows,
    kings and realms that pass to rise no more;

8

Now thy Forum roars no longer,
    fallen every purple Caesar's dome—   15
Though thine ocean-roll of rhythm
    sound forever of Imperial Rome—

9

Now the Rome of slaves hath perished,
    and the Rome of freemen[8] holds her place,
I, from out the Northern Island
    sundered once from all the human race,

10

I salute thee, Mantovano,[9]
    I that loved thee since my day began,
Wielder of the stateliest measure
    ever molded by the lips of man.   20

1882   1882

3. Hesiod, a Greek poet, whose *Works and Days* anticipated Virgil's *Georgics* in its pictures of farm life.
4. A shepherd in Virgil's *Eclogue* I.
5. Silenus, in *Eclogue* VI.
6. A friend of Virgil's who is celebrated in *Eclogue* IV.

7. A golden bough enabled Aeneas to enter the world of the shades. See *Aeneid* VI.208 ff.
8. Italy had only recently been liberated and unified.
9. Mantuan.

"Frater Ave atque Vale"[1]

Row us out from Desenzano,[2] to your Sirmione row!
So they rowed, and there we landed—"O venusta Sirmio!"
There to me through all the groves of olive in the summer glow,
There beneath the Roman ruin where the purple flowers grow,
Came that "Ave atque Vale" of the Poet's hopeless woe,   5
Tenderest of Roman poets nineteen hundred years ago,
"Frater Ave atque Vale"—as we wandered to and fro
Gazing at the Lydian[3] laughter of the Garda Lake below
Sweet Catullus's all-but-island, olive-silvery Sirmio!
1880   1883

To E. FitzGerald[1]

Old Fitz, who from your suburb grange,
    Where once I tarried for a while,
Glance at the wheeling orb of change,
    And greet it with a kindly smile;
Whom yet I see as there you sit   5
    Beneath your sheltering garden-tree,
And watch your doves about you flit,
    And plant on shoulder, hand, and knee,
Or on your head their rosy feet,
    As if they knew your diet spares   10
Whatever moved in that full sheet
    Let down to Peter at his prayers;[2]
Who live on milk and meal and grass;
    And once for ten long weeks I tried
Your table of Pythagoras,[3]   15
    And seemed at first "a thing enskied,"
As Shakespeare has it,[4] airy-light
    To float above the ways of men,
Then fell from that half-spiritual height

---

1. "Brother, hail and farewell," a line from an elegy by the Roman poet Catullus on the death of his brother (CI.10). Tennyson himself had recently lost his brother Charles.
2. A town on Lake Garda in Italy, which Tennyson visited in 1880. Sirmione is a beautiful peninsula jutting into the lake, on which Catullus had his summer home. Catullus' poem in honor of the locality includes the phrase "*O venusta Sirmio!*" ("O lovely Sirmio!").
3. The Etruscans, who settled near Lake Garda, were thought to be descended from the Lydians of Asia Minor.
1. Edward FitzGerald, translator of the *Rubáiyát of Omar Khayyám* (the "golden Eastern lay"), was an early admirer of Tennyson's poetry and a friend of long standing. This dedication in the form of a verse letter was to introduce an early poem by Tennyson entitled *Tiresias*. Before the letter and poem reached him in 1883 FitzGerald died.
2. I.e., meat, fish, or fowl. See Acts x.11–12.
3. Greek philosopher and vegetarian. FitzGerald made several unsuccessful attempts to regulate Tennyson's eating habits as well as to diminish his daily consumption of a pint of port wine and vast quantities of pipe tobacco.
4. *Measure for Measure* I.iv.34.

Chilled, till I tasted flesh again 20
One night when earth was winter-black,
    And all the heavens flashed in frost;
And on me, half-asleep, came back
    That wholesome heat the blood had lost,
And set me climbing icy capes 25
    And glaciers, over which there rolled
To meet me long-armed vines with grapes
    Of Eshcol hugeness;[5] for the cold
Without, and warmth within me, wrought
    To mold the dream; but none can say 30
That Lenten fare makes Lenten thought
    Who reads your golden Eastern lay,
Than which I know no version done
    In English more divinely well;
A planet equal to the sun 35
    Which cast it, that large infidel
Your Omar; and your Omar drew
    Full-handed plaudits from our best
In modern letters, and from two,
    Old friends outvaluing all the rest, 40
Two voices heard on earth no more;
    But we old friends are still alive,
And I am nearing seventy-four,
    While you have touched at seventy-five,
And so I send a birthday line 45
    Of greeting; and my son, who dipped
In some forgotten book of mine
    With sallow scraps of manuscript,
And dating many a year ago,
    Has hit on this, which you will take, 50
My Fitz, and welcome, as I know,
    Less for its own than for the sake
Of one recalling gracious times,
    When, in our younger London days,
You found some merit in my rhymes, 55
    And I more pleasure in your praise.

1883   1885

Locksley Hall Sixty Years After[1]

Late, my grandson! half the morning have I paced these sandy tracts,
Watched again the hollow ridges roaring into cataracts,

Wandered back to living boyhood while I heard the curlews call,
I myself so close on death, and death itself in Locksley Hall.

5. See Numbers xiii.23.
1. Tennyson insisted that this poem was a "dramatic impersonation," not an autobiography. The ranting tone is therefore as appropriate to the lonely 80-year-old speaker of 1886 as it was for the jilted young man in the original *Locksley Hall* (published in 1842 but

So—your happy suit was blasted—she the faultless, the divine;   5
And you liken—boyish babble—this boy-love of yours with mine.

I myself have often babbled doubtless of a foolish past;
Babble, babble; our old England may go down in babble at last.

"Curse him!" curse your fellow-victim? call him dotard in your rage?
Eyes that lured a doting boyhood well might fool a dotard's age.   10

Jilted for a wealthier! wealthier? yet perhaps she was not wise;
I remember how you kissed the miniature with those sweet eyes.

In the hall there hangs a painting—Amy's arms about my neck—
Happy children in a sunbeam sitting on the ribs of wreck.

In my life there was a picture, she that clasped my neck had flown; 15
I was left within the shadow sitting on the wreck alone.

Yours has been a slighter ailment, will you sicken for her sake?
You, not you! your modern amorist is of easier, earthlier make.

Amy loved me, Amy failed me, Amy was a timid child;
But your Judith—but your worldling—*she* had never driven me wild. 20

She that holds the diamond necklace dearer than the golden ring,
She that finds a winter sunset[2] fairer than a morn of spring.

She that in her heart is brooding on his briefer lease of life,
While she vows "till death shall part us," she the would-be-widow
wife.

She the worldling born of worldlings—father, mother—be content, 25
Even the homely farm can teach us there is something in descent.

Yonder in that chapel, slowly sinking now into the ground,
Lies the warrior, my forefather, with his feet upon the hound.

Crossed![3] for once he sailed the sea to crush the Moslem in his
pride;
Dead the warrior, dead his glory, dead the cause in which he died. 30

Yet how often I and Amy in the moldering aisle have stood,
Gazing for one pensive moment on that founder of our blood.

There again I stood today, and where of old we knelt in prayer,
Close beneath the casement crimson with the shield of Locksley—
there,

---

presumably set in 1826). Although the speaker's tone has remained the same during the 60 years that have passed, his attitudes towards progress, immortality, and democracy have changed considerably. Also changed is his view of the Squire of Locksley Hall, who has just died—the feudal past as represented by his former rival for the hand of his cousin Amy.

Tennyson told his son that later gener-ations of readers might find that the two poems were his "most historically interesting" productions, in their descriptions of his century at two different points in its development.

2. The elderly man whom Judith chose to marry.

3. The crossed feet of the statue on top of the tomb indicate that the speaker's ancestor had served in the Crusades.

All in white Italian marble, looking still as if she smiled,   35
Lies my Amy dead in childbirth, dead the mother, dead the child.

Dead—and sixty years ago, and dead her aged husband now—
I, this old white-headed dreamer, stoopt and kissed her marble brow.

Gone the fires of youth, the follies, furies, curses, passionate tears,
Gone like fires and floods and earthquakes of the planet's dawning
    years.   40

Fires that shook me once, but now to silent ashes fallen away.
Cold upon the dead volcano sleeps the gleam of dying day.

Gone the tyrant of my youth,[4] and mute below the chancel stones,
All his virtues—I forgive them—black in white above his bones.[5]

Gone the comrades of my bivouac, some in fight against the foe,   45
Some through age and slow diseases, gone as all on earth will go.

Gone with whom for forty years my life in golden sequence ran,
She with all the charm of woman, she with all the breadth of man,

Strong in will and rich in wisdom, Edith, yet so lowly-sweet,
Woman to her inmost heart, and woman to her tender feet,   50

Very woman of very woman, nurse of ailing body and mind,
She that linked again the broken chain that bound me to my kind.

Here today was Amy with me, while I wandered down the coast,
Near us Edith's holy shadow, smiling at the slighter ghost.

Gone our sailor son thy father, Leonard early lost at sea;   55
Thou alone, my boy, of Amy's kin and mine are left to me.

Gone thy tender-natured mother, wearying to be left alone,
Pining for the stronger heart that once had beat beside her own.

Truth, for truth is truth, he worshiped, being true as he was brave;
Good, for good is good, he followed, yet he looked beyond the
    grave.[6]   60

Wiser there than you, that crowning barren Death as lord of all,
Deem this over-tragic drama's closing curtain is the pall!

Beautiful was death in him, who saw the death, but kept the deck,
Saving women and their babes, and sinking with the sinking wreck,

Gone forever! Ever? no—for since our dying race began,   65
Ever, ever, and forever was the leading light of man.

---

4. A "selfish uncle" who became his guardian after the death of his father. See *Locksley Hall*, line 156.
5. I.e., black-lettered inscription carved on a slab of white marble set into the floor of the church.

6. These lines were written in April, 1886, after Tennyson received news of the death of his 32 year old son, Lionel, who had been returning from India to England.

Those that in barbarian burials killed the slave, and slew the wife
Felt within themselves the sacred passion of the second life.

Indian warriors dream of ampler hunting grounds beyond the night;
Even the black Australian dying hopes he shall return, a white.   70

Truth for truth, and good for good! The good, the true, the pure,
    the just—
Take the charm "Forever" from them, and they crumble into dust.

Gone the cry of "Forward, Forward," lost within a growing gloom;
Lost, or only heard in silence from the silence of a tomb.

Half the marvels of my morning, triumphs over time and space,   75
Staled by frequence, shrunk by usage into commonest common-
    place!

"Forward" rang the voices then, and of the many mine was one.
Let us hush this cry of "Forward" till ten thousand years have gone.

Far among the vanished races, old Assyrian kings would flay
Captives whom they caught in battle—iron-hearted victors they.   80

Ages after, while in Asia, he that led the wile Moguls
Timur built his ghastly tower of eighty thousand human skulls,[7]

Then, and here in Edward's time, an age of noblest English names,
Christian conquerors took and flung the conquered Christian into
    flames.[8]

Love your enemy, bless your haters, said the Greatest of the great;   85
Christian love among the Churches looked the twin of heathen hate.

From the golden alms of Blessing man had coined himself a curse:
Rome of Caesar, Rome of Peter, which was crueler? which was
    worse?

France had shown a light to all men, preached a Gospel, all men's
    good;
Celtic Demos[9] rose a Demon, shrieked and slaked the light with
    blood.   90

Hope was ever on her mountain, watching till the day begun—
Crowned with sunlight—over darkness—from the still unrisen sun.

Have we grown at last beyond the passions of the primal clan?
"Kill your enemy, for you hate him," still, "your enemy" was a man.

Have we sunk below them? peasants maim the helpless horse, and
    drive   95
Innocent cattle under thatch, and burn the kindlier brutes alive.[1]

7. Timur or Tamerlane (1336–1405), Mogul ruler whose conquests included the Persian City, Isfahan, where the skulls of thousands of the slaughtered inhabitants were piled up.
8. In the reign of Edward VI (1547–53), Catholics were persecuted; in the reign of Mary (1553–58), Protestants were persecuted.
9. I.e., the common people; here, the reference is to the mass executions and slaughterings during the French Revolution.
1. In the 1880's, peasants agitating against landlords in Ireland destroyed cattle and farm buildings.

916 · Alfred, Lord Tennyson

Brutes, the brutes are not your wrongers—burnt at midnight, found
at morn,
Twisted hard in mortal agony with their offspring, born-unborn,

Clinging to the silent mother! Are we devils? are we men?
Sweet Saint Francis of Assisi, would that he were here again,[2]   100

He that in his Catholic wholeness used to call the very flowers
Sisters, brothers—and the beasts—whose pains are hardly less than
ours!

Chaos, Cosmos! Cosmos, Chaos! who can tell how all will end?
Read the wide world's annals, you, and take their wisdom for your
friend.

Hope the best, but hold the Present fatal daughter of the Past,   105
Shape your heart to front the hour, but dream not that the hour will
last.

Aye, if dynamite and revolver [3] leave you courage to be wise—
When was age so crammed with menace? madness? written, spoken
lies?

Envy wears the mask of Love, and, laughing sober fact to scorn,
Cries to weakest as to strongest, "Ye are equals, equal-born."   110

Equal-born? O, yes, if yonder hill be level with the flat.
Charm us, orator, till the lion look no larger than the cat,

Till the cat through that mirage of overheated language loom
Larger than the lion—Demos end in working its own doom.

Russia bursts our Indian barrier,[4] shall we fight her? shall we yield?   115
Pause! before you sound the trumpet, hear the voices from the field.

Those three hundred millions under one Imperial scepter now,
Shall we hold them? shall we loose them? take the suffrage of the
plow.[5]

Nay, but these [6] would feel and follow Truth if only you and you,
Rivals of realm-ruining party, when you speak were wholly true.   120

Plowmen, shepherds, have I found, and more than once, and still
could find,
Sons of God, and kings of men in utter nobleness of mind,

2. St. Francis (1182–1226), whose
fondness for animals and birds was noteworthy.
3. Bombings and shootings, as in the
Anarchist Riot in Haymarket Square,
Chicago, May 4, 1886.
4. The British regarded Afghanistan as
a buffer between Russia and India; in
1885 a Russian attack against an Afghan
border force (an incident known as the
Panjdeh scare) brought Britain and Russia to the brink of war.
5. I.e., let the farm laborers' vote decide
whether Britain should try to hold India
as part of Queen Victoria's Empire
(which it had become in 1877) or to
withdraw and let the 300 million people
of India confront the threat of Russian
invasion on their own.
6. Farm laborers, to whom Parliament
granted the right to vote in 1884. As a
member of the House of Lords Tennyson himself had voted for this measure
but with considerable reluctance because
it seemed to him premature.

Truthful, trustful, looking upward to the practiced hustings-liar; [7]
So the higher wields the lower, while the lower is the higher.

Here and there a cotter's babe is royal-born by right divine;   125
Here and there my lord is lower than his oxen or his swine.

Chaos, Cosmos! Cosmos, Chaos! once again the sickening game;
Freedom, free to slay herself, and dying while they shout her name.

Step by step we gained a freedom known to Europe, known to all;
Step by step we rose to greatness—through the tonguesters we may
    fall.   130

You that woo the Voices [8]—tell them "old experience is a fool,"
Teach your flattered kings that only those who cannot read can rule.

Pluck the mighty from their seat, but set no meek ones in their
    place;
Pillory Wisdom in your markets, pelt your offal at her face.

Tumble Nature heel o'er head, and, yelling with the yelling street,   135
Set the feet above the brain and swear the brain is in the feet.

Bring the old dark ages back without the faith, without the hope,
Break the State, the Church, the Throne, and roll their ruins down
    the slope.

Authors—essayist, atheist, novelist, realist, rhymester, play your part,
Paint the mortal shame of nature with the living hues of art.   140

Rip your brothers' vices open, strip your own foul passions bare;
Down with Reticence, down with Reverence—forward—naked—let
    them stare.

Feed the budding rose of boyhood with the drainage of your sewer;
Send the drain into the fountain, lest the stream should issue pure.

Set the maiden fancies wallowing in the troughs of Zolaism [9]—   145
Forward, forward, aye, and backward, downward too into the abysm!

Do your best to charm the worst, to lower the rising race of men;
Have we risen from out the beast, then back into the beast again?

Only "dust to dust" for me that sicken at your lawless din,
Dust in wholesome old-world dust before the newer world begin.   150

Heated am I? you—you wonder—well, it scarce becomes mine age—
Patience! let the dying actor mouth his last upon the stage.

Cries of unprogressive dotage ere the dotard fall asleep?
Noises of a current narrowing, not the music of a deep?

Aye, for doubtless I am old, and think gray thoughts, for I am gray;   155
After all the stormy changes shall we find a changeless May?

After madness, after massacre, Jacobinism and Jacquerie,[1]
Some diviner force to guide us through the days I shall not see?

When the schemes and all the systems, kingdoms and republics fall,
Something kindlier, higher, holier—all for each and each for all?   160

All the full-brain, half-brain races, led by Justice, Love, and Truth;
All the millions one at length, with all the visions of my youth?

All diseases quenched by Science, no man halt, or deaf or blind;
Stronger ever born of weaker, lustier body, larger mind?

Earth at last a warless world, a single race, a single tongue—   165
I have seen her far away—for is not Earth as yet so young?—

Every tiger madness muzzled, every serpent passion killed,
Every grim ravine a garden, every blazing desert tilled,

Robed in universal harvest up to either pole she smiles,
Universal ocean softly washing all her warless isles.   170

Warless? when her tens are thousands, and her thousands millions, then—
All her harvest all too narrow—who can fancy warless men?

Warless? war will die out late then. Will it ever? late or soon?
Can it, till this outworn earth be dead as yon dead world the moon?

Dead the new astronomy calls her.—On this day and at this hour,   175
In this gap between the sandhills, whence you see the Locksley
  tower,

Here we met, our latest meeting—Amy—sixty years ago—
She and I—the moon was falling greenish through a rosy glow,

Just above the gateway tower, and even where you see her now—
Here we stood and clasped each other, swore the seeming-deathless
  vow.—   180

Dead, but how her living glory lights the hall, the dune, the grass!
Yet the moonlight is the sunlight, and the sun himself will pass.

Venus near her! smiling downward at this earthlier earth of ours,
Closer on the sun, perhaps a world of never fading flowers.[2]

1. The Jacobins were an extremist Revolutionary party in France; a "Jacquerie" is an uprising of peasants against
landholders, the name being derived
from a peasants' revolt against the nobles of Northern France in 1358.
2. The evening star, being closer to the
sun, may be a more perfect planet than
ours, but as the speaker also speculates
(line 192), its beautiful appearance may
be deceptive and life there be troubled
by war and other evils as is life on
earth.

Hesper, whom the poet called the Bringer home of all good things[3]—   185
All good things may move in Hesper, perfect peoples, perfect kings.

Hesper—Venus—were we native to that splendor or in Mars,
We should see the globe we groan in, fairest of their evening stars.

Could we dream of wars and carnage, craft and madness, lust and
    spite,
Roaring London, raving Paris, in that point of peaceful light?   190

Might we not in glancing heavenward on a star so silver-fair,
Yearn, and clasp the hands and murmur, "Would to God that we
    were there"?

Forward, backward, backward, forward, in the immeasurable sea,
Swayed by vaster ebbs and flows than can be known to you or me.

All the suns—are these but symbols of innumerable man,   195
Man or Mind that sees a shadow of the planner or the plan?

Is there evil but on earth? or pain in every peopled sphere?
Well, be grateful for the sounding watchword "Evolution" here,

Evolution ever climbing after some ideal good,
And Reversion ever dragging Evolution in the mud.   200

What are men that He should heed us? cried the king of sacred
    song;[4]
Insects of an hour, that hourly work their brother insect wrong,

While the silent heavens roll, and suns along their fiery way,
All their planets whirling round them, flash a million miles a day.

Many an aeon moulded earth before her highest, man, was born,   205
Many an aeon too may pass when earth is manless and forlorn,

Earth so huge, and yet so bounded—pools of salt, and plots of
    land—
Shallow skin of green and azure—chains of mountain, grains of
    sand!

Only That which made us meant us to be mightier by and by,
Set the sphere of all the boundless heavens within the human eye,   210

Sent the shadow of Himself, the boundless, through the human
    soul;
Boundless inward in the atom, boundless outward in the Whole.

·   ·   ·   ·   ·   ·   ·   ·   ·

Here is Locksley Hall, my grandson, here the lion-guarded gate.
Not tonight in Locksley Hall—tomorrow—you, you come so late.

---

3. Hesper or Venus, was addressed by
the Greek poet Sappho "Oh, Hesperus!
Thou bringest all things home." Cf. *The*

Wasteland, line 221-222 and see also
In Memoriam, sec. 121.
4. King David. See Psalm viii.4.

Wrecked—your train—or all but wrecked? a shattered wheel? a vicious boy!   215
Good, this forward,[5] you that preach it, is it well to wish you joy?

Is it well that while we range with Science, glorying in the Time,
City children soak and blacken soul and sense in city slime?

There among the glooming alleys Progress halts on palsied feet,
Crime and hunger cast our maidens by the thousand on the street.   220

There the master scrimps his haggard sempstress of her daily bread,
There a single sordid attic holds the living and the dead.

There the smoldering fire of fever creeps across the rotted floor,
And the crowded couch of incest in the warrens of the poor.

Nay, your pardon, cry your "Forward," yours are hope and youth,
but I—   225
Eighty winters leave the dog too lame to follow with the cry,

Lame and old, and past his time, and passing now into the night;
Yet I would the rising race were half as eager for the light.

Light the fading gleam of even? light the glimmer of the dawn?
Aged eyes may take the growing glimmer for the gleam withdrawn.   2

Far away beyond her myriad coming changes earth will be
Something other than the wildest modern guess of you and me.

Earth may reach her earthly-worst, of if she gain her earthly-best,
Would she find her human offspring this ideal man at rest?

Forward then, but still remember how the course of Time will swerve,
Crook and turn upon itself in many a backward streaming curve.

Not the Hall tonight, my grandson! Death and Silence hold their own.
Leave the master [6] in the first dark hour of his last sleep alone.

Worthier soul was he than I am, sound and honest, rustic Squire,
Kindly landlord, boon companion—youthful jealousy is a liar.

Cast the poison from your bosom, oust the madness from your brain.
Let the trampled serpent show you that you have not lived in vain.

Youthful! youth and age are scholars yet but in the lower school,
Nor is he the wisest man who never proved himself a fool.

5. Cf. *Locksley Hall*, line 181. "Forward" had been the young man's watchword for progress into the future, a progress associated with railway journeys. Now his grandson's railway journey has been disrupted by the vandalism of "a vicious boy" (line 215), an embodiment of the underprivileged classes of modern industrial society who may wreck the progress that Science seemed to promise.
6. Amy's husband, the feudal-style master and squire of Locksley Hall, as contrasted with the master as capitalist employer of line 221.

Yonder lies our young sea village—Art and Grace are less and less: 245
Science grows and Beauty dwindles—roofs of slated hideousness!

There is one old hostel left us where they swing the Locksley shield,
Till the peasant cow shall butt the "lion passant" from his field.[7]

Poor old Heraldry, poor old History, poor old Poetry, passing hence,
In the common deluge drowning old political common sense! 250

Poor old voice of eighty crying after voices that have fled!
All I loved are vanished voices, all my steps are on the dead.

All the world is ghost to me, and as the phantom disappears,
Forward far and far from here is all the hope of eighty years.

  •   •   •   •   •   •

In this hostel—I remember—I repent it o'er his grave— 255
Like a clown—by chance he met me—I refused the hand he gave.

From that casement where the trailer mantles all the moldering
    bricks—
I was then in early boyhood, Edith but a child of six—

While I sheltered in this archway from a day of driving showers—
Peeped the winsome face of Edith like a flower among the flowers. 260

Here tonight! the Hall tomorrow, when they toll the chapel bell!
Shall I hear in one dark room a wailing, "I have loved thee well"?

Then a peal that shakes the portal—one has come to claim his bride,
Her that shrank, and put me from her, shrieked, and started from
    my side—

Silent echoes! You, my Leonard, use and not abuse your day, 265
Move among your people, know them, follow him [8] who led the way,

Strove for sixty widowed years to help his homelier brother men,
Served the poor, and built the cottage, raised the school, and drained
    the fen.

Hears he now the voice that wronged him? who shall swear it cannot
    be?
Earth would never touch her worst, were one in fifty such as he. 270

Ere she gain her heavenly-best, a God must mingle with game.
Nay, there may be those about us whom we neither see nor name,

Felt within us as ourselves, the Powers of Good, the Powers of Ill,
Strowing balm, or shedding poison in the fountains of the will.

Follow you the star that lights a desert pathway, yours or mine. 275
Forward, till you see the Highest Human Nature is divine.

---

7. In heraldry "field" refers to the entire surface of the shield on which the coat-of-arms was painted. The Locksley shield, featuring a running lion ("lion passant"), appears on the signboard outside the old inn. On the "peasant cow" see lines 95–99 and 118.
8. Amy's husband.

Follow Light, and do the Right—for man can half-control his
doom—
Till you find the deathless Angel seated in the vacant tomb.[9]

Forward, let the stormy moment fly and mingle with the past.
I that loathed have come to love him. Love will conquer at the last. 280

Gone at eighty, mine own age, and I and you will bear the pall;
Then I leave thee lord and master, latest lord of Locksley Hall.
1886   1886

By an Evolutionist

The Lord let the house of a brute to the soul of a man,
  And the man said, "Am I your debtor?"
And the Lord—"Not yet: but make it as clean as you can,
  And then I will let you a better."

1

If my body come from brutes, my soul uncertain, or a fable,   5
  Why not bask amid the senses while the sun of morning shines,
I, the finer brute rejoicing in my hounds, and in my stable,
  Youth and health, and birth and wealth, and choice of women
  and of wines?

2

What has thou done for me, grim Old Age, save breaking my bones
  on the rack?
  Would I had passed in the morning that looks so bright from
  afar!   10

OLD AGE

Done for thee? starved the wild beast that was linked with thee
  eighty years back.
  Less weight now for the ladder-of-heaven that hangs on a star.

1

If my body come from brutes, though somewhat finer than their
  own,
  I am heir, and this my kingdom. Shall the royal voice be mute?
No, but if the rebel subject seek to drag me from the throne,   15
  Hold the scepter, Human Soul, and rule thy province of the brute.

2

I have climbed to the snows of Age, and I gaze at a field in the
  Past,
  Where I sank with the body at times in the sloughs of a low
  desire,

---

9. The angel who rolled back the stone from the tomb of Christ. See Matthew,
28—1–7.

But I hear no yelp of the beast, and the Man is quiet at last
  As he stands on the heights of his life with a glimpse of a height
    that is higher.
                             20
                            1889

June Bracken and Heather

TO ———[1]

There on the top of the down,
The wild heather round me and over me June's high blue,
When I looked at the bracken so bright and the heather so brown,
I thought to myself I would offer this book to you,
This, and my love together,   5
To you that are seventy-seven,
With a faith as clear as the heights of the June-blue heaven,
And a fancy as summer-new
As the green of the bracken amid the gloom of the heather.
                            1892

The Dawn

"You are but children."
—EGYPTIAN PRIEST TO SOLON

        Red of the Dawn!
Screams of a babe in the red-hot palms of a Moloch [2] of Tyre,
  Man with his brotherless dinner on man in the tropical wood,
  Priests in the name of the Lord passing souls through fire to the
    fire,
Head-hunters and boats of Dahomey [3] that float upon human blood!

        Red of the Dawn!   6
Godless fury of peoples, and Christless frolic of kings,
  And the bolt of war dashing down upon cities and blazing farms,
  For Babylon was a child newborn, and Rome was a babe in arms,
And London and Paris and all the rest are as yet but in leading
    strings.   10

        Dawn not Day,
While scandal is mouthing a bloodless name at *her* cannibal feast,
  And rake-ruined bodies and souls go down in a common wreck,
  And the Press of a thousand cities is prized for it smells of the
    beast,
Or easily violates virgin Truth for a coin or a check.   15

        Dawn not Day!
Is it Shame, so few should have climbed from the dens in the level

---

1. Addressed to Tennyson's wife as a dedication to a volume of poems.
2. A god to whom children were sacrificed as burnt offerings.

3. West African country in which the custom of human sacrifice persisted in the 19th century. In 1892, after a war, Dahomey became a French colony.

below,
Men, with a heart and a soul, no slaves of a four-footed will?
But if twenty million of summers are stored in the sunlight still,
We are far from the noon of man, there is time for the race to grow.

Red of the Dawn!   21
Is it turning a fainter red? So be it, but when shall we lay
    The Ghost of the Brute that is walking and haunting us yet, and
        be free?
In a hundred, a thousand winters? Ah, what will *our* children be?
The men of a hundred thousand, a million summers away?   25

1892

The Silent Voices

When the dumb Hour, clothed in black,
Brings the Dreams about my bed,
Call me not so often back,
Silent Voices of the dead,
Toward the lowland ways behind me,   5
And the sunlight that is gone!
Call me rather, silent voices,
Forward to the starry track
Glimmering up the heights beyond me
On, and always on!   10

1892

Crossing the Bar[1]

Sunset and evening star,
    And one clear call for me!
And may there be no moaning of the bar,[2]
    When I put out to sea,

But such a tide as moving seems asleep,   5
    Too full for sound and foam,
When that which drew from out the boundless deep
    Turns again home.

Twilight and evening bell,
    And after that the dark!   10
And may there be no sadness of farewell,
    When I embark;

For though from out our bourne[3] of Time and Place
    The flood may bear me far,
I hope to see my Pilot face to face   15
    When I have crossed the bar.

1889   1889

1. Although not the last poem written
by Tennyson, *Crossing the Bar* appears,
at his request, as the final poem in all
collections of his work.

2. Mournful sound of the ocean beating
on a sand bar at the mouth of a harbor.
3. Boundary.

ROBERT BROWNING
(1812–1889)

1846:   Marriage to Elizabeth Barrett and residence in Italy.
1855:   *Men and Women* published.
1861:   Death of Elizabeth Barrett Browning.
1868–69: *The Ring and the Book* published.

During the years of his marriage Robert Browning was sometimes referred to as "Mrs. Browning's husband." Elizabeth Barrett, who seems to us now a minor figure, was at that time a famous poet while her husband was a relatively unknown experimenter whose poems were greeted with misunderstanding or indifference. Not until the 1860's did he at last gain a public and become recognized as the rival or equal of Tennyson. In the 20th century his reputation has persisted, but in an unusual way: his poetry is admired by two groups of readers widely different in tastes. To one group his work is a moral tonic. Such readers appreciate him as a man who lived bravely and as a writer who showed life to be a joyful battle, the imperfections of this world being remedied, under the dispensations of an all-loving God, by the perfections of the next. Typical of this group are the Browning Societies which have flourished in England and America. Members of these societies usually regard their poet as a wise philosopher and religious teacher who resolved the doubts which had troubled Arnold and Tennyson and which have continued to trouble later generations of less confident writers.

A second group of readers enjoy Browning less for his attempt to solve problems of religious doubt than for his attempt to solve the problems of how poetry should be written. Such poets as Ezra Pound and Robert Lowell value him as a major artist. These readers recognize that more than any other 19th-century poet (even including Hopkins), it was Browning who energetically hacked through a trail that has subsequently become the main road of 20th-century poetry. In *Poetry and the Age* Randall Jarrell, speaking of present-day poetry, remarks how "the dramatic monologue, which once had depended for its effect upon being a departure from the norm of poetry, now became in one form or another the norm." Browning did not invent the dramatic monologue, but he established it as a norm.

The dramatic monologue, as Browning uses it, enables the reader, speaker, and poet to be located at an appropriate distance from each other, aligned in such a way that the reader must work *through* the words of the speaker toward the meaning of the poet himself. For example, in the well-known early monologue *My Last Duchess*, we listen to the Duke as he speaks of his dead wife, and it is almost as if we were overhearing a man talking into the telephone of a booth adjacent to ours. From his one-sided conversation we piece together the situation, both past and present, and we infer what sort of woman the Duchess really was, and what sort of man is the Duke. Ultimately we may also infer what the poet himself thinks of the speaker he has created. In this instance, from evidence outside the poem we know that Browning had a special aversion for domestic tyrants. His own father-in-law was to provide him with a striking example of the breed, and it is revealing that in his longest poem, *The Ring and the Book*, he once more explored the story of another domestic tyrant who, like the Duke, was irritated by his wife's virtues. Yet from *My Last Duchess* itself, if we exclude external evidence, it is interesting to note how persuasive is the Duke's own side of the story:

> She had
> A heart—how shall I say?—too soon made glad,
> Too easily impressed; she liked whate'er
> She looked on, and her looks went everywhere.

Although Browning contrives that our verdict as jurymen will be a just one, he does allow us a considerable amount of latitude. And in some of his later monologues we are really obliged to grope toward a choice. In reading *A Grammarian's Funeral*, for example, can we be sure that the central character is a hero? Or is he merely a fool? Browning has not made the answer easy for us.

In addition to his experiments with the dramatic monologue Browning also made experiments with language and syntax. The grotesque rhymes and jaw-breaking diction which he often employs have been repugnant to some critics; George Santayana, for instance, dismissed him as a clumsy barbarian. But to those who understand Browning's aims, the incongruities of language are not literally incongruous but functional, a humorous and appropriate counterpart to an imperfect world. Ezra Pound's tribute to "Old Hippety-Hop o' the accents," as he addresses Browning, is both affectionate and memorable:

> Heart that was big as the bowels of Vesuvius
> Words that were winged as her sparks in eruption,
> Eagled and thundered as Jupiter Pluvius
> Sound in your wind past all signs o' corruption.

This capacity to attract the admiration of such a diversity of readers, sophisticated and unsophisticated, is one of several ways in which Browning's writings can be likened to those of Dickens and Shakespeare.

The personal life of Robert Browning falls into three phases: his years as a child and young bachelor, as a husband, and as a widower. Each of these phases is most appropriately considered in relation to his development as a poet.

He was born in Camberwell, a London suburb, within a few months of the births of Dickens and Thackeray. His father, a bank clerk, was a learned man with an extensive library. His mother was a kindly, religious-minded woman, interested in music, whose love for her brilliant son was warmly reciprocated. Until the time of his marriage at the age of 34 Browning was rarely absent from his parents' home. He attended a boarding school near Camberwell, traveled a little, and was a student at the University of London for a short period, but he preferred to pursue his education at home where he was tutored in foreign languages, music, boxing, and horsemanship, and where he read omnivorously. From this unusual education he acquired a store of knowledge upon which to draw for the background of his poems.

The "obscurity" of which his contemporaries complained in his earlier poetry may be partly accounted for by the circumstances of Browning's education. He was inclined to assume that his out-of-the-ordinary learning was generally shared by educated readers. Often it was not. But the obscurity of such poems as *Sordello* is attributable not only to the nature of Browning's learning but to the poet's anxious desire to avoid exposing himself too explicitly before his readers. His first poem, *Pauline,* published when he was 21, had been modeled on the example of Shelley, the most personal of poets. When a review by John Stuart Mill pointed out that the young author was parading a "morbid state" of self-worship, Browning was overwhelmed with embarrassment. He resolved to avoid confessional writings thereafter.

One way of reducing the personal element in his poetry was to write plays instead of soul-searching narratives or lyrics. In 1836, encouraged by the actor W. C. Macready, Browning began work on his first play, *Strafford,* a historical tragedy that lasted only four nights when it was produced at a London theater in 1837. For ten years the young writer struggled to produce other plays that would better hold the attention of an audience, but as stage productions they all remained failures. Browning nevertheless profited from this otherwise disheartening experience. Writing dialogue for actors led him to explore another form more congenial to his genius, the dramatic monologue, a form that enabled him through imaginary speakers to avoid explicit autobiography and yet did not demand that these speakers act out their story with the speed or the simplifications that stage production demands.

Browning's resolution to avoid the subjective manner of Shelley did not preclude his being influenced by the earlier poet in other ways. At 14, when he first discovered Shelley's works, he became an atheist and liberal. Although he outgrew the atheism, after a struggle, and also the extreme phases of his liberalism, he retained from Shelley's influence something permanent and more difficult to define: an ardent dedication to ideals (often undefined ideals) and an energetic striving toward goals (often undefined goals). This quality of aspiration is much more mixed with earthiness—even worldliness—in Browning's character than in Shelley's. To soar upwards on a skylark's wing was not to Browning's taste. He is more like Robert Frost's swinger of birches who climbs a tree toward heaven but is anxious to swing down to earth again before getting too far away.

Yet the element of worldliness should not obscure from us Browning's ardent romanticism. His love affair with Elizabeth Barrett was romantic in several of the senses of that hard-worked adjective. It is easy to see why the well-known story of their courtship has been retold by novelists, dramatists, and movie-producers, for the situation had the dramatic ingredients of Browning's own favorite story of St. George rescuing the maiden from the dragon. Almost everything seemed unpropitious when Browning met Elizabeth Barrett in 1845. She was six years older than he was, a semi-invalid, jealously guarded by her possessively tyrannical father. But love, as the poet was to say later, is best, and love swept aside all obstacles. After their elopement to Italy, the former semi-invalid was soon enjoying good health and a full life. The husband likewise seemed to thrive during the years of this remarkable marriage. Like many English poets he was especially at ease in the warm lands of the Mediterranean. His most memorable volume of poems, *Men and Women* (1855), reflects his enjoyment of Italy: its picturesque landscapes and lively street scenes as well as its monuments from the past—its Renaissance past in particular, a period of expanding energies which was congenial to his own expansive temperament.

The happy fifteen-year sojourn in Italy ended in 1861 with Elizabeth's death. The widower returned to London with his son. During the 28 years remaining to him, the quantity of verse he produced did not diminish. Nor, during the first decade, did it decrease in quality. His greatest single work, *The Ring and the Book*, a poem on the vast scale of a long novel, was published in 1868. His later writings, however, suffer from a certain mechanical repetition of mannerism and an excess of argumentation—faults into which he may have been lead by the unqualified enthusiasm of his admirers, for it was during this period that he gained his great following. When he died, in 1889, he was buried in Westminster Abbey.

During these London years Browning became abundantly fond of social life. He dined at the homes of friends and at clubs, where he enjoyed port wine and conversation. He would talk loudly and emphatically about many topics—except his own poetry, about which he was usually reticent. His reticence bothered many of his admirers. American women visiting in London, after having looked forward to meeting the author whose 'poems had inspired them to higher things, were disappointed—almost appalled—when they met the man at a dinner party. He did not "look like a poet." His late poem *House* may show why he gave such an impression. Behind the façade of the hearty diner-out, Browning could live and think as he pleased, just as he had discovered in writing his monologues the advantage, for him, of indirect speaking. Each speaker of monologue provides a mask for the poet.

Despite his bursts of outspokenness, Browning's character is thus not so clearly known to us as that of Tennyson or Arnold or Carlyle. Hardy once said that Browning's character seemed to him "*the* literary puzzle of the 19th century." To solve the puzzle one biographer, Mrs. Betty Miller, has tried to show that Browning was not such a happy and confident person as he is usually represented to have been, an impression that can be reinforced by the note of desperation in such poems as *Childe Roland*. This eccentric interpretation has at least the merit of suggesting that like Yeats (a poet preoccupied with masks) Browning was a more complex man than some of his admirers have been willing to recognize.

Just as Browning's character is harder to identify than that of Tennyson, so also are his poems more difficult to relate to the age in which they were written than are the sometimes topical poems of Tennyson. Our first impression may be that there is no connection whatever. Bishops and painters of the Renaissance, physicians of the Roman Empire, musicians of 18th-century Germany—as we explore this gallery of talking portraits we seem to be in a world of time long past, remote from the world of steam engines and disputes about man's descent from the ape.

Yet our first impression is misleading. Many of these portraits explore problems that confronted Browning's contemporaries, especially problems of faith and doubt, good and evil, and problems of the function of the artist in modern life. *Caliban upon Setebos*, for example, is a highly topical critique of Darwinism and of natural (as opposed to supernatural) religions. Browning's own attitude towards these topics is partially concealed because of his use of speakers and of settings from earlier ages, yet we do encounter certain recurrent religious assumptions that we can safely assign to the poet himself. The most recurrent is that God has created an imperfect world as a kind of testing-ground, a "vale of soul-making," as Keats had said. It followed, for Browning's purposes, that man's soul must be immortal and that heaven itself be perfect. As Abt Vogler affirms: "On the earth the broken arcs; in the heaven, a perfect round." Armed with such a faith, Browning gives the impression that he was himself untroubled by the doubts that gnawed at the hearts of Arnold and Clough and Tennyson. The "evidence" presented by historical criticism of the Bible he could dismiss as simply irrelevant, just as D. H. Lawrence, a later romantic, disposed of evolution by contending that he did not feel the evidence for it in his solar plexus.

This kind of religious conviction attracts many readers who expect poetry to provide uplift and reassurances. Other readers find it an insurmountable obstacle, as fatuous as Macaulay's faith in progress. To what extent our capacity to enjoy the writings of an author is hindered if his religious position seems repellent to us is one of the most important problems in modern criticism. The problem is much too vast to explore here, but there is at least room to insert a qualifying clause to modify the indictment that Browning's critics too hastily draw up against his cheerful religious position. A blind optimist might be simply unreadable, but Browning's optimism was not blind. Few writers, in fact, seem to have been more aware of the existence of evil. His gallery of villains—murderers, sadistic husbands, mean and petty manipulators—is an extraordinary one. Nothing is more essential to a fair-minded study of his poetry than our recognition that his apparent optimism is consistently being tested by his bringing to light the evils of man's nature. Readers who prefer to dispose of his writings by pinning them down in a formulated phrase, instead of reading them with attention, invariably cite the following lines as summing up all of Browning:

> God's in his heaven—
> All's right with the world!

But if we turn to the poem in which these lines appear, we have to modify our formulation. *Pippa Passes* is a collection of sordid tales such as one encounters on the front page of the most lurid style of newspaper. The heroine, who works in a sweatshop 364 days a year, is about to be sent to Rome as a prostitute; a man and woman living in adultery have just murdered the woman's husband; a waspish set of Bohemians have tricked a youth into marriage. Because Pippa's innocence seems to counteract the sordidness of the other scenes, we may say afterwards that God is in his heaven. But that all's right with the world is merely affirmed by the girl; the poem does not show it.

A second aspect of Browning's poetry that separates it from the Victorian age is its style. The most representative Victorian poets such as Tennyson or Dante Gabriel Rossetti write in the manner of Keats, Milton, Spenser, and of classical poets such as Virgil. Theirs is the central stylistic tradition in English poetry, one which favors smoothly polished texture and pleasing liquidity of sound. Browning draws from a different tradition, more colloquial and discordant, a tradition which includes the poetry of John Donne, the soliloquies of Shakespeare, the comic verse of the early 19th-century poet Thomas Hood, and certain features of the narrative style of Chaucer. Of most significance are Browning's affinities with Donne. Both poets sacrifice, on occasion, the pleasures of harmony and of a consistent elevation of tone by using a harshly discordant style and unexpected juxtapositions that startle us into an awareness of a world of everyday realities and trivialities. Browning's late poem, *The Householder*, is an excellent example of this Donne-like vein. Readers who dislike this kind of poetry in Browning or in Donne argue that it suffers from prosiness. Oscar Wilde once described the novelist George Meredith as "a prose Browning." And so, he added, was Browning. Wilde's joke may help us to relate Browning to his contemporaries. For if Browning seems out of step with his fellow Victorian poets, he is by no means out of step with his contemporaries in prose. The grotesque, which plays such a prominent role in the style and subject matter of Carlyle and Dickens, and in the aesthetic theories of John Ruskin, is equally prominent in Browning's verse:

> Fee, faw, fum! bubble and squeak!
> Blessedest Thursday's the fat of the week.
> Rumble and tumble, sleek and rough,
> Stinking and savory, smug and gruff.

These opening lines of *Holy-Cross Day* display a similar kind of noisy jocularity in presenting a situation of grave seriousness as that used by Carlyle in his *French Revolution*.

The link between Browning and the Victorian prose writers is not limited to style. With the later generation of Victorian novelists, George Eliot, George Meredith, and Henry James, Browning shares a central pre-occupation. Like Eliot in particular, he was interested in exposing the devious ways in which our minds work and the complexity of our motives. "My stress lay on incidents in the development of a human soul," he wrote; "little else is worth study." His psychological insights can be illustrated in such poems as *The Bishop Orders His Tomb* or *Fra Lippo Lippi*. Although these are spoken monologues, not inner monologues in the manner of James Joyce, yet the insight into the workings of the minds of men is similarly acute. As in reading Joyce, we must be on our guard to follow the rapid shifts of the speaker's mental processes as jumps are made from one cluster of associations to another.

But Browning's role as a forerunner of 20th-century literature should not blind us to his essential Victorianism. Energy is the most characteristic aspect of his writing, and energy is perhaps the most characteristic aspect of Victorian literature in general. Often, of course, such energy was misdirected. Gerard Manley Hopkins identified this failing precisely when he complained of Browning's "Broad Church" way of talking, like "a man bouncing up from table with his mouth full of bread and cheese and saying that he meant to stand no blasted nonsense." At its best, however, such buoyancy is a virtue imparting a creative vitality to all of Browning's writings.

Porphyria's Lover[1]

The rain set early in tonight,
    The sullen wind was soon awake,
It tore the elm-tops down for spite,
    And did its worst to vex the lake:
    I listened with heart fit to break.   5
When glided in Porphyria; straight
    She shut the cold out and the storm,
And kneeled and made the cheerless grate
    Blaze up, and all the cottage warm;
    Which done, she rose, and from her form   10
Withdrew the dripping cloak and shawl,
    And laid her soiled gloves by, untied
Her hat and let the damp hair fall,
    And, last, she sat down by my side
    And called me. When no voice replied,   15
She put my arm about her waist,
    And made her smooth white shoulder bare,
And all her yellow hair displaced,
    And, stooping, made my cheek lie there,
    And spread, o'er all, her yellow hair,   20
Murmuring how she loved me—she
    Too weak, for all her heart's endeavor,
To set its struggling passion free
    From pride, and vainer ties dissever,
    And give herself to me forever.   25
But passion sometimes would prevail,
    Nor could tonight's gay feast restrain
A sudden thought of one so pale
    For love of her, and all in vain:
    So, she was come through wind and rain.   30
Be sure I looked up at her eyes
    Happy and proud; at last I knew
Porphyria worshiped me: surprise
    Made my heart swell, and still it grew
    While I debated what to do.   35
That moment she was mine, mine, fair,
    Perfectly pure and good: I found
A thing to do, and all her hair
    In one long yellow string I wound
    Three times her little throat around,   40
And strangled her. No pain felt she;
    I am quite sure she felt no pain.
As a shut bud that holds a bee,

1. One of a pair of monologues originally published under the title *Mad-*
house Cells, a title that emphasized the
abnormal state of mind of the speaker.

I warily oped her lids: again
　　Laughed the blue eyes without a stain. 45
And I untightened next the tress
　　About her neck; her cheek once more
Blushed bright beneath my burning kiss:
　　I propped her head up as before,
　　Only, this time my shoulder bore 50
Her head, which droops upon it still:
　　The smiling rosy little head,
So glad it has its utmost will,
　　That all it scorned at once is fled,
　　And I, its love, am gained instead! 55
Porphyria's love: she guessed not how
　　Her darling one wish would be heard.
And thus we sit together now,
　　And all night long we have not stirred,
　　And yet God has not said a word! 60

1834　　　　　　　　　　　　　　　　　　　1836, 1842

Soliloquy of the Spanish Cloister[1]

1

Gr-r-r—there go, my heart's abhorrence!
　　Water your damned flowerpots, do!
If hate killed men, Brother Lawrence,
　　God's blood, would not mine kill you!
What? your myrtle bush wants trimming? 5
　　Oh, that rose has prior claims—
Needs its leaden vase filled brimming?
　　Hell dry you up with its flames!

2

At the meal we sit together:
　　Salve tibi![2] I must hear 10
Wise talk of the kind of weather,
　　Sort of season, time of year:
Not a plenteous cork crop: scarcely
　　Dare we hope oak-galls,[3] *I doubt:*
What's the Latin name for "parsley"? 15
　　What's the Greek name for Swine's Snout?

3

Whew! We'll have our platter burnished,
　　Laid with care on our own shelf!
With a fire-new spoon we're furnished,
　　And a goblet for ourself, 20

1. No period of history is specified in this poem. The monastery setting is timeless and serves to intensify the pressure of meanness and hatred that is boiling up in the speaker.

2. "Hail to thee!" This and other speeches in italics are supposed to be the words of Brother Lawrence.
3. Abnormal outgrowths on oak trees, used for tanning.

Rinsed like something sacrificial
    Ere 'tis fit to touch our chaps[4]—
Marked with L. for our initial!
    (He-he! There his lily snaps!)

4

Saint, forsooth! While brown Dolores   25
    Squats outside the Convent bank
With Sanchicha, telling stories,
    Steeping tresses in the tank,
Blue-black, lustrous, thick like horsehairs,
    —Can't I see his dead eye glow,   30
Bright as 'twere a Barbary corsair's?[5]
    (That is, if he'd let it show!)

5

When he finishes refection,[6]
    Knife and fork he never lays
Cross-wise, to my recollection,   35
    As do I, in Jesu's praise.
I the Trinity illustrate,
    Drinking watered orange pulp—
In three sips the Arian[7] frustrate;
    While he drains his at one gulp.   40

6

Oh, those melons? If he's able
    We're to have a feast! so nice!
One goes to the Abbot's table,
    All of us get each a slice.
How go on your flowers? None double?   45
    Not one fruit-sort can you spy?
Strange!—And I, too, at such trouble,
    Keep them close-nipped on the sly!

7

There's a great text in Galatians,[8]
    Once you trip on it, entails   50
Twenty-nine distinct damnations,
    One sure, if another fails:
If I trip him just a-dying,
    Sure of heaven as sure can be,
Spin him round and send him flying
    Off to hell, a Manichee?[9]   55

8

Or, my scrofulous French novel
    On gray paper with blunt type!

4. Jaws.
5. Pirate of the Barbary Coast of northern Africa, renowned for fierceness and lechery.
6. Dinner.
7. Heretical followers of Arius (256–336), who denied the doctrine of the Trinity.
8. The speaker hopes to obtain Lawrence's damnation by luring him into a heresy, this to be accomplished by exposing him to the difficult task of interpreting "Galatians" in an unswervingly orthodox way. In Galatians v.15–23, St. Paul specifies an assortment of "works of the flesh" that lead to damnation, which could make up a total of "twenty-nine."
9. A heretic, a follower of the Persian prophet of the 3rd century, Mani.

Simply glance at it, you grovel
    Hand and foot in Belial's gripe: 60
If I double down its pages
    At the woeful sixteenth print,
When he gathers his greengages,
    Ope a sieve and slip it in't?

          9
Or, there's Satan!—one might venture   65
    Pledge one's soul to him,[1] yet leave
Such a flaw in the indenture
    As he'd miss till, past retrieve,
Blasted lay that rose-acacia
    We're so proud of! *Hy, Zy, Hine* . . .[2]   70
'St, there's Vespers! *Plena gratiá*
    Ave, Virgo![3] Gr-r-r—you swine!

ca. 1839   1842

My Last Duchess[1]

FERRARA

That's my last Duchess painted on the wall,
Looking as if she were alive. I call
That piece a wonder, now: Frà Pandolf's[2] hands
Worked busily a day, and there she stands.
Will't please you sit and look at her? I said   5
"Frà Pandolf" by design, for never read
Strangers like you that pictured countenance,
The depth and passion of its earnest glance,
But to myself they turned (since none puts by
The curtain I have drawn for you, but I)   10
And seemed as they would ask me, if they durst,
How such a glance came there; so, not the first
Are you to turn and ask thus Sir, 'twas not
Her husband's presence only, called that spot
Of joy into the Duchess' cheek: perhaps   15
Frà Pandolf chanced to say "Her mantle laps
Over my lady's wrist too much," or "Paint
Must never hope to reproduce the faint
Half-flush that dies along her throat": such stuff
Was courtesy, she thought, and cause enough   20

1. The speaker would pledge his own soul to Satan in return for blasting Lawrence and his "rose-acacia," but the pledge would be so cleverly worded that the speaker would not have to pay, himself, his debt to Satan. There would be an escape-clause, a "flaw in the indenture," for himself.
2. Perhaps the opening of a mysterious curse against Lawrence.
3. "Full of grace, Hail, Virgin!" The speaker's twisted state of mind may be reflected in his mixed-up version of the prayer to Mary: "Ave, Maria, gratia plena."

1. The poem is based on incidents in the life of Alfonso II, Duke of Ferrara in Italy, whose first wife, Lucrezia, a young girl, died in 1561 after three years of marriage. Following her death, the Duke negotiated through an agent to marry a niece of the Count of Tyrol. Browning represents the Duke as addressing this agent.
2. Brother Pandolf, an imaginary painter.

For calling up that spot of joy. She had
A heart—how shall I say?—too soon made glad,
Too easily impressed; she liked whate'er
She looked on, and her looks went everywhere.
Sir, 'twas all one! My favor at her breast,   25
The dropping of the daylight in the West,
The bough of cherries some officious fool
Broke in the orchard for her, the white mule
She rode with round the terrace—all and each
Would draw from her alike the approving speech,   30
Or blush, at least. She thanked men—good! but thanked
Somehow—I know not how—as if she ranked
My gift of a nine-hundred-years-old name
With anybody's gift. Who'd stoop to blame
This sort of trifling? Even had you skill   35
In speech—(which I have not)—to make your will
Quite clear to such an one, and say, "Just this
Or that in you disgusts me; here you miss,
Or there exceed the mark"—and if she let
Herself be lessoned so, nor plainly set   40
Her wits to yours, forsooth, and made excuse
—E'en then would be some stooping, and I choose
Never to stoop. Oh sir, she smiled, no doubt,
Whene'er I passed her; but who passed without
Much the same smile? This grew; I gave commands;   45
Then all smiles stopped together. There she stands
As if alive. Will't please you rise? We'll meet
The company below, then. I repeat,
The Count your master's known munificence
Is ample warrant that no just pretense   50
Of mine for dowry will be disallowed;
Though his fair daughter's self, as I avowed
At starting, is my object. Nay, we'll go
Together down, sir. Notice Neptune, though,
Taming a sea horse, thought a rarity,   55
Which Claus of Innsbruck[3] cast in bronze for me!

1842   1842

The Laboratory
Ancien Régime

1

Now that I, tying thy glass mask tightly,
May gaze thro' these faint smokes curling whitely,
As thou pliest thy trade in this devil's-smithy—
Which is the poison to poison her, prithee?

2

He is with her, and they know that I know   5
Where they are, what they do: they believe my tears flow
While they laugh, laugh at me, at me fled to the drear
Empty church, to pray God in, for them!—I am here.

3. An unidentified or imaginary sculptor. The Count of Tyrol had his capital at
Innsbruck.

3

Grind away, moisten and mash up thy paste,
Pound at thy powder—I am not in haste!   10
Better sit thus, and observe thy strange things,
Than go where men wait me and dance at the King's.

4

That in the mortar—you call it a gum?
Ah, the brave tree whence such gold oozings come!
And yonder soft phial, the exquisite blue,   15
Sure to taste sweetly, is that poison too?

5

Had I but all of them, thee and thy treasures,
What a wild crowd of invisible pleasures!
To carry pure death in an earring, a casket,
A signet, a fan-mount, a filigree basket!   20

6

Soon, at the King's,[1] a mere lozenge to give,
And Pauline should have just thirty minutes to live!
But to light a pastile, and Elise, with her head
And her breast and her arms and her hands, should drop dead!

7

Quick—is it finished? The color's too grim!   25
Why not soft like the phial's, enticing and dim?
Let it brighten her drink, let her turn it and stir,
And try it and taste, ere she fix and prefer!

8

What a drop! She's not little, no minion[2] like me!
That's why she ensnared him: this never will free   30
The soul from those masculine eyes—say, "no!"
To that pulse's magnificent come-and-go.

9

For only last night, as they whispered, I brought
My own eyes to bear on her so, that I thought
Could I keep them one half minute fixed, she would fall   35
Shriveled; she fell not; yet this does it all!

10

Not that I bid you spare her the pain;
Let death be felt and the proof remain:
Brand, burn up, bite into its grace—
He is sure to remember her dying face!   40

11

Is it done? Take my mask off! Nay, be not morose;
It kills her, and this prevents seeing it close:
The delicate droplet, my whole fortune's fee!
If it hurts her, beside, can it ever hurt me?

---

1. Probably King Louis XIV of France (1643–1715). In the 1670's a police investigation disclosed that an extraordinary number of women and men attached to the King's court had been disposing of rivals and enemies by poisonings. Some 36 of the accused courtiers and the dealers from whom they had purchased poisons were punished by torture and burnt to death. 2. A dainty and delicate person.

12

Now, take all my jewels, gorge gold to your fill,45
You may kiss me, old man, on my mouth if you will!
But brush this dust off me, lest horror it brings
Ere I know it—next moment I dance at the King's!

ca. 18441844

The Lost Leader[1]

1

Just for a handful of silver he left us,
Just for a riband to stick in his coat—
Found the one gift of which fortune bereft us,
Lost all the others she lets us devote;
They, with the gold to give, doled him out silver,5
So much was theirs who so little allowed:
How all our copper had gone for his service!
Rags—were they purple, his heart had been proud!
We that had loved him so, followed him, honored him,
Lived in his mild and magnificent eye,10
Learned his great language, caught his clear accents,
Made him our pattern to live and to die!
Shakespeare was of us, Milton was for us,
Burns, Shelley, were with us—they watch from their graves!
He alone breaks from the van[2] and the freemen15
—He alone sinks to the rear and the slaves!

2

We shall march prospering—not through his presence;
Songs may inspirit us—not from his lyre;
Deeds will be done—while he boasts his quiescence,
Still bidding crouch whom the rest bade aspire:20
Blot out his name, then, record one lost soul more,
One task more declined, one more footpath untrod,
One more devils'-triumph and sorrow for angels,
One wrong more to man, one more insult to God!
Life's night begins: let him never come back to us!25
There would be doubt, hesitation and pain,
Forced praise on our part—the glimmer of twilight,
Never glad confident morning again!
Best fight on well, for we taught him—strike gallantly,
Menace our heart ere we master his own;30
Then let him receive the new knowledge and wait us,
Pardoned in heaven, the first by the throne!

18431845

---

1. William Wordsworth, who had been an ardent liberal in his youth, had become a political conservative in later years. In old age, when he accepted a grant of money from the government ("a handful of silver") and also the office of poet laureate ("a riband to stick in his coat"), he alienated some of his young admirers such as Browning, whose liberalism was then as ardent as Wordsworth's had once been.

Cf. J. G. Whittier's poem *Ichabod*, which embodies a similar sense of sorrowful indignation over the apostasy of Daniel Webster, a great leader formerly admired by the poet.

2. Vanguard of the army of liberalism.

How They Brought the Good News from Ghent to Aix[1]

(16—)

1

I sprang to the stirrup, and Joris, and he;
I galloped, Dirck galloped, we galloped all three;
"Good speed!" cried the watch, as the gate-bolts undrew;
"Speed!" echoed the wall to us galloping through;
Behind shut the postern, the lights sank to rest,   5
And into the midnight we galloped abreast.

2

Not a word to each other; we kept the great pace
Neck by neck, stride by stride, never changing our place;
I turned in my saddle and made its girths tight,
Then shortened each stirrup, and set the pique[2] right,   10
Rebuckled the cheek-strap, chained slacker the bit,
Nor galloped less steadily Roland a whit.

3

'Twas moonset at starting; but while we drew near
Lokeren, the cocks crew and twilight dawned clear;
At Boom, a great yellow star came out to see;   15
At Düffeld, 'twas morning as plain as could be;
And from Mecheln church-steeple we heard the half-chime,
So, Joris broke silence with, "Yet there is time!"

4

At Aershot, up leaped of a sudden the sun,
And against him the cattle stood black every one,   20
To stare through the mist at us galloping past,
And I saw my stout galloper Roland at last,
With resolute shoulders, each butting away
The haze, as some bluff river headland its spray:

5

And his low head and crest, just one sharp ear bent back   25
For my voice, and the other pricked out on his track;
And one eye's black intelligence—ever that glance
O'er its white edge at me, his own master, askance!
And the thick heavy spume-flakes which ay and anon
His fierce lips shook upwards in galloping on.   30

6

By Hasselt, Dirck groaned; and cried Joris, "Stay spur!
Your Roos galloped bravely, the fault's not in her,
We'll remember at Aix"—for one heard the quick wheeze
Of her chest, saw the stretched neck and staggering knees,
And sunk tail, and horrible heave of the flank,   35
As down on her haunches she shuddered and sank.

1. The distance between Ghent, in Flanders, and Aix-la-Chapelle is about one hundred miles. Browning said that the incident, occurring during the wars between Flanders and Spain, was an imaginary one.
2. Spur or pommel.

7

So, we were left galloping, Joris and I,
Past Looz and past Tongres, no cloud in the sky;
The broad sun above laughed a pitiless laugh,
'Neath our feet broke the brittle bright stubble like chaff;   40
Till over by Dalhem a dome-spire sprang white,
And "Gallop," gasped Joris, "for Aix is in sight!"

8

"How they'll greet us!"—and all in a moment his roan
Rolled neck and croup over, lay dead as a stone;
And there was my Roland to bear the whole weight   45
Of the news which alone could save Aix from her fate,
With his nostrils like pits full of blood to the brim,
And with circles of red for his eye-sockets' rim.

9

Then I cast loose my buffcoat, each holster let fall,
Shook off both my jack boots, let go belt and all,   50
Stood up in the stirrup, leaned, patted his ear,
Called my Roland his pet name, my horse without peer;
Clapped my hands, laughed and sang, any noise, bad or good,
Till at length into Aix Roland galloped and stood.

10

And all I remember is—friends flocking round   55
As I sat with his head 'twixt my knees on the ground;
And no voice but was praising this Roland of mine,
As I poured down his throat our last measure of wine,
Which (the burgesses voted by common consent)
Was no more than his due who brought good news from Ghent. 60
ca. 1844   1845

Home-Thoughts, from Abroad

1

Oh, to be in England
Now that April's there,
And whoever wakes in England
Sees, some morning, unaware,
That the lowest boughs and the brushwood sheaf   5
Round the elm-tree bole are in tiny leaf,
While the chaffinch sings on the orchard bough
In England—now!

2

And after April, when May follows,
And the whitethroat builds, and all the swallows!   10
Hark, where my blossomed peartree in the hedge
Leans to the field and scatters on the clover
Blossoms and dewdrops—at the bent spray's edge—
That's the wise thrush; he sings each song twice over,

Lest you should think he never could recapture   15
The first fine careless rapture!
And though the fields look rough with hoary dew,
All will be gay when noontide wakes anew
The buttercups, the little children's dower
—Far brighter than this gaudy melon-flower!   20
ca. 1845   1845

Home-Thoughts, from the Sea

Nobly, nobly Cape Saint Vincent[1] to the northwest died away;
Sunset ran, one glorious blood-red, reeking into Cadiz Bay;
Bluish 'mid the burning water, full in face Trafalgar[2] lay;
In the dimmest northeast distance dawned Gibraltar grand and gray;
"Here and here did England help me: how can I help England?"—
          say,   5
Whoso turns as I, this evening, turn to God to praise and pray,
While Jove's planet[3] rises yonder, silent over Africa.
1844   1845

The Bishop Orders His Tomb at Saint Praxed's Church[1]

ROME, 15—

Vanity, saith the preacher, vanity![2]
Draw round my bed: is Anselm keeping back?
Nephews—sons mine . . . ah God, I know not! Well—
She, men would have to be your mother once,
Old Gandolf envied me, so fair she was!   5
What's done is done, and she is dead beside,
Dead long ago, and I am Bishop since,
And as she died so must we die ourselves,
And thence ye may perceive the world's a dream.
Life, how and what is it? As here I lie   10

1. Off the coast of Portugal, scene of British naval victory under Admiral Nelson (1797).
2. A cape in Spain, where Nelson won his great victory over Napoleon's fleets (1805).
3. Jupiter.
1. In *Fra Lippo Lippi* Browning represents the dawn of the Renaissance in Italy, with its fresh zest for "the beauty and the wonder and the power" of man's experiences in this world. In the present monologue he portrays a later stage of the Renaissance when such worldliness, full-blown, had infected even some of the leading churchmen of Italy. Browning's portrait of the dying bishop is, however, not primarily a satire against corruption in the church. It is a brilliant exposition of the workings of a mind, a mind that has been conditioned by special historical circumstances. The Victorian historian of art, John Ruskin, said of this poem: "I know of no other piece of modern English, prose or poetry, in which there is so much told, as in these lines, of the Renaissance spirit—its worldliness, inconsistency, pride, hypocrisy, ignorance of itself, love of art, of luxury, and of good Latin. It is nearly all that I have said of the central Renaissance in thirty pages of the *Stones of Venice*, put into as many lines, Browning's also being the antecedent work."
   St. Praxed's Church was named in honor of St. Praxedes, a Roman virgin of the 2nd century who gave her riches to poor Christians. Both the bishop and his predecessor, Gandolf, are imaginary persons.
2. Cf. Ecclesiastes i.2.

In this state chamber, dying by degrees,
Hours and long hours in the dead night, I ask
"Do I live, am I dead?" Peace, peace seems all.
Saint Praxed's ever was the church for peace;
And so, about this tomb of mine. I fought   15
With tooth and nail to save my niche, ye know:
—Old Gandolf cozened[3] me, despite my care;
Shrewd was that snatch from out the corner south
He graced his carrion with, God curse the same!
Yet still my niche is not so cramped but thence   20
One sees the pulpit o' the epistle side,[4]
And somewhat of the choir, those silent seats,
And up into the aery dome where live
The angels, and a sunbeam's sure to lurk:
And I shall fill my slab of basalt[5] there,   25
And 'neath my tabernacle[6] take my rest,
With those nine columns round me, two and two,
The odd one at my feet where Anselm stands:
Peach-blossom marble all, the rare, the ripe
As fresh-poured red wine of a mighty pulse.[7]   30
—Old Gandolf with his paltry onion-stone,[8]
Put me where I may look at him! True peach,
Rosy and flawless: how I earned the prize!
Draw close: that conflagration of my church
—What then? So much was saved if aught were missed!   35
My sons, ye would not be my death? Go dig
The white-grape vineyard where the oil-press stood,
Drop water gently till the surface sink,
And if ye find . . . Ah God, I know not, I! . . .
Bedded in store of rotten fig leaves soft,   40
And corded up in a tight olive-frail,[9]
Some lump, ah God, of *lapis lazuli*,[1]
Big as a Jew's head cut off at the nape,
Blue as a vein o'er the Madonna's breast . . .
Sons, all have I bequeathed you, villas, all,   45
That brave Frascati[2] villa with its bath,
So, let the blue lump poise between my knees,
Like God the Father's globe on both his hands
Ye worship in the Jesu Church[3] so gay,
For Gandolf shall not choose but see and burst!   50
Swift as a weaver's shuttle fleet our years:[4]
Man goeth to the grave, and where is he?

3. Cheated.
4. The Epistles of the New Testament are read from the right-hand side of the altar (as one faces it).
5. Dark-colored igneous rock.
6. Stone canopy or tentlike roof, presumably supported by the "nine columns" under which the sculptured effigy of the Bishop would lie on the slab of basalt.
7. Browning uses "pulse" in the special sense of a pulpy mash of fermented grapes from which a strong wine might be poured off. In a later poem, the *Epilogue* to *Pacchiarotto,* he likens such wine to "viscous blood" that has been "squeezed gold" from the "pulp" of the grapes.
8. An inferior marble that peels in layers.
9. Basket for holding olives.
1. Valuable bright blue stone.
2. Suburb of Rome, used as a resort by wealthy Italians.
3. Il Gesù, a Jesuit church in Rome.
4. Cf. Job vii.6.

Did I say basalt for my slab, sons? Black[5]—
'Twas ever antique-black I meant! How else
Shall ye contrast my frieze[6] to come beneath?   55
The bas-relief in bronze ye promised me,
Those Pans and Nymphs ye wot of, and perchance
Some tripod, thyrsus, with a vase or so,
The Saviour at his sermon on the mount,
Saint Praxed in a glory, and one Pan   60
Ready to twitch the Nymph's last garment off,
And Moses with the tables[7] . . . but I know
Ye mark me not! What do they whisper thee,
Child of my bowels, Anselm? Ah, ye hope
To revel down my villas while I gasp   65
Bricked o'er with beggar's moldy travertine[8]
Which Gandolf from his tomb-top chuckles at!
Nay, boys, ye love me—all of jasper, then!
'Tis jasper ye stand pledged to, lest I grieve
My bath must needs be left behind, alas!   70
One block, pure green as a pistachio nut,
There's plenty jasper somewhere in the world—
And have I not Saint Praxed's ear to pray
Horses for ye, and brown Greek manuscripts,
And mistresses with great smooth marbly limbs?   75
—That's if ye carve my epitaph aright,
Choice Latin, picked phrase, Tully's[9] every word,
No gaudy ware like Gandolf's second line—
Tully, my masters? Ulpian[1] serves his need!
And then how I shall lie through centuries,   80
And hear the blessed mutter of the mass,
And see God made and eaten all day long,[2]
And feel the steady candle flame, and taste
Good strong thick stupefying incense-smoke!
For as I lie here, hours of the dead night,   85
Dying in state and by such slow degrees,
I fold my arms as if they clasped a crook,[3]
And stretch my feet forth straight as stone can point,
And let the bedclothes, for a mortcloth,[4] drop
Into great laps and folds of sculptor's-work: 90
And as yon tapers dwindle, and strange thoughts
Grow, with a certain humming in my ears,

5. Black marble.
6. Continuous band of sculpture.
7. The "bas-relief" (or sculpture in which the figures do not project far from the background surface) would consist of a mixture of pagan and religious scenes (lines 57–62). Among the former would be a "tripod," on which priestesses at the oracle of Delphi sat to make their prophecies, and a "thyrsus," a long staff carried in processions in honor of Bacchus, the god of wine. The religious scenes would include St. Praxed with her halo ("a glory") and Moses with the stone tablets ("tables") on which the Ten Commandments were written. Such intermingling of classical and Christian traditions is characteristic of the Renaissance.
8. Italian limestone.
9. A familiar name for Marcus Tullius Cicero, whose writing was the model, during the Renaissance, of classical Latin prose.
1. Late Latin prose-writer, not considered a model of good style.
2. Reference to the doctrine of transubstantiation.
3. Bishop's staff or crozier.
4. Rich cloth spread over a dead body or coffin.

About the life before I lived this life,
And this life too, popes, cardinals, and priests,
Saint Praxed at his sermon on the mount,[5]   95
Your tall pale mother with her talking eyes,
And new-found agate urns as fresh as day,
And marble's language, Latin pure, discreet
—Aha, ELUCESCEBAT[6] quoth our friend?
No Tully, said I, Ulpian at the best!   100
Evil and brief hath been my pilgrimage.
All *lapis*, all, sons! Else I give the Pope
My villas! Will ye ever eat my heart?
Ever your eyes were as a lizard's quick,
They glitter like your mother's for my soul,   105
Or ye would heighten my impoverished frieze,
Piece out its starved design, and fill my vase
With grapes, and add a vizor and a Term,[7]
And to the tripod ye would tie a lynx
That in his struggle throws the thyrsus down,   110
To comfort me on my entablature[8]
Whereon I am to lie till I must ask
"Do I live, am I dead?" There, leave me, there!
For ye have stabbed me with ingratitude
To death—ye wish it—God, ye wish it! Stone—   115
Gritstone,[9] a-crumble! Clammy squares which sweat
As if the corpse they keep were oozing through—
And no more *lapis* to delight the world!
Well go! I bless ye. Fewer tapers there,
But in a row: and, going, turn your backs   120
—Aye, like departing altar-ministrants,
And leave me in my church, the church for peace,
That I may watch at leisure if he leers—
Old Gandolf, at me, from his onion-stone,
As still he envied me, so fair she was!   125

1844   1845

Meeting at Night[1]

1

The gray sea and the long black land;
And the yellow half-moon large and low;
And the startled little waves that leap

---

5. The bishop is confusing St. Praxed (a woman) with Christ—an indication that his mind is wandering.
6. Word from Gandolf's epitaph meaning "he was illustrious." The bishop considers the form of the verb to be in "gaudy" bad taste. If the epitaph had been copied from Cicero instead of from Ulpian, the word would have been *elucebat*.
7. "Vizor": part of a helmet, often represented in sculpture. "Term": statue of Terminus, the Roman god of boundaries, usually represented without arms.
8. Horizontal platform supporting a statue or effigy.
9. Coarse sandstone such as that used for grindstones.
1. This poem and the one which follows it appeared originally under the single title *Night and Morning*. The speaker in both is a man.

In fiery ringlets from their sleep,
As I gain the cove with pushing prow,   5
And quench its speed i' the slushy sand.

2

Then a mile of warm sea-scented beach;
Three fields to cross till a farm appears;
A tap at the pane, the quick sharp scratch
And blue spurt of a lighted match,   10
And a voice less loud, through its joys and fears,
Than the two hearts beating each to each!

1845

Parting at Morning

Round the cape of a sudden came the sea,
And the sun looked over the mountain's rim:
And straight was a path of gold for him,[2]
And the need of a world of men for me.

1845

A Toccata of Galuppi's[1]

1

Oh, Galuppi, Baldassaro, this is very sad to find!
I can hardly misconceive you; it would prove me deaf and blind;
But although I take your meaning, 'tis with such a heavy mind!

2

Here you come with your old music, and here's all the good it brings.
What, they lived once thus at Venice where the merchants were
      the kings,   5
Where Saint Mark's is, where the Doges used to wed the sea with
      rings?[2]

2. The sun.
1. There are three speakers in this short poem. The first is a 19th-century scientist in England who is listening to a musical composition by Baldassaro Galuppi (1706–85), a Venetian. The music evokes for this scientist the voice of the dead composer (the third speaker) who comments upon the pointless and butterfly-like frivolity of his 18th-century contemporaries. The second group of voices is made up of comments by members of Galuppi's audience as they respond to the different moods of his clavichord-playing during a party which the scientist imagines to have taken place in Venice.
  A "toccata" is defined in Grove's *Dictionary of Music* as a "touch-piece, or a composition intended to exhibit the touch and execution of the performer." The same authority states that "no particular composition was taken as the basis of the poem," but Browning is known to have himself played on the organ some unpublished compositions by Galuppi, and one of these, not yet identified, may have occasioned the poem. Browning's interest in music was keen, and his knowledge of the art was more extensive than that of most English poets.
2. An annual ceremony in which the Doge, the Venetian chief magistrate, threw a ring into the water to symbolize the bond between his city, with its maritime empire, and the sea.

3

Aye, because the sea's the street there; and 'tis arched by . . . what
  you call
. . . Shylock's bridge[3] with houses on it, where they kept the carnival:
I was never out of England—it's as if I saw it all.

4

Did young people take their pleasure when the sea was warm in
  May?   10
Balls and masks[4] begun at midnight, burning ever to midday,
When they made up fresh adventures for the morrow, do you say?

5

Was a lady such a lady, cheeks so round and lips so red—
On her neck the small face buoyant, like a bellflower on its bed,
O'er the breast's superb abundance where a man might base his
  head?   15

6

Well, and it was graceful of them—they'd break talk off and afford
—She, to bite her mask's black velvet—he, to finger on his sword,
While you sat and played toccatas, stately at the clavichord?[5]

7

What? Those lesser thirds so plaintive, sixths diminished, sigh on
  sigh,
Told them something? Those suspensions, those solutions—"Must
  we die?"   20
Those commiserating sevenths[6]—"Life might last! we can but
  try!"

8

"Were you happy?"—"Yes."—"And are you still as happy?"—
  "Yes. And you?"
—"Then, more kisses!"—"Did *I* stop them, when a million seemed
  so few?"
Hark, the dominant's persistence till it must be answered to!

9

So, an octave struck the answer. Oh, they praised you, I dare say! 25
"Brave Galuppi! that was music; good alike at grave and gay!
I can always leave off talking when I hear a master play!"

10

Then they left you for their pleasure: till in due time, one by one,
Some with lives that came to nothing, some with deeds as well un-
  done,   29
Death stepped tacitly and took them where they never see the sun.

---

3. The Rialto, a bridge over the Grand
Canal.
4. Masquerades.
5. A keyboard instrument in which the
strings are struck by metal hammers.
As a mechanism it resembles a piano,
but the sound is more like that of a
harpsichord.
6. This term and others in these lines
all refer to the technical devices used
by Galuppi to produce alternating moods
in his music, conflict in each instance
being resolved into harmony. Thus the
"dominant" (the fifth note of the
scale), after being persistently sounded,
is answered by a resolving chord (lines
24–25).

11

But when I sit down to reason, think to take my stand nor swerve,
While I triumph o'er a secret wrung from nature's close reserve,
In you come with your cold music till I creep through every nerve.

12

Yes, you, like a ghostly cricket, creaking where a house was burned:
"Dust and ashes, dead and done with, Venice spent what Venice
    earned.   35
The soul, doubtless, is immortal—where a soul can be discerned.

13

"Yours for instance: you know physics, something of geology,
Mathematics are your pastime; souls shall rise in their degree;
Butterflies may dread extinction—you'll not die, it cannot be!

14

"As for Venice and her people, merely born to bloom and drop,   40
Here on earth they bore their fruitage, mirth and folly were the
    crop:
What of soul was left, I wonder, when the kissing had to stop?

15

"Dust and ashes!" So you creak it, and I want the heart to scold.
Dear dead women, with such hair, too—what's become of all the
    gold   44
Used to hang and brush their bosoms? I feel chilly and grown old.
ca. 1847   1855

Memorabilia[1]

1

Ah, did you once see Shelley plain,
    And did he stop and speak to you
And did you speak to him again?
    How strange it seems and new!

2

But you were living before that,   5
    And also you are living after;
And the memory I started at—
    My starting moves your laughter.

3

I crossed a moor, with a name of its own
    And a certain use in the world no doubt,   10
Yet a hand's-breadth of it shines alone
    'Mid the blank miles round about:

1. The title means "things worth remembering." Browning reports that he once met a stranger in a bookstore who mentioned having talked with Shelley. "Suddenly the stranger paused, and burst into laughter as he observed me staring at him with blanched face. * * * I still vividly remember how strangely the presence of a man who had seen and spoken with Shelley affected me."

4
For there I picked up on the heather
And there I put inside my breast
A molted feather, an eagle feather! 15
Well, I forget the rest.

ca. 1851   1855

Love Among the Ruins[1]

1
Where the quiet-colored end of evening smiles,
    Miles and miles
On the solitary pastures where our sheep
    Half-asleep
Tinkle homeward through the twilight, stray or stop 5
    As they crop—
Was the site once of a city great and gay
    (So they say),
Of our country's very capital, its prince
    Ages since 10
Held his court in, gathered councils, wielding far
    Peace or war.

2
Now—the country does not even boast a tree,
    As you see,
To distinguish slopes of verdure, certain rills 15
    From the hills
Intersect and give a name to (else they run
    Into one),
Where the domed and daring palace shot its spires
    Up like fires 20
O'er the hundred-gated circuit of a wall
    Bounding all,
Made of marble, men might march on nor be pressed,
    Twelve abreast.

3
And such plenty and perfection, see, of grass 25
    Never was!
Such a carpet as, this summertime, o'erspreads
    And embeds
Every vestige of the city, guessed alone,
    Stock or stone— 30
Where a multitude of men breathed joy and woe
    Long ago;
Lust of glory pricked their hearts up, dread of shame
    Struck them tame;

1. The ruins may be those of such cities as Babylon or Nineveh or one of the Etruscan cities of Italy.
    The unusual stanza used in this poem was invented by Browning. The contrast between past and present, which is the core of the poem, is reinforced by devoting one half of each stanza to the past and the other half to the present.

And that glory and that shame alike, the gold 35
    Bought and sold.

4
Now—the single little turret that remains
    On the plains,
By the caper overrooted, by the gourd
    Overscored, 40
While the patching houseleek's[2] head of blossom winks
    Through the chinks—
Marks the basement whence a tower in ancient time
    Sprang sublime,
And a burning ring, all round, the chariots traced 45
    As they raced,
And the monarch and his minions and his dames
    Viewed the games.

5
And I know, while thus the quiet-colored eve
    Smiles to leave 50
To their folding, all our many-tinkling fleece
    In such peace,
And the slopes and rills in undistinguished gray
    Melt away—
That a girl with eager eyes and yellow hair 55
    Waits me there
In the turret whence the charioteers caught soul
    For the goal,
When the king looked, where she locks now, breathless, dumb
    Till I come. 60

6
But he looked upon the city, every side,
    Far and wide,
All the mountains topped with temples, all the glades'
    Colonnades,
All the causeys,[3] bridges, aqueducts—and then, 65
    All the men!
When I do come, she will speak not, she will stand,
    Either hand
On my shoulder, give her eyes the first embrace
    Of my face, 70
Ere we rush, ere we extinguish sight and speech
    Each on each.

7
In one year they sent a million fighters forth
    South and north,
And they built their gods a brazen pillar high 75
    As the sky,
Yet reserved a thousand chariots in full force—
    Gold, of course,

2. Common European plant, with petals clustered in the shape of rosettes.

3. Causeways or roads raised above low ground.

Oh heart! oh blood that freezes, blood that burns!
    Earth's returns   80
For whole centuries of folly, noise, and sin!
    Shut them in,
With their triumphs and their glories and the rest!
    Love is best.

1852   1855

Women and Roses[1]

1

I dream of a red-rose tree.
And which of its roses three
Is the dearest rose to me?

2

Round and round, like a dance of snow
In a dazzling drift, as its guardians, go   5
Floating the women faded for ages,
Sculptured in stone, on the poet's pages.
Then follow women fresh and gay,
Living and loving and loved today.
Last, in the rear, flee the multitude of maidens,   10
Beauties yet unborn. And all, to one cadence,
They circle their rose on my rose tree.

3

Dear rose, thy term is reached,
Thy leaf hangs loose and bleached:
Bees pass it unimpeached.[2]   15

4

Stay then, stoop, since I cannot climb,
You, great shapes of the antique time!
How shall I fix you, fire you, freeze you,
Break my heart at your feet to please you?
Oh, to possess and be possessed!   20
Hearts that beat 'neath each pallid breast!
Once but of love, the poesy, the passion,
Drink but once and die!—In vain, the same fashion,
They circle their rose on my rose tree.

5

Dear rose, thy joy's undimmed,   25
Thy cup is ruby-rimmed,
Thy cup's heart nectar-brimmed.

6

Deep, as drops from a statue's plinth[3]
The bee sucked in by the hyacinth,

1. Like Chaucer in the *Romaunt of the Rose* and also like Tennyson in *Maud*, the speaker in the following dream lyric associates roses with fair women and a garden of roses with the garden of love. The beautiful women of the past are first evoked (stanzas 3, 4); then those of the present (stanzas 5, 6); and finally those of the future (stanzas 7, 8). All, however, elude him.
2. Unhindered.
3. Base.

So will I bury me while burning, 30
Quench like him at a plunge my yearning,
Eyes in your eyes, lips on your lips!
Fold me fast where the cincture⁴ slips,
Prison all my soul in eternities of pleasure,
Girdle me for once! But no—the old measure, 35
They circle their rose on my rose tree.

7

Dear rose without a thorn,
Thy bud's the babe unborn:
First streak of a new morn.

8

Wings, lend wings for the cold, the clear! 40
What is far conquers what is near.
Roses will bloom nor want beholders,
Sprung from the dust where our flesh molders.
What shall arrive with the cycle's change?
A novel grace and a beauty strange. 45
I will make an Eve, be the artist that began her,
Shaped her to his mind!—Alas! in like manner
They circle their rose on my rose tree.

1852   1855

"Childe Roland to the Dark Tower Came"¹
(SEE EDGAR'S SONG IN "LEAR")

1

My first thought was, he lied in every word,
    That hoary cripple, with malicious eye
    Askance² to watch the working of his lie
On mine, and mouth scarce able to afford

4. Ornamental belt worn by women, usually across the hips.
1. Browning stated that this poem "came upon me as a kind of dream," and that it was written in one day. Although the poem was among those of his own writings that pleased him most, he was reluctant to explain what the dream (or nightmare) signified. He once agreed with a friend's suggestion that the meaning might be expressed in the statement: "He that endureth to the end shall be saved." Most readers have responded to the poem in this way, finding in the story of Roland's quest an inspiring expression of defiance and courage. Other readers find the poem to be more expressive of despair than of enduring hope, and it is at least true that the landscape is as grim and nightmarelike as in such 20th-century writings as T. S. Eliot's *Hollow Men* or Franz Kafka's *Penal Colony*. It has been said of *Childe Roland* that every reader can be his own allegorist, and such a poem thus poses a further large question of whether or not total comprehension of a work is always essential for appreciation of literature.

The lines from Shakespeare's *King Lear* (III.iv.187–90), from which the title is taken, are spoken when Lear is about to enter a hovel on the heath, and Edgar, feigning madness, chants the fragment of a song reminiscent of quests and challenges in fairly tales: "Child Rowland to the dark tower came; / His word was still / 'Fie, foh, and fum! / I smell the blood of a British man.'" A "childe" is a youth of gentle birth, usually a candidate for knighthood.
2. Squinting sidewise.

Suppression of the glee, that pursed and scored   5
   Its edge, at one more victim gained thereby.

2

What else should he be set for, with his staff?
   What, save to waylay with his lies, ensnare
   All travelers who might find him posted there,
And ask the road? I guessed what skull-like laugh   10
Would break, what crutch 'gin write my epitaph
   For pastime in the dusty thoroughfare,

3

If at his counsel I should turn aside
   Into that ominous tract which, all agree,
   Hides the Dark Tower. Yet acquiescingly   15
I did turn as he pointed: neither pride
Nor hope rekindling at the end descried,
   So much as gladness that some end might be.

4

For, what with my whole world-wide wandering,
   What with my search drawn out through years, my hope   20
   Dwindled into a ghost not fit to cope
With that obstreperous joy success would bring,
I hardly tried now to rebuke the spring
   My heart made, finding failure in its scope.

5

As when a sick man very near to death[3]   25
   Seems dead indeed, and feels begin and end
   The tears and takes the farewell of each friend,
And hears one bid the other go, draw breath
Freelier outside ("since all is o'er," he saith,
   "And the blow fallen no grieving can amend"),   30

6

While some discuss if near the other graves
   Be room enough for this, and when a day
   Suits best for carrying the corpse away,
With care about the banners, scarves and staves:
And still the man hears all, and only craves   35
   He may not shame such tender love and stay.

7

Thus, I had so long suffered in this quest,
   Heard failure prophesied so oft, been writ
   So many times among "The Band"—to wit,
The knights who to the Dark Tower's search addressed   40
Their steps—that just to fail as they, seemed best,
   And all the doubt was now—should I be fit?

8

So, quiet as despair, I turned from him,
   That hateful cripple, out of his highway
   Into the path he pointed. All the day   45

---

3. Cf. *A Valediction: Forbidding Mourning*, lines 1–4, by John Donne, a poet much admired by Browning.

Had been a dreary one at best, and dim
  Was settling to its close, yet shot one grim
  Red leer to see the plain catch its estray.[4]

9

For mark! no sooner was I fairly found
  Pledged to the plain, after a pace or two,
  Than, pausing to throw backward a last view   50
O'er the safe road, 'twas gone; gray plain all round:
Nothing but plain to the horizon's bound.
  I might go on; naught else remained to do.

10

So, on I went. I think I never saw   55
  Such starved ignoble nature; nothing throve:
  For flowers—as well expect a cedar grove!
But cockle,[5] spurge, according to their law
Might propagate their kind, with none to awe,
  You'd think; a burr had been a treasure trove.   60

11

No! penury, inertness and grimace,
  In some strange sort, were the land's portion. "See
  Or shut your eyes," said Nature peevishly,
"It nothing skills: I cannot help my case;
'Tis the Last Judgment's fire must cure this place,   65
  Calcine[6] its clods and set my prisoners free."

12

If there pushed any ragged thistle stalk
  Above its mates, the head was chopped; the bents[7]
  Were jealous else. What made those holes and rents
In the dock's[8] harsh swarth leaves, bruised as to balk   70
All hope of greenness? 'tis a brute must walk
  Pashing their life out, with a brute's intents.

13

As for the grass, it grew as scant as hair
  In leprosy; thin dry blades pricked the mud
  Which underneath looked kneaded up with blood.   75
One stiff blind horse, his every bone a-stare,
Stood stupefied, however he came there:
  Thrust out past service from the devil's stud!

14

Alive? he might be dead for aught I know,
  With that red gaunt and colloped[9] neck a-strain,   80
  And shut eyes underneath the rusty mane;
Seldom went such grotesqueness with such woe;
I never saw a brute I hated so;
  He must be wicked to deserve such pain.

---

4. Literally, a domestic animal that has strayed away from its home.
5. A weed that bears burrs. "Spurge" is a bitter-juiced weed.
6. Turn to powder by heat.
7. Coarse, stiff grasses.
8. Coarse plant.
9. Ridged.

15

I shut my eyes and turned them on my heart.   85
 As a man calls for wine before he fights,
 I asked one draught of earlier, happier sights,
Ere fitly I could hope to play my part.
Think first, fight afterwards—the soldier's art:
 One taste of the old time sets all to rights.   90

16

Not it! I fancied Cuthbert's reddening face
 Beneath its garniture of curly gold,
 Dear fellow, till I almost felt him fold
An arm in mine to fix me to the place,
That way he used. Alas, one night's disgrace!   95
 Out went my heart's new fire and left it cold.

17

Giles then, the soul of honor—there he stands
 Frank as ten years ago when knighted first.
 What honest man should dare (he said) he durst.
Good—but the scene shifts—faugh! what hangman hands   100
Pin to his breast a parchment? His own bands
 Read it. Poor traitor, spit upon and cursed!

18

Better this present than a past like that;
 Back therefore to my darkening path again!
 No sound, no sight as far as eye could strain.   105
Will the night send a howlet[1] or a bat?
I asked: when something on the dismal flat
 Came to arrest my thoughts and change their train.

19

A sudden little river crossed my path
 As unexpected as a serpent comes.
 No sluggish tide congenial to the glooms;   110
This, as it frothed by, might have been a bath
For the fiend's glowing hoof—to see the wrath
 Of its black eddy bespate[2] with flakes and spumes.

20

So petty yet so spiteful! All along,   115
 Low scrubby alders kneeled down over it;
 Drenched willows flung them headlong in a fit
Of mute despair, a suicidal throng:
The river which had done them all the wrong,
 Whate'er that was, rolled by, deterred no whit.   120

21

Which, while I forded—good saints, how I feared
 To set my foot upon a dead man's cheek,
 Each step, or feel the spear I thrust to seek
For hollows, tangled in his hair or beard!
—It may have been a water rat I speared,   125
 But, ugh! it sounded like a baby's shriek.

1. Owl.   2. Bespattered.

22

Glad was I when I reached the other bank.
    Now for a better country. Vain presage!
    Who were the strugglers, what war did they wage,
Whose savage trample thus could pad the dank   130
Soil to a plash? Toads in a poisoned tank,
    Or wild cats in a red-hot iron cage—

23

The fight must so have seemed in that fell cirque.[3]
    What penned them there, with all the plain to choose?
    No footprint leading to that horrid mews,[4]   135
None out of it. Mad brewage set to work
Their brains, no doubt, like galley slaves the Turk
    Pits for his pastime, Christians against Jews.

24

And more than that—a furlong on—why, there!
    What bad use was that engine for, that wheel,   140
    Or brake,[5] not wheel—that harrow fit to reel
Men's bodies out like silk? with all the air
Of Tophet's[6] tool, on earth left unaware,
    Or brought to sharpen its rusty teeth of steel.

25

Then came a bit of stubbed ground, once a wood,   145
    Next a marsh, it would seem, and now mere earth
    Desperate and done with; (so a fool finds mirth,
Makes a thing and then mars it, till his mood
Changes and off he goes!) within a rood[7]—
    Bog, clay and rubble, sand and stark black dearth.   150

26

Now blotches rankling, colored gay and grim,
    Now patches where some leanness of the soil's
    Broke into moss or substances like boils;
Then came some palsied oak, a cleft in him
Like a distorted mouth that splits its rim   155
    Gaping at death, and dies while it recoils.

27

And just as far as ever from the end!
    Naught in the distance but the evening, naught
    To point my footstep further! At the thought,
A great black bird, Apollyon's[8] bosom friend,   160
Sailed past, nor beat his wide wing dragon-penned[9]
    That brushed my cap—perchance the guide I sought.

28

For, looking up, aware I somehow grew,
    'Spite of the dusk, the plain had given place
    All round to mountains—with such name to grace   165

3. Dreadful arena.
4. Enclosed stable yard.
5. A toothed machine used for separating the fibers of flax or hemp. Here an instrument of torture.
6. Hell's.
7. A distance of sixteen feet.
8. The devil's.
9. With wings or pinions like those of a dragon.

Mere ugly heights and heaps now stolen in view.
How thus they had surprised me—solve it, you!
    How to get from them was no clearer case.

29

Yet half I seemed to recognize some trick
    Of mischief happened to me, God knows when—
    In a bad dream perhaps. Here ended, then,
Progress this way. When, in the very nick
Of giving up, one time more, came a click
    As when a trap shuts—you're inside the den!

30

Burningly it came on me all at once,
    This was the place! those two hills on the right,
    Crouched like two bulls locked horn in horn in fight;
While to the left, a tall scalped mountain . . . Dunce,
Dotard, a-dozing at the very nonce,[1]
    After a life spent training for the sight!

31

What in the midst lay but the Tower itself?
    The round squat turret, blind as the fool's heart,
    Built of brown stone, without a counterpart
In the whole world. The tempest's mocking elf
Points to the shipman thus the unseen shelf
    He strikes on, only when the timbers start.

32

Not see? because of night perhaps? why, day
    Came back again for that! before it left,
    The dying sunset kindled through a cleft:
The hills, like giants at a hunting, lay,
Chin upon hand, to see the game at bay—
    "Now stab and end the creature—to the heft!"[2]

33

Not hear? when noise was everywhere! it tolled
    Increasing like a bell. Names in my ears
    Of all the lost adventurers my peers—
How such a one was strong, and such was bold,
And such was fortunate, yet each of old
    Lost, lost! one moment knelled the woe of years.

34

There they stood, ranged along the hillsides, met
    To view the last of me, a living frame
    For one more picture! in a sheet of flame
I saw them and I knew them all. And yet
Dauntless the slug-horn[3] to my lips I set,
    And blew. *Childe Roland to the Dark Tower came.*

1852   1855

170

175

180

185

190

195

200

---

1. Moment.
2. Handle of dagger or sword.

3. A trumpet, probably made from the horn of an ox.

Up at a Villa—Down in the City
(AS DISTINGUISHED BY AN ITALIAN PERSON OF QUALITY)

1

Had I but plenty of money, money enough and to spare,
The house for me, no doubt, were a house in the city square;
Ah, such a life, such a life, as one leads at the window there!

2

Something to see, by Bacchus, something to hear, at least!
There, the whole day long, one's life is a perfect feast;   5
While up at a villa one lives, I maintain it, no more than a beast.

3

Well now, look at our villa! stuck like the horn of a bull
Just on a mountain edge as bare as the creature's skull,
Save a mere shag of a bush with hardly a leaf to pull!
—I scratch my own,[1] sometimes, to see if the hair's turned wool.   10

4

But the city, oh the city—the square with the houses! Why?
They are stone-faced, white as a curd, there's something to take the
    eye!
Houses in four straight lines, not a single front awry;
You watch who crosses and gossips, who saunters, who hurries by;
Green blinds, as a matter of course, to draw when the sun gets
    high;   15
And the shops with fanciful signs which are painted properly.

5

What of a villa? Though winter be over in March by rights,
'Tis May perhaps ere the snow shall have withered well off the
    heights:
You've the brown plowed land before, where the oxen steam and
    wheeze,
And the hills over-smoked behind by the faint gray olive trees.   20

6

Is it better in May, I ask you? You've summer all at once;
In a day he leaps complete with a few strong April suns.
'Mid the sharp short emerald wheat, scarce risen three fingers well,
The wild tulip, at end of its tube, blows out its great red bell
Like a thin clear bubble of blood, for the children to pick and
    sell.   25

7

Is it ever hot in the square? There's a fountain to spout and splash!
In the shade it sings and springs; in the shine such foam-bows flash
On the horses with curling fish-tails, that prance and paddle and
    pash

1. I.e., my own skull.

Round the lady atop in her conch—fifty gazers do not abash,
Though all that she wears is some weeds round her waist in a sort
of sash.   30

8

All the year long at the villa, nothing to see though you linger,
Except yon cypress that points like death's lean lifted forefinger.
Some think fireflies pretty, when they mix i' the corn and mingle,
Or thrid[2] the stinking hemp till the stalks of it seem a-tingle.
Late August or early September, the stunning cicala is shrill,   35
And the bees keep their tiresome whine round the resinous firs on
the hill.
Enough of the seasons—I spare you the months of the fever and
chill.

9

Ere you open your eyes in the city, the blessed church bells begin:
No sooner the bells leave off than the diligence[3] rattles in:
You get the pick of the news, and it costs you never a pin.   40
By-and-by there's the traveling doctor gives pills, lets blood, draws
teeth;
Or the Pulcinello-trumpet[4] breaks up the market beneath.
At the post office such a scene-picture[5]—the new play, piping hot!
And a notice how, only this morning, three liberal thieves[6] were
shot.
Above it, behold the Archbishop's most fatherly of rebukes,   45
And beneath, with his crown and his lion, some little new law of
the Duke's!
Or a sonnet with flowery marge, to the Reverend Don So-and-so
Who is Dante, Boccaccio, Petrarca, Saint Jerome, and Cicero,
"And moreover," (the sonnet goes rhyming) "the skirts of Saint
Paul has reached,
Having preached us those six Lent-lectures more unctuous than
ever he preached."   50
Noon strikes—here sweeps the procession; our Lady borne smiling
and smart
With a pink gauze gown all spangles, and seven swords[7] stuck in
her heart!
Bang-whang-whang goes the drum, *tootle-te-tootle* the fife;
No keeping one's haunches still: it's the greatest pleasure in life.

10

But bless you, it's dear—it's dear! fowls, wine, at double the rate. 55
They have clapped a new tax upon salt, and what oil pays passing
the gate[8]
It's a horror to think of. And so, the villa for me, not the city!

2. Thread their way through.
3. Stagecoach.
4. Trumpet announcing the puppet show, in which Pulcinello is the clown.
5. Picture advertising a coming play.
6. The men were republicans, opposed to Austrian rule, but "thieves" in the eyes of the speaker.
7. The swords symbolize the seven sorrows of Our Lady, the Virgin Mary.
8. Inside the gates of the city, produce was subject to special taxes.

Beggars can scarcely be choosers: but still—ah, the pity, the pity!
Look, two and two go the priests, then the monks with cowls and
  sandals,   60
And the penitents dressed in white shirts, a-holding the yellow
  candles;
One, he carries a flag up straight, and another a cross with handles,
And the Duke's guard brings up the rear, for the better prevention
  of scandals:
Bang-whang-whang goes the drum, *tootle-te-tootle* the fife.
Oh, a day in the city square, there is no such pleasure in life!   65

                                                                1855

Respectability

1

Dear, had the world in its caprice
    Deigned to proclaim "I know you both,
    Have recognized your plighted troth,
Am sponsor for you: live in peace!"—
How many precious months and years   5
    Of youth had passed, that speed so fast,
    Before we found it out at last,
The world, and what it fears?

2

How much of priceless life were spent
    With men that every virtue decks,   10
    And women models of their sex,
Society's true ornament—
Ere we dared wander, nights like this,
    Through wind and rain, and watch the Seine,
    And feel the Boulevard break again   15
To warmth and light and bliss?

3

I know! the world proscribes not love;
    Allows my fingers to caress
    Your lips' contour and downiness,
Provided it supply a glove.   20
    The world's good word!—the Institute![1]
        Guizot receives Montalembert!
        Eh? Down the court three lampions[2] flare:
Put forward your best foot!

ca. 1852   1855

1. A building in Paris, which the
lovers are approaching in their walk.
The speaker is reminded that at a
meeting of the French Academy, held
in the Institute, occurred a glaring instance of the hypocrisy which he thinks
is characteristic of all social relations.

In 1852, François Guizot had delivered
a flowery speech of welcome in honor
of Charles Montalembert, an author
whom Guizot at heart despised.
2. Ornamental lamps illuminating the
courtyard of the Institute.

Fra Lippo Lippi[1]

I am poor brother Lippo, by your leave!
You need not clap your torches to my face.
Zooks,[2] what's to blame? you think you see a monk!
What, 'tis past midnight, and you go the rounds,
And here you catch me at an alley's end   5
Where sportive ladies leave their doors ajar?
The Carmine's[3] my cloister: hunt it up,
Do—harry out, if you must show your zeal,
Whatever rat, there, haps on his wrong hole,
And nip each softling of a wee white mouse,   10
Weke, weke, that's crept to keep him company!
Aha, you know your betters! Then, you'll take
Your hand away that's fiddling on my throat,
And please to know me likewise. Who am I?
Why, one, sir, who is lodging with a friend   15
Three streets off—he's a certain . . . how d'ye call?
Master—a . . . Cosimo of the Medici,[4]
I' the house that caps the corner. Boh! you were best!
Remember and tell me, the day you're hanged,
How you affected such a gullet's gripe![5]   20
But you,[6] sir, it concerns you that your knaves
Pick up a manner nor discredit you.
Zooks, are we pilchards,[7] that they sweep the streets
And count fair prize what comes into their net?
He's Judas to a tittle, that man is![8]   25
Just such a face! Why, sir, you make amends.
Lord, I'm not angry! Bid your hangdogs go
Drink out this quarter-florin to the health
Of the munificent House that harbors me
(And many more beside, lads! more beside!)   30
And all's come square again. I'd like his face—
His, elbowing on his comrade in the door

1. This monologue portrays the dawn of the Renaissance in Italy at a point when the medieval attitude towards life and art was about to be displaced by a fresh appreciation of earthly pleasures. It was from Giorgio Vasari's *Lives of the Painters* that Browning derived most of his information about the life of the Florentine painter and friar, Lippo Lippi (1406–69), but the theory of art propounded by Lippi in the poem was developed by the poet himself. Browning's own partiality for this poem may be attributed, in part, to his having identified himself with his hero, an artist whose aesthetic principles made him a misfit among his more pharisaical contemporaries.

2. A shortened version of "Gadzooks," a mild oath now obscure in meaning but perhaps resembling a phrase still in use: "God's truth."
3. Italian for "Carmelite," an order of mendicant friars to which Lippi belongs.
4. Lippi's patron, banker and virtual ruler of Florence.
5. I.e., how you had the arrogance to choke the gullet of someone with my connections.
6. The officer in charge of the patrol of policemen or watchmen.
7. Small fish.
8. I.e., one of the watchmen has a face that would serve as a model for a painting of Judas.

With the pike and lantern—for the slave that holds
John Baptist's head a-dangle by the hair
With one hand ("Look you, now," as who should say)   35
And his weapon in the other, yet unwiped!
It's not your chance to have a bit of chalk,
A wood-coal or the like? or you should see!
Yes, I'm the painter, since you style me so.
What, brother Lippo's doings, up and down,   40
You know them and they take you? like enough!
I saw the proper twinkle in your eye—
'Tell you, I liked your looks at very first.
Let's sit and set things straight now, hip to haunch.
Here's spring come, and the nights one makes up bands   45
To roam the town and sing out carnival,[9]
And I've been three weeks shut within my mew,[1]
A-painting for the great man, saints and saints
And saints again. I could not paint all night—
Ouf! I leaned out of window for fresh air.   50
There came a hurry of feet and little feet,
A sweep of lute-strings, laughs, and whiffs of song—
Flower o' the broom,
Take away love, and our earth is a tomb!
Flower o' the quince,   55
I let Lisa go, and what good in life since?[2]
Flower o' the thyme—and so on. Round they went.
Scarce had they turned the corner when a titter
Like the skipping of rabbits by moonlight—three slim shapes,
And a face that looked up . . . zooks, sir, flesh and blood, 60
That's all I'm made of! Into shreds it went,
Curtain and counterpane and coverlet,
All the bed-furniture—a dozen knots,
There was a ladder! Down I let myself,
Hands and feet, scrambling somehow, and so dropped,   65
And after them. I came up with the fun
Hard by Saint Laurence,[3] hail fellow, well met—
Flower o' the rose,
If I've been merry, what matter who knows?
And so as I was stealing back again   70
To get to bed and have a bit of sleep
Ere I rise up tomorrow and go work
On Jerome knocking at his poor old breast
With his great round stone to subdue the flesh,[4]
You snap me of the sudden. Ah, I see!   75
Though your eye twinkles still, you shake your head—
Mine's shaved—a monk, you say—the sting's in that!
If Master Cosimo announced himself,

9. Season of revelry before the commencement of Lent.
1. Private den.
2. This and other interspersed flower-songs are called *stornelli* in Italy.
3. San Lorenzo, a church in Florence.
4. A picture of St. Jerome (ca. 340–420), whose ascetic observances were hardly a congenial subject for such a painter as Lippi.

Mum's the word naturally; but a monk!
Come, what am I a beast for? tell us, now!   80
I was a baby when my mother died
And father died and left me in the street.
I starved there, God knows how, a year or two
On fig skins, melon parings, rinds and shucks,
Refuse and rubbish. One fine frosty day,   85
My stomach being empty as your hat,
The wind doubled me up and down I went.
Old Aunt Lapaccia trussed me with one hand
(Its fellow was a stinger as I knew),
And so along the wall, over the bridge,   90
By the straight cut to the convent. Six words there,
While I stood munching my first bread that month:
"So, boy, you're minded," quoth the good fat father
Wiping his own mouth, 'twas refection time[5]—
"To quit this very miserable world?   95
Will you renounce" . . . "the mouthful of bread?" thought I;
By no means! Brief, they made a monk of me;
I did renounce the world, its pride and greed,
Palace, farm, villa, shop, and banking house,
Trash, such as these poor devils of Medici   100
Have given their hearts to—all at eight years old.
Well, sir, I found in time, you may be sure,
'Twas not for nothing—the good bellyful,
The warm serge and the rope that goes all round,
And day-long blessed idleness beside!   105
"Let's see what the urchin's fit for"—that came next.
Not overmuch their way, I must confess.
Such a to-do! They tried me with their books:
Lord, they'd have taught me Latin in pure waste!
Flower o' the clove,   110
All the Latin I construe is "amo," I love!
But, mind you, when a boy starves in the streets
Eight years together, as my fortune was,
Watching folk's faces to know who will fling
The bit of half-stripped grape bunch he desires,   115
And who will curse or kick him for his pains—
Which gentleman processional and fine,
Holding a candle to the Sacrament,
Will wink and let him lift a plate and catch
The droppings of the wax to sell again,   120
Or holla for the Eight[6] and have him whipped—
How say I?—nay, which dog bites, which lets drop
His bone from the heap of offal in the street—
Why, soul and sense of him grow sharp alike,
He learns the look of things, and none the less   125
For admonition from the hunger-pinch.
I had a store of such remarks, be sure,

5. Mealtime.   6. Florentine magistrates.

Which, after I found leisure, turned to use.
I drew men's faces on my copybooks,
Scrawled them within the antiphonary's marge,[7]
Joined legs and arms to the long music-notes,
Found eyes and nose and chin for A's and B's,
And made a string of pictures of the world
Betwixt the ins and outs of verb and noun,
On the wall, the bench, the door. The monks looked black.
"Nay," quoth the Prior,[8] "turn him out, d' ye say?
In no wise. Lose a crow and catch a lark.
What if at last we get our man of parts,
We Carmelites, like those Camaldolese
And Preaching Friars,[9] to do our church up fine
And put the front on it that ought to be!"
And hereupon he bade me daub away.
Thank you! my head being crammed, the walls a blank,
Never was such prompt disemburdening.
First, every sort of monk, the black and white,
I drew them, fat and lean: then, folk at church,
From good old gossips waiting to confess
Their cribs of barrel droppings, candle ends—
To the breathless fellow at the altar-foot,
Fresh from his murder, safe and sitting there
With the little children round him in a row
Of admiration, half for his beard and half
For that white anger of his victim's son
Shaking a fist at him with one fierce arm,
Signing himself with the other because of Christ
(Whose sad face on the cross sees only this
After the passion[1] of a thousand years)
Till some poor girl, her apron o'er her head
(Which the intense eyes looked through), came at eve
On tiptoe, said a word, dropped in a loaf,
Her pair of earrings and a bunch of flowers
(The brute took growling), prayed, and so was gone.
I painted all, then cried " 'Tis ask and have;
Choose, for more's ready!"—laid the ladder flat,
And showed my covered bit of cloister wall.
The monks closed in a circle and praised loud
Till checked, taught what to see and not to see,
Being simple bodies—"That's the very man!
Look at the boy who stoops to pat the dog!
That woman's like the Prior's niece who comes
To care about his asthma: it's the life!"
But there my triumph's straw-fire flared and funked;[2]
Their betters took their turn to see and say:
The Prior and the learned pulled a face

130

135

140

145

150

155

160

165

170

---

7. Margin of music book used for choral singing.
8. Head of a Carmelite convent.
9. Benedictine and Dominican reli-gious orders, respectively.
1. Sufferings.
2. Went up in smoke.

And stopped all that in no time. "How? what's here?   175
Quite from the mark of painting, bless us all!
Faces, arms, legs and bodies like the true
As much as pea and pea! it's devil's game!
Your business is not to catch men with show,
With homage to the perishable clay,   180
But lift them over it, ignore it all,
Make them forget there's such a thing as flesh.
Your business is to paint the souls of men—
Man's soul, and it's a fire, smoke . . . no, it's not . . .
It's vapor done up like a newborn babe—   185
(In that shape when you die it leaves your mouth)
It's . . . well, what matters talking, it's the soul!
Give us no more of body than shows soul!
Here's Giotto,[3] with his Saint a-praising God,
That sets us praising—why not stop with him?   190
Why put all thoughts of praise out of our head
With wonder at lines, colors, and what not?
Paint the soul, never mind the legs and arms!
Rub all out, try at it a second time.
Oh, that white smallish female with the breasts,   195
She's just my niece . . . Herodias,[4] I would say—
Who went and danced and got men's heads cut off!
Have it all out!" Now, is this sense, I ask?
A fine way to paint soul, by painting body
So ill, the eye can't stop there, must go further   200
And can't fare worse! Thus, yellow does for white
When what you put for yellow's simply black,
And any sort of meaning looks intense
When all beside itself means and looks naught.
Why can't a painter lift each foot in turn,   205
Left foot and right foot, go a double step,
Make his flesh liker and his soul more like,
Both in their order? Take the prettiest face,
The Prior's niece . . . patron-saint—is it so pretty
You can't discover if it means hope, fear,   210
Sorrow or joy? won't beauty go with these?
Suppose I've made her eyes all right and blue,
Can't I take breath and try to add life's flash,
And then add soul and heighten them threefold?
Or say there's beauty with no soul at all—   215
(I never saw it—put the case the same—)
If you get simple beauty and naught else,
You get about the best thing God invents:
That's somewhat: and you'll find the soul you have missed,
Within yourself, when you return him thanks.   220

3. Great Florentine painter (1276–1337), whose stylized pictures of religious subjects were admired as models of pre-Renaissance art.
4. See Matthew, xiv.1–12, for an account of John the Baptist's execution after he had aroused the displeasure of Herodias, sister-in-law of King Herod. It was her daughter, Salome, who performed the dance.

"Rub all out!" Well, well, there's my life, in short,
And so the thing has gone on ever since.
I'm grown a man no doubt, I've broken bounds:
You should not take a fellow eight years old
And make him swear to never kiss the girls. 225
I'm my own master, paint now as I please—
Having a friend, you see, in the Corner-house!5
Lord, it's fast holding by the rings in front—
Those great rings serve more purposes than just
To plant a flag in, or tie up a horse! 230
And yet the old schooling sticks, the old grave eyes
Are peeping o'er my shoulder as I work,
The heads shake still—"It's art's decline, my son!
You're not of the true painters, great and old;
Brother Angelico's the man, you'll find; 235
Brother Lorenzo stands his single peer:6
Fag on at flesh, you'll never make the third!"
Flower o' the pine,
You keep your mistr . . . manners, and I'll stick to mine!
I'm not the third, then: bless us, they must know! 240
Don't you think they're the likeliest to know,
They with their Latin? So, I swallow my rage,
Clench my teeth, suck my lips in tight, and paint
To please them—sometimes do and sometimes don't;
For, doing most, there's pretty sure to come 245
A turn, some warm eve finds me at my saints—
A laugh, a cry, the business of the world—
(*Flower o' the peach,*
Death for us all, and his own life for each!)
And my whole soul revolves, the cup runs over, 250
The world and life's too big to pass for a dream,
And I do these wild things in sheer despite,
And play the fooleries you catch me at,
In pure rage! The old mill-horse, out at grass
After hard years, throws up his stiff heels so, 255
Although the miller does not preach to him
The only good of grass is to make chaff.7
What would men have? Do they like grass or no—
May they or mayn't they? all I want's the thing
Settled forever one way. As it is, 260
You tell too many lies and hurt yourself:
You don't like what you only like too much,
You do like what, if given you at your word,
You find abundantly detestable.
For me, I think I speak as I was taught; 265
I always see the garden and God there
A-making man's wife: and, my lesson learned,

5. The Medici palace.
6. Fra Angelico (1387–1455) and Lorenzo Monaco (1370–1425), whose
paintings were in the approved traditional manner.
7. Straw.

The value and significance of flesh,
I can't unlearn ten minutes afterwards.

You understand me: I'm a beast, I know.   270
But see, now—why, I see as certainly
As that the morning star's about to shine,
What will hap some day. We've a youngster here
Comes to our convent, studies what I do,
Slouches and stares and lets no atom drop: 275
His name is Guidi[8]—he'll not mind the monks—
They call him Hulking Tom, he lets them talk—
He picks my practice up—he'll paint apace,
I hope so   though I never live so long,
I know what's sure to follow. You be judge!   280
You speak no Latin more than I, belike;
However, you're my man, you've seen the world
—The beauty and the wonder and the power,
The shapes of things, their colors, lights and shades,
Changes, surprises—and God made it all!   285
—For what? Do you feel thankful, aye or no,
For this fair town's face, yonder river's line,
The mountain round it and the sky above,
Much more the figures of man, woman, child,
These are the frame to? What's it all about?   290
To be passed over, despised? or dwelt upon,
Wondered at? oh, this last of course!—you say.
But why not do as well as say—paint these
Just as they are, careless what comes of it?
God's works—paint any one, and count it crime   295
To let a truth slip. Don't object, "His works
Are here already; nature is complete:
Suppose you reproduce her—(which you can't)
There's no advantage! You must beat her, then."
For, don't you mark? we're made so that we love   300
First when we see them painted, things we have passed
Perhaps a hundred times nor cared to see;
And so they are better, painted—better to us,
Which is the same thing. Art was given for that;
God uses us to help each other so,   305
Lending our minds out. Have you noticed, now,
Your cullion's[9] hanging face? A bit of chalk,
And trust me but you should, though! How much more,
If I drew higher things with the same truth!
That were to take the Prior's pulpit-place,   310
Interpret God to all of you! Oh, oh,
It makes me mad to see what men shall do
And we in our graves! This world's no blot for us,
Nor blank; it means intensely, and means good:

8. Guidi or Masaccio (1401–28), a painter who may have been Lippi's master rather than his pupil. Like Lippi he was in revolt against the medieval theory of art.
9. Rascal's.

To find its meaning is my meat and drink.   315
"Aye, but you don't so instigate to prayer!"
Strikes in the Prior: "when your meaning's plain
It does not say to folk—remember matins,
Or, mind you fast next Friday!" Why, for this
What need of art at all? A skull and bones,   320
Two bits of stick nailed crosswise, or, what's best,
A bell to chime the hour with, does as well.
I painted a Saint Laurence[1] six months since
At Prato, splashed the fresco in fine style:
"How looks my painting, now the scaffold's down?"   325
I ask a brother: "Hugely," he returns—
"Already not one phiz of your three slaves
Who turn the Deacon off his toasted side,
But's scratched and prodded to our heart's content,
The pious people have so eased their own   330
With coming to say prayers there in a rage:
We get on fast to see the bricks beneath.
Expect another job this time next year,
For pity and religion grow i' the crowd—
Your painting serves its purpose!" Hang the fools!   335

          —That is—you'll not mistake an idle word
Spoke in a huff by a poor monk, God wot,
Tasting the air this spicy night which turns
The unaccustomed head like Chianti wine!
Oh, the church knows! don't misreport me, now!   340
It's natural a poor monk out of bounds
Should have his apt word to excuse himself:
And hearken how I plot to make amends.
I have bethought me: I shall paint a piece
. . . There's for you! Give me six months, then go, see   345
Something in Sant' Ambrogio's![2] Bless the nuns!
They want a cast o' my office.[3] I shall paint
God in the midst, Madonna and her babe,
Ringed by a bowery flowery angel brood,
Lilies and vestments and white faces, sweet   350
As puff on puff of grated orris-root
When ladies crowd to Church at midsummer.
And then i' the front, of course a saint or two—
Saint John, because he saves the Florentines,
Saint Ambrose, who puts down in black and white   355
The convent's friends and gives them a long day,
And Job, I must have him there past mistake,
The man of Uz (and Us without the z,
Painters who need his patience). Well, all these
Secured at their devotion, up shall come   360

1. A scene representing the fiery martyr-dom of Saint Laurence; a "fresco" is painted quickly on fresh plaster over a surface of bricks. Prato is a town near Florence.
2. A convent church in Florence.
3. Sample of my work. The completed painting, which Browning saw in Florence, is Lippi's "Coronation of the Virgin."

Out of a corner when you least expect,
As one by a dark stair into a great light,
Music and talking, who but Lippo! I!—
Mazed, motionless and moonstruck—I'm the man!
Back I shrink—what is this I see and hear?   365
I, caught up with my monk's things by mistake,
My old serge gown and rope that goes all round,
I, in this presence, this pure company!
Where's a hole, where's a corner for escape?
Then steps a sweet angelic slip of a thing   370
Forward, puts out a soft palm—"Not so fast!"
—Addresses the celestial presence, "nay—
He made you and devised you, after all,
Though he's none of you! Could Saint John there draw—
His camel-hair⁴ make up a painting-brush?   375
We come to brother Lippo for all that,
Iste perfecit opus!"⁵ So, all smile—
I shuffle sideways with my blushing face
Under the cover of a hundred wings
Thrown like a spread of kirtles⁶ when you're gay   380
And play hot cockles,⁷ all the doors being shut,
Till, wholly unexpected, in there pops
The hothead husband! Thus I scuttle off
To some safe bench behind, not letting go
The palm of her, the little lily thing   385
That spoke the good word for me in the nick,
Like the Prior's niece . . . Saint Lucy, I would say.
And so all's saved for me, and for the church
A pretty picture gained. Go, six months hence!
Your hand, sir, and good-by: no lights, no lights!   390
The street's hushed, and I know my own way back,
Don't fear me! There's the gray beginning. Zooks!
ca. 1853   1855

In a Year

1

Never any more,
    While I live,
Need I hope to see his face
    As before.
Once his love grown chill,   5
    Mine may strive:
Bitterly we re-embrace,
    Single still.

4. "And John was clothed with camel's hair" (Mark i.6).
5. "This man made the work." In this painting, as later completed, these words appear beside a figure which Browning took to be Lippi's self-portrait.
6. Skirts.
7. A game in which a player wears a blindfold.

2

Was it something said,
    Something done,   10
Vexed him? was it touch of hand,
    Turn of head?
Strange! that very way
    Love begun:
I as little understand   15
    Love's decay.

3

When I sewed or drew,
    I recall
How he looked as if I sung
    —Sweetly too.   20
If I spoke a word,
    First of all
Up his cheek the color sprung,
    Then he heard.

4

Sitting by my side,   25
    At my feet,
So he breathed but air I breathed,
    Satisfied!
I, too, at love's brim
    Touched the sweet: 30
I would die if death bequeathed
    Sweet to him.

5

"Speak, I love thee best!"
    He exclaimed:
"Let thy love my own foretell!"   35
    I confessed:
"Clasp my heart on thine
    Now unblamed,
Since upon thy soul as well
    Hangeth mine!"   40

6

Was it wrong to own,
    Being truth?
Why should all the giving prove
    His alone?
I had wealth and ease,   45
    Beauty, youth:
Since my lover gave me love,
    I gave these.

7

That was all I meant
    —To be just,   50
And the passion I had raised,
    To content.

Since he chose to change
 Gold for dust,
If I gave him what he praised   55
 Was it strange?

8

Would he loved me yet,
 On and on,
While I found some way undreamed
 —Paid my debt!   60
Gave more life and more,
 Till, all gone,
He should smile, "She never seemed
 Mine before.

9

"What, she felt the while,   65
 Must I think?
Love's so different with us men!"
 He should smile:
"Dying for my sake—
 White and pink!   70
Can't we touch these bubbles then
 But they break?"

10

Dear, the pang is brief,
 Do thy part,
Have thy pleasure! How perplexed   75
 Grows belief!
Well, this cold clay clod
 Was man's heart:
Crumble it, and what comes next?
 Is it God?   80

1855

The Last Ride Together

1

I said—Then, dearest, since 'tis so,
Since now at length my fate I know,
Since nothing all my love avails,
Since all, my life seemed meant for, fails,
 Since this was written and needs must be—   5
My whole heart rises up to bless
Your name in pride and thankfulness!
Take back the hope you gave—I claim
Only a memory of the same,
 —And this beside, if you will not blame,
  Your leave for one more last ride with me.   10

2

My mistress bent that brow of hers;
Those deep dark eyes where pride demurs
When pity would be softening through,
Fixed me a breathing-while or two   15
    With life or death in the balance: right!
The blood replenished me again;
My last thought was at least not vain:
I and my mistress, side by side
Shall be together, breathe and ride,   20
So, one day more am I deified.
    Who knows but the world may end tonight?

3

Hush! if you saw some western cloud
All billowy-bosomed, over-bowed
By many benedictions—sun's   25
And moon's and evening star's at once—
    And so, you, looking and loving best,
Conscious grew, your passion drew
Cloud, sunset, moonrise, star-shine too,
Down on you, near and yet more near,   30
Till flesh must fade for heaven was here!—
Thus leant she and lingered[1]—joy and fear!
    Thus lay she a moment on my breast.

4

Then we began to ride. My soul
Smoothed itself out, a long-cramped scroll   35
Freshening and fluttering in the wind.
Past hopes already lay behind.
    What need to strive with a life awry?
Had I said that, had I done this,
So might I gain, so might I miss.   40
Might she have loved me? just as well
She might have hated, who can tell!
Where had I been now if the worst befell?
    And here we are riding, she and I.

5

Fail I alone, in words and deeds?   45
Why, all men strive and who succeeds?
We rode; it seemed my spirit flew,
Saw other regions, cities new,
    As the world rushed by on either side.
I thought—All labor, yet no less   50
Bear up beneath their unsuccess.
Look at the end of work, contrast
The petty done, the undone vast,
This present of theirs with the hopeful past!
    I hoped she would love me; here we ride.   55

1. Before she mounts her horse.

6

What hand and brain went ever paired?
What heart alike conceived and dared?
What act proved all its thought had been?
What will but felt the fleshly screen?
    We ride and I see her bosom heave.   60
There's many a crown for who can reach.
Ten lines, a statesman's life in each![2]
The flag stuck on a heap of bones,
A soldier's doing! what atones?
They scratch his name on the Abbey stones.   65
    My riding is better, by their leave.

7

What does it all mean, poet? Well,
Your brains beat into rhythm, you tell
What we felt only; you expressed
You hold things beautiful the best,   70
    And pace them in rhyme so, side by side.
'Tis something, nay 'tis much: but then,
Have you yourself what's best for men?
Are you—poor, sick, old ere your time—
Nearer one whit your own sublime   75
Than we who never have turned a rhyme?
    Sing, riding's a joy! For me, I ride.

8

And you, great sculptor—so, you gave
A score of years to Art, her slave,
And that's your Venus, whence we turn   80
To yonder girl that fords the burn![3]
    You acquiesce, and shall I repine?
What, man of music, you grown gray
With notes and nothing else to say,
Is this your sole praise from a friend,   85
"Greatly his opera's strains intend,
But in music we know how fashions end!"
    I gave my youth; but we ride, in fine.[4]

9

Who knows what's fit for us? Had fate
Proposed bliss here should sublimate   90
My being—had I signed the bond—
Still one must lead some life beyond,
    Have a bliss to die with, dim-descried.
This foot once planted on the goal,
This glory-garland round my soul,   95
Could I descry such? Try and test!
I sink back shuddering from the quest.

2. If a man tries hard enough, he may be crowned with what seems to be success. He might become, for example, an eminent "statesman." Yet his only memorial would be a short sketch of his career ("ten lines") in some history or biographical dictionary.
3. Crosses the brook.
4. In short.

Earth being so good, would Heaven seem best?[5]
Now, Heaven and she are beyond this ride.

10

And yet—she has not spoke so long!   100
What if heaven be that, fair and strong
At life's best, with our eyes upturned
Whither life's flower is first discerned,
   We, fixed so, ever should so abide?
What if we still ride on, we two   105
With life forever old yet new,
Changed not in kind but in degree,
The instant made eternity—
And heaven just prove that I and she
   Ride, ride together, forever ride?   110

1855

Andrea del Sarto[1]
(CALLED "THE FAULTLESS PAINTER")

But do not let us quarrel any more,
No, my Lucrezia; bear with me for once:
Sit down and all shall happen as you wish.
You turn your face, but does it bring your heart?
I'll work then for your friend's friend, never fear,   5
Treat his own subject after his own way,
Fix his own time, accept too his own price,
And shut the money into this small hand
When next it takes mine. Will it? tenderly?
Oh, I'll content him—but tomorrow, Love!   10
I often am much wearier than you think,

5. If fate had decreed that he could possess his mistress fully, life on earth would have been so blissful that heaven could offer nothing for him to look forward to after death. Hence (he argues) to preserve "a bliss to die with" (line 93), it is better that she never really became his on earth.

1. This portrait of Andrea del Sarto (1486–1531) was derived from a biography written by his pupil, Giorgio Vasari, author of *The Lives of the Painters*. Vasari's account seeks to explain why his Florentine master, one of the most skillful painters of the Renaissance, never altogether fulfilled the promise he had shown early in his career and why he had never arrived (in Vasari's opinion) at the level of such artists as Raphael. Vasari noted that Andrea suffered from "a certain timidity of mind * * * which rendered it impossible that those evidences of ardor and animation, which are proper to the more exalted character, should

ever appear in him."

Browning also follows Vasari's account of Andrea's marriage to a beautiful widow, Lucrezia, "an artful woman who made him do as she pleased in all things." Vasari reports that Andrea's "immoderate love for her soon caused him to neglect the studies demanded by his art," and that this infatuation had "more influence over him than the glory and honor towards which he had begun to make such hopeful advances."

Browning's poem has often been praised for its exposition of a paradoxical theory of success and failure, but it has other qualities as well. Its slow-paced, enervated blank-verse line, its setting of a quiet evening in autumn, its comparative lack of the movement and noise that we expect in Browning's energetic verse create a unity of impression that is unobtrusive yet effective.

This evening more than usual, and it seems
As if—forgive now—should you let me sit
Here by the window with your hand in mine
And look a half-hour forth on Fiesole,[2]   15
Both of one mind, as married people use,
Quietly, quietly the evening through,
I might get up tomorrow to my work
Cheerful and fresh as ever. Let us try.
Tomorrow, how you shall be glad for this!   20
Your soft hand is a woman of itself,
And mine the man's bared breast she curls inside.
Don't count the time lost, neither; you must serve
For each of the five pictures we require:
It saves a model. So! keep looking so—   25
My serpentining beauty, rounds on rounds![3]
—How could you ever prick those perfect ears,
Even to put the pearl there! oh, so sweet—
My face, my moon, my everybody's moon,
Which everybody looks on and calls his,   30
And, I suppose, is looked on by in turn,
While she looks—no one's: very dear, no less.[4]
You smile? why, there's my picture ready made,
There's what we painters call our harmony!
A common grayness silvers everything[5]—   35
All in a twilight, you and I alike
—You, at the point of your first pride in me
(That's gone you know)—but I, at every point;
My youth, my hope, my art, being all toned down
To yonder sober pleasant Fiesole.   40
There's the bell clinking from the chapel top;
That length of convent wall across the way
Holds the trees safer, huddled more inside;
The last monk leaves the garden; days decrease,
And autumn grows, autumn in everything.   45
Eh? the whole seems to fall into a shape
As if I saw alike my work and self
And all that I was born to be and do,
A twilight-piece. Love, we are in God's hand.
How strange now, looks the life he makes us lead;   50
So free we seem, so fettered fast we are!
I feel he laid the fetter: let it lie!
This chamber for example—turn your head—
All that's behind us! You don't understand
Nor care to understand about my art,   55
But you can hear at least when people speak:
And that cartoon,[6] the second from the door

---

2. A suburb on the hills overlooking
Florence.
3. Coils of hair like the coils of a serpent.
4. Her affections are centered upon no
one person, not even upon her husband,
yet she is nevertheless dear to him.
Cf. *My Last Duchess*, lines 23–24.
5. The predominant color in many of
Andrea's paintings is silver gray.
6. Drawing.

—It is the thing, Love! so such things should be—
Behold Madonna!—I am bold to say.
I can do with my pencil what I know,   60
What I see, what at bottom of my heart
I wish for, if I ever wish so deep—
Do easily, too—when I say, perfectly,
I do not boast, perhaps: yourself are judge,
Who listened to the Legate's[7] talk last week,   65
And just as much they used to say in France.
At any rate 'tis easy, all of it!
No sketches first, no studies, that's long past:
I do what many dream of, all their lives,
—Dream? strive to do, and agonize to do,   70
And fail in doing. I could count twenty such
On twice your fingers, and not leave this town,
Who strive—you don't know how the others strive
To paint a little thing like that you smeared
Carelessly passing with your robes afloat—   75
Yet do much less, so much less, Someone[8] says
(I know his name, no matter)—so much less!
Well, less is more, Lucrezia: I am judged.
There burns a truer light of God in them,
In their vexed beating stuffed and stopped-up brain,   80
Heart, or whate'er else, than goes on to prompt
This low-pulsed forthright craftsman's hand of mine.
Their works drop groundward, but themselves, I know,
Reach many a time a heaven that's shut to me,
Enter and take their place there sure enough,   85
Though they come back and cannot tell the world.
My works are nearer heaven, but I sit here.
The sudden blood of these men! at a word—
Praise them, it boils, or blame them, it boils too.
I, painting from myself and to myself,   90
Know what I do, am unmoved by men's blame
Or their praise either. Somebody remarks
Morello's[9] outline there is wrongly traced,
His hue mistaken; what of that? or else,
Rightly traced and well ordered; what of that?   95
Speak as they please, what does the mountain care?
Ah, but a man's reach should exceed his grasp,
Or what's a heaven for? All is silver-gray
Placid and perfect with my art: the worse!
I know both what I want and what might gain,   100
And yet how profitless to know, to sigh
"Had I been two, another and myself,
Our head would have o'erlooked the world!"[1] No doubt.
Yonder's a work now, of that famous youth

7. A deputy of the Pope.
8. Probably Michelangelo (1475–1564).
9. A mountain peak outside Florence.
1. I.e., if I had been both an aspiring, dedicated, and soul-conscious artist as well as a faultless craftsman, the combination would have been unsurpassable. See also line 140 ("we half-men").

The Urbinate[2] who died five years ago. 105
('Tis copied, George Vasari sent it me.)[3]
Well, I can fancy how he did it all,
Pouring his soul, with kings and popes to see,
Reaching, that heaven might so replenish him,
Above and through his art—for it gives way; 110
That arm is wrongly put—and there again—
A fault to pardon in the drawing's lines,
Its body, so to speak: its soul is right,
He means right—that, a child may understand.
Still, what an arm! and I could alter it: 115
But all the play, the insight and the stretch—
Out of me, out of me! And wherefore out?
Had you enjoined them on me, given me soul,
We might have risen to Rafael, I and you!
Nay, Love, you did give all I asked, I think— 120
More than I merit, yes, by many times.
But had you—oh, with the same perfect brow,
And perfect eyes, and more than perfect mouth,
And the low voice my soul hears, as a bird
The fowler's pipe,[4] and follows to the snare— 125
Had you, with these the same, but brought a mind!
Some women do so. Had the mouth there urged
"God and the glory! never care for gain.
The present by the future, what is that?
Live for fame, side by side with Agnolo![5] 130
Rafael is waiting. up to God, all three!"
I might have done it for you. So it seems:
Perhaps not. All is as God overrules.
Beside, incentives come from the soul's self;
The rest avail not. Why do I need you? 135
What wife had Rafael, or has Agnolo?
In this world, who can do a thing, will not;
And who would do it, cannot, I perceive:
Yet the will's somewhat—somewhat, too, the power—
And thus we half-men struggle. At the end, 140
God, I conclude, compensates, punishes.
'Tis safer for me, if the award be strict,
That I am something underrated here.
Poor this long while, despised, to speak the truth.
I dared not, do you know, leave home all day, 145
For fear of chancing on the Paris lords.
The best is when they pass and look aside;
But they speak sometimes; I must bear it all.
Well may they speak! That Francis,[6] that first time,

---

2. Raphael (1483–1520), born at Urbino.
3. In saying that the painting is a copy, Andrea may perhaps be concerned to prevent Lucrezia from selling it.
4. Whistle or call used by hunters to lure wildfowl into range.

5. Michelangelo.
6. King Francis I of France had invited Andrea to his court at Fontainebleau and warmly encouraged him in his painting. On returning to Florence, however, Andrea is reputed to have stolen some funds entrusted to him by

And that long festal year at Fontainebleau!   150
I surely then could sometimes leave the ground,
Put on the glory, Rafael's daily wear,
In that humane great monarch's golden look—
One finger in his beard or twisted curl
Over his mouth's good mark that made the smile,   155
One arm about my shoulder, round my neck,
The jingle of his gold chain in my ear,
I painting proudly with his breath on me,
All his court round him, seeing with his eyes,
Such frank French eyes, and such a fire of souls   160
Profuse, my hand kept plying by those hearts—
And, best of all, this, this, this face beyond,
This in the background, waiting on my work,
To crown the issue with a last reward!
A good time, was it not, my kingly days?   165
And had you not grown restless . . . but I know—
'Tis done and past; 'twas right, my instinct said;
Too live the life grew, golden and not gray,
And I'm the weak-eyed bat no sun should tempt
Out of the grange whose four walls make his world.[7]   170
How could it end in any other way?
You called me, and I came home to your heart.
The triumph was—to reach and stay there; since
I reached it ere the triumph, what is lost?
Let my hands frame your face in your hair's gold,   175
You beautiful Lucrezia that are mine!
"Rafael did this, Andrea painted that;
The Roman's is the better when you pray,
But still the other's Virgin was his wife—"
Men will excuse me. I am glad to judge   180
Both pictures in your presence; clearer grows
My better fortune, I resolve to think.
For, do you know, Lucrezia, as God lives,
Said one day Agnolo, his very self,
To Rafael . . . I have known it all these years . . .   185
(When the young man was flaming out his thoughts
Upon a palace wall for Rome to see,
Too lifted up in heart because of it)
"Friend, there's a certain sorry little scrub
Goes up and down our Florence, none cares how,   190
Who, were he set to plan and execute
As you are, pricked on by your popes and kings,
Would bring the sweat into that brow of yours!"
To Rafael's—And indeed the arm is wrong.
I hardly dare . . . yet, only you to see,   195

Francis, and to please Lucrezia he built
a house with the money. Now he is
afraid of being insulted by "Paris lords"
on the streets.
7. The bat, a creature of evening,
thrives best in the confines of the
"four walls" of a farm building
("grange"). See also line 261 in which
Andrea thinks of heaven as a place of
four walls.

Give the chalk here—quick, thus the line should go!
Aye, but the soul! he's Rafael! rub it out!
Still, all I care for, if he spoke the truth,
(What he? why, who but Michel Agnolo?
Do you forget already words like those?)   200
If really there was such a chance, so lost—
Is, whether you're—not grateful—but more pleased.
Well, let me think so. And you smile indeed!
This hour has been an hour! Another smile?
If you would sit thus by me every night   205
I should work better, do you comprehend?
I mean that I should earn more, give you more.
See, it is settled dusk now; there's a star;
Morello's gone, the watch-lights show the wall,
The cue-owls[8] speak the name we call them by.   210
Come from the window, love—come in, at last,
Inside the melancholy little house
We built to be so gay with. God is just.
King Francis may forgive me: oft at nights
When I look up from painting, eyes tired out,   215
The walls become illumined, brick from brick
Distinct, instead of mortar, fierce bright gold,
That gold of his I did cement them with!
Let us but love each other. Must you go?
That Cousin here again? he waits outside?   220
Must see you—you, and not with me? Those loans?
More gaming debts to pay?[9] you smiled for that?
Well, let smiles buy me! have you more to spend?
While hand and eye and something of a heart
Are left me, work's my ware, and what's it worth?   225
I'll pay my fancy. Only let me sit
The gray remainder of the evening out,
Idle, you call it, and muse perfectly
How I could paint, were I but back in France,
One picture, just one more—the Virgin's face,   230
Not yours this time! I want you at my side
To hear them—that is, Michel Agnolo—
Judge all I do and tell you of its worth.
Will you? Tomorrow, satisfy your friend.
I take the subjects for his corridor,   235
Finish the portrait out of hand—there, there,
And throw him in another thing or two
If he demurs; the whole should prove enough
To pay for this same Cousin's freak. Beside,
What's better and what's all I care about,   240
Get you the thirteen scudi[1] for the ruff!

---

8. An owl whose cry sounds like the Italian word *ciù*.
9. Lucrezia's "Cousin" (or lover or "friend") owes gambling debts to a creditor. Andrea has already contracted (lines 5–10) to pay off these debts by painting some pictures according to the creditor's specifications. Now he agrees to pay off further debts.
1. Italian coins.

Love, does that please you? Ah, but what does he,
The Cousin! What does he to please you more?

I am grown peaceful as old age tonight.
I regret little, I would change still less.   245
Since there my past life lies, why alter it?
The very wrong to Francis!—it is true
I took his coin, was tempted and complied,
And built this house and sinned, and all is said.
My father and my mother died of want.[2]   250
Well, had I riches of my own? you see
How one gets rich! Let each one bear his lot.
They were born poor, lived poor, and poor they died:
And I have labored somewhat in my time
And not been paid profusely. Some good son   255
Paint my two hundred pictures—let him try!
No doubt, there's something strikes a balance. Yes,
You loved me quite enough, it seems tonight.
This must suffice me here. What would one have?
In heaven, perhaps, new chances, one more chance—   260
Four great walls in the New Jerusalem,
Meted on each side by the angel's reed,[3]
For Leonard,[4] Rafael, Agnolo and me
To cover—the three first without a wife,
While I have mine! So—still they overcome   265
Because there's still Lucrezia—as I choose.

Again the Cousin's whistle! Go, my Love.

ca. 1853   1855

Two in the Campagna[1]

1

I wonder do you feel today
        As I have felt since, hand in hand,
We sat down on the grass, to stray
        In spirit better through the land,
This morn of Rome and May?   5

2

For me, I touched a thought, I know,
        Has tantalized me many times,
(Like turns of thread the spiders throw
        Mocking across our path) for rhymes
To catch at and let go.   10

2. According to Vasari, Andrea's infatuation for Lucrezia prompted him
to stop supporting his poverty-stricken
parents.
3. Measuring rod. For "New Jerusalem," see Revelation xxi.10–21.

4. Leonardo da Vinci (1452–1519).
1. The Campagna is the name for the
level plains and pasture lands near
Rome where the ruins of ancient cities
are overrun with wild flowers.

3

Help me to hold it! First it left
    The yellowing fennel,[2] run to seed
There, branching from the brickwork's cleft,
    Some old tomb's ruin: yonder weed
Took up the floating weft,[3]   15

4

Where one small orange cup amassed
    Five beetles—blind and green they grope
Among the honey-meal: and last,
    Everywhere on the grassy slope
I traced it. Hold it fast!   20

5

The champaign[4] with its endless fleece
    Of feathery grasses everywhere!
Silence and passion, joy and peace,
    An everlasting wash of air—
Rome's ghost since her decease.   25

6

Such life here, through such lengths of hours,
    Such miracles performed in play,
Such primal naked forms of flowers,
    Such letting nature have her way
While heaven looks from its towers!   30

7

How say you? Let us, O my dove,
    Let us be unashamed of soul,
As earth lies bare to heaven above!
    How is it under our control
To love or not to love?   35

8

I would that you were all to me,
    You that are just so much, no more.
Nor yours nor mine, nor slave nor free!
    Where does the fault lie? What the core
O' the wound, since wound must be?   40

9

I would I could adopt your will,
    See with your eyes, and set my heart
Beating by yours, and drink my fill
    At your soul's springs—your part my part
In life, for good and ill.   45

10

No. I yearn upward, touch you close,
    Then stand away. I kiss your cheek,
Catch your soul's warmth—I pluck the rose
    And love it more than tongue can speak—
Then the good minute goes.   50

2. A yellow-flowered plant from which
a pungent spice is derived.
3. Threads crossing from side to side
of a web.
4. Here, the Campagna.

11

Already how am I so far
    Out of that minute? Must I go
Still like the thistle-ball, no bar,
    Onward, whenever light winds blow,
Fixed by no friendly star?   55

12

Just when I seemed about to learn!
    Where is the thread now? Off again!
The old trick! Only I discern—
    Infinite passion, and the pain
Of finite hearts that yearn.   60

1854   1855

A Grammarian's Funeral[1]

SHORTLY AFTER THE REVIVAL OF LEARNING IN EUROPE

Let us begin and carry up this corpse,
    Singing together.
Leave we the common crofts, the vulgar thorpes[2]
    Each in its tether[3]
Sleeping safe on the bosom of the plain,   5
    Cared for till cock-crow:
Look out if yonder be not day again
    Rimming the rock-row!
That's the appropriate country; there, man's thought,
    Rarer, intenser,   10
Self-gathered for an outbreak, as it ought,
    Chafes in the censer.
Leave we the unlettered plain its herd and crop;[4]
    Seek we sepulture
On a tall mountain, citied to the top,   15
    Crowded with culture!
All the peaks soar, but one the rest excels;
    Clouds overcome it;
No! yonder sparkle is the citadel's
    Circling its summit.   20

1. The speaker is one of the students who are bearing the body of their scholarly master to the mountaintop for burial. The student's defense of the dead grammarian's idealistic dedication to knowledge and faith in a future life is expressed in some of the harshest-sounding and most laborious verse ever written by Browning. It is this grotesque combination of opposites (soaring idealism in conjunction with harsh or petty realities) that gives *A Grammarian's Funeral* its distinctive tone.

No model for the grammarian has been specifically identified. Browning seems to have had in mind the kind of early Renaissance scholar whose devotion to the Greek language made it possible for others to enjoy the more recognizably significant aspects of the revival of learning.

2. "Crofts" are small tracts of land farmed by peasants; "thorpes" are villages.

3. Restricted to a narrow sphere like an animal tied to a stake.

4. Flatlands at the base of the mountain which are populated by illiterate shepherds and peasants. "Sepulture": burial place.

Thither our path lies; wind we up the heights:
  Wait ye the warning?
Our low life was the level's and the night's;
  He's for the morning.
Step to a tune, square chests, erect each head,   25
  'Ware[5] the beholders!
This is our master, famous, calm, and dead,
  Borne on our shoulders.

Sleep, crop and herd! sleep, darkling thorpe and croft,
  Safe from the weather!   30
He, whom we convoy to his grave aloft,
  Singing together,
He was a man born with thy face and throat,
  Lyric Apollo![6]
Long he lived nameless: how should spring take note 35
  Winter would follow?
Till lo, the little touch, and youth was gone!
  Cramped and diminished,
Moaned he, "New measures, other feet anon!
  My dance is finished?"   40
No, that's the world's way: (keep the mountain-side,
  Make for the city!)
He knew the signal, and stepped on with pride
  Over men's pity;
Left play for work, and grappled with the world   45
  Bent on escaping:
"What's in the scroll," quoth he, "thou keepest furled?
  Show me their shaping,
Theirs who most studied man, the bard and sage—
  Give!"—So, he gowned him,[7]   50
Straight got by heart that book to its last page:
  Learned, we found him.
Yea, but we found him bald too, eyes like lead,
  Accents uncertain:
"Time to taste life," another would have said,   55
  "Up with the curtain!"
This man said rather, "Actual life comes next?
  Patience a moment!
Grant I have mastered learning's crabbed text,
  Still there's the comment.[8]   60
Let me know all! Prate not of most or least,
  Painful or easy!
Even to the crumbs I'd fain eat up the feast,
  Aye, nor feel queasy."
Oh, such a life as he resolved to live,   65
  When he had learned it,

---

5. Look out for!
6. God of music and embodiment of male beauty.
7. Dressed in academic gown; became a scholar.
8. Commentaries or annotations upon a text.

When he had gathered all books had to give!
    Sooner, he spurned it.
Image the whole, then execute the parts—
    Fancy the fabric   70
Quite, ere you build, ere steel strike fire from quartz,
    Ere mortar dab brick!

(Here's the town gate reached: there's the market place
    Gaping before us.)
Yea, this in him was the peculiar grace   75
    (Hearten our chorus!)
That before living he'd learn how to live—
    No end to learning:
Earn the means first—God surely will contrive
    Use for our earning.   80
Others mistrust and say, "But time escapes:
    Live now or never!"
He said, "What's time? Leave Now for dogs and apes!
    Man has Forever."
Back to his book then: deeper drooped his head: 85
    Calculus[9] racked him:
Leaden before, his eyes grew dross of lead:
    Tussis[1] attacked him.
"Now, master, take a little rest!"—not he!
    (Caution redoubled,   90
Step two abreast, the way winds narrowly!)
    Not a whit troubled
Back to his studies, fresher than at first,
    Fierce as a dragon
He (soul-hydroptic[2] with a sacred thirst)   95
    Sucked at the flagon.
Oh, if we draw a circle premature,
    Heedless of far gain,
Greedy for quick returns of profit, sure
    Bad is our bargain!   100
Was it not great? did not he throw on God
    (He loves the burthen)—
God's task to make the heavenly period
    Perfect the earthen?
Did not he magnify the mind, show clear   105
    Just what it all meant?
He would not discount life, as fools do here,
    Paid by installment.
He ventured neck or nothing—heaven's success
    Found, or earth's failure: 110
"Wilt thou trust death or not?" He answered "Yes:
    Hence with life's pale lure!"
That low man seeks a little thing to do,
    Sees it and does it:

9. A stone such as a gallstone.   2. Insatiably soul-thirsty.
1. A cough.

This high man, with a great thing to pursue,   115
   Dies ere he knows it.
That low man goes on adding one to one,
   His hundred's soon hit:
This high man, aiming at a million,
   Misses an unit.[3]   120
That, has the world here—should he need the next,
   Let the world mind him!
This, throws himself on God, and unperplexed
   Seeking shall find him.
So, with the throttling hands of death at strife,   125
   Ground he at grammar;
Still, through the rattle, parts of speech were rife:
   While he could stammer
He settled *Hoti's* business—let it be!—
   Properly based *Oun*—   130
Gave us the doctrine of the enclitic *De*,[4]
   Dead from the waist down.
Well, here's the platform, here's the proper place:
   Hail to your purlieus,
All ye highfliers of the feathered race,   135
   Swallows and curlews!
Here's the top peak; the multitude below
   Live, for they can, there:
This man decided not to Live but Know—
   Bury this man there?   140
Here—here's his place, where meteors shoot, clouds form,
   Lightnings are loosened,
Stars come and go! Let joy break with the storm,
   Peace let the dew send!
Lofty designs must close in like effects: 145
   Loftily lying,
Leave him—still loftier than the world suspects,
   Living and dying.

ca. 1854   1855

Confessions

1

What is he buzzing in my ears?
   "Now that I come to die,
Do I view the world as a vale of tears?"
   Ah, reverend sir, not I!

2

What I viewed there once, what I view again   5
   Where the physic bottles stand

3. A small item such as some trifling worldly pleasure.
4. "*Hoti*," "*Oun*," and "*De*" are Greek particles meaning "that," "then," and "towards." An unaccented word such as *de* is "enclitic" when it affects the accentuation of a word adjacent to it.

On the table's edge—is a suburb lane,
    With a wall to my bedside hand.

3

That lane sloped, much as the bottles do,
    From a house you could descry   10
O'er the garden wall: is the curtain blue
    Or green to a healthy eye?

4

To mine, it serves for the old June weather
    Blue above lane and wall;
And that farthest bottle labeled "Ether"   15
    Is the house o'ertopping all.

5

At a terrace, somewhere near the stopper,
    There watched for me, one June,
A girl: I know, sir, it's improper,
    My poor mind's out of tune.   20

6

Only, there was a way . . . you crept
    Close by the side to dodge
Eyes in the house, two eyes except:
    They styled their house "The Lodge."

7

What right had a lounger up their lane?   25
    But, by creeping very close,
With the good wall's help—their eyes might strain
    And stretch themselves to O's,

8

Yet never catch her and me together,
    As she left the attic, there,   30
By the rim of the bottle labeled "Ether,"
    And stole from stair to stair,

9

And stood by the rose-wreathed gate. Alas,
    We loved, sir—used to meet:
How sad and bad and mad it was—   35
    But then, how it was sweet!

ca. 1859   1864

Youth and Art

1

It once might have been, once only:
    We lodged in a street together,
You, a sparrow on the housetop lonely,
    I, a lone she-bird of his feather.

2

Your trade was with sticks and clay,   5
    You thumbed, thrust, patted, and polished,
Then laughed, "They will see some day
    Smith made, and Gibson[1] demolished."

3

My business was song, song, song;
    I chirped, cheeped, trilled, and twittered,   10
"Kate Brown's on the boards ere long,
    And Grisi's[2] existence embittered!"

4

I earned no more by a warble
    Than you by a sketch in plaster;
You wanted a piece of marble,   15
    I needed a music master.

5

We studied hard in our styles,
    Chipped each at a crust like Hindoos,
For air looked out on the tiles,
    For fun watched each other's windows.   20

6

You lounged, like a boy of the South,
    Cap and blouse—nay, a bit of beard, too;
Or you got it, rubbing your mouth
    With fingers the clay adhered to.

7

And I—soon managed to find   25
    Weak points in the flower-fence facing,
Was forced to put up a blind
    And be safe in my corset lacing.

8

No harm! It was not my fault
    If you never turned your eye's tail up,   30
As I shook upon E *in alt*,[3]
    Or ran the chromatic scale up:

9

For spring bade the sparrows pair,
    And the boys and girls gave guesses,
And stalls in our street looked rare   35
    With bulrush and watercresses.

10

Why did not you pinch a flower
    In a pellet of clay and fling it?
Why did not I put a power
    Of thanks in a look, or sing it?   40

11

I did look, sharp as a lynx,
    (And yet the memory rankles)

1. John Gibson (1790–1866), English
sculptor.
2. Giulia Grisi (1811–69), a famous
Italian soprano.
3. High E.

When models arrived, some minx
  Tripped upstairs, she and her ankles.

12

But I think I gave you as good!   45
  "That foreign fellow—who can know
How she pays, in a playful mood,
  For his tuning her that piano?"

13

Could you say so, and never say
  "Suppose we join hands and fortunes,   50
And I fetch her from over the way,
  Her, piano, and long tunes and short tunes"?

14

No, no: you would not be rash,
  Nor I rasher and something over:
You've to settle yet Gibson's hash,   55
  And Grisi yet lives in clover.

15

But you meet the Prince[4] at the Board,
  I'm queen myself at *bals-paré*,[5]
I've married a rich old lord,
  And you're dubbed knight and an R. A.   60

16

Each life unfulfilled, you see;
  It hangs still, patchy and scrappy:
We have not sighed deep, laughed free,
  Starved, feasted, despaired—been happy.

17

And nobody calls you a dunce,   65
  And people suppose me clever:
This could but have happened once,
  And we missed it, lost it forever.

ca. 1860   1864

4. Perhaps Prince Albert, a patron of the arts. Now that the sculptor has acquired a title and is an "R. A." (a member of the respectable Royal Academy of Arts), he serves on committees or boards with the prince.
5. Fancy-dress balls.

Caliban upon Setebos

Two closely related controversies of the Victorian period led Browning to write this poem (whose title means "Caliban's thoughts about Setebos"). The first, stimulated by Darwin, was concerned with man's origins and his relation to other animals. Caliban, the half-man and half-monster of Shakespeare's *Tempest*, provided the poet with a model of how the mind of a primitive creature may operate. The second controversy concerned the nature of God and God's responsibility for the existence of suffering in the world. Like many men, Caliban thinks of God's nature as similar to his own. His anthropomorphic conception of the deity, whom he calls Setebos, is confined to what he has observed of life on his island and to what he has observed of himself. From the former derives his "natural theology," that is, his identifying the character of God from evidences provided by nature rather than from the evidence of supernatural revelation. From the latter, his observation of his own character, derives Caliban's conception of God's willful power. Caliban himself admires power and thinks of God in Calvinistic terms as a being who selects at random some creatures who are to be saved and others who are to be condemned to suffer.

An obstacle for the reader is Caliban's use of the third person pronoun. He says that he "never speaks his mind save housed as now"— that is, he thinks if he is adequately hidden under the slush in his cave, the deity will not catch him thinking; he may remind us of the hero of George Orwell's 1984 trying to evade the Thought Police. But to make especially sure of not being caught, Caliban refers to himself in the third person. Thus " 'Will sprawl" means "Caliban will sprawl" (an apostrophe before the verb usually indicates that Caliban himself is the implied subject). Only occasionally does he slip into the first person (e.g., line 56 or 68), when he feels sure that Setebos will not hear him. The deity is also referred to in the third person but with an initial capital letter ("He").

Caliban upon Setebos

OR NATURAL THEOLOGY IN THE ISLAND

"Thou thoughtest that I was altogether such a one as thyself."[1]

['Will sprawl, now that the heat of day is best,
Flat on his belly in the pit's much mire,
With elbows wide, fists clenched to prop his chin.
And, while he kicks both feet in the cool slush,
And feels about his spine small eft-things[2] course,   5
Run in and out each arm, and make him laugh:
And while above his head a pompion plant,[3]
Coating the cave-top as a brow its eye,
Creeps down to touch and tickle hair and beard,
And now a flower drops with a bee inside,   10
And now a fruit to snap at, catch and crunch—
He looks out o'er yon sea which sunbeams cross
And recross till they weave a spider web
(Meshes of fire, some great fish breaks at times)
And talks to his own self, howe'er he please,   15
Touching that other, whom his dam[4] called God.
Because to talk about Him, vexes—ha,
Could He but know! and time to vex is now,
When talk is safer than in wintertime.
Moreover Prosper[5] and Miranda sleep   20

1. Psalm l.21. The speaker is God.
2. Water lizards.
3. Pumpkin plant.
4. Caliban's mother, Sycorax.

5. Prospero the magician, who is Caliban's master in *The Tempest*. Miranda is Prospero's daughter.

In confidence he drudges at their task,
And it is good to cheat the pair, and gibe,
Letting the rank tongue blossom into speech.]

Setebos, Setebos, and Setebos!
'Thinketh, He dwelleth i' the cold o' the moon.   25

'Thinketh He made it, with the sun to match,
But not the stars; the stars came otherwise;
Only made clouds, winds, meteors, such as that:
Also this isle, what lives and grows thereon,
And snaky sea which rounds and ends the same.   30

'Thinketh, it came of being ill at ease:
He hated that He cannot change His cold,
Nor cure its ache. 'Hath spied an icy fish
That longed to 'scape the rock-stream where she lived,
And thaw herself within the lukewarm brine   35
O' the lazy sea her stream thrusts far amid,
A crystal spike 'twixt two warm walls of wave;[6]
Only, she ever sickened, found repulse
At the other kind of water, not her life,
(Green-dense and dim-delicious, bred o' the sun)   40
Flounced back from bliss she was not born to breathe,
And in her old bounds buried her despair,
Hating and loving warmth alike: so He.

'Thinketh, He made thereat the sun, this isle,
Trees and the fowls here, beast and creeping thing.   45
Yon otter, sleek-wet, black, lithe as a leech;
Yon auk,[7] one fire-eye in a ball of foam,
That floats and feeds; a certain badger brown
He hath watched hunt with that slant white-wedge eye
By moonlight; and the pie[8] with the long tongue   50
That pricks deep into oakwarts for a worm,
And says a plain word when she finds her prize,
But will not eat the ants; the ants themselves
That build a wall of seeds and settled stalks
About their hole—He made all these and more,   55
Made all we see, and us, in spite: how else?
He could not, Himself, make a second self
To be His mate; as well have made Himself:
He would not make what he mislikes or slights,
An eyesore to Him, or not worth His pains: 60
But did, in envy, listlessness, or sport,
Make what Himself would fain, in a manner, be—
Weaker in most points, stronger in a few,
Worthy, and yet mere playthings all the while,
Things He admires and mocks too—that is it.   65

6. I.e., the thin stream of cold water   7. Sea bird.
which is driven into the warm ocean   8. Magpie.
like a spike between walls.

Because, so brave, so better though they be,
It nothing skills if He begin to plague.[9]
Look now, I melt a gourd-fruit into mash,
Add honeycomb and pods, I have perceived,
Which bite like finches when they bill and kiss—   70
Then, when froth rises bladdery,[1] drink up all,
Quick, quick, till maggots scamper through my brain;
Last, throw me on my back i' the seeded thyme,
And wanton, wishing I were born a bird.
Put case, unable to be what I wish,   75
I yet could make a live bird out of clay:
Would not I take clay, pinch my Caliban
Able to fly?—for, there, see, he hath wings,
And great comb like the hoopoe's[2] to admire,
And there, a sting to do his foes offense,   80
There, and I will that he begin to live,
Fly to yon rock-top, nip me off the horns
Of grigs[3] high up that make the merry din,
Saucy through their veined wings, and mind me not.
In which feat, if his leg snapped, brittle clay,   85
And he lay stupid-like—why, I should laugh;
And if he, spying me, should fall to weep,
Beseech me to be good, repair his wrong,
Bid his poor leg smart less or grow again—
Well, as the chance were, this might take or else   90
Not take my fancy: I might hear his cry,
And give the mankin three sound legs for one,
Or pluck the other off, leave him like an egg,
And lessoned he was mine and merely clay.
Were this no pleasure, lying in the thyme,   95
Drinking the mash, with brain become alive,
Making and marring clay at will? So He.

'Thinketh, such shows nor right nor wrong in Him,
Nor kind, nor cruel: He is strong and Lord.
'Am strong myself compared to yonder crabs   100
That march now from the mountain to the sea;
'Let twenty pass, and stone the twenty-first,
Loving not, hating not, just choosing so.
'Say, the first straggler that boasts purple spots
Shall join the file, one pincer twisted off;   105
'Say, this bruised fellow shall receive a worm,
And two worms he whose nippers end in red;
As it likes me each time, I do: so He.

Well then, 'supposeth He is good i' the main,
Placable if His mind and ways were guessed,   110
But rougher than His handiwork, be sure!

9. I.e., our superior virtues are of no
help to us if God elects to inflict plagues
upon us.

1. Bubbly.
2. Bird with bright plumage.
3. Grasshoppers.

Oh, He hath made things worthier than Himself,
And envieth that, so helped, such things do more
Than He who made them! What consoles but this?
That they, unless through Him, do naught at all,   115
And must submit: what other use in things?
'Hath cut a pipe of pithless elder-joint
That, blown through, gives exact the scream o' the jay
When from her wing you twitch the feathers blue:
Sound this, and little birds that hate the jay   120
Flock within stone's throw, glad their foe is hurt:
Put case such pipe could prattle and boast forsooth,
"I catch the birds, I am the crafty thing,
I make the cry my maker cannot make
With his great round mouth; he must blow through mine!"   125
Would not I smash it with my foot? So He.

But wherefore rough, why cold and ill at ease?
Aha, that is a question! Ask, for that,
What knows—the something over Setebos
That made Him, or He, may be, found and fought,   130
Worsted, drove off and did to nothing,[4] perchance.
There may be something quiet o'er His head,
Out of His reach, that feels nor joy nor grief,
Since both derive from weakness in some way.
I joy because the quails come; would not joy   135
Could I bring quails here when I have a mind:
This Quiet, all it hath a mind to, doth.
'Esteemeth stars the outposts of its couch,
But never spends much thought nor care that way.
It may look up, work up—the worse for those   140
It works on! 'Careth but for Setebos[5]
The many-handed as a cuttlefish,
Who, making Himself feared through what He does,
Looks up, first, and perceives he cannot soar
To what is quiet and hath happy life;   145
Next looks down here, and out of very spite
Makes this a bauble-world to ape yon real,
These good things to match those as hips[6] do grapes.
'Tis solace making baubles, aye, and sport.
Himself peeped late, eyed Prosper at his books   150
Careless and lofty, lord now of the isle:
Vexed, 'stitched a book of broad leaves, arrow-shaped,
Wrote thereon, he knows what, prodigious words;
Has peeled a wand and called it by a name;
Weareth at whiles for an enchanter's robe   155
The eyed skin of a supple oncelot;[7]

4. Completely overcame.
5. Caliban is concerned to appease only Setebos, not the other deity— the Quiet.
6. Hard fruits produced by wild roses.
7. Browning may have invented this term from the Spanish *oncela* or from the French *ocelot*. Both words signify a leopard or spotted wildcat.

And hath an ounce[8] sleeker than youngling mole,
A four-legged serpent he makes cower and couch,
Now snarl, now hold its breath and mind his eye,
And saith she is Miranda and my wife: 160
'Keeps for his Ariel[9] a tall pouch-bill crane
He bids go wade for fish and straight disgorge;
Also a sea beast, lumpish, which he snared,
Blinded the eyes of, and brought somewhat tame,
And split its toe-webs, and now pens the drudge 165
In a hole o' the rock and calls him Caliban;
A bitter heart that bides its time and bites.
'Plays thus at being Prosper in a way,
Taketh his mirth with make-believes: so He.

His dam held that the Quiet made all things 170
Which Setebos vexed only: 'holds not so.
Who made them weak, meant weakness He might vex.
Had He meant other, while His hand was in,
Why not make horny eyes no thorn could prick,
Or plate my scalp with bone against the snow, 175
Or overscale my flesh 'neath joint and joint,
Like an orc's[1] armor? Aye—so spoil His sport!
He is the One now: only He doth all.

'Saith, He may like, perchance, what profits Him.
Aye, himself loves what does him good; but why? 180
'Gets good no otherwise. This blinded beast
Loves whoso places flesh-meat on his nose,
But, had he eyes, would want no help, but hate
Or love, just as it liked him: He hath eyes.
Also it pleaseth Setebos to work, 185
Use all His hands, and exercise much craft,
By no means for the love of what is worked.
'Tasteth, himself, no finer good i' the world
When all goes right, in this safe summertime,
And he wants little, hungers, aches not much, 190
Than trying what to do with wit and strength.
'Falls to make something: 'piled yon pile of turfs,
And squared and stuck there squares of soft white chalk,
And, with a fish-tooth, scratched a moon on each,
And set up endwise certain spikes of tree, 195
And crowned the whole with a sloth's skull a-top,
Found dead i' the woods, too hard for one to kill.
No use at all i' the work, for work's sole sake;
'Shall some day knock it down again: so He.

'Saith He is terrible: watch His feats in proof! 200
One hurricane will spoil six good months' hope.
He hath a spite against me, that I know,

8. A large, ferocious leopard, six or
seven feet in length.
9. In *The Tempest*, a spirit who serves
Prospero.
1. Killer whale's.

Just as He favors Prosper, who knows why?
So it is, all the same, as well I find.
'Wove wattles half the winter, fenced them firm   205
With stone and stake to stop she-tortoises
Crawling to lay their eggs here: well, one wave,
Feeling the foot of Him upon its neck,
Gaped as a snake does, lolled out its large tongue,
And licked the whole labor flat; so much for spite.   210
'Saw a ball[2] flame down late (yonder it lies)
Where, half an hour before, I slept i' the shade:
Often they scatter sparkles: there is force!
'Dug up a newt He may have envied once
And turned to stone, shut up inside a stone.   215
Please Him and hinder this?—What Prosper does?[3]
Aha, if He would tell me how! Not He!
There is the sport: discover how or die!
All need not die, for of the things o' the isle
Some flee afar, some dive, some run up trees;   220
Those at His mercy—why, they please Him most
When . . . when . . . well, never try the same way twice!
Repeat what act has pleased, He may grow wroth.
You must not know His ways, and play Him off,
Sure of the issue. 'Doth the like himself: 225
'Spareth a squirrel that it nothing fears
But steals the nut from underneath my thumb,
And when I threat, bites stoutly in defense:
'Spareth an urchin[4] that contrariwise
Curls up into a ball, pretending death   230
For fright at my approach: the two ways please.
But what would move my choler more than this,
That either creature counted on its life
Tomorrow and next day and all days to come,
Saying, forsooth, in the inmost of its heart,   235
"Because he did so yesterday with me,
And otherwise with such another brute,
So must he do henceforth and always."—Aye?
Would teach the reasoning couple what "must" means!
'Doth as he likes, or wherefore Lord? So He.   240

'Conceiveth all things will continue thus,
And we shall have to live in fear of Him
So long as He lives, keeps His strength: no change,
If He have done His best, make no new world
To please Him more, so leave off watching this—   245
If He surprise not even the Quiet's self
Some strange day—or, suppose, grow into it
As grubs grow butterflies: else, here are we,
And there is He, and nowhere help at all.

2. Meteorite.
3. I.e., shall I please Setebos, as
Prospero does, and thus prevent my
being punished as the newt was punished?
4. Hedgehog.

'Believeth with the life, the pain shall stop. 250
His dam held different, that after death
He both plagued enemies and feasted friends:
Idly![5] He doth His worst in this our life,
Giving just respite lest we die through pain,
Saving last pain for worst—with which, an end. 255
Meanwhile, the best way to escape His ire
Is, not to seem too happy. 'Sees, himself,
Yonder two flies, with purple films and pink,
Bask on the pompion-bell above: kills both.
'Sees two black painful beetles roll their ball 260
On head and tail as if to save their lives:
Moves them the stick away they strive to clear.

Even so, 'would have Him misconceive, suppose
This Caliban strives hard and ails no less,
And always, above all else, envies Him; 265
Wherefore he mainly dances on dark nights,
Moans in the sun, gets under holes to laugh,
And never speaks his mind save housed as now:
Outside, 'groans, curses. If He caught me here,
O'erheard this speech, and asked "What chucklest at?" 270
'Would, to appease Him, cut a finger off,
Or of my three kid yearlings burn the best,
Or let the toothsome apples rot on tree,
Or push my tame beast for the orc to taste:
While myself lit a fire, and made a song 275
And sung it, *"What I hate, be consecrate
To celebrate Thee and Thy state, no mate
For Thee; what see for envy in poor me?"*
Hoping the while, since evils sometimes mend,
Warts rub away and sores are cured with slime, 280
That some strange day, will either the Quiet catch
And conquer Setebos, or likelier He
Decrepit may doze, doze, as good as die.

———————

[What, what? A curtain o'er the world at once!
Crickets stop hissing; not a bird—or, yes, 285
There scuds His raven that has told Him all!
It was fool's play this prattling! Ha! The wind
Shoulders the pillared dust, death's house o' the move,
And fast invading fires begin! White blaze—
A tree's head snaps—and there, there, there, there, there, 290
His thunder follows! Fool to gibe at Him!
Lo! 'Lieth flat and loveth Setebos!
'Maketh his teeth meet through his upper lip,

---

5. I.e., Caliban thinks his mother's opinion was wrong or idle. God's sport with man is confined to this world; there is no afterlife.

Will let those quails fly, will not eat this month
  One little mess of whelks,[6] so he may 'scape!]   295
ca. 1860   1864

Prospice[7]

Fear death?—to feel the fog in my throat,
    The mist in my face,
When the snows begin, and the blasts denote
    I am nearing the place,
The power of the night, the press of the storm,   5
    The post of the foe;
Where he stands, the Arch Fear in a visible form,
    Yet the strong man must go:
For the journey is done and the summit attained,
    And the barriers fall,   10
Though a battle's to fight ere the guerdon be gained,
    The reward of it all.
I was ever a fighter, so—one fight more,
    The best and the last!
I would hate that death bandaged my eyes, and forbore,   15
    And bade me creep past.
No! let me taste the whole of it, fare like my peers
    The heroes of old,
Bear the brunt, in a minute pay glad life's arrears
    Of pain, darkness, and cold.   20
For sudden the worst turns the best to the brave,
    The black minute's at end,
And the elements' rage, the fiend-voices that rave,
    Shall dwindle, shall blend,
Shall change, shall become first a peace out of pain,   25
    Then a light, then thy breast,
O thou soul of my soul![8] I shall clasp thee again,
    And with God be the rest!
ca. 1861   1864

Abt Vogler[1]

(AFTER HE HAS BEEN EXTEMPORIZING UPON THE MUSICAL
INSTRUMENT OF HIS INVENTION)

1

Would that the structure brave, the manifold music I build,
    Bidding my organ obey, calling its keys to their work,

6. Shellfish.
7. The title means "Look forward."
8. Browning's wife.
1. Georg Joseph Vogler (1749–1814), a German priest and musician, held the honorary title of *Abbé* or *Abt*. As a composer, teacher, and designer of musical instruments he was well known

Claiming each slave of the sound, at a touch, as when Solomon
   willed
   Armies of angels that soar, legions of demons that lurk,
Man, brute, reptile, fly—alien of end and of aim,   5
   Adverse, each from the other heaven-high, hell-deep removed—
Should rush into sight at once as he named the ineffable Name,[2]
   And pile him a palace straight, to pleasure the princess he
   loved!

2

Would it might tarry like his, the beautiful building of mine,
   This which my keys in a crowd pressed and importuned to
   raise!   10
Ah, one and all, how they helped, would dispart now and now com-
   bine,
   Zealous to hasten the work, heighten their master his praise!
And one would bury his brow with a blind plunge down to hell,
   Burrow awhile and build, broad on the roots of things,
Then up again swim into sight, having based me my palace well, 15
   Founded it, fearless of flame, flat on the nether springs.

3

And another would mount and march, like the excellent minion he
   was,
   Aye, another and yet another, one crowd but with many a crest,
Raising my rampired walls of gold as transparent as glass,
   Eager to do and die, yield each his place to the rest: 20
For higher still and higher (as a runner tips with fire,
   When a great illumination surprises a festal night—
Outlining round and round Rome's dome from space to spire)[3]
   Up, the pinnacled glory reached, and the pride of my soul was
   in sight.

4

In sight? Not half! for it seemed, it was certain, to match man's
   birth,   25
   Nature in turn conceived, obeying an impulse as I;
And the emulous heaven yearned down, made effort to reach the
   earth,
   As the earth had done her best, in my passion, to scale the sky:

in his own day, but he was most famous
as an extemporizer at the organ. Browning's soliloquy represents Vogler at
the organ joyfully improvising a piece
of music and then reflecting upon the
ephemeral existence of such a unique
work of art and of its possible relation
to God's purposes in heaven and on
earth. In this connection, a suggestive
comparison can be made between Browning's conception of a palace of music
inhabited by the "wonderful Dead" and
W. B. Yeats's conception of a heaven
of art in his Byzantium poems.

   A characteristic feature of *Abt Vogler*
is the use of exceptionally long sentences, densely packed with details,

which may evoke for us the effects of
rolling organ music. The resulting movement is markedly different from the brisk
staccato rhythms of *A Toccata of
Galuppi's.*

   The "musical instrument of his invention" is a compact organ called the
Orchestrion.

2. According to Jewish legend, King
Solomon (because he possessed a seal
inscribed with the "ineffable Name" of
God) had the power of compelling the
demons of earth and air to perform his
bidding.

3. On festival nights the dome of St.
Peter's in Rome is illuminated by a series
of lights ignited by a torchbearer.

Novel splendors burst forth, grew familiar and dwelt with mine,

    Not a point nor peak but found and fixed its wandering star;   30

Meteor-moons, balls of blaze: and they did not pale nor pine,

    For earth had attained to heaven, there was no more near nor
    far.

5

Nay more; for there wanted not who walked in the glare and glow,

    Presences plain in the place; or, fresh from the Protoplast,[4]

Furnished for ages to come, when a kindlier wind should blow,   35

    Lured now to begin and live, in a house to their liking at last;

Or else the wonderful Dead who have passed through the body and
    gone,

    But were back once more to breathe in an old world worth
    their new:

What never had been, was now; what was, as it shall be anon;

    And what is—shall I say, matched both? for I was made per-
    fect too.   40

6

All through my keys that gave their sounds to a wish of my soul,

    All through my soul that praised as its wish flowed visibly forth,

All through music and me! For think, had I painted the whole,

    Why, there it had stood, to see, nor the process so wonder-
    worth:

Had I written the same, made verse—still, effect proceeds from
    cause,   45

    Ye know why the forms are fair, ye hear how the tale is told;

It is all triumphant art, but art in obedience to laws,

    Painter and poet are proud in the artist-list enrolled—

7

But here is the finger of God, a flash of the will that can,

    Existent behind all laws, that made them and, lo, they are!   50

And I know not if, save in this, such gift be allowed to man,

    That out of three sounds he frame, not a fourth sound, but a
    star.[5]

Consider it well: each tone of our scale in itself is naught;

    It is everywhere in the world—loud, soft, and all is said:

Give it to me to use! I mix it with two in my thought: 55

    And, there! Ye have heard and seen: consider and bow the
    head!

8

Well, it is gone at last, the palace of music I reared;

    Gone! and the good tears start, the praises that come too slow;

For one is assured at first, one scarce can say that he feared,

    That he even gave it a thought, the gone thing was to go.   60

Never to be again! But many more of the kind

    As good, nay, better perchance: is this your comfort to me?

---

4. The original or archetypal form of a species. The "presences" from this source are beings of the future, not yet existing, who are "lured" into life by the music. Cf. *Women and Roses*, stanzas 7 and 8.

5. I.e., the musician's combining of three notes into a new harmonic unit is a creative act as miraculous as the creation of a star.

To me, who must be saved because I cling with my mind
    To the same, same self, same love, same God: aye, what was,
        shall be.

9

Therefore to whom turn I but to thee, the ineffable Name?   65
    Builder and maker, thou, of houses not made with hands![6]
What, have fear of change from thee who art ever the same?
    Doubt that thy power can fill the heart that thy power expands?
There shall never be one lost good! What was, shall live as before;
    The evil is null, is naught, is silence implying sound;   70
What was good shall be good, with, for evil, so much good more;
    On the earth the broken arcs; in the heaven, a perfect round.

10

All we have willed or hoped or dreamed of good shall exist;
    Not its semblance, but itself; no beauty, nor good, nor power
Whose voice has gone forth, but each survives for the melodist   75
    When eternity affirms the conception of an hour.
The high that proved too high, the heroic for earth too hard,
    The passion that left the ground to lose itself in the sky,
Are music sent up to God by the lover and the bard;
    Enough that he heard it once: we shall hear it by-and-by.   80

11

And what is our failure here but a triumph's evidence
    For the fullness of the days? Have we withered or agonized?
Why else was the pause prolonged but that singing might issue
        thence?
    Why rushed the discords in but that harmony should be
        prized?
Sorrow is hard to bear, and doubt is slow to clear,   85
    Each sufferer says his say, his scheme of the weal and woe:
But God has a few of us whom he whispers in the ear;
    The rest may reason and welcome: 'tis we musicians know.

12

Well, it is earth with me; silence resumes her reign:
    I will be patient and proud, and soberly acquiesce.   90
Give me the keys. I feel for the common chord again,
    Sliding by semitones, till I sink to the minor—yes,
And I blunt it into a ninth, and I stand on alien ground,
    Surveying awhile the heights I rolled from into the deep;
Which, hark, I have dared and done, for my resting place is
        found,   95
    The C Major of this life:[7] so, now I will try to sleep.

1864

6. See II Corinthians v.1, in which St. Paul speaks of "a building of God, an house not made with hands, eternal in the heavens."

7. Vogler's last moments of playing express first his sadness that he cannot remain forever among the "heights" of the music he has temporarily created, and afterwards his acceptance of this return to man's ordinary existence. Thus he plays in a "minor" key, pauses for a short space on the "alien ground" of a "ninth" (a discord which requires a resolution), and finally concludes in "C Major," a key without sharps or flats and representing the plane of ordinary life.

Rabbi Ben Ezra[1]

1

Grow old along with me!
The best is yet to be,
The last of life, for which the first was made:
Our times are in His hand
Who saith, "A whole I planned,   5
Youth shows but half; trust God: see all nor be afraid!"

2

Not that, amassing flowers,
Youth sighed, "Which rose make ours,
Which lily leave and then as best recall?"
Not that, admiring stars,   10
It yearned, "Nor Jove, nor Mars;
Mine be some figured flame which blends, transcends them all!"

3

Not for such hopes and fears
Annulling youth's brief years,
Do I remonstrate: folly wide the mark!   15
Rather I prize the doubt
Low kinds exist without,
Finished and finite clods, untroubled by a spark.

4

Poor vaunt of life indeed,
Were man but formed to feed   20
On joy, to solely seek and find and feast:
Such feasting ended, then
As sure an end to men;
Irks care the crop-full bird? Frets doubt the maw-crammed beast?[2]

5

Rejoice we are allied   25
To That which doth provide
And not partake, effect and not receive!
A spark disturbs our clod;
Nearer we hold of God
Who gives, than of His tribes that take, I must believe.   30

6

Then, welcome each rebuff
That turns earth's smoothness rough,
Each sting that bids nor sit nor stand but go!
Be our joys three parts pain!

---

1. The speaker, Abraham Ibn Ezra (ca. 1092–1167), was an eminent Biblical scholar of Spain, but Browning makes little attempt to present him as a distinct individual or to relate him to the age in which he lived. Unlike the more characteristic monologues, *Rabbi Ben Ezra* is not dramatic but declamatory.
2. I.e., does care disturb a bird whose gullet ("crop") is full of food? does doubt trouble an animal whose stomach ("maw") is full?

Strive, and hold cheap the strain; 35
Learn, nor account the pang; dare, never grudge the throe![3]

7

For thence—a paradox
Which comforts while it mocks—
Shall life succeed in that it seems to fail:
What 1 aspired to be, 40
And was not, comforts me:
A brute I might have been, but would not sink i' the scale.

8

What is he but a brute
Whose flesh has soul to suit,
Whose spirit works lest arms and legs want play? 45
To man, propose this test—
Thy body at its best,
How far can that project thy soul on its lone way?

9

Yet gifts should prove their use:
I own the Past profuse 50
Of power each side, perfection every turn:
Eyes, ears took in their dole,
Brain treasured up the whole;
Should not the heart beat once, "How good to live and learn"?

10

Not once beat, "Praise be Thine! 55
I see the whole design,
I, who saw power, see now love perfect too:
Perfect I call Thy plan:
Thanks that I was a man!
Maker, remake, complete—I trust what Thou shalt do!" 60

11

For pleasant is this flesh;
Our soul, in its rose-mesh[4]
Pulled ever to the earth, still yearns for rest;
Would we some prize might hold
To match those manifold 65
Possessions of the brute—gain most, as we did best!

12

Let us not always say,
"Spite of this flesh today
I strove, made head, gained ground upon the whole!"
As the bird wings and sings, 70
Let us cry, "All good things
Are ours, nor soul helps flesh more, now, than flesh helps soul!"

13

Therefore I summon age
To grant youth's heritage,
Life's struggle having so far reached its term: 75

---

3. Anguish.   4. The body which holds the soul in
                                  its net.

Thence shall I pass, approved
A man, for aye removed
From the developed brute; a god though in the germ.

14

And I shall thereupon
Take rest, ere I be gone   80
Once more on my adventure brave and new:[5]
Fearless and unperplexed,
When I wage battle next,
What weapons to select, what armor to indue.[6]

15

Youth ended, I shall try   85
My gain or loss thereby;
Leave the fire ashes,[7] what survives is gold:
And I shall weigh the same,
Give life its praise or blame:
Young, all lay in dispute; I shall know, being old.   90

16

For note, when evening shuts,
A certain moment cuts
The deed off, calls the glory from the gray:
A whisper from the west
Shoots—"Add this to the rest,   95
Take it and try its worth: here dies another day."

17

So, still within this life,
Though lifted o'er its strife,
Let me discern, compare, pronounce at last,
"This rage was right i' the main,   100
That acquiescence vain:
The Future I may face now I have proved the Past."

18

For more is not reserved
To man, with soul just nerved
To act tomorrow what he learns today: 105
Here, work enough to watch
The Master work, and catch
Hints of the proper craft, tricks of the tool's true play.

19

As it was better, youth
Should strive, through acts uncouth,   110
Toward making, than repose on aught found made:
So, better, age, exempt
From strife, should know, than tempt[8]
Further. Thou waitedst age: wait death nor be afraid!

20

Enough now, if the Right   115
And Good and Infinite

---

5. In the next life.   7. If the fire leaves ashes.
6. Put on.   8. Attempt.

Be named here, as thou callest thy hand thine own,
  With knowledge absolute,
  Subject to no dispute
From fools that crowded youth, nor let thee feel alone.[9]   120

21

  Be there, for once and all,
  Severed great minds from small,
Announced to each his station in the Past!
  Was I, the world arraigned,[1]
  Were they, my soul disdained,   125
Right? Let age speak the truth and give us peace at last!

22

  Now, who shall arbitrate?
  Ten men love what I hate,
Shun what I follow, slight what I receive;
  Ten, who in ears and eyes   130
  Match me: we all surmise,
They this thing, and I that: whom shall my soul believe?

23

  Not on the vulgar mass
  Called "work," must sentence pass,
Things done, that took the eye and had the price;   135
  O'er which, from level stand,
  The low world laid its hand,
Found straightway to its mind, could value in a trice:

24

  But all, the world's coarse thumb
  And finger failed to plumb,   140
So passed in making up the main account;
  All instincts immature,
  All purposes unsure,
That weighed not as his work, yet swelled the man's amount:

25

  Thoughts hardly to be packed   145
  Into a narrow act,
Fancies that broke through language and escaped;
  All I could never be,
  All, men ignored in me,
This, I was worth to God, whose wheel[2] the pitcher shaped.   150

26

  Aye, note that Potter's wheel,
  That metaphor! and feel
Why time spins fast, why passive lies our clay—
  Thou, to whom fools propound,[3]

9. Stanzas 20 and 21 affirm that in age we can more readily think independently than in youth. Maturity enables us to ignore the pressure of having to conform to the thinking of the crowd of small-minded people.
1. Was I, whom the world arraigned.
2. The potting-wheel on which the speaker's highest qualities of soul were shaped into an enduring "pitcher" by God. See Isaiah lxiv.8.
3. Perhaps addressed to Omar Khayyám, whose poem, *The Rubáiyát*, urged men to eat, drink, and be merry. Edward FitzGerald's translation of Omar's poem had appeared in 1859.

When the wine makes its round, 155
"Since life fleets, all is change; the Past gone, seize today!"

27

Fool! All that is, at all,
Lasts ever, past recall;
Earth changes, but thy soul and God stand sure:
What entered into thee, 160
That was, is, and shall be:
Time's wheel runs back or stops: Potter and clay endure.

28

He fixed thee 'mid this dance
Of plastic circumstance,
This Present, thou, forsooth, wouldst fain arrest:[4] 165
Machinery just meant
To give thy soul its bent,
Try thee and turn thee forth, sufficiently impressed.

29

What though the earlier grooves
Which ran the laughing loves
Around thy base,[5] no longer pause and press? 170
What though, about thy rim,
Skull-things in order grim
Grow out, in graver mood, obey the sterner stress?

30

Look not thou down but up! 175
To uses of a cup,
The festal board, lamp's flash, and trumpet's peal,
The new wine's foaming flow,
The Master's lips a-glow!
Thou, heaven's consummate cup, what need'st thou with earth's
wheel? 180

31

But I need, now as then,
Thee, God, who moldest men;
And since, not even while the whirl was worst,
Did I—to the wheel of life
With shapes and colors rife, 185
Bound dizzily—mistake my end, to slake Thy thirst:

32

So, take and use Thy work:
Amend what flaws may lurk,
What strain o' the stuff, what warpings past the aim!
My times be in Thy hand! 190
Perfect the cup as planned!
Let age approve of youth, and death complete the same!
ca. 1862

1864

4. I.e., you would be glad to stop ("arrest") time at this present point of your life.
5. Base of the clay pitcher.

Apparent Failure

"We shall soon lose a celebrated building."
PARIS NEWSPAPER

1

No, for I'll save it! Seven years since,
    I passed through Paris, stopped a day
To see the baptism of your Prince;[1]
    Saw, made my bow, and went my way:
Walking the heat and headache off,   5
    I took the Seine-side, you surmise,
Thought of the Congress, Gortschakoff,
    Cavour's appeal and Buol's replies,[2]
So sauntered till—what met my eyes?

2

Only the Doric little Morgue!   10
    The dead-house where you show your drowned:
Petrarch's Vaucluse makes proud the Sorgue,[3]
    Your Morgue has made the Seine renowned.
One pays one's debt in such a case;
    I plucked up heart and entered—stalked,   15
Keeping a tolerable face
    Compared with some whose cheeks were chalked:
Let them! No Briton's to be balked!

3

First came the silent gazers; next,
    A screen of glass, we're thankful for;   20
Last, the sight's self, the sermon's text,
    The three men who did most abhor
Their life in Paris yesterday,
    So killed themselves: and now, enthroned
Each on his copper couch, they lay   25
    Fronting me, waiting to be owned.
I thought, and think, their sin's atoned.

4

Poor men, God made, and all for that!
    The reverence struck me; o'er each head
Religiously was hung its hat,   30
    Each coat dripped by the owner's bed,
Sacred from touch: each had his berth,
    His bounds, his proper place of rest,
Who last night tenanted on earth

1. Prince Louis, son of Napoleon III, was baptized in June, 1856. Browning had witnessed the event.
2. The Congress of Paris which met in 1856 to establish peace terms after the Crimean War. Russia was represented by Prince Alexander Gortschakoff, Piedmont by Count Cavour, and Austria by Count von Buol-Schauenstein.
3. The Sorgue River is renowned because the poet Petrarch lived in Vaucluse, a village on its banks.

Some arch, where twelve such slept abreast—   35
Unless the plain asphalt seemed best.

5

How did it happen, my poor boy?
    You wanted to be Buonaparte
And have the Tuileries[4] for toy,
    And could not, so it broke your heart?   40
You, old one by his side, I judge,
    Were, red as blood, a socialist,
A leveler! Does the Empire grudge
    You've gained what no Republic missed?
Be quiet, and unclench your fist!   45

6

And this—why, he was red in vain,
    Or black[5]—poor fellow that is blue!
What fancy was it turned your brain?
    Oh, women were the prize for you!
Money gets women, cards and dice   50
    Get money, and ill luck gets just
The copper couch and one clear nice
    Cool squirt of water o'er your bust,
The right thing to extinguish lust!

7

It's wiser being good than bad;   55
    It's safer being meek than fierce:
It's fitter being sane than mad.
    My own hope is, a sun will pierce
The thickest cloud earth ever stretched;
    That, after Last, returns the First,   60
Though a wide compass round be fetched;
    That what began best, can't end worst,
Nor what God blessed once, prove accursed.

1863   1864

O Lyric Love[1]

O lyric Love, half angel and half bird
And all a wonder and a wild desire—
Boldest of hearts that ever braved the sun,
Took sanctuary within the holier blue,
And sang a kindred soul out to his face—   5
Yet human at the red-ripe of the heart—

---

4. The palace in Paris where the kings of France had resided.
5. Reference to a gambling game, *rouge-et-noir*, in which red or black may win the stakes.
1. These lines, which conclude Book I of *The Ring and the Book*, are addressed to the poet's wife, who had died in 1861. Ten out of the twelve books of this long poem are dramatic monologues, each speaker commenting upon the murder of Pompilia Franceschini by her husband, Guido. In Books I and XII, however, Browning usually speaks, as in this dedicatory passage, in his own person.

When the first summons from the darkling earth
Reached thee amid thy chambers, blanched their blue,
And bared them of the glory—to drop down,
To toil for man, to suffer or to die—   10
This is the same voice: can thy soul know change?
Hail then, and hearken from the realms of help!
Never may I commence my song, my due
To God who best taught song by gift of thee,
Except with bent head and beseeching hand—   15
That still, despite the distance and the dark,
What was, again may be; some interchange
Of grace, some splendor once thy very thought,
Some benediction anciently thy smile:
—Never conclude, but raising hand and head   20
Thither where eyes, that cannot reach, yet yearn
For all hope, all sustainment, all reward,
Their utmost up and on—so blessing back
In those thy realms of help, that heaven thy home,
Some whiteness which, I judge, thy face makes proud,   25
Some wanness where, I think, thy foot may fall!

                                                         1868

The Householder

[*Epilogue to* Fifine at the Fair]

1

Savage I was sitting in my house, late, lone:
    Dreary, weary with the long day's work:
Head of me, heart of me, stupid as a stone:
    Tongue-tied now, now blaspheming like a Turk;
When, in a moment, just a knock, call, cry,   5
    Half a pang and all a rapture, there again were we!—
"What, and is it really you again?" quoth I:
    "I again, what else did you expect?" quoth She.

2

"Never mind, hie away from this old house—
    Every crumbling brick embrowned with sin and shame!   10
Quick, in its corners ere certain shapes arouse!
    Let them—every devil of the night—lay claim,
Make and mend, or rap and rend, for me! Good-by!
    God be their guard from disturbance at their glee,
Till, crash, comes down the carcass in a heap!" quoth I: 15
    "Nay, but there's a decency required!" quoth She.

3

"Ah, but if you knew how time has dragged, days, nights!
    All the neighbor-talk with man and maid—such men!
All the fuss and trouble of street sounds, window sights:
    All the worry of flapping door and echoing roof; and then, 20

All the fancies . . . Who were they had leave, dared try
  Darker arts that almost struck despair in me?
If you knew but how I dwelt down here!" quoth I:
  "And was I so better off up there?" quoth She.

4

"Help and get it over! *Reunited to his wife*   25
  (How draw up the paper lets the parish-people know?)
Lies M., or N., departed from this life,
  Day the this or that, month and year the so and so.
What i' the way of final flourish? Prose, verse? Try!
  Affliction sore long time he bore, or, what is it to be?   30
Till God did please to grant him ease. Do end!" quoth I:
  "I end with—Love is all and Death is naught!" quoth She.

1872   1872

House

1

Shall I sonnet-sing you about myself?
  Do I live in a house you would like to see?
Is it scant of gear, has it store of pelf?
  "Unlock my heart with a sonnet-key?"

2

Invite the world, as my betters have done?   5
  "Take notice: this building remains on view,
Its suites of reception every one,
  Its private apartment and bedroom too;

3

"For a ticket, apply to the Publisher."
  No: thanking the public, I must decline.   10
A peep through my window, if folk prefer;
  But, please you, not foot over threshold of mine!

4

I have mixed with a crowd and heard free talk
  In a foreign land where an earthquake chanced:
And a house stood gaping, naught to balk   15
  Man's eye wherever he gazed or glanced.

5

The whole of the frontage shaven sheer,
  The inside gaped: exposed to day,
Right and wrong and common and queer,
  Bare, as the palm of your hand, it lay.   20

6

The owner? Oh, he had been crushed, no doubt!
  "Odd tables and chairs for a man of wealth!
What a parcel of musty old books about!
  He smoked—no wonder he lost his health!

7

"I doubt if he bathed before he dressed.   25
  A brazier?—the pagan, he burned perfumes!

You see it is proved, what the neighbors guessed:
    His wife and himself had separate rooms."
                            8
Friends, the goodman of the house at least
    Kept house to himself till an earthquake came: 30
'Tis the fall of its frontage permits you feast
    On the inside arrangement you praise or blame.
                            9
Outside should suffice for evidence:
    And whoso desires to penetrate
Deeper, must dive by the spirit-sense—   35
    No optics like yours, at any rate!
                           10
"Hoity toity! A street to explore,
    Your house the exception! '*With this same key
Shakespeare unlocked his heart,*' once more!" [2]
    Did Shakespeare? If so, the less Shakespeare he!   40

                                                            1876

To Edward FitzGerald[1]

I chanced upon a new book yesterday;
    I opened it, and, where my finger lay
'Twixt page and uncut page, these words I read—
Some six or seven at most—and learned thereby
That you, FitzGerald, whom by ear and eye   5
    She never knew, "thanked God my wife was dead."
Aye, dead! and were yourself alive, good Fitz,
How to return you thanks would task my wits.
    Kicking you seems the common lot of curs—
While more appropriate greeting lends you grace,   10
Surely to spit there glorifies your face—
    Spitting from lips once sanctified by hers.

1889   1889

---

2. The quotation is from Wordsworth's *Scorn Not the Sonnet,* which praises the sonnet form as the one in which Shakespeare had revealed his true self. In theory, if not in practice, Browning strongly disapproved of a poet who "unlocked his heart" in public. A striking example of this failing was *The House of Life,* a sonnet sequence by D. G. Rossetti, published in 1870. It has been conjectured that the glimpses into the intimacies of domestic life and love relations, featured in Rossetti's sonnets, probably prompted Browning to present his case on behalf of an artist's right to privacy and need for reticence.

1. In 1861 FitzGerald wrote to a friend: "Mrs. Browning's death is rather a relief to me, I must say: no more *Aurora Leighs* [title of a popular poem by Mrs. Browning], thank God! * * * She and her sex had better mind the kitchen and the children." Browning discovered the passage among FitzGerald's posthumously published letters and in white heat wrote this rejoinder which was published in the *Athenaeum.* In defense of his poem, Browning wrote a long and eloquent letter to the Tennysons (who had been close friends of FitzGerald) which has been published in the *Times Literary Supplement* (June 3, 1965), 464.

Epilogue to *Asolando*[2]

At the midnight in the silence of the sleep-time,
    When you[3] set your fancies free,
Will they pass to where—by death, fools think, imprisoned—
Low he lies who once so loved you, whom you loved so,
      —Pity me?   5
Oh to love so, be so loved, yet so mistaken!
    What had I on earth to do
With the slothful, with the mawkish, the unmanly?
Like the aimless, helpless, hopeless, did I drivel
      —Being—who?   10

One who never turned his back but marched breast forward,
    Never doubted clouds would break,
Never dreamed, though right were worsted, wrong would triumph,
Held we fall to rise, are baffled to fight better,
    Sleep to wake.   15

No, at noonday in the bustle of man's work-time
    Greet the unseen[4] with a cheer!
Bid him forward, breast and back as either should be,
"Strive and thrive!" cry, "Speed—fight on, fare ever
    There as here!"   20
1889   1890

2. The final poem in *Asolando*, a volume published on the day of Browning's death. Browning is said to have recognized that because the third stanza sounded "like bragging" he ought to consider canceling it. "But it's the simple truth," he added, "and as it's true, it shall stand."
3. Any loved person who survives the speaker.
4. The speaker, after he is dead.

MATTHEW ARNOLD
(1822–1888)

1853: *Poems* (with Preface) published.
1857: Elected Professor of Poetry at Oxford.
1869: *Culture and Anarchy* published.

How is a full and enjoyable life to be lived in a modern industrial society? This was the recurrent topic in the poetry and prose of Matthew Arnold. In his poetry the question itself is raised; in his prose some answers are attempted. Arnold's mode of posing such questions may not always satisfy us, and his answers may sometimes be simply wrong. What is less excusable, as he himself said of Ruskin, is that he could be not only wrong but dogmatic when he was wrong. On the whole, however, his writings have fared well with posterity. "The misapprehensiveness of his age is exactly what a poet is sent to remedy," wrote Browning. Oddly enough it is to Arnold's work rather than to Browning's that the statement seems more appropriate. And its applicability to Arnold has persisted from Victorian times to ours, in part because the "misapprehensiveness" has also persisted. Of all the major Victorian writers, as F. R. Leavis has said, it is Arnold who, "because of the peculiar quality of his intelligence and the peculiar nature of his relation to his time, will repay special study in a way no others will."

Matthew Arnold was born in Laleham, a village in the valley of the Thames. That his childhood was spent in the vicinity of a river seems appropriate, for clear-flowing streams were later to appear in his poems as symbols of serenity. At 6, Arnold was moved to Rugby School where his father, Dr. Thomas Arnold, had become headmaster. As a clergyman Dr. Arnold was a leader of the liberal or Broad Church and hence one of the principal opponents of John Henry Newman. As a headmaster he became famous as an educational reformer, a teacher who instilled into his pupils an earnest preoccupation with moral and social issues and also an awareness of the connection between liberal studies and modern life. At Rugby his eldest son, Matthew, was directly exposed to the powerful force of the father's mind and character. The son's attitude towards this force was a mixture of attraction and repulsion. That he was permanently influenced by his father is evident in his poems and in his writings on religion and politics, but like many sons of clergymen, he made a determined effort in his youth to be different. At Oxford he behaved like a character from one of Evelyn Waugh's early novels. Elegantly and colorfully dressed, alternately languid or merry in manner, he attracted attention as a dandy whose irreverent jokes irritated his more solemn undergraduate friends and acquaintances. With Rugby standards he appeared to have no connection. Even his studies did not seem to occupy him seriously. By a session of cramming, he managed to earn second-class honors in his final examinations, a near disaster that was redeemed by his election to a fellowship at Oriel College.

Arnold's biographers usually dismiss his youthful frivolity of spirit as a temporary pose or mask, but it was more. It remained to color his prose style, brightening his most serious criticism with geniality and wit. For most readers the jauntiness of his prose is a virtue, although for others it is offensive. Anyone suspicious of urbanity and irony would applaud Whitman's sour comment that Arnold is "one of the dudes of literature." A more appropriate estimate of his manner is provided by Arnold's own description of Sainte-Beuve as a critic: "a critic of measure, not exuberant; of the center, not provincial * * * with gay and amiable temper, his manner as good as his matter—the *'critique souriant'* [smiling critic]."

Unlike Tennyson or Carlyle, Arnold had to confine his writing and reading to his spare time. In 1847 he took the post of private secretary to Lord Lansdowne, and in 1851, the year of his marriage, he became an inspector of schools, a position which he held for 35 years. Although his work as an inspector may have reduced his output as a writer, it had several advantages. His extensive traveling in England took him to the homes of the more ardently Protestant middle classes, and when he criticized the dullness of middle-class life (as he often did), Arnold knew his subject intimately. His position also led to travel on the Continent to study the schools of Europe. As a critic of English education he was thus able to make helpful comparisons and to draw on a stock of fresh ideas in the same way as in his literary criticism he used his knowledge of French, German, Italian, and classical literatures to measure the achievements of English writers. Despite the monotony of much of his work as an inspector, Arnold became convinced of its importance. It was work that contributed to what he regarded as the most important need of his century: the development of a satisfactory system of education for the middle classes.

In 1849 Arnold published *The Strayed Reveler*, the first of his volumes of poetry. Eight years later, as a tribute to his poetic achievement, he was elected to the Professorship of Poetry at Oxford, a part-time position which he held for ten years. Later, like Dickens and Thackeray before him, Arnold toured America in order to make money by lecturing. For his two visits (1883 and 1886) there was the further inducement of seeing his daughter Lucy, who had married an American. Two years after his second visit to the United States, Arnold died of a sudden heart attack.

Arnold's career as a writer can be divided roughly into four periods. In the 1850's appeared most of his poems; in the 1860's, his literary criticism and social criticism; in the 1870's, his religious and educational writings, and in the 1880's, his second set of essays in literary criticism.

About his career as a poet, two questions are repeatedly asked. The first is whether his poetry is as effective or better than his prose; the second is why he virtually stopped writing poetry after 1860. The first has, of course, been variously answered. Many would endorse Tennyson's request in a letter: "Tell Mat not to write any more of those prose things like *Literature and Dogma*, but to give us something like his *Thyrsis, Scholar Gypsy*, or *Forsaken Merman*." At the opposite extreme is a recent critic, J. D. Jump, who has a high regard for Arnold's prose but considers only one of the poems to have merit: *Dover Beach*. Such readers complain, and with good cause, of Arnold's bad habits as a poet: for example, his excessive reliance upon italics instead of upon meter as a method of emphasizing the meaning of a line. Or they cite the prosy flatness with which he opens his fine sonnet *To a Friend:* "Who prop, thou ask'st, in these bad days, my mind?" Contrariwise, when Arnold leaves the flat plane of versified reflections and attempts to scale the heights of what he called "the grand style," there is a different kind of uncertainty which becomes evident, as in *Sohrab and Rustum*, in the over-elaborated similes. Yet the success of such lovely poems as *Thyrsis* is more than enough to overcome the indictments of the critics. Often, as in *Thyrsis*, he is at his best as a poet of nature. Settings of seashore or river or mountaintop provide something more than picturesque backdrops for these poems; they function to draw the meaning together. A concern for rendering outdoor nature may seem a curious accomplishment for so sophisticated a writer, but as his contemporaries noted, Arnold is in this respect, as in several others, similar to Thomas Gray.

Arnold's own verdict on the qualities of his poetry is a reasonable one. In a letter to his mother, in 1869, he writes: "My poems represent, on the whole, the main movement of mind of the last quarter of a century, and thus they will probably have their day as people become conscious to themselves of what that movement of mind is, and interested in the literary productions which reflect it. It might be fairly urged that I have less poetical sentiment than Tennyson, and less intellectual vigor and abundance that Browning; yet, because I have perhaps more of a fusion of the two than either of them, and have more regularly applied that fusion to the main line of modern development, I am likely enough to have my turn, as they have had theirs."

The emphasis in the letter upon "movement of mind" suggests that Arnold's poetry and prose should be studied together. Such an approach can be fruitful provided that it does not obscure the important difference between Arnold the poet and Arnold the critic. T. S. Eliot once said of his own writings that "in one's prose reflections one may be legitimately occupied with ideals, whereas in the writing of verse, one can deal only with actuality." Arnold's writings provide a nice verification of Eliot's seeming paradox. As a poet he usually records his own experiences, his own feelings of loneliness and isolation as a lover, his longing for a serenity that he cannot find, his melancholy sense of the passing of youth (more than for many men, Arnold's thirtieth birthday was an awesome landmark after which he felt, he said, "three parts iced over"). Above all he records his despair in a universe in which man's role seemed as incongruous as it was later to seem to Thomas Hardy. In a memorable passage of his *Stanzas from the Grande Chartreuse* he describes himself as "wandering between two worlds, one dead, / The other powerless to be born." And addressing the representatives of a faith which seems to him dead, he cries: "Take me, cowled forms, and fence me round, / Till I possess my soul again."

As a poet, then, like T. S. Eliot and W. H. Auden, Arnold provides a record of a sick individual in a sick society. This was "actuality" as he experienced it. As a prose-writer, a formulator of "ideals," he seeks a different role. It is the role of what Auden calls the "healer" of a sick society, or as he himself called Goethe, the "Physician of the iron age." And in this difference we have a clue to the question previously raised: why did Arnold virtually abandon the writing of poetry and shift into criticism? Among other reasons he abandoned it because he was dissatisfied with the kind of poetry he himself was writing.

In one of his excellent letters to his friend Arthur Hugh Clough in the 1850's (letters which provide the best insight we have into Arnold's mind and tastes) this note of dissatisfaction is struck: "I am glad you like the *Gypsy Scholar*—but what does it *do* for you? Homer *animates*—Shakespeare *animates*—in its poor way I think *Sohrab and Rustum animates*—the *Gypsy Scholar* at best awakens a pleasing melancholy. But this is not what we want." It is evident that early in his career Arnold had evolved a theory of what poetry should do for its readers, a theory based, in part, on his impression of what classical poetry had achieved. To help make life bearable, poetry, in Arnold's view, must bring joy. As he says in the Preface to his *Poems* in 1853, it must "inspirit and rejoice the reader"; it must "convey a charm, and infuse delight." Such a demand does not exclude tragic poetry but does exclude works "in which suffering finds no vent in action; in which a continual state of mental distress is prolonged." Of Charlotte Brontë's novel *Villette* he says witheringly: "The writer's mind contains nothing but hunger, rebellion, and rage. * * * No fine writing can hide this thoroughly, and it will be fatal to her in the long run." Judged by such a standard, most 19th-century poems, including *Empedocles on Etna* and others by Arnold, were unsatisfactory. And when Arnold tried himself to write poems which would meet his own requirements—*Sohrab* *and Rustum* or *Balder Dead*—he was not at his best. By the late 1850's he thus found himself at a dead end. By turning aside to literary criticism he was able partially to escape the dilemma. In his prose his melancholy and "morbid" personality was subordinated to the resolutely cheerful and purposeful character he had created for himself by an effort of will.

Arnold's two volumes of *Essays in Criticism* (1865 and 1888) repeatedly shows how authors as different as Marcus Aurelius, Tolstoy, Homer, and Wordsworth provide the virtues he sought in his reading. Among these virtues was plainness of style. Although he could on occasion recommend the richness of language of such poets as Keats or Tennyson—their "natural magic" as he himself called it—Arnold's usual preference was for literature that was unadorned. And beyond stylistic excellences the principal virtue he admired as a critic was what he called the quality of "high seriousness." Given a world in which formal religion appeared to be of subordinate importance, it became increasingly important to Arnold that the poet must be a serious thinker who could offer guidance for his readers. Arnold's attitude towards religion helps to account for his finally asking perhaps too much from literature. Excessive expectations underlie his most glaring blunder as a critic: his solemnly inadequate discussion of Chaucer's lack of high seriousness in *The Study of Poetry.*

In *The Function of Criticism* it is apparent that Arnold regarded good literary criticism, as he regarded literature itself, as a potent force in producing a civilized society. From a close study of this basic essay one could forecast the third stage of his career: his excursion into the criticism of society which was to culminate in *Culture and Anarchy* (1869) and *Friendship's Garland* (1871).

Arnold's starting point as a critic of society is different from that of Carlyle and John Ruskin. The older prophets attacked the Victorian middle classes on the grounds of their materialism, their selfish indifference to the sufferings of the poor—their immorality, in effect. Arnold argued instead that the "Philistines," as he called them, were not so much wicked as ignorant, narrow-minded, and suffering from the dullness of their private lives. This novel analysis was reinforced by Arnold's conviction that the world of the future would be a middle-class world, a world dominated therefore by a class inadequately equipped for leadership and inadequately equipped to enjoy civilized living.

To establish this point, Arnold employed cajolery, satire, and even quotations from the newspapers with considerable effect. He also employed catchwords (such as "sweetness and light") which have remained useful slogans even though they are an obstacle to understanding the complexities of his position. His view of civilization, for example, was pared down to a four-point formula of the four "powers": conduct, intellect and knowledge, beauty, social life and manners. The formula was simple and workable. Applying it to French or American civilizations, he had a scale by which to show up the virtues of different countries as well as their inadequacies. Applying the formula to his own country, Arnold usually awarded the Victorian middle classes an "A" in the first category (of conduct) but a failing grade in the other three categories.

Arnold's relentless exposure of middle-class narrow-mindedness eventually led him into the arena of religious controversy. As a critic of religious institutions he was arguing, in effect, that just as the middle classes did not know how to lead full lives, so also did they not know how to read the Bible intelligently or attend church intelligently. His three full-length studies of the Bible, including *Literature and Dogma* (1873), are best considered in this way as a postscript to his social criticism. The Bible, to Arnold, was a great work of literature like the *Odyssey*, and the Church of England was a great national institution like Parliament. Both Bible and church must be preserved not because historical Christianity was credible but because both, when properly understood, were agents of what he called "culture"—they contributed to making mankind more civilized.

The term *culture* is perhaps Arnold's most familiar catchword, although what he meant by it has sometimes been misunderstood. For him the term connotes the qualities of an open-minded intelligence (as described in *The Function of Criticism*)—a refusal to take things on authority. In this respect, Arnold appears close to T. H. Huxley and J. S. Mill. But the word also connotes a full awareness of man's past and a capacity to enjoy the best works of art, literature, history, and philosophy that have come down to us from that past. As a way of viewing life in all its aspects, including the social, political, and religious, culture represents for Arnold the most effective way of curing the ills of a sick society. It is his principal prescription.

To attempt to define culture brings one to a final aspect of Arnold's career as a critic: his writings on education, in which he sought to make cultural values, as he said, "prevail." Most obviously these writings comprise his reply to Huxley in his admirably reasoned essay, *Literature and Science*, as well as his volumes of official reports written as an inspector of schools. Less obviously they comprise all of his prose. At the core of these writings is his belief that good education is the crucial need for modern man. Arnold was essentially a great teacher raised to the nth degree. He has the faults of a teacher: a tendency to repeat himself, to lean too hard on formulated phrases, and he displays something of the lectern manner at times. He also has the great teacher's virtues, in particular the virtue of skillfully conveying to us the conviction on which all his arguments are based. This conviction is that the humanist tradition of which he is the expositor can enable the individual man or woman to live life more fully as well as to change the course of society. For these values Arnold fought. He boxed with the gloves on—kid gloves, his opponents used to say—and he provided a lively exhibition of footwork that is a pleasure in itself for us to witness. Yet the gracefulness of the display should not obscure the fact that he is landing hard blows squarely on what Carlyle called the vast blockheadism.

Although his lifelong attacks against the inadequacies of puritanism make Arnold one of the most anti-Victorian figures of the Victorian age, there is an assumption behind his attacks that is itself characteristically Victorian. This assumption is that the puritan middle classes *can* be changed, that they are, as we would more clumsily say, educable. In 1852, writing to Clough on the subject of equality (a political objective in which he believed by conviction if not by instinct), he observed: "I am more and more convinced that the world tends to become more comfortable for the mass, and more uncomfortable for those of any natural gift or distinction—and it is as well perhaps that it should be so—for hitherto the gifted have astonished and delighted the world, but not trained or inspired or in any real way changed it." Arnold's gifts as a poet and critic enabled him to do both: to delight the world and also to change it.

Shakespeare

Others abide our question. Thou art free.
We ask and ask—Thou smilest and art still,
Out-topping knowledge. For the loftiest hill,
Who to the stars uncrowns his majesty,

Planting his steadfast footsteps in the sea,[1]   5
Making the heaven of heavens his dwelling place,
Spares but the cloudy border of his base
To the foiled searching of mortality;
And thou, who didst the stars and sunbeams know,
Self-schooled, self-scanned, self-honored, self-secure,   10
Didst tread on earth unguessed at.—Better so!

All pains the immortal spirit must endure,
All weakness which impairs, all griefs which bow,
Find their sole speech in that victorious brow.

1844   1849

In Harmony with Nature[2]

TO A PREACHER

"In harmony with Nature?" Restless fool,
Who with such heat dost preach what were to thee,
When true, the last impossibility—
To be like Nature strong, like Nature cool!

Know, man hath all which Nature hath, but more,   5
And in that *more* lie all his hopes of good.
Nature is cruel, man is sick of blood;
Nature is stubborn, man would fain adore;

Nature is fickle, man hath need of rest;
Nature forgives no debt, and fears no grave;   10
Man would be mild, and with safe conscience blest.

Man must begin, know this, where Nature ends;
Nature and man can never be fast friends.
Fool, if thou canst not pass her, rest her slave!

1844(?)   1849

---

1. Cf. William Cowper's Olney Hymn 35: "God moves in a mysterious way / His wonders to perform; / He plants his footsteps in the sea, / And rides upon the storm."
2. Originally entitled: "To an Independent Preacher, who preached that we should be 'In Harmony with Nature.'"

To a Friend

Who prop, thou ask'st, in these bad days, my mind?—
He much, the old man,[3] who, clearest-souled of men,
Saw The Wide Prospect, and the Asian Fen,
And Tmolus hill, and Smyrna bay, though blind.

Much he, whose friendship I not long since won,   5
That halting slave, who in Nicopolis [4]
Taught Arrian, when Vespasian's brutal son [5]
Cleared Rome of what most shamed him. But be his

My special thanks, whose even-balanced soul,
From first youth tested up to extreme old age,   10
Business could not make dull, nor passion wild;

Who saw life steadily, and saw it whole;
The mellow glory of the Attic stage,
Singer of sweet Colonus,[4] and its child.

1849

The Forsaken Merman[1]

Come, dear children, let us away;
Down and away below!
Now my brothers call from the bay,
Now the great winds shoreward blow,
Now the salt tides seaward flow;   5
Now the wild white horses play,
Champ and chafe and toss in the spray.
Children dear, let us away!
This way, this way!

Call her once before you go—   10
Call once yet!
In a voice that she will know:
"Margaret! Margaret!"
Children's voices should be dear
(Call once more) to a mother's ear;   15

3. Homer, who was reputed to have been born in Smyrna, a seaport of what is now Turkey. From Smyrna he saw across the sea to Europe ("The Wide Prospect") as well as to the nearby marshes ("Fen") and mountain ranges ("Tmolus hill") of Asia Minor.
4. Epictetus, a lame philosopher who was exiled to Nicopolis where he taught Stoicism to Arrian, a Greek historian.
5. I.e., the Emperor Domitian (81–96). Because the philosophers had "shamed" him, he had ordered their expulsion from Rome.
4. Sophocles (496–406 B.C.), a native of Colonus, sang of his town in his *Oedipus at Colonus*.
1. For a comparison of Arnold's skillful telling of this story with the Danish version from which he derived it, see C. B. Tinker and H. F. Lowry: *The Poetry of Arnold: A Commentary* (1940), pp. 129–132.

Children's voices, wild with pain—
Surely she will come again!
Call her once and come away;
This way, this way!
"Mother dear, we cannot stay!   20
The wild white horses foam and fret."
Margaret! Margaret!

Come, dear children, come away down;
Call no more!
One last look at the white-walled town,   25
And the little gray church on the windy shore,
Then come down!
She will not come though you call all day;
Come away, come away!

Children dear, was it yesterday   30
We heard the sweet bells over the bay?
In the caverns where we lay,
Through the surf and through the swell,
The far-off sound of a silver bell?
Sand-strewn caverns, cool and deep,   35
Where the winds are all asleep;
Where the spent lights quiver and gleam,
Where the salt weed sways in the stream,
Where the sea beasts, ranged all round,
Feed in the ooze of their pasture ground;   40
Where the sea snakes coil and twine,
Dry their mail and bask in the brine;
Where great whales come sailing by,
Sail and sail, with unshut eye,
Round the world for ever and aye?   45
When did music come this way?
Children dear, was it yesterday?

Children dear, was it yesterday
(Call yet once) that she went away?
Once she sate with you and me,   50
On a red gold throne in the heart of the sea,
And the youngest sate on her knee.
She combed its bright hair, and she tended it well,
When down swung the sound of a far-off bell.
She sighed, she looked up through the clear green sea;   55
She said: "I must go, for my kinsfolk pray
In the little gray church on the shore today.
'Twill be Easter time in the world—ah me!
And I lose my poor soul, Merman! here with thee."
I said: "Go up, dear heart, through the waves;   60
Say thy prayer, and come back to the kind sea caves!"
She smiled, she went up through the surf in the bay.
Children dear, was it yesterday?

Children dear, were we long alone?
"The sea grows stormy, the little ones moan;   65
Long prayers," I said, "in the world they say;
Come!" I said; and we rose through the surf in the bay.
We went up the beach, by the sandy down
Where the sea stocks bloom, to the white-walled town;
Through the narrow paved streets, where all was still,   70
To the little gray church on the windy hill.
From the church came a murmur of folk at their prayers,
But we stood without in the cold blowing airs.
We climbed on the graves, on the stones worn with rains,
And we gazed up the aisle through the small leaded panes.   75
She sate by the pillar; we saw her clear:
"Margaret, hist! come quick, we are here!
Dear heart," I said, "we are long alone;
The sea grows stormy, the little ones moan."
But, ah, she gave me never a look,   80
For her eyes were sealed to the holy book!
Loud prays the priest; shut stands the door.
Come away, children, call no more!
Come away, come down, call no more!

    Down, down, down!   85
Down to the depths of the sea!
She sits at her wheel in the humming town,
Singing most joyfully.
Hark what she sings: "O joy, O joy,
For the humming street, and the child with its toy!   90
For the priest, and the bell, and the holy well;
For the wheel where I spun,
And the blessed light of the sun!"
And so she sings her fill,
Singing most joyfully,   95
Till the spindle drops from her hand,
And the whizzing wheel stands still.
She steals to the window, and looks at the sand,
And over the sand at the sea;
And her eyes are set in a stare;   100
And anon there breaks a sigh,
And anon there drops a tear,
From a sorrow-clouded eye,
And a heart sorrow-laden,
A long, long sigh;   105
For the cold strange eyes of a little Mermaiden
And the gleam of her golden hair.

    Come away, away children;
Come children, come down!
The hoarse wind blows coldly;   110
Lights shine in the town.
She will start from her slumber

When gusts shake the door;
She will hear the winds howling,
Will hear the waves roar.   115
We shall see, while above us
The waves roar and whirl,
A ceiling of amber,
A pavement of pearl.
Singing: "Here came a mortal,   120
But faithless was she!
And alone dwell forever
The kings of the sea."

But, children, at midnight,
When soft the winds blow,   125
When clear falls the moonlight,
When spring tides are low;
When sweet airs come seaward
From heaths starred with broom,
And high rocks throw mildly   130
On the blanched sands a gloom;
Up the still, glistening beaches,
Up the creeks we will hie,
Over banks of bright seaweed
The ebb tide leaves dry.   135
We will gaze, from the sand hills,
At the white, sleeping town;
At the church on the hillside—
And then come back down.
Singing: "There dwells a loved one,   140
But cruel is she!
She left lonely forever
The kings of the sea."

                                        1849

Isolation. To Marguerite[1]

We were apart; yet, day by day,
I bade my heart more constant be.
I bade it keep the world away,
And grow a home for only thee;
Nor feared but thy love likewise grew,   5
Like mine, each day, more tried, more true.

The fault was grave! I might have known,
What far too soon, alas! I learned—
The heart can bind itself alone,
And faith may oft be unreturned.   10

1. Addressed to a girl Arnold is reputed to have met in Switzerland in the late 1840's.

Self-swayed our feelings ebb and swell—
Thou lov'st no more—Farewell! Farewell!

Farewell!—and thou, thou lonely heart,[2]
Which never yet without remorse
Even for a moment didst depart   15
From thy remote and spheréd course
To haunt the place where passions reign—
Back to thy solitude again!

Back! with the conscious thrill of shame
Which Luna[3] felt, that summer night,   20
Flash through her pure immortal frame,
When she forsook the starry height
To hang over Endymion's sleep
Upon the pine-grown Latmian steep.

Yet she, chaste queen, had never proved   25
How vain a thing is mortal love,
Wandering in Heaven, far removed.
But thou hast long had place to prove
This truth—to prove, and make thine own:
"Thou hast been, shalt be, art, alone."   30

Or, if not quite alone, yet they
Which touch thee are unmating things—
Ocean and clouds and night and day;
Lorn autumns and triumphant springs;
And life, and others' joy and pain,   35
And love, if love, of happier men.

Of happier men—for they, at least,
Have *dreamed* two human hearts might blend
In one, and were through faith released
From isolation without end   40
Prolonged; nor knew, although not less
Alone than thou, their loneliness.

                                           1857

To Marguerite—Continued

Yes! in the sea of life enisled,
With echoing straits between us thrown,
Dotting the shoreless watery wild,
We mortal millions live *alone*.
The islands feel the enclasping flow,   5
And then their endless bounds they know.

---

2. Presumably the speaker's heart, not
Marguerite's.
3. Luna (or Diana), the goddess of
chastity and of the moon, fell in love
with Endymion, a handsome shepherd,
whom she discovered asleep on Mt.
Latmos.

But when the moon their hollows lights,
And they are swept by balms of spring,
And in their glens, on starry nights,
The nightingales divinely sing;   10
And lovely notes, from shore to shore,
Across the sounds and channels pour—

Oh! then a longing like despair
Is to their farthest caverns sent;
For surely once, they feel, we were   15
Parts of a single continent!
Now round us spreads the watery plain—
Oh might our marges meet again!

Who ordered that their longing's fire
Should be, as soon as kindled, cooled?   20
Who renders vain their deep desire?—
A God, a God their severance ruled!
And bade betwixt their shores to be
The unplumbed, salt, estranging sea.

ca. 1849   1852

The Buried Life

Light flows our war of mocking words, and yet,
Behold, with tears mine eyes are wet!
I feel a nameless sadness o'er me roll.
Yes, yes, we know that we can jest,
We know, we know that we can smile!   5
But there's a something in this breast,
To which thy light words bring no rest,
And thy gay smiles no anodyne.
Give me thy hand, and hush awhile,
And turn those limpid eyes on mine,   10
And let me read there, love! thy inmost soul.

Alas! is even love too weak
To unlock the heart, and let it speak?
Are even lovers powerless to reveal
To one another what indeed they feel?   15
I knew the mass of men concealed
Their thoughts, for fear that if revealed
They would by other men be met
With blank indifference, or with blame reproved;
I knew they lived and moved   20
Tricked in disguises, alien to the rest
Of men, and alien to themselves—and yet
The same heart beats in every human breast!

But we, my love!—doth a like spell benumb
Our hearts, our voices?—must we too be dumb?   25

Ah! well for us, if even we,
Even for a moment, can get free
Our heart, and have our lips unchained;
For that which seals them hath been deep-ordained!

Fate, which foresaw   30
How frivolous a baby man would be—
By what distractions he would be possessed,
How he would pour himself in every strife,
And well-nigh change his own identity—
That it might keep from his capricious play   35
His genuine self, and force him to obey
Even in his own despite his being's law,
Bade through the deep recesses of our breast
The unregarded river of our life
Pursue with indiscernible flow its way;   40
And that we should not see
The buried stream, and seem to be
Eddying at large in blind uncertainty,
Though driving on with it eternally.

But often, in the world's most crowded streets,[1]   45
But often, in the din of strife,
There rises an unspeakable desire
After the knowledge of our buried life;
A thirst to spend our fire and restless force
In tracking out our true, original course;   50
A longing to inquire
Into the mystery of this heart which beats
So wild, so deep in us—to know
Whence our lives come and where they go.
And many a man in his own breast then delves,   55
But deep enough, alas! none ever mines.
And we have been on many thousand lines,
And we have shown, on each, spirit and power;
But hardly have we, for one little hour,
Been on our own line, have we been ourselves—   60
Hardly had skill to utter one of all
The nameless feelings that course through our breast,
But they course on forever unexpressed.
And long we try in vain to speak and act
Our hidden self, and what we say and do   65
Is eloquent, is well—but 'tis not true!
And then we will no more be racked
With inward striving, and demand

---

1. This passage, like many others in Arnold's poetry, illustrates the impact on his writings of Wordsworth. In this instance cf. Wordsworth's *Tintern Ab-* *bey*, lines 25–27: "But oft, in lonely rooms, and 'mid the din / Of towns and cities, I have owed to them, / In hours of weariness, sensations sweet."

Of all the thousand nothings of the hour
Their stupefying power;   70
Ah yes, and they benumb us at our call!
Yet still, from time to time, vague and forlorn,
From the soul's subterranean depth upborne
As from an infinitely distant land,
Come airs, and floating echoes, and convey   75
A melancholy into all our day.[2]

Only—but this is rare—
When a beloved hand is laid in ours,
When, jaded with the rush and glare
Of the interminable hours,   80
Our eyes can in another's eyes read clear,
When our world-deafened ear
Is by the tones of a loved voice caressed—
A bolt is shot back somewhere in our breast,
And a lost pulse of feeling stirs again.   85
The eye sinks inward, and the heart lies plain,
And what we mean, we say, and what we would, we know.
A man becomes aware of his life's flow,
And hears its winding murmur; and he sees
The meadows where it glides, the sun, the breeze.   90

And there arrives a lull in the hot race
Wherein he doth forever chase
That flying and elusive shadow, rest.
An air of coolness plays upon his face,
And an unwonted calm pervades his breast.   95
And then he thinks he knows
The hills where his life rose,
And the sea where it goes.

1852

Stanzas in Memory of the Author of *Obermann*[3]

NOVEMBER, 1849

In front the awful Alpine track
Crawls up its rocky stair;

2. Cf. Wordsworth's *Ode: Intimations of Immortality*, lines 151–53: "Those shadowy recollections, / Which, be they what they may, / Are yet the fountain light of all our day."
3. The author of *Obermann* (1804), an epistolary novel, was a French essayist, E. P. de Senancour (1770–1846). The hero is a recluse living in a mountain chalet in the Lake Geneva district of Switzerland. The book's melancholy reflections and its celebration of Alpine scenery combined to establish its vogue among a select group of readers. When Arnold discovered the book in 1847 it made "an extraordinary impression" on him. In 1869 he published an essay on Senancour, and his poems refer often to *Obermann* as representative of qualities Arnold sometimes admired in writers of the Romantic Movement. In a note of 1868 he wrote: "The influence of Rousseau, and certain affinities with more famous and fortunate authors of his own day—Chateaubriand and Madame de Staël—are everywhere visible in Senancour. * * * The stir of all the main forces, by which modern life is and has been impelled, lives in the letters of *Obermann;* the dissolving agencies of the

The autumn storm-winds drive the rack,[4]
Close o'er it, in the air.

Behind are the abandoned baths [5]   5
Mute in their meadows lone;
The leaves are on the valley paths,
The mists are on the Rhone—

The white mists rolling like a sea!
I hear the torrents roar.   10
—Yes, Obermann, all speaks of thee;
I feel thee near once more!

I turn thy leaves! I feel their breath
Once more upon me roll;
That air of languor, cold, and death,   15
Which brooded o'er thy soul.

Fly hence, poor wretch, whoe'er thou art,
Condemned to cast about,
All shipwreck in thy own weak heart,
For comfort from without!   20

A fever in these pages burns
Beneath the calm they feign;
A wounded human spirit turns,
Here, on its bed of pain.

Yes, though the virgin mountain air   25
Fresh through these pages blows;
Though to these leaves the glaciers spare
The soul of their white snows;

Though here a mountain murmur swells
Of many a dark-boughed pine;   30
Though, as you read, you hear the bells
Of the high-pasturing kine—

Yet, through the hum of torrent lone,
And brooding mountain bee,
There sobs I know not what ground tone   35
Of human agony.

Is it for this, because the sound
Is fraught too deep with pain,
That, Obermann! the world around
So little loves thy strain?   40

eighteenth century, the fiery storm of the
French Revolution, the first faint promise
and dawn of that new world which our
own time is but now more fully bringing
to light—all these are to be felt * * *
there. To me, indeed, it will always seem
that the impressiveness of this production can hardly be rated too high."
Arnold composed his elegy during a visit
to Switzerland in the autumn of 1849.

Eighteen years later he stated in a letter
that the poem records "my separation of
myself, finally, from him [Senancour]
and his influence."
4. Mass of clouds.
5. The Baths of Leuk. This poem was
conceived, and partly composed, in the
valley going down from the foot of the
Gemmi Pass towards the Rhone [Ar-
nold's note].

Some secrets may the poet tell,
For the world loves new ways;
To tell too deep ones is not well—
It knows not what he says.

Yet of the spirits who have reigned   45
In this our troubled day,
I know but two, who have attained,
Save thee, to see their way.

By England's lakes, in gray old age,
His quiet home one keeps;   50
And one, the strong much toiling sage,
In German Weimar sleeps.

But Wordsworth's eyes avert their ken
From half of human fate;
And Goethe's course few sons of men   55
May think to emulate.

For he pursued a lonely road,
His eyes on Nature's plan;
Neither made man too much a God,
Nor God too much a man.   60

Strong was he, with a spirit free
From mists, and sane, and clear;
Clearer, how much! than ours—yet we
Have a worse course to steer.

For though his manhood bore the blast   65
Of a tremendous time,
Yet in a tranquil world was passed
His tender youthful prime.[6]

But we, brought forth and reared in hours
Of change, alarm, surprise—   70
What shelter to grow ripe is ours?
What leisure to grow wise?

Like children bathing on the shore,
Buried a wave beneath,
The second wave succeeds, before   75
We have had time to breathe.

Too fast we live, too much are tried,
Too harassed, to attain
Wordsworth's sweet calm, or Goethe's wide
And luminous view to gain.   80

And then we turn, thou sadder sage,
To thee! we feel thy spell!

6. Goethe (1749–1832) lived 40 years before the outbreak of the French Revolution.

—The hopeless tangle of our age,
Thou too hast scanned it well!

Immovable thou sittest, still   85
As death, composed to bear!
Thy head is clear, thy feeling chill,
And icy thy despair.

Yes, as the son of Thetis [7] said,
I hear thee saying now: 90
Greater by far than thou are dead;
Strive not! die also thou!

Ah! two desires toss about
The poet's feverish blood.
One drives him to the world without,   95
And one to solitude.

The glow, he cries, *the thrill of life,*
Where, where do these abound?—
Not in the world, not in the strife
Of men, shall they be found.   100

He who hath watched, not shared, the strife,
Knows how the day hath gone.
He only lives with the world's life,
Who hath renounced his own.

To thee we come, then! Clouds are rolled   105
Where thou, O seer! art set;
Thy realm of thought is drear and cold—
The world is colder yet!

And thou hast pleasures, too, to share
With those who come to thee—   110
Balms floating on thy mountain air,
And healing sights to see.

How often, where the slopes are green
On Jaman,[8] hast thou sate
By some high chalet door, and seen   115
The summer day grow late;

And darkness steal o'er the wet grass
With the pale crocus starred,
And reach that glimmering sheet of glass
Beneath the piny sward,   120

Lake Leman's waters, far below!
And watched the rosy light
Fade from the distant peaks of snow;
And on the air of night

7. Achilles. See *Iliad* XXI. 106–13.   8. A mountain on the shores of Lake
Geneva.

Heard accents of the eternal tongue 125
Through the pine branches play—
Listened, and felt thyself grow young!
Listened and wept—Away!

Away the dreams that but deceive
And thou, sad guide, adieu! 130
I go, fate drives me; but I leave
Half of my life with you.

We, in some unknown Power's employ,
Move on a rigorous line;
Can neither, when we will, enjoy, 135
Nor, when we will, resign.

I in the world must live; but thou,
Thou melancholy shade!
Wilt not, if thou canst see me now,
Condemn me, nor upbraid. 140

For thou art gone away from earth,
And place with those dost claim,
The Children of the Second Birth,[9]
Whom the world could not tame;

And with that small, transfigured band, 145
Whom many a different way
Conducted to their common land,
Thou learn'st to think as they.

Christian and pagan, king and slave,
Soldier and anchorite, 150
Distinctions we esteem so grave,
Are nothing in their sight.

They do not ask, who pined unseen,
Who was on action hurled,
Whose one bond is, that all have been 155
Unspotted by the world.

There without anger thou wilt see
Him who obeys thy spell
No more, so he but rest, like thee,
Unsoiled!—and so, farewell. 160

Farewell!—Whether thou now liest near
That much-loved inland sea,
The ripples of whose blue waves cheer
Vevey and Meillerie:[1]

And in that gracious region bland, 165
Where with clear rustling wave

9. "Except a man be born again, he cannot see the kingdom of God" (John iii.3).
1. Towns in the Lake Geneva region.

Senancour, as Arnold learned later, had been buried in a suburb of Paris, "The Capital of Pleasure" (line 179).

The scented pines of Switzerland
Stand dark round thy green grave,

Between the dusty vineyard walls
Issuing on that green place   170
The early peasant still recalls
The pensive stranger's face,

And stoops to clear thy moss-grown date
Ere he plods on again—
Or whether, by maligner fate,   175
Among the swarms of men,

Where between granite terraces
The blue Seine rolls her wave,
The Capital of Pleasure sees
The hardly-heard-of grave—   180

Farewell! Under the sky we part,
In this stern Alpine dell.
O unstrung will! O broken heart!
A last, a last farewell!

1849   1852

Memorial Verses[1]

APRIL, 1850

Goethe in Weimar sleeps, and Greece,
Long since, saw Byron's struggle cease.
But one such death remained to come;
The last poetic voice is dumb—
We stand today by Wordsworth's tomb.   5

When Byron's eyes were shut in death,
We bowed our head and held our breath.
He taught us little; but our soul
Had *felt* him like the thunder's roll.
With shivering heart the strife we saw   10
Of passion with eternal law;
And yet with reverential awe
We watched the fount of fiery life
Which served for that Titanic strife.

When Goethe's death was told, we said: 15
Sunk, then, is Europe's sagest head.
Physician of the iron age,

1. This elegy was written shortly after
Wordsworth had died in April, 1850, at
the age of 80. Arnold had known the
poet as a man and deeply admired his
writings—as is evident not only in this
poem but in his late essay, *Wordsworth*.
Byron, who died in Greece in 1824, had
affected Arnold profoundly in his youth,
but later that strenuous "Titanic" poetry seemed to him less satisfactory,
its value limited by its lack of serenity.
His final verdict on Byron can be encountered in his essay in *Essays in
Criticism: Second Series*. Goethe, who
died in 1832, was regarded by Arnold
as a great philosophical poet and the
most significant man of letters of the
early 19th century.

Goethe has done his pilgrimage.
He took the suffering human race,
He read each wound, each weakness clear;   20
And struck his finger on the place,
And said: *Thou ailest here, and here!*
He looked on Europe's dying hour
Of fitful dream and feverish power;
His eye plunged down the weltering strife,   25
The turmoil of expiring life—
He said: *The end is everywhere,*
Art still has truth, take refuge there!
And he was happy, if to know
Causes of things, and far below   30
His feet to see the lurid flow
Of terror, and insane distress,
And headlcng fate, be happiness.

    And Wordsworth!—Ah, pale ghosts, rejoice!
For never has such soothing voice   35
Been to your shadowy world conveyed,
Since erst, a morn, some wandering shade
Heard the clear song of Orpheus[2] come
Through Hades, and the mournful gloom.
Wordsworth has gone from us—and ye,   40
Ah, may ye feel his voice as we!
He too upon a wintry clime
Had fallen—on this iron time
Of doubts, disputes, distractions, fears.
He found us when the age had bound   45
Our souls in its benumbing round;
He spoke, and loosed our heart in tears.
He laid us as we lay at birth
On the cool flowery lap of earth,
Smiles broke from us and we had ease;   50
The hills were round us, and the breeze
Went o'er the sunlit fields again;
Our foreheads felt the wind and rain.
Our youth returned; for there was shed
On spirits that had long been dead,   55
Spirits dried up and closely furled,
The freshness of the early world.

    Ah! since dark days still bring to light
Man's prudence and man's fiery might,
Time may restore us in his course   60
Goethe's sage mind and Byron's force;
But where will Europe's latter hour
Again find Wordsworth's healing power?
Others will teach us how to dare,
And against fear our breast to steel;   65

2. By means of his beautiful music, in his search for the shade of his dead
Orpheus won his way through Hades wife, Eurydice.

Others will strengthen us to bear—
But who, ah! who, will make us feel?
The cloud of mortal destiny,
Others will front it fearlessly—
But who, like him, will put it by?   70

　　Keep fresh the grass upon his grave
O Rotha,[3] with thy living wave!
Sing him thy best! for few or none
Hears thy voice right, now he is gone.

1850   1850

Longing

　　Come to me in my dreams, and then
　　By day I shall be well again!
　　For then the night will more than pay
　　The hopeless longing of the day.

　　Come, as thou cam'st a thousand times,   5
　　A messenger from radiant climes,
　　And smile on thy new world, and be
　　As kind to others as to me!

　　Or, as thou never cam'st in sooth,
　　Come now, and let me dream it truth;   10
　　And part my hair, and kiss my brow,
　　And say: *My love! why sufferest thou?*

　　Come to me in my dreams, and then
　　By day I shall be well again!
　　For then the night will more than pay   15
　　The hopeless longing of the day.

                                                           1852

Lines Written in Kensington Gardens[4]

In this lone, open glade I lie,
Screened by deep boughs on either hand;
And at its end, to stay the eye,
Those black-crowned, red-boled pine trees stand!

Birds here make song, each bird has his,   5
Across the girdling city's hum.
How green under the boughs it is!
How thick the tremulous sheep-cries come![5]

---

3. A river near Wordsworth's burial
place.
4. A park in the heart of London.

5. Sheep are sometimes grazed in London parks.

Sometimes a child will cross the glade
To take his nurse his broken toy;   10
Sometimes a thrush flit overhead
Deep in her unknown day's employ.

Here at my feet what wonders pass,
What endless, active life is here!
What blowing daisies, fragrant grass!   15
An air-stirred forest, fresh and clear.

Scarce fresher is the mountain sod
Where the tired angler lies, stretched out,
And, eased of basket and of rod,
Counts his day's spoil, the spotted trout.   20

In the huge world, which roars hard by,
Be others happy if they can!
But in my helpless cradle I
Was breathed on by the rural Pan.

I, on men's impious uproar hurled,   25
Think often, as I hear them rave,
That peace has left the upper world
And now keeps only in the grave.

Yet here is peace forever new!
When I who watch them am away,   30
Still all things in this glade go through
The changes of their quiet day.

Then to their happy rest they pass!
The flowers upclose, the birds are fed,
The night comes down upon the grass,   35
The child sleeps warmly in his bed.

Calm soul of all things! make it mine
To feel, amid the city's jar,
That there abides a piece of thine,
Man did not make, and cannot mar.   40

The will to neither strive nor cry,
The power to feel with others give!
Calm, calm me more! nor let me die
Before I have begun to live.

                               1852

Philomela[1]

    Hark! ah, the nightingale—
    The tawny-throated!

1. The Greek tale of violence evoked by the song of the nightingale concerned two sisters, Philomela and Procne. In Arnold's version, Philomela was married to a king of Thrace. After learning that her husband had raped

Hark, from that moonlit cedar what a burst!
What triumph! hark!—what pain!

O wanderer from a Grecian shore,   5
Still, after many years, in distant lands,
Still nourishing in thy bewildered brain
That wild, unquenched, deep-sunken, old-world pain—
Say, will it never heal?
And can this fragrant lawn   10
With its cool trees, and night,
And the sweet, tranquil Thames,
And moonshine, and the dew,
To thy racked heart and brain
Afford no balm?   15

Dost thou tonight behold,
Here, through the moonlight on this English grass,
The unfriendly palace in the Thracian wild?
Dost thou again peruse
With hot cheeks and seared eyes   20
The too clear web,² and thy dumb sister's shame?
Dost thou once more assay
Thy flight, and feel come over thee,
Poor fugitive, the feathery change
Once more, and once more seem to make resound   25
With love and hate, triumph and agony,
Lone Daulis, and the high Cephissian vale?³
Listen, Eugenia⁴—
How thick the bursts come crowding through the leaves!
Again—thou hearest?   30
Eternal passion!
Eternal pain!

1848   1853

Requiescat⁵

Strew on her roses, roses,
    And never a spray of yew!
In quiet she reposes;
    Ah, would that I did too!

Her mirth the world required;   5
    She bathed it in smiles of glee.

Procne and cut out her tongue to prevent the outrage being discovered, Philomela was transformed into a nightingale.
2. A picture in needlework made by
Procne to tell what had happened to
her.

3. Daulis, a city in Phocis, where
Philomela's transformation took place;
the "Cephissian vale" was a river valley in Phocis.
4. Unidentified listener.
5. "May she rest."

But her heart was tired, tired,
And now they let her be.

Her life was turning, turning,
In mazes of heat and sound.   10
But for peace her soul was yearning,
And now peace laps her round.

Her cabined, ample spirit,
It fluttered and failed for breath.
Tonight it doth inherit   15
The vasty hall of death.

1853

The Scholar Gypsy   The story of a 17th-century student who left
Oxford and joined a band of gypsies had made a strong impression on
Arnold. In the poem he wistfully imagines that the spirit of this scholar
is still to be encountered in the Cumner countryside near Oxford, having achieved immortality by a serene pursuit of the secret of human existence. Like Keats's nightingale, the scholar has escaped "the weariness,
the fever, and the fret" of modern life.

At the outset, the poet addresses a shepherd who has been helping him
in his search for traces of the scholar. The shepherd is addressed as "you."
After line 61, with the shift to "thou" and "thy," the person addressed
is the scholar himself, and the poet thereafter sometimes uses the pronoun "we" to indicate he is speaking for all mankind of later generations.

About the setting Arnold wrote to his brother Tom on May 15, 1857:
"You alone of my brothers are associated with that life at Oxford, the
freest and most delightful part, perhaps, of my life, when with you and
Clough and Walrond I shook off all the bonds and formalities of the place,
and enjoyed the spring of life and that unforgotten Oxfordshire and
Berkshire country. Do you remember a poem of mine called 'The Scholar
Gipsy'? It was meant to fix the remembrance of those delightful wanderings
of ours in the Cumner Hills."

The passage from Joseph Glanvill's *Vanity of Dogmatizing* (1661)
which inspired the poem was included by Arnold as a note:

There was very lately a lad in the University of Oxford, who was by his
poverty forced to leave his studies there; and at last to join himself to a
company of vagabond gypsies. Among these extravagant people, by the
insinuating subtilty of his carriage, he quickly got so much of their love and
esteem as that they discovered to him their mystery. After he had been
a pretty while exercised in the trade, there chanced to ride by a couple of
scholars, who had formerly been of his acquaintance. They quickly spied
out their old friend among the gypsies; and he gave them an account of
the necessity which drove him to that kind of life, and told them that
the people he went with were not such imposters as they were taken for,
but that they had a traditional kind of learning among them, and could
do wonders by the power of imagination, their fancy binding that of
others: that himself had learned much of their art, and when he had
compassed the whole secret, he intended, he said, to leave their company, and give the world an account of what he had learned.

The Scholar Gypsy

Go, for they call you, shepherd, from the hill;
  Go, shepherd, and untie the wattled cotes![1]
  No longer leave thy wistful flock unfed,
  Nor let thy bawling fellows rack their throats,
  Nor the cropped herbage shoot another head.   5
    But when the fields are still,
  And the tired men and dogs all gone to rest,
  And only the white sheep are sometimes seen
  Cross and recross the strips of moon-blanched green,
Come, shepherd, and again begin the quest!   10

Here, where the reaper was at work of late—
  In this high field's dark corner, where he leaves
  His coat, his basket, and his earthen cruse,[2]
  And in the sun all morning binds the sheaves,
  Then here, at noon, comes back his stores to use—   15
    Here will I sit and wait,
  While to my ear from uplands far away
  The bleating of the folded[3] flocks is borne,
  With distant cries of reapers in the corn[4]—
All the live murmur of a summer's day.   20

Screened is this nook o'er the high, half-reaped field,
  And here till sundown, shepherd! will I be.
  Through the thick corn the scarlet poppies peep,
  And round green roots and yellowing stalks I see
  Pale pink convolvulus in tendrils creep;   25
    And air-swept lindens yield
  Their scent, and rustle down their perfumed showers
  Of bloom on the bent grass[5] where I am laid,
  And bower me from the August sun with shade;
And the eye travels down to Oxford's towers.   30

And near me on the grass lies Glanvill's book—
  Come, let me read the oft-read tale again!
  The story of the Oxford scholar poor,
  Of pregnant parts[6] and quick inventive brain,
  Who, tired of knocking at preferment's door,   35
    One summer morn forsook
  His friends, and went to learn the gypsy lore,
  And roamed the world with that wild brotherhood,
  And came, as most men deemed, to little good,
But came to Oxford and his friends no more.   40

But once, years after, in the country lanes,
  Two scholars, whom at college erst he knew,

1. Sheepfolds woven from sticks.   4. Grain or wheat.
2. Pot or jug for carrying his drink.   5. A stiff kind of grass.
3. Penned up.   6. Teeming with ideas.

Met him, and of his way of life inquired;
   Whereat he answered, that the gypsy crew,
      His mates, had arts to rule as they desired
         The workings of men's brains,   45
And they can bind them to what thoughts they will.
   "And I," he said, "the secret of their art,
      When fully learned, will to the world impart;
But it needs heaven-sent moments for this skill."   50

This said, he left them, and returned no more.—
   But rumors hung about the countryside,
      That the lost Scholar long was seen to stray,
Seen by rare glimpses, pensive and tongue-tied,
      In hat of antique shape, and cloak of gray,   55
         The same the gypsies wore.
Shepherds had met him on the Hurst [7] in spring;
   At some lone alehouse in the Berkshire moors,
      On the warm ingle-bench,[8] the smock-frocked boors
Had found him seated at their entering,   60

But, 'mid their drink and clatter, he would fly.
   And I myself seem half to know thy looks,
      And put the shepherds, wanderer! on thy trace;
And boys who in lone wheatfields scare the rooks[9]
      I ask if thou hast passed their quiet place;   65
         Or in my boat I lie
Moored to the cool bank in the summer heats,
   'Mid wide grass meadows which the sunshine fills,
      And watch the warm, green-muffled Cumner hills,
And wonder if thou haunt'st their shy retreats.   70

For most, I know, thou lov'st retired ground!
   Thee at the ferry Oxford riders blithe,
      Returning home on summer nights, have met
Crossing the stripling Thames[1] at Bab-lock-hithe,
   Trailing in the cool stream thy fingers wet,   75
      As the punt's rope chops round;[2]
And leaning backward in a pensive dream,
   And fostering in thy lap a heap of flowers
      Plucked in shy fields and distant Wychwood bowers,
And thine eyes resting on the moonlit stream.   80

And then they land, and thou art seen no more!—

---

7. A hill near Oxford. All the place names in the poem (except those in the final two stanzas) refer to the countryside near Oxford.
8. Fireside bench. "Boors," here, are rustics.
9. Boys hired to frighten crows away from eating wheat grains. See Hardy's novel *Jude the Obscure*, I.ii.
1. I.e., the narrow upper reaches of the river before it broadens out to its full width.
2. The scholar's flat-bottomed boat ("punt") is tied up by a rope at the river bank near the ferry-crossing like the speaker's boat (in the previous stanza), which was "moored to the cool bank." The motion of the boat as it is stirred by the current of the river causes the chopping sound of the rope in the water.

Maidens, who from the distant hamlets come
 To dance around the Fyfield elm in May,
  Oft through the darkening fields have seen thee roam,
   Or cross a stile into the public way.   85
    Oft thou hast given them store
  Of flowers—the frail-leafed, white anemone,
   Dark bluebells drenched with dews of summer eves,
   And purple orchises with spotted leaves—
But none hath words she can report of thee.   90

And, above Godstow Bridge, when hay time's here
 In June, and many a scythe in sunshine flames,
  Men who through those wide fields of breezy grass
   Where black-winged swallows haunt the glittering Thames,
    To bathe in the abandoned lasher pass,[3]   95
    Have often passed thee near
  Sitting upon the river bank o'ergrown;
   Marked thine outlandish garb, thy figure spare,
   Thy dark vague eyes, and soft abstracted air—
But, when they came from bathing, thou wast gone!   100

At some lone homestead in the Cumner hills,
 Where at her open door the housewife darns,
  Thou hast been seen, or hanging on a gate
   To watch the threshers in the mossy barns.
    Children, who early range these slopes and late   105
    For cresses from the rills,
  Have known thee eying, all an April day,
   The springing pastures and the feeding kine;
   And marked thee, when the stars come out and shine,
Through the long dewy grass move slow away.   110

In autumn, on the skirts of Bagley Wood—
 Where most the gypsies by the turf-edged way
  Pitch their smoked tents, and every bush you see
   With scarlet patches tagged and shreds of gray,
    Above the forest ground called Thessaly—   115
    The blackbird, picking food,
  Sees thee, nor stops his meal, nor fears at all;
   So often has he known thee past him stray,
   Rapt, twirling in thy hand a withered spray,
And waiting for the spark from heaven to fall.   120

And once, in winter, on the causeway chill
 Where home through flooded fields foot-travelers go,
  Have I not passed thee on the wooden bridge,
   Wrapped in thy cloak and battling with the snow,
    Thy face tow'rd Hinksey and its wintry ridge?   125
    And thou hast climbed the hill,
  And gained the white brow of the Cumner range;

3. Water that spills over a dam or weir.

Turned once to watch, while thick the snowflakes fall,
The line of festal light in Christ Church hall[4]—
Then sought thy straw in some sequestered grange.   130

But what—I dream! Two hundred years are flown
Since first thy story ran through Oxford halls,
And the grave Glanvill did the tale inscribe
That thou wert wandered from the studious walls
To learn strange arts, and join a gypsy tribe;   135
And thou from earth art gone
Long since, and in some quiet churchyard laid—
Some country nook, where o'er thy unknown grave
Tall grasses and white flowering nettles wave,
Under a dark, red-fruited yew tree's shade.   140

—No, no, thou hast not felt the lapse of hours!
For what wears out the life of mortal men?
'Tis that from change to change their being rolls;
'Tis that repeated shocks, again, again,
Exhaust the energy of strongest souls   145
And numb the elastic powers.
Till having used our nerves with bliss and teen,[5]
And tired upon a thousand schemes our wit,
To the just-pausing Genius[6] we remit
Our worn-out life, and are—what we have been.   150

Thou hast not lived, why should'st thou perish, so?
Thou hadst *one* aim, *one* business, *one* desire;
Else wert thou long since numbered with the dead!
Else hadst thou spent, like other men, thy fire!
The generations of thy peers are fled,   155
And we ourselves shall go;
But thou possessest an immortal lot,
And we imagine thee exempt from age
And living as thou liv'st on Glanvill's page,
Because thou hadst—what we, alas! have not.   160

For early didst thou leave the world, with powers
Fresh, undiverted to the world without,
Firm to their mark, not spent on other things;
Free from the sick fatigue, the languid doubt,
Which much to have tried, in much been baffled, brings. 165
O life unlike to ours!
Who fluctuate idly without term or scope,
Of whom each strives, nor knows for what he strives,
And each half[7] lives a hundred different lives;
Who wait like thee, but not, like thee, in hope.   170

Thou waitest for the spark from heaven! and we,
Light half-believers of our casual creeds,
Who never deeply felt, nor clearly willed,

4. The dining hall of an Oxford college.   which pauses briefly to receive back
5. Vexation.   the life given to us.
6. Perhaps the spirit of the universe,   7. An adverb modifying "lives."

Whose insight never has borne fruit in deeds,
   Whose vague resolves never have been fulfilled;   175
      For whom each year we see
Breeds new beginnings, disappointments new;
     Who hesitate and falter life away,
     And lose tomorrow the ground won today—
Ah! do not we, wanderer! await it too?   180
Yes, we await it!—but it still delays,
   And then we suffer! and amongst us one,[8]
     Who most has suffered, takes dejectedly
His seat upon the intellectual throne;
     And all his store of sad experience he   185
      Lays bare of wretched days;
Tells us his misery's birth and growth and signs,
     And how the dying spark of hope was fed,
     And how the breast was soothed, and how the head,
   And all his hourly varied anodynes.   190

This for our wisest! and we others pine,
   And wish the long unhappy dream would end,
     And waive all claim to bliss, and try to bear;
With close-lipped patience for our only friend,
     Sad patience, too near neighbor to despair—   195
      But none has hope like thine!
Thou through the fields and through the woods dost stray,
   Roaming the countryside, a truant boy,
     Nursing thy project in unclouded joy,
And every doubt long blown by time away.   200

O born in days when wits were fresh and clear,
   And life ran gaily as the sparkling Thames;
     Before this strange disease of modern life,
With its sick hurry, its divided aims,
     Its heads o'ertaxed, its palsied hearts, was rife—   205
      Fly hence, our contact fear!
Still fly, plunge deeper in the bowering wood!
   Averse, as Dido[9] did with gesture stern
     From her false friend's approach in Hades turn,
Wave us away, and keep thy solitude!   210

Still nursing the unconquerable hope,
   Still clutching the inviolable shade,
     With a free, onward impulse brushing through,
By night, the silvered branches of the glade—
     Far on the forest skirts, where none pursue.   215
      On some mild pastoral slope
Emerge, and resting on the moonlit pales
     Freshen thy flowers as in former years
     With dew, or listen with enchanted ears,

8. Probably Tennyson, whose *In Memoriam* had appeared in 1850, or perhaps Goethe.
9. Dido committed suicide after her lover, Aeneas, deserted her. When he later encountered her in Hades, she turned sternly away from him.

From the dark dingles,[10] to the nightingales!   220

But fly our paths, our feverish contact fly!
 For strong the infection of our mental strife,
  Which, though it gives no bliss, yet spoils for rest;
 And we should win thee from thy own fair life,
  Like us distracted, and like us unblest.   225
   Soon, soon thy cheer would die,
 Thy hopes grow timorous, and unfixed thy powers,
 And thy clear aims be cross and shifting made;
 And then thy glad perennial youth would fade,
 Fade, and grow old at last, and die like ours.   230

Then fly our greetings, fly our speech and smiles!
 —As some grave Tyrian trader, from the sea,
  Descried at sunrise an emerging prow
 Lifting the cool-haired creepers stealthily,
  The fringes of a southward-facing brow   235
   Among the Aegean isles;
 And saw the merry Grecian coaster come,
  Freighted with amber grapes, and Chian wine,
  Green, bursting figs, and tunnies[1] steeped in brine—
 And knew the intruders on his ancient home,   240

The young lighthearted masters of the waves—
 And snatched his rudder, and shook out more sail;
 And day and night held on indignantly
 O'er the blue Midland waters with the gale,
  Betwixt the Syrtes[2] and soft Sicily,   245
   To where the Atlantic raves
 Outside the western straits; and unbent sails
  There, where down cloudy cliffs, through sheets of foam,
  Shy traffickers, the dark Iberians[3] come;
 And on the beach undid his corded bales.[4]   250

           1853

10. Small deep valleys.
1. Tuna fish.
2. Shoals off the coast of North Africa.
3. Dark inhabitants of Spain and Portugal—perhaps associated with gypsies.
4. The elaborate simile of the final two stanzas has been variously interpreted and misinterpreted. The trader from Tyre is disconcerted when, peering out through the foliage ("fringes") that screens his hiding place, he sees noisy intruders entering his harbor. Like the Scholar Gypsy, when similarly intruded upon by hearty extroverts, he resolves to flee and seek a new home.
 The reference (line 249) to the Iberians as "*shy* traffickers" (traders) is explained by Kenneth Allott as having been derived from Herodotus' *History* (IV.196). Herodotus describes a distinctive method of selling goods established by Carthaginian merchants who used to sail through the straits of Gibraltar to trade with the inhabitants of the coast of West Africa.

The Carthaginians would leave bales of their merchandise on display along the beaches and, without having seen their prospective customers, would return to their ships. The shy natives would then come down from their inland hiding places and set gold beside the bales they wished to buy. When the natives withdrew in their turn, the Carthaginians would return to the beach and decide whether payments were adequate, a process repeated until agreement was reached. On the Atlantic coasts this method of bargaining persisted into the 19th century. As William Beloe, a translator of Herodotus, noted in 1844: "In this manner they transact their exchange without seeing one another, or without the least instance of dishonesty * * * on either side." For the solitary Tyrian trader such a procedure, with its avoidance of *contact* (line 221), would have been especially appropriate.

Dover Beach

The sea is calm tonight.
The tide is full, the moon lies fair
Upon the straits—on the French coast the light
Gleams and is gone; the cliffs of England stand,
Glimmering and vast, out in the tranquil bay.   5
Come to the window, sweet is the night air!
Only, from the long line of spray
Where the sea meets the moon-blanched land,
Listen! you hear the grating roar[1]
Of pebbles which the waves draw back, and fling,   10
At their return, up the high strand,
Begin, and cease, and then again begin,
With tremulous cadence slow, and bring
The eternal note of sadness in.

Sophocles long ago   15
Heard it on the Aegean, and it brought
Into his mind the turbid ebb and flow
Of human misery;[2] we
Find also in the sound a thought,
Hearing it by this distant northern sea.   20

The Sea of Faith
Was once, too, at the full, and round earth's shore
Lay like the folds of a bright girdle furled.[3]
But now I only hear
Its melancholy, long, withdrawing roar,   25
Retreating, to the breath
Of the night wind, down the vast edges drear
And naked shingles[4] of the world.

Ah, love, let us be true
To one another! for the world, which seems   30
To lie before us like a land of dreams,
So various, so beautiful, so new,
Hath really neither joy, nor love, nor light,
Nor certitude, nor peace, nor help for pain;
And we are here as on a darkling plain   35

---

1. Cf. Wordsworth's *It Is a Beauteous Evening*: "Listen! the mighty Being is awake, / And doth with his eternal motion make / A sound like thunder—everlastingly."
2. See Sophocles' *Antigone*, lines 583 ff.
3. This difficult line means, in general, that at high tide the sea envelops the land closely. Its forces are "gathered" up (to use Wordsworth's term for it) like the "folds" of bright clothing ("girdle") which have been compressed ("furled"). At ebb tide, as the sea retreats, it is unfurled and spread out. It still surrounds the shoreline but not as an "enclasping flow" (as Arnold speaks of the sea in *To Marguerite, Continued*). See also 2 *Henry IV*, III.i.49–51: "to see / The beachy girdle of the ocean / Too wide for Neptune's hips."
4. Beaches covered with pebbles.

Swept with confused alarms of struggle and flight,
Where ignorant armies [5] clash by night.
ca. 1851   1867

Stanzas from the Grande Chartreuse[1]

Through Alpine meadows soft-suffused
With rain, where thick the crocus blows,
Past the dark forges long disused,
The mule track from Saint Laurent goes.
The bridge is crossed, and slow we ride,   5
Through forest, up the mountainside.

The autumnal evening darkens round,
The wind is up, and drives the rain;
While, hark! far down, with strangled sound
Doth the Dead Guier's[2] stream complain,   10
Where that wet smoke, among the woods,
Over his boiling cauldron broods.

Swift rush the spectral vapors white
Past limestone scars [3] with ragged pines,
Showing—then blotting from our sight!—   15
Halt—through the cloud-drift something shines!
High in the valley, wet and drear,
The huts of Courrerie appear.

Strike leftward! cries our guide; and higher
Mounts up the stony forest way.   20
At last the encircling trees retire;
Look! through the showery twilight gray
What pointed roofs are these advance?—
A palace of the Kings of France?

Approach, for what we seek is here!   25
Alight, and sparely sup, and wait
For rest in this outbuilding near;
Then cross the sward and reach that gate.
Knock; pass the wicket! Thou art come
To the Carthusians' world-famed home.   30

5. Perhaps the revolutions of 1848 or a reference to the siege of Rome by the French in 1849. The date of composition of the poem is unknown, although generally assumed to be 1851.
1. A monastery situated high in the French Alps. It was established in 1084 by St. Bruno, founder of the Carthusians (line 30), whose austere regimen of solitary contemplation, fasting, and religious exercises (lines 37–44) had remained virtually unchanged for centuries.

Arnold visited the site September 7, 1851, accompanied by his bride. His account may be compared with that by Wordsworth (*Prelude* VI. 416–88) who had made a similar visit in 1790.
2. The Guiers Mort river flows down from the monastery and joins the Guiers Vif in the valley below. Wordsworth speaks of the two rivers as "the sister streams of Life and Death."
3. Precipices.

The silent courts, where night and day
Into their stone-carved basins cold
The splashing icy fountains play—
The humid corridors behold!
Where, ghostlike in the deepening night,   35
Cowled forms brush by in gleaming white.

The chapel, where no organ's peal
Invests the stern and naked prayer—
With penitential cries they kneel
And wrestle; rising then, with bare   40
And white uplifted faces stand,
Passing the Host from hand to hand;[4]

Each takes, and then his visage wan
Is buried in his cowl once more.
The cells!—the suffering Son of Man   45
Upon the wall—the knee-worn floor—
And where they sleep, that wooden bed,
Which shall their coffin be, when dead![5]

The library, where tract and tome
Not to feed priestly pride are there,   50
To hymn the conquering march of Rome,
Nor yet to amuse, as ours are!
They paint of souls the inner strife,
Their drops of blood, their death in life.

The garden, overgrown—yet mild,   55
See, fragrant herbs[6] are flowering there!
Strong children of the Alpine wild
Whose culture is the brethren's care;
Of human tasks their only one,
And cheerful works beneath the sun.   60

Those halls, too, destined to contain
Each its own pilgrim-host of old,
From England, Germany, or Spain—
All are before me! I behold
The House, the Brotherhood austere!   65
—And what am I, that I am here?

For rigorous teachers seized my youth,
And purged its faith, and trimmed its fire,
Showed me the high, white star of Truth,

---

4. Arnold, during his short visit, may not actually have witnessed the service of the Mass in the monastery. The consecrated wafer (the Host) is not passed from the hand of the officiating priest to the hands of the communicant (as is the practice in Arnold's own Anglican church) but placed, instead, on the tongue of the communicant (who kneels rather than stands). See Tinker and Lowry, *The Poetry of Matthew Arnold: A Commentary*, pp. 249–51.
5. A Carthusian is buried on a wooden plank but does not sleep in a coffin.
6. From which the liqueur, Chartreuse, is manufactured. Sales of this liqueur provide the principal revenues for upkeep of the monastery.

There bade me gaze, and there aspire.   70
Even now their whispers pierce the gloom:
What dost thou in this living tomb?

Forgive me, masters of the mind![7]
At whose behest I long ago
So much unlearnt, so much resigned—   75
I come not here to be your foe!
I seek these anchorites, not in ruth,[8]
To curse and to deny your truth;

Not as their friend, or child, I speak!
But as, on some far northern strand,   80
Thinking of his own Gods, a Greek
In pity and mournful awe might stand
Before some fallen Runic stone—[9]
For both were faiths, and both are gone.

Wandering between two worlds, one dead,   85
The other powerless to be born,
With nowhere yet to rest my head,
Like these, on earth I wait forlorn.
Their faith, my tears, the world deride—
I come to shed them at their side.   90

Oh, hide me in your gloom profound,
Ye solemn seats of holy pain!
Take me, cowled forms, and fence me round,
Till I possess my soul again;
Till free my thoughts before me roll,   95
Not chafed by hourly false control!

For the world cries your faith is now
But a dead time's exploded dream;
My melancholy, sciolists[1] say,
Is a passed mode, an outworn theme—   100
As if the world had ever had
A faith, or sciolists been sad!

Ah, if it *be* passed, take away,
At least, the restlessness, the pain;
Be man henceforth no more a prey   105
To these out-dated stings again!
The nobleness of grief is gone—
Ah, leave us not the fret alone!

7. Writers whose insistence upon testing religious beliefs in the light of fact and reason persuaded Arnold that faith in Christianity (especially in the Roman Catholic or Anglo Catholic forms) was no longer tenable in the modern world.
8. Remorse for having adopted the rationalist view of Christianity.
9. A monument inscribed in Teutonic letters (runes), emblematic of a Nordic religion that has become extinct. The relic reminds the Greek that his own religion is likewise dying and will soon be extinct. See Arnold's *Preface* of 1853, second paragraph.
1. Superficial-minded persons who pretend to know the answers to all questions.

But—if you[2] cannot give us ease—
Last of the race of them who grieve   110
Here leave us to die out with these
Last of the people who believe!
Silent, while years engrave the brow;
Silent—the best are silent now.

Achilles[3] ponders in his tent,   115
The kings of modern thought[4] are dumb;
Silent they are, though not content,
And wait to see the future come.
They have the grief men had of yore,
But they contend and cry no more.   120

Our fathers[5] watered with their tears
This sea of time whereon we sail,
Their voices were in all men's ears
Who passed within their puissant hail.
Still the same ocean round us raves,   125
But we stand mute, and watch the waves.

For what availed it, all the noise
And outcry of the former men?—
Say, have their sons achieved more joys,
Say, is life lighter now than then?   130
The sufferers died, they left their pain—
The pangs which tortured them remain.

What helps it now, that Byron bore,
With haughty scorn which mocked the smart,
Through Europe to the Aetolian shore[6]   135
The pageant of his bleeding heart?
That thousands counted every groan,
And Europe made his woe her own?

What boots it, Shelley! that the breeze
Carried thy lovely wail away,   140
Musical through Italian trees
Which fringe thy soft blue Spezzian bay?[7]
Inheritors of thy distress
Have restless hearts one throb the less?

---

2. It is not clear whether the speaker has resumed addressing his "rigorous teachers" (line 67) or (as would seem more likely) a combination of the sciolists, who scorn the speaker's melancholy and the worldly, who scorn the faith of the monks. See his address to the "sons of the world" (lines 160–68).
3. Achilles, after the death of Patroclus, refused to participate in the Trojan war; hence similar to modern intellectual leaders who refuse to speak out about their frustrated sense of alienation.
4. Variously but never satisfactorily identified as Newman or Carlyle (the latter was said to have preached the gospel of silence in 40 volumes). Another advocate of stoical silence was the French poet, Alfred de Vigny (1797–1863).
5. Predecessors among the Romantic writers such as Byron.
6. Region in Greece where Byron died.
7. The Gulf of Spezzia in Italy where Shelley was drowned.

Or are we easier, to have read,   145
O Obermann![8] the sad, stern page,
Which tells us how thou hidd'st thy head
From the fierce tempest of thine age
In the lone brakes of Fontainebleau,
Or chalets near the Alpine snow?   150

Ye slumber in your silent grave!—
The world, which for an idle day
Grace to your mood of sadness gave,
Long since hath flung her weeds[9] away.
The eternal trifler[1] breaks your spell;   155
But we—we learnt your lore too well!

Years hence, perhaps, may dawn an age,
More fortunate, alas! than we,
Which without hardness will be sage,
And gay without frivolity.   160
Sons of the world, oh, speed those years;
But, while we wait, allow our tears!

Allow them! We admire with awe
The exulting thunder of your race;
You give the universe your law,   165
You triumph over time and space!
Your pride of life, your tireless powers,
We laud them, but they are not ours.

We are like children reared in shade
Beneath some old-world abbey wall,   170
Forgotten in a forest glade,
And secret from the eyes of all.
Deep, deep the greenwood round them waves,
Their abbey, and its close[2] of graves!

But, where the road runs near the stream,   175
Oft through the trees they catch a glance
Of passing troops in the sun's beam—
Pennon, and plume, and flashing lance!
Forth to the world those soldiers fare,
To life, to cities, and to war!   180

And through the wood, another way,
Faint bugle notes from far are borne,
Where hunters gather, staghounds bay,[3]
Round some fair forest-lodge at morn.
Gay dames are there, in sylvan green;   185
Laughter and cries—those notes between!

8. Melancholy hero of *Obermann* (1804),
a novel by Senancour.
9. Mourning clothes.
1. The sciolist, as in line 99.

2. Enclosure.
3. Cf. the contrast between recluses and
hunters in *The Scholar Gypsy*, lines 71–
81.

The banners flashing through the trees
Make their blood dance and chain their eyes;
That bugle music on the breeze
Arrests them with a charmed surprise. 190
Banner by turns and bugle woo:
Ye shy recluses, follow too!

O children, what do ye reply?—
"Action and pleasure, will ye roam
Through these secluded dells to cry 195
And call us?—but too late ye come!
Too late for us your call ye blow,
Whose bent was taken long ago.

"Long since we pace this shadowed nave;
We watch those yellow tapers shine, 200
Emblems of hope over the grave,
In the high altar's depth divine;
The organ carries to our ear
Its accents of another sphere.

"Fenced early in this cloistral round 205
Of reverie, of shade, of prayer,
How should we grow in other ground?
How can we flower in foreign air?
—Pass, banners, pass, and bugles, cease;
And leave our desert to its peace!" 210

1852(?)   1855

Thyrsis[1]

A MONODY, TO COMMEMORATE THE AUTHOR'S FRIEND,
ARTHUR HUGH CLOUGH, WHO DIED AT FLORENCE, 1861

How changed is here each spot man makes or fills!
In the two Hinkseys[2] nothing keeps the same;

1. In the 1840's, at Oxford, Clough had been one of Arnold's closest friends. After the death of this fellow poet, twenty years later, Arnold revisited the Thames-valley countryside which they had explored together. The familiar scenes prompted him to review the changes wrought by time on the ideals shared in his Oxford days with Clough, ideals symbolized, in part, by a distant elm and by the story of the Scholar Gypsy. The survival of these ideals in the face of the difficulties of modern life is the subject of this elegy. Unlike Tennyson in such elegies as *In Memoriam*, Arnold rarely touches here upon other kinds of immortality.

As a framework for his elegy, Arnold draws on the same Greek and Latin pastoral tradition from which Milton's *Lycidas* and Shelley's *Adonais* were derived. Hence Clough is referred to by one of the traditional names for a shepherd-poet, Thyrsis, and Arnold himself as Corydon. The sense of distancing which results from this traditional elegiac mode is reduced considerably by the realism of the setting with its bleak wintry landscape at twilight, a landscape which is brightened, in turn, by evocations of the return of hopeful springtime.
2. The villages of North Hinksey and South Hinksey.

The village street its haunted mansion lacks,
And from the sign is gone Sibylla's name,[3]
And from the roofs the twisted chimney stacks—   5
    Are ye too changed, ye hills?
See, 'tis no foot of unfamiliar men
    Tonight from Oxford up your pathway strays!
Here came I often, often, in old days—
Thyrsis and I; we still had Thyrsis then.   10

Runs it not here, the track by Childsworth Farm,
    Past the high wood, to where the elm tree crowns
The hill behind whose ridge the sunset flames?
    The signal-elm, that looks on Ilsley Downs,
    The Vale, the three lone weirs, the youthful Thames?—   15
        This winter eve is warm,
Humid the air! leafless, yet soft as spring,
    The tender purple spray on copse and briers!
And that sweet city with her dreaming spires,
She needs not June for beauty's heightening,   20

Lovely all times she lies, lovely tonight!—
    Only, methinks, some loss of habit's power
Befalls me wandering through this upland dim.
    Once passed I blindfold here, at any hour;
    Now seldom come I, since I came with him.   25
        That single elm tree bright
Against the west—I miss it! is it gone?
    We prized it dearly; while it stood, we said,
Our friend, the Gypsy Scholar, was not dead;
While the tree lived, he in these fields lived on.   30

Too rare, too rare, grow now my visits here,
    But once I knew each field, each flower, each stick;
And with the countryfolk acquaintance made
    By barn in threshing time, by new-built rick.
    Here, too, our shepherd pipes we first assayed.   35
        Ah me! this many a year
My pipe is lost, my shepherd's holiday!
    Needs must I lose them, needs with heavy heart
Into the world and wave of men depart;
But Thyrsis of his own will went away.[4]   40

It irked him to be here, he could not rest.
    He loved each simple joy the country yields,
He loved his mates; but yet he could not keep,[5]
    For that a shadow loured on the fields,
    Here with the shepherds and the silly[6] sheep.   45
        Some life of men unblest

---

3. Sibylla Kerr had been the proprietress of a tavern in South Hinksey.
4. Arnold left Oxford out of the necessity for earning a living; Clough left as a matter of principle when in 1848 he resigned a fellowship rather than subscribe to the creed of the Anglican Church.
5. Stay.
6. Innocent.

He knew, which made him droop, and filled his head.
  He went; his piping took a troubled sound
  Of storms[7] that rage outside our happy ground;
He could not wait their passing, he is dead. 50

So, some tempestuous morn in early June,
  When the year's primal burst of bloom is o'er,
  Before the roses and the longest day—
When garden walks and all the grassy floor
  With blossoms red and white of fallen May 55
  And chestnut flowers are strewn—
So have I heard the cuckoo's parting cry,
  From the wet field, through the vexed garden trees,
  Come with the volleying rain and tossing breeze:
The bloom is gone, and with the bloom go I! 60

Too quick despairer, wherefore wilt thou go?
  Soon will the high Midsummer pomps come on,
  Soon will the musk carnations break and swell,
Soon shall we have gold-dusted snapdragon,
  Sweet-william with his homely cottage smell, 65
  And stocks in fragrant blow;
Roses that down the alleys shine afar,
  And open, jasmine-muffled lattices,
  And groups under the dreaming garden trees,
And the full moon, and the white evening star. 70

He hearkens not! light comer, he is flown!
  What matters it? next year he will return,
  And we shall have him in the sweet spring days,
With whitening hedges, and uncrumpling fern,
  And bluebells trembling by the forest ways, 75
  And scent of hay new-mown.
But Thyrsis never more we swains shall see;
  See him come back, and cut a smoother reed,
  And blow a strain the world at last shall heed—
For Time, not Corydon, hath conquered thee! 80

Alack, for Corydon no rival now!—
  But when Sicilian shepherds lost a mate,
  Some good survivor with his flute would go,
Piping a ditty sad for Bion's fate;[8]
  And cross the unpermitted ferry's flow,[9] 85
  And relax Pluto's brow,
And make leap up with joy the beauteous head
  Of Proserpine, among whose crownéd hair
  Are flowers first opened on Sicilian air,
And flute his friend, like Orpheus, from the dead.[1] 90

7. Religious and political controversies.
8. Moschus, a Greek poet, composed a pastoral elegy upon the death of the poet Bion in Sicily.
9. The river Styx across which the dead were ferried to the underworld where Pluto ruled with his queen, Proserpine.
In spring, Proserpine's returning above ground in Sicily would cause the flowers to blossom.
1. Orpheus' music enabled him to enter the "unpermitted" realms of the dead and to bring his wife, Eurydice, back with him to the land of the living.

O easy access to the hearer's grace
  When Dorian shepherds[2] sang to Proserpine!
    For she herself had trod Sicilian fields,
    She knew the Dorian water's gush divine,
      She knew each lily white which Enna yields,[3]   95
        Each rose with blushing face;
  She loved the Dorian pipe, the Dorian strain.
      But ah, of our poor Thames she never heard!
      Her foot the Cummer cowslips never stirred;
  And we should tease her with our plaint in vain!   100

Well! wind-dispersed and vain the words will be,
  Yet, Thyrsis, let me give my grief its hour
    In the old haunt, and find our tree-topped hill!
  Who, if not I, for questing here hath power?
      I know the wood which hides the daffodil,   105
        I know the Fyfield tree,
  I know what white, what purple fritillaries[4]
    The grassy harvest of the river fields,
    Above by Ensham, down by Sandford, yields,
  And what sedged brooks are Thames's tributaries;   110

I know these slopes; who knows them if not I?—
  But many a dingle[5] on the loved hillside,
    With thorns once studded, old, white-blossomed trees,
    Where thick the cowslips grew, and far descried
      High towered the spikes of purple orchises,   115
        Hath since our day put by
  The coronals of that forgotten time;
    Down each green bank hath gone the plowboy's team,
    And only in the hidden brookside gleam
  Primroses, orphans of the flowery prime.   120

Where is the girl, who by the boatman's door,
  Above the locks, above the boating throng,
    Unmoored our skiff when through the Wytham flats,
  Red loosestrife[6] and blond meadowsweet among
      And darting swallows and light water-gnats,   125
        We tracked the shy Thames shore?
  Where are the mowers, who, as the tiny swell
    Of our boat passing heaved the river grass,
    Stood with suspended scythe to see us pass?—
  They all are gone, and thou art gone as well!   130

Yes, thou art gone! and round me too the night
  In ever-nearing circle weaves her shade.
    I see her veil draw soft across the day,

2. The Dorian Greeks had colonized Sicily, the home of pastoral poetry.
3. From a meadow near Enna, a Sicilian town, Proserpine had been carried off to the underworld by Pluto (or Dis). Cf. the touchstone lines admired by Arnold in *Paradise Lost* (IV.268–71): "that fair field / Of Enna, where Proserpine gathering flowers, / Herself a fairer flower, by gloomy Dis / Was gathered * * * "
4. Flowers commonly found in moist meadows.
5. Small deep valley.
6. Flowers which grow on banks of streams.

I feel her slowly chilling breath invade
    The cheek grown thin, the brown hair sprent[7] with gray;   135
      I feel her finger light
Laid pausefully upon life's headlong train;
    The foot less prompt to meet the morning dew,
    The heart less bounding at emotion new,
And hope, once crushed, less quick to spring again.   140

And long the way appears, which seemed so short
    To the less practiced eye of sanguine youth;
    And high the mountaintops, in cloudy air,
The mountaintops where is the throne of Truth,[8]
    Tops in life's morning sun so bright and bare!   145
      Unbreachable the fort
Of the long-battered world uplifts its wall;
    And strange and vain the earthly turmoil grows,
    And near and real the charm of thy repose,
And night as welcome as a friend would fall.   150

But hush! the upland hath a sudden loss
    Of quiet!—Look, adown the dusk hillside,
    A troop of Oxford hunters going home,
As in old days, jovial and talking, ride!
    From hunting with the Berkshire hounds they come.   155
      Quick! let me fly, and cross
Into yon farther field!—'Tis done; and see,
    Backed by the sunset, which doth glorify
    The orange and pale violet evening sky,
Bare on its lonely ridge, the Tree! the Tree!   160

I take the omen! Eve lets down her veil,
    The white fog creeps from bush to bush about,
    The west unflushes, the high stars grow bright,
And in the scattered farms the lights come out.
    I cannot reach the signal-tree tonight,   165
      Yet, happy omen, hail!
Hear it from thy broad lucent Arno vale[9]
    (For there thine earth-forgetting eyelids keep
    The morningless and unawakening sleep
Under the flowery oleanders pale),   170

Hear it, O Thyrsis, still our tree is there!—
    Ah, vain! These English fields, this upland dim,
    These brambles pale with mist engarlanded,
That lone, sky-pointing tree, are not for him;
    To a boon southern country he is fled,   175
      And now in happier air,
Wandering with the great Mother's[1] train divine

---

7. Sprinkled.
8. Cf. Pope's *Essay on Criticism*, II.220–32.
9. Clough was buried in Florence, which is situated in the valley of the Arno River.

1. Demeter (whose name may mean Earth Mother) was worshiped as the goddess of agriculture. The "immortal chants" (line 181) would be sung in her honor by her followers, members of the "train divine" (line 176).

(And purer or more subtle soul than thee,
I trow, the mighty Mother doth not see)
Within a folding of the Apennine,[2]   180

Thou hearest the immortal chants of old!—
Putting his sickle to the perilous grain
  In the hot cornfield of the Phrygian king,[3]
For thee the Lityerses song again
  Young Daphnis with his silver voice doth sing;   185
    Sings his Sicilian fold,
His sheep, his hapless love, his blinded eyes—
  And how a call celestial round him rang,
  And heavenward from the fountain brink he sprang,
And all the marvel of the golden skies.   190

There thou art gone, and me thou leavest here
Sole in these fields! yet will I not despair.
  Despair I will not, while I yet descry
  'Neath the mild canopy of English air
    That lonely tree against the western sky.   195
    Still, still these slopes, 'tis clear,
Our Gypsy Scholar haunts, outliving thee!
  Fields where soft sheep from cages pull the hay,
  Woods with anemones in flower till May,
Know him a wanderer still; then why not me?   200

A fugitive and gracious light he seeks,
Shy to illumine; and I seek it too.
  This does not come with houses or with gold,
  With place, with honor, and a flattering crew;
    'Tis not in the world's market bought and sold—   205
    But the smooth-slipping weeks
Drop by, and leave its seeker still untired;
  Out of the heed of mortals he is gone,
  He wends unfollowed, he must house alone;
Yet on he fares, by his own heart inspired.   210

Thou too, O Thyrsis, on like quest wast bound;
Thou wanderedst with me for a little hour!
  Men gave thee nothing; but this happy quest,
  If men esteemed thee feeble, gave thee power,

2. Mountains near Florence.
3. Arnold includes a note from Servius' commentary on Virgil's *Eclogues:* "Daphnis, the ideal Sicilian shepherd of Greek pastoral poetry, was said to have followed into Phrygia his mistress Piplea, who had been carried off by robbers, and to have found her in the power of the king of Phrygia, Lityerses. Lityerses used to make strangers try a contest with him in reaping corn, and to put them to death if he overcame them. Hercules arrived in time to save Daphnis, took upon himself the reaping contest with Lityerses, overcame him, and slew him. The Lityerses song connected with this tradition was, like the Linus song, one of the early plaintive strains of Greek popular poetry, and used to be sung by corn reapers. Other traditions represented Daphnis as beloved by a nymph who exacted from him an oath to love no one else. He fell in love with a princess, and was struck blind by the jealous nymph. Mercury, who was his father, raised him to heaven, and made a fountain spring up in the place from which he ascended. At this fountain the Sicilians offered yearly sacrifices."

If men procured thee trouble, gave thee rest.   215
    And this rude Cumner ground,
Its fir-topped Hurst, its farms, its quiet fields,
    Here cam'st thou in thy jocund youthful time,
    Here was thine height of strength, thy golden prime!
And still the haunt beloved a virtue yields.   220

What though the music of thy rustic flute
    Kept not for long its happy, country tone;
    Lost it too soon, and learnt a stormy note[4]
Of men contention-tossed, of men who groan,
    Which tasked thy pipe too sore, and tired thy throat—   225
    It failed, and thou wast mute!
Yet hadst thou alway visions of our light,
    And long with men of care thou couldst not stay,
    And soon thy foot resumed its wandering way,
Left human haunt, and on alone till night.   230

Too rare, too rare, grow now my visits here!
    'Mid city noise, not, as with thee of yore,
    Thyrsis! in reach of sheep-bells is my home.
—Then through the great town's harsh, heart-wearying roar,
    Let in thy voice a whisper often come,   235
        To chase fatigue and fear:
Why faintest thou? I wandered till I died.
    Roam on! The light we sought is shining still.
    Dost thou ask proof? Our tree yet crowns the hill,
Our Scholar travels yet the loved hillside.   240

1866

Palladium

Set where the upper streams of Simois[5] flow
Was the Palladium,[6] high 'mid rock and wood;
And Hector was in Ilium, far below,
And fought, and saw it not—but there it stood!

It stood, and sun and moonshine rained their light   5
On the pure columns of its glen-built hall.
Backward and forward rolled the waves of fight
Round Troy—but while this stood, Troy could not fall.

So, in its lovely moonlight, lives the soul.
Mountains surround it, and sweet virgin air;   10
Cold plashing, past it, crystal waters roll;
We visit it by moments, ah, too rare!

4. Clough's poetry often dealt with contemporary religious problems
5. A river near Troy.
6. An ancient statue of the goddess
·Pallas Athena. The safety of Troy
(Ilium) was thought to depend upon the
statue's being retained in the city.

We shall renew the battle in the plain
Tomorrow—red with blood will Xanthus[7] be;
Hector and Ajax will be there again,   15
Helen will come upon the wall to see.

Then we shall rust in shade, or shine in strife,
And fluctuate 'twixt blind hopes and blind despairs,
And fancy that we put forth all our life,
And never know how with the soul it fares.   20

Still doth the soul, from its lone fastness high,
Upon our life a ruling effluence send.
And when it fails, fight as we will, we die;
And while it lasts, we cannot wholly end.

1867

The Better Part

Long fed on boundless hopes, O race of man,
How angrily thou spurn'st all simpler fare!
"Christ," someone says, "was human as we are;
No judge eyes us from Heaven, our sin to scan;

"We live no more, when we have done our span."—   5
"Well, then, for Christ," thou answerest, "who can care?
From sin, which Heaven records not, why forbear?
Live we like brutes our life without a plan!"

So answerest thou; but why not rather say:
"Hath man no second life?—*Pitch this one high!*   10
Sits there no judge in Heaven, our sin to see?—

"*More strictly, then, the inward judge obey!*
Was Christ a man like us? *Ah! let us try*
If we, then, too, can be such men as he!"

1867

Growing Old[1]

What is it to grow old?
Is it to lose the glory of the form,
The luster of the eye?
Is it for beauty to forego her wreath?
—Yes, but not this alone.   5

7. A river near Troy.
1. Arnold's poem may have been
prompted as a rejoinder to Browning's
enthusiastic picture of old age in
Rabbi Ben Ezra (1864).

Is it to feel our strength—
Not our bloom only, but our strength—decay?
Is it to feel each limb
Grow stiffer, every function less exact,
Each nerve more loosely strung?   10

Yes, this, and more; but not
Ah, 'tis not what in youth we dreamed 'twould be!
'Tis not to have our life
Mellowed and softened as with sunset glow, -
A golden day's decline.   15

'Tis not to see the world
As from a height, with rapt prophetic eyes,
And heart profoundly stirred;
And weep, and feel the fullness of the past,[2]
The years that are no more.   20

It is to spend long days
And not once feel that we were ever young;
It is to add, immured
In the hot prison of the present, month
To month with weary pain.   25

It is to suffer this,
And feel but half, and feebly, what we feel.
Deep in our hidden heart
Festers the dull remembrance of a change,
But no emotion—none.   30

It is—last stage of all—
When we are frozen up within, and quite
The phantom of ourselves,
To hear the world applaud the hollow ghost
Which blamed the living man.   35
                                                                1867

The Last Word

Creep into thy narrow bed,
Creep, and let no more be said!
Vain thy onset! all stands fast.
Thou thyself must break at last.

Let the long contention cease!   5
Geese are swans, and swans are geese.
Let them have it how they will!
Thou art tired; best be still.

---

2. Cf. Tennyson's *Tears, Idle Tears.*

They out-talked thee, hissed thee, tore thee?
Better men fared thus before thee;   10
Fired their ringing shot and passed,
Hotly charged—and sank at last.

Charge once more, then, and be dumb!
Let the victors, when they come,
When the forts of folly fall,
Find thy body by the wall!

1867

Preface to *Poems* (1853)

In two small volumes of poems, published anonymously, one in
1849, the other in 1852, many of the poems which compose the
present volume have already appeared. The rest are now published
for the first time.

I have, in the present collection, omitted the poem from which
the volume published in 1852 took its title.[1] I have done so, not
because the subject of it was a Sicilian Greek born between two and
three thousand years ago, although many persons would think this a
sufficient reason. Neither have I done so because I had, in my own
opinion, failed in the delineation which I intended to effect. I intended to delineate the feelings of one of the last of the Greek religious philosophers, one of the family of Orpheus and Musaeus,[2]
having survived his fellows, living on into a time when the habits of
Greek thought and feeling had begun fast to change, character to
dwindle, the influence of the Sophists[3] to prevail. Into the feelings of
a man so situated there entered much that we are accustomed
to consider as exclusively modern; how much, the fragments[4] of
Empedocles himself which remain to us are sufficient at least to
indicate. What those who are familiar only with the great monuments of early Greek genius suppose to be its exclusive character-

1. *Empedocles on Etna*, the long poem
that supplied the title for Arnold's second collection of poems, portrays the
disillusioned reflections of the Greek
philosopher and scientist Empedocles and
culminates in the speaker's suicide on
Mount Etna in Sicily, in the 5th century
B.C. Because of his dissatisfaction with
what he calls the "morbid" tone of
Empedocles on Etna Arnold continued to
exclude it from his volumes of poetry
until 1867 when he reprinted it at the
request, he said, "of a man of genius,
whom it had the honor and good fortune
to interest—Mr. Robert Browning." It
should be noted that in the arguments
developed in the *Preface* against his own
poem (and against 19th-century poetry
in general) Arnold is exclusively concerned with narrative and dramatic poetry. The *Preface*, as he himself remarked
in 1854, "leaves * * * untouched the
question, how far, and in what manner,
the opinions there expressed respecting
the choice of subjects apply to lyric poetry; that region of the poetical field
which is chiefly cultivated at present."
2. Pupil of the poet and musician Orpheus. The latter was the legendary
founder of the Orphic religion that flourished in 6th-century Greece and later declined.
3. Greek rhetoricians, often criticized because of their reputed concern for niceties
of expression over substance of knowledge.
4. Empedocles' writings (medical and
scientific treatises in verse) have survived only in fragments.

istics, have disappeared; the calm, the cheerfulness, the disinterested objectivity have disappeared; the dialogue of the mind with itself has commenced; modern problems have presented themselves, we hear already the doubts, we witness the discouragement, of Hamlet and of Faust.

The representation of such a man's feelings must be interesting, if consistently drawn. We all naturally take pleasure, says Aristotle, in any imitation or representation whatever;[5] this is the basis of our love of poetry; and we take pleasure in them, he adds, because all knowledge is naturally agreeable to us; not to the philosopher only, but to mankind at large. Every representation therefore which is consistently drawn may be supposed to be interesting, inasmuch as it gratifies this natural interest in knowledge of all kinds. What is *not* interesting is that which does not add to our knowledge of any kind; that which is vaguely conceived and loosely drawn; a representation which is general, indeterminate, and faint, instead of being particular, precise, and firm.

Any accurate representation may therefore be expected to be interesting; but, if the representation be a poetical one, more than this is demanded. It is demanded, not only that it shall interest, but also that it shall inspirit and rejoice the reader; that it shall convey a charm, and infuse delight. For the Muses, as Hesiod says, were born that they might be "a forgetfulness of evils, and a truce from cares":[6] and it is not enough that the poet should add to the knowledge of men, it is required of him also that he should add to their happiness. "All art," says Schiller, "is dedicated to Joy, and there is no higher and no more serious problem, than how to make men happy. The right art is that alone, which creates the highest enjoyment."[7]

A poetical work, therefore, is not yet justified when it has been shown to be an accurate, and therefore interesting representation; it has to be shown also that it is a representation from which men can derive enjoyment. In presence of the most tragic circumstances, represented in a work of Art, the feeling of enjoyment, as is well known, may still subsist; the representation of the most utter calamity, of the liveliest anguish, is not sufficient to destroy it; the more tragic the situation, the deeper becomes the enjoyment; and the situation is more tragic in proportion as it becomes more terrible.

What then are the situations, from the representation of which, though accurate, no poetical enjoyment can be derived? They are those in which the suffering finds no vent in action; in which a continuous state of mental distress is prolonged, unrelieved by

5. See Aristotle, *Poetics*, especially 1, 2, 4, 7, 14.
6. From *Theogony* 52–56, by the early Greek poet Hesiod.
7. J. C. F. von Schiller, *On the Use of* the Chorus in Tragedy, prefatory essay to *The Bride of Messina* (1803). See *Friedrich Schiller's Works* (1903), VIII, 224.

incident, hope, or resistance; in which there is everything to be endured, nothing to be done. In such situations there is inevitably something morbid, in the description of them something monotonous. When they occur in actual life, they are painful, not tragic; the representation of them in poetry is painful also.

To this class of situations, poetically faulty as it appears to me, that of Empedocles, as I have endeavored to represent him, belongs; and I have therefore excluded the poem from the present collection.

And why, it may be asked, have I entered into this explanation respecting a matter so unimportant as the admission or exclusion of the poem in question? I have done so, because I was anxious to avow that the sole reason for its exclusion was that which has been stated above; and that it has not been excluded in deference to the opinion which many critics of the present day appear to entertain against subjects chosen from distant times and countries: against the choice, in short, of any subjects but modern ones.

"The poet," it is said, and by an intelligent critic, "the poet who would really fix the public attention must leave the exhausted past, and draw his subjects from matters of present import, and *therefore* both of interest and novelty."[8]

Now this view I believe to be completely false. It is worth examining, inasmuch as it is a fair sample of a class of critical dicta everywhere current at the present day, having a philosophical form and air, but no real basis in fact; and which are calculated to vitiate the judgment of readers of poetry, while they exert, so far as they are adopted, a misleading influence on the practice of those who write it.

What are the eternal objects of poetry, among all nations and at all times? They are actions; human actions; possessing an inherent interest in themselves, and which are to be communicated in an interesting manner by the art of the poet.[9] Vainly will the latter imagine that he has everything in his own power; that he can make an intrinsically inferior action equally delightful with a more excellent one by his treatment of it; he may indeed compel us to admire his skill, but his work will possess, within itself, an incurable defect.

The poet, then, has in the first place to select an excellent action; and what actions are the most excellent? Those, certainly, which most powerfully appeal to the great primary human affections: to those elementary feelings which subsist permanently in the race, and which are independent of time. These feelings are permanent and the same; that which interests them is permanent and the same also. The modernness or antiquity of an action, therefore, has nothing to do with its fitness for poetical representation; this de-

8. In the *Spectator* of April 2nd, 1853. The words quoted were not used with reference to poems of mine [Arnold's note]. According to Arnold the "intel- ligent critic" was R. S. Rintoul, editor of the *Spectator*.
9. Cf. Aristotle, *Poetics* 6.

pends upon its inherent qualities. To the elementary part of our nature, to our passions, that which is great and passionate is eternally interesting; and interesting solely in proportion to its greatness and to its passion. A great human action of a thousand years ago is more interesting to it than a smaller human action of today, even though upon the representation of this last the most consummate skill may have been expended, and though it has the advantage of appealing by its modern language, familiar manners, and contemporary allusions, to all our transient feelings and interests. These, however, have no right to demand of a poetical work that it shall satisfy them; their claims are to be directed elsewhere. Poetical works belong to the domain of our permanent passions; let them interest these, and the voice of all subordinate claims upon them is at once silenced.

Achilles, Prometheus, Clytemnestra, Dido—what modern poem presents personages as interesting, even to us moderns, as these personages of an "exhausted past"? We have the domestic epic dealing with the details of modern life which pass daily under our eyes;[1] we have poems representing modern personages in contact with the problems of modern life, morel, intellectual, and social; these works have been produced by poets the most distinguished of their nation and time; yet I fearlessly assert that *Hermann and Dorothea, Childe Harold, Jocelyn, The Excursion*,[2] leave the reader cold in comparison with the effect produced upon him by the latter books of the *Iliad*, by the *Oresteia*,[3] or by the episode of Dido.[4] And why is this? Simply because in the three last-named cases the action is greater, the personages nobler, the situations more intense: and this is the true basis of the interest in a poetical work, and this alone.

It may be urged, however, that past actions may be interesting in themselves, but that they are not to be adopted by the modern poet, because it is impossible for him to have them clearly present to his own mind, and he cannot therefore feel them deeply, nor represent them forcibly. But this is not necessarily the case. The externals of a past action, indeed, he cannot know with the precision of a contemporary; but his business is with its essentials. The outward man of Oedipus or of Macbeth, the houses in which they lived, the ceremonies of their courts, he cannot accurately figure to himself; but neither do they essentially concern him. His business is with their inward man; with their feelings and behavior in certain tragic situations, which engage their passions as men; these have in them nothing local and casual; they are as accessible to the modern poet as to a contemporary.

1. Perhaps alluding to such poems as Tennyson's *The Princess* (1847) and Alexander Smith's *Life Drama* (1853).
2. Long poems by Goethe (1797), Byron (1818), Lamartine (1836), and Words-worth (1814), respectively.
3. A trilogy of plays by Aeschylus concerned with the stories of Agamemnon, Clytemnestra, and their son, Orestes.
4. See Virgil's *Aeneid* IV.

The date of an action, then, signifies nothing: the action itself, its selection and construction, this is what is all-important. This the Greeks understood far more clearly than we do. The radical difference between their poetical theory and ours consists, as it appears to me, in this: that, with them, the poetical character of the action in itself, and the conduct of it, was the first consideration; with us, attention is fixed mainly on the value of the separate thoughts and images which occur in the treatment of an action. They regarded the whole; we regard the parts. With them, the action predominated over the expression of it; with us, the expression predominates over the action. Not that they failed in expression, or were inattentive to it; on the contrary, they are the highest models of expression, the unapproached masters of the *grand style*: but their expression is so excellent because it is so admirably kept in its right degree of prominence; because it is so simple and so well subordinated; because it draws its force directly from the pregnancy of the matter which it conveys. For what reason was the Greek tragic poet confined to so limited a range of subjects? Because there are so few actions which unite in themselves, in the highest degree, the conditions of excellence: and it was not thought that on any but an excellent subject could an excellent poem be constructed. A few actions, therefore, eminently adapted for tragedy, maintained almost exclusive possession of the Greek tragic stage; their significance appeared inexhaustible; they were as permanent problems, perpetually offered to the genius of every fresh poet. This too is the reason of what appears to us moderns a certain baldness of expression in Greek tragedy; of the triviality with which we often reproach the remarks of the chorus, where it takes part in the dialogue: that the action itself, the situation of Orestes, or Merope, or Alcmaeon,[5] was to stand the central point of interest, unforgotten, absorbing, principal; that no accessories were for a moment to distract the spectator's attention from this; that the tone of the parts was to be perpetually kept down, in order not to impair the grandiose effect of the whole. The terrible old mythic story on which the drama was founded stood, before he entered the theater, traced in its bare outlines upon the spectator's mind; it stood in his memory, as a group of statuary, faintly seen, at the end of a long and dark vista: then came the poet, embodying outlines, developing situations, not a word wasted, not a sentiment capriciously thrown in: stroke upon stroke, the drama proceeded: the light deepened upon the group; more and more it revealed itself to the riveted gaze of the spectator: until at last, when the final words were spoken, it stood before him in broad sunlight, a model of immortal beauty.

5. Merope, queen of Messene in Greece, appears in plays by Euripides and in Arnold's own play *Merope* (1858). Alcmaeon was the son of a legendary Greek hero, who like Orestes, avenged his father's death by killing his mother. He was the subject of several Greek plays now lost.

This was what a Greek critic demanded; this was what a Greek poet endeavored to effect. It signified nothing to what time an action belonged; we do not find that the *Persae* occupied a particularly high rank among the dramas of Aeschylus, because it represented a matter of contemporary interest:[6] this was not what a cultivated Athenian required, he required that the permanent elements of his nature should be moved; and dramas of which the action, though taken from a long-distant mythic time, yet was calculated to accomplish this in a higher degree than that of the *Persae*, stood higher in his estimation accordingly. The Greeks felt, no doubt, with their exquisite sagacity of taste, that an action of present times was too near them, too much mixed up with what was accidental and passing, to form a sufficiently grand, detached, and self-subsistent object for a tragic poem: such objects belonged to the domain of the comic poet, and of the lighter kinds of poetry. For the more serious kinds, for *pragmatic* poetry, to use an excellent expression of Polybius,[7] they were more difficult and severe in the range of subjects which they permitted. Their theory and practice alike, the admirable treatise of Aristotle, and the unrivaled works of their poets, exclaim with a thousand tongues—"All depends upon the subject; choose a fitting action, penetrate yourself with the feeling of its situations; this done, everything else will follow."

But for all kinds of poetry alike there was one point on which they were rigidly exacting; the adaptability of the subject to the kind of poetry selected, and the careful construction of the poem.

How different a way of thinking from this is ours! We can hardly at the present day understand what Menander[8] meant when he told a man who inquired as to the progress of his comedy that he had finished it, not having yet written a single line, because he had constructed the action of it in his mind. A modern critic would have assured him that the merit of his piece depended on the brilliant things which arose under his pen as he went along. We have poems which seem to exist merely for the sake of single lines and passages; not for the sake of producing any total impression. We have critics who seem to direct their attention merely to detached expressions, to the language about the action, not to the action itself. I verily think that the majority of them do not in their hearts believe that there is such a thing as a total impression to be derived from a poem at all, or to be demanded from a poet; they think the term a commonplace of metaphysical criticism. They will permit the poet to select any action he pleases, and to suffer that action to go as it will, provided he gratifies them with occasional bursts of fine writing, and with a shower of isolated

6. Aeschylus' *Persians* (472 B.C.) portrays the Greek victory over the Persian invaders, which had occurred only a few years before the play was produced.

7. Greek historian (202–120 B.C.).
8. Greek writer of comedies (342–292 B.C.).

thoughts and images. That is, they permit him to leave their poetical sense ungratified, provided that he gratifies their rhetorical sense and their curiosity. Of his neglecting to gratify these, there is little danger. He needs rather to be warned against the danger of attempting to gratify these alone; he needs rather to be perpetually reminded to prefer his action to everything else; so to treat this, as to permit its inherent excellences to develop themselves, without interruption from the intrusion of his personal peculiarities; most fortunate, when he most entirely succeeds in effecting himself, and in enabling a noble action to subsist as it did in nature.

But the modern critic not only permits a false practice; he absolutely prescribes false aims.—"A true allegory of the state of one's own mind in a representative history," the poet is told, "is perhaps the highest thing that one can attempt in the way of poetry." [9] And accordingly he attempts it. An allegory of the state of one's own mind, the highest problem of an art which imitates actions! No assuredly, it is not, it never can be so: no great poetical work has ever been produced with such an aim. *Faust* itself, in which something of the kind is attempted, wonderful passages as it contains, and in spite of the unsurpassed beauty of the scenes which relate to Margaret, *Faust* itself, judged as a whole, and judged strictly as a poetical work, is defective: its illustrious author, the greatest poet of modern times, the greatest critic of all times, would have been the first to acknowledge it; he only defended his work, indeed, by asserting it to be "something incommensurable."[1]

The confusion of the present times is great, the multitude of voices counseling different things bewildering, the number of existing works capable of attracting a young writer's attention and of becoming his models, immense. What he wants is a hand to guide him through the confusion, a voice to prescribe to him the aim which he should keep in view, and to explain to him that the value of the literary works which offer themselves to his attention is relative to their power of helping him forward on his road towards this aim. Such a guide the English writer at the present day will nowhere find. Failing this, all that can be looked for, all indeed that can be desired is, that his attention should be fixed on excellent models; that he may reproduce, at any rate, something of their excellence, by penetrating himself with their works and by catching their spirit, if he cannot be taught to produce what is excellent independently.

Foremost among these models for the English writer stands Shakespeare: a name the greatest perhaps of all poetical names;

9. *North British Review*, XIX (August, 1853), 180 (U.S. edition). Arnold seems not to have noticed that Goethe (a critic he revered) had been cited earlier in the article as the authority for this critical generalization.
1. J. Eckermann, *Conversations with Goethe*, Jan. 3, 1830.

a name never to be mentioned without reverence. I will venture, however, to express a doubt, whether the influence of his works, excellent and fruitful for the readers of poetry, for the great majority, has been of unmixed advantage to the writers of it. Shakespeare indeed chose excellent subjects; the world could afford no better than Macbeth, or Romeo and Juliet, or Othello: he had no theory respecting the necessity of choosing subjects of present import, or the paramount interest attaching to allegories of the state of one's own mind; like all great poets, he knew well what constituted a poetical action; like them, wherever he found such an action, he took it; like them, too, he found his best in past times. But to these general characteristics of all great poets he added a special one of his own; a gift, namely, of happy, abundant, and ingenious expression, eminent and unrivaled; so eminent as irresistibly to strike the attention first in him, and even to throw into comparative shade his other excellences as a poet. Here has been the mischief. These other excellences were his fundamental excellences *as a poet*; what distinguishes the artist from the mere amateur, says Goethe, is *Architectonicè* in the highest sense,[2] that power of execution, which creates, forms, and constitutes: not the profoundness of single thoughts, not the richness of imagery, not the abundance of illustration. But these attractive accessories of a poetical work being more easily seized than the spirit of the whole, and these accessories being possessed by Shakespeare in an unequaled degree, a young writer having recourse to Shakespeare as his model runs great risk of being vanquished and absorbed by them, and, in consequence, of reproducing, according to the measure of his power, these, and these alone.[3] Of this preponderating quality of Shakespeare's genius, accordingly almost the whole of modern English poetry has, it appears to me, felt the influence. To the exclusive attention on the part of his imitators to this it is in a great degree owing, that of the majority of modern poetical works the details alone are valuable, the composition worthless. In reading them one is perpetually reminded of that terrible sentence on a modern French poet: *Il dit tout ce qu'il veut, mais malheureusement il n'a rien à dire.*[4]

Let me give an instance of what I mean. I will take it from the works of the very chief among those who seem to have been formed in the school of Shakespeare: of one whose exquisite

2. In Goethe's essay *Concerning the So-called Dilettantism* (1799) in his *Werke*, 1851, XXV, 322.

3. Cf. Arnold's letter to Clough (Oct. 28, 1852): "More and more I feel that the difference between a mature and a youthful age of the world compels the poetry of the former to use great plainness of speech * * * and that Keats and Shelley were on a false track when they set themselves to reproduce the exuberance of expression, the charm, the richness of images, and the felicity, of the Elizabethan poets."

4. "He says everything he wishes to, but unfortunately he has nothing to say"— a comment on Théophile Gautier (1811–72) whose emphasis on style was severely criticized by Arnold in his late essay *Wordsworth* (see below).

genius and pathetic death render him forever interesting. I will
take the poem of *Isabella, or the Pot of Basil,* by Keats. I choose
this rather than the *Endymion,* because the latter work (which a
modern critic has classed with the *Fairy Queen!* [5]) although undoubtedly there blows through it the breath of genius, is yet as a
whole so utterly incoherent, as not strictly to merit the name of a
poem at all. The poem of *Isabella,* then, is a perfect treasure-
house of graceful and felicitous words and images: almost in
every stanza there occurs one of those vivid and picturesque turns
of expression, by which the object is made to flash upon the eye
of the mind, and which thrill the reader with a sudden delight.
This one short poem contains, perhaps, a greater number of
happy single expressions which one could quote than all the extant tragedies of Sophocles. But the action, the story? The action in
itself is an excellent one; but so feebly is it conceived by the poet,
so loosely constructed, that the effect produced by it, in and for itself, is absolutely null. Let the reader, after he has finished the poem
of Keats, turn to the same story in the *Decameron:* [6] he will then
feel how pregnant and interesting the same action has become in the
hands of a great artist, who above all things delineates his object;
who subordinates expression to that which it is designed to express.

I have said that the imitators of Shakespeare, fixing their attention on his wonderful gift of expression, have directed their imitation to this, neglecting his other excellences. These excellences,
the fundamental excellences of poetical art, Shakespeare no doubt
possessed them—possessed many of them in a splendid degree;
but it may perhaps be doubted whether even he himself did not
sometimes give scope to his faculty of expression to the prejudice
of a higher poetical duty. For we must never forget that Shakespeare is the great poet he is from his skill in discerning and firmly
conceiving an excellent action, from his power of intensely feeling
a situation, of intimately associating himself with a character; not
from his gift of expression, which rather even leads him astray,
degenerating sometimes into a fondness for curiosity of expression,
into an irritability of fancy, which seems to make it impossible
for him to say a thing plainly, even when the press of the action
demands the very directest language, or its level character the
very simplest. Mr. Hallam, than whom it is impossible to find a
saner and more judicious critic, has had the courage (for at the
present day it needs courage) to remark, how extremely and faul-
tily difficult Shakespeare's language often is.[7] It is so: you may
find main scenes in some of his greatest tragedies, *King Lear* for
instance, where the language is so artificial, so curiously tortured,

---

5. In the *North British Review,* XIX
(Aug., 1853), 172, 74, Keats' *Endymion*
is twice linked with Spenser's *Faerie
Queene* as "leisurely compositions of the
sweet sensuous order."

6. Boccaccio's *Decameron,* 4th day, 5th
novel.
7. Henry Hallam, historian (1779–
1859), *Introduction to the Literature of
Europe* (1838–39), Ch. 23.

and so difficult, that every speech has to be read two or three times before its meaning can be comprehended. This over-curiousness of expression is indeed but the excessive employment of a wonderful gift—of the power of saying a thing in a happier way than any other man; nevertheless, it is carried so far that one understands what M. Guizot meant, when he said that Shakespeare appears in his language to have tried all styles except that of simplicity.[8] He has not the severe and scrupulous self-restraint of the ancients, partly no doubt, because he had a far less cultivated and exacting audience. He has indeed a far wider range than they had, a far richer fertility of thought; in this respect he rises above them. In his strong conception of his subject, in the genuine way in which he is penetrated with it, he resembles them, and is unlike the moderns. But in the accurate limitation of it, the conscientious rejection of superfluities, the simple and rigorous development of it from the first line of his work to the last, he falls below them, and comes nearer to the moderns. In his chief works, besides what he has of his own, he has the elementary soundness of the ancients; he has their important action and their large and broad manner; but he has not their purity of method. He is therefore a less safe model; for what he has of his own is personal, and inseparable from his own rich nature; it may be imitated and exaggerated, it cannot be learned or applied as an art. He is above all suggestive; more valuable, therefore, to young writers as men than as artists. But clearness of arrangement, rigor of development, simplicity of style—these may to a certain extent be learned; and these may, I am convinced, be learned best from the ancients, who although infinitely less suggestive than Shakespeare, are thus, to the artist, more instructive.

What, then, it will be asked, are the ancients to be our sole models? the ancients with their comparatively narrow range of experience, and their widely different circumstances? Not, certainly, that which is narrow in the ancients, nor that in which we can no longer sympathize. An action like the action of the *Antigone* of Sophocles, which turns upon the conflict between the heroine's duty to her brother's corpse and that to the laws of her country, is no longer one in which it is possible that we should feel a deep interest. I am speaking too, it will be remembered, not of the best sources of intellectual stimulus for the general reader, but of the best models of instruction for the individual writer. This last may certainly learn of the ancients, better than anywhere else, three things which it is vitally important for him to know: the all-importance of the choice of a subject; the necessity of accurate construction; and the subordinate character of expression. He will learn from them how unspeakably superior

8. F. P. G. Guizot, French historian (1787–1874), discussing Shakespeare's sonnets in his *Shakespeare et son Temps* (1852), p. 114.

is the effect of the one moral impression left by a great action treated as a whole, to the effect produced by the most striking single thought or by the happiest image. As he penetrates into the spirit of the great classical works, as he becomes gradually aware of their intense significance, their noble simplicity, and their calm pathos, he will be convinced that it is this effect, unity and profoundness of moral impression, at which the ancient poets aimed; that it is this which constitutes the grandeur of their works, and which makes them immortal. He will desire to direct his own efforts towards producing the same effect. Above all, he will deliver himself from the jargon of modern criticism, and escape the danger of producing poetical works conceived in the spirit of the passing time, and which partake of its transitoriness.

The present age makes great claims upon us; we owe it service, it will not be satisfied without our admiration. I know not how it is, but their commerce with the ancients appears to me to produce, in those who constantly practice it, a steadying and composing effect upon their judgment, not of literary works only, but of men and events in general. They are like persons who have had a very weighty and impressive experience; they are more truly than others under the empire of facts, and more independent of the language current among those with whom they live. They wish neither to applaud nor to revile their age; they wish to know what it is, what it can give them, and whether this is what they want. What they want, they know very well; they want to educe and cultivate what is best and noblest in themselves; they know, too, that this is no easy task—χαλεπὸν, as Pittacus said, χαλεπὸν ἐσθλὸν ἔμμεναι⁹—and they ask themselves sincerely whether their age and its literature can assist them in the attempt. If they are endeavoring to practice any art, they remember the plain and simple proceedings of the old artists, who attained their grand results by penetrating themselves with some noble and significant action, not by inflating themselves with a belief in the pre-eminent importance and greatness of their own times. They do not talk of their mission, nor of interpreting their age, nor of the coming poet; all this, they know, is the mere delirium of vanity; their business is not to praise their age, but to afford to the men who live in it the highest pleasure which they are capable of feeling. If asked to afford this by means of subjects drawn from the age itself, they ask what special fitness the present age has for supplying them. They are told that it is an era of progress, an age commissioned to carry out the great ideas of industrial development and social amelioration. They reply that with all this they can do nothing; that the elements they need for the exercise of their art are great actions, calculated powerfully and delightfully to affect what is permanent in the human soul;

9. "It is hard to be good." An aphorism of Pittacus, a Greek sage, 7th century B.C.

that so far as the present age can supply such actions, they will gladly make use of them; but that an age wanting in moral grandeur can with difficulty supply such, and an age of spiritual discomfort with difficulty be powerfully and delightfully affected by them.

A host of voices will indignantly rejoin that the present age is inferior to the past neither in moral grandeur nor in spiritual health. He who possesses the discipline I speak of will content himself with remembering the judgments passed upon the present age, in this respect, by the two men, the one of strongest head, the other of widest culture, whom it has produced; by Goethe and by Niebuhr.[1] It will be sufficient for him that he knows the opinions held by these two great men respecting the present age and its literature; and that he feels assured in his own mind that their aims and demands upon life were such as he would wish, at any rate, his own to be; and their judgment as to what is impeding and disabling such as he may safely follow. He will not, however, maintain a hostile attitude towards the false pretensions of his age: he will content himself with not being overwhelmed by them. He will esteem himself fortunate if he can succeed in banishing from his mind all feelings of contradiction, and irritation, and impatience; in order to delight himself with the contemplation of some noble action of a heroic time, and to enable others, through his representation of it, to delight in it also.

I am far indeed from making any claim, for myself, that I possess this discipline; or for the following poems, that they breathe its spirit. But I say, that in the sincere endeavor to learn and practice, amid the bewildering confusion of our times, what is sound and true in poetical art, I seemed to myself to find the only sure guidance, the only solid footing, among the ancients. They, at any rate, knew what they wanted in art, and we do not. It is this uncertainty which is disheartening, and not hostile criticism. How often have I felt this when reading words of disparagement or of cavil: that it is the uncertainty as to what is really to be aimed at which makes our difficulty, not the dissatisfaction of the critic, who himself suffers from the same uncertainty. *Non me tua fervida terrent Dicta; . . . Dii me terrent, et Jupiter hostis.*[2]

Two kinds of *dilettanti*, says Goethe, there are in poetry: he who neglects the indispensable mechanical part, and thinks he has done enough if he shows spirituality and feeling; and he who seeks to arrive at poetry merely by mechanism, in which he can acquire an artisan's readiness, and is without soul and matter.[3] And he adds, that the first does most harm to art, and the last to

---

1. B. G. Niebuhr (1776–1831), German historian.
2. Virgil, *Aeneid* XII. 894–95: "Your fiery speeches do not frighten me; it is the gods and the enmity of Jupiter that frighten me" (Turnus, a warrior abandoned by the gods, is replying to Aeneas who has taunted him with being afraid).
3. See note 2, Goethe's essay, above.

himself. If we must be *dilettanti;* if it is impossible for us, under the circumstances amidst which we live, to think clearly, to feel nobly, and to delineate firmly; if we cannot attain to the mastery of the great artists; let us, at least, have so much respect for our art as to prefer it to ourselves. Let us not bewilder our successors; let us transmit to them the practice of poetry, with its boundaries and wholesome regulative laws, under which excellent works may again, perhaps, at some future time, be produced, not yet fallen into oblivion through our neglect, not yet condemned and canceled by the influence of their eternal enemy, caprice.

From The Function of Criticism at the Present Time[1]

Many objections have been made to a proposition which, in some remarks of mine on translating Homer,[2] I ventured to put forth; a proposition about criticism, and its importance at the present day. I said: "Of the literature of France and Germany, as of the intellect of Europe in general, the main effort, for now many years, has been a critical effort; the endeavor, in all branches of knowledge, theology, philosophy, history, art, science, to see the object as in itself it really is." I added, that owing to the operation in English literature of certain causes, "almost the last thing for which one would come to English literature is just that very thing which now Europe most desires—criticism"; and that the power and value of English literature was thereby impaired. More than one rejoinder declared that the importance I here assigned to criticism was excessive, and asserted the inherent superiority of the creative effort of the human spirit over its critical effort. And the other day, having been led by a Mr. Shairp's excellent notice of Wordsworth[3] to turn again to his biography, I found, in the words of this great man, whom I, for one, must always listen to with the profoundest respect,

1. This essay served as an introduction to Arnold's volume of *Essays in Criticism* (1865). As a declaration of intentions, it can serve as a standard for measuring his total accomplishment in criticism. The essay makes us aware that criticism, for Arnold, meant a great deal more than casual book-reviewing or mere censoriousness. He was not a Utilitarian, yet his object in this essay is to show that good criticism is useful. Creative writers, he argues, can profit in a special way from good criticism, but all of us can also derive from it benefits of the greatest value. In particular, we may develop a civilized attitude of mind in which to examine the social, political, aesthetic, and religious problems which confront us.
2. *On Translating Homer* (1861).
3. J. C. Shairp's essay *Wordsworth:*

The Man and the Poet was published in 1864. Arnold comments in a footnote: "I cannot help thinking that a practice, common in England during the last century, and still followed in France, of printing a notice of this kind—a notice by a competent critic—to serve as an introduction to an eminent author's works, might be revived among us with advantage. To introduce all succeeding editions of Wordsworth, Mr. Shairp's notice might, it seems to me, excellently serve; it is written from the point of view of an admirer, nay, of a disciple, and that is right; but then the disciple must be also, as in this case he is, a critic, a man of letters, not, as too often happens, some relation or friend with no qualification for his task except affection for his author."

a sentence passed on the critic's business, which seems to justify every possible disparagement of it. Wordsworth says in one of his letters:

"The writers in these publications (the Reviews), while they prosecute their inglorious employment, cannot be supposed to be in a state of mind very favorable for being affected by the finer influences of a thing so pure as genuine poetry."

And a trustworthy reporter of his conversation quotes a more elaborate judgment to the same effect:

"Wordsworth holds the critical power very low, infinitely lower than the inventive; and he said today that if the quantity of time consumed in writing critiques on the works of others were given to original composition, of whatever kind it might be, it would be much better employed; it would make a man find out sooner his own level, and it would do infinitely less mischief. A false or malicious criticism may do much injury to the minds of others; a stupid invention, either in prose or verse, is quite harmless."

It is almost too much to expect of poor human nature, that a man capable of producing some effect in one line of literature, should, for the greater good of society, voluntarily doom himself to impotence and obscurity in another. Still less is this to be expected from men addicted to the composition of the "false or malicious criticism" of which Wordsworth speaks. However, everybody would admit that a false or malicious criticism had better never have been written. Everybody, too, would be willing to admit, as a general proposition, that the critical faculty is lower than the inventive. But is it true that criticism is really, in itself, a baneful and injurious employment; is it true that all time given to writing critiques on the works of others would be much better employed if it were given to original composition, of whatever kind this may be? Is it true that Johnson had better have gone on producing more *Irenes*[4] instead of writing his *Lives of the Poets*; nay, is it certain that Wordsworth himself was better employed in making his Ecclesiastical Sonnets[5] than when he made his celebrated Preface so full of criticism, and criticism of the works of others? Wordsworth was himself a great critic, and it is to be sincerely regretted that he has not left us more criticism; Goethe was one of the greatest of critics, and we may sincerely congratulate ourselves that he has left us so much criticism. Without wasting time over the exaggeration which Wordsworth's judgment on criticism clearly contains, or over an attempt to trace the causes—not difficult, I think, to be traced— which may have led Wordsworth to this exaggeration, a critic may

4. *Irene* is the name of a clumsy play by Samuel Johnson.
5. A sonnet sequence by Wordsworth, usually regarded as minor verse. The Preface is to his *Lyrical Ballads* of 1800.

with advantage seize an occasion for trying his own conscience, and for asking himself of what real service, at any given moment, the practice of criticism either is or may be made to his own mind and spirit, and to the minds and spirits of others.

The critical power is of lower rank than the creative. True; but in assenting to this proposition, one or two things are to be kept in mind. It is undeniable that the exercise of a creative power, that a free creative activity, is the highest function of man; it is proved to be so by man's finding in it his true happiness. But it is undeniable, also, that men may have the sense of exercising this free creative activity in other ways than in producing great works of literature or art; if it were not so, all but a very few men would be shut out from the true happiness of all men. They may have it in well-doing, they may have it in learning, they may have it even in criticizing. This is one thing to be kept in mind. Another is, that the exercise of the creative power in the production of great works of literature or art, however high this exercise of it may rank, is not at all epochs and under all conditions possible; and that therefore labor may be vainly spent in attempting it, which might with more fruit be used in preparing for it, in rendering it possible. This creative power works with elements, with materials; what if it has not those materials, those elements, ready for its use? In that case it must surely wait till they are ready. Now, in literature—I will limit myself to literature, for it is about literature that the question arises—the elements with which the creative power works are ideas; the best ideas on every matter which literature touches, current at the time. At any rate we may lay it down as certain that in modern literature no manifestation of the creative power not working with these can be very important or fruitful. And I say *current* at the time, not merely accessible at the time; for creative literary genius does not principally show itself in discovering new ideas, that is rather the business of the philosopher. The grand work of literary genius is a work of synthesis and exposition, not of analysis and discovery; its gift lies in the faculty of being happily inspired by a certain intellectual and spiritual atmosphere, by a certain order of ideas, when it finds itself in them; of dealing divinely with these ideas, presenting them in the most effective and attractive combinations—making beautiful works with them, in short. But it must have the atmosphere, it must find itself amidst the order of ideas, in order to work freely; and these it is not so easy to command. This is why great creative epochs in literature are so rare, this is why there is so much that is unsatisfactory in the productions of many men of real genius; because, for the creation of a masterwork of literature two powers must concur, the power of the man and the power of the moment, and the man is not enough without the moment; the creative power has, for its happy exercise, appointed elements, and those elements are not in its own control.

Nay, they are more within the control of the critical power. It is the business of the critical power, as I said in the words already quoted, "in all branches of knowledge, theology, philosophy, history, art, science, to see the object as in itself it really is." Thus it tends, at last, to make an intellectual situation of which the creative power can profitably avail itself. It tends to establish an order of ideas, if not absolutely true, yet true by comparison with that which it displaces; to make the best ideas prevail. Presently these new ideas reach society, the touch of truth is the touch of life, and there is a stir and growth everywhere; out of this stir and growth come the creative epochs of literature.

Or, to narrow our range, and quit these considerations of the general march of genius and of society—considerations which are apt to become too abstract and impalpable—everyone can see that a poet, for instance, ought to know life and the world before dealing with them in poetry; and life and the world being in modern times very complex things, the creation of a modern poet, to be worth much, implies a great critical effort behind it; else it must be a comparatively poor, barren, and short-lived affair. This is why Byron's poetry had so little endurance in it, and Goethe's so much; both Byron and Goethe had a great productive power, but Goethe's was nourished by a great critical effort providing the true materials for it, and Byron's was not; Goethe knew life and the world, the poet's necessary subjects, much more comprehensively and thoroughly than Byron. He knew a great deal more of them, and he knew them much more as they really are.

It has long seemed to me that the burst of creative activity in our literature, through the first quarter of this century, had about it in fact something premature; and that from this cause its productions are doomed, most of them, in spite of the sanguine hopes which accompanied and do still accompany them, to prove hardly more lasting than the productions of far less splendid epochs. And this prematureness comes from its having proceeded without having its proper data, without sufficient materials to work with. In other words, the English poetry of the first quarter of this century, with plenty of energy, plenty of creative force, did not know enough. This makes Byron so empty of matter, Shelley so incoherent, Wordsworth even, profound as he is, yet so wanting in completeness and variety. Wordsworth cared little for books, and disparaged Goethe. I admire Wordsworth, as he is, so much that I cannot wish him different; and it is vain, no doubt, to imagine such a man different from what he is, to suppose that he *could* have been different. But surely the one thing wanting to make Wordsworth an even greater poet than he is—his thought richer, and his influence of wider application—was that he should have read more books,

among them, no doubt, those of that Goethe whom he disparaged
without reading him.

But to speak of books and reading may easily lead to a misunderstanding here. It was not really books and reading that lacked to
our poetry at this epoch: Shelley had plenty of reading, Coleridge
had immense reading. Pindar and Sophocles—as we all say so glibly,
and often with so little discernment of the real import of what we
are saying—had not many books; Shakespeare was no deep reader.
True; but in the Greece of Pindar and Sophocles, in the England
of Shakespeare, the poet lived in a current of ideas in the highest
degree animating and nourishing to the creative power; society was,
in the fullest measure, permeated by fresh thought, intelligent and
alive. And this state of things is the true basis for the creative
power's exercise, in this it finds its data, its materials, truly ready
for its hand; all the books and reading in the world are only valuable
as they are helps to this. Even when this does not actually exist,
books and reading may enable a man to construct a kind of semblance of it in his own mind, a world of knowledge and intelligence
in which he may live and work. This is by no means an equivalent
to the artist for the nationally diffused life and thought of the
epochs of Sophocles or Shakespeare; but, besides that it may be a
means of preparation for such epochs, it does really constitute, if
many share in it, a quickening and sustaining atmosphere of great
value. Such an atmosphere the many-sided learning and the long
and widely combined critical effort of Germany formed for Goethe,
when he lived and worked. There was no national glow of life and
thought there as in the Athens of Pericles[6] or the England of Elizabeth. That was the poet's weakness. But there was a sort of equivalent for it in the complete culture and unfettered thinking of a
large body of Germans. That was his strength. In the England of
the first quarter of this century there was neither a national glow
of life and thought, such as we had in the age of Elizabeth, nor
yet a culture and a force of learning and criticism such as were to
be found in Germany. Therefore the creative power of poetry
wanted, for success in the highest sense, materials and a basis; a
thorough interpretation of the world was necessarily denied to it.

At first sight it seems strange that out of the immense stir of the
French Revolution and its age should not have come a crop of
works of genius equal to that which came out of the stir of the great
productive time of Greece, or out of that of the Renascence, with
its powerful episode the Reformation. But the truth is that the stir
of the French Revolution took a character which essentially distinguished it from such movements as these. These were, in the
main, disinterestedly intellectual and spiritual movements; movements in which the human spirit looked for its satisfaction in itself

6. Pericles (d. 429 B.C.), the leading
statesman of Athens during a period of
the city's most outstanding achievements
in art, literature, and politics.

and in the increased play of its own activity. The French Revolution took a political, practical character. The movement, which went on in France under the old *régime*, from 1700 to 1789, was far more really akin than that of the Revolution itself to the movement of the Renascence; the France of Voltaire and Rousseau told far more powerfully upon the mind of Europe than the France of the Revolution. Goethe reproached this last expressly with having "thrown quiet culture back." Nay, and the true key to how much in our Byron, even in our Wordsworth, is this!—that they had their source in a great movement of feeling, not in a great movement of mind. The French Revolution, however—that object of so much blind love and so much blind hatred—found undoubtedly its motive power in the intelligence of men, and not in their practical sense; this is what distinguishes it from the English Revolution of Charles the First's time. This is what makes it a more spiritual event than our Revolution, an event of much more powerful and worldwide interest, though practically less successful; it appeals to an order of ideas which are universal, certain, permanent. 1789 asked of a thing, Is it rational? 1642 asked of a thing, Is it legal? or, when it went furthest, Is it according to conscience? This is the English fashion, a fashion to be treated, within its own sphere, with the highest respect; for its success, within its own sphere, has been prodigious. But what is law in one place is not law in another; what is law here today is not law even here tomorrow; and as for conscience, what is binding on one man's conscience is not binding on another's. The old woman who threw her stool at the head of the surpliced minister in St. Giles's Church at Edinburgh[7] obeyed an impulse to which millions of the human race may be permitted to remain strangers. But the prescriptions of reason are absolute, unchanging, of universal validity; *to count by tens is the easiest way of counting*—that is a proposition of which everyone, from here to the Antipodes, feels the force; at least I should say so if we did not live in a country where it is not impossible that any morning we may find a letter in the *Times* declaring that a decimal coinage is an absurdity.[7a] That a whole nation should have been penetrated with an enthusiasm for pure reason, and with an ardent zeal for making its prescriptions triumph, is a very remarkable thing, when we consider how little of mind, or anything so worthy and quickening as mind, comes into the motives which alone, in general, impel great masses of men. In spite of the extravagant direction given to this enthusiasm, in spite of the crimes and follies in which it lost itself, the French Revolution derives from the force, truth, and universality of the ideas which it took for its law, and from the passion

7. In 1637 rioting broke out in Scotland against a new kind of church service prescribed by Charles I. The riot was started by an old woman hurling a stool at a clergyman.
7a. In 1863 a proposal in Parliament to introduce the French decimal system for weights and measures had provoked articles in the *Times* defending the English system (of ounces and pounds or inches and feet) as more practical.

with which it could inspire a multitude for these ideas, a unique and still living power; it is—it will probably long remain—the greatest, the most animating event in history. And as no sincere passion for the things of the mind, even though it turn out in many respects an unfortunate passion, is ever quite thrown away and quite barren of good, France has reaped from hers one fruit—the natural and legitimate fruit though not precisely the grand fruit she expected: she is the country in Europe where *the people* is most alive.

But the mania for giving an immediate political and practical application to all these fine ideas of the reason was fatal. Here an Englishman is in his element: on this theme we can all go on for hours. And all we are in the habit of saying on it has undoubtedly a great deal of truth. Ideas cannot be too much prized in and for themselves, cannot be too much lived with; but to transport them abruptly into the world of politics and practice, violently to revolutionize this world to their bidding—that is quite another thing. There is the world of ideas and there is the world of practice; the French are often for suppressing the one and the English the other; but neither is to be suppressed. A member of the House of Commons said to me the other day: "That a thing is an anomaly, I consider to be no objection to it whatever." I venture to think he was wrong; that a thing is an anomaly *is* an objection to it, but absolutely and in the sphere of ideas: it is not necessarily, under such and such circumstances, or at such and such a moment, an objection to it in the sphere of politics and practice. Joubert[8] has said beautifully: "*C'est la force et le droit qui règlent toutes choses dans le monde; la force en attendant le droit.*"—"Force and right are the governors of this world; force till right is ready." *Force till right is ready*; and till right is ready, force, the existing order of things, is justified, is the legitimate ruler. But right is something moral, and implies inward recognition, free assent of the will; we are not ready for right—*right*, so far as we are concerned, *is not ready*—until we have attained this sense of seeing it and willing it. The way in which for us it may change and transform force, the existing order of things, and become, in its turn, the legitimate ruler of the world, should depend on the way in which, when our time comes, we see it and will it. Therefore for other people enamored of their own newly discerned right, to attempt to impose it upon us as ours, and violently to substitute their right for our force, is an act of tyranny, and to be resisted. It sets at nought the second great half of our maxim, *force till right is ready.* This was the grand error of the French Revolution; and its movement of ideas, by quitting the intellectual sphere and rushing furiously into the political sphere, ran, indeed, a prodigious and memorable course, but produced no such intellectual fruit as the movement of ideas of the Renascence,

8. Joseph Joubert (1754–1824), French moralist about whom Arnold wrote one of his *Essays in Criticism*.

and created, in opposition to itself, what I may call an *epoch of concentration*. The great force of that epoch of concentration was England; and the great voice of that epoch of concentration was Burke.[9] It is the fashion to treat Burke's writings on the French Revolution as superannuated and conquered by the event; as the eloquent but unphilosophical tirades of bigotry and prejudice. I will not deny that they are often disfigured by the violence and passion of the moment, and that in some directions Burke's view was bounded, and his observation therefore at fault. But on the whole, and for those who can make the needful corrections, what distinguishes these writings is their profound, permanent, fruitful, philosophical truth. They contain the true philosophy of an epoch of concentration, dissipate the heavy atmosphere which its own nature is apt to engender round it, and make its resistance rational instead of mechanical.

But Burke is so great because, almost alone in England, he brings thought to bear upon politics, he saturates politics with thought. It is his accident that his ideas were at the service of an epoch of concentration, not of an epoch of expansion; it is his characteristic that he so lived by ideas, and had such a source of them welling up within him, that he could float even an epoch of concentration and English Tory politics with them. It does not hurt him that Dr. Price[1] and the Liberals were enraged with him; it does not even hurt him that George the Third and the Tories were enchanted with him. His greatness is that he lived in a world which neither English Liberalism nor English Toryism is apt to enter—the world of ideas, not the world of catchwords and party habits. So far is it from being really true of him that he "to party gave up what was meant for mankind,"[2] that at the very end of his fierce struggle with the French Revolution, after all his invectives against its false pretensions, hollowness, and madness, with his sincere convictions of its michievousness, he can close a memorandum on the best means of combating it, some of the last pages [2a] he ever wrote—the *Thoughts on French Affairs*, in December 1791—with these striking words:

"The evil is stated, in my opinion, as it exists. The remedy must be where power, wisdom, and information, I hope, are more united with good intentions than they can be with me. I have done with this subject, I believe, forever. It has given me many anxious moments for the last two years. *If a great change is to be made in human affairs, the minds of men will be fitted to it; the general opinions and feelings will draw that way. Every fear, every hope will*

9. Edmund Burke (1729–97), prominent statesman and author of *Reflections on the French Revolution* (1790), which expressed the conservative opposition to revolutionary theories.
1. Richard Price (1723–91), a prorevolutionary clergyman who was an opponent of Burke's.

2. See Oliver Goldsmith's poem, *Retaliation* (1774).
2a. Arnold was mistaken; Burke continued to write for another six years after 1791. According to Arnold's editor, R. H. Super, the mistake was caused by misunderstanding a passage in one of Burke's letters.

forward it; and then they who persist in opposing this mighty current in human affairs, will appear rather to resist the decrees of Providence itself, than the mere designs of men. They will not be resolute and firm, but perverse and obstinate."

That return of Burke upon himself has always seemed to me one of the finest things in English literature, or indeed in any literature. That is what I call living by ideas: when one side of a question has long had your earnest support, when all your feelings are engaged, when you hear all round you no language but one, when your party talks this language like a steam engine and can imagine no other— still to be able to think, still to be irresistibly carried, if so it be, by the current of thought to the opposite side of the question, and, like Balaam,[3] to be unable to speak anything *but what the Lord has put in your mouth.* I know nothing more striking, and I must add that I know nothing more un-English.

For the Englishman in general is like my friend the Member of Parliament, and believes, point-blank, that for a thing to be an anomaly is absolutely no objection to it whatever. He is like the Lord Auckland of Burke's day, who, in a memorandum on the French Revolution, talks of certain "miscreants, assuming the name of philosophers, who have presumed themselves capable of establishing a new system of society." The Englishman has been called a political animal, and he values what is political and practical so much that ideas easily become objects of dislike in his eyes, and thinkers, "miscreants," because ideas and thinkers have rashly meddled with politics and practice. This would be all very well if the dislike and neglect confined themselves to ideas transported out of their own sphere, and meddling rashly with practice; but they are inevitably extended to ideas as such, and to the whole life of intelligence; practice is everything, a free play of the mind is nothing. The notion of the free play of the mind upon all subjects being a pleasure in itself, being an object of desire, being an essential provider of elements without which a nation's spirit, whatever compensations it may have for them, must, in the long run, die of inanition, hardly enters into an Englishman's thoughts. It is noticeable that the word *curiosity*, which in other languages is used in a good sense, to mean, as a high and fine quality of man's nature, just this disinterested love of a free play of the mind on all subjects, for its own sake—it is noticeable, I say, that this word has in our language no sense of the kind, no sense but a rather bad and disparaging one. But criticism, real criticism, is essentially the exercise of this very quality. It obeys an instinct prompting it to try to know the best that is known and thought in the world, irrespectively of practice, politics, and everything of the kind; and to value knowledge and thought as they approach this best, without the intrusion

3. Cf. Numbers xxii.38.

of any other considerations whatever. This is an instinct for which there is, I think, little original sympathy in the practical English nature, and what there was of it has undergone a long benumbing period of blight and suppression in the epoch of concentration which followed the French Revolution.

But epochs of concentration cannot well endure forever; epochs of expansion, in the due course of things, follow them. Such an epoch of expansion seems to be opening in this country. In the first place all danger of a hostile forcible pressure of foreign ideas upon our practice has long disappeared; like the traveler in the fable, therefore, we begin to wear our cloak a little more loosely.[4] Then, with a long peace, the ideas of Europe steal gradually and amicably in, and mingle, though in infinitesimally small quantities at a time, with our own notions. Then, too, in spite of all that is said about the absorbing and brutalizing influence of our passionate material progress, it seems to me indisputable that this progress is likely, though not certain, to lead in the end to an apparition of intellectual life; and that man, after he has made himself perfectly comfortable and has now to determine what to do with himself next, may begin to remember that he has a mind, and that the mind may be made the source of great pleasure. I grant it is mainly the privilege of faith, at present, to discern this end to our railways, our business, and our fortune-making; but we shall see if, here as elsewhere, faith is not in the end the true prophet. Our ease, our traveling, and our unbounded liberty to hold just as hard and securely as we please to the practice to which our notions have given birth, all tend to beget an inclination to deal a little more freely with these notions themselves, to canvass them a little, to penetrate a little into their real nature. Flutterings of curiosity, in the foreign sense of the word, appear amongst us, and it is in these that criticism must look to find its account. Criticism first; a time of true creative activity, perhaps—which, as I have said, must inevitably be preceded amongst us by a time of criticism—hereafter, when criticism has done its work.

It is of the last importance that English criticism should clearly discern what rule for its course, in order to avail itself of the field now opening to it, and to produce fruit for the future, it ought to take. The rule may be summed up in one word—*disinterestedness*.[5] And how is criticism to show disinterestedness? By keeping aloof from what is called "the practical view of things"; by resolutely following the law of its own nature, which is to be a free play of the mind on all subjects which it touches. By steadily refusing to lend itself to any of those ulterior, political, practical considerations about ideas, which plenty of people will be sure to attach to them,

4. See Aesop's fable of the wind and the sun.
5. This key word in Arnold's argument connotes independence and objectivity of mind. It should not be confused, as it often is, with mere lack of interest.

which perhaps ought often to be attached to them, which in this country at any rate are certain to be attached to them quite sufficiently, but which criticism has really nothing to do with. Its business is, as I have said, simply to know the best that is known and thought in the world, and by in its turn making this known, to create a current of true and fresh ideas. Its business is to do this with inflexible honesty, with due ability; but its business is to do no more, and to leave alone all questions of practical consequences and applications, questions which will never fail to have due prominence given to them. Else criticism, besides being really false to its own nature, merely continues in the old rut which it has hitherto followed in this country, and will certainly miss the chance now given to it. For what is at present the bane of criticism in this country? It is that practical considerations cling to it and stifle it. It subserves interests not its own. Our organs of criticism are organs of men and parties having practical ends to serve, and with them those practical ends are the first thing and the play of mind the second; so much play of mind as is compatible with the prosecution of those practical ends is all that is wanted. An organ like the *Revue des Deux Mondes*,[6] having for its main function to understand and utter the best that is known and thought in the world, existing, it may be said, as just an organ for a free play of the mind, we have not. But we have the *Edinburgh Review*, existing as an organ of the old Whigs, and for as much play of mind as may suit its being that; we have the *Quarterly Review*, existing as an organ of the Tories, and for as much play of mind as may suit its being that; we have the *British Quarterly Review*, existing as an organ of the political Dissenters, and for as much play of mind as may suit its being that; we have the *Times*, existing as an organ of the common, satisfied, well-to-do Englishman, and for as much play of mind as may suit its being that. And so on through all the various fractions, political and religious, of our society; every fraction has, as such, its organ of criticism, but the notion of combining all fractions in the common pleasure of a free disinterested play of mind meets with no favor. Directly this play of mind wants to have more scope, and to forget the pressure of practical considerations a little, it is checked, it is made to feel the chain. We saw this the other day in the extinction, so much to be regretted, of the *Home and Foreign Review*.[6a] Perhaps in no organ of criticism in this country was there so much knowledge, so much play of mind; but these could not save it. The *Dublin Review* subordinates play of mind to the practical business of English and Irish Catholicism, and lives. It must needs be that men should act in sects and parties, that each of these sects and parties should have its organ, and should make

---

6. An international magazine of exceptionally high quality, founded in Paris in 1829.

6a. A liberal Catholic periodical, founded in 1862, which ceased publication in 1864.

this organ subserve the interests of its action; but it would be well, too, that there should be a criticism, not the minister of these interests, not their enemy, but absolutely and entirely independent of them. No other criticism will ever attain any real authority or make any real way towards its end—the creating a current of true and fresh ideas.

It is because criticism has so little kept in the pure intellectual sphere, has so little detached itself from practice, has been so directly polemical and controversial, that it has so ill accomplished, in this country, its best spiritual work; which is to keep man from a self-satisfaction which is retarding and vulgarizing, to lead him towards perfection, by making his mind dwell upon what is excellent in itself, and the absolute beauty and fitness of things. A polemical practical criticism makes men blind even to the ideal imperfection of their practice, makes them willingly assert its ideal perfection, in order the better to secure it against attack; and clearly this is narrowing and baneful for them. If they were reassured on the practical side, speculative considerations of ideal perfection they might be brought to entertain, and their spiritual horizon would thus gradually widen. Sir Charles Adderley[7] says to the Warwickshire farmers:

"Talk of the improvement of breed! Why, the race we ourselves represent, the men and women, the old Anglo-Saxon race, are the best breed in the whole world. . . . The absence of a too enervating climate, too unclouded skies, and a too luxurious nature, has produced so vigorous a race of people, and has rendered us so superior to all the world."

Mr. Roebuck[8] says to the Sheffield cutlers:

"I look around me and ask what is the state of England? Is not property safe? Is not every man able to say what he likes? Can you not walk from one end of England to the other in perfect security? I ask you whether, the world over or in past history, there is anything like it? Nothing. I pray that our unrivaled happiness may last."

Now obviously there is a peril for poor human nature in words and thoughts of such exuberant self-satisfaction, until we find ourselves safe in the streets of the Celestial City.

Das wenige verschwindet leicht dem Blicke
Der vorwärts sieht, wie viel noch übrig bleibt—[9]

says Goethe; "the little that is done seems nothing when we look forward and see how much we have yet to do." Clearly this is a

---

7. 1814–1905; conservative politician and wealthy landowner.
8. John Arthur Roebuck (1801–79), radical politician and representative in Parliament for the industrial city of Sheffield.
9. Goethe's *Iphigenie auf Tauris* I.ii.91–92.

better line of reflection for weak humanity, so long as it remains on this earthly field of labor and trial.

But neither Sir Charles Adderley nor Mr. Roebuck is by nature inaccessible to considerations of this sort. They only lose sight of them owing to the controversial life we all lead, and the practical form which all speculation takes with us. They have in view opponents whose aim is not ideal, but practical; and in their zeal to uphold their own practice against these innovators, they go so far as even to attribute to this practice an ideal perfection. Somebody has been wanting to introduce a six-pound franchise,[1] or to abolish church-rates, or to collect agricultural statistics by force, or to diminish local self-government. How natural, in reply to such proposals, very likely improper or ill-timed, to go a little beyond the mark and to say stoutly, "Such a race of people as we stand, so superior to all the world! The old Anglo-Saxon race, the best breed in the whole world! I pray that our unrivaled happiness may last! I ask you whether, the world over or in past history, there is anything like it?" And so long as criticism answers this dithyramb by insisting that the old Anglo-Saxon race would be still more superior to all others if it had no church-rates, or that our unrivaled happiness would last yet longer with a six-pound franchise, so long will the strain, "The best breed in the whole world!" swell louder and louder, everything ideal and refining will be lost out of sight, and both the assailed and their critics will remain in a sphere, to say the truth, perfectly unvital, a sphere in which spiritual progression is impossible. But let criticism leave church-rates and the franchise alone, and in the most candid spirit, without a single lurking thought of practical innovation, confront with our dithyramb this paragraph on which I stumbled in a newspaper immediately after reading Mr. Roebuck:

"A shocking child murder has just been committed at Nottingham. A girl named Wragg left the workhouse there on Saturday morning with her young illegitimate child. The child was soon afterwards found dead on Mapperly Hills, having been strangled. Wragg is in custody."

Nothing but that; but, in juxtaposition with the absolute eulogies of Sir Charles Adderley and Mr. Roebuck, how eloquent, how suggestive are those few lines! "Our old Anglo-Saxon breed, the best in the whole world!"—how much that is harsh and ill-favored there is in this best! *Wragg!* If we are to talk of ideal perfection, of "the best in the whole world," has anyone reflected what a touch of grossness in our race, what an original shortcoming in the more delicate spiritual perceptions, is shown by the natural growth amongst us of such hideous names—Higginbottom, Stiggins, Bugg!

1. A radical proposal to extend the right to vote to anyone owning land worth £6 annual rent. "Church-rates": taxes supporting the Church of England.

In Ionia and Attica they were luckier in this respect than "the best race in the world"; by the Ilissus[2] there was no Wragg, poor thing! And "our unrivaled happiness"—what an element of grimness, bareness, and hideousness mixes with it and blurs it; the workhouse, the dismal Mapperly Hills[2a]—how dismal those who have seen them will remember—the gloom, the smoke, the cold, the strangled illegitimate child! "I ask you whether, the world over or in past history, there is anything like it?" Perhaps not, one is inclined to answer; but at any rate, in that case, the world is very much to be pitied. And the final touch—short, bleak and inhuman: *Wragg is in custody.* The sex lost in the confusion of our unrivaled happiness; or (shall I say?) the superfluous Christian name lopped off by the straightforward vigor of our old Anglo-Saxon breed! There is profit for the spirit in such contrasts as this; criticism serves the cause of perfection by establishing them. By eluding sterile conflict, by refusing to remain in the sphere where alone narrow and relative conceptions have any worth and validity, criticism may diminish its momentary importance, but only in this way has it a chance of gaining admittance for those wider and more perfect conceptions to which all its duty is really owed. Mr. Roebuck will have a poor opinion of an adversary who replies to his defiant songs of triumph only by murmuring under his breath, *Wragg is in custody*; but in no other way will these songs of triumph be induced gradually to moderate themselves, to get rid of what in them is excessive and offensive, and to fall into a softer and truer key.

It will be said that it is a very subtle and indirect action which I am thus prescribing for criticism, and that, by embracing in this manner the Indian virtue of detachment and abandoning the sphere of practical life, it condemns itself to a slow and obscure work. Slow and obscure it may be, but it is the only proper work of criticism. The mass of mankind will never have any ardent zeal for seeing things as they are; very inadequate ideas will always satisfy them. On these inadequate ideas reposes, and must repose, the general practice of the world. That is as much as saying that whoever sets himself to see things as they are will find himself one of a very small circle; but it is only by this small circle resolutely doing its own work that adequate ideas will ever get current at all. The rush and roar of practical life will always have a dizzying and attracting effect upon the most collected spectator, and tend to draw him into its vortex; most of all will this be the case where that life is so powerful as it is in England. But it is only by remaining collected, and refusing to lend himself to the point of view of the practical man, that the critic can do the practical man any service; and it is only by the greatest sincerity in pursuing his own course, and by at last convincing even the practical man of his sin-

2. A stream in Attica, Greece.
2a. Adjacent to the coal-mining and industrial area of Nottingham (later associated with the writings of D. H. Lawrence).

cerity, that he can escape misunderstandings which perpetually threaten him.

For the practical man is not apt for fine distinctions, and yet in these distinctions truth and the highest culture greatly find their account. But it is not easy to lead a practical man—unless you reassure him as to your practical intentions, you have no chance of leading him—to see that a thing which he has always been used to look at from one side only, which he greatly values, and which, looked at from that side, quite deserves, perhaps, all the prizing and admiring which he bestows upon it—that this thing, looked at from another side, may appear much less beneficent and beautiful, and yet retain all its claims to our practical allegiance. Where shall we find language innocent enough, how shall we make the spotless purity of our intentions evident enough, to enable us to say to the political Englishman that the British Constitution itself, which, seen from the practical side, looks such a magnificent organ of progress and virtue, seen from the speculative side—with its compromises, its love of facts, its horror of theory, its studied avoidance of clear thoughts—that, seen from this side, our august Constitution sometimes looks—forgive me, shade of Lord Somers![3]—a colossal machine for the manufacture of Philistines?[4] How is Cobbett[5] to say this and not be misunderstood, blackened as he is with the smoke of a lifelong conflict in the field of political practice? how is Mr. Carlyle to say it and not be misunderstood, after his furious raid into this field with his *Latter-day Pamphlets?* how is Mr. Ruskin, after his pugnacious political economy?[6] I say, the critic must keep out of the region of immediate practice in the political, social, humanitarian sphere if he wants to make a beginning for that more free speculative treatment of things, which may perhaps one day make its benefits felt even in this sphere, but in a natural and thence irresistible manner.

Do what he will, however, the critic will still remain exposed to frequent misunderstandings, and nowhere so much as in this country. For here people are particularly indisposed even to comprehend that without this free disinterested treatment of things, truth and the highest culture are out of the question. So immersed are they in practical life, so accustomed to take all their notions from this life and its processes, that they are apt to think that truth and culture themselves can be reached by the processes of this life, and that it is an impertinent singularity to think of reaching them in

3. John Somers (1651–1716), statesman responsible for formulating the Declaration of Rights.
4. The unenlightened middle classes whose opposition to the men of culture is parallel to the Biblical tribe which fought against the people of Israel, "the children of light." Arnold's repeated use of this parallel has established the term in our language.
5. William Cobbett (1762–1835), vehement reformer whose political position anticipated that of Dickens.
6. Reference to *Unto this Last* (1862) in which Ruskin shifted from art criticism to an attack on traditional theories of economics.

any other. "We are all *terrae filii*,"[7] cries their eloquent advocate; "all Philistines together. Away with the notion of proceeding by any other course than the course dear to the Philistines; let us have a social movement, let us organize and combine a party to pursue truth and new thought, let us call it *the liberal party*, and let us all stick to each other, and back each other up. Let us have no nonsense about independent criticism, and intellectual delicacy, and the few and the many. Don't let us trouble ourselves about foreign thought; we shall invent the whole thing for ourselves as we go along. If one of us speaks well, applaud him; if one of us speaks ill, applaud him too; we are all in the same movement, we are all liberals, we are all in pursuit of truth." In this way the pursuit of truth becomes really a social, practical, pleasurable affair, almost requiring a chairman, a secretary, and advertisements; with the excitement of an occasional scandal, with a little resistance to give the happy sense of difficulty overcome; but, in general, plenty of bustle and very little thought. To act is so easy, as Goethe says; to think is so hard! It is true that the critic has many temptations to go with the stream, to make one of the party movement, one of these *terrae filii*; it seems ungracious to refuse to be a *terrae filius* when so many excellent people are; but the critic's duty is to refuse, or, if resistance is vain, at least to cry with Obermann: *Périssons en résistant.*[8] * * *

For criticism, these are elementary laws; but they never can be popular, and in this country they have been very little followed, and one meets with immense obstacles in following them. That is a reason for asserting them again and again. Criticism must maintain its independence of the practical spirit and its aims. Even with well-meant efforts of the practical spirit it must express dissatisfaction, if in the sphere of the ideal they seem impoverishing and limiting. It must not hurry on to the goal because of its practical importance. It must be patient, and know how to wait; and flexible, and know how to attach itself to things and how to withdraw from them. It must be apt to study and praise elements that for the fullness of spiritual perfection are wanted, even though they belong to a power which in the practical sphere may be maleficent. It must be apt to discern the spiritual shortcomings or illusions of powers that in the practical sphere may be beneficent. And this without any notion of favoring or injuring, in the practical sphere, one power or the other; without any notion of playing off, in this sphere, one power against the other. When one looks, for instance, at the English Divorce Court—an institution which perhaps has its practical conveniences, but which in the

---

7. "Sons of the earth."
8. "Let us die resisting." Three paragraphs are omitted here. They consist of a highly allusive account of a controversy concerning Biblical history. The discussion further illustrates the difficulties of a critic's remaining impartial.

ideal sphere is so hideous; an institution which neither makes divorce impossible nor makes it decent, which allows a man to get rid of his wife, or a wife of her husband, but makes them drag one another first, for the public edification, through a mire of unutterable infamy—when one looks at this charming institution, I say, with its crowded trials, its newspaper reports, and its money compensations, this institution in which the gross unregenerate British Philistine has indeed stamped an image of himself—one may be permitted to find the marriage theory of Catholicism refreshing and elevating. Or when Protestantism, in virtue of its supposed rational and intellectual origin, gives the law to criticism too magisterially, criticism may and must remind it that its pretensions, in this respect, are illusive and do it harm; that the Reformation was a moral rather than an intellectual event; that Luther's theory of grace no more exactly reflects the mind of the spirit than Bossuet's philosophy of history[9] reflects it; and that there is no more antecedent probability of the Bishop of Durham's[1] stock of ideas being agreeable to perfect reason than of Pope Pius the Ninth's. But criticism will not on that account forget the achievements of Protestantism in the practical and moral sphere; nor that, even in the intellectual sphere, Protestantism, though in a blind and stumbling manner, carried forward the Renascence, while Catholicism threw itself violently across its path.

I lately heard a man of thought and energy contrasting the want of ardor and movement which he now found amongst young men in this country with what he remembered in his own youth, twenty years ago. "What reformers we were then!" he exclaimed; "What a zeal we had! how we canvassed every institution in Church and State, and were prepared to remodel them all on first principles!" He was inclined to regret, as a spiritual flagging, the lull which he saw. I am disposed rather to regard it as a pause in which the turn to a new mode of spiritual progress is being accomplished. Everything was long seen, by the young and ardent amongst us, in inseparable connection with politics and practical life. We have pretty well exhausted the benefits of seeing things in this connection, we have got all that can be got by so seeing them. Let us try a more disinterested mode of seeing them; let us betake ourselves more to the serener life of the mind and spirit. This life, too, may have its excesses and dangers; but they are not for us at present. Let us think of quietly enlarging our stock of true and fresh ideas, and not, as soon as we get an idea or half an idea, be running out with it into the street, and trying to make it rule there. Our ideas will, in the end, shape the world all the better for matur-

9. Bishop Jacques Bossuet (1627–1704) whose theory of history is limited by its Roman Catholic bias (in Arnold's view), just as Martin Luther's exclusive view of grace reflects the bias of extreme Protestantism.
1. An Anglican bishop.

ing a little. Perhaps in fifty years' time it will in the English House of Commons be an objection to an institution that it is an anomaly, and my friend the Member of Parliament will shudder in his grave. But let us in the meanwhile rather endeavor that in twenty years' time it may, in English literature, be an objection to a proposition that it is absurd. That will be a change so vast, that the imagination almost fails to grasp it. *Ab integro saeclorum nascitur ordo.*[2]

If I have insisted so much on the course which criticism must take where politics and religion are concerned, it is because, where these burning matters are in question, it is most likely to go astray. I have wished, above all, to insist on the attitude which criticism should adopt towards things in general; on its right tone and temper of mind. But then comes another question as to the subject matter which literary criticism should most seek. Here, in general, its course is determined for it by the idea which is the law of its being; the idea of a disinterested endeavor to learn and propagate the best that is known and thought in the world, and thus to establish a current of fresh and true ideas. By the very nature of things, as England is not all the world, much of the best that is known and thought in the world cannot be of English growth, must be foreign; by the nature of things, again, it is just this that we are least likely to know, while English thought is streaming in upon us from all sides, and takes excellent care that we shall not be ignorant of its existence. The English critic of literature, therefore, must dwell much on foreign thought, and with particular heed on any part of it, which, while significant and fruitful in itself, is for any reason specially likely to escape him. Again, judging is often spoken of as the critic's one business, and so in some sense it is; but the judgment which almost insensibly forms itself in a fair and clear mind, along with fresh knowledge, is the valuable one; and thus knowledge, and ever fresh knowledge, must be the critic's great concern for himself. And it is by communicating fresh knowledge, and letting his own judgment pass along with it—but insensibly, and in the second place, not the first, as a sort of companion and clue, not as an abstract lawgiver—that the critic will generally do most good to his readers. Sometimes, no doubt, for the sake of establishing an author's place in literature, and his relation to a central standard (and if this is not done, how are we to get at our *best in the world?*) criticism may have to deal with a subject matter so familiar that fresh knowledge is out of the question, and then it must be all judgment; an enunciation and detailed application of principles. Here the great safeguard is never to let oneself become abstract, always to retain an intimate and lively consciousness of the truth of what one is saying, and, the moment this fails us, to be sure that something is wrong. Still under all circumstances,

2. "Order is born from the renewal of the ages" (Virgil, *Eclogues* IV.5).

this mere judgment and application of principles is, in itself, not the most satisfactory work to the critic; like mathematics, it is tautological, and cannot well give us, like fresh learning, the sense of creative activity.

But stop, some one will say; all this talk is of no practical use to us whatever; this criticism of yours is not what we have in our minds when we speak of criticism; when we speak of critics and criticism, we mean critics and criticism of the current English literature of the day; when you offer to tell criticism its function, it is to this criticism that we expect you to address yourself. I am sorry for it, for I am afraid I must disappoint these expectations. I am bound by my own definition of criticism: *a disinterested endeavor to learn and propagate the best that is known and thought in the world.* How much of current English literature comes into this "best that is known and thought in the world"? Not very much I fear; certainly less, at this moment, than of the current literature of France or Germany. Well, then, am I to alter my definition of criticism, in order to meet the requirements of a number of practicing English critics, who, after all, are free in their choice of a business? That would be making criticism lend itself just to one of those alien practical considerations, which, I have said, are so fatal to it. One may say, indeed, to those who have to deal with the mass—so much better disregarded—of current English literature, that they may at all events endeavor, in dealing with this, to try it, so far as they can, by the standard of the best that is known and thought in the world; one may say, that to get anywhere near this standard, every critic should try and possess one great literature, at least, besides his own; and the more unlike his own, the better. But, after all, the criticism I am really concerned with—the criticism which alone can much help us for the future, the criticism which, throughout Europe, is at the present day meant, when so much stress is laid on the importance of criticism and the critical spirit—is a criticism which regards Europe as being, for intellectual and spiritual purposes, one great confederation, bound to a joint action and working to a common result; and whose members have, for their proper outfit, a knowledge of Greek, Roman, and Eastern antiquity, and of one another. Special, local, and temporary advantages being put out of account, that modern nation will in the intellectual and spiritual sphere make most progress, which most thoroughly carries out this program. And what is that but saying that we too, all of us, as individuals, the more thoroughly we carry it out, shall make the more progress?

There is so much inviting us!—what are we to take? what will nourish us in growth towards perfection? That is the question which, with the immense field of life and of literature lying before him, the critic has to answer; for himself first, and afterwards for others. In this idea of the critic's business the essays brought together in the following pages have had their origin; in this idea, widely different as are their subjects, they have, perhaps, their unity.

I conclude with what I said at the beginning: to have the sense of creative activity is the great happiness and the great proof of being alive, and it is not denied to criticism to have it; but then criticism must be sincere, simple, flexible, ardent, ever widening its knowledge. Then it may have, in no contemptible measure, a joyful sense of creative activity; a sense which a man of insight and conscience will prefer to what he might derive from a poor, starved, fragmentary, inadequate creation. And at some epochs no other creation is possible.

Still, in full measure, the sense of creative activity belongs only to genuine creation; in literature we must never forget that. But what true man of letters ever can forget it? It is no such common matter for a gifted nature to come into possession of a current of true and living ideas, and to produce amidst the inspiration of them, that we are likely to underrate it. The epochs of Aeschylus and Shakespeare make us feel their pre-eminence. In an epoch like those is, no doubt, the true life of literature; there is the promised land, towards which criticism can only beckon. That promised land it will not be ours to enter, and we shall die in the wilderness: but to have desired to enter it, to have saluted it from afar, is already, perhaps, the best distinction among contemporaries; it will certainly be the best title to esteem with posterity.

1864, 1865

From Maurice de Guérin[1]
[A Definition of Poetry]

The grand power of poetry is its interpretative power; by which I mean, not a power of drawing out in black and white an explanation of the mystery of the universe, but the power of so dealing with things as to awaken in us a wonderfully full, new, and intimate sense of them, and of our relations with them. When this sense is awakened in us, as to objects without us, we feel ourselves to be in contact with the essential nature of those objects, to be no longer bewildered and oppressed by them, but to have their secret, and to be in harmony with them; and this feeling calms and satisfies us as no other can. Poetry, indeed, interprets in another way besides this; but one of its two ways of interpreting, of exercising its highest power, is by awakening this sense in us. I will not now inquire whether this sense is illusive, whether it can be proved not to be

---

1. 1810–39; a minor French poet. The essay was included in *Essays in Criticism: First Series*.

illusive, whether it does absolutely make us possess the real nature
of things; all I say is, that poetry can awaken it in us, and that to
awaken it is one of the highest powers of poetry. The interpretations of science do not give us this intimate sense of objects as the
interpretations of poetry give it; they appeal to a limited faculty,
and not to the whole man. * * *

I have said that poetry interprets in two ways; it interprets by
expressing, with magical felicity, the physiognomy and movement
of the outward world, and it interprets by expressing, with inspired conviction, the ideas and laws of the inward world of man's
moral and spiritual nature. In other words, poetry is interpretative
both by having *natural magic* in it, and by having *moral profundity*. In both ways it illuminates man; it gives him a satisfying sense
of reality; it reconciles him with himself and the universe. Thus
Aeschylus's "δράσαντι παθεῖν"[2] and his "ἀνήριθμον γέλασμα"[3] are
alike interpretative. Shakespeare interprets both when he says,

> Full many a glorious morning have I seen,
> Flatter the mountaintops with sovereign eye;[4]

and when he says,

> There's a divinity that shapes our ends,
> Rough-hew them as we will.[5]

These great poets unite in themselves the faculty of both kinds
of interpretation, the naturalistic and the moral. But it is observable
that in the poets who unite both kinds, the latter (the moral) usually ends by making itself the master. In Shakespeare the two kinds
seem wonderfully to balance one another; but even in him the balance leans; his expression tends to become too little sensuous and
simple, too much intellectualized. The same thing may be yet more
strongly affirmed of Lucretius and of Wordsworth. In Shelley there
is not a balance of the two gifts, nor even a coexistence of them,
but there is a passionate straining after them both, and this is
what makes Shelley, as a man, so interesting; I will not now inquire how much Shelley achieves as a poet, but whatever he
achieves, he in general fails to achieve natural magic in his expression; in Mr. Palgrave's charming *Treasury*[6] may be seen a gallery
of his failures.[7] But in Keats and Guérin, in whom the faculty of

2. "The doer must suffer." From
Aeschylus' *Choephori* (line 313).
3. "Countless laughter." From Aeschylus' *Prometheus Bound* (line 90).
4. Shakespeare, *Sonnets* XXXIII.1–2.
5. *Hamlet* V.ii.10–11.
6. Francis Palgrave's anthology of
poems, *The Golden Treasury*, was first
published in 1861.
7. "Compare, for example, his *Lines
Written in the Euganean Hills*, with
Keats's *Ode to Autumn* . . . The latter
piece *renders* Nature; the former *tries
to render* her. I will not deny, however,
that Shelley has natural magic in his
rhythm; what I deny is, that he has it
in his language. It always seems to me
that the right sphere for Shelley's genius
was the sphere of music, not of poetry;
the medium of sounds he can master,
but to master the more difficult medium
of words he has neither intellectual
force enough nor sanity enough" [Ar-
nold's note].

naturalistic interpretation is overpoweringly predominant, the natural magic is perfect; when they speak of the world they speak like Adam naming by divine inspiration the creatures; their expression corresponds with the thing's essential reality.

1863, 1865

From Culture and Anarchy[1]
From *Chapter I. Sweetness and Light*

[PURITANISM AND CULTURE]

The impulse of the English race towards moral development and self-conquest has nowhere so powerfully manifested itself as in Puritanism. Nowhere has Puritanism found so adequate an expression as in the religious organization of the Independents.[2] The modern Independents have a newspaper, the *Nonconformist*, written with great sincerity and ability. The motto, the standard, the profession of faith which this organ of theirs carries aloft, is: "The Dissidence of Dissent and the Protestantism of the Protestant religion." There is sweetness and light, and an ideal of complete harmonious human perfection! One need not go to culture and poetry to find language to judge it. Religion, with its instinct for perfection, supplies language to judge it, language, too, which is in our mouths every day. "Finally, be of one mind, united in feeling," says St. Peter.[3] There is an ideal which judges the Puritan ideal: "The Dissidence of Dissent and the Protestantism of the Protestant religion!" And religious organizations like this are what people believe in, rest in, would give their lives for! Such, I say, is the wonderful virtue of even the beginnings of perfection, of having conquered even the plain faults of our animality, that the religious organization which has helped us to do it can seem to us some-

---

1. As a critic of social life, Arnold sought to test Victorian institutions according to whether they seemed to him civilized. A characteristic quality of the civilized state of mind is summed up, for his purposes, in his formula "sweetness and light," a phrase suggesting reasonableness of temper and intellectual insight. Arnold derived the phrase from a fable contrasting the spider with the bee in Swift's *Battle of the Books*. The spider (representing a narrow, self-centered, and uncultured mind) spins out of itself "nothing at all but flybane and cobweb." The bee (representing a cultured mind that has drawn nourishment from the humanist tradition) ranges far and wide and brings to its hive honey and also wax out of which candles may be made. Therefore the bee, Swift says, furnishes mankind "with the two noblest of things, which are sweetness and light."

The three following excerpts illustrate aspects of Arnold's indictment of the middle classes for their lack of sweetness and light. The first and third expose the narrowness and dullness of middle-class Puritan religious institutions in both the 17th and 19th centuries. The second, "Doing As One Likes," shows the limitations of the middle-class political bias and the irresponsibility of *laissez faire*. Here Arnold is most close to Carlyle and Ruskin. These three extracts indicate why it has been said that Matthew Arnold discovered the foibles of Main Street fifty years before Sinclair Lewis exposed them in his novels of American life.
2. A 17th-century Puritan group (of which Cromwell was an adherent), allied with the Congregationalists.
3. Cf. I Peter iii.8.

thing precious, salutary, and to be propagated, even when it wears such a brand of imperfection on its forehead as this. And men have got such a habit of giving to the language of religion a special application, of making it a mere jargon, that for the condemnation which religion itself passes on the shortcomings of their religious organizations they have no ear; they are sure to cheat themselves and to explain this condemnation away. They can only be reached by the criticism which culture, like poetry, speaking a language not to be sophisticated, and resolutely testing these organizations by the ideal of a human perfection complete on all sides, applies to them.

But men of culture and poetry, it will be said, are again and again failing, and failing conspicuously, in the necessary first stage to a harmonious perfection, in the subduing of the great obvious faults of our animality, which it is the glory of these religious organizations to have helped us to subdue. True, they do often so fail. They have often been without the virtues as well as the faults of the Puritan; it has been one of their dangers that they so felt the Puritan's faults that they too much neglected the practice of his virtues. I will not, however, exculpate them at the Puritan's expense. They have often failed in morality, and morality is indispensable. And they have been punished for their failure, as the Puritan has been rewarded for his performance. They have been punished wherein they erred; but their ideal of beauty, of sweetness and light, and a human nature complete on all its sides, remains the true ideal of perfection still; just as the Puritan's ideal of perfection remains narrow and inadequate, although for what he did well he has been richly rewarded. Notwithstanding the mighty results of the Pilgrim Fathers' voyage, they and their standard of perfection are rightly judged when we figure to ourselves Shakespeare or Virgil—souls in whom sweetness and light, and all that in human nature is most humane, were eminent—accompanying them on their voyage, and think what intolerable company Shakespeare and Virgil would have found them! In the same way let us judge the religious organizations which we see all around us. Do not let us deny the good and the happiness which they have accomplished; but do not let us fail to see clearly that their idea of human perfection is narrow and inadequate, and that the Dissidence of Dissent and the Protestantism of the Protestant religion will never bring humanity to its true goal. As I said with regard to wealth: Let us look at the life of those who live in and for it—so I say with regard to the religious organizations. Look at the life imaged in such a newspaper as the *Nonconformist*—a life of jealousy of the Establishment,[4] disputes, tea-meetings, openings of chapels, sermons; and then think of it as an ideal of a human life completing

4. The Church of England or the Established Church.

itself on all sides, and aspiring with all its organs after sweetness, light, and perfection!

1867, 1869

From *Chapter II. Doing As One Likes*

* * * When I began to speak of culture, I insisted on our bondage to machinery, on our proneness to value machinery as an end in itself, without looking beyond it to the end for which alone, in truth, it is valuable. Freedom, I said, was one of those things which we thus worshiped in itself, without enough regarding the ends for which freedom is to be desired. In our common notions and talk about freedom, we eminently show our idolatry of machinery. Our prevalent notion is—and I quoted a number of instances to prove it—that it is a most happy and important thing for a man merely to be able to do as he likes. On what he is to do when he is thus free to do as he likes, we do not lay so much stress. Our familiar praise of the British Constitution under which we live, is that it is a system of checks—a system which stops and paralyzes any power in interfering with the free action of individuals. To this effect Mr. Bright,[1] who loves to walk in the old ways of the Constitution, said forcibly in one of his great speeches, what many other people are every day saying less forcibly, that the central idea of English life and politics is *the assertion of personal liberty*. Evidently this is so; but evidently, also, as feudalism, which with its ideas, and habits of subordination was for many centuries silently behind the British Constitution, dies out, and we are left with nothing but our system of checks, and our notion of its being the great right and happiness of an Englishman to do as far as possible what he likes, we are in danger of drifting towards anarchy. We have not the notion, so familiar on the Continent and to antiquity, of *the State*—the nation in its collective and corporate character, entrusted with stringent powers for the general advantage, and controlling individual wills in the name of an interest wider than that of individuals. We say, what is very true, that this notion is often made instrumental to tyranny; we say that a State is in reality made up of the individuals who compose it, and that every individual is the best judge of his own interests. Our leading class is an aristocracy, and no aristocracy likes the notion of a State-authority greater than itself, with a stringent administrative machinery superseding the decorative inutilities of lord-lieutenancy, deputy-lieutenancy, and the *posse comitatus*,[2] which are all in its own hands. Our middle class, the great representative of trade and Dissent, with its maxims of every man for himself in business, every man for himself in religion, dreads

---

1. John Bright, 19th-century orator and reformer.
2. I.e., "power of the county"—a feudal method of enforcing law by local authorities instead of by agencies of the central government.

a powerful administration which might somehow interfere with it; and besides, it has its own decorative inutilities of vestrymanship and guardianship, which are to this class what lord-lieutenancy and the county magistracy are to the aristocratic class, and a stringent administration might either take these functions out of its hands, or prevent its exercising them in its own comfortable, independent manner, as at present.

Then as to our working class. This class, pressed constantly by the hard daily compulsion of material wants, is naturally the very center and stronghold of our national idea, that it is man's ideal right and felicity to do as he likes. I think I have somewhere related how M. Michelet[3] said to me of the people of France, that it was "a nation of barbarians civilized by the conscription." He meant that through their military service the idea of public duty and of discipline was brought to the mind of these masses, in other respects so raw and uncultivated. Our masses are quite as raw and uncultivated as the French; and so far from their having the idea of public duty and of discipline, superior to the individual's self-will, brought to their mind by a universal obligation of military service, such as that of the conscription—so far from their having this, the very idea of a conscription is so at variance with our English notion of the prime right and blessedness of doing as one likes, that I remember the manager of the Clay Cross works in Derbyshire told me during the Crimean war, when our want of soldiers was much felt and some people were talking of a conscription, that sooner than submit to a conscription the population of that district would flee to the mines, and lead a sort of Robin Hood life underground.

For a long time, as I have said, the strong feudal habits of subordination and deference continued to tell upon the working class. The modern spirit has now almost entirely dissolved those habits, and the anarchical tendency of our worship of freedom in and for itself, of our superstitious faith, as I say, in machinery, is becoming very manifest. More and more, because of this our blind faith in machinery, because of our want of light to enable us to look beyond machinery to the end for which machinery is valuable, this and that man, and this and that body of men, all over the country, are beginning to assert and put in practice an Englishman's right to do what he likes; his right to march where he likes, meet where he likes, enter where he likes, hoot as he likes, threaten as he likes, smash as he likes.[4] All this, I say, tends to anarchy; and though a number of excellent people, and particularly my friends of the Liberal or progressive party, as they call themselves, are kind enough to reassure us by saying that these are trifles, that a few

3. Jules Michelet (1798–1874), French historian.
4. Reference to the riots of 1866 in which a London mob demolished the iron railings enclosing Hyde Park.

transient outbreaks of rowdyism signify nothing, that our system of liberty is one which itself cures all the evils which it works, that the educated and intelligent classes stand in overwhelming strength and majestic repose, ready, like our military force in riots, to act at a moment's notice—yet one finds that one's Liberal friends generally say this because they have such faith in themselves and their nostrums, when they shall return, as the public welfare requires, to place and power. But this faith of theirs one cannot exactly share, when one has so long had them and their nostrums at work, and see that they have not prevented our coming to our present embarrassed condition. And one finds, also, that the outbreaks of rowdyism tend to become less and less of trifles, to become more frequent rather than less frequent; and that meanwhile our educated and intelligent classes remain in their majestic repose, and somehow or other, whatever happens, their overwhelming strength, like our military force in riots, never does act.

How, indeed, *should* their overwhelming strength act, when the man who gives an inflammatory lecture, or breaks down the park railings, or invades a Secretary of State's office, is only following an Englishman's impulse to do as he likes; and our own conscience tells us that we ourselves have always regarded this impulse as something primary and sacred? Mr. Murphy[5] lectures at Birmingham, and showers on the Catholic population of that town "words," says the Home Secretary, "only fit to be addressed to thieves or murderers." What then? Mr. Murphy has his own reasons of several kinds. He suspects the Roman Catholic Church of designs upon Mrs. Murphy; and he says if mayors and magistrates do not care for their wives and daughters, he does. But, above all, he is doing as he likes; or, in worthier language, asserting his personal liberty. "I will carry out my lectures if they walk over my body as a dead corpse, and I say to the Mayor of Birmingham that he is my servant while I am in Birmingham, and as my servant he must do his duty and protect me." Touching and beautiful words, which find a sympathetic chord in every British bosom! The moment it is plainly put before us that a man is asserting his personal liberty, we are half disarmed; because we are believers in freedom, and not in some dream of a right reason to which the assertion of our freedom is to be subordinated. Accordingly, the Secretary of State had to say that although the lecturer's language was "only fit to be addressed to thieves or murderers," yet, "I do not think he is to be deprived, I do not think that anything I have said could justify the inference that he is to be deprived, of the right of protection in a place built by him for the purpose of these lectures; because the language was not language which afforded grounds for a criminal

5. An orator whose inflammatory anti-Catholic public speech *The Errors of* *the Roman Church* led to rioting in Birmingham and other cities in 1867.

prosecution." No, nor to be silenced by Mayor, or Home Secretary, or any administrative authority on earth, simply on their notion of what is discreet and reasonable! This is in perfect consonance with our public opinion, and with our national love for the assertion of personal liberty. * * *

From *Chapter V. Porro Unum Est Necessarium* [1]

* * *Sweetness and light evidently have to do with the bent or side in humanity which we call Hellenic. Greek intelligence has obviously for its essence the instinct for what Plato calls the true, firm, intelligible law of things; the law of light, of seeing things as they are. Even in the natural sciences, where the Greeks had not time and means adequately to apply this instinct, and where we have gone a great deal further than they did, it is this instinct which is the root of the whole matter and the ground of all our success; and this instinct the world has mainly learnt of the Greeks, inasmuch as they are humanity's most signal manifestation of it. Greek art, again, Greek beauty, have their root in the same impulse to see things as they really are, inasmuch as Greek art and beauty rest on fidelity to nature—the *best* nature—and on a delicate discrimination of what this best nature is. To say we work for sweetness and light, then, is only another way of saying that we work for Hellenism. But, oh! cry many people, sweetness and light are not enough; you must put strength or energy along with them, and make a kind of trinity of strength, sweetness and light, and then, perhaps, you may do some good. That is to say, we are to join Hebraism, strictness of the moral conscience, and manful walking by the best light we have, together with Hellenism, inculcate both, and rehearse the praises of both.

Or, rather, we may praise both in conjunction, but we must be careful to praise Hebraism most. "Culture," says an acute, though somewhat rigid critic, Mr. Sidgwick,[2] "diffuses sweetness and light. I do not undervalue these blessings, but religion gives fire and strength, and the world wants fire and strength even more than sweetness and light." By religion, let me explain, Mr. Sidgwick here means particularly that Puritanism on the insufficiency of which I have been commenting and to which he says I am unfair. Now, no doubt, it is possible to be a fanatical partisan of light and the instincts which push us to it, a fanatical enemy of strict-

---

1. Luke x.42: "But one thing is needful." This chapter develops a contrast established in Ch. IV between *Hebraism* (Puritan morality and energetic devotion to work) and *Hellenism* (cultivation of the aesthetic and intellectual understanding of life). The Puritan middle classes, according to Arnold, think that the "one thing needful" is the Hebraic form of virtue.
2. Henry Sidgwick, philosopher (1838–1900), whose article on Arnold appeared in *Macmillan's Magazine*, Aug., 1867.

ness of moral conscience and the instincts which push us to it. A fanaticism of this sort deforms and vulgarizes the well-known work, in some respects so remarkable, of the late Mr. Buckle.[3] Such a fanaticism carries its own mark with it, in lacking sweetness; and its own penalty, in that, lacking sweetness, it comes in the end to lack light too. And the Greeks—the great exponents of humanity's bent for sweetness and light united, of its perception that the truth of things must be at the same time beauty—singularly escaped the fanaticism which we moderns, whether we Hellenize or whether we Hebraize, are so apt to show. They arrived—though failing, as has been said, to give adequate practical satisfaction to the claims of man's moral side—at the idea of a comprehensive adjustment of the claims of both the sides in man, the moral as well as the intellectual, of a full estimate of both, and of a reconciliation of both; an idea which is philosophically of the greatest value, and the best of lessons for us moderns. So we ought to have no difficulty in conceding to Mr. Sidgwick that manful walking by the best light one has—fire and strength as he calls it—has its high value as well as culture, the endeavor to see things in their truth and beauty, the pursuit of sweetness and light. But whether at this or that time, and to this or that set of persons, one ought to insist most on the praises of fire and strength, or on the praises of sweetness and light, must depend, one would think, on the circumstances and needs of that particular time and those particular persons. And all that we have been saying, and indeed any glance at the world around us, shows that with us, with the most respectable and strongest part of us, the ruling force is now, and long has been, a Puritan force—the care for fire and strength, strictness of conscience, Hebraism, rather than the care for sweetness and light, spontaneity of consciousness, Hellenism.

Well, then, what is the good of our now rehearsing the praises of fire and strength to ourselves, who dwell too exclusively on them already? When Mr. Sidgwick says so broadly, that the world wants fire and strength even more than sweetness and light, is he not carried away by a turn for broad generalization? does he not forget that the world is not all of one piece, and every piece with the same needs at the same time? It may be true that the Roman world at the beginning of our era, or Leo the Tenth's Court at the time of the Reformation, or French society in the eighteenth century,[4] needed fire and strength even more than sweetness and light. But can it be said that the Barbarians who overran the empire needed fire and strength even more than sweetness and light; or

3. Henry Thomas Buckle (1821–62), author of *A History of Civilization*.
4. Societies representing an excess of sophisticated worldliness as at the courts of such a Roman emperor as Nero (A.D. 54–68), or Pope Leo X (1513–21), or Louis XV (1715–74).

that the Puritans needed them more; or that Mr. Murphy, the Birmingham lecturer, and the Rev. W. Cattle[5] and his friends, need them more?

The Puritan's great danger is that he imagines himself in possession of a rule telling him the *unum necessarium,* or one thing needful, and that he then remains satisfied with a very crude conception of what this rule really is and what it tells him, thinks he has now knowledge and henceforth needs only to act, and, in this dangerous state of assurance and self-satisfaction, proceeds to give full swing to a number of the instincts of his ordinary self. Some of the instincts of his ordinary self he has, by the help of his rule of life, conquered; but others which he has not conquered by this help he is so far from perceiving to need subjugation, and to be instincts of an inferior self, that he even fancies it to be his right and duty, in virtue of having conquered a limited part of himself, to give unchecked swing to the remainder. He is, I say, a victim of Hebraism, of the tendency to cultivate strictness of conscience rather than spontaneity of consciousness. And what he wants is a larger conception of human nature, showing him the number of other points at which his nature must come to its best, besides the points which he himself knows and thinks of. There is no *unum necessarium,* or one thing needful, which can free human nature from the obligation of trying to come to its best at all these points. The real *unum necessarium* for us is to come to our best at all points. Instead of our "one thing needful," justifying in us vulgarity, hideousness, ignorance, violence— our vulgarity, hideousness, ignorance, violence, are really so many touchstones which try our one thing needful, and which prove that in the state, at any rate, in which we ourselves have it, it is not all we want. And as the force which encourages us to stand staunch and fast by the rule and ground we have is Hebraism, so the force which encourages us to go back upon this rule, and to try the very ground on which we appear to stand, is Hellenism —a turn for giving our consciousness free play and enlarging its range. And what I say is, not that Hellenism is always for everybody more wanted than Hebraism, but that for the Rev. W. Cattle at this particular moment, and for the great majority of us his fellow countrymen, it is more wanted.

* * *

The newspapers a short time ago contained an account of the suicide of a Mr. Smith, secretary to some insurance company, who, it was said, "labored under the apprehension that he would come

5. A Nonconformist clergyman who was chairman of the anti-Catholic meeting addressed by Murphy in 1867. See "Doing As One Likes," above.

to poverty, and that he was eternally lost." And when I read these words, it occurred to me that the poor man who came to such a mournful end was, in truth, a kind of type—by the selection of his two grand objects of concern, by their isolation from everything else, and their juxtaposition to one another—of all the strongest, most respectable, and most representative part of our nation. "He labored under the apprehension that he would come to poverty, and that he was eternally lost." The whole middle class have a conception of things—a conception which makes us call them Philistines—just like that of this poor man; though we are seldom, of course, shocked by seeing it take the distressing, violently morbid, and fatal turn, which it took with him. But how generally, with how many of us, are the main concerns of life limited to these two: the concern for making money, and the concern for saving our souls! And how entirely does the narrow and mechanical conception of our secular business proceed from a narrow and mechanical conception of our religious business! What havoc do the united conceptions make of our lives! It is because the second-named of these two master-concerns presents to us the one thing needful in so fixed, narrow, and mechanical a way, that so ignoble a fellow master-concern to it as the first-named becomes possible; and, having been once admitted, takes the same rigid and absolute character as the other.

Poor Mr. Smith had sincerely the nobler master-concern as well as the meaner—the concern for saving his soul (according to the narrow and mechanical conception which Puritanism has of what the salvation of the soul is), as well as the concern for making money. But let us remark how many people there are, especially outside the limits of the serious and conscientious middle class to which Mr. Smith belonged, who take up with a meaner master-concern—whether it be pleasure, or field sports, or bodily exercises, or business, or popular agitation—who take up with one of these exclusively, and neglect Mr. Smith's nobler master-concern, because of the mechanical form which Hebraism has given to this noble master-concern. Hebraism makes it stand, as we have said, as something talismanic, isolated, and all-sufficient, justifying our giving our ordinary selves free play in bodily exercises, or business, or popular agitation, if we have made our account square with this master-concern; and, if we have not, rendering other things indifferent, and our ordinary self all we have to follow, and to follow with all the energy that is in us, till we do. Whereas the idea of perfection at all points, the encouraging in ourselves spontaneity of consciousness, the letting a free play of thought live and flow around all our activity, the indisposition to allow one side of our activity to stand as so all-important and all-sufficing that it makes other sides indifferent—this bent of mind in us may not only check us in following unreservedly a mean master-concern of any kind, but may even, also, bring new life and movement into that side of us with which alone Hebraism concerns itself, and awaken a healthier and less mechanical activity there. Hellenism may thus actually serve to further the designs of Hebraism.

* * *

1868, 1869

From Wordsworth[1]

* * * Wordsworth has been in his grave for some thirty years, and certainly his lovers and admirers cannot flatter themselves that this great and steady light of glory as yet shines over him. He is not fully recognized at home; he is not recognized at all abroad. Yet I firmly believe that the poetical performance of Wordsworth is, after that of Shakespeare and Milton, of which all the world now recognizes the worth, undoubtedly the most considerable in our language from the Elizabethan age to the present time. Chaucer is anterior; and on other grounds, too, he cannot well be brought into the comparison. But taking the roll of our chief poetical names, besides Shakespeare and Milton, from the age of Elizabeth downwards, and going through it—Spenser, Dryden, Pope, Gray, Goldsmith, Cowper, Burns, Coleridge, Scott, Campbell, Moore, Byron, Shelley, Keats (I mention those only who are dead)—I think it certain that Wordsworth's name deserves to stand, and will finally stand, above them all. Several of the poets named have gifts and excellences which Wordsworth has not. But taking the performance of each as a whole, I say that Wordsworth seems to me to have left a body of poetical work superior in power, in interest, in the qualities which give enduring freshness, to that which any one of the others has left.

But this is not enough to say. I think it certain, further, that if we take the chief poetical names of the Continent since the death of Molière, and, omitting Goethe, confront the remaining names with that of Wordsworth, the result is the same. Let us take Klopstock, Lessing, Schiller, Uhland, Rückert, and Heine for Germany; Filicaia, Alfieri, Manzoni, and Leopardi for Italy; Racine, Boileau, Voltaire, André Chénier, Béranger, Lamartine, Musset, M. Victor

1. In one of his letters to Clough, Arnold remarked that those who cannot read Greek literature "should read nothing but Milton and parts of Wordsworth: the state should see to it." The following essay, which served as the introduction to a volume of Words-worth's poems selected by Arnold, demonstrates the reasons for this admiration. A further tribute to Wordsworth is expressed in Arnold's poem *Memorial Verses*. The opening paragraphs of the essay, which are omitted here, review the history of Wordsworth's reputation.

Hugo (he has been so long celebrated that although he still lives I may be permitted to name him) for France. Several of these, again, have evidently gifts and excellences to which Wordsworth can make no pretension. But in real poetical achievement it seems to me indubitable that to Wordsworth, here again, belongs the palm. It seems to me that Wordsworth has left behind him a body of poetical work which wears, and will wear, better on the whole than the performance of any one of these personages, so far more brilliant and celebrated, most of them, than the homely poet of Rydal.[2] Wordsworth's performance in poetry is on the whole, in power, in interest, in the qualities which give enduring freshness, superior to theirs.

This is a high claim to make for Wordsworth. But if it is a just claim, if Wordsworth's place among the poets who have appeared in the last two or three centuries is after Shakespeare, Molière, Milton, Goethe, indeed, but before all the rest, then in time Wordsworth will have his due. We shall recognize him in his place, as we recognize Shakespeare and Milton; and not only we ourselves shall recognize him, but he will be recognized by Europe also. Meanwhile, those who recognize him already may do well, perhaps, to ask themselves whether there are not in the case of Wordsworth certain special obstacles which hinder or delay his due recognition by others, and whether these obstacles are not in some measure removable.

The *Excursion* and the *Prelude*, his poems of greatest bulk, are by no means Wordsworth's best work. His best work is in his shorter pieces, and many indeed are there of these which are of first-rate excellence. But in his seven volumes the pieces of high merit are mingled with a mass of pieces very inferior to them; so inferior to them that it seems wonderful how the same poet should have produced both. Shakespeare frequently has lines and passages in a strain quite false, and which are entirely unworthy of him. But one can imagine him smiling if one could meet him in the Elysian Fields and tell him so; smiling and replying that he knew it perfectly well himself, and what did it matter? But with Wordsworth the case is different. Work altogether inferior, work quite uninspired, flat, and dull, is produced by him with evident unconsciousness of its defects, and he presents it to us with the same faith and seriousness as his best work. Now a drama or an epic fill the mind, and one does not look beyond them; but in a collection of short pieces the impression made by one piece requires to be continued and sustained by the piece following. In reading Wordsworth the impression made by one of his fine pieces is too often dulled and

2. Rydal Mount, Wordsworth's home in the Lake District.

spoiled by a very inferior piece coming after it.

Wordsworth composed verses during a space of some sixty years; and it is no exaggeration to say that within one single decade of those years, between 1798 and 1808, almost all his really first-rate work was produced. A mass of inferior work remains, work done before and after this golden prime, imbedding the first-rate work and clogging it, obstructing our approach to it, chilling, not unfrequently, the high-wrought mood with which we leave it. To be recognized far and wide as a great poet, to be possible and receivable as a classic, Wordsworth needs to be relieved of a great deal of the poetical baggage which now encumbers him. To administer this relief is indispensable, unless he is to continue to be a poet for the few only—a poet valued far below his real worth by the world.[3] * * *

Disengaged from the quantity of inferior work which now obscures them, the best poems of Wordsworth, I hear many people say, would indeed stand out in great beauty, but they would prove to be very few in number, scarcely more than a half a dozen. I maintain, on the other hand, that what strikes me with admiration, what establishes in my opinion Wordsworth's superiority, is the great and ample body of powerful work which remains to him, even after all his inferior work has been cleared away. He gives us so much to rest upon, so much which communicates his spirit and engages ours!

This is of very great importance. If it were a comparison of single pieces, or of three or four pieces, by each poet, I do not say that Wordsworth would stand decisively above Gray, or Burns, or Coleridge, or Keats, or Manzoni, or Heine. It is in his ampler body of powerful work that I find his superiority. His good work itself, his work which counts, is not all of it, of course, of equal value. Some kinds of poetry are in themselves lower kinds than others. The ballad kind is a lower kind: the didactic kind, still more, is a lower kind. Poetry of this latter sort counts, too, sometimes, by its biographical interest partly, not by its poetical interest pure and simple; but then this can only be when the poet producing it has the power and importance of Wordsworth, a power and importance which he assuredly did not establish by such didactic poetry alone. Altogether, it is, I say, by the great body of powerful and significant work which remains to him, after every reduction and deduction has been made, that Wordsworth's superiority is proved.

To exhibit this body of Wordsworth's best work, to clear away obstructions from around it, and to let it speak for itself, is what every lover of Wordsworth should desire. Until this has been done,

---

3. Two paragraphs, here omitted, criticize Wordsworth's system of classifying his poems.

Wordsworth, whom we, to whom he is dear, all of us know and feel to be so great a poet, has not had a fair chance before the world. When once it has been done, he will make his way best, not by our advocacy of him, but by his own worth and power. We may safely leave him to make his way thus, we who believe that a superior worth and power in poetry finds in mankind a sense responsive to it and disposed at last to recognize it. Yet at the outset, before he has been duly known and recognized, we may do Wordsworth a service, perhaps, by indicating in what his superior power and worth will be found to consist, and in what it will not.

Long ago, in speaking of Homer, I said that the noble and profound application of ideas to life is the most essential part of poetic greatness. I said that a great poet receives his distinctive character of superiority from his application, under the conditions immutably fixed by the laws of poetic beauty and poetic truth, from his application, I say, to his subject, whatever it may be, of the ideas

On man, on nature, and on human life,[4]

which he has acquired for himself. The line quoted is Wordsworth's own; and his superiority arises from his powerful use, in his best pieces, his powerful application to his subject, of ideas "on man, on nature, and on human life."

Voltaire, with his signal acuteness, most truly remarked that "no nation has treated in poetry moral ideas with more energy and depth than the English nation." And he adds: "There, it seems to me, is the great merit of the English poets." Voltaire does not mean, by "treating in poetry moral ideas," the composing moral and didactic poems—that brings us but a very little way in poetry. He means just the same thing as was meant when I spoke above "of the noble and profound application of ideas to life"; and he means the application of these ideas under the conditions fixed for us by the laws of poetic beauty and poetic truth. If it is said that to call these ideas *moral* ideas is to introduce a strong and injurious limitation, I answer that it is to do nothing of the kind, because moral ideas are really so main a part of human life. The question, *how to live*, is itself a moral idea; and it is the question which most interests every man, and with which, in some way or other, he is perpetually occupied. A large sense is of course to be given to the term *moral*. Whatever bears upon the question, "how to live," comes under it.

Nor love thy life, nor hate; but, what thou liv'st,
Live well; how long or short, permit to heaven.[5]

4. *The Recluse*, line 754.   5. *Paradise Lost* XI.553–54.

In those fine lines Milton utters, as everyone at once perceives, a moral idea. Yes, but so too, when Keats consoles the forward-bending lover on the Grecian Urn, the lover arrested and presented in immortal relief by the sculptor's hand before he can kiss, with the line,

> Forever wilt thou love, and she be fair,[6]

he utters a moral idea. When Shakespeare says that

> We are such stuff
> As dreams are made on, and our little life
> Is rounded with a sleep,[7]

he utters a moral idea.

Voltaire was right in thinking that the energetic and profound treatment of moral ideas, in this large sense, is what distinguishes the English poetry. He sincerely meant praise, not dispraise or hint of limitation; and they err who suppose that poetic limitation is a necessary consequence of the fact, the fact being granted as Voltaire states it. If what distinguishes the greatest poets is their powerful and profound application of ideas to life, which surely no good critic will deny, then to prefix to the term ideas here the term moral makes hardly any difference, because human life itself is in so preponderating a degree moral.

It is important, therefore, to hold fast to this: that poetry is at bottom a criticism of life; that the greatness of a poet lies in his powerful and beautiful application of ideas to life—to the question: How to live. Morals are often treated in a narrow and false fashion; they are bound up with systems of thought and belief which have had their day; they are fallen into the hands of pedants and professional dealers; they grow tiresome to some of us. We find attraction, at times, even in a poetry of revolt against them; in a poetry which might take for its motto Omar Khayyám's words: "Let us make up in the tavern for the time which we have wasted in the mosque." Or we find attractions in a poetry indifferent to them: in a poetry where the contents may be what they will, but where the form is studied and exquisite. We delude ourselves in either case; and the best cure for our delusion is to let our minds rest upon that great and inexhaustible word *life*, until we learn to enter into its meaning. A poetry of revolt against moral ideas is a poetry of revolt against life; a poetry of indifference towards moral ideas is a poetry of indifference towards *life*.

Epictetus had a happy figure for things like the play of the senses, or literary form and finish, or argumentative ingenuity, in compari-

---

6. *Ode on a Grecian Urn*, line 20.   7. *The Tempest* IV.i.156–58.

son with "the best and master thing" for us, as he called it, the concern, how to live. Some people were afraid of them, he said, or they disliked and undervalued them. Such people were wrong; they were unthankful or cowardly. But the things might also be over-prized, and treated as final when they are not. They bear to life the relation which inns bear to home. "As if a man, journeying home, and finding a nice inn on the road, and liking it, were to stay forever at the inn! Man, thou hast forgotten thine object; thy journey was not *to* this, but *through* this. 'But this inn is taking.' And how many other inns, too, are taking, and how many fields and meadows! but as places of passage merely. You have an object, which is this: to get home, to do your duty to your family, friends, and fellow-countrymen, to attain inward freedom, serenity, happi-ness, contentment. Style takes your fancy, arguing takes your fancy, and you forget your home and want to make your abode with them and to stay with them, on the plea that they are taking. Who denies that they are taking? but as places of passage, as inns. And when I say this, you suppose me to be attacking the care for style, the care for argument. I am not; I attack the resting in them, the not looking to the end which is beyond them."

Now, when we come across a poet like Théophile Gautier[8] we have a poet who has taken up his abode at an inn, and never got farther. There may be inducements to this or that one of us, at this or that moment, to find delight in him, to cleave to him; but after all, we do not change the truth about him—we only stay ourselves in his inn along with him. And when we come across a poet like Wordsworth, who sings

> Of truth, of grandeur, beauty, love, and hope,
> And melancholy fear subdued by faith,
> Of blessed consolations in distress,
> Of moral strength and intellectual power,
> Of joy in widest commonalty spread—[9]

then we have a poet intent on "the best and master thing," and who prosecutes his journey home. We say, for brevity's sake, that he deals with *life*, because he deals with that in which life really con-sists. This is what Voltaire means to praise in the English poets—this dealing with what is really life. But always it is the mark of the greatest poets that they deal with it; and to say that the English

---

8. Théophile Gautier (1811–72), a poet whose preoccupation with "literary form and finish" and indifference towards edification in literature made him an important exponent of art for art's sake in France, like D. G. Rossetti in Eng-land. Arnold often deplored his fellow Victorians' fondness for the stunning phrasemaking of such poets as Tenny-son, Keats, and Rossetti.
9. *The Recluse*, lines 767–71.

poets are remarkable for dealing with it, is only another way of saying, what is true, that in poetry the English genius has especially shown its power.

Wordsworth deals with it, and his greatness lies in his dealing with it so powerfully. I have named a number of celebrated poets above all of whom he, in my opinion, deserves to be placed. He is to be placed above poets like Voltaire, Dryden, Pope, Lessing, Schiller, because these famous personages, with a thousand gifts and merits, never, or scarcely ever, attain the distinctive accent and utterance of the high and genuine poets—

> *Quique pii vates et Phoebo digna locuti,*[1]

at all. Burns, Keats, Heine, not to speak of others in our list, have this accent—who can doubt it? And at the same time they have treasures of humor, felicity, passion, for which in Wordsworth we shall look in vain. Where, then, is Wordsworth's superiority? It is here; he deals with more of *life* than they do; he deals with *life*, as a whole, more powerfully.

No Wordsworthian will doubt this. Nay, the fervent Wordsworthian will add, as Mr. Leslie Stephen does, that Wordsworth's poetry is precious because his philosophy is sound; that his "ethical system is as distinctive and capable of exposition as Bishop Butler's"; that his poetry is informed by ideas which "fall spontaneously into a scientific system of thought."[2] But we must be on our guard against the Wordsworthians, if we want to secure for Wordsworth his due rank as a poet. The Wordsworthians are apt to praise him for the wrong things, and to lay far too much stress upon what they call his philosophy. His poetry is the reality, his philosophy—so far, at least, as it may put on the form and habit of "a scientific system of thought," and the more that it puts them on—is the illusion. Perhaps we shall one day learn to make this proposition general, and to say: Poetry is the reality, philosophy the illusion. But in Wordsworth's case, at any rate, we cannot do him justice until we dismiss his formal philosophy.

The *Excursion* abounds with philosophy and therefore the *Excursion* is to the Wordsworthian what it never can be to the disinterested lover of poetry—a satisfactory work. "Duty exists," says Wordsworth, in the *Excursion;* and then he proceeds thus—

> . . . Immutably survive,
> For our support, the measures and the forms,
> Which an abstract Intelligence supplies,

---

1. "Those devout bards who utter things worthy of Phoebus" (Virgil, *Aeneid* VI.662).

2. From an essay on "Wordsworth's Ethics" in *Hours in a Library* by Leslie Stephen (1832–1904).

Whose kingdom is, where time and space are not.[3]

And the Wordsworthian is delighted, and thinks that here is a sweet union of philosophy and poetry. But the disinterested lover of poetry will feel that the lines carry us really not a step farther than the proposition which they would interpret; that they are a tissue of elevated but abstract verbiage, alien to the very nature of poetry.

Or let us come direct to the center of Wordsworth's philosophy, as "an ethical system, as distinctive and capable of systematical exposition as Bishop Butler's"—

> . . . One adequate support
> For the calamities of mortal life
> Exists, one only—an assured belief
> That the procession of our fate, howe'er
> Sad or disturbed, is ordered by a Being
> Of infinite benevolence and power;
> Whose everlasting purposes embrace
> All accidents, converting them to good.[4]

That is doctrine such as we hear in church too, religious and philosophic doctrine; and the attached Wordsworthian loves passages of such doctrine, and brings them forward in proof of his poet's excellence. But however true the doctrine may be, it has, as here presented, none of the characters of *poetic* truth, the kind of truth which we require from a poet, and in which Wordsworth is really strong.

Even the "intimations" of the famous *Ode*, those cornerstones of the supposed philosophic system of Wordsworth—the idea of the high instincts and affections coming out in childhood, testifying of a divine home recently left, and fading away as our life proceeds—this idea, of undeniable beauty as a play of fancy, has itself not the character of poetic truth of the best kind; it has no real solidity. The instinct of delight in Nature and her beauty had no doubt extraordinary strength in Wordsworth himself as a child. But to say that universally this instinct is mighty in childhood, and tends to die away afterwards, is to say what is extremely doubtful. In many people, perhaps with the majority of educated persons, the love of nature is nearly imperceptible at ten years old, but strong and operative at thirty. In general we may say of these high instincts of early childhood, the base of the alleged systematic philosophy of Wordsworth, what Thucydides says of the early achievements of the Greek race: "It is impossible to speak with certainty of what is so remote; but from all that we can really investigate, I should say

---

3. *The Excursion* IV.73–76.   4. *The Excursion* IV.10–17.

that they were no very great things."

Finally, the "scientific system of thought" in Wordsworth gives us at least such poetry as this, which the devout Wordsworthian accepts—

> O for the coming of that glorious time
> When, prizing knowledge as her noblest wealth
> And best protection, this Imperial Realm,
> While she exacts allegiance, shall admit
> An obligation, on her part, to *teach*
> Them who are born to serve her and obey;
> Binding herself by statute to secure,
> For all the children whom her soil maintains,
> The rudiments of letters, and inform
> The mind with moral and religious truth.[5]

Wordsworth calls Voltaire dull, and surely the production of these un-Voltairian lines must have been imposed on him as a judgment! One can hear them being quoted at a Social Science Congress; one can call up the whole scene. A great room in one of our dismal provincial towns; dusty air and jaded afternoon daylight; benches full of men with bald heads and women in spectacles; an orator lifting up his face from a manuscript written within and without to declaim these lines of Wordsworth; and in the soul of any poor child of nature who may have wandered in thither, an unutterable sense of lamentation, and mourning, and woe!

"But turn we," as Wordsworth says, "from these bold, bad men,"[6] the haunters of Social Science Congresses. And let us be on our guard, too, against the exhibitors and extollers of a "scientific system of thought" in Wordsworth's poetry. The poetry will never be seen aright while they thus exhibit it. The cause of its greatness is simple, and may be told quite simply. Wordsworth's poetry is great because of the extraordinary power with which Wordsworth feels the joy offered to us in nature, the joy offered to us in the simple primary affections and duties; and because of the extraordinary power with which, in case after case, he shows us this joy, and renders it so as to make us share it.

The source of joy from which he thus draws is the truest and most unfailing source of joy accessible to man. It is also accessible universally. Wordsworth brings us word, therefore, according to his own strong and characteristic line, he brings us word

> Of joy in widest commonalty spread.[7]

Here is an immense advantage for a poet. Wordsworth tells of what all seek, and tells of it at its truest and best source, and yet a

5. *The Excursion* IX.293–302.
6. In Wordsworth's poem *To the Lady*   *Fleming.*
7. *The Recluse,* line 771.

source where all may go and draw for it.

Nevertheless, we are not to suppose that everything is precious which Wordsworth, standing even at this perennial and beautiful source, may give us. Wordsworthians are apt to talk as if it must be. They will speak with the same reverence of *The Sailor's Mother*, for example, as of *Lucy Gray*. They do their master harm by such lack of discrimination. *Lucy Gray* is a beautiful success; *The Sailor's Mother* is a failure. To give aright what he wishes to give, to interpret and render successfully, is not always within Wordsworth's own command. It is within no poet's command; here is the part of the Muse, the inspiration, the God, the "not ourselves." In Wordsworth's case, the accident, for so it may almost be called, of inspiration, is of peculiar importance. No poet, perhaps, is so evidently filled with a new and sacred energy when the inspiration is upon him; no poet, when it fails him, is so left "weak as is a breaking wave."[8] I remember hearing him say that "Goethe's poetry was not inevitable enough." The remark is striking and true; no line in Goethe, as Goethe said himself, but its maker knew well how it came there. Wordsworth is right, Goethe's poetry is not inevitable; not inevitable enough. But Wordsworth's poetry, when he is at his best, is inevitable, as inevitable as Nature herself. It might seem that Nature not only gave him the matter for his poem, but wrote his poem for him. He has no style. He was too conversant with Milton not to catch at times his master's manner, and he has fine Miltonic lines; but he has no assured poetic style of his own, like Milton. When he seeks to have a style he falls into ponderosity and pomposity. In the *Excursion* we have his style, as an artistic product of his own creation; and although Jeffrey[9] completely failed to recognize Wordsworth's real greatness, he was yet not wrong in saying of the *Excursion*, as a work of poetic style: "This will never do." And yet magical as is that power, which Wordsworth has not, of assured and possessed poetic style, he has something which is an equivalent for it.

Everyone who has any sense for these things feels the subtle turn, the heightening, which is given to a poet's verse by his genius for style. We can feel it in the

> After life's fitful fever he sleeps well[1]—

of Shakespeare; in the

> . . . though fall'n on evil days,
> On evil days though fall'n, and evil tongues[2]—

8. Wordsworth, *A Poet's Epitaph,* line 58.
9. Francis Jeffrey (1773–1850), con-tributor to the *Edinburgh Review.*
1. *Macbeth* III.ii.23.
2. *Paradise Lost* VII.25–26.

of Milton. It is the incomparable charm of Milton's power of poetic style which gives such worth to *Paradise Regained*, and makes a great poem of a work in which Milton's imagination does not soar high. Wordsworth has in constant possession, and at command, no style of this kind; but he had too poetic a nature, and had read the great poets too well, not to catch, as I have already remarked, something of it occasionally. We find it not only in his Miltonic lines; we find it in such a phrase as this, where the manner is his own, not Milton's—

> the fierce confederate storm
> Of sorrow barricadoed evermore
> Within the walls of cities;[3]

although even here, perhaps, the power of style which is undeniable, is more properly that of eloquent prose than the subtle heightening and change wrought by genuine poetic style. It is style, again, and the elevation given by style, which chiefly makes the effectiveness of *Laodameia*. Still the right sort of verse to choose from Wordsworth, if we are to seize his true and most characteristic form of expression, is a line like this from *Michael*—

> And never lifted up a single stone.

There is nothing subtle in it, no heightening, no study of poetic style, strictly so called, at all; yet it is expression of the highest and most truly expressive kind.

Wordsworth owed much to Burns, and a style of perfect plainness, relying for effect solely on the weight and force of that which with entire fidelity it utters, Burns could show him.

> The poor inhabitant below
> Was quick to learn and wise to know,
> And keenly felt the friendly glow
> And softer flame;
> But thoughtless follies laid him low
> And stained his name.[4]

Everyone will be conscious of a likeness here to Wordsworth; and if Wordsworth did great things with this nobly plain manner, we must remember, what indeed he himself would always have been forward to acknowledge, that Burns used it before him.

Still Wordsworth's use of it has something unique and unmatchable. Nature herself seems, I say, to take the pen out of his hand, and to write for him with her own bare, sheer, penetrating power. This arises from two causes: from the profound sincereness with which Wordsworth feels his subject, and also from the profoundly sincere and natural character of his subject itself. He can and will treat such a subject with nothing but the most plain, first-hand, al-

3. *The Recluse*, lines 831–33.   4. From Burns's *A Bard's Epitaph*.

most austere naturalness. His expression may often be called bald, as, for instance, in the poem of *Resolution and Independence;* but it is bald as the bare mountaintops are bald, with a baldness which is full of grandeur.

Wherever we meet with the successful balance, in Wordsworth, of profound truth of subject with profound truth of execution, he is unique. His best poems are those which most perfectly exhibit this balance. I have a warm admiration for *Laodameia* and for the great *Ode;* but if I am to tell the very truth, I find *Laodameia* not wholly free from something artificial, and the great *Ode* not wholly free from something declamatory. If I had to pick out poems of a kind most perfectly to show Wordsworth's unique power, I should rather choose poems such as *Michael, The Fountain, The Highland Reaper.*[5] And poems with the peculiar and unique beauty which distinguishes these, Wordsworth produced in considerable number; besides very many other poems of which the worth, although not so rare as the worth of these, is still exceedingly high.

On the whole, then, as I said at the beginning, not only is Wordsworth eminent by reason of the goodness of his best work, but he is eminent also by reason of the great body of good work which he has left to us. With the ancients I will not compare him. In many respects the ancients are far above us, and yet there is something that we demand which they can never give. Leaving the ancients, let us come to the poets and poetry of Christendom. Dante, Shakespeare, Molière, Milton, Goethe are altogether larger and more splendid luminaries in the poetical heaven than Wordsworth. But I know not where else, among the moderns, we are to find his superiors.

To disengage the poems which show his power, and to present them to the English-speaking public and to the world, is the object of this volume. I by no means say that it contains all which in Wordsworth's poems is interesting. Except in the case of *Margaret,* a story composed separately from the rest of the *Excursion,* and which belongs to a different part of England, I have not ventured on detaching portions of poems, or on giving any piece otherwise than as Wordsworth himself gave it. But under the conditions imposed by this reserve, the volume contains, I think, everything, or nearly everything, which may best serve him with the majority of lovers of poetry, nothing which may disserve him.

I have spoken lightly of Wordsworthians; and if we are to get Wordsworth recognized by the public and by the world, we must recommend him not in the spirit of a clique, but in the spirit of disinterested lovers of poetry. But I am a Wordsworthian myself. I can read with pleasure and edification *Peter Bell,* and the whole series of *Ecclesiastical Sonnets,* and the address to Mr. Wilkinson's

5. I.e., *The Solitary Reaper.*

spade, and even the *Thanksgiving Ode*—everything of Wordsworth, I think, except *Vaudracour and Julia*. It is not for nothing that one has been brought up in the veneration of a man so truly worthy of homage; that one has seen him and heard him, lived in his neighborhood, and been familiar with his country. No Wordsworthian has a tenderer affection for this pure and sage master than I, or is less really offended by his defects. But Wordsworth is something more than the pure and sage master of a small band of devoted followers, and we ought not to rest satisfied until he is seen to be what he is. He is one of the very chief glories of English Poetry; and by nothing is England so glorious as by her poetry. Let us lay aside every weight which hinders our getting him recognized as this, and let our one study be to bring to pass, as widely as possible and as truly as possible, his own word concerning his poems: "They will co-operate with the benign tendencies in human nature and society, and will, in their degree, be efficacious in making men wiser, better, and happier."[6]

1879

The Study of Poetry[1]

"The future of poetry is immense, because in poetry, where it is worthy of its high destinies, our race, as time goes on, will find an ever surer and surer stay. There is not a creed which is not shaken, not an accredited dogma which is not shown to be questionable, not a received tradition which does not threaten to dissolve. Our religion has materialized itself in the fact, in the supposed fact; it has attached its emotion to the fact, and now the fact is failing it. But for poetry the idea is everything; the rest is a world of illusion, of divine illusion. Poetry attaches its emotion to the idea; the idea *is* the fact. The strongest part of our religion today is its unconscious poetry."

Let me be permitted to quote these words of my own, as uttering the thought which should, in my opinion, go with us and govern

6. Wordsworth's letter to Lady Beaumont, May 21, 1807.
1. Aside from its vindication of the importance of literature, this essay is an interesting example of the variety of Arnold's own reading. To know literature in only one language seemed to him not to know literature. His personal *Notebooks* show that throughout his active life he continued to read books in French, German, Italian, Latin, and Greek. His favorite authors in these languages are used by him as a means of testing English poetry. The testing is sometimes a severe one. Readers may also protest that despite Arnold's own wit, his essay is limited by an incomplete recognition of the values of comic literature, a shortcoming abundantly evident in the discussion of Chaucer. Nevertheless, whether we agree or disagree with some of Arnold's verdicts, we can be attracted by the combination of traditionalism and impressionism on which these verdicts are based, and we can enjoy the memorable phrasemaking in which the verdicts are expressed. *The Study of Poetry* has been extraordinarily potent in shaping literary tastes in England and in America.

us in all our study of poetry. In the present work[2] it is the course of one great contributory stream to the world-river of poetry that we are invited to follow. We are here invited to trace the stream of English poetry. But whether we set ourselves, as here, to follow only one of the several streams that make the mighty river of poetry, or whether we seek to know them all, our governing thought should be the same. We should conceive of poetry worthily, and more highly than it has been the custom to conceive of it. We should conceive of it as capable of higher uses, and called to higher destinies, than those which in general men have assigned to it hitherto. More and more mankind will discover that we have to turn to poetry to interpret life for us, to console us, to sustain us. Without poetry, our science will appear incomplete; and most of what now passes with us for religion and philosophy will be replaced by poetry. Science, I say, will appear incomplete without it. For finely and truly docs Wordsworth call poetry "the impassioned expression which is in the countenance of all science";[3] and what is a countenance without its expression? Again, Wordsworth finely and truly calls poetry "the breath and finer spirit of all knowledge": our religion, parading evidences such as those on which the popular mind relies now; our philosophy, pluming itself on its reasonings about causation and finite and infinite being; what are they but the shadows and dreams and false shows of knowledge? The day will come when we shall wonder at ourselves for having trusted to them, for having taken them seriously; and the more we perceive their hollowness, the more we shall prize "the breath and finer spirit of knowledge" offered to us by poetry.

But if we conceive thus highly of the destinies of poetry, we must also set our standard for poetry high, since poetry, to be capable of fulfilling such high destinies, must be poetry of a high order of excellence. We must accustom ourselves to a high standard and to a strict judgment. Sainte-Beuve[4] relates that Napoleon one day said, when somebody was spoken of in his presence as a charlatan: "Charlatan as much as you please; but where is there *not* charlatanism?"—"Yes," answers Sainte-Beuve, "in politics, in the art of governing mankind, that is perhaps true. But in the order of thought, in art, the glory, the eternal honor is that charlatanism shall find no entrance; herein lies the inviolableness of that noble portion of man's being." It is admirably said, and let us hold fast to it. In poetry, which is thought and art in one, it is the glory, the eternal honor, that charlatanism shall find no entrance; that this noble sphere be kept inviolate and inviolable. Charlatanism is for confusing or obliterating the distinctions between excellent and in-

---

2. An anthology of English poetry for which Arnold's essay served as the introduction.
3. See Wordsworth's Preface to *Lyrical Ballads*.
4. Charles Augustin Sainte-Beuve (1804–69), French critic who influenced Arnold.

ferior, sound and unsound or only half-sound, true and untrue or
only half-true. It is charlatanism, conscious or unconscious, whenever we confuse or obliterate these. And in poetry, more than anywhere else, it is unpermissible to confuse or obliterate them. For in
poetry the distinction between excellent and inferior, sound and
unsound or only half-sound, true and untrue or only half-true, is
of paramount importance. It is of paramount importance because
of the high destinies of poetry. In poetry, as a criticism of life under
the conditions fixed for such a criticism by the laws of poetic truth
and poetic beauty, the spirit of our race will find, we have said, as
time goes on and as other helps fail, its consolation and stay. But
the consolation and stay will be of power in proportion to the power
of the criticism of life. And the criticism of life will be of power in
proportion as the poetry conveying it is excellent rather than inferior, sound rather than unsound or half-sound, true rather than
untrue or half-true.

The best poetry is what we want; the best poetry will be found
to have a power of forming, sustaining, and delighting us, as nothing else can. A clearer, deeper sense of the best in poetry, and of
the strength and joy to be drawn from it, is the most precious benefit which we can gather from a poetical collection such as the
present. And yet in the very nature and conduct of such a collection
there is inevitably something which tends to obscure in us the consciousness of what our benefit should be, and to distract us from the
pursuit of it. We should therefore steadily set it before our minds
at the outset, and should compel ourselves to revert constantly to
the thought of it as we proceed.

Yes; constantly in reading poetry, a sense for the best, the really
excellent, and of the strength and joy to be drawn from it, should
be present in our minds and should govern our estimate of what we
read. But this real estimate, the only true one, is liable to be superseded, if we are not watchful, by two other kinds of estimate, the
historic estimate and the personal estimate, both of which are fallacious. A poet or a poem may count to us historically, they may
count to us on grounds personal to ourselves, and they may count
to us really. They may count to us historically. The course of development of a nation's language, thought, and poetry, is profoundly interesting; and by regarding a poet's work as a stage in
this course of development we may easily bring ourselves to make
it of more importance as poetry than in itself it really is, we may
come to use a language of quite exaggerated praise in criticizing
it; in short, to overrate it. So arises in our poetic judgments the
fallacy caused by the estimate which we may call historic. Then,
again, a poet or a poem may count to us on grounds personal to ourselves. Our personal affinities, likings, and circumstances, have great
power to sway our estimate of this or that poet's work, and to make

us attach more importance to it as poetry than in itself it really possesses, because to us it is, or has been, of high importance. Here also we overrate the object of our interest, and apply to it a language of praise which is quite exaggerated. And thus we get the source of a second fallacy in our poetic judgments—the fallacy caused by an estimate which we may call personal.

Both fallacies are natural. It is evident how naturally the study of the history and development of a poetry may incline a man to pause over reputations and works once conspicuous but now obscure, and to quarrel with a careless public for skipping, in obedience to mere tradition and habit, from one famous name or work in its national poetry to another, ignorant of what it misses, and of the reason for keeping what it keeps, and of the whole process of growth in its poetry. The French have become diligent students of their own early poetry, which they long neglected; the study makes many of them dissatisfied with their so-called classical poetry, the court-tragedy of the seventeenth century, a poetry which Pellisson[5] long ago reproached with its want of the true poetic stamp, with its *politesse stérile et rampante*,[6] but which nevertheless has reigned in France as absolutely as if it had been the perfection of classical poetry indeed. The dissatisfaction is natural; yet a lively and accomplished critic, M. Charles d'Héricault, the editor of Clément Marot,[7] goes too far when he says that "the cloud of glory playing round a classic is a mist as dangerous to the future of a literature as it is intolerable for the purposes of history." "It hinders," he goes on, "it hinders us from seeing more than one single point, the culminating and exceptional point; the summary, fictitious and arbitrary, of a thought and of a work. It substitutes a halo for a physiognomy, it puts a statue where there was once a man, and hiding from us all trace of the labor, the attempts, the weaknesses, the failures, it claims not study but veneration; it does not show us how the thing is done, it imposes upon us a model. Above all, for the historian this creation of classic personages is inadmissible; for it withdraws the poet from his time, from his proper life, it breaks historical relationships, it blinds criticism by conventional admiration, and renders the investigation of literary origins unacceptable. It gives us a human personage no longer, but a God seated immovable amidst His perfect work, like Jupiter on Olympus; and hardly will it be possible for the young student, to whom such work is exhibited at such a distance from him, to believe that it did not issue ready made from that divine head."

All this is brilliantly and tellingly said, but we must plead for a

5. Paul Pellison, 17th-century French critic.
6. "Conventionality that is barren and bombastic."
7. D'Héricault's edition of Marot was published in 1868. The graceful poetry of Clément Marot (ca. 1495–1544) was admired and imitated in late 19th-century England, sometimes at the expense of overlooking the excellences of the more severely classical 17th-century French poets such as Racine.

distinction. Everything depends on the reality of a poet's classic character. If he is a dubious classic, let us sift him; if he is a false classic, let us explode him. But if he is a real classic, if his work belongs to the class of the very best (for this is the true and right meaning of the word *classic, classical*), then the great thing for us is to feel and enjoy his work as deeply as ever we can, and to appreciate the wide difference between it and all work which has not the same high character. This is what is salutary, this is what is formative; this is the great benefit to be got from the study of poetry. Everything which interferes with it, which hinders it, is injurious. True, we must read our classic with open eyes, and not with eyes blinded with superstition; we must perceive when his work comes short, when it drops out of the class of the very best, and we must rate it, in such cases, at its proper value. But the use of this negative criticism is not in itself, it is entirely in its enabling us to have a clearer sense and a deeper enjoyment of what is truly excellent. To trace the labor, the attempts, the weaknesses, the failures of a genuine classic, to acquaint oneself with his time and his life and his historical relationships, is mere literary dilettantism unless it has that clear sense and deeper enjoyment for its end. It may be said that the more we know about a classic the better we shall enjoy him; and, if we lived as long as Methuselah and had all of us heads of perfect clearness and wills of perfect steadfastness, this might be true in fact as it is plausible in theory. But the case here is much the same as the case with the Greek and Latin studies of our schoolboys. The elaborate philological groundwork which we require them to lay is in theory an admirable preparation for appreciating the Greek and Latin authors worthily. The more thoroughly we lay the groundwork, the better we shall be able, it may be said, to enjoy the authors. True, if time were not so short, and schoolboys' wits not so soon tired and their power of attention exhausted; only, as it is, the elaborate philological preparation goes on, but the authors are little known and less enjoyed. So with the investigator of "historic origins" in poetry. He ought to enjoy the true classic all the better for his investigations; he often is distracted from the enjoyment of the best, and with the less good he overbusies himself, and is prone to overrate it in proportion to the trouble which it has cost him.

The idea of tracing historic origins and historical relationships cannot be absent from a compilation like the present. And naturally the poets to be exhibited in it will be assigned to those persons for exhibition who are known to prize them highly, rather than to those who have no special inclination towards them. Moreover the very occupation with an author, and the business of exhibiting him, disposes us to affirm and amplify his importance. In the present work, therefore, we are sure of frequent temptation to adopt the historic estimate, or the personal estimate, and to forget the real estimate; which latter, nevertheless, we must employ if we are to make poetry yield us its full benefit. So high is that benefit, the benefit of clearly feeling and of deeply enjoying the really excellent, the truly classic in poetry, that we do well, I say, to set it fixedly before our minds as our object in studying poets and poetry, and to make the desire of attaining it the one principle to which, as the *Imitation* says, whatever we may read or come to know, we always return. *Cum multa legeris et cognoveris, ad unum semper oportet redire principium.*[8]

The historic estimate is likely in especial to affect our judgment and our language when we are dealing with ancient poets; the personal estimate when we are dealing with poets our contemporaries, or at any rate modern. The exaggerations due to the historic estimate are not in themselves, perhaps, of very much gravity. Their report hardly enters the general ear; probably they do not always impose even on the literary men who adopt them. But they lead to a dangerous abuse of language. So we hear Cædmon,[9] amongst our own poets, compared to Milton. I have already noticed the enthusiasm of one accomplished French critic for "historic origins." Another eminent French critic, M. Vitet, comments upon that famous document of the early poetry of his nation, the *Chanson de Roland*.[1] It is indeed a most interesting document. The *joculator* or *jongleur*[2] Taillefer, who was with William the Conqueror's army at Hastings, marched before the Norman troops, so said the tradition, singing "of Charlemagne and of Roland and of Oliver, and of the vassals who died at Roncevaux"; and it is suggested that in the *Chanson de Roland* by one Turoldus or *Théroulde*, a poem preserved in a manuscript of the twelfth century in the Bodleian Library at Oxford, we have certainly the matter, perhaps even some of the words, of the chant which Taillefer sang. The poem has vigor and freshness; it is not without pathos. But M. Vitet is not satisfied with seeing in it a document of some poetic value, and of very high historic and linguistic value; he sees in it a grand and beautiful work, a monument of epic genius. In its general design he finds the grandiose conception, in its details he finds the constant union of simplicity with greatness, which are the marks, he truly says, of the genuine epic, and distinguish it from the artificial epic of literary ages. One thinks of Homer; this is the sort of praise which is given to Homer, and justly given. Higher praise there cannot well be, and it is the praise due to epic poetry of the highest order only, and to no other. Let us try, then, the *Chanson de Ro-*

---

8. "When you have read and learned many things, you ought always to return to the one principle" (*The Imitation of Christ* III.43, famous devotional work by Thomas à Kempis, 1380–1471).
9. 7th-century Old English poet.

1. 11th-century epic poem in Old French which tells of the wars of Charlemagne against the Moors in Spain, and of the bravery of the French leaders, Roland and Oliver.
2. I.e., minstrel.

land at its best. Roland, mortally wounded, lays himself down under a pine tree, with his face turned towards Spain and the enemy—

> De plusurs choses à remembrer li prist,
> De tantes teres cume li bers cunquist,
> De dulce France, des humes de sun lign,
> De Carlemagne sun seignor ki l'nurrit.³

That is primitive work, I repeat, with an undeniable poetic quality of its own. It deserves such praise, and such praise is sufficient for it. But now turn to Homer—

> Ὡς φάτο τοὺς δ' ἤδη κάτεχεν φυσίζοος αἶα
> ἐν Λακεδαίμονι αὖθι, φίλῃ ἐν πατρίδι γαίῃ.⁴

We are here in another world, another order of poetry altogether; here is rightly due such supreme praise as that which M. Vitet gives to the *Chanson de Roland*. If our words are to have any meaning, if our judgments are to have any solidity, we must not heap that supreme praise upon poetry of an order immeasurably inferior.

Indeed there can be no more useful help for discovering what poetry belongs to the class of the truly excellent, and can therefore do us most good, than to have always in one's mind lines and expressions of the great masters, and to apply them as a touchstone to other poetry. Of course we are not to require this other poetry to resemble them; it may be very dissimilar. But if we have any tact we shall find them, when we have lodged them well in our minds, an infallible touchstone for detecting the presence or absence of high poetic quality, and also the degree of this quality, in all other poetry which we may place beside them. Short passages, even single lines, will serve our turn quite sufficiently. Take the two lines which I have just quoted from Homer, the poet's comment on Helen's mention of her brothers—or take his

> Ἀ δειλώ, τί σφῶϊ δόμεν Πηλῆϊ ἄνακτι
> θνητῷ; ὑμεῖς δ' ἐστὸν ἀγήρω τ' ἀθανάτω τε.
> ἦ ἵνα δυστήνοισι μετ' ἀνδράσιν ἄλγε' ἔχητον;⁵

the address of Zeus to the horses of Peleus—or take finally his

> Καὶ σέ, γέρον, τὸ πρὶν μὲν ἀκούομεν ὄλβιον εἶναι⁶

3. " 'Then began he to call many things to remembrance—all the lands which his valor conquered and pleasant France, and the men of his lineage, and Charlemagne his liege lord who nourished him.' *Chanson de Roland* III.939–42" [Arnold's note].
4. " 'So said she; they long since in Earth's soft arms were reposing, / There, in their own dear land, their fatherland, Lacedaemon.' *Iliad* III.243–

44 (translated by Dr. Hawtrey)" [Arnold's note].
5. " 'Ah, unhappy pair, why gave we you to King Peleus, to a mortal? but ye are without old age, and immortal. Was it that with men born to misery ye might have sorrow?' *Iliad* XVII.443–45" [Arnold's note].
6. " 'Nay, and thou too, old man, in former days wast, as we hear, happy.' *Iliad* XXIV.543" [Arnold's note].

the words of Achilles to Priam, a suppliant before him Take that incomparable line and a half of Dante, Ugolino's tremendous words—

> Io no piangeva; sì dentro impietrai.
> Piangevan elli . . .[7]

take the lovely words of Beatrice to Virgil—

> Io son fatta da Dio, sua mercè, tale,
> Che la vostra miseria non mi tange,
> Nè fiamma d'esto incendio non m'assale . . .[8]

take the simple, but perfect, single line—

> In la sua volontade è nostra pace.[9]

Take of Shakespeare a line or two of Henry the Fourth's expostulation with sleep—

> Wilt thou upon the high and giddy mast
> Seal up the shipboy's eyes, and rock his brains
> In cradle of the rude imperious surge . . .[1]

and take, as well, Hamlet's dying request to Horatio—

> If thou didst ever hold me in thy heart,
> Absent thee from felicity awhile,
> And in this harsh world draw thy breath in pain,
> To tell my story . . .[2]

Take of Milton that Miltonic passage—

> Darkened so, yet shone
> Above them all the archangel; but his face
> Deep scars of thunder had intrenched, and care
> Sat on his faded cheek . . .[3]

add two such lines as—

> And courage never to submit or yield
> And what is else not to be overcome . . .[4]

and finish with the exquisite close to the loss of Proserpine, the loss

> . . . which cost Ceres all that pain
> To seek her through the world.[5]

---

7. " 'I wailed not, so of stone I grew within; *they* wailed.' *Inferno* XXXIII. 49–50" [Arnold's note].
8. " 'Of such sort hath God, thanked be His mercy, made me, that your misery toucheth me not, neither doth the flame of this fire strike me.' *Inferno* II.91–93" [Arnold's note].

9. " 'In His will is our peace.' *Paradiso* III.85" [Arnold's note].
1. *2 Henry IV* III.i.18–20.
2. *Hamlet* V.ii.357–60.
3. *Paradise Lost* I.599–602.
4. *Ibid.* I.108–9.
5. *Ibid.* IV.271–72.

These few lines, if we have tact and can use them, are enough even of themselves to keep clear and sound our judgments about poetry, to save us from fallacious estimates of it, to conduct us to a real estimate.

The specimens I have quoted differ widely from one another, but they have in common this: the possession of the very highest poetical quality. If we are thoroughly penetrated by their power, we shall find that we have acquired a sense enabling us, whatever poetry may be laid before us, to feel the degree in which a high poetical quality is present or wanting there. Critics give themselves great labor to draw out what in the abstract constitutes the characters of a high quality of poetry. It is much better simply to have recourse to concrete examples—to take specimens of poetry of the high, the very highest quality, and to say: The characters of a high quality of poetry are what is expressed *there*. They are far better recognized by being felt in the verse of the master, than by being perused in the prose of the critic. Nevertheless if we are urgently pressed to give some critical account of them, we may safely, perhaps, venture on laying down, not indeed how and why the characters arise, but where and in what they arise. They are in the matter and substance of the poetry, and they are in its manner and style. Both of these, the substance and matter on the one hand, the style and manner on the other, have a mark, an accent, of high beauty, worth, and power. But if we are asked to define this mark and accent in the abstract, our answer must be: No, for we should thereby be darkening the question, not clearing it. The mark and accent are as given by the substance and matter of that poetry, by the style and manner of that poetry, and of all other poetry which is akin to it in quality.

Only one thing we may add as to the substance and matter of poetry, guiding ourselves by Aristotle's profound observation that the superiority of poetry over history consists in its possessing a higher truth and a higher seriousness ($\phi\iota\lambda\sigma\sigma\phi\dot{\omega}\tau\epsilon\rho\sigma\nu$ $\kappa\alpha\grave{\iota}$ $\sigma\pi\sigma\upsilon\delta\alpha\iota\dot{\sigma}\tau\epsilon\rho\sigma\nu$).[6] Let us add, therefore, to what we have said, this: that the substance and matter of the best poetry acquire their special character from possessing, in an eminent degree, truth and seriousness. We may add yet further, what is in itself evident, that to the style and manner of the best poetry their special character, their accent, is given by their diction, and, even yet more, by their movement. And though we distinguish between the two characters, the two accents, of superiority, yet they are nevertheless vitally connected one with the other. The superior character of truth and seriousness, in the matter and substance of the best poetry, is inseparable from the superiority of diction and movement marking its style and manner. The two superiorities are closely related, and

6. Aristotle, *Poetics* IX.

are in steadfast proportion one to the other. So far as high poetic truth and seriousness are wanting to a poet's matter and substance, so far also, we may be sure, will a high poetic stamp of diction and movement be wanting to his style and manner. In proportion as this high stamp of diction and movement, again, is absent from a poet's style and manner, we shall find, also, that high poetic truth and seriousness are absent from his substance and matter.

So stated, these are but dry generalities; their whole force lies in their application. And I could wish every student of poetry to make the application of them for himself. Made by himself, the application would impress itself upon his mind far more deeply than made by me. Neither will my limits allow me to make any full application of the generalities above propounded; but in the hope of bringing out, at any rate, some significance in them, and of establishing an important principle more firmly by their means, I will, in the space which remains to me, follow rapidly from the commencement the course of our English poetry with them in my view.

Once more I return to the early poetry of France, with which our own poetry, in its origins, is indissolubly connected. In the twelfth and thirteenth centuries, that seed time of all modern language and literature, the poetry of France had a clear predominance in Europe. Of the two divisions of that poetry, its productions in the *langue d'oïl* and its productions in the *langue d'oc*,[7] the poetry of the *langue d'oc*, of southern France, of the troubadours, is of importance because of its effect on Italian literature—the first literature of modern Europe to strike the true and grand note, and to bring forth, as in Dante and Petrarch it brought forth, classics. But the predominance of French poetry in Europe, during the twelfth and thirteenth centuries, is due to its poetry of the *langue d'oïl*, the poetry of northern France and of the tongue which is now the French language. In the twelfth century the bloom of this romance poetry was earlier and stronger in England, at the court of our Anglo-Norman kings, than in France itself. But it was a bloom of French poetry; and as our native poetry formed itself, it formed itself out of this. The romance poems which took possession of the heart and imagination of Europe in the twelfth and thirteenth centuries are French; "they are," as Southey justly says, "the pride of French literature, nor have we anything which can be placed in competition with them." Themes were supplied from all quarters: but the romance setting which was common to them all, and which gained the ear of Europe, was French. This constituted for the French poetry, literature, and language, at the height of the Middle Age, an unchallenged predominance. The

7. Medieval dialects of France; in the northern dialect, from which modern French derives, the word *oui* ("yes") was pronounced *oïl;* in the southern dialect it was pronounced *oc.*

Italian Brunetto Latini, the master of Dante, wrote his *Treasure* in French because, he says, "*la parleure en est plus délitable et plus commune à toutes gens.*"[8] In the same century, the thirteenth, the French romance writer, Christian of Troyes, formulates the claims, in chivalry and letters, of France, his native country, as follows:

> *Or vous ert par ce livre apris,*
> *Que Gresse ot de chevalerie*
> *Le premier los et de clergie;*
> *Puis vint chevalerie à Rome,*
> *Et de la clergie la some,*
> *Qui ore est en France venue.*
> *Diex doinst qu'ele i soit retenue*
> *Et que li lius li abelisse*
> *Tant que de France n'isse*
> *L'onor qui s'i est arestée!*

"Now by this book you will learn that first Greece had the renown for chivalry and letters; then chivalry and the primacy in letters passed to Rome, and now it is come to France. God grant it may be kept there; and that the place may please it so well, that the honor which has come to make stay in France may never depart thence!"

Yet it is now all gone, this French romance poetry, of which the weight of substance and the power of style are not unfairly represented by this extract from Christian of Troyes. Only by means of the historic estimate can we persuade ourselves now to think that any of it is of poetical importance.

But in the fourteenth century there comes an Englishman nourished on this poetry; taught his trade by this poetry, getting words, rhyme, meter from this poetry; for even of that stanza which the Italians used, and which Chaucer derived immediately from the Italians, the basis and suggestion was probably given in France. Chaucer (I have already named him) fascinated his contemporaries, but so too did Christian of Troyes and Wolfram of Eschenbach.[9] Chaucer's power of fascination, however, is enduring; his poetical importance does not need the assistance of the historic estimate; it is real. He is a genuine source of joy and strength, which is flowing still for us and will flow always. He will be read, as time goes on, far more generally than he is read now. His language is a cause of difficulty for us; but so also, and I think in quite as great a degree, is the language of Burns. In Chaucer's case, as in that of Burns, it is a difficulty to be unhesitatingly accepted and overcome.

If we ask ourselves wherein consists the immense superiority of Chaucer's poetry over the romance poetry—why it is that in passing from this to Chaucer we suddenly feel ourselves to be in an-

---

8. "French speech is more delightful and more commonly known to all peoples."

9. 12th-century German poet.

other world, we shall find that his superiority is both in the substance of his poetry and in the style of his poetry. His superiority in substance is given by his large, free, simple, clear yet kindly view of human life—so unlike the total want, in the romance poets, of all intelligent command of it. Chaucer has not their helplessness; he has gained the power to survey the world from a central, a truly human point of view. We have only to call to mind the Prologue to *The Canterbury Tales*. The right comment upon it is Dryden's: "It is sufficient to say, according to the proverb, that *here is God's plenty*." And again: "He is a perpetual fountain of good sense."[1] It is by a large, free, sound representation of things, that poetry, this high criticism of life, has truth of substance; and Chaucer's poetry has truth of substance.

Of his style and manner, if we think first of the romance poetry and then of Chaucer's divine liquidness of diction, his divine fluidity of movement, it is difficult to speak temperately. They are irresistible, and justify all the rapture with which his successors speak of his "gold dewdrops of speech."[2] Johnson misses the point entirely when he finds fault with Dryden for ascribing to Chaucer the first refinement of our numbers, and says that Gower[3] also can show smooth numbers and easy rhymes. The refinement of our numbers means something far more than this. A nation may have versifiers with smooth numbers and easy rhymes, and yet may have no real poetry at all. Chaucer is the father of our splendid English poetry; he is our "well of English undefiled,"[4] because by the lovely charm of his diction, the lovely charm of his movement, he makes an epoch and founds a tradition. In Spenser, Shakespeare, Milton, Keats, we can follow the tradition of the liquid diction, the fluid movement, of Chaucer; at one time it is his liquid diction of which in these poets we feel the virtue, and at another time it is his fluid movement. And the virtue is irresistible.

Bounded as is my space, I must yet find room for an example of Chaucer's virtue, as I have given examples to show the virtue of the great classics. I feel disposed to say that a single line is enough to show the charm of Chaucer's verse; that merely one line like this—

> O martyr souded[5] in virginitee!

has a virtue of manner and movement such as we shall not find in all the verse of romance poetry—but this is saying nothing. The

---

1. Both quotations are from Dryden's Preface to his *Fables* (1700).
2. *The Life of Our Lady*, a poem by John Lydgate (ca. 1370–ca. 1451).
3. John Gower (ca. 1325–1408), friend of Chaucer and author of the *Confessio Amantis*, a long poem in octosyllabic couplets.
4. Said of Chaucer by Spenser (*Faerie Queene* IV.ii.32).
5. "The French *soudé*: soldered, fixed fast" [Arnold's note]. The line is from the Prioress's Tale (line 127): Chaucer wrote "souded to" rather than "souded in."

virtue is such as we shall not find, perhaps, in all English poetry, outside the poets whom I have named as the special inheritors of Chaucer's tradition. A single line, however, is too little if we have not the strain of Chaucer's verse well in our memory; let us take a stanza. It is from *The Prioress's Tale*, the story of the Christian child murdered in a Jewry—

> My throte is cut unto my nekke-bone
> Saidè this child, and as by way of kinde
> I should have deyd, yea, longè time agone;
> But Jesu Christ, as ye in bookès finde,
> Will that his glory last and be in minde,
> And for the worship of his mother dere
> Yet may I sing O *Alma* loud and clere.

Wordsworth has modernized this Tale, and to feel how delicate and evanescent is the charm of verse, we have only to read Wordsworth's first three lines of this stanza after Chaucer's—

> My throat is cut unto the bone, I trow,
> Said this young child, and by the law of kind
> I should have died, yea, many hours ago.

The charm is departed. It is often said that the power of liquidness and fluidity in Chaucer's verse was dependent upon a free, a licentious dealing with language, such as is now impossible; upon a liberty, such as Burns too enjoyed, of making words like *neck*, *bird*, into a dissyllable by adding to them, and words like *cause*, *rhyme*, into a dissyllable by sounding the *e* mute. It is true that Chaucer's fluidity is conjoined with this liberty, and is admirably served by it; but we ought not to say that it was dependent upon it. It was dependent upon his talent. Other poets with a like liberty do not attain to the fluidity of Chaucer; Burns himself does not attain to it. Poets, again, who have a talent akin to Chaucer's, such as Shakespeare or Keats, have known how to attain to his fluidity without the like liberty.

And yet Chaucer is not one of the great classics. His poetry transcends and effaces, easily and without effort, all the romance poetry of Catholic Christendom; it transcends and effaces all the English poetry contemporary with it, it transcends and effaces all the English poetry subsequent to it down to the age of Elizabeth. Of such avail is poetic truth of substance, in its natural and necessary union with poetic truth of style. And yet, I say, Chaucer is not one of the great classics. He has not their accent. What is wanting to him is suggested by the mere mention of the name of the first great classic of Christendom, the immortal poet who died eighty years before Chaucer—Dante. The accent of such verse as

In la sua volontade è nostra pace . . .

is altogether beyond Chaucer's reach; we praise him, but we feel that this accent is out of the question for him. It may be said that it was necessarily out of the reach of any poet in the England of that stage of growth. Possibly; but we are to adopt a real, not a historic, estimate of poetry. However we may account for its absence, something is wanting, then, to the poetry of Chaucer, which poetry must have before it can be placed in the glorious class of the best. And there is no doubt what that something is. It is the σπουδαιότης, the high and excellent seriousness, which Aristotle assigns as one of the grand virtues of poetry. The substance of Chaucer's poetry, his view of things and his criticism of life, has largeness, freedom, shrewdness, benignity; but it has not this high seriousness. Homer's criticism of life has it, Dante's has it, Shakespeare's has it. It is this chiefly which gives to our spirits what they can rest upon; and with the increasing demands of our modern ages upon poetry, this virtue of giving us what we can rest upon will be more and more highly esteemed. A voice from the slums of Paris, fifty or sixty years after Chaucer, the voice of poor Villon[6] out of his life of riot and crime, has at its happy moments (as, for instance, in the last stanza of *La Belle Heaulmière*[7]) more of this important poetic virtue of seriousness than all the productions of Chaucer. But its apparition in Villon, and in men like Villon, is fitful; the greatness of the great poets, the power of their criticism of life, is that their virtue is sustained.

To our praise, therefore, of Chaucer as a poet there must be this limitation: he lacks the high seriousness of the great classics, and therewith an important part of their virtue. Still, the main fact for us to bear in mind about Chaucer is his sterling value according to that real estimate which we firmly adopt for all poets. He has poetic truth of substance, though he has not high poetic seriousness, and corresponding to his truth of substance he has an exquisite virtue of style and manner. With him is born our real poetry.

For my present purpose I need not dwell on our Elizabethan poetry, or on the continuation and close of this poetry in Milton. We all of us profess to be agreed in the estimate of this poetry; we all of us recognize it as great poetry, our greatest, and Shake-

6. François Villon (1431–84), French poet and vagabond.
7. "The name *Heaulmière* is said to be derived from a headdress (helm) worn as a mask by courtesans. In Villon's ballad, a poor old creature of this class laments her days of youth and beauty. The last stanza of the ballad runs thus —'*Ainsi le bon temps regretons / Entre nous, pauvres vieilles sottes, / Assises bas, à croppetons, / Tout en ung tas comme pelottes; / A petit feu de chenevottes / Tost allumées, tost estainctes, / Et jadis fusmes si mignottes! / Ainsi en prend à maintz et maintes.'* [It may be translated:] 'Thus amongst ourselves we regret the good time, poor silly old things, low-seated on our heels, all in a heap like so many balls; by a little fire of hemp stalks, soon lighted, soon spent. And once we were such darlings! So fares it with many and many a one'" [Arnold's note].

speare and Milton as our poetical classics. The real estimate, here, has universal currency. With the next age of our poetry divergency and difficulty begin. An historic estimate of that poetry has established itself; and the question is, whether it will be found to coincide with the real estimate.

The age of Dryden, together with our whole eighteenth century which followed it, sincerely believed itself to have produced poetical classics of its own, and even to have made advance, in poetry, beyond all its predecessors. Dryden regards as not seriously disputable the opinion "that the sweetness of English verse was never understood or practiced by our fathers."[8] Cowley could see nothing at all in Chaucer's poetry. Dryden heartily admired it, and, as we have seen, praised its matter admirably; but of its exquisite manner and movement all he can find to say is that "there is the rude sweetness of a Scotch tune in it, which is natural and pleasing, though not perfect."[9] Addison, wishing to praise Chaucer's numbers, compares them with Dryden's own. And all through the eighteenth century, and down even into our own times, the stereotyped phrase of approbation for good verse found in our early poetry has been, that it even approached the verse of Dryden, Addison, Pope, and Johnson.

Are Dryden and Pope poetical classics? Is the historic estimate, which represents them as such, and which has been so long established that it cannot easily give way, the real estimate? Wordsworth and Coleridge, as is well known, denied it; but the authority of Wordsworth and Coleridge does not weigh much with the young generation, and there are many signs to show that the eighteenth century and its judgments are coming into favor again. Are the favorite poets of the eighteenth century classics?

It is impossible within my present limits to discuss the question fully. And what man of letters would not shrink from seeming to dispose dictatorially of the claims of two men who are, at any rate, such masters in letters as Dryden and Pope; two men of such admirable talent, both of them, and one of them, Dryden, a man, on all sides, of such energetic and genial power? And yet, if we are to gain the full benefit from poetry, we must have the real estimate of it. I cast about for some mode of arriving, in the present case, at such an estimate without offense. And perhaps the best way is to begin, as it is easy to begin, with cordial praise.

When we find Chapman, the Elizabethan translator of Homer, expressing himself in his preface thus: "Though truth in her very nakedness sits in so deep a pit, that from Gades to Aurora and Ganges few eyes can sound her, I hope yet those few here will so

8. Dryden's *Essay on Dramatic Poesy.* (1618–67).
Cowley is the poet Abraham Cowley 9. Dryden's Preface to his *Fables.*

discover and confirm that, the date being out of her darkness in this morning of our poet, he shall now gird his temples with the sun," we pronounce that such a prose is intolerable. When we find Milton writing: "And long it was not after, when I was confirmed in this opinion, that he, who would not be frustrate of his hope to write well hereafter in laudable things, ought himself to be a true poem"[1]—we pronounce that such a prose has its own grandeur, but that it is obsolete and inconvenient. But when we find Dryden telling us: "What Virgil wrote in the vigor of his age, in plenty and at ease, I have undertaken to translate in my declining years; struggling with wants, oppressed with sickness, curbed in my genius, liable to be misconstrued in all I write"[2]—then we exclaim that here at last we have the true English prose, a prose such as we would all gladly use if we only knew how. Yet Dryden was Milton's contemporary.

But after the Restoration the time had come when our nation felt the imperious need of a fit prose. So, too, the time had likewise come when our nation felt the imperious need of freeing itself from the absorbing preoccupation which religion in the Puritan age had exercised. It was impossible that this freedom should be brought about without some negative excess, without some neglect and impairment of the religious life of the soul; and the spiritual history of the eighteenth century shows us that the freedom was not achieved without them. Still, the freedom was achieved; the preoccupation, an undoubtedly baneful and retarding one if it had continued, was got rid of. And as with religion amongst us at that period, so it was also with letters. A fit prose was a necessity; but it was impossible that a fit prose should establish itself amongst us without some touch of frost to the imaginative life of the soul. The needful qualities for a fit prose are regularity, uniformity, precision, balance. The men of letters, whose destiny it may be to bring their nation to the attainment of a fit prose, must of necessity, whether they work in prose or in verse, give a predominating, an almost exclusive attention to the qualities of regularity, uniformity, precision, balance. But an almost exclusive attention to these qualities involves some repression and silencing of poetry.

We are to regard Dryden as the puissant and glorious founder, Pope as the splendid high priest, of our age of prose and reason, of our excellent and indispensable eighteenth century. For the purposes of their mission and destiny their poetry, like their prose, is admirable. Do you ask me whether Dryden's verse, take it almost where you will, is not good?

> A milk-white Hind, immortal and unchanged,
> Fed on the lawns and in the forest ranged.[3]

1. Milton's *Apology for Smectymnuus.*   in his translation of Virgil.
2. Dryden's *Postscript to the Reader*   3. *The Hind and the Panther* I.1–2.

I answer: Admirable for the purposes of the inaugurator of an age of prose and reason. Do you ask me whether Pope's verse, take it almost where you will, is not good?

> To Hounslow Heath I point, and Banstead Down;
> Thence comes your mutton, and these chicks my own.[4]

I answer: Admirable for the purposes of the high priest of an age of prose and reason. But do you ask me whether such verse proceeds from men with an adequate poetic criticism of life, from men whose criticism of life has a high seriousness, or even, without that high seriousness, has poetic largeness, freedom, insight, benignity? Do you ask me whether the application of ideas to life in the verse of these men, often a powerful application, no doubt, is a powerful *poetic* application? Do you ask me whether the poetry of these men has either the matter or the inseparable manner of such an adequate poetic criticism; whether it has the accent of

> Absent thee from felicity awhile . . .

or of

> And what is else not to be overcome . . .

or of

> O martyr souded in virginitee!

I answer: It has not and cannot have them; it is the poetry of the builders of an age of prose and reason. Though they may write in verse, though they may in a certain sense be masters of the art of versification, Dryden and Pope are not classics of our poetry, they are classics of our prose.

Gray is our poetical classic of that literature and age; the position of Gray is singular, and demands a word of notice here. He has not the volume or the power of poets who, coming in times more favorable, have attained to an independent criticism of life. But he lived with the great poets, he lived, above all, with the Greeks, through perpetually studying and enjoying them; and he caught their poetic point of view for regarding life, caught their poetic manner. The point of view and the manner are not self-sprung in him, he caught them of others; and he had not the free and abundant use of them. But whereas Addison and Pope never had the use of them, Gray had the use of them at times. He is the scantiest and frailest of classics in our poetry, but he is a classic.

And now, after Gray, we are met, as we draw towards the end of the eighteenth century, we are met by the great name of Burns. We enter now on times where the personal estimate of poets begins to be rife, and where the real estimate of them is not reached

4. *Imitations of Horace*, Satire II.ii.143–44.

without difficulty. But in spite of the disturbing pressures of personal partiality, of national partiality, let us try to reach a real estimate of the poetry of Burns.

By his English poetry Burns in general belongs to the eighteenth century, and has little importance for us.

> Mark ruffian Violence, distained with crimes,
> Rousing elate in these degenerate times;
> View unsuspecting Innocence a prey,
> As guileful Fraud points out the erring way;
> While subtle Litigation's pliant tongue
> The life-blood equal sucks of Right and Wrong![5]

Evidently this is not the real Burns, or his name and fame would have disappeared long ago. Nor is Clarinda's love-poet, Sylvander,[6] the real Burns either. But he tells us himself: "These English songs gravel me to death. I have not the command of the language that I have of my native tongue. In fact, I think that my ideas are more barren in English than in Scotch. I have been at *Duncan Gray* to dress it in English, but all I can do is desperately stupid."[7] We English turn naturally, in Burns, to the poems in our own language, because we can read them easily; but in those poems we have not the real Burns.

The real Burns is of course in his Scotch poems. Let us boldly say that of much of this poetry, a poetry dealing perpetually with Scotch drink, Scotch religion, and Scotch manners, a Scotchman's estimate is apt to be personal. A Scotchman is used to this world of Scotch drink, Scotch religion, and Scotch manners; he has a tenderness for it; he meets its poet half way. In this tender mood he reads pieces like the *Holy Fair* or *Halloween*. But this world of Scotch drink, Scotch religion, and Scotch manners is against a poet, not for him, when it is not a partial countryman who reads him; for in itself it is not a beautiful world, and no one can deny that it is of advantage to a poet to deal with a beautiful world. Burns's world of Scotch drink, Scotch religion, and Scotch manners, is often a harsh, a sordid, a repulsive world; even the world of his *Cotter's Saturday Night* is not a beautiful world. No doubt a poet's criticism of life may have such truth and power that it triumphs over its world and delights us. Burns may triumph over his world, often he does triumph over his world, but let us observe how and where. Burns is the first case we have had where the bias of the personal estimate tends to mislead; let us look at him closely, he can bear it.

Many of his admirers will tell us that we have Burns, convivial, genuine, delightful, here—

5. *On the Death of Lord President Dundas*, lines 25–30.
6. Burns, styling himself Sylvander, carried on an idyllic correspondence with a Mrs. Maclehose, addressing her as Clarinda.
7. Letter to George Thomson, October 19, 1794.

> Leeze me on drink! it gies us mair
>   Than either school or college;
> It kindles wit, it waukens lair,
>   It pangs us fou o' knowledge.
> Be't whisky gill or penny wheep
>   Or ony stronger potion,
> It never fails, on drinking deep,
>   To kittle up our notion
>   By night or day.[8]

There is a great deal of that sort of thing in Burns, and it is unsatisfactory, not because it is bacchanalian poetry, but because it has not that accent of sincerity which bacchanalian poetry, to do it justice, very often has. There is something in it of bravado, something which makes us feel that we have not the man speaking to us with his real voice; something, therefore, poetically unsound.

With still more confidence will his admirers tell us that we have the genuine Burns, the great poet, when his strain asserts the independence, equality, dignity, of men, as in the famous song *For A' That and A' That—*

> A prince can mak' a belted knight,
>   A marquis, duke, and a' that;
> But an honest man's aboon his might,
>   Guid faith he mauna fa' that!
>   For a' that, and a' that,
>   Their dignities, and a' that,
>   The pith o' sense, and pride o' worth,
>   Are higher rank than a' that.

Here they find his grand, genuine touches; and still more, when this puissant genius, who so often set morality at defiance, falls moralizing—

> The sacred lowe o' weel-placed love
>   Luxuriantly indulge it;
> But never tempt th' illicit rove,
>   Though naething should divulge it.
>   I waive the quantum o' the sin,
>   The hazard o' concealing,
>   But och! it hardens a' within,
>   And petrifies the feeling.[9]

Or in a higher strain—

> Who made the heart, 'tis He alone
>   Decidedly can try us;
> He knows each chord, its various tone;
>   Each spring, its various bias.
>   Then at the balance let's be mute,

8. *The Holy Fair*, lines 163–71.   9. *Epistle to a Young Friend*, lines 41–48.

We never can adjust it;
What's *done* we partly may compute,
But know not what's resisted.[1]

Or in a better strain yet, a strain, his admirers will say, unsurpassable—

To make a happy fireside clime
To weans and wife,
That's the true pathos and sublime
Of human life.[2]

There is criticism of life for you, the admirers of Burns will say to
us; there is the application of ideas to life! There is, undoubtedly.
The doctrine of the last-quoted lines coincides almost exactly with
what was the aim and end, Xenophon tells us, of all the teaching
of Socrates. And the application is a powerful one; made by a
man of vigorous understanding, and (need I say?) a master of
language.

But for supreme poetical success more is required than the powerful application of ideas to life; it must be an application under
the conditions fixed by the laws of poetic truth and poetic beauty.
Those laws fix as an essential condition, in the poet's treatment of
such matters as are here in question, high seriousness—the high
seriousness which comes from absolute sincerity. The accent of
high seriousness, born of absolute sincerity, is what gives to such
verse as

In la sua volontade è nostra pace . . .

to such criticism of life as Dante's, its power. Is this accent felt
in the passages which I have been quoting from Burns? Surely not;
surely, if our sense is quick, we must perceive that we have not
in those passages a voice from the very inmost soul of the genuine
Burns; he is not speaking to us from these depths, he is more or
less preaching. And the compensation for admiring such passages
less, for missing the perfect poetic accent in them, will be that
we shall admire more the poetry where that accent is found.

No; Burns, like Chaucer, comes short of the high seriousness
of the great classics, and the virtue of matter and manner which
goes with that high seriousness is wanting to his work. At moments
he touches it in a profound and passionate melancholy, as in those
four immortal lines taken by Byron as a motto for *The Bride of
Abydos*, but which have in them a depth of poetic quality such as
resides in no verse of Byron's own—

Had we never loved sae kindly,
Had we never loved sae blindly,

1. *Address to the Unco Guid*, lines 57–64. 2. *Epistle to Dr. Blacklock*, lines 51–54.

> Never met, or never parted,
> We had ne'er been broken-hearted.[3]

But a whole poem of that quality Burns cannot make; the rest, in the *Farewell to Nancy*, is verbiage.

We arrive best at the real estimate of Burns, I think, by conceiving his work as having truth of matter and truth of manner, but not the accent or the poetic virtue of the highest masters. His genuine criticism of life, when the sheer poet in him speaks, is ironic; it is not—

> Thou Power Supreme, whose mighty scheme
> These woes of mine fulfill,
> Here firm I rest, they must be best
> Because they are Thy will![4]

It is far rather: "Whistle owre the lave o't!"[5] Yet we may say of him as of Chaucer, that of life and the world, as they come before him, his view is large, free, shrewd, benignant—truly poetic, therefore; and his manner of rendering what he sees is to match. But we must note, at the same time, his great difference from Chaucer. The freedom of Chaucer is heightened, in Burns, by a fiery, reckless energy; the benignity of Chaucer deepens, in Burns, into an overwhelming sense of the pathos of things—of the pathos of human nature, the pathos, also, of nonhuman nature. Instead of the fluidity of Chaucer's manner, the manner of Burns has spring, bounding swiftness. Burns is by far the greater force, though he has perhaps less charm. The world of Chaucer is fairer, richer, more significant than that of Burns; but when the largeness and freedom of Burns get full sweep, as in *Tam o' Shanter*, or still more in that puissant and splendid production, *The Jolly Beggars*, his world may be what it will, his poetic genius triumphs over it. In the world of *The Jolly Beggars* there is more than hideousness and squalor, there is bestiality; yet the piece is a superb poetic success. It has a breadth, truth, and power which make the famous scene in Auerbach's Cellar, of Goethe's *Faust*, seem artificial and tame beside it, and which are only matched by Shakespeare and Aristophanes.

Here, where his largeness and freedom serve him so admirably, and also in those poems and songs where to shrewdness he adds infinite archness and wit, and to benignity infinite pathos, where his manner is flawless, and a perfect poetic whole is the result— in things like the address to the mouse whose home he had ruined, in things like *Duncan Gray, Tam Glen, Whistle and I'll Come to You, My Lad, Auld Lang Syne* (this list might be made much longer)—here we have the genuine Burns, of whom the real esti-

---

3. *Ae Fond Kiss* (also called *A Farewell to Nancy*), lines 13–16.
4. *Winter: A Dirge*, lines 17–20.

5. "Whistle over what's left of it." The phrase is a refrain from one of Burns's poems.

mate must be high indeed. Not a classic, nor with the excellent σπουδαιότης[6] of the great classics, nor with a verse rising to a criticism of life and a virtue like theirs; but a poet with thorough truth of substance and an answering truth of style, giving us a poetry sound to the core. We all of us have a leaning towards the pathetic, and may be inclined perhaps to prize Burns most for his touches of piercing, sometimes almost intolerable, pathos; for verse like—

> We twa hae paidl't i' the burn
> From mornin' sun till dine;
> But seas between us braid hae roared
> Sin auld lang syne . . .[7]

where he is as lovely as he is sound. But perhaps it is by the perfection of soundness of his lighter and archer masterpieces that he is poetically most wholesome for us. For the votary misled by a personal estimate of Shelley, as so many of us have been, are, and will be—of that beautiful spirit building his many-colored haze of words and images

> Pinnacled dim in the intense inane[8]—

no contact can be wholesomer than the contact with Burns at his archest and soundest. Side by side with the

> On the brink of the night and the morning
> My coursers are wont to respire,
> But the Earth has just whispered a warning
> That their flight must be swifter than fire . . .[9]

of *Prometheus Unbound*, how salutary, how very salutary, to place this from *Tam Glen*—

> My minnie does constantly deave me
> And bids me beware o' young men;
> They flatter, she says, to deceive me;
> But wha can think sae o' Tam Glen?

But we enter on burning ground as we approach the poetry of times so near to us—poetry like that of Byron, Shelley, and Wordsworth—of which the estimates are so often not only personal, but personal with passion. For my purpose, it is enough to have taken the single case of Burns, the first poet we come to of whose work the estimate formed is evidently apt to be personal, and to have suggested how we may proceed, using the poetry of the great classics as a sort of touchstone, to correct this estimate, as we had previously corrected by the same means the historic estimate where we met with it. A collection like the present, with its succession of cele-

---

6. "High seriousness."
7. *Auld Lang Syne*, lines 17–20.
8. Shelley, *Prometheus Unbound* III.

iv.204.
9. *Ibid*. II.v.1–4.

brated names and celebrated poems, offers a good opportunity to us for resolutely endeavoring to make our estimates of poetry real. I have sought to point out a method which will help us in making them so, and to exhibit it in use so far as to put anyone who likes in a way of applying it for himself.

At any rate the end to which the method and the estimate are designed to lead, and from leading to which, if they do lead to it, they get their whole value—the benefit of being able clearly to feel and deeply to enjoy the best, the truly classic, in poetry—is an end, let me say it once more at parting, of supreme importance. We are often told that an era is opening in which we are to see multitudes of a common sort of readers, and masses of a common sort of literature; that such readers do not want and could not relish anything better than such literature, and that to provide it is becoming a vast and profitable industry. Even if good literature entirely lost currency with the world, it would still be abundantly worth while to continue to enjoy it by oneself. But it never will lose currency with the world, in spite of momentary appearances; it never will lose supremacy. Currency and supremacy are insured to it, not indeed by the world's deliberate and conscious choice, but by something far deeper—by the instinct of self-preservation in humanity.

1880

Literature and Science[1]

Practical people talk with a smile of Plato and of his absolute ideas: and it is impossible to deny that Plato's ideas do often seem unpractical and unpracticable, and especially when one views them in connection with the life of a great work-a-day world like the United States. The necessary staple of the life of such a world Plato regards with disdain; handicraft and trade and the working professions he regards with disdain; but what becomes of the life of an industrial modern community if you take handicraft and trade and the working professions out of it? The base mechanic arts and handicrafts, says Plato, bring about a natural weakness in the principle of excellence in a man, so that he cannot govern the ignoble growths in him, but nurses them, and cannot understand fostering any other. Those who exercise such arts and trades, as they have their bodies, he says, marred by their vulgar businesses,

1. Delivered as a lecture during Arnold's tour of the United States in 1883, and published in *Discourses in America* (1885), this essay has become a classic contribution to a subject endlessly debated. Its main argument was summed up by Stuart P. Sherman: "If Arnold had said outright that the study of letters helps us to *bear* the grand results of science, he would not have been guilty of a superficial epigram; he would have spoken from the depths of his experience."

so they have their souls, too, bowed and broken by them. And if one of these uncomely people has a mind to seek self-culture and philosophy, Plato compares him to a bald little tinker, who has scraped together money, and has got his release from service, and has had a bath, and bought a new coat, and is rigged out like a bridegroom about to marry the daughter of his master who has fallen into poor and helpless estate.

Nor do the working professions fare any better than trade at the hands of Plato. He draws for us an inimitable picture of the working lawyer, and of his life of bondage; he shows how this bondage from his youth up has stunted and warped him, and made him small and crooked of soul, encompassing him with difficulties which he is not man enough to rely on justice and truth as means to encounter, but has recourse, for help out of them, to falsehood and wrong. And so, says Plato, this poor creature is bent and broken, and grows up from boy to man without a particle of soundness in him, although exceedingly smart and clever in his own esteem.

One cannot refuse to admire the artist who draws these pictures. But we say to ourselves that his ideas show the influence of a primitive and obsolete order of things, when the warrior caste and the priestly caste were alone in honor, and the humble work of the world was done by slaves. We have now changed all that; the modern majesty consists in work, as Emerson declares; and in work, we may add, principally of such plain and dusty kind as the work of cultivators of the ground, handicraftsmen, men of trade and business, men of the working professions. Above all is this true in a great industrious community such as that of the United States.

Now education, many people go on to say, is still mainly governed by the ideas of men like Plato, who lived when the warrior caste and the priestly or philosophical class were alone in honor, and the really useful part of the community were slaves. It is an education fitted for persons of leisure in such a community. This education passed from Greece and Rome to the feudal communities of Europe, where also the warrior caste and the priestly caste were alone held in honor, and where the really useful and working part of the community, though not nominally slaves as in the pagan world, were practically not much better off than slaves, and not more seriously regarded. And how absurd it is, people end by saying, to inflict this education upon an industrious modern community, where very few indeed are persons of leisure, and the mass to be considered has not leisure, but is bound, for its own great good, and for the great good of the world at large, to plain labor and to industrial pursuits, and the education in question tends necessarily to make men dissatisfied with these pursuits and unfitted for them!

That is what is said. So far I must defend Plato, as to plead that his view of education and studies is in the general, as it seems to me, sound enough, and fitted for all sorts and conditions of men, whatever their pursuits may be. "An intelligent man," says Plato, "will prize those studies which result in his soul getting soberness, righteousness, and wisdom, and will less value the others."[2] I cannot consider *that* a bad description of the aim of education, and of the motives which should govern us in the choice of studies, whether we are preparing ourselves for a hereditary seat in the English House of Lords or for the pork trade in Chicago.

Still I admit that Plato's world was not ours, that his scorn of trade and handicraft is fantastic, that he had no conception of a great industrial community such as that of the United States, and that such a community must and will shape its education to suit its own needs. If the usual education handed down to it from the past does not suit it, it will certainly before long drop this and try another. The usual education in the past has been mainly literary. The question is whether the studies which were long supposed to be the best for all of us are practically the best now; whether others are not better. The tyranny of the past, many think, weighs on us injuriously in the predominance given to letters in education. The question is raised whether, to meet the needs of our modern life, the predominance ought not now to pass from letters to science; and naturally the question is nowhere raised with more energy than here in the United States. The design of abasing what is called "mere literary instruction and education," and of exalting what is called "sound, extensive, and practical scientific knowledge," is, in this intensely modern world of the United States, even more perhaps than in Europe, a very popular design, and makes great and rapid progress.

I am going to ask whether the present movement for ousting letters from their old predominance in education, and for transferring the predominance in education to the natural sciences, whether this brisk and flourishing movement ought to prevail, and whether it is likely that in the end it really will prevail. An objection may be raised which I will anticipate. My own studies have been almost wholly in letters, and my visits to the field of the natural sciences have been very slight and inadequate, although those sciences have always strongly moved my curiosity. A man of letters, it will perhaps be said, is not competent to discuss the comparative merits of letters and natural science as means of education. To this objection I reply, first of all, that his incompetence, if he attempts the discussion but is really incompetent for it, will be abundantly visible; nobody will be taken in; he will have plenty of sharp observers and critics to save mankind from that danger. But the line I am going to follow is, as you will soon discover, so extremely

2. Plato, *Republic* IX.591.

simple, that perhaps it may be followed without failure even by one who for a more ambitious line of discussion would be quite incompetent.

Some of you may possibly remember a phrase of mine which has been the object of a good deal of comment; an observation to the effect that in our culture, the aim being *to know ourselves and the world*, we have, as the means to this end, *to know the best which has been thought and said in the world*.[3] A man of science, who is also an excellent writer and the very prince of debaters, Professor Huxley, in a discourse at the opening of Sir Josiah Mason's college at Birmingham,[4] laying hold of this phrase, expanded it by quoting some more words of mine, which are these: "The civilized world is to be regarded as now being, for intellectual and spiritual purposes, one great confederation, bound to a joint action and working to a common result; and whose members have for their proper outfit a knowledge of Greek, Roman, and Eastern antiquity, and of one another. Special local and temporary advantages being put out of account, that modern nation will in the intellectual and spiritual sphere make most progress, which most thoroughly carries out this program."

Now on my phrase, thus enlarged, Professor Huxley remarks that when I speak of the above-mentioned knowledge as enabling us to know ourselves and the world, I assert *literature* to contain the materials which suffice for thus making us know ourselves and the world. But it is not by any means clear, says he, that after having learnt all which ancient and modern literatures have to tell us, we have laid a sufficiently broad and deep foundation for that criticism of life, that knowledge of ourselves and the world, which constitutes culture. On the contrary, Professor Huxley declares that he finds himself "wholly unable to admit that either nations or individuals will really advance, if their outfit draws nothing from the stores of physical science. An army without weapons of precision, and with no particular base of operations, might more hopefully enter upon a campaign on the Rhine, than a man, devoid of a knowledge of what physical science has done in the last century, upon a criticism of life."

This shows how needful it is for those who are to discuss any matter together, to have a common understanding as to the sense of the terms they employ—how needful, and how difficult. What Professor Huxley says, implies just the reproach which is so often brought against the study of belles-lettres, as they are called: that the study is an elegant one, but slight and ineffectual; a smattering of Greek and Latin and other ornamental things, of little use for anyone whose object is to get at truth, and to be a practical man.

3. See *The Function of Criticism at the Present Time.* 4. See T. H. Huxley's lecture *Science and Culture.*

So, too, M. Renan[5] talks of the "superficial humanism" of a school course which treats us as if we were all going to be poets, writers, preachers, orators, and he opposes this humanism to positive science, or the critical search after truth. And there is always a tendency in those who are remonstrating against the predominance of letters in education, to understand by letters belles-lettres, and by belles-lettres a superficial humanism, the opposite of science or true knowledge.

But when we talk of knowing Greek and Roman antiquity, for instance, which is the knowledge people have called the humanities, I for my part mean a knowledge which is something more than a superficial humanism, mainly decorative. "I call all teaching *scientific*," says Wolf,[6] the critic of Homer, "which is systematically laid out and followed up to its original sources. For example: a knowledge of classical antiquity is scientific when the remains of classical antiquity are correctly studied in the original languages." There can be no doubt that Wolf is perfectly right; that all learning is scientific which is systematically laid out and followed up to its original sources, and that a genuine humanism is scientific.

When I speak of knowing Greek and Roman antiquity, therefore, as a help to knowing ourselves and the world, I mean more than a knowledge of so much vocabulary, so much grammar, so many portions of authors in the Greek and Latin languages, I mean knowing the Greeks and Romans, and their life and genius, and what they were and did in the world; what we get from them, and what is its value. That, at least, is the ideal; and when we talk of endeavoring to know Greek and Roman antiquity, as a help to knowing ourselves and the world, we mean endeavoring so to know them as to satisfy this ideal, however much we may still fall short of it.

The same also as to knowing our own and other modern nations, with the like aim of getting to understand ourselves and the world. To know the best that has been thought and said by the modern nations, is to know, says Professor Huxley, "only what modern *literatures* have to tell us; it is the criticism of life contained in modern literature." And yet "the distinctive character of our times," he urges, "lies in the vast and constantly increasing part which is played by natural knowledge." And how, therefore, can a man, devoid of knowledge of what physical science has done in the last century, enter hopefully upon a criticism of modern life?

Let us, I say, be agreed about the meaning of the terms we are using. I talk of knowing the best which has been thought and uttered in the world; Professor Huxley says this means knowing *literature*. Literature is a large word; it may mean everything writ-

5. Ernest Renan (1823–92), French religious philosopher and author of *The Life of Jesus*.   6. Friedrich August Wolf (1759–1824), German scholar.

ten with letters or printed in a book. Euclid's *Elements* and Newton's *Principia* are thus literature. All knowledge that reaches us through books is literature. But by literature Professor Huxley means belles-lettres. He means to make me say, that knowing the best which has been thought and said by the modern nations is knowing their belles-lettres and no more. And this is no sufficient equipment, he argues, for a criticism of modern life. But as I do not mean, by knowing ancient Rome, knowing merely more or less of Latin belles-lettres, and taking no account of Rome's military, and political, and legal, and administrative work in the world; and as, by knowing ancient Greece, I understand knowing her as the giver of Greek art, and the guide to a free and right use of reason and to scientific method, and the founder of our mathematics and physics and astronomy and biology—I understand knowing her as all this, and not merely knowing certain Greek poems, and histories, and treatises, and speeches—so as to the knowledge of modern nations also. By knowing modern nations, I mean not merely knowing their belles-lettres, but knowing also what has been done by such men as Copernicus, Galileo, Newton, Darwin. "Our ancestors learned," says Professor Huxley, "that the earth is the center of the visible universe, and that man is the cynosure of things terrestrial; and more especially was it inculcated that the course of nature had no fixed order, but that it could be, and constantly was, altered." "But for us now," continues Professor Huxley, "the notions of the beginning and the end of the world entertained by our forefathers are no longer credible. It is very certain that the earth is not the chief body in the material universe, and that the world is not subordinated to man's use. It is even more certain that nature is the expression of a definite order, with which nothing interferes." "And yet," he cries, "the purely classical education advocated by the representatives of the humanists in our day gives no inkling of all this."

In due place and time I will just touch upon that vexed question of classical education; but at present the question is as to what is meant by knowing the best which modern nations have thought and said. It is not knowing their belles-lettres merely which is meant. To know Italian belles-lettres is not to know Italy, and to know English belles-lettres is not to know England. Into knowing Italy and England there comes a great deal more, Galileo and Newton amongst it. The reproach of being a superficial humanism, a tincture of belles-lettres, may attach rightly enough to some other disciplines; but to the particular discipline recommended when I proposed knowing the best that has been thought and said in the world, it does not apply. In that best I certainly include what in modern times has been thought and said by the great observers and knowers of nature.

There is, therefore, really no question between Professor Huxley and me as to whether knowing the great results of the modern scientific study of nature is not required as a part of our culture, as well as knowing the products of literature and art. But to follow the processes by which those results are reached, ought, say the friends of physical science, to be made the staple of education for the bulk of mankind. And here there does arise a question between those whom Professor Huxley calls with playful sarcasm "the Levites of culture," and those whom the poor humanist is sometimes apt to regard as its Nebuchadnezzars.[7]

The great results of the scientific investigation of nature we are agreed upon knowing, but how much of our study are we bound to give to the processes by which those results are reached? The results have their visible bearing on human life. But all the processes, too, all the items of fact, by which those results are reached and established, are interesting. All knowledge is interesting to a wise man, and the knowledge of nature is interesting to all men. It is very interesting to know, that, from the albuminous white of the egg, the chick in the egg gets the materials for its flesh, bones, blood, and feathers; while, from the fatty yolk of the egg, it gets the heat and energy which enable it at length to break its shell and begin the world. It is less interesting, perhaps, but still it is interesting, to know that when a taper burns, the wax is converted into carbonic acid and water. Moreover, it is quite true that the habit of dealing with facts, which is given by the study of nature, is, as the friends of physical science praise it for being, an excellent discipline. The appeal, in the study of nature, is constantly to observation and experiment; not only is it said that the thing is so, but we can be made to see that it is so. Not only does a man tell us that when a taper burns the wax is converted into carbonic acid and water, as a man may tell us, if he likes, that Charon[8] is punting his ferry boat on the river Styx, or that Victor Hugo is a sublime poet, or Mr. Gladstone the most admirable of statesmen; but we are made to see that the conversion into carbonic acid and water does actually happen. This reality of natural knowledge it is, which makes the friends of physical science contrast it, as a knowledge of things, with the humanist's knowledge, which is, say they, a knowledge of words. And hence Professor Huxley is moved to lay it down that, "for the purpose of attaining real culture, an exclusively scientific education is at least as effectual as an exclusively literary education." And a certain President of the Section for Mechanical Science in the British Association is, in Scripture phrase, "very bold," and de-

<hr />

7. Huxley implied that the humanists are hidebound conservatives like the Levites, priests who were preoccupied with traditional ritual observances. Arnold implies that the scientists may be like Nebuchadnezzar, a Babylonian king who destroyed the temple of Jerusalem.
8. Boatman in Greek mythology who conducted the souls of the dead across the river Styx.

clares that if a man, in his mental training, "has substituted literature and history for natural science, he has chosen the less useful
alternative." But whether we go these lengths or not, we must all
admit that in natural science the habit gained of dealing with facts
is a most valuable discipline, and that everyone should have some
experience of it.

More than this, however, is demanded by the reformers. It is
proposed to make the training in natural science the main part of
education, for the great majority of mankind at any rate. And here,
I confess, I part company with the friends of physical science, with
whom up to this point I have been agreeing. In differing from
them, however, I wish to proceed with the utmost caution and diffidence. The smallness of my own acquaintance with the disciplines
of natural science is ever before my mind, and I am fearful of doing
these disciplines an injustice. The ability and pugnacity of the
partisans of natural science make them formidable persons to contradict. The tone of tentative inquiry, which befits a being of dim
faculties and bounded knowledge, is the tone I would wish to take
and not to depart from. At present it seems to me, that those who
are for giving to natural knowledge, as they call it, the chief place
in the education of the majority of mankind, leave one important
thing out of their account: the constitution of human nature. But
I put this forward on the strength of some facts not at all recondite,
very far from it; facts capable of being stated in the simplest possible fashion, and to which, if I so state them, the man of science
will, I am sure, be willing to allow their due weight.

Deny the facts altogether, I think, he hardly can. He can hardly
deny, that when we set ourselves to enumerate the powers which
go to the building up of human life, and say that they are the
power of conduct, the power of intellect and knowledge, the power
of beauty, and the power of social life and manners—he can hardly
deny that this scheme, though drawn in rough and plain lines
enough, and not pretending to scientific exactness, does yet give a
fairly true representation of the matter. Human nature is built up
by these powers; we have the need for them all. When we have
rightly met and adjusted the claims of them all, we shall then be in
a fair way for getting soberness and righteousness, with wisdom.
This is evident enough, and the friends of physical science would
admit it.

But perhaps they may not have sufficiently observed another
thing: namely, that the several powers just mentioned are not isolated, but there is, in the generality of mankind, a perpetual tendency to relate them one to another in divers ways. With one such
way of relating them I am particularly concerned now. Following
our instinct for intellect and knowledge, we acquire pieces of knowledge; and presently, in the generality of men, there arises the desire

to relate these pieces of knowledge to our sense for conduct, to our sense for beauty—and there is weariness and dissatisfaction if the desire is balked. Now in this desire lies, I think, the strength of that hold which letters have upon us.

All knowledge is, as I said just now, interesting; and even items of knowledge which from the nature of the case cannot well be related, but must stand isolated in our thoughts, have their interest. Even lists of exceptions have their interest. If we are studying Greek accents, it is interesting to know that *pais* and *pas*, and some other monosyllables of the same form of declension, do not take the circumflex upon the last syllable of the genitive plural, but vary, in this respect, from the common rule. If we are studying physiology, it is interesting to know that the pulmonary artery carries dark blood and the pulmonary vein carries bright blood, departing in this respect from the common rule for the division of labor between the veins and the arteries. But everyone knows how we seek naturally to combine the pieces of our knowledge together, to bring them under general rules, to relate them to principles; and how unsatisfactory and tiresome it would be to go on forever learning lists of exceptions, or accumulating items of fact which must stand isolated.

Well, that same need of relating our knowledge, which operates here within the sphere of our knowledge itself, we shall find operating, also, outside that sphere. We experience, as we go on learning and knowing—the vast majority of us experience—the need of relating what we have learnt and known to the sense which we have in us for conduct, to the sense which we have in us for beauty.

A certain Greek prophetess of Mantineia in Arcadia, Diotima by name, once explained to the philosopher Socrates that love, and impulse, and bent of all kinds, is, in fact, nothing else but the desire in men that good should forever be present to them. This desire for good, Diotima assured Socrates, is our fundamental desire, of which fundamental desire every impulse in us is only some one particular form.[9] And therefore this fundamental desire it is, I suppose—this desire in men that good should be forever present to them—which acts in us when we feel the impulse for relating our knowledge to our sense for conduct and to our sense for beauty. At any rate, with men in general the instinct exists. Such is human nature. And the instinct, it will be admitted, is innocent, and human nature is preserved by our following the lead of its innocent instincts. Therefore, in seeking to gratify this instinct in question, we are following the instinct of self-preservation in humanity.

But, no doubt, some kinds of knowledge cannot be made to directly serve the instinct in question, cannot be directly related to the sense for beauty, to the sense for conduct. These are instrument

9. Plato, *Symposium* 201–7.

knowledges; they lead on to other knowledges, which can. A man who passes his life in instrument knowledges is a specialist. They may be invaluable as instruments to something beyond, for those who have the gift thus to employ them; and they may be disciplines in themselves wherein it is useful for everyone to have some schooling. But it is inconceivable that the generality of men should pass all their mental life with Greek accents or with formal logic. My friend Professor Sylvester,[1] who is one of the first mathematicians in the world, holds transcendental doctrines as to the virtue of mathematics, but those doctrines are not for common men. In the very Senate House and heart of our English Cambridge[2] I once ventured, though not without an apology for my profaneness, to hazard the opinion that for the majority of mankind a little of mathematics, even, goes a long way. Of course this is quite consistent with their being of immense importance as an instrument to something else; but it is the few who have the aptitude for thus using them, not the bulk of mankind.

The natural sciences do not, however, stand on the same footing with these instrument knowledges. Experience shows us that the generality of men will find more interest in learning that, when a taper burns, the wax is converted into carbonic acid and water, or in learning the explanation of the phenomenon of dew, or in learning how the circulation of the blood is carried on, than they find in learning that the genitive plural of *pais* and *pas* does not take the circumflex on the termination. And one piece of natural knowledge is added to another, and others are added to that, and at last we come to propositions so interesting as Mr. Darwin's famous proposition that "our ancestor was a hairy quadruped furnished with a tail and pointed ears, probably arboreal in his habits." Or we come to propositions of such reach and magnitude as those which Professor Huxley delivers, when he says that the notions of our forefathers about the beginning and the end of the world were all wrong, and that nature is the expression of a definite order with which nothing interferes.

Interesting, indeed, these results of science are, important they are, and we should all of us be acquainted with them. But what I now wish you to mark is, that we are still, when they are propounded to us and we receive them, we are still in the sphere of intellect and knowledge. And for the generality of men there will be found, I say, to arise, when they have duly taken in the proposition that their ancestor was "a hairy quadruped furnished with a tail and pointed ears, probably arboreal in his habits," there will be found to arise an invincible desire to relate this proposition to

1. James T. Sylvester, professor of mathematics at Johns Hopkins University.
2. At Cambridge University, mathematics have been traditionally emphasized. In its original form, *Literature and Science* had been delivered as a lecture at Cambridge.

the sense in us for conduct, and to the sense in us for beauty. But this the men of science will not do for us, and will hardly even profess to do. They will give us other pieces of knowledge, other facts, about other animals and their ancestors, or about plants, or about stones, or about stars; and they may finally bring us to those great "general conceptions of the universe, which are forced upon us all," says Professor Huxley, "by the progress of physical science." But still it will be *knowledge* only which they give us; knowledge not put for us into relation with our sense for conduct, our sense for beauty, and touched with emotion by being so put; not thus put for us, and therefore, to the majority of mankind, after a certain while, unsatisfying, wearying.

Not to the born naturalist, I admit. But what do we mean by a born naturalist? We mean a man in whom the zeal for observing nature is so uncommonly strong and eminent, that it marks him off from the bulk of mankind. Such a man will pass his life happily in collecting natural knowledge and reasoning upon it, and will ask for nothing, or hardly anything, more. I have heard it said that the sagacious and admirable naturalist whom we lost not very long ago, Mr. Darwin, once owned to a friend that for his part he did not experience the necessity for two things which most men find so necessary to them—religion and poetry; science and the domestic affections, he thought, were enough. To a born naturalist, I can well understand that this should seem so. So absorbing is his occupation with nature, so strong his love for his occupation, that he goes on acquiring natural knowledge and reasoning upon it, and has little time or inclination for thinking about getting it related to the desire in man for conduct, the desire in man for beauty. He relates it to them for himself as he goes along, so far as he feels the need; and he draws from the domestic affections all the additional solace necessary. But then Darwins are extremely rare. Another great and admirable master of natural knowledge, Faraday,[3] was a Sandemanian. That is to say, he related his knowledge to his instinct for conduct and to his instinct for beauty, by the aid of that respectable Scottish sectary,[4] Robert Sandeman. And so strong, in general, is the demand of religion and poetry to have their share in a man, to associate themselves with his knowing, and to relieve and rejoice it, that, probably, for one man amongst us with the disposition to do as Darwin did in this respect, there are at least fifty with the disposition to do as Faraday.

Education lays hold upon us, in fact, by satisfying this demand. Professor Huxley holds up to scorn medieval education, with its neglect of the knowledge of nature, its poverty even of literary studies, its formal logic devoted to "showing how and why that

3. Michael Faraday (1791–1867), famous chemist.
4. I.e., a zealous member of a sect.

Robert Sandeman (1718–71) was the founder of a Scottish sect bearing his name.

which the Church said was true must be true." But the great medieval Universities were not brought into being, we may be sure, by the zeal for giving a jejune and contemptible education. Kings have been their nursing fathers, and queens have been their nursing mothers, but not for this. The medieval Universities came into being, because the supposed knowledge, delivered by Scripture and the Church, so deeply engaged men's hearts, by so simply, easily, and powerfully relating itself to their desire for conduct, their desire for beauty. All other knowledge was dominated by this supposed knowledge and was subordinated to it, because of the surpassing strength of the hold which it gained upon the affections of men, by allying itself profoundly with their sense for conduct, their sense for beauty.

But now, says Professor Huxley, conceptions of the universe fatal to the notions held by our forefathers have been forced upon us by physical science. Grant to him that they are thus fatal, that the new conceptions must and will soon become current everywhere, and that everyone will finally perceive them to be fatal to the beliefs of our forefathers. The need of humane letters, as they are truly called, because they serve the paramount desire in men that good should be forever present to them—the need of humane letters, to establish a relation between the new conceptions, and our instinct for beauty, our instinct for conduct, is only the more visible. The Middle Age could do without humane letters, as it could do without the study of nature, because its supposed knowledge was made to engage its emotions so powerfully. Grant that the supposed knowledge disappears, its power of being made to engage the emotions will of course disappear along with it—but the emotions themselves, and their claim to be engaged and satisfied, will remain. Now if we find by experience that humane letters have an undeniable power of engaging the emotions, the importance of humane letters in a man's training becomes not less, but greater, in proportion to the success of modern science in extirpating what it calls "medieval thinking."

Have humane letters, then, have poetry and eloquence, the power here attributed to them of engaging the emotions, and do they exercise it? And if they have it and exercise it, *how* do they exercise it, so as to exert an influence upon man's sense for conduct, his sense for beauty? Finally, even if they both can and do exert an influence upon the senses in question, how are they to relate to them the results—the modern results—of natural science? All these questions may be asked. First, have poetry and eloquence the power of calling out the emotions? The appeal is to experience. Experience shows that for the vast majority of men, for mankind in general, they have the power. Next, do they exercise it? They do. But then, *how* do they exercise it so as to affect man's sense for conduct, his sense for beauty? And this is perhaps a case for applying the Preacher's words: "Though a man labor to seek it out, yet he shall not find it; yea, farther, though a wise man think to know it, yet shall he not be able to find it."[5] Why should it be one thing, in its effect upon the emotions, to say, "Patience is a virtue," and quite another thing, in its effect upon the emotions, to say with Homer,

τλητὸν γὰρ Μοῖραι θυμὸν θέσαν ἀνθρώποισιν[6]—

"for an enduring heart have the destinies appointed to the children of men"? Why should it be one thing, in its effect upon the emotions, to say with the philosopher Spinoza, *Felicitas in eo consistit quod homo suum esse conservare potest*—"Man's happiness consists in his being able to preserve his own essence,"[7] and quite another thing, in its effect upon the emotions, to say with the Gospel, "What is a man advantaged, if he gain the whole world, and lose himself, forfeit himself?" [8] How does this difference of effect arise? I cannot tell, and I am not much concerned to know; the important thing is that it does arise, and that we can profit by it. But how, finally, are poetry and eloquence to exercise the power of relating the modern results of natural science to man's instinct for conduct, his instinct for beauty? And here again I answer that I do not know *how* they will exercise it, but that they can and will exercise it I am sure. I do not mean that modern philosophical poets and modern philosophical moralists are to come and relate for us, in express terms, the results of modern scientific research to our instinct for conduct, our instinct for beauty. But I mean that we shall find, as a matter of experience, if we know the best that has been thought and uttered in the world, we shall find that the art and poetry and eloquence of men who lived, perhaps, long ago, who had the most limited natural knowledge, who had the most erroneous conceptions about many important matters, we shall find that this art, and poetry, and eloquence, have in fact not only the power of refreshing and delighting us, they have also the power— such is the strength and worth, in essentials, of their authors' criticism of life—they have a fortifying, and elevating, and quickening, and suggestive power, capable of wonderfully helping us to relate the results of modern science to our need for conduct, our need for beauty. Homer's conceptions of the physical universe were, I imagine, grotesque; but really, under the shock of hearing from modern science that "the world is not subordinated to man's use, and that man is not the cynosure of things terrestrial," I could, for my own part, desire no better comfort than Homer's line which I quoted just now,

5. "*Ecclesiastes* viii.17" [Arnold's note].   7. Spinoza, *Ethics* IV.xviii.
6. "*Iliad* XXIV.49" [Arnold's note].   8. Cf. Luke ix.25.

τλητὸν γὰρ Μοῖραι θυμὸν θέσαν ἀνθρώποισιν—

"for an enduring heart have the destinies appointed to the children of men"!

And the more that men's minds are cleared, the more that the results of science are frankly accepted, the more that poetry and eloquence come to be received and studied as what in truth they really are—the criticism of life by gifted men, alive and active with extraordinary power at an unusual number of points—so much the more will the value of humane letters, and of art also, which is an utterance having a like kind of power with theirs, be felt and acknowledged, and their place in education be secured.

Let us therefore, all of us, avoid indeed as much as possible any invidious comparison between the merits of humane letters, as means of education, and the merits of the natural sciences. But when some President of a Section for Mechanical Science insists on making the comparison, and tells us that "he who in his training has substituted literature and history for natural science has chosen the less useful alternative," let us make answer to him that the student of humane letters only, will, at least, know also the great general conceptions brought in by modern physical science; for science, as Professor Huxley says, forces them upon us all. But the student of the natural sciences only, will, by our very hypothesis, know nothing of humane letters; not to mention that in setting himself to be perpetually accumulating natural knowledge, he sets himself to do what only specialists have in general the gift for doing genially. And so he will probably be unsatisfied, or at any rate incomplete, and even more incomplete than the student of humane letters only.

I once mentioned in a school report, how a young man in one of our English training colleges having to paraphrase the passage in *Macbeth* beginning,

> Can'st thou not minister to a mind diseased?[9]

turned this line into, "Can you not wait upon the lunatic?" And I remarked what a curious state of things it would be, if every pupil of our national schools knew, let us say, that the moon is two thousand one hundred and sixty miles in diameter, and thought at the same time that a good paraphrase for

> Can'st thou not minister to a mind diseased?

was, "Can you not wait upon the lunatic?" If one is driven to choose, I think I would rather have a young person ignorant about the moon's diameter, but aware that "Can you not wait upon the lunatic?" is bad, than a young person whose education had been

9. *Macbeth* V.iii.40.

such as to manage things the other way.

Or to go higher than the pupils of our national schools. I have in my mind's eye a member of our British Parliament who comes to travel here in America, who afterwards relates his travels, and who shows a really masterly knowledge of the geology of this great country and of its mining capabilities, but who ends by gravely suggesting that the United States should borrow a prince from our Royal Family, and should make him their king, and should create a House of Lords of great landed proprietors after the pattern of ours; and then America, he thinks, would have her future happily and perfectly secured. Surely, in this case, the President of the Section for Mechanical Science would himself hardly say that our member of Parliament, by concentrating himself upon geology and mineralogy, and so on, and not attending to literature and history, had "chosen the more useful alternative."

If then there is to be separation and option between humane letters on the one hand, and the natural sciences on the other, the great majority of mankind, all who have not exceptional and overpowering aptitudes for the study of nature, would do well, I cannot but think, to chose to be educated in humane letters rather than in the natural sciences. Letters will call out their being at more points, will make them live more.

I said that before I ended I would just touch on the question of classical education, and I will keep my word. Even if literature is to retain a large place in our education, yet Latin and Greek, say the friends of progress, will certainly have to go. Greek is the grand offender in the eyes of these gentlemen. The attackers of the established course of study think that against Greek, at any rate, they have irresistible arguments. Literature may perhaps be needed in education, they say; but why on earth should it be Greek literature? Why not French or German? Nay, "has not an Englishman models in his own literature of every kind of excellence?"[1] As before, it is not on any weak pleadings of my own that I rely for convincing the gainsayers; it is on the constitution of human nature itself, and on the instinct of self-preservation in humanity. The instinct for beauty is set in human nature, as surely as the instinct for knowledge is set there, or the instinct for conduct. If the instinct for beauty is served by Greek literature and art as it is served by no other literature and art, we may trust to the instinct of self-preservation in humanity for keeping Greek as part of our culture. We may trust to it for even making the study of Greek more prevalent than it is now. Greek will come, I hope, some day to be studied more rationally than at present; but it will be increasingly studied as men increasingly feel the need in them for beauty, and how powerfully Greek art and Greek literature can serve this need.

1. Quoted from Huxley's *Science and Culture.*

Women will again study Greek, as Lady Jane Grey[2] did; I believe
that in that chain of forts, with which the fair host of the Amazons
are now engirdling our English universities,[3] I find that here in
America, in colleges like Smith College in Massachusetts, and
Vassar College in the State of New York, and in the happy families
of the mixed universities out West, they are studying it already.

Defuit una mihi symmetria prisca—"The antique symmetry was
the one thing wanting to me," said Leonardo da Vinci; and he
was an Italian. I will not presume to speak for the Americans, but
I am sure that, in the Englishman, the want of this admirable symmetry of the Greeks is a thousand times more great and crying than
in any Italian. The results of the want show themselves most glar-
ingly, perhaps, in our architecture, but they show themselves, also,
in all our art. *Fit details strictly combined, in view of a large general
result nobly conceived;* that is just the beautiful *symmetria prisca*
of the Greeks, and it is just where we English fail, where all our
art fails. Striking ideas we have, and well-executed details we have;
but that high symmetry which, with satisfying and delightful effect,
combines them, we seldom or never have. The glorious beauty of
the Acropolis at Athens did not come from single fine things stuck
about on that hill, a statue here, a gateway there—no, it arose from
all things being perfectly combined for a supreme total effect. What
must not an Englishman feel about our deficiencies in this respect,
as the sense for beauty, whereof this symmetry is an essential element, awakens and strengthens within him! what will not one day
be his respect and desire for Greece and its *symmetria prisca*, when
the scales drop from his eyes as he walks the London streets, and
he sees such a lesson in meanness as the Strand, for instance, in its
true deformity! But here we are coming to our friend Mr. Ruskin's
province,[4] and I will not intrude upon it, for he is its very sufficient
guardian.

And so we at last find, it seems, we find flowing in favor of the
humanities the natural and necessary stream of things, which
seemed against them when we started. The "hairy quadruped furnished with a tail and pointed ears, probably arboreal in his habits,"
this good fellow carried hidden in his nature, apparently, something
destined to develop into a necessity for humane letters. Nay, more;
we seem finally to be even led to the further conclusion that our
hairy ancestor carried in his nature, also, a necessity for Greek.

And therefore, to say the truth, I cannot really think that humane
letters are in much actual danger of being thrust out from their
leading place in education, in spite of the array of authorities against

2. Lady Jane Grey (1537–54) was reputed to be a learned scholar in Greek.
She was proclaimed Queen of England
in 1553, but was forced to abdicate the
throne nine days afterwards. Later she
was executed by order of Queen Mary.

3. Colleges for women at Oxford and
Cambridge.
4. In such books as *The Stones of
Venice* John Ruskin (1819–1900) had
criticized the "meanness" of Victorian
architecture.

them at this moment. So long as human nature is what it is, their attractions will remain irresistible. As with Greek, so with letters generally: they will some day come, we may hope, to be studied more rationally, but they will not lose their place. What will happen will rather be that there will be crowded into education other matters besides, far too many; there will be, perhaps, a period of unsettlement and confusion and false tendency; but letters will not in the end lose their leading place. If they lose it for a time, they will get it back again. We shall be brought back to them by our wants and aspirations. And a poor humanist may possess his soul in patience, neither strive nor cry, admit the energy and brilliancy of the partisans of physical science, and their present favor with the public, to be far greater than his own, and still have a happy faith that the nature of things works silently on behalf of the studies which he loves, and that, while we shall all have to acquaint ourselves with the great results reached by modern science, and to give ourselves as much training in its disciplines as we can conveniently carry, yet the majority of men will always require humane letters; and so much the more, as they have the more and the greater results of science to relate to the need in man for conduct, and to the need in him for beauty.

1882, 1885

Lyric and Narrative Poetry

For the early part of the 19th century, the Romantic period, it is relatively easy to decide which of the English poets were the major ones. For the later part of the century, the ranking is much less fixed. Tennyson and Browning and perhaps Arnold come first to mind, but after these three there remain a number of other interesting poets whose stature is still a matter of dispute. Algernon Charles Swinburne, for example, is regarded by some critics as the major Victorian poet, towering over Tennyson and Browning not only in bulk but in quality. Others have discovered the highest merits in the delicate art of Christina Rossetti or in the philosophical verses of George Meredith. Although such attempts to reclassify writers into major or minor categories can develop into a trifling game, they help to indicate the vitality of the ten poets represented below. To read this group of writers enhances our realization of the total achievement of the Victorian age in poetry. And this realization would be further enhanced if to this group were added the names of some of the late Victorian poets whose writings are included in the 20th-century section of the present anthology, in particular, Gerard Manley Hopkins, A. E. Housman, and Thomas Hardy.

Aside from their having published their poems between 1837 and 1901, what have these ten poets in common? Our first impression may be that it is impossible to yoke any of them together. In their marked differences of manner and subject, they illustrate the variety and individualism in Victorian literature already discussed in the introduction to this period. Certain recurrences and similarities can, nevertheless, be detected. One topic that is unexpectedly prominent (unexpected because of the reputed strain of puritanism in the age) is love. In Victorian poetry love is as recurrently written about as it had been in the age of Donne and his followers. Unlike their 17th-century predecessors, however, the Victorian poets rarely made witty proposals for gathering rosebuds; they explored other aspects of the love relationship. In Dante Gabriel Rossetti's poems, for example, the union of lovers is distinctively pictured as a state of timeless equilibrium, lushly sensual and yet beyond the senses. And in Meredith's poems we encounter a subtle analysis of states of mind of lovers who have become incompatible. The prominent role of love in the lyrics and narratives of these ten writers also provides a link with a major Victorian love poet, Robert Browning, analyst and celebrator of the relations between men and women. As a love poem *The Last Ride Together* was ranked by George Saintsbury (often a severe critic of Browning) as "perhaps the very best that we have produced for two hundred years."

Another recurring subject with which most of these ten poets were preoccupied is religious faith and doubt. Here the link with the major figures is with Tennyson and Arnold. After a reading of *In Memoriam* or of *Dover Beach*, it is instructive to turn to Edward FitzGerald's *Rubáiyát* or Swinburne's *Hymn to Proserpine* to discover how the dilemmas that concerned the major poets concerned the lesser-known poets as well. The range of religious positions exemplified by the ten writers is remarkable. The spectrum extends from the negative fatalism expressed in FitzGerald's translation, through Arthur Hugh Clough's jocular yet earnest skepticism, to the religious affirmations of Christina Rossetti or Francis Thompson.

The styles and forms employed by these poets may likewise impress us at first as being so diverse as to have nothing in common, but again certain unifying recurrences can be detected. In style it is evident that although several of the poets resolved to escape the magnetic attraction of Tennyson's manner, they were usually drawn into its powerful field. In versification, although making considerable use of traditional lyric forms such as the sonnet, most of the poets preferred experimenting with new or unusual metrical patterns. In line with their metrical experiments are their experiments in the art of narrative poetry. During an age which witnessed the emergence of the novel as one of the dominant forms of literature, the poets, like Tennyson in *Maud*, sought new ways of telling stories in verse. Some of them, such as Emily Brontë, George Meredith, and William Morris, were novelists as well as poets, and were therefore especially aware that poetry can offer unusual resources for the writer of narratives, as the compression and intensification achieved in Morris's early poems or in Meredith's *Modern Love* will illustrate. Others, in particular Clough, sought to write narrative poems as if they were novels, poems that are long, casual in tone, and usually prosaic in style. Once again the diversity of the Victorian effort in poetry is evident, yet also evident is that these two different kinds of narrative poems, each being a response to the same challenge offered by the prose fiction of the age, are in fact closely related to each other.

ELIZABETH BARRETT BROWNING
(1806–1861)

Elizabeth Barrett's poetry, much of it ardently concerned with liberal causes, was popular during the Victorian age. Today her name is remembered primarily for the sequence of sonnets in which she recorded the stages of her love for her husband, Robert Browning, a sequence she presented under the guise of a translation from the Portuguese language.

From Sonnets from the Portuguese

22

When our two souls stand up erect and strong,
Face to face, silent, drawing nigh and nigher,

Until the lengthening wings break into fire
At either curvéd point—what bitter wrong
Can the earth do to us, that we should not long   5
Be here contented? Think! In mounting higher,
The angels would press on us and aspire
To drop some golden orb of perfect song
Into our deep, dear silence. Let us stay
Rather on earth, Beloved—where the unfit,   10
Contrarious moods of men recoil away
And isolate pure spirits, and permit
A place to stand and love in for a day,
With darkness and the death-hour rounding it.

43

How do I love thee? Let me count the ways.
I love thee to the depth and breadth and height
My soul can reach, when feeling out of sight
For the ends of Being and ideal Grace.
I love thee to the level of everyday's   5
Most quiet need, by sun and candle light.
I love thee freely, as men strive for Right;
I love thee purely, as they turn from Praise.
I love thee with the passion put to use
In my old griefs, and with my childhood's faith.   10
I love thee with a love I seemed to lose
With my lost saints—I love thee with the breath,
Smiles, tears, of all my life!—and, if God choose,
I shall but love thee better after death.

                                                  1850

EMILY BRONTË
(1818–1848)

Before completing her famous novel, *Wuthering Heights*, Emily Brontë
wrote a number of poems recording experiences of love which often seem
similar to the strange passion of Heathcliff and Catherine Earnshaw in
her novel. Such lyrics were part of a long narrative concerning Gondal,
an imaginary kingdom the scenery of which resembled the locality in
Yorkshire where Emily had grown up with her two sisters, Charlotte and
Anne. Various pairs of lovers are the speakers in the poems. At the time
of their first publication in 1846 these unsual poems, with their hymnlike
stanzas, were ignored. In the 20th century, however, their haunting picture
of a love that defies death has aroused considerable interest.

Remembrance

Cold in the earth—and the deep snow piled above thee,
Far, far removed, cold in the dreary grave!
Have I forgot, my only Love, to love thee,
Severed at last by Time's all-severing wave?

Now, when alone, do my thoughts no longer hover   5
Over the mountains, on that northern shore,
Resting their wings where heath and fern leaves cover
Thy noble heart forever, ever more?

Cold in the earth—and fifteen wild Decembers,
From those brown hills, have melted into spring;   10
Faithful, indeed, is the spirit that remembers
After such years of change and suffering!

Sweet Love of youth, forgive, if I forget thee,
While the world's tide is bearing me along;
Other desires and other hopes beset me,   15
Hopes which obscure, but cannot do thee wrong!

No later light has lightened up my heaven,
No second morn has ever shone for me;
All my life's bliss from thy dear life was given,
All my life's bliss is in the grave with thee.   20

But, when the days of golden dreams had perished,
And even Despair was powerless to destroy,
Then did I learn how existence could be cherished,
Strengthened, and fed without the aid of joy.

Then did I check the tears of useless passion—   25
Weaned my young soul from yearning after thine;
Sternly denied its burning wish to hasten
Down to that tomb already more than mine.

And, even yet, I dare not let it languish,
Dare not indulge in memory's rapturous pain;   30
Once drinking deep of that divinest anguish,
How could I seek the empty world again?

1846

No Coward Soul Is Mine[4]

No coward soul is mine,
No trembler in the world's storm-troubled sphere;
I see Heaven's glories shine,
And faith shines equal, arming me from fear.

4. According to Charlotte Brontë, these are the last lines written by her sister.

O God within my breast,   5
Almighty, ever-present Deity!
Life—that in me has rest,
As I—undying Life—have power in Thee!

Vain are the thousand creeds
That move men's hearts—unutterably vain;   10
Worthless as withered weeds,
Oridlest froth amid the boundless main,

To waken doubt in one
Holding so fast by Thine infinity;
So surely anchored on   15
The steadfast rock of immortality.

With wide-embracing love
Thy spirit animates eternal years
Pervades and broods above,
Changes, sustains, dissolves, creates, and rears.   20

Though earth and man were gone,
And suns and universes ceased to be,
And Thou were left alone,
Every existence would exist in Thee.

There is not room for Death,   25
Nor atom that his might could render void;
Thou—Thou art Being and Breath,
And what Thou art may never be destroyed.

1850

DANTE GABRIEL ROSSETTI
(1828–1882)

Rossetti was the son of an Italian patriot whose political activities had
led to his being exiled to England. The Rossetti household in London
was one in which liberal politics and other controversial topics were hotly
debated, but the son did not catch the infection. Displaying extraordinary
early promise both as a painter and as a poet, Dante Gabriel Rossetti confined his interest to art. The beauty of colors and textures, above all the
beauty of a woman's face and figure, made up for him a world isolated
from the Victorian scene. His view of life and art, derived in part from
his close study of Keats's poems and letters, anticipated by many years
the aesthetic movement later to be represented by such men as Walter
Pater, Oscar Wilde, and the painter James McNeill Whistler, who were
to insist that art must be exclusively concerned with the beautiful, not with
the useful or didactic.

The beauty that Rossetti admired in the faces of women was of a distinctive kind. In at least two of his models he found what he sought. The first was his wife, Elizabeth Siddal, whose suicide in 1862 haunted him with a sense of guilt for the rest of his life. The other was Jane Morris, the wife of his friend William Morris. In Rossetti's paintings both of these models are shown with dreamy stares, as if they were breathless from visions of heaven, but counteracting this impression is an emphasis on parted lips and fully rounded curves suggesting a more earthly kind of ecstasy. A similar combination is to be found in Rossetti's poems. *The Blessed Damozel*, first written when he was 18, portrays a heaven that is warm with physical bodies. And *The House of Life* (1870), his sonnet sequence, undertakes to explore the relationship of spirit to body in love. Some Victorian readers saw no Dante-like spirituality in *The House of Life*. Robert Buchanan saw in the poem nothing but lewd sensuality, and in 1871 he published a pamphlet, *The Fleshly School of Poetry*, which treated Rossetti's poetry to the most severe abuse. Buchanan's attack hurt the poet profoundly and contributed to the recurring seizures of nervous depression from which he suffered in the remaining years of his life.

Rossetti and his artist friends used to call such women as Jane Morris "stunners." The epithet can also be applied to Rossetti's own poetry, especially his later writings. In his maturity he used stunning polysyllabic diction to give an effect of opulence and density to his lines. His earlier poems such as *My Sister's Sleep* are usually much less elaborate in manner and can be related to the Pre-Raphaelite movement of which, in 1848, he became a founder and energetic leader.

This Pre-Raphaelite Brotherhood, as it was called, was a group of young artists and writers. The most prominent members were painters such as John Everett Millais, William Holman Hunt, and Rossetti himself. Their principal object was to reform English painting by repudiating the established academic style in favor of a revival of the simplicity and pure colors of pre-Renaissance art. Because each artist preferred to develop his own individual manner, the Brotherhood did not cohere for more than a few years. Rossetti himself grew away from the Pre-Raphaelite manner and cultivated a more richly ornate style of painting. In both the early and late phases of his writing and painting, however, it can be said that he remained a poet in his painting and a painter in his poetry. "Color and meter," he once said, "these are the true patents of nobility in painting and poetry, taking precedence of all intellectual claims."

The Blessed Damozel[1]

The blessed damozel leaned out
From the gold bar of heaven;
Her eyes were deeper than the depth

1. "Damozel," a poetic version of the word "damsel," signifying a young un-married lady. Rossetti once explained that *The Blessed Damozel* is related .to Poe's *Raven*, a poem which he admired. "I saw that Poe had done the utmost it was possible to do with the grief of the lover on earth, and so I determined to reverse the conditions, and give utter-ance to the yearning of the loved one in heaven."

Of waters stilled at even;
She had three lilies in her hand,   5
   And the stars in her hair were seven.

Her robe, ungirt from clasp to hem,
   No wrought flowers did adorn,
But a white rose of Mary's gift,
   For service meetly worn;   10
Her hair that lay along her back
   Was yellow like ripe corn.[2]

Herseemed[3] she scarce had been a day
   One of God's choristers;
The wonder was not yet quite gone   15
   From that still look of hers;
Albeit, to them she left, her day
   Had counted as ten years.

(To one it is ten years of years.
   . . . Yet now, and in this place,   20
Surely she leaned o'er me—her hair
   Fell all about my face. . . .
Nothing: the autumn fall of leaves.
   The whole year sets apace.)

It was the rampart of God's house   25
   That she was standing on;
By God built over the sheer depth
   The which is Space begun;
So high, that looking downward thence
   She scarce could see the sun.   30

It lies in heaven, across the flood
   Of ether, as a bridge.
Beneath the tides of day and night
   With flame and darkness ridge
The void, as low as where this earth   35
   Spins like a fretful midge.

Around her, lovers, newly met
   'Mid deathless love's acclaims,
Spoke evermore among themselves
   Their heart-remembered names;   40
And the souls mounting up to God
   Went by her like thin flames.

And still she bowed herself and stooped
   Out of the circling charm;
Until her bosom must have made   45
   The bar she leaned on warm,
And the lilies lay as if asleep
   Along her bended arm.

2. Grain.   3. It seemed to her.

From the fixed place of heaven she saw
   Time like a pulse shake fierce   50
Through all the worlds. Her gaze still strove
   Within the gulf to pierce
Its path; and now she spoke as when
   The stars sang in their spheres.

The sun was gone now; the curled moon   55
   Was like a little feather
Fluttering far down the gulf; and now
   She spoke through the still weather.
Her voice was like the voice the stars
   Had when they sang together.   60

(Ah, sweet! Even now, in that bird's song,
   Strove not her accents there,
Fain to be harkened? When those bells
   Possessed the midday air,
Strove not her steps to reach my side   65
   Down all the echoing stair?)

"I wish that he were come to me,
   For he will come," she said.
"Have I not prayed in heaven?—on earth,
   Lord, Lord, has he not prayed?   70
Are not two prayers a perfect strength?
   And shall I feel afraid?

"When round his head the aureole clings,
   And he is clothed in white,
I'll take his hand and go with him   75
   To the deep wells of light;
As unto a stream we will step down,
   And bathe there in God's sight.

"We two will stand beside that shrine,
   Occult, withheld, untrod,   80
Whose lamps are stirred continually
   With prayer sent up to God;
And see our old prayers, granted, melt
   Each like a little cloud.

"We two will lie i' the shadow of   85
   That living mystic tree[4]
Within whose secret growth the Dove
   Is sometimes felt to be,
While every leaf that His plumes touch
   Saith His Name audibly.   90

"And I myself will teach to him,
   I myself, lying so,
The songs I sing here; which his voice

---

4. See Revelation xxii.2.

Shall pause in, hushed and slow,
And find some knowledge at each pause, 95
Or some new thing to know."

(Alas! We two, we two, thou say'st!
Yea, one wast thou with me
That once of old. But shall God lift
To endless unity 100
The soul whose likeness with thy soul
Was but its love for thee?)

"We two," she said, "will seek the groves
Where the lady Mary is,
With her five handmaidens, whose names 105
Are five sweet symphonies,
Cecily, Gertrude, Magdalen,
Margaret, and Rosalys.

"Circlewise sit they, with bound locks
And foreheads garlanded; 110
Into the fine cloth white like flame
Weaving the golden thread,
To fashion the birth-robes for them
Who are just born, being dead.

"He shall fear, haply, and be dumb; 115
Then will I lay my cheek
To his, and tell about our love,
Not once abashed or weak;
And the dear Mother will approve
My pride, and let me speak. 120

"Herself shall bring us, hand in hand,
To Him round whom all souls
Kneel, the clear-ranged unnumbered heads
Bowed with their aureoles;
And angels meeting us shall sing 125
To their citherns and citoles.[5]

"There will I ask of Christ the Lord
Thus much for him and me—
Only to live as once on earth
With Love—only to be, 130
As then awhile, forever now,
Together, I and he."

She gazed and listened and then said,
Less sad of speech than mild—
"All this is when he comes." She ceased. 135
The light thrilled toward her, filled
With angels in strong, level flight.
Her eyes prayed, and she smiled.

5. Guitar-like instruments.

(I saw her smile.) But soon their path
   Was vague in distant spheres;   140
And then she cast her arms along
   The golden barriers,
And laid her face between her hands,
   And wept. (I heard her tears.)

1846   1850

My Sister's Sleep[6]

She fell asleep on Christmas Eve.
   At length the long-ungranted shade
   Of weary eyelids overweighed
The pain nought else might yet relieve.

Our mother, who had leaned all day   5
   Over the bed from chime to chime,
   Then raised herself for the first time,
And as she sat her down, did pray.

Her little worktable was spread
   With work to finish. For the glare   10
   Made by her candle, she had care
To work some distance from the bed.

Without, there was a cold moon up,
   Of winter radiance sheer and thin;
   The hollow halo it was in   15
Was like an icy crystal cup.

Through the small room, with subtle sound
   Of flame, by vents the fireshine drove
   And reddened. In its dim alcove
The mirror shed a clearness round.   20

I had been sitting up some nights,
   And my tired mind felt weak and blank;
   Like a sharp strengthening wine it drank
The stillness and the broken lights.

Twelve struck. That sound, by dwindling years   25
   Heard in each hour, crept off; and then
   The ruffled silence spread again,
Like water that a pebble stirs.

Our mother rose from where she sat;
   Her needles, as she laid them down,   30
   Met lightly, and her silken gown
Settled—no other noise than that.

6. The incident in this poem is imaginary, not autobiographical.

"Glory unto the Newly Born!"
   So, as said angels, she did say,   35
   Because we were in Christmas Day,
Though it would still be long till morn.

Just then in the room over us
   There was a pushing back of chairs,
   As some who had sat unawares
So late, now heard the hour, and rose.   40

With anxious softly-stepping haste
   Our mother went where Margaret lay,
   Fearing the sounds o'erhead—should they
Have broken her long watched-for rest!

She stooped an instant, calm, and turned,   45
   But suddenly turned back again;
   And all her features seemed in pain
With woe, and her eyes gazed and yearned.

For my part, I but hid my face,
   And held my breath, and spoke no word.   50
   There was none spoken; but I heard
The silence for a little space.

Our mother bowed herself and wept;
   And both my arms fell, and I said,
   "God knows I knew that she was dead."   55
And there, all white, my sister slept.

Then kneeling, upon Christmas morn
   A little after twelve o'clock,
   We said, ere the first quarter struck,
"Christ's blessing on the newly born!"   60

1847   1850

The Woodspurge

The wind flapped loose, the wind was still,
Shaken out dead from tree and hill;
I had walked on at the wind's will—
I sat now, for the wind was still.

Between my knees my forehead was—   5
My lips, drawn in, said not Alas!
My hair was over in the grass,
My naked ears heard the day pass.

My eyes, wide open, had the run
Of some ten weeds to fix upon;   10
Among those few, out of the sun,
The woodspurge flowered, three cups in one.

From perfect grief there need not be
Wisdom or even memory;
One thing then learned remains to me—   15
The woodspurge has a cup of three.

1856   1870

From The House of Life
The Sonnet

A Sonnet is a moment's monument—
    Memorial from the Soul's eternity
    To one dead deathless hour. Look that it be,
Whether for lustral[7] rite or dire portent,
Of its own arduous fullness reverent;   5
    Carve it in ivory or in ebony,
    As Day or Night may rule; and let Time see
Its flowering crest impearled and orient.

A Sonnet is a coin; its face reveals
    The soul—its converse, to what Power 'tis due—   10
Whether for tribute to the august appeals
    Of Life, or dower in Love's high retinue,
It serve; or, 'mid the dark wharf's cavernous breath,
In Charon's[8] palm it pay the toll to Death.

4. Lovesight

When do I see thee most, belovéd one?
    When in the light the spirits of mine eyes
    Before thy face, their altar, solemnize
The worship of that Love through thee made known?
Or when in the dusk hours (we two alone)   5
    Close-kissed and eloquent of still replies
    Thy twilight-hidden glimmering visage lies,
And my soul only sees thy soul its own?

O love, my love! if I no more should see
Thyself, nor on the earth the shadow of thee,   10
    Nor image of thine eyes in any spring—
How then should sound upon Life's darkening slope
The ground-whirl of the perished leaves of Hope,
    The wind of Death's imperishable wing?

19. Silent Noon

Your hands lie open in the long fresh grass—
    The finger-points look through like rosy blooms;
    Your eyes smile peace. The pasture gleams and glooms

---

7. Purification.
8. The ferryman who, for a fee, rowed the souls of the dead across the river Styx.

'Neath billowing skies that scatter and amass.
All round our nest, far as the eye can pass, 5
    Are golden kingcup-fields with silver edge
    Where the cow-parsley skirts the hawthorn hedge.
'Tis visible silence, still as the hourglass.

Deep in the sun-searched growths the dragonfly
Hangs like a blue thread loosened from the sky— 10
    So this winged hour is dropped to us from above.
Oh! clasp we to our hearts, for deathless dower,
This close-companioned inarticulate hour
    When twofold silence was the song of love.

49. *Willowwood—I*

I sat with Love upon a woodside well,
    Leaning across the water, I and he;
    Nor ever did he speak nor looked at me,
But touched his lute wherein was audible
The certain secret thing he had to tell. 5
    Only our mirrored eyes met silently
    In the low wave; and that sound came to be
The passionate voice I knew; and my tears fell.

And at their fall, his eyes beneath grew hers;
And with his foot and with his wing feathers 10
    He swept the spring that watered my heart's drouth.
Then the dark ripples spread to waving hair,
And as I stooped, her own lips rising there
    Bubbled with brimming kisses at my mouth.

63. *Inclusiveness*

The changing guests, each in a different mood,
    Sit at the roadside table and arise;
    And every life among them in like wise
Is a soul's board set daily with new food.
What man has bent o'er his son's sleep, to brood 5
    How that face shall watch his when cold it lies?—
    Or thought, as his own mother kissed his eyes,
Of what her kiss was when his father wooed?

May not this ancient room thou sitt'st in dwell
    In separate living souls for joy or pain? 10
    Nay, all its corners may be painted plain
Where Heaven shows pictures of some life spent well;
    And may be stamped, a memory all in vain,
Upon the sight of lidless eyes in Hell.

71. *The Choice—I*

Eat thou and drink; tomorrow thou shalt die.
    Surely the earth, that's wise being very old,
    Needs not our help. Then loose me, love, and hold

Thy sultry hair up from my face; that I
May pour for thee this golden wine, brim-high,   5
　Till round the glass thy fingers glow like gold.
　We'll drown all hours: thy song, while hours are tolled,
Shall leap, as fountains veil the changing sky.

Now kiss, and think that there are really those,
　My own high-bosomed beauty, who increase   10
　　Vain gold, vain lore, and yet might choose our way!
　　Through many years they toil; then on a day
　They die not—for their life was death—but cease;
And round their narrow lips the mold falls close.

72. The Choice—II

Watch thou and fear; tomorrow thou shalt die.
　Or art thou sure thou shalt have time for death?
　Is not the day which God's word promiseth
To come man knows not when? In yonder sky,
Now while we speak, the sun speeds forth; can I   5
　Or thou assure him of his goal? God's breath
　Even at this moment haply quickeneth
The air to a flame; till spirits, always nigh

Though screened and hid, shall walk the daylight here.
　And dost thou prate of all that man shall do?   10
　　Canst thou, who hast but plagues, presume to be
　　Glad in his gladness that comes after thee?
　Will *his* strength slay *thy* worm in Hell? Go to:
Cover thy countenance, and watch, and fear.

73. The Choice—III

Think thou and act; tomorrow thou shalt die.
　Outstretched in the sun's warmth upon the shore,
　Thou say'st: "Man's measured path is all gone o'er:
Up all his years, steeply, with strain and sigh,
Man clomb until he touched the truth; and I,   5
　Even I, am he whom it was destined for."
　How should this be? Art thou then so much more
Than they who sowed, that thou shouldst reap thereby?

Nay, come up hither. From this wave-washed mound
　Unto the furthest flood-brim look with me;   10
　Then reach on with thy thought till it be drowned.
　　Miles and miles distant though the last line be,
　And though thy soul sail leagues and leagues beyond—
　　Still, leagues beyond those leagues, there is more sea.

97. A Superscription

Look in my face; my name is Might-have-been;
　I am also called No-more, Too-late, Farewell;

Unto thine ear I hold the dead-sea shell
Cast up thy Life's foam-fretted feet between;
Unto thine eyes the glass⁹ where that is seen   5
    Which had Life's form and Love's, but by my spell
    Is now a shaken shadow intolerable,
Of ultimate things unuttered the frail screen.

Mark me, how still I am! But should there dart
    One moment through thy soul the soft surprise   10
    Of that winged Peace which lulls the breath of sighs—
Then shalt thou see me smile, and turn apart
Thy visage to mine ambush at thy heart
    Sleepless with cold commemorative eyes.

101. *The One Hope*

When vain desire at last and vain regret
    Go hand in hand to death, and all is vain,
    What shall assuage the unforgotten pain
And teach the unforgetful to forget?
Shall Peace be still a sunk stream long unmet—   5
    Or may the soul at once in a green plain
    Stoop through the spray of some sweet life-fountain
And cull the dew-drenched flowering amulet?¹
Ah! when the wan soul in that golden air
    Between the scriptured petals softly blown   10
    Peers breathless for the gift of grace unknown,
Ah! let none other alien spell soe'er
But only the one Hope's one name be there—
    Not less nor more, but even that word alone.

1848–80   1870, 1881

She Bound Her Green Sleeve

A FRAGMENT

She bound her green sleeve on my helm,
    Sweet pledge of love's sweet meed;²
Warm was her bared arm round my neck
    As well she bade me speed;
And her kiss clings still between my lips,   5
    Heart's beat and strength at need.

1870   1886

9. Mirror.   harm.
1. A charm to protect the wearer from   2. Reward.

The Orchard-Pit

A FRAGMENT

Piled deep below the screening apple branch
  They lie with bitter[3] apples in their hands:
And some are only ancient bones that blanch,
And some had ships that last year's wind did launch,
  And some were yesterday the lords of lands.   5

In the soft dell, among the apple trees,
  High up above the hidden pit she stands,[4]
And there forever sings, who gave to these,
That lie below, her magic hour of ease,
  And those her apples holden in their hands.   10

This in my dreams is shown me; and her hair
  Crosses my lips and draws my burning breath;
Her song spreads golden wings upon the air,
Life's eyes are gleaming from her forehead fair,
  And from her breasts the ravishing eyes of Death.   15

Men say to me that sleep hath many dreams,
  Yet I knew never but this dream alone:
There, from a dried-up channel, once the stream's,
The glen slopes up; even such in sleep it seems
  As to my waking sight the place well known.   20

My love I call her, and she loves me well:
  But I love her as in the maelstrom's cup
The whirled stone loves the leaf inseparable
That clings to it round all the circling swell,
  And that the same last eddy swallows up.   25

1869   1886

3. There is some evidence that Rossetti wrote "bitten" rather than "bitter"—a misprint that would affect our interpretation of the poem. See Oswald Doughty's edition of the *Poems* (1957), p. 307.
4. Cf. Swinburne's *Garden of Proserpine*, lines 49–50: "Pale, beyond porch and portal, / Crowned with calm leaves, she stands."

CHRISTINA ROSSETTI
(1830–1894)

Christina, the sister of Dante Gabriel Rossetti, was a devout High Church Anglican whose quiet life was dedicated to the care of relatives and to good works for church and charity. On two occasions her religious principles were responsible for breaking off plans for marriage. Her first fiancé reverted to Roman Catholicism, and in the second case the lover seemed insufficiently concerned with religion. In both instances she suffered painfully, and, as might be expected, most of her love lyrics are records of frustration and parting. Only rarely does she write of the happiness of union.

Her volume of 1862, *Goblin Market and Other Poems*, was the first collection of poetry in the Pre-Raphaelite manner to gain recognition from the public. Her affinity with the early aims of the Pre-Raphaelite group can be detected in the deceptively simple style of her writings, but her lyric gift is distinctive enough to defy historical classification. England, the birthplace of poets, has produced few women poets of note, but of these few Christina Rossetti is perhaps the finest.

Song

When I am dead, my dearest,
  Sing no sad songs for me;
Plant thou no roses at my head,
  Nor shady cypress tree.
Be the green grass above me   5
  With showers and dewdrops wet;
And if thou wilt, remember,
  And if thou wilt, forget.

I shall not see the shadows,
  I shall not feel the rain;   10
I shall not hear the nightingale
  Sing on as if in pain.
And dreaming through the twilight
  That doth not rise nor set,
Haply I may remember,   15
  And haply may forget.

1848   1862

After Death

The curtains were half drawn; the floor was swept
  And strewn with rushes; rosemary and may
  Lay thick upon the bed on which I lay,
Where, through the lattice, ivy-shadows crept.
He leaned above me, thinking that I slept   5
  And could not hear him; but I heard him say,
  "Poor child, poor child"; and as he turned away
Came a deep silence, and I knew he wept.
He did not touch the shroud, or raise the fold
  That hid my face, or take my hand in his,   10
  Or ruffle the smooth pillows for my head.

He did not love me living; but once dead
He pitied me; and very sweet it is
To know he still is warm though I am cold.

1849   1862

A Birthday

My heart is like a singing bird
    Whose nest is in a watered shoot:
My heart is like an apple tree
    Whose boughs are bent with thickset fruit;
My heart is like a rainbow shell   5
    That paddles in a halcyon sea;
My heart is gladder than all these
    Because my love is come to me.

Raise me a dais of silk and down;
    Hang it with vair[1] and purple dyes;   10
Carve it in doves and pomegranates,
    And peacocks with a hundred eyes;
Work it in gold and silver grapes,
    In leaves and silver fleurs-de-lys;
Because the birthday of my life   15
    Is come, my love is come to me.

1857   1861

An Apple Gathering

I plucked pink blossoms from mine apple tree
    And wore them all that evening in my hair:
Then in due season when I went to see
    I found no apples there.

With dangling basket all along the grass   5
    As I had come I went the selfsame track:
My neighbors mocked me while they saw me pass
    So empty-handed back.

Lilian and Lilias smiled in trudging by,
    Their heaped-up basket teased me like a jeer;   10
Sweet-voiced they sang beneath the sunset sky,
    Their mother's home was near.

Plump Gertrude passed me with her basket full,
    A stronger hand than hers helped it along;
A voice talked with her through the shadows cool   15
    More sweet to me than song.

---

1. Squirrel fur.

Ah Willie, Willie, was my love less worth
  Than apples with their green leaves piled above?
I counted rosiest apples on the earth
  Of far less worth than love.   20

So once it was with me you stooped to talk
  Laughing and listening in this very lane;
To think that by this way we used to walk
  We shall not walk again!

I let my neighbors pass me, ones and twos   25
  And groups; the latest said the night grew chill,
And hastened: but I loitered; while the dews
  Fell fast I loitered still.

1857   1861

Uphill

Does the road wind uphill all the way?
  Yes, to the very end.
Will the day's journey take the whole long day?
  From morn to night, my friend.

But is there for the night a resting place?   5
  A roof for when the slow dark hours begin.
May not the darkness hide it from my face?
  You cannot miss that inn.

Shall I meet other wayfarers at night?
  Those who have gone before.   10
Then must I knock, or call when just in sight?
  They will not keep you standing at that door.

Shall I find comfort, travel-sore and weak?
  Of labor you shall find the sum.
Will there be beds for me and all who seek?   15
  Yea, beds for all who come.

1858   1861

A Life's Parallels

Never on this side of the grave again,
  On this side of the river,
On this side of the garner of the grain,
  Never.

Ever while time flows on and on and on,   5
  That narrow noiseless river,

Ever while corn bows heavy-headed, wan,
    Ever.

Never despairing, often fainting, ruing,
    But looking back, ah never!
Faint yet pursuing, faint yet still pursuing   10
    Ever.

ca. 1881   1893

Cardinal Newman[1]

In the grave whither thou goest.

O weary Champion of the Cross, lie still:
    Sleep thou at length the all-embracing sleep;
    Long was thy sowing day, rest now and reap:
Thy fast was long, feast now thy spirit's fill.
Yea take thy fill of love, because thy will   5
    Chose love not in the shallows but the deep:
    Thy tides were spring tides, set against the neap[2]
Of calmer souls: thy flood rebuked their rill.
Now night has come to thee—please God, of rest:
    So some time must it come to every man;   10
    To first and last, where many last are first.
    Now fixed and finished thine eternal plan,
    Thy best has done its best, thy worst its worst:
Thy best its best, please God, thy best its best.

1890   1893

Sleeping at Last

Sleeping at last, the trouble and tumult over,
    Sleeping at last, the struggle and horror past,
Cold and white, out of sight of friend and of lover,
    Sleeping at last.

No more a tired heart downcast or overcast,   5
No more pangs that wring or shifting fears that hover,
    Sleeping at last in a dreamless sleep locked fast.

Fast asleep. Singing birds in their leafy cover
    Cannot wake her, nor shake her the gusty blast.
Under the purple thyme and the purple clover   10
    Sleeping at last.

1893   1896

1. Written on the occasion of the death of John Henry Newman. For an account of the theological controversies in which Newman had been involved, see the Critical and Controversial Prose section below. The epigraph is from Ecclesiastes ix.10.
2. Tides which do not rise to the high-water mark of the spring tides.

GEORGE MEREDITH
(1828–1909)

Like Thomas Hardy, George Meredith preferred writing poetry to writing novels, but it was as the author of *The Ordeal of Richard Feverel* (1859), *The Egoist* (1879), and other novels that he made his mark. His poems nevertheless deserve more attention than they have yet received, especially *Modern Love* (1862). This sequence of sixteen-line sonnets is a kind of novel in verse which analyzes the sufferings of a man and wife whose marriage is breaking up. *Modern Love* was probably derived, in part, from Meredith's own experiences. At 21, at the outset of his career as a writer in London, he married a daughter of the satirist Thomas Love Peacock. Nine years later, after a series of quarrels, his wife eloped to Europe with another artist. The Merediths were never reconciled, and in 1861 she died.

Meredith's second marriage was a happier one and reinforced his optimistic assumptions that the order of nature is good, assumptions that are sometimes developed in his poems.

From Modern Love

1

By this he knew she wept with waking eyes;
That, at his hand's light quiver by her head,
The strange low sobs that shook their common bed
Were called into her with a sharp surprise,
And strangled mute, like little gaping snakes,   5
Dreadfully venomous to him. She lay
Stone-still, and the long darkness flowed away
With muffled pulses. Then, as midnight makes
Her giant heart of Memory and Tears
Drink the pale drug of silence, and so beat   10
Sleep's heavy measure, they from head to feet
Were moveless, looking through their dead black years
By vain regret scrawled over the blank wall.
Like sculptured effigies they might be seen
Upon their marriage tomb, the sword between;[1]   15
Each wishing for the sword that severs all.

2

It ended, and the morrow brought the task.
Her eyes were guilty gates, that let him in
By shutting all too zealous for their sin:
Each sucked a secret, and each wore a mask.

1. The now silent couple are as motionless as recumbent stone statues on top of a tomb. In medieval legend, a naked sword between lovers ensured chastity.

But, oh, the bitter taste her beauty had!   5
He sickened as at breath of poison-flowers:
A languid humor stole among the hours,
And if their smiles encountered, he went mad,
And raged deep inward, till the light was brown
Before his vision, and the world, forgot,   10
Looked wicked as some old dull murder spot.
A star with lurid beams, she seemed to crown
The pit of infamy: and then again
He fainted on his vengefulness, and strove
To ape the magnanimity of love,   15
And smote himself, a shuddering heap of pain.

3

This was the woman; what now of the man?[2]
But pass him. If he comes beneath a heel,
He shall be crushed until he cannot feel,
Or, being callous, haply till he can.
But he is nothing—nothing? Only mark   5
The rich light striking out from her on him!
Ha! what a sense it is when her eyes swim
Across the man she singles, leaving dark
All else! Lord God, who mad'st the thing so fair,
See that I am drawn to her even now!   10
It cannot be such harm on her cool brow
To put a kiss? Yet if I meet him there!
But she is mine! Ah, no! I know too well
I claim a star whose light is overcast:
I claim a phantom woman in the Past.   15
The hour has struck, though I heard not the bell!

15

I think she sleeps: it must be sleep, when low
Hangs that abandoned arm toward the floor;
The face turned with it. Now make fast the door.
Sleep on: it is your husband, not your foe.
The Poet's black stage-lion[3] of wronged love   5
Frights not our modern dames—well if he did!
Now will I pour new light upon that lid,
Full-sloping like the breasts beneath. "Sweet dove,
Your sleep is pure. Nay, pardon: I disturb.
I do not? good!" Her waking infant-stare   10
Grows woman to the burden[4] my hands bear:
Her own handwriting to me when no curb
Was left on Passion's tongue. She trembles through;
A woman's tremble—the whole instrument—

---

2. I.e., a rival with whom the wife has fallen in love.
3. Probably a reference to Shakespeare's portrait of a jealous husband in *Othello*.
4. A letter once written by the wife to the husband.

I show another letter[5] lately sent.   15
The words are very like: the name is new.

16

In our old shipwrecked days there was an hour,
When in the firelight steadily aglow,
Joined slackly, we beheld the red chasm grow
Among the clicking coals. Our library bower
That eve was left to us: and hushed we sat   5
As lovers to whom Time is whispering.
From sudden-opened doors we heard them sing:
The nodding elders mixed good wine with chat.
Well knew we that Life's greatest treasure lay
With us, and of it was our talk. "Ah, yes!   10
Love dies!" I said: I never thought it less.
She yearned to me that sentence to unsay.
Then when the fire domed blackening, I found
Her cheek was salt against my kiss, and swift
Up the sharp scale of sobs her breast did lift—   15
Now am I haunted by that taste! that sound!

17

At dinner, she is hostess, I am host.
Went the feast ever cheerfuller? She keeps
The Topic over intellectual deeps
In buoyancy afloat. They see no ghost.
With sparkling surface-eyes we ply the ball: 5
It is in truth a most contagious game:
HIDING THE SKELETON, shall be its name.
Such play as this the devils might appall!
But here's the greater wonder: in that we,
Enamored of an acting naught can tire,   10
Each other, like true hypocrites, admire;
Warm-lighted looks, Love's ephemeridae,[6]
Shoot gayly o'er the dishes and the wine.
We waken envy of our happy lot.
Fast, sweet, and golden, shows the marriage knot.   15
Dear guests, you now have seen Love's corpse-light[7] shine.

50

Thus piteously Love closed[8] what he begat:
The union of this ever diverse pair!
These two were rapid falcons in a snare,
Condemned to do the flitting of the bat.
Lovers beneath the singing sky of May,   5
They wandered once; clear as the dew on flowers:

5. A letter she has recently written to
the man she now loves.
6. Insects which live for one day only.
7. Phosphorescent light such as seen in
marshes. When appearing in a cemetery it was believed to portend a
funeral.
8. The wife has died.

But they fed not on the advancing hours:
Their hearts held cravings for the buried day.
Then each applied to each that fatal knife,
Deep questioning, which probes to endless dole.   10
Ah, what a dusty answer gets the soul
When hot for certainties in this our life!—
In tragic hints here see what evermore
Moves dark as yonder midnight ocean's force,
Thundering like ramping hosts of warrior horse,   15
To throw that faint thin line upon the shore!

1862

Dirge in Woods

A wind sways the pines,
    And below
Not a breath of wild air;
Still as the mosses that glow
On the flooring and over the lines   5
Of the roots here and there.
The pine tree drops its dead;
They are quiet, as under the sea.
Overhead, overhead
Rushes life in a race,   10
As the clouds the clouds chase;
    And we go,
And we drop like the fruits of the tree,
    Even we,
    Even so.   15

1870

Lucifer in Starlight

On a starred night Prince Lucifer uprose.
Tired of his dark dominion, swung the fiend
Above the rolling ball, in cloud part screened,
Where sinners hugged their specter of repose.
Poor prey to his hot fit of pride were those.   5
And now upon his western wing he leaned,
Now his huge bulk o'er Afric's sands careened,
Now the black planet shadowed Arctic snows.
Soaring through wider zones that pricked his scars[9]
With memory of the old revolt from Awe,   10
He reached a middle height, and at the stars,
Which are the brain of heaven, he looked, and sank.
Around the ancient track marched, rank on rank,
The army of unalterable law.

1883

9. The vast expanse of sky reminds Satan of the wounds he suffered when his revolt against God was crushed and he was hurled from heaven to hell.

WILLIAM MORRIS
(1834–1896)

In his Apology to *The Earthly Paradise* Morris described himself as "the idle singer of an empty day," yet the word "idle," applied to him, seems incongruous or comic. Painter, businessman, poet, designer of furniture, printer, weaver, and political agitator, Morris was one of the most active men of his century.

Although anthologies usually feature his incidental lyrics, Morris was primarily, like Chaucer, a narrative poet. His early volume *The Defense of Guenevere* (1858) contains his most effective narratives: poems such as *The Haystack in the Floods* illustrate his flair for intense and concentrated storytelling. In his later volumes Morris abandons this promising vein and presents more diffuse and easily readable retellings of the sagas of Iceland as in *Sigurd the Volsung* (1876) or of classical legends as in *The Life and Death of Jason* (1867) and *The Earthly Paradise* (1868). The readability of these popular classical narratives is partly attributable to Morris's treatment of the rhymed couplet, a form he preferred to blank verse. In his hands the rhyming is so contrivedly unobtrusive that the narrative seems to flow without interruption. The following passage is representative (on a starlit night Medea first declares her love for Jason):

> "Upon the day thou weariest of me,
> I wish that thou mayst somewhat think of this,
> And 'twixt thy new-found kisses, and the bliss
> Of something sweeter than thine old delight,
> Remember thee a little of this night
> Of marvels, and this starlit, silent place,
> And these two lovers standing face to face."

Such poems had a marked influence on the early poetry of W. B. Yeats, who was honored when Morris said of his early volume of poems (*The Wanderings of Oisin*, 1889): "You write my kind of poetry."

Morris, in turn, was deeply attached to his own literary master, John Ruskin. Like Ruskin he became progressively dissatisfied with the drabness of the modern industrial world, and in later years became convinced that a political revolution was needed to restore mankind to a state in which work could once more be enjoyed, without the exploitation of workers that seemed to him prevalent in Victorian England. His prose narrative, *News from Nowhere* (1891), embodies his ideal of such a state, an ideal dependent partly on his study of Karl Marx but more upon his lifelong love for the color and vitality of medieval life.

Christ Keep the Hollow Land[1]

Christ keep the Hollow Land
All the summertide;

1. From a song sung by the heroine of a prose story, *The Hollow Land*, which was published in the *Oxford and Cambridge Magazine*.

Still we cannot understand
Where the waters glide:

Only dimly seeing them
Coldly slipping through
Many green-lipped cavern mouths
Where the hills are blue.

1856

The Haystack in the Floods[2]

Had she come all the way for this,
To part at last without a kiss?
Yea, had she borne the dirt and rain
That her own eyes might see him slain
Beside the haystack in the floods?   5

Along the dripping leafless woods,
The stirrup touching either shoe,
She rode astride as troopers do;
With kirtle kilted to her knee,
To which the mud splashed wretchedly;   10
And the wet dripped from every tree
Upon her head and heavy hair,
And on her eyelids broad and fair;
The tears and rain ran down her face.
By fits and starts they rode apace,   15
And very often was his place
Far off from her; he had to ride
Ahead, to see what might betide
When the roads crossed; and sometimes, when
There rose a murmuring from his men,   20
Had to turn back with promises.
Ah me! she had but little ease;
And often for pure doubt and dread
She sobbed, made giddy in the head
By the swift riding; while, for cold,   25
Her slender fingers scarce could hold
The wet reins; yea, and scarcely, too,
She felt the foot within her shoe
Against the stirrup: all for this,
To part at last without a kiss   30
Beside the haystack in the floods.

For when they neared that old soaked hay,
They saw across the only way
That Judas, Godmar, and the three

2. After the defeat of the French at
Poitiers in 1356, an English knight, Sir
Robert de Marny, is riding with Jehane, his mistress, to reach the frontier of
Gascony, which was in English hands.

Red running lions dismally   35
Grinned from his pennon, under which
In one straight line along the ditch,
They counted thirty heads.

          So then
While Robert turned round to his men,
She saw at once the wretched end,   40
And, stooping down, tried hard to rend
Her coif the wrong way from her head,
And hid her eyes; while Robert said:
"Nay, love, 'tis scarcely two to one;
At Poictiers where we made them run   45
So fast—why, sweet my love, good cheer,
The Gascon frontier is so near,
Nought after this."

          But: "O!" she said,
"My God! my God! I have to tread
The long way back without you; then   50
The court at Paris; those six men;[3]
The gratings of the Chatelet;
The swift Seine on some rainy day
Like this, and people standing by,
And laughing, while my weak hands try   55
To recollect how strong men swim.[4]
All this, or else a life with him,
For which I should be damned at last,
Would God that this next hour were past!"

He answered not, but cried his cry,   60
"St. George for Marny!" cheerily;
And laid his hand upon her rein.
Alas! no man of all his train
Gave back that cheery cry again;
And, while for rage his thumb beat fast   65
Upon his sword hilt, someone cast
About his neck a kerchief long,
And bound him.

          Then they went along
To Godmar; who said: "Now, Jehane,
Your lover's life is on the wane
So fast, that, if this very hour   70
You yield not as my paramour,
He will not see the rain leave off:
Nay, keep your tongue from gibe and scoff,
Sir Robert, or I slay you now."   75

3. The judges. The "Chatelet" is a prison in Paris.
4. In trial by water, a woman accused of witchcraft was thrown into the river to determine guilt or innocence. If she swam she would be judged guilty and thereafter burned. If she sank and drowned she was innocent.

She laid her hand upon her brow,
Then gazed upon the palm, as though
She thought her forehead bled, and: "No!"
She said, and turned her head away,
As there was nothing else to say,   80
And everything were settled: red
Grew Godmar's face from chin to head:
"Jehane, on yonder hill there stands
My castle, guarding well my lands;
What hinders me from taking you,   85
And doing that I list to do
To your fair willful body, while
Your knight lies dead?"

           A wicked smile
Wrinkled her face, her lips grew thin,
A long way out she thrust her chin: 90
"You know that I should strangle you
While you were sleeping; or bite through
Your throat, by God's help: ah!" she said,
"Lord Jesus, pity your poor maid!
For in such wise they hem me in,   95
I cannot choose but sin and sin,
Whatever happens: yet I think
They could not make me eat or drink,
And so should I just reach my rest."

"Nay, if you do not my behest,   100
O Jehane! though I love you well,"
Said Godmar, "would I fail to tell
All that I know?" "Foul lies," she said.
"Eh? lies, my Jehane? by God's head,
At Paris folks would deem them true!   105
Do you know, Jehane, they cry for you:
'Jehane the brown! Jehane the brown!
Give us Jehane to burn or drown!'
Eh!—gag me Robert!—sweet my friend,
This were indeed a piteous end   110
For those long fingers, and long feet,
And long neck, and smooth shoulders sweet;
An end that few men would forget
That saw it. So, an hour yet:
Consider, Jehane, which to take   115
Of life or death!"

         So, scarce awake,
Dismounting, did she leave that place,
And totter some yards: with her face
Turned upward to the sky she lay,

Her head on a wet heap of hay, 120
And fell asleep: and while she slept,
And did not dream, the minutes crept
Round to the twelve again; but she,
Being waked at last, sighed quietly,
And strangely childlike came, and said: 125
"I will not." Straightway Godmar's head,
As though it hung on strong wires, turned
Most sharply round, and his face burned.

For Robert, both his eyes were dry,
He could not weep, but gloomily 130
He seemed to watch the rain; yea, too,
His lips were firm; he tried once more
To touch her lips; she reached out, sore
And vain desire so tortured them,
The poor gray lips, and now the hem 135
Of his sleeve brushed them.

                  With a start
Up Godmar rose, thrust them apart;
From Robert's throat he loosed the bands
Of silk and mail; with empty hands
Held out, she stood and gazed, and saw, 140
The long bright blade without a flaw
Glide out from Godmar's sheath, his hand
In Robert's hair; she saw him bend
Back Robert's head; she saw him send
The thin steel down; the blow told well, 145
Right backward the knight Robert fell,
And moaned as dogs do, being half dead,
Unwitting, as I deem: so then
Godmar turned grinning to his men,
Who ran, some five or six, and beat 150
His head to pieces at their feet.

Then Godmar turned again and said:
"So, Jehane, the first fitte[5] is read!
Take note, my lady, that your way
Lies backward to the Chatelet!" 155
She shook her head and gazed awhile
At her cold hands with a rueful smile,
As though this thing had made her mad.

This was the parting that they had
Beside the haystack in the floods. 160
1858

5. Section or canto of a poem.

From The Earthly Paradise
An Apology

Of Heaven or Hell I have no power to sing,
I cannot ease the burden of your fears,
Or make quick-coming death a little thing,
Or bring again the pleasure of past years,
Nor for my words shall ye forget your tears,   5
Or hope again for aught that I can say,
The idle singer of an empty day.

But rather, when, aweary of your mirth,
From full hearts still unsatisfied ye sigh,
And, feeling kindly unto all the earth,   10
Grudge every minute as it passes by,
Made the more mindful that the sweet days die—
Remember me a little then, I pray,
The idle singer of an empty day.

The heavy trouble, the bewildering care   15
That weighs us down who live and earn our bread,
These idle verses have no power to bear;
So let me sing of names rememberéd,
Because they, living not, can ne'er be dead,
Or long time take their memory quite away   20
From us poor singers of an empty day.

Dreamer of dreams, born out of my due time,
Why should I strive to set the crooked straight?[6]
Let it suffice me that my murmuring rhyme
Beats with light wing against the ivory gate,[7]   25
Telling a tale not too importunate
To those who in the sleepy region stay,
Lulled by the singer of an empty day.

Folk say a wizard to a northern king
At Christmastide such wondrous things did show,   30
That through one window men beheld the spring,
And through another saw the summer glow,
And through a third the fruited vines a-row,
While still, unheard, but in its wonted way,
Piped the drear wind of that December day.   35

So with this Earthly Paradise it is,
If ye will read aright, and pardon me,
Who strive to build a shadowy isle of bliss
Midmost the beating of the steely sea,

6. In 1856, when Morris was an undergraduate, he wrote in a letter: "I can't enter into politico-social subjects with any interest, for on the whole I see that things are in a muddle, and I have no power or vocation to set them right in ever so little a degree. My work is the embodiment of dreams in one form or another."
7. At the cave of Morpheus, god of dreams, were two gates: through the gate of horn came prophetic dreams, and through the ivory gate came fictitious dreams.

Where tossed about all hearts of men must be;   40
Whose ravening monsters mighty men shall slay,
Not the poor singer of an empty day.

                                1868–70

A Death Song[8]

What cometh here from west to east a-wending?
And who are these, the marchers stern and slow?
We bear the message that the rich are sending
Aback to those who bade them wake and know.
Not one, not one, nor thousands must they slay,   5
But one and all if they would dusk the day.

We asked them for a life of toilsome earning—
They bade us bide their leisure for our bread;
We craved to speak to tell our woeful learning—
We come back speechless, bearing back our dead.   10
Not one, not one, nor thousands must they slay,
But one and all if they would dusk the day.

They will not learn; they have no ears to hearken;
They turn their faces from the eyes of fate;
Their gay lit halls shut out the skies that darken.   15
But, lo! this dead man knocking at the gate.
Not one, not one, nor thousands must they slay,
But one and all if they would dusk the day.

Here lies the sign that we shall break our prison;
Amidst the storm he won a prisoner's rest;   20
But in the cloudy dawn the sun arisen
Brings us our day of work to win the best.
Not one, not one, nor thousands must they slay,
But one and all if they would dusk the day.

                                1891

For the Bed at Kelmscott[9]

      The wind's on the wold
      And the night is a-cold,
      And Thames runs chill
      'Twixt mead and hill;
      But kind and dear   5
      Is the old house here,
      And my heart is warm
      'Midst winter's harm.

8. In a Socialist parade of 1887, in which Morris was one of the marchers, his friend Alfred Linnell was beaten by the police and died of injuries. Morris printed this poem as a penny pamphlet to raise money for Linnell's family.
9. Kelmscott Manor was owned by Morris. The bed itself is the speaker.

Rest, then, and rest,
And think of the best
'Twixt summer and spring,   10
When all birds sing
In the town of the tree,
And ye lie in me
And scarce dare move,
Lest the earth and its love   15
Should fade away
Ere the full of the day.
I am old and have seen
Many things that have been—   20
Both grief and peace
And wane and increase.
No tale I tell
Of ill or well,
But this I say,   25
Night treadeth on day.
And for worst and best
Right good is rest.

1893

EDWARD FITZGERALD
(1809–1883)

Omar Khayyám was a 12th-century mathematician, astronomer, and teacher, from Nishapur in Persia. He was also the author of numerous rhymed quatrains, a verse form called *rubā'i* in Persian. Omar's four-lined epigrams were subsequently brought together in collections called *Rubáiyát* and recorded in various manuscripts.

Over 700 years later, in 1857, one such Omar manuscript came into the hands of Edward FitzGerald, a Victorian man of letters, who made from it one of the most popular poems in the English language. FitzGerald was a scholar of comfortable means who lived in the country reading the classics and cultivating his garden. He also cultivated his friendships with writers like Tennyson, Thackeray, and Carlyle, to whom he wrote charming letters. His translations from Greek and Latin were largely ignored, and so too, at first, was his translation of Omar's Persian verses, which he published anonymously. In 1859, only two reviewers noticed the appearance of the *Rubáiyát*, and the edition was soon remaindered. Two years later the volume was discovered by D. G. Rossetti, and enthusiasm for it gradually spread, until edition after edition was called for. The demand for the poem led FitzGerald to revise his translation considerably by further polishing his already finely polished stanzas (the fifth version of these revisions appears below).

The Italians have a witty saying that translations are like wives: a beautiful translation is apt to be unfaithful, and a faithful translation is apt to be ugly. Experts have argued at great length whether FitzGerald's adaptation of Omar's poem is a faithful translation, but no one argues its beauty.

One reader said of FitzGerald's witty and melancholy masterpiece: "It reads like the latest and freshest expression of the perplexity and of the doubt of the generation to which we ourselves belong." This comment was made by the American critic Charles Eliot Norton, a late Victorian writing in 1888. Norton's favorable opinion has been endorsed by later generations as well. The *Rubáiyát* has much in common with another late Victorian volume, *The Shropshire Lad* by A. E. Housman, and the remarkable popularity of these two collections of nostalgic lyrics is a reminder that to be popular, especially among young readers, poetry does not have to offer optimistic edification. As George Moore said, "The sadness of life is the joy of art."

The Rubáiyát of Omar Khayyám

1

Wake! For the Sun, who scattered into flight
The Stars before him from the Field of Night,
   Drives Night along with them from Heav'n and strikes
The Sultán's Turret with a Shaft of Light.

2

Before the phantom of False morning[1] died,   5
Methought a Voice within the Tavern cried,
   "When all the Temple is prepared within,
Why nods the drowsy Worshiper outside?"

3

And, as the Cock crew, those who stood before
The Tavern shouted—"Open, then, the Door!   10
   You know how little while we have to stay,
And, once departed, may return no more."

4

Now the New Year[2] reviving old Desires,
The thoughtful Soul to Solitude retires,
   Where the WHITE HAND OF MOSES on the Bough
Puts out, and Jesus from the Ground suspires.[3]   15

5

Iram[4] indeed is gone with all his Rose,
And Jamshyd's[5] Sev'n-ringed Cup where no one knows;
   But still a Ruby kindles in the Vine,
And many a Garden by the Water blows.   20

6

And David's lips are locked; but in divine
High-piping Pehleví,[6] with "Wine! Wine! Wine!

---

1. "A transient Light on the Horizon about an hour before the * * * True Dawn" [FitzGerald's note].
2. In Persia, the beginning of spring.
3. Breathes. "Moses" and "Jesus": plants named in honor of prophets who came before Mohammed. The Persians believed that the healing power of Jesus was in his breath.
4. "A royal Garden now sunk somewhere in the Sands of Arabia" [FitzGerald's note].
5. Legendary king.
6. The classical language of Persia.

Red Wine!"—the Nightingale cries to the Rose
That sallow cheek of hers to incarnadine.

7

Come, fill the Cup, and in the fire of Spring   25
Your Winter-garment of Repentance fling;
   The Bird of Time has but a little way
To flutter—and the Bird is on the Wing.

8

Whether at Naishápur or Babylon,
Whether the Cup with sweet or bitter run,   30
   The Wine of Life keeps oozing drop by drop,
The Leaves of Life keep falling one by one.

9

Each Morn a thousand Roses brings, you say;
Yes, but where leaves the Rose of Yesterday?
   And this first Summer month that brings the Rose   35
Shall take Jamshyd and Kaikobád[7] away.

10

Well, let it take them! What have we to do
With Kaikobád the Great, or Kaikhosrú?
   Let Zál and Rustum bluster as they will,[8]
Or Hátim[9] call to Supper—heed not you.   40

11

With me along the strip of Herbage strown
That just divides the desert from the sown,
   Where name of Slave and Sultán is forgot—
And Peace to Mahmúd[1] on his golden Throne!

12

A Book of Verses underneath the Bough,   45
A Jug of Wine, a Loaf of Bread—and Thou
   Beside me singing in the Wilderness—
Oh, Wilderness were Paradise enow!

13

Some for the Glories of This World; and some
Sigh for the Prophet's[2] Paradise to come;   50
   Ah, take the Cash, and let the Credit go,
Nor heed the rumble of a distant Drum!

14

Look to the blowing Rose about us—"Lo,
Laughing," she says, "into the world I blow,
   At once the silken tassel of my Purse   55
Tear, and its Treasure on the Garden throw."

15

And those who husbanded the Golden Grain,
And those who flung it to the winds like Rain,
   Alike to no such aureate Earth are turned
As, buried once, Men want dug up again.   60

---

7. Founder of a line of Persian kings.
8. Kaikhosrú: a king; Zál and Rustum: son and father who were warriors.
9. A generous host.
1. A sultan who conquered India.
2. Mohammed's.

16

The Worldly Hope men set their Hearts upon
Turns Ashes—or it prospers; and anon,
   Like Snow upon the Desert's dusty Face,
Lighting a little hour or two—is gone.

17

Think, in this battered Caravanscrai[3]
Whose Portals are alternate Night and Day,
   How Sultán after Sultán with his Pomp
Abode his destined Hour, and went his way.

18

They say the Lion and the Lizard keep
The Courts where Jamshyd gloried and drank deep;
   And Bahrám,[4] that great Hunter—the Wild Ass
Stamps o'er his Head, but cannot break his Sleep.

19

I sometimes think that never blows so red
The Rose as where some buried Caesar bled;
   That every Hyacinth[5] the Garden wears
Dropped in her Lap from some once lovely Head.

20

And this reviving Herb whose tender Green
Fledges the River-Lip on which we lean—
   Ah, lean upon it lightly! for who knows
From what once lovely Lip it springs unseen!

21

Ah, my Belovéd, fill the Cup that clears
TODAY of past Regrets and future Fears:
   Tomorrow!—Why, Tomorrow I may be
Myself with Yesterday's Sev'n thousand Years.

22

For some we loved, the loveliest and the best
That from his Vintage rolling Time hath pressed,
   Have drunk their Cup a Round or two before,
And one by one crept silently to rest.

23

And we, that now make merry in the Room
They left, and Summer dresses in new bloom,
   Ourselves must we beneath the Couch of Earth
Descend—ourselves to make a Couch—for whom?

24

Ah, make the most of what we yet may spend,
Before we too into the Dust descend;
   Dust into Dust, and under Dust to lie,
Sans Wine, sans Song, sans Singer, and—sans End!

3. Inn.
4. A king who was lost while hunting a wild ass.
5. In classical myth, the hyacinth had associations of sadness because the plant was supposed to have sprung from the blood of Hyacinthus, a beautiful youth who was killed in an accident. Its petals were marked AI, meaning "alas." FitzGerald, however, seems to be referring more particularly to the shape of the flower, as in Homer's *Odyssey* VI.231, where locks of hair are likened to hyacinth clusters.

25

Alike for those who for TODAY prepare,
And those that after some TOMORROW stare,
    A Muezzín[6] from the Tower of Darkness cries,
"Fools, your Reward is neither Here nor There."   100

26

Why, all the Saints and Sages who discussed
Of the Two Worlds so wisely—they are thrust
    Like foolish Prophets forth; their Words to Scorn
Are scattered, and their Mouths are stopped with Dust.

27

Myself when young did eagerly frequent   105
Doctor and Saint, and heard great argument
    About it and about; but evermore
Came out by the same door where in I went.

28

With them the seed of Wisdom did I sow,
And with mine own hand wrought to make it grow;   110
    And this was all the Harvest that I reaped—
"I came like Water, and like Wind I go."

29

Into this Universe, and *Why* not knowing
Nor *Whence*, like Water willy-nilly flowing;
    And out of it, as Wind along the Waste,   115
I know not *Whither*, willy-nilly blowing.

30

What, without asking, hither hurried *Whence?*
And, without asking, *Whither* hurried hence!
    Oh, many a Cup of this forbidden Wine[7]
Must drown the memory of that insolence!   120

31

Up from the Earth's Center through the Seventh Gate
I rose, and on the Throne of Saturn[8] sate,
    And many a Knot unraveled by the Road;
But not the Master-knot of Human Fate.

32

There was the Door to which I found no Key;   125
There was the Veil through which I might not see;
    Some little talk awhile of ME and THEE
There was—and then no more of THEE and ME.

33

Earth could not answer; nor the Seas that mourn
In flowing Purple, of their Lord forlorn;   130
    Nor rolling Heaven, with all his Signs[9] revealed
And hidden by the sleeve of Night and Morn.

34

Then of the THEE IN ME who works behind
The Veil, I lifted up my hands to find

6. One who calls the hour of prayer from the tower of a mosque.
7. Alcohol is forbidden to strict Moslems.
8. The seat of knowledge. According to a note by FitzGerald, Saturn was lord of the seventh heaven.
9. I.e., of the zodiac.

A lamp amid the Darkness; and I heard,   135
As from Without—"THE ME WITHIN THEE BLIND!"

35

Then to the Lip of this poor earthen Urn
I leaned, the Secret of my Life to learn;
   And Lip to Lip it murmured—"While you live,
Drink!—for, once dead, you never shall return."   140

36

I think the Vessel, that with fugitive
Articulation answered, once did live,
   And drink; and Ah! the passive Lip I kissed,
How many Kisses might it take—and give!

37

For I remember stopping by the way   145
To watch a Potter thumping his wet Clay;
   And with its all-obliterated Tongue
It murmured—"Gently, Brother, gently, pray!"

38

And has not such a Story from of Old
Down Man's successive generations rolled   150
   Of such a clod of saturated Earth
Cast by the Maker into Human mold?

39

And not a drop that from our Cups we throw
For Earth to drink of,[1] but may steal below
   To quench the fire of Anguish in some Eye   155
There hidden—far beneath, and long ago.

40

As then the Tulip, for her morning sup
Of Heav'nly Vintage, from the soil looks up,
   Do you devoutly do the like, till Heav'n
To Earth invert you—like an empty Cup.   160

41

Perplexed no more with Human or Divine,
Tomorrow's tangle to the winds resign,
   And lose your fingers in the tresses of
The Cypress-slender Minister of Wine.[2]

42

And if the Wine you drink, the Lip you press,   165
End in what All begins and ends in—Yes;
   Think then you are TODAY what YESTERDAY
You were—TOMORROW you shall not be less.

43

So when that Angel of the darker Drink
At last shall find you by the river brink,   170
   And offering his Cup, invite your Soul
Forth to your Lips to quaff—you shall not shrink.

44

Why, if the Soul can fling the Dust aside,

1. A reference to the custom of pour-   and buried wine-drinker.
ing some wine on the ground before   2. Maiden who serves the wine.
drinking in order to refresh some dead

And naked on the Air of Heaven ride,
    Were 't not a Shame—were 't not a Shame for him   175
In this clay carcass crippled to abide?

45

'Tis but a Tent where takes his one day's rest
A Sultán to the realm of Death addressed;
    The Sultán rises, and the dark Ferrásh³
Strikes, and prepares it for another Guest.   180

46

And fear not lest Existence closing your
Account, and mine, should know the like no more;
    The Eternal Sákí⁴ from that Bowl has poured
Millions of Bubbles like us, and will pour.

47

When You and I behind the Veil are past,   185
Oh, but the long, long while the World shall last,
    Which of our Coming and Departure heeds
As the Sea's self should heed a pebble-cast.

48

A Moment's Halt—a momentary taste
Of BEING from the Well amid the Waste—   190
    And Lo!—the phantom Caravan has reached
The NOTHING it set out from—Oh, make haste!

49

Would you that spangle of Existence spend
About THE SECRET—quick about it, Friend!
    A Hair perhaps divides the False and True—   195
And upon what, prithee, may life depend?

50

A Hair perhaps divides the False and True—
Yes; and a single Alif⁵ were the clue—
    Could you but find it—to the Treasure-house,
And peradventure to THE MASTER too;   200

51

Whose secret Presence, through Creation's veins
Running Quicksilver-like, eludes your pains;
    Taking all shapes from Máh to Máhi;⁶ and
They change and perish all—but He remains;

52

A moment guessed—then back behind the Fold   205
Immersed of Darkness round the Drama rolled
    Which, for the Pastime of Eternity,
He doth Himself contrive, enact, behold.

53

But if in vain, down on the stubborn floor
Of Earth, and up to Heav'n's unopening Door,   210
    You gaze TODAY, while You are You—how then
TOMORROW, when You shall be You no more?

---

3. Servant who takes down ("strikes") a tent.
4. Servant who passes the wine.
5. The first letter of the Arabic alphabet, represented by a single vertical line.
6. I.e., from lowest to highest.

54

Waste not your Hour, nor in the vain pursuit
Of This and That endeavor and dispute;
    Better be jocund with the fruitful Grape
Than sadden after none, or bitter, Fruit.

215

55

You know, my Friends, with what a brave Carouse
I made a Second Marriage in my house;
    Divorced old barren Reason from my Bed,
And took the Daughter of the Vine to Spouse.

220

56

For "Is" and "Is-NOT" though with Rule and Line,
And "UP-AND-DOWN" by Logic, I define,
    Of all that one should care to fathom, I
Was never deep in anything but—Wine.

57

Ah, but my Computations, People say,
Reduced the Year to better reckoning?[7]—Nay,
    'Twas only striking from the Calendar
Unborn Tomorrow, and dead Yesterday.

225

58

And lately, by the Tavern Door agape,
Came shining through the Dusk an Angel Shape
    Bearing a Vessel on his Shoulder; and
He bid me taste of it; and 'twas—the Grape!

230

59

The Grape that can with Logic absolute
The Two-and-Seventy jarring Sects[8] confute;
    The sovereign Alchemist that in a trice
Life's leaden metal into Gold transmute;

235

60

The mighty Mahmúd, Allah-breathing Lord,
That all the misbelieving and black Horde[9]
    Of Fears and Sorrows that infest the Soul
Scatters before him with his whirlwind Sword.

240

61

Why, be this Juice the growth of God, who dare
Blaspheme the twisted tendril as a Snare?
    A Blessing, we should use it, should we not?
And if a Curse—why, then, Who set it there?

62

I must abjure the Balm of Life, I must,
Scared by some After-reckoning ta'en on trust
    Or lured with Hope of some Diviner Drink,
To fill the Cup—when crumbled into Dust!

245

---

7. As a mathematician, Omar had devised an improved calendar.
8. "The 72 religions supposed to divide the world" [FitzGerald's note].

9. "Alluding to Sultan Mahmúd's Conquest of India and its dark people" [FitzGerald's note].

63

Oh threats of Hell and Hopes of Paradise!
One thing at least is certain—*This* Life flies;
   One thing is certain and the rest is Lies—
The Flower that once has blown forever dies.   250

64

Strange, is it not? that of the myriads who
Before us passed the door of Darkness through,
   Not one returns to tell us of the Road,   255
Which to discover we must travel too.

65

The Revelations of Devout and Learn'd
Who rose before us, and as Prophets burned,[1]
   Are all but Stories, which, awoke from Sleep,
They told their comrades, and to Sleep returned.   260

66

I sent my Soul through the Invisible,
Some letter of that After-life to spell;
   And by and by my Soul returned to me,
And answered, "I Myself am Heav'n and Hell"—

67

Heaven but the Vision of fulfilled Desire,   265
And Hell the Shadow from a Soul on fire
   Cast on the Darkness into which Ourselves,
So late emerged from, shall so soon expire.

68

We are no other than a moving row
Of Magic Shadow-shapes that come and go   270
   Round with the Sun-illumined Lantern held
In Midnight by the Master of the Show;

69

But helpless Pieces of the Game He plays
Upon this Checkerboard of Nights and Days;
   Hither and thither moves, and checks, and slays,   275
And one by one back in the Closet lays.

70

The Ball no question makes of Ayes and Noes,
But Here or There as strikes the Player[2] goes;
   And He that tossed you down into the Field,
He knows about it all—HE knows—HE knows!   280

71

The Moving Finger writes, and, having writ,
Moves on; nor all your Piety nor Wit
   Shall lure it back to cancel half a Line,
Nor all your Tears wash out a Word of it.

72

And that inverted Bowl they call the Sky,   285
Whereunder crawling cooped we live and die,

1. Inspired by burning zeal to spread   2. Polo player.
their prophecies.

Lift not your hands to *It* for help—for It
As impotently moves as you or I.

73

With Earth's first Clay They did the Last Man knead,
And there of the Last Harvest sowed the Seed;   290
   And the first Morning of Creation wrote
What the Last Dawn of Reckoning shall read.

74

YESTERDAY *This* Day's Madness did prepare;
TOMORROW's Silence, Triumph, or Despair.
   Drink! for you know not whence you came, nor why;   295
Drink, for you know not why you go, nor where.

75

I tell you this—When, started from the Goal,
Over the flaming shoulders of the Foal
   Of Heav'n Parwín and Mushtarí they flung,
In my predestined Plot of Dust and Soul[3]   300

76

The Vine had struck a fiber; which about
If clings my Being—let the Dervish[4] flout;
   Of my Base metal may be filed a Key,
That shall unlock the Door he howls without.

77

And this I know: whether the one True Light   305
Kindle to Love, or Wrath—consume me quite,
   One Flash of It within the Tavern caught
Better than in the Temple lost outright.

78

What! out of senseless Nothing to provoke
A conscious Something to resent the yoke   310
   Of unpermitted Pleasure, under pain
Of Everlasting Penalties, if broke!

79

What! from his helpless Creature be repaid
Pure Gold for what he lent him dross-allayed—
   Sue for a Debt he never did contract,   315
And cannot answer—Oh, the sorry trade!

80

O Thou, who didst with pitfall and with gin[5]
Beset the Road I was to wander in,
   Thou wilt not with Predestined Evil round
Enmesh, and then impute my Fall to Sin!   320

---

3. The speaker asserts that his fate was predestined in accordance with the relationship of the stars and planets at the moment of his birth when he "started from the Goal." In his horoscope, the particular relationship involved the Pleiades ("Parwín") and the planet Jupiter ("Mushtarí") which were "flung" by the gods into a special position in relation to the place in the sky of the constellation Equuleus ("the Foal" or Colt).
4. Ascetic, who would despise ("flout") wine as a means of discovering truth.
5. Trap.

81

O Thou, who Man of Baser Earth didst make,
And ev'n with Paradise devise the Snake,
   For all the Sin wherewith the Face of Man
Is blackened—Man's forgiveness give—and take!

82

As under cover of departing Day   325
Slunk hunger-stricken Ramazán[6] away,
   Once more within the Potter's house alone
I stood, surrounded by the Shapes of Clay—

83

Shapes of all Sorts and Sizes, great and small,
That stood along the floor and by the wall;   330
   And some loquacious Vessels were; and some
Listened perhaps, but never talked at all.

84

Said one among them—"Surely not in vain
My substance of the common Earth was ta'en
   And to this Figure molded, to be broke,   335
Or trampled back to shapeless Earth again."

85

Then said a Second—"Ne'er a peevish Boy
Would break the Bowl from which he drank in joy;
   And He that with his hand the Vessel made
Will surely not in after Wrath destroy."   340

86

After a momentary silence spake
Some Vessel of a more ungainly Make:
   "They sneer at me for leaning all awry;
What! did the Hand, then, of the Potter shake?"

87

Whereat someone of the loquacious Lot—   345
I think a Súfi[7] pipkin—waxing hot—
   "All this of Pot and Potter—Tell me then,
Who is the Potter, pray, and who the Pot?"

88

"Why," said another, "Some there are who tell
Of one who threatens he will toss to Hell   350
   The luckless Pots he marred in making—Pish!
He's a Good Fellow, and 'twill all be well."

89

"Well," murmured one, "Let whoso make or buy,
My Clay with long Oblivion is gone dry;
   But fill me with the old familiar Juice,   355
Methinks I might recover by and by."

6. The month of fasting—during which   7. Mystic.
no food is eaten from sunrise to sunset.

90

So while the Vessels one by one were speaking
The little Moon looked in that all were seeking;[8]
    And then they jogged each other, "Brother! Brother!
Now for the Porter's shoulder-knot[9] a-creaking!"   360

91

Ah, with the Grape my fading Life provide,
And wash the Body whence the Life has died,
    And lay me, shrouded in the living Leaf,
By some not unfrequented Garden-side—

92

That ev'n my buried Ashes such a snare   365
Of Vintage shall fling up into the Air
    As not a True-believer passing by
But shall be overtaken unaware.

93

Indeed the Idols I have loved so long
Have done my credit in this World much wrong,   370
    Have drowned my Glory in a shallow Cup,
And sold my Reputation for a Song.

94

Indeed, indeed, Repentance oft before
I swore—but was I sober when I swore?
    And then and then came Spring, and Rose-in-hand   375
My threadbare Penitence apieces tore.

95

And much as Wine has played the Infidel,
And robbed me of my Robe of Honor—Well,
    I wonder often what the Vintners buy
One-half so precious as the stuff they sell.   380

96

Yet Ah, that Spring should vanish with the Rose!
That Youth's sweet-scented manuscript should close!
    The Nightingale that in the branches sang,
Ah whence, and whither flown again, who knows!

97

Would but the Desert of the Fountain yield   385
One glimpse—if dimly, yet indeed, revealed,
    To which the fainting Traveler might spring,
As springs the trampled herbage of the field.

98

Would but some wingéd Angel ere too late
Arrest the yet unfolded Roll of Fate,   390
    And make the stern Recorder otherwise
Enregister, or quite obliterate!

8. "At the close of the Fasting Month,
Ramazán * * * the first Glimpse of
the New Moon * * * is looked for
with the utmost Anxiety and hailed
with all Acclamation" [FitzGerald's
note].
9. The rope or strap on which were
hung the wine jars carried by the
porter.

99
Ah, Love! could you and I with Him conspire
To grasp this sorry Scheme of Things entire,
    Would not we shatter it to bits—and then
Remold it nearer to the Heart's Desire!   395

———————

100
Yon rising Moon that looks for us again—
How oft hereafter will she wax and wane;
    How oft hereafter rising look for us
Through this same Garden—and for *one* in vain!   400
101
And when like her, O Sákí, you shall pass
Among the Guests Star-scattered on the Grass,
    And in your joyous errand reach the spot
Where I made One—turn down an empty Glass!

TAMÁM[1]

1857   1859, 1889
1. "It is ended."

ARTHUR HUGH CLOUGH
(1819–1861)

The writings of Clough (whose name is pronounced so as to rhyme with
rough) are usually treated as a kind of footnote to those of his friend
Matthew Arnold. Read in this way they can indeed add to our understanding of Arnold's early poems written during the phase of religious
stress shared by both young men. Some of Clough's admirers argue, however, that such a reading is to be deplored because Clough, despite his
frequent clumsiness in versification, is a poet of considerable stature in his
own right. What is beyond dispute is that he provides exceptional insights
into the intellectual history of his century.

    Like many Victorians, Clough was permanently influenced by his mother's
pious religious convictions, her influence being reinforced by his years at
Rugby School, where he was the prize pupil of Dr. Thomas Arnold. Later,
at Oxford, his earnest preoccupation with religious duty was undermined
by a number of different intellectual developments. He was forced to
think through questions of High Church authoritarianism and traditionalism—provoked by Cardinal Newman's presence at Oxford—and to confront
the evidence of scientific critics who challenged the authority and authenticity of the Scriptures. Clough emerged as a skeptic in the real sense of the
word. In a letter to his sister in 1847, speaking of the Atonement as an
article of Christian faith, he remarks: "I think others are more right who
say boldly. We don't understand it, and therefore we *won't* fall down
and worship it. Though there is no occasion for adding—'there *is* noth-

ing in it—' I should say, Until I know, I will wait: and if I am not born with the power to discover, I will do what I can * * * and neither pretend to know, nor without knowing, pretend to embrace: nor yet oppose those who by whatever means are increasing or trying to increase knowledge." A year later, reflections of this kind led Clough to resign his fellowship at Oxford where he was expected to subscribe to the doctrines of the Church of England. For the rest of his life he held various educational posts and also traveled extensively—to the United States, where his early childhood had been spent, and in Italy, a country which served as the setting of several of his poems.

Much of Clough's poetry was published posthumously. His first volume, *The Bothie of Tober-na-Vuolich* (1848), is a delightful novel in verse, an undergraduate love story exhibiting aspects of his character omitted in Arnold's picture of him in *Thyrsis*. For despite his painful exposure to religious uncertainties, Clough had a strain of high spirits and fun that gives flavor to his best poems. In his later poems, including *Dipsychus* (1850), the strains of earnestness, uncertainty, and humor are blended into an ironic point of view different from Matthew Arnold's and, in fact, different from the characteristic tone of most of his contemporaries. Perhaps one of the reasons that Clough's poetry has been inadequately appreciated is that this distinctive tone of his is most evident in his full-length poems rather than in the short hymnlike verses by which he is usually represented in anthologies.

Epi-strauss-ium[1]

Matthew and Mark and Luke and holy John
Evanished all and gone!
Yea, he[2] that erst, his dusky curtains quitting,
Through Eastern pictured panes his level beams transmitting,
With gorgeous portraits blent, 5
On them his glories intercepted spent,
Southwestering now, through windows plainly glassed,
On the inside face his radiance keen hath cast,
And in the luster lost, invisible, and gone,
Are, say you, Matthew, Mark, and Luke and holy John? 10
Lost, is it? lost, to be recovered never?
However,
The place of worship the meantime with light
Is, if less richly, more sincerely bright,
And in blue skies the Orb is manifest to sight. 15

1847 1869

1. The title is a play on *epi-thalamium*, which means "concerning the bridal chamber." The word usually refers to a song in honor of a bride and bridegroom (as in Spenser's poem). Clough's title means "concerning Strauss-ism," a reference to D. F. Strauss, a German Biblical scholar whose *Life of Jesus* was translated into English by George Eliot in 1846. The "light" of Strauss's analysis reputedly showed up the historical inaccuracy of parts of the Gospels in the Bible.
2. The sun. Cf. lines 13–16 of *Say Not the Struggle*, below.

The Latest Decalogue

Thou shalt have one God only; who
Would be at the expense of two?
No graven images may be
Worshiped, except the currency.
Swear not at all; for, for thy curse   5
Thine enemy is none the worse.
At church on Sunday to attend
Will serve to keep the world thy friend.
Honor thy parents; that is, all
From whom advancement may befall.   10
Thou shalt not kill; but need'st not strive
Officiously to keep alive.
Do not adultery commit;
Advantage rarely comes of it.
Thou shalt not steal; an empty feat,   15
When it's so lucrative to cheat.
Bear not false witness; let the lie
Have time on its own wings to fly.
Thou shalt not covet, but tradition
Approves all forms of competition.   20

The sum of all is, thou shalt love,
If anybody, God above:
At any rate shall never labor
More than thyself to love thy neighbor.[3]

1862

Say Not the Struggle Nought Availeth

Say not the struggle nought availeth,
    The labor and the wounds are vain,
The enemy faints not, nor faileth,
    And as things have been they remain.

If hopes were dupes, fears may be liars;   5
    It may be, in yon smoke concealed,
Your comrades chase e'en now the fliers,
    And, but for you, possess the field.

For while the tired waves, vainly breaking,
    Seem here no painful inch to gain,   10
Far back, through creeks and inlets making,
    Comes silent, flooding in, the main.

3. Lines 21–24 were discovered in one of Clough's manuscripts and were not originally included in published versions of the poem.

And not by eastern windows only,
  When daylight comes, comes in the light,
In front, the sun climbs slow, how slowly,   15
  But westward, look, the land is bright.

1849   1862

From Dipsychus
I Dreamt a Dream[4]

I dreamt a dream; till morning light
A bell rang in my head all night,
Tinkling and tinkling first, and then
Tolling; and tinkling; tolling again.
So brisk and gay, and then so slow!   5
O joy, and terror! mirth, and woe!
Ting, ting, there is no God; ting, ting—
Dong, there is no God; dong,
There is no God; dong, dong!

Ting, ting, there is no God; ting, ting;   10
Come dance and play, and merrily sing—
Ting, ting a ding; ting, ting a ding!
O pretty girl who trippest along,
Come to my bed—it isn't wrong.
Uncork the bottle, sing the song!   15
Ting, ting a ding: dong, dong.
Wine has dregs; the song an end;
A silly girl is a poor friend
And age and weakness who shall mend?
Dong, there is no God; Dong!   20

Ting, ting a ding! Come dance and sing!
Staid Englishmen, who toil and slave
From your first breeching[5] to your grave,
And seldom spend and always save,
And do your duty all your life   25
By your young family and wife;
Come, be 't not said you ne'er had known
What earth can furnish you alone.
The Italian, Frenchman, German even,
Have given up all thoughts of heaven;   30
And you still linger—oh, you fool!
Because of what you learnt at school.
You should have gone at least to college,

---

4. Dipsychus, the Faust-like hero of Clough's long poem, is in Venice, a city of many bells, where he reports observations and reflections to a companion. The hero's name means "two-souled," a reference to the split between his worldliness and his idealism. This selection is from Scene V, lines 7–92 and 120–29.
5. First wearing of trousers or breeches by a boy.

And got a little ampler knowledge.
Ah well, and yet—dong, dong, dong: 35
Do, if you like, as now you do;
If work's a cheat, so's pleasure too;
And nothing's new and nothing's true;
Dong, there is no God; dong!

O Rosalie, my precious maid,   40
I think thou thinkest love is true;
And on thy fragrant bosom laid
I almost could believe it too.
O in our nook, unknown, unseen,
We'll hold our fancy like a screen,   45
Us and the dreadful fact between.
And it shall yet be long, aye, long,
The quiet notes of our low song
Shall keep us from that sad dong, dong.
Hark, hark, hark! O voice of fear![6]   50
It reaches us here, even here!
Dong, there is no God; dong!

Ring ding, ring ding, tara, tara,
To battle, to battle—haste, haste—
To battle, to battle—aha, aha!   55
On, on, to the conqueror's feast.
From east and west, and south and north,
Ye men of valor and of worth,
Ye mighty men of arms, come forth,
And work your will, for that is just;   60
And in your impulse put your trust,
Beneath your feet the fools are dust.
Alas, alas! O grief and wrong,
The good are weak, the wicked strong;
And O my God, how long, how long?   65
Dong, there is no God; dong!

Ring, ting; to bow before the strong,
There is a rapture too in this;
Speak, outraged maiden, in thy wrong
Did terror bring no secret bliss?   70
Were boys' shy lips worth half a song
Compared to the hot soldier's kiss?
Work for thy master, work, thou slave
He is not merciful, but brave.
Be 't joy to serve, who free and proud   75
Scorns thee and all the ignoble crowd;
Take that, 'tis all thou art allowed,
Except the snaky hope that they
May sometime serve, who rule today,
When, by hell-demons, shan't they pay?   80

6. Cf. *Love's Labour's Lost* (V.ii.911–12): "'Cuckoo, cuckoo!' O word of fear, / Unpleasing to a married ear!"

O wickedness, O shame and grief,
And heavy load, and no relief!
O God, O God! and which is worst,
To be the curser or the cursed,
The victim or the murderer? Dong   85
Dong, there is no God; dong!

* * *

I had a dream, from eve to light
A bell went sounding all the night.
Gay mirth, black woe, thin joys, huge pain:
I tried to stop it, but in vain.   90
It ran right on, and never broke;
Only when day began to stream
Through the white curtains to my bed,
And like an angel at my head
Light stood and touched me—I awoke,   95
And looked, and said, "It is a dream."

"There Is No God," the Wicked Saith[7]

"There is no God," the wicked saith,
    "And truly it's a blessing,
For what he might have done with us
    It's better only guessing."

"There is no God," a youngster thinks,   5
    "Or really, if there may be,
He surely didn't mean a man
    Always to be a baby."

"There is no God, or if there is,"
    The tradesman thinks, " 'twere funny   10
If he should take it ill in me
    To make a little money."

"Whether there be," the rich man says,
    "It matters very little,
For I and mine, thank somebody,   15
    Are not in want of victual."

Some others, also, to themselves
    Who scarce so much as doubt it,
Think there is none, when they are well,
    And do not think about it.   20

But country folks who live beneath
    The shadow of the steeple;
The parson and the parson's wife,
    And mostly married people;

Youths green and happy in first love,   25
    So thankful for illusion;

7. From *Dipsychus* V.152 ff.

And men caught out in what the world
Calls guilt, in first confusion;

And almost everyone when age,
Disease, or sorrows strike him,   30
Inclines to think there is a God,
Or something very like Him.

1850   1865

ALGERNON CHARLES SWINBURNE
(1837–1909)

Swinburne's writings are of interest in their own right and also as evidence
of the breakdown of conventional Victorian standards during the latter
part of the 19th century. Like the fat boy in *Pickwick Papers* who terrified the old lady by announcing: "I wants to make your flesh creep,"
Swinburne set about shocking his elders by a variety of rebellious gestures.
In religion he appeared to be a pagan; in politics, a liberal republican
dedicated to the overthrow of established governments. And on the subject of love he was often preoccupied with the pleasures of the lover who
inflicts pain or accepts pain, pleasures of which he had read in the writings
of the Marquis de Sade. As Arnold Bennett said of *Anactoria*, Swinburne
played "a rare trick" on England by "enshrining in the topmost heights
of its literature a lovely poem that cannot be discussed."

To a more limited extent Swinburne also expressed his rebellion against
established codes by his personal behavior. He came from a distinguished
family and attended Eton and Oxford, but sought the company of the
bohemians of Paris and of London where he became temporarily associated
with D. G. Rossetti and other Pre-Raphaelites. By 1879 his dissipations
had profoundly affected his frail physique, and he was obliged to put
himself into the protective custody of a friend, Theodore Watts-Dunton,
who removed him to the countryside and kept him alive although sobered
and tamed.

Swinburne continued to write voluminously, but most of his best poetry
is in his early publications. His early play, *Atalanta in Calydon* (1865), was
described by Swinburne himself as "pure Greek." Yet the kind of spirit
which he found in Greek literature was not the traditional quality of classic
serenity admired by Matthew Arnold. Like Shelley (the poet he most
closely resembles), Swinburne loved Greece as a land of liberty in which
men had expressed themselves with the most complete unrestraint. To call
such an ardently romantic poet "classical" requires a series of qualifying
clauses that make the term meaningless.

In his play and in the volume which followed it, *Poems and Ballads*
(1866), Swinburne demonstrated a metrical virtuosity which dazzled his
early readers and may still dazzle us. Those who demand that poetry
should make sense, first and foremost, will find little in Swinburne to

their taste. What he offers, instead, are heady rhythmical patterns in which words are relished primarily for sound rather than for sense.

> There lived a singer in France of old
> By the tideless dolorous midland sea.
> In a land of sand and ruin and gold
> There shone one woman, and none but she.

These lines from *The Triumph of Time* have often been cited to illustrate Swinburne's qualities. Like some of the poems of the later French Symbolists, such passages defy traditional kinds of critical analysis and oblige us to reconsider the variety of ways in which poetry may achieve its effects.

Choruses from Atalanta in Calydon
When the Hounds of Spring[1]

When the hounds of spring are on winter's traces,
    The mother of months in meadow or plain
Fills the shadows and windy places
    With lisp of leaves and ripple of rain;
And the brown bright nightingale[2] amorous   5
Is half assuaged for Itylus,
For the Thracian ships and the foreign faces,
    The tongueless vigil and all the pain.

Come with bows bent and with emptying of quivers,
    Maiden most perfect, lady of light,   10
With a noise of winds and many rivers,
    With a clamor of waters, and with might;
Bind on thy sandals, O thou most fleet,
Over the splendor and speed of thy feet;
For the faint east quickens, the wan west shivers,   15
    Round the feet of the day and the feet of the night.

Where shall we find her, how shall we sing to her,
    Fold our hands round her knees, and cling?
O that man's heart were as fire and could spring to her,
    Fire, or the strength of the streams that spring!   20
For the stars and the winds are unto her
As raiment, as songs of the harp player;
For the risen stars and the fallen cling to her,
    And the southwest wind and the west wind sing.

For winter's rains and ruins are over,   25
    And all the season of snows and sins;

1. This choral hymn, with which Swinburne's tragedy opens, is addressed to Artemis (or Diana), virgin goddess and huntress. Artemis was also goddess of the moon and hence, as affecting the seasons, the "mother of months" (line 2).

2. Philomela, after being raped by her brother-in-law and having her tongue cut out, was changed into a nightingale. To obtain revenge, her sister, Procne, killed her own son, Itylus, and fed the child's body to her husband, Tereus, a Thracian king.

The days dividing lover and lover,
　　The light that loses, the night that wins;
And time remembered is grief forgotten,
And frosts are slain and flowers begotten,　　　　　　30
And in green underwood and cover
　　Blossom by blossom the spring begins.

The full streams feed on flower of rushes,
　　Ripe grasses trammel a traveling foot,
The faint fresh flame of the young year flushes　　35
　　From leaf to flower and flower to fruit;
And fruit and leaf are as gold and fire,
And the oat[3] is heard above the lyre,
And the hooféd heel of a satyr crushes
　　The chestnut husk at the chestnut root.　　　　40

And Pan by noon and Bacchus by night,
　　Fleeter of foot than the fleet-foot kid,
Follows with dancing and fills with delight
　　The Maenad and the Bassarid;[4]
And soft as lips that laugh and hide,　　　　　　45
The laughing leaves of the trees divide,
And screen from seeing and leave in sight
　　The god pursuing, the maiden hid.

The ivy falls with the Bacchanal's hair
　　Over her eyebrows hiding her eyes;　　　　　　50
The wild vine slipping down leaves bare
　　Her bright breast shortening into sighs;
The wild vine slips with the weight of its leaves,
But the berried ivy catches and cleaves
To the limbs that glitter, the feet that scare　　55
　　The wolf that follows, the fawn that flies.

Before the Beginning of Years

Before the begining of years
　　There came to the making of man
Time, with a gift of tears;
　　Grief, with a glass that ran;
Pleasure, with pain for leaven;　　　　　　　　5
　　Summer, with flowers that fell;
Remembrance fallen from heaven,
　　And madness risen from hell;
Strength without hands to smite;
　　Love that endures for a breath;　　　　　　10
Night, the shadow of light,
　　And life, the shadow of death.

---

3. Musical pipe made from an oaten
straw.
4. Participants in the spring festival

honoring Dionysus (or Bacchus). Such
festivals sometimes developed into frenzied sexual orgies.

And the high gods took in hand
  Fire, and the falling of tears,
And a measure of sliding sand   15
  From under the feet of the years;
And froth and drift of the sea;
  And dust of the laboring earth;
And bodies of things to be
  In the houses of death and of birth;   20
And wrought with weeping and laughter,
  And fashioned with loathing and love,
With life before and after
  And death beneath and above,
For a day and a night and a morrow,   25
  That his strength might endure for a span
With travail and heavy sorrow,
  The holy spirit of man.

From the winds of the north and the south
  They gathered as unto strife;   30
They breathed upon his mouth,
  They filled his body with life;
Eyesight and speech they wrought
  For the veils of the soul therein,
A time for labor and thought,   35
  A time to serve and to sin;
They gave him light in his ways,
  And love, and a space for delight,
And beauty and length of days,
  And night, and sleep in the night.   40
His speech is a burning fire;
  With his lips he travaileth;
In his heart is a blind desire,
  In his eyes foreknowledge of death;
He weaves, and is clothed with derision;   45
  Sows, and he shall not reap;
His life is a watch or a vision
  Between a sleep and a sleep.

               1865

In the Orchard

(Provençal Burden)[5]

Leave go my hands, let me catch breath and see,
Let the dew-fall drench either side of me;
  Clear apple leaves are soft upon that moon
Seen sidelong like a blossom in the tree;
  Ah God, ah God, that day should be so soon.   5

5. The refrain in the final line of each stanza (termed a *burden*) is used here in the manner of poets of southeastern France (Provence) during the medieval period.

The grass is thick and cool, it lets us lie.
Kissed upon either cheek and either eye,
　I turn to thee as some green afternoon
Turns toward sunset, and is loth to die;
　Ah God, ah God, that day should be so soon.　　　10

Lie closer, lean your face upon my side,
Feel where the dew fell that has hardly dried,
　Hear how the blood beats that went nigh to swoon;
The pleasure lives there when the sense has died;
　Ah God, ah God, that day should be so soon.　　　15

O my fair lord, I charge you leave me this:
Is it not sweeter than a foolish kiss?
　Nay take it then, my flower, my first in June,
My rose, so like a tender mouth it is:
　Ah God, ah God, that day should be so soon.　　　20

Love, till dawn sunder night from day with fire,
Dividing my delight and my desire,
　The crescent life and love the plenilune,[6]
Love me though dusk begin and dark retire;
　Ah God, ah God, that day should be so soon.　　　25

Ah, my heart fails, my blood draws back; I know,
When life runs over, life is near to go;
　And with the slain of love love's ways are strewn,
And with their blood, if love will have it so;
　Ah God, ah God, that day should be so soon.　　　30

Ah, do thy will now; slay me if thou wilt;
There is no building now the walls are built,
　No quarrying now the cornerstone is hewn,
No drinking now the vine's whole blood is spilt;
　Ah God, ah God, that day should be so soon.　　　35

Nay, slay me now; nay, for I will be slain;
Pluck thy red pleasure from the teeth of pain,
　Break down thy vine ere yet grape-gatherers prune,
Slay me ere day can slay desire again;
　Ah God, ah God, that day should be so soon.　　　40

Yea, with thy sweet lips, with thy sweet sword; yea,
Take life and all, for I will die, I say;
　Love, I gave love, is life a better boon?
For sweet night's sake I will not live till day;
　Ah God, ah God, that day should be so soon.　　　45

Nay, I will sleep then only; nay, but go.
Ah sweet, too sweet to me, my sweet, I know
　Love, sleep, and death go to the sweet same tune;
Hold my hair fast, and kiss me through it so.
　Ah God, ah God, that day should be so soon.　　　50

1865

6. Full moon.

From The Triumph of Time
I Will Go Back to the Great Sweet Mother

33

I will go back to the great sweet mother,
    Mother and lover of men, the sea.
I will go down to her, I and none other,
    Close with her, kiss her, and mix her with me;
Cling to her, strive with her, hold her fast.
O fair white mother, in days long past   5
Born without sister, born without brother,
    Set free my soul as thy soul is free.

34

O fair green-girdled mother of mine,
    Sea, that art clothed with the sun and the rain,   10
Thy sweet hard kisses are strong like wine,
    Thy large embraces are keen like pain.
Save me and hide me with all thy waves,
Find me one grave of thy thousand graves,
Those pure cold populous graves of thine   15
    Wrought without hand in a world without stain.

35

I shall sleep, and move with the moving ships,
    Change as the winds change, veer in the tide;
My lips will feast on the foam of thy lips,
    I shall rise with thy rising, with thee subside;   20
Sleep, and not know if she[b] be, if she were,
Filled full with life to the eyes and hair,
As a rose is fulfilled to the roscleaf tips
    With splendid summer and perfume and pride.

36

This woven raiment of nights and days,   25
    Were it once cast off and unwound from me,
Naked and glad would I walk in thy ways,
    Alive and aware of thy ways and thee;
Clear of the whole world, hidden at home,
Clothed with the green and crowned with the foam,   30
A pulse of the life of thy straits and bays,
    A vein in the heart of the streams of the sea.

37

Fair mother, fed with the lives of men,
    Thou art subtle and cruel of heart, men say.
Thou hast taken, and shalt not render again;   35
    Thou art full of thy dead, and cold as they.
But death is the worst that comes of thee;
Thou art fed with our dead, O mother, O sea,
But when hast thou fed on our hearts? or when,
    Having given us love, hast thou taken away?   40

---

5. The woman to whom the poem is addressed. She had deserted the speaker
for another man.

38

O tender-hearted, O perfect lover,
   Thy lips are bitter, and sweet thine heart.
The hopes that hurt and the dreams that hover,
   Shall they not vanish away and apart?
But thou, thou art sure, thou art older than earth;   45
Thou art strong for death and fruitful of birth;
Thy depths conceal and thy gulfs discover;
   From the first thou wert; in the end thou art.

1862–66   1866

Hymn to Proserpine

(AFTER THE PROCLAMATION IN ROME OF THE CHRISTIAN FAITH)

Vicisti, Galilaee[6]

I have lived long enough, having seen one thing, that love hath an
   end;
Goddess and maiden and queen, be near me now and befriend.
Thou art more than the day or the morrow, the seasons that laugh
   or that weep;
For these give joy and sorrow; but thou, Proserpina, sleep.
Sweet is the treading of wine, and sweet the feet of the dove;   5
But a goodlier gift is thine than foam of the grapes or love.
Yea, is not even Apollo, with hair and harpstring of gold,
A bitter god to follow, a beautiful god to behold?
I am sick of singing; the bays[7] burn deep and chafe. I am fain
To rest a little from praise and grievous pleasure and pain.   10
For the gods we know not of, who give us our daily breath,
We know they are cruel as love or life, and lovely as death.

O gods dethroned and deceased, cast forth, wiped out in a day!
From your wrath is the world released, redeemed from your chains,
   men say.
New gods are crowned in the city; their flowers have broken your
   rods;   15
They are merciful, clothed with pity, the young compassionate gods.
But for me their new device is barren, the days are bare;
Things long past over suffice, and men forgotten that were.
Time and the gods are at strife; ye dwell in the midst thereof,

6. "Thou hast conquered, O Galilean"
—words supposedly addressed to Christ
by the Roman emperor, Julian the
Apostate, on his deathbed in 363.
Julian had tried to revive paganism and
to discourage Christianity, which, after
a proclamation of 313, had been tolerated in Rome. His efforts, however,
were unsuccessful. The speaker of the
poem, a Roman patrician and also a
poet (line 9), is like the Emperor
Julian: he prefers the old order of
pagan gods. His hymn is addressed to
the goddess Proserpine, who was carried

off by Hades (or Pluto) to be queen
of the lower world. In this role she is
addressed in the poem as goddess of
death and of sleep. The speaker also
associates her with the earth itself
(line 93) because she was the daughter
of Demeter (or Ceres), goddess of agriculture, whose name means "earth-
mother." Swinburne may have derived
some details here from the 4th-century
Latin poet Claudian, whose long narrative *The Rape of Proserpine* provides
helpful background for this hymn.
7. Laurel leaves of a poet's crown.

Draining a little life from the barren breasts of love.   20
I say to you, cease, take rest; yea, I say to you all, be at peace,
Till the bitter milk of her breast and the barren bosom shall cease.

Wilt thou yet take all, Galilean? But these thou shalt not take—
The laurel, the palms, and the paean, the breasts of the nymphs in
     the brake,
Breasts more soft than a dove's, that tremble with tenderer breath;
And all the wings of the Loves, and all the joy before death;   26
All the feet of the hours that sound as a single lyre,
Dropped and deep in the flowers, with strings that flicker like fire.
More than these wilt thou give, things fairer than all these things?
Nay, for a little we live, and life hath mutable wings.   30
A little while and we die; shall life not thrive as it may?
For no man under the sky lives twice, outliving his day.
And grief is a grievous thing, and a man hath enough of his tears;
Why should he labor, and bring fresh grief to blacken his years?

Thou hast conquered, O pale Galilean; the world has grown gray
     from thy breath;   35
We have drunken of things Lethean,[8] and fed on the fullness of
     death.
Laurel is green for a season, and love is sweet for a day;
But love grows bitter with treason, and laurel outlives not May.
Sleep, shall we sleep after all? for the world is not sweet in the end;
For the old faiths loosen and fall, the new years ruin and rend.   40
Fate is a sea without shore, and the soul is a rock that abides;
But her ears are vexed with the roar and her face with the foam of
     the tides.
O lips that the live blood faints in, the leavings of racks and rods!
O ghastly glories of saints, dead limbs of gibbeted gods!
Though all men abase them before you in spirit, and all knees bend,
I kneel not, neither adore you, but standing look to the end.   46

All delicate days and pleasant, all spirits and sorrows are cast
Far out with the foam of the present that sweeps to the surf of the
     past;
Where beyond the extreme sea wall, and between the remote sea
     gates,
Waste water washes, and tall ships founder, and deep death waits;
Where, mighty with deepening sides, clad about with the seas as
     with wings,   51
And impelled of invisible tides, and fulfilled of unspeakable things,
White-eyed and poisonous-finned, shark-toothed and serpentine-
     curled,
Rolls, under the whitening wind of the future, the wave of the
     world.
The depths stand naked in sunder behind it, the storms flee away;
In the hollow before it the thunder is taken and snared as a prey;   56
In its sides is the north wind bound; and its salt is of all men's tears,

8. I.e., of Lethe, a river in the lower world. By drinking its waters the dead forgot
the past.

With light of ruin, and sound of changes, and pulse of years;
With travail of day after day, and with trouble of hour upon hour.
And bitter as blood is the spray; and the crests are as fangs that devour;   60
And its vapor and storm of its steam as the sighing of spirits to be;
And its noise as the noise in a dream; and its depths as the roots of
  the sea;
And the height of its heads as the height of the utmost stars of the
  air;
And the ends of the earth at the might thereof tremble, and time
  is made bare.
Will ye bridle the deep sea with reins, will ye chasten the high sea
  with rods?   65
Will ye take her to chain her with chains, who is older than all ye
  gods?
All ye as a wind shall go by, as a fire shall ye pass and be past;
Ye are gods, and behold, ye shall die, and the waves be upon you
  at last.
In the darkness of time, in the deeps of the years, in the changes
  of things,
Ye shall sleep as a slain man sleeps, and the world shall forget you
  for kings.   70
Though the feet of thine high priests tread where thy lords and our
  forefathers trod,
Though these that were gods are dead, and thou being dead art a
  god,
Though before thee the throned Cytherean[9] be fallen, and hidden
  her head,
Yet thy kingdom shall pass, Galilean, thy dead shall go down to
  thee dead.

Of the maiden thy mother men sing as a goddess with grace clad
  around;   75
Thou art throned where another was king; where another was queen
  she is crowned.
Yea, once we had sight of another; but now she is queen, say these.
Not as thine, not as thine was our mother, a blossom of flowering
  seas,
Clothed round with the world's desire as with raiment, and fair as
  the foam,
And fleeter than kindled fire, and a goddess, and mother of Rome.[1]
For thine came pale and a maiden, and sister to sorrow; but ours, 81
Her deep hair heavily laden with odor and color of flowers,
White rose of the rose-white water, a silver splendor, a flame,
Bent down unto us that besought her, and earth grew sweet with
  her name.

---

9. Aphrodite (or Venus), who was
born from the waves near the island of
Cythera.

1. Aeneas, the founder of Rome, was
reputed to have been the son of Aphrodite.

For thine came weeping, a slave among slaves, and rejected; but she
Came flushed from the full-flushed wave, and imperial, her foot on
   the sea.   86
And the wonderful waters knew her, the winds and the viewless
   ways,
And the roses grew rosier, and bluer the sea-blue stream of the bays.

Ye are fallen, our lords, by what token? we wist that ye should not
   fall.
Ye were all so fair that are broken; and one more fair than ye all. 90
But I turn to her[2] still, having seen she shall surely abide in the end;
Goddess and maiden and queen, be near me now and befriend.
O daughter of earth, of my mother, her crown and blossom of birth,
I am also, I also, thy brother; I go as I came unto earth.
In the night where thine eyes are as moons are in heaven, the night
   where thou art,   95
Where the silence is more than all tunes, where sleep overflows
   from the heart,
Where the poppies are sweet as the rose in our world, and the red
   rose is white,
And the wind falls faint as it blows with the fume of the flowers of
   the night,
And the murmur of spirits that sleep in the shadow of gods from
   afar
Grows dim in thine ears and deep as the deep dim soul of a star, 100
In the sweet low light of thy face, under heavens untrod by the sun,
Let my soul with their souls find place, and forget what is done and
   undone.
Thou art more than the gods who number the days of our temporal
   breath;
For these give labor and slumber; but thou, Proserpina, death.
Therefore now at thy feet I abide for a season in silence. I know 105
I shall die as my fathers died, and sleep as they sleep; even so.
For the glass of the years is brittle wherein we gaze for a span.
A little soul for a little bears up this corpse which is man.
So long I endure, no longer; and laugh not again, neither weep. 109
For there is no god found stronger than death; and death is a sleep.

1866

The Garden of Proserpine[3]

Here, where the world is quiet;
Here, where all trouble seems

---

2. Proserpine.
3. Or Proserpina, the goddess who was carried off by Hades (or Pluto) to be queen of the lower world. According to some accounts, she had there a

Dead winds' and spent waves' riot
  In doubtful dreams of dreams;
I watch the green field growing   5
  For reaping folk and sowing,
  For harvest time and mowing,
  A sleepy world of streams.

I am tired of tears and laughter,
  And men that laugh and weep;   10
Of what may come hereafter
  For men that sow to reap;
I am weary of days and hours,
Blown buds of barren flowers,
Desires and dreams and powers   15
  And everything but sleep.

Here life has death for neighbor,
  And far from eye or ear
Wan waves and wet winds labor,
  Weak ships and spirits steer;   20
They drive adrift, and whither
They wot not who make thither;
But no such winds blow hither,
  And no such things grow here.

No growth of moor or coppice,   25
  No heather flower or vine,
But bloomless buds of poppies,
  Green grapes of Proserpine,
Pale beds of blowing rushes,
Where no leaf blooms or blushes   30
Save this whereout she crushes
  For dead men deadly wine.

Pale, without name or number,
  In fruitless fields of corn,[4]
They bow themselves and slumber   35
  All night till light is born;
And like a soul belated,
In hell and heaven unmated,
By cloud and mist abated
  Comes out of darkness morn.   40

Though one were strong as seven,
  He too with death shall dwell,
Nor wake with wings in heaven,
  Nor weep for pains in hell;
Though one were fair as roses,   45

garden of ever-blooming flowers. The
Greek and Roman festivals honoring her
and her mother, Ceres, emphasized
Proserpine's return to the upper world
in spring. In Swinburne's poems, however, the emphasis is on her role as

goddess of death and eternal sleep. Swinburne also associates her with the sea,
which he usually represents as eternally
unchanging despite its surface change-
fulness.
4. Wheat or grain.

His beauty clouds and closes;
  And well though love reposes,
    In the end it is not well.

Pale, beyond porch and portal,
  Crowned with calm leaves, she stands 50
Who gathers all things mortal
  With cold immortal hands;
Her languid lips are sweeter
Than love's who fears to greet her
To men that mix and meet her 55
  From many times and lands.

She waits for each and other,
  She waits for all men born;
Forgets the earth her mother,
  The life of fruits and corn; 60
And spring and seed and swallow
Take wing for her and follow
Where summer song rings hollow
  And flowers are put to scorn.

There go the loves that wither, 65
  The old loves with wearier wings;
And all dead years draw thither,
  And all disastrous things;
Dead dreams of days forsaken,
Blind buds that snows have shaken, 70
Wild leaves that winds have taken,
  Red strays of ruined springs.

We are not sure of sorrow,
  And joy was never sure;
Today will die tomorrow; 75
  Time stoops to no man's lure;
And love, grown faint and fretful,
With lips but half regretful
Sighs, and with eyes forgetful
  Weeps that no loves endure. 80

From too much love of living,
  From hope and fear set free,
We thank with brief thanksgiving
  Whatever gods may be
That no life lives forever; 85
That dead men rise up never;
That even the weariest river
  Winds somewhere safe to sea.

Then star nor sun shall waken,
  Nor any change of light: 90
Nor sound of waters shaken,
  Nor any sound or sight:

Nor wintry leaves nor vernal,
Nor days nor things diurnal;
Only the sleep eternal   95
In an eternal night.

1866

An Interlude

In the greenest growth of the Maytime,
I rode where the woods were wet,
Between the dawn and the daytime;
The spring was glad that we met.

There was something the season wanted,   5
Though the ways and the woods smelt sweet;
The breath at your lips that panted,
The pulse of the grass at your feet.

You came, and the sun came after,
And the green grew golden above;   10
And the flag flowers lightened with laughter,
And the meadowsweet shook with love.

Your feet in the full-grown grasses
Moved soft as a weak wind blows;
You passed me as April passes,   15
With face made out of a rose.

By the stream where the stems were slender,
Your bright foot paused at the sedge;
It might be to watch the tender
Light leaves in the springtime hedge,   20

On boughs that the sweet month blanches
With flowery frost of May:
It might be a bird in the branches,
It might be a thorn in the way.

I waited to watch you linger   25
With foot drawn back from the dew,
Till a sunbeam straight like a finger
Struck sharp through the leaves at you.

And a bird overhead sang *Follow*,
And a bird to the right sang *Here*;   30
And the arch of the leaves was hollow,
And the meaning of May was clear.

I saw where the sun's hand pointed,
I knew what the bird's note said;
By the dawn and the dewfall anointed,   35
You were queen by the gold on your head.

As the glimpse of a burnt-out ember
  Recalls a regret of the sun,
I remember, forget, and remember
  What Love saw done and undone.   40

I remember the way we parted,
  The day and the way we met;
You hoped we were both brokenhearted,
  And knew we should both forget.

And May with her world in flower   45
  Seemed still to murmur and smile
As you murmured and smiled for an hour;
  I saw you turn at the stile.

A hand like a white wood-blossom
  You lifted, and waved, and passed   50
With head hung down to the bosom,
  And pale, as it seemed, at last.

And the best and the worst of this is
  That neither is most to blame
If you've forgotten my kisses   55
  And I've forgotten your name.

                                        1866

FRANCIS THOMPSON
(1859–1907)

Francis Thompson's career seems like a tale from one of the novels of
Graham Greene. The son of Roman Catholic converts, he was anxious to
enter the priesthood but was not considered to be an eligible candidate.
Later, after an unsuccessful attempt to complete medical school, he moved
to London. Here he lived for several years as a tramp, suffering painfully
not only from poverty but from an addiction to opium: when in his poems
Thompson speaks of being an outcast, he speaks with the authority of
experience. In 1888 he was rescued by a magazine editor, Wilfred Meynell,
who recognized his literary talents and encouraged him to publish his
poems. Owing to shattered health and also to a marked streak of indolence,
Thompson's output in poetry was not extensive, but in his few best poems
his achievement is impressive and distinctive. As his friend Coventry Pat-
more noted, *The Hound of Heaven* is one of the finest odes in English
literature. In its fast-paced passages it may remind us of the odes of Shelley,
about whom Thompson wrote an appreciative essay. An even more important influence than Shelley upon Thompson was that of the 17th-century
metaphysical poets, and his poetry is therefore, like Browning's, a bridge
to much of the poetry of the 20th century. Thompson was especially attracted by the 17th-century Roman Catholic poet Richard Crashaw. The
Crashaw-like blending of religious fervor and striking conceits (such as

"traitorous trueness"), evident in the very title of *The Hound of Heaven*, seemed merely fantastic to some of Thompson's readers in the 1890's. To later readers, accustomed to the metaphysical devices of much 20th-century poetry, it has seemed less bizarre. Interesting comparisons may also be made between Thompson and Gerard Manley Hopkins, another Roman Catholic writer who likewise demonstrated, as the 19th century drew to its close, the exceptional variety of achievements in the poetry of the Victorian age.

The Hound of Heaven

I fled Him,[1] down the nights and down the days;
   I fled Him, down the arches of the years;
I fled Him, down the labyrinthine ways
   Of my own mind; and in the mist of tears
I hid from Him, and under running laughter.   5
        Up vistaed hopes I sped;
        And shot, precipitated,
Adown Titanic glooms of chasmèd fears,
   From those strong Feet that followed, followed after.
        But with unhurrying chase,   10
        And unperturbèd pace,
   Deliberate speed, majestic instancy,[2]
        They beat—and a Voice beat
        More instant than the Feet—
"All things betray thee, who betrayest Me."   15

        I pleaded, outlaw-wise,
By many a hearted casement, curtained red,
   Trellised with intertwining charities
(For, though I knew His love Who followed,
        Yet was I sore adread   20
Lest, having Him, I must have nought beside);[3]
But, if one little casement parted wide,
   The gust of His approach would clash it to.
   Fear wist not to evade, as Love wist to pursue.[4]
Across the margent[5] of the world I fled,   25
   And troubled the gold gateways of the stars,
   Smiting for shelter on their clangèd bars;
        Fretted to dulcet jars
And silvern chatter the pale ports o' the moon.[6]
I said to dawn, Be sudden; to eve, Be soon;   30

1. Cf. St. Augustine, *Confessions* IV.iv. 7: "And lo, Thou wert close on the heels of those fleeing from Thee, God of vengeance and fountain of mercies, both at the same time, who turnest us to Thyself by most wonderful means."
2. Urgency.
3. The speaker, afraid that love of God will exclude other kinds of love, is seeking shelter in one of the warm dwellings associated with human love. But his pursuer cuts off his escape, forcing him to remain outside, an outcast (lines 22–23).
4. This line apparently means that Fear did not know how to escape so effectively as Love knew how to pursue.
5. Boundary.
6. I.e., shook the gates of the moon until they gave forth soft and silvery sounds.

With thy young skyey blossoms heap me over
   From this tremendous Lover!
Float thy vague veil about me, lest He see!
   I tempted all His servitors, but to find
My own betrayal in their constancy,   35
In faith to Him their fickleness to me,
   Their traitorous trueness, and their loyal deceit.
To all swift things for swiftness did I sue;
   Clung to the whistling mane of every wind.
         But whether they swept, smoothly fleet,   40
        The long savannahs[7] of the blue;
         Or whether, Thunder-driven,
        They clanged his chariot 'thwart a heaven
Plashy with flying lightnings round the spurn o' their feet—
   Fear wist not to evade as Love wist to pursue.   45
         Still with unhurrying chase,
         And unperturbéd pace,
       Deliberate speed, majestic instancy,
         Came on the following Feet,
         And a Voice above their beat—   50
       "Nought shelters thee, who wilt not shelter Me."

I sought no more that after which I strayed
        In face of man or maid;
But still within the little children's eyes
       Seems something, something that replies;   55
They at least are for me, surely for me!
I turned me to them very wistfully;
But, just as their young eyes grew sudden fair
       With dawning answers there,
Their angel plucked them from me by the hair.   60
"Come then, ye other children, Nature's—share
With me" (said I) "your delicate fellowship;
       Let me greet you lip to lip,
       Let me twine with you caresses,
         Wantoning   65
       With our Lady-Mother's[8] vagrant tresses,
         Banqueting
       With her in her wind-walled palace,
       Underneath her azured daïs,[9]
       Quaffing, as your taintless way is,   70
         From a chalice
Lucent-weeping out of the dayspring."[1]
         So it was done;
I in their delicate fellowship was one—
Drew the bolt of Nature's secrecies.   75
      I knew all the swift importings[2]
      On the willful face of skies;

Plains.
Mother Nature's.
Blue canopy of the sky.
Overflowing with shining light from
the sun (i.e., the children of Nature
drink the sunshine).
2. Meanings.

I knew how the clouds arise
Spuméd of the wild sea-snortings;
All that's born or dies
Rose and drooped with—made them shapers   80
Of mine own moods, or wailful or divine—
With them joyed and was bereaven.
I was heavy with the even,
When she lit her glimmering tapers   85
Round the day's dead sanctities.
I laughed in the morning's eyes.
I triumphed and I saddened with all weather,
Heaven and I wept together,
And its sweet tears were salt with mortal mine;   90
Against the red throb of its sunset-heart
I laid my own to beat,
And share commingling heat;
But not by that, by that, was eased my human smart.
In vain my tears were wet on Heaven's gray cheek.   95
For ah! we know not what each other says,
These things and I; in sound *I* speak—
Their sound is but their stir, they speak by silences.
Nature, poor stepdame, cannot slake my drouth;
Let her, if she would owe[3] me,   100
Drop yon blue bosom-veil of sky, and show me
The breasts o' her tenderness;
Never did any milk of hers once bless
My thirsting mouth.
Nigh and nigh draws the chase,   105
With unperturbéd pace,
Deliberate speed, majestic instancy;
And past those noiséd Feet
A voice comes yet more fleet—
"Lo nought contents thee, who content'st not Me."   110

Naked I wait Thy love's uplifted stroke!
My harness[4] piece by piece Thou hast hewn from me,
And smitten me to my knee;
I am defenseless utterly.
I slept, methinks, and woke,   115
And, slowly gazing, find me stripped in sleep.
In the rash lustihead of my young powers,
I shook the pillaring hours
And pulled my life upon me;[5] grimed with smears,
I stand amid the dust o' the mounded years—   120
My mangled youth lies dead beneath the heap.
My days have crackled and gone up in smoke,
Have puffed and burst as sun-starts[6] on a stream.
Yea, faileth now even dream

3. Own.
4. Armor.
5. Like Samson when he shook the pillars of the temple of Dagon and pulled down the roof on his head (Judges xvi).
6. Bubbles.

The dreamer, and the lute the lutanist;   125
Even the linked fantasies, in whose blossomy twist
I swung the earth a trinket at my wrist,
Are yielding;[7] cords of all too weak account
For earth with heavy griefs so overplussed.
        Ah! is Thy love indeed   130
A weed, albeit an amaranthine[8] weed,
Suffering no flowers except its own to mount?
        Ah! must—
        Designer infinite!—
Ah! must Thou char the wood ere Thou canst limn[9] with it? 135
My freshness spent its wavering shower i' the dust;
And now my heart is as a broken fount,
Wherein tear-drippings stagnate, spilt down ever
      From the dank thoughts that shiver
Upon the sightful branches of my mind.   140
      Such is; what is to be?
The pulp so bitter, how shall taste the rind?
I dimly guess what Time in mists confounds;
Yet ever and anon a trumpet sounds
From the hid battlements of Eternity;   145
Those shaken mists a space unsettle, then
Round the half-glimpsèd turrets slowly wash again.
      But not ere him who summoneth
      I first have seen, enwound
With glooming robes purpureal, cypress-crowned; 150
His name I know, and what his trumpet saith.
Whether man's heart or life it be which yields
      Thee harvest, must Thy harvest fields
      Be dunged with rotten death?

        Now of that long pursuit   155
        Comes on at hand the bruit;[1]
      That Voice is round me like a bursting sea:
        "And is thy earth so marred,
        Shattered in shard[2] on shard?
Lo, all things fly thee, for thou fliest Me!   160
      Strange, piteous, futile thing,
Wherefore should any set thee love apart?
Seeing none but I makes much of nought" (He said)
"And human love needs human meriting,
        How hast thou merited—   165
Of all man's clotted clay the dingiest clot?
      Alack, thou knowest not
How little worthy of any love thou art!
Whom wilt thou find to love ignoble thee
      Save Me, save only Me?   170

7. I.e., even his power of creating an imaginary world by poetry and song ("linked fantasies") is now inadequate.
8. Unfading and immortal.
9. Draw, as with charcoal.
1. Noise.
2. Fragment, as of broken pottery.

All which I took from thee I did but take,
Not for thy harms,
But just that thou might'st seek it in My arms.
All which thy child's mistake
Fancies as lost, I have stored for thee at home; 175
Rise, clasp My hand, and come!"

Halts by me that footfall;
Is my gloom, after all,
Shade of His hand, outstretched caressingly?
"Ah, fondest,[3] blindest, weakest, 180
I am He Whom thou seekest!
Thou dravest love from thee, who dravest Me."

1890–92 1893

The Kingdom of God[4]

"IN NO STRANGE LAND"

O world invisible, we view thee,
O world intangible, we touch thee,
O world unknowable, we know thee,
Inapprehensible, we clutch thee!

Does the fish soar to find the ocean, 5
The eagle plunge to find the air—
That we ask of the stars in motion
If they have rumor of thee there?

Not where the wheeling systems darken,
And our benumbed conceiving soars!— 10
The drift of pinions, would we hearken,
Beats at our own clay-shuttered doors.

The angels keep their ancient places—
Turn but a stone and start a wing!
'Tis ye, 'tis your estrangéd faces, 15
That miss the many-splendored thing.

But (when so sad thou canst not sadder)
Cry—and upon thy so sore loss
Shall shine the traffic of Jacob's ladder
Pitched betwixt Heaven and Charing Cross.[5] 20

Yea, in the night, my Soul, my daughter,
Cry—clinging Heaven by the hems;
And lo, Christ walking on the water,
Not of Genesareth,[6] but Thames!

1908

---

3. Most foolish (archaic meaning).
4. Cf. Luke xvii.21: "The Kingdom of God is within you." See also Exodus ii.22, and Psalms cxxxvii.4.
5. An intersection in London.
6. The Sea of Galilee (cf. Matthew xiv.25–33).

Nonsense Verse

Despite its later reputation as an age of gloom, the Victorian age featured a remarkable outburst of humorous prose and verse from the time of Dickens' *Pickwick Papers* at the beginning of the period to the Gilbert and Sullivan operas near the end. The following selections are restricted to one kind of humor—a Victorian specialty—nonsense-writing. Shakespeare had exploited nonsense on occasion, and so have James Joyce and James Thurber, but the Victorians were more adept in this genre than any other generation has been. Freudian explanations can be devised to account for its appearance during this particular period, and indeed if nonsense-writing does originate in a writer's repressions we may have a clue to the undertone of melancholy that some readers detect in the verses of Edward Lear and Lewis Carroll. The best nonsense-writing, however, raises its own less solemn problems. Lear and Carroll created a zany upside-down world full of puzzles: the attempt to solve such puzzles, even when they cannot be solved, is in itself a perennial satisfaction.

EDWARD LEAR
(1812–1888)

Edward Lear was a landscape painter who spent much of his life in Mediterranean countries. In 1846 he published his first *Book of Nonsense*, a collection of limericks for children. The form of the limerick was not invented by Lear, but his use of it served to establish its popularity. In later volumes of the *Book of Nonsense* he used other forms of verse, some of them modeled on rhythms which had been developed by his close friend Tennyson. All of his own poems were characteristically classified by Lear as "nonsense pure and absolute," yet it is as the author of *The Owl and the Pussy-Cat, The Jumblies*, and other poems that Lear is remembered. Evidently pure and absolute nonsense is a rare art.

How Pleasant to Know Mr. Lear

"How pleasant to know Mr. Lear!"
  Who has written such volumes of stuff!
Some think him ill-tempered and queer,
  But a few think him pleasant enough.
1215

His mind is concrete and fastidious,
   His nose is remarkably big;
His visage is more or less hideous,
   His beard it resembles a wig.

He has ears, and two eyes, and ten fingers,
   Leastways if you reckon two thumbs;
Long ago he was one of the singers,
   But now he is one of the dumbs.

He sits in a beautiful parlor,
   With hundreds of books on the wall;
He drinks a great deal of Marsala,
   But never gets tipsy at all.

He has many friends, lay men and clerical,
   Old Foss is the name of his cat;
His body is perfectly spherical,
   He weareth a runcible[1] hat.

When he walks in waterproof white,
   The children run after him so!
Calling out, "He's come out in his night-
   Gown, that crazy old Englishman, oh!"

He weeps by the side of the ocean,
   He weeps on the top of the hill;
He purchases pancakes and lotion,
   And chocolate shrimps from the mill.

He reads, but he cannot speak, Spanish,
   He cannot abide ginger beer:
Ere the days of his pilgrimage vanish,
   How pleasant to know Mr. Lear!

5

10

15

20

25

30

1871

Limerick

There was a young man in Iowa
Who exclaimed, "Where on earth shall I stow her!"
Of his sister he spoke, who was felled by an Oak
      Which abound in the plains of Iowa.

1933

The Jumblies

They went to sea in a sieve, they did;
   In a sieve they went to sea;

1. A runcible spoon is a spoon-shaped fork with a cutting edge.

In spite of all their friends could say,
On a winter's morn, on a stormy day,
  In a sieve they went to sea.
And when the sieve turned round and round,
And everyone cried, "You'll be drowned!"
They called aloud, "Our sieve ain't big,
But we don't care a button; we don't care a fig—
  In a sieve we'll go to sea!"
    Far and few, far and few,
      Are the lands where the Jumblies live.
      Their heads are green, and their hands are blue;
        And they went to sea in a sieve.

They sailed away in a sieve, they did,
  In a sieve they sailed so fast,
With only a beautiful pea-green veil
Tied with a ribbon, by way of a sail,
  To a small tobacco-pipe mast.
And everyone said who saw them go,
"Oh! won't they be soon upset, you know,
For the sky is dark, and the voyage is long;
And, happen what may, it's extremely wrong
  In a sieve to sail so fast."

The water it soon came in, it did;
  The water it soon came in.
So, to keep them dry, they wrapped their feet
In a pinky paper all folded neat;
  And they fastened it down with a pin.
And they passed the night in a crockery-jar;
And each of them said, "How wise we are!
Though the sky be dark, and the voyage be long,
Yet we never can think we were rash or wrong,
  While round in our sieve we spin."

And all night long they sailed away;
  And, when the sun went down,
They whistled and warbled a moony song
To the echoing sound of a coppery gong,
  In the shade of the mountains brown,
"O Timballoo! how happy we are
When we live in a sieve and a crockery-jar!
And all night long, in the moonlight pale,
We sail away with a pea-green sail
  In the shade of the mountains brown."

They sailed to the Western Sea, they did—
  To a land all covered with trees;
And they bought an owl, and a useful cart,
And a pound of rice, and a cranberry tart,
  And a hive of silvery bees;
And they bought a pig, and some green jackdaws,

And a lovely monkey with lollipop paws,
And seventeen bags of edelweiss tea,
And forty bottles of ring-bo-ree,
  And no end of Stilton cheese.

And in twenty years they all came back—   55
  In twenty years or more;
And everyone said, "How tall they've grown!
For they've been to the Lakes, and the Torrible Zone,
  And the hills of the Chankly Bore."
And they drank their health, and gave them a feast   60
Of dumplings made of beautiful yeast;
And everyone said, "If we only live,
We, too, will go to sea in a sieve,
  To the hills of the Chankly Bore."
    Far and few, far and few,   65
      Are the lands where the Jumblies live.
    Their heads are green, and their hands are blue;
      And they went to sea in a sieve.

                                                          1871

Cold Are the Crabs

Cold are the crabs that crawl on yonder hills,
Colder the cucumbers that grow beneath,
And colder still the brazen chops that wreathe
  The tedious gloom of philosophic pills!
For when the tardy film of nectar fills   5
The ample bowls of demons and of men,
There lurks the feeble mouse, the homely hen,
  And there the porcupine with all her quills.
Yet much remains—to weave a solemn strain
That lingering sadly—slowly dies away,   10
Daily departing with departing day.
A pea-green gamut on a distant plain
When wily walruses in congress meet—
  Such such is life—

                                                          1953

LEWIS CARROLL
(1832–1898)

Charles Lutwidge Dodgson was a deacon in the Anglican Church and a
lecturer in mathematics at Oxford. Most of his publications were mathematical treatises, but his fame rests on the strange pair of books he wrote

for children: *Alice in Wonderland* (1865) and *Through the Looking-Glass* (1871), both published under the pseudonym Lewis Carroll. Like *Gulliver's Travels* these narratives have long been enjoyed, at different levels, by both children and adults. The various songs scattered through the stories are sometimes parodies, as, for example, *The Aged, Aged Man*, but more often they are classic examples of nonsense verse. Poems such as *Jabberwocky* exhibit a mathematician's fondness for puzzles combined with a literary man's fondness for word games. At this level *Jabberwocky* can be enjoyed as a small-scale *Finnegans Wake*.

Carroll learned something of his art from Edward Lear, also an eccentric Victorian bachelor, but Carroll's nonsense, hovering often on the brink of satire, has more edge to it.

Jabberwocky[1]

'Twas brillig, and the slithy toves
    Did gyre and gimble in the wabe;
All mimsy were the borogoves,
    And the mome raths outgrabe.

"Beware the Jabberwock, my son!   5
    The jaws that bite, the claws that catch!
Beware the Jubjub bird, and shun
    The frumious Bandersnatch!"

He took his vorpal sword in hand;
    Long time the manxome foe he sought—   10
So rested he by the Tumtum tree,
    And stood awhile in thought.

And, as in uffish thought he stood,
    The Jabberwock, with eyes of flame,
Came whiffling through the tulgey wood,   15
    And burbled as it came!

One, two! One, two! And through and through
    The vorpal blade went snicker-snack!
He left it dead, and with its head
    He went galumphing back.   20

"And hast thou slain the Jabberwock?
    Come to my arms, my beamish boy!
O frabjous day! Callooh! Callay!"
    He chortled in his joy.

'Twas brillig, and the slithy toves   25
    Did gyre and gimble in the wabe;

1. From *Through the Looking-Glass,* Chapter I.

> All mimsy were the borogoves,
> And the mome raths outgrabe.

1855   1871

[*Humpty Dumpty's Explication of* Jabberwocky][2]

"You seem very clever at explaining words, Sir," said Alice. "Would you kindly tell me the meaning of the poem *Jabberwocky?*"

"Let's hear it," said Humpty Dumpty. "I can explain all the poems that ever were invented—and a good many that haven't been invented just yet."

This sounded very hopeful, so Alice repeated the first verse:

> " 'Twas brillig, and the slithy toves
> Did gyre and gimble in the wabe;
> All mimsy were the borogoves,
> And the mome raths outgrabe."

"That's enough to begin with," Humpty Dumpty interrupted: "there are plenty of hard words there. 'Brillig' means four o'clock in the afternoon—the time when you begin *broiling* things for dinner."

"That'll do very well," said Alice: "and 'slithy'?"[3]

"Well, 'slithy' means 'lithe and slimy.' 'Lithe' is the same as 'active.' You see it's like a portmanteau—there are two meanings packed up into one word."

"I see it now," Alice remarked thoughtfully: "and what are 'toves'?"

"Well, 'toves' are something like badgers—they're something like lizards—and they're something like corkscrews."

"They must be very curious creatures."

"They are that," said Humpty Dumpty: "also they make their nests under sundials—also they live on cheese."

"And what's to 'gyre' and to 'gimble'?"

"To 'gyre' is to go round and round like a gyroscope. To 'gimble' is to make holes like a gimlet."

"And the 'wabe' is the grass plot round a sundial, I suppose?" said Alice, surprised at her own ingenuity.

"Of course it is. It's called 'wabe,' you know, because it goes a long way before it, and a long way behind it——"

"And a long way beyond it on each side," Alice added.

"Exactly so. Well then, 'mimsy' is 'flimsy and miserable' (there's another portmanteau for you). And a 'borogove' is a thin shabby-looking bird with its feathers sticking out all round—something like a live mop."

2. From *Through the Looking-Glass,* Chapter VI.
3. Concerning the pronunciation of these words, Carroll later said: "The 'i' in 'slithy' is long, as in 'writhe'; and 'toves' is pronounced so as to rhyme with 'groves.' Again, the first 'o' in 'borogroves' is pronounced like the 'o' in 'borrow.' I have heard people try to give it the sound of the 'o' in 'worry.' Such is Human Perversity."

"And then 'mome raths'?" said Alice. "If I'm not giving you too much trouble."

"Well, a 'rath' is a sort of green pig: but 'mome' I'm not certain about. I think it's short for 'from home'—meaning that they'd lost their way, you know."

"And what does 'outgrabe' mean?"

"Well, 'outgribing' is something between bellowing and whistling, with a kind of sneeze in the middle: however, you'll hear it done, maybe—down in the wood yonder—and when you've once heard it you'll be *quite* content. Who's been repeating all that hard stuff to you?"

"I read it in a book," said Alice.

1871

The White Knight's Song[4]

I'll tell thee everything I can;
    There's little to relate.
I saw an aged, aged man,
    A-sitting on a gate.
"Who are you, aged man?" I said.   5
    "And how is it you live?"
And his answer trickled through my head
    Like water through a sieve.

He said "I look for butterflies
    That sleep among the wheat;   10
I make them into mutton-pies,
    And sell them in the street.
I sell them unto men," he said,
    "Who sail on stormy seas;
And that's the way I get my bread—   15
    A trifle, if you please."

But I was thinking of a plan
    To dye one's whiskers green,
And always use so large a fan
    That they could not be seen.   20
So, having no reply to give
    To what the old man said,
I cried, "Come, tell me how you live!"
    And thumped him on the head.

His accents mild took up the tale;   25
    He said, "I go my ways,
And when I find a mountain-rill,

4. From Chapter VIII of *Through the Looking-Glass*. Cf. Wordsworth's poem concerning the aged leech-gatherer: *Resolution and Independence.*

I set it in a blaze;
And thence they make a stuff they call
  Rowland's Macassar Oil—   30
Yet twopence-halfpenny is all
  They give me for my toil."

But I was thinking of a way
  To feed oneself on batter,
And so go on from day to day   35
  Getting a little fatter.
I shook him well from side to side,
  Until his face was blue;
"Come, tell me how you live," I cried
  "And what it is you do!"   40

He said, "I hunt for haddocks' eyes
  Among the heather bright,
And work them into waistcoat-buttons
  In the silent night.
And these I do not sell for gold   45
  Or coin of silvery shine,
But for a copper halfpenny,
  And that will purchase nine.

"I sometimes dig for buttered rolls,
  Or set limed twigs for crabs;   50
I sometimes search the grassy knolls
  For wheels of hansom-cabs.
And that's the way" (he gave a wink)
  "By which I get my wealth—
And very gladly will I drink   55
  Your Honor's noble health."

I heard him then, for I had just
  Completed my design
To keep the Menai bridge[5] from rust
  By boiling it in wine.   60
I thanked him much for telling me
  The way he got his wealth,
But chiefly for his wish that he
  Might drink my noble health.

And now, if e'er by chance I put   65
  My fingers into glue,
Or madly squeeze a right-hand foot
  Into a left-hand shoe,
Or if I drop upon my toe
  A very heavy weight,   70
I weep, for it reminds me so
Of that old man I used to know—
Whose look was mild, whose speech was slow,

5. Railway bridge in Wales (completed in 1850).

Whose hair was whiter than the snow,
Whose face was very like a crow,   75
With eyes, like cinders, all aglow,
Who seemed distracted with his woe.
Who rocked his body to and fro,
And muttered mumblingly and low,
As if his mouth were full of dough,   80
Who snorted like a buffalo—
That summer evening long ago
    A-sitting on a gate.

1856   1871

The Walrus and the Carpenter[6]

The sun was shining on the sea,
    Shining with all his might;
He did his very best to make
    The billows smooth and bright—
And this was odd, because it was   5
    The middle of the night.

The moon was shining sulkily,
    Because she thought the sun
Had got no business to be there
    After the day was done—   10
"It's very rude of him," she said,
    "To come and spoil the fun!"

The sea was wet as wet could be,
    The sands were dry as dry.
You could not see a cloud, because   15
    No cloud was in the sky;
No birds were flying overhead—
    There were no birds to fly.

The Walrus and the Carpenter
    Were walking close at hand;   20
They wept like anything to see
    Such quantities of sand.
"If this were only cleared away,"
    They said, "it *would* be grand!"

"If seven maids with seven mops   25
    Swept it for half a year,
Do you suppose," the Walrus said,
    "That they could get it clear?"
"I doubt it," said the Carpenter,
    And shed a bitter tear.   30

6. Recited by Tweedledee in Chapter IV of *Through the Looking-Glass.*

"O Oysters, come and walk with us!"
　　The Walrus did beseech.
"A pleasant walk, a pleasant talk,
　　Along the briny beach;
We cannot do with more than four,　　　　35
　　To give a hand to each."

The eldest Oyster looked at him,
　　But never a word he said;
The eldest Oyster winked his eye,
　　And shook his heavy head—　　　　　40
Meaning to say he did not choose
　　To leave the oyster-bed.

But four young Oysters hurried up,
　　All eager for the treat;
Their coats were brushed, their faces washed,　　45
　　Their shoes were clean and neat—
And this was odd, because, you know,
　　They hadn't any feet.

Four other Oysters followed them,
　　And yet another four;　　　　　　50
And thick and fast they came at last,
　　And more, and more, and more—
All hopping through the frothy waves,
　　And scrambling to the shore.

The Walrus and the Carpenter　　　　55
　　Walked on a mile or so,
And then they rested on a rock
　　Conveniently low;
And all the little Oysters stood
　　And waited in a row.　　　　　60

"The time has come," the Walrus said,
　　"To talk of many things:
Of shoes—and ships—and sealing-wax—
　　Of cabbages—and kings—
And why the sea is boiling hot—　　　　65
　　And whether pigs have wings."

"But wait a bit," the Oysters cried,
　　"Before we have our chat;
For some of us are out of breath,
　　And all of us are fat!"　　　　　70
"No hurry!" said the Carpenter.
　　They thanked him much for that.

"A loaf of bread," the Walrus said,
　　"Is what we chiefly need;
Pepper and vinegar besides　　　　75
　　Are very good indeed—

Now, if you're ready, Oysters dear,
    We can begin to feed."

"But not on us!" the Oysters cried,
    Turning a little blue.   80
"After such kindness, that would be
    A dismal thing to do!"
"The night is fine," the Walrus said,
    "Do you admire the view?

"It was so kind of you to come!   85
    And you are very nice!"
The Carpenter said nothing but
    "Cut us another slice.
I wish you were not quite so deaf—
    I've had to ask you twice!"   90

"It seems a shame," the Walrus said,
    "To play them such a trick,
After we've brought them out so far,
    And made them trot so quick!"
The Carpenter said nothing but   95
    "The butter's spread too thick!"

"I weep for you," the Walrus said;
    "I deeply sympathize."
With sobs and tears he sorted out
    Those of the largest size,   100
Holding his pocket-handkerchief
    Before his streaming eyes.

"O Oysters," said the Carpenter,
    "You've had a pleasant run!
Shall we be trotting home again?"   105
    But answer came there none—
And this was scarcely odd, because
    They'd eaten every one.

1871

From The Hunting of the Snark
The Baker's Tale

They roused him[7] with muffins—they roused him with ice—
    They roused him with mustard and cress—
They roused him with jam and judicious advice—
    They set him conundrums to guess.

7. I.e., the Baker, a member of the Snark-hunting expedition. He had fainted when the leader of the crew, the Bellman, had mentioned that one species of Snark is called Boojum. The name-less Baker's fear of Boojums turns out later to have been well founded: at the end of the poem he encounters a Boojum and is never seen again.

When at length he sat up and was able to speak,　　　　　5
　　His sad story he offered to tell;
And the Bellman cried, "Silence! Not even a shriek!"
　　And excitedly tingled his bell.

There was silence supreme! Not a shriek, not a scream,
　　Scarcely even a howl or a groan,　　　　　10
As the man they called "Ho!" told his story of woe
　　In an antediluvian tone.

"My father and mother were honest though poor—"
　　"Skip all that!" cried the Bellman in haste.
"If it once becomes dark, there's no chance of a Snark—　　15
　　We have hardly a minute to waste!"

"I skip forty years," said the Baker, in tears,
　　"And proceed without further remark
To the day when you took me aboard of your ship
　　To help you in hunting the Snark.　　　　　20

"A dear uncle of mine (after whom I was named)
　　Remarked, when I bade him farewell—"
"Oh, skip your dear uncle!" the Bellman exclaimed,
　　As he angrily tingled his bell.

"He remarked to me then," said that mildest of men,　　25
　　" 'If your Snark be a Snark, that is right;
Fetch it home by all means—you may serve it with greens,
　　And it's handy for striking a light.

" 'You may seek it with thimbles—and seek it with care;
　　You may hunt it with forks and hope;　　　　　30
You may threaten its life with a railway-share;
　　You may charm it with smiles and soap—' "

("That's exactly the method," the Bellman bold
　　In a hasty parenthesis cried,
"That's exactly the way I have always been told　　35
　　That the capture of Snarks should be tried!")

" 'But oh, beamish[8] nephew, beware of the day,
　　If your Snark be a Boojum! For then
You will softly and suddenly vanish away,
　　And never be met with again!'　　　　　40

"It is this, it is this that oppresses my soul,
　　When I think of my uncle's last words;
And my heart is like nothing so much as a bowl
　　Brimming over with quivering curds!

"It is this, it is this—" "We have had that before!"　　45
　　The Bellman indignantly said.
And the Baker replied, "Let me say it once more.
　　It is this, it is this that I dread!

8. See *Jabberwocky*, line 22.

"I engage with the Snark—every night after dark—
  In a dreamy, delirious fight;
I serve it with greens in those shadowy scenes,
  And I use it for striking a light;

"But if ever I meet with a Boojum, that day,
  In a moment (of this I am sure),
I shall softly and suddenly vanish away—
  And the notion I cannot endure!"

1874–76   1876

Critical and Controversial Prose

In his essay on *Style* (1889), Walter Pater argued that prose was "the special and opportune art of the modern world." His contention was not that prose is superior to verse but that it more readily conveys the "chaotic variety and complexity" of modern life, the "incalculable" intellectual diversity of the "master currents of the present time." Whether prose is a more appropriate medium than verse to communicate the "chaotic variety" of an age remains a matter of dispute, but what Pater says of the age itself would be much more generally agreed upon. Toward this condition of their age the Victorian writers of nonfictional prose responded in a variety of ways and in a variety of styles. Each sought in his distinctive manner to create some sort of order out of the chaos. Pater himself, coming to maturity late in the century, differs from the others in his distaste for controversy. By writing critical essays celebrating a beautifully ordered world of art and literature, Pater sought to rise above the flux and chaos which he saw as characteristic of his century. His four predecessors (featured in the following selections) were more engaged in shaping and reconstructing the social order. John Henry Newman, John Stuart Mill, John Ruskin, and T. H. Huxley use prose primarily as an instrument of persuasion and argument. Mill generally relies most upon logical argument, Ruskin upon a thunderous rhetoric, Huxley upon what seems to be common sense, and Newman upon a variety of persuasive devices, but however different their tools of argument, the writings of all four men can be appropriately grouped under the heading of "controversial prose."

The essays and treatises of each of these writers can be independently enjoyed in their own right. Even more effectively, however, each can be profitably related to the others and also to Carlyle and Arnold, two masters of nonfictional prose who are represented at length in the present anthology. Such a comparative study reduces our sense of chaotic diversity by making us aware that the Victorian prose writers were linked by a common concern for the fate of man in an industrial, democratic, and increasingly secularized society. Of their interlocking debates on education, leadership, and the role of science and religion, C. F. Harrold aptly says: "What they wrote constitutes a fascinating chapter in the history of the English mind, and also provides a perspective for viewing much that continues to perplex the world. Above all, a survey of their beliefs and assumptions will illuminate the richness of their prose, a prose which is often highly allusive, sometimes deceptively simple, and always susceptible to fresh and profitable interpretation as the symbol of their thought and the eloquent expression of their convictions."

JOHN HENRY CARDINAL NEWMAN
(1801–1890)

Newman's writings may be appropriately classified under the heading of
"controversial prose," for at several points in his long lifetime he found
himself at the center of some of the most intense disputes that stirred
Victorian England, disputes in which he himself emerged as a controversialist of great skill—engagingly persuasive in defense of his position
and devastatingly effective in disposing of opponents. Thomas Hardy,
whose position was at the opposite extreme from Newman's, paid him a
high compliment when he noted in his diary: "Worked at J. H. Newman's *Apologia* which we have all been talking about lately. * * * Style
charming and his logic really human, being based not on syllogisms but
on converging probabilities. Only—and here comes the fatal catastrophe—
there is no first link to his excellent chain of reasoning, and down you
come headlong."

Newman was born in London, the son (like Browning) of a banker.
In his spiritual autobiography, *Apologia Pro Vita Sua* (in effect, his vindication of his life), he traces the principal stages of his religious development from the strongly Protestant period of his youth to his conversion
to Roman Catholicism in 1845. Along the way, after being elected to a
fellowship at Oriel College in Oxford and becoming an Anglican clergyman, he was attracted briefly into the orbit of religious liberalism. Gradually coming to realize, however, that liberalism, with its reliance upon
human reason, would be powerless to defend traditional religion from
attack, Newman shifted over into the new High Church wing of the Anglican Church and soon was recognized as the leading figure of the Oxford
Movement. During the 1830's he attracted a large and influential following
by his sermons at Oxford and his writing of tracts. His efforts to demonstrate the dogmatic and authoritative tradition of Anglicanism finally provoked so much opposition that he was reduced to silence. After much
reflection he took the final step. At the age of 44 he entered the Roman
Catholic priesthood and moved to Birmingham where he spent the rest
of his life. In 1879 he was created Cardinal.

Despite his mastery of prose style, Newman found the act of composition to be even more painfully difficult than most of us do. During his
years at Birmingham he was nevertheless prompted to write several books
including works of religious poetry and fiction. Most celebrated is the
series of articles, published as his *Apologia* in 1864, in which he replied
to an attack upon his intellectual honesty made by Charles Kingsley. Although parts of the *Apologia*, being devoted to fine points of theological
doctrine and church history, are difficult for the ordinary reader to follow,
the main argument is clearly and persuasively developed. The dignity and
candor with which Newman reviewed the stages of his religious development, the repeated appeals to his fellow countrymen's sense of honesty
and fair play, the unobtrusively beautiful prose style, gained for his master-

piece a sympathetic audience even among those who had been least disposed to listen to his side of the dispute with Kingsley.

Seemingly less controversial than the *Apologia* are Newman's lectures on the aims of education which were delivered in Dublin at the newly-founded Catholic University of Ireland, a university of which he was for a few years the rector. These lectures, published in 1852 and later entitled *The Idea of a University,* are a classic statement of the value of "the disciplined intellect" which can be developed by a liberal education rather than by a technical training. The lectures may be compared with the later lectures of Matthew Arnold and T. H. Huxley.

It should be noted that Newman's view of a liberal education is largely independent of his religious position. Such an education, he said, could form the minds of profligates and anticlericals as well as of saints and priests of the church. In considerable measure his view reflects his admiration for the kind of intellectual enlargement he had himself enjoyed as an undergraduate at Trinity College, Oxford. One of the most touching passages in the *Apologia* is Newman's account of his farewell to an Oxford friend, in February, 1846, as he was preparing his final departure from the precincts of the university he loved:

In him I took leave of my first College, Trinity, which was so dear to me. * * * There used to be much snapdragon growing on the walls opposite my freshman's rooms there, and I had taken it as the emblem of my perpetual residence even unto death in my University.

On the morning of the 23rd I left the Observatory. I have never seen Oxford since, excepting its spires, as they are seen from the railway.

From The Idea of a University
From *Discourse* V. *Knowledge Its Own End*

6

Now bear with me, Gentlemen, if what I am about to say has at first sight a fanciful appearance. Philosophy, then, or Science, is related to Knowledge in this way: Knowledge is called by the name of Science or Philosophy, when it is acted upon, informed, or if I may use a strong figure, impregnated by Reason. Reason is the principle of that intrinsic fecundity of Knowledge, which, to those who possess it, is its especial value, and which dispenses with the necessity of their looking abroad for any end to rest upon external to itself. Knowledge, indeed, when thus exalted into a scientific form, is also power; not only is it excellent in itself, but whatever such excellence may be, it is something more, it has a result beyond itself. Doubtless; but that is a further consideration, with which I am not concerned. I only say that, prior to its being a power, it is a good; that it is, not only an instrument, but an end. I know well it may resolve itself into an art, and terminate in a mechanical process, and in tangible fruit; but it also may fall back upon that Reason which informs it, and resolve itself into Philosophy. In one case it is called Useful Knowledge, in the other Liberal. The same person may cultivate it in both ways at once; but this again is a matter foreign to my subject; here I do but say that there are two ways of using Knowledge, and in matter of fact those who use it in one way are not likely to use it in the other, or at least in a very limited measure. You see, then, here are two methods of Education; the end of the one is to be philosophical, of the other to be mechanical; the one rises towards general ideas, the other is exhausted upon what is particular and external. Let me not be thought to deny the necessity, or to decry the benefit, of such attention to what is particular and practical, as belongs to the useful or mechanical arts; life could not go on without them; we owe our daily welfare to them; their exercise is the duty of the many, and we owe to the many a debt of gratitude for fulfilling that duty. I only say that Knowledge, in proportion as it tends more and more to be particular, ceases to be Knowledge. It is a question whether Knowledge can in any proper sense be predicated of the brute creation; without pretending to metaphysical exactness of phraseology, which would be unsuitable to an occasion like this, I say, it seems to me improper to call that passive sensation, or perception of things, which brutes seem to possess, by the name of Knowledge. When I speak of Knowledge, I mean something intellectual, something which grasps what it perceives through the senses; something which takes a view of things; which sees more than the senses convey; which reasons upon what it sees, and while it sees; which invests it with an idea. It expresses itself, not in a mere enunciation, but by an enthymeme:[1] it is of the nature of science from the first, and in this consists its dignity. The principle of real dignity in Knowledge, its worth, its desirableness, considered irrespectively of its results, is this germ within it of a scientific or a philosophical process. This is how it comes to be an end in itself; this is why it admits of being called Liberal. Not to know the relative disposition of things is the state of slaves or children; to have mapped out the Universe is the boast, or at least the ambition, of Philosophy.

Moreover, such knowledge is not a mere extrinsic or accidental advantage, which is ours today and another's tomorrow, which may be got up from a book, and easily forgotten again, which we can command or communicate at our pleasure, which we can borrow for the occasion, carry about in our hand, and take into the market; it is an acquired illumination, it is a habit, a personal possession, and an inward endowment. And this is the reason why it is more correct, as well as more usual, to speak of a University as a place of education than of instruction, though, when knowledge is concerned, instruction would at first sight have seemed the more appropriate word. We are instructed, for instance, in manual exercises,

1. A syllogism in which one of the premises is understood but not stated.

in the fine and useful arts, in trades, and in ways of business; for these are methods, which have little or no effect upon the mind itself, are contained in rules committed to memory, to tradition, or to use, and bear upon an end external to themselves. But education is a higher word; it implies an action upon our mental nature, and the formation of a character; it is something individual and permanent, and is commonly spoken of in connection with religion and virtue. When, then, we speak of the communication of Knowledge as being Education, we thereby really imply that that Knowledge is a state or condition of mind; and since cultivation of mind is surely worth seeking for its own sake, we are thus brought once more to the conclusion, which the word "Liberal" and the word "Philosophy" have already suggested, that there is a Knowledge, which is desirable, though nothing come of it, as being of itself a treasure, and a sufficient remuneration of years of labor. * * *

From *Discourse VII. Knowledge Viewed in Relation to Professional Skill*

1

I have been insisting, in my two preceding Discourses, first, on the cultivation of the intellect, as an end which may reasonably be pursued for its own sake; and next, on the nature of that cultivation, or what that cultivation consists in. Truth of whatever kind is the proper object of the intellect; its cultivation then lies in fitting it to apprehend and contemplate truth. Now the intellect in its present state, with exceptions which need not here be specified, does not discern truth intuitively, or as a whole. We know, not by a direct and simple vision, not at a glance, but, as it were, by piece-meal and accumulation, by a mental process, by going round an object, by the comparison, the combination, the mutual correction, the continual adaptation, of many partial notions, by the employment, concentration, and joint action of many faculties and exercises of mind. Such a union and concert of the intellectual powers, such an enlargement and development, such a comprehensiveness, is necessarily a matter of training. And again, such a training is a matter of rule; it is not mere application, however exemplary, which introduces the mind to truth, nor the reading many books, nor the getting up many subjects, nor the witnessing many experiments, nor the attending many lectures. All this is short of enough; a man may have done it all, yet be lingering in the vestibule of knowledge: he may not realize what his mouth utters; he may not see with his mental eye what confronts him; he may have no grasp of things as they are; or at least he may have no power at all of advancing one step forward of himself, in consequence of what he has already acquired, no power of discriminating between truth and falsehood, of sifting out the grains of truth from the mass, of arranging things according to their real value, and, if I may use the phrase, of building up ideas. Such a power is the result of a scientific formation of mind; it is an acquired faculty of judgment, of clearsightedness, of sagacity, of wisdom, of philosophical reach of mind, and of intellectual self-possession and repose—qualities which do not come of mere acquirement. The bodily eye, the organ for apprehending material objects, is provided by nature; the eye of the mind, of which the object is truth, is the work of discipline and habit.

This process of training, by which the intellect, instead of being formed or sacrificed to some particular or accidental purpose, some specific trade or profession, or study or science, is disciplined for its own sake, for the perception of its own proper object, and for its own highest culture, is called Liberal Education; and though there is no one in whom it is carried as far as is conceivable, or whose intellect would be a pattern of what intellects should be made, yet there is scarcely anyone but may gain an idea of what real training is, and at least look towards it, and make its true scope and result, not something else, his standard of excellence; and numbers there are who may submit themselves to it, and secure it to themselves in good measure. And to set forth the right standard, and to train according to it, and to help forward all students toward it according to their various capacities, this I conceive to be the business of a University.

2

Now this is what some great men are very slow to allow; they insist that Education should be confined to some particular and narrow end, and should issue in some definite work, which can be weighed and measured. They argue as if every thing, as well as every person, had its price; and that where there has been a great outlay, they have a right to expect a return in kind. This they call making Education and Instruction "useful," and "Utility" becomes their watchword. With a fundamental principle of this nature, they very naturally go on to ask what there is to show for the expense of a University; what is the real worth in the market of the article called "a Liberal Education," on the supposition that it does not teach us definitely how to advance our manufactures, or to improve our lands, or to better our civil economy; or again, if it does not at once make this man a lawyer, that an engineer, and that a surgeon; or at least if it does not lead to discoveries in chemistry, astronomy, geology, magnetism, and science of every kind. * * *

5

* * * This is the obvious answer which may be made to those who urge upon us the claims of Utility in our plans of Education;[2]

2. The Utilitarians argued that a useful education would be one which trained the mind in the "habit of pushing things up to their first principles." Newman had earlier pointed out that a liberal education does exactly that and is hence useful.

but I am not going to leave the subject here: I mean to take a wider view of it. Let us take "useful," as Locke[3] takes it, in its proper and popular sense, and then we enter upon a large field of thought, to which I cannot do justice in one Discourse, though to-day's is all the space that I can give to it. I say, let us take "useful" to mean, not what is simply good, but what *tends* to good, or is the *instrument* of good; and in this sense also, Gentlemen, I will show you how a liberal education is truly and fully a useful, though it be not a professional, education. "Good" indeed means one thing, and "useful" means another; but I lay it down as a principle, which will save us a great deal of anxiety, that, though the useful is not always good, the good is always useful. Good is not only good, but re-productive of good; this is one of its attributes; nothing is ex-cellent, beautiful, perfect, desirable for its own sake, but it overflows, and spreads the likeness of itself all around it. Good is prolific; it is not only good to the eye, but to the taste; it not only attracts us, but it communicates itself; it excites first our admiration and love, then our desire and our gratitude, and that, in proportion to its intense-ness and fullness in particular instances. A great good will impart great good. If then the intellect is so excellent a portion of us, and its cultivation so excellent, it is not only beautiful, perfect, admirable, and noble in itself, but in a true and high sense it must be useful to the possessor and to all around him; not useful in any low, me-chanical, mercantile sense, but as diffusing good, or as a blessing, or a gift, or power, or a treasure, first to the owner, then through him to the world. I say then, if a liberal education be good, it must necessarily be useful too.

6

You will see what I mean by the parallel of bodily health. Health is a good in itself, though nothing came of it, and is especially worth seeking and cherishing; yet, after all, the blessings which attend its presence are so great, while they are so close to it and so redound back upon it and encircle it, that we never think of it except as useful as well as good, and praise and prize it for what it does, as well as for what it is, though at the same time we cannot point out any definite and distinct work or production which it can be said to effect. And so as regards intellectual culture, I am far from denying utility in this large sense as the end of Education, when I lay it down that the culture of the intellect is a good in itself and its own end; I do not exclude from the idea of intellectual culture what it cannot but be, from the very nature of things; I only deny that we must be able to point out, before we have any right to call it useful, some art, or business, or profession, or trade, or work, as resulting from it, and as its real and complete end. The parallel is

---

3. John Locke (1632–1704), whose treatise *Of Education* advocated a utilitarian concept of education.

exact: As the body may be sacrificed to some manual or other toil, whether moderate or oppressive, so may the intellect be devoted to some specific profession; and I do not call *this* the culture of the intellect. Again, as some member or organ of the body may be inordinately used and developed, so may memory, or imagination, or the reasoning faculty; and *this* again is not intellectual culture. On the other hand, as the body may be tended, cherished, and exercised with a simple view to its general health, so may the intellect also be generally exercised in order to its perfect state; and this *is* its cultivation.

Again, as health ought to precede labor of the body, and as a man in health can do what an unhealthy man cannot do, and as of this health the properties are strength, energy, agility, graceful carriage and action, manual dexterity, and endurance of fatigue, so in like manner general culture of mind is the best aid to professional and scientific study, and educated men can do what illiterate cannot; and the man who has learned to think and to reason and to compare and to discriminate and to analyze, who has refined his taste, and formed his judgment, and sharpened his mental vision, will not indeed at once be a lawyer, or a pleader, or an orator, or a statesman, or a physician, or a good landlord, or a man of business, or a soldier, or an engineer, or a chemist, or a geologist, or an antiquarian, but he will be placed in that state of intellect in which he can take up any one of the sciences or callings I have referred to, or any other for which he has a taste or special talent, with an ease, a grace, a versatility, and a success, to which another is a stranger. In this sense then, and as yet I have said but a very few words on a large subject, mental culture is emphatically *useful*.

If then I am arguing, and shall argue, against Professional or Scientific knowledge as the sufficient end of a University Education, let me not be supposed, Gentlemen, to be disrespectful towards particular studies, or arts, or vocations, and those who are engaged in them. In saying that Law or Medicine is not the end of a University course, I do not mean to imply that the University does not teach Law or Medicine. What indeed can it teach at all, if it does not teach something particular? It teaches *all* knowledge by teaching all *branches* of knowledge, and in no other way. I do but say that there will be this distinction as regards a Professor of Law, or of Medicine, or of Geology, or of Political Economy, in a University and out of it, that out of a University he is in danger of being absorbed and narrowed by his pursuit, and of giving Lectures which are the Lectures of nothing more than a lawyer, physician, geologist, or political economist; whereas in a University he will just know where he and his science stand, he has come to it, as it were, from a height, he has taken a survey of all knowledge, he is kept from extravagance by the very rivalry of other studies, he has gained from them a special illumination and largeness of mind and freedom and self-possession, and he treats his own in consequence with a philosophy and a resource, which belongs not to the study itself, but to his liberal education.

This then is how I should solve the fallacy, for so I must call it, by which Locke and his disciples would frighten us from cultivating the intellect, under the notion that no education is useful which does not teach us some temporal calling, or some mechanical art, or some physical secret. I say that a cultivated intellect, because it is a good in itself, brings with it a power and a grace to every work and occupation which it undertakes, and enables us to be more useful, and to a greater number. There is a duty we owe to human society as such, to the state to which we belong, to the sphere in which we move, to the individuals towards whom we are variously related, and whom we successively encounter in life; and that philosophical or liberal education, as I have called it, which is the proper function of a University, if it refuses the foremost place to professional interests, does but postpone them to the formation of the citizen, and, while it subserves the larger interests of philanthropy, prepares also for the successful prosecution of those merely personal objects which at first sight it seems to disparage. * * *

10

But I must bring these extracts[4] to an end. Today I have confined myself to saying that that training of the intellect, which is best for the individual himself, best enables him to discharge his duties to society. The Philosopher, indeed, and the man of the world differ in their very notion, but the methods, by which they are respectively formed, are pretty much the same. The Philosopher has the same command of matters of thought, which the true citizen and gentleman has of matters of business and conduct. If then a practical end must be assigned to a University course, I say it is that of training good members of society. Its art is the art of social life, and its end is fitness for the world. It neither confines its views to particular professions on the one hand, nor creates heroes or inspires genius on the other. Works indeed of genius fall under no art; heroic minds come under no rule; a University is not a birthplace of poets or of immortal authors, of founders of schools, leaders of colonies, or conquerors of nations. It does not promise a generation of Aristotles or Newtons, of Napoleons or Washingtons, or Raphaels or Shakespeares, though such miracles of nature it has before now contained within its precincts. Nor is it content on the other hand with forming the critic or the experimentalist, the economist or the engineer, though such too it includes within its scope. But a University training is the great ordinary means to a great but ordinary

4. Quotations cited from other authorities on education.

end; it aims at raising the intellectual tone of society, at cultivating the public mind, at purifying the national taste, at supplying true principles to popular enthusiasm and fixed aims to popular aspiration, at giving enlargement and sobriety to the ideas of the age, at facilitating the exercise of political power, and refining the intercourse of private life. It is the education which gives a man a clear conscious view of his own opinions and judgments, a truth in developing them, an eloquence in expressing them, and a force in urging them. It teaches him to see things as they are, to go right to the point, to disentangle a skein of thought, to detect what is sophistical, and to discard what is irrelevant. It prepares him to fill any post with credit, and to master any subject with facility. It shows him how to accommodate himself to others, how to throw himself into their state of mind, how to bring before them his own, how to influence them, how to come to an understanding with them, how to bear with them. He is at home in any society, he has common ground with every class; he knows when to speak and when to be silent; he is able to converse, he is able to listen; he can ask a question pertinently, and gain a lesson seasonably, when he has nothing to impart himself; he is ever ready, yet never in the way; he is a pleasant companion, and a comrade you can depend upon; he knows when to be serious and when to trifle, and he has a sure tact which enables him to trifle with gracefulness and to be serious with effect. He has the repose of a mind which lives in itself, while it lives in the world, and which has resources for its happiness at home when it cannot go abroad. He has a gift which serves him in public, and supports him in retirement,[5] without which good fortune is but vulgar, and with which failure and disappointment have a charm. The art which tends to make a man all this is in the object which it pursues as useful as the art of wealth or the art of health, though it is less susceptible of method, and less tangible, less certain, less complete in its result.

1852, 1873

5. In one of his later works, *The Grammar of Assent* (1870), Newman enlarges upon this aspect of his subject in a passage describing the impact that classical literature may have on us at different ages of our lives, a passage admired by James Joyce. "Let us consider, too, how differently young and old are affected by the words of some classic author, such as Homer or Horace. Passages, which to a boy are but rhetorical commonplaces, neither better nor worse than a hundred others which any clever writer might supply, which he gets by heart and thinks very fine, and imitates, as he thinks, successfully, in his own flowing versification, at length come home to him, when long years have passed, and he has had experience of life, and pierce him, as if he had never before known them, with their sad earnestness and vivid exactness. Then he comes to understand how it is that lines, the birth of some chance morning or evening at an Ionian festival, or among the Sabine hills, have lasted generation after generation, for thousands of years, with a power over the mind, and a charm, which the current literature of his own day, with all its obvious advantages, is utterly unable to rival. Perhaps this is the reason of the medieval opinion about Virgil, as if a prophet or magician; his single words and phrases, his pathetic half lines, giving utterance, as the voice of Nature herself, to that pain and weariness, yet hope of better things, which is the experience of her children in every time."

From Apologia Pro Vita Sua

From *Chapter III. History of My Religious Opinions from 1839 to 1841*

And now that I am about to trace, as far as I can, the course of that great revolution of mind, which led me to leave my own home, to which I was bound by so many strong and tender ties, I feel overcome with the difficulty of satisfying myself in my account of it, and have recoiled from the attempt, till the near approach of the day, on which these lines must be given to the world, forces me to set about the task. For who can know himself, and the multitude of subtle influences which act upon him? And who can recollect, at the distance of twenty-five years, all that he once knew about his thoughts and his deeds, and that, during a portion of his life, when, even at the time, his observation, whether of himself or of the external world, was less than before or after, by very reason of the perplexity and dismay which weighed upon him, when, in spite of the light given to him according to his need amid his darkness, yet a darkness it emphatically was? And who can suddenly gird himself to a new and anxious undertaking, which he might be able indeed to perform well, were full and calm leisure allowed him to look through every thing that he had written, whether in published works or private letters? yet again, granting that calm contemplation of the past, in itself so desirable, who could afford to be leisurely and deliberate, while he practices on himself a cruel operation, the ripping up of old griefs, and the venturing again upon the *infandum dolorem* [1] of years, in which the stars of this lower heaven were one by one going out? I could not in cool blood, nor except upon the imperious call of duty, attempt what I have set myself to do. It is both to head and heart an extreme trial, thus to analyze what has so long gone by, and to bring out the results of that examination. I have done various bold things in my life; this is the boldest, and, were I not sure I should after all succeed in my object, it would be madness to set about it.

In the spring of 1839 my position in the Anglican Church was at its height. I had supreme confidence in my controversial *status*, and I had a great and still growing success, in recommending it to others. I had in the foregoing autumn been somewhat sore at the Bishop's Charge,[2] but I have a letter which shows that all annoyance had passed from my mind. In January, if I recollect aright, in order to meet the popular clamor against myself and others, and to satisfy the Bishop, I had collected into one all the strong things

---

1. "Grief beyond words" (*Aeneid* II.3).
2. In 1838 Newman had been hurt when his Bishop, Richard Bagot of Oxford (whom he admired), criticized some of the Tracts published by the Anglo-Catholic group.

which they, and especially I, had said against the Church of Rome, in order to their insertion among the advertisements appended to our publications.[3] Conscious as I was that my opinions in religion were not gained, as the world said, from Roman sources, but were, on the contrary, the birth of my own mind and of the circumstances in which I had been placed, I had a scorn of the imputations which were heaped upon me. It was true that I held a large bold system of religion, very unlike the Protestantism of the day, but it was the concentration and adjustment of the statements of great Anglican authorities, and I had as much right to hold it, as the Evangelical, and more right than the Liberal party could show, for asserting their own respective doctrines. As I declared on occasion of Tract 90,[4] I claimed, in behalf of who would in the Anglican Church, the right of holding with Bramhall a comprecation with the Saints, and the Mass all but Transubstantiation with Andrewes, or with Hooker that Transubstantiation itself is not a point for Churches to part communion upon, or with Hammond that a General Council, truly such, never did, never shall err in a matter of faith, or with Bull that man had in paradise and lost on the fall, a supernatural habit of grace, or with Thorndike that penance is a propitiation for post-baptismal sin, or with Pearson [5] that the all powerful name of Jesus is no otherwise given than in the Catholic Church. "Two can play at that," was often in my mouth, when men of Protestant sentiments appealed to the Articles, Homilies, or Reformers; in the sense that, if they had a right to speak loud, I had the liberty to speak out as well as they, and had the means, by the same or parallel appeals, of giving them tit for tat. I thought that the Anglican Church was tyrannized over by a mere party, and I aimed at bringing into effect the promise contained in the motto to the *Lyra,* "They shall know the difference now." [6] I only asked to be allowed to show them the difference.

What will best describe my state of mind at the early part of 1839 is an Article in the *British Critic* for that April. I have looked over it now, for the first time since it was published; and have been struck by it for this reason: it contains the last words which I ever spoke as an Anglican to Anglicans. It may now be

3. Tracts and articles written by High Church Anglican clergymen who made up the Tractarian Anglo-Catholic party or Oxford Movement. Their opponents, the Evangelicals and also the Broad Church liberals, accused them of favoring Roman Catholic doctrines.
4. An interpretation of Anglicanism by Newman, published in 1841, which provoked an acrimonious controversy.
5. All the names here are those of Anglican clergymen of the 16th and 17th centuries. Newman and his Anglo-Catholic party frequently reinforced their theological arguments by drawing from the writings of these earlier divines, especially from Richard Hooker's *The Laws of Ecclesiastical Polity* (1593), a defense of the Anglican position as a *via media* (middle way) between Roman Catholicism and Protestantism. See Vol. 1 of the present anthology.
6. On returning to battle the Trojans Achilles had boasted: "You shall know the difference now that I am back again." (*Iliad* XXVIII.125). His words served as the motto for *Lyra Apostolica,* a series of Anglo-Catholic articles published in the *British Magazine* of which Newman served as editor.

read as my parting address and valediction, made to my friends. I little knew it at the time. It reviews the actual state of things, and it ends by looking toward the future. It is not altogether mine; for my memory goes to this, that I had asked a friend to do the work; that then, the thought came on me, that I would do it myself; and that he was good enough to put into my hands what he had with great appositeness written, and that I embodied it in my Article. Every one, I think, will recognize the greater part of it as mine. It was published two years before the affair of Tract 90, and was entitled "The State of Religious Parties."

In this Article, I begin by bringing together testimonies from our enemies to the remarkable success of our exertions. One writer said: "Opinions and views of a theology of a very marked and peculiar kind have been extensively adopted and strenuously upheld, and are daily gaining ground among a considerable and influential portion of the members, as well as ministers of the Established Church." * * *

After thus stating the phenomenon of the time, as it presented itself to those who did not sympathize in it, the Article proceeds to account for it; and this it does by considering it as a reaction from the dry and superficial character of the religious teaching and the literature of the last generation, or century, and as a result of the need which was felt both by the hearts and the intellects of the nation for a deeper philosophy, and as the evidence and as the partial fulfillment of that need, to which even the chief authors of the then generation had borne witness. First, I mentioned the literary influence of Walter Scott, who turned men's minds in the direction of the middle ages. "The general need," I said, "of something' deeper and more attractive, than what had offered itself elsewhere, may be considered to have led to his popularity; and by means of his popularity he reacted on his readers, stimulating their mental thirst, feeding their hopes, setting before them visions, which, when once seen, are not easily forgotten, and silently indoctrinating them with nobler ideas, which might afterwards be appealed to as first principles."

Then I spoke of Coleridge, thus: "While history in prose and verse was thus made the instrument of Church feelings and opinions, a philosophical basis for the same was laid in England by a very original thinker, who, while he indulged a liberty of speculation, which no Christian can tolerate, and advocated conclusions which were often heathen rather than Christian, yet after all installed a higher philosophy into inquiring minds, than they had hitherto been accustomed to accept. In this way he made trial of his age, and succeeded in interesting its genius in the cause of Catholic truth."

Then come Southey and Wordsworth, "two living poets, one of

whom in the department of fantastic fiction, the other in that of philosophical meditation, have addressed themselves to the same high principles and feelings, and carried forward their readers in the same direction."

* * *

These being the circumstances under which the Movement began and progressed, it was absurd to refer it to the act of two or three individuals. It was not so much a movement as a "spirit afloat"; it was within us, "rising up in hearts where it was least suspected, and working itself, though not in secret, yet so subtly and impalpably, as hardly to admit of precaution or encounter on any ordinary human rules of opposition. It is," I continued, "an adversary in the air, a something one and entire, a whole wherever it is, unapproachable and incapable of being grasped, as being the result of causes far deeper than political or other visible agencies, the spiritual awakening of spiritual wants."

* * *

Lastly, I proceeded to the question of that future of the Anglican Church, which was to be a new birth of the Ancient Religion. And I did not venture to pronounce upon it. "About the future, we have no prospect before our minds whatever, good or bad. Ever since that great luminary, Augustine, proved to be the last bishop of Hippo, Christians have had a lesson against attempting to foretell, *how* Providence will prosper and" [or?] "bring to an end, what it begins." Perhaps the lately revived principles would prevail in the Anglican Church; perhaps they would be lost in some miserable schism, or some more miserable compromise; but there was nothing rash in venturing to predict that "neither Puritanism nor Liberalism had any permanent inheritance within her."

Then I went on: "As to Liberalism, we think the formularies of the Church will ever, with the aid of a good Providence, keep it from making any serious inroads upon the clergy. Besides, it is too cold a principle to prevail with the multitude." But as regarded what was called Evangelical Religion or Puritanism, there was more to cause alarm. I observed upon its organization; but on the other hand it had no intellectual basis; no internal idea, no principle of unity, no theology. "Its adherents," I said, "are already separating from each other; they will melt away like a snowdrift. It has no straightforward view on any one point, on which it professes to teach, and to hide its poverty, it has dressed itself out in a maze of words. We have no dread of it at all; we only fear what it may lead to. It does not stand on intrenched ground, or make any pretense to a position; it does but occupy the space between contending powers, Catholic Truth and Rationalism. Then indeed will be the stern encounter, when two real and living principles, simple, entire, and consistent, one in the Church, the other out of it, at length rush upon each other, contending not for names and words, or half-views, but for elementary notions and distinctive moral characters."

Whether the ideas of the coming age upon religion were true or false, at least they would be real. "In the present day," I said, "mistiness is the mother of wisdom. A man who can set down a half-a-dozen general propositions, which escape from destroying one another only by being diluted into truisms, who can hold the balance between opposites so skillfully as to do without fulcrum or beam, who never enunciates a truth without guarding himself against being supposed to exclude the contradictory—who holds that Scripture is the only authority, yet that the Church is to be deferred to, that faith only justifies, yet that it does not justify without works, that grace does not depend on the sacraments, yet is not given without them, that bishops are a divine ordinance, yet those who have them not are in the same religious condition as those who have—this is your safe man and the hope of the Church; this is what the Church is said to want, not party men, but sensible, temperate, sober, well-judging persons, to guide it through the channel of no-meaning, between the Scylla and Charybdis of Aye and No."

This state of things, however, I said, could not last, if men were to read and think. They "will not keep in that very attitude which you call sound Church-of-Englandism or orthodox Protestantism. They cannot go on forever standing on one leg, or sitting without a chair, or walking with their feet tied, or like Tityrus's stags grazing in the air.[7] They will take one view or another, but it will be a consistent view. It may be Liberalism, or Erastianism, or Popery, or Catholicity; but it will be real."

I concluded the Article by saying, that all who did not wish to be "democratic, or pantheistic, or popish," must "look out for *some* Via Media which will perserve us from what threatens, though it cannot restore the dead. The spirit of Luther is dead; but Hildebrand and Loyola are alive.[8] Is it sensible, sober, judicious, to be so very angry with those writers of the day, who point to the fact, that our divines of the seventeenth century have occupied a ground which is the true and intelligible mean between extremes? Is it wise to quarrel with this ground, because it is not exactly what we should choose, had we the power of choice? Is it true moderation, instead of trying to fortify a middle doctrine, to fling stones at those who do? . . . Would you rather have your sons and daughters members of the Church of England or of the Church of Rome?"

And thus I left the matter. But, while I was thus speaking of the future of the Movement, I was in truth winding up my accounts

7. Virgil, *Eclogues* I.59.
8. Hildebrand (Pope Gregory VII) and St. Ignatius of Loyola, representing medieval and modern Catholicism.

with it, little dreaming that it was so to be; while I was still, in some way or other, feeling about for an available *Via Media*, I was soon to receive a shock which was to cast out of my imagination all middle courses and compromises forever.[9] As I have said, this Article appeared in the April number of the *British Critic*; in the July number, I cannot tell why, there is no Article of mine; before the number for October, the event had happened to which I have alluded.

But before I proceed to describe what happened to me in the summer of 1839, I must detain the reader for a while, in order to describe the *issue* of the controversy between Rome and the Anglican Church, as I viewed it. This will involve some dry discussion; but it is as necessary for my narrative, as plans of buildings and homesteads are at times needed in the proceedings of our law courts.

* * *

From *Chapter V. Position of My Mind Since 1845*

Starting then with the being of a God (which, as I have said, is as certain to me as the certainty of my own existence, though when I try to put the grounds of that certainty into logical shape I find a difficulty in doing so in mood and figure to my satisfaction), I look out of myself into the world of men, and there I see a sight which fills me with unspeakable distress. The world seems simply to give the lie to that great truth, of which my whole being is so full; and the effect upon me is, in consequence, as a matter of necessity, as confusing as if it denied that I am in existence myself. If I looked into a mirror, and did not see my face, I should have the sort of feeling which actually comes upon me, when I look into this living busy world, and see no reflection of its Creator. This is, to me, one of the great difficulties of this absolute primary truth, to which I referred just now. Were it not for this voice, speaking so clearly in my conscience and my heart, I should be an atheist, or a pantheist, or a polytheist when I looked into the world. I am speaking for myself only; and I am far from denying the real force of the arguments in proof of a God, drawn from the general facts of human society, but these do not warm me or enlighten me; they do not take away the winter of my desolation, or make the buds unfold and the leaves grow within me, and my moral being rejoice. The sight of the world is nothing else than the prophet's scroll, full of "lamentations, and mourning, and woe."[2]

To consider the world in its length and breadth, its various history, the many races of man, their starts, their fortunes, their

9. The "shock" was prompted by his discovery in 1839, in the course of studying church history, that the Anglican position seemed to be identical with that of a heretical movement of the 5th century.
2. Ezekiel ii.9–10.

mutual alienation, their conflicts; and then their ways, habits, governments, forms of worship; their enterprises, their aimless courses, their random achievements and acquirements, the impotent conclusion of long-standing facts, the tokens so faint and broken, of a superintending design, the blind evolution of what turn out to be great powers or truth, the progress of things, as if from un-reasoning elements, not towards final causes, the greatness and little-ness of man, his far-reaching aims, his short duration, the curtain hung over his futurity, the disappoinments of life, the defeat of good, the success of evil, physical pain, mental anguish, the preva-lence and intensity of sin, the pervading idolatries, the corruptions, the dreary hopeless irreligion, that condition of the whole race, so fearfully yet exactly described in the Apostle's words, "having no hope and without God in the world"[3]—all this is a vision to dizzy and appall; and inflicts upon the mind the sense of a profound mystery which is absolutely beyond human solution.

What shall be said to this heart-piercing, reason-bewildering fact? I can only answer that either there is no Creator, or this living society of men is in a true sense discarded from His presence. Did I see a boy of good make and mind, with the tokens on him of a refined nature, cast upon the world without provision, unable to say whence he came, his birthplace or his family connections, I should conclude that there was some mystery connected with his history, and that he was one, of whom, from one cause or other, his parents were ashamed. Thus only should I be able to account for the contrast between the promise and condition of his being. And so I argue about the world—*if* there be a God, *since* there is a God, the human race is implicated in some terrible aboriginal calamity. It is out of joint with the purposes of its Creator. This is a fact, a fact as true as the fact of its existence; and thus the doctrine of what is theologically called original sin becomes to me almost as certain as that the world exists, and as the existence of God.

And now, supposing it were the blessed and loving will of the Creator to interfere in this anarchical condition of things, what are we to suppose would be the methods which might be necessarily or naturally involved in His object of mercy? Since the world is in so abnormal a state, surely it would be no surprise to me if the in-terposition were of necessity equally extraordinary—or what is called miraculous. But that subject does not directly come into the scope of my present remarks. Miracles as evidence involve an argu-ment; and of course I am thinking of some means which does not immediately run into argument. I am rather asking what must be the face-to-face antagonist, by which to withstand and baffle the fierce energy of passion and the all-corroding, all-dissolving skep-ticism of the intellect in religious inquiries? I have no intention at

3. Ephesians ii.12.

all to deny that truth is the real object of our reason, and that, if it does not attain to truth, either the premise or the process is in fault; but I am not speaking of right reason, but of reason as it acts in fact and concretely in fallen man. I know that even the unaided reason, when correctly exercised, leads to a belief in God, in the immortality of the soul, and in a future retribution; but I am considering it actually and historically; and in this point of view, I do not think I am wrong in saying that its tendency is towards a simple unbelief in matters of religion. No truth, however sacred, can stand against it, in the long run; and hence it is that in the pagan world, when our Lord came, the last traces of the religious knowledge of former times were all but disappearing from those portions of the world in which the intellect had been active and had had a career.

And in these latter days, in like manner, outside the Catholic Church things are tending, with far greater rapidity than in that old time from the circumstance of the age, to atheism in one shape or other. What a scene, what a prospect, does the whole of Europe present at this day! and not only Europe, but every government and every civilization through the world, which is under the influence of the European mind! Especially, for it most concerns us, how sorrowful, in the view of religion, even taken in its most elementary, most attenuated form, is the spectacle presented to us by the educated intellect of England, France, and Germany! Lovers of their country and of their race, religious men, external to the Catholic Church, have attempted various expedients to arrest fierce willful human nature in its onward course, and to bring it into subjection. The necessity of some form of religion for the interests of humanity has been generally acknowledged: but where was the concrete representative of things invisible, which would have the force and the toughness necessary to be a breakwater against the deluge? Three centuries ago the establishment of religion, material, legal, and social was generally adopted as the best expedient for the purpose, in those countries which separated from the Catholic Church; and for a long time it was successful; but now the crevices of those establishments are admitting the enemy. Thirty years ago, education was relied upon: ten years ago there was a hope that wars would cease forever, under the influence of commercial enterprise and the reign of the useful and fine arts;[4] but will anyone venture to say that there is anything anywhere on this earth, which will afford a fulcrum for us, whereby to keep the earth from moving onwards?

The judgment, which experience passes on establishments or

4. A reference to the optimism generated at the time of the Great Exhibition of 1851, a mood which was sobered by the sufferings endured during the Crimean War (1854–56).

education, as a means of maintaining religious truth in this anarchical world, must be extended even to Scripture, though Scripture be divine. Experience proves surely that the Bible does not
answer a purpose, for which it was never intended. It may be accidentally the means of the conversion of individuals; but a book,
after all, cannot make a stand against the wild living intellect of
man, and in this day it begins to testify, as regards its own structure and contents, to the power of that universal solvent,[5] which is
so successfully acting upon religious establishments.

Supposing then it to be the Will of the Creator to interfere in
human affairs, and to make provisions for retaining in the world a
knowledge of Himself, so definite and distinct as to be proof against
the energy of human skepticism, in such a case—I am far from saying that there was no other way—but there is nothing to surprise
the mind, if He should think fit to introduce a power into the
world, invested with the prerogative of infallibility in religious matters. Such a provision would be a direct, immediate, active, and
prompt means of withstanding the difficulty; it would be an instrument suited to the need; and, when I find that this is the very claim
of the Catholic Church, not only do I feel no difficulty in admitting
the idea, but there is a fitness in it, which recommends it to my
mind. And thus I am brought to speak of the Church's infallibility,
as a provision, adapted by the mercy of the Creator, to preserve religion in the world, and to restrain that freedom of thought, which
of course in itself is one of the greatest of our natural gifts, and to
rescue it from its own suicidal excesses. And let it be observed that,
neither here nor in what follows, shall I have occasion to speak
directly of the revealed body of truths, but only as they bear upon
the defense of natural religion. I say that a power, possessed of infallibility in religious teaching, is happily adapted to be a working
instrument, in the course of human affairs, for smiting hard and
throwing back the immense energy of the aggressive intellect—and
in saying this, as in the other things that I have to say, it must still
be recollected that I am all along bearing in mind my main purpose,
which is a defense of myself.

I am defending myself here from a plausible charge brought
against Catholics, as will be seen better as I proceed. The charge is
this: that I, as a Catholic, not only make profession to hold doctrines which I cannot possibly believe in my heart, but that I also
believe in the existence of a power on earth, which at its own will
imposes upon men any new set of *credenda*,[6] when it pleases, by a
claim to infallibility; in consequence, that my own thoughts are
not my own property; that I cannot tell that tomorrow I may not
have to give up what I hold today, and that the necessary effect of

5. Allusion to the Higher Criticism, a   tory.
method of analyzing the Bible as his-   6. Beliefs.

such a condition of mind must be a degrading bondage, or a bitter inward rebellion relieving itself in secret infidelity, or the necessity of ignoring the whole subject of religion in a sort of disgust, and of mechanically saying everything that the Church says, and leaving to others the defense of it. As then I have above spoken of the relation of my mind towards the Catholic Creed, so now I shall speak of the attitude which it takes up in the view of the Church's infallibility.

And first, the initial doctrine of the infallible teacher must be an emphatic protest against the existing state of mankind. Man had rebelled against his Maker. It was this that caused the divine interposition: and the first act of the divinely accredited messenger must be to proclaim it. The Church must denounce rebellion as of all possible evils the greatest. She must have no terms with it; if she would be true to her Master, she must ban and anathematize it. This is the meaning of a statement which has furnished matter for one of those special accusations to which I am at present replying: I have, however, no fault at all to confess in regard to it; I have nothing to withdraw, and in consequence I here deliberately repeat it. I said, "The Catholic Church holds it better for the sun and moon to drop from heaven, for the earth to fail, and for all the many millions on it to die of starvation in extremest agony, as far as temporal affliction goes, than that one soul, I will not say, should be lost, but should commit one single venial sin, should tell one willful untruth, or should steal one poor farthing without excuse." I think the principle here enunciated to be the mere preamble in the formal credentials of the Catholic Church, as an Act of Parliament might begin with a "*Whereas.*" It is because of the intensity of the evil which has possession of mankind that a suitable antagonist has been provided against it; and the initial act of that divinely-commissioned power is of course to deliver her challenge and to defy the enemy. Such a preamble then gives a meaning to her position in the world, and an interpretation to her whole course of teaching and action.

From *Liberalism*

I have been asked to explain more fully what it is I mean by "Liberalism," because merely to call it the Antidogmatic Principle is to tell very little about it. * * * Now by Liberalism I mean false liberty of thought, or the exercise of thought upon matters, in which, from the constitution of the human mind, thought cannot be brought to any successful issue, and therefore is out of place. Among such matters are first principles of whatever kind; and of these the most sacred and momentous are especially to be reckoned the truths of Revelation. Liberalism then is the mistake of subjecting to human judgment those revealed doctrines which are in their nature beyond and independent of it, and of claiming to determine on intrinsic grounds the truth and value of propositions which rest for their reception simply on the external authority of the Divine Word. * * *

I conclude this notice of Liberalism in Oxford, and the party which was antagonistic to it,[7] with some propositions in detail, which, as a member of the latter, and together with the High Church, I earnestly denounced and abjured.

1. No religious tenet is important, unless reason shows it to be so.

Therefore, e.g., the doctrine of the Athanasian Creed[8] is not to be insisted on, unless it tends to convert the soul; and the doctrine of the Atonement is to be insisted on, if it does convert the soul.

2. No one can believe what he does not understand.

Therefore, e.g., there are no mysteries in true religion.

3. No theological doctrine is anything more than an opinion which happens to be held by bodies of men.

Therefore, e.g., no creed, as such, is necessary for salvation.

4. It is dishonest in a man to make an act of faith in what he has not had brought home to him by actual proof.

Therefore, e.g., the mass of men ought not absolutely to believe in the divine authority of the Bible.

5. It is immoral in a man to believe more than he can spontaneously receive as being congenial to his moral and mental nature.

Therefore, e.g., a given individual is not bound to believe in eternal punishment.

6. No revealed doctrines or precepts may reasonably stand in the way of scientific conclusions.

Therefore, e.g., Political Economy may reverse our Lord's declarations about poverty and riches, or a system of Ethics may teach that the highest condition of body is ordinarily essential to the highest state of mind.

7. Christianity is necessarily modified by the growth of civilization, and the exigencies of times.

Therefore, e.g., the Catholic priesthood, though necessary in the Middle Ages, may be superseded now.

8. There is a system of religion more simply true than Christianity as it has ever been received.

Therefore, e.g., we may advance that Christianity is the "corn of wheat" which has been dead for 1800 years, but at length will bear fruit; and that Mahometanism is the manly religion, and existing Christianity the womanish.

9. There is a right of Private Judgment: that is, there is no existing authority on earth competent to interfere with the liberty of individuals in reasoning and judging for themselves about the Bible

7. The Tractarians or Party of the Oxford Movement.　　8. Belief in the Trinity.

and its contents, as they severally please.

Therefore, e.g., religious establishments requiring subscription are Antichristian.

10. There are rights of conscience such that everyone may lawfully advance a claim to profess and teach what is false and wrong in matters, religious, social, and moral, provided that to his private conscience it seems absolutely true and right.

Therefore, e.g., individuals have a right to preach and practice fornication and polygamy.

11. There is no such thing as a national or state conscience.

Therefore, e.g., no judgments can fall upon a sinful or infidel nation.

12. The civil power has no positive duty, in a normal state of things, to maintain religious truth.

Therefore, e.g., blasphemy and sabbath-breaking are not rightly punishable by law.

13. Utility and expedience are the measure of political duty.

Therefore, e.g., no punishment may be enacted, on the ground that God commands it: e.g., on the text, "Whoso sheddeth man's blood, by man shall his blood be shed." [9]

14. The Civil Power may dispose of Church property without sacrilege.

Therefore, e.g., Henry VIII committed no sin in his spoliations.[1]

15. The Civil Power has the right of ecclesiastical jurisdiction and administration.

Therefore, e.g., Parliament may impose articles of faith on the Church or suppress Dioceses.[2]

16. It is lawful to rise in arms against legitimate princes.

Therefore, e.g., the Puritans in the seventeenth century, and the French in the eighteenth, were justified in their Rebellion and Revolution respectively.

17. The people are the legitimate source of power.

Therefore, e.g., Universal Suffrage is among the natural rights of man.

18. Virtue is the child of knowledge, and vice of ignorance.

Therefore, e.g., education, periodical literature, railroad traveling, ventilation, drainage, and the arts of life, when fully carried out, serve to make a population moral and happy.

All of these propositions, and many others too, were familiar to me thirty years ago, as in the number of the tenets of Liberalism, and, while I gave in to none of them except No. 12, and perhaps No. 11, and partly No. 1, before I began to publish, so afterwards

---

9. Genesis ix.6.
1. The dissolution of the monasteries by Henry VIII.
2. Allusion to the abolishing of ten Irish bishoprics by liberal reformers in Parliament in 1833. This instance of interference by the state in affairs of the church had prompted Newman and his associates into organizing a "party of opposition": the Oxford Movement.

I wrote against most of them in some part or other of my Anglican works. * * *

I need hardly say that the above Note is mainly historical. How far the Liberal party of 1830–40 really held the above eighteen Theses, which I attributed to them, and how far and in what sense I should oppose those Theses now, could scarcely be explained without a separate Dissertation.

1864–65

JOHN STUART MILL
(1806–1873)

In many American colleges the writings of J. S. Mill are studied in courses in government or in philosophy, and it may therefore be asked why they should also have a place in the study of literature. It is evident that Mill is the least literary of the important Victorian prose writers. His analytic mind, preoccupied with abstractions rather than with the concrete details that are the concern of the more typical man of letters, his self-effacing manner, and his relatively colorless style are the marks of a writer whose value lies in his generalizations from experience rather than in the rendering of particular experiences for their own sake. Yet a knowledge of Mill's writings is essential to our understanding of Victorian literature. He is one of the leading figures in the intellectual history of his century, a thinker whose honest grappling with the political and religious problems of his age was to have a profound influence on writers as diverse as Arnold, Swinburne, and Hardy.

Mill was educated at home in London under the direction of his father, James Mill, a leader of the Utilitarians. James Mill believed that ordinary schooling fails to develop our intellectual capacities early enough, and he demonstrated his point by the extraordinary results he achieved in training his son. As a child John Stuart Mill read Greek and Latin, and as a boy he could carry on intelligent discussions of problems in mathematics, philosophy, and economics. By the time he was 14, as he reports in his *Autobiography*, his intensive education enabled him to start his career "with an advantage of a quarter of a century" over his contemporaries.

Mill worked in the office of the East India Company for many years and also served a term in Parliament in the 1860's, but his principal energies were devoted to his writings on such subjects as logic and philosophy, political principles, and economics. He began as a disciple of the Utilitarian theories of his father and of Jeremy Bentham but became gradually dissatisfied with the narrowness of their conception of human motives. His honesty and open-mindedness enabled him to appreciate the values of such anti-Utilitarians as Coleridge and Carlyle, and, whenever possible, to incorporate some of these values into the Utilitarian system. His essay on Coleridge's enlightened conservatism in politics and religion is a striking example of Mill's capacity for sympathetic understanding. In part this sympathy was gained by the lesson he learned through experiencing a nervous breakdown during his early 20's. This painful event, described in the chapter of his *Autobiography* included below, taught him that the lack of concern for the affections and emotions of men, characteristic of the Utilitarian system of thought (and typified by his own education), was a fatal flaw in that system. His tribute to the therapeutic value of art (because of its effect on human emotions), both in his *Autobiography* and in his early essay *What Is Poetry*, would have astonished Mill's master, Bentham, who had equated poetry with pushpin, a trifling game.

Mill's emotional life was also broadened by his love for Harriet Taylor, a married woman who eventually became his wife. Under her influence he became an advocate for the cause of female emancipation, one of several unpopular causes to which he was dedicated. The subjection of women was, however, only one aspect of the tyranny against which he fought. His fundamental concern was to prevent the subjection of individuals in a democracy. His classic treatise *On Liberty* (1859) is not a traditional liberal attack against tyrannical kings or dictators; it is an attack against tyrannical majorities. Mill foresaw that in democracies such as America, the pressure toward conformity might crush all individualists (intellectual individualists in particular) to the level of what he called a "collective mediocrity." Throughout all of his writings, even in his discussions of the advantages of socialism, Mill is concerned with demonstrating that the individual is more important than institutions such as church or state. In *On Liberty* we find a characteristic example of the sequence of his reasoning, but here, where the theme of individualism is central, his logic is charged with eloquence.

A similar eloquence is evident in a passage from his *Principles of Political Economy* (1848), a prophetic comment on the fate of the individual in an overpopulated world:

There is room in the world, no doubt, and even in old countries, for a great increase of population, supposing the arts of life go on improving, and capital to increase. But even if innocuous, I confess I see very little reason for desiring it. * * * It is not good for a man to be kept perforce at all times in the presence of his species. A world from which solitude is extirpated, is a very poor ideal. Solitude, in the sense of being often alone, is essential to any depth of meditation or of character: and solitude in the presence of natural beauty and grandeur, is the cradle of thoughts and aspirations which are not only good for the individual, but which society could ill do without. Nor is there much satisfaction in contemplating the world with nothing left to the spontaneous activity of nature; with every rood of land brought into cultivation, which is capable of growing food for human beings; every flowery waste or natural pasture ploughed up, all quadrupeds or birds which are not domesticated for man's use exterminated as his rivals for food, every hedgerow or superfluous tree rooted out, and scarcely a place left where a wild shrub or flower could grow without being eradicated as a weed in the name of improved agriculture. If the earth must lose that great portion of its pleasantness which it owes to things that the unlimited increase of wealth and population would extirpate from it, for the mere purpose of enabling it to support a larger, but not a better or a happier population, I sincerely hope, for the sake of posterity, that they will be content to be stationary, long before necessity compels them to it.

What Is Poetry?

It has often been asked, What Is Poetry? And many and various are the answers which have been returned. The vulgarest of all—one with which no person possessed of the faculties to which poetry addresses itself can ever have been satisfied—is that which confounds poetry with metrical composition; yet to this wretched mockery of a definition many have been led back by the failure of all their attempts to find any other that would distinguish what they have been accustomed to call poetry from much which they have known only under other names.

That, however, the word "poetry" imports something quite peculiar in its nature; something which may exist in what is called prose as well as in verse; something which does not even require the instrument of words, but can speak through the other audible symbols called musical sounds, and even through the visible ones which are the language of sculpture, painting, and architecture—all this, we believe, is and must be felt, though perhaps indistinctly, by all upon whom poetry in any of its shapes produces any impression beyond that of tickling the ear. The distinction between poetry and what is not poetry, whether explained or not, is felt to be fundamental; and, where every one feels a difference, a difference there must be. All other appearances may be fallacious; but the appearance of a difference is a real difference. Appearances too, like other things, must have a cause; and that which can cause anything, even an illusion, must be a reality. And hence, while a half-philosophy disdains the classifications and distinctions indicated by popular language, philosophy carried to its highest point frames new ones, but rarely sets aside the old, content with correcting and regularizing them. It cuts fresh channels for thought, but does not fill up such as it finds ready-made: it traces, on the countrary, more deeply, broadly, and distinctly, those into which the current has spontaneously flowed.

Let us then attempt, in the way of modest inquiry, not to coerce and confine Nature within the bounds of an arbitrary definition, but rather to find the boundaries which she herself has set, and erect a barrier round them; not calling mankind to account for having misapplied the word "poetry," but attempting to clear up the conception which they already attach to it, and to bring forward as a distinct principle that which, as a vague feeling, has really guided them in their employment of the term.

The object of poetry is confessedly to act upon the emotions; and therein is poetry sufficiently distinguished from what Wordsworth affirms to be its logical opposite; namely, not prose, but matter of fact, or science.[1] The one addresses itself to the belief; the other, to the feelings. The one does its work by convincing or persuading; the other, by moving. The one acts by presenting a proposition to the understanding; the other, by offering interesting objects of contemplation to the sensibilities.

This, however, leaves us very far from a definition of poetry. This distinguishes it from one thing; but we are bound to distinguish it from everything. To bring thoughts or images before the mind, for the purpose of acting upon the emotions, does not belong to poetry alone. It is equally the province (for example) of the novelist: and yet the faculty of the poet and that of the novelist are as distinct as any other two faculties; as the faculties of the novelist and of the orator, or of the poet and the metaphysician. The two characters may be united, as characters the most disparate may; but they have no natural connection.

Many of the greatest poems are in the form of fictitious narratives; and, in almost all good serious fictions, there is true poetry. But there is a radical distinction between the interest felt in a story as such, and the interest excited by poetry; for the one is derived from incident, the other from the representation of feeling. In one, the source of the emotion excited is the exhibition of a state or states of human sensibility; in the other, of a series of states of mere outward circumstances. Now, all minds are capable of being affected more or less by representations of the latter kind, and all, or almost all, by those of the former; yet the two sources of interest correspond to two distinct and (as respects their greatest development) mutually exclusive characters of mind.

At what age is the passion for a story, for almost any kind of story, merely as a story, the most intense? In childhood. But that also is the age at which poetry, even of the simplest description, is least relished and least understood; because the feelings with which it is especially conversant are yet undeveloped, and, not having been even in the slightest degree experienced, cannot be sympathized with. In what stage of the progress of society, again, is storytelling most valued, and the storyteller in greatest request and honor? In a rude state like that of the Tartars and Arabs at this day, and of almost all nations in the earliest ages. But, in this state of society, there is little poetry except ballads, which are mostly narrative—that is, essentially stories—and derive their principal interest from the incidents. Considered as poetry, they are of the lowest and most elementary kind: the feelings depicted, or rather indicated, are the simplest our nature has; such joys and griefs as the immediate pressure of some outward event excites in rude minds, which live wholly immersed in outward things, and have never, either from choice or a force they could not resist,

1. See above, Wordsworth's Preface to *Lyrical Ballads*.

turned themselves to the contemplation of the world within. Passing now from childhood, and from the childhood of society, to the grown-up men and women of this most grown-up and unchildlike age, the minds and hearts of greatest depth and elevation are commonly those which take greatest delight in poetry: the shallowest and emptiest, on the contrary, are, at all events, not those least addicted to novel-reading. This accords, too, with all analogous experience of human nature. The sort of persons whom not merely in books, but in their lives, we find perpetually engaged in hunting for excitement from without, are invariably those who do not possess, either in the vigor of their intellectual powers or in the depth of their sensibilities, that which would enable them to find ample excitement nearer home. The most idle and frivolous persons take a natural delight in fictitious narrative: the excitement it affords is of the kind which comes from without. Such persons are rarely lovers of poetry, though they may fancy themselves so because they relish novels in verse. But poetry, which is the delineation of the deeper and more secret workings of human emotion, is interesting only to those to whom it recalls what they have felt, or whose imagination it stirs up to conceive what they could feel, or what they might have been able to feel, had their outward circumstances been different.

Poetry, when it is really such, is truth; and fiction also, if it is good for anything, is truth: but they are different truths. The truth of poetry is to paint the human soul truly: the truth of fiction is to give a true picture of life. The two kinds of knowledge are different, and come by different ways, come mostly to different persons. Great poets are often proverbially ignorant of life. What they know has come by observation of themselves: they have found within them one highly delicate and sensitive specimen of human nature, on which the laws of emotion are written in large characters, such as can be read off without much study. Other knowledge of mankind, such as comes to men of the world by outward experience, is not indispensable to them as poets: but, to the novelist, such knowledge is all in all; he has to describe outward things, not the inward man; actions and events, not feelings; and it will not do for him to be numbered among those, who, as Madame Roland said of Brissot, know man, but not *men*.[2]

All this is no bar to the possibility of combining both elements, poetry and narrative or incident, in the same work, and calling it either a novel or a poem; but so may red and white combine on the same human features or on the same canvas. There is one order of composition which requires the union of poetry and incident, each in its highest kind—the dramatic. Even there, the two elements are perfectly distinguishable, and may exist of un-

---

2. Jacques Pierre Brissot (1754–93), a leading reformer during the French Revolution, is characterized in the *Mém-* *oires* of Jeanne Manon Roland (1754–93).

equal quality and in the most various proportion. The incidents of a dramatic poem may be scanty and ineffective, though the delineation of passion and character may be of the highest order, as in Goethe's admirable "Torquato Tasso"; or, again, the story as a mere story may be well got up for effect, as is the case with some of the most trashy productions of the Minerva Press:[3] it may even be, what those are not, a coherent and probable series of events, though there be scarcely a feeling exhibited which is not represented falsely, or in a manner absolutely commonplace. The combination of the two excellences is what renders Shakespeare so generally acceptable, each sort of readers finding in him what is suitable to their faculties. To the many, he is great as a storyteller; to the few, as a poet.

In limiting poetry to the delineation of states of feeling, and denying the name where nothing is delineated but outward objects, we may be thought to have done what we promised to avoid— to have not found, but made, a definition in opposition to the usage of language, since it is established by common consent that there is a poetry called descriptive. We deny the charge. Description is not poetry because there is descriptive poetry, no more than science is poetry because there is such a thing as a didactic poem. But an object which admits of being described, or a truth which may fill a place in a scientific treatise, may also furnish an occasion for the generation of poetry, which we thereupon choose to call descriptive or didactic. The poetry is not in the object itself, nor in the scientific truth itself, but in the state of mind in which the one and the other may be contemplated. The mere delineation of the dimensions and colors of external objects is not poetry, no more than a geometrical ground-plan of St. Peter's or Westminster Abbey is painting. Descriptive poetry consists, no doubt, in description, but in description of things as they appear, not as they are; and it paints them, not in their bare and natural lineaments, but seen through the medium and arrayed in the colors of the imagination set in action by the feelings. If a poet describes a lion, he does not describe him as a naturalist would, nor even as a traveler would, who was intent upon stating the truth, the whole truth, and nothing but the truth. He describes him by imagery, that is, by suggesting the most striking likenesses and contrasts which might occur to a mind contemplating a lion, in the state of awe, wonder, or terror, which the spectacle naturally excites, or is, on the occasion, supposed to excite. Now, this is describing the lion professedly, but the state of excitement of the spectator really. The lion may be described falsely or with exaggeration and the poetry be all the better: but, if the human emotion be not painted with scrupulous truth, the poetry is bad poetry; i.e., is not poetry at all, but a failure.

Thus far, our progress towards a clear view of the essentials of

3. Early 19th-century publishing house that fostered the production of sentimental novels.

poetry has brought us very close to the last two attempts at a definition of poetry which we happen to have seen in print, both of them by poets, and men of genius. The one is by Ebenezer Elliott, the author of "Corn-law Rhymes," and other poems of still greater merit. "Poetry," says he, "is impassioned truth." [4] The other is by a writer in "Blackwood's Magazine," and comes, we think, still nearer the mark. He defines poetry, "man's thoughts tinged by his feelings." There is in either definition a near approximation to what we are in search of. Every truth which a human being can enunciate, every thought, even every outward impression, which can enter into his consciousness, may become poetry, when shown through any impassioned medium; when invested with the coloring of joy, or grief, or pity, or affection, or admiration, or reverence, or awe, or even hatred or terror; and, unless so colored, nothing, be it as interesting as it may, is poetry. But both these definitions fail to discriminate between poetry and eloquence. Eloquence, as well as poetry, is impassioned truth; eloquence, as well as poetry, is thoughts colored by the feelings. Yet common apprehension and philosophic criticism alike recognize a distinction between the two: there is much that everyone would call eloquence, which no one would think of classing as poetry. A question will sometimes arise, whether some particular author is a poet; and those who maintain the negative commonly allow, that, though not a poet, he is a highly eloquent writer. The distinction between poetry and eloquence appears to us to be equally fundamental with the distinction between poetry and narrative, or between poetry and description, while it is still farther from having been satisfactorily cleared up than either of the others.

Poetry and eloquence are both alike the expression or utterance of feeling: but, if we may be excused the antithesis, we should say that eloquence is *heard*; poetry is *over*heard. Eloquence supposes an audience. The peculiarity of poetry appears to us to lie in the poet's utter unconsciousness of a listener. Poetry is feeling confessing itself to itself in moments of solitude, and embodying itself in symbols which are the nearest possible representations of the feeling in the exact shape in which it exists in the poet's mind. Eloquence is feeling pouring itself out to other minds, courting their sympathy, or endeavoring to influence their belief, or move them to passion or to action.

All poetry is of the nature of soliloquy. It may be said that poetry which is printed on hot-pressed paper, and sold at a bookseller's shop, is a soliloquy in full dress and on the stage. It is so; but there is nothing absurd in the idea of such a mode of soliloquizing. What we have said to ourselves we may tell to others afterwards; what we have said or done in solitude we may voluntarily reproduce when we know that other eyes are upon us. But

4. Preface to *Corn-Law Rhymes* (1828) by Ebenezer Elliot (1781–1849).

no trace of consciousness that any eyes are upon us must be visible in the work itself. The actor knows that there is an audience present: but, if he act as though he knew it, he acts ill. A poet may write poetry, not only with the intention of printing it, but for the express purpose of being paid for it. That it should *be* poetry, being written under such influences, is less probable, not, however, impossible; but no otherwise possible than if he can succeed in excluding from his work every vestige of such lookings-forth into the outward and every-day world, and can express his emotions exactly as he has felt them in solitude, or as he is conscious that he should feel them, though they were to remain for ever unuttered, or (at the lowest) as he knows that others feel them in similar circumstances of solitude. But when he turns round, and addresses himself to another person; when the act of utterance is not itself the end, but a means to an end—viz., by the feelings he himself expresses, to work upon the feelings, or upon the belief or the will of another; when the expression of his emotions, or of his thoughts tinged by his emotions, is tinged also by that purpose, by that desire of making an impression upon another mind—then it ceases to be poetry, and becomes eloquence.

Poetry, accordingly, is the natural fruit of solitude and meditation; eloquence, of intercourse with the world. The persons who have most feeling of their own, if intellectual culture has given them a language in which to express it, have the highest faculty of poetry: those who best understand the feelings of others are the most eloquent. The persons and the nations who commonly excel in poetry are those whose character and tastes render them least dependent upon the applause or sympathy or concurrence of the world in general. Those to whom that applause, that sympathy, that concurrence, are most necessary, generally excel most in eloquence. And hence, perhaps, the French, who are the least poetical of all great and intellectual nations, are among the most eloquent; the French also being the most sociable, the vainest, and the least self-dependent.

If the above be, as we believe, the true theory of the distinction commonly admitted between eloquence and poetry, or even though it be not so, yet if, as we cannot doubt, the distinction above stated be a real bona fide distinction, it will be found to hold, not merely in the language of words, but in all other language, and to intersect the whole domain of art.

Take, for example, music. We shall find in that art, so peculiarly the expression of passion, two perfectly distinct styles—one of which may be called the poetry, the other the oratory, of music. This difference, being seized, would put an end to much musical sectarianism. There has been much contention whether the music of the modern Italian school, that of Rossini,[5] and his suc-

5. G. A. Rossini (1792–1868), composer of operas.

cessors, be impassioned or not. Without doubt, the passion it expresses is not the musing, meditative tenderness or pathos or grief of Mozart or Beethoven; yet it is passion, but garrulous passion, the passion which pours itself into other ears, and therein the better calculated for dramatic effect, having a natural adaptation for dialogue. Mozart also is great in musical oratory; but his most touching compositions are in the opposite style, that of soliloquy. Who can imagine "Dove sono" [6] *heard?* We imagine it *over*heard.

Purely pathetic music commonly partakes of soliloquy. The soul is absorbed in its distress and, though there may be bystanders, it is not thinking of them. When the mind is looking within, and not without, its state does not often or rapidly vary; and hence the even, uninterrupted flow, approaching almost to monotony, which a good reader or a good singer will give to words or music of a pensive or melancholy cast. But grief, taking the form of a prayer or of a complaint, becomes oratorical: no longer low and even and subdued, it assumes a more emphatic rhythm, a more rapidly returning accent; instead of a few slow, equal notes, following one after another at regular intervals, it crowds note upon note, and often assumes a hurry and bustle like joy. Those who are familiar with some of the best of Rossini's serious compositions, such as the air "Tu che i miseri conforti," [7] in the opera of "Tancredi," or the duet "Ebben per mia memoria," [8] in "La Gazza Ladra," will at once understand and feel our meaning. Both are highly tragic and passionate: the passion of both is that of oratory, not poetry. The like may be said of that most moving invocation in Beethoven's "Fidelio,"

> "Komm, Hoffnung, lass das letzte Stern
> Der Müde nicht erbleichen "—[9]

in which Madame Schröder Devrient exhibited such consummate powers of pathetic expression. How different from Winter's beautiful "Paga fui," [1] the very soul of melancholy exhaling itself in solitude! fuller of meaning, and therefore more profoundly poetical, than the words for which it was composed; for it seems to express, not simple melancholy, but the melancholy of remorse.

If from vocal music we now pass to instrumental, we may have a specimen of musical oratory in any fine military symphony or march; while the poetry of music seems to have attained its consummation in Beethoven's "Overture to Egmont," so wonderful in its mixed expression of grandeur and melancholy.

6. "Where are fled [the lovely moments?]"—soprano aria from Act III of Mozart's opera *The Marriage of Figaro*.
7. "You, who give comfort to the wretched," soprano aria from Rossini's *Tancredi* (1813).
8. "Indeed according to my memory," soprano aria from Rossini's *La Gazza Ladra* (1817).
9. "Come, Hope, let not the weary person's last star fade out." Aria from *Fidelio* (1805). Mill seems to be quoting from memory. The passage should read: "Komm, Hoffnung, lass den letzten Stern / Der Müden nicht erbleichen."
1. "I have been contented." Aria from the once-popular opera *Il Ratto di Proserpina* by Peter Winter (1775–1825), first performed in London in 1804.

In the arts which speak to the eye, the same distinctions will be found to hold, not only between poetry and oratory, but between poetry, oratory, narrative, and simple imitation or description.

Pure description is exemplified in a mere portrait or a mere landscape, productions of art, it is true, but of the mechanical rather than of the fine arts; being works of simple imitation, not creation. We say, a mere portrait or a mere landscape; because it is possible for a portrait or a landscape, without ceasing to be such, to be also a picture, like Turner's [2] landscapes, and the great portraits by Titian or Vandyke.

Whatever in painting or sculpture expresses human feeling— or character, which is only a certain state of feeling grown habitual —may be called, according to circumstances, the poetry or the eloquence of the painter's or the sculptor's art: the poetry, if the feeling declares itself by such signs as escape from us when we are unconscious of being seen; the oratory, if the signs are those we use for the purpose of voluntary communication.

The narrative style answers to what is called historical painting, which it is the fashion among connoisseurs to treat as the climax of the pictorial art. That it is the most difficult branch of the art, we do not doubt, because, in its perfection, it includes the perfection of all the other branches; as, in like manner, an epic poem, though, in so far as it is epic (i.e., narrative), it is not poetry at all, is yet esteemed the greatest effort of poetic genius, because there is no kind whatever of poetry which may not appropriately find a place in it. But an historical picture as such, that is, as the representation of an incident, must necessarily, as it seems to us, be poor and ineffective. The narrative powers of painting are extremely limited. Scarcely any picture, scarcely even any series of pictures, tells its own story without the aid of an interpreter. But it is the single figures, which, to us, are the great charm even of an historical picture. It is in these that the power of the art is really seen. In the attempt to narrate, visible and permanent signs are too far behind the fugitive audible ones, which follow so fast one after another; while the faces and figures in a narrative picture, even though they be Titian's, stand still. Who would not prefer one "Virgin and Child" of Raphael to all the pictures which Rubens, with his fat, frouzy Dutch Venuses, ever painted?—though Rubens, besides excelling almost everyone in his mastery over the mechanical parts of his art, often shows real genius in *grouping* his figures, the peculiar problem of historical painting. But then, who, except a mere student of drawing and coloring, ever cared to look twice at any of the figures themselves? The power of painting lies in poetry, of which Rubens had not the slightest tincture, not in narrative, wherein he might have excelled.

2. J. W. M. Turner (1775–1851), English landscape painter.

The single figures, however, in an historical picture, are rather the eloquence of painting than the poetry. They mostly (unless they are quite out of place in the picture) express the feelings of one person as modified by the presence of others. Accordingly, the minds whose bent leads them rather to eloquence than to poetry rush to historical painting. The French painters, for instance, seldom attempt, because they could make nothing of, single heads, like those glorious ones of the Italian masters with which they might feed themselves day after day in their own Louvre. They must all be historical; and they are, almost to a man, attitudinizers. If we wished to give any young artist the most impressive warning our imagination could devise against that kind of vice in the pictorial which corresponds to rant in the histrionic art, we would advise him to walk once up and once down the gallery of the Luxembourg.[3] Every figure in French painting or statuary seems to be showing itself off before spectators. They are not poetical, but in the worst style of corrupted eloquence.

1833, 1859

From Coleridge[1]

The name of Coleridge is one of the few English names of our time which are likely to be oftener pronounced, and to become symbolical of more important things, in proportion as the inward workings of the age manifest themselves more and more in outward facts. Bentham[2] excepted, no Englishman of recent date has left his impress so deeply in the opinions and mental tendencies of those among us who attempt to enlighten their practice by philosophical meditation. If it be true, as Lord Bacon affirms, that a knowledge of the speculative opinions of the men between twenty and thirty years of age is the great source of political prophecy, the existence of Coleridge will show itself by no slight or ambiguous traces in the coming history of our country; for no one has contributed more to shape the opinions of those among its younger men, who can be said to have opinions at all.

The influence of Coleridge, like that of Bentham, extends far beyond those who share in the peculiarities of his religious or philosophical creed. He has been the great awakener in this country of the spirit of philosophy, within the bounds of traditional opinions. He has been, almost as truly as Bentham, "the great questioner of things established"; for a questioner needs not necessarily

---

3. A palace in Paris, where paintings of scenes from French history were exhibited.
1. In his *Autobiography* Mill discusses Samuel Taylor Coleridge as a poet. In the present essay he discusses Coleridge as a political and religious philosopher whose conversation and writings on conservatism had a profound influence on Mill's contemporaries in the 1820's and 1830's.
2. Jeremy Bentham (1748–1832), originator of Utilitarian theories of politics and ethics.

be an enemy. By Bentham, beyond all others, men have been led to ask themselves, in regard to any ancient or received opinion, Is it true? and by Coleridge, What is the meaning of it? The one took his stand *outside* the received opinion, and surveyed it as an entire stranger to it: the other looked at it from within, and endeavored to see it with the eyes of a believer in it; to discover by what apparent facts it was at first suggested, and by what appearances it has ever since been rendered continually credible— has seemed, to a succession of persons, to be a faithful interpretation of their experience. Bentham judged a proposition true or false as it accorded or not with the result of his own inquiries; and did not search very curiously into what might be meant by the proposition, when it obviously did not mean what he thought true. With Coleridge, on the contrary, the very fact that any doctrine had been believed by thoughtful men, and received by whole nations or generations of mankind, was part of the problem to be solved; was one of the phenomena to be accounted for. And, as Bentham's short and easy method of referring all to the selfish interests of aristocracies or priests or lawyers, or some other species of imposters, could not satisfy a man who saw so much farther into the complexities of the human intellect and feelings, he considered the long or extensive prevalence of any opinion as a presumption that it was not altogether a fallacy; that, to its first authors at least, it was the result of a struggle to express in words something which had a reality to them, though perhaps not to many of those who have since received the doctrine by mere tradition. The long duration of a belief, he thought, is at least proof of an adaptation in it to some portion or other of the human mind: and if, on digging down to the root, we do not find, as is generally the case, some truth, we shall find some natural want or requirement of human nature which the doctrine in question is fitted to satisfy; among which wants the instincts of selfishness and of credulity have a place, but by no means an exclusive one. From this difference in the points of view of the two philosophers, and from the too rigid adherence of each to his own, it was to be expected that Bentham should continually miss the truth which is in the traditional opinions, and Coleridge that which is out of them and at variance with them. But it was also likely that each would find, or show the way to finding, much of what the other missed.

It is hardly possible to speak of Coleridge, and his position among his contemporaries, without reverting to Bentham: they are connected by two of the closest bonds of association—resemblance and contrast. It would be difficult to find two persons of philosophic eminence more exactly the contrary of one another. Compare their modes of treatment of any subject, and you might fancy them inhabitants of different worlds. They seem to have scarcely a principle or a premise in common. Each of them sees scarcely any thing but what the other does not see. Bentham would have regarded Coleridge with a peculiar measure of the good-humored contempt with which he was accustomed to regard all modes of philosophizing different from his own. Coleridge would probably have made Bentham one of the exceptions to the enlarged and liberal appreciation which (to the credit of *his* mode of philosophizing) he extended to most thinkers of any eminence from whom he differed. But contraries, as logicians say, are but *quae in eodem genere maxime distant*—the things which are farthest from one another in the same kind. These two agreed in being the men, who, in their age and country, did most to enforce, by precept and example, the necessity of a philosophy. They agreed in making it their occupation to recall opinions to first principles; taking no proposition for granted without examining into the grounds of it, and ascertaining that it possessed the kind and degree of evidence suitable to its nature. They agreed in recognizing that sound theory is the only foundation for sound practice; and that whoever despises theory, let him give himself what airs of wisdom he may, is self-convicted of being a quack. If a book were to be compiled containing all the best things ever said on the rule-of-thumb school of political craftsmanship, and on the insufficiency for practical purposes of what the mere practical man calls experience, it is difficult to say whether the collection would be more indebted to the writings of Bentham or of Coleridge. They agreed, too, in perceiving that the groundwork of all other philosophy must be laid in the philosophy of the mind. To lay this foundation deeply and strongly, and to raise a superstructure in accordance with it, were the objects to which their lives were devoted. They employed, indeed, for the most part, different materials; but as the materials of both were real observations, the genuine product of experience, the results will, in the end, be found, not hostile, but supplementary, to one another. Of their methods of philosophizing, the same thing may be said: they were different, yet both were legitimate logical processes. In every respect, the two men are each other's "completing counterpart": the strong points of each correspond to the weak points of the other. Whoever could master the premises and combine the methods of both would possess the entire English philosophy of his age. Coleridge used to say that every one is born either a Platonist or an Aristotelian: it may be similarly affirmed that every Englishman of the present day is by implication either a Benthamite or a Coleridgian; holds views of human affairs which can only be proved true on the principles either of Bentham or of Coleridge. * * *

1840

From On Liberty

From *Chapter III. Of Individuality As One of the Elements of Well-Being*

* * * Few persons, out of Germany, even comprehend the meaning of the doctrine which Wilhelm von Humboldt, so eminent both as a savant and as a politician, made the text of a treatise—that "the end of man, or that which is prescribed by the eternal or immutable dictates of reason, and not suggested by vague and transient desires, is the highest and most harmonious development of his powers to a complete and consistent whole"; that, therefore, the object "towards which every human being must ceaselessly direct his efforts, and on which especially those who design to influence their fellow men must ever keep their eyes, is the individuality of power and development"; that for this there are two requisites, "freedom, and variety of situations"; and that from the union of these arise "individual vigor and manifold diversity," which combine themselves in "originality."[1]

Little, however, as people are accustomed to a doctrine like that of Von Humboldt, and surprising as it may be to them to find so high a value attached to individuality, the question, one must nevertheless think, can only be one of degree. No one's idea of excellence in conduct is that people should do absolutely nothing but copy one another. No one would assert that people ought not to put into their mode of life, and into the conduct of their concerns, any impress whatever of their own judgment, or of their own individual character. On the other hand, it would be absurd to pretend that people ought to live as if nothing whatever had been known in the world before they came into it; as if experience had as yet done nothing towards showing that one mode of existence, or conduct, is preferable to another. Nobody denies that people should be so taught and trained in youth, as to know and benefit by the ascertained results of human experience. But it is the privilege and proper condition of a human being, arrived at the maturity of his faculties, to use and interpret experience in his own way. It is for him to find out what part of recorded experience is properly applicable to his own circumstances and character. The traditions and customs of other people are, to a certain extent, evidence of what their experience has taught *them;* presumptive evidence, and as such, have a claim to his deference: but, in the first place, their experience may be too narrow; or they may not have interpreted it rightly. Secondly, their interpretation of experience may be

1. From *The Sphere and Duties of Government,* by Baron Wilhelm von Humboldt (1767–1835), Prussian statesman and man of letters. Orig-inally written in 1791, this treatise was first published in Germany in 1852 and was translated into English in 1854.

correct, but unsuitable to him. Customs are made for customary circumstances, and customary characters; and his circumstances or his character may be uncustomary. Thirdly, though the customs be both good as customs, and suitable to him, yet to conform to custom, merely *as* custom, does not educate or develop in him any of the qualities which are the distinctive endowment of a human being. The human faculties of perception, judgment, discriminative feeling, mental activity, and even moral preference are exercised only in making a choice. He who does anything because it is the custom makes no choice. He gains no practice either in discerning or in desiring what is best. The mental and moral, like the muscular powers, are improved only by being used. The faculties are called into no exercise by doing a thing merely because others do it, no more than by believing a thing only because others believe it. If the grounds of an opinion are not conclusive to the person's own reason, his reason cannot be strengthened, but is likely to be weakened, by his adopting it: and if the inducements to an act are not such as are consentaneous[2] to his own feelings and character (where affection, or the rights of others, are not concerned) it is so much done towards rendering his feelings and character inert and torpid, instead of active and energetic.

He who lets the world, or his own portion of it, choose his plan of life for him has no need of any other faculty than the apelike one of imitation. He who chooses his plan for himself employs all his faculties. He must use observation to see, reasoning and judgment to foresee, activity to gather materials for decision, discrimination to decide, and when he has decided, firmness and self-control to hold to his deliberate decision. And these qualities he requires and exercises exactly in proportion as the part of his conduct which he determines according to his own judgment and feelings is a large one. It is possible that he might be guided in some good path, and kept out of harm's way, without any of these things. But what will be his comparative worth as a human being? It really is of importance, not only what men do, but also what manner of men they are that do it. Among the works of man, which human life is rightly employed in perfecting and beautifying, the first in importance surely is man himself. Supposing it were possible to get houses built, corn grown, battles fought, causes tried, and even churches erected and prayers said, by machinery—by automatons in human form—it would be a considerable loss to exchange for these automatons even the men and women who at present inhabit the more civilized parts of the world, and who assuredly are but starved specimens of what nature can and will produce. Human nature is not a machine to be built after a model, and set to do exactly the work prescribed for it, but a tree, which requires to grow and develop itself on all sides, according to the tendency of the inward forces

2. Agreeable.

which make it a living thing.

It will probably be conceded that it is desirable people should exercise their understandings, and that an intelligent following of custom, or even occasionally an intelligent deviation from custom, is better than a blind and simply mechanical adhesion to it. To a certain extent it is admitted that our understanding should be our own: but there is not the same willingness to admit that our desires and impulses should be our own likewise; or that to possess impulses of our own, and of any strength, is anything but a peril and a snare. Yet desires and impulses are as much a part of a perfect human being, as beliefs and restraints: and strong impulses are only perilous when not properly balanced; when one set of aims and inclinations is developed into strength, while others, which ought to coexist with them, remain weak and inactive. It is not because men's desires are strong that they act ill; it is because their consciences are weak. There is no natural connection between strong impulses and a weak conscience. The natural connection is the other way. To say that one person's desires and feelings are stronger and more various than those of another is merely to say that he has more of the raw material of human nature, and is therefore capable, perhaps of more evil, but certainly of more good. Strong impulses are but another name for energy. Energy may be turned to bad uses; but more good may always be made of an energetic nature than of an indolent and impassive one. Those who have most natural feeling are always those whose cultivated feelings may be made the strongest. The same strong susceptibilities which make the personal impulses vivid and powerful are also the source from whence are generated the most passionate love of virture, and the sternest self-control. It is through the cultivation of these that society both does its duty and protects its interests: not by rejecting the stuff of which heroes are made, because it knows not how to make them. A person whose desires and impulses are his own—are the expression of his own nature, as it has been developed and modified by his own culture—is said to have a character. One whose desires and impulses are not his own, has no character, no more than a steam engine has a character. If, in addition to being his own, his impulses are strong, and are under the government of a strong will, he has an energetic character. Whoever thinks that individuality of desires and impulses should not be encouraged to unfold itself must maintain that society has no need of strong natures—is not the better for containing many persons who have much character—and that a high general average of energy is not desirable.

In some early states of society, these forces might be, and were, too much ahead of the power which society then possessed of disciplining and controlling them. There has been a time when the element of spontaneity and individuality was in excess, and the social principle had a hard struggle with it. The difficulty then was to induce men of strong bodies or minds to pay obedience to any rules which required them to control their impulses. To overcome this difficulty, law and discipline, like the Popes struggling against the Emperors, asserted a power over the whole man, claiming to control all his life in order to control his character—which society had not found any other sufficient means of binding. But society has now fairly got the better of individuality; and the danger which threatens human nature is not the excess, but the deficiency, of personal impulses and preferences. Things are vastly changed, since the passions of those who were strong by station or by personal endowment were in a state of habitual rebellion against laws and ordinances, and required to be rigorously chained up to enable the persons within their reach to enjoy any particle of security. In our times, from the highest class of society down to the lowest, everyone lives as under the eye of a hostile and dreaded censorship. Not only in what concerns others, but in what concerns only themselves, the individual or the family do not ask themselves—what do I prefer? or, what would suit my character and disposition? or, what would allow the best and highest in me to have fair play, and enable it to grow and thrive? They ask themselves, what is suitable to my position? what is usually done by persons of my station and pecuniary circumstances? or (worse still) what is usually done by persons of a station and circumstances superior to mine? I do not mean that they choose what is customary, in preference to what suits their own inclination. It does not occur to them to have any inclination, except for what is customary. Thus the mind itself is bowed to the yoke: even in what people do for pleasure, conformity is the first thing thought of; they like in crowds; they exercise choice only among things commonly done: peculiarity of taste, eccentricity of conduct, are shunned equally with crimes: until by dint of not following their own nature, they have no nature to follow: their human capacities are withered and starved: they become incapable of any strong wishes or native pleasures, and are generally without either opinions or feelings of home growth, or properly their own. Now is this, or is it not, the desirable condition of human nature?

It is so, on the Calvinistic theory. According to that, the one great offense of man is self-will. All the good of which humanity is capable is comprised in obedience. You have no choice; thus you must do, and no otherwise: "whatever is not a duty is a sin." Human nature being radically corrupt, there is no redemption for anyone until human nature is killed within him. To one holding this theory of life, crushing out any of the human faculties, capacities, and susceptibilities is no evil: man needs no capacity but that of surrendering himself to the will of God: and if he uses any of his faculties for any other purpose but to do that supposed will more effectually, he is better without them. This is the theory of Calvinism; and it is held, in a mitigated form, by many who do not consider themselves Calvinists; the mitigation consisting in giving a less ascetic interpretation to the alleged will of God; asserting it to be his will that mankind should gratify some of their inclinations; of course not in the manner they themselves prefer, but in the way of obedience, that is, in a way prescribed to them by authority; and, therefore, by the necessary conditions of the case, the same for all.

In some such insidious form there is at present a strong tendency to this narrow theory of life, and to the pinched and hidebound type of human character which it patronizes. Many persons, no doubt, sincerely think that human beings thus cramped and dwarfed are as their Maker designed them to be; just as many have thought that trees are a much finer thing when clipped into pollards,[3] or cut out into figures of animals, than as nature made them. But if it be any part of religion to believe that man was made by a good Being, it is more consistent with that faith to believe that this Being gave all human faculties that they might be cultivated and unfolded, not rooted out and consumed, and that he takes delight in every nearer approach made by his creatures to the ideal conception embodied in them, every increase in any of their capabilities of comprehension, of action, or of enjoyment. There is a different type of human excellence from the Calvinistic; a conception of humanity as having its nature bestowed on it for other purposes than merely to be abnegated. "Pagan self-assertion" is one of the elements of human worth, as well as "Christian self-denial."[4] There is a Greek ideal of self-development, which the Platonic and Christian ideal of self-government blends with, but does not supersede. It may be better to be a John Knox than an Alcibiades, but it is better to be a Pericles than either;[5] nor would a Pericles, if we had one in these days, be without anything good which belonged to John Knox.

It is not by wearing down into uniformity all that is individual in themselves, but by cultivating it and calling it forth, within the limits imposed by the rights and interests of others, that human beings become a noble and beautiful object of contemplation; and as the works partake the character of those who do them, by the same process human life also becomes rich, diversified, and animating, furnishing more abundant aliment to high thoughts and elevating feelings, and strengthening the tie which binds every individual to the race, by making the race infinitely better worth belonging to. In proportion to the development of his individuality, each person becomes more valuable to himself, and is therefore capable of being more valuable to others. There is a greater fullness

3. Trees that acquire an artificial shape by being cut back so as to produce a mass of dense foliage.
4. From the *Essays* (1848) of John Sterling, a minor writer and friend of Thomas Carlyle's.

5. John Knox (1505–72) was the stern Scottish Calvinist reformer; Alcibiades (450–404 B.C.) was a dissolute Athenian commander, and Pericles (500–429 B.C.) was a model statesman in Athens.

of life about his own existence, and when there is more life in the units there is more in the mass which is composed of them. As much compression as is necessary to prevent the stronger specimens of human nature from encroaching on the rights of others cannot be dispensed with; but for this there is ample compensation even in the point of view of human development. The means of development which the individual loses by being prevented from gratifying his inclinations to the injury of others are chiefly obtained at the expense of the development of other people. And even to himself there is a full equivalent in the better development of the social part of his nature, rendered possible by the restraint put upon the selfish part. To be held to rigid rules of justice for the sake of others develops the feelings and capacities which have the good of others for their object. But to be restrained in things not affecting their good, by their mere displeasure, develops nothing valuable, except such force of character as may unfold itself in resisting the restraint. If acquiesced in, it dulls and blunts the whole nature. To give any fair play to the nature of each, it is essential that different persons should be allowed to lead different lives. In proportion as this latitude has been exercised in any age, has that age been noteworthy to posterity. Even despotism does not produce its worst effects, so long as individuality exists under it; and whatever crushes individuality is despotism, by whatever name it may be called, and whether it professes to be enforcing the will of God or the injunctions of men.

Having said that Individuality is the same thing with development, and that it is only the cultivation of individuality which produces, or can produce, well-developed human beings, I might here close the argument: for what more or better can be said of any condition of human affairs than that it brings human beings themselves nearer to the best thing they can be? or what worse can be said of any obstruction to good than that it prevents this? Doubtless, however, these considerations will not suffice to convince those who most need convincing; and it is necessary further to show that these developed human beings are of some use to the undeveloped— to point out to those who do not desire liberty, and would not avail themselves of it, that they may be in some intelligible manner rewarded for allowing other people to make use of it without hindrance.

In the first place, then, I would suggest that they might possibly learn something from them. It will not be denied by anybody, that originality is a valuable element in human affairs. There is always need of persons not only to discover new truths, and point out when what were once truths are true no longer, but also to commence new practices, and set the example of more enlightened conduct, and better taste and sense in human life. This cannot well be gainsaid by anybody who does not believe that the world has already attained perfection in all its ways and practices. It is true that this benefit is not capable of being rendered by everybody alike: there are but few persons, in comparison with the whole of mankind, whose experiments, if adopted by others, would be likely to be any improvement on established practice. But these few are the salt of the earth; without them, human life would become a stagnant pool. Not only is it they who introduce good things which did not before exist; it is they who keep the life in those which already existed. If there were nothing new to be done, would human intellect cease to be necessary? Would it be a reason why those who do the old things should forget why they are done, and do them like cattle, not like human beings? There is only too great a tendency in the best beliefs and practices to degenerate into the mechanical; and unless there were a succession of persons whose ever-recurring originality prevents the grounds of those beliefs and practices from becoming merely traditional, such dead matter would not resist the smallest shock from anything really alive, and there would be no reason why civilization should not die out, as in the Byzantine Empire. Persons of genius, it is true, are, and are always likely to be, a small minority; but in order to have them, it is necessary to preserve the soil in which they grow. Genius can only breathe freely in an *atmosphere* of freedom. Persons of genius are, *ex vi termini*,[6] *more* individual than any other people—less capable, consequently, of fitting themselves, without hurtful compression, into any of the small number of molds which society provides in order to save its members the trouble of forming their own character. If from timidity they consent to be forced into one of these molds, and to let all that part of themselves which cannot expand under the pressure remain unexpanded, society will be little the better for their genius. If they are of a strong character, and break their fetters, they become a mark for the society which has not succeeded in reducing them to commonplace, to point at with solemn warning as "wild," "erratic," and the like; much as if one should complain of the Niagara River for not flowing smoothly between its banks like a Dutch canal.

I insist thus emphatically on the importance of genius, and the necessity of allowing it to unfold itself freely both in thought and in practice, being well aware that no one will deny the position in theory, but knowing also that almost everyone, in reality, is totally indifferent to it. People think genius a fine thing if it enables a man to write an exciting poem, or paint a picture. But in its true sense, that of originality in thought and action, though no one says that it is not a thing to be admired, nearly all, at heart, think that they can do very well without it. Unhappily this is too natural to be wondered at. Originality is the one thing which unoriginal minds cannot feel the use of. They cannot see what it is to do for

6. Latin for "by force of the term," i.e., by definition.

them: how should they? If they could see what it would do for them, it would not be originality. The first service which originality has to render them is that of opening their eyes: which being once fully done, they would have a chance of being themselves original. Meanwhile, recollecting that nothing was ever yet done which some-one was not the first to do, and that all good things which exist are the fruits of originality, let them be modest enough to believe that there is something still left for it to accomplish, and assure themselves that they are more in need of originality, the less they are conscious of the want.

In sober truth, whatever homage may be professed, or even paid, to real or supposed mental superiority, the general tendency of things throughout the world is to render mediocrity the ascendant power among mankind. In ancient history, in the middle ages, and in a diminishing degree through the long transition from feudality to the present time, the individual was a power in himself; and if he had either great talents or a high social position, he was a considerable power. At present individuals are lost in the crowd. In politics it is almost a triviality to say that public opinion now rules the world. The only power deserving the name is that of masses, and of governments while they make themselves the organ of the tendencies and instincts of masses. This is as true in the moral and social relations of private life as in public transactions. Those whose opinions go by the name of public opinion, are not always the same sort of public: in America they are the whole white population; in England, chiefly the middle class. But they are always a mass, that is to say, collective mediocrity. And what is a still greater novelty, the mass do not now take their opinions from dignitaries in Church or State, from ostensible leaders, or from books. Their thinking is done for them by men much like themselves, addressing them or speaking in their name, on the spur of the moment, through the newspapers. I am not complaining of all this. I do not assert that anything better is compatible, as a general rule, with the present low state of the human mind. But that does not hinder the government of mediocrity from being mediocre government. No government by a democracy or a numerous aristocracy, either in its political acts or in the opinions, qualities, and tone of mind which it fosters, ever did or could rise above mediocrity, except in so far as the sovereign Many have let themselves be guided (which in their best times they always have done) by the counsels and influence of a more highly gifted and instructed One or Few. The initiation of all wise or noble things, comes and must come from individuals; generally at first from some one individual. The honor and glory of the average man is that he is capable of following that initiative; that he can respond internally to wise and noble things, and be led to them with his eyes open. I am not countenancing the sort of "hero worship" which applauds the strong man of genius for forcibly

seizing on the government of the world and making it do his bidding in spite of itself. All he can claim is freedom to point out
the way. The power of compelling others into it is not only inconsistent with the freedom and development of all the rest, but corrupting to the strong man himself. It does seem, however, that
when the opinions of masses of merely average men are everywhere
become or becoming the dominant power, the counterpoise and
corrective to that tendency would be the more and more pronounced
individuality of those who stand on the higher eminences of thought.
It is in these circumstances most especially that exceptional individuals, instead of being deterred, should be encouraged in acting
differently from the mass. In other times there was no advantage in
their doing so, unless they acted not only differently, but better. In
this age, the mere example of nonconformity, the mere refusal to
bend the knee to custom, is itself a service. Precisely because the
tyranny of opinion is such as to make eccentricity a reproach, it is
desirable, in order to break through that tyranny, that people
should be eccentric. Eccentricity has always abounded when and
where strength of character has abounded; and the amount of eccentricity in a society has generally been proportional to the amount
of genius, mental vigor, and moral courage which it contained. That
so few now dare to be eccentric marks the chief danger of the
time. * * *

There is one characteristic of the present direction of public
opinion, peculiarly calculated to make it intolerant of any marked
demonstration of individuality. The general average of mankind
are not only moderate in intellect, but also moderate in inclinations: they have no tastes or wishes strong enough to incline them
to do anything unusual, and they consequently do not understand
those who have, and class all such with the wild and intemperate
whom they are accustomed to look down upon. Now, in addition to
this fact which is general, we have only to suppose that a strong
movement has set in towards the improvement of morals, and it is
evident what we have to expect. In these days such a movement has
set in; much has actually been effected in the way of increased
regularity of conduct, and discouragement of excesses; and there
is a philanthropic spirit abroad, for the exercise of which there
is no more inviting field than the moral and prudential improvement of our fellow creatures. These tendencies of the times cause
the public to be more disposed than at most former periods to prescribe general rules of conduct, and endeavor to make everyone
conform to the approved standard. And that standard, express or
tacit, is to desire nothing strongly. Its ideal of character is to be
without any marked character; to maim by compression, like a
Chinese lady's foot, every part of human nature which stands out
prominently, and tends to make the person markedly dissimilar in
outline to commonplace humanity.

As is usually the case with ideals which exclude one half of what is desirable, the present standard of approbation produces only an inferior imitation of the other half. Instead of great energies guided by vigorous reason, and strong feelings strongly controlled by a conscientious will, its result is weak feelings and weak energies, which therefore can be kept in outward conformity to rule without any strength either of will or reason. Already energetic characters on any large scale are becoming merely traditional. There is now scarcely any outlet for energy in this country except business. The energy expended in this may still be regarded as considerable. What little is left from that employment, is expended on some hobby; which may be a useful, even a philanthropic hobby, but is always some one thing, and generally a thing of small dimensions. The greatness of England is now all collective: individually small, we only appear capable of anything great by our habit of combining; and with this our moral and religious philanthropies are perfectly contented. But it was men of another stamp than this that made England what it has been; and men of another stamp will be needed to prevent its decline.

The despotism of custom is everywhere the standing hindrance to human advancement, being in unceasing antagonism to that disposition to aim at something better than customary, which is called, according to circumstances, the spirit of liberty, or that of progress or improvement. The spirit of improvement is not always a spirit of liberty, for it may aim at forcing improvements on an unwilling people; and the spirit of liberty, in so far as it resists such attempts, may ally itself locally and temporarily with the opponents of improvement; but the only unfailing and permanent source of improvement is liberty, since by it there are as many possible independent centers of improvement as there are individuals. The progressive principle, however, in either shape, whether as the love of liberty or of improvement, is antagonistic to the sway of Custom, involving at least emancipation from that yoke; and the contest between the two constitutes the chief interest of the history of mankind. The greater part of the world has, properly speaking, no history, because the depotism of Custom is complete. This is the case over the whole East. Custom is there, in all things, the final appeal; justice and right mean conformity to custom; the argument of custom no one, unless some tyrant intoxicated with power, thinks of resisting. And we see the result. Those nations must once have had originality; they did not start out of the ground populous, lettered, and versed in many of the arts of life; they made themselves all this, and were then the greatest and most powerful nations of the world. What are they now? The subjects or dependants of tribes whose forefathers wandered in the forests when theirs had magnificent palaces and gorgeous temples, but over whom custom exercised only a divided rule with liberty and progress. A people, it appears, may be progressive for a certain length of time, and then stop: when does it stop? When it ceases to possess individuality. If a similar change should befall the nations of Europe, it will not be in exactly the same shape: the despotism of custom with which these nations arc threatened is not precisely stationariness. It proscribes singularity, but it does not preclude change, provided all change together. We have discarded the fixed costumes of our forefathers; everyone must still dress like other people, but the fashion may change once or twice a year. We thus take care that when there is change it shall be for change's sake, and not from any idea of beauty or convenience; for the same idea of beauty or convenience would not strike all the world at the same moment, and be simultaneously thrown aside by all at another moment. But we are progressive as well as changeable: we continually make new inventions in mechanical things, and keep them until they are again superseded by better; we are eager for improvement in politics, in education, even in morals, though in this last our idea of improvement chiefly consists in persuading or forcing other people to be as good as ourselves. It is not progress that we object to; on the contrary, we flatter ourselves that we are the most progressive people who ever lived. It is individuality that we war against: we should think we had done wonders if we had made ourselves all alike; forgetting that the unlikeness of one person to another is generally the first thing which draws the attention of either to the imperfection of his own type, and the superiority of another, or the possibility, by combining the advantages of both, of producing something better than either. We have a warning example in China—a nation of much talent, and, in some respects, even wisdom, owing to the rare good fortune of having been provided at an early period with a particularly good set of customs, the work, in some measure, of men to whom even the most enlightened European must accord, under certain limitations, the title of sages and philosophers. They are remarkable, too, in the excellence of their apparatus for impressing, as far as possible, the best wisdom they possess upon every mind in the community, and securing that those who have appropriated most of it shall occupy the posts of honor and power. Surely the people who did this have discovered the secret of human progressiveness, and must have kept themselves steadily at the head of the movement of the world. On the contrary, they have become stationary—have remained so for thousands of years; and if they are ever to be farther improved, it must be by foreigners. They have succeeded beyond all hope in what English philanthropists are so industriously working at—in making a people all alike, all governing their thoughts and conduct by the same maxims and rules; and these are the fruits. The modern regime of public opinion is, in an unorganized form, what the Chinese educational and political systems are in an organized; and unless individuality shall be able successfully to assert itself against this yoke, Europe, notwithstanding its noble antecedents and its professed Christianity, will tend to become another China. * * *

1859

From Autobiography

From *Chapter V. A Crisis in My Mental History.*
One Stage Onward

For some years after this time[1] I wrote very little, and nothing regularly, for publication: and great were the advantages which I derived from the intermission. It was of no common importance to me, at this period, to be able to digest and mature my thoughts for my own mind only, without any immediate call for giving them out in print. Had I gone on writing, it would have much disturbed the important transformation in my opinions and character, which took place during those years. The origin of this transformation, or at least the process by which I was prepared for it, can only be explained by turning some distance back.

From the winter of 1821, when I first read Bentham, and especially from the commencement of the *Westminster Review*, I had what might truly be called an object in life; to be a reformer of the world. My conception of my own happiness was entirely identified with this object. The personal sympathies I wished for were those of fellow laborers in this enterprise. I endeavored to pick up as many flowers as I could by the way; but as a serious and permanent personal satisfaction to rest upon, my whole reliance was placed on this; and I was accustomed to felicitate myself on the certainty of a happy life which I enjoyed, through placing my happiness in something durable and distant, in which some progress might be always making, while it could never be exhausted by complete attainment. This did very well for several years, during which the general improvement going on in the world and the idea of myself as engaged with others in struggling to promote it, seemed enough to fill up an interesting and animated existence. But the time came when I awakened from this as from a dream. It was in the autumn of 1826. I was in a dull state of nerves, such as everybody is occasionally liable to; unsusceptible to enjoyment or pleasurable excitement; one of those moods when what is pleasure at other times becomes insipid or indifferent; the state, I should think, in which converts to Methodism usually are, when smitten by their first "conviction of sin." In this frame of mind it occurred to me to put

1. 1828. Mill had been contributing articles to the *Westminster Review*.

the question directly to myself: "Suppose that all your objects in life were realized; that all the changes in institutions and opinions which you are looking forward to could be completely effected at this very instant: would this be a great joy and happiness to you?" And an irrepressible self-consciousness distinctly answered, "No!" At this my heart sank within me: the whole foundation on which my life was constructed fell down. All my happiness was to have been found in the continual pursuit of this end. The end had ceased to charm, and how could there ever again be any interest in the means? I seemed to have nothing left to live for.

At first I hoped that the cloud would pass away of itself; but it did not. A night's sleep, the sovereign remedy for the smaller vexations of life, had no effect on it. I awoke to a renewed consciousness of the woeful fact. I carried it with me into all companies, into all occupations. Hardly anything had power to cause me even a few minutes' oblivion of it. For some months the cloud seemed to grow thicker and thicker. The lines in Coleridge's *Dejection*—I was not then acquainted with them—exactly describe my case:

> A grief without a pang, void, dark and drear,
> A drowsy, stifled, unimpassioned grief,
> Which finds no natural outlet or relief
> In word, or sigh, or tear.[2]

In vain I sought relief from my favorite books; those memorials of past nobleness and greatness from which I had always hitherto drawn strength and animation. I read them now without feeling, or with the accustomed feeling minus all its charm; and I became persuaded that my love of mankind, and of excellence for its own sake, had worn itself out. I sought no comfort by speaking to others of what I felt. If I had loved anyone sufficiently to make confiding my griefs a necessity, I should not have been in the condition I was. I felt, too, that mine was not an interesting, or in any way respectable distress. There was nothing in it to attract sympathy. Advice, if I had known where to seek it, would have been most precious. The words of Macbeth to the physician[3] often occurred to my thoughts. But there was no one on whom I could build the faintest hope of such assistance. My father, to whom it would have been natural to me to have recourse in any practical difficulties, was the last person to whom, in such a case as this, I looked for help. Everything convinced me that he had no knowledge of any such mental state as I was suffering from, and that even if he could be made to understand it, he was not the physician who could heal it. My education, which was wholly his work, had been conducted without any regard to the possibility of its ending in this result; and I saw no use in giving him the pain of thinking

2. *Dejection: An Ode*, lines 21–24.
3. "Canst thou not minister to a   mind   diseas'd * * * ?" (*Macbeth* V.iii.40–44).

that his plans had failed, when the failure was probably irremediable, and, at all events, beyond the power of *his* remedies. Of other friends, I had at that time none to whom I had any hope of making my condition intelligible. It was however abundantly intelligible to myself; and the more I dwelt upon it, the more hopeless it appeared.

My course of study had led me to believe that all mental and moral feelings and qualities, whether of a good or of a bad kind, were the results of association; that we love one thing, and hate another, take pleasure in one sort of action or contemplation, and pain in another sort, through the clinging of pleasurable or painful ideas to those things, from the effect of education or of experience. As a corollary from this, I had always heard it maintained by my father, and was myself convinced, that the object of education should be to form the strongest possible associations of the salutary class; associations of pleasure with all things beneficial to the great whole, and of pain with all things hurtful to it. This doctrine appeared inexpugnable; but it now seemed to me, on retrospect, that my teachers had occupied themselves but superficially with the means of forming and keeping up these salutary associations. They seemed to have trusted altogether to the old familiar instruments, praise and blame, reward and punishment. Now, I did not doubt that by these means, begun early, and applied unremittingly, intense associations of pain and pleasure, especially of pain, might be created, and might produce desires and aversions capable of lasting undiminished to the end of life. But there must always be something artificial and casual in associations thus produced. The pains and pleasures thus forcibly associated with things are not connected with them by any natural tie; and it is therefore, I thought, essential to the durability of these associations that they should have beome so intense and inveterate as to be practically indissoluble, before the habitual exercise of the power of analysis had commenced. For I now saw, or thought I saw, what I had always before received with incredulity—that the habit of analysis has a tendency to wear away the feelings: as indeed it has, when no other mental habit is cultivated, and the analyzing spirit remains without its natural complements and correctives. The very excellence of analysis (I argued) is that it tends to weaken and undermine whatever is the result of prejudice; that it enables us mentally to separate ideas which have only casually clung together: and no associations whatever could ultimately resist this dissolving force, were it not that we owe to analysis our clearest knowledge of the permanent sequences in nature; the real connections between Things, not dependent on our will and feelings; natural laws, by virtue of which, in many cases, one thing is inseparable from another in fact; which laws, in proportion as they are clearly perceived and imaginatively realized, cause our ideas of things which are always joined together in Nature to cohere more and more closely in our thoughts. Analytic habits may thus even strengthen the associations between causes and effects, means and ends, but tend altogether to weaken those which are, to speak familiarly, a *mere* matter of feeling. They are therefore (I thought) favorable to prudence and clear-sightedness, but a perpetual worm at the root both of the passions and of the virtues; and, above all, fearfully undermine all desires, and all pleasures, which are the effects of association, that is, according to the theory I held, all except the purely physical and organic; of the entire insufficiency of which to make life desirable, no one had a stronger conviction than I had. These were the laws of human nature, by which, as it seemed to me, I had been brought to my present state. All those to whom I looked up were of opinion that the pleasure of sympathy with human beings, and the feelings which made the good of others, and especially of mankind on a large scale, the object of existence, were the greatest and surest sources of happiness. Of the truth of this I was convinced, but to know that a feeling would make me happy if I had it, did not give me the feeling. My education, I thought, had failed to create these feelings in sufficient strength to resist the dissolving influence of analysis, while the whole course of my intellectual cultivation had made precocious and premature analysis the inveterate habit of my mind. I was thus, as I said to myself, left stranded at the commencement of my voyage, with a well-equipped ship and a rudder, but no sail; without any real desire for the ends which I had been so carefully fitted out to work for: no delight in virtue, or the general good, but also just as little in anything else. The fountains of vanity and ambition seemed to have dried up within me, as completely as those of benevolence. I had had (as I reflected) some gratification of vanity at too early an age: I had obtained some distinction, and felt myself of some importance, before the desire of distinction and of importance had grown into a passion: and little as it was which I had attained, yet having been attained too early, like all pleasures enjoyed too soon, it had made me *blasé* and indifferent to the pursuit. Thus neither selfish nor unselfish pleasures were pleasures to me. And there seemed no power in nature sufficient to begin the formation of my character anew, and create in a mind now irretrievably analytic, fresh associations of pleasure with any of the objects of human desire.

These were the thoughts which mingled with the dry heavy dejection of the melancholy winter of 1826–7. During this time I was not incapable of my usual occupations. I went on with them mechanically, by the mere force of habit. I had been so drilled in a certain sort of mental exercise that I could still carry it on when all the spirit had gone out of it. I even composed and spoke several speeches at the debating society, how, or with what degree of success, I know not. Of four years continual speaking at that society, this is the only year of which I remember next to nothing. Two lines of Coleridge, in whom alone of all writers I have found a true description of what I felt, were often in my thoughts, not at this time (for I had never read them), but in a later period of the same mental malady:

> Work without hope draws nectar in a sieve,
> And hope without an object cannot live.[4]

In all probability my case was by no means so peculiar as I fancied it, and I doubt not that many others have passed through a similar state; but the idiosyncrasies of my education had given to the general phenomenon a special character, which made it seem the natural effect of causes that it was hardly possible for time to remove. I frequently asked myself if I could, or if I was bound to go on living, when life must be passed in this manner. I generally answered to myself, that I did not think I could possibly bear it beyond a year. When, however, not more than half that duration of time had elapsed, a small ray of light broke in upon my gloom. I was reading, accidentally, Marmontel's *Mémoires*,[5] and came to the passage which relates his father's death, the distressed position of the family, and the sudden inspiration by which he, then a mere boy, felt and made them feel that he would be everything to them—would supply the place of all that they had lost. A vivid conception of that scene and its feelings came over me, and I was moved to tears. From this moment my burden grew lighter. The oppression of the thought that all feeling was dead within me was gone. I was no longer hopeless: I was not a stock or a stone. I had still, it seemed, some of the material out of which all worth of character, and all capacity for happiness, are made. Relieved from my ever present sense of irremediable wretchedness, I gradually found that the ordinary incidents of life could again give me some pleasure; that I could again find enjoyment, not intense, but sufficient for cheerfulness, in sunshine and sky, in books, in conversation, in public affairs; and that there was, once more, excitement, though of a moderate kind, in exerting myself for my opinions, and for the public good. Thus the cloud gradually drew off, and I again enjoyed life: and though I had several relapses, some of which lasted many months, I never again was as miserable as I had been.

The experiences of this period had two very marked effects on my opinions and character. In the first place, they led me to adopt a theory of life, very unlike that on which I had before acted, and

---

4. From Coleridge's short poem *Work Without Hope.*   5. J. F. Marmontel (1723–99), whose *Mémoires* were published in 1804.

having much in common with what at that time I certainly had never heard of, the anti-self-consciousness theory of Carlyle.[6] I never, indeed, wavered in the conviction that happiness is the test of all rules of conduct, and the end of life. But I now thought that this end was only to be attained by not making it the direct end. Those only are happy (I thought) who have their minds fixed on some object other than their own happiness; on the happiness of others, on the improvement of mankind, even on some art or pursuit, followed not as a means, but as itself an ideal end. Aiming thus at something else, they find happiness by the way. The enjoyments of life (such was now my theory) are sufficient to make it a pleasant thing, when they are taken *en passant*, without being made a principal object. Once make them so, and they are immediately felt to be insufficient. They will not bear a scrutinizing examination. Ask yourself whether you are happy, and you cease to be so. The only chance is to treat, not happiness, but some end external to it, as the purpose of life. Let your self-consciousness, your scrutiny, your self-interrogation exhaust themselves on that; and if otherwise fortunately circumstanced you will inhale happiness with the air you breathe, without dwelling on it or thinking about it, without either forestalling it in imagination, or putting it to flight by fatal questioning. This theory now became the basis of my philosophy of life. And I still hold to it as the best theory for all those who have but a moderate degree of sensibility and of capacity for enjoyment, that is, for the great majority of mankind.

The other important change which my opinions at this time underwent was that I, for the first time, gave its proper place, among the prime necessities of human well-being, to the internal culture of the individual. I ceased to attach almost exclusive importance to the ordering of outward circumstances, and the training of the human being for speculation and for action.

I had now learnt by experience that the passive susceptibilities needed to be cultivated as well as the active capacities, and required to be nourished and enriched as well as guided. I did not, for an instant, lose sight of, or undervalue, that part of the truth which I had seen before; I never turned recreant to intellectual culture, or ceased to consider the power and practice of analysis as an essential condition both of individual and of social improvement. But I thought that it had consequences which required to be corrected, by joining other kinds of cultivation with it. The maintenance of a due balance among the faculties now seemed to me of primary importance. The cultivation of the feelings became one of the cardinal points in my ethical and philosophical creed. And my thoughts and inclinations turned in an increasing degree toward

---

6. See Carlyle's *Characteristics* and Chapter IX of *Sartor Resartus,* "The Everlasting Yea."

whatever seemed capable of being instrumental to that object.

I now began to find meaning in the things which I had read or heard about the importance of poetry and art as instruments of human culture. But it was some time longer before I began to know this by personal experience. The only one of the imaginative arts in which I had from childhood taken great pleasure was music; the best effect of which (and in this it surpasses perhaps every other art) consists in exciting enthusiasm; in winding up to a high pitch those feelings of an elevated kind which are already in the character, but to which this excitement gives a glow and a fervor, which, though transitory at its utmost height, is precious for sustaining them at other times. This effect of music I had often experienced; but like all my pleasurable susceptibilities it was suspended during the gloomy period. I had sought relief again and again from this quarter, but found none. After the tide had turned, and I was in process of recovery, I had been helped forward by music, but in a much less elevated manner. I at this time first became acquainted with Weber's *Oberon*,[7] and the extreme pleasure which I drew from its delicious melodies did me good, by showing me a source of pleasure to which I was as susceptible as ever. The good, however, was much impaired by the thought that the pleasure of music (as is quite true of such pleasure as this was, that of mere tune) fades with familiarity, and requires either to be revived by intermittence, or fed by continual novelty. And it is very characteristic both of my then state, and of the general tone of my mind at this period of my life, that I was seriously tormented by the thought of the exhaustibility of musical combinations. The octave consists only of five tones and two semitones, which can be put together in only a limited number of ways, of which but a small proportion are beautiful: most of these, it seemed to me, must have been already discovered, and there could not be room for a long succession of Mozarts and Webers, to strike out, as these had done, entirely new and surpassingly rich veins of musical beauty. This source of anxiety may, perhaps, be thought to resemble that of the philosophers of Laputa,[8] who feared lest the sun should be burnt out. It was, however, connected with the best feature in my character, and the only good point to be found in my very unromantic and in no way honorable distress. For though my dejection, honestly looked at, could not be called other than egotistical, produced by the ruin, as I thought, of my fabric of happiness, yet the destiny of mankind in general was ever in my thoughts, and could not be separated from my own. I felt that the flaw in my life must be a flaw in life itself; that the question was whether, if the reformers of society and government could succeed in their objects, and every person in the

---

7. A romantic opera composed by Carl Maria von Weber (1786–1826).   8. See *Gulliver's Travels*, Part III.

community were free and in a state of physical comfort, the pleasures of life, being no longer kept up by struggle and privation, would cease to be pleasures. And I felt that unless I could see my way to some better hope than this for human happiness in general, my dejection must continue; but that if I could see such an outlet, I should then look on the world with pleasure; content as far as I was myself concerned, with any fair share of the general lot.

This state of my thoughts and feelings made the fact of my reading Wordsworth for the first time (in the autumn of 1828), an important event in my life. I took up the collection of his poems from curiosity, with no expectation of mental relief from it, though I had before resorted to poetry with that hope. In the worst period of my depression, I had read through the whole of Byron (then new to me), to try whether a poet, whose peculiar department was supposed to be that of the intenser feelings, could rouse any feeling in me. As might be expected, I got no good from this reading, but the reverse. The poet's state of mind was too like my own. His was the lament of a man who had worn out all pleasures, and who seemed to think that life, to all who possess the good things of it, must necessarily be the vapid, uninteresting thing which I found it. His Harold and Manfred had the same burden on them which I had; and I was not in a frame of mind to desire any comfort from the vehement sensual passion of his Giaours, or the sullenness of his Laras.[9] But while Byron was exactly what did not suit my condition, Wordsworth was exactly what did. I had looked into *The Excursion*[1] two or three years before, and found little in it; and I should probably have found as little had I read it at this time. But the miscellaneous poems, in the two-volume edition of 1815 (to which little of value was added in the latter part of the author's life), proved to be the precise thing for my mental wants at that particular juncture.

In the first place, these poems addressed themselves powerfully to one of the strongest of my pleasurable susceptibilities, the love of rural objects and natural scenery; to which I had been indebted not only for much of the pleasure of my life, but quite recently for relief from one of my longest relapses into depression. In this power of rural beauty over me, there was a foundation laid for taking pleasure in Wordsworth's poetry; the more so, as his scenery lies mostly among mountains, which, owing to my early Pyrenean excursion,[2] were my ideal of natural beauty. But Wordsworth would never have had any great effect on me, if he had merely placed

9. The heroes of some of Byron's early poems were usually gloomy and self-preoccupied. Mill refers here to *Childe Harold's Pilgrimage* (1812–18), *Manfred* (1817), *The Giaour* (1813) and *Lara* (1814).
1. A long meditative poem by Wordsworth, published in 1814.
2. At 15 Mill had been deeply affected by the landscape of the Pyrenees in Spain, a mountainous region which also made a strong impression upon Tennyson.

before me beautiful pictures of natural scenery. Scott does this still better than Wordsworth, and a very second-rate landscape does it more effectually than any poet. What made Wordsworth's poems a medicine for my state of mind, was that they expressed, not mere outward beauty, but states of feeling, and of thought colored by feeling, under the excitement of beauty. They seemed to be the very culture of the feelings, which I was in quest of. In them I seemed to draw from a source of inward joy, of sympathetic and imaginative pleasure, which could be shared in by all human beings; which had no connection with struggle or imperfection, but would be made richer by every improvement in the physical or social condition of mankind. From them I seemed to learn what would be the perennial sources of happiness, when all the greater evils of life shall have been removed. And I felt myself at once better and happier as I came under their influence. There have certainly been, even in our own age, greater poets than Wordsworth; but poetry of deeper and loftier feeling could not have done for me at that time what his did. I needed to be made to feel that there was real, permanent happiness in tranquil contemplation. Wordsworth taught me this, not only without turning away from, but with a greatly increased interest in the common feelings and common destiny of human beings. And the delight which these poems gave me proved that with culture of this sort, there was nothing to dread from the most confirmed habit of analysis. At the conclusion of the Poems came the famous *Ode*, falsely called Platonic, *Intimations of Immortality:* in which, along with more than his usual sweetness of melody and rhythm, and along with the two passages of grand imagery but bad philosophy so often quoted, I found that he too had had similar experience to mine; that he also had felt that the first freshness of youthful enjoyment of life was not lasting; but that he had sought for compensation, and found it, in the way in which he was now teaching me to find it. The result was that I gradually, but completely, emerged from my habitual depression, and was never again subject to it. I long continued to value Wordsworth less according to his intrinsic merits than by the measure of what he had done for me. Compared with the greatest poets, he may be said to be the poet of unpoetical natures, possessed of quiet and contemplative tastes. But unpoetical natures are precisely those which require poetic cultivation. This cultivation Wordsworth is much more fitted to give than poets who are intrinsically far more poets than he. * * *

1873

JOHN RUSKIN

(1819–1900)

John Ruskin was the leading Victorian critic of art and also an important
critic of society. These two roles can be traced back to two important influences of his childhood. His father, a wealthy wine merchant, was fond
of travel, and on tours of the Continent he introduced his son to beautiful
landscape, architecture, and art. From this exposure John Ruskin acquired
a zest for beauty that animates even the most theoretical of his discussions
of aesthetics. The second influence, often at variance with the first, was
his mother's exposing him to daily readings from the Bible. From this
Biblical indoctrination, Ruskin derived some elements of his lush and
highly rhythmical prose style, but more especially his sense of prophecy
and mission as a critic of modern society.

Ruskin's life was spent in traveling, lecturing, and writing. His prodigious
literary output can be roughly divided into three phases. In the first phase
he was preoccupied with problems of art. *Modern Painters,* which he began
writing at the age of 23 after his graduation from Oxford, was a defense
of the English landscape painter J. M. W. Turner (1775–1851). This defense (which was to extend to five volumes) involved Ruskin in problems
of truth in art (as in his chapter on the "Pathetic Fallacy") and in the
ultimate importance of imagination (as in his discussion of Turner's painting, "The Slave Ship").

During the 1850's Ruskin's principal interest shifted from art to architecture, especially to the problem of determining what kind of society is capable of producing great buildings. His enthusiasm for Gothic architecture
was infectious, and he has sometimes been blamed for the prevalence of
Gothic buildings on college campuses in America. A study of *The Stones
of Venice* (1851–53), however (especially the chapter included below),
will show that merely to revive the Gothic style was not his concern. What
he wanted to revive was the kind of society that had produced such architecture, a society in which the individual workman could express himself and
enjoy what Ruskin's disciple, William Morris, called "work-pleasure." A
mechanized production-line society, such as Ruskin's or our own, could
not produce Gothic architecture but only imitations of its mannerisms.
Ruskin's concern was to change industrial society, not to decorate concrete
towers with gargoyles.

This interest in the stultifying effects of industrialism led Ruskin finally
into economics. After 1860 the critic of art became (like his master,
Carlyle) an outspoken critic of laissez-faire economics. His conception of
the responsibilities of employers towards their workmen, as expounded in
Unto This Last (1860), was dismissed by his contemporaries as an absurdity. Although his position was essentially conservative, in the proper
sense of the word, he was regarded as a radical eccentric. Ruskin's realization that despite his fame he was becoming isolated and that the world
was continuing to move in directions opposite from those to which he

pointed may have contributed to the recurrent mental breakdowns from
which he suffered between 1870 and 1900. Also contributory may have
been his unhappiness in his relations with women. His marriage had ended
in 1854 when his wife left him to marry the Pre-Raphaelite painter John
Millais, and in later years he fell pathetically in love with a young girl,
Rose La Touche, from whom he was divided not only by the gap of age
but by religious differences.

During the last thirty years of his life, in spite of periods of mental illness, Ruskin remained active and productive. His publications during this
period include six volumes of his lectures on art which he had delivered
as Slade Professor of Fine Arts at Oxford, as well as his letters to workmen, *Fors Clavigera* (1871–84), and his autobiography, *Praeterita* (1885–
89).

Ruskin's fame as a critic of art and architecture was firmly established
during the mid-Victorian period. It was only at a later date, however, that
his influence as a critic of society was to make itself felt. Upon the founders of the British Labour Party as well as upon writers as diverse as William Morris, George Bernard Shaw, and D. H. Lawrence, his writings were
to have a profound effect.

From Modern Painters
["The Slave Ship"][1]

But I think the noblest sea that Turner has ever painted, and,
if so, the noblest certainly ever painted by man, is that of "The
Slave Ship," the chief Academy picture of the exhibition of 1840.[2]
It is a sunset on the Atlantic after prolonged storm; but the storm is
partially lulled, and the torn and streaming rain clouds are moving
in scarlet lines to lose themselves in the hollow of the night. The
whole surface of sea included in the picture is divided into two
ridges of enormous swell, not high, nor local, but a low, broad
heaving of the whole ocean, like the lifting of its bosom by deep-
drawn breath after the torture of the storm. Between these two
ridges the fire of the sunset falls along the trough of the sea, dyeing
it with an awful but glorious light, the intense and lurid splendor
which burns like gold and bathes like blood. Along this fiery path
and valley the tossing waves by which the swell of the sea is restlessly divided lift themselves in dark, indefinite, fantastic forms,
each casting a faint and ghastly shadow behind it along the illumined
foam. They do not rise everywhere, but three or four together in
wild groups, fitfully and furiously, as the under-strength of the swell
compels or permits them; leaving between them treacherous spaces
of level and whirling water, now lighted with green and lamplike

1. From Volume I, Part II, Section
v, Chapter 3.
2. The painting is of a ship in which
slaves are being transported. Victims
who have died during the passage are
being thrown overboard at sunset: as
Ruskin noted, "the near sea is encumbered with corpses." The "Academy" is the Royal Academy of Arts,
founded in London in 1768.

fire, now flashing back the gold of the declining sun, now fearfully dyed from above with the indistinguishable images of the burning clouds, which fall upon them in flakes of crimson and scarlet and give to the reckless waves the added motion of their own fiery flying. Purple and blue, the lurid shadows of the hollow breakers are cast upon the mist of night, which gathers cold and low, advancing like the shadow of death upon the guilty ship as it labors amidst the lightning of the sea, its thin masts written upon the sky in lines of blood, girded with condemnation in that fearful hue which signs the sky with horror, and mixes its flaming flood with the sunlight, and, cast far along the desolate heave of the sepulchral waves, incarnadines the multitudinous sea.[3]

I believe, if I were reduced to rest Turner's immortality upon any single work, I should choose this. Its daring conception—ideal in the highest sense of the word—is based on the purest truth, and wrought out with the concentrated knowledge of a life; its color is absolutely perfect, not one false or morbid hue in any part or line, and so modulated that every square inch of canvas is a perfect composition; its drawing as accurate as fearless; the ship buoyant, bending, and full of motion; its tones as true as they are wonderful; and the whole picture dedicated to the most sublime of subjects and impressions—completing thus the perfect system of all truth which we have shown to be formed by Turner's works—the power, majesty, and deathfulness of the open, deep, illimitable Sea.

1843

From *Of the Pathetic Fallacy*[4]

* * * Now, therefore, putting these tiresome and absurd words[5] quite out of our way, we may go on at our ease to examine the point in question—namely, the difference between the ordinary, proper, and true appearances of things to us; and the extraordinary, or false appearances, when we are under the influence of emotion, or contemplative fancy; false appearances, I say, as being entirely unconnected with any real power or character in the object, and only imputed to it by us.

For instance—

> The spendthrift crocus, bursting through the mold
> Naked and shivering, with his cup of gold.[6]

This is very beautiful, and yet very untrue. The crocus is not a spendthrift, but a hardy plant; its yellow is not gold, but saffron. How is it that we enjoy so much the having it put into our heads that it is anything else than a plain crocus?

3. See *Macbeth* II.ii.62.
4. From Volume III, Part IV, Chapter 12.
5. The metaphysical terms "objective" and "subjective" as applied to kinds of truth.
6. From a poem by Oliver Wendell Holmes.

It is an important question. For, throughout our past reasonings about art, we have always found that nothing could be good or useful, or ultimately pleasurable, which was untrue. But here is something pleasurable in written poetry, which is nevertheless *un-true*. And what is more, if we think over our favorite poetry, we shall find it full of this kind of fallacy, and that we like it all the more for being so.

It will appear also, on consideration of the matter, that this fallacy is of two principal kinds. Either, as in this case of the crocus, it is the fallacy of willful fancy, which involves no real expectation that it will be believed; or else it is a fallacy caused by an excited state of the feelings, making us, for the time, more or less irrational. Of the cheating of the fancy we shall have to speak presently; but, in this chapter, I want to examine the nature of the other error, that which the mind admits when affected strongly by emotion. Thus, for instance, in *Alton Locke*—

> They rowed her in across the rolling foam—
> The cruel, crawling foam.[7]

The foam is not cruel, neither does it crawl. The state of mind which attributes to it these characters of a living creature is one in which the reason is unhinged by grief. All violent feelings have the same effect. They produce in us a falseness in all our impressions of external things, which I would generally characterize as the "pathetic fallacy."

Now we are in the habit of considering this fallacy as eminently a character of poetical description, and the temper of mind in which we allow it, as one eminently poetical, because passionate. But, I believe, if we look well into the matter, that we shall find the greatest poets do not often admit this kind of falseness—that it is only the second order of poets who much delight in it.

Thus, when Dante describes the spirits falling from the bank of Acheron "as dead leaves flutter from a bough," [8] he gives the most perfect image possible of their utter lightness, feebleness, passiveness, and scattering agony of despair, without, however, for an instant losing his own clear perception that *these* are souls, and *those* are leaves: he makes no confusion of one with the other. But when Coleridge speaks of

> The one red leaf, the last of its clan,
> That dances as often as dance it can,[9]

he has a morbid, that is to say, a so far false, idea about the leaf: he fancies a life in it, and will, which there are not; confuses its powerlessness with choice, its fading death with merriment, and the wind that shakes it with music. Here, however, there is some

---

7. From Charles Kingsley's novel, *Al-ton Locke* (1850).
8. Dante, *Inferno* III.112.
9. *Christabel*, lines 49–50.

beauty, even in the morbid passage; but take an instance in Homer and Pope. Without the knowledge of Ulysses, Elpenor, his youngest follower, has fallen from an upper chamber in the Circean palace, and has been left dead, unmissed by his leader or companions, in the haste of their departure. They cross the sea to the Cimmerian land; and Ulysses summons the shades from Tartarus. The first which appears is that of the lost Elpenor. Ulysses, amazed, and in exactly the spirit of bitter and terrified lightness which is seen in Hamlet, addresses the spirit with the simple, startled words: "Elpenor! How camest thou under the shadowy darkness? Hast thou come faster on foot than I in my black ship?"[1] Which Pope renders thus:

> O, say, what angry power Elpenor led
> To glide in shades, and wander with the dead?
> How could thy soul, by realms and seas disjoined,
> Outfly the nimble sail, and leave the lagging wind?

I sincerely hope the reader finds no pleasure here, either in the nimbleness of the sail, or the laziness of the wind! And yet how is it that these conceits are so painful now, when they have been pleasant to us in the other instances?

For a very simple reason. They are not a *pathetic* fallacy at all, for they are put into the mouth of the wrong passion—a passion which never could possibly have spoken them—agonized curiosity. Ulysses wants to know the facts of the matter, and the very last thing his mind could do at the moment would be to pause, or suggest in anywise what was *not* a fact. The delay in the first three lines, and conceit in the last, jar upon us instantly, like the most frightful discord in music. No poet of true imaginative power could possibly have written the passage.

Therefore, we see that the spirit of truth must guide us in some sort, even in our enjoyment of fallacy. Coleridge's fallacy has no discord in it, but Pope's has set our teeth on edge. * * *

1856

From The Stones of Venice
[*The Savageness of Gothic Architecture*][2]

* * * I am not sure when the word "Gothic" was first generically applied to the architecture of the North; but I presume that, whatever the date of its original usage, it was intended to imply reproach, and express the barbaric character of the nations among whom that architecture arose. It never implied that they were literally of Gothic lineage, far less that their architecture had been

---

1. *Odyssey* XI.57.　　　　2. From Volume II, Chapter 6.

originally invented by the Goths themselves; but it did imply that they and their buildings together exhibited a degree of sternness and rudeness, which, in contradistinction to the character of Southern and Eastern nations, appeared like a perpetual reflection of the contrast between the Goth and the Roman in their first encounter. And when that fallen Roman, in the utmost impotence of his luxury, and insolence of his guilt, became the model for the imitation of civilized Europe,[3] at the close of the so-called Dark Ages, the word Gothic became a term of unmitigated contempt, not unmixed with aversion. From that contempt, by the exertion of the antiquaries and architects of this century, Gothic architecture has been sufficiently vindicated; and perhaps some among us, in our admiration of the magnificent science of its structure, and sacredness of its expression, might desire that the term of ancient reproach should be withdrawn, and some other, of more apparent honorableness, adopted in its place. There is no chance, as there is no need, of such a substitution. As far as the epithet was used scornfully, it was used falsely; but there is no reproach in the word, rightly understood; on the contrary, there is a profound truth, which the instinct of mankind almost unconsciously recognizes. It is true, greatly and deeply true, that the architecture of the North is rude and wild; but it is not true that, for this reason, we are to condemn it, or despise. Far otherwise: I believe it is in this very character that it deserves our profoundest reverence.

The charts of the world which have been drawn up by modern science have thrown into a narrow space the expression of a vast amount of knowledge, but I have never yet seen any one pictorial enough to enable the spectator to imagine the kind of contrast in physical character which exists between Northern and Southern countries. We know the differences in detail, but we have not that broad glance and grasp which would enable us to feel them in their fullness. We know that gentians grow on the Alps, and olives on the Apennines; but we do not enough conceive for ourselves that variegated mosaic of the world's surface which a bird sees in its migration, that difference between the district of the gentian and of the olive which the stork and the swallow see far off, as they lean upon the sirocco wind.[4] Let us, for a moment, try to raise ourselves even above the level of their flight, and imagine the Mediterranean lying beneath us like an irregular lake, and all its ancient promontories sleeping in the sun: here and there an angry spot of thunder, a gray stain of storm, moving upon the burning field; and here and

there a fixed wreath of white volcano smoke, surrounded by its circle
of ashes; but for the most part a great peacefulness of light, Syria
and Greece, Italy and Spain, laid like pieces of a golden pavement
into the sea-blue, chased, as we stoop nearer to them, with bossy
beaten work of mountain chains, and glowing softly with terraced
gardens, and flowers heavy with frankincense, mixed among masses
of laurel, and orange, and plumy palm, that abate with their gray-
green shadows the burning of the marble rocks, and of the ledges
of porphyry sloping under lucent sand. Then let us pass farther
towards the north, until we see the orient colors change gradually
into a vast belt of rainy green, where the pastures of Switzerland,
and poplar valleys of France, and dark forests of the Danube and
Carpathians stretch from the mouths of the Loire to those of
the Volga, seen through clefts in gray swirls of rain cloud and flaky
veils of the mist of the brooks, spreading low along the pasture
lands: and then, farther north still, to see the earth heave into
mighty masses of leaden rock and heathy moor, bordering with a
broad waste of gloomy purple that belt of field and wood, and
splintering into irregular and grisly islands amidst the northern
seas, beaten by storm, and chilled by ice drift, and tormented by
furious pulses of contending tide, until the roots of the last forests
fail from among the hill ravines, and the hunger of the north wind
bites their peaks into barrenness; and, at last, the wall of ice, durable
like iron, sets, deathlike, its white teeth against us out of the polar
twilight. And, having once traversed in thought this gradation of
the zoned iris of the earth in all its material vastness, let us go
down nearer to it, and watch the parallel change in the belt of
animal life: the multitudes of swift and brilliant creatures that
glance in the air and sea, or tread the sands of the southern zone;
striped zebras and spotted leopards, glistening serpents, and birds
arrayed in purple and scarlet. Let us contrast their delicacy and
brilliancy of color, and swiftness of motion, with the frost-cramped
strength, and shaggy covering, and dusky plumage of the northern
tribes; contrast the Arabian horse with the Shetland, the tiger and
leopard with the wolf and bear, the antelope with the elk, the bird
of paradise with the osprey: and then, submissively acknowledging
the great laws by which the earth and all that it bears are ruled
throughout their being, let us not condemn, but rejoice in the
expression by man of his own rest in the statutes of the lands that
gave him birth. Let us watch him with reverence as he sets side by
side the burning gems, and smooths with soft sculpture the jasper
pillars, that are to reflect a ceaseless sunshine, and rise into a cloudless sky: but not with less reverence let us stand by him, when, with
rough strength and hurried stroke, he smites an uncouth animation
out of the rocks which he has torn from among the moss of the
moorland, and heaves into the darkened air the pile of iron buttress

and rugged wall, instinct with work of an imagination as wild and wayward as the northern sea; creations of ungainly shape and rigid limb, but full of wolfish life; fierce as the winds that beat, and changeful as the clouds that shade them.

There is, I repeat, no degradation, no reproach in this, but all dignity and honorableness: and we should err grievously in refusing either to recognize as an essential character of the existing architecture of the North, or to admit as a desirable character in that which it yet may be, this wildness of thought, and roughness of work; this look of mountain brotherhood between the cathedral and the Alp; this magnificence of sturdy power, put forth only the more energetically because the fine finger-touch was chilled away by the frosty wind, and the eye dimmed by the moor mist, or blinded by the hail; this outspeaking of the strong spirit of men who may not gather redundant fruitage from the earth, nor bask in dreamy benignity of sunshine, but must break the rock for bread, and cleave the forest for fire, and show, even in what they did for their delight, some of the hard habits of the arm and heart that grew on them as they swung the ax or pressed the plow.

If, however, the savageness of Gothic architecture, merely as an expression of its origin among Northern nations, may be considered, in some sort, a noble character, it possesses a higher nobility still, when considered as an index, not of climate, but of religious principle.

In the 13th and 14th paragraphs of Chapter XXI of the first volume of this work, it was noticed that the systems of architectural ornament, properly so called, might be divided into three: (1) Servile ornament, in which the execution or power of the inferior workman is entirely subjected to the intellect of the higher; (2) Constitutional ornament, in which the executive inferior power is, to a certain point, emancipated and independent, having a will of its own, yet confessing its inferiority and rendering obedience to higher powers; and (3) Revolutionary ornament, in which no executive inferiority is admitted at all. I must here explain the nature of these divisions at somewhat greater length.

Of Servile ornament, the principal schools are the Greek, Ninevite, and Egyptian; but their servility is of different kinds. The Greek master-workman was far advanced in knowledge and power above the Assyrian or Egyptian. Neither he nor those for whom he worked could endure the appearance of imperfection in anything; and, therefore, what ornament he appointed to be done by those beneath him was composed of mere geometrical forms—balls, ridges, and perfectly symmetrical foliage—which could be executed with absolute precision by line and rule, and were as perfect in their way, when completed, as his own figure sculpture. The Assyrian and Egyptian, on the contrary, less cognizant of accurate form in anything, were content to allow their figure sculpture to be executed by inferior workmen, but lowered the method of its treatment to a standard which every workman could reach, and then trained him by discipline so rigid that there was no chance of his falling beneath the standard appointed. The Greek gave to the lower workman no subject which he could not perfectly execute. The Assyrian gave him subjects which he could only execute imperfectly, but fixed a legal standard for his imperfection. The workman was, in both systems, a slave.

But in the medieval, or especially Christian, system of ornament, this slavery is done away with altogether; Christianity having recognized, in small things as well as great, the individual value of every soul. But it not only recognizes its value; it confesses its imperfection, in only bestowing dignity upon the acknowledgment of unworthiness. That admission of lost power and fallen nature, which the Greek or Ninevite felt to be intensely painful, and, as far as might be, altogether refused, the Christian makes daily and hourly, contemplating the fact of it without fear, as tending, in the end, to God's greater glory. Therefore, to every spirit which Christianity summons to her service, her exhortation is: Do what you can, and confess frankly what you are unable to do; neither let your effort be shortened for fear of failure, nor your confession silenced for fear of shame. And it is, perhaps, the principal admirableness of the Gothic schools of architecture, that they thus receive the results of the labor of inferior minds; and out of fragments full of imperfection, and betraying that imperfection in every touch, indulgently raise up a stately and unaccusable whole.

But the modern English mind has this much in common with that of the Greek, that it intensely desires, in all things, the utmost completion or perfection compatible with their nature. This is a noble character in the abstract, but becomes ignoble when it causes us to forget the relative dignities of that nature itself, and to prefer the perfectness of the lower nature to the imperfection of the higher; not considering that as, judged by such a rule, all the brute animals would be preferable to man, because more perfect in their functions and kind, and yet are always held inferior to him, so also in the works of man, those which are more perfect in their kind are always inferior to those which are, in their nature, liable to more faults and shortcomings. For the finer the nature, the more flaws it will show through the clearness of it; and it is a law of this universe that the best things shall be seldomest seen in their best form. The wild grass grows well and strongly, one year with another; but the wheat is, according to the greater nobleness of its nature, liable to the bitterer blight. And therefore, while in all things that we see, or do, we are to desire perfection, and strive for it, we are nevertheless not to set the meaner thing, in its narrow accomplishment, above the nobler thing, in its mighty progress; not to esteem smooth minuteness above shattered majesty; not to prefer mean victory to honorable defeat; not to lower the level of our aim, that we may the more surely enjoy the complacency of success. But above all, in our dealings with the souls of other men, we are to take care how we check, by severe requirement or narrow caution, efforts which might otherwise lead to a noble issue; and, still more, how we withhold our admiration from great excellencies, because they are mingled with rough faults. Now, in the make and nature of every man, however rude or simple, whom we employ in manual labor, there are some powers for better things: some tardy imagination, torpid capacity of emotion, tottering steps of thought, there are, even at the worst; and in most cases it is all our own fault that they *are* tardy or torpid. But they cannot be strengthened, unless we are content to take them in their feebleness, and unless we prize and honor them in their imperfection above the best and most perfect manual skill. And this is what we have to do with all our laborers; to look for the *thoughtful* part of them, and get that out of them, whatever we lose for it, whatever faults and errors we are obliged to take with it. For the best that is in them cannot manifest itself, but in company with much error. Understand this clearly: You can teach a man to draw a straight line, and to cut one; to strike a curved line, and to carve it; and to copy and carve any number of given lines or forms, with admirable speed and perfect precision; and you find his work perfect of its kind: but if you ask him to think about any of those forms, to consider if he cannot find any better in his own head, he stops; his execution becomes hesitating; he thinks, and ten to one he thinks wrong; ten to one he makes a mistake in the first touch he gives to his work as a thinking being. But you have made a man of him for all that. He was only a machine before, an animated tool.

And observe, you are put to stern choice in this matter. You must either make a tool of the creature, or a man of him. You cannot make both. Men were not intended to work with the accuracy of tools, to be precise and perfect in all their actions. If you will have that precision out of them, and make their fingers measure degrees like cogwheels, and their arms strike curves like compasses, you must unhumanize them. All the energy of their spirits must be given to make cogs and compasses of themselves. All their attention and strength must go to the accomplishment of the mean act. The eye of the soul must be bent upon the finger point, and the soul's force must fill all the invisible nerves that guide it, ten hours a day, that it may not err from its steely precision, and so soul and sight be worn away, and the whole human being be lost at last—a heap of sawdust, so far as its intellectual work in this world is concerned; saved only by its Heart, which cannot go into the form of cogs and compasses, but expands, after the ten hours are over, into fireside humanity. On the other hand, if you will make a man of the working creature, you cannot make a tool. Let him but begin to imagine, to think, to try to do anything worth doing; and the engine-turned precision is lost at once. Out come all his roughness, all his dullness, all his incapability; shame upon shame, failure upon failure, pause after pause: but out comes the whole majesty of him also; and we know the height of it only, when we see the clouds settling upon him. And, whether the clouds be bright or dark, there will be transfiguration behind and within them.

And now, reader, look round this English room of yours, about which you have been proud so often, because the work of it was so good and strong, and the ornaments of it so finished. Examine again all those accurate moldings, and perfect polishings, and unerring adjustments of the seasoned wood and tempered steel. Many a time you have exulted over them, and thought how great England was, because her slightest work was done so thoroughly. Alas! if read rightly, these perfectnesses are signs of a slavery in our England a thousand times more bitter and more degrading than that of the scourged African, or helot[5] Greek. Men may be beaten, chained, tormented, yoked like cattle, slaughtered like summer flies, and yet remain in one sense, and the best sense, free. But to smother their souls within them, to blight and hew into rotting pollards[6] the suckling branches of their human intelligence, to make the flesh and skin which, after the worm's work on it, is to see God, into leathern thongs to yoke machinery with—this is to be slave-masters indeed; and there might be more freedom in England, though her feudal lords' lightest words were worth men's lives, and though the blood of the vexed husbandman dropped in the furrows of her fields, than there is while the animation of her multitudes is sent like fuel to feed the factory smoke, and the strength of them is given daily to be wasted into the fineness of a web, or racked into the exactness of a line.

And, on the other hand, go forth again to gaze upon the old cathedral front, where you have smiled so often at the fantastic ignorance of the old sculptors: examine once more those ugly goblins, and formless monsters, and stern statues, anatomiless and rigid; but do not mock at them, for they are signs of the life and liberty of every workman who struck the stone; a freedom of thought, and rank in scale of being, such as no laws, no charters, no charities can secure; but which it must be the first aim of all Europe at this day to regain for her children.

Let me not be thought to speak wildly or extravagantly. It is verily this degradation of the operative into a machine, which, more

5. A class of serfs in Sparta.   6. Trees with top branches cut back to the trunk.

than any other evil of the times, is leading the mass of the nations
everywhere into vain, incoherent, destructive struggling for a freedom of which they cannot explain the nature to themselves. Their
universal outcry against wealth, and against nobility, is not forced
from them either by the pressure of famine, or the sting of mortified
pride. These do much, and have done much in all ages; but the
foundations of society were never yet shaken as they are at this
day. It is not that men are ill fed, but that they have no pleasure
in the work by which they make their bread, and therefore look to
wealth as the only means of pleasure. It is not that men are pained
by the scorn of the upper classes, but they cannot endure their own;
for they feel that the kind of labor to which they are condemned
is verily a degrading one, and makes them less than men. Never had
the upper classes so much sympathy with the lower, or charity for
them, as they have at this day, and yet never were they so much
hated by them: for, of old, the separation between the noble and the
poor was merely a wall built by law; now it is a veritable difference
in level of standing, a precipice between upper and lower grounds
in the field of humanity, and there is pestilential air at the bottom of
it. I know not if a day is ever to come when the nature of right
freedom will be understood, and when men will see that to obey
another man, to labor for him, yield reverence to him or to his
place, is not slavery. It is often the best kind of liberty—liberty from
care. The man who says to one, Go, and he goeth, and to another,
Come, and he cometh, has, in most cases, more sense of restraint
and difficulty than the man who obeys him. The movements of the
one are hindered by the burden on his shoulder; of the other, by the
bridle on his lips: there is no way by which the burden may be
lightened; but we need not suffer from the bridle if we do not champ
at it. To yield reverence to another, to hold ourselves and our lives
at his disposal, is not slavery; often, it is the noblest state in which
a man can live in this world. There is, indeed, a reverence which is
servile, that is to say irrational or selfish: but there is also noble
reverence, that is to say, reasonable and loving; and a man is never
so noble as when he is reverent in this kind; nay, even if the feeling
pass the bounds of mere reason, so that it be loving, a man is raised
by it. Which had, in reality, most of the serf nature in him—the
Irish peasant who was lying in wait yesterday for his landlord, with
his musket muzzle thrust through the ragged hedge; or that old
mountain servant, who, 200 years ago, at Inverkeithing, gave up his
own life and the lives of his seven sons for his chief?[7]—as each
fell, calling forth his brother to the death, "Another for Hector!"
And therefore, in all ages and all countries, reverence has been paid
and sacrifice made by men to each other, not only without com-

7. An incident described in the Preface to Walter Scott's novel, *The Fair Maid
of Perth*.

plaint, but rejoicingly; and famine, and peril, and sword, and all evil, and all shame, have been borne willingly in the causes of masters and kings; for all these gifts of the heart ennobled the men who gave not less than the men who received them, and nature prompted, and God rewarded the sacrifice. But to feel their souls withering within them, unthanked, to find their whole being sunk into an unrecognized abyss, to be counted off into a heap of mechanism, numbered with its wheels, and weighed with its hammer strokes—this nature bade not—this God blesses not—this humanity for no long time is able to endure.

We have much studied and much perfected, of late, the great civilized invention of the division of labor; only we give it a false name. It is not, truly speaking, the labor that is divided; but the men: Divided into mere segments of men—broken into small fragments and crumbs of life; so that all the little piece of intelligence that is left in a man is not enough to make a pin, or a nail, but exhausts itself in making the point of a pin, or the head of a nail. Now it is a good and desirable thing, truly, to make many pins in a day; but if we could only see with what crystal sand their points were polished—sand of human soul, much to be magnified before it can be discerned for what it is—we should think there might be some loss in it also. And the great cry that rises from all our manufacturing cities, louder than their furnace blast, is all in very deed for this—that we manufacture everything there except men; we blanch cotton, and strengthen steel, and refine sugar, and shape pottery; but to brighten, to strengthen, to refine, or to form a single living spirit, never enters into our estimate of advantages. And all the evil to which that cry is urging our myriads can be met only in one way: not by teaching nor preaching, for to teach them is but to show them their misery, and to preach to them, if we do nothing more than preach, is to mock at it. It can be met only by a right understanding, on the part of all classes, of what kinds of labor are good for men, raising them, and making them happy; by a determined sacrifice of such convenience, or beauty, or cheapness as is to be got only by the degradation of the workman; and by equally determined demand for the products and results of healthy and ennobling labor.

And how, it will be asked, are these products to be recognized, and this demand to be regulated? Easily: by the observance of three broad and simple rules:

1. Never encourage the manufacture of any article not absolutely necessary, in the production of which *Invention* has no share.

2. Never demand an exact finish for its own sake, but only for some practical or noble end.

3. Never encourage imitation or copying of any kind, except for the sake of preserving record of great works.

The second of these principles is the only one which directly rises out of the consideration of our immediate subject; but I shall briefly explain the meaning and extent of the first also, reserving the enforcement of the third for another place.

1. Never encourage the manufacture of anything not necessary, in the production of which invention has no share.

For instance. Glass beads are utterly unnecessary, and there is no design or thought employed in their manufacture. They are formed by first drawing out the glass into rods; these rods are chopped up into fragments of the size of beads by the human hand, and the fragments are then rounded in the furnace. The men who chop up the rods sit at their work all day, their hands vibrating with a perpetual and exquisitely timed palsy, and the beads dropping beneath their vibration like hail. Neither they, nor the men who draw out the rods or fuse the fragments, have the smallest occasion for the use of any single human faculty; and every young lady, therefore, who buys glass beads is engaged in the slave trade, and in a much more cruel one than that which we have so long been endeavoring to put down.

But glass cups and vessels may become the subjects of exquisite invention; and if in buying these we pay for the invention, that is to say for the beautiful form, or color, or engraving, and not for mere finish of execution, we are doing good to humanity.

So, again, the cutting of precious stones, in all ordinary cases, requires little exertion of any mental faculty; some tact and judgment in avoiding flaws, and so on, but nothing to bring out the whole mind. Every person who wears cut jewels merely for the sake of their value is, therefore, a slave driver.

But the working of the goldsmith, and the various designing of grouped jewelry and enamel-work, may become the subject of the most noble human intelligence. Therefore, money spent in the purchase of well-designed plate, of precious engraved vases, cameos, or enamels, does good to humanity; and, in work of this kind, jewels may be employed to heighten its splendor; and their cutting is then a price paid for the attainment of a noble end, and thus perfectly allowable.

I shall perhaps press this law farther elsewhere, but our immediate concern is chiefly with the second, namely, never to demand an exact finish, when it does not lead to a noble end. For observe, I have only dwelt upon the rudeness of Gothic, or any other kind of imperfectness, as admirable, where it was impossible to get design or thought without it. If you are to have the thought of a rough and untaught man, you must have it in a rough and untaught way; but from an educated man, who can without effort express his thoughts in an educated way, take the graceful expression, and be thankful. Only *get* the thought, and do not silence the peasant because he cannot speak good grammar, or until you have taught him his grammar. Grammar and refinement are good things, both, only be sure of the better thing first. And thus in art, delicate finish is desirable from the greatest masters, and is always given by them. In some places Michael Angelo, Leonardo, Phidias, Perugino, Turner all finished with the most exquisite care; and the finish they give always leads to the fuller accomplishment of their noble purposes. But lower men than these cannot finish, for it requires consummate knowledge to finish consummately, and then we must take their thoughts as they are able to give them. So the rule is simple: Always look for invention first, and after that, for such execution as will help the invention, and as the inventor is capable of without painful effort, and *no more*. Above all, demand no refinement of execution where there is no thought, for that is slaves' work, unredeemed. Rather choose rough work than smooth work, so only that the practical purpose be answered, and never imagine there is reason to be proud of anything that may be accomplished by patience and sandpaper.

I shall only give one example, which however will show the reader what I mean, from the manufacture already alluded to, that of glass. Our modern glass is exquisitely clear in its substance, true in its form, accurate in its cutting. We are proud of this. We ought to be ashamed of it. The old Venice glass was muddy, inaccurate in all its forms, and clumsily cut, if at all. And the old Venetian was justly proud of it. For there is this difference between the English and Venetian workman, that the former thinks only of accurately matching his patterns, and getting his curves perfectly true and his edges perfectly sharp, and becomes a mere machine for rounding curves and sharpening edges, while the old Venetian cared not a whit whether his edges were sharp or not, but he invented a new design for every glass that he made, and never molded a handle or a lip without a new fancy in it. And therefore, though some Venetian glass is ugly and clumsy enough, when made by clumsy and uninventive workmen, other Venetian glass is so lovely in its forms that no price is too great for it; and we never see the same form in it twice. Now you cannot have the finish and the varied form too. If the workman is thinking about his edges, he cannot be thinking of his design; if of his design, he cannot think of his edges. Choose whether you will pay for the lovely form or the perfect finish, and choose at the same moment whether you will make the worker a man or a grindstone.

Nay, but the reader interrupts me—"If the workman can design beautifully, I would not have him kept at the furnace. Let him be taken away and made a gentleman, and have a studio, and design his glass there, and I will have it blown and cut for him by common workmen, and so I will have my design and my finish too."

All ideas of this kind are founded upon two mistaken suppositions: the first, that one man's thoughts can be, or ought to be, executed by another man's hands; the second, that manual labor is a degradation, when it is governed by intellect.

On a large scale, and in work determinable by line and rule, it is indeed both possible and necessary that the thoughts of one man should be carried out by the labor of others; in this sense I have already defined the best architecture to be the expression of the mind of manhood by the hands of childhood. But on a smaller scale, and in a design which cannot be mathematically defined, one man's thoughts can never be expressed by another: and the difference between the spirit of touch of the man who is inventing, and of the man who is obeying directions, is often all the difference between a great and a common work of art. How wide the separation is between original and secondhand execution, I shall endeavor to show elsewhere; it is not so much to our purpose here as to mark the other and more fatal error of despising manual labor when governed by intellect; for it is no less fatal an error to despise it when thus regulated by intellect, than to value it for its own sake. We are always in these days endeavoring to separate the two; we want one man to be always thinking, and another to be always working, and we call one a gentleman, and the other an operative; whereas the workman ought often to be thinking, and the thinker often to be working, and both should be gentlemen, in the best sense. As it is, we make both ungentle, the one envying, the other despising, his brother; and the mass of society is made up of morbid thinkers, and miserable workers. Now it is only by labor that thought can be made healthy, and only by thought that labor can be made happy, and the two cannot be separated with impunity. It would be well if all of us were good handicraftsmen in some kind, and the dishonor of manual labor done away with altogether; so that though there should still be a trenchant distinction of race between nobles and commoners, there should not, among the latter, be a trenchant distinction of employment, as between idle and working men, or between men of liberal and illiberal professions. All professions should be liberal, and there should be less pride felt in peculiarity of employment, and more in excellence of achievement. And yet more, in each several profession, no master should be too proud to do its hardest work. The painter should grind his own colors; the architect work in the mason's yard with his men; the master manufacturer be himself a more skillful operative than any man in his mills; and the distinction between one man and another be only in experience and skill, and the authority and wealth which these must naturally and justly obtain.

I should be led far from the matter in hand, if I were to pursue this interesting subject. Enough, I trust, has been said to show the reader that the rudeness or imperfection which at first rendered the term "Gothic" one of reproach is indeed, when rightly understood, one of the most noble characters of Christian architecture, and not only a noble but an *essential* one. It seems a fantastic paradox, but it is nevertheless a most important truth, that no architecture can be truly noble which is *not* imperfect. And this is easily demonstrable. For since the architect, whom we will suppose capable of doing all in perfection, cannot execute the whole with his own hands, he must either make slaves of his workmen in the old Greek, and present English fashion, and level his work to a slave's capacities, which is to degrade it; or else he must take his workmen as he finds them, and let them show their weaknesses together with their strength, which will involve the Gothic imperfection, but render the whole work as noble as the intellect of the age can make it.

But the principle may be stated more broadly still. I have confined the illustration of it to architecture, but I must not leave it as if true of architecture only. Hitherto I have used the words imperfect and perfect merely to distinguish between work grossly unskillful, and work executed with average precision and science; and I have been pleading that any degree of unskillfulness should be admitted, so only that the laborer's mind had room for expression. But, accurately speaking, no good work whatever can be perfect, and *the demand for perfection is always a sign of a misunderstanding of the ends of art.*

This for two reasons, both based on everlasting laws. The first, that no great man ever stops working till he has reached his point of failure; that is to say, his mind is always far in advance of his powers of execution, and the latter will now and then give way in trying to follow it; besides that he will always give to the inferior portions of his work only such inferior attention as they require; and according to his greatness he becomes so accustomed to the feeling of dissatisfaction with the best he can do, that in moments of lassitude or anger with himself he will not care though the beholder be dissatisfied also. I believe there has only been one man who would not acknowledge this necessity, and strove always to reach perfection, Leonardo; the end of his vain effort being merely that he would take ten years to a picture, and leave it unfinished. And therefore, if we are to have great men working at all, or less men doing their best, the work will be imperfect, however beautiful. Of human work none but what is bad can be perfect, in its own bad way.[8]

8. "The Elgin marbles are supposed by many persons to be 'perfect.' In the most important portions they indeed approach perfection, but only there. The draperies are unfinished, the hair and wool of the animals are unfinished, and the entire bas-reliefs of the frieze are roughtly cut" [Ruskin's note]. Ruskin is referring to the collection of statues brought from Athens to England by Lord Elgin, statues which were considered models of perfect realism.

The second reason is that imperfection is in some sort essential to all that we know of life. It is the sign of life in a mortal body, that is to say, of a state of progress and change. Nothing that lives is, or can be, rigidly perfect; part of it is decaying, part nascent. The foxglove blossom—a third part bud, a third part past, a third part in full bloom—is a type of the life of this world. And in all things that live there are certain irregularities and deficiencies which are not only signs of life, but sources of beauty. No human face is exactly the same in its lines on each side, no leaf perfect in its lobes, no branch in its symmetry. All admit irregularity as they imply change; and to banish imperfection is to destroy expression, to check exertion, to paralyze vitality. All things are literally better, lovelier, and more beloved for the imperfections which have been divinely appointed, that the law of human life may be Effort, and the law of human judgment, Mercy.

Accept this then for a universal law, that neither architecture nor any other noble work of man can be good unless it be imperfect; and let us be prepared for the otherwise strange fact, which we shall discern clearly as we approach the period of the Renaissance, that the first cause of the fall of the arts of Europe was a relentless requirement of perfection, incapable alike either of being silenced by veneration for greatness, or softened into forgiveness of simplicity.

Thus far then of the Rudeness or Savageness, which is the first mental element of Gothic architecture. It is an element in many other healthy architectures also, as in Byzantine and Romanesque; but true Gothic cannot exist without it. * * *

1851–53

THOMAS HENRY HUXLEY
(1825–1895)

In Victorian controversies over religion and education, one of the most distinctive participants was Thomas Henry Huxley, a scientist who wrote clear, readable, and very persuasive English prose. Huxley's literary skill was responsible for his being lured out of his laboratory onto the platforms of public debate where his role was to champion, as he said, "the application of scientific methods of investigation to all the problems of life."

Huxley, a schoolmaster's son, was born in a London suburb. Until beginning the study of medicine, at 17, he had had little formal education, having taught himself classical and modern languages as well as the rudiments of scientific theory. In 1846, after receiving his degree in medicine, he embarked on a long voyage to the South Seas during which he studied the marine life of the tropical oceans and established a considerable reputation as a zoologist. Later he made investigations in geology and physiology, completing a total of 250 research papers during his lifetime. He also held teaching positions and served on public committees, but it was as a popularizer of science that he made his real mark. His popularizing was of two kinds. The first was to make the results of scientific investigations intelligible to a large audience. Such lectures as *On a Piece of Chalk* (too long to include here) are models of clear, vivid exposition that can be studied with profit by anyone interested in the art of teaching. His second kind of popularizing consisted of expounding the values of scientific education or of the application of scientific thinking to problems in religion. Here Huxley excels not so much as a teacher as a debater. In 1860 he demonstrated his argumentative skill when, as Darwin's defender or "Bulldog," he demolished Bishop Wilberforce in a battle over *The Origin of Species*. In the 1870's, in such lectures as *Science and Culture*, he engaged in more genial fencing with Matthew Arnold concerning the relative importance of the study of science or the humanities in education. And in the 1880's he debated with Gladstone on the topic of interpreting the Bible. His essay *Agnosticism and Christianity* indicates his premises in this controversy.

Summing up his own career in his *Autobiography*, Huxley noted that he had subordinated his ambition for scientific fame to other ends: "to the popularization of science; to the development and organization of scientific education; to the endless series of battles and skirmishes over evolution; and to untiring opposition to that ecclesiastical spirit, that clericalism, which * * * to whatever denomination it may belong, is the deadly enemy of science." In fighting these "battles" Huxley operated from different bases. Most of the time he wrote as a biologist engaged in assessing all assumptions by the tests of laboratory science. In this role he argued that man is merely an animal and that traditional religion is a tissue of superstitions and lies. At other times, however, Huxley wrote as a humanist and even as a follower of Carlyle. As he stated in a letter: "*Sartor Resartus* led me to know that a deep sense of religion was compatible with the entire absence of theology." In this second role he argued that man is a very special kind of animal whose great distinction is that he is endowed with a moral sense and with freedom of the will, a creature who is admirable not for following nature but for departing from nature. The humanistic streak muddies the seemingly clear current of Huxley's thinking yet makes him a more interesting figure than he might otherwise have been. It is noteworthy that in the writings of his grandsons, Julian Huxley, the biologist, and Aldous Huxley, the novelist, a similar division of mind can once more be detected.

Even in his dying, T. H. Huxley continued his role as controversialist. The words he asked to be engraved on his tomb are typical of his view of life and typical, also, in the effect they had on his contemporaries, some of whom found the epitaph to be shocking:

> Be not afraid, ye waiting hearts that weep
> For still he giveth His beloved sleep,
> And if an endless sleep He wills, so best.

From A Liberal Education[1]
[A Game of Chess]

Suppose it were perfectly certain that the life and fortune of every one of us would, one day or other, depend upon his winning or losing a game of chess. Don't you think that we should all consider it to be a primary duty to learn at least the names and the moves of the pieces; to have a notion of a gambit,[2] and a keen eye for all the means of giving and getting out of check? Do you not think that we should look with a disapprobation amounting to scorn, upon the father who allowed his son, or the state which allowed its members, to grow up without knowing a pawn from a knight?

Yet it is a very plain and elementary truth that the life, the fortune, and the happiness of every one of us, and, more or less, of those who are connected with us, do depend upon our knowing something of the rules of a game infinitely more difficult and complicated than chess. It is a game which has been played for untold ages, every man and woman of us being one of the two players in a game of his or her own. The chessboard is the world, the pieces are the phenomena of the universe, the rules of the game are what we call the laws of Nature. The player on the other side is hidden from us. We know that his play is always fair, just, and patient. But also we know, to our cost, that he never overlooks a mistake, or makes the smallest allowance for ignorance. To the man who plays well, the highest stakes are paid, with that sort of overflowing generosity with which the strong shows delight in strength. And one who plays ill is checkmated—without haste, but without remorse.

My metaphor will remind some of you of the famous picture in which Retzsch[3] has depicted Satan playing at chess with man for his soul. Substitute for the mocking fiend in that picture a calm, strong angel who is playing for love, as we say, and would rather lose than win—and I should accept it as an image of human life.

Well, what I mean by Education is learning the rules of this mighty game. In other words, education is the instruction of the intellect in the laws of Nature, under which name I include not merely things and their forces, but men and their ways; and the fashioning of the affections and of the will into an earnest and loving desire to move in harmony with those laws. For me, education means neither more nor less than this. Anything which professes to call itself education must be tried by this standard, and if it

1. Originally an address, delivered at the South London Working Men's College in 1868.
2. Opening move in chess.
3. Friedrich A. M. Retzsch (1779–1857), German painter.

fails to stand the test, I will not call it education, whatever may be the force of authority, or of numbers, upon the other side.

It is important to remember that, in strictness, there is no such thing as an uneducated man. Take an extreme case. Suppose that an adult man, in the full vigor of his faculties, could be suddenly placed in the world, as Adam is said to have been, and then left to do as he best might. How long would he be left uneducated? Not five minutes. Nature would begin to teach him, through the eye, the ear, the touch, the properties of objects. Pain and pleasure would be at his elbow telling him to do this and avoid that; and by slow degrees the man would receive an education which, if narrow, would be thorough, real, and adequate to his circumstances, though there would be no extras and very few accomplishments.

And if to this solitary man entered a second Adam or, better still, an Eve, a new and greater world, that of social and moral phenomena, would be revealed. Joys and woes, compared with which all others might seem but faint shadows, would spring from the new relations. Happiness and sorrow would take the place of the coarser monitors, pleasure and pain; but conduct would still be shaped by the observation of the natural consequences of actions; or, in other words, by the laws of the nature of man.

To every one of us the world was once as fresh and new as to Adam. And then, long before we were susceptible of any other mode of instruction, Nature took us in hand, and every minute of waking life brought its educational influence, shaping our actions into rough accordance with Nature's laws, so that we might not be ended untimely by too gross disobedience. Nor should I speak of this process of education as past for anyone, be he as old as he may. For every man the world is as fresh as it was at the first day, and as full of untold novelties for him who has the eyes to see them. And Nature is still continuing her patient education of us in that great university, the universe, of which we are all members—Nature having no Test Acts.[4]

Those who take honors in Nature's university, who learn the laws which govern men and things and obey them, are the really great and successful men in this world. The great mass of mankind are the "Poll," [5] who pick up just enough to get through without much discredit. Those who won't learn at all are plucked;[6] and then you can't come up again. Nature's pluck means extermination.

Thus the question of compulsory education is settled so far as Nature is concerned. Her bill on that question was framed and passed long ago. But, like all compulsory legislation, that of Nature

4. Legislation (repealed in 1854) which excluded from Oxford and Cambridge any student who would not profess faith in the 39 Articles of the Church of England.

5. English slang term describing the mass of students who get through college with very low (but passing) grades.
6. Failed.

is harsh and wasteful in its operation. Ignorance is visited as sharply as willful disobedience—incapacity meets with the same punishment as crime. Nature's discipline is not even a word and a blow, and the blow first; but the blow without the word. It is left to you to find out why your ears are boxed.

The object of what we commonly call education—that education in which man intervenes and which I shall distinguish as artificial education—is to make good these defects in Nature's methods; to prepare the child to receive Nature's education, neither incapably nor ignorantly, nor with willful disobedience; and to understand the preliminary symptoms of her pleasure, without waiting for the box on the ear. In short, all artificial education ought to be an anticipation of natural education. And a liberal education is an artificial education which has not only prepared a man to escape the great evils of disobedience to natural laws, but has trained him to appreciate and to seize upon the rewards which Nature scatters with as free a hand as her penalties.

That man, I think, has had a liberal education who has been so trained in youth that his body is the ready servant of his will, and does with ease and pleasure all the work that, as a mechanism, it is capable of; whose intellect is a clear, cold, logic engine, with all its parts of equal strength, and in smooth working order; ready, like a steam engine, to be turned to any kind of work, and spin the gossamers as well as forge the anchors of the mind; whose mind is stored with a knowledge of the great and fundamental truths of Nature and of the laws of her operations; one who, no stunted ascetic, is full of life and fire, but whose passions are trained to come to heel by a vigorous will, the servant of a tender conscience; who has learned to love all beauty, whether of Nature or of art, to hate all vileness, and to respect others as himself.

Such a one and no other, I conceive, has had a liberal education; for he is, as completely as a man can be, in harmony with Nature. He will make the best of her, and she of him. They will get on together rarely; she as his ever beneficent mother; he as her mouthpiece, her conscious self, her minister and interpreter. * * *

1868, 1870

From An Address on University Education[1]
[*The Function of a Professor*]

Up to this point I have considered only the teaching aspect of your great foundation, that function of the university in virtue of

1. During a visit to the United States in 1876 Huxley delivered an address in Baltimore on the occasion of the founding of the Johns Hopkins University, a newly endowed institution which encouraged research.

which it plays the part of a reservoir of ascertained truth, so far as our symbols can ever interpret nature. All can learn; all can drink of this lake. It is given to few to add to the store of knowledge, to strike new springs of thought, or to shape new forms of beauty. But so sure as it is that men live not by bread, but by ideas, so sure is it that the future of the world lies in the hands of those who are able to carry the interpretation of nature a step further than their predecessors; so certain is it that the highest function of a university is to seek out those men, cherish them, and give their ability to serve their kind full play.

I rejoice to observe that the encouragement of research occupies so prominent a place in your official documents, and in the wise and liberal inaugural address of your president. This subject of the encouragement, or, as it is sometimes called, the endowment of research, has of late years greatly exercised the minds of men in England. It was one of the main topics of discussion by the members of the Royal Commission of whom I was one, and who not long since issued their report, after five years' labor. Many seem to think that this question is mainly one of money; that you can go into the market and buy research, and that supply will follow demand, as in the ordinary course of commerce. This view does not commend itself to my mind. I know of no more difficult practical problem than the discovery of a method of encouraging and supporting the original investigator without opening the door to nepotism and jobbery. My own conviction is admirably summed up in the passage of your president's address, "that the best investigators are usually those who have also the responsibilities of instruction, gaining thus the incitement of colleagues, the encouragement of pupils, and the observation of the public." * * *

It appears to me that what I have ventured to lay down as the principles which should govern the relations of a university to education in general, are entirely in accordance with the measures you have adopted. You have set no restrictions upon access to the instruction you propose to give; you have provided that such instruction, either as given by the university or by associated institutions, should cover the field of human intellectual activity. You have recognized the importance of encouraging research. You propose to provide means by which young men, who may be full of zeal for a literary or for a scientific career, but who also may have mistaken aspiration for inspiration, may bring their capacities to a test, and give their powers a fair trial. If such a one fail, his endowment terminates and there is no harm done. If he succeed, you may give power of flight to the genius of a Davy or a Faraday,[2] a Carlyle or a Locke, whose influence on the future of his fellow

---

2. Sir Humphry Davy (1778–1829), English chemist and inventor; Michael Faraday (1791–1867), at one time Davy's laboratory assistant, who became famous for his discovery of the induction of electric currents.

men shall be absolutely incalculable.

You have enunciated the principle that "the glory of the university should rest upon the character of the teachers and scholars, and not upon their numbers of buildings constructed for their use." And I look upon it as an essential and most important feature of your plan that the income of the professors and teachers shall be independent of the number of students whom they can attract. In this way you provide against the danger, patent elsewhere, of finding attempts at improvement obstructed by vested interests; and, in the department of medical education especially, you are free of the temptation to set loose upon the world men utterly incompetent to perform the serious and responsible duties of their profession.

1876–77

From Science and Culture[1]

From the time that the first suggestion to introduce physical science into ordinary education was timidly whispered, until now, the advocates of scientific education have met with opposition of two kinds. On the one hand, they have been pooh-poohed by the men of business who pride themselves on being the representatives of practicality; while, on the other hand, they have been excommunicated by the classical scholars, in their capacity of Levites in charge of the ark of culture[2] and monopolists of liberal education.

The practical men believed that the idol whom they worship—rule of thumb—has been the source of the past prosperity, and will suffice for the future welfare of the arts and manufactures. They are of opinion that science is speculative rubbish; that theory and practice have nothing to do with one another; and that the scientific habit of mind is an impediment, rather than an aid, in the conduct of ordinary affairs.

I have used the past tense in speaking of the practical men—for although they were very formidable thirty years ago, I am not sure that the pure species has not been extirpated. In fact, so far as mere argument goes, they have been subjected to such a *feu d'enfer*[3] that it is a miracle if any have escaped. But I have remarked that your typical practical man has an unexpected resemblance to one of Milton's angels. His spiritual wounds, such as are inflicted by logical weapons, may be as deep as a well and as wide as a church

1. This essay was first delivered as an address in 1880. The occasion had been the opening of a new Scientific College at Birmingham which had been endowed by Sir Josiah Mason (1795–1881), a self-made businessman. For Matthew Arnold's reply to Huxley's argument see his essay *Literature and Science*.

2. In the Old Testament, the Levites were the priests preoccupied with traditional ritual observances (see Joshua vi).

3. Hell-fire.

door, but beyond shedding a few drops of ichor,[4] celestial or otherwise, he is no whit the worse. So, if any of these opponents be left, I will not waste time in vain repetition of the demonstrative evidence of the practical value of science; but knowing that a parable will sometimes penetrate where syllogisms fail to effect an entrance, I will offer a story for their consideration.

Once upon a time, a boy, with nothing to depend upon but his own vigorous nature, was thrown into the thick of the struggle for existence in the midst of a great manufacturing population. He seems to have had a hard fight, inasmuch as, by the time he was thirty years of age, his total disposable funds amounted to twenty pounds. Nevertheless, middle life found him giving proof of his comprehension of the practical problems he had been roughly called upon to solve, by a career of remarkable prosperity.

Finally, having reached old age with its well-earned surroundings of "honor, troops of friends,"[5] the hero of my story bethought himself of those who were making a like start in life, and how he could stretch out a helping hand to them.

After long and anxious reflection this successful practical man of business could devise nothing better than to provide them with the means of obtaining "sound, extensive, and practical scientific knowledge." And he devoted a large part of his wealth and five years of incessant work to this end.

I need not point the moral of a tale which, as the solid and spacious fabric of the Scientific College assures us, is no fable, nor can anything which I could say intensify the force of this practical answer to practical objections.

We may take it for granted then, that, in the opinion of those best qualified to judge, the diffusion of thorough scientific education is an absolutely essential condition of industrial progress; and that the College which has been opened today will confer an inestimable boon upon those whose livelihood is to be gained by the practice of the arts and manufactures of the district.

The only question worth discussion is whether the conditions under which the work of the College is to be carried out are such as to give it the best possible chance of achieving permanent success.

Sir Josiah Mason, without doubt most wisely, has left very large freedom of action to the trustees, to whom he proposes ultimately to commit the administration of the College, so that they may be able to adjust its arrangements in accordance with the changing conditions of the future. But, with respect to three points, he has laid most explicit injunctions upon both administrators and teachers.

4. Ethereal fluid which supposedly flows through the veins of the gods.   5. Cf. *Macbeth* V.iii.25.

Party politics are forbidden to enter into the minds of either, so far as the work of the College is concerned; theology is as sternly banished from its precincts; and finally, it is especially declared that the College shall make no provision for "mere literary instruction and education."

It does not concern me at present to dwell upon the first two injunctions any longer than may be needful to express my full conviction of their wisdom. But the third prohibition brings us face to face with those other opponents of scientific education, who are by no means in the moribund condition of the practical man, but alive, alert, and formidable.

It is not impossible that we shall hear this express exclusion of "literary instruction and education" from a College which, nevertheless, professes to give a high and efficient education, sharply criticized. Certainly the time was that the Levites of culture would have sounded their trumpets against its walls as against an educational Jericho.[6]

How often have we not been told that the study of physical science is incompetent to confer culture; that it touches none of the higher problems of life; and, what is worse, that the continual devotion to scientific studies tends to generate a narrow and bigoted belief in the applicability of scientific methods to the search after truth of all kinds? How frequently one has reason to observe that no reply to a troublesome argument tells so well as calling its author a "mere scientific specialist." And, as I am afraid it is not permissible to speak of this form of opposition to scientific education in the past tense; may we not expect to be told that this, not only omission, but prohibition, of "mere literary instruction and education" is a patent example of scientific narrow-mindedness?

I am not acquainted with Sir Josiah Mason's reasons for the action which he has taken; but if, as I apprehend is the case, he refers to the ordinary classical course of our schools and universities by the name of "mere literary instruction and education," I venture to offer sundry reasons of my own in support of that action.

For I hold very strongly by two convictions: The first is that neither the discipline nor the subject matter of classical education is of such direct value to the student of physical science as to justify the expenditure of valuable time upon either; and the second is that for the purpose of attaining real culture, an exclusively scientific education is at least as effectual as an exclusively literary education.

I need hardly point out to you that these opinions, especially the latter, are diametrically opposed to those of the great majority of educated Englishmen, influenced as they are by school and university traditions. In their belief, culture is obtainable only by a

6. See Joshua vi.

liberal education; and a liberal education is synonymous, not merely with education and instruction in literature, but in one particular form of literature, namely, that of Greek and Roman antiquity. They hold that the man who has learned Latin and Greek, however little, is educated; while he who is versed in other branches of knowledge, however deeply, is a more or less respectable specialist, not admissible into the cultured caste. The stamp of the educated man, the University degree, is not for him.

I am too well acquainted with the generous catholicity of spirit, the true sympathy with scientific thought, which pervades the writings of our chief apostle of culture[7] to identify him with these opinions; and yet one may cull from one and another of those epistles to the Philistines, which so much delight all who do not answer to that name, sentences which lend them some support.

Mr. Arnold tells us that the meaning of culture is "to know the best that has been thought and said in the world." It is the criticism of life contained in literature. That criticism regards "Europe as being, for intellectual and spiritual purposes, one great confederation, bound to a joint action and working to a common result; and whose members have, for their common outfit, a knowledge of Greek, Roman, and Eastern antiquity, and of one another. Special, local, and temporary advantages being put out of account, that modern nation will in the intellectual and spiritual sphere make most progress, which most thoroughly carries out this program. And what is that but saying that we too, all of us, as individuals, the more thoroughly we carry it out, shall make the more progress?"[8]

We have here to deal with two distinct propositions. The first, that a criticism of life is the essence of culture; the second, that literature contains the materials which suffice for the construction of such criticism.

I think that we must all assent to the first proposition. For culture certainly means something quite different from learning or technical skill. It implies the possession of an ideal, and the habit of critically estimating the value of things by comparison with a theoretic standard. Perfect culture should supply a complete theory of life, based upon a clear knowledge alike of its possibilities and of its limitations.

But we may agree to all this, and yet strongly dissent from the assumption that literature alone is competent to supply this knowledge. After having learnt all that Greek, Roman, and Eastern antiquity have thought and said, and all that modern literature have to tell us, it is not self-evident that we have laid a sufficiently broad and deep foundation for that criticism of life which constitutes culture.

7. I.e., Matthew Arnold. For his discussion of the Philistines, see *Culture and Anarchy*.

8. From Arnold's *Function of Criticism*, fourth paragraph from the end.

Indeed, to anyone acquainted with the scope of physical science, it is not at all evident. Considering progress only in the "intellectual and spiritual sphere," I find myself wholly unable to admit that either nations or individuals will really advance, if their common outfit draws nothing from the stores of physical science. I should say that an army, without weapons of precision and with no particular base of operations, might more hopefully enter upon a campaign on the Rhine than a man, devoid of a knowledge of what physical science has done in the last century, upon a criticism of life.

When a biologist meets with an anomaly, he instinctively turns to the study of development to clear it up. The rationale of contradictory opinions may with equal confidence be sought in history.

It is, happily, no new thing that Englishmen should employ their wealth in building and endowing institutions for educational purposes. But, five or six hundred years ago, deeds of foundation expressed or implied conditions as nearly as possible contrary to those which have been thought expedient by Sir Josiah Mason. That is to say, physical science was practically ignored, while a certain literary training was enjoined as a means to the acquirement of knowledge which was essentially theological.

The reason of this singular contradiction between the actions of men alike animated by a strong and disinterested desire to promote the welfare of their fellows, is easily discovered.

At that time, in fact, if anyone desired knowledge beyond such as could be obtained by his own observation, or by common conversation, his first necessity was to learn the Latin language, inasmuch as all the higher knowledge of the western world was contained in works written in that language. Hence, Latin grammar, with logic and rhetoric, studied through Latin, were the fundamentals of education. With respect to the substance of the knowledge imparted through this channel, the Jewish and Christian Scriptures, as interpreted and supplemented by the Romish Church, were held to contain a complete and infallibly true body of information.

Theological dicta were, to the thinkers of those days, that which the axioms and definitions of Euclid are to the geometers of these. The business of the philosophers of the Middle Ages was to deduce from the data furnished by the theologians, conclusions in accordance with ecclesiastical decrees. They were allowed the high privilege of showing, by logical process, how and why that which the Church said was true, must be true. And if their demonstrations fell short of or exceeded this limit, the Church was maternally ready to check their aberrations; if need were, by the help of the secular arm.

Between the two, our ancestors were furnished with a compact and complete criticism of life. They were told how the world began and how it would end; they learned that all material existence was but a base and insignificant blot upon the fair face of the spiritual world, and that nature was, to all intents and purposes, the playground of the devil; they learned that the earth is the center of the visible universe, and that man is the cynosure of things terrestrial, and more especially was it inculcated that the course of nature had no fixed order, but that it could be, and constantly was, altered by the agency of innumerable spiritual beings, good and bad, according as they were moved by the deeds and prayers of men. The sum and substance of the whole doctrine was to produce the conviction that the only thing really worth knowing in this world was how to secure that place in a better which, under certain conditions, the Church promised.

Our ancestors had a living belief in this theory of life, and acted upon it in their dealings with education, as in all other matters. Culture meant saintliness—after the fashion of the saints of those days; the education that led to it was, of necessity, theological; and the way to theology lay through Latin.

That the study of nature—further than was requisite for the satisfaction of everyday wants—should have any bearing on human life was far from the thoughts of men thus trained. Indeed, as nature had been cursed for man's sake, it was an obvious conclusion that those who meddled with nature were likely to come into pretty close contact with Satan. And, if any born scientific investigator followed his instincts, he might safely reckon upon earning the reputation, and probably upon suffering the fate, of a sorcerer.

Had the western world been left to itself in Chinese isolation, there is no saying how long this state of things might have endured. But, happily, it was not left to itself. Even earlier than the thirteenth century, the development of Moorish civilization in Spain and the great movement of the Crusades had introduced the leaven which, from that day to this, has never ceased to work. At first, through the intermediation of Arabic translations, afterwards by the study of the originals, the western nations of Europe became acquainted with the writings of the ancient philosophers and poets, and, in time, with the whole of the vast literature of antiquity.

Whatever there was of high intellectual aspiration or dominant capacity in Italy, France, Germany, and England, spent itself for centuries in taking possession of the rich inheritance left by the dead civilizations of Greece and Rome. Marvelously aided by the invention of printing,[9] classical learning spread and flourished. Those who possessed it prided themselves on having attained the

9. In the mid-15th century.

highest culture then within the reach of mankind.

And justly. For, saving Dante on his solitary pinnacle, there was no figure in modern literature at the time of the Renaissance to compare with the men of antiquity; there was no art to compete with their sculpture; there was no physical science but that which Greece had created. Above all, there was no other example of perfect intellectual freedom—of the unhesitating acceptance of reason as the sole guide to truth and the supreme arbiter of conduct.

The new learning necessarily soon exerted a profound influence upon education. The language of the monks and schoolmen[1] seemed little better than gibberish to scholars fresh from Virgil and Cicero, and the study of Latin was placed upon a new foundation. Moreover, Latin itself ceased to afford the sole key to knowledge. The student who sought the highest thought of antiquity found only a secondhand reflection of it in Roman literature, and turned his face to the full light of the Greeks. And after a battle, not altogether dissimilar to that which is at present being fought over the teaching of physical science, the study of Greek was recognized as an essential element of all higher education.

Then the Humanists, as they were called, won the day; and the great reform which they effected was of incalculable service to mankind. But the nemesis of all reformers is finality; and the reformers of education, like those of religion, fell into the profound, however common, error of mistaking the beginning for the end of the work of reformation.

The representatives of the Humanists, in the nineteenth century, take their stand upon classical education as the sole avenue to culture as firmly as if we were still in the age of Renaissance. Yet, surely, the present intellectual relations of the modern and the ancient worlds are profoundly different from those which obtained three centuries ago. Leaving aside the existence of a great and characteristically modern literature, of modern painting, and, especially, of modern music, there is one feature of the present state of the civilized world which separates it more widely from the Renaissance than the Renaissance was separated from the Middle Ages.

This distinctive character of our own times lies in the vast and constantly increasing part which is played by natural knowledge. Not only is our daily life shaped by it; not only does the prosperity of millions of men depend upon it, but our whole theory of life has long been influenced, consciously or unconsciously, by the general conceptions of the universe which have been forced upon us by physical science.

In fact, the most elementary acquaintance with the results of scientific investigation shows us that they offer a broad and striking

---

1. Exponents of the theology, philosophy, and logic of the medieval period in Europe.

contradiction to the opinion so implicitly credited and taught in the Middle Ages.

The notions of the beginning and the end of the world entertained by our forefathers are no longer credible. It is very certain that the earth is not the chief body in the material universe, and that the world is not subordinated to man's use. It is even more certain that nature is the expression of a definite order with which nothing interferes, and that the chief business of mankind is to learn that order and govern themselves accordingly. Moreover this scientific "criticism of life" presents itself to us with different credentials from any other. It appeals not to authority, nor to what anybody may have thought or said, but to nature. It admits that all our interpretations of natural fact are more or less imperfect and symbolic, and bids the learner seek for truth not among words but among things. It warns us that the assertion which outstrips evidence is not only a blunder but a crime.

The purely classical education advocated by the representatives of the Humanists in our day gives no inkling of all this. A man may be a better scholar than Erasmus,[2] and know no more of the chief causes of the present intellectual fermentation than Erasmus did. Scholarly and pious persons, worthy of all respect, favor us with allocutions upon the sadness of the antagonism of science to their medieval way of thinking, which betray an ignorance of the first principles of scientific investigation, an incapacity for understanding what a man of science means by veracity, and an unconsciousness of the weight of established scientific truths, which is almost comical. * * *

Thus I venture to think that the pretensions of our modern Humanists to the possession of the monopoly of culture and to the exclusive inheritance of the spirit of antiquity must be abated, if not abandoned. But I should be very sorry that anything I have said should be taken to imply a desire on my part to depreciate the value of classical education, as it might be and as it sometimes is. The native capacities of mankind vary no less than their opportunities; and while culture is one, the road by which one man may best reach it is widely different from that which is most advantageous to another. Again, while scientific education is yet inchoate and tentative, classical education is thoroughly well organized upon the practical experience of generations of teachers. So that, given ample time for learning and estimation for ordinary life, or for a literary career, I do not think that a young Englishman in search of culture can do better than follow the course usually marked out for him, supplementing its deficiencies by his own efforts.

But for those who mean to make science their serious occupation; or who intend to follow the profession of medicine; or who have to

2. Eminent Dutch humanist and scholar (1466–1536).

enter early upon the business of life; for all these, in my opinion, classical education is a mistake; and it is for this reason that I am glad to see "mere literary education and instruction" shut out from the curriculum of Sir Josiah Mason's College, seeing that its inclusion would probably lead to the introduction of the ordinary smattering of Latin and Greek.

Nevertheless, I am the last person to question the importance of genuine literatary education, or to suppose that intellectual culture can be complete without it. An exclusively scientific training will bring about a mental twist as surely as an exclusively literary training. The value of the cargo does not compensate for a ship's being out of trim; and I should be very sorry to think that the Scientific College would turn out none but lopsided men.

There is no need, however, that such a catastrophe should happen. Instruction in English, French, and German is provided, and thus the three greatest literatures of the modern world are made accessible to the student.

French and German, and especially the latter language, are absolutely indispensable to those who desire full knowledge in any department of science. But even supposing that the knowledge of these languages acquired is not more than sufficient for purely scientific purposes, every Englishman has, in his native tongue, an almost perfect instrument of literary expression; and, in his own literature, models of every kind of literary excellence. If an Englishman cannot get literary culture out of his Bible, his Shakespeare, his Milton, neither, in my belief, will the profoundest study of Homer and Sophocles, Virgil and Horace, give it to him.

Thus, since the constitution of the College makes sufficient provision for literary as well as for scientific education, and since artistic instruction is also contemplated, it seems to me that a fairly complete culture is offered to all who are willing to take advantage of it. * * *

1880, 1881

From Agnosticism and Christianity[1]

Nemo ergo ex me scire quaerat, quod me nescire scio, nisi forte ut nescire discat.
—AUGUSTINUS, *De Civ. Dei*, XII.7.[2]

The present discussion has arisen out of the use, which has become general in the last few years, of the terms "Agnostic" and

1. This essay appeared in a magazine in 1889 as a reply to critics who had argued that agnostics were simply infidels under a new name. It was later included in Huxley's volume, *Essays on Some Controverted Questions*

(1892).
2. "No one, therefore, should seek to learn knowledge from me, for I know that I do not know—unless indeed he wishes to learn that he does not know." St. Augustine, *City of God* XII.7.

"Agnosticism."[3]

The people who call themselves "Agnostics" have been charged with doing so because they have not the courage to declare themselves "Infidels." It has been insinuated that they have adopted a new name in order to escape the unpleasantness which attaches to their proper denomination. To this wholly erroneous imputation I have replied by showing that the term "Agnostic" did, as a matter of fact, arise in a manner which negatives it; and my statement has not been, and cannot be, refuted. Moreover, speaking for myself, and without impugning the right of any other person to use the term in another sense, I further say that Agnosticism is not properly described as a "negative" creed, nor indeed as a creed of any kind, except in so far as it expresses absolute faith in the validity of a principle, which is as much ethical as intellectual. This principle may be stated in various ways, but they all amount to this: that it is wrong for a man to say that he is certain of the objective truth of any proposition unless he can produce evidence which logically justifies that certainty. This is what Agnosticism asserts; and, in my opinion, it is all that is essential to Agnosticism. That which Agnostics deny and repudiate, as immoral, is the contrary doctrine, that there are propositions which men ought to believe, without logically satisfactory evidence; and that reprobation ought to attach to the profession of disbelief in such inadequately supported propositions. The justification of the Agnostic principle lies in the success which follows upon its application, whether in the field of natural, or in that of civil, history; and in the fact that, so far as these topics are concerned, no sane man thinks of denying its validity.

Still speaking for myself, I add that though Agnosticism is not, and cannot be, a creed, except in so far as its general principle is concerned; yet that the application of that principle results in the denial of, or the suspension of judgment concerning, a number of propositions respecting which our contemporary ecclesiastical "gnostics" profess entire certainty. And, in so far as these ecclesiastical persons can be justified in their old-established custom (which many nowadays think more honored in the breach than the observance) of using opprobrious names to those who differ from them, I fully admit their right to call me and those who think with me "Infidels"; all I have ventured to urge is that they must not expect us to speak of ourselves by that title.

The extent of the region of the uncertain, the number of the problems the investigation of which ends in a verdict of not proven, will vary according to the knowledge and the intellectual habits of the individual Agnostic. I do not very much care to speak of anything as "unknowable." What I am sure about is that there are many topics about which I know nothing; and which, so far as I

3. The term "agnostic" was coined by Huxley.

can see, are out of reach of my faculties. But whether these things are knowable by anyone else is exactly one of those matters which is beyond my knowledge, though I may have a tolerably strong opinion as to the probabilities of the case. Relatively to myself, I am quite sure that the region of uncertainty—the nebulous country in which words play the part of realities—is far more extensive than I could wish. Materialism and Idealism; Theism and Atheism; the doctrine of the soul and its mortality or immortality—appear in the history of philosophy like the shades of Scandinavian heroes, eternally slaying one another and eternally coming to life again in a metaphysical "Nifelheim."[4] It is getting on for twenty-five centuries, at least, since mankind began seriously to give their minds to these topics. Generation after generation, philosophy has been doomed to roll the stone uphill; and, just as all the world swore it was at the top, down it has rolled to the bottom again.[5] All this is written in innumerable books; and he who will toil through them will discover that the stone is just where it was when the work began. Hume saw this; Kant saw it; since their time, more and more eyes have been cleansed of the films which prevented them from seeing it; until now the weight and number of those who refuse to be the prey of verbal mystifications has begun to tell in practical life.

It was inevitable that a conflict should arise between Agnosticism and Theology; or rather, I ought to say, between Agnosticism and Ecclesiasticism. For Theology, the science, is one thing; and Ecclesiasticism, the championship of a foregone conclusion[6] as to the truth of a particular form of Theology, is another. With scientific Theology, Agnosticism has no quarrel. On the contrary, the Agnostic, knowing too well the influence of prejudice and idiosyncrasy, even on those who desire most earnestly to be impartial, can wish for nothing more urgently than that the scientific theologian should not only be at perfect liberty to thresh out the matter in his own fashion; but that he should, if he can, find flaws in the Agnostic position; and, even if demonstration is not to be had, that he should put, in their full force, the grounds of the conclusions he thinks probable. The scientific theologian admits the Agnostic principle, however widely his results may differ from those reached by the majority of Agnostics.

But, as between Agnosticism and Ecclesiasticism, or, as our neighbors across the Channel call it, Clericalism, there can be neither peace nor truce. The Cleric asserts that it is morally wrong not to believe certain propositions, whatever the results of a strict

4. Realms of cold and darkness in Norse mythology.
5. Cf. the Greek story of Sisyphus in Hades, who was condemned to keep rolling a stone uphill which always rolled downhill again before it reached the summit.
6. "Let us maintain, before we have proved. This seeming paradox is the secret of happiness. (Dr. Newman, *Tract 85*)" [Huxley's note].

scientific investigation of the evidence of these propositions. He tells us "that religious error is, in itself, of an immoral nature."[7] He declares that he has prejudged certain conclusions, and looks upon those who show cause for arrest of judgment as emissaries of Satan. It necessarily follows that, for him, the attainment of faith, not the ascertainment of truth, is the highest aim of mental life. And, on careful analysis of the nature of this faith, it will too often be found to be, not the mystic process of unity with the Divine, understood by the religious enthusiast; but that which the candid simplicity of a Sunday scholar once defined it to be. "Faith," said this unconscious plagiarist of Tertullian,[8] "is the power of saying you believe things which are incredible."

Now I, and many other Agnostics, believe that faith, in this sense, is an abomination; and though we do not indulge in the luxury of self-righteousness so far as to call those who are not of our way of thinking hard names, we do feel that the disagreement between ourselves and those who hold this doctrine is even more moral than intellectual. It is desirable there should be an end of any mistakes on this topic. If our clerical opponents were clearly aware of the real state of the case, there would be an end of the curious delusion, which often appears between the lines of their writings, that those whom they are so fond of calling "Infidels" are people who not only ought to be, but in their hearts are, ashamed of themselves. It would be discourteous to do more than hint the antipodal opposition of this pleasant dream of theirs to facts.

The clerics and their lay allies commonly tell us that if we refuse to admit that there is good ground for expressing definite convictions about certain topics, the bonds of human society will dissolve and mankind lapse into savagery. There are several answers to this assertion. One is that the bonds of human society were formed without the aid of their theology; and, in the opinion of not a few competent judges, have been weakened rather than strengthened by a good deal of it. Greek science, Greek art, the ethics of old Israel, the social organization of old Rome, contrived to come into being, without the help of anyone who believed in a single distinctive article of the simplest of the Christian creeds. The science, the art, the jurisprudence, the chief political and social theories, of the modern world have grown out of those of Greece and Rome— not by favor of, but in the teeth of, the fundamental teachings of early Christianity, to which science, art, and any serious occupation with the things of this world, were alike despicable.

Again, all that is best in the ethics of the modern world, in so far as it has not grown out of Greek thought, or Barbarian manhood, is the direct development of the ethics of old Israel. There

7. "Dr Newman, *Essay on Development*" [Huxley's note].

8. Roman author and Church Father (ca. 155–ca. 222).

is no code of legislation, ancient or modern, at once so just and so merciful, so tender to the weak and poor, as the Jewish law; and, if the Gospels are to be trusted, Jesus of Nazareth himself declared that he taught nothing but that which lay implicitly, or explicitly, in the religious and ethical system of his people.

"And the scribe said unto him, Of a truth, Teacher, thou hast well said that he is one; and there is none other but he and to love him with all the heart, and with all the understanding, and with all the strength, and to love his neighbour as himself, is much more than all whole burnt offerings and sacrifices." (Mark xii.32–33)

Here is the briefest of summaries of the teaching of the prophets of Israel of the eighth century; does the Teacher, whose doctrine is thus set forth in his presence, repudiate the exposition? Nay; we are told, on the contrary, that Jesus saw that he "answered discreetly," and replied, "Thou art not far from the kingdom of God."

So that I think that even if the creeds,[9] from the so-called "Apostles'" to the so-called "Athanasian," were swept into oblivion; and even if the human race should arrive at the conclusion that, whether a bishop washes a cup or leaves it unwashed, is not a matter of the least consequence, it will get on very well. The causes which have led to the development of morality in mankind, which have guided or impelled us all the way from the savage to the civilized state, will not cease to operate because a number of ecclesiastical hypotheses turn out to be baseless. And, even if the absurd notion that morality is more the child of speculation than of practical necessity and inherited instinct, had any foundation; if all the world is going to thieve, murder, and otherwise misconduct itself as soon as it discovers that certain portions of ancient history are mythical; what is the relevance of such arguments to any one who holds by the Agnostic principle?

Surely, the attempt to cast out Beelzebub by the aid of Beelzebub is a hopeful procedure as compared to that of preserving morality by the aid of immorality. For I suppose it is admitted that an Agnostic may be perfectly sincere, may be competent, and may have studied the question at issue with as much care as his clerical opponents. But, if the Agnostic really believes what he says, the "dreadful consequence" argufier (consistently, I admit, with his own principles) virtually asks him to abstain from telling the truth, or to say what he believes to be untrue, because of the supposed injurious consequences to morality. "Beloved brethren, that we may be spotlessly moral, before all things let us lie," is the sum total of many an exhortation addressed to the "Infidel." Now, as I have already pointed out, we cannot oblige our exhorters. We leave the practical application of the convenient doctrines of "Reserve" and

9. Summaries of Christian doctrine.

"Non-natural interpretation" to those who invented them.

I trust that I have now made amends for any ambiguity, or want of fullness, in my previous exposition of that which I hold to be the essence of the Agnostic doctrine. Henceforward, I might hope to hear no more of the assertion that we are necessarily Materialists, Idealists, Atheists, Theists, or any other ists, if experience had led me to think that the proved falsity of a statement was any guarantee against its repetition. And those who appreciate the nature of our position will see, at once, that when Ecclesiasticism declares that we ought to believe this, that, and the other, and are very wicked if we don't, it is impossible for us to give any answer but this: We have not the slightest objection to believe anything you like, if you will give us good grounds for belief; but, if you cannot, we must respectfully refuse, even if that refusal should wreck morality and insure our own damnation several times over. We are quite content to leave that to the decision of the future. The course of the past has impressed us with the firm conviction that no good ever comes of falsehood, and we feel warranted in refusing even to experiment in that direction. * * *

1889, 1892

WALTER PATER
(1839–1894)

Studies in the History of the Renaissance, a collection of essays published in 1873, was the first of several volumes which established Walter Pater as the most important critical writer of the late Victorian period. A shy bachelor who spent his life as a tutor of classics at Oxford, Pater was surprised and even alarmed by the impact made by his books on young readers of the 1870's and 1880's. Some of his younger followers such as Oscar Wilde and George Moore may have misread him. It can be demonstrated that Pater's writings (especially his historical novel *Marius the Epicurean*, 1885) have much in common with his earnest-minded mid-Victorian predecessors, but his disciples overlooked these similarities. To them, his work seemed strikingly different and, in its quiet way, more subversive than the head-on attacks against traditional Victorianism made by Swinburne or Samuel Butler. Instead of recommending a continuation of the painful quest for Truth that had dominated Oxford in the days of Newman, Pater assured his readers that the quest was pointless. Truth, he said, is relative. And instead of echoing Carlyle's call to duty and social responsibilities, Pater reminded his readers that life passes quickly and that our only responsibility is to enjoy fully "this short day of frost and sun," to relish its sensations, especially those sensations provoked by works of art.

This epicurean gospel was conveyed in a highly-wrought prose style that baffles anyone who likes to read quickly. Pater believed that prose was as difficult an art as poetry, and he expected his own elaborate sentences to be savored. Like Flaubert, the French novelist whom he admired, Pater painstakingly revised his sentences with special attention to their rhythms and seeking always the right word, *le mot juste*, as Flaubert had called it. What Pater said of Dante is an apt description of his own polished style: "He is one of those artists whose general effect largely depends on vocabulary, on the minute particles of which his work is wrought, on the color and outline of single words and phrases."

Aside from his interest as a key figure in the transition from mid-Victorianism to the decadence of the 1890's, Pater's essays also command our attention as examples of impressionistic criticism at its best. In each of his essays he seeks to communicate what he called the "special unique impression of pleasure" made upon him by the works of some artist or writer. His range of subjects included the dialogues of Plato, the paintings of Leonardo da Vinci, the plays of Shakespeare, and the writings of the French Romantic school of the 19th century. Of particular value to students of English literature are his discriminating studies of Wordsworth, Coleridge, Lamb, and Sir Thomas Browne in his volume of *Appreciations* (1889).

The final sentences of his *Appreciations* volume are a revealing indication of Pater's critical position. After having attempted to show the differences between the classical and romantic schools of art, he concludes that most great artists combine the qualities of both. "To discriminate schools, of art, of literature," he writes, "is, of course, part of the obvious business of literary criticism: but, in the work of literary production, it is easy to be overmuch occupied concerning them. For, in truth, the legitimate contention is, not of one age or school of literary art against another, but of all successive schools alike, against the stupidity which is dead to the substance, and the vulgarity which is dead to form."

From The Renaissance
Preface

Many attempts have been made by writers on art and poetry to define beauty in the abstract, to express it in the most general terms, to find some universal formula for it. The value of these attempts has most often been in the suggestive and penetrating things said by the way. Such discussions help us very little to enjoy what has been well done in art or poetry, to discriminate between what is more and what is less excellent in them, or to use words like beauty, excellence, art, poetry, with a more precise meaning than they would otherwise have. Beauty, like all other qualities presented to human experience, is relative; and the definition of it becomes unmeaning and useless in proportion to its abstractness. To define beauty, not in the most abstract but in the most concrete terms possible, to find not its universal formula, but the formula which expresses most adequately this or that special manifestation of it, is the aim of the true student of aesthetics.

"To see the object as in itself it really is,"[1] has been justly said to be the aim of all true criticism whatever; and in aesthetic criticism the first step towards seeing one's object as it really is, is to know one's own impression as it really is, to discriminate it, to realize it distinctly. The objects with which aesthetic criticism deals —music, poetry, artistic and accomplished forms of human life— are indeed receptacles of so many powers or forces: they possess, like the products of nature, so many virtues or qualities. What is this song or picture, this engaging personality presented in life or in a book, to *me*? What effect does it really produce on me? Does it give me pleasure? and if so, what sort or degree of pleasure? How is my nature modified by its presence, and under its influence? The answers to these questions are the original facts with which the aesthetic critic has to do; and, as in the study of light, of morals, of number, one must realize such primary data for one's self, or not at all. And he who experiences these impressions strongly, and drives directly at the discrimination and analysis of them, has no need to trouble himself with the abstract question what beauty is in itself, or what its exact relation to truth or experience—metaphysical questions, as unprofitable as metaphysical questions elsewhere. He may pass them all by as being, answerable or not, of no interest to him.

The aesthetic critic, then, regards all the objects with which he has to do, all works of art, and the fairer forms of nature and human life, as powers or forces producing pleasurable sensations, each of a more or less peculiar or unique kind. This influence he feels, and wishes to explain, by analyzing and reducing it to its elements. To him, the picture, the landscape, the engaging personality in life or in a book, "La Gioconda," the hills of Carrara, Pico of Mirandola,[2] are valuable for their virtues, as we say, in speaking of a herb, a wine, a gem; for the property each has of affecting one with a special, a unique, impression of pleasure. Our education becomes complete in proportion as our susceptibility to these impressions increases in depth and variety. And the function of the aesthetic critic is to distinguish, to analyze, and separate from its adjuncts, the virtue by which a picture, a landscape, a fair personality in life or in a book, produces this special impression of beauty or pleasure, to indicate what the source of that impression is, and under what conditions it is experienced. His end is reached when he has disengaged that virtue, and noted it, as a chemist notes some natural element, for himself and others; and the rule for those who

1. See Matthew Arnold, *The Function of Criticism*, opening paragraph.
2. "La Gioconda" is Leonardo da Vinci's famous painting, the "Mona Lisa"; "the hills of Carrara" are marble quarries in Italy; Pico of Mirandola (or Pico della Mirandola) was an Italian philosopher and classical scholar (1463–94), subject of an essay by Pater which was included in *The Renaissance*.

would reach this end is stated with great exactness in the words of a recent critic of Sainte-Beuve: *De se borner à connaître de près les belles choses, et à s'en nourrir en exquis amateurs, en humanistes accomplis.*[3]

What is important, then, is not that the critic should possess a correct abstract definition of beauty for the intellect, but a certain kind of temperament, the power of being deeply moved by the presence of beautiful objects. He will remember always that beauty exists in many forms. To him all periods, types, schools of taste, are in themselves equal. In all ages there have been some excellent workmen, and some excellent work done. The question he asks is always: In whom did the stir, the genius, the sentiment of the period find itself? where was the receptacle of its refinement, its elevation, its taste? "The ages are all equal," says William Blake, "but genius is always above its age."

Often it will require great nicety to disengage this virtue from the commoner elements with which it may be found in combination. Few artists, not Goethe or Byron even, work quite cleanly, casting off all debris, and leaving us only what the heat of their imagination has wholly fused and transformed. Take, for instance, the writings of Wordsworth. The heat of his genius, entering into the substance of his work, has crystallized a part, but only a part, of it; and in that great mass of verse there is much which might well be forgotten. But scattered up and down it, sometimes fusing and transforming entire compositions, like the stanzas on *Resolution and Independence*, or the *Ode on the Recollections of Childhood*,[4] sometimes, as if at random, depositing a fine crystal here or there, in a matter it does not wholly search through and transmute, we trace the action of his unique, incommunicable faculty, that strange, mystical sense of a life in natural things, and of man's life as a part of nature, drawing strength and color and character from local influences, from the hills and streams, and from natural sights and sounds. Well! that is the *virtue*, the active principle in Wordsworth's poetry; and then the function of the critic of Wordsworth is to follow up that active principle, to disengage it, to mark the degree in which it penetrates his verse.

The subjects of the following studies are taken from the history of the *Renaissance*, and touch what I think the chief points in that complex, many-sided movement. I have explained in the first of them what I understand by the word, giving it a much wider scope than was intended by those who originally used it to denote that revival of classical antiquity in the fifteenth century which was only one of many results of a general excitement and enlightening of the

---

3. "To confine themselves to knowing beautiful things intimately, and to sustain themselves by these, as sensitive amateurs and accomplished humanists do."
4. Wordsworth's *Ode* was entitled *Intimations of Immortality from Recollections of Early Childhood*.

human mind, but of which the great aim and achievements of what, as Christian art, is often falsely opposed to the Renaissance, were another result. This outbreak of the human spirit may be traced far into the Middle Age itself, with its motives already clearly pronounced, the care for physical beauty, the worship of the body, the breaking down of those limits which the religious system of the Middle Age imposed on the heart and the imagination. I have taken as an example of this movement, this earlier Renaissance within the Middle Age itself, and as an expression of its qualities, two little compositions in early French; not because they constitute the best possible expression of them, but because they help the unity of my series, inasmuch as the Renaissance ends also in France, in French poetry, in a phase of which the writings of Joachim du Bellay[5] are in many ways the most perfect illustration. The Renaissance, in truth, put forth in France an aftermath, a wonderful later growth, the products of which have to the full that subtle and delicate sweetness which belongs to a refined and comely decadence, just as its earliest phases have the freshness which belongs to all periods of growth in art, the charm of *ascêsis*,[6] of the austere and serious girding of the loins in youth.

But it is in Italy, in the fifteenth century, that the interest of the Renaissance mainly lies—in that solemn fifteenth century which can hardly be studied too much, not merely for its positive results in the things of the intellect and the imagination, its concrete works of art, its special and prominent personalities, with their profound aesthetic charm, but for its general spirit and character, for the ethical qualities of which it is a consummate type.

The various forms of intellectual activity which together make up the culture of an age, move for the most part from different starting points, and by unconnected roads. As products of the same generation they partake indeed of a common character, and unconsciously illustrate each other; but of the producers themselves, each group is solitary, gaining what advantage or disadvantage there may be in intellectual isolation. Art and poetry, philosophy and the religious life, and that other life of refined pleasure and action in the conspicuous places of the world, are each of them confined to its own circle of ideas, and those who prosecute either of them are generally little curious of the thoughts of others. There come, however, from time to time, eras of more favorable conditions, in which the thoughts of men draw nearer together than is their wont, and the many interests of the intellectual world combine in one complete type of general culture. The fifteenth century in Italy is one of these happier eras, and what is sometimes said of the age of Pericles is true of that of Lorenzo: it is an age productive in personalities,

---

5. French poet and critic (1524–60), subject of another essay in *The Ren-*   *aissance.*
6. Asceticism.

many-sided, centralized, complete. Here, artists and philosophers and those whom the action of the world has elevated and made keen, do not live in isolation, but breathe a common air, and catch light and heat from each other's thoughts. There is a spirit of general elevation and enlightenment in which all alike communicate. The unity of this spirit gives unity to all the various products of the Renaissance; and it is to this intimate alliance with mind, this participation in the best thoughts which that age produced, that the art of Italy in the fifteenth century owes much of its grave dignity and influence.

I have added an essay on Winckelmann,[7] as not incongruous with the studies which precede it, because Winckelmann, coming in the eighteenth century, really belongs in spirit to an earlier age. By his enthusiasm for the things of the intellect and the imagination for their own sake, by his Hellenism, his lifelong struggle to attain to the Greek spirit, he is in sympathy with the humanists of a previous century. He is the last fruit of the Renaissance, and explains in a striking way its motive and tendencies.

["La Gioconda"][8]

"La Gioconda" is, in the truest sense, Leonardo's masterpiece, the revealing instance of his mode of thought and work. In suggestiveness, only the "Melancholia" of Dürer[9] is comparable to it; and no crude symbolism disturbs the effect of its subdued and graceful mystery. We all know the face and hands of the figure, set in its marble chair, in that circle of fantastic rocks, as in some faint light under sea. Perhaps of all ancient pictures time has chilled it least. As often happens with works in which invention seems to reach its limit, there is an element in it given to, not invented by, the master. In that inestimable folio of drawings, once in the possession of Vasari, were certain designs by Verrocchio,[1] faces of such impressive beauty that Leonardo in his boyhood copied them many times. It is hard not to connect with these designs of the elder, by-past master, as with its germinal principle, the unfathomable smile, always with a touch of something sinister in it, which plays over all Leonardo's work. Besides, the picture is a portrait. From childhood we see this image defining itself on the fabric of his dreams, and but for express historical testimony, we might fancy

7. Johann Joachim Winckelmann (1717–68), German classicist.
8. "La Gioconda" or "Mona Lisa," famous painting by Leonardo da Vinci which now hangs in the Louvre in Paris. The sitter for the portrait may have been Lisa, the third wife of the Florentine Francesco del Giocondo (to whom Pater refers as "Il Giocondo") —hence her title, La Gioconda. *Mona* (more correctly *Monna*) *Lisa* means "Madonna Lisa" or "My Lady Lisa."

This selection is drawn from the essay on Leonardo da Vinci.
9. Albrecht Dürer (1471–1528), German artist whose picture of the spirit of Melancholy is full of details which may stimulate reflection in the spectator.
1. Andrea del Verrocchio (1435–88), Florentine painter and sculptor. Giorgio Vasari, author of *Lives of the Most Excellent Italian Painters* (1550).

that this was but his ideal lady, embodied and beheld at last. What was the relationship of a living Florentine to this creature of his thought? By what strange affinities had the dream and the person grown up thus apart, and yet so closely together? Present from the first incorporeally in Leonardo's brain, dimly traced in the designs of Verrocchio, she is found present at last in Il Giocondo's house. That there is much of mere portraiture in the picture is attested by the legend that by artificial means, the presence of mimes[2] and flute-players, that subtle expression was protracted on the face. Again, was it in four years and by renewed labor never really completed, or in four months and as by stroke of magic, that the image was projected?

The presence that rose thus so strangely beside the waters, is expressive of what in the ways of a thousand years men had come to desire. Hers is the head upon which all "the ends of the world are come,"[3] and the eyelids are a little weary. It is a beauty wrought out from within upon the flesh, the deposit, little cell by cell, of strange thoughts and fantastic reveries and exquisite passions. Set it for a moment beside one of those white Greek goddesses or beautiful women of antiquity, and how would they be troubled by this beauty, into which the soul with all its maladies has passed! All the thoughts and experience of the world have etched and molded there, in that which they have of power to refine and make expressive the outward form, the animalism of Greece, the lust of Rome, the mysticism of the Middle Age with its spiritual ambition and imaginative loves, the return of the Pagan world, the sins of the Borgias.[4] She is older than the rocks among which she sits; like the vampire,[5] she has been dead many times, and learned the secrets of the grave; and has been a diver in deep seas, and keeps their fallen day about her; and trafficked for strange webs with Eastern merchants, and, as Leda, was the mother of Helen of Troy,[6] and, as Saint Anne, the mother of Mary; and all this has been to her but as the sound of lyres and flutes, and lives only in the delicacy with which it has molded the changing lineaments, and tinged the eyelids and the hands. The fancy of a perpetual life, sweeping together ten thousand experiences, is an old one; and modern philosophy has conceived the idea of humanity as wrought upon by, and summing up in itself, all modes of thought and life. Certainly Lady Lisa might stand as the embodiment of the old fancy, the symbol of the modern idea.

2. Mimics or clowns.
3. I Corinthians x.11.
4. The Borgias were an Italian family during the Renaissance whose reputation for scandalous conduct was notorious.

5. A dead body which, according to widespread legends, returns from the grave to prey upon the living.
6. Leda's union with Zeus (who approached her in the form of a swan) produced Helen of Troy.

Conclusion[7]

Δέγει που Ἡράκλειτος ὅτι πάντα χωρεῖ καὶ οὐδὲν μένει[8]

To regard all things and principles of things as inconstant modes or fashions has more and more become the tendency of modern thought. Let us begin with that which is without—our physical life. Fix upon it in one of its more exquisite intervals, the moment, for instance, of delicious recoil from the flood of water in summer heat. What is the whole physical life in that moment but a combination of natural elements to which science gives their names? But those elements, phosphorus and lime and delicate fibers, are present not in the human body alone: we detect them in places most remote from it. Our physical life is a perpetual motion of them—the passage of the blood, the waste and repairing of the lenses of the eye, the modification of the tissues of the brain under every ray of light and sound—processes which science reduces to simpler and more elementary forces. Like the elements of which we are composed, the action of these forces extends beyond us: it rusts iron and ripens corn. Far out on every side of us those elements are broadcast, driven in many currents; and birth and gesture and death and the springing of violets from the grave are but a few out of ten thousand resultant combinations. That clear, perpetual outline of face and limb is but an image of ours, under which we group them— a design in a web, the actual threads of which pass out beyond it. This at least of flamelike our life has, that it is but the concurrence, renewed from moment to moment, of forces parting sooner or later on their ways.

Or, if we begin with the inward world of thought and feeling, the whirlpool is still more rapid, the flame more eager and devouring. There it is no longer the gradual darkening of the eye, the gradual fading of color from the wall—movements of the shore-side, where the water flows down indeed, though in apparent rest—but the race of the midstream, a drift of momentary acts of sight and passion and thought. At first sight experience seems to bury us under a flood of external objects, pressing upon us with a sharp and importunate reality, calling us out of ourselves in a thousand forms of action. But when reflection begins to play upon those objects they are dissipated under its influence; the cohesive force seems suspended like some trick of magic; each object is loosed into a group of impressions—color, odor, texture—in the mind of the observer.

7. "This brief 'Conclusion' was omitted in the second edition of this book, as I conceived it might possibly mislead some of those young men into whose hands it might fall. On the whole, I have thought it best to reprint it here, with some slight changes which bring it closer to my original meaning. I have dealt more fully in *Marius the Epicurean* with the thoughts suggested by it" [Pater's note to the third edition, 1888].
8. "Heraclitus says, 'All things give way; nothing remaineth'" [Pater's translation].

And if we continue to dwell in thought on this world, not of objects in the solidity with which language invests them, but of impressions, unstable, flickering, inconsistent, which burn and are extinguished with our consciousness of them, it contracts still further: the whole scope of observation is dwarfed into the narrow chamber of the individual mind. Experience, already reduced to a group of impressions, is ringed round for each one of us by that thick wall of personality through which no real voice has ever pierced on its way to us, or from us to that which we can only conjecture to be without. Every one of those impressions is the impression of the individual in his isolation, each mind keeping as a solitary prisoner its own dream of a world. Analysis goes a step farther still, and assures us that those impressions of the individual mind to which, for each one of us, experience dwindles down, are in perpetual flight; that each of them is limited by time, and that as time is infinitely divisible, each of them is infinitely divisible also; all that is actual in it being a single moment, gone while we try to apprehend it, of which it may ever be more truly said that it has ceased to be than that it is. To such a tremulous wisp constantly reforming itself on the stream, to a single sharp impression, with a sense in it, a relic more or less fleeting, of such moments gone by, what is real in our life fines itself down. It is with this movement, with the passage and dissolution of impressions, images, sensations, that analysis leaves off—that continual vanishing away, that strange, perpetual weaving and unweaving of ourselves.

Philosophiren, says Novalis, *ist dephlegmatisiren, vivificiren.*[9] The service of philosophy, of speculative culture, towards the human spirit is to rouse, to startle it to a life of constant and eager observation. Every moment some form grows perfect in hand or face; some tone on the hills or the sea is choicer than the rest; some mood of passion or insight or intellectual excitement is irresistibly real and attractive to us—for that moment only. Not the fruit of experience, but experience itself, is the end. A counted number of pulses only is given to us of a variegated, dramatic life. How may we see in them all that is to be seen in them by the finest senses? How shall we pass most swiftly from point to point, and be present always at the focus where the greatest number of vital forces unite in their purest energy?

To burn always with this hard, gemlike flame, to maintain this ecstasy, is success in life. In a sense it might even be said that our failure is to form habits: for, after all, habit is relative to a stereotyped world, and meantime it is only the roughness of the eye that makes any two persons, things, situations, seem alike. While all

---

9. "To philosophize is to cast off inertia, to make oneself alive." "Novalis" was the pseudonym of Friedrich von Hardenberg (1772–1801), German Romantic writer.

melts under our feet, we may well grasp at any exquisite passion, or any contribution to knowledge that seems by a lifted horizon to set the spirit free for a moment, or any stirring of the senses, strange dyes, strange colors, and curious odors, or work of the artist's hands, or the face of one's friend. Not to discriminate every moment some passionate attitude in those about us, and in the very brilliancy of their gifts some tragic dividing of forces on their ways, is, on this short day of frost and sun, to sleep before evening. With this sense of the splendor of our experience and of its awful brevity, gathering all we are into one desperate effort to see and touch, we shall hardly have time to make theories about the things we see and touch. What we have to do is to be forever curiously testing new opinions and courting new impressions, never acquiescing in a facile ortho- doxy of Comte, or of Hegel,[1] or of our own. Philosophical theories or ideas, as points of view, instruments of criticism, may help us to gather up what might otherwise pass unregarded by us. "Philosophy is the microscope of thought." The theory or idea or system which requires of us the sacrifice of any part of this experience, in con- sideration of some interest into which we cannot enter, or some abstract theory we have not identified with ourselves, or of what is only conventional, has no real claim upon us.

One of the most beautiful passages of Rousseau is that in the sixth book of the *Confessions,* where he describes the awakening in him of the literary sense. An undefinable taint of death had clung always about him, and now in early manhood he believed himself smitten by mortal disease. He asked himself how he might make as much as possible of the interval that remained; and he was not biased by anything in his previous life when he decided that it must be by intellectual excitement, which he found just then in the clear, fresh writings of Voltaire. Well! we are all *condamnés* as Victor Hugo says: we are all under sentence of death but with a sort of indefinite reprieve—*les hommes sont tous condamnés à mort avec des sursis indéfinis:* we have an interval, and then our place knows us no more. Some spend this interval in listlessness, some in high passions, the wisest, at least among "the children of this world," in art and song. For our one chance lies in expanding that interval, in getting as many pulsations as possible into the given time Great passions may give us this quickened sense of life, ecstasy and sorrow of love, the various forms of enthusiastic activity, dis- interested or otherwise, which come naturally to many of us. Only be sure it is passion—that it does yield you this fruit of a quickened, multiplied consciousness. Of such wisdom, the poetic passion, the desire of beauty, the love of art for its own sake, has most. For art comes to you proposing frankly to give nothing but the highest

---

1. Auguste Comte (1798–1857), French founder of positivism; Georg W. F. Hegel (1770–1831), German idealistic philosopher.

quality to your moments as they pass, and simply for those moments' sake.

1868   1873

From Appreciations
From *Style*

Since all progress of mind consists for the most part in differentiation, in the resolution of an obscure and complex object into its component aspects, it is surely the stupidest of losses to confuse things which right reason has put asunder, to lose the sense of achieved distinctions, the distinction between poetry and prose, for instance, or, to speak more exactly, between the laws and characteristic excellences of verse and prose composition. On the other hand, those who have dwelt most emphatically on the distinction between prose and verse, prose and poetry, may sometimes have been tempted to limit the proper functions of prose too narrowly; and this again is at least false economy, as being, in effect, the renunciation of a certain means or faculty, in a world where after all we must needs make the most of things. Critical efforts to limit art *a priori*,[1] by anticipations regarding the natural incapacity of the material with which this or that artist works, as the sculptor with solid form, or the prose-writer with the ordinary language of men, are always liable to be discredited by the facts of artistic production; and while prose is actually found to be a colored thing with Bacon, picturesque with Livy and Carlyle, musical with Cicero and Newman, mystical and intimate with Plato and Michelet[2] and Sir Thomas Browne, exalted or florid, it may be, with Milton and Taylor,[3] it will be useless to protest that it can be nothing at all, except something very tamely and narrowly confined to mainly practical ends—a kind of "good round hand"; as useless as the protest that poetry might not touch prosaic subjects as with Wordsworth, or an abstruse matter as with Browning, or treat contemporary life nobly as with Tennyson. In subordination to one essential beauty in all good literary style, in all literature as a fine art, as there are many beauties of poetry so the beauties of prose are many, and it is the business of criticism to estimate them as such; as it is good in the criticism of verse to look for those hard, logical, and quasi-prosaic excellences which that too has, or needs. To find in the poem, amid the flowers, the allusions, the mixed perspectives, of *Lycidas* for instance, the thought, the logical structure: how wholesome! how delightful! as to identify in prose what we call the poetry,

---

1. Prior to experience.
2. Jules Michelet (1798–1874), French historian.

3. Jeremy Taylor (1613–67), famous for the elaborate style of his sermons.

the imaginative power, not treating it as out of place and a kind of vagrant intruder, but by way of an estimate of its rights, that is, of its achieved powers, there.

Dryden, with the characteristic instinct of his age, loved to emphasize the distinction between poetry and prose, the protest against their confusion with each other, coming with somewhat diminished effect from one whose poetry was so prosaic. In truth, his sense of prosaic excellence affected his verse rather than his prose, which is not only fervid, richly figured, poetic, as we say, but vitiated, all unconsciously, by many a scanning line. Setting up correctness, that humble merit of prose, as the central literary excellence, he is really a less correct writer than he may seem, still with an imperfect mastery of the relative pronoun. It might have been foreseen that, in the rotations of mind, the province of poetry in prose would find its assertor; and, a century after Dryden, amid very different intellectual needs, and with the need therefore of great modifications in literary form, the range of the poetic force in literature was effectively enlarged by Wordsworth. The true distinction between prose and poetry he regarded as the almost technical or accidental one of the absence or presence of metrical beauty, or, say! metrical restraint; and for him the opposition came to be between verse and prose of course; but, as the essential dichotomy in this matter, between imaginative and unimaginative writing, parallel to De Quincey's distinction between "the literature of power and the literature of knowledge,"[4] in the former of which the composer gives us not fact, but his peculiar sense of fact, whether past or present.

Dismissing then, under sanction of Wordsworth, that harsher opposition of poetry to prose, as savoring in fact of the arbitrary psychology of the last century, and with it the prejudice that there can be but one only beauty of prose style, I propose here to point out certain qualities of all literature as a fine art, which, if they apply to the literature of fact, apply still more to the literature of the imaginative sense of fact, while they apply indifferently to verse and prose, so far as either is really imaginative—certain conditions of true art in both alike, which conditions may also contain in them the secret of the proper discrimination and guardianship of the peculiar excellences of either.

The line between fact and something quite different from external fact is, indeed, hard to draw. In Pascal,[5] for instance, in the persuasive writers generally, how difficult to define the point where, from time to time, argument which, if it is to be worth anything at all, must consist of facts or groups of facts, becomes a pleading—a theorem no longer, but essentially an appeal to the reader to catch the writer's spirit, to think with him, if one can or will—an expres-

4. De Quincey's essay on this topic appeared in 1848.

5. Blaise Pascal (1623–62), French scientist, philosopher, and theologian.

sion no longer of fact but of his sense of it, his peculiar intuition of a world, prospective, or discerned below the faulty conditions of the present, in either case changed somewhat from the actual world. In science, on the other hand, in history so far as it conforms to scientific rule, we have a literary domain where the imagination may be thought to be always an intruder. And as, in all science, the functions of literature reduce themselves eventually to the transcribing of fact, so all the excellences of literary form in regard to science are reducible to various kinds of painstaking; this good quality being involved in all "skilled work" whatever, in the drafting of an act of parliament, as in sewing. Yet here again, the writer's sense of fact, in history especially, and in all those complex subjects which do but lie on the borders of science, will still take the place of fact, in various degrees. Your historian, for instance, with absolutely truthful intention, amid the multitude of facts presented to him must needs select, and in selecting assert something of his own humor, something that comes not of the world without but of a vision within. So Gibbon molds his unwieldy material to a preconceived view. Livy, Tacitus, Michelet, moving full of poignant sensibility amid the records of the past, each, after his own sense, modifies—who can tell where and to what degree?—and becomes something else than a transcriber; each, as he thus modifies, passing into the domain of art proper. For just in proportion as the writer's aim, consciously or unconsciously, comes to be the transcribing, not of the world, not of mere fact, but of his sense of it, he becomes an artist, his work *fine* art; and good art (as I hope ultimately to show) in proportion to the truth of his presentment of that sense; as in those humbler or plainer functions of literature also, truth— truth to bare fact, there—is the essence of such artistic quality as they may have. Truth! there can be no merit, no craft at all, without that. And further, all beauty is in the long run only *fineness* of truth, or what we call expression, the finer accommodation of speech to that vision within.

—The transcript of his sense of fact rather than the fact, as being preferable, pleasanter, more beautiful to the writer himself. In literature, as in every other product of human skill, in the molding of a bell or a platter for instance, wherever this sense asserts itself, wherever the producer so modifies his work as, over and above its primary use or intention, to make it pleasing (to himself, of course, in the first instance) there, "fine" as opposed to merely serviceable art, exists. Literary art, that is, like all art which is in any way imitative or reproductive of fact—form, or color, or incident—is the representation of such fact as connected with soul, of a specific personality, in its preferences, its volition and power.

Such is the matter of imaginative or artistic literature—this transcript, not of mere fact, but of fact in its infinite variety, as modified by human preference in all its infinitely varied forms. It will be good literary art not because it is brilliant or sober, or rich, or impulsive, or severe, but just in proportion as its representation of that sense, that soul-fact, is true, verse being only one department of such literature, and imaginative prose, it may be thought, being the special art of the modern world. That imaginative prose should be the special and opportune art of the modern world results from two important facts about the latter: first, the chaotic variety and complexity of its interests, making the intellectual issue, the really master currents of the present time incalculable—a condition of mind little susceptible of the restraint proper to verse form, so that the most characteristic verse of the nineteenth century has been lawless verse; and secondly, an all-pervading naturalism, a curiosity about everything whatever as it really is, involving a certain humility of attitude, cognate to what must, after all, be the less ambitious form of literature. And prose thus asserting itself as the special and privileged artistic faculty of the present day, will be, however critics may try to narrow its scope, as varied in its excellence as humanity itself reflecting on the facts of its latest experience—an instrument of many stops, meditative, observant, descriptive, eloquent, analytic, plaintive, fervid. Its beauties will be not exclusively "pedestrian": it will exert, in due measure, all the varied charms of poetry, down to the rhythm which, as in Cicero, or Michelet, or Newman, at their best, gives its musical value to every syllable. * * *

If the style be the man, in all the color and intensity of a veritable apprehension, it will be in a real sense "impersonal."

I said, thinking of books like Victor Hugo's *Les Misérables*, that prose literature was the characteristic art of the nineteenth century, as others, thinking of its triumphs since the youth of Bach, have assigned that place to music. Music and prose literature are, in one sense, the opposite terms of art; the art of literature presenting to the imagination, through the intelligence, a range of interests, as free and various as those which music presents to it through sense. And certainly the tendency of what has been here said is to bring literature too under those conditions, by conformity to which music takes rank as the typically perfect art. If music be the ideal of all art whatever, precisely because in music it is impossible to distinguish the form from the substance or matter, the subject from the expression, then, literature, by finding its specific excellence in the absolute correspondence of the term to its import, will be but fulfilling the condition of all artistic quality in things everywhere, of all good art.

Good art, but not necessarily great art; the distinction between great art and good art depending immediately, as regards literature at all events, not on its form, but on the matter. Thackeray's *Esmond*, surely, is greater art than *Vanity Fair*, by the greater dignity of its interests. It is on the quality of the matter it informs or controls, its compass, its variety, its alliance to great ends, or the depth of the note of revolt, or the largeness of hope in it, that the greatness of literary art depends, as *The Divine Comedy, Paradise Lost, Les Misérables,* the English Bible, are great art. Given the conditions I have tried to explain as constituting good art—then, if it be devoted further to the increase of men's happiness, to the redemption of the oppressed, or the enlargement of our sympathies with each other, or to such presentment of new or old truth about ourselves and our relation to the world as may ennoble and fortify us in our sojourn here, or immediately, as with Dante, to the glory of God, it will be also great art; if, over and above those qualities I summed up as mind and soul—that color and mystic perfume, and that reasonable structure, it has something of the soul of humanity in it, and finds its logical, architectural place, in the great structure of human life.

1889

Topics in Victorian Literature

EVOLUTION

One of the most dramatic controversies in the Victorian age concerned theories of evolution. This controversy exploded into prominence in 1859 when Charles Darwin's *Origin of Species* was published, but it had been rumbling for many years previously. Sir Charles Lyell's *Principles of Geology* (1830) and Robert Chambers' popular book, *Vestiges of Creation* (1843–46), had already raised issues which Tennyson aired in his *In Memoriam* (1850). It was Darwin, however, with his monumental marshaling of evidence to establish his theory of natural selection, who finally brought the topic fully into the open, and the public, as well as the experts, took sides.

The opposition aroused by Darwin's treatise came from two different quarters. The first consisted of some of his fellow scientists who affirmed that his theory was unsound. The second consisted of religious leaders who attacked his theory because it seemed to contradict a literal interpretation of the Bible. Sometimes the two kinds of opposition combined forces as in 1860 when his scientific opponents selected Bishop Wilberforce to be their spokesman in spearheading their attack on *The Origin of Species*. In replying to such attacks, Darwin had the good fortune to be supported by two of the ablest popularizers of science in his day, T. H. Huxley and John Tyndall. Moreover, although shy by temperament, Darwin was himself (as Tyndall affirms and the following selections will illustrate) an exceptionally effective expositor of his own theories.

For other discussions of this topic of evolution, see, in the present volume, Arnold's *Literature and Science*, p. 1130; Browning's *Caliban Upon Setebos*, p. 986; T. H. Huxley's essays, p. 1300; Tennyson's *Locksley Hall*, p. 845, *In Memoriam*, p. 856, and *The Dawn*, p. 923.

CHARLES DARWIN: *From* The Descent of Man
[*Natural Selection and Sexual Selection*][1]

A brief summary will here be sufficient to recall to the reader's mind the more salient points in this work. Many of the views which

---

1. Charles Darwin (1809–82) developed an interest in geology and biology at Cambridge where he was studying to become a clergyman. Aided by a private income, he resolved to devote the rest of his life to scientific research. The observations he made during a long voyage to the South Seas on H.M.S. *Beagle* (on which he served as a naturalist) led Darwin to construct hypotheses about evolution. In 1858, more than twenty years after his re-

have been advanced are highly speculative, and some no doubt will prove erroneous; but I have in every case given the reasons which have led me to one view rather than to another. It seemed worth while to try how far the principle of evolution would throw light on some of the more complex problems in the natural history of man. False facts are highly injurious to the progress of science, for they often long endure; but false views, if supported by some evidence, do little harm, as everyone takes a salutary pleasure in proving their falseness; and when this is done, one path towards error is closed and the road to truth is often at the same time opened.

The main conclusion arrived at in this work, and now held by many naturalists who are well competent to form a sound judgment, is that man is descended from some less highly organized form. The grounds upon which this conclusion rests will never be shaken, for the close similarity between man and the lower animals in embryonic development, as well as in innumerable points of structure and constitution, both of high and of the most trifling importance—the rudiments which he retains, and the abnormal reversions to which he is occasionally liable—are facts which cannot be disputed. They have long been known, but until recently they told us nothing with respect to the origin of man. Now when viewed by the light of our knowledge of the whole organic world, their meaning is unmistakable. The great principle of evolution stands up clear and firm, when these groups of facts are considered in connection with others, such as the mutual affinities of the members of the same group, their geographical distribution in past and present times, and their geological succession. It is incredible that all these facts should speak falsely. He who is not content to look, like a savage, at the phenomena of nature as disconnected cannot any longer believe that man is the work of a separate act of creation. He will be forced to admit that the close resemblance of the embryo of man to that, for instance, of a dog—the construction of his skull, limbs, and whole frame, independently of the uses to which the parts may be put, on the same plan with that of other mammals—the occasional reappearance of various structures, for instance of several distinct muscles, which man does not normally possess, but which are common to the Quadrumana[2]—and a crowd of analogous facts—all point in the plainest manner to the conclusion that man is the codescendant with other mammals of a common pro-

turn to England from his voyage, he ventured to submit a paper developing his theory of the origin of species. A year later, when his theory appeared in book form, Darwin emerged as a famous and controversial figure. During the remainder of his life he published several treatises, some of which develop and clarify the theory of *The Origin of Species*. One of these works, *The Descent of Man* (1871) was espe-

cially provocative in its stress on the similarities between men and animals and in its naturalistic explanations of the beautiful colorings of birds, insects, and flowers. The present selection is from Chapter XXI of *The Descent of Man*.

2. Animals such as monkeys whose hind feet and forefeet can be used as hands—hence "four-handed."

genitor. * * *

By considering the embryological structure of man—the homologies which he presents with the lower animals, the rudiments which he retains, and the reversions to which he is liable—we can partly recall in imagination the former condition of our early progenitors; and can approximately place them in their proper position in the zoological series. We thus learn that man is descended from a hairy quadruped, furnished with a tail and pointed ears, probably arboreal in its habits, and an inhabitant of the Old World. This creature, if its whole structure had been examined by a naturalist, would have been classed amongst the Quadrumana, as surely as would the common and still more ancient progenitor of the Old and New World monkeys. The Quadrumana and all the higher mammals are probably derived from an ancient marsupial animal, and this through a long line of diversified forms, either from some reptile-like or some amphibianlike creature, and this again from some fishlike animal. In the dim obscurity of the past we can see that the early progenitor of all the Vertebrata must have been an aquatic animal, provided with branchae, with the two sexes united in the same individual, and with the most important organs of the body (such as the brain and heart) imperfectly developed. This animal seems to have been more like the larvae of our existing marine ascidians[3] than any other known form. * * *

Sexual selection has been treated at great length in these volumes; for, as I have attempted to show, it has played an important part in the history of the organic world. * * *

The belief in the power of sexual selection rests chiefly on the following considerations. The characters which we have the best reason for supposing to have been thus acquired are confined to one sex; and this alone renders it probable that they are in some way connected with the act of reproduction. These characters in innumerable instances are fully developed only at maturity; and often during only a part of the year, which is always the breeding season. The males (passing over a few exceptional cases) are the most active in courtship; they are the best armed, and are rendered the most attractive in various ways. It is to be especially observed that the males display their attractions with elaborate care in the presence of the females; and that they rarely or never display them excepting during the season of love. It is incredible that all this display should be purposeless. Lastly we have distinct evidence with some quadrupeds and birds that the individuals of the one sex are capable of feeling a strong antipathy or preference for certain individuals of the opposite sex.

Bearing these facts in mind, and not forgetting the marked re-

3. Part of a group of marine animals called Tunicata, or popularly "sea squirts," sometimes assumed to be ancestors of the vertebrate animals.

sults of man's unconscious selection, it seems to me almost certain that if the individuals of one sex were during a long series of generations to prefer pairing with certain individuals of the other sex, characterized in some peculiar manner, the offspring would slowly but surely become modified in this same manner. I have not attempted to conceal that, excepting when the males are more numerous than the females, or when polygamy prevails, it is doubtful how the more attractive males succeed in leaving a larger number of offspring to inherit their superiority in ornaments or other charms than the less attractive males; but I have shown that this would probably follow from the females—especially the more vigorous females which would be the first to breed, preferring not only the more attractive but at the same time the more vigorous and victorious males.

Although we have some positive evidence that birds appreciate bright and beautiful objects, as with the bowerbirds of Australia, and although they certainly appreciate the power of song, yet I fully admit that it is an astonishing fact that the females of many birds and some mammals should be endowed with sufficient taste for what has apparently been effected through sexual selection; and this is even more astonishing in the case of reptiles, fish, and insects. But we really know very little about the minds of the lower animals. It cannot be supposed that male birds of paradise or peacocks, for instance, should take so much pains in erecting, spreading, and vibrating their beautiful plumes before the females for no purpose. We should remember the fact given on excellent authority in a former chapter, namely that several peahens, when debarred from an admired male, remained widows during a whole season rather than pair with another bird.

Nevertheless I know of no fact in natural history more wonderful than that the female argus pheasant should be able to appreciate the exquisite shading of the ball-and-socket ornaments and the elegant patterns on the wing feathers of the male. He who thinks that the male was created as he now exists must admit that the great plumes, which prevent the wings from being used for flight, and which, as well as the primary feathers, are displayed in a manner quite peculiar to this one species during the act of courtship, and at no other time, were given to him as an ornament. If so, he must likewise admit that the female was created and endowed with the capacity of appreciating such ornaments. I differ only in the conviction that the male argus pheasant acquired his beauty gradually, through the females having preferred during many generations the more highly ornamented males; the aesthetic capacity of the females having been advanced through exercise or habit in the same manner as our own taste is gradually improved. In the male, through the fortunate chance of a few feathers not having been modified, we can distinctly see how simple spots with a little fulvous[4] shading on one side might have been developed by small and graduated steps into the wonderful ball-and-socket ornaments; and it is probable that they were actually thus developed. * * *

He who admits the principle of sexual selection will be led to the remarkable conclusion that the cerebral system not only regulates most of the existing functions of the body, but has indirectly influenced the progressive development of various bodily structures and of certain mental qualities. Courage, pugnacity, perseverance, strength and size of body, weapons of all kinds, musical organs, both vocal and instrumental, bright colors, stripes and marks, and ornamental appendages have all been indirectly gained by the one sex or the other, through the influence of love and jealousy, through the appreciation of the beautiful in sound, color or form, and through the exertion of a choice; and these powers of the mind manifestly depend on the development of the cerebral system. * * *

The main conclusion arrived at in this work, namely that man is descended from some lowly-organized form, will, I regret to think, be highly distasteful to many persons. But there can hardly be a doubt that we are descended from barbarians. The astonishment which I felt on first seeing a party of Fuegians[5] on a wild and broken shore will never be forgotten by me, for the reflection at once rushed into my mind—such were our ancestors. These men were absolutely naked and bedaubed with paint, their long hair was tangled, their mouths frothed with excitement, and their expression was wild, startled, and distrustful. They possessed hardly any arts, and like wild animals lived on what they could catch; they had no government, and were merciless to everyone not of their own small tribe. He who has seen a savage in his native land will not feel much shame, if forced to acknowledge that the blood of some more humble creature flows in his veins. For my own part I would as soon be descended from that heroic little monkey, who braved his dreaded enemy in order to save the life of his keeper; or from that old baboon, who, descending from the mountains, carried away in triumph his young comrade from a crowd of astonished dogs[6]— as from a savage who delights to torture his enemies, offers up bloody sacrifices, practices infanticide without remorse, treats his wives like slaves, knows no decency, and is haunted by the grossest superstitions.

Man may be excused for feeling some pride at having risen, though not through his own exertions, to the very summit of the

---

4. Dull yellow.
5. Savages inhabiting the islands off the southern tip of South America. Tierra del Fuego, which Darwin had visited in 1832. See his *Voyage of the*

Beagle. Chapter X.
6. Incidents described in Chapter IV of *The Descent of Man* to demonstrate that animals may be endowed with a moral sense.

organic scale; and the fact of his having thus risen, instead of having been aboriginally placed there, may give him hopes for a still higher destiny in the distant future. But we are not here concerned with hopes or fears, only with the truth as far as our reason allows us to discover it. I have given the evidence to the best of my ability; and we must acknowledge, as it seems to me, that man with all his noble qualities, with sympathy which feels for the most debased, with benevolence which extends not only to other men but to the humblest living creature, with his godlike intellect which has penetrated into the movements and constitution of the solar system— with all these exalted powers—Man still bears in his bodily frame the indelible stamp of his lowly origin.

JOHN TYNDALL: *From* The Belfast Address
[*Darwin's Method of Argument*][7]

Mr. Darwin shirks no difficulty; and, saturated as the subject was with his own thought, he must have known, better than his critics, the weakness as well as the strength of his theory. This of course would be of little avail were his object a temporary dialectic victory, instead of the establishment of a truth which he means to be everlasting. But he takes no pains to disguise the weakness he has discerned; nay, he takes every pains to bring it into the strongest light. His vast resources enable him to cope with objections started by himself and others, so as to leave the final impression upon the reader's mind that, if they be not completely answered, they certainly are not fatal. Their negative force being thus destroyed, you are free to be influenced by the vast positive mass of evidence he is able to bring before you. This largeness of knowledge, and readiness of resource, render Mr. Darwin the most terrible of antagonists. Accomplished naturalists have leveled heavy and sustained criticisms against him—not always with the view of fairly weighing his theory, but with the express intention of exposing its weak points only. This does not irritate him. He treats every objection with a soberness and thoroughness which even Bishop Butler [8] might be proud to imitate, surrounding each fact with its appropriate detail, placing it in its proper relations, and usually giving it a significance which, as long as it was kept isolated, failed to appear. This is done without a trace of ill temper. He moves over the subject with the passionless strength of a glacier; and the

7. John Tyndall (1820–93) was a physicist and popularizer of science. In 1874 he delivered an address on religion and science entitled *The Belfast Address*, later published in his collection of essays, *Fragments of Science* (1899).

8. Joseph Butler (1692–1752), Bishop of Durham. In his book *The Analogy of Religion* (1736), objections to religious faith are aired calmly and fully before being answered by the author.

grinding of the rocks is not always without a counterpart in the logical pulverization of the objector. But though in handling this mighty theme all passion has been stilled, there is an emotion of the intellect, incident to the discernment of new truth, which often colors and warms the pages of Mr. Darwin. His success has been great; and this implies not only the solidity of his work, but the preparedness of the public mind for such a revelation. On this head, a remark of Agassiz[9] impressed me more than anything else. Sprung from a race of theologians, this celebrated man combated to the last the theory of natural selection. One of the many times I had the pleasure of meeting him in the United States was at Mr. Winthrop's beautiful residence at Brookline, near Boston. Rising from luncheon, we all halted as if by common consent, in front of a window, and continued there a discussion which had been started at table. The maple was in its autumn glory, and the exquisite beauty of the scene outside seemed, in my case, to interpenetrate without disturbance the intellectual action. Earnestly, almost sadly, Agassiz turned, and said to the gentlemen standing round, "I confess that I was not prepared to see this theory received as it has been by the best intellects of our time. Its success is greater than I could have thought possible."

1874, 1899

LEONARD HUXLEY: *From* The Life and Letters
of Thomas Henry Huxley
[*The Huxley-Wilberforce Debate at Oxford*][1]

The famous Oxford Meeting of 1860 was of no small importance in Huxley's career. It was not merely that he helped to save a great cause from being stifled under misrepresentation and ridicule— that he helped to extort for it a fair hearing; it was now that he first made himself known in popular estimation as a dangerous adversary in debate—a personal force in the world of science which

9. Louis Agassiz (1807–73), Swiss naturalist who became professor of zoology and geology at Harvard. He refused to accept the concept of evolution.
1. At meetings of the British Association for the Advancement of Science, the reading of a paper is followed by a discussion. In 1860, at Oxford, this discussion developed into a debate between Thomas Henry Huxley, a defender of Darwin's theories, and Bishop Samuel Wilberforce (1805–73). Although he had majored in mathematics as an undergraduate, Wilberforce could hardly lay claim to be a scientist. He was willing, nevertheless, to serve as a spokesman for those scientists who dis-

agreed with *The Origin of Species*, and he reportedly came to the meeting ready to "smash Darwin." The bishop's principal qualifications for this role were his great powers as a smoothly persuasive orator (he was commonly known by his detractors as "Soapy Sam"), but he met more than his match in Huxley.
Because no complete transcript of this celebrated debate was made at the time, Huxley's son Leonard, had to reconstruct the scene by combining quotations from reports made by magazine writers and other witnesses. The account given here is from Chapter XIV.

could not be neglected. From this moment he entered the front fighting line in the most exposed quarter of the field. * * *

It was the merest chance, as I have already said, that Huxley attended the meeting of the section that morning. Dr. Draper of New York was to read a paper on the *Intellectual Development of Europe considered with reference to the views of Mr. Darwin.* "I can still hear," writes one who was present, "the American accents of Dr. Draper's opening address when he asked 'Air we a fortuitous concourse of atoms?' " However, it was not to hear him, but the eloquence of the Bishop, that the members of the Association crowded in such numbers into the Lecture Room of the Museum, that this, the appointed meeting place of the section, had to be abandoned for the long west room, since cut in two by a partition for the purposes of the library. It was not term time, nor were the general public admitted; nevertheless the room was crowded to suffocation long before the protagonists appeared on the scene, 700 persons or more managing to find places. The very windows by which the room was lighted down the length of its west side were packed with ladies, whose white handkerchiefs, waving and fluttering in the air at the end of the Bishop's speech, were an unforgettable factor in the acclamation of the crowd.

On the east side between the two doors was the platform. Professor Henslow, the President of the section, took his seat in the center; upon his right was the Bishop, and beyond him again Dr. Draper; on his extreme left was Mr. Dingle, a clergyman from Lanchester, near Durham, with Sir J. Hooker and Sir J. Lubbock in front of him, and nearer the center, Professor Beale of King's College, London, and Huxley.

The clergy, who shouted lustily for the Bishop, were massed in the middle of the room; behind them in the northwest corner a knot of undergraduates (one of these was T. H. Green, who listened but took no part in the cheering) had gathered together beside Professor Brodie, ready to lift their voices, poor minority though they were, for the opposite party. Close to them stood one of the few men among the audience already in Holy orders, who joined in—and indeed led—the cheers for the Darwinians.

So "Dr. Draper droned out his paper, turning first to the right hand and then to the left, of course bringing in a reference to the *Origin of Species* which set the ball rolling."

An hour or more that paper lasted, and then discussion began. The President "wisely announced *in limine*[2] that none who had not valid arguments to bring forward on one side or the other would be allowed to address the meeting; a caution that proved necessary, for no fewer than four combatants had their utterances burked by him, because of their indulgence in vague declamation."

2. As a starting point.

"First spoke" (writes Professor Farrar) "a layman from Brompton, who gave his name as being one of the Committee of the (newly formed) Economic section of the Association. He, in a stentorian voice, let off his theological venom. Then jumped up Richard Greswell with a thin voice, saying much the same, but speaking as a scholar; but we did not merely want any theological discussion, so we shouted them down. Then a Mr. Dingle got up and tried to show that Darwin would have done much better if he had taken him into consultation. He used the blackboard and began a mathematical demonstration on the question—'Let this point A be man, and let that point B be the mawnkey.' He got no further; he was shouted down with cries of 'mawnkey.' None of these had spoken more than three minutes. It was when these were shouted down that Henslow said he must demand that the discussion should rest on *scientific* grounds only.

"Then there were calls for the Bishop, but he rose and said he understood his friend Professor Beale had something to say first. Beale, who was an excellent histologist,[3] spoke to the effect that the new theory ought to meet with fair discussion, but added, with great modesty, that he himself had not sufficient knowledge to discuss the subject adequately. Then the Bishop spoke the speech that you know, and the question about his mother being an ape, or his grandmother."

From the scientific point of view, the speech was of small value. It was evident from his mode of handling the subject that he had been "crammed up to the throat," and knew nothing at first hand; he used no argument beyond those to be found in his *Quarterly* article, which appeared a few days later, and is now admitted to have been inspired by Owen.[4] "He ridiculed Darwin badly and Huxley savagely; but," confesses one of his strongest opponents, "all in such dulcet tones, so persuasive a manner, and in such well turned periods, that I who had been inclined to blame the President for allowing a discussion that could serve no scientific purpose, now forgave him from the bottom of my heart."

The Bishop spoke thus "for full half an hour with inimitable spirit, emptiness and unfairness." "In a light, scoffing tone, florid and fluent, he assured us there was nothing in the idea of evolution; rock pigeons were what rock pigeons had always been. Then, turning to his antagonist with a smiling insolence, he begged to know, was it through his grandfather or his grandmother that he claimed his descent from a monkey?"

This was the fatal mistake of his speech. Huxley instantly grasped the tactical advantage which the descent to personalities gave him. He turned to Sir Benjamin Brodie, who was sitting beside him, and emphatically striking his hand upon his knee, exclaimed, "The

3. Biologist specializing in the study of the minute structure of the tissues of plants and animals.

4. Sir Richard Owen (1804–92), a leading zoologist and paleontologist, was opposed to Darwin's theories.

Lord hath delivered him into mine hands." The bearing of the exclamation did not dawn upon Sir Benjamin until after Huxley had completed his "forcible and eloquent" answer to the scientific part of the Bishop's argument, and proceeded to make his famous retort.

"On this" (continues the writer in *Macmillan's Magazine*) "Mr. Huxley slowly and deliberately arose. A slight tall figure, stern and pale, very quiet and very grave, he stood before us and spoke those tremendous words—words which no one seems sure of now, nor, I think, could remember just after they were spoken, for their meaning took away our breath, though it left us in no doubt as to what it was. He was not ashamed to have a monkey for his ancestor; but he would be ashamed to be connected with a man who used great gifts to obscure the truth. No one doubted his meaning, and the effect was tremendous. One lady fainted and had to be carried out; I, for one, jumped out of my seat."

The fullest and probably most accurate account of these concluding words is the following, from a letter of the late John Richard Green, then an undergraduate, to his friend, afterwards Professor Boyd Dawkins·

"I asserted—and I repeat—that a man has no reason to be ashamed of having an ape for his grandfather. If there were an ancestor whom I should feel shame in recalling it would rather be a man—a man of restless and versatile intellect—who, not content with an equivocal success in his own sphere of activity, plunges into scientific questions with which he has no real acquaintance, only to obscure them by an aimless rhetoric, and distract the attention of his hearers from the real point at issue by eloquent digressions and skilled appeals to religious prejudice."

The result of this encounter, though a check to the other side, cannot, of course, be represented as an immediate and complete triumph for evolutionary doctrine. This was precluded by the character and temper of the audience, most of whom were less capable of being convinced by the arguments than shocked by the boldness of the retort, although, being gentlefolk, as Professor Farrar remarks, they were disposed to admit on reflection that the Bishop had erred on the score of taste and good manners. Nevertheless, it was a noticeable feature of the occasion, Sir M. Foster tells me, that when Huxley rose he was received coldly, just a cheer of encouragement from his friends, the audience as a whole not joining in it. But as he made his points the applause grew and widened, until, when he sat down, the cheering was not very much less than that given to the Bishop. To that extent he carried an unwilling audience with him by the force of his speech. The debate on the ape question, however, was continued elsewhere during the next two years, and the evidence was completed by the unanswerable demonstrations of Sir W. H. Flower at the Cambridge meeting of the Association in 1862.

The importance of the Oxford meeting lay in the open resistance that was made to authority, at a moment when even a drawn battle was hardly less effectual than acknowledged victory. Instead of being crushed under ridicule, the new theories secured a hearing, all the wider, indeed, for the startling nature of their defense.

1901

SIR EDMUND GOSSE: *From* Father and Son[5]
[*The Dilemma of the Fundamentalist and Scientist*]

So, through my Father's brain, in that year of scientific crisis, 1857, there rushed two kinds of thought, each absorbing, each convincing, yet totally irreconcilable. There is a peculiar agony in the paradox that truth has two forms, each of them indisputable, yet each antagonistic to the other. It was this discovery, that there were two theories of physical life, each of which was true, but the truth of each incompatible with the truth of the other, which shook the spirit of my Father with perturbation. It was not, really, a paradox, it was a fallacy, if he could only have known it, but he allowed the turbid volume of superstition to drown the delicate stream of reason. He took one step in the service of truth, and then he drew back in an agony, and accepted the servitude of error.

This was the great moment in the history of thought when the theory of the mutability of species was preparing to throw a flood of light upon all departments of human speculation and action. It was becoming necessary to stand emphatically in one army or the other. Lyell was surrounding himself with disciples, who were making strides in the direction of discovery. Darwin had long been collecting facts with regard to the variation of animals and plants. Hooker and Wallace, Asa Gray and even Agassiz, each in his own sphere, were coming closer and closer to a perception of that secret which was first to reveal itself clearly to the patient and humble genius of Darwin. In the year before, in 1856, Darwin, under pressure from Lyell, had begun that modest statement of the new revelation, that "abstract of an essay," which developed so mightily into *The Origin of Species*. Wollaston's *Variation of Species* had just appeared, and had been a nine days' wonder in the wilderness.

5. Philip Henry Gosse (1810–88) was a zoologist of some repute and also an ardent adherent of a strict Protestant sect, the Plymouth Brethren. To reconcile his scientific knowledge with his fundamentalist position in religion, Gosse published a book called *Omphalos* which pleased no one. His dilemma is described by his son, the literary critic Sir Edmund Gosse (1849–1928), in an autobiography published in 1907. The present selection is from Chapter V.

On the other side, the reactionaries, although never dreaming of the fate which hung over them, had not been idle. In 1857 the astounding question had for the first time been propounded with contumely, "What, then, did we come from orangoutang?" The famous *Vestiges of Creation* had been supplying a sugar-and-water panacea for those who could not escape from the trend of evidence, and who yet clung to revelation. Owen was encouraging reaction by resisting, with all the strength of his prestige, the theory of the mutability of species.

In this period of intellectual ferment, as when a great political revolution is being planned, many possible adherents were confidentially tested with hints and encouraged to reveal their bias in a whisper. It was the notion of Lyell, himself a great mover of men, that, before the doctrine of natural selection was given to a world which would be sure to lift up at it a howl of execration, a certain bodyguard of sound and experienced naturalists, expert in the description of species, should be privately made aware of its tenor. Among those who were thus initiated, or approached with a view towards possible illumination, was my Father. He was spoken to by Hooker, and later on by Darwin, after meetings of the Royal Society in the summer of 1857.

My Father's attitude towards the theory of natural selection was critical in his career, and oddly enough, it exercised an immense influence on my own experience as a child. Let it be admitted at once, mournful as the admission is, that every instinct in his intelligence went out at first to greet the new light. It had hardly done so, when a recollection of the opening chapter of Genesis checked it at the outset. He consulted with Carpenter, a great investigator, but one who was fully as incapable as himself of remodeling his ideas with regard to the old, accepted hypotheses. They both determined, on various grounds, to have nothing to do with the terrible theory, but to hold steadily to the law of the fixity of species. * * *

My Father had never admired Sir Charles Lyell. I think that the famous Lord Chancellor manner of the geologist intimidated him, and we undervalue the intelligence of those whose conversation puts us at a disadvantage. For Darwin and Hooker, on the other hand, he had a profound esteem, and I know not whether this had anything to do with the fact that he chose, for his impetuous experiment in reaction, the field of geology, rather than that of zoology or botany. Lyell had been threatening to publish a book on the geological history of Man, which was to be a bombshell flung into the camp of the catastrophists. My Father, after long reflection, prepared a theory of his own, which, as he fondly hoped, would take the wind out of Lyell's sails, and justify geology to godly readers of Genesis. It was, very briefly, that there had been no gradual modification of the surface of the earth, or slow development of organic forms, but that when the catastrophic act of creation took place, the world presented, instantly, the structural appearance of a planet on which life had long existed.

The theory, coarsely enough, and to my Father's great indignation, was defined by a hasty press as being this—that God hid the fossils in the rocks in order to tempt geologists into infidelity. In truth, it was the logical and inevitable conclusion of accepting, literally, the doctrine of a sudden act of creation; it emphasized the fact that any breach in the circular course of nature could be conceived only on the supposition that the object created bore false witness to past processes, which had never taken place.

Never was a book cast upon the waters with greater anticipations of success than was this curious, this obstinate, this fanatical volume. My Father lived in a fever of suspense, waiting for the tremendous issue. This *Omphalos* of his, he thought, was to bring all the turmoil of scientific speculation to a close, fling geology into the arms of Scripture, and make the lion eat grass with the lamb. It was not surprising, he admitted, that there had been experienced an ever-increasing discord between the facts which geology brings to light and the direct statements of the early chapters of Genesis. Nobody was to blame for that. My Father, and my Father alone, possessed the secret of the enigma; he alone held the key which could smoothly open the lock of geological mystery. He offered it, with a glowing gesture, to atheists and Christians alike. This was to be the universal panacea; this the system of intellectual therapeutics which could not but heal all the maladies of the age. But, alas! atheists and Christians alike looked at it, and laughed, and threw it away.

In the course of that dismal winter, as the post began to bring in private letters, few and chilly, and public reviews, many and scornful, my Father looked in vain for the approval of the churches, and in vain for the acquiescence of the scientific societies, and in vain for the gratitude of those "thousands of thinking persons," which he had rashly assured himself of receiving. As his reconciliation of Scripture statements and geological deductions was welcomed nowhere; as Darwin continued silent, and the youthful Huxley was scornful, and even Charles Kingsley,[6] from whom my Father had expected the most instant appreciation, wrote that he could not "give up the painful and slow conclusion of five and twenty years' study of geology, and believe that God has written on the rocks one enormous and superfluous lie"—as all this happened or failed to happen, a gloom, cold and dismal, descended upon our morning teacups. * * *

1907

6. Charles Kingsley (1819–75), clergyman and novelist.

INDUSTRIALISM: PROGRESS OR DECLINE?

Was the machine age a blessing or a curse? Was the middle-class economic system making mankind happier or more wretched? Was human progress probable, and how, in fact, is progress to be defined? In confronting these questions, Victorian writers were generally divided into two camps. The changes brought about by industrialism impressed one group of writers as an appalling retrogression. They pointed to the dreadful living and working conditions of the industrial classes, and they deplored the disappearance of what Karl Marx called the "feudal, patriarchal, idyllic relations" between employer and employee which, they believed, had existed in earlier economics. These critics are represented by essayists such as Carlyle, Ruskin, and Morris (see pp. 746, 1283, and 1171), and by novelists such as Charles Kingsley and Charles Dickens, whose pictures of a London slum and of an industrial town are included in the following selections. On this topic Dickens' position was actually a mixed one. He was aware that the past had its imperfections and that the colorful stagecoach (affectionately pictured in the first selection below) had to be superseded by the grim and grimy railway engine. Because of this awareness he was once accused by Ruskin of being "the leader of the steam whistle party *par excellence.*" In general, however, Dickens belonged in Ruskin's own camp; the ugliness of the machine age and, more specially, what seemed to him its hardheartedness, were deeply offensive to him and were consistently treated as targets for his satire. Related to this essentially conservative group, although working from assumptions and to conclusions altogether different from theirs, is Karl Marx. In his *Communist Manifesto* of 1848 Marx does not repudiate industrialism, but he does seek to expose what he and Friedrich Engels considered to be the inadequacies and iniquities of middle-class industrial society. In the opposite camp from Carlyle or Marx were writers who found the new society an unqualified improvement over societies of earlier ages. The historian Thomas Babington Macaulay was the most effective Victorian spokesman for this view. A masterful debater and a memorable prose stylist, Macaulay sought to show up the absurdity of anyone who did not share his satisfaction in the accomplishments of his own century. The popularity of his writings suggests that his position was shared by many of his contemporaries. One of these was the sociologist Herbert Spencer, an extreme example of a writer whose faith in the advantages of the new system was unbounded. The "advancement" of mankind toward a state of "perfection" was, according to Spencer, a "certainty." Basing his observations on the industrial development of England, Spencer argued that future human advancement would be accelerated by individual enterprise, whereas government control was almost invariably an obstacle to progress.

CHARLES DICKENS: *From* Martin Chuzzlewit[1]

[*A Journey by Stagecoach*]

When the coach came round at last, with "London" blazoned in letters of gold upon the boot,[2] it gave Tom such a turn, that he was half disposed to run away. But he didn't do it; for he took his seat upon the box instead, and looking down upon the four grays, felt as if he were another gray himself, or, at all events, a part of the turnout; and was quite confused by the novelty and splendor of his situation.

And really it might have confused a less modest man than Tom to find himself sitting next that coachman; for of all the swells that ever flourished a whip, professionally, he might have been elected emperor. He didn't handle his gloves like another man, but put them on—even when he was standing on the pavement, quite detached from the coach—as if the four grays were, somehow or other, at the ends of the fingers. It was the same with his hat. He did things with his hat, which nothing but an unlimited knowledge of horses and the wildest freedom of the road, could ever have made him perfect in. Valuable little parcels were brought to him with particular instructions, and he pitched them into this hat, and stuck it on again; as if the laws of gravity did not admit of such an event as its being knocked off or blown off and nothing like an accident could befall it. The guard, too! Seventy breezy miles a day were written in his very whiskers. His manners were a canter; his conversation a round trot. He was a fast coach upon a downhill turnpike road; he was all pace. A wagon couldn't have moved slowly, with that guard and his key bugle on the top of it.

These were all foreshadowings of London, Tom thought, as he sat upon the box, and looked about him. Such a coachman, and such a guard, never could have existed between Salisbury and any other place. The coach was none of your steady-going, yokel coaches, but a swaggering, rakish, dissipated London coach; up all night, and lying by all day, and leading a devil of a life. It cared no more for Salisbury than if it had been a hamlet. It rattled noisily through the best streets, defied the Cathedral, took the worst corners sharpest, went cutting in everywhere, making everything get out of its way; and spun along the open country road, blowing a lively defiance out of its key bugle, as its last glad parting legacy.

1. The passage is from Chapter XXXVI of the novel by Charles Dickens (1812–70). Tom Pinch, an unsophisticated architectural student from the cathedral town of Salisbury, is traveling to London by one of the fast coaches that had their heyday in the early decades of the 19th century. By 1843 coaches were rapidly being displaced by railways.
2. Luggage compartment.

It was a charming evening. Mild and bright. And even with the weight upon his mind which arose out of the immensity and uncertainty of London, Tom could not resist the captivating sense of rapid motion through the pleasant air. The four grays skimmed along, as if they liked it quite as well as Tom did; the bugle was in as high spirits as the grays; the coachman chimed in sometimes with his voice; the wheels hummed cheerfully in unison; the brass work on the harness was an orchestra of little bells; and thus, as they went clinking, jingling, rattling smoothly on, the whole concern, from the buckles of the leaders' coupling reins, to the handle of the hind boot, was one great instrument of music.

Yoho, past hedges, gates, and trees; past cottages and barns, and people going home from work. Yoho, past donkey chaises, drawn aside into the ditch, and empty carts with rampant horses, whipped up at a bound upon the little watercourse, and held by struggling carters close to the five-barred gate, until the coach had passed the narrow turning in the road. Yoho, by churches dropped down by themselves in quiet nooks, with rustic burial grounds about them, where the graves are green, and daisies sleep—for it is evening—on the bosoms of the dead. Yoho, past streams, in which the cattle cool their feet, and where the rushes grow; past paddock fences, farms, and rickyards; past last year's stacks, cut, slice by slice, away, and showing, in the waning light, like ruined gables, old and brown. Yoho, down the pebbly dip, and through the merry water splash, and up at a canter to the level road again. Yoho! Yoho!

1843

CHARLES DICKENS: *From* Dombey and Son

[*Railway-Construction in a London Suburb*][3]

The first shock of a great earthquake had, just at that period, rent the whole neighborhood to its center. Traces of its course were visible on every side. Houses were knocked down; streets broken through and stopped; deep pits and trenches dug in the ground; enormous heaps of earth and clay thrown up; buildings that were undermined and shaking, propped by great beams of wood. Here, a chaos of carts, overthrown and jumbled together, lay topsy-turvy at the bottom of a steep unnatural hill; there, confused treasures of iron soaked and rusted in something that had accidentally become a pond. Everywhere were bridges that led nowhere; thoroughfares that were wholly impassable; Babel towers of chimneys, want-

3. The year 1846, when *Dombey and Son* was being written, was a high point in the railway boom in England. This passage, from Chapter VI, pictures a housing complex, Staggs's Gardens, in Camden Town, a lower-class suburb of London.

ing half their height; temporary wooden houses and enclosures, in the most unlikely situations; carcases of ragged tenements, and fragments of unfinished walls and arches, and piles of scaffolding, and wildernesses of bricks, and giant forms of cranes, and tripods straddling above nothing. There were a hundred thousand shapes and substances of incompleteness, wildly mingled out of their places, upside down, burrowing in the earth, aspiring in the air, mouldering in the water, and unintelligible as any dream. Hot springs and fiery eruptions, the usual attendants upon earthquakes, lent their contributions of confusion to the scene. Boiling water hissed and heaved within dilapidated walls; whence, also, the glare and roar of flames came issuing forth; and mounds of ashes blocked up rights of way, and wholly changed the law and custom of the neighborhood.

In short, the yet unfinished and unopened Railroad was in progress; and, from the very core of all this dire disorder, trailed smoothly away, upon its mighty course of civilization and improvement.

But as yet, the neighborhood was shy to own the Railroad. One or two bold speculators had projected streets; and one had built a little, but had stopped among the mud and ashes to consider farther of it. A bran-new Tavern, redolent of fresh mortar and size, and fronting nothing at all, had taken for its sign The Railway Arms; but that might be rash enterprise—and then it hoped to sell drink to the workmen. So, the Excavators' House of Call had sprung up from a beer shop; and the old established Ham and Beef Shop had become the Railway Eating House, with a roast leg of pork daily, through interested motives of a similar immediate and popular description. Lodginghouse keepers were favorable in like manner; and for the like reasons were not to be trusted. The general belief was very slow. There were frowzy fields, and cow houses, and dunghills, and dustheaps, and ditches, and gardens, and summer houses, and carpet-beating grounds, at the very door of the Railway. Little tumuli of oyster shells in the oyster season, and of lobster shells in the lobster season, and of broken crockery and faded cabbage leaves in all seasons, encroached upon its high places. Posts, and rails, and old cautions to trespassers, and backs of mean houses, and patches of wretched vegetation, stared it out of countenance. Nothing was the better for it, or thought of being so. If the miserable waste ground lying near it could have laughed, it would have laughed it to scorn, like many of the miserable neighbors.

Staggs's Gardens was uncommonly incredulous. It was a little row of houses, with little squalid patches of ground before them, fenced off with old doors, barrel staves, scraps of tarpaulin, and dead bushes; with bottomless tin kettles and exhausted iron fenders, thrust into the gaps. Here, the Staggs's Gardeners trained scarlet beans, kept fowls and rabbits, erected rotten summer houses (one was an old boat), dried clothes, and smoked pipes. Some were of opinion that Staggs's Gardens derived its name from a deceased capitalist, one Mr. Staggs, who had built it for his delectation. Others, who had a natural taste for the country, held that it dated from those rural times when the antlered herd, under the familiar denomination of Staggses, had resorted to its shady precincts. Be this as it may, Staggs's Gardens was regarded by its population as a sacred grove not to be withered by railroads; and so confident were they generally of its long outliving any such ridiculous inventions, that the master chimney sweeper at the corner, who was understood to take the lead in the local politics of the Gardens, had publicly declared that on the occasion of the Railroad opening, if ever it did open, two of his boys should ascend the flues of his dwelling, with instructions to hail the failure with derisive jeers from the chimney pots.

[A Journey by Railway][4]

Through the hollow, on the height, by the heath, by the orchard, by the park, by the garden, over the canal, across the river, where the sheep are feeding, where the mill is going, where the barge is floating, where the dead are lying, where the factory is smoking, where the stream is running, where the village clusters, where the great cathedral rises, where the bleak moor lies, and the wild breeze smooths or ruffles it at its inconstant will; away, with a shriek, and a roar, and a rattle, and no trace to leave behind but dust and vapor: like as in the track of the remorseless monster, Death!

Breasting the wind and light, the shower and sunshine, away, and still away, it rolls and roars, fierce and rapid, smooth and certain, and great works and massive bridges crossing up above, fall like a beam of shadow an inch broad upon the eye, and then are lost. Away, and still away, onward and onward ever: glimpses of cottage homes, of houses, mansions, rich estates, of husbandry and handicraft, of people, of old roads and paths that look deserted, small, and insignificant as they are left behind: and so they do, and what else is there but such glimpses, in the track of the indomitable monster, Death!

Away, with a shriek, and a roar, and a rattle, plunging down into the earth again, and working on in such a storm of energy and perseverance, that amidst the darkness and whirlwind the motion seems reversed, and to tend furiously backward, until a ray of light upon the wet wall shows its surface flying past like a fierce

4. From Chapter XX, an account of Mr. Dombey on a trip after the death of his son, Paul.

stream. Away once more into the day, and through the day, with a shrill yell of exultation, roaring, rattling, tearing on, spurning everything with its dark breath, sometimes pausing for a minute where a crowd of faces are, that in a minute more are not: sometimes lapping water greedily, and before the spout at which it drinks has ceased to drip upon the ground, shrieking, roaring, rattling through the purple distance!

Louder and louder yet, it shrieks and cries as it comes tearing on resistless to the goal: and now its way, still like the way of Death, is strewn with ashes thickly. Everything around is blackened. There are dark pools of water, muddy lanes, and miserable habitations far below. There are jagged walls and falling houses close at hand, and through the battered roofs and broken windows, wretched rooms are seen, where want and fever hide themselves in many wretched shapes, while smoke and crowded gables, and distorted chimneys, and deformity of brick and mortar penning up deformity of mind and body, choke the murky distance. As Mr. Dombey looks out of his carriage window, it is never in his thoughts that the monster who has brought him there has let the light of day in on these things: not made or caused them. It was the journey's fitting end, and might have been the end of everything; it was so ruinous and dreary.

1846–48

CHARLES DICKENS: *From* Hard Times[1]
[*Coketown*]

It was a town of red brick, or of brick that would have been red if the smoke and ashes had allowed it; but, as matters stood, it was a town of unnatural red and black, like the painted face of a savage. It was a town of machinery and tall chimneys, out of which interminable serpents of smoke trailed themselves for ever and ever, and never got uncoiled. It had a black canal in it, and a river that ran purple with ill-smelling dye, and vast piles of building full of windows where there was a rattling and a trembling all day long, and where the piston of the steam engine worked monotonously up and down, like the head of an elephant in a state of melancholy madness. It contained several large streets all very like one another, and many small streets still more like one another, inhabited by people equally like one another, who all went in and

---

1. The picture of Coketown (from Chapter V of the novel) was based on Dickens' impressions of the raw industrial towns of central and northern England such as Birmingham and, in particular, Preston, a cotton-manufacturing center in Lancashire.

out at the same hours, with the same sound upon the same pavements, to do the same work, and to whom every day was the same as yesterday and tomorrow, and every year the counterpart of the last and the next.

These attributes of Coketown were in the main inseparable from the work by which it was sustained; against them were to be set off, comforts of life which found their way all over the world, and elegancies of life which made, we will not ask how much of the fine lady, who could scarcely bear to hear the place mentioned. The rest of its features were voluntary, and they were these.

You saw nothing in Coketown but what was severely workful. If the members of a religious persuasion built a chapel there—as the members of eighteen religious persuasions had done—they made it a pious warehouse of red brick, with sometimes (but this only in highly ornamented examples) a bell in a birdcage on the top of it. The solitary exception was the New Church; a stuccoed edifice with a square steeple over the door, terminating in four short pinnacles like florid wooden legs. All the public inscriptions in the town were painted alike, in severe characters of black and white. The jail might have been the infirmary, the infirmary might have been the jail, the town hall might have been either, or both, or anything else, for anything that appeared to the contrary in the graces of their construction. Fact, fact, fact, everywhere in the material aspect of the town; fact, fact, fact, everywhere in the immaterial. The M'Choakumchild school was all fact, and the school of design was all fact, and the relations between master and man were all fact, and everything was fact between the lying-in hospital and the cemetery, and what you couldn't state in figures, or show to be purchasable in the cheapest market and saleable in the dearest, was not, and never should be, world without end, Amen.

1854

CHARLES KINGSLEY: *From* Alton Locke[2]

[*A London Slum*]

It was a foul, chilly, foggy Saturday night. From the butchers and greengrocers' shops the gaslights flared and flickered, wild and ghastly, over haggard groups of slipshod dirty women, bargaining for scraps of stale meat and frostbitten vegetables, wrangling about short weight and bad quality. Fish stalls and fruit stalls lined the

2. From Chapter VIII of *Alton Locke*, a novel by Charles Kingsley (1819–75). Under the influence of Carlyle's writings and also as a result of his own observations, Kingsley, a clergy-man, became deeply concerned with the sufferings of the working classes. The speaker here is a young tailor who is accompanied by an elderly Scottish bookseller, Sandy Mackaye.

edge of the greasy pavement, sending up odors as foul as the language of sellers and buyers. Blood and sewer water crawled from under doors and out of spouts, and reeked down the gutters among offal, animal and vegetable, in every stage of putrefaction. Foul vapors rose from cow sheds and slaughterhouses, and the doorways of undrained alleys, where the inhabitants carried the filth out on their shoes from the backyard into the court, and from the court up into the main street; while above, hanging like cliffs over the streets—those narrow, brawling torrents of filth, and poverty, and sin—the houses with their teeming load of life were piled up into the dingy, choking night. A ghastly, deafening, sickening sight it was. Go, scented Belgravian![3] and see what London is! and then go to the library which God has given thee—one often fears in vain—and see what science says this London might be! * * *

We went on through a back street or two, and then into a huge, miserable house, which, a hundred years ago, perhaps, had witnessed the luxury, and rung to the laughter of some one great fashionable family, alone there in their glory. Now every room of it held its family, or its group of families—a phalanstery[4] of all the fiends—its grand staircase, with the carved balustrades rotting and crumbling away piecemeal, converted into a common sewer for all its inmates. Up stair after stair we went, while wails of children, and curses of men, steamed out upon the hot stifling rush of air from every doorway, till, at the topmost story, we knocked at a garret door. We entered. Bare it was of furniture, comfortless, and freezing cold; but, with the exception of the plaster dropping from the roof, and the broken windows, patched with rags and paper, there was a scrupulous neatness about the whole, which contrasted strangely with the filth and slovenliness outside. There was no bed in the room—no table. On a broken chair by the chimney sat a miserable old woman, fancying that she was warming her hands over embers which had long been cold, shaking her head, and muttering to herself, with palsied lips, about the guardians and the workhouse; while upon a few rags on the floor lay a girl, ugly, smallpox-marked, hollow-eyed, emaciated, her only bedclothes the skirt of a large handsome new riding habit, at which two other girls, wan and tawdry, were stitching busily, as they sat right and left of her on the floor. The old woman took no notice of us as we entered; but one of the girls looked up, and, with a pleased gesture of recognition, put her finger up to her lips, and whispered, "Ellen's asleep."

"I'm not asleep, dears," answered a faint unearthly voice; "I was only praying. Is that Mr. Mackaye?"

3. Inhabitant of Belgravia, a wealthy residential district of London.
4. A kind of model housing develop-ment proposed by the French socialist François Fourier (1772–1830).

"Aye, my lassies; but ha' ye gotten na fire the nicht?"

"No," said one of them, bitterly, "we've earned no fire tonight, by fair trade or foul either."

1850

KARL MARX *and* FRIEDRICH ENGELS:
From The Communist Manifesto[5]
[Bourgeois and Proletarians]

The history of all hitherto existing society is the history of class struggles.

Freeman and slave, patrician and plebeian, lord and serf, guildmaster and journeyman, in a word, oppressor and oppressed, stood in constant opposition to one another, carried on an uninterrupted, now hidden, now open fight, a fight that each time ended, either in a revolutionary reconstitution of society at large, or in the common ruin of the contending classes.

In the earlier epochs of history we find almost everywhere a complicated arrangement of society into various orders, a manifold gradation of social rank. In ancient Rome we have patricians, knights, plebeians, slaves; in the Middle Ages, feudal lords, vassals, guildmasters, journeymen, apprentices, serfs; in almost all of these classes, again, subordinate gradations.

The modern bourgeois society that has sprouted from the ruins of feudal society has not done away with class antagonisms. It has but established new classes, new conditions of oppression, new forms of struggle in place of the old ones.

Our epoch, the epoch of the bourgeoisie, possesses, however, this distinctive feature; it has simplified the class antagonisms. Society as a whole is more and more splitting up into two great hostile camps, into two great classes directly facing each other: Bourgeoisie and Proletariat.

From the serfs of the Middle Ages sprang the chartered burghers of the earliest towns. From these burgesses the first elements of the bourgeoisie were developed.

5. From Chapter I of the *Communist Manifesto*, first printed in London in 1848 in German and translated into English in 1850. This pamphlet was jointly written by Karl Marx (1818–83) and Friedrich Engels (1820–95) as a program for the Communist League. Engels later stated in a note that their history of the economic development of the middle classes was based primarily on the example of England, and their history of political developments on the example of France. "By bourgeoisie" he said, "is meant the class of modern Capitalists, owners of the means of social production and employers of wage labor. By proletariat, the class of modern wage laborers who, having no means of production of their own, are reduced to selling their labor power in order to live."

The discovery of America, the rounding of the Cape, opened up fresh ground for the rising bourgeoisie. The East Indian and Chinese markets, the colonization of America, trade with the colonies, the increase in the means of exchange and in commodities generally, gave to commerce, to navigation, to industry, an impulse never before known, and thereby, to the revolutionary element in the tottering feudal society, a rapid development.

The feudal system of industry, under which industrial production was monopolized by close guilds, now no longer sufficed for the growing wants of the new market. The manufacturing system took its place. The guildmasters were pushed on one side by the manufacturing middle class; division of labor between the different corporate guilds vanished in the face of division of labor in each single workshop.

Meantime the markets kept ever growing, the demand ever rising. Even manufacture no longer sufficed. Thereupon, steam and machinery revolutionized industrial production. The place of manufacture was taken by the giant Modern Industry, the place of the industrial middle class, by industrial millionaires, the leaders of whole industrial armies, the modern bourgeois.

Modern industry has established the world market, for which the discovery of America paved the way. This market has given an immense development to commerce, to navigation, to communication by land. This development has, in its turn, reacted on the extension of industry; and in proportion as industry, commerce, navigation, railways extended, in the same proportion the bourgeoisie developed, increased its capital, and pushed into the background every class handed down from the Middle Ages.

We see, therefore, how the modern bourgeoisie is itself the product of a long course of development, of a series of revolutions in the modes of production and of exchange.

Each step in the development of the bourgeoisie was accompanied by a corresponding political advance of that class. An oppressed class under the sway of the feudal nobility; an armed and self-governing association in the medieval commune,[6] (here independent urban republic, as in Italy and Germany, there taxable "third estate" of the monarchy, as in France); afterwards, in the period of manufacture proper, serving either the semi-feudal or the absolute monarchy as a counterpoise against the nobility, and, in fact, cornerstone of the great monarchies in general—the bourgeoisie has at last, since the establishment of modern industry and of the

6. Small-sized French municipality. Engels notes that the name *Commune* was adopted in France "by the nascent towns even before they had conquered from their feudal lords and masters local self-government and political rights as 'the Third Estate.'" The Third Estate in France corresponded roughly to the Commons in England, comprising that part of the body politic not represented by the nobility and the clergy.

world market, conquered for itself, in the modern representative State, exclusive political sway. The executive of the modern State is but a committee for managing the common affairs of the whole bourgeoisie.

The bourgeoisie, historically, has played a most revolutionary part.

The bourgeoisie, wherever it has got the upper hand, has put an end to all feudal, patriarchal, idyllic relations. It has pitilessly torn asunder the motley feudal ties that bound man to his "natural superiors," and has left no other nexus between man and man than naked self-interest, than callous "cash payment." It has drowned the most heavenly ecstasies of religious fervor, of chivalrous enthusiasm, of philistine sentimentalism, in the icy water of egotistical calculation. It has resolved personal worth into exchange value, and in place of the numberless indefeasible chartered freedoms, has set up that single, unconscionable freedom—Free Trade. In one word, for exploitation, veiled by religious and political illusions, it has substituted naked, shameless, direct, brutal exploitation.

The bourgeoisie has stripped of its halo every occupation hitherto honored and looked up to with reverent awe. It has converted the physician, the lawyer, the priest, the poet, the man of science, into its paid wage laborers.

The bourgeoisie has torn away from the family its sentimental veil, and has reduced the family relation to a mere money relation.

The bourgeoisie has disclosed how it came to pass that the brutal display of vigor in the Middle Ages, which reactionists so much admire, found its fitting complement in the most slothful indolence. It has been the first to show what man's activity can bring about. It has accomplished wonders far surpassing Egyptian pyramids, Roman aqueducts, and Gothic cathedrals; it has conducted expeditions that put in the shade all former Exoduses of nations and crusades.

The bourgeoisie cannot exist without constantly revolutionizing the instruments of production, and thereby the relations of production, and with them the whole relations of society. Conservation of the old modes of production in unaltered form was, on the contrary, the first condition of existence for all earlier industrial classes. Constant revolutionizing of production, uninterrupted disturbance of all social conditions, everlasting uncertainty and agitation distinguished the bourgeois epoch from all earlier ones. All fixed, fast-frozen relations, with their train of ancient and venerable prejudices and opinions, are swept away, all new-formed ones become antiquated before they can ossify. All that is solid melts into the air, all that is holy is profaned, and man is at last compelled to face with sober senses his real conditions of life, and his relations with his kind.

The need of a constantly expanding market for its products drives the bourgeoisie over the whole surface of the globe. It must elbow-in everywhere, settle everywhere, establish connections everywhere.

The bourgeoisie has through its exploitation of the world market given a cosmopolitan character to production and consumption in every country. To the great chagrin of reactionists, it has drawn from under the feet of industry the national ground on which it stood. All old-established national industries have been destroyed or are daily being destroyed. They are dislodged by new industries, whose introduction becomes a life and death question for all civilized nations, by industries that no longer work up indigenous raw material, but raw material drawn from the remotest zones; industries whose products are consumed, not only at home, but in every quarter of the globe. In place of the old wants, satisfied by the productions of the country, we find new wants, requiring for their satisfaction the products of distant lands and climes. In place of the old local and national seclusion and self-sufficiency, we have intercourse in every direction, universal interdependence of nations. And as in material, so also in intellectual production. The intellectual creations of individual nations become common property. National one-sidedness and narrow-mindedness become more and more impossible, and from the numerous national and local literatures there arises a world literature.

The bourgeoisie, by the rapid improvement of all instruments of production, by the immensely facilitated means of communication, draws all, even the most barbarian nations, into civilization. The cheap prices of its commodities are the heavy artillery with which it batters down all Chinese walls, with which it forces the barbarians' intensely obstinate hatred of foreigners to capitulate. It compels all nations, on pain of extinction, to adopt the bourgeois mode of production; it compels them to introduce what it calls civilization into their midst, i.e., to become bourgeois themselves. In a word, it creates a world after its own image.

The bourgeoisie has subjected the country to the rule of the towns. It has created enormous cities, has greatly increased the urban population as compared with the rural, and has thus rescued a considerable part of the population from the idiocy of rural life. Just as it has made the country dependent on the towns, so it has made barbarian and semi-barbarian countries dependent on civilized ones, nations of peasants on nations of bourgeois, the East on the West.

The bourgeoisie keeps more and more doing away with the scattered state of the population, of the means of production, and of property. It has agglomerated population, centralized means of production, and has concentrated property in a few hands. The necessary consequence of this was political centralization. Independent, or but loosely connected provinces, with separate interests, laws, governments, and systems of taxation, became lumped together in one nation, with one government, one code of laws, one national class interest, one frontier and one customs' tariff.

The bourgeoisie, during its rule of scarce one hundred years, has created more massive and more colossal productive forces than have all preceding generations together. Subjection of nature's forces to man, machinery, application of chemistry to industry and agriculture, steam navigation, railways, electric telegraphs, clearing of whole continents for cultivation, canalization of rivers, whole populations conjured out of the ground—what earlier century had even a presentiment that such productive forces slumbered in the lap of social labor?

We see then: the means of production and of exchange on whose foundation the bourgeoisie built itself up were generated in feudal society. At a certain stage in the development of these means of production and of exchange, the conditions under which feudal society produced and exchanged, the feudal organization of agriculture and manufacturing industry—in one word, the feudal relations of property—became no longer compatible with the already developed productive forces; they became so many fetters. They had to burst asunder; they were burst asunder.

Into their places stepped free competition, accompanied by a social and political constitution adapted to it, and by the economical and political sway of the bourgeois class.

A similar movement is going on before our own eyes. Modern bourgeois society with its relations of production, of exchange, and of property, a society that has conjured up such gigantic means of production and of exchange, is like the sorcerer, who is no longer able to control the powers of the nether world whom he has called up by his spells. For many a decade past, the history of industry and commerce is but the history of the revolt of modern productive forces against modern conditions of production, against the property relations that are the conditions for the existence of the bourgeoisie and of its rule. It is enough to mention the commercial crises that by their periodical return put on its trial, each time more threateningly, the existence of the entire bourgeois society. In these crises a great part not only of the existing products, but also of the previously created productive forces, are periodically destroyed. In these crises there breaks out an epidemic that, in all earlier epochs, would have seemed an absurdity—the epidemic of overproduction. Society suddenly finds itself put back into a state of momentary barbarism; it appears as if a famine, a universal war of devastation, had cut off the supply of every means of subsistence; industry and commerce seem to be destroyed; and why? Because there is too much civilization, too much means of subsistence, too much industry, too much commerce. The productive forces at the disposal of society no longer tend to further the development of the conditions of bourgeois property; on the contrary, they have become too powerful for these conditions by which they are confined, and as soon as they overcome these limitations they bring disorder into the whole bourgeois society, endanger the existence of bourgeois property. The conditions of bourgeois society are too narrow to comprise the wealth created by them. And how does the bourgeoisie get over these crises? On the one hand by enforced destruction of a mass of productive forces; on the other, by the conquest of new markets, and by the more thorough exploitation of the old ones. That is to say, by paving the way for more extensive and more destructive crises, and by diminishing the means whereby crises are prevented.

The weapons with which the bourgeoisie felled feudalism to the ground are now turned against the bourgeoisie itself.

But not only has the bourgeoisie forged the weapons that bring death to itself; it has also called into existence the men who are to wield those weapons—the modern working class—the proletarians.

In proportion as the bourgeoisie, that is, capital, is developed, in the same proportion is the proletariat, the modern working class, developed, a class of laborers who live only so long as they find work, and who find work only so long as their labor increases capital. These laborers, who must sell themselves piecemeal, are a commodity, like every other article of commerce, and are consequently exposed to all the vicissitudes of competition, to all the fluctuations of the market.

Owing to the extensive use of machinery and to division of labor, the work of the proletarians has lost all individual character, and, consequently, all charm for the workman. He becomes an appendage of the machine, and it is only the most simple, most monotonous, and most easily acquired knack that is required of him. Hence, the cost of production of a workman is restricted almost entirely to the means of subsistence that he requires for his maintenance, and for the propagation of his race. But the price of a commodity and also of labor is equal to its cost of production. In proportion, therefore, as the repulsiveness of the work increases, the wage decreases. Nay more, in proportion as the use of machinery and division of labor increase, in the same proportion of burden of toil increases, whether by prolongation of the working hours, by increase of the work enacted in a given time, or by increased speed of the machinery, and so forth.

Modern industry has converted the little workshop of the patriarchal master into the great factory of the industrial capitalist. Masses of laborers, crowded into factories, are organized like soldiers. As privates of the industrial army they are placed under the command of a perfect hierarchy of officers and sergeants. Not only are they the slaves of the bourgeois class and of the bourgeois state, they are daily and hourly enslaved by the machine, by the foreman, and, above all, by the individual bourgeois manufacturer himself. The more openly this despotism proclaims gain to be its end and aim, the more petty, the more hateful and the more embittering it is.

The less the skill and exertion or strength implied in manual labor, in other words, the more modern industry becomes developed, the more is the labor of men superseded by that of women. Differences of age and sex have no longer any distinctive social validity for the working class. All are instruments of labor, more or less expensive to use, according to their age and sex.

No sooner is the exploitation of the laborer by the manufacturer so far at an end that he receives his wages in cash, than he is set upon by the other portions of the bourgeoisie, the landlord, the shopkeeper, the pawnbroker, and so forth.

The lower strata of the middle class—the small tradespeople, shopkeepers and retired tradesmen generally, the handicraftsmen and peasants—all these sink gradually into the proletariat, partly because their diminutive capital does not suffice for the scale on which modern industry is carried on, and is swamped in the competition with the large capitalists, partly because their specialized skill is rendered worthless by new methods of production. Thus the proletariat is recruited from all classes of the population.

The proletariat goes through various stages of development. With its birth begins its struggle with the bourgeoisie. At first the contest is carried on by individual laborers, then by the workpeople of a factory, then by the operatives of one trade, in one locality, against the individual bourgeois who directly exploits them. They direct their attacks not against the bourgeois conditions of production, but against the instruments of production themselves; they destroy imported wares that compete with their labor, they smash machinery, they set factories ablaze, they seek to restore by force the vanished status of the workman of the Middle Ages.

At this stage the laborers still form an incoherent mass scattered over the whole country, and broken up by their mutual competition.

If anywhere they unite to form more compact bodies, this is not yet the consequence of their own active union, but of the union of the bourgeoisie, which class, in order to attain its own political ends, is compelled to set the whole proletariat in motion, and is moreover, for a time, still able to do so. At this stage, therefore, the proletarians do not fight their enemies, but the enemies of their enemies, the remnants of absolute monarchy, the landowners, the nonindustrial bourgeois, the petty bourgeoisie. Thus the whole historical movement is concentrated in the hands of the bourgeoisie, every victory so obtained is a victory for the bourgeoisie.

But with the development of industry the proletariat not only increases in number; it becomes concentrated in greater masses, its strength grows and it feels that strength more. The various interests and conditions of life within the ranks of the proletariat are more and more equalized, in proportion as machinery obliterates all distinctions of labor, and nearly everywhere reduces wages to the same low level. The growing competition among the bourgeois, and the resulting commercial crises make the wages of the workers ever more fluctuating; the unceasing improvement of machinery, ever more rapidly developing, makes their livelihood more and more precarious; the collisions between individual workmen and individual bourgeois take more and more the character of collisions between two classes. Thereupon the workers begin to form combinations (trade unions) against the bourgeois; they club together in order to keep up the rate of wages; they found permanent associations in order to make provision beforehand for these occasional revolts. Here and there the contest breaks out into riots.

Now and then the workers are victorious, but only for a time. The real fruit of their battle lies not in the immediate result, but in the ever expanding union of workers. This union is helped on by the improved means of communication that are created by modern industry, and that places the workers of different localities in contact with one another. It was just this contact that was needed to centralize the numerous local struggles, all of the same character, into one national struggle between classes. But every class struggle is a political struggle. And that union, to attain which the burghers of the Middle Ages with their miserable highways, required centuries, the modern proletarians, thanks to railways, achieve in a few years.

This organization of the proletarians into a class, and consequently into a political party, is continually being upset again by the competition between the workers themselves. But it ever rises up again, stronger, firmer, mightier. It compels legislative recognition of particular interests of the workers by taking advantage of the divisions among the bourgeoisie itself. Thus the Ten Hours Bill in England was carried.

Altogether collisions between the classes of the old society further, in many ways, the development of the proletariat. The bourgeoisie finds itself involved in a constant battle—at first with the aristocracy; later on, with those portions of the bourgeoisie itself whose interests have become antagonistic to the progress of industry; at all times, with the bourgeoisie of foreign countries. In all these battles it sees itself compelled to appeal to the proletariat, to ask for its help, and thus to drag it into the political arena. The bourgeoisie itself, therefore, supplies the proletariat with its own elements of political and general education; in other words, it furnishes the proletariat with weapons for fighting the bourgeoisie.

Further, as we have already seen, entire sections of the ruling classes are, by the advance of industry, precipitated into the proletariat, or are at least threatened in their conditions of existence. These also supply the proletariat with fresh elements of enlightenment and progress.

Finally, in times when the class struggle nears the decisive hour, the process of dissolution going on within the ruling class, in fact within the whole range of an old society, assumes such a violent, glaring character that a small section of the ruling class cuts itself adrift and joins the revolutionary class, the class that holds the future in its hands. Just as, therefore, at an earlier period, a section of the nobility went over to the bourgeoisie, so now a portion of the bourgeoisie goes over to the proletariat, and in particular, a portion of the bourgeois ideologists, who have raised themselves to the level of comprehending theoretically the historical movements as a whole.

Of all the classes that stand face to face with the bourgeoisie today the proletariat alone is a really revolutionary class. The other classes decay and finally disappear in the face of modern industry; the proletariat is its special and essential product.

The lower middle class, the small manufacturer, the shopkeeper, the artisan, the peasant, all these fight against the bourgeoisie, to save from extinction their existence as fractions of the middle class. They are therefore not revolutionary, but conservative. Nay, more; they are reactionary, for they try to roll back the wheel of history. If by chance they are revolutionary, they are so only in view of their impending transfer into the proletariat; they thus defend not their present, but their future interests; they desert their own standpoint to place themselves at that of the proletariat.

The "dangerous class," the social scum, that passively rotting mass thrown off by the lowest layers of the old society, may here and there be swept into the movement by a proletarian revolution; its conditions of life, however, prepare it far more for the part of a bribed tool of reactionary intrigue.

In the conditions of the proletariat, those of old society at large are already virtually swamped. The proletarian is without property; his relation to his wife and children has no longer anything in common with the bourgeois family relations; modern industrial labor, modern subjection to capital, the same in England as in France, in America as in Germany, has stripped him of every trace of national character. Law, morality, religion are to him so many bourgeois prejudices, behind which lurk in ambush just as many bourgeois interests.

All the preceding classes that got the upper hand sought to fortify their already acquired status by subjecting society at large to their conditions of appropriation. The proletarians cannot become masters of the productive forces of society, except by abolishing their own previous mode of appropriation, and thereby also every other previous mode of appropriation. They have nothing of their own to secure and to fortify; their mission is to destroy all previous securities for and insurances of individual property.

All previous historical movements were movements of minorities, or in the interest of minorities. The proletarian movement is the self-conscious, independent movement of the immense majority. The proletariat, the lowest stratum of our present society, cannot stir, cannot raise itself up without the whole superincumbent strata of official society being sprung into the air.

Though not in substance, yet in form, the struggle of the proletariat with the bourgeoisie is at first a national struggle. The proletariat of each country must, of course, first of all settle matters with its own bourgeoisie.

In depicting the most general phases of the development of the proletariat, we have traced the more or less veiled civil war, raging within existing society, up to the point where that war breaks out into open revolution, and where the violent overthrow of the bourgeoisie, lays the foundation for the sway of the proletariat.

Hitherto every form of society has been based, as we have already seen, on the antagonism of oppressing and oppressed classes. But in order to oppress a class, certain conditions must be assured to it under which it can at least continue its slavish existence. The serf in the period of serfdom raised himself to membership in the commune, just as the petty bourgeois, under the yoke of feudal absolutism, managed to develop into a bourgeois. The modern laborer, on the contrary, instead of rising with the progress of industry, sinks deeper and deeper below the conditions of existence of his own class. He becomes a pauper, and pauperism develops more rapidly than population and wealth. And here it becomes evident that the bourgeoisie is unfit any longer to be the ruling class in society, and to impose its conditions of existence upon society as an overriding law. It is unfit to rule, because it is incompetent to assure an existence to its slave within his slavery, because it cannot help letting him sink into such a state that it has to feed him, instead of being fed by him. Society can no longer live under this bourgeoisie; in other words, its existence is no longer compatible with society.

The essential condition for the existence, and for the sway of the bourgeois class, is the formation and augmentation of capital; the condition for capital is wage labor. Wage labor rests exclusively on competition between the laborers. The advance of industry, whose involuntary promoter is the bourgeoisie, replaces the isolation of the laborers, due to competition, by their revolutionary combination, due to association. The development of modern industry, therefore, cuts from under its feet the very foundation on which the bourgeoisie produces and appropriates products. What the bourgeoisie therefore produces, above all, are its own gravediggers. Its fall and the victory of the proletariat are equally inevitable.

1848

THOMAS BABINGTON MACAULAY: *From* A Review of Southey's *Colloquies*[7]
[Evidence of Progress]

* * * Perhaps we could not select a better instance of the spirit which pervades the whole book than the passages in which Mr. Southey gives his opinion of the manufacturing system. There is nothing which he hates so bitterly. It is, according to him, a system more tyrannical than that of the feudal ages, a system of actual servitude, a system which destroys the bodies and degrades the minds of those who are engaged in it. He expresses a hope that the competition of other nations may drive us out of the field; that our foreign trade may decline; and that we may thus enjoy a restoration of national sanity and strength. But he seems to think that the extermination of the whole manufacturing population would be a blessing, if the evil could be removed in no other way.

Mr. Southey does not bring forward a single fact in support of these views; and, as it seems to us, there are facts which lead to a

7. Published in the *Edinburgh Review* (1830). In a book entitled *Colloquies on the Progress and Prospects of Society* (1829), the poet and man of letters Robert Southey (1774–1843) had sought to expose the evils of industrialism and to assert the superiority of the traditional feudal and agricultural way of life of England's past. His romantic Toryism provoked Ma- cauley (1800–59) to review the book in a long and characteristic essay. As in his popular *History of England* (1849–61), Macaulay seeks here to demolish his opponent with a bombardment of facts and figures demonstrating that industrialism and middle-class government have resulted in progress and increased comforts for mankind.

very different conclusion. In the first place, the poor rate[8] is very decidedly lower in the manufacturing than in the agricultural districts. If Mr. Southey will look over the Parliamentary returns on this subject, he will find that the amount of parochial relief required by the laborers in the different counties of England is almost exactly in inverse proportion to the degree in which the manufacturing system has been introduced into those counties. The returns for the years ending in March, 1825, and in March, 1828, are now before us. In the former year we find the poor rate highest in Sussex,[9] about twenty shillings to every inhabitant. Then come Buckinghamshire, Essex, Suffolk, Bedfordshire, Huntingdonshire, Kent, and Norfolk. In all these the rate is above fifteen shillings a head. We will not go through the whole. Even in Westmoreland and the North Riding of Yorkshire, the rate is at more than eight shillings. In Cumberland and Monmouthshire, the most fortunate of all the agricultural districts, it is at six shillings. But in the West Riding of Yorkshire,[1] it is as low as five shillings: and when we come to Lancashire, we find it at four shillings, one-fifth of what it is in Sussex. The returns of the year ending in March, 1828, are a little, and but a little, more unfavorable to the manufacturing districts. Lancashire, even in that season of distress, required a smaller poor rate than any other district, and little more than one-fourth of the poor rate raised in Sussex. Cumberland alone, of the agricultural districts, was as well off as the West Riding of Yorkshire. These facts seem to indicate that the manufacturer is both in a more comfortable and in a less dependent situation than the agricultural laborer.

As to the effect of the manufacturing system on the bodily health, we must beg leave to estimate it by a standard far too low and vulgar for a mind so imaginative as that of Mr. Southey, the proportion of births and deaths. We know that, during the growth of this atrocious system, this new misery, to use the phrases of Mr. Southey, this new enormity, this birth of a portentous age, this pest which no man can approve whose heart is not seared or whose understanding has not been darkened, there has been a great diminution of mortality, and that this diminution has been greater in the manufacturing towns than anywhere else. The mortality still is, as it always was, greater in towns than in the country. But the difference has diminished in an extraordinary degree. There is the best reason to believe that the annual mortality of Manchester, about the middle of the last century, was one in twenty-eight. It is now reckoned at one in forty-five. In Glasgow and Leeds a similar improvement has taken place. Nay, the rate of mortality in those

---

8. Taxes on property, to provide food and lodging for the unemployed or unemployable. The amount or rate of such taxes varied from district to district in England, depending upon local conditions of unemployment.
9. A predominantly agricultural district.
1. A manufacturing district.

three great capitals of the manufacturing districts is now considerably less than it was, fifty years ago, over England and Wales, taken together, open country and all. We might with some plausibility maintain that the people live longer because they are better fed, better lodged, better clothed, and better attended in sickness, and that these improvements are owing to that increase of national wealth which the manufacturing system has produced.

Much more might be said on this subject. But to what end? It is not from bills of mortality and statistical tables that Mr. Southey has learned his political creed. He cannot stoop to study the history of the system which he abuses, to strike the balance between the good and evil which it has produced, to compare district with district, or generation with generation. We will give his own reason for his opinion, the only reason which he gives for it, in his own words:

"We remained a while in silence looking upon the assemblage of dwellings below. Here, and in the adjoining hamlet of Millbeck, the effects of manufactures and of agriculture may be seen and compared. The old cottages are such as the poet and the painter equally delight in beholding. Substantially built of the native stone without mortar, dirtied with no white lime, and their long low roofs covered with slate, if they had been raised by the magic of some indigeneous Amphion's[2] music, the materials could not have adjusted themselves more beautifully in accord with the surrounding scene; and time has still further harmonized them with weather stains, lichens, and moss, short grasses, and short fern, and stoneplants of various kinds. The ornamented chimneys, round or square, less adorned than those which, like little turrets, crest the houses of the Portuguese peasantry, and yet not less happily suited to their place; the hedge of clipped box beneath the windows, the rose bushes beside the door, the little patch of flower ground, with its tall hollyhocks in front, the garden beside, the beehives, and the orchard with its bank of daffodils and snowdrops, the earliest and the profusest in these parts, indicate in the owners some portion of ease and leisure, some regard to neatness and comfort, some sense of natural, and innocent, and healthful enjoyment. The new cottages of the manufacturers are upon the manufacturing pattern —naked, and in a row.

" 'How is it,' said I, 'that everything which is connected with manufactures presents such features of unqualified deformity? From the largest of Mammon's temples down to the poorest hovel in which his helotry are stalled, these edifices have all one character. Time will not mellow them; nature will neither clothe nor conceal them; and they will remain always as offensive to the eye as to the mind.' "

Here is wisdom. Here are the principles on which nations are to be governed. Rosebushes and poor rates, rather than steam engines

2. According to Greek mythology, Amphion's magical skill as a harp player caused the walls of Thebes to be erected without human aid.

and independence. Mortality and cottages with weather stains, rather than health and long life with edifices which time cannot mellow. We are told that our age has invented atrocities beyond the imagination of our fathers; that society has been brought into a state compared with which extermination would be a blessing; and all because the dwellings of cotton-spinners are naked and rectangular. Mr. Southey has found out a way, he tells us, in which the effects of manufactures and agriculture may be compared. And what is this way? To stand on a hill, to look at a cottage and a factory, and to see which is the prettier. Does Mr. Southey think that the body of the English peasantry live, or ever lived, in substantial or ornamented cottages, with boxhedges, flower gardens, beehives, and orchards? If not, what is his parallel worth? We despise those mock philosophers,[3] who think that they serve the cause of science by depreciating literature and the fine arts. But if anything could excuse their narrowness of mind, it would be such a book as this. It is not strange that, when one enthuisast makes the picturesque the test of political good, another should feel inclined to proscribe altogether the pleasures of taste and imagination. * * *

It is not strange that, differing so widely from Mr. Southey as to the past progress of society, we should differ from him also as to its probable destiny. He thinks, that to all outward appearance, the country is hastening to destruction; but he relies firmly on the goodness of God. We do not see either the piety or the rationality of thus confidently expecting that the Supreme Being will interfere to disturb the common succession of causes and effects. We, too, rely on his goodness, on his goodness as manifested, not in extraordinary interpositions, but in those general laws which it has pleased him to establish in the physical and in the moral world. We rely on the natural tendency of the human intellect to truth, and on the natural tendency of society to improvement. We know no well-authenticated instance of a people which has decidedly retrograded in civilization and prosperity, except from the influence of violent and terrible calamities, such as those which laid the Roman Empire in ruins, or those which, about the beginning of the sixteenth century, desolated Italy. We know of no country which, at the end of fifty years of peace and tolerably good government, has been less prosperous than at the beginning of that period. The political importance of a state may decline, as the balance of power is disturbed by the introduction of new forces. Thus the influence of Holland and of Spain is much diminished. But are Holland and Spain poorer than formerly? We doubt it. Other countries have outrun them. But we suspect that they have been positively, though

---

3. Presumably such Utilitarian philosophers as Jeremy Bentham, who had equated poetry with pushpin, a trifling game. It should be noted, however, that although Macaulay often attacked the Utilitarians for their narrow preoccupation with theory, his own position has much in common with theirs.

not relatively, advancing. We suspect that Holland is richer than when she sent her navies up the Thames,[4] that Spain is richer than when a French king was brought captive to the footstool of Charles the Fifth.[5]

History is full of the signs of this natural progress of society. We see in almost every part of the annals of mankind how the industry of individuals, struggling up against wars, taxes, famines, conflagrations, mischievous prohibitions, and more mischievous protections, creates faster than governments can squander, and repairs whatever invaders can destroy. We see the wealth of nations increasing, and all the arts of life approaching nearer and nearer to perfection, in spite of the grossest corruption and the wildest profusion on the part of rulers.

The present moment is one of great distress. But how small will that distress appear when we think over the history of the last forty years; a war,[6] compared with which all other wars sink into insignificance; taxation, such as the most heavily taxed people of former times could not have conceived; a debt larger than all the public debts that ever existed in the world added together; the food of the people studiously rendered dear; the currency imprudently debased, and imprudently restored. Yet is the country poorer than in 1790? We firmly believe that, in spite of all the misgovernment of her rulers, she has been almost constantly becoming richer and richer. Now and then there has been a stoppage, now and then a short retrogression; but as to the general tendency there can be no doubt. A single breaker may recede; but the tide is evidently coming in.

If we were to prophesy that in the year 1930 a population of fifty millions, better fed, clad, and lodged than the English of our time, will cover these islands, that Sussex and Huntingdonshire will be wealthier than the wealthiest parts of the West Riding of Yorkshire now are, that cultivation, rich as that of a flower garden, will be carried up to the very tops of Ben Nevis and Helvellyn,[7] that machines constructed on principles yet undiscovered will be in every house, that there will be no highways but railroads, no traveling but by steam, that our debt, vast as it seems to us, will appear to our great-grandchildren a trifling encumbrance, which might easily be paid off in a year or two, many people would think us insane. We prophesy nothing; but this we say: If any person had told the Parliament which met in perplexity and terror after the crash in 1720 that in 1830 the wealth of England would surpass all their wildest dreams, that the annual revenue would equal the principal

---

4. In 1667 a Dutch fleet displayed its power by sailing up the river Thames without being challenged by the English navy.
5. The Spanish king, Charles V, captured the king of France, Francis I,
in the battle of Pavia (1525).
6. The wars against France and Napoleon, extending, with some interruptions, from 1792 to 1815.
7. Mountains, in Scotland and in the English Lake District, respectively.

of that debt which they considered as an intolerable burden, that for one man of ten thousand pounds then living there would be five men of fifty thousand pounds, that London would be twice as large and twice as populous, and that nevertheless the rate of mortality would have diminished to one-half of what it then was, that the post office would bring more into the exchequer than the excise and customs had brought in together under Charles the Second, that stage coaches would run from London to York in twenty-four hours, that men would be in the habit of sailing without wind, and would be beginning to ride without horses, our ancestors would have given as much credit to the prediction as they gave to *Gulliver's Travels.* Yet the prediction would have been true; and they would have perceived that it was not altogether absurd, if they had considered that the country was then raising every year a sum which would have purchased the fee-simple[8] of the revenue of the Plantagenets, ten times what supported the Government of Elizabeth, three times what, in the time of Cromwell, had been thought intolerably oppressive. To almost all men the state of things under which they have been used to live seems to be the necessary state of things. We have heard it said that five per cent is the natural interest of money, that twelve is the natural number of a jury, that forty shillings is the natural qualification of a county voter. Hence it is that, though in every age everybody knows that up to his own time progressive improvement has been taking place, nobody seems to reckon on any improvement during the next generation. We cannot absolutely prove that those are in error who tell us that society has reached a turning point, that we have seen our best days. But so said all who came before us, and with just as much apparent reason. "A million a year will beggar us," said the patriots of 1640. "Two millions a year will grind the country to powder," was the cry in 1660. "Six millions a year, and a debt of fifty millions!" exclaimed Swift, "the high allies have been the ruin of us." "A hundred and forty millions of debt!" said Junius;[9] "well may we say that we owe Lord Chatham more than we shall ever pay, if we owe him such a load as this." "Two hundred and forty millions of debt!" cried all the statesmen of 1783 in chorus; "what abilities, or what economy on the part of a minister, can save a country so burdened?" We know that if, since 1783, no fresh debt had been incurred, the increased resources of the country would have enabled us to defray that debt at which Pitt, Fox, and Burke stood aghast, nay, to defray it over and over again, and that with much lighter taxation than what we have actually borne. On what principle is it that, when

8. Absolute ownership of their estates. The Plantagenet family provided the monarchs of England from 1145 to 1485.
9. Pseudonym of a political commentator whose letters (1769–72) usu-

ally praised William Pitt, Earl of Chatham. Pitt, as leader of the war against France, which gained Canada for England, could have been blamed for running his country into debt.

we see nothing but improvement behind us, we are to expect nothing but deterioration before us?

It is not by the intermeddling of Mr. Southey's idol, the omniscient and omnipotent State, but by the prudence and energy of the people, that England has hitherto been carried forward in civilization; and it is to the same prudence and the same energy that we now look with comfort and good hope. Our rulers will best promote the improvement of the nation by strictly confining themselves to their own legitimate duties, by leaving capital to find its most lucrative course, commodities their fair price, industry and intelligence their natural reward, idleness and folly their natural punishment, by maintaining peace, by defending property, by diminishing the price of law, and by observing strict economy in every department of the State. Let the Government do this: the People will assuredly do the rest.

1830

HERBERT SPENCER: *From* Social Statics[1]
[*Progress Through Individual Enterprise*]

* * * Under the natural order of things, the unfolding of an intelligent, self-helping character, must keep pace with the amelioration of physical circumstances—the advance of the one with the exertions put forth to achieve the other; so that in establishing arrangements conducive to robustness of body, robustness of mind must be insensibly acquired. Contrariwise, to whatever extent activity of thought and firmness of purpose are made less needful by an artificial performance of their work, to that same extent must their increase, and the dependent social improvements be retarded.

Should proof of this be asked for, it may be found in the contrast between English energy and Continental helplessness. English engineers (Manby, Wilson, and Co.) established the first gasworks in Paris, after the failure of a French company;[2] and many of the gasworks throughout Europe have been constructed by Englishmen. An English engineer (Miller) introduced steam navigation on the Rhône; another English engineer (Pritchard) succeeded in ascending the Danube by steam, after the French and Germans had failed. The first steamboats on the Loire were built by Englishmen (Fawcett and Preston); the great suspension bridge at Pesth[3] has been

1. From Chapter XXVIII. Herbert Spencer (1820–1903) was a philosopher and sociologist.
2. A demonstration of the commercial possibilities of gas for lighting was first made by a Frenchman, Philippe Lebon (1767–1804), but it was in England that his discoveries were first exploited successfully. By 1812 a gas company was chartered in London, and miles of pipes were soon laid down. English companies thereafter were frequently employed to install gas lines and fixtures in Europe and in America.
3. In Hungary.

built by an Englishman (Tierney Clarke); and an Englishman (Vignolles) is now building a still greater suspension bridge over the Dnieper; many continental railways have had Englishmen as consulting engineers; and in spite of the celebrated Mining College at Freyburg, several of the mineral fields along the Rhine have been opened up by English capital employing English skill. Now why is this? Why were our coaches so superior to the diligences and eilwagen[4] of our neighbours? Why did our railway system develop so much faster? Why are our towns better drained, better paved, and better supplied with water? There was originally no greater mechanical aptitude, and no greater desire to progress in us than in the connate nations of northern Europe. If anything, we were comparatively deficient in these respects. Early improvements in the arts of life were imported. The germs of our silk and woolen manufactures came from abroad. The first waterworks in London were erected by a Dutchman. How happens it, then, that we have now reversed the relationship? How happens it, that instead of being dependent on continental skill and enterprise, our skill and enterprise are at a premuim on the Continent? Manifestly the change is due to difference of discipline. Having been left in a greater degree than others to manage their own affairs, the English people have become self-helping, and have acquired great practical ability. Whilst conversely that comparative helplessness of the paternally-governed nations of Europe, illustrated in the above facts, and commented upon by Laing, in his *Notes of a Traveler*, and by other observers, is a natural result of the state-superintendence policy—is the reaction attendant on the action of official mechanisms —is the atrophy corresponding to some artificial hypertrophy.

1850

4. Stage coaches.

The Twentieth Century

(1890 to the Present)

1914–18: World War I.
1918: Gerard Manley Hopkins' poetry published.
1922: T. S. Eliot's *The Waste Land*.
1922: James Joyce's *Ulysses*.
1928: W. B. Yeats's *The Tower*.
1930: Period of depression and unemployment begins.
1939–45: World War II.

THE END OF VICTORIANISM

Cultural movements do not proceed neatly by centuries, and this section, which for convenience we call "the twentieth century," begins really with the late 19th, when the sense of the passing of a major phase of English history was already in the air. Queen Victoria's Jubilee in 1887 and, even more, her Diamond Jubilee in 1897 were felt even by contemporaries to mark the end of an era. As the 19th century drew to a close there were many manifestations of a weakening of traditional stabilities. The aesthetic movement, with its insistence on "art for art's sake," assaulted the assumptions about the nature and function of art held by ordinary middle-class readers, deliberately, provocatively. It helped to widen the breach between artists and writers on the one hand and the "Philistine" public on the other —a breach whose earlier symptom was Matthew Arnold's war on the Philistines in *Culture and Anarchy* and which was later to result in the "alienation of the artist" that is now a commonplace of criticism. This was more than a purely English matter. From France came the tradition of the bohemian life that scorned the limits imposed by conventional ideas of respectability, together with other notions of the artist as rejecting and rejected by ordinary society, which in different ways fostered the view of the alienated artist. The life and work of the French Symbolist poets in France, the early novels of Thomas Mann in Germany (especially *Buddenbrooks*, 1901), and Joyce's *Portrait of the Artist as a Young Man* (1916) show some of the very different ways in which this attitude revealed itself in literature all over Europe. In England, the growth of popular education as a result of the Education Act of 1870, which finally made elementary education compulsory and universal, led to the rapid emergence of a large, unsophisticated literary public at whom new kinds of journalism, in particular the cheap "yellow press," were directed. A public that was literate but not in any real sense educated increased steadily throughout the 19th century, and one result of this was the splitting up of the audience for literature into "highbrows," "lowbrows," and "middlebrows." Although in earlier periods there had been different kinds of audience for different kinds of writing, the split now developed with unprecedented speed and to an unprecedented degree because of the mass production of "popular" literature for the semiliterate. The fragmentation of the reading public now merged with the artist's war on the Philistine (and indeed was one of the causes of that war in the first place) to widen the gap between popular art and art esteemed only by the sophisticated and the expert. This is part of the background of modern literature all over the Western world.

Another manifestation—or at least accompaniment—of the end of the Victorian age was the rise of various kinds of pessimism and stoicism. The novels and poetry of Thomas Hardy show one kind of pessimism (and it *was* pessimism, even if Hardy himself repudiated the term), and the poems of A. E. Housman show another variety, while a real or affected stoicism is to be found not only in these writers but also in many minor writers of the last decade of the 19th century and the first decade of the 20th. Examples of this stoicism—the determination to stand for human dignity by enduring bravely, with a "stiff upper lip," whatever fate may bring—range from Robert Louis Stevenson's essays and the rhetorically assertive poems of the editor and journalist W. E. Henley, to Rudyard Kipling's *Jungle Books* and many of his short stories, the last stanza of Housman's *The Chestnut Casts His Flambeaux* ("Bear them we can, and if we can we must") and Yeats's "They know that Hamlet and Lear are gay."

Although the high tide of anti-Victorianism was marked by the publication in 1918 of that classic of ironic debunking, *Eminent Victorians* by Lytton Strachey (1880–1932), the criticism of the normal attitudes and preconceptions of the Victorian middle classes first became really violent in the last two decades of the 19th century. No one could have been more savage in his attacks on the Victorian conceptions of the family, education, and religion than Samuel Butler, whose novel *The Way of All Flesh* (completed in 1884, posthumously published in 1903) is still the bitterest indictment in English literature of the Victorian way of life. The chorus of questioning of Victorian assumptions grew ever louder as the century drew to an end; sounding prominently in it was the voice of the young Bernard Shaw, one of Butler's greatest admirers. The position of women, too, was rapidly changing during this period. The Married Woman's Property Act of 1882, which allowed married women to own property in their own right; the admission of women to the universities at different times during the latter part of the century; the fight for women's suffrage, which was not won until 1918 (and not fully won until 1928)—these events marked a change in the attitude to women and in the part they played in the national life as well as in the relation between the sexes, which is reflected in a variety of ways in the literature of the period.

The Boer War (1899–1902), fought by the British to establish political and economic control over the Boer republics of South Africa, marked both the high point of and the reaction against British imperialism. It was a war against which many British intellectuals protested and one which the British in the end were slightly ashamed of having won. The development

of the British Empire into the British Commonwealth (i.e., into an association of self-governing countries) continued in fits and starts throughout
the first half of the 20th century, with imperialist and anti-imperialist
sentiment often meeting head on; writers as far apart as Kipling and E. M.
Forster occupied themselves with the problem. The Irish question also
caused a great deal of excitement from the beginning of the period until
well into the 1920's. A steadily rising Irish nationalism protested with increasing violence against the political subordination of Ireland to the
British Crown and government. In World War I some Irish nationalists
sought German help in rebelling against Britain, and this exacerbated feeling on both sides. No one can fully understand William Butler Yeats or
James Joyce without some awareness of the Irish struggle for independence,
the feelings of Anglo-Irish men of letters on this burning topic, and the
way in which the Irish Literary Revival of the late 19th and early 20th
centuries (with which Yeats was much concerned) reflected a determination
to achieve a vigorous national life culturally even if the road seemed
blocked politically.

THE IMPACT OF WORLD WAR I

Edwardian England (1901–10) was very conscious of being no longer
Victorian. Edward VII stamped his character on the decade in which
he reigned. It was a vulgar age of conspicuous enjoyment by those who
could afford it, and writers and artists kept well away from implication in
high society (though there were some conspicuous exceptions): in general,
there was no equivalent in this period of Queen Victoria's interest in Tennyson. The alienation of artists and intellectuals was proceeding apace. From
1910 (when George V came to the throne) until war broke out in August,
1914, Britain achieved a temporary equilibrium between Victorian earnestness and Edwardian flashiness; in retrospect that "Georgian" period seems
peculiarly golden, the last phase of assurance and stability before the old
order throughout Europe broke up in violence with results that are still
with us. Yet even then, under the surface, there was restlessness and experimentation. If this was the age of Rupert Brooke, it was also the age of
T. S. Eliot's first experiments in a disturbingly new kind of poetry.

"Edwardian" as a term applied to English cultural history suggests a
period in which the social and economic stabilities of the Victorian age—
country houses with numerous servants, a flourishing and confident middle
class, a strict hierarchy of social classes—remained unimpaired, though on
the level of ideas there was a sense of change and liberation. "Georgian"
refers largely to the lull before the storm of World War I.

The quiet traditionalism of much of the verse that appeared in the volumes of *Georgian Poetry* edited by Edward Marsh between 1911 and 1920
represented an attempt to wall in the garden of English poetry against the
disruptive forces of modern civilization. Cultured meditations on the
English countryside ("I love the mossy quietness / That grows upon the
great stone flags") alternated with self-conscious exercises in the exotic
("When I was but thirteen or so / I went into a golden land, / Chim-
borazo, Cotopaxi, / Took me by the hand"). Sometimes the magical note
was authentic, as in many of Walter de la Mare's poems, and sometimes
the meditative strain was original and impressive, as in the poetry of Edward Thomas. But as World War I went on, with more and more poets

killed and the survivors increasingly disillusioned, the whole world on which the Georgian imagination rested came to appear unreal. A patriotic poem such as Rupert Brooke's *The Soldier* became a ridiculous anachronism in the face of modern trench warfare, and the even more blatantly patriotic note sounded by other Georgian poets (as in John Freeman's *Happy Is England Now,* which claimed that "there's not a nobleness of heart, hand, brain / But shines the purer; happiest is England now / In those that fight") came to seem positively obscene. The savage ironies of Siegfried Sassoon's war poems and the combination of pity and irony in those of Wilfred Owen portrayed a world undreamed of in the golden years from 1910 to 1914. Over four years of tremendous slaughter under appalling conditions (the battle casualties were many times greater than those in World War II), the wiping out of virtually a whole generation of young men, the shattering of so many illusions and ideals made World War I a watershed in European civilization. No one had been prepared for what actually happened in that war—in contrast to World War II, so long anticipated and predicted by a generation brought up on the grim war books of World War I. The experience was traumatic. It left throughout all Europe a sense that the bases of civilization had been destroyed, that all traditional values had been wiped out, and we see this reflected in different ways in *The Waste Land* of Eliot and the early novels and stories of Aldous Huxley.

THE POETIC REVOLUTION

A technical revolution in poetry was going on side by side with shifts in attitude. The Imagist movement, influenced by T. E. Hulme's insistence on hard, clear, precise images and encouraged by Ezra Pound when he lived in London just before World War I, fought against romantic fuzziness and facile emotionalism in poetry. The movement developed simultaneously on both sides of the Atlantic, and its early members included Amy Lowell, Richard Aldington, Hilda Doolittle, John Gould Fletcher, and F. S. Flint. As Flint explained in an article in March, 1913, Imagists insisted on "direct treatment of the 'thing,' whether subjective or objective," on the avoidance of all words "that did not contribute to the presentation," and on a freer metrical movement than a strict adherence to "the sequence of a metronome" could allow. All this encouraged precision in imagery and freedom of rhythmic movement, but more was required for the production of poetry of any real scope and interest. Imagism went in for the short, sharply etched, descriptive lyric, but it had no technique for the production of longer and more complex poems. Other new ideas about poetry helped to provide this technique. Sir Herbert Grierson's great edition of the poems of John Donne in 1912 both reflected and helped to encourage a new enthusiasm for 17th-century metaphysical poetry. The revival of interest in metaphysical wit brought with it a desire on the part of some pioneering poets to introduce into their poetry a much higher degree of intellectual complexity than had been found among the Victorians or the Georgians. The full subtlety of French Symbolist poetry also now came to be appreciated; it had been admired in the 90's, but for its dreamy suggestiveness rather than for its imagistic precision and complexity. At the same time a need was felt to bring poetic language and rhythms closer to those of conversation, or at least to spice the formalities of poetic utterance with echoes of the colloquial and even the slangy. Irony, which made possible several levels of discourse simultaneously, and wit, with the use of puns (banished from serious poetry for over 200 years), helped to achieve that union of thought and passion which T. S. Eliot, in his review of Grierson's anthology of metaphysical poetry (1921), saw as characteristic of the metaphysicals and wished to bring back into modern poetry. A new critical and a new creative movement in poetry went hand in hand, with Eliot the high priest of both. It was Eliot who extended the scope of Imagism by bringing the English metaphysicals and the French Symbolists (as well as the English Jacobean dramatists) to the rescue, thus adding new criteria of complexity and allusiveness to the criteria of concreteness and precision stressed by the Imagists. It was Eliot, too, who introduced into modern English and American poetry the kind of irony achieved by shifting suddenly from the formal to the colloquial or by oblique allusions to objects or ideas that contrasted sharply with those carried by the surface meaning of the poem. Thus between, say, 1911 (the first year of the Georgian poets) and 1922 (the year of the publication of *The Waste Land*) a major revolution occurred in English—and for that matter American—poetic theory and practice—a revolution which determined the way in which most serious poets and critics now think about their art. If one compares the poems in Palgrave's *Golden Treasury*, a Victorian anthology which was still used as a basic school text in Britain in the 1930's, with those in a number of academic anthologies of the mid-20th century, the change in poetic taste will become startlingly apparent. In the critical discussion, if not always in the allotment of space, Donne rather than Spenser becomes the great poet of the 16th- and 17th-century period; Gerard Manley Hopkins replaces Tennyson as the great 19th-century poet; and in general what one might call the metaphysical-Symbolist tradition predominates over both the cultivated self-pity of the Romantic-Victorian tradition and the Platonic-meditative strain of both the Elizabethans and (in his own way) Wordsworth.

The posthumous publication by Robert Bridges in 1918 of the poetry of Gerard Manley Hopkins encouraged further experimentation in language and rhythms. Hopkins combined absolute precision of the individual image with a complex ordering of images and a new kind of metrical patterning. The young poets of the early 1930's—W. H. Auden, Stephen Spender, C. Day Lewis—were much influenced by Hopkins as well as by Eliot (now the presiding genius of modern English and American poetry) and by a variety of other poets from the 16th-century John Skelton to Wilfred Owen. And even when the almost flamboyant new tones of Dylan Thomas were first sounded in the late 1930's, the influence of Hopkins could still be heard. It is only since World War II that a new generation of young English poets (including Donald Davie, Elizabeth Jennings, and Philip Larkin), searching for what has been called "purity of diction," have turned away from both the 17th century and the poetry of Hopkins and Eliot to seek a poetry which avoids all kinds of verbal excess in its desire for quiet luminosity and unpretentious truth.

Meanwhile the remarkable career of W. B. Yeats, stretching across the whole modern period, showed how a truly great poet can at the same time reflect the varying developments of his age and maintain an unmistakably individual accent. Beginning among the aesthetes of the 90's, turning later to a more tough and spare ironic language without losing his characteristic verbal magic, working out his own notions of symbolism and bringing them in different ways into his poetry, developing in his full maturity a rich symbolic and metaphysical poetry with its own curiously haunting cadences and its imagery both shockingly realistic and movingly suggestive, Yeats's work is itself a history of English poetry between 1890 and 1939. Yet he is always Yeats, unique and inimitable—without doubt the greatest English-speaking poet of his age.

Two important 20th-century poets stand somewhat apart from the main map of English poetry in the first half of the century. They are Robert Graves and Edwin Muir. Each has a highly individual voice and, the latter especially, a limited range. But they both show that there were strengths in the English poetic tradition untapped by Eliot and his followers. Graves, with a strong sense of tradition combined with a highly idiosyncratic poetic personality, has played a part in English poetry comparable to that played by Robert Frost in American. Muir's more quietist and mystical temperament was nourished by the unusual circumstances of his life, and his childhood in Orkney. In him, awareness of his native Scotland and a response to the heroic stories of ancient Greece were linked. Both poets were much concerned with time and the human response to time, and both had a deep sense of history.

BETWEEN THE WARS

The postwar disillusion of the 1920's was, it might be said, a spiritual matter, just as Eliot's Waste Land was a spiritual and not a literal wasteland. Depression and unemployment in the early 1930's, followed by the rise of Hitler and the cruel shadow of Fascism and Nazism over Europe, with its threat of another war, represented another sort of wasteland which produced another sort of effect on poets and novelists. The impotence of capitalist governments in the face of Hitlerism combined with economic dislocation to turn the majority of young intellectuals (and not only intellectuals) in the 1930's to the political Left. The 1930's were the Red decade, because only the Left seemed to offer any solution. The early poetry of W. H. Auden and his contemporaries cried out for "the death of the old gang" (in Auden's phrase) and a clean sweep politically and economically, while the Franco rebellion against the republican government in Spain, which started in the summer of 1936 and soon led to full-scale civil war, was regarded as a rehearsal for an inevitable second world war and thus further emphasized the inadequacy of politicians. Yet though all this is reflected passionately in the literature of the period, particularly in the poetry, it was not accompanied by any interesting developments in technique; many younger writers were more anxious to express their attitudes than to construct new kinds of works of art. The outbreak of World War II in September, 1939, following very shortly on Hitler's pact with Russia, which shocked and disillusioned so many of the young Left-wing writers, marked the sudden end of the Red decade; the concern of writers in Britain now was to maintain their integrity and indeed their existence in what was from the beginning expected to be a long and destructive war. This they did surprisingly well, but nevertheless this second war brought inevitable exhaustion: English literature has never quite recovered the vitality and interest in technical experimentation that marked the twenty years after about 1912.

These years—roughly 1912 to 1930—were the Heroic Age of the modern English novel. Joseph Conrad, James Joyce, and D. H. Lawrence are the giants, with Virginia Woolf and E. M. Forster brilliant minor figures— to name only the most outstanding writers. An important novelist of this period who stands rather apart from any of the movements discussed here is Ford Madox Ford (1873–1939), whose four novels about Christopher Tietjens published in the 1920's (and republished in a single volume as *Parade's End* in 1950) show meticulous craftsmanship and a deep sense of the changes wrought by the war on English life and character. The poet Robert Graves is similarly independent of movements and fashions in 20th-century literature: he developed and subtilized the Georgian tradition instead of adopting that of Eliot.

NEW METHODS IN FICTION

One can trace three major influences on the changes in attitude and technique in the modern novel. The first is the novelist's realization that the general background of belief which united him with his public in a common sense of what was significant in experience had disappeared. The public values of the Victorian novel, in which major crises of plot could be shown through changes in the social or financial or marital status of the chief characters, gave way to more personally conceived notions of value, dependent on the novelist's intuitions and sensibilities rather than on public agreement. "To believe that your impressions hold good for others," Virginia Woolf once wrote (discussing Jane Austen), "is to be released from the cramp and confinement of personality." The modern novelist could no longer believe this: he had to fall back on personality, drawing his criterion of significance in human affairs (and thus his principle of selection) from his own intuitions, so that he needed to find ways of convincing the reader that his own private sense of what was significant in experience was truly valid. A new technical burden was thus imposed on the novelist's prose, for it had now to build up a world of values instead of drawing on an existing world of values. Virginia Woolf tried to solve the problem by using some of the devices of poetry in order to suggest the novelist's own sense of value and vision of the world. Joyce, on the other hand, made no attempt to convey a single personal attitude, but reacted to the breakdown of public values by employing a kind of writing so multiple in its implications that it conveyed numerous points of view simultaneously, the author being totally objective and committed to none of them—a mode which required remarkable technical virtuosity.

The second influence on the changes in attitude and technique in the modern novel was a new view of time; time was not a series of chronological moments to be presented by the novelist in sequence with an occasional deliberate retrospect ("this reminded him of," "he recalled that"), but as a continuous flow in the consciousness of the individual, with the "already" continuously merging into the "not yet" and retrospect merging into anticipation. This influence is closely bound up with a third: the new notions of the nature of consciousness, which derived in a general way from Sigmund Freud and Carl Jung but were also part of the spirit of the age and discernible even in those novelists who had not read either psychologist. Consciousness is multiple; the past is always present in it at some level and is continually coloring one's present reaction. Marcel Proust in France, in his great novel sequence *Remembrance of Things Past* (1913–28), had explored the ways in which the past impinges on the present and consciousness is determined by memory. The view that a man *is* his memories, that his present is the sum of his past, that if we dig into a man's consciousness we can tell the whole truth about him without waiting for a chronological sequence of time to take him through a series of testing circumstances, inevitably led to a technical revolution in the novel. For now, by exploring in depth into consciousness and memory rather than proceeding lengthwise along the dimension of time, a novelist could write a novel concerned ostensibly with only one day of the hero's life (Joyce's *Ulysses* and Virginia Woolf's *Mrs. Dalloway*). This view of multiple levels of consciousness existing simultaneously, coupled with the view of time as a constant flow rather than a series of separate moments, meant that a novelist preferred to plunge into the consciousness of his characters in order to tell his story rather than to provide an external framework of chronological narrative. The "stream-of-consciousness" technique, where the author tries to render directly the very fabric of his character's consciousness without reporting it in formal, quoted remarks, was developed in the 1920's as an important new technique of the English novel. It made for more difficult reading, at least for those accustomed only to the methods of the older English novel. No "porch" was constructed at the front of the novel to put the reader in possession of necessary preliminary information: such information emerged, as the novel progressed, from the consciousness of each character as it responded to the present with echoes of its past. No conventional signposts were put up to tell the reader where he was, for that was felt to interfere with the immediacy of the impression. But once the reader learns how to find his way in this unsignposted territory, he is rewarded by new delicacies of perception and new subtleties of presentation.

Concentration on the "stream of consciousness" and on the association of ideas within the individual consciousness led inevitably to stress on the essential loneliness of the individual. For all consciousnesses are unique and isolated, and if this unique, private world is the real world in which men live, if the public values to which they must pay lip service in the social world in which they move are not the real values which give meaning to their personality, then each man is condemned to live in the prison of his own incommunicable consciousness. How is true communication possible in such a world? The public gestures imposed upon us by society never correspond to our real inward needs. They are conventional in the bad sense, mechanical, imposing a crude standardization on the infinite subtlety of experience. If we do try to give out a sign from our real selves, that sign is bound to be misunderstood when read by some other self in the light of that self's quite other personality. The theme of such modern fiction is thus the possibility of love, the establishment of emotional communication, in a community of private consciousnesses. This, is, in different ways, the theme of Joyce, of Lawrence, of Virginia Woolf, and of Forster, and (on a rather different scale and not always so directly) of Conrad. The search for communion and the inevitable isolation of Leopold Bloom in *Ulysses* is symbolic of the human condition as seen by the modern novelist. Similar investigations of this basic condition are Forster's explorations of the conventions which seem to be helps to living but which in fact prevent true human contacts, and Virginia Woolf's delicate projections of the relation between the self's need for privacy and the self's need for genuine communication. The theme of all Lawrence's novels is human relationships, the ideal of which he restlessly explored with shifting emphasis throughout his career; such relationships can be all too easily distorted by the mechanical conventions of society, by notions of respectability or propriety, by all the shams and frauds of middle-class life, by the demands of power or money or success. One might almost say that the greatest modern novels are about the difficulty, and at the same time the inevitability, of being human. The dilemma of the human condition is never really solved in these novelists; but knowledge that the dilemma is shared— a knowledge so brilliantly conveyed in *Ulysses* and so wryly proffered by Forster—can both illuminate and comfort.

Not all the novelists of the period, of course, were concerned with these themes or employed the new techniques appropriate to them. The "documentary" novelists, such as Arnold Bennett and John Galsworthy (and, in some at least of his novels, H. G. Wells), presented, often with great skill, the changing social scene, showing considerable insight and sympathy in recording aspects of it through the behavior of their imagined characters. Virginia Woolf called these writers "materialists," maintaining that they were content to deal with externals and did not go on to explore those aspects of consciousness, of the true inward life of men, in which human reality resides. She was perhaps judging unfairly, by standards that were not applicable to their sort of fiction; but modern criticism has on the whole agreed with her.

The short story in this period benefited from the new techniques of exploration in depth. A greater consciousness of the symbolic uses to which objects and incidents can be put and a greater subtlety in the ways in which patterns of suggestiveness are built up below the quietly realistic surface can be found in the short stories of writers so different from each other as Joyce, Katherine Mansfield, Lawrence, and Forster. Katherine Mansfield learned from the Russian short-story writer Anton Chekhov how to use the casual-seeming incidents of ordinary life in such a way as to set up haunting overtones of meaning. The apparently inconsequential surface masking the carefully organized substructure is found in much modern fiction (perhaps most of all in *Ulysses*): it is one of the results of the coming together, in the novel and the short story, of realism and symbolism, of contemporary probability and timeless significance. These things of course come together in great fiction of all ages; but the modern writer contrives their coexistence with greater self-consciousness than his predecessors.

THE DRAMA

Modern drama begins in a sense with the witty drawing-room comedies of Oscar Wilde; yet Wilde founded no dramatic school. His wit was per-

sonal and irresponsible, unlike the wit of Restoration comedy, which reflected an attitude to the relation between the sexes which was part of a
view of society held by a whole (if a small) social class. Bernard Shaw
brought still another kind of wit into drama—not Wilde's exhibitionist
sparkle nor yet the assured sophistication of the Restoration dramatists,
but the provocative paradox that was meant to tease and disturb, to challenge the complacency of the audience. Shaw's discussion plays were given
dramatic life through the mastery of theatrical techniques which he
learned during his years as a dramatic critic. In his general attitudes Shaw
represents the anti-Victorianism of the late Victorians; his long life should
not obscure the fact that his first—and some of his best—plays belong to
the 90's. Other attempts by 20th-century dramatists to debate social questions on the stage—by Galsworthy, for example—deserve respect for their
humanity and intelligence and sometimes for their theatrical craftsmanship, but they lack Shaw's verbal and intellectual brilliance and his superb
capacity to entertain. We must turn to Ireland to find another really impressive variety of dramatic activity. The Irish Literary Theatre was founded
in 1899, with Yeats's early play *The Countess Cathleen* as its first production. The founders—Yeats, Lady Gregory, George Moore, and Edward
Martyn—wanted to make a contribution to an Irish literary revival, but
they were influenced also by the Independent Theatre in London, founded
in 1891 by J. T. Grein in order to encourage new developments in the
drama. In 1902 the Irish Literary Theatre was able to maintain a permanent all-Irish company and changed its name to the Irish National Theatre,
which moved in 1904 to the Abbey Theatre, by which name it has since
been known. Many of the plays produced at the Abbey Theatre were only
of local and ephemeral interest, but J. M. Synge's use of the speech and
imagination of Irish country people, Yeats's powerful symbolic use of
themes from old Irish legend, and Sean O'Casey's use of the Irish civil
war as a background for plays combining tragic melodrama, humor of
character, and irony of circumstance, brought new kinds of vitality to the
theater. T. S. Eliot attempted with considerable success to revive a ritual
poetic drama in England with his *Murder in the Cathedral* (1935). His
later attempts to combine religious symbolism with the box-office appeal
of amusing society comedy (as in *The Cocktail Party*, 1950), though impressive technical achievements, were not wholly successful: the combination
of contemporary social chatter with profound religious symbolism produces
an unevenness of tone and disturbing shifts in levels of realism. Elsewhere
in modern drama the conflict between realism and symbolism (first clearly
seen in Ibsen) is acted out in a variety of ways.

In spite of the achievements of Shaw, Yeats, and Eliot, it cannot be
said of the drama as it can of poetry and fiction in this period that a technical revolution occurred which changed the whole course of literary history
with respect to that particular literary form. The reformers of the 1890's
invoked the name of the great Norwegian playwright Henrik Ibsen: like
Shaw they saw him as essentially a critic of middle-class society rather than
(as critics tend to see him today) as an essentially poetic dramatist experimenting with symbolic modes of expression. This may be the reason why
the influence of Ibsen soon petered out in run-of-the-mill plays of humanitarian social concern. Harley Granville-Barker, actor, director, and Shake-

speare scholar and critic as well as playwright, wrote four interesting and thoughtful plays in 1909 and 1910, but for all their intelligence they never really come alive theatrically. The staple of the London West End theater remained social comedy stiffened by occasional irony and sweetened by sentimentality (Noel Coward is one of the best purveyors of this sort of fare). The cleverly contrived sentimentalities of J. M. Barrie (1860–1937) were highly popular in their day; Barrie's plays showed a high theatrical skill and a determined cunning in the exploitation of the audience's reaction. That audience consisted for the most part of tired Philistines, and it was they who determined what was to be a box-office success. An original Scottish dramatist, who at one time appeared to be achieving singlehanded a new awakening in the Scottish theater but who in the end failed to do so, was James Bridie (pseudonym of Dr. O. H. Mavor, 1885–1951), whose witty and inventive plays show an intellectual liveliness sometimes reminiscent of Shaw.

The energy which the Irish movement gave to English drama has not lasted. Sean O'Casey's later plays, where he is influenced by expressionist techniques suggested by German dramatists as well as by Eugene O'Neill, have neither the vitality nor the vivid humor of those earlier plays in which he was able to give tragic meaning to the realities of contemporary Dublin life without denying its comic elements. Another Irish playwright, William Denis Johnston, has also experimented with expressionist techniques and has achieved in some of his plays a remarkable combination of the grotesque and the ironic. But vitality has not been coming into the English theater in the 1950's and early 1960's from this direction.

In the late 1940's and early 1950's it seemed that the verse plays of Christopher Fry were about to bring a new kind of poetic life into English drama. But Fry's exuberantly witty use of metaphor soon lost its appeal, and by the late 1950's a very different kind of drama brought vitality to the British theater. John Osborne's *Look Back in Anger* was produced at the Royal Court Theatre in 1956. Angrily, violently, and in an unadorned and sometimes brutally colloquial dialogue, it thrust upon the audience the revelation of psychological and social problems left unresolved, or even exacerbated, by the welfare state. *The Entertainer* (1957) was similar in its brash virtuosity; Osborne's third play, *Luther* (1960), shows him moving out of a preoccupation with a restricted part of the contemporary social scene to wider concerns and a freer use of imagination. Arnold Wesker was another Royal Court discovery. In a trilogy that began with *Chicken Soup with Barley* (1958), he explored, though less stridently than Osborne, related social and psychological problems. Joan Littlewood's Theatre Workshop introduced another kind of vigorous new theatricalism, with an impromptu-seeming kind of play made up of numerous small scenes; distinctive examples are Brendan Behan's *The Quare Fellow* (1956) and Shelagh Delaney's *A Taste of Honey* (1958). A third significant influence on recent English drama has been the director Peter Hall, who commissioned a number of important plays for his Aldwych productions, including Robert Bolt's *A Man for All Seasons* (1960) and John Arden's *Live Like Pigs* (1958). The man, however, who is emerging as the most important and individual dramatist is Harold Pinter, whose plays, including *The Birthday Party* (1958), *The Caretaker* (1960), and *The Homecoming*

(1966), project disturbing symbolic meanings in a quietly colloquial language. These playwrights have the advantage of working with lively and innovative talent in the practical theater. In addition there is a constant and fruitful interaction between drama on the stage and drama in the film, the playwright himself usually working in both media. It is too early to say how much this dramatic revival will endure as literature, but clearly the drama and the theater is the place in contemporary Britain where the artistic action is.

LITERARY CRITICISM

Criticism occupies a much larger place on the map of modern literary culture than it has ever occupied before. New psychological and anthropological ideas have stimulated new kinds of critical activity; tools of critical analysis have been sharpened by the impact of linguistic philosophy; the increased difficulty of much modern writing, itself the result of the fragmentation of the audience for literature and the consequent withdrawal of serious writers into coteries using a more or less private symbolism, has increased the demand for critical interpretation. This is the great critical age, and criticism and creation have marched together (in Eliot's work, for example) to an unusual degree, although modern America has placed more emphasis on criticism than has modern Britain.

From one point of view, it could be maintained that Matthew Arnold is the father of modern literary criticism. Arnold thought literature was bound to replace religion as a source of inspiration and spiritual refreshment, and as a result insisted that we must have "the best" literature. If literature, rather than religion, is central to a civilization, and not a mere relaxation or optional pleasure, discrimination between good and bad literature is of the first importance, and critics become in a sense the equivalent of priests. F. R. Leavis, who edited the influential critical review *Scrutiny* from its foundation in 1932 until its demise in 1953, inherited from Arnold this view of the need to discover and proclaim "the best." His and his contributors' essays in *Scrutiny* were devoted to what they called "discrimination," to a determined winnowing of the little wheat from the abundant chaff by a careful technique of practical criticism which at first owed a great deal to I. A. Richards' methods in his Cambridge lectures. Leavis also inherited from Arnold his war against the Philistines and the view that the quality of literature which is produced and esteemed by a generation is bound up with the whole quality of its culture, of the way in which people live and work as well as think. *Culture and Environment*, by Leavis and Denys Thompson (1933), is similar in more than title to Arnold's *Culture and Anarchy*: it is an examination of the way in which the conditions of living imposed by some elements in modern civilization inhibit proper discrimination in literature as in other spheres. But Leavis repudiates any such simple ethical criterion as Arnold's "high seriousness," and sees the true moral vision of a writer embodied much more subtly and often indirectly in his work than Arnold did. In this view he has been influenced by Eliot's repudiation (in *Tradition and the Individual Talent*) of "any semi-ethical criterion of 'sublimity.'"

In general there has been in the last forty years or so—but again not to the same degree as in America—a repudiation of the older view of criticism as gentlemanly chat about books, the "hours in a library" sort of thing, in favor of a criticism much more rigorous and analytic. The revolution in taste proclaimed in the antiromantic essays of T. E. Hulme and developed in the influential essays of Eliot inevitably demanded a more strenuous kind of criticism. If poetic imagery was to be hard, dry, and precise and at the same time impregnated with metaphysical wit and irony, and if a new degree of intellectual complexity was to be demanded of poetry, then the critic had to provide himself with tools for the careful analysis of meaning and structure in order to demonstrate these qualities or the lack of them. Similarly, critics who agreed with Eliot that "the poet has, not a 'personality' to express, but a particular medium," became suspicious alike of autobiographical and exclamatory responses to literature and of the biographical approach which tended to assess literary quality in terms of the degree to which the writer genuinely expressed himself.

Thus the Arnoldian insistence on discrimination combined with the Hulme-Eliot tradition of precision and complexity to demand a more searchingly analytic kind of critical description and evaluation. At the same time I. A. Richards, interested in problems of communication and the different ways in which words work to communicate different sorts of meaning, developed his own technique of analysis of poetic imagery and structure, which had considerable influence on practical (i.e., applied) criticism. Richards turned to psychology for aid in his investigation of meaning and also for the construction of a theory of literary value. Psychology came into modern criticism in many other ways. Although the old-fashioned kind of biographical approach was now out of favor, the examination of the psychology of poetic creation became a respectable branch of criticism, sometimes used to reinforce an analytic account of how imagery works in a poem. On the whole, however, what might be called "genetic" criticism—explanation of the origins and development of a work, rather than of its present nature and value—went on apart from analytic and evaluative criticism. "Genetic" criticism could use psychology, with all the new resources brought in by Freud and Jung, or it could use sociology, studying the social factors that helped to condition particular writers and their works.

Psychology came into criticism in other ways also. Together with anthropology it helped to investigate the ways in which myth and symbol work in literature. Eliot had confessedly drawn on anthropological works in *The Waste Land*, thus virtually asking the critics to use such aids in examining the poem. They were not slow to take him up. Here Jung rather than Freud was the major influence, for Jung's view of racial memory (akin to Yeats's view of the "Great Memory," which preserved the meaning of symbols) was obviously relevant to any investigation of the way in which the mythical element in literature operates. Maud Bodkin's *Archetypal Patterns in Poetry* (1934) was a pioneer work in this field; it stimulated a host of further studies of myth and symbol on both sides of the Atlantic.

At the same time techniques of the analysis of meaning developed by Richards in his practical criticism were being developed to greater and sometimes provocative lengths by his onetime pupil, William Empson. Semantics was now an established tool of the analytic critic, used in many different ways. So the pattern is this: first, the necessity for discrimination (because we must have "the best") through rigorous critical analysis; further emphasis on critical rigor by the Hulme-Eliot tradition of precision, impersonality, and complexity; new tools for critical analysis through the study of semantics and linguistic philosophy; an interest in archetypal images through the psychological and anthropological incitements to the study of myth and symbol; side by side with all this, and sometimes interacting with it, psychological and sociological investigation of the way the creative process operates in given instances. All these elements are present in what has for many years now been called in America the "new criticism," for American critics, more than British critics, have taken up and developed, sometimes with great originality and persuasiveness, all of these critical strains.

BRITISH-AMERICAN LITERARY RELATIONS

The relationship between British and American literature has been closer in the present century than at any other time. It is true that American dependence on English literature in earlier periods resulted in a certain kind of closeness of relationship, but the really individual American writers—Walt Whitman, Herman Melville, Mark Twain, for example—turned deliberately away from the English literary scene in order to avoid this dependence. Henry James, who lived mainly in England from 1876 until his death in 1916, becoming a British citizen in 1915, was a pioneer in the development of what might be called an Anglo-American sensibility. The American poet Robert Frost lived in England from 1912 to 1915, published his first book of poems there, and had a close literary and personal association with the English poet Edward Thomas. A more revolutionary American poet, Ezra Pound, lived in England from 1908 to 1920, and it was from England that he launched the Imagist movement, which proved equally influential on both sides of the Atlantic. In the modern period most of the significant literary movements have been common to the two countries; indeed, the most significant movement of all—the revolution in poetic taste and practice associated with the work of T. S. Eliot—was an Anglo-American phenomenon. The American Eliot turned British subject and the English Auden turned American citizen are symbolic of the whole literary situation—as is I. A. Richards, who, after years in Cambridge, England, now teaches at Harvard in Cambridge, Massachusetts. In poetry and criticism, at least, the modern achievement has been in considerable degree Anglo-American (although the individuality and uniqueness of each poet is, of course, undeniable—Yeats on one side of the Atlantic and Wallace Stevens on the other, for example).

The Nineties

The last decade of the 19th century saw the culmination of a movement toward a self-conscious aestheticism that was partly a revolt against the moral earnestness of such Victorian prophets as Carlyle and Ruskin and partly a development of ideas implicit in the writings of Walter Pater (see, for example, the conclusion to *The Renaissance*). Ruskin, too, had insisted on beauty, but he had linked it with morality, and the Pre-Raphaelites had turned to medieval art and religion to find beauty and controlled ecstasy in clarity of detail and precision of sensation. The aesthetes of the 90's, while learning from Ruskin and the Pre-Raphaelites, preached and practiced a more self-indulgent doctrine. Art for them represented not only the embodiment of beauty but also the search for new kinds of sensation and of emotional experience. The doctrine of "art for art's sake," so often preached during this period, really meant art for the sake of the sensations and experiences it could induce, with no reference to any standard of morality or utility. The artist was in rebellion against the Victorian middle-class way of life and of thought and took a peculiar pleasure in shocking middle-class opinion.

The writers who took part in this movement were very much aware of living at the end of a great century and often cultivated a deliberately *fin-de-siècle* ("end-of-century") pose. A studied languor, a weary sophistication, a search for new ways of titillating jaded palates can be found in both the poetry and the prose of the period. *The Yellow Book*, a periodical devoted entirely to art and letters which ran from 1894 to 1897, is generally taken to represent the aestheticism of the 90's. The startling black-and-white drawings and designs of its art editor, Aubrey Beardsley (1872–98), the prose of George Moore and Max Beerbohm, and the poetry of Ernest Dowson illustrate different aspects of the movement. But *The Yellow Book* also printed Lionel Johnson and the young W. B. Yeats, naturalistic stories of contemporary life by Arnold Bennett and others, as well as essays by respectable academic critics such as George Saintsbury and Sir Edmund Gosse. It was thus not entirely the organ of the aesthetic movement, but appealed to a variety of kinds of sophistication, from the latest in aestheticism to the latest in realism.

The poets of the aesthetic movement were in a sense the last heirs of the Romantics; the appeal to sensation in their imagery goes back through Rossetti and Tennyson to Keats. They developed this sensationalism, however, much more histrionically than their predecessors, seeking compensation for the drabness of ordinary life in melancholy suggestiveness, antibourgeois sensationalism, heady ritualism, histrionic world-weariness, or mere emotional debauchery. At their best they have considerable emotional power and a certain incantatory persuasiveness. At their worst, the sensationalism of their imagery becomes merely ludicrous. Even Dowson's *To One in Bedlam*, an adroit and moving poem in its way, is spoiled by "thy moon-kissed roses" and "star-crowned solitude"—images which come out of the property-room of the 90's.

What makes the 90's important as a period of English literary history is not, however, its writers' sensationalism and desire to shock. It is their strongly held belief in the independence of art, their view that a work of art has its own unique kind of value—that, in T. S. Eliot's phrase, poetry must be judged "as poetry and not another thing"—which has most strongly influenced later generations. Not only did the aesthetic movement nurse the young Yeats and provide him with his lifelong belief in poetry as poetry rather than as a means to some moral or other end; it also provided modern criticism with its basic assumptions. "Art for art's sake" was in the 90's a provocative slogan; today it is a commonplace, and there are few significant critics who would not accept some version of it. The whole modern movement in criticism, as well as the new poetic techniques associated with it, has been largely concerned with demonstrating the uniqueness of the literary use of language and with training us to see works of literary art as possessing their special kind of form, their special kind of meaning, and hence their special kind of value. In this it is the heir of the 90's, however much it may have modified or enriched the legacy. It was the poets of the 90's, too, who first absorbed the influence of the French *symbolistes* poets, an influence which has proved pervasive in the 20th century and is especially strong (though in different ways) in the poetry of Yeats and of Eliot.

OSCAR WILDE
(1856–1900)

Oscar Fingall O'Flahertie Wills Wilde was born in Dublin; his father was a distinguished eye and ear surgeon who had been knighted for his work, his mother a minor poetess who ran a well-known literary salon. He was educated at Trinity College, Dublin, where his success in classical studies enabled him to win a scholarship to Magdalen College, Oxford. At Oxford he soon won a reputation for his brilliant conversation and studied eccentricities in dress and manner of living. He was much influenced by Walter Pater, particularly by *The Renaissance*, "that book which has had such strange influence over my life," as he later recalled, and he read, too, Rossetti and Swinburne and the work of the French poet Charles Baudelaire. He left Oxford in 1878 already known as a champion of the aesthetic movement and of the creed of "art for art's sake," and settled in London, where he published stories and poems in periodicals and continued his exhibitionist behavior. Gilbert and Sullivan's opera *Patience* (1881) satirized Wilde in the character of the poet Bunthorne, and though this satire tended to run together the earlier Pre-Raphaelite movement with the aesthetic movement of the following decades, it represented the popular view of Wilde and his activities:

Though the Philistines may jostle, you will rank as an apostle in the high
　　aesthetic band,
If you walk down Piccadilly with a poppy or a lily in your medieval hand.
　　　　　　And everyone will say,
　　　　　　As you walk your flowery way,
"If he's content with a vegetable love which would certainly not suit *me*,
Why, what a most particularly pure young man this pure young man must
　　be!"

Wilde did in fact walk in London wearing velvet knee breeches, silk stockings, and a velveteen coat with an exotic flower in the buttonhole.

　　Wilde continued his writing for periodicals while his rapidly growing
reputation as a brilliant wit made him the most sought-after dinner guest
in London. He edited *The Woman's World* (1887–89), and in 1888
brought out a volume of fairy tales, *The Happy Prince and Other Tales*,
a curiously stylized cross-breeding of Hans Andersen and Pater. The following year *The Decay of Lying* appeared in *The Nineteenth Century*;
here he presented with glittering paradoxes his view of the autonomy of the
artistic imagination:

Many a young man starts in life with a natural gift for exaggeration which,
if nurtured in congenial and sympathetic surroundings, or by the imitation
of the best models, might grow into something really great and wonderful.
But, as a rule, he comes to nothing. * * * He either falls into careless
habits of accuracy, or takes to frequenting the society of the aged and the
well-informed. Both things are equally fatal to his imagination, as indeed
they would be fatal to the imagination of anybody, and in a short time he
develops a morbid and unhealthy faculty of truth-telling, begins to verify all
statements made in his presence, * * * and often ends by writing novels
which are so lifelike that no one can possibly believe in their probability.

Wilde insisted that imitation was not the function of art. "Art finds her
own perfection within, and not outside of, herself. She is not to be judged
by any external standard of resemblance." He argued, too, that Nature imitates Art, rather than the other way round. "Things are because we see
them, and what we see, and how we see it, depends on the Arts that have
influenced us."

　　Wilde's first published book of *Poems* (1881) showed the influence of
Elizabethan, Romantic, Pre-Raphaelite, and 19th-century French poets,
and he continued to write for periodicals poems exploring the momentary
sensation or emotion or impression. But his most important work was in
his critical and dramatic prose and his curiously mannered prose fable,
The Picture of Dorian Gray (1891). This is the story of a young man
who, in his desire to carry out Pater's advice to savor every kind of beauty
in experience, is led into a great variety of vice with no visible sign of age
or degeneration, while his portrait gradually changes to show the corruption of his soul. The equation of the pursuit of beauty with involvement in
vice was curiously Philistine; it revealed a contradiction in Wilde's attitude, since for him art and beauty ought logically to have had no relation
to morality one way or the other. *Intentions*, published in the same year,
contained a number of dialogues in which Wilde's aesthetic philosophy was
given its most eloquent expression: *The Critic as Artist*, which first appeared in this volume, maintains that the critic's "sole aim is to chronicle

his own impressions," and not to give an objective account or estimate of the work criticized.

Wilde's greatest successes were his plays—*Lady Windermere's Fan* (1892), *A Woman of No Importance* (1893), *An Ideal Husband* (1895), and, best and most brilliant, *The Importance of Being Earnest*, written in 1894 and produced in 1895. It was while these last two plays were running simultaneously and enjoying phenomenal success—they were artificial social comedies whose verbal wit and shocking paradoxes still astonish and delight—that Wilde's spectacular fall took place. The Marquis of Queensberry had accused Wilde of homosexuality; Wilde rashly brought a libel suit against the Marquis, and lost, since it was proved that the Marquis had spoken the truth. Wilde now found himself accused of what (under a law of 1885) was a crime punishable by imprisonment. He could have left the country after the Queensberry case, but, fascinated by the melodrama of his own fate, he stayed to face the charge, defending himself with wit and confidence. The result was, however, a foregone conclusion: Wilde lost and was sentenced to two years imprisonment with hard labor. The revulsion of feeling against him in England was tremendous; his name became a bad word, and the aesthetic movement which he had championed fell—at least so far as its externals went—into immediate oblivion. Literary men and others did everything to demonstrate their healthy normality, and the public turned to the more virile writings of men like W. E. Henley and Rudyard Kipling. Wilde wrote the melodramatic but genuinely powerful *Ballad of Reading Gaol* and the searchingly autobiographical *De Profundis* as a result of his experience in prison, and after his release he lived in France under an assumed name, a ruined man, until his death three years later.

The gods had given me almost everything. I had a genius, a distinguished name, high social position, brilliancy, intellectual daring * * * I treated art as the supreme reality and life as a mere mode of fiction. * * * But I let myself be lured into long spells of senseless and sensual ease. * * * Tired of being on the heights, I deliberately went to the depths in the search for new sensation. What the paradox was to me in the sphere of thought, perversity became to me in the sphere of passion. * * * I ended in horrible disgrace. There is only one thing for me now, absolute humility.

So Wilde wrote in *De Profundis*, when he was still in prison. "Oscar Wilde's greatest play was his own life," remarked Frank Harris. "It was a five-act tragedy with Greek implications and he was its most ardent spectator."

Impression du Matin[1]

The Thames nocturne of blue and gold
    Changed to a harmony in gray;
    A barge with ocher-colored hay
Dropped from the wharf:[2] and chill and cold

The yellow fog came creeping down
    The bridges, till the houses' walls   5

---

1. "Impression of the Morning."
2. Left the wharf and went down river with the ebb tide.

Seemed changed to shadows, and St. Paul's
Loomed like a bubble o'er the town.

Then suddenly arose the clang
  Of waking life; the streets were stirred   10
  With country wagons; and a bird
Flew to the glistening roofs and sang.

But one pale woman all alone,
  The daylight kissing her wan hair,
  Loitered beneath the gas lamps' flare,   15
With lips of flame and heart of stone.

1881

Hélas[3]

To drift with every passion till my soul
Is a stringed lute on which all winds can play,
Is it for this that I have given away
Mine ancient wisdom, and austere control?
Methinks my life is a twice-written scroll   5
Scrawled over on some boyish holiday
With idle songs for pipe and virelay,[4]
Which do but mar the secret of the whole.
Surely there was a time I might have trod
The sunlit heights, and from life's dissonance   10
Struck one clear chord to reach the ears of God:
Is that time dead? lo! with a little rod
I did but touch the honey of romance—
And must I lose a soul's inheritance?

1881

E Tenebris[1]

Come down, O Christ, and help me! reach thy hand,
  For I am drowning in a stormier sea
  Than Simon on thy lake of Galilee:[2]
The wine of life is spilt upon the sand,
My heart is as some famine-murdered land   5
  Whence all good things have perished utterly,
  And well I know my soul in Hell must lie
If I this night before God's throne should stand.
"He sleeps perchance, or rideth to the chase,
  Like Baal, when his prophets howled that name   10

3. "Alas!"
4. A song or short lyric in stanzas.
1. "Out of Darkness."
2. Simon, surnamed Peter, one of the twelve apostles, was a fisherman on Lake Galilee when found there by Jesus.

From morn to noon on Carmel's smitten height."[3]
Nay, peace, I shall behold, before the night,
    The feet of brass,[4] the robe more white than flame,
The wounded hands, the weary human face.

1881

The Harlot's House

We caught the tread of dancing feet,
We loitered down the moonlit street,
And stopped beneath the harlot's house.

Inside, above the din and fray,
We heard the loud musicians play   5
The "Treues Liebes Herz" of Strauss.[5]

Like strange mechanical grotesques,
Making fantastic arabesques,
The shadows raced across the blind.

We watched the ghostly dancers spin   10
To sound of horn and violin,
Like black leaves wheeling in the wind.

Like wire-pulled automatons,
Slim silhouetted skeletons
Went sidling through the slow quadrille.[6]   15

They took each other by the hand,
And danced a stately saraband;[7]
Their laughter echoed thin and shrill.

Sometimes a clockwork puppet pressed
A phantom lover to her breast,   20
Sometimes they seemed to try to sing.

Sometimes a horrible marionette
Came out, and smoked its cigarette
Upon the steps like a live thing.

Then, turning to my love, I said,   25
"The dead are dancing with the dead,
The dust is whirling with the dust."

But she—she heard the violin,
And left my side, and entered in:
Love passed into the house of lust.   30

3. The poet imagines an ironic voice discouraging him; it uses the language of Elijah when he mocked the priests of Baal for their god's impotence by suggesting that perhaps Baal was on a journey or asleep (see I Kings xviii.19–40).
4. Cf. Revelation i ff., where the "Son of man" is seen in a vision, "his feet like unto fine brass, as if they burned in a furnace."
5. "Heart of True Love," a waltz by the Austrian composer and "Waltz King," Johann Strauss (1825–99).
6. A square dance.
7. A slow and stately dance, originating in Spain.

Then suddenly the tune went false,
The dancers wearied of the waltz,
The shadows ceased to wheel and whirl.

And down the long and silent street,
The dawn, with silver-sandaled feet,   35
Crept like a frightened girl.

1885, 1908

From The Critic as Artist[1]
[*Criticism Itself an Art*]

ERNEST. Gilbert, you sound too harsh a note. Let us go back to the more gracious fields of literature. What was it you said? That it was more difficult to talk about a thing than to do it?

GILBERT. [*after a pause*] Yes: I believe I ventured upon that simple truth. Surely you see now that I am right? When man acts he is a puppet. When he describes he is a poet. The whole secret lies in that. It was easy enough on the sandy plains by windy Ilion[2] to send the notched arrow from the painted bow, or to hurl against the shield of hide and flamelike brass the long ash-handled spear. It was easy for the adulterous queen[3] to spread the Tyrian carpets for her lord, and then, as he lay couched in the marble bath, to throw over his head the purple net, and call to her smooth-faced lover to stab through the meshes at the heart that should have broken at Aulis.[4] For Antigone[5] even, with Death waiting for her as her bridegroom, it was easy to pass through the tainted air at noon, and climb the hill, and strew with kindly earth the wretched naked corse that had no tomb. But what of those who wrote about these things? What of those who gave them reality, and made them live forever? Are they not greater than the men and women they sing of? "Hector that sweet knight is dead."[6] and Lucian[7] tells us

1. In "the library of a house in Piccadilly" Gilbert and Ernest, two sophisticated young men, are talking about the use and function of criticism. Earlier in the dialogue, Ernest had complained that criticism is officious and useless: "Why should the artist be troubled by the shrill clamor of criticism? Why should those who cannot create take upon themselves to estimate the value of creative work?" Gilbert, in his reply, argues that criticism is creative in its own right. He digresses to compare the life of action unfavorably to the life of art: actions are dangerous and their results unpredictable; "if we lived long enough to see the results of our actions it may be that those who call themselves good would be sickened by a dull remorse, and those whom the world calls evil stirred by a noble joy." The ex-cerpt printed here begins immediately following this digression.
2. Troy. Gilbert is referring to Homer's *Iliad*.
3. Clytemnestra, whose murder of her husband Agamemnon provides the plot for Aeschylus' tragedy of that name.
4. Where Agamemnon sacrificed his daughter Iphigenia, thus incurring Clytemnestra's wrath.
5. Antigone defied Creon, king of Thebes, by burying the body of her brother, an act which Creon had forbidden, and was punished by death; see Sophocles' play *Antigone*.
6. Cf. Shakespeare's *Love's Labor's Lost* V.ii.666: "The sweet war-man [Hector] is dead and rotten."
7. Late Greek satirical writer, influenced by the earlier Greek seriocomic writer Menippus.

how in the dim underworld Menippus saw the bleaching skull of Helen, and marveled that it was for so grim a favor that all those horned ships were launched, those beautiful mailed men laid low, those towered cities brought to dust. Yet, every day the swanlike daughter of Leda comes out on the battlements, and looks down at the tide of war. The graybeards wonder at her loveliness, and she stands by the side of the king.[8] In his chamber of stained ivory lies her leman.[9] He is polishing his dainty armor, and combing the scarlet plume. With squire and page, her husband passes from tent to tent. She can see his bright hair, and hears, or fancies that she hears, that clear cold voice. In the courtyard below, the son of Priam is buckling on his brazen cuirass. The white arms of Andromache[1] are around his neck. He sets his helmet on the ground, lest their babe should be frightened. Behind the embroidered curtains of his pavilion sits Achilles,[2] in perfumed raiment, while in harness of gilt and silver the friend of his soul[3] arrays himself to go forth to the fight. From a curiously carven chest that his mother Thetis had brought to his shipside, the Lord of the Myrmidons takes out that mystic chalice that the lip of man had never touched, and cleanses it with brimstone, and with fresh water cools it, and, having washed his hands, fills with black wine its burnished hollow, and spills the thick grape-blood upon the ground in honor of Him whom at Dodona[4] barefooted prophets worshiped, and prays to Him, and knows not that he prays in vain, and that by the hands of two knights from Troy, Panthous' son, Euphorbus, whose lovelocks were looped with gold, and the Priamid,[5] the lion-hearted, Patroclus, the comrade of comrades, must meet his doom. Phantoms, are they? Heroes of mist and mountain? Shadows in a song? No: they are real. Action! What is action? It dies at the moment of its energy. It is a base concession to fact. The world is made by the singer for the dreamer.

ERNEST. While you talk it seems to me to be so.

GILBERT. It is so in truth. On the moldering citadel of Troy lies the lizard like a thing of green bronze. The owl has built her nest in the palace of Priam. Over the empty plain wander shepherd and goatherd with their flocks, and where, on the wine-surfaced, oily sea, οἶνοψ πόντος,[6] as Homer calls it, copper-prowed and streaked with vermilion, the great galleys of the Danaoi[7] came in their

8. Priam. Homer in the *Iliad* describes the old men of Troy admiring the beauty of Helen, "swanlike daughter of Leda" and of Zeus (Zeus came to Leda in the form of a swan).
9. Lover (i.e., Paris).
1. Wife of Hector, one of the sons of Priam.
2. Achilles, son of Peleus and of the sea nymph Thetis, was the Greek hero, opposite number of Hector, the Trojan hero, in the Trojan War. The scene set here is a tissue of recollections from the *Iliad*.
3. I.e., Patroclus.
4. Seat of a very ancient oracle of Zeus.
5. "Son of Priam," i.e., Hector. With the help of Euphorbus, one of the bravest of the Trojans, he slew Patroclus and was in turn slain by Achilles.
6. "Wine-dark sea."
7. Greeks.

gleaming crescent, the lonely tunny-fisher sits in his little boat and watches the bobbing corks of his net. Yet, every morning the doors of the city are thrown open, and on foot, or in horse-drawn chariot, the warriors go forth to battle, and mock their enemies from behind their iron masks. All day long the fight rages, and when night comes the torches gleam by the tents, and the cresset[8] burns in the hall. Those who live in marble or on painted panel know of life but a single exquisite instant, eternal indeed in its beauty, but limited to one note of passion or one mood of calm. Those whom the poet makes live have their myriad emotions of joy and terror, of courage and despair, of pleasure and of suffering. The seasons come and go in glad or saddening pageant, and with winged or leaden feet the years pass by before them. They have their youth and their manhood, they are children, and they grow old. It is always dawn for St. Helena, as Veronese saw her at the window.[9] Through the still morning air the angels bring her the symbol of God's pain. The cool breezes of the morning lift the gilt threads from her brow. On that little hill by the city of Florence, where the lovers of Giorgione[1] are lying, it is always the solstice of noon, made so languorous by summer suns that hardly can the slim naked girl dip into the marble tank the round bubble of clear glass, and the long fingers of the lute player rest idly upon the chords. It is twilight always for the dancing nymphs whom Corot[2] set free among the silver poplars of France. In eternal twilight they move, those frail diaphanous figures, whose tremulous white feet seem not to touch the dew-drenched grass they tread on. But those who walk in epos,[3] drama, or romance, see through the laboring months the young moons wax and wane, and watch the night from evening unto morning star, and from sunrise unto sunsetting can note the shifting day with all its gold and shadow. For them, as for us, the flowers bloom and wither, and the Earth, that Green-tressed Goddess as Coleridge calls her, alters her raiment for their pleasure. The statue is concentrated to one moment of perfection. The image stained upon the canvas possesses no spiritual element of growth or change. If they know nothing of death, it is because they know little of life, for the secrets of life and death belong to those, and those only, whom the sequence of time affects, and who possess not merely the present but the future, and can rise or fall from a past of glory or of shame. Movement, that problem of the visible arts, can be truly realized by Literature alone. It is Literature that shows us the body in its swiftness and the soul in its unrest.

ERNEST. Yes; I see now what you mean. But, surely, the higher

8. Metal basket holding fuel burned for illumination, often hung from the ceiling.
9. One of the best-known paintings of the 16th-century Italian Paolo Veronese is "Helena's Vision."

1. Italian painter (ca. 1477–1511), the most brilliant colorist of his time.
2. Jean Baptiste Camille Corot, 19th-century French painter, best-known for his shimmering trees.
3. Epic poetry.

you place the creative artist, the lower must the critic rank.

GILBERT. Why so?

ERNEST. Because the best that he can give us will be but an echo of rich music, a dim shadow of clear-outlined form. It may, indeed, be that life is chaos, as you tell me that it is; that its martyrdoms are mean and its heroisms ignoble; and that it is the function of Literature to create, from the rough material of actual existence, a new world that will be more marvelous, more enduring, and more true than the world that common eyes look upon, and through which common natures seek to realize their perfection. But surely, if this new world has been made by the spirit and touch of a great artist, it will be a thing so complete and perfect that there will be nothing left for the critic to do. I quite understand now, and indeed admit most readily, that it is far more difficult to talk about a thing than to do it. But it seems to me that this sound and sensible maxim, which is really extremely soothing to one's feelings, and should be adopted as its motto by every Academy of Literature all over the world, applies only to the relations that exist between Art and Life, and not to any relations that there may be between Art and Criticism.

GILBERT. But, surely, Criticism is itself an art. And just as artistic creation implies the working of the critical faculty, and, indeed, without it cannot be said to exist at all, so Criticism is really creative in the highest sense of the word. Criticism is, in fact, both creative and independent.

ERNEST. Independent?

GILBERT. Yes; independent. Criticism is no more to be judged by any low standard of imitation or resemblance than is the work of poet or sculptor. The critic occupies the same relation to the work of art that he criticizes as the artist does to the visible world of form and color, or the unseen world of passion and of thought. He does not even require for the perfection of his art the finest materials. Anything will serve his purpose. And just as out of the sordid and sentimental amours of the silly wife of a small country doctor in the squalid village of Yonville-l'Abbaye, near Rouen, Gustave Flaubert[4] was able to create a classic, and make a masterpiece of style, so, from subjects of little or of no importance, such as the pictures in this year's Royal Academy, or in any year's Royal Academy for that matter, Mr. Lewis Morris's poems, M. Ohnet's novels, or the plays of Mr. Henry Arthur Jones,[5] the true critic can, if it be his pleasure so to direct or waste his faculty of contemplation, produce work that will be flawless in beauty and instinct with

---

4. French novelist; the reference is to his novel, *Madame Bovary* (1857).
5. Wilde is mischievously suggesting his low opinion of the contemporary writers just named: Lewis Morris was a Welsh poet and essayist often ridi-culed by the critics; Georges Ohnet was a French novelist and dramatist; Henry Arthur Jones was one of the leading English playwrights of his time.

intellectual subtlety. Why not? Dullness is always an irresistible temptation for brilliancy, and stupidity is the permanent *Bestia Trionfans*[6] that calls wisdom from its cave. To an artist so creative as the critic, what does subject matter signify? No more and no less than it does to the novelist and the painter. Like them, he can find his motives everywhere. Treatment is the test. There is nothing that has not in it suggestion or challenge.

ERNEST. But is Criticism really a creative art?

GILBERT. Why should it not be? It works with materials, and puts them into a form that is at once new and delightful. What more can one say of poetry? Indeed, I would call criticism a creation within a creation. For just as the great artists, from Homer and Aeschylus, down to Shakespeare and Keats, did not go directly to life for their subject matter, but sought for it in myth, and legend, and ancient tale, so the critic deals with materials that others have, as it were, purified for him, and to which imaginative form and color have been already added. Nay, more, I would say that the highest Criticism, being the purest form of personal impression, is in its way more creative than creation, as it has least reference to any standard external to itself, and is, in fact, its own reason for existing, and, as the Greeks would put it, in itself, and to itself, an end. Certainly, it is never trammeled by any shackles of verisimilitude. No ignoble considerations of probability, that cowardly concession to the tedious repetitions of domestic or public life, affect it ever. One may appeal from fiction unto fact. But from the soul there is no appeal.

ERNEST. From the soul?

GILBERT. Yes, from the soul. That is what the highest criticism really is, the record of one's own soul. It is more fascinating than history, as it is concerned simply with oneself. It is more delightful than philosophy, as its subject is concrete and not abstract, real and not vague. It is the only civilized form of autobiography, as it deals not with the events, but with the thoughts of one's life, not with life's physical accidents of deed or circumstance, but with the spiritual moods and imaginative passions of the mind. I am always amused by the silly vanity of those writers and artists of our day who seem to imagine that the primary function of the critic is to chatter about their second-rate work. The best that one can say of most modern creative art is that it is just a little less vulgar than reality, and so the critic, with his fine sense of distinction and sure instinct of delicate refinement, will prefer to look into the silver mirror or through the woven veil, and will turn his eyes away from the chaos and clamor of actual existence, though the mirror be tarnished and the veil be torn. His sole aim is to chronicle his

6. "Triumphant Beast." A reference to *Spaccio della Bestia Trionfante* ("Expulsion of the Triumphant Beast," 1584), a philosophical allegory by the Italian philosopher Giordano Bruno.

own impressions. It is for him that pictures are painted, books written, and marble hewn into form.

ERNEST. I seem to have heard another theory of Criticism.

GILBERT. Yes: it has been said by one who gracious memory we all revere, and the music of whose pipe once lured Proserpina from her Sicilian fields, and made those white feet stir, and not in vain, the Cumnor cowslips, that the proper aim of Criticism is to see the object as in itself it really is.[7] But this is a very serious error, and takes no cognizance of Criticism's most perfect form, which is in its essence purely subjective, and seeks to reveal its own secret and not the secret of another. For the highest Criticism deals with art not as expressive but as impressive purely.

ERNEST. But is that really so?

GILBERT. Of course it is. Who cares whether Mr. Ruskin's views on Turner are sound or not?[8] What does it matter? That mighty and majestic prose of his, so fervid and so fiery-colored in its noble eloquence, so rich in its elaborate symphonic music, so sure and certain, at its best, in subtle choice of word and epithet, is at least as great a work of art as any of those wonderful sunsets that bleach or rot on their corrupted canvases in England's Gallery; greater indeed, one is apt to think at times, not merely because its equal beauty is more enduring, but on account of the fuller variety of its appeal, soul speaking to soul in those long-cadenced lines, not through form and color alone, though through these, indeed, completely and without loss, but with intellectual and emotional utterance, with lofty passion and with loftier thought, with imaginative insight, and with poetic aim; greater, I always think, even as Literature is the greater art. Who, again, cares whether Mr. Pater has put into the portrait of Mona Lisa something that Leonardo never dreamed of? The painter may have been merely the slave of an archaic smile, as some have fancied, but whenever I pass into the cool galleries of the Palace of the Louvre, and stand before that strange figure "set in its marble chair in that cirque of fantastic rocks, as in some faint light under sea," I murmur to myself, "She is older than the rocks among which she sits; like the vampire, she has been dead many times, and learned the secrets of the grave; and has been a diver in deep seas, and keeps their fallen day about her: and trafficked for strange webs with Eastern merchants; and, as Leda, was the mother of Helen of Troy, and, as St. Anne, the

---

7. The "one whose gracious memory we all revere" is Matthew Arnold; the references are (a) to his poem *Empedocles on Etna*, set in Sicily, where the god of the underworld carried off Proserpine; (b) to his two poems *The Scholar Gypsy* and *Thyrsis*, set in the Cumner (or Cumnor) hills, the district westward across the Thames from Oxford; (c) to his critical essay *The Function of Criticism at the Present Time*, in which he noted with approval of French and German literature that it showed "the endeavor * * * to see the object as in itself it really is"— an endeavor which Arnold continually advocated as the true aim of literary criticism.

8. The English landscape painter J. M. W. Turner (1775–1851) was passionately defended by Ruskin, especially in his *Modern Painters*.

mother of Mary; and all this has been to her but as the sound of lyres and flutes, and lives only in the delicacy with which it has molded the changing lineaments, and tinged the eyelids and the hands." And I say to my friend, "The presence that thus so strangely rose beside the waters is expressive of what in the ways of a thousand years man had come to desire"; and he answers me, "Hers is the head upon which all 'the ends of the world are come,' and the eyelids are a little weary."[9]

And so the picture becomes more wonderful to us than it really is, and reveals to us a secret of which, in truth, it knows nothing, and the music of the mystical prose is as sweet in our ears as was that flute-player's music that lent to the lips of La Gioconda[1] those subtle and poisonous curves. Do you ask me what Leonardo would have said had any one told him of this picture that "all the thoughts and experience of the world had etched and molded therein that which they had of power to refine and make expressive the outward form, the animalism of Greece, the lust of Rome, the reverie of the Middle Age with its spiritual ambition and imaginative loves, the return of the Pagan world, the sins of the Borgias?" He would probably have answered that he had contemplated none of these things, but had concerned himself simply with certain arrangements of lines and masses, and with new and curious color-harmonies of blue and green. And it is for this very reason that the criticism which I have quoted is criticism of the highest kind. It treats the work of art simply as a starting point for a new creation. It does not confine itself—let us at least suppose so for the moment—to discovering the real intention of the artist and accepting that as final. And in this it is right, for the meaning of any beautiful created thing is, at least, as much in the soul of him who looks at it, as it was in his soul who wrought it. Nay, it is rather the beholder who lends to the beautiful thing its myriad meanings, and makes it marvelous for us, and sets it in some new relation to the age, so that it becomes a vital portion of our lives, and symbol of what we pray for, or perhaps of what, having prayed for, we fear that we may receive. The longer I study, Ernest, the more clearly I see that the beauty of the visible arts is, as the beauty of music, impressive[2] primarily, and that it may be marred, and indeed often is so, by any excess of intellectual intention on the part of the artist. For when the work is finished it has, as it were, an independent life of its own, and may deliver a message far other than that which was put into its lips to say. Sometimes, when I listen to the overture to *Tannhäuser*,[3] I seem indeed to see that comely knight treading

9. Wilde is quoting from Pater's *The Renaissance.*
1. I.e., the "Mona Lisa" (she was the wife of Francesco del Gioconda—hence "La Gioconda").
2. I.e., designed to create an impression on the senses.
3. Opera by Richard Wagner (1845) based on the legend of a 14th-century German poet who fell under the spell of Lady Venus and lived with her in the Venusberg.

delicately on the flower-strewn grass, and to hear the voice of Venus calling to him from the caverned hill. But at other times it speaks to me of a thousand different things, of myself, it may be, and my own life, or of the lives of others whom one has loved and grown weary of loving, or of the passions that man has known, or of the passions that man has not known, and so has sought for. Tonight it may fill one with that ΕΡΩΣ ΤΩΝ ΑΔΥΝΑΤΩΝ, that *amour de l'impossible*,[4] which falls like a madness on many who think they live securely and out of reach of harm, so that they sicken suddenly with the poison of unlimited desire, and, in the infinite pursuit of what they may not obtain, grow faint and swoon or stumble. Tomorrow, like the music of which Aristotle and Plato tell us, the noble Dorian music of the Greek, it may perform the office of a physician, and give us an anodyne against pain, and heal the spirit that is wounded, and "bring the soul into harmony with all right things." And what is true about music is true about all the arts. Beauty has as many meanings as man has moods. Beauty is the symbol of symbols. Beauty reveals everything, because it expresses nothing. When it shows us itself, it shows us the whole fiery-colored world.

ERNEST. But is such work as you have talked about really criticism?

GILBERT. It is the highest Criticism, for it criticizes not merely the individual work of art, but Beauty itself, and fills with wonder a form which the artist may have left void, or not understood, or understood incompletely.

ERNEST. The highest Criticism, then, is more creative than creation, and the primary aim of the critic is to see the object as in itself it really is not; that is your theory, I believe?

GILBERT. Yes, that is my theory. To the critic the work of art is simply a suggestion for a new work of his own, that need not necessarily bear any obvious resemblance to the thing it criticizes. The one characteristic of a beautiful form is that one can put into it whatever one wishes, and see in it whatever one chooses to see; and the Beauty, that gives to creation its universal and aesthetic element, makes the critic a creator in his turn, and whispers of a thousand different things which were not present in the mind of him who carved the statue or painted the panel or graved the gem.

It is sometimes said by those who understand neither the nature of the highest Criticism nor the charm of the highest Art, that the pictures that the critic loves most to write about are those that belong to the anecdotage of painting, and that deal with scenes taken out of literature or history. But this is not so. Indeed, pictures of this kind are far too intelligible. As a class, they rank with illustrations,

---

4. The Greek (in capital letters, perhaps to give the effect of an inscrip-tion) means the same as the French phrase: "love of the impossible."

and even considered from this point of view are failures, as they do not stir the imagination, but set definite bounds to it. For the domain of the painter is, as I suggested before, widely different from that of the poet. To the latter belongs life in its full and absolute entirety; not merely the beauty that men look at, but the beauty that men listen to also; not merely the momentary grace of form or the transient gladness of color, but the whole sphere of feeling, the perfect cycle of thought. The painter is so far limited that it is only through the mask of the body that he can show us the mystery of the soul; only through conventional images that he can handle ideas; only through its physical equivalents that he can deal with psychology. And how inadequately does he do it then, asking us to accept the torn turban of the Moor for the noble rage of Othello, or a dotard in a storm for the wild madness of Lear! Yet it seems as if nothing could stop him. Most of our elderly English painters spend their wicked and wasted lives in poaching upon the domain of the poets, marring their motives by clumsy treatment, and striving to render, by visible form or color, the marvel of what is invisible, the splendor of what is not seen. Their pictures are, as a natural consequence, insufferably tedious. They have degraded the invisible arts into the obvious arts, and the one thing not worth looking at is the obvious. I do not say that poet and painter may not treat of the same subject. They have always done so, and will always do so. But while the poet can be pictorial or not, as he chooses, the painter must be pictorial always. For a painter is limited, not to what he sees in nature, but to what upon canvas may be seen.

And so, my dear Ernest, pictures of this kind will not really fascinate the critic. He will turn from them to such works as make him brood and dream and fancy, to works that possess the subtle quality of suggestion, and seem to tell one that even from them there is an escape into a wider world. It is sometimes said that the tragedy of an artist's life is that he cannot realize his ideal. But the true tragedy that dogs the steps of most artists is that they realize their ideal too absolutely. For, when the ideal is realized, it is robbed of its wonder and its mystery, and becomes simply a new starting point for an ideal that is other than itself. This is the reason why music is the perfect type of art. Music can never reveal its ultimate secret. This, also, is the explanation of the value of limitations in art. The sculptor gladly surrenders imitative color, and the painter the actual dimensions of form, because by such renunciations they are able to avoid too definite a presentation of the Real, which would be mere imitation, and too definite a realization of the Ideal, which would be too purely intellectual. It is through its very incompleteness that Art becomes complete in beauty, and so addresses itself, not to the faculty of recognition nor to the faculty of reason, but to the aesthetic sense alone, which, while accepting both reason and recognition as stages of apprehension, subordinates them both to a pure synthetic impression of the work of art as a whole, and, taking whatever alien emotional elements the work may possess, uses their very complexity as a means by which a richer unity may be added to the ultimate impression itself. You see, then, how it is that the aesthetic critic rejects these obvious modes of art that have but one message to deliver, and having delivered it become dumb and sterile, and seeks rather for such modes as suggest reverie and mood, and by their imaginative beauty make all interpretations true, and no interpretation final. Some resemblance, no doubt, the creative work of the critic will have to the work that has stirred him to creation, but it will be such resemblance as exists, not between Nature and the mirror that the painter of landscape or figure may be supposed to hold up to her, but between Nature and the work of the decorative artist. Just as on the flowerless carpets of Persia, tulip and rose blossom indeed and are lovely to look on, though they are not reproduced in visible shape or line; just as the pearl and purple of the sea shell is echoed in the church of St. Mark at Venice; just as the vaulted ceiling of the wondrous chapel at Ravenna is made gorgeous by the gold and green and sapphire of the peacock's tail, though the birds of Juno fly not across it; so the critic reproduces the work that he criticizes in a mode that is never imitative, and part of whose charm may really consist in the rejection of resemblance, and shows us in this way not merely the meaning but also the mystery of Beauty, and, by transforming each art into literature, solves once for all the problem of Art's unity.

But I see it is time for supper. After we have discussed some Chambertin [5] and a few ortolans, we will pass on to the question of the critic considered in the light of the interpreter.

ERNEST. Ah! you admit, then, that the critic may occasionally be allowed to see the object as in itself it really is.

GILBERT. I am not quite sure. Perhaps I may admit it after supper. There is a subtle influence in supper.

1890, 1891

Preface to *The Picture of Dorian Gray*

The artist is the creator of beautiful things.
To reveal art and conceal the artist is art's aim.
The critic is he who can translate into another manner or a new material his impression of beautiful things.

5. One of the finest wines of Burgundy; "ortolans" are birds esteemed by epicures for their delicate flavor.

The highest, as the lowest, form of criticism is a mode of autobiography.

Those who find ugly meaning in beautiful things are corrupt without being charming. This is a fault.

Those who find beautiful meanings in beautiful things are the cultivated. For these there is hope.

They are the elect to whom beautiful things mean only Beauty.

There is no such thing as a moral or an immoral book.

Books are well written, or badly written. That is all.

The nineteenth-century dislike of Realism is the rage of Caliban[1] seeing his own face in a glass.

The nineteenth-century dislike of Romanticism is the rage of Caliban not seeing his own face in a glass.

The moral life of man forms part of the subject matter of the artist, but the morality of art consists in the perfect use of an imperfect medium. No artist desires to prove anything. Even things that are true can be proved.

No artist has ethical sympathies. An ethical sympathy in an artist is an unpardonable mannerism of style.

No artist is ever morbid. The artist can express everything.

Thought and language are to the artist instruments of an art.

Vice and virtue are to the artist materials for an art.

From the point of view of form, the type of all the arts is the art of the musician. From the point of view of feeling, the actor's craft is the type.

All art is at once surface and symbol.

Those who go beneath the surface do so at their peril.

Those who read the symbol do so at their peril.

It is the spectator, and not life, that art really mirrors.

Diversity of opinion about a work of art shows that the work is new, complex, and vital.

When critics disagree the artist is in accord with himself.

We can forgive a man for making a useful thing as long as he does not admire it. The only excuse for making a useless thing is that one admires it intensely.

All art is quite useless.

1891

1.This character in Shakespeare's *Tempest* is half-man, half-monster.

ERNEST DOWSON
(1867–1900)

Ernest Christopher Dowson spent much of his childhood traveling with his father on the Continent, mostly in France. His education was thus irregular and informal, but he acquired a thorough knowledge of French and of his favorite French writers Gustave Flaubert, Honoré de Balzac, and Paul Verlaine, and a good knowledge of Latin poetry, especially Catullus, Propertius, and Horace. Dowson went to Oxford in 1886, but he did not take to regular academic instruction and left after a year. Though nominally assisting his father to manage a dock in the London district of Limehouse, Dowson spent most of his time writing poetry, stories, and essays, and talking with Lionel Johnson, W. B. Yeats, and other members of the Rhymers' Club, in which he played a prominent part. Between 1890 and 1894 Dowson, though leading the irregular life of so many of the 90's poets, produced his best work, and his volume of *Verses* came out in 1896. Late nights and excessive drinking impaired a constitution already threatened by tuberculosis. He moved to France in 1894, making a living by translating from the French for an English publisher, but growing steadily worse in health. After his return to England he was discovered in a dying condition by a friend, who took him to his home and nursed him until his death six weeks later.

Dowson was a member of what Yeats called "the tragic generation" of poets in the 90's who seemed to be driven by their own restless energies to dissipation and premature death. As a poet he was considerably influenced by Swinburne (whose feverish emotional tone he often captures very skillfully), but he learned also from Latin lyric poetry and from contemporary French poetry. He experimented with a variety of meters, and in *Cynara* used the alexandrine as the normal line of a six-line stanza in a manner more common in French than in English poetry. He shared with his fellow members of the Rhymers' Club a belief in the pursuit of beauty, verbal sensation, the haunting cadence, the cultivated languor. He was also interested in the work of the French Symbolist poets and in their theories of verbal suggestiveness and of poetry as incantation: he believed (as he once wrote in a letter) that a finer poetry could sometimes be achieved by "mere sound and music, with just a suggestion of sense."

[Cynara]

Non sum qualis eram bonae sub regno Cynarae[1]

Last night, ah, yesternight, betwixt her lips and mine
There fell thy shadow, Cynara! thy breath was shed

1. "I am not as I was under the reign of the good Cynara." This is the third and part of the fourth line of an ode of Horace (IV.1) in which the poet

Upon my soul between the kisses and the wine;
And I was desolate and sick of an old passion,
    Yea, I was desolate and bowed my head: 5
I have been faithful to thee, Cynara! in my fashion.

All night upon mine heart I felt her warm heart beat,
Night-long within mine arms in love and sleep she lay;
Surely the kisses of her bought red mouth were sweet;
But I was desolate and sick of an old passion,   10
    When I awoke and found the dawn was gray:
I have been faithful to thee, Cynara! in my fashion.

I have forgot much, Cynara! gone with the wind,
Flung roses, roses riotously with the throng,
Dancing, to put thy pale, lost lilies out of mind;   15
But I was desolate and sick of an old passion,
    Yea, all the time, because the dance was long:
I have been faithful to thee, Cynara! in my fashion.

I cried for madder music and for stronger wine,
But when the feast is finished and the lamps expire,   20
Then falls thy shadow, Cynara! the night is thine;
And I am desolate and sick of an old passion,
    Yea, hungry for the lips of my desire:
I have been faithful to thee, Cynara! in my fashion.

                            1891, 1896

Flos Lunae[1]

FOR YVANHOÉ RAMBOSSON[2]

I would not alter thy cold eyes,
Nor trouble the calm fount of speech
With aught of passion or surprise.
The heart of thee I cannot reach:
I would not alter thy cold eyes!   5

I would not alter thy cold eyes;
Nor have thee smile, nor make thee weep:
Though all my life droops down and dies,
Desiring thee, desiring sleep,
I would not alter thy cold eyes.   10

pleads with Venus to stop tormenting him with love since he is growing old and is no longer what he was when under the sway of Cynara (*Sin-ah-rah*), the girl he used to love. Of Dowson's "Cynara" Yeats later wrote: "Dowson, who seemed to drink so little and had so much dignity and reserve, was breaking his heart for the daughter of the keeper of an Italian eating house, in dissipation and drink * * * " Dowson's "Cynara" was, in fact, a Polish girl by the name of Adelaide Foltinowicz.
1. "Flower of the moon."
2. This name sounds too good to be true, and perhaps is. Desmond Flower's annotated edition of Dowson's poetical works identifies the other characters to whom Dowson dedicated poems but is silent on this one.

I would not alter thy cold eyes;
I would not change thee if I might,
To whom my prayers for incense rise,
Daughter of dreams! my moon of night!
I would not alter thy cold eyes.   15

I would not alter thy cold eyes,
With trouble of the human heart:
Within their glance my spirit lies,
A frozen thing, alone, apart;
I would not alter thy cold eyes.   20

1891, 1896

To One in Bedlam[1]

FOR HENRY DAVRAY[2]

With delicate, mad hands, behind his sordid bars,
Surely he hath his posies, which they tear and twine;
Those scentless wisps of straw, that miserably line
His strait, caged universe, whereat the dull world stares,

Pedant and pitiful. O, how his rapt gaze wars   5
With their stupidity! Know they what dreams divine
Lift his long, laughing reveries like enchanted wine,
And make his melancholy germane to the stars'?

O lamentable brother! if those pity thee,
Am I not fain of all thy lone eyes promise me;   10
Half a fool's kingdom, far from men who sow and reap,
All their days, vanity?[3] Better than mortal flowers,
Thy moon-kissed roses seem: better than love or sleep,
The star-crowned solitude of thine oblivious hours!

1892, 1896

A Last Word

Let us go hence: the night is now at hand;
The day is overworn, the birds all flown;

1. Insane asylum (specifically, an ancient madhouse in London).
2. Henry Davray was a French critic and great friend of Dowson's; he reviewed English books for the *Mercure de France.* The habit of dedicating individual poems to particular friends Dowson and Lionel Johnson picked up from the French poet Paul Verlaine (1844–96), who entitled one of his volumes of poetry *Dédicaces* ("Dedications"), and explained in the introduction that "these ballads and sonnets are all intimate and are directed only to certain friends and good companions of the author who *dedicates* the poems to them exclusively, without any other intention than of pleasing them."
3. The sense of lines 10–12 is: "Would I not be glad to have all that your eyes promise me—namely, half a fool's kingdom—far from men who are engaged in ordinary mundane activities and who thus pass their days in vanity?" The "fool's kingdom" is the lunatic's world of imagination; the lunatic's eyes promise to share that kingdom with the poet.

And we have reaped the crops the gods have sown;
Despair and death; deep darkness o'er the land,
Broods like an owl; we cannot understand 5
Laughter or tears, for we have only known
Surpassing vanity: vain things alone
Have driven our perverse and aimless band.
Let us go hence, somewhither strange and cold,
To Hollow Lands where just men and unjust 10
Find end of labor, where's rest for the old,
Freedom to all from love and fear and lust.
Twine our torn hands! O pray the earth enfold
Our life-sick hearts and turn them into dust.

1896, 1899

Spleen

FOR ARTHUR SYMONS[1]

I was not sorrowful, I could not weep,
And all my memories were put to sleep.

I watched the river grow more white and strange,
All day till evening I watched it change.

All day till evening I watched the rain 5
Beat wearily upon the window pane.

I was not sorrowful, but only tired
Of everything that ever I desired.

Her lips, her eyes, all day became to me
The shadow of a shadow utterly. 10

All day mine hunger for her heart became
Oblivion, until the evening came,

And left me sorrowful, inclined to weep,
With all my memories that could not sleep.

1896

Dregs

The fire is out, and spent the warmth thereof,
(This is the end of every song man sings!)
The golden wine is drunk, the dregs remain,
Bitter as wormwood and as salt as pain;
And health and hope have gone the way of love 5

1. 1865–1945. English poet and critic influential in spreading knowledge in England of the French symbolist poets.

Into the drear oblivion of lost things.
Ghosts go along with us until the end;
This was a mistress, this, perhaps, a friend.
With pale, indifferent eyes, we sit and wait
For the dropped curtain and the closing gate: 10
This is the end of all the songs man sings.

1899

Exchanges

All that I had brought,
   Little enough I know;
A poor rhyme roughly wrought,
   A rose to match thy snow:
All that I had I brought.   5

Little enough I sought:
   But a word compassionate,
A passing glance, or thought,
   For me outside the gate:
Little enough I sought.   10

Little enough I found:
   All that you had, perchance!
With the dead leaves on the ground,
   I dance the devil's dance.
   All that you had I found.   15

1899

THOMAS HARDY
(1840–1928)

1872–96: Career as novelist, ending with *Jude the Obscure*.
1898:   *Wessex Poems*, first collection of poetry.

Thomas Hardy was born near Dorchester, in that area of southwest England that he was to make the "Wessex" of his novels. He attended local schools until the age of 15, when he was articled to a Dorchester architect with whom he worked for six years. In 1861 he went to London to continue his studies and to practice as an architect. Meanwhile he was completing his general education informally through his own erratic reading, and becoming more and more interested in both fiction and poetry. After some early attempts at writing both short stories and poems, he decided to concentrate on fiction. His first novel was rejected by the publishers in 1868 on the advice of George Meredith, who nevertheless advised Hardy to write another. The result was *Desperate Remedies*, published anonymously in 1871, followed the next year by his first real success (also published anonymously), *Under the Greenwood Tree*. Hardy's career as a novelist was now well launched; he gave up his architectural work and produced a series of novels that ended with *Jude the Obscure* in 1896. The hostile reception of this novel sent him back to poetry. His remarkable epic-drama of the Napoleonic Wars, *The Dynasts*, came out in three parts between 1903 and 1908; after this he wrote mostly lyric poetry.

Hardy's novels, set in a predominantly rural "Wessex," show the forces of nature outside and inside man combining to shape human destiny. Against a background of immemorial agricultural labor, with ancient monuments such as Stonehenge or an old Roman amphitheater reminding us of the human past, he presents characters at the mercy of their own passions or finding temporary salvation in the age-old rhythms of rural work or rural recreation. Men in Hardy's fiction are not masters of their fates; they are at the mercy of the indifferent forces which manipulate their behavior and their relations with others; but they can achieve dignity through endurance, and heroism through simple strength of character. The characteristic Victorian novelist—e.g., Dickens and Thackeray —was concerned with the behavior and problems of men in a given social milieu, which he described in detail; Hardy preferred to go directly for the elemental in human behavior with a minimum of contemporary social detail. Most of Hardy's novels are tragic, though *Under the Greenwood Tree* has an idyllic character possessed by no other of his novels. But even here the happy ending is achieved only by ending the story with the marriage of the hero and heroine and refusing to go further; the texture of the narrative, for all its moments of gaiety and charm, has already suggested the bitter ironies of which life is capable. His later work explores those ironies with sometimes an almost malevolent staging of coincidence in order to emphasize the disparity between human desire and ambition on the one hand and what fate has in store for the characters on the other. But fate is not a wholly external force. Men are driven by the demands of their own nature as much as by anything from outside them. *Tess of the D'Urbervilles* (1891) is the story of an intelligent and sensitive girl, daughter of a poor family, driven to murder and so to death by hanging, by a concatenation of events and circumstances so bitterly ironic that many readers find it the darkest of Hardy's novels, while others would award that distinction to *Jude the Obscure*, the disturbingly powerful account of an ambitious rustic trapped between his intellect and his sensuality and as a result delivered to destruction.

Hardy himself denied that he was a pessimist, calling himself a "meliorist," i.e., one who believes that the world may be made better by human effort. But there is little sign of "meliorism" in either his most important novels or his lyric poetry. In his poems—which alone are represented here because no extract could do justice to Hardy's power as a novelist—many of his characteristic attitudes and ideas and many of his favorite situations can be found. A number of his poems are verse anecdotes illustrating the perversity of fate, the disastrous or ironic coincidence. But his best poems go beyond this mood to present with quiet gravity and a carefully controlled elegiac feeling some aspect of human sorrow or loss or frustration or regret, always projected through a particular, fully realized situation. *Hap* shows Hardy in the characteristic mood of complaining about the irony of human destiny in a universe ruled by chance; but a poem such as *The Walk* (one of a group of poems written after the death of his first wife in 1912) gives, with remarkable power, concrete embodiment to a sense of loss. That power—we see it also in *A Broken Appointment* and *She Hears the Storm*—is achieved through a kind of verbal as well as an emotional integrity. Hardy's poetry, like his prose, often has a self-taught air about it; both can be odd or pretentious or awkward or clumsy. But at their best both his poetry and his prose have an air of persuasive authenticity. The association of a given emotion with particular visual memories in *Neutral Tones*, for example, is impressive because it carries such extraordinary conviction; and it carries that conviction because the rhythms and rhymes are handled so as to suggest the kind of utterance actually wrung from the poet (consider, e.g., the curious dead fall of "They had fallen from an ash, and were gray"). At the same time, Hardy will use an antique or a poetic word or phrase ("thereby," "a-wing") if it fits in with the movement of the poem and keeps him from having to stop and search for something more deft: the result is an effect not of artificiality but of spontaneity. Hardy's use of ballad rhythms often helps to give an elemental quality to his poetry, suggesting that this incident or situation, carefully particularized though it is, nevertheless stands for some profound and recurring themes in human experience.

Sometimes in Hardy's poetry the quiet lilt of the verse and the fall of the rhymes convey a deep but controlled emotion, as in *Drummer Hodge*, where the sense of a simple English soldier buried in a far distant land and mingling with an earth that will produce vegetation so different from anything known in England is poignantly expressed. *In Time of "The Breaking of Nations"* conveys with stark clarity the same awareness of the processes of nature continuing in spite of cataclysms caused by human folly in the novels. The sadness in Hardy—his inability to believe in the government of the world by a benevolent God, his sense of the waste and frustration involved in human life, his insistent irony when faced with moral or metaphysical questions—is part of the late Victorian mood. We can see something like it in A. E. Housman, and there is an earlier version of Victorian pessimism in Edward FitzGerald's *Rubáiyát of Omar Khayyám*, published when Hardy was 19. Yet Hardy's characteristic themes and attitudes cannot be related simply to the reaction to new scientific and philosophical ideas (Darwin's theory of evolution, for example) that we see in so many forms in late 19th-century literature. The favorite poetic mood of both Tennyson and Arnold was also an elegiac one (e.g., in Tennyson's *Break, Break, Break* and Arnold's *Dover Beach*), but this is not Hardy's mood. The sad-sweet cadences of Victorian self-pity are not to be found in Hardy's poetry, which is sterner, as though braced by a long look at the worst. It is this sternness—sometimes amounting to ruggedness—together with his verbal and emotional integrity, his refusal ever to surrender to mere poetic fashion, his quietly searching individual accent, that has helped to bring about the steady rise in Hardy's poetic reputation in recent years, so that today he is regarded not only as a distinguished novelist but also as a great English poet.

Hap[1]

If but some vengeful god would call to me
From up the sky, and laugh: "Thou suffering thing,
Know that thy sorrow is my ecstasy,
That thy love's loss is my hate's profiting!"

Then would I bear it, clench myself, and die,   5
Steeled by the sense of ire unmerited;
Half-eased in that a Powerfuller than I
Had willed and meted me the tears I shed.

But not so. How arrives it joy lies slain,
And why unblooms the best hope ever sown?   10
—Crass Casualty obstructs the sun and rain,
And dicing Time for gladness casts a moan. . . .
These purblind Doomsters[2] had as readily strown
Blisses about my pilgrimage as pain.

1866   1898

The Impercipient

(AT A CATHEDRAL SERVICE)

That with this bright believing band
    I have no claim to be,
That faiths by which my comrades stand
    Seem fantasies to me,

1. I.e., chance (as also "Casualty," line 11).
2. Half-blind judges.

And mirage-mists their Shining Land,   5
    Is a strange destiny.

Why thus my soul should be consigned
    To infelicity,
Why always I must feel as blind
    To sights my brethren see,   10
Why joys they've found I cannot find,
    Abides a mystery.

Since heart of mine knows not that ease
    Which they know; since it be
That He who breathes All's Well to these   15
    Breathes no All's-Well to me,
My lack might move their sympathies
    And Christian charity!

I am like a gazer who should mark
    An inland company   20
Standing upfingered, with, "Hark! hark!
    The glorious distant sea!"
And feel, "Alas, 'tis but yon dark
    And wind-swept pine to me!"

Yet I would bear my shortcomings   25
    With meet tranquillity,
But for the charge that blessed things
    I'd liefer not have be.
O, doth a bird deprived of wings
    Go earth-bound willfully!   30

.   .   .   .   .

Enough. As yet disquiet clings
    About us. Rest shall we.

1898

Neutral Tones

We stood by a pond that winter day,
And the sun was white, as though chidden of God,
And a few leaves lay on the starving sod;
    —They had fallen from an ash, and were gray.

Your eyes on me were as eyes that rove   5
Over tedious riddles of years ago;
And some words played between us to and fro
    On which lost the more by our love.

The smile on your mouth was the deadest thing
Alive enough to have strength to die;   10

And a grin of bitterness swept thereby
   Like an ominous bird a-wing. . . .
Since then, keen lessons that love deceives,
And wrings with wrong, have shaped to me
Your face, and the God-cursed sun, and a tree,   15
   And a pond edged with grayish leaves.

1867   1898

I Look into My Glass

I look into my glass,
And view my wasting skin,
And say, "Would God it came to pass
My heart had shrunk as thin!"

For then, I, undistressed   5
By hearts grown cold to me,
Could lonely wait my endless rest
With equanimity.

But Time, to make me grieve,
Part steals, lets part abide;   10
And shakes this fragile frame at eve
With throbbings of noontide.

1898

A Broken Appointment

    You did not come,
And marching Time drew on, and wore me numb.—
Yet less for loss of your dear presence there
Than that I thus found lacking in your make
That high compassion which can overbear   5
Reluctance for pure loving-kindness' sake
Grieved I, when, as the hope-hour stroked its sum,
    You did not come.

    You love not me,
And love alone can lend you loyalty;   10
—I know and knew it. But, unto the store
Of human deeds divine in all but name,
Was it not worth a little hour or more
To add yet this: Once you, a woman, came
To soothe a time-torn man; even though it be   15
    You love not me?

1902

Drummer Hodge

1

They throw in Drummer Hodge, to rest
  Uncoffined—just as found:
His landmark is a kopje-crest[1]
  That breaks the veldt around;
And foreign constellations west[2]   5
  Each night above his mound.

2

Young Hodge the Drummer never knew—
  Fresh from his Wessex home—
The meaning of the broad Karoo,[3]
  The Bush, the dusty loam,   10
And why uprose to nightly view
  Strange stars amid the gloam.

3

Yet portion of that unknown plain
  Will Hodge forever be;
His homely Northern breast and brain   15
  Grow to some Southern tree,
And strange-eyed constellations reign
  His stars eternally.

1902

Lausanne[4]

IN GIBBON'S OLD GARDEN: 11–12 P.M.
JUNE 27, 1897

(The 110th anniversary of the completion of the Decline and Fall *at the same hour and place)*

A spirit seems to pass,
  Formal in pose, but grave withal and grand:
  He contemplates a volume in his hand,
And far lamps fleck him through the thin acacias.

1. South African Dutch (Afrikaans) word for a small hill. "Veldt": Afrikaans for a plain or prairie. The poem is a lament for an English soldier killed in the Boer War (1899–1902).
2. Set. The "foreign constellations" are those visible only in the southern hemisphere.
3. A dry table-land region in South Africa (usually spelled "Karroo"). "The Bush": British Colonial word for an uncleared area of land.
4. Edward Gibbon finished his monumental *History of the Decline and Fall of the Roman Empire* (6 vols., 1776–88) in Lausanne, Switzerland, where he lived from 1783 until his death. Gibbon records in his *Memoirs of My Life and Writings* that "It was on the day, or rather night, of the 27th of June, 1787, that I wrote the last lines of the last page, in a summer-house in my garden," and goes on to describe his emotions on having completed his life's work. Gibbon, a skeptic, saw himself fighting for truth against prejudice and superstition.

Anon the book is closed, 5
With "It is finished!" And at the alley's end
He turns, and when on me his glances bend
As from the Past comes speech—small, muted, yet composed.

"How fares the Truth now?—Ill?
—Do pens but slily further her advance? 10
May one not speed her but in phrase askance?[5]
Do scribes aver the Comic to be Reverend still?[6]

"Still rule those minds on earth
At whom sage Milton's wormwood words were hurled:
'Truth like a bastard comes into the world 15
Never without ill fame to him who gives her birth'?"[7]
1897   1902

The Darkling[1] Thrush

I leant upon a coppice gate[2]
    When Frost was specter-gray,
And Winter's dregs made desolate
    The weakening eye of day.
The tangled bine-stems[3] scored the sky 5
    Like strings of broken lyres,
And all mankind that haunted nigh
    Had sought their household fires.

The land's sharp features seemed to be
    The Century's corpse[4] outleant, 10
His crypt the cloudy canopy,
    The wind his death-lament.
The ancient pulse of germ and birth
    Was shrunken hard and dry,
And every spirit upon earth 15
    Seemed fervorless as I.

At once a voice arose among
    The bleak twigs overhead
In a fullhearted evensong
    Of joy illimited; 20
An aged thrush, frail, gaunt, and small,
    In blast-beruffled plume,
Had chosen thus to fling his soul
    Upon the growing gloom.

5. Oblique.
6. I.e., do theological writers still claim respect for what is ridiculous on the grounds that it is ancient and venerable?
7. From Milton's *Areopagitica* (1644), defending liberty of the press.

1. In the dark.
2. Gate leading to a small wood or thicket.
3. Twining stems of shrubs.
4. This poem was written on December 31, 1900, the last day of the 19th century.

So little cause for carolings   25
  Of such ecstatic sound
Was written on terrestrial things
  Afar or nigh around,
That I could think there trembled through
  His happy good-night air   30
Some blessed Hope, whereof he knew
  And I was unaware.

1900   1902

A Trampwoman's Tragedy

(182–)

1

From Wynyard's Gap [1] the livelong day,
  The livelong day,
We beat afoot the northward way
  We had traveled times before.
The sun-blaze burning on our backs,   5
Our shoulders sticking to our packs,
By fosseway,[2] fields, and turnpike tracks
  We skirted sad Sedge-Moor.

2

Full twenty miles we jaunted on,
  We jaunted on—   10
My fancy-man, and jeering John,
  And Mother Lee, and I.
And, as the sun drew down to west,
We climbed the toilsome Poldon [3] crest,
And saw, of landskip sights the best,   15
  The inn that beamed thereby.

3

For months we had padded side by side,
  Ay, side by side
Through the Great Forest, Blackmoor wide,
  And where the Parret ran.   20
We'd faced the gusts on Mendip ridge,
Had crossed the Yeo unhelped by bridge,
Been stung by every Marshwood midge,
  I and my fancy-man.

---

1. The places here named are in Somerset, in southwest England on the northern edge of the area which Hardy called "Wessex" and of which his native Dorset, the county south and southwest of Somerset, reaching to the English Channel, was the major part.
2. Path running along a ditch. See note 4 below.
3. Sad (line 8) because of the Battle of Sedgemoor (1685) when the rebellion of the Duke of Monmouth against James

II was crushed with excessive cruelty. "This plain [Sedgemoor], intersected by ditches known as *rhines,* * * * is broken by isolated hills and lower ridges, of which the most conspicuous are Brent Knoll near Burnham, the Isle of Avalon, rising with Glastonbury Tor as its highest point, and the long low ridge of Polden ending to the west in a steep bluff." *Encyclopaedia Britannica,* 11th edition, 1911.

4

Lone inns we loved, my man and I,   25
 My man and I;
"King's Stag," "Windwhistle"[4] high and dry,
 "The Horse" on Hintock Green.
The cosy house at Wynyard's Gap,
"The Hut" renowned on Bredy Knap,   30
And many another wayside tap
 Where folk might sit unseen.

5

Now as we trudged—O deadly day,
 O deadly day!—
I teased my fancy-man in play   35
 And wanton idleness.
I walked alongside jeering John,
I laid his hand my waist upon;
I would not bend my glances on
 My lover's dark distress.   40

6

Thus Poldon top at last we won,
 At last we won,
And gained the inn at sink of sun
 Far-famed as "Marshal's Elm."[5]
Beneath us figured tor and lea,   45
From Mendip to the western sea—
I doubt if finer sight there be
 Within this royal realm.

7

Inside the settle all a-row—
 All four a-row   50
We sat, I next to John, to show
 That he had wooed and won.
And then he took me on his knee,
And swore it was his turn to be
My favored mate, and Mother Lee   55
 Passed to my former one.

8

Then in a voice I had never heard,
 I had never heard,
My only Love to me: "One word,
 My lady, if you please!   60
Whose is the child you are like to bear?—
His? After all my months o' care?"
God knows 'twas not! But, O despair!
 I nodded—still to tease.

---

4. "The highness and dryness of Windwhistle Inn was impressed upon the writer two or three years ago, when, after climbing on a hot afternoon to the beautiful spot near which it stands and entering the inn for tea, he was informed by the landlady that none could be had, unless he would fetch water from a valley half a mile off, the house containing not a drop, owing to its situation. However, a tantalizing row of full barrels behind her back testified to a wetness of a certain sort, which was not at that time desired" [Hardy's note].

5. " 'Marshal's Elm,' so picturesquely situated, is no longer an inn, though the house, or part of it, still remains. It used to exhibit a fine old swinging sign" [Hardy's note].

9
Then up he sprung, and with his knife—   65
    And with his knife
He let out jeering Johnny's life,
    Yes; there, at set of sun.
The slant ray through the window nigh
Gilded John's blood and glazing eye,   70
Ere scarcely Mother Lee and I
    Knew that the deed was done.

10
The taverns tell the gloomy tale,
    The gloomy tale,
How that at Ivel-chester jail   75
    My Love, my sweetheart swung;
Though stained till now by no misdeed
Save one horse ta'en in time o' need;
(Blue Jimmy stole right many a steed
    Ere his last fling he flung).⁶   80

11
Thereaft I walked the world alone,
    Alone, alone!
On his death-day I gave my groan
    And dropt his dead-born child.
'Twas nigh the jail, beneath a tree,   85
None tending me; for Mother Lee
Had died at Glaston, leaving me
    Unfriended on the wild.

12
And in the night as I lay weak,
    As I lay weak,   90
The leaves a-falling on my cheek,
    The red moon low declined—
The ghost of him I'd die to kiss
Rose up and said: "Ah, tell me this!
Was the child mine, or was it his?   95
    Speak, that I rest may find!"

13
O doubt not but I told him then,
    I told him then,
That I had kept me from all men
    Since we joined lips and swore.   100
Whereat he smiled, and thinned away
As the wind stirred to call up day . . .
—'Tis past! And here alone I stray
    Haunting the Western Moor.

April, 1902   1909

6. " 'Blue Jimmy ' was a notorious horse stealer of Wessex in those days, who appropriated more than a hundred horses before he was caught, among others one belonging to a neighbor of the writer's grandfather. He was hanged at the now demolished Ivel-chester or Ilchester jail above mentioned—that building formerly of so many sinister associations in the minds of the local peasantry, and the continual haunt of fever, which at last led to its condemnation. Its site is now an innocent-looking green meadow" [Hardy's note].

Let Me Enjoy

(MINOR KEY)

1

Let me enjoy the earth no less
Because the all-enacting Might
That fashioned forth its loveliness
Had other aims than my delight.

2

About my path there flits a Fair,
Who throws me not a word or sign;
I'll charm me with her ignoring air,
And laud the lips not meant for mine.

3

From manuscripts of moving song
Inspired by scenes and dreams unknown
I'll pour out raptures that belong
To others, as they were my own.

4

And some day hence, towards Paradise
And all its blest—if such should be—
I will lift glad, afar-off eyes,
Though it contain no place for me.

1909

The Rash Bride

AN EXPERIENCE OF THE MELLSTOCK QUIRE[1]

1

We Christmas-caroled down the Vale, and up the Vale, and
  round the Vale,
We played and sang that night as we were yearly wont to do—
A carol in a minor key, a carol in the major D,
Then at each house: "Good wishes: many Christmas joys to you!"

2

Next, to the widow's John and I and all the rest drew on.
  And I
Discerned that John could hardly hold the tongue of him for joy.
The widow was a sweet young thing whom John was bent on
  marrying,
And quiring at her casement seemed romantic to the boy.

3

"She'll make reply, I trust," said he, "to our salute? She must!"
  said he,
"And then I will accost her gently—much to her surprise!—
For knowing not I am with you here, when I speak up and call
  her dear
A tenderness will fill her voice, a bashfulness her eyes."

4

So, by her window-square we stood; ay, with our lanterns there
  we stood,

1. Choir.

And he along with us—not singing, waiting for a sign;
And when we'd quired her carols three a light was lit and out
    looked she,   15
A shawl about her bedgown, and her color red as wine.

5

And sweetly then she bowed her thanks, and smiled, and
    spoke aloud her thanks;
When lo, behind her back there, in the room, a man appeared.
I knew him—one from Woolcomb way—Giles Swetman—
    honest as the day,
But eager, hasty; and I felt that some strange trouble neared.   20

6

"How comes he there? . . . Suppose," said we, "she's wed of
    late! Who knows?" said we.
—"She married yestermorning—only mother yet has known
The secret o't!" shrilled one small boy. "But now I've told,
    let's wish 'em joy!"
A heavy fall aroused us: John had gone down like a stone.

7

We rushed to him and caught him round, and lifted him, and
    brought him round,   25
When, hearing something wrong had happened, oped the
    window she:
"Has one of you fallen ill?" she asked, "by these night
    labors overtasked?"
None answered. That she'd done poor John a cruel turn felt we.

8

Till up spoke Michael: "Fie, young dame! You've broke your
    promise, sly young dame,
By forming this new tie, young dame, and jilting John so true,   30
Who trudged tonight to sing to 'ee because he thought he'd
    bring to 'ee
Good wishes as your coming spouse. May ye such trifling rue!"

9

Her man had said no word at all; but being behind had heard
    it all,
And now cried: "Neighbors, on my soul I knew not 'twas
    like this!"
And then to her: "If I had known you'd had in tow not me
    alone,   35
No wife should you have been of mine. It is a dear bought bliss!"

10

She changed death-white, and heaved a cry: we'd never heard
    so grieved a cry
As came from her at this from him: heartbroken quite seemed
    she;
And suddenly, as we looked on, she turned, and rushed; and
    she was gone,
Whither, her husband, following after, knew not; nor knew we. 40

11

We searched till dawn about the house; within the house,
    without the house,

We searched among the laurel boughs that grew beneath the
    wall,
And then among the crocks and things, and stores for winter
    junketings,
In linhay,[2] loft, and dairy; but we found her not at all.

12

Then John rushed in: "O friends," he said, "hear this, this,
    this!" and bends his head: 45
"I've—searched round by the—*well*, and find the cover open
    wide!
I am fearful that—I can't say what . . . Bring lanterns, and
    some cords to knot."
We did so, and we went and stood the deep dark hole beside.

13

And then they, ropes in hand, and I—ay, John, and all the
    band, and I
Let down a lantern to the depths—some hundred feet and
    more;   50
It glimmered like a fog-dimmed star; and there, beside its light,
    afar,
White drapery floated, and we knew the meaning that it bore.

14

The rest is naught. . . . We buried her o' Sunday. Neighbors
    carried her;
And Swetman—he who'd married her—now miserablest
    of men,
Walked mourning first; and then walked John; just quivering,
    but composed anon;   55
And we the quire formed round the grave, as was the custom
    then.

15

Our old bass player, as I recall—his white hair blown—but why
    recall!—
His viol upstrapped, bent figure—doomed to follow her full
    soon—
Stood bowing, pale and tremulous; and next to him the rest
    of us. . . .
We sang the Ninetieth Psalm [3] to her—set to Saint Stephen's
    tune.   60

1909

One We Knew

(M. H.[4] 1772–1857)

She told how they used to form for the country dances—
    "The Triumph," "The New-rigged Ship"—
To the light of the guttering wax in the paneled manses
    And in cots to the blink of a dip.[5]

---

2. Shed.
3. A favorite psalm at funerals, contrasting God's eternity with the brevity of human life.
4. Hardy's grandmother.
5. I.e., in cottages by the light of a candle.

She spoke of the wild "poussetting" and "allemanding" [6] 5
    On carpet, on oak, and on sod;
And the two long rows of ladies and gentlemen standing,
    And the figures the couples trod.

She showed us the spot where the maypole was yearly planted,
    And where the bandsmen stood 10
While breeched and kerchiefed partners whirled, and panted
    To choose each other for good.

She told of that far-back day when they learnt astounded
    Of the death of the King of France:
Of the Terror; and then of Bonaparte's unbounded 15
    Ambition and arrogance.

Of how his threats woke warlike preparations
    Along the southern strand,
And how each night brought tremors and trepidations
    Lest morning should see him land. 20

She said she had often heard the gibbet creaking
    As it swayed in the lightning flash,
Had caught from the neighboring town a small child's shrieking
    At the cart tail under the lash. . . .

With cap-framed face and long gaze into the embers— 25
    We seated around her knees—
She would dwell on such dead themes, not as one who remembers,
    But rather as one who sees.

She seemed one left behind of a band gone distant
    So far that no tongue could hail: 30
Past things retold were to her as things existent,
    Things present but as a tale.
May 20, 1902   1909

She Hears the Storm

There was a time in former years—
    While my rooftree was his—
When I should have been distressed by fears
    At such a night as this!

I should have murmured anxiously, 5
    "The pricking rain strikes cold;
His road is bare of hedge or tree,
    And he is getting old."

But now the fitful chimney-roar,
    The drone of Thorncombe trees, 10

6. To pousette is to dance round with hands joined; allemande is the name of a
dance originating in Germany.

The Froom in flood upon the moor,
   The mud of Mellstock Leaze,[7]
The candle slanting sooty wicked,
   The thuds upon the thatch,
The eaves-drops on the window flicked,   15
   The clacking garden-hatch,[8]
And what they mean to wayfarers,
   I scarcely heed or mind;
He has won that storm-tight roof of hers
   Which Earth grants all her kind.   20

1909

Channel Firing[1]

That night your great guns, unawares,
Shook all our coffins as we lay,
And broke the chancel window-squares,
We thought it was the Judgment Day
And sat upright. While drearisome   5
Arose the howl of wakened hounds:
The mouse let fall the altar-crumb,
The worms drew back into the mounds,

The glebe cow[2] drooled. Till God called, "No;
It's gunnery practice out at sea   10
Just as before you went below;
The world is as it used to be:

"All nations striving strong to make
Red war yet redder. Mad as hatters
They do no more for Christés[3] sake   15
Than you who are helpless in such matters.

"That this is not the judgment hour
For some of them's a blessed thing,
For if it were they'd have to scour
Hell's floor for so much threatening. . . .   20

"Ha, ha. It will be warmer when
I blow the trumpet (if indeed
I ever do; for you are men,
And rest eternal sorely need)."

---

7. The place names in Hardy's fictional "Wessex" were often invented ("Thorncombe," "Mellstock Leaze"), but he also used the names of real locations, as in "A Trampwoman's Tragedy." The standard edition of Hardy's novels has a map of "Wessex" showing the locale of both the real and the invented names. "The Froom" is presumably the river Frome, flowing through Dorsetshire and Somerset.
8. Gate.

1. Written in April, 1914, when Anglo-German naval rivalry was growing steadily more acute; the title refers to gunnery practice in the English Channel. Four months later (August 4) World War I broke out.
2. I.e., cow on a small plot of land belonging to a cottage (a "glebe" is a small field).
3. The archaic spelling and pronunciation suggests a ballad note of doom.

So down we lay again. "I wonder,   25
Will the world ever saner be,"
Said one, "than when He sent us under
In our indifferent century!"

And many a skeleton shook his head.
"Instead of preaching forty year,"   30
My neighbor Parson Thirdly said,
"I wish I had stuck to pipes and beer."

Again the guns disturbed the hour,
Roaring their readiness to avenge,
As far inland as Stourton Tower,   35
And Camelot, and starlit Stonehenge.[4]

1914   1914

The Convergence of the Twain

(LINES ON THE LOSS OF THE "TITANIC")[1]

1

In a solitude of the sea
Deep from human vanity,
And the Pride of Life that planned her, stilly couches she.

2

Steel chambers, late the pyres
Of her salamandrine fires,[2]   5
Cold currents thrid, and turn to rhythmic tidal lyres.

3

Over the mirrors meant
To glass the opulent
The sea worm crawls—grotesque, slimed, dumb, indifferent.

4

Jewels in joy designed   10
To ravish the sensuous mind
Lie lightless, all their sparkles bleared and black and blind.

5

Dim moon-eyed fishes near
Gaze at the gilded gear
And query: "What does this vaingloriousness down here?" . . . 15

---

4. Again the "Wessex" place names from various sources: Stonehenge is the famous prehistoric stone circle on Salisbury Plain; Camelot was the legendary location of King Arthur's court and the Round Table. There is a real river Stour in Dorset, and a town called Stour Head, which Hardy calls "Stourton."
1. The *Titanic* was the largest and most luxurious ocean liner of her day. Considered unsinkable, she sank with great loss of life on April 15, 1912, on her maiden voyage from Southampton to America, after colliding with an iceberg.
2. Probably "fires in which nothing could survive" (although, since the salamander is a lizardlike animal supposed to be able to live in fire, "salamandrine" usually means "able to resist or to live in fire"). In the next line, "thrid" is the archaic past tense of the verb "thread."

6

Well: while was fashioning
This creature of cleaving wing,
The Immanent Will[3] that stirs and urges everything

7

Prepared a sinister mate
For her—so gaily great—   20
A Shape of Ice, for the time far and dissociate.

8

And as the smart ship grew
In stature, grace, and hue,
In shadowy silent distance grew the Iceberg too.

9

Alien they seemed to be: 25
No mortal eye could see
The intimate welding of their later history,

10

Or sign that they were bent
By paths coincident
On being anon twin halves of one august event,   30

11

Till the Spinner of the Years
Said "Now!" And each one hears,
And consummation comes, and jars two hemispheres.

1912   1912, 1914

Ah, Are You Digging on My Grave?

"Ah, are you digging on my grave,
    My loved one?—planting rue?"[1]
—"No: yesterday he went to wed
One of the brightest wealth has bred.
'It cannot hurt her now,' he said,   5
    'That I should not be true.' "

"Then who is digging on my grave?
    My nearest dearest kin?"
—"Ah, no: they sit and think, 'What use!
What good will planting flowers produce?   10
No tendance of her mound can loose
    Her spirit from Death's gin.' "[2]

"But someone digs upon my grave?
    My enemy?—prodding sly?"
—"Nay: when she heard you had passed the Gate   15
That shuts on all flesh soon or late,
She thought you no more worth her hate,
    And cares not where you lie."

3. The force (blind, but slowly gaining consciousness throughout history) which drives the world, according to Hardy's philosophy.

1. A yellow-flowered herb, traditionally an emblem of sorrow ("rue" is also an archaic word for "sorrow").
2. Trap.

"Then, who is digging on my grave?
    Say—since I have not guessed!"   20
—"O it is I, my mistress dear,
Your little dog, who still lives near,
And much I hope my movements here
    Have not disturbed your rest?"

"Ah yes! *You* dig upon my grave . . .   25
    Why flashed it not on me
That one true heart was left behind!
What feeling do we ever find
To equal among human kind
    A dog's fidelity!"   30

"Mistress, I dug upon your grave
    To bury a bone, in case
I should be hungry near this spot
When passing on my daily trot.
I am sorry, but I quite forgot   35
    It was your resting place."

          1914

Under the Waterfall

"Whenever I plunge my arm, like this,
In a basin of water, I never miss
The sweet sharp sense of a fugitive day
Fetched back from its thickening shroud of gray.
    Hence the only prime   5
    And real love-rhyme
    That I know by heart,
    And that leaves no smart,
Is the purl of a little valley fall
About three spans wide and two spans tall   10
Over a table of solid rock,
And into a scoop of the self-same block;
The purl of a runlet that never ceases
In stir of kingdoms, in wars, in peaces;
With a hollow boiling voice it speaks   15
And has spoken since hills were turfless peaks."

"And why gives this the only prime
Idea to you of a real love rhyme?
And why does plunging your arm in a bowl
Full of spring water, bring throbs to your soul?"   20

"Well, under the fall, in a crease of the stone,
Though where precisely none ever has known,
Jammed darkly, nothing to show how prized,
And by now with its smoothness opalized,

Is a drinking glass: 25
For, down that pass
My lover and I
Walked under a sky
Of blue with a leaf-wove awning of green,
In the burn of August, to paint the scene,   30
And we placed our basket of fruit and wine
By the runlet's rim, where we sat to dine;
And when we had drunk from the glass together,
Arched by the oak-copse from the weather,
I held the vessel to rinse in the fall,   35
Where it slipped, and sank, and was past recall,
Though we stooped and plumbed the little abyss
With long bared arms. There the glass still is.
And, as said, if I thrust my arm below
Cold water in basin or bowl, a throe   40
From the past awakens a sense of that time,
And the glass we used, and the cascade's rhyme.
The basin seems the pool, and its edge
The hard smooth face of the brookside ledge,
And the leafy pattern of chinaware   45
The hanging plants that were bathing there.

"By night, by day, when it shines or lours,
There lies intact that chalice of ours,
And its presence adds to the rhyme of love
Persistently sung by the fall above.   50
No lip has touched it since his and mine
In turns therefrom sipped lovers' wine."

                                                    1914

The Walk

You did not walk with me
Of late to the hilltop tree
    By the gated ways,
    As in earlier days;
    You were weak and lame,   5
    So you never came,
And I went alone, and I did not mind,
Not thinking of you as left behind.

    I walked up there today
    Just in the former way;   10
    Surveyed around
    The familiar ground
    By myself again:
    What difference, then?
Only that underlying sense   15
Of the look of a room on returning thence.

                                                    1914

During Wind and Rain

They sing their dearest songs—
He, she, all of them—yea,
Treble and tenor and bass,
    And one to play;
With the candles mooning each face. . . .   5
    Ah, no; the years O!
How the sick leaves reel down in throngs!

They clear the creeping moss—
Elders and juniors—aye,
Making the pathways neat   10
    And the garden gay;
And they build a shady seat. . . .
    Ah, no; the years, the years;
See, the white stormbirds wing across!

They are blithely breakfasting all—   15
Men and maidens—yea,
Under the summer tree,
    With a glimpse of the bay,
While pet fowl come to the knee. . . .
    Ah, no; the years O!   20
And the rotten rose is ripped from the wall.

They change to a high new house,
He, she, all of them—aye,
Clocks and carpets and chairs
    On the lawn all day,
And brightest things that are theirs. . . .   25
    Ah, no; the years, the years;
Down their carved names the raindrop plows.

        1917

In Time of "The Breaking of Nations"[1]

1
Only a man harrowing clods
    In a slow silent walk
With an old horse that stumbles and nods
    Half asleep as they stalk.

2
Only thin smoke without flame   5
    From the heaps of couch-grass;
Yet this will go onward the same
    Though Dynasties pass.

3
Yonder a maid and her wight
    Come whispering by;   10
War's annals will cloud into night
    Ere their story die.

1915   1916

1. Cf. "Thou art my battle ax and weapons of war: for with thee will I break in pieces the nations" (Jeremiah li.20). The poem was written during World War I.

GERARD MANLEY HOPKINS

(1844–1889)

1866: Joins the Roman Catholic Church.
1877: Ordained.
1918: Posthumous publication of his poems by Bridges.

Gerard Manley Hopkins was educated at Highgate School, London, and at Balliol College, Oxford, where he studied classics and was influenced by the Oxford Movement, that revival of the ritualistic and dogmatic side of Christianity which began as a movement within the Church of England but which ended by taking many of its adherents, including the leading figure in the movement, John Henry Newman, to the Roman Catholic Church. After a period of spiritual turmoil Hopkins joined the Roman Catholic Church in 1866, sponsored by Newman, and two years later entered the Society of Jesus. He was ordained in 1877, and after serving as priest in a number of parishes, including one in a working-class area of Liverpool where the squalor disturbed him deeply, he was in 1884 appointed Professor of Classics at University College, Dublin.

A devoted Jesuit performing faithfully the duties assigned to him by his superiors, Hopkins was also a sensitive poet fascinated by language and rhythm and a passionately keen observer of the color and form and detail of the world of nature. The claims of religion and the duties of his religious profession were paramount, but his aesthetic interests (which included an interest in painting and music) asserted themselves with sometimes painful force, and it was not always easy for him to reconcile his religious vocation with his poetic genius. Before entering the Society of Jesus he burned his finished poems (though working copies survive) and did not write poetry again until late in 1875 or early in 1876. Hopkins went through periods of deep depression, of a listless sense of failure, and of that deep spiritual emptiness which mystics know as "the dark night of the soul" and see as one of the necessary stages on the road to spiritual fulfillment. This mood of spiritual desolation is expressed in the so-called "terrible sonnets," written between 1885 and 1889. But Hopkins also enjoyed moods of intense pleasure in the natural world, linked with a profound sense of natural beauty as a reflection of divine reality, and it is this combination of the most passionate and particularized apprehension of the sounds, shapes, and colors of the English countryside with the religious awareness of God as revealed through these sounds, shapes and colors, that is the theme of much of his poetry.

Hopkins' poems were never published in his lifetime. In spite of his eager interest in poetry and in technical problems of writing verse—an interest which is reflected in all its variety and intensity in the letters he wrote to his friends Robert Bridges (later poet laureate) and R. W. Dixon—Hopkins subordinated his poetry to his duties as a Jesuit and never sought any public fame as a poet. He resisted the suggestion made by Bridges and others in 1879 that he publish some of his poems, as he felt that his religious superiors would not approve. It is doubtful in any case whether his poetry would have been appreciated or even understood in the 19th century, for it flouted most of the contemporary expectations of what poetry should be. One of his aims was to rejuvenate the language of poetry, and he did so in a variety of ways. Sometimes he placed a familiar and much-used word in a new and startling context to bring out a lost aspect of its original meaning (e.g., addressing God as "sir" in *Thou Art Indeed Just, Lord*); sometimes he revived older words or used dialect words or phrases (such as "all road ever" in *Felix Randal*); sometimes he coined new words on the analogy of existing ones (e.g., "leafmeal" in *Spring and Fall*). He also employed devices found in other poetic modes, such as Anglo-Saxon and Welsh, to find new ways of giving exact and arresting expression to an impression or an idea or a combination of both; and he used unusual combinations of words and unusual word order to achieve the exact curve of the meaning. His study of the medieval philosopher Duns Scotus had encouraged this interest in "individuation" or "this-ness" (*haecceitas*) as a clue to the nature of reality. The essential inward pattern of the expression, what he called "inscape," was his primary concern. "No doubt," he wrote to Bridges, "my poetry errs on the side of oddness * * * but as air, melody, is what strikes me most of all in music and design in painting, so design, pattern, or what I am in the habit of calling 'inscape' is what I above all aim at in poetry. Now it is the virtue of design, pattern, or inscape to be distinctive and it is the vice of distinctiveness to become queer. This vice I cannot have escaped." Bridges, though recognizing his friend's genius, was often more aware of the oddness than of the distinctiveness; a later generation, reacting against the mellifluous poeticizings of an attenuated Romantic tradition, saw in the power and originality of Hopkins' expression not only something tremendously impressive in itself but also an invitation to experiment in new uses of language and new poetic rhythms.

Hopkins' interest in rhythms was as great as his interest in words. In his letters he developed a theory of "sprung rhythm" which broke away from the standard conception of poetic rhythms as consisting of a number of metrical feet, each having a fixed number of syllables, some stressed and some unstressed, with a limited number of possible variations and substitutions. Intead, he saw rhythm in poetry as much more flexible, much more like time and tempo in music, where the rhythmic effects are controlled by the number of beats in the measure (rather than the number of notes) and the general pattern of rising or falling movement. He also experimented with various ways of running lines into each other and of manipulating groups of "slack" or unaccented syllables within the line. He often used accent marks, which draw the reader's attention to the way the stresses fall in the line. All these devices help to produce his characteristic "sprung rhythm," which gives his poetry a different sound from that of other Victorian verse, a sound in many respects more like that of English and American poetry since Eliot.

The remarkable swinging movement of the opening of *The Windhover* is a characteristic triumph of Hopkins' rhythmic effects. He called the rhythm here "falling," meaning that the stress comes first in each foot. (The first word, "I," is conceived of as an introductory light beat outside the main movement of the line.) Hopkins himself scanned the first four lines in this way:

I caught this morning morning's minion, king-
　　dom of daylight's dauphin, dapple-dawn-drawn Falcon, in his riding
　　Of the rolling level underneath him steady air, and striding
High there, how he rung upon the rein of a wimpling wing * * *

The stressed syllables are marked /, while the curved line underneath a
syllable marks what he called "hangers" or "outriders," which he defined
as "one, two, or three slack syllables added to a foot and not counted in
the nominal scanning." He remarked elsewhere that "the strong syllable
in an outriding foot has always a great stress and after the outrider follows
a short pause." Thus the first syllable in "dauphin" and in "Falcon" is
marked with a double stress-mark. The curious plunging effect which this
rhythm achieves—reproducing so effectively the movement of the bird
which is being described—is heightened by the sense of urgent forward
movement achieved by splitting "kingdom" between two lines and rhyming the first syllable ("king-") with the unstressed syllable "ing" of "riding" in the next line as well as, more obviously, with "wing" in line 4.
The hyphenating of groups of words, as in "dapple-dawn-drawn," is another common device of Hopkins: it can achieve a variety of effects, with
each word in the hyphenated group modifying and coloring the other to
achieve a simultaneous blend of meaning both more immediate and more
subtle in its impact on the reader than the same words could produce if
linked more conventionally by conjunctions. Hopkins always tried to
squeeze all water out of his language, to avoid all unnecessary words that
are required only as grammatical signs and so are liable to dissipate the
meaning. To concentrate meaning (so that when the poem is finally made
out its meaning "explodes," as he once put it) rather than to dissipate it
was always Hopkins' aim.

Other devices used by Hopkins include patterns of alliteration (e.g.,
God's Grandeur, line 3: "It gathers to a greatness, like the ooze of oil");
internal rhymes (line 6: "And all is *seared* with trade; *bleared, smeared*
with toil"); varieties of assonance (lines 11–14: "West," "went,"
"breast"); and different kinds of sound patterns which he adapted from
the traditions of Welsh poetry.

In its kind of imagery, too, and in the way in which the imagery works,
Hopkins' poetry differs sharply from that of, say, Tennyson or Rossetti.
In such a poem as *The Starlight Night* we are struck not only by the
arresting imperatives with which it opens and the echoes of Anglo-Saxon
poetic devices in "fire-folk" and "circle-citadel" but also by the remarkable way in which excitement at an aspect of the natural world moves
into a religious affirmation. This is achieved partly by a punning use of
language unknown in serious English poetry since the 17th century. In
line 13, for example, the harvested sheaves ("shocks") are to be safely
housed in the barn. But "shocks" also suggests the other and more familiar
sense of the word—"the thousand natural shocks that flesh is heir to"
(*Hamlet*). By buying the beauty of nature with prayer (lines 8 ff.), we
learn to see God in nature and to possess both nature and God. Thus by
"owning" nature we have a home for it—and for ourselves, protecting

both the "shocks" of corn and ourselves from the shocks of life. At the conclusion Christ and his saints are brought into this communion of the sheltered and protected: it becomes now the communion of saints and that, we now learn, is what "the fire-folk sitting in the air" really suggested. And what other 19th-century poet would have used the language of the auction room in talking of the beauty of nature and its relation to religious practices? ("Buy then! bid then!—What?—Prayer, patience, alms, vows.")

This combination of the startlingly colloquial and the strikingly unusual is an important feature of Hopkins' poetry. *The Lantern Out of Doors* begins with a simple, colloquial use of English ("And who goes there? / I think * * * "). The surface thought is also simple: we meet people in daily life who interest us momentarily, but our paths cross briefly and they disappear and we forget about them, because "out of sight is out of mind" (and notice the way Hopkins introduces a homely proverb here). Christ, on the other hand, never forgets people; He is always interested in them; He is their ransom, their rescue, and their eternal friend. There is, however, much more than this in the poem. The word "interests" in line 2 is not a normal poetic word; it arrests us by its very ordinariness. As the poem develops, it comes to suggest not only its obvious, primary meaning but its financial meaning (as in "to lend at interest"). The thought is: people whose character makes them valuable pass by but soon disappear when they are bought by death or distance. Although death or distance buys or consumes them, so that they are lost to sight, Christ continues to "mind" them—in the sense (still common in Scotland) of "remember" them as well as "look after" them, as a man minds his property. Christ's *interest* is their *ransom:* the implication is that Christ gives the interest on his property to ransom man—but of course the word "interest" is also used in its more obvious meaning. Or consider lines 5 and following. The sense is that men beautiful in "mould" (shape) disappear in the "mould" (the earth of the grave): their very beauty suggests their mortality. Or we could follow out the double meaning of "kind" in the phrase "foot follows kind." This combination of the colloquial and the formal, the building up of complex patterns of meaning through the multiple suggestiveness given to words in their poetic context, is what so excited 20th-century poets when they discovered Hopkins.

This discovery was made in 1918, long after Hopkins' death, when Bridges first brought out an edition of Hopkins' poems. By the time the second edition appeared, with an introduction by Charles Williams, in 1930, Hopkins' position was established; the younger poets, such as W. H. Auden and later Dylan Thomas, turned to him enthusiastically as one of their masters. Hopkins is thus in a sense a 20-century poet born out of his time who had to wait until the present century for posthumous appreciation and influence.

The text of the selections given here follows that of the third edition of Hopkins' poems (1948), edited by W. H. Gardner, which is now the standard text.

God's Grandeur

The world is charged with the grandeur of God.
   It will flame out, like shining from shook foil;[1]
   It gathers to a greatness, like the ooze of oil
Crushed.[2] Why do men then now not reck his rod?
Generations have trod, have trod, have trod;   5
   And all is seared with trade; bleared, smeared with toil;
   And wears man's smudge and shares man's smell: the soil
Is bare now, nor can foot feel, being shod.

And for all this, nature is never spent;
   There lives the dearest freshness deep down things;   10
And though the last lights off the black West went
Oh, morning, at the brown brink eastward, springs—
Because the Holy Ghost over the bent
   World broods with warm breast and with ah! bright wings.

1877   1918

The Starlight Night

Look at the stars! look, look up at the skies!
   O look at all the fire-folk sitting in the air!
   The bright boroughs, the circle-citadels there!
Down in dim woods the diamond delves! the elves'-eyes!
The grey lawns cold where gold,[3] where quickgold lies!
   Wind-beat whitebeam! airy abeles [4] set on a flare!
   Flake-doves sent floating forth at a farmyard scare!—
Ah well! it is all a purchase, all is a prize.

Buy then! bid then!—What?—Prayer, patience, alms, vows.
Look, look: a May-mess,[5] like on orchard boughs!
Look! March-bloom, like on mealed-with-yellow[6] sallows!
These are indeed the barn; withindoors house
   The shocks.[7] This piece-bright paling[8] shuts the spouse
   Christ home, Christ and his mother and all his hallows.[9]

1877   1918

1. "I mean foil in the sense of leaf or tinsel * * * Shaken goldfoil gives off broad glares like sheet lightning and also, and this is true of nothing else, owing to its zigzag dints and creasings and network of small many cornered facets, a sort of fork lightning too" (Hopkins, *Letters*).
2. From olives.
3. Dewdrops, referred to also as "quickgold" (a word coined by analogy with "quicksilver" and thus suggesting the gleaming and volatile nature of dewdrops).
4. White poplars.
5. A profusion of May—i.e., suggesting a mass of May blossoms, such as pear blossoms ("like on orchard boughs"). "May" is also another name for the white hawthorn. There may be religious overtones, with "May" suggesting "Mary" (the Virgin) and "mess" suggesting "Mass" (the Catholic rite).
6. Yellow-spotted. "Sallows" are a variety of willow tree.
7. Sheaves of corn: see discussion of this poem in the Hopkins introduction.
8. Fencing. It is "piece-bright," i.e., bright as a gold or silver coin. "Piece" in this sense suggests the thirty pieces of silver for which Judas betrayed Christ: but line 9 implies that we can buy both Christ and the beauty of nature with a very different kind of coin.
9. Saints.

Spring

Nothing is so beautiful as spring—
  When weeds, in wheels, shoot long and lovely and lush;
  Thrush's eggs look little low heavens, and thrush
Through the echoing timber does so rinse and wring
The ear, it strikes like lightnings to hear him sing;   5
  The glassy peartree leaves and blooms, they brush
  The descending blue; that blue is all in a rush
With richness; the racing lambs too have fair their fling.

What is all this juice and all this joy?
  A strain of the earth's sweet being in the beginning   10
In Eden garden.—Have, get, before it cloy,
  Before it cloud, Christ, lord, and sour with sinning,
Innocent mind and Mayday in girl and boy,
  Most, O maid's[1] child, thy choice and worthy the winning. .
1877   1918

The Lantern Out of Doors

Sometimes a lantern moves along the night,
  That interests our eyes. And who goes there?
  I think; where from and bound, I wonder, where,
With, all down darkness wide, his wading light?

Men go by me whom either beauty bright   5
  In mould or mind or what not else makes rare:
  They rain against our much-thick and marsh air
Rich beams, till death or distance buys them quite.

Death or distance soon consumes them: wind
  What most I may eye after,[2] be in at the end   10
I cannot, and out of sight is out of mind.

Christ minds; Christ's interest, what to avow or amend
  There, éyes them, heart wánts, care haúnts, foot fóllows kínd,
Their ránsom, théir rescue, ánd first, fást, last friénd.[3]
1877   1918

1. The Virgin Mary's. May is a popular form of the word "Mary," so "Mayday" in line 13 also suggests "Mary's day," day of innocence and purity. Cf. note 3 to *The Starlight Night*.
2. W. H. Gardner notes that the entire verb in this passage is "wind eye after." "I mean that the eye winds only in the sense that its focus or point of sight winds and that coincides with a point of the object and winds with that. For the object, a lantern passing further and further away and bearing now east now west of one right line, is truly and properly described as winding" (Hopkins, *Letters*).
3. For a discussion of the language in this poem, see the Hopkins introduction.

The Windhover[1]

TO CHRIST OUR LORD

I caught this morning morning's minion,[2] king-
   dom of daylight's dauphin,[3] dapple-dawn-drawn Falcon, in
     his riding
Of the rolling level underneath him steady air, and striding
High there, how he rung upon the rein[4] of a wimpling wing
In his ecstasy! then off, off forth on swing,
   As a skate's heel sweeps smooth on a bow-bend: the hurl
     and gliding   5
Rebuffed the big wind. My heart in hiding
Stirred for a bird,—the achieve of, the mastery of the thing!

Brute beauty and valour and act, oh, air, pride, plume, here
   Buckle![5] AND[6] the fire that breaks from thee then, a billion   10
Times told lovelier, more dangerous, O my chevalier!

No wonder of it: shéer plód makes plough down sillion[7]
Shine, and blue-bleak embers, ah my dear,
   Fall, gall themselves, and gash gold-vermilion.

1877   1918

Pied Beauty

Glory be to God for dappled things—
   For skies of couple-colour as a brinded[1] cow;
     For rose-moles all in stipple[2] upon trout that swim;

1. Kestrel, called "windhover" because it hovers in the air, head to wind. This poem, which Hopkins considered "the best thing I ever wrote" (*Letters*), has been variously explicated. The main thought seems to be that the ecstatic flying of the bird stirs the poet's heart ("in hiding," for the poet is a priest, with his heart hidden away from earthly things in the service of God). In the combination of beauty, strength, and glory which the poet sees in the bird, he sees an emblem of the beauty, strength, and glory of Christ, whom he addresses as "my chevalier" (line 11). It is "dangerous" to see these qualities in Christ, for we look to Christ for lessons in humility and the enduring of suffering. But it is "no wonder" (lines 12–14) that Christ's humility and suffering are bound up with His glory and pride; many things include their opposites; "sheer plod" can make the ploughshare shine, as it cuts its furrow, and a black coal in a fire can fall over and break and reveal its red-hot interior, its "gold-vermilion" gashes suggesting *both* beauty and pride *and* Christ's wounds and suffering.
2. Darling.
3. Heir (literally, the title of the eldest son of the king of France); the word carries overtones of chivalry and splendor.
4. There is an implied comparison to a horse circling around its trainer at the end of a long rein. "Wimpling": rippling.
5. The obvious sense here is "join," though some critics have understood it as "bend" or "break" and some have taken it as an imperative in that sense. But see note 1. Hopkins is celebrating the point at which animal beauty, strength, bearing, and fine display all join.
6. Hopkins emphasizes the "AND" to draw attention from the admiration of the bird to the sense of Christ behind it which that admiration brings. A movement from appreciation of the life of nature to a religious sense of the God reflected in nature is found in very many of Hopkins' poems.
7. The ridge between two furrows of a plowed field. Hopkins uses this archaic word perhaps to suggest an overtone from "silica" (the mineral which in the form of gleaming particles of quartz often makes dull rocks shine).
1. Brindled, streaked.
2. Dots or small spots.

Fresh-firecoal chestnut-falls;[3] finches' wings;
   Landscape plotted and pieced[4]—fold, fallow, and plough;   5
   And áll trádes, their gear and tackle and trim.[5]

All things counter,[6] original, spare, strange;
   Whatever is fickle, freckled (who knows how?)
     With swift, slow; sweet, sour; adazzle, dim;
He fathers-forth whose beauty is past change: 10
            Praise him.

1877   1918

Hurrahing in Harvest

Summer ends now; now, barbarous in beauty, the stocks[7] arise
   Around; up above, what wind-walks! what lovely
     behaviour
Of silk-sack clouds! has wilder, wilful-wavier

Meal-drift moulded ever and melted across skies?
I walk, I lift up, I lift up heart, eyes,
   Down all that glory in the heavens to glean our Saviour;   5
   And, éyes, heárt, what looks, what lips yet gave you a
Rapturous love's greeting of realer, of rounder replies?

And the azurous hung hills are his world-wielding shoulder
   Majestic—as a stallion stalwart, very-violet-sweet!—   10
These things, these things were here and but the beholder
   Wanting; which two when they once meet,
The heart rears wings bold and bolder
   And hurls for him, O half hurls earth for him off under
     his feet.

1877   1918

Binsey Poplars

FELLED 1879

My aspens dear, whose airy cages quelled,
Quelled or quenched in leaves the leaping sun,
All felled, felled, are all felled;
   Of a fresh and following folded rank[1]
       Not spared, not one   5
       That dandled a sandalled
     Shadow that swam or sank
On meadow and river and wind-wandering weed-winding bank.

---

3. Chestnuts stripped of their husks after being roasted in "fresh-firecoal."
4. Divided into rectangles of different colors, as the English landscape appears. "Fold": enclosure for animals; "fallow": a field plowed but left unsown for a season.
5. Equipment.
6. Contrary, i.e., in contrasted patterns or colors. "Spare": rare.
7. Stooks (or shocks: see "The Starlight Night") are sheaves of corn placed upright, supporting each other at an angle, for drying.
1. Row of trees with alternate trees set off at an angle, making the row "folded."

O if we but knew what we do
    When we delve[2] or hew—   10
Hack and rack[3] the growing green!
    Since country is so tender
To touch, her being só slender,
That, like this sleek and seeing ball[4]
But a prick will make no eye at all,   15
    Where we, even where we mean
        To mend her we end her,
    When we hew or delve:
After-comers cannot guess the beauty been.
    Ten or twelve, only ten or twelve   20
      Strokes of havoc únselve[5]
      The sweet especial scene,
    Rural scene, a rural scene,
    Sweet especial rural scene.

1879   1918

Duns Scotus's Oxford[6]

Towery city and branchy between towers;
Cuckoo-echoing, bell-swarmèd, lark-charmèd, rook-racked, river-
    rounded;
The dapple-eared lily below thee; that country and town did
Once encounter in, here coped[7] and poisèd powers;

Thou hast a base and brickish skirt[8] there, sours   5
That neighbour-nature thy grey beauty is grounded
Best in; graceless growth, thou hast confounded
Rural rural keeping[9]—folk, flocks, and flowers.

Yet ah! this air I gather and I release
He lived on; these weeds and waters, these walls are what   10
He haunted who of all men most sways my spirits to peace;

Of realty[1] the rarest-veinèd unraveller; a not
Rivalled insight, be rival Italy or Greece;
Who fired France for Mary without spot.[2]

1879   1918

2. Dig.
3. Torture.
4. The eye.
5. Rob it of its "self" or individuality.
6. Duns Scotus, the 13th-century Scholastic philosopher, is supposed to have taught at Oxford ca. 1301. Hopkins admired him greatly; when he came upon two of Scotus's commentaries in 1872 he was "flush with a new stroke of enthusiasm. * * * When I took in any inscape of the sky or sea I thought of Scotus" (*Note-books*). In this poem he builds up an impression of medieval Oxford, then links this to Scotus through himself ("this air I gather and I release / He lived on") to end with a tribute to him.
7. Set off one against the other.
8. Refers to the appearance of 19th-century brick houses in north Oxford. Note the characteristic omission of the relative pronoun before "sours."
9. I.e., you have spoiled the effect of a rural city presiding over its rural environment.
1. Reality.
2. Reference to Scotus's work in spreading the cult of the Virgin Mary in France.

Felix Randal

Felix Randal the farrier,[1] O he is dead then? my duty all ended,
Who have watched his mould of man, big-boned and hardy-handsome
Pining, pining, till time when reason rambled in it and some
Fatal four disorders, fleshed there, all contended?

Sickness broke him. Impatient he cursed at first, but mended   5
Being anointed and all; though a heavenlier heart began some
Months earlier, since I had our sweet reprieve and ransom
Tendered to him.[2] Ah well, God rest him all road ever[3] he offended!

This seeing the sick endears them to us, us too it endears.
My tongue had taught thee comfort, touch had quenched thy
    tears,   10
Thy tears that touched my heart, child, Felix, poor Felix Randal;

How far from then forethought of, all thy more boisterous years,
When thou at the random[4] grim forge, powerful amidst peers,
Didst fettle[5] for the great grey drayhorse his bright and battering
    sandal!
1880   1918

Spring and Fall

TO A YOUNG CHILD

Márgarét, are you grieving
Over Goldengrove unleaving?
Leáves, líke the things of man, you
With your fresh thoughts care for, can you?
Áh! ás the heart grows older   5
It will come to such sights colder
By and by, nor spare a sigh
Though worlds of wanwood leafmeal[6] lie;
And yet you wíll weep and know why.
Now no matter, child, the name: 10
Sórrow's spríngs áre the same.

---

1. Blacksmith.
2. Had heard his confession and given him absolution.
3. In whatever way.
4. Built with stones of irregular shapes and sizes.
5. Prepare.
6. "I take *wanwood* to be a noun (the meaning 'bloodless' being combined with the older meaning 'dark,' 'livid' —O.E. *wann*). *Leafmeal* I take for an adverb, made 'by substitution' from *piecemeal* on the analogy of Shakespeare's *inch-meal* and *limb-meal:* hence it suggests the leaves falling one by one, then rotting to form pale, mealy fragments" [W. H. Gardner's note].

Nor mouth had, no nor mind, expressed
What heart heard of, ghost guessed: [7]
It ís the blight man was born for,
It is Margaret you mourn for.

1880

15

1918

Inversnaid [8]

This darksome burn,[9] horseback brown,
His rollrock highroad roaring down,
In coop and in comb [1] the fleece of his foam
Flutes and low to the lake falls home.

A windpuff-bonnet of fáwn-fróth   5
Turns and twindles [2] over the broth
Of a pool so pitchblack, féll-frówning,
It rounds and rounds Despair to drowning.

Degged [3] with dew, dappled with dew
Are the groins of the braes [4] that the brook treads through,   10
Wiry heathpacks, flitches [5] of fern,
And the beadbonny ash that sits over the burn.

What would the world be, once bereft
Of wet and of wildness? Let them be left,
O let them be left, wildness and wet;   15
Long live the weeds and the wilderness yet.

1881

1918

[Carrion Comfort] [6]

Not, I'll not, carrion comfort, Despair, not feast on thee;
Not untwist—slack they may be—these last strands of man
In me ór, most weary, cry *I can no more*. I can;
Can something, hope, wish day come, not choose not to be.
But ah, but O thou terrible, why wouldst thou rude on me   5
Thy wring-world right foot rock?[7] lay a lionlimb against me? scan

---

7. *Ghost,* spirit (of the living), with a proleptic suggestion of 'phantom'—the living spirit foreknowing, through sensory experience, its own state after death. Lines 8 and 14 connect the Fall of the Leaf with the Fall of Man: 'and unto dust shalt thou return' (Genesis iii.18)" [W. H. Gardner's note].
8. On Loch Lomondside, Scotland, famous for its rushing stream and waterfall.
9. Stream.
1. "Coop": hollow; "comb": crest.

2. Apparently Hopkins' coinage: twists and dwindles.
3. Sprinkled.
4. Hills.
5. Tufts, clumps.
6. Title supplied by Bridges in the 1918 edition. This is one of the "terrible sonnets," as are the two poems that follow.
7. Why wouldst thou turn roughly against me thy right foot that wrings the world?

With darksome devouring eyes my bruisèd bones? and fan,
O in turns of tempest, me heaped there; me frantic to avoid thee
    and flee?

  Why? That my chaff might fly; my grain lie, sheer and clear.
Nay in all that toil, that coil,[8] since (seems) I kissed the rod,   10
Hand rather, my heart lo! lapped strength, stole joy, would laugh,
    chéer.
Cheer whom though? the hero whose heaven-handling flung me,
    fóot tród
Me? or me that fought him? O which one? is it each one? That
    night, that year
Of now done darkness I wretch lay wrestling with (my God!) my
    God.
1885   1918

[No Worst, There Is None][9]

No worst, there is none. Pitched past pitch of grief,
More pangs will, schooled at forepangs, wilder wring.
Comforter, where, where is your comforting?
Mary, mother of us, where is your relief?

My cries heave, herds-long,[1] huddle in a main, a chief   5
Woe, world-sorrow; on an age-old anvil wince and sing—
Then lull, then leave off. Fury had shrieked "No ling-
ering! Let me be fell:[2] force I must be brief."

  O the mind, mind has mountains; cliffs of fall
Frightful, sheer, no-man-fathomed. Hold them cheap   10
May who ne'er hung there. Nor does long our small
Durance[3] deal with that steep or deep. Here! creep,
Wretch, under a comfort serves in a whirlwind: all
Life death does end and each day dies with sleep.
1885   1918

[Thou Art Indeed Just, Lord]

*Justus quidem tu es, Domine, si disputem tecum: verumtamen
justa loquar ad te: Quare via impiorum prosperatur? etc.*[4]

---

8. Disturbance.
9. Untitled by Hopkins. Cf. the description of "desolation" in the *Spiritual Exercises* of St. Ignatius Loyola, founder of the Jesuit order: "a darkening of the soul, trouble of mind, movement to base and earthly things, restlessness of various agitations and temptations, moving to distrust, loss of hope, loss of love; when the soul feels herself thoroughly apathetic, sad, and as it were separated from her Creator and Lord."
1. Coming in large numbers and in a long series, like herds of cattle following each other. "Main" (like "chief") is an adjective, qualifying "woe."
2. Fierce. "Force" means here "perforce."
3. Endurance.
4. The Latin is the Vulgate version of Jeremiah xii.1, which reads in the King James version: "Righteous art thou, O Lord, when I plead with thee: yet let me talk with thee of thy judgments: Wherefore doth the way of the wicked prosper? * * * " This Latin quotation was Hopkins' title.

Thou art indeed just, Lord, if I contend
With thee; but, sir, so what I plead is just.
Why do sinners' ways prosper? and why must
Disappointment all I endeavour end?
　　Wert thou my enemy, O thou my friend, 　　　　　　5
How wouldst thou worse, I wonder, than thou dost
Defeat, thwart me? Oh, the sots and thralls of lust
Do in spare hours more thrive than I that spend,
Sir, life upon thy cause. See, banks and brakes[5]
Now, leavèd how thick! lacèd they are again 　　　　10
With fretty[6] chervil, look, and fresh wind shakes
Them; birds build—but not I build; no, but strain,
Time's eunuch, and not breed one work that wakes.
Mine,[7] O thou lord of life, send my roots rain.

1889 　　　　　　　　　　　　　　　　　　　　1918

5. Clumps of fern.
6. Fretted, with interlacing pattern. "Chervil" is a member of the parsley family.
7. "Mine" may refer to "roots," em-

phasizing that the poet wants God to send "*my* roots rain" since every other creature is flourishing, or it may mean "my God."

GEORGE BERNARD SHAW
(1856–1950)

1876: Settles in London.
1892: *Widowers' Houses* produced.
1898: Publication of *Plays Pleasant and Unpleasant,* including *Arms and the Man.*
1923: *Saint Joan.*

Bernard Shaw was born in Dublin of English stock, one of the galaxy of Anglo-Irishmen (they include Swift, Sheridan, Edmund Burke, and Yeats) who have contributed so brilliantly to English literature. He left school at the age of 14 and worked for five years (1871–76) in a land agent's office. He went to London in 1876, his mother having settled there in order to improve her prospects as a music teacher, and began his literary career as a writer of unsuccessful novels. He soon became interested in social reform: in 1884 he was one of the founders of the Fabian Society, an organization dedicated to the promotion of socialism by gradual stages. Although he was friendly with the most important socialist thinkers in England in the late 19th century, including Sidney and Beatrice Webb and William Morris, Shaw was never a conventional socialist. His social and political attitude was affected by his belief in an active and individually *willed* kind of evolution, urged on by what he called the Life Force, and by his admiration of vitality and power. He inherited from his gifted mother a love of music and learned from her to know and admire Mozartian opera; he also became a great champion of Richard Wagner, and in his regular music criticism, first for the London *Star* and then for the *World,* not only displayed his enthusiasms with lively wit but also introduced a new standard in judging both performers and composers, often mocking conventional taste and fashionable preferences. In 1895 he became dramatic critic for the *Saturday Review* (a London periodical): his deliberately provocative reviews stirred up contemporary English ideas about plays and acting and enlarged the intellectual horizons of his readers. He championed Henrik Ibsen as well as Wagner, and published in 1891 a study of Ibsen entitled *The Quintessence of Ibsenism* which presented the Norwegian dramatist as a realistic and reforming playwright who addressed himself to the problems of modern life and introduced genuine *discussion* in his dialogue. The more profound and symbolic Ibsen whom we admire today was not Shaw's Ibsen, and it is significant that for him the great plays were those which attacked middle-class conventionality and hypocrisy rather than those which probed more subtly and poetically into deeper aspects of experience.

His training in music and dramatic criticism, his interest in social reform, his admiration for Wagner and Ibsen, the influence of Samuel Butler (author of *Erewhon* and *The Way of All Flesh* and the great satirist of Victorian life and thought) helped to make Shaw a playwright who on the one hand knew all the conventional tricks of the theater and on the other was determined to use the drama as he conceived Ibsen to have used it—as a means of shaking theater audiences out of their complacencies, hypocrisies, and thoughtless acquiescence in all kinds of social evil.

Reviewing new plays over a period of years had given Shaw an expert knowledge of the structural devices employed by the authors of the "well-made play" (adroitly plotted theatrical entertainment) of the late 19th century; and when he came to write his own plays he was able to use conventional dramatic structure and even conventional themes for highly unconventional purposes. From the beginning his aim as a dramatist was to shock his audiences into taking a new view of their society and the moral problems that arose out of it. "I must warn my readers," he wrote, "that my attacks are directed against themselves, not against my stage figures." Not only did he delight in standing the popular view on its head, but he went further: beginning by persuading his audience by means of dramatic action and dialogue that the conventional hero was the villain and the conventional villain was the hero, he would swing everything around again to show that the conventional hero was the hero after all, but in a very different sense from that which the audience had originally thought. He followed this pattern in *Man and Superman, Major Barbara,* and *Arms and the Man.* He used paradox, both in the action and even more in the dialogue, to dazzle and even bewilder his audiences—only to demonstate that their absurd conventional views and unconscious hypocrisies were responsible for their bewilderment. Having thus destroyed the audience's self-confidence he would organize the dialogue (or sometimes a monologue) in order to allow one of his splendidly vital (but never conventionally heroic) heroes to put across the Shavian vision of society or politics or religion or whatever was the main theme of the play. And all the time he entertained and fascinated by his wit as well as by his sheer sense of fun. Sometimes this sense of fun led him to conclude a serious critical comedy in sheer farce—as in *You Never Can Tell* (1900)—but on the whole Shaw combined entertainment and intellectual provocation to bring a new kind of critical wit into English drama. The wit of Oscar Wilde's comedies had no specific critical implications; it drew on the conventions of society not in order to expose them but in order to get the maximum number of epigrams out of their delightful inconsistencies and absurdities. Shaw's wit was put at the service of a genuine passion for reform, and even if he sometimes assumed the posture of a licensed clown—a posture which members of the public were all too ready to accept as his natural one, for it enabled them to laugh off the disturbing paradoxes he thrust at them—he remained to the end a crusader as well as an entertainer.

Shaw's first play, *Widowers' Houses* (produced in 1892), dealt in a characteristically provocative manner with the problem of slum landlordism: even here, with a subject easily compartmentalized into moral blacks and whites, Shaw's techniques of reversal and inversion keep revealing new aspects of the problem, so that, instead of merely condemning the landlord, the audience is forced to comprehend the entire complex of social and economic conditions that produced the problem. *Mrs. Warren's Profession*, written in 1893, was for a long time banned from the public theater because of its concern with the tabooed subject of prostitution; it is not, however, simply about prostitution, but about well-meaning brothel-keepers and the laws of supply and demand, which it explores with boldness and wit, again substituting the revelation of causes and consequences for simple moral indignation. In 1898 Shaw published *Plays Pleasant and Unpleasant*, with long provocative prefaces attacking a great variety of things, including theatrical censorship; the plays included *Arms and the Man, Candida, The Man of Destiny*, and (among the "unpleasant") *Widowers' Houses* and *Mrs. Warren's Profession*. Among his later plays, *John Bull's Other Island* (1904) is a characteristic contribution to the discussion of Ireland's grievances against the English; *Man and Superman* (1904) is an ambitious attempt to project through comedy his views of how the Life Force works in ordinary life and contains some brilliant scenes, though the play as a whole is rather too long and too talkative; *The Doctor's Dilemma* (1906) exposes both doctors and artists while exploring some of the moral problems in which they can become involved; *Major Barbara* (1907) shows Shaw's characteristic admiration of success and energy and his contempt for those evangelists who attempt to promote religion by giving soup to the poor instead of trying to convert the strong and successful; *Pygmalion* (1912) is a brilliant exploration of the relation between social class and accent in England, which has since been made into the extraordinarily popular musical comedy, *My Fair Lady*. *Heartbreak House* (1917), subtitled "a fantasia in the Russian manner on English themes," suggests the Russian dramatist Chekhov in its depiction of the imminent collapse of a civilization, but it is essentially Shavian, and the finest example of what Eric Bentley has called the "disquisitory" Shavian play, based on the interplay of ideas in dialogue. *The Apple Cart* (1929) is a paradoxical treatment of the problems of monarchy and democracy done with a mischievous desire to shock equally both Left- and Right-wing thinkers and again shows that admiration of the strong man which is Shaw's personal heresy and goes oddly with his socialism.

Back to Methuselah (1921) was Shaw's most ambitious work, and the one which he considered his masterpiece. But it is in fact the dullest of his plays. Shaw's picture of the Life Force eventually enabling men to improve the human species to the point where they can live long enough to become little more than disembodied intellects reveals a curious coldness and abstraction at the heart of his thought. *Saint Joan* (1923), his one tragedy and often regarded as his finest play, is brilliant in its way, but it is really a comedy containing one tragic scene rather than a tragedy. Shaw had no historical imagination. He makes the past interesting by analogizing it to the present and gets his comic effects by interpreting historical characters as though they were the kind of characters who would be doing the same sort of thing today. The result is often very amusing, but it yields no real insight. Saint Joan as a girl with inspired common sense is a refreshing, funny, and, up to a point, a persuasive portrait—but this portrait is not compatible with the image of Joan as religious martyr, which Shaw does not know how to paint. Similarly, in that most entertaining play *Caesar and Cleopatra* (which is, incidentally, most brilliant theatrically) Shaw's wit takes the form of interpreting the main characters as though they lived in the 19th century. Caesar becomes a 19th-century liberal and his secretary Britannicus is a Victorian Philistine: this gives a kind of reality to the past, but at the cost of losing a dimension.

Shaw continued throughout his long and active career to tease and provoke the public with his plays and prefaces. He is at his best when he uses effective dramatic devices and brilliantly entertaining dialogue in order to expose contradictions, inconsistencies, gaps between the pretended and the real, in contemporary attitudes and behavior. In *Arms and the Man* he does this admirably. It is a deliberately antiromantic play, if by romanticism one means "fictitious morals and fictitious good conduct, shedding fictitious glory on overcrowding, disease, crime, drink, war, cruelty, infant mortality * * *" It exhibits what Shaw called "natural morality" as against the "romantic morality" of those who objected to it. We see in this play Shaw's characteristic device of continually transposing the parts of conventional hero and conventional villain. First we think Bluntschli, the soldier in danger of capture and death, is a military hero; then we see him as a coward who prefers chocolate to bullets; then we find that he is capable of a brave resignation to death; and in the end, after many further transformations, he emerges as a new sort of hero—the *efficient* man. And it is he who wins the heroine, who also keeps changing before our eyes until we finally see her—as we do so many of Shaw's heroines —as the girl led by the Life Force to seek out as her mate the most efficient and vital man available. Similar transformations occur in our view of Louka and Sergius. These teasing shifts in ways of presenting a character represent more than a successful dramatic trick: this is how Shaw makes his audiences look again and again at the particular situation he is presenting, until they have shed all illusions bred either by convention or by facile anticonventionality.

Shaw was an ardent believer in spelling reform, and, while awaiting a reformed alphabet and phonetic spelling, introduced some minor simplifications in his own spelling which he insisted on his publishers retaining. These simplifications (omission of the apostrophe in a number of contractions, for example) are retained in the text here printed.

From Preface to *Plays Pleasant*[1]
[*Arms and the Man*]

* * * There is no reason, however, why I should take this haughty attitude towards those representative critics whose complaint is that my plays, though not unentertaining, lack the elevation of sentiment and seriousness of purpose of Shakespear and Ibsen. They can find, under the surface brilliancy for which they give me credit, no coherent thought or sympathy, and accuse me, in various terms and degrees, of an inhuman and freakish wantonness; of preoccupation with "the seamy side of life"; of paradox, cynicism, and eccentricity, reducible, as some contend, to a trite formula of treating bad as good, and good as bad, important as trivial, and trivial as important, serious as laughable, and laughable as serious, and so forth. As to this formula I can only say that if any gentleman is simple enough to think that even a good comic opera can be produced by it, I invite him to try his hand, and see whether anything remotely resembling one of my plays will result.

I could explain the matter easily enough if I chose; but the result would be that the people who misunderstand the plays would misunderstand the explanation ten times more. The particular exceptions taken are seldom more than symptoms of the underlying fundamental disagreement between the romantic morality of the critics and the realistic morality of the plays. For example, I am quite aware that the much criticized Swiss officer in *Arms and the Man* is not a conventional stage soldier. He suffers from want of food and sleep; his nerves go to pieces after three days under fire, ending in the horrors of a rout and pursuit; he has found by experience that it is more important to have a few bits of chocolate to eat in the field than cartridges for his revolver. When many of my critics rejected these circumstances as fantastically improbable and cynically unnatural, it was not necessary to argue them into common sense: all I had to do was to brain them, so to speak, with the first half dozen military authorities at hand, beginning with the present Commander in Chief. But when it proved that such unromantic (but all the more dramatic) facts implied to them a denial of the existence of courage, patriotism, faith, hope, and charity, I saw that it was not really mere matter of fact that was at issue between us. One strongly Liberal critic, who had received my first play with the most generous encouragement, declared, when *Arms and the Man* was produced, that I had struck a wanton blow at the cause of liberty in the Balkan Peninsula by mentioning that it was

1. First printed in the second volume ("Containing the Four Pleasant Plays") of *Plays Pleasant and Unpleasant* (1898), this Preface later, with some changes, became the Preface to *Arms and the Man*. The earlier text is followed here.

not a matter of course for a Bulgarian in 1885 to wash his hands every day. My Liberal critic no doubt saw soon afterwards the squabble, reported all through Europe, between Stambouiloff[2] and an eminent lady of the Bulgarian court who took exception to his neglect of his fingernails. After that came the news of his ferocious assassination, and a description of the room prepared for the reception of visitors by his widow, who draped it with black, and decorated it with photographs of the mutilated body of her husband. Here was a sufficiently sensational confirmation of the accuracy of my sketch of the theatrical nature of the first apings of western civilization by spirited races just emerging from slavery. But it had no bearing on the real issue between my critic and myself, which was, whether the political and religious idealism which had inspired the rescue of these Balkan principalities from the despotism of the Turk, and converted miserably enslaved provinces into hopeful and gallant little states, will survive the general onslaught on idealism which is implicit, and indeed explicit, in *Arms and the Man* and the realistic plays of the modern school. For my part I hope not; for idealism, which is only a flattering name for romance in politics and morals, is as obnoxious to me as romance in ethics or religion. In spite of a Liberal Revolution or two, I can no longer be satisfied with fictitious morals and fictitious good conduct, shedding fictitious glory on overcrowding, disease, crime, drink, war, cruelty, infant mortality, and all the other commonplaces of civilization which drive men to the theatre to make foolish pretences that these things are progress, science, morals, religion, patriotism, imperial supremacy, national greatness and all the other names the newspapers call them. On the other hand, I see plenty of good in the world working itself out as fast as the idealist will allow it; and if they would only let it alone and learn to respect reality, which would include the beneficial exercise of respecting themselves, and incidentally respecting me, we should all get along much better and faster. At all events, I do not see moral chaos and anarchy as the alternative to romantic convention; and I am not going to pretend that I do to please the less clear-sighted people who are convinced that the world is only held together by the force of unanimous, strenuous, eloquent, trumpet-tongued lying. To me the tragedy and comedy of life lie in the consequences, sometimes terrible, sometimes ludicrous, of our persistent attempts to found our institutions on the ideals suggested to our imaginations by our half-satisfied passions, instead of on a genuinely scientific natural history. And with that hint as to what I am driving at, I withdraw and ring up the curtain.

2. Stefan Stambolov (Stambouiloff), was a Bulgarian politician, nationalist leader and premier from 1887 to 1894. He was fatally wounded by an assassin on July 15, 1895.

Arms and the Man[1]

Act I

Night: *A lady's bedchamber in Bulgaria, in a small town near the Dragoman Pass, late in November in the year 1885. Through an open window with a little balcony a peak of the Balkans, wonderfully white and beautiful in the starlit snow, seems quite close at hand, though it is really miles away. The interior of the room is not like anything to be seen in the west of Europe. It is half rich Bulgarian, half cheap Viennese. Above the head of the bed, which stands against a little wall cutting off the left-hand corner of the room, is a painted wooden shrine, blue and gold, with an ivory image of Christ, and a light hanging before it in a pierced metal ball suspended by three chains. The principal seat, placed towards the other side of the room and opposite the window, is a Turkish ottoman. The counterpane and hangings of the bed, the window curtains, the little carpet, and all the ornamental textile fabrics in the room are oriental and gorgeous; the paper on the walls is occidental and paltry. The washstand, against the wall on the side nearest the ottoman and window, consists of an enamelled iron basin with a pail beneath it in a painted metal frame, and a single towel on the rail at the side. The dressing table, between the bed and the window, is a common pine table, covered with a cloth of many colours, with an expensive toilet mirror on it. The door is on the side nearest the bed; and there is a chest of drawers between. This chest of drawers is also covered by a variegated native cloth; and on it there is a pile of paper-backed novels, a box of chocolate creams, and a miniature easel with a large photograph of an extremely handsome officer, whose lofty bearing and magnetic glance can be felt even from the portrait. The room is lighted by a candle on the chest of drawers, and another on the dressing table with a box of matches beside it.*

The window is hinged doorwise and stands wide open. Outside, a pair of wooden shutters, opening outwards, also stand open. On the balcony a young lady, intensely conscious of the romantic beauty of the night, and of the fact that her own youth and beauty

---

1. The title comes from the first line of Virgil's *Aeneid, Arma virumque cano,* "Arms and the man I sing." The play takes place in 1885 and 1886, during the last days of the Serbo-Bulgarian War (Act I) and the ensuing Treaty of Bucharest (Acts II and III). Less than twenty years before, Bulgaria had at last achieved a measure of proud independence after five centuries of oppressive Turkish rule, although Eastern Rumelia (formerly southern Bulgaria) remained subject to the sultan. In 1885 nationalist leaders in Eastern Rumelia revolted in an attempt to unite the two Bulgarias. The neighboring kingdom of Serbia, ostensibly fearing an upset of the balance of power in the Balkans, proclaimed war, but its army was brilliantly defeated by the largely untrained Bulgarian army in November of 1885—shortly before the beginning of Shaw's play. The Bulgarians were, however, prevented from pursuing their victory by the intervention of Austria and the Treaty of Bucharest (March 3, 1886). The interest of the larger powers in Balkan affairs explains the presence of or allusion to Russian and Austrian officers in the play.

Since later printings of the play contain some inaccuracies, our text has been collated with that of the Ayot St. Lawrence edition (1930–32).

are part of it, is gazing at the snowy Balkans. She is in her night-gown, well covered by a long mantle of furs, worth, on a moderate estimate, about three times the furniture of the room.

Her reverie is interrupted by her mother, Catherine Petkoff, a woman over forty, imperiously energetic, with magnificent black hair and eyes, who might be a very splendid specimen of the wife of a mountain farmer, but is determined to be a Viennese lady, and to that end wears a fashionable tea gown on all occasions.

CATHERINE. [*entering hastily, full of good news*] Raina! [*She pronounces it Rah-eena, with the stress on the ee.*] Raina! [*She goes to the bed, expecting to find Raina there.*] Why, where—? [*Raina looks into the room*]. Heavens, child! are you out in the night air instead of in your bed? Youll catch your death. Louka told me you were asleep.

RAINA. [*dreamily*] I sent her away. I wanted to be alone. The stars are so beautiful! What is the matter?

CATHERINE. Such news! There has been a battle.

RAINA. [*her eyes dilating*] Ah! [*She comes eagerly to Catherine.*]

CATHERINE. A great battle at Slivnitza! A victory! And it was won by Sergius.

RAINA. [*with a cry of delight*] Ah! [*They embrace rapturously*] Oh, mother! [*Then, with sudden anxiety*] Is father safe?

CATHERINE. Of course: he sends me the news. Sergius is the hero of the hour, the idol of the regiment.

RAINA. Tell me, tell me. How was it? [*Ecstatically*] Oh, mother! mother! mother! [*She pulls her mother down on the ottoman; and they kiss one another frantically.*]

CATHERINE. [*with surging enthusiasm*] You cant guess how splendid it is. A cavalry charge! think of that! He defied our Russian commanders—acted without orders—led a charge on his own responsibility—headed it himself—was the first man to sweep through their guns. Cant you see it, Raina: our gallant splendid Bulgarians with their swords and eyes flashing, thundering down like an avalanche and scattering the wretched Serbs and their dandified Austrian officers like chaff. And you! you kept Sergius waiting a year before you would be betrothed to him. Oh, if you have a drop of Bulgarian blood in your veins, you will worship him when he comes back.

RAINA. What will he care for my poor little worship after the acclamations of a whole army of heroes? But no matter: I am so happy! so proud! [*She rises and walks about excitedly.*] It proves that all our ideas were real after all.

CATHERINE. [*indignantly*] Our ideas real! What do you mean?

RAINA. Our ideas of what Sergius would do. Our patriotism. Our heroic ideals. I sometimes used to doubt whether they were anything but dreams. Oh, what faithless little creatures girls are! When I buckled on Sergius's sword he looked so noble: it was treason to think of disillusion or humiliation or failure. And yet —and yet—[*She sits down again suddenly*] Promise me youll never tell him.

CATHERINE. Dont ask me for promises until I know what I'm promising.

RAINA. Well, it came into my head just as he was holding me in his arms and looking into my eyes, that perhaps we only had our heroic ideas because we are so fond of reading Byron and Pushkin,[2] and because we were so delighted with the opera that season at Bucharest. Real life is so seldom like that! indeed never, as far as I knew it then. [*Remorsefully*] Only think, mother: I doubted him: I wondered whether all his heroic qualities and his soldiership might not prove mere imagination when he went into a real battle. I had an uneasy fear that he might cut a poor figure there beside all those clever officers from the Tsar's court.

CATHERINE. A poor figure! Shame on you! The Serbs have Austrian officers who are just as clever as the Russians; but we have beaten them in every battle for all that.

RAINA. [*laughing and snuggling against her mother*] Yes: I was only a prosaic little coward. Oh, to think that it was all true! that Sergius is just as splendid and noble as he looks! that the world is really a glorious world for women who can see its glory and men who can act its romance! What happiness! what unspeakable fulfilment!

They are interrupted by the entry of Louka, a handsome proud girl in a pretty Bulgarian peasant's dress with double apron, so defiant that her servility to Raina is almost insolent. She is afraid of Catherine, but even with her goes as far as she dares.

LOUKA. If you please, madam, all the windows are to be closed and the shutters made fast. They say there may be shooting in the streets. [*Raina and Catherine rise together, alarmed.*] The Serbs are being chased right back through the pass; and they say they may run into the town. Our cavalry will be after them; and our people will be ready for them, you may be sure, now theyre running away. [*She goes out on the balcony, and pulls the outside shutters to; then steps back into the room.*]

CATHERINE. [*businesslike, housekeeping instincts aroused*] I must see that everything is made safe downstairs.

RAINA. I wish our people were not so cruel. What glory is there in killing wretched fugitives?

CATHERINE. Cruel! Do you suppose they would hesitate to kill you —or worse?

RAINA. [*to Louka*] Leave the shutters so that I can just close them if I hear any noise.

CATHERINE. [*authoritatively, turning on her way to the door*] Oh no, dear: you must keep them fastened. You would be sure to drop off to sleep and leave them open. Make them fast, Louka.

LOUKA. Yes, madam. [*She fastens them.*]

RAINA. Dont be anxious about me. The moment I hear a shot, I shall blow out the candles and roll myself up in bed with my ears well covered.

---

2. Alexander Pushkin (1799–1837), generally recognized as the great Russian Romantic poet; he was influenced by Byron.

CATHERINE. Quite the wisest thing you can do, my love. Goodnight.

RAINA. Goodnight. [*Her emotion comes back for a moment.*] Wish me joy [*They kiss.*] This is the happiest night of my life—if only there are no fugitives.

CATHERINE. Go to bed, dear; and dont think of them. [*She goes out.*]

LOUKA. [*secretly to Raina*] If you would like the shutters open, just give them a push like this [*she pushes them: they open: she pulls them to again*]. One of them ought to be bolted at the bottom; but the bolt's gone.

RAINA. [*with dignity, reproving her*] Thanks, Louka; but we must do what we are told. [*Louka makes a grimace.*] Goodnight.

LOUKA. [*carelessly*] Goodnight. [*She goes out, swaggering.*]

Raina, left alone, takes off her fur cloak and throws it on the ottoman. Then she goes to the chest of drawers, and adores the portrait there with feelings that are beyond all expression. She does not kiss it or press it to her breast, or shew it any mark of bodily affection; but she takes it in her hands and elevates it, like a priestess.

RAINA. [*looking up at the picture*] Oh, I shall never be unworthy of you any more, my soul's hero: never, never, never. [*She replaces it reverently. Then she selects a novel from the little pile of books. She turns over the leaves dreamily; finds her page; turns the book inside out at it; and, with a happy sigh, gets into bed and prepares to read herself to sleep. But before abandoning herself to fiction, she raises her eyes once more, thinking of the blessed reality, and murmurs*] My hero! my hero!

A distant shot breaks the quiet of the night. She starts, listening; and two more shots, much nearer, follow, startling her so that she scrambles out of bed, and hastily blows out the candle on the chest of drawers. Then, putting her fingers in her ears, she runs to the dressing table, blows out the light there, and hurries back to bed in the dark, nothing being visible but the glimmer of the light in the pierced ball before the image, and the starlight seen through the slits at the top of the shutters. The firing breaks out again: there is a startling fusillade quite close at hand. Whilst it is still echoing, the shutters disappear, pulled open from without; and for an instant the rectangle of snowy starlight flashes out with the figure of a man silhouetted in black upon it. The shutters close immediately; and the room is dark again. But the silence is now broken by the sound of panting. Then there is a scratch; and the flame of a match is seen in the middle of the room.

RAINA. [*crouching on the bed*] Who's there? [*The match is out instantly.*] Who's there? Who is that?

A MAN'S VOICE. [*in the darkness, subduedly, but threateningly*] Sh —sh! Dont call out; or youll be shot. Be good; and no harm will happen to you. [*She is heard leaving her bed, and making for the door.*] Take care: it's no use trying to run away.

RAINA. But who——

THE VOICE. [*warning*] Remember: if you raise your voice my revolver will go off. [*Commandingly*] Strike a light and let me see you. Do you hear. [*Another moment of silence and darkness as she retreats to the chest of drawers. Then she lights a candle; and the mystery is at an end. He is a man of about 35, in a deplorable plight, bespattered with mud and blood and snow, his belt and the strap of his revolver case keeping together the torn ruins of the blue tunic of a Serbian artillery officer. All that the candlelight and his unwashed unkempt condition make it possible to discern is that he is of middling stature and undistinguished appearance, with strong neck and shoulders, roundish obstinate looking head covered with short crisp bronze curls, clear quick eyes and good brows and mouth, hopelessly prosaic nose like that of a strong minded baby, trim soldierlike carriage and energetic manner, and with all his wits about him in spite of his desperate predicament: even with a sense of the humor of it, without, however, the least intention of trifling with it or throwing away a chance. Reckoning up what he can guess about Raina: her age, her social position, her character, and the extent to which she is frightened, he continues, more politely but still most determinedly*] Excuse my disturbing you; but you recognize my uniform? Serb! If I'm caught I shall be killed. [*Menacingly*] Do you understand that?

RAINA. Yes.

THE MAN. Well, I dont intend to get killed if I can help it. [*Still more formidably*] Do you understand that? [*He locks the door quickly but quietly.*]

RAINA. [*disdainfully*] I suppose not. [*She draws herself up superbly, and looks him straight in the face, adding, with cutting emphasis*] Some soldiers, I know, are afraid to die.

THE MAN. [*with grim goodhumor*] All of them, dear lady, all of them, believe me. It is our duty to live as long as we can. Now, if you raise an alarm—

RAINA. [*cutting him short*] You will shoot me. How do you know that I am afraid to die?

THE MAN. [*cunningly*] Ah; but suppose I dont shoot you, what will happen then? A lot of your cavalry will burst into this pretty room of yours and slaughter me here like a pig; for I'll fight like a demon: they shant get me into the street to amuse themselves with: I know what they are. Are you prepared to receive that sort of company in your present undress? [*Raina, suddenly conscious of her nightgown, instinctively shrinks and gathers it more closely about her neck. He watches her and adds pitilessly*] Hardly presentable, eh? [*She turns to the ottoman. He raises his pistol instantly, and cries*] Stop! [*She stops.*] Where are you going?

RAINA. [*with dignified patience*] Only to get my cloak.

THE MAN. [*passing swiftly to the ottoman and snatching the cloak*] A good idea! I'll keep the cloak; and youll take care that nobody comes in and sees you without it. This is a better weapon than the revolver: eh? [*He throws the pistol down on the ottoman.*]

RAINA. [*revolted*] It is not the weapon of a gentleman!

THE MAN. It's good enough for a man with only you to stand between him and death. [*As they look at one another for a moment, Raina hardly able to believe that even a Serbian officer can be so cynically and selfishly unchivalrous, they are startled by a sharp fusillade in the street. The chill of imminent death hushes the man's voice as he adds*] Do you hear? If you are going to bring those blackguards in on me you shall receive them as you are.

Clamor and disturbance. The pursuers in the street batter at the house door, shouting Open the door! Open the door! Wake up, will you! *A man servant's voice calls to them angrily from within* This is Major Petkoff's house: you cant come in here; *but a renewal of the clamor, and a torrent of blows on the door, end with his letting a chain down with a clank, followed by a rush of heavy footsteps and a din of triumphant yells, dominated at last by the voice of Catherine, indignantly addressing an officer with* What does this mean, sir? Do you know where you are? *The noise subsides suddenly.*

LOUKA. [*outside, knocking at the bedroom door*] My lady! my lady! get up quick and open the door. If you dont they will break it down.

The fugitive throws up his head with the gesture of a man who sees that it is all over with him, and drops the manner he has been assuming to intimidate Raina.

THE MAN. [*sincerely and kindly*] No use, dear: I'm done for. [*Flinging the cloak to her*] Quick! wrap yourself up: theyre coming.

RAINA. Oh, thank you. [*She wraps herself up with intense relief*].

THE MAN. [*between his teeth*] Dont mention it.

RAINA. [*anxiously*] What will you do?

THE MAN. [*grimly*] The first man in will find out. Keep out of the way; and dont look. It wont last long; but it will not be nice. [*He draws his sabre and faces the door, waiting.*]

RAINA. [*impulsively*] I'll help you. I'll save you.

THE MAN. You cant.

RAINA. I can. I'll hide you. [*She drags him towards the window*]. Here! behind the curtains.

THE MAN. [*yielding to her*] Theres just half a chance, if you keep your head.

RAINA. [*drawing the curtain before him*] S-sh! [*She makes for the ottoman.*]

THE MAN. [*putting out his head*] Remember—

RAINA. [*running back to him*] Yes?

THE MAN.—nine soldiers out of ten are born fools.

RAINA. Oh! [*She draws the curtain angrily before him.*]

THE MAN. [*looking out at the other side*] If they find me, I promise you a fight: a devil of a fight.

She stamps at him. He disappears hastily. She takes off her cloak, and throws it across the foot of the bed. Then, with a sleepy, disturbed air, she opens the door. Louka enters excitedly.

LOUKA. One of those beasts of Serbs has been seen climbing up the waterpipe to your balcony. Our men want to search for him; and they are so wild and drunk and furious. [*She makes for the other side of the room to get as far from the door as possible.*] My lady says you are to dress at once and to—[*She sees the revolver lying on the ottoman, and stops, petrified.*]

RAINA. [*as if annoyed at being disturbed*] They shall not search here. Why have they been let in?

CATHERINE. [*coming in hastily*] Raina, darling, are you safe? Have you seen anyone or heard anything?

RAINA. I heard the shooting. Surely the soldiers will not dare come in here?

CATHERINE. I have found a Russian officer, thank Heaven: he knows Sergius. [*Speaking through the door to someone outside*] Sir: will you come in now. My daughter will receive you.

A young Russian officer, in Bulgarian uniform, enters, sword in hand.

OFFICER. [*with soft feline politeness and stiff military carriage*] Good evening, gracious lady. I am sorry to intrude; but there is a Serb hiding on the balcony. Will you and the gracious lady your mother please to withdraw whilst we search?

RAINA. [*petulantly*] Nonsense, sir: you can see that there is no one on the balcony. [*She throws the shutters wide open and stands with her back to the curtain where the man is hidden, pointing to the moonlit balcony. A couple of shots are fired right under the window; and a bullet shatters the glass opposite Raina, who winks and gasps, but stands her ground; whilst Catherine screams, and the officer, with a cry of* Take care! *rushes to the balcony.*]

THE OFFICER. [*on the balcony, shouting savagely down to the street*] Cease firing there, you fools: do you hear? Cease firing, damn you! [*He glares down for a moment; then turns to Raina, trying to resume his polite manner.*] Could anyone have got in without your knowledge? Were you asleep?

RAINA. No: I have not been to bed.

THE OFFICER. [*impatiently, coming back into the room*] Your neighbors have their heads so full of runaway Serbs that they see them everywhere. [*Politely*] Gracious lady: a thousand pardons. Goodnight. [*Military bow, which Raina returns coldly. Another to Catherine, who follows him out.*]

Raina closes the shutters. She turns and sees Louka, who has been watching the scene curiously.

RAINA. Dont leave my mother, Louka, until the soldiers go away.

Louka glances at Raina, at the ottoman, at the curtain; then purses her lips secretively, laughs insolently, and goes out. Raina, highly offended by this demonstration, follows her to the door, and shuts it behind her with a slam, locking it violently. The man immediately steps out from behind the curtain, sheathing his sabre. Then, dismissing the danger from his mind in a businesslike way, he comes affably to Raina.

THE MAN. A narrow shave; but a miss is as good as a mile. Dear young lady: your servant to the death. I wish for your sake I had joined the Bulgarian army instead of the other one. I am not a native Serb.

RAINA. [*haughtily*] No: you are one of the Austrians who set the Serbs on to rob us of our national liberty, and who officer their army for them. We hate them!

THE MAN. Austrian! not I. Dont hate me, dear young lady. I am a Swiss, fighting merely as a professional soldier. I joined the Serbs because they came first on the road from Switzerland. Be generous: youve beaten us hollow.

RAINA. Have I not been generous?

THE MAN. Noble! Heroic! But I'm not saved yet. This particular rush will soon pass through; but the pursuit will go on all night by fits and starts. I must take my chance to get off in a quiet interval. [*Pleasantly*] You dont mind my waiting just a minute or two, do you?

RAINA. [*putting on her most genteel society manner*] Oh, not at all. Wont you sit down?

THE MAN. Thanks. [*He sits on the foot of the bed.*]

Raina walks with studied elegance to the ottoman and sits down. Unfortunately she sits on the pistol, and jumps up with a shriek. The man, all nerves, shies like a frightened horse to the other side of the room.

THE MAN. [*irritably*] Dont frighten me like that. What is it?

RAINA. Your revolver! It was staring that officer in the face all the time. What an escape!

THE MAN. [*vexed at being unnecessarily terrified*] Oh, is that all?

RAINA. [*staring at him rather superciliously as she conceives a poorer and poorer opinion of him, and feels proportionately more and more at her ease*] I am sorry I frightened you. [*She takes up the pistol and hands it to him.*] Pray take it to protect yourself against me.

THE MAN. [*grinning wearily at the sarcasm as he takes the pistol*] No use, dear young lady: theres nothing in it. It's not loaded. [*He makes a grimace at it, and drops it disparagingly into his revolver case.*]

RAINA. Load it by all means.

THE MAN. Ive no ammunition. What use are cartridges in battle? I always carry chocolate instead; and I finished the last cake of that hours ago.

RAINA. [*outraged in her most cherished ideals of manhood*] Chocolate! Do you stuff your pockets with sweets—like a schoolboy—even in the field?

THE MAN. [*grinning*] Yes: isnt it contemptible? [*Hungrily*] I wish I had some now.

RAINA. Allow me. [*She sails away scornfully to the chest of drawers, and returns with the box of confectionery in her hand.*] I am sorry I have eaten them all except these. [*She offers him the box.*]

THE MAN. [*ravenously*] Youre an angel! [*He gobbles the contents.*] Creams! Delicious! [*He looks anxiously to see whether there are any more. There are none: he can only scrape the box with his fingers and suck them. When that nourishment is exhausted he accepts the inevitable with pathetic goodhumor, and says, with grateful emotion*] Bless you, dear lady! You can always tell an old soldier by the inside of his holsters and cartridge boxes. The young ones carry pistols and cartridges: the old ones, grub. Thank you. [*He hands back the box. She snatches it contemptuously from him and throws it away. He shies again, as if she had meant to strike him.*] Ugh! Dont do things so suddenly, gracious lady. It's mean to revenge yourself because I frightened you just now.

RAINA. [*loftily*] Frighten me! Do you know, sir, that though I am only a woman, I think I am at heart as brave as you.

THE MAN. I should think so. You havnt been under fire for three days as I have. I can stand two days without shewing it much; but no man can stand three days: I'm as nervous as a mouse. [*He sits down on the ottoman, and takes his head in his hands.*] Would you like to see me cry?

RAINA. [*alarmed*] No.

THE MAN. If you would, all you have to do is to scold me just as if I were a little boy and you my nurse. If I were in camp now, theyd play all sorts of tricks on me.

RAINA. [*a little moved*] I'm sorry. I wont scold you. [*Touched by the sympathy in her tone, he raises his head and looks gratefully at her: she immediately draws back and says stiffly*] You must excuse me: our soldiers are not like that. [*She moves away from the ottoman.*]

THE MAN. Oh yes they are. There are only two sorts of soldiers: old ones and young ones. Ive served fourteen years: half of your fellows never smelt powder before. Why, how is it that youve just beaten us? Sheer ignorance of the art of war, nothing else. [*Indignantly*] I never saw anything so unprofessional.

RAINA. [*ironically*] Oh! was it unprofessional to beat you?

THE MAN. Well, come! is it professional to throw a regiment of cavalry on a battery of machine guns, with the dead certainty that if the guns go off not a horse or man will ever get within fifty yards of the fire? I couldnt believe my eyes when I saw it.

RAINA. [*eagerly turning to him, as all her enthusiasm and her dreams of glory rush back on her*] Did you see the great cavalry charge? Oh, tell me about it. Describe it to me.

THE MAN. You never saw a cavalry charge, did you?

RAINA. How could I?

THE MAN. Ah, perhaps not. No: of course not! Well, it's a funny sight. It's like slinging a handful of peas against a window pane: first one comes; then two or three close behind him; and then all the rest in a lump.

RAINA. [*her eyes dilating as she raises her clasped hands ecstatically*] Yes, first One! the bravest of the brave!

THE MAN. [*prosaically*] Hm! you should see the poor devil pulling at his horse.

RAINA. Why should he pull at his horse?

THE MAN. [*impatient of so stupid a question*] It's running away with him, of course: do you suppose the fellow wants to get there before the others and be killed? Then they all come. You can tell the young ones by their wildness and their slashing. The old ones come bunched up under the number one guard: they know that theyre mere projectiles, and that it's no use trying to fight. The wounds are mostly broken knees, from the horses cannoning together.

RAINA. Ugh! But I dont believe the first man is a coward. I know he is a hero!

THE MAN. [*goodhumoredly*] Thats what youd have said if youd seen the first man in the charge today.

RAINA. [*breathless, forgiving him everything*] Ah, I knew it! Tell me. Tell me about him.

THE MAN. He did it like an operatic tenor. A regular handsome fellow, with flashing eyes and lovely moustache, shouting his war-cry and charging like Don Quixote at the windmills. We did laugh.

RAINA. You dared to laugh!

THE MAN. Yes; but when the sergeant ran up as white as a sheet, and told us theyd sent us the wrong ammunition, and that we couldnt fire a round for the next ten minutes, we laughed at the other side of our mouths. I never felt so sick in my life; though Ive been in one or two very tight places. And I hadnt even a revolver cartridge: only chocolate. We'd no bayonets: nothing. Of course, they just cut us to bits. And there was Don Quixote flourishing like a drum major, thinking he'd done the cleverest thing ever known, whereas he ought to be courtmartialled for it. Of all the fools ever let loose on a field of battle, that man must be the very maddest. He and his regiment simply committed suicide; only the pistol missed fire: thats all.

RAINA. [*deeply wounded, but steadfastly loyal to her ideals*] Indeed! Would you know him again if you saw him?

THE MAN. Shall I ever forget him!

She again goes to the chest of drawers. He watches her with a vague hope that she may have something more for him to eat. She takes the portrait from its stand and brings it to him.

RAINA. That is a photograph of the gentleman—the patriot and hero—to whom I am betrothed.

THE MAN. [*recognizing it with a shock*] I'm really very sorry. [*Looking at her*] Was it fair to lead me on? [*He looks at the portrait again*] Yes: thats Don Quixote: not a doubt of it. [*He stifles a laugh.*]

RAINA. [*quickly*] Why do you laugh?

THE MAN. [*apologetic, but still greatly tickled*] I didnt laugh, I assure you. At least I didnt mean to. But when I think of him charging the windmills and imagining he was doing the finest thing—[*He chokes with suppressed laughter.*]

RAINA. [*sternly*] Give me back the portrait, sir.

THE MAN. [*with sincere remorse*] Of course. Certainly. I'm really very sorry. [*He hands her the picture. She deliberately kisses it and looks him straight in the face before returning to the chest of drawers to replace it. He follows her, apologizing.*] Perhaps

I'm quite wrong, you know: no doubt I am. Most likely he had got wind of the cartridge business somehow, and knew it was a safe job.

RAINA. That is to say, he was a pretender and a coward! You did not dare say that before.

THE MAN. [*with a comic gesture of despair*] It's no use, dear lady: I cant make you see it from the professional point of view. [*As he turns away to get back to the ottoman, a couple of distant shots threaten renewed trouble.*]

RAINA. [*sternly, as she sees him listening to the shots*] So much the better for you!

THE MAN. [*turning*] How?

RAINA. You are my enemy; and you are at my mercy. What would I do if I were a professional soldier?

THE MAN. Ah, true, dear young lady: youre always right. I know how good youve been to me: to my last hour I shall remember those three chocolate creams. It was unsoldierly; but it was angelic.

RAINA. [*coldly*] Thank you. And now I will do a soldierly thing. You cannot stay here after what you have just said about my future husband; but I will go out on the balcony and see whether it is safe for you to climb down into the street. [*She turns to the window.*]

THE MAN. [*changing countenance*] Down that waterpipe! Stop! Wait! I cant! I darent! The very thought of it makes me giddy. I came up it fast enough with death behind me. But to face it now in cold blood—! [*He sinks on the ottoman.*] It's no use: I give up: I'm beaten. Give the alarm. [*He drops his head on his hands in the deepest dejection.*]

RAINA. [*disarmed by pity*] Come: dont be disheartened. [*She stoops over him almost maternally: he shakes his head.*] Oh, you are a very poor soldier: a chocolate cream soldier! Come, cheer up! it takes less courage to climb down than to face capture: remember that.

THE MAN. [*dreamily, lulled by her voice*] No: capture only means death; and death is sleep: oh, sleep, sleep, sleep, undisturbed sleep! Climbing down the pipe means doing something—exerting myself—thinking! Death ten times over first.

RAINA. [*softly and wonderingly, catching the rhythm of his weariness*] Are you as sleepy as that?

THE MAN. Ive not had two hours undisturbed sleep since I joined. I havnt closed my eyes for forty-eight hours.

RAINA. [*at her wit's end*] But what am I to do with you?

THE MAN. [*staggering up, roused by her desperation*] Of course. I must do something. [*He shakes himself; pulls himself together; and speaks with rallied vigor and courage.*] You see, sleep or no sleep, hunger or no hunger, tired or not tired, you can always do a thing when you know it must be done. Well, that pipe must be got down: [*he hits himself on the chest*] do you hear that, you chocolate cream soldier? [*He turns to the window.*]

RAINA. [*anxiously*] But if you fall?

THE MAN. I shall sleep as if the stones were a feather bed. Goodbye. [*He makes boldly for the window; and his hand is on the shutter when there is a terrible burst of firing in the street beneath.*]

RAINA. [*rushing to him*] Stop! [*She seizes him recklessly, and pulls him quite round.*] Theyll kill you.

THE MAN. [*coolly, but attentively*] Never mind: this sort of thing is all in my day's work. I'm bound to take my chance. [*Decisively*] Now do what I tell you. Put out the candle; so that they shant see the light when I open the shutters. And keep away from the window, whatever you do. If they see me theyre sure to have a shot at me.

RAINA. [*clinging to him*] Theyre sure to see you: it's bright moonlight. I'll save you. Oh, how can you be so indifferent! You want me to save you, dont you?

THE MAN. I really dont want to be troublesome. [*She shakes him in her impatience.*] I am not indifferent, dear young lady, I assure you. But how is it to be done?

RAINA. Come away from the window. [*She takes him firmly back to the middle of the room. The moment she releases him he turns mechanically towards the window again. She seizes him and turns him back, exclaiming*] Please! [*He becomes motionless, like a hypnotized rabbit, his fatigue gaining fast on him. She releases him, and addresses him patronizingly.*] Now listen. You must trust to our hospitality. You do not yet know in whose house you are. I am a Petkoff.

THE MAN. A pet what?

RAINA. [*rather indignantly*] I mean that I belong to the family of the Petkoffs, the richest and best known in our country.

THE MAN. Oh yes, of course. I beg your pardon. The Petkoffs, to be sure. How stupid of me!

RAINA. You know you never heard of them until this moment. How can you stoop to pretend!

THE MAN. Forgive me: I'm too tired to think; and the change of subject was too much for me. Dont scold me.

RAINA. I forgot. It might make you cry. [*He nods, quite seriously. She pouts and then resumes her patronizing tone.*] I must tell you that my father holds the highest command of any Bulgarian in our army. He is [*proudly*] a Major.

THE MAN. [*pretending to be deeply impressed*] A Major! Bless me! Think of that!

RAINA. You shewed great ignorance in thinking that it was necessary to climb up to the balcony because ours is the only private house that has two rows of windows. There is a flight of stairs inside to get up and down by.

THE MAN. Stairs! How grand! You live in great luxury indeed, dear young lady.

RAINA. Do you know what a library is?

THE MAN. A library? A roomful of books?

RAINA. Yes. We have one, the only one in Bulgaria.

THE MAN. Actually a real library! I should like to see that.

RAINA. [*affectedly*] I tell you these things to shew you that you are not in the house of ignorant country folk who would kill you the moment they saw your Serbian uniform, but among civilized people. We go to Bucharest every year for the opera season; and I have spent a whole month in Vienna.

THE MAN. I saw that, dear young lady. I saw at once that you knew the world.

RAINA. Have you ever seen the opera of Ernani?[3]

THE MAN. Is that the one with the devil in it in red velvet, and a soldiers' chorus?

RAINA. [*contemptuously*] No!

THE MAN. [*stifling a heavy sigh of weariness*] Then I dont know it.

RAINA. I thought you might have remembered the great scene where Ernani, flying from his foes just as you are tonight, takes refuge in the castle of his bitterest enemy, an old Castilian noble. The noble refuses to give him up. His guest is sacred to him.

THE MAN. [*quickly, waking up a little*] Have your people got that notion?

RAINA. [*with dignity*] My mother and I can understand that notion, as you call it. And if instead of threatening me with your pistol as you did you had simply thrown yourself as a fugitive on our hospitality, you would have been as safe as in your father's house.

THE MAN. Quite sure?

RAINA. [*turning her back on him in disgust*] Oh, it is useless to try to make you understand.

THE MAN. Dont be angry: you see how awkward it would be for me if there was any mistake. My father is a very hospitable man: he keeps six hotels; but I couldnt trust him as far as that. What about your father?

RAINA. He is away at Slivnitza fighting for his country. I answer for your safety. There is my hand in pledge of it. Will that reassure you? [*She offers him her hand.*]

THE MAN. [*looking dubiously at his own hand*] Better not touch my hand, dear young lady. I must have a wash first.

RAINA. [*touched*] That is very nice of you. I see that you are a gentleman.

THE MAN. [*puzzled*] Eh?

RAINA. You must not think I am surprised. Bulgarians of really good standing—people in our position—wash their hands nearly every day. So you see I can appreciate your delicacy. You may take my hand. [*She offers it again.*]

THE MAN. [*kissing it with his hands behind his back*] Thanks, gracious young lady: I feel safe at last. And now would you mind breaking the news to your mother? I had better not stay here secretly longer than is necessary.

RAINA. If you will be so good as to keep perfectly still whilst I am away.

THE MAN. Certainly. [*He sits down on the ottoman.*]

    Raina goes to the bed and wraps herself in the fur cloak. His eyes

3. Opera by Verdi, first produced in 1844, based on Victor Hugo's tragedy *Hernani*.

close. She goes to the door. Turning for a last look at him, she sees that he is dropping off to sleep.

RAINA. [*at the door*] You are not going asleep, are you? [*He murmurs inarticulately: she runs to him and shakes him.*] Do you hear? Wake up: you are falling asleep.

THE MAN. Eh? Falling aslee—? Oh no: not the least in the world: I was only thinking. It's all right: I'm wide awake.

RAINA. [*severely*] Will you please stand up while I am away. [*He rises reluctantly.*] All the time, mind.

THE MAN. [*standing unsteadily*] Certainly. Certainly: you may depend on me.

Raina looks doubtfully at him. He smiles weakly. She goes reluctantly, turning again at the door, and almost catching him in the act of yawning. She goes out.

THE MAN. [*drowsily*] Sleep, sleep, sleep, sleep, slee—[*The words trail off into a murmur. He wakes again with a shock on the point of falling.*] Where am I? Thats what I want to know: where am I? Must keep awake. Nothing keeps me awake except danger: remember that: [*intently*] danger, danger, danger, dan—[*trailing off again: another shock*] Wheres danger? Mus' find it. [*He starts off vaguely round the room in search of it*] What am I looking for? Sleep—danger—dont know. [*He stumbles against the bed.*] Ah yes: now I know. All right now. I'm to go to bed, but not to sleep. Be sure not to sleep, because of danger. Not to lie down either, only sit down. [*He sits on the bed. A blissful expression comes into his face.*] Ah! [*With a happy sigh he sinks back at full length; lifts his boots into the bed with a final effort; and falls fast asleep instantly.*]

Catherine comes in, followed by Raina.

RAINA. [*looking at the ottoman*] He's gone! I left him here.

CATHERINE. Here! Then he must have climbed down from the—

RAINA. [*seeing him*] Oh! [*She points.*]

CATHERINE. [*scandalized*] Well! [*She strides to the bed, Raina following until she is opposite her on the other side.*] He's fast asleep. The brute!

RAINA. [*anxiously*] Sh!

CATHERINE. [*shaking him*] Sir! [*Shaking him again, harder*] Sir!! [*Vehemently, shaking very hard*] Sir!!!

RAINA. [*catching her arm*] Dont, mamma; the poor darling is worn out. Let him sleep.

CATHERINE. [*letting him go, and turning amazed to Raina*] The poor darling! Raina!!! [*She looks sternly at her daughter.*] *The man sleeps profoundly.*

Act II

The sixth of March, 1886. In the garden of Major Petkoff's house. It is a fine spring morning: the garden looks fresh and pretty. Beyond the paling the tops of a couple of minarets can be seen, shewing that there is a valley there, with the little town in it. A few miles further the Balkan mountains rise and shut in the land-

scape. Looking towards them from within the garden, the side of the house is seen on the left, with a garden door reached by a little flight of steps. On the right the stable yard, with its gateway, encroaches on the garden. There are fruit bushes along the paling and house, covered with washing spread out to dry. A path runs by the house, and rises by two steps at the corner, where it turns out of sight. In the middle, a small table, with two bent wood chairs at it, is laid for breakfast with Turkish coffee pot, cups, rolls, etc.; but the cups have been used and the bread broken. There is a wooden garden seat against the wall on the right.

Louka, smoking a cigaret, is standing between the table and the house, turning her back with angry disdain on a man servant who is lecturing her. He is a middle-aged man of cool temperament and low but clear and keen intelligence, with the complacency of the servant who values himself on his rank in servitude, and the imperturbability of the accurate calculator who has no illusions. He wears a white Bulgarian costume: jacket with embroidered border, sash, wide knickerbockers, and decorated gaiters. His head is shaved up to the crown, giving him a high Japanese forehead. His name is Nicola.

NICOLA. Be warned in time, Louka: mend your manners. I know the mistress. She is so grand that she never dreams that any servant could dare be disrespectful to her; but if she once suspects that you are defying her, out you go.

LOUKA. I do defy her. I will defy her. What do I care for her?

NICOLA. If you quarrel with the family, I never can marry you. It's the same as if you quarrelled with me!

LOUKA. You take her part against me, do you?

NICOLA. [*sedately*] I shall always be dependent on the good will of the family. When I leave their service and start a shop in Sofia, their custom will be half my capital: their bad word would ruin me.

LOUKA. You have no spirit. I should like to catch them saying a word against me!

NICOLA. [*pityingly*] I should have expected more sense from you, Louka. But youre young: youre young!

LOUKA. Yes; and you like me the better for it, dont you? But I know some family secrets they wouldnt care to have told, young as I am. Let them quarrel with me if they dare!

NICOLA. [*with compassionate superiority*] Do you know what they would do if they heard you talk like that?

LOUKA. What could they do?

NICOLA. Discharge you for untruthfulness. Who would believe any stories you told after that? Who would give you another situation? Who in this house would dare be seen speaking to you ever again? How long would your father be left on his little farm? [*She impatiently throws away the end of her cigaret, and stamps on it.*] Child: you dont know the power such high people have over the like of you and me when we try to rise out of our poverty against them. [*He goes close to her and lowers his voice.*] Look at me, ten years in their service. Do you think I know no secrets? I know things about the mistress that she wouldnt have the master know for a thousand levas.[4] I know things about him that she wouldnt let him hear the last of for six months if I blabbed them to her. I know things about Raina that would break off her match with Sergius if—

LOUKA. [*turning on him quickly*] How do you know? I never told you!

NICOLA. [*opening his eyes cunningly*] So thats your little secret, is it? I thought it might be something like that. Well, you take my advice and be respectful; and make the mistress feel that no matter what you know or dont know, she can depend on you to hold your tongue and serve the family faithfully. Thats what they like; and thats how youll make most out of them.

LOUKA. [*with searching scorn*] You have the soul of a servant, Nicola.

NICOLA. [*complacently*] Yes: thats the secret of success in service.

A loud knocking with a whip handle on a wooden door is heard from the stable yard.

MALE VOICE OUTSIDE. Hollo! Hollo there! Nicola!

LOUKA. Master! back from the war!

NICOLA. [*quickly*] My word for it, Louka, the war's over. Off with you and get some fresh coffee. [*He runs out into the stable yard.*]

LOUKA. [*as she collects the coffee pot and cups on the tray, and carries it into the house*] Youll never put the soul of a servant into me.

Major Petkoff comes from the stable yard, followed by Nicola. He is a cheerful, excitable, insignificant, unpolished man of about 50, naturally unambitious except as to his income and his importance in local society, but just now greatly pleased with the military rank which the war has thrust on him as a man of consequence in his town. The fever of plucky patriotism which the Serbian attack roused in all the Bulgarians has pulled him through the war; but he is obviously glad to be home again.

PETKOFF. [*pointing to the table with his whip*] Breakfast out here, eh?

NICOLA. Yes, sir. The mistress and Miss Raina have just gone in.

PETKOFF. [*sitting down and taking a roll*] Go in and say Ive come; and get me some fresh coffee.

NICOLA. It's coming, sir. [*He goes to the house door. Louka, with fresh coffee, a clean cup, and a brandy bottle on her tray, meets him.*] Have you told the mistress?

LOUKA. Yes: she's coming.

Nicola goes into the house. Louka brings the coffee to the table.

PETKOFF. Well: the Serbs havnt run away with you, have they?

LOUKA. No, sir.

PETKOFF. Thats right. Have you brought me some cognac?

LOUKA. [*putting the bottle on the table*] Here, sir.

PETKOFF. Thats right. [*He pours some into his coffee.*]

4. The *lev* was the Bulgarian monetary unit, equal to about a cent (Shaw apparently thought the plural, *leva*, was the singular).

Catherine, who, having at this early hour made only a very perfunctory toilet, wears a Bulgarian apron over a once brilliant but now half worn-out dressing gown, and a colored handkerchief tied over her thick black hair, comes from the house with Turkish slippers on her bare feet, looking astonishingly handsome and stately under all the circumstances. Louka goes into the house.

CATHERINE. My dear Paul: what a surprise for us! [*She stoops over the back of his chair to kiss him.*] Have they brought you fresh coffee?

PETKOFF. Yes: Louka's been looking after me. The war's over. The treaty was signed three days ago at Bucharest; and the decree for our army to demobilize was issued yesterday.

CATHERINE. [*springing erect, with flashing eyes*] Paul: have you let the Austrians force you to make peace?

PETKOFF. [*submissively*] My dear: they didnt consult me. What could I do? [*She sits down and turns away from him.*] But of course we saw to it that the treaty was an honorable one. It declares peace—

CATHERINE. [*outraged*] Peace!

PETKOFF. [*appeasing her*]—but not friendly relations: remember that. They wanted to put that in; but I insisted on its being struck out. What more could I do?

CATHERINE. You could have annexed Serbia and made Prince Alexander[5] Emperor of the Balkans. Thats what I would have done.

PETKOFF. I dont doubt it in the least, my dear. But I should have had to subdue the whole Austrian Empire first; and that would have kept me too long away from you. I missed you greatly.

CATHERINE. [*relenting*] Ah! [*She stretches her hand affectionately across the table to squeeze his.*]

PETKOFF. And how have you been, my dear?

CATHERINE. Oh, my usual sore throats: thats all.

PETKOFF. [*with conviction*] That comes from washing your neck every day. Ive often told you so.

CATHERINE. Nonsense, Paul!

PETKOFF. [*over his coffee and cigaret*] I dont believe in going too far with these modern customs. All this washing cant be good for the health: it's not natural. There was an Englishman at Philippopolis who used to wet himself all over with cold water every morning when he got up. Disgusting! It all comes from the English: their climate makes them so dirty that they have to be perpetually washing themselves. Look at my father! he never had a bath in his life; and he lived to be ninety-eight, the healthiest man in Bulgaria. I dont mind a good wash once a week to keep up my position; but once a day is carrying the thing to a ridiculous extreme.

CATHERINE. You are a barbarian at heart still, Paul. I hope you behaved yourself before all those Russian officers.

PETKOFF. I did my best. I took care to let them know that we have a library.

5. Prince Alexander of Battenberg, first elected ruler of Bulgaria (reigned 1879–86).

CATHERINE. Ah; but you didnt tell them that we have an electric bell in it? I have had one put up.

PETKOFF. Whats an electric bell?

CATHERINE. You touch a button; something tinkles in the kitchen; and then Nicola comes up.

PETKOFF. Why not shout for him?

CATHERINE. Civilized people never shout for their servants. Ive learnt that while you were away.

PETKOFF. Well, I'll tell you something Ive learnt too. Civilized people dont hang out their washing to dry where visitors can see it; so youd better have all that [*indicating the clothes on the bushes*] put somewhere else.

CATHERINE. Oh, thats absurd, Paul: I dont believe really refined people notice such things.

SERGIUS. [*knocking at the stable gates*] Gate, Nicola!

PETKOFF. Theres Sergius. [*Shouting*] Hollo, Nicola!

CATHERINE. Oh, dont shout, Paul: it really isnt nice.

PETKOFF. Bosh! [*He shouts louder than before*] Nicola!

NICOLA. [*appearing at the house door*] Yes, sir.

PETKOFF. Are you deaf? Dont you hear Major Saranoff knocking? Bring him round this way. [*He pronounces the name with the stress on the second syllable: Sarahnoff*].

NICOLA. Yes, major. [*He goes into the stable yard.*]

PETKOFF. You must talk to him, my dear, until Raina takes him off our hands. He bores my life out about our not promoting him. Over my head, if you please.

CATHERINE. He certainly ought to be promoted when he marries Raina. Besides, the country should insist on having at least one native general.

PETKOFF. Yes; so that he could throw away whole brigades instead of regiments. It's no use, my dear: he hasnt the slightest chance of promotion until we're quite sure that the peace will be a lasting one.

NICOLA. [*at the gate, announcing*] Major Sergius Saranoff! [*He goes into the house and returns presently with a third chair, which he places at the table. He then withdraws.*]

Major Sergius Saranoff, the original of the portrait in Raina's room, is a tall romantically handsome man, with the physical hardihood, the high spirit, and the susceptible imagination of an untamed mountaineer chieftain. But his remarkable personal distinction is of a characteristically civilized type. The ridges of his eyebrows, curving with an interrogative twist round the projections at the outer corners; his jealously observant eye; his nose, thin, keen, and apprehensive in spite of the pugnacious high bridge and large nostril; his assertive chin would not be out of place in a Parisian salon, shewing that the clever imaginative barbarian has an acute critical faculty which has been thrown into intense activity by the arrival of western civilization in the Balkans. The result is precisely what the advent of nineteenth century thought first produced in England: to wit, Byronism. By his brooding on the perpetual failure, not only of others, but of himself, to live up to his ideals; by his consequent cynical scorn for humanity; by his jejune credulity as to the absolute validity of his concepts and the unworthiness of the world in disregarding them; by his wincings and mockeries under the sting of the petty disillusions which every hour spent among men brings to his sensitive observation, he has acquired the half tragic, half ironic air, the mysterious moodiness, the suggestion of a strange and terrible history that has left nothing but undying remorse, by which Childe Harold[6] fascinated the grandmothers of his English contemporaries. It is clear that here or nowhere is Raina's ideal hero. Catherine is hardly less enthusiastic about him than her daughter, and much less reserved in shewing her enthusiasm. As he enters from the stable gate, she rises effusively to greet him. Petkoff is distinctly less disposed to make a fuss about him.

PETKOFF. Here already, Sergius! Glad to see you.

CATHERINE. My dear Sergius! [She holds out both her hands.]

SERGIUS. [kissing them with scrupulous gallantry] My dear mother, if I may call you so.

PETKOFF. [drily] Mother-in-law, Sergius: mother-in-law! Sit down; and have some coffee.

SERGIUS. Thank you: none for me. [He gets away from the table with a certain distaste for Petkoff's enjoyment of it, and posts himself with conscious dignity against the rail of the steps leading to the house.]

CATHERINE. You look superb. The campaign has improved you, Sergius. Everybody here is mad about you. We were all wild with enthusiasm about that magnificent cavalry charge.

SERGIUS. [with grave irony] Madam: it was the cradle and the grave of my military reputation.

CATHERINE. How so?

SERGIUS. I won the battle the wrong way when our worthy Russian generals were losing it the right way. In short, I upset their plans, and wounded their self-esteem. Two Cossack colonels had their regiments routed on the most correct principles of scientific warfare. Two major-generals got killed strictly according to military etiquette. The two colonels are now major-generals; and I am still a simple major.

CATHERINE. You shall not remain so, Sergius. The women are on your side; and they will see that justice is done you.

SERGIUS. It is too late. I have only waited for the peace to send in my resignation.

PETKOFF. [dropping his cup in his amazement] Your resignation!

CATHERINE. Oh, you must withdraw it!

SERGIUS. [with resolute measured emphasis, folding his arms] I never withdraw.

PETKOFF. [vexed] Now who could have supposed you were going to do such a thing?

---

6. Hero of Byron's famous travel poem, *Childe Harold* (1812, 1816, 1818), an epitome of the Romantic Man of Feeling.

SERGIUS. [*with fire*] Everyone that knew me. But enough of myself and my affairs. How is Raina; and where is Raina?

RAINA. [*suddenly coming round the corner of the house and standing at the top of the steps in the path*] Raina is here.

She makes a charming picture as they turn to look at her. She wears an underdress of pale green silk, draped with an overdress of thin ecru canvas embroidered with gold. She is crowned with a dainty eastern cap of gold tinsel. Sergius goes impulsively to meet her. Posing regally, she presents her hand: he drops chivalrously on one knee and kisses it.

PETKOFF. [*aside to Catherine, beaming with parental pride*] Pretty, isnt it? She always appears at the right moment.

CATHERINE. [*impatiently*] Yes; she listens for it. It is an abominable habit.

Sergius leads Raina forward with splendid gallantry. When they arrive at the table, she turns to him with a bend of the head: he bows; and thus they separate, he coming to his place and she going behind her father's chair.

RAINA. [*stooping and kissing her father*] Dear father! Welcome home!

PETKOFF. [*patting her cheek*] My little pet girl. [*He kisses her. She goes to the chair left by Nicola for Sergius, and sits down.*]

CATHERINE. And so youre no longer a soldier, Sergius.

SERGIUS. I am no longer a soldier. Soldiering, my dear madam, is the coward's art of attacking mercilessly when you are strong, and keeping out of harm's way when you are weak. That is the whole secret of successful fighting. Get your enemy at a disadvantage; and never, on any account, fight him on equal terms.

PETKOFF. They wouldnt let us make a fair stand-up fight of it. However, I suppose soldiering has to be a trade like any other trade.

SERGIUS. Precisely. But I have no ambition to shine as a tradesman; so I have taken the advice of that bagman of a captain that settled the exchange of prisoners with us at Pirot, and given it up.

PETKOFF. What! that Swiss fellow? Sergius: Ive often thought of that exchange since. He over-reached us about those horses.

SERGIUS. Of course he over-reached us. His father was a hotel and livery stable keeper; and he owed his first step to his knowledge of horse-dealing. [*With mock enthusiasm*] Ah, he was a soldier: every inch a soldier! If only I had bought the horses for my regiment instead of foolishly leading it into danger, I should have been a field-marshal now!

CATHERINE. A Swiss? What was he doing in the Serbian army?

PETKOFF. A volunteer, of course: keen on picking up his profession. [*Chuckling*] We shouldnt have been able to begin fighting if these foreigners hadnt shewn us how to do it: we knew nothing about it; and neither did the Serbs. Egad, thered have been no war without them!

RAINA. Are there many Swiss officers in the Serbian Army?

PETKOFF. No. All Austrians, just as our officers were all Russians. This was the only Swiss I came across. I'll never trust a Swiss again. He humbugged us into giving him fifty ablebodied men for two hundred worn out chargers. They werent even eatable!

SERGIUS. We were two children in the hands of that consummate soldier, major: simply two innocent little children.

RAINA. What was he like?

CATHERINE. Oh, Raina, what a silly question!

SERGIUS. He was like a commercial traveller in uniform. Bourgeois to his boots!

PETKOFF. [*grinning*] Sergius: tell Catherine that queer story his friend told us about how he escaped after Slivnitza. You remember. About his being hid by two women.

SERGIUS. [*with bitter irony*] Oh yes: quite a romance! He was serving in the very battery I so unprofessionally charged. Being a thorough soldier, he ran away like the rest of them, with our cavalry at his heels. To escape their sabres he climbed a waterpipe and made his way into the bedroom of a young Bulgarian lady. The young lady was enchanted by his persuasive commercial traveller's manners. She very modestly entertained him for an hour or so, and then called in her mother lest her conduct should appear unmaidenly. The old lady was equally fascinated; and the fugitive was sent on his way in the morning, disguised in an old coat belonging to the master of the house, who was away at the war.

RAINA. [*rising with marked stateliness*] Your life in the camp has made you coarse, Sergius. I did not think you would have repeated such a story before me. [*She turns away coldly.*]

CATHERINE. [*also rising*] She is right, Sergius. If such women exist, we should be spared the knowledge of them.

PETKOFF. Pooh! nonsense! what does it matter?

SERGIUS. [*ashamed*] No, Petkoff: I was wrong. [*To Raina, with earnest humility*] I beg your pardon. I have behaved abominably. Forgive me, Raina. [*She bows reservedly.*] And you too, madam. [*Catherine bows graciously and sits down. He proceeds solemnly, again addressing Raina*] The glimpses I have had of the seamy side of life during the last few months have made me cynical; but I should not have brought my cynicism here: least of all into your presence, Raina. I— [*Here, turning to the others, he is evidently going to begin a long speech when the Major interrupts him.*]

PETKOFF. Stuff and nonsense, Sergius! Thats quite enough fuss about nothing: a soldier's daughter should be able to stand up without flinching to a little strong conversation. [*He rises.*] Come: it's time for us to get to business. We have to make up our minds how those three regiments are to get back to Philippopolis: theres no forage for them on the Sofia route. [*He goes towards the house.*] Come along. [*Sergius is about to follow him when Catherine rises and intervenes.*]

CATHERINE. Oh, Paul, cant you spare Sergius for a few moments? Raina has hardly seen him yet. Perhaps I can help you to settle about the regiments.

SERGIUS. [*protesting*] My dear madam, impossible: you—

CATHERINE. [*stopping him playfully*] You stay here, my dear Sergius: theres no hurry. I have a word or two to say to Paul. [*Sergius instantly bows and steps back.*] Now, dear [*taking Petkoff's arm*]: come and see the electric bell.

PETKOFF. Oh, very well, very well.

They go into the house together affectionately. Sergius, left alone with Raina, looks anxiously at her, fearing that she is still offended. She smiles, and stretches out her arms to him.

SERGIUS. [*hastening to her*] Am I forgiven?

RAINA. [*placing her hands on his shoulders as she looks up at him with admiration and worship*] My hero! My king!

SERGIUS. My queen! [*He kisses her on the forehead.*]

RAINA. How I have envied you, Sergius! You have been out in the world, on the field of battle, able to prove yourself there worthy of any woman in the world; whilst I have had to sit at home inactive—dreaming—useless—doing nothing that could give me the right to call myself worthy of any man.

SERGIUS. Dearest: all my deeds have been yours. You inspired me. I have gone through the war like a knight in a tournament with his lady looking down at him!

RAINA. And you have never been absent from my thoughts for a moment. [*Very solemnly*] Sergius: I think we two have found the higher love. When I think of you, I feel that I could never do a base deed, or think an ignoble thought.

SERGIUS. My lady and my saint! [*He clasps her reverently.*]

RAINA. [*returning his embrace*] My lord and my—

SERGIUS. Sh—sh! Let me be the worshipper, dear. You little know how unworthy even the best man is of a girl's pure passion!

RAINA. I trust you. I love you. You will never disappoint me, Sergius. [*Louka is heard singing within the house. They quickly release each other.*] I cant pretend to talk indifferently before her: my heart is too full. [*Louka comes from the house with her tray. She goes to the table, and begins to clear it, with her back turned to them.*] I will get my hat; and then we can go out until lunch time. Wouldnt you like that?

SERGIUS. Be quick. If you are away five minutes, it will seem five hours. [*Raina runs to the top of the steps, and turns there to exchange looks with him and wave him a kiss with both hands. He looks after her with emotion for a moment; then turns slowly away, his face radiant with the loftiest exaltation. The movement shifts his field of vision, into the corner of which there now comes the tail of Louka's double apron. His attention is arrested at once. He takes a stealthy look at her, and begins to twirl his moustache mischievously, with his left hand akimbo on his hip. Finally, striking the ground with his heels in something of a cavalry swagger, he strolls over to the other side of the table, opposite her, and says*] Louka: do you know what the higher love is?

LOUKA. [*astonished*] No, sir.

SERGIUS. Very fatiguing thing to keep up for any length of time,

Louka. One feels the need of some relief after it.

LOUKA. [*innocently*] Perhaps you would like some coffee, sir? [*She stretches her hand across the table for the coffee pot.*]

SERGIUS. [*taking her hand*] Thank you, Louka.

LOUKA. [*pretending to pull*] Oh, sir, you know I didnt mean that. I'm surprised at you!

SERGIUS. [*coming clear of the table and drawing her with him*] I am surprised at myself, Louka. What would Sergius, the hero of Slivnitza, say if he saw me now? What would Sergius, the apostle of the higher love, say if he saw me now? What would the half dozen Sergiuses who keep popping in and out of this handsome figure of mine say if they caught us here? [*Letting go her hand and slipping his arm dexterously round her waist*] Do you consider my figure handsome, Louka?

LOUKA. Let me go, sir. I shall be disgraced. [*She struggles: he holds her inexorably.*] Oh, will you let go?

SERGIUS. [*looking straight into her eyes*] No.

LOUKA. Then stand back where we cant be seen. Have you no common sense?

SERGIUS. Ah! thats reasonable. [*He takes her .., the stableyard gateway, where they are hidden from the house.*]

LOUKA. [*plaintively*] I may have been seen from the windows: Miss Raina is sure to be spying about after you.

SERGIUS. [*stung: letting her go*] Take care, Louka. I may be worthless enough to betray the higher love; but do not you insult it.

LOUKA. [*demurely*] Not for the world, sir, I'm sure. May I go on with my work, please, now?

SERGIUS. [*again putting his arm round her*] You are a provoking little witch, Louka. If you were in love with me, would you spy out of windows on me?

LOUKA. Well, you see, sir, since you say you are half a dozen different gentlemen all at once, I should have a great deal to look after.

SERGIUS. [*charmed*] Witty as well as pretty. [*He tries to kiss her.*]

LOUKA. [*avoiding him*] No: I dont want your kisses. Gentlefolk are all alike: you making love to me behind Miss Raina's back; and she doing the same behind yours.

SERGIUS. [*recoiling a step*] Louka!

LOUKA. It shews how little you really care.

SERGIUS. [*dropping his familiarity, and speaking with freezing politeness*] If our conversation is to continue, Louka, you will please remember that a gentleman does not discuss the conduct of the lady he is engaged to with her maid.

LOUKA. It's so hard to know what a gentleman considers right. I thought from your trying to kiss me that you had given up being so particular.

SERGIUS. [*turning from her and striking his forehead as he comes back into the garden from the gateway*] Devil! devil!

LOUKA. Ha! ha! I expect one of the six of you is very like me, sir; though I am only Miss Raina's maid. [*She goes back to her work at the table, taking no further notice of him.*]

SERGIUS. [*speaking to himself*] Which of the six is the real man? thats the question that torments me. One of them is a hero, another a buffoon, another a humbug, another perhaps a bit of a blackguard. [*He pauses, and looks furtively at Louka as he adds, with deep bitterness*] And one, at least, is a coward: jealous, like all cowards. [*He goes to the table.*] Louka.

LOUKA. Yes?

SERGIUS. Who is my rival?

LOUKA. You shall never get that out of me, for love or money.

SERGIUS. Why?

LOUKA. Never mind why. Besides, you would tell that I told you; and I should lose my place.

SERGIUS. [*holding out his right hand in affirmation*] No! on the honor of a—[*He checks himself; and his hand drops, nerveless, as he concludes sardonically*]—of a man capable of behaving as I have been behaving for the last five minutes. Who is he?

LOUKA. I dont know. I never saw him ⟨ ⟩ only heard his voice through the door of her room. ⟨ ⟩ow dare you?

SERGIUS. Damnati⟨ ⟩ Oh, I mean no harm: youve no right to take up
LOUKA words like that. The mistress knows all about it. And I tell you that if that gentleman ever comes here again, Miss Raina will marry him, whether he likes it or not. I know the difference between the sort of manner you and she put on before one another and the real manner.

Sergius shivers as if she had stabbed him. Then, setting his face like iron, he strides grimly to her, and grips her above the elbows with both hands.

SERGIUS. Now listen you to me.

LOUKA. [*wincing*] Not so tight: youre hurting me.

SERGIUS. That doesn't matter. You have stained my honor by making me a party to your eavesdropping. And you have betrayed your mistress.

LOUKA. [*writhing*] Please—

SERGIUS. That shews that you are an abominable little clod of common clay, with the soul of a servant. [*He lets her go as if she were an unclean thing, and turns away, dusting his hands of her, to the bench by the wall, where he sits down with averted head, meditating gloomily.*]

LOUKA. [*whimpering angrily with her hands up her sleeves, feeling her bruised arms*] You know how to hurt with your tongue as well as with your hands. But I dont care, now Ive found out that whatever clay I'm made of, youre made of the same. As for her, she's a liar; and her fine airs are a cheat; and I'm worth six of her. [*She shakes the pain off hardily; tosses her head; and sets to work to put the things on the tray.*]

He looks doubtfully at her. She finishes packing the tray, and laps the cloth over the edges, so as to carry all out together. As she stoops to lift it, he rises.

SERGIUS. Louka! [*She stops and looks defiantly at him.*] A gentleman has no right to hurt a woman under any circumstances. [*With profound humility, uncovering his head*] I beg your pardon.

LOUKA. That sort of apology may satisfy a lady. Of what use is it to a servant?

SERGIUS. [*rudely crossed in his chivalry, throws it off with a bitter laugh, and says slightingly*] Oh! you wish to be paid for the hurt! [*He puts on his shako, and takes some money from his pocket.*]

LOUKA. [*her eyes filling with tears in spite of herself*] No: I want my hurt made well.

SERGIUS. [*sobered by her tone*] How?

She rolls up her left sleeve; clasps her arm with the thumb and fingers of her right hand; and looks down at the bruise. Then she raises her head and looks straight at him. Finally, with a superb gesture, she presents her arm to be kissed. Amazed, he looks at her; at the arm; at her again; hesitates; and then, with shuddering intensity, exclaims Never! *and gets away as far as possible from her.*

Her arm drops. Without a word, and with unaffected dignity, she takes her tray, and is approaching the house when Raina returns, wearing a hat and jacket in the height of the Vienna fashion of the previous year, 1885. Louka makes way proudly for her, and then goes into the house.

RAINA. I'm ready. Whats the matter? [*Gaily*] Have you been flirting with Louka?

SERGIUS. [*hastily*] No, no. How can you think such a thing?

RAINA. [*ashamed of herself*] Forgive me, dear: it was only a jest. I am so happy today.

He goes quickly to her, and kisses her hand remorsefully. Catherine comes out and calls to them from the top of the steps.

CATHERINE. [*coming down to them*] I am sorry to disturb you, children; but Paul is distracted over those three regiments. He doesnt know how to send them to Philippopolis; and he objects to every suggestion of mine. You must go and help him, Sergius. He is in the library.

RAINA. [*disappointed*] But we are just going out for a walk.

SERGIUS. I shall not be long. Wait for me just five minutes. [*He runs up the steps to the door.*]

RAINA. [*following him to the foot of the steps and looking up at him with timid coquetry*] I shall go round and wait in full view of the library windows. Be sure you draw father's attention to me. If you are a moment longer than five minutes, I shall go in and fetch you, regiments or no regiments.

SERGIUS. [*laughing*] Very well. [*He goes in.*]

Raina watches him until he is out of her sight. Then, with a perceptible relaxation of manner, she begins to pace up and down the garden in a brown study.

CATHERINE. Imagine their meeting that Swiss and hearing the whole story! The very first thing your father asked for was the old coat we sent him off in. A nice mess you have got us into!

RAINA. [*gazing thoughtfully at the gravel as she walks*] The little beast!

CATHERINE. Little beast! What little beast?

RAINA. To go and tell! Oh, if I had him here, I'd cram him with chocolate creams til he couldnt ever speak again!

CATHERINE. Dont talk such stuff. Tell me the truth, Raina. How long was he in your room before you came to me?

RAINA. [*whisking round and recommencing her march in the opposite direction*] Oh, I forget.

CATHERINE. You cannot forget! Did he really climb up after the soldiers were gone; or was he there when that officer searched the room?

RAINA. No. Yes: I think he must have been there then.

CATHERINE. You think! Oh, Raina! Raina! Will anything ever make you straightforward? If Sergius finds out, it will be all over between you.

RAINA. [*with cool impertinence*] Oh, I know Sergius is your pet. I sometimes wish you could marry him instead of me. You would just suit him. You would pet him, and spoil him, and mother him to perfection.

CATHERINE. [*opening her eyes very widely indeed*] Well, upon my word!

RAINA. [*capriciously: half to herself*] I always feel a longing to do or say something dreadful to him—to shock his propriety—to scandalize the five senses out of him. [*To Catherine, perversely*] I dont care whether he finds out about the chocolate cream soldier or not. I half hope he may.[*She again turns and strolls flippantly away up the path to the corner of the house.*]

CATHERINE. And what should I be able to say to your father, pray?

RAINA. [*over her shoulder, from the top of the two steps*] Oh, poor father! As if he could help himself! [*She turns the corner and passes out of sight.*]

CATHERINE. [*looking after her, her fingers itching*] Oh, if you were only ten years younger! [*Louka comes from the house with a salver, which she carries hanging down by her side.*] Well?

LOUKA. Theres a gentleman just called, madam. A Serbian officer.

CATHERINE. [*flaming*] A Serb! And how dare he—[*checking herself bitterly*] Oh, I forgot. We are at peace now. I suppose we shall have them calling every day to pay their compliments. Well: if he is an officer why dont you tell your master? He is in the library with Major Saranoff. Why do you come to me?

LOUKA. But he asks for you, madam. And I dont think he knows who you are: he said the lady of the house. He gave me this little ticket for you. [*She takes a card out of her bosom; puts it on the salver; and offers it to Catherine.*]

CATHERINE. [*reading*] "Captain Bluntschli"? Thats a German name.

LOUKA. Swiss, madam, I think.

CATHERINE. [*with a bound that makes Louka jump back*] Swiss! What is he like?

LOUKA. [*timidly*] He has a big carpet bag, madam.

CATHERINE. Oh Heavens! he's come to return the coat. Send him away: say we're not at home: ask him to leave his address and I'll write to him. Oh stop: that will never do. Wait! [*She throws herself into a chair to think it out. Louka waits.*] The master and Major Saranoff are busy in the library, arnt they?

LOUKA. Yes, madam.

CATHERINE. [*decisively*] Bring the gentleman out here at once. [*Peremptorily*] And be very polite to him. Dont delay. Here [*impatiently snatching the salver from her*]: leave that here; and go straight back to him.

LOUKA. Yes, madam [*going*].

CATHERINE. Louka!

LOUKA. [*stopping*] Yes, madam.

CATHERINE. Is the library door shut?

LOUKA. I think so, madam.

CATHERINE. If not, shut it as you pass through.

LOUKA. Yes, madam [*going.*]

CATHERINE. Stop [*Louka stops*]. He will have to go that way [*indicating the gate of the stable yard*]. Tell Nicola to bring his bag here after him. Dont forget.

LOUKA. [*surprised*] His bag?

CATHERINE. Yes: here: as soon as possible. [*Vehemently*] Be quick! [*Louka runs into the house. Catherine snatches her apron off and throws it behind a bush. She then takes up the salver and uses it as a mirror, with the result that the handkerchief tied round her head follows the apron. A touch to her hair and a shake to her dressing gown make her presentable.*] Oh, how? how? how can a man be such a fool! Such a moment to select! [*Louka appears at the door of the house, announcing Captain Bluntschli. She stands aside at the top of the steps to let him pass before she goes in again. He is the man of the midnight adventure in Raina's room, clean, well brushed, smartly uniformed, and out of trouble, but still unmistakably the same man. The moment Louka's back is turned, Catherine swoops on him with impetuous, urgent, coaxing appeal.*] Captain Bluntschli: I am very glad to see you; but you must leave this house at once. [*He raises his eyebrows.*] My husband has just returned with my future son-in-law; and they know nothing. If they did, the consequences would be terrible. You are a foreigner: you do not feel our national animosities as we do. We still hate the Serbs: the effect of the peace on my husband has been to make him feel like a lion baulked of his prey. If he discovers our secret, he will never forgive me; and my daughter's life will hardly be safe. Will you, like the chivalrous gentleman and soldier you are, leave at once before he finds you here?

BLUNTSCHLI. [*disappointed, but philosophical*] At once, gracious lady. I only came to thank you and return the coat you lent me. If you will allow me to take it out of my bag and leave it with your servant as I pass out, I need detain you no further. [*He turns to go into the house.*]

CATHERINE. [catching him by the sleeve] Oh, you must not think of going back that way. [Coaxing him across to the stable gates] This is the shortest way out. Many thanks. So glad to have been of service to you. Good-bye.

BLUNTSCHLI. But my bag?

CATHERINE. It shall be sent on. You will leave me your address.

BLUNTSCHLI. True. Allow me. [He takes out his cardcase, and stops to write his address, keeping Catherine in an agony of impatience. As he hands her the card, Petkoff, hatless, rushes from the house in a fluster of hospitality, followed by Sergius.]

PETKOFF. [as he hurries down the steps] My dear Captain Bluntschli—

CATHERINE. Oh Heavens! [She sinks on the seat against the wall.]

PETKOFF. [too preoccupied to notice her as he shakes Bluntschli's hand heartily] Those stupid people of mine thought I was out here, instead of in the—haw!—library [he cannot mention the library without betraying how proud he is of it]. I saw you through the window. I was wondering why you didnt come in. Saranoff is with me: you remember him, dont you?

SERGIUS. [saluting humorously, and then offering his hand with great charm of manner] Welcome, our friend the enemy!

PETKOFF. No longer the enemy, happily. [Rather anxiously] I hope youve called as a friend, and not about horses or prisoners.

CATHERINE. Oh, quite as a friend, Paul. I was just asking Captain Bluntschli to stay to lunch; but he declares he must go at once.

SERGIUS. [sardonically] Impossible, Bluntschli. We want you here badly. We have to send on three cavalry regiments to Philippopolis; and we dont in the least know how to do it.

BLUNTSCHLI. [suddenly attentive and businesslike] Philippopolis? The forage is the trouble, I suppose.

PETKOFF. [eagerly] Yes: thats it. [To Sergius] He sees the whole thing at once.

BLUNTSCHLI. I think I can shew you how to manage that.

SERGIUS. Invaluable man! Come along! [Towering over Bluntschli, he puts his hand on his shouder and takes him to the steps, Petkoff following.]

Raina comes from the house as Bluntschli puts his foot on the first step.

RAINA. Oh! The chocolate cream soldier!

Bluntschli stands rigid. Sergius, amazed, looks at Raina, then at Petkoff, who looks back at him and then at his wife.

CATHERINE. [with commanding presence of mind] My dear Raina, dont you see that we have a guest here? Captain Bluntschli: one of our new Serbian friends.

Raina bows: Bluntschli bows.

RAINA. How silly of me! [She comes down into the centre of the group, between Bluntschli and Petkoff.] I made a beautiful ornament this morning for the ice pudding; and that stupid Nicola has just put down a pile of plates on it and spoilt it. [To Bluntschli, winningly] I hope you didn't think that you were the chocolate cream soldier, Captain Bluntschli.

BLUNTSCHLI. [*laughing*] I assure you I did. |*Stealing a whimsical glance at her*] Your explanation was a relief.

PETKOFF. [*suspiciously, to Raina*] And since when, pray, have you taken to cooking?

CATHERINE. Oh, whilst you were away. It is her latest fancy.

PETKOFF. [*testily*] And has Nicola taken to drinking? He used to be careful enough. First he shews Captain Bluntschli out here when he knew quite well I was in the library; and then he goes downstairs and breaks Raina's chocolate soldier. He must— [*Nicola appears at the top of the steps with the bag. He descends; places it respectfully before Bluntschli; and waits for further orders. General amazement. Nicola, unconscious of the effect he is producing, looks perfectly satisfied with himself. When Petkoff recovers his power of speech, he breaks out at him with*] Are you mad, Nicola?

NICOLA. [*taken aback*] Sir?

PETKOFF. What have you brought that for?

NICOLA. My lady's orders, major. Louka told me that—

CATHERINE. [*interrupting him*] My orders! Why should I order you to bring Captain Bluntschli's luggage out here? What are you thinking of, Nicola?

NICOLA. [*after a moment's bewilderment, picking up the bag as he addresses Bluntschli with the very perfection of servile discretion*] I beg your pardon, captain, I am sure. [*To Catherine*] My fault, madam: I hope youll overlook it. [*He bows, and is going to the steps with the bag, when Petkoff addresses him angrily.*]

PETKOFF. Youd better go and slam that bag, too, down on Miss Raina's ice pudding! [*This is too much for Nicola. The bag drops from his hand almost on his master's toes, eliciting a roar of*] Begone, you butter-fingered donkey.

NICOLA. [*snatching up the bag, and escaping into the house*] Yes, major.

CATHERINE. Oh, never mind. Paul: dont be angry.

PETKOFF. [*blustering*] Scoundrel! He's got out of hand while I was away. I'll teach him. Infernal blackguard! The sack next Saturday! I'll clear out the whole establishment—[*He is stifled by the caresses of his wife and daughter, who hang round his neck, petting him*].

CATHERINE.⎱ [*together*] ⎰Now, now, now, it mustnt be angry. He
RAINA. ⎰ ⎱Wow, wow, wow: not on your first day at
⎰meant no harm. Be good to please me, dear.
⎰home. I'll make another ice pudding. Tch-
⎱Sh-sh-sh-sh!
⎰ch-ch!

PETKOFF. [*yielding*] Oh well, never mind. Come, Bluntschli: lets have no more nonsense about going away. You know very well youre not going back to Switzerland yet. Until you do go back youll stay with us.

RAINA. Oh, do, Captain Bluntschli.

PETKOFF. [*to Catherine*] Now, Catherine: it's of you he's afraid. Press him: and he'll stay.

CATHERINE. Of course I shall be only too delighted if [*appealingly*] Captain Bluntschli really wishes to stay. He knows my wishes.

BLUNTSCHLI. [*in his driest military manner*] I am at madam's orders.

SERGIUS. [*cordially*] That settles it!

PETKOFF. [*heartily*] Of course!

RAINA. You see you must stay.

BLUNTSCHLI. [*smiling*] Well, if I must, I must.

Gesture of despair from Catherine.

Act III

In the library after lunch. It is not much of a library. Its literary equipment consists of a single fixed shelf stocked with old paper covered novels, broken backed, coffee stained, torn and thumbed; and a couple of little hanging shelves with a few gift books on them: the rest of the wall space being occupied by trophies of war and the chase. But it is a most comfortable sitting room. A row of three large windows shews a mountain panorama, just now seen in one of its friendliest aspects in the mellowing afternoon light. In the corner next the right-hand window a square earthenware stove, a perfect tower of glistening pottery, rises nearly to the ceiling and guarantees plenty of warmth. The ottoman is like that in Raina's room, and similarly placed; and the window seats are luxurious with decorated cushions. There is one object, however, hopelessly out of keeping with its surroundings. This is a small kitchen table, much the worse for wear, fitted as a writing table with an old canister full of pens, an eggcup filled with ink, and a deplorable scrap of heavily used pink blotting paper.

At the side of this table, which stands to the left of anyone facing the window, Bluntschli is hard at work with a couple of maps before him, writing orders. At the head of it sits Sergius, who is supposed to be also at work, but is actually gnawing the feather of a pen, and contemplating Bluntschli's quick, sure, businesslike progress with a mixture of envious irritation at his own incapacity and awestruck wonder at an ability which seems to him almost miraculous, though its prosaic character forbids him to esteem it. The Major is comfortably established on the ottoman, with a newspaper in his hand and the tube of his hookah within easy reach. Catherine sits at the stove, with her back to them, embroidering. Raina, reclining on the divan, is gazing in a daydream out at the Balkan landscape, with a neglected novel in her lap.

The door is on the same side as the stove, farther from the window. The button of the electric bell is at the opposite side, behind Bluntschli.

PETKOFF. [*looking up from his paper to watch how they are getting on at the table*] Are you sure I cant help in any way, Bluntschli?

BLUNTSCHLI. [*without interrupting his writing or looking up*] Quite sure, thank you. Saranoff and I will manage it.

SERGIUS. [*grimly*] Yes: we'll manage it. He finds out what to do; draws up the orders; and I sign em. Division of labor! [*Bluntschli passes him a paper.*] Another one? Thank you. [*He plants the paper squarely before him; sets his chair carefully parallel to it; and signs with his cheek on his elbow and his protruded tongue following the movements of his pen.*] This hand is more accustomed to the sword than to the pen.

PETKOFF. It's very good of you, Bluntschli: it is indeed, to let yourself be put upon in this way. Now are you quite sure I can do nothing?

CATHERINE. [*in a low warning tone*] You can stop interrupting, Paul.

PETKOFF. [*starting and looking round at her*] Eh? Oh! Quite right, my love: quite right. [*He takes his newspaper up again, but presently lets it drop.*] Ah, you havnt been campaigning, Catherine: you dont know how pleasant it is for us to sit here, after a good lunch, with nothing to do but enjoy ourselves. Theres only one thing I want to make me thoroughly comfortable.

CATHERINE. What is that?

PETKOFF. My old coat. I'm not at home in this one: I feel as if I were on parade.

CATHERINE. My dear Paul, how absurd you are about that old coat! It must be hanging in the blue closet where you left it.

PETKOFF. My dear Catherine, I tell you Ive looked there. Am I to believe my own eyes or not? [*Catherine rises and crosses the room to press the button of the electric bell.*] What are you shewing off that bell for? [*She looks at him majestically, and silently resumes her chair and her needlework.*] My dear: if you think the obstinacy of your sex can make a coat out of two old dressing gowns of Raina's, your waterproof, and my mackintosh, youre mistaken. Thats exactly what the blue closet contains at present. *Nicola presents himself.*

CATHERINE. Nicola: go to the blue closet and bring your master's old coat here: the braided one he wears in the house.

NICOLA. Yes, madame. [*He goes out.*]

PETKOFF. Catherine.

CATHERINE. Yes, Paul.

PETKOFF. I bet you any piece of jewellery you like to order from Sofia against a week's housekeeping money that the coat isnt there.

CATHERINE. Done, Paul!

PETKOFF. [*excited by the prospect of a gamble*] Come: heres an opportunity for some sport. Wholl bet on it? Bluntschli: I'll give you six to one.

BLUNTSCHLI. [*imperturbably*] It would be robbing you, major. Madame is sure to be right. [*Without looking up, he passes another batch of papers to Sergius.*]

SERGIUS. [*also excited*] Bravo, Switzerland! Major: I bet my best charger against an Arab mare for Raina that Nicola finds the coat in the blue closet.

PETKOFF. [*eagerly*] Your best char—

CATHERINE. [*hastily interrupting him*] Dont be foolish, Paul. An

Arabian mare will cost you 50,000 levas.

RAINA. [*suddenly coming out of her picturesque revery*] Really, mother, if you are going to take the jewellery, I dont see why you should grudge me my Arab.

Nicola comes back with the coat, and brings it to Petkoff, who can hardly believe his eyes.

CATHERINE. Where was it, Nicola?

NICOLA. Hanging in the blue closet, madame.

PETKOFF. Well, I am d—

CATHERINE. [*stopping him*] Paul!

PETKOFF. I could have sworn it wasnt there. Age is beginning to tell on me. I'm getting hallucinations. [*To Nicola*] Here: help me to change. Excuse me, Bluntschli. [*He begins changing coats, Nicola acting as valet.*] Remember: I didnt take that bet of yours, Sergius. Youd better give Raina that Arab steed yourself, since youve roused her expectations. Eh, Raina? [*He looks round at her; but she is again rapt in the landscape. With a little gush of parental affection and pride, he points her out to them, and says*] She's dreaming, as usual.

SERGIUS. Assuredly she shall not be the loser.

PETKOFF. So much the better for her. I shant come off so cheaply, I expect. [*The change is now complete. Nicola goes out with the discarded coat.*] Ah, now I feel at home at last. [*He sits down and takes his newspaper with a grunt of relief.*]

BLUNTSCHLI. [*to Sergius, handing a paper*] Thats the last order.

PETKOFF. [*jumping up*] What! Finished?

BLUNTSCHLI. Finished.

PETKOFF. [*with childlike envy*] Havnt you anything for me to sign?

BLUNTSCHLI. Not necessary. His signature will do.

PETKOFF. [*inflating his chest and thumping it*] Ah well, I think weve done a thundering good day's work. Can I do anything more?

BLUNTSCHLI. You had better both see the fellows that are to take these. [*Sergius rises*] Pack them off at once; and shew them that Ive marked on the orders the time they should hand them in by. Tell them that if they stop to drink or tell stories—if theyre five minutes late, theyll have the skin taken off their backs.

SERGIUS. [*stiffening indignantly*] I'll say so. [*He strides to the door.*] And if one of them is man enough to spit in my face for insulting him, I'll buy his discharge and give him a pension. [*He goes out.*]

BLUNTSCHLI. [*confidentially*] Just see that he talks to them properly, major, will you?

PETKOFF. [*officiously*] Quite right, Bluntschli, quite right. I'll see to it. [*He goes to the door importantly, but hesitates on the threshold.*] By the bye, Catherine, you may as well come too. Theyll be far more frightened of you than of me.

CATHERINE. [*putting down her embroidery*] I daresay I had better. You would only splutter at them. [*She goes out, Petkoff holding the door for her and following her.*]

BLUNTSCHLI. What an army! They make cannons out of cherry trees; and the officers send for their wives to keep discipline! [*He begins to fold and docket the papers.*]

Raina, who has risen from the divan, marches slowly down the room with her hands clasped behind her, and looks mischievously at him.

RAINA. You look ever so much nicer than when we last met. [*He looks up, surprised.*] What have you done to yourself?

BLUNTSCHLI. Washed; brushed; good night's sleep and breakfast. Thats all.

RAINA. Did you get back safely that morning?

BLUNTSCHLI. Quite, thanks.

RAINA. Were they angry with you for running away from Sergius's charge?

BLUNTSCHLI [*grinning*] No: they were glad; because theyd all just run away themselves.

RAINA. [*going to the table, and leaning over it towards him*] It must have made a lovely story for them: all that about me and my room.

BLUNTSCHLI. Capital story. But I only told it to one of them: a particular friend.

RAINA. On whose discretion you could absolutely rely?

BLUNTSCHLI. Absolutely.

RAINA. Hm! He told it all to my father and Sergius the day you exchanged the prisoners. [*She turns away and strolls carelessly across to the other side of the room.*]

BLUNTSCHLI. [*deeply concerned, and half incredulous*] No! You dont mean that, do you?

RAINA. [*turning, with sudden earnestness*] I do indeed. But they dont know that it was in this house you took refuge. If Sergius knew, he would challenge you and kill you in a duel.

BLUNTSCHLI. Bless me! then dont tell him.

RAINA. Please be serious, Captain Bluntschli. Can you not realize what it is to me to deceive him? I want to be quite perfect with Sergius: no meanness, no smallness, no deceit. My relation to him is the one really beautiful and noble part of my life. I hope you can understand that.

BLUNTSCHLI. [*sceptically*] You mean that you wouldnt like him to find out that the story about the ice pudding was a—a—a—You know.

RAINA. [*wincing*] Ah, dont talk of it in that flippant way. I lied: I know it. But I did it to save your life. He would have killed you. That was the second time I ever uttered a falsehood. [*Bluntschli rises quickly and looks doubtfully and somewhat severely at her.*] Do you remember the first time?

BLUNTSCHLI. I! No. Was I present?

RAINA. Yes; and I told the officer who was searching for you that you were not present.

BLUNTSCHLI. True. I should have remembered it.

RAINA. [*greatly encouraged*] Ah, it is natural that you should forget it first. It cost you nothing: it cost me a lie! A lie!

She sits down on the ottoman, looking straight before her with her hands clasped around her knee. Bluntschli, quite touched, goes to the ottoman with a particularly reassuring and considerate air, and sits down beside her.

BLUNTSCHLI. My dear young lady, dont let this worry you. Remember: I'm a soldier. Now what are the two things that happen to a soldier so often that he comes to think nothing of them? One is hearing people tell lies [*Raina recoils*]: the other is getting his life saved in all sorts of ways by all sorts of people.

RAINA. [*rising in indignant protest*] And so he becomes a creature incapable of faith and of gratitude.

BLUNTSCHLI. [*making a wry face*] Do you like gratitude? I dont. If pity is akin to love, gratitude is akin to the other thing.

RAINA. Gratitude! [*Turning on him*] If you are incapable of gratitude you are incapable of any noble sentiment. Even animals are grateful. Oh, I see now exactly what you think of me! You were not surprised to hear me lie. To you it was something I probably did every day! every hour! That is how men think of women. [*She paces the room tragically.*]

BLUNTSCHLI. [*dubiously*] Theres reason in everything. You said youd told only two lies in your whole life. Dear young lady: isnt that rather a short allowance? I'm quite a straightforward man myself; but it wouldnt last me a whole morning.

RAINA. [*staring haughtily at him*] Do you know, sir, that you are insulting me?

BLUNTSCHLI. I cant help it. When you strike that noble attitude and speak in that thrilling voice, I admire you; but I find it impossible to believe a single word you say.

RAINA. [*superbly*] Captain Bluntschli!

BLUNTSCHLI. [*unmoved*] Yes?

RAINA. [*standing over him, as if she could not believe her senses*] Do you mean what you said just now? Do you know what you said just now?

BLUNTSCHLI. I do.

RAINA. [*gasping*] I! I!!! [*She points to herself incredulously, meaning "I, Raina Petkoff, tell lies!" He meets her gaze unflinchingly. She suddenly sits down beside him, and adds, with a complete change of manner from the heroic to a babyish familiarity*] How did you find me out?

BLUNTSCHLI [*promptly*] Instinct, dear young lady. Instinct, and experience of the world.

RAINA. [*wonderingly*] Do you know, you are the first man I ever met› who did not take me seriously?

BLUNTSCHLI. You mean, dont you, that I am the first man that has ever taken you quite seriously?

RAINA. Yes: I suppose I do mean that. [*Cosily, quite at her ease with him*] How strange it is to be talked to in such a way! You know, Ive always gone on like that.

BLUNTSCHLI. You mean the——?

RAINA. I mean the noble attitude and the thrilling voice. [*They laugh together.*] I did it when I was a tiny child to my nurse. She believed in it. I do it before my parents. They believe in it. I do it before Sergius. He believes in it.

BLUNTSCHLI. Yes: he's a little in that line himself, isnt he?

RAINA. [*startled*] Oh! Do you think so?

BLUNTSCHLI. You know him better than I do.

RAINA. I wonder—I wonder is he? If I thought that—! [*Discouraged*] Ah, well: what does it matter? I suppose, now youve found me out, you despise me.

BLUNTSCHLI. [*warmly, rising*] No, my dear young lady, no, no, no a thousand times. It's part of your youth: part of your charm. I'm like all the rest of them: the nurse, your parents, Sergius: I'm your infatuated admirer.

RAINA. [*pleased*] Really?

BLUNTSCHLI. [*slapping his breast smartly with his hand, German fashion*] Hand aufs Herz![7] Really and truly.

RAINA. [*very happy*] But what did you think of me for giving you my portrait?

BLUNTSCHLI. [*astonished*] Your portrait! You never gave me your portrait.

RAINA. [*quickly*] Do you mean to say you never got it?

BLUNTSCHLI. No. [*He sits down beside her, with renewed interest, and says, with some complacency*] When did you send it to me?

RAINA. [*indignantly*] I did not send it to you. [*She turns her head away, and adds, reluctantly*] It was in the pocket of that coat.

BLUNTSCHLI. [*pursing his lips and rounding his eyes*] Oh-o oh! I never found it. It must be there still.

RAINA. [*springing up*] There still! for my father to find the first time he puts his hand in his pocket! Oh, how could you be so stupid?

BLUNTSCHLI. [*rising also*] It doesnt matter: I suppose it's only a photograph: how can he tell who it was intended for? Tell him he put it there himself.

RAINA. [*bitterly*] Yes: that is so clever! isnt it? [*Distractedly*] Oh! what shall I do?

BLUNTSCHLI. Ah, I see. You wrote something on it. That was rash.

RAINA. [*vexed almost to tears*] Oh, to have done such a thing for you, who care no more—except to laugh at me—oh! Are you sure nobody has touched it?

BLUNTSCHLI. Well, I cant be quite sure. You see, I couldnt carry it about with me all the time: one cant take much luggage on active service.

RAINA. What did you do with it?

BLUNTSCHLI. When I got through to Pirot I had to put it in safe keeping somehow. I thought of the railway cloak room; but thats the surest place to get looted in modern warfare. So I pawned it.

RAINA. Pawned it!!!

BLUNTSCHLI. I know it doesnt sound nice; but it was much the safest

7. "Hand on heart" (German).

plan. I redeemed it the day before yesterday. Heaven only knows whether the pawnbroker cleared out the pockets or not.

RAINA. [*furious: throwing the words right into his face*] You have a low shopkeeping mind. You think of things that would never come into a gentleman's head.

BLUNTSCHLI. [*phlegmatically*] Thats the Swiss national character, dear lady. [*He returns to the table.*]

RAINA. Oh, I wish I had never met you. [*She flounces away, and sits at the window fuming.*]

Louka comes in with a heap of letters and telegrams on her salver, and crosses, with her bold free gait, to the table. Her left sleeve is looped up to the shoulder with a brooch, shewing her naked arm, with a broad gilt bracelet covering the bruise.

LOUKA. [*to Bluntschli*] For you. [*She empties the salver with a fling on to the table.*] The messenger is waiting. [*She is determined not to be civil to an enemy, even if she must bring him his letters.*]

BLUNTSCHLI. [*to Raina*] Will you excuse me: the last postal delivery that reached me was three weeks ago. These are the subsequent accumulations. Four telegrams: a week old. [*He opens one.*] Oho! Bad news!

RAINA. [*rising and advancing a little remorsefully*] Bad news?

BLUNTSCHLI. My father's dead. [*He looks at the telegram with his lips pursed, musing on the unexpected change in his arrangements. Louka crosses herself hastily.*]

RAINA. Oh, how very sad!

BLUNTSCHLI. Yes: I shall have to start for home in an hour. He has left a lot of big hotels behind him to be looked after. [*He takes up a fat letter in a long blue envelope.*] Here's a whacking letter from the family solicitor. [*He puts out the enclosures and glances over them.*] Great Heavens! Seventy! Two hundred! [*In a crescendo of dismay*] Four hundred! Four thousand!! Nine thousand six hundred!!! What on earth am I to do with them all?

RAINA. [*timidly*] Nine thousand hotels?

BLUNTSCHLI. Hotels! nonsense. If you only knew! Oh, it's too ridiculous! Excuse me: I must give my fellow orders about starting. [*He leaves the room hastily, with the documents in his hand.*]

LOUKA. [*knowing instinctively that she can annoy Raina by disparaging Bluntschli*] He has not much heart, that Swiss. He has not a word of grief for his poor father.

RAINA. [*bitterly*] Grief! A man who has been doing nothing but killing people for years! What does he care? What does any soldier care? [*She goes to the door, restraining her tears with difficulty.*]

LOUKA. Major Saranoff has been fighting too; and he has plenty of heart left. [*Raina, at the door, draws herself up haughtily and goes out.*] Aha! I thought you wouldnt get much feeling out of your soldier. [*She is following Raina when Nicola enters with an armful of logs for the stove.*]

NICOLA. [*grinning amorously at her*] Ive been trying all the afternoon to get a minute alone with you, my girl. [*His countenance changes as he notices her arm.*] Why, what fashion is that of wearing your sleeve, child?

LOUKA. [*proudly*] My own fashion.

NICOLA. Indeed! If the mistress catches you, she'll talk to you. [*He puts the logs down, and seats himself comfortably on the ottoman.*]

LOUKA. Is that any reason why you should take it on yourself to talk to me?

NICOLA. Come! dont be so contrairy with me. Ive some good news for you. [*She sits down beside him. He takes out some paper money. Louka, with an eager gleam in her eyes, tries to snatch it; but he shifts it quickly to his left hand, out of her reach.*] See! a twenty leva bill! Sergius gave me that, out of pure swagger. A fool and his money are soon parted. Theres ten levas more. The Swiss gave me that for backing up the mistress's and Raina's lies about him. He's no fool, he isnt. You should have heard old Catherine downstairs as polite as you please to me, telling me not to mind the Major being a little impatient; for they knew what a good servant I was—after making a fool and a liar of me before them all! The twenty will go to our savings; and you shall have the ten to spend if youll only talk to me so as to remind me I'm a human being. I get tired of being a servant occasionally.

LOUKA. Yes: sell your manhood for 30 levas, and buy me for 10! [*Rising scornfully*] Keep your money. You were born to be a servant. I was not. When you set up your shop you will only be everybody's servant instead of somebody's servant. [*She goes moodily to the table and seats herself regally in Sergius's chair.*]

NICOLA. [*picking up his logs, and going to the stove*] Ah, wait til you see. We shall have our evenings to ourselves; and I shall be master in my own house, I promise you. [*He throws the logs down and kneels at the stove.*]

LOUKA. You shall never be master in mine.

NICOLA. [*turning, still on his knees, and squatting down rather forlornly on his calves, daunted by her implacable disdain*] You have a great ambition in you, Louka. Remember: if any luck comes to you, it was I that made a woman of you.

LOUKA. You!

NICOLA. [*scrambling up and going to her*] Yes, me. Who was it made you give up wearing a couple of pounds of false black hair on your head and reddening your lips and cheeks like any other Bulgarian girl! I did. Who taught you to trim your nails, and keep your hands clean, and be dainty about yourself, like a fine Russian lady! Me: do you hear that? me! [*She tosses her head defiantly; and he turns away, adding more coolly*] Ive often thought that if Raina were out of the way, and you just a little less of a fool and Sergius just a little more of one, you might come to be one of my grandest customers, instead of only being my wife and costing me money.

LOUKA. I believe you would rather be my servant than my husband. You would make more out of me. Oh, I know that soul of yours.

NICOLA. [*going closer to her for greater emphasis*] Never you mind my soul; but just listen to my advice. If you want to be a lady, your present behavior to me wont do at all, unless when we're alone. It's too sharp and impudent; and impudence is a sort of familiarity: it shews affection for me. And dont you try being high and mighty with me, either. Youre like all country girls: you think it's genteel to treat a servant the way I treat a stableboy. Thats only your ignorance; and dont you forget it. And dont be so ready to defy everybody. Act as if you expected to have your own way, not as if you expected to be ordered about. The way to get on as a lady is the same as the way to get on as a servant: youve got to know your place: thats the secret of it. And you may depend on me to know my place if you get promoted. Think over it, my girl. I'll stand by you: one servant should always stand by another.

LOUKA. [*rising impatiently*] Oh, I must behave in my own way. You take all the courage out of me with your cold-blooded wisdom. Go and put those logs in the fire: thats the sort of thing you understand.

Before Nicola can retort, Sergius comes in. He checks himself a moment on seeing Louka; then goes to the stove.

SERGIUS. [*to Nicola*] I am not in the way of your work, I hope.

NICOLA. [*in a smooth, elderly manner*] Oh no, sir: thank you kindly. I was only speaking to this foolish girl about her habit of running up here to the library whenever she gets a chance, to look at the books. Thats the worst of her education, sir: it gives her habits above her station. [*To Louka*] Make that table tidy, Louka, for the Major. [*He goes out sedately.*]

Louka, without looking at Sergius, pretends to arrange the papers on the table. He crosses slowly to her, and studies the arrangement of her sleeve reflectively.

SERGIUS. Let me see: is there a mark there? [*He turns up the bracelet and sees the bruise made by his grasp. She stands motionless, not looking at him: fascinated, but on her guard*] Ffff! Does it hurt?

LOUKA. Yes.

SERGIUS. Shall I cure it?

LOUKA. [*instantly withdrawing herself proudly, but still not looking at him*] No. You cannot cure it now.

SERGIUS. [*masterfully*] Quite sure? [*He makes a movement as if to take her in his arms.*]

LOUKA. Dont trifle with me, please. An officer should not trifle with a servant.

SERGIUS. [*indicating the bruise with a merciless stroke of his forefinger*] That was no trifle, Louka.

LOUKA. [*flinching; then looking at him for the first time*] Are you sorry?

SERGIUS. [*with measured emphasis, folding his arms*] I am never sorry.

LOUKA. [*wistfully*] I wish I could believe a man could be as unlike a woman as that. I wonder are you really a brave man?

SERGIUS. [*unaffectedly, relaxing his attitude*] Yes: I am a brave man. My heart jumped like a woman's at the first shot; but in the charge I found that I was brave. Yes: that at least is real about me.

LOUKA. Did you find in the charge that the men whose fathers are poor like mine were any less brave than the men who are rich like you?

SERGIUS. [*with bitter levity*] Not a bit. They all slashed and cursed and yelled like heroes. Psha! the courage to rage and kill is cheap. I have an English bull terrier who has as much of that sort of courage as the whole Bulgarian nation, and the whole Russian nation at its back. But he lets my groom thrash him, all the same. Thats your soldier all over! No, Louka: your poor men can cut throats; but they are afraid of their officers; they put up with insults and blows; they stand by and see one another punished like children: aye, and help to do it when they are ordered. And the officers!!! Well [*with a short harsh laugh*] I am an officer. Oh, [*fervently*] give me the man who will defy to the death any power on earth or in heaven that sets itself up against his own will and conscience: he alone is the brave man.

LOUKA. How easy it is to talk! Men never seem to me to grow up: they all have schoolboy's ideas. You dont know what true courage is.

SERGIUS. [*ironically*] Indeed! I am willing to be instructed. [*He sits on the ottoman, sprawling magnificently.*]

LOUKA. Look at me! How much am I allowed to have my own will? I have to get your room ready for you: to sweep and dust, to fetch and carry How could that degrade me if it did not degrade you to have it done for you? But [*with subdued passion*] if I were Empress of Russia, above everyone in the world, then!! Ah then, though according to you I could shew no courage at all, you should see, you should see.

SERGIUS. What would you do, most noble Empress?

LOUKA. I would marry the man I loved, which no other queen in Europe has the courage to do. If I loved you, though you would be as far beneath me as I am beneath you, I would dare to be the equal of my inferior. Would you dare as much if you loved me? No: if you felt the beginnings of love for me you would not let it grow. You would not dare: you would marry a rich man's daughter because you would be afraid of what other people would say of you.

SERGIUS. [*bounding up*] You lie: it is not so, by all the stars! If I loved you, and I were the Tsar himself, I would set you on the throne by my side. You know that I love another woman, a woman as high above you as heaven is above earth. And you are jealous of her.

LOUKA. I have no reason to be. She will never marry you now. The man I told you of has come back. She will marry the Swiss.

SERGIUS. [*recoiling*] The Swiss!

LOUKA. A man worth ten of you. Then you can come to me; and I will refuse you. You are not good enough for me. [*She turns to the door.*]

SERGIUS. [*springing after her and catching her fiercely in his arms*] I will kill the Swiss; and afterwards I will do as I please with you.

LOUKA. [*in his arms, passive and steadfast*] The Swiss will kill you, perhaps. He has beaten you in love. He may beat you in war.

SERGIUS. [*tormentedly*] Do you think I believe that she—she! whose worst thoughts are higher than your best ones, is capable of trifling with another man behind my back?

LOUKA. Do you think she would believe the Swiss if he told her now that I am in your arms?

SERGIUS. [*releasing her in despair*] Damnation! Oh, damnation! Mockery! mockery everywhere! everything I think is mocked by everything I do. [*He strikes himself frantically on the breast.*] Coward! liar! fool! Shall I kill myself like a man, or live and pretend to laugh at myself? [*She again turns to go.*] Louka! [*She stops near the door.*] Remember: you belong to me.

LOUKA. [*turning*] What does that mean? An insult?

SERGIUS. [*commandingly*] It means that you love me, and that I have had you here in my arms, and will perhaps have you there again. Whether that is an insult I neither know nor care: take it as you please. But [*vehemently*] I will not be a coward and a trifler. If I choose to love you, I dare marry you, in spite of all Bulgaria. If these hands ever touch you again, they shall touch my affianced bride.

LOUKA. We shall see whether you dare keep your word. And take care. I will not wait long.

SERGIUS. [*again folding his arms and standing motionless in the middle of the room*] Yes: we shall see. And you shall wait my pleasure.

Bluntschli, much preoccupied, with his papers still in his hand, enters, leaving the door open for Louka to go out. He goes across to the table, glancing at her as he passes. Sergius, without altering his resolute attitude, watches him steadily. Louka goes out, leaving the door open.

BLUNTSCHLI. [*absently, sitting at the table as before, and putting down his papers*] Thats a remarkable looking young woman.

SERGIUS. [*gravely, without moving*] Captain Bluntschli.

BLUNTSCHLI. Eh?

SERGIUS. You have deceived me. You are my rival. I brook no rivals. At six o'clock I shall be in the drilling-ground on the Klissoura road, alone, on horseback, with my sabre. Do you understand?

BLUNTSCHLI. [*staring, but sitting quite at his ease*] Oh, thank you: thats a cavalry man's proposal. I'm in the artillery; and I have the choice of weapons. If I go, I shall take a machine gun. And there shall be no mistake about the cartridges this time.

SERGIUS. [*flushing, but with deadly coldness*] Take care, sir. It is not our custom in Bulgaria to allow invitations of that kind to be trifled with.

BLUNTSCHLI. [*warmly*] Pooh! dont talk to me about Bulgaria. You dont know what fighting is. But have it your own way. Bring your sabre along. I'll meet you.

SERGIUS. [*fiercely delighted to find his opponent a man of spirit*] Well said, Switzer. Shall I lend you my best horse?

BLUNTSCHLI. No: damn your horse! thank you all the same, my dear fellow. [*Raina comes in, and hears the next sentence.*] I shall fight you on foot. Horseback's too dangerous; I dont want to kill you if I can help it.

RAINA. [*hurrying forward anxiously*] I have heard what Captain Bluntschli said, Sergius. You are going to fight. Why? [*Sergius turns away in silence, and goes to the stove, where he stands watching her as she continues, to Bluntschli*] What about?

BLUNTSCHLI. I dont know: he hasnt told me. Better not interfere, dear young lady. No harm will be done: Ive often acted as sword instructor. He wont be able to touch me; and I'll not hurt him. It will save explanations. In the morning I shall be off home; and youll never see me or hear of me again. You and he will then make it up and live happily ever after.

RAINA. [*turning away deeply hurt, almost with a sob in her voice*] I never said I wanted to see you again.

SERGIUS. [*striding forward*] Ha! That is a confession.

RAINA. [*haughtily*] What do you mean?

SERGIUS. You love that man!

RAINA. [*scandalized*] Sergius!

SERGIUS. You allow him to make love to you behind my back, just as you treat me as your affianced husband behind his. Bluntschli: you knew our relations; and you deceived me. It is for that that I call you to account, not for having received favors I never enjoyed.

BLUNTSCHLI. [*jumping up indignantly*] Stuff! Rubbish! I have received no favors. Why, the young lady doesnt even know whether I'm married or not.

RAINA. [*forgetting herself*] Oh! [*Collapsing on the ottoman*] Are you?

SERGIUS. You see the young lady's concern, Captain Bluntschli. Denial is useless. You have enjoyed the privilege of being received in her own room, late at night—

BLUNTSCHLI. [*interrupting him pepperily*] Yes, you blockhead! she received me with a pistol at her head. Your cavalry were at my heels. I'd have blown out her brains if she'd uttered a cry.

SERGIUS. [*taken aback*] Bluntschli! Raina: is this true?

RAINA. [*rising in wrathful majesty*] Oh, how dare you, how dare you?

BLUNTSCHLI. Apologize, man: apologize. [*He resumes his seat at the table.*]

SERGIUS [*with the old measured emphasis, folding his arms*] I never apologize!

RAINA. [*passionately*] This is the doing of that friend of yours, Captain Bluntschli. It is he who is spreading this horrible story about me. [*She walks about excitedly.*]

BLUNTSCHLI. No: he's dead. Burnt alive!

RAINA. [*stopping, shocked*] Burnt alive!

BLUNTSCHLI. Shot in the hip in a woodyard. Couldnt drag himself out. Your fellows' shells set the timber on fire and burnt him, with half a dozen other poor devils in the same predicament.

RAINA. How horrible!

SERGIUS. And how ridiculous! Oh, war! war! the dream of patriots and heroes! A fraud, Bluntschli. A hollow sham, like love.

RAINA. [*outraged*] Like love! You say that before me!

BLUNTSCHLI. Come, Saranoff: that matter is explained.

SERGIUS. A hollow sham, I say. Would you have come back here if nothing had passed between you except at the muzzle of your pistol? Raina is mistaken about your friend who was burnt. He was not my informant.

RAINA. Who then? [*Suddenly guessing the truth*] Ah, Louka! my maid! my servant! You were with her this morning all that time after—after—Oh, what sort of god is this I have been worshipping! [*He meets her gaze with sardonic enjoyment of her disenchantment. Angered all the more, she goes closer to him, and says, in a lower, intenser tone*] Do you know that I looked out of the window as I went upstairs, to have another sight of my hero; and I saw something I did not understand then. I know now that you were making love to her.

SERGIUS. [*with grim humor*] You saw that?

RAINA. Only too well. [*She turns away, and throws herself on the divan under the centre window, quite overcome.*]

SERGIUS. [*cynically*] Raina: our romance is shattered. Life's a farce.

BLUNTSCHLI. [*to Raina, whimsically*] You see: he's found himself out now.

SERGIUS. [*going to him*] Bluntschli: I have allowed you to call me a blockhead. You may now call me a coward as well. I refuse to fight you. Do you know why?

BLUNTSCHLI. No; but it doesnt matter. I didnt ask the reason when you cried on; and I dont ask the reason now that you cry off. I'm a professional soldier! I fight when I have to, and am very glad to get out of it when I havnt to. Youre only an amateur: you think fighting's an amusement.

SERGIUS. [*sitting down at the table, nose to nose with him*] You shall hear the reason all the same, my professional. The reason is that it takes two men—real men—men of heart, blood and honor—to make a genuine combat. I could no more fight with you than I could make love to an ugly woman. Youve no magnetism: youre not a man: youre a machine.

BLUNTSCHLI. [*apologetically*] Quite true, quite true. I always was that sort of chap. I'm very sorry.

SERGIUS. Psha!

BLUNTSCHLI. But now that youve found that life isnt a farce, but something quite sensible and serious, what further obstacle is there to your happiness?

RAINA. [*rising*] You are very solicitous about my happiness and his.

Do you forget his new love—Louka? It is not you that he must
fight now, but his rival, Nicola.

SERGIUS. Rival!! [bounding half across the room]

RAINA. Dont you know that theyre engaged?

SERGIUS. Nicola! Are fresh abysses opening? Nicola!!

RAINA. [sarcastically] A shocking sacrifice, isnt it? Such beauty! such
intellect! such modesty! wasted on a middle-aged servant man.
Really, Sergius, you cannot stand by and allow such a thing. It
would be unworthy of your chivalry.

SERGIUS. [losing all self-control] Viper! Viper! [He rushes to and
fro, raging.]

BLUNTSCHLI. Look here, Saranoff: youre getting the worst of this.

RAINA. [getting angrier] Do you realize what he has done, Captain
Bluntschli? He has set this girl as a spy on us; and her reward is
that he makes love to her.

SERGIUS. False! Monstrous!

RAINA. Monstrous! [Confronting him] Do you deny that she told
you about Captain Bluntschli being in my room?

SERGIUS. No; but—

RAINA. [interrupting] Do you deny that you were making love to her
when she told you?

SERGIUS. No; but I tell you—

RAINA. [cutting him short contemptuously] It is unnecessary to tell
us anything more. That is quite enough for us. [She turns away
from him and sweeps majestically back to the window.]

BLUNTSCHLI. [quietly, as Sergius, in an agony of mortification, sinks
on the ottoman, clutching his averted head between his fists] I
told you you were getting the worst of it, Saranoff.

SERGIUS. Tiger cat!

RAINA. [running excitedly to Bluntschli] You hear this man calling
me names, Captain Bluntschli?

BLUNTSCHLI. What else can he do, dear lady? He must defend himself somehow. Come [very persuasively]: dont quarrel. What
good does it do?

Raina, with a gasp, sits down on the ottoman, and after a vain
effort to look vexedly at Bluntschli, falls a victim to her sense of
humor, and actually leans back babyishly against the writhing
shoulder of Sergius.

SERGIUS. Engaged to Nicola! Ha! ha! Ah well, Bluntschli, you are
right to take this huge imposture of a world coolly.

RAINA. [quaintly to Bluntschli, with an intuitive guess at his state
of mind] I daresay you think us a couple of grown-up babies,
dont you?

SERGIUS. [grinning savagely] He does: he does. Swiss civilization
nursetending Bulgarian barbarism, eh?

BLUNTSCHLI. [blushing] Not at all, I assure you. I'm only very glad
to get you two quieted. There! there! let's be pleasant and talk it
over in a friendly way. Where is this other young lady?

RAINA. Listening at the door, probably.

SERGIUS. [shivering as if a bullet had struck him, and speaking with *quiet but deep indignation*] I will prove that that, at least, is a calumny. [*He goes with dignity to the door and opens it. A yell of fury bursts from him as he looks out. He darts into the passage, and returns dragging in Louka, whom he flings violently against the table, exclaiming*] Judge her, Bluntschli. You, the cool impartial man: judge the eavesdropper.

Louka stands her ground, proud and silent.

BLUNTSCHLI. [*shaking his head*] I mustnt judge her. I once listened myself outside a tent when there was a mutiny brewing. It's all a question of the degree of provocation. My life was at stake.

LOUKA. My love was at stake. I am not ashamed.

RAINA. [*contemptuously*] Your love! Your curiosity, you mean.

LOUKA. [*facing her and returning her contempt with interest*] My love, stronger than anything you can feel, even for your chocolate cream soldier.

SERGIUS. [*with quick suspicion, to Louka*] What does that mean?

LOUKA. [*fiercely*] I mean—

SERGIUS [*interrupting her slightingly*] Oh, I remember: the ice pudding. A paltry taunt, girl!

Major Petkoff enters, in his shirtsleeves.

PETKOFF. Excuse my shirtsleeves, gentlemen. Raina: somebody has been wearing that coat of mine: I'll swear it. Somebody with a differently shaped back. It's all burst open at the sleeve. Your mother is mending it. I wish she'd make haste: I shall catch cold. [*He looks more attentively at them.*] Is anything the matter?

RAINA. No. [*She sits down at the stove, with a tranquil air.*]

SERGIUS. Oh no.[*He sits down at the end of the table, as at first.*]

BLUNTSCHLI. [*who is already seated*] Nothing. Nothing.

PETKOFF. [*sitting down on the ottoman in his old place*] Thats all right. [*He notices Louka.*] Anything the matter, Louka?

LOUKA. No, sir.

PETKOFF. [*genially*] Thats all right. [*He sneezes.*] Go and ask your mistress for my coat, like a good girl, will you?

Nicola enters with the coat. Louka makes a pretence of having business in the room by taking the little table with the hookah away to the wall near the windows.

RAINA. [*rising quickly as she sees the coat on Nicola's arm*] Here it is, papa. Give it to me, Nicola; and do you put some more wood on the fire. [*She takes the coat, and brings it to the Major, who stands up to put it on. Nicola attends to the fire.*]

PETKOFF. [*to Raina, teasing her affectionately*] Aha! Going to be very good to poor old papa just for one day after his return from the wars, eh?

RAINA. [*with solemn reproach*] Ah, how can you say that to me, father?

PETKOFF. Well, well, only a joke, little one. Come: give me a kiss. [*She kisses him.*] Now give me the coat.

RAINA. No: I am going to put it on for you. Turn your back. [*He turns his back and feels behind him with his arms for the sleeves. She dexterously takes the photograph from the pocket and throws it on the table before Bluntschli, who covers it with a sheet of paper under the very nose of Sergius, who looks on amazed, with his suspicions roused in the highest degree. She then helps Petkoff on with his coat.*] There, dear! Now are you comfortable?

PETKOFF. Quite, little love. Thanks. [*He sits down; and Raina returns to her seat near the stove.*] Oh, by the bye, Ive found something funny. Whats the meaning of this? [*He puts his hand into the picked pocket.*] Eh? Hallo! [*He tries the other pocket.*] Well, I could have sworn—! [*Much puzzled, he tries the breast pocket.*] I wonder—[*trying the original pocket*] Where can it—? [*He rises, exclaiming*] Your mother's taken it!

RAINA. [*very red*] Taken what?

PETKOFF. Your photograph, with the inscription: "Raina, to her Chocolate Cream Soldier: a Souvenir." Now you know theres something more in this than meets the eye; and I'm going to find it out. [*Shouting*] Nicola!

NICOLA. [*coming to him*] Sir!

PETKOFF. Did you spoil any pastry of Miss Raina's this morning?

NICOLA. You heard Miss Raina say that I did, sir.

PETKOFF. I know that, you idiot. Was it true?

NICOLA. I am sure Miss Raina is incapable of saying anything that is not true, sir.

PETKOFF. Are you? Then I'm not. [*Turning to the others*] Come: do you think I dont see it all? [*He goes to Sergius, and slaps him on the shoulder.*] Sergius: youre the chocolate cream soldier, arnt you?

SERGIUS. [*starting up*] I! A chocolate cream soldier! Certainly not.

PETKOFF. Not! [*He looks at them. They are all very serious and very conscious.*] Do you mean to tell me that Raina sends things like that to other men?

SERGIUS. [*enigmatically*] The world is not such an innocent place as we used to think, Petkoff.

BLUNTSCHLI. [*rising*] It's all right, major. I'm the chocolate cream soldier. [*Petkoff and Sergius are equally astonished.*] The gracious young lady saved my life by giving me chocolate creams when I was starving: shall I ever forget their flavour! My late friend Stolz told you the story at Pirot. I was the fugitive.

PETKOFF. You! [*He gasps.*] Sergius: do you remember how those two women went on this morning when we mentioned it? [*Sergius smiles cynically. Petkoff confronts Raina severely.*] Youre a nice young woman, arnt you?

RAINA. [*bitterly*] Major Saranoff has changed his mind. And when I wrote that on the photograph, I did not know that Captain Bluntschli was married.

BLUNTSCHLI. [*startled into vehement protest*] I'm not married.

RAINA. [*with deep reproach*] You said you were.

BLUNTSCHLI. I did not. I positively did not. I never was married in my life.

PETKOFF. [*exasperated*] Raina: will you kindly inform me, if I am not asking too much, which of these gentlemen you are engaged to?

RAINA. To neither of them. This young lady [*introducing Louka, who faces them all proudly*] is the object of Major Saranoff's affections at present.

PETKOFF. Louka! Are you mad, Sergius? Why, this girl's engaged to Nicola.

NICOLA. I beg your pardon, sir. There is a mistake. Louka is not engaged to me.

PETKOFF. Not engaged to you, you scoundrel! Why, you had twenty-five levas from me on the day of your betrothal; and she had that gilt bracelet from Miss Raina.

NICOLA. [*with cool unction*] We gave it out so, sir. But it was only to give Louka protection. She had a soul above her station; and I have been no more than her confidential servant. I intend, as you know, sir, to set up a shop later on in Sofia; and I look forward to her custom and recommendation should she marry into the nobility. [*He goes out with impressive discretion, leaving them all staring after him.*]

PETKOFF. [*breaking the silence*] Well, I am—hm!

SERGIUS. This is either the finest heroism or the most crawling baseness. Which is it, Bluntschli?

BLUNTSCHLI. Never mind whether it's heroism or baseness. Nicola's the ablest man Ive met in Bulgaria. I'll make him manager of a hotel if he can speak French and German.

LOUKA. [*suddenly breaking out at Sergius*] I have been insulted by everyone here. You set them the example. You owe me an apology.

Sergius, like a repeating clock of which the spring has been touched, immediately begins to fold his arms.

BLUNTSCHLI. [*before he can speak*] It's no use. He never apologizes.

LOUKA. Not to you, his equal and his enemy. To me, his poor servant, he will not refuse to apologize.

SERGIUS. [*approvingly*] You are right. [*He bends his knee in his grandest manner*] Forgive me.

LOUKA. I forgive you. [*She timidly gives him her hand, which he kisses.*] That touch makes me your affianced wife.

SERGIUS. [*springing up*] Ah! I forgot that.

LOUKA. [*coldly*] You can withdraw if you like.

SERGIUS. Withdraw! Never! You belong to me. [*He puts his arm about her.*]

Catherine comes in and finds Louka in Sergius's arms, with all the rest gazing at them in bewildered astonishment.

CATHERINE. What does this mean?

Sergius releases Louka.

PETKOFF. Well, my dear, it appears that Sergius is going to marry Louka instead of Raina. [*She is about to break out indignantly at him: he stops her by exclaiming testily*] Dont blame me: Ive nothing to do with it. [*He retreats to the stove.*]

CATHERINE. Marry Louka! Sergius: you are bound by your word to us!

SERGIUS. [*folding his arms*] Nothing binds me.

BLUNTSCHLI. [*much pleased by this piece of common sense*] Saranoff: your hand. My congratulations. These heroics of yours have their practical side after all. [*To Louka*] Gracious young lady: the best wishes of a good Republican! [*He kisses her hand, to Raina's great disgust, and returns to his seat.*]

CATHERINE. Louka: you have been telling stories.

LOUKA. I have done Raina no harm.

CATHERINE. [*haughtily*] Raina!

Raina, equally indignant, almost snorts at the liberty.

LOUKA. I have a right to call her Raina: she calls me Louka. I told Major Saranoff she would never marry him if the Swiss gentleman came back.

BLUNTSCHLI. [*rising, much surprised*] Hallo!

LOUKA. [*turning to Raina*] I thought you were fonder of him than of Sergius. You know best whether I was right.

BLUNTSCHLI. What nonsense! I assure you, my dear major, my dear madame, the gracious young lady simply saved my life, nothing else. She never cared two straws for me. Why, bless my heart and soul, look at the young lady and look at me. She, rich, young, beautiful, with her imagination full of fairy princes and noble natures and cavalry charges and goodness knows what! And I, a commonplace Swiss soldier who hardly knows what a decent life is after fifteen years of barracks and battles: a vagabond, a man who has spoiled all his chances in life through an incurably romantic disposition, a man—

SERGIUS. [*starting as if a needle had pricked him and interrupting Bluntschli in incredulous amazement*] Excuse me, Bluntschli: what did you say had spoiled your chances in life?

BLUNTSCHLI. [*promptly*] An incurably romantic disposition. I ran away from home twice when I was a boy. I went into the army instead of into my father's business. I climbed the balcony of this house when a man of sense would have dived into the nearest cellar. I came sneaking back here to have another look at the young lady when any other man of my age would have sent the coat back—

PETKOFF. My coat!

BLUNTSCHLI.—yes: thats the coat I mean—would have sent it back and gone quietly home. Do you suppose I am the sort of fellow a young girl falls in love with? Why, look at our ages! I'm thirty-four: I dont suppose the young lady is much over seventeen. [*This estimate produces a marked sensation, all the rest turning and staring at one another. He proceeds innocently*] All that adventure which was life or death to me, was only a schoolgirl's game to her—chocolate creams and hide and seek. Heres the proof! [*He takes the photograph from the table.*] Now, I ask you, would a woman who took the affair seriously have sent me this and written on it "Raina, to her Chocolate Cream Soldier: a Souvenir"? [*He exhibits the photograph triumphantly, as if it settled the matter beyond all possibility of refutation.*]

PETKOFF. Thats what I was looking for. How the deuce did it get there? [*He comes from the stove to look at it, and sits down on the ottoman.*]

BLUNTSCHLI. [*to Raina, complacently*] I have put everything right, I hope, gracious young lady.

RAINA. [*going to the table to face him*] I quite agree with your account of yourself. You are a romantic idiot. [*Bluntschli is unspeakably taken aback.*] Next time, I hope you will know the difference between a schoolgirl of seventeen and a woman of twenty-three.

BLUNTSCHLI. [*stupefied*] Twenty-three!

Raina snaps the photograph contemptuously from his hand; tears it up; throws the pieces in his face; and sweeps back to her former place.

SERGIUS. [*with grim enjoyment of his rival's discomfiture*] Bluntschli: my one last belief is gone. Your sagacity is a fraud, like everything else. You have less sense than even I!

BLUNTSCHLI. [*overwhelmed*] Twenty-three! Twenty-three!! [*He considers.*] Hm! [*swiftly making up his mind and coming to his host*] In that case, Major Petkoff, I beg to propose formally to become a suitor for your daughter's hand, in place of Major Saranoff retired.

RAINA. You dare!

BLUNTSCHLI. If you were twenty-three when you said those things to me this afternoon, I shall take them seriously.

CATHERINE. [*loftily polite*] I doubt, sir, whether you quite realize either my daughter's position or that of Major Sergius Saranoff, whose place you propose to take. The Petkoffs and the Saranoffs are known as the richest and most important families in the country. Our position is almost historical: we can go back for twenty years.

PETKOFF. Oh, never mind that, Catherine. [*To Bluntschli*] We should be most happy, Bluntschli, if it were only a question of your position; but hang it, you know, Raina is accustomed to a very comfortable establishment. Sergius keeps twenty horses.

BLUNTSCHLI. But who wants twenty horses? We're not going to keep a circus.

CATHERINE. [*severely*] My daughter, sir, is accustomed to a first-rate stable.

RAINA. Hush, mother: youre making me ridiculous.

BLUNTSCHLI. Oh well, if it comes to a question of an establishment, here goes! [*He darts impetuously to the table; seizes the papers in the blue envelope; and turns to Sergius.*] How many horses did you say?

SERGIUS. Twenty, noble Switzer.

BLUNTSCHLI. I have two hundred horses. [*They are amazed.*] How many carriages?

SERGIUS. Three.

BLUNTSCHLI. I have seventy. Twenty-four of them will hold twelve inside, besides two on the box, without counting the driver and conductor. How many tablecloths have you?

SERGIUS. How the deuce do I know?

BLUNTSCHLI. Have you four thousand?

SERGIUS. No.

BLUNTSCHLI. I have. I have nine thousand six hundred pairs of sheets and blankets, with two thousand four hundred eider-down quilts. I have ten thousand knives and forks, and the same quantity of dessert spoons. I have three hundred servants. I have six palatial establishments, besides two livery stables, a tea garden, and a private house. I have four medals for distinguished services; I have the rank of an officer and the standing of a gentleman; and I have three native languages. Shew me any man in Bulgaria that can offer as much!

PETKOFF. [*with childish awe*] Are you Emperor of Switzerland?

BLUNTSCHLI. My rank is the highest known in Switzerland: I am a free citizen.

CATHERINE. Then, Captain Bluntschli, since you are my daughter's choice—

RAINA. [*mutinously*] He's not.

CATHERINE. [*ignoring her*]—I shall not stand in the way of her happiness. [*Petkoff is about to speak*] That is Major Petkoff's feeling also.

PETKOFF. Oh, I shall be only too glad. Two hundred horses! Whew!

SERGIUS. What says the lady?

RAINA. [*pretending to sulk*] The lady says that he can keep his tablecloths and his omnibuses. I am not here to be sold to the highest bidder. [*She turns her back on him.*]

BLUNTSCHLI. I wont take that answer. I appealed to you as a fugitive, a beggar, and a starving man. You accepted me. You gave me your hand to kiss, your bed to sleep in, and your roof to shelter me.

RAINA. I did not give them to the Emperor of Switzerland.

BLUNTSCHLI. Thats just what I say. [*He catches her by the shoulders and turns her face-to-face with him.*] Now tell us whom you did give them to.

RAINA. [*succumbing with a shy smile*] To my chocolate cream soldier.

BLUNTSCHLI. [*with a boyish laugh of delight*] Thatll do. Thank you. [*He looks at his watch and suddenly becomes businesslike.*] Time's up, major. Youve managed those regiments so well that youre sure to be asked to get rid of some of the infantry of the Timok division. Send them home by way of Lom Palanka. Saranoff: dont get married until I come back: I shall be here punctually at five in the evening on Tuesday fortnight. Gracious ladies [*his heels click*] good evening. [*He makes them a military bow, and goes.*]

SERGIUS. What a man! Is he a man?

1894   1898

JOSEPH CONRAD
(1857–1924)

1875–94: Career as a seaman.
1895:   *Almayer's Folly.*
1904:   *Nostromo.*

Joseph Conrad was born Jozef Teodor Konrad Nalecz Korzeniowski in Poland (then under Russian rule), son of a Polish patriot who suffered exile in Russia for his Polish nationalist activities and died in 1869, leaving Conrad to be brought up by a maternal uncle. At the age of 15 he amazed everybody by announcing his passionate desire to go to sea; he was eventually allowed to go to Marseilles in 1874, and from there he made a number of voyages on French merchant ships to Martinique and the West Indies. In 1878 he signed on an English ship which brought him to the east coast English port of Lowestoft, where (still as an ordinary seaman) he joined the crew of a small coasting vessel plying between Lowestoft and Newcastle. In six voyages between these two ports he learned English. Thus launched on a career in the British merchant service, Conrad sailed on a variety of British ships to the Orient and elsewhere and eventually gained his master's certificate in 1886, the year when he became a naturalized British subject. He received his first command in 1888, and in 1890 took a steamboat up the Congo River in nightmarish circumstances (described in *Heart of Darkness*) which produced severe illness and permanently haunted his imagination. In the early 1890's he was already thinking of turning some of his Malayan experiences into English fiction, and in 1892–93, when serving as first mate on the *Torrens* sailing from London to Adelaide, he revealed to a sympathetic passenger that he had begun a novel (*Almayer's Folly*), while on the return journey he impressed John Galsworthy, who was a passenger, with his conversation. Though possessed of a master's certificate, Conrad found it difficult to get the kind of job as master that he wished, and occasionally he had to serve in lesser capacities. His difficulty in obtaining a command, together with the interest aroused by *Almayer's Folly* when it was published in 1895, helped to turn him away from the sea to a career as a writer. He settled in London and in 1896 married an English girl; this son of a Polish patriot turned merchant seaman turned writer was henceforth an English novelist.

Conrad was for a long time regarded as a sea writer whose exotic descriptions of eastern landscapes and exploitation of the romantic atmosphere of Malaya and other unfamiliar regions gave his work a special kind of richness and splendor. But this is only one, and not in the last analysis the most important, aspect of his work. More and more Conrad used the sea and the circumstances of life on shipboard or in remote eastern settlements as means of exploring certain profound moral ambiguities in human experience. In *The Nigger of the "Narcissus"* (1897) he shows how a dying Negro seaman corrupts the morale of a ship's crew by the very fact that his plight produces sympathy, thus symbolically presenting one of his commonest themes—the necessity and at the same time the dangers of human contact. In *Lord Jim* (1900), using the device of an intermediate narrator, he probes the meaning of a gross failure of duty on the part of a romantic and idealistic young sailor, and by presenting the hero's history from a series of different points of view keeps the moral questioning continuing to the end. The use of intermediate narrators and multiple points of view is common in Conrad; it is his favorite way of suggesting the complexity of experience and the difficulty of judging human actions. In *Heart of Darkness* he draws on his Congo River experience to create an atmosphere of darkness and horror in the midst of which the hero recognizes a deep inner kinship with the corrupt villain, the Belgian trader who has lost all his earlier ideals to succumb to the worst elements in the native life he had hoped to improve.

This notion of the difficulty of true communion, coupled with the idea that communion can be unexpectedly forced on us—sometimes with someone who may be on the surface our moral opposite, so that we can at times be compelled into a mysterious recognition of our opposite as our true self—is found in many of Conrad's works; it provides one of the underlying themes of *The Secret Sharer* (1912). This story can be enjoyed for the clarity and power with which Conrad renders the atmosphere of the Gulf of Siam as felt by a young sea captain on taking on his first command, but it also uses situation and incident symbolically in order to suggest some of the paradoxes of identity and sympathy.

Other stories and novels explore the ways in which the codes we live by are tested in moments of crisis, revealing either their inadequacy or our own. Imagination can corrupt (as with Lord Jim), or save (as in *The Shadow Line*, 1917); and there are times when total lack of it can see a man through (Captain M'Whirr in *Typhoon*, 1902), though a similar lack in other circumstances can render a man comically ridiculous (Captain Mitchell in *Nostromo*, 1904).

Nostromo, a profound and subtle study of the corrupting effects of politics and "material interests" on personal relationships (set in an imaginary South American republic), is now generally regarded as Conrad's greatest work. His two other political novels—*The Secret Agent* (1906) and *Under Western Eyes* (1910)—have also recently come into their own. The latter is the story of a Russian student who becomes involuntarily associated with antigovernment violence in Czarist Russia and is irresistibly maneuvered by circumstances into a position where, although a government spy, he has to pretend to be a revolutionary among revolutionaries. This is the ultimate in human loneliness and incommunicability— when you must consistently pretend to be the opposite of what you are. It is a story of Dostoievskian power, and shows a very different Conrad from the picturesque sea-dreamer pictured by the earlier critics. Conrad was as much a pessimist as Hardy, but he projected his pessimism in subtler ways. He was also a great master of English prose, an astonishing fact when we realize that he was 21 before he learned any English, and that to the end of his life he spoke English with a thick foreign accent.

Preface to *The Nigger of the "Narcissus"* [1]

[The Task of the Artist]

A work that aspires, however humbly, to the condition of art should carry its justification in every line. And art itself may be defined as a single-minded attempt to render the highest kind of justice to the visible universe, by bringing to light the truth, manifold and one, underlying its every aspect. It is an attempt to find in its forms, in its colors, in its light, in its shadows, in the aspects of matter and in the facts of life, what of each is fundamental, what is enduring and essential—their one illuminating and convincing quality—the very truth of their existence. The artist, then, like the thinker or the scientist, seeks the truth and makes his appeal. Impressed by the aspect of the world the thinker plunges into ideas, the scientist into facts—whence, presently, emerging they make their appeal to those qualities of our being that fit us best for the hazardous enterprise of living. They speak authoritatively to our common-sense, to our intelligence, to our desire of peace or to our desire of unrest; not seldom to our prejudices, sometimes to our fears, often to our egoism—but always to our credulity. And their words are heard with reverence, for their concern is with weighty matters: with the cultivation of our minds and the proper care of our bodies, with the attainment of our ambitions, with the perfection of the means and the glorification of our precious aims.

It is otherwise with the artist.

Confronted by the same enigmatical spectacle the artist descends within himself, and in that lonely region of stress and strife, if he be deserving and fortunate, he finds the terms of his appeal. His appeal is made to our less obvious capacities: to that part of our nature which, because of the warlike conditions of existence, is necessarily kept out of sight within the more resisting and hard qualities—like the vulnerable body within a steel armor. His appeal is less loud, more profound, less distinct, more stirring—and sooner forgotten. Yet its effect endures forever. The changing wisdom of successive generations discards ideas, questions facts, demolishes theories. But the artist appeals to that part of our being which is not dependent on wisdom: to that in us which is a gift and not an acquisition—and, therefore, more permanently enduring. He

---

1. *The Nigger of the "Narcissus"* was written in 1896–97, shortly after his marriage, and published first in *The New Review*, August–December 1897, and then in book form in 1898. The novel, in the words of Jocelyn Baines, Conrad's biographer, "is the culmination of Conrad's apprenticeship as a novelist." Conrad took particular pleasure in writing the book, and later called it "the story by which, as a creative artist, I stand or fall." It was with the feeling that he was now wholly dedicated to writing and had finally (in his own words) "done with the sea" that, a few months after finishing the novel, he wrote the preface in which he defined his aims as an artist. The preface first appeared in the 1898 edition.

speaks to our capacity for delight and wonder, to the sense of mystery surrounding our lives; to our sense of pity, and beauty, and pain; to the latent feeling of fellowship with all creation—and to the subtle but invincible conviction of solidarity that knits together the loneliness of innumerable hearts, to the solidarity in dreams, in joy, in sorrow, in aspirations, in illusions, in hope, in fear, which binds men to each other, which binds together all humanity—the dead to the living and the living to the unborn.

It is only some such train of thought, or rather of feeling, that can in a measure explain the aim of the attempt, made in the tale which follows,[2] to present an unrestful episode in the obscure lives of a few individuals out of all the disregarded multitude of the bewildered, the simple and the voiceless. For, if any part of truth dwells in the belief confessed above, it becomes evident that there is not a place of splendor or a dark corner of the earth that does not deserve if only a passing glance of wonder and pity. The motive, then, may be held to justify the matter of the work; but this preface, which is simply an avowal of endeavor, cannot end here—for the avowal is not yet complete.

Fiction—if it at all aspires to be art—appeals to temperament. And in truth it must be, like painting, like music, like all art, the appeal of one temperament to all the other innumerable temperaments whose subtle and resistless power endows passing events with their true meaning, and creates the moral, the emotional atmosphere of the place and time. Such an appeal, to be effective, must be an impression conveyed through the senses; and, in fact, it cannot be made in any other way, because temperament, whether individual or collective, is not amenable to persuasion. All art, therefore, appeals primarily to the senses, and the artistic aim when expressing itself in written words must also make its appeal through the senses, if its high desire is to reach the secret spring of responsive emotions. It must strenuously aspire to the plasticity of sculpture, to the color of painting, and to the magic suggestiveness of music—which is the art of arts. And it is only through complete, unswerving devotion to the perfect blending of form and substance; it is only through an unremitting, never-discouraged care for the shape and ring of sentences that an approach can be made to plasticity, to color, and that the light of magic suggestiveness may be brought to play for an evanescent instant over the commonplace surface of words: of the old, old words, worn thin, defaced by ages of careless usage.

The sincere endeavor to accomplish that creative task, to go as far on that road as his strength will carry him, to go undeterred by faltering, weariness, or reproach, is the only valid justification for the worker in prose. And if his conscience is clear, his answer to

2. I.e., *The Nigger of the "Narcissus."*

those who in the fullness of a wisdom which looks for immediate profit, demand specifically to be edified, consoled, amused; who demand to be promptly improved, or encouraged, or frightened, or shocked, or charmed, must run thus:—My task which I am trying to achieve is, by the power of the written word, to make you hear, to make you feel—it is, before all, to make you *see*. That—and no more, and it is everything. If I succeed, you shall find there, according to your deserts, encouragement, consolation, fear, charm—all you demand—and, perhaps, also that glimpse of truth for which you have forgotten to ask.

To snatch, in a moment of courage, from the remorseless rush of time a passing phase of life, is only the beginning of the task. The task approached in tenderness and faith is to hold up unquestioningly, without choice and without fear, the rescued fragment before all eyes in the light of a sincere mood. It is to show its vibration, its color, its form; and through its movement, its form, and its color, reveal the substance of its truth—disclose its inspiring secret: the stress and passion within the core of each convincing moment. In a single-minded attempt of that kind, if one be deserving and fortunate, one may perchance attain to such clearness of sincerity that at last the presented vision of regret or pity, of terror or mirth, shall awaken in the hearts of the beholders that feeling of unavoidable solidarity; of the solidarity in mysterious origin, in toil, in joy, in hope, in uncertain fate, which binds men to each other and all mankind to the visible world.

It is evident that he who, rightly or wrongly, holds by the convictions expressed above cannot be faithful to any one of the temporary formulas of his craft. The enduring part of them—the truth which each only imperfectly veils—should abide with him as the most precious of his possessions, but they all—Realism, Romanticism, Naturalism, even the unofficial sentimentalism (which, like the poor,[3] is exceedingly difficult to get rid of)—all these gods must, after a short period of fellowship, abandon him—even on the very threshold of the temple—to the stammerings of his conscience and to the outspoken consciousness of the difficulties of his work. In that uneasy solitude the supreme cry of Art for Art, itself, loses the exciting ring of its apparent immorality. It sounds far off. It has ceased to be a cry, and is heard only as a whisper, often incomprehensible, but at times and faintly encouraging.

Sometimes, stretched at ease in the shade of a roadside tree, we watch the motions of a laborer in a distant field, and after a time, begin to wonder languidly as to what the fellow may be at. We watch the movements of his body, the waving of his arms; we see him bend down, stand up, hesitate, begin again. It may add to the charm of an idle hour to be told the purpose of his exertions. If we

---

3. "For the poor always ye have with you." John xii.8.

know he is trying to lift a stone, to dig a ditch, to uproot a stump, we look with a more real interest at his efforts; we are disposed to condone the jar of his agitation upon the restfulness of the land-scape; and even, if in a brotherly frame of mind, we may bring our-selves to forgive his failure. We understand his object, and, after all, the fellow has tried, and perhaps he had not the strength—and perhaps he had not the knowledge. We forgive, go on our way—and forget.

And so it is with the workmen of art. Art is long and life is short,[4] and success is very far off. And thus, doubtful of strength to travel so far, we talk a little about the aim—the aim of art, which, like life itself, is inspiring, difficult—obscured by mists. It is not in the clear logic of a triumphant conclusion; it is not in the unveiling of one of those heartless secrets which are called the Laws of Nature. It is not less great, but only more difficult.

To arrest, for the space of a breath, the hands busy about the work of the earth, and compel men entranced by the sight of dis-tant goals to glance for a moment at the surrounding vision of form and color, of sunshine and shadows, to make them pause for a look, for a sigh, for a smile—such is the aim, difficult and evanescent, and reserved only for a very few to achieve. But sometimes, by the deserving and the fortunate, even that task is accomplished. And when it is accomplished—behold!—all the truth of life is there: a moment of vision, a sigh, a smile—and the return to an eternal rest.

1897   1898

Youth[1]

This could have occurred nowhere but in England, where men and sea interpenetrate, so to speak—the sea entering into the life of most men, and the men knowing something or everything about the sea, in the way of amusement, of travel, or of bread-winning.

We were sitting round a mahogany table that reflected the bottle, the claret-glasses, and our faces as we leaned on our elbows. There was a director of companies, an accountant, a lawyer, Marlow, and myself. The director had been a *Conway*[2] boy, the accountant had served four years at sea, the lawyer—a fine crusted Tory, High Churchman, the best of old fellows, the soul of honor—had been

---

4. Cf. the Latin proverb (deriving from a dictum of the Greek physician Hip-pocrates) *ars longa, vita brevis,* "art is long and life is short." Chaucer ren-dered it, "The lyf so short, the craft so long to lerne" (*The Parlement of Foules*) and Longfellow, "Art is long, and Time is fleeting" (*A Psalm of Life*).
1. This story is derived from Conrad's own experience at sea. In an "author's note," written in 1917, Conrad re-marked that " 'Youth' is a feat of mem-ory. It is a record of experience; but that experience, in its facts, in its in-wardness and in its outward coloring, begins and ends in myself." The real ship was called the *Palestine,* and Con-rad changed the name to *Judea;* he did not alter the name of the captain, Beard, or that of the mate, Mahon.
2. The *Conway* was a training ship on which student officers for the British merchant marine gained sea experience.

chief officer in the P. & O.[3] service in the good old days when mail-
boats were square-rigged at least on two masts, and used to come
down the China Sea before a fair monsoon with stun'sails set alow
and aloft. We all began life in the merchant service. Between the
five of us there was the strong bond of the sea, and also the fellowship of the craft, which no amount of enthusiasm for yachting,
cruising, and so on can give, since one is only the amusement of
life and the other is life itself.

Marlow (at least I think that is how he spelt his name) told the
story, or rather the chronicle, of a voyage:

"Yes, I have seen a little of the Eastern seas; but what I remember best is my first voyage there. You fellows know there are those
voyages that seem ordered for the illustration of life, that might
stand for a symbol of existence. You fight, work, sweat, nearly kill
yourself, sometimes do kill yourself, trying to accomplish something—and you can't. Not from any fault of yours. You simply can
do nothing, neither great nor little—not a thing in the world—not
even marry an old maid, or get a wretched 600-ton cargo of coal to
its port of destination.

"It was altogether a memorable affair. It was my first voyage to
the East, and my first voyage as second mate; it was also my skipper's first command. You'll admit it was time. He was sixty if a day;
a little man, with a broad, not very straight back, with bowed
shoulders and one leg more bandy than the other, he had that queer
twisted-about appearance you see so often in men who work in the
fields. He had a nutcracker face—chin and nose trying to come
together over a sunken mouth—and it was framed in iron-gray fluffy
hair, that looked like a chin-strap of cotton-wool sprinkled with
coal-dust. And he had blue eyes in that old face of his, which were
amazingly like a boy's, with that candid expression some quite
common men preserve to the end of their days by a rare internal
gift of simplicity of heart and rectitude of soul. What induced him
to accept me was a wonder. I had come out of a crack Australian
clipper, where I had been third officer, and he seemed to have a
prejudice against crack clippers as aristocratic and high-toned. He
said to me, 'You know, in this ship you will have to work.' I said I
had to work in every ship I had ever been in. 'Ah, but this is different, and you gentlemen out of them big ships; . . . but there!
I dare say you will do. Join tomorrow.'

"I joined tomorrow. It was twenty-two years ago; and I was just
twenty. How time passes! It was one of the happiest days of my life.
Fancy! Second mate for the first time—a really responsible officer!
I wouldn't have thrown up my new billet for a fortune. The mate
looked me over carefully. He was also an old chap, but of another
stamp. He had a Roman nose, a snow-white, long beard, and his

3. "Pacific and Oriental," a famous British line shipping to the Far East.

name was Mahon, but he insisted that it should be pronounced Mann. He was well connected; yet there was something wrong with his luck, and he had never got on.

"As to the captain, he had been for years in coasters, then in the Mediterranean, and last in the West Indian trade. He had never been round the Capes.[4] He could just write a kind of sketchy hand, and didn't care for writing at all. Both were thorough good seamen of course, and between those two old chaps I felt like a small boy between two grandfathers.

"The ship also was old. Her name was the *Judea*. Queer name, isn't it? She belonged to a man Wilmer, Wilcox—some name like that; but he has been bankrupt and dead these twenty years or more, and his name don't matter. She had been laid up in Shadwell basin for ever so long. You may imagine her state. She was all rust, dust, grime—soot aloft, dirt on deck. To me it was like coming out of a palace into a ruined cottage. She was about 400 tons, had a primitive windlass, wooden latches to the doors, not a bit of brass about her, and a big square stern. There was on it, below her name in big letters, a lot of scrollwork, with the gilt off, and some sort of a coat of arms, with the motto 'Do or Die' underneath. I remember it took my fancy immensely. There was a touch of romance in it, something that made me love the old thing—something that appealed to my youth!

"We left London in ballast—sand ballast—to load a cargo of coal in a northern port for Bangkok. Bangkok! I thrilled. I had been six years at sea, but had only seen Melbourne and Sydney, very good places, charming places in their way—but Bangkok!

"We worked out of the Thames under canvas, with a North Sea pilot on board. His name was Jermyn, and he dodged all day long about the galley drying his handkerchief before the stove. Apparently he never slept. He was a dismal man, with a perpetual tear sparkling at the end of his nose, who either had been in trouble, or was in trouble, or expected to be in trouble—couldn't be happy unless something went wrong. He mistrusted my youth, my common sense, and my seamanship, and made a point of showing it in a hundred little ways. I dare say he was right. It seems to me I knew very little then, and I know not much more now; but I cherish a hate for that Jermyn to this day.

"We were a week working up as far as Yarmouth Roads, and then we got into a gale—the famous October gale of twenty-two years ago. It was wind, lightning, sleet, snow, and a terrific sea. We were flying light, and you may imagine how bad it was when I tell you we had smashed bulwarks and a flooded deck. On the second night she shifted her ballast into the lee bow, and by that time we

4. The Cape of Good Hope, at the southwestern tip of the African continent, and Cape Horn, the southernmost point of South America.

had been blown off somewhere on the Dogger Bank. There was nothing for it but go below with shovels and try to right her, and there we were in that vast hold, gloomy like a cavern, the tallow dips stuck and flickering on the beams, the gale howling above, the ship tossing about like mad on her side; there we all were, Jermyn, the captain, everyone, hardly able to keep our feet, engaged on that gravedigger's work, and trying to toss shovelfuls of wet sand up to windward. At every tumble of the ship you could see vaguely in the dim light men falling down with a great flourish of shovels. One of the ship's boys (we had two), impressed by the weirdness of the scene, wept as if his heart would break. We could hear him blubbering somewhere in the shadows.

"On the third day the gale died out, and by and by a north-country tug picked us up. We took sixteen days in all to get from London to the Tyne![5] When we got into dock we had lost our turn for loading, and they hauled us off to a pier where we remained for a month. Mrs. Beard (the captain's name was Beard) came from Colchester to see the old man. She lived on board. The crew of runners had left, and there remained only the officers, one boy and the steward, a mulatto who answered to the name of Abraham. Mrs. Beard was an old woman, with a face all wrinkled and ruddy like a winter apple, and the figure of a young girl. She caught sight of me once, sewing on a button, and insisted on having my shirts to repair. This was something different from the captains' wives I had known on board crack clippers. When I brought her the shirts, she said: 'And the socks? They want mending, I am sure, and John's—Captain Beard's—things are all in order now. I would be glad of something to do.' Bless the old woman. She overhauled my outfit for me, and meantime I read for the first time *Sartor Resartus* and Burnaby's *Ride to Khiva*.[6] I didn't understand much of the first then; but I remember I preferred the soldier to the philosopher at the time; a preference which life has only confirmed. One was a man, the other was either more—or less. However, they are both dead and Mrs. Beard is dead, and youth, strength, genius, thoughts, achievements, simple hearts—all dies. . . . No matter.

"They loaded us at last. We shipped a crew. Eight able seamen and two boys. We hauled off one evening to the buoys at the dock-gates, ready to go out, and with a fair prospect of beginning the voyage next day. Mrs. Beard was to start for home by a late train.

5. A river in the northeast of England, on which the port of Newcastle-on-Tyne is situated. It flows into the North Sea at Tynemouth, nearly 300 miles north of London.
6. A once-popular travel book, published in 1876, by the English soldier and traveler Frederick Gustavus Barnaby (1842–85), describing his 300-mile winter journey on horseback across the Russian steppes. Khiva is now in the Uzbek Soviet Socialist Republic of the U.S.S.R.

When the ship was fast we went to tea. We sat rather silent through the meal—Mahon, the old couple, and I. I finished first, and slipped away for a smoke, my cabin being in a deckhouse just against the poop.[7] It was high water, blowing fresh with a drizzle; the double dock-gates were opened, and the steam colliers were going in and out in the darkness with their lights burning bright, a great plashing of propellers, rattling of winches, and a lot of hailing on the pierheads. I watched the procession of head-lights gliding high and of green lights gliding low in the night, when suddenly a red gleam flashed at me, vanished, came into view again, and remained. The fore-end of a steamer loomed up close. I shouted down the cabin, 'Come up, quick!' and then heard a startled voice saying afar in the dark, 'Stop her, sir.' A bell jingled. Another voice cried warningly, 'We are going right into that bark, sir.' The answer to this was a gruff 'All right,' and the next thing was a heavy crash as the steamer struck a glancing blow with the bluff of her bow about our fore-rigging. There was a moment of confusion, yelling, and running about. Steam roared. Then somebody was heard saying, 'All clear, sir.' . . . 'Are you all right?' asked the gruff voice. I had jumped forward to see the damage, and hailed back, 'I think so.' 'Easy astern,' said the gruff voice. A bell jingled. 'What steamer is that?' screamed Mahon. By that time she was no more to us than a bulky shadow maneuvering a little way off. They shouted at us some name—a woman's name, Miranda or Melissa—or some such thing. 'This means another month in this beastly hole,' said Mahon to me, as we peered with lamps about the splintered bulwarks and broken braces. 'But where's the captain?'

"We had not heard or seen anything of him all that time. We went aft to look. A doleful voice arose hailing somewhere in the middle of the dock, '*Judea* ahoy!' . . . How the devil did he get there? . . . 'Hallo!' we shouted. 'I am adrift in our boat without oars,' he cried. A belated water-man offered his services, and Mahon struck a bargain with him for a half crown to tow our skipper alongside; but it was Mrs. Beard that came up the ladder first. They had been floating about the dock in that mizzly cold rain for nearly an hour. I was never so surprised in my life.

"It appears that when he heard my shout 'Come up' he understood at once what was the matter, caught up his wife, ran on deck, and across, and down into our boat, which was fast to the ladder. Not bad for a sixty-year-old. Just imagine that old fellow saving heroically in his arms that old woman—the woman of his life. He set her down on a thwart, and was ready to climb back on board when the painter came adrift somehow, and away they went together. Of course in the confusion we did not hear him shouting.

7. Raised deck, often forming the roof of the cabin, at ship's stern.

He looked abashed. She said cheerfully, 'I suppose it does not matter my losing the train now?' 'No, Jenny—you go below and get
warm,' he growled. Then to us: 'A sailor has no business with a
wife—I say. There I was, out of the ship. Well, no harm done this
time. Let's go and look at what that fool of a steamer smashed.'

"It wasn't much, but it delayed us three weeks. At the end of that
time, the captain being engaged with his agents, I carried Mrs.
Beard's bag to the railway station and put her all comfy into a
third-class carriage. She lowered the window to say, 'You are a
good young man. If you see John—Captain Beard—without his
muffler at night, just remind him from me to keep his throat well
wrapped up.' 'Certainly, Mrs. Beard,' I said. 'You are a good young
man; I noticed how attentive you are to John—to Captain——' The
train pulled out suddenly; I took my cap off to the old woman: I
never saw her again. . . . Pass the bottle.

"We went to sea next day. When we made that start for Bangkok
we had been already three months out of London. We had expected to be a fortnight or so—at the outside.

"It was January, and the weather was beautiful—the beautiful
sunny winter weather that has more charm than in the summertime,
because it is unexpected, and crisp, and you know it won't, it can't,
last long. It's like a windfall, like a godsend, like an unexpected
piece of luck.

"It lasted all down the North Sea, all down Channel; and it
lasted till we were three hundred miles or so to the westward of
the Lizards; [8] then the wind went round to the sou'west and began
to pipe up. In two days it blew a gale. The *Judea*, hove to, wallowed
on the Atlantic like an old candle-box. It blew day after day: it blew
with spite, without interval, without mercy, without rest. The
world was nothing but an immensity of great foaming waves rushing
at us, under a sky low enough to touch with the hand and dirty like
a smoked ceiling. In the stormy space surrounding us there was as
much flying spray as air. Day after day and night after night there
was nothing round the ship but the howl of the wind, the tumult
of the sea, the noise of water pouring over her deck. There was no
rest for her and no rest for us. She tossed, she pitched, she stood on
her head, she sat on her tail, she rolled, she groaned, and we had to
hold on while on deck and cling to our bunks when below, in a
constant effort of body and worry of mind.

"One night Mahon spoke through the small window of my berth.
It opened right into my very bed, and I was lying there sleepless, in
my boots, feeling as though I had not slept for years, and could not
if I tried. He said excitedly:

8. Lizard Head, peninsula in southwest England, on the coast of Cornwall, terminating in Lizard Point, the southern-most point in England.

" 'You got the sounding-rod in here, Marlow? I can't get the pumps to suck. By God! It's no child's play.'

"I gave him the sounding rod and lay down again, trying to think of various things—but I thought only of the pumps. When I came on deck they were still at it, and my watch relieved at the pumps. By the light of the lantern brought on deck to examine the sounding rod I caught a glimpse of their weary, serious faces. We pumped all the four hours. We pumped all night, all day, all the week—watch and watch. She was working herself loose, and leaked badly—not enough to drown us at once, but enough to kill us with the work at the pumps. And while we pumped the ship was going from us piecemeal: the bulwarks went, the stanchions were torn out, the ventilators smashed, the cabin door burst in. There was not a dry spot in the ship. She was being gutted bit by bit. The long-boat changed, as if by magic, into matchwood where she stood in her gripes. I had lashed her myself, and was rather proud of my handiwork, which had withstood so long the malice of the sea. And we pumped. And there was no break in the weather. The sea was white like a sheet of foam, like a caldron of boiling milk; there was not a break in the clouds, no—not the size of a man's hand—no, not for so much as ten seconds. There was for us no sky, there were for us no stars, no sun, no universe—nothing but angry clouds and an infuriated sea. We pumped watch and watch, for dear life; and it seemed to last for months, for years, for all eternity, as though we had been dead and gone to a hell for sailors. We forgot the day of the week, the name of the month, what year it was, and whether we had ever been ashore. The sails blew away, she lay broadside on under a weather cloth, the ocean poured over her, and we did not care. We turned those handles, and had the eyes of idiots. As soon as we had crawled on deck I used to take a round turn with a rope about the men, the pumps, and the mainmast, and we turned, we turned incessantly, with the water to our waists, to our necks, over our heads. It was all one. We had forgotten how it felt to be dry.

"And there was somewhere in me the thought: By Jove! this is the deuce of an adventure—something you read about; and it is my first voyage as second mate—and I am only twenty—and here I am lasting it out as well as any of these men, and keeping my chaps up to the mark. I was pleased. I would not have given up the experience for worlds. I had moments of exultation. Whenever the old dismantled craft pitched heavily with her counter high in the air, she seemed to me to throw up, like an appeal, like a defiance, like a cry to the clouds without mercy, the words written on her stern: 'Judea, London: Do or Die.'

"O youth! The strength of it, the faith of it, the imagination of it! To me she was not an old rattletrap carting about the world a lot of coal for a freight—to me she was the endeavor, the test, the trial of life. I think of her with pleasure, with affection, with regret —as you would think of someone dead you have loved. I shall never forget her. . . . Pass the bottle.

"One night when tied to the mast, as I explained, we were pumping on, deafened with the wind, and without spirit enough in us to wish ourselves dead, a heavy sea crashed aboard and swept clean over us. As soon as I got my breath I shouted, as in duty bound, 'Keep on, boys!' when suddenly I felt something hard floating on deck strike the calf of my leg. I made a grab at it and missed. It was so dark we could not see each other's faces within a foot—you understand.

"After that thump the ship kept quiet for a while, and the thing, whatever it was, struck my leg again. This time I caught it— and it was a saucepan. At first, being stupid with fatigue and thinking of nothing but the pumps, I did not understand what I had in my hand. Suddenly it dawned upon me, and I shouted, 'Boys, the house on deck is gone. Leave this, and let's look for the cook.'

"There was a deck-house forward, which contained the galley, the cook's berth, and the quarters of the crew. As we had expected for days to see it swept away, the hands had been ordered to sleep in the cabin—the only safe place in the ship. The steward, Abraham, however, persisted in clinging to his berth, stupidly, like a mule— from sheer fright I believe, like an animal that won't leave a stable falling in an earthquake. So we went to look for him. It was chancing death, since once out of our lashings we were as exposed as if on a raft. But we went. The house was shattered as if a shell had exploded inside. Most of it had gone overboard—stove, men's quarters, and their property, all was gone; but two posts, holding a portion of the bulkhead to which Abraham's bunk was attached, remained as if by a miracle. We groped in the ruins and came upon this, and there he was, sitting in his bunk, surrounded by foam and wreckage, jabbering cheerfully to himself. He was out of his mind; completely and forever mad, with this sudden shock coming upon the fag-end of his endurance. We snatched him up, lugged him aft, and pitched him headfirst down the cabin companion. You understand there was no time to carry him down with infinite precautions and wait to see how he got on. Those below would pick him up at the bottom of the stairs all right. We were in a hurry to go back to the pumps. That business could not wait. A bad leak is an inhuman thing.

"One would think that the sole purpose of that fiendish gale had been to make a lunatic of that poor devil of a mulatto. It eased before morning, and next day the sky cleared, and as the sea went down the leak took up. When it came to bending a fresh set of sails the crew demanded to put back—and really there was nothing else to do. Boats gone, decks swept clean, cabin gutted, men without a stitch but what they stood in, stores spoiled, ship strained. We put her head for home, and—would you believe it? The wind came east right in our teeth. It blew fresh, it blew continuously. We had to beat up every inch of the way, but she did not leak so badly, the water keeping comparatively smooth. Two hours' pumping in every four is no joke—but it kept her afloat as far as Falmouth.[9]

"The good people there live on casualties of the sea, and no doubt were glad to see us. A hungry crowd of shipwrights sharpened their chisels at the sight of that carcass of a ship. And, by Jove! they had pretty pickings off us before they were done. I fancy the owner was already in a tight place. There were delays. Then it was decided to take part of the cargo out and caulk her topsides. This was done, the repairs finished, cargo reshipped; a new crew came on board, and we went out—for Bangkok. At the end of a week we were back again. The crew said they weren't going to Bangkok—a hundred and fifty days' passage—in a something hooker that wanted pumping eight hours out of the twenty-four; and the nautical papers inserted again the little paragraph: '*Judea.* Bark. Tyne to Bangkok; coals; put back to Falmouth leaky and with crew refusing duty.'

"There were more delays—more tinkering. The owner came down for a day, and said she was as right as a little fiddle. Poor old Captain Beard looked like the ghost of a Geordie [1] skipper— through the worry and humiliation of it. Remember he was sixty, and it was his first command. Mahon said it was a foolish business, and would end badly. I loved the ship more than ever, and wanted awfully to get to Bangkok. To Bangkok! Magic name, blessed name. Mesopotamia wasn't a patch on it.[2] Remember I was twenty, and it was my first second-mate's billet, and the East was waiting for me.

"We went out and anchored in the outer roads with a fresh crew—the third. She leaked worse than ever. It was as if those confounded shipwrights had actually made a hole in her. This time we did not even go outside. The crew simply refused to man the windlass.

"They towed us back to the inner harbor, and we became a fixture, a feature, an institution of the place. People pointed us out to visitors as 'That 'ere barque that's going to Bangkok—has been here six months—put back three times.' On holidays the small

---

9. Port on southwest English coast, in Cornwall.
1. A "Geordie" is a native of Tyneside, in northeast England. (See note 5 above.)
2. David Garrick, the 18th-century English actor, said that "that blessed word Mesopotamia" in the mouth of the famous preacher George Whitefield had the power of making people laugh or cry.

boys pulling about in boats would hail, '*Judea*, ahoy!' and if a head showed above the rail shouted, 'Where you bound to?—Bangkok?' and jeered. We were only three on board. The poor old skipper mooned in the cabin. Mahon undertook the cooking, and unexpectedly developed all a Frenchman's genius for preparing nice little messes. I looked languidly after the rigging. We became citizens of Falmouth. Every shopkeeper knew us. At the barber's or tobacconist's they asked familiarly, 'Do you think you will ever get to Bangkok?' Meantime the owner, the underwriters, and the charterers squabbled amongst themselves in London, and our pay went on. . . . Pass the bottle.

"It was horrid. Morally it was worse than pumping for life. It seemed as though we had been forgotten by the world, belonged to nobody, would get nowhere; it seemed that, as if bewitched, we would have to live for ever and ever in that inner harbor, a derision and a byword to generations of long-shore loafers and dishonest boatmen. I obtained three months' pay and a five days' leave, and made a rush for London. It took me a day to get there and pretty well another to come back—but three months' pay went all the same. I don't know what I did with it. I went to a music-hall, I believe, lunched, dined, and supped in a swell place in Regent Street, and was back on time, with nothing but a complete set of Byron's works and a new railway rug to show for three months' work. The boatman who pulled me off to the ship said: 'Hallo! I thought you had left the old thing. *She* will never get to Bangkok.' 'That's all *you* know about it,' I said, scornfully—but I didn't like that prophecy at all.

"Suddenly a man, some kind of agent to somebody, appeared with full powers. He had grog blossoms all over his face, an indomitable energy, and was a jolly soul. We leaped into life again. A hulk came alongside, took our cargo, and then we went into dry dock to get our copper stripped. No wonder she leaked. The poor thing, strained beyond endurance by the gale, had, as if in disgust, spat out all the oakum of her lower seams. She was recaulked, new-coppered, and made as tight as a bottle. We went back to the hulk and reshipped our cargo.

"Then, on a fine moonlight night, all the rats left the ship.

"We had been infested with them. They had destroyed our sails, consumed more stores than the crew, affably shared our beds and our dangers, and now, when the ship was made seaworthy, concluded to clear out. I called Mahon to enjoy the spectacle. Rat after rat appeared on our rail, took a last look over his shoulder, and leaped with a hollow thud into the empty hulk. We tried to count them, but soon lost the tale. Mahon said: 'Well, well! don't talk to me about the intelligence of rats. They ought to have left before, when we had that narrow squeak from foundering. There you have the proof how silly is the superstition about them. They leave a good ship for an old rotten hulk, where there is nothing to eat, too, the fools! . . . I don't believe they know what is safe or what is good for them, any more than you or I.'

"And after some more talk we agreed that the wisdom of rats had been grossly overrated, being in fact no greater than that of men.

"The story of the ship was known, by this, all up the Channel from Land's End to the Forelands, and we could get no crew on the south coast. They sent us one all complete from Liverpool, and we left once more—for Bangkok.

"We had fair breezes, smooth water right into the tropics, and the old *Judea* lumbered along in the sunshine. When she went eight knots everything cracked aloft, and we tied our caps to our heads; but mostly she strolled on at the rate of three miles an hour. What could you expect? She was tired—that old ship. Her youth was where mine is—where yours is— you fellows who listen to this yarn; and what friend would throw your years and your weariness in your face? We didn't grumble at her. To us aft, at least, it seemed as though we had been born in her, reared in her, had lived in her for ages, had never known any other ship. I would just as soon have abused the old village church at home for not being a cathedral.

"And for me there was also my youth to make me patient. There was all the East before me, and all life, and the thought that I had been tried in that ship and had come out pretty well. And I thought of men of old who, centuries ago, went that road in ships that sailed no better, to the land of palms, and spices, and yellow sands, and of brown nations ruled by kings more cruel than Nero the Roman, and more splendid than Solomon the Jew. The old barque lumbered on, heavy with her age and the burden of her cargo, while I lived the life of youth in ignorance and hope. She lumbered on through an interminable procession of days; and the fresh gilding flashed back at the setting sun, seemed to cry out over the darkening sea the words painted on her stern, '*Judea*, London. Do or Die.'

"Then we entered the Indian Ocean and steered northerly for Java Head. The winds were light. Weeks slipped by. She crawled on, do or die, and people at home began to think of posting us as overdue.

"One Saturday evening, I being off duty, the men asked me to give them an extra bucket of water or so—for washing clothes. As I did not wish to screw on the fresh-water pump so late, I went forward whistling, and with a key in my hand to unlock the forepeak scuttle, [3] intending to serve the water out of a spare tank we kept there.

"The smell down below was as unexpected as it was frightful. One would have thought hundreds of paraffin lamps had been flaring and smoking in that hole for days. I was glad to get out. The man with me coughed and said, 'Funny smell, sir.' I answered negligently, 'It's good for the health, they say,' and walked aft.

"The first thing I did was to put my head down the square of the midship ventilator. As I lifted the lid a visible breath, something like a thin fog, a puff of faint haze, rose from the opening. The ascending air was hot, and had a heavy, sooty, paraffiny smell. I gave one sniff, and put down the lid gently. It was no use choking myself. The cargo was on fire.

"Next day she began to smoke in earnest. You see it was to be expected, for though the coal was of a safe kind, that cargo had been so handled, so broken up with handling, that it looked more like smithy coal than anything else. Then it had been wetted—more than once. It rained all the time we were taking it back from the hulk, and now with this long passage it got heated, and there was another case of spontaneous combustion.

"The captain called us into the cabin. He had a chart spread on the table, and looked unhappy. He said, 'The coast of West Australia is near, but I mean to proceed to our destination. It is the hurricane month, too; but we will just keep her head for Bangkok, and fight the fire. No more putting back anywhere, if we all get roasted. We will try first to stifle this 'ere damned combustion by want of air.'

"We tried. We battened down everything, and still she smoked. The smoke kept coming out through imperceptible crevices; it forced itself through bulkheads and covers; it oozed here and there and everywhere in slender threads, in an invisible film, in an incomprehensible manner. It made its way into the cabin, into the forecastle; it poisoned the sheltered places on the deck; it could be sniffed as high as the mainyard. It was clear that if the smoke came out the air came in. This was disheartening. This combustion refused to be stifled.

"We resolved to try water, and took the hatches off. Enormous volumes of smoke, whitish, yellowish, thick, greasy, misty, choking, ascended as high as the trucks. All hands cleared out aft. Then the poisonous cloud blew away, and we went back to work in a smoke that was no thicker now than that of an ordinary factory chimney.

"We rigged the force pump, got the hose along, and by and by it burst. Well, it was as old as the ship—a prehistoric hose, and

3. A covered hatchway (small opening) in the deck of a ship.

past repair. Then we pumped with the feeble head pump, drew water with buckets, and in this way managed in time to pour lots of Indian Ocean into the main hatch. The bright stream flashed in sunshine, fell into a layer of white crawling smoke, and vanished on the black surface of coal. Steam ascended mingling with the smoke. We poured salt water as into a barrel without a bottom. It was our fate to pump in that ship, to pump out of her, to pump into her; and after keeping water out of her to save ourselves from being drowned, we frantically poured water into her to save ourselves from being burnt.

"And she crawled on, do or die, in the serene weather. The sky was a miracle of purity, a miracle of azure. The sea was polished, was blue, was pellucid, was sparkling like a precious stone, extending on all sides, all round to the horizon—as if the whole terrestrial globe had been one jewel, one colossal sapphire, a single gem fashioned into a planet. And on the luster of the great calm waters the *Judea* glided imperceptibly, enveloped in languid and unclean vapors, in a lazy cloud that drifted to leeward, light and slow; a pestiferous cloud defiling the splendor of sea and sky.

"All this time of course we saw no fire. The cargo smoldered at the bottom somewhere. Once Mahon, as we were working side by side, said to me with a queer smile: 'Now, if she would only spring a tidy leak—like that time when we first left the Channel—it would put a stopper on this fire. Wouldn't it?' I remarked irrelevantly, 'Do you remember the rats?'

"We fought the fire and sailed the ship too as carefully as though nothing had been the matter. The steward cooked and attended on us. Of the other twelve men, eight worked while four rested. Everyone took his turn, captain included. There was equality, and if not exactly fraternity, then a deal of good feeling. Sometimes a man, as he dashed a bucketful of water down the hatchway, would yell out, 'Hurrah for Bangkok!' and the rest laughed. But generally we were taciturn and serious—and thirsty. Oh! how thirsty! And we had to be careful with the water. Strict allowance. The ship smoked, the sun blazed. . . . Pass the bottle.

"We tried everything. We even made an attempt to dig down to the fire. No good, of course. No man could remain more than a minute below. Mahon, who went first, fainted there, and the man who went to fetch him out did likewise. We lugged them out on deck. Then I leaped down to show how easily it could be done. They had learned wisdom by that time, and contented themselves by fishing for me with a chainhook tied to a broom handle, I believe. I did not offer to go and fetch up my shovel, which was left down below.

"Things began to look bad. We put the longboat into the

water. The second boat was ready to swing out. We had also another, a fourteen-foot thing, on davits aft, where it was quite safe.

"Then, behold, the smoke suddenly decreased. We redoubled our efforts to flood the bottom of the ship. In two days there was no smoke at all. Everybody was on the broad grin. This was on a Friday. On Saturday no work, but sailing the ship of course, was done. The men washed their clothes and their faces for the first time in a fortnight, and had a special dinner given them. They spoke of spontaneous combustion with contempt, and implied *they* were the boys to put out combustions. Somehow we all felt as though we each had inherited a large fortune. But a beastly smell of burning hung about the ship. Captain Beard had hollow eyes and sunken cheeks. I had never noticed so much before how twisted and bowed he was. He and Mahon prowled soberly about hatches and ventilators, sniffing. It struck me suddenly poor Mahon was a very, very old chap. As to me, I was as pleased and proud as though I had helped to win a great naval battle. O! Youth!

"The night was fine. In the morning a homeward-bound ship passed us hull down—the first we had seen for months; but we were nearing the land at last, Java Head being about 190 miles off, and nearly due north.

"Next day it was my watch on deck from eight to twelve. At breakfast the captain observed, 'It's wonderful how that smell hangs about the cabin.' About ten, the mate being on the poop, I stepped down on the main deck for a moment. The carpenter's bench stood abaft the mainmast: I leaned against it sucking at my pipe, and the carpenter, a young chap, came to talk to me. He remarked, 'I think we have done very well, haven't we?' and then I perceived with annoyance the fool was trying to tilt the bench. I said curtly, 'Don't, Chips,' and immediately became aware of a queer sensation, of an absurd delusion—I seemed somehow to be in the air. I heard all round me like a pent-up breath released—as if a thousand giants simultaneously had said Phoo!—and felt a dull concussion which made my ribs ache suddenly. No doubt about it—I was in the air, and my body was describing a short parabola. But short as it was, I had the time to think several thoughts in, as far as I can remember, the following order: 'This can't be the carpenter—What is it?—Some accident—Submarine volcano?—Coals, gas!—By Jove! We are being blown up—Everybody's dead—I am falling into the after-hatch—I see fire in it.'

"The coaldust suspended in the air of the hold had glowed dull-red at the moment of the explosion. In the twinkling of an eye, in an infinitesimal fraction of a second since the first tilt of the bench, I was sprawling full length on the cargo. I picked myself up and scrambled out. It was quick like a rebound. The deck was a wilderness of smashed timber, lying crosswise like trees in a wood after a hurricane; an immense curtain of solid rags waved gently before me—it was the mainsail blown to strips. I thought: the masts will be toppling over directly; and to get out of the way bolted on all fours towards the poop ladder. The first person I saw was Mahon, with eyes like saucers, his mouth open, and the long white hair standing straight on end round his head like a silver halo. He was just about to go down when the sight of the main deck stirring, heaving up, and changing into splinters before his eyes, petrified him on the top step. I stared at him in unbelief, and he stared at me with a queer kind of shocked curiosity. I did not know that I had no hair, no eyebrows, no eyelashes, that my young mustache was burnt off, that my face was black, one cheek laid open, my nose cut, and my chin bleeding. I had lost my cap, one of my slippers, and my shirt was torn to rags. Of all this I was not aware. I was amazed to see the ship still afloat, the poop deck whole—and, most of all, to see anybody alive. Also the peace of the sky and the serenity of the sea were distinctly surprising. I suppose I expected to see them convulsed with horror. . . . Pass the bottle.

"There was a voice hailing the ship from somewhere—in the air, in the sky—I couldn't tell. Presently I saw the captain—and he was mad. He asked me eagerly, 'Where's the cabin table?' and to hear such a question was a frightful shock. I had just been blown up, you understand, and vibrated with that experience—I wasn't quite sure whether I was alive. Mahon began to stamp with both feet and yelled at him, 'Good God! don't you see the deck's blown out of her?' I found my voice, and stammered out as if conscious of some gross neglect of duty, 'I don't know where the cabin table is.' It was like an absurd dream.

"Do you know what he wanted next? Well, he wanted to trim the yards. Very placidly, and as if lost in thought, he insisted on having the foreyard squared. 'I don't know if there's anybody alive,' said Mahon, almost tearfully. 'Surely,' he said gently, 'there will be enough left to square the foreyard.'

"The old chap, it seems, was in his own berth winding up the chronometers, when the shock sent him spinning. Immediately it occurred to him—as he said afterwards—that the ship had struck something, and ran out into the cabin. There, he saw, the cabin table had vanished somewhere. The deck being blown up, it had fallen down into the lazarette [4] of course. Where we had our breakfast that morning he saw only a great hole in the floor. This appeared to him so awfully mysterious, and impressed him so immensely, that what he saw and heard after he got on deck were

4. Space between decks.

mere trifles in comparison. And, mark, he noticed directly the wheel deserted and his bark off her course—and his only thought was to get that miserable, stripped, undecked, smoldering shell of a ship back again with her head pointing at her port of destination. Bangkok! That's what he was after. I tell you this quiet, bowed, bandy-legged, almost deformed little man was immense in the singleness of his idea and in his placid ignorance of our agitation. He motioned us forward with a commanding gesture, and went to take the wheel himself.

"Yes; that was the first thing we did—trim the yards of that wreck! No one was killed, or even disabled, but everyone was more or less hurt. You should have seen them! Some were in rags, with black faces, like coal heavers, like sweeps, and had bullet heads that seemed closely cropped, but were in fact singed to the skin. Others, of the watch below, awakened by being shot out from their collapsing bunks, shivered incessantly, and kept on groaning even as we went about our work. But they all worked. That crew of Liverpool hard cases had in them the right stuff. It's my experience they always have. It is the sea that gives it—the vastness, the loneliness surrounding their dark stolid souls. Ah! Well! We stumbled, we crept, we fell, we barked our shins on the wreckage, we hauled. The masts stood, but we did not know how much they might be charred down below. It was nearly calm, but a long swell ran from the west and made her roll. They might go at any moment. We looked at them with apprehension. One could not foresee which way they would fall.

"Then we retreated aft and looked about us. The deck was a tangle of planks on edge, of planks on end, of splinters, of ruined woodwork. The masts rose from that chaos like big trees above a matted undergrowth. The interstices of that mass of wreckage were full of something whitish, sluggish, stirring—of something that was like a greasy fog. The smoke of the invisible fire was coming up again, was trailing, like a poisonous thick mist in some valley choked with dead wood. Already lazy wisps were beginning to curl upwards amongst the mass of splinters. Here and there a piece of timber, stuck upright, resembled a post. Half of a fife-rail had been shot through the foresail, and the sky made a patch of glorious blue in the ignobly soiled canvas. A portion of several boards holding together had fallen across the rail, and one end protruded overboard, like a gangway leading upon nothing, like a gangway leading over the deep sea, leading to death—as if inviting us to walk the plank at once and be done with our ridiculous troubles. And still the air, the sky—a ghost, something invisible was hailing the ship.

"Someone had the sense to look over, and there was the

helmsman, who had impulsively jumped overboard, anxious to come back. He yelled and swam lustily like a merman, keeping up with the ship. We threw him a rope, and presently he stood amongst us streaming with water and very crestfallen. The captain had surrendered the wheel, and apart, elbow on rail and chin in hand, gazed at the sea wistfully. We asked ourselves, What next? I thought, Now, this is something like. This is great. I wonder what will happen. O youth!

"Suddenly Mahon sighted a steamer far astern. Captain Beard said, 'We may do something with her yet.' We hoisted two flags, which said in the international language of the sea, 'On fire. Want immediate assistance.' The steamer grew bigger rapidly, and by and by spoke with two flags on her foremast, 'I am coming to your assistance.'

"In half an hour she was abreast, to windward, within hail, and rolling slightly, with her engines stopped. We lost our composure, and yelled all together with excitement, 'We've been blown up.' A man in a white helmet, on the bridge, cried, 'Yes! All right! all right!' and he nodded his head, and smiled, and made soothing motions with his hand as though at a lot of frightened children. One of the boats dropped in the water, and walked towards us upon the sea with her long oars. Four Calashes pulled a swinging stroke. This was my first sight of Malay seamen. I've known them since, but what struck me then was their unconcern; they came alongside, and even the bowman standing up and holding to our main-chains with the boat-hook did not deign to lift his head for a glance. I thought people who had been blown up deserved more attention.

"A little man, dry like a chip and agile like a monkey, clambered up. It was the mate of the steamer. He gave one look, and cried, 'O boys—you had better quit!'

"We were silent. He talked apart with the captain for a time—seemed to argue with him. Then they went away together to the steamer.

"When our skipper came back we learned that the steamer was the *Somerville*, Captain Nash, from West Australia to Singapore via Batavia with mails, and that the agreement was she should tow us to Anjer or Batavia, if possible, where we could extinguish the fire by scuttling,[5] and then proceed on our voyage—to Bangkok! The old man seemed excited. 'We will do it yet,' he said to Mahon, fiercely. He shook his fist at the sky. Nobody else said a word.

"At noon the steamer began to tow. She went ahead slim and high, and what was left of the *Judea* followed at the end of seventy

5. I.e., sinking the boat by cutting a hole in the side or bottom.

fathom of tow-rope—followed her swiftly like a cloud of smoke with mastheads protruding above. We went aloft to furl the sails. We coughed on the yards, and were careful about the bunts.[6] Do you see the lot of us there, putting a neat furl on the sails of that ship doomed to arrive nowhere? There was not a man who didn't think that at any moment the masts would topple over. From aloft we could not see the ship for smoke, and they worked carefully, passing the gaskets with even turns. 'Harbor furl—aloft there!' cried Mahon from below.

"You understand this? I don't think one of those chaps expected to get down in the usual way. When we did I heard them saying to each other, 'Well, I thought we would come down overboard, in a lump—sticks and all—blame me if I didn't.' 'That's what I was thinking to myself,' would answer wearily another battered and bandaged scarecrow. And, mind, these were men without the drilled-in habit of obedience. To an onlooker they would be a lot of profane scallywags without a redeeming point. What made them do it—what made them obey me when I, thinking consciously how fine it was, made them drop the bunt of the foresail twice to try and do it better? What? They had no professional reputation—no examples, no praise. It wasn't a sense of duty; they all knew well enough how to shirk, and laze, and dodge—when they had a mind to it—and mostly they had. Was it the two pounds ten a month that sent them there? They didn't think their pay half good enough. No; it was something in them, something inborn and subtle and everlasting. I don't say positively that the crew of a French or German merchantman wouldn't have done it, but I doubt whether it would have been done in the same way. There was a completeness in it, something solid like a principle, and masterful like an instinct—a disclosure of something secret—of that hidden something, that gift of good or evil that makes racial difference, that shapes the fate of nations.

"It was that night at ten that, for the first time since we had been fighting it, we saw the fire. The speed of the towing had fanned the smoldering destruction. A blue gleam appeared forward, shining below the wreck of the deck. It wavered in patches, it seemed to stir and creep like the light of a glowworm. I saw it first, and told Mahon. 'Then the game's up,' he said. 'We had better stop this towing, or she will burst out suddenly fore and aft before we can clear out.' We set up a yell; rang bells to attract their attention; they towed on. At last Mahon and I had to crawl forward and cut the rope with an ax. There was no time to cast off the lashings. Red tongues could be seen licking the wilderness of splinters under our feet as we made our way back to the poop.

6. The middle part of a furled sail, gathered into a bunch.

"Of course they very soon found out in the steamer that the rope was gone. She gave a loud blast of her whistle, her lights were seen sweeping in a wide circle, she came up ranging close alongside, and stopped. We were all in a tight group on the poop looking at her. Every man had saved a little bundle or a bag. Suddenly a conical flame with a twisted top shot up forward and threw upon the black sea a circle of light, with the two vessels side by side and heaving gently in its center. Captain Beard had been sitting on the gratings still and mute for hours, but now he rose slowly and advanced in front of us, to the mizzen-shrouds. Captain Nash hailed: 'Come along! Look sharp. I have mailbags on board. I will take you and your boats to Singapore.'

" 'Thank you! No!' said our skipper. 'We must see the last of the ship.'

" 'I can't stand by any longer,' shouted the other. 'Mails—you know.'

" 'Ay! ay! We are all right.'

" 'Very well! I'll report you in Singapore. . . . Good-by!'

"He waved his hands. Our men dropped their bundles quietly. The steamer moved ahead, and passing out of the circle of light, vanished at once from our sight, dazzled by the fire which burned fiercely. And then I knew that I would see the East first as commander of a small boat. I thought it fine; and the fidelity to the old ship was fine. We should see the last of her. Oh, the glamor of youth! Oh, the fire of it, more dazzling than the flames of the burning ship, throwing a magic light on the wide earth, leaping audaciously to the sky, presently to be quenched by time, more cruel, more pitiless, more bitter than the sea—and like the flames of the burning ship surrounded by an impenetrable night.

"The old man warned us in his gentle and inflexible way that it was part of our duty to save for the underwriters as much as we could of the ship's gear. Accordingly we went to work aft, while she blazed forward to give us plenty of light. We lugged out a lot of rubbish. What didn't we save? An old barometer fixed with an absurd quantity of screws nearly cost me my life: a sudden rush of smoke came upon me, and I just got away in time. There were various stores, bolts of canvas, coils of rope; the poop looked like a marine bazaar, and the boats were lumbered to the gunwales. One would have thought the old man wanted to take as much as he could of his first command with him. He was very, very quiet, but off his balance evidently. Would you believe it? He wanted to take a length of old stream-cable and a kedge anchor with him in the longboat. We said, 'Ay, ay, sir,' deferentially, and

on the quiet let the things slip overboard. The heavy medicine
chest went that way, two bags of green coffee, tins of paint—fancy,
paint!—a whole lot of things. Then I was ordered with two hands
into the boats to make a stowage and get them ready against the
time it would be proper for us to leave the ship.

"We put everything straight, stepped the long-boat's mast for
our skipper, who was to take charge of her, and I was not sorry to
sit down for a moment. My face felt raw, every limb ached as if
broken, I was aware of all my ribs, and would have sworn to a
twist in the backbone. The boats, fast astern, lay in a deep
shadow, and all around I could see the circle of the sea lighted by
the fire. A gigantic flame arose forward straight and clear. It
flared fierce, with noises like the whirr of wings, with rumbles as
of thunder. There were cracks, detonations, and from the cone of
flame the sparks flew upwards, as man is born to trouble,[7] to leaky
ships, and to ships that burn.

"What bothered me was that the ship, lying broadside to the
swell and to such wind as there was—a mere breath—the boats
would not keep astern where they were safe, but persisted, in a
pig-headed way boats have, in getting under the counter and then
swinging alongside. They were knocking about dangerously and
coming near the flame, while the ship rolled on them, and, of
course, there was always the danger of the masts going over the
side at any moment. I and my two boat-keepers kept them off as
best as we could, with oars and boat-hooks; but to be constantly at
it became exasperating, since there was no reason why we should
not leave at once. We could not see those on board, nor could we
imagine what caused the delay. The boat-keepers were swearing
feebly, and I had not only my share of the work but also had to
keep at it two men who showed a constant inclination to lay
themselves down and let things slide.

"At last I hailed, 'On deck there,' and someone looked over.
'We're ready here,' I said. The head disappeared, and very soon
popped up again. 'The captain says, All right, sir, and to keep the
boats well clear of the ship.'

"Half an hour passed. Suddenly there was a frightful racket,
rattle, clanking of chain, hiss of water, and millions of sparks
flew up into the shivering column of smoke that stood leaning
slightly above the ship. The cat-heads had burned away, and the
two red-hot anchors had gone to the bottom, tearing out after
them two hundred fathom of red-hot chain. The ship trembled,
the mass of flame swayed as if ready to collapse, and the fore-
topgallant mast fell. It darted down like an arrow of fire, shot
under, and instantly leaping up within an oar's-length of the

7. "Yet man is born unto trouble as the sparks fly upward." Job v.7.

boats, floated quietly, very black on the luminous sea. I hailed the deck again. After some time a man in an unexpectedly cheerful but also muffled tone, as though he had been trying to speak with his mouth shut, informed me, 'Coming directly, sir,' and vanished. For a long time I heard nothing but the whirr and roar of the fire. There were also whistling sounds. The boats jumped, tugged at the painters, ran at each other playfully, knocked their sides together, or, do what we would, swung in a bunch against the ship's side. I couldn't stand it any longer, and swarming up a rope, clambered aboard over the stern.

"It was as bright as day. Coming up like this, the sheet of fire facing me was a terrifying sight, and the heat seemed hardly bearable at first. On a settee cushion dragged out of the cabin Captain Beard, his legs drawn up and one arm under his head, slept with the light playing on him. Do you know what the rest were busy about? They were sitting on deck right aft, round an open case, eating bread and cheese and drinking bottled stout.

"On the background of flames twisting in fierce tongues above their heads they seemed at home like salamanders, and looked like a band of desperate pirates. The fire sparkled in the whites of their eyes, gleamed on patches of white skin seen through the torn shirts. Each had the marks as of a battle about him—bandaged heads, tied-up arms, a strip of dirty rags around a knee—and each man had a bottle between his legs and a chunk of cheese in his hand. Mahon got up. With his handsome and disreputable head, his hooked profile, his long white beard, and with an uncorked bottle in his hand, he resembled one of those reckless sea robbers of old making merry amidst violence and disaster. 'The last meal on board,' he explained solemnly. 'We had nothing to eat all day, and it was no use leaving all this.' He flourished the bottle and indicated the sleeping skipper. 'He said he couldn't swallow anything, so I got him to lie down,' he went on; and as I stared, 'I don't know whether you are aware, young fellow, the man had no sleep to speak of for days—and there will be dam' little sleep in the boats.' 'There will be no boats by and by if you fool about much longer,' I said, indignantly. I walked up to the skipper and shook him by the shoulder. At last he opened his eyes, but did not move. 'Time to leave her, sir,' I said quietly.

"He got up painfully, looked at the flames, at the sea sparkling round the ship, and black, black as ink farther away; he looked at the stars shining dim through a thin veil of smoke in a sky black, black as Erebus.[8]

" 'Youngest first,' he said.

"And the ordinary seaman, wiping his mouth with the back of

8. In Greek mythology, the entry to Hades, the underworld; hence, total darkness.

his hand, got up, clambered over the taffrail and vanished. Others followed. One, on the point of going over, stopped short to drain his bottle, and with a great swing of his arm flung it at the fire. 'Take this!' he cried.

"The skipper lingered disconsolately, and we left him to commune alone for a while with his first command. Then I went up again and brought him away at last. It was time. The ironwork on the poop was hot to the touch.

"Then the painter of the long-boat was cut, and the three boats, tied together, drifted clear of the ship. It was just sixteen hours after the explosion when we abandoned her. Mahon had charge of the second boat, and I had the smallest—the fourteen-foot thing. The long-boat would have taken the lot of us; but the skipper said we must save as much property as we could—for the underwriters—and so I got my first command. I had two men with me, a bag of biscuits, a few tins of meat, and a breaker of water. I was ordered to keep close to the long-boat, that in case of bad weather we might be taken into her.

"And do you know what I thought? I thought I would part company as soon as I could. I wanted to have my first command all to myself. I wasn't going to sail in a squadron if there were a chance for independent cruising. I would make land by myself. I would beat the other boats. Youth! All youth! The silly, charming, beautiful youth.

"But we did not make a start at once. We must see the last of the ship. And so the boats drifted about that night, heaving and setting on the swell. The men dozed, waked, sighed, groaned. I looked at the burning ship.

"Between the darkness of earth and heaven she was burning fiercely upon a disc of purple sea shot by the blood-red play of gleams; upon a disc of water glittering and sinister. A high, clear flame, an immense and lonely flame, ascended from the ocean, and from its summit the black smoke poured continuously at the sky. She burned furiously; mournful and imposing like a funeral pile kindled in the night, surrounded by the sea, watched over by the stars. A magnificent death had come like a grace, like a gift, like a reward to that old ship at the end of her laborious days. The surrender of her weary ghost to the keeping of stars and sea was stirring like the sight of a glorious triumph. The masts fell just before daybreak, and for a moment there was a burst and turmoil of sparks that seemed to fill with flying fire the night patient and watchful, the vast night lying silent upon the sea. At daylight she was only a charred shell, floating still under a cloud of smoke and bearing a glowing mass of coal within.

"Then the oars were got out, and the boats forming in a line

moved round her remains as if in procession—the long-boat leading. As we pulled across her stern a slim dart of fire shot out
viciously at us, and suddenly she went down, head first, in a great
hiss of steam. The unconsumed stern was the last to sink; but
the paint had gone, had cracked, had peeled off, and there were
no letters, there was no word, no stubborn device that was like
her soul, to flash at the rising sun her creed and her name.

"We made our way north. A breeze sprang up, and about noon
all the boats came together for the last time. I had no mast or
sail in mine, but I made a mast out of a spare oar and hoisted
a boat-awning for a sail, with a boathook for a yard. She was
certainly over-masted, but I had the satisfaction of knowing that
with the wind aft I could beat the other two. I had to wait for
them. Then we all had a look at the captain's chart, and, after a
sociable meal of hard bread and water, got our last instructions.
These were simple: steer north, and keep together as much as
possible. 'Be careful with that jury-rig,⁹ Marlow,' said the captain;
and Mahon, as I sailed proudly past his boat, wrinkled his curved
nose and hailed, 'You will sail that ship of yours under water, if
you don't look out, young fellow.' He was a malicious old man—
and may the deep sea where he sleeps now rock him gently, rock
him tenderly to the end of time!

"Before sunset a thick rain-squall passed over the two boats,
which were far astern, and that was the last I saw of them for a
time. Next day I sat steering my cockle-shell—my first command—
with nothing but water and sky round me. I did sight in the
afternoon the upper sails of a ship far away, but said nothing, and
my men did not notice her. You see I was afraid she might be
homeward bound, and I had no mind to turn back from the
portals of the East. I was steering for Java—another blessed name—
like Bangkok, you know. I steered many days.

"I need not tell you what it is to be knocking about in an open
boat. I remember nights and days of calm, when we pulled, we
pulled, and the boat seemed to stand still, as if bewitched within
the circle of the sea horizon. I remember the heat, the deluge of
rain-squalls that kept us baling for dear life (but filled our water-
cask), and I remember sixteen hours on end with a mouth dry as a
cinder and a steering-oar over the stern to keep my first command
head on to a breaking sea. I did not know how good a man I was
till then. I remember the drawn faces, the dejected figures of my
two men, and I remember my youth and the feeling that will
never come back any more—the feeling that I could last forever,
outlast the sea, the earth, and all men; the deceitful feeling that
lures us on to joys, to perils, to love, to vain effort—to death;
the triumphant conviction of strength, the heat of life in the

9. Temporary rig.

handful of dust, the glow in the heart that with every year grows dim, grows cold, grows small, and expires—and expires, too soon, too soon—before life itself.

"And this is how I see the East. I have seen its secret places and have looked into its very soul; but now I see it always from a small boat, a high outline of mountains, blue and afar in the morning; like faint mist at noon; a jagged wall of purple at sunset. I have the feel of the oar in my hand, the vision of a scorching blue sea in my eyes. And I see a bay, a wide bay, smooth as glass and polished like ice, shimmering in the dark. A red light burns far off upon the gloom of the land, and the night is soft and warm. We drag at the oars with aching arms, and suddenly a puff of wind, a puff faint and tepid and laden with strange odors of blossoms, of aromatic wood, comes out of the still night—the first sigh of the East on my face. That I can never forget. It was impalpable and enslaving, like a charm, like a whispered promise of mysterious delight.

"We had been pulling this finishing spell for eleven hours. Two pulled, and he whose turn it was to rest sat at the tiller. We had made out the red light in that bay and steered for it, guessing it must mark some small coasting port. We passed two vessels, outlandish and high-sterned, sleeping at anchor, and, approaching the light, now very dim, ran the boat's nose against the end of a jutting wharf. We were blind with fatigue. My men dropped the oars and fell off the thwarts as if dead. I made fast to a pile. A current rippled softly. The scented obscurity of the shore was grouped into vast masses, a density of colossal clumps of vegetation, probably—mute and fantastic shapes. And at their foot the semicircle of a beach gleamed faintly, like an illusion. There was not a light, not a stir, not a sound. The mysterious East faced me, perfumed like a flower, silent like death, dark like a grave.

"And I sat weary beyond expression, exulting like a conqueror, sleepless and entranced as if before a profound, a fateful engima.

"A splashing of oars, a measured dip reverberating on the level of water, intensified by the silence of the shore into loud claps, made me jump up. A boat, a European boat, was coming in. I invoked the name of the dead; I hailed: '*Judea* ahoy!' A thin shout answered.

"It was the captain. I had beaten the flagship by three hours, and I was glad to hear the old man's voice again, tremulous and tired. 'Is it you, Marlow?' 'Mind the end of that jetty, sir,' I cried.

"He approached cautiously, and brought up with the deep-sea lead-line which we had saved—for the underwriters. I eased my painter and fell alongside. He sat, a broken figure at the stern, wet with dew, his hands clasped in his lap. His men were asleep already. 'I had a terrible time of it,' he murmured. 'Mahon is behind—not very far.' We conversed in whispers, in low whispers, as if afraid to wake up the land. Guns, thunder, earthquakes would not have awakened the men just then.

"Looking round as we talked, I saw away at sea a bright light traveling in the night. 'There's a steamer passing the bay,' I said. She was not passing, she was entering, and she even came close and anchored. 'I wish,' said the old man, 'you would find out whether she is English. Perhaps they could give us a passage somewhere.' He seemed nervously anxious. So by dint of punching and kicking I started one of my men into a state of somnambulism, and giving him an oar, took another and pulled towards the lights of the steamer.

"There was a murmur of voices in her, metallic hollow clangs of the engine-room, footsteps on the deck. Her ports shone, round like dilated eyes. Shapes moved about, and there was a shadowy man high up on the bridge. He heard my oars.

"And then, before I could open my lips, the East spoke to me, but it was in a Western voice. A torrent of words was poured into the enigmatical, the fateful silence; outlandish, angry words, mixed with words and even whole sentences of good English, less strange but even more surprising. The voice swore and cursed violently; it riddled the solemn peace of the bay by a volley of abuse. It began by calling me Pig, and from that went crescendo into unmentionable adjectives—in English. The man up there raged aloud in two languages, and with a sincerity in his fury that almost convinced me I had, in some way, sinned against the harmony of the universe. I could hardly see him, but began to think he would work himself into a fit.

"Suddenly he ceased, and I could hear him snorting and blowing like a porpoise. I said:

" 'What steamer is this, pray?'

" 'Eh? What's this? And who are you?'

" 'Castaway crew of an English barque burnt at sea. We came here tonight. I am the second mate. The captain is in the long-boat, and wishes to know if you would give us a passage somewhere.'

" 'Oh, my goodness! I say. . . . This is the *Celestial* from Singapore on her return trip. I'll arrange with your captain in the morning, . . . and, . . . I say, . . . did you hear me just now?'

" 'I should think the whole bay heard you.'

" 'I thought you were a shore-boat. Now, look here—this infernal lazy scoundrel of a caretaker has gone to sleep again—curse him. The light is out, and I nearly ran foul of the end of this damned jetty. This is the third time he plays me this trick. Now, I ask you, can anybody stand this kind of thing? It's enough to drive a man out of his mind. I'll report him. . . . I'll get the Assistant Resident to give him the sack, by—! See—there's no light. It's out, isn't it? I take you to witness the light's out. There should be a light, you know. A red light on the—'

" 'There was a light,' I said mildly.

" 'But it's out, man! What's the use of talking like this? You can see for yourself it's out—don't you? If you had to take a valuable steamer along this God-forsaken coast you would want a light, too. I'll kick him from end to end of his miserable wharf. You'll see if I don't. I will—'

" 'So I may tell my captain you'll take us?' I broke in.

" 'Yes, I'll take you. Good night,' he said, brusquely.

"I pulled back, made fast again to the jetty, and then went to sleep at last. I had faced the silence of the East. I had heard some of its language. But when I opened my eyes again the silence was as complete as though it had never been broken. I was lying in a flood of light, and the sky had never looked so far, so high, before. I opened my eyes and lay without moving.

"And then I saw the men of the East—they were looking at me. The whole length of the jetty was full of people. I saw brown, bronze, yellow faces, the black eyes, the glitter, the color of an Eastern crowd. And all these beings stared without a murmur, without a sigh, without a movement. They stared down at the boats, at the sleeping men who at night had come to them from the sea. Nothing moved. The fronds of palms stood still against the sky. Not a branch stirred along the shore, and the brown roofs of hidden houses peeped through the green foliage, through the big leaves that hung shining and still like leaves forged of heavy metal. This was the East of the ancient navigators, so old, so mysterious, resplendent and somber, living and unchanged, full of danger and promise. And these were the men. I sat up suddenly. A wave of movement passed through the crowd from end to end, passed along the heads, swayed the bodies, ran along the jetty like a ripple on the water, like a breath of wind on a field—and all was still again. I see it now—the wide sweep of the bay, the glittering sands, the wealth of green infinite and varied, the sea blue like the sea of a dream, the crowd of attentive faces, the blaze of vivid color—the water reflecting it all, the curve of the shore, the jetty, the high-sterned outlandish craft floating still, and the three boats with the tired men from the West sleeping, unconscious of the land and the people and of the violence of sunshine. They slept thrown across the thwarts, curled on bottom-boards, in the careless attitudes of death. The head of the old skipper, leaning back in the stern of the long-boat, had fallen on his breast, and he looked as though he would never wake. Farther out old Mahon's face was upturned to the sky, with the long white beard spread out on his breast, as though he had been shot where he sat at the tiller; and a man, all in a heap in the bows of the boat, slept with both arms embracing the stem-head and with his cheek laid on the gunwale. The East looked at them without a sound.

"I have known its fascination since; I have seen the mysterious shores, the still water, the lands of brown nations, where a stealthy Nemesis lies in wait, pursues, overtakes so many of the conquering race, who are proud of their wisdom, of their knowledge, of their strength. But for me all the East is contained in that vision of my youth. It is all in that moment when I opened my young eyes on it. I came upon it from a tussle with the sea—and I was young—and I saw it looking at me. And this is all that is left of it! Only a moment; a moment of strength, of romance, glamor—of youth! . . . A flick of sunshine upon a strange shore, the time to remember, the time for a sigh, and—good-bye!—Night—Good-bye . . . !"

He drank.

"Ah! The good old time—the good old time. Youth and the sea. Glamor and the sea! The good, strong sea, the salt, bitter sea, that could whisper to you and roar at you and knock your breath out of you."

He drank again.

"By all that's wonderful it is the sea, I believe, the sea itself—or is it youth alone? Who can tell? But you here—you all had something out of life: money, love—whatever one gets on shore—and, tell me, wasn't that the best time, that time when we were young at sea; young and had nothing, on the sea that gives nothing, except hard knocks—and sometimes a chance to feel your strength—that only—that you all regret?"

And we all nodded at him: the man of finance, the man of accounts, the man of law, we all nodded at him over the polished table that like a still sheet of brown water reflected our faces, lined, wrinkled; our faces marked by toil, by deceptions, by success, by love; our weary eyes looking still, looking always, looking anxiously for something out of life, that while it is expected is already gone—has passed unseen, in a sigh, in a flash—together with the youth, with the strength, with the romance of illusions.

1898   1898, 1902

The Secret Sharer

I

On my right hand there were lines of fishing stakes resembling a mysterious system of half-submerged bamboo fences, incomprehensible in its division of the domain of tropical fishes, and crazy of aspect as if abandoned forever by some nomad tribe of fishermen now gone to the other end of the ocean; for there was no sign of human habitation as far as the eye could reach. To the left a group of barren islets, suggesting ruins of stone walls, towers, and blockhouses, had its foundations set in a blue sea that itself looked solid, so still and stable did it lie below my feet; even the track of light from the westering sun shone smoothly, without that animated glitter which tells of an imperceptible ripple. And when I turned my head to take a parting glance at the tug which had just left us anchored outside the bar, I saw the straight line of the flat shore joined to the stable sea, edge to edge, with a perfect and unmarked closeness, in one leveled floor half brown, half blue under the enormous dome of the sky. Corresponding in their insignificance to the islets of the sea, two small clumps of trees, one on each side of the only fault in the impeccable joint, marked the mouth of the river Meinam we had just left on the first preparatory stage of our homeward journey; and, far back on the inland level, a larger and loftier mass, the grove surrounding the great Paknam pagoda, was the only thing on which the eye could rest from the vain task of exploring the monotonous sweep of the horizon. Here and there gleams as of a few scattered pieces of silver marked the windings of the great river; and on the nearest of them, just within the bar, the tug steaming right into the land become lost to my sight, hull and funnel and masts, as though the impassive earth had swallowed her up without an effort, without a tremor. My eye followed the light cloud of her smoke, now here, now there, above the plain, according to the devious curves of the stream, but always fainter and farther away, till I lost it at last behind the miter-shaped hill of the great pagoda. And then I was left alone with my ship, anchored at the head of the Gulf of Siam.

She floated at the starting point of a long journey, very still in an immense stillness, the shadows of her spars flung far to the eastward by the setting sun. At that moment I was alone on her decks. There was not a sound in her—and around us nothing moved, nothing lived, not a canoe on the water, not a bird in the air, not a cloud in the sky. In this breathless pause at the threshold of a long passage we seemed to be measuring our fitness for a long and arduous enterprise, the appointed task of both our existences to be carried out, far from all human eyes, with only sky and sea for spectators and for judges.

There must have been some glare in the air to interfere with one's sight, because it was only just before the sun left us that my roaming eyes made out beyond the highest ridge of the principal islet of the group something which did away with the solemnity of perfect solitude. The tide of darkness flowed on swiftly; and with tropical suddenness a swarm of stars came out above the shadowy earth, while I lingered yet, my hand resting lightly on my ship's rail as if on the shoulder of a trusted friend. But, with all that multitude of celestial bodies staring down at one, the comfort of quiet communion with her was gone for good. And there were also disturbing sounds by this time—voices, footsteps forward; the steward flitted along the main deck, a busily ministering spirit; a hand bell tinkled urgently under the poop deck. . . .

I found my two officers waiting for me near the supper table, in the lighted cuddy.[1] We sat down at once, and as I helped the chief mate, I said:

"Are you aware that there is a ship anchored inside the islands? I saw her mastheads above the ridge as the sun went down."

He raised sharply his simple face, overcharged by a terrible growth of whisker, and emitted his usual ejaculations: "Bless my soul, sir! You don't say so!"

My second mate was a round-cheeked, silent young man, grave beyond his years, I thought; but as our eyes happened to meet I detected a slight quiver on his lips. I looked down at once. It was not my part to encourage sneering on board my ship. It must be said, too, that I knew very little of my officers. In consequence of certain events of no particular significance, except to myself, I had been appointed to the command only a fortnight before. Neither did I know much of the hands forward. All these people had been together for eighteen months or so, and my position was that of the only stranger on board. I mention this because it has some bearing on what is to follow. But what I felt most was my being a stranger to the ship; and if all the truth must be told, I was somewhat of a stranger to myself. The youngest man on board (barring the second mate), and untried as yet by a position of the fullest responsibility, I was willing to take the adequacy of the others for granted. They had simply to be equal to their tasks: but I wondered how far I should turn out faithful to that ideal conception of one's own personality every man sets up for himself secretly.

Meantime the chief mate, with an almost visible effect of collaboration on the part of his round eyes and frightful whiskers, was

1. Cabin.

trying to evolve a theory of the anchored ship. His dominant trait was to take all things into earnest consideration. He was of a painstaking turn of mind. As he used to say, he "liked to account to himself" for practically everything that came in his way, down to a miserable scorpion he had found in his cabin a week before. The why and the wherefore of that scorpion—how it got on board and came to select his room rather than the pantry (which was a dark place and more what a scorpion would be partial to), and how on earth it managed to drown itself in the inkwell of his writing desk —had exercised him infinitely. The ship within the islands was much more easily accounted for; and just as we were about to rise from the table he made his pronouncement. She was, he doubted not, a ship from home lately arrived. Probably she drew too much water to cross the bar except at the top of spring tides. Therefore she went into that natural harbor to wait for a few days in preference to remaining in an open roadstead.

"That's so," confirmed the second mate, suddenly, in his slightly hoarse voice. "She draws over twenty feet. She's the Liverpool ship *Sephora* with a cargo of coal. Hundred and twenty-three days from Cardiff."

We looked at him in surprise.

"The tugboat skipper told me when he came on board for your letters, sir," explained the young man. "He expects to take her up the river the day after tomorrow."

After thus overwhelming us with the extent of his information he slipped out of the cabin. The mate observed regretfully that he "could not account for that young fellow's whims." What prevented him telling us all about it at once, he wanted to know.

I detained him as he was making a move. For the last two days the crew had had plenty of hard work, and the night before they had very little sleep. I felt painfully that I—a stranger—was doing something unusual when I directed him to let all hands turn in without setting an anchor watch.[2] I proposed to keep on deck myself till one o'clock or thereabouts. I would get the second mate to relieve me at that hour.

"He will turn out the cook and the steward at four," I concluded, "and then give you a call. Of course at the slightest sign of any sort of wind we'll have the hands up and make a start at once."

He concealed his astonishment. "Very well, sir." Outside the cuddy he put his head in the second mate's door to inform him of my unheard-of caprice to take a five hours' anchor watch on myself. I heard the other raise his voice incredulously: "What? The captain himself?" Then a few more murmurs, a door closed, then another. A few moments later I went on deck.

2. I.e., a part of the ship's crew kept on duty while the ship lies at anchor.

My strangeness, which had made me sleepless, had prompted that unconventional arrangement, as if I had expected in those solitary hours of the night to get on terms with the ship of which I knew nothing, manned by men of whom I knew very little more. Fast alongside a wharf, littered like any ship in port with a tangle of unrelated things, invaded by unrelated shore people, I had hardly seen her yet properly. Now, as she lay cleared for sea, the stretch of her main deck seemed to me very fine under the stars. Very fine, very roomy for her size, and very inviting. I descended the poop and paced the waist, my mind picturing to myself the coming passage through the Malay Archipelago, down the Indian Ocean, and up the Atlantic. All its phases were familiar enough to me, every characteristic, all the alternatives which were likely to face me on the high seas—everything! . . . except the novel responsibility of command. But I took heart from the reasonable thought that the ship was like other ships, the men like other men, and that the sea was not likely to keep any special surprises expressly for my discomfiture.

Arrived at that comforting conclusion, I bethought myself of a cigar and went below to get it. All was still down there. Everybody at the after end of the ship was sleeping profoundly. I came out again on the quarter-deck, agreeably at ease in my sleeping suit on that warm breathless night, barefooted, a glowing cigar in my teeth, and, going forward, I was met by the profound silence of the fore end of the ship. Only as I passed the door of the forecastle I heard a deep, quiet, trustful sigh of some sleeper inside. And suddenly I rejoiced in the great security of the sea as compared with the unrest of the land, in my choice of that untempted life presenting no disquieting problems, invested with an elementary moral beauty by the absolute straightforwardness of its appeal and by the singleness of its purpose.

The riding light in the fore-rigging burned with a clear, untroubled, as if symbolic, flame, confident and bright in the mysterious shades of the night. Passing on my way aft along the other side of the ship, I observed that the rope side ladder, put over, no doubt, for the master of the tug when he came to fetch away our letters, had not been hauled in as it should have been. I became annoyed at this, for exactitude in small matters is the very soul of discipline. Then I reflected that I had myself peremptorily dismissed my officers from duty, and by my own act had prevented the anchor watch being formally set and things properly attended to. I asked myself whether it was wise ever to interfere with the established routine of duties even from the kindest of motives. My action might have made me appear eccentric. Goodness only knew how that absurdly whiskered mate would "account" for my conduct, and what the whole ship thought of that informality of their new captain. I was vexed with myself.

Not from compunction certainly, but, as it were mechanically, I proceeded to get the ladder in myself. Now a side ladder of that sort is a light affair and comes in easily, yet my vigorous tug, which should have brought it flying on board, merely recoiled upon my body in a totally unexpected jerk. What the devil! . . . I was so astounded by the immovableness of that ladder that I remained stock-still, trying to account for it to myself like that imbecile mate of mine. In the end, of course, I put my head over the rail.

The side of the ship made an opaque belt of shadow on the darkling glassy shimmer of the sea. But I saw at once something elongated and pale floating very close to the ladder. Before I could form a guess a faint flash of phosphorescent light, which seemed to issue suddenly from the naked body of a man, flickered in the sleeping water with the elusive, silent play of summer lightning in a night sky. With a gasp I saw revealed to my stare a pair of feet, the long legs, a broad livid back immersed right up to the neck in a greenish cadaverous glow. One hand, awash, clutched the bottom rung of the ladder. He was complete but for the head. A headless corpse! The cigar dropped out of my gaping mouth with a tiny plop and a short hiss quite audible in the absolute stillness of all things under heaven. At that I suppose he raised up his face, a dimly pale oval in the shadow of the ship's side. But even then I could only barely make out down there the shape of his black-haired head. However, it was enough for the horrid, frost-bound sensation which had gripped me about the chest to pass off. The moment of vain exclamations was past, too. I only climbed on the spare spar and leaned over the rail as far as I could, to bring my eyes nearer to that mystery floating alongside.

As he hung by the ladder, like a resting swimmer, the sea lightning played about his limbs at every stir; and he appeared in it ghastly, silvery, fishlike. He remained as mute as a fish, too. He made no motion to get out of the water, either. It was inconceivable that he should not attempt to come on board, and strangely troubling to suspect that perhaps he did not want to. And my first words were prompted by just that troubled incertitude.

"What's the matter?" I asked in my ordinary tone, speaking down to the face upturned exactly under mine.

"Cramp," it answered, no louder. Then slightly anxious, "I say, no need to call anyone."

"I was not going to," I said.

"Are you alone on deck?"

"Yes."

I had somehow the impression that he was on the point of letting go the ladder to swim away beyond my ken—mysterious as he came. But, for the moment, this being appearing as if he had risen from the bottom of the sea (it was certainly the nearest land to the ship) wanted only to know the time. I told him. And he, down there, tentatively:

"I suppose your captain's turned in?"

"I am sure he isn't," I said.

He seemed to struggle with himself, for I heard something like the low, bitter murmur of doubt. "What's the good?" His next words came out with a hesitating effort.

"Look here, my man. Could you call him out quietly?"

I thought the time had come to declare myself.

"I am the captain."

I heard a "By Jove!" whispered at the level of the water. The phosphorescence flashed in the swirl of the water all about his limbs, his other hand seized the ladder.

"My name's Leggatt."

The voice was calm and resolute. A good voice. The self-possession of that man had somehow induced a corresponding state in myself. It was very quietly that I remarked:

"You must be a good swimmer."

"Yes. I've been in the water practically since nine o'clock. The question for me now is whether I am to let go this ladder and go on swimming till I sink from exhaustion, or—to come on board here."

I felt this was no mere formula of desperate speech, but a real alternative in the view of a strong soul. I should have gathered from this that he was young; indeed, it is only the young who are ever confronted by such clear issues. But at the time it was pure intuition on my part. A mysterious communication was established already between us two—in the face of that silent, darkened tropical sea. I was young, too; young enough to make no comment. The man in the water began suddenly to climb up the ladder, and I hastened away from the rail to fetch some clothes.

Before entering the cabin I stood still, listening in the lobby at the foot of the stairs. A faint snore came through the closed door of the chief mate's room. The second mate's door was on the hook, but the darkness in there was absolutely soundless. He, too, was young and could sleep like a stone. Remained the steward, but he was not likely to wake up before he was called. I got a sleeping suit out of my room and, coming back on deck, saw the naked man from the sea sitting on the main hatch, glimmering white in the darkness, his elbows on his knees and his head in his hands. In a moment he had concealed his damp body in a sleeping suit of the same gray-stripe pattern as the one I was wearing and followed me like my double on the poop. Together we moved right aft, bare-footed, silent.

"What is it?" I asked in a deadened voice, taking the lighted lamp out of the binnacle,[3] and raising it to his face.

"An ugly business."

He had rather regular features; a good mouth; light eyes under somewhat heavy, dark eyebrows; a smooth, square forehead; no growth on his cheeks; a small, brown mustache, and a well-shaped, round chin. His expression was concentrated, meditative, under the inspecting light of the lamp I held up to his face; such as a man thinking hard in solitude might wear. My sleeping suit was just right for his size. A well-knit young fellow of twenty-five at most. He caught his lower lip with the edge of white, even teeth.

"Yes," I said, replacing the lamp in the binnacle. The warm, heavy tropical night closed upon his head again.

"There's a ship over there," he murmured.

"Yes, I know. The *Sephora*. Did you know of us?"

"Hadn't the slightest idea. I am the mate of her—" He paused and corrected himself. "I should say I *was*."

"Aha! Something wrong?"

"Yes. Very wrong indeed. I've killed a man."

"What do you mean? Just now?"

"No, on the passage. Weeks ago. Thirty-nine south. When I say a man—"

"Fit of temper," I suggested, confidently.

The shadowy, dark head, like mine, seemed to nod imperceptibly above the ghostly gray of my sleeping suit. It was, in the night, as though I had been faced by my own reflection in the depths of a somber and immense mirror.

"A pretty thing to have to own up to for a Conway boy,"[4] murmured my double, distinctly.

"You're a Conway boy?"

"I am," he said, as if startled. Then, slowly . . . "Perhaps you too—"

It was so; but being a couple of years older I had left before he joined. After a quick interchange of dates a silence fell; and I thought suddenly of my absurd mate with his terrific whiskers and the "Bless my soul—you don't say so" type of intellect. My double gave me an inkling of his thoughts by saying:

"My father's a parson in Norfolk. Do you see me before a judge and jury on that charge? For myself I can't see the necessity. There are fellows that an angel from heaven—— And I am not that. He was one of those creatures that are just simmering all the time with

---

3. A stand on the deck, near the helm, on which the compass rests.   4. See footnote 2 to *Youth*, above.

a silly sort of wickedness. Miserable devils that have no business to live at all. He wouldn't do his duty and wouldn't let anybody else do theirs. But what's the good of talking! You know well enough the sort of ill-conditioned snarling cur—"

He appealed to me as if our experiences had been as identical as our clothes. And I knew well enough the pestiferous danger of such a character where there are no means of legal repression. And I knew well enough also that my double there was no homicidal ruffian. I did not think of asking him for details, and he told me the story roughly in brusque, disconnected sentences. I needed no more. I saw it all going on as though I were myself inside that other sleeping suit.

"It happened while we were setting a reefed foresail, at dusk. Reefed foresail! You understand the sort of weather. The only sail we had left to keep the ship running; so you may guess what it had been like for days. Anxious sort of job, that. He gave me some of his cursed insolence at the sheet. I tell you I was overdone with this terrific weather that seemed to have no end to it. Terrific, I tell you—and a deep ship. I believe the fellow himself was half crazed with funk. It was no time for gentlemanly reproof, so I turned round and felled him like an ox. He up and at me. We closed just as an awful sea made for the ship. All hands saw it coming and took to the rigging, but I had him by the throat, and went on shaking him like a rat, the men above us yelling, 'Look out! look out!' Then a crash as if the sky had fallen on my head. They say that for over ten minutes hardly anything was to be seen of the ship—just the three masts and a bit of the forecastle head and of the poop all awash driving along in a smother of foam. It was a miracle that they found us, jammed together behind the fore-bits. It's clear that I meant business, because I was holding him by the throat still when they picked us up. He was black in the face. It was too much for them. It seems they rushed us aft together, gripped as we were, screaming 'Murder!' like a lot of lunatics, and broke into the cuddy. And the ship running for her life, touch and go all the time, any minute her last in a sea fit to turn your hair gray only a-looking at it. I understand that the skipper, too, started raving like the rest of them. The man had been deprived of sleep for more than a week, and to have this sprung on him at the height of a furious gale nearly drove him out of his mind. I wonder they didn't fling me overboard after getting the carcass of their precious shipmate out of my fingers. They had rather a job to separate us, I've been told. A sufficiently fierce story to make an old judge and a respectable jury sit up a bit. The first thing I heard when I came to myself was the maddening howling of that endless gale, and on that the voice of the old man. He was hanging on to my bunk, staring into my face out of his sou'wester.

" 'Mr. Leggatt, you have killed a man. You can act no longer as chief mate of this ship.' "

His care to subdue his voice made it sound monotonous. He rested a hand on the end of the skylight to steady himself with, and all that time did not stir a limb, so far as I could see. "Nice little tale for a quiet tea party," he concluded in the same tone.

One of my hands, too, rested on the end of the skylight; neither did I stir a limb, so far as I knew. We stood less than a foot from each other. It occurred to me that if old "Bless my soul—you don't say so" were to put his head up the companion and catch sight of us, he would think he was seeing double, or imagine himself come upon a scene of weird witchcraft; the strange captain having a quiet confabulation by the wheel with his own gray ghost. I became very much concerned to prevent anything of the sort. I heard the other's soothing undertone.

"My father's a parson in Norfolk," it said. Evidently he had forgotten he had told me this important fact before. Truly a nice little tale.

"You had better slip down into my stateroom now," I said, moving off stealthily. My double followed my movements; our bare feet made no sound; I let him in, closed the door with care, and, after giving a call to the second mate, returned on deck for my relief.

"Not much sign of any wind yet," I remarked when he approached.

"No, sir. Not much," he assented, sleepily, in his hoarse voice, with just enough deference, no more, and barely suppressing a yawn.

"Well, that's all you have to look out for. You have got your orders."

"Yes, sir."

I paced a turn or two on the poop and saw him take up his position face forward with his elbow in the rat-lines of the mizzen-rigging before I went below. The mate's faint snoring was still going on peacefully. The cuddy lamp was burning over the table on which stood a vase with flowers, a polite attention from the ships' provision merchant—the last flowers we should see for the next three months at the very least. Two bunches of bananas hung from the beam symmetrically, one on each side of the rudder casing. Everything was as before in the ship—except that two of her captain's sleeping suits were simultaneously in use, one motionless in the cuddy, the other keeping very still in the captain's stateroom.

It must be explained here that my cabin had the form of the capital letter L, the door being within the angle and opening into the short part of the letter. A couch was to the left, the bed-place to the right; my writing desk and the chronometers' table faced the door. But anyone opening it, unless he stepped right inside, had no view of what I call the long (or vertical) part of the letter. It contained some lockers surmounted by a bookcase; and a few clothes, a thick jacket or two, caps, oilskin coat, and such like, hung on hooks. There was at the bottom of that part a door opening into my bathroom, which could be entered also directly from the saloon.[5] But that way was never used.

The mysterious arrival had discovered the advantage of this particular shape. Entering my room, lighted strongly by a big bulkhead lamp swung on gimbals[6] above my writing desk, I did not see him anywhere till he stepped out quietly from behind the coats hung in the recessed part.

"I heard somebody moving about, and went in there at once," he whispered.

I, too, spoke under my breath.

"Nobody is likely to come in here without knocking and getting permission."

He nodded. His face was thin and the sunburn faded, as though he had been ill. And no wonder. He had been, I heard presently, kept under arrest in his cabin for nearly seven weeks. But there was nothing sickly in his eyes or in his expression. He was not a bit like me, really; yet, as we stood leaning over my bed-place, whispering side by side, with our dark heads together and our backs to the door, anybody bold enough to open it stealthily would have been treated to the uncanny sight of a double captain busy talking in whispers with his other self.

"But all this doesn't tell me how you came to hang on to our side ladder," I inquired, in the hardly audible murmurs we used, after he had told me something more of the proceedings on board the *Sephora* once the bad weather was over.

"When we sighted Java Head I had had time to think all those matters out several times over. I had six weeks of doing nothing else, and with only an hour or so every evening for a tramp on the quarter-deck."

He whispered, his arms folded on the side of my bed-place, staring through the open port. And I could imagine perfectly the manner of this thinking out—a stubborn if not a steadfast operation; something of which I should have been perfectly incapable.

"I reckoned it would be dark before we closed with the land," he continued, so low that I had to strain my hearing, near as we were to each other, shoulder touching shoulder almost. "So I asked to speak to the old man. He always seemed very sick when he came to see me—as if he could not look me in the face. You know, that foresail saved the ship. She was too deep to have run long under bare poles. And it was I that managed to set it for him. Anyway,

---

5. I.e., the officers' dining room.
6. Device for suspending articles in order to keep them in a horizontal position whatever the ship's motion.

he came. When I had him in my cabin—he stood by the door looking at me as if I had the halter around my neck already—I asked
him right away to leave my cabin door unlocked at night while the
ship was going through Sunda Straits.[7] There would be the Java
coast within two or three miles, off Angier Point. I wanted nothing
more. I've had a prize for swimming my second year in the Conway.'

"I can believe it," I breathed out.

"God only knows why they locked me in every night. To see
some of their faces you'd have thought they were afraid I'd go
about at night strangling people. Am I a murdering brute? Do I
look it? By Jove! if I had been he wouldn't have trusted himself like
that into my room. You'll say I might have chucked him aside and
bolted out, there and then—it was dark already. Well, no. And
for the same reason I wouldn't think of trying to smash the door.
There would have been a rush to stop me at the noise, and I did
not mean to get into a confounded scrimmage. Somebody else
might have got killed—for I would not have broken out only to
get chucked back, and I did not want any more of that work. He
refused, looking more sick than ever. He was afraid of the men, and
also of that old second mate of his who had been sailing with him
for years—a gray-headed old humbug; and his steward, too, had
been with him devil knows how long—seventeen years or more—a
dogmatic sort of loafer who hated me like poison, just because I was
the chief mate. No chief mate ever made more than one voyage in
the *Sephora*, you know. Those two old chaps ran the ship. Devil
only knows what the skipper wasn't afraid of (all his nerve went to
pieces altogether in that hellish spell of bad weather we had)—of
what the law would do to him—of his wife, perhaps. Oh, yes!
she's on board. Though I don't think she. would have meddled.
She would have been only too glad to have me out of the ship in
any way. The 'brand of Cain'[8] business, don't you see. That's all
right. I was ready enough to go off wandering on the face of the
earth—and that was price enough to pay for an Abel of that sort.
Anyhow, he wouldn't listen to me. 'This thing must take its course.
I represent the law here.' He was shaking life a leaf. 'So you won't?'
'No!' 'Then I hope you will be able to sleep on that,' I said, and
turned my back on him. 'I wonder that *you* can,' cries he, and
locks the door.

"Well, after that, I couldn't. Not very well. That was three weeks
ago. We have had a slow passage through the Java Sea; drifted
about Carimata[9] for ten days. When we anchored here they

7. Narrow passage between the islands
of Sumatra and Java in the East Indies;
the *Sephora* has been heading up from
the Indian Ocean into the Java Sea.
8. After Cain killed his brother Abel,
"the Lord set a mark upon Cain, lest
any finding him should kill him"
(Genesis iv.15).
9. Carimata (or Karimata) Strait, between the islands of Borneo and Billi-
ton, connects the Java Sea with the
South China Sea.

thought, I suppose, it was all right. The nearest land (and that's five miles) is the ship's destination; the consul would soon set about catching me; and there would have been no object in bolting to these islets there. I don't suppose there's a drop of water on them. I don't know how it was, but tonight that steward, after bringing me my supper, went out to let me eat it, and left the door unlocked. And I ate it—all there was, too. After I had finished I strolled out on the quarter-deck. I don't know that I meant to do anything. A breath of fresh air was all I wanted, I believe. Then a sudden temptation came over me. I kicked off my slippers and was in the water before I had made up my mind fairly. Somebody heard the splash and they raised an awful hullabaloo. 'He's gone! Lower the boats! He's committed suicide! No, he's swimming.' Certainly I was swimming. It's not so easy for a swimmer like me to commit suicide by drowning. I landed on the nearest islet before the boat left the ship's side. I heard them pulling about in the dark, hailing, and so on, but after a bit they gave up. Everything quieted down and the anchorage became as still as death. I sat down on a stone and began to think. I felt certain they would start searching for me at daylight. There was no place to hide on those stony things—and if there had been, what would have been the good? But now I was clear of that ship, I was not going back. So after a while I took off all my clothes, tied them up in a bundle with a stone inside, and dropped them in the deep water on the outer side of that islet. That was suicide enough for me. Let them think what they liked, but I didn't mean to drown myself. I meant to swim till I sank—but that's not the same thing. I struck out for another of these little islands, and it was from that one that I first saw your riding light. Something to swim for. I went on easily, and on the way I came upon a flat rock a foot or two above water. In the daytime, I dare say, you might make it out with a glass from your poop. I scrambled up on it and rested myself for a bit. Then I made another start. That last spell must have been over a mile."

His whisper was getting fainter and fainter, and all the time he stared straight out through the porthole, in which there was not even a star to be seen. I had not interrupted him. There was something that made comment impossible in his narrative, or perhaps in himself; a sort of feeling, a quality, which I can't find a name for. And when he ceased, all I found was a futile whisper: "So you swam for our light?"

"Yes—straight for it. It was something to swim for. I couldn't see any stars low down because the coast was in the way, and I couldn't see the land, either. The water was like glass. One might have been swimming in a confounded thousand-feet deep cistern with no place for scrambling out anywhere; but what I didn't like was the notion of swimming round and round like a crazed bullock

before I gave out; and as I didn't mean to go back . . . No. Do
you see me being hauled back, stark naked, off one of these little
islands by the scruff of the neck and fighting like a wild beast?
Somebody would have got killed for certain, and I did not want
any of that. So I went on. Then your ladder—"

"Why didn't you hail the ship?" I asked, a little louder.

He touched my shoulder lightly. Lazy footsteps came right over
our heads and stopped. The second mate had crossed from the other
side of the poop and might have been hanging over the rail, for
all we knew.

"He couldn't hear us talking—could he?" My double breathed
into my very ear, anxiously.

His anxiety was an answer, a sufficient answer, to the question
I had put to him. An answer containing all the difficulty of that
situation. I closed the porthole quietly, to make sure. A louder
word might have been overheard.

"Who's that?" he whispered then.

"My second mate. But I don't know much more of the fellow
than you do."

And I told him a little about myself. I had been appointed to
take charge while I least expected anything of the sort, not quite
a fortnight ago. I didn't know either the ship or the people. Hadn't
had the time in port to look about me or size anybody up. And as
to the crew, all they knew was that I was appointed to take the
ship home. For the rest, I was almost as much of a stranger on
board as himself, I said. And at the moment I felt it most acutely.
I felt that it would take very little to make me a suspect person
in the eyes of the ship's company.

He had turned about meantime; and we, the two strangers in
the ship, faced each other in identical attitudes.

"Your ladder—" he murmured, after a silence. "Who'd have
thought of finding a ladder hanging over at night in a ship anchored
out here! I felt just then a very unpleasant faintness. After the life
I've been leading for nine weeks, anybody would have got out of
condition. I wasn't capable of swimming round as far as your rudder chains. And, lo and behold! there was a ladder to get hold of.
After I gripped it I said to myself, 'What's the good?' When I saw
a man's head looking over I thought I would swim away presently
and leave him shouting—in whatever language it was. I didn't mind
being looked at. I—I liked it. And then you speaking to me so
quietly—as if you had expected me—made me hold on a little
longer. It had been a confounded lonely time—I don't mean while
swimming. I was glad to talk a little to somebody that didn't belong to the *Sephora*. As to asking for the captain, that was a mere
impulse. It could have been no use, with all the ship knowing about
me and the other people pretty certain to be round here in the

morning. I don't know—I wanted to be seen, to talk with some-body, before I went on. I don't know what I would have said. . . . 'Fine night, isn't it?' or something of the sort."

"Do you think they will be round here presently?" I asked with some incredulity.

"Quite likely," he said, faintly.

He looked extremely haggard all of a sudden. His head rolled on his shoulders.

"H'm. We shall see then. Meantime get into that bed," I whispered. "Want help? There."

It was a rather high bed-place with a set of drawers underneath. This amazing swimmer really needed the lift I gave him by seizing his leg. He tumbled in, rolled over on his back, and flung one arm across his eyes. And then, with his face nearly hidden, he must have looked exactly as I used to look in that bed. I gazed upon my other self for a while before drawing across carefully the two green serge curtains which ran on a brass rod. I thought for a moment of pinning them together for greater safety, but I sat down on the couch, and once there I felt unwilling to rise and hunt for a pin. I would do it in a moment. I was extremely tired, in a peculiarly intimate way, by the strain of stealthiness, by the effort of whisper-ing and the general secrecy of this excitement. It was three o'clock by now and I had been on my feet since nine, but I was not sleepy; I could not have gone to sleep. I sat there, fagged out, looking at the curtains, trying to clear my mind of the confused sensation of being in two places at once, and greatly bothered by an exasperating knocking in my head. It was a relief to discover suddenly that it was not in my head at all, but on the outside of the door. Before I could collect myself the words "Come in" were out of my mouth, and the steward entered with a tray, bringing in my morning coffee. I had slept, after all, and I was so frightened that I shouted, "This way! I am here, steward," as though he had been miles away. He put down the tray on the table next the couch and only then said, very quietly, "I can see you are here, sir." I felt him give me a keen look, but I dared not meet his eyes just then. He must have wondered why I had drawn the curtains of my bed before going to sleep on the couch. He went out, hooking the door open as usual.

I heard the crew washing decks above me. I knew I would have been told at once if there had been any wind. Calm, I thought, and I was doubly vexed. Indeed, I felt dual more than ever. The steward reappeared suddenly in the doorway. I jumped up from the couch so quickly that he gave a start.

"What do you want here?"

"Close your port, sir—they are washing decks."

"It is closed," I said, reddening.

"Very well, sir." But he did not move from the doorway and returned my stare in an extraordinary, equivocal manner for a time. Then his eyes wavered, all his expression changed, and in a voice unusually gentle, almost coaxingly:

"May I come in to take the empty cup away, sir?"

"Of course!" I turned my back on him while he popped in and out. Then I unhooked and closed the door and even pushed the bolt. This sort of thing could not go on very long. The cabin was as hot as an oven, too. I took a peep at my double, and discovered that he had not moved, his arm was still over his eyes; but his chest heaved; his hair was wet; his chin glistened with perspiration. I reached over him and opened the port.

"I must show myself on deck," I reflected.

Of course, theoretically, I could do what I liked, with no one to say nay to me within the whole circle of the horizon; but to lock my cabin door and take the key away I did not dare. Directly I put my head out of the companion I saw the group of my two officers, the second mate barefooted, the chief mate in long india-rubber boots, near the break of the poop, and the steward halfway down the poop ladder talking to them eagerly. He happened to catch sight of me and dived, the second ran down on the main deck shouting some order or other, and the chief mate came to meet me, touching his cap.

There was a sort of curiosity in his eye that I did not like. I don't know whether the steward had told them that I was "queer" only, or downright drunk, but I know the man meant to have a good look at me. I watched him coming with a smile which, as he got into point-blank range, took effect and froze his very whiskers. I did not give him time to open his lips.

"Square the yards by lifts and braces before the hands go to breakfast."

It was the first particular order I had given on board that ship; and I stayed on deck to see it executed, too. I had felt the need of asserting myself without loss of time. That sneering young cub got taken down a peg or two on that occasion, and I also seized the opportunity of having a good look at the face of every foremast man as they filed past me to go to the after braces. At breakfast time, eating nothing myself, I presided with such frigid dignity that the two mates were only too glad to escape from the cabin as soon as decency permitted; and all the time the dual working of my mind distracted me almost to the point of insanity. I was constantly watching myself, my secret self, as dependent on my actions as my own personality, sleeping in that bed, behind that door which faced me as I sat at the head of the table. It was very much like being mad, only it was worse because one was aware of it.

I had to shake him for a solid minute, but when at last he

opened his eyes it was in the full possession of his senses, with an inquiring look.

"All's well so far," I whispered. "Now you must vanish into the bathroom."

He did so, as noiseless as a ghost, and I then rang for the steward, and facing him boldly, directed him to tidy up my stateroom while I was having my bath—" and be quick about it." As my tone admitted of no excuses, he said, "Yes, sir," and ran off to fetch his dustpan and brushes. I took a bath and did most of my dressing, splashing, and whistling softly for the steward's edification, while the secret sharer of my life stood drawn up bolt upright in that little space, his face looking very sunken in daylight, his eyelids lowered under the stern, dark line of his eyebrows drawn together by a slight frown.

When I left him there to go back to my room the steward was finishing dusting. I sent for the mate and engaged him in some insignificant conversation. It was, as it were, trifling with the terrific character of his whiskers; but my object was to give him an opportunity for a good look at my cabin. And then I could at last shut, with a clear conscience, the door of my stateroom and get my double back into the recessed part. There was nothing else for it. He had to sit still on a small folding stool, half smothered by the heavy coats hanging there. We listened to the steward going into the bathroom out of the saloon, filling the water bottles there, scrubbing the bath, setting things to rights, whisk, bang, clatter—out again into the saloon—turn the key—click. Such was my scheme for keeping my second self invisible. Nothing better could be contrived under the circumstances. And there we sat; I at my writing desk ready to appear busy with some papers, he behind me, out of sight of the door. It would not have been prudent to talk in daytime; and I could not have stood the excitement of that queer sense of whispering to myself. Now and then, glancing over my shoulder, I saw him far back there, sitting rigidly on the low stool, his bare feet close together, his arms folded, his head hanging on his breast—and perfectly still. Anybody would have taken him for me.

I was fascinated by it myself. Every moment I had to glance over my shoulder. I was looking at him when a voice outside the door said:

"Beg pardon, sir."

"Well!" . . . I kept my eyes on him, and so, when the voice outside the door announced, "There's a ship's boat coming our way, sir," I saw him give a start—the first movement he had made for hours. But he did not raise his bowed head.

"All right. Get the ladder over."

I hesitated. Should I whisper something to him? But what? His immobility seemed to have been never disturbed. What could I tell him he did not know already? . . . Finally I went on deck.

II

The skipper of the *Sephora* had a thin red whisker all round his face, and the sort of complexion that goes with hair of that color; also the particular, rather smeary shade of blue in the eyes. He was not exactly a showy figure; his shoulders were high, his stature but middling—one leg slightly more bandy than the other. He shook hands, looking vaguely around. A spiritless tenacity was his main characteristic, I judged. I behaved with a politeness which seemed to disconcert him. Perhaps he was shy. He mumbled to me as if he were ashamed of what he was saying; gave his name (it was something like Archbold—but at this distance of years I hardly am sure), his ship's name, and a few other particulars of that sort, in the manner of a criminal making a reluctant and doleful confession. He had had terrible weather on the passage out— terrible—terrible—wife aboard, too.

By this time we were seated in the cabin and the steward brought in a tray with a bottle and glasses. "Thanks! No." Never took liquor. Would have some water, though. He drank two tumblerfuls. Terrible thirsty work. Ever since daylight had been exploring the islands round his ship.

"What was that for—fun?" I asked, with an appearance of polite interest.

"No!" He sighed. "Painful duty."

As he persisted in his mumbling and I wanted my double to hear every word, I hit upon the notion of informing him that I regretted to say I was hard of hearing.

"Such a young man, too!" he nodded, keeping his smeary blue, unintelligent eyes fastened upon me. What was the cause of it— some disease? he inquired, without the least sympathy and as if he thought that, if so, I'd got no more than I deserved.

"Yes; disease," I admitted in a cheerful tone which seemed to shock him. But my point was gained, because he had to raise his voice to give me his tale. It is not worth while to record that version. It was just over two months since all this had happened, and he had thought so much about it that he seemed completely muddled as to its bearings, but still immensely impressed.

"What would you think of such a thing happening on board your own ship? I've had the *Sephora* for these fifteen years. I am a well-known shipmaster."

He was densely distressed—and perhaps I should have sympathized with him if I had been able to detach my mental vision from the unsuspected sharer of my cabin as though he were my second self. There he was on the other side of the bulkhead, four or five feet from us, no more, as we sat in the saloon. I looked politely at

Captain Archbold (if that was his name), but it was the other I saw, in a gray sleeping suit, seated on a low stool, his bare feet close together, his arms folded, and every word said between us falling into the ears of his dark head bowed on his chest.

"I have been at sea now, man and boy, for seven-and-thirty years, and I've never heard of such a thing happening in an English ship. And that it should be my ship. Wife on board, too."

I was hardly listening to him.

"Don't you think," I said, "that the heavy sea which, you told me, came aboard just then might have killed the man? I have seen the sheer weight of a sea kill a man very neatly, by simply breaking his neck."

"Good God!" he uttered, impressively, fixing his smeary blue eyes on me. "The sea! No man killed by the sea ever looked like that." He seemed positively scandalized at my suggestion. And as I gazed at him, certainly not prepared for anything original on his part, he advanced his head close to mine and thrust his tongue out at me so suddenly that I couldn't help starting back.

After scoring over my calmness in this graphic way he nodded wisely. If I had seen the sight, he assured me, I would never forget it as long as I lived. The weather was too bad to give the corpse a proper sea burial. So next day at dawn they took it up on the poop, covering its face with a bit of bunting; he read a short prayer, and then, just as it was, in its oilskins and long boots, they launched it amongst those mountainous seas that seemed ready every moment to swallow up the ship herself and the terrified lives on board of her.

"That reefed foresail saved you," I threw in.

"Under God—it did," he exclaimed fervently. "It was by a special mercy, I firmly believe, that it stood some of those hurricane squalls."

"It was the setting of that sail which—" I began.

"God's own hand in it," he interrupted me. "Nothing less could have done it. I don't mind telling you that I hardly dared give the order. It seemed impossible that we could touch anything without losing it, and then our last hope would have been gone."

The terror of that gale was on him yet. I let him go on for a bit, then said, casually—as if returning to a minor subject:

"You were very anxious to give up your mate to the shore people, I believe?"

He was. To the law. His obscure tenacity on that point had in it something incomprehensible and a little awful; something, as it were, mystical, quite apart from his anxiety that he should not be suspected of "countenancing any doings of that sort." Seven-and-thirty virtuous years at sea, of which over twenty of immaculate command, and the last fifteen in the *Sephora*, seemed to have laid him under some pitiless obligation.

"And you know," he went on, groping shamefacedly amongst his feelings, "I did not engage that young fellow. His people had some interest with my owners. I was in a way forced to take him on. He looked very smart, very gentlemanly, and all that. But do you know —I never liked him, somehow. I am a plain man. You see, he wasn't exactly the sort for the chief mate of a ship like the *Sephora*."

I had become so connected in thoughts and impressions with the secret sharer of my cabin that I felt as if I, personally, were being given to understand that I, too, was not the sort that would have done for the chief mate of a ship like the *Sephora*. I had no doubt of it in my mind.

"Not at all the style of man. You understand," he insisted, superfluously, looking hard at me.

I smiled urbanely. He seemed at a loss for a while.

"I suppose I must report a suicide."

"Beg pardon?"

"Sui-cide! That's what I'll have to write to my owners directly I get in."

"Unless you manage to recover him before tomorrow," I assented, dispassionately. . . . "I mean, alive."

He mumbled something which I really did not catch, and I turned my ear to him in a puzzled manner. He fairly bawled:

"The land—I say, the mainland is at least seven miles off my anchorage."

"About that."

My lack of excitement, of curiosity, of surprise, of any sort of pronounced interest, began to arouse his distrust. But except for the felicitous pretense of deafness I had not tried to pretend anything. I had felt utterly incapable of playing the part of ignorance properly, and therefore was afraid to try. It is also certain that he had brought some ready-made suspicions with him, and that he viewed my politeness as a strange and unnatural phenomenon. And yet how else could I have received him? Not heartily! That was impossible for psychological reasons, which I need not state here. My only object was to keep off his inquiries. Surlily? Yes, but surliness might have provoked a point-blank question. From its novelty to him and from its nature, punctilious courtesy was the manner best calculated to restrain the man. But there was the danger of his breaking through my defense bluntly. I could not, I think, have met him by a direct lie, also for psychological (not moral) reasons. If he had only known how afraid I was of his putting my feeling of identity with the other to the test! But, strangely enough—(I thought of it only afterward)—I believe that he was not a little disconcerted by the reverse side of that weird situation, by something in me that reminded him of the man he was seeking—suggested a mysterious similitude to the young fellow he had distrusted and disliked from the first.

However that might have been, the silence was not very prolonged. He took another oblique step.

"I reckon I had no more than a two-mile pull to your ship. Not a bit more."

"And quite enough, too, in this awful heat," I said.

Another pause full of mistrust followed. Necessity, they say, is mother of invention, but fear, too, is not barren of ingenious suggestions. And I was afraid he would ask me point-blank for news of my other self.

"Nice little saloon, isn't it?" I remarked, as if noticing for the first time the way his eyes roamed from one closed door to the other. "And very well fitted out, too. Here, for instance," I continued, reaching over the back of my seat negligently and flinging the door open, "is my bathroom."

He made an eager movement, but hardly gave it a glance. I got up, shut the door of the bathroom, and invited him to have a look round, as if I were very proud of my accommodation. He had to rise and be shown round, but he went through the business without any raptures whatever.

"And now we'll have a look at my stateroom," I declared, in a voice as loud as I dared to make it, crossing the cabin to the starboard side with purposely heavy steps.

He followed me in and gazed around. My intelligent double had vanished. I played my part.

"Very convenient—isn't it?"

"Very nice. Very comf . . ." He didn't finish, and went out brusquely as if to escape from some unrighteous wiles of mine. But it was not to be. I had been too frightened not to feel vengeful; I felt I had him on the run, and I meant to keep him on the run. My polite insistence must have had something menacing in it, because he gave in suddenly. And I did not let him off a single item; mate's room, pantry, storerooms, the very sail locker which was also under the poop—he had to look into them all. When at last I showed him out on the quarter-deck he drew a long, spiritless sigh, and mumbled dismally that he must really be going back to his ship now. I desired my mate, who had joined us, to see to the captain's boat.

The man of whiskers gave a blast on the whistle which he used to wear hanging round his neck, and yelled, "*Sephora's* away!" My double down there in my cabin must have heard, and certainly could not feel more relieved than I. Four fellows came running out from somewhere forward and went over the side, while my own men, appearing on deck too, lined the rail. I escorted my visitor to the gangway ceremoniously, and nearly overdid it. He was a tenacious beast. On the very ladder he lingered, and in that unique, guiltily conscientious manner of sticking to the point:

"I say . . . you . . . you don't think that—"

I covered his voice loudly:

"Certainly not. . . . I am delighted. Good-by."

I had an idea of what he meant to say, and just saved myself by the privilege of defective hearing. He was too shaken generally to insist, but my mate, close witness of that parting, looked mystified and his face took on a thoughtful cast. As I did not want to appear as if I wished to avoid all communication with my officers, he had the opportunity to address me.

"Seems a very nice man. His boat's crew told our chaps a very extraordinary story, if what I am told by the steward is true. I suppose you had it from the captain, sir?"

"Yes. I had a story from the captain."

"A very horrible affair—isn't it, sir?"

"It is."

"Beats all these tales we hear about murders in Yankee ships."

"I don't think it beats them. I don't think it resembles them in the least."

"Bless my soul—you don't say so! But of course I've no ac-quaintance whatever with American ships, not I, so I couldn't go against your knowledge. It's horrible enough for me. . . . But the queerest part is that these fellows seemed to have some idea the man was hidden aboard here. They had really. Did you ever hear of such a thing?"

"Preposterous—isn't it?"

We were walking to and fro athwart the quarter-deck. No one of the crew forward could be seen (the day was Sunday), and the mate pursued:

"There was some little dispute about it. Our chaps took offense. 'As if we would harbor a thing like that,' they said. 'Wouldn't you like to look for him in our coal hole?' Quite a tiff. But they made it up in the end. I suppose he did drown himself. Don't you, sir?"

"I don't suppose anything."

"You have no doubt in the matter, sir?"

"None whatever."

I left him suddenly. I felt I was producing a bad impression, but with my double down there it was most trying to be on deck. And it was almost as trying to be below. Altogether a nerve-trying situa-tion. But on the whole I felt less torn in two when I was with him. There was no one in the whole ship whom I dared take into my confidence. Since the hands had got to know his story, it would have been impossible to pass him off for anyone else, and an ac-cidental discovery was to be dreaded now more than ever. . . .

The steward being engaged in laying the table for dinner, we could talk only with our eyes when I first went down. Later in the afternoon we had a cautious try at whispering. The Sunday quietness of the ship was against us; the stillness of air and water around her was against us; the elements, the men were against us—everything was against us in our secret partnership; time itself—for this could not go on forever. The very trust in Providence was, I suppose, denied to his guilt. Shall I confess that this thought cast me down very much? And as to the chapter of accidents which counts for so much in the book of success, I could only hope that it was closed. For what favorable accident could be expected?

"Did you hear everything?" were my first words as soon as we took up our position side by side, leaning over my bed-place.

He had. And the proof of it was his earnest whisper, "The man told you he hardly dared to give the order."

I understood the reference to be to that saving foresail.

"Yes. He was afraid of it being lost in the setting."

"I assure you he never gave the order. He may think he did, but he never gave it. He stood there with me on the break of the poop after the maintopsail blew away, and whimpered about our last hope—positively whimpered about it and nothing else—and the night coming on! To hear one's skipper go on like that in such weather was enough to drive any fellow out of his mind. It worked me up into a sort of desperation. I just took it into my own hands and went away from him, boiling, and— But what's the use telling you? *You* know! . . . Do you think that if I had not been pretty fierce with them I should have got the men to do anything? Not it! The bosun perhaps? Perhaps! It wasn't a heavy sea—it was a sea gone mad! I suppose the end of the world will be something like that; and a man may have the heart to see it coming once and be done with it—but to have to face it day after day— I don't blame anybody. I was precious little better than the rest. Only—I was an officer of that old coal-wagon, anyhow—"

"I quite understand," I conveyed that sincere assurance into his ear. He was out of breath with whispering; I could hear him pant slightly. It was all very simple. The same strung-up force which had given twenty-four men a chance, at least, for their lives, had, in a sort of recoil, crushed an unworthy mutinous existence.

But I had no leisure to weigh the merits of the matter—footsteps in the saloon, a heavy knock. "There's enough wind to get under way with, sir." Here was the call of a new claim upon my thoughts and even upon my feelings.

"Turn the hands up," I cried through the door. "I'll be on deck directly."

I was going out to make the acquaintance of my ship. Before I left the cabin our eyes met—the eyes of the only two strangers on board. I pointed to the recessed part where the little campstool

awaited him and laid my finger on my lips. He made a gesture—
somewhat vague—a little mysterious, accompanied by a faint smile,
as if of regret.

This is not the place to enlarge upon the sensations of a man
who feels for the first time a ship move under his feet to his own
independent word. In my case they were not unalloyed. I was not
wholly alone with my command; for there was that stranger in
my cabin. Or rather, I was not completely and wholly with her.
Part of me was absent. That mental feeling of being in two places
at once affected me physically as if the mood of secrecy had penetrated my very soul. Before an hour had elapsed since the ship had
begun to move, having occasion to ask the mate (he stood by my
side) to take a compass bearing of the Pagoda, I caught myself
reaching up to his ear in whispers. I say I caught myself, but enough
had escaped to startle the man. I can't describe it otherwise than
by saying that he shied. A grave, preoccupied manner, as though he
were in possession of some perplexing intelligence, did not leave
him henceforth. A little later I moved away from the rail to look
at the compass with such a stealthy gait that the helmsman noticed it—and I could not help noticing the unusual roundness of
his eyes. These are trifling instances, though it's to no commander's
advantage to be suspected of ludicrous eccentricities. But I was
also more seriously affected. There are to a seaman certain words,
gestures, that should in given conditions come as naturally, as instinctively as the winking of a menaced eye. A certain order should
spring on to his lips without thinking; a certain sign should get itself made, so to speak, without reflection. But all unconscious alertness had abandoned me. I had to make an effort of will to recall
myself back (from the cabin) to the conditions of the moment. I
felt that I was appearing an irresolute commander to those people
who were watching me more or less critically.

And, besides, there were the scares. On the second day out, for
instance, coming off the deck in the afternoon (I had straw slippers on my bare feet) I stopped at the open pantry door and spoke
to the steward. He was doing something there with his back to
me. At the sound of my voice he nearly jumped out of his skin, as
the saying is, and incidentally broke a cup.

"What on earth's the matter with you?" I asked, astonished.

He was extremely confused. "Beg your pardon, sir. I made sure
you were in your cabin."

"You see I wasn't."

"No, sir. I could have sworn I had heard you moving in there
not a moment ago. It's most extraordinary . . . very sorry, sir."

I passed on with an inward shudder. I was so identified with my
secret double that I did not even mention the fact in those scanty,
fearful whispers we exchanged. I suppose he had made some slight

noise of some kind or other. It would have been miraculous if he hadn't at one time or another. And yet, haggard as he appeared, he looked always perfectly self-controlled, more than calm—almost invulnerable. On my suggestion he remained almost entirely in the bathroom, which, upon the whole, was the safest place. There could be really no shadow of an excuse for anyone ever wanting to go in there, once the steward had done with it. It was a very tiny place. Sometimes he reclined on the floor, his legs bent, his head sustained on one elbow. At others I would find him on the campstool, sitting in his gray sleeping suit and with his cropped dark hair like a patient, unmoved convict. At night I would smuggle him into my bed-place, and we would whisper together, with the regular footfalls of the officer of the watch passing and repassing over our heads. It was an infinitely miserable time. It was lucky that some tins of fine preserves were stowed in a locker in my stateroom; hard bread I could always get hold of; and so he lived on stewed chicken, paté de foie gras, asparagus, cooked oysters, sardines—on all sorts of abominable sham delicacies out of tins. My early morning coffee he always drank; and it was all I dared do for him in that respect.

Every day there was the horrible maneuvering to go through so that my room and then the bathroom should be done in the usual way. I came to hate the sight of the steward, to abhor the voice of that harmless man. I felt that it was he who would bring on the disaster of discovery. It hung like a sword over our heads.

The fourth day out, I think (we were then working down the east side of the Gulf of Siam, tack for tack, in light winds and smooth water)—the fourth day, I say, of this miserable juggling with the unavoidable, as we sat at our evening meal, that man, whose slightest movement I dreaded, after putting down the dishes ran up on deck busily. This could not be dangerous. Presently he came down again; and then it appeared that he had remembered a coat of mine which I had thrown over a rail to dry after having been wetted in a shower which had passed over the ship in the afternoon. Sitting stolidly at the head of the table I became terrified at the sight of the garment on his arm. Of course he made for my door. There was no time to lose.

"Steward," I thundered. My nerves were so shaken that I could not govern my voice and conceal my agitation. This was the sort of thing that made my terrifically whiskered mate tap his forehead with his forefinger. I had detected him using that gesture while talking on deck with a confidential air to the carpenter. It was too far to hear a word, but I had no doubt that this pantomime could only refer to the strange new captain.

"Yes, sir," the pale-faced steward turned resignedly to me. It was this maddening course of being shouted at, checked without rhyme or reason, arbitrarily chased out of my cabin, suddenly called into it, sent flying out of his pantry on incomprehensible errands, that accounted for the growing wretchedness of his expression.

"Where are you going with that coat?"

"To your room, sir."

"Is there another shower coming?"

"I'm sure I don't know, sir. Shall I go up again and see, sir?"

"No! never mind."

My object was attained, as of course my other self in there would have heard everything that passed. During this interlude my two officers never raised their eyes off their respective plates; but the lip of that confounded cub, the second mate, quivered visibly.

I expected the steward to hook my coat on and come out at once. He was very slow about it; but I dominated my nervousness sufficiently not to shout after him. Suddenly I became aware (it could be heard plainly enough) that the fellow for some reason or other was opening the door of the bathroom. It was the end. The place was literally not big enough to swing a cat in. My voice died in my throat and I went stony all over. I expected to hear a yell of surprise and terror, and made a movement, but had not the strength to get on my legs. Everything remained still. Had my second self taken the poor wretch by the throat? I don't know what I would have done next moment if I had not seen the steward come out of my room, close the door, and then stand quietly by the sideboard.

Saved, I thought. But, no! Lost! Gone! He was gone!

I laid my knife and fork down and leaned back in my chair. My head swam. After a while, when sufficiently recovered to speak in a steady voice, I instructed my mate to put the ship round at eight o'clock himself.

"I won't come on deck," I went on. "I think I'll turn in, and unless the wind shifts I don't want to be disturbed before midnight. I feel a bit seedy."

"You did look middling bad a little while ago," the chief mate remarked without showing any great concern.

They both went out, and I stared at the steward clearing the table. There was nothing to be read on that wretched man's face. But why did he avoid my eyes I asked myself. Then I thought I should like to hear the sound of his voice.

"Steward!"

"Sir!" Startled as usual.

"Where did you hang up that coat?"

"In the bathroom, sir." The usual anxious tone. "It's not quite dry yet, sir."

For some time longer I sat in the cuddy. Had my double vanished as he had come? But of his coming there was an explanation, whereas his disappearance would be inexplicable. . . . I went slowly into my dark room, shut the door, lighted the lamp, and for a time dared not turn round. When at last I did I saw him standing bolt upright in the narrow recessed part. It would not be true to say I had a shock, but an irresistible doubt of his bodily existence flitted through my mind. Can it be, I asked myself, that he is not visible to other eyes than mine? It was like being haunted. Motionless, with a grave face, he raised his hands slightly at me in a gesture which meant clearly, "Heavens! what a narrow escape!" Narrow indeed. I think I had come creeping quietly as near insanity as any man who has not actually gone over the border. That gesture restrained me, so to speak.

The mate with the terrific whiskers was now putting the ship on the other tack. In the moment of profound silence which follows upon the hands going to their stations I heard on the poop his raised voice: "Hard alee!" and the distant shout of the order repeated on the maindeck. The sails, in that light breeze, made but a faint fluttering noise. It ceased. The ship was coming round slowly; I held my breath in the renewed stillness of expectation; one wouldn't have thought that there was a single living soul on her decks. A sudden brisk shout, "Mainsail haul!" broke the spell, and in the noisy cries and rush overhead of the men running away with the main brace we two, down in my cabin, came together in our usual position by the bed-place.

He did not wait for my question. "I heard him tumbling here and just managed to squat myself down in the bath," he whispered to me. "The fellow only opened the door and put his arm in to hang the coat up. All the same—"

"I never thought of that," I whispered back, even more appalled than before at the closeness of the shave, and marveling at that something unyielding in his character which was carrying him through so finely. There was no agitation in his whisper. Whoever was being driven distracted, it was not he. He was sane. And the proof of his sanity was continued when he took up the whispering again.

"It would never do for me to come to life again."

It was something that a ghost might have said. But what he was alluding to was his old captain's reluctant admission of the theory of suicide. It would obviously serve his turn—if I had understood at all the view which seemed to govern the unalterable purpose of his action.

"You must maroon me as soon as ever you can get amongst these islands off the Cambodje[1] shore," he went on.

"Maroon you! We are not living in a boy's adventure tale," I protested. His scornful whispering took me up.

1. I.e., Cambodia.

"We aren't indeed! There's nothing of a boy's tale in this. But there's nothing else for it. I want no more. You don't suppose I am afraid of what can be done to me? Prison or gallows or whatever they may please. But you don't see me coming back to explain such things to an old fellow in a wig and twelve respectable tradesmen, do you? What can they know whether I am guilty or not—or of *what* I am guilty, either? That's my affair. What does the Bible say? 'Driven off the face of the earth.'[2] Very well. I am off the face of the earth now. As I came at night so I shall go."

"Impossible!" I murmured. "You can't."

"Can't? . . . Not naked like a soul on the Day of Judgment. I shall freeze on to this sleeping suit. The Last Day is not yet—and . . . you have understood thoroughly. Didn't you?"

I felt suddenly ashamed of myself. I may say truly that I understood—and my hesitation in letting that man swim away from my ship's side had been a mere sham sentiment, a sort of cowardice.

"It can't be done now till next night," I breathed out. "The ship is on the offshore tack and the wind may fail us."

"As long as I know that you understand," he whispered. "But of course you do. It's a great satisfaction to have got somebody to understand. You seem to have been there on purpose." And in the same whisper, as if we two whenever we talked had to say things to each other which were not fit for the world to hear, he added, "It's very wonderful."

We remained side by side talking in our secret way—but sometimes silent or just exchanging a whispered word or two at long intervals. And as usual he stared through the port. A breath of wind came now and again into our faces. The ship might have been moored in dock, so gently and on an even keel she slipped through the water, that did not murmur even at our passage, shadowy and silent like a phantom sea.

At midnight I went on deck, and to my mate's great surprise put the ship round on the other tack. His terrible whiskers flitted round me in silent criticism. I certainly should not have done it if it had been only a question of getting out of that sleepy gulf as quickly as possible. I believe he told the second mate, who relieved him, that it was a great want of judgment. The other only yawned. That intolerable cub shuffled about so sleepily and lolled against the rails in such a slack, improper fashion that I came down on him sharply.

"Aren't you properly awake yet?"

"Yes, sir! I am awake."

"Well, then, be good enough to hold yourself as if you were. And keep a lookout. If there's any current we'll be closing with

2. "And Cain said unto the Lord, '* * * Behold, thou hast driven me out this day from the face of the earth * * * '" (Genesis iv.13–14).

some islands before daylight."

The east side of the gulf is fringed with islands, some solitary, others in groups. On the blue background of the high coast they seem to float on silvery patches of calm water, arid and gray, or dark green and rounded like clumps of evergreen bushes, with the larger ones, a mile or two long, showing the outlines of ridges, ribs of gray rock under the dark mantle of matted leafage. Unknown to trade, to travel, almost to geography, the manner of life they harbor is an unsolved secret. There must be villages—settlements of fishermen at least—on the largest of them, and some communication with the world is probably kept up by native craft. But all that forenoon, as we headed for them, fanned along by the faintest of breezes, I saw no sign of man or canoe in the field of the telescope I kept on pointing at the scattered group.

At noon I gave no orders for a change of course, and the mate's whiskers became much concerned and seemed to be offering themselves unduly to my notice. At last I said:

"I am going to stand right in. Quite in—as far as I can take her."

The stare of extreme surprise imparted an air of ferocity also to his eyes, and he looked truly terrific for a moment.

"We're not doing well in the middle of the gulf," I continued, casually. "I am going to look for the land breezes tonight."

"Bless my soul! Do you mean, sir, in the dark amongst the lot of all them islands and reefs and shoals?"

"Well—if there are any regular land breezes at all on this coast one must get close inshore to find them, mustn't one?"

"Bless my soul!" he exclaimed again under his breath. All that afternoon he wore a dreamy, contemplative appearance which in him was a mark of perplexity. After dinner I went into my stateroom as if I meant to take some rest. There we two bent our dark heads over a half-unrolled chart lying on my bed.

"There," I said. "It's got to be Koh-ring. I've been looking at it ever since sunrise. It has got two hills and a low point. It must be inhabited. And on the coast opposite there is what looks like the mouth of a biggish river—with some town, no doubt, not far up. It's the best chance for you that I can see."

"Anything. Koh-ring let it be."

He looked thoughtfully at the chart as if surveying chances and distances from a lofty height—and following with his eyes his own figure wandering on the blank land of Cochin China,[3] and then passing off that piece of paper clean out of sight into uncharted regions. And it was as if the ship had two captains to plan her course for her. I had been so worried and restless running up and down that I had not had the patience to dress that day. I had remained in my sleeping suit, with straw slippers and a soft floppy

3. South of Cambodia, with coast on the Gulf of Siam and the South China Sea.

hat. The closeness of the heat in the gulf had been most oppressive, and the crew were used to see me wandering in that airy attire.

"She will clear the south point as she heads now," I whispered into his ear. "Goodness only knows when, though, but certainly after dark. I'll edge her in to half a mile, as far as I may be able to judge in the dark—"

"Be careful," he murmured, warningly—and I realized suddenly that all my future, the only future for which I was fit, would perhaps go irretrievably to pieces in any mishap to my first command.

I could not stop a moment longer in the room. I motioned him to get out of sight and made my way on the poop. That unplayful cub had the watch. I walked up and down for a while thinking things out, then beckoned him over.

"Send a couple of hands to open the two quarter-deck ports," I said, mildly.

He actually had the impudence, or else so forgot himself in his wonder at such an incomprehensible order, as to repeat:

"Open the quarter-deck ports! What for, sir?"

"The only reason you need concern yourself about is because I tell you to do so. Have them open wide and fastened properly."

He reddened and went off, but I believe made some jeering remark to the carpenter as to the sensible practice of ventilating a ship's quarter-deck. I know he popped into the mate's cabin to impart the fact to him because the whiskers came on deck, as it were by chance, and stole glances at me from below—for signs of lunacy or drunkenness, I suppose.

A little before supper, feeling more restless than ever, I rejoined, for a moment, my second self. And to find him sitting so quietly was surprising, like something against nature, inhuman.

I developed my plan in a hurried whisper.

"I shall stand in as close as I dare and then put her round. I shall presently find means to smuggle you out of here into the sail locker, which communicates with the lobby. But there is an opening, a sort of square for hauling the sails out, which gives straight on the quarter-deck and which is never closed in fine weather, so as to give air to the sails. When the ship's way is deadened in stays and all the hands are aft at the main braces you shall have a clear road to slip out and get overboard through the open quarter-deck port. I've had them both fastened up. Use a rope's end to lower yourself into the water so as to avoid a splash—you know. It could be heard and cause some beastly complication."

He kept silent for a while, then whispered, "I understand."

"I won't be there to see you go," I began with an effort. "The rest . . . I only hope I have understood, too."

"You have. From first to last," and for the first time there seemed to be a faltering, something strained in his whisper. He caught hold of my arm, but the ringing of the supper bell made me start. He didn't, though; he only released his grip.

After supper I didn't come below again till well past eight o'clock. The faint, steady breeze was loaded with dew; and the wet, darkened sails held all there was of propelling power in it. The night, clear and starry, sparkled darkly, and the opaque, lightless patches shifting slowly against the low stars were the drifting islets. On the port bow there was a big one more distant and shadowily imposing by the great space of sky it eclipsed.

On opening the door I had a back view of my very own self looking at a chart. He had come out of the recess and was standing near the table.

"Quite dark enough," I whispered.

He stepped back and leaned against my bed with a level, quiet glance. I sat on the couch. We had nothing to say to each other. Over our heads the officer of the watch moved here and there. Then I heard him move quickly. I knew what that meant. He was making for the companion; and presently his voice was outside my door.

"We are drawing in pretty fast, sir. Land looks rather close."

"Very well," I answered. "I am coming on deck directly."

I waited till he was gone out of the cuddy, then rose. My double moved too. The time had come to exchange our last whispers, for neither of us was ever to hear each other's natural voice.

"Look here!" I opened a drawer and took out three sovereigns. "Take this, anyhow. I've got six and I'd give you the lot, only I must keep a little money to buy some fruit and vegetables for the crew from native boats as we go through Sunda Straits."

He shook his head.

"Take it," I urged him, whispering desperately. "No one can tell what—"

He smiled and slapped meaningly the only pocket of the sleeping jacket. It was not safe, certainly. But I produced a large old silk handkerchief of mine, and tying the three pieces of gold in a corner, pressed it on him. He was touched, I suppose, because he took it at last and tied it quickly round his waist under the jacket, on his bare skin.

Our eyes met; several seconds elapsed, till, our glances still mingled, I extended my hand and turned the lamp out. Then I passed through the cuddy, leaving the door of my room wide open. . . . "Steward!"

He was still lingering in the pantry in the greatness of his zeal, giving a rub-up to a plated cruet stand the last thing before going to bed. Being careful not to wake up the mate, whose room was opposite, I spoke in an undertone.

He looked round anxiously. "Sir!"

"Can you get me a little hot water from the galley?"

"I am afraid, sir, the galley fire's been out for some time now."

"Go and see."

He fled up the stairs.

"Now," I whispered, loudly, into the saloon—too loudly, perhaps, but I was afraid I couldn't make a sound. He was by my side in an instant—the double captain slipped past the stairs—through the tiny dark passage . . . a sliding door. We were in the sail locker, scrambling on our knees over the sails. A sudden thought struck me. I saw myself wandering barefooted, bareheaded, the sun beating on my dark poll. I snatched off my floppy hat and tried hurriedly in the dark to ram it on my other self. He dodged and fended off silently. I wonder what he thought had come to me before he understood and suddenly desisted. Our hands met gropingly, lingered united in a steady, motionless clasp for a second. . . . No word was breathed by either of us when they separated.

I was standing quietly by the pantry door when the steward returned.

"Sorry, sir. Kettle barely warm. Shall I light the spirit lamp?"

"Never mind."

I came out on deck slowly. It was now a matter of conscience to shave the land as close as possible—for now he must go overboard whenever the ship was put in stays. Must! There could be no going back for him. After a moment I walked over to leeward and my heart flew into my mouth at the nearness of the land on the bow. Under any other circumstances I would not have held on a minute longer. The second mate had followed me anxiously.

I looked on till I felt I could command my voice.

"She will weather," I said then in a quiet tone.

"Are you going to try that, sir?" he stammered out incredulously.

I took no notice of him and raised my tone just enough to be heard by the helmsman.

"Keep her good full."

"Good full, sir."

The wind fanned my cheek, the sails slept, the world was silent. The strain of watching the dark loom of the land grow bigger and denser was too much for me. I had shut my eyes—because the ship must go closer. She must! The stillness was intolerable. Were we standing still?

When I opened my eyes the second view started my heart with a thump. The black southern hill of Koh-ring seemed to hang right over the ship like a towering fragment of the everlasting night. On that enormous mass of blackness there was not a gleam to be seen, not a sound to be heard. It was gliding irresistibly toward us and yet seemed already within reach of the hand. I saw the vague figures of the watch grouped in the waist, gazing in awed silence.

"Are you going on, sir?" inquired an unsteady voice at my elbow. I ignored it. I had to go on.

"Keep her full. Don't check her way. That won't do now," I said warningly.

"I can't see the sails very well," the helmsman answered me, in strange, quavering tones.

Was she close enough? Already she was, I won't say in the shadow of the land, but in the very blackness of it, already swallowed up as it were, gone too close to be recalled, gone from me altogether.

"Give the mate a call," I said to the young man who stood at my elbow still as death. "And turn all hands up."

My tone had a borrowed loudness reverberated from the height of the land. Several voices cried out together: "We are all on deck, sir."

Then stillness again, with the great shadow gliding closer, towering higher, without a light, without a sound. Such a hush had fallen on the ship that she might have been a bark of the dead floating in slowly under the very gate of Erebus.[4]

"My God! Where are we?"

It was the mate moaning at my elbow. He was thunderstruck, and as it were deprived of the moral support of his whiskers. He clapped his hands and absolutely cried out, "Lost!"

"Be quiet," I said sternly.

He lowered his tone, but I saw the shadowy gesture of his despair. "What are we doing here?"

"Looking for the land wind."

He made as if to tear his hair, and addressed me recklessly.

"She will never get out. You have done it, sir. I knew it'd end in something like this. She will never weather, and you are too close now to stay. She'll drift ashore before she's round. O my God!"

I caught his arm as he was raising it to batter his poor devoted head, and shook it violently.

"She's ashore already," he wailed, trying to tear himself away.

"Is she? . . . Keep good full there!"

"Good full, sir," cried the helmsman in a frightened, thin, childlike voice.

I hadn't let go the mate's arm and went on shaking it. "Ready about, do you hear? You go forward"—shake—"and stop there" —shake—"and hold your noise"—shake—"and see these head sheets properly overhauled"—shake, shake—shake.

And all the time I dared not look toward the land lest my heart should fail me. I released my grip at last and he ran forward as if

4. Entry to Hades; place of pitch darkness.

fleeing for dear life.

I wondered what my double there in the sail locker thought of this commotion. He was able to hear everything—and perhaps he was able to understand why, on my conscience, it had to be thus close—no less. My first order "Hard alee!" re-echoed ominously under the towering shadow of Koh-ring as if I had shouted in a mountain gorge. And then I watched the land intently. In that smooth water and light wind it was impossible to feel the ship coming-to. No! I could not feel her. And my second self was making now ready to slip out and lower himself overboard. Perhaps he was gone already . . . ?

The great black mass brooding over our very mastheads began to pivot away from the ship's side silently. And now I forgot the secret stranger ready to depart, and remembered only that I was a total stranger to the ship. I did not know her. Would she do it? How was she to be handled?

I swung the mainyard and waited helplessly. She was perhaps stopped, and her very fate hung in the balance, with the black mass of Koh-ring like the gate of the everlasting night towering over her taffrail.[5] What would she do now? Had she way on her yet? I stepped to the side swiftly, and on the shadowy water I could see nothing except a faint phosphorescent flash revealing the glassy smoothness of the sleeping surface. It was impossible to tell—and I had not learned yet the feel of my ship. Was she moving? What I needed was something easily seen, a piece of paper, which I could throw overboard and watch. I had nothing on me. To run down for it I didn't dare. There was no time. All at once my strained, yearning stare distinguished a white object floating within a yard of the ship's side. White on the black water. A phosphorescent flash passed under it. What was that thing? . . . I recognized my own floppy hat. It must have fallen off his head . . . and he didn't bother. Now I had what I wanted—the saving mark for my eyes. But I hardly thought of my other self, now gone from the ship, to be hidden forever from all friendly faces, to be a fugitive and a vagabond on the earth, with no brand of the curse on his sane forehead to stay a slaying hand . . . too proud to explain.

And I watched the hat—the expression of my sudden pity for his mere flesh. It had been meant to save his homeless head from the dangers of the sun. And now—behold—it was saving the ship, by serving me for a mark to help out the ignorance of my strangeness. Ha! It was drifting forward, warning me just in time that the ship had gathered sternway.

"Shift the helm," I said in a low voice to the seaman standing still like a statue.

5. Rail across the stern.

The man's eyes glistened wildly in the binnacle light as he jumped round to the other side and spun round the wheel.

I walked to the break of the poop. On the overshadowed deck all hands stood by the forebraces waiting for my order. The stars ahead seemed to be gliding from right to left. And all was so still in the world that I heard the quiet remark "She's round," passed in a tone of intense relief between two seamen.

"Let go and haul."

The foreyards ran round with a great noise, amidst cheery cries. And now the frightful whiskers made themselves heard giving various orders. Already the ship was drawing ahead. And I was alone with her. Nothing! no one in the world should stand now between us, throwing a shadow on the way of silent knowledge and mute affection, the perfect communion of a seaman with his first command.

Walking to the taffrail, I was in time to make out, on the very edge of a darkness thrown by a towering black mass like the very gateway of Erebus—yes, I was in time to catch an evanescent glimpse of my white hat left behind to mark the spot where the secret sharer of my cabin and of my thoughts, as though he were my second self, had lowered himself into the water to take his punishment: a free man, a proud swimmer striking out for a new destiny.

1909   1912

WILLIAM BUTLER YEATS
(1865–1939)

1891: Organization of the Rhymers' Club.
1899: Launching of the Irish National Theatre.
1914: *Responsibilities*.
1923: Nobel Prize.
1928: *The Tower*.

William Butler Yeats was born in Sandymount, Dublin. His father's family, of English stock, had been in Ireland for at least 200 years; his mother's, the Pollexfens, hailing originally from Devon, had been for some generations in Sligo, in the west of Ireland. J. B. Yeats, his father, had abandoned the law to take up painting, at which he made a somewhat precarious living. The Yeatses were in London from 1874 until 1883, when they returned to Ireland—to Howth, a few miles from Dublin. On leaving high school in Dublin in 1883 Yeats decided to be an artist, with poetry as his avocation, and attended art school; but he soon left, to concentrate on poetry. His first published poems appeared in the *Dublin University Review* in 1885.

Yeats's father was a religious skeptic, but he believed in the "religion of art." Yeats himself, religious by temperament but unable to believe in Christian orthodoxy, sought all his life for traditions of esoteric thought that would compensate for a lost religion. This search led him to various kinds of mysticism, to folklore, theosophy, spiritualism, and Neo-Platonism—not in any strict chronological order, for he kept returning to and reworking earlier aspects of his thought. In middle life he elaborated a symbolic system of his own, based on a variety of sources, which enabled him to strengthen the pattern and coherence of his poetic imagery. The student of Yeats is constantly coming up against this willful and sometimes baffling esotericism which he cultivated sometimes playfully, sometimes earnestly, sometimes treating it as though it were a body of truths and sometimes as though it were a convenient language of symbols. Modern scholarship has traced most of Yeats's mystical and quasi-mystical ideas to sources that were common to Blake and Shelley and which sometimes go far back into pre-Platonic beliefs and traditions. But his greatness as a poet lies in his ability to communicate the power and significance of his symbols, by the way he expresses and organizes them, even to readers who know nothing of his system.

Yeats's childhood and young manhood were spent between Dublin, London, and Sligo, and each of these places contributed something to his poetic development. In London in the 1890's he met the important poets of the day, and in 1891 was one of the founders of the Rhymers' Club, whose members included Lionel Johnson, Ernest Dowson, and many other characteristic figures of the 90's. Here he acquired ideas of poetry which were vaguely Pre-Raphaelite: he believed, in this early stage of his career, that a poet's language should be dreamy, evocative, and ethereal. From the countryside around Sligo he got something much more vigorous and earthy—a knowledge of the life of the peasantry and of their folklore. In Dublin he was influenced by the currents of Irish nationalism and, while often in disagreement with those who wished to use literature for crude political ends, he nevertheless learned to see his poetry as a contribution to a rejuvenated Irish culture. The three influences of Dublin, London, and Sligo did not develop in chronological order—he was going to and fro between these places throughout his early life—and we sometimes find a poem based on Sligo folklore in the midst of a group of dreamy poems written under the influence of the Rhymers' Club or an echo of Irish nationalist feeling in a lyric otherwise wholly Pre-Raphaelite in tone.

We can distinguish quite clearly, however, the main periods into which Yeats's poetic career falls. He began in the tradition of self-conscious romanticism which he learned from the London poets of the 90's. Spenser and Shelley, and a little later Blake, were also important influences. One of his early verse plays ends with a song:

> The woods of Arcady are dead
> And over is their antique joy;
> Of old the world on dreaming fed;
> Gray Truth is now her painted toy.

About the same time he was writing poems (e.g., *The Stolen Child*) deriving from his Sligo experience, with a quiet precision of natural imagery, country place names, and themes from folklore. A little later—i.e., in the latter part of his first period—Dublin literary circles sent him to Standish O'Grady's *History of Ireland: Heroic Period*, where he found the great stories of the heroic age of Irish history, and to George Sigerson's and Douglas Hyde's translations of Gaelic poetry into "that dialect which gets from Gaelic its syntax and keeps its still partly Tudor vocabulary." Even when he plays with Neo-Platonic ideas, as in *The Rose of the World* (also the product of the latter part of his early period), he can link them with Irish heroic themes and so give a dignity and a *style* to his imagery not normally associated with this sort of poetic dreaminess. Thus the heroic legends of old Ireland and the folk traditions of the modern Irish countryside provided Yeats with a stiffening for his early dreamlike imagery, which is why even his first, "90's" phase is productive of interesting poems. *The Lake Isle of Innisfree*, spoiled for some by overanthologizing, is nevertheless a fine poem of its kind: it is the clarity and control shown in the handling of the imagery which keeps all romantic fuzziness out of it and gives it its haunting quality. In *The Man Who Dreamed of Faeryland* he makes something peculiarly effective out of the contrast between human activities and the strangeness of nature. In *The Madness of King Goll* the disturbing sense of the *otherness* of the natural world drives the king mad. (Such contrasts are common in the early Yeats; in his later poetry he tries to resolve what he called these "antinomies" in inclusive symbols. See, for example, *Crazy Jane Talks to the Bishop*.)

It is important to realize that Yeats had a habit of revising his earlier poems in later printings, tightening up the language and getting rid of the more self-indulgent romantic imagery. The revised versions are found in his *Collected Poems*, which therefore present a somewhat muted picture of his poetic development. For the complete picture one should consult the Variorum Edition edited by Peter Allt and Russell K. Alspach, 1957.

It was Irish nationalism that first sent Yeats in search of a consistently simpler and more popular style. He tells in one of his autobiographical essays how he sought for a style in which to express the elemental facts about Irish life and aspirations. This led him to the concrete image, as did Hyde's translations from Gaelic folk songs, in which "nothing * * * was abstract, nothing worn-out." But other forces were also working on him. He began to feel more and more that his earlier poetic styles could not speak for the whole self. Looking back in 1906, he found that he had mistaken the poetic ideal. "Without knowing it, I had come to care for nothing but impersonal beauty. * * * We should ascend out of common interests, the thoughts of the newspapers, of the market place, but only so far as we can carry the normal, passionate, reasoning self, the personality as a whole." The result of the abandonment of "impersonal beauty," and of the desire to "carry the normal, passionate, reasoning self" into his poetry, is seen in the volumes of collected poems, *In the Seven Woods* (1903) and *The Green Helmet and Other Poems* (1910). *The Folly of Being Comforted, Adam's Curse*, and *The Old Men Admiring Themselves* are from the former of these, and one can see immediately how Yeats here combines the colloquial with the formal. This is characteristic of his "second period."

By this time Yeats had met the beautiful actress and violent Irish nationalist Maud Gonne, with whom he was desperately in love for many years, but who persistently refused to marry him. This affair is reflected in many of the poems of his second period, notably *No Second Troy*, published in *The Green Helmet*. He had also met Lady Gregory, Irish writer and promoter of Irish literature, in 1896 and she invited him to spend the following summer at her country house, Coole Park, in Galway. Yeats spent many holidays with Lady Gregory and discovered the attractiveness of the "country house ideal," seeing in an aristocratic life of elegance and leisure in a great house a method of imposing order on chaos and a symbol of the Neo-Platonic dance of life. He expresses this view many times in his poetry—e.g., at the end of *A Prayer for My Daughter*—and it became an important part of Yeats's complex of attitudes. The middle classes, with their Philistine money-grubbing, he detested, and for his ideal characters he looked either below them, to peasants and beggars, or above them, to the aristocracy, for each of these had their own traditions and lived according to them.

It was under Lady Gregory's influence that Yeats became involved in the founding of the Irish National Theatre in 1899. This led to his active participation in problems of play production, which included political problems of censorship, economic problems of paying carpenters and actors, and other aspects of "theater business, management of men." All this had an effect on his style. The reactions of Dublin audiences did not encourage Yeats's trust in popular judgment, and his bitterness with the "Paudeens," middle-class shopkeepers—who seemed to him to be without any dignity, or understanding, or nobility of spirit—produced some of the most effective poems (e.g., *September 1913* and *To a Shade*) of his third or middle period. This period is best represented by the volume *Responsibilities* (1914), whose title is significant of the change in Yeats's view of the poetic function. Yeats was now becoming more and more of a public figure. In 1922 he was appointed a senator of the recently established Irish Free State and served until 1928, playing an active part not only in promoting the arts but also in general political affairs, in which he supported the views of the Protestant landed class.

Meanwhile Yeats was responding in his own way to the change in poetic taste represented in the poetry and criticism of Ezra Pound and T. S. Eliot immediately before World War I. A gift for epigram had already begun to emerge in his poetry: in the volume entitled *The Wild Swans at Coole* (1919) he has a poem citing Walter Savage Landor (the 19th-century poet who wrote some fine lapidary verse) and John Donne as masters. To the precision, and the combination of colloquial and formal, which he had achieved early in the century, he now added a "metaphysical" as well as an epigrammatic element, and this is seen in the later poems of his third period. He also continued his experiments with different kinds of rhythm. At the same time he was continuing his search for a language of symbols and pursuing his esoteric studies. Yeats married in 1917, and his wife proved so sympathetic to his imaginative needs that the automatic writing which she produced (believed by Yeats to have been dictated by spirits, but apparently faked by Mrs. Yeats to help her husband) gave him the elements of a symbolic system which he later worked out in his book *A Vision* (1925, 1937) and which he used in all sorts of ways in much of his later poetry. The system was both a theory of the movements of history and a theory of the different types of personality, each movement and type being related in various complicated ways to a different phase of the moon. Some of Yeats's poetry is unintelligible without a knowledge of A *Vision;* but the better poems, such as the two on Byzantium, can be appreciated without such knoweldge by the experienced reader who responds sensitively to the patterning of the imagery reinforced by the incantatory effect of the rhythms. Some recent criticism decries attempts by those who are not experts in the background of Yeats's esoteric thought to discuss his poetry and insists that only a detailed knowledge of Yeats's sources can yield his poetic meaning; but while it is true that some particular images do not yield all their significance to whose who are ignorant of the background, it is also true that too literal a paraphase of the symbolism in the light of the sources robs the poems of their power by reducing them to mere exercises in the use of a code.

The Tower (1928) and *The Winding Stair* (1933), from which the poems from *Sailing to Byzantium* through *After Long Silence* have been here selected, represent the mature Yeats at his very best—a realist-symbolist-metaphysical poet with an uncanny power over words. These volumes represent his fourth and greatest period. Here, in his poems of the 1920's and 1930's, winding stairs, spinning tops, "gyres," spirals of all kinds, are important symbols; not only are they connected with Yeats's philosophy of history and of personality, but they also serve as a means of resolving some of those contraries that had arrested him from the beginning. Life is a journey up a spiral staircase; as we grow older we cover the ground we have covered before, only higher up; as we look down the winding stair below us we measure our progress by the number of places where we were but no longer are. The journey is both repetitious and progressive; we go both round and upward. Through symbolic images of this kind Yeats explores the paradoxes of time and change, of growth and identity, of love and age, of life and art, of madness and wisdom.

The Byzantium poems show Yeats trying to escape from the turbulence of life to the calm eternity of art. But in his fifth and final period he returned to the turbulence after (if only partly as a result of) undergoing the Steinach glandular operations in 1934, and his last poems have a controlled yet startling wildness. Yeats's return to life, to "the foul rag-and-bone shop of the heart," is one of the most impressive final phases of any poet's career. "I shall be a sinful man to the end, and think upon my deathbed of all the nights I wasted in my youth," he wrote in old age to a correspondent, and in his very last letter he wrote: "When I try to put all into a phrase I say, 'Man can embody truth but he cannot know it.' * * * The abstract is not life and everywhere draws out its contradictions. You can refute Hegel but not the Saint or the Song of Sixpence." When he died in January , 1939, he left a body of verse which, in variety and power, makes him beyond question the greatest 20th-century poet of the English language.

The Madness of King Goll[1]

I sat on cushioned otter skin:
My word was law from Ith to Emain,
And shook at Inver Amergin [2]
The hearts of the world-troubling seamen,
And drove tumult and war away   5
From girl and boy and man and beast;
The fields grew fatter day by day,
The wild fowl of the air increased;
And every ancient Ollave [3] said,
While he bent down his fading head,   10
'He drive away the Northern cold.'
*They will not hush, the leaves a-flutter round me, the
    beech leaves old.*

I sat and mused and drank sweet wine;
A herdsman came from inland valleys,
Crying, the pirates drove his swine   15
To fill their dark-beaked hollow galleys.
I called my battle-breaking men
And my loud brazen battle cars
From rolling vale and rivery glen;
And under the blinking of the stars   20
Fell on the pirates by the deep,
And hurled them in the gulph of sleep:
These hands won many a torque of gold.
*They will not hush, the leaves a-flutter round me, the
    beech leaves old.*

But slowly, as I shouting slew   25
And trampled in the bubbling mire,
In my most secret spirit grew
A whirling and a wandering fire:
I stood: keen stars above me shone,
Around me shone keen eyes of men: 30
I laughed aloud and hurried on
By rocky shore and rushy fen;
I laughed because birds fluttered by,
And starlight gleamed, and clouds flew high,
And rushes waved and waters rolled.   35
*They will not hush, the leaves a-flutter round me, the
    beech leaves old.*

1. Yeats's first poem to be published in England (in *The Leisure Hour*, September, 1887). Its original title was *King Goll, An Irish Legend*. Like most of Yeats's early poems, the text was later much revised, and it is the revised version that is printed here. (In all cases of revision, we print the version revised by Yeats for his *Collected Poems*.) The legend tells of an ancient Irish king, who went mad and hid himself in a valley near Cork, where all the madmen of Ireland were believed to wish to gather if they were free. Yeats's father painted his son (in the latter's words) "as King Goll, tearing the strings out of a harp, being insane with youth."
2. The ancient Irish place names evoke the old heroic legends of Ireland. Emain, said to have been founded by Queen Macha of the Golden Hair (4th century), was in County Armagh (Armagh-Ard-macha, hill of Macha); it is now Navan Rath.
3. Learned man.

And now I wander in the woods
When summer gluts the golden bees,
Or in autumnal solitudes
Arise the leopard-colored trees;   40
Or when along the wintry strands
The cormorants shiver on their rocks;
I wander on, and wave my hands,
And sing, and shake my heavy locks.
The gray wolf knows me; by one ear   45
I lead along the woodland deer;
The hares run by me growing bold.
*They will not hush, the leaves a-flutter round me, the
    beech leaves old.*

I came upon a little town
That slumbered in the harvest moon,   50
And passed a-tiptoe up and down,
Murmuring, to a fitful tune,
How I have followed, night and day,
A tramping of tremendous feet,
And saw where this old tympan lay   55
Deserted on a doorway seat,
And bore it to the woods with me;
Of some inhuman misery
Our married voices wildly trolled.
*They will not hush, the leaves a-flutter round me, the
    beech leaves old.*   60

I sang how, when day's toil is done,
Orchil shakes out her long dark hair
That hides away the dying sun
And sheds faint odors through the air:
When my hand passed from wire to wire   65
It quenched, with sound like falling dew,
The whirling and the wandering fire;
But lift a mournful ulalu,
For the kind wires are torn and still,
And I must wander wood and hill   70
Through summer's heat and winter's cold.
*They will not hush, the leaves a-flutter round me, the
    beech leaves old.*

                                                    1887, 1888

The Stolen Child

Where dips the rocky highland
Of Sleuth Wood [4] in the lake,
There lies a leafy island

4. This and other places mentioned in
the poem are in County Sligo, in northwestern Ireland, where Yeats spent much
of his childhood.

Where flapping herons wake
The drowsy water rats;   5
There we've hid our faery vats,
Full of berries
And of reddest stolen cherries.
Come away, O human child!
To the waters and the wild   10
With a faery, hand in hand,
For the world's more full of weeping than you can understand.

Where the wave of moonlight glosses
The dim gray sands with light,
Far off by furthest Rosses   15
We foot it all the night,
Weaving olden dances
Mingling hands and mingling glances
Till the moon has taken flight;
To and fro we leap   20
And chase the frothy bubbles,
While the world is full of troubles
And is anxious in its sleep.
Come away, O human child!
To the waters and the wild   25
With a faery, hand in hand,
For the world's more full of weeping than you can understand.

Where the wandering water gushes
From the hills above Glen-Car,
In pools among the rushes   30
That scarce could bathe a star,
We seek for slumbering trout
And whispering in their ears
Give them unquiet dreams;
Leaning softly out   35
From ferns that drop their tears
Over the young streams.
Come away, O human child!
To the waters and the wild
With a faery, hand in hand,   40
For the world's more full of weeping than you can understand.

Away with us he's going,
The solemn-eyed:
He'll hear no more the lowing
Of the calves on the warm hillside   45
Or the kettle on the hob
Sing peace into his breast,
Or see the brown mice bob
Round and round the oatmeal chest.
For he comes, the human child,   50
To the waters and the wild

With a faery, hand in hand,
From a world more full of weeping than he can understand.

1886, 1889

Down by the Salley Gardens[5]

Down by the salley gardens my love and I did meet;
She passed the salley gardens with little snow-white feet.
She bid me take love easy, as the leaves grow on the tree;
But I, being young and foolish, with her would not agree.

In a field by the river my love and I did stand,   5
And on my leaning shoulder she laid her snow-white hand.
She bid me take life easy, as the grass grows on the weirs;
But I was young and foolish, and now am full of tears.

1889

The Rose of the World[1]

Who dreamed that beauty passes like a dream?
For these red lips, with all their mournful pride,
Mournful that no new wonder may betide,
Troy passed away in one high funeral gleam,
And Usna's children died.[2]   5

We and the laboring world are passing by:
Amid men's souls, that waver and give place
Like the pale waters in their wintry race,
Under the passing stars, foam of the sky,
Lives on this lonely face.   10

Bow down, archangels, in your dim abode:
Before you were, or any hearts to beat,
Weary and kind one lingered by His seat;
He made the world to be a grassy road
Before her wandering feet.   15

1892

5. Originally entitled *An Old Song Re-sung*, with Yeats's footnote: "This is an attempt to reconstruct an old song from three lines imperfectly remembered by an old peasant woman in the village of Ballysodare, Sligo, who often sings them to herself." "Salley" is a variant of "sallow," a species of willow tree.
1. The Platonic Idea of eternal Beauty. "I notice upon reading these poems for the first time for several years that the quality symbolized as The Rose differs from the Intellectual Beauty of Shelley and of Spenser in that I have imagined it as suffering with man and not as something pursued and seen from afar" (Yeats, in 1925).
2. In Old Irish legend, the Ulster warrior Naoise, son of Usna or Usnach (pronounced *Úshna*), carried off the beautiful Deirdre, whom King Conchubar of Ulster had intended to marry, and with his two brothers took her to Scotland. Eventually Conchubar lured the four of them back to Ireland and killed the three brothers.

The Lake Isle of Innisfree[3]

I will arise and go now, and go to Innisfree,
And a small cabin build there, of clay and wattles[4] made:
Nine bean-rows will I have there, a hive for the honeybee,
And live alone in the bee-loud glade.

And I shall have some peace there, for peace comes dropping slow, 5
Dropping from the veils of the morning to where the cricket sings;
There midnight's all a glimmer, and noon a purple glow,
And evening full of the linnet's wings.

I will arise and go now, for always night and day
I hear lake water lapping with low sounds by the shore;   10
While I stand on the roadway, or on the pavements gray,
I hear it in the deep heart's core.

                                                    1890, 1892

The Sorrow of Love

The brawling of a sparrow in the eaves,
The brilliant moon and all the milky sky,
And all that famous harmony of leaves,
Had blotted out man's image and his cry.

A girl arose that had red mournful lips   5
And seemed the greatness of the world in tears,
Doomed like Odysseus and the laboring ships
And proud as Priam murdered with his peers;[5]

Arose, and on the instant clamorous eaves,
A climbing moon upon an empty sky,   10
And all that lamentation of the leaves,
Could but compose man's image and his cry.

                                                    1892

When You Are Old[6]

When you are old and gray and full of sleep,
And nodding by the fire, take down this book,

3. Island in Lough Gill, County Sligo. "My father had read to me some passage out of [Thoreau's] *Walden*, and I planned to live some day in a cottage on a little island called Innisfree * * * "
4. Stakes interwoven with twigs or branches.
5. Odysseus (whom the Romans called Ulysses), hero of Homer's *Odyssey* which describes how, after having fought in the siege of Troy, he wandered for ten years before reaching his home, the Greek island of Ithaca. Priam was king of Troy at the time of the siege and was killed when the Greeks captured the city.
6. A poem suggested by a sonnet of the 16th-century French poet Pierre de Ronsard; it begins "*Quand vous serez bien vieille, au soir, à la chandelle*" ("When you are old, sitting at evening by candle light"), but ends very differently from Yeats's poem.

And slowly read, and dream of the soft look
Your eyes had once, and of their shadows deep;

How many loved your moments of glad grace,　　　　5
And loved your beauty with love false or true,
But one man loved the pilgrim soul in you,
And loved the sorrows of your changing face;

And bending down beside the glowing bars,
Murmur, a little sadly, how Love fled　　　　10
And paced upon the mountains overhead
And hid his face amid a crowd of stars.

　　　　　　　　　　　　　　　　　1892

Who Goes with Fergus?[7]

Who will go drive with Fergus now,
And pierce the deep wood's woven shade,
And dance upon the level shore?
Young man, lift up your russet brow,
And lift your tender eyelids, maid,　　　　5
And brood on hopes and fear no more.

And no more turn aside and brood
Upon love's bitter mystery;
For Fergus rules the brazen cars,
And rules the shadows of the wood,　　　　10
And the white breast of the dim sea
And all disheveled wandering stars.

　　　　　　　　　　　　　　　　　1893

The Man Who Dreamed of Faeryland

He stood among a crowd at Dromahair;[8]
His heart hung all upon a silken dress,
And he had known at last some tenderness,
Before earth took him to her stony care;
But when a man poured fish into a pile,　　　　5
It seemed they raised their little silver heads,
And sang what gold morning or evening sheds
Upon a woven world-forgotten isle
Where people love beside the raveled[9] seas;

7. Fergus, in Irish heroic legend, "king of the proud Red Branch Kings," gave up his throne voluntarily to Conchubar to learn by dreaming and meditating the bitter wisdom of the poet and philosopher. This poem is quoted by Buck Mulligan in *Ulysses*, and a line of it also comes into Stephen Dedalus' mind. 8. This and other place names in the poem refer to places in County Sligo. 9. Tangled; hence here "turbulent."

That Time can never mar a lover's vows   10
Under that woven changeless roof of boughs:
The singing shook him out of his new ease.

He wandered by the sands of Lissadell;
His mind ran all on money cares and fears,
And he had known at last some prudent years   15
Before they heaped his grave under the hill;
But while he passed before a plashy place,
A lugworm with its gray and muddy mouth
Sang that somewhere to north or west or south
There dwelt a gay, exulting, gentle race   20
Under the golden or the silver skies;
That if a dancer stayed his hungry foot
It seemed the sun and moon were in the fruit:
And at that singing he was no more wise.

He mused beside the well of Scanavin,   25
He mused upon his mockers: without fail
His sudden vengeance were a country tale,
When earthy night had drunk his body in;
But one small knotgrass growing by the pool
Sang where—unnecessary cruel voice—   30
Old silence bids its chosen race rejoice,
Whatever raveled waters rise and fall
Or stormy silver fret the gold of day,
And midnight there enfold them like a fleece
And lover there by lover be at peace.   35
The tale drove his fine angry mood away.

He slept under the hill of Lugnagall;
And might have known at last unhaunted sleep
Under that cold and vapor-turbaned steep,
Now that the earth had taken man and all: 40
Did not the worms that spired about his bones
Proclaim with that unwearied, reedy cry
That God has laid his fingers on the sky,
That from those fingers glittering summer runs
Upon the dancer by the dreamless wave.   45
Why should those lovers that no lovers miss
Dream, until God burn Nature with a kiss?
The man has found no comfort in the grave.

                                        1891, 1892

The Secret Rose[1]

Far-off, most secret, and inviolate Rose,
Enfold me in my hour of hours; where those

1. The Rose is a symbol of beauty (see "The Rose of the World," below), and in this poem "this spiritual beauty was seen as part of Yeats's own belief that there would be a revelation due to the creation of Celtic mysteries (and a complete understanding between Yeats and Maud Gonne)" [A. N. Jeffares]. Yeats

Who sought thee in the Holy Sepulcher,
Or in the wine-vat, dwell beyond the stir
And tumult of defeated dreams; and deep 5
Among pale eyelids, heavy with the sleep
Men have named beauty. Thy great leaves enfold
The ancient beards, the helms of ruby and gold
Of the crowned Magi;[2] and the king whose eyes
Saw the Pierced Hands and Rood of elder rise 10
In Druid vapor and make the torches dim;
Till vain frenzy awoke and he died;[3] and him
Who met Fand walking among flaming dew
By a gray shore where the wind never blew,
And lost the world and Emer for a kiss;[4] 15
And him who drove the gods out of their liss,[5]
And till a hundred morns had flowered red
Feasted, and wept the barrows of his dead;
And the proud dreaming king who flung the crown
And sorrow away, and calling bard and clown 20
Dwelt among wine-stained wanderers in deep woods;[6]
And him who sold tillage, and house, and goods,
And sought through lands and islands numberless years,
Until he found, with laughter and with tears,
A woman of so shining loveliness 25
That men threshed corn at midnight by a tress,
A little stolen tress.[7] I, too, await

reveals how he used his sources in an interesting note: "I find that I have unintentionally changed the old story of Conchubar's death. He did not see the Crucifixion in a vision but was told of it * * * I have imagined Cuchulain meeting Fand 'walking among the flaming dew,' because, I think, of something in Mr. Standish O'Grady's books. [See above, p. 1563.] I have founded the man 'who drove the gods out of their liss,' or fort, upon something I have read about Caoilte after the battle of Gabhra, when almost all his companions were killed, driving the gods out of their liss, * * * I have founded 'the proud dreaming king' upon Fergus, the son of Rogh, but when I wrote my poem here, and in the song in my early book, 'Who will drive with Fergus now?' I only knew him in Mr. Standish O'Grady, * * * I have founded 'him who sold tillage, and house, and goods,' upon something in 'The Red Pony,' a folktale in Mr. Larminie's *West Irish Folk Tales*. A young man 'saw a light before him on the high-road. When he came as far, there was an open box on the road, and a light coming up out of it. He took up the box. There was a lock of hair in it. Presently he had to go to become the servant of a king for his living. There were eleven boys. When they were going out into the stable at ten o'clock, each of them took a light but he. He took no candle at all with him. Each of them went into his own stable. When he went into his stable he opened the box. He left it in a hole in the wall. The light was great. It was twice as much as in the other stables.' The king hears of it, and makes him show him the box. The king says, 'You must go and bring me the woman to whom the hair belongs.' In the end the young man, and not the king, marries the woman."

2. The Magi are of course the "wise men" from the East who came to do homage to the infant Jesus. Mrs. Yeats told T. R. Henn that the image in lines 7–9 was "perhaps based on Botticelli's 'Adoration of the Magi,' with a Pre-Raphaelite overlay."

3. King Conchubar, in early Christian legend, is said to have died on the day of Christ's crucifixion in a fit of rage at hearing the news. Yeats, as his note explains, makes Conchubar see the crucifixion in a vision raised by the magic of the ancient Celtic priests, or Druids. The "Pierced Hands" are, of course, Christ's, and the "Rood" is the Cross.

4. The ancient Irish hero Cuchulain was seduced by Fand away from his wife Emer.

5. Fort. This is Caoilte, legendary Irish hero and companion of Oisin, son of Finn, poet and warrior.

6. The "proud dreaming king" is Fergus. See Yeats's note.

7. Yeats describes this tale in his note.

The hour of thy great wind of love and hate.
When shall the stars be blown about the sky,
Like the sparks blown out of a smithy, and die?
Surely thine hour has come, thy great wind blows,
Far-off, most secret, and inviolate Rose?

30

1896, 1897

The Folly of Being Comforted

One that is ever kind said yesterday:
"Your well-beloved's hair has threads of gray,
And little shadows come about her eyes;
Time can but make it easier to be wise
Though now it seem impossible, and so
All that you need is patience."

5

                                    Heart cries, "No,
I have not a crumb of comfort, not a grain.
Time can but make her beauty over again:
Because of that great nobleness of hers
The fire that stirs about her, when she stirs,
Burns but more clearly. O she had not these ways
When all the wild summer was in her gaze."

10

O heart! O heart! if she'd but turn her head,
You'd know the folly of being comforted.

1902, 1903

Adam's Curse[1]

We sat together at one summer's end,
That beautiful mild woman, your close friend,
And you and I, and talked of poetry.
I said: "A line will take us hours maybe;
Yet if it does not seem a moment's thought,
Our stitching and unstitching has been naught.
Better go down upon your marrowbones
And scrub a kitchen pavement, or break stones
Like an old pauper, in all kinds of weather;
For to articulate sweet sounds together
Is to work harder than all these, and yet
Be thought an idler by the noisy set
Of bankers, schoolmasters, and clergymen
The martyrs call the world."

5

10

---

1. To work for a living was the curse imposed by God upon Adam after the Fall (see Genesis iii.17–19). The poem reflects an incident in Yeats's passionate but hopeless love for the beautiful actress Maud Gonne (see A. N. Jeffares, *W. B. Yeats: Man and Poet*, 1949, pp. 128–29).

And thereupon 15
That beautiful mild woman for whose sake
There's many a one shall find out all heartache
On finding that her voice is sweet and low
Replied: "To be born woman is to know—
Although they do not talk of it at school— 20
That we must labor to be beautiful."

I said: "It's certain there is no fine thing
Since Adam's fall but needs much laboring.
There have been lovers who thought love should be
So much compounded of high courtesy 25
That they would sigh and quote with learned looks
Precedents out of beautiful old books;
Yet now it seems an idle trade enough."

We sat grown quiet at the name of love;
We saw the last embers of daylight die, 30
And in the trembling blue-green of the sky
A moon, worn as if it had been a shell
Washed by time's waters as they rose and fell
About the stars and broke in days and years.

I had a thought for no one's but your ears: 35
That you were beautiful, and that I strove
To love you in the old high way of love;
That it had all seemed happy, and yet we'd grown
As weary-hearted as that hollow moon.

1902, 1903

The Old Men Admiring Themselves in the Water

I heard the old, old men say,
"Everything alters,
And one by one we drop away."
They had hands like claws, and their knees
Were twisted like the old thorn trees 5
By the waters.
I heard the old, old men say,
"All that's beautiful drifts away
Like the waters."

1903

No Second Troy[1]

Why should I blame her that she filled my days
With misery, or that she would of late
Have taught to ignorant men most violent ways,
Or hurled the little streets upon the great,
Had they but courage equal to desire? 5

1. Another poem about Maud Gonne, who was a passionate Irish nationalist, preaching violence to achieve Irish independence (see lines 3–5).

What could have made her peaceful with a mind
That nobleness made simple as a fire,
With beauty like a tightened bow, a kind
That is not natural in an age like this,
Being high and solitary and most stern?   10
Why, what could she have done, being what she is?
Was there another Troy for her to burn?[2]

1910

The Fascination of What's Difficult[3]

The fascination of what's difficult
Has dried the sap out of my veins, and rent
Spontaneous joy and natural content
Out of my heart. There's something ails our colt
That must, as if it had not holy blood   5
Nor on Olympus leaped from cloud to cloud,
Shiver under the lash, strain, sweat and jolt
As though it dragged road-metal. My curse on plays
That have to be set up in fifty ways,
On the day's war with every knave and dolt,   10
Theater business, management of men.
I swear before the dawn comes round again
I'll find the stable and pull out the bolt.

1910

September 1913[4]

What need you, being come to sense,
But fumble in a greasy till
And add the halfpence to the pence
And prayer to shivering prayer, until
You have dried the marrow from the bone?   5
For men were born to pray and save:
Romantic Ireland's dead and gone,
It's with O'Leary[5] in the grave.

Yet they were of a different kind,
The names that stilled your childish play,   10
They have gone about the world like wind,
But little time had they to pray

2. Helen of Troy was, of course, the cause of the destruction of the "first" Troy. The mixture of admiration and bitterness reflected here is characteristic of many of Yeats's poems about Maud Gonne.
3. Written when Yeats was director-manager of the Abbey Theatre. "Subject. To complain of the fascination of what's difficult. It spoils spontaneity and pleasure, and wastes time. Repeat the line ending difficult three times and rhyme on bolt, exalt, colt, jolt" (Yeats's diary for September, 1909).
4. The poem reflects Yeats's disillusion with the state of the Irish national movement (for independence from Great Britain). Contrast *Easter 1916*, where the heroism of the Easter Rebellion, 1916, has led him to withdraw his criticism.
5. John O'Leary, Irish nationalist of great spirit and integrity who died in 1907.

For whom the hangman's rope was spun,
And what, God help us, could they save?
Romantic Ireland's dead and gone,   15
It's with O'Leary in the grave.

Was it for this the wild geese spread
The gray wing upon every tide;
For this that all that blood was shed,
For this Edward Fitzgerald[6] died,   20
And Robert Emmet and Wolfe Tone,
All that delirium of the brave?
Romantic Ireland's dead and gone,
It's with O'Leary in the grave.

Yet could we turn the years again,   25
And call those exiles as they were
In all their loneliness and pain,
You'd cry, "Some woman's yellow hair
Has maddened every mother's son":
They weighed so lightly what they gave.   30
But let them be, they're dead and gone,
They're with O'Leary in the grave.

1913

To a Shade[1]

If you have revisited the town, thin Shade,
Whether to look upon your monument
(I wonder if the builder has been paid)
Or happier-thoughted when the day is spent
To drink of that salt breath out of the sea   5
When gray gulls flit about instead of men,
And the gaunt houses put on majesty:
Let these content you and be gone again;
For they are at their old tricks yet.
                              A man
Of your own passionate serving kind who had brought   10
In his full hands what, had they only known,
Had given their children's children loftier thought,
Sweeter emotion, working in their veins
Like gentle blood, has been driven from the place,
And insult heaped upon him for his pains,   15

6. Lord Edward Fitzgerald (1763–98), a British officer who, after being dismissed from the army for disloyal activities, joined the United Irishmen (an Irish nationalist organization), was arrested, and died in prison. Robert Emmet (1778–1803) was also an Irish patriot, executed for treason after a heroic career. Theobald Wolfe Tone (1763–98), one of the chief founders of the United Irishmen, committed suicide in prison in Dublin.

1. I.e., the spirit of the great Irish nationalist leader, Charles Stewart Parnell (1846–91). Yeats is here expressing his disgust at the grubby materialism and Philistinism of the Dublin middle classes.

And for his openhandedness, disgrace;[2]
Your enemy, an old foul mouth, had set
The pack upon him.
                    Go, unquiet wanderer,
And gather the Glasnevin[3] coverlet
About your head till the dust stops your ear,   20
The time for you to taste of that salt breath
And listen at the corners has not come;
You had enough of sorrow before death—
Away, away! You are safer in the tomb.

1913   1913

The Cold Heaven[4]

Suddenly I saw the cold and rook-delighting heaven
That seemed as though ice burned and was but the more ice,
And thereupon imagination and heart were driven
So wild that every casual thought of that and this
Vanished, and left but memories, that should be out of season   5
With the hot blood of youth, of love crossed long ago;
And I took all the blame out of all sense and reason,
Until I cried and trembled and rocked to and fro,
Riddled with light. Ah! when the ghost begins to quicken,[5]
Confusion of the deathbed over, is it sent   10
Out naked on the roads, as the books say, and stricken
By the injustice of the skies for punishment?

1912

The Wild Swans at Coole[1]

The trees are in their autumn beauty,
The woodland paths are dry,
Under the October twilight the water
Mirrors a still sky;
Upon the brimming water among the stones   5
Are nine-and-fifty swans.

2. Sir Hugh Lane, Lady Gregory's nephew, had collected a number of important modern French paintings which he wished to give to the city of Dublin, provided they were permanently housed in a suitable building. Fierce abuse of the paintings and of the proposed design of the gallery in the Dublin nationalist press caused Lane to send the pictures to the London National Gallery. (Lane was drowned on the *Lusitania* in 1915; after years of bitter court dispute over an unwitnessed codicil to his will bequeathing the paintings to Dublin, an arrangement was reached in 1959 for the pictures to hang first in Dublin and then in London, for five years at a time.)
3. The cemetery where Parnell is buried.

4. Yeats told Maud Gonne, in answer to her inquiry. that this poem "was an attempt to describe the feelings aroused in him by the cold and detachedly beautiful winter sky. He felt alone and responsible in that loneliness for all the past mistakes that tortured his peace of mind. It was a momentary intensity of dreamlike perception, where physical surroundings remained fixed clear in the mind, to accentuate the years of thought and reality that passed in review in an instantaneous and yet eternal suspension of time" (A. N. Jeffares).
5. Come alive.
1. I.e., Coole Park, Lady Gregory's country estate, where Yeats was a frequent guest.

The nineteenth autumn has come upon me
Since I first made my count;[2]
I saw, before I had well finished,
All suddenly mount   10
And scatter wheeling in great broken rings
Upon their clamorous wings.

I have looked upon those brilliant creatures,
And now my heart is sore.
All's changed since I, hearing at twilight,   15
The first time on this shore,
The bell-beat of their wings above my head,
Trod with a lighter tread.

Unwearied still, lover by lover,
They paddle in the cold   20
Companionable streams or climb the air;
Their hearts have not grown old;
Passion or conquest, wander where they will,
Attend upon them still.

But now they drift on the still water,   25
Mysterious, beautiful;
Among what rushes will they build,
By what lake's edge or pool
Delight men's eyes when I awake some day
To find they have flown away?

1916   1917

Easter 1916[1]

I have met them at close of day
Coming with vivid faces
From counter or desk among gray
Eighteenth-century houses.
I have passed with a nod of the head   5
Or polite meaningless words,
Or have lingered awhile and said
Polite meaningless words,
And thought before I had done
Of a mocking tale or a gibe   10
To please a companion
Around the fire at the club,
Being certain that they and I
But lived where motley is worn:

2. His first visit had been in 1897 (nineteen years earlier).
1. On Easter Sunday of 1916, Irish nationalists launched a heroic but unsuccessful revolt against the British government; the week of street fighting that followed is known as the Easter Rebellion. As a result, a number of the nationalists were executed: Britain, at war with Germany, was in no mood to tolerate Irish agitation for independence —which was supported, for obvious reasons, by Germany. Yeats knew the chief rebels personally.

All changed, changed utterly: 15
A terrible beauty is born.

That woman's days were spent
In ignorant good will,
Her nights in argument
Until her voice grew shrill.   20
What voice more sweet than hers
When, young and beautiful,
She rode to harriers?[2]
This man had kept a school
And rode our wingéd horse;[3]   25
This other his helper and friend
Was coming into his force;
He might have won fame in the end,
So sensitive his nature seemed,
So daring and sweet his thought.   30
This other man I had dreamed
A drunken, vainglorious lout.[4]
He had done most bitter wrong
To some who are near my heart,
Yet I number him in the song;   35
He, too, has resigned his part
In the casual comedy;
He, too, has been changed in his turn,
Transformed utterly:
A terrible beauty is born.   40

Hearts with one purpose alone
Through summer and winter seem
Enchanted to a stone
To trouble the living stream.
The horse that comes from the road,   45
The rider, the birds that range
From cloud to tumbling cloud,
Minute by minute they change;
A shadow of cloud on the stream
Changes minute by minute;   50
A horse-hoof slides on the brim,
And a horse plashes within it;
The long-legged moorhens dive,
And hens to moorcocks call;
Minute by minute they live: 55
The stone's in the midst of all.

Too long a sacrifice
Can make a stone of the heart.
O when may it suffice?

2. Constance Gore-Booth (afterwards Countess Markiewicz), a member of the Sligo county aristocracy. A gay and beautiful girl she had annoyed Yeats by becoming an embittered nationalist.
3. Patrick Pearse, who was a schoolmaster, a leader in the movement to restore the Gaelic language in Ireland, and a poet (hence the reference to "our wingéd horse"—Pegasus, the horse of the Muses). "His helper and friend" was Thomas MacDonagh.
4. Major John MacBride. Maud Gonne, to Yeats's great disgust, had married MacBride in 1903, only to be separated from him after two years.

That is Heaven's part, our part   60
To murmur name upon name,
As a mother names her child
When sleep at last has come
On limbs that had run wild.
What is it but nightfall?   65
No, no, not night but death;
Was it needless death after all?
For England may keep faith
For all that is done and said.
We know their dream; enough   70
To know they dreamed and are dead;
And what if excess of love
Bewildered them till they died?
I write it out in a verse—
MacDonagh and MacBride   75
And Connolly[5] and Pearse
Now and in time to be,
Wherever green is worn,
Are changed, changed utterly:
A terrible beauty is born.   80

                                    1916, 1920

On a Political Prisoner[1]

She that but little patience knew,
From childhood on, had now so much
A gray gull lost its fear and flew
Down to her cell and there alit,
And there endured her fingers' touch   5
And from her fingers ate its bit.

Did she in touching that lone wing
Recall the years before her mind
Became a bitter, an abstract thing,
Her thought some popular enmity: 10
Blind and leader of the blind
Drinking the foul ditch where they lie?

When long ago I saw her ride
Under Ben Bulben[2] to the meet,
The beauty of her countryside
With all youth's lonely wildness stirred,   15
She seemed to have grown clean and sweet
Like any rock-bred, sea-borne bird:

Sea-borne, or balanced on the air
When first it sprang out of the nest   20

5. James Connolly, Pearse's partner in leading the insurrection. Like the other rebels named here, he was executed by shooting.
1. Constance Gore-Booth Markiewicz, who was imprisoned after the Easter Rebellion. She also figures in *Easter 1916*.
2. Mountain in County Sligo. The Gore-Booths lived at Lissadell, not far from Ben Bulben.

Upon some lofty rock to stare
Upon the cloudy canopy,
While under its storm-beaten breast
Cried out the hollows of the sea.

1920, 1921

The Second Coming[1]

Turning and turning in the widening gyre
The falcon cannot hear the falconer;
Things fall apart; the center cannot hold;
Mere anarchy is loosed upon the world,
The blood-dimmed tide is loosed, and everywhere   5
The ceremony of innocence is drowned;
The best lack all conviction, while the worst
Are full of passionate intensity.[2]

Surely some revelation is at hand;   10
Surely the Second Coming is at hand.
The Second Coming! Hardly are those words out
When a vast image out of *Spiritus Mundi*[3]
Troubles my sight: somewhere in sands of the desert
A shape with lion body and the head of a man,
A gaze blank and pitiless as the sun,   15
Is moving its slow thighs, while all about it
Reel shadows of the indignant desert birds.
The darkness drops again; but now I know
That twenty centuries of stony sleep
Were vexed to nightmare by a rocking cradle,[4]   20

1. This poem expresses Yeats's sense of the dissolution of the civilization of his time, the end of one cycle of history and the approach of another. He called each cycle of history a "gyre" (line 1) —literally a circular or spiral turn (Yeats pronounced it with a hard *g*). He imagines a falconer losing control of the falcon which sweeps in ever widening circles around him until it breaks away altogether, and sees this as a symbol of the end of the present gyre of civilization—what he once described as "all our scientific democratic fact-finding heterogeneous civilization." The birth of Christ brought to an end the cycle that had lasted from what Yeats called the "Babylonian mathematical starlight" (2000 B.C.) to the dissolution of Greco-Roman culture. "What if the irrational return?" Yeats asked in his prose work *A Vision*. "What if the circle begin again?" He speculates that "we may be about to accept the most implacable authority the world has known." The new Nativity ("the rough beast" of lines 21–22) is deliberately mysterious, both terrible and regenerative.

2. Lines 4–8 refer to the Russian Revolution of 1917, seen as a portent, but later Yeats accepted the poem as an unconscious prophecy of the rise of Fascism also. Speaking in 1924, Yeats declared: "It is impossible not to ask oneself to what great task of the nations we have been summoned in this transformed world where there is so much that is obscure and terrible." "The ceremony of innocence" suggests Yeats's view of ritual as the basis of civilized living. Cf. the last stanza of *A Prayer for My Daughter*.

3. The Spirit or Soul of the Universe, with which all individual souls are connected through the "Great Memory," which Yeats held to be a universal subconscious in which the human race preserves its past memories. It is thus a source of symbolic images for the poet.

4. I.e., the cradle of the infant Christ.

And what rough beast, its hour come round at last,
Slouches towards Bethlehem to be born?

1920, 1921

A Prayer for My Daughter[1]

Once more the storm is howling, and half hid
Under this cradle-hood and coverlid
My child sleeps on. There is no obstacle
But Gregory's wood[2] and one bare hill
Whereby the haystack- and roof-leveling wind,   5
Bred on the Atlantic, can be stayed;
And for an hour I have walked and prayed
Because of the great gloom that is in my mind.

I have walked and prayed for this young child an hour
And heard the sea-wind scream upon the tower,   10
And under the arches of the bridge, and scream
In the elms above the flooded stream;
Imagining in excited reverie
That the future years had come,
Dancing to a frenzied drum,   15
Out of the murderous innocence of the sea.[3]

May she be granted beauty and yet not
Beauty to make a stranger's eye distraught,
Or hers before a looking glass, for such,
Being made beautiful overmuch,   20
Consider beauty a sufficient end,
Lose natural kindness and maybe
The heart-revealing intimacy
That chooses right, and never find a friend.

Helen being chosen found life flat and dull   25
And later had much trouble from a fool,[4]
While that great Queen, that rose out of the spray,[5]
Being fatherless could have her way
Yet chose a bandy-leggéd smith for man.
It's certain that fine women eat   30
A crazy salad with their meat
Whereby the Horn of Plenty[6] is undone.

1. Yeats's daughter, christened Anne Butler, was born on February 26, 1919, in the refitted Norman tower of Thoor Ballylee (Ballylee Castle) in Galway, where Yeats lived: it is not far from Coole Park. The wind from the Atlantic roared in constantly (lines 1, 5–6).
2. Originally part of the Gregory estate, which had once also included Thoor Ballylee.
3. A reference to Yeats's visions of the future (cf. *The Second Coming*).
4. Presumably Paris, who carried Helen off from her husband.
5. Venus, wife (in the *Odyssey* and later accounts) of Vulcan, "bandy-legged" god of fire and forge (line 29).
6. The traditional image of the "Horn of Plenty" is generally associated by Yeats not only with abundance of the good things of the earth but also with the good life, conceived to be based on order and elegance (see concluding lines).

In courtesy I'd have her chiefly learned;
Hearts are not had as a gift but hearts are earned
By those that are not entirely beautiful;   35
Yet many, that have played the fool
For beauty's very self, has charm made wise,
And many a poor man that has roved,
Loved and thought himself beloved,
From a glad kindness cannot take his eyes.   40

May she become a flourishing hidden tree
That all her thoughts may like the linnet[7] be,
And have no business but dispensing round
Their magnanimities of sound,
Nor but in merriment begin a chase,   45
Nor but in merriment a quarrel.
O may she live like some green laurel
Rooted in one dear perpetual place.

My mind, because the minds that I have loved,
The sort of beauty that I have approved,   50
Prosper but little, has dried up of late,
Yet knows that to be choked with hate
May well be of all evil chances chief.
If there's no hatred in a mind
Assault and battery of the wind   55
Can never tear the linnet from the leaf.

An intellectual hatred is the worst,
So let her think opinions are accursed.
Have I not seen the loveliest woman born[8]
Out of the mouth of Plenty's horn,   60
Because of her opinionated mind
Barter that horn and every good
By quiet natures understood
For an old bellows full of angry wind?

Considering that, all hatred driven hence,   65
The soul recovers radical innocence
And learns at last that it is self-delighting,
Self-appeasing, self-affrighting,
And that its own sweet will is Heaven's will;
She can, though every face should scowl   70
And every windy quarter howl
Or every bellows burst, be happy still.

And may her bridegroom bring her to a house
Where all's accustomed, ceremonious;
For arrogance and hatred are the wares   75
Peddled in the thoroughfares.
How but in custom and in ceremony
Are innocence and beauty born?

7. A small European songbird.   8. Maud Gonne.

Ceremony's a name for the rich horn,
And custom for the spreading laurel tree.   80
June, 1919   1919, 1921

Sailing to Byzantium[1]

1

That is no country for old men. The young
In one another's arms, birds in the trees
—Those dying generations—at their song,
The salmon-falls, the mackerel-crowded seas,
Fish, flesh, or fowl, commend all summer long   5
Whatever is begotten, born, and dies.
Caught in that sensual music all neglect
Monuments of unaging intellect.

2

An aged man is but a paltry thing,
A tattered coat upon a stick, unless   10
Soul clap its hands and sing, and louder sing
For every tatter in its mortal dress,
Nor is there singing school but studying
Monuments of its own magnificence;
And therefore I have sailed the seas and come   15
To the holy city of Byzantium.

3

O sages standing in God's holy fire
As in the gold mosaic of a wall,[2]
Come from the holy fire, perne in a gyre,[3]
And be the singing-masters of my soul.   20
Consume my heart away; sick with desire

1. This poem should be read together with *Byzantium*. Byzantium had become for Yeats the symbol of art or artifice as opposed to the natural world of biological activity, and as he grew older he turned away from the sensual world of growth and change to the timeless world of art (though he returned to the sensual world later on). He wrote in *A Vision:* "I think that if I could be given a month of antiquity and leave to spend it where I chose, I would spend it in Byzantium [modern Istanbul] a little before Justinian opened St. Sophia and closed the Academy of Plato [i.e., ca. A.D. 535]. * * * I think that in early Byzantium, maybe never before or since in recorded history, religious, aesthetic, and practical life were one, that architects and artificers * * * spoke to the multitude in gold and silver. The painter, the mosaic worker, the worker in gold and silver, the illuminator of sacred books were almost impersonal, almost perhaps without the consciousness of individual design, absorbed in their subject matter and that the vision of a whole people." In his old age, the poet repudiates the world of biological change (of birth, growth, and death), putting behind him images of breeding and sensuality to turn to "monuments of unaging intellect," in a world of art and artifice outside of time. The theme of this poem, though not the treatment, is similar to that of Keats's *Ode on a Grecian Urn.* Note that the stanza form is *ottava rima,* used with great originality in the placing of pauses.
2. Like the mosaic figures on the walls of the Church of Hagia Sophia ("Holy Wisdom") in Byzantium.
3. I.e., whirl round in a spiral motion. "Perne" (or "pirn") is literally a bobbin, reel, or spool, on which something is wound. It became a favorite word of Yeats's, used as a verb meaning "to spin round"; he associated the spinning with the spinning of fate. Here he asks the saints on the wall to descend in this symbolic spinning motion and help him to enter into their state.

And fastened to a dying animal
It knows not what it is; and gather me
Into the artifice of eternity.

4

Once out of nature I shall never take   25
My bodily form from any natural thing,
But such a form as Grecian goldsmiths make
Of hammered gold and gold enameling
To keep a drowsy Emperor awake;[4]
Or set upon a golden bough to sing   30
To lords and ladies of Byzantium
Of what is past, or passing, or to come.

1927   1927

Leda and the Swan[1]

A sudden blow: the great wings beating still
Above the staggering girl, her thighs caressed
By the dark webs, her nape caught in his bill,
He holds her helpless breast upon his breast.

How can those terrified vague fingers push   5
The feathered glory from her loosening thighs?
And how can body, laid in that white rush,
But feel the strange heart beating where it lies?

A shudder in the loins engenders there
The broken wall, the burning roof and tower[2]   10
And Agamemnon dead.
                              Being so caught up,
So mastered by the brute blood of the air,
Did she put on his knowledge with his power
Before the indifferent beak could let her drop?

1923   1924, 1928

4. "I have read somewhere," Yeats wrote, "that in the Emperor's palace at Byzantium was a tree made of gold and silver, and artificial birds that sang." Cf. also Hans Christian Andersen's *Emperor's Nightingale*, which may have been in Yeats's mind at the time.
1. In Greek mythology Zeus visited Leda in the form of a swan. As a result of the union Leda gave birth to Helen and to Clytemnestra (wife of Agamemnon). Yeats saw Zeus's visit to Leda as an "annunciation," marking the beginning of Greek civilization: "I imagine the annunciation that founded Greece as made to Leda, remembering that they showed in a Spartan temple, strung up to the roof as a holy relic, an unhatched egg of hers, and that from one of her eggs came love and from the other war" (*A Vision*). In the original Cuala Press edition Yeats noted: "I wrote *Leda and the Swan* because the editor of a political review asked me for a poem. I thought, 'After the individualist, demagogic movement, founded by Hobbes and popularized by the Encyclopedists and the French Revolution, we have a soil so exhausted that it cannot grow that crop again for centuries.' Then I thought, 'Nothing is now possible but some movement from above preceded by some violent annunciation.' My fancy began to play with Leda and the Swan for metaphor, and I began this poem; but as I wrote, bird and lady took such possession of the scene that all politics went out of it, and my friend tells me that his 'conservative readers would misunderstand the poem.'" Note that this poem is in sonnet form; the placing of the pauses gives it a rhetorical pattern not normally associated with the sonnet.
2. I.e., the destruction of Troy, caused by Helen's elopement with the Trojan Paris. Agamemnon was murdered by his wife Clytemnestra, the other daughter of Leda and the Swan.

Among School Children

1

I walk through the long schoolroom questioning;
A kind old nun in a white hood replies;
The children learn to cipher and to sing,
To study reading-books and history,
To cut and sew, be neat in everything   5
In the best modern way—the children's eyes
In momentary wonder stare upon
A sixty-year-old smiling public man.

2

I dream of a Ledaean body,[1] bent
Above a sinking fire, a tale that she   10
Told of a harsh reproof, or trivial event
That changed some childish day to tragedy—
Told, and it seemed that our two natures blent
Into a sphere from youthful sympathy,
Or else, to alter Plato's parable,   15
Into the yolk and white of the one shell.[2]

3

And thinking of that fit of grief or rage
I look upon one child or t'other there
And wonder if she stood so at that age—
For even daughters of the swan can share   20
Something of every paddler's heritage—
And had that color upon cheek or hair,
And thereupon my heart is driven wild:
She stands before me as a living child.

4

Her present image floats into the mind—   25
Did Quattrocento[3] finger fashion it
Hollow of cheek as though it drank the wind
And took a mess of shadows for its meat?
And I though never of Ledaean kind
Had pretty plumage once—enough of that,   30
Better to smile on all that smile, and show
There is a comfortable kind of old scarecrow.

5

What youthful mother, a shape upon her lap
Honey of generation had betrayed,

---

1. "Ledaean": adjective from "Leda," meaning "like Helen of Troy" (Leda's daughter). The reference is to Maud Gonne (as also in lines 19–28).
2. In Plato's *Symposium* Aristophanes explains Love by supposing that "the primeval man was round and had four hands and four feet, back and sides forming a circle, one head with two faces," and was subsequently divided into two. "After the division, the two parts of man, each desiring his other half, came together, and threw their arms about one another eager to grow into one." The fact that Helen was born from an egg (as the daughter of Leda and the Swan) suggests Yeats's image for such a union.
3. 15th-century; a reference to Italian painters of the period, especially Botticelli (ca. 1444–1510).

And that must sleep, shriek, struggle to escape   35
As recollection or the drug decide,[4]
Would think her son, did she but see that shape
With sixty or more winters on its head,
A compensation for the pang of his birth,
Or the uncertainty of his setting forth?   40

6

Plato thought nature but a spume that plays
Upon a ghostly paradigm of things;
Solider Aristotle played the taws
Upon the bottom of a king of kings;[5]
World-famous golden-thighed Pythagoras[6]   45
Fingered upon a fiddle-stick or strings
What a star sang and careless Muses heard:
Old clothes upon old sticks to scare a bird.[7]

7

Both nuns and mothers worship images,[8]
But those the candles light are not as those   50
That animate a mother's reveries,
But keep a marble or a bronze repose.
And yet they too break hearts—O Presences
That passion, piety, or affection knows,
And that all heavenly glory symbolize—   55
O self-born mockers of man's enterprise;

8

Labor is blossoming or dancing where
The body is not bruised to pleasure soul,
Nor beauty born out of its own despair,
Nor blear-eyed wisdom out of midnight oil.   60
O chestnut tree, great-rooted blossomer,
Are you the leaf, the blossom, or the bole?
O body swayed to music, O brightening glance,
How can we know the dancer from the dance?[9]

1927

4. "I have taken the 'honey of genera-tion' from Porphyry's essay on 'The Cave of the Nymphs,' but find no war-rant in Porphyry for considering it the 'drug' that destroys the 'recollection' of prenatal freedom" [Yeats's note]. Por-phyry was a Neo-Platonic philosopher of the 3rd century A.D. "Honey of gen-eration," by blotting out the memory of prenatal happiness, "betrays" an in-fant to be born into this world. The infant will either "sleep" or "struggle to escape" (from this world) depending on whether the drug works or the recol-lection of blissful prenatal life over-comes the oblivion caused by the drug.
5. Plato thought nature was a mere appearance ("spume") veiling the ulti-mate spiritual and mathematical reality ("ghostly paradigm"); Aristotle was "solider" in that he believed that form really inhered in the matter of nature, and thus that nature itself had reality.

Aristotle was tutor to Alexander the Great, and disciplined him by applying the "taws" or strap.
6. Greek philosopher (early 6th cen-tury B.C.), interested in mathematics and the mathematical study of acous-tics and music; his disciples, the Py-thagoreans, developed a mystical phi-losophy of numerical relations and united the notions of astronomical and mathematical relations in the theory of the music of the spheres. Pythagoreans regarded their master with veneration as a god with a golden thigh.
7. A contemptuous description of the philosophies of Plato, Aristotle, and Pythagoras.
8. Nuns worship images of Christ or the Virgin; mothers worship their own in-ward images of their children.
9. Yeats's view of life as a cosmic dance, in which every human faculty joins harmoniously. The individual be-

A Dialogue of Self and Soul[1]

1

MY SOUL. I summon to the winding ancient stair;
Set all your mind upon the steep ascent,
Upon the broken, crumbling battlement,
Upon the breathless starlit air,
Upon the star that marks the hidden pole;　　　　　5
Fix every wandering thought upon
That quarter where all thought is done:
Who can distinguish darkness from the soul?

MY SELF. The consecrated blade upon my knees
Is Sato's ancient blade,[2] still as it was,　　　　　10
Still razor-keen, still like a looking glass
Unspotted by the centuries;
That flowering, silken, old embroidery, torn
From some court lady's dress and round
The wooden scabbard bound and wound,　　　　　15
Can, tattered, still protect, faded adorn.

MY SOUL. Why should the imagination of a man
Long past his prime remember things that are
Emblematical of love and war?
Think of ancestral night that can,　　　　　20
If but imagination scorn the earth
And intellect its wandering
To this and that and t'other thing,
Deliver from the crime of death and birth.

MY SELF. Montashigi, third of his family, fashioned it　　　　25
Five hundred years ago, about it lie
Flowers from I know not what embroidery—
Heart's purple—and all these I set
For emblems of the day against the tower
Emblematical of the night,　　　　　30
And claim as by a soldier's right
A charter to commit the crime once more.

comes involved in the process, as the dancer becomes part of the dance. Yeats relates the idea of the cosmic dance to his views of ritual, elegance, and order (cf. "the ceremony of innocence" in *The Second Coming* and the end of *Prayer for my Daughter*), and sees it as a means of reconciling the conflicting opposites of ordinary life.
1. Yeats here debates two opposing claims: the soul's summons to wisdom, resignation from an active life, the spiritual ascent—symbolized by the winding stair, a symbol similar to that of Byzantium—against the summons to the life of action and passion, symbolized by the sword of the second stanza and championed by the "Self."
2. A Japanese called Sato had given Yeats a sword, telling him that it was a symbol of life and that its silk-embroidered sheath was a symbol of beauty. Thus the sword in its scabbard is "emblematical of love and war" (line 19) and represents the "day," as opposed to the "night" represented by the tower and the winding stair (lines 29–30).

MY SOUL. Such fullness in that quarter overflows
And falls into the basin of the mind
That man is stricken deaf and dumb and blind,   35
For intellect no longer knows
Is from the *Ought*, or *Knower* from the *Known*—
That is to say, ascends to Heaven;
Only the dead can be forgiven;
But when I think of that my tongue's a stone.   40

2

MY SELF. A living man is blind and drinks his drop.
What matter if the ditches are impure?
What matter if I live it all once more?
Endure that toil of growing up;
The ignominy of boyhood; the distress   45
Of boyhood changing into man;
The unfinished man and his pain
Brought face to face with his own clumsiness;

The finished man among his enemies?—
How in the name of Heaven can he escape   50
That defiling and disfigured shape
The mirror of malicious eyes
Casts upon his eyes until at last
He thinks that shape must be his shape?
And what's the good of an escape   55
If honor find him in the wintry blast?

I am content to live it all again
And yet again, if it be life to pitch
Into the frog-spawn of a blind man's ditch,
A blind man battering blind men;   60
Or into that most fecund ditch of all,
The folly that man does
Or must suffer, if he woos
A proud woman not kindred of his soul.

I am content to follow to its source   65
Every event in action or in thought;
Measure the lot; forgive myself the lot!
When such as I cast out remorse
So great a sweetness flows into the breast
We must laugh and we must sing,   70
We are blest by everything,
Everything we look upon is blest.

1929

For Anne Gregory

"Never shall a young man,
Thrown into despair
By those great honey-colored

Ramparts at your ear,
Love you for yourself alone   5
And not your yellow hair."

"But I can get a hair-dye
And set such color there,
Brown, or black, or carrot,
That young men in despair   10
May love me for myself alone
And not my yellow hair."

"I heard an old religious man
But yesternight declare
That he had found a text to prove   15
That only God, my dear,
Could love you for yourself alone
And not your yellow hair."

1931, 1932

Byzantium[1]

The unpurged images of day recede;
The Emperor's drunken soldiery are abed;
Night resonance recedes, night-walkers' song
After great cathedral gong;
A starlit or a moonlit dome[2] disdains   5

1. The world of artifice and eternity to
which Yeats journeyed in *Sailing to
Byzantium* is now seen also as the
world of death and spiritual purification
from the "mire or blood" of life. As the
poem opens, the "unpurged images of
day" and then "night resonance" recede after the sounding of the gong
at midnight (symbolic of the summons
to death)—i.e., images of both the
conscious (day) mind and the subconscious (night) mind depart, leaving
the self in the hushed starlight or moonlight, purged of the "mere complexities" of flesh-and-blood life. This purified self "disdains" the confusion and
murkiness of the unpurified self. In the
second stanza the soul, released from
what Yeats once called "the strain one
upon another of opposites" of ordinary
life, sees his spirit-guide leading him to
the world of changelessness and purity.
He hails this guide (a mediating figure
between man, image, and shade) because he is now far enough beyond life
to be able to do so. The third stanza
shows the poet in the midst of the
death-world of artifice and eternity,
admiring the golden artifacts which, "in
glory of changeless metal" (line 22),
scorn the "complexities" and impurities of earthly creatures. In the next
stanza the poet sees purgatorial fires

burning away the "complexities" of
bodily life; yet, unlike earthly flame
which consumes as it burns, this flame
"cannot singe a sleeve" (line 32). Finally, the poet finds himself no longer
clearly in the world of pure spirit: he
is pulled back by the tug of human
emotion. He sees the smithies of the
metalworkers buttressing the city against
the dark tides of impurity and lust,
while the dance of eternal life on the
cold marble floor similarly helps to
stem the flood (these are Platonic and
Neo-Platonic images). But art and
artifice cannot succeed in repelling the
sensual life that beats against the city
walls: in the end, human images break
through and "beget" yet further images
(cf. *Sailing to Byzantium*, in which he
wanted to escape from "whatever is begotten, born, and dies"). The poem
concludes on a note of human passion,
"that dolphin-torn, that gong-tormented
sea." In this instance, the gong is calling
the poet back to life, not from life to
death. He has discovered that art is
nourished by life and in the end leads
back to it. Yeats himself said that this
poem was written "to warm myself
back to life" after a serious illness.
2. "Starlit" and "moonlit" had a special
symbolic significance for Yeats, as part
of his theory of history and personality

All that man is,
All mere complexities,
The fury and the mire of human veins.

Before me floats an image, man or shade,
Shade more than man, more image than a shade;   10
For Hades' bobbin bound in mummy-cloth
May unwind the winding path;[3]
A mouth that has no moisture and no breath
Breathless mouths may summon;
I hail the superhuman;   15
I call it death-in-life and life-in-death.

Miracle, bird or golden handiwork,
More miracle than bird or handiwork,
Planted on the starlit golden bough,[4]
Can like the cocks of Hades crow,   20
Or, by the moon embittered, scorn aloud
In glory of changeless metal
Common bird or petal
And all complexities of mire or blood.

At midnight on the Emperor's pavement flit   25
Flames that no faggot feeds, nor steel has lit,
Nor storm disturbs, flames begotten of flame,
Where blood-begotten spirits come
And all complexities of fury leave,
Dying into a dance,   30
An agony of trance,
An agony of flame[5] that cannot singe a sleeve.

Astraddle on the dolphin's mire and blood,[6]
Spirit after spirit! The smithies break the flood,

in terms of the phases of the moon (in *A Vision*). The first phase—that of the dark of the moon, when only the stars shine—is the phase when "body is completely absorbed in its supernatural environment." The fifteenth phase—the full moon—is the phase of complete subjectivity, where the mind is "completely absorbed by being." Thus both phases are states of *being:* they reject the complexities of the world of *becoming* and change.

In the Cuala Press edition of 1932, "disdains" is printed as "distains" (i.e., discolors, pollutes); all subsequent printings, however, read "disdains." It has been argued that the first reading must be correct, but it makes less sense, and Yeats never corrected the "disdains" in later printings.
3. The spool of man's fate, which spins his destiny and which is symbolized by the wrappings around a mummy, may lead man, as it unwinds, to the realm of pure spirit (or up the winding stair, in another of Yeats's favorite images).
4. The "starlit golden bough" is part of the death-world of artifice and eter-

nity; it is opposed to a real, living bough, which would be lighted by the sun or the moon (cf. note 2). The bough is also associated with the mystical tree of the esoteric Hebrew doctrine of the cabala, in whose branches "the birds lodge and build their nests; that is, the souls or angels have their place." The "cocks of Hades" are the birds standing outside time whose crowing proclaims the cycles of rebirth to mortal beings: the golden birds of art, who live in the same tree, are similarly eternal.
5. The "agony of flame" was suggested to Yeats by a Japanese *Nō* play, *Motomezulka*, wherein a young girl suffers from perpetual burning, which is a sense of her own guilt. A priest tells her that the flames will cease if she no longer believes in their reality; she finds herself incapable of disbelief, however, and the play ends in "the dance of her agony."
6. The dolphin, in ancient art, was a symbol of the soul in transit from one state to another. Mounted on its back, the poet here is able to ride over the

The golden smithies of the Emperor!   35
Marbles of the dancing floor
Break bitter furies of complexity,
Those images that yet
Fresh images beget,
That dolphin-torn, that gong-tormented sea.   40

1930   1932

Crazy Jane Talks with the Bishop[1]

I met the Bishop on the road
And much said he and I.
"Those breasts are flat and fallen now,
Those veins must soon be dry;
Live in a heavenly mansion,   5
Not in some foul sty."

"Fair and foul are near of kin,
And fair needs foul," I cried.
"My friends are gone, but that's a truth
Nor grave nor bed denied,   10
Learned in bodily lowliness
And in the heart's pride.

"A woman can be proud and stiff
When on love intent;
But Love has pitched his mansion in   15
The place of excrement;
For nothing can be sole or whole
That has not been rent."

1932

After Long Silence

Speech after long silence; it is right,
All other lovers being estranged or dead,
Unfriendly lamplight hid under its shade,
The curtains drawn upon unfriendly night,
That we descant and yet again descant   5
Upon the supreme theme of Art and Song:
Bodily decrepitude is wisdom; young
We loved each other and were ignorant.

1932

sea of human passions—except that the dolphin itself is made of "mire or blood."
1. One of a series of poems dealing with the paradox that wisdom may reside with fools and beggars (such as Jane) rather than with the respectable representatives of orthodoxy (such as the Bishop). This poem also deals with a favorite Yeatsian theme, the resolution of opposites, of what he called elsewhere "all those antinomies / Of day and night."

Lapis Lazuli[1]

(FOR HARRY CLIFTON)

I have heard that hysterical women say
They are sick of the palette and fiddle bow,
Of poets that are always gay,
For everybody knows or else should know
That if nothing drastic is done   5
Aeroplane and Zeppelin will come out,
Pitch like King Billy[2] bomb-balls in
Until the town lie beaten flat.

All perform their tragic play,
There struts Hamlet, there is Lear,   10
That's Ophelia, that Cordelia;
Yet they, should the last scene be there,
The great stage curtain about to drop,
If worthy their prominent part in the play,
Do not break up their lines to weep.   15
They know that Hamlet and Lear are gay;
Gaiety transfiguring all that dread.
All men have aimed at, found and lost;
Black out; Heaven blazing into the head:
Tragedy wrought to its uttermost.   20
Though Hamlet rambles and Lear rages,
And all the drop-scenes drop at once
Upon a hundred thousand stages,
It cannot grow by an inch or an ounce.

On their own feet they came, or on shipboard,   25
Camel-back, horse-back, ass-back, mule-back,
Old civilizations put to the sword.
Then they and their wisdom went to rack:
No handiwork of Callimachus,[3]
Who handled marble as if it were bronze,   30

1. A deep blue stone. "I notice that you have much lapis lazuli; someone has sent me a present of a great piece carved by some Chinese sculptor into the semblance of a mountain with temple, trees, paths, and an ascetic and pupil about to climb the mountain. Ascetic, pupil, hard stone, eternal theme of the sensual east. The heroic cry in the midst of despair. But no, I am wrong, the east has its solutions always and therefore knows nothing of tragedy. It is we, not the east, that must raise the heroic cry" (Yeats to Dorothy Wellesley, July 6, 1935).
2. King William III (William of Orange), who defeated the army of King James II at the Battle of the Boyne in 1690.
3. Greek sculptor (5th century B.C.), supposedly the originator of the Corinthian column and of the use of the running drill to imitate folds in drapery in statues. Yeats wrote of him: "With Callimachus pure Ionic revives again * * * and upon the only example of his work known to us, a marble chair, a Persian is represented, and may one not discover a Persian symbol in that bronze lamp, shaped like a palm * * * ? But he was an archaistic workman, and those who set him to work brought back public life to an older form" (*A Vision*).

Made draperies that seemed to rise
When sea wind swept the corner, stands;
His long lamp chimney shaped like the stem
Of a slender palm, stood but a day;
All things fall and are built again,   35
And those that build them again are gay.

Two Chinamen, behind them a third,
Are carved in lapis lazuli,
Over them flies a long-legged bird,
A symbol of longevity;   40
The third, doubtless a servingman,
Carries a musical instrument.

Every discoloration of the stone,
Every accidental crack or dent,
Seems a watercourse or an avalanche,   45
Or lofty slope where it still snows
Though doubtless plum or cherry branch
Sweetens the little halfway house
Those Chinamen climb towards, and I
Delight to imagine them seated there;   50
There, on the mountain and the sky,
On all the tragic scene they stare.
One asks for mournful melodies;
Accomplished fingers begin to play.
Their eyes mid many wrinkles, their eyes,   55
Their ancient, glittering eyes, are gay.

                                                          1938

Long-legged Fly[1]

That civilization may not sink,
Its great battle lost,
Quiet the dog, tether the pony
To a distant post;
Our master Caesar is in the tent   5
Where the maps are spread,
His eyes fixed upon nothing,
A hand under his head.
Like a long-legged fly upon the stream
His mind moves upon silence.   10

1. The first stanza shows Caesar planning one of his history-making campaigns: any disturbing noise now will alter the course of civilization. In the next stanza Helen of Troy as a child practices a part: the future of Troy and of the ancient world depends on her being allowed to train herself to be a woman. Finally, Michelangelo works in the Sistine Chapel in Rome: he must be undisturbed if his art is to be unspoiled, so that it can give to future generations of "girls at puberty" their first disturbing thoughts of men.

That the topless towers[2] be burnt
And men recall that face,
Move most gently if move you must
In this lonely place.
She thinks, part woman, three parts a child,   15
That nobody looks; her feet
Practice a tinker shuffle
Picked up on a street.
Like a long-legged fly upon the stream
Her mind moves upon silence.   20

That girls at puberty may find
The first Adam in their thought,
Shut the door of the Pope's chapel,
Keep those children out.
There on that scaffolding reclines   25
Michael Angelo.
With no more sound than the mice make
His hand moves to and fro.
Like a long-legged fly upon the stream
His mind moves upon silence.   30

1939

The Circus Animals' Desertion[1]

1

I sought a theme and sought for it in vain,
I sought it daily for six weeks or so.
Maybe at last, being but a broken man,
I must be satisfied with my heart, although
Winter and summer till old age began   5
My circus animals were all on show,
Those stilted boys, that burnished chariot,
Lion and woman[2] and the Lord knows what.

2

What can I but enumerate old themes?
First that sea-rider Oisin[3] led by the nose   10
Through three enchanted islands, allegorical dreams,
Vain gaiety, vain battle, vain repose,
Themes of the embittered heart, or so it seems,
That might adorn old songs or courtly shows;

2. Of Troy. Cf. "Was this the face that launched a thousand ships / And burnt the topless towers of Ilium?" (Marlowe, *Dr. Faustus*).

1. Yeats in old age looks back on some of the main themes of his poems and plays as circus animals that have now deserted him, leaving him with only the refuse of his human passions.

2. Cf. "On the gray rock of Cashel I suddenly saw / A Sphinx with woman breast and lion paw * * * " (Yeats, *The Double Vision of Michael Robartes*).

3. Pronounced *Ushéen*. Hero of an Old Irish legend, he was beguiled by a fairy woman to the fairy world and returned 150 years later to find his friends dead and Ireland Christian. Subject of an early long poem by Yeats (1889).

But what cared I that set him on to ride,   15
I, starved for the bosom of his faery bride?

And then a counter-truth filled out its play,
The Countess Cathleen was the name I gave it;
She, pity-crazed, had given her soul away,
But masterful Heaven had intervened to save it.[4]   20
I thought my dear must her own soul destroy,
So did fanaticism and hate enslave it,
And this brought forth a dream and soon enough
This dream itself had all my thought and love.

And when the Fool and Blind Man stole the bread   25
Cuchulain fought the ungovernable sea;[5]
Heart-mysteries there, and yet when all is said
It was the dream itself enchanted me:
Character isolated by a deed
To engross the present and dominate memory.   30
Players and painted stage took all my love,
And not those things that they were emblems of.

3

Those masterful images because complete
Grew in pure mind, but out of what began?
A mound of refuse or the sweepings of a street,   35
Old kettles, old bottles, and a broken can,
Old iron, old bones, old rags, that raving slut
Who keeps the till. Now that my ladder's gone,
I must lie down where all the ladders start,
In the foul rag-and-bone shop of the heart.   40

1939

Under Ben Bulben[1]

1

Swear by what the sages spoke
Round the Mareotic Lake[2]

4. Title of an early Yeats play (1892) about an Irish countess who, although she sold her soul to the devil to get food for the starving people, goes to Heaven anyway, for God looks "on the motive, not the deed."
5. In Yeats's play *On Baile's Strand* (1904), where he probes for symbolic meanings in an old Irish legend.
1. One of Yeats's last poems, ending with the epitaph he wrote for himself. He wished to be buried in the churchyard of the village of Drumcliff, which lies "under Ben Bulben," mountain in County Sligo. Although he died on the French Riviera, his body was later brought back and buried at Drumcliff.

2. Lake Mareotis, bordering the city of Alexandria where a school of Neo-Pythagorean philosophers flourished in the 1st century A.D. By Lake Mareotis also flourished (3rd century A.D.) the Christian Neo-Platonists, in whom Yeats was much interested. The lake is mentioned in Shelley's poem *The Witch of Atlas*, a poem which Yeats admired and interpreted in his own way, seeing the Witch as a symbol of timeless, absolute beauty; hence what she "knew" and "spoke" and what "set the cocks a-crow" can be related to the "miracle" that "can like the cocks of Hades crow" in *Byzantium*.

That the Witch of Atlas knew,
Spoke and set the cocks a-crow.

Swear by those horsemen, by those women   5
Complexion and form prove superhuman,[3]
That pale, long-visaged company
That air in immortality
Completeness of their passions won;
Now they ride the wintry dawn   10
Where Ben Bulben sets the scene.

Here's the gist of what they mean.

2

Many times man lives and dies
Between his two eternities,
That of race and that of soul,   15
And ancient Ireland knew it all.
Whether man die in his bed
Or the rifle knocks him dead,
A brief parting from those dear
Is the worst man has to fear.   20
Though gravediggers' toil is long,
Sharp their spades, their muscles strong,
They but thrust their buried men
Back in the human mind again.

3

You that Mitchel's prayer have heard,   25
"Send war in our time, O Lord!"[4]
Know that when all words are said
And a man is fighting mad,
Something drops from eyes long blind,
He completes his partial mind,   30
For an instant stands at ease,
Laughs aloud, his heart at peace.
Even the wisest man grows tense
With some sort of violence
Before he can accomplish fate,   35
Know his work or choose his mate.

4

Poet and sculptor, do the work,
Nor let the modish painter shirk
What his great forefathers did,
Bring the soul of man to God,   40
Make him fill the cradles right.

Measurement began our might:
Forms a stark Egyptian thought,

3. The *sidhe* or fairy folk, who were believed to ride through the countryside near Ben Bulben. The gist of Yeats's thought here is: "Swear by those who speak superhuman, eternal truths." These truths are summed up in the second section of the poem: man has an afterlife both in the future of his individual soul and in the memory he leaves behind on earth.
4. John Mitchel, an Irish patriot imprisoned for his activities, wrote in his *Jail Journal:* "Give us war in our time, O Lord!"

Forms that gentler Phidias wrought.[5]
Michael Angelo left a proof   45
On the Sistine Chapel roof,
Where but half-awakened Adam
Can disturb globe-trotting Madam
Till her bowels are in heat,[6]
Proof that there's a purpose set   50
Before the secret working mind:
Profane perfection of mankind.

Quattrocento[7] put in paint
On backgrounds for a God or Saint
Gardens where a soul's at ease;   55
Where everything that meets the eye,
Flowers and grass and cloudless sky,
Resemble forms that are or seem
When sleepers wake and yet still dream,
And when it's vanished still declare,   60
With only bed and bedstead there,
That heavens had opened.

           Gyres run on;
When that greater dream had gone
Calvert and Wilson, Blake and Claude,[8]
Prepared a rest for the people of God,   65
Palmer's phrase, but after that
Confusion fell upon our thought.

                            5
Irish poets, learn your trade,
Sing whatever is well made,
Scorn the sort now growing up   70
All out of shape from toe to top,
Their unremembering hearts and heads
Base-born products of base beds.
Sing the peasantry, and then
Hard-riding country gentlemen,   75
The holiness of monks, and after
Porter-drinkers' randy laughter;
Sing the lords and ladies gay
That were beaten into the clay
Through seven heroic centuries;   80

5. Greek sculptor (5th century B.C.), generally thought to have raised the classical ideal in art to its highest culmination. Yeats here itemizes steps in his history of knowledge and the arts, beginning with Babylonian mathematics ("measurement"), through "stark Egyptian thought," to the Renaissance of Michelangelo. Each of these steps is related to Yeats's cyclical theory of history.
6. Cf. *Long-Legged Fly*, stanza 3.
7. 15th-century Italian art.
8. Works by the five artists mentioned in lines 64–66 all provided images for Yeats's poetry: Edward Calvert, 19th-century wood-engraver; Richard Wilson, 18th-century landscape painter; William Blake, "one of the great mythmakers and mask-makers"; Claude Lorrain, 17th-century landscape painter; and (in line 66) Samuel Palmer, 19th-century landscape painter and etcher, one of whose works was "The Lonely Tower." Calvert, Blake, and Palmer knew each other and shared a view of the holiness of art. (See T. R. Henn, *The Lonely Tower*, 1950.)

Cast your mind on other days
That we in coming days may be
Still the indomitable Irishry.
6
Under bare Ben Bulben's head
In Drumcliff churchyard Yeats is laid.   85
An ancestor was rector there
Long years ago, a church stands near,
By the road an ancient cross.
No marble, no conventional phrase;
On limestone quarried near the spot   90
By his command these words are cut:
        Cast a cold eye
        On life, on death.
        Horseman, pass by!

September 4, 1938   1939

From Reveries over Childhood and Youth[1]
[*The Yeats Family*]

Some six miles off towards Ben Bulben and beyond the Channel,[2] as we call the tidal river between Sligo and the Rosses, and on top of a hill there was a little square two-storied house covered with creepers and looking out upon a garden where the box borders were larger than any I had ever seen, and where I saw for the first time the crimson steak of the gladiolus and awaited its blossom with excitement. Under one gable a dark thicket of small trees made a shut-in mysterious place, where one played and believed that something was going to happen. My great-aunt Micky lived there. Micky was not her right name for she was Mary Yeats and her father had been my great-grandfather, John Yeats, who had been Rector of Drumcliffe, a few miles further off, and died in 1847. She was a spare, high-colored, elderly woman and had the oldest-looking cat I had ever seen, for its hair had grown into matted locks of yellowy white. She farmed and had one old manservant, but could not have farmed at all, had not neighboring farmers helped to gather in the crops, in return for the loan of her farm implements and "out of respect for the family," for as Johnny Mac-Gurk, the Sligo barber said to me, "The Yeatses were always very respectable." She was full of family history; all her dinner knives were pointed like daggers through much cleaning, and there was a little

1. Yeats wrote a variety of autobiographical essays between 1914 and 1928: these were originally published separately and later collected as *The Autobiography of W. B. Yeats* (1936, 1953). The selections given here are from *Reveries over Childhood and Youth*, first published in 1915, and *The Trembling of the Veil*, first published in 1922.
2. Yeats's favorite County Sligo landscape. Cf. the places named in *The Stolen Child*.

James the First cream-jug with the Yeats motto and crest, and on her dining-room mantelpiece a beautiful silver cup that had belonged to my great-great-grandfather, who had married a certain Mary Butler. It had upon it the Butler crest and had been already old at the date 1534, when the initials of some bride and bridegroom were engraved under the lip. All its history for generations was rolled up inside it upon a piece of paper yellow with age, until some caller took the paper to light his pipe.

Another family of Yeats, a widow and her two children on whom I called sometimes with my grandmother, lived near in a long low cottage, and owned a very fierce turkey cock that did battle with their visitors; and some miles away lived the secretary to the Grand Jury and Land Agent, my great-uncle Mat Yeats and his big family of boys and girls; but I think it was only in later years that I came to know them well. I do not think any of these liked the Pollexfens, who were well off and seemed to them purse-proud, whereas they themselves had come down in the world. I remember them as very well-bred and very religious in the Evangelical way and thinking a good deal of Aunt Micky's old histories. There had been among our ancestors a King's County soldier, one of Marlborough's[3] generals, and when his nephew came to dine he gave him boiled pork, and when the nephew said he disliked boiled pork he had asked him to dine again and promised him something he would like better. However, he gave him boiled pork again and the nephew took the hint in silence. The other day as I was coming home from America, I met one of his descendants whose family has not another discoverable link with ours, and he too knew the boiled pork story and nothing else. We have the General's portrait, and he looks very fine in his armor and his long curly wig, and underneath it, after his name, are many honors that have left no tradition among us. Were we country people, we could have summarized his life in a legend. Other ancestors or great-uncles bore a part in Irish history; one saved the life of Sarsfield[4] at the battle of Sedgemoor; another, taken prisoner by King James's army, owed his to Sarsfield's gratitude; another, a century later, roused the gentlemen of Meath[5] against some local Jacquère,[6] and was shot dead upon a county road, and yet another "chased the United Irishmen[7] for a fortnight, fell into their hands and was hanged." The notorious

3. John Churchill, Duke of Marlborough (1650–1722), English general in the War of the Spanish Succession (1702–13).
4. Patrick Sarsfield (d. 1693), Irish Jacobite general who served in the battle of Sedgemoor (1685) when the Duke of Monmouth, illegitimate son of Charles II who was claiming the throne from his uncle James II, was defeated and captured.
5. Maritime county in province of Leinster, in the east of Ireland.
6. Peasant revolutionary. The "Jacquerie" was a peasants' revolt (1358) against the nobles in northern France (the term derived from *Jacques Bonhomme*, the nobility's contemptuous name for a peasant).
7. Irish society founded 1791 by Theobald Wolfe Tone which later was influential in causing the Irish rebellion of 1798.

Major Sirr, who arrested Lord Edward Fitzgerald[8] and gave him the bullet wound he died of in the jail, was godfather to several of my great-great-grandfather's children; while to make a balance, my great-grandfather had been Robert Emmett's[9] friend and was suspected and imprisoned though but for a few hours. One great-uncle fell at New Orleans in 1813, while another, who became Governor of Penang,[1] led the forlorn hope at the taking of Rangoon, and even in the last generation of all there had been lives of some power and pleasure. An old man who had entertained many famous people, in his eighteenth-century house, where battlement and tower showed the influence of Horace Walpole,[2] had but lately, after losing all his money, drowned himself, first taking off his rings and chain and watch as became a collector of many beautiful things; and once to remind us of more passionate life, a gunboat put into Rosses, commanded by the illegitimate son of some great-uncle or other. Now that I can look at their miniatures, turning them over to find the name of soldier, or lawyer, or Castle official,[3] and wondering if they cared for good books or good music, I am delighted with all that joins my life to those who had power in Ireland or with those anywhere that were good servants and poor bargainers, but I cared nothing as a child for Micky's tales. I could see my grandfather's ships come up the bay or the river, and his sailors treated me with deference, and a ship's carpenter made and mended my toy boats and I thought that nobody could be so important as my grandfather. Perhaps, too, it is only now that I can value those more gentle natures so unlike his passion and violence. An old Sligo priest has told me how my great-grandfather John Yeats always went into his kitchen rattling the keys, so much did he fear finding some one doing wrong, and of a speech of his when the agent of the great landowner of his parish brought him from cottage to cottage to bid the women send their children to the Protestant school. All promised till they came to one who cried, "Child of mine will never darken your door." "Thank you, my woman," he said, "you are the first honest woman I have met today." My uncle, Mat Yeats, the Land Agent, had once waited up every night for a week to catch some boys who stole his apples and when he caught them had given them sixpence and told them not to do it again. Perhaps it is only fancy or the softening touch of the miniaturist that makes me discover in their faces some courtesy and much gentleness. Two eighteenth-century faces interest me the

8. British officer (1763–98) who, after dismissal from the army for disloyal activities, joined the United Irishmen. Cf. *September 1913*, lines 19–22.
9. 1778–1803; Irish patriot, hanged at Dublin for treason.
1. Island in Malaya. Rangoon, capital of Burma, was taken by the British in 1824.

2. The 18th-century English author whose pseudo-Gothic house, Strawberry Hill, much influenced subsequent "Gothic" architecture in England and elsewhere.
3. I.e., official at Dublin Castle, where the Viceroy (representing the British Crown) lived with his staff before Irish independence was achieved in 1922.

most, one that of a great-great-grandfather, for both have under
their powdered curling wigs a half-feminine charm, and as I look
at them I discover a something clumsy and heavy in myself. Yet it
was a Yeats who spoke the only eulogy that turns my head: "We
have ideas and no passions, but by marriage with a Pollexfen we
have given a tongue to the sea cliffs."

Among the miniatures there is a larger picture, an admirable
drawing by I know not what master, that is too harsh and merry for
its company. He was a connection and close friend of my great-
grandmother Corbet, and though we spoke of him as "Uncle Beat-
tie" in our childhood, no blood relation. My great-grandmother
who died at ninety-three had many memories of him. He was the
friend of Goldsmith and was accustomed to boast, clergyman though
he was, that he belonged to a hunt club of which every member
but himself had been hanged or transported for treason, and that
it was not possible to ask him a question he could not reply to with
a perfectly appropriate blasphemy or indecency.

[An Irish Literature]

From these debates, from O'Leary's[4] conversation, and from the
Irish books he lent or gave me has come all I have set my hand to
since. I had begun to know a great deal about the Irish poets who
had written in English. I read with excitement books I should find
unreadable today, and found romance in lives that had neither wit
nor adventure. I did not deceive myself, I knew how often they
wrote a cold and abstract language, and yet I who had never wanted
to see the houses where Keats and Shelley lived would ask everybody what sort of place Inchedony was, because Callanan[5] had
named after it a bad poem in the manner of *Childe Harold*. Walking home from a debate, I remember saying to some college student, "Ireland cannot put from her the habits learned from her
old military civilization and from a church that prays in Latin.
Those popular poets have not touched her heart, her poetry when
it comes will be distinguished and lonely." O'Leary had once said
to me, "Neither Ireland nor England knows the good from the
bad in any art, but Ireland unlike England does not hate the good
when it is pointed out to her." I began to plot and scheme how one
might seal with the right image the soft wax before it began to
harden. I had noticed that Irish Catholics among whom had been
born so many political martyrs had not the good taste, the household courtesy and decency of the Protestant Ireland I had known,
yet Protestant Ireland seemed to think of nothing but getting on
in the world. I thought we might bring the halves together if we

4. John O'Leary (d. 1907), an Irish nationalist, for whom Yeats had great respect. Cf. *September 1913* ("Romantic
Ireland's dead and gone, / It's with
O'Leary in the grave").
5. Jeremiah John Callanan, Anglo-Irish
poet, published *The Recluse of Inchedony and Other Poems* in 1830.

had a national literature that made Ireland beautiful in the memory, and yet had been freed from provincialism by an exacting criticism, an European pose.

1915

From The Trembling of the Veil
[*London and Pre-Raphaelitism*]

At the end of the 'eighties my father and mother, my brother and sisters and myself, all newly arrived from Dublin, were settled in Bedford Park in a red-brick house with several mantelpieces of wood, copied from marble mantelpieces designed by the brothers Adam,[1] a balcony and a little garden shadowed by a great horse-chestnut tree. Years before we had lived there, when the crooked ostentatiously picturesque streets with great trees casting great shadows had been a new enthusiasm: the Pre-Raphaelite movement at last affecting life. But now exaggerated criticism had taken the place of enthusiasm, the tiled roofs, the first in modern London, were said to leak, which they did not, and the drains to be bad, though that was no longer true; and I imagine that houses were cheap. I remember feeling disappointed because the co-operative stores, with their little seventeenth-century panes, had lost the romance I saw there when I passed them still unfinished on my way to school; and because the public-house, called The Tabard after Chaucer's Inn, was so plainly a common public-house; and because the great sign of a trumpeter designed by Rooke, the Pre-Raphaelite artist, had been freshened by some inferior hand. The big red-brick church had never pleased me, and I was accustomed, when I saw the wooden balustrade that ran along the slanting edge of the roof where nobody ever walked or could walk, to remember the opinion of some architect friend of my father's, that it had been put there to keep the birds from falling off. Still, however, it had some village characters and helped us to feel not wholly lost in the metropolis. I no longer went to church as a regular habit, but go I sometimes did, for one Sunday morning I saw these words painted on a board in the porch: "The congregation are requested to kneel during prayers; the kneelers are afterwards to be hung upon pegs provided for the purpose." In front of every seat hung a little cushion and these cushions were called "kneelers." Presently the joke ran through the community, where there were many artists who considered religion at best an unimportant accessory to good architecture and who disliked that particular church.

1. James and Robert, 18th-century Scottish architects and furniture designers who successfully adapted ancient Roman style in their work in England and Scotland.

I could not understand where the charm had gone that I had felt, when as a schoolboy of twelve or thirteen I had played among the unfinished houses, once leaving the marks of my two hands, blacked by a fall among some paint, upon a white balustrade.

Yet I was in all things Pre-Raphaelite. When I was fifteen or sixteen my father had told me about Rossetti and Blake and given me their poetry to read; and once at Liverpool on my way to Sligo I had seen Dante's *Dream* in the gallery there, a picture painted when Rossetti had lost his dramatic power and today not very pleasing to me, and its color, its people, its romantic architecture had blotted all other pictures away. It was a perpetual bewilderment that when my father, moved perhaps by some memory of his youth, chose some theme from poetic tradition, he would soon weary and leave it unfinished. I had seen the change coming bit by bit and its defense elaborated by young men fresh from the Paris art schools. "We must paint what is in front of us," or "A man must be of his own time," they would say, and if I spoke of Blake or Rossetti they would point out his bad drawing and tell me to admire Carolus Duran and Bastien-Lepage.[2] Then, too, they were very ignorant men; they read nothing, for nothing mattered but "knowing how to paint," being in reaction against a generation that seemed to have wasted its time upon so many things. I thought myself alone in hating these young men, their contempt for the past, their monopoly of the future, but in a few months I was to discover others of my own age, who thought as I did, for it is not true that youth looks before it with the mechanical gaze of a well-drilled soldier. Its quarrel is not with the past, but with the present, where its elders are so obviously powerful and no cause seems lost if it seem to threaten that power. Does cultivated youth ever really love the future, where the eye can discover no persecuted Royalty hidden among oak leaves,[3] though from it certainly does come so much proletarian rhetoric?

I was unlike others of my generation in one thing only. I am very religious, and deprived by Huxley and Tyndall,[4] whom I detested, of the simple-minded religion of my childhood, I had made a new religion, almost an infallible church of poetic tradition, of a fardel[5] of stories, and of personages, and of emotions, inseparable from their first expression, passed on from generation to generation by poets and painters with some help from philosophers and theologians. I wished for a world where I could discover this tradition

2. Carolus Duran (1837–1917) and Jules Bastien-Lepage (1848–84), French painters.
3. Charles II, after the decisive defeat of his father Charles I by the Parliamentarians at Naseby in 1645, hid in an oak tree before escaping abroad.
4. Thomas Henry Huxley (1825–95), biologist and popularizer of Darwin's ideas; John Tyndall (1820–93), physicist and active propagandist for science and materialism.
5. Bundle. This archaic word suggests Yeats's poetic attitude at the stage in his life which he is describing.

perpetually, and not in pictures and in poems only, but in tiles round the chimney piece and in the hangings that kept out the draft. I had even created a dogma: "Because those imaginary people are created out of the deepest instinct of man, to be his measure and his norm, whatever I can imagine those mouths speaking may be the nearest I can go to truth." When I listened they seemed always to speak of one thing only: they, their loves, every incident of their lives, were steeped in the supernatural. Could even Titian's "Ariosto"[6] that I loved beyond other portraits have its grave look, as if waiting for some perfect final event, if the painters before Titian had not learned portraiture, while painting into the corner of compositions full of saints and Madonnas, their kneeling patrons? At seventeen years old I was already an old-fashioned brass cannon full of shot, and nothing had kept me from going off but a doubt as to my capacity to shoot straight.

[Oscar Wilde]

My first meeting with Oscar Wilde was an astonishment. I never before heard a man talking with perfect sentences, as if he had written them all overnight with labor and yet all spontaneous. There was present that night at Henley's,[7] by right of propinquity or of accident, a man full of the secret spite of dullness, who interrupted from time to time, and always to check or disorder thought; and I noticed with what mastery he was foiled and thrown. I noticed, too, that the impression of artificiality that I think all Wilde's listeners have recorded came from the perfect rounding of the sentences and from the deliberation that made it possible. That very impression helped him, as the effect of meter, or of the antithetical prose of the seventeenth century, which is itself a true meter, helped its writers, for he could pass without incongruity from some unforeseen, swift stroke of wit to elaborate reverie. I heard him say a few nights later: "Give me *The Winter's Tale*, 'Daffodils that come before the swallow dare' but not *King Lear*. What is *King Lear* but poor life staggering in the fog?" and the slow, carefully modulated cadence sounded natural to my ears. That first night he praised Walter Pater's *Studies in the History of the Renaissance*: "It is my golden book; I never travel anywhere without it; but it is the very flower of decadence: the last trumpet should have sounded the moment it was written." "But," said the dull man, "would you not have given us time to read it?" "Oh no," was the retort, "there would have been plenty of time afterwards—in either world." I think he seemed to us, baffled as we were by youth, or by infirmity, a triumphant figure, and to some of us a figure from another age,

---

6. Titian (ca. 1477–1576), a Venetian painter, was thought to have painted a portrait of Lodovico Ariosto, the Italian poet and author of *Orlando Furioso*. The painting is now described simply as "Portrait of a Man."
7. William Ernest Henley (1849–1903), poet, critic, and editor.

an audacious Italian fifteenth-century figure. A few weeks before I had heard one of my father's friends, an official in a publishing firm that had employed both Wilde and Henley as editors, blaming Henley who was "no use except under control" and praising Wilde, "so indolent but such a genius"; and now the firm became the topic of our talk. "How often do you go to the office?" said Henley. "I used to go three times a week," said Wilde, "for an hour a day but I have since struck off one of the days." "My God," said Henley, "I went five times a week for five hours a day and when I wanted to strike off a day they had a special committee meeting." "Furthermore," was Wilde's answer, "I never answered their letters. I have known men come to London full of bright prospects and seen them complete wrecks in a few months through a habit of answering letters." He too knew how to keep our elders in their place, and his method was plainly the more successful, for Henley had been dismissed. "No he is not an aesthete," Henley commented later, being somewhat embarrassed by Wilde's Pre-Raphaelite entanglement; "one soon finds that he is a scholar and a gentleman." And when I dined with Wilde a few days afterwards he began at once, "I had to strain every nerve to equal that man at all"; and I was too loyal to speak my thought: "You and not he said all the brilliant things." He like the rest of us had felt the strain of an intensity that seemed to hold life at the point of drama. He had said on that first meeting, "The basis of literary friendship is mixing the poisoned bowl"; and for a few weeks Henley and he became close friends till, the astonishment of their meeting over, diversity of character and ambition pushed them apart, and, with half the cavern helping, Henley began mixing the poisoned bowl for Wilde. Yet Henley never wholly lost that first admiration, for after Wilde's downfall he said to me: "Why did he do it? I told my lads to attack him and yet we might have fought under his banner."

[The Handiwork of Art]

Though I went to Sligo every summer, I was compelled to live out of Ireland the greater part of every year, and was but keeping my mind upon what I knew must be the subject matter of my poetry. I believed that if Morris[8] had set his stories amid the scenery of his own Wales, for I knew him to be of Welsh extraction and supposed wrongly that he had spent his childhood there, that if Shelley had nailed his *Prometheus*,[9] or some equal symbol, upon some Welsh or Scottish rock, their art would have entered more intimately, more microscopically, as it were, into our thought and given perhaps to modern poetry a breadth and stability like that

8. William Morris (1834–96), the poet, painter, and socialist.

9. A reference to Shelley's lyrical drama, *Prometheus Unbound*.

of ancient poetry. The statues of Mausolus and Artemisia[1] at the British Museum, private, half-animal, half-divine figures, all unlike the Grecian athletes and Egyptian kings in their near neighborhood, that stand in the middle of the crowd's applause, or sit above measuring it out unpersuadable justice, became to me, now or later, images of an unpremeditated joyous energy, that neither I nor any other man, racked by doubt and inquiry, can achieve; and that yet, if once achieved, might seem to men and women of Connemara or of Galway their very soul. In our study of that ruined tomb raised by a queen to her dead lover, and finished by the unpaid labor of great sculptors, after her death from grief, or so runs the tale, we cannot distinguish the handiwork of Scopas from that of Praxiteles,[2] and I wanted to create once more an art where the artist's handiwork would hide as under those half-anonymous chisels or as we find it in some old Scots ballads, or in some twelfth- or thirteenth-century Arthurian Romance. That handiwork assured, I had martyred no man for modeling his own image upon Pallas Athena's buckler; for I took great pleasure in certain allusions to the singer's life, one finds in old romances and ballads, and thought his presence there all the more poignant because we discover it half lost, like portly Chaucer, behind his own maunciple and pardoner upon the Canterbury roads. Wolfram von Eschenbach,[3] singing his German Parsifal, broke off some description of a famished city to remember that in his own house at home the very mice lacked food, and what old ballad singer was it who claimed to have fought by day in the very battle he sang by night? So masterful indeed was that instinct that when the minstrel knew not who his poet was, he must needs make up a man: "When any stranger asks who is the sweetest of singers, answer with one voice: 'A blind man; he dwells upon rocky Chios;[4] his songs shall be the most beautiful forever.'" Elaborate modern psychology sounds egotistical, I thought, when it speaks in the first person, but not those simple emotions which resemble the more, the more powerful they are, everybody's emotion, and I was soon to write many poems where an always personal emotion was woven into a general pattern of myth and symbol. When the Fenian poet[5] says that his heart has grown cold and callous—"For thy hapless fate, dear Ireland, and sorrows of my own"—he but follows tradition and if he does not move us deeply, it is because he has no sensuous musical vocabulary

---

1. Mausolus, king of Caria (in Asia Minor) in 4th century B.C. He married his sister Artemisia, who after his death built the famous monument named after him, the Mausoleum; a Greek statue of Mausolus and other sculptures from the Mausoleum is in the British Museum.
2. Greek sculptor of late 5th and early 4th century B.C. Scopas was a Greek sculptor of the 4th century B.C. who

went to Halicarnassus to superintend the sculpture of the Mausoleum (see previous note).
3. German poet of late 12th and early 13th century, who wrote the epic poem *Parzival*.
4. Greek island in the Aegean—one of the seven places which claimed Homer as its son.
5. I.e., a poet of Irish nationalism.

that comes at need, without compelling him to sedentary toil and so driving him out from his fellows. I thought to create that sensuous, musical vocabulary, and not for myself only, but that I might leave it to later Irish poets, much as a medieval Japanese painter left his style as an inheritance to his family, and I was careful to use a traditional manner and matter, yet changed by that toil, impelled by my share in Cain's curse,[6] by all that sterile modern complication, by my "originality," as the newspapers call it, did something altogether different. Morris set out to make a revolution that the persons of his *Well at the World's End* or his *Waters of the Wondrous Isles,* always, to my mind, in the likeness of Artemisia and her man, might walk his native scenery; and I, that my native scenery might find imaginary inhabitants, half-planned a new method and a new culture. My mind began drifting vaguely towards that doctrine of "the mask" which has convinced me that every passionate man (I have nothing to do with mechanist, or philanthropist, or man whose eyes have no preference) is, as it were, linked with another age, historical or imaginary, where alone he finds images that rouse his energy. Napoleon was never of his own time, as the naturalistic writers and painters bid all men be, but had some Roman emperor's image in his head and some condottiere's[7] blood in his heart; and when he crowned that head at Rome with his own hands he had covered, as may be seen from David's[8] painting, his hesitation with that emperor's old suit.

[*The Origin of* The Lake Isle of Innisfree]

I had various women friends on whom I would call towards five o'clock mainly to discuss my thoughts that I could not bring to a man without meeting some competing thought, but partly because their tea and toast saved my pennies for the bus ride home; but with women, apart from their intimate exchanges of thought, I was timid and abashed. I was sitting on a seat in front of the British Museum feeding pigeons when a couple of girls sat near and began enticing my pigeons away, laughing and whispering to one another, and I looked straight in front of me, very indignant, and presently went into the Museum without turning my head towards them. Since then I have often wondered if they were pretty or merely very young. Sometimes I told myself very adventurous love stories with myself for hero, and at other times I planned out a life of lonely austerity, and at other times mixed the ideals and planned a life of lonely austerity mitigated by periodical lapses. I had still

---

6. The curse imposed on Cain for killing his brother was to be "a fugitive and a vagabond" (Genesis iv.12). Yeats seems to be thinking of the curse imposed on *Adam,* that he should have to work (Genesis iii.19).

7. Mercenary soldier (14th- and 15th-century Italy)—usually hired as a leader with a band of his followers.

8. Jacques Louis David (1748–1825), French historical painter, court painter to Napoleon: he painted a picture of Napoleon's coronation.

the ambition, formed in Sligo in my teens, of living in imitation of Thoreau on Innisfree, a little island in Lough Gill,[9] and when walking through Fleet Street very homesick I heard a little tinkle of water and saw a fountain in a shop window which balanced a little ball upon its jet, and began to remember lake water. From the sudden remembrance came my poem *Innisfree*, my first lyric with anything in its rhythm of my own music. I had begun to loosen rhythm as an escape from rhetoric and from that emotion of the crowd that rhetoric brings, but I only understood vaguely and occasionally that I must for my special purpose use nothing but the common syntax. A couple of years later I would not have written that first line with its conventional archaism—"Arise and go"— nor the inversion in the last stanza. * * *

[The Rhymers' Club]

I had already met most of the poets of my generation. I had said, soon after the publication of *The Wanderings of Usheen*,[1] to the editor of a series of shilling reprints, who had set me to compile tales of the Irish fairies, "I am growing jealous of other poets and we will all grow jealous of each other unless we know each other and so feel a share in each other's triumph." He was a Welshman, lately a mining engineer, Ernest Rhys,[2] a writer of Welsh translations and original poems, that have often moved me greatly though I can think of no one else who has read them. He was perhaps a dozen years older than myself and through his work as editor knew everybody who would compile a book for seven or eight pounds. Between us we founded The Rhymers' Club, which for some years was to meet every night in an upper room with a sanded floor in an ancient eating-house in the Strand called The Cheshire Cheese. Lionel Johnson, Ernest Dowson, Victor Plarr, Ernest Radford, John Davidson, Richard le Gallienne, T. W. Rolleston, Selwyn Image, Edwin Ellis, and John Todhunter came constantly for a time, Arthur Symons and Herbert Horne, less constantly, while William Watson joined but never came and Francis Thompson[3] came once but never joined; and sometimes if we met in a private house, which we did occasionally, Oscar Wilde came. It had been useless to invite him to The Cheshire Cheese for he hated Bohemia. "Olive Schreiner,"[4] he said once to me, "is staying in the East End because that is the only place where people do not wear masks upon their faces, but I have told her that I live in the West

---

9. See *The Lake Isle of Innisfree*, above, and the note on it.
1. An early long poem by Yeats (1889). Yeats later spelled the name of the hero "Oisin."
2. 1859–1946; Welsh writer and editor; original editor of Everyman's Library.
3. The names here are of poets and

writers of the 90's who were fellow members with Yeats of the Rhymers' Club. Francis Thompson (1859–1907), who "never joined," was the author of *The Hound of Heaven*.
4. South African novelist, author of *The Story of an African Farm* (1883).

End because nothing in life interests me but the mask."

We read our poems to one another and talked criticism and drank a little wine. I sometimes say when I speak of the club, "We had such and such ideas, such and such a quarrel with the great Victorians, we set before us such and such aims," as though we had many philosophical ideas. I say this because I am ashamed to admit that I had these ideas and that whenever I began to talk of them a gloomy silence fell upon the room. A young Irish poet, who wrote excellently but had the worst manners, was to say a few years later, "You do not talk like a poet, you talk like a man of letters," and if all the Rhymers had not been polite, if most of them had not been to Oxford or Cambridge, the greater number would have said the same thing. I was full of thought, often very abstract thought, longing all the while to be full of images, because I had gone to the art school instead of a university. Yet even if I had gone to a university, and learned all the classical foundations of English literature and English culture, all that great erudition which once accepted frees the mind from restlessness, I should have had to give up my Irish subject matter, or attempt to found a new tradition. Lacking sufficient recognized precedent I must needs find out some reason for all I did. * * *

1922

JAMES JOYCE
(1882–1941)

1915: *Dubliners.*
1916: *A Portrait of the Artist as a Young Man.*
1922: *Ulysses.*
1939: *Finnegans Wake.*

James Joyce was born in Dublin, son of a talented but feckless father who is accurately described by Stephen Dedalus in *A Portrait of the Artist as a Young Man* as a man who had in his time been "a medical student, an oarsman, a tenor, an amateur actor, a shouting politician, a small land-lord, a small investor, a drinker, a good fellow, a storyteller, somebody's secretary, something in a distillery, a tax-gatherer, a bankrupt, and at present a praiser of his own past." The elder Joyce drifted steadily down the financial and social scale, his family moving from house to house, each one less genteel and more shabby than the previous. James Joyce's whole education was Catholic, from the age of 6 to the age of 9 at Clongowes Wood College, and from 11 to 16 at Belvedere College, Dublin. Both were Jesuit institutions, and were normal roads to the priesthood. He then studied modern languages at University College, Dublin.

From a comparatively early age Joyce regarded himself as a rebel against the shabbiness and Philistinism of Dublin. In his early youth he was very religious, but in his last year at Belvedere he began to reject his Catholic faith in favor of a literary mission which he saw as involving rebellion and exile. He refused to play any part in the nationalist or other popular activities of his fellow students, and created some stir by his outspoken articles, one of which, on the Norwegian playwright Henrik Ibsen, appeared in the *Fortnightly Review* for April, 1900. He taught himself Norwegian to be able to read Ibsen and to write to him. When an article by Joyce, significantly entitled *The Day of the Rabblement*, was refused, on instructions of the faculty adviser, by the student magazine that had commissioned it, he had it printed privately. By 1902, when he received his B.A. degree, he was already committed to a career as exile and writer. For Joyce, as for his character Stephen Dedalus, the latter implied the former. To preserve his integrity, to avoid involvement in popular sentimentalities and dishonesties, and above all to be able to re-create with both total understanding and total objectivity the Dublin life he knew so well, he felt that he had to go abroad.

Joyce went to Paris after graduation, was recalled to Dublin by his mother's fatal illness, had a short spell there as a schoolteacher, then returned to the Continent in 1904 to teach English at Trieste and then at Zurich. He took with him Nora Barnacle, an uneducated Galway girl with no interest in literature; her native vivacity and peasant wit charmed Joyce, and the two lived in devoted companionship until Joyce's death, though they were not married until 1931. In 1920 Joyce settled in Paris, where he lived until December, 1940, when the war forced him to take refuge in Switzerland; he died in Zurich a few weeks later.

Proud, obstinate, absolutely convinced of his genius, given to fits of sudden gaiety and of sudden silence, Joyce was not always an easy person to get on with, yet he never lacked friends and throughout his 36 years on the Continent was always the center of a literary circle. Life was hard at first. At Trieste he had very little money, and he did not improve matters by drinking heavily, a habit checked somewhat by his brother Stanislaus who came out from Dublin to act (as Stanislaus put it much later) as his "brother's keeper." His financial position was much improved by the patronage of Mrs. Harold McCormick (Edith Rockefeller), who provided him with a monthly stipend from March, 1917, until September, 1919, when they quarreled, apparently because Joyce refused to submit to psychoanalysis by Carl Jung, who had been heavily endowed by Mrs. McCormick. The New York lawyer and art patron John Quinn, steered in Joyce's direction by Ezra Pound, also helped Joyce financially in 1917. A more permanent benefactor was the English feminist and editor Harriet Shaw Weaver, who not only subsidized Joyce generously from 1917 to the end of his life, but occupied herself indefatigably with arrangements for publishing his work.

Joyce's almost life-long exile from his native Ireland has something paradoxical about it. No writer has ever been more soaked in Dublin, its atmosphere, its history, its topography; in spite of doing most of his writing in Trieste, Zurich, and Paris, he wrote only and always about Dublin. He devised ways of expanding his accounts of Dublin, however, so that they became microcosms, small-scale models, of all human life, of all history and all geography. Indeed that was his life's work: to write about Dublin in such a way that he was writing about all of human experience.

Joyce began his career by writing a series of stories etching with extraordinary clarity aspects of Dublin life. But these stories—published as *Dubliners* in 1915—are more than sharp realistic sketches. In each, the detail is so chosen and organized that carefully interacting symbolic meanings are set up, and as a result *Dubliners* is a book about man's fate as well as a series of sketches of Dublin. (*Araby*, for example, is meticulously accurate in every physical detail, yet it is also a symbolic story about the relation between dreams and reality.) Further, the stories are presented in a particular order so that new meanings arise from the relation between them.

This was Joyce's first phase: he had to come directly to terms with the life he had rejected, to see it for what it was and for what it meant. Next, he had to come to terms with the meaning of his own development as a man dedicated to writing. He did this by weaving his autobiography into a novel so finely chiseled and carefully organized, so stripped of everything superfluous, that each word contributes to the presentation of the theme: the parallel movement toward art and toward exile. A part of Joyce's first draft has been posthumously published under the original title of *Stephen Hero* (1944): a comparison between it and the final version which Joyce gave to the world, *A Portrait of the Artist as a Young Man* (1916), will show how carefully Joyce reworked and compressed his material for maximum effect. The *Portrait* is not literally true as autobiography, though it has many autobiographical elements; but it is representatively true not only of Joyce but of the relation between the artist and society in the modern world.

In the *Portrait* Stephen worked out a theory of art which considers that art moves from the lyrical form—which is the simplest, the personal expression of an instant of emotion—through the narrative form—no longer purely personal—to the dramatic—the highest and most perfect form, where "the artist, like the God of creation, remains within or behind or beyond or above his handiwork, invisible, refined out of existence, indifferent, paring his fingernails." This view of art, which involves the objectivity, even the exile, of the artist (even though the artist uses only the materials provided for him by his own life) is related to that held by the poets of the 90's. More widely, it is related to the rejection by the artist of the ordinary world of middleclass values and activities which we see equally, though in different ways, in Matthew Arnold's war against the Philistines and in the concept (very un-Arnoldian) of the artist as bohemian. Joyce's career belongs to that long chapter in the history of the arts in Western civilization which begins with the artist's declaring his independence and ends with his feeling his inevitable "alienation." But if Joyce was alienated, as in certain ways he clearly was, he made his alienation serve his art: the kinds of writing represented by *Ulysses* and *Finnegans Wake* represent the most consummate craftsmanship put at the service of a humanely comic vision of all life. Some (though surprisingly few) of Joyce's innovations in organization and style have been imitated by other writers, but these books are, and will probably remain, unique in our literature. They are not freaks or historical oddities, but serious and exciting works.

From the beginning Joyce had trouble with the Philistines. Publication of *Dubliners* was held up for many years while he fought with both English and Irish publishers about certain words and phrases which they wished to eliminate. (It was the former who finally published the book.) His masterpiece *Ulysses* was banned in both Britain and America on its first appearance in 1922, its earlier serialization in the *Little Review* (March 1918–December 1920) having had to stop abruptly when the U.S. Post Office brought a charge of obscenity against it. Fortunately, Judge Woolsey's history-making decision in favor of *Ulysses* in the United States District Court on December 6, 1933, resulted in the lifting of the ban and the free circulation of the work first in America and soon afterwards in Britain.

ULYSSES

Ulysses is an account of one day in the lives of citizens of Dublin in the year 1904: it is thus the description of a limited number of events involving a limited number of people in a limited environment. Yet Joyce's ambition—which took him seven years to realize—is to make his action into a microcosm of all human experience. The events are not therefore told on a single level; the story is presented in such a manner that depth and implication are given to them and they become symbolic of the activity of Man in the World. The most obvious of the devices which Joyce employs in order to make clear the microcosmic aspect of his story is the parallel with Homer's *Odyssey*: every episode in *Ulysses* corresponds in some way to an episode in the *Odyssey*. Joyce regarded Homer's Ulysses as the most "complete" man in literature, a man who is shown in all his aspects—both coward and hero, cautious and reckless, weak and strong, husband and lover, father and son, sublime and ridiculous; so he makes his hero, Leopold Bloom, an Irish Jew, into a modern Ulysses, and by so doing helps to make him Everyman and to make Dublin the world.

The book opens at eight o'clock on the morning of June 16, 1904. Stephen Dedalus (the same character we saw in the *Portrait*, but this is two years after our last glimpse of him there) had been summoned back to Dublin by his mother's fatal illness and now lives in an old military tower on the shore with Buck Mulligan, a rollicking medical student, and an Englishman called Haines. In the first three episodes of *Ulysses*, which concentrate on Stephen, he is built up as an aloof, uncompromising artist, rejecting all advances by representatives of the normal world, the incomplete man, to be contrasted later with the complete Leopold Bloom, who is much more "normal" and conciliatory. After tracing Stephen through his early-morning activities and learning the main currents of his mind, we go, in the fourth episode, to the home of Bloom. We follow closely his every activity: attending a funeral, transacting his business, eating his lunch, walking through the Dublin streets, worrying about his wife's infidelity with Blazes Boylan—and at each point the contents of his mind, including retrospect and anticipation, are presented to the reader, until all his past history is revealed. Finally, Bloom and Stephen, who have just been missing each other all day, get together. By this time it is late, and Stephen, who has been drinking with some medical students, is the worse for liquor. Bloom, moved by a paternal feeling towards Stephen (his own son had died in infancy and in a symbolic way Stephen takes his place), follows him during subsequent adventures in the role of protector. The climax of the book comes when Stephen, far gone in drink, and Bloom, worn out with fatigue, succumb to a series of hallucinations where their subconscious and unconscious come to the surface in dramatic form and their whole personalities are revealed with a completeness and a frankness unique in literature. Then Bloom takes the unresponsive Stephen home and gives him a meal. After Stephen's departure Bloom retires to bed—it is now 2 A.M. on June 17—while his wife Molly, representing the principles of sex and reproduction on which all human life is based, closes the book with a long monologue in which her experiences as woman are remembered.

On the level of realistic description, *Ulysses* pulses with life and can be enjoyed for its evocation of early 20th-century Dublin. On the level of psychological exploration, it gives a profound and moving presentation of the personality and consciousness of Leopold Bloom and (to a lesser extent) Stephen Dedalus. On the level of style, it exhibits the most fascinating linguistic virtuosity. On a deeper symbolic level, the novel explores the paradoxes of human loneliness and sociability (for Bloom is both Jew and Dubliner, both exile and citizen, just as all men are in a sense both exiles and citizens), and it explores the problems posed by the relations between parent and child, between the generations, and between the sexes. At the same time, through its use of themes from Homer, Dante, and Shakespeare, from literature, philosophy, and history, the book weaves a subtle pattern of allusion and suggestion which illuminates many aspects of human experience. The more one reads *Ulysses* the more one finds in it, but at the same time one does not need to probe into the symbolic meaning in order to relish both its literary artistry and its human feeling. At the forefront stands Leopold Bloom, from one point of view a frustrated and confused outsider in the society in which he moves, from another a champion of kindness and justice whose humane curiosity about his fellows redeems him from mere vulgarity and gives the book its positive human foundation.

Readers who come to *Ulysses* with expectations about the way the story is to be presented derived from their reading of Victorian novels or even of such 20th-century novelists as Conrad and Lawrence will find much that is at first puzzling. Joyce presents the consciousness of his characters directly, without any explanatory comment which tells the reader whose consciousness is being rendered (this is the "stream-of-consciousness" method). He may move, in the same paragraph and without any sign that he is making such a transition, from a description of a character's action—e.g., Stephen walking along the shore or Bloom entering a restaurant —to an evocation of the character's mental response to this action. That response is always multiple: it derives partly from the character's immediate situation and partly from the whole complex of attitudes which his past history has created in him. To suggest this multiplicity, Joyce may vary his style, from the flippant to the serious or from a realistic description to a suggestive set of images which indicate what might be called the general tone of the character's consciousness. Past and present mingle in the texture of the prose because they mingle in the texture of consciousness; and this mingling can be indicated by puns, by sudden breaks into a new kind of style or a new kind of subject matter, or by some other device for keeping the reader constantly in sight of the shifting, kaleidoscopic nature of human awareness. With a little experience, the reader learns to follow the implications of Joyce's shifts in manner and content—even to follow that at first sight bewildering passage in the "Proteus" episode where Stephen does not go to visit his uncle and aunt but, passing the road that leads to their house, imagines the kind of conversation that would take place in his home *if* he had gone to visit his uncle and had then returned home and reported that he had done so. *Ulysses* must not be approached as though it were a novel written in a traditional manner; all preconceptions must be set aside and we must follow wherever the author leads us and let the language tell us what it has to say without our troubling whether language is being used "properly" or not.

FINNEGANS WAKE

Joyce's last work, *Finnegans Wake*, was published in 1939; it took more than fourteen years to write, and Joyce considered it his masterpiece. In *Ulysses* he had made the symbolic aspect of the novel at least as important as the realistic aspect, but in *Finnegans Wake* he gave up realism altogether. This vast story of a symbolic Irishman's cosmic dream develops by enormous reverberating puns a continuous expansion of meaning, the elements in the puns deriving from every conceivable source in history, literature, mythology, and Joyce's personal experience. The whole book being (on one level at least) a dream, Joyce invents his own dream language in which words are combined, distorted, created by fitting together bits of other words, used with several different meanings at once, often drawn from several different languages at once, and fused in all sorts of ways to achieve whole clusters of meaning simultaneously. In fact, so many echoing suggestions can be found in every word or phrase that a full annotation of even a few pages would require a large book. It has taken the co-operative work of a number of devoted readers to make clear the complex interactions of the multiple puns and pun-clusters through which the ideas are projected, and every rereading reveals new meanings. It is true that many readers find the efforts of explication demanded by *Finnegans Wake* too arduous; some, indeed, feel that the law of diminishing returns has now begun to operate, and that the effort of both author and reader is disproportionate. Nevertheless, the book has great beauty and fascination even for the casual reader. Students are advised to read aloud—or to listen to the record of Joyce reading aloud—the extract printed in this anthology, in order to appreciate the degree to which the rhythms of the prose assist in conveying the meaning.

To an even greater extent than *Ulysses*, *Finnegans Wake* aims at embracing all of human history. The title is from an Irish-American ballad about Tom Finnegan, a hod carrier who falls off a ladder when drunk and is apparently killed, but who revives when during the "wake" (the watch by the dead body) someone spills whiskey on him. The theme of death and resurrection, of cycles of change coming round in the course of history, is central to *Finnegans Wake*, which derives one of its main principles of organization from the cyclical theory of history put forward in 1725 by the Italian philosopher Giambattista Vico. Vico held that history passes through four phases: the divine or theocratic, when people are governed by their awe of the supernatural; the aristocratic (the "heroic age" reflected in Homer and in *Beowulf*); the democratic and individualistic; and the final stage of chaos, a fall into confusion which startles man back into supernatural reverence and starts the process once again. Joyce, like Yeats, saw his own generation as in the final stage awaiting the shock that will bring man back to the first.

A mere account of the narrative line of *Finnegans Wake* cannot, of course, give any idea of the content of the work. If one explains that it opens with Finnegan's fall, then introduces his successor Humphrey Chimpden Earwicker, who is Everyman, and whose dream constitutes the novel; that he is presented as having guilt feelings about an indecency he committed (or may have committed) in Phoenix Park, Dublin; that his wife Anna Livia Plurabelle or ALP (who is also Eve, Iseult, Ireland, the River Liffey) changes her role just as he does; that he has two sons Shem and Shaun (or Jerry and Kevin), who represent introvert and extrovert, artist and practical man, creator and popularizer, and symbolize this basic dichotomy in human nature by all kinds of metamorphoses; and if one adds that, in the four books into which *Finnegans Wake* is divided (after Vico's pattern), actions comic or grotesque or sad or tender or desperate or passionate or terribly ordinary (and very often several of these things at the same time) take place with all the shifting meanings of a dream, so that characters change into others or into inanimate objects and the setting keeps shifting—if we explain all this, we still have said very little about what makes *Finnegans Wake* what it is. The dreamer, whose initials HCE indicate his universality ("Here Comes Everybody"), is at the same time a particular person, who keeps a pub in Chapelizod, a Dublin suburb on the River Liffey near Phoenix Park. His mysterious misdemeanor in Phoenix Park is in a sense Original Sin: Earwicker is Adam as well as a primeval giant, the Hill of Howth, the Great Parent ("Haveth Childers Everywhere" is another expansion of HCE), and Man in History. Other characters who flit and change through the book, such as the Twelve Customers (who are also twelve jurymen and public opinion) and the Four Old Men (who are also judges, the authors of the four Gospels, and the four elements), help to weave the texture of multiple significance so characteristic of the work. But always it is the punning language, extending significance downwards—rather than the plot, developing it lengthwise— that bears the main load of meaning.

Araby[1]

North Richmond Street, being blind, was a quiet street except at the hour when the Christian Brothers' School set the boys free.[2]

1. The third of the fifteen stories in *Dubliners*. This tale of the frustrated quest for beauty in the midst of drabness is both meticulously realistic in its handling of details of Dublin life and the Dublin scene and highly symbolic in that almost every image and incident suggests some particular aspect of the theme (e.g., the suggestion of the Holy Grail in the image of the chalice, mentioned in the fifth paragraph). Joyce was drawing on his own childhood

An uninhabited house of two storeys stood at the blind end, detached from its neighbours in a square ground. The other houses of the street, conscious of decent lives within them, gazed at one another with brown imperturbable faces.

The former tenant of our house, a priest, had died in the back drawing-room. Air, musty from having been long enclosed, hung in all the rooms, and the waste room behind the kitchen was littered with old useless papers. Among these I found a few paper-covered books, the pages of which were curled and damp: *The Abbot*, by Walter Scott, *The Devout Communicant* and *The Memoirs of Vidocq*.[3] I liked the last best because its leaves were yellow. The wild garden behind the house contained a central apple-tree and a few straggling bushes under one of which I found the late tenant's rusty bicycle-pump. He had been a very charitable priest; in his will he had left all his money to institutions and the furniture of his house to his sister.

When the short days of winter came dusk fell before we had well eaten our dinners. When we met in the street the houses had grown sombre. The space of sky above us was the colour of ever-changing violet and towards it the lamps of the street lifted their feeble lanterns. The cold air stung us and we played till our bodies glowed. Our shouts echoed in the silent street. The career of our play brought us through the dark muddy lanes behind the houses where we ran the gauntlet of the rough tribes from the cottages, to the back doors of the dark dripping gardens where odours arose from the ashpits, to the dark odorous stables where a coachman smoothed and combed the horse or shook music from the buckled harness. When we returned to the street light from the kitchen windows had filled the areas. If my uncle was seen turning the corner we hid in the shadow until we had seen him safely housed. Or if Mangan's sister came out on the doorstep to call her brother in to his tea we watched her from our shadow peer up and down the street. We waited to see whether she would remain or go in and, if she remained, we left our shadow and walked up to Mangan's steps resignedly. She was waiting for us, her figure defined by the light from the half-opened door. Her brother always teased her before he obeyed and I stood by the railings looking at

recollections, and the uncle in the story is a reminiscence of Joyce's father. But in all the stories in *Dubliners* dealing with childhood, the child lives not with his parents but with an uncle and aunt —a symbol of that isolation and lack of proper relation between "consubstantial" ("in the flesh") parents and children which is a major theme in Joyce's work.

2. The Joyce family moved to 17 North Richmond Street, Dublin, in 1894, and Joyce had earlier briefly attended the Christian Brothers' school a few doors away (The Christian Brothers are a Catholic religious community). The details of the house described here correspond exactly to those of No. 17.

3. François Eugène Vidocq (1775–1857) had an extraordinary career as soldier, thief, chief of the French detective force, and private detective. *The Abbot* is a historical novel dealing with Mary Queen of Scots, *The Devout Communicant* a Catholic religious manual.

her. Her dress swung as she moved her body and the soft rope of her hair tossed from side to side.

Every morning I lay on the floor in the front parlour watching her door. The blind was pulled down to within an inch of the sash so that I could not be seen. When she came out on the doorstep my heart leaped. I ran to the hall, seized my books and followed her. I kept her brown figure always in my eye and, when we came near the point at which our ways diverged, I quickened my pace and passed her. This happened morning after morning. I had never spoken to her, except for a few casual words, and yet her name was like a summons to all my foolish blood.

Her image accompanied me even in places the most hostile to romance. On Saturday evenings when my aunt went marketing I had to go to carry some of the parcels. We walked through the flaring streets, jostled by drunken men and bargaining women, amid the curses of labourers, the shrill litanies of shop-boys who stood on guard by the barrels of pigs' cheeks, the nasal chanting of street-singers, who sang a *come-all-you*[4] about O'Donovan Rossa, or a ballad about the troubles in our native land. These noises converged in a single sensation of life for me: I imagined that I bore my chalice safely through a throng of foes. Her name sprang to my lips at moments in strange prayers and praises which I myself did not understand. My eyes were often full of tears (I could not tell why) and at times a flood from my heart seemed to pour itself out into my bosom. I thought little of the future. I did not know whether I would ever speak to her or not or, if I spoke to her, how I could tell her of my confused adoration. But my body was like a harp and her words and gestures were like fingers running upon the wires.

One evening I went into the back drawing-room in which the priest had died. It was a dark rainy evening and there was no sound in the house. Through one of the broken panes I heard the rain impinge upon the earth, the fine incessant needles of water playing in the sodden beds. Some distant lamp or lighted window gleamed below me. I was thankful that I could see so little. All my senses seemed to desire to veil themselves and, feeling that I was about to slip from them, I pressed the palms of my hands together until they trembled, murmuring: "*O love! O love!*" many times.

At last she spoke to me. When she addressed the first words to me I was so confused that I did not know what to answer. She asked me was I going to *Araby.*[5] I forgot whether I answered yes

---

4. Street ballad, so called from its opening words. This one was about the 19th-century Irish nationalist Jeremiah Donovan, popularly known as O'Donovan Rossa.

5. The bazaar, described by its "official catalogue" as a "Grand Oriental Fête," was actually held in Dublin on May 14–19, 1894.

or no. It would be a splendid bazaar, she said she would love to go.

"And why can't you?" I asked.

While she spoke she turned a silver bracelet round and round her wrist. She could not go, she said, because there would be a retreat[6] that week in her convent. Her brother and two other boys were fighting for their caps and I was alone at the railings. She held one of the spikes, bowing her head towards me. The light from the lamp opposite our door caught the white curve of her neck, lit up her hair that rested there and, falling, lit up the hand upon the railing. It fell over one side of her dress and caught the white border of a petticoat, just visible as she stood at ease.

"It's well for you," she said.

"If I go," I said, "I will bring you something."

What innumerable follies laid waste my waking and sleeping thoughts after that evening! I wished to annihilate the tedious intervening days. I chafed against the work of school. At night in my bedroom and by day in the classroom her image came between me and the page I strove to read. The syllables of the word *Araby* were called to me through the silence in which my soul luxuriated and cast an Eastern enchantment over me. I asked for leave to go to the bazaar on Saturday night. My aunt was surprised and hoped it was not some Freemason affair.[7] I answered few questions in class. I watched my master's face pass from amiability to sternness; he hoped I was not beginning to idle. I could not call my wandering thoughts together. I had hardly any patience with the serious work of life which, now that it stood between me and my desire, seemed to me child's play, ugly monotonous child's play.

On Saturday morning I reminded my uncle that I wished to go to the bazaar in the evening. He was fussing at the hallstand, looking for the hat-brush, and answered me curtly:

"Yes, boy, I know."

As he was in the hall I could not go into the front parlour and lie at the window. I left the house in bad humour and walked slowly towards the school. The air was pitilessly raw and already my heart misgave me.

When I came home to dinner my uncle had not yet been home. Still it was early. I sat staring at the clock for some time and, when its ticking began to irritate me, I left the room. I mounted the staircase and gained the upper part of the house. The high cold empty gloomy rooms liberated me and I went from room to room singing. From the front window I saw my companions playing below in the street. Their cries reached me weakened and indistinct and, leaning my forehead against the cool glass, I looked over at the

---

6. Period of seclusion from ordinary activities devoted to religious exercises; "her convent" is, of course, her convent school.

7. His aunt shares her church's distrust of the Freemasons, an old European secret society, reputedly anti-Catholic.

dark house where she lived. I may have stood there for an hour, seeing nothing but the brown-clad figure cast by my imagination, touched discreetly by the lamplight at the curved neck, at the hand upon the railings and at the border below the dress.

When I came downstairs again I found Mrs. Mercer sitting at the fire. She was an old garrulous woman, a pawnbroker's widow, who collected used stamps for some pious purpose. I had to endure the gossip of the tea-table. The meal was prolonged beyond an hour and still my uncle did not come. Mrs. Mercer stood up to go: she was sorry she couldn't wait any longer, but it was after eight o'clock and she did not like to be out late, as the night air was bad for her. When she had gone I began to walk up and down the room, clenching my fists. My aunt said:

"I'm afraid you may put off your bazaar for this night of Our Lord."

At nine o'clock I heard my uncle's latchkey in the halldoor. I heard him talking to himself and heard the hallstand rocking when it had received the weight of his overcoat. I could interpret these signs. When he was midway through his dinner I asked him to give me the money to go to the bazaar. He had forgotten.

"The people are in bed and after their first sleep now," he said.

I did not smile. My aunt said to him energetically:

"Can't you give him the money and let him go? You've kept him late enough as it is."

My uncle said he was very sorry he had forgotten. He said he believed in the old saying: "All work and no play makes Jack a dull boy." He asked me where I was going and, when I had told him a second time he asked me did I know *The Arab's Farewell to his Steed.*[8] When I left the kitchen he was about to recite the opening lines of the piece to my aunt.

I held a florin tightly in my hand as I strode down Buckingham Street towards the station. The sight of the streets thronged with buyers and glaring with gas recalled to me the purpose of my journey. I took my seat in a third-class carriage of a deserted train. After an intolerable delay the train moved out of the station slowly. It crept onward among ruinous houses and over the twinkling river. At Westland Row Station a crowd of people pressed to the carriage doors; but the porters moved them back, saying that it was a special train for the bazaar. I remained alone in the bare carriage. In a few minutes the train drew up beside an improvised wooden platform. I passed out on to the road and saw by the lighted dial of a clock that it was ten minutes to ten. In front of me was a large building which displayed the magical name.

I could not find any sixpenny entrance and, fearing that the bazaar would be closed, I passed in quickly through a turnstile,

8. Once-popular sentimental poem by Caroline Norton.

handing a shilling to a weary-looking man. I found myself in a big hall girdled at half its height by a gallery. Nearly all the stalls were closed and the greater part of the hall was in darkness. I recognised a silence like that which pervades a church after a service. I walked into the centre of the bazaar timidly. A few people were gathered about the stalls which were still open. Before a curtain, over which the words *Café Chantant*[9] were written in coloured lamps, two men were counting money on a salver. I listened to the fall of the coins.

Remembering with difficulty why I had come I went over to one of the stalls and examined porcelain vases and flowered tea-sets. At the door of the stall a young lady was talking and laughing with two young gentlemen. I remarked their English accents and listened vaguely to their conversation.

"O, I never said such a thing!"

"O, but you did!"

"O, but I didn't!"

"Didn't she say that?"

"Yes. I heard her."

"O, there's a . . . fib!"

Observing me the young lady came over and asked me did I wish to buy anything. The tone of her voice was not encouraging: she seemed to have spoken to me out of a sense of duty. I looked humbly at the great jars that stood like eastern guards at either side of the dark entrance to the stall and murmured:

"No, thank you."

The young lady changed the position of one of the vases and went back to the two young men. They began to talk of the same subject. Once or twice the young lady glanced at me over her shoulder.

I lingered before her stall, though I knew my stay was useless, to make my interest in her wares seem the more real. Then I turned away slowly and walked down the middle of the bazaar. I allowed the two pennies to fall against the sixpence in my pocket. I heard a voice call from one end of the gallery that the light was out. The upper part of the hall was now completely dark.

Gazing up into the darkness I saw myself as a creature driven and derided by vanity; and my eyes burned with anguish and anger.

1905   1914

9. Literally "singing café" (café providing musical entertainment, popular early in this century).

From A Portrait of the Artist as a Young Man[1]
[*The Interview with the Director*]

The director stood in the embrasure of the window, his back to the light, leaning an elbow on the brown crossblind, and, as he spoke and smiled, slowly dangling and looping the cord of the other blind, Stephen stood before him, following for a moment with his eyes the waning of the long summer daylight above the roofs or the slow deft movements of the priestly fingers. The priest's face was in total shadow, but the waning daylight from behind him touched the deeply grooved temples and the curves of the skull. Stephen followed also with his ears the accents and intervals of the priest's voice as he spoke gravely and cordially of indifferent themes, the vacation which had just ended, the colleges of the order abroad, the transference of masters. The grave and cordial voice went on easily with its tale, and in the pauses Stephen felt bound to set it on again with respectful questions. He knew that the tale was a prelude and his mind waited for the sequel. Ever since the message of summons had come for him from the director his mind had struggled to find the meaning of the message; and during the long restless time he had sat in the college parlour waiting for the director to come in his eyes had wandered from one

---

1. *A Portrait of the Artist as a Young Man* is the story of the development of Stephen Dedalus from earliest childhood until his full realization of his destiny as artist and of the implications of that destiny. There is a considerable amount of autobiography in the book, but it is far from straight autobiography. Everything is organized to show the parallel development of artist and exile: for Joyce, the writer can only achieve the objectivity proper to an artist by totally withdrawing from all implication in the life of the community from which he is to draw his material. In the novel Stephen rejects one by one his home, his religion, his country, growing ever more aloof and independent, exclaiming *"Non serviam"* ("I will not serve") to all the representatives of orthodoxy and convention, and even to the claims of friendship and personal affection. Stephen the artist comes into being at the moment when he has successfully resisted the temptation to enter the Jesuit order: he suddenly realizes that he is born to dwell apart, to look objectively on the world of men and record their doings with the artist's disinterested craftsmanship. He might well have become a priest, but the choice lay only between priest and artist, between "the

power of the keys, the power to bind and loose from sin," and the artist's godlike power to re-create the world with the word. That is why Stephen's rejection of the call to join the Jesuit order preludes the climax of the *Portrait* (which comes at the end of the second extract here printed). The first extract shows Stephen's response to that call, and the second shows him shortly afterwards experiencing his first true aesthetic vision as he looks at the girl standing with kilted skirts in the water and sees her without the desire either to possess or to convert but with the artist's joy in the presence of her reality.

As so often, Joyce in this book combines meticulous realism of detail with a persistent symbolism. The hero's name, for example, is itself symbolic. Stephen was the first Christian martyr, and in Greek mythology Daedalus was the first craftsman (or artist: the Greeks had one word for both), who made the labyrinth for King Minos at Crete; later, when Minos turned against him, he made himself wings and escaped by flying across the sea—symbol for Joyce of the artist's flight into necessary exile. The name "Daedalus" means "cunning craftsman": the artist for Joyce was both martyr and pioneer craftsman.

sober picture to another around the walls and his mind wandered from one guess to another until the meaning of the summons had almost become clear. Then, just as he was wishing that some unforeseen cause might prevent the director from coming, he had heard the handle of the door turning and the swish of a soutane.[2]

The director had begun to speak of the Dominican and Franciscan orders and of the friendship between Saint Thomas and Saint Bonaventure.[3] The Capuchin dress, he thought, was rather too . . .

Stephen's face gave back the priest's indulgent smile and, not being anxious to give an opinion, he made a slight dubitative movement with his lips.

—I believe, continued the director, that there is some talk now among the Capuchins themselves of doing away with it and following the example of the other Franciscans.

—I suppose they would retain it in the cloisters? said Stephen.

—O, certainly, said the director. For the cloister it is all right, but for the street I really think it would be better to do away with, don't you?

—It must be troublesome, I imagine?

—Of course it is, of course. Just imagine when I was in Belgium I used to see them out cycling in all kinds of weather with this thing up about their knees! It was really ridiculous. *Les jupes,*[4] they call them in Belgium.

The vowel was so modified as to be indistinct.

—What do they call them?

—*Les jupes.*

—O!

Stephen smiled again in answer to the smile which he could not see on the priest's shadowed face, its image or spectre only passing rapidly across his mind as the low discreet accent fell upon his ear. He gazed calmly before him at the waning sky, glad of the cool of the evening and the faint yellow glow which hid the tiny flame kindling upon his cheek.

The names of articles of dress worn by women or of certain soft and delicate stuffs used in their making brought always to his mind a delicate and sinful perfume. As a boy he had imagined the reins by which horses are driven as slender silken bands and it shocked him to feel at Stradbrooke the greasy leather of harness. It had shocked him, too, when he had felt for the first time beneath his tremulous fingers the brittle texture of a woman's stocking for, retaining nothing of all he read save that which seemed to him an

2. Cassock.
3. St. Bonaventure, Italian Scholastic philosopher (known as "the seraphic doctor"), became general of the Franciscan order in 1256; his contemporary, St. Thomas Aquinas (*doctor angelicus,* or "the angelic doctor"), leading Scholastic philosopher, was a member of the Dominican order. The Capuchins were a special order of Franciscans, so called from the long pointed "capuche," or hood, which they wore.
4. Skirts.

echo or a prophecy of his own state, it was only amid softworded phrases or within rosesoft stuffs that he dared to conceive of the soul or body of a woman moving with tender life.

But the phrase on the priest's lips was disingenuous for he knew that a priest should not speak lightly on that theme. The phrase had been spoken lightly with design and he felt that his face was being searched by the eyes in the shadow. Whatever he had heard or read of the craft of jesuits he had put aside frankly as not borne out by his own experience. His masters, even when they had not attracted him, had seemed to him always intelligent and serious priests, athletic and highspirited prefects. He thought of them as men who washed their bodies briskly with cold water and wore clean cold linen. During all the years he had lived among them in Clongowes[5] and in Belvedere he had received only two pandies[6] and, though these had been dealt him in the wrong, he knew that he had often escaped punishment. During all those years he had never heard from any of his masters a flippant word: it was they who had taught him christian doctrine and urged him to live a good life and, when he had fallen into grievous sin, it was they who had led him back to grace. Their presence had made him diffident of himself when he was a muff in Clongowes and it had made him diffident of himself also while he had held his equivocal position in Belvedere. A constant sense of this had remained with him up to the last year of his school life. He had never once disobeyed or allowed turbulent companions to seduce him from his habit of quiet obedience: and, even when he doubted some statement of a master, he had never presumed to doubt openly. Lately some of their judgments had sounded a little childish in his ears and had made him feel a regret and pity as thought he were slowly passing out of an accustomed world and were hearing its language for the last time. One day when some boys had gathered round a priest under the shed near the chapel, he heard the priest say:

—I believe that Lord Macaulay was a man who probably never committed a mortal sin in his life, that is to say, a deliberate mortal sin.[7]

Some of the boys had then asked the priest if Victor Hugo were not the greatest French writer. The priest had answered that Victor Hugo had never written half so well when he had turned against the church as he had written when he was a catholic.

—But there are many eminent French critics, said the priest, who consider that even Victor Hugo, great as he certainly was, had not so pure a French style as Louis Veuillot.[8]

---

5. The Jesuit school which Stephen (and the young Joyce) attended before going to Belvedere College.
6. Hard blows on the palm of the hand (for punishment).

7. The life of the Whig historian Thomas Babington Macaulay (1800–59) was noted for its purity.
8. A 19th-century French journalist and leader of the French "Ultramon-

The tiny flame which the priest's allusion had kindled upon Stephen's cheek had sunk down again and his eyes were still fixed calmly on the colourless sky. But an unresting doubt flew hither and thither before his mind. Masked memories passed quickly before him: he recognised scenes and persons yet he was conscious that he had failed to perceive some vital circumstance in them. He saw himself walking about the grounds watching the sports in Clongowes and eating slim jim out of his cricket-cap. Some jesuits were walking round the cycletrack in the company of ladies. The echoes of certain expressions used in Clongowes sounded in remote caves of his mind.

His ears were listening to these distant echoes amid the silence of the parlour when he became aware that the priest was addressing him in a different voice.

—I sent for you today, Stephen, because I wished to speak to you on a very important subject.

—Yes, sir.

—Have you ever felt that you had a vocation?

Stephen parted his lips to answer yes and then withheld the word suddenly. The priest waited for the answer and added:

—I mean have you ever felt within yourself, in your soul, a desire to join the order. Think.

—I have sometimes thought of it, said Stephen.

The priest let the blindcord fall to one side and, uniting his hands, leaned his chin gravely upon them, communing with himself.

—In a college like this, he said at length, there is one boy or perhaps two or three boys whom God calls to the religious life. Such a boy is marked off from his companions by his piety, by the good example he shows to others. He is looked up to by them; he is chosen perhaps as prefect by his fellow sodalists. And you, Stephen, have been such a boy in this college, prefect of Our Blessed Lady's sodality.[9] Perhaps you are the boy in this college whom God designs to call to Himself.

A strong note of pride reinforcing the gravity of the priest's voice made Stephen's heart quicken in response. —To receive that call, Stephen, said the priest, is the greatest honour that the Almighty God can bestow upon a man. No king or emperor on this earth has the power of the priest of God. No angel or archangel in heaven, no saint, not even the Blessed Virgin herself has the power of a priest of God: the power of the keys, the power to bind and to loose from sin, the power of exorcism, the power to cast out from the creatures of God the evil spirits that have power over them, the power, the authority, to make the great God of Heaven come down

tanes" (who supported the Pope's claim to be spiritual head of the church everywhere).

9. A religious fellowship.

upon the altar and take the form of bread and wine. What an awful power, Stephen!

A flame began to flutter again on Stephen's cheek as he heard in this proud address an echo of his own proud musings. How often had he seen himself as a priest wielding calmly and humbly the awful power of which angels and saints stood in reverence! His soul had loved to muse in secret on this desire. He had seen himself, a young and silentmannered priest, entering a confessional swiftly, ascending the altarsteps, incensing, genuflecting, accomplishing the vague acts of the priesthood which pleased him by reason of their semblance of reality and of their distance from it. In that dim life which he had lived through in his musings he had assumed the voices and gestures which he had noted with various priests. He had bent his knee sideways like such a one, he had shaken the thurible[1] only slightly like such a one, his chasuble[2] had swung open like that of such another as he turned to the altar again after having blessed the people. And above all it had pleased him to fill the second place in those dim scenes of his imagining. He shrank from the dignity of celebrant because it displeased him to imagine that all the vague pomp should end in his own person or that the ritual should assign to him so clear and final an office. He longed for the minor sacred offices, to be vested with the tunicle of subdeacon at high mass, to stand aloof from the altar, forgotten by the people, his shoulders covered with a humeral veil,[3] holding the paten within its folds or, when the sacrifice had been accomplished, to stand as deacon in a dalmatic of cloth of gold on the step below the celebrant, his hands joined and his face towards the people, and sing the chant, *Ite missa est*.[4] If ever he had seen himself celebrant it was as in the pictures of the mass in his child's massbook, in a church without worshippers, save for the angel of the sacrifice, at a bare altar and served by an acolyte scarcely more boyish than himself. In vague sacrificial or sacramental acts alone his will seemed drawn to go forth to encounter reality: and it was partly the absence of an appointed rite which had always constrained him to inaction whether he had allowed silence to cover his anger or pride or had suffered only an embrace he longed to give.

He listened in reverent silence now to the priest's appeal and through the words he heard even more distinctly a voice bidding him approach, offering him secret knowledge and secret power. He would know then what was the sin of Simon Magus[5] and what the

---

1. Censer (container in which incense is burned).
2. Sleeveless outer garment worn by celebrant at Mass.
3. Veil covering the shoulders. "Paten": plate on which bread is placed in celebration of the Eucharist (Holy Communion).
4. "Go; it is sent forth." The traditional formula of dismissal at the end of the Mass.
5. The Simon who offered money in order to be given the power of laying on of hands possessed by the apostles (see Acts viii.18–19).

sin against the Holy Ghost for which there was no forgiveness. He would know obscure things, hidden from others, from those who were conceived and born children of wrath. He would know the sins, the sinful longings and sinful thoughts and sinful acts, of others, hearing them murmured into his ears in the confessional under the shame of a darkened chapel by the lips of women and of girls: but rendered immune mysteriously at his ordination by the imposition of hands his soul would pass again uncontaminated to the white peace of the altar. No touch of sin would linger upon the hands with which he would elevate and break the host; no touch of sin would linger on his lips in prayer to make him eat and drink damnation to himself not discerning the body of the Lord. He would hold his secret knowledge and secret power, being as sinless as the innocent: and he would be a priest for ever according to the order of Melchisedec.[6]

—I will offer up my mass tomorrow morning, said the director, that Almighty God may reveal to you His holy will. And let you, Stephen, make a novena[7] to your holy patron saint, the first martyr who is very powerful with God, that God may enlighten your mind. But you must be quite sure, Stephen, that you have a vocation because it would be terrible if you found afterwards that you had none. Once a priest always a priest, remember. Your catechism tells you that the sacrament of Holy Orders is one of those which can be received only once because it imprints on the soul an indelible spiritual mark which can never be effaced. It is before you must weigh well, not after. It is a solemn question, Stephen, because on it may depend the salvation of your eternal soul. But we will pray to God together.

He held open the heavy hall door and gave his hand as if already to a companion in the spiritual life. Stephen passed out on to the wide platform above the steps and was conscious of the caress of mild evening air. Towards Findlater's church a quartette of young men were striding along with linked arms, swaying their heads and stepping to the agile melody of their leader's concertina. The music passed in an instant, as the first bars of sudden music always did, over the fantastic fabrics of his mind, dissolving them painlessly and noiselessly as a sudden wave dissolves the sandbuilt turrets of children. Smiling at the trivial air he raised his eyes to the priest's face and, seeing in it a mirthless reflection of the sunken day, detached his hand slowly which had acquiesced faintly in that companionship.

As he descended the steps the impression which effaced his troubled selfcommunion was that of a mirthless mask reflecting a sunken

---

6. "Thou art a priest forever after the order of Melchisedec" (Hebrews v.6). Cf. Genesis xiv.18: "And Melchizedek king of Salem brought forth bread and wine: and he was the priest of the most high God."

7. Devotion consisting of prayers on nine consecutive days.

day from the threshold of the college. The shadow, then, of the life of the college passed gravely over his consciousness. It was a grave and ordered and passionless life that awaited him, a life without material cares. He wondered how he would pass the first night in the novitiate and with what dismay he would wake the first morning in the dormitory. The troubling odour of the long corridors of Clongowes came back to him and he heard the discreet murmur of the burning gasflames. At once from every part of his being unrest began to irradiate. A feverish quickening of his pulses followed and a din of meaningless words drove his reasoned thoughts hither and thither confusedly. His lungs dilated and sank as if he were inhaling a warm moist unsustaining air, and he smelt again the moist warm air which hung in the bath in Clongowes above the sluggish turfcoloured water.

Some instinct, waking at these memories, stronger than education or piety quickened within him at every near approach to that life, an instinct subtle and hostile, and armed him against acquiescence. The chill and order of the life repelled him. He saw himself rising in the cold of the morning and filing down with the others to early mass and trying vainly to struggle with his prayers against the fainting sickness of his stomach. He saw himself sitting at dinner with the community of a college. What, then, had become of that deeprooted shyness of his which had made him loth to eat or drink under a strange roof? What had come of the pride of his spirit which had always made him conceive himself as a being apart in every order?

The Reverend Stephen Dedalus, S. J.[8]

His name in that new life leaped into characters before his eyes and to it there followed a mental sensation of an undefined face or colour of a face. The colour faded and became strong like a changing glow of pallid brick red. Was it the raw reddish glow he had so often seen on wintry mornings on the shaven gills of the priests? The face was eyeless and sourfavoured and devout, shot with pink tinges of suffocated anger. Was it not a mental spectre of the face of one of the jesuits whom some of the boys called Lantern Jaws and others Foxy Campbell?

He was passing at that moment before the jesuit house in Gardiner Street, and wondered vaguely which window would be his if he ever joined the order. Then he wondered at the vagueness of his wonder, at the remoteness of his soul from what he had hitherto imagined her sanctuary, at the frail hold which so many years of order and obedience had of him when once a definite and irrevocable act of his threatened to end for ever, in time and in eternity, his freedom. The voice of the director urging upon him the proud claims of the church and the mystery and power of the priestly

8. Society of Jesus (the Jesuit order).

office repeated itself idly in his memory. His soul was not there to hear and greet it and he knew now that the exhortation he had listened to had already fallen into an idle formal tale. He would never swing the thurible before the tabernacle as priest. His destiny was to be elusive of social or religious orders. The wisdom of the priest's appeal did not touch him to the quick. He was destined to learn his own wisdom apart from others or to learn the wisdom of others himself wandering among the snares of the world.

The snares of the world were its ways of sin. He would fall. He had not yet fallen but he would fall silently, in an instant. Not to fall was too hard, too hard: and he felt the silent lapse of his soul, as it would be at some instant to come, falling, falling, but not yet fallen, still unfallen, but about to fall.

[*The Walk on the Shore*]

He could wait no longer.

From the door of Byron's publichouse to the gate of Clontarf Chapel, from the gate of Clontarf Chapel to the door of Byron's publichouse, and then back again to the chapel and then back again to the publichouse he had paced slowly at first, planting his steps scrupulously in the spaces of the patchwork of the footpath, then timing their fall to the fall of verses. A full hour had passed since his father had gone in with Dan Crosby, the tutor, to find out for him something about the university. For a full hour he had paced up and down, waiting: but he could wait no longer.

He set off abruptly for the Bull,[9] walking rapidly lest his father's shrill whistle might call him back; and in a few moments he had rounded the curve at the police barrack and was safe.

Yes, his mother was hostile to the idea, as he had read from her listless silence. Yet her mistrust pricked him more keenly than his father's pride and he thought coldly how he had watched the faith which was fading down in his soul aging and strengthening in her eyes. A dim antagonism gathered force within him and darkened his mind as a cloud against her disloyalty: and when it passed, cloudlike, leaving his mind serene and dutiful towards her again, he was made aware dimly and without regret of a first noiseless sundering of their lives.

The university! So he had passed beyond the challenge of the sentries who had stood as guardians of his boyhood and had sought to keep him among them that he might be subject to them and serve their ends. Pride after satisfaction uplifted him like long slow waves. The end he had been born to serve yet did not see had led him to escape by an unseen path: and now it beckoned to him once more and a new adventure was about to be opened to him.

---

9. The places and buildings referred to in this extract are all in Dublin. The Bull is a long tongue of land by the sea, fortified to form a protecting sea wall.

It seemed to him that he heard notes of fitful music leaping upwards a tone and downwards a diminished fourth, upwards a tone
and downwards a major third, like triple-branching flames leaping
fitfully, flame after flame, out of a midnight wood. It was an elfin
prelude, endless and formless; and, as it grew wilder and faster, the
flames leaping out of time, he seemed to hear from under the
boughs and grasses wild creatures racing, their feet pattering like
rain upon the leaves. Their feet passed in pattering tumult over his
mind, the feet of hares and rabbits, the feet of harts and hinds and
antelopes, until he heard them no more and remembered only a
proud cadence from Newman:[1]—

—Whose feet are as the feet of harts and underneath the everlasting arms.

The pride of that dim image brought back to his mind the dignity of the office he had refused. All through his boyhood he had
mused upon that which he had so often thought to be his destiny
and when the moment had come for him to obey the call he had
turned aside, obeying a wayward instinct. Now time lay between:
the oils of ordination would never anoint his body. He had refused.
Why?

He turned seaward from the road at Dollymount and as he passed
on to the thin wooden bridge he felt the planks shaking with the
tramp of heavily shod feet. A squad of Christian Brothers was on
its way back from the Bull and had begun to pass, two by two,
across the bridge. Soon the whole bridge was trembling and resounding. The uncouth faces passed him two by two, stained yellow or red or livid by the sea, and as he strove to look at them with
ease and indifference, a faint stain of personal shame and com-
miseration rose to his own face. Angry with himself he tried to hide
his face from their eyes by gazing down sideways into the shallow
swirling water under the bridge but he still saw a reflection therein
of their tophcavy silk hats, and humble tapelike collars and loosely
hanging clerical clothes.

—Brother Hickey.
Brother Quaid.
Brother MacArdle.
Brother Keogh.

Their piety would be like their names, like their faces, like their
clothes; and it was idle for him to tell himself that their humble
and contrite hearts,[2] it might be, paid a far richer tribute of devotion than his had ever been, a gift tenfold more acceptable than
his elaborate adoration. It was idle for him to move himself to be
generous towards them, to tell himself that if he ever came to their
gates, stripped of his pride, beaten and in beggar's weeds, that they

1. John Henry Cardinal Newman.
2. "The sacrifices of God are a broken
spirit: a broken and a contrite heart,

O God, thou wilt not despise" (Psalms
li.17).

would be generous towards him, loving him as themselves. Idle and embittering, finally, to argue, against his own dispassionate certitude, that the commandment of love bade us not to love our neighbour as ourselves with the same amount and intensity of love but to love him as ourselves with the same kind of love.

He drew forth a phrase from his treasure and spoke it softly to himself:

—A day of dappled seaborne clouds.—

The phrase and the day and the scene harmonised in a chord. Words. Was it their colours? He allowed them to glow and fade, hue after hue: sunrise gold, the russet and green of apple orchards, azure of waves, the greyfringed fleece of clouds. No, it was not their colours: it was the poise and balance of the period itself. Did he then love the rhythmic rise and fall of words better than their associations of legend and colour? Or was it that, being as weak of sight as he was shy of mind, he drew less pleasure from the reflection of the glowing sensible world through the prism of a language manycoloured and richly storied than from the contemplation of an inner world of individual emotions mirrored perfectly in a lucid supple periodic prose?

He passed from the trembling bridge on to firm land again. At that instant, as it seemed to him, the air was chilled; and looking askance towards the water he saw a flying squall darkening and crisping suddenly the tide. A faint click at his heart, a faint throb in his throat told him once more of how his flesh dreaded the cold infra-human odour of the sea: yet he did not strike across the downs on his left but held straight on along the spine of rocks that pointed against the river's mouth.

A veiled sunlight lit up faintly the grey sheet of water where the river was embayed. In the distance along the course of the slow-flowing Liffey slender masts flecked the sky and, more distant still, the dim fabric of the city lay prone in haze. Like a scene on some vague arras, old as man's weariness, the image of the seventh city of Christendom was visible to him across the timeless air, no older nor more weary nor less patient of subjection than in the days of the thingmote.[3]

Disheartened, he raised his eyes towards the slowdrifting clouds, dappled and seaborne. They were voyaging across the deserts of the sky, a host of nomads on the march, voyaging high over Ireland, westward bound. The Europe they had come from lay out there beyond the Irish Sea, Europe of strange tongues and valleyed and woodbegirt and citadelled and of entrenched and marshalled races. He heard a confused music within him as of memories and names which he was almost conscious of but could not capture even for

3. Ancient Scandinavian public assembly; Dublin, "the seventh city of Christendom," was settled and ruled by the Danes in the 9th and 10th centuries.

an instant; then the music seemed to recede, to recede, to recede: and from each receding trail of nebulous music there fell always one long-drawn calling note, piercing like a star the dusk of silence. Again! Again! Again! A voice from beyond the world was calling.

—Hello, Stephanos!

—Here comes The Dedalus!

—Ao! . . . Eh, give it over, Dwyer, I'm telling you or I'll give you a stuff in the kisser for yourself. . . . Ao!

—Good man, Towser! Duck him!

—Come along, Dedalus! Bous Stephanoumenos![4] Bous Stephaneforos!

—Duck him! Guzzle him now, Towser!

—Help! Help! . . . Ao!

He recognised their speech collectively before he distinguished their faces. The mere sight of that medley of wet nakedness chilled him to the bone. Their bodies, corpsewhite or suffused with a pallid golden light or rawly tanned by the suns, gleamed with the wet of the sea. Their divingstone, poised on its rude supports and rocking under their plunges, and the rough-hewn stones of the sloping breakwater over which they scrambled in their horseplay, gleamed with cold wet lustre. The towels with which they smacked their bodies were heavy with cold seawater: and drenched with cold brine was their matted hair.

He stood still in deference to their calls and parried their banter with easy words. How characterless they looked: Shuley without his deep unbuttoned collar, Ennis without his scarlet belt with the snaky clasp, and Connolly without his Norfolk coat with the flapless sidepockets! It was a pain to see them and a sword-like pain to see the signs of adolescence that made repellent their pitiable nakedness. Perhaps they had taken refuge in number and noise from the secret dread in their souls. But he, apart from them and in silence, remembered in what dread he stood of the mystery of his own body.

—Stephanos Dedalos! Bous Stephanoumenos! Bous Stephaneforos!

Their banter was not new to him and now it flattered his mild proud sovereignty. Now, as never before, his strange name seemed to him a prophecy. So timeless seemed the grey warm air, so fluid and impersonal his own mood, that all ages were as one to him. A moment before the ghost of the ancient kingdom of the Danes had looked forth through the vesture of the hazewrapped city. Now, at the name of the fabulous artificer,[5] he seemed to hear the noise of dim waves and to see a winged form flying above the waves and

---

4. Greek, "garlanded ox." "Stephanos" is the Greek for "crown," and sacrificial animals were crowned with garlands. "Bous Stephaneforos" means similarly "crown-bearing (or garland-bearing) ox."
5. The Greek craftsman Daedalus: see introductory note to *A Portrait*.

slowly climbing the air. What did it mean? Was it a quaint device opening a page of some medieval book of prophecies and symbols, a hawklike man flying sunward above the sea, a prophecy of the end he had been born to serve and had been following through the mists of childhood and boyhood, a symbol of the artist forging anew in his workshop out of the sluggish matter of the earth a new soaring impalpable imperishable being?

His heart trembled; his breath came faster and a wild spirit passed over his limbs as though he were soaring sunward. His heart trembled in an ecstasy of fear and his soul was in flight. His soul was soaring in an air beyond the world and the body he knew was purified in a breath and delivered of incertitude and made radiant and commingled with the element of the spirit. An ecstasy of flight made radiant his eyes and wild his breath and tremulous and wild and radiant his windswept limbs.

—One! Two! . . . Look out!

—O, Cripes, I'm drownded!

—One! Two! Three and away!

—The next! The next!

—One! . . . Uk!

—Stephaneforos!

His throat ached with a desire to cry aloud, the cry of a hawk or eagle on high, to cry piercingly of his deliverance to the winds. This was the call of life to his soul not the dull gross voice of the world of duties and despair, not the inhuman voice that had called him to the pale service of the altar. An instant of wild flight had delivered him and the cry of triumph which his lips withheld cleft his brain.

—Stephaneforos!

What were they now but the cerements shaken from the body of death—the fear he had walked in night and day, the incertitude that had ringed him round, the shame that had abased him within and without—cerements, the linens of the grave?

His soul had arisen from the grave of boyhood, spurning her graveclothes. Yes! Yes! Yes! He would create proudly out of the freedom and power of his soul, as the great artificer whose name he bore, a living thing, new and soaring and beautiful, impalpable, imperishable.

He started up nervously from the stoneblock for he could no longer quench the flame in his blood. He felt his cheeks aflame and his throat throbbing with song. There was a lust of wandering in his feet that burned to set out for the ends of the earth. On! On! his heart seemed to cry. Evening would deepen above the sea, night fall upon the plains, dawn glimmer before the wanderer and show him strange fields and hills and faces. Where?

He looked northward towards Howth. The sea had fallen below

the line of seawrack on the shallow side of the breakwater and already the tide was running out fast along the foreshore. Already one long oval bank of sand lay warm and dry amid the wavelets. Here and there warm isles of sand gleamed above the shallow tides and about the isles and around the long bank and amid the shallow currents of the beach were lightclad figures, wading and delving.

In a few moments he was barefoot, his stockings folded in his pockets, and his canvas shoes dangling by their knotted laces over his shoulders and, picking a pointed salteaten stick out of the jetsam among the rocks, he clambered down the slope of the breakwater.

There was a long rivulet in the strand and, as he waded slowly up its course, he wondered at the endless drift of seaweed. Emerald and black and russet and olive, it moved beneath the current, swaying and turning. The water of the rivulet was dark with endless drift and mirrored the highdrifting clouds. The clouds were drifting above him silently and silently the seatangle was drifting below him; and the grey warm air was still: and a new wild life was singing in his veins.

Where was his boyhood now? Where was the soul that had hung back from her destiny, to brood alone upon the shame of her wounds and in her house of squalor and subterfuge to queen it in faded cerements and in wreaths that withered at the touch? Or where was he?

He was alone. He was unheeded, happy, and near to the wild heart of life. He was alone and young and wilful and wildhearted, alone amid a waste of wild air and brackish waters and the seaharvest of shells and tangle and veiled grey sunlight and gayclad lightclad figures of children and girls and voices childish and girlish in the air.

A girl stood before him in midstream, alone and still, gazing out to sea. She seemed like one whom magic had changed into the likeness of a strange and beautiful seabird. Her long slender bare legs were delicate as a crane's and pure save where an emerald trail of seaweed had fashioned itself as a sign upon the flesh. Her thighs, fuller and softhued as ivory, were bared almost to the hips where the white fringes of her drawers were like feathering of soft white down. Her slateblue skirts were kilted boldly about her waist and dovetailed behind her. Her bosom was as a bird's, soft and slight, slight and soft as the breast of some darkplumaged dove. But her long fair hair was girlish: and girlish, and touched with the wonder of mortal beauty, her face.

She was alone and still, gazing out to sea; and when she felt his presence and the worship of his eyes her eyes turned to him in quiet sufferance of his gaze, without shame or wantonness. Long, long she suffered his gaze and then quietly withdrew her eyes from his and bent them towards the stream, gently stirring the water with her foot hither and thither. The first faint noise of gently moving water broke the silence, low and faint and whispering, faint as the bells of sleep; hither and thither, hither and thither: and a faint flame trembled on her cheek.

—Heavenly God! cried Stephen's soul, in an outburst of profane joy.

He turned away from her suddenly and set off across the strand. His cheeks were aflame; his body was aglow; his limbs were trembling. On and on and on and on he strode, far out over the sands, singing wildly to the sea, crying to greet the advent of the life that had cried to him.

Her image had passed into his soul for ever and no word had broken the holy silence of his ecstasy. Her eyes had called him and his soul had leaped at the call. To live, to err, to fall, to triumph, to recreate life out of life! A wild angel had appeared to him, the angel of mortal youth and beauty, an envoy from the fair courts of life, to throw open before him in an instant of ecstasy the gates of all the ways of error and glory. On and on and on and on!

He halted suddenly and heard his heart in the silence. How far had he walked? What hour was it?

There was no human figure near him nor any sound borne to him over the air. But the tide was near the turn and already the day was on the wane. He turned landward and ran towards the shore and, running up the sloping beach, reckless of the sharp shingle, found a sandy nook amid a ring of tufted sandknolls and lay down there that the peace and silence of the evening might still the riot of his blood.

He felt above him the vast indifferent dome and the calm processes of the heavenly bodies; and the earth beneath him, the earth that had borne him, had taken him to her breast.

He closed his eyes in the languor of sleep. His eyelids trembled as if they felt the vast cyclic movement of the earth and her watchers, trembled as if they felt the strange light of some new world. His soul was swooning into some new world, fantastic, dim, uncertain as under sea, traversed by cloudy shapes and beings. A world, a glimmer, or a flower? Glimmering and trembling, trembling and unfolding, a breaking light, an opening flower, it spread in endless succession to itself, breaking in full crimson and unfolding and fading to palest rose, leaf by leaf and wave of light by wave of light, flooding all the heavens with its soft flushes, every flush deeper than other.

Evening had fallen when he woke and the sand and arid grasses of his bed glowed no longer. He rose slowly and, recalling the rapture of his sleep, sighed at its joy.

He climbed to the crest of the sandhill and gazed about him. Evening had fallen. A rim of the young moon cleft the pale waste of sky like the rim of a silver hoop embedded in grey sand; and the tide was flowing in fast to the land with a low whisper of her waves, islanding a few last figures in distant pools.

1904–14   1916

From Ulysses

[Proteus]¹

Ineluctable modality of the visible: at least that if no more, thought through my eyes.² Signatures of all things I am here to read, seaspawn and seawrack, the nearing tide, that rusty boot. Snotgreen, bluesilver, rust: coloured signs. Limits of the diaphane.³ But

---

1. "Proteus" is so titled because of the deliberate analogies that exist between it and the description of Proteus in *Odyssey* IV. (Joyce did not title any of the episodes in *Ulysses*, but the names are his; he used them in correspondence and in talk with friends.) In Homer's *Odyssey*, Proteus is the changing sea god who continually alters his shape: when Telemachus, the son of Ulysses, asks Menelaus for help in finding his father, Menelaus tells him that he encountered Proteus on the seashore on the island of Pharos "in front of Egypt," and that, by holding on to him while he changed from one shape to another, he was able to force him to tell what had happened to Ulysses and the other Greek heroes of the Trojan war. In Joyce's narrative, Stephen Dedalus (who, like Homer's Telemachus, is looking for a father, but not in the literal "consubstantial" sense) is walking by the Dublin shore alone, "along Sandymount strand," speculating on the shifting shapes of things and the possibility of knowing truth by mere appearances.

First Stephen meditates on the "modality of the visible" and on the mystical notion that God writes his signature on all His works; then on the "modality of the audible," closing his eyes and trying to know reality simply through the sense of hearing. As he continues his walk, the people and objects he sees mingle in his thoughts with memories of his past relations with his family, of his schooldays, his residence in Paris whence he was recalled by his mother's fatal illness, his feel-

ing of guilt about his mother's death (he had refused to kneel down and pray at her bedside, since he considered it would be a betrayal of his integrity as an unbeliever), and a variety of speculations about life and reality often derived from mystical works he had read "in the stagnant bay of Marsh's library" (in Dublin). This episode gives the reader a profound awareness of the nature of Stephen's sensibility and the contents of his conscious and subconscious mind and also sets going themes to be developed later in other episodes of *Ulysses*. The highly theoretical, inquiring, musing, speculating mind of Stephen is in sharp contrast to the practical, humane, sensual, concrete imagination of the book's real hero, Leopold Bloom, but there are also significant parallels between the streams of consciousness of the two. Some of the more important themes which emerge in Stephen's reverie are pointed out in footnotes.

The text given here has been collated with the Odyssey Press edition of *Ulysses* (1932), which is accepted as the "definitive standard edition."

2. I.e., the sense of sight provides an unavoidable way ("ineluctable modality") of knowing reality, the knowledge thus provided being a kind of "thought through [the] eyes." The phrase "signature of all things" comes from the German mystic Jakob Böhme, (1575–1624).

3. Transparency. Stephen is speculating on Aristotle's view of perception as developed in his *De Anima*.

he adds: in bodies. Then he was aware of them bodies before of them coloured. How? By knocking his sconce against them, sure. Go easy. Bald he was and a millionaire, *maestro di color che sanno.*[4] Limit of the diaphane in. Why in? Diaphane, adiaphane.[5] If you can put your five fingers through it, it is a gate, if not a door. Shut your eyes and see.

Stephen closed his eyes to hear his boots crush crackling wrack and shells. You are walking through it howsomever. I am, a stride at a time. A very short space of time through very short times of space. Five, six: the *nacheinander.*[6] Exactly: and that is the ineluctable modality of the audible. Open your eyes. No. Jesus! If I fell over a cliff that beetles o'er his base,[7] fell through the *nebeneinander* ineluctably. I am getting on nicely in the dark. My ash sword hangs at my side. Tap with it: they do.[8] My two feet in his boots are at the end of his legs, *nebeneinander.* Sounds solid: made by the mallet of *Los Demiurgos.*[9] Am I walking into eternity along Sandymount strand? Crush, crack, crik, crick. Wild sea money. Dominie[1] Deasy kens them a'.

> *Won't you come to Sandymount,*
> *Madeline the mare?*

Rhythm begins, you see. I hear. A catalectic tetrameter[2] of iambs marching. No, agallop: *deline the mare.*

Open your eyes now. I will. One moment. Has all vanished since? If I open and am for ever in the black adiaphane. *Basta!*[3] I will see

---

4. There was a tradition that Aristotle was bald, with thin legs, small eyes, and a lisp. Aristotle is also traditionally supposed to have inherited considerable wealth and to have been presented with a fortune by his former pupil Alexander the Great. The Italian phrase is Dante's description of Aristotle in the *Inferno*, and means "the master of them that know."
5. What is not transparent (opposite of "diaphane").
6. "After one another." Stephen, with eyes shut, is now sensing reality through the sense of sound only: unlike sight, sound falls on the sense of hearing in chronological sequence, one sound after another.
7. "What if it tempt you toward the flood, my lord, / Or to the dreadful summit of the cliff / That beetles o'er his base into the sea * * * " (*Hamlet* I.iv.69–71). "*Nebeneinander*": beside one another.
8. Stephen is still walking with his eyes shut, tapping with his "ash sword" (the walking stick of ash wood he always carried), as "they" (i.e., blind

people) do. "His boots": Buck Mulligan's. Stephen, lacking boots of his own, had borrowed a castoff pair of Mulligan's.
9. The Demiurge, supernatural being who made the world in subordination to God. The mystical notion of the Demiurge who created the world haunts Stephen's mind; it is the Demiurge who writes his signature on created objects and whose mallet fashioned them. The world, sensed by the ear only, "sounds solid," as though made by the Demiurge's hammer.
1. Schoolmaster. Mr. Deasy was the headmaster of the school where Stephen taught (the previous episode has shown Stephen teaching). "Kens them a'": knows them all; Stephen is putting Deasy into a mock-Scottish folk song.
2. The first of the two lines of popular verse which have come into Stephen's head consists metrically of four iambic feet ("tetrameter") with the unstressed syllable of the first iamb missing ("catalectic").
3. Italian, "Enough!"

if I can see.

See now. There all the time without you: and ever shall be, world without end.

They came down the steps from Leahy's terrace prudently, *Frauenzimmer:*[4] and down the shelving shore flabbily their splayed feet sinking in the silted sand. Like me, like Algy,[5] coming down to our mighty mother. Number one swung lourdily[6] her midwife's bag, the other's gamp poked in the beach. From the liberties, out for the day. Mrs. Florence MacCabe,[7] relict of the late Patk Mac-Cabe, deeply lamented, of Bride Street. One of her sisterhood lugged me squealing into life. Creation from nothing. What has she in the bag? A misbirth with a trailing navelcord, hushed in ruddy wool. The cords of all link back, strandentwining cable of all flesh. That is why mystic monks. Will you be as gods? Gaze in your omphalos. Hello. Kinch here. Put me on to Edenville. Aleph, alpha: nought, nought, one.[8]

Spouse and helpmate of Adam Kadmon:[9] Heva, naked Eve. She had no navel. Gaze. Belly without blemish, bulging big, a buckler of taut vellum, no, whiteheaped corn, orient and immortal, standing from everlasting to everlasting.[1] Womb of sin.

Wombed in sin darkness I was too, made not begotten. By them, the man with my voice and my eyes and a ghostwoman with ashes on her breath.[2] They clasped and sundered, did the coupler's will. From before the ages He willed me and now may not will me away

4. "Midwives"; Stephen sees them coming from Leahy's Terrace, which runs by the beach.
5. Algernon Charles Swinburne, who wrote: "I will go back to the great sweet mother, / Mother and lover of men, the sea. I will go down to her, I and none other * * * " (*The Triumph of Time*).
6. Heavily (coined by Stephen from the French *lourd*). Stephen, like Joyce, had studied modern languages at University College, Dublin, and his preoccupation with words and languages is part of his character as potential literary artist. "Gamp": umbrella; and perhaps reference to Mrs. Gamp, the nurse in Dickens' *Martin Chuzzlewit*.
7. Stephen imagines the first midwife is called Mrs. MacCabe. "Relict": widow.
8. Stephen is speculating on the mystical significance of the navel cord, seeing it as linking the generations, the combined navel cords stretching back to Adam and Eve. A mystic gazed in his *omphalos* (navel) to make contact with the first man. Stephen thinks of himself ("Kinch," his nickname) calling up Adam in "Edenville" through his navel,

using the line of linked navel cords as a telephone line. Adam's telephone number, "Aleph, alpha: nought, nought, one," begins with the first letters of the Hebrew and of the Greek alphabet to suggest the great primeval number.
9. "Adam the Beginner," so called in Hebrew cabalistic literature of the Middle Ages; "Heva" is Hebrew for Eve. Because she was not born in the regular way, but created from Adam's rib, she had no navel.
1. Stephen is led, through reflection on Eve's navel-less "belly without blemish," to a recollection of the description of the original Eden (Paradise) by Thomas Traherne (ca. 1637–74), from whose prose *Centuries of Meditation* he quotes: "The corn was orient and immortal wheat, which should never be reaped, nor was ever sown. I thought it had stood from everlasting to everlasting. * * * " But immediately afterwards Stephen reflects that such language is inappropriate to Eve's body, as hers was the "womb of sin"—i.e., she first ate the fatal apple and brought forth sin.
2. Stephen is haunted by thoughts of his mother in this guise.

or ever. A *lex eterna*[3] stays about Him. Is that then the divine substance wherein Father and Son are consubstantial? Where is poor dear Arius[4] to try conclusions? Warring his life long on the contransmagnificandjewbangtantiality.[5] Illstarred heresiarch.[6] In a Greek watercloset he breathed his last: euthanasia. With beaded mitre and with crozier, stalled upon his throne, widower of a widowed see, with upstiffed omophorion, with clotted hinderparts.

Airs romped around him, nipping and eager airs. They are coming, waves. The whitemaned seahorses, champing, brightwindbridled, the steeds of Mananaan.[7]

I mustn't forget his letter for the press. And after? The Ship, half twelve. By the way go easy with that money like a good young imbecile. Yes, I must.[8]

His pace slackened. Here. Am I going to Aunt Sara's or not? My consubstantial father's voice. Did you see anything of your artist brother Stephen lately? No? Sure he's not down in Strasburg terrace with his aunt Sally? Couldn't he fly a bit higher than that, eh? And and and and tell us Stephen, how is uncle Si? O weeping God, the things I married into. De boys up in de hayloft. The drunken little costdrawer and his brother, the cornet player. Highly respectable gondoliers. And skeweyed Walter sirring his father, no less. Sir. Yes, sir. No, sir. Jesus wept: and no wonder, by Christ.[9]

I pull the wheezy bell of their shuttered cottage: and wait. They take me for a dun, peer out from a coign of vantage.[1]

—It's Stephen, sir.

3. Eternal law. God's eternal law, Stephen reflects, willed his birth from the beginning. He then goes on to speculate on the nature of the divine substance and whether God the Father and God the Son are of the same substance ("consubstantial").

4. 3rd-century theologian who "tried conclusions" on this matter, maintaining that Christ was less divine than God (Arius' views were condemned as heretical by the Council of Nicaea in 325).

5. Ironic "portmanteau word" made up of terms connected with the Arian controversy—"consubstantial," "transubstantial" (of a substance that changes into another)—and with the facts of Christ's nature (e.g., "Jew"; Jesus was a Jew, as Leopold Bloom in a later episode reminds an anti-Semitic Irishman).

6. Arch-heretic. Arius died suddenly in Constantinople in 336. He was never a bishop, and Stephen's image of him at the moment of death in full episcopal attire seems to combine recollections of other early "heresiarchs." In an earlier reverie Stephen had conjured up in his mind "a horde of heresies fleeing with mitres awry." These heretics are connected in Stephen's mind with argument about the relation between God the Father and God the Son and so

with the problem of the true nature of paternity, which haunts him constantly.

7. Mananaan MacLir, Celtic sea god; his steeds are the "white horses" (still the name in Britain for the white foam on top of waves).

8. Mr. Deasy had given Stephen a letter to the press to be taken to the newspaper office. After that he has an appointment with Mulligan at The Ship, a tavern. "That money" is Mr. Deasy's last payment to him.

9. Stephen has been wondering whether to call on his uncle and aunt, Richie and Sara Goulding. He imagines his father interrogating him about the visit as if he had gone, and then pictures his cousins asking after his father, Simon Dedalus (his cousins' "uncle Si"). Simon Dedalus is contemptuous of his wife's relations (Sara Goulding is his wife's sister). Stephen knows that any mention of them will bring on the familiar abuse of "the things I married into"—at best "highly respectable gondoliers" (from Gilbert and Sullivan's opera *The Gondoliers*). The scene that follows is also Stephen's purely imaginary picture of what the visit would be like.

1. Favorable corner.

—Let him in. Let Stephen in.

A bolt drawn back and Walter welcomes me.

—We thought you were someone else.

In his broad bed nuncle Richie, pillowed and blanketed, extends over the hillock of his knees a sturdy forearm. Clean chested. He has washed the upper moiety.

—Morrow, nephew.

He lays aside the lapboard whereon he drafts his bills of costs for the eyes of Master Goff and Master Shapland Tandy, filing consents and common searches and a writ of *Duces Tecum.*[2] A bogoak frame over his bald head: Wilde's *Requiescat.*[3] The drone of his misleading whistle brings Walter back.

—Yes, sir?

—Malt[4] for Richie and Stephen, tell mother. Where is she?

—Bathing Crissie, sir.

Papa's little bedpal. Lump of love.

—No, uncle Richie. . .

—Call me Richie. Damn your lithia water. It lowers. Whusky!

—Uncle Richie, really. . .

—Sit down or by the law Harry I'll knock you down.

Walter squints vainly for a chair.

—He has nothing to sit down on, sir.

—He has nowhere to put it, you mug. Bring in our Chippendale chair. Would you like a bite of something? None of your damned lawdeedaw air here; the rich of a rasher fried with a herring? Sure? So much the better. We have nothing in the house but backache pills.

All'erta![5]

He drones bars of Ferrando's *aria di sortita.* The grandest number, Stephen, in the whole opera. Listen.

His tuneful whistle sounds again, finely shaded, with rushes of the air, his fists bigdrumming on his padded knees.

This wind is sweeter.

Houses of decay, mine, his and all. You told the Clongowes gentry you had an uncle a judge and an uncle a general in the army.[6] Come out of them, Stephen. Beauty is not there. Nor in the stagnant bay of Marsh's library where you read the fading prophecies of Joachim Abbas.[7] For whom? The hundredheaded

2. "You shall take with you": opening words of search warrant. Goulding was a law clerk with Messrs. Goff and Tandy.
3. Poem by Oscar Wilde.
4. Whisky.
5. "Look out!" The first words of the *aria di sortita* (aria of a singer's entrance) sung by Ferrando, captain of the guard, in Verdi's opera *Il Trovatore.*
6. Stephen, reflecting on the steady so-

cial decline of his family, is remembering that, while at school at Clongowes Wood College, he had pretended to have important relations.
7. Abbot Joachim of Floris (the monastery of San Giovanni in Fiore, Italy), 12th-century mystic and theologian, whose prophetic work *Expositio in Apocalypsin* Stephen (i.e., Joyce) had read in Marsh's Library.

rabble of the cathedral close.[8] A hater of his kind ran from them to the wood of madness, his mane foaming in the moon, his eyeballs stars. Houyhnhnm, horsenostrilled.[9] The oval equine faces, Temple, Buck Mulligan, Foxy Campbell. Lantern jaws. Abbas father,[1] furious dean, what offence laid fire to their brains? Paff! *Descende, calve, ut ne nimium decalveris.*[2] A garland of grey hair on his comminated head see him me clambering down to the footpace (*descende*), clutching a monstrance, basiliskeyed. Get down, bald poll! A choir gives back menace and echo, assisting about the altar's horns, the snorted Latin of jackpriests moving burly in their albs, tonsured and oiled and gelded, fat with the fat of kidneys of wheat.

And at the same instant perhaps a priest round the corner is elevating it. Dringdring! And two streets off another locking it into a pyx.[3] Dringadring! And in a ladychapel another taking housel all to his own cheek. Dringdring! Down, up, forward, back. Dan Occam[4] thought of that, invincible doctor. A misty English morning the imp hypostasis tickled his brain. Bringing his host down and kneeling he heard twine with his second bell the first bell in the transept (he is lifting his) and, rising, heard (now I am lifting) their two bells (he is kneeling) twang in diphthong.

Cousin Stephen, you will never be a saint.[5] Isle of saints.[6] You were awfully holy, weren't you? You prayed to the Blessed Virgin that you might not have a red nose. You prayed to the devil in Serpentine avenue that the fubsy widow in front might lift her clothes still more from the wet street. O *si, certo!*[7] Sell your soul for that, do, dyed rags pinned round a squaw. More tell me, more still! On the top of the Howth tram alone crying to the rain: *naked women!* What about that, eh?

What about what? What else were they invented for?

8. I.e., the precinct of a cathedral (Marsh's Library is in the close of St. Patrick's Cathedral).
9. St. Patrick's Close has recalled Jonathan Swift (who was Dean of St. Patrick's). Stephen remembers Swift's misanthropy (he was "a hater of his kind") and his creation of the Houyhnhnms (noble horses) in Book IV of *Gulliver's Travels*. Then he thinks of people he knew who have horse-faces.
1. "Abbas" means literally "father."
2. "Go down, bald-head, lest you become even balder." This sentence, from Joachim's *Concordia* of the Old and New Testaments, is based on the mocking cry of the children to the prophet Elisha (II Kings ii.23: "Go up, thou bald head"); Joachim saw Elisha as a forerunner of St. Benedict—both had shaven or baldish heads. Stephen imagines the "comminated" (i.e., threatened) head of Joachim descending, clutching a "monstrance" (receptacle in which the consecrated host is exposed for adoration), in the midst of a nightmare church service.
3. Vessel in which the Host (consecrated bread or wafer) is kept. Stephen is imagining such a service, with himself officiating (he almost became a priest).
4. William of Occam or Ockham ("Dan" means "master"), 14th-century English theologian, who held that the individual thing is the reality and its name, the universal, an abstraction; he was concerned with "hypostasis"— the essential part of a thing as distinct from its attributes.
5. A parody of the words of Dryden to his distant relative Swift: "Cousin, you will never make a poet."
6. Ireland was called "*insula sanctorum,*" ("isle of saints") in the Middle Ages.
7. "Oh yes, certainly!"

Reading two pages apiece of seven books every night, eh? I was young. You bowed to yourself in the mirror, stepping forward to applause earnestly, striking face. Hurray for the Goddamned idiot! Hray! No-one saw: tell no-one. Books you were going to write with letters for titles. Have you read his F? O yes, but I prefer Q. Yes, but W is wonderful. O yes, W. Remember your epiphanies[8] on green oval leaves, deeply deep, copies to be sent if you died to all the great libraries of the world, including Alexandria? Someone was to read them there after a few thousand years, a mahamanvantara.[9] Pico della Mirandola like. Ay, very like a whale.[1] When one reads these strange pages of one long gone one feels that one is at one with one who once. . .

The grainy sand had gone from under his feet. His boots trod again a damp crackling mast, razorshells, squeaking pebbles, that on the unnumbered pebbles beats, wood sieved by the shipworm, lost Armada. Unwholesome sandflats waited to suck his treading soles, breathing upward sewage breath. He coasted them, walking warily. A porterbottle stood up, stogged to its waist, in the cakey sand dough. A sentinel: isle of dreadful thirst.[2] Broken hoops on the shore; at the land a maze of dark cunning nets; farther away chalkscrawled backdoors and on the higher beach a dryingline with two crucified shirts. Ringsend: wigwams of brown steersmen and master mariners. Human shells.

He halted. I have passed the way to aunt Sara's. Am I not going there? Seems not. No-one about. He turned northeast and crossed the firmer sand towards the Pigeonhouse.[3]

—*Qui vous a mis dans cette fichue position?*
—*C'est le pigeon, Joseph.*

8. Joyce's own term for the prose poems he wrote as a young man. An epiphany, he said, was the sudden "revelation of the whatness of a thing" —of a gesture, a phrase, or a thought which he had experienced; he attempted to express, in the writing, the moment at which "the soul of the commonest object * * * seems to us radiant." Stephen's recollection of early and exotic literary ambitions is drawn directly from Joyce's own ambitions at the same age.
9. Cycle of change and recurrence, in Indian mystical thought. It is connected in Stephen's mind with the constant ebb and flow of the sea by which he is walking. Pico della Mirandola was a 15th-century mystical philosopher; his *Heptaplus* is a mystical account of the creation, much influenced by Jewish cabalistic thought.
1. Polonius to Hamlet (*Hamlet* III.ii.399) with reference to the changing shape of a cloud. The Protean theme of constant change, of ebb and flow, and of metempsychosis (i.e., trans-

migration of souls: a major theme in *Ulysses*), is working in Stephen's mind. The following sentence is a parody of an elegant, condescending modern essay on Pico or some other early mystic.
2. The atmosphere of the sandflats reminds Stephen of a desert island where men die of thirst. (The island of Pharos, where Menelaus found Proteus, was an "island of dreadful hunger.")
3. The Pigeon house in Ringsend, an old structure built on a breakwater in Dublin Bay and which in the course of time has served a great variety of purposes, suggests to Stephen the Dove which is the symbol of the Holy Spirit, and this in turn suggests an irreverent dialogue (supposedly between Joseph and Mary when Mary is found to be pregnant: "Who has got you into this wretched condition?" "It was the pigeon [i.e., the Holy Dove], Joseph"). This he had picked up in Paris from the blasphemous M. Léo Taxil, whose book *La Vie de Jésus* ("The Life of Jesus") is mentioned in the next paragraph.

Patrice, home on furlough, lapped warm milk with me in the bar MacMahon. Son of the wild goose, Kevin Egan of Paris. My father's a bird, he lapped the sweet *lait chaud* with pink young tongue, plump bunny's face. Lap, *lapin*. He hopes to win in the *gros lots*. About the nature of women he read in Michelet. But he must send me *La Vie de Jésus* by M. Léo Taxil. Lent it to his friend.[4]

—*C'est tordant, vous savez. Moi je suis socialiste. Je ne crois pas en l'existence de Dieu. Faut pas le dire à mon père.*

—*Il croit?*

—*Mon père, oui.*

Schluss. He laps.[5]

My Latin quarter hat. God, we simply must dress the character. I want puce gloves. You were a student, weren't you? Of what in the other devil's name? Paysayenn. P. C. N., you know: *physiques, chimiques et naturelles.*[6] Aha. Eating your groatsworth of *mou en civet*, fleshpots of Egypt, elbowed by belching cabmen. Just say in the most natural tone: when I was in Paris, *boul' Mich',*[7] I used to. Yes, used to carry punched tickets to prove an alibi if they arrested you for murder somewhere. Justice. On the night of the seventeenth of February 1904 the prisoner was seen by two witnesses. Other fellow did it: other me. Hat, tie, overcoat, nose. *Lui, c'est moi.*[8] You seem to have enjoyed yourself.

Proudly walking. Whom were you trying to walk like? Forget: a dispossessed. With mother's money order, eight shillings, the banging door of the post office slammed in your face by the usher. Hunger toothache. *Encore deux minutes.* Look clock. Must get. *Fermé.* Hired dog! Shoot him to bloody bits with a bang shotgun, bits man spattered walls all brass buttons. Bits all khrrrrklak in place clack back. Not hurt? O, that's all right. Shake hands. See what I meant, see? O, that's all right. Shake a shake. O, that's all only all right.[9]

4. Stephen had first met Léo Taxil through Patrice, the son of "Kevin Egan of Paris," who in real life was the exiled nationalist Joseph Casey. The phrase "my father's a bird" comes from *The Song of the Cheerful Jesus,* a blasphemous poem by Buck Mulligan (actually Oliver Gogarty, who really wrote the poem); Stephen recalls Patrice reciting it as he drank warm milk (*"lait chaud"*), lapping it like a *"lapin"* ("rabbit"), and expressing the hope that he would win something substantial in the French national lottery (*gros lot:* "first prize"). Jules Michelet (1798–1874) was a French historian.
5. Conversation between Stephen and Patrice: "It's screamingly funny, you know. I'm a socialist myself. I don't believe in the existence of God. Mustn't tell my father." "He is a believer?"

"My father, yes." *"Schluss":* end.
6. I.e., the faculty of physics, chemistry, and biology at the École de Médecine in Paris, where Stephen, like Joyce, took a premedical course for a short time. The faculty was popularly known as "P. C. N." (pronounced "Paysayenn"). *"Mou en civet":* stew.
7. Popular Parisian abbreviation for the Boulevard Saint Michel.
8. "He is me"—a parody of Louis XIV's remark, *"L'état c'est moi"* ("I am the state").
9. A recollection of the occasion when, desperate for money, Stephen had received a money order for eight shillings from his mother. Afflicted with both hunger and toothache, he had gone to cash it at the post office—which was closed, even though, as he expostulated with the man at the door, there were still two minutes (*"encore deux min-*

You were going to do wonders, what? Missionary to Europe after fiery Columbanus.[1] Fiacre and Scotus on their creepystools in heaven spilt from their pintpots, loudlatinlaughing: *Euge! Euge!*[2] Pretending to speak broken English as you dragged your valise, porter threepence, across the slimy pier at Newhaven. *Comment?* Rich booty you brought back; *Le tutu*, five tattered numbers of *Pantalon Blanc et Culotte Rouge*,[3] a blue French telegram, curiosity to show:

—Mother dying come home father.[4]

The aunt thinks you killed your mother. That's why she won't.[5]

> *Then here's a health to Mulligan's aunt*
> *And I'll tell you the reason why.*
> *She always kept things decent in*
> *The Hannigan famileye.*

His feet marched in sudden proud rhythm over the sand furrows, along by the boulders of the south wall. He stared at them proudly, piled stone mammoth skulls. Gold light on sea, on sand, on boulders. The sun is there, the slender trees, the lemon houses.

Paris rawly waking, crude sunlight on her lemon streets. Moist pith of farls[6] of bread, the froggreen wormwood, her matin incense, court the air. Belluomo rises from the bed of his wife's lover's wife, the kerchiefed housewife is astir, a saucer of acetic acid in her hands. In Rodot's Yvonne and Madeleine newmake their tumbled beauties, shattering with gold teeth *chaussons* of pastry, their mouths yellowed with the *pus* of *flan breton*.[7] Faces of Paris men go by, their wellpleased pleasers, curled conquistadores.[8]

Noon slumbers. Kevin Egan rolls gunpowder cigarettes through fingers smeared with printer's ink,[9] sipping his green fairy as Patrice his white. About us gobblers fork spiced beans down their gullets. *Un demi setier!*[1] A jet of coffee steam from the burnished caldron. She serves me at his beck. *Il est irlandais. Hollandais? Non fromage. Deux irlandais, nous, Irlande, vous savez? Ah oui!*[2] She thought you wanted a cheese *hollandais*. Your postprandial, do you know

---

utes") until the official closing time. In his retrospective rage he imagines himself shooting the "hired dog" to bits, and then in a revulsion of feeling has a mental reconciliation with him.

1. 6th-century Irish missionary on the Continent. Fiacre was a 6th-century Irish saint. Duns Scotus (ca. 1265–1308): Scholastic theologian and philosopher. "Creepystools": low stools.

2. "Well done!"

3. Like the preceding name, name of French popular periodical.

4. This telegram was actually received by Joyce in Paris.

5. Stephen recalls Buck Mulligan's telling him that his (Mulligan's) aunt disapproved of Stephen because, by refusing to pray at his dying mother's bedside, he had hastened her death.

Stephen then tries to laugh away his feeling of guilt by quoting mentally a (slightly parodied) verse of a popular song.

6. Thin circular cakes.

7. Memories of a restaurant in Paris: "*chaussons*" are pastry turnovers; "*flan breton*" is a pastry filled with custard.

8. Conquerors (Spanish).

9. Egan (i.e., Joseph Casey) became a typesetter for the Parisian edition of the *New York Herald*.

1. Abusive Parisian slang for a liquid measure (about one fourth of a liter) —here, presumably, of wine or beer.

2. "He is Irish. Dutch? Not cheese. We are two Irishmen, Ireland, you understand? Oh, yes!"

that word? Postprandial. There was a fellow I knew once in Barcelona, queer fellow, used to call it his postprandial. Well: *slainte!*[3] Around the slabbed tables the tangle of wined breaths and grumbling gorges. His breath hangs over our saucestained plates, the green fairy's fang thrusting between his lips. Of Ireland, the Dalcassions, of hopes, conspiracies, of Arthur Griffith now.[4] To yoke me as his yokefellow, our crimes our common cause. You're your father's son. I know the voice. His fustian shirt, sanguineflowered, trembles its Spanish tassels at his secrets. M. Drumont,[5] famous journalist, Drumont, know what he called queen Victoria? Old hag with the yellow teeth. *Vieille ogresse* with the *dents jaunes.* Maud Gonne, beautiful woman, *La Patrie,* M. Millevoye, Félix Faure,[6] know how he died? Licentious men. The froeken, *bonne à tout faire,*[7] who rubs male nakedness in the bath at Upsala. *Moi faire,* she said. *Tous les messieurs.*[8] Not this *Monsieur,* I said. Most licentious custom. Bath a most private thing. I wouldn't let my brother, not even my own brother, most lascivious thing. Green eyes, I see you. Fang, I feel. Lascivious people.

The blue fuse burns deadly between hands and burns clear. Loose tobacco shreds catch fire: a flame and acrid smoke light our corner. Raw facebones under his peep of day boy's hat. How the head centre got away, authentic version. Got up as a young bride, man, veil, orangeblossoms, drove out the road to Malahide. Did, faith. Of lost leaders, the betrayed, wild escapes. Disguises, clutched at, gone, not here.[9]

Spurned lover. I was a strapping young gossoon[1] at that time, I tell you, I'll show you my likeness one day. I was, faith. Lover, for her love he prowled with colonel Richard Burke, tanist[2] of his sept, under the walls of Clerkenwell[3] and, crouching, saw a flame of vengeance hurl them upward in the fog. Shattered glass and toppling masonry. In gay Paree he hides, Egan of Paris, unsought by any save by me. Making his day's stations, the dingy printingcase, his three taverns, the Montmartre lair he sleeps short night in, rue de la Goutte-d'Or, damascened with flyblown faces of the

3. Gaelic, "Your health!"
4. Two extremes of Irish history: from the Dalcassian line came the early kings of Munster (from A.D. 300 on); Arthur Griffith (1872–1922) was an Irish revolutionary leader, founder of the Sinn Fein ("We Ourselves") movement.
5. Édouard Drumont (1844–1917), French politician and bitter anti-Semite.
6. Maud Gonne, the beautiful actress and violent Irish nationalist whom Yeats loved; "*La Patrie*": the Fatherland; Charles Millevoye (1782–1816), French poet; Félix Faure, 19th-century French statesman.
7. Maid-of-all-work (French, translating the preceding Swedish word).
8. "I do all the gentlemen" (in broken French).
9. Another Protean theme of change. Egan had told Stephen of his cousin James Stephens' escape from prison disguised as a bride (Stephens was really the cousin of Casey, the original of Egan in this episode).
1. Boy.
2. Successor-apparent to a Celtic chief. "Sept": clan.
3. District in east central London. Stephen is recalling Egan's conversation about the Fenian violence in London which necessitated his fleeing to France.

gone. Loveless, landless, wifeless. She is quite nicey comfy without her outcast man,⁴ madame, in rue Gît-le-Coeur, canary and two buck lodgers. Peachy cheeks, a zebra skirt, frisky as a young thing's. Spurned and undespairing. Tell Pat⁵ you saw me, won't you? I wanted to get poor Pat a job one time. *Mon fils*, soldier of France. I taught him to sing. *The boys of Kilkenny are stout roaring blades.* Know that old lay? I taught Patrice that. Old Kilkenny:⁶ saint Canice, Strongbow's castle on the Nore. Goes like this. O, O. He takes me, Napper Tandy,⁷ by the hand.

> O, O the boys of
> Kilkenny. . .

Weak wasting hand on mine. They have forgotten Kevin Egan, not he them. Remembering thee, O Sion.⁸

He had come nearer the edge of the sea and wet sand slapped his boots. The new air greeted him, harping in wild nerves, wind of wild air of seeds of brightness. Here, I am not walking out to the Kish lightship, am I? He stood suddenly, his feet beginning to sink slowly in the quaking soil. Turn back.

Turning, he scanned the shore south, his feet sinking again slowly in new sockets. The cold domed room of the tower⁹ waits. Through the barbicans¹ the shafts of light are moving ever, slowly ever as my feet are sinking, creeping duskward over the dial floor. Blue dusk, nightfall, deep blue night. In the darkness of the dome they wait, their pushedback chairs, my obelisk valise, around a board of abandoned platters. Who to clear it? He has the key.² I will not sleep there when this night comes. A shut door of a silent tower entombing their blind bodies, the panthersahib and his pointer.³ Call: no answer. He lifted his feet up from the suck and turned back by the mole of boulders. Take all, keep all. My soul walks with me, form of forms. So in the moon's midwatches I pace the path above the rocks, in sable silvered, hearing Elsinore's tempting flood.⁴

4. I.e., Egan's wife, who is "quite nicey comfy" in the metaphorical "rue Git-le-Cœur" (i.e., the street where the heart lies dead) back home in Ireland.
5. Patrice, Egan's son.
6. Kilkenny is called after the Irish St. Canice (its Irish name is Cill Chainnigh), on the river Nore, where Strongbow (the second Earl of Pembroke, who invaded Ireland in the 12th century), had his stronghold.
7. James Napper Tandy (1740–1803), Irish revolutionary, hero of the song *The Wearing of the Green.*
8. Cf. Psalm cxxxvii.1 (in the King James Bible): "we wept, when we remembered Zion." But "Zion" in the Douay (Roman Catholic) Bible, is spelled "Sion," and the Book of Common Prayer has "When we remembered thee, O Sion."

9. Where Stephen lived with Buck Mulligan.
1. Outworks of a castle.
2. In the preceding episode, Mulligan asked for and got the key of the tower from Stephen.
3. I.e., Mulligan and the Englishman Haines, who live with Stephen in the tower. Stephen thinks of them as calling for him in vain, since he has decided not to return.
4. Cf. *Hamlet* I.ii.242, where the ghost of Hamlet's murdered father is described as having a beard of "sable silver'd." Allusions to *Hamlet* occur often in *Ulysses;* in a later episode Stephen expounds the theory that Shakespeare is to be identified, not with Hamlet himself, but with his betrayed father.

The flood is following me. I can watch it flow past from here. Get back then by the Poolbeg road to the strand there. He climbed over the sedge and eely oarweeds and sat on a stool of rock, resting his ashplant in a grike.

A bloated carcass of a dog lay lolled on bladderwrack. Before him the gunwale of a boat, sunk in sand. *Un coche ensablé.*[5] Louis Veuillot called Gautier's prose. These heavy sands are language tide and wind have silted here. And there, the stoneheaps of dead builders, a warren of weasel rats. Hide gold there. Try it. You have some. Sands and stones. Heavy of the past. Sir Lout's toys. Mind you don't get one bang on the ear. I'm the bloody well gigant rolls all them bloody well boulders, bones for my steppingstones. Feefawfum. I zmells de bloodz oldz an Iridzman.[6]

A point, live dog, grew into sight running across the sweep of sand. Lord, is he going to attack me? Respect his liberty. You will not be master of others or their slave. I have my stick. Sit tight. From farther away, walking shoreward across from the crested tide, figures, two. The two maries. They have tucked it safe among the bulrushes. Peekaboo. I see you. No, the dog. He is running back to them. Who?

Galleys of the Lochlanns[7] ran here to beach, in quest of prey, their bloodbeaked prows riding low on a molten pewter surf. Dane vikings, torcs of tomahawks aglitter on their breasts when Malachi wore the collar of gold. A school of turlehide whales stranded in hot noon, spouting, hobbling in the shallows. Then from the starving cagework city a horde of jerkined dwarfs, my people, with flayers' knives, running, scaling, hacking in green blubbery whalemeat. Famine, plague and slaughters. Their blood is in me, their lusts my waves. I moved among them on the frozen Liffey, that I, a changeling, among the spluttering resin fires. I spoke to no-one: none to me.

The dog's bark ran towards him, stopped, ran back.[8] Dog of my enemy. I just simply stood pale, silent, bayed about. *Terribilia meditans.*[9] A primrose doublet, fortune's knave, smiled on my fear. For that are you pining, the bark of their applause? Pretenders: live their lives. The Bruce's brother, Thomas Fitzgerald, silken knight, Perkin Warbeck, York's false scion, in breeches of silk of whiterose ivory, wonder of a day, and Lambert Simnel, with a tail

5. "A coach embedded in the sand." Louis Veuillot was a 19th-century French journalist; Théophile Gautier, a 19th-century French poet, novelist, and critic.
6. Stephen is thinking of the boulders on the shore as the work of a large but clumsy giant ("Sir Lout"). "They [Sir Lout and his family] were giants right enough * * * My Sir Lout has rocks in his mouth instead of teeth. He articulates badly" (Joyce to Frank Budgen, reported in Budgen's *James*

Joyce and the Making of Ulysses, 1934).
7. Scandinavians (Gaelic). Stephen is meditating on the Vikings who settled Dublin; it was here that they came ashore, he thinks.
8. The dog in this and subsequent paragraphs keeps changing in appearance; he "is the mummer among beasts—the Protean animal" (Joyce to Budgen). Joyce himself was afraid of dogs.
9. "Meditating terrible things."

of naus and sutlers, a scullion crowned.[1] All kings' sons. Paradise
of pretenders then and now. He saved men from drowning[2] and
you shake at a cur's yelping. But the courtiers who mocked Guido
in Or san Michele were in their own house. House of . . . We
don't want any of your medieval abstrusiosities. Would you do what
he did? A boat would be near, a lifebuoy. *Natürlich*,[3] put there for
you. Would you or would you not? The man that was drowned nine
days ago off Maiden's rock. They are waiting for him now. The
truth, spit it out. I would want to. I would try. I am not a strong
swimmer. Water cold soft. When I put my face into it in the basin
at Clongowes. Can't see! Who's behind me? Out quickly, quickly!
Do you see the tide flowing quickly in on all sides, sheeting the
lows of sands quickly, shellcocoacoloured? If I had land under my
feet. I want his life still to be his, mine to be mine. A drowning
man. His human eyes scream to me out of horror of his death.
I. . . With him together down . . . I could not save her.[4] Waters: bitter death: lost.

A woman and a man. I see her skirties. Pinned up, I bet.

Their dog ambled about a bank of dwindling sand, trotting,
sniffing on all sides. Looking for something lost in a past life. Suddenly he made off like a bounding hare, ears flung back, chasing
the shadow of a lowskimming gull. The man's shrieked whistle
struck his limp ears. He turned, bounded back, came nearer, trotted
on twinkling shanks. On a field tenney a buck, trippant, proper,
unattired.[5] At the lacefringe of the tide he halted with stiff fore-
hoofs, seawardpointed ears. His snout lifted barked at the wave-
noise, herds of seamorse. They serpented towards his feet, curling,
unfurling many crests, every ninth, breaking, plashing, from far,
from farther out, waves and waves.

Cocklepickers.[6] They waded a little way in the water and, stooping, soused their bags, and, lifting them again, waded out. The dog
yelped running to them, reared up and pawed them, dropping on
all fours, again reared up at them with mute bearish fawning. Unheeded he kept by them as they came towards the drier sand, a
rag of wolf's tongue redpanting from his jaws. His speckled body
ambled ahead of them and then loped off at a calf's gallop. The
carcass lay on his path. He stopped, sniffed, stalked round it,

1. Stephen is meditating on pretenders (i.e., false claimants): the names
here are those of pretenders who have
figured in English history. This is the
Proteus theme again—disguises and
changes.
2. Mulligan had saved a man from
drowning.
3. Of course.
4. A man had been drowned off the
coast, and his body had not yet been
recovered. As Stephen thinks of the
horror of drowning he recalls once
again his mother's death.

5. At this point in its constantly changing appearance the dog looks like a
heraldic animal and is described in the
language of heraldry; the sentence "On
a field * * * unattired" means: "On
an orange-brown (tawny) background,
a buck, tripping, in natural colors, without horns."
6. Stephen recognizes the man and
woman on the beach as gypsy cockle-
pickers (cockles are edible shellfish,
like mussels).

brother, nosing closer, went round it, sniffling rapidly like a dog all over the dead dog's bedraggled fell. Dogskull, dogsniff, eyes on the ground, moves to one great goal. Ah, poor dogsbody. Here lies poor dogsbody's body.

—Tatters! Out of that, you mongrel.

The cry brought him skulking back to his master and a blunt bootless kick sent him unscathed across a spit of sand, crouched in flight. He slunk back in a curve. Doesn't see me. Along by the edge of the mole he lolloped, dawdled, smelt a rock and from under a cocked hindleg pissed against it. He trotted forward and, lifting his hindleg, pissed quick short at an unsmelt rock. The simple pleasures of the poor. His hindpaws then scattered sand: then his forepaws dabbled and delved. Something he buried there, his grandmother.[7] He rooted in the sand, dabbling, delving and stopped to listen to the air, scraped up the sand again with a fury of his claws, soon ceasing, a pard,[8] a panther, got in spousebreach,[9] vulturing the dead.

After he woke me up last night same dream or was it? Wait. Open hallway. Street of harlots. Remember. Haroun al Raschid.[1] I am almosting it. That man led me, spoke. I was not afraid. The melon he had he held against my face. Smiled: creamfruit smell. That was the rule, said. In. Come. Red carpet spread. You will see who.

Shouldering their bags they trudged, the red Egyptians.[2] His blued feet out of turnedup trousers slapped the clammy sand, a dull brick muffler strangling his unshaven neck. With woman steps she followed: the ruffian and his strolling mort.[3] Spoils slung at her back. Loose sand and shellgrit crusted her bare feet. About her windraw face her hair trailed. Behind her lord his helpmate, bing awast, to Romeville.[4] When night hides her body's flaws calling under her brown shawl from an archway where dogs have mired. Her fancyman is treating two Royal Dublins in O'Loughlin's of Blackpitts. Buss her, wap in rogue's rum lingo, for, O, my dimber wapping dell.[5] A shefiend's whiteness under her rancid rags. Fumbally's lane that night: the tanyard smells.

7. Reference to a joke Stephen had made to his pupils in school that morning about "the fox burying his grandmother under a hollybush." This has many symbolic reverberations throughout *Ulysses*. The buried grandmother suggests Stephen's mother, the Church, and Ireland (the "Poor Old Woman"), while the hollybush, evergreen tree of life, represents resurrection in which, in spite of his religious disbelief, Stephen is much interested and about which (as about metempsychosis) he is continually brooding.
8. Leopard or panther.
9. I.e., begotten in adultery.
1. Stephen's dream of the famous Caliph of Baghdad, of the "street of harlots," and of his meeting a man with a melon, foreshadows his meeting later in the day with Leopold Bloom and his visit to the brothel area of Dublin.
2. I.e., gypsies. As Stephen watches the gypsy cockle-pickers with their dog he imagines their vagabond life and recalls fragments of gypsy speech and of thieves' slang.
3. Gypsies' "freewoman" (i.e., a harlot). "Spoils": the association gypsy-Egyptian reminds Stephen of the Israelites "spoiling the Egyptians" in Exodus xii.36.
4. Go away to London.
5. 17th-century thieves' slang—"buss":

> *White thy fambles, red thy gan*
> *And thy quarrons dainty is.*
> *Couch a hogshead with me then.*
> *In the darkmans clip and kiss.*[6]

Morose delectation Aquinas tunbelly calls this, *frate porcospino.*[7] Unfallen Adam rode and not rutted. Call away let him:[8] *thy quarrons dainty is.* Language no whit worse than his. Monkwords, marybeads jabber on their girdles: roguewords, tough nuggets patter in their pockets.

Passing now.

A side-eye at my Hamlet hat. If I were suddenly naked here as I sit? I am not. Across the sands of all the world, followed by the sun's flaming sword, to the west, trekking to evening lands. She trudges, schlepps, trains, drags, trascines her load.[9] A tide westering, moondrawn, in her wake. Tides, myriadislanded, within her, blood not mine, *oinopa ponton,*[1] a winedark sea. Behold the handmaid of the moon. In sleep the wet sign calls her hour, bids her rise. Bridebed, childbed, bed of death, ghostcandled.[2] *Omnis caro ad te veniet.* He comes, pale vampire, through storm his eyes, his bat sails bloodying the sea, mouth to her mouth's kiss.[3]

Here. Put a pin in that chap, will you? My tablets.[4] Mouth to her kiss. No. Must be two of em. Glue 'em well. Mouth to her mouth's kiss.

His lips lipped and mouthed fleshless lips of air: mouth to her womb. Oomb, allwombing tomb.[5] His mouth moulded issuing breath, unspeeched: ooeeehah: roar of cataractic planets, globed, blazing, roaring wayawayawayawayawayaway. Paper. The banknotes, blast them. Old Deasy's letter. Here. Thanking you for hospitality tear the blank end off. Turning his back to the sun he bent over far to a table of rock and scribbled words.[6] That's twice I forgot to take slips from the library counter.

His shadow lay over the rocks as he bent, ending. Why not endless till the farthest star? Darkly they are there behind this light,

kiss; "wap": copulate with; "rum": good; "dimber": pretty; "wapping dell": whore.
6. More thieves' slang: "fambles": hands; "gan": mouth; "quarrons": body; "couch a hogshead": come to bed; "darkmans": night; "clip": kiss. These four lines and some of the phrases in the preceding paragraph are quoted from a song of the period, *The Rogue's Delight in Praise of His Strolling Mort* (cf. note 3).
7. "Brother porcupine" (Italian), a reference to the fat ("tunbelly") but prickly philosopher, St. Thomas Aquinas.
8. The gypsy is calling his dog.
9. All words suggesting moving or dragging. " 'I like that crescendo of verbs,' he [Joyce] said. 'The irresistible tug of the tides' " (Budgen).

1. "Winedark sea" (Homer).
2. He is thinking of his mother again. The Latin (from the burial service) means: "All flesh will come to thee."
3. Death comes like the Flying Dutchman in a phantom ship to give the fatal kiss.
4. Cf. Hamlet I.v.107: "My tablets!"
5. Stephen's consciousness here can be illuminated with reference to Blake's poem *The Gates of Paradise,* which concludes: "The door of death I open found / And the worm weaving in the ground: / Thou'rt my mother from the womb, / Wife, sister, daughter, to the tomb * * * " Cf. also "the earth that's nature's mother is her tomb. / What is her burying ground that is her womb * * * " (*Romeo and Juliet,* II.iii.9–10).
6. Stephen tears off the blank end of Mr. Deasy's letter to the press and

darkness shining in the brightness, delta of Cassiopeia, worlds. Me sits there with his augur's rod of ash, in borrowed sandals, by day beside a livid sea, unbeheld, in violet night walking beneath a reign of uncouth stars.[7] I throw this ended shadow from me, man-shape ineluctable, call it back. Endless, would it be mine, form of my form? Who watches me here? Who ever anywhere will read these written words? Signs on a white field. Somewhere to someone in your flutiest voice. The good bishop of Cloyne[8] took the veil of the temple out of his shovel hat: veil of space with coloured emblems hatched on its field. Hold hard. Coloured on a flat: yes, that's right. Flat I see, then think distance, near, far, flat I see, east, back. Ah, see now. Falls back suddenly, frozen in stereoscope. Click does the trick. You find my words dark. Darkness is in our souls, do you not think? Flutier. Our souls, shamewounded by our sins, cling to us yet more, a woman to her lover clinging, the more the more.

She trusts me, her hand gentle, the longlashed eyes. Now where the blue hell am I bringing her beyond the veil?[9] Into the ineluctable modality of the ineluctable visuality. She, she, she. What she? The virgin at Hodges Figgis' window on Monday looking in for one of the alphabet books you were going to write. Keen glance you gave her. Wrist through the braided jess of her sunshade. She lives in Leeson park, with a grief and kickshaws, a lady of letters. Talk that to some else, Stevie: a pickmeup. Bet she wears those curse of God stays suspenders and yellow stockings, darned with lumpy wool. Talk about apple dumplings, *piuttosto*.[1] Where are your wits?

Touch me. Soft eyes. Soft soft soft hand. I am lonely here. O, touch me soon, now. What is that word known to all men? I am quiet here alone. Sad too. Touch, touch me.

He lay back at full stretch over the sharp rocks, cramming the scribbled note and pencil into a pocket, his hat tilted down on his eyes. That is Kevin Egan's movement I made nodding for his nap, sabbath sleep. *Et vidit Deus. Et erant valde bona.*[2] Alo! *Bonjour,* welcome as the flowers in May. Under its leaf he watched through peacocktwittering lashes the southing sun. I am caught in this burn-

---

writes a poem that will be quoted later in the novel.
7. He imagines himself as the constellation Cassiopeia, supposed to represent the wife of Cepheus (an Ethiopian king) seated in a chair and holding up her arms. His ash walking stick he thinks of as an "augur's [Roman soothsayer's] rod of ash."
8. George Berkeley, Bishop of Cloyne (in Ireland), 1685-1753, who argued that the external world has no objective reality but exists only in the mind of the perceiver. Stephen (as at the opening of this episode) is experimenting again with ways of sensing reality.
9. "She" is Psyche, the soul, whom he is bringing from "beyond the veil." But from metaphysical speculations on reality and the soul Stephen is led (by the Psyche association) to think of "the virgin at Hodges Figgis' window."
1. Rather, sooner.
2. Connecting two phrases from the Vulgate: "And God saw" (Genesis i.4) and "And they were very good" (Genesis i.31).

ing scene. Pan's hour, the faunal noon. Among gumheavy serpent-
plants, milkoozing fruits, where on the tawny waters leaves lie wide.
Pain is far.

And no more turn aside and brood.[3]

His gaze brooded on his broadtoed boots, a buck's castoffs
nebeneinander. He counted the creases of rucked leather wherein
another's foot had nested warm. The foot that beat the ground
in tripudium, foot I dislove. But you were delighted when Esther
Osvalt's shoe went on you: girl I knew in Paris. *Tiens, quel petit
pied!*[4] Staunch friend, a brother soul: Wilde's love that dare not
speak its name. He now will leave me. And the blame? As I am.
As I am. All or not at all.

In long lassoes from the Cock lake the water flowed full, covering greengoldenly lagoons of sand, rising, flowing. My ashplant will
float away. I shall wait. No, they will pass on, passing chafing
against the low rocks, swirling, passing. Better get this job over
quick. Listen: a fourworded wavespeech: seesoo, hrss, rsseeiss ooos.
Vehement breath of waters amid seasnakes, rearing horses, rocks.
In cups of rocks it slops: flop, slop, slap: bounded in barrels. And,
spent, its speech ceases. It flows purling, widely flowing, floating
foampool, flower unfurling.

Under the upswelling tide he saw the writhing weeds lift languidly and sway reluctant arms, hising up their petticoats,[5] in
whispering water swaying and upturning coy silver fronds. Day by
day: night by night: lifted, flooded and let fall. Lord, they are
weary: and, whispered to, they sigh. Saint Ambrose heard it, sigh
of leaves and waves, waiting, awaiting the fullness of their times,
diebus ac noctibus iniurias patiens ingemiscit.[6] To no end gathered:
vainly then released, forth flowing, wending back: loom of the
moon. Weary too in sight of lovers, lascivious men, a naked woman
shining in her courts, she draws a toil of waters.

Five fathoms out there. Full fathom five thy father lies.[7] At once
he said. Found drowned. High water at Dublin bar. Driving before it a loose drift of rubble, fanshoals of fishes, silly shells. A
corpse rising saltwhite from the undertow, bobbing landward, a
pace a pace a porpoise. There he is. Hook it quick. Sunk though
he be beneath the watery floor. We have him. Easy now.

3. The first line of the second (and last) stanza of Yeats's poem *Who Goes with Fergus,* which is often in Stephen's mind. The line expresses for him the mood of noontide stillness and of lotos-eating in a lush oriental scene which overcomes him momentarily when he realizes that it is 12 o'clock, the hour of the Greek nature god Pan, "faunal noon." This oriental lotos-eating theme, which is associated also with Bloom, is important in the *Ulysses.*
4. "Look, what a little foot!"
5. A phrase from a vulgar song sung by Mulligan earlier that morning.
6. "Night and day he patiently groaned forth his wrongs" (St. Ambrose).
7. The theme of the drowned man is important in this episode (cf. the drowned sailor in Eliot's *Waste Land*). This line is from Ariel's song in *The Tempest* (I.ii.396).

Bag of corpsegas sopping in foul brine. A quiver of minnows, fat of a spongy titbit, flash though the slits of his buttoned trouserfly. God becomes man becomes fish becomes barnacle goose becomes featherbed mountain. Dead breaths I living breathe, tread dead dust, devour a urinous offal from all dead. Hauled stark over the gunwale he breathes upward the stench of his green grave, his leprous nosehole snoring to the sun.

A seachange this, brown eyes saltblue. Seadeath, mildest of all deaths known to man. Old Father Ocean. *Prix de Paris:*[8] beware of imitations. Just you give it a fair trial. We enjoyed ourselves immensely.

Come. I thirst. Clouding over. No black clouds anywhere, are there?[9] Thunderstorm. Allbright he falls, proud lightning of the intellect, *Lucifer, dico, qui nescit occasum.*[1] No. My cockle hat and staff and his my sandal shoon.[2] Where? To evening lands. Evening will find itself.

He took the hilt of his ashplant, lunging with it softly, dallying still. Yes, evening will find itself in me, without me. All days make their end. By the way next when is it? Tuesday will be the longest day. Of all the glad new year, mother,[3] the rum tum tiddledy tum. Lawn Tennyson, gentleman poet. *Già.*[4] For the old hag with the yellow teeth. And Monsieur Drumont, gentleman journalist. *Già.* My teeth are very bad. Why, I wonder? Feel. That one is going too. Shells. Ought I go to a dentist, I wonder, with what money? That one. Toothless Kinch, the superman. Why is that, I wonder, or does it mean something perhaps?

My handkerchief. He threw it. I remember. Did I not take it up?

His hand groped vainly in his pockets. No, I didn't. Better buy one.

He laid the dry snot picked from his nostril on a ledge of rock, carefully. For the rest let look who will.

Behind. Perhaps there is someone.

He turned his face over a shoulder, rere regardant.[5] Moving

8. "Prize of Paris"; the reference is probably to the Paris Exposition of 1889, where prizes were awarded in various categories of food, etc.: the prize-winning commodities bear the seal of the prize on the label (hence, "beware of imitations"). Stephen mentally awards the prize to death by drowning. "Seachange" is from Ariel's song, once more.
9. Stephen is looking up to make sure the sky does not threaten a thunderstorm; like Joyce, he hates thunder.
1. Thunder and lightning recall the Fall of Lucifer, "Lucifer, I say, who knows not his fall."
2. From Ophelia's mad song (*Hamlet*, IV.v.23–26): "How should I your true-love know / From another one? / By his cockle hat and staff, / And his sandal shoon." Ophelia, too, was drowned.
3. "You must wake and call me early, call me early, mother dear; / Tomorrow 'ill be the happiest time of all the glad New Year * * * " From *The May Queen* by Alfred, Lord Tennyson ("Lawn Tennyson").
4. Of course!
5. Looking behind him (heraldic terminology). Stephen, as we leave him sitting by the shore, is described in a highly stylized, heraldic language, as though he had himself become a work of art.

through the air high spars of a threemaster, her sails brailed up on the crosstrees,[6] homing, upstream, silently moving, a silent ship.

[*Lestrygonians*][1]

Pineapple rock, lemon platt, butter scotch. A sugarsticky girl shovelling scoopfuls of creams for a christian brother. Some school treat. Bad for their tummies. Lozenge and comfit manufacturer to His Majesty the King. God. Save. Our. Sitting on his throne, sucking red jujubes white.

A sombre Y. M. C. A. young man, watchful among the warm sweet fumes of Graham Lemon's, placed a throwaway in a hand of Mr Bloom.

Heart to heart talks.

Bloo . . . Me? No.

Blood of the Lamb.[2]

His slow feet walked him riverward, reading. Are you saved? All are washed in the blood of the lamb. God wants blood victim. Birth, hymen, martyr, war, foundation of a building, sacrifice, kidney burntoffering, druid's altars. Elijah is coming. Dr John Alex-

---

6. When Budgen pointed out to Joyce that "crosstrees" was not the proper nautical term for the spars to which the sails are bent Joyce thanked him but added: "But the word 'crosstrees' is essential. It comes in later on and I can't change it. After all, a yard is also a crosstree for the onlooking landlubber." Joyce later uses "crosstree" in a reference to the crucifixion of Christ, so that the suggestion here is of Stephen as both artist and martyr (as his name implies). But the ship is also a real ship, which actually arrived in Dublin on June 16, 1904.

1. It is lunch time in Dublin and Leopold Bloom, as he walks through the city in no great hurry (for he likes to linger and watch what goes on around him), thinks of food. The Lestrygonians in Book X of the *Odyssey* are cannibals, and throughout this episode there are suggestions of the slaughter of living creatures for food, or of food as something disgusting, which make somewhat tenuous contact with Homer's description of the cannibals spearing Ulysses' men for food; the parallel is not, however, profound or very important. What is most important about this episode is that it shows us Bloom's consciousness responding to the sights and sounds of Dublin. His humane curiosity, his desire to learn and to improve the human lot, his sympathetic concern for Mrs. Breen and Mrs. Purefoy, his feeding the gulls, his recollections of a happier time when his daugh-

ter was a baby and his relations with his wife Molly were thoroughly satisfactory, his interest in opera, his continuous obying away from thoughts of his wife's rendezvous with the dashing Blazes Boylan—all this helps to build up his character in depth and to differentiate him sharply from Stephen. Unlike Stephen, Bloom's interest in language is confined to simple puns and translations, his interest in poetry is obvious and sentimental; his interest in the nature of reality takes the form of half-forgotten fragments of science remaining in his mind from schooldays. Everything about him is concrete, practical, sensual, and middlebrow or lowbrow, as distinct from the abstract, theoretical, esoteric speculations of Stephen in the "Proteus" episode. For example, when Stephen saw seagulls, he speculated on Daedalus and on flying as a symbol of the artist going into exile; when Bloom sees them, he thinks they must be hungry and buys a bun to feed them. There are parallels between their two streams of consciousness. Bloom's thoughts, in a sense, include Stephen's, but in a popularized and even vulgarized form.

The text of this selection has also been collated with the Odyssey Press edition of 1932.

2. Bloom has been handed a religious leaflet ("throwaway") containing the phrase "Blood of the Lamb." He at first mistakes "Blood" for "Bloom."

ander Dowie, restorer of the church in Zion, is coming.[3]

Is coming! Is coming!! Is coming!!!
All heartily welcome.

Paying game. Torry and Alexander last year. Polygamy. His wife will put the stopper on that. Where was that ad some Birmingham firm the luminous crucifix? Our Saviour. Wake up in the dead of night and see him on the wall, hanging. Pepper's ghost idea. Iron nails ran in.

Phosphorous it must be done with. If you leave a bit of codfish for instance. I could see the bluey silver over it. Night I went down to the pantry in the kitchen. Don't like all the smells in it waiting to rush out. What was it she wanted?[4] The Malaga raisins. Thinking of Spain. Before Rudy[5] was born. The phosphorescence, that bluey greeny. Very good for the brain.

From Butler's monument house corner he glanced along Bachelor's walk. Dedalus' daughter there still outside Dillon's auction-rooms. Must be selling off some old furniture. Knew her eyes at once from the father. Lobbing about waiting for him. Home always breaks up when the mother goes. Fifteen children he had. Birth every year almost. That's in their theology or the priest won't give the poor woman the confession, the absolution. Increase and multiply. Did you ever hear such an ïdea? Eat you out of house and home. No families themselves to feed. Living on the fat of the land. Their butteries and larders. I'd like to see them do the black fast Yom Kippur.[6] Crossbuns. One meal and a collation for fear he'd collapse on the altar. A housekeeper of one of those fellows if you could pick it out of her. Never pick it out of her. Like getting L s. d.[7] out of him. Does himself well. No guests. All for number one. Watching his water. Bring your own bread and butter. His reverence. Mum's the word.

Good Lord, that poor child's dress is in flitters. Underfed she looks too. Potatoes and marge, marge and potatoes. It's after they feel it. Proof of the pudding. Undermines the constitution.

As he set foot on O'Connell bridge a puffball of smoke plumed up from the parapet. Brewery barge with export stout. England. Sea air sours it, I heard. Be interesting some day get a pass through Hancock to see the brewery. Regular world in itself. Vats of porter, wonderful. Rats get in too. Drink themselves bloated as big as a collie floating. Dead drunk on the porter. Drink till they puke again

---

3. Dowie was a Scottish-American evangelist who established the "Christian Catholic Apostolic Church in Zion" (i.e., Zion City, Illinois) in 1901.
4. "She" is Bloom's wife Molly, born in Gibraltar.

5. Their son, who had died in infancy eleven years before.
6. Jewish Day of Atonement.
7. I.e., cash: £, s., d. are the abbreviations, respectively, for pounds, shillings, and pence.

like christians. Imagine drinking that! Rats: vats. Well of course
if we knew all the things.

Looking down he saw flapping strongly, wheeling between the
gaunt quay walls, gulls. Rough weather outside. If I threw myself
down? Reuben J's son must have swallowed a good bellyful of that
sewage.[8] One and eightpence too much. Hhhhm. It's the droll way
he comes out with the things. Knows how to tell a story too.

They wheeled lower. Looking for grub. Wait.

He threw down among them a crumpled paper ball. Elijah
thirtytwo feet per sec is com.[9] Not a bit. The ball bobbed unheeded on the wake of swells, floated under by the bridge piers.
Not such damn fools. Also the day I threw that stale cake out of
the Erin's King picked it up in the wake fifty yards astern. Live
by their wits. They wheeled, flapping.

> *The hungry famished gull*
> *Flaps o'er the waters dull.*

That is how poets write, the similar sounds. But then Shakespeare has no rhymes. blank verse. The flow of the language it
is. The thoughts. Solemn.

> *Hamlet, I am thy father's spirit*
> *Doomed for a certain time to walk the earth.*[1]

—Two apples a penny! Two for a penny!

His gaze passed over the glazed apples serried on her stand.
Australians they must be this time of year. Shiny peels: polishes
them up with a rag or a handkerchief.

Wait. Those poor birds.

He halted again and bought from the old applewoman two Ban-
bury cakes for a penny and broke the brittle paste and threw its
fragments down into the Liffey. See that? The gulls swooped silently two, then all, from their heights, pouncing on prey. Gone.
Every morsel.

Aware of their greed and cunning he shook the powdery crumb
from his hands. They never expected that. Manna.[2] Live on fishy
flesh they have to, all sea birds, gulls, seagoose. Swans from Anna

8. Reuben J. Dodd, Dublin solicitor
(lawyer), whose son had been rescued
from the Liffey River by a man to
whom Reuben J. had given two shillings as a reward—"one and eightpence
too much," as Simon Dedalus had remarked to Bloom earlier that morning
when they were discussing the incident.
It is Dedalus' comment that Bloom is
thinking of in the following sentences.

9. I.e., Elijah is coming, accelerating
at the rate of 32 feet per second per
second, the acceleration rate of falling
bodies. ("Elijah is coming" is the legend
on the handbill Bloom is tossing away).
1. *Hamlet* I.v.9–10 (slightly misquoted).
2. The divine food (small, round, and
white) which the children of Israel ate
in the wilderness (Exodus xvi.14–15).

Liffey[3] swim down here sometimes to preen themselves. No accounting for tastes. Wonder what kind is swanmeat. Robinson Crusoe had to live on them.

They wheeled, flapping weakly. I'm not going to throw any more. Penny quite enough. Lot of thanks I get. Not even a caw. They spread foot and mouth disease too. If you cram a turkey, say, on chestnut meal it tastes like that. Eat pig like pig. But then why is it that saltwater fish are not salty? How is that?

His eyes sought answer from the river and saw a rowboat rock at anchor on the treacly swells lazily its plastered board.

Kino's
11/–
Trousers.[4]

Good idea that. Wonder if he pays rent to the corporation. How can you own water really? It's always flowing in a stream, never the same, which in the stream of life we trace. Because life is a stream. All kinds of places are good for ads. That quack doctor for the clap used to be stuck up in all the greenhouses. Never see it now. Strictly confidential. Dr Hy Franks. Didn't cost him a red like Maginni the dancing master self advertisement. Got fellows to stick them up or stick them up himself for that matter on the q. t. running in to loosen a button. Fly by night. Just the place too. Post No Bills. Post No Pills. Some chap with a dose burning him. If he. . .

O!

Eh?

No . . . No.

No, no. I don't believe it. He wouldn't surely?

No, no.[5]

Mr Bloom moved forward raising his troubled eyes. Think no more about that. After one. Timeball on the ballast office is down. Dunsink time. Fascinating little book that is of Sir Robert Ball's.[6] Parallax. I never exactly understood. There's a priest. Could ask

3. The Liffey flows from the Wicklow Mountains northeast and east to Dublin Bay.
4. I.e., eleven shillings ("11/–") for Kino's Trousers. Bloom is a canvasser for advertisements: he receives commissions from newspapers for getting tradesmen to place advertisements with them.
5. Blazes Boylan, flashy philanderer, is due to call on Molly Bloom that afternoon, to discuss the program of a concert which he is managing for her (Molly is a singer). Bloom knows that Boylan and his wife will commit adultery together. Here it suddenly occurs to him that Boylan might give Molly

a "dose" of venereal disease, but he puts the thought from him as incredible.
6. The "timeball on the ballastoffice" registers the official time of the observatory at Dunsink. Noticing that the timeball is down, which means that it is after 1 o'clock, Bloom is reminded of the observatory, then of the Irish astronomer Sir Robert Ball's popular book on astronomy, *The Story of the Heavens* (1886), and of the astronomical term "parallax" he found in the book but which he "never exactly understood."

him. Par it's Greek: parallel, parallax. Met him pikehoses[7] she called it till I told her about the transmigration. O rocks!

Mr Bloom smiled O rocks at two windows of the ballast office. She's right after all. Only big words for ordinary things on account of the sound. She's not exactly witty. Can be rude too. Blurt out what I was thinking. Still I don't know. She used to say Ben Dollard had a base barreltone voice. He has legs like barrels and you'd think he was singing into a barrel. Now, isn't that wit? They used to call him big Ben. Not half as witty as calling him base barreltone. Appetite like an albatross. Get outside of a baron of beef. Powerful man he was at storing away number one Bass.[8] Barrel of Bass. See? It all works out.

A procession of whitesmocked men marched slowly towards him along the gutter, scarlet sashes across their boards. Bargains. Like that priest they are this morning: we have sinned: we have suffered. He read the scarlet letters on their five tall white hats: H. E. L. Y. S. Wisdom Hely's. Y lagging behind drew a chunk of bread from under his foreboard, crammed it into his mouth and munched as he walked. Our staple food. Three bob a day, walking along the gutters, street after street. Just keep skin and bone together, bread and skilly. They are not Boyl: no: M'Glade's men. Doesn't bring in any business either. I suggested to him about a transparent show cart with two smart girls sitting inside writing letters, copybooks, envelopes, blotting paper. I bet that would have caught on. Smart girls writing something catch the eye at once. Everyone dying to know what she's writing. Get twenty of them round you if you stare at nothing. Have a finger in the pie. Women too. Curiosity. Pillar of salt. Wouldn't have it of course because he didn't think of it himself first. Or the inkbottle I suggested with a false stain of black celluloid. His ideas for ads like Plumtree's potted under the obituaries, cold meat department. You can't lick 'em. What? Our envelopes. Hello! Jones, where are you going? Can't stop, Robinson, I am hastening to purchase the only reliable inkeraser *Kansell,* sold by Hely's Ltd, 85 Dame Street. Well out of that ruck I am. Devil of a job it was collecting accounts of those convents. Tranquilla convent. That was a nice nun there, really sweet face. Wimple suited her small head. Sister? Sister? I am sure she was crossed in love by her eyes. Very hard to bargain with that sort of woman. I disturbed her at her devotions that morning. But glad to communicate with the outside world. Our great day, she said.

7. Molly's way of pronouncing "metempsychosis." When Bloom had explained metempsychosis to her that morning, she had exclaimed "O rocks" at the pretentious term. He now mentally repeats "O rocks!" at the thought of the word "parallax."
8. A popular British beer.

Feast of Our Lady of Mount Carmel. Sweet name too: caramel. She knew, I think she knew by the way she. If she had married she would have changed. I suppose they really were short of money. Fried everything in the best butter all the same. No lard for them. My heart's broke eating dripping. They like buttering themselves in an out. Molly tasting it, her veil up. Sister? Pat Claffey, the pawnbroker's daughter. It was a nun they say invented barbed wire.

He crossed Westmoreland street when apostrophe S had plodded by. Rover cycleshop. Those races are on today. How long ago is that? Year Phil Gilligan died. We were in Lombard street west. Wait, was in Thom's. Got the job in Wisdom Hely's year we married. Six years. Ten years ago: ninetyfour he died, yes that's right, the big fire at Arnott's. Val Dillon was lord mayor. The Glencree dinner. Alderman Robert O'Reilly emptying the port into his soup before the flag fell, Bobbob lapping it for the inner alderman. Couldn't hear what the band played. For what we have already received may the Lord make us. Milly[9] was a kiddy then. Molly had that elephantgrey dress with the braided frogs. Mantailored with selfcovered buttons. She didn't like it because I sprained my ankle first day she wore choir picnic at the Sugarloaf. As if that. Old Goodwin's tall hat done up with some sticky stuff. Flies' picnic too. Never put a dress on her back like it. Fitted her like a glove, shoulder and hips. Just beginning to plump it out well. Rabbit pie we had that day. People looking after her.

Happy. Happier then. Snug little room that was with the red wallpaper, Dockrell's, one and ninepence a dozen. Milly's tubbing night. American soap I bought: elderflower. Cosy smell of her bathwater. Funny she looked soaped all over. Shapely too. Now photography.[1] Poor papa's daguerreotype atelier he told me of. Hereditary taste.

He walked along the curbstone.

Stream of life. What was the name of that priestlylooking chap was always squinting in when he passed? Weak eyes, woman. Stopped in Citron's saint Kevin's parade. Pen something. Pendennis? My memory is getting. Pen . . . ? of course it's years ago. Noise of the trams probably. Well, if he couldn't remember the dayfather's name that he sees every day.

Bartell d'Arcy was the tenor, just coming out then. Seeing her home after practice. Conceited fellow with his waxedup moustache. Gave her that song *Winds that blow from the south*.

Windy night that was I went to fetch her there was that lodge meeting on about those lottery tickets after Goodwin's concert in the supper room or oakroom of the mansion house. He and I be-

---

9. Bloom's 15-year-old daughter.   1. Milly is working at a photographer's.

hind. Sheet of her music blew out of my hand against the high
school railings. Lucky it didn't. Thing like that spoils the effect
of a night for her. Professor Goodwin linking her in front. Shaky
on his pins, poor old sot. His farewell concerts. Positively last appearance on any stage. May be for months and may be for never.
Remember her laughing at the wind, her blizzard collar up. Corner
of Harcourt road remember that gust? Brrfoo! Blew up all her skirts
and her boa nearly smothered old Goodwin. She did get flushed
in the wind. Remember when we got home raking up the fire and
frying up those pieces of lap of mutton for her supper with the
Chutney sauce she liked. And the mulled rum. Could see her in the
bedroom from the hearth unclamping the busk of her stays. White.

Swish and soft flop her stays made on the bed. Always warm
from her. Always liked to let herself out. Sitting there after till near
two, taking out her hairpins. Milly tucked up in beddyhouse. Happy.
Happy. That was the night. . .

—O, Mr Bloom, how do you do?

—O, how do you do, Mrs Breen?[2]

—No use complaining. How is Molly those times? Haven't seen
her for ages.

—In the pink, Mr Bloom said gaily, Milly has a position down
in Mullingar, you know.

—Go away! Isn't that grand for her?

—Yes, in a photographer's there. Getting on like a house on fire.
How are all your charges?

—All on the baker's list, Mrs Breen said.

How many has she? No other in sight.

—You're in black I see. You have no. . .

—No, Mr Bloom said. I have just come from a funeral.

Going to crop up all day, I foresee. Who's dead, when and what
did he die of? Turn up like a bad penny.

—O dear me, Mrs Breen said, I hope it wasn't any near relation.

May as well get her sympathy.

—Dignam, Mr Bloom said. An old friend of mine. He died quite
suddenly, poor fellow. Heart trouble, I believe. Funeral was this
morning.

> *Your funeral's tomorrow*
> *While you're coming through the rye.*
> *Diddlediddle dumdum*
> *Diddlediddle. . .*

—Sad to lose the old friends, Mrs Breen's woman eyes said mel-
ancholily.

Now that's quite enough about that. Just quietly: husband.

2. Mrs. Breen had been an old sweetheart of Bloom's.

—And your lord and master?

Mrs Breen turned up her two large eyes. Hasn't lost them anyhow.

—O, don't be talking, she said. He's a caution to rattlesnakes. He's in there now with his lawbooks finding out the law of libel. He has me heartscalded. Wait till I show you.

Hot mockturtle vapour and steam of newbaked jampuffs rolypoly poured out from Harrison's. The heavy noonreek tickled the top of Mr Bloom's gullet. Want to make good pastry, butter, best flour, Demerara sugar, or they'd taste it with the hot tea. Or is it from her? A barefoot arab stood over the grating, breathing in the fumes. Deaden the gnaw of hunger that way. Pleasure or pain is it? Penny dinner. Knife and fork chained to the table.

Opening her handbag, chipped leather, hatpin: ought to have a guard on those things. Stick it in a chap's eye in the tram. Rummaging. Open. Money. Please take one. Devils if they lose sixpence. Raise Cain. Husband barging. Where's the ten shillings I gave you on Monday? Are you feeding your little brother's family? Soiled handkerchief: medicinebottle. Pastille that was fell. What is she? . . .

—There must be a new moon out, she said. He's always bad then.[3] Do you know what he did last night?

Her hand ceased to rummage. Her eyes fixed themselves on him, wide in alarm, yet smiling.

—What? Mr Bloom asked.

Let her speak. Look straight in her eyes. I believe you. Trust me.

—Woke me up in the night, she said. Dream he had, a nightmare.

Indiges.

—Said the ace of spades[4] was walking up the stairs.

—The ace of spades! Mr Bloom said.

She took a folded postcard from her handbag.

—Read that, she said. He got it this morning.

—What is it? Mr Bloom asked, taking the card. U. P.?

—U. P.: up, she said. Someone taking a rise out of him. It's a great shame for them whoever he is.

—Indeed it is, Mr Bloom said.

She took back the card, sighing.

—And now he's going round to Mr Menton's office. He's going to take an action for ten thousand pounds, he says.

She folded the card into her untidy bag and snapped the catch.

Same blue serge dress she had two years ago, the nap bleaching. Seen its best days. Wispish hair over her ears. And that dowdy

3. Mr. Breen is mentally disturbed.   4. Symbol of death.

toque, three old grapes to take the harm out of it. Shabby genteel. She used to be a tasty dresser. Lines round her mouth. Only a year or so older than Molly.

See the eye that woman gave her, passing. Cruel. The unfair sex.

He looked still at her, holding back behind his look his discontent. Pungent mockturtle oxtail mulligatawny. I'm hungry too. Flakes of pastry on the gusset of her dress: daub of sugary flour stuck to her cheek. Rhubarb tart with liberal fillings, rich fruit interior. Josie Powell that was. In Luke Doyle's long ago, Dolphin's Barn, the charades. U. P.: up.

Change the subject.

—Do you ever see anything of Mrs Beaufoy, Mr Bloom asked.

—Mina Purefoy? she said.

Philip Beaufoy I was thinking. Playgoer's club.[5] Matcham often thinks of the masterstroke. Did I pull the chain? Yes. The last act.

—Yes.

—I just called to ask on the way in is she over it. She's in the lying-in hospital in Holles street. Dr Horne got her in. She's three days bad now.

—O, Mr Bloom said. I'm sorry to hear that.

—Yes, Mrs Breen said. And a houseful of kids at home. It's a very stiff birth, the nurse told me.

—O, Mr Bloom said.

His heavy pitying gaze absorbed her news. His tongue clacked in compassion. Dth! Dth!

—I'm sorry to hear that, he said. Poor thing! Three days! That's terrible for her.

Mrs Breen nodded.

—She was taken bad on the Tuesday. . .

Mr Bloom touched her funnybone gently, warning her.

—Mind! Let this man pass.

A bony form strode along the curbstone from the river, staring with a rapt gaze into the sunlight through a heavy stringed glass. Tight as a skullpiece a tiny hat gripped his head. From his arm a folded dustcoat, a stick and an umbrella dangled to his stride.

—Watch him, Mr Bloom said. He always walks outside the lampposts. Watch!

—Who is he if it's a fair question, Mrs. Breen asked. Is he dotty?

—His name is Cashel Boyle O'Connor Fitzmaurice Tisdall Farrell, Mr Bloom said, smiling. Watch!

---

5. Bloom is thinking of the story *Matcham's Masterstroke*, by "Mr. Philip Beaufoy, Playgoers' club, Lon-don," which he had read in the toilet that morning. He then mentally quotes the opening sentence.

—He has enough of them, she said. Denis will be like that one of these days.

She broke off suddenly.

—There he is, she said. I must go after him. Goodbye. Remember me to Molly, won't you?

—I will, Mr Bloom said.

He watched her dodge through passers towards the shopfronts. Denis Breen in skimpy frockcoat and blue canvas shoes shuffled out of Harrison's hugging two heavy tomes to his ribs. Blown in from the bay. Like old times. He suffered her to overtake him without surprise and thrust his dull grey beard towards her, his loose jaw wagging as he spoke earnestly.

Meshuggah.[6] Off his chump.

Mr Bloom walked on again easily, seeing ahead of him in sunlight the tight skullpiece, the dangling stick, umbrella, dustcoat. Going the two days. Watch him! Out he goes again. One way of getting on in the world. And that other old mosey lunatic in those duds. Hard time she must have with him.

U. P.: up. I'll take my oath that's Alf Bergan or Richie Goulding. Wrote it for a lark in the Scotch house, I bet anything. Round to Menton's office. His oyster eyes staring at the postcard. Be a feast for the gods.

He passed the *Irish Times*. There might be other answers lying there. Like to answer them all. Good system for criminals. Code. At their lunch now. Clerk with the glasses there doesn't know me. O, leave them there to simmer. Enough bother wading through fortyfour of them. Wanted smart lady typist to aid gentleman in literary work. I called you naughty darling because I do not like that other world. Please tell me what is the meaning. Please tell me what perfume does your wife.[7] Tell me who made the world. The way they spring those questions on you. And the other one Lizzie Twigg. My literary efforts have had the good fortune to meet with the approval of the eminent poet A. E. (Mr Geo Russell).[7a] No time to do her hair drinking sloppy tea with a book of poetry.

Best paper by long chalks for a small ad. Got the provinces now. Cook and general, exc cuisine, housemaid kept. Wanted live man for spirit counter. Resp girl (R. C.) wishes to hear of post in fruit or pork shop. James Carlisle made that. Six and a half per cent

---

6. Yiddish, "mad."
7. Bloom is mentally quoting a letter written to him by the typist Martha Clifford, with whom he is carrying on a purely epistolary love affair (she had misspelled "word" as "world": "I do not like that other *world*"). Lizzie Twigg was one of the other typists who had answered his advertisement for a

secretary "to aid gentleman in literary work" (Bloom's pretext for beginning such an affair).
7a. A. E. (George Russell, 1867–1935), the Irish poet mentioned as a reference by Lizzie Twigg when she answered Bloom's advertisement, is later encountered by Bloom with a woman who Bloom speculates might be Lizzie.

dividend. Made a big deal on Coates's shares. Ca'canny. Cunning old Scotch hunks. All the toady news. Our gracious and popular vicereine.[8] Bought the *Irish Field* now. Lady Mountcashel has quite recovered after her confinement and rode out with the Ward Union staghounds at the enlargement yesterday at Rathoath. Uneatable fox. Pothunters too. Fear injects juices make it tender enough for them. Riding astride. Sit her horse like a man. Weightcarrying huntress. No sidesaddle or pillion for her, not for Joe. First to the meet and in at the death. Strong as a brood mare some of those horsey women. Swagger around livery stables. Toss off a glass of brandy neat while you'd say knife. That one at the Grosvenor this morning. Up with her on the car: wishwish. Stonewall or fivebarred gate put her mount to it. Think that pugnosed driver did it out of spite. Who is this she was like? O yes! Mrs Miriam Dandrade that sold me her old wraps and black underclothes in the Shelbourne hotel. Divorced Spanish American. Didn't take a feather out of her my handling them. As if I was her clotheshorse. Saw her in the viceregal party when Stubbs the park ranger got me in with Whelan of the *Express*. Scavenging what the quality left. High tea. Mayonnaise I poured on the plums thinking it was custard. Her ears ought to have tingled for a few weeks after. Want to be a bull for her. Born courtesan. No nursery work for her, thanks.

Poor Mrs Purefoy! Methodist husband. Method in his madness. Saffron bun and milk and soda lunch in the educational dairy. Eating with a stopwatch, thirtytwo chews to the minute. Still his muttonchop whiskers grew. Supposed to be well connected. Theodore's cousin in Dublin Castle. One tony relative in every family. Hardy annuals he presents her with. Saw him out at the Three Jolly Topers marching along bareheaded and his eldest boy carrying one in a marketnet. The squallers. Poor thing! Then having to give the breast year after year all hours of the night. Selfish those t.t's are. Dog in the manger. Only one lump of sugar in my tea, if you please.

He stood at Fleet street crossing. Luncheon interval a six penny at Rowe's? Must look up that ad in the national library.[9] An eightpenny in the Burton. Better. On my way.

He walked on past Bolton's Westmoreland house. Tea. Tea. Tea. I forgot to tap Tom Kernan.[1]

Sss. Dth, dth, dth! Three days imagine groaning on a bed with a vinegared handkerchief round her forehead, her belly swollen out!

8. Wife of the Viceroy, who represented the British Crown in Ireland; Bloom is thinking of the society column in the *Irish Times.*
9. Bloom's goal, on his walk through Dublin, is the National Library, where he wants to look up an advertisement in a back number of the *Kilkenny People.*
1. A Dublin tea merchant and friend of Bloom's, whom Bloom had earlier intended to ask ("tap") for some tea.

Phew! Dreadful simply! Child's head too big: forceps. Doubled up inside her trying to butt its way out blindly, groping for the way out. Kill me that would. Lucky Molly got over hers lightly. They ought to invent something to stop that. Life with hard labour. Twilight-sleep idea: queen Victoria was given that. Nine she had. A good layer. Old woman that lived in a shoe she had so many children. Suppose he was consumptive. Time someone thought about it instead of gassing about the what was it the pensive bosom of the silver effulgence. Flapdoodle to feed fools on. They could easily have big establishments. Whole thing quite painless out of all the taxes give every child born five quid at compound interest up to twentyone, five per cent is a hundred shillings and five tiresome pounds, multiply by twenty decimal system, encourage people to put by money save hundred and ten and a bit twentyone years want to work it out on paper come to a tidy sum, more than you think.

Not stillborn of course. They are not even registered. Trouble for nothing.

Funny sight two of them together, their bellies out. Molly and Mrs Moisel. Mothers' meeting. Phthisis retires for the time being, then returns. How flat they look after all of a sudden! Peaceful eyes. Weight off their minds. Old Mrs Thornton was a jolly old soul. All my babies, she said. The spoon of pap in her mouth before she fed them. O, that's nyumyum. Got her hand crushed by old Tom Wall's son. His first bow to the public. Head like a prize pumpkin. Snuffy Dr Murren. People knocking them up at all hours. For God's sake doctor. Wife in her throes. Then keep them waiting months for their fee. To attendance on your wife. No gratitude in people. Humane doctors, most of them.

Before the huge high door of the Irish house of parliament a flock of pigeons flew. Their little frolic after meals. Who will we do it on? I pick the fellow in black. Here goes. Here's good luck. Must be thrilling from the air. Apjohn, myself and Owen Goldberg up in the trees near Goose green playing the monkeys. Mackerel they called me.

A squad of constables debouched from College street, marching in Indian file. Goose step. Foodheated faces, sweating helmets, patting their truncheons. After their feed with a good load of fat soup under their belts. Policeman's lot is oft a happy one. They split up into groups and scattered, saluting towards their beats. Let out to graze. Best moment to attack one in pudding time. A punch in his dinner. A squad of others, marching irregularly, rounded Trinity railings, making for the station. Bound for their troughs. Prepare to receive cavalry. Prepare to receive soup.

He crossed under Tommy Moore's roguish finger. They did right to put him up over a urinal: meeting of the waters.[2] Ought to be places for women. Running into cakeshops. Settle my hat straight. *There is not in this wide world a vallee.* Great song of Julia Morkan's. Kept her voice up to the very last. Pupil of Michael Balfe's wasn't she?

He gazed after the last broad tunic. Nasty customers to tackle. Jack Power could a tale unfold: father a G man. If a fellow gave them trouble being lagged they let him have it hot and heavy in the bridewell.[3] Can't blame them after all with the job they have especially the young hornies. That horse policeman the day Joe Chamberlain was given his degree in Trinity he got a run for his money.[4] My word he did! His horse's hoofs clattering after us down Abbey street. Luck I had the presence of mind to dive into Manning's or I was souped. He did come a wallop, by George. Must have cracked his skull on the cobblestones. I oughtn't to have got myself swept along with those medicals. And the Trinity jibs[5] in their mortarboards. Looking for trouble. Still I got to know that young Dixon who dressed that sting for me in the Mater and now he's in Holles street where Mrs Purefoy. Wheels within wheels. Police whistle in my ears still. All skedaddled. Why he fixed on me. Give me in charge. Right here it began.

—Up the Boers!

—Three cheers for De Wet![6]

—We'll hang Joe Chamberlain on a sourapple tree.

Silly billies: mob of young cubs yelling their guts out. Vinegar hill The Butter exchange band. Few years time half of them magistrates and civil servants. War comes on: into the army helterskelter: same fellows used to whether on the scaffold high.

Never know who you're talking to. Corney Kelleher he has Harvey Duff in his eye. Like that Peter or Denis or James Carey that blew the gaff on the invincibles. Member of the corporation too. Egging raw youths on to get in the know. All the time drawing secret service pay from the castle.[7] Drop him like a hot potato. Why those plain clothes men are always courting slaveys. Easily twig a man used to uniform. Squarepushing up against a backdoor. Maul her a bit. Then the next thing on the menu. And who is the gentleman does be visiting there? Was the young master saying anything? Peeping Tom through the keyhole. Decoy duck. Hotblooded young student fooling round her fat arms ironing.

---

2. *The Meeting of the Waters* was a famous poem by the much-loved Irish poet Thomas Moore (1779–1852) whose statue Bloom now passes.
3. Prison.
4. When Joseph Chamberlain, the British Colonial Secretary, came to Dublin to receive an honorary degree from Trinity College, a group of medical students rioted against him and against the Boer War.
5. Trinity College students.
6. Boer general.
7. I.e., from the British government, whose representative lived at Dublin Castle.

—Are those yours, Mary?

—I don't wear such things. . . Stop or I'll tell the missus on you. Out half the night.

—There are great times coming, Mary. Wait till you see.

—Ah, get along with your great times coming.

Barmaids too. Tobacco shopgirls.

James Stephens'[8] idea was the best. He knew them. Circles of ten so that a fellow couldn't round on more than his own ring. Sinn Fein.[9] Back out you get the knife. Hidden hand. Stay in. The firing squad. Turnkey's daughter got him out of Richmond, off from Lusk. Putting up in the Buckingham Palace hotel under their very noses. Garibaldi.[1]

You must have a certain fascination: Parnell.[2] Arthur Griffith is a squareheaded fellow but he has no go in him for the mob. Want to gas about our lovely land. Gammon and spinach. Dublin Bakery Company's tearoom. Debating societies. That republicanism is the best form of government. That the language question should take precedence of the economic question. Have your daughters inveigling them to your house. Stuff them up with meat and drink. Michaelmas goose. Here's a good lump of thyme seasoning under the apron for you. Have another quart of goosegrease before it gets too cold. Halffed enthusiastists. Penny roll and a walk with the band. No grace for the carver. The thought that the other chap pays best sauce in the world. Make themselves thoroughly at home. Shove us over those apricots, meaning peaches. The not far distant day. Home Rule sun rising up in the northwest.[3]

His smile faded as he walked, a heavy cloud hiding the sun slowly, shadowing Trinity's surly front. Trams passed one another, ingoing, outgoing, clanging. Useless words. Things go on same; day after day: squads of police marching out, back: trams in, out. Those two loonies mooching about. Dignam carted off. Mina Purefoy swollen belly on a bed groaning to have a child tugged out of her. One born every second somewhere. Other dying every second. Since I fed the birds five minutes. Three hundred kicked the bucket. Other three hundred born, washing the blood off, all are washed in the blood of the lamb, bawling maaaaaa.

Cityful passing away, other cityful coming, passing away too: other coming on, passing on. Houses, lines of houses, streets, miles

8. Irish nationalist revolutionary.
9. Irish revolutionary movement; the Gaelic words mean "We Ourselves."
1. Bloom is thinking of a variety of nationalist conspirators who escaped from danger, among them the 19th-century Italian patriot and general Giuseppe Garibaldi.

2. Charles Stewart Parnell (1846–91), Irish nationalist political leader. Arthur Griffith was founder of the Sinn Fein
3. Reference to Arthur Griffith's comment on the *Freeman* masthead, which showed the sun rising in the northwest from behind the bank of Ireland. Bloom has a *Freeman* in his pocket.

of pavements, piledup bricks, stones. Changing hands. This owner, that. Landlord never dies they say. Other steps into his shoes when he gets his notice to quit. They buy the place up with gold and still they have all the gold. Swindle in it somewhere. Piled up in cities, worn away age after age. Pyramids in sand. Built on bread and onions. Slaves Chinese wall. Babylon. Big stones left. Round towers. Rest rubble, sprawling suburbs, jerrybuilt, Kerwan's mushroom houses, built of breeze. Shelter for the night.

No one is anything.

This is the very worst hour of the day. Vitality. Dull, gloomy: hate this hour. Feel as if I had been eaten and spewed.

Provost's house. The reverend Dr Salmon: tinned salmon. Well tinned in there. Wouldn't live in it if they paid me. Hope they have liver and bacon today. Nature abhors a vacuum.

The sun freed itself slowly and lit glints of light among the silver ware in Walter Sexton's window opposite by which John Howard Parnell[4] passed, unseeing.

There he is: the brother. Image of him. Haunting face. Now that's a coincidence. Course hundreds of times you think of a person and don't meet him. Like a man walking in his sleep. No-one knows him. Must be a corporation meeting today. They say he never put on the city marshal's uniform since he got the job. Charley Boulger used to come out on his high horse, cocked hat, puffed, powdered and shaved. Look at the woebegone walk of him. Eaten a bad egg. Poached eyes on ghost. I have a pain. Great man's brother. His brother's brother. He'd look nice on the city charger. Drop into the D. B. C. probably for his coffee, play chess there. His brother used men as pawns. Let them all go to pot. Afraid to pass a remark on him. Freeze them up with that eye of his. That's the fascination: the name. All a bit touched. Mad Fanny and his other sister Mrs Dickinson driving about with scarlet harness. Bolt upright like surgeon M'Ardle. Still David Sheehy beat him for south Meath. Apply for the Chiltern Hundreds and retire into public life. The patriot's banquet. Eating orangepeels in the park. Simon Dedalus said when they put him in parliament that Parnell would come back from the grave and lead him out of the House of Commons by the arm.

—Of the twoheaded octopus, one of whose heads is the head upon which the ends of the world have forgotten to come while the other speaks with a Scotch accent. The tentacles. . .

They passed from behind Mr Bloom along the curbstone. Beard and bicycle. Young woman.

And there he is too. Now that's really a coincidence: secondtime. Coming events cast their shadows before. With the approval of the

4. C. S. Parnell's brother.

eminent poet Mr Geo Russell.[5] That might be Lizzie Twigg with him. A. E.: what does that mean? Initials perhaps. Albert Edward, Arthur Edmund, Alphonsus Eb Ed El Esquire. What was he saying? The ends of the world with a Scotch accent. Tentacles: octopus. Something occult: symbolism. Holding forth. She's taking it all in. Not saying a word. To aid gentleman in literary work.

His eyes followed the high figure in homespun, beard and bicycle, a listening woman at his side. Coming from the vegetarian. Only weggebobbles and fruit. Don't eat a beefsteak. If you do the eyes of that cow will pursue you through all eternity. They say it's healthier. Wind and watery though. Tried it. Keep you on the run all day. Bad as a bloater. Dreams all night. Why do they call that thing they gave me nutsteak? Nutarians. Fruitarians. To give you the idea you are eating rumpsteak. Absurd. Salty too. They cook in soda. Keep you sitting by the tap all night.

Her stockings are loose over her ankles. I detest that: so tasteless. Those literary ethereal people they are all. Dreamy, cloudy, symbolistic. Esthetes they are. I wouldn't be surprised if it was that kind of food you see produces the like waves of the brain the poetical. For example one of those policemen sweating Irish stew into their shirts; you couldn't squeeze a line of poetry out of him. Don't know what poetry is even. Must be in a certain mood.

> *The dreamy cloudy gull*
> *Waves o'er the waters dull.*

He crossed at Nassau street corner and stood before the window of Yeates and Son, pricing the field glasses. Or will I drop into old Harris's and have a chat with young Sinclair? Wellmannered fellow. Probably at his lunch. Must get those old glasses of mine set right. Gœrz lenses, six guineas. Germans making their way everywhere. Sell on easy terms to capture trade. Undercutting. Might chance on a pair in the railway lost property office. Astonishing the things people leave behind them in trains and cloak rooms. What do they be thinking about? Women too. Incredible. Last year travelling to Ennis had to pick up that farmer's daughter's bag and hand it to her at Limerick junction. Unclaimed money too. There's a little watch up there on the roof of the bank to test those glasses by.

His lids came down on the lower rims of his irides. Can't see it. If you imagine it's there you can almost see it. Can't see it.

He faced about and, standing between the awnings, held out his right hand at arm's length towards the sun. Wanted to try that often. Yes: completely. The tip of his little finger blotted out the

---

5. Bloom wonders whether the woman with A.E. might be Lizzie Twigg and then goes on to speculate on the meaning of "A.E." and on Russell's mystical ideas.

sun's disk. Must be the focus where the rays cross. If I had black glasses. Interesting. There was a lot of talk about those sunspots when we were in Lombard street west. Terrific explosions they are. There will be a total eclipse this year: autumn some time.

Now that I come to think of it, that ball falls at Greenwich time. It's the clock is worked by an electric wire from Dunsink. Must go out there some first Saturday of the month. If I could get an introduction to professor Joly or learn up something about his family. That would do to: man always feels complimented. Flattery where least expected. Nobleman proud to be descended from some king's mistress. His foremother. Lay it on with a trowel. Cap in hand goes through the land. Not go in and blurt out what you know you're not to: what's parallax? Show this gentleman the door.

Ah.

His hand fell again to his side.

Never know anything about it. Waste of time. Gasballs spinning about, crossing each other, passing. Same old dingdong always. Gas, then solid, then world, then cold, then dead shell drifting around, frozen rock like that pineapple rock. The moon. Must be a new moon out, she said. I believe there is.

He went on by la Maison Claire.

Wait. The full moon was the night we were Sunday fortnight exactly there is a new moon. Walking down by the Tolka. Not bad for a Fairview moon. She was humming: The young May moon she's beaming, love. He other side of her. Elbow, arm. He. Glowworm's la-amp is gleaming, love. Touch. Fingers. Asking. Answer. Yes.

Stop. Stop. If it was it was.[6] Must.

Mr Bloom, quick breathing, slowlier walking, passed Adam court.

With a deep quiet relief, his eyes took note: this is street here middle of the day Bob Doran's bottle shoulders. On his annual bend, M'Coy said. They drink in order to say or do something or *cherchez la femme*.[7] Up in the Coombe with chummies and streetwalkers and then the rest of the year as sober as a judge.

Yes. Thought so. Sloping into the Empire. Gone. Plain soda would do him good. Where Pat Kinsella had his Harp theater before Whitbread ran the Queen's.[8] Broth of a boy. Dion Boucicault business with his harvestmoon face in a poky bonnet. Three Purty Maids from School. How time flies eh? Showing long red pantaloons under his skirts. Drinkers, drinking, laughed spluttering, their drink against their breath. More power, Pat. Coarse red: fun for drunkards: guffaw and smoke. Take off that white hat. His parboiled eyes. Where is he now? Beggar somewhere. The harp that

---

6. Bloom is thinking again of his wife's infidelities.
7. "Look for the woman" (in the case).

8. The Queen's Theatre. Dion Boucicault was an Irish-born American dramatist, manager, and actor.

once did starve us all.[9]

I was happier then. Or was that I? Or am I now I? Twentyeight I was. She twentythree when we left Lombard street west something changed. Could never like it again after Rudy. Can't bring back time. Like holding water in your hand. Would you go back to then? Just beginning then. Would you? Are you not happy in your home, you poor little naughty boy? Wants to sew on buttons for me. I must answer. Write it in the library.

Grafton street gay with housed awnings lured his senses. Muslin prints silk, dames and dowagers, jingle of harnesses, hoofthuds lowringing in the baking causeway. Thick feet that woman has in the white stockings. Hope the rain mucks them up on her. Country bred chawbacon. All the beef to the heels were in. Always gives a woman clumsy feet. Molly looks out of plumb.

He passed, dallying, the windows of Brown Thomas, silk mercers. Cascades of ribbons. Flimsy China silks. A tilted urn poured from its mouth a flood of bloodhued poplin: lustrous blood. The huguenots brought that here. *La causa è santa!*[1] Tara tara. Great chorus that. Tara. Must be washed in rainwater. Meyerbeer. Tara: bom bom bom.

Pincushions. I'm a long time threatening to buy one. Stick them all over the place. Needles in window curtains.

He bared slightly his left forearm. Scrape: nearly gone. Not today anyhow. Must go back for that lotion. For her birthday perhaps. Junejuly augseptember eighth. Nearly three months off. Then she mightn't like it. Women won't pick up pins. Say it cuts lo.

Gleaming silks, petticoats on slim brass rails, rays of flat silk stockings.

Useless to go back. Had to be. Tell me all.

High voices. Sunwarm silk. Jingling harnesses. All for a woman, home and houses, silk webs, silver, rich fruits, spicy from Jaffa. Agendath Netaim.[2] Wealth of the world.

A warm human plumpness settled down on his brain. His brain yielded. Perfume of embraces all him assailed. With hungered flesh obscurely, he mutely craved to adore.

Duke street. Here we are. Must eat. The Burton. Feel better then. He turned Combridge's corner, still pursued. Jingling hoofthuds. Perfumed bodies, warm, full. All kissed, yielded: in deep summer fields, tangled pressed grass, in trickling hallways of tenements, along sofas, creaking beds.

---

9. A reference to the lack of financial success of the Harp Theatre through a punning reworking (almost worthy of Stephen Dedalus) of Tom Moore's famous *Harp That Once Through Tara's Halls*.
1. "The cause is sacred," chorus from Meyerbeer's opera *Les Huguenots*, which Bloom is recalling. The Huguenots were 16th- and 17th-century French Protestants, many of whom fled to Britain to escape persecution.
2. "Planters' Company" (Hebrew). Bloom recalls a leaflet advertising an early Zionist settlement which he had seen that morning and is still carrying in his pocket.

—Jack, love!
—Darling!
—Kiss me, Reggy!
—My boy!
—Love![3]

His heart astir he pushed in the door of the Burton restaurant. Stink gripped his trembling breath: pungent meatjuice, slop of greens. See the animals feed.

Men, men, men.

Perched on high stools by the bar, hats shoved back, at the tables calling for more bread no charge, swilling, wolfing gobfuls of sloppy food, their eyes bulging, wiping wetted moustaches. A pallid suetfaced young man polished his tumbler knife fork and spoon with his napkin. New set of microbes. A man with an infant's saucestained napkin tucked round him shovelled gurgling soup down his gullet. A man spitting back on his plate: halfmasticated gristle: no teeth to chewchewchew it. Chump chop from the grill. Bolting to get it over. Sad booser's eyes. Bitten off more than he can chew. Am I like that? See ourselves as others see us. Hungry man is an angry man. Working tooth and jaw. Don't! O! A bone! That last pagan king of Ireland Cormac in the schoolpoem choked himself at Sletty southward of the Boyne.[4] Wonder what he was eating. Something galoptious. Saint Patrick converted him to Christianity. Couldn't swallow it all however.

—Roast beef and cabbage.
—One stew.

Smells of men. His gorge rose. Spaton sawdust, sweetish warmish cigarette smoke, reek of plug, spilt beer, men's beery piss, the stale of ferment.

Couldn't eat a morsel here. Fellow sharpening knife and fork, to eat all before him, old chap picking his tootles. Slight spasm, full, chewing the cud. Before and after. Grace after meals. Look on this picture then on that. Scoffing up stewgravy with sopping sippets of bread. Lick it off the plate, man! Get out of this.

He gazed round the stooled and tabled eaters, tightening the wings of his nose.

—Two stouts here.
—One corned and cabbage.

That fellow ramming a knifeful of cabbage down as if his life depended on it. Good stroke. Give me the fidgets to look. Safer to eat from his three hands. Tear it limb from limb. Second nature to

3. Sensual images are leading Bloom to imagine love scenes from a sentimental novel. The cannibal Lestrygonians had used "the handsome daughter of Lestrygonian Antiphates" as a decoy to lure Ulysses' men to her father, and Bloom is drawn by his sensual and sexual imagination to enter Burton's restaurant —only to be disgusted by the grossness of the atmosphere.
4. Bloom is recalling a "schoolpoem" about a legendary incident in Irish history.

him. Born with a silver knife in his mouth. That's witty, I think.
Or no. Silver means born rich. Born with a knife. But then the
allusion is lost.

An illgirt server gathered sticky clattering plates. Rock, the bailiff,
standing at the bar blew the foamy crown from his tankard. Well
up: it splashed yellow near his boot. A diner, knife and fork upright,
elbows on table, ready for a second helping stared towards the food-
lift across his stained square of newspaper. Other chap telling him
something with his mouth full. Sympathetic listener. Table talk.
I munched hum un thu Unchster Bunk un Munchday. Ha? Did
you, faith?

Mr Bloom raised two fingers doubtfully to his lips. His eyes said.

—Not here. Don't see him.[5]

Out. I hate dirty eaters.

He backed towards the door. Get a light snack in Davy Byrne's.
Stopgap. Keep me going. Had a good breakfast.

—Roast and mashed here.

—Pint of stout.

Every fellow for his own, tooth and nail. Gulp. Grub. Gulp.
Gobstuff.

He came out into clearer air and turned back towards Grafton
street. Eat or be eaten. Kill! Kill!

Suppose that communal kitchen years to come perhaps. All
trotting down with porringers and tommycans to be filled. Devour
contents in the street. John Howard Parnell example the provost
of Trinity every mother's son don't talk of your provosts and provost
of Trinity women and children, cabmen, priests, parsons, field-
marshals, archbishops. From Ailesbury road, Clyde road, artisan's
dwellings north Dublin union, lord mayor in his gingerbread coach,
old queen in a bathchair. My plate's empty. After you with our incorporated drinkingcup. Like sir Philip Crampton's fountain. Rub
off the microbes with your handkerchief. Next chap rubs on a new
batch with his. Father O'Flynn would make hares of them all. Have
rows all the same. All for number one. Children fighting for the
scrapings of the pot. Want a soup pot as big as the Phoenix Park.
Harpooning flitches and hindquarters out of it. Hate people all
around you. City Arms hotel *table d'hôte* she called it. Soup, joint
and sweet. Never know whose thoughts you're chewing. Then who'd
wash up all the plates and forks? Might be all feeding on tabloids
that time. Teeth getting worse and worse.

After all there's a lot in that vegetarian fine flavour of things
from the earth garlic, of course, it stinks Italian organgrinders crisp
of onions, mushrooms truffles. Pain to animal too. Pluck and draw
fowl. Wretched brutes there at the cattlemarket waiting for the

5. He pretends he is looking for someone he cannot see, so that he has an excuse
to leave without eating.

poleaxe to split their skulls open. Moo. Poor trembling calves. Meh. Staggering bob. Bubble and squeak. Butchers' buckets wobble lights. Give us that brisket off the hook. Plup. Rawhead and bloody bones. Flayed glasseyed sheep hung from their haunches, sheepsnouts bloodypapered sniveling nosejam on sawdust. Top and lashers going out. Don't maul them pieces, young one.

Hot fresh blood they prescribe for decline. Blood always needed. Insidious. Lick it up, smoking hot, thick sugary. Famished ghosts.

Ah, I'm hungry.

He entered Davy Byrne's. Moral pub. He doesn't chat. Stands a drink now and then. But in leapyear once in four. Cashed a cheque for me once.

What will I take now? He drew his watch. Let me see now. Shandygaff?

—Hello, Bloom! Nosey Flynn said from his nook.

—Hello, Flynn.

—How's things?

—Tiptop . . . Let me see. I'll take a glass of burgundy and . . . let me see.

Sardines on the shelves. Almost taste them by looking. Sandwich? Ham and his descendants musteied and bred there. Potted meats. What is home without Plumtree's potted meat? Incomplete. What a stupid ad! Under the obituary notices they stuck it. All up a plumtree. Dignam's potted meat. Cannibals would with lemon and rice. White missionary too salty. Like pickled pork. Except the chief consumes the parts of honour. Ought to be tough from exercise. His wives in a row to watch the effect. *There was a right royal old nigger. Who ate or something the somethings of the reverend Mr MacTrigger.* With it an abode of bliss. Lord knows what concoction. Cauls mouldy tripes windpipes faked and minced up. Puzzle find the meat. Kosher. No meat and milk together. Hygiene that was what they call now. Yom kippur fast spring cleaning of inside. Peace and war depend on some fellow's digestion. Religions. Christmas turkeys and geese. Slaughter of innocents. Eat, drink and be merry. Then casual wards full after. Heads bandaged. Cheese digests all but itself. Mighty cheese.

—Have you a cheese sandwich?

—Yes, sir.

Like a few olives too if they had them. Italian I prefer. Good glass of burgundy; take away that. Lubricate. A nice salad, cool as a cucumber. Tom Kernan can dress. Puts gusto into it. Pure olive oil. Milly served me that cutlet with a sprig of parsley. Take one Spanish onion. God made food, the devil the cooks. Devilled crab.

—Wife well?

—Quite well, thanks . . . A cheese sandwich, then. Gorgonzola, have you?

—Yes, sir.

Nosey Flynn sipped his grog.

—Doing any singing those times?

Look at his mouth. Could whistle in his own ear. Flap ears to match. Music. Knows as much about it as my coachman. Still better tell him. Does no harm. Free ad.

—She's engaged for a big tour end of this month. You may have heard perhaps.

—No. O, that's the style. Who's getting it up?

The curate[6] served.

—How much is that?

—Seven d., sir . . . Thank you, sir.

Mr Bloom cut his sandwich into slender strips. *Mr MacTrigger.* Easier than the dreamy creamy stuff. *His five hundred wives. Had the time of their lives.*

—Mustard, sir?

—Thank you.

He studded under each lifted strip yellow blobs. *Their lives.* I have it. *It grew bigger and bigger and bigger.*

—Getting it up? he said. Well, it's like a company idea, you see. Part shares and part profits.

—Ay, now I remember, Nosey Flynn said, putting his hand in his pocket to scratch his groin. Who is this was telling me? Isn't Blazes Boylan mixed up in it?

A warm shock of air heat of mustard haunched on Mr Bloom's heart. He raised his eyes and met the stare of a bilious clock. Two. Pub clock five minutes fast. Time going on. Hands moving. Two. Not yet.[7]

His midriff yearned then upward, sank within him, yearned more longly, longingly.

Wine.

He smellsipped the cordial juice and, bidding his throat strongly to speed it, set his wineglass delicately down.

—Yes, he said. He's the organiser in point of fact.

No fear. No brains.

Nosey Flynn snuffed and scratched. Flea having a good square meal.

—He had a good slice of luck, Jack Mooney was telling me, over that boxing match Myler Keogh won again that soldier in the Portobello barracks. By God, he had the little kipper down in the county Carlow he was telling me. . . .

Hope that dewdrop doesn't come down into his glass. No, snuffled it up.

—For near a month, man, before it came off. Sucking duck eggs

---

6. Bartender.

7. I.e., not yet time for Boylan to visit Molly.

by God till further orders. Keep him off the boose, see? O, by God, Blazes is a hairy chap.

Davy Byrne came forward from the hindbar in tuckstitched shirt-sleeves, cleaning his lips with two wipes of his napkin. Herring's blush. Whose smile upon each feature plays with such and such replete. Too much fat on the parsnips.

—And here's himself and pepper on him, Nosey Flynn said. Can you give us a good one for the Gold cup?

—I'm off that, Mr Flynn, Davy Byrne answered. I never put anything on a horse.

—You're right there, Nosey Flynn said.

Mr Bloom ate his strips of sandwich, fresh clean bread, with relish of disgust, pungent mustard, the feety savour of green cheese. Sips of his wine soothed his palate. Not logwood that. Tastes fuller this weather with the chill off.

Nice quiet bar. Nice piece of wood in that counter. Nicely planed. Like the way it curves there.

—I wouldn't do anything at all in that line, Davy Byrne said. It ruined many a man the same horses.

Vintners' sweepstake. Licensed for the sale of beer, wine and spirits for consumption on the premises. Heads I win tails you lose.

—True for you, Nosey Flynn said. Unless you're in the know. There's no straight sport going now. Lenehan gets some good ones. He's giving Sceptre today. Zinfandel's the favourite, lord Howard de Walden's, won at Epsom. Morny Cannon is riding him. I could have got seven to one against Saint Amant a fortnight before.

—That so? Davy Byrne said.

He went towards the window and, taking up the pettycash book, scanned its pages.

—I could, faith, Nosey Flynn said, snuffling. That was a rare bit of horseflesh. Saint Frusquin was her sire. She won in a thunderstorm, Rothschild's filly, with wadding in her ears. Blue jacket and yellow cap. Bad luck to big Ben Dollard and his John O'Gaunt. He put me off it. Ay.

He drank resignedly from his tumbler, running his fingers down the flutes.

—Ay, he said, sighing.

Mr Bloom, champing, standing, looked upon his sigh. Nosey numbskull. Will I tell him that horse Lenehan?[8] He knows already. Better let him forget. Go and lose more. Fool and his money. Dewdrop coming down again. Cold nose he'd have kissing a woman. Still they might like. Prickly beards they like. Dogs' cold noses. Old Mrs Riordan with the rumbling stomach's Skye terrier in the City Arms hotel. Molly fondling him in her lap. O

8. Bloom is wondering whether to pass on a tip from Lenehan, who wrote for the racing paper *Sport*.

wowsywowsy!

Wine soaked and softened rolled pith of bread mustard a moment mawkish cheese. Nice wine it is. Taste it better because I'm not thirsty. Bath of course does that. Just a bite or two. Then about six o'clock I can. Six, six. Time will be gone then. She. . .

Mild fire of wine kindled his veins. I wanted that badly. Felt so off colour. His eyes unhungrily saw shelves of tins, sardines, gaudy lobster's claws. All the odd things people pick up for food. Out of shells, periwinkles with a pin, off trees, snails out of the ground the French eat, out of the sea with bait on a hook. Silly fish learn nothing in a thousand years. If you didn't know risky putting anything into your mouth. Poisonous berries. Johnny Magories. Roundness you think good. Gaudy colour warns you off. One fellow told another and so on. Try it on the dog first. Led on by the smell or the look. Tempting fruit. Ice cones. Cream. Instinct. Orangegroves for instance. Need artificial irrigation. Bleibtreustrasse.[9] Yes but what about oysters. Unsightly like a clot of phlegm. Filthy shells. Devil to open them too. Who found them out? Garbage, sewage they feed on. Fizz and Red bank oysters. Effect on the sexual. Aphrodis. He was in the Red bank this morning. Was he oyster old fish at table. Perhaps he young flesh in bed. No. June has no ar no oysters. But there are people like tainted game. Jugged hare. First catch your hare. Chinese eating eggs fifty years old, blue and green again. Dinner of thirty courses. Each dish harmless might mix inside. Idea for a poison mystery. That archduke Leopold was it. No. Yes, or was it Otto one of those Habsburgs? Or who was it used to eat the scruff off his own head? Cheapest lunch in town. Of course, aristocrats. Then the others copy to be in the fashion. Milly too rock oil and flour. Raw pastry I like myself. Half the catch of oysters they throw back in the sea to keep up the price. Cheap. No one would buy. Caviare. Do the grand. Hock in green glasses. Swell blowout. Lady this. Powdered bosom pearls. The *élite*. *Crème de la crème*.[1] They want special dishes to pretend they're. Hermit with a platter of pulse keep down the stings of the flesh. Know me come eat with me. Royal sturgeon. High sheriff, Coffey, the butcher, right to venisons of the forest from his ex.[2] Send him back the half of a cow. Spread I saw down in the Master of the Rolls' kitchen area. Whitehatted *chef* like a rabbi. Combustible duck. Curly cabbage *à la duchesse de Parme*. Just as well to write it on the bill of fare so you can know what you've eaten too many drugs spoil the broth. I know it myself. Dosing it with Edward's desiccated soup. Geese stuffed silly for them. Lobsters boiled alive. Do ptake some

9. The Berlin street which contained the offices of the "Planters' Company."
1. "Cream of the cream" (i.e., the very best, socially).
2. All sturgeon caught in or off Britain were the property of the king, according to the ancient traditional rights to certain kinds of fish or game. Bloom goes on to imagine a Dublin butcher having a "right to venisons of the forest from his ex[cellency]"—i.e., the Viceroy.

ptarmigan. Wouldn't mind being a waiter in a swell hotel. Tips, evening dress, halfnaked ladies. May I tempt you to a little more filleted lemon sole, miss Dubedat? Yes, do bedad. And she did bedad. Huguenot name I expect that. A miss Dubedat lived in Killiney I remember. *Du, de la,* French. Still it's the same fish, perhaps old Micky Hanlon of Moore street ripped the guts out of making money, hand over fist, finger in fishes' gills, can't write his name on a cheque, think he was painting the landscape with his mouth twisted. Moooikill A Aitcha Ha. Ignorant as a kish of brogues,[3] worth fifty thousand pounds.

Stuck on the pane two flies buzzed, stuck.

Glowing wine on his palate lingered swallowed. Crushing in the winepress grapes of Burgundy. Sun's heat it is. Seems to a secret touch telling me memory. Touched his sense moistened remembered. Hidden under wild ferns on Howth. Below us bay sleeping sky. No sound. The sky. The bay purple by the Lion's head. Green by Drumleck. Yellowgreen towards Sutton. Fields of undersea, the lines faint brown in grass, buried cities. Pillowed on my coat she had her hair, earwigs in the heather scrub my hand under her nape, you'll toss me all. O wonder! Coolsoft with ointments her hand touched me, caressed: her eyes upon me did not turn away. Ravished over her I lay, full lips full open, kissed her mouth. Yum. Softly she gave me in my mouth the seedcake warm and chewed. Mawkish pulp her mouth had mumbled sweet and sour with spittle. Joy. I ate it: joy. Young life, her lips that gave me pouting. Soft, warm, sticky gumjelly lips. Flowers her eyes were, take me, willing eyes. Pebbles fell. She lay still. A goat. No-one. High on Ben Howth rhododendrons a nannygoat walking surefooted, dropping currants. Screened under ferns she laughed warmfolded. Wildly I lay on her, kissed her; eyes, her lips, her stretched neck, beating, woman's breasts full in her blouse of nun's veiling, fat nipples upright. Hot I tongued her. She kissed me. I was kissed. All yielding she tossed my hair. Kissed, she kissed me.[4]

Me. And me now.

Stuck, the flies buzzed.

His downcast eyes followed the silent veining of the oaken slab. Beauty: it curves: curves are beauty. Shapely goddesses, Venus, Juno: curves the world admires. Can see them library museum standing in the round hall, naked goddesses. Aids to digestion. They don't care what man looks. All to see. Never speaking, I mean to

---

3. A basket of shoes.
4. Bloom is remembering when he first proposed to Molly, on the Hill of Howth, near Dublin. Molly also recalls this in the final "Penelope" episode, which is her soliloquy: " * * * we were lying on the rhododendrons on Howth head in the grey tweed suit and his straw hat the day I got him to propose to me yes * * * my God after that long kiss I near lost my breath * * * I saw he understood or felt what a woman is and I knew I could always get round him and I gave him all the pleasure I could leading him on * * * "

say to fellows like Flynn. Suppose she did Pygmalion and Galatea[5]
what would she say first? Mortal! Put you in your proper place.
Quaffing nectar at mess with gods, golden dishes, all ambrosial.
Not like a tanner lunch we have, boiled mutton, carrots and turnips,
bottle of Allsop. Nectar, imagine it drinking electricity: god's food.
Lovely forms of woman sculped Junonian. Immortal lovely. And
we stuffing food in one hole and out behind: food, chyle, blood,
dung, earth, food: have to feed it like stoking an engine. They have
no. Never looked. I'll look today. Keeper won't see. Bend down let
something fall see if she.

Dribbling a quiet message from his bladder came to go to do not
to do there to do. A man and ready he drained his glass to the lees
and walked, to men too they gave themselves, manly conscious, lay
with men lovers, a youth enjoyed her, to the yard.

When the sound of his boots had ceased Davy Byrne said from
his book:

—What is this he is? Isn't he in the insurance line?

—He's out of that long ago, Nosey Flynn said. He does canvassing for the *Freeman*.

—I know him well to see, Davy Byrne said. Is he in trouble?

—Trouble? Nosey Flynn said. Not that I heard of. Why?

—I noticed he was in mourning.

—Was he? Nosey Flynn said. So he was, faith. I asked him how
was all at home. You're right, by God. So he was.

—I never broach the subject, Davy Byrne said humanely, if I
see a gentleman is in trouble that way. It only brings it up fresh in
their minds.

—It's not the wife anyhow, Nosey Flynn said. I met him the
day before yesterday and he coming out of that Irish farm dairy
John Wyse Nolan's wife has in Henry street with a jar of cream
in his hand taking it home to his better half. She's well nourished,
I tell you. Plovers on toast.

—And is he doing for the *Freeman?* Davy Byrne said.

Nosey Flynn pursed his lips.

—He doesn't buy cream on the ads he picks up. You can make
bacon of that.

—How so? Davy Byrne asked, coming from his book.

Nosey Flynn made swift passes in the air with juggling fingers. He
winked.

—He's in the craft,[6] he said.

—Do you tell me so? Davy Byrne said.

—Very much so, Nosey Flynn said. Ancient free and accepted

order. Light, life and love, by God. They give him a leg up. I was told that by a, well, I won't say who.

—Is that a fact?

—O, it's a fine order, Nosey Flynn said. They stick to you when you're down. I know a fellow was trying to get into it, but they're as close as damn it. By God they did right to keep the women out of it.

Davy Byrne smiledyawnednodded all in one:

—Iiiiiichaaaaaaach!

—There was one woman, Nosey Flynn said, hid herself in a clock to find out what they do be doing. But be damned but they smelt her out and swore her in on the spot a master mason. That was one of the Saint Legers of Doneraile.

Davy Byrne, sated after his yawn, said with tearwashed eyes:

—And is that a fact? Decent quiet man he is. I often saw him in here and I never once saw him, you know, over the line.

—God Almighty couldn't make him drunk, Nosey Flynn said firmly. Slips off when the fun gets too hot. Didn't you see him look at his watch? Ah, you weren't there. If you ask him to have a drink first thing he does he outs with the watch to see what he ought to imbibe. Declare to God he does.

—There are some like that, Davy Byrne said. He's a safe man, I'd say.

—He's not too bad, Nosey Flynn said, snuffling it up. He has been known to put his hand down too to help a fellow. Give the devil his due. O, Bloom has his good points. But there's one thing he'll never do.

His hand scrawled a dry pen signature beside his grog.

—I know, Davy Byrne said.

—Nothing in black and white, Nosey Flynn said.

Paddy Leonard and Bantam Lyons came in. Tom Rochford followed, a plaining hand on his claret waistcoat.

—Day, Mr. Byrne.

—Day, gentlemen.

They paused at the counter.

—Who's standing? Paddy Leonard asked.

—I'm sitting anyhow, Nosey Flynn answered.

—Well, what'll it be? Paddy Leonard asked.

—I'll take a stone ginger, Bantam Lyons said.

—How much? Paddy Leonard cried. Since when, for God's sake? What's yours, Tom?

—How is the main drainage? Nosey Flynn asked, sipping.

For answer Tom Rochford pressed his hand to his breastbone and hiccupped.

—Would I trouble you for a glass of fresh water, Mr Byrne? he said.

—Certainly, sir.

Paddy Leonard eyed his alemates.

—Lord love a duck, he said, look at what I'm standing drinks to! Cold water and gingerpop! Two fellows that would suck whisky off a sore leg. He has some bloody horse up his sleeve for the Gold cup. A dead snip.

—Zinfandel is it? Nosey Flynn asked.

Tom Rochford spilt powder from a twisted paper into the water set before him.

—That cursed dyspepsia, he said before drinking.

—Breadsoda is very good, Davy Byrne said.

Tom Rochford nodded and drank.

—Is it Zinfandel?

—Say nothing, Bantam Lyons winked. I'm going to plunge five bob on my own.

—Tell us if you're worth your salt and be damned to you, Paddy Leonard said. Who gave it to you?

Mr Bloom on his way out raised three fingers in greeting.

—So long, Nosey Flynn said.

The others turned.

—That's the man now that gave it to me, Bantam Lyons whispered.

—Prrwht! Paddy Leonard said with scorn. Mr Byrne, sir, we'll take two of your small Jamesons after that and a. . .

—Stone ginger, Davy Byrne added civilly.

—Ay, Paddy Leonard said. A suckingbottle for the baby.

Mr Bloom walked towards Dawson street, his tongue brushing his teeth smooth. Something green it would have to be: spinach say. Then with those Röntgen rays searchlight you could.

At Duke lane a ravenous terrier choked up a sick knuckly cud on the cobble stones and lapped it with new zest. Surfeit. Returned with thanks having fully digested the contents. First sweet then savoury. Mr Bloom coasted warily. Ruminants. His second course. Their upper jaw they move. Wonder if Tom Rochford will do anything with that invention of his. Wasting time explaining it to Flynn's mouth. Lean people long mouths. Ought to be a hall or a place where inventors could go in and invent free. Course then you'd have all the cranks pestering.

He hummed, prolonging in solemn echo, the closes of the bars:

Don Giovanni, a cenar teco
M'invitasti.[8]

8. Since Molly is a singer, Bloom is familiar with opera. Here he recalls the song sung by the Commendatore's statue in Mozart's *Don Giovanni*, and translates accurately the Italian words he quotes, except for "*teco*" ("with you"). This opera supplies some of the key themes in *Ulysses*, and the famous duet between Don Giovanni and Zerlina, "*Là ci darèm la mano*" ("There we will join hands"), haunts Bloom's mind continually throughout the day. It is on the program of Molly's concert which she is discussing with Boylan that after-

Feel better. Burgundy. Good pick me up. Who distilled first? Some chap in the blues. Dutch courage. That *Kilkenny People* in the national library now I must.

Bare clean closestools, waiting, in the window of William Miller, plumber, turned back his thoughts. They could: and watch it all the way down, swallow a pin sometimes come out of the ribs years after, tour round the body, changing biliary duct, spleen squirting liver, gastric juice coils of intestines like pipes. But the poor buffer would have to stand all the time with his insides entrails on show. Science.

—A *cenar teco.*

What does that *teco* mean? Tonight perhaps.

> *Don Giovanni, thou hast me invited*
> *To come to supper tonight,*
> *The rum the rumdum.*

Doesn't go properly.

Keyes: two months if I get Nannetti[9] to. That'll be two pounds ten, about two pounds eight. Three Hynes owes me. Two eleven. Presscott's ad. Two fifteen. Five guineas about. On the pig's back.

Could buy one of those silk petticoats for Molly, colour of her new garters.

Today. Today. Not think.[1]

Tour the south then. What about English watering places? Brighton, Margate. Piers by moonlight. Her voice floating out. Those lovely sideside girls. Against John Long's a drowsing loafer lounged in heavy thought, gnawing a crusted knuckle. Handy man wants job. Small wages. Will eat anything.

Mr Bloom turned at Gray's confectioner's window of unbought tarts and passed the reverend Thomas Connellan's bookstore. *Why I left the church of Rome? Bird's Nest.* Women run him. They say they used to give pauper children soup to change to protestants in the time of the potato blight. Society over the way papa went to for the conversion of poor jews. Same bait. Why we left the church of Rome?

A blind stripling stood tapping the curbstone with his slender cane. No tram in sight. Wants to cross.

—Do you want to cross? Mr Bloom asked.

The blind stripling did not answer. His wall face frowned weakly. He moved his head uncertainly.

—You're in Dawson street, Mr Bloom said. Molesworth street is opposite. Do you want to cross? There's nothing in the way.

noon, and Bloom associates it with her adultery with Boylan.
9. Proofreader and business manager of the *Freeman's Journal*, and in charge of the advertising Bloom is trying to get for the paper. If he will add a complimentary reference to Keyes, a grocer, in a gossip column, Keyes promises to renew his advertisement, which means a commission for Bloom.
1. I.e., of Molly and Boylan.

The cane moved out trembling to the left. Mr Bloom's eye followed its line and saw again the dyeworks' van drawn up before Drago's. Where I saw his brilliantined hair just when I was. Horse drooping. Driver in John Long's. Slaking his drouth.

—There's a van there, Mr Bloom said, but it's not moving. I'll see you across. Do you want to go to Molesworth street?

—Yes, the stripling answered. South Frederick street.

—Come, Mr Bloom said.

He touched the thin elbow gently: then took the limp seeing hand to guide it forward.

Say something to him. Better not do the condescending. They mistrust what you tell them. Pass a common remark.

—The rain kept off.

No answer.

Stains on his coat. Slobbers his food, I suppose. Tastes all different for him. Have to be spoonfed first. Like a child's hand his hand. Like Milly's was. Sensitive. Sizing me up I daresay from my hand. Wonder if he has a name. Van. Keep his cane clear of the horse's legs tired drudge get his doze. That's right. Clear. Behind a bull: in front of a horse.

—Thanks, sir.

Knows I'm a man. Voice.

—Right now? First turn to the left.

The blind stripling tapped the curbstone and went on his way, drawing his cane back, feeling again.

Mr Bloom walked behind the eyeless feet, a flatcut suit of herringbone tweed. Poor young fellow! How on earth did he know that van was there? Must have felt it. See things in their foreheads perhaps. Kind of sense of volume. Weight would he feel it if something was removed. Feel a gap. Queer idea of Dublin he must have, tapping his way round by the stones. Could he walk in a beeline if he hadn't that cane? Bloodless pious face like a fellow going in to be a priest.

Penrose! That was that chap's name.

Look at all the things they can learn to do. Read with their fingers. Tune pianos. Or we are surprised they have any brains. Why we think a deformed person or a hunchback clever if he says something we might say. Of course the other senses are more. Embroider. Plait baskets. People ought to help. Work basket I could buy Molly's birthday. Hates sewing. Might take an objection. Dark men they call them.

Sense of smell must be stronger too. Smells on all sides bunched together. Each person too. Then the spring, the summer: smells. Tastes. They say you can't taste wines with your eyes shut or a cold in the head. Also smoke in the dark they say get no pleasure.

And with a woman, for instance. More shameless not seeing.

That girl passing the Stewart institution, head in the air. Look at me. I have them all on. Must be strange not to see her. Kind of a form in his mind's eye. The voice temperature when he touches her with fingers must almost see the lines, the curves. His hands on her hair, for instance. Say it was black for instance. Good. We call it black. Then passing over her white skin. Different feel perhaps. Feeling of white.

Postoffice. Must answer.[2] Fag today. Send her a postal order two shillings half a crown. Accept my little present. Stationer's just here too. Wait. Think over it.

With a gentle finger he felt ever so slowly the hair combed back above his ears. Again. Fibres of fine fine straw. Then gently his finger felt the skin of his right cheek. Downy hair there too. Not smooth enough. The belly is the smoothest. No-one about. There he goes into Frederick street. Perhaps to Levenston's dancing academy piano. Might be settling my braces.

Walking by Doran's public house he slid his hand between waistcoat and trousers and, pulling aside his shirt gently, felt a slack fold of his belly. But I know it's whiteyellow. Want to try in the dark to see.

He withdrew his hand and pulled his dress to.

Poor fellow! Quite a boy. Terrible. Really terrible. What dreams would he have, not seeing. Life a dream for him. Where is the justice being born that way. All those women and children excursion beanfeast burned and drowned in New York.[3] Holocaust. Karma they call that transmigration for sins you did in a past life the reincarnation met him pikehoses.[4] Dear, dear, dear. Pity of course: but somehow you can't cotton on to them someway.

Sir Frederick Falkiner going into the freemasons' hall. Solemn as Troy. After his good lunch in Earlsfort terrace. Old legal cronies cracking a magnum. Tales of the bench and assizes and annals of the bluecoat school.[5] I sentenced him to ten years. I suppose he'd turn up his nose at that stuff I drank. Vintage wine for them, the year marked on a dusty bottle. Has his own ideas of justice in the recorder's court. Wellmeaning old man. Police chargesheets crammed with cases get their percentage manufacturing crime. Sends them to the rightabout. The devil on moneylenders. Gave Reuben J. a great strawcalling. Now he's really what they call a dirty jew. Power those judges have. Crusty old topers in wigs. Bear with a sore paw. And may the Lord have mercy on your soul.

Hello, placard. Mirus bazaar. His excellency the lord lieuten-

2. Martha Clifford's letter.
3. This terrible disaster on an excursion steamer on the Hudson took place on June 15, 1904, and was reported in the Dublin papers on June 16.
4. I.e., metempsychosis: Bloom is remembering again their morning conversation on this subject, when Molly exclaimed "O rocks!"
5. Sir Frederick Falkiner wrote the history of the "bluecoat school" in Oxmantown, Dublin. The Dublin "bluecoat school" was founded by Charles II for poor children.

ant. Sixteenth today it is. In aid of funds for Mercer's hospital. *The Messiah* was first given for that. Yes. Handel. What about going out there. Ballsbridge. Drop in on Keyes. No use sticking to him like a leech. Wear out my welcome. Sure to know someone on the gate.

Mr Bloom came to Kildare street. First I must. Library.

Straw hat in sunlight. Tan shoes. Turnedup trousers. It is. It is.[6]

His heart quopped softly. To the right. Museum. Goddesses. He swerved to the right.

Is it? Almost certain. Won't look. Wine in my face. Why did I? Too heady. Yes, it is. The walk. Not see. Not see. Get on.

Making for the museum gate with long windy strides he lifted his eyes. Handsome building. Sir Thomas Deane designed. Not following me?

Didn't see me perhaps. Light in his eyes.

The flutter of his breath came forth in short sighs. Quick. Cold statues: quiet there. Safe in a minute.

No, didn't see me. After two. Just at the gate.

My heart!

His eyes beating looked steadfastly at cream curves of stone. Sir Thomas Deane was the Greek architecture.

Look for something I.

His hasty hand went quick into a pocket, took out, read unfolded Agendath Netaim. Where did I?

Busy looking for.

He thrust back quickly Agendath.

Afternoon she said.

I am looking for that. Yes, that. Try all pockets. Handker. *Freeman*. Where did I? Ah, yes. Trousers. Purse. Potato. Where did I?

Hurry. Walk quietly. Moment more. My heart.

His hand looking for the where did I put found in his hip pocket soap lotion have to call tepid paper stuck. Ah, soap there! Yes. Gate.[7]

Safe!

1914–21   1922

6. Bloom catches a glimpse of Boylan and tries to avoid an encounter.
7. Anxious to avoid Boylan, Bloom pretends to admire the architecture of the Museum and National Library building, and then pretends to be looking for something in his pockets, where he finds the "Agendath Netaim" leaflet. He continues to search desperately in his pock-ets to avoid looking up and seeing Boylan, discovers the potato he carries as a remedy against rheumatism and a cake of soap he had bought that morning (the soap reminds him that he must call at the chemist's to collect a face lotion he had ordered for Molly). At last he goes through the National Library gate and feels safe.

From Finnegans Wake[1]

From *Anna Livia Plurabelle*

* * * Well, you know or don't you kennet[2] or haven't I told
you every telling has a taling and that's the he and the she of it.
Look, look, the dusk is growing! My branches lofty are taking root.
And my cold cher's[3] gone ashley. Fieluhr?[4] Filou! What age is at? It
saon[5] is late. 'Tis endless now senne[6] eye or erewone[7] last saw
Waterhouse's clogh.[8] They took it asunder, I hurd thum sigh.
When will they reassemble it? O, my back, my back, my bach![9]
I'd want to go to Aches-les-Pains.[10] Pingpong! There's the Belle
for Sexaloitez![11] And Concepta de Send-us-pray! Pang! Wring out
the clothes! Wring in the dew![12] Godavari,[13] vert the showers! And

1. Because the meanings in *Finnegans Wake* are developed not by action but by language—a great network of multiple puns that echo themes back and forth throughout the book—the careful reading of a single passage, even out of context, will convey more than any summary of the "plot" (some discussion of the general plan of the work is given in the Joyce introduction). The particular passage selected here was one of Joyce's favorites, and there exists a phonograph recording of it made by himself. It consists of the closing pages of the eighth chapter of Book I; the chapter was published separately as *Anna Livia Plurabelle* in 1928 and 1930, although the finished book omits this title.

The entire chapter is a dialogue, and the scene is the river Liffey: two washerwomen are washing in public the dirty linen of HCE and ALP (the "hero" and "heroine"; see the Joyce introduction), and gossiping as they work. As this excerpt opens, it is growing dark; things become gradually less and less distinct, so that the washerwomen cannot be sure what the objects seen in the dusk really are. As it grows darker, the river becomes wider (we get nearer its mouth) and the wind rises, so that the women have more and more difficulty hearing each other. At last, as night falls, they become part of the landscape, an elm tree and a stone on the river bank. Toward the end of the dialogue they ask to hear a tale of Shem and Shaun (HCE's two sons), and this question points the way to Book II, which opens with the two boys (metamorphosed for the moment into Glugg and Chuff) playing in front of the tavern in the evening.

A complete annotation of even this brief passage is, of course, a physical impossibility in this anthology. The notes that are provided are intended to indicate the nature of what Joyce does with language and to enable the reader

to see what is going on. But there are all sorts of suggestions built up in the language that are not referred to in the notes: each reader will find some for himself.

2. Ken it ("know it") + Kennet (river in England). Rivers in *Finnegans Wake* symbolize the flow of life, and thousands of river names are suggested throughout the book in allusive pun-combinations, as here.

3. Cold cheer (i.e., cold comfort) + cold chair + (perhaps) culture. "Gone ashley": gone to ashes. Going to ashes suggests the fiery death and rebirth of the mythical phoenix. From the ashes of the dead phoenix rises a new one. Modern culture, which can provide only cold cheer, is in the state of decay, the "going to ashes," which precedes the stage of rebirth into a new cultural cycle (according to Giambattista Vico's cyclical theory of history, which is important to *Finnegans Wake*). "Gone ashley" also means "turned into an ash tree" (i.e., it is so cold that the speaker feels herself turning into a tree).

4. *Viel Uhr?* (German, "What's the time?") "Filou": pickpocket, thief (French). The question echoes so as to suggest that time is a thief.

5. Soon + Saône (river in France).

6. Since + Senne (river in Belgium).

7. E'er a one + *Erewhon* (novel by Samuel Butler—"Nowhere" spelled backwards).

8. Clock or bell (Irish) + the name of an Irish river.

9. Brook (German) + dear (Welsh).

10. Cf. Aix-les-Bains, France.

11. *Sex* (Latin, "six") + *laüten* (German, "to ring [the bells]"). The Angelus bell is rung every six hours.

12. Cf. "Ring out the old, ring in the new" (Tennyson, *In Memoriam*).

13. God of Eire; also the name of a river in India. "Vert": avert + *vert* (French, "green"), for "the showers" make grass green.

grant thaya grace! Aman. Will we spread them here now? Ay, we will. Flip! Spread on your bank and I'll spread mine on mine. Flep! It's what I'm doing. Spread! It's churning chill. Der went[14] is rising. I'll lay a few stones on the hostel sheets. A man and his bride embraced between them. Else I'd have sprinkled and folded them only. And I'll tie my butcher's apron here. It's suety yet. The strollers will pass it by. Six shifts, ten kerchiefs, nine to hold to the fire and this for the code,[15] the convent napkins, twelve, one baby's shawl. Good mother Jossiph[16] knows, she said. Whose head? Mutter snores? Deataceas![17] Wharnow are alle her childer, say? In kingdome gone or power to come or gloria be to them farther? Allalivial, allalluvial![18] Some here, more no more, more again lost alla stranger.[19] I've heard tell that same brooch of the Shannons[20] was married into a family in Spain. And all the Dunders de Dunnes[21] in Markland's[22] Vineland beyond Brendan's herring pool[23] takes number nine in yangsee's[24] hats. And one of Biddy's[25] beads went bobbing till she rounded up lost histereve[26] with a marigold and a cobbler's candle in a side strain of a main drain of a manzinahurries[27] off Bachelor's Walk. But all that's left to the last of the Meaghers[28] in the loup of the years prefixed and between is one kneebuckle and two hooks in the front. Do you tell me that now? I do in troth. Orara por Orbe and poor Las Animas![29]

---

14. *Der Wind* (German, "the wind") + Derwent (river in England).
15. Cold + code (i.e., the code in which the book is written). The numbers in this sentence have special meanings indicated in other episodes.
16. Joseph + *joss* (pidgin English, "God") + gossip (which derives from *god-sib*, Middle English, "godparent").
17. Latin, "Goddess, may you be silent!" Dea Tacita, in Roman mythology, is the name sometimes given to Acca Laurentia, mistress of Hercules and foster-mother of Romulus and Remus.
18. Multiple punning—Anna Livia + all alive + *la lluvia* (Spanish, "rain") + alluvial—suggesting the mother-river-fertility associations of ALP. At least two other meanings are also present: All alive O! (street cry of shellfish vendors) + Alleluia (Vulgate Latin form of "Hallelujah").
19. Cf. *à l'étranger* (French, "abroad").
20. Ornament and branch of the Shannons (family and river).
21. The form of the name suggests an aristocratic Anglo-Norman family. "Dunder" suggests thunder; *dun* is an Irish word meaning "hill," "fort on a hill."
22. Borderland + land of the mark (i.e., land of money, or America; "Vineland" or Vinland was the Norse name for America). Both King Mark of Cornwall (a character in the Tristan and Iseult story) and Mark of the Gospels are primary symbolic characters in *Finnegans Wake*.
23. The Atlantic Ocean; St. Brendan was an Irish monk who sailed out into the Atlantic to find the terrestrial paradise.
24. Yankees' + Yangtze (river in China). The de Dunnes have swollen heads now that they have emigrated to America.
25. Diminutive form of the name Bridget; St. Brigid (or Bridget) is a patron saint of Ireland. "Biddy" is also a term for an Irish maidservant.
26. Yester eve (last night) + eve of history. The sentence may be paraphrased: "Irish history got lost when she went off in a side branch of the main Roman Catholic Church, and Biddy (i.e., Ireland) landed herself in the dirt." There are also Freudian implications here.
27. Man's in a hurry + Manzanares (river in Spain).
28. Thomas Francis Meagher, Irish patriot and revolutionary, who was transported to Van Diemen's Land in 1849 and escaped to America in 1852. "Loup": loop + *loup* (French, "wolf" and also "solitary man"). Cf. Wolfe Tone, the ill-fated Irish revolutionist.
29. *Ora pro nobis* (Latin, "pray for us") + Orara (river in New South Wales) + *pro orbe* (Latin, "for the world") + Orbe (river in France). "Las Animas": souls (Spanish); also

Ussa, Ulla, we're umbas[30] all! Mezha, didn't you hear it a deluge of times, ufer[31] and ufer, respund to spond?[32] You deed, you deed! I need, I need! It's that irrawaddyng[33] I've stoke in my aars. It all but husheth the lethest zswound. Oronoko![34] What's your trouble? Is that the great Finnleader[35] himself in his joakimono on his statue riding the high horse there forehengist?[36] Father of Otters,[37] it is himself! Yonne there! Isset that? On Fallareen Common? You're thinking of Astley's Amphitheayter where the bobby restrained you making sugarstuck pouts to the ghostwhite horse of the Peppers.[38] Throw the cobwebs from your eyes, woman, and spread your washing proper! It's well I know your sort of slop. Flap! Ireland sober is Ireland stiff. Lord help you, Maria, full of grease, the load is with me! Your prayers. I sonht zo![39] Madammangut! Were you lifting your elbow, tell us, glazy cheeks, in Conway's Carrigacurra canteen? Was I what, hobbledyhips?[40] Flop! Your rcrc gait's creakorheuman bitts your butts disagrees.[41] Amn't I up since the damp dawn, marthared mary allacook, with Corrigan's pulse and varicoarse veins, my pramaxle smashed, Alice Jane in decline and my onceyed mongrel twice run over, soaking and bleaching boiler rags, and sweating cold, a widow like me, for to deck my tennis champion son, the laundryman with the lavandier flannels? You won your limpopo[42] limp fron the husky[43] hussars when Collars and Cuffs was heir to the town and your slur gave the stink to Carlow.[44] Holy Scamander,[45] I sar it again! Near the golden falls. Icis on us! Seints of light! Zezere![46] Subdue your noisc, you hamble creature! What

---

the name of a river in Colorado. The entire sentence may be read: "Pray for us and for all souls."
30. *Umbra* (Latin, "shade") + Umba (river in Africa). "Ussa," "Ulla," and "Mezha" are also river names; each contains a number of other meanings.
31. Bank (of river).
32. *Spund* (German, "bung").
33. A multiple pun: Irrawady (river in Burma) + irritating + wadding. This and the following sentence may be paraphrased: "It's that wadding I've stuck in my ears. It hushes the least sound."
34. *Oroonoko* (novel by Mrs. Aphra Behn about a "noble savage," published ca. 1678).
35. Fionn mac Cumhail (Finn MacCool), legendary hero of ancient Ireland. "Joakimono": i.e., comic kimono; *joki* is the Finnish word for river; the name Joachim is perhaps also implied.
36. Hengist was the Jute invader of England (with Horsa), ca. 449; he founded the kingdom of Kent.
37. Father of Waters (i.e., the Mississippi) + Father of Orders (i.e., Saint Patrick).
38. Philip Astley's Royal Amphitheatre was a famous late 18th-century English circus, specializing in trained

horses; "Pepper's Ghost" was a popular circus act. One of the washerwomen has been reproving the other, who thought she saw the great Finn himself riding his high horse, by telling her that once before she had to be restrained by a policeman for making "sugarstuck pouts" at a circus horse.
39. I thought so + Izontzo (river in Italy).
40. Hobbledehoy + wobbly hips.
41. The sentence is a punning discussion of her hard work and ailments. The first four words may also be read: "Your rear get (i.e., your last child) is Greek or Roman."
42. Name of a river in south Africa.
43. Cf. *uisge* (Gaelic, "whisky," but literally, "water [of life]").
44. I.e., "You got a slur on your reputation carrying on with soldiers in the Age of Elegance, and the scandal was all over Ireland" (ALP is being addressed, and some of her many lovers are mentioned). "Carlow" is a county in Ireland.
45. River near Troy, famous in classical legend. "I sar": I saw + Isar (river in Germany).
46. See there + Zezere (river in Portugal).

is it but a blackburry growth or the dwyergray ass them four old codgers[47] owns. Are you meanam[48] Tarpey and Lyons and Gregory? I meyne now, thank all, the four of them, and the roar of them, that draves[49] that stray in the mist and old Johnny MacDougal along with them. Is that the Poolbeg flasher beyant,[50] pharphar, or a fireboat coasting nyar[51] the Kishtna or a glow I behold within a hedge or my Garry come back from the Indes? Wait till the honeying of the lune,[52] love! Die eve, little eve, die![53] We see that wonder in your eye. We'll meet again, we'll part once more. The spot I'll seek if the hour you'll find. My chart shines high where the blue milk's upset. Forgivemequick, I'm going! Bubye! And you, pluck your watch, forgetmenot. Your evenlode.[54] So save to jurna's[55] end! My sights are swimming thicker on me by the shadows to this place. I sow[56] home slowly now by own way, moyvalley way. Towy[57] I too, rathmine.

Ah, but she was the queer old skeowsha anyhow, Anna Livia, trinkettoes! And sure he was the quare old buntz too, Dear Dirty Dumpling,[58] foostherfather of fingalls[59] and dottergills. Gammer and gaffer we're all their gangsters. Hadn't he seven dams to wive him? And every dam had her seven crutches. And every crutch had its seven hues.[60] And each hue had a differing cry. Sudds[61] for me and supper for you and the doctor's bill for Joe John. Befor! Bifur![62] He married his markets, cheap by foul, I know, like any Etrurian

47. The Four Old Men, who represent, among other things, the authors of the Gospels and the four elements.
48. Meaning + Menam (river in Thailand). The precise connotations of the three proper names that follow escape the present annotator.
49. Drives + Drave (river in Hungary).
50. I.e., the Poolbeg Lighthouse beyond (this lighthouse is in Dublin Bay); "pharphar": far far + Pharphar (river in Damascus) + *pharos* (Greek, "lighthouse").
51. Near + Nyar (river in India). "Kishtna": Kish (city in ancient Mesopotamia, traditionally the ruling city after the Flood) + Krishna (Hindu god of joy) + Kistna (river in India) + the Kish lightship (in Dublin Bay).
52. Loon (Scottish, "boy") + *luna* (Latin, "moon"). "Honeying of the lune": honeymoon, etc.
53. This sentence suggests traditional lovers' prayers for the day to die and night to come, and it also recalls the death of "little Eva" in *Uncle Tom's Cabin*. The sentences that follow are echoes of popular songs.
54. Evening load + Evenlode (river in England).
55. Journey + Jurna (river in Brazil).
56. Sow (river in England).
57. Name of a river in Wales. Moy is the name of an Irish river, and Moyvalley and Rathmine are names of Dublin suburbs.
58. "Dumpling" suggests Humpty Dumpty, whose fall is one of the many involved in the vastly symbolic fall of Finnegan. The phrase "Dear Dirty Dublin" occurs in *Ulysses*.
59. A pun-cluster: Fine Gael (the United Ireland Party) + fine Gaels + Fingal (river in Tasmania) + *Fingal* (the poem by James Macpherson, supposedly a translation from the Gaelic original of Ossian, an ancient Gaelic poet and son of Fingal—who is the same as Fionn mac Cumhail or Finn MacCool).
60. Colors of the rainbow (suggested a few lines later by "pinky limony creamy" and "turkiss indienne mauves"). In these sentences Joyce is punningly parodying the nursery rhyme, "As I was going to St. Ives / I met a man with seven wives * * * "
61. Suds (slang term for beer) + soapsuds + sudd (the floating vegetable matter which often obstructs navigation on the White Nile).
62. Bifurcated creature! This image of man as a forked being suggests HCE (cf. "*Etrurian Catholic Heathen*"). HCE's marital history, in his role as the Great Parent or generator, is one of the themes in this passage.

Catholic Heathen, in their pinky limony creamy birnies[63] and their turkiss indienne mauves. But at milkidmass[64] who was the spouse? Then all that was was fair. Tys Elvenland![65] Teems of times and happy returns. The seim anew.[66] Ordovico[67] or viricordo. Anna was, Livia is, Plurabelle's to be. Northmen's thing made southfolk's place but howmulty plurators made eachone in person?[68] Latin me that, my trinity scholard, out of eure sanscreed into oure eryan![69] *Hircus Civis Eblanensis!*[70] He had buckgoat paps on him, soft ones for orphans. Ho,[71] Lord! Twins of his bosom. Lord save us! And ho! Hey? What all men. Hot? His tittering daughters of. Whawk?

Can't hear with the waters of. The chittering waters of. Flittering bats, fieldmice bawk talk. Ho! Are you not gone ahome? What Thom Malone? Can't hear with bawk of bats, all thim liffeying waters of. Ho, talk save us! My foos won't moos.[72] I feel as old as yonder elm. A tale told of Shaun or Shem? All Livia's daughter-sons. Dark hawks hear us. Night! Night! My ho head halls. I feel as heavy as yonder stone. Tell me of John or Shaun? Who were Shem and Shaun the living sons or daughters of? Night now! Tell me, tell me, tell me, elm! Night night! Telmetale of stem or stone.[73] Beside the rivering waters of, hitherandthithering waters of. Night!

1923-38   1939

63. Coats of mail.
64. Milking time + Michaelmas (September 29).
65. 'Tis the land of Elves + Tys Elv (Norway).
66. The same again + Seim (river in Ireland).
67. The Ordovices were an ancient British tribe in northern Wales, and Ordovician is a term for a geological period. "Ordovico" is also a pun on Vico and his order of historical phases. Joyce is here suggesting the cyclical nature of things: the marital history of HCE is the history of ever-renewing life ("the seim anew"), and HCE's bride is Everywoman, past, present, and future ("Anna was, Livia is, Plurabelle's to be"). "Viricordo" is another verbal twist to Vico and his cycles, suggesting his *ricorso* ("recurrence," i.e., the 4th stage of the cycle which brings back the 1st), as well as overtones from the Latin *vir* (man) and *cor* (heart): the heart of man beats on, through all phases of civilization.
68. This sentence may be paraphrased: "The assembly of the Norsemen made the South-folk's place (i.e., as the Vikings settled Dublin), but how many marital pluralists (the word 'plurators' suggests men who had many wives or mistresses) went into the making of each of us?" The question is another link with the theme of HCE as the Great Parent.
69. I.e., out of your Sanskrit into your Aryan. "Sanscreed" has further punning meanings: *sans* screed (without script) + *sans* creed (without faith). Thus the phrase can read: "out of your illiteracy or faithlessness into Irish" (Eire-an). The greatest skeptic must pause in reverence before the endless flow of life, represented by Irish history.
70. Latin, "The Goat-Citizen of Dublin!" The goat is the symbol of lust and so of fecundity; *"Eblanensis"* is the adjective form of Eblana, the name given by the 3rd-century Alexandrian geographer Ptolemy to what may have been the site of the modern Dublin.
71. Chinese, "river."
72. Move + *Moos* (German, "moss"). Her foot ("foos") won't move; it is also turning to moss.
73. Stone and elm tree are important symbols in *Finnegans Wake*. Signifying permanence and change, time and space, mercy and justice, they undergo many changes of symbolic meaning throughout the book.

D. H. LAWRENCE
(1885–1930)

1912: Gives up school teaching for literature.
1915: *The Rainbow*, first of the "new" novels.

David Herbert Lawrence was born in the Midland mining village of East-wood, Nottinghamshire. His father was a miner; his mother, better educated than her husband and self-consciously genteel, fought all her married life to lift her children out of the working class. Lawrence was aware from an early age of the struggle between his parents; he was very much on his mother's side during his childhood, resenting his father's coarse and sometimes drunken behavior and allying himself with his mother's delicacy and refinement. After the death of an elder brother he became the center of his mother's emotional life and played in his own relation to her a loving and protective role. His mother's claims on him kept frustrating his relationships with girls, and the personal problems and conflicts that resulted are presented in his first really distinguished novel, *Sons and Lovers* (1913), where, against a background of paternal coarseness and vitality conflicting with maternal refinement and gentility, he sets the theme of the demanding mother who has given up the prospect of achieving a true emotional life with her husband and turns to her sons with a stultifying and possessive love. Many years later Lawrence came to feel that he had misjudged his father, whose coarseness represented after all a genuine vitality and some wholeness of personality, even if these qualities were impoverished and distorted by the civilization in which he lived.

Spurred on by his mother, Lawrence escaped through education from the mining world of his father. He won a scholarship to Nottingham high school and later, after working first as a clerk and then as an elementary school teacher (1902–6), studied for two years at Nottingham University College, where he obtained his teacher's certificate in 1908. Meanwhile he was reading on his own a great deal of literature and some philosophy and was working on his first novel, encouraged (as he was in all his early writing) by Jessie Chambers, the "Miriam" of *Sons and Lovers*. His first published work was a group of poems which appeared in the *English Review* for November, 1909. The following February the same periodical published his first short story. He was now regarded in London literary circles as a promising young writer; his first novel, *The White Peacock* (1910), was received with respect. From 1908 to 1912 he taught school in Croydon, a southern suburb of London, but he gave this up after falling in love with Frieda von Richthofen, the German wife of a Professor of French at Nottingham. They went to Germany together and married in 1914, after Frieda had been divorced by her first husband.

Abroad with Frieda, Lawrence finished *Sons and Lovers*, the autobiographical novel at which he had been working off and on for years. The
war brought them back to England, where Frieda's German origins and
Lawrence's fierce objection to the war gave him trouble with the authorities.
More and more—especially after the banning of his next novel, *The Rainbow*, in 1915—Lawrence came to feel that the forces of modern civilization
were arrayed against him. As soon as he could leave England after the war
he sought refuge in Italy, Australia, Mexico, then again in Italy, and finally
in the south of France, often desperately ill, restlessly searching for an ideal,
or at least a tolerable, community in which to live. He died of tuberculosis
in the south of France on the 2nd of March, 1930, at the early age of 44.

Shortly before his death he had written:

> Give me the moon at my feet
> Put my feet upon the crescent, like a Lord!
> O let my ankles be bathed in moonlight, that I may go
> sure and moon-shod, cool and bright-footed
> towards my goal.
>
> For the sun is hostile, now
> his face is like the red lion . . .

In these elemental images he invoked his end, a gesture at once heroic and
desperate. It was typical of him to symbolize his passing with reference to
the sun and moon, for Lawrence was at home with such cosmic images as
no other English writer except Blake has ever been; he was at home, one
might say, with the universe, with all that is deep-rooted and elemental in
man and nature, and at constant war with the mechanical and artificial,
with the constraints and hypocrisies that civilization imposes on man's
fundamental self. His most characteristic writings are essentially a record in
symbolic terms of his explorations of human individuality and of all that
hindered it and all that might fulfill it, whether in the natural world or in
the world of other individuals.

This is not what the English novel is generally supposed to do, and
Lawrence, with new things to say and a new way of using the novel form,
was not easily or quickly appreciated. His early novels, *The White Peacock*,
The Trespasser, and even the original and impressive *Sons and Lovers*, were
more conventional in style and treatment; they aroused contemporary interest and even acclaim, and it appeared that he might be on his way to becoming one of the acknowledged and popular Georgian novelists. But with
the publication of *The Rainbow* in 1915 the true, original Lawrence first
emerged clearly, and the critics turned away in bewilderment and condemnation. *The Rainbow* was suppressed as indecent a month after its publication,
and the war between Lawrence and the world of timid convention was on.
The rest of his life, during which he produced about a dozen more novels
and many poems, short stories, sketches, and miscellaneous articles, was, in
his own words, "a savage enough pilgrimage," marked by incessant struggle

and by moments of frustration and despair. Lawrence was one of those artists who had to create the taste by which he could be appreciated. He had no gift for explaining his attitude and literary technique in simple expository prose. He could explain himself only by performing, by operating in his own way as an artist, letting the work of art speak with its own voice and pulse with its own life. When he tried to talk *about* his ideas, instead of projecting them symbolically in art, he was often irritatingly and vaguely rhetorical. "Sense of truth," "supreme impulse" are phrases characteristic of Lawrence's belief in intuition, in the dark forces of the inner self, that must not be allowed to be swamped by the rational faculties but must be brought into a harmonious relation with them. It was a point of view—or rather, a perception, a passionate insight—which could not be convincingly expressed in argument, but demanded direct projection in art.

The genteel culture of Lawrence's mother came more and more to represent death for Lawrence. In much of his later work, and especially in some of his short stories, he sets the deadening restrictiveness of middle-class conventional living against the forces of liberation that are often represented by an outsider—a peasant, a gypsy, a working man, a primitive of some kind, someone free by circumstance or personal effort. The recurring theme of his short stories—which contain some of his best work—is the distortion of love by possessiveness or gentility or a false romanticism or a false conception of the life of the artists, and the achievement of a living relation between a man and a woman against the pressure of class-feeling or tradition or habit or prejudice.

His two masterpieces, *The Rainbow* and *Women in Love* (both of which developed out of what was originally conceived as a single novel to be called *The Sisters*), are to be read as symbolic and dramatic poems in prose. In these novels Lawrence probes with both subtlety and power into various aspects of relationship—the relationship between man and his environment, the relationship between the generations, the relationship between man and woman, the relationship between instinct and intellect, and above all the proper basis for the marriage relationship as he conceived it. He is concerned too with the impact of modern industrial civilization on human sensibility, and finds many ways, at once realistic and symbolic, of projecting this. At the very opening of *The Rainbow*, where Lawrence is dealing with the family history of the Brangwens, whose annals he is about to tell, he makes clear even by the rhythms of his prose, as well as by his tone and imagery, that this is not to be a chronicle family novel like Galsworthy's *Forsyte Saga*.

The Rainbow is built on sets of human relationships, both horizontal and vertical. Thus we first see the marriage of Tom Brangwen with the Polish widow Lydia Lensky; then Tom's relationship with his step-daughter Anna; then Anna's relationship with her husband Will; then Will's relationship with his daughters Ursula and Gudrun; and so on. The truth of emotional detail in the presentation of these developing relationships is rendered with extraordinary force and subtlety. A fine example is in the extract below, which shows Tom Brangwen comforting his little step-daughter Anna.

In the relationship of Anna and Will in marriage we begin to find the true Laurentian doctrine that marriage is a fight and at the same time, if properly realized, a means of mystic knowledge through the awareness by one partner (in ultimate intimacy) of the essential *otherness* of the other. After the amorous luxury and mutual discovery of the first few days of marriage, Anna suddenly turns into the brisk housewife and sends the bewildered Will out of doors while she sets about her housework. Lawrence's view of marriage as a struggle derived from his own relationship with his strong-minded German-born wife Frieda. There are more and bitterer lovers' quarrels in Lawrence's novels than anywhere else in English literature. Lawrence's "crockery-throwing" view of love could become tedious, except that, as he presents it, it is bound up with the deepest rhythms and most profound instincts of the man-woman relationship. It is even more strong in *Women in Love*, which deals with Ursula and Gudrun Brangwen and their search for an adequate love relationship. The novel is, however, very much more than the traditional love quest, the developing relationships of Ursula and Rupert Birkin on the one hand and Gudrun and Gerald Crich on the other.

In Rupert there is more than a little of Lawrence himself, yet Lawrence is still able occasionally to laugh at him. Gerald, coldly handsome son of a powerful Midland mineowner, accumulates for himself, as the novel progresses, all the deadening and distorting effects of modern industrial civilization. Lawrence does not simply make Gerald's behavior inadequate or offensive; he is able to invent for his characters actions which while wholly realistic on the surface, or social level, are at the same time profoundly symbolic. This symbolism does not always come off, but when it does the effect is remarkable, as in a scene where Gerald forces his terrified mare to stand by the railway line while a shunting train hisses and clanks back and forth, or in the extraordinary scene with the rabbit (reprinted below). The novel as a whole reveals a deep sense of English provincial life, in which—in spite of all Lawrence's wanderings abroad and of the foreign setting of many of his novels—his sensibility was really deeply rooted, much as George Eliot's was. His intimacy with the English scene, especially with provincial middle-class and working-class patterns of thought and feeling and the relation between them, is revealed again and again in the short stories, notably in "Fanny and Annie," "Daughters of the Vicar," "The Fox," "The Christening," and "Tickets Please."

In *The Rainbow* and *Women in Love*, then, Lawrence is developing a radically new kind of novel in which he explores kinds of human relationships with a combination of uncanny psychological precision and intense poetic feeling. They have an acute surface realism, a sharp sense of time and place, and brilliant topographical detail, and at the same time their high poetic symbolism, both of the total pattern of action and of incidents and objects within it, establishes a rhythm of meaning that is missed by those who read the novels with the conventional categories of "plot" and "characters" in mind. His next novel, *Aaron's Rod* (1922), is more uneven; in it Lawrence, employing many of his own experiences, explores problems of human relations under the question of moral and political leadership, which for a time obsessed him. He was concerned with the struggle for leadership in marriage as well as in politics. Two other novels on the theme of leadership, *Kangaroo* (1923), set in Australia, and *The Plumed Serpent* (1926), set in Mexico, similarly uneven, show him trying to give symbolic fictional form to his own problems and preoccupations. But *Kangaroo* in particular has its moments of uncanny perceptiveness, and it is extraordinary how Lawrence, drawing on his experiences during a short stay in Australia, was able to get beneath the skin of the country and evoke so much of the essential reality of both place and people.

It is hard to think of another English novelist whose best and most characteristic work makes such a disquieting assault on our normal patterns of thought and feeling. It is not simply that Lawrence is a rebel against convention—many writers have been that—or that his views are startling, though they sometimes are. It is rather that the whole response to life, and in particular to the problems posed by human relationships, that emerges from his novels and stories seems to come so profoundly from the deepest recesses of his being and therefore assault the deepest recesses of *our* being, that the challenge seems to go beyond that which is normally asserted by a work of art. It is difficult to escape the challenge; to make any attempt to respond fully to what he is saying is to be drawn into his world, forced to share his vision.

Although there are complex critical reasons for the posthumous triumph of this writer who was so much reviled in his lifetime, there is also a simple and striking reason that must not be forgotten. Lawrence had vision; he had a poetic sense of life; he had a keen ear and a piercing eye for every kind of vitality and color and sound in the world, for landscape—be it of England or Italy or New Mexico—for the individuality and concreteness of things in nature, and for the individuality and concreteness of people. His travel sketches are as impressive in their way as his novels; he seizes both on the symbolic incident and on the concrete reality, and each is interpreted in terms of the other. He looked at the world freshly, with his own eyes, avoiding formulas and clichés; and he forged for himself a kind of utterance which, at his best, was able to convey powerfully and vividly what his fresh, original vision showed him. This kind of originality has its drawbacks; he was sometimes shrill, sometimes repetitive, sometimes almost hysterical; some scenes in his novels are murky with unachieved symbolism or splutter with unresolved passion. But the great Lawrence remains.

This restless pilgrim with his uncanny perceptions into the depths of physical things, with his uncompromising honesty and originality in his view of men and the world, cannot be dismissed as merely a great eccentric. Nor is he a great prophet. He is essentially an artist; it is his *rendering* of life in his art, not his preaching about life's meaning, that matters.

Odor of Chrysanthemums

I

The small locomotive engine, Number 4, came clanking, stumbling down from Selston with seven full wagons. It appeared round the corner with loud threats of speed, but the colt that it startled from among the gorse,[1] which still flickered indistinctly in the raw afternoon, out-distanced it at a canter. A woman, walking up the railway line to Underwood, drew back into the hedge, held her basket aside, and watched the footplate of the engine advancing. The trucks [2] thumped heavily past, one by one, with slow inevitable movement, as she stood insignificantly trapped between the jolting black wagons and the hedge; then they curved away towards the coppice [3] where the withered oak leaves dropped noiselessly, while the birds, pulling at the scarlet hips beside the track, made off into the dusk that had already crept into the spinney.[4] In the open, the smoke from the engine sank and cleaved to the rough grass. The fields were dreary and forsaken, and in the marshy strip that led to the whimsey,[5] a reedy pit pond, the fowls had already abandoned their run among the alders, to roost in the tarred fowl house. The pit bank loomed up beyond the pond, flames like red sores licking its ashy sides, in the afternoon's stagnant light. Just beyond rose the tapering chimneys and the clumsy black head-stocks of Brinsley Colliery.[6] The two wheels were spinning fast up against the sky, and the winding engine rapped out its little spasms. The miners were being turned up.

The engine whistled as it came into the wide bay of railway lines beside the colliery, where rows of trucks stood in harbor.

Miners, single, trailing, and in groups, passed like shadows diverging home. At the edge of the ribbed level of sidings squat a low cottage, three steps down from the cinder track. A large bony vine clutched at the house, as if to claw down the tiled roof. Round the bricked yard grew a few wintry primroses. Beyond, the long garden sloped down to a bush-covered brook course. There were some twiggy apple trees, winter-crack trees, and ragged cabbages. Beside the path hung disheveled pink chrysanthemums, like pink cloths hung on bushes. A woman came stooping out of the felt-covered fowl house, halfway down the garden. She closed and

---

1. Also known as furze or whin, a prickly bush with yellow flowers common on heaths, moors, and hillsides all over Britain.
2. Open freight cars.
3. A wood of small trees or shrubs.

4. Copse, thicket.
5. Machine for raising ore or water from a mine.
6. Coal mine; "headstocks" support revolving parts of a machine.

padlocked the door, then drew herself erect, having brushed some bits from her white apron.

She was a tall woman of imperious mien, handsome, with definite black eyebrows. Her smooth black hair was parted exactly. For a few moments she stood steadily watching the miners as they passed along the railway: then she turned towards the brook course. Her face was calm and set, her mouth was closed with disillusionment. After a moment she called:

"John!" There was no answer. She waited, and then said distinctly:

"Where are you?"

"Here!" replied a child's sulky voice from among the bushes. The woman looked piercingly through the dusk.

"Are you at that brook?" she asked sternly.

For answer the child showed himself before the raspberry canes that rose like whips. He was a small, sturdy boy of five. He stood quite still, defiantly.

"Oh!" said the mother, conciliated. "I thought you were down at that wet brook—and you remember what I told you——"

The boy did not move or answer.

"Come, come on in," she said more gently, "it's getting dark. There's your grandfather's engine coming down the line!"

The lad advanced slowly, with resentful, taciturn movement. He was dressed in trousers and waistcoat of cloth that was too thick and hard for the size of the garments. They were evidently cut down from a man's clothes.

As they went slowly towards the house he tore at the ragged wisps of chrysanthemums and dropped the petals in handfuls among the path.

"Don't do that—it does look nasty," said his mother. He refrained, and she, suddenly pitiful, broke off a twig with three or four wan flowers and held them against her face. When mother and son reached the yard her hand hesitated, and instead of laying the flower aside, she pushed it in her apron-band. The mother and son stood at the foot of the three steps looking across the bay of lines at the passing home of the miners. The trundle of the small train was imminent. Suddenly the engine loomed past the house and came to a stop opposite the gate.

The engine-driver, a short man with round gray beard, leaned out of the cab high above the woman.

"Have you got a cup of tea?" he said in a cheery, hearty fashion.

It was her father. She went in, saying she would mash.[7] Directly,

---

7. Infuse the tea, i.e., let it stand after pouring boiling water over the tea leaves in order to gain strength.

she returned.

"I didn't come to see you on Sunday," began the little gray-bearded man.

"I didn't expect you," said his daughter.

The engine driver winced; then, reassuming his cheery, airy manner, he said:

"Oh, have you heard then? Well, and what do you think——?"

"I think it is soon enough," she replied.

At her brief censure the little man made an impatient gesture, and said coaxingly, yet with dangerous coldness:

"Well, what's a man to do? It's no sort of life for a man of my years, to sit at my own hearth like a stranger. And if I'm going to marry again it may as well be soon as late—what does it matter to anybody?"

The woman did not reply, but turned and went into the house. The man in the engine-cab stood assertive, till she returned with a cup of tea and a piece of bread and butter on a plate. She went up the steps and stood near the footplate of the hissing engine.

"You needn't 'a' brought me bread an' butter," said her father. "But a cup of tea"—he sipped appreciatively—"it's very nice." He sipped for a moment or two, then: "I hear as Walter's got another bout on," he said.

"When hasn't he?" said the woman bitterly.

"I heerd tell of him in the Lord Nelson braggin' as he was going to spend that h—— afore he went: half a sovereign that was."

"When?" asked the woman.

"A' Sat'day night—I know that's true."

"Very likely," she laughed bitterly. "He gives me twenty-three shillings."

"Aye, it's a nice thing, when a man can do nothing with his money but make a beast of himself!" said the gray-whiskered man. The woman turned her head away. Her father swallowed the last of his tea and handed her the cup.

"Aye," he sighed, wiping his mouth. "It's a settler,[8] it is——"

He put his hand on the lever. The little engine strained and groaned, and the train rumbled towards the crossing. The woman again looked across the metals. Darkness was settling over the spaces of the railway and trucks: the miners, in gray somber groups, were still passing home. The winding engine pulsed hurriedly, with brief pauses. Elizabeth Bates looked at the dreary flow of men, then she went indoors. Her husband did not come.

The kitchen was small and full of firelight; red coals piled glowing up the chimney mouth. All the life of the room seemed in the

8. Crushing (or final) blow.

white, warm hearth and the steel fender reflecting the red fire. The cloth was laid for tea; cups glinted in the shadows. At the back, where the lowest stairs protruded into the room, the boy sat struggling with a knife and a piece of white wood. He was almost hidden in the shadow. It was half-past four. They had but to await the father's coming to begin tea. As the mother watched her son's sullen little struggle with the wood, she saw herself in his silence and pertinacity; she saw the father in her child's indifference to all but himself. She seemed to be occupied by her husband. He had probably gone past his home, slunk past his own door, to drink before he came in, while his dinner spoiled and wasted in waiting. She glanced at the clock, then took the potatoes to strain them in the yard. The garden and fields beyond the brook were closed in uncertain darkness. When she rose with the saucepan, leaving the drain steaming into the night behind her, she saw the yellow lamps were lit along the high road that went up the hill away beyond the space of the railway lines and the field.

Then again she watched the men trooping home, fewer now and fewer.

Indoors the fire was sinking and the room was dark red. The woman put her saucepan on the hob, and set a batter pudding near the mouth of the oven. Then she stood unmoving. Directly, gratefully, came quick young steps to the door. Someone hung on the latch a moment, then a little girl entered and began pulling off her outdoor things, dragging a mass of curls, just ripening from gold to brown, over her eyes with her hat.

Her mother chid her for coming late from school, and said she would have to keep her at home the dark winter days.

"Why, mother, it's hardly a bit dark yet. The lamp's not lighted, and my father's not home."

"No, he isn't. But it's a quarter to five! Did you see anything of him?"

The child became serious. She looked at her mother with large, wistful blue eyes.

"No, mother, I've never seen him. Why? Has he come up an' gone past, to Old Brinsley? He hasn't, mother, 'cos I never saw him."

"He'd watch that," said the mother bitterly, "he'd take care as you didn't see him. But you may depend upon it, he's seated in the Prince o' Wales. He wouldn't be this late."

The girl looked at her mother piteously.

"Let's have our teas, mother, should we?" said she.

The mother called John to table. She opened the door once more and looked out across the darkness of the lines. All was deserted:

she could not hear the winding-engines.

"Perhaps," she said to herself, "he's stopped to get some rip-ping [9] done."

They sat down to tea. John, at the end of the table near the door, was almost lost in the darkness. Their faces were hidden from each other. The girl crouched against the fender slowly moving a thick piece of bread before the fire. The lad, his face a dusky mark on the shadow, sat watching her who was transfigured in the red glow.

"I do think it's beautiful to look in the fire," said the child.

"Do you?" said her mother. "Why?"

"It's so red, and full of little caves—and it feels so nice, and you can fair smell it."

"It'll want mending directly," replied her mother, "and then if your father comes he'll carry on and say there never is a fire when a man comes home sweating from the pit. A public house is always warm enough."

There was silence till the boy said complainingly: "Make haste, our Annie."

"Well, I am doing! I can't make the fire do it no faster, can I?"

"She keeps wafflin' it about so's to make 'er slow," grumbled the boy.

"Don't have such an evil imagination, child," replied the mother.

Soon the room was busy in the darkness with the crisp sound of crunching. The mother ate very little. She drank her tea deter-minedly, and sat thinking. When she rose her anger was evident in the stern unbending of her head. She looked at the pudding in the fender, and broke out:

"It is a scandalous thing as a man can't even come home to his dinner! If it's crozzled up to a cinder I don't see why I should care. Past his very door he goes to get to a public house, and here I sit with his dinner waiting for him——"

She went out. As she dropped piece after piece of coal on the red fire, the shadows fell on the walls, till the room was almost in total darkness.

"I canna see," grumbled the invisible John. In spite of herself, the mother laughed.

"You know the way to your mouth," she said. She set the dust-pan outside the door. When she came again like a shadow on the hearth, the lad repeated, complaining sulkily:

"I canna see."

"Good gracious!" cried the mother irritably, "you're as bad as your father if it's a bit dusk!"

9. Taking out or cutting away coal or stone (a mining and quarrying term).

Nevertheless, she took a paper spill from a sheaf on the mantelpiece and proceeded to light the lamp that hung from the ceiling
in the middle of the room. As she reached up, her figure displayed itself just rounding with maternity.

"Oh, mother——!" exclaimed the girl.

"What?" said the woman, suspended in the act of putting the
lamp glass over the flame. The copper reflector shone handsomely
on her, as she stood with uplifted arm, turning to face her daughter.

"You've got a flower in your apron!" said the child, in a little
rapture at this unusual event.

"Goodness me!" exclaimed the woman, relieved. "One would
think the house was afire." She replaced the glass and waited a
moment before turning up the wick. A pale shadow was seen
floating vaguely on the floor.

"Let me smell!" said the child, still rapturously, coming forward and putting her face to her mother's waist.

"Go along, silly!" said the mother, turning up the lamp. The
light revealed their suspense so that the woman felt it almost unbearable. Annie was still bending at her waist. Irritably, the mother
took the flowers out from her apron band.

"Oh, mother—don't take them out!" Annie cried, catching her
hand and trying to replace the sprig.

"Such nonsense!" said the mother, turning away. The child
put the pale chrysanthemums to her lips, murmuring:

"Don't they smell beautiful!"

Her mother gave a short laugh.

"No," she said, "not to me. It was chrysanthemums when I married him, and chrysanthemums when you were born, and the first
time they ever brought him home drunk, he'd got brown chrysanthemums in his buttonhole."

She looked at the children. Their eyes and their parted lips were
wondering. The mother sat rocking in silence for some time. Then
she looked at the clock.

"Twenty minutes to six!" In a tone of fine bitter carelessness she
continued: "Eh, he'll not come now till they bring him. There he'll
stick! But he needn't come rolling in here in his pit dirt, for *I* won't
wash him. He can lie on the floor——Eh, what a fool I've been,
what a fool! And this is what I came here for, to this dirty hole, rats
and all, for him to slink past his very door. Twice last week—he's
begun now——"

She silenced herself, and rose to clear the table.

While for an hour or more the children played, subduedly intent, fertile of imagination, united in fear of the mother's wrath,
and in dread of their father's home-coming, Mrs. Bates sat in her

rocking chair making a "singlet" of thick cream-colored flannel, which gave a dull wounded sound as she tore off the gray edge. She worked at her sewing with energy, listening to the children, and her anger wearied itself, lay down to rest, opening its eyes from time to time and steadily watching, its ears raised to listen. Sometimes even her anger quailed and shrank, and the mother suspended her sewing, tracing the footsteps that thudded along the sleepers outside; she would lift her head sharply to bid the children "hush," but she recovered herself in time, and the footsteps went past the gate, and the children were not flung out of their play-world.

But at last Annie sighed, and gave in. She glanced at her wagon of slippers, and loathed the game. She turned plaintively to her mother.

"Mother!"—but she was inarticulate.

John crept out like a frog from under the sofa. His mother glanced up.

"Yes," she said, "just look at those shirt-sleeves!"

The boy held them out to survey them, saying nothing. Then somebody called in a hoarse voice away down the line, and suspense bristled in the room, till two people had gone by outside, talking.

"It is time for bed," said the mother.

"My father hasn't come," wailed Annie plaintively. But her mother was primed with courage.

"Never mind. They'll bring him when he does come—like a log." She meant there would be no scene. "And he may sleep on the floor till he wakes himself. I know he'll not go to work to-morrow after this!"

The children had their hands and faces wiped with a flannel. They were very quiet. When they had put on their nightdresses, they said their prayers, the boy mumbling. The mother looked down at them, at the brown silken bush of intertwining curls in the nape of the girl's neck, at the little black head of the lad, and her heart burst with anger at their father, who caused all three such distress. The children hid their faces in her skirts for comfort.

When Mrs. Bates came down, the room was strangely empty, with a tension of expectancy. She took up her sewing and stitched for some time without raising her head. Meantime her anger was tinged with fear.

II

The clock struck eight and she rose suddenly, dropping her sewing on her chair. She went to the stair-foot door, opened it, listening. Then she went out, locking the door behind her.

Something scuffled in the yard, and she started, though she knew it was only the rats with which the place was over-run. The night was very dark. In the great bay of railway lines, bulked with trucks, there was no trace of light, only away back she could see a few yellow lamps at the pit top, and the red smear of the burning pit bank on the night. She hurried along the edge of the track, then, crossing the converging lines, came to the stile by the white gates, whence she emerged on the road. Then the fear which had led her shrank. People were walking up to New Brinsley; she saw the lights in the houses; twenty yards farther on were the broad windows of the Prince of Wales, very warm and bright, and the loud voices of men could be heard distinctly. What a fool she had been to imagine that anything had happened to him! He was merely drinking over there at the Prince of Wales. She faltered. She had never yet been to fetch him, and she never would go. So she continued her walk towards the long straggling line of houses, standing back on the highway. She entered a passage between the dwellings.

"Mr. Rigley?—Yes! Did you want him? No, he's not in at this minute."

The raw-boned woman leaned forward from her dark scullery and peered at the other, upon whom fell a dim light through the blind of the kitchen window.

"Is it Mrs. Bates?" she asked in a tone tinged with respect.

"Yes. I wondered if your Master was at home. Mine hasn't come yet."

" 'Asn't 'e! Oh, Jack's been 'ome an' 'ad 'is dinner an' gone out. 'E's just gone for 'alf an hour afore bedtime. Did you call at the Prince of Wales?"

"No——"

"No, you didn't like——! It's not very nice." The other woman was indulgent. There was an awkward pause. "Jack never said nothink about—about your Master," she said.

"No!—I expect he's stuck in there!"

Elizabeth Bates said this bitterly, and with recklessness. She knew that the woman across the yard was standing at her door listening, but she did not care. As she turned:

"Stop a minute! I'll just go an' ask Jack if 'e knows anythink," said Mrs. Rigley.

"Oh no—I wouldn't like to put——!"

"Yes, I will, if you'll just step inside an' see as th' childer doesn't come downstairs and set theirselves afire."

Elizabeth Bates, murmuring a remonstrance, stepped inside. The other woman apologized for the state of the room.

The kitchen needed apology. There were little frocks and trousers and childish undergarments on the squab and on the floor, and a litter of playthings everywhere. On the black American cloth [1] of the table were pieces of bread and cake, crusts, slops, and a teapot with cold tea.

"Eh, ours is just as bad," said Elizabeth Bates, looking at the woman, not at the house. Mrs. Rigley put a shawl over her head and hurried out, saying:

"I shanna be a minute."

The other sat, noting with faint disapproval the general untidiness of the room. Then she fell to counting the shoes of various sizes scattered over the floor. There were twelve. She sighed and said to herself: "No wonder!"—glancing at the litter. There came the scratching of two pairs of feet on the yard, and the Rigleys entered. Elizabeth Bates rose. Rigley was a big man, with very large bones. His head looked particularly bony. Across his temple was a blue scar, caused by a wound got in the pit, a wound in which the coal dust remained blue like tattooing.

" 'Asna 'e come whoam yit?" asked the man, without any form of greeting, but with deference and sympathy. "I couldna say wheer he is—'e's non ower theer!"—he jerked his head to signify the Prince of Wales.

" 'E's 'appen gone up to th' Yew," said Mrs. Rigley.

There was another pause. Rigley had evidently something to get off his mind:

"Ah left 'im finishin' a stint," he began. "Loose-all [2] 'ad bin gone about ten minutes when we com'n away, an' I shouted: 'Are ter comin', Walt?' an' 'e said: 'Go on, Ah shanna be but a'ef a minnit,' so we com'n ter th' bottom, me an' Bowers, thinkin' as 'e wor just behint, an' 'ud come up i' th' next bantle [3]——"

He stood perplexed, as if answering a charge of deserting his mate. Elizabeth Bates, now again certain of disaster, hastened to reassure him:

"I expect 'e's gone up to th' Yew Tree, as you say. It's not the first time. I've fretted myself into a fever before now. He'll come home when they carry him."

"Ay, isn't it too bad!" deplored the other woman.

"I'll just step up to Dick's an' see if 'e *is* theer," offered the man, afraid of appearing alarmed, afraid of taking liberties.

"Oh, I wouldn't think of bothering you that far," said Elizabeth Bates, with emphasis, but he knew she was glad of his offer.

As they stumbled up the entry, Elizabeth Bates heard Rigley's wife run across the yard and open her neighbor's door. At this, suddenly all the blood in her body seemed to switch away from her

1. Oilcloth.　　　　3. Group.
2. Signal for end of work.

heart.

"Mind!" warned Rigley. "Ah've said many a time as Ah'd fill up them ruts in this entry, sumb'dy 'll be breakin' their legs yit."

She recovered herself and walked quickly along with the miner.

"I don't like leaving the children in bed, and nobody in the house," she said.

"No, you dunna!" he replied courteously. They were soon at the gate of the cottage.

"Well, I shanna be many minnits. Dunna you be frettin' now, 'e'll be all right," said the butty.[4]

"Thank you very much, Mr. Rigley," she replied.

"You're welcome!" he stammered, moving away. "I shanna be many minnits."

The house was quiet. Elizabeth Bates took off her hat and shawl, and rolled back the rug. When she had finished, she sat down. It was a few minutes past nine. She was startled by the rapid chuff of the winding engine at the pit, and the sharp whirr of the brakes on the rope as it descended. Again she felt the painful sweep of her blood, and she put her hand to her side, saying aloud: "Good gracious!—it's only the nine o'clock deputy [5] going down," rebuking herself.

She sat still, listening. Half an hour of this, and she was wearied out.

"What am I working myself up like this for?" she said pitiably to herself, "I s'll only be doing myself some damage."

She took out her sewing again.

At a quarter to ten there were footsteps. One person! She watched for the door to open. It was an elderly woman, in a black bonnet and a black woolen shawl—his mother. She was about sixty years old, pale, with blue eyes, and her face all wrinkled and lamentable. She shut the door and turned to her daughter-in-law peevishly.

"Eh, Lizzie, whatever shall we do, whatever shall we do!" she cried.

Elizabeth drew back a little, sharply.

"What is it, mother?" she said.

The elder woman seated herself on the sofa.

"I don't know, child, I can't tell you!"—she shook her head slowly. Elizabeth sat watching her, anxious and vexed.

"I don't know," replied the grandmother, sighing very deeply. "There's no end to my troubles, there isn't. The things I've gone through, I'm sure it's enough——!" She wept without wiping her

4. Workmate (cf. "buddy"). 5. Minor coal-mine official.

eyes, the tears running.

"But, mother," interrupted Elizabeth, "what do you mean? What is it?"

The grandmother slowly wiped her eyes. The fountains of her tears were stopped by Elizabeth's directness. She wiped her eyes slowly.

"Poor child! Eh, you poor thing!" she moaned. "I don't know what we're going to do, I don't—and you as you are—it's a thing, it is indeed!"

Elizabeth waited.

"Is he dead?" she asked, and at the words her heart swung violently, though she felt a slight flush of shame at the ultimate extravagance of the question. Her words sufficiently frightened the old lady, almost brought her to herself.

"Don't say so, Elizabeth! We'll hope it's not as bad as that; no, may the Lord spare us that, Elizabeth. Jack Rigley came just as I was sittin' down to a glass afore going to bed, an' 'e said: ' 'Appen you'll go down th' line, Mrs. Bates. Walt's had an accident. 'Appen you'll go an' sit wi' 'er till we can get him home.' I hadn't time to ask him a word afore he was gone. An' I put my bonnet on an' come straight down, Lizzie. I thought to myself: 'Eh, that poor blessed child, if anybody should come an' tell her of a sudden, there's no knowin' what'll 'appen to 'er.' You mustn't let it upset you, Lizzie —or you know what to expect. How long is it, six months—or is it five, Lizzie? Ay!"—the old woman shook her head—"time slips on, it slips on! Ay!"

Elizabeth's thoughts were busy elsewhere. If he was killed— would she be able to manage on the little pension and what she could earn?—she counted up rapidly. If he was hurt—they wouldn't take him to the hospital—how tiresome he would be to nurse!—but perhaps she'd be able to get him away from the drink and his hateful ways. She would—while he was ill. The tears offered to come to her eyes at the picture. But what sentimental luxury was this she was beginning? She turned to consider the children. At any rate she was absolutely necessary for them. They were her business.

"Ay!" repeated the old woman, "it seems but a week or two since he brought me his first wages. Ay—he was a good lad, Elizabeth, he was, in his way. I don't know why he got to be such a trouble, I don't. He was a happy lad at home, only full of spirits. But there's no mistake he's been a handful of trouble, he has! I hope the Lord'll spare him to mend his ways. I hope so, I hope so. You've had a sight o' trouble with him, Elizabeth, you have indeed. But he was a jolly enough lad wi' me, he was, I can assure you. I don't know how it is. . . ."

The old woman continued to muse aloud, a monotonous irritating sound, while Elizabeth thought concentratedly, startled once, when she heard the winding engine chuff quickly, and the brakes skirr with a shriek. Then she heard the engine more slowly, and the brakes made no sound. The old woman did not notice. Elizabeth waited in suspense. The mother-in-law talked, with lapses into silence.

"But he wasn't your son, Lizzie, an' it makes a difference. Whatever he was, I remember him when he was little, an' I learned to understand him and to make allowances. You've got to make allowances for them——"

It was half-past ten, and the old woman was saying: "But it's trouble from beginning to end; you're never too old for trouble, never too old for that——" when the gate banged back, and there were heavy feet on the steps.

"I'll go, Lizzie, let me go," cried the old woman, rising. But Elizabeth was at the door. It was a man in pit clothes.

"They're bringin' 'im, Missis," he said. Elizabeth's heart halted a moment. Then it surged on again, almost suffocating her.

"Is he—is it bad?" she asked.

The man turned away, looking at the darkness:

"The doctor says 'e'd been dead hours. 'E saw 'im i' th' lamp-cabin."

The old woman, who stood just behind Elizabeth, dropped into a chair, and folded her hands, crying: "Oh, my boy, my boy!"

"Hush!" said Elizabeth, with a sharp twitch of a frown. "Be still, mother, don't waken th' children: I wouldn't have them down for anything!"

The old woman moaned softly, rocking herself. The man was drawing away. Elizabeth took a step forward.

"How was it?" she asked.

"Well, I couldn't say for sure," the man replied, very ill at ease. " 'E wor finishin' a stint an' th' butties 'ad gone, an' a lot o' stuff come down atop 'n 'im."

"And crushed him?" cried the widow, with a shudder.

"No," said the man, "it fell at th' back of 'im. 'E wor under th' face an' it niver touched 'im. It shut 'im in. It seems 'e wor smothered."

Elizabeth shrank back. She heard the old woman behind her cry:

"What?—what did 'e say it was?"

The man replied, more loudly: " 'E wor smothered!"

Then the old woman wailed aloud, and this relieved Elizabeth.

"Oh, mother," she said, putting her hand on the old woman, "don't waken th' children, don't waken th' children."

She wept a little, unknowing, while the old mother rocked herself and moaned. Elizabeth remembered that they were bringing him home, and she must be ready. "They'll lay him in the parlor," she said to herself, standing a moment pale and perplexed.

Then she lighted a candle and went into the tiny room. The air was cold and damp, but she could not make a fire, there was no fireplace. She set down the candle and looked round. The candlelight glittered on the luster-glasses, on the two vases that held some of the pink chrysanthemums, and on the dark mahogany. There was a cold, deathly smell of chrysanthemums in the room. Elizabeth stood looking at the flowers. She turned away, and calculated whether there would be room to lay him on the floor, between the couch and the chiffonier. She pushed the chairs aside. There would be room to lay him down and to step round him. Then she fetched the old red tablecloth, and another old cloth, spreading them down to save her bit of carpet. She shivered on leaving the parlor; so, from the dresser drawer she took a clean shirt and put it at the fire to air. All the time her mother-in-law was rocking herself in the chair and moaning.

"You'll have to move from there, mother," said Elizabeth. "They'll be bringing him in. Come in the rocker."

The old mother rose mechanically, and seated herself by the fire, continuing to lament. Elizabeth went into the pantry for another candle, and there, in the little penthouse under the naked tiles, she heard them coming. She stood still in the pantry doorway, listening. She heard them pass the end of the house, and come awkwardly down the three steps, a jumble of shuffling footsteps and muttering voices. The old woman was silent. The men were in the yard.

Then Elizabeth heard Matthews, the manager of the pit, say: "You go in first, Jim. Mind!"

The door came open, and the two women saw a collier backing into the room, holding one end of a stretcher, on which they could see the nailed pit boots of the dead man. The two carriers halted, the man at the head stooping to the lintel of the door.

"Wheer will you have him?" asked the manager, a short, white-bearded man.

Elizabeth roused herself and came from the pantry carrying the unlighted candle.

"In the parlor," she said.

"In there, Jim!" pointed the manager, and the carriers backed round into the tiny room. The coat with which they had covered

the body fell off as they awkwardly turned through the two doorways, and the women saw their man, naked to the waist, lying
stripped for work. The old woman began to moan in a low voice
of horror.

"Lay th' stretcher at th' side," snapped the manager, "an' put
'im on th' cloths. Mind now, mind! Look you now——!"

One of the men had knocked off a vase of chrysanthemums. He
stared awkwardly, then they set down the stretcher. Elizabeth did
not look at her husband. As soon as she could get in the room, she
went and picked up the broken vase and the flowers.

"Wait a minute!" she said.

The three men waited in silence while she mopped up the
water with a duster.

"Eh, what a job, what a job, to be sure!" the manager was
saying, rubbing his brow with trouble and perplexity. "Never
knew such a thing in my life, never! He'd no business to ha' been
left. I never knew such a thing in my life! Fell over him clean
as a whistle, an' shut him in. Not four foot of space, there wasn't—
yet it scarce bruised him."

He looked down at the dead man, lying prone, half naked, all
grimed with coal dust.

"''Sphyxiated', the doctor said. It *is* the most terrible job I've
ever known. Seems as if it was done o' purpose. Clean over him,
an' shut 'im in, like a mouse-trap"—he made a sharp, descending
gesture with his hand.

The colliers standing by jerked aside their heads in hopeless
comment.

The horror of the thing bristled upon them all.

Then they heard the girl's voice upstairs calling shrilly: "Mother,
mother—who is it? Mother, who is it?"

Elizabeth hurried to the foot of the stairs and opened the door:

"Go to sleep!" she commanded sharply. "What are you shouting
about? Go to sleep at once—there's nothing——"

Then she began to mount the stairs. They could hear her on
the boards, and on the plaster floor of the little bedroom. They
could hear her distinctly:

"What's the matter now?—what's the matter with you, silly
thing?"—her voice was much agitated, with an unreal gentleness.

"I thought it was some men come," said the plaintive voice of
the child. "Has he come?"

"Yes, they've brought him. There's nothing to make a fuss
about. Go to sleep now, like a good child."

They could hear her voice in the bedroom, they waited whilst
she covered the children under the bedclothes.

"Is he drunk?" asked the girl, timidly, faintly.

"No! No—he's not! He—he's asleep."

"Is he asleep downstairs?"

"Yes—and don't make a noise."

There was silence for a moment, then the men heard the frightened child again:

"What's that noise?"

"It's nothing, I tell you, what are you bothering for?"

The noise was the grandmother moaning. She was oblivious of everything, sitting on her chair rocking and moaning. The manager put his hand on her arm and bade her "Sh—sh! !"

The old woman opened her eyes and looked at him. She was shocked by this interruption, and seemed to wonder.

"What time is it?" the plaintive thin voice of the child, sinking back unhappily into sleep, asked this last question.

"Ten o'clock," answered the mother more softly. Then she must have bent down and kissed the children.

Matthews beckoned to the men to come away. They put on their caps and took up the stretcher. Stepping over the body, they tiptoed out of the house. None of them spoke till they were far from the wakeful children.

When Elizabeth came down she found her mother alone on the parlor floor, leaning over the dead man, the tears dropping on him.

"We must lay him out," the wife said. She put on the kettle, then returning knelt at the feet, and began to unfasten the knotted leather laces. The room was clammy and dim with only one candle, so that she had to bend her face almost to the floor. At last she got off the heavy boots and put them away.

"You must help me now," she whispered to the old woman. Together they stripped the man.

When they arose, saw him lying in the naïve dignity of death, the woman stood arrested in fear and respect. For a few moments they remained still, looking down, the old mother whimpering. Elizabeth felt countermanded. She saw him, how utterly inviolable he lay in himself. She had nothing to do with him. She could not accept it. Stooping, she laid her hand on him, in claim. He was still warm, for the mine was hot where he had died. His mother had his face between her hands, and was murmuring incoherently. The old tears fell in succession as drops from wet leaves; the mother was not weeping, merely her tears flowed. Elizabeth embraced the body of her husband, with cheek and lips. She seemed to be listening, inquiring, trying to get some connection. But she could not. She was driven away. He was impregnable.

She rose, went into the kitchen, where she poured warm water into a bowl, brought soap and flannel and a soft towel. "I must wash him," she said.

Then the old mother rose stiffly, and watched Elizabeth as she carefully washed his face, carefully brushing his big blond moustache from his mouth with the flannel. She was afraid with a bottomless fear, so she ministered to him. The old woman, jealous, said:

"Let me wipe him!"—and she kneeled on the other side drying slowly as Elizabeth washed, her big black bonnet sometimes brushing the dark head of her daughter-in-law. They worked thus in silence for a long time. They never forgot it was death, and the touch of the man's dead body gave them strange emotions, different in each of the women; a great dread possessed them both, the mother felt the lie was given to her womb, she was denied; the wife felt the utter isolation of the human soul, the child within her was a weight apart from her.

At last it was finished. He was a man of handsome body, and his face showed no traces of drink. He was blond, full fleshed, with fine limbs. But he was dead.

"Bless him," whispered his mother, looking always at his face, and speaking out of sheer terror. "Dear lad—bless him!" She spoke in a faint, sibilant ecstasy of fear and mother love.

Elizabeth sank down again to the floor, and put her face against his neck, and trembled and shuddered. But she had to draw away again. He was dead, and her living flesh had no place against his. A great dread and weariness held her: she was so unavailing. Her life was gone like this.

"White as milk he is, clear as a twelve-month baby, bless him, the darling!" the old mother murmured to herself. "Not a mark on him, clear and clean and white, beautiful as ever a child was made," she murmured with pride. Elizabeth kept her face hidden.

"He went peaceful, Lizzie—peaceful as sleep. Isn't he beautiful, the lamb? Ay—he must ha' made his peace, Lizzie. 'Appen he made it all right, Lizzie, shut in there. He'd have time. He wouldn't look like this if he hadn't made his peace. The lamb, the dear lamb. Eh, but he had a hearty laugh. I loved to hear it. He had the heartiest laugh, Lizzie, as a lad——"

Elizabeth looked up. The man's mouth was fallen back, slightly open under the cover of the moustache. The eyes, half shut, did not show glazed in the obscurity. Life with its smoky burning gone from him, had left him apart and utterly alien to her. And she knew what a stranger he was to her. In her womb was ice of fear, because of this separate stranger with whom she had been living as one flesh. Was this what it all meant—utter, intact

separateness, obscured by heat of living? In dread she turned her
face away. The fact was too deadly. There had been nothing
between them, and yet they had come together, exchanging their
nakedness repeatedly. Each time he had taken her, they had been
two isolated beings, far apart as now. He was no more responsible
than she. The child was like ice in her womb. For as she looked at
the dead man, her mind, cold and detached, said clearly: "Who am
I? What have I been doing? I have been fighting a husband who
did not exist. *He* existed all the time. What wrong have I done?
What was that I have been living with? There lies the reality,
this man." And her soul died in her for fear: she knew she had
never seen him, he had never seen her, they had met in the dark
and had fought in the dark, not knowing whom they met or whom
they fought. And now she saw, and turned silent in seeing. For
she had been wrong. She had said he was something he was not;
she had felt familiar with him. Whereas he was apart all the
while, living as she never lived, feeling as she never felt.

In fear and shame she looked at his naked body, that she had
known falsely. And he was the father of her children. Her soul
was torn from her body and stood apart. She looked at his naked
body and was ashamed, as if she had denied it. After all, it was
itself. It seemed awful to her. She looked at his face, and she
turned her own face to the wall. For his look was other than hers,
his way was not her way. She had denied him what he was—she
saw it now. She had refused him as himself. And this had been her
life, and his life. She was grateful to death, which restored the
truth. And she knew she was not dead.

And all the while her heart was bursting with grief and pity for
him. What had he suffered? What stretch of horror for this helpless
man! She was rigid with agony. She had not been able to help him.
He had been cruelly injured, this naked man, this other being,
and she could make no reparation. There were the children—but
the children belonged to life. This dead man had nothing to do
with them. He and she were only channels through which life
had flowed to issue in the children. She was a mother—but how
awful she knew it now to have been a wife. And he, dead now,
how awful he must have felt it to be a husband. She felt that in
the next world he would be a stranger to her. If they met there, in
the beyond, they would only be ashamed of what had been before.
The children had come, for some mysterious reason, out of both
of them. But the children did not unite them. Now he was dead,
she knew how eternally he was apart from her, how eternally he
had nothing more to do with her. She saw this episode of her
life closed. They had denied each other in life. Now he had with-

drawn. An anguish came over her. It was finished then: it had become hopeless between them long before he died. Yet he had been her husband. But how little!

"Have you got his shirt, 'Lizabeth?"

Elizabeth turned without answering, though she strove to weep and behave as her mother-in-law expected. But she could not, she was silenced. She went into the kitchen and returned with the garment.

"It is aired," she said, grasping the cotton shirt here and there to try. She was almost ashamed to handle him; what right had she or anyone to lay hands on him; but her touch was humble on his body. It was hard work to clothe him. He was so heavy and inert. A terrible dread gripped her all the while: that he could be so heavy and utterly inert, unresponsive, apart. The horror of the distance between them was almost too much for her—it was so infinite a gap she must look across.

At last it was finished. They covered him with a sheet and left him lying, with his face bound. And she fastened the door of the little parlor, lest the children should see what was lying there. Then, with peace sunk heavy on her heart, she went about making tidy the kitchen. She knew she submitted to life, which was her immediate master. But from death, her ultimate master, she winced with fear and shame.

1911, 1914

The Horse Dealer's Daughter

"Well, Mabel, and what are you going to do with yourself?" asked Joe, with foolish flippancy. He felt quite safe himself. Without listening for an answer, he turned aside, worked a grain of tobacco to the tip of his tongue, and spat it out. He did not care about anything, since he felt safe himself.

The three brothers and the sister sat round the desolate breakfast-table, attempting some sort of desultory consultation. The morning's post had given the final tap to the family fortunes, and all was over. The dreary dining-room itself, with its heavy mahogany furniture, looked as if it were waiting to be done away with.

But the consultation amounted to nothing. There was a strange air of ineffectuality about the three men, as they sprawled at table, smoking and reflecting vaguely on their own condition. The girl was alone, a rather short, sullen-looking young woman of twenty-seven. She did not share the same life as her brothers. She would have been good-looking, save for the impressive fixity of her face, "bull-dog," as her brothers called it.

There was a confused tramping of horses' feet outside. The three men all sprawled round in their chairs to watch. Beyond the dark holly bushes that separated the strip of lawn from the highroad, they could see a cavalcade of shire horses swinging out of their own yard, being taken for exercise. This was the last time. These were the last horses that would go through their hands. The young men watched with critical, callous look. They were all frightened at the collapse of their lives, and the sense of disaster in which they were involved left them no inner freedom.

Yet they were three fine, well-set fellows enough. Joe, the eldest, was a man of thirty-three, broad and handsome in a hot, flushed way. His face was red, he twisted his black moustache over a thick finger, his eyes were shallow and restless. He had a sensual way of uncovering his teeth when he laughed, and his bearing was stupid. Now he watched the horses with a glazed look of helplessness in his eyes, a certain stupor of downfall.

The great draught horses swung past. They were tied head to tail, four of them, and they heaved along to where a lane branched off from the highroad, planting their great hoofs floutingly in the fine black mud, swinging their great rounded haunches sumptuously, and trotting a few sudden steps as they were led into the lane, round the corner. Every movement showed a massive, slumbrous strength, and a stupidity which held them in subjection. The groom at the head looked back, jerking the leading rope. And the cavalcade moved out of sight up the lane, the tail of the last horse, bobbed up tight and stiff, held out taut from the swinging great haunches as they rocked behind the hedges in a motion-like sleep.

Joe watched with glazed hopeless eyes. The horses were almost like his own body to him. He felt he was done for now. Luckily he was engaged to a woman as old as himself, and therefore her father, who was steward of a neighboring estate, would provide him with a job. He would marry and go into harness. His life was over, he would be a subject animal now.

He turned uneasily aside, the retreating steps of the horses echoing in his ears. Then, with foolish restlessness, he reached for the scraps of bacon rind from the plates, and making a faint whistling sound, flung them to the terrier that lay against the fender. He watched the dog swallow them, and waited till the creature looked into his eyes. Then a faint grin came on his face, and in a high, foolish voice he said:

"You won't get much more bacon, shall you, you little b——?"

The dog faintly and dismally wagged its tail, then lowered its haunches, circled round, and lay down again.

There was another helpless silence at the table. Joe sprawled uneasily in his seat, not willing to go till the family conclave was dissolved. Fred Henry, the second brother, was erect, clean-limbed, alert. He had watched the passing of the horses with more *sang froid*. If he was an animal, like Joe, he was an animal which controls, not one which is controlled. He was master of any horse, and he carried himself with a well-tempered air of mastery. But he was not master of the situations of life. He pushed his coarse brown moustache upwards, off his lip, and glanced irritably at his sister, who sat impassive and inscrutable.

"You'll go and stop with Lucy for a bit, shan't you?" he asked. The girl did not answer.

"I don't see what else you can do," persisted Fred Henry.

"Go as a skivvy," [1] Joe interpolated laconically.

The girl did not move a muscle.

"If I was her, I should go in for training for a nurse," said Malcolm, the youngest of them all. He was the baby of the family, a young man of twenty-two, with a fresh, jaunty *museau*.[2]

But Mabel did not take any notice of him. They had talked at her and round her for so many years, that she hardly heard them at all.

The marble clock on the mantelpiece softly chimed the half-hour, the dog rose uneasily from the hearth-rug and looked at the party at the breakfast-table. But still they sat on an ineffectual conclave.

"Oh, all right," said Joe suddenly, apropos of nothing. "I'll get a move on."

He pushed back his chair, straddled his knees with a downward jerk, to get them free, in horsey fashion, and went to the fire. Still he did not go out of the room; he was curious to know what the others would do or say. He began to charge his pipe, looking down at the dog and saying in a high, affected voice:

"Going wi' me? Going wi' me are ter? Tha'rt goin' further than tha counts on just now, dost hear?"

The dog faintly wagged his tail, the man stuck out his jaw and covered his pipe with his hands, and puffed intently, losing himself in the tobacco, looking down all the while at the dog with an absent brown eye. The dog looked up at him in mournful distrust. Joe stood with his knees stuck out, in real horsey fashion.

"Have you had a letter from Lucy?" Fred Henry asked of his sister.

1. Servant girl.   2. Face (French slang).

"Last week," came the neutral reply.

"And what does she say?"

There was no answer.

"Does she *ask* you to go and stop there?" persisted Fred Henry.

"She says I can if I like."

"Well, then, you'd better. Tell her you'll come on Monday." This was received in silence.

"That's what you'll do then, is it?" said Fred Henry, in some exasperation.

But she made no answer. There was a silence of futility and irritation in the room. Malcolm grinned fatuously.

"You'll have to make up your mind between now and next Wednesday," said Joe loudly, "or else find yourself lodgings on the curbstone."

The face of the young woman darkened, but she sat on immutable.

"Here's Jack Ferguson!" exclaimed Malcolm, who was looking aimlessly out of the window.

"Where?" exclaimed Joe loudly.

"Just gone past."

"Coming in?"

Malcolm craned his neck to see the gate.

"Yes," he said.

There was a silence. Mabel sat on like one condemned, at the head of the table. Then a whistle was heard from the kitchen. The dog got up and barked sharply. Joe opened the door and shouted:

"Come on."

After a moment a young man entered. He was muffled up in overcoat and a purple woolen scarf, and his tweed cap, which he did not remove, was pulled down on his head. He was of medium height, his face was rather long and pale, his eyes looked tired.

"Hello, Jack! Well, Jack!" exclaimed Malcolm and Joe. Fred Henry merely said: "Jack."

"What's doing?" asked the newcomer, evidently addressing Fred Henry.

"Same. We've got to be out by Wednesday. Got a cold?"

"I have—got it bad, too."

"Why don't you stop in?"

"*Me* stop in? When I can't stand on my legs, perhaps I shall have a chance." The young man spoke huskily. He had a slight Scotch accent.

"It's a knockout, isn't it," said Joe, boisterously, "if a doctor goes round croaking with a cold. Looks bad for the patients, doesn't it?"

The young doctor looked at him slowly.

"Anything the matter with *you*, then?" he asked sarcastically.

"Not as I know of. Damn your eyes, I hope not. Why?"

"I thought you were very concerned about the patients, wondered if you might be one yourself."

"Damn it, no, I've never been patient to no flaming doctor, and hope I never shall be," returned Joe.

At this point Mabel rose from the table, and they all seemed to become aware of her existence. She began putting the dishes together. The young doctor looked at her, but did not address her. He had not greeted her. She went out of the room with the tray, her face impassive and unchanged.

"When are you off then, all of you?" asked the doctor.

"I'm catching the eleven-forty," replied Malcolm. "Are you goin' down wi' th' trap, Joe?"

"Yes, I've told you I'm going down wi' th' trap, haven't I?"

"We'd better be getting her in then. So long, Jack, if I don't see you before I go," said Malcolm, shaking hands.

He went out, followed by Joe, who seemed to have his tail between his legs.

"Well, this is the devil's own," exclaimed the doctor, when he was left alone with Fred Henry. "Going before Wednesday, are you?"

"That's the orders," replied the other.

"Where, to Northampton?"

"That's it."

"The devil!" exclaimed Ferguson, with quiet chagrin.

And there was silence between the two.

"All settled up, are you?" asked Ferguson.

"About."

There was another pause.

"Well, I shall miss yer, Freddy, boy," said the young doctor.

"And I shall miss thee, Jack," returned the other.

"Miss you like hell," mused the doctor.

Fred Henry turned aside. There was nothing to say. Mabel came in again, to finish clearing the table.

"What are *you* going to do, then, Miss Pervin?" asked Ferguson. "Going to your sister's, are you?"

Mabel looked at him with her steady, dangerous eyes, that always made him uncomfortable, unsettling his superficial ease.

"No," she said.

"Well, what in the name of fortune *are* you going to do? Say what you mean to do," cried Fred Henry, with futile intensity.

But she only averted her head, and continued her work. She folded the white table cloth, and put on the chenille cloth.

"The sulkiest bitch that ever trod!" muttered her brother.

But she finished her task with perfectly impassive face, the young doctor watching her interestedly all the while. Then she went out.

Fred Henry stared after her, clenching his lips, his blue eyes fixing in sharp antagonism, as he made a grimace of sour exasperation.

"You could bray her into bits, and that's all you'd get out of her," he said, in a small, narrowed tone.

The doctor smiled faintly.

"What's she *going* to do, then?" he asked.

"Strike me if *I* know!" returned the other.

There was a pause. Then the doctor stirred.

"I'll be seeing you tonight, shall I?" he said to his friend.

"Ay—where's it to be? Are we going over to Jessdale?"

"I don't know. I've got such a cold on me. I'll come round to the Moon and Stars, anyway."

"Let Lizzie and May miss their night for once, eh?"

"That's it—if I feel as I do now."

"All's one——"

The two young men went through the passage and down to the back door together. The house was large, but it was servantless now, and desolate. At the back was a small bricked house yard and beyond that a big square, graveled fine and red, and having stables on two sides. Sloping, dank, winter-dark fields stretched away on the open sides.

But the stables were empty. Joseph Pervin, the father of the family, had been a man of no education, who had become a fairly large horse dealer. The stables had been full of horses, there was a great turmoil and come-and-go of horses and of dealers and grooms. Then the kitchen was full of servants. But of late things had declined. The old man had married a second time, to retrieve his fortunes. Now he was dead and everything was gone to the dogs, there was nothing but debt and threatening.

For months, Mabel had been servantless in the big house, keeping the home together in penury for her ineffectual brothers. She had kept house for ten years. But previously it was with unstinted means. Then, however brutal and coarse everything was, the sense of money had kept her proud, confident. The men might be foul-mouthed, the women in the kitchen might have had reputations, her brothers might have illegitimate children.

But so long as there was money, the girl felt herself established, and brutally proud, reserved.

No company came to the house, save dealers and coarse men. Mabel had no associates of her own sex, after her sister went away. But she did not mind. She went regularly to church, she attended to her father. And she lived in the memory of her mother, who had died when she was fourteen, and whom she had loved. She had loved her father, too, in a different way, depending upon him, and feeling secure in him, until at the age of fifty-four, he married again. And then she had set hard against him. Now he had died and left them all hopelessly in debt.

She had suffered badly during the period of poverty. Nothing, however, could shake the curious, sullen, animal pride that dominated each member of the family. Now, for Mabel, the end had come. Still she would not cast about her. She would follow her own way just the same. She would always hold the keys of her own situation. Mindless and persistent, she endured from day to day. Why should she think? Why should she answer anybody? It was enough that this was the end, and there was no way out. She need not pass any more darkly along the main street of the small town, avoiding every eye. She need not demean herself any more, going into the shops and buying the cheapest food. This was at an end. She thought of nobody, not even of herself. Mindless and persistent, she seemed in a sort of ecstasy to be coming nearer to her fulfilment, her own glorification, approaching her dead mother, who was glorified.

In the afternoon, she took a little bag, with shears and sponge and a small scrubbing-brush, and went out. It was a gray, wintry day, with saddened, dark green fields and an atmosphere blackened by the smoke of foundries not far off. She went quickly, darkly along the causeway, heeding nobody, through the town to the churchyard.

There she always felt secure, as if no one could see her, although as a matter of fact she was exposed to the stare of everyone who passed along under the churchyard wall. Nevertheless, once under the shadow of the great looming church, among the graves, she felt immune from the world, reserved within the thick churchyard wall as in another country.

Carefully she clipped the grass from the grave, and arranged the pinky-white, small chrysanthemums in the tin cross. When this was done, she took an empty jar from a neighboring grave, brought water, and carefully, most scrupulously sponged the marble headstone and the coping-stone.

It gave her sincere satisfaction to do this. She felt in immediate contact with the world of her mother. She took minute pains, went through the park in a state bordering on pure happiness, as if in performing this task she came into a subtle, intimate connection with her mother. For the life she followed here in the world was far less real than the world of death she inherited from her mother.

The doctor's house was just by the church. Ferguson, being a mere hired assistant, was slave to the countryside. As he hurried now to attend to the out-patients in the surgery, glancing across the graveyard with his quick eye, he saw the girl at her task at the grave. She seemed so intent and remote, it was like looking into another world. Some mystical element was touched in him. He slowed down as he walked, watching her as if spellbound.

She lifted her eyes, feeling him looking. Their eyes met. And each looked again at once, each feeling, in some way, found out by the other. He lifted his cap and passed on down the road. There remained distinct in his consciousness, like a vision, the memory of her face, lifted from the tombstone in the churchyard, and looking at him with slow, large, portentous eyes. It *was* portentous, her face. It seemed to mesmerize him. There was a heavy power in her eyes which laid hold of his whole being, as if he had drunk some powerful drug. He had been feeling weak and done before. Now the life came back into him, he felt delivered from his own fretted, daily self.

He finished his duties at the surgery as quickly as might be, hastily filling up the bottles of the waiting people with cheap drugs. Then, in perpetual haste, he set off again to visit several cases in another part of his round, before tea-time. At all times he preferred to walk if he could, but particularly when he was not well. He fancied the motion restored him.

The afternoon was falling. It was gray, deadened, and wintry, with a slow, moist, heavy coldness sinking in and deadening all the faculties. But why should he think or notice? He hastily climbed the hill and turned across the dark green fields, following the black cinder-track. In the distance, across a shallow dip in the country, the small town was clustered like smouldering ash, a tower, a spire, a heap of low, raw, extinct houses. And on the nearest fringe of the town, sloping into the dip, was Oldmeadow, the Pervins' house. He could see the stables and the outbuildings distinctly, as they lay towards him on the slope. Well, he would not go there many more times! Another resource would be lost to him, another place gone: the only company he cared for in the alien, ugly little town he was losing. Nothing but work, drudgery, constant hastening from dwelling to dwelling among the colliers and the iron-workers. It wore him out, but at the same time he had a craving for it. It was a stimulant to him to be in the homes of the working people, moving, as it were, through the innermost body of their life. His nerves were excited and gratified. He could come so near, into the very lives of the rough, inarticulate, powerfully emotional men and women. He grumbled, he said he hated the hellish hole. But as a matter of fact it excited him, the contact with the rough, strongly-feeling people was a stimulant applied direct to his nerves.

Below Oldmeadow, in the green, shallow, soddened hollow of fields, lay a square, deep pond. Roving across the landscape, the doctor's quick eye detected a figure in black passing through the gate of the field, down towards the pond. He looked again. It would be Mabel Pervin. His mind suddenly became alive and attentive.

Why was she going down there? He pulled up on the path on the slope above, and stood staring. He could just make sure of the small black figure moving in the hollow of the failing day. He seemed to see her in the midst of such obscurity, that he was like a clairvoyant, seeing rather with the mind's eye than with ordinary sight. Yet he could see her positively enough, whilst he kept his eye attentive. He felt, if he looked away from her, in the thick, ugly falling dusk, he would lose her altogether.

He followed her minutely as she moved, direct and intent, like something transmitted rather than stirring in voluntary activity, straight down the field towards the pond. There she stood on the bank for a moment. She never raised her head. Then she waded slowly into the water.

He stood motionless as the small black figure walked slowly and deliberately towards the center of the pond, very slowly, gradually moving deeper into the motionless water, and still moving forward as the water got up to her breast. Then he could see her no more in the dusk of the dead afternoon.

"There!" he exclaimed. "Would you believe it?"

And he hastened straight down, running over the wet, soddened fields, pushing through the hedges, down into the depression of callous wintry obscurity. It took him several minutes to come to the pond. He stood on the bank, breathing heavily. He could see nothing. His eyes seemed to penetrate the dead water. Yes, perhaps that was the dark shadow of her black clothing beneath the surface of the water.

He slowly ventured into the pond. The bottom was deep, soft clay, he sank in, and the water clasped dead cold round his legs. As he stirred he could smell the cold, rotten clay that fouled up into the water. It was objectionable in his lungs. Still, repelled and yet not heeding, he moved deeper into the pond. The cold water rose over his thighs, over his loins, upon his abdomen. The lower part of his body was all sunk in the hideous cold element. And the bottom was so deeply soft and uncertain, he was afraid of pitching with his mouth underneath. He could not swim, and was afraid.

He crouched a little, spreading his hands under the water and moving them round, trying to feel for her. The dead cold pond swayed upon his chest. He moved again, a little deeper, and again, with his hands underneath, he felt all around under the water. And he touched her clothing. But it evaded his fingers. He made a desperate effort to grasp it.

And so doing he lost his balance and went under, horribly, suffocating in the foul earthy water, struggling madly for a few moments. At last, after what seemed an eternity, he got his footing, rose again into the air and looked around. He gasped, and knew he was in the world. Then he looked at the water. She had risen near him. He grasped her clothing, and drawing her nearer, turned to take his way to land again.

He went very slowly, carefully, absorbed in the slow progress. He rose higher, climbing out of the pond. The water was now only about his legs; he was thankful, full of relief to be out of the clutches of the pond. He lifted her and staggered on to the bank, out of the horror of wet, gray clay.

He laid her down on the bank. She was quite unconscious and running with water. He made the water come from her mouth, he worked to restore her. He did not have to work very long before he could feel the breathing begin again in her; she was breathing naturally. He worked a little longer. He could feel her live beneath his hands; she was coming back. He wiped her face, wrapped her in his overcoat, looked round into the dim, dark gray world, then lifted her and staggered down the bank and across the fields.

It seemed an unthinkably long way, and his burden so heavy he felt he would never get to the house. But at last he was in the stable yard, and then in the house yard. He opened the door and went into the house. In the kitchen he laid her down on the hearth-rug and called. The house was empty. But the fire was burning in the grate.

Then again he kneeled to attend to her. She was breathing regularly, her eyes were wide open and as if conscious, but there seemed something missing in her look. She was conscious in herself, but unconscious of her surroundings.

He ran upstairs, took blankets from a bed, and put them before the fire to warm. Then he removed her saturated, earthy-smelling clothing, rubbed her dry with a towel, and wrapped her naked in the blankets. Then he went into the dining room, to look for spirits. There was a little whisky. He drank a gulp himself, and put some into her mouth.

The effect was instantaneous. She looked full into his face, as if she had been seeing him for some time, and yet had only just become conscious of him.

"Dr. Ferguson?" she said.

"What?" he answered.

He was divesting himself of his coat, intending to find some dry clothing upstairs. He could not bear the smell of the dead, clayey water, and he was mortally afraid for his own health.

"What did I do?" she asked.

"Walked into the pond," he replied. He had begun to shudder like one sick, and could hardly attend to her. Her eyes remained full on him, he seemed to be going dark in his mind, looking back at her helplessly. The shuddering became quieter in him, his life came back to him, dark and unknowing, but strong again.

"Was I out of my mind?" she asked, while her eyes were fixed on him all the time.

"Maybe, for the moment," he replied. He felt quiet, because his strength had come back. The strange fretful strain had left him.

"Am I out of my mind now?" she asked.

"Are you?" he reflected a moment. "No," he answered truthfully. "I don't see that you are." He turned his face aside. He was afraid now, because he felt dazed, and felt dimly that her power was stronger than his, in this issue. And she continued to look at him fixedly all the time. "Can you tell me where I shall find some dry things to put on?" he asked.

"Did you dive into the pond for me?" she asked.

"No," he answered. "I walked in. But I went in overhead as well."

There was silence for a moment. He hesitated. He very much wanted to go upstairs to get into dry clothing. But there was another desire in him. And she seemed to hold him. His will seemed to have gone to sleep, and left him, standing there slack before her. But he felt warm inside himself. He did not shudder at all, though his clothes were sodden on him.

"Why did you?" she asked.

"Because I didn't want you to do such a foolish thing," he said.

"It wasn't foolish," she said, still gazing at him as she lay on the floor, with a sofa cushion under her head. "It was the right thing to do. *I* knew best, then."

"I'll go and shift these wet things," he said. But still he had not the power to move out of her presence, until she sent him. It was as if she had the life of his body in her hands, and he could not extricate himself. Or perhaps he did not want to.

Suddenly she sat up. Then she became aware of her own immediate condition. She felt the blankets about her, she knew her own limbs. For a moment it seemed as if her reason were going. She looked round, with wild eye, as if seeking something. He stood still with fear. She saw her clothing lying scattered.

"Who undressed me?" she asked, her eyes resting full and inevitable on his face.

"I did," he replied, "to bring you round."

For some moments she sat and gazed at him awfully, her lips parted.

"Do you love me, then?" she asked.

He only stood and stared at her, fascinated. His soul seemed to melt.

She shuffled forward on her knees, and put her arms round him, round his legs, as he stood there, pressing her breasts against his knees and thighs, clutching him with strange, convulsive certainty, pressing his thighs against her, drawing him to her face, her throat, as she looked up at him with flaring, humble eyes of transfiguration, triumphant in first possession.

"You love me," she murmured, in strange transport, yearning and triumphant and confident. "You love me. I know you love me, I know."

And she was passionately kissing his knees, through the wet clothing, passionately and indiscriminately kissing his knees, his legs, as if unaware of everything.

He looked down at the tangled wet hair, the wild, bare, animal shoulders. He was amazed, bewildered, and afraid. He had never thought of loving her. He had never wanted to love her. When he rescued her and restored her, he was a doctor, and she was a patient. He had had no single personal thought of her. Nay, this introduction of the personal element was very distasteful to him, a violation of his professional honor. It was horrible to have her there embracing his knees. It was horrible. He revolted from it, violently. And yet—and yet—he had not the power to break away.

She looked at him again, with the same supplication of powerful love, and that same transcendent, frightening light of triumph. In view of the delicate flame which seemed to come from her face like a light, he was powerless. And yet he had never intended to love her. He had never intended. And something stubborn in him could not give way.

"You love me," she repeated, in a murmur of deep, rhapsodic assurance. "You love me."

Her hands were drawing him, drawing him down to her. He was afraid, even a little horrified. For he had, really, no intention of loving her. Yet her hands were drawing him towards her. He put out his hand quickly to steady himself, and grasped her bare shoulder. A flame seemed to burn the hand that grasped her soft shoulder. He had no intention of loving her: his whole will was against his yielding. It was horrible. And yet wonderful was the touch of her shoulders, beautiful the shining of her face. Was she perhaps mad? He had a horror of yielding to her. Yet something in him ached also.

He had been staring away at the door, away from her. But his hand remained on her shoulder. She had gone suddenly very still. He looked down at her. Her eyes were now wide with fear, with doubt, the light was dying from her face, a shadow of terrible grayness was returning. He could not bear the touch of her eyes' question upon him, and the look of death behind the question.

With an inward groan he gave way, and let his heart yield towards her. A sudden gentle smile came on his face. And her eyes, which never left his face, slowly, slowly filled with tears. He watched the strange water rise in her eyes, like some slow fountain coming up. And his heart seemed to burn and melt away in his breast.

He could not bear to look at her any more. He dropped on his knees and caught her head with his arms and pressed her face against his throat. She was very still. His heart, which seemed to have broken, was burning with a kind of agony in his breast. And he felt her slow, hot tears wetting his throat. But he could not move.

He felt the hot tears wet his neck and the hollows of his neck, and he remained motionless, suspended through one of man's eternities. Only now it had become indispensable to him to have her face pressed close to him; he could never let her go again. He could never let her head go away from the close clutch of his arm. He wanted to remain like that for ever, with his heart hurting him in a pain that was also life to him. Without knowing, he was looking down on her damp, soft brown hair.

Then, as it were suddenly, he smelt the horrid stagnant smell of that water. And at the same moment she drew away from him and looked at him. Her eyes were wistful and unfathomable. He was afraid of them, and he fell to kissing her, not knowing what he was doing. He wanted her eyes not to have that terrible, wistful, unfathomable look.

When she turned her face to him again, a faint delicate flush was glowing, and there was again dawning that terrible shining of joy in her eyes, which really terrified him, and yet which he now wanted to see, because he feared the look of doubt still more.

"You love me?" she said, rather faltering.

"Yes." The word cost him a painful effort. Not because it wasn't true. But because it was too newly true, the *saying* seemed to tear open again his newly torn heart. And he hardly wanted it to be true, even now.

She lifted her face to him, and he bent forward and kissed her on the mouth, gently, with the one kiss that is an eternal pledge. And as he kissed her his heart strained again in his breast. He never intended to love her. But now it was over. He had crossed over the gulf to her, and all that he had left behind had shriveled and become void.

After the kiss, her eyes again slowly filled with tears. She sat still, away from him, with her face drooped aside, and her hands folded in her lap. The tears fell very slowly. There was complete silence. He too sat there motionless and silent on the hearth rug. The strange pain of his heart that was broken seemed to consume him. That he should love her? That this was love! That he should be ripped open in this way! Him, a doctor! How they would all jeer if they knew! It was agony to him to think they might know.

In the curious naked pain of the thought he looked again to her. She was sitting there drooped into a muse. He saw a tear fall, and his heart flared hot. He saw for the first time that one of her shoulders was quite uncovered, one arm bare, he could see one of her small breasts; dimly, because it had become almost dark in the room.

"Why are you crying?" he asked, in an altered voice.

She looked up at him, and behind her tears the consciousness of her situation for the first time brought a dark look of shame to her eyes.

"I'm not crying, really," she said, watching him, half frightened.

He reached his hand, and softly closed it on her bare arm.

"I love you! I love you!" he said in a soft, low vibrating voice, unlike himself.

She shrank, and dropped her head. The soft, penetrating grip of his hand on her arm distressed her. She looked up at him.

"I want to go," she said. "I want to go and get you some dry things."

"Why?" he said. "I'm all right."

"But I want to go," she said. "And I want you to change your things."

He released her arm, and she wrapped herself in the blanket, looking at him, rather frightened. And still she did not rise.

"Kiss me," she said wistfully.

He kissed her, but briefly, half in anger.

Then, after a second, she rose nervously, all mixed up in the blanket. He watched her in her confusion as she tried to extricate herself and wrap herself up so that she could walk. He watched her relentlessly, as she knew. And as she went, the blanket trailing, and as he saw a glimpse of her feet and her white leg, he tried to remember her as she was when he had wrapped her in the blanket. But then he didn't want to remember, because she had been nothing to him then, and his nature revolted from remembering her as she was when she was nothing to him.

A tumbling muffled noise from within the dark house startled him. Then he heard her voice: "There are clothes." He rose and went to the foot of the stairs, and gathered up the garments she had thrown down. Then he came back to the fire, to rub himself down and dress. He grinned at his own appearance when he had finished.

The fire was sinking, so he put on coal. The house was now quite dark, save for the light of a street-lamp that shone in faintly from beyond the holly trees. He lit the gas with matches he found on the mantelpiece. Then he emptied the pockets of his own clothes, and threw all his wet things in a heap into the scullery. After which he gathered up her sodden clothes, gently, and put them in a separate heap on the copper-top in the scullery.

It was six o'clock on the clock. His own watch had stopped. He ought to go back to the surgery. He waited, and still she did not come down. So he went to the foot of the stairs and called:

"I shall have to go."

Almost immediately he heard her coming down. She had on her best dress of black voile, and her hair was tidy, but still damp. She looked at him—and in spite of herself, smiled.

"I don't like you in those clothes," she said.

"Do I look a sight?" he answered.

They were shy of one another.

"I'll make you some tea," she said.

"No, I must go."

"Must you?" And she looked at him again with the wide, strained, doubtful eyes. And again, from the pain of his breast, he knew how he loved her. He went and bent to kiss her, gently, passionately, with his heart's painful kiss.

"And my hair smells so horrible," she murmured in distraction. "And I'm so awful, I'm so awful! Oh no, I'm too awful." And she broke into bitter, heart-broken sobbing. "You can't want to love me, I'm horrible."

"Don't be silly, don't be silly," he said, trying to comfort her, kissing her, holding her in his arms. "I want you, I want to marry you, we're going to be married, quickly, quickly—tomorrow if I can."

But she only sobbed terribly, and cried:

"I feel awful. I feel awful. I feel I'm horrible to you."

"No, I want you, I want you," was all he answered, blindly, with that terrible intonation which frightened her almost more than her horror lest he should *not* want her.

1922

From The Rainbow

From *Chapter II. They Live at the Marsh* [1]

One afternoon, the pains began, Mrs. Brangwen was put to bed, the midwife came. Night fell, the shutters were closed, Brangwen came in to tea, to the loaf and the pewter teapot, the child, silent and quivering, playing with glass beads, the house, empty, it seemed, or exposed to the winter night, as if it had no walls.

Sometimes there sounded, long and remote in the house, vibrating through everything, the moaning cry of a woman in labor. Brangwen, sitting downstairs, was divided. His lower, deeper self was with her, bound to her, suffering. But the big shell of his body remembered the sound of owls that used to fly round the farmstead when he was a boy. He was back in his youth, a boy, haunted by the sound of the owls, waking up his brother to speak to him. And his mind drifted away to the birds, their solemn, dignified faces, their flight so soft and broad-winged. And then to the birds his brother had shot, fluffy, dust-colored, dead heaps of softness with faces absurdly asleep. It was a queer thing, a dead owl.

He lifted his cup to his lips, he watched the child with the beads. But his mind was occupied with owls, and the atmosphere of his boyhood, with his brothers and sisters. Elsewhere, fundamental, he was with his wife in labor, the child was being brought forth out of their one flesh. He and she, one flesh, out of which life must be put forth. The rent was not in his body, but it was of his body. On her the blows fell, but the quiver ran through to him, to his last fiber. She must be torn asunder for life to come forth, yet still they were one flesh, and still, from further back, the life came out of him to her, and still he was the unbroken that has the broken rock in its arms, their flesh was one rock from which the life gushed, out of her who was smitten and rent, from him who quivered and yielded.

He went upstairs to her. As he came to the bedside she spoke to him in Polish.

---

1. Tom Brangwen, a Nottinghamshire farmer, married Lydia Lensky, widow of a Polish émigré doctor. Anna is Lydia's child by her first marriage. The scene is Marsh Farm, a few miles south of East- wood, where Lawrence was born, and just across the Nottinghamshire-Derbyshire border from the town of Ilkeston where Lawrence trained as a teacher. Lydia is about to have her first child by Tom.

"Is it very bad?" he asked.

She looked at him, and oh, the weariness to her, of the effort to understand another language, the weariness of hearing him, attending to him, making out who he was, as he stood there fair-bearded and alien, looking at her. She knew something of him, of his eyes. But she could not grasp him. She closed her eyes.

He turned away, white to the gills.

"It's not so very bad," said the midwife.

He knew he was a strain on his wife. He went downstairs.

The child glanced up at him, frightened.

"I want my mother," she quavered.

"Ay, but she's badly," he said mildly, unheeding.

She looked at him with lost, frightened eyes.

"Has she got a headache?"

"No—she's going to have a baby."

The child looked round. He was unaware of her. She was alone again in terror.

"I want my mother," came the cry of panic.

"Let Tilly undress you," he said. "You're tired."

There was another silence. Again came the cry of labor.

"I want my mother," rang automatically from the wincing, panic-stricken child, that felt cut off and lost in a horror of desolation.

Tilly came forward, her heart wrung.

"Come an' let me undress her then, pet lamb," she crooned. "You s'll have your mother in th' mornin', don't you fret, my duckie; never mind, angel."

But Anna stood upon the sofa, her back to the wall.

"I want my mother," she cried, her little face quivering, and the great tears of childish, utter anguish falling.

"She's poorly, my lamb, she's poorly tonight, but she'll be better by mornin'. Oh, don't cry, don't cry, love, she doesn't want you to cry, precious little heart, no, she doesn't."

Tilly took gently hold of the child's skirts. Anna snatched back her dress, and cried, in a little hysteria:

"No, you're not to undress me—I want my mother,"—and her child's face was running with grief and tears, her body shaken.

"Oh, but let Tilly undress you. Let Tilly undress you, who loves you, don't be wilful tonight. Mother's poorly, she doesn't want you to cry."

The child sobbed distractedly, she could not hear.

"I want my mother," she wept.

"When you're undressed, you s'll go up to see your mother—when you're undressed, pet, when you've let Tilly undress you, when you're a little jewel in your nightie, love. Oh, don't you cry, don't you——"

Brangwen sat stiff in his chair. He felt his brain going tighter. He crossed over the room, aware only of the maddening sobbing.

"Don't make a noise," he said.

And a new fear shook the child from the sound of his voice. She cried mechanically, her eyes looking watchful through her tears, in terror, alert to what might happen.

"I want—my—mother," quavered the sobbing, blind voice.

A shiver of irritation went over the man's limbs. It was the utter, persistent unreason, the maddening blindness of the voice and the crying.

"You must come and be undressed," he said, in a quiet voice that was thin with anger.

And he reached his hand and grasped her. He felt her body catch in a convulsive sob. But he too was blind, and intent, irritated into mechanical action. He began to unfasten her little apron. She would have shrunk from him, but could not. So her small body remained in his grasp, while he fumbled at the little buttons and tapes, unthinking, intent, unaware of anything but the irritation of her. Her body was held taut and resistant, he pushed off the little dress and the petticoats, revealing the white arms. She kept stiff, overpowered, violated, he went on with his task. And all the while she sobbed, choking:

"I want my mother."

He was unheedingly silent, his face stiff. The child was now incapable of understanding, she had become a little, mechanical thing of fixed will. She wept, her body convulsed, her voice repeating the same cry.

"Eh, dear o' me!" cried Tilly, becoming distracted herself. Brangwen, slow, clumsy, blind, intent, got off all the little garments, and stood the child naked in its shift upon the sofa.

"Where's her nightie?" he asked.

Tilly brought it, and he put it on her. Anna did not move her limbs to his desire. He had to push them into place. She stood, with fixed, blind will, resistant, a small, convulsed, unchangeable thing weeping ever and repeating the same phrase. He lifted one foot after the other, pulled off slippers and socks. She was ready.

"Do you want a drink?" he asked.

She did not change. Unheeding, uncaring, she stood on the sofa, standing back, alone, her hands shut and half lifted, her face, all tears, raised and blind. And through the sobbing and choking came the broken:

"I—want—my—mother."

"Do you want a drink?" he said again.

There was no answer. He lifted the stiff, denying body between his hands. Its stiff blindness made a flash of rage go through him. He would like to break it.

He set the child on his knee, and sat again in his chair beside the fire, the wet, sobbing, inarticulate noise going on near his ear, the child sitting stiff, not yielding to him or anything, not aware.

A new degree of anger came over him. What did it all matter? What did it matter if the mother talked Polish and cried in labor, if this child were stiff with resistance, and crying? Why take it to heart? Let the mother cry in labor, let the child cry in resistance, since they would do so. Why should he fight against it, why resist? Let it be, if it were so. Let them be as they were, if they insisted.

And in a daze he sat, offering no fight. The child cried on, the minutes ticked away, a sort of torpor was on him.

It was some little time before he came to, and turned to attend to the child. He was shocked by her little wet, blinded face. A bit dazed, he pushed back the wet hair. Like a living statue of grief, her blind face cried on.

"Nay," he said, "not as bad as that. It's not as bad as that, Anna, my child. Come, what are you crying for so much? Come, stop now, it'll make you sick. I wipe you dry, don't wet your face any more. Don't cry any more wet tears, don't, it's better not to. Don't cry—it's not so bad as all that. Hush now, hush—let it be enough."

His voice was queer and distant and calm. He looked at the child. She was beside herself now. He wanted her to stop, he wanted it all to stop, to become natural.

"Come," he said, rising to turn away, "we'll go an' supper-up the beast."

He took a big shawl, folded her round, and went out into the kitchen for a lantern.

"You're never taking the child out, of a night like this," said Tilly.

"Ay, it'll quieten her," he answered.

It was raining. The child was suddenly still, shocked, finding the rain on its face, the darkness.

"We'll just give the cows their something-to-eat, afore they go to bed," Brangwen was saying to her, holding her close and sure.

There was a trickling of water into the butt, a burst of raindrops sputtering on to her shawl, and the light of the lantern swinging, flashing on a wet pavement and the base of a wet wall. Otherwise it was black darkness: one breathed darkness.

He opened the doors, upper and lower, and they entered into the high, dry barn, that smelled warm even if it were not warm. He hung the lantern on the nail and shut the door. They were in another world now. The light shed softly on the timbered barn, on the whitewashed walls, and the great heap of hay; instruments cast their shadows largely, a ladder rose to the dark arch of a loft. Outside there was the driving rain, inside, the softly illuminated stillness and calmness of the barn.

Holding the child on one arm, he set about preparing the food for the cows, filling a pan with chopped hay and brewer's grains and a little meal. The child, all wonder, watched what he did. A new being was created in her for the new conditions. Sometimes, a little spasm, eddying from the bygone storm of sobbing, shook her small body. Her eyes were wide and wondering, pathetic. She was silent, quite still.

In a sort of dream, his heart sunk to the bottom, leaving the surface of him still, quite still, he rose with the panful of food, carefully balancing the child on one arm, the pan in the other hand. The silky fringe of the shawl swayed softly, grains and hay trickled to the floor; he went along a dimly lit passage behind the mangers, where the horns of the cows pricked out of the obscurity. The child shrank, he balanced stiffly, rested the pan on the manger wall, and tipped out the food, half to this cow, half to the next. There was a noise of chains running, as the cows lifted or dropped their heads sharply; then a contented, soothing sound, a long snuffing as the beasts ate in silence.

The journey had to be performed several times. There was the rhythmic sound of the shovel in the barn, then the man returned walking stiffly between the two weights, the face of the child peering out from the shawl. Then the next time, as he stooped, she freed her arm and put it round his neck, clinging soft and warm, making all easier.

The beasts fed, he dropped the pan and sat down on a box, to arrange the child.

"Will the cows go to sleep now?" she said, catching her breath as she spoke.

"Yes."

"Will they eat all their stuff up first?"

"Yes. Hark at them."

And the two sat still listening to the snuffing and breathing of cows feeding in the sheds communicating with this small barn. The lantern shed a soft, steady light from one wall. All outside was still in the rain. He looked down at the silky folds of the paisley shawl. It reminded him of his mother. She used to go to church in it. He was back again in the old irresponsibility and security, a boy at home.

The two sat very quiet. His mind, in a sort of trance, seemed to become more and more vague. He held the child close to him. A quivering little shudder, re-echoing from her sobbing, went down her limbs. He held her closer. Gradually she relaxed, the eyelids began to sink over her dark, watchful eyes. As she sank to sleep, his mind became blank.

When he came to, as if from sleep, he seemed to be sitting in a timeless stillness. What was he listening for? He seemed to be listening for some sound a long way off, from beyond life. He remembered his wife. He must go back to her. The child was asleep, the eyelids not quite shut, showing a slight film of black pupil between. Why did she not shut her eyes? Her mouth was also a little open.

He rose quickly and went back to the house.

"Is she asleep?" whispered Tilly.

He nodded. The servant woman came to look at the child who slept in the shawl, with cheeks flushed hot and red, and a whiteness, a wanness round the eyes.

"God-a-mercy!" whispered Tilly, shaking her head.

He pushed off his boots and went upstairs with the child. He became aware of the anxiety grasped tight at his heart, because of his wife. But he remained still. The house was silent save for the wind outside, and the noisy trickling and splattering of water in the water butts. There was a slit of light under his wife's door.

He put the child into bed wrapped as she was in the shawl, for the sheets would be cold. Then he was afraid that she might not be able to move her arms, so he loosened her. The black eyes opened, rested on him vacantly, sank shut again. He covered her up. The last little quiver from the sobbing shook her breathing.

This was his room, the room he had had before he married. It was familiar. He remembered what it was to be a young man, untouched.

He remained suspended. The child slept, pushing her small fists from the shawl. He could tell the woman her child was asleep. But he must go to the other landing. He started. There was the sound of the owls—the moaning of the woman. What an uncanny sound! It was not human—at least to a man.

He went down to her room, entering softly. She was lying still, with eyes shut, pale, tired. His heart leapt, fearing she was dead. Yet he knew perfectly well she was not. He saw the way her hair went loose over her temples, her mouth was shut with suffering in a sort of grin. She was beautiful to him—but it was not human. He had a dread of her as she lay there. What had she to do with him? She was other than himself.

Something made him go and touch her fingers that were still grasped on the sheet. Her brown-gray eyes opened and looked at him. She did not know him as himself. But she knew him as the man. She looked at him as a woman in childbirth looks at the man who begot the child in her: an impersonal look, in the extreme hour, female to male. Her eyes closed again. A great, scalding peace went over him, burning his heart and his entrails, passing off into the infinite.

When her pains began afresh, tearing her, he turned aside, and could not look. But his heart in torture was at peace, his bowels were glad. He went downstairs, and to the door, outside, lifted his face to the rain, and felt the darkness striking unseen and steadily upon him.

The swift, unseen threshing of the night upon him silenced him and he was overcome. He turned away indoors, humbly. There was the infinite world, eternal, unchanging, as well as the world of life.

1912–14   1915

From Women in Love

Chapter XVIII. Rabbit[1]

Gudrun knew that it was a critical thing for her to go to Shortlands. She knew it was equivalent to accepting Gerald Crich as a lover. And though she hung back, disliking the condition, yet she knew she would go on. She equivocated. She said to herself, in torment recalling the blow and the kiss, "After all, what is it? What is a kiss? What even is a blow? It is an instant, vanished at once. I can go to Shortlands just for a time, before I go away, if only to see what it is like." For she had an insatiable curiosity to see and to know everything.

She also wanted to know what Winifred was really like. Having heard the child calling from the steamer in the night, she felt some mysterious connection with her.

Gudrun talked with the father in the library. Then he sent for his daughter. She came accompanied by Mademoiselle.

"Winnie, this is Miss Brangwen, who will be so kind as to help you with your drawing and making models of your animals," said the father.

The child looked at Gudrun for a moment with interest, before she came forward, and with face averted offered her hand. There was a complete *sang froid* and indifference under Winifred's childish reserve, a certain irresponsible callousness.

"How do you do?" said the child, not lifting her face.

"How do you do?" said Gudrun.

Then Winifred stood aside, and Gudrun was introduced to Mademoiselle.

1. Anna (of *The Rainbow*) eventually married her stepfather's nephew Will Brangwen. *Women in Love* is largely the story of Anna and Will's two daughters Ursula and Gudrun and their attempts to establish successful relationships with their lovers Rupert Birkin and Gerald Crich respectively. As this chapter opens Gudrun, on the brink of a serious love affair with Gerald, has accepted an invitation from Gerald's father to stay at Shortlands, the Criches' luxurious home, in order to tutor Gerald's younger sister Winifred.

"You have a fine day for your walk," said Mademoiselle, in a bright manner.

"*Quite* fine," said Gudrun.

Winifred was watching from her distance. She was as if amused, but rather unsure as yet what this new person was like. She saw so many new persons, and so few who became real to her. Mademoiselle was of no count whatever, the child merely put up with her, calmly and easily, accepting her little authority with faint scorn, compliant out of childish arrogance of indifference.

"Well, Winifred," said the father, "aren't you glad Miss Brangwen has come? She makes animals and birds in wood and in clay, that the people in London write about in the papers, praising them to the skies."

Winifred smiled slightly.

"Who told you, Daddie?" she asked.

"Who told me? Hermione told me, and Rupert Birkin."

"Do you know them?" Winifred asked of Gudrun, turning to her with faint challenge.

"Yes," said Gudrun.

Winifred readjusted herself a little. She had been ready to accept Gudrun as a sort of servant. Now she saw it was on terms of friendship they were intended to meet. She was rather glad. She had so many half inferiors, whom she tolerated with perfect good-humor.

Gudrun was very calm. She also did not take these things very seriously. A new occasion was mostly spectacular to her. However, Winifred was a detached, ironic child, she would never attach herself. Gudrun liked her and was intrigued by her. The first meetings went off with a certain humiliating clumsiness. Neither Winifred nor her instructress had any social grace.

Soon, however, they met in a kind of make-believe world. Winifred did not notice human beings unless they were like herself, playful and slightly mocking. She would accept nothing but the world of amusement, and the serious people of her life were the animals she had for pets. On those she lavished, almost ironically, her affection and her companionship. To the rest of the human scheme she submitted with a faint bored indifference.

She had a Pekinese dog called Looloo, which she loved.

"Let us draw Looloo," said Gudrun, "and see if we can get his Looliness, shall we?"

"Darling!" cried Winifred, rushing to the dog, that sat with contemplative sadness on the hearth, and kissing its bulging brow. "Darling one, will you be drawn? Shall its mummy draw its portrait?" Then she chuckled gleefully, and turning to Gudrun, said: "Oh, let's!"

They proceeded to get pencils and paper, and were ready.

"Beautifullest," cried Winifred, hugging the dog, "sit still while its mummy draws its beautiful portrait." The dog looked up at her with grievous resignation in its large, prominent eyes. She kissed it fervently, and said: "I wonder what mine will be like. It's sure to be awful."

As she sketched she chuckled to herself, and cried out at times: "Oh, darling, you're so beautiful!"

And again chuckling, she rushed to embrace the dog, in penitence, as if she were doing him some subtle injury. He sat all the time with the resignation and fretfulness of ages on his dark velvety face. She drew slowly, with a wicked concentration in her eyes, her head on one side, an intense stillness over her. She was as if working the spell of some enchantment. Suddenly she had finished. She looked at the dog, and then at her drawing, and then cried, with real grief for the dog, and at the same time with wicked exultation:

"My beautiful, why did they?"

She took her paper to the dog, and held it under his nose. He turned his head aside as in chagrin and mortification, and she impulsively kissed his velvety bulging forehead.

" 'S a Loolie, 's a little Loozie! Look at his portrait, darling, look at his portrait, that his mother has done of him." She looked at her paper and chuckled. Then, kissing the dog once more, she rose and came gravely to Gudrun, offering her the paper.

It was a grotesque little diagram of a grotesque little animal, so wicked and so comical, a slow smile came over Gudrun's face, unconsciously. And at her side Winifred chuckled with glee, and said:

"It isn't like him, is it? He's much lovelier than that. He's so beautiful—mmm, Looloo, my sweet darling." And she flew off to embrace the chagrined little dog. He looked up at her with reproachful, saturnine eyes, vanquished in his extreme agedness of being. Then she flew back to her drawing, and chuckled with satisfaction.

"It isn't like him, is it?" she said to Gudrun.

"Yes, it's very like him," Gudrun replied.

The child treasured her drawing, carried it about with her, and showed it, with a silent embarrassment, to everybody.

"Look," she said, thrusting the paper into her father's hand.

"Why, that's Looloo!" he exclaimed. And he looked down in surprise, hearing the almost inhuman chuckle of the child at his side.

Gerald was away from home when Gudrun first came to Shortlands. But the first morning he came back he watched for her. It was a sunny, soft morning, and he lingered in the garden paths, looking at the flowers that had come out during his absence. He was clean and fit as ever, shaven, his fair hair scrupulously parted at the side, bright in the sunshine, his short, fair moustache closely clipped, his eyes with their humorous kind twinkle, which was so deceptive. He was dressed in black, his clothes sat well on his well-nourished body. Yet as he lingered before the flower-beds in the morning sunshine, there was a certain isolation, a fear about him, as of something wanting.

Gudrun came up quickly, unseen. She was dressed in blue, with woolen yellow stockings, like the Bluecoat boys.[2] He glanced up in surprise. Her stockings always disconcerted him, the pale-yellow stockings and the heavy, heavy black shoes. Winifred, who had been playing about the garden with Mademoiselle and the dogs, came flitting towards Gudrun. The child wore a dress of black-and-white stripes. Her hair was rather short, cut round and hanging level in her neck.

"We're going to do Bismarck, aren't we?" she said, linking her hand through Gudrun's arm.

"Yes, we're going to do Bismarck. Do you want to?"

"Oh yes—oh, I do! I want most awfully to do Bismarck. He looks *so* splendid this morning, so *fierce*. He's almost as big as a lion." And the child chuckled sardonically at her own hyperbole. "He's a real king, he really is."

"Bonjour, Mademoiselle," said the little French governess, wavering up with a slight bow, a bow of the sort that Gudrun loathed, insolent.

"Winifred veut tant faire le portrait de Bismarck——! Oh, mais toute la matinée—'We will do Bismarck this morning!'—Bismarck, Bismarck, toujours Bismarck! C'est un lapin, n'est-ce pas, mademoiselle?"

"Oui, c'est un grand lapin blanc et noir. Vous ne l'avez pas vu?" said Gudrun in her good, but rather heavy French.

"Non, mademoiselle, Winifred n'a jamais voulu me le faire voir. Tant de fois je le lui ai demandé, 'Qu'est ce donc que ce Bismarck, Winifred?' Mais elle n'a pas voulu me le dire. Son Bismarck, c'était un mystère."

"Oui, c'est un mystère, vraiment un mystère! Miss Brangwen, say that Bismarck is a mystery," cried Winifred.

"Bismarck is a mystery, Bismarck, c'est un mystère, der Bismarck, er ist ein Wunder," said Gudrun, in mocking incantation.

"Ja, er ist ein Wunder," repeated Winifred, with odd seriousness, under which lay a wicked chuckle.

"Ist er auch ein Wunder?" came the slightly insolent sneering of Mademoiselle.

"Doch!" said Winifred briefly, indifferent.

"Doch ist er nicht ein König. Beesmarck, he was not a king,

2. The boys at Christ's Hospital (a secondary school) wear a traditional uniform of blue gowns and yellow stockings.

Winifred, as you have said. He was only—il n'était que chancelier."

"Qu'est ce qu'un chancelier?"[3] said Winifred, with slightly contemptuous indifference.

"A chancelier is a chancellor, and a chancellor is, I believe, a sort of judge," said Gerald, coming up and shaking hands with Gudrun. "You'll have made a song of Bismarck soon," said he.

Mademoiselle waited, and discreetly made her inclination, and her greeting.

"So they wouldn't let you see Bismarck, Mademoiselle?" he said.

"Non, Monsieur."

"Ay, very mean of them. What are you going to do to him, Miss Brangwen? I want him sent to the kitchen and cooked."

"Oh no," cried Winifred.

"We're going to draw him," said Gudrun.

"Draw him and quarter him and dish him up," he said, being purposely fatuous.

"Oh no," cried Winifred with emphasis, chuckling.

Gudrun detected the tang of mockery in him, and she looked up and smiled into his face. He felt his nerves caressed. Their eyes met in knowledge.

"How do you like Shortlands?" he asked.

"Oh, very much," she said, with nonchalance.

"Glad you do. Have you noticed these flowers?"

He led her along the path. She followed intently. Winifred came, and the governess lingered in the rear. They stopped before some veined calpiglossis flowers.

"Aren't they wonderful?" she cried, looking at them absorbedly. Strange how her reverential, almost ecstatic admiration of the flowers caressed his nerves. She stooped down, and touched the trumpets, with infinitely fine and delicate-touching finger tips. It filled him with ease to see her. When she rose, her eyes, hot with the beauty of the flowers, looked into his.

"What are they?" she asked.

"Sort of petunia, I suppose," he answered. "I don't really know them."

"They are quite strangers to me," she said.

They stood together in a false intimacy, a nervous contact. And he was in love with her.

She was aware of Mademoiselle standing near, like a little

3. "Winifred wants so much to do a portrait of Bismarck——! Oh, but all morning * * * Bismarck, Bismarck, always Bismarck! He's a rabbit, isn't he, mademoiselle?" "Yes, he's a big white-and-black rabbit. Haven't you seen him?" * * * "No, mademoiselle, Winifred has never wanted to have me see him. I've so often asked her, 'What is this Bismarck, then, Winifred?' But she wouldn't tell me. Her Bismarck remained a mystery." "Yes, he's a mystery, truly a mystery! * * *" "Bismarck is a mystery, Bismarck is a mystery, Bismarck is a marvel," * * * "Yes, he is a marvel," * * * "Is he a marvel, too?" * * * "Indeed!" * * * "But he is not a king * * *—he was only chancellor." "What is a chancellor?"

French beetle, observant and calculating. She moved away with Winifred, saying they would go to find Bismarck.

Gerald watched them go, looking all the while at the soft, full, still body of Gudrun, in its silky cashmere. How silky and rich and soft her body must be. An excess of appreciation came over his mind, she was the all-desirable, the all-beautiful. He wanted only to come to her, nothing more. He was only this, this being that should come to her, and be given to her.

At the same time he was finely and acutely aware of Mademoiselle's neat, brittle finality of form. She was like some elegant beetle with thin ankles, perched on her high heels, her glossy black dress perfectly correct, her dark hair done high and admirably. How repulsive her completeness and her finality was! He loathed her.

Yet he did admire her. She was perfectly correct. And it did rather annoy him, that Gudrun came dressed in startling colors, like a macaw, when the family was in mourning. Like a macaw she was! He watched the lingering way she took her feet from the ground. And her ankles were pale yellow, and her dress a deep blue. Yet it pleased him. It pleased him very much. He felt the challenge in her very attire—she challenged the whole world. And he smiled as to the note of a trumpet.

Gudrun and Winifred went through the house to the back, where were the stables and the outbuildings. Everywhere was still and deserted. Mr. Crich had gone out for a short drive, the stableman had just led round Gerald's horse. The two girls went to the hutch that stood in a corner, and looked at the great black-and-white rabbit.

"Isn't he beautiful! Oh, do look at him listening! Doesn't he look silly!" she laughed quickly, then added: "Oh, do let's do him listening, do let us, he listens with so much of himself;—don't you, darling Bismarck?"

"Can we take him out?" said Gudrun.

"He's very strong. He really is extremely strong." She looked at Gudrun, her head on one side, in odd calculating mistrust.

"But we'll try, shall we?"

"Yes, if you like. But he's a fearful kicker!"

They took the key to unlock the door. The rabbit exploded in a wild rush round the hutch.

"He scratches most awfully sometimes," cried Winifred in excitement. "Oh, do look at him, isn't he wonderful!" The rabbit tore round the hutch in a flurry. "Bismarck!" cried the child, in rousing excitement. "How *dreadful* you are! You are beastly." Winifred looked up at Gudrun with some misgiving in her wild excitement. Gudrun smiled sardonically with her mouth. Winifred made a strange crooning noise of unaccountable excitement. "Now he's still!" she cried, seeing the rabbit settled down in a far corner of the hutch. "Shall we take him now?" she whispered excitedly, mysteriously, looking up at Gudrun and edging very close. "Shall we get him now?——" she chuckled wickedly to herself.

They unlocked the door of the hutch. Gudrun thrust in her arm and seized the great, lusty rabbit as it crouched still, she grasped its long ears. It set its four feet flat, and thrust back. There was a long scraping sound as it was hauled forward, and in another instant it was in mid-air, lunging wildly, its body flying like a spring coiled and released, as it lashed out, suspended from the ears. Gudrun held the black-and-white tempest at arms' length, averting her face. But the rabbit was magically strong, it was all she could do to keep her grasp. She almost lost her presence of mind.

"Bismarck, Bismarck, you are behaving terribly," said Winifred in a rather frightened voice. "Oh, do put him down, he's beastly."

Gudrun stood for a moment astounded by the thunderstorm that had sprung into being in her grip. Then her color came up, a heavy rage came over her like a cloud. She stood shaken as a house in a storm, and utterly overcome. Her heart was arrested with fury at the mindlessness and the bestial stupidity of this struggle, her wrists were badly scored by the claws of the beast, a heavy cruelty welled up in her.

Gerald came round as she was trying to capture the flying rabbit under her arm. He saw, with subtle recognition, her sullen passion of cruelty.

"You should let one of the men do that for you," he said, hurrying up.

"Oh, he's so horrid!" cried Winifred, almost frantic.

He held out his nervous, sinewy hand and took the rabbit by the ears from Gudrun.

"It's most *fearfully* strong," she cried in a high voice, like the crying of a seagull, strange and vindictive.

The rabbit made itself into a ball in the air and lashed out, flinging itself into a bow. It really seemed demoniacal. Gudrun saw Gerald's body tighten, saw a sharp blindness come into his eyes.

"I know these beggars of old," he said.

The long, demon-like beast lashed out again, spread on the air as if it were flying, looking something like a dragon, then closing up again, inconceivably powerful and explosive. The man's body, strung to its efforts, vibrated strongly. Then a sudden sharp, white-edged wrath came up in him. Swift as lightning he drew back and brought his free hand down like a hawk on the neck of the rabbit. Simultaneously, there came the unearthly abhorrent scream of a rabbit in the fear of death. It made one immense writhe, tore his wrists and his sleeves in a final convulsion, all its belly flashed white in a whirlwind of paws, and then he had slung it round and had it under his arm, fast. It cowered and skulked. His face was gleaming with a smile.

"You wouldn't think there was all that force in a rabbit," he said, looking at Gudrun. And he saw her eyes black as night in her pallid face, she looked almost unearthly. The scream of the rabbit, after the violent tussle, seemed to have torn the veil of her consciousness. He looked at her, and the whitish, electric gleam in his face intensified.

"I don't really like him," Winifred was crooning. "I don't care for him as I do for Loozie. He's hateful really."

A smile twisted Gudrun's face as she recovered. She knew she was revealed.

"Don't they make the most fearful noise when they scream?" she cried, the high note in her voice like a seagull's cry.

"Abominable," he said.

"He shouldn't be so silly when he has to be taken out," Winifred was saying, putting out her hand and touching the rabbit tentatively, as it skulked under his arm, motionless as if it were dead.

"He's not dead, is he, Gerald?" she asked.

"No, he ought to be," he said.

"Yes, he ought!" cried the child, with a sudden flush of amusement. And she touched the rabbit with more confidence. "His heart is beating so fast. Isn't he funny? He really is."

"Where do you want him?" asked Gerald.

"In the little green court," she said.

Gudrun looked at Gerald with strange, darkened eyes, strained with underworld knowledge, almost supplicating, like those of a creature which is at his mercy, yet which is his ultimate victor. He did not know what to say to her. He felt the mutual hellish recognition. And he felt he ought to say something to cover it. He had the power of lightning in his nerves, she seemed like a soft recipient of his magical, hideous white fire. He was unconfident, he had qualms of fear.

"Did he hurt you?" he asked.

"No," she said.

"He's an insensible beast," he said, turning his face away.

They came to the little court, which was shut in by old red walls in whose crevices wallflowers were growing. The grass was soft and fine and old, a level floor carpeting the court, the sky was blue overhead. Gerald tossed the rabbit down. It crouched still and would not move. Gudrun watched it with faint horror.

"Why doesn't it move?" she cried.

"It's skulking," he said.

She looked up at him, and a slight sinister smile contracted her white face.

"Isn't it a *fool!*" she cried. "Isn't it a sickening *fool?*" The vindictive mockery in her voice made his brain quiver. Glancing up at him, into his eyes, she revealed again the mocking, white-cruel recognition. There was a league between them, abhorrent to them both. They were implicated with each other in abhorrent mysteries.

"How many scratches have you?" he asked, showing his hard forearm, white and hard and torn in red gashes.

"How really vile!" she cried, flushing with a sinister vision. "Mine is nothing."

She lifted her arm and showed a deep red score down the silken white flesh.

"What a devil!" he exclaimed. But it was as if he had had knowledge of her in the long red rent of her forearm, so silken and soft. He did not want to touch her. He would have to make himself touch her, deliberately. The long, shallow red rip seemed torn across his own brain, tearing the surface of his ultimate consciousness, letting through the forever unconscious, unthinkable red ether of the beyond, the obscene beyond.

"It doesn't hurt you very much, does it?" he asked, solicitous.

"Not at all," she cried.

And suddenly the rabbit, which had been crouching as if it were a flower, so still and soft, suddenly burst into life. Round and round the court it went, as if shot from a gun, round and round like a furry meteorite, in a tense hard circle that seemed to bind their brains. They all stood in amazement, smiling uncannily, as if the rabbit were obeying some unknown incantation. Round and round it flew, on the grass under the old red walls like a storm.

And then quite suddenly it settled down, hobbled among the grass, and sat considering, its nose twitching like a bit of fluff in the wind. After having considered for a few minutes, a soft bunch with a black, open eye, which perhaps was looking at them, perhaps was not, it hobbled calmly forward and began to nibble the grass with that mean motion of a rabbit's quick eating.

"It's mad," said Gudrun. "It is most decidedly mad."

He laughed.

"The question is," he said, "what is madness? I don't suppose it is rabbit-mad."

"Don't you think it is?" she asked.

"No. That's what it is to be a rabbit."

There was a queer, faint, obscene smile over his face. She looked at him and saw him, and knew that he was initiate as she was initiate. This thwarted her, and contravened her, for the moment.

"God be praised we aren't rabbits," she said in a high, shrill voice.

The smile intensified a little on his face.

"Not rabbits?" he said, looking at her fixedly.

Slowly her face relaxed into a smile of obscene recognition.

"Ah, Gerald," she said in a strong, slow, almost manlike way. "—All that, and more." Her eyes looked up at him with shocking nonchalance.

He felt again as if she had hit him across the face—or rather as if she had torn him across the breast, dully, finally. He turned aside.

"Eat, eat, my darling!" Winifred was softly conjuring the rabbit, and creeping forward to touch it. It hobbled away from her. "Let its mother stroke its fur then, darling, because it is so mysterious——"

1916   1920

From Etruscan Places

Tarquinia[1]

In Cerveteri there is nowhere to sleep, so the only thing to do is to go back to Rome, or forwards to Città Vecchia. The bus landed us at the station of Palo at about five o'clock: in the midst of nowhere: to meet the Rome train. But we were going on to Tarquinia, not back to Rome, so we must wait two hours, till seven.

In the distance we could see the concrete villas and new houses of what was evidently Ladispoli, a seaside place, some two miles away. So we set off to walk to Ladispoli, on the flat sea road. On the left, in the wood that forms part of the great park, the nightingales had already begun to whistle, and looking over the wall one could see many little rose-colored cyclamens glowing on the earth in the evening light.

We walked on, and the Rome train came surging round the bend. It misses Ladispoli, whose two miles of branch line runs only in the hot bathing months. As we neared the first ugly villas on the road the ancient wagonette drawn by the ancient white horse, both

1. Long before 1927, when Lawrence made his Etruscan journey with his American friend Earl Brewster, he had been interested in the Etruscans and their art. The Etruscans were the most important of the pre-Roman inhabitants of Italy; they spread out from their original territory (modern Tuscany, region in Central Italy) to dominate about a third of Italy, but were in their turn conquered by the Romans. Scholars are still uncertain about the precise identity of the Etruscans, and inscriptions in their language have never been deciphered. Of their twelve cities, Lawrence visited and describes Caere (modern Cervetri, Cerveteri), Tarquinii (later Corneto Tarquinia, now Tarquinia), Vulci (modern Volci), Volaterrae (modern Volterra). Tarquinia is some fifty miles northwest of Rome, up the Italian west coast, and the Italian towns mentioned by Lawrence in this essay are in this area of Italy: Città Vecchia is north of Rome, about half way between Rome and Tarquinia, on the coast.

looking sun-bitten almost to ghostliness, clattered past. It just beat us.

Ladispoli is one of those ugly little places on the Roman coast, consisting of new concrete villas, new concrete hotels, kiosks, and bathing establishments; bareness and non-existence for ten months in the year, seething solid with fleshy bathers in July and August. Now it was deserted, quite deserted, save for two or three officials and four wild children.

B. and I lay on the gray-black lava sand, by the flat, low sea, over which the sky, gray and shapeless, emitted a flat, wan evening light. Little waves curled green out of the sea's dark grayness, from the curious low flatness of the water. It is a peculiarly forlorn coast, the sea peculiarly flat and sunken, lifeless-looking, the land as if it had given its last gasp, and was now forever inert.

Yet this is the Tyrrhenian sea of the Etruscans, where their shipping spread sharp sails, and beat the sea with slave-oars, roving in from Greece and Sicily, Sicily of the Greek tyrants; from Cumae, the city of the old Greek colony of Campania, where the province of Naples now is; and from Elba, where the Etruscans mined their iron ore. The Etruscans sailed the seas. They are even said to have come by sea, from Lydia in Asia Minor, at some date far back in the dim mists before the eighth century B.C. But that a whole people, even a whole host, sailed in the tiny ships of those days, all at once, to people a sparsely peopled central Italy, seems hard to imagine. Probably ships did come— even before Ulysses. Probably men landed on the strange flat coast, and made camps, and then treated with the natives. Whether the newcomers were Lydians or Hittites with hair curled in a roll behind, or men from Mycenae or Crete, who knows. Perhaps men of all these sorts came, in batches. For in Homeric days a restlessness seems to have possessed the Mediterranean basin, and ancient races began shaking ships like seeds over the sea. More people than Greeks, or Hellenes, or Indo-Germanic groups, were on the move.[2]

2. Lawrence is casting his mind's eye over the Tyrrhenian Sea, which is that very roughly circular area of the Mediterranean bounded on the east by the west coast of Italy, on the south by Sicily, and on the west by the islands of Sardinia and Corsica, with the little island of Elba lying between Corsica and the Italian mainland. On this sea the Etruscans plied their trade, sailing south to Sicily, which had been colonized by Greece from the 8th century B.C. and where in the 5th and 6th centuries B.C., under the Greek tyrants Hippocrates of Gela, Gelon, and Hieron, Greek civilization in Sicily reached its peak. The Greeks colonized not only Sicily but part of the mainland of Italy, notably the fertile region of Campania (lying between the Appenines and the Tyrrhenian Sea) with its city of Cumae, the first Greek colony in Italy. Etruscan forces in Campania were crushed by the forces of Cumae, aided by those of the Greek Sicilian colony Syracuse, in 474 B.C. Lawrence then extends his vision further east, where he speculates the Etruscans might have come from—perhaps from Lydia, the territory in Asia Minor which dominated trade routes both eastward to the Orient and westward to Greece and Italy, a great entrepot of trade in the ancient Mediterranean world, a pioneer in music, and the first state to use coined money. The Hittites were an ancient people in Asia Minor (c. 2000 to 1200 B.C.). Mycenae is one of the most ancient of Greek cities some fourteen miles south-

But whatever little ships were run ashore on the soft, deep, gray-black volcanic sand of this coast, three thousand years ago, and earlier, their mariners certainly did not find those hills inland empty of people. If the Lydians or Hittites pulled up their long little two-eyed ships on to the beach, and made a camp behind a bank, in shelter from the wet strong wind, what natives came down curiously to look at them? For natives there were, of that we may be certain. Even before the fall of Troy, before even Athens was dreamed of, there were natives here. And they had huts on the hills, thatched huts in clumsy groups most probably; with patches of grain, and flocks of goats and probably cattle. Probably it was like coming on an old Irish village, or a village in the Scottish Hebrides in Prince Charlie's day,[3] to come upon a village of these Italian aborigines, by the Tyrrhenian sea, three thousand years ago. But by the time Etruscan history starts in Caere, some eight centuries B.C., there was certainly more than a village on the hill. There was a native city, of that we may be sure; and a busy spinning of linen and beating of gold, long before the Regolini-Galassi tomb was built.[4]

However that may be, somebody came, and somebody was already here, of that we may be certain, and, in the first place, none of them were Greeks or Hellenes. It was the days before Rome rose up: probably when the first comers arrived it was the days even before Homer. The newcomers, whether they were few or many, seem to have come from the east, Asia Minor or Crete or Cyprus. They were, we must feel, of an old, primitive Mediterranean and Asiatic or Aegean stock. The twilight of the beginning of our history was the nightfall of some previous history, which will never be written. Pelasgian is but a shadow-word.[5] But Hittite and Minoan, Lydian, Carian, Etruscan, these words emerge from shadow, and perhaps from one and the same great shadow come the peoples to whom the names belong.

west of Corinth. Crete is the Mediterranean island (southeast of Greece and southwest of Asia Minor) colonized by Greeks after an earlier flourishing Bronze Age culture. It was a great center of commerce. Lawrence's history is perhaps vague here, as he imagines ancient peoples migrating across the Mediterranean. The phrase "Homeric days" can have little specific meaning, for the Homeric poems deal with the siege of Troy (mid-13th century B.C.) but are the result of centuries of oral poetry composed, recited and transmitted by later professional bards living in a very different civilization from that of Troy and its age, and were finally written down in a third and still more different phase of civilization some time between the late 9th and early 7th centuries B.C. The Hellenes are the ancient Greeks. Indo-Germanic (more usually, Indo-European) is not a term for a race, but for a group of languages (which include the Greek, Italic, Celtic, Germanic, and Slavic).

3. Prince Charles Edward led his unsuccessful Jacobite rebellion in 1745.

4. The most important of the ancient Etruscan tombs in the necropolis in the hill to the northwest of Caere (Cervetri), dating from around the mid-7th century B.C. The name comes from the tomb's discoverers.

5. Pelasgians are mentioned by Homer as Trojan allies "from afar," and the name came to be used by the Greeks to denote the aboriginal inhabitants of Greece. All accounts of the Pelasgians which we have are legendary and modern scholars have come to no certain conclusion about their identity.

The Etruscan civilization seems a shoot, perhaps the last, from the prehistoric Mediterranean world, and the Etruscans, new-comers and aborigines alike, probably belonged to that ancient world, though they were of different nations and levels of culture. Later, of course, the Greeks exerted a great influence. But that is another matter.

Whatever happened, the newcomers in ancient central Italy found many natives flourishing in possession of the land. These aboriginals, now ridiculously called Villanovans, were neither wiped out nor suppressed. Probably they welcomed the strangers, whose pulse was not hostile to their own. Probably the more highly de-veloped religion of the newcomers was not hostile to the primitive religion of the aborigines; no doubt the two religions had the same root. Probably the aborigines formed willingly a sort of religious aristocracy from the newcomers; the Italians might almost do the same today. And so the Etruscan world arose. But it took centuries to arise. Etruria was not a colony, it was a slowly developed country.

There was never an Etruscan nation: only, in historical times, a great league of tribes or nations using the Etruscan language and the Etruscan script—at least officially—and uniting in their religious feeling and observances. The Etruscan alphabet seems to have been borrowed from the old Greeks, apparently from the Chal-cidians of Cumae—the Greek colony just north of where Naples now is. But the Etruscan language is not akin to any of the Greek dialects, nor, apparently, to the Italic. But we don't know. It is probably to a great extent the language of the old aboriginals of southern Etruria, just as the religion is in all probability basically aboriginal, belonging to some vast old religion of the prehistoric world. From the shadow of the prehistoric world emerge dying re-ligions that have not yet invented gods or goddesses, but live by the mystery of the elemental powers in the Universe, the complex vitalities of what we feebly call Nature. And the Etruscan religion was certainly one of these. The gods and goddesses don't seem to have emerged in any sharp definiteness.

But it is not for me to make assertions. Only, that which half emerges from the dim background of time is strangely stirring; and after having read all the learned suggestions, most of them contra-dicting one another; and then having looked sensitively at the tombs and the Etruscan things that are left, one must accept one's own resultant feeling.

Ships came along this low, inconspicuous sea, coming up from the Near East, we should imagine, even in the days of Solomon—even, maybe, in the days of Abraham.[6] And they kept on coming.

6. The age of the Old Testament patri-archs cannot be certainly dated: proba-bly between the 18th and 16th centuries B.C. (the second quarter of the 2nd mil-lennium B.C.). King Solomon reigned over Israel in the 10th century B.C.

As the light of history dawns and brightens, we see them winging along with their white or scarlet sails. Then, as the Greeks came crowding into colonies in Italy, and the Phoenicians began to exploit the western Mediterranean, we begin to hear of the silent Etruscans, and to see them.

Just north of here Caere founded a port called Pyrgi, and we know that the Greek vessels flocked in, with vases and stuffs and colonists coming from Hellas or from Magna Graecia, and that Phoenician ships came rowing sharply, over from Sardinia, up from Carthage, round from Tyre and Sidon; while the Etruscans had their own fleets, built of timber from the mountains, caulked with pitch from northern Volterra, fitted with sails from Tarquinia, filled with wheat from the bountiful plains, or with the famous Etruscan articles of bronze and iron, which they carried away to Corinth or to Athens or to the ports of Asia Minor. We know of the great and finally disastrous sea-battles with the Phoenicians and the tyrant of Syracuse. And we know that the Etruscans, all except those of Caere, became ruthless pirates, almost like the Moors and the Barbary corsairs later on. This was part of their viciousness, a great annoyance to their loving and harmless neighbors, the law-abiding Romans—who believed in the supreme law of conquest.

However, all this is long ago. The very coast has changed since then. The smitten sea has sunk and fallen back, and weary land has emerged when, apparently, it didn't want to, and the flowers of the coastline are miserable bathing places such as Ladispoli and seaside Ostia, desecration put upon desolation, to the triumphant trump of the mosquito.

The wind blew flat and almost chill from the darkening sea, the dead waves lifted small bits of pure green out of the leaden grayness, under the leaden sky. We got up from the dark gray but soft sand, and went back along the road to the station, peered at by the few people and officials who were holding the place together till the next bathers came.

At the station there was general desertedness. But our things still lay untouched in a dark corner of the buffet, and the man gave us a decent little meal of cold meats and wine and oranges. It was already night. The train came rushing in, punctually.

It is an hour or more to Cività Vecchia, which is a port of not much importance, except that from here the regular steamer sails to Sardinia. We gave our things to a friendly old porter, and told him to take us to the nearest hotel. It was night, very dark as we emerged from the station.

And a fellow came furtively shouldering up to me.

"You are foreigners, aren't you?"

"Yes."

"What nationality?"

"English."

"You have your permission to reside in Italy—or your passport?"

"My passport I have—what do you want?"

"I want to look at your passport."

"It's in the valise! And why? Why is this?"

"This is a port, and we must examine the papers of foreigners."

"And why? Genoa is a port, and no one dreams of asking for papers."

I was furious. He made no answer. I told the porter to go on to the hotel, and the fellow furtively followed at our side, half-a-pace to the rear, in the mongrel way these spy-louts have.

In the hotel I asked for a room and registered, and then the fellow asked again for my passport. I wanted to know why he demanded it, what he meant by accosting me outside the station as if I was a criminal, what he meant by insulting us with his requests, when in any other town in Italy one went unquestioned—and so forth, in considerable rage.

He did not reply, but obstinately looked as though he would be venomous if he could. He peered at the passport—though I doubt if he could make head or tail of it—asked where we were going, peered at B.'s passport, half excused himself in a whining, disgusting sort of fashion, and disappeared into the night. A real lout.

I was furious. Supposing I had not been carrying my passport—and usually I don't dream of carrying it—what amount of trouble would that lout have made me! Probably I should have spent the night in prison, and been bullied by half-a-dozen low bullies.

Those poor rats at Ladispoli had seen me and B. go to the sea and sit on the sand for half-an-hour, then go back to the train. And this was enough to rouse their suspicions, I imagine, so they telegraphed to Cività Vecchia. Why are officials always fools? Even when there is no war on? What could they imagine we were doing?

The hotel manager, propitious, said there was a very interesting museum in Cività Vecchia, and wouldn't we stay the next day and see it. "Ah!" I replied. "But all it contains is Roman stuff, and we don't want to look at that." It was malice on my part, because the present regime considers itself purely ancient Roman. The man looked at me scared, and I grinned at him. "But what do they mean," I said, "behaving like this to a simple traveler, in a country where foreigners are invited to travel!" "Ah!" said the porter softly and soothingly. "It is the Roman province. You will have no more of it when you leave the Provincia di Roma." And when the Italians give the soft answer to turn away wrath, the wrath somehow turns away.

We walked for an hour in the dull street of Cività Vecchia. There

seemed so much suspicion, one would have thought there were
several wars on. The hotel manager asked if we were staying. We
said we were leaving by the eight-o'clock train in the morning, for
Tarquinia.

And, sure enough, we left by the eight-o'clock train. Tarquinia is
only one station from Cività Vecchia—about twenty minutes over
the flat Maremma country, with the sea on the left, and the green
wheat growing luxuriantly, the asphodel sticking up its spikes.

We soon saw Tarquinia, its towers pricking up like antennae on
the side of a low bluff of a hill, some few miles inland from the sea.
And this was once the metropolis of Etruria, chief city of the great
Etruscan League. But it died like all the other Etruscan cities, and
had a more or less medieval rebirth, with a new name. Dante knew
it, as it was known for centuries, as Corneto—Corgnetum or Corne-
tium—and forgotten was its Etruscan past. Then there was a feeble
sort of wakening to remembrance a hundred years ago, and the
town got Tarquinia tacked on to its Corneto: Corneto-Tarquinia.
The Fascist regime,[7] however, glorying in the Italian origins of
Italy, has now struck out the Corneto, so the town is once more,
simply, Tarquinia. As you come up in the motor-bus from the station you see the great black letters, on a white ground, painted on
the wall by the city gateway: *Tarquinia*. So the wheel of revolution
turns. There stands the Etruscan word—Latinized Etruscan—beside the medieval gate, put up by the Fascist power to name and
unname.

But the Fascists, who consider themselves in all things Roman,
Roman of the Caesars, heirs of Empire and world power, are beside
the mark restoring the rags of dignity to Etruscan places. For of all
the Italian people that ever lived, the Etruscans were surely the
least Roman. Just as, of all the people that ever rose up in Italy, the
Romans of ancient Rome were surely the most un-Italian, judging
from the natives of today.

Tarquinia is only about three miles from the sea. The omnibus
soon runs one up, charges through the widened gateway, swirls
round in the empty space inside the gateway, and is finished. We
descend in the bare place, which seems to expect nothing. On the
left is a beautiful stone palazzo—on the right is a café, upon the
low ramparts above the gate. The man of the *Dazio*, the town customs, looks to see if anybody has brought foodstuffs into the town
—but it is a mere glance. I ask him for the hotel. He says: "Do you
mean to sleep?" I say I do. Then he tells a small boy to carry my
bag and take us to Gentile's.

Nowhere is far off, in these small wall-girdled cities. In the warm
April morning the stony little town seems half asleep. As a matter

7. A right-wing totalitarian system of government established in Italy by Benito Mussolini in 1922 and surviving there until his overthrow in 1943.

of fact, most of the inhabitants are out in the fields, and won't come in through the gates again till evening. The slight sense of deserted-ness is everywhere—even in the inn, when we have climbed up the stairs to it, for the ground floor does not belong. A little lad in long trousers, who would seem to be only twelve years old but who has the air of a mature man, confronts us with his chest out. We ask for rooms. He eyes us, darts away for the key, and leads us off upstairs another flight, shouting to a young girl, who acts as chambermaid, to follow on. He shows us two small rooms, opening off a big, desert sort of general assembly room common in this kind of inn. "And you won't be lonely," he says briskly, "because you can talk to one another through the wall. *Toh! Lina!*" He lifts his finger and listens. "*Eh!*" comes through the wall, like an echo, with startling nearness and clearness. "*Fai presto!*" says Albertino. "*È pronto!*" comes the voice of Lina. "*Ecco!*" says Albertino to us.[8] "You hear!" We cer-tainly did. The partition wall must have been butter muslin. And Albertino was delighted, having reassured us we should not feel lonely nor frightened in the night.

He was, in fact, the most manly and fatherly little hotel manager I have ever known, and he ran the whole place. He was in reality fourteen years old, but stunted. From five in the morning till ten at night he was on the go, never ceasing, and with a queer, abrupt, sideways-darting alacrity that must have wasted a great deal of energy. The father and mother were in the background—quite young and pleasant. But they didn't seem to exert themselves. Albertino did it all. How Dickens would have loved him! But Dickens would not have seen the queer wistfulness, and trustful-ness, and courage in the boy. He was absolutely unsuspicious of us strangers. People must be rather human and decent in Tarquinia, even the commercial travelers: who, presumably, are chiefly buyers of agricultural produce, and sellers of agricultural implements and so forth.

We sallied out, back to the space by the gate, and drank coffee at one of the tin tables outside. Beyond the wall there were a few new villas—the land dropped green and quick, to the strip of coast plain and the indistinct, faintly gleaming sea, which seemed some-how not like a sea at all.

I was thinking, if this were still an Etruscan city, there would still be this cleared space just inside the gate. But instead of a rather forlorn vacant lot it would be a sacred clearing, with a little temple to keep it alert.

Myself, I like to think of the little wooden temples of the early Greeks and of the Etruscans: small, dainty, fragile, and evanescent as flowers. We have reached the stage when we are weary of huge

8. "Hey, Lina!" "What!" "Hurry up!"   "Right away!" "There you are!"

stone erections, and we begin to realize that it is better to keep life fluid and changing than to try to hold it fast down in heavy monuments. Burdens on the face of the earth are man's ponderous erections.

The Etruscans made small temples, like little houses with pointed roofs, entirely of wood. But then, outside, they had friezes and cornices and crests of terra cotta, so that the upper part of the temple would seem almost made of earthenware, terra-cotta plaques fitted neatly, and alive with freely modeled painted figures in relief, gay dancing creatures, rows of ducks, round faces like the sun, and faces grinning and putting out a big tongue, all vivid and fresh and unimposing. The whole thing small and dainty in proportion, and fresh, somehow charming instead of impressive. There seems to have been in the Etruscan instinct a real desire to preserve the natural humor of life. And that is a task surely more worthy, and even much more difficult in the long run, than conquering the world or sacrificing the self or saving the immortal soul.

Why has mankind had such a craving to be imposed upon? Why this lust after imposing creeds, imposing deeds, imposing buildings, imposing language, imposing works of art? The thing becomes an imposition and a weariness at last. Give us things that are alive and flexible, which won't last too long and become an obstruction and a weariness. Even Michelangelo becomes at last a lump and a burden and a bore. It is so hard to see past him.

Across the space from the café is the Palazzo Vitelleschi, a charming building, now a national museum—so the marble slab says. But the heavy doors are shut. The place opens at ten, a man says. It is nine-thirty. We wander up the steep but not very long street, to the top.

And the top is a fragment of public garden, and a look-out. Two old men are sitting in the sun, under a tree. We walk to the parapet, and suddenly are looking into one of the most delightful landscapes I have ever seen: as it were, into the very virginity of hilly green country. It is all wheat—green and soft and swooping, swooping down and up, and glowing with green newness, and no houses. Down goes the declivity below us, then swerving the curve and up again, to the neighboring hill that faces in all its greenness and long-running immaculateness. Beyond, the hills ripple away to the mountains, and far in the distance stands a round peak, that seems to have an enchanted city on its summit.

Such a pure, uprising, unsullied country, in the greenness of wheat on an April morning!—and the queer complication of hills! There seems nothing of the modern world here—no houses, no contrivances, only a sort of fair wonder and stillness, an openness which has not been violated.

The hill opposite is like a distinct companion. The near end is quite steep and wild, with evergreen oaks and scrub, and specks of black-and-white cattle on the slopes of common. But the long crest is green again with wheat, running and drooping to the south. And immediately one feels: that hill has a soul, it has a meaning.

Lying thus opposite to Tarquinia's long hill, a companion across a suave little swing of valley, one feels at once that, if this is the hill where the living Tarquinians had their gay wooden houses, then that is the hill where the dead lie buried and quick, as seeds, in their painted houses underground. The two hills are as inseparable as life and death, even now, on the sunny, green-filled April morning with the breeze blowing in from the sea. And the land beyond seems as mysterious and fresh as if it were still the morning of Time.

But B. wants to go back to the Palazzo Vitelleschi: it will be open now. Down the street we go, and sure enough the big doors are open, several officials are in the shadowy courtyard entrance. They salute us in the Fascist manner: *alla Romana!* Why don't they discover the Etruscan salute, and salute us *all'Etrusca!* But they are perfectly courteous and friendly. We go into the court-yard of the palace.

The museum is exceedingly interesting and delightful, to anyone who is even a bit aware of the Etruscans. It contains a great number of things found at Tarquinia, and important things.

If only we would realize it, and not tear things from their settings. Museums anyhow are wrong. But if one must have museums, let them be small, and above all, let them be local. Splendid as the Etruscan museum is in Florence, how much happier one is in the museum at Tarquinia, where all the things are Tarquinian, and at least have some association with one another, and form some sort of *organic* whole.

In the entrance room from the cortile [9] lie a few of the long sar-cophagi in which the nobles were buried. It seems as if the primi-tive inhabitants of this part of Italy always burned their dead, and then put the ashes in a jar, sometimes covering the jar with the dead man's helmet, sometimes with a shallow dish for a lid, and then laid the urn with its ashes in a little round grave like a little well. This is called the Villanovan way of burial, in the well-tomb.

The newcomers to the country, however, apparently buried their dead whole. Here, at Tarquinia, you may still see the hills where the well-tombs of the aboriginal inhabitants are discovered, with the urns containing the ashes inside. Then come the graves where the dead were buried unburned, graves very much like those of today. But tombs of the same period with cinerary urns are found

9. Courtyard.

near to, or in connection. So that the new people and the old apparently lived side by side in harmony, from very early days, and the two modes of burial continued side by side, for centuries, long before the painted tombs were made.

At Tarquinia, however, the main practice seems to have been, at least from the seventh century on, that the nobles were buried in the great sarcophagi, or laid out on biers, and placed in chamber-tombs, while the slaves apparently were cremated, their ashes laid in urns, and the urns often placed in the family tomb, where the stone coffins of the masters rested. The common people, on the other hand, were apparently sometimes cremated, sometimes buried in graves very much like our graves of today, though the sides were lined with stone. The mass of the common people was mixed in race, and the bulk of them were probably serf-peasants, with many half-free artisans. These must have followed their own desire in the matter of burial: some had graves, many must have been cremated, their ashes saved in an urn or jar which takes up little room in a poor man's burial place. Probably even the less important members of the noble families were cremated, and their remains placed in the vases, which became more beautiful as the connection with Greece grew more extensive.

It is a relief to think that even the slaves—and the luxurious Etruscans had many, in historical times—had their remains decently stored in jars and laid in a sacred place. Apparently the "vicious Etruscans" had nothing comparable to the vast dead-pits which lay outside Rome, beside the great highway, in which the bodies of slaves were promiscuously flung.

It is all a question of sensitiveness. Brute force and overbearing may make a terrific effect. But in the end, that which lives lives by delicate sensitiveness. If it were a question of brute force, not a single human baby would survive for a fortnight. It is the grass of the field, most frail of all things, that supports all life all the time. But for the green grass, no empire would rise, no man would eat bread: for grain is grass; and Hercules or Napoleon or Henry Ford would alike be denied existence.

Brute force crushes many plants. Yet the plants rise again. The Pyramids will not last a moment compared with the daisy. And before Buddha or Jesus spoke the nightingale sang, and long after the words of Jesus and Buddha are gone into oblivion the nightingale still will sing. Because it is neither preaching nor teaching nor commanding nor urging. It is just singing. And in the beginning was not a Word, but a chirrup.

Because a fool kills a nightingale with a stone, is he therefore greater than the nightingale? Because the Roman took the life out of the Etruscan, was he therefore greater than the Etruscan? Not he! Rome fell, and the Roman phenomenon with it. Italy today is far more Etruscan in its pulse than Roman: and will always be so. The Etruscan element is like the grass of the field and the sprouting of corn, in Italy: it will always be so. Why try to revert to the Latin-Roman mechanism and suppression?

In the open room upon the courtyard of the Palazzo Vitelleschi lie a few sarcophagi of stone, with the effigies carved on top, something as the dead crusaders in English churches. And here, in Tarquinia, the effigies are more like crusaders than usual, for some lie flat on their backs, and have a dog at their feet; whereas usually the carved figure of the dead rears up as if alive, from the lid of the tomb, resting upon one elbow, and gazing out proudly, sternly. If it is a man, his body is exposed to just below the navel, and he holds in his hand the sacred *patera*, or *mundum*, the round saucer with the raised knob in the center, which represents the round germ of heaven and earth. It stands for the plasm, also, of the living cell, with its nucleus, which is the indivisible God of the beginning, and which remains alive and unbroken to the end, the eternal quick of all things, which yet divides and subdivides, so that it becomes the sun of the firmament and the lotus of the waters under the earth, and the rose of all existence upon the earth; and the sun maintains its own quick, unbroken for ever; and there is a living quick of the sea, and of all the waters; and every living created thing has its own unfailing quick. So within each man is the quick of him, when he is a baby, and when he is old, the same quick; some spark, some unborn and undying vivid life-electron. And this is what is symbolized in the *patera*, which may be made to flower like a rose or like the sun, but which remains the same, the germ central within the living plasm.

And this *patera*, this symbol, is almost invariably found in the hand of a dead man. But if the dead is a woman her dress falls in soft gathers from her throat, she wears splendid jewelry, and she holds in her hand not the *mundum*, but the mirror, the box of essence, the pomegranate, some symbols of her reflected nature, or of her woman's quality. But she, too, is given a proud, haughty look, as is the man: for she belongs to the sacred families that rule and that read the signs.

These sarcophagi and effigies here all belong to the centuries of the Etruscan decline, after there had been long intercourse with the Greeks, and perhaps most of them were made after the conquest of Etruria by the Romans. So that we do not look for fresh, spontaneous works of art, any more than we do in modern memorial stones. The funerary arts are always more or less commercial. The rich man orders his sarcophagus while he is still alive, and the monument carver makes the work more or less elaborate, according to the price. The figure is supposed to be a portrait of the man who orders it, so we see well enough what the later Etruscans look like. In the third and second centuries B.C., at the fag end of their existence as a people, they look very like the Romans of the same day, whose busts we know so well. And often they are given the tiresomely haughty air of people who are no longer rulers indeed, only by virtue of wealth.

Yet, even when the Etruscan art is Romanized and spoilt, there still flickers in it a certain naturalness and feeling. The Etruscan *Lucumones*, or prince-magistrates, were in the first place religious seers, governors in religion, then magistrates; then princes. They were not aristocrats in the Germanic sense, nor even patricians in the Roman. They were first and foremost leaders in the sacred mysteries, then magistrates, then men of family and wealth. So there is always a touch of vital life, of life-significance. And you may look through modern funerary sculpture in vain for anything so good even as the Sarcophagus of the Magistrate, with his written scroll spread before him, his strong, alert old face gazing sternly out, the necklace of office round his neck, the ring of rank on his finger. So he lies, in the museum at Tarquinia. His robe leaves him naked to the hip, and his body lies soft and slack, with the soft effect of relaxed flesh the Etruscan artists render so well, and which is so difficult. On the sculptured side of the sarcophagus the two death dealers wield the hammer of death, the winged figures wait for the soul, and will not be persuaded away. Beautiful it is, with the easy simplicity of life. But it is late in date. Probably this old Etruscan magistrate is already an official under Roman authority: for he does not hold the sacred *mundum*, the dish, he has only the written scroll, probably of laws. As if he were no longer the religious lord or Lucumo. Though possibly, in this case, the dead man was not one of the Lucumones anyhow.

Upstairs in the museum are many vases, from the ancient crude pottery of the Villanovans to the early black ware decorated in scratches, or undecorated, called *bucchero*, and on the painted bowls and dishes and amphoras which came from Corinth or Athens, or to those painted pots made by the Etruscans themselves more or less after the Greek patterns. These may or may not be interesting: the Etruscans are not at their best, painting dishes. Yet they must have loved them. In the early days these great jars and bowls, and smaller mixing bowls, and drinking cups and pitchers, and flat wine cups formed a valuable part of the household treasure. In very early times the Etruscans must have sailed their ships to Corinth and to Athens, taking perhaps wheat and honey, wax and bronze ware, iron and gold, and coming back with these precious jars, and stuffs, essences, perfumes and spice. And jars brought from overseas for the sake of their painted beauty must have been household treasures.

But then the Etruscans made pottery of their own, and by the thousand they imitated the Greek vases. So that there must have been millions of beautiful jars in Etruria. Already in the first century B.C. there was a passion among the Romans for collecting Greek and Etruscan painted jars from the Etruscans, particularly from the Etruscan tombs: jars and the little bronze votive figures and statuettes, the *sigilla Tyrrhena*[1] of the Roman luxury. And when the tombs were first robbed, for gold and silver treasure, hundreds of fine jars must have been thrown over and smashed. Because even now, when a part-rifled tomb is discovered and opened, the fragments of smashed vases lie around.

As it is, however, the museums are full of vases. If one looks for the Greek form of elegance and convention, those elegant "still-unravished brides of quietness," one is disappointed. But get over the strange desire we have for elegant convention, and the vases and dishes of the Etruscans, especially many of the black bucchero ware, begin to open out like strange flowers, black flowers with all the softness and the rebellion of life against convention, or red-and-black flowers painted with amusing free, bold designs. It is there nearly always in Etruscan things, the naturalness verging on the commonplace, but usually missing it, and often achieving an originality so free and bold, and so fresh, that we, who love convention and things "reduced to a norm," call it a bastard art, and commonplace.

It is useless to look in Etruscan things for "uplift." If you want uplift, go to the Greek and the Gothic. If you want mass, go to the Roman. But if you love the odd spontaneous forms that are never to be standardized, go to the Etruscans. In the fascinating little Palazzo Vitelleschi one could spend many an hour, but for the fact that the very fullness of museums makes one rush through them.

1932

Why the Novel Matters

We have curious ideas of ourselves. We think of ourselves as a body with a spirit in it, or a body with a soul in it, or a body with a mind in it. *Mens sana in corpore sano.* The years drink up the wine, and at last throw the bottle away, the body, of course, being the bottle.

It is a funny sort of superstition. Why should I look at my hand, as it so cleverly writes these words, and decide that it is a mere nothing compared to the mind that directs it? Is there really any

1. Tyrrhenian statuettes.

huge difference between my hand and my brain? Or my mind? My hand is alive, it flickers with a life of its own. It meets all the strange universe in touch, and learns a vast number of things, and knows a vast number of things. My hand, as it writes these words, slips gaily along, jumps like a grasshopper to dot an *i*, feels the table rather cold, gets a little bored if I write too long, has its own rudiments of thought, and is just as much *me* as is my brain, my mind, or my soul. Why should I imagine that there is a *me* which is more *me* than my hand is? Since my hand is absolutely alive, me alive.

Whereas, of course, as far as I am concerned, my pen isn't alive at all. My pen *isn't me* alive. Me alive ends at my finger tips.

Whatever is me alive is me. Every tiny bit of my hands is alive, every little freckle and hair and fold of skin. And whatever is me alive is me. Only my fingernails, those ten little weapons between me and an inanimate universe, they cross the mysterious Rubicon [1] between me alive and things like my pen, which are not alive, in my own sense.

So, seeing my hand is all alive, and me alive, wherein is it just a bottle, or a jug, or a tin can, or a vessel of clay, or any of the rest of that nonsense? True, if I cut it it will bleed, like a can of cherries. But then the skin that is cut, and the veins that bleed, and the bones that should never be seen, they are all just as alive as the blood that flows. So the tin can business, or vessel of clay, is just bunk.

And that's what you learn, when you're a novelist. And that's what you are very liable *not* to know, if you're a parson, or a philosopher, or a scientist, or a stupid person. If you're a parson, you talk about souls in heaven. If you're a novelist, you know that paradise is in the palm of your hand, and on the end of your nose, because both are alive; and alive, and man alive, which is more than you can say, for certain, of paradise. Paradise is after life, and I for one am not keen on anything that is *after* life. If you are a philosopher, you talk about infinity, and the pure spirit which knows all things. But if you pick up a novel, you realize immediately that infinity is just a handle to this self-same jug of a body of mine; while as for knowing, if I find my finger in the fire, I know that fire burns, with a knowledge so emphatic and vital, it leaves Nirvana merely a conjecture. Oh, yes, my body, me alive, *knows*, and knows intensely. And as for the sum of all knowledge, it can't be anything more than an accumulation of all the things I know in the body, and you, dear reader, know in the body.

1. When Julius Caesar crossed the River Rubicon (near Rimini, Italy) in 49 B.C., in defiance of the Senate's orders, this indicated his intention of advancing against Pompey and thus involving the country in civil war. Hence to "cross the Rubicon" means to take an important and irrevocable decision.

These damned philosophers, they talk as if they suddenly went off in steam, and were then much more important than they are when they're in their shirts. It is nonsense. Every man, philosopher included, ends in his own finger tips. That's the end of his man alive. As for the words and thoughts and sighs and aspirations that fly from him, they are so many tremulations in the ether, and not alive at all. But if the tremulations reach another man alive, he may receive them into his life, and his life may take on a new color, like a chameleon creeping from a brown rock on to a green leaf. All very well and good. It still doesn't alter the fact that the so-called spirit, the message or teaching of the philosopher or the saint, isn't alive at all, but just a tremulation upon the ether, like a radio message. All this spirit stuff is just tremulations upon the ether. If you, as man alive, quiver from the tremulation of the ether into new life, that is because you are man alive, and you take sustenance and stimulation into your alive man in a myriad ways. But to say that the message, or the spirit which is communicated to you, is more important than your living body, is nonsense. You might as well say that the potato at dinner was more important.

Nothing is important but life. And for myself, I can absolutely see life nowhere but in the living. Life with a capital L is only man alive. Even a cabbage in the rain is cabbage alive. All things that are alive are amazing. And all things that are dead are subsidiary to the living. Better a live dog than a dead lion. But better a live lion than a live dog. *C'est la vie!*

It seems impossible to get a saint, or a philosopher, or a scientist, to stick to this simple truth. They are all, in a sense, renegades. The saint wishes to offer himself up as spiritual food for the multitude. Even Francis of Assisi turns himself into a sort of angel-cake, of which anyone may take a slice. But an angel-cake is rather less than man alive. And poor St. Francis might well apologize to his body, when he is dying: "Oh, pardon me, my body, the wrong I did you through the years!" It was no wafer, for others to eat.

The philosopher, on the other hand, because he can think, decides that nothing but thoughts matter. It is as if a rabbit, because he can make little pills, should decide that nothing but little pills matter. As for the scientist, he has absolutely no use for me so long as I am man alive. To the scientist, I am dead. He puts under the microscope a bit of dead me, and calls it me. He takes me to pieces, and says first one piece, and then another piece, is me. My heart, my liver, my stomach have all been scientifically me, according to the scientist; and nowadays I am either a brain, or nerves, or glands, or something more up-to-date in the tissue line.

Now I absolutely flatly deny that I am a soul, or a body, or a mind, or an intelligence, or a brain, or a nervous system, or a bunch of glands, or any of the rest of these bits of me. The whole is greater than the part. And therefore, I, who am man alive, am greater than my soul, or spirit, or body, or mind, or consciousness, or anything else that is merely a part of me. I am a man, and alive. I am man alive, and as long as I can, I intend to go on being man alive.

For this reason I am a novelist. And being a novelist, I consider myself superior to the saint, the scientist, the philosopher, and the poet, who are all great masters of different bits of man alive, but never get the whole hog.

The novel is the one bright book of life. Books are not life. They are only tremulations on the ether. But the novel as a tremulation can make the whole man alive tremble. Which is more than poetry, philosophy, science, or any other book-tremulation can do.

The novel is the book of life. In this sense, the Bible is a great confused novel. You may say, it is about God. But it is really about man alive. Adam, Eve, Sarai, Abraham, Isaac, Jacob, Samuel, David, Bath-Sheba, Ruth, Esther, Solomon, Job, Isaiah, Jesus, Mark, Judas, Paul, Peter: what is it but man alive, from start to finish? Man alive, not mere bits. Even the Lord is another man alive, in a burning bush, throwing the tablets of stone at Moses's head.

I do hope you begin to get my idea, why the novel is supremely important, as a tremulation on the ether. Plato makes the perfect ideal being tremble in me. But that's only a bit of me. Perfection is only a bit, in the strange make-up of man alive. The Sermon on the Mount makes the selfless spirit of me quiver. But that, too, is only a bit of me. The Ten Commandments set the old Adam shivering in me, warning me that I am a thief and a murderer, unless I watch it. But even the old Adam is only a bit of me.

I very much like all these bits of me to be set trembling with life and the wisdom of life. But I do ask that the whole of me shall tremble in its wholeness, some time or other.

And this, of course, must happen in me, living.

But as far as it can happen from a communication, it can only happen when a whole novel communicates itself to me. The Bible —but *all* the Bible—and Homer, and Shakespeare: these are the supreme old novels. These are all things to all men. Which means that in their wholeness they affect the whole man alive, which is the man himself, beyond any part of him. They set the whole tree trembling with a new access of life, they do not just stimulate growth in one direction.

I don't want to grow in any one direction any more. And, if I can help it, I don't want to stimulate anybody else into some particular direction. A particular direction ends in a *cul-de-sac*. We're in a *cul-de-sac* at present.

I don't believe in any dazzling revelation, or in any supreme

Word. "The grass withereth, the flower fadeth, but the Word of the Lord shall stand for ever." That's the kind of stuff we've drugged ourselves with. As a matter of fact, the grass withereth, but comes up all the greener for that reason, after the rains. The flower fadeth, and therefore the bud opens. But the Word of the Lord, being man-uttered and a mere vibration on the ether, becomes staler and staler, more and more boring, till at last we turn a deaf ear and it ceases to exist, far more finally than any withered grass. It is grass that renews its youth like the eagle, not any Word.

We should ask for no absolutes, or absolute. Once and for all and for ever, let us have done with the ugly imperialism of any absolute. There is no absolute good, there is nothing absolutely right. All things flow and change, and even change is not absolute. The whole is a strange assembly of apparently incongruous parts, slipping past one another.

Me, man alive, I am a very curious assembly of incongruous parts. My yea! of today is oddly different from my yea! of yesterday. My tears of tomorrow will have nothing to do with my tears of a year ago. If the one I love remains unchanged and unchanging, I shall cease to love her. It is only because she changes and startles me into change and defies my inertia, and is herself staggered in her inertia by my changing, that I can continue to love her. If she stayed put, I might as well love the pepper pot.

In all this change, I maintain a certain integrity. But woe betide me if I try to put my finger on it. If I say of myself, I am this, I am that!—then, if I stick to it, I turn into a stupid fixed thing like a lamp-post. I shall never know wherein lies my integrity, my individuality, my me. I *can* never know it. It is useless to talk about my ego. That only means that I have made up an *idea* of myself, and that I am trying to cut myself out to pattern. Which is no good. You can cut your cloth to fit your coat, but you can't clip bits off your living body, to trim it down to your idea. True, you can put yourself into ideal corsets. But even in ideal corsets, fashions change.

Let us learn from the novel. In the novel, the characters can do nothing but *live*. If they keep on being good, according to pattern, or bad, according to pattern, or even volatile, according to pattern, they cease to live, and the novel falls dead. A character in a novel has got to live, or it is nothing.

We, likewise, in life have got to live, or we are nothing.

What we mean by living is, of course, just as indescribable as what we mean by *being*. Men get ideas into their heads, of what they mean by Life, and they proceed to cut life out to pattern. Sometimes they go into the desert to seek God, sometimes they go into the desert to seek cash, sometimes it is wine, woman, and song, and again it is water, political reform, and votes. You never know what it will be next: from killing your neighbor with hideous bombs and gas that tears the lungs, to supporting a Foundlings Home and preaching infinite Love, and being co-respondent in a divorce.

In all this wild welter, we need some sort of guide. It's no good inventing Thou Shalt Nots!

What then? Turn truly, honorably to the novel, and see wherein you are man alive, and wherein you are dead man in life. You may love a woman as man alive, and you may be making love to a woman as sheer dead man in life. You may eat your dinner as man alive, or as a mere masticating corpse. As man alive you may have shot at your enemy. But as a ghastly simulacrum of life you may be firing bombs into men who are neither your enemies nor your friends, but just things you are dead to. Which is criminal, when the things happen to be alive.

To be alive, to be man alive, to be whole man alive: that is the point. And at its best, the novel, and the novel supremely, can help you. It can help you not to be dead man in life. So much of a man walks about dead and a carcass in the street and house, today: so much of women is merely dead. Like a pianoforte with half the notes mute.

But the novel you can see, plainly, when the man goes dead, the woman goes inert. You can develop an instinct for life, if you will, instead of a theory of right and wrong, good and bad.

In life, there is right and wrong, good and bad, all the time. But what is right in one case is wrong in another. And in the novel you see one man becoming a corpse, because of his so-called good-ness, another going dead because of his so-called wickedness. Right and wrong is an instinct: but an instinct of the whole consciousness in a man, bodily, mental, spiritual at once. And only in the novel are *all* things given full play, or at least, they may be given full play, when we realize that life itself, and not inert safety, is the reason for living. For out of the full play of all things emerges the only thing that is anything, the wholeness of a man, the wholeness of a woman, man alive, and live woman.

1936

Piano

Softly, in the dusk, a woman is singing to me;
Taking me back down the vista of years, till I see
A child sitting under the piano, in the boom of the tingling
    strings
And pressing the small, poised feet of a mother who smiles
    as she sings.

In spite of myself, the insidious mastery of song
Betrays me back, till the heart of me weeps to belong
To the old Sunday evenings at home, with winter outside
And hymns in the cozy parlor, the tinkling piano our guide.

So now it is vain for the singer to burst into clamor
With the great black piano appassionato. The glamor
Of childish days is upon me, my manhood is cast
Down in the flood of remembrance, I weep like a child for the
    past.

1918

Bavarian Gentians

Not every man has gentians in his house
in Soft September, at slow, Sad Michaelmas.

Bavarian gentians, big and dark, only dark
darkening the daytime torchlike with the smoking blueness of
    Pluto's gloom,[1]
ribbed and torchlike, with their blaze of darkness spread blue   5
down flattening into points, flattened under the sweep of white day
torch-flower of the blue-smoking darkness, Pluto's dark-blue daze,
black lamps from the halls of Dis, burning dark blue,
giving off darkness, blue darkness, as Demeter's pale lamps give off
    light,
lead me then, lead me the way.   10

Reach me a gentian, give me a torch
let me guide myself with the blue, forked torch of this flower
down the darker and darker stairs, where blue is darkened on blue-
    ness.
even where Persephone[2] goes, just now, from the frosted September
to the sightless realm where darkness was awake upon the dark   15
and Persephone herself is but a voice
or a darkness invisible enfolded in the deeper dark
of the arms Plutonic, and pierced with the passion of dense gloom,
among the splendor of torches of darkness, shedding darkness on
    the lost bride and her groom.

1923

---

1. Pluto was god of the underworld in classical mythology; he was also called "Dis" (line 8).
2. Bride of Pluto, who abducted her from the earth, and daughter of Demeter, goddess of the fruits of the earth (line 14). She was allowed to return to earth every spring but had to descend again to Hades in the autumn, "the frosted September." Demeter and Persephone were central figures in ancient fertility myths, where Persephone's annual descent and return were linked with the death and rebirth of vegetation.

Snake

A snake came to my water trough
On a hot, hot day, and I in pajamas for the heat,
To drink there.

In the deep, strange-scented shade of the great dark carob tree
I came down the steps with my pitcher   5
And must wait, must stand and wait, for there he was at the trough
    before me.

He reached down from a fissure in the earth-wall in the gloom
And trailed his yellow-brown slackness soft-bellied down, over the
    edge of the stone trough
And rested his throat upon the stone bottom,
And where the water had dripped from the tap, in a small clear-
    ness,   10
He sipped with his straight mouth,
Softly drank through his straight gums, into his slack long body,
Silently.

Someone was before me at my water trough,
And I, like a second-comer, waiting.   15

He lifted his head from his drinking, as cattle do,
And looked at me vaguely, as drinking cattle do,
And flickered his two-forked tongue from his lips, and mused a
    moment,
And stooped and drank a little more,
Being earth-brown, earth-golden from the burning bowels of the
    earth   20
On the day of Sicilian July, with Etna smoking.

The voice of my education said to me
He must be killed,
For in Sicily the black black snakes are innocent, the gold are veno-
    mous.

And voices in me said, If you were a man   25
You would take a stick and break him now, and finish him off.

But must I confess how I liked him,
How glad I was he had come like a guest in quiet, to drink at my
    water trough
And depart peaceful, pacified, and thankless
Into the burning bowels of this earth?   30

Was it cowardice, that I dared not kill him?
Was it perversity, that I longed to talk to him?
Was it humility, to feel so honored?
I felt so honored.

And yet those voices: 35
If you were not afraid, you would kill him!

And truly I was afraid, I was most afraid,
But even so, honored still more
That he should seek my hospitality
From out the dark door of the secret earth. 40

He drank enough
And lifted his head, dreamily, as one who has drunken,
And flickered his tongue like a forked night on the air, so black,
Seeming to lick his lips,
And looked around like a god, unseeing, into the air, 45
And slowly turned his head,
And slowly, very slowly, as if thrice adream
Proceeded to draw his slow length curving round
And climb the broken bank of my wall-face.

And as he put his head into that dreadful hole, 50
And as he slowly drew up, snake-easing his shoulders, and entered
further,
A sort of horror, a sort of protest against his withdrawing into that
horrid black hole,
Deliberately going into the blackness, and slowly drawing himself
after,
Overcame me now his back was turned.

I looked round, I put down my pitcher, 55
I picked up a clumsy log
And threw it at the water trough with a clatter.

I think it did not hit him;
But suddenly that part of him that was left behind convulsed in un-
dignified haste,
Writhed like lightning, and was gone 60
Into the black hole, the earth-lipped fissure in the wall-front
At which, in the intense still noon, I stared with fascination.

And immediately I regretted it.
I thought how paltry, how vulgar, what a mean act!
I despised myself and the voices of my accursed human education. 65

And I thought of the albatross,[1]
And I wished he would come back, my snake.

For he seemed to me again like a king,
Like a king in exile, uncrowned in the underworld,
Now due to be crowned again. 70

And so, I missed my chance with one of the lords
Of life.
And I have something to expiate:
A pettiness.

1923

1. Coleridge's *Ancient Mariner*.

The Ship of Death

1

Now it is autumn and the falling fruit
and the long journey towards oblivion.

The apples falling like great drops of dew
to bruise themselves an exit from themselves.

And it is time to go, to bid farewell   5
to one's own self, and find an exit
from the fallen self.

2

Have you built your ship of death, O have you?
O build your ship of death, for you will need it.

The grim frost is at hand, when the apples will fall   10
thick, almost thundrous, on the hardened earth.

And death is on the air like a smell of ashes!
Ah! can't you smell it?

And in the bruised body, the frightened soul
finds itself shrinking, wincing from the cold   15
that blows upon it through the orifices.

3

And can a man his own quietus make
with a bare bodkin?

With daggers, bodkins, bullets, man can make
a bruise or break of exit for his life;   20
but is that a quietus, O tell me, is it quietus?

Surely not so! for how could murder, even self-murder
ever a quietus make?

4

O let us talk of quiet that we know,
that we can know, the deep and lovely quiet   25
of a strong heart at peace!

How can we this, our own quietus, make?

5

Build then the ship of death, for you must take
the longest journey, to oblivion.

And die the death, the long and painful death   30
that lies between the old self and the new.

Already our bodies are fallen, bruised, badly bruised,
already our souls are oozing through the exit
of the cruel bruise.

Already the dark and endless ocean of the end   35
is washing in through the breaches of our wounds,
already the flood is upon us.

Oh build your ship of death, your little ark
and furnish it with food, with little cakes, and wine
for the dark flight down oblivion.   40

6

Piecemeal the body dies, and the timid soul
has her footing washed away, as the dark flood rises.

We are dying, we are dying, we are all of us dying
and nothing will stay the death-flood rising within us
and soon it will rise on the world, on the outside world.   45

We are dying, we are dying, piecemeal our bodies are
          dying
and our strength leaves us,
and our soul cowers naked in the dark rain over the flood,
cowering in the last branches of the tree of our life.

7

We are dying, we are dying, so all we can do   50
is now to be willing to die, and to build the ship
of death to carry the soul on the longest journey.

A little ship, with oars and food
and little dishes, and all accoutrements
fitting and ready for the departing soul.   55

Now launch the small ship, now as the body dies
and life departs, launch out, the fragile soul
in the fragile ship of courage, the ark of faith
with its store of food and little cooking pans
and change of clothes,   60
upon the flood's back waste
upon the waters of the end
upon the sea of death, where still we sail
darkly, for we cannot steer, and have no port.

There is no port, there is nowhere to go   65
only the deepening blackness darkening still
blacker upon the soundless, ungurgling flood
darkness at one with darkness, up and down
and sideways utterly dark, so there is no direction any
          more
and the little ship is there; yet she is gone.   70
She is not seen, for there is nothing to see her by.
She is gone! gone! and yet
somewhere she is there.
Nowhere!

8

And everything is gone, the body is gone   75
completely under, gone, entirely gone.
The upper darkness is heavy as the lower,
between them the little ship
is gone
It is the end, it is oblivion.

9

And yet out of eternity a thread   80
separates itself on the blackness,
a horizontal thread
that fumes a little with pallor upon the dark.

Is it illusion? or does the pallor fume
A little higher?
Ah wait, wait, for there's the dawn,   85
the cruel dawn of coming back to life
out of oblivion

Wait, wait, the little ship
drifting, beneath the deathly ashy gray
of a flood-dawn.   90

Wait, wait! even so, a flush of yellow
and strangely, O chilled wan soul, a flush of rose.

A flush of rose, and the whole thing starts again.

10

The flood subsides, and the body, like a worn sea-shell
emerges strange and lovely.
And the little ship wings home, faltering and lapsing   95
on the pink flood,
and the frail soul steps out, into her house again
filling the heart with peace.

Swings the heart renewed with peace   100
even of oblivion.

Oh build your ship of death, oh build it!
for you will need it.
For the voyage of oblivion awaits you.

1929–30   1933

T. S. ELIOT
(1888–1965)

1915: Settles in London.
1917: *Prufrock and Other Observations.*
1922: *The Waste Land.*
1927: Becomes British subject; confirmed in Anglican Church.
1944: *Four Quartets.*

Thomas Stearns Eliot was born in St. Louis, Missouri, of New England
stock. He entered Harvard in 1906, and was influenced there by the anti-
romanticism of Irving Babbitt and the philosophical and critical interests

of George Santayana, as well as by the enthusiasm that prevailed in certain Harvard circles for Elizabethan and Jacobean literature, the Italian Renaissance, and Indian mystical philosophy. His philosophical studies included intensive work on the English idealist philosopher F. H. Bradley, on whom he eventually wrote his Harvard dissertation. (Bradley's emphasis on the private nature of individual experience, "a circle enclosed on the outside," had considerable influence on the private imagery of Eliot's poetry and on the view of the relation between the individual and other individuals reflected in much of his poetry.) Later Eliot studied literature and philosophy in France and Germany, before going to England shortly after the outbreak of World War I in 1914. He studied Greek philosophy at Oxford, taught school in London, and then obtained a position with Lloyd's Bank which he held until 1925, when he joined the London publishing firm of Faber and Gwyer, becoming a director when the firm became Faber and Faber in 1929.

Eliot started writing literary and philosophical reviews soon after settling in London. He wrote for the *Athenaeum* and the *Times Literary Supplement*, among other periodicals, and was assistant editor of the *Egoist* from 1917 to 1919. In 1922 he founded the influential quarterly, the *Criterion*, which he edited until it ceased publication in 1939. His poetry first appeared in 1915, when *The Love Song of J. Alfred Prufrock* was printed in *Poetry* magazine (Chicago) and a few other short poems were published in the short-lived periodical, *Blast*. His first published collection of poems was *Prufrock and Other Observations*, 1917; two other small collections followed in 1919 and 1920; in 1922 *The Waste Land* appeared, first in the *Criterion* in October, then in the *Dial* (in America) in November, and finally in book form. *Poems 1909–25* (1925) collected these earlier poems. Meanwhile he was also publishing collections of his critical essays, notably *The Sacred Wood* in 1920 and *Homage to John Dryden* in 1924. *For Lancelot Andrewes* followed in 1928 and in 1932 he included most of these earlier essays with some new ones in *Selected Essays*. Eliot became a British subject and joined the Church of England in 1927.

"Our civilization comprehends great variety and complexity, and this variety and complexity, playing upon a refined sensibility, must produce various and complex results. The poet must become more and more comprehensive, more allusive, more indirect, in order to force, to dislocate if necessary, language into his meaning." This remark, from Eliot's essay on *The Metaphysical Poets* (1921), gives one clue to his poetic method from *Prufrock* through *The Waste Land*. In the attenuated romantic tradition of the Georgian poets who were active when he settled in London, in their quietly meditative pastoralism, faded exoticism, or self-consciously realistic descriptions of urban life, he saw an exhausted poetic mode being employed, with no verbal excitement or original craftsmanship. He sought to make poetry more subtle, more suggestive, and at the same time more precise. He had learned from the Imagists the necessity of clear and precise images, and he learned, too, from T. E. Hulme and from his early supporter and adviser Ezra Pound to fear romantic softness and to regard the poetic medium rather than the poet's personality as the important factor. At the same time, the "hard dry" images advocated by Hulme were not enough for him; he wanted wit, allusiveness, irony. He saw in the metaphysical poets how wit and passion could be combined, and he saw in the French Symbolists how an image could be both absolutely precise in what it referred to physically and at the same time endlessly suggestive in the meanings it set up because of its relationship to other images. The combination of precision, symbolic suggestion, and ironic mockery in the poetry of the late 19th-century French poet Jules Laforgue attracted and influenced him, and he was influenced too by other 19th-century French poets: by Théophile Gautier's artful carving of impersonal shapes of meaning; by Charles Baudelaire's strangely evocative explorations of the symbolic suggestions of objects and images; by the Symbolist poets Paul Verlaine, Arthur Rimbaud, and Stéphane Mallarmé. He also found in the Jacobean dramatists a flexible blank verse with overtones of colloquial movement: Middleton, Tourneur, Webster, and others, taught him as much—in the way of verse movement, imagery, the counterpointing of the accent of conversation and the note of terror—as either the metaphysicals or the French Symbolists.

Hulme's protests against the romantic concept of poetry fitted in well enough with what Eliot had learned from Irving Babbitt at Harvard; yet for all his severity with such poets as Shelley, for all his conscious cultivation of a classical viewpoint and his insistence on order and discipline rather than on mere self-expression in art, one side of Eliot's poetic genius is, in one sense of the word, romantic. The Symbolist influence on his imagery, his interest in the evocative and the suggestive, such lines as "And fiddled whisper music on those strings / And bats with baby faces in the violet light / Whistled, and beat their wings," and such recurring images as the hyacinth girl and the rose garden, all show what could be called a romantic element in his poetry. But it is combined with a dry ironic allusiveness, a play of wit, and a colloquial element, which are not normally found in poets of the romantic tradition.

Eliot's real novelty—and the cause of much bewilderment when his poems first appeared—was his deliberate elimination of all merely connective and transitional passages, his building up of the total pattern of meaning through the immediate juxtaposition of images without overt explanation of what they are doing, together with his use of oblique references to other works of literature (some of them quite obscure to most contemporary readers). *Prufrock* presents a symbolic landscape where the meaning emerges from the mutual interaction of the images, and that meaning is enlarged by echoes, often ironic, of Hesiod and Dante and Shakespeare. *The Waste Land* is a series of scenes and images with no author's voice intervening to tell us where we are, but with the implications developed through multiple contrasts and through analogies with older literary works often referred to in a distorted quotation or half-concealed allusion. Further, the works referred to are not necessarily works which are central in the Western literary tradition: besides Dante and Shakespeare there are pre-Socratic philosophers, minor (as well as major) 17th-century poets and dramatists, works of anthropology, history, and philosophy, and other echoes of the poet's private reading. In a culture

where there is no longer any assurance on the part of the poet that his
public has a common cultural heritage, a common knowledge of works of
the past, Eliot felt it necessary to build up his own body of references.
It is this which marks the difference between Eliot's use of earlier literature and, say, Milton's. Both poets are difficult to the modern reader,
who needs editorial assistance in recognizing and understanding many of
the allusions—but Milton was drawing on a body of knowledge common
to educated men in his day. Nevertheless, this aspect of Eliot can be
exaggerated: the fact remains that the nature of his imagery together with
the movement of his verse generally succeed in setting the tone he requires, in establishing the area of meaning to be developed, so that even
a reader ignorant of most of the literary allusions can often get the "feel"
of the poem and achieve some understanding of what it says.

Eliot's early poetry, until at least the middle 1920's, is mostly concerned in one way or another with the Waste Land, with aspects of the
decay of culture in the modern Western world. After his formal acceptance
of Anglican Christianity we find a penitential note in much of his verse,
a note of quiet searching for spiritual peace, with considerable allusion
to Biblical, liturgical, and mystical religious literature and to Dante.
Ash Wednesday (1930), a poem in six parts, much less fiercely concentrated in style than the earlier poetry, explores with gentle insistence a
mood both penitential and questioning. The so-called "Ariel" poems (the
title is accidental, and has nothing to do with their form or content)
present or explore aspects of religious doubt or discovery or revelation,
sometimes, as in *Marina*, using a purely secular imagery and sometimes, as
in *Journey of the Magi*, drawing on Biblical incident. In *Four Quartets*
(of which the first, *Burnt Norton*, appeared in the *Collected Poems* of
1935, though all four were not completed until 1943, when they were
published together) Eliot further explored essentially religious moods, dealing with the relation between time and eternity and the cultivation of
that selfless passivity which can yield the moment of timeless revelation
in the midst of time. The mocking irony, the savage humor, the deliberately startling juxtaposition of the sordid and the romantic, give way
in these later poems to a quieter poetic idiom, often still complexly allusive
but never deliberately shocking.

Eliot's criticism was the criticism of a practicing poet who worked out in
relation to his reading of older literature what he needed to hold and to admire. He lent the growing weight of his authority to that shift in literary
taste that replaced Milton by Donne as the great 17th-century English
poet, and replaced Tennyson in the 19th century by Hopkins. His often-
quoted description of the late 17th-century "dissociation of sensibility"—
keeping wit and passion in separate compartments—which he saw as determining the course of English poetry throughout the 18th and 19th
centuries, is both a contribution to the rewriting of English literary history and an explanation of what he was aiming at in his own poetry: the
re-establishment of that *unified* sensibility he found in Donne and other
early 17th-century poets and dramatists. His view of tradition, his dislike
of the poetic exploitation of the author's own personality, his advocacy of
what he called "orthodoxy," made him suspicious of what he considered

eccentric geniuses such as Blake and D. H. Lawrence. On the other side, his dislike of the grandiloquent and his insistence on complexity and on the mingling of the formal with the conversational made him distrustful of the influence of Milton on English poetry. He considered himself "classicist in literature, royalist in politics, and Anglo-Catholic in religion" (*For Lancelot Andrewes*, 1928), in favor of order against chaos, tradition against eccentricity, authority against rampant individualism; yet his own poetry is in many respects untraditional and certainly highly individual in tone. His conservative and even authoritarian habit of mind has alienated some who admire—and some whose own poetry has been much influenced by—his poetry.

Eliot's plays have all been, directly or indirectly, on religious themes. *Murder in the Cathedral* (1935) deals with the murder of Archbishop Thomas à Becket in an appropriately ritual manner, with much use of a chorus and with the central speech in the form of a sermon by the archbishop in his cathedral shortly before his murder. *The Family Reunion* (1939) deals with the problem of guilt and redemption in a modern upper-class English family; it makes a deliberate attempt to combine choric devices from Greek tragedy with a poetic idiom subdued to the accents of drawing-room conversation. In his three later plays, all written in the 1950's, *The Cocktail Party, The Confidential Clerk,* and *The Elder Statesman,* he achieved popular success by casting a serious religious theme in the form of a sophisticated modern social comedy, using a verse that is so conversational in movement that when spoken in the theater it does not sound like verse at all.

Critics differ on the degree to which Eliot succeeded in his last plays in combining box-office success with dramatic effectiveness. But there is no disagreement on his importance as one of the great renovators of the English poetic dialect, whose influence on a whole generation of poets, critics, and intellectuals generally was enormous. His range as a poet is limited, and his interest in the great middle ground of human experience (as distinct from the extremes of saint and sinner) deficient: but when in 1948 he was awarded the rare honor of the Order of Merit by King George VI and also gained the Nobel Prize in literature, his positive qualities were widely and fully recognized—his poetic cunning, his fine craftsmanship, his original accent, his historical and representative importance as *the* poet of the modern Symbolist-metaphysical tradition.

The Love Song of J. Alfred Prufrock[1]

*S'io credesse che mia risposta fosse
A persona che mai tornasse al mondo,
Questa fiamma staria senza piu scosse.
Ma perciocche giammai di questo fondo
Non torno vivo alcun, s'i'odo il vero,
Senza tema d'infamia ti rispondo.*[2]

Let us go then, you and I,
When the evening is spread out against the sky
Like a patient etherized[3] upon a table;
Let us go, through certain half-deserted streets,
The muttering retreats   5
Of restless nights in one-night cheap hotels
And sawdust restaurants with oyster shells:
Streets that follow like a tedious argument
Of insidious intent
To lead you to an overwhelming question . . .   10
Oh, do not ask, "What is it?"
Let us go and make our visit.

In the room the women come and go
Talking of Michelangelo.

The yellow fog that rubs its back upon the windowpanes,   15
The yellow smoke that rubs its muzzle on the windowpanes
Licked its tongue into the corners of the evening,
Lingered upon the pools that stand in drains,
Let fall upon its back the soot that falls from chimneys,
Slipped by the terrace, made a sudden leap,   20

1. A dramatic monologue in which the speaker builds up a mood of social futility and inadequacy through the thoughts and images which haunt his consciousness and by means of the symbolic landscape in which he moves. The title implies an ironic contrast between the romantic suggestions of "love song" and the dully prosaic name, "J. Alfred Prufrock." The quotation from Dante's *Inferno* which stands at the head of the poem adds to this contrast a note of profound hopelessness. Prufrock himself, middle-aged and unhappy, is not really at home in the society in which he is condemned to live; he is aware of the futility of such visits as he is paying, of his own awkwardness and maladjustment, and his self-conscious response to the demands made on him. He is haunted not only by a knowledge of the pettiness and triviality of this world, but also by a sense of his own sexual inadequacy and a feeling that once, somewhere, he had had a vision of a life more real and more beautiful, but that he has long since strayed from that reality to the artificial and barren existence in which he now suffocates. The lost dream-world was paradoxically the only real world, man's true element, and out of it he drowns.

2. "If I thought that my reply would be to one who would ever return to the world, this flame would stay without further movement; but since none has ever returned alive from this depth, if what I hear is true, I answer you without fear of infamy." Dante, *Inferno* XXVII.61–66. Guido da Montefeltro, shut up in his flame (the punishment given to false counselors), tells the shame of his evil life to Dante because he believes Dante will never return to earth to report it.

3. A contrast is perhaps here implied between "ether" as the free sky or the heavens and the word's medical connotations—helplessness, disease, the elimination of consciousness and personality.

And seeing that it was a soft October night,
Curled once about the house, and fell asleep.

And indeed there will be time[4]
For the yellow smoke that slides along the street,
Rubbing its back upon the windowpanes;   25
There will be time, there will be time
To prepare a face to meet the faces that you meet;
There will be time to murder and create,
And time for all the works and days of hands[5]
That lift and drop a question on your plate;   30
Time for you and time for me,
And time yet for a hundred indecisions,
And for a hundred visions and revisions,
Before the taking of a toast and tea.

In the room the women come and go   35
Talking of Michelangelo.

And indeed there will be time
To wonder, "Do I dare?" and, "Do I dare?"
Time to turn back and descend the stair,
With a bald spot in the middle of my hair—   40
(They will say: "How his hair is growing thin!")
My morning coat, my collar mounting firmly to the chin,
My necktie rich and modest, but asserted by a simple pin—
(They will say: "But how his arms and legs are thin!")
Do I dare   45
Disturb the universe?
In a minute there is time
For decisions and revisions which a minute will reverse.

For I have known them all already, known them all—
Have known the evenings, mornings, afternoons,   50
I have measured out my life with coffee spoons;
I know the voices dying with a dying fall[6]
Beneath the music from a farther room.
    So how should I presume?

And I have known the eyes already, known them all—   55
The eyes that fix you in a formulated phrase,
And when I am formulated, sprawling on a pin,
When I am pinned and wriggling on the wall,
Then how should I begin
To spit out all the butt-ends of my days and ways?   60
    And how should I presume?

And I have known the arms already, known them all—
Arms that are braceleted and white and bare

4. Cf. Andrew Marvell's *To His Coy Mistress:* "Had we but world enough and time * * * "
5. *Works and Days* is a poem about the farming year by Hesiod, Greek poet of 8th century B.C. Eliot's contrast is between useful agricultural labor and the futile "works and days of hands" engaged in meaningless social gesturing.
6. Ironic recollection of Orsino's speech in *Twelfth Night* (I.i.4): "That strain again! It had a dying fall."

(But in the lamplight, downed with light brown hair!)
Is it perfume from a dress   65
That makes me so digress?
Arms that lie along a table, or wrap about a shawl.
    And should I then presume?
    And how should I begin?

         .   .   .   .   .

Shall I say, I have gone at dusk through narrow streets   70
And watched the smoke that rises from the pipes
Of lonely men in shirt-sleeves, leaning out of windows? . . .

I should have been a pair of ragged claws
Scuttling across the floors of silent seas.[7]

         .   .   .   .   .

And the afternoon, the evening, sleeps so peacefully!   75
Smoothed by long fingers,
Asleep . . . tired . . . or it malingers,
Stretched on the floor, here beside you and me.
Should I, after tea and cakes and ices,
Have the strength to force the moment to its crisis?   80
But though I have wept and fasted, wept and prayed,
Though I have seen my head (grown slightly bald) brought in upon
    a platter,[8]
I am no prophet—and here's no great matter;
I have seen the moment of my greatness flicker,
And I have seen the eternal Footman hold my coat, and snicker,   85
And in short, I was afraid.

And would it have been worth it, after all,
After the cups, the marmalade, the tea,
Among the porcelain, among some talk of you and me,
Would it have been worth while,   90
To have bitten off the matter with a smile,
To have squeezed the universe into a ball
To roll it toward some overwhelming question,
To say: "I am Lazarus,[9] come from the dead,
Come back to tell you all, I shall tell you all"—   95
If one, settling a pillow by her head,
    Should say: "That is not what I meant at all.
    That is not it, at all."

And would it have been worth it, after all,
Would it have been worth while,   100
After the sunsets and the dooryards and the sprinkled streets,

7. I.e., he would have been better as a crab on the ocean bed. Perhaps, too, the motion of a crab suggests futility and growing old; cf. *Hamlet* II.ii.205–6: "for you yourself, sir, should be old as I am, if, like a crab, you could go backward."
8. Like that of John the Baptist. See Mark vi.17–28 and Matthew xiv.3–11.
9. Cf. Luke xvi.19–31 and John xi.1–44.

After the novels, after the teacups, after the skirts that trail along
    the floor—
And this, and so much more?—
It is impossible to say just what I mean!
But as if a magic lantern threw the nerves in patterns on a
    screen: 105
Would it have been worth while
If one, settling a pillow or throwing off a shawl,
And turning toward the window, should say:
    "That is not it at all,
    That is not what I meant, at all."   110

. . . . .

No! I am not Prince Hamlet, nor was meant to be;
Am an attendant lord, one that will do
To swell a progress,[1] start a scene or two,
Advise the prince; no doubt, an easy tool,
Deferential, glad to be of use,   115
Politic, cautious, and meticulous;
Full of high sentence,[2] but a bit obtuse;
At times, indeed, almost ridiculous—
Almost, at times, the Fool.

I grow old . . . I grow old . . .   120
I shall wear the bottoms of my trousers rolled.

Shall I part my hair behind? Do I dare to eat a peach?
I shall wear white flannel trousers, and walk upon the beach.
I have heard the mermaids singing, each to each.

I do not think that they will sing to me.   125

I have seen them riding seaward on the waves
Combing the white hair of the waves blown back
When the wind blows the water white and black.

We have lingered in the chambers of the sea
By sea-girls wreathed with seaweed red and brown   130
Till human voices wake us, and we drown.
1910–11   1915, 1917

From Landscapes[3]
Rannoch, by Glencoe[4]

Here the crow starves, here the patient stag
Breeds for the rifle. Between the soft moor

1. In the Elizabethan sense of a state journey made by a royal or noble person. Elizabethan plays sometimes showed such "progresses" crossing the stage.
2. In its older meanings, "opinions,"
"sententiousness."
3. Under this title Eliot grouped five short poems, each dealing with a specific place. The last two are reprinted here.
4. In Scotland.

And the soft sky, scarcely room
To leap or soar. Substance crumbles, in the thin air
Moon cold or moon hot. The road winds in   5
Listlessness of ancient war
Languor of broken steel,
Clamor of confused wrong, apt
In silence. Memory is strong
Beyond the bone. Pride snapped,   10
Shadow of pride is long, in the long pass
No concurrence of bone.

Cape Ann⁵

O quick quick quick, quick hear the song sparrow,
Swamp sparrow, fox sparrow, vesper sparrow
At dawn and dusk. Follow the dance
Of the goldfinch at noon. Leave to chance
The Blackburnian warbler, the shy one. Hail   5
With shrill whistle the note of the quail, the bobwhite
Dodging by baybush. Follow the feet
Of the walker, the water thrush. Follow the flight
Of the dancing arrow, the purple martin. Greet
In silence the bullbat. All are delectable. Sweet sweet sweet   10
But resign this land at the end, resign it
To its true owner, the tough one, the sea gull.
The palaver is finished.

1933–34   1936

Sweeney Among the Nightingales¹

ὤμοι, πέπληγμαι καιρίαν πληγὴν ἔσω.²

Apeneck Sweeney spreads his knees
Letting his arms hang down to laugh,
The zebra stripes along his jaw
Swelling to maculate³ giraffe.

5. On the northern coast of Massachusetts, not far from the New Hampshire border; a wilderness area in the middle of the cape is inhabited by the birds Eliot here describes.

1. This poem shows Eliot's characteristic method of presenting his meaning through multiple parallels and contrasts. Lust, cruelty, and violence have always existed in the world; but in heroic periods of history they have sprung from grand passions of love or hate and have later been embodied in meaningful myths. The nightingale, in Greek myth, was the symbol of the transformation of human lust into art: Philomela, having been ravished and had her tongue cut out by her sister's husband Tereus, was turned into a nightingale and sings eternally. The horrors of Agamemnon's murder are similarly subsumed in the search for and achievement of divine justice (cf. Aeschylus' dramatic trilogy, the *Oresteia*). But the shabby animality of Sweeney and his drunken lady friend (significantly anonymous), frolicking lewdly in a restaurant, is unrelieved by any such transmutation. In Sweeney's world violence is limited to overturning a coffee cup and tearing at grapes, and lust has become only a "gambit," easily "declined."

2. "Alas, I am struck with a mortal blow within" (Aeschylus, *Agamemnon*, line 1343). The voice of Agamemnon heard crying out from the palace as he is murdered by his wife Clytemnestra.

3. Spotted, stained.

The circles of the stormy moon   5
Slide westward toward the River Plate,[4]
Death and the Raven drift above
And Sweeney guards the hornéd gate.[5]

Gloomy Orion and the Dog
Are veiled;[6] and hushed the shrunken seas;   10
The person in the Spanish cape
Tries to sit on Sweeney's knees

Slips and pulls the tablecloth
Overturns a coffee cup,
Reorganized upon the floor   15
She yawns and draws a stocking up;

The silent man in mocha brown
Sprawls at the window sill and gapes;
The waiter brings in oranges
Bananas figs and hothouse grapes;   20

The silent vertebrate in brown
Contracts and concentrates, withdraws;
Rachel *née* Rabinovitch
Tears at the grapes with murderous paws;

She and the lady in the cape   25
Are suspect, thought to be in league;
Therefore the man with heavy eyes
Declines the gambit, shows fatigue,

Leaves the room and reappears
Outside the window, leaning in,   30
Branches of wistaria
Circumscribe a golden grin;

The host with someone indistinct
Converses at the door apart,
The nightingales are singing near   35
The Convent of the Sacred Heart,

And sang within the bloody wood
When Agamemnon cried aloud,[7]
And let their liquid siftings fall
To stain the stiff dishonored shroud.   40

1918, 1919

4. Estuary on South American coast
between Argentina and Uruguay, formed
by the Uruguay and Paraná rivers.
5. The gates of horn, in Hades, through
which true dreams come to the upper
world.
6. "Orion" and the "Dog" are the
constellations. For Sweeney and his
friend, the gate of vision is blocked and
the great mythmaking constellations are
"veiled."
7. Agamemnon was not murdered in a
"bloody wood," but in his bath. Eliot
is here telescoping Agamemnon's murder with the wood where Philomela was
ravished and also with the "bloody
wood" of Nemi, where, in ancient times,
the old priest was slain by his successor (as described in the first chapter
of Sir James Frazer's *Golden Bough*).
The great myths of regeneration represented by this ritual slaying are meaningless for Sweeney and his friends, as
are the song of the nightingales and the
spiritual reality represented by the
Convent of the Sacred Heart.

Whispers of Immortality[1]

Webster[2] was much possessed by death
And saw the skull beneath the skin;
And breastless creatures under ground
Leaned backward with a lipless grin.

Daffodil bulbs instead of balls   5
Stared from the sockets of the eyes!
He knew that thought clings round dead limbs
Tightening its lusts and luxuries.

Donne,[3] I suppose, was such another
Who found no substitute for sense,   10
To seize and clutch and penetrate;
Expert beyond experience,

He knew the anguish of the marrow
The ague of the skeleton;
No contact possible to flesh   15
Allayed the fever of the bone.

. . . . .

Grishkin is nice: her Russian eye
Is underlined for emphasis;
Uncorseted, her friendly bust
Gives promise of pneumatic bliss.   20

The couched Brazilian jaguar
Compels the scampering marmoset
With subtle effluence of cat;
Grishkin has a maisonette;

The sleek Brazilian jaguar   25
Does not in its arboreal gloom
Distil so rank a feline smell
As Grishkin in a drawing room.

And even the Abstract Entities
Circumambulate her charm;   30
But our lot crawls between dry ribs
To keep our metaphysics warm.

1918, 1919

1. The effects are here again achieved by contrasts and parallels. The Elizabethan and Jacobean poets and dramatists were obsessed by death and suffered the anguish of those for whom all knowledge comes through the senses but who know that the senses, doomed to decay, cannot satisfy the ultimate longings. By contrast Grishkin, high-class prostitute, is wholly committed to the flesh, like an animal; even abstract philosophy is seduced by her charms.
2. John Webster, Jacobean dramatist, author of *The Duchess of Malfi* and *The White Devil*.
3. The poet John Donne (1572–1631).

The Waste Land is a poem about spiritual dryness, about the kind of existence in which no regenerating belief gives significance and value to men's daily activities, sex brings no fruitfulness, and death heralds no resurrection. Eliot himself gives one of the main clues to the theme and structure of the poem in a general note, in which he stated that "not only the title, but the plan and a good deal of the symbolism of the poem were suggested by Miss Jessie L. Weston's book on the Grail legend: *From Ritual to Romance*" (1920). He further acknowledged a general indebtedness to Sir James Frazer's *Golden Bough* (12 volumes, 1890–1915), "especially the two volumes *Adonis, Attis, Osiris*," in which Frazer deals with ancient vegetation myths and fertility ceremonies. Miss Weston's study, drawing on material from Frazer and other anthropologists, traced the relationship of these myths and rituals to Christianity and most especially to the legend of the Holy Grail. She found an archetypal fertility myth in the story of the Fisher King whose death, infirmity, or impotence (there are many forms of the myth) brought drought and desolation to the land and failure of the power to reproduce themselves among both men and beasts. This symbolic Waste Land can be revived only if a "questing knight" goes to the Chapel Perilous, situated in the heart of it, and there asks certain ritual questions about the Grail (or Cup) and the Lance— originally fertility symbols, female and male respectively. The proper asking of these questions revives the king and restores fertility to the land. The relation of this original Grail myth to fertility cults and rituals found in many different civilizations, and represented by stories of a dying god who is later resurrected (e.g., Tammuz, Adonis, Attis), shows their common origin in a response to the cyclical movement of the seasons, with vegetation dying in winter to be resurrected again in the spring. Christianity, according to Miss Weston, gave its own spiritual meaning to the myth; it "did not hesitate to utilize the already existing medium of instruction, but boldly identified the Deity of Vegetation, regarded as Life Principle, with the God of the Christian Faith." The Fisher King is related to the use of the fish symbol in early Christianity. Miss Weston states "with certainty that the Fish is a Life symbol of immemorial antiquity, and that the title of Fisher has, from the earliest ages, been associated with the Deities who were held to be specially connected with the origin and preservation of Life." Eliot, following Miss Weston, thus uses a great variety of mythological and religious material, both occidental and oriental, in order to paint a symbolic picture of the modern Waste Land and the need for regeneration. Eliot's use of anthropological material must not blind us to his stress on the religious consolation available to those who live in the inferno of modern life. The terror of that life—its loneliness, emptiness, and irrational apprehensions—as well as its misuse of sexuality are vividly presented, but the poem ends with a benediction. Another significant general source for the poem is the composer Richard Wagner, some of whose operas (*Götterdämmerung* ["Twilight of the Gods"], *Parsifal, Rheingold*, and *Tristan and Isolde*) are drawn on.

When the poem was first published in book form in 1922, Eliot added a series of notes identifying some of his sources or suggesting relationships between various images or allusions; these notes are quoted in the present editor's footnotes to the poem.

The Waste Land

"Nam Sibyllam quidem Cumis ego ipse oculis meis vidi in ampulla pendere, et cum illi pueri dicerent: Σίβυλλα τί θέλεις; respondebat illa: ἀποθανεῖν θέλω."[1]

FOR EZRA POUND[2]

il miglior fabbro

I. The Burial of the Dead[3]

April is the cruelest month, breeding
Lilacs out of the dead land, mixing
Memory and desire, stirring
Dull roots with spring rain.
Winter kept us warm, covering   5
Earth in forgetful snow, feeding
A little life with dried tubers.
Summer surprised us, coming over the Starnbergersee[4]
With a shower of rain; we stopped in the colonnade,
And went on in sunlight, into the Hofgarten,[5]   10
And drank coffee, and talked for an hour.
Bin gar keine Russin, stamm' aus Litauen, echt deutsch.[6]
And when we were children, staying at the archduke's,

1. From the *Satyricon* of Petronius (1st century A.D.): "For once I myself saw with my own eyes the Sibyl at Cumae hanging in a cage, and when the boys said to her 'Sibyl, what do you want?' she replied, 'I want to die.'" The Cumaean Sibyl was the most famous of the Sibyls, the prophetic old women of Greek mythology: she guided Aeneas through Hades in the *Aeneid*. She had been granted immortality by Apollo, but since she forgot to ask for perpetual youth, she shrank into withered old age and her authority declined. Cf. other prophets in the poem: Madame Sosostris and Tiresias.
2. Ezra Pound (1885–), the American expatriate poet who was a key figure in the modern movement in poetry, helped Eliot with the final revisions. "*Il miglior fabbro*" (i.e., the better craftsman) was a tribute originally paid to the Provencal poet Arnaut Daniel in Dante's *Purgatorio* XXVI.117.
3. The title comes from the Anglican burial service. April is the cruelest month because it brings no true renewal but instead tortures us with vain recollections. The seasons as they are here described do not form part of a living cycle; the people whose chatter we hear in international holiday resorts do not wish a really new life, and April is thus cruel in another sense because it suggests resurrection to those who do

not wish it. With a sudden shift in tone the voice becomes suggestive of the prophet Ezekiel announcing the dryness and hopeless fragmentation of civilization; then this voice gives way to songs of romantic passion and memories of lost opportunities for love. We next see the mysteries of ancient religion transformed into fashionable fortune-telling by a fake Egyptian clairvoyante; the elemental symbols of the ancient Tarot pack of cards have degenerated into a trickster's patter (but still immensely evocative, and with each character in the pack related to themes to be developed later in the the poem). Then the vision changes to a more direct picture of modern civilization: Baudelaire's Paris, modern London, Dante's Limbo, all three seen as really the same; the feverish speaker turns the great resurrection ritual into a mad and sinister question about gardening; and the author rounds on the reader to insist that he see himself in the same situation.
4. Lake near Munich. The scene in this and the following eight lines was suggested by Countess Marie Larisch, *My Past* as a means of evoking European decadence before World War I.
5. Public park in Munich, with a zoo and cafés.
6. "I am not Russian at all; I come from Lithuania, a true German."

My cousin's, he took me out on a sled,
And I was frightened. He said, Marie,   15
Marie, hold on tight. And down we went.
In the mountains, there you feel free.
I read, much of the night, and go south in the winter.

What are the roots that clutch, what branches grow
Out of this stony rubbish? Son of man,[7]   20
You cannot say, or guess, for you know only
A heap of broken images, where the sun beats,
And the dead tree gives no shelter, the cricket no relief,[8]
And the dry stone no sound of water. Only
There is shadow under this red rock,[9]   25
(Come in under the shadow of this red rock),
And I will show you something different from either
Your shadow at morning striding behind you
Or your shadow at evening rising to meet you;
I will show you fear in a handful of dust.   30
            Frisch weht der Wind
            Der Heimat zu
            Mein Irisch Kind,
            Wo weilest du?[1]
"You gave me hyacinths first a year ago;   35
They called me the hyacinth girl."
—Yet when we came back, late, from the Hyacinth garden,
Your arms full, and your hair wet, I could not
Speak, and my eyes failed, I was neither
Living nor dead, and I knew nothing,   40
Looking into the heart of light, the silence.
Oed' und leer das Meer.[2]

Madame Sosostris,[3] famous clairvoyante,
Had a bad cold, nevertheless
Is known to be the wisest woman in Europe,   45

7. "Cf. Ezekiel II, i" [Eliot's note].
Here God is addressing Ezekiel, "Son
of man." God continues, "stand upon
thy feet, and I will speak unto thee."
8. "Cf. Ecclesiastes XII, v" [Eliot's
note]. The verse cited by Eliot is part
of the Preacher's picture of the desolation of old age, "when they shall
be afraid of that which is high, and
fears shall be in the way, and the almond tree shall flourish, and the grasshopper shall be a burden, and desire
shall fail * * * "
9. Cf. Isaiah xxxii.2: the "righteous
king" "shall be * * * as rivers of
water in a dry place, as the shadow of
a great rock in a weary land."
1. "V. *Tristan und Isolde*, I, verses
5–8"[Eliot's note]. In Wagner's opera,
a sailor recalls the girl he has left be-

hind: "Fresh blows the wind to the
homeland; my Irish child, where are
you waiting?"
2. "Id. III, verse 24" [Eliot's note].
In Act III of *Tristan und Isolde*, Tristan lies dying. He is waiting for Isolde
to come to him from Cornwall, but a
shepherd, appointed to watch for her
sail, can only report, "Waste and empty
is the sea."
3. A mock Egyptian name (suggested
to Eliot by "Sesostris, the Sorceress of
Ecbatana," the name assumed by a
character in Aldous Huxley's novel
Crome Yellow who dresses up as a
gypsy to tell fortunes at a fair). The
anticlimactic effect of "had a bad
cold" is deliberate; it is intended to be
ironic and debunking.

With a wicked pack of cards.[4] Here, said she,
Is your card, the drowned Phoenician Sailor,[5]
(Those are pearls that were his eyes. Look!)
Here is Belladonna, the Lady of the Rocks,[6]
The lady of situations.   50
Here is the man with three staves,[7] and here the Wheel,
And here is the one-eyed merchant,[8] and this card,
Which is blank, is something he carries on his back,
Which I am forbidden to see. I do not find
The Hanged Man.[9] Fear death by water.   55
I see crowds of people, walking round in a ring.
Thank you. If you see dear Mrs. Equitone,
Tell her I bring the horoscope myself:
One must be so careful these days.

4. I.e., the Tarot deck of cards. The four suits of the Tarot pack, discussed by Jessie Weston in *From Ritual to Romance*, are the cup, lance, sword, and dish—the life symbols found in the Grail story. Miss Weston noted that "today the Tarot has fallen somewhat into disrepute, being principally used for purposes of divination." Some of the cards mentioned in lines 46–56 are discussed by Eliot in his note to this passage: "I am not familiar with the exact constitution of the Tarot pack of cards, from which I have obviously departed to suit my own convenience. The Hanged Man, a member of the traditional pack, fits my purpose in two ways: because he is associated in my mind with the Hanged God of Frazer, and because I associate him with the hooded figure in the passage of the disciples to Emmaus in Part V. The Phoenician Sailor and the Merchant appear later; also the 'crowds of people,' and Death by Water is executed in Part IV. The Man with Three Staves (an authentic member of the Tarot pack) I associate, quite arbitrarily, with the Fisher King himself."
5. See Part IV. Phlebas the Phoenician and Mr. Eugenides, the Smyrna merchant—both of whom appear later in the poem—are different phases of the same symbolic character, here identified as the "Phoenician Sailor." Mr. Eugenides exports "currants" (line 210); the drowned Phlebas floats in the "current" (line 315). The line that follows is from Shakespeare's *Tempest* (I.ii.398). Ariel's song to the shipwrecked Ferdinand, who was "sitting on a bank / Weeping again the King my father's wrack," when "this music crept by me on the waters." The song is about the supposed drowning of Ferdinand's father, Alonso. *The Waste Land* contains many references to *The Tempest*: the supposed drowning of Alonso and Ferdinand is regarded as their purification by water, and the

"sea change" suffered by Alonso typifies, from one point of view, suffering transmuted into art (Eliot was impressed by the ritual element in Shakespeare's last plays). Ferdinand is also associated with Phlebas and Mr. Eugenides and therefore with the "drowned Phoenician Sailor." Drowning and sea change are both, of course, the work of water. Symbol of purification, baptism, refreshment, and growth, water plays diverse roles in the poem.
6. "Belladonna": beautiful lady. The word also suggests Madonna (the Virgin Mary) and therefore the Madonna of the Rocks (as in Leonardo da Vinci's painting); the rocks symbolize the Church. But there are other rocks—the rocks of dryness, of the Waste Land (e.g., lines 331 ff.). Belladonna is also an eye-cosmetic and a poison—the "deadly" nightshade. In the next line, the woman-figure of the Virgin becomes "the lady of situations," foreshadowing the neurasthenic lady of intrigue in Part II.
7. Life-force symbol, associated by Eliot with the Fisher King. The "Wheel" is the wheel of fortune, whose turning represents the reversals of human life.
8. Mr. Eugenides, "one-eyed" because the figure is in profile on the card and also as a suggestion of evil or crookedness. The mysterious burden on his back may be the mysteries of the fertility cults which, Miss Weston emphasizes, Phoenician merchants carried throughout the Mediterranean, or simply "the burthen of the mystery," "the heavy and the weary weight / Of all this unintelligible world" in Wordsworth's *Tintern Abbey*.
9. On his card in the Tarot pack he is shown hanging from one point from a T-shaped cross. He symbolizes the self-sacrifice of the fertility god who is killed in order that his resurrection may bring fertility once again to land and people.

Unreal City,[1]   60
Under the brown fog of a winter dawn,
A crowd flowed over London Bridge, so many,[2]
I had not thought death had undone so many.
Sighs, short and infrequent, were exhaled,[3]
And each man fixed his eyes before his feet.   65
Flowed up the hill and down King William Street,
To where Saint Mary Woolnoth kept the hours
With a dead sound on the final stroke of nine.[4]
There I saw one I knew, and stopped him, crying: "Stetson![5]
You who were with me in the ships at Mylae![6]   70
That corpse you planted last year in your garden,
Has it begun to sprout?[7] Will it bloom this year?
Or has the sudden frost disturbed its bed?
Oh keep the Dog far hence, that's friend to men,
Or with his nails he'll dig it up again![8]   75
You! hypocrite lecteur!—mon semblable—mon frère!"[9]

1. "Cf. Baudelaire: 'Fourmillante cité, cité pleine de rêves, / Où le spectre en plein jour raccroche le passant" [Eliot's note]. The lines are quoted from Les Sept Vieillards ("The Seven Old Men") by Charles Baudelaire (1821–67); it is poem XCIII of Les Fleurs du Mal ("The Flowers of Evil"). The lines may be translated: "Swarming city, city full of dreams, / Where the specter in broad daylight accosts the passerby."
2. "Cf. Inferno III, 55–57 * * * " [Eliot's note]. The note goes on to quote Dante's lines, which may be translated: "So long a train of people, / that I should never have believed / That death had undone so many." Dante, just outside the gate of Hell, has seen "the wretched souls of those who lived without disgrace and without praise." In his essay on Baudelaire Eliot argued that in a sense it was better to be positively evil than to be neither good nor evil.
3. "Cf. Inferno IV, 25–27 * * * " [Eliot's note]. In Limbo, the first circle of Hell, Dante has found the virtuous heathen, who lived before Christianity and are therefore eternally unable to achieve their desire of seeing God. Dante's lines, cited by Eliot, mean: "Here, so far as I could tell by listening, / there was no lamentation except sighs, / which caused the eternal air to tremble."
4. "A phenomenon which I have often noticed" [Eliot's note]. St. Mary Woolnoth is a church in the "City" of London (the financial district); the crowd is flowing across London Bridge to work in the City.
5. Presumably representing the "aver-

age businessman."
6. The battle of Mylae (260 B.C.) in the First Punic War, which, like World War I, was fought for economic reasons.
7. A distortion of the ritual death of the fertility god.
8. "Cf. the Dirge in Webster's White Devil" [Eliot's note]. In the play by John Webster (d. 1625), the dirge, sung by Cornelia, has the lines: "But keep the wolf far thence, that's foe to men, / For with his nails he'll dig them up again." Eliot makes the "wolf" into a "Dog," which is not a "foe" but a "friend" to man. The image may be intended to suggest the ultimate degeneration of the fertility ritual, where the dying god is something buried in a suburban back garden to be dug up again by a friendly dog. There may be a reference to Sirius, the Dog Star, which is important in Egyptian mythology as heralding the fertilizing floods of the Nile (this is discussed by Miss Weston). But most important in this passage is the feverish nightmare atmosphere which it develops.
9. "V. Baudelaire, Preface to Fleurs du Mal" [Eliot's note]. The passage is the last line of the introductory poem Au Lecteur ("To the Reader") in Baudelaire's Fleurs du Mal; it may be translated: "Hypocrite reader!—my likeness —my brother!" Au Lecteur describes man as sunk in stupidity, sin, and evil; but the worst in "each man's foul menagerie of sin" is Boredom, the "monstre délicat"—"You know him, reader * * * " Like Baudelaire, Eliot is here shocking the reader into full participation in the poem.

II. A Game of Chess[1]

The Chair she sat in, like a burnished throne,[2]
Glowed on the marble, where the glass
Held up by standards wrought with fruited vines
From which a golden Cupidon peeped out   80
(Another hid his eyes behind his wing)
Doubled the flames of sevenbranched candelabra
Reflecting light upon the table as
The glitter of her jewels rose to meet it,
From satin cases poured in rich profusion;   85
In vials of ivory and colored glass
Unstoppered, lurked her strange synthetic perfumes,
Unguent, powdered, or liquid—troubled, confused
And drowned the sense in odors; stirred by the air
That freshened from the window, these ascended   90
In fattening the prolonged candle flames,
Flung their smoke into the laquearia,[3]
Stirring the pattern on the coffered ceiling.
Huge sea-wood fed with copper
Burned green and orange, framed by the colored stone,   95
In which sad light a carvéd dolphin swam.
Above the antique mantel was displayed
As though a window gave upon the sylvan scene[4]
The change of Philomel,[5] by the barbarous king

1. The title suggests two plays by Thomas Middleton (1580–1627): *A Game at Chess* and, more significantly, *Women Beware Women*, which has a scene in which a mother-in-law is distracted by a game of chess while her daughter-in-law is seduced: every move in the chess game represents a move in the seduction. Section II opens with a bored woman of leisure sitting before her dressing table in an atmosphere where the ornaments, the perfumes, the sheer excess of objects stifle the senses, while works of art emphasize the distinction between grandeur and futility. The neurasthenia and mounting hysteria revealed by the dialogue (or an interior monologue, or the remarks in quotation marks may be spoken by the lady and those not in quotation marks may represent her husband's unspoken answers) and the degeneration of culture through parody and jazzing up of lines from Shakespeare culminate in the meaningless yet terrifying "knock." This at once becomes the barman's knock on the counter as he calls closing time, and thus the scene changes to the lower end of the social scale, with women talking in a pub about methods of abortion—another aspect of that sterility and misuse of sex which help to make up the modern Waste Land.
2. "Cf. *Antony and Cleopatra*, II, ii, 1. 190" [Eliot's note]. In Shakespeare's play, Enobarbus' famous description of the first meeting of Antony and Cleopatra begins, "The barge she sat in, / like a burnish'd throne, / Burn'd on the water. * * * " Eliot's language in the opening lines of Part II is full of ironic distortions of Enobarbus' speech.
3. "Laquearia. V. *Aeneid*, I, 726 * * * " [Eliot's note]. *Laquearia* means "a paneled ceiling," and Eliot's note quotes the passage in the *Aeneid* which was his source for the word. The passage may be translated: "Blazing torches hang from the gold-paneled ceiling [*laquearibus aureis*], and torches conquer the night with flames." Virgil is here describing the banquet given by Dido, queen of Carthage, for Aeneas, with whom she fell in love. (Carthage is the scene of more "unholy loves" later in the poem; cf. line 307 and Eliot's note on it.)
4. "Sylvan scene. V. Milton, *Paradise Lost*, IV, 140" [Eliot's note]. The phrase is part of the first description of Eden, which we see through Satan's eyes.
5. "V. Ovid, *Metamorphoses*, VI, Philomela" [Eliot's note]. The note is a reference to Ovid's version of the Greek myth of the rape of Philomela by "the barbarous king" Tereus, husband of her sister Procne. Philomela was transformed into a nightingale. Eliot's note for line 100 refers ahead to his elaboration of the nightingale's song.

So rudely forced; yet there the nightingale   100
Filled all the desert with inviolable voice
And still she cried, and still the world pursues,
"Jug Jug"[6] to dirty ears.
And other withered stumps of time
Were told upon the walls; staring forms   105
Leaned out, leaning, hushing the room enclosed.
Footsteps shuffled on the stair.
Under the firelight, under the brush, her hair
Spread out in fiery points
Glowed into words, then would be savagely still.   110

"My nerves are bad tonight. Yes, bad. Stay with me.
Speak to me. Why do you never speak. Speak.
       What are you thinking of? What thinking? What?
I never know what you are thinking. Think."

I think we are in rats' alley[7]   115
Where the dead men lost their bones.

"What is that noise?"
                    The wind under the door.[8]
"What is that noise now? What is the wind doing?"
                    Nothing again nothing.   120
                       "Do
You know nothing? Do you see nothing? Do you remember
Nothing?"

       I remember
Those are pearls that were his eyes.   125
"Are you alive, or not? Is there nothing in your head?"
                                   But

O O O O that Shakespeherian Rag—
It's so elegant
So intelligent
"What shall I do now? What shall I do?"   130
"I shall rush out as I am, and walk the street
With my hair down, so. What shall we do tomorrow?
What shall we ever do?"
                    The hot water at ten.   135
And if it rains, a closed car at four.
And we shall play a game of chess,[1]
Pressing lidless eyes and waiting for a knock upon the door.

When Lil's husband got demobbed,[2] I said—
I didn't mince my words, I said to her myself,   140

6. Conventional representation of nightingale's song in Elizabethan poetry. The
tragic myth has become degraded into
a dirty story.
7. "Cf. Part III, l. 195" [Eliot's note].
8. "Cf. Webster: 'Is the wind in that
door still?'" [Eliot's note]. The line
cited in the note is from John Webster's *The Devil's Law Case* (III.ii.162).
1. "Cf. the game of chess in Middleton's *Women Beware Women*" [Eliot's
note]. The significance of this chess
game is discussed in note 1 for this section.
2. British slang for "demobilized" (dis-
charged from the army).

HURRY UP PLEASE ITS TIME[3]
Now Albert's coming back, make yourself a bit smart.
He'll want to know what you done with that money he gave you
To get yourself some teeth. He did, I was there.
You have them all out, Lil, and get a nice set,   145
He said, I swear, I can't bear to look at you.
And no more can't I, I said, and think of poor Albert,
He's been in the army four years, he wants a good time,
And if you don't give it him, there's others will, I said.
Oh is there, she said. Something o' that, I said.   150
Then I'll know who to thank, she said, and give me a straight look.
HURRY UP PLEASE ITS TIME
If you don't like it you can get on with it, I said.
Others can pick and choose if you can't.
But if Albert makes off, it won't be for lack of telling.   155
You ought to be ashamed, I said, to look so antique.
(And her only thirty-one.)
I can't help it, she said, pulling a long face,
It's them pills I took, to bring it off, she said.
(She's had five already, and nearly died of young George.)   160
The chemist[4] said it would be all right, but I've never been the
      same.
You *are* a proper fool, I said.
Well, if Albert won't leave you alone, there it is, I said,
What you get married for if you don't want children?
HURRY UP PLEASE ITS TIME   165
Well, that Sunday Albert was home, they had a hot gammon,[5]
And they asked me in to dinner, to get the beauty of it hot—
HURRY UP PLEASE ITS TIME
HURRY UP PLEASE ITS TIME
Goonight Bill. Goonight Lou. Goonight May. Goonight.   170
Ta ta. Goonight. Goonight.
Good night, ladies, good night, sweet ladies, good night, good night.[6]

III. *The Fire Sermon*[7]

The river's tent is broken: the last fingers of leaf
Clutch and sink into the wet bank. The wind

3. The traditional call of the British bartender at closing time.
4. Druggist.
5. Ham or bacon.
6. Cf. the mad Ophelia's departing words (*Hamlet* IV.v.72). Ophelia, too, met "death by water."
7. Just as water both purifies and drowns, so fire both purges and destroys: in this part, the roles of fire are emphasized. The Fire Sermon itself was preached by the Buddha against the fires of lust and other passions which destroy men and prevent their regeneration. The section opens with an autumn scene on the Thames, which is made increasingly sinister by such devices as ironic references to or distortions of famous passages in literature and the mocking equation of noble rituals of the past with modern trivialities and obscenities. We turn briefly to Mr. Eugenides, degenerate descendant of the Syrian merchants who had once spread the fertility cults throughout the Mediterranean, and then to the deliberately horrible scene of modern lust, sex without meaning. Seductions on the Thames, old and new, with parodic echoes of Wagner, Shakespeare, and Dante, lead to a further expression of the sense of nothingness and meaninglessness that characterizes the modern Waste Land, and the section ends with the Occidental St. Augustine echoing the Oriental Buddha in a call for the renunciation of lust.

Crosses the brown land, unheard. The nymphs are departed. 175
Sweet Thames, run softly, till I end my song.[8]
The river bears no empty bottles, sandwich papers,
Silk handkerchiefs, cardboard boxes, cigarette ends
Or other testimony of summer nights. The nymphs are departed.
And their friends, the loitering heirs of city directors; 180
Departed, have left no addresses.
By the waters of Leman I sat down and wept . . .[9]
Sweet Thames, run softly till I end my song,
Sweet Thames, run softly, for I speak not loud or long.
But at my back in a cold blast I hear[1] 185
The rattle of the bones, and chuckle spread from ear to ear.
A rat crept softly through the vegetation
Dragging its slimy belly on the bank
While I was fishing[2] in the dull canal
On a winter evening round behind the gashouse 190
Musing upon the king my brother's wreck[3]
And on the king my father's death before him.
White bodies naked on the low damp ground
And bones cast in a little low dry garret,
Rattled by the rat's foot only, year to year. 195
But at my back from time to time I hear[4]
The sound of horns and motors, which shall bring
Sweeney to Mrs. Porter in the spring.[5]
O the moon shone bright on Mrs. Porter
And on her daughter 200
They wash their feet in soda water[6]
Et O ces voix d'enfants, chantant dans la coupole![7]

8. "V. Spenser, *Prothalamion*" [Eliot's note]. Eliot's line is the refrain from Spenser's marriage song, which is also set by the Thames in London—but a very different Thames from the modern littered river.
9. Cf. Psalms cxxxvii.1, in which the exiled Hebrews mourn for their homeland: "By the rivers of Babylon, there we sat down, yea, we wept, when we remembered Zion." Lake Leman is another name for Lake Geneva; Eliot wrote *The Waste Land* in Lausanne, by that lake. The common noun "leman" is an archaic word meaning, in the bad sense, an illicit sweetheart or mistress; hence "the waters of Leman" become associated with the fires of lust.
1. An ironic distortion of Andrew Marvell's famous lines from *To His Coy Mistress:* "But at my back I always hear / Time's wingéd chariot hurrying near * * * " Cf. line 196.
2. To fish is to seek eternity and salvation (cf. the Fisher King), but this activity is now degraded and dirtied.
3. "Cf. *The Tempest*, I, ii" [Eliot's note]. See line 48.
4. "Cf. Marvell, *To His Coy Mistress*" [Eliot's note].
5. "Cf. Day, *Parliament of Bees:* 'When

of the sudden, listening, you shall hear, / A noise of horns and hunting, which shall bring / Actaeon to Diana in the spring, / Where all shall see her naked skin . . .' " [Eliot's note]. Actaeon was changed to a stag and hunted to death after he saw Diana, the goddess of chastity, bathing with her nymphs. In parodying the poem by John Day (1574–ca. 1640), Eliot is implying that Actaeon's fate indicates a very different set of values from those represented by the association of Sweeney and Mrs. Porter.
6. "I do not know the origin of the ballad from which these lines are taken: it was reported to me from Sydney, Australia" [Eliot's note]. One of the less vulgar versions of the song, which was popular among Australian troops in World War I, went as follows: "O the moon shines bright on Mrs. Porter / And on the daughter / Of Mrs. Porter. / They wash their feet in soda water / And so they oughter / To keep them clean."
7. "V. Verlaine, *Parsifal*" [Eliot's note]. The line is translated, "And O those children's voices singing in the dome!" Verlaine's sonnet describes Parsifal, the questing knight, resisting all

Twit twit twit
Jug jug jug jug jug jug
So rudely forc'd.   205
Tereu[8]

Unreal City
Under the brown fog of a winter noon
Mr. Eugenides, the Smyrna[9] merchant
Unshaven, with a pocket full of currants   210
C.i.f.[1] London: documents at sight,
Asked me in demotic French[2]
To luncheon at the Cannon Street Hotel[3]
Followed by a weekend at the Metropole.

At the violet hour, when the eyes and back   215
Turn upward from the desk, when the human engine waits
Like a taxi throbbing waiting,
I Tiresias,[4] though blind, throbbing between two lives,
Old man with wrinkled female breasts, can see
At the violet hour, the evening hour that strives   220
Homeward, and brings the sailor home from sea,[5]
The typist home at teatime, clears her breakfast, lights

sensual temptations to keep himself pure for the Grail; Wagner's Parsifal had his feet washed before entering the castle of the Grail
8. "Tereu" is a reference to Tereus, who "rudely forc'd" Philomela; it was also one of the conventional words for a nightingale's song in Elizabethan poetry. Cf. the song from John Lyly's *Alexander and Campaspe* (1564): "Oh, 'tis the ravished nightingale. / *Jug, jug, jug, jug, tereu!* she cries," and lines 100 ff.
9. Seaport in western Turkey; here associated with Carthage and the ancient Phoenician and Syrian merchants (unlike those of modern Smyrna), who spread the old mystery cults. The sort of cult spread by Mr. Eugenides is indicated by his suggestion of "a weekend at the Metropole" (a luxury hotel at Brighton).
1. "The currants were quoted at a price 'carriage and insurance free to London'; and the Bill of Lading etc. were to be handed to the buyer upon payment of the sight draft" [Eliot's note].
2. Popular, vulgar French.
3. By the station which was then chief terminus for travelers to the continent; hence, a favorite meeting place for businessmen going or coming from abroad.
4. "Tiresias, although a mere spectator and not indeed a 'character,' is yet the most important personage in the poem, uniting all the rest. Just as the one-eyed merchant, seller of currants, melts into the Phoenician Sailor, and the latter is not wholly distinct from Ferdinand Prince of Naples, so all the women are one woman, and the two

sexes meet in Tiresias. What Tiresias sees, in fact, is the substance of the poem. The whole passage from Ovid is of great anthropological interest * * * " [Eliot's note]. The note then quotes the Latin text of Ovid's *Metamorphoses* which tells the story of Tiresias' change of sex. The Latin may be translated: "[The story goes that once Jove, having drunk a great deal,] jested with Juno. He said, 'Your pleasure in love is really greater than that enjoyed by men.' She denied it; so they decided to seek the opinion of the wise Tiresias, for he knew both aspects of love. For once, with a blow of his staff, he had committed violence on two huge snakes as they copulated in the green forest; and—wonderful to tell—was turned from a man into a woman and thus spent seven years. In the eighth year he saw the same snakes again and said: 'If a blow struck at you is so powerful that it changes the sex of the giver, I will now strike at you again.' With these words he struck the snakes, and his former shape was restored to him and he became as he had been born. So he was appointed arbitrator in the playful quarrel, and supported Jove's statement. It is said that Saturnia [i.e., Juno] was quite disproportionately upset, and condemned the arbitrator to perpetual blindness. But the almighty father (for no god may undo what has been done by another god), in return for the sight that was taken away, gave him the power to know the future and so lightened the penalty paid by the honor."
5. "This may not appear as exact as Sappho's lines, but I had in mind the

Her stove, and lays out food in tins.
Out of the window perilously spread
Her drying combinations touched by the sun's last rays.[5a]   225
On the divan are piled (at night her bed)
Stockings, slippers, camisoles, and stays.
I Tiresias, old man with wrinkled dugs
Perceived the scene, and foretold the rest—
I too awaited the expected guest.   230
He, the young man carbuncular,[6] arrives,
A small house agent's clerk, with one bold stare,
One of the low on whom assurance sits
As a silk hat on a Bradford[7] millionaire.
The time is now propitious, as he guesses,   235
The meal is ended, she is bored and tired,
Endeavors to engage her in caresses
Which still are unreproved, if undesired.
Flushed and decided, he assaults at once;
Exploring hands encounter no defense;   240
His vanity requires no response,
And makes a welcome of indifference.
(And I Tiresias have foresuffered all
Enacted on this same divan or bed;
I who have sat by Thebes[8] below the wall   245
And walked among the lowest of the dead.)
Bestows one final patronizing kiss,
And gropes his way, finding the stairs unlit . . .

She turns and looks a moment in the glass,
Hardly aware of her departed lover;   250
Her brain allows one half-formed thought to pass;
"Well now that's done: and I'm glad it's over."
When lovely woman stoops to folly and
Paces about her room again, alone,
She smoothes her hair with automatic hand,   255
And puts a record on the gramophone.[9]

"This music crept by me upon the waters"[1]
And along the Strand, up Queen Victoria Street.

'longshore' or 'dory' fisherman, who returns at nightfall" [Eliot's note]. Sappho's poem addressed Hesperus, the evening star, as the star that brings everyone home from work to evening rest; her poem is here distorted by Eliot. There is also an echo of Robert Louis Stevenson's *Requiem* in line 221 ("Home is the sailor, home from sea").
5a. The present editor has been informed that this and the preceding line constitute a "great allusion" to Keats's lines "Charmed magic casements, opening on the foam/ Of perilous seas, in faery lands forlorn" (*Ode to a Nightingale*, lines 69–70) but he remains skeptical. It is, however, certainly a powerful antiromantic image.
6. Pimply.

7. A Yorkshire woolen-manufacturing town, where many rapid fortunes were made in World War I.
8. Tiresias lived in Thebes for many generations, where he witnessed the tragic fates of Oedipus and Creon; he prophesied in the market place by the wall of Thebes.
9. "V. Goldsmith, the song in *The Vicar of Wakefield*" [Eliot's note]. Olivia, a character in Oliver Goldsmith's novel, sings the following song when she returns to the place where she was seduced: "When lovely woman stoops to folly / And finds too late that men betray / What charm can soothe her melancholy, / What art can wash her guilt away? / The only art her guilt to cover, / To hide her shame from every

O City city, I can sometimes hear
Beside a public bar in Lower Thames Street,   260
The pleasant whining of a mandolin
And a clatter and a chatter from within
Where fishmen lounge at noon: where the walls
Of Magnus Martyr hold
Inexplicable splendor of Ionian white and gold [2]   265

> The river sweats[3]
> Oil and tar
> The barges drift
> With the turning tide
> Red sails   270
> Wide
> To leeward, swing on the heavy spar.
> The barges wash
> Drifting logs
> Down Greenwich reach   275
> Past the Isle of Dogs.[4]
>> Weialala leia
>> Wallala leialala

> Elizabeth and Leicester[5]
> Beating oars   280
> The stern was formed
> A gilded shell
> Red and gold
> The brisk swell
> Rippled both shores   285
> Southwest wind
> Carried down stream
> The peal of bells

eye, / To give repentance to her lover / And wring his bosom—is to die."
1. "V. *The Tempest*, as above" [Eliot's note]. Cf. line 48. (The line is from Ferdinand's speech, continuing after "weeping again the King my father's wrack.")
2. "The interior of St. Magnus Martyr is to my mind one of the finest among [Sir Christopher] Wren's interiors. * * * " [Eliot's note]. In these lines, the "pleasant" music, the "fishmen" resting after labor, and the splendor of the church interior all suggest a world of true values, where work and relaxation are both real and take place in a context of religious meaning. It is but a momentary glimpse of an almost lost world.
3. "The Song of the (three) Thames-daughters begins here. From line 292 to 306 inclusive they speak in turn. V. *Götterdämmerung*, III, i: the Rhine-daughters" [Eliot's note]. The Thames-daughters, both old and new, reflect a barren world of shabbiness and lust. Eliot parallels them with the Rhine-maidens in Wagner's opera *Die Götter-*

dämmerung ("The Twilight of the Gods") who lament that, with the gold of the Nibelungs stolen, the beauty of the river is gone. The refrain in lines 277–78 is borrowed from Wagner.
4. Greenwich is a borough in London on the south side of the Thames; opposite is the Isle of Dogs (a peninsula): Eliot presumably intends a reference to the earlier theme of the Dog.
5. The fruitless love of Queen Elizabeth and the Earl of Leicester (Sir Robert Dudley) is recalled in Eliot's note: "V. [J. A.] Froude, *Elizabeth*, Vol. I, ch. iv, letter of De Quadra to Philip of Spain: 'In the afternoon we were in a barge, watching the games on the river. (The queen) was alone with Lord Robert and myself on the poop, when they began to talk nonsense, and went so far that Lord Robert at last said, as I was on the spot there was no reason why they should not be married if the queen pleased.'" Even these two great figures from the 16th century represent no past glory and no contrast to present sordidness. (Queen Elizabeth was born in the old Green-

White towers

> Weialala leia   290
> Wallala leialala

"Trams and dusty trees.
Highbury bore me. Richmond and Kew
Undid me.[6] By Richmond I raised my knees
Supine on the floor of a narrow canoe."   295

"My feet are at Moorgate,[7] and my heart
Under my feet. After the event
He wept. He promised 'a new start.'
I made no comment. What should I resent?"

"On Margate[8] Sands.   300
I can connect
Nothing with nothing.
The broken fingernails of dirty hands.
My people humble people who expect
Nothing."   305

> la la

To Carthage then I came[9]

Burning burning burning burning[1]
O Lord Thou pluckest me out[2]
O Lord Thou pluckest   310

burning

IV. Death by Water[3]

Phlebas the Phoenician, a fortnight dead,
Forgot the cry of gulls, and the deep sea swell

wich House, by the river, where Greenwich Hospital now stands.)
6. "Cf. *Purgatorio*, V, 133 * * * " [Eliot's note]. The *Purgatorio* lines, which Eliot here parodies, may be translated: "Remember me, who am La Pia. / Siena made me, Maremma undid me." Highbury is a residential London suburb; Richmond is a pleasant part of London westward up the Thames, with boating and riverside hotels; Kew, adjoining Richmond, has the famous Kew Gardens.
7. Slum area in east London.
8. Popular seaside resort on Thames estuary.
9. "V. St. Augustine's *Confessions*: 'to Carthage then I came, where a caldron of unholy loves sang all about mine ears' " [Eliot's note]. The passage from the *Confessions* quoted here occurs in St. Augustine's account of his youthful life of lust. Cf. line 92 and its note.
1. "The complete text of the Buddha's Fire Sermon (which corresponds in importance to the Sermon on the Mount) from which these words are taken, will be found translated in the late Henry

Clarke Warren's *Buddhism in Translation* (Harvard Oriental Series). * * * " [Eliot's note]. In the sermon, the Buddha instructs his priests that all things "are on fire. * * * The eye * * * is on fire; forms are on fire; eye-consciousness is on fire; impressions received by the eye are on fire; and whatever sensation, pleasant, unpleasant, or indifferent, originates in dependence on impressions received by the eye, that also is on fire. And with what are these on fire? With the fire of passion, say I, with the fire of hatred, with the fire of infatuation * * * " For Christ's Sermon on the Mount see Matthew v-vii.
2. "From St. Augustine's *Confessions* again. The collocation of these two representatives of eastern and western asceticism, as the culmination of this part of the poem, is not an accident" [Eliot's note]. Cf. also Zechariah iii.2, where God, rebuking Satan, speaks of Joshua the high priest as "a brand plucked out of the fire."
3. This section has been interpreted in two ways: either it signifies death by water without resurrection (water *mis-*

And the profit and loss.
        A current under sea   315
Picked his bones in whispers. As he rose and fell
He passed the stages of his age and youth
Entering the whirlpool.
        Gentile or Jew
O you who turn the wheel and look to windward,   320
Consider Phlebas, who was once handsome and tall as **you**.

V. *What the Thunder Said*[4]

After the torchlight red on sweaty faces
After the frosty silence in the gardens
After the agony in stony places
The shouting and the crying   325
Prison and palace and reverberation
Of thunder of spring over distant mountains
He who was living is now dead[5]
We who were living are now dying
With a little patience   330

Here is no water but only rock
Rock and no water and the sandy road
The road winding above among the mountains
Which are mountains of rock without water
If there were water we should stop and drink   335
Amongst the rock one cannot stop or think
Sweat is dry and feet are in the sand
If there were only water amongst the rock
Dead mountain mouth of carious teeth that cannot spit
Here one can neither stand nor lie nor sit   340

used), or it symbolizes the sacrificial death which precedes rebirth. It is true that Phlebas is purged of his commercial interests and vanities when he suffers a sea change, and Miss Weston tells of the annual casting into the sea at Alexandria of an effigy of the head of Adonis—to be taken out after seven days by jubilant celebrators of the cult. The majority of interpreters, however, see Phlebas' drowning as a death by water which brings no resurrection, although there is a strange sense of peace in the death. Cf. line 47 and its note.

4. "In the first part of Part V three themes are employed: the journey to Emmaus, the approach to the Chapel Perilous (see Miss Weston's book), and the present decay of eastern Europe" [Eliot's note]. The journey to Emmaus (see line 360 and its note) is a significant feature in the story of Christ, and in this section the Waste Land is more clearly related to that story. Christ is associated with the slain fertility god, but there is still no resurrection. The rocky landscape is described with a new and agonizing intensity until everything breaks down in

hallucination in which visions of the decay of the great cities of Western civilization give way to nightmare images of horror. Then the scene changes to the Chapel Perilous in the midst of the Waste Land: it seems empty and derelict and apparently the quest has been in vain. But suddenly the cock crows, the lightning flashes, and the fertilizing rain falls. The thunder peals and gives its message of salvation in terms of Oriental wisdom, the Sanskrit words for "Give, Sympathize, Control." But we are too timidly prudent to give properly, too shut in within our own individualities to be able to sympathize properly, and we can more easily respond to control than exercise it. Salvation remains problematical.

5. These lines, containing allusions to Christ's imprisonment and trial, and to Gethsemane and Golgotha, suggest the hopeless days between Good Friday and Easter, between the Crucifixion and the Resurrection—associated with the death of the Fisher King and the moment of despair in the Waste Land when regeneration seems impossible.

There is not even silence in the mountains
But dry sterile thunder without rain
There is not even solitude in the mountains
But red sullen faces sneer and snarl
From doors of mudcracked houses   345
                If there were water

    And no rock
    If there were rock
    And also water
    And water   350
    A spring
    A pool among the rock
    If there were the sound of water only
    Not the cicada[6]
    And dry grass singing   355
    But sound of water over a rock
    Where the hermit thrush[7] sings in the pine trees
    Drip drop drip drop drop drop drop
    But there is no water

Who is the third who walks always beside you?[8]   360
When I count, there are only you and I together
But when I look ahead up the white road
There is always another one walking beside you
Gliding wrapped in a brown mantle, hooded
I do not know whether a man or a woman   365
—But who is that on the other side of you?

What is that sound high in the air[9]
Murmur of maternal lamentation
Who are those hooded hordes swarming
Over endless plains, stumbling in cracked earth   370
Ringed by the flat horizon only
What is the city over the mountains
Cracks and reforms[1] and bursts in the violet air
Falling towers

6. Grasshopper. Cf. the prophecy of Ecclesiastes, "the grasshopper shall be a burden, and desire shall fail * * * " (and cf. also line 23 and its note).

7. "This is * * * the hermit thrush which I have heard in Quebec County. * * * Its 'water-dripping song' is justly celebrated" [Eliot's note].

8. "The following lines were stimulated by the account of one of the Antarctic expeditions (I forget which, but I think one of Shackleton's): it was related that the party of explorers, at the extremity of their strength, had the constant delusion that there was *one more member* than could actually be counted" [Eliot's note]. This reminiscence is associated with the journey of Christ's disciples to Emmaus given in Luke xxiv.13–16: "And it came to pass, that, while they communed together and reasoned, Jesus himself drew near, and went with them. But their eyes were holden that they should not know him."

9. Eliot's note for lines 367–77 is: "Cf. Herman Hesse, *Blick ins Chaos* ["A Glimpse into Chaos"] * * * " The note then quotes a passage from the German text, which is translated: "Already half of Europe, already at least half of Eastern Europe, on the way to Chaos, drives drunk in sacred infatuation along the edge of the precipice, sings drunkenly, as though hymn singing, as Dmitri Karamazov [in Dostoyevski's *Brothers Karamazov*] sang. The offended bourgeois laughs at the songs; the saint and the seer hear them with tears."

1. Used ironically.

Jerusalem Athens Alexandria   375
Vienna London
Unreal

A woman drew her long black hair out tight
And fiddled whisper music on those strings
And bats with baby faces in the violet light   380
Whistled, and beat their wings
And crawled head downward down a blackened wall
And upside down in air were towers
Tolling reminiscent bells, that kept the hours
And voices singing out of empty cisterns and exhausted wells.   385

In this decayed hole among the mountains
In the faint moonlight, the grass is singing
Over the tumbled graves, about the chapel
There is the empty chapel, only the wind's home.[2]
It has no windows, and the door swings,   390
Dry bones can harm no one.
Only a cock stood on the rooftree
Co co rico co co rico[3]
In a flash of lightning. Then a damp gust
Bringing rain   395

Ganga[4] was sunken, and the limp leaves
Waited for rain, while the black clouds
Gathered far distant, over Himavant.[5]
The jungle crouched, humped in silence.
Then spoke the thunder   400
DA[6]
Datta: what have we given?
My friend, blood shaking my heart
The awful daring of a moment's surrender
Which an age of prudence can never retract   405
By this, and this only, we have existed
Which is not to be found in our obituaries
Or in memories draped by the beneficent spider[7]
Or under seals broken by the lean solicitor

2. Suggesting the moment of near despair before the Chapel Perilous, when
the questing knight sees nothing there
but decay. This illusion of nothingness
is the knight's final test.
3. The crowing of the cock signals the
departure of ghosts and evil spirits.
Cf. *Hamlet* I.i.157 ff.
4. The river Ganges.
5. I.e., snowy mountain; the name of
a peak in the Himalayas.
6. " 'Datta, dayadhvam, damyata'
(Give, sympathize, control). The fable
of the meaning of the Thunder is found
in the *Brihadaranyaka—Upanishad*, 5,
1. * * * " [Eliot's note]. The Hindu
fable referred to is that of gods, men,
and demons each in turn asking of

their father Prajapati, "Speak to us,
O Lord." To each he replied with the
one syllable "*DA*," and each group interpreted it in a different way: "*Datta*,"
to give alms; "*Dayadhvam*," to have
compassion; "*Damyata*," to practice
self-control. The fable concludes, "This
is what the divine voice, the Thunder,
repeats when he says: *DA, DA, DA*:
'Control yourselves; give alms; be compassionate.' Therefore one should practice these three things: self-control,
alms-giving, and compassion."
7. "Cf. Webster, *The White Devil*, V,
vi: ' . . . they'll remarry / Ere the
worm pierce your winding-sheet, ere
the spider / Make a thin curtain for
your epitaphs' " [Eliot's note].

In our empty rooms $\qquad$ 410
DA
Dayadhvam: I have heard the key[8]
Turn in the door once and turn once only
We think of the key, each in his prison
Thinking of the key, each confirms a prison $\qquad$ 415
Only at nightfall, ethereal rumours
Revive for a moment a broken Coriolanus[9]
DA
Damyata: The boat responded
Gaily, to the hand expert with sail and oar $\qquad$ 420
The sea was calm, your heart would have responded
Gaily, when invited, beating obedient
To controlling hands

$\qquad$ I sat upon the shore
Fishing,[1] with the arid plain behind me $\qquad$ 425
Shall I at least set my lands in order?[2]
London Bridge is falling down falling down falling down[3]
Poi s'ascose nel foco che gli affina[4]
Quando fiam uti chelidon[5]—O swallow swallow

8. "Cf. *Inferno*, XXXIII, 46 * * * "
[Eliot's note]. In this passage from
the *Inferno* Ugolino recalls his imprisonment in the tower with his children,
where they starved to death: "And I
heard below the door of the horrible
tower being locked up." Eliot implies
that we cannot obey the command to
sympathize because we are imprisoned
within the circle of our own egotism.
Eliot's note for this line goes on to
quote F. H. Bradley, *Appearance and
Reality*, p. 346, as follows: " 'My external sensations are no less private
to myself than are my thoughts or my
feelings. In either case my experience
falls within my own circle, a circle
closed on the outside; and, with all its
elements alike, every sphere is opaque
to the others which surround it. . . .
In brief, regarded as an existence which
appears in a soul, the whole world for
each is peculiar and private to that
soul.' "
9. Coriolanus, who acted out of pride
rather than duty, is an obvious example of a man locked in the prison of
his own self. He led the enemy against
his native city out of injured pride
(cf. Shakespeare's *Coriolanus*).
1. "V. Weston: *From Ritual to Romance;* chapter on the Fisher King"
[Eliot's note].
2. The inclusive "I," who sits in the
symbolic act of fishing (seeking salvation, regeneration, eternity) with the
Waste Land behind him, wonders how
far he can order his affairs. There is
a note of subdued hope or at least of
determination in these lines. The "at
least" suggests a reasonable minimum
of achievement.

3. One of the later lines of this nursery
rhyme is: "Take the key and lock her
up, my fair lady."
4. "V. *Purgatorio*, XXVI, 148 * * * "
[Eliot's note]. The note goes on to
quote lines 145–48 of the *Purgatorio*,
in which Arnaut Daniel, the Provençal
poet, addresses Dante: " 'Now I pray
you, by that virtue which guides you
to the summit of the stairway, be mindful in due time of my pain.' " Then
(in the line Eliot quotes here) "he
hid himself in the fire which refines
them." The purgatorial vision of refining fire—as distinct from the fires
of lust—represents one of the hopeful
fragments shored up by the seeker for
regeneration and order.
5. "V. *Pervigilium Veneris*. Cf. Philomela in Parts II and III" [Eliot's
note]. The Latin phrase in the text
means, "When shall I be as the swallow?" It comes from the *Pervigilium
Veneris* ("Vigil of Venus"), an anonymous late Latin poem combining a
hymn to Venus with a description of
spring. In the last two stanzas of the
Pervigilium occurs a recollection of the
Tereus-Procne-Philomela myth (except
that in this version the swallow is identified with Philomela); the anonymous
poet's mood changes to one of sadness,
combined with hope for renewal: "The
maid of Tereus sings under the poplar
shade, so that you would think musical
trills of love came from her mouth and
not a sister's complaint of a barbarous
husband. * * * She sings, we are silent. When will my spring come? When
shall I be as the swallow that I may
cease to be silent? I have lost the Muse
in silence, and Apollo regards me not

Le Prince d'Aquitaine à la tour abolie[6]   430
These fragments I have shored against my ruins[7]
Why then Ile fit you. Hieronymo's mad againe.[8]
Datta. Dayadhvam. Damyata.
     Shantih   shantih   shantih[9]
1921   1922

Journey of the Magi[1]

"A cold coming we had of it,
Just the worst time of the year
For a journey, and such a long journey:
The ways deep and the weather sharp,
The very dead of winter."[2]   5
And the camels galled, sore-footed, refractory,
Lying down in the melting snow.
There were times we regretted
The summer palaces on slopes, the terraces,
And the silken girls bringing sherbet.   10
Then the camel men cursing and grumbling
And running away, and wanting their liquor and women,
And the night-fires going out, and the lack of shelters,
And the cities hostile and the towns unfriendly
And the villages dirty and charging high prices: 15
A hard time we had of it.

* * * " For "O swallow swallow" cf.
Swinburne's *Itylus*, which begins, "Swallow, my sister, O sister swallow, /
How can thine heart be full of spring?"
and Tennyson's lyric in *The Princess:*
"O Swallow, Swallow, flying, flying south
* * * "
6. "V. Gerard de Nerval, Sonnet *El
Desdichado*" [Eliot's note]. The French
line may be translated, "The Prince of
Aquitaine in the ruined tower." One of
the cards in the Tarot pack is "the
tower struck by lightning." The ruined
tower is symbolic of a decayed tradition.
7. This may refer to the whole poem
—fragments assembled by the poet in
the attempt to come to terms with
his situation.
8. "V. Kyd's *Spanish Tragedy*" [Eliot's
note]. Subtitled "Hieronymo's Mad
Againe," Kyd's play (1594) is an early
example of the Elizabethan tragedy of
revenge. Hieronymo, driven mad by
the murder of his son, has his revenge
when he is asked to write a court entertainment. He replies, "Why then Ile
fit you!" (i.e., accommodate you), and
assigns the parts in the entertainment
so that, in the course of the action,
his son's murderers are killed.
9. "Shantih. Repeated as here, a formal

ending to an Upanishad. 'The Peace
which passeth understanding' is our
equivalent to this word" [Eliot's note].
The Upanishads are poetic dialogues on
Hindu metaphysics, written after the
Vedas, the ancient Hindu scriptures, and
in part commenting on them. The fact
that the benediction is in a language
so foreign to Western tradition may indicate that the solution is willed, not
achieved. The fragments with which the
poem ends seem like a desperate attempt at ordering chaos, but it breaks
down in madness ("Hieronymo's mad
againe"). We end with the threefold
message repeated and the benediction
uttered; but the issue remains in doubt.
1. One of the three wise men who came
from the east to Jerusalem to do homage to the infant Jesus (Matthew
ii.1–12) is recalling in old age the
meaning of the experience.
2. Adapted from a passage in a Nativity sermon by the 17th-century divine
Lancelot Andrewes: "A cold coming
they had of it at this time of the year,
just the worst time of the year to take
a journey, and specially a long journey
in. The ways deep, the weather sharp,
the days short, the sun farthest off, *in
solstitio brumali*, 'the very dead of
winter.'"

At the end we preferred to travel all night,
Sleeping in snatches,
With the voices singing in our ears, saying
That this was all folly. 20

Then at dawn we came down to a temperate valley,
Wet, below the snow line, smelling of vegetation;
With a running stream and a water mill beating the darkness,
And three trees on the low sky,
And an old white horse galloped away in the meadow.[3] 25
Then we came to a tavern with vine-leaves over the lintel,
Six hands at an open door dicing for pieces of silver,[4]
And feet kicking the empty wineskins.
But there was no information, and so we continued
And arrived at evening, not a moment too soon 30
Finding the place; it was (you may say) satisfactory.

All this was a long time ago, I remember,
And I would do it again, but set down
This set down
This: were we led all that way for 35
Birth or Death? There was a Birth, certainly,
We had evidence and no doubt. I had seen birth and death,
But had thought they were different; this Birth was
Hard and bitter agony for us, like Death, our death.
We returned to our places, these Kingdoms, 40
But no longer at ease here, in the old dispensation,
With an alien people clutching their gods.
I should be glad of another death.

1927

Marina[1]

Quis hic locus, quae regio, quae mundi plaga?[2]

What seas what shores what gray rocks and what islands
What water lapping the bow

3. A series of images of freshness and renewal, combined with anticipations of disaster. The "three trees on the low sky" suggest the three crosses, with Christ crucified on the center one; the men dicing for pieces of silver suggest the soldiers dicing for Christ's garments and Judas' betrayal of him for thirty pieces of silver.
4. "Why, for all of us, out of all that we have heard, seen, felt, in a lifetime, do certain images recur, charged with emotion, rather than others? * * * six ruffians seen through an open window playing cards at night at a small French railway junction where there was a water mill" (Eliot, *The Use of*

Poetry and the Use of Criticism).
1. Marina is Pericles' daughter in Shakespeare's play *Pericles Prince of Tyre:* she was born at sea, lost to her father, then as a young woman found by him again. This poem evokes the mood of hushed wonder with which Pericles rediscovered his daughter, who had almost miraculously preserved her innocence and virtue through harrowing experiences. The situation is of course symbolic: a mood is established of regeneration, of escape from lust into love and from violence and confusion into peace. The symbolic boat on which the reunion takes place was originally made by the speaker, but for

And scent of pine and the woodthrush singing through the fog
What images return
O my daughter.   5

Those who sharpen the tooth of the dog, meaning
Death
Those who glitter with the glory of the hummingbird, meaning
Death
Those who sit in the sty of contentment, meaning   10
Death
Those who suffer the ecstasy of the animals, meaning
Death

Are become unsubstantial, reduced by a wind,
A breath of pine, and the woodsong fog   15
By this grace dissolved in place

What is this face, less clear and clearer
The pulse in the arm, less strong and stronger—
Given or lent? more distant than stars and nearer than the eye

Whispers and small laughter between leaves and hurrying feet   20
Under sleep, where all the waters meet.

Bowsprit cracked with ice and paint cracked with heat.
I made this, I have forgotten
And remember.
The rigging weak and the canvas rotten   25
Between one June and another September.
Made this unknowing, half conscious, unknown, my own.
The garboard strake[3] leaks, the seams need calking.
This form, this face, this life
Living to live in a world of time beyond me; let me   30
Resign my life for this life, my speech for that unspoken,
The awakened, lips parted, the hope, the new ships.

What seas what shores what granite islands towards my timbers
And woodthrush calling through the fog
My daughter.   35
                                                                      1930

a purpose he cannot remember; it is battered and frail; but it serves its purpose, having led him to this moment of grace, dedication, and new hope. One must not be too literal in pressing a meaning on each of the images: this is the most delicately evocative of all Eliot's poems.
2. "What place is this, what country, what region of the world?" Spoken by Hercules on regaining sanity after having killed his children in his madness, in Seneca's play *Hercules Furens* ("The Mad Hercules"). This is a situation contrary to the one evoked in the poem. Eliot once wrote to a correspondent that he wished to achieve a "crisscross" between the scenes in the Senecan and the Shakespearean plays. He appears to be making that association between birth and death which he uses so often (as in *The Waste Land* and *Journey of the Magi*).
3. The planking nearest to the boat's keel—hence its most vital spot.

From FOUR QUARTETS
Little Gidding[1]

I

Midwinter spring is its own season
Sempiternal[2] though sodden towards sundown,
Suspended in time, between pole and tropic.
When the short day is brightest, with frost and fire,
The brief sun flames the ice, on pond and ditches,   5
In windless cold that is the heart's heat,
Reflecting in a watery mirror
A glare that is blindness in the early afternoon.
And glow more intense than blaze of branch, or brazier,
Stirs the dumb spirit: no wind, but pentecostal fire[3]   10
In the dark time of the year. Between melting and freezing

1. This is the fourth of Eliot's *Four Quartets,* four related poems each divided into five "movements" in a manner reminiscent of the structure of a quartet or a sonata and each dealing with some aspect of the relation of time and eternity, the meaning of history, the achievement of the moment of timeless insight. Though the *Four Quartets* constitute a unified sequence, they were each written separately and can be read as individual poems. "*Little Gidding* can be understood by itself, without reference to the preceding poems, which it yet so beautifully completes" (Helen Gardner). Each of the four is named after a place. Little Gidding is a village in Huntingdonshire where in 1625 Nicholas Ferrar established an Anglican religious community; it was broken up in 1647, toward the end of the Civil War, by the victorious Puritans; the chapel, however, was rebuilt in the 19th century and still exists. The poet recalls a midwinter visit to the chapel; he evokes the scene and uses it for a starting point for a meditation on England's past and present, on the possibility of redemption through purgation. Eliot wrote the poem in 1942, when he was a fire-watcher during World War II, and he looks back at the history and meaning of Little Gidding from his own war experience in order to project its present significance.

The first section or movement is itself in three parts of which the first sets the scene and the season, the second asserts the significance of this place at any season, and the third reminds us of the original purpose of the community and suggests what these dead can communicate to us now, to achieve "the intersection of the timeless moment." The second movement is much more lyrical in tone, and broods over change and decay. It then changes to a Dan-tesque verse form (suggesting Dante's *terza rima,* but unrhymed) in which the poet describes himself walking at dawn after an air raid and encountering a "dead master" returned temporarily from Purgatory. (The scene also recalls Dante's meeting his own dead master Brunetto Latini in Hell.) The spirit talks of the relation between past and present, their common concern with language, and the slow and difficult progress toward purgation; he disappears when the All Clear sounds. The third movement broods over the uses of memory and attitudes toward history; recalls that the combatants in that earlier war are now "folded in a single party"; concedes that one cannot revive lost causes; and suggests that in detachment and in the view of past suffering as purgation a sense of peace and of renewal might be achieved. The short lyrical fourth movement elaborates the notion of purgation (the dove of peace has become the bombing plane), sees fire as purgative as well as destructive, and emphasizes the dual nature of love and the alternative of the two kinds of fire. The final movement accepts the movements of history and sees history as "a pattern of timeless moments," so that here at this moment in Little Gidding "while the light fails / On a winter afternoon, in a secluded chapel / History is now and England." The poet now sees the rose of life and the yew tree of death interpenetrating at each moment and ends with a vision of suffering and love, the fire and the rose, as one.

2. Eternal, everlasting.

3. On the Pentecost day after the death and resurrection of Christ, there appeared to His apostles "cloven tongues like as of fire * * * And they were all filled with the Holy Ghost" (Acts ii).

The soul's sap quivers. There is no earth smell
Or smell of living thing. This is the springtime
But not in time's covenant. Now the hedgerow
Is blanched for an hour with transitory blossom   15
Of snow, a bloom more sudden
Than that of summer, neither budding nor fading,
Not in the scheme of generation.
Where is the summer, the unimaginable
Zero summer?   20

            If you came this way,
Taking the route you would be likely to take
From the place you would be likely to come from,
If you came this way in may time, you would find the hedges
White again, in May, with voluptuary sweetness.   25
It would be the same at the end of the journey,
If you came at night like a broken king,[4]
If you came by day not knowing what you came for,
It would be the same, when you leave the rough road
And turn behind the pigsty to the dull façade   30
And the tombstone. And what you thought you came for
Is only a shell, a husk of meaning
From which the purpose breaks only when it is fulfilled
If at all. Either you had no purpose
Or the purpose is beyond the end you figured   35
And is altered in fulfillment. There are other places
Which also are the world's end, some at the sea jaws,
Or over a dark lake, in a desert or a city—
But this is the nearest, in place and time,
Now and in England.   40

            If you came this way,
Taking any route, starting from anywhere,
At any time or at any season,
It would always be the same: you would have to put off
Sense and notion. You are not here to verify,   45
Instruct yourself, or inform curiosity
Or carry report. You are here to kneel
Where prayer has been valid. And prayer is more
Than an order of words, the conscious occupation
Of the praying mind, or the sound of the voice praying. 50
And what the dead had no speech for, when living,
They can tell you, being dead: the communication
Of the dead is tongued with fire beyond the language of the living.
Here, the intersection of the timeless moment
Is England and nowhere. Never and always.   55

                    II

Ash on an old man's sleeve
Is all the ash the burnt roses leave.

4. I.e., Charles I. King Charles visited Ferrar's community more than once, and is said to have paid his last visit in secret after his final defeat in the Civil War.

Dust in the air suspended
Marks the place where a story ended.
Dust inbreathed was a house—   60
The wall, the wainscot, and the mouse.
The death of hope and despair,
        This is the death of air.[5]

There are flood and drouth
Over the eyes and in the mouth,   65
Dead water and dead sand
Contending for the upper hand.
The parched eviscerate soil
Gapes at the vanity of toil,
Laughs without mirth.   70
        This is the death of earth.

Water and fire succeed
The town, the pasture, and the weed.
Water and fire deride
The sacrifice that we denied.   75
Water and fire shall rot
The marred foundations we forgot,
Of sanctuary and choir.
        This is the death of water and fire.

In the uncertain hour before the morning   80
        Near the ending of interminable night
        At the recurrent end of the unending
After the dark dove with the flickering tongue
        Had passed below the horizon of his homing
        While the dead leaves still rattled on like tin   85
Over the asphalt where no other sound was
        Between three districts whence the smoke arose
        I met one walking, loitering and hurried
As if blown towards me like the metal leaves
        Before the urban dawn wind unresisting.   90
        And as I fixed upon the down-turned face
That pointed scrutiny with which we challenge
        The first-met stranger in the waning dusk
        I caught the sudden look of some dead master
Whom I had known, forgotten, half recalled   95
        Both one and many; in the brown baked features
        The eyes of a familiar compound ghost[6]
Both intimate and unidentifiable.

5. "The death of air," like that of "earth" and of "water and fire" in the succeeding stanzas, recalls the theory of the creative strife of the four elements propounded by Heraclitus (Greek philosopher of 4th and 5th centuries B.C.): "Fire lives in the death of air; air lives in the death of fire; water lives in the death of earth; and earth lives in the death of water." But at this point in the poem, unlike Heraclitus' theory, death is not intermingled with life.
6. Cf. Shakespeare, *Sonnet* LXXXVI, line 9: "that affable familiar ghost." W. B. Yeats is the "dead master" who is an important part of this "compound ghost."

So I assumed a double part,[7] and cried
And heard another's voice cry: "What! are *you* here?"   100
Although we were not. I was still the same,
  Knowing myself yet being someone other—
  And he a face still forming; yet the words sufficed
To compel the recognition they preceded.
  And so, compliant to the common wind,   105
  Too strange to each other for misunderstanding,
In concord at this intersection time
  Of meeting nowhere, no before and after,
  We trod the pavement in a dead patrol.
I said: "The wonder that I feel is easy,   110
  Yet ease is cause of wonder. Therefore speak:
  I may not comprehend, may not remember."
And he: "I am not eager to rehearse
  My thought and theory which you have forgotten.
  These things have served their purpose: let them be.   115
So with your own, and pray they be forgiven
  By others, as I pray you to forgive
  Both bad and good. Last season's fruit is eaten
And the fullfed beast shall kick the empty pail.
  For last year's words belong to last year's language   120
  And next year's words await another voice.
But, as the passage now presents no hindrance
  To the spirit unappeased and peregrine[8]
  Between two worlds become much like each other,
So I find words I never thought to speak   125
  In streets I never thought I should revisit
  When I left my body on a distant shore.
Since our concern was speech, and speech impelled us
  To purify the dialect of the tribe[9]
  And urge the mind to aftersight and foresight,   130
Let me disclose the gifts reserved for age
  To set a crown upon your lifetime's effort.
  First, the cold friction of expiring sense
Without enchantment, offering no promise
  But bitter tastelessness of shadow fruit   135
  As body and soul begin to fall asunder.
Second, the conscious impotence of rage
  At human folly, and the laceration
  Of laughter at what ceases to amuse.
And last, the rending pain of re-enactment   140
  Of all that you have done, and been; the shame
  Of motives late revealed, and the awareness
Of things ill done and done to others' harm

7. Two interpretations have been suggested: either the poet assumes the part of Dante as he accosted people in Hell or Purgatory, or else he assumes the part of his own other self.
8. Foreign, coming from abroad.
9. A rendering of the line *"Donner un sens plus pur aux mots de la tribu"* in Stéphane Mallarmé's sonnet *Le Tombeau d'Edgar Poe* ("The Tomb of Edgar Poe"). There are many less direct literary echoes in this passage, some recalling Milton, some various Jacobean dramatists, some Dante.

Which once you took for exercise of virtue.
Then fools' approval strings, and honor stains.   145
From wrong to wrong the exasperated spirit
   Proceeds, unless restored by that refining fire[1]
   Where you must move in measure, like a dancer."
The day was breaking. In the disfigured street
   He left me, with a kind of valediction,   150
   And faded on the blowing of the horn.[2]

III

There are three conditions which often look alike
Yet differ completely, flourish in the same hedgerow:
Attachment to self and to things and to persons, detachment
From self and from things and from persons; and, growing between
   them, indifference   155
Which resembles the others as death resembles life,
Being between two lives—unflowering, between
The live and the dead nettle. This is the use of memory:
For liberation—not less of love but expanding
Of love beyond desire, and so liberation   160
From the future as well as the past. Thus, love of a country
Begins as attachment to our own field of action
And comes to find that action of little importance
Though never indifferent. History may be servitude,
History may be freedom. See, now they vanish,   165
The faces and places, with the self which, as it could, loved them,
To become renewed, transfigured, in another pattern.

Sin is Behovely, but
All shall be well, and
All manner of things shall be well.[3]   170
If I think, again, of this place,
And of people, not wholly commendable,
Of no immediate kin or kindness,
But some of peculiar genius,
All touched by a common genius,   175
United in the strife which divided them;
If I think of a king at nightfall,[4]

1. Cf. *The Waste Land*, line 428 and its note.
2. Cf. *Hamlet*, I.ii.157. "It faded on the crowing of the cock." The horn is the All Clear signal after an air raid (the dialogue has taken place between the dropping of the last bomb and the sounding of the All Clear). Eliot called the section which ends with this line "the nearest equivalent to a canto of the *Inferno* or *Purgatorio*" that he could achieve, and spoke of his intention to present "a parallel, by means of contrast, between the *Inferno* and the *Purgatorio* * * * and a hallucinated scene after an air raid."
3. A quotation from the 14th-century English mystic, Dame Juliana of Norwich: "Sin is behovabil [inevitable], but all shall be well and all shall be

well and all manner of thing shall be well." It is the accent of genuine mystical experience and authority that Eliot wishes to convey in using Dame Juliana's words. The thought expressed—that in spite of sin or even through sin all shall be well—is a variation of the "fortunate fall" (*felix culpa*) idea found in Milton and elsewhere.
4. Charles I. He died "on the scaffold" in 1649, while his principal advisers, Archbishop Laud and Thomas Wentworth, Earl of Strafford, were both executed earlier by the victorious Parliamentary forces. Eliot is here meditating on the English Civil War and refusing to take sides, for history subsumes both sides. The war becomes a symbol of purgation through suffering. Cf. conclusion of this section.

Of three men, and more, on the scaffold
And a few who died forgotten
In other places, here and abroad,   180
And of one who died blind and quiet[4a]
Why should we celebrate
These dead men more than the dying?
It is not to ring the bell backward
Nor is it an incantation   185
To summon the specter of a Rose.
We cannot revive old factions
We cannot restore old policies
Or follow an antique drum.
These men, and those who opposed them   190
And those whom they opposed
Accept the constitution of silence
And are folded in a single party.
Whatever we inherit from the fortunate
We have taken from the defeated   195
What they had to leave us—a symbol:
A symbol perfected in death.
And all shall be well and
All manner of thing shall be well
By the purification of the motive   200
In the ground of our beseeching.

IV

The dove descending breaks the air
With flame of incandescent terror
Of which the tongues declare
The one discharge from sin and error.   205
The only hope, or else despair
    Lies in the choice of pyre or pyre—
    To be redeemed from fire by fire.

Who then devised the torment? Love.
Love is the unfamiliar Name   210
Behind the hands that wove
The intolerable shirt of flame[5]
Which human power cannot remove.
    We only live, only suspire
    Consumed by either fire or fire.   215

V

What we call the beginning is often the end
And to make an end is to make a beginning.
The end is where we start from. And every phrase
And sentence that is right (where every word is at home,
Taking its place to support the others,   220
The word neither diffident nor ostentatious,

4a. Milton.
5. Out of love for her husband Hercules, Deianira gave him the poisoned shirt of Nessus. She had been told that it would increase his love for her, but instead it so corroded his flesh that in his agony he mounted a funeral pyre and burned himself to death.

An easy commerce of the old and the new,
The common word exact without vulgarity,
The formal word precise but not pedantic,
The complete consort[6] dancing together)   225
Every phrase and every sentence is an end and a beginning,
Every poem an epitaph. And any action
Is a step to the block, to the fire, down the sea's throat
Or to an illegible stone: and that is where we start.
We die with the dying: 230
See, they depart, and we go with them.
We are born with the dead:
See, they return, and bring us with them.
The moment of the rose and the moment of the yew tree
Are of equal duration. A people without history   235
Is not redeemed from time, for history is a pattern
Of timeless moments. So, while the light fails
On a winter's afternoon, in a secluded chapel
History is now and England.
With the drawing of this Love and the voice of this Calling[7]   240

We shall not cease from exploration
And the end of all our exploring
Will be to arrive where we started
And know the place for the first time.
Through the unknown, remembered gate   245
When the last of earth left to discover
Is that which was the beginning;
At the source of the longest river
The voice of the hidden waterfall
And the children in the apple tree   250
Not known, because not looked for
But heard, half-heard, in the stillness
Between two waves of the sea.[8]
Quick now, here, now, always—
A condition of complete simplicity   255
(Costing not less than everything)
And all shall be well and
All manner of thing shall be well
When the tongues of flame are in-folded
Into the crowned knot of fire   260
And the fire and the rose are one.
1942   1942, 1943

6. The word means both "company" and "harmony of sounds."
7. This line is from an anonymous 14th-century mystical work, the *Cloud of Unknowing*.
8. The voice of the children in the apple tree symbolizes the sudden moment of insight. Cf. the conclusion to *Burnt Norton* (the first of the *Four Quartets*), where the laughter of the children in the garden has a like meaning: "Sudden in a shaft of sunlight / Even while the dust moves / There rises the hidden laughter / Of children in the foliage / Quick now, here, now, always * * * "

Tradition and the Individual Talent[1]

I

In English writing we seldom speak of tradition, though we occasionally apply its name in deploring its absence. We cannot refer to "the tradition" or to "a tradition"; at most, we employ the adjective in saying that the poetry of So-and-so is "traditional" or even "too traditional." Seldom, perhaps, does the word appear except in a phrase of censure. If otherwise, it is vaguely approbative, with the implication, as to the work approved, of some pleasing archaeological reconstruction. You can hardly make the word agreeable to English ears without this comfortable reference to the reassuring science of archaeology.

Certainly the word is not likely to appear in our appreciations of living or dead writers. Every nation, every race, has not only its own creative, but its own critical turn of mind; and is even more oblivious of the shortcomings and limitations of its critical habits than of those of its creative genius. We know, or think we know, from the enormous mass of critical writing that has appeared in the French language the critical method or habit of the French; we only conclude (we are such unconscious people) that the French are "more critical" than we, and sometimes even plume ourselves a little with the fact, as if the French were the less spontaneous. Perhaps they are; but we might remind ourselves that criticism is as inevitable as breathing, and that we should be none the worse for articulating what passes in our minds when we read a book and feel an emotion about it, for criticizing our own minds in their work of criticism. One of the facts that might come to light in this process is our tendency to insist, when we praise a poet, upon those aspects of his work in which he least resembles anyone else. In these aspects or parts of his work we pretend to find what is individual, what is the peculiar essence of the man. We dwell with satisfaction upon the poet's difference from his predecessors, especially his immediate predecessors; we endeavor to find something that can be isolated in order to be enjoyed. Whereas if we approach a poet without this prejudice we shall often find that not only the best, but the most individual parts of his work may be those in which the dead poets, his ancestors, assert their immortality most vigorously. And I do not mean the impressionable period of adolescence, but the period of full maturity.

Yet if the only form of tradition, of handing down, consisted in

1. First published in the *Egoist* (1919) and later collected in *The Sacred Wood* (1920), this essay is one of Eliot's most influential pieces of criticism.

following the ways of the immediate generation before us in a blind or timid adherence to its successes, "tradition" should positively be discouraged. We have seen many such simple currents soon lost in the sand; and novelty is better than repetition. Tradition is a matter of much wider significance. It cannot be inherited, and if you want it you must obtain it by great labor. It involves, in the first place, the historical sense, which we may call nearly indispensable to any one who would continue to be a poet beyond his twenty-fifth year; and the historical sense involves a perception, not only of the pastness of the past, but of its presence; the historical sense compels a man to write not merely with his own generation in his bones, but with a feeling that the whole of the literature of Europe from Homer and within it the whole of the literature of his own country has a simultaneous existence and composes a simultaneous order. This historical sense, which is a sense of the timeless as well as of the temporal and of the timeless and of the temporal together, is what makes a writer traditional. And it is at the same time what makes a writer most acutely conscious of his place in time, of his own contemporaneity.

No poet, no artist of any art, has his complete meaning alone. His significance, his appreciation is the appreciation of his relation to the dead poets and artists. You cannot value him alone; you must set him, for contrast and comparison, among the dead. I mean this as a principle of aesthetic, not merely historical, criticism. The necessity that he shall conform, that he shall cohere, is not one-sided; what happens when a new work of art is created is something that happens simultaneously to all the works of art which preceded it. The existing monuments form an ideal order among themselves, which is modified by the introduction of the new (the really new) work of art among them. The existing order is complete before the new work arrives; for order to persist after the supervention of novelty, the *whole* existing order must be, if ever so slightly, altered; and so the relations, proportions, values of each work of art toward the whole are readjusted; and this is conformity between the old and the new. Whoever has approved this idea of order, of the form of European, of English literature will not find it preposterous that the past should be altered by the present as much as the present is directed by the past. And the poet who is aware of this will be aware of great difficulties and responsibilities.

In a peculiar sense he will be aware also that he must inevitably be judged by the standards of the past. I say judged, not amputated, by them; not judged to be as good as, or worse or better than, the dead; and certainly not judged by the canons of dead critics. It is a judgment, a comparison, in which two things are measured by each other. To conform merely would be for the new work not really to conform at all; it would not be new, and would therefore not be a work of art. And we do not quite say that the new is more valuable because it fits in; but its fitting in is a test of its value—a test, it is true, which can only be slowly and cautiously applied, for we are none of us infallible judges of conformity. We say: it appears to conform, and is perhaps individual, or it appears individual, and may conform; but we are hardly likely to find that it is one and not the other.

To proceed to a more intelligible exposition of the relation of the poet to the past: he can neither take the past as a lump, an indiscriminate bolus,[2] nor can he form himself wholly on one or two private admirations, nor can he form himself wholly upon one preferred period. The first course is inadmissible, the second is an important experience of youth, and the third is a pleasant and highly desirable supplement. The poet must be very conscious of the main current, which does not at all flow invariably through the most distinguished reputations. He must be quite aware of the obvious fact that art never improves, but that the material of art is never quite the same. He must be aware that the mind of Europe—the mind of his own country—a mind which he learns in time to be much more important than his own private mind—is a mind which changes, and that this change is a development which abandons nothing en route, which does not superannuate either Shakespeare, or Homer, or the rock drawing of the Magdalenian[3] draftsmen. That this development, refinement perhaps, complication certainly, is not, from the point of view of the artist, any improvement. Perhaps not even an improvement from the point of view of the psychologist or not to the extent which we imagine; perhaps only in the end based upon a complication in economics and machinery. But the difference between the present and the past is that the conscious present is an awareness of the past in a way and to an extent which the past's awareness of itself cannot show.

Someone said: "The dead writers are remote from us because we *know* so much more than they did." Precisely, and they are that which we know.

I am alive to a usual objection to what is clearly part of my program for the métier of poetry. The objection is that the doctrine requires a ridiculous amount of erudition (pedantry), a claim which can be rejected by appeal to the lives of poets in any pantheon. It will even be affirmed that much learning deadens or perverts poetic sensibility. While, however, we persist in believing that a poet ought to know as much as will not encroach upon his necessary receptivity and necessary laziness, it is not desirable to confine knowledge to whatever can be put into a useful shape for examinations, drawing rooms, or the still more pretentious modes of pub-

2. A round mass of anything: a large pill.
3. The most advanced culture of the European Paleolithic period (from discoveries at La Madeleine, France).

licity. Some can absorb knowledge, the more tardy must sweat for it. Shakespeare acquired more essential history from Plutarch[4] than most men could from the whole British Museum. What is to be insisted upon is that the poet must develop or procure the consciousness of the past and that he should continue to develop this consciousness throughout his career.

What happens is a continual surrender of himself as he is at the moment to something which is more valuable. The progress of an artist is a continual self-sacrifice, a continual extinction of personality.

There remains to define this process of depersonalization and its relation to the sense of tradition. It is in this depersonalization that art may be said to approach the condition of science. I, therefore, invite you to consider, as a suggestive analogy, the action which takes place when a bit of finely filiated[5] platinum is introduced into a chamber containing oxygen and sulphur dioxide.

II

Honest criticism and sensitive appreciation are directed not upon the poet but upon the poetry. If we attend to the confused cries of the newspaper critics and the *susurrus*[6] of popular repetition that follows, we shall hear the names of poets in great numbers; if we seek not Blue-book[7] knowledge but the enjoyment of poetry, and ask for a poem, we shall seldom find it. I have tried to point out the importance of the relation of the poem to other poems by other authors, and suggested the conception of poetry as a living whole of all the poetry that has ever been written. The other aspect of this Impersonal theory of poetry is the relation of the poem to its author. And I hinted, by an analogy, that the mind of the mature poet differs from that of the immature one not precisely in any valuation of "personality," not being necessarily more interesting, or having "more to say," but rather by being a more finely perfected medium in which special, or very varied, feelings are at liberty to enter into new combinations.

The analogy was that of the catalyst.[8] When the two gases previously mentioned are mixed in the presence of a filament of platinum, they form sulphurous acid. This combination takes place only if the platinum is present; nevertheless the newly formed acid contains no trace of platinum, and the platinum itself is apparently unaffected; has remained inert, neutral, and unchanged. The mind of the poet is the shred of platinum. It may partly or exclusively operate upon the experience of the man himself; but, the more perfect the artist, the more completely separate in him will be the

4. Greek biographer (1st century A.D.) of Greek and Roman celebrities, from whose work Shakespeare drew the plots of his Roman plays.
5. Drawn out like a thread.
6. Murmuring, buzzing.

7. British official government publication.
8. Substance that triggers a chemical change without itself being affected by the reaction.

man who suffers and the mind which creates; the more perfectly will the mind digest and transmute the passions which are its material.

The experience, you will notice, the elements which enter the presence of the transforming catalyst, are of two kinds: emotions and feelings. The effect of a work of art upon the person who enjoys it is an experience different in kind from any experience not of art. It may be formed out of one emotion, or may be a combination of several; and various feelings, inhering for the writer in particular words or phrases or images, may be added to compose the final result. Or great poetry may be made without the direct use of any emotion whatever: composed out of feelings solely. Canto XV of the *Inferno* (Brunetto Latini)[9] is a working up of the emotion evident in the situation; but the effect, though single as that of any work of art, is obtained by considerable complexity of detail. The last quatrain gives an image, a feeling attaching to an image, which "came," which did not develop simply out of what precedes, but which was probably in suspension in the poet's mind until the proper combination arrived for it to add itself to.[1] The poet's mind is in fact a receptacle for seizing and storing up numberless feelings, phrases, images, which remain there until all the particles which can unite to form a new compound are present together.

If you compare several representative passages of the greatest poetry you see how great is the variety of types of combination, and also how completely any semi-ethical criterion of "sublimity" misses the mark. For it is not the "greatness," the intensity, of the emotions, the components, but the intensity of the artistic process, the pressure, so to speak, under which the fusion takes place, that counts. The episode of Paolo and Francesca[2] employs a definite emotion, but the intensity of the poetry is something quite different from whatever intensity in the supposed experience it may give the impression of. It is no more intense, furthermore, than Canto XXVI,[3] the voyage of Ulysses, which has not the direct dependence upon an emotion. Great variety is possible in the process of transmutation of emotion: the murder of Agamemnon,[4] or the agony of Othello, gives an artistic effect apparently closer to a possible

9. Dante meets in Hell his old master Brunetto Latini, suffering eternal punishment for unnatural lust, yet still loved and admired by Dante, who addresses him with affectionate courtesy. It is one of the most moving passages in the *Inferno.*
1. Dante's strange interview with Brunetto is over, and Brunetto moves off to continue his punishment: "Then he turned round, and seemed like one of those / Who run for the green cloth [in the footrace] at Verona / In the field; and he seemed among them / Not the loser but the winner."
2. Illicit lovers whom Dante meets in the second circle of Hell (*Inferno* V) and at whose punishment and sorrows he swoons with pity.
3. Of the *Inferno.* Ulysses, suffering in Hell for "false counseling," tells Dante of his final voyage.
4. By his wife Clytemnestra; the central action of Aeschylus' play *Agamemnon.*

original than the scenes from Dante. In the *Agamemnon*, the artistic emotion approximates to the emotion of an actual spectator; in *Othello* to the emotion of the protagonist himself. But the difference between art and the event is always absolute; the combination which is the murder of Agamemnon is probably as complex as that which is the voyage of Ulysses. In either case there has been a fusion of elements. The ode of Keats contains a number of feelings which have nothing particular to do with the nightingale, but which the nightingale, partly, perhaps, because of its attractive name, and partly because of its reputation, served to bring together.

The point of view which I am struggling to attack is perhaps related to the metaphysical theory of the substantial unity of the soul: for my meaning is, that the poet has, not a "personality" to express, but a particular medium, which is only a medium and not a personality, in which impressions and experiences combine in peculiar and unexpected ways. Impressions and experiences which are important for the man may take no place in the poetry, and those which become important in the poetry may play quite a negligible part in the man, the personality.

I will quote a passage which is unfamiliar enough to be regarded with fresh attention in the light—or darkness—of these observations:

> And now methinks I could e'en chide myself
> For doting on her beauty, though her death
> Shall be revenged after no common action.
> Does the silkworm expend her yellow labors
> For thee? For thee does she undo herself?
> Are lordships sold to maintain ladyships
> For the poor benefit of a bewildering minute?
> Why does yon fellow falsify highways,
> And put his life between the judge's lips,
> To refine such a thing—keeps horse and men
> To beat their valors for her? . . .[5]

In this passage (as is evident if it is taken in its context) there is a combination of positive and negative emotions: an intensely strong attraction toward beauty and an equally intense fascination by the ugliness which is contrasted with it and which destroys it. This balance of contrasted emotion is in the dramatic situation to which the speech is pertinent, but that situation alone is inadequate to it. This is, so to speak, the structural emotion, provided by the drama. But the whole effect, the dominant tone, is due to the fact that a number of floating feelings, having an affinity to this emotion by no means superficially evident, have combined with it to give us a new art emotion.

It is not in his personal emotions, the emotions provoked by par-

5. From Cyril Tourneur's *The Revenger's Tragedy* (1607), III.iv.

ticular events in his life, that the poet is in any way remarkable or interesting. His particular emotions may be simple, or crude, or flat. The emotion in his poetry will be a very complex thing, but not with the complexity of the emotions of people who have very complex or unusual emotions in life. One error, in fact, of eccentricity in poetry is to seek for new human emotions to express; and in this search for novelty in the wrong place it discovers the perverse. The business of the poet is not to find new emotions, but to use the ordinary ones and, in working them up into poetry, to express feelings which are not in actual emotions at all. And emotions which he has never experienced will serve his turn as well as those familiar to him. Consequently, we must believe that "emotion recollected in tranquility"[6] is an inexact formula. For it is neither emotion, nor recollection, nor, without distortion of meaning, tranquility. It is a concentration, and a new thing resulting from the concentration, of a very great number of experiences which to the practical and active person would not seem to be experiences at all; it is a concentration which does not happen consciously or of deliberation. These experiences are not "recollected," and they finally unite in an atmosphere which is "tranquil" only in that it is a passive attending upon the event. Of course this is not quite the whole story. There is a great deal, in the writing of poetry, which must be conscious and deliberate. In fact, the bad poet is usually unconscious where he ought to be conscious, and conscious where he ought to be unconscious. Both errors tend to make him "personal." Poetry is not a turning loose of emotion, but an escape from emotion; it is not the expression of personality, but an escape from personality. But, of course, only those who have personality and emotions know what it means to want to escape from these things.

III

ὁ δὲ νοῦς ἴσως θειότερόν τι χαὶ ἀπαθές ἐστιν.[7]

This essay proposes to halt at the frontier of metaphysics or mysticism, and confine itself to such practical conclusions as can be applied by the responsible person interested in poetry. To divert interest from the poet to the poetry is a laudable aim: for it would conduce to a juster estimation of actual poetry, good and bad. There are many people who appreciate the expression of sincere emotion in verse, and there is a smaller number of people who can appreciate technical excellence. But very few know when there is an expression of *significant* emotion, emotion which has its life in the poem and not in the history of the poet. The emotion of art is impersonal. And the poet cannot reach this impersonality with-

6. Wordsworth, Preface to *Lyrical Ballads*, 2nd edition (1800). Wordsworth said that poetry "takes its origin from emotion recollected in tranquility."

7. "The mind is doubtless something more divine and unimpressionable." Aristotle, *De Anima* ("On the Soul"), I.4.

out surrendering himself wholly to the work to be done. And he is not likely to know what is to be done unless he lives in what is not merely the present, but the present moment of the past, unless he is conscious, not of what is dead, but of what is already living.

1919, 1920

The Metaphysical Poets

By collecting these poems[1] from the work of a generation more often named than read, and more often read than profitably studied, Professor Grierson has rendered a service of some importance. Certainly the reader will meet with many poems already preserved in other anthologies, at the same time that he discovers poems such as those of Aurelian Townshend or Lord Herbert of Cherbury here included. But the function of such an anthology as this is neither that of Professor Saintsbury's admirable edition of Caroline poets nor that of the *Oxford Book of English Verse*. Mr. Grierson's book is in itself a piece of criticism and a provocation of criticism; and we think that he was right in including so many poems of Donne, elsewhere (though not in many editions) accessible, as documents in the case of "metaphysical poetry." The phrase has long done duty as a term of abuse or as the label of a quaint and pleasant taste. The question is to what extent the so-called metaphysicals formed a school (in our own time we should say a "movement"), and how far this so-called school or movement is a digression from the main current.

Not only is it extremely difficult to define metaphysical poetry, but difficult to decide what poets practice it and in which of their verses. The poetry of Donne (to whom Marvell and Bishop King are sometimes nearer than any of the other authors) is late Elizabethan, its feeling often very close to that of Chapman. The "courtly" poetry is derivative from Jonson, who borrowed liberally from the Latin; it expires in the next century with the sentiment and witticism of Prior. There is finally the devotional verse of Herbert, Vaughan, and Crashaw (echoed long after by Christina Rossetti and Francis Thompson); Crashaw, sometimes more profound and less sectarian than the others, has a quality which returns through the Elizabethan period to the early Italians. It is difficult to find any precise use of metaphor, simile, or other conceit, which is common to all the poets and at the same time important enough as an element of style to isolate these poets as a group. Donne, and

1. *Metaphysical Lyrics and Poems of the Seventeenth Century:* Donne to Butler. Selected and edited, with an Essay, by Herbert J. C. Grierson (1921). Eliot's essay was originally a review of this book in the London *Times Literary Supplement*.

often Cowley, employ a device which is sometimes considered characteristically "metaphysical"; the elaboration (contrasted with the condensation) of a figure of speech to the farthest stage to which ingenuity can carry it. Thus Cowley develops the commonplace comparison of the world to a chessboard through long stanzas (*To Destiny*), and Donne, with more grace, in *A Valediction*,[2] the comparison of two lovers to a pair of compasses. But elsewhere we find, instead of the mere explication of the content of a comparison, a development by rapid association of thought which requires considerable agility on the part of the reader.

> On a round ball
> A workman that hath copies by, can lay
> An Europe, Afrique, and an Asia,
> And quickly make that which was nothing, all;
> > So doth each tear,
> > Which thee doth wear,
> A globe, yea world, by that impression grow,
> Till thy tears mixed with mine do overflow
> This world; by waters sent from thee, my heaven dissolvéd so.[3]

Here we find at least two connections which are not implicit in the first figure, but are forced upon it by the poet: from the geographer's globe to the tear, and the tear to the deluge. On the other hand, some of Donne's most successful and characteristic effects are secured by brief words and sudden contrasts:

> A bracelet of bright hair about the bone,[4]

where the most powerful effect is produced by the sudden contrast of associations of "bright hair" and of "bone." This telescoping of images and multiplied associations is characteristic of the phrase of some of the dramatists of the period which Donne knew: not to mention Shakespeare, it is frequent in Middleton, Webster, and Tourneur, and is one of the sources of the vitality of their language.

Johnson, who employed the term "metaphysical poets," apparently having Donne, Cleveland, and Cowley chiefly in mind, remarks of them that "the most heterogeneous ideas are yoked by violence together."[5] The force of this impeachment lies in the failure of the conjunction, the fact that often the ideas are yoked but not united; and if we are to judge of styles of poetry by their abuse, enough examples may be found in Cleveland to justify Johnson's condemnation. But a degree of heterogeneity of material compelled into unity by the operation of the poet's mind is omnipresent in poetry. We need not select for illustration such a line as:

---

2. I.e., *A Valediction: Forbidding Mourning.*
3. Donne's *A Valediction: Of Weeping*, lines 10–18.
4. *The Relique*, line 6.
5. See Samuel Johnson's *Life of Cowley.*

Notre âme est un trois-mâts cherchant son Icarie;[6]

we may find it in some of the best lines of Johnson himself (*The Vanity of Human Wishes*):

> His fate was destined to a barren strand,
> A petty fortress, and a dubious hand;
> He left a name at which the world grew pale,
> To point a moral, or adorn a tale.

where the effect is due to a contrast of ideas, different in degree but the same in principle, as that which Johnson mildly reprehended. And in one of the finest poems of the age (a poem which could not have been written in any other age), the *Exequy* of Bishop King, the extended comparison is used with perfect success: the idea and the simile become one, in the passage in which the Bishop illustrates his impatience to see his dead wife, under the figure of a journey:

> Stay for me there; I will not fail
> To meet thee in that hollow Vale.
> And think not much of my delay;
> I am already on the way,
> And follow thee with all the speed
> Desire can make, or sorrows breed.
> Each minute is a short degree,
> And ev'ry hour a step towards thee.
> At night when I betake to rest,
> Next morn I rise nearer my West
> Of life, almost by eight hours sail,
> Than when sleep breathed his drowsy gale. . . .
> But hark! My pulse, like a soft drum
> Beats my approach, tells Thee I come;
> And slow howe'er my marches be,
> I shall at last sit down by Thee.

(In the last few lines there is that effect of terror which is several times attained by one of Bishop King's admirers, Edgar Poe.) Again, we may justly take these quatrains from Lord Herbert's Ode,[7] stanzas which would, we think, be immediately pronounced to be of the metaphysical school:

> So when from hence we shall be gone,
> And be no more, nor you, nor I,
> As one another's mystery,
> Each shall be both, yet both but one.

---

6. "Our soul is a three-masted ship searching for her Icarie"; a line from Charles Baudelaire's poem, *Le Voyage* (Icarie is an imaginary utopia in *Voyage en Icarie*, 1840, a novel by the French socialist Etienne Cabet).

7. Lord Herbert of Cherbury (1583–1648), brother of George Herbert. The "Ode" is his *Ode upon a Question moved, whether Love should continue forever?*

> This said, in her uplifted face,
>   Her eyes, which did that beauty crown,
>   Were like two stars, that having faln down,
> Look up again to find their place:
>
> While such a moveless silent peace
>   Did seize on their becalméd sense,
>   One would have thought some influence
> Their ravished spirits did possess.

There is nothing in these lines (with the possible exception of the stars, a simile not at once grasped, but lovely and justified) which fits Johnson's general observations on the metaphysical poets in his essay on Cowley. A good deal resides in the richness of association which is at the same time borrowed from and given to the word "becalmed"; but the meaning is clear, the language simple and elegant. It is to be observed that the language of these poets is as a rule simple and pure; in the verse of George Herbert this simplicity is carried as far as it can go—a simplicity emulated without success by numerous modern poets. The *structure* of the sentences, on the other hand, is sometimes far from simple, but this is not a vice; it is a fidelity to thought and feeling. The effect, at its best, is far less artificial than that of an ode by Gray. And as this fidelity induces variety of thought and feeling, so it induces variety of music. We doubt whether, in the eighteenth century, could be found two poems in nominally the same meter, so dissimilar as Marvell's *Coy Mistress* and Crashaw's *Saint Teresa*; the one producing an effect of great speed by the use of short syllables, and the other an ecclesiastical solemnity by the use of long ones:

> Love, thou art absolute sole lord
>   Of life and death.

If so shrewd and sensitive (though so limited) a critic as Johnson failed to define metaphysical poetry by its faults, it is worth while to inquire whether we may not have more success by adopting the opposite method: by assuming that the poets of the seventeenth century (up to the Revolution[8]) were the direct and normal development of the precedent age; and, without prejudicing their case by the adjective "metaphysical," consider whether their virtue was not something permanently valuable, which subsequently disappeared, but ought not to have disappeared. Johnson has hit, perhaps by accident, on one of their peculiarities, when he observes that "their attempts were always analytic"; he would not agree that, after the dissociation, they put the material together again in a new unity.

It is certain that the dramatic verse of the later Elizabethan and early Jacobean poets expresses a degree of development of sensibil-

8. Of 1688; when James II was replaced by William and Mary.

ity which is not found in any of the prose, good as it often is. If
we except Marlowe, a man of prodigious intelligence, these dramatists were directly or indirectly (it is at least a tenable theory)
affected by Montaigne. Even if we except also Jonson and Chapman, these two were probably erudite, and were notably men who
incorporated their erudition into their sensibility: their mode of
feeling was directly and freshly altered by their reading and thought.
In Chapman especially there is a direct sensuous apprehension of
thought, or a recreation of thought into feeling, which is exactly
what we find in Donne:

> in this one thing, all the discipline
> Of manners and of manhood is contained;
> A man to join himself with th' Universe
> In his main sway, and make in all things fit
> One with that All, and go on, round as it;
> Not plucking from the whole his wretched part,
> And into straits, or into nought revert,
> Wishing the complete Universe might be
> Subject to such a rag of it as he;
> But to consider great Necessity.[9]

We compare this with some modern passage:

> No, when the fight begins within himself,
> A man's worth something. God stoops o'er his head,
> Satan looks up between his feet—both tug—
> He's left, himself, i' the middle; the soul wakes
> And grows. Prolong that battle through his life![1]

It is perhaps somewhat less fair, though very tempting (as both
poets are concerned with the perpetuation of love by offspring),
to compare with the stanzas already quoted from Lord Herbert's
Ode the following from Tennyson:

> One walked between his wife and child,
> With measured footfall firm and mild,
> And now and then he gravely smiled.
> The prudent partner of his blood
> Leaned on him, faithful, gentle, good,
> Wearing the rose of womanhood.
> And in their double love secure,
> The little maiden walked demure,
> Pacing with downward eyelids pure.
> These three made unity so sweet,
> My frozen heart began to beat,
> Remembering its ancient heat.[2]

9. From *The Revenge of Bussy d'Am-
bois* (IV.i.137–46).
1. Robert Browning's *Bishop Blou-
gram's Apology*, lines 693–97.
2. Tennyson's *The Two Voices*, lines
412–23.

The difference is not a simple difference of degree between poets. It is something which had happened to the mind of England between the time of Donne or Lord Herbert of Cherbury and the time of Tennyson and Browning; it is the difference between the intellectual poet and the reflective poet. Tennyson and Browning are poets, and they think; but they do not feel their thought as immediately as the odor of a rose. A thought to Donne was an experience; it modified his sensibility. When a poet's mind is perfectly equipped for its work, it is constantly amalgamating disparate experience; the ordinary man's experience is chaotic, irregular, fragmentary. The latter falls in love, or reads Spinoza, and these two experiences have nothing to do with each other, or with the noise of the typewriter or the smell of cooking; in the mind of the poet these experiences are always forming new wholes.

We may express the difference by the following theory: The poets of the seventeenth century, the successors of the dramatists of the sixteenth, possessed a mechanism of sensibility which could devour any kind of experience. They are simple, artificial, difficult, or fantastic, as their predecessors were; no less nor more than Dante, Guido Cavalcanti, Guinicelli, or Cino.[3] In the seventeenth century a dissociation of sensibility set in, from which we have never recovered; and this dissociation, as is natural, was aggravated by the influence of the two most powerful poets of the century, Milton and Dryden. Each of these men performed certain poetic functions so magnificently well that the magnitude of the effect concealed the absence of others. The language went on and in some respects improved; the best verse of Collins, Gray, Johnson, and even Goldsmith satisfies some of our fastidious demands better than that of Donne or Marvell or King. But while the language became more refined, the feeling became more crude. The feeling, the sensibility, expressed in the *Country Churchyard* (to say nothing of Tennyson and Browning) is cruder than that in the *Coy Mistress*.

The second effect of the influence of Milton and Dryden followed from the first, and was therefore slow in manifestation. The sentimental age began early in the eighteenth century, and continued. The poets revolted against the ratiocinative, the descriptive; they thought and felt by fits, unbalanced; they reflected. In one or two passages of Shelley's *Triumph of Life*, in the second *Hyperion*, there are traces of a struggle toward unification of sensibility. But Keats and Shelley died, and Tennyson and Browning ruminated.

After this brief exposition of a theory—too brief, perhaps, to

3. These last three poets, all of whom lived in the 13th century, were members of the Tuscan school of lyric love poets (Guido Guinicelli was hailed by Dante in the *Purgatorio* as "father of Italian poets"; Cino da Pistoia was a friend of Dante and Petrarch).

carry conviction—we may ask, what would have been the fate of the "metaphysical" had the current of poetry descended in a direct line from them, as it descended in a direct line to them? They would not, certainly, be classified as metaphysical. The possible interests of a poet are unlimited; the more intelligent he is the better; the more intelligent he is the more likely that he will have interests: our only condition is that he turn them into poetry, and not merely meditate on them poetically. A philosophical theory which has entered into poetry is established, for its truth or falsity in one sense ceases to matter, and its truth in another sense is proved. The poets in question have, like other poets, various faults. But they were, at best, engaged in the task of trying to find the verbal equivalent for states of mind and feeling. And this means both that they are more mature, and that they wear better, than later poets of certainly not less literary ability.

It is not a permanent necessity that poets should be interested in philosophy, or in any other subject. We can only say that it appears likely that poets in our civilization, as it exists at present, must be *difficult*. Our civilization comprehends great variety and complexity, and this variety and complexity, playing upon a refined sensibility, must produce various and complex results. The poet must become more and more comprehensive, more allusive, more indirect, in order to force, to dislocate if necessary, language into his meaning. (A brilliant and extreme statement of this view, with which it is not requisite to associate oneself, is that of M. Jean Epstein, *La Poésie d'aujourd'hui*.[4]) Hence we get something which looks very much like the conceit—we get, in fact, a method curiously similar to that of the "metaphysical poets," similar also in its use of obscure words and of simple phrasing.

> O géraniums diaphanes, guerroyeurs sortilèges,
> Sacrilèges monomanes!
> Emballages, dévergondages, douches! O pressoirs
> Des vendanges des grands soirs!
> Layettes aux abois,
> Thyrses au fond des bois!
> Transfusions, représailles,
> Relevailles, compresses et l'éternal potion,
> Angélus! n'en pouvoir plus
> De débâcles nuptiales! de débâcles nuptiales![5]

4. "Poetry of Today."
5. "O transparent geraniums, warrior incantations, / Monomaniac sacrileges! / Packing materials, shamelessnesses, shower baths! O wine presses / Of great evening vintages! / Hard-pressed baby linen, / Thyrsis in the depths of the woods! / Transfusions, reprisals, / Churchings, compresses, and the eternal potion, / Angelus! no longer to be borne [are] / Catastrophic marriages! catastrophic marriages!" This passage is from *Derniers vers X* ("Last Poems," 1890), by Jules Laforgue (1860–87). Eliot oddly sees a similarity between this kind of hysterical free association and the strictly ordered imagery of the metaphysicals. But it is the combination of "obscure words and simple phrasing" that strikes him in both.

The same poet could write also simply:

> *Elle est bien loin, elle pleure,*
> *Le grand vent se lamente aussi . . .*[6]

Jules Laforgue, and Tristan Corbière[7] in many of his poems, are nearer to the "school of Donne" than any modern English poet. But poets more classical than they have the same essential quality of transmuting ideas into sensations, of transforming an observation into a state of mind.

> *Pour l'enfant, amoureux de cartes et d'estampes,*
> *L'univers est égal à son vaste appétit.*
> *Ah, que le monde est grand à la clarté des lampes!*
> *Aux yeux du souvenir que le monde est petit!*[8]

In French literature the great master of the seventeenth century —Racine—and the great master of the nineteenth—Baudelaire— are in some ways more like each other than they are like any one else. The greatest two masters of diction are also the greatest two psychologists, the most curious explorers of the soul. It is interesting to speculate whether it is not a misfortune that two of the greatest masters of diction in our language, Milton and Dryden, triumph with a dazzling disregard of the soul. If we continued to produce Miltons and Drydens it might not so much matter, but as things are it is a pity that English poetry has remained so incomplete. Those who object to the "artificiality" of Milton or Dryden sometimes tell us to "look into our hearts and write." But that is not looking deep enough; Racine or Donne looked into a good deal more than the heart. One must look into the cerebral cortex, the nervous system, and the digestive tracts.

May we not conclude, then, that Donne, Crashaw, Vaughan, Herbert and Lord Herbert, Marvell, King, Cowley at his best, are in the direct current of English poetry, and that their faults should be reprimanded by this standard rather than coddled by antiquarian affection? They have been enough praised in terms which are implicit limitations because they are "metaphysical" or "witty," "quaint" or "obscure," though at their best they have not these attributes more than other serious poets. On the other hand, we must not reject the criticism of Johnson (a dangerous person to disagree with) without having mastered it, without having assimilated the Johnsonian canons of taste. In reading the celebrated passage in his essay on Cowley we must remember that by wit he clearly means something more serious than we usually mean today;

6. "She is far away, she weeps, / The great wind mourns also." From *Derniers vers XI, Sur une défunte* ("On a Dead Woman").
7. 1845–75; also a French Symbolist poet.

8. From Baudelaire's *Le Voyage:* "For the child, in love with maps and prints, / The universe matches his vast appetite. / Ah, how big the world is by lamplight! How small the world is to the eyes of memory!"

in his criticism of their versification we must remember in what a narrow discipline he was trained, but also how well trained; we must remember that Johnson tortures chiefly the chief offenders, Cowley and Cleveland. It would be a fruitful work, and one requiring a substantial book, to break up the classification of Johnson (for there has been none since) and exhibit these poets in all their difference of kind and of degree, from the massive music of Donne to the faint, pleasing tinkle of Aurelian Townshend—whose *Dialogue Between a Pilgrim and Time* is one of the few regrettable omissions from the excellent anthology of Professor Grierson.

1921

Ulysses, Order, and Myth

Mr. Joyce's book has been out long enough for no more general expression of praise, or expostulation with its detractors, to be necessary; and it has not been out long enough for any attempt at a complete measurement of its place and significance to be possible. All that one can usefully do at this time, and it is a great deal to do, for such a book, is to elucidate any aspect of the book—and the number of aspects is indefinite—which has not yet been fixed. I hold this book to be the most important expression which the present age has found; it is a book to which we are all indebted, and from which none of us can escape. These are postulates for anything that I have to say about it, and I have no wish to waste the reader's time by elaborating my eulogies; it has given me all the surprise, delight, and terror that I can require, and I will leave it at that.

Amongst all the criticisms I have seen of the book, I have seen nothing—unless we except, in its way, M. Valéry Larbaud's[1] valuable paper which is rather an Introduction than a criticism—which seemed to me to appreciate the significance of the method employed—the parallel to the Odyssey, and the use of appropriate styles and symbols to each division. Yet one might expect this to be the first peculiarity to attract attention; but it has been treated as an amusing dodge, or scaffolding erected by the author for the purpose of disposing his realistic tale, of no interest in the completed structure. The criticism which Mr. Aldington[2] directed upon *Ulysses* several years ago seems to me to fail by this oversight—but, as Mr. Aldington wrote before the complete work had appeared, fails more honorably than the attempts of those who had the whole book before them. Mr. Aldington treated Mr. Joyce as a

1. French writer (1881–1957) important in the modern movement, translator of *Ulysses*.   2. Richard Aldington (1892–   ), English poet, novelist, and critic.

prophet of chaos; and wailed at the flood of Dadaism [3] which his prescient eye saw bursting forth at the tap of the magician's rod. Of course, the influence which Mr. Joyce's book may have is from my point of view an irrelevance. A very great book may have a very bad influence indeed; and a mediocre book may be in the event most salutary. The next generation is responsible for its own soul; a man of genius is responsible to his peers, not to a studio-full of uneducated and undisciplined coxcombs. Still, Mr. Aldington's apathetic solicitude for the half-witted seems to me to carry implications about the nature of the book itself to which I cannot assent; and this is the important issue. He finds the book, if I understand him, to be an invitation to chaos, and an expression of feelings which are perverse, partial, and a distortion of reality. But unless I quote Mr. Aldington's words I am likely to falsify. "I say, moreover," he says,[4] "that when Mr. Joyce, with his marvelous gifts, uses them to disgust us with mankind, he is doing something which is false and a libel on humanity." It is somewhat similar to the opinion of the urbane Thackeray upon Swift. "As for the moral, I think it horrible, shameful, unmanly, blasphemous; and giant and great as this Dean is, I say we should hoot him." (This, of the conclusion of the Voyage to the Houyhnhnms—which seems to me one of the greatest triumphs that the human soul has ever achieved.)—It is true that Thackeray later pays Swift one of the finest tributes that a man has ever given or received: "So great a man he seems to me that thinking of him is like thinking of an empire falling." (And Mr. Aldington, in his time, is almost equally generous.)

Whether it is possible to libel humanity (in distinction to libel in the usual sense, which is libeling an individual or a group in contrast with the rest of humanity) is a question for philosophical societies to discuss; but of course if *Ulysses* were a "libel" it would simply be a forged document, a powerless fraud, which would never have extracted from Mr. Aldington a moment's attention. I do not wish to linger over this point: the interesting question is that begged by Mr. Aldington when he refers to Mr. Joyce's "great *undisciplined* talent."

I think that Mr. Aldington and I are more or less agreed as to what we want in principle, and agreed to call it classicism. It is because of this agreement that I have chosen Mr. Aldington to attack on the present issue. We are agreed as to what we want, but not as to how to get it, or as to what contemporary writing exhibits

3. Dadaism, founded in Zurich, Switzerland, during World War I, aimed at showing contempt for all traditional aesthetic and moral values and bourgeois institutions by random, illogical, spontaneous reflection (both in literature and in the visual arts) of the casual happenings of experience. The language was often deliberately infantile. Surrealism developed from one wing of the Dadaist movement.
4. *English Review*, April, 1921 [Eliot's note].

a tendency in that direction. We agree, I hope, that "classicism" is not an alternative to "romanticism," as of political parties, Conservative and Liberal, Republican and Democrat, on a "turn-the-rascals-out" platform. It is a goal toward which all good literature strives, so far as it is good, according to the possibilities of its place and time. One can be "classical," in a sense, by turning away from nine-tenths of the material which lies at hand, and selecting only mummified stuff from a museum—like some contemporary writers, about whom one could say some nasty things in this connection, if it were worth while (Mr. Aldington is not one of them). Or one can be classical in tendency by doing the best one can with the material at hand. The confusion springs from the fact that the term is applied to literature and to the whole complex of interests and modes of behavior and society of which literature is a part; and it has not the same bearing in both applications. It is much easier to be a classicist in literary criticism than in creative art—because in criticism you are responsible only for what you want, and in creation you are responsible for what you can do with material which you must simply accept. And in this material I include the emotions and feelings of the writer himself, which, for that writer, are simply material which he must accept—not virtues to be enlarged or vices to be diminished. The question, then, about Mr. Joyce, is: how much living material does he deal with, and how does he deal with it: deal with, not as a legislator or exhorter, but as an artist?

It is here that Mr. Joyce's parallel use of the Odyssey has a great importance. It has the importance of a scientific discovery. No one else has built a novel upon such a foundation before: it has never before been necessary. I am not begging the question in calling *Ulysses* a "novel"; and if you call it an epic it will not matter. If it is not a novel, that is simply because the novel is a form which will no longer serve; it is because the novel, instead of being a form, was simply the expression of an age which had not sufficiently lost all form to feel the need of something stricter. Mr. Joyce has written one novel—*The Portrait*; Mr. Wyndham Lewis has written one novel—*Tarr* [5]. I do not suppose that either of them will ever write another "novel." The novel ended with Flaubert and with James. It is, I think, because Mr. Joyce and Mr. Lewis, being "in advance" of their time, felt a conscious or probably unconscious dissatisfaction with the form, that their novels are more formless than those of a dozen clever writers who

5. First novel (1918) of Percy Wyndham Lewis (1884–1957), English novelist, poet, critic, painter, who denounced his contemporaries' interest in the flux of time and the stream of consciousness and advocated "conceptual quality, hard exact outline, grand architectural propor- tion." A strong satirical novel, *Tarr* is in a way the antithesis of *Ulysses* in its rejection of interior monologue and of submergence in the drift of time and consciousness. Edwin Muir once called Lewis "the hair of the dog that bit Lawrence and Joyce."

are unaware of its obsolescence.

In using the myth, in manipulating a continuous parallel between contemporaneity and antiquity, Mr. Joyce is pursuing a method which others must pursue after him. They will not be imitators, any more than the scientist who uses the discoveries of an Einstein in pursuing his own, independent, further investigations. It is simply a way of controlling, of ordering, of giving a shape and a significance to the immense panorama of futility and anarchy which is contemporary history. It is a method already adumbrated by Mr. Yeats, and of the need for which I believe Mr. Yeats to have been the first contemporary to be conscious. It is a method for which the horoscope is auspicious. Psychology (such as it is, and whether our reaction to it be comic or serious), ethnology, and *The Golden Bough* have concurred to make possible what was impossible even a few years ago. Instead of narrative method, we may now use the mythical method. It is, I seriously believe, a step toward making the modern world possible for art, toward that order and form which Mr. Aldington so earnestly desires. And only those who have won their own discipline in secret and without aid, in a world which offers very little assistance to that end, can be of any use in furthering this advance.

1923, 1948

Yeats[1]

The generations of poetry in our age seem to cover a span of about twenty years. I do not mean that the best work of any poet is limited to twenty years: I mean that it is about that length of time before a new school or style of poetry appears. By the time, that is to say, that a man is fifty, he has behind him a kind of poetry written by men of seventy, and before him another kind written by men of thirty. That is my position at present, and if I live another twenty years I shall expect to see still another younger school of poetry. One's relation to Yeats, however, does not fit into this scheme. When I was a young man at the university, in America, just beginning to write verse, Yeats was already a considerable figure in the world of poetry, and his early period was well defined. I cannot remember that his poetry at that stage made any deep impression upon me. A very young man, who is himself stirred to write, is not primarily critical or even widely appreciative. He is looking for masters who will elicit his consciousness of what he wants to say himself, of the kind of poetry that is in him to write. The taste of an adolescent writer is intense, but narrow: it is determined by personal needs. The kind of poetry that I needed, to teach me the use

1. The first annual Yeats Lecture, delivered to the Friends of the Irish Academy at the Abbey Theatre, Dublin, in 1940.

of my own voice, did not exist in English at all; it was only to be found in French. For this reason the poetry of the young Yeats hardly existed for me until after my enthusiasm had been won by the poetry of the older Yeats; and by that time—I mean, from 1919 on—my own course of evolution was already determined. Hence, I find myself regarding him, from one point of view, as a contemporary and not a predecessor; and from another point of view, I can share the feelings of younger men, who came to know and admire him by that work from 1919 on, which was produced while they were adolescent.

Certainly, for the younger poets of England and America, I am sure that their admiration for Yeats's poetry has been wholly good. His idiom was too different for there to be any danger of imitation, his opinions too different to flatter and confirm their prejudices. It was good for them to have the spectacle of an unquestionably great living poet, whose style they were not tempted to echo and whose ideas opposed those in vogue among them. You will not see, in their writing, more than passing evidences of the impression he made, but the work, and the man himself as poet, have been of the greatest significance to them for all that. This may seem to contradict what I have been saying about the kind of poetry that a young poet chooses to admire. But I am really talking about something different. Yeats would not have this influence had he not become a great poet; but the influence of which I speak is due to the figure of the poet himself, to the integrity of his passion for his art and his craft which provided such an impulse for his extraordinary development. When he visited London he liked to meet and talk to younger poets. People have sometimes spoken of him as arrogant and overbearing. I never found him so; in his conversations with a younger writer I always felt that he offered terms of equality, as to a fellow worker, a practitioner of the same mistery.[2] It was, I think, that, unlike many writers, he cared more for poetry than for his own reputation as a poet or his picture of himself as a poet. Art was greater than the artist: and this feeling he communicated to others; which was why younger men were never ill at ease in his company.

This, I am sure, was part of the secret of his ability, after becoming unquestionably the master, to remain always a contemporary. Another is the continual development of which I have spoken. This has become almost a commonplace of criticism of his work. But while it is often mentioned, its causes and its nature have not been often analyzed. One reason, of course, was simply concentration and hard work. And behind that is character: I mean

---

2. The original spelling of a word later confused with "mystery" (of different origin and meaning); it means an art, skill, or craft with the implication that the practitioners belong to a closed corporation.

the special character of the artist as artist—that is, the force of character by which Dickens, having exhausted his first inspiration, was able in middle age to proceed to such a masterpiece, so different from his early work, as *Bleak House*. It is difficult and unwise to generalize about ways of composition—so many men, so many ways—but it is my experience that toward middle age a man has three choices: to stop writing altogether, to repeat himself with perhaps an increasing skill of virtuosity, or by taking thought to adapt himself to middle age and find a different way of working. Why are the later long poems of Browning and Swinburne mostly unread? It is, I think, because one gets the essential Browning or Swinburne entire in earlier poems; and in the later, one is reminded of the early freshness which they lack, without being made aware of any compensating new qualities. When a man is engaged in work of abstract thought—if there is such a thing as wholly abstract thought outside of the mathematical sciences—his mind can mature, while his emotions either remain the same or only atrophy, and it will not matter. But maturing as a poet means maturing as the whole man, experiencing new emotions appropriate to one's age, and with the same intensity as the emotions of youth.

One form, a perfect form, of development is that of Shakespeare, one of the few poets whose work of maturity is just as exciting as that of their early manhood. There is, I think, a difference between the development of Shakespeare and Yeats, which makes the latter case still more curious. With Shakespeare, one sees a slow, continuous development of mastery of his craft of verse, and the poetry of middle age seems implicit in that of early maturity. After the first few verbal exercises you say of each piece of work: "This is the perfect expression of the sensibility of that stage of his development." That a poet should develop at all, that he should find something new to say, and say it equally well, in middle age, has always something miraculous about it. But in the case of Yeats the kind of development seems to me different. I do not want to give the impression that I regard his earlier and his later work almost as if they had been written by two different men. Returning to his earlier poems after making a close acquaintance with the later, one sees, to begin with, that in technique there was a slow and continuous development of what is always the same medium and idiom. And when I say development, I do not mean that many of the early poems, for what they are, are not as beautifully written as they could be. There are some, such as *Who Goes with Fergus?*, which are as perfect of their kind as anything in the language. But the best, and the best known of them, have this limitation: that they are as satisfactory in isolation, as "anthology pieces," as they are in the context of his other poems of the same period.

I am obviously using the term "anthology piece" in a rather special sense. In any anthology, you find some poems which give you complete satisfaction and delight in themselves, such that you are hardly curious who wrote them, hardly want to look further into the work of that poet. There are others, not necessarily so perfect or complete, which make you irresistibly curious to know more of that poet through his other work. Naturally, this distinction applies only to short poems, those in which a man has been able to put only a part of his mind, if it is a mind of any size. With some such you feel at once that the man who wrote them must have had a great deal more to say, in different contexts, of equal interest. Now among all the poems in Yeats's earlier volumes I find only in a line here or there, that sense of a unique personality which makes one sit up in excitement and eagerness to learn more about the author's mind and feelings. The intensity of Yeats's own emotional experience hardly appears. We have sufficient evidence of the intensity of experience of his youth, but it is from the retrospections in some of his later work that we have our evidence.

I have, in early essays, extolled what I called impersonality in art, and it may seem that, in giving as a reason for the superiority of Yeats's later work the greater expression of personality in it, I am contradicting myself. It may be that I expressed myself badly, or that I had only an adolescent grasp of that idea—as I can never bear to re-read my own prose writings, I am willing to leave the point unsettled—but I think now, at least, that the truth of the matter is as follows. There are two forms of impersonality: that which is natural to the mere skillful craftsman, and that which is more and more achieved by the maturing artist. The first is that of what I have called the "anthology piece," of a lyric by Lovelace or Suckling, or of Campion,[3] a finer poet than either. The second impersonality is that of the poet who, out of intense and personal experience, is able to express a general truth; retaining all the particularity of his experience, to make of it a general symbol. And the strange thing is that Yeats, having been a great craftsman in the first kind, became a great poet in the second. It is not that he became a different man, for, as I have hinted, one feels sure that the intense experience of youth had been lived through—and indeed, without this early experience he could never have attained anything of the wisdom which appears in his later writing. But he had to wait for a later maturity to find expression of early experience; and this makes him, I think, a unique and especially interesting poet.

3. Thomas Campion (1567–1619), poet and musician, known for his song lyrics. Richard Lovelace (1618–58) and Sir John Suckling (1609–42) were Cavalier poets of considerable charm and limited range. All three are best known for a few individual poems.

Consider the early poem which is in every anthology, *When you are old and gray and full of sleep*, or *A Dream of Death* in the same volume of 1893. They are beautiful poems, but only craftsman's work, because one does not feel present in them the particularity which must provide the material for the general truth. By the time of the volume of 1904 there is a development visible in a very lovely poem, *The Folly of Being Comforted*, and in *Adam's Curse*; something is coming through, and in beginning to speak as a particular man he is beginning to speak for man. This is clearer still in the poem *Peace*, in the 1910 volume. But it is not fully evinced until the volume of 1914, in the violent and terrible epistle dedicatory of *Responsibilities*, with the great lines

> *Pardon that for a barren passion's sake,*
> *Although I have come close on forty-nine. . . .*[4]

And the naming of his age in the poem is significant. More than half a lifetime to arrive at this freedom of speech. It is a triumph.

There was much also for Yeats to work out of himself, even in technique. To be a younger member of a group of poets, none of them certainly of anything like his stature, but further developed in their limited path, may arrest for a time a man's development of idiom. Then again, the weight of the pre-Raphaelite prestige must have been tremendous. The Yeats of the Celtic twilight—who seems to me to have been more the Yeats of the pre-Raphaelite twilight— uses Celtic folklore almost as William Morris uses Scandinavian folklore. His longer narrative poems bear the mark of Morris. Indeed, in the pre-Raphaelite phase, Yeats is by no means the least of the pre-Raphaelites. I may be mistaken, but the play, *The Shadowy Waters*, seems to me one of the most perfect expressions of the vague enchanted beauty of that school: yet it strikes me—this may be an impertinence on my part—as the western seas described through the back window of a house in Kensington,[5] an Irish myth for the Kelmscott Press; and when I try to visualize the speakers in the play, they have the great dim, dreamy eyes of the knights and ladies of Burne-Jones.[6] I think the phase in which he treated Irish legend in the manner of Rossetti or Morris is a phase of confusion. He did not master this legend until he made it a vehicle for his own creation of character—not, really, until he began to write the *Plays for Dancers*.[7] The point is, that in becoming more Irish, not

---

4. Lines 19 and 20 of this 22-line poem.
5. This genteel residential section of West London is contrasted with the romantic vision supposedly seen from its windows. The Kelmscott Press was founded in 1890 by William Morris to bring back good design to printing.

6. Sir Edward Coley Burne-Jones (1833– 1898), pre-Raphaelite painter.
7. The first of these, *At the Hawk's Well*, was performed in March 1916. Two volumes of *Plays for Dancers* were published, the first in 1919 and the second (containing this play) in 1921.

in subject matter but in expression, he became at the same time universal.

The points that I particularly wish to make about Yeats's development are two. The first, on which I have already touched, is that to have accomplished what Yeats did in the middle and later years is a great and permanent example—which poets-to-come should study with reverence—of what I have called Character of the Artist: a kind of moral, as well as intellectual, excellence. The second point, which follows naturally after what I have said in criticism of the lack of complete emotional expression in his early work, is that Yeats is preeminently the poet of middle age. By this I am far from meaning that he is a poet only for middle-aged readers: the attitude towards him of younger poets who write in English, the world over, is enough evidence to the contrary. Now, in theory, there is no reason why a poet's inspiration or material should fail, in middle age or at any time before senility. For a man who is capable of experience finds himself in a different world in every decade of his life; as he sees it with different eyes, the material of his art is continually renewed. But in fact, very few poets have shown this capacity of adaptation to the years. It requires, indeed, an exceptional honesty and courage to face the change. Most men either cling to the experiences of youth, so that their writing becomes an insincere mimicry of their earlier work, or they leave their passion behind, and write only from the head, with a hollow and wasted virtuosity. There is another and even worse temptation: that of becoming dignified, of becoming public figures with only a public existence—coatracks hung with decorations and distinctions, doing, saying, and even thinking and feeling only what they believe the public expects of them. Yeats was not that kind of poet: and it is, perhaps, a reason why young men should find his later poetry more acceptable than older men easily can. For the young man can see him as a poet who in his work remained in the best sense always young, who even in one sense became young as he aged. But the old, unless they are stirred to something of the honesty with oneself expressed in the poetry, will be shocked by such a revelation of what a man really is and remains. They will refuse to believe that *they* are like that.

> *You think it horrible that lust and rage*
> *Should dance attendance upon my old age;*
> *They were not such a plague when I was young:*
> *What else have I to spur me into song?* [8]

These lines are very impressive and not very pleasant, and the

---

8. These four lines are a complete poem, "The Spur," first published in *The Lon-* *don Mercury*, March 1938, and then in *Last Poems and Plays*, 1940.

sentiment has recently been criticized by an English critic whom I generally respect. But I think he misread them. I do not read them as a personal confession of a man who differed from other men, but of a man who was essentially the same as most other men; the only difference is in the greater clarity, honesty and vigor. To what honest man, old enough, can these sentiments be entirely alien? They can be subdued and disciplined by religion, but who can say that they are dead? Only those to whom the maxim of La Rochefoucauld applies: "Quand les vices nous quittent, nous nous flattons de la créance que c'est nous qui les quittons." [9] The tragedy of Yeats's epigram is all in the last line.

Similarly, the play *Purgatory* [1] is not very pleasant, either. There are aspects of it which I do not like myself. I wish he had not given it this title, because I cannot accept a purgatory in which there is no hint, or at least no emphasis upon Purgation. But, apart from the extraordinary theatrical skill with which he has put so much action within the compass of a very short scene of but little movement, the play gives a masterly exposition of the emotions of an old man. I think that the epigram I have just quoted seems to me just as much to be taken in a dramatic sense as the play *Purgatory*. The lyric poet—and Yeats was always lyric, even when dramatic—can speak for every man, or for men very different from himself; but to do this he must for the moment be able to identify himself with every man or other men; and it is only his imaginative power of becoming this that deceives some readers into thinking that he is speaking for and of himself alone—especially when they prefer not to be implicated.

I do not wish to emphasize this aspect only of Yeats's poetry of age. I would call attention to the beautiful poem in *The Winding Stair*, in memory of Eva Gore-Booth and Con Markicwicz,[2] in which the picture at the beginning, of:

> *Two girls in silk kimonos, both*
> *Beautiful, one a gazelle,*

gets great intensity from the shock of the later line;

> *When withered, old and skeleton gaunt,*

and also to *Coole Park*, beginning

> *I meditate upon a swallow's flight,*
> *Upon an aged woman and her house.*

9. "When our vices abandon us, we flatter ourselves with the belief that it is we who are abandoning them."
1. 1938.

2. Two sisters of the Sligo county aristocracy. Eva was a poetess. See *Easter 1916*, note 2.

In such poems one feels that the most lively and desirable emotions of youth have been preserved to receive their full and due expression in retrospect. For the interesting feelings of age are not just different feelings; they are feelings into which the feelings of youth are integrated.

Yeats's development in his dramatic poetry is as interesting as that in his lyrical poetry. I have spoken of him as having been a lyric poet—in a sense in which I should not think of myself, for instance, as lyric; and by this I mean rather a certain kind of selection of emotion rather than particular metrical forms. But there is no reason why a lyric poet should not also be a dramatic poet; and to me Yeats is the type of lyrical dramatist. It took him many years to evolve the dramatic form suited to his genius. When he first began to write plays, poetic drama meant plays written in blank verse. Now, blank verse has been a dead meter for a long time. It would be outside of my frame to go into all the reasons for that now: but it is obvious that a form which was handled so supremely well by Shakespeare has its disadvantages. If you are writing a play of the same type as Shakespeare's, the reminiscence is oppressive; if you are writing a play of a different type, it is distracting. Furthermore, as Shakespeare is so much greater than any dramatist who has followed him, blank verse can hardly be dissociated from the life of the sixteenth and seventeenth centuries: it can hardly catch the rhythms with which English is spoken nowadays. I think that if anything like regular blank verse is ever to be reestablished, it can be after a long departure from it, during the course of which it will have liberated itself from period associations. At the time of Yeats's early plays it was not possible to use anything else for a poetry play: that is not criticism of Yeats himself, but an assertion that changes in verse forms come at one moment and not at another. His early verse-plays, including the *Green Helmet*, which is written in a kind of irregular rhymed fourteener, have a good deal of beauty in them and, at least, they are the best verse-plays written in their time. And even in these, one notices some development of irregularity in the metric. Yeats did not quite invent a new meter, but the blank verse of his later plays shows a great advance toward one; and what is most astonishing is the virtual abandonment of blank verse meter in *Purgatory*. One device used with great success in some of the later plays is the lyrical choral interlude. But another, and important, cause of improvement is the gradual purging out of poetical ornament. This, perhaps, is the most painful part of the labor, so far as the versification goes, of the modern poet who tries to write a play in verse. The course of improvement is toward a greater and greater starkness. The beautiful line for its own sake is a luxury dangerous even for the poet who has made himself a virtuoso of the technique of the theater. What is necessary is a beauty which shall not be in the line or the isolable passage, but woven into the dramatic texture itself; so that you can hardly say whether the lines give grandeur to the drama, or whether it is the drama which turns the words into poetry. (One of the most thrilling lines in *King Lear* is the simple:

> *Never, never, never, never, never* [3]

but, apart from a knowledge of the context, how can you say that it is poetry, or even competent verse?) Yeats's purification of his verse becomes much more evident in the four *Plays for Dancers* and in the two in the posthumous volume: those, in fact, in which he had found his right and final dramatic form.

It is in the first three of the *Plays for Dancers*, also, that he shows the internal, as contrasted with the external, way of handling Irish myth of which I have spoken earlier. In the earlier plays, as in the earlier poems, about legendary heroes and heroines, I feel that the characters are treated, with the respect that we pay to legend, as creatures of a different world from ours. In the later plays they are universal men and women. I should, perhaps, not include *The Dreaming of the Bones* [4] quite in this category, because Dermott and Devorgilla are characters from modern history, not figures of pre-history; but I would remark in support of what I have been saying that in this play these two lovers have something of the universality of Dante's Paolo and Francesca, and this the younger Yeats could not have given them. So with the Cuchulain of *The Hawk's Well*, [5] the Cuchulain, Emer and Eithne of *The Only Jealousy of Emer*; [6] the myth is not presented for its own sake, but as a vehicle for a situation of universal meaning.

I see at this point that I may have given the impression, contrary to my desire and my belief, that the poetry and the plays of Yeats's earlier period can be ignored in favor of his later work. You cannot divide the work of a great poet so sharply as that. Where there is the continuity of such a positive personality and such a single purpose, the later work cannot be understood, or properly enjoyed, without a study and appreciation of the earlier; and the later work again reflects light upon the earlier, and shows us beauty and significance not before perceived. We have also to take account of the historical conditions. As I have said above, Yeats was born into the end of a literary movement, and an English movement at that: only those who have toiled with

---

3. *Lear*, V. 3. 308.
4. Written 1917, first published in *Two Plays for Dancers*, 1919.

5. See footnote 7 above.
6. Written 1917–1918, first published in *Four Plays for Dancers*, 1921.

language know the labor and constancy required to free oneself
from such influences—yet, on the other hand, once we are familiar with the older voice, we can hear its individual tones even
in his earliest published verse. In my own time of youth there
seemed to be no immediate great powers of poetry either to
help or to hinder, either to learn from or to rebel against, yet I
can understand the difficulty of the other situation, and the magnitude of the task. With the verse-play, on the other hand, the
situation is reversed, because Yeats had nothing, and we have
had Yeats. He started writing plays at a time when the prose-play
of contemporary life seemed triumphant, with an infinite future
stretching before it, when the comedy of light farce dealt only
with certain privileged strata of metropolitan life; and when the
serious play tended to be an ephemeral tract on some transient
social problem. We can begin to see now that even the imperfect
early attempts he made are probably more permanent literature
than the plays of Shaw; and that his dramatic work as a whole may
prove a stronger defense against the successful urban Shaftesbury
Avenue [7] vulgarity which he opposed as stoutly as they. Just as,
from the beginning, he made and thought his poetry in terms of
speech and not in terms of print, so in the drama he always
meant to write plays to be played and not merely to be read. He
cared, I think, more for the theater as an organ for the expression
of the consciousness of a people, than as a means to his own fame
or achievement; and I am convinced that it is only if you serve it
in this spirit that you can hope to accomplish anything worth
doing with it. Of course, he had some great advantages, the recital
of which does not rob him of any of his glory: his colleagues, a
people with a natural and unspoiled gift for speech and for acting.
It is impossible to disentangle what he did for the Irish theater
from what the Irish theater did for him. From this point of
advantage, the idea of the poetic drama was kept alive when
everywhere else it had been driven underground. I do not know
where our debt to him as a dramatist ends—and in time, it will
not end until that drama itself ends. In his occasional writings on
dramatic topics he has asserted certain principles to which we
must hold fast: such as the primacy of the poet over the actor,
and of the actor over the scene-painter; and the principle that
the theater, while it need not be concerned only with "the
people" in the narrow Russian sense, must be for the people;
that to be permanent it must concern itself with fundamental
situations. Born into a world in which the doctrine of "Art for
Art's sake" was generally accepted, and living on into one in
which art has been asked to be instrumental to social purposes, he

7. London theater district, thus signifying the commercial theater.

held firmly to the right view which is between these, though not in any way a compromise between them, and showed that an artist, by serving his art with entire integrity, is at the same time rendering the greatest service he can to his own nation and to the whole world.

To be able to praise, it is not necessary to feel complete agreement; and I do not dissimulate the fact that there are aspects of Yeats's thought and feeling which to myself are unsympathetic. I say this only to indicate the limits which I have set to my criticism. The questions of difference, objection and protest arise in the field of doctrine, and these are vital questions. I have been concerned only with the poet and dramatist, so far as these can be isolated. In the long run they cannot be wholly isolated. A full and elaborate examination of the total work of Yeats must some day be undertaken; perhaps it will need a longer perspective. There are some poets whose poetry can be considered more or less in isolation, for experience and delight. There are others whose poetry, though giving equally experience and delight, has a larger historical importance. Yeats was one of the latter: he was one of those few whose history is the history of their own time, who are a part of the consciousness of an age which cannot be understood without them. This is a very high position to assign to him: but I believe that it is one which is secure.

1940, 1957

Distinctive Voices in Poetry and Fiction

A. E. HOUSMAN
(1859–1936)

Alfred Edward Housman was born in Fockbury, Worcestershire (close to the Shropshire border). After attending school at the nearby town of Bromsgrove he proceeded to Oxford where he studied classics and philosophy and in 1881 shocked his friends and teachers by failing his final examinations (he was at the time in a state of psychological turmoil resulting from his suppressed homosexual love for a fellow student). He obtained a civil service job and pursued his classical studies alone, gradually building up a reputation as a great textual critic of Latin literature by his contributions to learned periodicals. In 1892 he was appointed to the Chair of Latin at University College, London, and from 1911 until his death he was professor of Latin at Cambridge.

It was characteristic of Housman that his classical studies consisted of meticulous, impersonal textual investigations; there was something reserved and solitary about his life as there was about his scholarship, in which he allowed no trace of his feeling for literature to appear. That feeling nevertheless ran strong and deep, and in his lecture *The Name and Nature of Poetry* (1933) he expressed the view that poetry cannot be explained or analyzed, but is recognized by its almost physical effects on the reader as he reads. His own poetry was limited both in quantity and in range. Two "slim volumes"—*A Shropshire Lad* (1896) and *Last Poems* (1922) —were all that appeared during his lifetime, and after his death his brother Laurence Housman, playwright and poet, brought out another small book of *More Poems* (1936), on the whole inferior in quality to the first two.

Housman's writings on classical subjects consisted of articles and reviews marked by bitterly sarcastic exposure of the work of inferior editors punctuated by gloomy remarks about life. He was a very great textual critic of Latin poetry, but his remarks on the folly and incompetence of other textual critics go far beyond anything normally expected of superior scholarship talking of inferior. "If a man will comprehend the richness and variety of the universe, and inspire his mind with a due measure of wonder and of awe, he must contemplate the human intellect not only on its heights of genius but in its abysses of ineptitude. * * * Elias Stoeber['s] reprint * * * saw the light in 1767 at Strasburg, a city still famous for its geese. * * * Stoeber's mind, though that is no name to call it by, was one which turned as unswervingly to the false, the meaningless, the unmetrical, and the ungrammatical, as the needle to the pole" (Preface to *Manilius*, 1903).

Housman's aim as a poet was not to expand or develop the resources of English poetry but by limitation and concentration to achieve an utterance both compact and moving. He was influenced by Greek and Latin lyric poetry, by the traditional ballad, and by the lyrics of the early 19th-century German poet Heinrich Heine. His favorite theme is that of the doomed youth acting out the tragedy of his brief life in a context of agricultural activity and against a specific English background containing visual reminders of man's long history there. Nature is beautiful but indifferent and is to be enjoyed while we are still able to enjoy it. Love, friendship, and conviviality cannot last and may well result in betrayal or death, but are likewise to be relished while there is time. The wryly ironic tone sometimes degenerates into melodrama, and the stoicism seems at time histrionic, but at his best Housman's control of cadence enabled him to sound the note of resigned wisdom with quiet poignancy. Housman avoids self-pity by projecting the emotion through an imagined character, notably the "Shropshire lad," so that even the first-person poems seem to be distanced in some degree. At the same time the poems are distinguished sharply from the "gather ye rosebuds" tradition by the undertones of fatalism and even of doom.

Loveliest of Trees

Loveliest of trees, the cherry now
Is hung with bloom along the bough,
And stands about the woodland ride
Wearing white for Eastertide.

Now, of my threescore years and ten,   5
Twenty will not come again,
And take from seventy springs a score,
It only leaves me fifty more.

And since to look at things in bloom
Fifty springs are little room,   10
About the woodlands I will go
To see the cherry hung with snow.

1896

When I Was One-and-Twenty

When I was one-and-twenty
    I heard a wise man say,
"Give crowns and pounds and guineas
    But not your heart away;
Give pearls away and rubies   5
    But keep your fancy free."
But I was one-and-twenty,
    No use to talk to me.

When I was one-and-twenty
    I heard him say again,   10

"The heart out of the bosom
    Was never given in vain;
'Tis paid with sighs a plenty
    And sold for endless rue."
And I am two-and-twenty,   15
    And oh, 'tis true, 'tis true.

                                            1896

To an Athlete Dying Young

The time you won your town the race
We chaired you through the market place;
Man and boy stood cheering by,
And home we brought you shoulder-high.

Today, the road all runners come,   5
Shoulder-high we bring you home,
And set you at your threshold down,
Townsman of a stiller town.

Smart lad, to slip betimes away
From fields where glory does not stay   10
And early though the laurel grows
It withers quicker than the rose.

Eyes the shady night has shut
Cannot see the record cut,
And silence sounds no worse than cheers   15
After earth has stopped the ears:

Now you will not swell the rout
Of lads that wore their honors out,
Runners whom renown outran
And the name died before the man.   20

So set, before its echoes fade,
The fleet foot on the sill of shade,
And hold to the low lintel up
The still defended challenge cup.

And round that early laureled head   25
Will flock to gaze the strengthless dead
And find unwithered on its curls
The garland briefer than a girl's.

                                            1896

Bredon[1] Hill

In summertime on Bredon
    The bells they sound so clear;

1. "Pronounced Breedon" [Housman's note]. The hill is in Worcestershire, adjacent to Shropshire.

Round both the shires they ring them
   In steeples far and near,
A happy noise to hear.   5

Here of a Sunday morning
   My love and I would lie,
And see the colored counties,
   And hear the larks so high
   About us in the sky.   10

The bells would ring to call her
   In valleys miles away:
"Come all to church, good people;
   Good people, come and pray."
   But here my love would stay.   15

And I would turn and answer
   Among the springing thyme,
"O, peal upon our wedding,
   And we will hear the chime,
   And come to church in time."   20

But when the snows at Christmas
   On Bredon top were strown,
My love rose up so early
   And stole out unbeknown
   And went to church alone.   25

They tolled the one bell only,
   Groom there was none to see,
The mourners followed after,
   And so to church went she,
   And would not wait for me.   30

The bells they sound on Bredon,
   And still the steeples hum,
"Come all to church, good people"—
   Oh, noisy bells, be dumb;   35
   I hear you, I will come.

                    1896

The Lent Lily

'Tis spring; come out to ramble
   The hilly brakes[1] around,
For under thorn and bramble
   About the hollow ground
   The primroses are found.   5

And there's the windflower[2] chilly
   With all the winds at play,

---

1. Clumps of bushes.   2. Anemone.

And there's the Lenten lily
  That has not long to stay
  And dies on Easter day.   10

And since till girls go maying
  You find the primrose still,
And find the windflower playing
  With every wind at will,
  But not the daffodil,   15

Bring baskets now, and sally
  Upon the spring's array,
And bear from hill and valley
  The daffodil away
  That dies on Easter day.   20

1896

On Wenlock Edge[3]

On Wenlock Edge the wood's in trouble;
  His forest fleece the Wrekin[4] heaves;
The gale, it plies the saplings double,
  And thick on Severn[5] snow the leaves.

'Twould blow like this through holt[6] and hanger   5
  When Uricon[7] the city stood:
'Tis the old wind in the old anger,
  But then it threshed another wood.

Then, 'twas before my time, the Roman
  At yonder heaving hill would stare: 10
The blood that warms an English yeoman,
  The thoughts that hurt him, they were there.

There, like the wind through woods in riot,
  Through him the gale of life blew high;
The tree of man was never quiet: 15
  Then 'twas the Roman, now 'tis I.

The gale, it plies the saplings double,
  It blows so hard, 'twill soon be gone:
Today the Roman and his trouble
  Are ashes under Uricon.   20

1896

3. A sharp ridge, twenty miles long, in southeastern Shropshire.
4. A sugar-loaf hill at the northeast end of the Caradoc Hills in Shropshire.
5. The Severn River flows through Shropshire past the Wrekin into Wales.
6. Wooded hill; "hanger": wood on the side of a steep hill.
7. The Roman city of Uriconium (whose site is near Shrewsbury, the county seat of Shropshire).

With Rue My Heart Is Laden

With rue my heart is laden
  For golden friends I had,
For many a rose-lipped maiden
  And many a lightfoot lad.

By brooks too broad for leaping   5
  The lightfoot boys are laid;
The rose-lipped girls are sleeping
  In fields where roses fade.

              1896

Terence,[1] This Is Stupid Stuff

"Terence, this is stupid stuff:
You eat your victuals fast enough;
There can't be much amiss, 'tis clear,
To see the rate you drink your beer.
But oh, good Lord, the verse you make,   5
It gives a chap the bellyache.
The cow, the old cow, she is dead;
It sleeps well, the hornéd head:
We poor lads, 'tis our turn now
To hear such tunes as killed the cow.   10
Pretty friendship 'tis to rhyme
Your friends to death before their time
Moping melancholy mad:
Come, pipe a tune to dance to, lad."

Why, if 'tis dancing you would be,   15
There's brisker pipes than poetry.
Say, for what were hopyards meant,
Or why was Burton built on Trent?[2]
Oh many a peer of England brews
Livelier liquor than the Muse,   20
And malt does more than Milton can
To justify God's ways to man.
Ale, man, ale's the stuff to drink
For fellows whom it hurts to think:
Look into the pewter pot   25
To see the world as the world's not.
And faith, 'tis pleasant till 'tis past:

1. *The Poems of Terence Hearsay* was Housman's intended title for *The Shropshire Lad*.
2. Burton-on-Trent is the most famous of all English brewing towns; "many a peer" refers to the "beer barons," brewery magnates raised to the peerage.

The mischief is that 'twill not last.
Oh I have been to Ludlow[3] fair
And left my necktie God knows where,   30
And carried halfway home, or near,
Pints and quarts of Ludlow beer:
Then the world seemed none so bad,
And I myself a sterling lad;
And down in lovely muck I've lain,   35
Happy till I woke again.
Then I saw the morning sky.
Heigho, the tale was all a lie;
The world, it was the old world yet,
I was I, my things were wet,   40
And nothing now remained to do
But begin the game anew.

Therefore, since the world has still
Much good, but much less good than ill,
And while the sun and moon endure   45
Luck's a chance, but trouble's sure,
I'd face it as a wise man would,
And train for ill and not for good.
'Tis true the stuff I bring for sale
Is not so brisk a brew as ale: 50
Out of a stem that scored[4] the hand
I wrung it in a weary land.
But take it: if the smack is sour,
The better for the embittered hour;
It should do good to heart and head   55
When your soul is in my soul's stead;
And I will friend you, if I may,
In the dark and cloudy day.

There was a king reigned in the East:
There, when kings will sit to feast,   60
They get their fill before they think
With poisoned meat and poisoned drink.
He gathered all that springs to birth
From the many-venomed earth;
First a little, thence to more,   65
He sampled all her killing store;
And easy, smiling, seasoned sound,
Sate the king when healths went round.
They put arsenic in his meat
And stared aghast to watch him eat;   70
They poured strychnine in his cup
And shook to see him drink it up:
They shook, they stared as white's their shirt.
Them it was their poison hurt.

3. A market town in Shropshire.   4. Cut.

—I tell the tale that I heard told.   75
Mithridates, he died old.⁵

                                              1896

The Chestnut Casts His Flambeaux¹

The chestnut casts his flambeaux, and the flowers
    Stream from the hawthorn on the wind away,
The doors clap to, the pane is blind with showers.
    Pass me the can, lad; there's an end of May.

There's one spoilt spring to scant our mortal lot,   5
    One season ruined of our little store.
May will be fine next year as like as not:
    Oh ay, but then we shall be twenty-four.

We for a certainty are not the first
    Have sat in taverns while the tempest hurled   10
Their hopeful plans to emptiness, and cursed
    Whatever brute and blackguard made the world.

It is in truth iniquity on high
    To cheat our sentenced souls of aught they crave,
And mar the merriment as you and I   15
    Fare on our long fool's-errand to the grave.

Iniquity it is; but pass the can.
    My lad, no pair of kings our mothers bore;
Our only portion is the estate of man:
    We want the moon, but we shall get no more.   20

If here today the cloud of thunder lours
    Tomorrow it will hie on far behests;
The flesh will grieve on other bones than ours
    Soon, and the soul will mourn in other breasts.

The troubles of our proud and angry dust   25
    Are from eternity, and shall not fail.
Bear them we can, and if we can we must.
    Shoulder the sky, my lad, and drink your ale.

                                              1922

Could Man Be Drunk Forever

        Could man be drunk forever
          With liquor, love, or fights,

---

5. The story of Mithridates, king of
Pontus, who made himself immune to
poison by taking small doses daily, is
told in Pliny's *Natural History*.

1. Literally, torches. Housman is here
referring to the erect flower-clusters
(white, dashed with red and yellow)
of the horse-chestnut tree.

Lief should I rouse at morning
And lief lie down of nights.

But men at whiles are sober   5
And think by fits and starts,
And if they think, they fasten
Their hands upon their hearts.

1896   1922

Epitaph on an Army of Mercenaries

These, in the day when heaven was falling,
The hour when earth's foundations fled,
Followed their mercenary calling
And took their wages and are dead.

Their shoulders held the sky suspended;   5
They stood, and earth's foundations stay;
What God abandoned, these defended,
And saved the sum of things for pay.

1922

RUDYARD KIPLING
(1865–1936)

Kipling was born in Bombay, India; his father was the curator of the
Lahore Museum and a well-known illustrator. He went to school in Eng-
land, and returned to India as a journalist in 1882, coming back again to
England in 1889 to achieve rapid fame as a poet and short-story writer.
He married an American in 1892 and lived in Vermont until driven out
in 1897 by a violent quarrel with his brother-in-law; he spent the rest of
his life in England. He was the first Englishman to receive the Nobel
Prize for Literature (1907).

Kipling's poetry owed much to the strong rhythms of the Methodist
hymns he heard in his childhood. He had a real gift for communal poetic
utterance, creating what might be called a public emotion by swinging
movement carefully varied in accordance with the demands of the particular theme. He is often thought of as the poet of British imperialism,
but in fact he looked at the British Empire from the point of view of the
ordinary "tommy" (private soldier) doing his duty in a distant outpost
without any awareness of the policies or problems which determined it,
and thus gave a new vividness and reality to the subject. This approach,
together with his rhythmic skill, won an immediate audience for his *Bar-
rack-Room Ballads* (1890, 1892). At the same time he was gaining a
reputation as a gifted story-teller whose tales of military life in India again

stressed the unconscious heroism of the "tommy" and explored some of the psychological and moral problems of a white community living in the midst of a subject people. Gradually Kipling built up a code of honor and duty which combined something from the English public school, something from the English code of fair play in sport, something from biological notions of the survival of the fittest, and something from the idea of "the white man's burden." *Plain Tales from the Hills* (1888) are stories of India; later he extended his scope and wrote a great variety of stories and novels in which he applied his ethical code to many different kinds of modern societies and situations. At his best, his stories possess vividness, strength, and real narrative cunning; at his worst, the code becomes intrusive and (to modern minds) offensive. The two *Jungle Books* (1894, 1895) apply the code with real brilliance to the animals of the Indian jungle; *Captains Courageous* (1897) applies it to life at sea and the education, through such a life, of a spoiled millionaire's son. *Stalky and Co.* (1899), which draws on his own schooldays, applies the code to boys' boarding-school life, and *Puck of Pook's Hill* (1906) applies it with unusual subtlety and a fine historical imagination to Roman and Anglo-Saxon Britain. *Kim* (1901), set in India, transcends the bounds of the normal Kipling formula. It presents the interrelations of two vocations, the active and imperialist (British) and the contemplative and religious (Indian); each is treated with equal sympathy, and the result is the most complex of Kipling's novels and his masterpiece.

Kipling's poetry is far removed from the poetry of the modern movement associated with the name of T. S. Eliot. His vigorous rhythms, relatively simple moral and psychological diagnosis, and simplicity of verbal texture account for the natural reaction against him in the 1920's and 1930's. It is true that some of his verse is both jingling and jingoist; but much, too, shows a power to handle elemental themes, such as loyalty or endurance or loss or fear, with remarkable power. He is now recognized as a considerable craftsman in verse; a selection of his poetry has, in fact, been edited by Eliot himself.

Danny Deever

"What are the bugles blowin' for?" said Files-on-Parade.[1]
"To turn you out, to turn you out," the Color-Sergeant said.
"What makes you look so white, so white?" said Files-on-Parade.
"I'm dreadin' what I've got to watch," the Color-Sergeant said.
  For they're hangin' Danny Deever, you can hear the Dead
    March play,   5
  The regiment's in 'ollow square—they're hangin' him today;
  They've taken of his buttons off an' cut his stripes away,
  An they're hangin' Danny Deever in the mornin'.

"What makes the rear rank breathe so 'ard?" said Files-on-Parade.
"It's bitter cold, it's bitter cold," the Color-Sergeant said.   10
"What makes that front-rank man fall down?" said Files-on-Parade.

1. Private soldier.

"A touch o' sun, a touch o' sun," the Color-Sergeant said.
  They are hangin' Danny Deever, they are marchin' of 'im round,
  They 'ave 'alted Danny Deever by 'is coffin on the ground;
  An' 'e'll swing in 'arf a minute for a sneakin' shootin' hound— 15
  O they're hangin' Danny Deever in the mornin'!

" 'Is cot was right-'and cot to mine," said Files-on-Parade.
" 'E's sleepin' out an' far tonight," the Color-Sergeant said.
"I've drunk 'is beer a score o' times," said Files-on-Parade.
" 'E's drinkin' bitter beer[2] alone," the Color-Sergeant said. 20
  They are hangin' Danny Deever, you must mark 'im to 'is place,
  For 'e shot a comrade sleepin'—you must look 'im in the face;
  Nine 'undred of 'is county an' the Regiment's disgrace,
  While they're hangin' Danny Deever in the mornin'.

"What's that so black agin the sun?" said Files-on-Parade. 25
"It's Danny fightin' 'ard for life," the Color-Sergeant said.
"What's that that whimpers over'ead?" said Files-on-Parade.
"It's Danny's soul that's passin' now," the Color-Sergeant said.
  For they're done with Danny Deever, you can 'ear the quickstep
    play,
  The regiment's in column, an' they're marchin' us away; 30
  Ho! the young recruits are shakin', an' they'll want their beer
    today,
  After hangin' Danny Deever in the mornin'.

1890

Recessional[3]

1897

God of our fathers, known of old—
  Lord of our far-flung battle-line—
Beneath whose awful Hand we hold
  Dominion over palm and pine—
Lord God of Hosts, be with us yet 5
Lest we forget—lest we forget!

The tumult and the shouting dies—
  The Captains and the Kings depart—
Still stands Thine ancient Sacrifice,
  An humble and a contrite heart.[4] 10

2. "Bitter beer" or simply "bitter" is one of the favorite varieties of draught beer drunk in English pubs; the word "bitter" thus becomes a grim pun.
3. A hymn for Queen Victoria's Diamond Jubilee, first published near the close of the celebrations. It has a simple gravity of utterance appropriate to such an occasion, and in reversing the coin of imperial self-congratulation strikes a note peculiarly fitting in a "recessional" (technically a hymn sung at the end of a church service, as the clergy and choir leave the church in procession).
4. "The sacrifices of God are a broken spirit: a broken and a contrite heart, O God, thou wilt not despise" (Psalms li.17).

Lord God of Hosts, be with us yet,
 Lest we forget—lest we forget!

Far-called, our navies melt away—
 On dune and headland sinks the fire—
Lo, all our pomp of yesterday   15
 Is one with Nineveh and Tyre![5]
Judge of the Nations, spare us yet,
 Lest we forget—lest we forget!

If, drunk with sight of power, we loose
 Wild tongues that have not Thee in awe—   20
Such boasting as the Gentiles use
 Or lesser breeds without the Law[6]—
Lord God of Hosts, be with us yet,
 Lest we forget—lest we forget!

For heathen heart that puts her trust   25
 In reeking tube and iron shard—
All valiant dust that builds on dust,
 And guarding calls not Thee to guard—
For frantic boast and foolish word,
 Thy mercy on Thy People, Lord!   30

1897   1897, 1899

Edgehill Fight[1]

(CIVIL WARS, 1642)

Naked and gray the Cotswolds[2] stand
 Beneath the summer sun,
And the stubble fields on either hand
 Where Stour and Avon[3] run.
There is no change in the patient land   5
 That has bred us every one.

She should have passed in cloud and fire
 And saved us from this sin
Of war—red war—'twixt child and sire,
 Household and kith and kin,   10
In the heart of a sleepy Midland shire,
 With the harvest scarcely in.

---

5. Once-great cities of Assyria and Phoenicia, respectively; Nineveh is now buried in the desert; Tyre is a small Lebanese town.
6. "For when the Gentiles, which have not the law, do by nature the things contained in the law, these, having not the law, are a law unto themselves" (Romans ii.14).
1. Edgehill was the first battle in the English Civil War, between the Royalists under Charles I and the Parliamentarians under the Earl of Essex. The result was indecisive. Edgehill itself is a ridge in the western English county of Warwickshire.
2. The Cotswold Hills lie south of Edgehill, in Gloucestershire.
3. Rivers that flow through this part of England (Shakespeare's Stratford is on the Avon).

But there is no change as we meet at last
  On the brow-head or the plain,
And the raw astonished ranks stand fast   15
  To slay or to be slain
By the men they knew in the kindly past
  That shall never come again—

By the men they met at dance or chase,
  In the tavern or the hall,   20
At the justice bench and the market place,
  At the cudgel play or brawl—
Of their own blood and speech and race,
  Comrades or neighbors all!

More bitter than death this day must prove   25
  Whichever way it go,
For the brothers of the maids we love
  Make ready to lay low
Their sisters' sweethearts, as we move
  Against our dearest foe.   30

Thank Heaven! At last the trumpets peal
  Before our strength gives way.
For King or for the Commonweal—
  No matter which they say,
The first dry rattle of new-drawn steel   35
  Changes the world today!

1903

RUPERT BROOKE
(1887–1915)

Rupert Brooke was educated at Rugby School and at King's College, Cambridge. Thereafter he traveled extensively in Europe, America, Canada, and the South Seas, writing poems and essays. In 1914, when World War I broke out, he saw service in Belgium; the next year he was dead of a fever on the Greek island of Skyros.

Brooke is often, and with considerable justice, taken as representative of the golden world of liberal culture immediately before World War I. His early death was symbolic of the death of a whole generation of dedicated English youth—brilliant and beautiful youth as they seemed in retrospect, for Brooke was noted for his physical beauty as well as for his talents. The irony of his poem *Heaven* is much more genial and contentedly civilized than anything in Eliot, while *The Soldier*, traditional both in its sonnet form and its idealistic patriotic mood, represents the last significant expression of an attitude that could not survive the horrors of trench warfare. The war poets who followed Brooke expressed extreme bitterness and showed a much more savage irony, manifesting the disillusion, the sense of a whole world of values having disappeared, that influenced every aspect of serious English literature in the immediate postwar period.

Brooke is the one poet represented here to whom the term "Georgian" can be applied without qualification. George V succeeded Edward VII in 1910 and "Georgian" refers to the early years of his reign, up to the 1914–18 World War. This term was first used of poets when Edward Marsh brought out in 1912 the first of a series of volumes, *Georgian Poetry.* For the most part, the poets represented in these anthologies were not interested in major changes in poetic technique and attitude; their subject matter was often the English countryside or else the exotic and the magical; their craftsmanship was on the whole traditional; their mood tended to be quietly meditative. Yet, though essentially conservative in his poetic tastes, Marsh was reasonably catholic in his choices: some of D. H. Lawrence's poems appeared first in *Georgian Poetry* (though Lawrence called Marsh a "bit of a policeman in poetry"). Brooke, however, was more at home in Marsh's poetic environment. Both the poems printed below first appeared in *Georgian Poetry 1913–15* (1915).

Heaven

Fish (fly-replete, in depth of June,
Dawdling away their wat'ry noon)
Ponder deep wisdom, dark or clear,
Each secret fishy hope or fear.
Fish say, they have their Stream and Pond;   5
But is there anything Beyond?
This life cannot be All, they swear,
For how unpleasant, if it were!
One may not doubt that, somehow, Good
Shall come of Water and of Mud;   10
And, sure, the reverent eye must see
A Purpose in Liquidity.
We darkly know, by Faith we cry,
The future is not Wholly Dry.
Mud unto mud!—Death eddies near—   15
Not here the appointed End, not here!
But somewhere, beyond Space and Time,
Is wetter water, slimier slime!
And there (they trust) there swimmeth One
Who swam ere rivers were begun,   20
Immense, of fishy form and mind,
Squamous,[1] omnipotent, and kind;
And under that Almighty Fin,
The littlest fish may enter in.
Oh! never fly conceals a hook,   25
Fish say, in the Eternal Brook,
But more than mundane weeds are there,
And mud, celestially fair;

1. Scaly.

Fat caterpillars drift around,
And Paradisal grubs are found;   30
Unfading moths, immortal flies,
And the worm that never dies.
And in that Heaven of all their wish,
There shall be no more land, say fish.

1913   1915

The Soldier[2]

If I should die, think only this of me,
    That there's some corner of a foreign field
That is forever England. There shall be

    In that rich earth a richer dust concealed,
A dust whom England bore, shaped, made aware,   5
    Gave, once, her flowers to love, her ways to roam,
A body of England's, breathing English air,
    Washed by the rivers, blest by suns of home.

And think, this heart, all evil shed away,
    A pulse in the Eternal mind, no less   10
        Gives somewhere back the thoughts by England given,
    Her sights and sounds; dreams happy as her day;
And laughter, learnt of friends; and gentleness,
    In hearts at peace, under an English heaven.

1914   1915

2. The text given here follows Brooke's MS. in the British Museum.

EDWARD THOMAS
(1878–1917)

Edward Thomas was one of many English poets whose lives were cut short
by World War I. He began his literary career as a writer for the *Manchester Guardian*, but turned to serious poetry under the influence of his
close friend Robert Frost, with whose work his poems have some affinity.
He was able to bring out two books of poems (1916, 1917) before his
death in France. *Last Poems* was published posthumously in 1918.

Thomas's poetry manages to distill an extraordinary intensity of meaning and atmosphere out of quite ordinary experiences by a quiet precision
of imagery, a careful placing of words and phrases where they will take
on an intriguing light from their context, and a combination of simplicity
of surface meaning with an echoing suggestiveness. Thomas is one "Georgian" poet who, while never moving beyond the accepted limits of Georgian
poetry in either subject or technique, enjoys a reputation today as a minor
poet of distinction.

Tears

It seems I have no tears left. They should have fallen—
Their ghosts, if tears have ghosts, did fall—that day
When twenty hounds streamed by me, not yet combed out
But still all equals in their rage of gladness
Upon the scent, made one, like a great dragon   5
In Blooming Meadow that bends towards the sun
And once bore hops: and on that other day
When I stepped out from the double-shadowed Tower
Into an April morning, stirring and sweet
And warm. Strange solitude was there and silence.   10
A mightier charm than any in the Tower
Possessed the courtyard. They were changing guard,
Soldiers in line, young English countrymen,
Fair-haired and ruddy, in white tunics. Drums
And fifes were playing "The British Grenadiers."   15
The men, the music piercing that solitude
And silence, told me truths I had not dreamed,
And have forgotten since their beauty passed.

                                                    1917

The Owl

Downhill I came, hungry, and yet not starved;
Cold, yet had heat within me that was proof
Against the north wind; tired, yet so that rest
Had seemed the sweetest thing under a roof.

Then at the inn I had food, fire, and rest,   5
Knowing how hungry, cold, and tired was I.
All of the night was quite barred out except
An owl's cry, a most melancholy cry

Shaken out long and clear upon the hill,
No merry note, nor cause of merriment,   10
But one telling me plain what I escaped
And others could not, that night, as in I went.

And salted was my food, and my repose,
Salted and sobered, too, by the bird's voice
Speaking for all who lay under the stars,   15
Soldiers and poor, unable to rejoice.

                                                    1917

The Path

Running along a bank, a parapet
That saves from the precipitous wood below

The level road, there is a path. It serves
Children for looking down the long smooth steep,
Between the legs of beech and yew, to where   5
A fallen tree checks the sight: while men and women
Content themselves with the road and what they see
Over the bank, and what the children tell.
The path, winding like silver, trickles on,
Bordered and even invaded by thinnest moss   10
That tries to cover roots and crumbling chalk
With gold, olive, and emerald, but in vain.
The children wear it. They have flattened the bank
On top, and silvered it between the moss
With the current of their feet, year after year.   15
But the road is houseless, and leads not to school.
To see a child is rare there, and the eye
Has but the road, the wood that overhangs
And underyawns it, and the path that looks
As if it led on to some legendary   20
Or fancied place where men have wished to go
And stay; till, sudden, it ends where the wood ends.

                                                         1917

Adlestrop [1]

Yes. I remember Adlestrop—
The name, because one afternoon
Of heat the express train drew up there
Unwontedly. It was late June.
The steam hissed. Someone cleared his throat.   5
No one left and no one came
On the bare platform. What I saw
Was Adlestrop—only the name.

And willows, willow herb, and grass,
And meadowsweet, and haycocks dry,   10
No whit less still and lonely fair
Than the high cloudlets in the sky.

And for that minute a blackbird sang
Close by, and round him, mistier,
Farther and farther, all the birds   15
Of Oxfordshire and Gloucestershire.

                                                         1917

The Gallows

There was a weasel lived in the sun
With all his family,
Till a keeper shot him with his gun
And hung him up on a tree,

---

1. A small town in Gloucestershire.

Where he swings in the wind and rain,   5
In the sun and in the snow,
Without pleasure, without pain,
On the dead oak tree bough.

There was a crow who was no sleeper,
But a thief and a murderer   10
Till a very late hour; and this keeper
Made him one of the things that were,
To hang and flap in rain and wind,
In the sun and in the snow.
There are no more sins to be sinned   15
On the dead oak tree bough.

There was a magpie, too,
Had a long tongue and a long tail;
He could both talk and do—
But what did that avail?   20
He, too, flaps in the wind and rain
Alongside weasel and crow,
Without pleasure, without pain,
On the dead oak tree bough.

And many other beasts   25
And birds, skin, bone, and feather,
Have been taken from their feasts
And hung up there together,
To swing and have endless leisure
In the sun and in the snow,   30
Without pain, without pleasure,
On the dead oak tree bough.

                                            1917

Ambition

Unless it was that day I never knew
Ambition. After a night of frost, before
The March sun brightened and the Southwest blew,
Jackdaws began to shout and float and soar
Already, and one was racing straight and high   5
Alone, shouting like a black warrior
Challenges and menaces to the wide sky.
With loud long laughter then a woodpecker
Ridiculed the sadness of the owl's last cry.
And through the valley where all the folk astir 10
Made only plumes of pearly smoke to tower
Over dark trees and white meadows happier
Than was Elysium in that happy hour,
A train that roared along raised after it

And carried with it a motionless white bower   15
Of purest cloud, from end to end close-knit,
So fair it touched the roar with silence. Time
Was powerless while that lasted. I could sit
And think I had made the loveliness of prime,
Breathed its life into it and were its lord,   20
And no mind lived save this 'twixt clouds and rime.[1]
Omnipotent I was, nor even deplored
That I did nothing. But the end fell like a bell:
The bower was scattered; far off the train roared.
But if this was ambition I cannot tell.   25
What 'twas ambition for I know not well.

                                                      1918

1. Hoarfrost.

WILFRED OWEN
(1893–1918)

Wilfred Owen was the most brilliantly promising of all the English poets
who were killed in World War I. In his early poems he had experimented
with new varieties of Keatsian sensuousness, but, under the influence of
his war experiences, he matured rapidly and remarkably. His powerful and
concentrated poems transcend bitterness to evoke what he called "the pity
of war" and to suggest the human waste and confusions involved in modern warfare.

Owen was also concerned to expand the resources of English poetic expression, but in a different way from Eliot and those influenced by Eliot.
His "pararhymes"—imperfect or half rhymes—and his flexible stanza forms
show him adapting rather than abandoning traditional techniques, while
his attitude, combining irony, compassion, and a sense of personal involvement in all human suffering, differs from characteristic Victorian poetic
attitudes without showing the studied objectivity of the early Eliot. Had
he lived, English poetry would almost certainly have been less dependent
upon the Eliot school; indeed, there might have developed an alternative
and equally valuable new tradition in postwar English poetry.

Owen's poems were collected and published posthumously (1920) by
his friend Siegfried Sassoon.

Greater Love

Red lips are not so red
   As the stained stones kissed by the English dead.
Kindness of wooed and wooer
Seems shame to their love pure.
O Love, your eyes lose lure   5
   When I behold eyes blinded in my stead!

Your slender attitude
   Trembles not exquisite like limbs knife skewed,
Rolling and rolling there
Where God seems not to care;   10
Till the fierce love they bear
   Cramps them in death's extreme decrepitude.

Your voice sings not so soft—
   Though even as wind murmuring through raftered loft—
Your dear voice is not dear,   15
Gentle, and evening clear,
As theirs whom none now hear,
   Now earth has stopped their piteous mouths that coughed.

Heart, you were never hot
   Nor large, nor full like hearts made great with shot;   20
And though your hand be pale,
Paler are all which trail
Your cross through flame and hail:
   Weep, you may weep, for you may touch them not.

                                       1920

Futility

Move him into the sun—
Gently its touch awoke him once,
At home, whispering of fields unsown.
Always it woke him, even in France,
Until this morning and this snow.   5
If anything might rouse him now
The kind old sun will know.

Think how it wakes the seeds—
Woke, once, the clays of a cold star.
Are limbs, so dear-achieved, are sides,   10
Full-nerved—still warm—too hard to stir?
Was it for this the clay grew tall?
—O what made fatuous sunbeams toil
To break earth's sleep at all?

                                       1920

Sonnet

On Seeing a Piece of Our Artillery Brought Into Action

Be slowly lifted up, thou long black arm,
Great gun towering towards Heaven, about to curse;
Sway steep against them, and for years rehearse
Huge imprecations like a blasting charm!   5
Reach at that Arrogance which needs thy harm,
And beat it down before its sins grow worse;

Spend our resentment, cannon—yea, disburse
Our gold in shapes of flame, our breaths in storm.

Yet, for men's sakes whom thy vast malison [1]   10
Must wither innocent of enmity,
Be not withdrawn, dark arm, thy spoilure done,
Safe to the bosom of our prosperity.
But when thy spell be cast complete and whole,
May God curse thee, and cut thee from our soul!   15

1920

Anthem for Doomed Youth

What passing-bells for these who die as cattle?
Only the monstrous anger of the guns.
Only the stuttering rifles' rapid rattle
Can patter out their hasty orisons.
No mockeries for them from prayers or bells,   5
Nor any voice of mourning save the choirs—
The shrill, demented choirs of wailing shells;
And bugles calling for them from sad shires.

What candles may be held to speed them all?
Not in the hands of boys, but in their eyes   10
Shall shine the holy glimmers of good-byes.
The pallor of girls' brows shall be their pall;
Their flowers the tenderness of patient minds,
And each slow dusk a drawing-down of blinds.

1920

Apologia Pro Poemate Meo [2]

I, too, saw God through mud—
The mud that cracked on cheeks when wretches smiled.
War brought more glory to their eyes than blood,
And gave their laughs more glee than shakes a child.

Merry it was to laugh there—   5
Where death becomes absurd and life absurder.
For power was on us as we slashed bones bare
Not to feel sickness or remorse of murder.

I, too, have dropped off fear—
Behind the barrage, dead as my platoon,   10
And sailed my spirit surging light and clear
Past the entanglement where hopes lay strewn;

1. Curse, malediction.   2. "Apology for My Poem."

And witnessed exultation—
    Faces that used to curse me, scowl for scowl,
    Shine and lift up with passion of oblation,   15
    Seraphic for an hour; though they were foul.

I have made fellowships—
    Untold of happy lovers in old song.
    For love is not the binding of fair lips
    With the soft silk of eyes that look and long,   20

By Joy, whose ribbon slips,
    But wound with war's hard wire whose stakes are strong;
    Bound with the bandage of the arm that drips;
    Knit in the webbing of the rifle thong.

I have perceived much beauty   25
    In the hoarse oaths that kept our courage straight;
    Heard music in the silentness of duty;
    Found peace where shell-storms spouted reddest spate.

Nevertheless, except you share
    With them in hell the sorrowful dark of hell,   30
    Whose world is but the trembling of a flare,
    And heaven but as the highway for a shell,

You shall not hear their mirth:
    You shall not come to think them well content
    By any jest of mine. These men are worth   35
    Your tears. You are not worth their merriment.

November, 1917   1920

Strange Meeting[1]

It seemed that out of the battle I escaped
Down some profound dull tunnel, long since scooped
Through granites which titanic wars had groined.
Yet also there encumbered sleepers groaned,
Too fast in thought or death to be bestirred.   5
Then, as I probed them, one sprang up, and stared
With piteous recognition in fixed eyes,
Lifting distressful hands as if to bless.
And by his smile, I knew that sullen hall;
By his dead smile I knew we stood in Hell.   10

1. This poem, one of the last that Owen wrote, is unfinished. It shows his use of "pararhyme" (e.g., "groined," "groaned"; "hall," "Hell"), one of his technical experiments which have influenced later poets. The poem is "peculiarly a poem of the Western Front; it is a dream only a stage further on than the actuality of the tunneled dugouts with their muffled security, their smoky dimness, their rows of soldiers painfully sleeping, their officers and sergeants and corporals attempting to awaken those for duty, and the sense presently of 'going up' the ugly stairway to do someone in the uglier mud above a good turn. Out of these and similar materials Owen's transforming spirit has readily created his wonderful phantasma" (Edmund Blunden).

With a thousand pains that vision's face was grained;
Yet no blood reached there from the upper ground,
And no guns thumped, or down the flues made moan.
"Strange friend," I said, "here is no cause to mourn."
"None," said the other, "save the undone years,   15
The hopelessness. Whatever hope is yours,
Was my life also; I went hunting wild
After the wildest beauty in the world,
Which lies not calm in eyes, or braided hair,
But mocks the steady running of the hour,   20
And if it grieves, grieves richlier than here.
For by my glee might many men have laughed,
And of my weeping something had been left,
Which must die now. I mean the truth untold,
The pity of war, the pity war distilled.   25
Now men will go content with what we spoiled,
Or, discontent, boil bloody, and be spilled.
They will be swift with swiftness of the tigress,
None will break ranks, though nations trek from progress.
Courage was mine, and I had mystery,   30
Wisdom was mine, and I had mastery;
To miss the march of this retreating world
Into vain citadels that are not walled.
Then when much blood had clogged their chariot wheels
I would go up and wash them from sweet wells,   35
Even with truths that lie too deep for taint.
I would have poured my spirit without stint
But not through wounds; not on the cess[2] of war.
Foreheads of men have bled where no wounds were.
I am the enemy you killed, my friend.   40
I knew you in this dark; for so you frowned
Yesterday through me as you jabbed and killed.
I parried; but my hands were loath and cold.
Let us sleep now. . . ."

1918   1920

2. A somewhat archaic Anglo-Irish word meaning either "tax, levy" or (more probably, here) "luck"—as used in the phrase "bad cess to you" (may evil befall you).

E. M. FORSTER
(1879–)

Edward Morgan Forster was born in London; his father was an architect of Welsh extraction and his mother a member of a family distinguished during several generations for its evangelical religion and its philanthropic activities. He was educated at Tonbridge School (the "Sawston" of *The Longest Journey*), where he suffered the tribulations of a day boy at a boarding school, and King's College, Cambridge. The friends he made and the intellectual companionship he found at Cambridge have influenced his entire life. He visited Greece and spent some time in Italy in 1901, and this experience also had a permanent influence on him; throughout his life he has tended to set Greek and Italian peasant life in symbolic contrast to the stuffy and repressed life of middle-class England. Both Greek mythology and Italian Renaissance art opened up to him a world of what Matthew Arnold called "spontaneity of consciousness," and most of his work is concerned with ways of discovering such a quality in personal relationships amid the complexities and distortions of modern life. He began writing as a contributor to the newly founded liberal *Independent Review* in 1903, and in 1905 published his first novel, *Where Angels Fear to Tread*, a tragicomic projection of conflicts between refined English gentility and coarse Italian vitality.

English tutoring in Germany; an extended visit to India in 1912 and a shorter one in 1922; continuous intellectual companionship with members of the "Bloomsbury group" and others; and in 1946 an honorary fellowship at King's College, Cambridge, where he has mostly lived since, though with a good deal of traveling abroad—all this adds up to a civilized and humane existence, and (as Forster himself insists) an unusually happy one. His main interest has always been in personal relations, the "little society" we make for ourselves with our friends. But he has also cast a critical and reforming eye on the abuses of the world, his point of view being always that of the independent liberal, suspicious of all political slogans and catchwords.

Forster's second novel, *The Longest Journey* (1907), explores the differences between living and dead relationships with much incidental satire of English public-school education and English notions of respectability. A *Room with a View* (1908) explores the nature of love with a great deal of subtlety, using (as with his first novel) Italy as a liberating agent. *Howards End* (1910) probes the relation between inward feeling and outward action, between the kinds of reality in which people get involved in living. "Only connect!" exclaims one of the characters. "Only connect the prose and the passion, and both will be exalted, and human love will soon be at its height." But no one knew better than Forster that this is more easily said than done, and that false or premature connections, connections made by rule and not achieved through total realization of the personality, can destroy and corrupt. The halfway house to salvation is often grimmer than the starting point. In his last novel (for Forster has written no more fiction), *A Passage to India* (1924), he takes the relations between the English and the Indians in India in the early 1920's as a background against which to erect the most searching and complex of all his explorations of the possibilities and the limitations, the promises and the pitfalls, of human relationships. This remains his best-known novel, as well as his best.

Forster's short stories are as a rule much simpler in theme and treatment than his novels; many of them draw on Greek mythology to project the moment of escape or illumination for a character struggling against the meshes of convention. *The Road from Colonus* draws on themes from Greek tragedy to present a modern ironic picture of the moment of escape seen but not seized, with the inevitable consequence of loss and degeneration. There is a conscious use of symbolism here (for example, in the running water that so enchants Mr. Lucas in the magical spot in Greece, and his horror of the noise of running tap water at the end of the story) which is more successful than in most of his other short stories. Forster has also written critical, autobiographical and descriptive prose, notably *Aspects of the Novel* (1927), which, as a discussion of the techniques of fiction by a practicing novelist, has become a minor classic of criticism.

The Road from Colonus[1]

I

For no very intelligible reason, Mr. Lucas had hurried ahead of his party. He was perhaps reaching the age at which independence becomes valuable, because it is so soon to be lost. Tired of attention and consideration, he liked breaking away from the younger members, to ride by himself, and to dismount unassisted. Perhaps he also relished that more subtle pleasure of being kept waiting for lunch, and of telling the others on their arrival that it was of no consequence.

So, with childish impatience, he battered the animal's sides with his heels, and made the muleteer bang it with a thick stick and prick it with a sharp one, and jolted down the hillsides through clumps of flowering shrubs and stretches of anemones and asphodel, till he heard the sound of running water, and came in sight of the group of plane trees where they were to have their meal.

Even in England those trees would have been remarkable, so huge were they, so interlaced, so magnificently clothed in quivering green. And here in Greece they were unique, the one cool spot in that hard brilliant landscape, already scorched by the heat of an April sun. In their midst was hidden a tiny Khan or country inn, a frail and mud building with a broad wooden balcony in which sat an old woman spinning, while a small brown pig, eating orange peel, stood beside her. On the wet earth below squatted two children, playing some primeval game with their fingers; and their mother, none too clean either, was messing with some rice inside. As Mrs. Forman would have said, it was all very Greek, and the fastidious Mr. Lucas felt thankful that they were bringing their own food with them, and should eat it in the open air.

Still, he was glad to be there—the muleteer had helped him

1. Having been banished from Thebes on the discovery that he had unwittingly killed his father and married his mother, Oedipus wandered until he came to Colonus, and there with his daughter Antigone he rested on a rock within the sacred grove of the Furies. A passing native bade him depart, but, knowing that he had reached the last resting place appointed for him, he refused, and was eventually allowed to stay by Theseus, king of Athens. Shortly afterward he met his death mysteriously, having been taken by the gods in some unknown way to final rest. See Sophocles' play, *Oedipus at Colonus*.

off—and glad that Mrs. Forman was not there to forestall his opinions—glad even that he should not see Ethel for quite half an hour. Ethel was his youngest daughter, still unmarried. She was unselfish and affectionate, and it was generally understood that she was to devote her life to her father, and be the comfort of his old age. Mrs. Forman always referred to her as Antigone, and Mr. Lucas tried to settle down to the role of Oedipus, which seemed the only one that public opinion allowed him.

He had this in common with Oedipus, that he was growing old. Even to himself it had become obvious. He had lost interest in other people's affairs, and seldom attended when they spoke to him. He was fond of talking himself but often forgot what he was going to say, and even when he succeeded, it seldom seemed worth the effort. His phrases and gestures had become stiff and set, his anecdotes, once so successful, fell flat, his silence was as meaningless as his speech. Yet he had led a healthy, active life, had worked steadily, made money, educated his children. There was nothing and no one to blame: he was simply growing old.

At the present moment, here he was in Greece, and one of the dreams of his life was realized. Forty years ago he had caught the fever of Hellenism, and all his life he had felt that could he but visit that land, he would not have lived in vain. But Athens had been dusty, Delphi wet, Thermopylae flat, and he had listened with amazement and cynicism to the rapturous exclamations of his companions. Greece was like England: it was a man who was growing old, and it made no difference whether that man looked at the Thames or the Eurotas.[2] It was his last hope of contradicting that logic of experience, and it was failing.

Yet Greece had done something for him, though he did not know it. It had made him discontented, and there are stirrings of life in discontent. He knew that he was not the victim of continual ill-luck. Something great was wrong, and he was pitted against no mediocre or accidental enemy. For the last month a strange desire had possessed him to die fighting.

"Greece is the land for young people," he said to himself as he stood under the plane trees, "but I will enter into it, I will possess it. Leaves shall be green again, water shall be sweet, the sky shall be blue. They were so forty years ago; and I will win them back. I do mind being old, and I will pretend no longer."

He took two steps forward, and immediately cold waters were gurgling over his ankle.

"Where does the water come from?" he asked himself. "I do not even know that." He remembered that all the hillsides were dry; yet here the road was suddenly covered with flowing streams.

2. In ancient times, the river on which Sparta stood, in southern Greece (now the Iri or Iris).

He stopped still in amazement, saying: "Water out of a tree—out of a hollow tree? I never saw nor thought of that before."

For the enormous plane that leant towards the Khan was hollow—it had been burnt out for charcoal—and from its living trunk there gushed an impetuous spring, coating the bark with fern and moss, and flowing over the mule track to create fertile meadows beyond. The simple country folk had paid to beauty and mystery such tribute as they could, for in the rind of the tree a shrine was cut, holding a lamp and a little picture of the Virgin, inheritor of the Naiad's[3] and Dryad's joint abode.

"I never saw anything so marvelous before," said Mr. Lucas. "I could even step inside the trunk and see where the water comes from."

For a moment he hesitated to violate the shrine. Then he remembered with a smile his own thought—"the place shall be mine; I will enter it and possess it"—and leapt almost aggressively onto a stone within.

The water pressed up steadily and noiselessly from the hollow roots and hidden crevices of the plane, forming a wonderful amber pool ere it spilt over the lip of bark on to the earth outside. Mr. Lucas tasted it and it was sweet, and when he looked up the black funnel of the trunk he saw sky which was blue, and some leaves which were green; and he remembered, without smiling, another of his thoughts.

Others had been before him—indeed he had a curious sense of companionship. Little votive offerings to the presiding Power were fastened on to the bark—tiny arms and legs and eyes in tin, grotesque models of the brain or the heart—all tokens of some recovery of strength or wisdom or love. There was no such thing as the solitude of nature, for the sorrows and joys of humanity had pressed even into the bosom of a tree. He spread out his arms and steadied himself against the soft charred wood, and then slowly leant back, till his body was resting on the trunk behind. His eyes closed, and he had the strange feeling of one who is moving, yet at peace—the feeling of the swimmer, who, after long struggling with chopping seas, finds that after all the tide will sweep him to his goal.

So he lay motionless, conscious only of the stream below his feet, and that all things were a stream, in which he was moving.

He was aroused at last by a shock—the shock of an arrival perhaps, for when he opened his eyes, something unimagined, indefinable, had passed over all things, and made them intelligible and good.

There was meaning in the stoop of the old woman over her work, and in the quick motions of the little pig, and in her diminishing globe of wool. A young man came singing over the streams on a

3. Water nymph. "Dryad": wood nymph.

mule, and there was beauty in his pose and sincerity in his greeting. The sun made no accidental patterns upon the spreading roots of the trees, and there was intention in the nodding clumps of asphodel, and in the music of the water. To Mr. Lucas, who, in a brief space of time, had discovered not only Greece, but England and all the world and life, there seemed nothing ludicrous in the desire to hang within the tree another votive offering—a little model of an entire man.

"Why, here's papa, playing at being Merlin."

All unnoticed they had arrived—Ethel, Mrs. Forman, Mr. Graham, and the English-speaking dragoman.[4] Mr. Lucas peered out at them suspiciously. They had suddenly become unfamiliar, and all that they did seemed strained and coarse.

"Allow me to give you a hand," said Mr. Graham, a young man who was always polite to his elders.

Mr. Lucas felt annoyed. "Thank you, I can manage perfectly well by myself," he replied. His foot slipped as he stepped out of the tree, and went into the spring.

"Oh papa, my papa!" said Ethel, "what are you doing? Thank goodness I have got a change for you on the mule."

She tended him carefully, giving him clean socks and dry boots, and then sat him down on the rug beside the lunch basket, while she went with the others to explore the grove.

They came back in ecstasies, in which Mr. Lucas tried to join. But he found them intolerable. Their enthusiasm was superficial, commonplace, and spasmodic. They had no perception of the coherent beauty that was flowering around them. He tried at least to explain his feelings, and what he said was:

"I am altogether pleased with the appearance of this place. It impresses me very favorably. The trees are fine, remarkably fine for Greece, and there is something very poetic in the spring of clear running water. The people too seem kindly and civil. It is decidedly an attractive place."

Mrs. Forman upbraided him for his tepid praise.

"Oh, it is a place in a thousand!" she cried, "I could live and die here! I really would stop if I had not to be back at Athens! It reminds me of the Colonus of Sophocles."

"Well, I must stop," said Ethel. "I positively must."

"Yes, do! You and your father! Antigone and Oedipus. Of course you must stop at Colonus!"

Mr. Lucas was almost breathless with excitement. When he stood within the tree, he had believed that his happiness would be independent of locality. But these few minutes' conversation had undeceived him. He no longer trusted himself to journey through the world, for old thoughts, old wearinesses might be waiting to rejoin

4. Interpreter.

him as soon as he left the shade of the planes, and the music of the virgin water. To sleep in the Khan with the gracious, kind-eyed country people, to watch the bats flit about within the globe of shade, and see the moon turn the golden patterns into silver—one such night would place him beyond relapse, and confirm him forever in the kingdom he had regained. But all his lips could say was: "I should be willing to put in a night here."

"You mean a week, papa! It would be sacrilege to put in less."

"A week then, a week," said his lips, irritated at being corrected, while his heart was leaping with joy. All through lunch he spoke to them no more, but watched the place he should know so well, and the people who would so soon be his companions and friends. The inmates of the Khan only consisted of an old woman, a middle-aged woman, a young man and two children, and to none of them had he spoken, yet he loved them as he loved everything that moved or breathed or existed beneath the benedictory shade of the planes.

"En route!" said the shrill voice of Mrs. Forman. "Ethel! Mr. Graham! The best of things must end."

"Tonight," thought Mr. Lucas, "they will light the little lamp by the shrine. And when we all sit together on the balcony, perhaps they will tell me which offerings they put up."

"I beg your pardon, Mr. Lucas," said Graham, "but they want to fold up the rug you are sitting on."

Mr. Lucas got up, saying to himself: "Ethel shall go to bed first, and then I will try to tell them about my offering too—for it is a thing I must do. I think they will understand if I am left with them alone."

Ethel touched him on the cheek. "Papa! I've called you three times. All the mules are here."

"Mules? What mules?"

"Our mules. We're all waiting. Oh, Mr. Graham, do help my father on."

"I don't know what you're talking about, Ethel."

"My dearest papa, we must start. You know we have to get to Olympia tonight."

Mr. Lucas in pompous, confident tones replied: "I always did wish, Ethel, that you had a better head for plans. You know perfectly well that we are putting in a week here. It is your own suggestion."

Ethel was startled into impoliteness. "What a perfectly ridiculous idea. You must have known I was joking. Of course I meant I wished we could."

"Ah! if we could only do what we wished!" sighed Mrs. Forman, already seated on her mule.

"Surely," Ethel continued in calmer tones, "you didn't think I meant it."

"Most certainly I did. I have made all my plans on the supposition that we are stopping here, and it will be extremely inconvenient, indeed, impossible for me to start."

He delivered this remark with an air of great conviction, and Mrs. Forman and Mr. Graham had to turn away to hide their smiles.

"I am sorry I spoke so carelessly; it was wrong of me. But, you know, we can't break up our party, and even one night here would make us miss the boat at Patras."

Mrs. Forman, in an aside, called Mr. Graham's attention to the excellent way in which Ethel managed her father.

"I don't mind about the Patras boat. You said that we should stop here, and we are stopping."

It seemed as if the inhabitants of the Khan had divined in some mysterious way that the altercation touched them. The old woman stopped her spinning, while the young man and the two children stood behind Mr. Lucas, as if supporting him.

Neither arguments nor entreaties moved him. He said little, but he was absolutely determined, because for the first time he saw his daily life aright. What need had he to return to England? Who would miss him? His friends were dead or cold. Ethel loved him in a way, but, as was right, she had other interests. His other children he seldom saw. He had only one other relative, his sister Julia, whom he both feared and hated. It was no effort to struggle. He would be a fool as well as a coward if he stirred from the place which brought him happiness and peace.

At last Ethel, to humor him, and not disinclined to air her modern Greek, went into the Khan with the astonished dragoman to look at the rooms. The woman inside received them with loud welcomes, and the young man, when no one was looking, began to lead Mr. Lucas' mule to the stable.

"Drop it, you brigand!" shouted Graham, who always declared that foreigners could understand English if they chose. He was right, for the man obeyed, and they all stood waiting for Ethel's return.

She emerged at last, with close-gathered skirts, followed by the dragoman bearing the little pig, which he had bought at a bargain.

"My dear papa, I will do all I can for you, but stop in that Khan—no."

"Are there—fleas?" asked Mrs. Forman.

Ethel intimated that "fleas" was not the word.

"Well, I am afraid that settles it," said Mrs. Forman, "I know how particular Mr. Lucas is."

"It does not settle it," said Mr. Lucas. "Ethel, you go on. I do not want you. I don't know why I ever consulted you. I shall stop here alone."

"That is absolute nonsense," said Ethel, losing her temper. "How can you be left alone at your age? How would you get your meals or your bath? All your letters are waiting for you at Patras. You'll miss the boat. That means missing the London operas, and upsetting all your engagements for the month. And as if you could travel by yourself!"

"They might knife you," was Mr. Graham's contribution.

The Greeks said nothing; but whenever Mr. Lucas looked their way, they beckoned him towards the Khan. The children would even have drawn him by the coat, and the old woman on the balcony stopped her almost completed spinning, and fixed him with mysterious appealing eyes. As he fought, the issue assumed gigantic proportions, and he believed that he was not merely stopping because he had regained youth or seen beauty or found happiness, but because in that place and with those people a supreme event was awaiting him which would transfigure the face of the world. The moment was so tremendous that he abandoned words and arguments as useless, and rested on the strength of his mighty unrevealed allies: silent men, murmuring water, and whispering trees. For the whole place called with one voice, articulate to him, and his garrulous opponents became every minute more meaningless and absurd. Soon they would be tired and go chattering away into the sun, leaving him to the cool grove and the moonlight and the destiny he foresaw.

Mrs. Forman and the dragoman had indeed already started, amid the piercing screams of the little pig, and the struggle might have gone on indefinitely if Ethel had not called in Mr. Graham.

"Can you help me?" she whispered. "He is absolutely unmanageable."

"I'm no good at arguing—but if I could help you in any other way—" and he looked down complacently at his well-made figure.

Ethel hesitated. Then she said: "Help me in any way you can. After all, it is for his good that we do it."

"Then have his mule led up behind him."

So when Mr. Lucas thought he had gained the day, he suddenly felt himself lifted off the ground, and sat sideways on the saddle, and at the same time the mule started off at a trot. He said nothing, for he had nothing to say, and even his face showed little emotion as he felt the shade pass and heard the sound of the water cease. Mr. Graham was running at his side, hat in hand, apologizing.

"I know I had no business to do it, and I do beg your pardon awfully. But I do hope that some day you too will feel that I was— damn!"

A stone had caught him in the middle of the back. It was thrown by the little boy, who was pursuing them along the mule track. He was followed by his sister, also throwing stones.

Ethel screamed to the dragoman, who was some way ahead with Mrs. Forman, but before he could rejoin them, another adversary appeared. It was the young Greek, who had cut them off in front, and now dashed down at Mr. Lucas' bridle. Fortunately Graham was an expert boxer, and it did not take him a moment to beat down the youth's feeble defense, and to send him sprawling with a bleeding mouth into the asphodel. By this time the dragoman had arrived, the children, alarmed at the fate of their brother, had desisted, and the rescue party, if such it is to be considered, retired in disorder to the the trees.

"Little devils!" said Graham, laughing with triumph. "That's the modern Greek all over. Your father meant money if he stopped, and they consider we were taking it out of their pocket."

"Oh, they are terrible—simple savages! I don't know how I shall ever thank you. You've saved my father."

"I only hope you didn't think me brutal."

"No," replied Ethel with a little sigh. "I admire strength."

Meanwhile the cavalcade reformed, and Mr. Lucas, who, as Mrs. Forman said, bore his disappointment wonderfully well, was put comfortably on to his mule. They hurried up the opposite hillside, fearful of another attack, and it was not until they had left the eventful place far behind that Ethel found an opportunity to speak to her father and ask his pardon for the way she had treated him.

"You seemed so different, dear father, and you quite frightened me. Now I feel that you are your old self again."

He did not answer, and she concluded that he was not unnaturally offended at her behavior.

By one of those curious tricks of mountain scenery, the place they had left an hour before suddenly reappeared far below them. The Khan was hidden under the green dome, but in the open there still stood three figures, and through the pure air rose up a faint cry of defiance or farewell.

Mr. Lucas stopped irresolutely, and let the reins fall from his hand.

"Come, father dear," said Ethel gently.

He obeyed, and in another moment a spur of the hill hid the dangerous scene forever.

II

It was breakfast time, but the gas was alight, owing to the fog. Mr. Lucas was in the middle of an account of a bad night he had spent. Ethel, who was to be married in a few weeks, had her arms on the table, listening.

"First the door bell rang, then you came back from the theater. Then the dog started, and after the dog the cat. And at three in the morning a young hooligan passed by singing. Oh yes: then there was the water gurgling in the pipe above my head."

"I think that was only the bath water running away," said Ethel, looking rather worn.

"Well, there's nothing I dislike more than running water. It's perfectly impossible to sleep in the house. I shall give it up. I shall give notice next quarter. I shall tell the landlord plainly, 'The reason I am giving up the house is this: it is perfectly impossible to sleep in it.' If he says—says—well, what has he got to say?"

"Some more toast, father?"

"Thank you, my dear." He took it, and there was an interval of peace.

But he soon recommenced. "I'm not going to submit to the practicing next door as tamely as they think. I wrote and told them so—didn't I?"

"Yes," said Ethel, who had taken care that the letter should not reach. "I have seen the governess, and she has promised to arrange it differently. And Aunt Julia hates noise. It will be sure to be all right."

Her aunt, being the only unattached member of the family, was coming to keep house for her father when she left him. The reference was not a happy one, and Mr. Lucas commenced a series of half articulate sighs, which was only stopped by the arrival of the post.

"Oh, what a parcel!" cried Ethel. "For me! What can it be! Greek stamps. This is most exciting!"

It proved to be some asphodel bulbs, sent by Mrs. Forman from Athens for planting in the conservatory.

"Doesn't it bring it all back! You remember the asphodels, father. And all wrapped up in Greek newspapers. I wonder if I can read them still. I used to be able to, you know."

She rattled on, hoping to conceal the laughter of the children next door—a favorite source of querulousness at breakfast time.

"Listen to me! 'A rural disaster.' Oh, I've hit on something sad. But never mind. 'Last Tuesday at Plataniste, in the province of Messenia, a shocking tragedy occurred. A large tree'—aren't I getting on well?—'blew down in the night and'—wait a minute—oh, dear! 'crushed to death the five occupants of the little Khan there, who had apparently been sitting in the balcony. The bodies of Maria Rhomaides, the aged proprietress, and of her daughter, aged forty-six, were easily recognizable, whereas that of her grandson'—oh, the rest is really too horrid; I wish I had never tried it, and what's more I feel to have heard the name Plataniste before. We didn't stop there, did we, in the spring?"

"We had lunch," said Mr. Lucas, with a faint expression of trouble on his vacant face. "Perhaps it was where the dragoman bought the pig."

"Of course," said Ethel in a nervous voice. "Where the dragoman bought the little pig. How terrible!"

"Very terrible!" said her father, whose attention was wandering to the noisy children next door. Ethel suddenly started to her feet with genuine interest.

"Good gracious!" she exclaimed. "This is an old paper. It happened not lately but in April—the night of Tuesday the eighteenth —and we—we must have been there in the afternoon."

"So we were," said Mr. Lucas. She put her hand to her heart, scarcely able to speak.

"Father, dear father, I must say it: you wanted to stop there. All those people, those poor half savage people, tried to keep you, they're dead. The whole place, it says, is in ruins, and even the stream has changed its course. Father, dear, if it had not been for me, and if Arthur had not helped me, you must have been killed."

Mr. Lucas waved his hand irritably. "It is not a bit of good speaking to the governess, I shall write to the landlord and say, 'The reason I am giving up the house is this: the dog barks, the children next door are intolerable, and I cannot stand the noise of running water.' "

Ethel did not check his babbling. She was aghast at the narrowness of the escape, and for a long time kept silence. At last she said: "Such a marvelous deliverance does make one believe in Providence."

Mr. Lucas, who was still composing his letter to the landlord, did not reply.

1911

VIRGINIA WOOLF
(1882–1941)

Virginia Woolf was born in London, daughter of Leslie Stephen, the late Victorian critic, philosopher, biographer, and scholar. She grew up as a member of a large and talented family, educating herself in her father's magnificent library, meeting in childhood many eminent Victorians, learning Greek from Walter Pater's sister. After her father's death in 1904 she settled with her sister and two brothers in Bloomsbury, that district of London which later was to become associated with her and the group among whom she moved. The "Bloomsbury group" included Lytton Strachey, the biographer; J. M. Keynes, the eminent economist; Roger Fry, an art critic; and E. M. Forster. When her sister Vanessa married Clive Bell, an art critic, in 1907, Virginia and her brother took together another house in Bloomsbury, and there they entertained their literary and artistic friends at evening gatherings where the conversation sparkled. In 1912 she married Leonard Woolf, journalist, essayist, and political thinker; together they founded the Hogarth Press in 1917—a press which has published some of the most interesting literature of our time, including an early volume of Eliot's poems (1919) and his *Homage to John Dryden* (1924) as well as her own novels. Virginia Woolf's suicide in March, 1941, resulting from the fear that she was about to lose her mind and become a burden on her husband, first revealed to the public that she had been subject to periods of nervous depression, particularly after finishing a book, and that underneath the liveliness and wit so well known among the Bloomsbury group lay disturbing psychological tensions.

Virginia Woolf came naturally into the profession of writing. Moving among writers and artists, her world was from the beginning the cultured world of the middle-class and upper-middle-class London intelligentsia. She was comfortably off, she had leisure to cultivate her sensibility, she wrote because she wanted to. She rebelled against what she called the "materialism" of such novelists as Arnold Bennett and John Galsworthy, and sought a more delicate rendering of those aspects of consciousness in which she felt that the truth of human experience really lay. After two novels cast rather cumbersomely in traditional form, she developed her own subtle style, which handled the "stream of consciousness" with a carefully modulated poetic flow and brought into prose fiction something of the rhythms and the imagery of lyric poetry. The sketches in which she explored the possibilities of moving between action and contemplation, between specific external events in time and delicate tracings of the flow of consciousness where the mind moves between retrospect and anticipation, were collected in *Monday or Tuesday* (1921), from which *The Mark on the Wall* is printed below. These were technical experiments, and they made possible those later novels where her characteristic method is fully developed—*Jacob's Room* (1922); *Mrs. Dalloway* (1925), the first completely successful novel in her "new" style; *To the Lighthouse* (1927); *The Waves* (1931), the most stylized of her novels; and *Between the Acts* (1941), published after her death. Virginia Woolf was a skilled exponent of the "stream of consciousness" technique in her novels, exploring with great subtlety problems of personal identity and personal relationships as well as the significance of time, change, and memory for human personality. The delicate, lyrical prose of her finest novels was a remarkable technical achievement. Virginia Woolf also wrote a great many reviews and critical essays, collected in *The Common Reader* (1925) and *The Second Common Reader* (1932); informal and personal in tone, her criticism is suggestive rather than authoritative and has an engaging air of spontaneity.

The Mark on the Wall

Perhaps it was the middle of January in the present year that I first looked up and saw the mark on the wall. In order to fix a date it is necessary to remember what one saw. So now I think of the fire; the steady film of yellow light upon the page of my book; the three chrysanthemums in the round glass bowl on the mantelpiece. Yes, it must have been the wintertime, and we had just finished our tea, for I remember that I was smoking a cigarette when I looked up and saw the mark on the wall for the first time. I looked up through the smoke of my cigarette and my eye lodged for a moment upon the burning coals, and that old fancy of the crimson flag flapping from the castle tower came into my mind, and I thought of the cavalcade of red knights riding up the side of the black rock. Rather to my relief the sight of the mark interrupted the fancy, for it is an old fancy, an automatic fancy, made as a child perhaps. The mark was a small round mark, black upon the white wall, about six or seven inches above the mantelpiece.

How readily our thoughts swarm upon a new object, lifting it a little way, as ants carry a blade of straw so feverishly, and then leave it. . . . If that mark was made by a nail, it can't have been for a picture, it must have been for a miniature—the miniature of a lady with white powdered curls, powder-dusted cheeks, and lips like red carnations. A fraud of course, for the people who had this house before us would have chosen pictures in that way—an old picture for an old room. That is the sort of people they were—very interesting people, and I think of them so often, in such queer places, because one will never see them again, never know what happened next. They wanted to leave this house because they wanted to change their style of furniture, so he said, and he was in process of saying that in his opinion art should have ideas behind it when we were torn asunder, as one is torn from the old lady about to pour out tea and the young man about to hit the tennis ball in the back garden of the suburban villa as one rushes past in the train.

But for that mark, I'm not sure about it; I don't believe it was made by a nail after all; it's too big, too round, for that. I might get up, but if I got up and looked at it, ten to one I shouldn't be able to say for certain; because once a thing's done, no one ever knows how it happened. Oh! dear me, the mystery of life; the inaccuracy of thought! The ignorance of humanity! To show how very little control of our possessions we have—what an accidental affair this living is after all our civilization—let me just count over a few of the things lost in one lifetime, beginning, for that seems always the most mysterious of losses—what cat would gnaw, what rat would nibble—three pale blue canisters of bookbinding tools? Then there were the bird cages, the iron hoops, the steel skates, the Queen Anne coal scuttle, the bagatelle board, the hand organ—all gone, and jewels, too. Opals and emeralds, they lie about the roots of turnips. What a scraping paring affair it is to be sure! The wonder is that I've any clothes on my back, that I sit surrounded by solid furniture at this moment. Why, if one wants to compare life to anything, one must liken it to being blown through the Tube[1] at fifty miles an hour—landing at the other end without a single hairpin in one's hair! Shot out at the feet of God entirely naked! Tumbling head over heels in the asphodel meadows[2] like brown paper parcels pitched down a shoot in the post office! With one's hair flying back like the tail of a race horse. Yes, that seems to express the rapidity of life, the perpetual waste and repair; all so casual, all so haphazard. . . .

But after life. The slow pulling down of thick green stalks so that the cup of the flower, as it turns over, deluges one with purple and red light. Why, after all, should one not be born there as one is born here, helpless, speechless, unable to focus one's eyesight, groping at the roots of the grass, at the toes of the Giants? As for saying which are trees, and which are men and women, or whether there are such things, that one won't be in a condition to do for fifty years or so. There will be nothing but spaces of light and dark, intersected by thick stalks, and rather higher up perhaps, rose-shaped blots of an indistinct color—dim pinks and blues— which will, as time goes on, become more definite, become—I don't know what. . . .

And yet that mark on the wall is not a hole at all. It may even be caused by some round black substance, such as a small rose leaf, left over from the summer, and I, not being a very vigilant housekeeper—look at the dust on the mantelpiece, for example, the dust which, so they say, buried Troy three times over, only fragments of pots utterly refusing annihilation, as one can believe.

The tree outside the window taps very gently on the pane. . . . I want to think quietly, calmly, spaciously, never to be interrupted, never to have to rise from my chair, to slip easily from one thing to another, without any sense of hostility, or obstacle. I want to sink deeper and deeper, away from the surface, with its hard separate facts. To steady myself, let me catch hold of the first idea that passes . . . Shakespeare. . . . Well, he will do as well as another. A man who sat himself solidly in an armchair, and looked into the fire, so— A shower of ideas fell perpetually from some very high Heaven down through his mind. He leant his forehead on his hand, and people, looking in through the open door—for this scene is supposed to take place on a summer's evening— But how dull this is, this historical fiction! It doesn't interest me at all. I wish I could hit upon a pleasant track of thought, a track indirectly reflecting credit upon myself, for those are the pleasantest thoughts, and very frequent even in the minds of modest mouse-colored people, who believe genuinely that they dislike to hear their own praises. They are not thoughts directly praising oneself; that is the beauty of them; they are thoughts like this:

"And then I came into the room. They were discussing botany.

1. London underground railway.
2. I.e., heaven, the next world (in

Greek mythology, asphodel flowers grow in the Elysian fields).

I said how I'd seen a flower growing on a dust heap on the site of an old house in Kingsway.[3] The seed, I said, must have been sown in the reign of Charles the First. What flowers grew in the reign of Charles the First?" I asked— (But I don't remember the answer.) Tall flowers with purple tassels to them perhaps. And so it goes on. All the time I'm dressing up the figure of myself in my own mind, lovingly, stealthily, not openly adoring it, for if I did that, I should catch myself out, and stretch my hand at once for a book in self-protection. Indeed, it is curious how instinctively one protects the image of oneself from idolatry or any other handling that could make it ridiculous, or too unlike the original to be believed in any longer. Or is it not so very curious after all? It is a matter of great importance. Suppose the looking glass smashes, the image disappears, and the romantic figure with the green of forest depths all about it is there no longer, but only that shell of a person which is seen by other people—what an airless, shallow, bald, prominent world it becomes! A world not to be lived in. As we face each other in omnibuses and underground railways we are looking into the mirror; that accounts for the vagueness, the gleam of glassiness, in our eyes. And the novelists in future will realize more and more the importance of these reflections, for of course there is not one reflection but an almost infinite number; those are the depths they will explore, those the phantoms they will pursue, leaving the description of reality more and more out of their stories, taking a knowledge of it for granted, as the Greeks did and Shakespeare perhaps—but these generalizations are very worthless. The military sound of the word is enough. It recalls leading articles, cabinet ministers—a whole class of things indeed which, as a child, one thought the thing itself, the standard thing, the real thing, from which one could not depart save at the risk of nameless damnation. Generalizations bring back somehow Sunday in London, Sunday afternoon walks, Sunday luncheons, and also ways of speaking of the dead, clothes, and habits—like the habit of sitting all together in one room until a certain hour, although nobody liked it. There was a rule for everything. The rule for tablecloths at that particular period was that they should be made of tapestry with little yellow compartments marked upon them, such as you may see in photographs of the carpets in the corridors of the royal palaces. Tablecloths of a different kind were not real tablecloths. How shocking, and yet how wonderful it was to discover that these real things, Sunday luncheons, Sunday walks, country houses, and tablecloths were not entirely real, were indeed half phantoms, and the damnation which visited the disbeliever in them was only a sense of illegitimate freedom. What now takes the place of those things I wonder, those real standard things?

3. Street in London.

Men perhaps, should you be a woman; the masculine point of view which governs our lives, which sets the standard, which establishes Whitaker's Table of Precedency,[4] which has become, I suppose, since the war, half a phantom to many men and women, which soon, one may hope, will be laughed into the dustbin where the phantoms go, the mahogany sideboards and the Landseer[5] prints, Gods and Devils, Hell and so forth, leaving us all with an intoxicating sense of illegitimate freedom—if freedom exists. . . .

In certain lights that mark on the wall seems actually to project from the wall. Nor is it entirely circular. I cannot be sure, but it seems to cast a perceptible shadow, suggesting that if I ran my finger down that strip of the wall it would, at a certain point, mount and descend a small tumulus, a smooth tumulus like those barrows[6] on the South Downs which are, they say, either tombs or camps. Of the two I should prefer them to be tombs, desiring melancholy like most English people, and finding it natural at the end of a walk to think of the bones stretched beneath the turf. . . . There must be some book about it. Some antiquary must have dug up those bones and given them a name. . . . What sort of a man is an antiquary, I wonder? Retired Colonels for the most part, I daresay, leading parties of aged laborers to the top here, examining clods of earth and stone, and getting into correspondence with the neighboring clergy, which, being opened at breakfast time, gives them a feeling of importance, and the comparison of arrowheads necessitates cross-country journeys to the county towns, an agreeable necessity both to them and to their elderly wives, who wish to make plum jam or to clean out the study, and have every reason for keeping that great question of the camp or the tomb in perpetual suspension, while the Colonel himself feels agreeably philosophic in accumulating evidence on both sides of the question. It is true that he does finally incline to believe in the camp; and, being opposed, indites a pamphlet which he is about to read at the quarterly meeting of the local society when a stroke lays him low, and his last conscious thoughts are not of wife or child, but of the camp and that arrowhead there, which is now in the case at the local museum, together with the foot of a Chinese murderess, a handful of Elizabethan nails, a great many Tudor clay pipes, a piece of Roman pottery, and the wineglass that Nelson drank out of—proving I really don't know what.

4. Whitaker's Almanack, an annual compendium of information, prints a "Table of Precedency," which shows the order in which the various ranks in public life and society proceed on formal occasions.
5. Edwin Henry Landseer, 19th-century animal painter, reproductions of whose "Stag at Bay," "Monarch of the Glen," and similar paintings were often found in Victorian homes.
6. Mounds of earth or stones erected by prehistoric peoples, usually as burial places; the South Downs are a range of low hills in southeastern England.

No, no, nothing is proved, nothing is known. And if I were to get up at this very moment and ascertain that the mark on the wall is really—what shall we say?—the head of a gigantic old nail, driven in two hundred years ago, which has now, owing to the patient attrition of many generations of housemaids, revealed its head above the coat of paint, and is taking its first view of modern life in the sight of a white-walled firelit room, what should I gain? —Knowledge? Matter for further speculation? I can think sitting still as well as standing up. And what is knowledge? What are our learned men save the descendants of witches and hermits who crouched in caves and in woods brewing herbs, interrogating shrew-mice and writing down the language of the stars? And the less we honor them as our superstitions dwindle and our respect for beauty and health of mind increases. . . . Yes, one could imagine a very pleasant world. A quiet, spacious world, with the flowers so red and blue in the open fields. A world without professors or specialists or housekeepers with the profiles of policemen, a world which one could slice with one's thought as a fish slices the water with his fin, grazing the stems of the water lilies, hanging suspended over nests of white sea eggs. . . . How peaceful it is down here, rooted in the center of the world and gazing up through the gray waters, with their sudden gleams of light, and their reflections—if it were not for Whitaker's Almanack—if it were not for the Table of Precedency!

I must jump up and see for myself what that mark on the wall really is—a nail, a rose leaf, a crack in the wood?

Here is nature once more at her old game of self-preservation. This train of thought, she perceives, is threatening mere waste of energy, even some collision with reality, for who will ever be able to lift a finger against Whitaker's Table of Precedency? The Archbishop of Canterbury is followed by the Lord High Chancellor; the Lord High Chancellor is followed by the Archbishop of York. Everybody follows somebody, such is the philosophy of Whitaker; and the great thing is to know who follows whom. Whitaker knows, and let that, so Nature counsels, comfort you, instead of enraging you; and if you can't be comforted, if you must shatter this hour of peace, think of the mark on the wall.

I understand Nature's game—her prompting to take action as a way of ending any thought that threatens to excite or to pain. Hence, I suppose, comes our slight contempt for men of action— men, we assume, who don't think. Still, there's no harm in putting a full stop to one's disagreeable thoughts by looking at a mark on the wall.

Indeed, now that I have fixed my eyes upon it, I feel that I have grasped a plank in the sea; I feel a satisfying sense of reality which at once turns the two Archbishops and the Lord High Chancellor to the shadows of shades. Here is something definite, something real. Thus, waking from a midnight dream of horror, one hastily turns on the light and lies quiescent, worshiping the chest of drawers, worshiping solidity, worshiping reality, worshiping the impersonal world which is a proof of some existence other than ours. That is what one wants to be sure of. . . . Wood is a pleasant thing to think about. It comes from a tree; and trees grow, and we don't know how they grow. For years and years they grow, without paying any attention to us, in meadows, in forests, and by the side of rivers —all things one likes to think about. The cows swish their tails beneath them on hot afternoons; they paint rivers so green that when a moorhen dives one expects to see its feathers all green when it comes up again. I like to think of the fish balanced against the stream like flags blown out; and of water beetles slowly raising domes of mud upon the bed of the river. I like to think of the tree itself: first of the close dry sensation of being wood; then the grinding of the storm; then the slow, delicious ooze of sap; I like to think of it, too, on winter's nights standing in the empty field with all leaves close-furled, nothing tender exposed to the iron bullets of the moon, a naked mast upon an earth that goes tumbling, tumbling, all night long. The song of birds must sound very loud and strange in June; and how cold the feet of insects must feel upon it, as they make laborious progresses up the creases of the bark, or sun themselves upon the thin green awning of the leaves, and look straight in front of them with diamond-cut red eyes. . . . One by one the fibers snap beneath the immense cold pressure of the earth, than the last storm comes and, falling, the highest branches drive deep into the ground again. Even so, life isn't done with; there are a million patient, watchful lives still for a tree, all over the world, in bedrooms, in ships, on the pavement, living rooms, where men and women sit after tea, smoking cigaretts. It is full of peaceful thoughts, happy thoughts, this tree. I should like to take each one separately—but something is getting in the way. . . . Where was I? What has it all been about? A tree? A river? The Downs? Whitaker's Almanack? The fields of asphodel? I can't remember a thing. Everything's moving, falling, slipping, vanishing. . . . There is a vast upheaval of matter. Someone is standing over me and saying:

"I'm going out to buy a newspaper."

"Yes?"

"Though it's no good buying newspapers. . . . Nothing ever happens. Curse this war; God damn this war! . . . All the same, I don't see why we should have a snail on our wall."

Ah, the mark on the wall! It was a snail.

1919, 1921

EDWIN MUIR
(1887–1959)

Edwin Muir was born on a farm in the Orkney Islands, Scotland, but moved with his family to Glasgow at the age of 14. This move from a simple farming community with deep roots in the past to a large, dirty, industrial city represented a change that haunted his imagination for the rest of his life and which he described vividly in his autobiography, *The Story and the Fable*, 1940. His life in Glasgow was for some years wretched and poverty-stricken. Father, mother, and two brothers died in rapid succession. Muir worked at a variety of jobs in the city—officeboy in a law office, then with an engineering firm, then with a publishing firm, clerk in the office of a beer-bottling factory—before getting a job in a bone factory in Fairport where "except for making a return of the weight of the bones and enduring their stench during the various stages they passed through, I had nothing to do with the stuff out of which the firm ground its profits." Meanwhile he was reading widely and educating himself in both literature and politics. In 1919 he married the novelist and critic Willa Anderson and moved to London. He was by now making his living as a literary journalist on the staff of the periodical *The New Age*. The Muirs lived on the continent for a while, then settled in St. Andrews, still making a precarious living by writing. After World War II Muir was head of the British Council in Prague until the Communists took over Czechoslovakia; he then became Warden of Newbattle Abbey, near Edinburgh. The last few years of his life he spent in a small village near Cambridge.

Muir published his first volume of poems in 1925, and thereafter his poems were to be found regularly (though never in any great number) in periodicals and in nine further slim volumes. He also published several books of criticism, notably *The Structure of the Novel* (1928) and *Scott and Scotland* (1936). He also, with his wife, translated Kafka's novels from the German. It was only on the publication of his last book of poems, *One Foot in Eden* (1956), that more than a small minority of perceptive critics came to recognize his poetic stature. With the posthumous publication of his *Collected Poems* in 1960 his reputation as one of the most original poets of the 20th century was assured.

Muir's range is limited: he was always fascinated by time, by links between generations, by the modern meaning of ancient myths, by the question of identity and change. These interests provide the themes of almost all his poetry. Yet if he had but few themes, the grave precision of his language, the translucent quality of his imagery, the supple, unforced rhythms, and the delicacy of observation and of sensibility that underlies all this, combine to make poetry of remarkable individuality and power. Writing in his autobiography of his first few years in Glasgow, Muir described them as "so stupidly wretched, such a meaningless waste of inherited virtue, that I cannot write of them even now without confused grief and anger." "Inherited virtue" meant much to him, and its waste was to him always a tragedy. For all the sophistication and the knowledge of modern psychology and political theory that Muir acquired, he never ceased to be aware that his roots had been torn from the primitive traditions of Orkney,

and he sought to replant these with new ways. He was far from being a
rustic escapist or an idealizer of the country life. His poetry is often grim
and sometimes nightmarish. But the integrity of feeling, the delicacy and
precision of awareness, and the quiet, seemingly effortless, mastery of a
supple language that we find in his poetry produce in the end a reassurance. Muir belonged to no modern school and followed no contemporary
fashion. Like Graves, but in a very different manner, he found his own
way of relating traditional myth to the tensions of modern life.

Troy[1]

He all that time among the sewers of Troy
Scouring for scraps. A man so venerable
He might have been Priam's self, but Priam was dead,
Troy taken. His arms grew meager as a boy's,
And all that flourished in that hollow famine   5
Was his long, white, round beard. Oh, sturdily
He swung his staff and sent the bold rats skipping
Across the scurfy hills and worm-wet valleys,
Crying: "Achilles, Ajax, turn and fight!
Stop cowards!" Till his cries, dazed and confounded,   10
Flew back at him with: "Coward, turn and fight!"
And the wild Greeks yelled round him.
Yet he withstood them, a brave, mad old man,
And fought the rats for Troy. The light was rat-gray,
The hills and dells, the common drain, his Simois,   15
Rat-gray. Mysterious shadows fell
Affrighting him whenever a cloud offended
The sun up in the other world. The rat-hordes,
Moving, were gray dust shifting in gray dust.
Proud history has such sackends. He was taken   20
At last by some chance robber seeking treasure
Under Troy's riven roots. Dragged to the surface.
And there he saw Troy like a burial ground
With tumbled walls for tombs, the smooth sward wrinkled
As Time's last wave had long since passed that way,   25
The sky, the sea, Mount Ida and the islands,
No sail from edge to edge, the Greeks clean gone.
They stretched him on a rock and wrenched his limbs,
Asking: "Where is the treasure?" till he died.

1937

1. Priam was king of Troy at the time
it was besieged and finally captured and
destroyed by the Greeks. He himself was
killed by the victorious Greek army.
Achilles (hero of Homer's *Iliad*) and
Ajax were Greek heroes in the Trojan
War. Simois (line 15) was the river
that flowed across the Trojan plain.

The Return

I see myself sometimes, an old old man
Who has walked so long with time as time's true servant,
That he's grown strange to me—who was once myself—
Almost as strange as time, and yet familiar
With old man's staff and legendary cloak,   5
For see, it is I, it is I. And I return
So altered, so adopted, to the house
Of my own life. There all the doors stand open
Perpetually, and the rooms ring with sweet voices,
And there my long life's seasons sound their changes,   10
Childhood and youth and manhood all together,
And welcome waits, and not a room but is
My own, beloved and longed for. And the voices,
Sweeter than any sound dreamt of or known,
Call me, recall me. I draw near at last,   15
An old old man, and scan the ancient walls
Rounded and softened by the compassionate years,
The old and heavy and long-leaved trees that watch
This my inheritance in friendly darkness.
And yet I cannot enter, for all within   20
Rises before me there, rises against me,
A sweet and terrible labyrinth of longing,
So that I turn aside and take the road
That always, early or late, runs on before.

                                                    1947, 1949

The Animals

They do not live in the world,
Are not in time and space.
From birth to death hurled
No word do they have, not one
To plant a foot upon,   5
Were never in any place.

For with names the world was called
Out of the empty air,
With names was built and walled,
Line and circle and square,   10
Dust and emerald;
Snatched from deceiving death
By the articulate breath.

But these have never trod
Twice the familiar track,   15
Never never turned back
Into the memoried day.
All is new and near

In the unchanging Here
Of the fifth great day of God,[2]   20
That shall remain the same,
Never shall pass away.

On the sixth day we came.

1949, 1952

Adam's Dream

They say the first dream Adam our father had
After his agelong daydream in the Garden [3]
When heaven and sun woke in his wakening mind,
The earth with all its hills and woods and waters,
The friendly tribes of trees and animals,   5
And earth's last wonder Eve (the first great dream
Which is the ground of every dream since then)—
They say he dreamt lying on the naked ground,
The gates shut fast behind him as he lay
Fallen in Eve's fallen arms, his terror drowned   10
In her engulfing terror, in the abyss
Whence there's no further fall, and comfort is—
That he was standing on a rocky ledge
High on the mountainside, bare crag behind,
In front a plain as far as eye could reach,   15
And on the plain a few small figures running
That were like men and women, yet were so far away
He could not see their faces. On they ran,
And fell, and rose again, and ran, and fell,
And rising were the same yet not the same,   20
Identical or interchangeable,
Different in indifference. As he looked
Still there were more of them, the plain was filling
As by an alien arithmetical magic
Unknown in Eden, a mechanical   25
Addition without meaning, joining only
Number to number in no mode or order,
Weaving no pattern. For these creatures moved
Towards no fixed mark even when in growing bands
They clashed against each other and clashing fell   30
In mounds of bodies. For they rose again,
Identical or interchangeable,
And went their way that was not like a way;

2. God created fish and fowl on the
fifth day; then he created the land
animals on the sixth day, and after that
(still on the sixth day) created man
(Genesis i). Muir seems to have put the
animals together with the birds and
fishes in the fifth day.

3. I.e., after the Fall. After they had
eaten of the forbidden Tree of the Knowledge of Good and Evil, Adam and Eve
were expelled from the Garden of Eden:
Muir here imagines Adam's first dream
after the expulsion.

Some back and forward, back and forward, some
In a closed circle, wide or narrow, others　　　　　　35
In zigzags on the sand. Yet all were busy,
And tense with purpose as they cut the air
Which seemed to press them back. Sometimes they paused
While one stopped one—fortuitous assignations
In the disorder, whereafter two by two　　　　　　40
They ran awhile,
Then parted and again were single. Some
Ran straight against the frontier of the plain
Till the horizon drove them back. A few
Stood still and never moved. Then Adam cried　　　　45
Out of his dream, "What are you doing there?"
And the crag answered "Are you doing there?"
"What are you doing there?"—"you doing there?"
The animals had withdrawn and from the caves
And woods stared out in fear or condemnation,　　　50
Like outlaws or like judges. All at once
Dreaming or half-remembering, "This is time,"
Thought Adam in his dream, and time was strange
To one lately in Eden. "I must see,"
He cried, "the faces. Where are the faces? Who　　　55
Are you all out there?" Then in his changing dream
He was a little nearer, and he saw
They were about some business strange to him
That had a form and sequence past their knowledge;
And that was why they ran so frenziedly.　　　　　60
Yet all, it seemed, made up a story, illustrated
By these the living, the unknowing, cast
Each singly for his part. But Adam longed
For more, not this mere moving pattern, not
This illustrated storybook of mankind　　　　　　65
Always a-making, improvised on nothing.
At that he was among them, and saw each face
Was like his face, so that he would have hailed them
As sons of God but that something restrained him.
And he remembered all, Eden, the Fall,　　　　　　70
The Promise, and his place, and took their hands
That were his hands, his and his children's hands,
Cried out and was at peace, and turned again
In love and grief in Eve's encircling arms.

　　　　　　　　　　　　　　　　　1950, 1952

ROBERT GRAVES
(1895–)

Robert Ranke Graves was born in London of partly Anglo-Irish and partly
German descent—his great-uncle was the distinguished German historian
Leopold von Ranke—but his voice is peculiarly English. He left Charter-

house School to go immediately into the army, serving in World War I until he was invalided out in 1917. After the war he went to Oxford, took a B.Litt. degree and in 1926 began a brief period as Professor of English at the Egyptian University in Cairo. In 1929 he published *Goodbye to All That*, an account of his experiences in the war, which, as he himself put it, "paid my debts and enabled me to set up in Majorca as a writer." He returned to Majorca after World War II and has made his home there ever since.

Graves began as a Georgian poet, but from an early stage it was clear that he was a Georgian with a difference. The mingling of the colloquial and the visionary in his vocabulary, the accent of conversation underlying the regular rhythms of his stanzas, the tension between a romantic indulgence in emotion and a cool appraisal of its significance—these are qualities found even in his early poetry, though it is only in his later work that we find them more consistently employed and effectively disciplined. His best work combines the ironic and the visionary in a highly individual manner, and he is also capable of a down-to-earth poetry, often ironical and mocking in tone and dealing with simple domestic facts or the more annoying of personal relationships, which nevertheless is seen on further reading to reach out to ever wider and deeper implications. He himself has said: "I write poems for poets, and satires or grotesques for wits. For people in general I write prose, and am content that they should be unaware that I do anything else. To write poems for other than poets is wasteful" (Foreword to *Poems 1938–45*). But this is mischievous exaggeration. "What Mr. Graves means," Lionel Trilling has observed, "is that, in our day, only poets can be counted on not to be misled by the lightness and clarity of his verse, by the irony and the humor; that only poets will be sufficiently aware of the tradition in which he writes, and of hearing the truth that lies not only in the doctrinal statements that the poem makes but also in the justice of its diction, in the pitch and tone of its voice * * * " (*A Gathering of Fugitives*, p. 23).

Graves has long made his living by his prose, which is extensive and varied and includes, in addition to *Goodbye to All That*, a number of historical novels in which characters and events from the classical or Biblical past are reconstructed in a lively modern idiom: the most notable of his historical novels are *I, Claudius* (1934), *Claudius the God* (1934), and *King Jesus* (1946). Graves is a good classical and Biblical scholar, though an eccentric one. His interest in classical and Biblical myth is closely related to his theory of poetry and of poetic inspiration, which he expressed in *The White Goddess* (1948), a study of mythology drawn from a great variety of sources but essentially original in its main emphases and interpretations. The book begins as a history of myth, develops into an attack on fashionable kinds of poetry, and ends with his own view of poetry. It preserves the secret wisdom of a people and derives from the great female inspirational principle which he called the White Goddess. Only a return to goddess-worship and an abandonment of patriarchal in favor of matriarchal society can help modern poetry to recover its lost force, clarity, and mythic wisdom. There is often a note of willful exaggeration or mocking mischief in Graves' criticism: he loves to flutter the academic dovecotes, and in the lectures he gave as Clark Lecturer at Cambridge in 1954–55

(*The Crowning Privilege*, 1955) and as Professor of Poetry at Oxford (the professorship of poetry at Oxford is not a regular academic appointment but a visiting lectureship chosen by the vote of all Oxford M.A.'s) in 1964–65 (*Poetic Craft and Principle*, 1967) he deliberately provoked the local academics by contemptuously dismissing most of the accepted great figures of English poetry.

Among the early influences on Graves' poetry were the late 15th- and early 16th-century poet John Skelton, the ballads, Welsh and Irish heroic and popular poetry, and Thomas Hardy (one of the few poets surviving into his own lifetime whom he admired). From 1925 to 1939 the American poet Laura Riding was in Europe and Graves worked closely with and was much influenced by her: they collaborated in the influential critical work, *A Survey of Modernist Poetry* (1927). But for Graves modernism was not represented by the later Yeats or by Pound or Eliot; it had more in common with the work of the American poets John Crowe Ransom, E. E. Cummings, and William Carlos Williams. In his own later poetry Graves becomes more and more the poet of personal relationships, especially of love between the sexes.

In successive editions of his poems Graves has ruthlessly pruned away what he has come to dislike or believes to represent a phase of his poetic career that he has outgrown. He has published over 15 volumes of poetry, of which *Collected Poems* 1959 represents most of what he wants to preserve. He has continued to publish slim volumes of new poetry (*New Poems 1961*; *New Poems 1962*), but the 1959 volume well represents the range and quality of his genius. Its publication was the sign for clear critical affirmation, on both sides of the Atlantic, that Graves is a major English poet of our time. He won the Russell Loines Award for Poetry in 1958 and the Gold Medal of the National Poetry Society of America in 1960.

Flying Crooked

The butterfly, a cabbage-white,
(His honest idiocy of flight)
Will never now, it is too late,
Master the art of flying straight,
Yet has—who knows so well as I?—   5
A just sense of how not to fly:
He lurches here and here by guess
And God and hope and hopelessness.
Even the aerobatic swift [1]
Has not his flying-crooked gift.   10

1931

1. A bird outwardly resembling the swallow, conspicuous for rushing through the air with vigorous wheeling; it is constantly in flight and is only accidentally on the ground.

Down, Wanton, Down!

Down, wanton, down! Have you no shame
That at the whisper of Love's name,
Or Beauty's, presto! up you raise
Your angry head and stand at gaze?

Poor bombard-captain, sworn to reach   5
The ravelin and effect a breach—
Indifferent what you storm or why,
So be that in the breach you die!

Love may be blind, but Love at least
Knows what is man and what mere beast;   10
Or Beauty wayward, but requires
More delicacy from her squires.

Tell me, my witless, whose one boast
Could be your staunchness at the post,
When were you made a man of parts   15
To think fine and profess the arts?

Will many-gifted Beauty come
Bowing to your bald rule of thumb,
Or Love swear loyalty to your crown?
Be gone, have done! Down, wanton, down!   20

                                                             1933

The Reader Over My Shoulder

You, reading over my shoulder, peering beneath
My writing arm—I suddenly feel your breath
    Hot on my hand or on my nape,
So interrupt my theme, scratching these few
Words on the margin for you, namely you,   5
    Too-human shape fixed in that shape:—

All the saying of things against myself
And for myself I have well done myself.
    What now, old enemy, shall you do
But quote and underline, thrusting yourself   10
Against me, as ambassador of myself,
    In damned confusion of myself and you?

For you in strutting, you in sycophancy,
Have played too long this other self of me,
    Doubling the part of judge and patron   15
With that of creaking grind-stone to my wit.
Know me, have done: I am a proud spirit
    And you forever clay. Have done.

                                                             1938

The Devil's Advice to
Story-tellers

Lest men suspect your tale to be untrue,
Keep probability—some say—in view.
But my advice to story-tellers is:
Weigh out no gross of probabilities,
Nor yet make diligent transcriptions of   5
Known instances of virtue, crime or love.
To forge a picture that will pass for true,
Do conscientiously what liars do—
Born liars, not the lesser sort that raid
The mouths of others for their stock-in-trade: 10
Assemble, first, all casual bits and scraps
That may shake down into a world perhaps;
People this world, by chance created so,
With random persons whom you do not know—
The teashop sort, or travelers in a train   15
Seen once, guessed idly at, not seen again;
Let the erratic course they steer surprise
Their own and your own and your readers' eyes;
Sigh then, or frown, but leave (as in despair)
Motive and end and moral in the air;   20
Nice contradiction between fact and fact
Will make the whole read human and exact.

1938

A Civil Servant

While in this cavernous place employed
    Not once was I aware
Of my officious other-self
    Poised high above me there,

My self reversed, my rage-less part,   5
    A slimy yellowish cone—
Drip, drip; drip, drip—so down the years
    I stalagmized in stone.

Now pilgrims to the cave, who come
    To chip off what they can,   10
Prod me with child-like merriment:
    "Look, look! It's like a man!"

1948

Gulls and Men

The naturalists of the Bass Rock [2]
On this vexatious point agree:

2. A small, roughly circular, rocky island in the Firth of Forth, Scotland,
on which there are a lighthouse and
huge numbers of sea birds.

That sea-birds of all sorts that flock
  About the Bass, repeatedly
    Collide in mid-flight,   5

And neither by design, in play,
  Nor by design, in shrewd assault,
But (as these patient watchers say,
    Eyes that are seldom proved at fault)
      By lack of foresight.   10

Stupidity, which poor and rich
  Hold the recognizance of man,
Precious stupidity, of which
    Let him denude himself who can
      And stand at God's height—   15

Stupidity that brings to birth
  More, always more, than to the grave,
The burden of all songs on earth,
    And by which men are brave
      And women contrite—   20

This jewel bandied from a cliff
  By gulls and razor-bills and such!
Where is man's vindication if
    Perfectibility's as much
      Bird-right as man-right?   25

1947, 1948

The White Goddess[3]

All saints revile her, and all sober men
Ruled by the God Apollo's golden mean—
In scorn of which we sailed to find her
In distant regions likeliest to hold her
Whom we desired above all things to know,   5
Sister of the mirage and echo.

It was a virtue not to stay,
To go our headstrong and heroic way
Seeking her out at the volcano's head,
Among pack ice, or where the track had faded   10
Beyond the cavern of the seven sleepers: [4]
Whose broad high brow was white as any leper's,
Whose eyes were blue, with rowan-berry lips,
With hair curled honey-colored to white hips.

Green sap of Spring in the young wood astir   15
Will celebrate the Mountain Mother,
And every song-bird shout awhile for her;

3. The significance of the White Goddess for Graves is explained in the introductory headnote.

4. Cf. Donne, *The Good-Morrow*—"Or snorted we in the seven sleepers' den,"

But we are gifted, even in November
Rawest of seasons, with so huge a sense
Of her nakedly worn magnificence   20
We forget cruelty and past betrayal,
Heedless of where the next bright bolt may fall.

1953

The Straw

Peace, the wild valley streaked with torrents,
A hoopoe [5] perched on his warm rock. Then why
This tremor of the straw between my fingers?

What should I fear? Have I not testimony
In her own hand, signed with her own name   5
That my love fell as lightning on her heart?

These questions, bird, are not rhetorical.
Watch how the straw twitches and leaps
As though the earth quaked at a distance.

Requited love; but better unrequited   10
If this chance instrument gives warning
Of cataclysmic anguish far away.

Were she at ease, warmed by the thought of me,
Would not my hand stay steady as this rock?
Have I undone her by my vehemence?   15

1951, 1953

Dialogue on the Headland

SHE: You'll not forget these rocks and what I told you?
HE: How could I? Never: whatever happens.
SHE: What do you think might happen?
      Might you fall out of love?—did you mean that?
HE: Never, never! "Whatever" was a sop   5
      For jealous listeners in the shadows.
SHE: You haven't answered me. I asked:
      "What do you think might happen?"
HE: Whatever happens: though the skies should fall
      Raining their larks and vultures in our laps—   10
SHE: "Though the seas turn to slime"—say that—
      "Though water-snakes be hatched with six heads."
HE: Though the seas turn to slime, or tower
      In an arching wave above us, three miles high—
SHE: "Though she should break with you," —dare you say that?— 15
      "Though she deny her words on oath."

5. Bird with pinkish-cinnamon mantle and breast, prominent black-tipped crest, and barred black-and-white wings and tail.

HE: I had that in my mind to say, or nearly;
          It hurt so much I choked it back.
SHE: How many other days can't you forget?
          How many other loves and landscapes?   20
HE: You are jealous?
SHE: Damnably.
HE: The past is past.
SHE: And this?
HE: Whatever happens, this goes on.   25
SHE: Without a future? Sweetheart, tell me now:
          What do you want of me? I must know that.
HE: Nothing that isn't freely mine already.
SHE: Say what is freely yours and you shall have it.
HE: Nothing that, loving you, I could dare take.   30
SHE: O, for an answer with no "nothing" in it!
HE: Then give me everything that's left.
SHE: Left after what?
HE: After whatever happens:
          Skies have already fallen, seas are slime,
          Water-snakes poke and peer six-headedly—   35
SHE: And I lie snugly in the Devil's arms.
HE: I said: "Whatever happens." Are you crying?
SHE: You'll not forget me—ever, ever, ever?

                              1952, 1953

The Blue-fly

Five summer days, five summer nights,
The ignorant, loutish, giddy blue-fly
Hung without motion on the cling peach,
Humming occasionally: "O my love, my fair one!"
    As in the Canticles.[6]   5

Magnified one thousand times, the insect
Looks farcically human; laugh if you will!
Bald head, stage-fairy wings, blear eyes,
A caved-in chest, hairy black mandibles,
    Long spindly thighs.   10

The crime was detected on the sixth day.
What then could be said or done? By anyone?
It would have been vindictive, mean and what-not
To swat that fly for being a blue-fly,
    For debauch of a peach.   15

Is it fair, either, to bring a microscope
To bear on the case, even in search of truth?

6. The Biblical Song of Songs, or Song
of Solomon.

Nature, doubtless, has some compelling cause
To glut the carriers of her epidemics—
    Nor did the peach complain.   20

                                                        1952, 1953

A Plea to Boys and Girls

You learned Lear's *Nonsense Rhymes* by heart, not rote;
    You learned Pope's *Iliad* by rote, not heart;
These terms should be distinguished if you quote
    My verses, children—keep them poles apart—
And call the man a liar who says I wrote   5
    All that I wrote in love, for love of art.

                                                        1956, 1958

Friday Night

Love, the sole Goddess fit for swearing by,
Concedes us graciously the little lie:
The white lie, the half-lie, the lie corrective
Without which love's exchange might prove defective,
Confirming hazardous relationships   5
By kindly *maquillage* [7] of Truth's pale lips.
This little lie was first told, so they say,
On the sixth day (Love's planetary day)
When, meeting her full-bosomed and half dressed,
Jove roared out suddenly: "Hell take the rest!   10
Six hard days of Creation are enough"—
And clasped her to him, meeting no rebuff.

Next day he rested, and she rested too.
The busy little lie between them flew:
"If this be not perfection," Love would sigh,   15
"Perfection is a great, black, thumping lie . . ."
Endearments, kisses, grunts, and whispered oaths;
But were her thoughts on breakfast, or on clothes?

                                                        1957, 1958

The Naked and the Nude

    For me, the naked and the nude
    (By lexicographers construed
    As synonyms that should express
    The same deficiency of dress
    Or shelter) stand as wide apart   5
    As love from lies, or truth from art.

7. Make-up (French).

Lovers without reproach will gaze
On bodies naked and ablaze;
The Hippocratic [8] eye will see
In nakedness, anatomy;   10
And naked shines the Goddess when
She mounts her lion among men.

The nude are bold, the nude are sly
To hold each treasonable eye.
While draping by a showman's trick   15
Their dishabille in rhetoric,
They grin a mock-religious grin
Of scorn at those of naked skin.

The naked, therefore, who compete
Against the nude may know defeat;   20
Yet when they both together tread
The briary pastures of the dead,
By Gorgons [9] with long whips pursued,
How naked go the sometime nude!

1957, 1958

A Slice of Wedding Cake

Why have such scores of lovely, gifted girls
    Married impossible men?
Simple self-sacrifice may be ruled out,
    And missionary endeavor, nine times out of ten.

Repeat "impossible men": not merely rustic,   5
    Foul-tempered or depraved
(Dramatic foils chosen to show the world
    How well women behave, and always have behaved).

Impossible men: idle, illiterate,
    Self-pitying, dirty, sly,
For whose appearance even in City parks   10
    Excuses must be made to casual passers-by.

Has God's supply of tolerable husbands
    Fallen, in fact, so low?
Or do I always over-value woman
    At the expense of man?   15
                Do I?
                    It might be so.

1959

8. Medical: Hippocrates, the "Father of Medicine," was a Greek physician, 5th–4th century B.C.

9. Monsters in Greek mythology: three horrible sisters with hair composed of snakes, brazen claws, and staring eyes.

W. H. AUDEN

(1907–)

Wystan Hugh Auden was born in York and educated at Gresham's School, Holt, Cheshire, and Christ Church, Oxford. After leaving Oxford he taught school from 1930 to 1935 and later worked for a government film unit. His sympathies in the 1930's were with the Left, like those of most intellectuals of his age, and he spent a short time as an ambulance driver on the republican side in the Spanish Civil War. He traveled in Iceland and China before coming to America in 1939; in 1946 he became an American citizen. He has taught at a number of American colleges, and was elected Professor of Poetry at Oxford for the 1956–60 tenure (the position requires the giving of only a few lectures a year).

Auden was the most active of the group of young English poets who, in the late 1920's and early 1930's, saw themselves bringing new techniques and attitudes to English poetry. Stephen Spender and Cecil Day Lewis were at the time the most prominent of the other members of the new school, which soon afterward fell apart, each poet going his own separate way. Like all his generation, Auden learned poetic wit and irony from Eliot, and he also learned metrical and verbal techniques from Hopkins and from Wilfred Owen. His English studies at Oxford familiarized him with the rhythms and long alliterative line of Anglo-Saxon poetry as well as with the rapid and rollicking short lines (a sort of inspired doggerel) of the early 16th-century poet John Skelton: both influenced his own versification. He learned, too, from the songs of the English music hall and, later, from American blues singers.

The depression which upset America in 1929 hit England soon afterwards, and Auden and his contemporaries looked out at an England of industrial stagnation and mass unemployment, seeing not the metaphorical Waste Land of Eliot but a more literal Waste Land of poverty and "depressed areas." His early poetry is much concerned with a diagnosis of the ills of his country. This diagnosis, conducted in a verse which combined deliberate irreverence and sometimes even clowning with a cunning verbal craftsmanship, drew on both Freud and Marx to show England now as a nation of neurotic invalids who must learn to "throw away their rugs," and now as the victim of an antiquated economic system. The liveliness and nervous force of this early poetry of Auden's made a great impression, even though an uncertainty about his audience led him to introduce purely private symbols, intelligible only to a few friends, in some of his poems.

Gradually, Auden learned to clarify his imagery and control his desire to shock, and he produced, in the years around 1940, some poems (such as *Lay Your Sleeping Head, My Love*) of finely disciplined movement, pellucid clarity, and deep yet unsentimental feeling. At the same time he was developing a more complex view of the world, moving from his earlier diagnosis of modern ills in terms of Freud and Marx to a more religious view of personal responsibility and traditional value without, however, abandoning the ideas and terms he had learned from modern psychology. But he has never lost his ear for popular speech or his ability to combine elements from popular art with an extreme technical formality. He is always the experimenter, particularly in ways of bringing together high artifice and a colloquial tone.

Some of Auden's most exciting work is found in his early volumes, *Poems* (1930) and *On This Island* (1937). *Another Time* (1940) shows greater control and less violence. Of his later volumes, *Nones* (1951) shows most clearly his characteristic ways of combining or alternating the grave and the flippant. Auden is very much the poet of his times: first of the Depression and then of the Age of the Refugee. Unlike Eliot, he has preferred to confront modern problems directly, not to filter them through symbolic situations. For all the brilliance of his achievement, he still gives the impression of never having really found himself, never having fully established his mode and come to rest in it; it is his restlessness and energy which make his career as a poet seem somehow so tentative, as though he were always just about to produce the great poetry of which he is capable.

This Lunar Beauty[1]

This lunar beauty
Has no history
Is complete and early;
If beauty later
Bear any feature   5
It had a lover
And is another.

This like a dream
Keeps other time
And daytime is   10
The loss of this;
For time is inches
And the heart's changes
Where ghost has haunted
Lost and wanted.   15

But this was never
A ghost's endeavor
Nor finished this,
Was ghost at ease;
And till it pass   20
Love shall not near
The sweetness here
Nor sorrow take
His endless look.

1930

1. The poem contrasts "lunar beauty," which is complete, changeless, and impersonal, to the beauty of daylight, which is involved in time and changing human passion.

Petition

Sir, no man's enemy, forgiving all
But will its negative inversion, be prodigal:
Send to us power and light, a sovereign touch[1]
Curing the intolerable neural itch,
The exhaustion of weaning, the liar's quinsy,[2]   5
And the distortions of ingrown virginity.
Prohibit sharply the rehearsed response
And gradually correct the coward's stance;
Cover in time with beams those in retreat
That, spotted, they turn though the reverse were great;   10
Publish each healer that in city lives
Or country houses at the end of drives;
Harrow the house of the dead; look shining at
New styles of architecture, a change of heart.

1930

Look, Stranger

Look, stranger, on this island now
The leaping light for your delight discovers,
Stand stable here
And silent be,
That through the channels of the ear   5
May wander like a river
The swaying sound of the sea.

Here at the small field's ending pause
When the chalk wall falls to the foam, and its tall ledges
Oppose the pluck   10
And knock of the tide,
And the shingle scrambles after the suck-
-ing surf, and the gull lodges
A moment on its sheer side.

Far off like floating seeds the ships   15
Diverge on urgent voluntary errands;
And the full view
Indeed may enter
And move in memory as now these clouds do,
That pass the harbor mirror   20
And all the summer through the water saunter.

1936

1. The "king's touch" was often re-   meaning "the best").
garded as a miraculous cure for dis-   2. Tonsillitis.
ease (cf. "sovereign" as an adjective,

Spain 1937[1]

Yesterday all the past. The language of size
Spreading to China along the trade routes; the diffusion
　　　　　Of the counting-frame and the cromlech;[2]
Yesterday the shadow-reckoning in the sunny climates.

Yesterday the assessment of insurance by cards,　　　　　5
The divination of water; yesterday the invention
　　　　　Of cart wheels and clocks, the taming of
Horses; yesterday the bustling world of the navigators.

Yesterday the abolition of fairies and giants;
The fortress like a motionless eagle eyeing the valley,　　　10
　　　　　The chapel built in the forest;
Yesterday the carving of angels and of frightening gargoyles.

The trial of heretics among the columns of stone;
Yesterday the theological feuds in the taverns
　　　　　And the miraculous cure at the fountain;　　　15
Yesterday the Sabbath of Witches. But today the struggle.

Yesterday the installation of dynamos and turbines;
The construction of railways in the colonial desert;
　　　　　Yesterday the classic lecture
On the origin of Mankind. But today the struggle.　　　　20

Yesterday the belief in the absolute value of Greek;
The fall of the curtain upon the death of a hero;
　　　　　Yesterday the prayer to the sunset,
And the adoration of madmen. But today the struggle.

As the poet whispers, startled among the pines　　　　　25
Or, where the loose waterfall sings, compact, or upright
　　　　　On the crag by the leaning tower:
"O my vision. O send me the luck of the sailor."

And the investigator peers through his instruments
At the inhuman provinces, the virile bacillus　　　　　30
　　　　　Or enormous Jupiter finished:
"But the lives of my friends. I inquire, I inquire."

And the poor in their fireless lodgings dropping the sheets
Of the evening paper: "Our day is our loss. O show us
　　　　　History the operator, the　　　　　35
Organizer, Time the refreshing river."

---

1. Written when the Spanish Civil War was raging. The rebellion by General Franco's Right-wing army against the Left-wing Spanish government, which broke out in 1936 and provoked full-scale civil war, was viewed by British liberal intellectuals at the time as a testing struggle between fascism and democracy. The poem first appeared separately in 1937, the proceeds of its sale going to "Medical Aid for Spain." This is Auden's revised version of 1940. 2. Ancient stone circle (archaeological term).

And the nations combine each cry, invoking the life
That shapes the individual belly and orders
      The private nocturnal terror:
"Did you not found once the city-state of the sponge,   40

"Raise the vast military empires of the shark
And the tiger, establish the robin's plucky canton?[3]
      Intervene. O descend as a dove or
A furious papa or a mild engineer: but descend."

And the life, if it answers at all, replies from the heart   45
And the eyes and the lungs, from the shops and squares of the city:
      "O no, I am not the Mover,
Not today, not to you. To you I'm the
"Yes-man, the bar-companion, the easily-duped:
I am whatever you do; I am your vow to be   50
      Good, your humorous story;
I am your business voice; I am your marriage.

"What's your proposal? To build the Just City? I will.
I agree. Or is it the suicide pact, the romantic
      Death? Very well, I accept, for   55
I am your choice, your decision: yes, I am Spain."

Many have heard it on remote peninsulas,
On sleepy plains, in the aberrant fishermen's islands,
      In the corrupt heart of the city;
Have heard and migrated like gulls or the seeds of a flower.   60

They clung like burrs to the long expresses that lurch
Through the unjust lands, through the night, through the alpine
    tunnel;
      They floated over the oceans;
They walked the passes: they came to present their lives.

On that arid square, that fragment nipped off from hot   65
Africa, soldered so crudely to inventive Europe,
      On that tableland scored by rivers,
Our fever's menacing shapes are precise and alive.

Tomorrow, perhaps, the future: the research on fatigue
And the movements of packers; the gradual exploring of all the   70
      Octaves of radiation;
Tomorrow the enlarging of consciousness by diet and breathing.

Tomorrow the rediscovery of romantic love;
The photographing of ravens; all the fun under
      Liberty's masterful shadow;   75
Tomorrow the hour of the pageant-master and the musician.

Tomorrow, for the young, the poets exploding like bombs,
The walks by the lake, the winter of perfect communion;

3. District.

Tomorrow the bicycle races
Through the suburbs on summer evenings: but today the struggle. 80

Today the inevitable increase in the chances of death;
The conscious acceptance of guilt in the fact of murder;
Today the expending of powers
On the flat ephemeral pamphlet and the boring meeting.

Today the makeshift consolations; the shared cigarette;   85
The cards in the candle-lit barn and the scraping concert,
The masculine jokes; today the
Fumbled and unsatisfactory embrace before hurting.

The stars are dead; the animals will not look:
We are left alone with our day, and the time is short and   90
History to the defeated
May say Alas but cannot help or pardon.
1937   1937, 1940

Musée des Beaux Arts[1]

About suffering they were never wrong,
The Old Masters: how well they understood
Its human position; how it takes place
While someone else is eating or opening a window or just walking
    dully along;
How, when the aged are reverently, passionately waiting   5
For the miraculous birth, there always must be
Children who did not specially want it to happen, skating
On a pond at the edge of the wood:
They never forgot
That even the dreadful martyrdom must run its course   10
Anyhow in a corner, some untidy spot
Where the dogs go on with their doggy life and the torturer's horse
Scratches its innocent behind on a tree.

In Brueghel's *Icarus*,[2] for instance: how everything turns away
Quite leisurely from the disaster; the plowman may   15
Have heard the splash, the forsaken cry,
But for him it was not an important failure; the sun shone
As it had to on the white legs disappearing into the green
Water; and the expensive delicate ship that must have seen

1. "Museum of Fine Arts." The reference is to the Museum of Fine Arts in Brussels, which contains Brueghel's *Icarus*.
2. Icarus was the son of Daedalus, the cunning craftsman of ancient legend. Together they flew on artificial wings fastened to their shoulders with wax, but Icarus ventured too near the sun, which melted the wax, and so he fell and perished. The painting of the fall of Icarus is by the Flemish painter Pieter Brueghel (ca. 1520–69): Icarus' legs are disappearing into the sea in one corner of the picture, the rest of which has nothing to do with him.

Something amazing, a boy falling out of the sky,   20
Had somewhere to get to and sailed calmly on.

1940

Lay Your Sleeping Head, My Love

Lay your sleeping head, my love,
Human on my faithless arm;
Time and fevers burn away
Individual beauty from
Thoughtful children, and the grave   5
Proves the child ephemeral:
But in my arms till break of day
Let the living creature lie,
Mortal, guilty, but to me
The entirely beautiful.   10

Soul and body have no bounds:
To lovers as they lie upon
Her tolerant enchanted slope
In their ordinary swoon,
Grave the vision Venus sends   15
Of supernatural sympathy,
Universal love and hope;
While an abstract insight wakes
Among the glaciers and the rocks
The hermit's sensual ecstasy.   20

Certainty, fidelity
On the stroke of midnight pass
Like vibrations of a bell,
And fashionable madmen raise
Their pedantic boring cry: 25
Every farthing of the cost,
All the dreaded cards foretell,
Shall be paid, but from this night
Not a whisper, not a thought,
Not a kiss nor look be lost.   30

Beauty, midnight, vision dies:
Let the winds of dawn that blow
Softly round your dreaming head
Such a day of sweetness show
Eye and knocking heart may bless,   35
Find the mortal world enough;
Noons of dryness see you fed
By the involuntary powers,
Nights of insult let you pass
Watched by every human love.   40

1940

In Memory of W. B. Yeats

(D. JAN. 1939)

1

He disappeared in the dead of winter:
The brooks were frozen, the airports almost deserted,
And snow disfigured the public statues;
The mercury sank in the mouth of the dying day.
O all the instruments agree   5
The day of his death was a dark cold day.

Far from his illness
The wolves ran on through the evergreen forests,
The peasant river was untempted by the fashionable quays;
By mourning tongues   10
The death of the poet was kept from his poems.

But for him it was his last afternoon as himself,
An afternoon of nurses and rumors;
The provinces of his body revolted,
The squares of his mind were empty,   15
Silence invaded the suburbs,
The current of his feeling failed: he became his admirers.

Now he is scattered among a hundred cities
And wholly given over to unfamiliar affections;
To find his happiness in another kind of wood   20
And be punished under a foreign code of conscience.
The words of a dead man
Are modified in the guts of the living.

But in the importance and noise of tomorrow
When the brokers are roaring like beasts on the floor of the
        Bourse,[1]   25
And the poor have the sufferings to which they are fairly
        accustomed,
And each in the cell of himself is almost convinced of his freedom;
A few thousand will think of this day
As one thinks of a day when one did something slightly unusual.
O all the instruments agree   30
The day of his death was a dark cold day.

2

You were silly like us: your gift survived it all;
The parish of rich women, physical decay,
Yourself; mad Ireland hurt you into poetry.
Now Ireland has her madness and her weather still,   35
For poetry makes nothing happen: it survives
In the valley of its saying where executives
Would never want to tamper; it flows south

---

1. Stock exchange.

From ranches of isolation and the busy griefs,
Raw towns that we believe and die in; it survives,   40
A way of happening, a mouth.

3

Earth, receive an honored guest;
William Yeats is laid to rest:
Let the Irish vessel lie
Emptied of its poetry.   45

Time that is intolerant
Of the brave and innocent,
And indifferent in a week
To a beautiful physique,

Worships language and forgives   50
Everyone by whom it lives;
Pardons cowardice, conceit,
Lays its honours at their feet.

Time that with this strange excuse
Pardoned Kipling and his views,   55
And will pardon Paul Claudel,
Pardons him for writing well.[4]

In the nightmare of the dark
All the dogs of Europe bark,
And the living nations wait,   60
Each sequestered in its hate;

Intellectual disgrace
Stares from every human face,
And the seas of pity lie
Locked and frozen in each eye.   65

Follow, poet, follow right
To the bottom of the night,
With your unconstraining voice
Still persuade us to rejoice;

With the farming of a verse   70
Make a vineyard of the curse,
Sing of human unsuccess
In a rapture of distress;

In the deserts of the heart
Let the healing fountain start,   75
In the prison of his days
Teach the free man how to praise.

1940

---

4. Kipling's "views" were imperialistic and jingoistic; Paul Claudel (1868–1955), French poet, dramatist, and diplomat, was an extreme Right-winger in his political ideas. Yeats's own politics were at times antidemocratic and appeared to favor dictatorship.

Their Lonely Betters

As I listened from a beach-chair in the shade
To all the noises that my garden made,
It seemed to me only proper that words
Should be withheld from vegetables and birds.

A robin with no Christian name ran through   5
The Robin-Anthem which was all it knew,
And rustling flowers for some third party waited
To say which pairs, if any, should get mated.

No one of them was capable of lying,
There was not one which knew that it was dying   10
Or could have with a rhythm or a rhyme
Assumed responsibility for time.

Let them leave language to their lonely betters
Who count some days and long for certain letters;
We, too, make noises when we laugh or weep,   15
Words are for those with promises to keep.

                                                    1951

In Praise of Limestone

If it form the one landscape that we the inconstant ones
    Are consistently homesick for, this is chiefly
Because it dissolves in water. Mark these rounded slopes
    With their surface fragrance of thyme and beneath
A secret system of caves and conduits; hear these springs   5
    That spurt out everywhere with a chuckle
Each filling a private pool for its fish and carving
    Its own little ravine whose cliffs entertain
The butterfly and the lizard; examine this region
    Of short distances and definite places: 10
What could be more like Mother or a fitter background
    For her son, for the nude young male who lounges
Against a rock displaying his dildo, never doubting
    That for all his faults he is loved, whose works are but
Extensions of his power to charm? From weathered outcrop   15
    To hill-top temple, from appearing waters to
Conspicuous fountains, from a wild to a formal vineyard,
    Are ingenious but short steps that a child's wish
To receive more attention than his brothers, whether
    By pleasing or teasing, can easily take.   20

Watch, then, the band of rivals as they climb up and down
    Their steep stone gennels [1] in twos and threes, sometimes

1. A "gennel," in the dialect of Auden's native Yorkshire and other northern counties, is a long narrow passage between houses. Here it is a passage between rocks.

Arm in arm, but never, thank God, in step; or engaged
   On the shady side of a square at midday in
Voluble discourse, knowing each other too well to think   25
   There are any important secrets, unable
To conceive a god whose temper-tantrums are moral
   And not to be pacified by a clever line
Or a good lay: for, accustomed to a stone that responds,
   They have never had to veil their faces in awe   30
Of a crater whose blazing fury could not be fixed;
   Adjusted to the local needs of valleys
Where everything can be touched or reached by walking,
   Their eyes have never looked into infinite space
Through the lattice-work of a nomad's comb;[2] born lucky,   35
   Their legs have never encountered the fungi
And insects of the jungle, the monstrous forms and lives
   With which we have nothing, we like to hope, in common.
So, when one of them goes to the bad, the way his mind works
   Remains comprehensible: to become a pimp   40
Or deal in fake jewelry or ruin a fine tenor voice
   For effects that bring down the house could happen to all
But the best and the worst of us . . .
                         That is why, I suppose,
   The best and worst never stayed here long but sought   45
Immoderate soils where the beauty was not so external,
   The light less public and the meaning of life
Something more than a mad camp. "Come!" cried the granite wastes,
   "How evasive is your humor, how accidental
Your kindest kiss, how permanent is death." (Saints-to-be
   Slipped away sighing.) "Come!" purred the clays and gravels.   50
"On our plains there is room for armies to drill; rivers
   Wait to be tamed and slaves to construct you a tomb
In the grand manner: soft as the earth is mankind and both
   Need to be altered." (Intendant Caesars rose and
Left, slamming the door.) But the really reckless were fetched   55
   By an older colder voice, the oceanic whisper:
"I am the solitude that asks and promises nothing;
   That is how I shall set you free. There is no love;
There are only the various envies, all of them sad."

They were right, my dear, all those voices were right   60
And still are; this land is not the sweet home that it looks,
   Nor its peace the historical calm of a site
Where something was settled once and for all: A backward
   And delapidated province, connected
To the big busy world by a tunnel, with a certain   65
   Seedy appeal, is that all it is now? Not quite:
It has a worldly duty which in spite of itself

2. The context suggests that this might be a popular name for a plant or tree (cf. "traveler's joy" and "traveler's palm"), but Auden is probably using the phrase quite literally to suggest that these people have never led a nomad's (wanderer's) life. The "nomad's comb" might be the fringe of unkempt hair through which the nomad peers at wild landscapes.

It does not neglect, but calls into question
All the Great Powers assumed; it disturbs our rights. The poet,
  Admired for his earnest habit of calling   70
The sun the sun, his mind Puzzle, is made uneasy
  By these solid statues which so obviously doubt
His antimythological myth; and these gamins,
  Pursuing the scientist down the tiled colonnade
With such lively offers,[3] rebuke his concern for Nature's   75
  Remotest aspects: I, too, am reproached, for what
And how much you know. Not to lose time, not to get caught,
  Not to be left behind, not, please! to resemble
The beasts who repeat themselves, or a thing like water
  Or stone whose conduct can be predicted, these   80
Are our Common Prayer, whose greatest comfort is music
  Which can be made anywhere, is invisible,
And does not smell. In so far as we have to look forward
  To death as a fact, no doubt we are right: But if
Sins can be forgiven, if bodies rise from the dead,   85
  These modifications of matter into
Innocent athletes and gesticulating fountains,
  Made solely for pleasure, make a further point:
The blessed will not care what angle they are regarded from,
  Having nothing to hide. Dear, I know nothing of   90
Either, but when I try to imagine a faultless love
  Or the life to come, what I hear is the murmur
Of underground streams, what I see is a limestone landscape.

                                                              1948, 1951

3. These are not to be taken as literal statues of gamins (urchins) or man-made colonnades; they suggest rather that limestone is easily worked (by nature as well as by art) into shapes that remind us of familiar objects in the customary human world, unlike the "granite wastes" (line 47) and other sterner landscapes with which the limestone landscape is contrasted. The scientist, concerned with "Nature's remotest aspects," is "rebuked" by the familiar limestone shapes which suggest that man and his ordinary needs are more important. A basic theme of the poem is that easily weathered and easily worked limestone joins the natural to the human world, so that there is an easy transition "From weathered outcrop / To hilltop temple, from appearing waters to / Conspicuous fountains, from a wild to a formal vineyard" (lines 15–18). Saints, would-be world conquerors, and solitary mystics prefer less comfortable landscapes; and even the limestone landscape is not as reassuring as it may seem ("this land is not the sweet home that it looks," line 61). But it asserts the primacy of the ordinary human, and as an ordinary man, not a saint, the poet finds in it the only satisfactory symbol of the good life. The landscape of this poem derives from Auden's native Yorkshire. Cf. "New Year Letter": "I see the nature of my kind / As a locality I love / Those limestone moors that stretch from Brough / To Hexham on the Roman Wall / That is my symbol of us all."

LOUIS MacNEICE
(1907–1963)

Louis MacNeice was born in Belfast, Northern Ireland, and educated at
Marlborough and at Merton College, Oxford, where he studied classics.

For the next ten years he lectured in classics—at the University of Birmingham from 1930 to 1936, and at Bedford College for Women, London, from 1936 to 1940. He was feature-writer and producer for the British Broadcasting Corporation from 1941 to 1949, and after that became director of the British Institute in Athens.

MacNeice uses the modern tradition of irony in his own way. His dry, precise style has none of Auden's verbal brilliance, but it can be highly effective through its very restraint. He has never joined any of the movements in modern English poetry. A carefully controlled melancholy underlies much of his poetry; he has a somber sense of modern life, of its tragicomedies and futilities, and above all of the sadness that underlies all modern attempts to recapture, in memories of youth or by sudden emotion when listening to a street singer or watching a landscape, a sense of significance in daily living. His best poetry has always been fairly low-pressured, sardonic in a subdued manner, but with an occasional burst of wild Celtic irony. There is an integrity of feeling and a consistently high level of craftsmanship in his work that give his poems their special air of full realization: one never finds on a second reading that one had been taken in by an initial showiness. MacNeice is coming to be regarded more and more in England as second only to Auden among poets of his generation.

Sunday Morning

Down the road someone is practicing scales,
The notes like little fishes vanish with a wink of tails,
Man's heart expands to tinker with his car
For this is Sunday morning, Fate's great bazaar,
Regard these means as ends, concentrate on this Now,   5
And you may grow to music or drive beyond Hindhead[1] anyhow,
Take corners on two wheels until you go so fast
That you can clutch a fringe or two of the windy past,
That you can abstract this day and make it to the week of time
A small eternity, a sonnet self-contained in rhyme.   10

But listen, up the road, something gulps, the church spire
Opens its eight bells out, skulls' mouths which will not tire
To tell how there is no music or movement which secures
Escape from the weekday time. Which deadens and endures.

1935

The Sunlight on the Garden

The sunlight on the garden
Hardens and grows cold,

1. This upland district in Surrey is a usual place to stop on the typical Sunday outing.

We cannot cage the minute
Within its nets of gold;
When all is told   5
We cannot beg for pardon.

Our freedom as free lances
Advances towards its end;
The earth compels, upon it
Sonnets and birds descend;   10
And soon, my friend,
We shall have no time for dances.

The sky was good for flying
Defying the church bells
And every evil iron   15
Siren and what it tells:
The earth compels,
We are dying, Egypt, dying[2]

And not expecting pardon,
Hardened in heart anew,   20
But glad to have sat under
Thunder and rain with you,
And grateful too
For sunlight on the garden.

1937   1938

Bagpipe Music

It's no go the merrygoround, it's no go the rickshaw,
All we want is a limousine and a ticket for the peepshow.
Their knickers are made of crepe-de-chine, their shoes are made of
    python,
Their halls are lined with tiger rugs and their walls with heads of
    bison.

John MacDonald found a corpse, put it under the sofa,   5
Waited till it came to life and hit it with a poker,
Sold its eyes for souvenirs, sold its blood for whisky,
Kept its bones for dumbbells to use when he was fifty.

It's no go the Yogi-Man, it's no go Blavatsky,[3]
All we want is a bank balance and a bit of skirt in a taxi.   10

---

2. Cf. Antony's speech in *Antony and Cleopatra:* "I am dying, Egypt, dying" (IV.xv.41).
3. **Madame Blavatsky (1831–91),** the famous theosophist whose ideas were popular in some quarters in Britain in the 1930's.

Annie MacDougall went to milk, caught her foot in the heather,
Woke to hear a dance record playing of Old Vienna.
It's no go your maidenheads, it's no go your culture,
All we want is a Dunlop tire and the devil mend the puncture.

The Laird o' Phelps spent Hogmanay [5] declaring he was sober,   15
Counted his feet to prove the fact and found he had one foot over.
Mrs. Carmichael had her fifth, looked at the job with repulsion,
Said to the midwife, "Take it away; I'm through with overproduc-
tion."

It's no go the gossip column, it's no go the Ceilidh,[6]
All we want is a mother's help and a sugar-stick for the baby.   20

Willie Murray cut his thumb, couldn't count the damage,
Took the hide of an Ayrshire cow and used it for a bandage.
His brother caught three hundred cran [7] when the seas were lavish,
Threw the bleeders back in the sea and went upon the parish.[8]

It's no go the Herring Board, it's no go the Bible,   25
All we want is a packet of fags when our hands are idle.

It's no go the picture palace, it's no go the stadium,
It's no go the country cot with a pot of pink geraniums,
It's no go the Government grants, it's no go the elections,
Sit on your arse for fifty years and hang your hat on a pension.   30

It's no go my honey love, it's no go my poppet;
Work your hands from day to day, the winds will blow the profit.
The glass is falling hour by hour, the glass will fall forever,
But if you break the bloody glass you won't hold up the weather.

                                                                  1938

Good Dream

He woke in his usual room, decided
Feeling completely awake to switch
The reading lamp on and read—but where
Is the switch? No switch no light. No light
No chapter nor verse. Competely awake   5
He gropes for the switch and finds the book
He left in the dark but what is a book
Left in the dark? He feels the book
Suddenly gently taken away
By someone's hand and warm voice   10
Begins, beginneth, aloud in the dark:

---

5. New Year's Eve.
6. Pronounced *kaley:* a Scottish Gaelic word meaning a social evening spent in singing and story-telling.
7. A measure of fresh herrings, about 750 fish. The Scottish herring industry failed in the 1930's; the Herring Board (line 25) was a government attempt to provide helpful direction.
8. I.e., "went on the county" (on re-lief).

Here beginneth the first chapter—
But it wasn't the first, he was half way through.
No, says the voice, *the first chapter*
At the first verse in the first voice,
Which is mine, none other's: Here beginneth— 15
But I tell you, he says, I was half way through,
I am completely awake, I can prove it;
Where is the switch? I will show you the place
Half way through.
          There is no switch, 20
The voice replies; *in the beginning*
Is darkness upon the face of the earth
In which you must wait for me till I
Show you the place not half way through
But just begun, the place you never 25
Knew was here.
        But I know this place,
It is my usual room, except
The switch has gone.
        The switch was never
There to start with; which is why
You refuse to wake.
        But I am completely 30
Awake, I told you.
        You will tell me
Once you are. Here beginneth—
I tell you this is my usual room;
I can put my hand from the bed and feel the . . .
Yes?
    The wall—but I can't. Where 35
Has the wall gone? My bed was against it.
What was against it?
        Why is your voice
Moving away? Why do I hear
Water over it?
        There is water
Between us, I am here on the bank, 40
You will have to row.
        Row?
           What
Is a boat for? I am here on the bank
But I need light to row.
        No.
No light until you reach this bank.
Feel for your oars.
        Here are my oars. 45
Then loose that rope. Are you ready? Row.
Here beginneth. . . .
        He dips his oars
And knows the walls receding, hears

The ripples round the chair legs, hears
Larksong high in the chimney, hears   50

Rustling leaves in the wardrobe, smells
All the smells of a river, and yet
Feeling, smelling, hearing, knowing,
Still cannot see. This boat has no
Switch. No switch no light.
> No light?   55
> *Pull on your oars. I am here.*
> He pulls.
Splutter of water, crackle and grinding
Of reeds and twigs; then bump. The hand
That stole the book that was left in the dark
Comes out of the dark, the hand that is hers,   60
Hers, none other's, and seizes his
To help him on to the bank.
> "And God

Said Let there be light" [9]

> His usual room

Has lost its usual walls and found
Four walls of sky, incredible blue   65
Enclosing incredible green enclosing
Her, none other.
> Completely awake.

9. Genesis 1.3. "And God said, let there
be light: and there was light."

1961

DYLAN THOMAS
(1914–1953)

Dylan Thomas was born in Swansea, Wales, and educated at Swansea
Grammar School. After working for a time as a newspaper reporter, he
was "discovered" as a poet in 1933 through a poetry contest in a popular
newspaper. The following year his *Eighteen Poems* caused considerable
excitement because of the strange violence of their imagery and their
powerfully suggestive obscurity. It looked as though a new kind of strength
and romantic picturesqueness had been restored to English poetry after
the deliberately muted tones of Eliot and his followers. Thomas did not,
however, turn out to be the founder of a neo-romantic movement, though
some early critics took him to be so. As his poetry became better known,
and after he had clarified the somewhat clotted imagery of his early style
in his later volumes—*The Map of Love* (1939), *Deaths and Entrances*
(1946), *Collected Poems* (1953)—it became clear that Thomas was an
extremely craftsmanlike poet, and not the shouting rhapsodist that some

had taken him to be. His images were most carefully ordered in a pat-terned sequence, and his major theme was the unity of all life, the con-tinuing *process* of life and death and new life which linked the generations to each other. Thomas saw the workings of biology as a magical transform-ation producing unity out of diversity, and again and again in his poetry he sought a poetic ritual to celebrate this unity ("The force that through the green fuse drives the flower / Drives my green age"). He saw man locked in a round of identities—with the beginning of growth also the first movement toward death, the beginning of love leading to procreation, new growth, and so in turn to death again and to life again, and because of this view he comforted himself with the unity of man and nature, of past and present, of life and death, and so "refused to mourn the death of a child." In his best poems the closely woven imagery (deriving from the Bible, Welsh folklore and preaching, and Freud) is organized to pre-sent aspects of this theme. His more open-worked poems of reminiscence and autobiographical emotion, such as *Poem in October*, communicate more immediately to the reader through their fine lyrical feeling and com-pelling use of simple natural images. His autobiographical work *Portrait of the Artist as a Young Dog* and his radio play *Under Milk Wood* reveal a vividness of observation and a combination of violence and tenderness in expression that shows he could handle prose as excitingly as verse.

Thomas was a brilliant talker (when he felt like it), a considerable drinker, a reckless and impulsive man whose short life was packed with emotional ups and downs. His poetry readings in America between 1950 and 1953 were enormous successes, in spite of his sometimes reckless antics and his deliberately offensive behavior to academic stuffed shirts or those he imagined to be such. He died suddenly in New York, on his third American trip, in November 1953. He acted the bohemian poet as that role had not been played since the 90's; some thought this be-havior wonderful, though others deplored it. He was a brilliant reader of his own and others' poems, and many people who do not normally read poetry were drawn to Thomas's by the magic of his own reading. After his premature death a reaction set in: some critics declared that he had been overrated as a poet because of the sensational role he had played in life. But a balanced view is now possible; it is clear that at his best he was an original poet of great power and beauty.

The Force That Through the Green Fuse
Drives the Flower

The force that through the green fuse drives the flower
Drives my green age; that blasts the roots of trees
Is my destroyer.
And I am dumb to tell the crooked rose
My youth is bent by the same wintry fever.

5

The force that drives the water through the rocks
Drives my red blood; that dries the mouthing streams
Turns mine to wax.
And I am dumb to mouth unto my veins
How at the mountain spring the same mouth sucks.   10

The hand that whirls the water in the pool
Stirs the quicksand; that ropes the blowing wind
Hauls my shroud sail.
And I am dumb to tell the hanging man
How of my clay is made the hangman's lime.   15

The lips of time leech to the fountain head;
Love drips and gathers, but the fallen blood
Shall calm her sores.
And I am dumb to tell a weather's wind
How time has ticked a heaven round the stars.   20

And I am dumb to tell the lover's tomb
How at my sheet goes the same crooked worm.

1934

After the Funeral[1]

(IN MEMORY OF ANN JONES)

After the funeral, mule praises, brays,
Windshake of sailshaped ears, muffle-toed tap
Tap happily of one peg in the thick
Grave's foot, blinds down the lids, the teeth in black,
The spittled eyes, the salt ponds in the sleeves,   5
Morning smack of the spade that wakes up sleep,
Shakes a desolate boy who slits his throat
In the dark of the coffin and sheds dry leaves,
That breaks one bone to light with a judgment clout,
After the feast of tear-stuffed time and thistles   10
In a room with a stuffed fox and a stale fern,
I stand, for this memorial's sake, alone
In the sniveling hours with dead, humped Ann
Whose hooded, fountain heart once fell in puddles
Round the parched worlds of Wales and drowned each sun   15
(Though this for her is a monstrous image blindly
Magnified out of praise; her death was a still drop;
She would not have me sinking in the holy
Flood of her heart's fame; she would lie dumb and deep
And need no druid[2] of her broken body).   20

---

1. Ann Jones was Thomas's aunt; she lived in a farmhouse in the Welsh landscape described in *Poem in October*. The opening lines of the poem describe, in deliberately mixed metaphors and "transferred epithets," the insincerity of the behavior at the funeral in contrast to the genuine grief of the "desolate boy" who in imagination is already dead (lines 7 ff.).
2. Priest of the ancient Celtic pagans (forefathers of the modern Welsh).

But I, Ann's bard on a raised hearth, call all
The seas to service that her wood-tongued virtue
Babble like a bellbuoy over the hymning heads,
Bow down the walls of the ferned and foxy woods
That her love sing and swing through a brown chapel,   25
Bless her bent spirit with four, crossing birds.
Her flesh was meek as milk, but this skyward statue
With the wild breast and blessed and giant skull
Is carved from her in a room with a wet window
In a fiercely mourning house in a crooked year.   30
I know her scrubbed and sour humble hands
Lie with religion in their cramp, her threadbare
Whisper in a damp word, her wits drilled hollow,
Her fist of a face died clenched on a round pain;
And sculptured Ann is seventy years of stone.   35
These cloud-sopped, marble hands, this monumental
Argument of the hewn voice, gesture and psalm,
Storm me forever over her grave until
The stuffed lung of the fox twitch and cry Love
And the strutting fern lay seeds on the black sill.   40

                                        1938, 1939

In My Craft or Sullen Art

In my craft or sullen art
Exercised in the still night
When only the moon rages
And the lovers lie abed
With all their griefs in their arms,   5
I labor by singing light
Not for ambition or bread
Or the strut and trade of charms
On the ivory stages
But for the common wages   10
Of their most secret heart.

Not for the proud man apart
From the raging moon I write
On these spindrift pages
Nor for the towering dead   15
With their nightingales and psalms
But for the lovers, their arms
Round the griefs of the ages,
Who pay no praise or wages
Nor heed my craft or art.   20

                                        1945, 1946

A Refusal to Mourn the Death, by Fire, of a Child in London

Never until the mankind making
Bird beast and flower
Fathering and all humbling darkness
Tells with silence the last light breaking
And the still hour   5
Is come of the sea tumbling in harness

And I must enter again the round
Zion of the water bead
And the synagogue of the ear of corn
Shall I let pray the shadow of a sound   10
Or sow my salt seed
In the least valley of sackcloth to mourn

The majesty and burning of the child's death.
I shall not murder
The mankind of her going with a grave truth   15
Nor blaspheme down the stations [3] of the breath
With any further
Elegy of innocence and youth.

Deep with the first dead lies London's daughter,
Robed in the long friends,   · 20
The grains beyond age, the dark veins of her mother,
Secret by the unmourning water
Of the riding Thames.
After the first death, there is no other.

                                   1945, 1946

Poem in October

It was my thirtieth year to heaven
Woke to my hearing from harbor and neighbor wood
And the mussel pooled and the heron
                Priested shore
                The morning beckon   5
With water praying and call of seagull and rook
And the knock of sailing boats on the net webbed wall

---

3. Suggesting stations of the cross, a traditional series of representations in painting or sculpture of the stages (generally fourteen) of Christ's passion.

Myself to set foot
That second
In the still sleeping town and set forth.   10

My birthday began with the water-
Birds and the birds of the winged trees flying my name
Above the farms and the white horses
And I rose
In rainy autumn   15
And walked abroad in a shower of all my days.
High tide and the heron dived when I took the road
Over the border
And the gates
Of the town closed as the town awoke.   20

A springful of larks in a rolling
Cloud and the roadside bushes brimming with whistling
Black birds and the sun of October
Summery
On the hill's shoulder,   25
Here were fond climates and sweet singers suddenly
Come in the morning where I wandered and listened
To the rain wringing
Wind blow cold
In the wood faraway under me.   30

Pale rain over the dwindling harbor
And over the sea wet church the size of a snail
With its horns through mist and the castle
Brown as owls
But all the gardens   35
Of spring and summer were blooming in the tall tales
Beyond the border and under the lark full cloud.
There could I marvel
My birthday
Away but the weather turned around.   40

It turned away from the blithe country
And down the other air and the blue altered sky
Streamed again a wonder of summer
With apples
Pears and red currants   45
And I saw in the turning so clearly a child's
Forgotten mornings when he walked with his mother
Through the parables
Of sun light
And the legends of the green chapels   50

And the twice told fields of infancy
That his tears burned my cheeks and his heart moved in mine.
These were the woods the river and sea
Where a boy

> In the listening
> Summertime of the dead whispered the truth of his joy   55
> To the trees and the stones and the fish in the tide.
>> And the mystery
>> Sang alive
> Still in the water and singingbirds.   60
>
> And there could I marvel my birthday
> Away but the weather turned around. And the true
>> Joy of the long dead child sang burning
>> In the sun.
>> It was my thirtieth   65
> Year to heaven stood there then in the summer noon
> Though the town below lay leaved with October blood.
>> O may my heart's truth
>> Still be sung
> On this high hill in a year's turning.   70

1945, 1946

Fern Hill

Now as I was young and easy under the apple boughs
About the lilting house and happy as the grass was green,
  The night above the dingle[4] starry,
    Time let me hail and climb
  Golden in the heydays of his eyes,   5
And honored among wagons I was prince of the apple towns
And once below a time I lordly had the trees and leaves
    Trail with daisies and barley
  Down the rivers of the windfall light.

And as I was green and carefree, famous among the barns   10
About the happy yard and singing as the farm was home,
  In the sun that is young once only,
    Time let me play and be
  Golden in the mercy of his means,
And green and golden I was huntsman and herdsman, the
    calves   15
Sang to my horn, the foxes on the hills barked clear and cold,
    And the sabbath rang slowly
  In the pebbles of the holy streams.

All the sun long it was running, it was lovely, the hay
Fields high as the house, the tunes from the chimneys, it
    was air   20
    And playing, lovely and watery
    And fire green as grass.

---

4. Narrow wooded valley.

And nightly under the simple stars
As I rode to sleep the owls were bearing the farm away,
All the moon long I heard, blessed among stables, the nightjars[5]   25
   Flying with the ricks, and the horses
    Flashing into the dark.

And then to awake, and the farm, like a wanderer white
With the dew, come back, the cock on his shoulder: it was all
   Shining, it was Adam and maiden,   30
    The sky gathered again
   And the sun grew round that very day.
So it must have been after the birth of the simple light
In the first, spinning place, the spellbound horses walking
   warm
   Out of the whinnying green stable   35
    On to the fields of praise.

And honored among foxes and pheasants by the gay house
Under the new made clouds and happy as the heart was long,
   In the sun born over and over,
    I ran my heedless ways,   40
   My wishes raced through the house high hay
And nothing I cared, at my sky blue trades, that time allows
In all his tuneful turning so few and such morning songs
   Before the children green and golden
    Follow him out of grace,   45

Nothing I cared, in the lamb white days, that time would
   take me
Up to the swallow thronged loft by the shadow of my hand,
   In the moon that is always rising,
    Nor that riding to sleep
   I should hear him fly with the high fields   50
And wake to the farm forever fled from the childless land.
Oh as I was young and easy in the mercy of his means,
    Time held me green and dying
   Though I sang in my chains like the sea.

                        1945, 1946

Do Not Go Gentle into That Good Night

Do not go gentle into that good night,
Old age should burn and rave at close of day;
Rage, rage against the dying of the light.

Though wise men at their end know dark is right,
Because their words had forked no lightning they   5
Do not go gentle into that good night.

5. Nightjars are nocturnal migratory birds.

Good men, the last wave by, crying how bright
Their frail deeds might have danced in a green bay,
Rage, rage against the dying of the light.

Wild men who caught and sang the sun in flight,   10
And learn, too late, they grieved it on its way,
Do not go gentle into that good night.

Grave men, near death, who see with blinding sight
Blind eyes could blaze like meteors and be gay,
Rage, rage against the dying of the light.   15

And you, my father, there on the sad height,
Curse, bless, me now with your fierce tears, I pray.
Do not go gentle into that good night.
Rage, rage against the dying of the light.

1951, 1952

Topics in
Twentieth-Century Literature

THE CRITICAL REVOLT AGAINST
ROMANTICISM AND IMPRESSIONISM

The most important critical movement of the 20th century has been closely connected with the new ideals of precision of poetic imagery and complexity of poetic organization advocated and practiced by T. S. Eliot. This movement is first clearly discernible in the critical essays of T. E. Hulme (pronounced *Hume*; 1883–1917), most of which appeared in periodicals between 1909 and 1915. Hulme considered that the view of art as self-expression was the prime romantic heresy, and insisted that only through discipline and formality could adequate artistic expression be achieved. He traced the origins of this view to the Renaissance, when individualism was first encouraged, and he considered himself therefore anti-Renaissance as well as anti-romantic. From Renaissance individualism, he believed, sprang those features of modern culture which he deplored— humanism, romanticism, "utopianism," democracy, belief in inevitable progress, pacifism, and relativism. It is an odd collection of heresies, and against them Hulme set (as objects of admiration, to be aimed at): the "religious" attitude (which sees all human endeavor as strictly limited and capable of realizing a particular end only by external discipline); belief in "original sin" (an aspect of the religious attitude, with stress on human limitations); belief in what he somewhat vaguely called "violence"; militarism; "nonvitalistic" geometrical art; and, in poetry, dry, precise language. He prophesied, and he welcomed, an end of the view of life that had come with the Renaissance. In his violent repudiation of all kinds of sloppiness and self-pity in art he proclaimed his belief in authority, order, and impersonality in the fields of art and politics, as well as in religion.

Hulme's influence has been out of all proportion to the consistency or the profundity of his somewhat confused philosophical and aesthetic position. His insistence on clear, dry, hard images helped to bring about the Imagist movement in poetry, which advocated exactly that. His attack on self-expression as an ideal in art fitted in with a widespread feeling that the romantic movement had finally run down and a new type of artistic discipline must be found. Few of those who were influenced by him accepted all the elements in his complex antithesis, although Eliot came closer than most, as his position in matters of Church and State suggest. But his condemnation of the gentle mood-poetry of the Georgians as "romantic," in the sense that it was not sufficiently precise in its imagery or disciplined in its expression, helped to spark that revolution in poetic taste which was to lead to the supplanting of Tennyson by Hopkins

1916

as the great Victorian poet.

These ideas were in the air at the time. Yeats had come by a very different route to a belief in the importance of a ritual stylization in poetry and in the necessity of employing a sharper and clearer imagery than that of his earliest poems. Ezra Pound, who had come to London from America, was inveighing against looseness of poetic expression and demanding sharpness and clear visualization. Eliot had brought with him from America Irving Babbitt's view of the degeneracy of the romantic ideal of self-expression and the need for classical discipline, and was thus ready to be influenced by Hulme and Pound. Eliot also developed Hulme's notions of the impersonality of art, and in his influential essay *Tradition and the Individual Talent* argued not only for "the conception of poetry as a living whole of all the poetry that has ever been written"—which was really the poet's charter of freedom to embody in his own work quotations from or references to any work of the past—but also for the view that "the poet has, not a 'personality' to express, but a particular medium, which is only a medium and not a personality * * * " In objecting to Wordsworth's famous romantic formulation, "emotion recollected in tranquility," Eliot argued that the process of poetic creation involved "neither emotion, nor recollection, nor, without distortion of meaning, tranquility." "Poetry is not a turning loose of emotion, but an escape from emotion." Eliot also insisted on the necessity of the poet's combining wit and passion, and looked back to the metaphysical poets of the 17th century as examples of that "unified sensibility" (where thought and emotion go together) which, he maintained, had unhappily given way in the 18th and 19th centuries to a "dissociated sensibility." In the age of dissociated sensibility, a poet would be likely to be either solemn and passionate or flippant and witty, whereas Eliot wanted him to be both passionate and witty at the same time. Hulme insisted on clarity, objectivity, and discipline; Eliot accepted these and added wit, irony, and intellectual complexity. It is hardly an exaggeration to say that the result was modern poetry, as well as modern criticism.

What the Hulme-Eliot movement achieved in criticism can be better understood if we realize that the most popular kind of criticism (both journalistic and academic) of the late 19th and early 20th centuries took the form of chatty, impressionistic essays, in which the critic talked about the effect a particular work had on himself, threw in remarks about the author's life and times, and in general moved discursively between autobiography, biography, rhapsody, and generalization. At its best, the kind of criticism which tries to demonstrate the value of a work by recording the critic's own impressions of it can be highly effective. Hazlitt, earlier in the 19th century, could convey remarkably persuasively his own mood and excitement on reading a work and so suggest to the reader what its significant qualities were. But even Hazlitt depended to a large degree on generalized and vaguely evocative statements. "Spenser was the poet of our waking dreams; and he has invented not only a language but a music of his own for them. The undulations are infinite, like those of the waves of the sea; but the effect is still the same, lulling the senses into a deep oblivion of the jarring noises of the world, from which we have no wish to be ever recalled." Critics were still writing like that, or trying to, when

Hulme composed his essays.

The impressionist mode of criticism took on a new lease of life under the impact of the aesthetic movement of the late 19th century. Oscar Wilde maintained, in his essay on *The Critic as Artist*, that the function of criticism is not to describe and assess the work, but to use the work as an excuse for projecting the critic's own sensibility. Wilde's master, Walter Pater, in his appreciation of Leonardo da Vinci's great painting "La Gioconda" (the "Mona Lisa"), produced a classic of impressionist criticism: "The presence that thus rose so strangely beside the waters, is expressive of what in the ways of a thousand years men had come to desire. Here is the head upon which all 'the ends of the world are come,' and the eyelids are a little weary. * * * " (See page 1325 for the entire passage.) If we put this side by side with Eliot on the metaphysical poets, or F. R. Leavis on Shelley, we can see clearly the revolution that has occurred in critical thought and methods.

The modern critical movement is indebted also to I. A. Richards (1893–), who began his career as critic with an investigation into the difference between scientific and poetic meaning (*The Meaning of Meaning*, 1922) which developed the view that "a poem has no concern with limited or directed reference. *It tells us, or should tell us, nothing.*" Richards distinguished between "referential" (scientific) and "emotive" (poetic) meaning, and expanded the distinction in his influential *Principles of Literary Criticism* (1924). Here he developed also a psychological theory of value: a valuable state of consciousness is that which involves the satisfaction of the greatest number of "appetencies" (or "impulses") consistent with the least number of frustrations of other "appetencies." He went on to show how poetry, by its special use of nonreferential language, can communicate such a valuable state of mind from poet to reader, provided that the reader has the proper kind of experience in reading. The value of poetry thus consists in its ability to produce in the properly qualified reader the valuable kind of psychological adjustment which existed in the poet at the time of his writing the poem: the organization of the imagery reflects the organization in the nervous system of the poet. If the function of poetry is to communicate to the qualified reader a valuable state of consciousness, then it is important that we learn how to respond properly to it if we are to receive its benefits. How do most readers actually respond to poetry? Richards set himself to investigate this, and in the course of his investigation he tested the responses to particular poems of his students at Cambridge in the 1920's and 1930's. He set before them a mixed collection of good and bad poems, with no indication of date or authorship, and asked them to write critical analyses. The results of his investigation were given in his *Practical Criticism* (1929). In the part of the book from which the extract below is taken, Richards was concerned with explaining and correcting defective ways of reading poetry, preparatory to showing how to read it properly. The list which he gives of the difficulties which lie in the way of adequate reading and evaluation have become part of the inheritance of modern criticism. The "new criticism" in America, with its analytical techniques and suspicion of "stock responses," owes much to Richards.

Thus Richards' work has led to the development of new techniques of analysis and the recognition of complexities in poetic expression which were ignored for the most part by the late 19th-century critics. The necessity of precision and complexity which the Hulme-Eliot approach stressed is now further emphasized by a critic anxious to correlate the subtleties of poetic organization with the subtleties of valuable states of consciousness which poetry, when properly read, can communicate. Once again, we have different currents flowing into the same critical stream.

Meanwhile, another Cambridge critic, F. R. Leavis (1895–), influenced by both Eliot and Richards, and influenced too by Matthew Arnold's insistence that, since poetry was central to a civilization and not an optional luxury, it is of vital importance to discriminate between good and bad poetry, was developing his own contribution to the attack on romanticism and impressionism. With an acerbity of tone deriving from his deep conviction of the importance to civilization of making proper literary evaluations, Leavis subjected both earlier and contemporary literature to close scrutiny, rejecting everything that did not seem to him to be a fully realized expression of a mature attitude. His attack on Shelley set the tone for a host of similar attacks by other critics; it reveals both the insistence on clear and fully visualized images which we find in Hulme (though Leavis has never admired Hulme), the demand for a complexly organized poetic structure made by Eliot and Richards, and the distrust of romantic excess that is part of the spirit of the age. Leavis's single-mindedness, his devotion to what he likes to call *discrimination*, his pursuit of the critic's vocation with a positively priestly sense of dedication, and the vigor and integrity with which he writes, have helped to make him one of the most influential critics of our time, and perhaps (after Eliot) the most powerful single representative of the modern movement.

The analytic techniques encouraged or developed by Eliot, Richards, and Leavis were raised to a new level of sophistication by Richards' pupil William Empson (1906–), the first of the critics represented below to have grown up with the movement; he thus represents the second generation of modern criticism. Empson pursues complexity and multiplicity of meaning (which he called "ambiguity") in poetry with an almost facile, and at times even irresponsible, ingenuity. It is perhaps worth observing that *Seven Types of Ambiguity* (1930; revised edition, 1954) was first produced as an undergraduate essay for Richards at Cambridge. Empson's tendency to regard any given poem as though it were contemporary and anonymous, a timeless "structure of meanings," has had considerable influence on the "new criticism"; it has also brought him into collision with more historically minded critics who have pointed out that unless one pays attention to the different meanings of words in particular times and places, and to the changing intellectual climates and modes of sensibility of different periods, one is bound to misread works written in a previous age. But the verve and high spirits as well as the brilliant ingenuity of Empson's analytic criticism give it an excitement and interest which account for its influence.

One important result of the whole modern movement has been to favor the close reading of literary texts, and this seems to be a permanent contribution to critical method. It is hard to believe that, whatever changes of taste or method may develop, critics will return to the kind of exclamatory generalization that was so common at the beginning of this century. The anti-romantic mood of modern criticism will probably not, in the nature of things, be permanent; but once the responsibility of the reader to read properly what is before him has been established, it is not likely to be challenged. Analytic criticism has had its excesses of ingenuity, but—and perhaps this is its most important achievement—it has taught us to *read* the text which is before us.

So far as the effect of the modern critical movement on poets goes, it must be remembered that one of the streams flowing into 20th-century poetry has derived from the French Symbolist poets, and the Symbolist use of imagery, especially when it involves private associations, is romantic in the sense that it derives from personal feeling rather than from an ideal of impersonal form working on material common to a culture. There is thus, paradoxically, a romantic element in the anti-romantic movement, which is clearly illustrated in Eliot.

T. E. HULME: *From* Romanticism and Classicism

I want to maintain that after a hundred years of romanticism, we are in for a classical revival, and that the particular weapon of this new classical spirit, when it works in verse, will be fancy.[1] And in this I imply the superiority of fancy—not superior generally or absolutely, for that would be obvious nonsense, but superior in the sense that we use the word good in empirical ethics—good for something, superior for something. I shall have to prove then two things, first that a classical revival is coming, and, secondly, for its particular purposes, fancy will be superior to imagination. * * *

What I mean by classical in verse, then, is this. That even in the most imaginative flights there is always a holding back, a reservation. The classical poet never forgets this finiteness, this limit of man. He remembers always that he is mixed up with earth. He may jump, but he always returns back; he never flies away into the circumambient gas.

You might say if you wished that the whole of the romantic attitude seems to crystallize in verse round metaphors of flight. Hugo[2] is always flying, flying over abysses, flying up into the eternal gases. The word infinite in every other line.

In the classical attitude you never seem to swing right along to the infinite nothing. If you say an extravagant thing which does exceed the limits inside which you know man to be fastened, yet there is always conveyed in some way at the end an impression of yourself standing outside it, and not quite believing it, or con-

1. Hulme is here deliberately reversing Coleridge's "romantic" elevation of imagination over fancy in his *Biographia* *Literaria.*
2. Victor Hugo (1802–85), the French poet and novelist.

sciously putting it forward as a flourish. You never go blindly into an atmosphere more than the truth, an atmosphere too rarefied for man to breathe for long. You are always faithful to the conception of a limit. It is a question of pitch; in romantic verse you move at a certain pitch of rhetoric which you know, man being what he is, to be a little highfalutin. The kind of thing you get in Hugo or Swinburne. In the coming classical reaction that will feel just wrong. For an example of the opposite thing, a verse written in the proper classical spirit, I can take the song from *Cymbeline* beginning with "Fear no more the heat of the sun." I am just using this as a parable. I don't quite mean what I say here. Take the last two lines:

> Golden lads and girls all must,
> Like chimney sweepers come to dust.

Now, no romantic would have ever written that. Indeed, so ingrained is romanticism, so objectionable is this to it, that people have asserted that these were not part of the original song.

Apart from the pun, the thing that I think quite classical is the word lad. Your modern romantic could never write that. He would have to write golden youth, and take up the thing at least a couple of notes in pitch.

I want now to give the reasons which make me think that we are nearing the end of the romantic movement

The first lies in the nature of any convention or tradition in art. A particular convention or attitude in art has a strict analogy to the phenomena of organic life. It grows old and decays. It has a definite period of life and must die. All the possible tunes get played on it and then it is exhausted; moreover its best period is its youngest. Take the case of the extraordinary efflorescence of verse in the Elizabethan period. All kinds of reasons have been given for this —the discovery of the new world and all the rest of it. There is a much simpler one. A new medium had been given them to play with—namely, blank verse. It was new and so it was easy to play new tunes on it.

The same law holds in other arts. All the masters of painting are born into the world at a time when the particular tradition from which they start is imperfect. The Florentine tradition was just short of full ripeness when Raphael came to Florence, the Bellinesque[3] was still young when Titian was born in Venice. Landscape was still a toy or an appanage of figure-painting when Turner and Constable[4] arose to reveal its independent power. When Turner and Constable had done with landscape they left little or

---

3. Jacopo Bellini, Venetian painter, died in 1470; his two sons continued the Bellinesque tradition into the 16th century. Titian was born ca. 1477.

4. J. M. Turner (1775–1851) and John Constable (1776–1837), British landscape painters.

nothing for their successors to do on the same lines. Each field of artistic activity is exhausted by the first great artist who gathers a full harvest from it.

This period of exhaustion seems to me to have been reached in romanticism. We shall not get any new efflorescence of verse until we get a new technique, a new convention, to turn ourselves loose in. * * *

I object even to the best of the romantics. I object still more to the receptive attitude. I object to the sloppiness which doesn't consider that a poem is a poem unless it is moaning or whining about something or other. I always think in this connection of the last line of a poem of John Webster's which ends with a request I cordially endorse:

> End your moan and come away.[5]

The thing has got so bad now that a poem which is all dry and hard, a properly classical poem, would not be considered poetry at all. How many people now can lay their hands on their hearts and say they like either Horace or Pope? They feel a kind of chill when they read them.

The dry hardness which you get in the classics is absolutely repugnant to them. Poetry that isn't damp isn't poetry at all. They cannot see that accurate description is a legitimate object of verse. Verse to them always means a bringing in of some of the emotions that are grouped round the word infinite.

The essence of poetry to most people is that it must lead them to a beyond of some kind. Verse strictly confined to the earthly and the definite (Keats is full of it) might seem to them to be excellent writing, excellent craftsmanship, but not poetry. So much has romanticism debauched us, that, without some form of vagueness, we deny the highest.

In the classic it is always the light of ordinary day, never the light that never was on land or sea. It is always perfectly human and never exaggerated: man is always man and never a god.

But the awful result of romanticism is that, accustomed to this strange light, you can never live without it. Its effect on you is that of a drug.

There is a general tendency to think that verse means little else than the expression of unsatisfied emotion. People say: "But how can you have verse without sentiment?" You see what it is: the prospect alarms them. A classical revival to them would mean the prospect of an arid desert and the death of poetry as they understand it, and could only come to fill the gap caused by that death.

5. From a song in *The Duchess of Malfi* (IV.ii). The line is misquoted: Hulme substituted "moan" for the original "groan."

Exactly why this dry classical spirit should have a positive and legitimate necessity to express itself in poetry is utterly inconceivable to them. What this positive need is, I shall show later. It follows from the fact that there is another quality, not the emotion produced, which is at the root of excellence in verse. Before I get to this I am concerned with a negative thing, a theoretical point, a prejudice that stands in the way and is really at the bottom of this reluctance to understand classical verse.

It is an objection which ultimately I believe comes from a bad metaphysic of art. You are unable to admit the existence of beauty without the infinite being in some way or another dragged in. * * * It is essential to prove that beauty may be in small, dry things.

The great aim is accurate, precise and definite description. The first thing is to recognize how extraordinarily difficult this is. It is no mere matter of carefulness; you have to use language, and language is by its very nature a communal thing; that is, it expresses never the exact thing but a compromise—that which is common to you, me and everybody. But each man sees a little differently, and to get out clearly and exactly what he does see, he must have a terrific struggle with language, whether it be with words or the technique of other arts. Language has its own special nature, its own conventions and communal ideas. It is only by a concentrated effort of the mind that you can hold it fixed to your own purpose. * * *

This is the point I aim at, then, in my argument. I prophesy that a period of dry, hard, classical verse is coming. I have met the preliminary objection founded on the bad romantic aesthetic that in such verse, from which the infinite is excluded, you cannot have the essence of poetry at all. * * *

1913   1924

I. A. RICHARDS: *From* Practical Criticism

From *Part I. Introductory*

* * * Whenever we hear or read any not too nonsensical opinion, a tendency so strong and so automatic that it must have been formed along with our earliest speech-habits leads us to consider *what seems to be said* rather than the *mental operations* of the person who said it. If the speaker is a recognized and obvious liar this tendency is, of course, arrested. We do then neglect what he has said and turn our attention instead to the motives or mechanisms that have caused him to say it. But ordinarily we at once try to consider the objects his words seem to stand for and not the mental goings-on that led him to use the words. We say that we "follow his thought" and mean, not that we have traced what

happened in his mind, but merely that we have gone through a train of thinking that seems to end where he ended. We are in fact so anxious to discover whether we agree or not with what is being said that we overlook the mind that says it, unless some very special circumstance calls us back.

Compare now the attitude to speech of the alienist attempting to "follow" the ravings of mania or the dream maunderings of a neurotic. I do not suggest that we should treat one another altogether as "mental cases" but merely that for some subject matters and some types of discussion the alienist's attitude, his direction of attention, his order or plan of interpretation, is far more fruitful, and would lead to better understanding on both sides of the discussion, than the usual method that our language habits force upon us. For normal minds are easier to "follow" than diseased minds, and even more can be learned by adopting the psychologist's attitude to ordinary speech-situations than by studying aberrations.

It is very strange that we have no simple verbal means by which to describe these two different kinds of "meaning." Some device as unmistakable as the "up" or "down" of a railway signal ought to be available. But there is none. Clumsy and pedantic looking psychological periphrases have to be employed instead. I shall, however, try to use one piece of shorthand consistently. In handling the piles of material supplied by the protocols[1] I shall keep the term "statement" for those utterances whose "meaning" in the sense of what they *say*, or purport to say, is the prime object of interest. I shall reserve the term "expression" for those utterances where it is the mental operations of the writers which are to be considered.

When the full range of this distinction is realized the study of criticism takes on a new significance. But the distinction is not easy to observe. Even the firmest resolution will be constantly broken down, so strong are our native language habits. When views that seem to conflict with our own prepossessions are set before us, the impulse to refute, to combat, or to reconstruct them, rather than to investigate them, is all but overwhelming. So the history of criticism,[2] like the history of all the middle subjects alluded to above, is a history of dogmatism and argumentation rather than a history of research. And like all such histories the chief lesson to be learnt from it is the futility of all argumentation that precedes understanding. We cannot profitably attack any opinion until we have discovered what it expresses as well as what it states; and our present technique for investigating opinions must be ad-

1. Richards' term for the critiques written by his students on the unidentified poems which he asked them to comment on. The opinions expressed in the protocols are discussed and quoted extensively in *Practical Criticism;* they are the data upon which Richards bases his critical conclusions.

2. "We shall meet in the protocols plenty of living instances of famous critical doctrines that are often thought to be now merely curiosities of opinion long since extinct" [Richards' note].

mitted, for all these middle subjects, to be woefully inadequate.

Therefore, the second aim of this book is to improve this technique. We shall have before us several hundreds of opinions upon particular aspects of poetry, and the poems themselves to help us to examine them. We shall have the great advantage of being able to compare numbers of extremely different opinions upon the same point. We shall be able to study what may be called the same opinion in different stages of development as it comes from different minds. And further, we shall be able in many instances to see what happens to a given opinion, when it is applied to a different detail or a different poem.

The effect of all this is remarkable. When the first dizzy bewilderment has worn off, as it very soon does, it is as though we were strolling through and about a building that hitherto we were only able to see from one or two distant standpoints. We gain a much more intimate understanding both of the poem and of the opinions it provokes.[3] Something like a plan of the most usual approaches can be sketched and we learn what to expect when a new object, a new poem, comes up for discussion.

It is as a step towards another training and technique in discussion that I would best like this book to be regarded. If we are to begin to understand half the opinions which appear in the protocols we shall need no little mental plasticity. And in the course of our comparisons, interpretations, and extrapolations something like a plan of the ways in which the likely ambiguities of any given term or opinion-formula may radiate will make itself apparent. For the hope of a new technique in discussion lies in this: that the study of the ambiguities of one term assists in the elucidation of another. To trace the meanings of "sentimentality," "truth," "sincerity," or "meaning" itself, as these terms are used in criticism, can help us with other words used in other topics. Ambiguity in fact is systematic; the separate senses that a word may have are related to one another, if not as strictly as the various aspects of a building, at least to a remarkable extent. Something comparable to a "perspective" which will include and enable us to control and "place" the rival meanings that bewilder us in discussion and hide our minds from one another can be worked out. Perhaps every intelligence that has ever reflected upon this matter will agree that this may be so. Everyone agrees but no one does any research into the matter, although this is an affair in which even the slightest step forward affects the whole frontier line of human thought and discussion.

3. "A strange light, incidentally, is thrown upon the sources of popularity for poetry. Indeed I am not without fears that my efforts may prove of assistance to young poets (and others) desiring to increase their sales. A set of formulae for 'nation-wide appeal' seems to be a just possible outcome" [Richards' note].

The indispensable instrument for this inquiry is psychology. I am anxious to meet as far as may be the objection that may be brought by some psychologists, and these the best, that the protocols do not supply enough evidence for us really to be able to make out the motives of the writers and that therefore the whole investigation is superficial. But the *beginning* of every research ought to be superficial, and to find something to investigate that is accessible and detachable is one of the chief difficulties of psychology. I believe the chief merit of the experiment here made is that it gives us this. Had I wished to plumb the depths of these writers' Unconscious, where I am quite willing to agree the real motives of their likings and dislikings would be found, I should have devised something like a branch of psychoanalytic technique for the purpose. But it was clear that little progress would be made if we attempted to drag too deep a plow. However, even as it is, enough strange material is turned up.

After these explanations the reader will be prepared to find little argumentation in these pages, but much analysis, much rather strenuous exercise in changing our ground, and a good deal of rather intricate navigation. Navigation, in fact—the art of knowing where we are wherever, as mental travelers, we may go—is the main subject of the book. To discuss poetry and the ways in which it may be approached, appreciated and judged is, of course, its prime purpose. But poetry itself is a mode of communication. What it communicates and how it does so and the worth of what is communicated form the subject matter of criticism. It follows that criticism itself is very largely, though not wholly, an exercise in navigation. It is all the more surprising then that no treatise on the art and science of intellectual and emotional navigation has yet been written; for logic, which might appear to cover part of this field, in actuality hardly touches it.

That the one and only goal of all critical endeavors, of all interpretation, appreciation, exhortation, praise, or abuse, is improvement in communication may seem an exaggeration. But in practice it is so. The whole apparatus of critical rules and principles is a means to the attainment of finer, more precise, more discriminating communication. There is, it is true, a valuation side to criticism. When we have solved, completely, the communication problem, when we have got, perfectly, the experience, *the mental condition* relevant to the poem, we have still to judge it, still to decide upon its worth. But the later question nearly always settles itself; or rather, our own inmost nature and the nature of the world in which we live decide it for us. Our prime endeavor must be to get the relevant mental condition and then see what happens. If we cannot then decide whether it is good or bad, it is doubtful whether any principles, however refined and subtle, can help us much. Without the capacity to get the experience they cannot help us at all. This is still clearer if we consider the use of critical maxims in teaching. Value cannot be demonstrated except through the communication of what is valuable.

Critical principles, in fact, need wary handling. They can never be a substitute for discernment though they may assist us to avoid unnecessary blunders. There has hardly ever been a critical rule, principle, or maxim which has not been for wise men a helpful guide but for fools a will-o'-the-wisp. All the great watchwords of criticism, from Aristotle's "Poetry is an imitation" down to the doctrine that "Poetry is expression," are ambiguous pointers that different people follow to very different destinations. Even the most sagacious critical principles may, as we shall see, become merely a cover for critical ineptitude; and the most trivial or baseless generalization may really mask good and discerning judgment. Everything turns upon how the principles are applied. It is to be feared that critical formulas, even the best, are responsible for more bad judgment than good, because it is far easier to forget their subtle sense and apply them crudely than to remember it and apply them finely.

The astonishing variety of human responses makes irksome any too systematic scheme for arranging these extracts. I wish to present a sufficient selection to bring the situation concretely before the reader, reserving to the chapters of Part III any serious attempt to clear up the various difficulties with which the protocol-writers have been struggling. I shall proceed poem by poem, allowing the internal drama latent in every clash of opinion, of taste or temperament to guide the arrangement. Not all the poems, needless to say, raise the same problems in equal measure. In most, some one outstanding difficulty, some special occasion for a division of minds, takes precedence.

It is convenient therefore to place here a somewhat arbitrary list of the principal difficulties that may be encountered by one reader or another in the presence of almost any poem. This list is suggested by a study of the protocols themselves, and drawn up in an order which proceeds from the simplest, infant's, obstacle to successful reading up to the most insidious, intangible and bewildering of critical problems.

If some of these difficulties seem so simple as to be hardly worth discussion, I would beg my reader who feels a temptation to despise them not to leap lightly to his decision. Part of my purpose is *documentation* and I am confident of showing that the simple difficulties are those that most need attention as they are those that in fact receive least.

We soon advance, however, to points on which more doubt may be felt—where controversy, more and less enlightened, still continues—and we finish face to face with questions which no one will pretend are yet settled and with some which will not be settled till the Day of Judgment. In the memorable words of Benjamin Paul Blood,[4] "What is concluded that we should conclude anything about it?"

The following seem to be the chief difficulties of criticism or, at least, those which we shall have most occasion to consider here:

A. First must come the difficulty of *making out the plain sense* of poetry. The most disturbing and impressive fact brought out by this experiment is that a large proportion of average-to-good (and in some cases, certainly, devoted) readers of poetry frequently and repeatedly *fail to understand it*, both as a statement and as an expression. They fail to make out its prose sense, its plain, overt meaning, as a set of ordinary, intelligible, English sentences, taken quite apart from any further poetic significance. And equally, they misapprehend its feeling, its tone, and its intention. They would travesty it in a paraphrase. They fail to construe it just as a schoolboy fails to construe a piece of Caesar. How serious in its effects in different instances this failure may be, we shall have to consider with care. It is not confined to one class of readers; not only those whom we would suspect fall victims. Nor is it only the most abstruse poetry which so betrays us. In fact, to set down, for once, the brutal truth, no immunity is possessed on any occasion, not by the most reputable scholar, from this or any other of these critical dangers.

B. Parallel to, and not unconnected with, these difficulties of interpreting the meaning are the difficulties of *sensuous apprehension*. Words in sequence have a form to the mind's ear and the mind's tongue and larynx, even when silently read. They have a movement and may have a rhythm. The gulf is wide between a reader who naturally and immediately perceives this form and movement (by a conjunction of sensory, intellectual, and emotional sagacity) and another reader, who either ignores it or has to build it up laboriously with finger-counting, table-tapping and the rest; and this difference has most far-reaching effects.

C. Next may come those difficulties that are connected with the place of *imagery*, principally visual imagery, in poetic reading. They arise in part from the incurable fact that we differ immensely in our capacity to visualize, and to produce imagery of the other senses. Also the importance of our imagery as a whole, as well as of some pet particular type of image, in our mental lives varies surprisingly. Some minds can do nothing and get nowhere without images; others seem to be able to do everything and get anywhere, reach any and every state of thought and feeling without making use of

4. 1832–1919; American poet and philosopher.

them. Poets on the whole (though by no means all poets always) may be suspected of exceptional imaging capacity, and some readers are constitutionally prone to stress the place of imagery in reading, to pay great attention to it, and even to judge the value of the poetry by the images it excites in them. But images are erratic things; lively images aroused in one mind need have no similarity to the equally lively images stirred by the same line of poetry in another, and neither set need have anything to do with any images which may have existed in the poet's mind. Here is a troublesome source of critical deviations.

D. Thirdly, more obviously, we have to note the powerful very pervasive influence of *mnemonic irrelevances*. These are misleading effects of the reader's being reminded of some personal scene or adventure, erratic associations, the interference of emotional reverberations from a past which may have nothing to do with the poem. Relevance is not an easy notion to define or to apply, though some instances of irrelevant instrusions are among the simplest of all accidents to diagnose.

E. More puzzling and more interesting are the critical traps that surround what may be called *stock responses*. These have their opportunity whenever a poem seems to, or does, involve views and emotions already fully prepared in the reader's mind, so that what happens appears to be more of the reader's doing than the poet's. The button is pressed, and then the author's work is done, for immediately the record starts playing in quasi- (or total) independence of the poem which is supposed to be its origin or instrument.

Whenever this lamentable redistribution of the poet's and reader's share in the labor of poetry occurs, or is in danger of occurring, we require to be especially on our guard. Every kind of injustice may be committed as well by those who just escape as by those who are caught.

F. *Sentimentality* is a peril that needs less comment here. It is a question of the due measure of response. This overfacility in certain emotional directions is the Scylla[5] whose Charybdis is—

G. *Inhibition*. This, as much as Sentimentality, is a positive phenomenon, though less studied until recent years and somewhat masked under the title of Hardness of Heart. But neither can well be considered in isolation.

H. *Doctrinal adhesions* present another troublesome problem. Very much poetry—religious poetry may be instanced—seems to contain or imply views and beliefs, true or false, about the world. If this be so, what bearing has the truth-value of the views upon

5. Scylla and Charybdis were two rocks between Italy and Sicily. In classical legend, the first one contained the cave of a six-headed man-eating monster; in the other lived a monster who thrice daily swallowed and regurgitated the waters of the sea. It was extremely difficult to navigate between them.

the worth of the poetry? Even if it be not so, if the beliefs are not really contained or implied, but only seem so to a nonpoetical reading, what should be the bearing of the reader's conviction, if any, upon his estimate of the poetry? Has poetry anything to say; if not, why not, and if so, how? Difficulties at this point are a fertile source of confusion and erratic judgment.

I. Passing now to a different order of difficulties, the effects of *technical presuppositions* have to be noted. When something has once been well done in a certain fashion we tend to expect similar things to be done in the future in the same fashion, and are disappointed or do not recognize them if they are done differently. Conversely, a technique which has shown its ineptitude for one purpose tends to become discredited for all. Both are cases of mistaking means for ends. Whenever we attempt to judge poetry from outside by technical details we are putting means before ends, and—such is our ignorance of cause and effect in poetry—we shall be lucky if we do not make even worse blunders. We have to try to avoid judging pianists by their hair.

J. Finally, *general critical preconceptions* (prior demands made upon poetry as a result of theories—conscious or unconscious—about its nature and value), intervene endlessly, as the history of criticism shows only too well, between the reader and the poem. Like an unlucky dietetic formula they may cut him off from what he is starving for, even when it is at his very lips.

These difficulties, as will have been observed, are not unconnected with one another and indeed overlap. They might have been collected under more heads or fewer. Yet, if we set aside certain extreme twists or trends of the personality (for example, blinding narcissism or groveling self-abasement—aberrations, temporary or permanent, of the self-regarding sentiment) together with undue accumulations or depletions of energy, I believe that most of the principal obstacles and causes of failure in the reading and judgment of poetry may without much straining be brought under these ten heads. But they are too roughly sketched here for this to be judged. * * *

1929

F. R. LEAVIS: *From* Revaluation[1]

From *Chapter 6. Shelley*

* * * It will be well to start, in fact, by examining the working of Shelley's poetry—his characteristic modes of expression—as exemplified in one of his best poems.[2]

1. Leavis's complete title is *Revaluation: Tradition and Development in English Poetry*. The text is that of the 1949 edition.
2. Shelley's *Ode to the West Wind*, lines 15–23.

Thou on whose stream, mid the steep sky's commotion
Loose clouds like earth's decaying leaves are shed,
Shook from the tangled boughs of Heaven and Ocean,

Angels of rain and lightning: there are spread
On the blue surface of thine aëry surge,
Like the bright hair uplifted from the head

Of some fierce Maenad,[3] even from the dim verge
Of the horizon to the zenith's height,
The locks of the approaching storm.

The sweeping movement of the verse, with the accompanying plangency, is so potent that, as many can testify, it is possible to have been for years familiar with the *Ode*—to know it by heart—without asking the obvious questions. In what respects are the "loose clouds" like "decaying leaves"? The correspondence is certainly not in shape, color, or way of moving. It is only the vague general sense of windy tumult that associates the clouds and the leaves; and, accordingly, the appropriateness of the metaphor "stream" in the first line is not that it suggests a surface on which, like leaves, the clouds might be "shed," but that it contributes to the general "streaming" effect in which the inappropriateness of "shed" passes unnoticed. What again, are those "tangled boughs of Heaven and Ocean"? They stand for nothing that Shelley could have pointed to in the scene before him; the "boughs," it is plain, have grown out of the "leaves" in the previous line, and we are not to ask what the tree is. Nor are we to scrutinize closely the "stream" metaphor as developed: that "blue surface" must be the concave of the sky, an oddly smooth surface for a "surge"—if we consider a moment. But in this poetic surge, while we let ourselves be swept along, there is no considering, the image doesn't challenge any inconvenient degree of realization, and the oddness is lost. Then again, in what ways does the approach of a storm ("loose clouds like earth's decaying leaves," "like ghosts from an enchanter fleeing") suggest streaming hair? The appropriateness of the Maenad, clearly, lies in the pervasive suggestion of frenzied onset, and we are not to ask whether her bright hair is to be seen as streaming out in front of her (as, there is no need to assure ourselves, it might be doing if she were running before a still swifter gale: in the kind of reading that got so far as proposing to itself this particular reassurance no general satisfaction could be exacted from Shelley's imagery).

Here, clearly, in these peculiarities of imagery and sense, peculiarities analyzable locally in the mode of expression, we have the

---

3. Frenzied woman (specifically, attendant on and celebrator of the wine god Bacchus).

manifestation of essential characteristics—the Shelleyan characteristics as envisaged by the criticism that works on a philosophical plane and makes judgments of a moral order. In the growth of those "tangled boughs" out of the leaves, exemplifying as it does a general tendency of the images to forget the status of the metaphor or simile that introduced them and to assume an autonomy and a right to propagate, so that we lose in confused generations and perspectives the perception or thought that was the ostensible *raison d'être* of imagery, we have a recognized essential trait of Shelley's: his weak grasp upon the actual. This weakness, of course, commonly has more or less creditable accounts given of it—idealism, Platonism, and so on; and even as unsentimental a judge as Mr. Santayana[4] correlates Shelley's inability to learn from experience with his having been born a "nature preformed," a "spokesman of the *a priori*," "a dogmatic, inspired, perfect and incorrigible creature."[5] It seems to me that Mr. Santayana's essay, admirable as it is, rates the poetry too high. But for the moment it will be enough to recall limitations that are hardly disputed: Shelley was not gifted for drama or narrative. Having said this, I realize that I had forgotten the conventional standing of *The Cenci*;[6] but controversy may be postponed: it is at any rate universally agreed that (to shift tactfully to positive terms) Shelley's genius was "essentially lyrical."

This predicate would, in common use, imply a special emotional intensity—a vague gloss, but it is difficult to go further without slipping into terms that are immediately privative and limiting. Thus there is certainly a sense in which Shelley's poetry is peculiarly emotional, and when we try to define this sense we find ourselves invoking an absence of something. The point may be best made, perhaps, by recalling the observation noted above, that one may have been long familiar with the *Ode to the West Wind* without ever having asked the obvious questions; questions that propose themselves at the first critical inspection. This poetry induces—depends for its success on inducing—a kind of attention that doesn't bring the critical intelligence into play: the imagery feels right, the associations work appropriately, if (as it takes conscious resistance not to do) one accepts the immediate feeling and doesn't slow down to think.

Shelley himself can hardly have asked the questions. Not that he didn't expend a great deal of critical labor upon his verse. "He composed rapidly and attained to perfection by intensive correction. He would sometimes write down a phrase with alterations and rejections time after time until it came within a measure of satisfying

---

4. George Santayana (1863–1952), Spanish-born American critic and philosopher.

5. "See the essay on Shelley in *Winds of Doctrine*" [Leavis's note].
6. Poetic drama by Shelley.

him. Words are frequently substituted for others and lines interpolated." The *Ode to the West Wind* itself, as is shown in the re-
pository of fragments[7] the preface to which supplies these observations, profited by the process described, which must be allowed to
have been in some sense critical. But the critical part of Shelley's
creative labor was a matter of getting the verse to feel right, and
feeling, for Shelley as a poet, had—as the insistent concern for
"rightness," the typical final product being what it is, serves to emphasize—little to do with thinking (though Shelley was in some
ways a very intelligent man). * * *

The transition from the lighter concerns of literary criticism to
the diagnosis of radical disabilities and perversions, such as call
for moral comment, may be conveniently illustrated from a favorite anthology piece, *When the Lamp Is Shattered:*

> When the lamp is shattered
> The light in the dust lies dead—
> When the cloud is scattered
> The rainbow's glory is shed.
> When the lute is broken,
> Sweet tones are remembered not;
> When the lips have spoken,
> Loved accents are soon forgot.
>
> As music and splendor
> Survive not the lamp and the lute,
> The heart's echoes render
> No song when the spirit is mute—
> No song but sad dirges,
> Like the wind through a ruined cell;
> Or the mournful surges
> That ring the dead seaman's knell.
>
> When hearts have once mingled
> Love first leaves the well-built nest;
> The weak one is singled
> To endure what it once possessed.
> O Love! who bewailest
> The frailty of all things here,
> Why choose you the frailest
> For your cradle, your home, and your bier?
>
> Its passions will rock thee
> As the storms rock the ravens on high;
> Bright reason will mock thee,
> Like the sun from a wintry sky.

7. *"Verse and Prose from the Manuscripts of Percy Bysshe Shelley.* Edited by Sir
John C. E. Shelley-Rolls, Bart., and Roger Ingpen" [Leavis's note].

From thy nest every rafter
Will rot, and thine eagle home
Leave thee naked to laughter,
When leaves fall and cold winds come.

The first two stanzas call for no very close attention—to say so, indeed, is to make the main criticism, seeing that they offer a show of insistent argument. However, reading with an unsolicited closeness, one may stop at the second line and ask whether the effect got with "lies dead" is legitimate. Certainly, the emotional purpose of the poem is served, but the emotional purpose that went on being served in that way would be suspect. Leaving the question in suspense, perhaps, one passes to "shed"; "shed" as tears, petals, and coats are shed, or as light is shed? The latter would be a rather more respectable use of the word in connection with a rainbow's glory, but the context indicates the former. Only in the vaguest and slackest state of mind—if imagination and thought— could one so describe the fading of a rainbow; but for the right reader "shed" sounds right, the alliteration with "shattered" combining with the verse-movement to produce a kind of inevitability. And, of course, suggesting tears and the last rose of summer, it suits with the general emotional effect. The nature of this is by now so unmistakable that the complete nullity of the clinching "so," when it arrives—of the two lines that justify the ten preparatory lines of analogy—seems hardly worth stopping to note:

The heart's echoes render
No song when the spirit is mute.

Nor is it surprising that there should turn out to be a song after all, and a pretty powerful one—for those who like that sort of thing; the "sad dirges," the "ruined cell," the "mournful surges," and the "dead seamen's knell" being immediately recognizable as currency values. Those who take pleasure in recognizing and accepting them are not at the same time exacting about sense.

The critical interest up to this point has been to see Shelley, himself (when inspired) so unexacting about sense, giving himself so completely to sentimental banalities. With the next stanza it is much the same, though the emotional clichés take on a grosser unction and the required abeyance of thought (and imagination) becomes more remarkable. In what form are we to imagine Love leaving the well-built nest? For readers who get so far asking, there can be no acceptable answer. It would be unpoetically literal to suggest that, since the weak one is singled, the truant must be the mate, and, besides, it would raise unnecessary difficulties. Perhaps the mate, the strong one, is what the weak one, deserted by Love, whose alliance made possession once possible, now has to endure? But the suggestion is frivolous; the sense is plain enough—enough, that is, for those who respond to the sentiment. Sufficient recognition of the sense depends neither on thinking, nor on realization of the metaphors, but on response to the sentimental commonplaces: it is only when intelligence and imagination insist on intruding that difficulties arise. So plain is this that there would be no point in contemplating the metaphorical complexity that would develop if we could take the tropes seriously and tried to realize Love making of the weak one, whom it (if we evade the problem of sex) leaves behind in the well-built nest, a cradle, a home, and a bier.

The last stanza brings a notable change; it alone in the poem has any distinction, and its personal quality, characteristically Shelleyan, stands out against the sentimental conventionality of the rest. The result is to compel a more radical judgment on the poem than has yet been made. In "its passions will rock thee" the "passions" must be those of Love, so that it can no longer be Love that is being apostrophized. Who, then, is "thee"? The "frailest"—the "weak one"—it would appear. But any notion one may have had that the "weak one," as the conventional sentiments imply, is the woman must be abandoned: the "eagle home," to which the "well-built nest" so incongruously turns, is the Poet's. The familiar timbre, the desolate intensity (note particularly the use of "bright" in "bright reason"), puts it beyond doubt that Shelley is, characteristically, addressing himself—the "pardlike Spirit beautiful and swift," the "Love in desolation masked," the "Power girt round with weakness."

Characteristically: that is, Shelley's characteristic pathos is self-regarding, directed upon an idealized self in the way suggested by the tags just quoted. This is patently so in some of his best poetry; for instance, in the *Ode to the West Wind*. Even there, perhaps, one may find something too like an element of luxury in the poignancy (at any rate, one's limiting criticism of the *Ode* would move towards such a judgment); and that in general there must be dangers and weakness attending upon such a habit will hardly be denied. The poem just examined shows how gross may be, in Shelley, the corruptions that are incident. He can make self-pity a luxury at such a level that the conventional pathos of album poeticizing, not excluding the banalities about (it is plainly so in the third stanza) the sad lot of woman, can come in to gratify the appetite.

The abeyance of thought exhibited by the first three stanzas now takes on a more sinister aspect. The switching-off of intelligence that is necessary if the sentiments of the third stanza are to be accepted has now to be invoked in explanation of a graver matter—Shelley's ability to accept the grosser, the truly corrupt, gratifications that have just been indicated. The antipathy of his sensibility to any play of the critical mind, the uncongeniality of intelligence to inspiration, these clearly go in Shelley, not merely with a capacity for momentary self-deceptions and insincerities, but with a radical lack of self-knowledge. He could say of Wordsworth, implying the opposite of himself, that

> he never could
> Fancy another situation
> From which to dart his contemplation
> Than that wherein he stood.

But, for all his altruistic fervors and his fancied capacity for projecting his sympathies, Shelley is habitually—it is no new observation—his own hero: Alastor, Laon, The Sensitive Plant

> (It loves, even like Love, its deep heart is full,
> It desires what it has not, the Beautiful),

and Prometheus. It is characteristic that he should say to the West Wind,

> A heavy weight of hours has chained and bowed
> One too like thee: tameless, and swift, and proud,

and conclude:

> Be thou, Spirit fierce,
> My spirit! Be thou me, impetuous one!

1936

WILLIAM EMPSON: *From* Seven Types of Ambiguity[1]
[Wordsworth]

* * * Wordsworth was not an ambiguous poet, for reasons that I have discussed; the cult of simplicity moved its complexity back into the subconscious, poisoned only the sources of thought, in the high bogs of the mountains, and stated as simply as possible the fundamental disorders of the mind. But he sometimes uses what may be called philosophical ambiguities when he is not sure how far this process can tolerably be pushed. In the third type we were among the uses of ambiguity for jokes; the fourth type includes its electoral applications. Thus the degree of pantheism implied by some of Wordsworth's most famous passages depends very much on the taste of the reader, who can impose grammar without difficulty to uphold his own views.

> For I have learnt
> To look on nature, not as in the hour
> Of thoughtless youth, but hearing oftentimes
> The still, sad music of humanity,
> Not harsh nor grating, but of ample power
> To chasten and subdue. And I have felt
> A presence that disturbs me with the joy

1. The selection here reprinted is from the first edition of 1930, Chapter 4.

Of elevated thoughts; a sense sublime
Of something far more deeply interfused,
Whose dwelling is the light of setting suns,
And the round ocean, and the living air,
And the blue sky, and in the mind of man,
A motion and a spirit, that impels
All thinking things, all objects of all thought,
And rolls through all things.[2]

It is not sufficient to say that these lines convey with great beauty the mood intended; Wordsworth seems to have believed in his own doctrines and wanted his readers to know what they were. It is reasonable, then, to try to extract from this passage definite opinions on the relations of God, man, and nature, and on the means by which such relations can be known.

There are several points of difficulty in the grammar when one tries to do this. It is not certain what is *more deeply interfused* than what. It is not certain whether the *music of humanity* is the same as the *presence*; they are separated by the word *and* and a full stop. We may notice, too, that the word *in* seems to distinguish, though but faintly, the *mind of man* from the *light, the ocean,* the *air* and the *sky*; this tends to separate the *motion* and the *spirit* form from the *presence* and the *something*; but they may, again, all be identical with the *music*. Wordsworth may then have *felt a something far more deeply interfused* than the *presence* that *disturbed* him; we seem here to have God revealing himself in particular to the mystic, but being in a more fundamental sense immanent in his whole creation.[3] Or the *something* may be in apposition to the *presence* (the *sense* equal to the *joy*); so that both are *more deeply interfused* than the *music of humanity*, but apparently in the same way. This version only conceives God as immanent in his creation, and as affecting the poet in the same way as he affects everything else; or as only imagined by the poet as immanent in creation, in the same way as the *music of humanity* is imagined as immanent. Thus, the first version is Christian, the second in part pantheistic, in part agnostic. Again, the *something* may possibly dwell only in the natural objects mentioned, ending at *sky*; the *motion* and the *spirit* are then not thought of at all as *interfused* into nature, like the *something*; they are things active *in the mind of man*. At the same time they are similar to the *something*; thus Wordsworth either *feels* them or *feels a sense* of them. With this reading the voice would rise in some triumph at the words *mind of man*; man has a spirit immanent in nature in the same way as in the spirit of God, and is decently independent from him. Or the *something* may

2. Wordworth's *Tintern Abbey*, lines 88–102.
3. "Or one may stand for paganism (the local deity of a bit of lake scenery, say) and the other for the more puzzling doctrine (far more deeply interfused) on which Wordsworth would support it" [Empson's note, added to 2nd edition].

also *dwell in the mind of man,* and have the *motion* and the spirit in apposition to it; under this less fortunate arrangement a God who is himself nature subjects us at once to determinism and predestination.

So far I have been examining grammatical ambiguities, but the last three lines also admit of doubt, as to the purpose of what seems an irrelevant distinction. Whether man or some form of God is subject here, he distinguishes between *things* which are objects or subjects of *thought,* these he *impels,* and *things* which are neither objects nor subjects of *thought,* through these he merely *rolls.* (I am not sure what is the logical status of the *things* not the objects of *thought* about which Wordsworth is *thinking* here; after all, he is not thinking very hard, so it may be all right.) The only advantage I can see in this distinction is that it makes the *spirit* at once intelligent and without intelligence; at once God and nature; allows us to think of him as the second, without compromising his position as the first.[4]

And, indeed, whether or not a great deal of wisdom is enshrined in these lines, lines just as muddled, superficially speaking, may convey a mode of using their antinomies,[5] and so act as creeds. The reason why one grudges Wordsworth this source of strength is that he talks as if he owned a creed by which his half-statements might be reconciled, whereas, in so far as his creed was definite, he found these half-statements necessary to keep it at bay. There is something rather shuffling about this attempt to be uplifting yet nondenominational, to put across as much pantheism as would not shock his readers. I must protest again that I enjoy the lines very much, and find, like everybody else, that I remember them; probably it was necessary for Wordsworth to shuffle, if he was to maintain his peculiar poetical attitude. And, of course, by considering the example in this chapter, I have shown that I regard the shuffling as a deeply-rooted necessity, not conscious at the time when it was achieved. But, perhaps, this last example may serve as a sort of applied ambiguity, may show how these methods may be used to convict a poet of holding muddled opinions rather than to praise the complexity of the order of his mind. * * *

1930

4. "Critics have disliked the meanness and fussiness of this passage, and I wish that I had something wise and reconciling to say after all these years. Miss M. C. Bradbrook wrote that the nouns after the full stop are all obviously in apposition, because the theme is the transcendence of the subject-object relationship. It is, I suppose, almost certain that Wordsworth meant the grammar to run on like this. But surely, even if clauses are in apposition, they must be supposed to be somehow distinguishable, or why do they have to be said one after the other? One could give a much more sympathetic account of the philosophic background of Wordsworth, and no doubt if I. A. Richards' *Coleridge on Imagination* had been already published I would have written differently. But the more seriously one takes the doctrine, it seems to me, the more this expression of it seems loose rhetoric" [Empson's note, added to 2nd edition].
5. Contradictions.

LITERATURE SINCE MID-CENTURY: ANTI-CULTURE AND THE NEW TRADITIONALISM †

The literature of Great Britain since World War I can be seen as a ground on which two widely differing literary traditions have been struggling to come to terms. The line of poetic thought and feeling which a reader of this anthology can trace from Chaucer through Tennyson (though sinuous and various enough, it finds genuine continuity in an image of rational man adjusted to an ordered society) seems to weaken and grow slack in the 20th century. So too with the line a student of prose fiction can follow from Defoe through Trollope: the life seems to go out, and in novelists like Galsworthy or the lesser Arnold Bennett the characters degenerate into caricature and the manners into something close to mannerisms. At the same time, a powerful new tide of influence is making itself felt from the Continent. In poetry, we find Eliot saying explicitly that when he began to write he found few English authors who could suggest to him how to handle the language in order to represent modern experience. He turned instead for crucial examples of modern technique to Nerval, Baudelaire, Mallarmé, Laforgue—all accomplished ironists and many of them practitioners of the difficult art of symbolism. So, in the realm of prose fiction, with Joyce, who peremptorily dismissed Dickens, George Eliot, and the whole crew of late-19th-century English novelists, in order to ground himself in a tradition stemming from Flaubert and flowering into such diverse figures as Zola, the apostle of naturalism, and D'Annunzio, the flamboyant Italian poet-revolutionary.

The wave of continental influence that flooded English literature in the 1920's, followed by repeated breakers from the expressionist, surrealist, symbolist, and existentialist movements, constituted an extremely complex phenomenon; it struck upon an English society that was itself undergoing a series of complex and radical changes. Another crucial dividing line in English social life is World War II; but the end of empire and the coming of the welfare state simply augmented and deepened a process of literary revaluation already under way.

For an important characteristic of the continental traditions that for the last half century have been influencing traditionally English forms of feeling and expression (destroying, revitalizing, always challenging them) is their corrosive emphasis on alienation, negation, and emptiness. Partly this is a political phenomenon, resulting from wars, depressions, population increases, and a pervasive sense that both technological machinery and the machinery of public life are somehow out of control; on a deeper level, it derives from a cynicism about culture itself, stemming from the bold speculations and subtle insights of thinkers as diverse as Kierkegaard, Marx, Nietzsche, and Freud. To summarize these intricate, yet far-reaching, intellectual developments in a sentence or two is clearly a difficult undertaking; yet they do culminate, from one point of view, in a single gigantic question: Does not

---

† This Topic has been edited by David Daiches and Robert M. Adams, in collaboration.

modern man's culture constitute a band of glowing iron, constricting his instinctual life, and forcing him into a wasteland of frustration and falsity? Have not modern civilization and modern culture, between them, called into question the very idea of a human being? Franz Kafka follows his patient protagonists through inconceivable labyrinths of bureaucratic equivocation, toward some vague ultimate—love, god, happiness, or relief from guilt. The search is literally interminable—yet Kafka never fails to leave us with the sense that it may be completely unnecessary as well, that the good and true might be found at our feet if only we could escape the blinders of our conscious mind—the shackles of our will. Seen in this light, *Finnegans Wake* appears as a gigantic effort to tunnel through the century-old rubbish piles of history and culture to the instinctual giant Finn who lies sleeping in the lowest sedimentary level of us all—where culture has buried him. A thousand other examples could be adduced in the same vein; suffice it to say that a major feature of modernism, as it developed under the shifting currents of continental influence was the mind's often subtle and intricate attack on itself. To represent a late stage of this attack, we present the final portion of Samuel Beckett's one-act play, *Endgame*.

The title, of course, refers to the closing moves in a game of chess, where most of the pieces have been eliminated, and the contest reduces itself to a few stylized moves, the end of which is clearly foreseen. Of the four characters appearing on stage, three are paralyzed. The old folk, Nagg and Nell (whose names perhaps suggest, in degraded form, Agammenon and Helen), have been discarded to garbage cans, literally as well as symbolically. Hamm, whose name is that of Noah's accursed son, as well as that of a corny actor, plays out his game on a lonely throne from which, blind and despairing, he controls the last pawn remaining to him, his adopted son Clov. Little flurries of intermittent life are stirred up by the senile erotic memories of Nagg and Nell, by a possible flea in Clov's pants, by a possible rat in the kitchen, by a toy dog with three legs, and by Hamm's yearning for his pain-killer. But the attempt to fill time with words or actions fails again and again; the game against time is lost from the beginning. "If I don't kill that rat," Clov says earnestly at one point, "he'll die." Thought bound by its own helpless contradictions could not be more concisely illustrated. No exterior force confines the characters to the repetition of their ghastly routines in that icy, mist-bound room; they are like Sartre's characters in *Huis-Clos*, punishers of themselves in a do-it-yourself hell. Yet the play is also lit by a mocking and derisive humor; it is continually under-cutting itself by turning its irony in upon itself and juxtaposing, for grotesque effect, burlesque and vaudeville routines with moans of metaphysical anguish.

If World War I raised the curtain on a series of radically experimental and often shockingly unfamiliar literary works in English, World War II had in many respects precisely the opposite effect. After the transitory phenomenon of Dylan Thomas (who was himself a throwback to modes of unabashed romanticism), such relatively traditional craftsmen as Robert Graves and Edwin Muir enjoyed a revival of public interest. But the most striking examples of the new conservatism are found in fiction, where C. P. Snow has carried forward the Trollope tradition of large, interlinked social panoramas, and the so-called "angry young men" picked up a mode of social protest deriving from the early novels of H. G. Wells—but without Wells's assurance of inherited values. Books like John Wain's *Hurry on Down* (1953), Kingsley Amis's *Lucky Jim* (1954), John Braine's *Room at the Top* (1957), and Alan Sillitoe's *Loneliness of the Long-Distance Runner* (1959) all expressed a muffled and sometimes explosive protest against an Establishment which seemed to retain its power over their minds even as its outer forms were melting away. Perhaps this was why the social complaint in these novels seemed often to be weakened and rendered ineffectual by self-doubt or self-loathing. The most potent expression of this uneasy mixture took place on the stage.

John Osborne's *Look Back in Anger* (1956) focused on a young man with a virulent tongue and a complete loathing of the world in which he was forced to live. What wasn't represented on the stage was the paralyzing inertia or mental block which kept him from doing anything about his surroundings except yelp and complain about them. Jimmy Porter was a sick diagnostician, and the exposure of his hopeless case made for potent dramatic scenes which deliberately frustrated and provoked audiences. Similarly in the plays of Harold Pinter (*The Birthday Party*, 1959; *The Caretaker*, 1960; *The Homecoming*, 1965); a surface realism which is often violent and vulgar plays against symbolic suggestions and a multiplicity of motivations which are deliberately left obscure. In both these playwrights the form of the play includes a carefully managed irresolution about what used to be called "ultimate meanings," while the superficial violence of language conveys a sense of immense and undischarged anguish.

Less divided figures, of more modest dimensions, more clearly devoted to revivifying inherited artistic forms and the humanist tradition of Western cultural values are a group of young poets and critics known generically since the middle 1950's as "the Movement." These are not by any means the hardshelled traditionalists of the traditional Anglican royalist-and-classical persuasion; they reject the rigidity of the T. S. Eliot formulations as earnestly as the near-nihilism of the extreme existentialists, and have tried to carve out a middle course of their own. Perhaps the most significant critical champion of the Movement is the poet, critic and scholar Donald Davie whose revealingly entitled book, *Purity of Diction in English Verse* (1952), sets out to demonstrate the eighteenth-century virtues of plainness, clarity, economy of metaphor, and urbanity of statement in which the Augustan poets excelled and the romantic poets were often deficient. His second critical work, *Articulate Energy: An Inquiry into the Syntax of English Poetry* (1955) urges the advantages of retaining prose syntax in poetry and concludes with a frontal attack on Northrop Frye's view as expressed in the following quotation: "Language in a human mind is not a list of words with their customary meanings attached, but a single interlocking structure, one's total power of expressing oneself. Literature is the objective counterpart of this, a total form of verbal expression which is re-created in miniature whenever a new poem is written." Not so, argues Davie:

The appeal of theories such as Mr. Frye's is manifest in the loaded words that their promoters use, in recommending them. A poetry in which the syntax articulates only "the world of the poem" is said to be "pure," "absolute," "sheer," "self-sufficient." Wordsworth's poems are "impure" because they have about them the smell of soil and soiled flesh, the reek of humanity. Their syntax is not "pure" syntax because it refers to, it mimes, something outside itself and outside the world of its poem, something that smells of the human, of generation and hence of corruption. It is my case against the symbolist theorists that, in trying to remove the human smell from poetry, they are only doing harm. For poetry to be great, it must reek of the human as Wordsworth's poetry does. This is not a novel contention; but perhaps it is one of those things that cannot be said too often.

It was being said often enough in England in the late 1950's and early 1960's. Another English critic, Graham Hough, ended his discussion of the modern poetic movement in his book *Image and Experience* (1960) with exactly the same appeal to humanity and to Wordsworth: "For certain purposes and at a certain historical point it was doubtless very apt and very salutary to liken the poet to a finely filiated bit of platinum. At the present conjunction of the stars it might also be well to remember the quite unmetaphorical saying of an earlier writer [Wordsworth]—that the poet is a man speaking to men."

The miniature anthology of English poetry of the fifties and sixties below begins with some examples of Movement poets and then presents work by two poets generally considered in England to be the best of their generation—Thom Gunn and Ted Hughes. Gunn's poems (*The Sense of Movement*, 1957; *My Sad Captains*, 1961; *Touch*, 1967) show how the insistence on exactness of image and movement can produce something more than agreeable verse craftsmanship. Reminiscent sometimes of Graves, sometimes of Muir, sometimes of the American Yvor Winters (with whom Gunn studied in California), Gunn's poems have a special kind of modest and honest individuality which make them if not continuously exciting, at least always engaging. Ted Hughes' poems (*The Hawk in the Rain*, 1957; *Lupercal*, 1960; *Wodwo*, 1967) have a richer and more sensuous imagery than Gunn's: he is really farther away from the Movement. His poems show an inventiveness, a joy in the exercise of his art, that exist side by side with—and indeed are put at the service of—a compassionate curiosity. In his more recent work the control is firmer, the more riotous aspects of his imagery are subdued, and we have poetry of chastened purity enriched by a powerful and humane imagination.

SAMUEL BECKETT: *From* Endgame

[*The End*]

HAMM. Is it not time for my pain-killer?
CLOV. Yes.
HAMM. Ah! At last! Give it to me! Quick!
  (*Pause.*)
CLOV. There's no more pain-killer.
  (*Pause.*)

HAMM (*appalled*). Good. . . !
 (*Pause.*)
 No more pain-killer!
CLOV. No more pain-killer. You'll never get any more pain-killer.
 (*Pause.*)
HAMM. But the little round box. It was full!
CLOV. Yes. But now it's empty.
 (*Pause. Clov starts to move about the room. He is looking for a place to put down the alarm-clock.*)
HAMM (*soft*). What'll I do?
 (*Pause. In a scream.*)
 What'll I do?
 (*Clov sees the picture, takes it down, stands it on the floor with its face to the wall, hangs up the alarm-clock in its place.*)
 What are you doing?
CLOV. Winding up.
HAMM. Look at the earth.
CLOV. Again!
HAMM. Since it's calling to you.
CLOV. Is your throat sore?
 (*Pause.*)
 Would you like a lozenge?
 (*Pause.*)
 No.
 (*Pause.*)
 Pity.
 (*Clov goes, humming, towards window right, halts before it, looks up at it.*)
HAMM. Don't sing.
CLOV (*turning towards Hamm*). One hasn't the right to sing any more?
HAMM. No.
CLOV. Then how can it end?
HAMM. You want it to end?
CLOV. I want to sing.
HAMM. I can't prevent you.
 (*Pause. Clov turns towards window right.*)
CLOV. What did I do with that steps?
 (*He looks around for ladder.*)
 You didn't see that steps?
 (*He sees it.*)
 Ah, about time.
 (*He goes towards window left.*)
 Sometimes I wonder if I'm in my right mind. Then it passes over and I'm as lucid as before.
 (*He gets up on ladder, looks out of window.*)
 ·Christ, she's under water!
 (*He looks.*)
 How can that be?

(*He pokes forward his head, his hand above his eyes.*)
It hasn't rained.
(*He wipes the pane, looks. Pause.*)
Ah what a fool I am! I'm on the wrong side!
(*He gets down, takes a few steps towards window right.*)
Under water!
(*He goes back for ladder.*)
What a fool I am!
(*He carries ladder towards window right.*)
Sometimes I wonder if I'm in my right senses. Then it passes off and I'm as intelligent as ever.
(*He sets down ladder under window right, gets up on it, looks out of window. He turns towards Hamm.*)
Any particular sector you fancy? Or merely the whole thing?
HAMM. Whole thing.
CLOV. The general effect? Just a moment.
(*He looks out of window. Pause.*)
HAMM. Clov.
CLOV. (*absorbed*). Mmm.
HAMM. Do you know what it is?
CLOV. (*as before*). Mmm.
HAMM. I was never there.
(*Pause.*)
Clov!
CLOV (*turning towards Hamm, exasperated*). What is it?
HAMM. I was never there.
CLOV. Lucky for you.
(*He looks out of window.*)
HAMM. Absent, always. It all happened without me. I don't know what's happened.
(*Pause.*)
Do you know what's happened?
(*Pause.*)
Clov!
CLOV (*turning towards Hamm, exasperated*). Do you want me to look at this muckheap, yes or no?
HAMM. Answer me first.
CLOV. What?
HAMM. Do you know what's happened?
CLOV. When? Where?
HAMM (*violently*). When! What's happened? Use your head, can't you! What has happened?
CLOV. What for Christ's sake does it matter?
(*He looks out of window.*)
HAMM. I don't know.
(*Pause. Clov turns towards Hamm.*)
CLOV. (*harshly*). When old Mother Pegg asked you for oil for her lamp and you told her to get out to hell, you knew what was happening then, no?

(Pause.)

You know what she died of, Mother Pegg? Of darkness.

HAMM *(feebly)*. I hadn't any.

CLOV *(as before)*. Yes, you had.

(Pause.)

HAMM. Have you the glass?

CLOV. No, it's clear enough as it is.

HAMM. Go and get it.

(Pause. Clov casts up his eyes, brandishes his fists. He loses balance, clutches on to the ladder. He starts to get down, halts.)

CLOV. There's one thing I'll never understand.

(He gets down.)

Why I always obey you. Can you explain that to me?

HAMM. No. . . . Perhaps it's compassion.

(Pause.)

A kind of great compassion.

(Pause.)

Oh you won't find it easy, you won't find it easy.

(Pause. Clov begins to move about the room in search of the telescope.)

CLOV. I'm tired of our goings on, very tired.

(He searches.)

You're not sitting on it?

(He moves the chair, looks at the place where it stood, resumes his search.)

HAMM *(anguished)*. Don't leave me there!

(Angrily Clov restores the chair to its place.)

Am I right in the center?

CLOV. You'd need a microscope to find this—

(He sees the telescope.)

Ah, about time.

(He picks up the telescope, gets up on the ladder, turns the telescope on the without.)

HAMM. Give me the dog.

CLOV *(looking)*. Quiet!

HAMM *(angrily)*. Give me the dog!

(Clove drops the telescope, clasps his hands to his head. Pause. He gets down precipitately, looks for the dog, sees it, picks it up, hastens towards Hamm and strikes him violently on the head with the dog.)

CLOV. There's your dog for you!

(The dog falls to the ground. Pause.)

HAMM. He hit me!

CLOV. You drive me mad, I'm mad!

HAMM. If you must hit me, hit me with the axe.

(Pause.)

Or with the gaff, hit me with the gaff. Not with the dog. With the gaff. Or with the axe.

(Clov picks up the dog and gives it to Hamm who takes it in his arms.)

CLOV. *(imploringly).* Let's stop playing!

HAMM. Never!

(Pause.)

Put me in my coffin.

CLOV. There are no more coffins.

HAMM. Then let it end!

(Clov goes towards ladder.)

With a bang!

(Clov gets up on ladder, gets down again, looks for telescope, sees it, picks it up, gets up ladder, raises telescope.)

Of darkness! And me? Did anyone ever have pity on me?

CLOV *(lowering the telescope, turning towards Hamm).* What?

(Pause.)

Is it me you're referring to?

HAMM *(angrily).* An aside, ape! Did you never hear an aside before?

(Pause.)

I'm warming up for my last soliloquy.

CLOV. I warn you. I'm going to look at this filth since it's an order. But it's the last time.

(He turns the telescope on the without.)

Let's see.

(He moves the telescope.)

Nothing . . . nothing . . . good . . . good . . . nothing . . . goo—

(He starts, lowers the telescope, examines it, turns it again on the without. Pause.)

Bad luck to it!

HAMM. More complications!

(Clov gets down.)

Not an underplot, I trust.

(Clov moves ladder nearer window, gets up on it, turns telescope on the without.)

CLOV *(dismayed).* Looks like a small boy!

HAMM *(sarcastic).* A small . . . boy!

CLOV. I'll go and see.

(He gets down, drops the telescope, goes towards door, turns.)

I'll take the gaff.

(He looks for the gaff, sees it, picks it up, hastens towards door.)

HAMM. No!

(Clov halts.)

CLOV. No? A potential procreator?

HAMM. If he exists he'll die there or he'll come here. And if he doesn't . . .

(Pause.)

CLOV. You don't believe me? You think I'm inventing?

(Pause.)

HAMM. It's the end, Clov, we've come to the end. I don't need you any more.

(Pause.)

CLOV. Lucky for you.

(He goes towards door.)

HAMM. Leave me the gaff.

(Clov gives him the gaff, goes towards door, halts, looks at alarm-clock, takes it down, looks round for a better place to put it, goes to bins, puts it on lid of Nagg's bin. Pause.)

CLOV. I'll leave you.

(He goes towards door.)

HAMM. Before you go . . .

(Clov halts near door.)

. . . say something.

CLOV. There is nothing to say.

HAMM. A few words . . . to ponder . . . in my heart.

CLOV. Your heart!

HAMM. Yes.

(Pause. Forcibly.)

Yes!

(Pause.)

With the rest, in the end, the shadows, the murmurs, all the trouble, to end up with.

(Pause.)

Clov. . . . He never spoke to me. Then, in the end, before he went, without my having asked him, he spoke to me. He said . . .

CLOV *(despairingly).* Ah. . . !

HAMM. Something . . . from your heart.

CLOV. My heart!

HAMM. A few words . . . from your heart.

(Pause.)

CLOV *(fixed gaze, tonelessly, towards auditorium).* They said to me, That's love, yes, yes, not a doubt, now you see how—

HAMM. Articulate!

CLOV *(as before).* How easy it is. They said to me, That's friendship, yes, yes, no question, you've found it. They said to me, Here's the place, stop, raise your head and look at all that beauty. That order! They said to me, Come now, you're not a brute beast, think upon these things and you'll see how all becomes clear. And simple! They said to me, What skilled attention they get, all these dying of their wounds.

HAMM. Enough!

CLOV *(as before).* I say to myself—sometimes, Clov, you must learn to suffer better than that if you want them to weary of punishing you—one day. I say to myself—sometimes, Clov, you must be there better than that if you want them to let you go—one day. But I feel too old, and too far, to form new habits. Good, it'll never end, I'll never go.

(Pause.)

Then one day, suddenly, it ends, it changes, I don't understand, it dies, or it's me, I don't understand, that either. I ask the words that remain—sleeping, waking, morning, evening. They have nothing to say.

(*Pause.*)

I open the door of the cell and go. I am so bowed I only see my feet, if I open my eyes, and between my legs a little trail of black dust. I say to myself that the earth is extinguished, though I never saw it lit.

(*Pause.*)

It's easy going.

(*Pause.*)

When I fall I'll weep for happiness.

(*Pause. He goes towards door.*)

HAMM. Clov!

(*Clove halts, without turning.*)

Nothing.

(*Clov moves on.*)

Clov!

(*Clov halts, without turning.*)

CLOV. This is what we call making an exit.

HAMM. I'm obliged to you, Clov. For your services.

CLOV (*turning, sharply*). Ah pardon, it's I am obliged to you.

HAMM. It's we are obliged to each other.

(*Pause. Clov goes towards door.*)

One thing more.

(*Clov halts.*)

A last favor.

(*Exit Clov.*)

Cover me with the sheet.

(*Long pause.*)

No? Good.

(*Pause.*)

Me to play.

(*Pause. Wearily.*)

Old endgame lost of old, play and lose and have done with losing.

(*Pause. More animated.*)

Let me see.

(*Pause.*)

Ah yes!

(*He tries to move the chair, using the gaff as before. Enter Clov, dressed for the road. Panama hat, tweed coat, raincoat over his arm, umbrella, bag. He halts by the door and stands there, impassive and motionless, his eyes fixed on Hamm, till the end. Hamm gives up.*)

Good.

(*Pause.*)

Discard.

(*He throws away the gaff, makes to throw away the dog, thinks better of it.*)

Take it easy.

(Pause.)
And now?
(Pause.)
Raise hat.
(He raises his toque.)
Peace to our . . . arses.
(Pause.)
And put on again.
(He puts on his toque.)
Deuce.
(Pause. He takes off his glasses.)
Wipe.
(He takes out his handkerchief and, without unfolding it, wipes his glasses.)
And put on again.
(He puts on his glasses, puts back the handkerchief in his pocket.)
We're coming. A few more squirms like that and I'll call.
(Pause.)
A little poetry.
(Pause.)
You prayed—
(Pause. He corrects himself.)
You CRIED for night; it comes—
(Pause. He corrects himself.)
It FALLS: now cry in darkness.
(He repeats, chanting.)
You cried for night; it falls: now cry in darkness.
(Pause.)
Nicely put, that.
(Pause.)
And now?
(Pause.)
Moments for nothing, now as always, time was never and time is over, reckoning closed and story ended.
(Pause. Narrative tone.)
If he could have his child with him. . . .
(Pause.)
It was the moment I was waiting for.
(Pause.)
You don't want to abandon him? You want him to bloom while you are withering? Be there to solace your last million last moments?
(Pause.)
He doesn't realize, all he knows is hunger, and cold, and death to crown it all. But you! You ought to know what the earth is like, nowadays. Oh I put him before his responsibilities!
(Pause. Normal tone.)
Well, there we are, there I am, that's enough.
(He raises the whistle to his lips, hesitates, drops it. Pause.)

Yes, truly!
(He whistles. Pause. Louder. Pause.)
Good.
(Pause.)
Father!
(Pause. Louder.)
Father!
(Pause.)
Good.
(Pause.)
We're coming.
(Pause.)
And to end up with?
(Pause.)
Discard.
(He throws away the dog. He tears the whistle from his neck.)
With my compliments.
(He throws whistle towards auditorium. Pause. He sniffs. Soft.)
Clov!
(Long pause.)
No? Good.
(He takes out the handkerchief.)
Since that's the way we're playing it . . .
(he unfolds handkerchief)
. . . let's play it that way . . .
(he unfolds)
. . . and speak no more about it . . .
(he finishes unfolding)
. . . speak no more.
(He holds handkerchief spread out before him.)
Old stancher!
(Pause.)
You . . . remain.
(Pause. He covers his face with handkerchief, lowers his arms to armrests, remains motionless.)
(Brief tableau.)

1958

CURTAIN

DONALD DAVIE: A Voice from the Garden

We have a lawn of moss.
The next house is called The Beeches.
A towering squirrel-haunted
Trellis of trees, across
Our matt and trefoil, reaches
Shade where our guests have sauntered.

Cars snap by in the road.
In a famous photographed village
The High Street is our address.
Our guests write from abroad   10
Delighted to envisage
Rose-arbor and wilderness.

They get them, and the lilacs.
Some frenzy in us discards
Lilacs and all, and will harden,   15
However England stacks
Her dear discolored cards
Against us, us to her garden.

Anglophobia rises
In Brooklyn to hysteria   20
At some British verses.
British, one sympathizes.
Diesel-fumes cling to wistaria.
One conceives of worse reverses.

The sough of the power-brake   25
Makes every man an island;
But we are the island race.
We must be mad to take
Offense at our poisoned land
And the gardens that pock her face.   30

1963

ELIZABETH JENNINGS: An English Summer

An English summer—and a sense of form
Rides the five senses that dispute their claims.
Lawns leveled against nature, airs which warm
Each plant, perpetuate the hours and names.
We cannot see beyond the blue; no storm   5
Vies with the children ardent at their games.

Childhood returns with summer. It is strange
That such a season brings one's memories back.
Springs have their homesickness, autumns arrange
The sweet nostalgias that we long to lack.   10
But summer is itself; it's we who change
And lay our childhoods on the golden stack.

My fingers rest and eyes concern their sight
Simply with what would live were I not here.
It is the concentration of the light   15

That shows the other side of pain and fear.
I watch, incredulous of such delight,
Wanting the meaning not the landscape clear.

Was it for this the breath once breathed upon
The waters that we rose from? I can see   20
Only a summer with its shadows gone,
Skies that refuse an alien dignity.
But gardens, gardens echo. What sun shone
To make this truce with pain and ecstasy?

                                        1963

PHILIP LARKIN: Lines on a Young Lady's
              Photograph Album

At last you yielded up the album, which,
Once open, sent me distracted. All your ages
Matt and glossy on the thick black pages!
Too much confectionery, too rich:
I choke on such nutritious images.   5

My swivel eye hungers from pose to pose—
In pigtails, clutching a reluctant cat;
Or furred yourself, a sweet girl-graduate;
Or lifting a heavy-headed rose
Beneath a trellis, or in a trilby hat   10

(Faintly disturbing, that, in several ways)—
From every side you strike at my control,
Not least through these disquieting chaps who loll
At ease about your earlier days:
Not quite your class, I'd say, dear, on the whole. 15

But O, photography! as no art is,
Faithful and disappointing! that records
Dull days as dull, and hold-it smiles as frauds,
And will not censor blemishes
Like washing-lines, and Hall's-Distemper boards,   20

But shows the cat as disinclined, and shades
A chin as doubled when it is, what grace
Your candor thus confers upon her face!
How overwhelmingly persuades
That this is a real girl in a real place,   25

In every sense empirically true!
Or is it just *the past?* Those flowers, that gate,
These misty parks and motors, lacerate

Simply by being over; you
Contract my heart by looking out of date.   30

Yes, true; but in the end, surely, we cry
Not only at exclusion, but because
It leaves us free to cry. We know *what was*
Won't call on us to justify
Our grief, however hard we yowl across   35

The gap from eye to page. So I am left
To mourn (without a chance of consequence)
You, balanced on a bike against a fence;
To wonder if you'd spot the theft
Of this one of you bathing; to condense,   40

In short, a past that no one now can share,
No matter whose your future; calm and dry,
It holds you like a heaven, and you lie
Unvariably lovely there,
Smaller and clearer as the years go by.   45

1956

THOM GUNN: Human Condition

Now it is fog, I walk
Contained within my coat;
No castle more cut off
By reason of its moat:
Only the sentry's cough,   5
The mercenaries' talk.

The street lamps, visible,
Drop no light on the ground,
But press beams painfully
In a yard of fog around.   10
I am condemned to be
An individual.

In the established border
There balances a mere
Pinpoint of consciousness.   15
I stay, or start from, here:
No fog makes more or less
The neighboring disorder.

Particular, I must
Find out the limitation   20
Of mind and universe,

To pick thought and sensation
And turn to my own use
Disordered hate or lust.

I seek, to break, my span.   25
I am my one touchstone.
This is a test more hard
Than any ever known.
And thus I keep my guard
On that which makes me man.   30

Much is unknowable.
No problem shall be faced
Until the problem is;
I, born to fog, to waste,
Walk through hypothesis,   35
An individual.

                                        1957

TED HUGHES: Relic

I found this jawbone at the sea's edge:
There, crabs, dogfish, broken by the breakers or tossed
To flap for half an hour and turn to a crust
Continue the beginning. The deeps are cold:
In that darkness camaraderie does not hold: 5
Nothing touches but, clutching, devours. And the jaws,
Before they are satisfied or their stretched purpose
Slacken, go down jaws; go gnawn bare. Jaws
Eat and are finished and the jawbone comes to the beach:
This is the sea's achievement; with shells,   10
Vertebrae, claws, carapaces, skulls.

Time in the sea eats its tail, thrives, casts these
indigestibles, the spars of purposes
That failed far from the surface. None grow rich
In the sea. This curved jawbone did not laugh   15
But gripped, gripped and is now a cenotaph.

                                        1960

Selected Bibliographies

The symbol ‡ following a title indicates that the volume is available in a paperbound edition

SUGGESTED GENERAL READINGS

Histories of England and of English Literature

George Macaulay Trevelyan's *History of England*,‡ rev., 1945, is an excellent survey in one volume; for detailed studies of single periods, see *The Oxford History of England*, 1934– , by a variety of historians, to be published in 14 volumes. The projected 12-volume *Oxford History of English Literature*, edited by F. P. Wilson and Bonamy Dobrée, 1945–, is nearing completion; see the listings below. *A Guide to English Literature*, ed. Boris Ford (1954–61), is available in 6 paperback volumes. Up-to-date one-volume histories are Albert C. Baugh and others, *A Literary History of England*,‡ rev., 1967; Hardin Craig and others, *A History of English Literature*, 1950; and (less densely factual, and more a running literary appreciation) David Daiches, *A Critical History of English Literature*, 2 vols., 1961.

Drama

Allardyce Nicoll, *British Drama*, rev., 1957, and *A History of English Drama, 1660–1900*, 6 vols., rev., 1952–59.

The Novel

The most detailed history is Ernest A. Baker's *History of the English Novel*, 10 vols., 1924–39. Among the short histories are Walter A. Raleigh, *The English Novel*, rev., 1911, which stops at Walter Scott; Wilbur L. Cross, *The Development of the English Novel*, 1930, through R. L. Stevenson; and, more up-to-date, Arnold Kettle, *An Introduction to the English Novel*,‡ 2 vols., 1951–53, and Walter Allen, *The English Novel*,‡ 1954.

Poetry

W. J. Courthope, *A History of English Poetry*, 6 vols., 1895–1910, and H. J. C. Grierson and J. C. Smith, *A Critical History of English Poetry*, rev., 1947. In addition, Douglas Bush's two books, *Mythology and the Renaissance Tradition in English Poetry*,‡ 1932, and *Mythology and the Romantic Tradition in English Poetry*,‡ 1937, 1957, constitute an excellent running account, from their special perspective, of English poetry from the 16th century through T. S. Eliot. Another book which ranges widely in English poetry from the Middle Ages through the 18th century is E. M. W. Tillyard, *The English Epic and Its Background*,‡ 1954.

Literary Criticism

George Saintsbury, *A History of English Criticism*, 1911, is still referred to. More recent histories of English criticism are J. W. H. Atkins' three books on *The Medieval Phase*, 1943, *The Renascence*, 1947, and *17th and 18th Centuries*,‡ 1951; W. K. Wimsatt, Jr., and Cleanth Brooks, *Literary Criticism: A Short History*,‡ 1957; and René Wellek, *A History of Modern Criticism: 1750–1950*, 1955–, of which four of the projected five volumes have been published.

Reference Works

The Cambridge Bibliography of English Literature, edited by F. W. Bateson, 4 vols., 1941, lists all the books of the major and many minor British authors, together with a large selection from biographical, scholarly, and critical works written about these authors; a supplement edited by George Watson carries the listing of secondary materials to 1955. Literary biographies and critical books published since that time can be found in the "Annual Bibliography" *PMLA;* for separate periods, see the listings below. *Poetry Explication*,‡ rev. by Joseph M. Kuntz, 1962, lists close analyses of English poems, old and recent, and I. F. Bell and Donald Baird, *The English Novel, 1578–1956*,‡ 1958, provides a useful list of 20th-century criticisms of fiction. Further bibliographical aids are described in

Richard D. Altick and Andrew Wright, *Selective Bibliography for the Study of English and American Literature*,‡ 1960, and Arthur G. Kennedy, *A Concise Bibliography for Students of English*, rev., 1954.

For compact biographies of English authors see the multi-volumed *Dictionary of National Biography*, edited by Leslie Stephen and Sidney Lee in 1885–1900, with supplements that carry the work to persons who died up to 1950; condensed biographies will be found in the one-volume *Concise Dictionary of National Biography*, 1939. Handy reference books on authors, works, and various literary terms and allusions are *The Oxford Companion to English Literature*, edited by Paul Harvey, rev., 1946; *The Oxford Companion to the Theater*, edited by Phyllis Hartnoll, rev., 1957; *Dictionary of World Literature*,‡ edited by Joseph T. Shipley, rev., 1953; and *Encyclopedia of Poetry and Poetics*, ed. Alex Preminger and others, 1965. Low-priced handbooks which define and illustrate literary concepts and terms are: M. H. Abrams, *A Glossary of Literary Terms*, 1957; Carl Beckson and Arthur Ganz, *A Reader's Guide to Literary Terms*,‡ 1960; and W. F. Thrall and Addison Hibbard, *A Handbook to Literature*,‡ revised by G. Hugh Holman, 1960.

Albert C. Baugh, *A History of the English Language*, rev., 1957, will be found helpful, as will various treatments of English meters and stanza forms, such as: R. M. Alden, *English Verse*, 1903; T. S. Omond, *English Metrists*, 1921; George R. Stewart, *The Technique of English Verse*, 1930; Enid Hamer, *The Metres of English Verse*, 1930; Paul Fussell, Jr., *Poetic Meter and Poetic Form*,‡ 1966; and *The Structure of Verse: Modern Essays in Prosody*,‡ ed. Harvey Gross, 1966.

Intellectual History and Criticism

Students interested in intellectual history as a background for reading English literature will profit from Arthur O. Lovejoy, *The Great Chain of Being*,‡ 1936, and *Essays in the History of Ideas*,‡ 1948; Marjorie Nicolson, *The Breaking of the Circle*,‡ 1950, *Science and Imagination*,‡ 1956, and *Mountain Gloom and Mountain Glory*,‡ 1959; John Herman Randall, Jr., *The Making of the Modern Mind*, rev., 1940; Basil Willey, *The Seventeenth Century Background*, 1934, *The Eighteenth Century Background*, 1940, and *Nineteenth Century Studies*, 1949; and Joseph Warren Beach, *The Concept of Nature in 19th-Century English Poetry*, 1936, 1956. In addition, the following is a selection from those books in literary history and criticism which have been notably influential in shaping modern approaches to English literature and literary forms: Erich Auerbach, *Mimesis: The Representation of Reality in Western Literature*,‡ 1953; Maud Bodkin, *Archetypal Patterns in Poetry*,‡ 1934; Cleanth Brooks, *The Well Wrought Urn*,‡ 1947; Ronald Crane, *The Languages of Criticism and the Structure of Poetry*,‡ 1953, *The Idea of the Humanities*, 2 vols., 1967; and, as editor, *Critics and Criticism, Ancient and Modern*,‡ 1952; T. S. Eliot, *Selected Essays*,‡ 3rd edition, 1951, and *On Poetry and Poets*,‡ 1957; William Empson, *Seven Types of Ambiguity*,‡ 3rd edition, 1953; Francis Fergusson, *The Idea of a Theater*,‡ 1949; Northrop Frye, *Anatomy of Criticism*, 1957; Henry James, *The Art of the Novel: Critical Prefaces*,‡ 1934; F. R. Leavis, *Revaluation*,‡ 1936, and *The Great Tradition* ‡ (i.e., in the novel), 1948; C. S. Lewis, *The Allegory of Love*,‡ rev., 1938; John Livingston Lowes, *The Road to Xanadu*,‡ rev., 1930; Percy Lubbock, *The Craft of Fiction*,‡ 1926; I. A. Richards, *Principles of Literary Criticism*,‡ 5th edition, 1934, and *Practical Criticism*,‡ 1930; Caroline Spurgeon, *Shakespeare's Imagery*,‡ 1935; Lionel Trilling, *The Liberal Imagination*,‡ 1950, and *The Opposing Self*,‡ 1955; Edmund Wilson, *Axel's Castle: A Study in the Imaginative Literature of 1870–1930*,‡ 1936, and *The Wound and the Bow*,‡ 1941; and Wayne C. Booth, *The Rhetoric of Fiction*,‡ 1961.

THE ROMANTIC PERIOD

Succinct and reliable treatments of the political and social events in this period are the relevant chapters of G. M. Trevelyan's *British History of the Nineteenth Century*,‡ 2nd edition, 1937, and *English Social History*, 1942. More detailed histories are Elie Halévy, *England in 1815*,‡ rev., 1949, and *The Liberal Awakening*, 1815–1830, rev. ed., 1949, and J. Steven Watson, *The Reign of George III, 1760–1815*, 1960. Gilbert Slater, *The Growth of Modern England*, 1932, deals especially with the industrial revolution. For English literary relations to the French Revolution, see Edward Dowden, *The French Revolution and English Literature*, 1897, and A. E. Hancock, *The French Revolution and the English Poets*, 1899. Illuminating analyses of important intellectual movements will be found in A. O. Lovejoy's *The Great Chain of Being*,‡ 1936, Chapters IX and X, and *Essays in the History of Ideas*,‡ 1948. Other particularly useful works on intellectual history are Basil Willey, *Nineteenth-Century Studies: Coleridge to Matthew Arnold*,‡ 1949; Joseph

Warren Beach, *The Concept of Nature in Nineteenth-Century English Poetry*, 1936; Hoxie Neale Fairchild, *Religious Trends in English Poetry*, of which vol. III (1949) deals with 1780–1830; and H. W. Piper, *The Active Universe: Pantheism and the Concept of Imagination in the English Romantic Poets*, 1962. On Romantic literature in its social matrix, see the relevant chapters in Raymond Williams, *Culture and Society, 1780–1950*, 1960. In *Romanticism: Points of View*, 1962, Robert F. Gleckner and Gerald E. Enscoe present a selection of the attempts to define "Romanticism"; see also the essays in *Romanticism Reconsidered*, ed. Northrop Frye, 1963.

Among the histories of Romantic literature are: Oliver Elton, *A Survey of English Literature, 1780–1830*, 2 vols., 1928; W. L. Renwick's rather inadequate *English Literature, 1789–1815*, 1963; and Ian Jack's *English Literature, 1815–1832*, 1963. Mario Praz's *The Romantic Agony*,‡ 2nd ed. 1951, treats Satanism, sadism, vampirism, and others of the more exotic literary interests of the time; and Peter Thorslev's *The Byronic Hero*, 1962, discusses the solitary or alienated hero in other writers, as well as Byron. Douglas Bush's *Mythology and the Romantic Tradition in English Poetry*,‡ 1937, is so broad in its range that it constitutes an excellent survey of Romantic poetry in general, and *The Romantic Poets*,‡ by Graham Hough, 1953, provides a succinct introduction. The older negative appraisals of the Romantic achievement by the neohumanist, Irving Babbitt, in *Rousseau and Romanticism*,‡ 1919, and *On Being Creative and Other Essays*, 1932 have been taken up and expanded by Edward E. Bostetter in *The Romantic Ventriloquists*, 1963. G. Wilson Knight, *The Starlit Dome*, 1941, reprinted 1960, is an influential early example of the approach to Romantic poets by the analysis of characteristic patterns of imagery; and Harold Bloom, *The Visionary Company*, 1962, which relates these poets to the prophetic tradition of Spenser and Milton, includes brief and stimulating commentaries on each of the important poems. David Perkins, who treated *The Quest for Permanence* in Wordsworth, Shelley, and Keats, 1959, has also edited a remarkably inclusive anthology of *English Romantic Writers*, 1967. *English Romantic Poets: Modern Essays in Criticism*, ed. M. H. Abrams, 1960, is a collection of essays by major contemporary critics.

Following are studies of various forms of Romantic literature. On literary criticism: M. H. Abrams, *The Mirror and the Lamp: Romantic Theory and the Critical Tradition*,‡ 1953; René Wellek, *A History of Modern Criticism: 1750–1950*, Vol. II, *The Romantic Age*, 1955. On narrative poetry: Karl Kroeber, *Romantic Narrative Art*,‡ 1960, and Brian Wilkie, *Romantic Poets and Epic Tradition*, 1965. On the novel: Ernest A. Baker, *The History of the English Novel*, Vol. VI, 1961; Montague Summers, *The Gothic Quest: A History of the Gothic Novel*, 1938. On drama: Allardyce Nicoll, *History of Early Nineteenth-Century Drama, 1800–50*, 2 vols., rev. ed. 1955. On the essay: William F. Bryan and Ronald S. Crane, Introduction, *The English Familiar Essay*, 1916; Marie H. Law, *The English Familiar Essay in the Early Nineteenth Century*, 1934.

For further references on Romantic literature consult Ernest Bernbaum, *Guide Through the Romantic Movement*, 2nd edition, 1949; Thomas M. Raysor, ed., *The English Romantic Poets, A Review of Research*, rev., 1956, on Wordsworth, Coleridge, Byron, Shelley, and Keats; and Carolyn W. Houtchens and Lawrence H. Houtchens, *The English Romantic Poets and Essayists*, rev., 1966, on Blake, the lesser poets, and the major essayists. *Philological Quarterly* carries an annual bibliography of publications about this period through 1964, and thereafter, *English Language Notes*.

Robert Burns

The standard reference for Burns's poems is the Centenary Edition, edited in 4 vols. by W. E. Henley and T. F. Henderson, 1896–97. A good one-volume edition is that by Charles S. Dougall, *Robert Burns, The Poems*, 1927; and a useful selection has been edited by John DeLancey Ferguson, *Selected Poems of Robert Burns*, 1926. Ferguson has also given us a reliable edition of *The Letters of Robert Burns*, 2 vols., 1931, and a brilliant portrait of Burns, *Pride and Passion*, 1939. A detailed and thoroughly documented biography is by Franklyn Bliss Snyder, *The Life of Robert Burns*, 1932. James C. Dick has written an excellent study of the texts and music of *The Songs of Robert Burns*, 1903. David Daiches, *Robert Burns*, 1950, provides a critical analysis of all the major poems, while Thomas Crawford's *Burns: A Study of the Poems and Songs*,‡ 1960, is a detailed and comprehensive commentary. See also James Kinsley, ed., *Scottish Poetry, A Critical Survey*, 1955.

William Blake

The beautifully printed *The Complete Writings of William Blake*, edited by Geoffrey Keynes, 1957, has now been replaced as the scholar's edition by *The Poetry and Prose of William*

Blake, edited by David Erdman and Harold Bloom, 1965, which includes painstaking textual notes and brief commentaries on many of the poems. There is a good *Life of William Blake* by Mona Wilson, 1927, rev., 1948; but the first full account, Alexander Gilchrist's *The Life of William Blake,* which appeared in 1863, is a charming work which has been a source-book for all later biographers, and is available (expertly edited and supplemented by Ruthven Todd) in Everyman's Library, 1945.

The modern era of the scholarly explication of Blake symbolism was begun by S. Foster Damon's trail-blazing *William Blake: His Philosophy and Symbols,* 1924; the same scholar has also published an extremely helpful *Blake Dictionary: The Ideas and Symbols of William Blake,* 1965. Of more recent books perhaps the most useful are: Northrop Frye's classic analysis of Blake's moral allegory, *Fearful Symmetry,*‡ 1947; Mark Schoer's study emphasizing Blake's characteristic union of political, moral, and religious radicalism, *William Blake: The Politics of Vision,*‡ 1946; David V. Erdman's detailed investigation of the relation of Blake's poetry to the historical events of his time, *Blake: Prophet Against Empire,* 1954; Peter Fisher's incisive exposition of Blake's thought, *The Valley of Vision,* 1961; and Harold Bloom's illuminating commentaries on the individual poems, *Blake's Apocalypse: A Study in Poetic Argument,*‡ 1963. Modern critical essays are collected in *Blake,*‡ edited by Northrop Frye, 1966. H. M. Margoliouth's *William Blake,* 1951, is a concise introduction to the man and his work. Studies emphasizing the poems written before the long "prophetic books" are: Hazard Adams, *William Blake: A Reading of the Shorter Poems,* 1963. Robert F. Gleckner, *The Piper and the Bard,* 1959; and E. D. Hirsch, Jr., *Innocence and Experience: An Introduction to Blake,*‡ 1964. A *Concordance to the Writings of William Blake,* edited by David Erdman, 1967, is an important aid in elucidating his symbolism. Finally, there is a large and growing list of books which reproduce (some of them in splendid color) Blake's etched poems, drawings, and engravings. The excellent *Blake Bibliography,* edited by G. E. Bentley, Jr., and Martin K. Nurmi, 1964, includes an annotated list of all works by and about Blake, as well as Blake's illustrations for the work of others, published reproductions of his drawings, paintings, and engravings, and other Blakeana.

William Wordsworth

Ernest de Selincourt, the great Wordsworth scholar, has edited *The Poetical Works* (with Helen Darbishire), 5 vols., 1940–49; the variorum edition of *The Prelude,* with the texts of 1805 and 1850 on facing pages (revised by Helen Darbishire, 1959); and *The Letters of William and Dorothy Wordsworth,* 6 vols., 1935–39. He has also written the biography of Dorothy Wordsworth, 1933, and edited her *Journals,* 2 vols., 1941. A useful collection of Wordsworth's poems in one volume was edited for Oxford Standard Authors by Thomas Hutchinson and revised by Ernest de Selincourt,‡ 1950. Until recently, the standard biography was George McLean Harper, *William Wordsworth: His Life, Works, and Influence,* 2 vols., 1916, rev., 1929; Mary Moorman's *William Wordsworth,* 2 vols., 1957 and 1965, takes advantage of the greatly expanded scholarship of the last three decades. Edith Batho, *The Later Wordsworth,* 1933, is a detailed study of Wordsworth after 1805. H. M. Margoliouth deals briefly with the relations between two great poets in *Wordsworth and Coleridge, 1795–1835,* 1953.

Walter Raleigh's *Wordsworth,* 1903, H. W. Garrod's *Wordsworth, Lectures and Essays,* 1923, 2nd edition, 1927, Helen Darbishire's *The Poet Wordsworth,*‡ 1950, and Carl Woodring's, *Wordsworth,*‡ 1965, are useful introductions to Wordsworth's poetry. *The Mind of a Poet,* by Raymond D. Havens, 2 vols., 1941, is a detailed study of *The Prelude;* Herbert Lindenberger, *On Wordsworth's Prelude,*‡ 1963, is a more recent and lively exploration of the poem. Various aspects of Wordsworth's thought are discussed in M. M. Rader, *Presiding Ideas in Wordsworth's Poetry,* 1931; Basil Willey, *The Eighteenth Century Background,*‡ 1940; and N. P. Stallknecht, *Strange Seas of Thought,* 2nd ed., 1958. Prominent among the books which attest the growing interest in Wordsworth are John Jones, *The Egotistical Sublime,* 1954, and Geoffrey Hartman's impressive study of *Wordsworth's Poetry, 1787–1814,* 1964. A collection of recent critical essays is available in *Discussions of William Wordsworth,*‡ edited by J. M. Davis, 1964.

Samuel Taylor Coleridge

The *Complete Works,* ed. W. G. T. Shedd, 7 vols., 1853, 1884, though very far from complete, is the most inclusive collection of Coleridge's works; it will be superseded by the edition of Coleridge's writings now in process under the general editorship of Kathleen Coburn. The standard edition of the *Complete Poetical Works* is by E. H. Coleridge, 2 vols., 1912; a one-volume edition of *The Poems* by the same editor is available in Oxford Standard Authors. The most fully annotated edition of *Biographia Literaria* is by John Shawcross, 2 vols., 1907; a good reprint of the critical classic was edited by George Watson in 1956. Thomas Middleton Raysor has edited the fragmentary remains of *Coleridge's Shakespearean Criticism*, 2 vols., 1930, and *Coleridge's Miscellaneous Criticism*, 1936. The definitive edition of Coleridge's *Collected Letters* is now being issued by Earl Leslie Griggs: the first four volumes (covering 1785–1819) were published in 1956–1959. The first two volumes of Coleridge's extraordinary *Notebooks* are available, meticulously edited by Kathleen Coburn, 1957–61.

E. K. Chambers, *Samuel Taylor Coleridge*, 1938, gives a condensed and unsympathetic factual account of Coleridge's life. Lawrence Hanson, *The Life of S. T. Coleridge: The Early Years*, 1938, is an extensive study of the poet's life and writings to 1800; and H. M. Margoliouth has described the most fruitful literary association on record in his *Wordsworth and Coleridge, 1795–1834*, Home University Library, 1953. The best inclusive critique of Coleridge as poet is by Humphry House, *Coleridge*, 1953. *The Road to Xanadu*, 1927, rev.,‡ 1930, by J. L. Lowes, which investigates the sources and composition of *The Ancient Mariner* and *Kubla Khan*, has achieved the status of a critical classic. Recent discussion of Coleridge as philosopher and critic will be found in M. H. Abrams, *The Mirror and the Lamp*,‡ 1953, René Wellek, *A History of Modern Criticism 1750–1950*, Vol. II, 1955, Richard Harter Fogle, *The Idea of Coleridge's Criticism*, 1962, and J. A. Appleyard, *Coleridge's Philosophy of Literature*, 1965.

George Gordon, Lord Byron

The Works of Lord Byron, 1898–1904, contains seven volumes of *Poetry*, edited by Ernest Hartley Coleridge, and six volumes of *Letters and Journals*, edited by Rowland E. Prothero; the latter have been supplemented by *Lord Byron's Correspondence*, 2 vols., 1922, edited by Sir John Murray. There are numerous editions of the collected poems; a well-chosen and annotated selection has been published in two volumes in the Odyssey Press Series: *Don Juan and Other Satiric Poems*, edited by Louis I. Bredvold, 1935, and *Childe Harold's Pilgrimage and Other Romantic Poems*, edited by Samuel C. Chew, 1936. Selections from the letters have been prepared by V. H. Collins, *Lord Byron in His Letters*, 1927, and by R. G. Howarth, *Letters of Lord Byron*, 1933. *His Very Self and Voice*, by Ernest J. Lovell, Jr., 1954, is a compilation of Byron's conversations, and *Byron: A Self-Portrait*, edited by Peter Quennell, 2 vols., 1950, reprints selected letters and the text of his diaries.

The standard biography, a circumstantial and objective narrative, is Leslie A. Marchand's *Byron: A Biography*, 3 vols., 1957. Shorter and very readable lives are Ethel C. Mayne, *Byron*, one-volume edition, 1924, and Peter Quennell, *Byron*, 1934. Charles Du Bos' *Byron and the Need of Fatality*, trans. E. C. Mayne, 1932, attempts a depth analysis of Byron's temperament. The fascination of Byron the man and the apparent difficulty of saying unobvious things about his poetry have until recently made for a dearth of primarily critical writings about Byron. Among the criticism may be mentioned: William J. Calvert, *Byron: Romantic Paradox*, 1935; G. Wilson Knight's symbolic interpretations and praises of Byron, *The Burning Oracle*, 1939, and *Lord Byron: Christian Virtues*, 1954; E. J. Lovell, Jr., *Byron: The Record of a Quest*, 1950; Paul West, *Byron and the Spoiler's Art*, 1960; Andrew Rutherford, *Byron*, 1961; M. K. Joseph, *Byron, the Poet*, 1964, and L. A. Marchand, *Byron's Poetry: A Critical Introduction*,‡ 1965. *Byron*,‡ 1963, edited by Paul West, is a collection of twentieth-century essays in criticism.

An edition of *Don Juan* which incorporates the changes Byron made in his manuscripts is *Byron's Don Juan*, edited by T. G. Steffan and W. W. Pratt, 4 vols., 1957; the first volume, by Steffan, is a full and revealing commentary on his poem. Other discussions of Byron's masterpiece are: P. G. Trueblood, *The Flowering of Byron's Genius: Studies in Byron's Don Juan*, 1945; and E. F. Boyd, *Byron's Don Juan: A Critical Study*, 1945; and George M. Ridenour, *The Style of "Don Juan,"* 1960.

Percy Bysshe Shelley

The standard collection of Shelley's writings is *The Complete Works*, edited in 10 vols. by Roger Ingpen and Walter E. Peck, 1926–30. The most useful single volume of the poems is in the Oxford Standard Authors, edited by Thomas Hutchinson and reissued in 1933 with Introduction and Notes by Benjamin P. Kurtz. *Shelley's Prose* was collected by David Lee Clark in 1954; and *The Letters* were edited by Frederick L. Jones in 2 vols., 1964.

The classic life is Newman Ivey White's *Shelley*, 2 vols., 1940, which is also available in a condensed single volume under the title *Portrait of Shelley*, 1945. A graceful short biography and appreciation is Edmund

Blunden's *Shelley: A Life Story*,‡ 1946. Kenneth Neill Cameron, in *The Young Shelley*,‡ 1950, emphasizes the development of Shelley's radical social and political thinking. C. E. Pulos, *The Deep Truth: A Study of Shelley's Scepticism*,‡ 1954, a valuable corrective of standard views of Shelley, emphasizes the philosophic scepticism at the center of his idealism.

Shelley's Major Poetry,‡ by Carlos Baker, 1948, provides useful analyses of the longer poems which stress their ideational content; Carl H. Grabo, in *A Newton Among Poets*, 1930, and Desmond King-Hele, in *Shelley: His Thought and Work*, 1960, deal with Shelley's conversion of scientific knowledge into poetic imagery. *The Imagery of Keats and Shelley*, 1949, by Richard H. Fogle, is an analysis of the stylistic qualities of Shelley's poetry.

As early as 1900, W. B. Yeats, in "The Philosophy of Shelley's Poetry" (reprinted in *Essays*, 1924), dealt with Shelley as one of the great symbolist poets; the essay reveals the paradoxical position of modern critics who revere Yeats but condemn Shelley, one of Yeats's most important poetic models. Recent treatments of Shelley's symbolic imagery are Peter Butter, *Shelley's Idols of the Cave*, 1954, and Harold Bloom's innovative study, *Shelley's Mythmaking*, 1959, which puts Shelley in the line of the visionary poets whose imaginative processes were instinctively mythopeic. Earl Wasserman's *The Subtler Language*, 1959, includes detailed explications of *Mont Blanc*, *The Sensitive Plant*, and *Adonais*, and his *Shelley's Prometheus Unbound: A Critical Reading*, 1965, extends this close reading to Shelley's masterpiece. Other recent critiques are Milton Wilson, *Shelley's Later Poetry*, 1959, and R. G. Woodman, *The Apocalyptic Tradition in the Poetry of Shelley*, 1964. *Shelley*,‡ ed. George M. Ridenour, 1965, is an anthology of modern critical essays. Shelley's *Prometheus Unbound: A Variorum Edition*, edited by Lawrence J. Zillman, 1959, incorporates variant interpretations of the poem in general and of the details of its text.

John Keats

The two best editions of Keats's poems are Ernest de Selincourt's *Poems*, 5th edition, 1926, and H. W. Garrod's *Poetical Works*,‡ 2nd edition, 1958. Hyder E. Rollins's *The Letters of John Keats*, 2 vols., 1958, has now replaced M. B. Forman's earlier collection of the letters, 4th edition, 1952.

Sir Sidney Colvin's *John Keats*, 1917, and Amy Lowell's *John Keats*, 2 vols., 1925, have now been replaced by W. J. Bate's notable study of the poet's life, writings, and place in the English poetic tradition, *John Keats*,‡ 1963. Two shorter critical biographies, both valuable, are Aileen Ward, *John Keats: The Making of a Poet*,‡ 1963, and Douglas Bush, *John Keats*, 1966. Among the many critical writings on the poet, the following are especially useful: C. D. Thorpe, *The Mind of John Keats*, 1926 (on Keats's thought); M. R. Ridley, *Keats's Craftsmanship*,‡ 1933 (based on the revisions in Keats's manuscripts); W. J. Bate, *The Stylistic Development of Keats*, 1945, 1958; R. H. Fogle, *The Imagery of Keats and Shelley*, 1949 (a fine study of Keats's characteristic diction and figurative language); Earl Wasserman, *The Finer Tone*, 1953 (a close and sometimes oversubtle analysis of the major poems); and E. C. Pettet, *On the Poetry of Keats*, 1957. *Keats*,‡ edited by W. J. Bate, 1964, reprints a number of recent critical essays.

Sir Walter Scott

Scott's novels have been often reprinted, both collectively and individually, and most of the best ones are available in cheap editions. A useful collection of the *Poetical Works* is that in the Oxford Standard Authors, edited in 1904 by J. L. Robertson. The letters have been edited by H. J. C. Grierson in 12 vols., 1932–37, and the *Journal* has been edited by J. G. Tait in 3 vols., 1939–46. The official *Memoirs of the Life of Sir Walter Scott* by Scott's son-in-law, J. G. Lockhart, 7 vols., 1837–38, is an English classic; its facts and evaluations are supplemented by H. J. C. Grierson's *Sir Walter Scott, Bart.*, 1938. There is also a lively and engaging life, *Sir Walter Scott*, by the novelist John Buchan, 1932. See also James T. Hillhouse, *The Waverley Novels and their Critics*, 1936, and the many treatments of Scott as poet and novelist listed in Chapter IV of *The English Romantic Poets and Essayists*, edited by Carolyn W. and Lawrence H. Houtchens, 1957.

Robert Southey

The *Poetical Works*, edited by Southey himself, are in 10 vols., 1837–38, reprinted, 1860; the best one-volume selection is *Poems*, edited by M. H. Fitzgerald, 1909. The prose works have not been collected. There is a *Life and Correspondence*, edited in 6 vols. by C. C. Southey in 1849–50, and a selection of the *Letters*, edited by M. H. Fitzgerald for World's Classics, 1912. For biography see Edward Dowden's *Southey*, 1874; William Haller's *The Early Life*, 1917; Jack Simmons' *Southey*, 1945; and Robert Carnall's *Robert Southey and His Age*, 1960.

Walter Savage Landor

The Complete Works have been edited by T. E. Welby and Stephen Wheeler, 16 vols., 1927–36, and the poems alone by Stephen Wheeler in 3 vols., 1937. A more reliable edition of the prose writings is by C. G. Crump, 2 vols., 1891–93. There is a volume of selected *Poetry and Prose*, edited by E. K. Chambers, 1946. The official biography is *Walter Savage Landor*, by his friend, John Forster, 2 vols., 1869, but it is long and dull; a recent, full, and readable biography is R. H. Super's *Landor: A Biography*, 1954. For criticism, see also Malcolm Elwin, *Landor: A Rap-levin*, 1958, and Chapter VII in Douglas Bush, *Mythology and the Romantic Tradition*,‡ 1937.

Thomas Moore

Political Works, edited by A. D. Godley, 1910; a selection of *Lyrics and Satires*, edited by Sean O'Faolain, 1929; *Memoirs, Journals, and Correspondence,* edited by Lord John Russell, 8 vols., 1853–56. A selection from the memoirs was published as *Tom Moore's Diary*, edited by J. B. Priestley, 1925. The best biography is Howard M. Jones's lively *The Harp That Once—A Chronicle of the Life of Thomas Moore*, 1937.

Leigh Hunt

Hunt's complete journalistic output (it is estimated that it would take up between 50 and 60 volumes) has never been collected. Following are the best editions and useful selections of various types of his writing: *Poetical Works*, edited by H. S. Milford, Oxford Standard Authors, 1923; *Leigh Hunt's Literary Criticism*, edited by Carolyn W. and Lawrence H. Houtchens, 1956 (it includes a general appreciation of Hunt as a man of letters by C. D. Thorpe), and by the same editors, *Leigh Hunt's Dramatic Criticism, 1808–1831*, 1949; *Selected Essays*, edited by J. B. Priestley, 1929. Hunt's *Autobiography* is available in The World's Classics. The best English biography is Edmund Blunden's *Leigh Hunt: A Biography*, 1930, but the fullest and most scholarly is in French, the first volume of Louis Landré's monumental *Leigh Hunt* (1935–36); the second volume of this treatise constitutes the best critical survey of all of Hunt's writings.

Thomas Love Peacock

The Works have been edited by H. F. B. Brett-Smith and C. E. Jones in 10 vols., 1924–34, and the poems alone by R. B. Johnson, 1906. The novels have been often reprinted, singly and collectively. There are good lives of Peacock by Carl Van Doren, 1911, and by J. B. Priestley, 1927.

John Clare

The fullest selection from Clare's published poems and from the great mass of his unpublished remains is *The Poems of John Clare*, edited by J. W. Tibble, 2 vols., 1935. The same scholar, with Anne Tibble, has written *Clare: His Life and Poetry*, 1956, and has edited *The Prose*, 1951, and *The Letters*, 1951. A selection of the poems is that by Geoffrey Grigson in The Muses' Library, 1950. Another collection is *John Clare's Later Poetry*. The essays on Clare by J. M. Murry, collected in his *John Clare and Other Studies*, 1959, will indicate the sudden leap forward of Clare's reputation when he was "rediscovered" in the 1920's.

George Darley

Complete Poetical Works, edited by Ramsay Colles, 1908; C. C. Abbott, *The Life and Letters of George Darley*, 1928.

Thomas Lovell Beddoes

The standard edition of Beddoes' writings, including his manuscript remains, is the *Works*, edited by H. W. Donner, 1935. The same scholar has edited a good selection of the *Plays and Poems*, 1950, and has written the best biography, *Thomas Lovell Beddoes: The Making of a Poet*, 1935. See also R. H. Snow, *Thomas Lovell Beddoes*, 1928.

William Hazlitt

The Complete Works of William Hazlitt, 21 vols., 1930–34, is excellently edited by P. P. Howe; the final volume includes a full general index, as well as an index of Hazlitt's quotations. Useful selections of Hazlitt's writings are *Selected Essays*, edited by Geoffrey Keynes, 1930, and *Hazlitt on English Literature*, edited by Jacob Zeitlin, 1926. P. P. Howe's largely factual *Life of William Hazlitt*, revised ed., 1947, has been superseded by Herschel Baker's comprehensive study of his life, writings, and thought, *William Hazlitt*, 1962. Stewart C. Wilcox described *Hazlitt in the Workshop*, 1943. The chapter on Hazlitt in Oliver Elton's *A Survey of English Literature 1780–1830*, 2 vols., 1912, remains a useful comment on Hazlitt as essayist and prose stylist. Virginia Woolf includes an appreciation of Hazlitt in *The Second Common Reader*,‡ 1932. On Hazlitt as a critic of literature and the arts, see the Introduction in Jacob Zeitlin's anthology, *Hazlitt on English Literature*, 1913; Elizabeth Schneider, *The Aesthetics of William Hazlitt*, 1933; W. J. Bate's comments in *Criticism: The Major Texts*, 1952; and René Wellek, *A History of Modern Criticism 1750–1950*, Vol. II, 1955.

Thomas De Quincey

The Collected Writings, edited by David Masson, 14 vols., 1889–90, although incomplete, is still the standard edition of De Quincey's writings; other essays will be found in Uncollected Writings, ed. James Hogg, 2 vols., 1890, and Posthumous Writings, ed. A. H. Japp, 2 vols., 1891–93. There are numerous books of selections from De Quincey, and The Confessions of an English Opium-Eater,‡ has been frequently reprinted. Horace Ainsworth Eaton's Thomas De Quincey: A Biography, 1936, is a detailed and reliable biography; Edward Sackville-West's A Flame in Sunlight, 1936, offers a speculative depth-analysis of De Quincey's temperament. Good short biographies and critiques are Malcolm Elwin's DeQuincey, 1935, and J. C. Metcalf's DeQuincey: A Portrait, 1940. On his criticism see John E. Jordan, Thomas DeQuincey, Literary Critic, 1952, and on his thought, the section in J. Hillis Miller, The Disappearance of God: Five Nineteenth-Century Writers,‡ 1963.

Charles Lamb

We are indebted to E. V. Lucas for the standard Works of Charles and Mary Lamb, 7 vols., 1903–5; for the standard edition of their Letters, 3 vols., 1935; and for the standard Life of Charles Lamb, 2 vols., rev., 1921. The shorter work, Charles Lamb, written by Alfred Ainger for the English Men of Letters series in 1882, is still a useful critical biography. The influential essay on Lamb by Walter Pater in his Appreciations set the tone for much of the standard commentary on the essayist; Edmund Blunden's Charles Lamb and His Contemporaries, 1933, is an appreciation by a more recent devotee; Denys Thompson's "Our Debt to Lamb," in Determinations, ed. F. R. Leavis, 1934, offers a contrary view. A selection from his critical writings, Lamb's Criticism, 1923, was edited by E. M. W. Tillyard, and includes an introductory essay on "Lamb as a Literary Critic."

The Art of Romantic Poetry

Students interested in the process of composition, as this is discussed by poets and demonstrated in their manuscripts, may refer to: Charles D. Abbott, ed., Poets at Work, 1948; Phyllis Bartlett, Poems in Process, 1951; A. F. Scott, The Poet's Craft,‡ 1957.

THE VICTORIAN AGE

Studies of the Victorian age and its point of view include Asa Briggs, The Age of Improvement, 1962; W. L. Burn, The Age of Equipoise: A Study of the Mid-Victorian Generation,‡ 1964; Jerome Buckley, The Victorian Temper,‡ 1951; Walter E. Houghton, The Victorian Frame of Mind, 1830–1870, 1957; G. Kitson Clark, The Making of Victorian England, 1962; D. C. Somervell, English Thought in the Nineteenth Century,‡ 1929; and G. M. Young, Victorian England: Portrait of an Age,‡ 1936. Young's essay is a brilliant synthesis, but it can be incomprehensible to readers who are not yet adequately familiar with the history of the age. Such readers should consult G. M. Trevelyan's British History in the Nineteenth Century,‡ 1937, or David Thomson's England in the Nineteenth Century, 1950. For further information about the background of the age see Richard Altick, The English Common Reader,‡ 1957; Jerome Buckley, The Triumph of Time, 1966; Raymond Williams, Culture and Society 1780–1950, 1958.

Studies of Victorian literature include Joseph Warren Beach, The Concept of Nature in Nineteenth-Century English Poetry, 1936; Douglas Bush, Mythology and the Romantic Tradition,‡ 1937; Oliver Elton, A Survey of English Literature, 1920, Vols. III, IV; George Ford, Keats and the Victorians, 1944; Graham Hough, The Last Romantics,‡ 1949; E. D. H. Johnson, The Alien Vision of Victorian Poetry, 1952; F. L. Lucas, Ten Victorian Poets, 1940; Robert Langbaum, The Poetry of Experience,‡ 1957; J. Hillis Miller, The Disappearance of God: Five Nineteenth-Century Writers,‡ 1963; Morse Peckham, Beyond the Tragic Vision, 1962; René Wellek, A History of Modern Criticism, vol. IV, 1965. Helpful collections of critical essays have been compiled by Austin Wright in his Victorian Literature: Modern Essays in Criticism,‡ 1961, by Robert Preyer in his Victorian Literature: Selected Essays,‡ 1966, and by Richard Levine in his Backgrounds to Victorian Literature, 1967.

For classified lists of other books and articles, see The Victorian Poets, A Guide to Research, edited by F. E. Faverty, 1956 (a revised edition is to be published); and Bibliographies of Studies in Victorian Literature 1945–1954, edited by Austin Wright, 1956. Lists are also published in Studies in Philology and Victorian Studies.

For developments in prose fiction during the period see Walter Allen, The English Novel,‡ 1954; Lionel Stevenson, The English Novel: A Panorama,‡ 1960; and Kathleen Tillotson, The Novel of the Eighteen-Forties, 1956. Aspects of novel-criticism are surveyed in George Ford's Dickens and his Readers,‡ 1955, and in Richard Stang's

The Theory of the Novel in England, 1850–70, 1959. For a detailed review of scholarship and criticism see *Victorian Fiction: A Guide to Research,* edited by Lionel Stevenson, 1964.

Thomas Carlyle

The *Works* have been edited by H. D. Traill, 30 vols., 1898–1901, and a 30 volume collection of the *Letters* (edited by C. R. Sanders and others) is in process of being published. C. F. Harrold's edition of *Sartor Resartus* (1937) is helpful concerning Carlyle's debt to German literature, as is Louis Cazamian's *Carlyle,* translated in 1932, concerning his religious background. J. A. Froude's *Thomas Carlyle,* 1882–84, remains, despite its inaccuracies, the standard biography. A reasonable account of his marriage is given by Lawrence and Elizabeth Hanson in their *Necessary Evil: The Life of Jane Welsh Carlyle,* 1952. Emery Neff's *Carlyle and Mill,* 1926, and Eric Bentley's *A Century of Hero-Worship,‡* 1944, are recommended as studies of Carlyle's thought. John Holloway's *The Victorian Sage,‡* 1953, includes a chapter analyzing Carlyle's rhetoric. George B. Tennyson's *Sartor Called Resartus,* 1965, is an important critical study. For other discussions see Carlisle Moore's critical bibliography in *The English Romantic Poets and Essayists,* edited by Carolyn and Lawrence Houtchens (Revised edition), 1966.

Alfred, Lord Tennyson

Tennyson's *Works* were edited by his son Hallam, Lord Tennyson, in 9 vols., 1907–8. A readily available one-volume edition was edited by W. J. Rolfe, 1898. Hallam Tennyson's *Alfred Lord Tennyson: A Memoir,* 2 vols., 1897, is a mine of scattered anecdotes and valuable information. The best biography is Sir Charles Tennyson's *Alfred Tennyson,* 1949, Sir Harold Nicolson's *Tennyson,* 1923, a critical study more than a biography, gives a lively but distorted assessment of Tennyson's achievement. Also unsympathetic is Paull F. Baum's *Tennyson Sixty Years After,* 1948. A judicious corrective is supplied by Jerome H. Buckley's *Tennyson: The Growth of a Poet,‡* 1961, and also by Valerie Pitt's *Tennyson Laureate,* 1962.

Some of the most interesting discussions are in introductory essays to Tennyson's poems by T. S. Eliot, 1936; W. C. DeVane,‡ 1940; W. H. Auden, 1944; H. M. McLuhan,‡ 1956; and Jerome H. Buckley,‡ 1958. Also useful are *A Commentary on Tennyson's "In Memoriam,"* by A. C. Bradley, 1901; *The Formation of Tennyson's Style,* by J. F. A. Pyre, 1921; *The Alien Vision of Victorian Poetry,* by E. D. H. Johnson, 1952; and *Critical Essays on the*

Poetry of Tennyson, edited by John Kilham, 1960.

Robert Browning

A variorum edition of Browning's poetry, edited by Roma A. King Jr. and others, is projected to be published in 1969. Meanwhile a standard edition is that edited by F. G. Kenyon, 10 vols., 1912. Also projected is a collection of Browning's letters in 21 vols., to be edited by Philip Kelley and Ronald Hudson. W. Hall Griffin and H. C. Minchin's *The Life of Robert Browning,* 1910, rev., 1938, is the standard biography. It may be compared with Betty Miller's *Robert Browning: A Portrait,* 1952, a lively psychoanalytical study. W. C. DeVane's *A Browning Handbook,* rev., 1955, is a model compilation of factual data concerning each of Browning's poems: sources, composition, and reputation.

The critical assessments in G. K. Chesterton's *Robert Browning,* 1903, are colorfully expressed and often shrewd. Roma A. King, Jr.'s *The Bow and the Lyre,‡* 1957, contains detailed discussions of some of the principal monologues. Robert Langbaum's *The Poetry of Experience ‡* is an admirable attempt to relate Browning's monologues to some of the main developments in modern literature. For an understanding of Browning's ideas, W. O. Raymond's *The Infinite Moment,‡* 1965, is suggestive. Many of the best discussions of Browning's achievement, especially discussions of individual poems, have been conveniently assembled in two collections that rarely overlap each other: *Robert Browning: A Collection of Critical Essays,* edited by Philip Drew,‡ 1966, and *The Browning Critics,‡* edited by Boyd Litzinger and K. L. Knickerbocker, 1965. The latter collection also includes an extensive bibliography.

Matthew Arnold

The Works, 1903, is an incomplete collection of Arnold's writings; it must be supplemented by later editions such as *The Poetical Works,* edited by C. B. Tinker and H. F. Lowry, 1950, and the elaborately annotated *Poems of Arnold,* edited by Kenneth Allott, 1965; the *Note-Books,* edited by H. F. Lowry, Karl Young, and W. H. Dunn, 1952; and *The Letters of Arnold to * * * Clough,* edited by H. F. Lowry, 1932. Since 1960 several of the projected 10 volumes of Arnold's *Complete Prose Works,* edited by R. H. Super, have been published. For a study of these prose works see William Robbins' *The Ethical Idealism of Matthew Arnold,* 1959.

Lionel Trilling's excellent *Matthew Arnold ‡* (1949) remains a standard critical and biographical study but see also W. Stacy Johnson's *The Voices of Matthew Arnold,* 1961; Dwight Culler's *Imaginative Reason,* 1966, and G. Robert Stange's *Matthew Arnold: The Poet as Humanist,* 1967. Two useful investigations of Arnold's literary and intellectual background are Leon Gottfried's *Matthew Arnold and the Romantics,* 1963, and Warren D. Anderson's *Matthew Arnold and the Classical Tradition,* 1965. One of the best shorter essays is E. K. Brown's Introduction to *Representative Essays of Arnold,* 1936, and see also Geoffrey and Kathleen Tillotson, *Mid-Victorian Studies,* 1965, pp. 152–238.

Elizabeth Barrett Browning

The standard *Complete Works* were edited by Charlotte Porter and Helen Clarke, 6 vols., 1900. A reasonable biography is Gardner B. Taplin's *The Life of Elizabeth Barrett Browning,* 1957. An essay by L. E. Gates in his *Studies and Appreciations,* 1900, helps to relate her poems to those of her predecessors among the Romantics.

Emily Brontë

The Complete Poems were edited by C. W. Hatfield in 1941. Information about the Gondal narrative is supplied by Fannie E. Rotchford's *The Brontës' Web of Childhood,* 1941, and *Gondal's Queen, A Novel in Verse,‡* 1955. C. Day Lewis's lecture on the poems appears in his *Notable Images of Virtue,* 1954.

Dante Gabriel Rossetti

Rossetti's *Works* were edited by W. M. Rossetti, 1911; *The House of Life* was edited by P. F. Baum, 1928, and *The Letters* by Oswald Doughty and J. R. Wahl, 2 vols., 1965 and 2 vols., subsequently. See Oswald Doughty's *D. G. Rossetti: A Victorian Romantic,* 2nd ed., 1960; and G. H. Fleming, *Rossetti and the Pre-Raphaelite Brotherhood,* 1967.

Christina Rossetti

The standard edition of the *Poetical Works of Christina Rossetti* was edited by W. M. Rossetti in 1904. Virginia Woolf's *The Second Common Reader,‡* 1932, contains an essay on the poetess. Also useful are Marya Zaturenska, *Christina Rossetti: A Portrait,* 1949; H. N. Fairchild, *Religious Trends in English Poetry,* 1957, Vol. IV, Chapter 10, and Lona M. Packer, *Christina Rossetti,* 1963.

George Meredith

The Poetical Works were edited by G. M. Trevelyan in 1928. See Lionel Stevenson, *The Ordeal of George Meredith,* 1953, and C. Day Lewis, Introduction to *Modern Love,* 1948, and Norman Kelvin, *A Troubled Eden,* 1961.

William Morris

Collected Works, 24 vols., 1910–15; J. W. Mackail, *The Life of William Morris,* 2 vols., 1899; George Bernard Shaw, *William Morris, As I Knew Him,* 1936; Graham Hough, *The Last Romantics,‡* 1949; Peter Faulkner, *William Morris and William Butler Yeats,* 1962.

Edward FitzGerald

George Bentham edited *The Variorum Edition of the * * * Writings of Edward FitzGerald,* 7 vols., 1902. A. McKinley Terhune, *The Life of Edward Fitzgerald,* 1947; A. J. Arberry, *The Romance of the Rubáiyát,* 1959.

Arthur Hugh Clough

The Poems have been edited by H. F. Lowry, A. L. F. Norrington, and F. L. Mulhauser, 1951; *The Correspondence* by F. L. Mulhauser, 1957. *A. H. Clough: The Uncommitted Mind,* by Katherine Chorley, 1962, is a lively but frequently misleading study. *The Poetry of Clough* by Walter Houghton, 1963, contends that Clough is a major satirical poet. On Clough's religious and intellectual background see Paul Veyriras, *A. H. Clough,* 1965 (in French).

Algernon Charles Swinburne

Complete Works, edited by E. W. Gosse and T. J. Wise, 20 vols., 1925–27; *The Swinburne Letters,* edited by Cecil Y. Lang, 6 vols., 1959–62 (reviewed by Edmund Wilson in *The Bit Between My Teeth,* 1965); G. Lafourcade, *Swinburne: A Literary Biography,* 1932. Douglas Bush's chapter in *Mythology and the Romantic Tradition,‡* 1937, is highly informative if unsympathetic. Robert Peters' *The Crowns of Apollo,* 1965, is an attempt to show that Swinburne was a major literary critic.

Francis Thompson

Complete Poetical Works were edited by Wilfred Meynell, 3 vols., 1913. Biographies are Everard Meynell, *The Life of Francis Thompson,* 1913, and Paul van K. Thomson, *Francis Thompson: A Critical Biography,* 1961.

Edward Lear

The Complete Nonsense,‡ edited by Holbrook Jackson, 1947. Angus Davidson, *Edward Lear: Landscape Painter and Nonsense Poet,* 1938; Elizabeth Sewell, *The Field of Nonsense,* 1952.

Lewis Carroll

The Complete Works, 1949. See also Derek Hudson, *Lewis Carroll,* 1954; William Empson, *Some Versions of*

Pastoral,‡ 1935; Martin Gardner, *The Annotated Snark,* 1962; and Virginia Woolf, *The Moment and other Essays,* 1948.

John Henry Cardinal Newman

The 41 volumes of Newman's works were published over a period of years, but no standard edition has as yet appeared. Several of the projected 30 volumes of the *Letters and Diaries,* edited by C. S. Dessain, have been published since 1961. Meriol Trevor's *New man,* 2 vols., 1962, is a comprehensive biography. For Newman's religious background and development, two of the most helpful studies are R. W. Church's *The Oxford Movement,* 1891, and Charles F. Harold's *John Henry Newman,* 1945. His literary skill is analyzed in John Holloway's *The Victorian Sage,*‡ 1953, Chapter VI; Walter E. Houghton's *The Art of Newman's "Apologia,"* 1945; and Martin J. Svaglic's "The Structure of Newman's *Apologia,"* *PMLA,* LXVI (1951), 138–48. Especially recommended is Dwight Culler's *The Imperial Intellect,*‡ 1955.

John Stuart Mill

Since 1963 several of the projected 20 volumes of the *Collected Works,* edited by F. E. L. Priestly, have been published (including volumes of Mill's letters). A. W. Benn, *The History of English Rationalism in the Nineteenth Century,* 2 vols., 1906. Karl Britton, *John Stuart Mill,* 1953; Emery Neff, *Carlyle and Mill,* 1926; M. St. J. Packe, *The Life of J. S. Mill,* 1954.

John Ruskin

The *Works* were edited by E. T. Cook

and Alexander Wedderburn, 39 vols., 1903–12. Ruskin's biography is being at present rewritten, but meanwhile E. T. Cook's *The Life of Ruskin,* 2 vols., 1911, is informative. His *Diaries,* edited by Joan Evans and J. H. Whitehouse, were published in 1956. An interesting digest of his aesthetic theories was compiled by Joan Evans in *The Lamp of Beauty: Writings on Art by John Ruskin,* 1958. Also recommended are F. W. Roe, *The Social Philosophy of Carlyle and Ruskin,* 1921, R. H. Wilenski, *John Ruskin,* 1933, and John D. Rosenberg, *The Darkening Glass,* 1961.

Thomas Henry Huxley

The *Life and Letters of Thomas Henry Huxley* was edited by Leonard Huxley, 2 vols., 1900. William Irvine, *Apes, Angels, and Victorians,*‡ 1955, is lively and informative. See also *1859: Entering an Age of Crisis,* edited by P. Appleman, W. A. Madden, and M. Wolff, 1959.

Walter Pater

Works, 10 vols., 1910. Thomas Wright, *The Life of Walter Pater,* 2 vols., 1907; Germain d'Hangest, *Walter Pater: l'homme et l'oeuvre,* 2 vols., 1962. Critical essays include T. S. Eliot's "Arnold and Pater" in *Selected Essays 1917–32,* 1932; Graham Hough, *The Last Romantics,*‡ 1949, Chapter IV; Ruth Z. Temple, "The Ivory Tower as Lighthouse" in *Edwardians and Late Victorians,* edited by Richard Ellman, 1960, and U. C. Knoepflmacher, *Religious Humanism and the Victorian Novel,* 1965.

THE TWENTIETH CENTURY

The following critical works deal with some general aspects of modern English literature: *New Bearings in English Poetry,*‡ by F. R. Leavis, 2nd edition, 1950; *Forces in Modern British Literature,*‡ by William Y. Tindall, 1947, 1956; *The Modern Writer and His World,*‡ by G. S. Fraser, 1953; *The Present Age in British Literature,* by David Daiches, 1958; *The Novel and the Modern World,*‡ by David Daiches, 2nd edition, 1960; *The Modern Poets, A Critical Introduction,*‡ by M. L. Rosenthal, 1960; *Twentieth Century British Literature: A Reference Guide and Bibliography,* by Ruth Z. Temple, 1968. *Eight Modern Writers,* by J. I. M. Stewart (*Oxford History of English Literature* vol. XII), 1963, includes valuable chapters on Hardy, Shaw, Conrad, Kipling, Yeats, Joyce, and Lawrence, and a comprehensive bibliography. *The Modern Age,*‡ vol. 7 of *The Pelican Guide to English Literature,* 1961, edited by B. Ford, contains some helpful critical essays and a bibliography. *Contemporary British Lit-*

erature, by Fred B. Millett, 1935, contains bibliographies of modern British writers up to that date. Bibliographies also appear in the periodical *20th-Century Literature.* The first three chapters of *Image and Experience: Studies in a Literary Revolution,*‡ by Graham Hough, 1960, attempt to put the whole modern movement in perspective.

The Long Week-End: a Social History of Great Britain 1918–1939,‡ by Robert Graves and Alan Hodge, 1940; *The Thirties,* by Julian Symons, 1960; and *The Baldwin Age,* edited by John Raymond, 1960, give helpful social and political background.

The Nineties

Some helpful books on the period are: *The Last Romantics,*‡ by Graham Hough, 1947; *The Eighteen Nineties,*‡ by Holbrook Jackson, 1913; *The Beardsley Period,* by Osbert Burdett, 1925; *John Lane and the Nineties,* by J. L. May, 1936. Two useful anthologies of the poetry of the period are *An Anthology of 'Nineties' Verse*, by A. J. A. Symons, 1928, and *British Poetry of the Eighteen-Nineties*, edited by Donald Davidson, 1937.

Oscar Wilde

There are many modern editions of selections of Wilde's work, and a convenient one-volume edition of *The Works of Oscar Wilde*, edited by G. F. Maine, 1948, new ed. 1966. Maine's edition is virtually complete; it includes "everything written by Wilde that can be published at present" (for legal reasons) and everything of his that ever has been published. Wilde's *Letters* were edited by R. Hart-Davis, 1962. *Oscar Wilde and the Yellow Nineties*, by Frances Winwar, 1940, gives a picture of Wilde in his setting, and *The Life of Oscar Wilde, His Life and Wit* by Hesketh Pearson, 1946, is a lively biography. *Oscar Wilde*, by Edouard Roditi, 1947, is a critical study. Frank Harris's somewhat sensational biography,‡ first published in 1916, has been reprinted in 1960, together with G. B. Shaw's *Memories of Oscar Wilde* and Robert Ross's account of Wilde's last days. *Oscar Wilde, a Pictorial Biography*, 1960, by Vyvyan Holland, Oscar Wilde's son, has some splendid photographs of Wilde and his contemporaries and also provides a vivid narrative.

Ernest Dowson

The standard modern edition of Dowson's poems is *The Poetical Works of Ernest Christopher Dowson*, edited with an introduction by Desmond Flower, 1934, new edition with changes, 1967. Much lively and illuminating comment on Dowson will be found in W. B. Yeats's *Autobiography*,‡ 1955. *Ernest Dowson*, by J. M. Longaker, 1944, and *Ernest Dowson*, by T. B. Swann, 1965, are critical biographies; *Letters of Ernest Dowson*, edited by Desmond Flower and Henry Maas, was published in 1967.

Thomas Hardy

Hardy published about a dozen volumes of poetry in his lifetime; of these, the most important are *Wessex Poems and Other Verses*, 1898; *Poems of the Past and Present*, 1902; *Time's Laughingstocks*, 1909; *Satires of Circumstance*, 1914. The *Collected Poems* were issued in one volume in 1932 and have several times been reprinted. There are several collected editions of Hardy's works, notably the Wessex Edition, 21 vols., 1912–14, and the Mellstock Edition, 37 vols., 1919–20.

Hardy of Wessex, by Carl J. Weber, 1940, is the best general account of Hardy's life and work. The two biographical volumes by his wife—*The Early Life of Thomas Hardy*, 1928, and *The Later Years of Thomas Hardy*, 1930—are packed with information,

much of it dictated by Hardy himself. *Thomas Hardy*, by Douglas Brown, 1954, is an excellent critical study. "The Shorter Poems of Hardy," by R. P. Blackmur, to be found in Blackmur's *Language as Gesture*, 1952, is one of the finest critical discussions of Hardy's poetry. *Hardy: A Collection of Critical Essays*,‡ edited by A. J. Guerard, 1963, is a useful collection.

Gerard Manley Hopkins

Robert Bridges edited the first (posthumous) edition of Hopkins' poems in 1918; a second edition, with "An Appendix of Additional Poems," appeared with a critical introduction by Charles Williams in 1930; the third edition, adding some further unpublished poems, was edited by W. H. Gardner in 1948 with additional notes and a biographical introduction. This is now the standard edition.

In addition to the poems, Hopkins' letters and parts of his notebooks have been published, and these are of great interest to students of Hopkins' mind and of his poetic techniques: *The Letters of Gerard Manley Hopkins to Robert Bridges* and *The Correspondence of G. M. Hopkins and Richard Watson Dixon*, edited by C. C. Abbott, 2 vols., 1935; *Further Letters of Gerard Manley Hopkins*, edited by C. C. Abbott, 1937, rev., 1956; and *Notebooks and Papers of Gerard Manley Hopkins*, edited by Humphry House, 1937. House has also edited *Journals and Papers*, 1959; the edition was completed by Graham Storey. This, together with *Sermons and Devotional Writings*, edited by Christopher Devlin, 1959, constitutes a revised edition of the *Notebooks and Papers*. A useful selection of Hopkins' poetry and prose is *A Hopkins Reader*,‡ edited by John Pick, 1953.

The most elaborate study of Hopkins is *G. M. Hopkins: A Study of Poetic Idiosyncrasy in Relation to Poetic Tradition*, by W. H. Gardner, 2 vols., 1944, 1949. *Gerard Manley Hopkins*, by the Kenyon Critics, 1945, contains some helpful critical essays, and *The Shaping Vision of Gerard Manley Hopkins*, by Alan Heuser, 1958, is a careful study of the relation of certain of Hopkins' dominating ideas to his poetic theory and practice. *Gerard Manley Hopkins*, by G. F. Lahey, 1930, is a biography, as is *Gerard Manley Hopkins, Priest and Poet*,‡ by J. Pick, 2nd ed., 1966.

George Bernard Shaw

The Collected Works of Bernard Shaw, in the Ayot St. Lawrence Edition, 30 vols., appeared in 1930 ff. Selections of drama are *Nine Plays*, 1931; *Seven Plays*, 1951; and *Selected Plays*, 4 vols. (containing 27 plays), 1948–57. Many of the plays are also available in inexpensive reprints. Selections of his prose include *Bernard Shaw, Selected Prose,* edited by Diarmuid Russell, 1952; *Plays and Players* (drama criticism), edited by A. C. Ward, 1952; and *Shaw on Music,*‡ edited by Eric Bentley, 1955.

Of the many books on Shaw, the best critical study is Eric Bentley's *Bernard Shaw: A Reconsideration,*‡ 1947. Hesketh Pearson's biography, *Shaw: A Full-length Portrait,* was first published in 1942; Pearson added in 1950 *G.B.S.: A Postscript.* The two books are now available in a single volume. Edmund Wilson's essay, "Shaw at Eighty," in *The Triple Thinkers,*‡ 1938, 1952, is a stimulating discussion of Shaw as thinker and playwright. *G.B.S. 90: Aspects of Shaw's Life and Works,* edited by S. Winsten, 1946, contains essays by a variety of writers. *G. B. Shaw, A Collection of Critical Essays,*‡ edited by R. J. Kaufmann, 1965.

Joseph Conrad

Standard is *The Uniform Edition of the works of Joseph Conrad,* 22 vols., 1923–28, reprinted in 1946 ff, as *The Collected Edition of the Works of Joseph Conrad.* Other collections are the Concord Edition, 22 vols., 1923–28, and the Memorial Edition, 21 vols., 1925.

Two perceptive studies of Conrad are *Conrad the Novelist,*‡ by Albert J. Guerard, 1958, and *Joseph Conrad, Achievement and Decline,* by Thomas Mosher, 1957. *The Portable Conrad,*‡ edited by Morton D. Zabel, 1947, contains a good selection with a helpful introduction (Zabel has also edited *Tales of the East and West,* 1958; *Lord Jim,*‡ *Youth,* and *The Shadow-Line,* all 1959; and, in one volume, *The Shadow-Line, Typhoon,* and *The Secret Sharer,* under the title *The Shadow-Line and Two other Tales,*‡ 1959). *The Conrad Companion,* 1948 (originally published as *The Conrad Reader,* 1946), edited by A. J. Hoppé, contains a large selection from the stories and other writings with a biographical introduction. The discussion of Conrad in *The Great Tradition,*‡ by F. R. Leavis, 1949, is valuable. There is a chapter on Conrad in *The Novel and the Modern World,*‡ by D. Daiches, 2nd edition, 1960, which deals at length with *The Nigger of the "Narcissus," Lord Jim,* and *Nostromo. Joseph Conrad, Life and Letters,* edited by G. Jean-Aubry, 2 vols., 1927; *The Sea Dreamer,* by G. Jean-Aubry, 1957; and *Joseph Conrad,*‡ by Jocelyn Baines, 1960, are biographies. The last is now the standard biography.

William Butler Yeats

In addition to poems and verse plays,

Yeats published essays, short stories, and autobiographical writings, and produced editions of William Blake (with Edwin Ellis) and of some poems of Spenser. He also edited the *Oxford Book of Modern Verse. Collected Poems,* Definitive Edition, 1956, and *Collected Plays,* 2nd edition, 1952, collect Yeats's main work into two convenient volumes, while his letters are collected in *The Letters of W. B. Yeats,* edited by Allan Wade, 1954. Yeats's mystical work *A Vision* was first published in 1925; a new, much revised edition appeared in 1937. *Mythologies* was published in 1959. Yeats's autobiographical writings are combined in *The Autobiography of W. B. Yeats,*‡ 1938 ff. Peter Alt and Russell K. Alspach edited a variorum edition of the *Poems* in 1957.

Three helpful books on Yeats as both man and poet are: *Yeats, the Man and the Masks,*‡ by Richard Ellmann, 1948; *W. B. Yeats, Man and Poet,*‡ by Norman Jeffares, 1949; *The Lonely Tower: Studies in the Poetry of W. B. Yeats,* by T. R. Henn, 1950. *W. B. Yeats,*‡ by Joseph Hone, 1942, 2nd ed., 1962, is a biography. *The Permanence of Yeats,*‡ edited by James Hall and Martin Steinmann, 1950. *Yeats: A Collection of Critical Essays,*‡ edited by John Unterecker, 1963, and *In Excited Reverie,* edited by A. N. Jeffares and K. G. W. Cross, 1965, are three of several useful collections of critical essays on the poet.

James Joyce

Dubliners ‡ is available in various editions. A critical edition of *A Portrait of the Artist as a Young Man,*‡ based on the autograph manuscript, was published in 1964. *Ulysses* ‡ was first published in the United States in 1934; a greatly superior text was published in 1961. *Finnegans Wake* ‡ was published in 1939, and a revised text, incorporating the author's corrections, in 1958. There are three volumes of Joyce's *Letters,* the first edited by Stuart Gilbert, 1957, and the second and third by Richard Ellmann, 1966.

Good general accounts of Joyce's work will be found in *James Joyce,*‡ by Harry Levin, 1941, and *James Joyce,*‡ by William Y. Tindall, 1950. *James Joyce's Ulysses,*‡ by Stuart Gilbert, 1930, rev., 1952, and *James Joyce and the Making of Ulysses,*‡ by Frank Budgen, 1934, 1937, are almost necessary works for the reader of *Ulysses,* as are *A Skeleton Key to Finnegans Wake,*‡ by J. Campbell and H. M. Robinson, 1944, and *The Books at the Wake,* by J. S. Atherton, 1959, for the reader of *Finnegans Wake.* Four chapters in *The Novel and the Modern World,*‡ by David Daiches, 2nd ed., 1960, give a general critical account of

Joyce's work. *James Joyce: Two Decades of Criticism*, edited by Seon Givens, 1948, is a useful anthology of criticism. *James Joyce,‡* by Richard Ellmann, 1959, is the standard biography. *Surface and Symbol,‡* by Robert M. Adams, 1963, studies the raw material of actual Dublin life in *Ulysses*.

D. H. Lawrence

The standard edition of the collected works is the Phoenix Edition, 1955. *Collected Poems* appeared in 1928 and 1932, *Selected Poems* (selected by Richard Aldington) in 1934, and *Complete Poems*, 3 vols., in 1964. *Studies in Classic American Literature,‡* was published in 1923.

Lawrence was a highly controversial figure long before his death, and soon after it a spate of books about him by friends, enemies, and acquaintances began to pour from the press. Most of these are one-sided, but his wife's memoir, *Not I, But the Wind . . .* , by Frieda Lawrence, 1934, is an important and moving book. Two critical studies neatly supplement each other, *D. H. Lawrence: Novelist,‡* by F. R. Leavis, 1955, which is an impassioned argument for Lawrence's supreme greatness, and the much cooler, less "committed," but not unsympathetic *The Dark Sun*, by Graham Hough, 1956, which has a helpful chapter on Lawrence's poetry. *Double Measure*, by George Ford, 1965, is an excellent study of *Women in Love* and *The Rainbow*, and various short stories that illustrate the same themes. The best biography is *The Intelligent Heart,‡* by Harry T. Moore, 1954; but Lawrence's own *Letters*, ed. by Aldous Huxley, 1932, and much more fully but, still incompletely by Harry T. Moore in 1962, provide the best introduction to his life.

T. S. Eliot

The fullest one-volume collections of Eliot's poetry are *Collected Poems, 1909–1963*, 1963, and *The Complete Poems and Plays* (including the plays through *The Cocktail Party*), 1952. Some critical essays are in *Selected Essays*, 1932, and *On Poetry and Poets,‡* 1957.

Among the many books on Eliot, *The Achievement of T. S. Eliot,‡* by F. O. Matthiessen, rev., 1947, has the enthusiasm of a pioneer work; *T. S. Eliot: A Study of His Writings by Various Hands*, edited by B. Rajan, 1947, and *T. S. Eliot, a Selected Critique,‡* edited by Leonard Unger, 1948, bring together a variety of critical essays including some helpful explications of *The Waste Land* and *Four Quartets; The Art of T. S. Eliot,‡* by Helen Gardner, is a perceptive critical study of his poetry; *T. S. Eliot, the Design of his Poetry,‡* by Elizabeth Drew, 1950, is a systematic chrono-logical survey and explanation; *A Reader's Guide to T. S. Eliot,‡* by George Williamson, 1953, is thorough and informative in its explanation of obscurities and references; and *T. S. Eliot's Poetry and Plays,‡* by Grover Smith, Jr., 1956, goes through the poems and plays in an exhaustive and even exhausting manner. The best short critical book on Eliot is *T. S. Eliot*, by Northrop Frye, 1963.

A. E. Housman

Housman's three volumes of poetry —*A Shropshire Lad*, 1896; *Last Poems*, 1922; and the posthumous *More Poems*, 1936—were brought together in *Collected Poems*, 1939, 1953; the fourteenth (revised) impression is the most accurate text. A *Complete Poems*, edited by Basil Davenport, with a history of the text by Tom Burns Haber, was published in 1959. *Selected Prose,‡* ed. John Carter, 1961, includes some of the notorious prefaces.

There is an interesting critical essay on Housman by Edmund Wilson in *The Triple Thinkers,‡* 1952. "Housman: A Controversy," in *The Condemned Playground*, by Cyril Connolly, 1946, is a lively discussion of the case for and against Housman as poet. There is a critical essay on Housman in *Collected Essays*, by John P. Bishop, 1948. *A. E. Housman: A Divided Life*, by George L. Watson, 1957, is a biography.

Rudyard Kipling

The Sussex Edition of the complete works, 35 vols., 1937–39, is the standard complete edition. *Rudyard Kipling's Verse, 1885–1936* (Definitive Edition), 1940, contains all the poetry. T. S. Eliot has edited, with an appreciative and discerning introduction, *A Choice of Kipling's Verse,‡* 1941 (the introduction contains a valuable analysis of *Danny Deever*). Edmund Wilson's essay on Kipling in *The Wound and the Bow,‡* 1941, is stimulating and illuminating; so, in a very different way, is George Orwell's essay on Kipling in his *Critical Essays*, 1946. Lionel Trilling's essay on Kipling in *The Liberal Imagination,‡* 1950, is the third in an important trilogy of modern estimates. *Kipling's Mind and Art,‡* ed. A. Rutherford, 1964, is an important collection of critical essays. *Rudyard Kipling, Realist and Fabulist* by Bonamy Dobrée, 1967, is the fullest critical study. *Rudyard Kipling* by Charles E. Carrington, 1955, is the official biography.

Rupert Brooke

The Collected Poems of Rupert Brooke,‡ 1932, and *The Poetical Works*, edited by G. Keynes, 1946, 1960. Walter de la Mare wrote an essay on "Rupert Brooke and the Intellectual Imagination," which is collected in his *Pleasures and Speculations*, 1940. *Ru-*

pert *Brooke*, by Christopher Hassall, 1964, is a biography.

Edward Thomas

Collected Poems, with a foreword by Walter de la Mare, 1928, 1936. *Edward Thomas*, by Henry Coombes, 1956, is a critical study of the man, the poet, and the prose writer.

Wilfred Owen

The Collected Poems,‡ edited by C. Day Lewis, 1963, is the definitive edition. *The Poetry of Wilfred Owen* has been edited with a memoir by Edmund Blunden, 1931, 1933, 1949. D. S. R. Welland's *Wilfred Owen*, 1960, is a critical study. William Harold Owen, Wilfred's brother, has published two volumes of a projected trilogy on his brother's life—*Journey from Obscurity: Wilfred Owen 1893–1918* (vol. 1, 1963; vol. 2, 1965). *The Collected Letters*, edited by Harold Owen and John Bell, was published in 1967.

E. M. Forster

The Collected Tales of E. M. Forster appeared in 1947. Forster has also collected some eighty of his essays and articles in *Abinger Harvest*,‡ 1936. His study of fictional technique, *Aspects of the Novel*,‡ appeared in 1927, and other essays are included in *Two Cheers for Democracy*,‡ 1951. His novels are available in various editions. Two important critical studies are *E. M. Forster* ‡ by Lionel Trilling, 2nd rev. ed., 1965, and *The Cave and the Mountain: A Study of E. M. Forster*, by Wilfred Stone, 1966.

Virginia Woolf

Extracts from Virginia Woolf's fascinating journal were published by her husband, Leonard Woolf, after her death in 1953, under the title *A Writer's Diary*. *Virginia Woolf*, by E. M. Forster, 1942, is a brief personal account. *Virginia Woolf*,‡ by David Daiches, 1942; *Virginia Woolf: Her Art as a Novelist*,‡ by Joan Bennett, 1945; and *Virginia Woolf: A Commentary*, by Bernard Blackstone, 1949, are critical studies. *Virginia Woolf and her Works*, by Jean Guiget (trans. Jean Stewart), 1965, is the most detailed critical study of her works. Of interest also are Leonard Woolf's four volumes of autobiography, *Sowing*, 1960, *Growing*, 1961, *Beginning Again*, 1964, and *Downhill all the Way*, 1967. See also J. K. Johnstone, *The Bloomsbury Group*,‡ 1954.

Edwin Muir

Collected Poems 1921–1958, 1960, is the standard complete edition of the poems. Muir's important autobiography, *The Story and the Fable*, 1940, was reissued in a revised and enlarged form in 1954 entitled simply *An Autobiography*.

In addition to the works mentioned in the headnote, Muir has written *John Knox: Portrait of a Calvinist*, 1929, and two collections of critical essays, *Transition*, 1926, and *Essays on Literature and Society*, 1949. Peter Butter's *Edwin Muir*, 1962, is a critical study; Butter has also written a biography, *Edwin Muir, Man and Poet*, 1966.

Robert Graves

Collected Poems 1959, 1959, is the fullest of Graves's volumes, but he has published further slim volumes since. *Robert Graves: Poems Chosen by Himself*, 1957, provides an admirable introduction to his poetry. *The White Goddess* ‡ was first published in 1948, but the 1952 edition is amended and enlarged. *Robert Graves*, by J. M. Cohen, 1960, is a critical study. "A Ramble on Graves" by Lionel Trilling (in *A Gathering of Fugitives*,‡ 1956) is a highly agreeable critical essay.

W. H. Auden

The Collected Poetry of W. H. Auden, 1945, includes everything the poet wished to preserve up to that date; a more recent volume, edited by Auden on the same principle, is *Collected Shorter Poems 1927–1957*, 1966. Volumes published in the interim included *The Age of Anxiety*, 1947; *Nones*, 1951; *The Shield of Achilles*, 1955; and *Homage to Clio*, 1960. He has edited a number of anthologies, including (with Norman Pearson) *Poets of the English Language*,‡ 5 vols., 1950, and (with Noah Greenberg and Charles Kallman) *An Elizabethan Songbook*,‡ 1955. *Auden: An Introductory Essay*, by Richard Hoggart, 1951, *The Poetry of W. H. Auden*, by M. K. Spears, 1963, *Auden*, by Barbara Everett, 1964, and *The Poetic Art of W. H. Auden*,‡ by J. G. Blair, 1965, are critical studies.

Louis MacNeice

All of MacNeice's poetry has now been collected in one volume, *Collected Poems*, 1967. *The Strings are False*, 1966, is a posthumously published unfinished autobiography. *Varieties of Parable*, 1965, are lectures on poetry given at Cambridge. MacNeice made verse translations of Aeschylus' *Agamemnon*, 1937, and, with E. L. Stahl, of Goethe's *Faust* (an abridged version of parts I and II), 1951. A critical essay, "Feats on the Fjord," is in *Selected Criticism*, by Louise Bogan, 1955.

Dylan Thomas

Collected Poems, augmented edition, 1957, is the standard collection. In addition to his poetry Thomas wrote the autobiographical prose *Portrait of the Artist as a Young Dog*,‡ 1940, and *Adventures in the Skin Trade*,‡ 1955, as well as a radio play *Under Milk Wood*,‡ 1954, which has proved a great popular success. *Quite Early One Morn-*

ing,‡ 1954, is a collection of stories, essays, and minor pieces.

The Poetry of Dylan Thomas,‡ by Elder Olsen, 1954, is a helpful if somewhat over-systematized discussion of his poetry; *Dylan Thomas*, by Henry Treece, rev., 1956, is an account by a British fellow poet; *Dylan Thomas in America,*‡ by John M. Brinnin, 1955, is a moving if indiscreet account of Thomas's last years. In 1957 Vernon Watkins edited Thomas *Letters to Vernon Watkins*. "The Poetry of Dylan Thomas," in *Literary Essays*, by D. Daiches, 1956, is an appraisal of Thomas's poetic achievement, which includes an analysis and evaluation of *A Refusal to Mourn*. See also *The Craft and Art of Dylan Thomas*, by William T. Moynihan, 1966.

The Critical Revolt Against Romanticism and Impressionism

A general account of modern criticism, English and American, is *The Armed Vision,*‡ by Stanley Edgar Hyman, 1948. "Reflections on a Literary Revolution" (Chapter 1 of *Image and Experience*) ‡ by Graham Hough, 1960, is a helpful presentation of the modern critical movement. Two useful anthologies of modern criticism are *Critiques and Essays in Criticism, 1920–1948*, edited by R. W. Stallman, 1949, and *Critiques and Essays on Modern Fiction 1920–1951*, edited by J. W. Aldridge, 1952.

T. E. Hulme

Hulme's essays have been gathered and edited by Herbert Read under the title *Speculations,*‡ 1924; 2nd edition, 1936. A volume of *Further Speculations* ‡ appeared in 1955, edited by S. Hynes. A biography is *The Life and Opinions of T. E. Hulme*, by Alun R. Jones, 1960.

I. A. Richards

Richards collaborated with C. K. Ogden on *The Foundations of Aesthetics*, 1921 (2nd edition, 1948, with James Wood), and *The Meaning of Meaning,*‡ 1922, much reprinted since. Later books include *Principles of Literary Criticism,*‡ 1925; *Science and Poetry*, 1926, rev., 1935; *Practical*

Criticism,‡ 1929; *Mencius on the Mind,* 1932; *Coleridge on Imagination,*‡ 1935, 1950; and *Speculative Instruments,* 1955. A book of poems, *Goodbye, Earth*, was published in 1958; *The Screens and Other Poems*, 1960, is another book of verse.

William Empson

Among Empson's books are *Seven Types of Ambiguity,*‡ 1930, 1953; *Some Versions of Pastoral,*‡ 1935; and *The Structure of Complex Words,*‡ 1951. He published his *Collected Poems* ‡ in 1955.

F. R. Leavis

Among Leavis' important books are *Revaluation,*‡ 1936, 1950; *New Bearings in English Poetry,*‡ 1932; *For Continuity*, 1933; *The Great Tradition,*‡ 1948; and *The Common Pursuit,*‡ 1952. Leavis edited the critical periodical *Scrutiny* from 1932 to 1953.

Literature Since Mid-Century: Anti-Culture and the New Traditionalism

Critical materials may be found in Martin Esslin, *The Theatre of the Absurd,*‡ 1962; John Press, *Rule and Energy: Trends in British Poetry Since the Second World War*, 1963; and M. L. Rosenthal, *The New Poets,* 1967. Samuel Beckett has published novels, plays, and poetry, most of which are available in paperbound editions: *Samuel Beckett: A Collection of Critical Essays* ‡ was edited by Martin Esslin in 1965. Donald Davie's poems are collected in *New and Selected Poems,*‡ 1961, and *Events and Wisdoms,*‡ 1965; Elizabeth Jennings' in *Collected Poems*, 1967; and Philip Larkins' in *Girl in Winter*, 1963, *Jill*, 1964, and *Whitsun Weddings,*‡ 1964. Volumes of poetry by Thom Gunn and Ted Hughes are cited in the headnote. These poets and their contemporaries were first significantly anthologized in Robert Conquest's *New Lines*, 1957, and *New Lines 2*, 1963. Students will find good representations of their work in *New Poets of England and America,*‡ 1957, edited by Donald Hall, Robert Pack, and Louis Simpson, and *New Poets of England and America,*‡ Second Selection, 1962, edited by Hall and Pack.

Index